Dictionary of American Family Names

Dictionary of American Family Names

PATRICK HANKS

Editor

VOLUME THREE

O–Z

OXFORD

UNIVERSITY PRESS

2003

Oxford University Press

Oxford   New York
Auckland   Bangkok   Buenos Aires   Cape Town   Chennai
Dar es Salaam   Delhi   Hong Kong   Istanbul   Karachi   Kolkata
Kuala Lumpur   Madrid   Melbourne   Mexico City   Mumbai
Nairobi   São Paulo   Shanghai   Taipei   Tokyo   Toronto

Published by Oxford University Press, Inc.
198 Madison Avenue, New York, New York, 10016
http://www.oup-usa.org

Oxford is a registered trademark of Oxford University Press

Library of Congress Cataloging-in-Publication Data

Dictionary of American family names / Patrick Hanks, editor.
    p. cm.
Includes bibliographical references.
    ISBN 0-19-508137-4 (set : acid-free paper) — ISBN 0-19-516557-8 (v. 1
: acid free paper) — ISBN 0-19-516558-6 (v. 2 : acid free paper) —
ISBN 0-19-516559-4 (v. 3 : acid free paper)
    1. Names, Personal—United States—Dictionaries.   I. Hanks, Patrick.
    CS2485.D53 2003
    929.4′0973—dc21

                                                                2003003844

Printing number: 9 8 7 6 5 4 3 2 1

Printed in the United States of America
on acid-free paper

EDITORIAL STAFF

CONTRIBUTORS AND CONSULTANTS

For Names from the British Isles

English	David Mills, Patrick Hanks, Kate Hardcastle
Welsh	Hywel Wyn Owen
Scottish	William Nicolaisen, Patrick Hanks
Irish	Kay Muhr
Scottish Gaelic	Kay Muhr

For Names from Western Europe

French	Susan Whitebook
German	Edda Gentry, Jürgen Eichhoff
Dutch	Charles Gehring

For Scandinavian and Finnish Names

Norwegian and Danish	Olav Veka
Swedish	Lena Peterson
Finnish	Hannele Jönsson-Korhola, Kate Moore

For Names from Southern Europe

Spanish and other Iberian Languages	Dieter Kremer, Roser Saurí Colomer
Italian	Enzo Caffarelli
Greek	Nick Nicholas, Johanna Kolleca

For Jewish Names

Jewish	Alexander Beider

For Slavic and East European Names

Polish	Aleksandra Cieślikowa
Czech	Dobrana Moldanová
Slovak	Peter Ďurčo
Russian and Ukrainian	Alexander Beider
Armenian	Bert Vaux
Slovenian	Simon Lenarčič
Croatian	Dunja Brozović
Serbian	Svetozar Stijović, Tvrtko Prćić
Hungarian	Gábor Bátonyi
Latvian and Lithuanian	Laimute Balode

For Names from the Middle East and Indian Subcontinent

Indian	Rocky Miranda
Muslim names	Salahuddin Ahmed
Arabic names	Paul Roochnik

For Names from East Asia

Chinese	Mark Lewellen
Japanese	Fred Brady
Korean	Gary Mackelprang

Genealogical Notes
Project team; Additional notes: Marion Harris, M. Tracey Ober

KEY TO THE DICTIONARY

*Consult the General Introduction and the essay
by D. Kenneth Tucker for further explanation.*

Main entry (one of the more than 70,000 surnames listed in DAFN)

Frequency of this surname in the sample of 88.7 million listings in the DAFN database

Explanation and etymology

Register (3259) English: perhaps from Middle English, Old French *registre* 'register', 'book for recording enactments', hence perhaps a metonymic occupational name for a scribe or clerk.

Surname type (e.g., occupational, habitational, patronymic, nickname)

Language or culture of origin

Regner (420) German: **1.** (Bavarian): habitational name for someone from Regen (a place on the Regen river, for which it is named). **2.** from a Germanic personal name composed of the elements *ragin* 'counsel' + *hari*, *heri* 'army'.
GIVEN NAMES German 4%. *Alois* (2), *Kurt* (2), *Erwin*, *Franz*, *Otto*.

Region where this surname probably originated

Gloss on the etymon (in single quotation marks)

Etymon (a word or element from which the surname is derived; in italics)

Regnier (926) French (**Régnier**): from the personal name *Régnier*, of Germanic origin (see RAYNER 1).

Cross-reference to a related main entry (in capital and small capital letters)

Forebear note for an early bearer of this surname in North America

FOREBEARS A Regnier from La Rochelle, France, is documented in Pointe-aux-Trembles, Quebec, in 1708, with the secondary surname BRION or Brillon.
GIVEN NAMES French 6%. *Lucien* (2), *Micheline* (2), *Pierre* (2), *Andre*, *Celestine*, *Felicie*, *Guilene*, *Marcel*, *Marcelle*, *Patrice*, *Romain*.

Selection of diagnostic given names from U.S. telephone directories

Number of occurrences of this diagnostic given name with this particular surname in the DAFN database

Rego (1493) **1.** Portuguese and Galician: habitational name from any of the numerous places in Portugal and Galicia called Rego, named with *rego* 'ditch', 'channel', 'furrow'. **2.** Dutch: from a Germanic personal name with the first element *ragin* 'counsel' + *guda* 'god', or *gōda* 'good', or *gauta* 'Goth'. **3.** Dutch: variant of REGA 2. **4.** Hungarian (**Regő**): occupational name for a musician or poet, from *rege* 'song', 'tale'.

Multiple origins

Alternate form in the language of origin (usually with diacritics)

Statistical confidence measure that this surname is in fact Spanish, based on analysis of the associated given names

GIVEN NAMES Spanish 15%; Portuguese 9%. *Manuel* (32), *Jose* (25), *Armando* (5), *Eduardo* (5), *Carlos* (4), *Fernando* (4), *Francisco* (4), *Ramon* (4), *Humberto* (3), *Juan* (3), *Luis* (3), *Mario* (3); *Joao* (5), *Duarte* (2), *Adauto*, *Albano*, *Goncalo*, *Guilherme*, *Serafim*.

Diagnostic given names grouped by language or cultural group (separated by semicolons)

Dictionary of
American Family
Names

O

O (122) Variant of Korean and Chinese OH.
GIVEN NAMES Chinese/Korean 70%. *Young* (3), *Bo Young, Chae, Chong Hwan, Dong Kun, Ho, Hwan, Hyun, Jong, Jung, Ki Soon, Kwang*; *Min* (3), *Chong* (2), *Chol, Jung Ho, Myong, Sa, Sung Kyun*.

Oachs (112) Respelling of German and Jewish OCHS.

Oak (383) **1.** English: topographic name for someone who lived near an oak tree or in an oak wood, from Middle English *oke* 'oak', also used in the singular in a collective sense. In some cases the surname may be a habitational name from minor places named with this word, such as Oake in Somerset. It is possible that it was sometimes also used as a nickname for someone 'as strong as oak'. **2.** Indian (Maharashtra): Hindu (Brahman) name of unknown meaning.
GIVEN NAMES Indian 9%. *Suresh* (2), *Anjali, Milind, Nutan, Pooja, Raj, Raji, Shaila, Shilpa, Shrikant, Sudhir, Uday*.

Oakes (6698) **1.** English: topographic name, a plural variant of OAK. **2.** Irish: Anglicized form of Gaelic **Mac Dubhdara** 'son of *Dubhdara*', a personal name composed of the elements *dubh* 'dark' + *dara(ch)*, genitive of *dair* 'oak', by translation of the main element of the Gaelic name.

Oakey (265) English: **1.** from an ancient Scandinavian personal name, *Aki* (Old Danish, Old Swedish *Áki*), derived from *anu-* 'ancestor' (unattested) + the diminutive suffix *-k*. **2.** topographic name for someone who lived by a small oakwood, from Middle English *oke* 'oak' + *heye* 'enclosure'.

Oakland (533) English: topographic name for someone who lived on a patch of land marked by an oak tree or trees, from Middle English *oke* 'oak' + *land* 'land'.

Oakleaf (167) Probably an Americanized (translated) form of Swedish **Eklöf** (see EKLOF).

Oakley (6481) English: habitational name from any of the numerous places in southern and central England named with the Old English elements *āc* 'oak' + *lēah* 'wood', 'clearing'.

Oakman (331) **1.** English: from an Old English personal name, *Ācmann*, composed of the elements *āc* 'oak' + *mann* 'man'. **2.** Probably a translated form of Swedish EKMAN.

Oaks (2464) **1.** English: variant spelling of OAKES. **2.** Americanized form of Jewish OCHS.

Oard (127) Variant spelling of northern English and Scottish ORD.

Oare (131) English: variant spelling of ORE.

Oas (301) Altered spelling of Norwegian **Aas, Ås**, habitational names from any of numerous farmsteads so named from Old Norse *áss* 'hill', 'ridge'.
GIVEN NAMES Scandinavian 9%. *Egil, Erik, Eyvind, Nels*.

Oates (3731) English: patronymic from the Middle English personal name *Ode* (see OTT).

Oathout (232) Altered spelling of Dutch **Oudhout**, unexplained.

Oatis (270) Altered spelling of OTIS, itself a variant of OATES.

Oatley (208) English: **1.** habitational name from Oteley in Ellesmere, Shropshire, named with Old English *āte* 'oats' + *lēah* 'wood', 'clearing'. **2.** variant of OAKLEY.

Oatman (644) Altered form of Dutch **Oudeman, Oudmans**, or **Outmans**, nicknames denoting an old man, though the last may also be a variant of **Houtman**, a habitational name for someone from a place named Ter Hout or a topographic name for someone who lived by a wood or copse, from Middle Dutch *houte* 'wood'.

Oats (270) English: variant spelling of OATES.

Oatts (100) **1.** English: variant spelling of OATES. **2.** Frenchified spelling of English WATTS.

Oba (130) Japanese (**Ōba**): meaning 'large garden', the name is found mostly in the Ryūkyū Islands. One family of samurai by this name lived in Sagami (now part of Kanagawa prefecture).
GIVEN NAMES Japanese 55%. *Keiji* (2), *Takashi* (2), *Akio, Etsuko, Hideki, Hisako, Katsuko, Kazuhito, Kazuko, Kengi, Kenichi, Kenji*.

Obando (252) Spanish: habitational name from Obando in Extremadura province.
GIVEN NAMES Spanish 50%. *Carlos* (7), *Jose* (6), *Manuel* (4), *Jaime* (3), *Juan* (3), *Julio* (3), *Luis* (3), *Mario* (3), *Ricardo* (3), *Roberto* (3), *Fernando* (2), *Jairo* (2).

O'Banion (695) Irish: Anglicized form of Gaelic **Ó Banáin** (see O'BANNON).

O'Bannon (915) Irish: Anglicized form of Gaelic **Ó Banáin** 'descendant of *Banán*', a personal name representing a diminutive of *ban* 'white' (see BANNON).

O'Bar (225) Variant spelling of Irish O'BARR.

Obara (221) **1.** Japanese: from a common place name meaning 'small plain'. Some bearers are descended from the SASAKI or TAKEDA families. **2.** Polish: nickname for an indecisive person, from *obarać się* 'to hesitate or waver'.
GIVEN NAMES Japanese 14%; Polish 5%. *Mako* (2), *Akira, Asako, Goro, Kayoko, Kazuto, Makoto, Nobuhiro, Noriko, Seiji, Shigeru, Shinji*; *Grzegorz* (2), *Janusz, Kazimiera*.

O'Barr (289) Americanized form of Irish **Ó Bairr**, a variant of **Ó Báire** (see BARRY), which in Ireland is often Anglicized as BARR.

O'Bear (105) Irish: probably a variant of O'BERRY.

Obee (111) **1.** English (Kent): unexplained. Perhaps a variant of French OBIE. Compare OBEY. **2.** Possibly also of German origin, an altered spelling of German **Obbe**, from a short form of the Germanic personal name *Obbert*.
GIVEN NAME German 5%. *Kurt* (2).

Obeid (109) Muslim: from a personal name based on Arabic *'ubayd* 'inferior servant'. It is found in combinations such as *Obeidullah* 'humble servant of Allah'.
GIVEN NAMES Muslim 42%; French 5%. *Ali* (3), *Omar* (3), *Fouad* (2), *Nabil* (2), *Abdou, Anis, Diya, Erfan, Ghassan, Haytham, Jalal, Khaled*; *Antoine, Camil*.

O'Beirne (252) Irish: Anglicized form of Gaelic **Ó Broin** 'descendant of *Bran*' (see BYRNE).
GIVEN NAMES Irish 11%. *Ciaran, Declan, Maeve, Ronan*.

Obenauer (129) German: topographic name for someone who lived by or owned a water meadow at the upper end of a village, or held land there, from *oben* 'up', 'above' + *Au* 'water meadow' (Middle High German *oben* 'up', 'above' + *ouwe* 'water meadow') + the suffix *-er*, denoting an inhabitant.

Obenauf (139) German: **1.** topographic name for someone who lived 'up there'. **2.** alternatively, it may be a nickname for an upstart or a go-getter, from the same word in the sense 'up on top'.
GIVEN NAME German 4%. *Otto*.

Obenchain (251) German: unexplained.

Obenhaus (131) German: ostensibly a topographic name for someone who lived in a house that was situated higher than others nearby, e.g. at the upper end of a village, from *oben* 'up', 'above' + *Haus* 'house' (Middle High German *oben(e)* 'up', 'above' + *hūs* 'house'). However, it may actually be a hypercorrected form of **Obenaus**, a nickname for an upstart, a reduced form of *oben hinaus* (*oben* 'up', 'above' + *hinaus* 'out', indicating direction).
GIVEN NAME German 7%. *Otto* (2).

Obenour (130) Altered spelling of German OBENAUER.

Obenshain (156) Variant of OBENCHAIN.

Ober (1513) **1.** English: unexplained. **2.** South German: topographic name for someone who lived at the upper end of a village on a hill, from Middle High German *ober*, *obar* 'above'. In other cases, it may have denoted someone who lived on an upper floor of a building with two or more floors. **3.** North German: topographic for someone who lived on the bank of a river or stream name, standardized from Middle Low German *over* 'river bank'. **4.** Possibly a shortened form of any of various German compound names formed with *Ober-* (see entries below). **5.** Jewish (Ashkenazic): from German *Ober* 'senior', 'chief'. In some cases it can denote a rabbi; in others it is ornamental.
FOREBEARS A 17th-century American bearer of this name, Richard Ober (1641–1715/16), emigrated from Abbotsbury, Dorset, England, to the Salem colony and settled in Mackerel Cove, MA, later Beverly. His descendant Frederick Albion Ober, who was born in Beverly, MA, in 1849, was an ornithologist who discovered 22 new species of birds in the Lesser Antilles, the flycatcher *Myiarchus oberi*, and oriole *Icterus oberi*.

Oberbeck (183) German: **1.** topographic name from North German **Overbeck**, from Middle Low German *over de beke* 'across the creek'. **2.** distinguishing name for a baker (see BECK) who lived in the upper part of a village (see OBER).

Oberbroeckling (146) German (**Oberbröckling**): unexplained.

Oberdick (127) Variant of North German **Oberdieck**, a topographic name for someone who lived 'over the dike', from *ober* (standardized High German form of Low German *over*) + Low German *die(c)k* 'dike'.

Oberdorf (188) German: **1.** from a habitational name from any of several places so named in all parts of Germany. **2.** topographic name for someone who lived at the upper part of a village, from *ober* 'up', 'above' + *Dorf* 'village'.
GIVEN NAMES German 4%. *Bernd, Heinz.*

Oberg (2334) **1.** Americanized spelling of Swedish **Åberg** (see ABERG). **2.** Swedish

(**Öberg**): ornamental name composed of *ö* 'island' + *berg* 'mountain', 'hill'. **3.** German: habitational name from Oberg near Peine in Lower Saxony.
GIVEN NAMES Scandinavian 5%. *Erik* (7), *Nils* (2), *Thor* (2), *Ejnar, Hild, Lars, Nels, Sigfrid, Sven.*

Obergfell (122) German: perhaps a reduced form of the topographic name **Oberbergfels** 'upper mountain peak'.

Oberhaus (161) German: habitational name from either of two places named Oberhaus, in Rhineland and Bavaria, or a variant of OBERHAUSEN.
GIVEN NAMES German 4%. *Eldor, Erwin.*

Oberhausen (131) German: from any of numerous places named Oberhausen, literally 'upper houses'.

Oberhauser (127) German: habitational name for someone from a place called OBERHAUS or OBERHAUSEN.

Oberhelman (157) German (**Oberhellmann**): topographic name for someone who lived at the upper part of a wild and steep tract of land, from *ober* 'upper' + *Hell* (Middle High German *ober* 'upper' + *helle* 'hell', also 'steep, wild terrain') + *Mann* 'man'.

Oberholtzer (751) German: from Middle High German *ober* 'above' (or German *ober-* 'upper') + *holz* 'wood' + the suffix *-er*, denoting an inhabitant, a topographic name for someone who lived above a wood or on the far side of it, or alternatively a habitational name for someone who lived in a place known as Oberholtz ('upper wood').

Oberholzer (165) German: variant spelling of OBERHOLTZER.

Oberlander (790) German (**Oberländer**) and Jewish (Ashkenazic): topographic or habitational name from *Oberland*, meaning 'higher land', especially in the Alps, where it refers to a settled plateau above the valley bottom.
GIVEN NAMES Jewish 5%. *Sholem* (3), *Chaim* (2), *Moshe* (2), *Amnon, Amron, Benzion, Hadassa, Heshy, Miriam, Moishe, Mordchai, Sima.*

Oberle (947) German and Swiss German: **1.** from an Alemannic pet form of the personal name ALBRECHT. **2.** topographic name for someone who lived at the upper end of or above a settlement, from Middle High German *ober* 'upper one' + the diminutive suffix *-ele*.

Oberley (120) Respelling of German and Swiss OBERLE.

Oberlies (120) Probably German: unexplained.

Oberlin (653) German (mainly Swiss) and French (Alsace): from an Alemannic pet form of the German personal name ALBRECHT.

Oberly (290) Swiss German: variant of OBERLE.

Oberman (623) **1.** Jewish (Ashkenazic): elaborated form of OBER. **2.** German: variant of OBERMANN.
GIVEN NAMES Jewish 4%. *Dorit, Hershel, Isaak, Izya, Moshe, Yael.*

Obermann (148) German: **1.** topographic name from German *ober* 'upper', 'above' (see OBER), with the addition of *man* 'man'. This may have referred to someone living in an upper part of a village or to someone living on an upper story of an apartment block. **2.** status name for an overseer or arbitrator.

Obermark (110) German: topographic name from Middle High German *ober* 'upper' + *merc* 'boundary', 'fenced-off area'.

Obermeier (383) German: variant spelling of OBERMEYER.
GIVEN NAMES German 7%. *Klaus* (2), *Kurt* (2), *Manfred* (2), *Alfons, Irmgard.*

Obermeyer (621) German: distinguishing name for the tenant farmer (see MEYER) of the upper farm in a settlement (see OBER).

Obermiller (334) Partly Americanized form of German **Obermüller**, a topographic name for the miller at the 'upper mill'.

O'Berry (577) Irish: Anglicized form of Gaelic **Ó Béara** 'descendant of *Béara*', a personal name of unexplained origin.

Oberst (554) German: topographic name for someone who lived at the highest part of a village on a hillside, from Middle High German *obrist* 'uppermost' (later *oberst*), superlative form of OBER.

Oberstein (105) German: topographic name from Middle High German *ober* 'upper' + *stein* 'rock', 'stone'.

Obert (902) **1.** German (Swiss): variant of ALBERT. **2.** Dutch: from a Germanic personal name composed of Old High German *ōt*, 'wealth' + *berht* 'bright', 'famous'.

Oberto (141) Italian (chiefly Piedmont): from a personal name of Germanic origin, of which the medieval Latinate forms were *O(t)bertus, Ubertus.*

Obey (223) English: unexplained. Compare OBEE, of which this is probably a variant.

Obi (164) Japanese: written with characters meaning 'small tail', the name could possibly mean 'sash' as well. It is not common in Japan, and could be habitational, from a castle in Hyūga (now Miyazaki prefecture), though the castle's name was written with different characters.
GIVEN NAMES Japanese 5%. *Hideo* (2), *Naoki.*

Obie (202) French: altered spelling of **Aubé** (see AUBE) or of **Auby**, a southern variant of the personal name **Aubin** (Latin *Albinus*).
GIVEN NAMES French 7%. *Armand, Cecile, Marcel, Normand.*

Obier (134) French (Périgord): probably a variant of **Aubier**: **1.** from a Germanic personal name composed of the elements *albh* 'elf' + *heri, hari* 'army'. **2.** topographic name for someone who lived where white poplars grew, from Latin *albarius*, a derivative of *albus* 'white'.

Oblak (187) Slovenian: nickname from *oblak* 'cloud', probably denoting an ill-humored or gloomy person.

Oblander (144) German: topographic name for an upland dweller, from Middle High German *ob(e)* 'up', 'above' + *lant* 'land', 'terrain' + the suffix *-er* denoting an inhabitant. Compare OBERLANDER.

Oblinger (195) **1.** Swiss German: habitational name for someone from Oblikon, near Zürich. **2.** possibly a variant of **Obleier** 'almoner', someone who was in charge of the so-called *obleie* 'alms', contributions for spiritual purposes, from Late Latin *oblegium* 'offering'.
GIVEN NAME German 4%. *Kurt.*

Oborn (148) English (Somerset, Wiltshire, Dorset): unexplained.

Oborny (103) Origin unidentified.

O'Boyle (1311) Irish: Anglicized form of Gaelic **Ó Baoighill** 'descendant of *Baoigheall*' (see BOYLE).
GIVEN NAMES Irish 8%. *Seamus, Siobhan.*

Obradovich (216) Serbian (**Obradović**): patronymic from the personal name *Obrad*, a derivative of *obradovati* 'to give joy'.
GIVEN NAMES South Slavic 17%; Jewish 4%. *Milan* (4), *Aleksandar, Darinka, Dragan, Mihajlo, Milenko, Novak, Predrag, Radmilo, Radomir, Vojin, Zdravko; Miriam.*

Obray (116) English: variant of AUBREY.

Obrecht (367) **1.** German (Swiss): variant of ALBERT. **2.** Dutch: variant of OBERT 2.

Obregon (626) Spanish (**Obregón**): habitational name from Obregón in Santander province.
GIVEN NAMES Spanish 47%. *Jose* (15), *Carlos* (11), *Mario* (8), *Pedro* (8), *Juan* (7), *Arturo* (5), *Francisco* (4), *Jesus* (4), *Jorge* (4), *Roberto* (4), *Ruben* (4), *Alfonso* (3).

Obremski (215) Polish (also **Obrębski**) and Jewish (eastern Ashkenazic): habitational name for someone from any of the places called Obręb in Ciechanów, Siedlce, and Tarnobrzeg voivodeships, or from Obręby (*Obremby*, now in Lithuania), named with *obręb* 'precinct', 'sphere'.
GIVEN NAMES Polish 5%. *Karol, Zigmund, Zigmunt.*

O'Brian (870) Irish: variant spelling of O'BRIEN.
GIVEN NAME Irish 5%. *Liam.*

O'Briant (522) Irish: variant of O'BRIEN.

O'Brien (49025) Irish: Anglicized form of Gaelic **Ó Briain** 'descendant of *Brian*', a personal name probably based on the element *bre-* 'hill', with the transferred sense 'eminence', i.e. 'exalted one'. See also BRYAN. In Ireland there has also been some confusion with O'BYRNE (see BYRNE).
FOREBEARS This name is borne in particular by one of the greatest of Irish septs, descendants of Brian Boru, who rose to the high kingship of Ireland in 1002.

GIVEN NAMES Irish 6%. *Brendan* (34), *Dermot* (10), *Liam* (8), *Brigid* (5), *Declan* (5), *Donovan* (5), *John Patrick* (5), *Kieran* (5), *Colm* (4), *Donal* (4), *Brennan* (3), *Caitlin* (3).

Obringer (196) German: of uncertain origin: **1.** perhaps a habitational or topographic name of unidentified origin. **2.** alternatively, perhaps a variant of OBLINGER.

O'Brion (133) Irish: variant spelling of O'BRIEN.

Obrist (149) Swiss German: variant of OBERST.
GIVEN NAMES German 6%. *Fritz, Otto.*

Obrochta (136) Polish: Polonized form of German ALBRECHT.
GIVEN NAMES Polish 7%. *Wladyslaw* (2), *Eugeniusz.*

O'Bryan (2318) Irish: variant spelling of O'BRIEN.
GIVEN NAMES Irish 4%. *James Patrick, Padraic.*

O'Bryant (1270) Irish: variant of O'BRIEN.

O'Bryon (134) Irish: variant of O'BRIEN.
GIVEN NAME Irish 7%. *William Kevin.*

Obrzut (113) Polish: nickname from *obrzut* 'discontent'.
GIVEN NAME Polish 4%. *Wojciech.*

Obst (272) Eastern German (Silesia) and Jewish (Ashkenazic): from Middle High German *obez*, German *Obst* 'fruit', hence a metonymic occupational name for a fruit grower or seller, or perhaps a nickname. As a Jewish name, it may be of ornamental origin.
GIVEN NAMES German 6%. *Wolfgang* (3), *Armin, Manfred.*

Obuchowski (142) Polish and Ukrainian: habitational name for someone from Obuchowo in Suwałki and Olsztyn voivodeships, or from Obuchów, which is now in Lithuania, or (as a Ukrainian name) from Obukhov near Kiev. These places are named from the nickname *Obuch*, which is from the vocabulary word *obuch* 'back of an axe'.
GIVEN NAMES Polish 7%. *Casimir, Ignacy.*

O'Byrne (493) Irish: Anglicized form of Gaelic **Ó Broin** (see BYRNE).
GIVEN NAMES Irish 7%. *Brendan, Ciaran, Cormac, Grainne.*

O'Cain (307) Irish: reduced form of O'CALLAGHAN.

O'Callaghan (1129) Irish: from Gaelic **Ó Ceallacháin** 'descendant of *Ceallachán*', a diminutive of the personal name *Ceallach*, possibly meaning 'lover of churches', from *ceall* 'church', or (more likely) 'bright-headed', from *cen* 'head' + *lach* 'light'. This name was borne by a 10th-century king of Munster, from whom many present-day bearers of the surname claim descent.
GIVEN NAMES Irish 10%. *Liam* (4), *Dermot* (2), *Donal* (2), *Kiernan* (2), *Niall* (2), *Conor, Donovan, John Patrick, Kieran, Siobhan, Tiernan.*

O'Callahan (128) Irish: Anglicized form of Gaelic **Ó Ceallacháin** (see CALLAHAN).

Ocampo (1728) Galician: topographic name meaning 'the field', from the Galician definite article *o* (masculine singular) + *campo* 'field' (Latin *campus*), or habitational name from a town of this name in Lugo province, Galicia.
GIVEN NAMES Spanish 54%. *Jose* (37), *Carlos* (21), *Juan* (21), *Roberto* (16), *Luis* (15), *Francisco* (14), *Jesus* (13), *Manuel* (12), *Pedro* (11), *Jorge* (10), *Armando* (9), *Cesar* (9); *Antonio* (14), *Dario* (2), *Leonardo* (2), *Lorenzo* (2), *Romeo* (2), *Amadeo, Caesar, Carmel, Ciro, Clemente, Constantino, Dino.*

Ocana (198) Spanish (**Ocaña**): habitational name from Ocaña in Toledo province.
GIVEN NAMES Spanish 47%. *Juan* (6), *Jose* (3), *Raul* (3), *Angel* (2), *Blanca* (2), *Carlos* (2), *Javier* (2), *Jesus* (2), *Jorge* (2), *Manuel* (2), *Marta* (2), *Miguel* (2); *Marco* (2), *Antonio, Lorenzo.*

Ocanas (140) Spanish (**Ocañas**): apparently a variant of OCANA.
GIVEN NAMES Spanish 50%. *Jose* (4), *Enrique* (3), *Gilberto* (3), *Manuel* (3), *Carlos* (2), *Eleazar* (2), *Jorge* (2), *Juan* (2), *Juanita* (2), *Leticia* (2), *Ruben* (2), *Adriana.*

O'Carroll (219) Irish: Anglicized form of Gaelic **Ó Cearbhaill** 'descendant of *Cearbhall*' (see CARROLL). This is the name of several different Irish families.
GIVEN NAMES Irish 26%. *Brendan* (3), *Donal* (2), *Cian, Cormac, Fergus, Finbarr, James Patrick, Jarlath, John Patrick, Sinead, Siobhan.*

Ocasio (869) Hispanic (mainly Puerto Rico): apparently from Spanish *ocasión* 'time', 'occasion', but the meaning as a surname is unexplained.
GIVEN NAMES Spanish 44%. *Jose* (23), *Luis* (19), *Angel* (15), *Juan* (15), *Miguel* (11), *Ramon* (8), *Carlos* (6), *Francisco* (6), *Ruben* (6), *Ricardo* (5), *Wilfredo* (5), *Ana* (4).

Occhino (136) Italian: nickname for a one-eyed man or for someone with otherwise remarkable eyes, from a derivative of *occhio* 'eye' (Latin *oc(u)lus*).
GIVEN NAMES Italian 18%; Spanish 6%. *Antonio* (2), *Giovanni* (2), *Sebastiano* (2), *Carmela, Carmelo, Concetta, Filippo, Gaetano; Alicia, Jose, Placido, Victorio.*

Occhiogrosso (108) Italian: descriptive nickname meaning 'big eye'.
GIVEN NAMES Italian 17%. *Angelo* (2), *Gaetano, Vito.*

Occhipinti (455) Italian (Sicily): nickname from *occhi* 'eyes' + *pinti* 'painted', denoting someone with dark eyelashes or with flecked or blood-shot eyes.
GIVEN NAMES Italian 22%. *Salvatore* (5), *Angelo* (4), *Rosario* (4), *Sal* (4), *Cosimo* (2), *Saverio* (2), *Antonio, Carlo, Carmelo, Concetta, Concetto, Domenic, Emanuele, Mario.*

Ocegueda (150) Hispanic (Mexico): variant of the habitational name OSEGUERA. Compare OCEGUERA, OSEGUEDA.

GIVEN NAMES Spanish 61%. *Jesus* (4), *Jose* (4), *Carlos* (3), *Francisco* (3), *Javier* (3), *Rafael* (3), *Alberto* (2), *Alfredo* (2), *Fernando* (2), *Joaquin* (2), *Juan* (2), *Miguel* (2).

Ocegueda (180) Hispanic (Mexico): variant of the habitational name OSEGUERA. Compare OCEGUEDA, OSEGUEDA.

GIVEN NAMES Spanish 65%. *Jose* (9), *Juan* (9), *Jesus* (6), *Ramon* (4), *Carlos* (3), *Rafael* (3), *Salvador* (3), *Alejandro* (2), *Alfredo* (2), *Arturo* (2), *Blanca* (2), *Jaime* (2).

Och (181) **1.** German (southern and Silesian): variant of ACH. **2.** Belgian (**van Och**): habitational name for someone from Ogbrugga in Mark (East Flanders), or Ogmolen or Ogpoort in Sint-Renelde (Brabant).

Ocheltree (325) Scottish: variant of OGLE-TREE.

Ochman (114) Polish spelling of German **Achmann** 'water bailiff'.

GIVEN NAMES Polish 9%; French 4%. *Andrzej, Fryderyk; Armand, Cecile.*

Ochoa (6326) Spanish (of Basque origin): Castilianized form of the Basque personal name *Otxoa*, equivalent of Latin *lupus* 'wolf'.

GIVEN NAMES Spanish 51%. *Jose* (188), *Jesus* (85), *Juan* (84), *Carlos* (74), *Manuel* (70), *Luis* (53), *Francisco* (47), *Jorge* (45), *Javier* (37), *Rafael* (37), *Roberto* (33), *Raul* (32).

Ochocki (105) Polish: habitational name from a place called Ochota, now a suburb of Warsaw, or Ochociće in Piotrków voivodeship, named with the vocabulary word *ochota* 'willingness'.

GIVEN NAMES Polish 9%. *Jerzy, Wieslaw, Wojciech.*

Ochs (2535) German and Jewish (Ashkenazic): from German *Ochs* 'ox', Middle High German *ohse*; probably a nickname for a strong or lumbering individual, or a metonymic occupational name for someone who tended or drove oxen, or for a cattle dealer. In some cases the surname was a habitational name derived from an inn sign. As a Jewish name it is often ornamental.

FOREBEARS The *New York Times* publisher Adolph Simon Ochs (1858–1935), of German-Jewish stock, was a second-generation immigrant whose father, Julius Ochs, had come over from Fürth in Bavaria, Germany, in 1845 and settled in Louisville, KY, in the early 1800s.

Ochsner (863) German (also **Öchsner**): occupational name for someone who looked after or worked with oxen, from an agent derivative of Middle High German *ohse* 'ox'.

Ocken (103) German (Frisian): nickname or patronymic from an altered form of the personal name *Odeke*.

GIVEN NAME German 4%. *Lorenz.*

Ockenfels (101) German: habitational name from Ockenfels in Rhineland-Palatinate.

Ocker (489) German: **1.** topographic name for someone living by the Ocker river in the Harz Mountains, which perhaps derives its name from a Celtic word for 'salmon', cognate with Cornish *ehoc*. **2.** (**Öcker**): patronymic from a pet form of the personal name *Odo, Otto* (see OTT).

Ockerman (271) **1.** Dutch: topographic name, derived from a misdivision of *van den nokere* 'from the nut (tree)' (Middle Dutch *noker*) + *man* 'man'. **2.** Dutch: variant of **Ackerman**, from *akker* 'field' + *man* 'man', a topographic name, or an occupational name for a farmer. **3.** German (**Ockermann**): variant of OCKER 1.

Ockert (140) German: **1.** obscene nickname from Middle High German *ocker* 'penis'. **2.** variant of OCKER 1.

GIVEN NAME German 5%. *Otto.*

Oclair (240) Altered spelling of French AUCLAIR.

GIVEN NAMES French 4%. *Armand, Rolande.*

Ocon (234) Spanish (**Ocón**): habitational name from Ocón in La Rioja province, or possibly in some cases from Villafranca de Ocón in Burgos province.

GIVEN NAMES Spanish 42%. *Jose* (8), *Francisco* (4), *Alberto* (3), *Ernesto* (3), *Fernando* (3), *Jesus* (3), *Juan* (3), *Manuel* (3), *Guillermo* (2), *Jorge* (2), *Luis* (2), *Aida.*

O'Connell (15220) Irish: Anglicized form of Gaelic **Ó Conaill** 'descendant of *Conall*', a personal name, possibly composed of the elements *con*, from *cú* 'hound' or 'wolf' (genitive *con*) + *gal* 'valour'. It was borne by many early chieftains and warriors of Ireland, including the Ulster hero Conall Cearnach, one of the two sons of Niall of the Nine Hostages, who gave his name to Tirconell, otherwise known as Donegal. It was further popularized by the fame of a 7th-century Irish saint, abbot of Inis Caoil.

GIVEN NAMES Irish 6%. *Brendan* (16), *Liam* (7), *Donal* (3), *Finbarr* (3), *Malachy* (3), *Seamus* (2), *William Sean* (2), *Aileen, Aisling, Brian Patrick, Colm, Dermot.*

O'Conner (1453) Irish: variant spelling of O'CONNOR.

GIVEN NAMES Irish 5%. *Brendan, Finbarr.*

O'Connor (30953) Irish (Derry, Connacht, Munster): Anglicized form of Gaelic **Ó Conchobhair** 'descendant of *Conchobhar*', a personal name which is said to have begun as *Cú Chobhair*, from *cú* 'hound' (genitive *con*) + *cobhar* 'desiring', i.e. 'hound of desire'. Present-day bearers of the surname claim descent from a 10th-century king of Connacht of this name. In

Irish legend, Conchobhar was a king of Ulster who lived at around the time of Christ and who adopted the youthful Cú Chulainn.

GIVEN NAMES Irish 6%. *Brendan* (32), *Siobhan* (7), *Donal* (6), *Aileen* (5), *Kieran* (5), *Aidan* (4), *Colm* (4), *Fitzgerald* (4), *Liam* (4), *Caitlin* (3), *Eamon* (3), *Niall* (3).

O'Conor (183) Irish: variant spelling of O'CONNOR.

Oczkowski (124) Polish: habitational name for someone from Oczków in Bielsko-Biała voivodeship or Oczkowice in Leszno voivodeship, named with *oczko* 'little eye' 'eyelet'.

GIVEN NAMES Polish 11%. *Boguslaw, Henryk, Wladyslaw.*

Oda (613) Japanese: common place name and surname throughout Japan, meaning 'small rice paddy'. A less common but more famous Oda name, written with characters meaning 'woven rice paddy' (i.e. fields laid out evenly as woven cloth), was borne by the family of the famous conqueror Oda Nobunaga (1534–1582). Their name is taken from two Shintō shrines in Fukui prefecture; so an added meaning would be 'august rice paddy', denoting respect shown to a shrine's property.

GIVEN NAMES Japanese 42%. *Kenji* (4), *Kazuo* (3), *Kiyoshi* (3), *Tadashi* (3), *Hiromi* (2), *Hiroyuki* (2), *Iwao* (2), *Mayumi* (2), *Noboru* (2), *Nobuaki* (2), *Ryoko* (2), *Satoshi* (2).

O'Daniel (1052) Irish: variant of O'DONNELL, influenced by the Biblical name DANIEL, to which it is etymologically unrelated.

O'Day (2996) Irish: Anglicized form of Gaelic **Ó Deaghaidh** (see O'DEA).

GIVEN NAMES Irish 6%. *Brendan* (3), *Eamon, Sean Patrick, William Kevin.*

Odden (333) Norwegian: habitational name from any of numerous farmsteads, so named from the definite singular form of *odde*, from Old Norse *oddi* 'headland'.

GIVEN NAMES Scandinavian 4%. *Alf, Lars.*

Oddi (140) Italian: patronymic or plural form of ODDO.

GIVEN NAMES Italian 12%. *Concetta, Enio, Gino, Giovanni, Rocco.*

Oddo (950) Italian: from the Germanic personal name *Od(d)o, Otto* (see OTT).

GIVEN NAMES Italian 15%. *Salvatore* (11), *Vito* (7), *Angelo* (3), *Giuseppe* (3), *Annamarie* (2), *Antonio* (2), *Nicola* (2), *Sal* (2), *Santo* (2), *Alfonse, Baldassare, Carlo.*

Oddy (153) English: from the Middle English personal name *Ode* (see OTT).

Ode (170) **1.** North German: from a short form of the various Germanic personal names composed with *Ode* (see OTT), for example *Odebert, Oderich, Odeger.* **2.** Swedish: unexplained.

GIVEN NAME Scandinavian 4%. *Helmer.*

O'Dea (1253) Irish: Anglicized form of Gaelic **Ó Deaghaidh**, 'descendant of

Deaghadh', a personal name of uncertain origin. It may be a compound of *deagh-* 'good' + *ádh* 'luck', 'fate'.

GIVEN NAMES Irish 7%. *Brendan, Conor, Declan, Fergus, Maeve, Murphy.*

O'Dean (125) Irish: Anglicized form of Gaelic **Ó Déaghain** 'descendant of the deacon'.

Odegaard (596) Norwegian: habitational name from any of numerous farmsteads, chiefly in eastern Norway, named *Øygard, Øygarden, Ødegård, Ødegaard*, from *øyde* 'deserted' + *gård* 'enclosure', 'farm'. These, for the most part, are farmsteads that were left deserted after the Black Death of 1349.

GIVEN NAMES Scandinavian 11%. *Audun* (2), *Erik* (2), *Knute* (2), *Nils* (2), *Ordell* (2), *Alf, Fredrik, Helmer, Hjalmer, Iver, Lars, Per.*

Odegard (736) Variant spelling of Norwegian ODEGAARD.

GIVEN NAMES Scandinavian 4%. *Bernt, Erik, Gudrun, Helmer, Nils, Thorvald.*

Odeh (132) Muslim: probably a variant of Arabic *'Ā'idah* 'returning visitor'.

GIVEN NAMES Muslim 69%. *Munir* (3), *Sami* (3), *Bashar* (2), *Ibrahim* (2), *Jamel* (2), *Mohamad* (2), *Naser* (2), *Ziad* (2), *Abdalla, Abdel, Alaa, Ali.*

Odekirk (181) Dutch: habitational name of German origin, from Odenkirchen near Rheydt (North Rhine-Westphalia), or from Adinkerke, the spelling *Odekirk* being a reflection of the local pronunciation.

Odell (11610) English: **1.** habitational name from a place in Bedfordshire, also called Woodhill, from Old English *wād* 'woad' (a plant collected for the blue dye that could be obtained from it) + *hyll* 'hill'. Compare WADDELL. **2.** (**O'Dell**) of the same origin as 1, but altered by folk etymology as if of Irish origin.

Odem (228) German: variant of ADAM.

Oden (2492) **1.** North German and Dutch: patronymic from the personal name *Odo* (see OTT, or possibly a metronymic from *Oda*, a feminine form of the name). **2.** Swedish (**Odén**): ornamental name composed of the unexplained element *Od-* + the common surname suffix *-én*, from Latin *-enius.*

Odenbach (123) German: habitational name from Odenbach in Rhineland-Palatinate or in some cases possibly from Ödenbach in Baden-Württemberg.

GIVEN NAMES German 6%. *Fritz, Wolfgang.*

Odendahl (151) German: variant of ODENTHAL.

GIVEN NAMES German 10%. *Kurt* (2), *Otto* (2).

Odenthal (169) German: habitational name from Odenthal northeast of Cologne, formerly named *Udendar*, from a prehistoric creek name, *Udandra.*

GIVEN NAMES German 5%. *Gerhard, Kurt, Theodor.*

Odenwald (144) German: regional name for someone from the Odenwald mountains (between the rivers Main and Neckar).

GIVEN NAMES German 9%; Scandinavian 4%. *Kurt* (2), *Uwe*; *Sten.*

Odenweller (108) German: variant of **Odenwälder**, presumably a habitational name for someone from a place named Odenwald.

GIVEN NAME German 4%. *Liesl* (2).

Oder (373) **1.** German: from the river of this name in central Europe, denoting someone who lived on its banks. **2.** German (**Öder**): variant of EDER. **3.** Jewish (Ashkenazic): possibly as in 1, or from a western or northeastern Yiddish pronunciation of *adar*, the name of a month of the Jewish calendar. This is considered a happy time of year mainly because the festival of Purim is celebrated during this month and because Jewish tradition has it that Moses was born in this month.

Odermatt (103) Swiss German: Alemannic form of the habitational name **Andermatt**.

GIVEN NAMES French 9%; German 4%. *Andre, Gabrielle, Michel; Othmar.*

Odette (367) Probably an altered spelling of French **Odet**, from a pet form of the personal name *Odo* (see OTT).

Odgers (303) English: patronymic from *Odger*, from a continental Germanic equivalent of the personal name EDGAR, brought to England by the Normans.

Odham (119) English: variant of ODOM, altered by folk etymology as if derived from a place name formed with *-ham.*

Odierno (105) Italian: from the personal name *Odierno*, which is of uncertain origin, perhaps a nickname from Latin *hodiernus* 'of today', i.e. 'transient' or 'ephemeral'.

Odiorne (187) English: from an Old French feminine personal name, *Odierne, Hodierne*, from Germanic *Audigerna.*

Odland (285) Norwegian: habitational name from any of several farmsteads in Rogaland and Hordaland named Odland, from Old Norse *Árland*, a compound of *á* 'small river' (or another first element of uncertain origin) + *land* 'land', 'farm'.

GIVEN NAMES Scandinavian 6%. *Erik* (2), *Bjarne, Einar, Inger, Ingvald, Ole.*

Odle (1487) English (Surrey): possibly a variant of ODELL.

Odneal (176) Origin uncertain. Perhaps an irregular variant of Irish O'NEILL.

O'Doherty (626) Irish (Donegal): Anglicized form of Gaelic **Ó Dochartaigh** 'descendant of *Dochartach*' (see DOHERTY).

GIVEN NAMES Irish 23%. *Dermot* (3), *Liam* (3), *Eamonn* (2), *Brendan, Cathal, Donal, Fergal, Fergus, Niall, Paddy.*

Odom (11159) English: nickname for someone who had done well for himself by marrying the daughter of a prominent figure in the local community, from Middle English *odam* 'son-in-law' (Old English *āðum*).

Odoms (224) English: patronymic from ODOM.

O'Donald (178) Variant of Irish O'DONNELL, altered by influence of DONALD.

O'Donnel (155) Irish: variant spelling of O'DONNELL.

O'Donnell (17583) Irish (Donegal, Munster): Anglicized form of Gaelic **Ó Domhnaill** 'descendant of *Domhnall*' (see MCDONNELL). This name is borne by several different Irish families.

GIVEN NAMES Irish 6%. *Brendan* (19), *Brigid* (4), *Niall* (3), *Siobhan* (3), *Brennan* (2), *Bridie* (2), *Declan* (2), *Donal* (2), *Fergus* (2), *Jarlath* (2), *John Patrick* (2), *Padraic* (2).

O'Donoghue (722) Irish: Anglicized form of Gaelic **Ó Donnchadha** 'descendant of *Donnchadh*' (see DONAHUE).

GIVEN NAMES Irish 14%. *Brendan* (4), *Conor* (2), *Brigid, Eoin, Finbarr, Kieran, Mavourneen, Ronan, Siobhan, William Sean.*

O'Donohue (253) Irish: variant spelling of O'DONOGHUE.

O'Donovan (463) Irish: Anglicized form of Gaelic **Ó Donndubháin** 'descendant of *Donndubhán*' (see DONOVAN).

GIVEN NAMES Irish 13%. *Aidan, Aileen, Brendan, Colm, Cormac, Declan, Donal, Finbarr, Grainne, Kieran.*

Odor (177) Hungarian (**Ódor**): from the Hungarian personal name *Ódor*, a derivative of German *Oldrich*, Old High German *Odalrīc* (see ULRICH).

Odorizzi (133) Italian: from a variant of the Germanic personal name *Odorisio.*

GIVEN NAMES Italian 5%. *Leno, Ottavio.*

O'Dowd (709) Irish (Connacht and Ulster): Anglicized form of Gaelic **Ó Dubhda** 'descendant of *Dubhda*' (see DOWD).

GIVEN NAMES Irish 9%. *Cathal, Clancy, Eamon, Eamonn, Padraig, Ronan.*

O'Driscoll (530) Irish (western Cork): Anglicized form of Gaelic **Ó hEidirsceóil** 'descendant of the messenger' (see DRISCOLL).

GIVEN NAMES Irish 10%. *Donal* (3), *Colm, Conor, Liam.*

Odum (1426) Probably an altered spelling of English ODOM.

O'Dwyer (530) Southern Irish: Anglicized form of Gaelic **Ó Duibhuidhir** 'descendant of *Duibhuidhir*' (see DWYER).

GIVEN NAMES Irish 10%. *Aidan, Dermot, Eamonn, Kieran, Padraic, Ronan, Seamus.*

Oe (23) Japanese (**Ōe**): variously written, usually with characters meaning 'large inlet'; found mostly in western Japan and the Ryūkyūan island of Yaeyama. An ancient family of scholars and statesmen, one branch is ancestral to the MORI clan of Chōshū (now part of Yamaguchi prefecture). Listed in the Shinsen shōjiroku.

Oechsle (183) South German (**Öchsle**): from a diminutive of OCHS.

GIVEN NAMES German 4%. *Alois, Dieter.*

Oechsner (141) German (**Öchsner**): variant of OCHSNER.

Oeding (114) German: from a derivative of the personal name *Ode*, a short form of any of the various personal names beginning with *Ode* (for example, *Odebert*, *Oderich*, *Odewin*).
GIVEN NAMES German 5%. *Ernst, Jurgen.*

Oehl (123) German (**Öhl**): 1. short form of the personal name ULRICH. 2. possibly a habitational name from Oehle in Baden. 3. possibly a shortened form of any of various compound names or derivatives, e.g. **Öhlschäger, Oehlhoff, Oehlerking, Oehlerich**.
GIVEN NAMES German 7%. *Frieda, Ute, Wilhelm.*

Oehler (904) South German (**Öhler**): 1. occupational name, a variant of OHLER. 2. from a short form of a personal name formed with Old Saxon *ōd* 'possession'.
GIVEN NAMES German 5%. *Kurt* (2), *Bernd, Bodo, Eugen, Franz, Gerhard, Hans, Otto, Reinhold, Sieglinde.*

Oehlerking (139) German (**Öhlerking**): patronymic from the personal name *Öhlerke*, a derivative of *Ohlerich* (a variant of ULRICH).
GIVEN NAMES German 7%. *Erwin, Fritz, Gunter, Otto.*

Oehlert (214) German (**Öhlert**): from a reduced form of the personal name *Odalhard*, a personal name composed wih Old Saxon *ōd* 'possession'.

Oehlke (161) North German (**Öhlke**): from a pet form of OHL.
GIVEN NAMES German 4%. *Berthold, Ewald.*

Oehm (109) German: variant of OHM.
GIVEN NAME German 7%. *Ernst* (2).

Oehme (125) North German (**Öhme**): variant of OMMEN.
GIVEN NAMES German 14%. *Heinz* (2), *Gunter, Hans, Otto, Reinhard, Wolfgang.*

Oehmke (115) North German (**Öhmke**): from a diminutive of OMMEN.

Oehrlein (174) German (**Öhrlein**): 1. nickname, from a diminutive of OHR. 2. pet form of *Aurelius* (saint's name).

Oei (101) Malaysian or Indonesian: unexplained.
GIVEN NAMES Southeast Asian 19%. *Heng* (2), *Chun, Geng, Han, Hoo, Ik, Ming.*

Oelfke (140) North German (**Ölfke**): pet form (diminutive) of the Germanic personal name *Od(w)olf* or *Olf*.

Oelke (450) North German (**Ölke**): 1. short form of the female personal name *Olgardis*, hence a metronymic, or of the male personal name *Ulrich* (see OEHL). 2. nickname for a short person, from Low German *ölken* 'dwarf'. 3. possibly a habitational name from Oelken in Westphalia.
GIVEN NAMES German 4%. *Otto* (2), *Diethelm, Erwin, Oskar, Wilhelm.*

Oelkers (285) 1. German (**Ölkers**): patronymic from OELKE 1. 2. Dutch: patronymic from a pet form of ULRICH.

Oelrich (213) German (**Ölrich**): variant of ULRICH, from the Germanic personal name *Odalrich* (see OEHL 1).

Oelschlager (279) North German (**Ölschläger**): occupational name for a producer of oil from olives or the like, from Middle High German *öle* (from Latin *oleum*) + agent derivative of *slahen* (modern *schlagen*) 'to beat', 'pound'.
GIVEN NAMES German 6%. *Ralf* (2), *Hans, Kurt.*

Oeltjen (135) North German (**Öltjen**): patronymic from a pet form of ULRICH (from Germanic patronal name *Odalrich*).

Oeltjenbruns (101) Dutch: unexplained.
GIVEN NAME German 4%. *Gerhard.*

Oen (162) 1. Norwegian: habitational name from a farmstead in Hordaland named Oen, from Old Norse *Ó* (unexplained), or from any of several named Øen, most from the definite form of *øy* 'island'. 2. Dutch: variant of HOEN.
GIVEN NAME Scandinavian 5%. *Juel.*

Oertel (496) German: from a pet form of the medieval personal names *Ortolf* or *Ortwin*. Compare ERTEL.
GIVEN NAMES German 7%. *Fritz* (2), *Dieter, Gerhard, Hans, Heinz, Horst, Irmgard.*

Oertle (108) Respelling of German and Swiss German **Örtel**, a variant (unrounded) form of ERTEL.
GIVEN NAME German 8%. *Kurt* (2).

Oertli (105) Swiss German: variant of **Örtel** (see OERTLE).

Oesch (274) Swiss and German (**Ösch**): variant of ESCH.
GIVEN NAMES German 4%. *Fritz, Hans, Kurt.*

Oeser (174) North German: from the Germanic personal name *Ans-her*, composed of Old Saxon *ans* 'god' + *hari*, *heri* 'army'. The -*e* indicates lengthening of the preceding vowel, but since through humanist practice the umlaut *ö* was frequently rendered as *oe* it is mostly pronounced as an umlaut in modern German.
GIVEN NAMES German 6%. *Fritz, Gunter.*

Oest (129) North German (**Öst**): 1. from a Germanic personal name composed with a cognate of Old High German *ōst(an)*, which denoted the area and direction of sunrise and in various personal names took on the meaning 'shining', 'spring', later 'Easter' and the compass point; hence also a topographic name from Middle Low German *ōst* 'east'. Compare EAST. The -*e* indicates a lengthening of the preceding *ō*-, as the variant *Ohst* shows, but in more recent forms like *Öst*, *Östmann* the *oe* has been converted to an o-umlaut (*ö*). 2. habitational name from any of several places so named.
GIVEN NAMES German 7%. *Erwin, Heinz, Kurt.*

Oester (108) Swiss German: perhaps a shortened form of a compound name formed with *Öster*; see for example OESTERLING.

Oesterle (391) 1. South German (**Österle**): apparently from a diminutive of a base form *Oster*, which has two possible derivations: 2. 'eastern', denoting someone who lived to the east of a settlement or who came from the east. 3. from a personal name.
GIVEN NAMES German 5%. *Erwin, Fritz, Gerd, Horst, Kurt.*

Oesterling (231) German (**Östeling**): nickname from Middle Low German *österlinc* 'someone from the Baltic Sea' or 'someone from the East', and later 'citizen of a city belonging to the Hanseatic League'.

Oesterreich (142) German (**Österreich**) and Jewish (Ashkenazic): regional name from the province of Upper or Lower Austria, from German *Österreich* 'Austria', the name of which literally means 'the Eastern kingdom'.
GIVEN NAMES German 10%. *Gerhard, Kurt, Uwe, Wolfgang.*

Oestmann (137) North German (**Östmann**): variant of OEST.

Oestreich (979) German and Jewish (Ashkenazic): variant of OESTERREICH.

Oestreicher (238) German and Jewish (Ashkenazic): regional name for someone from the province of Upper or Lower Austria (see OESTERREICH).
GIVEN NAMES German 11%; Jewish 6%. *Ernst* (5), *Franz* (2), *Otto* (2), *Horst*; *Shloime* (2), *Chaim, Mendy.*

Oeth (103) German: unexplained.

Oetjen (116) North German and Frisian: patronymic from a pet form of the personal name *Odo*.
GIVEN NAMES German 12%. *Kurt* (2), *Elke, Erwin, Fritz.*

Oetken (251) North German and Dutch: patronymic from a pet form of the personal name *Odo* (see ODE).
GIVEN NAMES German 5%. *Erwin* (3), *Otto, Theresia.*

Oetting (378) German (**Ötting**): 1. habitational name for someone from places in Bavaria and East Prussia called Öttingen, or Ottingen in Lower Saxony. 2. patronymic from the personal name OTTO.
GIVEN NAMES German 5%. *Erwin* (4), *Fritz.*

Oettinger (328) German (**Öttinger**) and Jewish (Ashkenazic): habitational name from places in Bavaria and East Prussia called Öttingen.
GIVEN NAMES German 4%. *Hanni* (2), *Christoph, Siegbert.*

Oetzel (130) German (**Ötzel**): from a pet form of the medieval personal name *Oz(o)* or the modern name *Otzen*.
GIVEN NAME German 4%. *Monika.*

O'Fallon (229) Irish (Leinster and Connacht): Anglicized form of Gaelic **Ó Fallamhain** 'descendant of *Fallamhan*' (see FALLON).
GIVEN NAME Irish 7%. *Liam.*

O'Farrell (799) Irish: Anglicized form of Gaelic **Ó Fearghail** 'descendant of *Fearghal*' (see FARRELL). This name is borne by

several families in Ireland, in counties Longford, Tyrone, and Wicklow.
GIVEN NAMES Irish 8%. *Fergus* (2), *Kieran* (2), *Brendan, Finbarr, Niall, Sinead.*

Off (162) North German: from an old German personal name, *Offo*, from a Germanic form *Autfrid*, composed of a cognate of Old High German *ōt* 'wealth', 'possession' + *frid(u)* 'peace'.
GIVEN NAMES German 5%. *Dieter, Herta, Manfred.*

Offen (175) **1.** German: variant of OFF. **2.** German and Jewish (Ashkenazic): from Middle High German *oven*, German *Ofen* 'oven', a metonymic occupational name for a baker, or, as a German name, for someone who had charge of the communal village oven and was empowered to exact payment in kind for its use. It may also be a topographic name for someone who lived near a kiln or in an area or field named with this word. **3.** German and Jewish (Ashkenazic): habitational name for someone from Buda, now part of Budapest in Hungary, known in Middle High German as *Ofen*.

Offenbacher (142) German (also **Offenbächer**) and Jewish (western Ashkenazic): habitational name for someone from Offenbach in Hesse.
GIVEN NAME German 5%. *Klaus.*

Offenbacker (100) Americanized spelling of OFFENBACHER.

Offenberger (127) German: habitational name for someone from any of various places named Offenberg or from Offenburg in Baden.

Offer (237) **1.** English (of Norman origin): occupational name for a goldsmith, from Anglo-Norman French *orfrer*, Old French *orfevre*, Latin *aurifaber*, from *aurum* 'gold' + *faber* 'maker'. Compare French **Fèvre** (see LEFEVRE). **2.** German: variant of OFF. **3.** Jewish: unexplained.

Offerdahl (204) Norwegian: habitational name from farmstead in Sogn named Ofredal, probably from *Opra*, a river name of uncertain origin, + *dal* 'valley'.
GIVEN NAMES Scandinavian 9%. *Nels* (2), *Helmer.*

Offerman (331) **1.** Dutch: occupational name for a sexton or verger, Middle Dutch *offerman*. **2.** Respelling of German and Jewish OFFERMANN.

Offermann (179) **1.** North German: variant of OPPERMANN. **2.** Jewish (Ashkenazic): elaborated form of OFFER.
GIVEN NAMES German 13%. *Alphons, Gunther, Horst, Klaus, Kurt, Otto.*

Officer (507) English: **1.** occupational name for the holder of any office, from Anglo-Norman French *officer* (an agent derivative of Old French *office* 'duty', 'service', Latin *officium* 'service', 'task'). **2.** occupational name for a sewer of gold embroidery, from Anglo-Norman French *orfroiser* (an agent derivative of Old French *orfrois*, Late Latin *auriphyrigium*

'Phrygian gold'—the Phrygians being famed in antiquity for their gold embroidery).

Offield (212) English: variant of OLDFIELD.

Offill (188) Perhaps a respelling of German **Ophüls**, a topographic name for someone who lived on a site overgrown with thistles, from Low German *op* 'on (top)' + *hüls* 'wood thistle'.

Offner (240) German: metonymic occupational name for someone who made ovens or used one, for example, a baker, from an agent derivative of Middle High German *oven* 'oven', 'stove' (see OFFEN).
GIVEN NAMES German 4%. *Gunter, Johann.*

Offord (255) English (Essex): habitational name from a place in Cambridgeshire, called Offord, from Old English *uppe* 'up' (here 'upstream') + *ford* 'ford'.

Offutt (1078) Possibly a respelling of German **Auffahrt** 'ascension'.

O'Flaherty (493) Irish (Connacht): Anglicized form of Gaelic **Ó Flaithbheartaigh** 'descendant of *Flaithbheartach*' (see FLAHERTY).
GIVEN NAMES Irish 11%. *Brendan, Cathal, Clancy, Kieran, Liam, Ronan, Seamus, Siobhan.*

O'Flanagan (102) Irish: Anglicized form of Gaelic **Ó Flannagáin** 'descendant of *Flannagán*' (see FLANAGAN).

O'Flynn (231) Irish: Anglicized form of Gaelic **Ó Floinn** 'descendant of *Flann*' (see FLYNN). This is a name borne by several families in Ireland, in Connacht, Cork, and Tyrone.
GIVEN NAMES Irish 12%. *Brendan* (2), *Conor* (2), *Grainne, Sinead.*

Oftedahl (225) Norwegian: habitational name from farmsteads in Agder and Rogaland named Oftedal or Oltedal, from a river name derived from Old Norse *ǫlpt* 'swan' + *dalr* 'valley'.
GIVEN NAMES Scandinavian 6%. *Johan, Nels.*

Ogan (553) Irish (Counties Louth and Dublin): variant of WOGAN, found Gaelicized as **Úgán**.

Oganesyan (125) Armenian: Russianized form of **Ohanesian**.
GIVEN NAMES Armenian 62%; Russian 8%. *Anait* (4), *Grigor* (4), *Armen* (2), *Arutyun* (2), *Gagik* (2), *Gayane* (2), *Gevorg* (2), *Oganes* (2), *Srbui* (2), *Vigen* (2), *Adrine, Anush, Ambartsum, Andranik; Liliya, Sergey, Svetlana, Vladimir, Yekaterina, Yuriy, Zhanna.*

O'Gara (737) Irish: Anglicized form of Gaelic **Ó Gadhra** 'descendant of *Gadhra*', a personal name derived from *gadhar* 'hound', 'mastiff'.
GIVEN NAMES Irish 7%. *John Patrick* (2), *Niall, Tadhg.*

Ogas (114) Galician: habitational name from Ogas in A Coruña province, Galicia; an infrequent surname now in Spain, but well established in North America.

GIVEN NAMES Spanish 25%. *Alvaro* (2), *Jose* (2), *Manuel* (2), *Abelino, Ana, Apolonio, Efren, Felipa, Juanita, Lucila, Luis, Porfirio.*

Ogasawara (100) Japanese: 'plain of the small bamboo hat'. This name is found mostly in northeastern Japan. Two noble families bearing the name were descended from the MINAMOTO clan through the TAKEDA and Kagami families.
GIVEN NAMES Japanese 59%. *Kazuhiro* (2), *Minoru* (2), *Akiko, Atsushi, Chiaki, Chie, Hitoshi, Ikumi, Isamu, Kenichiro, Kiyoto, Megumi.*

Ogata (457) Japanese: **1.** in the island of Kyūshū it is written with characters meaning 'beginning' and 'direction'; this is the original form of the name, which is habitational, taken from Ogatagō in Bungo (now Ōita prefecture). **2.** in eastern Japan it is written with characters meaning 'tail' and 'form'.
GIVEN NAMES Japanese 44%. *Mitsuo* (3), *Yoshitaka* (3), *Akira* (2), *Kaoru* (2), *Kunio* (2), *Makoto* (2), *Manabu* (2), *Masako* (2), *Akihiko, Akio, Asao, Atsushi.*

Ogawa (662) Japanese: common place name and surname throughout Japan, written with characters meaning 'small river'; it is sometimes pronounced *Kogawa*.
GIVEN NAMES Japanese 60%. *Masao* (6), *Takashi* (5), *Takeshi* (5), *Hiroshi* (4), *Kazuo* (4), *Akira* (3), *Kenji* (3), *Kiyoshi* (3), *Susumu* (3), *Yasuo* (3), *Yuji* (3), *Hajime* (2).

Ogborn (290) English: habitational name from either of two villages in Wiltshire called Ogbourne, from the Old English personal name *Oc(c)a* + Old English *burna* 'stream', 'creek' (see BOURNE).

Ogburn (1217) English: variant of OGBORN.

Ogden (7272) English: habitational name from some minor place, probably the one in West Yorkshire, called Ogden, from Old English *āc* 'oak' + *denu* 'valley'.

Ogdon (129) English: variant spelling of OGDEN.

Oge (125) French (**Ogé**): variant of OGIER.
GIVEN NAMES French 8%. *Alphonse, Gesner, Jacques.*

Ogea (143) Origin uncertain; perhaps a variant of French OGIER.
GIVEN NAMES French 5%. *Aldes, Pierre.*

Ogg (1028) Scottish: Anglicized form of a nickname from the Gaelic adjective *óg* 'young', used to distinguish the junior of two bearers of the same personal name.

Ogier (195) **1.** French: from a Germanic personal name composed of the elements *aud* 'wealth' + *gār, gēr* 'spear'. This is a cognate of English EDGAR. **2.** Polish: nickname from *ogier* 'stallion', 'stud horse'.
GIVEN NAME French 4%. *Jean-Jacques* (2).

Ogilvie (1390) Scottish: habitational name from a place near Glamis in the former county of Angus, which is first recorded c.1205 in the form *Ogilvin*. It is probably named from an early British form of Welsh *uchel* 'high' + *ma* 'plain', 'place' (mutated to *fa*) or *ban* 'hill' (mutated to *fan*).

Ogino (100) Japanese: meaning 'reed plain', of which Japan has many. This name is not common; it is found mostly in eastern Japan.
GIVEN NAMES Japanese 69%. *Junichi* (2), *Yoshihiro* (2), *Haruo, Hideo, Hiroaki, Kaori, Katsumi, Kazuhide, Kazuhiko, Koichi, Maki, Masae.*

Ogle (5562) Scottish, English, and northern Irish: habitational name from a place in Northumbria, named with the Old English personal name *Ocga* + Old English *hyll* 'hill'.

Ogles (382) English: variant of OGLE.

Oglesbee (410) English: variant spelling of OGLESBY.

Oglesby (4079) English: habitational name, perhaps from Ugglebarnby (recorded in 1314 as *Oggelberdesby*) in North Yorkshire, named from an unattested Old Norse personal name *Uglubárthr* + *býr* 'farmstead', 'settlement'.

Ogletree (1453) Scottish: habitational name from Ochiltree in Ayrshire.

Ognibene (201) Italian: from a personal name, an omen name meaning '(may he have) all good', or '(he has) all good'.
GIVEN NAMES Italian 14%. *Sal* (4), *Salvatore* (3), *Angelo, Annamarie, Ignazio, Rocco, Santo, Stefano.*

Ogonowski (156) Polish: habitational name from places called Ogonowo in Ciechanów voivodeship or Ogonów in Częstochowa voivodeship, or any of several places so called in Kielce voivodeship. All are named with Polish *ogon* 'tail'.
GIVEN NAME Polish 7%. *Sylwester.*

Ogorek (107) Polish (**Ogórek**): from Polish *ogórek* 'cucumber', perhaps a metonymic occupational name for a grower or seller of cucumbers or a nickname for someone thought to resemble a cucumber.
GIVEN NAMES Polish 9%; German 4%. *Zbigniew* (2), *Casimir, Wieslaw; Kurt* (2).

O'Gorman (993) Irish: Anglicized form of Gaelic **Ó Gormáin** 'descendant of *Gormán*' (see GORMAN).
GIVEN NAMES Irish 7%. *John Patrick, Kieran, Maeve, Malachy, Niall.*

O'Grady (2965) Irish: Anglicized form of Gaelic **Ó Gráda** 'descendant of *Gráda*' (see GRADY).
GIVEN NAMES Irish 7%. *Brendan* (4), *Conn, Dermot, Eamon, Roisin, Siobhan.*

Ogren (1000) Swedish (**Ögren**): ornamental name from Swedish *ö* 'island' + *gren* 'branch'.
GIVEN NAMES Scandinavian 6%. *Helmer* (3), *Erik* (2), *Hilmer, Knute, Lennart, Nels, Nils.*

Ogrodnik (129) Polish: occupational name for a market gardener or owner of an orchard or market garden, Polish *ogród*.
GIVEN NAMES Polish 9%. *Ryszard* (2), *Malgorzata, Tadeusz, Witold.*

Ogrodowski (74) Polish: habitational name for someone from places called Ogrodowa in Chełm voivodeship or any of several places called Ogrody, all named with Polish *ogród* 'orchard', 'market garden'.

O'Guin (243) Irish: variant of O'QUINN.

O'Guinn (178) Irish: variant of O'QUINN.

Ogura (124) Japanese: 'small warehouse'; the name is found mostly in eastern Japan and the Ryūkyū Islands. Some families pronounce the name *Kogura*.
GIVEN NAMES Japanese 68%. *Seiki* (2), *Tatsuya* (2), *Yuzo* (2), *Akiyoshi, Harumi, Hiroshi, Hiroya, Ichiro, Katsuhiro, Kazuo, Keiji, Keiko.*

Oh (3170) **1.** Korean (**O**): historically, there were two Chinese characters for the O surname, but by the late Koryŏ period (14th century AD), one of them had disappeared. Some records indicate that there are as many as 210 different clans for the remaining character, but only sixteen can be positively documented. All sixteen of these clans originate from the same ancestor, O Ch'ŏm, who migrated to Korea from China during the reign of Shilla's King Chijŭng (500–514 AD). *Oh* is a common surname throughout Korea. **2.** Japanese: Romanization of Ō 'king', the Japanese pronunciation of the Chinese surname *Wang*. It is mostly borne by Japanese of Chinese descent or Chinese long-term residents in Japan.
GIVEN NAMES Korean 63%. *Young* (57), *Sung* (29), *Jung* (26), *Yong* (21), *Chang* (17), *Kwang* (17), *Sang* (17), *Dong* (15), *Hyun* (15), *Jae* (15), *Jin* (15), *Kyung* (15), *Jong* (13), *Chong* (11), *Chung* (10), *Byung* (9), *Jeong* (8), *Pyong* (6), *Myong* (5), *Hak* (4), *Jin Hwan* (4), *Sook* (4), *Yeong* (4), *Choon* (3).

O'Hagan (699) Irish: Anglicized form of Gaelic **Ó hÁgáin** 'descendant of *Ágán*' (see HAGAN).
GIVEN NAMES Irish 11%. *Liam* (3), *Brendan* (2), *Brigid, Dermot, Seamus.*

O'Hair (434) Irish (Ulster): Anglicized form of Gaelic **Ó hÍr** (see HARE).

O'Haire (150) Irish: variant spelling of O'HARE.

O'Halloran (1315) Irish: Anglicized form of Gaelic **Ó hAllmhuráin** 'descendant of *Allmhurán*' (see HALLORAN).
GIVEN NAMES Irish 7%. *Brendan* (2), *Dermot, Fergal, Liam.*

Ohanesian (174) Armenian: patronymic from the personal name *Yovhannēs*, Armenian form of JOHN.
GIVEN NAMES Armenian 22%. *Ohanes* (3), *Aram* (2), *Armen* (2), *Sarkis* (2), *Arsen, Garabet, Minas, Ohannes, Sahag, Vahik.*

Ohanian (368) Armenian: patronymic from the personal name *Ohan*, a variant of *Yovhannēs*, Armenian equivalent of JOHN.
GIVEN NAMES Armenian 34%. *Haig* (5), *Ara* (4), *Raffi* (3), *Vartan* (3), *Armen* (2), *Garbis*

(2), *Kevork* (2), *Ohan* (2), *Sarkis* (2), *Vigen* (2), *Adrine, Agop.*

O'Hanlon (799) Irish: Anglicized form of Gaelic **Ó hAnluain** (see HANLON).
GIVEN NAMES Irish 8%. *Eamonn* (2), *Dermot, Jarlath.*

Ohara (120) Japanese (**Ōhara**): 'large plain'; a common place name, mostly found as a surname in western and west-central Japan. Listed in the Shinsen shōjiroku.

O'Hara (8197) Irish: Anglicized form of Gaelic **Ó hEaghra** 'descendant of *Eaghra*', a personal name of uncertain derivation.
GIVEN NAMES Irish 6%. *Brendan* (13), *Kieran* (3), *Michael Patrick* (2), *Seamus* (2), *Brennan, Brigid, Cathal, Clancy, Colm, Conor, Donovan, Eamonn.*

O'Hare (2045) Irish: Anglicized form of Gaelic **Ó hAichir** 'descendant of *Aichear*' (see HARE).
GIVEN NAMES Irish 6%. *Brendan* (2), *Siobhan* (2), *Briana, Ciaran, Colm, Colum, Dermot, Donal, Eamon, Eamonn, Fintan.*

O'Harra (249) Irish: most likely a variant of O'HARA.

O'Harrow (113) Irish: variant of O'HARA.
GIVEN NAMES Irish 8%. *Conan, Siobhan.*

Ohashi (202) Japanese (**Ōhashi**): from a common habitational name meaning 'large bridge'. Many bearers may be unrelated; some have TAIRA or FUJIWARA connections. This surname is mostly found in central Japan.
GIVEN NAMES Japanese 65%. *Aki* (5), *Fumio* (2), *Jiro* (2), *Katsuo* (2), *Kunio* (2), *Masaaki* (2), *Takashi* (2), *Toshiyasu* (2), *Yoichi* (2), *Akemi, Akiko, Atsuko.*

O'Haver (287) Irish: Anglicized form either of Gaelic **Ó hÉibhir** 'descendant of *Éibhear*' (a personal name of unknown origin) or of Gaelic **Ó híomhair** 'descendant of *Íomhar*', Gaelic form of the Old Norse personal name *Ivarr*. This surname is no longer found in Ireland.

Ohayon (125) Jewish (Sephardic): from the male personal name *Hayon* (meaning 'quite vivid' in Hebrew), prefixed by Berber *au* 'son'.
GIVEN NAMES Jewish 30%; French 20%. *Avi* (2), *Meir* (2), *Yosi* (2), *Haim, Haya, Meyer, Moshe, Nir, Ovadia, Pnina, Shimon, Yitshak; Michel* (4), *Alain, Emile, Gabrielle, Henri, Laurent, Marcelle, Prosper, Stephane.*

Ohde (114) North German: variant of ODE.

O'Hearn (1190) Irish: Anglicized form of Gaelic **Ó hEachthighearna** 'descendant of *Eachthighearna*' (see HEARN). The surname **O'Hearn** is no longer found in Ireland.
GIVEN NAMES Irish 5%. *Sean Michael* (2), *Brendan.*

O'Hern (590) Irish: variant spelling of O'HEARN.
GIVEN NAME Irish 5%. *John Patrick.*

O'Herron (165) Irish: Anglicized form of Gaelic **Ó hEaráin** 'descendant of *Earán*' (see HERRON 2). The name O'Herron is no longer found in Ireland.

O'Higgins (63) Irish: Anglicized form of Gaelic **Ó hUiginn** 'descendant of *Uiginn*', a byname meaning 'viking', 'sea-rover' (from Old Norse *víkingr*).

Ohl (845) **1.** German: from a short form of a personal name beginning with *Ohl-*, such as *Ohlerich* (a variant of ULRICH), or *Ohlbrecht* (a compound of *Odal-* (from *od-* 'prosperity', 'riches') + *berht* 'bright', 'famous'). **2.** North German: habitational name from places in Westphalia and the Rhineland named Ohl, or a topographic name from Middle Low German *ōl* 'meadowland surrounded by water'.

Ohland (171) **1.** North German: possibly a habitational name from Oland, an island in the Husum district of Schleswig-Holstein, or Ohland in the Rhineland (near Geldern). **2.** Swedish: ornamental name composed of an unexplained first element + *land* 'land'.
GIVEN NAMES French 4%; German 4%. *Andre*; *Hans, Oskar, Theodor.*

Ohle (125) German: **1.** nickname from Middle High German *olt* 'old', dialect *öl*. **2.** habitational name from a place named Ohl(e), or a topographic name from Middle Low German *öl* 'mud'.
GIVEN NAME German 4%. *Otto.*

Ohlendorf (216) German: habitational name from any of several places in Lower Saxony, or possibly a topographic name, a reduced form of **Oldendorf** 'old village', denoting a former settlement or the oldest part of a settlement.
GIVEN NAMES German 7%. *Erwin* (2), *Guenter, Kurt.*

Ohler (736) German: **1.** (also **Öhler**) occupational name for an extractor or seller of culinary oil (typically from olives) or for a soap maker, from Middle High German *öler*, an agent derivative of *öl, ol* 'oil' (from Latin *oleum* '(olive) oil'). **2.** (in some western parts of Germany) occupational name for a potter, Middle High German *ollære*, from Latin *ollarius* 'potter', from *olla* 'pot'. **3.** (**Öhler**): patronymic from a short form of a personal name formed with Old Saxon *ōd* 'possession'.

Ohlhauser (125) German: unexplained; possibly a habitational name for someone from Aulhausen in Hesse or Alhausen in North Rhine-Westphalia.

Ohlin (179) Swedish: ornamental name composed of an unexplained first element + *-lin*, a common suffix of surnames.
GIVEN NAME Scandinavian 9%. *Erik* (3).

Ohlinger (338) German: **1.** topographic name from Ohling in Schleswig-Holstein. **2.** variant of **Ohliger**, a habitational name from a Rhineland town called Ohlig. **3.** variant of **Oehling**, a patronymic from the Germanic personal name *Odilo* (see OTTO).
GIVEN NAMES German 4%. *Klaus, Kurt, Wilhelm.*

Ohlman (152) **1.** Respelling of German **Öhlmann** or **Ohlmann** (see OHLMANN). **2.** Swedish form of German OHLMANN 1.

Ohlmann (164) **1.** German (**Öhlmann**): occupational name for a seller of culinary oil, from Middle High German *öl, ol* 'oil' + *man* 'man'. Compare OHLER. **2.** German: from a Germanic personal name derived from *Odal*, from *od* 'wealth'. **3.** North German: nickname from *ōle, olde* 'old' + *man* 'man'. Compare OLD.
GIVEN NAMES German 4%. *Erwin, Otto.*

Ohlrich (166) Dutch and German: variant of ULRICH.
GIVEN NAMES German 4%. *Fritz, Kurt.*

Ohlsen (380) **1.** Danish and Norwegian: variant of OLSEN. **2.** North German: patronymic from OHL.
GIVEN NAME Scandinavian 4%. *Nils* (2).

Ohlson (673) **1.** Scandinavian: variant of OHLSSON; or an Americanized spelling of OHLSEN. **2.** Dutch: patronymic from the name *Ole*, a short form of a Germanic compound personal name formed with the initial element *odal* (see OHL).
GIVEN NAMES German 5%; Scandinavian 4%. *Kurt* (5), *Hans, Otto; Nils* (2), *Knute.*

Ohlsson (152) Swedish: patronymic from the personal name *Olaf* (see OLSEN).
GIVEN NAMES Scandinavian 27%; German 6%. *Nils* (2), *Alvar, Anders, Bjorn, Bodil, Eskil, Lars, Lennart, Stellan; Erna, Kurt.*

Ohlund (106) Swedish: altered spelling of **Ålund**, an ornamental name from *å* 'river' + *lund* 'grove'.
GIVEN NAME Scandinavian 5%; German 4%. *Kurt.*

Ohm (815) **1.** North German (also **Öhm**): kinship name from Middle Low German *ōm* 'maternal uncle', 'relative', which was used as a respectful form of address for older people. Compare NEVE. **2.** Norwegian: habitational name from farmsteads on the west coast named Om or Åm, from Old Norse *áum*, dative plural of *á* 'small river'.
GIVEN NAMES German 6%. *Fritz* (3), *Otto* (2), *Eldred, Guenther, Heinrich, Kurt, Manfred, Reinhard, Reinhold.*

Ohman (793) Swedish (**Öhman**): variant spelling of OMAN.
GIVEN NAMES Scandinavian 7%. *Erik* (2), *Nils* (2), *Thor* (2), *Klas, Knute, Lars.*

Ohmann (179) North German: **1.** patronymic from ODE. **2.** topographic name from Low German *Ohe* 'water meadow', from Middle Low German *ō* 'island', or a habitational name for someone from a place named with this element, such as Ohe near Hamburg.
GIVEN NAMES German 4%. *Reinhardt.*

Ohmart (141) Possibly a respelling of German **O(h)merht**, a variant of OHMER 1.

Ohme (112) German (also **Öhme**): variant of OHM.
GIVEN NAMES Scandinavian 5%; German 4%. *Knut; Wilhelm.*

Ohmer (269) German: **1.** from an agent derivative of Middle High German *āme, ōme* 'standard measure', hence an occupational name for someone who checked and sealed weights and measures. **2.** (**Öhmer**): topographic name (mostly Swiss), for someone who lived or owned a farm in a wider, flat part of a valley, a variant of EBNER. **3.** status or occupational name from Middle High German *ebenære* 'arbitrator', 'judge'.

Ohmes (149) German: **1.** variant of OHMS. **2.** habitational name from a place so named in Hesse.

Ohms (159) North German (also **Öhms**): patronymic from OHM.
GIVEN NAMES French 5%; German 4%. *Matthias, Otto.*

Ohnemus (201) South German: reduced form of the personal name *Hieronymus* (see JEROME).

Ohnesorge (129) German: nickname for a carefree person, from Middle High German *ān(e)* 'without' + *sorge* 'care', 'worry', 'anxiety'.
GIVEN NAMES German 7%. *Armin* (2), *Helmut.*

Ohnstad (234) Norwegian: variant spelling of ONSTAD.

O'Hora (168) Irish: variant of O'HARA.

Ohr (170) German: **1.** from Middle High German *ær, ōr* 'ear', hence a nickname for someone with remarkable, for example prominent, ears. **2.** (**Öhr**) from a Low German (Frisian) personal name.
GIVEN NAMES German 6%. *Matthias, Otto.*

Ohren (116) German: possibly a habitational name from a place named Ohren, or from Ohron near Trier.
GIVEN NAMES German 4%. *Hans* (2), *Otto.*

Ohrn (105) Swedish: variant of ORN.
GIVEN NAME Scandinavian 15%; German 5%. *Holger.*

Ohrt (373) North German: **1.** from a short form of a Germanic personal name composed with a cognate of Old Saxon *ort* 'point', 'sharp weapon'. **2.** topographic name for someone who lived in a nook or on a corner, Middle Low German *ort*, or a habitational name from any of several places in Oldenburg named Ohrt.
GIVEN NAMES German 6%. *Gunther* (2), *Gerhard, Hans, Otto.*

Ohs (106) Swedish and North German: unexplained.

Ohta (168) Japanese: variant spelling of OTA.
GIVEN NAMES Japanese 53%. *Eiko* (2), *Hiroshi* (2), *Hitoshi* (2), *Tsutomu* (2), *Akihiko, Akiko, Chizuko, Fumiko, Hiro, Hirotaka, Ichiro, Itsuo.*

Oie (178) Norwegian: variant of OYE.
GIVEN NAMES Scandinavian 10%. *Lars, Svein.*

Oien (472) **1.** Dutch: metronymic from a Germanic female personal name, *Oda*, derived from *aud, od* 'wealth'. **2.** Dutch: from *oye* 'ewe', hence a metonymic occupational name for shepherd, or a nickname for a silly person. **3.** Norwegian: variant spelling of OYEN.

GIVEN NAMES Scandinavian 7%. *Anders, Gudrun, Hjalmer, Iver, Nels, Ordell.*

Oiler (337) **1.** Altered spelling of OYLER. **2.** Possibly a respelling of German EULER.

Oines (118) Norwegian: habitational name from any of several farmsteads named Øynes, from *øy* 'island' + *nes* 'headland', 'promontory'.

GIVEN NAME Scandinavian 12%. *Alf.*

Oishi (206) Japanese (**Ōishi**): from a common topographic name meaning 'large rock'. The surname is found mostly in eastern Japan and on the island of Okinawa. It is listed in the Shinsen shōjiroku.

GIVEN NAMES Japanese 57%. *Hiroshi* (3), *Isao* (2), *Kazuo* (2), *Kiyoshi* (2), *Masami* (2), *Noboru* (2), *Sadao* (2), *Takeshi* (2), *Yoshiro* (2), *Yutaka* (2), *Akio, Eiko.*

Oja (466) Finnish: from *oja* 'ditch', a habitational name from a farm so named for its situation. This name occurs chiefly in western Finland and can be traced back to the 15th century. In America, it may also be an abbreviation of OJALA.

GIVEN NAMES Finnish 9%; Scandinavian 6%. *Reino* (4), *Olavi* (2), *Onni* (2), *Toivo* (2), *Wilho* (2), *Arvo, Kaino, Niilo, Torsti, Veikko, Vieno, Waino; Erik* (2).

Ojala (365) Finnish: from *oja* 'ditch', 'channel' + the local suffix *-la*, a habitational name from any of the numerous farms so named throughout Finland, early settlement of the country having been concentrated along waterways. The oldest record of the family name is from the 15th century.

GIVEN NAMES Finnish 19%; Scandinavian 4%. *Eino* (4), *Reino* (3), *Aatos* (2), *Esa* (2), *Waino* (2), *Arvi, Arvo, Erkki, Jorma, Juha, Mikko, Niilo; Erik, Helmer.*

Ojeda (1819) Spanish: habitational name from Ojeda in Burgos province or from the valley of Ojeda in Palencia province, which is probably named with a reduced form of Latin *folia* 'leaves' + the collective suffix *-eta.*

GIVEN NAMES Spanish 49%. *Jose* (53), *Luis* (24), *Carlos* (22), *Francisco* (22), *Juan* (18), *Manuel* (18), *Rafael* (17), *Jesus* (15), *Pedro* (13), *Miguel* (12), *Ruben* (12), *Angel* (11).

Ok (163) Korean: unexplained.

GIVEN NAMES Korean 71%; Other Southeast Asian 5%. *Dong* (3), *Myung* (2), *Song* (2), *Sung* (2), *Bok, Chang Ho, Chol, Dong Suk, Doo, Eun Jung, Hee Young, Ho, Hyeong, Insung, Insup, Jae Won, Ji, Myong, Sung Do, Woon; Du, Phon, Savuth, Seong.*

Oka (280) Japanese: 'hill'; a name found mostly in western Japan.

GIVEN NAMES Japanese 54%. *Masao* (3), *Takashi* (3), *Kaoru* (2), *Makiko* (2), *Masahiko* (2), *Rieko* (2), *Shigeki* (2), *Shogo* (2), *Akio, Atsuhiko, Atsushi, Haruo.*

Okabe (112) Japanese: 'hill section'; the name is found mostly in eastern Japan. A noble family by that name, descended from the FUJIWARA, originated in Mikawa (now part of Aichi prefecture).

GIVEN NAMES Japanese 67%. *Akira* (3), *Hiroshi* (2), *Masayuki* (2), *Tomoko* (2), *Akio, Chiaki, Hideki, Hideo, Hiromi, Isamu, Kazuhiro, Kazuhito.*

Okada (668) Japanese: 'rice paddy on the hill'; variously written. This is a common place name throughout Japan, but the surname is mostly found in western Japan.

GIVEN NAMES Japanese 57%. *Keiko* (4), *Takeshi* (4), *Akira* (3), *Isao* (3), *Mitsuko* (3), *Naoko* (3), *Satoshi* (3), *Seiki* (3), *Shigeru* (3), *Susumu* (3), *Yuko* (3), *Aki* (2).

Okafor (146) African: unexplained.

GIVEN NAMES French 8%; African 7%; Jewish Biblical 4%. *Bonaventure; Osita* (2), *Emeka, Ndubuisi.*

Okamoto (772) Japanese: '(one who lives) at the base of the hill'. This is found mostly in western and central Japan, and the Ryūkyū Islands.

GIVEN NAMES Japanese 49%. *Masao* (8), *Takeo* (4), *Toru* (4), *Hiro* (3), *Hitomi* (3), *Keiji* (3), *Kenji* (3), *Koji* (3), *Minoru* (3), *Nobuko* (3), *Satoshi* (3), *Takashi* (3).

Okamura (422) Japanese: 'hill village'; found mostly in western Japan and the Ryūkyū Islands.

GIVEN NAMES Japanese 44%. *Takeo* (4), *Koji* (3), *Kenji* (2), *Masaichi* (2), *Masaye* (2), *Noboru* (2), *Yoshiharu* (2), *Yoshio* (2), *Akihide, Akira, Asao, Ayano.*

Okane (100) Japanese (**Ōkane**): 'great deity'; this is a rare surname in Japan. In America it could be a shortening of the Okinawan surname **Ōkaneku**, which is written (apparently phonetically) with characters meaning 'great' or 'combine' and 'long time'.

O'Kane (847) Irish: Anglicized form of Gaelic **Ó Catháin** 'descendant of *Cathán*', a personal name derived from *cath* 'battle'. As lords of Keenaght in County Derry the O'Kanes were a leading sept in Ulster up to the time of the plantation (early 17th century).

GIVEN NAMES Irish 9%. *Liam* (3), *Brendan, Brigid, Declan, Eoin, Seamus.*

Okano (208) Japanese: 'hill field'; found mostly around the Tōkyō and Nagoya regions.

GIVEN NAMES Japanese 55%. *Hiroshi* (3), *Masao* (3), *Fujio* (2), *Hitoshi* (2), *Kazuko* (2), *Koichi* (2), *Shigeki* (2), *Shigetaka* (2), *Toru* (2), *Akemi, Harumi, Hirotaka.*

Okawa (123) Japanese (**Ōkawa**): 'large river'; the name is found mostly in eastern Japan and the Ryūkyū Islands.

GIVEN NAMES Japanese 58%. *Hiroshi* (3), *Hiroya* (2), *Michiko* (2), *Akira, Hidefumi, Itsuo, Junichi, Junko, Kaoru, Kazushi, Kiyomi, Kiyoshi.*

Okazaki (375) Japanese: 'hill cape'; found mostly in northeastern Japan and the island of Shikoku. Some bearers have samurai connections.

GIVEN NAMES Japanese 48%. *Hiroshi* (3), *Mitsuo* (3), *Hiroaki* (2), *Isamu* (2), *Iwao* (2), *Masa* (2), *Masanori* (2), *Masao* (2), *Noboru* (2), *Takashi* (2), *Tomoko* (2), *Yuki* (2).

Oke (152) English (Devon): variant spelling of OAK.

O'Keefe (6956) Irish: Anglicized form of Gaelic **Ó Caoimh** 'descendant of *Caomh*', a personal name based on *caomh* 'gentle'.

GIVEN NAMES Irish 6%. *Brendan* (5), *Brigid* (2), *Conor, Dermot, Ethna, Fergus, James Patrick, Kieran.*

O'Keeffe (808) Irish: variant spelling of O'KEEFE.

GIVEN NAMES Irish 9%. *Brendan* (2), *Dermot* (2), *Declan, Eamon, Eamonn.*

Okeke (125) African: unexplained.

GIVEN NAMES African 8%. *Emeka* (2), *Ngozi* (2), *Ijeoma.*

O'Kelley (951) Irish: Anglicized form of Gaelic **Ó Ceallaigh** 'descendant of *Ceallach*' (see KELLY). This is the name of several Irish families, in Cork and counties Derry and Sligo.

O'Kelly (573) Irish: Anglicized form of Gaelic **Ó Ceallaigh** 'descendant of *Ceallach*' (see KELLY).

GIVEN NAMES Irish 8%. *Brendan* (2), *Conor, Dermot, Eoin.*

Oken (189) Apparently an altered spelling of Jewish OKIN, OKON, or OKUN.

GIVEN NAMES Jewish 5%. *Haskel, Hyman.*

Okerlund (202) Respelling of Swedish **Åkerlund**, an ornamental name composed of the elements *åker* 'field' + *lund* 'grove'.

Okerson (114) Respelling of Swedish **Åkerson** (see AKERSON).

Okerstrom (124) Respelling of Swedish **Åkerström**, an ornamental name composed of the elements *åker* 'field' + *ström* 'river'.

GIVEN NAMES Scandinavian 8%. *Erik* (2), *Lars.*

Okeson (229) Respelling of Swedish **Åkesson**, a patronymic from the personal name *Åke*, from Old Norse *Áki*, probably from Early Scandinavian *anu-* 'ancestor' + the diminutive suffix *-k*.

GIVEN NAMES Scandinavian 10%. *Lars* (2), *Nils* (2), *Dagny, Erik, Hilmer, Nels.*

Okey (274) English: variant spelling of OAKEY.

Oki (177) Japanese: 'offing'; a very old surname which is a component of the name of the island of Okinawa, as well as of the Oki Islands north of Shimane prefecture (though the latter is written phonetically with different characters). The surname is listed in the Shinsen shōjiroku, but written with different characters used phonetically.

GIVEN NAMES Japanese 55%. *Hideaki* (2), *Hiroko* (2), *Hiroshi* (2), *Ikumi* (2), *Megumi*

(2), *Tadashi* (2), *Akira, Chisako, Etsuko, Fumio, Goro, Hideo.*

Okimoto (221) Japanese: '(one who lives) near the offing' or '(one who comes) from the open sea'; mostly found in western Japan.
GIVEN NAMES Japanese 31%. *Takashi* (3), *Iwao* (2), *Minoru* (2), *Asako, Asami, Fujio, Hayato, Hiroshi, Kazuo, Keiji, Kiyoko, Kiyoshi.*

Okin (181) Jewish (eastern Ashkenazic): variant of OKUN.
GIVEN NAME Jewish 4%. *Aron.*

Okino (119) Japanese: 'field (fronting the) open sea'. The name is not common in Japan.
GIVEN NAMES Japanese 39%. *Hideo* (2), *Fujio, Haruo, Hatsuko, Hayato, Isami, Masaru, Nobuo, Saburo, Setsuo, Shigeo, Tadashi.*

Okita (99) Japanese: 'rice paddy near the offing'; mostly found in west-central Japan.
GIVEN NAMES Japanese 29%. *Mamoru* (2), *Atsushi, Fumio, Keizo, Kiyo, Kiyomi, Koichiro, Makoto, Masao, Shogo, Sumiye, Yosh.*

Okland (120) Norwegian: habitational name from any of about 10 farmsteads named Økland or Aukland, from a first element related to *auka* 'increase' + *land* 'land', i.e. a farm where the land under cultivation has been increased.
GIVEN NAMES Scandinavian 18%; Dutch 4%. *Erik, Hilmer, Kristoffer, Nils; Henrik* (3).

Okon (290) Polish (**Okoń**) and Jewish (from Poland): from *okoń, okuń* 'perch', metonymic occupational name for a freshwater fisherman or a nickname for someone thought to resemble a perch. As a Jewish name it is mainly ornamental.
GIVEN NAMES Jewish 5%; Polish 5%. *Dvora, Emanuel, Hyman, Sol; Andrzej, Casimir, Stanislaw.*

Okonek (133) Polish: pet form of **Okoń** (see OKON).

Okoniewski (168) Polish: habitational name for someone from places called Okuniew or Okuniewo in Warszawa and Gdańsk voivodeships.

Okonski (245) Polish (**Okoński**): habitational name for someone from Okoń in Kalisz voivodeship or Okońsk in Łuck, now in Belarus, both named with the Polish word *okoń* 'perch'.
GIVEN NAME French 4%. *Dreux.*

Okoro (104) African: unexplained.
GIVEN NAMES French 6%. *Gaston, Marcel.*

Okray (219) Americanized spelling of Polish **Okraj**, from *okraj* 'border', 'edge'. This is either a topographic name denoting someone living near a frontier, or a nickname for someone who used to cut something (e.g. a tailor).

Okubo (262) Japanese (**Ōkubo**): from a place name meaning 'large hollow', which is common in Japan and the Ryūkyū

Islands. This is a frequent surname in Japan and was taken by several samurai families.
GIVEN NAMES Japanese 55%. *Akira* (4), *Tadashi* (3), *Kenzo* (2), *Kiyoshi* (2), *Masashi* (2), *Ryuichi* (2), *Takayuki* (2), *Tomoyuki* (2), *Asako, Ayumi, Daisuke, Hajime.*

Okuda (229) Japanese: 'secluded rice paddy'; found mostly in western Japan and the Ryūkyū Islands. Some bearers have FUJIWARA or MINAMOTO connections.
GIVEN NAMES Japanese 64%. *Akira* (3), *Fumiyo* (2), *Hideki* (2), *Masako* (2), *Minoru* (2), *Naofumi* (2), *Shigeo* (2), *Shizuo* (2), *Tadashi* (2), *Yoko* (2), *Chikako, Eiichi.*

Okula (100) Polish (also **Okuła**): nickname for a lame person, from *okuleć* 'to stumble or founder', Old Polish *okułac.*
GIVEN NAMES Polish 22%. *Ryszard* (2), *Jadwiga, Jozef, Marzena, Stanislaw, Tadeusz, Wiktoria, Zygmunt.*

Okuma (113) Japanese: it is uncertain whether instances of this name in America are *Ōkuma* meaning 'large bear', found mostly in eastern Japan, or *Okuma*, meaning 'interior space', found mostly in the Ryūkyū Islands. One noble family bearing the former lived in the far west of Japan, in Hizen (now Nagasaki prefecture).
GIVEN NAMES Japanese 42%. *Yoshiaki* (2), *Ayako, Haru, Katsushi, Kei, Keiko, Kuni, Kunihiko, Maiko, Masahiro, Masao, Masayuki.*

Okumura (257) Japanese: 'secluded village'; mostly found in the Nagoya region and the island of Okinawa.
GIVEN NAMES Japanese 51%. *Yoshio* (3), *Akio* (2), *Haruo* (2), *Hideyuki* (2), *Kenichi* (2), *Koji* (2), *Masayuki* (2), *Shunji* (2), *Akinobu, Eiji, Hiroshi, Hiroyoshi.*

Okun (548) Jewish (eastern Ashkenazic): ornamental name from Russian and Belorussian *okun* 'perch' (the fish).
GIVEN NAMES Jewish 9%; Russian 4%. *Aviva* (2), *Meyer* (2), *Aron, Avi, Faina, Ilya, Isaak, Sol, Tema; Boris* (2), *Anatoly, Arkady, Ayzik, Fanya, Fedor, Galina, Grigoriy, Konstantin, Lev, Sofya, Vladimir.*

Okura (87) Japanese (**Ōkura**): 'large warehouse'; the name is found mostly in western Japan, and is listed in the Shinsen shōjiroku. There are many unrelated bearers, some with samurai connections, who took the name from places of residence.
GIVEN NAMES Japanese 47%. *Kazuo* (2), *Akira, Chiye, Gengo, Hiroko, Hiroshi, Iori, Kanae, Kazu, Kazuki, Kazumi, Masako.*

Ola (102) Basque and Aragonese (of Basque origin): habitational name from either of two places named Ola, in Navarre, Basque Country, and Uesca, Aragon, where Basque was spoken in pre-Roman times, from Basque *ola* 'forge' or 'cabin'.
GIVEN NAMES Spanish 16%. *Salvador* (2), *Diosdado, Jose, Luis Armando, Manuel, Marcelina, Marina, Paulino, Rosauro.*

Olafson (308) Scandinavian: patronymic from the common personal name *Olaf.*
GIVEN NAMES Scandinavian 8%. *Erik, Nels.*

Olague (283) Basque: habitational name from Olague in Navarre, named with Basque *ola* 'forge', 'ironworks' + the locative suffix *-gue.*
GIVEN NAMES Spanish 47%. *Juan* (5), *Javier* (4), *Lupe* (4), *Eduardo* (3), *Manuel* (3), *Alfonso* (2), *Diego* (2), *Domingo* (2), *Ignacio* (2), *Jaime* (2), *Jose* (2), *Jose Lopez* (2).

Olah (618) Hungarian (**Oláh**): ethnic name from Hungarian *oláh* 'Romanian', old form *volách*, from *vlach* 'Italian', 'speaker of a Romance language'. See also VLACH.
GIVEN NAMES Hungarian 9%. *Zoltan* (4), *Bela* (3), *Gabor* (3), *Tibor* (3), *Miklos* (2), *Csaba, Geza, Imre, Janos, Lajos, Laszio, Laszlo.*

Olan (120) **1.** Spanish (**Olán**): variant spelling of *holán* 'furbelow', a kind of delicate white fabric frill (originally from Holland, whence the name), used to adorn women's skirts; possibly therefore a metonymic occupational name for someone who made or sold such frills. This name is found mainly in Mexico and Caribbean Islands. **2.** Swedish: probably an ornamental name, but unexplained.
GIVEN NAMES Spanish 19%. *Jose* (4), *Pedro* (3), *Roberto* (2), *Aida, Juan, Juana, Luis, Marcelina, Marcelino, Mario, Miguel, Ramonita.*

Oland (201) Swedish (also **Öland**): possibly an ornamental name composed of the elements *ö* 'island' + *land* 'land' or possibly a habitational name taken from the name of an island, Öland.
GIVEN NAME Scandinavian 6%. *Erik.*

Olander (1014) Swedish: habitational name for someone from the island of Öland, or possibly a respelling of **Ålander**, a habitational name for someone from the island of Åland.
GIVEN NAMES Scandinavian 5%. *Lennart* (2), *Nels* (2), *Bjorn, Britt, Helmer, Holger, Lars, Majken.*

Olano (148) Basque: habitational name from Olano in the Basque province of Araba, so named from *ola* 'forge', 'ironworks' + the diminutive suffix *-no.*
GIVEN NAMES Spanish 40%. *Luis* (5), *Manuel* (3), *Rodolfo* (3), *Gerardo* (2), *Jose* (2), *Juan* (2), *Ricardo* (2), *Ana, Arturo, Carlos, Cristino, Edgardo.*

Olarte (118) Basque: topographic name from a derivative of Basque *ola* 'blacksmith' + *arte* 'space'.
GIVEN NAMES Spanish 49%. *Guillermo* (3), *Jorge* (3), *Francisco* (2), *Luis* (2), *Orlando* (2), *Pedro* (2), *Silvia* (2), *Adriana, Alberto, Alvaro, Carlos, Carlos Alfredo.*

O'Laughlin (661) Irish: Anglicized form of Gaelic **Ó Lochlainn** 'descendant of *Lochlann*' (see LAUGHLIN).

Olavarria (144) Spanish (of Basque origin): topographic name from Basque *ola* 'forge' + *berri* 'new' + the definite article -*a*, or possibly variant form of the habitational name from any of the places in Navarre named Olaberri.
GIVEN NAMES Spanish 45%. *Jose* (5), *Enrique* (3), *Juan* (3), *Angel* (2), *Jesus* (2), *Manuel* (2), *Rafael* (2), *Ramon* (2), *Alejandrina*, *Aurea*, *Baudilio*, *Evaristo*.

Olberding (441) German and Dutch: from a derivative of the personal name *Olbert* (see OLBRICH) or ALBERT.

Olbert (105) Variant (in Slavic-speaking regions) of North German ALBERT.
GIVEN NAMES German 7%; Polish 5%. *Dieter*, *Jochen*; *Zigmond* (2).

Olbrich (149) German and Dutch: **1.** from a Germanic personal name composed of the elements *odal* 'wealth', 'inheritance' + *berht* 'bright', 'famous'. **2.** Saxon and Silesian variant of ALBRECHT or ALBERT.
GIVEN NAMES German 12%. *Gunter* (2), *Alois*, *Franz*, *Gunther*, *Irmgard*.

Olbrys (108) Polish: variant of German ALBRECHT.
GIVEN NAMES Polish 9%. *Zygmunt* (2), *Gerzy*.

Olcott (557) Variant spelling of English ALCOTT.

Olczak (155) Polish: **1.** patronymic from the personal name *Olcza*, a pet form of OLEK. **2.** possibly also a topographic name for someone who lived by an alder tree, from a derivative of *olcza*, variant of *olsza* 'alder'.
GIVEN NAMES Polish 5%. *Wladyslaw*, *Wlodek*.

Old (496) **1.** English: from Middle English *old*, not necessarily implying old age, but rather used to distinguish an older from a younger bearer of the same personal name. **2.** North German form of ALT, like the English name a distinguishing name for the older of two bearers of a personal name. **3.** Americanized form of German ALT.

Oldaker (454) English: topographic name from Middle English *ald*, *old* 'old' + *aker* 'field'.

Oldakowski (133) Polish (**Ołdakowski**): habitational name for someone from places called Ołdaki in Ciechanów, Łomża, and Ostrołęka voivodeships.
GIVEN NAMES Polish 9%. *Czeslaw*, *Janusz*, *Leszek*, *Zdzislaw*.

Oldani (237) Italian (Lombardy): **1.** habitational name for someone from Olda in Bergamo, from an adjectival derivative of the place name. **2.** in some cases, possibly a patronymic from an old Germanic personal name, *Oldano*.
GIVEN NAMES Italian 8%. *Angelo* (5), *Caesar*, *Evo*, *Francesca*, *Guido*.

Olden (554) **1.** English: variant of ALDEN. **2.** North German: patronymic from OLD. **3.** Norwegian: habitational name from a farmstead in Trøndelag, probably taking its name from the Old Norse fjord name *Áldi*,

of unexplained etymology. **4.** Swedish (**Oldén**): unexplained.

Oldenburg (1226) North German, Danish, and Jewish (Ashkenazic): habitational name from Oldenburg, the capital of the former principality of the same name, from the weak dative case (originally used after a preposition and article) of Middle Low German *ald*, *old* 'old' + *burg* 'fortress', 'fortified town'.
GIVEN NAMES German 4%. *Kurt* (3), *Erwin* (2), *Fritz* (2), *Otto* (2), *Claus*, *Hans*, *Jurgen*, *Ruediger*.

Oldenkamp (219) North German: topographic name from *olden*, the weak dative case (originally used after a preposition and article) of Middle Low German *ald*, *old* 'old' + *kamp* 'enclosed field', 'domain' (from Latin *campus*), denoting someone who lived by a field or domain so named.

Older (231) North German: status name for an older man or alderman, chairman of a corporation or a city or church council. See OLD.

Oldfather (209) Literal translation of German ALTVATER or North German **Oldvader**, a kinship and status name from Middle High German *alt* 'old' + *vater* 'father', i.e. 'grandfather'.

Oldfield (1174) English (Yorkshire and Lancashire): habitational name from any of various minor places so called, from Old English *(e)ald* 'old' + *feld* 'open country'.

Oldford (107) English: perhaps a habitational name from Oldford in Somerset.

Oldham (4943) English: **1.** habitational name from the place in Lancashire, so named from Middle English *ald*, *old* 'old' + *holm* 'island', 'dry land in a fen', 'promontory'. **2.** topographic name from Old English *(e)ald* 'old' + *hamm* 'water meadow', 'low-lying land by a river'.
FOREBEARS Colonist and trader John Oldham was born in Lancashire, England, in about 1600 and emigrated to America in 1623, arriving at Plymouth, MA, in July on the ship *Anne*.

Olding (151) **1.** English (southern counties): unexplained. **2.** German: patronymic form of OLD 2.

Oldroyd (323) English (Yorkshire): habitational name from any of various minor places in northern England named Oldroyd, from Middle English *ald*, *old* 'old' + *royd* 'clearing'.

Olds (2747) English: patronymic from OLD.

Oldt (141) North German: variant of ALT.
FOREBEARS This name was estabished in PA in the 18th century. George Oldt arrived in Philadelphia from the Rhineland in Germany on the ship *Phoenix* in October 1744; he or his family eventually settled in Ruscomb Township, Berks Co., PA. Twenty years later, in 1766, Johannes Olt arrived in on the ship *Chance*, settling in Lehigh Co. There has been some confusion between the two immigrant families.

Olea (286) Spanish: habitational name from places in the provinces of Cantabria, Palencia, and Burgos named Olea, possibly from Basque *ola* 'forge', 'ironworks' + the definite article -*a*.
GIVEN NAMES Spanish 47%. *Jose* (5), *Juan* (5), *Carlos* (3), *Francisco* (3), *Mario* (3), *Ricardo* (3), *Agustin* (2), *Alvaro* (2), *Edmundo* (2), *Efren* (2), *Humberto* (2), *Javier* (2).

Olean (108) Respelling of French **Oléon**, which may be an altered form of **Auléon** '(son) of Léon'.
GIVEN NAME French 4%. *Normand*.

O'Lear (254) Variant of Irish O'LEARY.

O'Leary (9123) Irish (Munster): Americanized form of **Ó Laoghaire** 'descendant of *Laoghaire*', a byname originally meaning 'keeper of the calves', from *laogh* 'calf'. This was the name of a 5th-century king of Ireland.
GIVEN NAMES Irish 8%. *Brendan* (11), *Donal* (5), *Liam* (4), *Aileen* (3), *James Patrick* (3), *Siobhan* (3), *Conor* (2), *Kieran* (2), *Bridie*, *Brigid*, *Dermot*, *Eoin*.

Olech (96) Polish: from the personal name *Olech*, a pet form of *Oleksy* (see ALEXIS) or *Oleksander* (see ALEXANDER).

Olejniczak (490) Polish: patronymic from the occupational name OLEJNIK.
GIVEN NAMES Polish 7%. *Bogdan*, *Czeslaw*, *Jacek*, *Jadwiga*, *Kazimierz*, *Lech*, *Piotr*, *Tadeusz*, *Thadeus*, *Wladyslaw*.

Olejnik (247) Czech and Slovak (**Olejník**), Polish, Ukrainian, and Jewish (eastern Ashkenazic): occupational name for an extractor or seller of cooking oil, from *olej* 'oil' + -*ník* (Czech), -*nik* (Polish, Yiddish), or -*nyk* (Ukrainian), suffix of agent nouns. In at least one family, the name has been Americanized (or rather Gaelicized) as **O'Lennick**.
GIVEN NAMES Polish 12%. *Bogdan*, *Grzegorz*, *Janusz*, *Jaroslaw*, *Jerzy*, *Mieczyslaw*, *Stanislaw*, *Wladyslaw*, *Zbigniew*, *Zofia*.

Olek (110) Polish: short form of the personal name *Oleksander* (see ALEXANDER) or *Oleksy* (see ALEXIS).
GIVEN NAMES Polish 7%. *Alojzy*, *Irena*, *Zygmund*.

Oleksa (138) Polish: derivative of the personal name or *Oleksander* (see ALEXANDER) or *Oleksy* (see ALEXIS).

Oleksak (135) Polish: variant of OLEKSIAK.

Oleksiak (154) Polish: patronymic from a short form of the personal names *Oleksander* (see ALEXANDER) or *Oleksy* (see ALEXIS).
GIVEN NAMES Polish 6%. *Izabela*, *Mieczyslaw*, *Ryszard*.

Oleksy (235) Polish: from the personal name *Oleksy* (see ALEXIS).
GIVEN NAMES Polish 14%. *Andrzej* (2), *Slawomir* (2), *Darek*, *Halina*, *Jerzy*, *Jozef*, *Stanislaw*, *Wladyslawa*, *Zbigniew*, *Zigmund*.

Olen (280) **1.** Dutch: patronymic from *Oele*, *Oole*, a short form of any of the Germanic compound names with the first element *odal* 'wealth', e.g. *Odelbert* (with second element *berht* 'bright', 'famous'). **2.** Swedish (**Olén**, **Ölén**): probably an ornamental name; etymology unexplained.

Olender (243) Polish and Jewish (Ashkenazic): from German **Holländer** (see HOLLANDER), denoting a Dutch settler in Poland.
GIVEN NAMES Polish 8%; German 4%. *Casimir, Danuta, Dorota, Miroslaw, Stanislaw, Wieslaw; Kurt* (2).

Olenick (434) Americanized or Germanized spelling of Jewish and Slavic OLEJNIK.

Olenik (200) Americanized spelling of Jewish and Slavic OLEJNIK.

Olenski (110) Polish (**Oleński**): variant of OLINSKI.
GIVEN NAMES Polish 5%. *Andrzej, Michalina*.

Oler (475) Variant of German OHLER.

Oles (572) **1.** Polish (**Oleś**): from a pet form of the personal name *Oleksander* (see ALEXANDER) or *Oleksy* (see ALEXIS). **2.** Hungarian (**Öles**): nickname for a strong or big man from *öles* 'strong', 'well-built'.

Olesen (897) Danish and Norwegian: variant of OLSEN.
GIVEN NAMES Scandinavian 12%. *Erik* (5), *Jorgen* (2), *Niels* (2), *Per* (2), *Bjorn, Britt, Lars, Nels, Rigmor, Sven, Uffe*.

Oleski (142) Polish: habitational name from a lost place called Olsza, or from Oleszno (see OLCZAK).

Olesky (190) **1.** Polish: variant of OLESKI. **2.** Ukrainian: habitational name from Olewsk in Ukraine.

Oleson (1593) **1.** Dutch: patronymic from O(e)le (see OLEN). **2.** Americanized spelling of OLSEN.
GIVEN NAMES Scandinavian 4%. *Alf* (2), *Erik, Kristoffer, Nels, Niels*.

Olexa (226) Polish: variant of OLEKSA.

Oley (183) German (**Öley**): occupational name for an oil merchant, from Middle High German *oleier* 'oil miller' (i.e. someone who extracted olive oil from olives), or from *öl* 'oil' + *hey* 'administrator', 'ranger'. Compare OHLER.

Olgin (106) Spanish (**Olgín**): unexplained. Possibly a variant of **Olguín** (see OLGUIN).
GIVEN NAMES Spanish 32%; Jewish 4%. *Ramon* (3), *Alicia* (2), *Ruben* (2), *Alonzo, Cipriano, Corina, Cruz, Dionisia, Eduardo, Elidia, Felipe, Fernando; Hyman, Miriam*.

Olguin (982) Spanish (**Olguín**): variant of **Holguín** (see HOLGUIN).
GIVEN NAMES Spanish 40%. *Jose* (20), *Juan* (14), *Manuel* (9), *Jesus* (8), *Miguel* (8), *Jaime* (6), *Pedro* (6), *Francisco* (5), *Rogelio* (5), *Alejandro* (4), *Carlos* (4), *Mario* (4).

Olheiser (179) German: dialect form of **Althäuser**, a habitational name from the common place name Althausen or Althaus,

or from Ahlhausen or Alhausen in Lower Saxony.

Oliff (188) English: from the Old Norse personal name *Óleifr*, a variant of *Ólafr* 'Olaf' (see OLSEN). The name was always common in Scandinavia, and became popular also in northern Scotland and Ireland, which received Scandinavian colonists at an early date.
GIVEN NAMES French 4%. *Damien, Monique*.

Oliger (183) Respelling of German **Ohliger**: **1.** occupational name for an oil merchant, from Middle High German *oleier* 'oil miller' (i.e. someone who extracted olive oil from olives). **2.** habitational name for someone from either of two places called Ohlig, in the Sieg district or in the Rhineland.
GIVEN NAMES French 6%; German 4%. *Antoine* (2), *Marcel*; *Erwin, Otto*.

Olin (1743) **1.** French and Dutch: from a pet form of a Germanic compound personal name with the first element *odal*. Compare OHL. **2.** Jewish (from Ukraine): from Ukrainian *olin* 'stag'. This name is either ornamental or represents a calque of Yiddish personal name HIRSCH. **3.** Swedish: variant spelling of OHLIN.

Olinde (195) Origin unidentified.

Olinger (2093) **1.** German: variant of OHLINGER. **2.** German: habitational name for someone from Ölling in Bavaria or Öllingen near Ulm, or from Olingen near Betzdorf.

Olinski (103) Polish (**Oliński**): habitational name for someone from a place called Olin in Piła voivodeship, named with the personal name *Ola*, pet form of *Oleksander* (see ALEXANDER).

Oliphant (1993) English, Scottish, French, and German: from Middle English, Old French, Middle High German *olifant* 'elephant' (medieval Latin *olifantus*, from classical Latin *elephantus*, Greek *elephas*, genitive *elephantos*). The circumstances in which this word was applied as a surname are not clear. It may have been a nickname for a large, lumbering individual, or a metonymic occupational name for a worker in ivory, or a habitational name from a house distinguished by the sign of an elephant.

Oliva (2772) **1.** Catalan, Spanish, and Portuguese: habitational name from Oliva in Valencia, Santa Oliva in Girona, or possibly from any of the places in Extremadura named La Oliva, from Latin *oliva* 'olive'. **2.** Italian (mainly southern and Ligurian): from Latin *oliva* 'olive'; a topographic name for someone who lived by an olive tree or grove, or a metonymic occupational name for a gatherer or seller of olives or an extractor or seller of olive oil, or perhaps in some cases a nickname for someone with a sallow complexion. **3.** German: habitational name from Oliva, a place now in Gdańsk voivodeship, Poland.

GIVEN NAMES Spanish 33%; Italian 7%. *Jose* (39), *Carlos* (25), *Juan* (22), *Armando* (13), *Luis* (13), *Mario* (13), *Angel* (11), *Francisco* (11), *Jorge* (11), *Jesus* (10), *Roberto* (10), *Jaime* (8); *Salvatore* (8), *Antonio* (7), *Angelo* (6), *Carmine* (4), *Giovanni* (4), *Enrico* (3), *Aldo* (2), *Carlo* (2), *Dino* (2), *Elio* (2), *Gaetano* (2), *Lorenzo* (2).

Olivar (118) Spanish and Asturian-Leonese: topographic name meaning 'place of olives'.
GIVEN NAMES Spanish 45%. *Alberto* (2), *Carlos* (2), *Felipe* (2), *Jose* (2), *Juan* (2), *Pedro* (2), *Ramon* (2), *Adriano, Alfredo, Ana, Artemio, Benigno*.

Olivares (1940) Spanish: habitational name from any of several places named Olivares, from the plural of Spanish *olivar* 'olive grove'. Compare OLIVEIRA. The Spanish surname spread into Italy, becoming widespread in Milan and the Naples region.
GIVEN NAMES Spanish 51%. *Jose* (66), *Juan* (40), *Manuel* (25), *Luis* (23), *Jesus* (18), *Enrique* (14), *Miguel* (14), *Carlos* (13), *Francisco* (12), *Jorge* (12), *Pablo* (11), *Pedro* (11).

Olivarez (1196) Spanish (**Olivárez**): variant (hypercorrected form) of OLIVARES. In Spain itself this is an infrequent name.
GIVEN NAMES Spanish 49%. *Juan* (23), *Jose* (18), *Manuel* (14), *Guadalupe* (13), *Jesus* (10), *Cruz* (9), *Carlos* (8), *Juanita* (8), *Raul* (8), *Mario* (7), *Arturo* (6), *Ramiro* (6).

Olivas (2011) **1.** Catalan: variant spelling of **Olives**, habitational name from Olives in Girona province, or a topographic name from the plural of OLIVA. **2.** Spanish: plural form of OLIVA.
GIVEN NAMES Spanish 44%. *Jose* (40), *Manuel* (36), *Jesus* (31), *Juan* (23), *Ramon* (19), *Carlos* (17), *Armando* (10), *Jaime* (10), *Raul* (10), *Arturo* (9), *Ruben* (9), *Ernesto* (8).

Olive (2090) **1.** French: from *olive* 'olive' (see OLIVA). **2.** English: usually an Americanized form of a Romance name such as OLIVA, OLIVO, etc. **3.** Catalan (**Olivé**): variant spelling of OLIVER.

Oliveira (3313) Portuguese and Galician: habitational name from any of the numerous places named Oliveira, from Portuguese and Galician *oliveira* 'olive grove' (Late Latin *olivarius*, a derivative of Latin *oliva* 'olive'), or a topographic name from this word.
GIVEN NAMES Spanish 26%; Portuguese 17%. *Manuel* (115), *Jose* (89), *Carlos* (33), *Luis* (25), *Fernando* (24), *Mario* (14), *Luiz* (12), *Francisco* (9), *Sergio* (9), *Ana* (8), *Geraldo* (8), *Pedro* (8); *Joao* (24), *Paulo* (11), *Joaquim* (10), *Duarte* (7), *Agostinho* (4), *Guilherme* (3), *Marcio* (3), *Sebastiao* (3), *Anabela* (2), *Henrique* (2), *Messias* (2), *Ademir; Antonio* (77), *Angelo* (5), *Marco* (3), *Mauro* (3), *Filomena* (2), *Flavio* (2),

Caesar, Caio, Carmel, Clementino, Dante, Delio.

Oliver (37088) **1.** English, Scottish, Welsh, and German: from the Old French personal name *Olivier*, which was taken to England by the Normans from France. It was popular throughout Europe in the Middle Ages as having been borne by one of Charlemagne's paladins, the faithful friend of Roland, about whose exploits there were many popular romances. The name ostensibly means 'olive tree' (see OLIVEIRA), but this is almost certainly the result of folk etymology working on an unidentified Germanic personal name, perhaps a cognate of ALVARO. The surname is also borne by Jews, apparently as an adoption of the non-Jewish surname. **2.** Catalan and southern French (Occitan): generally a topographic name from *oliver* 'olive tree', but in some instances possibly related to the homonymous personal name (see 1 above).

Olivera (955) **1.** Catalan, Portuguese, and Spanish: topographic name from *olivera* 'olive tree'. **2.** In some cases a Castilianized spelling of Galician OLIVEIRA.
GIVEN NAMES Spanish 42%; Portuguese 11%. *Jose* (21), *Manuel* (13), *Carlos* (10), *Jorge* (9), *Luis* (9), *Jesus* (8), *Rafael* (7), *Ramon* (7), *Angel* (6), *Julio* (6), *Miguel* (6), *Arturo* (5); *Joao* (3), *Paulo* (2), *Joaquim*; *Antonio* (6), *Heriberto* (3), *Silvio* (2), *Angelo*, *Bartolo*, *Carmelo*, *Claudina*, *Donato*, *Gasper*, *Giovanna*, *Guido*, *Olivera*.

Oliveras (252) Catalan: variant spelling of the topographic name *Oliveres*, from the plural of *olivera* 'olive tree', or a habitational name from Las Oliveras in Murcia province.
GIVEN NAMES Spanish 41%. *Jose* (11), *Ana* (3), *Carlos* (3), *Luis* (3), *Geraldo* (2), *Juan* (2), *Marcos* (2), *Margarita* (2), *Pedro* (2), *Ramon* (2), *Roberto* (2), *Wilfredo* (2).

Oliveri (1021) Italian: **1.** patronymic form of *Oliverio*. **2.** habitational name from Oliveri in Messina province, Sicily.
GIVEN NAMES Italian 24%. *Salvatore* (9), *Rocco* (6), *Carmelo* (4), *Sal* (4), *Antonio* (3), *Dante* (3), *Marco* (3), *Angelo* (2), *Calogero* (2), *Caterina* (2), *Enrico* (2), *Mario* (2), *Vito* (2).

Oliveria (183) Variant spelling of Portuguese OLIVEIRA.
GIVEN NAMES Portuguese 14%; Spanish 11%. *Joao* (2), *Joaquim*, *Paulo*; *Manuel* (4), *Antonio* (2), *Jose* (2), *Domingos*, *Ernesto*, *Marta*, *Pedro*, *Raul*, *Ronaldo*, *Vicente*.

Oliverio (589) Italian: variant of the personal name OLIVIERO.
GIVEN NAMES Italian 18%; Spanish 7%. *Salvatore* (8), *Antonio* (4), *Carlo* (4), *Mario* (3), *Rocco* (3), *Angelo* (2), *Carmine* (2), *Francesco* (2), *Aldo*, *Concetta*, *Eduardo*, *Egidio*, *Ezio*; *Jose* (3), *Gutierrez*, *Juan*, *Maria Lucia*.

Olivero (352) **1.** Spanish and Italian: from the personal name *Olivero* (see OLIVER).

2. Catalan (**Oliveró**): topographic name, from a diminutive of *oliver* 'olive tree'.
3. Spanish: habitational name for someone from Oliva de la Frontera, in Badajoz province.
GIVEN NAMES Spanish 17%; Italian 5%. *Luis* (3), *Jose* (2), *Mercedes* (2), *Ana*, *Andres*, *Armando*, *Cesar*, *Domitila*, *Dulce*, *Feliciano*, *Fernanda*, *Fernando*; *Antonio* (4), *Aldo* (2), *Carlo*, *Carmela*, *Carmelo*, *Franco*, *Gabriele*, *Marco*.

Oliveros (371) Spanish: from an old form of the personal name *Olivero* (see OLIVER).
GIVEN NAMES Spanish 48%; Italian 6%. *Jose* (14), *Francisco* (5), *Pedro* (5), *Alfredo* (4), *Gilberto* (4), *Juan* (4), *Arturo* (3), *Carlos* (3), *Javier* (3), *Jesus* (3), *Jorge* (3), *Luis* (3); *Severino* (2), *Antonio*, *Fausto*, *Lorenzo*.

Oliverson (128) Scottish: patronymic from OLIVER.

Oliveto (216) Italian: habitational name from a place named with Oliveto (from Latin *olivetum* 'olive grove'), notably Oliveto Citra in Salerno province or Oliveto Lucano in Matera province.
GIVEN NAMES Italian 19%. *Salvatore* (4), *Carmelo*, *Carmine*, *Domenico*, *Fulvio*, *Pasquale*, *Rocco*, *Vincenzo*.

Olivier (2063) French: variant of OLIVER.
GIVEN NAMES French 11%. *Pierre* (10), *Jacques* (5), *Michel* (5), *Andre* (3), *Antoine* (3), *Julien* (3), *Marcel* (3), *Armand* (2), *Benoit* (2), *Edouard* (2), *Emile* (2), *Henri* (2).

Olivieri (991) Italian: patronymic from the personal name OLIVIERO.
GIVEN NAMES Italian 31%; Spanish 8%. *Mario* (9), *Rocco* (6), *Angelo* (4), *Salvatore* (4), *Antonio* (3), *Carmine* (3), *Elena* (3), *Emilio* (2), *Giovanni* (2), *Lucio* (2), *Luigi* (2), *Nunzio* (2), *Onofrio* (2), *Aldo*, *Alessandro*; *Jose* (5), *Carlos* (3), *Enrique* (2), *Pedro* (2), *Rosario* (2), *Abramo*.

Oliviero (104) Italian: from the personal name *Oliviero*, from the Old French personal name *Olivier* (see OLIVER).
GIVEN NAMES Italian 28%; Spanish 9%. *Antonio* (2), *Amedeo*, *Aniello*, *Ciro*, *Dante*, *Gennaro*, *Pasquale*, *Pietro*, *Rocco*, *Salvatore*, *Silvio*, *Ugo*; *Mario* (2), *Ademar*, *Guadalupe*, *Jose*, *Ricardo*.

Olivo (1237) Spanish and Italian: topographic name from *olivo* 'olive tree', or occupational name for a seller of olives.
GIVEN NAMES Spanish 35%; Italian 6%. *Jose* (15), *Juan* (14), *Jesus* (12), *Luis* (11), *Manuel* (6), *Juana* (5), *Rafael* (4), *Ana* (3), *Angel* (3), *Carlos* (3), *Cruz* (3), *Elena* (3); *Antonio* (10), *Angelo* (3), *Aldo* (2), *Ceasar* (2), *Sal* (2), *Carmela*, *Carmelo*, *Caterina*, *Dario*, *Domenic*, *Leonardo*, *Lucio*.

Olk (250) German: **1.** habitational name from any of several places so called (for example, near Trier, and in former East Prussia). The place name is probably formed with an element meaning 'dirty'.

2. from a Germanic personal name formed with *od-* 'property', 'riches'.
GIVEN NAMES German 4%. *Heinz*, *Jurgen*, *Math.*

Olkowski (243) Polish: habitational name for someone from places called Olkowice or Olkowo in Ostrołęka and Radom voivodeships, named with the personal name OLEK.
GIVEN NAMES Polish 5%. *Bronislaw*, *Stanislaw.*

Ollar (180) Probably a variant of OLLER.

Olle (129) **1.** German or Swedish: unexplained. **2.** Catalan (**Ollé**): variant spelling of OLLER 2.
GIVEN NAME German 5%. *Erwin.*

Oller (911) **1.** German (**Öller**): variant of **Öhler** (see OHLER) or of EULER. **2.** Catalan: occupational name for a potter, *oller* (from Late Latin *ollarius*, from *olla* 'pot').

Olley (154) English (East Anglia): variant of DULEY, without the preposition *d'*.

Ollie (265) Probably a variant spelling of English OLLEY.
GIVEN NAMES German 4%. *Arno* (3), *Hilde.*

Olliff (232) English: variant spelling of OLIFF.

Ollila (303) Finnish: from the Finnish personal name *Olli*, a pet form of Norse *Olav*, + the local ending *-la*, a habitational name from a farm named for its owner, i.e. 'Olav's place'. The surname occurs chiefly in western Finland.

Ollinger (201) German: variant of OHLINGER.

Ollis (671) English (Bristol and Bath): unexplained.

Ollison (209) Americanized form of OLESEN.

Ollmann (110) German: variant of OHLMANN.
GIVEN NAMES German 7%. *Horst*, *Kurt.*

Ollom (101) Origin unidentified.

Olm (131) **1.** German: habitational name from places near Mainz or in Lower Saxony (near Lüneburg), so named from an old element, *ulm* 'mud'. In some instances the surname may be topographic. **2.** Dutch and Catalan: topographic name from Dutch and Old Catalan *olm* 'elm', from Latin *ulmus*.

Olman (104) Respelling of German **Ölmann**, a variant of OHLMANN; possibly also a Jewish variant of the same name.

Olmeda (203) Spanish: habitational name from any of various places named Olmeda, from *olmeda* 'stand of elm trees'.
GIVEN NAMES Spanish 48%. *Juan* (5), *Jose* (4), *Luz* (3), *Rosario* (3), *Angel* (2), *Gerardo* (2), *Jaime* (2), *Luis* (2), *Manuel* (2), *Pedro* (2), *Rafael* (2), *Alfonso.*

Olmedo (379) Spanish: habitational name from any of the places named Olmedo in Burgos and Valladolid provinces, from *olmedo* 'stand of elm trees'.

GIVEN NAMES Spanish 51%. *Jose* (16), *Carlos* (8), *Luis* (6), *Miguel* (6), *Alfredo* (4), *Francisco* (4), *Javier* (4), *Jorge* (4), *Juan* (4), *Manuel* (4), *Mario* (4), *Pedro* (4); *Antonio* (5), *Lorenzo* (3), *Angelo, Carmela, Filomena, Leonardo, Lucio, Marcello, Vito.*

Olmo (250) Italian (mainly Tuscany and northern Italy) and Spanish: from *olmo* 'elm', Latin *ulmus*, topographic name for someone who lived by a conspicuous elm tree, or a habitational name from a place named Olmo, from the same word.
GIVEN NAMES Spanish 36%. *Jose* (8), *Carlos* (3), *Julio* (3), *Luis* (3), *Ernesto* (2), *Luz* (2), *Miguel* (2), *Orlando* (2), *Pedro* (2), *Rafael* (2), *Agustin, Alicia.*

Olmos (771) Spanish: habitational name from any of the places named Olmos, from the plural of *olmo* 'elm'.
GIVEN NAMES Spanish 54%. *Jose* (22), *Carlos* (11), *Jesus* (11), *Manuel* (9), *Juan* (8), *Lupe* (7), *Ruben* (7), *Guadalupe* (6), *Rafael* (6), *Ramon* (6), *Roberto* (6), *Salvador* (6).

Olmscheid (137) German: probably a Rhineland habitational or topographic name, from an old element *ul-m* 'mud' + *scheid* 'watershed area', 'mountain ridge', 'privately owned forest clearing'.

Olmstead (3245) English: habitational name from Olmstead Green in Cambridgeshire.

Olmsted (1493) English: variant spelling of OLMSTEAD.
FOREBEARS James Olmsted was one of the founders of Hartford, CT, (coming from Cambridge, MA, with Thomas Hooker) in 1635.

Olney (1274) English: habitational name from places called Olney in Buckinghamshire and Northamptonshire. The former is named in Old English as *Ollanēg* 'island of a man called Olla'; the latter is from Old English *āna* 'one', 'single', 'solitary' + *lēah* 'wood', 'clearing', with later metathesis of *-nl-* to *-ln-*.

Olofson (245) Respelling of Swedish **Olofsson**, equivalent of OLSEN.
GIVEN NAMES Scandinavian 9%; German 7%. *Erik* (2), *Berger, Iver; Kurt* (2), *Ewald, Franz.*

O'Loughlin (1334) Irish (Ulster and County Clare): Anglicized form of Gaelic **Ó Lochlainn** 'descendant of Lochlann' (see LAUGHLIN).
GIVEN NAMES Irish 6%. *Brendan, Bridie, Finian, Kieran, Liam, Roisin.*

Olp (149) German: **1.** from a short form of the personal name *Olbrecht*, a variant of *Albrecht* (see ALBERT), frequent in Württemberg. **2.** possibly a topographic name from a variant of Middle High German *albe* 'mountain pasture' (German *Alp*).

Olsavsky (110) Origin uncertain; perhaps a respelling of Jewish **Olshevsky**, habitational name from the village of Olshevo in Belarus. It also could be an Americanized form of Polish and Jewish OLSZEWSKI.

Olsen (24356) **1.** Danish and Norwegian: patronymic from the personal name *Olaf, Olav* (Old Norse *Óláfr, Ólafr,* variant *Óleifr,* earlier *Anleifr,* from proto-Scandinavian elements meaning 'ancestor' + 'heir', 'descendant'). Olaf has always been one of the most common Scandinavian names; it continued to be popular in the Middle Ages, in part as a result of the fame of St. Olaf, King of Norway, who brought Christianity to his country *c.*1030. This surname, the second most common in Norway, is also established in England, notably in the Newcastle upon Tyne area. **2.** German (**Ölsen**): habitational name from any of several places so named, in Saxony, Brandenburg, and the Rhineland.
GIVEN NAMES Scandinavian 7%. *Erik* (71), *Nels* (11), *Nils* (11), *Lars* (10), *Alf* (9), *Thor* (9), *Niels* (8), *Sven* (7), *Jorgen* (5), *Helmer* (4), *Iver* (4), *Arnfinn* (3).

Olshan (160) Shortened form of OLSHANSKY and related names.
GIVEN NAMES Jewish 7%. *Ilya, Mort.*

Olshansky (190) **1.** Jewish (from Ukraine and Belarus), Ukrainian, and Belorussian: habitational name for someone from Olshana or Olshanka in Ukraine, or Olshany in Belarus. **2.** Americanized form of Polish and Jewish (from Poland) OLSZANSKI.
GIVEN NAMES Russian 15%; Jewish 14%. *Leonid* (3), *Semyon* (3), *Lev* (2), *Boris, Grigoriy, Grigory, Mikhail, Savely, Vladimir, Vladmir, Yefim; Polina* (2), *Avrum, Gersh, Ilya, Izya, Naum, Sol, Yakov.*

Olshefski (188) Americanized spelling of Polish OLSZEWSKI.

Olson (72486) Americanized spelling of Swedish OLSSON or Danish and Norwegian OLSEN.
GIVEN NAMES Scandinavian 4%. *Erik* (109), *Nels* (38), *Lars* (19), *Thor* (16), *Helmer* (15), *Selmer* (12), *Bjorn* (10), *Nils* (10), *Elof* (7), *Einer* (6), *Lennart* (6), *Bertel* (5).

Olsson (1119) **1.** Swedish: patronymic from the personal name *Olaf* (see OLSEN). **2.** German (Eastphalia): patronymic from a short form of the personal name ULRICH.
GIVEN NAMES Scandinavian 20%; German 5%. *Lars* (10), *Lennart* (5), *Sven* (5), *Nils* (4), *Erik* (3), *Mats* (3), *Per* (3), *Anders* (2), *Bjorn* (2), *Fredrik* (2), *Nels* (2), *Olle* (2), *Hans* (3), *Kurt* (3), *Fritz* (2), *Ingeborg, Otto, Ute.*

Olstad (404) Norwegian: habitational name from any of ten farmsteads in southeastern Norway named Olstad, from a contracted form of Old Norse *Ólafsstaðir,* from the personal name *Ólaf* + *staðir,* plural of *staðr* 'farmstead', 'dwelling'.

Olszanski (56) Polish (**Olszański**): habitational name for someone from places called Olszany or Olszanica, named with Polish *olsza* 'alder'.
GIVEN NAMES Polish 10%. *Halina, Kazimierz.*

Olszewski (2112) Polish and Jewish (from Poland): habitational name for someone from any of the many places in Poland called Olsze, Olszew, Olszewa, or Olszewo, named with Polish *olsza* 'alder'.
GIVEN NAMES Polish 7%. *Jerzy* (4), *Casimir* (3), *Andrzej* (2), *Dariusz* (2), *Jacek* (2), *Lech* (2), *Mariusz* (2), *Stanislaw* (2), *Tadeusz* (2), *Wladyslaw* (2), *Aleksander, Boguslaw.*

Olszowy (117) Polish: topographic name for someone who lived where alders grew, from a derivative of Polish *olsza* 'alder'.
GIVEN NAMES Polish 8%. *Boleslaw, Jozef, Zdzislaw.*

Olt (159) German: variant spelling of ALT. See also OLDT.

Olthoff (223) North German and Dutch: topographic name or habitational name from Middle Low German *Olde hove* 'old farm'.

Oltman (661) Altered spelling of German OLTMANN.

Oltmann (240) North German form of ALTMANN.
GIVEN NAMES German 5%. *Erwin* (2), *Gerd, Kurt.*

Oltmanns (261) German: variant of OLTMANN.
GIVEN NAMES German 7%. *Fritz, Gerhard, Kurt, Otto.*

Oltmans (118) Respelling of German OLTMANNS.
GIVEN NAMES Dutch 6%. *Harm* (2), *Willem.*

Oltrogge (130) Possibly a variant of German **Olrogge**, an occupational name for a rye farmer.

Oltz (108) German and French (Alsace): unexplained; perhaps a respelling of German **Ohls**: a patronymic from the personal name *Ohl,* a short form of *Olrich* (see ULRICH).

Olund (181) Respelling of Swedish **Ålund** or **Ölund**, composed of *å* 'creek', 'river' or *ö* 'island' + *lund* 'grove'.
GIVEN NAMES Scandinavian 9%. *Lennart* (3), *Sven.*

Olver (286) English (Devon): variant of OLIVER.

Olvera (1849) Spanish: habitational name from Olvera in Cádiz province.
GIVEN NAMES Spanish 55%. *Jose* (49), *Juan* (35), *Jesus* (20), *Carlos* (18), *Manuel* (16), *Luis* (15), *Pedro* (13), *Felipe* (12), *Rafael* (12), *Raul* (12), *Francisco* (11), *Miguel* (11).

Olvey (181) Possibly an altered spelling of ALVEY.

Olwell (122) English: possibly a habitational name from Ulwell in Swanage, Dorset, named with Old English *ūle* 'owl' + *wella* 'stream'.

Om (126) **1.** Indian (Uttar Pradesh): Hindu (Brahman) name, from Sanskrit *om,* the Hindu sacred and mystic syllable uttered at the beginning of prayers, etc. **2.** Korean:

unexplained. **3.** Cambodian or other Southeast Asian: unexplained.

GIVEN NAMES Southeast Asian 44%; Indian 6%. *Kyong* (2), *Kyong Suk* (2), *Young* (2), *Chae, Chi Young, Hang, Kil, Rin, Sang Hun; Chang, Chong, Insoo, Kum, Sun Young, Yom, Young Hwan; Kiwan, Oeurn, Phoeun, Pich, Saroeuth, Seung, Sophath, Sophea, Yoeun, Phan, Son; Shanti* (2), *Harendra*.

O'Mahoney (184) Irish: Anglicized form of Gaelic **Ó Mathghamhna** 'descendant of *Mathghamhain*' (see MAHONEY). There are two families of this name, in Cork and Ulster, but the Ulster family name was usually Anglicized as McMAHON.

GIVEN NAMES Irish 9%. *Seamus* (2), *Senan*.

O'Mahony (236) Irish: variant spelling of O'MAHONEY.

GIVEN NAMES Irish 17%. *Conor* (2), *Aisling, Brendan, Ciaran, Eoin, Ronan, Siobhan*.

O'Maley (112) Irish: variant spelling of O'MALLEY.

O'Malley (6826) Irish (Connacht and Munster): Anglicized form of Gaelic **Ó Máille**. This is of uncertain derivation. Woulfe suggests a Celtic source *maglios* 'prince', 'champion', 'poet'. There is a Gaelic adjective *mall* 'slow', 'stately', and another, *málla*, meaning 'sedate', 'pleasant', and an abstract noun *máille* 'stateliness'; the source could be any of these.

GIVEN NAMES Irish 8%. *Brendan* (8), *Ronan* (3), *Colm* (2), *Cormac* (2), *Brigid, Cahal, Colum, Conal, Conor, Delma, Donal, Eamon*.

Oman (1370) **1.** Swedish (also **Öman**): ornamental name from Swedish *ö* 'island' + *man* 'man', in some cases adopted as a topographic name by someone who lived on an island. **2.** Scottish and English: variant of HAMMOND. **3.** Slovenian: topographic name from *oman*, the name of a plant (in English known as elecampane or meadow fleabane; Latin genus name *Inula*). **4.** Slovenian: perhaps a medieval status name from a Slovenian spelling of German Bavarian *Amtmann* 'official' (see AMMANN). Compare AMAN, AMON.

GIVEN NAMES Scandinavian 4%. *Nels* (2), *Sven* (2), *Erik, Kerstin, Obert*.

Omans (119) **1.** Scottish and English: patronymic from OMAN 2. **2.** Possibly an altered spelling of Dutch **Oomens**, a patronymic from a derivative of a Germanic personal name composed of *ōd* 'property', 'possession' + *māri, mēri* 'famous'.

Omar (601) **1.** Muslim (found almost exclusively among Sunni Muslims): from an Arabic personal name of uncertain etymology. It is thought to be related to Arabic *'āmir*, which means 'prosperous', 'full of life', 'large', 'substantial'. The root word *'umr* means 'life'. 'Umar bin al-Khaṭṭāb was the second of the 'rightly guided' khalifs (ruled 634–44). He was known by the title *al-Fārūq* 'the distinguisher', i.e. one

who distinguishes between truth and falsehood. He was one of the Companions of the Prophet Muhammad. The Persian poet 'Umar al-Khayyām (1048–1125), also known in English as Omar Khayyam, is the author of the classic poem, the *Rubaiyyat*. **2.** Catalan: topographic name for someone who lived by a group of elm trees, from the collective form of *om* 'elm'.

GIVEN NAMES Muslim 63%. *Mohammed* (9), *Mohamed* (8), *Ali* (7), *Omar* (7), *Ahmed* (6), *Ahmad* (5), *Hassan* (5), *Abdul* (3), *Husam* (3), *Khalid* (3), *Mohammad* (3), *Mohd* (3).

O'Mara (1752) Irish: Anglicized form of Gaelic **Ó Meadhra** 'descendant of *Meadhair*' a personal name derived from *meadhair* 'mirth'.

GIVEN NAME Irish 5%. *Brendan*.

O'Mary (220) Irish: probably an altered form of O'MARA, influenced by the cult of the Virgin Mary.

Omdahl (186) Norwegian: habitational name from any of several farmsteads, notably in Agder and Rogaland, named Omdal or Åmdal, from Old Norse *Almdalr*, a compound of *almr* 'elm' + *dalr* 'valley'.

GIVEN NAMES Scandinavian 9%. *Oyvind, Svein*.

O'Meara (2081) Irish: variant of O'MARA.

GIVEN NAMES Irish 6%. *Brendan* (2), *Maeve* (2), *Dermot, Liam, Patrick Do, Patrick James*.

O'Melia (284) Irish: Anglicized form of Gaelic **Ó Máille** (see O'MALLEY).

GIVEN NAMES Irish 7%. *Brendan, Ciaran*.

Omer (425) **1.** Muslim: variant of OMAR. **2.** French: from a Germanic personal name composed of the elements *aud* 'wealth' + *mari, meri* 'renowned'. As a Huguenot name, it is also found in Germany. **3.** Possibly a respelling of German OHMER.

GIVEN NAMES Muslim 25%. *Ahmed* (6), *Mohamed* (6), *Mohammed* (4), *Tarig* (3), *Mohammad* (2), *Murad* (2), *Abdirahman, Abdul, Abdulla, Abdulrahim, Ali, Amin*.

Omlor (191) Probably a respelling of German **Amler**, from a Germanic personal name formed with *Am-*, an unexplained stem, possibly cognate with Latin *amare* 'to love'.

Ommen (157) **1.** Frisian and North German: patronymic from the personal name *Ommo*. **2.** Dutch (**van Ommen**): habitational name for someone from Ommen in Overijssel.

Omo (119) Americanized spelling of the Norwegian habitational name **Åmo**, from a number of farmsteads so named from *á* 'small river' + *mo* 'plain', 'moor'.

Omohundro (237) Origin unidentified. Possibly of American Indian origin.

FOREBEARS Richard Omohundro is recorded in Westmoreland Co., VA, as early as December 30, 1670.

Omori (195) Japanese (**Ōmori**): 'large grove'; variously written. It is found most-

ly in eastern Japan and the island of Okinawa. Some bearers, of FUJIWARA origin, took the name from a district in Suruga (now part of Shizuoka prefecture).

GIVEN NAMES Japanese 53%. *Masao* (3), *Shigeru* (3), *Hideo* (2), *Keiko* (2), *Mika* (2), *Seijiro* (2), *Toshio* (2), *Akira, Chizuko, Hide, Hiromi, Hiroyuki*.

Omundson (122) Americanized spelling of Norwegian **Om(m)undsen**, a patronymic from *Om{m}und*, from the Nordic personal name *Ǫgmundr*, composed of the elements *agi* 'awe' (or possibly *ag* 'point of a sword') + *mund* 'protection'. Compare AMUNDSEN.

Omura (173) Japanese (**Ōmura**): 'large village'; a place name and surname found throughout Japan and the Ryūkyū Islands. The name listed in the Shinsen shōjiroku may be taken from a district in Hizen (now Nagasaki prefecture).

GIVEN NAMES Japanese 48%. *Akiko* (3), *Emiko* (2), *Hiroshi* (2), *Toshio* (2), *Akihiro, Akio, Asao, Atsushi, Azusa, Hiromi, Hisanori, Hisashi*.

On (209) **1.** Vietnamese: unexplained. **2.** Chinese 安: variant of AN 1.

GIVEN NAMES Vietnamese 34%; Chinese 18%. *Hung* (3), *Lam* (3), *Muoi* (3), *Hai* (2), *Hoa* (2), *Loc* (2), *Trung* (2), *Be Van, Binh, Ha, Huu, Phoung, Tong; Meng* (2), *Dung, Hong, Kin, Kwong, Kyung-Won, Mi Ok, Wing, Yan, Yon, Young*.

Onaga (110) Japanese: variously written with characters that can mean 'very old man', 'small eternity', or 'long tail'. Found mostly in the Ryūkyū Islands.

GIVEN NAMES Japanese 24%; Spanish 4%. *Atsuo, Kazumi, Koji, Kotaro, Kuniko, Matsuko, Satoru, Shinzo, Shizuo, Tetsuo, Toshio, Yasue; Ana, Elena, Jaime, Oswaldo, Ricardo, Sergio*.

Onan (444) Variant of Irish **Oonan**, itself a variant of **Honeen** (see HONAN 2).

FOREBEARS Alexander Onan (born in Ireland in about 1793) came to Kent Co., MI, in the early 19th century.

Onate (178) Spanish (**Oñate**): Castilianized form of Basque **Oñati**, habitational name from a place of this name in Gipuzkoa province, Basque Country. The place name is of Basque origin but disputed etymology.

GIVEN NAMES Spanish 51%. *Jose* (5), *Francisco* (4), *Manuel* (4), *Juan* (3), *Pedro* (3), *Ramon* (3), *Raul* (3), *Alfonso* (2), *Cesar* (2), *Gregorio* (2), *Luis* (2), *Pablo* (2).

Oncale (144) Origin unidentified. Possibly of French origin.

GIVEN NAMES French 7%. *Colette, Nolton, Patrice*.

Oncken (107) German (Frisian): patronymic from the personal name *Onno*.

GIVEN NAMES German 7%. *Benno, Ingeborg, Klaus*.

Onder (182) **1.** Dutch: topographic name from *onder* 'below', 'beneath'. **2.** Turkish

(Önder): from a personal name based on Turkish *önder* 'leader'.
GIVEN NAMES Muslim 6%. *Kemal* (3), *Ismet* (2), *Fatma, Ibrahim, Soner, Vedat.*

Onderdonk (222) Dutch: topographic name from *onder* 'below', 'under' + *donk* 'small hill'.

Onderko (138) Czech and Slovak: derivative of the personal name *Ondřej, Ondrej* (see ANDREAS).

Ondo (239) **1.** Basque: topographic name from Basque *ondo* 'deep valley', 'ravine', 'gully'. **2.** Hungarian (**Ondó**): from a pet form of the old secular personal name *Ond.*

Ondracek (150) Czech (**Ondráček**): from a pet form of the personal name *Ondřej* (see ANDREAS).
GIVEN NAME German 5%. *Otto* (2).

Ondrey (115) Americanized form of Czech *Ondřej* or Slovak *Ondej*, forms of ANDREAS.

Ondrus (108) Czech (**Ondruš**): from a variant of the personal name *Ondřej*, Czech form of ANDREAS.
GIVEN NAMES Czech and Slovak 4%. *Frantisek, Milan.*

O'Neal (15342) Irish: variant spelling of O'NEILL.

O'Neall (155) Irish: variant spelling of O'NEILL.

O'Neel (134) Respelling of Irish O'NEILL.

O'Neil (11840) Irish: variant of O'NEILL.
GIVEN NAMES Irish 5%. *Brendan* (6), *Conn* (2), *Donal* (2), *Liam* (2), *Siobhan* (2), *Aileen, Eamon, Michael Patrick, Seamus, Sean Patrick, William Sean.*

O'Neill (19940) Irish: Anglicized form of Gaelic **Ó Néill** 'descendant of *Niall*' (see NEILL).
GIVEN NAMES Irish 6%. *Brendan* (27), *Kieran* (4), *Seamus* (4), *Siobhan* (4), *Dermot* (3), *Liam* (3), *Nuala* (3), *Bridie* (2), *Brigid* (2), *Conor* (2), *Fintan* (2), *John Patrick* (2).

Oneto (187) Italian: unexplained. Perhaps a masculinized form the of habitational name **Oneta**, from any of several places so named, in particular the one in Bergamo province. The name is also found in Spain, notably in San Fernando in Cádiz province, and Portugal, apparently taken there from Italy.

O'Ney (1130) Irish: Anglicized form of Gaelic **Ó Niadh** 'descendant of *Nia(dh)*', a byname meaning 'champion'.

Ong (1871) **1.** English (mostly East Anglia): unexplained. **2.** Vietnamese (**Ông**): unexplained. **3.** Chinese 王: variant of WANG 1. **4.** Indonesian: unexplained. **5.** Filipino: unexplained.
GIVEN NAMES Vietnamese 10%; Chinese 7%; Spanish 6%. *Hung* (6), *Tuan* (5), *Quang* (4), *Lien* (3), *Minh* (3), *Nga* (3), *Binh* (2), *Chau* (2), *Chuoi* (2), *Cuong* (2), *Dung* (2), *Hien* (2); *Beng* (5), *Cheng* (5), *Boon* (4), *Eng* (3), *Kwok* (3), *Chee* (2), *Chiang* (2), *Chin* (2), *Ching* (2), *Hang* (2), *Hong* (2), *Jin* (2); *Francisco* (4), *Carlos* (3), *Ernesto* (3), *Manuel* (3), *Alejandro* (2), *Arsenio* (2),

Artemio (2), *Belita* (2), *Carmencita* (2), *Conrado* (2), *Edgardo* (2), *Eduardo* (2).

Ongaro (116) Italian: ethnic name for a Hungarian, from Old Italian *ongaro.*
GIVEN NAMES Italian 14%. *Aldo* (2), *Roberto* (2), *Sal* (2), *Massimo, Mauro.*

Onion (109) **1.** Welsh: variant of EYNON. **2.** English: metonymic occupational name for an onion grower or seller, from Old French *oignon* 'onion'.

Onishi (210) Japanese (**Ōnishi**): 'great west'; a habitational name taken from a village in Awa (now Tokushima prefecture) by members of the OGASAWARA family, who were of MINAMOTO descent. The name is also found on Okinawa Island.
GIVEN NAMES Japanese 65%. *Hideo* (3), *Hiromi* (3), *Shizuo* (3), *Akira* (2), *Hiroshi* (2), *Kazuyoshi* (2), *Kenichi* (2), *Masashi* (2), *Masato* (2), *Mayumi* (2), *Nobuhiro* (2), *Takehiro* (2).

Onken (529) Frisian, North German, and Dutch: patronymic from a pet form of the Frisian personal name *Onno.*
GIVEN NAMES German 4%. *Bernhard, Erwin, Frieda, Fritz, Hermann, Kurt, Reinold.*

Onley (272) English: habitational name from Onley or Olney in Northamptonshire, possibly also from Onneley in Staffordshire. Like Olney, Onley was named in Old English as 'lonely (*āna*, from *ān* 'one') glade (*lēah*)'; Onneley has the same second element, and possibly the same initial one, though this may alternatively have been a personal name, *Onna.*

Onnen (206) Frisian: patronymic from the personal name *Onno.*

Ono (678) Japanese: 'small field'; variously written, mostly found in western Japan. In its Romanized form, the surname is often confused with *Ōno*, which means 'large field' and is also a common place name and surname throughout Japan and in the Ryūkyū Islands. Some bearers of the surname are descended from the MINAMOTO. *Ōno* is listed in the Shinsen shōjiroku.
GIVEN NAMES Japanese 63%. *Akira* (8), *Hiroshi* (7), *Kenji* (7), *Makoto* (6), *Yoshi* (5), *Hiromi* (4), *Hisashi* (3), *Junji* (3), *Kazuo* (3), *Masaaki* (3), *Masao* (3), *Masaru* (3).

Onofre (156) Catalan: from the personal name *Onofre* (see ONOFRIO).
GIVEN NAMES Spanish 53%. *Juan* (5), *Alberto* (3), *Jose* (3), *Manuel* (3), *Felipe* (2), *Fernando* (2), *Francisco* (2), *Lourdes* (2), *Luz* (2), *Ricardo* (2), *Adan, Adriana.*

Onofrey (113) Altered spelling of Catalan ONOFRE.

Onofrio (324) Italian (mainly southern): from the personal name *Onofrio*, derived from Latin *Onnuphrius*, borrowed from an epithet of the Egyptian god Osiris, *Onnophris* 'always glad'. It gained popularity as a Christian name in Italy with the cult of St. Onofrio, a 5th-century Egyptian martyr.

GIVEN NAMES Italian 12%; French 6%. *Angelo* (2), *Dino* (2), *Pasquale* (2), *Salvatore* (2), *Carmine, Giovanni, Santo; Patrice* (2), *Armand, Josee.*

Onorati (110) Southern Italian: patronymic or plural form of ONORATO.
GIVEN NAMES Italian 20%. *Marino* (2), *Angelo, Enzo, Guido, Guilio, Lelio, Luigi, Piera, Remo.*

Onorato (642) Southern Italian: from the personal name *Onorato*, derived from Latin *Honoratus* 'honoured', 'worthy of respect'.
GIVEN NAMES Italian 14%. *Rocco* (7), *Angelo* (5), *Luigi* (2), *Sal* (2), *Salvatore* (2), *Antonio, Domenico, Donato, Geno, Gilda, Giovanni, Pasquale.*

Onsager (107) Norwegian: habitational name from a farmstead named with *Ons-* (from *Odin*, the name of a god) + *ager* 'cultivated field'.
GIVEN NAMES Scandinavian 16%; German 5%. *Lars* (2), *Nils* (2), *Erik; Frieda* (2), *Hans.*

Onstad (342) Norwegian: habitational name from the name of any of seven farmsteads, mainly in the southeast, most of them with names formed from any of various Old Norse personal names + *staðir* 'farmstead',as for example *Augunarstaðir*, from the personal name *Auðun* (from *Auð* 'wealth' + *un* 'friend').

Onstott (460) **1.** Probably an altered spelling of ONSTAD. **2.** Possibly an altered spelling of German **Amstad**, a topographic name from Middle High German *an, am* 'at (the)' + *stade* 'bank', 'shore'.

Ontiveros (1406) Spanish: of uncertain derivation; possibly from an old personal name of unexplained etymology.
GIVEN NAMES Spanish 45%. *Jose* (47), *Jesus* (20), *Juan* (20), *Manuel* (19), *Carlos* (9), *Francisco* (9), *Alfredo* (8), *Javier* (8), *Guadalupe* (7), *Pedro* (7), *Ramon* (7), *Ruben* (7).

Ontko (175) Ukrainian: unexplained. Compare ONDERKO.

Onufer (127) **1.** Hungarian: unexplained. **2.** Possibly also an Americanized spelling of Spanish ONOFRIO.

Ooi (109) Malaysian: unexplained.
GIVEN NAMES Southeast Asian 40%. *Boon* (3), *Joon* (2), *Beng, Chen, Cheng Hua, Chin, Han, Kuo, Leong, Liling, Seng, Sze, Siew, Wee, Yen.*

Ooley (219) Possibly an Americanized spelling of German UHLE.

Oommen (130) Indian (Kerala): variant of THOMAS among Kerala Christians, with the Tamil-Malayalam third person masculine singular suffix *-n*. It is only found as a personal name in Kerala, but in the U.S. has come to be used as a family name among Kerala Christians.
GIVEN NAMES Indian 42%. *Varughese* (4), *Cheriyan* (2), *Raju* (2), *Marykutty, Ninan, Oommen, Pothen, Preetha, Reji, Saji, Sanju, Smitha.*

Ooms (156) Dutch: patronymic from the kinship name *oom* 'uncle' (also 'grandfather' and 'brother-in-law'). Compare NEVE.

GIVEN NAMES Dutch 6%. *Dirk, Gerrit, Hendrik.*

Oosterhouse (109) Americanized form of a Dutch habitational name meaning 'the eastern dwelling', possibly from Oosterhuizen in Gelderland, Netherlands.

GIVEN NAMES Dutch 6%; German 4%. *Klaas* (2); *Kurt.*

Oosting (134) Dutch and North German: topographic name denoting someone who came from or lived in the eastern part of a region, from Middle Low German *oost(en)* 'eastern' + the suffix *-ing* denoting affiliation.

Ooten (325) Variant spelling of Dutch **Uten**, either a patronymic from the Middle Dutch personal name *Udin*, a derivative of Germanic *Udo* (see UDE), or a metronymic from the female personal name *Jutta.*

Opal (134) Polish: **1.** from *opał* 'combustible material', a derivative of *opić* 'to burn or singe' or 'to get sunburnt', hence a nickname for a sunburnt individual. **2.** nickname from *opal* 'opal' (the jewel).

GIVEN NAME French 5%. *Jacques* (2).

Opalinski (111) Polish: habitational name for someone from a place called Opalenica in Poznań voivodeship (see OPAL).

GIVEN NAMES Polish 9%. *Jerzy, Karol, Stanislaw, Zosia.*

Opalka (225) **1.** Polish (**Opałka**): nickname for a sunburnt individual (see OPAL). **2.** Czech (**Opálka**): metonymic occupational name for a basket maker, from *opálka* 'woven basket'.

GIVEN NAMES Polish 7%; German 4%. *Andrzej, Wieslaw, Zbigniew, Zofia; Helmuth, Klaus.*

Opat (112) Czech and Slovak: occupational name for someone in the service of an abbot, from *opat* 'abbot'.

Opatz (134) German (of Slavic origin): occupational name for someone in the service of an abbot, from Slavic *opat* 'abbot'.

Opdahl (280) Norwegian: **1.** habitational name from any of about fifteen farmsteads named Oppdal, from Old Norse *Uppdalr*, from *uppi* 'up' + *dalr* 'valley'. **2.** altered form of Øvstedal, the name of a farm in western Norway, composed of *øvste* 'upper' + *dal* 'valley'.

Opdycke (102) Variant spelling of Dutch OPDYKE.

Opdyke (350) Dutch: topographic name for someone who lived 'on the dike', from *op* 'up', 'on' + *dyck* 'dike'. Compare DYKE, UPDIKE.

Opel (378) German (Saxony): from a short form of ALBERT or *Adalbert*.

GIVEN NAMES German 4%. *Erwin* (2), *Kurt* (2), *Fritz, Gerhard, Inge.*

Opelt (119) German: variant of OPPELT.

Openshaw (350) English (Lancashire): habitational name from a place in Greater Manchester called Openshaw, from Old English *open* 'open' (i.e. not surrounded by a hedge) + *sceaga* 'copse'.

Opfer (357) Jewish (Ashkenazic): from German *Opfer* 'sacrifice'.

Opferman (101) German (**Opfermann**): occupational name for a churchwarden, one who took the collection in church, Middle High German *opferman*, a derivative of *ofper(gilt)* 'donation'. Compare North German OPPERMANN.

Opgenorth (104) Altered form of an unidentified Dutch or German name.

GIVEN NAMES German 6%. *Hermann, Kurt.*

Opheim (334) **1.** Norwegian: habitational name from any of about twenty farmsteads, chiefly in Hordaland, so named from Old Norse *Uppheimr*, a compound of *uppi* 'up' + *heimr* 'farmstead' (i.e. a farmstead situated on higher ground). **2.** German: habitational name from an unidentified place.

GIVEN NAMES Scandinavian 5%. *Knute, Lars, Selmer.*

Opie (406) Cornish: from the medieval personal name *Oppy, Obby*, a pet form of various personal names such as *Osborn, Osbert*, and *Osbald*.

Opiela (176) Polish: occupational name for a gardener, from an agent derivative of *opielać* 'to weed'.

GIVEN NAMES Polish 4%. *Beata, Jaroslaw.*

Opitz (720) Eastern German: **1.** from *Opecz* a medieval Silesian and Bohemian pet form of *Albrecht* (see ALBERT). **2.** habitational name from a place so named in Saxony.

GIVEN NAMES German 8%. *Erhard* (2), *Hans* (2), *Konrad* (2), *Wolfgang* (2), *Berthold, Dieter, Ernst, Erwin, Gerhard, Johann, Kurt, Manfred.*

Opland (161) Norwegian: habitational name from four farmsteads, notably in Trøndelag, named Oppland, from Old Norse *Upplandir*, a compound of *uppi* 'up' + *land* 'land', denoting a farmstead situated on relatively high ground.

GIVEN NAMES Scandinavian 5%. *Einar, Lars, Kari.*

Oplinger (276) Variant spelling of Swiss German OBLINGER.

Opolka (108) Polish: variant of **Opiołka**, nickname from Old Polish *opiołka* 'weed torn up by the roots', thus an occupational name for a plowman.

Opp (712) German: **1.** from a short form of a German personal name composed with a cognte of Old High German *ōt*, Old Saxon *ōel* 'possession', 'wealth'. **2.** possibly a shortening of any of numerous German compound names such as **Oppenberg**, **Oppendinger**, or *Oppenhäuser*.

GIVEN NAMES German 5%. *Reinhold* (2), *Eckhart, Erhard, Frieda, Kurt, Milbert, Otto, Reinhart.*

Oppedisano (210) Italian: habitational name for someone from Oppido Mamertino in Reggio Calabria, so named from Latin *oppidum* 'fortified place', 'stronghold'. The original settlement was destroyed by an earthquake in 1783; it was rebuilt on a site further south.

GIVEN NAMES Italian 31%. *Rocco* (6), *Salvatore* (4), *Carmelo* (2), *Cosimo* (2), *Vincenzo* (2), *Angelo, Antonio, Carlo, Filippo, Pierina, Pietro, Sal.*

Oppegard (131) Norwegian: habitational name from any of several farmsteads in southeastern Norway, so named from Old Norse *Uppigarðr*, a compound of *uppi* 'up' + *garðr* 'farmstead', denoting a farmstead situated on relatively high ground.

Oppel (238) **1.** German: from a pet form of a Germanic personal name formed with a cognate of Old High German *ōt*, Old Saxon *ōd* 'possession', 'wealth'. **2.** German: habitational name from a place so named near Löbau, or perhaps from Oppeln in Silesia.

GIVEN NAME German 4%. *Kurt.*

Oppelt (291) German: from the Germanic personal name *Otbald* composed of the elements *aud* 'wealth' + *bald* 'brave'.

GIVEN NAMES German 5%. *Hans* (4), *Erhardt, Kurt.*

Oppenheim (990) German and Jewish (Ashkenazic): habitational name from a place on the Rhine, between Mainz and Worms, so named from an unexplained first element + Old High German *heim* 'homestead'. There was an important Jewish settlement here before the Holocaust.

GIVEN NAMES German 5%; Jewish 4%. *Gerd* (4), *Kurt* (3), *Hedwig* (2), *Manfred* (2), *Erna, Heinz; Mendel, Miriam, Naftaly, Oded, Shmuel, Shoshana, Shoshanah, Shulamith, Yitzchok.*

Oppenheimer (1180) German and Jewish (western Ashkenazic): habitational name for someone from OPPENHEIM.

GIVEN NAMES German 7%. *Kurt* (5), *Franz* (3), *Ernst* (2), *Lothar* (2), *Otto* (2), *Erwin, Frieda, Gerhard, Hansi, Heinz, Ilse, Manfred.*

Oppenlander (113) German (**Oppenländer**): **1.** in the northwest, a topographic name for someone from a higher or more southerly part of the country, from Low German *op* 'up', 'on' + *land* 'land' + the agent suffix *-er*. **2.** in Württemberg, a topographic name from a field name, of unexplained etymology.

GIVEN NAMES German 13%. *Otto* (2), *Fritz, Horst, Karl Heinz.*

Opper (415) **1.** Dutch and German: from the Germanic personal name *Obrecht*, composed of the elements *aud* 'wealth' + *berht* 'bright', 'famous'. **2.** German: probably a variant of OPPERMANN.

Opperman (938) **1.** Dutch: occupational name for hod carrier for a bricklayer or roadbuilder. **2.** variant of German OPPER-MANN.

Oppermann (287) North German: occupational name for a churchwarden or sexton, with particular reference to his task of taking the collection, Middle Low German *opperman*, from *opper(gilt)* 'donation' (*oppern* 'to donate', 'to sacrifice', Late Latin *operari*) + *man* 'man'.
GIVEN NAMES German 8%. *Armin, Christoph, Erwin, Heinz, Siegfried, Theresia.*

Oppliger (140) Swiss German: variant of OBLINGER.

Oppy (104) Cornish: unexplained.

Oprea (109) Romanian: unexplained.
GIVEN NAMES Romanian 32%. *Florin* (4), *Radu* (4), *Anca, Danut, Dumitru, Gheorghe, Horia, Ilie, Liviu, Mihai, Mircea, Rodica.*

Opry (157) Origin uncertain; perhaps an Americanized form of Irish Gaelic **Ó Préith** (see PREY).
GIVEN NAMES French 5%. *Eugenie, Nolton, Vernice.*

Opsahl (388) Variant of Norwegian OPSAL.
GIVEN NAMES Scandinavian 7%; German 4%. *Erik, Ludvig; Kurt* (3), *Eldred, Erhard.*

Opsal (198) Norwegian: habitational name from any of about fifty farmsteads named Oppsal, from Old Norse *Uppsalir*, a compound of *uppi* 'up' + *salr* 'hall', 'house', 'farm', denoting a dwelling place situated relatively high up on a hillside.
GIVEN NAMES Scandinavian 11%. *Bernt, Knut, Nels.*

Oquendo (493) Spanish (of Basque origin): Castilianized form of **Okendo**, a habitational name from Okendo in Arava province, Basque Country.
GIVEN NAMES Spanish 46%. *Jose* (15), *Juan* (8), *Miguel* (8), *Angel* (6), *Luis* (5), *Raul* (5), *Alberto* (4), *Carlos* (4), *Carmelo* (4), *Pedro* (4), *Enrique* (3), *Fernando* (3), *Jesus* (3).

O'Quin (282) Variant spelling of Irish O'QUINN.

O'Quinn (1916) Irish: Anglicized form of Gaelic **Ó Coinn** 'descendant of *Conn*', a byname meaning 'head', 'sense', or 'reason'.

Oquist (137) Swedish: ornamental name composed of the elements *ö* 'island' + *quist*, an old or ornamental spelling of *kvist* 'twig'.
GIVEN NAME Scandinavian 5%. *Kjersten.*

Orahood (168) Said to be of Scottish origin, but the etymology is unexplained.

Oram (695) English: variant of ORME.

Oran (182) French: from the personal name *Orran*, an assimilated form of a Germanic personal name composed of the elements *aud* 'wealth' + *hramn* 'raven'.

Orand (131) French: variant of ORAN.

Orange (1160) **1.** English: of uncertain origin. A certain William de Orenge mentioned in Domesday Book probably derives his name from Orange in Mayenne. Later medieval examples probably come from a female personal , *Orenge*, of obscure derivation. **2.** French: habitational name from a place in Vaucluse.

Orantes (180) Spanish (Granada): unexplained. This name is well established in Mexico.
GIVEN NAMES Spanish 48%. *Jose* (7), *Juan* (4), *Julio* (3), *Manuel* (3), *Carlos* (2), *Cesar* (2), *Cristina* (2), *Jorge* (2), *Luis* (2), *Pedro* (2), *Ricardo* (2), *Roberto* (2).

Oravec (331) Slovak: regional name for someone from the region of Orava in northern Slovakia.

Oravetz (211) Germanized spelling of Slovak ORAVEC.

Orbach (177) **1.** Jewish (Ashkenazic): variant of AUERBACH, in which the first element has become associated with German *Ohr* 'ear'. **2.** Eastern German: variant of *Urbach*, a Sorbian pet form of URBAN. **3.** German: habitational name from Orbach in North Rhine-Westphalia.
GIVEN NAMES Jewish 12%. *Eliezer, Hyman, Moshe, Noam, Oded, Shlomo, Yael, Zeev, Zvi.*

Orban (687) **1.** Hungarian (**Orbán**): from the personal name *Orbán*, from Latin *Urbanus* (see URBAN). **2.** German and Dutch: variant of URBAN. **3.** French: habitational name from a place so named in Tarn.
GIVEN NAMES Hungarian 4%. *Istvan* (2), *Zoltan* (2), *Balazs, Csaba, Denes, Ferenc, Janos, Katalin, Tamas.*

Orbe (104) Spanish (of Basque origin): from Basque *oru(be)* 'of or relating to the sun'; probably a nickname.
GIVEN NAMES Spanish 36%. *Francisco* (2), *Juan* (2), *Marcelo* (2), *Orlando* (2), *Agusto, Angel, Arnulfo, Conrado, Cosme, Guillermo, Hernandez Jose, Luisa.*

Orbin (139) Probably a variant spelling of Dutch or German ORBAN.

Orchard (879) **1.** English: topographic name for someone who lived by an orchard, or a metonymic occupational name for a fruit grower, from Middle English *orchard*. **2.** English: habitational name from any of the places called Orchard. Those in Devon and Somerset are named from Old English *ortgeard, orceard* (a compound of *wort, wyrt* 'plant' (later associated with Latin *hortus* 'garden') + *geard* 'yard', 'enclosure'), while East and West Orchard near Shaftesbury in Dorset have a different origin, '(place) beside the wood', from Celtic *ar* + *cēd*. **3.** Scottish: English surname adopted as equivalent of URQUHART.

Orcutt (1963) English (Staffordshire): unexplained. Perhaps a much altered spelling of Scottish URQUHART.

Ord (384) **1.** English (Northumbria) and Scottish: habitational name from East Ord in Northumberland, named with Old English *ord* 'point'. Compare ORT 3. **2.** English: from a Germanic personal name (see ORT 2). **3.** Scottish: habitational name from various minor places named with Gaelic *ord* 'hammer', used as a topographical term for a rounded hill.

Ordaz (483) Spanish: variant of *Ordás*, habitational name from Santa María de Ordás in León province.
GIVEN NAMES Spanish 57%. *Jose* (14), *Jesus* (11), *Juan* (11), *Miguel* (9), *Francisco* (7), *Manuel* (7), *Raul* (6), *Pedro* (5), *Arturo* (4), *Carlos* (4), *Guadalupe* (4), *Jorge* (4).

Orders (141) Altered form of German **Örder**, itself a variant of ORT 3.

Ordiway (157) English: variant of ORDWAY.

Ordner (107) German: from Middle High German *ordenære*, an occupational name denoting someone who had something to arrange or put in order.

Ordonez (1375) Spanish (**Ordóñez**): patronymic from the medieval personal name *Ordoño*, of uncertain origin and meaning.
GIVEN NAMES Spanish 54%. *Jose* (32), *Carlos* (28), *Luis* (25), *Juan* (18), *Jorge* (15), *Manuel* (13), *Mario* (13), *Jesus* (12), *Miguel* (12), *Cesar* (8), *Javier* (8), *Fernando* (7).

Ordoyne (281) French?
GIVEN NAMES French 8%. *Lucien* (2), *Emile, Eulice, Oneil, Raoul, Remy.*

Orduna (146) Spanish (**Orduña**): habitational name from the Castilianized form of Basque Urduña, a town in Biscay, Basque Country.
GIVEN NAMES Spanish 56%. *Juan* (5), *Ruben* (5), *Jose* (4), *Alberto* (3), *Rafael* (3), *Andres* (2), *Felipe* (2), *Pilar* (2), *Alfonso, Alfredo, Alicia, Anastacia.*

Orduno (160) Spanish (**Orduño**): probably a variant of ORDUNA.
GIVEN NAMES Spanish 51%. *Jesus* (3), *Nacho* (3), *Armando* (2), *Guadalupe* (2), *Ignacio* (2), *Javier* (2), *Manuela* (2), *Miguel* (2), *Adela, Alicia, Arturo, Blanca.*

Ordway (1125) English: from a late Old English personal name, *Ordwīg*, composed of the elements *ord* 'point (especially of a spear or sword)' + *wīg* 'war'.

Ore (460) **1.** English: habitational name from any of the places called Oare in Berkshire, Kent, and Wiltshire, or Ore in East Sussex, all named with Old English *ōra* 'shore', 'hill-slope', 'flat-topped ridge'. It may also be a topographic name from the same element, though Reaney and Wilson consider that in general this would have had an initial *N-*. Compare NOAH 2. **2.** Scottish: possibly from the Sussex place name.

O'Rear (959) Apparently of Irish origin, but unexplained.

Orebaugh (212) Americanized spelling of German ORBACH or AUERBACH.
GIVEN NAME French 4%. *Valere.*

Orecchio (102) Italian: from *orecchio* 'ear', a nickname for someone with large or otherwise remarkable ears, or possibly for an eavesdropper.

GIVEN NAMES Italian 10%. *Alfredo, Angelo, Mario.*

Orefice (256) Southern Italian: occupational name for a jeweler, *orefice*, from Latin *aurifex*, genitive *aurificis*.

GIVEN NAMES Italian 17%. *Salvatore* (3), *Angelo* (2), *Corrado* (2), *Antonio, Attilio, Carmine, Ettore, Franco, Giuseppe, Italo, Sal, Santo.*

O'Regan (467) Irish: Anglicized form of Gaelic **Ó Riagáin** 'descendant of *Riagán*', a personal name of uncertain origin, perhaps akin to *ríodhgach* 'impulsive', 'furious'. There are two families of this surname, in Meath and Munster; traditionally they both claim descent from a nephew of Brian Boru called *Riagán* (see REGAN).

GIVEN NAMES Irish 14%. *Brendan* (2), *Aidan, Brennan, Briana, Colm, Conor, Declan, Donal.*

O'Reilly (4673) Irish: Anglicized form of Gaelic **Ó Raghailligh** 'descendant of *Raghailleach*', Old Irish *Roghallach*, a personal name of unexplained etymology. This is the name of a chieftain family in County Cavan, related to the O'Rourkes.

GIVEN NAMES Irish 9%. *Brendan* (11), *Mairead* (3), *Aidan* (2), *Colm* (2), *Declan* (2), *Dermot* (2), *Dympna* (2), *Eamon* (2), *Finbar* (2), *Brennan, Brian Patrick, Brid.*

Orel (139) **1.** Czech, Ukrainian, Slovenian, and Jewish (Ashkenazic): nickname from Czech, Ukrainian, and Slovenian *orel* 'eagle', or (in Czech) habitational name for someone who lived in a house distinguished by the sign of an eagle. **2.** Jewish (eastern Ashkenazic): from the Yiddish personal name *Orl*, a pet form of AARON.

GIVEN NAMES Russian 13%; Jewish 6%. *Mikhail* (2), *Grigoriy, Lyubov, Oksana, Sergei, Sergey, Serguei, Vladimir; Inna, Polina.*

Orell (103) **1.** Catalan and Swiss German: from a personal name derived from the Latin name *Aurelius*. **2.** Swedish: variant of ORRELL.

Orellana (1495) Spanish: habitational name from either of two places in Badajoz province, probably so called from Latin *villa Aureliana* 'estate of *Aurelius*' (see ORELL).

GIVEN NAMES Spanish 55%. *Jose* (60), *Carlos* (48), *Juan* (24), *Luis* (22), *Manuel* (22), *Jorge* (14), *Ana* (13), *Francisco* (10), *Mario* (10), *Pablo* (9), *Rafael* (9), *Ricardo* (9).

Orem (483) **1.** Scottish (Angus): of uncertain origin; Black suggests it may be a habitational name from a place in England called Oram or Orem, or possibly a variant of ORME. **2.** Probably also an altered spelling of German **Ohrem**, a habitational name from a place near Wolfenbüttel called O(h)rum.

Oren (647) **1.** Dutch: variant of HORN. **2.** Americanized form of Norwegian **Øren**, a habitational name from any of about thirty farmsteads, mainly on the west coast of Norway, named Øyra, from Old Norse *eyrr* 'delta', 'sandbank'. **3.** Americanized spelling of German OHREN. **4.** Jewish (Israeli): ornamental name from Hebrew *oren* 'pine tree'. In some cases it may be a substitute for some original Ashkenazic name of similar sound or meaning, e.g. TANNENBAUM or SOSNA.

GIVEN NAMES Jewish 7%. *Moshe* (2), *Ronen* (2), *Yoram* (2), *Ahuva, Arie, Avi, Avital, Ido, Meyer, Miriam, Nachum, Omri.*

Orender (149) Origin unidentified.

Orendorf (100) Variant of German **Ohrendorf** (see ORENDORFF).

Orendorff (260) Respelling of German **Ohrendorf**, a habitational name, perhaps from Ohrdruf, near Gotha, or alternatively a variant of **Ohrdorf**, from Ohrdorf, a place on the Ohre river in Lower Saxony.

Orenstein (745) Jewish (Ashkenazic): variant of ORNSTEIN.

GIVEN NAMES Jewish 8%. *Ari* (3), *Hyman* (2), *Aron, Aviva, Ben-Zion, Gershon, Hershel, Isadore, Shmuel, Sol, Zvi.*

Oreskovich (161) Croatian (northern and eastern Croatia; **Orešković**): habitational name for someone from any of the many places named with the dialect word *oreh* 'walnut', or possibly a topographic name for someone who lived by a walnut tree or an occupational name for someone who collected and sold walnuts.

Orey (109) **1.** English: unexplained. **2.** Belgian: habitational name from a place called Oreye or Oerle in Liège province.

Orf (478) German: possibly a metonymic occupational name for a fisherman, from *orfe*, a species of freshwater fish.

Orff (118) German: variant spelling of ORF.

Orfield (154) Possibly English: habitational name from Horfield, Gloucestershire, named with Old English *horu* 'mud', 'dirt' + *feld* 'open country'.

GIVEN NAMES German 4%. *Bernhard, Gerhard.*

Orgain (109) Variant of English ORGAN.

Organ (772) **1.** English: metonymic occupational name for a player of a musical instrument (any musical instrument, not necessarily what is now known as an organ), from Middle English *organ* (Old French *organe*, Late Latin *organum* 'device', '(musical) instrument', Greek *organon* 'tool', from *ergein* 'to work or do'). **2.** English: from a rare medieval personal name, attested only in the Latinized forms *Organus* (masculine) and *Organa* (feminine). Its etymology is obscure; it may be a reworking of a Celtic name. **3.** French: habitational name from a place in the Hautes Pyrénées named Organ.

Orgel (179) **1.** South German (**Örgel**): from Middle High German *erkelin* (a loan-

word from Latin *arca* 'grape bin', 'vat'), hence probably a metonymic occupational name for someone who worked in a vineyard. **2.** English: variant spelling of ORGILL. **3.** Jewish (Ashkenazic): from German *Orgel* 'organ'.

GIVEN NAME Jewish 6%. *Simcha.*

Orgeron (528) French?

GIVEN NAMES French 7%. *Clovis* (3), *Alphonse* (2), *Alcide, Camille, Gracien, Jean-Paul, Leonce.*

Orgill (228) English: nickname from Old French *orgueil* 'pride'. Compare PRIDE.

Ori (213) **1.** Southern Italian: from **Oro**, which Caracausi associates with medieval Greek *Oros*, or otherwise derives from a short form of the personal name *Orobello* or from *oro* 'gold' (from Latin *aurum*). **2.** Hungarian (**Őri**): habitational name for someone from any of several places in Hungary called **Őr**.

GIVEN NAMES Italian 16%. *Geno* (4), *Angelo* (2), *Deno, Dino, Domenic, Dominico, Edoardo, Egidio, Emelio, Lodovico, Renzo.*

Orians (114) German: variant of **Arians**, from the personal name *Hadrianus* (a Latin habitational name from Hadria), borne by a 4th-century Christian martyr.

GIVEN NAME French 4%. *Armand* (2).

Orick (278) Apparently an altered spelling of **Orrick**.

Origer (120) Probably a variant of French **Origier**, an occupational name for someone who fashioned braids and embroideries for offertory bags, from southern *origer*, a variant of Old French *orier*.

GIVEN NAMES French 6%. *Andre, Olivier.*

Orihuela (154) Spanish (from Catalan): habitational name from Orihuela in Alacant province, Spanish form of Catalan *Oriola*.

GIVEN NAMES Spanish 48%. *Carlos* (7), *Jose* (6), *Mario* (3), *Roberto* (3), *Armando* (2), *Arturo* (2), *Jorge* (2), *Alberto, Aldolfo, Alicia, Ana, Angel; Clemente* (2), *Antonio, Carmelo, Cecilio.*

O'Riley (342) Irish: variant spelling O'REILLY.

GIVEN NAME Irish 7%. *Eamonn.*

Orio (114) **1.** Italian: habitational name from any of various places named with *Orio*, for example Orio Canavese (Turni province, Piedmont), Orio al Serio (Bergamo province, Lombardy), Orio Litta (Milan province, Lombardy). **2.** Basque: habitational name from Orio in Gipuzkoa province. **3.** Japanese: not a common name in Japan. One version is written with a character pronounced *chisha* or *chisa*, a tree which is a sort of false persimmon. Other versions are written with characters used phonetically, or with a pair meaning 'hanging tail'.

GIVEN NAMES Italian 10%; Japanese 5%. *Cesare, Francesca, Salvatore, Vito; Shinichiro, Toru.*

Oriol (103) **1.** Catalan: from the old personal name *Oriol* (from Latin *Aureolus*), or in

some cases possibly a nickname from Catalan *oriol* 'oriole' (likewise from Latin *aureolus* 'golden'), denoting someone thought to resemble the bird. **2.** French: nickname, possibly for a flamboyant dresser or sweet singer, from *oriol, oriel* 'oriole', a species of bird of which the male has bright yellow and black plumage.
GIVEN NAMES Spanish 15%; French 11%; German 4%. *Alberto* (2), *Hipolito* (2), *Luis* (2), *Eriberto, Jose, Luisa, Ramon, Ricardo*; *Edwige, Serge, Yvrose*; *Fritz.*

O'Riordan (263) Irish: Anglicized form of Gaelic **Ó Ríoghbhárdáin** 'descendant of *Ríoghbhárdán*' (see RIORDAN). This family is probably descended from Ríoghbhardán Ó Cearbhaill, who fell in battle in 1058.
GIVEN NAMES Irish 18%. *Colm* (3), *Brigid, Cormac, Eamonn, Eithne, Eoin.*

Oris (100) French: **1.** topographic name from Old French *horis*, a hill name. **2.** from a Germanic personal name composed of the elements *ald* 'old' + *rīc* 'power', 'rule'.

Oritz (146) Basque: habitational name from Oritz, a town in Navarre province.
GIVEN NAMES Spanish 43%. *Jose* (6), *Carlos* (3), *Juan* (2), *Luis* (2), *Manuel* (2), *Margarita* (2), *Alejandro, Benito, Elba, Elena, Eloy, Eulalia.*

Orkin (213) Jewish (eastern Ashkenazic): patronymic from the Yiddish male personal name *Orke*, a pet form of AARON + the eastern Slavic possessive suffix *-in*.
GIVEN NAME Jewish 4%. *Lipman.*

Orland (163) **1.** Dutch: metathesized variant of the personal name *Roland*. Compare Italian ORLANDO. **2.** Jewish (from Ukraine): unexplained.

Orlandi (405) Italian: patronymic or plural form of ORLANDO.
GIVEN NAMES Italian 22%. *Aldo* (4), *Mario* (3), *Reno* (3), *Edgardo* (2), *Emilio* (2), *Enrico* (2), *Graziano* (2), *Palmira* (2), *Alberto, Alessio, Angelo, Aroldo, Attilio, Beniamino, Deno, Dino, Ezio, Fabio, Fernando, Orlando.*

Orlandini (106) Italian: patronymic or plural form of ORLANDO.
GIVEN NAMES Italian 10%. *Attilio, Premo, Rinaldo.*

Orlando (4191) Italian: from the personal name *Orlando*, earlier *Rolando* (see ROWLAND).
GIVEN NAMES Italian 14%. *Salvatore* (19), *Angelo* (17), *Rocco* (16), *Sal* (11), *Vito* (9), *Antonio* (7), *Carlo* (7), *Marco* (5), *Santo* (5), *Carmine* (4), *Giovanni* (4), *Cosimo* (3).

Orleans (124) French (**Orléans**): habitational name from the city so named in Loiret.
GIVEN NAME French 5%. *Magalie.*

Orlich (212) Polish: nickname from a derivative of *orzeł* 'eagle'.

Orlick (184) Germanized or Americanized spelling of ORLIK.

Orlicki (33) Polish: habitational name for someone from a place called Orlik in Bydgoszcz voivodeship.

Orlik (141) Czech, Slovak (**Orlík**), Polish, and Ukrainian: nickname from Slavic *orlik*, a diminutive of *orel* 'eagle' (Polish *orzeł*).
GIVEN NAMES Polish 9%; Russian 6%; Czech and Slovak 4%; German 4%. *Krzysztof* (2), *Aleksander, Kazimierz, Ryszard*; *Arkady, Grigoriy, Lidiya, Zoya*; *Bozena, Pavel, Vladislav*; *Otto.*

Orlikowski (137) Polish: habitational name for someone from a place called Orlikowo in Łomża voivodeship.
GIVEN NAMES German 5%. *Klaus, Kurt.*

Orlin (142) Jewish (from Lithuania): habitational name from places in Lithuania or Belarus called Orlany or Orlya.
GIVEN NAMES Jewish 7%. *Rivka* (2), *Hyman.*

Orloff (615) **1.** Russian (**Orlov**) and Jewish (eastern Ashkenazic): patronymic from the nickname *Oryol* 'eagle', or a Jewish ornamental name taken from the vocabulary word. **2.** Jewish (eastern Ashkenazic): patronymic from the Yiddish personal name *Orl*, taken as a pet form of AARON. **3.** Jewish (eastern Ashkenazic): habitational name from any of several villages called Orlovo, in Ukraine and Belarus.

Orloski (148) Polish and Jewish (from Poland): variant of ORLOWSKI.

Orlosky (155) Jewish (from Poland): variant of ORLOWSKI.

Orlov (153) Russian and Jewish (eastern Ashkenazic): variant spelling of ORLOFF.
GIVEN NAMES Russian 36%; Jewish 13%. *Mikhail* (4), *Sergei* (4), *Nikolay* (3), *Vladimir* (3), *Arkady* (2), *Dmitry* (2), *Aleksandra, Aleksey, Anatoliy, Anatoly, Andrei, Anisia*; *Irina* (2), *Sol, Yakov.*

Orlovsky (111) **1.** Russian and Jewish (eastern Ashkenazic): elaborated form of **Orlov** (see ORLOFF). **2.** Jewish (from Poland): variant of ORLOWSKI.
GIVEN NAMES Russian 16%; Jewish 6%. *Dmitry* (2), *Arkady, Efim, Mikhail, Pyotr, Yefim*; *Ilya, Semen.*

Orlow (136) German and Polish spelling of Russian and Jewish **Orlov** (see ORLOFF).
GIVEN NAME German 4%. *Manfred.*

Orlowski (1292) Polish (**Orłowski**) and Jewish (from Poland): habitational name for someone from any of the numerous places in Poland called Orłów, Orłowo, or Orły, named with Polish *orlów*, possessive case of *orzeł* 'eagle'.
GIVEN NAMES Polish 5%. *Andrzej* (3), *Witold* (2), *Czeslawa, Jacek, Janusz, Juliusz, Lucjan, Ludwik, Maciej, Marzena, Pawel, Zbigniew.*

Orlowsky (110) Jewish (eastern Ashkenazic): variant spelling of ORLOWSKI or ORLOVSKY.
GIVEN NAMES Jewish 6%. *Baruch, Nachman, Sol.*

Orman (1188) **1.** Irish: variant of ORMOND. **2.** Dutch: from a derivative of HORN suffixed by *man* 'man', or the topographic or habitational name **van Hoorn**, denoting someone who lived by a pointed or curved geographical feature (Dutch *hoorn*). **3.** Hungarian (**Ormán**): from *Ormán*, an old secular personal name. **4.** Jewish (Ashkenazic): of uncertain origin; perhaps a nickname from Yiddish *orem* 'poor' + *man* 'man'. **5.** Southern English: unexplained.

Ormand (255) Variant of Irish ORMOND.

Orme (953) **1.** Northern English: from the Old Norse personal name *Ormr*, originally a byname meaning 'snake', 'serpent', 'dragon'. **2.** French: topographic name for someone who lived near a conspicuous elm tree, from Old French *orme* (Latin *ulmus*).

Ormerod (178) English (Lancashire): habitational name from a place in Lancashire, called Ormerod, from the Old Norse personal name *Ormr* (see ORME 1) or *Ormarr* (a compound of *orm* 'serpent' + *herr* 'army') + Old English *rod* 'clearing'.

Ormes (151) English: patronymic from ORME 1.

Ormiston (405) Scottish: habitational name from places called Ormiston, in the former counties of Roxburgh and East Lothian, named with the genitive case of the Old Norse personal name *Ormr* (see ORME 1) + Old English *tūn* 'enclosure', 'settlement'.

Ormond (807) Irish (common in Cork and Waterford): Anglicized form of Gaelic **Ó Ruaidh** 'descendant of *Ruadh*', a byname meaning 'red', altered by folk etymology to resemble a regional name from the ancient region of East Munster known as *Ormond* (Gaelic *Ur Mhumhain*). Ó Ruaidh is also Anglicized as ROE.

Ormonde (153) Variant spelling of Irish ORMOND. The surname is also found in Portugal, having been taken there by an immigrant Irish family.
GIVEN NAMES Spanish 17%. *Jose* (4), *Manuel* (4), *Adelino, Ana, Avelino, Bernardo, Blanca, Eugenio, Filipe, Helio, Mario, Serafina*; *Antonio, Firmino.*

Orms (122) English: variant spelling of ORMES.

Ormsbee (354) Variant spelling of English ORMSBY.

Ormsby (1327) English: habitational name from Ormsby in Lincolnshire and North Yorkshire, or Ormesby in Norfolk, all named from the genitive case of the Old Norse personal name *Ormr* (see ORME 1) + Old Norse *býr* 'farm', 'settlement'.

Orn (154) Swedish (**Örn**): ornamental name from *örn* 'eagle'.

Orndoff (261) Variant of German ORENDORFF.

Orndorf (135) Variant of German ORENDORFF.
GIVEN NAME German 5%; Scandinavian 4%. *Mathias.*

Orndorff (1268) Probably a variant of German ORENDORFF.

Orne (245) **1.** Swedish (**Örne**): variant of ORN. **2.** French: topographic name from the river or department of this name.

Ornelas (1985) Portuguese: from a misinterpretation (as *d'Ornelas*) of **Dornelas**, a habitational name from any of several places called Dornelas, from the plural diminutive of *dorna* 'vat', 'tub'.
GIVEN NAMES Spanish 47%. *Jose* (56), *Juan* (29), *Jesus* (18), *Manuel* (17), *Francisco* (15), *Carlos* (14), *Raul* (14), *Miguel* (12), *Pedro* (10), *Javier* (9), *Ramon* (9), *Arturo* (8).

Ornellas (265) Portuguese: probably a variant of ORNELAS.
GIVEN NAMES Spanish 6%. *Manuel* (3), *Alberto* (2), *Alfredo*, *Joaquin*, *Rafael*, *Raul*, *Santiago*, *Yesenia*.

Orner (590) German and Swiss German: variant of ARNER.

Ornstein (481) Jewish (Ashkenazic): ornamental name composed of a variant of HORN (in regions where Yiddish has no *h*) + *stein* 'stone'.
GIVEN NAMES Jewish 4%. *Miriam* (2), *Avi*, *Golda*, *Sol*.

O'Roark (175) Irish: variant spelling of O'ROURKE.

Orona (688) Spanish: habitational name from a town of this name in Burgos province.
GIVEN NAMES Spanish 37%. *Juan* (9), *Manuel* (9), *Jose* (7), *Ruben* (6), *Armando* (5), *Ignacio* (4), *Fernando* (3), *Guadalupe* (3), *Jose Luis* (3), *Alejandro* (2), *Angelina* (2), *Arturo* (2).

Oropeza (560) Spanish: **1.** Castilianized spelling of Catalan **Orpesa**, a town in Castelló province. **2.** perhaps a habitational name from Oropesa in Toledo.
GIVEN NAMES Spanish 53%. *Jose* (18), *Manuel* (11), *Carlos* (9), *Juan* (9), *Luis* (8), *Enrique* (7), *Jesus* (6), *Rafael* (6), *Armando* (5), *Francisco* (5), *Ricardo* (5), *Miguel* (4).

O'Rorke (145) Irish: variant spelling of O'ROURKE.

Oros (486) **1.** Catalan (**Orós**): possibly from an old personal name name, *Orosius*, which was borne by a 4th-century theologian and disciple of St. Augustine. **2.** Aragonese (**Orós**): habitational name from Orós in Uesca province. **3.** Hungarian: from the old secular name *Oros*, or possibly an Americanized spelling of OROSZ.
GIVEN NAMES Spanish 9%. *Manuel* (3), *Juan* (2), *Miguel* (2), *Angelina*, *Armida*, *Candelario*, *Felipe*, *Francisco*, *Hilario*, *Humberto*, *Javier*, *Jose*.

Orosco (1007) Spanish (of Basque origin): variant of OROZCO.
GIVEN NAMES Spanish 46%. *Jesus* (15), *Jose* (14), *Juan* (12), *Manuel* (11), *Pedro* (8), *Rafael* (8), *Arturo* (7), *Carlos* (7), *Francisco* (7), *Roberto* (7), *Ramon* (6), *Salvador* (5).

Orosz (592) Hungarian: ethnic name for a Russian, *orosz*, from Turkish *urus*, in turn derived from Russian *Rusak* 'Russian', which owes its origin to a Scandinavian term meaning 'oarsman', 'rower' (a reference to the fact that the Russian state was first established by Scandinavians who rowed their ships inland from the Baltic sea).
GIVEN NAMES Hungarian 7%. *Laszlo* (3), *Imre* (2), *Miklos* (2), *Tibor* (2), *Akos*, *Andras*, *Arpad*, *Csaba*, *Csilla*, *Gabor*, *Lajos*, *Laszio*.

O'Rourke (6981) Irish: Anglicized form of Gaelic **Ó Ruairc** 'descendant of *Ruarc*', Old Gaelic *Ruadhrac*, a personal name from Norse *Hrothrekr* (see RODERICK). This is the name of chieftain family in counties Leitrim and Cavan.
GIVEN NAMES Irish 7%. *Brendan* (6), *Kieran* (3), *Dermot* (2), *Roisin* (2), *Siobhan* (2), *Aileen*, *Briana*, *Bridie*, *Brigid*, *Cait*, *Conal*, *Conan*.

Orozco (4388) Spanish (of Basque origin): habitational name from Orozco in Bilbao province.
GIVEN NAMES Spanish 55%. *Jose* (119), *Juan* (61), *Manuel* (49), *Jesus* (48), *Jorge* (39), *Francisco* (36), *Raul* (36), *Luis* (34), *Carlos* (30), *Salvador* (30), *Pedro* (28), *Guadalupe* (27).

Orr (16571) **1.** Northern English, Scottish, and northern Irish: from the Old Norse byname *Orri* 'blackcock' (the male black grouse). **2.** Scottish: nickname for someone with a sallow complexion, from Gaelic *odhar* 'pale', 'dun'. **3.** English: topographic name for someone who lived on a shore or ridge, from Old English *ōra* 'shore', 'hill-slope', 'flat-topped ridge', or a habitational name from a place named with this word (see ORE).

Orrantia (105) Spanish or Basque: possibly a topographic name from *orrantia* 'mountain pass'.
GIVEN NAMES Spanish 42%. *Angel* (3), *Luis* (3), *Fernando* (2), *Gustavo* (2), *Manuel* (2), *Alejandro*, *Alonso*, *Arturo*, *Elva*, *Francisco*, *Guillermo*, *Javier*.

Orrell (716) **1.** English (Lancashire): habitational name from either of two minor places in Lancashire called Orell, from Old English *ōra* 'ore' + *hyll* 'hill', probably denoting a hill with deposits of iron ore. Reaney and Wilson also mention a medieval female personal name, *Orella*, but there is no evidence of a link with the surname. **2.** Swedish: unexplained.

Orren (235) Possibly an altered spelling of OREN.

Orrick (507) **1.** English (Newcastle area): from a Middle English survival of the Old English personal name *Ordrīc*, composed of the elements *ord* 'point' (of a sword, spear) + *rīc* 'power'. **2.** Scottish: variant spelling of ORROCK.

Orrico (264) Italian: from a personal name derived from the Germanic personal name *Othalric* (see ULRICH).
GIVEN NAMES Italian 9%. *Aldo*, *Antonio*, *Benedetto*, *Carlo*, *Carmine*, *Pasquale*.

Orrill (139) Variant spelling of ORRELL.

Orris (671) English (Suffolk): from a vernacular form of the Latin name *Horatius*, which, according to Reaney and Wilson, was apparently taken to England during the Renaissance in the Italian form *Horatio*.

Orrison (271) Apparently an English patronymic from ORRIS; however, the surname does not occur in current British records.

Orrock (114) Scottish: habitational name from Orrock in Fife.
GIVEN NAME German 4%. *Kurt*.

Orsak (407) Czech: unexplained.

Orsborn (317) English: variant of OSBORNE.

Orsburn (222) English: variant of OSBORNE.

Orser (255) Americanized form of Dutch **Aertse** (see AERTS).

Orsi (450) **1.** Italian: patronymic or plural form of ORSO. **2.** It may also be an Italianized form of Slovenian **Uršič**, metronymic from the female personal name *Urša*, short form of *Uršula* (Latin *Ursula*), or a patronymic from the male personal name *Urh*, Slovenian vernacular form of *Ulrik*, German *Udalrich*. **3.** Hungarian (**Örsi**): habitational name for someone from any of several places called Örs in Hungary.
GIVEN NAMES Italian 20%; Spanish 5%. *Antonio* (4), *Mario* (3), *Aldo* (2), *Evo* (2), *Levio* (2), *Adriano*, *Armando*, *Federico*, *Florio*, *Gaetano*, *Gennaro*, *Geno*, *Guiseppe*, *Oreste*, *Oriano*, *Renato*; *Agueda*, *Alejandro*, *Carlos*.

Orsini (1071) Italian: patronymic or plural form of ORSINO.
GIVEN NAMES Italian 19%; Spanish 5%. *Rocco* (6), *Angelo* (5), *Armando* (4), *Donato* (4), *Orlando* (4), *Antonio* (3), *Mario* (3), *Carmine* (2), *Nunzio* (2), *Pasquale* (2), *Vittorio* (2), *Camillo*, *Dante*, *Domenic*; *Carlos* (3), *Domingo* (2), *Jose* (2), *Santos* (2), *Alejandro*, *Ana*, *Anacleto*.

Orsino (184) Italian: nickname from a diminutive of *orso* 'bear', or from a pet form of the personal name ORSO.
GIVEN NAMES Italian 11%. *Orlando* (6), *Annunziata*, *Salvatore*.

Orso (344) **1.** Italian: from the personal name *Orso* meaning 'bear' (from Latin *ursus*), or a nickname for someone thought to resemble a bear (e.g. a large, lumbering person). In some cases the name may be habitational, denoting someone who lived in a house distinguished by the sign of a bear. Compare URSO. **2.** Hungarian (**Orsó**): metonymic occupational name for a spinner, from *orsó* 'spinning wheel'.

Orszulak (131) Polish: metonymic from the female personal name *Urszula* (Latin *Ursula*, from a feminine diminutive of *ursus* 'bear'). St. Ursula was a 4th-century martyr who was put to death at Cologne and whose cult stretched far across north-central Europe.

GIVEN NAMES Polish 10%. *Casimir, Jacek, Jozef, Krzysztof, Miroslaw.*

Ort (756) **1.** Southern French: metonymic occupational name for a gardener or topographic name for someone who lived near an enclosed garden, Occitan *ort* (Latin *hortus*). **2.** German: from a Germanic personal name *Ort*, a short form of the various compound names with the first element *ord* 'point' (of a sword, spear). **3.** German: topographic name for someone who lived at the top of a hill or the end of a settlement, from Middle High German *ort* (see 2 above), in the transferred sense 'tip', 'extremity'. In modern German the word has come to mean 'point', 'spot', 'place'.

Orta (765) Portuguese, Galician, and Catalan: topographic name, from a variant of *horta* 'irrigated area' or 'kitchen garden'.

GIVEN NAMES Spanish 47%. *Jose* (17), *Manuel* (14), *Pedro* (10), *Juan* (9), *Carlos* (7), *Francisco* (6), *Angel* (5), *Armando* (5), *Roberto* (5), *Jesus* (4), *Jorge* (4), *Orlando* (4).

Ortega (10930) **1.** Spanish (from Galician): habitational name from Ortega in A Coruña province. **2.** Spanish: nickname from *ortega* '(female) black grouse' (from Greek *ortyx* 'quail'). **3.** Southern French (Occitan): topographic name from Occitan *ortiga* 'nettle' (Latin *urtica*, French *ortie*).

GIVEN NAMES Spanish 47%. *Jose* (293), *Juan* (156), *Manuel* (121), *Carlos* (107), *Jesus* (89), *Luis* (86), *Francisco* (83), *Miguel* (74), *Jorge* (68), *Pedro* (60), *Raul* (58), *Ramon* (57).

Ortego (814) Spanish: possibly a nickname from a variant of ORTEGA 2; from the masculine form, i.e. 'black cock'.

Ortegon (286) Spanish (**Ortegón**): from an augmentative of ORTEGA.

GIVEN NAMES Spanish 45%. *Manuel* (7), *Jose* (6), *Raul* (6), *Juan* (5), *Luis* (5), *Pedro* (4), *Francisco* (3), *Jorge* (3), *Alberto* (2), *Arturo* (2), *Blanca* (2), *Carlos* (2).

Ortel (137) German (**Örtel**): variant (unrounded) of ERTEL.

Orten (141) Norwegian: habitational name from a farmstead in Romsdal named Orten, probably originally an island name, from Old Norse *Urptir*, from an unrecorded word meaning 'place where seabirds lay their eggs'.

Ortez (314) Spanish: variant of ORTIZ or of Catalan *Ortes*, plural form of ORTA.

GIVEN NAMES Spanish 35%. *Jose* (9), *Juan* (5), *Ana* (2), *Carlos* (2), *Margarita* (2), *Mario* (2), *Sergio* (2), *Adela, Adriana, Amando, Aminta, Andres.*

Orth (2673) **1.** North German: variant spelling of ORT 3. **2.** German and French: from a short form of a compound personal name formed with *ort* 'point (of a

weapon)', as the first element (for example, ORTLIEB).

Ortis (132) Spanish: variant of ORTIZ.

GIVEN NAMES Spanish 23%. *Jose* (2), *Agustin, Ana, Arturo, Baldomero, Bicente, Consuelo, Emiliano, Ernestina, Gerardo, Jesus, Luis Enrique.*

Ortiz (24985) Spanish: patronymic from the Basque personal name *Orti* (Latin *Fortunius*).

FOREBEARS Nicolas Ortiz Ladron de Guevara, a native of Mexico City, came to Santa Fe, NM, in June 1694 with others, to re-establish Spanish rule in New Mexico after the Pueblo Indian revolt.

GIVEN NAMES Spanish 47%. *Jose* (688), *Juan* (342), *Carlos* (248), *Luis* (248), *Manuel* (222), *Francisco* (178), *Jesus* (171), *Miguel* (132), *Angel* (130), *Jorge* (126), *Pedro* (125), *Ramon* (121).

Ortlieb (293) German: from a Germanic personal name composed of the elements *ort* 'point' (of a weapon) + *lieb* 'dear' or *lif* 'life', 'body'.

GIVEN NAMES German 6%. *Kurt* (2), *Hans, Otto, Siegfried.*

Ortlip (116) Variant of German **Ortlipp**, itself probably a variant of **Otlepp**, a habitational name from a place called Ottleben.

Ortloff (210) Southern German: from the personal name *Ortolf*, composed of the Germanic elements *ord* 'point (of a weapon)' + *wulf* 'wolf'.

Ortman (1033) **1.** Jewish (Ashkenazic): ornamental from German *Ort* 'place' + *Mann* 'man'. **2.** Respelling of German ORTMANN.

Ortmann (396) German: **1.** variant of ORT 3. **2.** nickname for someone who acted as an arbitrator or judge casting the decisive vote in the event of a tie, Middle High German *ortman*.

GIVEN NAMES German 7%. *Erna, Erwin, Guenter, Hans, Klaus, Kurt, Manfred, Otto, Reinhard, Ursel.*

Ortmeier (134) German: distinguishing name for a tenant farmer (see MEYER) who worked an outlying farm (see ORT 3).

Ortner (555) German and Jewish (Ashkenazic): topographic name for someone who lived on the fringe of a village or settlement, from the oblique case of Middle High German *ort* in the sense 'tip', 'extremity' (see ORT 3) + the suffix *-er*, denoting an inhabitant. In the Austrian Tyrol the name denoted a person who worked in a salt mine.

GIVEN NAMES German 4%. *Georg, Horst, Inge, Johann, Konrad, Willi.*

Ortolani (127) Italian: patronymic or plural form of ORTOLANO.

GIVEN NAMES Italian 17%. *Aida, Alessia, Benito, Mario, Sergio, Viviana.*

Ortolano (194) **1.** Italian: occupational name for a cultivator or seller of vegetables, *ortolano*, from a derivative of *orto* 'vegetable garden' (from Latin *hortus*

'garden'). **2.** Italian: from a term denoting a kind of bunting (a small bird, *Emberiza hortulana*, prized as a delicacy by Mediterranean gourmets); the surname may alternatively be a nickname from this sense. **3.** Spanish: occupational name from a variant spelling of Old Spanish *hortolano* 'cultivator or seller of vegetables'.

GIVEN NAMES Italian 16%. *Angelo* (5), *Carmela, Francesca, Girolamo, Pasquale, Salvatore.*

Orton (2404) English and Scottish: habitational name from any of various places called Orton. All those in England share a second element from Old English *tūn* 'enclosure', 'settlement', but the first element in each case is more difficult to determine. Examples in Cambridgeshire and Warwickshire are on the banks of rivers, so that there it is probably Old English *ōfer* 'riverbank'; in other cases it is impossible to decide between *ofer* 'ridge' and *ufera* 'upper'. Orton in Cumbria is probably formed with the Old Norse byname *Orri* 'black-cock' (the male black grouse). Orton near Fochabers, Scotland, is of uncertain etymology.

Ortt (131) German: variant spelling of ORT.

Ortuno (108) Spanish (**Ortuño**): from the personal name *Ortuño* (Latin *Fortunius*).

GIVEN NAMES Spanish 57%. *Manuel* (7), *Carlos* (2), *Jorge* (2), *Jose* (2), *Amado, Araceli, Aracely, Arnoldo, Atanacio, Benito, Bolivar, Cesar.*

Ortwein (244) South German: from the Germanic personal name *Ortwin*, composed of the elements *ord* 'point (of a weapon)' + *wine* 'friend'.

GIVEN NAMES German 9%. *Otto* (4), *Juergen* (2), *Frieda, Mathias.*

Orum (292) **1.** Danish: habitational name from any of several places called Órum, named as a compound of *ór* 'gravel beach' + *hem* 'dwelling'. This name is also found in Norway, of Danish origin. **2.** English: variant of ORME 1.

Orvik (111) Norwegian (also **Ørvik**): habitational name from any of several farmsteads, mainly in Romsdal, so named from *or* 'alder' + *vik* 'bay'.

GIVEN NAME Scandinavian 4%. *Obert.*

Orvin (132) French (Normandy): metonymic occupational name for a flour merchant, from a diminutive of *orve* 'wheatflour'.

Orvis (635) English (Suffolk): unexplained.

Orwick (195) Americanized form of Norwegian ORVIK.

Orwig (604) Germanized form of Norwegian ORVIK.

Ory (476) **1.** French: habitational name from Orry-la-Ville in Oise, derived from the Latin personal name *Aurius, Orius* + suffix *-acum*, denoting the estate of a *villa*. **2.** German: from a personal name, *Ory* or *Olry*, derived from Latin *aureus* 'golden', which was borne by a 5th-century saint from Mainz. **3.** Hungarian (**Őry**): variant spelling of **Őri** (see ORI).

O'Ryan (106) Irish: **1.** (Leinster) Anglicized form of Gaelic **Ó Riagháin** (modern Irish **Ó Riain**) 'descendant of *Rian*, earlier *Riaghán*', a personal name of uncertain etymology. See also RYAN. **2.** (Munster) Anglicized form of Gaelic **Ó Maoilriain** 'descendant of *Maoilriaghain*', a personal name meaning 'follower of *Riaghán*'. **3.** (Connacht) Anglicized form of Gaelic **Ó Ruaidhín** 'descendant of the little red one', from a diminutive of *ruadh* 'red'.

Orzech (220) Polish and Jewish (from Poland): from *orzech* 'nut', a nickname for someone thought to resemble a nut, or a metonymic occupational name for someone who gathered and sold nuts. As a Jewish name it is mainly ornamental.
GIVEN NAMES Polish 6%; German 4%. *Jacek, Wladyslawa, Zigmund; Florian, Otto.*

Orzechowski (566) Polish: habitational name for someone from any of various places called Orzechów or Orzechowo, named with *orzech* 'nut', 'hazelnut'. It may also be a topographic name for someone living by a hazelnut tree, or a nickname for someone with light brown hair, from the adjective *orzechowy* 'hazel'.
GIVEN NAMES Polish 10%. *Casimir* (2), *Jerzy* (2), *Tadeusz* (2), *Wieslaw* (2), *Aleksander, Bogdan, Ewa, Henryk, Leszek, Mieczyslaw, Stanislaw, Zygmunt.*

Orzel (288) Polish (**Orzeł**) and Jewish (from Poland): Polish nickname or Jewish ornamental name from Polish *orzeł* 'eagle'.
GIVEN NAMES Polish 12%; Jewish 4%. *Janina* (2), *Casimir, Czeslaw, Elzbieta, Ignacy, Janusz, Krystian, Krzysztof, Malgorzata, Mieczyslaw, Slawomir, Zofia; Akiva* (2), *Feivel, Zelman.*

Osada (117) **1.** Japanese: an alternative pronunciation of the name NAGATA, also pronounced *Chōda* by some families. All three versions are found in eastern Japan. **2.** Polish: topographic name from *osada* 'settlement', 'colony'.
GIVEN NAMES Japanese 48%; Polish 5%. *Akinori, Fumi, Fumio, Hiro, Kaz, Kiyo, Kyoko, Masaaki, Masao, Masashi, Mikako, Minoru; Radoslaw, Zygmunt.*

Osaki (141) Japanese (**Ōsaki**): 'great cape'; a name found mostly in eastern Japan. An older family is listed in the Shinsen shōjiroku, and an apparently later family, descended from the MINAMOTO clan, took the name from their residence in Shimōsa (now part of Chiba prefecture).
GIVEN NAMES Japanese 50%. *Hiroshi* (3), *Toshio* (2), *Hiroto, Hisao, Jitsuo, Katsutoshi, Keichi, Keiko, Kimie, Koichi, Kunio, Masao.*

Osbeck (106) Swedish: probably a topographic or ornamental name from *os* 'river mouth' or *ås* 'hill', 'ridge' + *beck, bäck* 'brook', 'stream'. Alternatively, the first

element may be an altered spelling of *ås* 'ridge'.

Osberg (374) **1.** Norwegian and Swedish: topographic or ornamental name, from *os* 'river mouth' or *ås* 'hill', 'ridge' + *berg* 'hill', 'mountain'. **2.** Probably a respelling of Swedish **Åsberg**, an ornamental name composed of the elements *ås* 'ridge' + *berg* 'mountain', 'hill'.
GIVEN NAMES Scandinavian 5%. *Erik* (3), *Lars.*

Osbon (238) Variant of English OSBORNE.

Osborn (12622) English: variant spelling of OSBORNE.

Osborne (23343) English: from the Old Norse personal name *Ásbjorn*, composed of the elements *ás* 'god' + *björn* 'bear'. This was established in England before the Conquest, in the late Old English form *Ōsbern*, and was later reinforced by Norman *Osbern*. The surname *Osborne* has also been widely established in Ireland since the 16th century.

Osbourn (382) English: variant spelling of OSBORNE.

Osbourne (417) English: variant spelling of OSBORNE.

Osbun (125) English: variant spelling of OSBORNE.

Osburn (2814) English: variant spelling of OSBORNE.

Osby (335) English (Suffolk): presumably a habitational name from a lost or unidentified place.

Oscar (318) Scandinavian and English: from the personal name *Oscar*, which is of Gaelic origin, composed of the elements *os* 'deer' + *cara* 'friend'. The personal name owes its popularity in Scandinavia and elsewhere to the Ossian poems of James MacPherson (1760), which enjoyed a great vogue in the latter part of the 18th century.

Oscarson (254) Swedish: patronymic from a Scandinavian form of the Irish Gaelic personal name OSCAR.
GIVEN NAME Scandinavian 4%; German 4%. *Kurt* (2).

Ose (174) **1.** Norwegian: habitational name from any of three farmsteads, so named from the dative singular of Old Norse *óss* 'river mouth'. **2.** Hungarian (**Őse**): from a pet form of the old secular personal name *Ős*. **3.** Japanese: 'small strait' or (*Ōse*) 'large strait'. The latter is mostly found along the coast west of Tōkyō, but neither form is very common in Japan.
GIVEN NAMES Scandinavian 5%; Japanese 4%. *Erik; Jiro, Miho, Mitsunori.*

Osegueda (138) Spanish: variant of the habitational name OSEGUERA.
GIVEN NAMES Spanish 55%. *Jose* (5), *Guadalupe* (3), *Jesus* (3), *Margarita* (3), *Alejandro* (2), *Carlos* (2), *Francisco* (2), *Juan* (2), *Manuel* (2), *Marta* (2), *Adan, Ana Maria.*

Oseguera (279) Spanish: habitational name from Oseguera, a village in Burgos province.
GIVEN NAMES Spanish 63%. *Jose* (10), *Francisco* (7), *Jesus* (6), *Raul* (5), *Javier* (4), *Jose Luis* (4), *Juan* (4), *Miguel* (4), *Salvador* (4), *Alfredo* (3), *Guadalupe* (3), *Jaime* (3).

Osei (139) African: unexplained.
GIVEN NAMES African 16%. *Kofi* (2), *Kwaku* (2), *Kwame* (2), *Akwasi, Baffour, Kwabena, Yaa.*

Osen (147) **1.** English: from Old French *oison* 'gosling'. **2.** German (**Ösen**): patronymic from the personal name *Öser* (see OSER). **3.** German: habitational name from Oese near Hemer. **4.** Norwegian: habitational name from any of numerous farmsteads so named from the definite singular form of *os*, Old Norse *óss* 'river mouth'. **5.** Swedish: probably an ornamental name, of unexplained origin.
GIVEN NAMES Scandinavian 6%; German 4%. *Arlis, Berger, Lars; Bernhard.*

Osenbaugh (138) Altered form of German **Osenbach**, a habitational name from a place so named near Colmar in Alsace, France.

Osenga (124) Probably a variant of Frisian **Osinga**, an occupational name for a bleacher.

Osentoski (173) Polish: probably a variant of **Osędowski**, habitational name from Osędowice in Łęczyca province.

Oser (559) North German (also **Öser**): **1.** from a personal name composed of Germanic *ans* 'god' + *heri, hari* 'army'. **2.** habitational name for someone from any of several places called Oos, for example in Baden. **3.** (**Öser**): habitational name from any of several places called Oes or Öse.

Osgood (2605) **1.** English: from the Old Norse personal name *Ásgautr*, composed of the elements *ás* 'god' + the tribal name *Gaut* (see JOSLIN). This was established in England before the Conquest, in the late Old English forms *Ōsgot* or *Ōsgod*, and was later reinforced by the Norman *Ansgot*. **2.** Jewish: adoption of 1 in place of some like-sounding Ashkenazic surname.

O'Shaughnessy (1324) Irish (County Galway): Anglicized form of Gaelic **Ó Seachnasaigh** 'descendant of *Seachnasach*', a personal name of uncertain origin, perhaps derived from *seachnach* 'elusive'.
GIVEN NAMES Irish 9%. *Brendan* (2), *Kieran* (2), *Ciaran, Niall.*

O'Shea (3987) Irish (County Kerry): Anglicized form of Gaelic **Ó Séaghdha** 'descendant of *Séaghdha*', a byname meaning 'fine' or 'fortunate'.
GIVEN NAMES Irish 9%. *Brendan* (11), *Donal* (5), *Brennan* (2), *Colm, Finian, John Patrick, Kieran, Michael Patrick, Seamus.*

Oshel (188) South German (**Öschle**): from a pet form of Alemannic *Oschwald*, from the personal name OSWALD.

Oshell (161) Origin uncertain. Probably a respelling of South German **Öschle** (see OSHEL).

Osher (252) Jewish (Ashkenazic): from the Yiddish personal name *Osher* (Hebrew ASHER 'blessed').
GIVEN NAMES Jewish 4%. *Meyer, Yehuda.*

O'Shields (588) Irish: Anglicized form of Gaelic **Ó Siaghail** (modern Irish **Ó Siáil**) 'descendant of *Siadhal*', a well-attested personal name of unknown derivation.

Oshima (257) Japanese: **1.** (**Ōshima**): 'large island'. Japan has islands of all sizes and many families have taken the name. **2.** (**Oshima**): variant pronunciation of *Ojima* or KOJIMA.
GIVEN NAMES Japanese 56%. *Hiroshi* (3), *Haruo* (2), *Keiichi* (2), *Kiyoshi* (2), *Seiko* (2), *Shigeru* (2), *Yoshi* (2), *Yoshiko* (2), *Yukiko* (2), *Aki, Akira, Chiharu.*

Oshinsky (132) Jewish (Ashkenazic): variant spelling of OSINSKI.
GIVEN NAMES Jewish 6%. *Elihu, Isidor, Sol.*

Oshiro (903) Japanese: **1.** (**Ōshiro**): 'large castle'; found mostly in western Japan and the Ryūkyū Islands. **2.** (**Oshiro**): 'small castle', descended from the MINAMOTO clan. **3.** (**Oshiro**): (perhaps) a variant written with the characters for 'small' and 'generation'.
GIVEN NAMES Japanese 36%. *Yoshio* (7), *Masao* (6), *Shigeo* (4), *Teruo* (4), *Hideo* (3), *Hiroshi* (3), *Kaoru* (3), *Kiyoshi* (3), *Minoru* (3), *Mitsuo* (3), *Seichi* (3), *Toshio* (3).

Oshita (148) Japanese: (**Ōshita**): apparently a habitational or topographic name meaning '(one who lives) in the large (area) below'; it is found mainly in western Japan.
GIVEN NAMES Japanese 42%. *Hideo* (2), *Shigeru* (2), *Yutaka* (2), *Fumio, Goro, Harumi, Hiroshi, Ikuo, Isao, Itsuki, Kazuma, Kazumi.*

Oshman (143) Jewish (eastern Ashkenazic): habitational name from either of two places called Oshmyany, one now in Belarus, the other (Ašmena) in Lithuania in Vilnius region.

Osiecki (302) Polish: habitational name for someone from any of various places called Osieck, Osiecko, or Osiek, named with *osiek* a topographic term denoting low-lying fertile land, i.e. meadowland.
GIVEN NAMES Polish 6%. *Zygmunt* (2), *Kazimierz, Leszek, Stanislaw.*

Osier (449) French: from Old French *osier* 'willow' (of Gaulish origin), a topographic name for someone who lived near a willow tree or willow grove.

Osika (182) Polish and Ukrainian: from Polish *osika*, Ukrainian *osyka* 'aspen', either a nickname for someone who trembled like an aspen leaf, or a topographic term for someone who lived where aspens grew.

Osinski (450) Polish (**Osiński**) and Jewish (from Poland): habitational name for someone from any of numerous places in Poland called Osiny or Osina, named with Polish *osina* 'aspen (tree)'.
GIVEN NAMES Polish 8%. *Casimir* (2), *Darek, Ewa, Grzegorz, Jadwiga, Janusz, Jerzy, Ryszard, Waclaw, Witold.*

Oskey (121) Variant of English ASKEY.

Oskin (108) Variant of English HOSKIN.
GIVEN NAME French 7%. *Emile.*

Osland (243) **1.** Norwegian: habitational name from any of three farmsteads so named. Two of the farms, in Sogn og Fjordane, are named with Old Norse *Óðinsland*, a compound of *Óðinn* (the name of an important Norse god) + *land* 'land', 'farmstead'. The third, situated in Rogaland, has a first element of uncertain etymology. **2.** Americanized form of Norwegian **Åsland**, from Old Norse *áss* 'hill', 'ridge' + *land*.
GIVEN NAMES Scandinavian 7%. *Ketil, Knut, Nord.*

Osler (395) **1.** English: variant of OSTLER. **2.** Possibly an altered form of German OSTLER.

Osley (171) English: possibly a habitational name from Osterley in Middlesex, named with Old English *eowestre* 'sheepfold' + *lēah* '(woodland) clearing'.

Oslin (198) Swedish: variant of **Åslin** (see ASLIN).

Oslund (384) Americanized spelling of Swedish or Norwegian **Åslund**, composed of the elements *ås* 'ridge' + *lund* 'grove'.

Osman (1555) **1.** Turkish: from the Turkish personal name *Osman*, Turkish form of Arabic *'Uthmān*. This was the name of the third of the 'rightly guided' khalifs (ruled 644–656), one of the ten Companions of the Prophet Muhammad, to whom he gave the good news of entering into paradise. **2.** English: variant of OSMOND. **3.** Dutch: from a Germanic personal name composed of the elements *ans* 'god' + *man* 'man'. **4.** Dutch: occupational name for an ox driver, from *os* 'ox', 'bullock' + *man* 'man'. **5.** German (**Osmann**): variant of **Ossmann** (see OSSMANN). **6.** Jewish (eastern Ashkenazic): of uncertain origin; perhaps a variant of OSHMAN or HAUSMAN.
GIVEN NAMES Muslim 29%. *Mohamed* (27), *Mohammed* (9), *Ahmed* (7), *Hassan* (5), *Ibrahim* (4), *Mohammad* (4), *Said* (4), *Salah* (4), *Abdi* (3), *Abdulkadir* (3), *Ali* (3), *Khalid* (3).

Osmanski (166) **1.** Polish (**Osmański**): habitational name for someone from a place called Osmanka in Płock voivodeship. **2.** Possibly also a derivative of the German personal name OSMAN, which is also found in Poland.

Osment (262) English: variant of OSMOND.

Osmer (288) English and North German: from an Old English and Continental Germanic personal name composed of Old English, Old Saxon *ōs* 'god' + Old English *mǣr*, Old Saxon *mere* 'famous'.

Osmon (300) English: variant of OSMOND.

Osmond (448) English and French: from the Old Norse personal name *Ásmundr*, composed of the elements *ás* 'god' + *mund* 'protection'. This was established in England before the Conquest, coalescing with the independent Old English form *Ōsmund*, and was later reinforced by the Norman *Osmund*.

Osmun (338) Variant of French or English OSMOND.

Osmundsen (111) Danish or Norwegian: patronymic from the personal name *Ásmund* (see OSMOND).
GIVEN NAMES Scandinavian 10%. *Sigvald, Tor.*

Osmundson (330) Americanized spelling of OSMUNDSEN.
GIVEN NAMES Scandinavian 7%. *Juel* (2), *Obert* (2), *Jarl.*

Osness (120) Norwegian: habitational name from any of various farmsteads, most in western Norway, named from Old Norse *óss* 'river mouth' + *nes* 'headland', 'promontory'.

Osofsky (165) Jewish (eastern Ashkenazic): variant spelling of OSOWSKI.
GIVEN NAMES Jewish 7%. *Meyer* (2), *Azriel, Hyman, Sol.*

Osorio (1847) Portuguese (**Osório**) and Spanish: from a medieval personal name *Osorius*, of uncertain origin. It is perhaps a metathesized form of Latin *Orosius* (Greek *Orosios*, a derivative of *oros* 'mountain'), the name borne by a 4th-century Iberian theologian and historian, who was famous in Spain throughout the Middle Ages.
GIVEN NAMES Spanish 55%; Portuguese 11%. *Jose* (42), *Carlos* (36), *Juan* (27), *Luis* (20), *Francisco* (17), *Jorge* (15), *Miguel* (15), *Mario* (14), *Jaime* (10), *Manuel* (10), *Rafael* (10), *Ana* (9); *Agostinho, Marcio.*

Osowski (653) Polish and Jewish (eastern Ashkenazic): habitational name for someone from any of the various places named Osów, Osowa, Osowo, Ossowo, Ossowa, etc., all named either with *osowy* (adjective) 'aspen' or with *osa* 'wasp'.
GIVEN NAMES Polish 5%. *Henryk* (2), *Krystyna* (2), *Aleksander, Casimir, Danuta, Jozef, Tadeusz, Tadeuz, Teofil.*

Ospina (382) Hispanic: unexplained. This name is found mainly in Colombia.
GIVEN NAMES Spanish 55%. *Luis* (11), *Carlos* (10), *Luz* (8), *Jose* (7), *Diego* (5), *Jaime* (5), *Eduardo* (4), *Juan* (4), *Alvaro* (3), *Enrique* (3), *Gustavo* (3), *Jairo* (3).

Oss (164) **1.** North German: from Low German *oss* 'ox', hence a nickname for a farmer or a stupid person, or in some cases a habitational name for someone living at a house or inn distinguished by the sign of an ox. **2.** South German (especially southern Bavaria (Allgäu)): from a short form of the personal name OSWALD. **3.** Dutch (**van**

Oss): habitational name from Oss in North Brabant. **4.** Probably an Americanized form of any of a number of common Norwegian habitational names from farmsteads named with Old Norse *áss* 'hill', 'ridge' (see AAS).

Ossa (104) Spanish: **1.** variant of Basque **Osa** or **Otsa**, habitational name from a town in Navarre province. **2.** possibly also a habitational name from a place called Ossa de Montiel in Albacete province, Spain.
GIVEN NAMES Spanish 46%. *Jaime* (4), *Julio* (3), *Jairo* (2), *Jesus* (2), *Jose* (2), *Luis* (2), *Roberto* (2), *Adiela*, *Adriana*, *Alba*, *Alberto*, *Alejandro*.

Ossi (102) Italian: possibly from the plural of *osso* 'bone', hence a nickname for a skinny person. The form **Osso** is more frequent in Italy.
GIVEN NAMES Italian 6%. *Florio*, *Massimo*, *Vito*.

Ossman (251) **1.** Dutch: variant spelling of OSMAN 3 and 4. **2.** German (**Ossmann**): from a personal name composed of Germanic *ans* 'god' + *man* 'man'.

Osso (174) Italian: nickname from *osso* 'bone'.
GIVEN NAMES Italian 33%. *Mario* (3), *Salvatore* (3), *Francesco* (2), *Luigi* (2), *Nunzio* (2), *Antonio*, *Carmine*, *Enrico*, *Fiore*, *Gaetano*, *Gaspare*, *Italo*, *Marcello*, *Roberto*.

Ossowski (127) Polish: variant of OSOWSKI, associated in particular with Ossowa in Biała Podlaska voivodeship and Ossów in Warszawa voivodeship.
GIVEN NAMES Polish 9%. *Casimir*, *Jerzy*, *Maciej*, *Zbigniew*, *Zygmunt*.

Osswald (153) English: variant of OSWALD.
GIVEN NAMES German 9%. *Dieter* (2), *Ernst*, *Hartmut*, *Oskar*.

Ost (570) **1.** German, North German (also **Öst**), Swedish (also **Öst**), and Jewish (Ashkenazic): topographic name from German *Ost(en)*, Swedish *öst* 'east' denoting someone who lived to the east of a settlement or who had come there from the east. Compare EAST. As a Jewish name, as well as Swedish, it can be ornamental. **2.** German: from a short form of any of various Germanic personal names formed with this element (see OEST).

Ostberg (234) **1.** Swedish (**Östberg**) and Jewish (Ashkenazic): ornamental or topographic name composed of Swedish *öst*, German *Ost* 'east' + Swedish *berg*, German *Berg* 'mountain', 'hill'. **2.** Norwegian: habitational name from any of several farmsteads named Østberg (see 1).
GIVEN NAMES Scandinavian 10%. *Lennart* (2), *Mats*, *Petter*.

Ostby (465) Norwegian: habitational name from any of about forty farmsteads, mostly in southeastern Norway, named Østby or Austby, from Old Norse *Austbýr*, a compound of *aust* 'east' + *býr* 'farmstead'.

GIVEN NAMES Scandinavian 5%. *Gothard* (2), *Gunner*, *Jorun*.

Ostdiek (115) Variant of Dutch **Oostdijk**, **Oostdyk**, a habitational name from any of several places so named in the Netherlands and Belgium.

Osteen (2029) **1.** Swedish (**Östeen**): variant spelling of **Östén** (see OSTEN). **2.** alternatively it could be a hibernicization (**O'Steen**) of Scottish STEEN, which has long been established in Ireland.

Osten (317) **1.** German: mainly a topographic name derived from German *Ost(en)* 'east', but in some cases a shortened form of *von der Osten*, also a topographic name meaning 'from the Oste river', a name borne by an old Pomeranian noble family. **2.** German: habitational name from any of several places so named in northern Germany. **3.** Dutch: patronymic from a Germanic personal name *Austa*, meaning 'eastern'. **4.** Swedish (**Östén**, **Östen**): ornamental name from *öst* 'east' + the common surname suffix *-én*, from Latin *-enius*.

Ostendorf (728) German: habitational name from Ostendorf, a common place name in the region of Münster, Westphalia.
GIVEN NAMES German 4%. *Erhard*, *Erwin*, *Fritz*, *Hans*, *Wilhelm*.

Ostenson (185) Norwegian: patronymic from the personal name Østen, from Øystein, Old Norse *Eysteinn*, composed of the elements *ey* 'luck', 'gift' + *steinn* 'stone'.

Oster (2413) **1.** Swedish (**Öster**) and German: topographic name from Swedish *öster*, Middle Low German and Middle High German *öster* 'eastern', denoting someone who lived to the east of a settlement or who had come there from the east. In many cases the Swedish name is probably ornamental. **2.** German: nickname for someone who had a connection with the festival of Easter (for example, someone who was born or baptized at that time), from *Oster* 'Easter'. **3.** Jewish (Ashkenazic): topographic or ornamental name from German *Ost* 'east' or ornamental name from German *Oster* 'Easter'; compare 1 and 3. **4.** Jewish (eastern Ashkenazic): nickname from Polish *ostry* or Russian *ostryj* 'sharp', 'sharp-minded'. **5.** Dutch: from a Germanic personal name composed of *aust* 'east' + *heri*, *hari* 'army'.

Osterberg (675) **1.** German: habitational name from any of many places named with Middle Low German or Middle High German *öster* 'eastern' + *berg* 'mountain', 'hill'. Places so named are common in Bavaria, Westphalia, and Lower Saxony. **2.** Swedish (**Österberg**), Norwegian (**Østerberg**): ornamental or topographic name from *öster* 'eastern' + *berg* 'mountain', 'hill'.
GIVEN NAMES Scandinavian 8%. *Nils* (3), *Einer* (2), *Fredrik* (2), *Erik*, *Lars*, *Lennart*.

Ostergaard (235) Danish (**Østergaard**) and Swedish (**Östergaard**): habitational name from a place named with *øster* 'eastern' + *gård* 'farmstead'.
GIVEN NAMES Scandinavian 16%; German 6%. *Bent*, *Erik*, *Knud*, *Nels*, *Palle*; *Ewald*, *Hans*, *Kurt*, *Orlo*.

Ostergard (169) Danish and Swedish: see OSTERGAARD.

Ostergren (189) Swedish (**Östergren**): ornamental name composed of the elements *öster* 'eastern' + *gren* 'branch'.
GIVEN NAMES Scandinavian 11%. *Erik* (2), *Lennart*.

Osterhaus (291) North German: habitational name from a common place name, Osterhausen, from Middle Low German *öster* 'easterly' + *hūs* 'house'.

Osterholm (108) Swedish: ornamental name composed of the elements *öster* 'eastern' + *holm* 'islet'.
GIVEN NAME Scandinavian 5%. *Erik*.

Osterholt (181) **1.** North German: topographic name from *oster* 'east', 'easterly' + *holt* 'wood'. **2.** Norwegian: habitational name from either of two farmsteads named Østerholt, from Old Norse *Austrholtar*, composed of the elements *austr* 'east' + *holt* 'grove'.

Osterhoudt (405) Dutch: variant spelling of OSTERHOUT.

Osterhout (804) Dutch: topographic name from *oster* 'eastern' + *hout* 'wood'.

Osterkamp (205) North German: topographic name from *oster* 'east', 'easterly' + *kamp* 'enclosed field', 'domain'.

Osterland (110) German: regional or ethnic name, from Middle High German *österland* 'country or land lying to the east', also 'Austria'.
GIVEN NAMES German 7%. *Otto* (2), *Hans*.

Osterling (133) **1.** North German: variant of **Österling** (see OESTERLING). **2.** Swedish: (**Österling**): ornamental name from *öster* 'eastern' + *-ling*, a common suffix of Swedish surnames, denoting a person.
GIVEN NAME Scandinavian 8%. *Lars*.

Osterloh (289) North German: topographic name from Middle Low German *öster* 'eastern', 'easterly' + *loh* 'small wood'.
GIVEN NAMES German 5%. *Egon*, *Erhard*, *Othmar*, *Rainer*.

Osterlund (194) Swedish (**Österlund**) and Danish (**Østerlund**): ornamental or topographic name composed of the elements *öster* 'eastern' + *lund* 'grove'.
GIVEN NAMES Scandinavian 10%. *Erik*, *Holger*, *Johan*, *Sven*.

Osterman (1410) Swedish (also **Österman**) and Jewish (Ashkenazic): variant of OSTER with the addition of Swedish, Yiddish *man* 'man'.

Ostermann (407) German: topographic name denoting someone who lived to the east of a settlement or who had immigrated to it from the east, from Middle High German *oster* 'eastern' + *man* 'man', or an ethnic name from Middle High German *ōstermann* 'Austrian'.

GIVEN NAMES German 7%. *Hans* (2), *Bernd, Dietmar, Gerhardt, Klaus, Kurt, Meinrad, Wilfried.*

Ostermeier (206) German and Dutch: distinguishing name for a tenant farmer (MEYER) living to the east (see OSTER) of a settlement. In the Netherlands this surname is more commonly written **Oost(er)meyer**.

GIVEN NAMES German 8%. *Alfons, Alois, Kurt, Otto, Xaver.*

Ostermeyer (166) German: variant spelling of OSTERMEIER.

Ostermiller (205) Partly Americanized form of German **Ostermüller**, a distinguishing name for a miller (see MUELLER) whose mill was situated to the east (see OSTER) of a settlement.

GIVEN NAMES German 4%. *Gottlieb, Kurt.*

Ostertag (386) German: nickname for a person with a joyful nature, from Middle High German *ōstertac* 'Easter Day', signifying 'the greatest joy'.

GIVEN NAMES German 8%. *Erwin* (2), *Kurt* (2), *Alfons, Angelika, Armin, Eldred, Hans, Juergen, Wolfgang.*

Ostheimer (154) **1.** German and Jewish (western Ashkenazic): habitational name denoting someone from any of a number of places called Ostheim, in Hesse, Franconia and Thuringia. **2.** French (from German): habitational name for someone from Ostheim in Alsace.

GIVEN NAMES German 4%. *Heinz, Kurt.*

Osthoff (138) German and Dutch: habitational name meaning 'east farmstead', from places in northwestern Germany called Osthof or places in the Netherlands and Belgium called Oosthof or Oosthove.

GIVEN NAMES German 6%. *Ewald, Klaus.*

Ostiguy (145) French: unexplained.

GIVEN NAMES French 13%. *Jean Claude, Jean-Francois, Marcel, Normand, Raoul.*

Osting (155) North German (**Östing**): patronymic from a short form of a Germanic personal name formed with *Ost* (see OEST).

Ostler (586) **1.** English: occupational name for an innkeeper, from Middle English *(h)osteler* (Old French *(h)ostelier*, an agent derivative of *hostel*, meaning a sizeable house in which guests could be lodged in separate rooms, derived from Late Latin *hospitalis*, from the genitive case of *hospes* 'guest'). This term was at first applied to the secular officer in a monastery who was responsible for the lodging of visitors, but it was later extended to keepers of commercial hostelries, and this is probably the usual sense of the surname. The more restricted modern English sense, 'groom', is also a possible source. **2.** German: from a short form of a Germanic personal name formed with a cognate of Old High German *ōst(an)* (see OEST).

Ostlie (137) Origin unidentified.

Ostling (167) Swedish (**Östling**): ornamental name from *öst* 'east' + the common surname suffix *-ling* denoting a person, sometimes adopted as a topographic name by someone who lived to the east of a settlement or had come there from the east.

GIVEN NAMES Scandinavian 8%; German 4%. *Algot, Sven; Kurt.*

Ostlund (679) Swedish (**Östlund**) and Norwegian (**Østlund**): ornamental or topographic name composed of the elements *öst* 'east' + *lund* 'grove'.

GIVEN NAMES Scandinavian 7%. *Holger* (2), *Anders, Arlis, Bjorn, Knute, Lars, Maren, Per, Petter.*

Ostman (295) **1.** Swedish (**Östman**): ornamental or topographic name from *öst* ('east') + *man* 'man'. **2.** Respelling of North German OSTMANN.

GIVEN NAME Scandinavian 5%. *Per* (2).

Ostmann (108) North German: topographic name from OST ('east') + Low German *man* 'man'.

Ostrand (180) Respelling of Swedish **Åstrand** or **Östrand**, probably an ornamental name composed of the elements *å* 'creek' or *ö* 'island' + *strand* 'shore', 'beach'.

GIVEN NAMES German 7%; Scandinavian 6%. *Ernst* (3), *Hans; Maren, Sven.*

Ostrander (3457) Respelling of Swedish **Åstrander** or **Östrander**, probably of the same etymology as OSTRAND, the addition of the suffix *-er* giving the appearance of a name formed with *-ander* (from Greek *anēr, andros* 'man').

Ostreicher (124) Jewish (Ashkenazic): variant of OESTREICHER.

GIVEN NAMES Jewish 34%. *Aron* (2), *Cheskel* (2), *Avrom, Berish, Blima, Chaim, Chaya, Eliezer, Leser, Mendel, Meyer, Moric.*

Ostrem (383) Norwegian: habitational name from any of several farmsteads, particularly in Rogaland, named Austrheim, from *austr* 'east' + *heim* 'home', 'farmstead'.

GIVEN NAMES Scandinavian 6%. *Obert* (2), *Arnt, Knute, Peer, Sten.*

Ostrenga (111) Polish (**Ostręga**): from Polish dialect *ostręga* literally 'blackberry', a derivative of *ostry* 'sharp', probably a nickname for someone who had a sharp tongue or who was sharp-witted.

Ostroff (483) **1.** Jewish (Ashkenazic): alternative spelling of OSTROV. **2.** Shortened form of Jewish and Slavic OSTROVSKY.

GIVEN NAMES Jewish 6%. *Sol* (3), *Hyman, Isadore, Meyer, Miriam, Myer.*

Ostrofsky (98) French, German, or American spelling of Jewish and Eastern Slavic OSTROVSKY.

Ostrom (1507) Swedish (**Öström**): ornamental name composed of the elements *ö* 'island' + *ström* 'river'.

GIVEN NAMES Scandinavian 4%. *Erik* (2), *Lars* (2), *Hedvig, Nils.*

Ostroski (321) Polish: variant spelling of OSTROWSKI.

Ostrosky (207) Jewish (eastern Ashkenazic): variant spelling of OSTROVSKY.

Ostrov (128) Jewish (eastern Ashkenazic): **1.** habitational name from the village of Ostrov, now in Belarus, named with *ostrov* 'island'. **2.** variant of OSTROW.

GIVEN NAMES Jewish 11%; Russian 7%. *Herschel, Hyman, Ilya; Anatoly, Boris, Iosif, Mikhail, Vladimir.*

Ostrovsky (204) Russian, Ukrainian, Belorussian, and Jewish (eastern Ashkenazic): habitational name for someone from any of many places in different parts of eastern Europe named Ostrov, from Eastern Slavic *ostrov* 'island', 'water meadow'.

GIVEN NAMES Russian 27%; Jewish 19%. *Boris* (7), *Mikhail* (5), *Igor* (4), *Leonid* (3), *Lev* (3), *Vladimir* (3), *Grigory* (2), *Semyon* (2), *Svetlana* (2), *Arkady, Betya, Dmitri; Akiva, Aron, Irina, Isak, Moysey, Naum, Rimma, Uri, Yakov.*

Ostrow (699) **1.** Polish (**Ostrów**) and Jewish (from Poland): habitational name from any of several places called Ostrów, named with *ostrów* 'island', 'water meadow'. **2.** Jewish (American): shortened form of OSTROWSKI.

GIVEN NAMES Jewish 5%. *Hyman, Leib, Meyer, Miriam, Sol.*

Ostrowski (2601) Polish and Jewish (Ashkenazic): habitational name for someone from any of many places in Poland and adjacent parts of eastern Europe named Ostrów, named with Polish *ostrów* 'island', 'water meadow' (see OSTROW) or a cognate word in a related Slavic language.

GIVEN NAMES Polish 5%. *Casimir* (6), *Ewa* (3), *Bogdan* (2), *Jerzy* (2), *Stanislaw* (2), *Waclaw* (2), *Alicja, Andrzej, Boguslaw, Bronislaw, Danuta, Darek.*

Ostrowsky (164) Variant spelling of OSTROWSKI. This spelling can be Jewish, Russian, Ukrainian, or Americanized Polish.

Ostrum (244) Probably a respelling of Swedish **Öström** (see OSTROM).

GIVEN NAMES German 4%. *Eldred* (2), *Otto.*

Ostwald (238) **1.** German: variant of OSWALD. **2.** German: from the Germanic personal name *Ostold*, composed of the elements *Ost* (see OEST 1) + Old High German *walt(an)* 'to rule'. **3.** Jewish (Ashkenazic): ornamental name composed of German *Ost* 'east' + *Wald* 'forest'.

GIVEN NAME German 4%. *Kurt.*

Osuch (183) Polish: nickname from Polish dialect *osuch*, a word with several meanings: 'withered tree', 'dry bread', or 'withered old man'.

GIVEN NAME German 4%. *Kurt.*

O'Sullivan (4533) Irish (Munster): Anglicized form of Gaelic **Ó Súileabháin** 'descendant of *Súileabháin*' (see SULLIVAN).

GIVEN NAMES Irish 11%. *Brendan* (16), *Donal* (9), *Liam* (6), *Siobhan* (4), *Declan* (3), *Kieran* (3), *Cathal* (2), *Dermot* (2),

Eamon (2), *Fergus* (2), *Grainne* (2), *Seamus* (2).

Osuna (639) Spanish: habitational name from a place in the province of Seville, named from Arabic *Oxuna*, perhaps from Late Latin *Ursina (villa)* 'estate of *Ursus*', a byname meaning 'bear'.
GIVEN NAMES Spanish 46%. *Juan* (10), *Jose* (9), *Jesus* (7), *Jorge* (7), *Luis* (7), *Miguel* (6), *Rafael* (6), *Alicia* (5), *Manuel* (5), *Ramon* (5), *Raul* (5), *Carlos* (4).

Oswald (5620) **1.** Scottish, northern English, and German: from an Old English personal name composed of the elements *ōs* 'god' + *weald* 'power'. In the Middle English period, this fell together with the less common Old Norse cognate *Ásvaldr*. The name was introduced to Germany from England, as a result of the fame of St. Oswald, a 7th-century king of Northumbria, whose deeds were reported by Celtic missionaries to southern Germany. The name was also borne by a 10th-century English saint of Danish parentage, who was important as a monastic reformer. **2.** Irish: adopted as an English equivalent of Gaelic **Ó hEodhusa** (see HUSSEY 1).

Oswalt (2040) German: variant of OSWALD.

Osweiler (136) Respelling of German **Ossweiler**, a habitational name for someone from Osswil in Baden-Württemberg.

Oswell (156) **1.** English: of uncertain origin, possibly a habitational name, of which the second element appears to be Old English *well(a)* 'spring', 'creek'. The first element may be a short form of an Old English personal name containing the element *ōs* 'god' (see for example OSWALD) or its Old Norse cognate *ás* (see OSBORNE). However, the earliest known bearer of the name was Roger Wyswall, who was admitted as a burgess of Shrewsbury in 1450. The English name is found in various forms, including **Woosall** and **Wossald**. **2.** Irish (Ulster): adopted as an English equivalent of Gaelic **Ó hEodhusa** 'descendant of *Eodhus*' (see HUSSEY).

Ota (635) Japanese (**Ōta**): 'large rice paddy'; variously written and found mostly in western Japan and the Ryūkyū Islands. Some bearers are descended from the MINAMOTO and the surname is listed in the Shinsen shōjiroku. A village in Tōtōmi (now part of Shizuoka prefecture) gave its name to several families, but the village itself was originally named after a branch of the ancient *Ōta* clan which settled there.
GIVEN NAMES Japanese 52%. *Hiroshi* (8), *Kenji* (5), *Minoru* (4), *Nobuyuki* (4), *Takahiro* (4), *Tetsuo* (4), *Keiko* (3), *Makoto* (3), *Tsutomu* (3), *Hideko* (2), *Hiro* (2), *Hiroko* (2).

Otake (124) Japanese (**Ōtake**): 'large bamboo'; the name is found mostly along the southeastern seaboard and in the Ryūkyū Islands. Other names, much less common and probably unrelated but having the same

pronunciation, are written with characters meaning 'great warrior' and 'large residence'.
GIVEN NAMES Japanese 57%. *Atsushi* (2), *Hiromi* (2), *Norio* (2), *Ryuji* (2), *Shigemasa* (2), *Akihisa*, *Chihiro*, *Eiko*, *Hidenori*, *Hiroko*, *Hiroshi*, *Hitoshi*.

Otani (268) Japanese: **1.** (**Ōtani**): 'large valley'; mostly found in western Japan. Another pronunciation, **Ōya**, is found in eastern Japan. **2.** (**Otani**): 'small valley'; this is more usually pronounced *Kotani* or *Koya*; all three forms are from western Japan.
GIVEN NAMES Japanese 53%. *Kazuo* (3), *Akira* (2), *Hajime* (2), *Hideo* (2), *Hiromi* (2), *Ichiro* (2), *Masato* (2), *Masatoshi* (2), *Noboru* (2), *Noriko* (2), *Shigeo* (2), *Shozo* (2).

Oteri (153) Italian: from a Germanic personal name composed of the elements *aud* 'old' + *hari*, *heri* 'army'.
GIVEN NAMES Italian 8%. *Gaetano*, *Giuseppe*, *Salvatore*.

Otero (2587) Spanish: **1.** habitational name from any of various places so called, from Spanish *otero* 'height', 'hill' (Late Latin *altarium*, a derivative of *altus* 'high'). **2.** Castilianized form of the common Galician and Asturian-Leonese place names Outeiro and Uteru.
GIVEN NAMES Spanish 38%. *Jose* (86), *Luis* (30), *Manuel* (23), *Jorge* (19), *Angel* (17), *Juan* (16), *Carlos* (15), *Pablo* (13), *Pedro* (11), *Ruben* (11), *Jesus* (10), *Rafael* (10); *Antonio* (22), *Lorenzo* (7), *Dario* (4), *Angelo* (3), *Carmelo* (3), *Eliseo* (3), *Amadeo*, *Antoninette*, *Carlo*, *Carmello*, *Ceasar*, *Clemente*.

Otey (747) English: variant of OTTEY.

Othman (185) Muslim: variant of Arabic *'Uthmān*, a name of unknown etymology. This was the name of the third of the 'rightly guided' khalifs (ruled 644–656), one of the Companions of the Prophet Muhammad, to whom he gave the good news of entering into paradise.
GIVEN NAMES Muslim 76%. *Mohamed* (6), *Mahmoud* (5), *Ali* (4), *Khaled* (3), *Mohammad* (3), *Adnan* (2), *Aziz* (2), *Fahad* (2), *Hassan* (2), *Maher* (2), *Mohammed* (2), *Othman* (2).

Otis (2877) English: variant of OATES.
FOREBEARS John Otis emigrated from England in 1631 to Hingham, MA; he had many prominent descendants. His great grandson, James Otis (1725–83), was a Boston lawyer who played a major role in the development of opposition to the British crown and the establishment of the Fourth Amendment. Another descendant was Elisha Graves Otis (1811–61), inventor of the elevator, who was born on his father's farm at Halifax, Windham Co., VT.

Otley (137) English: variant spelling of OTTLEY.
GIVEN NAME German 4%. *Kurt*.

Otness (103) Norwegian: habitational name from any of three farmsteads named with *Ot* (probably from a river name related to *otte* 'fear') + *nes* 'headland', 'promontory'.
GIVEN NAMES Scandinavian 11%; German 4%. *Nels* (3); *Kurt*.

O'Tool (102) Irish: variant spelling of O'TOOLE.

O'Toole (4345) Irish: Anglicized form of Gaelic **Ó Tuathail** 'descendant of *Tuathal*', an old Celtic personal name composed of the elements *tuath* 'people' + *gal* 'mighty'. This is the name of distinct families in Leinster and Ulster.
GIVEN NAMES Irish 7%. *Brendan* (3), *Caitlin*, *Eamonn*, *Eoin*, *Kelan*, *Kieran*, *Michael Patrick*, *Niall*, *Patrick James*, *Peadar*, *Siobhan*.

Otradovec (103) Czech: habitational name for someone from any of four places in Bohemia called Otradov or Otradovice.

Otremba (192) Polish (also **Otręba**): from *otręba* 'chaff', 'husks', 'bran', either an occupational name for one who winnowed grain or an unflattering nickname for a worthless person.

Otsuka (226) Japanese (**Ōtsuka**): 'large (tomb) mound'; tomb mounds and places named after them are found in all but the far north of Japan, but the surname is found mostly in eastern Japan. Several families with this name have samurai connections of various origins.
GIVEN NAMES Japanese 64%. *Akira* (4), *Koji* (3), *Hiroyuki* (2), *Kazuo* (2), *Kenji* (2), *Kiyoshi* (2), *Noriko* (2), *Takashi* (2), *Tsutomu* (2), *Yoshihiko* (2), *Yukichi* (2), *Akemi*.

Ott (10452) English and German: from a Middle English personal name, *Ode*, in which personal names of several different origins have coalesced: principally Old English *Od(d)a*, Old Norse *Od(d)a* and Continental Germanic *Odo*, *Otto*. The first two are short forms of names with the first element Old English *ord*, Old Norse *odd* 'point of a weapon'. The Continental Germanic names are from a short form of compound names with the first element *od-* 'possessions', 'riches'. The situation is further confused by the fact that all of these names were Latinized as *Odo*. Odo was the name of the half-brother of the Conqueror, archbishop of Bayeux, who accompanied the Norman expedition to England and was rewarded with 439 confiscated manors. The German name Odo or Otto was a hereditary name in the Saxon ruling house, as well as being borne by Otto von Wittelsbach, who founded the Bavarian ruling dynasty in the 11th century, and the 12th-century Otto of Bamberg, apostle of Pomerania.

Ottaviani (155) Italian: patronymic or plural form of OTTAVIANO.
GIVEN NAMES Italian 16%. *Guido* (2), *Stefano* (2), *Amedeo*, *Angelo*, *Antonio*, *Dario*, *Giorgio*, *Marco*, *Marino*, *Silvio*.

Ottaviano (358) Italian: **1.** from the personal name *Ottaviano* (Latin *Octavianus*, meaning 'of the *gens Octavia*', a name derived from *octavus* 'eight'). **2.** (Neapolitan): habitational name from Ottaviano in the province of Naples, called Ottaiano until 1933.
GIVEN NAMES Italian 19%. *Antonio* (3), *Carlo* (2), *Luigi* (2), *Annamarie, Camillo, Dario, Dino, Gino, Gioia, Giovanni, Guido, Italia.*

Ottaway (308) English: from either of two Norman personal names: *Otoïs*, composed of the Germanic elements *od* 'prosperity', 'riches' + *widis* (from *wid* 'wide' or *witu* 'wood'), or *Otewi*, in which the second element is *wīg* 'war'.

Otte (1812) German, Danish, and Dutch: from the personal name *Otto* (see OTT).
GIVEN NAMES German 4%. *Kurt* (4), *Erwin* (3), *Armin, Bernd, Dieter, Friedhelm, Gerhard, Hans, Heinz, Klaus, Siegfried, Wilhelm.*

Otteman (111) Dutch and German (**Ottemann**): probably an occupational name meaning 'servant of *Otto*' (see OTT).

Otten (1613) **1.** English: variant of OTT, from the Old French oblique case. **2.** North German and Dutch: patronymic from the personal name *Otto* (see OTT).

Ottenbacher (111) German: habitational name for someone from either of two places (in Baden-Württemberg and Saxony) named Ottenbach.
GIVEN NAMES German 9%. *Aloysius, Gottlieb, Kurt, Otto.*

Ottens (205) North German and Dutch: patronymic from the personal name *Otto* (see OTT).
GIVEN NAMES German 7%; Dutch 4%. *Horst* (2), *Gunther; Dirk* (2), *Harm.*

Otter (484) **1.** English, German, Dutch, and Jewish (Ashkenazic): metonymic occupational name for an otter hunter, or nickname for someone supposedly resembling an otter, from Middle English, Middle High German *oter*, Middle Dutch *otter*, German *Otter* 'otter'. The Jewish surname can be ornamental. **2.** English: from the late Old English personal name *Ohthere*, a borrowing of Old Norse *Óttar*, composed of the elements *ótti* 'fear', 'dread' + *herr* 'army'. In Scotland the Old Norse name is the source. **3.** French: from a Germanic personal name composed of the elements *aud, od* 'wealth' + *hari, heri* 'army'.
GIVEN NAMES German 4%. *Horst, Johannes, Kurt, Monika, Otto, Wilhelm.*

Otterbein (153) German: nickname from Middle High German *oter* 'otter' + *bein* 'bone', 'leg'; its precise application is unclear.

Otterman (119) German (**Ottermann**) and Jewish (Ashkenazic): elaborated form of OTTER with the addition of Middle High German *man*, Yiddish *man* 'man'.

Otterness (200) Norwegian: habitational name from a farmstead in Trøndelag named from *oter* 'otter' + *nes* 'headland', 'point'.
GIVEN NAMES Scandinavian 6%. *Iver* (2), *Ole.*

Otterson (469) Americanized spelling of Norwegian **Ottersen**, a patronymic from the personal name *Ottar*, Old Norse *Óttarr*, from *ótt* 'something fearful', 'danger' + *-arr* 'warrior'.

Otterstrom (101) Swedish (**Otterström**): ornamental name composed of the elements *utter* (earlier *oter*) 'otter' + *ström* 'river'.

Ottesen (271) Dutch, Danish, and Norwegian: patronymic from the personal name *Otto* (see OTT).
GIVEN NAMES Scandinavian 11%; German 5%. *Jarl, Knud, Sven; Hans* (2), *Otto* (2).

Otteson (386) Americanized spelling of OTTESEN.
GIVEN NAMES German 4%. *Otto* (3), *Hans, Orlo.*

Ottey (166) English: unexplained.
GIVEN NAME French 4%. *Patrice.*

Otting (304) Dutch and German: patronymic from the Germanic personal name *Odo* (see OTT).

Ottinger (1182) **1.** German: variant of OTTING. **2.** German (also **Öttinger**) and Jewish (Ashkenazic): habitational name denoting someone from any of the places called Otting or Öttingen, in Swabia, Bavaria, and the French province of Lorraine. **3.** Swiss German: variant of **Ottiger**.

Ottis (106) Variant spelling of English OTIS, a variant of OATES.

Ottley (345) English: habitational name from places in West Yorkshire and Suffolk, named Otley, from an unattested Old English personal name, *Otta*, + *lēah* 'woodland' or 'clearing'.

Ottman (594) North German and Dutch: variant spelling of OTTMANN.

Ottmann (105) North German: from the Germanic personal name *Otman*, composed of the elements *aud, od* 'wealth' + *man* 'man'.
GIVEN NAMES German 6%. *Klaus, Kurt.*

Ottmar (149) South German and Swiss German: from a Germanic personal name composed of the elements *aud, od* 'wealth' + *māri, mēri* 'fame'.
GIVEN NAMES German 4%. *Monika, Otto.*

Ottmers (106) German: patronymic from the personal name OTTMAR.
GIVEN NAMES German 16%; Scandinavian 4%. *Guenther* (3), *Erwin, Ewald, Matthias.*

Otto (9090) German, Dutch, Hungarian (**Ottó**), Danish, and Swedish: from the personal name *Otto* (see OTT).
FOREBEARS This name was introduced to America by Bodo Otto, a senior surgeon of the Continental Army, who was born in Hannover, Germany, in 1711, came to

America in 1755, and practiced in NJ and PA. He died in Reading, PA, in 1787.

Ottosen (164) Danish and Norwegian: patronymic from the personal name *Otto* (see OTT).

Ottoson (265) **1.** Dutch: patronymic from the personal name *Otto* (see OTT). **2.** Respelling of OTTOSEN or the Swedish cognate **Ottosson**.
GIVEN NAMES Scandinavian 7%; German 5%. *Nels; Ernst, Fritz, Hans.*

Otts (487) Dutch: patronymic from the personal name *Otto* (see OTT).

Ottum (149) Norwegian: habitational name from a farmstead in Sogn named Ottum, probably from a river name derived from Old Norse *ótta* 'to frighten', denoting a dangerous river.
GIVEN NAME Scandinavian 4%. *Nordahl.*

Otwell (647) English (Oxfordshire): from a personal name based on Old French *Otuel*.

Ou (494) **1.** Chinese 欧: during the Spring and Autumn period (722–481 BC), a prince of the state of Yue was enfeoffed a region that included a mountain the name of which contained the Chinese character for *Ou*. Many of the prince's descendants adopted this character as their surname. Other descendants adopted the surname OU YANG (the most common of the two-character Chinese surnames), composed of this character together with a character meaning 'sunny', indicating the region to the south of the mountain. **2.** Cambodian or other Southeast Asian: unexplained.
GIVEN NAMES Chinese 41%; Other Southeast Asian 5%. *Wei* (3), *Ying* (3), *Ching* (2), *Heng* (2), *Hong* (2), *Jia* (2), *Kuang Yu* (2), *Li-Ching* (2), *Ming* (2), *Quan* (2), *Roeun* (2), *Sokhom* (2), *Chau, Hai, Leang, Ly, Nhanh, Phan, Pho, Tha.*

Oubre (695) Southern French (**Oubré**): occupational name from an Occitan form of Old French *ouvrier* 'craftsman', agent derivative of *ouvrer* 'to work or make'.
GIVEN NAMES French 8%. *Lucien* (3), *Emile* (2), *Pierre* (2), *Alcide, Antoine, Clovis, Felicie, Fernand, Marcel, Patrice.*

Ouchi (106) Japanese (**Ōuchi**): 'large house'; the name is found mostly in northeastern Japan. A noble family of Suō province (now part of Yamaguchi prefecture, in far western Japan) took the name from the village where they resided. According to legend, they were descended from a Korean prince who immigrated in 611.
GIVEN NAMES Japanese 62%. *Masahiro* (2), *Akiko, Akira, Chiaki, Harumi, Haruto, Hideo, Hiro, Ichiro, Ikuo, Isamu, Jiro.*

Ouderkirk (303) Dutch (also **Oudekerk**): topographic name for someone living by the 'old church'.
FOREBEARS This name is recorded in Beverwijck in New Netherland (Albany, NY) in the mid 17th century.

Ouelette (127) Canadian French: variant spelling of OUELLETTE.

Ouellet (436) Canadian French: variant spelling of OUELLETTE.

Ouellette (5713) Canadian spelling of French (Norman and Champenois) **Ouilet**, from a Frenchified form of WILLET, a pet form of WILLIAM.

Ough (105) English (Cornwall): unexplained.

Oughton (139) **1.** Scottish: Black quotes other sources which explain this as a variant of HOUGHTON, or of *Aughton*, which may be a form of *Acton*; but he offers the example of an Admiral Oughton of Cullen, Banff, who changed his name from *Haughty* to *Oughton* in the late 18th or early 19th century. **2.** Possibly an altered spelling of **Aughton**, an English habitational name from any of three places, in Humberside, Lancashire, and South Yorkshire, named with Old English *āc* 'oak' + *tūn* 'farmstead', 'settlement'.

Ouillette (131) Canadian French: variant spelling of OUELLETTE.

GIVEN NAMES French 7%. *Adelard, Armand, Lucienne.*

Ouimet (451) French (Norman and Champenois): from a Frenchified spelling of **Wimet**, a variant of **Willemet**, a pet form of WILLIAM.

GIVEN NAMES French 11%. *Marcel* (2), *Normand* (2), *Alain, Camille, Fernand, Gaetan, Henri, Jean Guy, Lucien, Yvan.*

Ouimette (380) Canadian spelling of French OUIMET.

GIVEN NAMES French 8%. *Laurent* (2), *Andre, Andree, Germaine, Gilles, Jean Guy, Martial.*

Ouk (176) **1.** Cambodian: unexplained. **2.** Other Southeast Asian: unexplained.

GIVEN NAMES Southeast Asian 35%; Cambodian 10%. *Chea* (3), *Eng* (2), *Sok* (2), *Chan, Chean, Hun, Rin, Rong, Sarin, Seng; Tha* (2), *Thon* (2), *Hai, Ly, Pha, Phon, Thong; Oeun* (2), *Sokhom* (2), *Chhoeun, Chhom, Moeun, Sambath, Samoeun, Sophal, Soun, Yoeum; Kok, Savuth, Youn.*

Oulton (100) English: habitational name from any of various places called Oulton, in particular those in Cheshire and Staffordshire.

Oum (118) Cambodian: unexplained.

GIVEN NAMES Cambodian 65%. *Heang, Hye, Kam, Kan, Kheng, Khin, Kun, Sang, Sok; Phong, Yom, Yoo, Youn; Cuong, Phal, Samnang, Tin; Sokha* (2), *Chheang, Choeun, Moeun, Roeun, Sambath, Samoeun, Savuth, Soeun, Sopheap.*

Ourada (290) Slavic: unexplained.

Ouradnik (105) Slavic: unexplained.

Ouren (113) Norwegian: habitational name from a farm named Auren in Toten, named with Old Norse *aurr* 'gravel' + *vin* 'meadow'.

Ours (582) French: **1.** from *ours* 'bear' (Latin *ursus*), hence a nickname for someone thought to resemble a bear (e.g. a large, lumbering person, or an unsociable one), or local name for someone who lived in a house distinguished with the sign of a bear. **2.** from the old personal name *Ours*, not common, derived from Latin *Ursus*, which was the name of some early saints in Gaul.

Oursler (261) Possibly an altered form of German **Ursler**, a habitational name for someone from Ursel near Wiesbaden (Hesse).

Ourso (229) Possibly an altered spelling of French **Orsaud** or **Orseau**, diminutive or pet forms of OURS.

Oury (182) French (Alsace-Lorraine): from a French pet form of the German personal name *Ulrich*.

Ousley (1384) Southern English: apparently a habitational name from an unidentified place, perhaps a compound of the river name *Ouse* (Old English *Usa*, of ancient British origin, from *ud-* 'water') + Old English *lēah* 'wood', 'clearing'.

FOREBEARS This surname was brought to North America by Major Thomas Owsley in about 1677; he was born in Stogursey in Somerset, England.

Outcalt (177) Origin uncertain; perhaps a respelling of German **Altgeld**, a nickname for a miser or money changer, from Middle High German *alt* 'old' + *geld* 'money'.

Outen (342) Dutch: see OOTEN.

Outerbridge (113) English: habitational name from Oughtibridge, South Yorkshire, which is probably named from an unattested Old English female personal name, *Ūhtgifu* + Old English *brycg* 'bridge'.

Outhouse (124) **1.** Americanized form of Norwegian **Uthus**, a habitational name from various farmsteads so named, from Old Norse *Uthúsar*, a compound of *ut* 'out(lying)' + *hús* 'farmstead'. **2.** Probably an Americanized form of North German *Uthoff*, a topographic or habitational name for someone living or working at an outlying farm, from Middle Low German *ūt* 'out', 'away' + *hove* 'farmstead'. **3.** Americanized form of Dutch **Outhof**, a topographic or habitational name, from *oude hove* 'old farm'.

Outland (652) Probably an Americanized form of Dutch **Uitland** or German **Ausland**, bynames for a foreigner or stranger, from Middle High German *ūz* 'out', 'away' + *land-* 'country'.

Outlaw (2349) English: nickname from Middle English *outlawe* 'outlaw' (from Old Norse *útlagi*). (When a sentence of outlawry was passed on someone in the Middle Ages it meant that they no longer had the protection of the law.) According to Reaney and Wilson this was also occasionally used as a personal name; they cite the example of someone called *Hutlage*.

Outler (196) Probably an altered form of English OUTLAW.

Outley (102) Probably an altered form of English OUTLAW.

Outman (219) Americanized form of Dutch *Uitman* or North German **Utmann**, from Middle Low German *ūtman* 'stranger', 'newcomer', or possibly from the South German cognate **Ussmann**, from Middle High German *ūzman* (as opposed to *Land(s)mann* 'fellow countryman').

Outten (410) Dutch: see OOTEN.

Outwater (155) Probably of Dutch origin, but unexplained. It may be a habitational name for someone who came from (*uit*) a place called *Water*, of which there are many in the Netherlands, or alternatively from a place named as the 'outer water'.

Ouverson (102) Probably an Americanized form of Danish or Norwegian **Ovesen** (see OVESON).

Ou Yang (242) Chinese 欧阳: a rare example of a two-character Chinese surname, from a phrase meaning 'the sunny (south) side of Ou mountain'. It was adopted by descendants of a prince who was enfeoffed to an area that included land to the south of a mountain whose name contains the character for OU.

GIVEN NAMES Chinese 60%. *Ming* (7), *Wei* (6), *Hui* (4), *Jian* (4), *Hong* (3), *Chieh* (2), *Chu* (2), *Xin* (2), *Zhuo* (2), *Baoping, Biao, Bin, Hai, Pu, Quan, Tuan.*

Ouzts (562) Altered form of German **Ütz**, from a pet form of the personal name ULRICH.

Ovadia (116) Jewish (Sephardic): from the Biblical male personal name *Ovadia*, Hebrew form of the name known in English as *Obadiah* 'servant of God'.

GIVEN NAMES Jewish 33%; Spanish 4%. *Moshe* (4), *Arie* (2), *Drora* (2), *Shlomo* (2), *Avi, Eliahu, Erez, Meir, Ravit, Shulamith, Yaakov, Yossi; Estrella, Rebeca, Ruben, Salomon.*

Ovalle (574) Galician: topographic name from *o vale* 'the valley' (Latin *uallis, ualles*).

GIVEN NAMES Spanish 52%. *Juan* (18), *Jose* (15), *Carlos* (10), *Manuel* (8), *Luis* (7), *Arturo* (4), *Jesus* (4), *Ana* (3), *Felipe* (3), *Francisco* (3), *Guadalupe* (3), *Juana* (3).

Ovalles (102) Spanish: variant of OVALLE.

GIVEN NAMES Spanish 58%. *Juan* (5), *Jose* (3), *Manuel* (3), *Arturo* (2), *Cesar* (2), *Milagros* (2), *Ramon* (2), *Roberto* (2), *Sergio* (2), *Vicente* (2), *Aida, Altagracia.*

Ovando (101) Spanish: variant of OBANDO.

Ovard (111) English (Midlands): unexplained.

Ovens (178) **1.** English and Scottish: from the plural of Middle English *oven* 'oven', 'furnace' (for lime, iron, charcoal, etc.), hence a topographic name or occupational name for someone who lived near or worked at an oven or furnace. According to MacLysaght this surname is found also in

County Fermanagh in Ireland. **2.** North German: patronymic from the Frisian personal name *Ove*.

Over (415) **1.** English: topographic name for someone who lived on the bank of a river or on a slope (from Old English *ōfer* 'seashore', 'riverbank', or from the originally distinct word *ofer* 'slope', 'bank', 'ridge'). The two terms, being of similar meaning as well as similar form, fell together in the Middle English period. The surname may also be a habitational name from places named with one or other of these words, which can only be distinguished with reference to their situation. Over in Cambridgeshire is on a riverbank, whereas examples in Cheshire and Derbyshire are not; Over in Gloucestershire is on the bank of the Severn, but also at the foot of a hill. **2.** North German: topographic name denoting someone who lived above or beyond a settlement or feature. **3.** Swedish (**Över**): ornamental name of unexplained origin.

Overacker (176) Partly Americanized form of South German **Überacker**, a habitational name from any of several places so named in Bavaria, from Middle High German *über* 'near', 'across from' + *acker* 'field', denoting the location of a farm. In some instances it may be topographic.

Overall (538) **1.** English: topographic name composed of Middle English *overe*, *uvere* 'upper' + *hall* 'hall'. **2.** Translated form (literal) of German **Überall**, a nickname for a know-it-all.

Overbaugh (268) Americanized form of German **Oberbach**, a topographic and perhaps a habitational name, from *ober* 'upper' + *Bach* 'stream', 'creek'.

Overbay (542) Norwegian or Danish: variant of OVERBY.

Overbeck (562) **1.** English and North German: topographic name for someone who lived 'over the creek', from Middle English and Middle Low German *over* 'over' + *beck* 'stream', 'creek'. **2.** Dutch: variant of OVERBEEK. **3.** Swedish (**Överbäck**): ornamental or topographic name from *över* 'over' + *bäck* 'stream', 'creek' (Old Norse *bekkr*). **4.** Altered form of German OBERBECK.

Overbeek (175) Dutch: habitational name from any of many places named Overbeke, meaning 'across the creek'.

Overberg (158) **1.** Dutch: habitational name from places named Overberg (for example to the east of Utrecht), meaning 'over the hill'. **2.** Swedish (**Överberg**): ornamental or topographic name from *över* 'over' + *berg* 'mountain'.
GIVEN NAMES German 7%; Scandinavian 4%. *Kurt* (2), *Heinz*.

Overbey (941) Norwegian or Danish: variant of OVERBY.

Overby (2397) **1.** Norwegian (**Øverby**): habitational name from any of some twenty farmsteads, chiefly in southeastern Norway, named Øverby, from Old Norse *Øfribýr*, a compound of *øfri* 'upper' + *býr* 'farmstead'. **2.** Danish: habitational name from any of several places so named.

Overcash (1109) Americanized form of South German **Oberkirch**, a habitational name meaning 'upper church' from a place so named in Baden (or possibly from places called Oberkirchen, in Westphalia and Saar district).

Overcast (187) Probably an Americanized spelling of German **Obergasser**, a topographic name from *ober* 'upper', 'above' + *Gasse* 'side street', 'lane'.

Overdorf (207) Altered form of German **Ober(n)dorf**, a habitational name, from any of many places in Germany and Austria called Oberndorf or Oberdorf, meaning 'upper village'.

Overdorff (128) German: variant spelling of OVERDORF.

Overend (149) English (Yorkshire): topographic name for someone who lived at the 'upper end' of a settlement, from Middle English *overe*, *uvere* 'upper' + *end* 'end'.

Overfelt (289) Dutch: habitational name from any of various minor places in Belgium and the Netherlands called Overveld, meaning 'across the field'.

Overfield (530) **1.** English: topographic name for someone who lived by the 'upper pasture', from Middle English *uvere* 'over', 'higher' + *feld(e)* 'pasture', 'open country', or a habitational name from a place named with these elements. **2.** Americanized form of Dutch OVERFELT or of German **Oberfeld**, a topographic name from *ober* 'upper', 'up above' + *feld* 'open country'.

Overgaard (284) Swedish (**Övergaard**): habitational name for someone who lived at 'the upper farm' or an ornamental name from *över* 'over' + *gård* 'farm'.
GIVEN NAMES Scandinavian 13%. *Nels* (2), *Anders*, *Borge*, *Jorgen*.

Overgard (100) Swedish (**Övergård**): see OVERGAARD.

Overholser (514) Altered form of German OBERHOLTZER.

Overholt (1080) **1.** Dutch: Americanized spelling of **Overhoud**, a topographic name for someone who lived 'across the woods'. **2.** Americanized spelling of German **Oberholz**, a topographic name from from Middle High German *ober* 'above' (or German *ober-* 'upper') + *holz* 'wood' (see OBERHOLTZER).

Overholtzer (184) Partly Americanized form of German OBERHOLTZER.

Overkamp (142) **1.** North German: habitational name from any of several places so named, or a topographic name from Middle Low German *over* 'over', 'across' + *kamp* 'field', 'domain' (originally denoting the location of a farmstead or settlement). **2.** Americanized form of North German

Oberkamp, a topographic name for someone living by an upper (*ober*) field.
GIVEN NAMES German 6%. *Aloys*, *Ewald*, *Gervas*.

Overland (460) **1.** Norwegian: habitational name from any of some twenty farmsteads, mainly in Telemark and on the west coast, named Øverland, from *øver* 'upper' + *land* 'land'. **2.** English: habitational name from Overland Farm in Kent, named with Old English *yfer* 'hill brow' + *land* 'land'.
GIVEN NAMES Scandinavian 6%. *Borge*, *Erik*, *Jan Erik*, *Nordahl*, *Tryg*.

Overley (269) English: variant of OVERLY.

Overlin (119) Variant of German OBERLIN.

Overlock (242) Altered form of German **Oberlack**, a topographic name for someone who lived beyond a pond or small lake, from Middle Low German *over* 'across' + Middle High German *lache*, Middle Low German *lake* 'pond' (dialect *la(c)ke*).

Overly (776) **1.** English: habitational name from a place named Overley or Overleigh, as for example Overleigh in Cheshire, named with Old English *uferra* 'higher' + *lēah* '(woodland) clearing', 'glade'. **2.** Americanized spelling of German OBERLE, or of **Oberley**, **Overley**, topographic names from *ober* 'up above' + Middle Low German *leie* 'rock', 'stone', 'shale'.

Overman (2029) **1.** Dutch: status name from Middle Dutch *overman* 'judge', 'arbitrator', 'go-between'. **2.** Respelling of German OVERMANN.

Overmann (113) North German: topographic name for someone who lived on the bank of a river, from Middle Low German *over* 'river bank' + *man* 'man'.

Overmeyer (136) Variant of German OBERMEYER. This is either a North German form or an Americanization.

Overmier (132) See OVERMEYER.

Overmiller (121) Americanized form of German **Obermüller**, distinguishing name for a miller, Middle High German *müller* (see MUELLER) who lived at the upper (Middle High German *ober*) mill.

Overmyer (803) Americanized spelling of German OBERMEYER, OBERMEIER.

Overpeck (183) Respelling of South German OBERBECK 2.

Overson (304) Altered spelling of OVESON.

Overstreet (4288) **1.** Americanized form of Dutch and Belgian **Overstraete**, a topographic name for someone who lived 'on the other side of the street', or a habitational name from a place so named. According to Debrabandere this is a Brabantine name, originating from the Hof ter Overstraeten in Sint-Martens-Lennik. **2.** Americanized form of German **Oberstrass** or Low German **Overstraat**, a topographic name from a field so named, in particular one near Wermelskirchen in Rhineland.

Overton (6201) English: habitational name from any of the numerous places so called.

Most are named from Old English *uferra* 'upper' + *tūn* 'enclosure', 'settlement'; others have Old English *ōfer* 'riverbank' or *ofer* 'slope' as the first element.

Overturf (806) Possibly an Americanized form of German OBERDORF.

Overway (123) Americanized form of Dutch OVERWEG.

Overweg (109) Dutch: topographic name for someone who lived across (Dutch *over*) the road or way (Dutch *weg*).
GIVEN NAMES Dutch 9%. *Dirk* (2), *Gerrit* (2), *Cornie*, *Gradus*.

Overy (195) English (mainly southeastern): habitational name from a place named with the Old English phrase *ofer īe* 'over, across the river', as for example Overy in Oxfordshire. In some cases the name may be topographic, with the same meaning, or with Old English *ēg* 'dry ground in a marsh', 'well-watered land' as the second element.

Oveson (178) Americanized spelling of Danish and Norwegian **Ovesen**, a patronymic from the personal name *Ove*, a Danish form of the older *Aghi*, with a second element which probably meant 'spear'.

Oviatt (513) English: probably a variant of **Ovett**, a name of unknown origin, which is found mainly in Sussex.

Oviedo (627) Spanish: habitational name from *Oviedo*, Spanish form of Asturian-Leonese *Uviéu*, name of the regional capital of Asturies, found in early records in the Latin form *Ovetum*.
GIVEN NAMES Spanish 53%. *Juan* (19), *Jose* (17), *Miguel* (6), *Eduardo* (5), *Manuel* (5), *Margarita* (5), *Rafael* (5), *Fernando* (4), *Jaime* (4), *Luis* (4), *Lupe* (4), *Mario* (4).

Ovington (119) English: habitational name from any of various places named Ovington, most notably those in Durham and Northumberland, where the surname is most common. The one in Durham is named in Old English as 'estate (*tūn*) associated with (*-ing-*) a man called *Wulfa*'; the one in Northumberland as 'hill (*dūn*) of the followers of (*-inga-*) a man called *Ofa*'.

Ovitt (317) English: variant of **Ovett** (see OVIATT).

Ow (123) Chinese 欧: variant of OU 1.
GIVEN NAMES Chinese 8%. *Cheng*, *Jing*, *Kam Fung*, *Wai Shing*, *Wing*, *Yali*, *Yuk*.

Owczarzak (173) Polish: patronymic from the occupational name *owczarz* 'shepherd'.

Owen (25394) **1.** Welsh: from the Welsh personal name *Owain*, probably a borrowing in Roman times of Latin *Eugenius* (see EUGENE), but possibly of more ancient Celtic origin, cognate with Gaelic *Eoghan*. **2.** Scottish and Irish: reduced Anglicized form of Gaelic **Mac Eoghain** 'son of *Eoghan*' (see MCEWEN).

Owenby (766) English: habitational name from one of three places in Lincolnshire: Aunby, Owmby, and Aunsby, all of which are named with the Old Norse personal name *Auðun* + *býr* 'farmstead', 'settlement'.

Owens (56055) **1.** Welsh: patronymic from OWEN, with English patronymic *-s*. **2.** Irish: adopted as an Anglicized form by bearers of the Gaelic surname **Mac Eoghain** (see MCEWEN).

Owensby (713) Probably English: habitational name from Aunsby in Lincolnshire, which has the same origin as **Aunby** (see OWENBY).

Owings (1765) Variant of Irish or Welsh OWENS.

Ownbey (456) Variant of OWENBY.

Ownby (838) Variant of OWENBY.

Ownes (105) Variant of Irish or Welsh OWENS.

Owsiany (118) Polish: nickname from the adjective *owsiany* 'oaten', a derivative of *owies* 'oats'.
GIVEN NAME Polish 4%. *Henryk*.

Owsley (1047) English: variant spelling of OUSLEY.

Owusu (237) African: unexplained.
GIVEN NAMES African 18%. *Kwame* (6), *Kofi* (3), *Kwabena* (2), *Kwaku* (2), *Afua*, *Akwasi*, *Kwadwo*, *Kwasi*, *Kwesi*, *Osei*.

Owyang (100) Chinese 欧阳: variant spelling of OU YANG.

Oxborrow (107) English (Suffolk): habitational name from a place in Norfolk named Oxborough, named with Old English *oxa* 'oxen' + *burh* 'fortification'.

Oxendine (1727) English: habitational name from places called Oxendean in East Sussex and Kent or Oxenden in Kent, all named in Old Englsih as 'valley of the oxen'.

Oxenford (162) English: from an old spelling of OXFORD.

Oxenreider (140) Americanized form of German **Ochsenreiter**, a topographic name from *Ochse* 'ox' + *Reute* 'forest clearing' + *-er* suffix denoting an inhabitant. See REUTER.

Oxenrider (104) See OXENREIDER.

Oxford (1722) English: habitational name from the city of Oxford, named in Old English with *ox(e)na* (genitive plural of *oxa* 'ox') + *ford* 'ford'.

Oxley (1697) **1.** English: habitational name from any of various places, for example Oxley in Staffordshire and Ox Lee near Hepworth (West Yorkshire), named with Old English *oxa* 'ox' + *lēah* '(woodland) clearing'. **2.** Probably a respelling of South German **Öchsle** (see OECHSLE).

Oxman (301) English and Jewish (Ashkenazic): occupational name for someone in charge of oxen, from Middle English *oxe* 'ox' + *man* 'man', or German *Ochs* + *Mann*, or Yiddish *oks* + *man*.
GIVEN NAMES Jewish 7%. *Meyer*, *Myer*.

Oxner (410) German: variant (**Öxner**) or Americanized spelling of German **Öchsner** (see OCHSNER).

Oxton (111) English: habitational name from Oxton in Nottinghamshire, named from Old English *oxa* 'oxen' + *tūn* 'farmstead', 'settlement'.

Oyama (308) Japanese: **1.** 'small mountain'; another common pronunciation is **Koyama**. Both are found throughout Japan. One Oyama family is descended from FUJIWARA no Hidesato (10th century). **2.** (**Ōyama**): 'large mountain'. Some modern bearers have samurai connections, and the name is listed in the Shinsen shōjiroku.
GIVEN NAMES Japanese 42%. *Hiroki* (2), *Junichi* (2), *Noboru* (2), *Shigeru* (2), *Tadao* (2), *Takashi* (2), *Akira*, *Chiaki*, *Fumio*, *Hideko*, *Hiroshi*, *Isami*.

Oye (143) **1.** Norwegian (**Øye**): habitational name from any of about twenty-five farmsteads, chiefly in Møre and Trøndelag, so named from *øy* 'island'. **2.** Japanese: Alternate Romanized spelling of OE. The *-ye* spelling represents a sound no longer used in modern Japanese.
GIVEN NAMES Japanese 7%. *Emiko*, *Fusae*, *Kaz*, *Naoto*, *Sho*.

Oyen (206) **1.** Dutch: variant of OIEN. **2.** Dutch and North German (Frisian): topographic name for someone who lived by a water meadow, Middle Dutch *ooye*, *oye*, Low German, Frisian *oje*, *oye*. **3.** Norwegian (**Øyen**): habitational name from any of various farmsteads named Øyen, from the definite singular form of *øy* 'island'.
GIVEN NAMES Scandinavian 9%. *Nels*, *Sig*, *Sigvald*.

Oyer (629) French: from the Old French agent derivative of *oie* 'goose', denoting someone who sold geese or roast meat.

Oyler (1350) **1.** English: occupational name for an extractor or seller of oil, from a metathesized form of Anglo-Norman French *olier* (from *oile* 'oil', Latin *oleum* '(olive) oil'; compare OLIVA). In northern England linseed oil obtained from locally grown flax was more common than olive oil. **2.** English: from the Continental Germanic personal name *Odilard*, *Oilard*, introduced by the Normans. **3.** Americanized spelling of German EULER or of Swabian **Äuler**, a topographic name for someone who lived by a water meadow, *Äule*, a diminutive of *Au*.

Oyola (192) Spanish or Basque: variant of LOYOLA.
GIVEN NAMES Spanish 46%. *Juan* (7), *Manuel* (4), *Carlos* (3), *Jose* (3), *Eduardo* (2), *Enrique* (2), *Julio* (2), *Luis* (2), *Raul* (2), *Alberto*, *Angel*, *Blanca*; *Antonio* (2), *Angelo*, *Benigna*, *Marco*, *Tarcisio*.

Oyster (267) Origin uncertain. Possibly an English occupational name for someone who cultivated and sold oysters, or a respelling of German AUSTER.

Oza (116) Indian (Rajasthan): Hindu (Brahman) name, probably from *Ojha*, a Hindu Brahman name found in Uttar

Pradesh and its neighborhood, derived ultimately from Sanskrit *upādhyāya* 'teacher'. GIVEN NAMES Indian 89%. *Amita* (3), *Kandarp* (3), *Ashutosh* (2), *Bharat* (2), *Chandrakant* (2), *Harish* (2), *Jayanti* (2), *Kaushik* (2), *Rajesh* (2), *Ratnam* (2), *Vibha* (2), *Anil.*

Ozaki (245) Japanese: 'end of the cape'; a topographic name from western Japan. Several bearers are of MINAMOTO descent. GIVEN NAMES Japanese 50%. *Minoru* (3), *Hiroshi* (2), *Mitsuru* (2), *Shoichi* (2), *Yuka* (2), *Yukio* (2), *Akira, Chieko, Fumiko, Hachiro, Hajime, Haruka.*

Ozan (100) Turkish: from the personal name *Ozan.*
GIVEN NAMES Muslim 5%. *Huseyin, Kerim, Mahmut.*

Ozanich (182) Bosnian (**Ozanić**): from the Turkish personal name OZAN.

Ozanne (119) **1.** English: from a female personal name, *Osanna,* derived from a Hebrew liturgical word rendered in Latin as *Hosanna* (see 2). **2.** French (Normandy): from a medieval personal name, derived from an old name for Palm Sunday, reflecting the liturgical chant of *Hosanna* used on that day to represent the acclamation of Jesus when he rode into Jerusalem (Matthew 21:8–9). **3.** Dutch and German: from a variant of the female personal name *Susanna,* influenced by the liturgical word *hosanna* (see 1 and 2).
GIVEN NAME French 4%. *Elodie.*

Ozark (100) Origin unidentified. Presumably it from *Ozark,* name of a region of southern Missouri. Most authorities give the etymology of this region as French *aux*

Arks 'in the country of the Arkansas Indians'. It could also be from French *aux arcs* 'at the bends (i.e. river bends)'.

Ozawa (199) Japanese: 'small swamp', a common place name all over Japan. As a surname, it is mostly found in eastern Japan, another pronunciation, *Kozawa,* being found in western Japan. Some families are of TAIRA descent.
GIVEN NAMES Japanese 65%. *Yuichi* (3), *Isao* (2), *Masashi* (2), *Tetsuo* (2), *Yasunori* (2), *Yasushi* (2), *Yoshihiro* (2), *Atsuhiko, Atsushi, Ayako, Eiichi, Fumihiro.*

Ozbirn (115) Variant of English OSBORNE.

Ozbun (200) Variant of English OSBORNE.

Ozburn (241) Variant of English OSBORNE.

Ozer (214) **1.** Jewish (eastern Ashkenazic): from the Yiddish personal name *Oyzer,* meaning 'helper' in Hebrew. **2.** Jewish (eastern Ashkenazic): habitational name from a place called Ozery, now in Belarus. **3.** Muslim: from the Turkish form of the Arabic personal name *'Uzayr,* the name of a prophet (the Biblical EZRA).
GIVEN NAMES Jewish 9%; Muslim 9%. *Hyman, Miriam, Nissim, Reuven, Zahava; Faruk* (2), *Ali, Aziz, Huseyin, Kadir, Kamil, Mumtaz, Pervin, Senol.*

Ozga (229) Polish (**Ożga**): nickname from Polish *ożga* 'fire', applied to a shabby person, metaphorically 'victim of a fire'.
GIVEN NAMES Polish 9%. *Andrzej, Beata, Casimir, Ewa, Jerzy, Jozefa, Ryszard.*

Ozier (257) English: variant spelling of OSIER.

Ozimek (207) **1.** Polish: habitational name from a place called Ozimek, which lies

southeast of Wrocław. **2.** Polish: nickname from *ozimek,* denoting a young animal born before winter. **3.** Slovenian: probably a nickname from *ozimek* 'winter crops', a derivative of *zima* 'winter'.
GIVEN NAMES Polish 6%. *Bronislaw, Bronislawa, Jolanta, Jozef.*

Ozment (623) Perhaps an altered form of English OSMOND.

Ozmun (127) Americanized form of English OSMOND.

Ozog (110) Polish (also **Ożóg**): nickname from *ożóg* 'poker'.
GIVEN NAMES Polish 13%. *Ewa, Franciszek, Janusz, Jolanta, Mieczyslaw.*

Ozolins (176) Latvian (**Ozoliņš**): patronymic from a nickname from Latvian *ozols* 'oak tree' + the suffix *-ins.*
GIVEN NAMES Latvian 45%. *Valdis* (5), *Velta* (5), *Uldis* (3), *Adolfs* (2), *Andrejs* (2), *Karlis* (2), *Martins* (2), *Valija* (2), *Aivars, Alberts, Arturs, Edmunds, Egils, Elmars, Girts, Gunars, Jekabs, Teodors.*

Ozols (157) Latvian: topographic name from *ozols* 'oak tree'.
GIVEN NAMES Latvian 47%. *Andris* (4), *Maris* (3), *Alberts* (2), *Atis* (2), *Gunars* (2), *Juris* (2), *Karlis* (2), *Valdis* (2), *Aija, Austra, Baiba, Daina, Adolfs, Egils, Eizens, Indulis, Ivars, Rudolfs, Vitauts, Voldemars.*

Ozuna (635) Spanish: Andalusian form of OSUNA.
GIVEN NAMES Spanish 50%. *Carlos* (8), *Jesus* (7), *Manuel* (7), *Domingo* (6), *Juan* (6), *Jose* (5), *Arturo* (4), *Guadalupe* (4), *Ruben* (4), *Alfredo* (3), *Armando* (3), *Emilio* (3).

P

Paap (182) North German and Dutch: variant of PAPE.

GIVEN NAMES German 7%. *Hans* (2), *Kurt, Manfred, Otto, Wolf.*

Paape (209) North German and Dutch: variant of PAPE.

Paar (323) North German, Dutch, and Belgian: topographic name from Middle Low German *pār* 'house of a priest', or a habitational name from any of various minor places named Parre or Perre, for example in Ruiselede or Hillegem in East Flanders or Noordewijk in Antwerp province.

Paas (102) German: variant of PAASCH.

GIVEN NAMES German 8%. *Arno, Guenter, Kurt.*

Paasch (354) North German: **1.** from a short form of the Latin personal name *Paschalis*. Compare Italian PASQUALE. **2.** nickname for someone with tax or service obligations at Easter time, from Middle Low German *pāsche(n)* 'Easter' (see PASCAL). In the Middle Ages the year of the influential archdiocese of Cologne, for instance, began officially at Easter.

GIVEN NAMES German 9%. *Erhardt* (3), *Bernd, Egon, Erwin, Fritz, Ilse, Kurt, Uwe, Wolfgang.*

Paavola (191) Finnish: habitational name, from a farm so named from the personal name *Paavo*, vernacular form of *Paulus* (see PAUL), + the locative ending -*la*. Both the farm name and the surname can be traced back to the 15th century. The surname occurs chiefly in western Finland.

GIVEN NAMES Finnish 10%; Scandinavian 5%. *Jouni* (2), *Osmo* (2), *Esko, Jouko, Sulo, Timo, Toivo, Waino; Nels.*

Paben (113) Variant of German PAPEN or from a personal name *Babo*, a nursery term.

Pabian (149) Polish: from the personal name *Pabian*, a variant of FABIAN.

GIVEN NAMES Polish 11%. *Henryk, Janina, Janusz, Jozef, Lucyna, Stanislaw, Zygmunt.*

Pabich (122) Polish: from a pet form of the personal name PABIAN.

GIVEN NAMES Polish 7%. *Andrzej, Ewa, Zigmond.*

Pabis (114) Polish (also **Pabiś, Pabisz**): from a pet form of PABIAN.

GIVEN NAMES Polish 6%. *Alojzy, Krzysztof.*

Pablo (360) Spanish: from the personal name *Pablo*, Spanish equivalent of PAUL.

GIVEN NAMES Spanish 37%. *Pedro* (4), *Alfredo* (3), *Cesar* (3), *Jaime* (3), *Manuel*

(3), *Vicente* (3), *Amado* (2), *Arturo* (2), *Corazon* (2), *Felipe* (2), *Jose* (2), *Juan* (2).

Pabon (725) Spanish (**Pabón**): variant of **Pavón** (see PAVON).

GIVEN NAMES Spanish 43%. *Luis* (17), *Jose* (11), *Angel* (10), *Juan* (8), *Pedro* (7), *Ramon* (7), *Enrique* (6), *Carlos* (5), *Luz* (5), *Pablo* (5), *Ana* (4), *Julio* (4).

Pabst (998) German: from Middle High German *bābes(t)* (modern German *Papst*) 'pope', a nickname for a self-important person, one who believed in the infallibility of his own opinions.

Pac (164) Polish, Belorussian, and Lithuanian: from a short form of a personal name beginning with or containing *Pa-*, for example Polish *Pakosław* or *Paweł*, Belorussian *Pavel* (see PAUL), of Lithuanian *Pacas* (from *Ipatijus*, Greek *Hypatios*).

GIVEN NAME Polish 4%. *Ryszard.*

Pacana (102) Spanish: from *pacana* 'pecan', 'pecan tree', a word of Algonquin origin. This name is also found in the Philippines.

GIVEN NAMES Spanish 7%. *Renato* (2), *Arturo, Francisca, Maria Teresa, Ronaldo.*

Paccione (254) Italian: augmentative of **Paccio**, either a central–southern nickname from *paccio* 'madman', or a patronymic from the personal name *Paccio*, a Tuscan reduced pet form, of, for example, *Filippaccio* (from FILIPPO), *Jacopaccio* (from *Jacopo*, an Italian equivalent of JACOB).

GIVEN NAMES Italian 11%. *Rocco* (4), *Angelo* (2), *Donato, Sal.*

Pace (14127) **1.** English: from a vernacular short form of the Latin personal name *Paschalis* (see PASCAL, Italian PASQUALE). **2.** nickname for a mild-mannered and peaceable person, from Middle English *pace, pece* 'peace', 'concord', 'amity' (via Anglo-Norman French from Latin *pax*, genitive *pacis*). **3.** Italian: from the medieval personal name *Pace*, used for both men and women, from the word *pace* 'peace' (see 1).

Pacek (119) **1.** Czech (**Paček**): from a pet form of the Old Czech personal name *Pačej*, shortened form of *Pačeslav*. **2.** Polish: from a pet form of any of various personal names beginning with *Pa-*, for example *Pakosław* or *Paweł* (see PAUL).

Pacella (404) Italian: from a female pet form of the personal name *Pace* (see PACE 2).

GIVEN NAMES Italian 18%. *Angelo* (3), *Antonio* (3), *Salvatore* (3), *Luciano* (2), *Nunzio* (2), *Querino* (2), *Rinaldo* (2), *Rocco* (2), *Dante, Donato, Giovanni, Guerino.*

Pacelli (411) Italian: patronymic from *Pacello*, a pet form of the personal name *Pace* (see PACE 2).

GIVEN NAMES Italian 14%. *Rocco* (4), *Nicola* (3), *Angelo* (2), *Dominico, Franco, Giovanni, Guido, Luca, Luigi, Remo, Romeo, Salvatore.*

Pacer (153) English: unexplained.

Pacetti (308) Italian: variant of **Pacetto**, a pet form of the personal name *Pace* (see PACE 2).

Pacey (219) English (of Norman origin): habitational name from Pacy-sur-Eure, which took its name from the Gallo-Roman personal name *Paccius* + the locative suffix -*acum*.

Pach (132) **1.** Polish, Czech, and Eastern German: from a pet form of any of various personal names beginning with *Pa-*, for example local forms of PAUL or any of the Old Slavic names represented by Czech *Pačeslav* and Polish *Pakosław* (see PACEK). **2.** German: from a pet form of the personal name *Bartholomäus* (see BARTHOLOMEW). **3.** South German: variant of BACH.

GIVEN NAMES Polish 8%. *Andrzej, Jozef, Pawel, Piotr.*

Pacha (152) **1.** Polish: from a derivative of the personal name PACH. **2.** Variant spelling in various eastern Mediterranean languages of Turkish PASHA.

Pache (101) Probably a variant, under French influence, of the Slavic name PACH.

GIVEN NAMES French 7%; German 5%; Spanish 4%. *Henri, Jean Claude; Klaus, Viktor; Ramona* (2), *Adriana, Osvaldo.*

Pacheco (8576) Spanish and Portuguese: from a personal name of uncertain, possibly pre-Roman, origin.

FOREBEARS Lieutenant of Engineers Romualdo Pacheco, a native of Guanajuato, Mexico, went to CA in 1825 as an aide-de-camp to Governor Echeandía. His son. also called Romualdo Pacheco was born in 1831 in Santa Barbara, CA, and went on to become governor of CA.

GIVEN NAMES Spanish 35%; Portuguese 9%. *Jose* (174), *Manuel* (146), *Carlos* (82), *Juan* (79), *Luis* (70), *Ramon* (32), *Rafael* (28), *Jorge* (26), *Jesus* (24), *Raul* (24), *Ana* (23), *Miguel* (23); *Joao* (8), *Paulo* (5), *Duarte* (2), *Fernandes* (2), *Agostinho,*

Albano, Anabela, Armanda, Joaquim, Marcio, Seraphine, Vasco.

Pachl (102) South German: pet form of PACH.

Pacholski (182) Polish: **1.** occupational name or nickname from *pachoł(ek)* 'servant' + *-ski*, suffix of surnames. **2.** habitational name, probably from Pachole, in Biała Podlaska voivodeship.

Pachter (156) German (also **Pächter**), Dutch, and Jewish (Ashkenazic): status name for a tenant farmer, from an agent derivative of Middle High German *phaht* 'contract' or 'rent' (from Late Latin *pacta* 'contract', 'tax'), Middle Dutch *pachtere* 'tenant', 'leaseholder', or modern German *Pächter* 'leaseholder'.
GIVEN NAMES Jewish 9%. *Meir, Meyer, Zeev.*

Pachucki (115) Polish: from the personal name *Pachuta*, a derivative of PACH.
GIVEN NAMES Polish 14%; German 4%. *Czeslaw (2), Casimir, Janusz, Kazimierz; Hedwig.*

Pachuta (150) Polish: from a derivative of the personal name PACH.

Paci (193) **1.** Italian: patronymic from PACE. **2.** Hungarian: habitational name for someone from a place called Pac in Bihar county.
GIVEN NAMES Italian 31%. *Salvatore (3), Domenic (2), Aldo, Arduino, Attilio, Dino, Domenico, Elisabetta, Enrico, Gino, Lamberto, Luigi, Mario, Sante.*

Paciello (121) Italian: diminutive of PACE.
GIVEN NAMES Italian 16%. *Rocco (3), Angelo, Attilio, Domenic, Sal, Salvatore.*

Pacific (171) Italian (Venetia): variant of PACIFICO.
GIVEN NAMES Italian 8%. *Franco, Nunzio.*

Pacifico (457) **1.** Italian, Spanish (**Pacífico**), and Portuguese: from the medieval personal name or nickname *Pacifico*, meaning 'peaceful', 'peace-loving' (Latin *pacificus*). **2.** Jewish (from Italy): adoption of the Italian surname as an approximate translation of the Hebrew name *Shelomo* (see SOLOMON).
GIVEN NAMES Italian 21%. *Dante (3), Vito (3), Alessandro (2), Angelo (2), Antonio (2), Bartolomeo (2), Luciano (2), Luigi (2), Sal (2), Vincenzo (2), Arduino, Biagio.*

Pacilio (117) Italian: from the personal name *Pacilio*, possibly a derivative of PACE.
GIVEN NAMES Italian 22%. *Angelo, Carlo (2), Carmine, Gennaro, Nino, Palma, Sal.*

Pacini (413) Italian: patronymic from a pet form of PACE.
GIVEN NAMES Italian 16%. *Aldo (2), Angelo (2), Dino (2), Edo (2), Franco (2), Giovanni (2), Alessandro, Antonio, Emo, Enrico, Ezio, Geno.*

Pacino (110) Italian: diminutive of PACE.
GIVEN NAMES Italian 12%. *Salvatore (2), Angelo, Franco, Vincenzo.*

Pacione (117) Italian: from an augmentative of the personal name PACE.

GIVEN NAMES Italian 34%. *Primo (3), Mario (2), Vito (2), Antonio, Carlo, Emilio, Enrico, Ernesto, Fernando, Franco, Guido, Luigi, Salvatore, Stefano.*

Paciorek (137) Polish: from *paciorek* 'rosary' (from *pacierz* 'prayer'), probably a nickname for a devout man.
GIVEN NAMES Polish 8%. *Ewa, Irena, Wieslaw, Zbigniew.*

Pacitti (210) Italian: patronymic or plural form of PACITTO.
GIVEN NAMES Italian 15%. *Domenic (4), Angelo, Antonio, Carlo, Carmela, Filomena, Luigi, Pasquale.*

Pacitto (134) Italian: from a pet form of the personal name PACE.
GIVEN NAMES Italian 19%. *Domenic (3), Angelo (2), Antonio, Pasquale, Salvatore.*

Pack (6109) **1.** English (Kentish): from a medieval personal name, *Pack*, possibly a survival of the Old English personal name *Pacca*, although this is found only as a place name element and appears to have died out fairly early on in the Old English period. The Middle English personal name is more likely to be a derivative of the Latin Christian name *Paschalis* (see PASCAL). **2.** Jewish (Ashkenazic): metonymic occupational name for a wholesale trader, from German *Pack* 'package' (see PACKER). **3.** Anglicized form of Dutch PAK.

Packard (3922) **1.** English: from Middle English *pa(c)k* 'pack', 'bundle' + the Anglo-Norman French pejorative suffix *-ard*, hence a derogatory occupational name for a peddler. **2.** English: pejorative derivative of the Middle English personal name PACK. **3.** English: from a Norman personal name, *Pachard*, *Baghard*, composed of the Germanic elements *pac*, *bag* 'fight' + *hard* 'hardy', 'brave', 'strong'. **4.** Probably an Americanized spelling of German **Packert**, **Päckert**, from Germanic personal names formed with a word meaning 'battle' or 'to fight'; or a variant of PACKER 2 (with excrescent *-t*).

Packer (3339) **1.** English: occupational name for a wool-packer, from an agent derivative of Middle English *pack(en)* 'to pack'. **2.** German and Jewish (Ashkenazic): from an agent derivative of Middle Low German *pak*, German *Pack* 'package', hence an occupational name for a wholesale trader, especially in the wool trade, one who sold goods in large packages rather than broken down into smaller quantities, or alternatively one who rode or drove pack animals to transport goods.

Packett (280) **1.** Americanized form of French PAQUETTE. **2.** Possibly also an Americanized form of German **Packert** (see PACKARD).

Packham (200) English: habitational name, either from Pagham in Sussex or from Pakenham in Suffolk, named in Old English from the personal names *Pæcga* and *Pacca* respectively, + *hām* 'homestead'.

Packman (254) **1.** English: occupational name for a peddler or hawker, Middle English *packeman*. **2.** English: occupational name for the servant (Middle English *man*) of someone called PACK. **3.** German (**Packmann**, **Päckmann**), Dutch (**Pakman**), and Jewish (Ashkenazic): occupational name for a packer (one who packed goods for shipping) or alternatively a rider or driver of pack animals, used for carrying comparatively light quantitites of goods at high speed, from a derivative of *packen* 'to pack'. **4.** German: variant of PACH 1, 2.
GIVEN NAMES Jewish 4%. *Galit, Hyman.*

Packwood (286) English: habitational name from a place in Warwickshire, so named from the Old English personal name *Pac(c)a* + *wudu* 'wood'.

Pacocha (103) Polish: from a derivative of the personal name PAC.

Pacyna (132) Polish (also **Paczyna**): unflattering nickname from *paczyna* 'clod', 'brickbat', or possibly a metonymic occupational name for a boatman, from the same word in the sense 'oar', 'rudder'.
GIVEN NAMES Polish 9%. *Andrzej, Benedykt, Kazimierz, Malgorzata.*

Paczkowski (350) Polish: habitational name for someone from places called Paczkowo or Paczków, in Poznań and Opole voivodeships, named with the personal name *Paczek* (see PACEK).
GIVEN NAMES Polish 5%. *Eugeniusz, Grzegorz, Jaroslaw, Lucjan, Piotr, Zbigniew.*

Padalino (118) Italian: metathesized variant of PALADINO.
GIVEN NAMES Italian 12%. *Bartolo, Carmela, Vita.*

Padberg (121) German: habitational name from a place so called in Waldeck district, or from the Padberg mountain near Horn in Lippe (with the first element *pad* 'mud', 'mire').

Paddack (201) Variant of English PADDOCK.

Padden (679) Irish: Anglicized form of Gaelic **Mac Páidín** (see McPADDEN).

Paddock (2142) English: **1.** from Middle English *parrock* 'paddock', 'small enclosure', hence a topographic name for a dweller by a paddock or enclosed meadow, or a habitational name from a place named with this word, as for example Paddock Wood in Kent. The change of *-rr-* to *-dd-* is an unexplained development which did not occur before the 17th century. **2.** from Middle English *paddock* 'toad', 'frog', a diminutive of *pad* (of Old Norse origin), hence a nickname for someone considered to resemble a toad or frog.

Paddy (131) English or Irish: unexplained. It is probably, but not certainly, from the familiar Irish pet form of PATRICK.
FOREBEARS William Paddy (d. 1657) is buried in the King's Chapel Burying Ground in Boston, MA.

Padelford (106) English: unexplained. Its form is that of an English habitational name but no place of this name has been identified in Britain. It may be an altered form of English **Puddiford**, itself probably a variant of **Puddefoot** or **Puddephat**, a nickname for a short, fat person or someone with a pot belly, from Middle English *puddy* 'round', 'rotund', + *vat* 'barrel'.
FOREBEARS Jonathan Paddleford is recorded in Cambridge, MA, in 1652.

Paden (1446) Irish and Scottish: reduced Anglicized form of Gaelic **Mac Páidín** 'son of *Páidín*', a pet form of the personal name *Pádraig* (see PATRICK).

Paderewski (26) Polish: habitational name, probably for someone from Paderew in Siedlce voivodeship, or possibly Padarew, now in Ukraine.
FOREBEARS This name, borne by a Polish noble family, is recorded from the 16th century. Ignacy Jan Paderewski (1860–1941), world-famous as a pianist and conductor, was also prime minister of Poland and minister of foreign affairs (1919–20), Polish delegate to the League of Nations, and president of the National Council of the Polish government in exile in London (1940–41).

Padfield (185) English: habitational name from a place in Derbyshire (or some other minor place with the same name), named in Old English with the personal name *Pad(d)a* + *feld* 'pasture', 'open country'.

Padget (335) English: variant of PADGETT.

Padgett (9046) English (mainly West Yorkshire): from a Middle English diminutive of *page*, a status name for a young servant.

Padgham (110) English: habitational name.

Padgitt (123) English: variant of PADGETT.

Padilla (10850) Spanish: habitational name from any of the various minor places, for example in the provinces of Burgos, Guadalajara, and Valladolid, named from Spanish *padilla* 'frying pan', 'breadpan' (Latin *patella*, a diminutive of *patina* 'shallow dish'), a word which was commonly used in the topographical sense of a gentle depression.
GIVEN NAMES Spanish 41%. *Jose* (268), *Juan* (96), *Manuel* (91), *Luis* (84), *Carlos* (78), *Jesus* (62), *Ramon* (55), *Pedro* (52), *Miguel* (51), *Ruben* (47), *Francisco* (46), *Jorge* (40).

Padin (148) Galician (**Padín**): habitational name from any of seven places in Galicia called Padin, from Latin *(villa) Palatini* 'estate of *Palatinus*', a personal name derived from *palatium* 'palace'.
GIVEN NAMES Spanish 50%. *Juan* (4), *Jose* (3), *Julio* (3), *Luis* (3), *Manuel* (3), *Jacinto* (2), *Miguel* (2), *Ramon* (2), *Wilfredo* (2), *Adalberto*, *Agustin*, *Aida*.

Padley (174) English: habitational name from Padley in Derbyshire or Padley Common in Devon. The place in Derby-

shire was named probably with the Old English personal name *Padda* + *lēah* 'glade', 'woodland clearing'. Alternatively, the first element may have been *padde* 'toad'.

Padlo (116) Polish (**Padło**): unflattering nickname from *padło*, an informal dialect variant of *padlina* 'carrion'.
GIVEN NAMES Polish 11%. *Andrzej*, *Stanislaw*, *Tadeusz*, *Waclaw*.

Padmanabhan (138) Indian (Kerala, Tamil Nadu): Hindu name from Sanskrit *padmanābha* 'lotus navel' (from *padma* 'lotus' + *nābha* 'navel'), an epithet of the god Vishnu + the Tamil-Malayalam third-person masculine singular suffix *-n*. This is only a given name in India, but has come to be used as a family name in the U.S.
GIVEN NAMES Indian 93%. *Geetha* (3), *Srinivasan* (3), *Anand* (2), *Arun* (2), *Bala* (2), *Gopal* (2), *Kumar* (2), *Lakshmanan* (2), *Mahesh* (2), *Pradeep* (2), *Prakash* (2), *Ram* (2).

Padmore (131) English: variant of PATMORE. This name is common in Barbados.

Pado (109) Filipino: unexplained.

Padon (137) Scottish: variant of PATON.

Padovani (147) Italian and Jewish (from Italy): see PADOVANO.
GIVEN NAMES Italian 13%; Spanish 12%; French 8%. *Guido* (2), *Stefano* (2), *Angelo*, *Giulio*; *Mario* (4), *Adalberto* (2), *Julio* (2), *Orlando* (2), *Alicia*, *Fabiola*, *Pedro*, *Renato*; *Armand*, *Francois*, *Pierre*.

Padovano (246) Italian and Jewish (from Italy): habitational name for someone from the city of Padua, Italian *Padova* (Latin *Patavium*).
GIVEN NAMES Italian 12%. *Carmine* (2), *Angelo*, *Carlo*, *Gino*, *Giuseppina*, *Marco*, *Salvatore*.

Padrick (181) Irish: variant of PATRICK.

Padro (192) Catalan (**Padró**): 1. variant spelling of the topographic name **Pedró**, from *pedró* 'memorial stone' (see PEDRO). 2. nickname or status name from *padró* 'master'. Compare PATRON.
GIVEN NAMES Spanish 43%. *Jose* (5), *Rafael* (4), *Carlos* (3), *Ramon* (3), *Andres* (2), *Angel* (2), *Efrain* (2), *Luz* (2), *Rolando* (2), *Ruben* (2), *Altagracia*, *Anabella*.

Padron (1316) 1. Spanish (Tenerife; **Padrón**): in some cases a variant of Catalan **Padró** (see PADRO); otherwise from the Spanish equivalent *padrón*, a variant of *patrón* 'master'. 2. Galician: habitational name from Padrón, a town in Galicia.
GIVEN NAMES Spanish 53%. *Jose* (34), *Juan* (23), *Luis* (20), *Carlos* (17), *Alberto* (12), *Mario* (12), *Raul* (12), *Jorge* (10), *Roberto* (10), *Manuel* (9), *Rafael* (9), *Jesus* (8); *Antonio* (15), *Angelo* (3), *Lorenzo* (3), *Cecilio* (2), *Cesario* (2), *Fausto* (2), *Gilda* (2), *Heriberto* (2), *Leonardo* (2), *Amelio* (2), *Annamarie*, *Antonino*.

Padua (309) Spanish, Portuguese (**De Pádua**), and Catalan: habitational name from the Italian city of Padua.
GIVEN NAMES Spanish 36%. *Manuel* (4), *Carlos* (3), *Jose* (3), *Roberto* (3), *Horacio* (2), *Pedro* (2), *Ruben* (2), *Adoracion*, *Aida*, *Alberto*, *Alejandro*, *Alejo*.

Paduano (290) Italian: 1. northern variant of PADOVANO. 2. in Naples and Campania, a variant of *Padulano*, a derivative of PADULA.
GIVEN NAMES Italian 17%. *Sal* (2), *Angelo*, *Antonio*, *Cosmo*, *Dominico*, *Donato*, *Gaetano*, *Giro*, *Giuseppe*, *Matteo*, *Nicolino*, *Onofrio*.

Paduch (107) Polish: unflattering nickname from *paduch* 'robber', 'predator', a derivative of *padać* 'to fall upon'.
GIVEN NAMES Polish 9%. *Boleslaw* (2), *Piotr*.

Padula (965) 1. Southern Italian (Campania): habitational name from places called Padula, in Salerno and Teramo, Paduli in Benevento, or various other places, all named from a metathesized form of *palude* 'swamp'. 2. Polish (**Paduła**): nickname for someone who was unsteady on his feet, from a derivative of *padać* 'to fall down'.
GIVEN NAMES Italian 16%. *Rocco* (7), *Angelo* (5), *Guido* (4), *Pasquale* (4), *Antonio* (3), *Caesar* (3), *Domenic* (3), *Nicola* (3), *Gino* (2), *Sal* (2), *Salvatore* (2), *Amedeo*.

Pae (301) Korean: there is only one Chinese character for the Pae surname. The only documented Pae clan is that of Kyŏngju. The founding ancestor of the Kyŏngju Pae clan, Ki-t'a, was one of the six elders who made Pak Hyŏkkŏse Shilla's first king. Afterwards, Ki-t'a received the surname of *Pae* during the 32nd year of the reign of the Shilla King Yuri Isagŭm (24–57 AD).
GIVEN NAMES Korean 48%. *Yong* (4), *Sung* (3), *Young* (3), *Kyung* (2), *Sang Suk* (2), *Yoon* (2), *Yun* (2), *Chae*, *Chang Ho*, *Chang Hui*, *Chee*, *Chun*; *Chong* (4), *Chang* (2), *Seong* (2), *Sung-Hoon* (2), *Byung Kyu*, *Chong Ho*, *Chong Hun*, *Eun Hee*, *Hae*, *Jae Hong*, *Jae Kun*, *Jae Sik*.

Paek (322) Korean: There is only one Chinese character for this surname. Although some sources indicate that there are 157 different clans of the *Paek* family, modern research has shown them all to have derived from a single clan, the Suwŏn Paek. The clan's founding ancestor was named Paek U-kyŏng; he migrated to Korea from China in 780.
GIVEN NAMES Korean 69%. *Sung* (7), *Sang* (6), *Young* (5), *Yong* (4), *Hyung* (3), *Seung* (3), *Won* (3), *Byong* (2), *Chae* (2), *Hyun* (2), *Jong* (2), *Jung* (2); *Chong* (10), *Nam* (4), *Byung* (2), *Chang* (2), *Min* (2), *Pong* (2), *Chong Nam*, *Chong Su*, *Dae*, *Dong Hyun*, *Hyum*, *Hyung Jin*.

Paepke (119) Dutch and North German: diminutive of PAPE. See also PAPKE.

Paes (104) Portuguese: variant of PAIS.

GIVEN NAMES Spanish 5%. *Fernanda, Jose, Orlando, Pedro, Renato.*

Paeth (153) German: of uncertain origin; perhaps an altered form of **Päthe**, from Middle Low German *pade* 'godfather', 'male relative', from Latin *pater*, or from the French name *Peteu*. Compare PATE.

Paetow (113) German (**Pätow**): habitational name from Pätow in Mecklenburg.

GIVEN NAME German 9%. *Claus.*

Paetz (150) German: from the personal name *Pätz*, a vernacular form of PETER.

GIVEN NAME German 6%. *Juergen* (2).

Paetzold (142) German (**Pätzold**): from the personal name **Pätzold**, a pet form of PETER.

GIVEN NAMES German 26%. *Armin* (3), *Hans* (2), *Heinz* (2), *Maximilian* (2), *Bernd, Dieter, Ernst, Friederike, Heiner, Horst, Markus, Oskar.*

Paez (1093) Spanish form (**Páez**) of Portuguese and Galician PAIS.

GIVEN NAMES Spanish 54%. *Jose* (27), *Juan* (20), *Luis* (17), *Jorge* (16), *Carlos* (14), *Jesus* (12), *Pedro* (8), *Rafael* (8), *Manuel* (7), *Miguel* (7), *Raul* (7), *Ricardo* (7).

Paff (409) Probably a variant of German PFAFF. However, *Paffen* is recorded as a variant of North German PAPE.

Pafford (587) English: **1.** from Old French *pafard* 'shield', hence a Norman nickname for a fighting man or metonymic occupational name for an armorer. **2.** probably a habitational name from either of two minor places in Devon: Pafford in Moretonhampstead or Parford in Drewsteignton, both named from Old English *pæð* 'path' + *ford* 'ford'.

Paffrath (118) German: habitational name from Paffrath in North Rhine-Westphalia.

Pagac (107) Slovak (**Pagáč**): nickname from *pagáč* 'clown', 'buffoon'.

Pagan (2877) **1.** Spanish (**Pagán**): Castilianized spelling of Catalan **Pagà**, from the Late Latin personal name *Paganus*, which originally meant 'dweller in an outlying village' (see PAINE). **2.** Spanish: in some cases it may be a topographic name from Catalan *pagà* 'heath', from Latin *pagus* 'district', 'outlying village'. **3.** Northern English and Scottish: probably from the Latin medieval personal name *Paganus*, the vernacular form of which was *Paine* (see PAINE).

GIVEN NAMES Spanish 35%. *Jose* (58), *Luis* (36), *Juan* (29), *Angel* (26), *Carlos* (22), *Rafael* (19), *Ramon* (17), *Pedro* (15), *Francisco* (14), *Jesus* (13), *Miguel* (13), *Julio* (12).

Paganelli (254) Italian: patronymic from *Paganello*, a pet form of the personal name PAGANO.

GIVEN NAMES Italian 8%. *Dino* (4), *Angelo, Caesar, Elvio, Marino, Vincenzo.*

Pagani (308) Italian: patronymic or plural form of PAGANO.

GIVEN NAMES Italian 12%; Spanish 7%. *Biagio, Carlo, Domenico, Gino, Italo, Leonardo, Livio, Manfredo, Nino, Santino; Luis* (7), *Graciela* (2), *Miguel* (2), *Aurelio.*

Paganini (152) Italian: patronymic from *Paganino*, a pet form of the personal name PAGANO.

GIVEN NAMES Italian 11%; Spanish 6%. *Adriano, Agostino, Alfonso, Angelo, Gino, Pietro; Aquiles, Exequiel, Fernando, Miguel.*

Pagano (2981) **1.** Italian: from the personal name *Pagano*, Latin *Paganus*, from a word meaning 'village dweller' (see PAINE). **2.** Spanish equivalent of Catalan **Pagà** (see PAGAN), cognate with 1.

GIVEN NAMES Italian 15%. *Angelo* (17), *Salvatore* (12), *Carmine* (10), *Antonio* (8), *Sal* (4), *Canio* (3), *Domenic* (3), *Filippo* (3), *Giovanni* (3), *Matteo* (3), *Rocco* (3), *Santo* (3).

Page (29192) **1.** English, Scottish, and French: status name for a young servant, Middle English and Old French *page* (from Italian *paggio*, ultimately from Greek *paidion*, diminutive of *pais* 'boy', 'child'). The surname is also common in Ireland (especially Ulster and eastern Galway), having been established there since the 16th century. **2.** North German: metonymic occupational name for a horse dealer, from Middle Low German *page* 'horse'. **3.** (**Pagé**): North American form of French PAGET.

FOREBEARS A Pagé, also known as Carsy, Quercy, and LAROSE, was documented in 1666 in Ange-Gardien, Quebec. Mann Page (1691–1730) was one of the largest land owners in VA.

Pageau (131) French: from a diminutive of PAGE.

GIVEN NAMES French 21%. *Armand* (2), *Stephane* (2), *Alphonse, Andre, Fernand, Gisele, Jean Claude, Lucien, Philippe.*

Pagel (2123) **1.** North German: from the personal name *Pagel*, a Low German form of PAUL. **2.** North German (**Pägel**): metonymic occupational name for a calibrator, from Low German *pegel* 'water level gauge', 'small container' (see PEGLER 3). **3.** French: diminutive of PAGE.

GIVEN NAMES German 4%. *Erwin* (4), *Kurt* (4), *Gerhard* (3), *Otto* (3), *Eldred* (2), *Ewald* (2), *Armin, Arno, Fritz, Hermann, Horst, Juergen.*

Pagels (382) North German: patronymic from PAGEL 1.

Pagenkopf (204) German: from Low German *page* 'horse' and *kopf* 'head', a nickname and probably an occupational nickname for a horse dealer; or alternatively a habitational or topographic name from a place so named in Pomerania or locations in the Oldenburg region.

Pages (176) Catalan (**Pagès**): occupational name for a peasant farmer or agricultural laborer, from *pagès* 'peasant' (Late Latin

pagensis, a derivative of *pagus* 'village', 'country district').

GIVEN NAMES Spanish 35%; French 6%. *Carlos* (4), *Mario* (4), *Eduardo* (3), *Jorge* (3), *Luis* (3), *Mauricio* (3), *Ramon* (3), *Fernando* (2), *Jose* (2), *Lazaro* (2), *Pedro* (2), *Alfredo; Jacques* (2), *Lucien, Michel.*

Paget (397) English and French: from a diminutive of PAGE.

Pagett (178) English: variant spelling of PAGET.

Paglia (565) Italian: from *paglia* 'straw', hence possibly a nickname or a metonymic occupational name for someone who gathered straw or used it to make hats or mattresses, or a topographic name.

GIVEN NAMES Italian 16%. *Angelo* (3), *Donato* (3), *Vito* (3), *Antonino* (2), *Carmela* (2), *Elio* (2), *Giuseppe* (2), *Rocco* (2), *Aldo, Antonio, Carlo, Carmelo.*

Pagliarini (113) Italian: from a diminutive of PAGLIARO.

GIVEN NAMES Italian 14%. *Carlo* (2), *Angelo, Domenic, Guido, Rocco.*

Pagliaro (551) Southern Italian (especially Sicily): **1.** occupational name for someone who gathered or used straw, from an agent derivative of *paglia* 'straw' or from *pagliaro* 'straw-rick'. **2.** topographic name for someone who lived near a straw-loft or barn (Late Latin *palearium*) or a habitational name from any of the places named Pagliaro, Pagliara, and Pagliare.

GIVEN NAMES Italian 17%. *Carmine* (3), *Salvatore* (3), *Antonio* (2), *Attilio* (2), *Domenic* (2), *Francesco* (2), *Antonino, Carlo, Emanuele, Filomena, Geno.*

Pagliarulo (205) Southern Italian: from a diminutive of PAGLIARO.

GIVEN NAMES Italian 18%. *Domenic* (2), *Enrico* (2), *Giuseppe* (2), *Angelo, Luciano, Marco, Nunzio, Pasquale, Rocco, Vito.*

Paglione (122) Italian: augmentative of **Paglia**, an occupational name for someone who gathered or used straw, from *paglia* 'straw' *paglia.*

GIVEN NAMES Italian 9%. *Antonio, Giancarlo, Luigi.*

Pagliuca (220) Variant of Italian **Pagliucca**, a southern diminutive of PAGLIA, in the sense 'straw', 'chaff'.

GIVEN NAMES Italian 36%. *Angelo* (4), *Domenic* (2), *Mario* (2), *Sal* (2), *Antonietta, Antonio, Arnoldo, Arturo, Basilio, Carlo, Cesare, Dante, Domenico, Emelio, Emilio, Ferdinando, Fiore.*

Pagni (133) Italian (Tuscany): patronymic from *Pagno*, a shortened form of the nicknames *Compagno* or *Boncompagno*, denoting someone who is a good neighbor or an amiable fellow worker.

Pagnotta (263) Italian (mostly Tuscany): from a feminine form of *Pagnotto*, which is either a diminutive of *Compagno* or *Boncompagno* (see PAGNI), or a metonymic occupational name for a baker or pantryman, from a diminutive of *pano* 'bread'.

GIVEN NAMES Italian 20%. *Domenico* (2), *Pasquale* (2), *Carmel, Carmine, Ceasar, Enrico, Filomena, Gaetano, Gasper, Gianni, Giovanni, Giuseppi.*

Pagnozzi (103) Italian: from a derivative of the personal name *Pagno* (see PAGNI).

GIVEN NAMES Italian 13%. *Orlando* (2), *Alfonso, Carmine, Gennaro, Rosaria.*

Pagonis (138) Greek: 1. from the vocabulary word *pagoni* 'peacock' (classical Greek *paōn*), nickname for a vain or showy man. 2. possibly also a metronymic from the related personal name *Pagona.*

GIVEN NAMES Greek 9%. *Konstantinos* (2), *Costas, Eleni, Georgios.*

Pahl (1502) 1. German: from a vernacular form of the personal name PAUL. 2. North German: metonymic occupational name for a pile driver, from Middle Low German *pāl* 'pile', 'post'.

GIVEN NAMES German 5%. *Hans* (3), *Kurt* (3), *Claus* (2), *Erwin, Fritz, Goetz, Gunther, Heinz, Helmut, Helmuth, Jochen, Juergen.*

Pahls (109) German: patronymic from PAHL.

GIVEN NAME German 4%. *Heinrich.*

Pahnke (107) Eastern German: Germanized form of PANEK.

GIVEN NAME German 4%. *Erwin.*

Pai (561) 1. Indian (Goa): Hindu (Brahman) name, from Sanskrit *pati* 'lord'. It is found among the Konkani-speaking Saraswat Brahmans, who were originally from Goa but are now found in larger numbers in coastal Karnataka. 2. Korean: variant of PAE.

GIVEN NAMES Indian 55%; Korean 4%. *Mohan* (6), *Suresh* (6), *Dinesh* (4), *Anil* (3), *Rajesh* (3), *Satish* (3), *Sunil* (3), *Ajith* (2), *Arun* (2), *Damodar* (2), *Jagdish* (2), *Kamalesh* (2); *Bok, Chang-Sheng, Chi, Chia, Ching, Chun, Dong, Doo, Feng, Jae Ho, Joong, Jui.*

Paice (122) Variant of PACE.

Paige (5164) English (mainly London): variant spelling of PAGE.

Paik (639) 1. Korean: variant of PAEK. 2. English: variant of PACK.

GIVEN NAMES Korean 57%. *Sung* (15), *Young* (14), *Jong* (8), *Seung* (6), *Eun* (4), *In* (4), *Kwang* (4), *Sun* (4), *Won* (4), *Yong* (4), *Jin* (3), *Jung* (3), *Byung* (2), *Chul* (2), *Moon* (2), *Moon Soo* (2), *Myong* (2), *Woon* (2), *Chang, Chang Hyun, Chong, Chong Hun, Chong Son.*

Paille (130) French: from Old French *paille* 'straw', hence a metonymic occupational name for someone who gathered straw or used it to make hats or mattresses. It may also have been a nickname for someone with straw-colored hair.

FOREBEARS A Paillé from the Poitou region of France is documented in Beauport, Quebec, in 1678; he was also known as Payer.

GIVEN NAMES French 20%. *Andre* (2), *Pierre* (2), *Michel, Raoul, Remy, Yves.*

Pain (169) Variant of PAINE.

GIVEN NAMES French 8%. *Jean-Luc, Normand, Reynald, Veronique.*

Painchaud (139) French: literally 'hot bread'; occupational nickname for a baker.

GIVEN NAMES French 22%. *Germain* (2), *Andre, Francois, Gilles, Gisele, Jacques, Laureat, Normand, Raynald.*

Paine (3641) English (mainly Kent and Sussex): from the Middle English personal name *Pain(e), Payn(e)* (Old French *Paien*, from Latin *Paganus*), introduced to Britain by the Normans. The Latin name is a derivative of *pagus* 'outlying village', and meant at first a person who lived in the country (as opposed to *Urbanus* 'city dweller'), then a civilian as opposed to a soldier, and eventually a heathen (one not enrolled in the army of Christ). This remained a popular name throughout the Middle Ages, but it died out in the 16th century.

FOREBEARS Thomas Payne, who was a freeman of the Plymouth Colony in 1639, was the founder of a large American family, which included Robert Treat Paine (1731–1814), one of the signers of the Declaration of Independence. The author of the republican treatise *The Rights of Man*, Thomas Paine (1737–1809), left England for North America in the mid 1770s, where he became involved in the movement that led to independence. His pamphlet of 1776, *Common Sense*, influenced the Declaration of Independence and furnished some of the arguments justifying it.

Paino (219) Italian: Frenchified variant (influenced by French *païen*) of PAGANO.

GIVEN NAMES Italian 7%. *Angelo* (2), *Domenic, Salvatore.*

Painter (8384) 1. English: from Middle English, Old French *peinto(u)r*, oblique case of *peintre* 'painter', hence an occupational name for a painter (normally of colored glass). In the Middle Ages the walls of both great and minor churches were covered with painted decorations, and Reaney and Wilson note that in 1308 Hugh le Peyntour and Peter the Pavier were employed 'making and painting the pavement' at St. Stephen's Chapel, Westminster. The name is widespread in central and southern England. 2. German: topographic name for someone living in a fenced enclosure (see BAINTER).

Painton (162) English: habitational name from Paignton in Devon, named with the Old English personal name *Pæga* (genitive *Pægan*) + *tūn* 'farmstead', 'settlement'.

GIVEN NAMES French 4%. *Monique, Patrice.*

Pair (778) Possibly a respelling of German BAER.

Pais (352) 1. Portuguese and Galician: patronymic from the personal name *Paio*, equivalent of Spanish PELAYO. 2. Italian: when not of the same origin as 1, a nick-

name from Greek *pais* 'boy', 'lad', 'servant'.

GIVEN NAMES Spanish 14%; Portuguese 8%; Italian 6%. *Fernando* (4), *Jose* (4), *Alberto* (2), *Ana* (2), *Ramon* (2), *Adelino, Alina, Altino, Angel, Armando, Armindo, Catalina; Joao, Joaquim, Sebastiao, Serafim; Antonio* (6), *Angelo* (2), *Silvio* (2), *Antonino, Ateo, Elio, Guido, Lia.*

Paisley (1118) Scottish and northern Irish: habitational name from a place in Renfrewshire, now a suburb of Glasgow. It is first recorded in 1157 as *Passeleth*, then in 1158 as *Paisleth* and in 1163 as *Passelet, Passelay*; it may be derived from Late Latin *basilica* 'church'.

Pait (367) Scottish: 1. from the personal name *Pait*, short form of PATRICK. 2. nickname for a man with a bald head, from Middle English *pate* 'head', 'skull'.

Paiva (807) Portuguese: habitational name from any of the places named Paiva, which all take their name from the Paiva river, a tributary of the Douro.

GIVEN NAMES Spanish 17%; Portuguese 11%. *Manuel* (18), *Jose* (14), *Carlos* (8), *Fernando* (5), *Luis* (3), *Mario* (3), *Ana* (2), *Angelino* (2), *Evodio* (2), *Jorge* (2), *Luiz* (2), *Adelina; Joao* (7), *Afonso, Agostinho, Albano, Guilherme, Paulo, Zulmira.*

Paiz (535) Spanish (**Páiz**): variant of Portuguese and Galician PAIS.

GIVEN NAMES Spanish 36%. *Manuel* (7), *Jorge* (6), *Jose* (6), *Carlos* (4), *Juan* (4), *Luis* (4), *Armando* (3), *Fernando* (3), *Alfonso* (2), *Alfredo* (2), *Andres* (2), *Ascension* (2).

Pajak (466) Polish (**Pająk**): nickname for someone thought to resemble a spider, from *pająk* 'spider'.

GIVEN NAMES Polish 9%. *Tadeusz* (4), *Alicja, Casimir, Danuta, Jerzy, Jolanta, Leszek, Tomasz, Urszula.*

Pajor (142) Polish: nickname of uncertain origin, perhaps from a derivative of Polish dialect *pajować* 'to shout or quarrel'.

GIVEN NAMES Polish 18%. *Stanislaw* (2), *Boguslaw, Grzegorz, Jadwiga, Janina, Jerzy, Miroslaw, Wieslaw, Zofia.*

Pak (2388) 1. Korean: there is only one Chinese character for this surname, which is the third most common in Korea, and can be found in every part of the peninsula. The *Pak* clans claim no founding ancestors from foreign lands. Although some sources indicate that there are 270 Pak clans, only 44 of these can be documented. All Pak clans spring from one common semi-mythological ancestor named Pak Hyŏkkŏse. Before the establishment of the Shilla Kingdom, the southern tip of the peninsula is said to have been ruled by six elders who led the six tribes which inhabited that part of the country. In answer to their prayer for a leader, Pak Hyŏkkŏse arrived at the foot of a distant mountain in 69 BC inside a golden gourd-shaped egg. When the egg was opened, Pak Hyŏkkŏse emerged and, after taking a wife (who was born on the back of a dragon), established and ruled the new Shilla kingdom. Supposedly, the surname *Pak* denoted either the gourd-shaped egg in which the youth was found or the light which is said to have radiated from the boy's head (the word *pak* in Korean can mean 'gourd' or 'to shine brightly'). **2.** Dutch: probably an occupational name for a rider or driver of pack animals (see PACKMAN).

GIVEN NAMES Korean 66%. *Chong* (47), *Yong* (45), *Young* (28), *Sung* (26), *Song* (21), *Sang* (20), *Kyong* (16), *Kwang* (15), *Chun* (13), *Chang* (12), *Sun* (12), *Jong* (10), *Jung* (10), *Chan* (9), *Chung* (9), *Byung* (5), *Nam* (5), *Myong* (4), *Pyong* (4), *Chol* (3), *Hae* (3), *Hyong* (3), *In Kyu* (3), *Tuk* (3).

Pake (130) German (Westphalian): of uncertain origin. Compound names such as *Pakebusch*, and *Pakedorf* indicate a topographic source.

Pakkala (118) Finnish: topographic name from *pakka* 'hill' (a derivative of Swedish *backe*) + the local suffix *-la*. This name is found mainly in western Finland.

GIVEN NAMES Finnish 12%. *Juhani*, *Olli*, *Pekka*, *Pentti*, *Seppo*, *Waino*.

Pakula (180) Polish (**Pakuła**): **1.** from Polish *pakuły* 'tow' (in the sense 'loose ends of linen or rope'), hence a nickname for someone with tow-colored hair, or perhaps a metonymic occupational name for someone who worked with linen or hemp. **2.** from a derivative of the personal name *Pakosław*, from Old Slavic *pače* 'more' + *slav* 'glory'. GIVEN NAMES Polish 10%; French 5%. *Krystyna*, *Krzysztof*, *Maciej*, *Tomasz*, *Waclaw*, *Zbigniew*; *Amie*, *Jean Pierre*.

Pakulski (137) Polish: habitational name for someone from either of two places named Pakuły, in Częstochowa and Kielce voivodeships.

GIVEN NAMES Polish 5%. *Janusz*, *Zbigniew*.

Pal (512) **1.** Indian (Bengal) and Bangladeshi: Hindu (Kayasth) name, from Sanskrit *pāla* 'protector', 'keeper', 'guard', 'herdsman' (compare *gopāla* 'cowherd'), an epithet of the god Krishna and a common personal name. A Pala dynasty that was founded by one Gopala in the 8th century ruled in Bengal and Bihar until the 12th century. **2.** Hungarian (**Pál**): from the personal name *Pál*, Hungarian form of PAUL. This name is also found, spelled **Pal**, in Slovenia (Prekmurje) and northern and eastern Croatia.

GIVEN NAMES Indian 61%. *Sat* (6), *Ram* (5), *Dharam* (4), *Raj* (4), *Yash* (4), *Dilip* (3), *Ajay* (2), *Anil* (2), *Aruna* (2), *Chandra* (2), *Gopal* (2), *Indar* (2).

Pala (107) **1.** Italian: topographic name from *pala* 'upland meadow'. **2.** Catalan: generally a habitational name from a place called Palà, in Barcelona province. **3.** Catalan: possibly a metonymic occupa-

tional from *pala* 'shovel' (Latin *pala*). **4.** Polish (also **Pała**): from a vernacular form of the personal name *Paweł*, Polish form of PAUL. **5.** Czech: nickname for an obstinate person, from Moravian dialect *pala* 'head'. **6.** Hawaiian: unexplained.

GIVEN NAMES Italian 9%; Spanish 7%; Polish 6%. *Severino* (3), *Antonio*, *Enio*; *Angel* (2), *Jorge*, *Juan*, *Manuel*; *Andrzej*, *Danuta*, *Zbigniew*.

Palace (140) Probably an Americanized form of Spanish PALACIO, Italian PALAZZO, or French **Palais**, which is in some cases a habitational name, from places in Morbihan and Haute-Vienne called Le Palais or from Palais-du-Cros in Puy-de-Dôme, but in the South is from a vernacular form of the Latin personal name *Palladius* (Greek *Palladios*).

Palacio (910) Spanish: habitational name from any of the many places in Spain, especially Galicia, called Palacio (alongside the Galician form *Pazo*), or from El Palacio, Castilianized form of El Palaciu, a town in Asturies. All are named with *palacio* 'palace', 'manor', 'great house', Latin *palatium*, a word derived from the *Palatium* or *mons Palatinus* in Rome, site of the emperor Augustus' golden house.

GIVEN NAMES Spanish 46%. *Carlos* (15), *Jose* (14), *Luis* (12), *Jaime* (7), *Jorge* (7), *Juan* (7), *Manuel* (7), *Francisco* (6), *Joaquin* (6), *Mario* (6), *Ricardo* (6), *Alfredo* (4).

Palacios (3341) Spanish: variant (plural) of PALACIO.

GIVEN NAMES Spanish 52%. *Jose* (91), *Juan* (56), *Carlos* (45), *Luis* (32), *Manuel* (32), *Jorge* (29), *Francisco* (25), *Miguel* (22), *Raul* (22), *Ramon* (19), *Enrique* (18), *Jesus* (18).

Paladini (117) Italian: patronymic or plural form of PALADINO.

GIVEN NAMES Italian 19%. *Achille*, *Aldo*, *Angelo*, *Arcangelo*, *Dino*, *Domenic*, *Giovanni*, *Luciano*, *Mario*, *Roberto*, *Umberto*.

Paladino (1080) Italian: from the 12th-century personal name *Paladino*, derived from tales of the Frankish king Charlemagne's legendary knights or paladins (from Latin *palatinus* 'of or pertaining to the palace').

GIVEN NAMES Italian 13%. *Angelo* (7), *Rocco* (5), *Domenic* (3), *Salvatore* (3), *Dino* (2), *Gaetano* (2), *Sal* (2), *Vito* (2), *Aldo*, *Biagio*, *Carlo*, *Carmello*.

Palafox (377) Castilianized form of Catalan **Palafolls**, habitational name from a place of this name in Catalonia. This form of the name is mainly found in Mexico.

GIVEN NAMES Spanish 53%. *Jose* (13), *Jesus* (7), *Francisco* (6), *Javier* (5), *Juan* (5), *Miguel* (4), *Guadalupe* (3), *Humberto* (3), *Lourdes* (3), *Manuel* (3), *Alberto* (2), *Armando* (2).

Palagi (105) Italian: plural form of the habitational name Palagio, from a place so named in Montaione in Florence province.

Palaia (126) Italian: apparently a habitational name from Palaia in Pisa province (Tuscany). However, the family name occurs chiefly in Calabria, suggesting perhaps that another source may be involved.

GIVEN NAMES Italian 22%. *Rocco* (3), *Saverio* (2), *Gerardo*, *Sal*.

Palamara (132) Southern Italian and Greek: occupational name for a sailor, from Greek *palamaras* 'cable', 'mooring rope'. The Greek verb *palamarein*, Italian *spalamare*, means 'to coat a ship's bottom with grease'.

GIVEN NAMES Italian 11%. *Guido*, *Rocco*, *Salvator*.

Palan (126) Indian: variant of BALAN in Tamil Nadu.

GIVEN NAMES Indian 4%; German 4%. *Praful*, *Prakash*; *Kurt* (2).

Palange (116) **1.** French: from *palange*, a regional variant of *palanche* 'yoke', hence a metonymic occupational name for a porter, someone who carried buckets or other loads suspended from a yoke. **2.** Italian: unexplained.

GIVEN NAME Italian 11%. *Angelo* (3).

Palardy (222) Respelling of French **Pallardy**, derogatory nickname denoting someone who slept on straw, from a derivative of *paille* 'straw'. This name occurs chiefly in New England.

FOREBEARS A bearer of the name Palardy is documented in Sillery, Quebec, in 1666. Another branch came from the Poitou region of France.

GIVEN NAMES French 13%. *Adrien* (2), *Laurent* (2), *Alphonse*, *Andre*, *Armand*, *Benoit*, *Lucien*.

Palas (119) **1.** Greek: variant of PALLAS. **2.** German: variant of **Balasch**, a Germanized form of Czech and Slovak **Balaš** or Hungarian BALAZS, vernacular forms of the Latin personal name BLASIUS.

GIVEN NAMES Greek 6%; German 4%. *Antonios*, *Panos*, *Takis*; *Bernhard*, *Fritz*.

Palau (145) Catalan: from *palau* 'palace', 'mansion' (see PALACIO).

GIVEN NAMES Spanish 34%; Italian 8%. *Julio* (4), *Jose* (3), *Luis* (3), *Guillermo* (2), *Gustavo* (2), *Manuel* (2), *Aida*, *Alejandro*, *Armando*, *Arturo*, *Augustina*, *Beatriz*; *Enzo* (2), *Leonardo* (2), *Antonio*, *Marco*.

Palazzi (179) Italian: patronymic or plural form of PALAZZO.

GIVEN NAMES Italian 7%. *Marco* (2), *Nino*, *Ugo*, *Vito*.

Palazzo (1068) Italian: habitational name from Palazzo Adriano in Palermo province, Sicily, Palazzo San Gervasio in Potenza province, Basilicata, or possibly from Palazzo Canavese in Turin province, all named with *palazzo* 'palace', 'noble mansion' (Latin *palatium*, a word derived from the *Palatium* or *mons Palatinus* in Rome, site of the emperor Augustus' golden house). In some instances the name may be topographic for someone who lived near a royal or noble mansion, or an occupational name for someone who was employed in one.

GIVEN NAMES Italian 18%. *Angelo* (11), *Antonio* (6), *Gasper* (4), *Biagio* (3), *Salvatore* (3), *Vito* (3), *Carlo* (2), *Natale* (2), *Nicola* (2), *Pasco* (2), *Pietro* (2), *Alesio, Arturo, Eduardo, Emilio, Fabio, Mario*.

Palazzola (191) Italian: variant (feminine form) of PALAZZOLO.

GIVEN NAMES Italian 21%. *Vito* (7), *Antonio, Carmela, Dino, Natale, Sal, Salvator, Salvatore, Santo*.

Palazzolo (1014) Italian: habitational name from any of numerous places named Palazzolo, in particular Palazzolo Acreide in Syracuse province, Sicily.

GIVEN NAMES Italian 33%. *Salvatore* (16), *Vito* (15), *Antonio* (9), *Gaspare* (5), *Mario* (5), *Angelo* (4), *Damiano* (4), *Natale* (4), *Pietro* (4), *Gasper* (3), *Giacomo* (3), *Giovanni* (3), *Giuseppe* (3).

Palcic (105) Slovenian (**Palčič**) and Croatian (**Palčić**): from a diminutive of *palec* (Slovenian), *palac* (Croatian) 'thumb', nickname for a small person, or perhaps a nickname from *palčič* (Slovenian) or *palčić* (Croatian) 'wren'. The bird was named with this word with reference to its small size.

Palczewski (117) Polish: habitational name for someone from either of two places called Palczew, in Kalisz and Radom voivodeships, or from Palczowice; derived from a nickname, *Palec*, from *palec* 'finger', 'toe'.

GIVEN NAMES Polish 16%. *Dariusz* (3), *Andrzej, Jacek, Wladyslaw, Wojciech*.

Palczynski (100) Polish (**Palczyński**): habitational name for someone from Palczyn in Bydgoszcz voivodeship, or from Pałczyn in Poznań voivodeship, named with *pałka* 'truncheon', 'club' (see PALKA).

GIVEN NAME Ukrainian 5%. *Taras* (2).

Palecek (237) Czech (**Paleček**): **1.** from a double diminutive of the personal name *Pavel* or some other personal name beginning with *Pa-*. **2.** from a diminutive of *palec* 'thumb', hence a nickname for a small person or a dwarf, or for someone with a deformed or missing thumb.

Palek (114) Czech: from a pet form of the personal name *Pavel* or some other personal name beginning with *Pa-*.

Palen (530) **1.** Variant of North German **Pahlen**, a topographic name from Middle Low German *pāl* 'post', 'stake', 'boundary marker'. **2.** French: variant of PALIN. **3.** Americanized spelling of Belgian **Peelen**, a habitational name for someone from either of two places called Peel, in North Brabant and Limburg.

FOREBEARS An early (1630s) immigrant from Nijkerk, Netherlands, to Rensselaerswijck, NY named *Peelen* was the ancestor of the present-day bearers of this surname. Palenville in Ulster Co., NY is named from the same source.

Palencia (245) Spanish: habitational name from the city or region of Palencia in northern Spain.

GIVEN NAMES Spanish 49%; Portuguese 10%. *Francisco* (5), *Jose* (5), *Cesar* (4), *Luis* (4), *Alfonso* (3), *Jorge* (3), *Ramon* (3), *Consuelo* (2), *Guillermo* (2), *Josue* (2), *Juan* (2), *Julio Cesar* (2); *Paulo; Dante, Dino, Enrico, Gino, Heriberto, Julieta, Leonardo, Lucio, Marco, Romeo, Tranquilino*.

Paler (108) **1.** Jewish (eastern Ashkenazic): occupational name for a distiller, a Yiddishized form of Ukrainian *palyar* 'distiller'. **2.** English: variant of PAYLOR.

GIVEN NAMES French 9%; Jewish 7%. *Simcha, Yitzchok*.

Palermo (2888) Italian and Jewish (from Italy): habitational name from the Sicilian city of Palermo, the Greek name of which is *Panormos*, from *pan* 'all' + *ormos* 'gulf', 'bay', probably in the sense 'wide gulf', but possibly 'well-protected bay'.

GIVEN NAMES Italian 13%. *Angelo* (22), *Rocco* (11), *Salvatore* (11), *Antonio* (4), *Sal* (4), *Vito* (4), *Ciro* (3), *Guido* (3), *Pasquale* (3), *Carlo* (2), *Carmine* (2).

Palese (184) Italian: possibly a habitational name from Palese in Bari province.

GIVEN NAMES Italian 12%. *Carmine, Gino, Guerino, Leonardo, Pasquale, Rocco, Umberto*.

Paletta (205) Italian: from a derivative of PALA.

GIVEN NAMES Italian 16%; Spanish 6%; French 4%. *Salvatore* (2), *Silvio* (2), *Adamo, Angelo, Domenic, Geno, Gino, Mario, Serafino; Angel, Juan, Luz; Alain, Jean Marie*.

Paley (788) **1.** English (Yorkshire): possibly a nickname for someone with pale or lustreless eyes, from Middle English *pale* 'pale' + *eye* 'eye'. **2.** English: from an Old Scandinavian personal name, Old Danish *Palli* or Old Swedish *Palle*, probably originally an ethnic name meaning 'Pole'. **3.** French: habitational name from a place in Seine-et-Marne, probably originally derived from Latin *palus* 'post', 'stake' + suffix *-etum*. **4.** Jewish (from Belarus), Belorussian, and Ukrainian: occupational name for a distiller, from an eastern Slavic word meaning 'to burn' (Russian *palit*, Ukrainian *palyty*) + the Slavic noun suffix *-ej*.

GIVEN NAMES Jewish 4%. *Dror* (2), *Semen* (2), *Yakov* (2), *Hyman, Miriam, Yitzchok, Zalmon*.

Palfrey (135) English (chiefly Devon): metonymic occupational name for a man responsible for the maintenance and provision of saddle-horses, from Middle English *palfrey* 'saddle-horse' (Old French *palefrei*).

Palfreyman (109) English: occupational name for a man responsible for the maintenance and provision of saddle-horses (see PALFREY).

Palik (114) Slovak (**Palík**) and German: probably a variant of PAULICK.

GIVEN NAME German 4%. *Kurt*.

Palin (433) **1.** Welsh: Anglicized form of the Welsh patronymic *ap Heilyn* 'son of *Heilyn*', which is probably a derivative of a word meaning 'to serve at table'. **2.** English: habitational name from Palling in Norfolk or Poling in Sussex. These were named in Old English with the personal names *Pælli* and *Pāl* respectively, + *-ingas* 'followers of', 'dependants of'. **3.** French: unexplained.

FOREBEARS A Palin, also written Palen and Pallin, from the Poitou region of France, is documented in Quebec City in 1692, with the secondary surname Dabonville.

Palinkas (172) Hungarian (**Pálinkás**): from Hungarian *pálinka* 'brandy', 'spirit'; a metonymic occupational name for a producer of brandy or an innkeeper, or possibly a nickname for a heavy drinker.

GIVEN NAMES German 5%. *Horst, Klaus, Wilhelm*.

Palinski (101) Polish (**Paliński**): habitational name from a place named with the nickname *Pała* (see PALA) + the common surname ending *-iński*.

GIVEN NAMES Polish 9%. *Jacek, Kazimier, Witold*.

Paliotta (117) Italian: unexplained.

GIVEN NAMES Italian 25%. *Angelo* (2), *Giuseppe* (2), *Antonio, Arduino, Concetta, Domenic, Erminio, Gianna, Guiseppe*.

Paliwoda (115) Polish: nickname from *paliwoda* 'uninhibited reveler', 'harum-scarum'.

GIVEN NAMES Polish 29%. *Andrzej* (2), *Wieslaw* (2), *Casimir, Czeslaw, Irena, Iwona, Jadwiga, Krzysztof, Mieczyslaw, Pawel, Stanislaw, Stanistaw*.

Palk (129) English (Devon): unexplained.

Palka (435) Polish (**Pałka**): from *pałka* 'truncheon', 'club', used as a nickname applied either to a thin or stiff person, or to one who used a truncheon as a weapon.

GIVEN NAMES Polish 6%. *Stanislaw* (2), *Elzbieta, Krystyna, Krzysztof, Rafal, Ryszard, Zbigniew*.

Palko (626) **1.** Hungarian (**Palkó**): from a pet form of the personal name *Pál*, Hungarian form of PAUL. **2.** Slovak and Ukrainian: derivative of the personal name *Palo, Pavel* (see PAUL).

Palkovic (151) Serbian and northeastern Croatian (**Palković**): patronymic from *Palko*, Hungarian pet form of PAL (see PAUL).

Palkowski (116) Polish (**Pałkowski**): habitational name for someone from a place called Pałkowa (now in Belarus), named with *pałka* 'stave', 'stick'.

Pall (235) **1.** Indian: variant spelling of PAL 1. **2.** Hungarian (**Páll**): variant spelling of **Pál** (see PAL 2).

GIVEN NAMES Indian 9%. *Gurmukh* (2), *Sat* (2), *Ajay, Chandrakant, Dharam*.

Palla (215) **1.** Italian: from *palla* 'ball', a metonymic occupational name for a maker of cannon balls or a nickname for a player of ball games or someone with a rotund figure. **2.** Catalan: habitational name from any of several places of this name in Catalonia. **3.** Catalan and Galician: also probably a derivative of *palla* 'straw'. **4.** Hungarian: from the personal name *Pál* (see PAL). **5.** Indian (Gujarat): Muslim name of unknown meaning. **6.** Indian (Panjab): Sikh name, probably from Panjabi *pəllā* 'edge of a garment', 'support'.

GIVEN NAMES Indian 6%. *Bhanu* (2), *Prasad* (2), *Anila, Kavita, Suvarna.*

Palladino (1481) Italian (mainly southern): variant of PALADINO.

GIVEN NAMES Italian 14%. *Angelo* (12), *Carmine* (7), *Rocco* (6), *Antonio* (4), *Nunzio* (4), *Carlo* (2), *Cataldo* (2), *Giuseppe* (2), *Salvatore* (2), *Adamo, Aldo, Augostino.*

Pallante (248) Italian: of uncertain derivation; possibly from a rare medieval personal name (compare modern Greek *Pallantios*).

GIVEN NAMES Italian 16%. *Angelo* (2), *Romeo* (2), *Sal* (2), *Domenic, Enrico, Franco, Lorenzo, Nicola, Rocco, Salvatore, Vito.*

Pallares (192) **1.** Catalan (**Pallarès**): regional name for someone from Pallars, a region in the Catalan Pyrenees. **2.** Galician: habitational name from a place in Galicia named Pallares, from a derivative of Galician *palla* 'straw'.

GIVEN NAMES Spanish 46%. *Jesus* (5), *Luis* (5), *Carlos* (4), *Raul* (3), *Alfredo* (2), *Cristina* (2), *Fernando* (2), *Gerardo* (2), *Jaime* (2), *Jose* (2), *Manuel* (2), *Reyna* (2).

Pallas (449) **1.** German (of Slavic origin): from a pet form of the personal name *Pavel* or *Paweł*, respectively the Czech and Polish forms of PAUL, or from a Sorbian cognate. **2.** German (of Slavic origin): nickname for a small man, from Slavic *palac* 'thumb'. **3.** Irish: MacLysaght ascribes the origin of this surname in Ireland to the arrival there in the 15th century of a Lombard family of bankers named **de Palatio**. **4.** English: from Old French *palis, paleis* 'palisade', 'fence', hence a topographic name for someone who lived by a palisade or a metonymic occupational name for a maker of fences. **5.** English: possibly a metonymic occupational name for someone who worked at a palace (bishop's, archbishop's, or royal), from Old French, Middle English *palais, paleis*. **6.** English: metonymic occupational name for a worker at a straw stack, from Old French *paille* 'straw' + Middle English *hous* 'house'. **7.** Greek: ornamental name or nickname from Albanian *pallë* 'sword'. **8.** Catalan (**Pallàs**): variant spelling of **Pallars**, a regional name from the Catalan district of Pallars, in the Pyrenees.

Pallay (108) Hungarian: habitational name for someone from a place called Palló in the former Hungarian county of Ung, now part of Ukraine.

Paller (152) **1.** Altered form of **Pfaller**, a South German variant of PFAHLER. **2.** Hungarian (**Pallér**) and Jewish (from Hungary): occupational name or status name from Hungarian *pallér* 'foreman'.

Palleschi (205) Italian: nickname for a follower of the Medicis, from *palla* 'ball' (here referring to the balls on the coat-of-arms of the Medici family) + the suffix *-eschi* denoting descendants, or retainers or followers.

GIVEN NAMES Italian 15%; French 4%. *Tullio* (2), *Angelo, Antonio, Arduino, Attilio, Dino, Domenic, Giancarlo, Marco, Rinaldo; Achille, Armand.*

Pallett (210) English (Leicestershire): metonymic occupational name for a maker of palliasses (straw mattresses), from Middle English, Old French *pa(i)llet* 'heap of straw', 'straw mattress', a diminutive of Old French *paille* 'straw'.

Palley (156) **1.** Swiss French: from Old French *palet*, a term with a variety of meanings, any of which could have contributed to the surname: 'post', 'paling'; 'military exercise'; it also denoted an item of head armor. **2.** Variant spelling of PALEY.

Pallister (148) Northern English: occupational name for someone who made palings and fences, from an agent derivative of Old French *pal(e)is* 'palisade' (from Late Latin *palicium*, a derivative of *palus* 'stake', 'pole').

Pallo (221) Hungarian (**Palló**): from a pet form of the personal name *Pál*, Hungarian form of PAUL.

Pallone (324) Italian: augmentative of PALLA.

GIVEN NAMES Italian 13%. *Angelo* (2), *Rocco* (2), *Antonio, Carmel, Carmine, Domenic.*

Pallotta (407) Italian: from a derivative of PALLA.

GIVEN NAMES Italian 16%. *Antonio* (2), *Salvatore* (2), *Agostino, Angelo, Benedetto, Carmela, Carmine, Dino, Gino, Pasquale, Rocco, Saverio.*

Palm (2738) **1.** German: from a medieval personal name *Palmatius*, borne by a saint who died in 286. **2.** Northwest German: topographic name from Middle High German *palme, balme* 'pussy willow', the tree that traditionally provided the branches for Palm Sunday processions, or habitational name from a house distinguished by the sign of a palm tree. **3.** German: from a reduced and altered form of a personal name formed with Old High German *bald* 'bold', 'brave' as its first element. **4.** Swedish: ornamental name from *palm* 'palm tree'. **5.** Dutch: nickname for someone who had been on pilgrimage to the Holy Land (see PALMER), from *palm* 'palm tree'. **6.** Dutch (**Van Palm**): habitational name denoting someone from any of several minor places called Palm or Palme. **7.** Translation of French LAPALME.

GIVEN NAMES Scandinavian 4%. *Nels* (7), *Erik* (3), *Anders, Kerstin, Per, Sig, Sigfrid, Thor.*

Palma (2349) **1.** Spanish, Catalan, Galician, Portuguese, and southern Italian: habitational name from any of various places named or named with Palma, from Latin *palma* 'palm'. **2.** Portuguese: habitational name for someone from Parma in Italy.

GIVEN NAMES Spanish 28%; Portuguese 6%; Italian 6%. *Jose* (26), *Carlos* (16), *Luis* (15), *Juan* (9), *Manuel* (9), *Mario* (9), *Miguel* (8), *Rafael* (8), *Ruben* (8), *Alfredo* (7), *Alfonso* (6), *Francisco* (6); *Godofredo, Joaquim, Ligia, Wenceslao; Antonio* (8), *Angelo* (4), *Lorenzo* (2), *Palma* (2), *Caesar, Carlo, Ceasar, Cecilio, Clemente, Constantino, Dino, Domenic.*

Palmateer (466) Most probably a variant of English PARMENTER.

Palmatier (504) Most probably a variant of English PARMENTER.

Palmberg (150) **1.** Swedish: ornamental name composed of the elements *palm* 'palm tree' + *berg* 'mountain', 'hill'. **2.** Dutch and German: habitational name from a place so called near Aachen and another in Bavaria.

GIVEN NAME Scandinavian 4%; German 4%. *Kurt.*

Palme (115) Swedish: name adopted by a notable Swedish family in honor of their founder Palme Lyder (died 1630), a merchant who came to Ystad in Sweden from the Netherlands or Germany around 1607.

GIVEN NAMES Scandinavian 6%; German 6%. *Johan, Lennart; Bernd.*

Palmer (54798) **1.** English: from Middle English, Old French *palmer, paumer* (from *palme, paume* 'palm tree', Latin *palma*), a nickname for someone who had been on a pilgrimage to the Holy Land. Such pilgrims generally brought back a palm branch as proof that they had actually made the journey, but there was a vigorous trade in false souvenirs, and the term also came to be applied to a cleric who sold indulgences. **2.** Swedish (**Palmér**): ornamental name formed with *palm* 'palm tree' + the suffix *-ér*, from Latin *-erius* 'descendant of'. **3.** Irish: when not truly of English origin (see 1 above), a surname adopted by bearers of Gaelic **Ó Maolfhoghmhair** (see MILFORD) perhaps because they were from an ecclesiastical family. **4.** German: topographic name for someone living among pussy willows (see PALM 2). **5.** German: from the personal name *Palm* (see PALM 3).

Palmeri (756) Italian (mainly Sicily): variant of PALMIERI (see PALMIERE).

GIVEN NAMES Italian 18%. *Salvatore* (12), *Vito* (4), *Angelo* (3), *Nicolo* (3), *Gasper* (2), *Giuseppe* (2), *Luigi* (2), *Sal* (2), *Santo* (2), *Vincenzo* (2), *Antonio, Domenica.*

Palmero (154) Spanish: nickname from *palmero* 'pilgrim (to the Holy Land)', a derivative of *palma* 'palm'.
GIVEN NAMES Spanish 23%. *Juan* (3), *Francisco* (2), *Jorge* (2), *Jose* (2), *Santiago* (2), *Angel, Aurelio, Carlos, Eduardo, Idania, Jesus, Luis.*

Palmersheim (123) German: habitational name from Palmersheim in North Rhine-Westphalia.

Palmerton (208) English: possibly a habitational name from a lost or unidentified place.

Palmertree (171) Jewish (American): partly translated form of the Ashkenazic surname **Palmenbaum**, an ornamental name meaning 'palm tree' in German.

Palmeter (113) Probably a variant of English PARMETER (see PARMENTER).

Palmgren (246) Swedish: ornamental name composed of the elements *palm* 'palm tree' + *gren* 'branch'.
GIVEN NAMES Scandinavian 5%. *Berndt, Einer, Erik, Tor.*

Palmiere (101) Italian: from *palmiere* 'palmer', 'pilgrim', an agent derivative of *palma* 'palm', influenced by Old French *palmier* (see PALMER).
GIVEN NAMES Italian 23%. *Angelo* (2), *Dante* (2), *Enrico, Nicola, Salvatore, Vittorio.*

Palmieri (2252) Italian: patronymic or plural form of PALMIERE.
GIVEN NAMES Italian 24%. *Salvatore* (18), *Angelo* (12), *Mario* (12), *Armando* (9), *Antonio* (8), *Pasquale* (7), *Rocco* (7), *Dante* (6), *Aldo* (5), *Vito* (5), *Carlo* (3), *Domenic* (3), *Giuseppe* (3), *Marco* (3).

Palmiero (120) Italian: from the personal name *Palmiero*, a personal name derived from the vocabulary word *palmiere* 'palmer' (see PALMIERE).
GIVEN NAMES Italian 20%. *Angelo, Antonio, Guiseppe, Nicola, Palma, Sal, Vincenza.*

Palmisano (1138) Southern Italian: habitational name principally denoting someone from Palmi in Reggio Calabria but occasionally from any of the numerous places in southern Italy called Palma (with the ethnic suffix *-sano*).
GIVEN NAMES Italian 12%. *Angelo* (11), *Salvatore* (4), *Vito* (4), *Sal* (3), *Enrico* (2), *Gasper* (2), *Giuseppe* (2), *Augustino, Carmine, Cosmo, Dino, Domenico.*

Palmiter (284) Variant of English PARMENTER.

Palmore (877) Probably an altered spelling of PALMER or an Americanized spelling of South German BALMER.

Palmour (112) Variant of PALMORE.

Palmquist (1012) Swedish: ornamental name composed of the elements *palm* 'palm tree' + *quist*, an old or ornamental spelling of *kvist* 'twig'.

Palms (164) Dutch: variant of PALM 5.

Palo (489) **1.** Finnish: topographic name from *palo* 'field cleared by burning', also 'beacon', 'signal fire'. This name is found chiefly in Western Finland. **2.** Italian: habitational name from any of numerous places named with Palo, as for example Palo del Colle in Baria province or Portopalo in Syracuse province, Sicily.
GIVEN NAMES Finnish 4%. *Arvi, Arvo, Eero, Eino, Reijo, Tauno, Toini.*

Palomar (128) Spanish: habitational name from any of the numerous places named Palomar, from *palomar* 'dovecote', a derivative of *paloma* 'dove'.
GIVEN NAMES Spanish 52%. *Jose* (5), *Juan* (5), *Luis* (3), *Carlos* (2), *Francisco* (2), *Jesus* (2), *Miguel* (2), *Rafael* (2), *Ramon* (2), *Adriana, Alejandro, Alfredo.*

Palomares (440) Spanish: variant (plural) of PALOMAR.
GIVEN NAMES Spanish 57%. *Jose* (13), *Juan* (9), *Miguel* (7), *Luis* (5), *Salvador* (4), *Carlos* (3), *Javier* (3), *Jesus* (3), *Manuel* (3), *Maria Elena* (3), *Raul* (3), *Ruben* (3).

Palomarez (116) Spanish (**Palomárez**): variant spelling of PALOMARES.
GIVEN NAMES Spanish 35%. *Manuel* (3), *Candido* (2), *Jose* (2), *Lazaro* (2), *Arcadio, Audelio, Concepcion, Diocelina, Ignacio, Jorge, Juanita, Lourdes.*

Palomba (229) Italian: nickname from *palomba* 'female dove'.
GIVEN NAMES Italian 22%. *Rocco* (3), *Antonio* (2), *Mauro* (2), *Remo* (2), *Salvatore* (2), *Aniello, Carlo, Ciro, Corrado, Enrico, Giovanni, Giuseppe.*

Palombi (203) Italian: patronymic or plural form of PALOMBO.
GIVEN NAMES Italian 13%. *Carlo* (3), *Angelo* (2), *Concetta, Enzo, Rocco, Silvio.*

Palombo (677) Italian: from the medieval personal name *Palombo*, from *palombo* 'dove' (Late Latin *palumbus*). The surname may also be derived directly from the vocabulary word, as a nickname for a mild and inoffensive individual, or a metonymic occupational name for a keeper of pigeons, which were an important source of food in the medieval period.
GIVEN NAMES Italian 14%; French 4%. *Antonio* (3), *Rocco* (3), *Aldo* (2), *Carmine* (2), *Donato* (2), *Gennaro* (2), *Gino* (2), *Silvio* (2), *Amerigo, Angelo, Antonietta, Dante; Armand* (2), *Camille* (2), *Dominique* (2), *Emile.*

Palomino (827) Spanish: from *palomino* 'squab', 'young pigeon', a derivative of *paloma* 'dove'.
GIVEN NAMES Spanish 48%. *Jose* (21), *Carlos* (11), *Jesus* (11), *Juan* (10), *Manuel* (8), *Luis* (7), *Pedro* (6), *Ricardo* (6), *Armando* (5), *Julio* (5), *Domingo* (4), *Francisco* (4).

Palomo (731) Spanish: from *palomo* 'pigeon', 'dove'. Compare PALOMBO.
GIVEN NAMES Spanish 50%. *Jose* (24), *Juan* (13), *Armando* (11), *Carlos* (10), *Luis* (9), *Andres* (8), *Francisco* (8), *Jesus* (8), *Jorge* (8), *Manuel* (8), *Ramon* (6), *Domingo* (5).

Palone (147) Italian (Lazio): unexplained.

Palos (291) **1.** Spanish: habitational name from Palos de la Frontera, the port in Huelva from which it is said Columbus' ships set sail. **2.** Hungarian (**Pálos**): from the personal name *Pál*, Hungarian form of PAUL.
GIVEN NAMES Spanish 43%. *Jesus* (6), *Manuel* (6), *Juan* (5), *Humberto* (4), *Jose* (3), *Agustin* (2), *Carlos* (2), *Felipe* (2), *Francisco* (2), *Homero* (2), *Miguel Angel* (2), *Salvador* (2).

Pals (390) Dutch: from a Brabantine dialect pronunciation of *Pauls*, patronymic from the personal name PAUL.

Palser (126) English: variant of PALLISTER.

Palsgrove (117) Americanized form of German PFALZGRAF.

Palu (100) Hawaiian: unexplained.
GIVEN NAMES Hawaiian 4%. *Sione, Tevita.*

Palubicki (132) Polish (**Pałubicki**): habitational name for someone from Pałubice in Gdańsk voivodeship.
GIVEN NAMES French 5%. *Constant, Germain.*

Paluch (512) Polish: from *paluch* 'thumb' (augmentative of *palec* 'finger'), hence a nickname used to denote a small person or a dwarf, or possibly a descriptive nickname for someone with a deformed or missing thumb.
GIVEN NAMES Polish 8%. *Zbigniew* (2), *Andrzej, Casimir, Franciszek, Katarzyna, Krystyna, Lech, Ludwik, Pawel, Piotr, Slawomir, Zdzislaw.*

Paluck (158) Probably an altered spelling of PALUCH.

Palumbo (4001) Southern Italian (especially Neapolitan): dialect variant of PALOMBO.
GIVEN NAMES Italian 14%. *Salvatore* (18), *Angelo* (16), *Vito* (13), *Pasquale* (10), *Sal* (9), *Antonio* (7), *Rocco* (5), *Carmine* (3), *Domenic* (3), *Domenico* (3), *Franco* (3), *Giuseppe* (3).

Paluska (106) Czech or Slovak (**Paluška**): unexplained.

Paluzzi (184) Italian: from either a derivative of PALO, or of the personal name PAOLO, Sicilian *Paluzzu*.
GIVEN NAMES Italian 16%. *Angelo* (2), *Gino* (2), *Ezio, Giuseppe, Guido, Marco, Rocco, Tosca.*

Palys (139) Polish (**Pałys**): variant of **Pałysz**, a derivative of *pała* 'staff', 'club', 'truncheon', which was also used metaphorically as an unflattering nickname meaning 'blockhead'.
GIVEN NAMES Polish 11%. *Andrzej, Henryk, Krzysztof, Michalina, Thadeus.*

Pam (111) **1.** Hispanic (Mexican): unexplained. **2.** English: unexplained.

Pamer (179) **1.** German (Tyrol): local form of BAUMER. **2.** Dutch: variant of PALMER.
GIVEN NAMES German 6%. *Erna, Florian, Ignatz.*

Pamperin (184) **1.** German: variant of **Bamberin**, a nickname from a feminine form of *bamber* denoting a short thickset man. **2.** German: habitational name from a place in Mecklenburg named Pamprin.

Pamplin (358) English: possibly from a pet form of an Old French personal name, *Pamphile*, from Greek *Pamphilos*, the name of a 4th-century martyr, from *pan* 'all' + -*philos* 'dear to', 'beloved of'.

Pan (1739) **1.** Chinese 潘: from the place name Pan, which existed in the state of Wei during the Zhou dynasty. Bi Gonggao, fifteenth son of the virtuous duke Wen Wang, was granted a state named Wei when the Zhou dynasty came to power in 1122 BC (see FENG 1). Bi Gonggao in turn granted the area called Pan to one of his sons, whose descendants eventually adopted Pan as their surname. This name is also Romanized as **Poon**, **Pun**, and **Pon**. **2.** Korean: There are two Chinese characters for this surname; only one of them, however, is common enough to warrant treatment here. There are three clans which use this character: the Kisŏng (also called the Kŏje), the Kwangju, and the Namp'yŏng. The founding ancestors of these clans were Koryŏ (918–1392) figures, and it is widely believed that they were related. **3.** Spanish and southern French (Occitan): metonymic occupational name for a baker or a pantryman, from Spanish and Occitan *pan* 'bread' (Latin *panis*). **4.** English and Dutch: metonymic occupational name for someone who cast pans, from Middle English, Middle Dutch *panne* 'pan'. **5.** Jewish (eastern Ashkenazic): from Polish, Ukrainian, Yiddish *pan* 'lord', 'master', 'landowner', hence a nickname for a haughty person. **6.** Perhaps also an Americanized spelling or translation of German **Pfann** (North German PANN).

GIVEN NAMES Chinese/Korean 36%. *Wei* (10), *Ying* (8), *Yong* (7), *Tao* (6), *Hong* (5), *Hui* (5), *Ming* (5), *Dong* (4), *Jing* (4), *Ning* (4), *Rong* (4), *Chen* (3).

Panagakos (127) Greek: from a pet form of the personal name *Panagiotis* 'All Holy' (an epithet of the Virgin Mary; see PANAGOS). The patronymic suffix -*akos* is particularly associated with the Mani Peninsula in southwestern Peloponnese.

GIVEN NAMES Greek 16%. *Ilias* (2), *Demetrios, Panagiotis, Panos, Pericles, Tassos.*

Panagopoulos (172) Greek: from the personal name PANAGOS + the patronymic ending -*poulos* . This ending occurs chiefly in the Peloponnese; it is derived from Latin *pullus* 'nestling', 'chick'.

GIVEN NAMES Greek 26%. *Angelos* (2), *Kostas* (2), *Nikolaos* (2), *Andreas, Antonios, Athanasia, Dimitrios, Eleni, Ioannis, Iraklis, Konstantions, Spiros.*

Panagos (168) Greek: from a short form of the personal name *Panagiotis* 'All Holy' (an epithet of the Virgin Mary).

GIVEN NAMES Greek 7%. *Christos, Panagiota, Panos, Sotirios, Spiros.*

Panarello (132) Italian: from a diminutive of PANARO.

GIVEN NAMES Italian 22%. *Salvatore* (3), *Sal* (2), *Albino, Alfonso, Cosimo, Domenico, Emilio, Fiore, Marcello.*

Panarese (107) Italian: habitational name for someone from a place named Panaro (from Latin *panarium* 'bread basket'), from an adjectival form of the place name.

GIVEN NAMES Italian 5%. *Delfino, Genaro, Silvia.*

Panariello (101) Italian: apparently a diminutive of PANARO.

GIVEN NAMES Italian 17%. *Angelo, Antonio, Carmine, Filippo, Salvatore.*

Panaro (282) Italian: metonymic occupational name for a baker, from Latin *panarium* 'bread basket'.

GIVEN NAMES Italian 13%. *Fausto, Gino, Nicola, Nino, Rocco, Salvatore, Vito.*

Panas (245) **1.** Greek: reduced form of any of the surnames derived from the personal name *Panagiotis* (see PANAGOS). **2.** Greek: occupational name for a cloth merchant, from Greek *pani* or *panna* 'cloth' + the occupational suffix -*as*. **3.** Ukrainian and Polish: from the personal name *Panas*, a Ukrainian pet form of *Afanasy*, a derivative of Greek *Athanasios* (see ATHANAS).

GIVEN NAMES Greek 5%. *Tassos* (2), *Konstantinos, Nikos, Spiro.*

Panasuk (137) Ukrainian: from the personal name *Panas*, a Ukrainian pet form of *Athanasios* (see ATHANAS), + the patronymic suffix -*uk*.

Pancake (383) Translation of German **Pfannkuch(e)**, North German **Pannkoke**, **Pankauke**, or Dutch **Pannekoek(e)**, metonymic occupational names for someone who made and sold pancakes.

Panchal (161) Indian (Gujarat): Hindu (Vishwakarma) name, probably from Sanskrit *pāñcāla* 'association of five guilds' (from *pañca* 'five').

GIVEN NAMES Indian 93%. *Dilip* (4), *Pravin* (3), *Ramesh* (3), *Ajay* (2), *Anil* (2), *Harish* (2), *Harshad* (2), *Jayesh* (2), *Madhu* (2), *Prakash* (2), *Rajendra* (2), *Ramanlal* (2).

Panciera (194) Italian: from *panciera* denoting a piece of armor for the stomach, a derivative of *pancia* 'belly', 'paunch'.

GIVEN NAMES Italian 6%. *Dino* (2), *Aldo, Angelo, Antonio, Primo, Romeo, Silvio.*

Pancoast (512) Probably a variant of English PENTECOST.

Pandey (211) Indian (northern states): Hindu (Brahman) name, Hindi *pāṇḍe*, from Sanskrit *paṇḍita* 'scholar'. Compare PANDIT. In Hindi *pāṇḍe*, as well as being a family name, also denotes a Brahman engaged in either of two traditional Brahman occupations: teaching and cooking.

GIVEN NAMES Indian 91%. *Rajiv* (5), *Ram* (4), *Ramesh* (4), *Ashok* (3), *Chandra* (3), *Kailash* (3), *Manish* (3), *Rajesh* (3), *Rakesh* (3), *Ravi* (3), *Vivek* (3), *Arun* (2).

Pandit (194) Indian (northern states): Hindu (chiefly Brahman) name, from Sanskrit *paṇḍita* 'scholar'. Compare PANDEY.

GIVEN NAMES Indian 93%. *Vijay* (7), *Milind* (4), *Ashok* (3), *Ajay* (2), *Anand* (2), *Anurag* (2), *Baburao* (2), *Benoy* (2), *Bharti* (2), *Hemant* (2), *Himanshu* (2), *Pradeep* (2).

Pando (436) Spanish, Portuguese, and Galician: habitational name from any of several places in Portugal, Galicia, and Asturies named Pando (the Asturian form being **Pandu**), from Spanish, Galician and Portuguese *pando* in the sense 'hollow', 'depression'.

GIVEN NAMES Spanish 41%. *Jose* (6), *Jesus* (5), *Raul* (5), *Carlos* (4), *Fernando* (4), *Jaime* (4), *Eugenio* (3), *Felipe* (3), *Jose Antonio* (3), *Pedro* (3), *Ramon* (3), *Roberto* (3).

Pandolfi (328) Italian: patronymic or plural form of PANDOLFO.

GIVEN NAMES Italian 22%. *Mario* (3), *Aldo* (2), *Dante* (2), *Alfonso, Alfonzo, Antonio, Arsenio, Carmela, Domenic, Francesco, Livio, Luca, Orlando, Rafael, Renato, Rico, Rocco, Santi, Siro.*

Pandolfo (290) Italian (Campania and Tuscany): from the Lombardic personal name *Pandulf*, composed of the Germanic elements *bandwo*- 'banner' + *wulfa* 'wolf'.

GIVEN NAMES Italian 21%. *Angelo* (3), *Mario* (3), *Giuseppe* (2), *Salvatore* (2), *Antonio, Carmine, Dino, Elio, Enrico, Luigi, Massimo, Nicola, Nino.*

Pandya (461) Indian (Gujarat): Hindu (Brahman) name, from Sanskrit *paṇḍita* 'scholar'. See also PANDEY, PANDIT.

GIVEN NAMES Indian 93%. *Bharat* (6), *Ramesh* (6), *Dilip* (5), *Jayesh* (5), *Raj* (5), *Dinesh* (4), *Jagdish* (4), *Mahesh* (4), *Manoj* (4), *Rajesh* (4), *Ashok* (3), *Ashvin* (3).

Pane (457) **1.** Italian: from *pane* 'bread', applied as a metonymic occupational name for a baker or as a nickname meaning 'a good thing'. **2.** Dutch: from a pet form of the personal name *Frans*, Dutch form of FRANCIS. **3.** Variant of English PAINE.

GIVEN NAMES Italian 23%. *Angelo* (4), *Antonio* (3), *Salvatore* (2), *Aldo, Carmela, Carmine, Ciro, Concetta, Enzo, Guiseppe, Mario* (3), *Armando, Claudio, Macario, Remigio.*

Panebianco (234) Italian: metonymic occupational name for a baker of fine breads, from *pane* 'bread' + *bianco* 'white'.

GIVEN NAMES Italian 24%. *Alessandro* (2), *Candido* (2), *Mario* (2), *Rosario* (2), *Salvatore* (2), *Vincenzo* (2), *Antonio, Caesar, Ignazio, Livio, Luigi, Sal, Serafino.*

Panek (1146) **1.** Czech (**Pánek**) and Polish: from a pet form of the personal name *Pankrać* (see PANKRATZ) or *Stípán* (see STEVEN). **2.** Polish: nickname from a diminutive of Polish *pan* 'master', used either affectionately, in the sense 'little master', or contemptuously, in the sense 'lordling'. **3.** Polish: from a pet form of the personal name *Panas*, a vernacular form of *Atanazy*, a derivative of Greek *Athanasios* (see ATHANAS).

GIVEN NAMES Polish 6%. *Zofia* (3), *Tadeusz* (2), *Andrzej*, *Beata*, *Bronislawa*, *Eugeniusz*, *Janina*, *Jerzy*, *Jolanta*, *Jozef*, *Kazimierz*, *Krystyna*.

Panella (499) Italian: from a diminutive of PANE.

GIVEN NAMES Italian 11%. *Rocco* (4), *Dante* (2), *Sante* (2), *Alessandro*, *Antonio*, *Carlo*, *Clementina*, *Fabrizio*, *Giovanna*, *Pellegrino*, *Remo*, *Silvio*.

Panelli (122) Italian: from a diminutive of PANE.

GIVEN NAMES Italian 22%. *Gino* (4), *Giulio* (2), *Renzo* (2), *Gabriella*, *Iolanda*, *Ivano*, *Reno*.

Panepinto (287) Italian: from a compound of *pane* 'bread' + *pinto* generally meaning 'painted', 'flecked' (i.e. 'mouldy'?), or possibly 'bad' (like Calabrian *pintu*), hence a derogatory nickname for a baker.

GIVEN NAMES Italian 15%. *Carlo* (3), *Salvatore* (3), *Angelo* (2), *Gino*, *Lia*, *Lorenzo*.

Panetta (593) Italian: from a diminutive of PANE.

GIVEN NAMES Italian 22%. *Rocco* (8), *Angelo* (5), *Cosimo* (4), *Salvatore* (4), *Ettore* (2), *Luigi* (2), *Marco* (2), *Pasquale* (2), *Sal* (2), *Aldo*, *Amedeo*, *Antonio*.

Panetti (104) Italian: from a diminutive of PANE.

GIVEN NAMES Italian 8%. *Nunzi* (2), *Angelo*, *Ettore*.

Panfil (235) **1.** Polish and Ukrainian: from the Slavic personal name *Panfil*, *Pamfil*, a derivative of Greek *Pamphilos* (see PAMPLIN). **2.** Jewish (from Poland): adoption of the Polish name.

GIVEN NAMES Polish 4%. *Andrzej*, *Zofia*.

Pang (1613) **1.** Chinese 庞: from the name of a village called Pang, which was granted to a descendant of Bi Gonggao, the 15th son of the virtuous duke Wu Wang, whose magnanimous rule led to the establishment of the Zhou dynasty in 1122 BC. Later descendants adopted the name of the village as their surname. **2.** Chinese 逄: from the name of a prince of the Yin dynasty (1401–1122 BC), Pang Boling. **3.** Chinese 彭: variant of PENG. **4.** Korean: there are five Chinese characters for this surname; only one, however, is common enough to warrant treatment here. The clan associated with this character is the Onyang Pang. The founding ancestor of this clan was a Tang Chinese named Pang Chi, who lived in Hunan province, China, until his migration to Shilla in 669. There is a gap in the records after Pang Chi. The ancestor who settled in the Onyang area was named Pang Un. He served the early Koryŏ Wang Dynasty faithfully, so when he retired to the Onyang area, local geographic features were named after him and many of his

descendants continued to live there, hence the name of their clan. **5.** Variant of German BANG.

GIVEN NAMES Chinese/Korean 20%. *Wai* (5), *Chi* (3), *Kam* (3), *Kwai* (3), *Siu* (3), *Sun* (3), *Yuan* (3), *Zhen* (3), *Chan* (2), *Huiling* (2), *Hyun* (2), *Ling* (2).

Pangallo (162) Southern Italian: from the Greek personal name *Pangalos*, composed of the elements *pan* 'all' + *kallos* 'beautiful', i.e. 'most beautiful'.

GIVEN NAMES Italian 25%. *Rocco* (8), *Marco* (3), *Carmelo*, *Marcellina*, *Salvatore*.

Panganiban (185) Filipino: unexplained. Compare PANGILINAN.

GIVEN NAMES Spanish 39%. *Pilar* (3), *Carmelita* (2), *Edgardo* (2), *Erlinda* (2), *Ernesto* (2), *Miguel* (2), *Rafael* (2), *Ramon* (2), *Ricardo* (2), *Romulo* (2), *Alicia*, *Antero*; *Antonio*, *Dario*, *Lia*, *Romeo*.

Pangborn (418) English: habitational name from Pangbourne in Berkshire, named with the Old English personal name *Pǣga* + -*inga* 'followers or dependants of' + *burna* 'creek'.

Pangburn (634) English: variant of PANGBORN.

Pangelinan (113) Filipino: unexplained. Compare PANGANIBAN, PANGILINAN. This name is also found in Mexico.

GIVEN NAMES Spanish 28%. *Jesus* (3), *Ignacio* (2), *Joaquin* (2), *Jose* (2), *Adriano*, *Alejandro*, *Eloy*, *Elvira*, *Francisco*, *Juan*, *Manuel*, *Marisa*.

Pangilinan (221) Filipino: unexplained. Compare PANGANIBAN, PANGELINAN.

GIVEN NAMES Spanish 35%. *Jose* (5), *Nestor* (3), *Angel* (2), *Francisco* (2), *Lauro* (2), *Mario* (2), *Roberto* (2), *Adoracion*, *Alberto*, *Amelita*, *Andres*, *Angelito*.

Pangle (403) German: altered form of **Bangel**, of unexplained origin, or of **Pangerl**, which is from a pet form of an old personal name, *Banager*, related to Old High German *bannan* 'to ban' or *ban* 'order', 'command'.

Paniagua (745) Spanish and Portuguese (**Paniágua**): status name for a servant who worked for his board (*pan* 'bread' and *agua* 'water') and lodging.

GIVEN NAMES Spanish 51%. *Jose* (22), *Juan* (13), *Carlos* (11), *Miguel* (10), *Luis* (8), *Armando* (7), *Jorge* (7), *Manuel* (7), *Raul* (6), *Francisco* (5), *Enrique* (4), *Guadalupe* (4).

Paniccia (219) Italian: from *paniccia* denoting a type of flat bread, hence a metonymic occupational name for a baker of such bread, or possibly a nickname.

GIVEN NAMES Italian 37%; Spanish 4%. *Angelo* (3), *Carlo* (3), *Egidio* (2), *Lorenzo* (2), *Luigi* (2), *Rocco* (2), *Umberto* (2), *Ambrogio*, *Antonio*, *Arduino*, *Dino*, *Domenic*; *Mario* (5), *Americo* (3), *Adolfo*, *Armando*, *Fernando*, *Julio*.

Panich (120) Serbian (**Panić**): patronymic from the personal name *Pane*, *Pano*, pet forms of *Panteleon* or *Pankracij*.

GIVEN NAMES South Slavic 19%. *Drago*, *Dragoljub*, *Marko*, *Ratko*, *Zarko*; *Boris* (2), *Dmitry*, *Gennadiy*, *Sofya*.

Panico (551) Italian: **1.** metonymic occupational name for a grower or seller of millet, from *panico* 'millet'. **2.** Italianized form of Serbian PANICH. **3.** from the Germanic personal name *Panico*.

GIVEN NAMES Italian 14%. *Salvatore* (5), *Carmine* (3), *Gennaro* (3), *Sal* (3), *Alfonse* (2), *Carmela*, *Ciro*, *Luciano*, *Nino*, *Vittorio*.

Panik (152) Polish, Czech, and Slovak (**Pánik**): nickname from a diminutive of *pan*, *pán* 'master'. Compare PANEK.

Panitz (104) Germanized form of Jewish (from Ukraine) **Panich**, a nickname from Ukrainian *panych* 'young nobleman'.

GIVEN NAME Jewish 8%. *Yitzchok*.

Panjwani (110) Hindu and Muslim name found among people from Sind, Pakistan, meaning '(descendant) of Panju'. *Panju* (probably from Sanskrit *pañca* 'five') appears to be the shortened form of an ancestral name.

GIVEN NAMES Muslim 70%; Indian 18%. *Abdul* (4), *Karim* (3), *Ahmed* (2), *Amin* (2), *Amirali* (2), *Javed* (2), *Mahmood* (2), *Nizar* (2), *Sadruddin* (2), *Shaukat* (2), *Siraj* (2), *Abdul Majid*; *Vishnu* (2), *Ajit*, *Anil*, *Bakul*, *Mahesh*, *Manju*, *Mohan*, *Nandlal*, *Narain*, *Prakash*, *Reshma*.

Pankau (184) German (of Slavic origin): variant of PANKOW.

Panke (116) German: variant of PAHNKE.

GIVEN NAMES German 8%. *Gerhardt*, *Kurt*, *Otto*.

Pankey (1181) Americanized form of German PAHNKE.

Pankiewicz (140) Polish: patronymic from PANEK.

GIVEN NAMES Polish 15%. *Krzysztof* (2), *Feliks*, *Janina*, *Jerzy*, *Katarzyna*, *Zbigniew*.

Panko (391) **1.** Hungarian (**Pankó**): from a pet form of the personal name *Pongrác*. Compare PANKRATZ. **2.** Ukrainian and Slovak: from the personal name *Panko*, a pet form of various names starting with *Pa-*. **3.** Ukrainian: nickname from a diminutive of Ukrainian *pan* 'lord', 'landlord'.

Pankonin (207) Polish: from *pan koni* 'Mr Horses', 'the horse man', a nickname for someone who was the owner of a great number of horses, with the possessive suffix -*in*.

Pankow (595) German (of Slavic origin): habitational name from a Slavic place name (several in Brandenburg) derived from the Slavic element *pank*, *penk* 'swamp' + -*ow* 'place' (German -*au*).

GIVEN NAMES German 4%. *Bernd* (3), *Dieter*, *Erwin*, *Gerhardt*, *Kurt*.

Pankowski (206) Polish: habitational name for someone from Panki in Częstochowa voivodeship or possibly from places called

Panków or Pankowo, now in Ukraine, named with PANEK.

GIVEN NAMES Polish 9%. *Dariusz, Franciszek, Jadwiga, Jozef, Zbigniew, Zdzislaw.*

Pankratz (1023) German: from the medieval personal name *Pankratz*, the vernacular form of Latin *Pancratius* (Greek *Pankratios*, from *pankratēs* 'all-in wrestler', from *pan* 'all', 'every' + *kratein* 'to conquer, subdue', re-analysed by early Christians as meaning 'Almighty' and thus a suitable epithet of Christ). The name was borne by a 4th-century Christian martyr in Rome, hence its popularity as a personal name in the Middle Ages.

Pann (130) **1.** North German: from Middle Low German *pann* 'pan', 'roof tile', hence a metonymic occupational name for a maker of either of these items. **2.** Altered spelling of German **Pfann**, a metonymic occupational name for a maker of pans, cognate with 1, from Middle High German *pfanne, phanne* 'pan', or a topographic name for someone living in low lying terrain, in a pan. *Pfann* sometimes denoted a salt panner.

GIVEN NAMES German 6%. *Hans* (2), *Dieter, Juergen.*

Pannebaker (118) North German: occupational names for a maker of roof tiles or a tiler, from Middle Low German *panne* 'pan', 'tile' + *backer* 'baker'. Compare PENNYPACKER.

Pannell (2625) English (Sussex): **1.** from Middle English *panel* 'panel', hence a metonymic occupational name for a maker of panels, for wainscoting or saddles for example. **2.** perhaps a variant of PARNELL.

Panneton (107) French: from a double diminutive of *pain* 'bread', hence a metonymic occupational name for a baker or someone who sold bread.

GIVEN NAMES French 24%. *Andre* (2), *Marcel* (2), *Armand, Colette, Octave, Raymonde, Serge, Yves.*

Pannier (193) **1.** French: occupational name for a baker or a pantryman, from an agent derivative of Old French *pain* 'bread'. **2.** French (Normandy): metonymic occupational name for a basket-maker or seller, from *panier* 'basket'.

GIVEN NAMES French 6%. *Dominique, Patrice.*

Panning (264) German: **1.** perhaps a habitational name from Panningen near Venlo. **2.** from a short form of an old personal name related to Old High German *bannan* 'to ban', *ban* 'order', 'command'.

GIVEN NAMES German 7%. *Armin, Eldor, Erwin, Kurt, Siegfried.*

Panno (150) Italian: from *panno* 'cloth', 'clothes', 'linen', hence probably a metonymic occupational name for someone who made cloth or clothes.

GIVEN NAMES Italian 15%. *Angelo* (2), *Domenic, Domenico, Enrico, Gino, Salvatore, Umberto, Vincenza.*

Pannone (298) Italian: probably from an augmentative of PANNO.

GIVEN NAMES Italian 14%. *Angelo* (2), *Antonio* (2), *Attilio, Carlo, Carmela, Carmine, Gennaro, Gino, Marino, Salvatore, Vito.*

Pannullo (147) Italian: probably from a derivative of PANNO.

GIVEN NAMES Italian 10%. *Antonietta, Pasquale, Vincenza.*

Panos (641) Greek: from a pet form of the personal name *Panayiotis* 'All Holy', a derivative of *Panagia* (from *pan* 'all' + *hagia* 'holy'), an epithet of the Virgin Mary (see PANAGOS).

GIVEN NAMES Greek 7%. *Costas* (3), *Anastasios, Andreas, Constantine, Demos, Dimitrios, Euripides, Joannis, Kosta, Labros, Lampros, Sotirios.*

Panozzo (323) Italian: from a derivative of PANE.

GIVEN NAMES Italian 12%. *Angelo* (2), *Romeo* (2), *Silvano* (2), *Silvio* (2), *Aldo, Attilio, Ennio, Geno, Gildo, Italo.*

Pant (116) Indian (Uttar Pradesh, Uttaranchal): Hindu (Brahman) name of unknown meaning.

GIVEN NAMES Indian 54%. *Ramesh* (3), *Ranjan* (3), *Rajiv* (2), *Ajay, Anandi, Anup, Anupama, Arun, Ashish, Bala, Bhanu, Bharat.*

Pantages (112) Americanized form of Greek **Pantazis**, from a personal name meaning 'may you live for ever', from *panta* 'always' + *zis* 'may you live' (an inflected form of the verb *zein* 'to live').

Pantaleo (388) Italian: from a personal name, Greek *Pantaleōn*, from *pas* 'all' (genitive *pantos*) + *leōn* 'lion'. In the altered form *Panteleēmōn* (from *pas* 'all' (genitive *pantos*) + *eleēmōn* 'merciful'), it was the name borne by a saint said to have been martyred under Diocletian Nicomedia. He is the patron of physicians, having apparently been one himself. He was honored in the Eastern Church as early as the 5th century, but his cult did not reach the Western Church until the 11th century, when he was adopted as the patron saint of Venice. In the 14th century the Italian name *Pantaleone* came to be used for a character in the Harlequinade, a foolish old Venetian, and in some later cases the surname may have arisen as a nickname for someone who played the part of this character. It was from his prototypical costume that the term *pantaloon* came to be used to denote a type of loose-fitting breeches, whence the modern English word *pants*.

GIVEN NAMES Italian 15%. *Vito* (4), *Edvige* (2), *Gasper* (2), *Nunzio* (2), *Angelo, Antonio, Domenic, Enrico, Giacomo, Nicola, Romeo.*

Pantaleon (145) Spanish (**Pantaleón**): from the personal name *Pantaleón*, Greek *Panteleōn* (see PANTALEO).

GIVEN NAMES Spanish 52%; Italian 7%. *Pedro* (5), *Jose* (3), *Manuel* (3), *Mario* (3), *Juan* (2), *Aida, Alberto, Andres, Angel, Angelina, Angelita, Armando; Antonio, Eliseo, Federico, Leonardo, Lucio, Romeo.*

Pantalone (257) Italian: variant of **Pantaleone** (see PANTALEO).

GIVEN NAMES Italian 14%. *Salvatore* (2), *Alfonse, Angelo, Carmine, Domenico, Fiore, Marco, Pasquale, Rocco, Sal, Vito.*

Pantano (489) Italian and Spanish: habitational name from any of numerous places in Italy and Spain named with *pantano* 'marsh', 'bog'.

GIVEN NAMES Italian 24%. *Salvatore* (9), *Angelo* (5), *Carlo* (4), *Sal* (4), *Biagio* (2), *Giuseppe* (2), *Santo* (2), *Aldo, Alessandra, Augostino, Carmelo, Carmine.*

Pantel (156) **1.** South German: from a pet form of the personal name *Pantaleon*, vernacular variant *Pantlen* (see PANTALEO). **2.** North German: from a Middle Low German word meaning 'panther' (see PANTER).

Panter (727) **1.** German: habitational name for someone who lived at a house distinguished by the sign of a panther, Middle High German *panter* (see PANTHER 1). **2.** North German: occupational name for a mortager or pawn broker, from a contracted form of *Pfandherr*. **3.** English (mainly Northamptonshire) and Scottish: occupational name for a servant in charge of the supply of bread and other provisions in a monastery or large household, Middle English *pan(e)ter* (Old French *panetier*).

Panther (345) **1.** German: variant of PANTER 1. **2.** English: variant of PANTER 3. **3.** English: possibly a habitational name from a house bearing the sign of a panther. In England this surname is mainly found in Northamptonshire.

Pantle (130) **1.** German: variant of PANTEL 1. **2.** Probably an altered spelling of South German **Pfandl**, a variant of **Pfann(e)** (see PANN 2).

Pantoja (997) Spanish: habitational name from a Pantoja in Toledo.

GIVEN NAMES Spanish 55%. *Jose* (37), *Jesus* (15), *Manuel* (15), *Juan* (14), *Carlos* (13), *Francisco* (8), *Rafael* (8), *Javier* (7), *Luis* (7), *Roberto* (7), *Salvador* (7), *Alfredo* (6).

Panton (277) English (mainly Cambridgeshire): habitational name from a place in Lincolnshire called Panton, from Old English *pamp* 'hill', 'ridge' or *panne* 'pan' + *tūn* 'enclosure', 'settlement'.

Pantone (108) **1.** Italian (Basilicata): perhaps from an inflected form of the Germanic personal name *Panto*, a variant of *Pando*. **2.** Dutch: unexplained.

GIVEN NAMES Italian 8%; Dutch 7%. *Giuseppe, Vincenza; Dirk* (3).

Pantuso (177) Italian: probably a nickname from Calabrian *pantu* 'stupid' or *pandu* 'myopic'.

GIVEN NAMES Italian 8%. *Amedeo, Carmine, Gildo.*

Panza (499) **1.** Italian and Spanish: nickname for a fat or greedy man, from *panza* 'belly', 'paunch' (in Italian a variant of *pancia*). **2.** Southern Italian (Naples): possibly a habitational name from Panza, a district of Forio.
GIVEN NAMES Italian 19%; Spanish 5%. *Prisco* (4), *Domenico* (3), *Rocco* (3), *Sabino* (3), *Salvatore* (3), *Mario* (2), *Angelo, Antonio, Domenic, Elio, Ennio, Fiorino, Gaetano; Humberto, Juan, Julio, Libia, Sancho.*

Panzarella (337) Italian: from a diminutive of PANZA.
GIVEN NAMES Italian 16%. *Angelo* (5), *Salvatore* (2), *Santo* (2), *Antonio, Attilio, Carlo, Nino, Saverio.*

Panzarino (133) Italian: from a diminutive of PANZA.
GIVEN NAMES Italian 37%. *Angelo* (4), *Domenico* (3), *Mario* (2), *Rocco* (2), *Vito* (2), *Fedele, Rino, Saverio.*

Panzer (748) **1.** German: metonymic occupational name for an armorer, from Middle High German *panzier* 'mailcoat' (from Old French *pancier* 'armor for the stomach', 'body armor', from Late Latin). **2.** Jewish (Ashkenazic): ornamental name from German *Panzer* 'armor' (see 1).
GIVEN NAMES German 4%. *Erwin* (2), *Otto* (2), *Hans, Kurt, Wolfgang.*

Panzera (133) Italian: variant of PANCIERA.
GIVEN NAMES Italian 21%. *Salvatore* (3), *Angelo, Carmelo, Filippo, Guido, Sandro, Santo.*

Panzica (233) Italian: nickname for a paunchy or pot-bellied person, from a derivative of PANZA 1 or from Sicilian *panzicu*.
GIVEN NAMES Italian 14%; Spanish 4%. *Augustino, Carmela, Leonardo, Palma, Salvatore, Saverio, Vincenzo; Carlos* (2), *Diego.*

Pao (280) **1.** Chinese: variant of BAO. **2.** Portuguese (**Pão**): metonymic occupational name for a baker, from *pão* 'bread'.
GIVEN NAMES Chinese 19%. *Hsien* (2), *Chen, Ching-I, Feng, Jia Ming, Jung, Ling, Lung, Minhui, Peiling, Po, Shu-Min.*

Paola (163) Italian: **1.** habitational name from Paola in Cosenza province. **2.** from the female personal name *Paola*, feminine form of *Paolo*, Italian equivalent of PAUL.
GIVEN NAMES Italian 13%. *Francesco* (2), *Angelo, Antonio, Pasquale, Pasqualina, Silvio.*

Paolantonio (108) Italian: from a compound personal name composed of PAOLO and ANTONIO.
GIVEN NAMES Italian 20%. *Vito* (3), *Silvio* (2), *Angelo, Dino, Rocco, Sal.*

Paolella (191) Italian: from a pet form of the female personal name PAOLA.
GIVEN NAMES Italian 19%. *Salvatore* (3), *Gennaro* (2), *Angelo, Antonio, Filomena, Giovanni, Nicola.*

Paoletta (115) Italian: from a pet form of the female personal name PAOLA.
GIVEN NAMES Italian 20%. *Angelo* (2), *Carmela, Carmine, Giovanni, Pasquale, Rocco, Sal, Vito.*

Paoletti (451) Italian: patronymic from *Paoletto*, a pet form of PAOLO.
GIVEN NAMES Italian 14%. *Antonio* (3), *Aldo* (2), *Domenic* (2), *Amadeo, Carlo, Carmela, Dino, Enzo, Ercole, Gianni, Gino, Giovanni.*

Paoli (449) Italian and Corsican: patronymic or plural form of PAOLO.
GIVEN NAMES Italian 15%; Spanish 7%. *Emilio* (2), *Ettore* (2), *Guido* (2), *Rafael* (2), *Antonino, Antonio, Attilio, Giovanni, Leopoldo, Lido, Luciano, Marco, Pasquale, Piera, Valentino; Angel, Celso, Clodomiro, Domingo, Juliano, Julio, Luis, Luz.*

Paolillo (327) Italian: from a pet form of PAOLO.
GIVEN NAMES Italian 18%. *Salvatore* (6), *Ciro* (3), *Marco* (2), *Antonio, Gaetano, Gennaro, Orazio, Pasquale, Stefano.*

Paolini (644) Italian: patronymic or plural form of PAOLINO.
GIVEN NAMES Italian 15%. *Angelo* (3), *Vito* (3), *Antonio* (2), *Camillo* (2), *Pasquale* (2), *Rocco* (2), *Salvatore* (2), *Agostino, Aldo, Carlo, Carmine, Deno.*

Paolino (460) Italian: from the personal name *Paolino*, a pet form of PAOLO.
GIVEN NAMES Italian 13%. *Angelo* (4), *Carmine* (3), *Rocco* (3), *Carmelina, Emelio, Enrico, Gaetano, Gilda, Pasquale, Vito.*

Paolo (178) Italian: from the personal name *Paolo*, Italian equivalent of PAUL.
GIVEN NAMES Italian 22%. *Antonio* (4), *Domenic* (4), *Pasquale* (2), *Angelo, Erasmo, Pasqualino, Silvestro, Vittoria.*

Paolucci (653) Italian: from *Paoluccio*, a pet form of PAOLO.
GIVEN NAMES Italian 17%. *Salvatore* (3), *Carlo* (2), *Carmine* (2), *Domenic* (2), *Nicola* (2), *Sante* (2), *Umberto* (2), *Aldo, Angelo, Arcangelo, Carmelina, Domenico.*

Paone (664) Italian: variant of PAVONE.
GIVEN NAMES Italian 24%. *Angelo* (8), *Domenic* (4), *Rocco* (4), *Sal* (4), *Carmela* (2), *Ottavio* (2), *Antonino, Carmello, Carmelo, Carmine, Ciriaco, Concetto.*

Paonessa (299) Italian: from *Pavonessa*, a feminine pet form of PAVONE.
GIVEN NAMES Italian 19%. *Sal* (3), *Angelo, Antonio, Cosimo, Fausto, Franco, Guido, Maurizio, Rafael, Rosario, Salvatore, Vito.*

Pap (122) Hungarian: from *pap* 'priest', variant of PAPP.
GIVEN NAMES Hungarian 13%. *Geza* (2), *Jeno* (2), *Arpad, Attila, Csaba.*

Papa (1981) **1.** Italian: nickname from *papa* 'father', 'priest', 'pope'. In southern Italy it is generally a nickname for someone thought to resemble a priest, or in some cases for the illegitimate child of a priest, but in the North it is more often a nickname

meaning 'pope', denoting a vain or pompous man. In Calabria it also means 'uncle'. **2.** Greek: shortened form of any of various names beginning with *papas* 'priest', for example PAPAGEORGIOU 'priest George'. Compare PAPAS. In the Eastern Church priests are allowed to marry and have children. **3.** French: from a dialect variant of French PAPE. **4.** Dutch: variant of PAPPERT. **5.** Hungarian: probably from the old secular personal name *Pápa*, but in some cases possibly a habitational name from a place called Pápa in Veszprém county, or some other place similarly named.
GIVEN NAMES Italian 28%; Spanish 4%. *Angelo* (11), *Salvatore* (10), *Mario* (8), *Rosario* (6), *Domenic* (5), *Alfonso* (4), *Eduardo* (4), *Antonio* (3), *Basilio* (3), *Carmelo* (3), *Emidio* (3), *Ettore* (2), *Gino* (2), *Marco* (2), *Pasquale* (2), *Pellegrino* (2), *Pietro* (2), *Ricardo* (2), *Rodolfo* (2); *Salvador* (3), *Joselito* (2), *Nicanor* (2), *Rolando* (2).

Papadakis (184) Greek: patronymic from *papas* 'priest' + the patronymic–diminutive ending *-akis*. The *-akis* patronymic is particularly common in Crete, where it was adopted massively in the 19th century.
GIVEN NAMES Greek 18%. *Spiros* (4), *Constantine* (2), *Spiro* (2), *Antigoni, Ioannis, Kostas, Panagiota, Spyros, Stavros, Toula.*

Papadopoulos (617) Greek: patronymic meaning 'son of the priest', from *papas* 'priest' + the patronymic ending *-poulos*, an ending that occurs mainly in the Peloponnese, derived from Latin *pullus* 'nestling', 'chick'. Greek Orthodox priests, unlike their Roman Catholic counterparts, were allowed to marry and have children. This is the commonest surname in Greece.
GIVEN NAMES Greek 38%. *Dimitrios* (8), *Christos* (6), *Panagiotis* (6), *Costas* (4), *Demos* (4), *Vasilios* (4), *Anastasios* (3), *Andreas* (3), *Athanasios* (3), *Kimon* (3), *Lazaros* (3), *Pavlos* (3).

Papageorge (237) Americanized form of Greek PAPAGEORGIOU.
GIVEN NAMES Greek 11%. *Christos, Demetre, Despina, Dimitrios, Eleni, Euripides, Fotios, Marios, Spiros, Themis.*

Papageorgiou (100) Greek: from the genitive case of the status name *Papagiorgios* 'George the priest'.
GIVEN NAMES Greek 47%. *Dimitrios* (3), *Christos* (2), *Demetrios* (2), *Dimitris* (2), *Andreas, Anthi, Antigoni, Apostolos, Demetris, Eleftherios, Eleni, Ioannis.*

Papale (193) Southern Italian: status name from Greek *Papales*, a shortened form of PAPALIA or PAPALEO.
GIVEN NAMES Italian 18%. *Angelo* (2), *Antonio* (2), *Agostino, Carmelo, Enrico, Franco, Gabriella, Marino, Nicola.*

Papaleo (195) Italian: status name from Greek *papa* 'priest', 'father' (see PAPA) + the personal name *Leo.*

GIVEN NAMES Italian 24%. *Rocco* (2), *Valentino* (2), *Angelo, Carlo, Carmela, Carmelo, Cosimo, Domenico, Luciano, Orlando, Rocci, Ronaldo, Tito.*

Papalia (176) Italian and Greek: status name meaning 'Elias the priest', from Italian *papa* 'priest', 'father' (see PAPA) or Greek *papas* 'priest' + the personal name *Elia* (see ELIAS).

GIVEN NAMES Italian 22%; French 4%. *Rocco* (4), *Angelo, Francesco, Nazareno, Orazio, Salvatore; Alphonse.*

Papandrea (211) Italian and Greek: from Italian *papa* 'priest', 'father' (see PAPA) or Greek *papas* 'priest' + the personal name *Andrea* (see ANDREAS).

GIVEN NAMES Italian 18%. *Rocco* (4), *Sal* (3), *Pasquale, Salvatore.*

Papania (172) Italian (Sicily): from *papa* 'priest', 'father' (see PAPA) + the personal name *Ania.*

Paparella (221) Italian: nickname from *paperella* 'little duck'.

GIVEN NAMES Italian 13%. *Domenica, Domenico, Giulio, Ignazio, Lucio, Luigi, Rosaria, Vito.*

Paparo (115) Italian (Sicilian): nickname from Sicilian *paparu* 'young gander', 'gosling'.

GIVEN NAMES Italian 29%; Jewish 6%. *Angelo* (2), *Vito* (2), *Domenic, Domenico, Raffaele, Saverio, Ugo, Vicenzo, Vincenza; Meyer* (2).

Papas (404) Greek: status name meaning 'priest' or, more usually, a reduced form of any of the numerous Greek patronymics starting with *Papa-* (see for example PAPAGEORGIOU). In the Eastern Church priests are allowed to marry and have children, so there is nothing unusual about this term having become a family name.

GIVEN NAMES Greek 11%. *Constantine* (4), *Costas* (3), *Andreas* (2), *Spiros* (2), *Emilios, Georgios, Ourania, Rigas, Sotiris, Spiro, Takis, Tasos.*

Papay (181) Hungarian (**Pápay**): habitational name for someone from any of various places called Pápa in western Hungary.

GIVEN NAMES Hungarian 4%. *Bela* (2), *Kalman.*

Papazian (385) Armenian: patronymic from Turkish *papaz* '(Orthodox) priest', 'father', from Greek *papas* (see PAPAS).

GIVEN NAMES Armenian 32%. *Ara* (5), *Aram* (4), *Armen* (3), *Anahit* (2), *Karapet* (2), *Shavarsh* (2), *Tigran* (2), *Vahan* (2), *Agop, Akop, Araxi, Armine.*

Papciak (108) Polish: nickname from Polish dialect *papciak* 'pulp', 'mash', also used to denote a kind of porridge or gruel.

GIVEN NAMES Polish 12%. *Zygmunt* (2), *Casimir, Piotr, Stanislaw.*

Pape (2753) **1.** English (mainly northern), North German, Dutch, and French: nickname for someone with a severe or pompous manner or perhaps a pageant name for someone who had played the part of a pope or priest, from Middle English *pope* or Old French *pape* 'pope', Middle Low German, Middle Dutch *pape* 'priest', Old French *pape* 'pope'. Compare PAPA. **2.** German: nickname from a baby word for 'father'. Compare BAAB.

Papen (105) **1.** North German: variant of PFAFF, from *pfaffe* 'priest', 'cleric'. **2.** German: variant of PAPE.

Papendick (114) Altered form of German **Papendieck**, a habitational name from a place so called in northern Germany.

GIVEN NAME German 5%. *Helmuth.*

Papenfus (115) Dutch (common in South Africa): variant of PAPENFUSS.

Papenfuss (266) Dutch and North German: nickname from Middle Low German *pape* 'priest' (genitive *papen*) + *fuss* 'foot' (standardized form of Middle Low German *vōt*, found in Low German names as *-fot(h)*).

GIVEN NAMES German 5%. *Kurt* (2), *Erhart, Gunter, Otto.*

Paper (156) **1.** English: unexplained. In part at least, the name appears to be of Dutch or French (possibly Huguenot) origin, perhaps a translation of **Papier**, a metonymic occupational name for a clerk or scribe, or perhaps a respelling of PAPE. **2.** Swiss German: variant spelling of **Papper**, probably from baby talk. Compare PABEN.

Papes (105) **1.** Dutch: patronymic from an old Germanic personal name, *Papo* (see PAPIN 2). **2.** Czech, Slovak, and Slovenian (**Papeš, Pápež, Papež**): ironic nickname for someone who behaved or looked like the Pope, from the vocabulary word *papež*. Compare German PABST.

Papesh (203) Americanized form of Czech or Slovenian **Papeš** or **Papežš**, Slovak **Pápež**, or German **Papesch**, a nickname from *papež* 'pope' (see PAPES).

Papetti (115) Italian: from the personal name *Papetto*, a pet form of *Papo* (see PAPI).

GIVEN NAMES Italian 17%. *Dino* (3), *Salvatore* (3).

Papi (107) Italian: **1.** patronymic from a pet form of the personal name *Iacopo, Giacopo*, Italian equivalents of JACOB. **2.** variant of PAPA 1. **3.** Hungarian: habitational name for someone from any of various places named with *pap* 'priest'.

GIVEN NAMES Italian 27%. *Caesar* (2), *Gino* (2), *Giuseppe* (2), *Aldo, Carlo, Dario, Enzo, Giovanni, Piero, Secondo, Tullio.*

Papier (110) Jewish (Ashkenazic) and German: metonymic occupational name for a paper maker or merchant, from German *Papier* 'paper'.

GIVEN NAMES Jewish 5%; German 4%. *Mayer, Yechiel; Wolfgang.*

Papillion (113) English: from Old French *papillon* 'butterfly' (Latin *papilio*), possibly applied as a nickname for a rash or inconstant person.

Papin (279) **1.** French: from Old French *paper* 'to munch or eat' (Late Latin *pappare*, in origin a nursery word); as a nickname its sense is uncertain, but possibly it referred to a glutton. The word *papin* also had the meaning 'pap', 'pulp'. **2.** Dutch: from a pet form of an old Germanic personal name, *Papo.*

FOREBEARS A Papin from the Maine region of France is documented in Montreal in 1665.

GIVEN NAMES French 4%. *Lucien, Pierre.*

Papineau (636) French: from a pet form of PAPIN.

FOREBEARS A Papineau from the Poitou region of France is recorded in Montreal in 1699, with the secondary surname DESLAURIERS. Another, also from Poitou, is documented in Rivière-des-Prairies, Quebec, in 1704.

GIVEN NAMES French 6%. *Andre* (3), *Adelard, Alain, Armand, Colette, Jean Guy, Michel, Normand.*

Papini (137) Italian: patronymic from the personal name *Papino*, a pet form of *Papo* (see PAPI).

GIVEN NAMES Italian 9%. *Carlo, Gino, Luca, Umberto.*

Papka (121) North German or Dutch: variant of PAPKE.

Papke (648) North German (also **Päpke**) and Dutch: nickname from a diminutive of Low German *pape*, Dutch *paepe* 'pope'. Compare POPE.

GIVEN NAMES German 5%. *Kurt* (4), *Bernhard, Erwin, Hans, Otto, Willi.*

Papp (1527) **1.** German (Bavaria, Tyrol) and Dutch: from Middle High German *pap* 'baby food' and Dutch *pap* 'porridge', 'pap', hence perhaps a nickname denoting someone who had lost his teeth or subsisted on a meagre diet. **2.** Hungarian: from *pap* 'priest', probably an occupational name for someone in the service of a priest or a nickname for a pious person.

GIVEN NAMES Hungarian 10%. *Laszlo* (10), *Zoltan* (8), *Geza* (7), *Istvan* (6), *Gabor* (4), *Miklos* (4), *Tibor* (3), *Arpad* (2), *Denes* (2), *Imre* (2), *Laszio* (2), *Attila.*

Pappa (245) Southern Italian: **1.** nickname for a greedy or voracious person, from *pappa* 'he eats', from *pappare* 'to munch or gobble', or from a short form of a compound of this verb + a noun, as for example PAPPALARDO, *Pappacoda* (*coda* 'tail'). **2.** possibly a variant of PAPA.

Pappalardo (740) Italian: from *pappa* 'he eats' (see PAPPA) + *lardo* 'lard', 'bacon fat'; a nickname for a glutton or someone who pretended to observe religious fasts but ate meat in secret.

GIVEN NAMES Italian 24%; Spanish 4%. *Angelo* (9), *Sal* (6), *Salvatore* (5), *Santo* (4), *Nunzio* (3), *Soccorso* (3), *Domenic* (2), *Gaetano* (2), *Rosaria* (2), *Amedeo, Annamarie, Antonio, Emilio, Rosario; Carlos, Enrique, Ramon.*

Pappan (136) Swiss French: probably a variant of **Papin**, a derivative of *paper* 'to eat gluttonously', which had the sense in Old French of 'baby's pap', or alternatively of **Papon**, from Old French and Occitan *papon* 'grandfather'.

Pappano (102) Italian (Campania): unexplained.
GIVEN NAMES Italian 12%. *Dante, Rino.*

Pappas (6524) Greek: variant spelling of PAPAS 'priest'.
GIVEN NAMES Greek 5%. *Constantine* (9), *Christos* (7), *Spiro* (6), *Demetrios* (5), *Dimitrios* (5), *Costas* (4), *Lambros* (4), *Spero* (4), *Spiros* (4), *Spyros* (4), *Alexandros* (3), *Anastasios* (2).

Pappert (192) **1.** Dutch: nickname from a derivative *pap* 'porridge', 'pap' (see PAPP). **2.** German: from a Germanic personal name formed with *badu* 'battle' + *berht* 'bright', 'famous'.

Paprocki (425) Polish: habitational name for someone from any of the many places called Paproć, Paprotki, Paprotno, or Paproty, named with *paproć* 'fern'. In some cases it may be a topographic name for someone who lived in a place where ferns grew in abundance.
FOREBEARS The surname Paprocki, borne by several Polish noble families, has been recorded since the 15th century. Bartosz Paprocki (1540–1614) was a heraldry expert, historian, and poet, and author of the armorial *Herby rycerstwa polskiego* "Coats of arms of Polish knighthood".
GIVEN NAMES Polish 4%. *Jacek* (2), *Andrzej, Grzegorz, Irena, Ryszard.*

Papson (134) Americanized form of Greek PAPAS 'priest', with the English patronymic ending -son.
GIVEN NAME Greek 4%. *Haralambos.*

Papst (106) German: nickname meaning 'pope'. Compare PABST.

Papuga (122) Polish: nickname from Polish *papuga* 'parrot'.
GIVEN NAME Polish 4%. *Marzanna.*

Papworth (138) English: habitational name from Papworth in Cambridgeshire, named with the Old English personal name *Papa* + *worþ* 'enclosure'. In England, the name still occurs chiefly in Cambridgeshire and adjoining counties.

Paquet (550) French: see PAQUETTE.
FOREBEARS A Paquet, also known as Pasquier and Pasquet, from the Poitou region of France, is recorded in Quebec City in 1668. Secondary surnames associated with Paquet are LAVALLEE and LARIVIERE.
GIVEN NAMES French 20%. *Marcel* (3), *Philippe* (3), *Camille* (2), *Luc* (2), *Rejean* (2), *Aime, Alain, Alphonse, Armand, Camil, Cecile, Damien.*

Paquette (3926) French: **1.** from the personal name *Pa(s)quet*, a pet form of PASCAL. **2.** from Old French *pacquet* 'bundle (of faggots)', a diminutive of *paque* 'parcel', hence a metonymic occupational

name for a gatherer or seller of firewood or kindling. In North America, spellings of surnames in -*ette* are not normally feminine, but reflects the practice of sounding the final -*t*, which is not the usual practice in European French.
GIVEN NAMES French 12%. *Lucien* (14), *Normand* (14), *Andre* (12), *Marcel* (12), *Armand* (11), *Cecile* (6), *Emile* (6), *Yvon* (6), *Adrien* (5), *Jacques* (4), *Adelard* (3), *Gilles* (3).

Paquin (1628) French: from a pet form of *Paque, Pasque*, a female personal name taken from *Pasques* 'Easter'. Compare PASCAL.
FOREBEARS A Paquin from Normandy, France is documented in Château Richier, Quebec, in 1676.
GIVEN NAMES French 13%. *Armand* (11), *Andre* (5), *Normand* (5), *Pierre* (5), *Jacques* (3), *Laurent* (3), *Colette* (2), *Emile* (2), *Julien* (2), *Marcel* (2), *Adrien, Armande.*

Para (325) **1.** Polish: nickname for a vigorous person, from *para* 'breath'. **2.** Spanish and Asturian-Leonese: habitational name from either of the places called Para, in Asturies and Burgos province.
GIVEN NAMES Polish 6%; Spanish 4%. *Andrzej, Casimir, Jacek, Ludwika, Ryszard, Zofia; Alba, Elena, Gustavo, Jaime, Jose, Josefina, Manuel, Marciano, Rigoberto, Santos, Tomas.*

Parada (674) Galician, Asturian-Leonese, and Portuguese: habitational name from any of numerous places called Parada, predominantly in Galicia, but also in Asturies, Lleón, and northern Portugal.
GIVEN NAMES Spanish 48%. *Jose* (33), *Luis* (12), *Manuel* (11), *Carlos* (10), *Juan* (8), *Ana* (5), *Julio* (5), *Alfonso* (4), *Armando* (4), *Jesus* (4), *Mario* (4), *Rafael* (4).

Paradee (149) Americanized spelling of French PARADIS.

Paradine (111) English (Buckinghamshire): unexplained.

Paradis (2418) French: **1.** from a learned variant of Old French *pareis* 'Paradise', Greek *paradeisos* (see PARADISE). As a toponym this was applied to verdant places, and it is quite common as a place name in Nord and Normandy; the surname, therefore, can be a topographic or habitational name. **2.** topographic name from Old French *parvis* 'square in front of a church'.
FOREBEARS A Paradis from the Perche region of France is documented in Quebec City in 1653.
GIVEN NAMES French 13%. *Armand* (10), *Fernand* (6), *Lucien* (5), *Normand* (4), *Raoul* (4), *Adelard* (3), *Andre* (3), *Laureat* (3), *Marcel* (3), *Philippe* (3), *Serge* (3), *Adrien* (2).

Paradise (1515) **1.** English and Scottish: from Old French *paradis*, denoting someone who lived by a park or pleasure garden, especially one attached to a monastery,

nunnery, or cathedral. **2.** Americanized form of French PARADIS or Italian PARADISO. **3.** Americanized form of a Greek family name such as **Paradissis, Paradissiadis**, or **Paradissopoulos**, from a personal name based on ancient Greek *paradeisos* 'paradise', 'pleasure garden', from Persian *pairidaesa* 'royal park'. **4.** Americanized form of German **Paradies**, a German topographic name and house name and an ornamental Ashkenazic Jewish name, from Middle High German *paradīs(e)*, German *Paradies* 'paradise', 'park', 'pleasure garden' (see 1 and 3).

Paradiso (614) Italian: from *paradiso* 'Paradise', applied as a topographic name for someone living in a verdant place where flowers grew in abundance, or near a pleasure garden, or from the same word used as a personal name.
GIVEN NAMES Italian 17%. *Angelo* (9), *Rocco* (6), *Carmine* (3), *Vito* (3), *Aldo, Antonino, Antonio, Biagio, Carlo, Domenico, Donato, Giovanni.*

Paradowski (191) Polish: **1.** habitational name for someone from either Paradów in Leszno voivodeship or Paradowo (also Poradowo) in Konin voivodeship. **2.** nickname for a swaggerer, from *paradować* 'to swagger', from *parada* 'parade', 'display', + the common surname suffix -*ski*.
GIVEN NAMES Polish 8%; German 4%. *Jacek, Jozef, Zigmont; Alois* (2), *Florian* (2).

Parady (243) **1.** Hungarian (**Párády**): habitational name for someone from Parád in Hever county, a place famous for the medicinal qualities of its foul-smelling mineral water. **2.** Americanized spelling of French PARADIS.
GIVEN NAME French 4%. *Emile.*

Paramo (240) Spanish and Galician (**Páramo**): habitational name from any of the numerous places named Paramo, in particular those in the provinces of Lugo (Galicia), Léon, Palencia, and Burgos, from *páramo* 'wasteland', 'bare plateau'.
GIVEN NAMES Spanish 52%. *Jose* (6), *Manuel* (6), *Jorge* (4), *Jesus* (3), *Arturo* (2), *Enrique* (2), *Felipe* (2), *Fidel* (2), *Javier* (2), *Jose Antonio* (2), *Juan* (2), *Margarita* (2).

Paramore (492) English: nickname from Middle English *paramour* 'lover' (Old French *par amour* 'with love').

Paras (449) probably Spanish or Asturian-Leonese, habitational name from a place named with the plural of PARA.
GIVEN NAMES Spanish 17%. *Armando* (3), *Fidel* (3), *Jose* (3), *Ricardo* (3), *Francisco* (2), *Mario* (2), *Modesto* (2), *Aida, Alberto, Alipio, Amado, Augusto.*

Paratore (301) Italian: occupational name for a fuller, from Late Latin *parator* (genitive *paratoris*) or Sicilian dialect *paratoris*.
GIVEN NAMES Italian 22%. *Salvatore* (4), *Paco* (2), *Vito* (2), *Alfredo, Bernardo, Carmelo, Dalia, Filippo.*

Parcel (204) English and Welsh: variant of PURCELL.

Parcell (498) English and Welsh: variant of PURCELL.

Parcells (192) English and Welsh: variant of PURCELL.

Parchem (107) East German: habitational name from a place in Mecklenburg called Parchim.

Parcher (254) Probably an altered form of German **Bartscher**, South German **Partscher**, an occupational name for a barber, from Middle High German *bart* 'beard' + *scher(er)* 'shearer', 'cropper' (from *scheren* 'to shear').

Parchman (428) German (**Parchmann**): habitational name for someone from Parchim in Mecklenburg, or Parchen or Parchau near Genthin.

Parchment (151) English: metonymic occupational name for a maker or seller of parchment (Old French *parcheminier*). This name is common in Jamaica.

Parco (108) **1.** Spanish, Portuguese, and Italian: nickname from *parco* 'thrifty', 'frugal', 'sober', 'moderate'. **2.** Italian: habitational name from any of various places named with *parco* 'game park'.
GIVEN NAMES Spanish 15%; Italian 10%. *Salvador* (2), *Abelardo, Candido, Delfin, Fernando, Luzviminda, Ruben, Sergio*; *Salvatore* (2), *Cosimo, Idolo.*

Parde (172) French (**Pardé**): from the oath *par Dieu* 'by God', hence a nickname for someone who used the expression to excess.

Pardee (1063) Probably a variant spelling of PARDY (see PERDUE).

Parden (162) English: variant spelling of PARDON.

Pardi (335) **1.** Italian: patronymic or plural form of PARDO. **2.** Hungarian: habitational name for someone from a place called Pardi, in Pest county.
GIVEN NAMES Italian 14%. *Angelo* (3), *Guido* (2), *Salvatore* (2), *Amedeo, Dino, Domenic, Giustino, Italo, Livio, Marco, Remo, Rocco.*

Pardini (345) Italian (mainly Liguria): patronymic from *Pardino*, a pet form of the personal name PARDO.
GIVEN NAMES Italian 20%; Spanish 5%. *Aldo* (2), *Angelo* (2), *Geno* (2), *Gino* (2), *Antonio, Arrigo, Carlo, Dino, Franca, Guido, Mario, Orlando, Rico, Silvio*; *Carlota* (2), *Julio* (2), *Luis, Manuel.*

Pardo (1754) **1.** Spanish and Portuguese: nickname for someone with tawny hair, from *pardo* 'dusky', 'brown', 'dark gray', (from Latin *pardus* 'leopard'). **2.** Italian: from a personal name, a variant of the Lombardic personal name **Bardo** (see BARDO). **3.** Italian and Greek: from the Greek personal name *Pardos* 'leopard', 'cheetah'.
GIVEN NAMES Spanish 36%. *Jose* (37), *Luis* (20), *Carlos* (14), *Juan* (11), *Julio* (11),

Manuel (11), *Raul* (9), *Pedro* (8), *Angel* (7), *Jaime* (7), *Jorge* (7), *Mario* (7).

Pardoe (280) English: variant of PERDUE.

Pardon (288) **1.** English (Norfolk): from Middle English *pardun, pardon* 'pardon', a metonymic occupational name for a pardoner, a person licensed to sell papal pardons or indulgences. **2.** German: either a cognate of 1 (also for a sexton), from Old French *pardon* 'pardon', or perhaps a nickname from Middle Low German *bardūn*, Middle High German *purdūne* 'pipe' (instrument), 'tenor' (voice).

Pardue (2284) English: variant of PERDUE.

Parduhn (101) German: variant of PARDON.
GIVEN NAMES German 10%. *Ewald, Kurt.*

Pardun (151) German: variant of PARDON.

Pardy (210) English (Dorset): variant of PERDUE.

Pare (1232) French (**Paré**): occupational name for someone who finished cloth, from the past participle of *parer* 'to prepare'. This is a frequent name in ME.
FOREBEARS A Paré from the Périgord region of France is recorded in Quebec City in 1653.
GIVEN NAMES French 19%. *Andre* (12), *Henri* (5), *Laurent* (5), *Normand* (5), *Fernand* (4), *Alphonse* (3), *Clermont* (3), *Elphege* (3), *Alain* (2), *Benoit* (2), *Gaston* (2), *Girard* (2).

Paredes (2126) Spanish, Galician and Portuguese: topographic name for someone who lived in a lean-to built against the wall of a larger building, from Spanish *pared*, Portuguese and Galician *parede* '(house) wall'. Servants often lived in buildings of this sort outside manor houses, and masons constructed huts of this kind on the site of their labors, making temporary use of the walls of the new building. There are also numerous places named with this word, and the surname may also be a habitational name from any of these.
GIVEN NAMES Spanish 50%. *Jose* (50), *Juan* (34), *Carlos* (28), *Manuel* (25), *Luis* (24), *Miguel* (20), *Jorge* (15), *Francisco* (13), *Mario* (12), *Pedro* (12), *Roberto* (12), *Ernesto* (11); *Antonio* (14), *Lorenzo* (3), *Clemente* (2), *Julieta* (2), *Leonardo* (2), *Marco Tulio* (2), *Angelo, Cecilio, Cesario, Clementina, Dante, Eliseo.*

Paredez (155) Variant spelling of Spanish, Galician and Portuguese PAREDES.
GIVEN NAMES Spanish 48%. *Eleno* (3), *Manuel* (3), *Armando* (2), *Carlos* (2), *Jose* (2), *Juan* (2), *Lupe* (2), *Pedro* (2), *Alfredo, Benito, Blanca, Cruz.*

Pareja (153) Spanish: habitational name from Pareja in Guadalajara province.
GIVEN NAMES Spanish 54%. *Carlos* (5), *Juan* (5), *Eduardo* (4), *Alfredo* (3), *Fernando* (3), *Jaime* (3), *Pedro* (3), *Ana* (2), *Esteban* (2), *Guillermo* (2), *Jorge* (2), *Jose* (2).

Parekh (549) Indian: variant of PARIKH.
GIVEN NAMES Indian 86%. *Dilip* (10), *Bharat* (8), *Rajesh* (8), *Ramesh* (8), *Mahendra* (7),

Prakash (7), *Ketan* (6), *Ashok* (5), *Dinesh* (5), *Kiran* (5), *Kirit* (5), *Kishor* (5).

Parella (176) **1.** Catalan: variant spelling of the habitational name PERELLA. **2.** Catalan: apparently also a habitational name, possibly from *pareja* 'pair', as a medieval land measurement denoting the area of land that could be plowed by a pair of oxen in one day. **3.** Italian: unexplained.
GIVEN NAMES Italian 22%. *Gaetano* (2), *Armando, Carmine, Gilberto, Mario, Rocco, Salvatore.*

Parent (4356) **1.** English and French: from Middle English, Old French *parent* 'parent', 'relative', hence a nickname for someone who was related to an important member of the community. **2.** English and French: nickname for someone of striking or imposing appearance, from Middle English, Old French *parent* 'notable', 'impressive'.
FOREBEARS A Parent from the Saintonge region of France is documented in Quebec City in 1654.
GIVEN NAMES French 10%. *Marcel* (7), *Normand* (7), *Fernand* (6), *Pierre* (5), *Rosaire* (5), *Andre* (4), *Armand* (4), *Gilles* (4), *Laurent* (4), *Alain* (3), *Chanel* (3), *Donat* (3).

Parente (1062) **1.** Italian: from the medieval personal name *Parente*, which originated as a reduced form of *Bonparente*, meaning 'good parent'. **2.** Portuguese: from Portuguese *parente* 'relative'.
GIVEN NAMES Italian 20%; Spanish 7%. *Antonio* (10), *Rocco* (8), *Angelo* (6), *Nicola* (5), *Nunzio* (4), *Vito* (4), *Armando* (3), *Pasquale* (3), *Amedeo* (2), *Americo* (2), *Carlo* (2), *Domenic* (2), *Emilio* (2), *Fiore* (2); *Gaeton* (3), *Jose* (3), *Aires, Alfonso, Alicia, Efren, Julio.*

Parenteau (909) French: diminutive of PARENT.
FOREBEARS A Parenteau from the Saintonge region of France, is documented in Quebec City in 1673, with the secondary surname LAFONTAINE.
GIVEN NAMES French 14%. *Andre* (4), *Marcel* (4), *Normand* (3), *Camille* (2), *Cecile* (2), *Florent* (2), *Paul Emile* (2), *Pierre* (2), *Yvan* (2), *Aime, Armand, Aurel.*

Parenti (615) Italian (mainly Emilia-Romagna and Tuscany): from a patronymic or plural form of PARENTE.
GIVEN NAMES Italian 13%. *Angelo* (4), *Rocco* (3), *Dante* (2), *Elio* (2), *Olindo* (2), *Pasquale* (2), *Vito* (2), *Alfonse, Antonella, Dino, Gino, Giulio.*

Paret (107) **1.** French: unexplained. **2.** Catalan: topographic name from Catalan *paret* 'wall' (compare PAREDES). **3.** Catalan: variant of **Peret**, diminutive of the personal name PERE, or from *paret*, a diminutive of *pare* 'father'.
GIVEN NAMES French 9%; Spanish 8%. *Andre, Philippe, Pierre*; *Joaquin* (2),

Alberto, Caridad, Eduardo, Eugenio, Lourdes, Patricio, Wilfredo.

Paretti (108) Italian: from a short form of **Gasparetti**, from a pet form of the personal name *Gaspare*.

GIVEN NAME Italian 5%. *Ettore.*

Parfait (156) French: nickname from Old French *parfit* 'complete(d)' (see PARFITT). This name is found chiefly in LA.

GIVEN NAMES French 8%. *Germaine, Homere, Jacques.*

Parfitt (430) English: from Middle English *parfit* 'fully trained', 'well versed' (Old French *parfit(e)* 'complete(d)', from Latin *perfectus*, past participle of *perficere* 'to finish or accomplish'), hence a nickname, probably originally denoting an apprentice who had completed his period of training. (The change from -er- to -ar- was a characteristic phonetic development in Old French and Middle English.) The modern English word *perfect* is a learned recoinage from Latin.

Parga (166) Galician: habitational name from any of various places named Parga, especially in Lugo province, Galicia.

GIVEN NAMES Spanish 49%. *Jose* (9), *Luis* (4), *Rodolfo* (4), *Ruben* (3), *Alfredo* (2), *Angel* (2), *Carlos* (2), *Eduardo* (2), *Guillermo* (2), *Manuel* (2), *Adriano, Alejandro; Antonio* (3).

Parham (4882) English (London): habitational name from places in Suffolk and Sussex, named in Old English with *pere* 'pear' + *hām* 'homestead'.

Pari (114) Southern Italian: either from *pari* 'equal', 'same', or from a short form of *Paribene* or some other omen name formed with this element.

GIVEN NAMES Italian 16%. *Angelo, Carmine, Geno, Luigi, Modesto, Nevio.*

Parikh (1246) Indian (Gujarat, Rajasthan): Hindu (Bania, Vania) and Jain name meaning 'assayer' in Gujarati, from Sanskrit *parīkṣaka* 'examiner'. The Oswal and Porwal Banias have clans called Parekh.

GIVEN NAMES Indian 92%. *Dilip* (16), *Ashok* (13), *Bharat* (11), *Sanjay* (10), *Girish* (9), *Kirit* (9), *Mahesh* (9), *Sudhir* (9), *Amit* (8), *Jayesh* (8), *Nilesh* (8), *Paresh* (8).

Parillo (367) Italian: from a derivative of PARI.

GIVEN NAMES Italian 9%. *Domenic* (2), *Antonio, Carlo, Carmel, Gaetano, Guido, Luciano.*

Paris (5856) **1.** French, English, and German: from the medieval personal name *Paris*, which is actually an Old French variant of **Patrice** (see PATRICK), but which became associated with the name of the Trojan prince *Paris* in Homer's Iliad. **2.** French, English, and German: habitational name from the French city of Paris or a nickname denoting someone who had Parisian connections, for example through trade. **3.** Catalan (**París**): from a reduced form of the personal name *Aparici*, which

was given to children born on the Feast of the Epiphany, 6th January (see APARICIO). **4.** Hungarian (**Páris**): from the personal name *Páris* or *Párizs*.

FOREBEARS The first bearer of the surname Paris documented in North America was in fact from Paris; he is recorded in 1668 in Quebec City. Another, from the Gascon region of France, was at Chambly, Quebec, in 1671, with the secondary surname CHAMPAGNE. Others came from Normandy, France.

Parise (933) Italian: from the personal name *Paris, Paride*, of Greek origin. A connection with the city of Paris (Italian *Parigi*, Latin *Parisium*) is unlikely.

GIVEN NAMES Italian 8%. *Rocco* (5), *Salvatore* (4), *Caesar* (2), *Luigi* (2), *Aldo, Angelo, Dante, Donato, Lucio, Sal.*

Pariseau (568) French: from a pet form of PARIS 1.

GIVEN NAMES French 9%. *Armand* (2), *Gilles* (2), *Michel* (2), *Adrien, Donat, Luc, Marcel, Normand, Paul Andre, Rosaire, Urbain, Yves.*

Pariser (133) Jewish (Ashkenazic): ornamental name from German *Pariser* 'person from Paris (France)'.

GIVEN NAMES Jewish 8%. *Avi* (3), *Emanuel* (3).

Parish (4962) English and Irish: variant spelling of PARRISH.

Parisi (2948) Italian: patronymic or plural form of PARISE.

GIVEN NAMES Italian 19%. *Salvatore* (24), *Angelo* (15), *Vito* (15), *Rocco* (11), *Antonio* (5), *Carmelo* (5), *Antonino* (4), *Sal* (4), *Domenic* (3), *Giacomo* (3), *Guiseppe* (3), *Mauro* (3).

Parisian (114) Variant of French PARISIEN.

Parisien (160) French: variant of PARIS 2, from the adjectival form.

GIVEN NAMES French 12%. *Germaine, Gilles, Gillis, Jean-Pierre, Yves.*

Pariso (120) Italian: variant of PARISE.

Parisot (112) French: from a pet form of the personal name PARIS.

GIVEN NAMES French 8%. *Dominique, Francoise, Jacques.*

Parizek (253) Czech (**Pařízek**): **1.** nickname for a dumpy, strong, obstinate, or tenacious person, from Czech *pařízek*, diminutive of *pařez* 'tree stump'. **2.** possibly also a habitational name from a place so called near Sobotka, which derives its name from *pařez* 'tree stump'.

Parizo (160) Altered spelling of French PARISEAU.

Park (23457) A name with many origins, to which other, rarer names have been assimilated. The principal sources are: **1.** English and Scottish: from Middle English, Old French *parc* 'park'; a metonymic occupational name for someone employed in a park or a topographic name for someone who lived in or near a park. In the Middle Ages a park was a large enclosed area

where the landowner could hunt game. **2.** English and Scottish: from a medieval pet form of the personal name PETER. Compare PARKIN. **3.** Swedish: ornamental name from *park* 'park'. **4.** Korean: variant of PAK.

GIVEN NAMES Korean 36%. *Young* (252), *Sang* (137), *Sung* (129), *Yong* (115), *Jung* (111), *Jong* (103), *Chan* (73), *Jae* (73), *Jin* (73), *Kwang* (62), *Kyung* (60), *Myung* (56); *Chong* (80), *Chang* (72), *Chung* (55), *Byung* (48), *Min* (29), *Moon* (28), *Chul* (27), *Hae* (24), *Jeong* (18), *Dae* (16), *Seong* (16), *Myong* (15).

Parke (1685) English: variant spelling of PARK, found mainly in northern Ireland.

Parker (112936) **1.** English: occupational name for a gamekeeper employed in a medieval park, from an agent derivative of Middle English *parc* 'park' (see PARK 1). This surname is also found in Ireland. **2.** Americanized form of one or more like-sounding Jewish names.

Parkerson (743) English: variant of PARKINSON.

Parkes (1017) English: **1.** variant of PARK 1. **2.** patronymic from PARK 2.

Parkey (394) English: possibly a habitational name from a lost or unidentified place.

Parkhill (612) English, Scottish, and northern Irish: habitational name from any of various minor places called Parkhill or Park Hill.

Parkhouse (143) English (mainly Devon): topographic name for someone who lived in a house, such as a warden's lodge, in a park (see PARK 1), from Middle English *parc + hous*.

Parkhurst (2281) English: habitational name from any of various minor places called Parkhurst, for example in Sussex, Surrey, and Hampshire.

Parkin (1496) English (mainly Yorkshire): from the Middle English personal name *Perkin, Parkin*, a pet form of PETER with the diminutive suffix -kin. (The change from -er- to -ar- was a characteristic phonetic development in Old French and Middle English.)

Parkins (926) **1.** English: patronymic from PARKIN. **2.** Americanized form of one or more like-sounding Jewish names.

Parkinson (3641) English (mainly northern): patronymic from PARKIN. This surname has been established in Ireland since the 17th century.

Parkison (393) Variant of PARKINSON.

Parkman (775) English: **1.** occupational name for a gamekeeper, from Middle English *park* 'park' + *man* 'man', 'servant', cognate with PARKER. **2.** occupational name denoting the servant (Middle English *man*) of someone called *Park* (see PARK 2). FOREBEARS Elias Parkman settled at Dorchester, MA, in or before 1633. He was the ancestor of a wealthy and influential Boston family.

Parkos (125) Czech: unexplained.

Parks (29378) English: patronymic from PARK 2.

Parlapiano (136) Italian: nickname for someone with a soft voice or possibly a smooth talker, from *parlare* 'to speak' + *piano* 'quietly', 'softly'.
GIVEN NAMES Italian 9%. *Angelo, Carmine, Clementina, Dino, Silvio.*

Parlato (254) Southern Italian: from a metathesized form (common in earlier and southern usage) of *prelato* 'prelate', apparently a status name or nickname for a high-ranking member of the clergy.
GIVEN NAMES Italian 11%. *Carmelo, Giovani, Salvatore, Vincenzo.*

Parlee (186) Dutch: variant of PARLIER.

Parler (144) German: from an agent derivative of Middle High German *perle* 'pearl', hence an occupational name for a bead-worker, embroiderer, or pearl trader. Compare PEARL. The presence of *-a-* where standard German would have *-e-* is a feature of former eastern (i.e. Bohemian, Silesian) dialects.
GIVEN NAME French 4%. *Camille.*

Parlett (290) **1.** English: from a double diminutive of the personal name *Per*. **2.** variant spelling of **Parlet** (see PARLETTE).

Parlette (202) Characteristic Canadian spelling of French **Parlet**, a nickname for a talkative person or a legal advocate or orator, from a derivative of *parler*, 'to speak'. This is a characteristic Canadian spelling reflecting the Canadian practice of sounding the final *-t*, which in France would normally be silent.

Parliament (100) English: presumably a nickname, or an occupational name for someone in the service of parliament, the British deliberative assembly. The name is recorded in northeast England in the 17th and 18th centuries, but appears to have died out there in the early 19th century. It is not found in the 1881 British census.

Parlier (453) French and Dutch: from Old French *parlier*, an agent derivative of *parler* 'to speak', nickname for a talkative person, or an orator or advocate.

Parlin (425) Irish: Anglicized form of Gaelic **Mac Parthaláin** 'son of *Parthalán*', a Gaelicized form of BARTHOLOMEW. Compare Scottish MCFARLANE.

Parlow (197) German: habitational name from any of several places so named in Brandenburg and Pomerania.

Parma (250) Italian: **1.** habitational name from Parma in northern Italy. **2.** from Sicilian *parma* 'palm', possibly denoting someone who had been on pilgrimage to the Holy Land.

Parmalee (104) English: variant spelling of PARMLEY. This spelling is recorded in England in the 17th century, but appears to have died out there in the 18th or 19th cen-

tury. It is not found in the 1881 British census.

Parman (721) **1.** German (**Parmann**): variant of PARR. **2.** Possibly an altered form of German **Bärmann** (see BARMANN).

Parmar (317) Indian (Rajasthan and neighboring states): Hindu (Rajput) name meaning 'one that strikes the enemy', from Sanskrit *para* 'alien', 'enemy' + *māra* 'strike', 'kill'. The Parmars ruled in Malwa, which is now part of Madhya Pradesh. They consider themselves one of the Agnikulas or 'Fire Tribes' (see CHAUHAN for the Agnikula legend).
GIVEN NAMES Indian 89%. *Kishor* (4), *Pankaj* (4), *Ramesh* (4), *Naresh* (3), *Prakash* (3), *Suresh* (3), *Chhagan* (2), *Deepak* (2), *Hasmukh* (2), *Laxman* (2), *Mahendra* (2), *Pravin* (2).

Parmele (181) Variant spelling of English PARMLEY.

Parmelee (856) Variant spelling of English PARMLEY.

Parmely (130) Variant spelling of English PARMLEY.

Parmenter (1329) English (mainly Essex): occupational name for a maker of facings and trimmings, Middle English, Old French *par(e)mentier* (from *parement* 'fitting', 'finishing', Late Latin *paramentum*, a derivative of *parare* 'to prepare or adorn').

Parmentier (394) French and English: occupational name for a maker of facings and trimmings, Old French *par(e)mentier*. Compare PARMENTER.
GIVEN NAMES French 7%. *Monique* (2), *Achille, Andre, Antoine, Henri, Marcel.*

Parmer (1505) **1.** variant of English PALMER. **2.** Indian (northern states): Hindu name, probably related to PARMAR.

Parmeter (344) English: variant of PARMENTER.

Parmiter (101) English: variant of PARMENTER.

Parmley (761) English (Cumberland and Durham): presumably a habitational name from a lost or unidentified place.

Parnell (4904) English (mainly Devon): from the medieval female personal name *Peronel, Pernel, Parnell*, a vernacular form of Latin *Petronilla*. This is a diminutive of *Petronia*, feminine of *Petronius*, a Roman family name of uncertain etymology. It was borne by an early Roman martyr about whom little is known.

Parnes (376) Jewish (eastern Ashkenazic): occupational name for the president of a Jewish community, Yiddish *parnes* (from Hebrew *parnas*).
GIVEN NAMES Jewish 12%. *Chaim* (4), *Herschel* (2), *Ari, Asher, Aviva, Avner, Chaya, Ido, Meyer, Sol, Uzi, Yehudah.*

Parness (173) Variant of PARNES.
GIVEN NAMES Jewish 10%. *Maer* (2), *Hillel, Hyman, Miriam, Sol.*

Parnham (102) English: habitational name from Parnham in Beaminster, Dorset.

Paro (389) Italian (Venice): unexplained.

Parodi (264) Italian (mainly central Liguria and Genoa): habitational name from Parodi Ligure in Alessandria region. There are early forms of the place name and surname spelt with *-l-* instead of *-r-* (e.g. *Castrum Palodium*, 12th century), a characteristic of Ligurian dialect. This name is now found in Mexico and South America.
GIVEN NAMES Spanish 20%; Italian 8%. *Jorge* (4), *Carlos* (3), *Juan* (3), *Blanca* (2), *Luis* (2), *Alfredo, Atilio, Francisca, Fulgencio, Gustavo, Guzman, Juan Carlos; Silvio* (3), *Angelo* (2), *Aldo, Antonio, Augustino, Duilio, Fabrizio, Flavio, Franco, Natale, Renzo.*

Parody (105) Spanish: apparently an altered form of Italian PARODI.

Parola (150) Italian: **1.** from *parola* 'word', 'talk', a nickname for a gossip or talkative person. **2.** shortened form of Calabrian *Bomparola*, a compound name composed of the elements *buona* 'good' + *parola* 'word', applied as a nickname for an honorable, trustworthy person, or as a personal name. **3.** from *parola*, which means 'kettle' in the dialect of Cremona, 'bucket' in that of Modena, hence probably a metonymic occupational name for someone whose work involved the use of such containers, as for example a kitchen scullion. **4.** possibly also a habitational name from Parola, a locality of Fidenza in Parma.
GIVEN NAMES Italian 7%. *Carlo* (2), *Primo* (2).

Parpart (174) German: habitational name from any of three places so called in Pomerania.

Parquette (131) French: variant of PAQUET.

Parr (6476) **1.** English: habitational name from Parr in Lancashire, which was named in Old English with *pearr* 'enclosure'. **2.** German: from Middle Low German *parre* 'parish', 'district', 'minister's house'; a metonymic occupational name for a parson or for someone who worked in a parsonage or manse. Compare PFARR.

Parra (3153) Spanish, Catalan, Portuguese, and Galician: from *parra* 'vine bower', 'trellis', a topographic name or a habitational name from any of the places named with this word.
GIVEN NAMES Spanish 48%. *Jose* (85), *Manuel* (39), *Juan* (33), *Luis* (33), *Carlos* (28), *Francisco* (20), *Jesus* (20), *Miguel* (20), *Ramon* (18), *Raul* (16), *Sergio* (16), *Armando* (15).

Parrack (232) English: variant of PARK 1, from a word related to Middle English *parc*.

Parramore (345) English (South Yorkshire): variant spelling of PARAMORE.

Parran (146) **1.** French: perhaps a variant of **Parrain**, relationship name from *parrain* 'godfather'. **2.** English: possibly a variant of PARENT.
GIVEN NAMES French 5%. *Andre, Monique.*

Parras (158) Spanish and Portuguese: topographic name meaning 'vine bowers', from the plural of PARRA.
GIVEN NAMES Spanish 32%; Portuguese 13%. *Jose* (3), *Manuel* (3), *Alfonso* (2), *Armando* (2), *Mario* (2), *Tiburcio* (2), *Armandina*, *Delfino*, *Enrique*, *Erasmo*, *Evaristo*, *Florentina*; *Damiao* (2), *Paulo* (2).

Parreira (107) Portuguese: variant of PEREIRA.
GIVEN NAMES Spanish 24%. *Manuel* (6), *Jose* (4), *Francisco* (2), *Avelina*, *Cesar*, *Helio*, *Herminia*, *Luis*, *Luisa*, *Pedro*, *Valentina*.

Parrella (327) **1.** Italian (mainly Campania): from a derivative of PARRA. **2.** Catalan: habitational name from La Parrella, a place in Valencia.
GIVEN NAMES Italian 11%. *Sal* (2), *Angelo*, *Carmine*, *Cosmo*, *Dino*, *Enrico*, *Gennaro*, *Martino*, *Rocco*.

Parrent (311) English: variant spelling of PARENT.

Parrett (1128) English (southern counties): from a Middle English personal name, a pet form of PETER. Compare PARROTT.

Parrick (105) English: variant of PARRACK.

Parrill (216) English: from a Middle English personal name, a pet form of PETER. Compare PARROTT.

Parrilla (265) **1.** Spanish: from a diminutive of PARRA; probably a habitational name from one of the places in southern Spain called Parrilla. **2.** Italian (Calabria): from the feminine form of PARRILLO or from *parrilla* 'titmouse', 'long-tailed tit' (a small bird), hence a nickname, perhaps for a small, lively, talkative person, though Fucilla refers to a Calabrian idiom, 'the titmouse has sung to him', indicating a person who has become rich.
GIVEN NAMES Spanish 34%. *Jose* (10), *Arturo* (3), *Carlos* (3), *Juan* (2), *Julio* (2), *Luis* (2), *Rafael* (2), *Ramon* (2), *Adela*, *Alejandro*, *Ana Maria*, *Angel*; *Antonio*, *Dario*, *Francesca*, *Ireneo*, *Lorenzo*.

Parrilli (129) Italian: patronymic or plural form of PARRILLO.
GIVEN NAMES Italian 7%; French 5%. *Giovanni*, *Paolo*, *Vito*; *Monique*.

Parrillo (389) Italian: **1.** from a pet form of the personal name *Gasparro*, a dialect variant of *Gaspare* (see JASPER). **2.** variant of PARRILLA.
GIVEN NAMES Italian 13%; French 4%. *Rocco* (3), *Carmine* (2), *Oreste* (2), *Pasquale* (2), *Vito* (2), *Antonio*, *Carlo*, *Enrico*, *Philomena*, *Rinaldo*; *Flore* (2), *Armand*, *Lucien*.

Parrinello (312) Italian: from a diminutive of PARRINO.
GIVEN NAMES Italian 17%. *Giovanni* (4), *Salvatore* (3), *Sal* (2), *Santi* (2), *Antonio*, *Carmella*, *Carolina*, *Domenico*, *Franco*, *Gaspare*, *Gasper*, *Ignazio*, *Matteo*, *Orazio*.

Parrino (480) Italian (Sicily): from a nickname from *parrino*, the Sicilian form of *padrino*, denoting a priest or any influential person who assumes the patronage and protection of a subordinate.
GIVEN NAMES Italian 19%. *Salvatore* (9), *Angelo* (4), *Carlo* (2), *Carmelo* (2), *Dino*, *Gaetano*, *Gaspare*, *Gasper*, *Giulio*, *Giuseppe*, *Luigi*, *Natale*.

Parriott (198) Probably English, a variant of PARROTT.

Parris (3965) **1.** English (Kent): variant of PARRISH. **2.** French: variant of PARIS 1.
FOREBEARS Samuel Parris, of Salem witchcraft fame, was a clergyman born in London and came to Boston, MA, in or before 1674. He had five children from two marriages and lived out his years in Sudbury, MA.

Parrish (18039) English (mainly southern): from the Old French habitational name and personal name *Paris* (see PARIS 1). *Parrish* is the most common form of the name in English, and is the result of confusion between -s and -sh (compare NORRIS), reinforced by folk etymological association with the modern English word *parish*. In the 17th and 18th centuries the surname was occasionally bestowed on foundlings brought up at the expense of the parish.

Parro (110) Italian: from a short form of the personal name GASPARRO.

Parrot (161) **1.** English: variant spelling of PARROTT 1. **2.** French: nickname from a derivative of a Celtic word, *perr* 'ram'. **3.** French: regional variant of the personal name *Perrot*, a pet form of the personal name *Pierre* (see PETER).

Parrott (5249) **1.** English: from a Middle English personal name which took various forms: e.g. *Perot*, *Parot*, *Paret*, all pet forms of PETER. The word *parrot*, denoting the talking bird, is most probably from the personal name (compare *robin*, which is from a diminutive of ROBERT; also *jackdaw* and *magpie*). The bird name is most unlikely to be the source of the surname. **2.** English: possibly a habitational name from North and South Perrott in Somerset, which are named for the river Parret, on which they stand.

Parrotta (148) Italian: from a derivative of the personal name PARRO.
GIVEN NAMES Italian 25%. *Nicola* (3), *Rocco* (3), *Umberto* (3), *Carlo*, *Dante*, *Domenic*, *Pasquale*, *Pietro*.

Parrotte (134) French Canadian spelling of PARROT, reflecting the Canadian practice of pronouncing the final -t, which differs from the practice in France.
GIVEN NAME French 4%. *Colette*.

Parrow (208) Americanized form of French PARROT.

Parry (3994) Welsh: Anglicized form of the patronymic *ap Harry* 'son of Harry' (see HARRIS).

Parsa (105) **1.** Muslim: from a personal name based on Persian *parsa* 'chaste', 'devout', 'pious'. **2.** Indian (Gujarat and Bombay city): Parsi and Muslim ethnic name meaning 'Persian'.
GIVEN NAMES Muslim 68%. *Ali* (4), *Hassan* (2), *Abbas* (2), *Afshin*, *Ahmad*, *Aref*, *Aziz*, *Bahram*, *Behzad*, *Ebrahim*, *Ehsan*, *Firouzeh*.

Parsell (471) English: probably a variant of PURCELL.

Parsells (142) English: see PARSELL.

Parshall (616) Americanized spelling of South German **Parschall**, a variant of **Parschalk**, a status name for a freeholder (a freeman with few service obligations), from Middle High German *bar* 'naked', 'free from', 'apparent' + *schalk* 'servant', 'man'.

Parshley (114) Variant of English PARSLEY.

Parsley (2217) English (of Norman origin): altered form of the medieval family name **Passelewe** (assimilated by folk etymology to the herb name *parsley*). The medieval name is from Old French *passe(r)* 'to pass or cross' + *l'ewe* 'the water', hence a nickname, probably for a ferryman or a merchant who was in the habit of traveling overseas, or else someone who had been on a pilgrimage or crusade. It may also have been used as a topographic name for someone who lived on the opposite side of a watercourse from the main settlement.

Parslow (270) English: variant of PARSLEY.

Parson (3943) **1.** English: from Middle English *persone*, *parsoun* 'parish priest', 'parson' (Old French *persone*, from Latin *persona* 'person', 'character'), hence a status name for a parish priest or perhaps a nickname for a devout man. The reasons for the semantic shift from 'person' to 'priest' are not certain; the most plausible explanation is that the local priest was regarded as the representative person of the parish. The phonetic change from -er- to -ar- was a regular development in Middle English. **2.** Americanized form of one or more like-sounding Jewish names. **3.** Americanized spelling of Swedish **Pärsson**, **Persson** (see PERSSON).

Parsons (25477) **1.** English: occupational name for the servant of a parish priest or parson, or a patronymic denoting the child of a parson, from the possessive case of Middle English *persone*, *parsoun* (see PARSON). **2.** English: many early examples are found with prepositions (e.g. Ralph *del Persones* 1323); these are habitational names, with the omission of *house*, hence in effect occupational names for servants employed at the parson's house. **3.** Irish: usually of English origin (see above), but sometimes a reduced Anglicized form of Gaelic **Mac an Phearsain**, which is of Highland Scottish origin (see McPHERSON).
FOREBEARS Members of an Irish family called Parsons were twice created earl of Rosse, first in 1718 and again in 1806. They settled in Ireland c.1590, when two

brothers, William and Laurence Parsons, were granted large estates. Birr Castle, Parsonstown, became the family seat. Samuel Holden Parsons, born Lyme, CT, in 1737 was a Connecticut legislator and revolutionary war officer. Theophilius Parsons (1750–1813) was born in Byfield, MA, and was chief justice of the MA supreme court (1806–13); his son, also Theophilius, was a professor at Harvard Law School (1848–1869).

Partain (1338) English: probably a variant spelling of PARTON.

Partch (231) Altered spelling of German **Partsch**, a variant of BARTSCH.

Partee (694) French: unexplained.
FOREBEARS Benjamin Partee (died 1764) came from France and settled first in Loudon Co., VA, and subsequently in Granville Co., NC.

Parten (486) **1.** German (of Slavic origin): from the personal name *Part(h)en*, ultimately derived from Greek *Parthenios*, from *parthenos* 'virginal', 'pure', 'undefiled'. This was a name borne by two martyrs of the early Christian Church. **2.** Variant of English PARTON.

Partenheimer (130) German: habitational name for someone from Partenheim in Rheinhessen.
GIVEN NAMES German 5%; Scandinavian 4%. *Dieter, Egon, Hans; Hedvig, Maren.*

Partida (698) Spanish: habitational name from any of the places named Partida, from *partida* 'departure'.
GIVEN NAMES Spanish 55%. *Jose* (19), *Juan* (13), *Francisco* (11), *Carlos* (8), *Manuel* (8), *Luis* (7), *Jose Luis* (6), *Ramon* (6), *Ricardo* (6), *Jorge* (5), *Leticia* (5), *Pedro* (5).

Partin (2669) English: probably a variant spelling of PARTON.

Partington (564) English (Lancashire): habitational name from a place in Greater Manchester (formerly in Cheshire) called Partington, from Old English *Peartingtūn* 'settlement (*tūn*) associated with *Pearta*', a personal name not independently recorded.

Partipilo (113) Italian: from *partire* 'to split' + Sicilian *pilu*, Italian *pelo* 'hair', i.e. 'to split hairs', hence probably a nickname for a pedantic or intransigent person.
GIVEN NAMES Italian 16%; French 7%; Spanish 4%. *Vito* (3), *Vincenzo; Michelin* (2), *Dominique.*

Partlo (109) See PARTLOW.
GIVEN NAMES German 4%. *Erwin, Kurt.*

Partlow (1151) **1.** Shortened form of Irish **McPartlow**, Anglicized form of Gaelic **Mac Pharthaláin**, a patronymic from *Parthalán* (see MCFARLANE). **2.** Variant of German **Bartlau**, a habitational name from Bartelow, a place in Pomerania no longer extant.

Partney (139) English: habitational name from Partney in Lincolnshire, named from

the Old English personal name *Pearta* + *ēg* 'island', 'dry ground in a marsh'.

Parton (1894) English (chiefly West Midlands): habitational name from any of various places called Parton; most are named with Old English *peretūn* 'pear orchard' (a compound of *pere* 'pear' + *tūn* 'enclosure', with later change of -*er*- to -*ar*-, a regular phonetic development in Middle English). There are examples in Gloucestershire, two in Cumbria, and one in Kircudbrightshire, Scotland.

Partridge (3832) English: from Middle English *pertriche* 'partridge' (via Old French and Latin from Greek *perdix*), either a metonymic occupational name for a hunter of the bird or a nickname for someone with some fancied resemblance to it, or a habitational name for someone living at a house distinguished by the sign of a partridge. This surname has been established in Ireland since the 17th century. As an American family name, it has probably absorbed some cases of other European surnames with the same meaning, e.g. Italian PERNICE.

Partsch (121) German: variant of BARTSCH, a vernacular derivative of the personal name *Bartholomaeus* (see BARTHOLOMEW).

Partyka (505) **1.** Polish: nickname from Polish dialect *partyka* 'chunk of bread', probably denoting an impoverished person, one who owned nothing but a chunk of bread. **2.** Czech: nickname from *partyka* 'obscure salesman'.
GIVEN NAMES Polish 8%. *Bogdan* (2), *Janusz* (2), *Andrzej, Danuta, Elzbieta, Henryk, Jadwiga, Jerzy, Piotr, Waclaw, Zdislaw.*

Parvin (724) **1.** English: unexplained. The name is now found only in Hampshire, but was formerly more widespread. **2.** Iranian: from a female personal name, *Parvin*, Persian name of the Pleiades (constellation).
FOREBEARS In the 1720s Francis (1700–67) Parvin came from Northallerton, Yorkshire, England to Berks County, PA. Notable bearers of the name in the U.S. have included Theodore Sutton Parvin (1817–1901), an IA lawyer, and Theodore Parvin (1829–98), a PA gynecologist and obstetrician.

Parvis (105) Variant of English PURVIS.

Parys (109) Polish: from the personal name *Parys*, Polish form of PARIS.
GIVEN NAMES Polish 5%. *Elzbieta, Mariusz.*

Parziale (275) Italian: nickname from *parziale* 'partial', 'biased'.
GIVEN NAMES Italian 12%. *Angelo* (3), *Carmine* (2), *Carmela, Ciro, Emidio, Salvatore.*

Parzych (282) Polish: nickname from a derivative of *parzyć* 'to burn or scald', also 'to copulate'.
GIVEN NAMES Polish 7%. *Boleslaw, Jozef, Krystyna, Witold, Zdzislaw, Zygmunt.*

Pas (124) Polish: from Polish *pas* 'belt', 'girdle', presumably either a nickname for someone who habitually wore a distinctive belt, or an occupational name for a maker of or dealer in belts and girdles.
GIVEN NAMES Polish 7%. *Kazimierz, Ryszard, Slawomir.*

Pascal (772) **1.** French and English: from the personal name *Pascal*, Latin *Paschalis*, a derivative of *pascha* 'Easter', via Greek and Aramaic from Hebrew *pesach* 'Passover'. Compare Italian PASQUALE. **2.** possibly also an Americanized form of Greek **Paskhalēs**, which has the same origin as 1.
FOREBEARS Blaise Pascal (1623–62), the French philosopher and mathematician, was born in Clermont-Ferrand, where his father was president of the tax court.
   The name Pascal is documented in Quebec City in 1698, with the secondary surname Brisefer.
GIVEN NAMES French 10%. *Andre* (3), *Camille* (2), *Jean Claude* (2), *Pierre* (2), *Benedicte, Berthony, Fernande, Francois, Georges, Jean-Pierre, Ketly, Maryse.*

Pascale (993) **1.** Southern Italian: from the personal name *Pascale*, southern form of PASQUALE. **2.** French: variant of PASCAL.
GIVEN NAMES Italian 13%. *Salvatore* (4), *Carmine* (3), *Domenic* (3), *Pietro* (3), *Amadeo* (2), *Angelo* (2), *Giuseppe* (2), *Palma* (2), *Rocco* (2), *Saverio* (2), *Antonio, Attilio.*

Pascarella (695) Italian: from the personal name *Pascarella*, a female pet form of PASCALE.
GIVEN NAMES Italian 18%. *Salvatore* (3), *Carmine* (2), *Luigi* (2), *Marco* (2), *Nunzio* (2), *Rocco* (2), *Sal* (2), *Vincenzo* (2), *Angelo, Antimo, Antonio, Carmela.*

Pascarelli (189) Italian: patronymic from the personal name *Pascarello*, a pet form of PASCALE.
GIVEN NAMES Italian 12%. *Dino, Gennaro, Matteo, Salvatore.*

Pasch (563) German: **1.** from a short form of the Latin personal name *Paschalis*. Compare Italian PASQUALE. **2.** (Westphalia): topographic name for a field or meadow which was used at Easter as a playground; etymologically two sources seem to be combined: Latin *pascuum* 'pasture' and Middle Low German *pāsche(n)* 'Easter' (see PAASCH).
GIVEN NAMES German 5%. *Hans* (4), *Kurt* (2), *Erwin, Grete, Merwin, Siegfried.*

Paschal (2005) French and English: variant of PASCAL.

Paschall (1671) English: variant of PASCAL.

Pasche (135) German: variant of PASCH.
GIVEN NAMES French 7%. *Marcel, Reynald.*

Paschen (203) German: variant of PASCH.

Paschke (665) German (of Slavic origin): variant spelling of **Paaschke**, from a pet form of the personal name PAUL.

Pasciak (125) Polish: **1.** patronymic from *Paszek*, a pet form of the personal name *Pawel* (see PAUL). **2.** perhaps a variant of **Paszczak**, patronymic from the nickname *Paszcza* meaning 'mouth' or 'jaw'. **3.** *Paszczak* also denotes a sea fish, known in English as the John Dory, and this too could be the origin of the surname.
GIVEN NAMES Polish 10%. *Andrzej, Casimir, Karol, Ryszard, Zdzislaw.*

Pasco (708) **1.** Italian: regularized (masculine) form of **Pasca**, a variant of PASQUA. **2.** Variant of English PASCOE.

Pascoe (1356) English (Cornwall): from a Cornish variant of the personal name PASCAL.

Pascua (492) Spanish: byname from *pascua* 'Easter' or from a short form of the personal name PASCUAL.
GIVEN NAMES Spanish 41%. *Jose* (9), *Manuel* (6), *Vicente* (5), *Cesar* (3), *Ernesto* (3), *Francisco* (3), *Jaime* (3), *Miguel* (3), *Santiago* (3), *Alfredo* (2), *Andres* (2), *Catalino* (2); *Antonio* (3), *Primo* (2), *Caesar, Cecilio, Dino, Emiliana, Federico, Filomena, Julieta, Leonardo, Lorenzo, Lucio.*

Pascual (1081) Spanish: from the personal name *Pascual*, Latin *Paschalis*, from *pascha* 'Easter'. Compare Italian PASQUALE.
GIVEN NAMES Spanish 46%. *Jose* (15), *Juan* (13), *Carlos* (10), *Domingo* (8), *Manuel* (8), *Miguel* (8), *Jorge* (7), *Alberto* (6), *Francisco* (6), *Luis* (6), *Mario* (6), *Rafael* (6).

Pascucci (635) Italian: patronymic from a pet form of PASQUA.
GIVEN NAMES Italian 17%. *Angelo* (8), *Antonio* (4), *Rocco* (4), *Carmine* (2), *Sal* (2), *Salvatore* (2), *Stefano* (2), *Aldo, Ambrogio, Carlo, Deno, Dino.*

Pascuzzi (249) Italian: from a diminutive of *Pasca* (see PASQUA).
GIVEN NAMES Italian 13%. *Angelo* (3), *Santo* (3), *Salvatore* (2), *Gabriele, Marco, Natale.*

Pase (134) Northern Italian: variant of PACE.

Pasek (422) **1.** Czech (**Pašek**) and Polish (**Paszek**): from a pet form of the personal name *Pavel* or *Pawel*, respectively the Czech and Polish forms of PAUL. **2.** Polish: nickname from *pasek* 'little belt', 'girdle', presumably applied to someone who wore a distinctive girdle.
GIVEN NAMES Polish 7%. *Alicja, Casimir, Czeslaw, Janina, Janusz, Jozefa, Kazimierz, Krzysztof, Marcin, Marzena.*

Paseur (106) French: probably a variant of **Passeur**, an occupational nickname for a ferryman or boatman, from the phrase *passer l'eau* 'cross the water'.

Pash (258) **1.** English: variant of PASK, from the byform *pasche*, Latin *pascha*. **2.** Americanized spelling of German PASCH.

Pasha (212) Muslim, Balkan, and eastern Mediterranean: status name or honorific title from Turkish *başa* 'pasha', a title of rank for a regional governor in the Ottoman Empire.
GIVEN NAMES Muslim 59%. *Mustafa* (5), *Syed* (5), *Kamal* (4), *Ali* (3), *Mohammad* (3), *Ibrahim* (2), *Imran* (2), *Iqbal* (2), *Levent* (2), *Mohammed* (2), *Muhammad* (2), *Abbas.*

Pashby (101) English (Yorkshire): unexplained; perhaps a habitational name from a lost or unidentified place in Yorkshire.

Pashia (122) Muslim, Balkan, and eastern Mediterranean: variant spelling of PASHA.

Pashley (181) English: **1.** habitational name from Pashley in the parish of Ticehurst, Sussex, named with an unattested Old English personal name *Pæcca* or *Pacca* (see PACKHAM) + Old English *lēah* 'wood', 'clearing'. A district of Eastbourne, Sussex, bearing this name derives it from the surname; a family called Pashley had moved there from Ticehurst by the later part of the 13th century. **2.** possibly a variant of PARSLEY. The surname now occurs chiefly in southern Yorkshire.

Pasierb (141) Polish: status name from Polish *pasierb* 'stepson'.
GIVEN NAMES Polish 10%. *Casimir, Jadwiga, Jozef, Ryszard.*

Pasillas (297) Spanish (from Mexico): from *chile pasillas*, a name given in Mexico to dry chile chilaca, probably a metonymic occupational name for a dryer or seller of chiles pasillas, or perhaps a nickname for a very skinny person. This name is not found in Spain but only in the American continent, mostly Mexico.
GIVEN NAMES Spanish 52%. *Manuel* (11), *Jose* (6), *Juan* (6), *Jesus* (4), *Miguel* (4), *Alberto* (3), *Carlos* (3), *Francisco* (3), *Guillermo* (2), *Joaquin* (2), *Juan Manuel* (2), *Lupe* (2); *Antonio* (5), *Eliseo, Federico, Leonardo, Lucio.*

Pasini (147) Italian: patronymic from a pet form of PACE.
GIVEN NAMES Italian 10%. *Luigi* (2), *Ezio, Giovanna, Giovanni, Lorenzo.*

Pasinski (102) Polish (**Pasiński**): habitational name for someone from a place called Paszyn in Nowy Sącz voivodeship, named with *Pasz*, a pet form of *Pawel* (see PAUL).
GIVEN NAMES Polish 16%. *Casimir* (2), *Jerzy* (2), *Kazimierz, Mariola.*

Pasion (200) Spanish (**Pasión**): from *pasión* 'suffering', referring to the Passion or suffering of Christ, and hence a name given to someone born on Good Friday.
GIVEN NAMES Spanish 41%. *Angelito* (2), *Juan* (2), *Roldan* (2), *Rosendo* (2), *Agustin, Alfredo, Ana, Andres, Angelita, Artemio, Bonifacio, Candelaria.*

Pask (193) English: from a medieval vernacular short form of the personal name *Pascal*, Latin *Paschalis* (see PASCAL).

Paske (273) **1.** English: variant spelling of PASK. **2.** Danish (**Paaske**): from a vernacular short form of the Latin personal name *Paschalis* (see PASCAL), or perhaps a nickname for someone who was born at Easter, *påske*, or had some other particular connection with that time of year, such as owing a feudal obligation then. **3.** German: from an eastern (Slavic) short form of the medieval personal names *Paschasius* or *Paschalis* (see PASCAL). **4.** German: habitational name from Paska in Thuringia. **5.** German (**Päske**): from an eastern (Slavic) short form of the personal name *Petrus* (see PETER).

Paskell (104) English: vernacular spelling of PASCAL.

Pasker (124) English: perhaps a derivative of the medieval personal name PASK.

Paskett (166) English: from a pet form of the medieval personal name PASK.

Paskey (160) **1.** English (Devon): from a pet form of the medieval personal name PASK. **2.** Perhaps an altered form of German PASKE.

Paskiewicz (152) Polish: patronymic from the personal names PASEK or PASZEK.
GIVEN NAMES Polish 5%. *Casimir, Jerzy.*

Paskin (100) English (Staffordshire): from the Welsh personal name *Pasgen*, a derivative of Latin *Pascentius*.

Pasko (515) **1.** Polish and Ukrainian: variant of PASZEK. **2.** Hungarian (**Paskó**): from a pet form of the ecclesiastical name *Paskál, Paszkál*, from Latin *Paschalis* (see PASCAL).

Paslay (245) Variant of Scottish PASLEY.

Pasley (1059) **1.** English: variant of PARSLEY. **2.** Scottish: variant of PAISLEY. Black suggests also that some examples of *Pasley* and *Paisley* may be derived from a place known as Pasley or Howpasley, in the Borders region. **3.** Possibly an altered spelling of German **Pasler**, a variant of BASLER, or of **Pässler**, an occupational name, from an agent derivative of *basteln* 'to do handicraft'.

Pasqua (331) Italian: from a personal name or nickname for someone who was born at Easter (Latin *pascua*), or had some other particular connection with that time of year, such as owing a feudal obligation then.
GIVEN NAMES Italian 27%. *Mario* (3), *Gaetano* (2), *Valerio* (2), *Alfredo, Angelo, Attilio, Carmel, Carmela, Carmine, Cono, Dino, Lucio, Luigi, Massimiliano, Mauro, Rosario.*

Pasqual (145) **1.** Spanish: Catalan variant of Spanish PASCUAL. **2.** Italian (Venice): variant of PASQUALE.
GIVEN NAMES Spanish 9%. *Andres, Bolivar, Esperanza, Francisco, Juan, Manuel.*

Pasquale (1244) Italian: from the personal name *Pasquale* (Latin *Paschalis*, from *pascha* 'Easter', via Greek and Aramaic from Hebrew *pesach* 'Passover'). This was popular as a given name throughout Christian Europe in the Middle Ages, mainly in honor of the festival of Christ's crucifixion and resurrection, but also in honor of a 9th-century pope and saint who bore the name.

GIVEN NAMES Italian 14%. *Angelo* (8), *Vito* (5), *Antonio* (3), *Gino* (3), *Luigi* (3), *Rocco* (2), *Salvatore* (2), *Amedeo*, *Carlo*, *Carmela*, *Carmine*.

Pasquali (116) Italian: patronymic or plural form of PASQUALE.

GIVEN NAMES Italian 16%. *Antonio* (2), *Francesca*, *Gino*, *Matteo*, *Pietro*, *Romolo*, *Ugo*.

Pasqualini (108) Italian: from a diminutive of PASQUALE.

GIVEN NAMES Italian 12%. *Carlo*, *Enrico*, *Luigi*, *Silvano*.

Pasqualone (121) Italian: from an augmentative of PASQUALE.

GIVEN NAMES Italian 21%; French 4%. *Attilio* (3), *Angelo* (2), *Antonio*, *Domenic*, *Gino*, *Pasquale*, *Raniero*; *Arianne*, *Patrice*.

Pasquarella (188) Italian: from a feminine form of PASQUARELLO.

GIVEN NAMES Italian 13%. *Angelo* (2), *Alfonse*, *Pasquale*, *Remo*, *Silvio*.

Pasquarelli (188) Italian: patronymic or plural form of PASQUARELLO.

GIVEN NAMES Italian 26%. *Donato* (2), *Gino* (2), *Alfio*, *Amato*, *Antonio*, *Armando*, *Carmine*, *Domenic*, *Gerardo*, *Giovanna*, *Guido*, *Mario*, *Rocco*, *Romolo*.

Pasquarello (179) Italian: from a pet form of the personal name PASQUALE.

GIVEN NAMES Italian 10%. *Concetta* (3), *Angelo*, *Rocco*.

Pasquariello (330) Italian: variant of PASQUARELLO.

GIVEN NAMES Italian 11%. *Angelo* (4), *Vito* (2), *Aldo*, *Donato*, *Francesco*, *Girolamo*, *Umberto*.

Pasquinelli (172) Italian: patronymic from a pet form of PASQUA.

GIVEN NAMES Italian 10%. *Aldo* (2), *Geno*, *Gino*.

Pasquini (337) Italian: patronymic from a pet form of PASQUA.

GIVEN NAMES Italian 18%. *Angelo* (3), *Domenic* (2), *Mauro* (2), *Amedeo*, *Antonio*, *Carmine*, *Dante*, *Dino*, *Elio*, *Enrico*, *Fiore*, *Italo*.

Pass (1589) **1.** English: from a pet form of the medieval personal name *Pascal*, which was brought to England from France. **2.** German: topographic name from *Pass* 'pass', 'passage' (from Middle Low German *pas* 'pace', 'passage way', 'water gauge'). **3.** Jewish (Ashkenazic): metonymic occupational name or nickname from Yiddish and Polish *pas* 'belt', 'girdle'.

Passafiume (192) Italian (Sicily): occupational nickname for a ferryman, from *passa fiume* '(he who) crosses the river'.

GIVEN NAMES Italian 13%. *Salvatore* (2), *Angelo*, *Federico*, *Gino*, *Pietro*, *Sal*, *Vincenzo*.

Passage (168) English: topographic name for someone who lived in a narrow lane or passage, Middle English *passage*.

GIVEN NAME French 4%. *Celine*.

Passalacqua (476) Italian: **1.** occupational nickname for a ferryman or boatman, from the phrase *passa l'aqua* '(one who) crosses the water'. Compare PASSAFIUME. **2.** perhaps also a habitational name from Passalacqua, a place near Alessandria.

GIVEN NAMES Italian 25%; Spanish 6%. *Salvatore* (12), *Vito* (3), *Enzo* (2), *Sal* (2), *Silvio* (2), *Angelo*, *Antonio*, *Carlo*, *Cosmo*, *Gaspare*, *Giancarlo*, *Guido*; *Jose* (3), *Rosario* (3), *Felipe*, *Raul*, *Rosalia*.

Passamonte (100) Italian: literally 'cross the mountain': perhaps an occupational name for a mountain guide, a topographic name for someone who lived by a mountain pass, or a nickname for a tall strong man.

GIVEN NAMES Italian 17%. *Salvatore* (2), *Antonino*, *Francesco*, *Santo*.

Passanante (127) Italian (Sicily): possibly a variant of **Passananti**, which may be a nickname from Sicilian *passannanti* 'passing stranger'.

GIVEN NAMES Italian 22%; French 4%; Spanish 4%. *Rocco* (2), *Angelo*, *Carlo*, *Natale*, *Salvatore*, *Vito*; *Girard*; *Isidoro*.

Passanisi (171) Italian: possibly a habitational name for someone from a place called Pasano or Passano (from an adjectival form of the place name), as for example Madonna di Pasano.

GIVEN NAMES Italian 25%. *Angelo* (2), *Domenic* (2), *Sal* (2), *Vincenzo* (2), *Carmel*, *Emanuele*, *Luigi*, *Mauro*, *Nunzio*, *Rosaria*, *Santo*, *Umberto*.

Passante (181) Southern Italian: occupational name from *passante* 'ferryman', a derivative of *passare* 'to pass or cross'.

GIVEN NAMES Italian 14%. *Angelo* (2), *Nicola* (2), *Aldo*, *Bruna*, *Rocco*, *Salvatore*.

Passantino (252) Italian: from a diminutive of PASSANTE.

GIVEN NAMES Italian 12%. *Sal* (2), *Vito* (2), *Antonella*, *Antonino*, *Carmela*, *Dante*, *Domenic*, *Salvatore*.

Passarella (285) Italian: from a diminutive of PASSARO. The ending in -*a*, typical of southern dialects, possibly arises from the vulgar Latin form, *passar*, of Latin *passer*, -*eris*.

GIVEN NAMES Italian 14%. *Salvatore* (4), *Rocco* (2), *Caesar*, *Carmine*, *Gilda*, *Rossano*.

Passarelli (539) Italian: patronymic or plural form of PASSARELLO.

GIVEN NAMES Italian 21%. *Angelo* (3), *Mario* (3), *Emilio* (2), *Horacio* (2), *Oreste* (2), *Rosario* (2), *Sal* (2), *Amedeo*, *Attilio*, *Camillo*, *Carmel*, *Carmino*, *Emelio*, *Enrico*, *Francesco*, *Fabricio*, *Gaetano*, *Gustavo*, *Orlando*.

Passarello (101) Italian: diminutive of PASSARO.

GIVEN NAMES Italian 18%. *Angelo*, *Lucio*, *Nunzio*, *Salvatore*, *Vito*.

Passaretti (164) Italian: from a diminutive of PASSARO.

GIVEN NAMES Italian 13%. *Salvatore* (2), *Ettore*, *Gaetano*, *Sal*.

Passariello (100) Italian (Naples): from a diminutive of PASSARO.

GIVEN NAMES Italian 24%. *Eduardo* (2), *Angelo*, *Bernardo*, *Emilio*, *Giovanna*, *Rocco*, *Salvatore*, *Vincenzo*, *Vito*.

Passaro (461) Southern Italian: **1.** variant of PASSERO. **2.** possibly from *Passarus*, a personal name recorded from the 10th century.

GIVEN NAMES Italian 12%. *Angelo* (2), *Antonio* (2), *Amerigo*, *Dario*, *Fiore*, *Giovanni*, *Marco*, *Paolo*, *Pasquale*, *Sal*, *Salvatore*, *Silvio*.

Passe (184) **1.** English: variant spelling of PASS. **2.** French: possibly a nickname from *passe* 'sparrow'.

Passehl (121) Eastern German (of Slavic origin): unexplained.

GIVEN NAME German 6%. *Armin* (2).

Passer (155) Danish: possibly of German origin, unexplained.

Passeri (129) Italian: patronymic or plural form of PASSERO.

GIVEN NAMES Italian 9%. *Aldo*, *Angelo*, *Antonio*, *Enio*, *Gino*.

Passero (349) Italian: from *passero* 'sparrow' (Latin *passer*), a nickname from the bird, to which slyness was often imputed.

GIVEN NAMES Italian 12%. *Domenic* (2), *Rocco* (2), *Angelo*, *Antonio*, *Carmine*, *Marino*, *Matteo*, *Philomena*, *Pietro*, *Silvio*, *Vito*.

Passey (291) English: unexplained.

Passini (122) Italian: patronymic or plural form of PASSINO.

GIVEN NAMES Italian 7%. *Primo* (2), *Angelo*, *Attilio*, *Massimo*.

Passino (202) Italian: from a derivative of *Passo*, which is of uncertain origin; most likely it is a topographic name from *passo* 'passage', 'way', but it could be a reduced form of TRAPASSO or CAPASSO.

Passman (429) English, German (**Passmann**), and Jewish (Ashkenazic): variant of PASS.

Passmore (2062) English (chiefly Devon): **1.** from Middle English *pass(en)* 'to pass or go across' + *more* 'marsh', 'fen', a nickname, bestowed no doubt on someone who lived on the far side of a tract of moorland near the main settlement, or for someone who was familiar with the safe routes across a moor. **2.** several early forms have -*e*- in place of -*o*- in the second syllable, and may have a different origin. They could derive from an Anglo-Norman French nickname for a seafarer, *Passemer*, from *passe(r)* 'to cross' (as above) + *mer* 'sea', 'ocean', or the second element could be from Old English *mere* 'lake', 'marsh'.

Passon (189) **1.** English: unexplained; possibly an altered spelling of PARSON. **2.** German: unexplained.

Passons (116) English: probably an altered spelling of PARSONS.

Passow (276) German: habitational name from a Slavic place name occurring in Mecklenburg, Brandenburg, and Pomerania.

Passwater (127) English (London): probably an occupational name for a ferryman.

Passwaters (192) Probably a variant of English PASSWATER, or perhaps a translation of Italian PASSALACQUA or an equivalent surname of non-English origin.

Paster (379) **1.** German: variant of PASTOR 2. **2.** Jewish (eastern Ashkenazic): occupational name from Polish *pasterz* 'shepherd'. **3.** English: generally a variant of PASTOR, but possibly in some cases an occupational name for a baker, from an agent derivative of Old French *paste* 'paste or dough'.

Pasternack (354) Americanized spelling of Slavic and Jewish PASTERNAK.

GIVEN NAMES Jewish 7%. *Mayer* (2), *Aron, Hyman.*

Pasternak (1020) Polish, Ukrainian, and Jewish (eastern Ashkenazic): from Polish, Ukrainian, and eastern Yiddish *pasternak* 'parsnip' (via Middle High German from Latin *pastinaca*), apparently a nickname or in the case of the Jewish surname, an ornamental name.

GIVEN NAMES Jewish 5%; Russian 4%. *Zev* (3), *Hersch* (2), *Mayer* (2), *Ari, Chana, Girsh, Hyman, Moishe, Mordechai, Rozalia, Semen; Mikhail* (4), *Gavril* (2), *Leonid* (2), *Anatoliy, Anatoly, Andrei, Efim, Fanya, Fedor, Galina, Igor, Lev.*

Pastor (1703) **1.** English, Portuguese, Galician, Spanish, Catalan, and French: occupational name for a shepherd, Anglo-Norman French *pastre* (oblique case *pastour*), Portuguese, Galician, Spanish, Catalan, *pastor* 'shepherd', from Latin *pastor*, an agent derivative of *pascere* 'to graze'. The religious sense of a spiritual leader was rare in the Middle Ages, and insofar as it occurs at all it seems always to be a conscious metaphor; it is unlikely, therefore, that this sense lies behind any examples of the surname. **2.** German and Dutch: humanistic name, a Latinized form of various vernacular names meaning 'shepherd', for example HIRT or **Schäfer** (see SCHAFER). **3.** Americanized spelling of Hungarian **Pásztor**, an occupational name from *pásztor* 'shepherd'.

GIVEN NAMES Spanish 13%. *Manuel* (14), *Carlos* (8), *Jose* (8), *Luis* (6), *Mario* (4), *Fernando* (3), *Mariano* (3), *Pedro* (3), *Ricardo* (3), *Santiago* (3), *Sergio* (3), *Alfonso* (2).

Pastore (1529) Italian: occupational name for a shepherd, *pastore.*

GIVEN NAMES Italian 12%. *Angelo* (6), *Antonio* (5), *Vito* (4), *Rocco* (3), *Dante* (2), *Domenic* (2), *Gaetano* (2), *Giuseppe* (2), *Salvatore* (2), *Amato, Biagio, Carlo.*

Pastorek (136) Czech: status name meaning 'stepson'.

Pastori (101) Italian: patronymic or plural form of PASTORE.

GIVEN NAME Italian 5%. *Angelo* (2).

Pastorino (167) Italian: from a diminutive of PASTORE. This surname is also common in Uruguay.

GIVEN NAMES Italian 14%; Spanish 5%. *Angelo* (2), *Alfredo, Costantino, Guido, Lorenzo, Nicolo, Rico, Sergio; Carlos, Marcelo, Pablo.*

Pastorius (257) German: humanistic name, a Latinized form of **Schäfer** 'shepherd' (see SCHAFER).

FOREBEARS Francis Daniel Pastorius (1651–1719), from Sommershausen near Frankfurt, Germany, arrived in Philadelphia in 1683. Under his leadership plans were made for the city of Germantown, PA, of which he became mayor in 1691. He was one of the signers of the first Quaker protest against slavery in America.

Pastrana (403) Spanish: habitational name from a place so called in Guadalajara province.

GIVEN NAMES Spanish 49%. *Jose* (9), *Carlos* (6), *Manuel* (6), *Miguel* (6), *Alfredo* (4), *Angel* (4), *Ana* (3), *Andres* (3), *Fernando* (3), *Jaime* (3), *Juan* (3), *Luis* (3); *Antonio* (4), *Eliseo* (2), *Carmelo, Leonardo.*

Pastrano (126) Spanish: unexplained, but apparently related to PASTRANA.

GIVEN NAMES Spanish 37%. *Manuel* (3), *Miguel* (3), *Francisco* (2), *Pedro* (2), *Alfredo, Ana Maria, Angel, Angelina, Bernabe, Cruz, Dominga, Emilia.*

Pastrick (124) Probably an Americanized form of Czech PASTOREK.

Pastula (156) Polish (**Pastuła**): probably a derivative of the occupational term *pastuch* 'herdsman'.

GIVEN NAMES Polish 6%. *Janina, Krzysztof, Urszula.*

Paszek (166) Polish: from a pet form of the personal name *Paweł*, Polish form of PAUL, or some other personal name beginning with *Pa-*. Compare PACEK.

GIVEN NAMES Polish 9%. *Casimir* (2), *Janina* (2), *Arkadiusz, Kazimierz.*

Paszkiewicz (209) Polish: patronymic from the personal name PASZEK.

GIVEN NAMES Polish 4%. *Andrzej, Zigmund.*

Paszkowski (118) Polish: habitational name from Paszków in Warszawa voivodeship or Paszkowice in Piotrków voivodeship.

GIVEN NAMES Polish 27%. *Andrzej* (3), *Casimir, Janina, Jaroslaw, Jerzy, Jozefa, Karol, Wieslaw, Zbigniew, Zygmunt.*

Pata (124) Italian: unexplained.

GIVEN NAMES Italian 7%; French 4%. *Angelo* (3), *Antonio, Soccorro; Nicolle* (2).

Patak (187) **1.** Hungarian: either a topographic name from *patak* 'creek' or a habitational name from any of several places named with this word. **2.** Czech (**Paták**): an old surname meaning 'five', probably from a house sign.

Pataki (137) Hungarian, Slovak, and Jewish: variant of PATAKY.

GIVEN NAMES Hungarian 11%. *Laszlo* (2), *Gabor, Imre, Jeno.*

Pataky (248) Hungarian and Jewish (from Hungary): habitational name for someone from any of several places in Hungary called Patak, or a topographic name for someone who lived near a creek (see PATAK). This name is also found in German-speaking countries.

Patalano (196) Italian: unexplained. This surname comes from the island of Ischia in the Gulf of Naples.

GIVEN NAMES Italian 24%. *Domenic* (2), *Domenico* (2), *Vito* (2), *Cosmo, Gaetano, Nicola, Ottavio, Rocco, Sal, Salvatore.*

Patane (359) Southern Italian (Sicily; **Patané**): habitational name from Patané, a district of Acireale in Catania province, Sicily.

GIVEN NAMES Italian 10%. *Angelo* (2), *Alfio, Camillo, Carlo, Carmela, Giovanni, Rocco, Sebastiano.*

Patania (114) Italian: variant of PLATANIA.

GIVEN NAMES Italian 25%. *Angelo* (3), *Giuseppe* (2), *Salvatore* (2), *Alfio, Carmelo.*

Patch (1645) **1.** Southwestern English: from a medieval personal name of uncertain origin. Compare PACK. **2.** Probably an altered spelling of German **Pätsch** or **Petsch** (from a pet form of PETER) or of **Patsch**, which is probably from a *Pazzo*, short form of a Germanic personal name meaning 'fight'.

Patchell (258) English: from the female personal name *Pechel*, a Middle English continuation of an Old English name, *Pæcchild*, which is not recorded independently.

Patchen (476) English: from a pet form of PATCH (see PACK).

Patchett (505) English: from a pet form of PATCH (see PACK).

Patchin (375) English: variant spelling of PATCHEN.

Pate (10186) **1.** English and Scottish: from the personal name *Pat(t)*, *Pate*, a short form of PATRICK. **2.** English and Scottish: nickname for a man with a bald head, from Middle English *pate* 'head', 'skull'. **3.** French (**Paté**): from Old French *pat(t)é* 'with paws', 'pawed' (from *pat(t)e* 'paw'), a nickname, applied presumably to a man with large and clumsy hands and feet. **4.** German: nickname for a trustworthy man, from Middle High German *pate*, Middle Low German *pade* 'godfather', 'male relative' (see PAETH), or alternatively from a personal name *Bado*, probably meaning 'battle', 'fight'.

Patek (286) **1.** Czech (**Pátek**): from the personal name *Pátek* 'Friday' (named as the fifth day of the week). Illegitimate children were sometimes given the name of the day of the week on which they were baptized. **2.** Jewish (from Poland): from Polish *patek* 'godfather', hence, as a Jewish name, perhaps a nickname for a person bringing a child in for circumcision.

Patel (22878) Indian (Gujarat, Maharashtra, Karnataka): Hindu and Parsi name which goes back to an official title meaning 'village headman', *paṭel* in Gujarati, Marathi, and Kannada (where it is *paṭēla*). It comes ultimately from Sanskrit *paṭṭakila* 'tenant of royal land'. Among the Indians in the U.S, it is the most common family name.
GIVEN NAMES Indian 93%. *Ramesh* (315), *Bharat* (251), *Pravin* (239), *Ashok* (226), *Mahesh* (188), *Dinesh* (186), *Mahendra* (183), *Arvind* (180), *Dilip* (177), *Suresh* (177), *Kirit* (170), *Mukesh* (161).

Patella (241) Italian: **1.** possibly from *patella* 'limpet', and hence a metonymic occupational name for someone who collected shell fish, or a nickname for a tenacious or withdrawn person. **2.** nickname or metonymic occupational name from a variant of *patella* 'porringer', 'frying pan'. In this sense, it is also found as a Greek name.
GIVEN NAMES Italian 13%; French 4%. *Salvatore* (3), *Rocco*, *Vito*; *Gaetan*.

Patenaude (940) French: from the Latin phrase *pater noster*, 'our father', an metonymic occupational name for a maker of rosary beads. Compare PATERNOSTER.
FOREBEARS A Patenaude, also known as Patenostre, from Normandy, France, was documented in Quebec City in 1651.
GIVEN NAMES French 10%. *Andre* (4), *Adrien* (2), *Monique* (2), *Normand* (2), *Alcide*, *Aldea*, *Armand*, *Berthe*, *Edmour*, *Emile*, *Fernand*, *Gaetane*.

Pater (476) Dutch, German, and Polish: from Latin *pater* 'father', also used to denote the father superior in a religious order, hence probably a nickname for a solemn or pompous man.
GIVEN NAMES Polish 5%. *Stanislaw* (2), *Tadeusz* (2), *Zbigniew* (2), *Mariusz*, *Wieslaw*, *Wieslawa*, *Wladyslaw*.

Patera (163) **1.** Czech: nickname for the illegitimate son of a priest, or for someone thought to resemble a priest, from Czech *pater* 'priest', from Latin *pater* 'father'. **2.** Greek: from the medieval and modern Greek vocabulary word *patera(s)* 'father', ancient Greek *patēr*.

Paterniti (127) Italian: habitational name for someone from the city of Paterno in Catania, Sicily, from an adjectival form of the place name.
GIVEN NAMES Italian 10%. *Angelo*, *Angelina*, *Carmelo*.

Paterno (467) Italian: habitational name from either of two places called Paterno, in Catania, Sicily, or in Potenza.
GIVEN NAMES Italian 23%; Spanish 5%. *Salvatore* (3), *Angelo* (2), *Carlo* (2), *Marco* (2), *Santo* (2), *Alberto*, *Alfredo*, *Carmine*, *Enrico*, *Gaetano*, *Ricardo*, *Rico*, *Roberto*, *Rosario*, *Sandro*; *Jose*, *Jose Maria*, *Juanita*, *Miguel*, *Ramon*.

Paternoster (358) **1.** English (Essex), French, German, and Italian (Apulia and Basilicata): from Latin *pater noster* 'Our Father', the opening words of the Lord's Prayer, which is represented by large beads punctuating the rosary. The surname was a metonymic occupational name for a maker of rosaries, often a shortened form of the Middle English, Middle High German occupational term *paternosterer*. It may also have been originally a nickname for an excessively pious individual or for someone who was under a feudal obligation to say paternosters for his master as part of the service by which he held land. **2.** Dutch: probably a habitational name from the name of a house in Delft, 'Int paternoster', built in 1600. In this case the derivation is from the word as a term for manacles which hold the hands together so that it appears that the restrained person is praying.
GIVEN NAMES Italian 13%. *Rocco* (4), *Guido* (3), *Elio* (2), *Angelo*, *Caesar*, *Carlo*, *Franco*, *Gennaro*, *Raffaela*, *Renzo*, *Vittorio*.

Paternostro (269) Italian (Sicily and Calabria): variant (Italianized) of PATERNOSTER.
GIVEN NAMES Italian 18%. *Angelo* (3), *Antonio*, *Dino*, *Donato*, *Enzo*, *Nicola*, *Nino*, *Orazio*, *Rocco*, *Sal*, *Salvatore*, *Santo*.

Paterson (2470) Scottish: patronymic from a pet form of PATE 1.

Pates (226) English: patronymic from PATE 1.

Patey (168) English: from a pet form of PATE 1.

Pathak (273) Indian (northern states): Hindu (Brahman) name, from Sanskrit *pāṭhaka* 'teacher', 'preceptor'.
GIVEN NAMES Indian 97%. *Anil* (6), *Anjali* (4), *Arvind* (4), *Pinakin* (4), *Radha* (4), *Ambarish* (3), *Chandra* (3), *Jagdish* (3), *Shyam* (3), *Yogesh* (3), *Ajay* (2), *Anant* (2).

Patience (156) English and Scottish: from Middle English, Old French *patience* (Latin *patientia*, a derivative of *patiens* 'patient'), hence a nickname, given perhaps to a notably long-suffering individual or to someone who had represented this abstract virtue in a morality play. However, this was also a personal name for men and women and the surname may derive from this use.
GIVEN NAMES German 4%. *Hansi*, *Kurt*.

Patierno (105) Italian: variant of PATERNO.
GIVEN NAMES Italian 9%. *Rocco*, *Vito*.

Patil (288) Indian: variant of PATEL, found in Maharashtra and Karnataka.

GIVEN NAMES Indian 95%. *Sunil* (6), *Ashok* (5), *Deepak* (4), *Dilip* (4), *Rajesh* (4), *Ramesh* (4), *Arun* (3), *Aruna* (3), *Arvind* (3), *Avinash* (3), *Jagdish* (3), *Raj* (3).

Patillo (399) Scottish: variant spelling of PATTILLO.

Patin (904) Probably a variant spelling of PATON or PATTEN.
GIVEN NAMES French 5%. *Alcide* (2), *Andre*, *Armand*, *Benoit*, *Gaston*, *Leonce*, *Oneil*, *Patrice*, *Pierre*.

Patino (1607) **1.** Galician (**Patiño**): from a diminutive of *pato* 'duck', hence a nickname, for instance denoting a person who waddled. **2.** Italian: unexplained.
GIVEN NAMES Spanish 51%; Italian 11%. *Jose* (49), *Carlos* (24), *Manuel* (23), *Juan* (20), *Luis* (18), *Jesus* (14), *Jorge* (12), *Raul* (11), *Francisco* (10), *Miguel* (10), *Ricardo* (10), *Javier* (8); *Antonio* (14), *Flavio* (6), *Federico* (4), *Filiberto* (2), *Francesca* (2), *Leonardo* (2), *Lucio* (2), *Angelo*, *Aureliano*, *Carmela*, *Constantino*, *Dario*.

Patitucci (128) Italian: patronymic from a derivative of **Patito**, a nickname from Italian *patito* 'sickly', 'suffering'; otherwise (**Patitò**) from Greek *Patētos* 'trampled', 'trodden underfoot'.
GIVEN NAMES Italian 20%. *Angelo* (2), *Rocco* (2), *Aldo*, *Gino*, *Luigi*, *Marco*, *Salvatore*.

Patla (106) **1.** Indian (Gujarat): Muslim name of unknown meaning. **2.** Indian (Rajasthan): Hindu name of unknown meaning. **3.** Polish: nickname from *patla*, a dialect variant of standard Polish *pętla* 'noose', 'loop'.
GIVEN NAMES Indian 7%. *Padma*, *Prem*.

Patlan (165) Nahuatl: probably a habitational name from an unidentified place, with the suffix *-tlan* 'place near where there is abundance of', or perhaps from *patlan* 'to fly'.
GIVEN NAMES Spanish 56%. *Jose* (8), *Juan* (4), *Ruben* (4), *Jesus* (3), *Lupe* (3), *Agustin* (2), *Arturo* (2), *Enrique* (2), *Luis* (2), *Oralia* (2), *Pedro* (2), *Adelita*.

Patman (180) English (Cambridgeshire): occupational name for the servant (Middle English *man*) of someone called *Pat(t)* or *Pate* (see PATE).
GIVEN NAME Irish 6%. *Connor* (2).

Patmon (135) Variant of English PATMAN.

Patmore (158) English: habitational name from Patmore in Hertfordshire, which appears in Domesday Book as *Patemere*, from an Old English personal name *P(e)atta* + Old English *mere* 'lake', 'pool'.

Patnaude (403) Variant of French PATENAUDE.
GIVEN NAMES French 5%. *Armand* (2), *Normand* (2), *Colette*, *Laurette*.

Patnode (882) Variant of French PATENAUDE.
GIVEN NAMES French 4%. *Andre* (2), *Adelard*, *Alcide*, *Jean-Paul*.

Patoka (111) Polish: nickname from Old Polish *patoka* 'liquid honey', or perhaps an occupational name for a seller of honey.
GIVEN NAME German 4%. *Wolf*.

Paton (1177) Scottish: from a pet form of the personal name *Pat* (short form of PATRICK), formed with the Old French diminutive suffix *-on*.

Patras (146) Greek: reduced form of **Patrinos**, habitational name from the city of Patras in northwestern Peloponnese.
GIVEN NAMES Greek 6%. *Costas, Efthimios, Pavlos, Stamatios*.

Patraw (100) Origin unidentified.

Patriarca (160) Southern Italian: from *patriarca* 'patriarch'.
GIVEN NAMES Italian 24%; Spanish 5%. *Antonio, Cosmo, Damiano, Dante, Grazia, Guido, Luigi, Remo, Renato, Roberto, Rocco, Rodolfo, Romeo; Angelito, Carlos, Carmelita*.

Patricelli (172) Italian: **1.** from a diminutive of Latin *pater* 'father', and hence related to *padre* 'priest'. **2.** possibly a nickname from Sicilian *patricu* 'adept', 'practical'.
GIVEN NAMES Italian 9%. *Dino, Rocco*.

Patricio (192) Spanish and Portuguese: from the personal name *Patricio*, Latin *Patricius* (see PATRICK).
GIVEN NAMES Spanish 39%; Portuguese 12%. *Jose (5), Manuel (5), Carlos (3), Alicia (2), Arturo (2), Enrique (2), Francisco (2), Agustin, Alejandra, Angeles, Blanca, Catalino; Joao (2), Joaquim*.

Patrick (19633) Scottish and Irish: reduced Anglicized form of Gaelic **Mac Phádraig** 'son of *Patrick*', a personal name derived from Latin *Patricius* 'son of a noble father', 'member of the patrician class'. This was the name of a 5th-century Romano-Briton who became the apostle and patron saint of Ireland, and it was largely as a result of his fame that the personal name was so popular from the Middle Ages onward. In Ireland the surname is usually Scottish in origin, but it is also found as a shortened form of *Mulpatrick* and FITZPATRICK.

Patridge (386) English: variant of PARTRIDGE.

Patrie (242) French: variant spelling of PATRY.

Patriquin (144) Probably a French spelling of Irish **Parrican**, an Anglicized form of Gaelic **Mac Pádraigín**, a patronymic from a pet form of *Pádraig* (see PATRICK).

Patrizi (124) Italian: patronymic or plural form of PATRIZIO.
GIVEN NAMES Italian 10%; German 4%. *Carmelo, Domenico, Ercole, Santino; Kurt*.

Patrizio (163) Italian: from the personal name *Patrizio*, Latin *Patricius* (see PATRICK).
GIVEN NAMES Italian 23%. *Antonio (2), Gino (2), Lelio (2), Angelo, Arduino, Carmino, Giuseppe, Italia, Pasquale, Sal, Salvatore*.

Patron (321) Spanish (**Patrón**) and northern Italian: from Spanish *patrón* 'master' (Latin *patronus*, a derivative of *pater* 'father'). The term had various senses in the Middle Ages; it was applied, for example, to the master of a ship, and also to the former owner of a freed serf, who still enjoyed certain rights over him.
GIVEN NAMES Spanish 25%. *Jose (5), Diego (3), Fernando (3), Francisco (3), Roberto (3), Carlos (2), Manuel (2), Marcelo (2), Mario (2), Miguel (2), Rafael (2), Ricardo (2)*.

Patrone (268) Italian: nickname or status name from *patrone* 'master' (Latin *patronus*, a derivative of *pater* 'father'). The term had various senses in the Middle Ages: it was applied, for example, to a householder, the master of a ship, and also to the former owner of a freed serf, who still enjoyed certain rights over him.
GIVEN NAMES Italian 15%. *Angelo (2), Antonio (2), Enrico (2), Aldo, Ettore, Leonardo, Lorenzo, Raffaele, Salvator, Salvatore*.

Patruno (102) Italian (Apulia): variant of PATRONE.
GIVEN NAMES Italian 34%. *Vito (2), Aldo, Dino, Luca, Luigi, Mario, Mauro, Nicola, Nunzio, Pasquale, Pietro, Sergio*.

Patry (263) **1.** French: from a variant of the personal name **Patrice** (see PATRICK). **2.** Variant of Scottish PETRIE.
FOREBEARS A Patry or Patrie from the Poitou region of France is documented in Quebec City in 1675.
GIVEN NAMES French 19%. *Adrien (2), Jean-Guy (2), Pierre (2), Benoit, Gaston, Gisele, Jean-Pierre, Julien, Luc, Lucien, Marcel, Michel*.

Patschke (148) German: **1.** habitational name from Patschkau in Upper Silesia or Patzschkau in Saxony. **2.** from a pet form of the personal name PAUL.

Patsy (114) Origin uncertain; possibly English, but unexplained.

Patt (720) English (mainly Devon): variant of PATE 1.

Pattee (594) Origin uncertain. Perhaps a variant of English PATTY or French PATY.

Patten (4553) **1.** English: metonymic occupational name for a maker or seller of clogs, from Middle English *paten* 'clog' (Old French *patin*). **2.** English: variant spelling of PATTON.

Patterson (67787) **1.** Scottish and northern English: patronymic from a pet form of PATE, a short form of PATRICK. **2.** Irish: in Ulster of English or Scottish origin; in County Galway, a surname taken by bearers of Gaelic **Ó Caisín** 'descendant of the little curly-headed one' (from Gaelic *casán*), which is usually Anglicized as **Cussane**.

Patteson (420) Scottish, northern English, or Irish: variant of PATTERSON.

Patti (1399) Italian (Sicily): habitational name from Patti in Messina province, Sicily.
GIVEN NAMES Italian 24%. *Salvatore (20), Angelo (12), Sal (5), Antonio (3), Augustino (3), Gasper (3), Lino (3), Mario (3), Carmelo (2), Mirta (2), Paolo (2), Placido (2), Antonino, Benedetto, Carlo, Cataldo, Isidoro, Nicasio, Orlando, Rosario*.

Pattie (238) Scottish: from a pet form of the personal name PATRICK.

Pattillo (798) Scottish: habitational name from either of two places, in the former counties of Fife and Perthshire, called Pittilloch, from the Pictish element *peit* 'portion' (of land) + Gaelic *tulach* 'hill'.

Pattinson (184) Variant of PATTISON.

Pattison (2106) English (northeastern) and Scottish: patronymic from a pet form of the personal name *Pat(t)* (see PATE 1).

Patton (22883) English, northern Irish, and Scottish: from a pet form of the personal name PATE.
FOREBEARS The American general George Patton (1885–1945) was born in San Gabriel, CA, into a family with a long military tradition. His earliest American ancestor, Robert Patton, had emigrated from Scotland to VA *c*.1770.

Patty (1086) English: probably from a pet form of the personal name PATRICK. Compare PADDY.

Paty (174) French: from a variant of *pâtis* 'pasture', hence a topographic name for someone living by grazing land, or a habitational name from a place so called in Puy-de-Dôme. .

Patyk (105) Polish: nickname for a thin man, from Polish *patyk* 'stick'.
GIVEN NAMES Polish 6%. *Isadore (2), Andrzej, Danuta*.

Patz (488) Eastern German: **1.** from a Sorbian pet form of the personal name BALTHAZAR. **2.** topographic name for someone living near a village bake oven, Sorbian *paz*. **3.** (**Pätz**): from a pet form of the personal name PETER.

Patzer (480) German: habitational name for someone from Patzau in Bohemia.
GIVEN NAMES German 5%. *Ewald, Helmut, Otto, Sigfried*.

Patzke (168) Eastern German: from a pet form of the personal name PATZ.

Patzner (133) German: **1.** habitational name (**Pätzner**) for someone from Pätz in Brandenburg. **2.** topographic name for someone who lived near the village bake oven.

Pau (112) **1.** Dutch: nickname for a flamboyant or haughty man, from Dutch *pauw* 'peacock' (see DE PAUW). **2.** Indian (Gujarat): Hindu (Lohana) name of unknown meaning. **3.** Chinese: variant of BAO. **4.** Catalan: from the personal name *Pau*, Catalan equivalent of PAUL.

GIVEN NAMES Chinese 12%; Indian 6%; Spanish 5%. *Hok* (2), *Kwan*, *Quang*, *Thang*, *Wai*, *Wing Hong*; *Dhirajlal*, *Prakash*; *Angeles*, *Carlos*, *Enrique*, *Margarita*.

Paugh (1175) Americanized form of German PACH.

Pauk (108) German: probably a metonymic occupational name for a drummer, from Middle High German *pauk* 'drum'. Compare PEIKERT.

Paukert (109) Variant of German PEIKERT 'drummer'.

Paul (25550) **1.** English, French, German, and Dutch: from the personal name *Paul* (Latin *Paulus* 'small'), which has always been popular in Christendom. It was the name adopted by the Pharisee Saul of Tarsus after his conversion to Christianity on the road to Damascus in about AD 34. He was a most energetic missionary to the Gentiles in the Roman Empire, and played a very significant role in establishing Christianity as a major world religion. The name was borne also by numerous other early saints. The American surname has absorbed cognates from other European languages, for example Greek *Pavlis* and its many derivatives. It is also occasionally borne by Jews; the reasons for this are not clear. **2.** Irish: reduced Anglicized form of Gaelic **Mac Phóil** 'son of Paul'. Compare MCFALL. **3.** Catalan (**Paül**): habitational name from any of several places named Paül. **4.** Spanish: topographic name from *paúl* 'marsh', 'lagoon'. **5.** Spanish: Castilianized form of Basque *Padul*, a habitational name from a town of this name in Araba province.

Paula (234) Portuguese and Spanish: possibly from the female personal name *Paula*, but more likely from a shortened form of *Francisco de Paula*, the name of a saint from Paola in Calabria (1416(?)–1507).
GIVEN NAMES Spanish 40%; Portuguese 8%. *Luis* (3), *Placido* (3), *Eduardo* (2), *Eleodoro* (2), *Enrique* (2), *Juan* (2), *Juana* (2), *Maribel* (2), *Mario* (2), *Rafael* (2), *Ruben* (2), *Adriano*; *Joaquim*.

Paulding (233) Apparently of Dutch origin, probably an altered form of **Paling**, a nickname for a lithe or devious man or a metonymic occupational name for a seller or catcher of eels, from *paling* 'eel'.
FOREBEARS The surname is common among the Dutch in the Tarrytown area of NY. The writer James Kirke Paulding (1778–1860) published a humorous periodical with the novelist Washington Irving.

Paule (295) **1.** English and German: variant of PAUL. **2.** Catalan (**Paüle**): habitational name from Paüle, a place in northern Catalonia. **3.** French: from a female personal name *Paule*, feminine form of PAUL, given in honor of St. Paula, a 4th-century Italian saint.

GIVEN NAMES Spanish 7%. *Jesus* (2), *Angel*, *Carlito*, *Consolacion*, *Efren*, *Ernesto*, *Felicidad*, *Jose*, *Maribel*, *Pepito*, *Raul*, *Renato*.

Paules (319) **1.** Basque, Aragonese and Spanish: habitational name from any of several places in the provinces of Biscay (Basque Country), Zaragoza, and Uesca (Aragon), and Albacete named Paules. **2.** Greek: variant transliteration of PAVLIS.

Paulette (322) Altered spelling of French **Paulet**, from a pet form of PAUL. The spelling reflects the Canadian pronunciation of the final *-t*, which is normally silent in standard French.
FOREBEARS A Paulet or Poulet from Normandy, France, is documented in Quebec City in 1655.

Pauley (3861) **1.** English: from a medieval pet form of PAUL. **2.** German: variant or derivative of PAUL. Compare POLEY.

Paulhamus (138) Americanized form of Dutch POLHEMUS.

Paulhus (214) French: from a fusion of the personal name *Paul* with the surname **Hus**, a topographic name of Norman origin, meaning 'house'. Thus Jean-Paul Hus became Jean Paulhus. It is still found as Paul-Hus in Montreal.
GIVEN NAMES French 20%. *Andre* (4), *Normand* (4), *Francois* (2), *Gabrielle*, *Jacques*, *Lucien*, *Raoul*.

Pauli (683) German and Swedish: humanistic name, a Latinized patronymic from the genitive case of the Latin personal name *Paulus* (see PAUL).
GIVEN NAMES German 4%. *Gerd* (2), *Benno*, *Franz*, *Heinrich*, *Kurt*, *Lutz*, *Meggan*, *Orlo*, *Rainer*.

Paulick (267) German (of Slavic origin): German spelling of PAVLIK, a Slavic derivative of PAUL.

Paulik (156) German (of Slavic origin): see PAULICK.

Paulin (1116) **1.** Scottish, English, and French: from a pet form of PAUL. In America, the French form has sometimes been Americanized as POLAND. **2.** German: derivative of the personal name *Paulinus*, found especially in the Rhineland.
GIVEN NAMES French 4%. *Aime* (2), *Armand*, *Emile*, *Georges*, *Marcel*, *Marceline*, *Monique*, *Raoul*, *Valmont*.

Pauline (278) French: variant of PAULIN or POULIN.

Pauling (508) English and German: patronymic from the personal name PAUL.

Paulino (926) Portuguese, Galician, and Spanish: from the personal name *Paulino* (from Latin *Paulinus*).
GIVEN NAMES Spanish 43%; Portuguese 8%. *Jose* (19), *Ana* (12), *Juan* (10), *Ramon* (10), *Francisco* (8), *Rafael* (7), *Juana* (6), *Milagros* (6), *Carlos* (5), *Luis* (5), *Manuel* (5), *Julio* (4); *Paulo*; *Antonio* (4), *Salvatore* (3), *Carlo* (2), *Leonardo* (2), *Adalgisa*,

Aldo, *Angelo*, *Canio*, *Carmine*, *Dino*, *Domenic*, *Enrico*.

Paulk (1679) **1.** Variant spelling of Scottish POLK, a reduced form of POLLOCK. **2.** Shortened form of German **Paulke**, a pet form PAUL.

Paull (1103) English and German: variant spelling of PAUL.

Paullin (252) Scottish, English, French, and German: variant of PAULIN.

Paullus (110) German: variant spelling of PAULUS.
GIVEN NAMES German 5%. *Fritz*, *Kurt*.

Paulman (120) Americanized spelling of **Paulmann**, which is from a North German pet form of PAUL.

Paulo (353) Portuguese and Basque: from the personal name *Paulo*, from Latin *Paulus* (see PAUL).
GIVEN NAMES Spanish 19%; Portuguese 9%; Italian 7%. *Jose* (3), *Luiz* (3), *Adelino* (2), *Alfredo* (2), *Ana* (2), *Herminio* (2), *Justino* (2), *Albino*, *Alipio*, *Americo*, *Angelina*, *Arnaldo*; *Joaquim* (2), *Paulo*; *Antonio* (7), *Romeo* (2), *Carmine*, *Dino*, *Geronimo*, *Lucio*.

Paulos (330) **1.** Portuguese: from the personal name *Paulo*, from the old Latinized form *Paulos*. **2.** Greek: variant transliteration of **Paulos** (see PAVLIS).

Pauls (888) **1.** Dutch and North German: patronymic from PAUL. **2.** Catalan (**Paüls**): habitational name from any of the places called Paüls in Catalonia.
GIVEN NAMES German 4%. *Otto* (6), *Claus* (2), *Heinz*, *Kurt*.

Paulsen (4900) North German, Frisian, Danish, and Norwegian: patronymic from PAUL.
GIVEN NAMES Scandinavian 4%. *Erik* (8), *Sven* (3), *Bent* (2), *Thor* (2), *Alf*, *Einer*, *Fredrik*, *Gudmund*, *Hjordis*, *Iver*, *Jorgen*, *Karsten*.

Paulson (8560) **1.** English (East Midlands): patronymic from PAUL. **2.** Respelling of any of a number of Scandinavian patronymics from the personal name *Paul*, for example PAULSEN.

Paulsrud (100) Norwegian: habitational from any of eight farmsteads in eastern Norway named 'Paul's clearing'.
GIVEN NAMES Scandinavian 8%. *Erik*, *Ottar*.

Paulus (1952) German and Dutch: humanistic name, a Latinized form of PAUL.

Pauly (1270) French, English, and German: from a pet form of PAUL.
GIVEN NAMES German 4%. *Otto* (2), *Erhardt*, *Erna*, *Erwin*, *Frieda*, *Hans*, *Helmuth*, *Kurt*, *Markus*, *Reinhard*, *Wolfgang*.

Paumen (101) Dutch and Belgian: from Middle Dutch *palme*, Old French *paume* 'palm', a nickname for a pilgrim or crusader who had brought back a palm from the Holy Land.

Paup (176) Origin unidentified.

Paus (102) **1.** Dutch, North German, and Scandinavian: from Middle Low German *paves*, *pawes* 'pope', pe₁haps applied as a nickname for someone renowned for his piety. **2.** North German and Dutch: a reduced form of PABST. **3.** Americanized form of South German **Pfaus**, a variant of PFAUTZ.

GIVEN NAMES Scandinavian 6%; German 4%. *Erik, Johan, Tollef; Franz, Monika.*

Paustian (299) German: variant short form of SEBASTIAN.

GIVEN NAMES German 4%. *Arno, Kurt.*

Pautler (210) German: variant of **Pfaudler**, a nickname for a sloppy worker or grumpy man, from an agent derivative of *pfaudlen*.

Pautsch (166) German: variant of **Pfautzsch** (see PFAUTZ).

GIVEN NAMES German 7%. *Arno* (2), *Kurt, Otto.*

Pautz (338) German: **1.** variant of PFAUTZ. **2.** of a different, but unexplained origin.

Pauwels (153) Dutch and North German: patronymic from the personal name *Pauwel*, a vernacular form of PAUL.

GIVEN NAMES French 7%. *Alberic, Jacques, Remi.*

Pavan (128) Italian (**Pavàn**): medieval variant of PADOVANO, habitational name for someone from Padua.

GIVEN NAMES Italian 21%. *Reginaldo* (2), *Aldo, Dino, Egidio, Francisco, Gildo, Gino, Guido, Lia, Luigi, Marcello, Nino, Tullio.*

Pavao (490) Portuguese (**pavão**): nickname from *pavão* 'peacock', probably denoting someone who was proud or self-important. Compare PAVON.

GIVEN NAMES Spanish 20%; Portuguese 12%. *Manuel* (27), *Jose* (8), *Carlos* (4), *Mario* (4), *Luis* (3), *Agusto* (2), *Dimas* (2), *Virgilio* (2), *Aires, Aurelio, Avelino, Bento; Joao* (2), *Albano, Duarte, Vasco.*

Pavek (335) Czech (**Pávek**): from a diminutive of *páv* 'peacock', hence a nickname for a pretentious or ostentatious person. The vocabulary word *pávek* or *pavák* also denotes a type of dove or pigeon, and this too may be the source of the surname in some cases.

Pavel (444) Czech, Slovak, and Romanian: from the personal name *Pavel*, Czech form of PAUL.

GIVEN NAMES Romanian 4%. *Petru* (2), *Alexandru, Doina, Dorel, Mihai, Octavian, Vasile.*

Pavelich (105) Croatian (**Pavelić**): patronymic from an old form of the personal name *Pavao*, Croatian form of PAUL.

Pavelka (532) Czech: from a pet form of the personal name *Pavel* (see PAUL).

Pavelko (210) Ukrainian and Slovak: from a pet form of the personal name *Pavel* (see PAUL).

Paver (170) English: occupational name for a layer of paving, from Middle English, Old French *pavier* 'paver', an agent derivative of Old French *paver* 'to pave' (though the Old French verb may be a back-formation from *pavement* 'laid floor').

Pavese (164) Italian: habitational name for someone from Pavia in Lombardy, from an adjectival derivative of the place name.

GIVEN NAMES Italian 15%. *Rocco* (4), *Antonella, Domenic, Leonardo, Lucio, Salvatore.*

Pavey (603) English (southern): **1.** from the medieval female personal name *Pavia*, which is of uncertain origin. Reaney and Wilson suggest it may be from Old French *pavie* 'peach' or *Pavie* 'woman from Pavia' (see 2). **2.** habitational name from Pavia in Lombardy, Italy. **3.** variant of PAVER.

Pavia (539) Italian and Jewish (from Italy): habitational name from the Italian city of Pavia. Compare PAVESE.

GIVEN NAMES Italian 21%; Spanish 6%. *Vito* (6), *Giovanni* (2), *Mario* (2), *Vincenzo* (2), *Antonio, Bernardo, Biagio, Carmine, Dante, Delfino, Ernesto, Gaspare, Leonardo, Marco, Marco Antonio; Fernando* (2), *Agustin, Angel, Francisco, Guadalupe, Hernan, Jesus.*

Pavich (264) Croatian (**Pavić**): patronymic from the personal names *Pavo* or *Pave*, pet forms of *Pavao*, Croatian form of PAUL.

Pavlak (324) Czech (**Pavlák**): derivative of the personal name *Pavel* (see PAUL).

Pavlas (111) Czech: derivative of the personal name *Pavel* (see PAUL).

Pavlat (103) Czech (**Pavlát**): from a derivative of the personal name *Pavel* (see PAUL).

Pavlic (167) Slovenian (**Pavlič**); Croatian and Serbian (**Pavlić**): patronymic from the personal names *Pavel* (Slovenian), *Pavle* (Slovenian, Serbian, and Croatian) or *Pavao* (Croatian) (see PAUL).

Pavlica (171) Czech: from a pet form of the personal names *Pavel* (see PAUL).

Pavlicek (384) Czech (**Pavlíček**): from a pet form of the personal name *Pavlík*, itself a pet form of *Pavel* (see PAUL).

Pavlich (229) Slovenian (**Pavlič**) or Serbian and Croatian (**Pavlić**): see PAVLIC.

Pavlick (605) Americanized spelling of Ukrainian or Czech PAVLIK or Polish PAWLIK.

Pavlik (1510) **1.** Czech (**Pavlík**) and Slovak: from a pet form of PAVEL. **2.** Ukrainian: from a pet form of the personal name *Pavlo*, Ukrainian equivalent of PAUL.

Pavlis (143) **1.** Greek: from a derivative of the personal name *Pavlos* (see PAUL). **2.** Czech (**Pavliš**, Moravia): from a variant of PAVEL. **3.** Lithuanian: from the personal name *Paulis*, Lithuanian form of PAUL.

GIVEN NAMES Greek 6%. *Despina, Nikolaos, Vasilios.*

Pavlock (223) Americanized form of Ukrainian PAWLUK.

Pavloff (151) Russian: alternative spelling of PAVLOV.

Pavlov (225) Russian and Croatian (Dalmatia): patronymic from the personal names *Pavel* (Russian) or *Pavao* and *Pavle* (Croatian) (see PAUL).

GIVEN NAMES Russian 29%; South Slavic 4%; German 4%. *Vladimir* (7), *Boris* (3), *Igor* (3), *Konstantin* (3), *Nikolay* (2), *Yuriy* (2), *Aleksandr, Anatoliy, Andrei, Dmitriy, Evgeni, Gennady; Atanas, Dimitar, Dusica, Slobodan, Velimir; Viktor* (3), *Florian, Reimund.*

Pavlovic (259) Croatian and Serbian (**Pavlović**); Slovenian (**Pavlovič**): patronymic from the personal names *Pavle* (Serbian and Croatian), *Pavao* (Croatian) and *Pavel* (Slovenian) (see PAUL).

GIVEN NAMES South Slavic 43%. *Dragan* (2), *Dusko* (2), *Petar* (2), *Savo* (2), *Slobodan* (2), *Vukasin* (2), *Zeljko* (2), *Aleksandar, Anka, Bojan, Bojana, Bozidar; Milan* (3), *Miroslav* (2), *Dusan, Radmila; Igor* (2), *Jelena, Josip, Tatjana, Vladimir.*

Pavlovich (469) **1.** Croatian, Serbian (**Pavlović**), or Slovenian (**Pavlovič**): see PAVLOVIC. **2.** Ukrainian and Belorussian: patronymic from the personal name *Pavlo* (see PAUL).

GIVEN NAMES South Slavic 8%. *Branko* (3), *Marko* (2), *Davor, Dragisa, Radomir, Ratko, Trifun, Zarko, Zika, Zivko, Zvonko.*

Pavlovsky (127) **1.** Ukrainian, Belorussian, and Jewish (from Ukraine and Belarus): habitational name for someone from any of the villages in Ukraine and Belarus called Pavlovka, from the eastern Slavic form of PAUL. **2.** Czech (**Pavlovský**): from a possessive derivative of the personal name *Pavel* (see PAUL), i.e. someone who is a member of Pavel's household.

GIVEN NAMES Russian 5%. *Fenya, Leonid, Yelena.*

Pavon (264) **1.** Spanish (**Pavón**): nickname for a proud, vain, or showy man, from *pavón* 'peacock'. **2.** Italian: northern variant of PAVONE.

GIVEN NAMES Spanish 46%. *Jose* (8), *Carlos* (6), *Jorge* (5), *Luis* (3), *Manuel* (3), *Mario* (3), *Cesar* (2), *Eduardo* (2), *Hernan* (2), *Jesus* (2), *Pedro* (2), *Ramon* (2).

Pavone (730) Italian: nickname for a proud or vain man, from *pavone* 'peacock'. Compare PEACOCK.

GIVEN NAMES Italian 14%. *Angelo* (2), *Gaetano* (2), *Luca* (2), *Luigi* (2), *Nicola* (2), *Antonio, Biagio, Carmelo, Concetta, Cono, Cosmo, Gino.*

Pavy (132) English: variant spelling of PAVEY.

GIVEN NAMES French 7%. *Laurent, Monique, Octave.*

Pawel (32) Polish: from the personal name *Paweł*, a vernacular form of Latin *Paulus* (see PAUL).

Pawelczyk (139) Polish (**Pawełczyk**): from a pet form of the personal name *Paweł* (see PAWEL).

GIVEN NAMES Polish 6%. *Casimir, Leszek.*

Pawelek (253) Polish (**Pawełek**): from a pet form of the personal name *Paweł* (see PAWEL).

GIVEN NAMES Polish 5%. *Alicja, Andrzej, Tadeusz, Wladyslawa.*

Pawelski (220) Polish: **1.** habitational name for someone from Pawły in Białystok voivodeship. **2.** from the personal name *Paweł* (see PAUL) + the surname suffix *-ski*.

Pawl (113) English: variant of PAUL.

Pawlaczyk (117) Polish: from a pet form of the personal name PAWLAK.

GIVEN NAMES Polish 8%. *Jacek, Tomasz.*

Pawlak (1501) Polish: patronymic from the personal name *Paweł* (see PAUL).

GIVEN NAMES Polish 6%. *Jaroslaw* (3), *Krzysztof* (2), *Zygmunt* (2), *Andrzej, Bogumil, Boguslaw, Casimir, Feliks, Janusz, Jerzy, Jozef, Karol.*

Pawley (335) **1.** English (of Norman origin): habitational name from Pavilly in Seine-Maritime, which is named with the Gallo-Roman personal name *Pavilius* + the locative suffix *-acum*. **2.** English: from a pet form of PAUL. **3.** Possibly an altered spelling of PAULI.

Pawlicki (302) Polish: habitational name for someone from a place called Pawliki in Nowy Sącz voivodeship, or possibly Pawlikowice in Kraków, Łódź, and Płock voivodeships, all named with the personal name *Paweł* (see PAUL).

Pawlik (662) Polish: from the personal name *Pawlik*, a pet form of *Paweł* (see PAUL).

GIVEN NAMES Polish 6%; German 5%. *Jozef* (2), *Tadeusz* (2), *Casimir, Franciszek, Irena, Kazimierz, Krzysztof, Leszek, Stanislaw, Wieslaw, Zbigniew; Klaus-Dieter* (2), *Monika* (2), *Aloysius, Florian, Gunter, Ignatz, Markus.*

Pawlikowski (282) Polish: habitational name for someone from a place called Pawlikowice; there is one near Kutno in Płock voivodeship, also one near Krakow.

GIVEN NAMES Polish 9%; French 4%; German 4%. *Beata, Bronislaw, Janusz, Piotr, Stanislaw, Tadeusz, Wieslaw, Witold; Andre, Michel; Erwin, Kurt, Wilhelm.*

Pawling (191) **1.** English: from a pet form of PAUL. **2.** Altered form, in the New Netherland Dutch community, of *Paling*. Compare PAULDING.

Pawloski (574) Polish: variant of **Pawłowski** (see PAWLOWSKI).

Pawlowicz (201) Polish (**Pawłowicz**): patronymic from the personal name *Pawel* (see PAUL).

GIVEN NAMES Polish 6%. *Leszek* (2), *Tadeusz.*

Pawlowski (1948) Polish (**Pawłowski**): habitational name for someone from any of various places called Pawłów and Pawłowo, named with the personal name *Paweł* (see PAUL).

GIVEN NAMES Polish 7%. *Andrzej* (4), *Casimir* (4), *Jerzy* (3), *Piotr* (3), *Ewa* (2), *Jadwiga* (2), *Mieczyslaw* (2), *Ryszard* (2),

Tadeusz (2), *Tomasz* (2), *Wieslaw* (2), *Zbigniew* (2).

Pawluk (210) Ukrainian: patronymic from the personal name *Pavlo*, Ukrainian form of PAUL.

GIVEN NAMES Polish 10%; Ukrainian 4%. *Wasyl* (3), *Andrzej, Boleslaw, Iwan, Stanislaw, Teofil; Borys* (3), *Oleh.*

Pawlus (136) Polish: Partially Latinized form of the Polish personal name *Paweł* (see PAWEL, PAUL).

GIVEN NAMES Polish 10%. *Czeslaw, Danuta, Grazyna, Janusz, Mieczyslaw, Stanislaw.*

Pawson (191) English (Yorkshire): patronymic from the personal name *Paw*, a variant of PAUL.

Pax (139) **1.** German: variant of BAX. Compare PAXMAN 2. Alternatively, it may be a Latinized form of FRIEDE 'peace'. **2.** Catalan: variant spelling of **Pacs**, a habitational name from Pacs in Catalonia.

Paxman (171) **1.** English: occupational name for the servant (Middle English *man*) of someone named PASK. **2.** German (**Paxmann**): perhaps from a Germanic personal name formed with *bag*, reflected by Old High German *bagan* 'to fight'.

Paxson (1063) English (Northumberland): patronymic from a medieval personal name, *Pack* (see PACK).

Paxton (4381) Scottish and English: habitational name from places in the former county of Berwickshire and in Cambridgeshire, so named from the Old English personal name *Pæcc + tūn* 'settlement'.

Pay (198) **1.** English (mainly Kent): nickname from Middle English *pē, pā* 'peacock' (see PEACOCK). **2.** English: from an early medieval personal name, apparently masculine, but of uncertain origin; perhaps derived from 1, or, as Reaney suggests, a survival of Old English *Pæga*. **3.** French: habitational name from places called Le Pay, in Indre, Rhône, and Vendée. This may also be a variant of *pays* 'region', 'country', used to denote a local person. **4.** Irish (County Kilkenny): apparently from the Old English female personal name *Pega*, taken to Ireland (Kilkenny) by English settlers. Peakirk in Northamptonshire, England, is named for St. Pega (died *c.* 719), who reputedly founded a cell there.

Payan (497) **1.** probably Spanish: unexplained. In Spain this name is mainly found in Andalusia. **2.** English: variant spelling of PAINE. **3.** Southern French: from Latin *paganus* 'country dweller', hence a nickname for a country-born person, or from its later sense of 'pagan', 'heathen', given to a child not yet baptized. Compare PAINE.

FOREBEARS A Payan, also called **Saintonge**, from the Saintonge region of France, is documented in Quebec City in 1699.

GIVEN NAMES Spanish 47%. *Jose* (13), *Manuel* (8), *Ramon* (6), *Carlos* (5), *Jesus* (5), *Leticia* (5), *Luis* (5), *Ana* (4), *Cruz* (4),

Juana (4), *Roberto* (4), *Rodolfo* (4); *Antonio* (6), *Heriberto* (2), *Sal* (2), *Ciro, Federico, Lorenzo, Lucio, Quirino.*

Payant (123) French: variant of PAYAN.

GIVEN NAMES French 5%. *Pierre, Romain.*

Paye (251) French: **1.** metonymic occupational name for an official responsible for settling accounts, from Old French *paie* 'payment'. Compare PAYEUR. **2.** (**Payé**): apparently a variant of PAILLE.

GIVEN NAME French 4%. *Girard.*

Payer (307) **1.** French: variant of **Paillé** (see PAILLE). **2.** German: variant of BAYER. **3.** Anglicized spelling of Slovenian **Pajer**, medieval Slovenian form of German BAYER, denoting a colonist from Bavaria brought to the Slovenian territory by feudal lords in the Middle Ages.

Payette (551) Variant of French **Payet**, from a diminutive of PAYEUR. The spelling reflects the Canadian practice of pronouncing the final *-t*, which is not the practice France.

FOREBEARS A Payet, also called Saint-Amour, from the Gascony region of France is documented in 1671 in Montreal.

GIVEN NAMES French 7%. *Aldor* (2), *Pierre* (2), *Camille, Emile, Fernand, Gervais, Raoul.*

Payeur (199) French: occupational name for an official responsible for settling accounts, from Old French *payeur* 'one who pays (money)' (agent derivative of *paie* 'payment' from Late Latin *pacare* 'to appease, require').

GIVEN NAMES French 9%. *Benoit* (2), *Marcel* (2), *Fernande.*

Paylor (414) English (Yorkshire): occupational name for a maker of pots and pans, from an agent derivative of Middle English *pail(e)* (Old French *paelle* 'frying pan', 'cooking pan').

Payment (234) French: from *paiement* 'payment', 'sum given to pay off a debt', hence a variant of PAYE.

FOREBEARS A Payment, also called LAFOREST, from the lower Limousine region of France, is documented in Ange-Gardien, Quebec, in 1698. Another, with the secondary surname of LARIVIERE, came from the Poitou region of France.

GIVEN NAME French 4%. *Napoleon.*

Payne (47739) English: variant spelling of PAINE. This is also a well-established surname in Ireland.

Paynter (1183) English: variant spelling of PAINTER.

Payseur (111) French: unexplained.

Paysinger (101) Americanized variant of the German habitational name **Bäsinger** (see BASINGER), or **Bösinger**, a habitational name from a place called Bösingen in Swabia.

Payson (603) German and Frisian: variant spelling of **Paysen**, a patronymic from the personal name PAUL.

Payton (6189) **1.** English (mainly West Midlands): habitational name from Peyton in Sussex, named the Old English personal name *Pǣga* + Old English *tūn* 'enclosure', 'settlement', or from some other place similarly named. Peyton in Essex has probably not contributed; it has a quite different early etymology, and even in the 16th century it was still *Pakenho* or *Patenhall*. **2.** Irish (mainly County Donegal): Anglicized form of Gaelic **Ó Peatáin** 'descendant of *Peatán*', a pet form of the personal name *Pádraig* (see PATRICK). Outside County Donegal, the name is apparently mainly of English origin (see 1).

Paz (2291) Spanish and Portuguese: from the Marian epithet *paz* 'peace' (Latin *pax*, genitive *pacis*): *María de la Paz* (Spanish), *Maria da Paz* (Portuguese). The name was often assumed, as an approximate translation of the Hebrew personal name *Shelomo*, by Jews converted to Christianity.

GIVEN NAMES Spanish 47%; Portuguese 11%. *Jose* (64), *Luis* (26), *Carlos* (23), *Mario* (22), *Juan* (21), *Jorge* (16), *Manuel* (16), *Miguel* (16), *Pedro* (13), *Francisco* (12), *Jesus* (12), *Julio* (12); *Albano, Joao*.

Pazienza (113) Italian: from the late Latin personal name *Patientia*.

GIVEN NAMES Italian 21%. *Angelo, Carlo, Cesare, Cosmo, Ercole, Marco, Rocco, Vincenzo, Vito*.

Pazmino (133) Hispanic: unexplained; mainly found in Ecuador.

GIVEN NAMES Spanish 43%. *Luis* (4), *Eduardo* (2), *Sergio* (2), *Alejandro, Alfredo, Ana, Aracelis, Aura, Bolivar, Carlos, Cesar, Enrique; Fausto, Giovanni*.

Pazos (196) Galician: habitational name from any of the numerous places named Pazos, from the plural of *pazo* 'palace', 'manor'. Compare Spanish PALACIOS.

GIVEN NAMES Spanish 49%. *Jose* (6), *Carlos* (4), *Manuel* (4), *Andres* (3), *Armando* (3), *Cesar* (3), *Julio* (3), *Felipe* (2), *Humberto* (2), *Jose Luis* (2), *Juan* (2), *Justo* (2); *Antonio* (2), *Enrico, Fausto, Lucio*.

Pea (258) English: from Middle English *pē* 'peacock' (see PEACOCK).

Peabody (2286) English: probably a nickname for a showy dresser, from Middle English *pe* 'peacock' (see PEACOCK) + *body* 'body', 'person'.

FOREBEARS The prominent financier and philanthropist George Peabody was born 1795 in South Danvers, now Peabody, MA. His first ancestor in America was Francis Peabody, who emigrated from England in 1635 and settled at Topsfield, MA.

Peace (2709) English: variant of PACE, found mainly in Yorkshire but also in Orkney.

Peach (1734) **1.** English: from Old French *pech(i)e*, Middle English *peche* 'sin', hence a nickname for a reprobate, probably given more often in jest than as a mark of cen-

sure. **2.** Probably an Americanized spelling of German PIETSCH.

Peacher (323) English: occupational name from Old French *pescheor, pecheour, pecher* 'fisherman'.

Peachey (714) **1.** Swiss German: probably an altered form of Swiss **Büchi**. However, in The Mennonite Encyclopedia **Bitsche** (or **Bitschi**) is proposed as the origin. See also BEACHY. **2.** English: variant of PEACH.

FOREBEARS *Swiss Surnames* shows numerous Büchis (mainly in Zürich and Toggenburg) and several variants (**Bücheli, Büchele, Bücheler, Büchler**, etc.), whereas **Bitsch(e)** is listed four times and was apparently taken to Switzerland from Germany at the end of the 19th and beginning of the 20th centuries. Peachey is most common in Mifflin Co., PA; other variants appear in various communities.

Peaco (103) Probably an altered form of English PEACOCK.

Peacock (7953) English: from Middle English *pe, pa, po* 'peacock', with the later disambiguating addition of *cok* 'male bird', hence a nickname for a vain, strutting person or for a dandy. In some cases it may be a habitational name from a house distinguished by the sign of a peacock. This surname is established in Ireland also.

Peaden (273) Irish: reduced Anglicized form of Gaelic **Mac Páidín** 'son of *Páidín*', a pet form of the personal name *Pádraig* (see PATRICK).

Peagler (237) Possibly an altered spelling of BIEGLER.

Peairs (111) English, Welsh, or Irish: variant spelling of PIERCE.

Peak (2727) **1.** English: topographic name for someone living by a pointed hill (or regional name from the Peak District (Old English *Pēaclond*) in Derbyshire), named with Old English *pēac* 'peak', 'pointed hill' (found only in place names). This word is not directly related to Old English *pīc* 'point', 'pointed hill', which yielded PIKE; there is, however, some evidence of confusion between the two surnames. **2.** Possibly also Irish: reduced form of MCPEAK.

FOREBEARS Major concentrations of the surname *Peak* are found in Staffordshire and the West Country of England. Among the earliest known bearers were Richard del Pech or del Pek (d. 1196), son of Rannulf, sheriff of Nottingham, and Willielmus Piec (Winchester 1194). A century later, c.1284, a certain Richard del Peke settled in Denbighshire (now part of Clwyd), Wales, receiving lands from Henry de Lacey, earl of Lincoln, in return for helping to control the region. His descendants, who bear the name Peak(e), can be traced to the present day, and are found in New Zealand and Canada as well as in Britain. Peake is also the name of a family descended from John Pyke, who paid rent to the abbot of

Leicester in 1477. The name took various forms, such as *Peke* and *Pick*, eventually becoming established as *Peak* in the 17th century.

Peake (1683) English and Irish: variant spelling of PEAK.

Peaks (266) Probably an altered spelling of German **Pix**, a name of uncertain origin (see PIXLER).

Peal (456) English: variant of PEEL.

Peale (198) English: variant of PEEL.

Pealer (185) Probably an Americanized spelling of German PIEHLER or BUEHLER.

Pean (100) French (**Péan**): from a regional form of *Payen*, an old personal name from Latin *Paganus*, a derivative of *pagus* 'of or relating to the countryside'.

GIVEN NAMES French 30%. *Georges* (2), *Michel* (2), *Colette, Fabienne, Herve, Jacques, Maryse, Pierre*.

Pear (203) **1.** English: from Middle English *pe(e)re* 'pear' (Old English *pere, peru*, from Latin *pirum*), a metonymic occupational name for a grower or seller of pears, or a topographic name for someone who lived by a pear tree or pear orchard. **2.** English: nickname from Middle English *pere* 'peer', 'companion' (Old French *pe(e)r*, from Latin *par* 'equal'). **3.** Jewish: Americanization of some like-sounding Ashkenazic surname; e.g. possibly a shortened form of a surname such as PEARL, PEARLMAN, or PEARLSTEIN.

GIVEN NAME Jewish 4%. *Dov*.

Pearce (12445) Welsh, English, and Irish: variant spelling of PIERCE.

Pearcey (114) English: variant of PERCY.

Pearcy (1070) English: variant of PERCY.

Peard (117) English (Devon): probably a variant of BEARD.

Peardon (144) English: probably a variant of BEARDEN.

Peare (122) English: variant spelling of PEAR.

Pearl (3043) **1.** English: metonymic occupational name for a trader in pearls, which in the Middle Ages were fashionable among the rich for the ornamentation of clothes, from Middle English, Old French *perle* (Late Latin *perla*). **2.** Americanized form of Jewish PEREL.

Pearlman (1668) Americanized form of Ashkenazic Jewish PERELMAN.

GIVEN NAMES Jewish 5%. *Sol* (7), *Hyman* (4), *Elihu* (3), *Emanuel* (3), *Meyer* (2), *Miriam* (2), *Avram, Elisheva, Galit, Golda, Ilissa, Kieve*.

Pearlstein (448) Partly Americanized form of Ashkenazic Jewish PERLSTEIN.

GIVEN NAMES Jewish 5%. *Avram, Isadore, Miriam*.

Pearman (1033) English: variant of PEAR 1, with the addition of *man* 'man'.

Pearo (117) Origin unidentified.

Pearre (142) English: perhaps an altered spelling of French PIERRE.
GIVEN NAME French 4%. *Andre.*

Pears (176) English: variant of PEARCE.

Pearsall (1865) English (West Midlands): habitational name from Pearshall in Staffordshire.

Pearse (515) English: variant of PEARCE.

Pearson (36555) **1.** English: patronymic from the Middle English personal name *Piers* (see PIERCE). The surname is also quite common in Ireland, where it has been established for many centuries. **2.** Americanized form of one or more like-sounding Ashkenazic Jewish surnames.

Peart (878) Scottish and English: **1.** perhaps a habitational name from Pert on the North Esk near Montrose, named with a Pictish term for a wood or copse. MacLysaght records this as a surname in Ireland, noting that the chief branch originated in Newark on Trent (Nottinghamshire) in the 18th century, though there are earlier instances of the name. **2.** variant spelling of PERT.

Peary (162) Northern English: variant spelling of PEERY.
FOREBEARS Robert E. Peary (1856–1920) was a U.S.-born explorer, who in 1909 led the first successful expedition to the North Pole. Peary Land in the north of Greenland is named after him, as he explored there in 1892 and 1900.

Pease (5128) English: from Middle English *pese* 'pea', hence a metonymic occupational name for a grower or seller of peas, or a nickname for a small and insignificant person. The word was originally a collective singular (Old English *peose, pise*, from Latin *pisa*) from which the modern English vocabulary word *pea* is derived by folk etymology, the singular having been taken as a plural.
FOREBEARS Robert and John Pease came from Great Baddow, Essex, England, to Salem, MA, in 1634. In 1644 Robert died, leaving a son (also called Robert) who was apprenticed as a weaver in Salem. By 1646 John Pease was living on Martha's Vineyard.

Peaslee (727) Altered spelling of PEASLEY.

Peasley (616) English (West Midlands): probably a variant of PAISLEY or BEASLEY.

Peaster (153) English (Somerset): unexplained; perhaps a variant of PASTER or PASTOR.

Peat (372) Northern English: from a short form of PETER.

Peatross (190) Origin unidentified. This name is concentrated in VA, where it was already established by 1677.

Peavey (770) English or Scottish: unexplained. Compare PEAVY.
FOREBEARS Edward Peavey is mentioned in the records of Portsmouth, NH, in 1691, as well as Abell, Nathaniel, Joseph, William, and Peter Peavey (probably his sons).

Peavler (534) Probably an altered spelling (resulting from altered pronunciation) of PEVELER.

Peavy (1613) English or Scottish: unexplained.

Peay (914) English: possibly a variant of PAY 1.

Pebbles (117) Possibly altered form of patronymic of German PEPPEL.

Pebley (231) English: probably from a place called Pebley in Derbyshire.

Pebworth (134) English: habitational name from a place in Herefordshire named Pebworth, from an unattested Old English personal name *Peobba* + *worþ* 'enclosure', 'settlement'.

Pecchia (118) Italian: nickname, probably for an industrious person, from *pecchia* 'bee'.
GIVEN NAMES Italian 17%. *Gino* (2), *Mauro* (2), *Amerigo, Angelo, Pasquale.*

Pecci (156) Italian: of uncertain derivation; possibly from *peccio, peccia*, which can have the meaning of 'paunch' (hence a nickname for a large-bellied man), or 'chicken', 'hen' (either a nickname for someone thought to resemble a chicken or a metonymic occupational name for a poultry keeper), or 'woodpecker' (applied as a nickname for someone considered to be a sneak, meddler, or a parasite, all apparently characteristics associated with the bird), but more likely a habitational name from a place named Peccia or similar for the presence of spruce trees (Latin *picea*).
GIVEN NAMES Italian 15%. *Luigi* (3), *Artilio* (2), *Domenic, Palma, Paolo.*

Pech (421) **1.** Mayan: nickname from Mayan *pech* 'tick'. **2.** German and Jewish (Ashkenazic): from Middle High German *pech*, German *Pech* 'pitch', 'tar', presumably a nickname for someone with exceptionally dark skin or hair, or a metonymic occupational name for someone who prepared, sold, or used pitch. **3.** Jewish (Ashkenazic): nickname from German *Pech*, Polish *pech* 'bad luck'. **4.** Czech (also well established in German-speaking lands): from the personal name *Pech*, a pet form of *Petr* (see PETER). **5.** Catalan: variant spelling of nickname from Catalan *pec* 'simple', 'naive'.
GIVEN NAMES Spanish 9%; German 4%. *Carlos* (2), *Jose* (2), *Manuel* (2), *Alvaro, Diego, Edelmira, Emilio, Francisco, Gilberto, Jorge, Jose Angel; Gerhard, Hans, Ilse, Lutz, Manfred, Wolf.*

Pecha (310) **1.** Czech: from a pet form of *Petr*, Czech form of PETER. **2.** Spanish (of Italian origin): nickname from Italian *pecchia* 'bee', taken to Spain from Tuscany in the 16th century.

Pechacek (350) Czech (**Pecháček**): from a pet form of the personal name *Petr*, Czech form of PETER.

Pecher (102) German: occupational name for someone who prepared, sold, or used

pitch, from an agent derivative of Middle High German *pech*, 'pitch'.
GIVEN NAMES German 6%; French 4%. *Hans, Reinhard, Theresia.*

Pechin (140) French (**Péchin**): from a diminutive of PETIT.
GIVEN NAMES French 7%. *Henri, Marcel, Pierre.*

Pechman (96) German (**Pechmann**): occupational name for someone who prepared, sold, or used pitch (see PECH 2).

Pechous (101) Czech: from a derivative of the personal name *Pech*, a vernacular form of *Petr* (see PETER).

Pecht (176) German (of Slavic origin): from a pet form of *Petr*, Czech form of PETER.

Pecina (258) **1.** Spanish and Galician (**Peciña**): habitational name from any of the places called Peciña, in Logroño, Aragon, and Lugo, Galicia. **2.** Spanish: nickname from *pecina* 'mud', 'slurry', commonly used to refer to shoemakers, with reference to the dark layer of polish covering their hands and clothes.
GIVEN NAMES Spanish 43%. *Jose* (6), *Pablo* (3), *Elvira* (2), *Francisca* (2), *Javier* (2), *Juan* (2), *Manuel* (2), *Maricela* (2), *Ramon* (2), *Agustin, Alejandro, Alvaro.*

Peck (16374) **1.** English (mainly East Anglia): metonymic occupational name for someone who dealt in weights and measures, for example a grain factor, from Middle English *pekke* 'peck' (an old measure of dry goods equivalent to eight quarts or a quarter of a bushel). **2.** English: variant of PEAK 1. **3.** Irish: variant of PEAK 2. **4.** South German: variant of BECK. **5.** North German and Dutch: metonymic occupational name for someone who prepared or sold pitch, from Middle Low German *pek*, Middle Dutch *pec, pic*. **6.** Dutch: from Middle Dutch *pec, pick* 'desperate straits', hence a nickname for a person in difficult circumstances or perhaps for someone with a gloomy disposition.

Pecka (186) Czech: nickname for a hard man, from *pecka* 'cherry stone', 'plum stone'.

Peckenpaugh (159) Altered spelling of German **Bickenbach**, a habitational name from any of three places so named in Bavaria, Hesse, and Rhineland.

Peckham (2140) Southern English: habitational name from Peckham in London or East or West Peckham in Kent, all named with Old English *pēac* 'hill' + *hām* 'homestead'.

Peckinpaugh (186) Variant of PECKENPAUGH.

Peckman (206) German (**Peckmann**): **1.** Low German variant of **Pechmann**, an elaborated form of PECH. **2.** variant of BECKMANN.

Pecor (363) Americanized spelling of French PICARD.

Pecora (834) Italian (mainly southern): metonymic occupational name for a keeper of sheep or goats, from *pecora* 'flock' (from Latin *pecus*, genitive *pecoris*).
GIVEN NAMES Italian 15%. *Angelo* (5), *Giovanni* (4), *Rocco* (3), *Sal* (3), *Salvatore* (3), *Santo* (3), *Cono* (2), *Giuseppe* (2), *Antonino*, *Antonio*, *Attilio*, *Cosimo*.

Pecoraro (1064) Italian: occupational name for a sheep or goat keeper, from an agent derivative of *pecora* 'flock'.
GIVEN NAMES Italian 18%. *Salvatore* (10), *Sal* (5), *Gaeton* (4), *Luigi* (4), *Angelo* (3), *Carmine* (3), *Cesare* (2), *Filippo* (2), *Gaetano* (2), *Onofrio* (2), *Stefano* (2), *Agostino*.

Pecore (173) Origin uncertain. It is an Italian name (unexplained), but there is little evidence of an Italian origin in the U.S. However, it is also recorded in French-speaking Canada and it may perhaps be a respelling of French **Pécour(t)**, a habitational name from Pécourt in Loiret or a nickname from *pied* 'foot' + *court* 'short'.

Pecorella (148) Italian: from a diminutive of PECORA.
GIVEN NAMES Italian 13%; Spanish 4%. *Salvatore* (3), *Gasper*, *Luciano*, *Matteo*; *Jaime* (2), *Rosario*.

Pecot (132) Americanized spelling of French PICOTTE.
GIVEN NAMES French 11%. *Fernand*, *Marcelle*, *Monique*, *Pierre*.

Pectol (111) Danish and North German: probably an Americanized form of German BECHTOLD.

Pedalino (122) Italian: either a diminutive of **Pedale**, a topographic name from *pedale* 'foot of the mountain' or a habitational name from a place named with this word, or alternatively a variant form of *Padalino* (see PALADINO).
GIVEN NAMES Italian 15%. *Salvatore* (2), *Francesca*.

Pedder (116) English: from a derivative of Middle English *pedder* 'pannier', hence a metonymic occupational name for a peddler or someone who carried a pannier. This name is now frequent in Australia.

Peddicord (508) English: perhaps a variant of PETTICREW.
FOREBEARS A family bearing this name was established in Baltimore, MD, in the 18th century.

Peddie (194) Scottish: from a pet form of PETER.

Peddle (178) Origin uncertain. Perhaps an Americanized spelling of South German BITTEL.

Peddy (228) Probably a variant spelling of PEDDIE.

Peddycoart (112) Variant of northern Irish PEDDICORD.
GIVEN NAME Irish 4%. *Loman*.

Peden (1847) Scottish and northern Irish: from a Gaelic pet form of PATRICK. Compare PADEN.

Pedersen (8424) Norwegian and Danish: patronymic from PETER.
GIVEN NAMES Scandinavian 13%. *Erik* (39), *Lars* (19), *Niels* (16), *Bjorn* (7), *Knud* (7), *Nils* (7), *Anders* (6), *Jorgen* (6), *Egil* (5), *Einer* (5), *Knut* (5), *Peer* (5).

Pederson (6616) Americanized spelling of PEDERSEN.
GIVEN NAMES Scandinavian 5%. *Erik* (12), *Nels* (4), *Hjalmer* (3), *Obert* (3), *Ove* (3), *Hilmer* (2), *Iver* (2), *Knud* (2), *Lars* (2), *Selmer* (2), *Alf*, *Anders*.

Pedicini (110) Southern Italian: from a diminutive of Sicilian *pedi* 'foot' or alternatively a nickname from Sicilian *pidicinu* denoting a short and angular person.
GIVEN NAMES Italian 27%. *Cosimo* (4), *Mario* (4), *Amadeo*, *Italo*, *Ofelia*, *Silvio*.

Pedigo (1723) Americanized form of French **Périgord**, a regional name of Gaulish origin.

Pedley (303) English (chiefly Midlands and West Yorkshire): **1.** (of Norman origin): nickname for a stealthy person, from Old French *pie de leu* 'wolf's foot'. **2.** habitational name from Pedley Barton in East Worlington, Devon, named from an Old English personal name *Pidda* + Old English *lēah* '(woodland) clearing'.

Pedone (433) Italian: occupational name from Old Italian *pedone* 'foot soldier', 'infantryman'. Later, this word came to be used to denote anyone who traveled about on foot.
GIVEN NAMES Italian 20%. *Angelo* (11), *Massimo* (2), *Salvatore* (2), *Vito* (2), *Carlo*, *Cesare*, *Giacomo*, *Giovanni*, *Luigi*, *Marco*, *Nicola*, *Paolo*.

Pedraza (992) Spanish: habitational name from any of the places called Pedraza, especially those in the provinces of Palencia, Salamanca, and Segovia.
GIVEN NAMES Spanish 53%. *Jose* (28), *Juan* (15), *Luis* (15), *Pedro* (10), *Rafael* (9), *Roberto* (9), *Francisco* (8), *Manuel* (8), *Alfonso* (7), *Arturo* (7), *Carlos* (7), *Mario* (7).

Pedregon (117) Spanish (**Pedregón**): possibly a topographic name from a derivative of *piedra* 'stone'.
GIVEN NAMES Spanish 38%. *Manuel* (4), *Arturo* (3), *Karina* (2), *Raul* (2), *Alfonso*, *Alonzo*, *Andres*, *Armando*, *Beatriz*, *Carlos*, *Diego*, *Eloy*; *Antonio*, *Lorenzo*, *Viterbo*.

Pedretti (231) Northern Italian: patronymic from a pet form of the personal name PIETRO.
GIVEN NAMES Italian 5%. *Gino* (2), *Angelo*, *Dante*, *Guido*, *Paride*.

Pedrick (539) Cornish: from the Cornish personal name *Petroc* or *Pedrek*, a pet form of PETER. St. Petroc is a local saint, who is commemorated in several place names, including Padstow (earlier *Sancte Petroces stow*).

Pedro (970) **1.** Spanish, Portuguese, and Galician: from the personal name *Pedro*, Spanish and Portuguese equivalent of PETER. **2.** Catalan (**Pedró**): topographic name from Catalan *pedró*, *padró* 'memorial stone', or a variant of PADRO.
GIVEN NAMES Spanish 16%; Portuguese 8%. *Manuel* (20), *Jose* (7), *Francisco* (5), *Juan* (5), *Carlos* (3), *Domingo* (3), *Alberto* (3), *Eduardo* (2), *Jaime* (2), *Julio* (2), *Luis* (2), *Orlando* (2); *Joao* (3), *Joaquim* (2), *Henrique*, *Ilidio*.

Pedroni (106) Swiss Italian: from an augmentative of the personal name PIETRO.
GIVEN NAMES Italian 12%. *Carlo* (2), *Emilio*, *Flavio*, *Gabriella*, *Guillermo*.

Pedrosa (170) Spanish, Catalan, Portuguese, and Galician: habitational name from any of numerous places named Pedrosa, from *pedroso*, *pedrosa* 'stoney', an adjectival derivative of *pedra* 'stone'.
GIVEN NAMES Spanish 42%; Portuguese 17%. *Jose* (5), *Juan* (3), *Manuel* (3), *Marcos* (3), *Alicia* (2), *Carlos* (2), *Luis* (2), *Rafael* (2), *Ramon* (2), *Alba*, *Alejandro*, *Amalia*; *Amadeu* (2), *Joao*, *Joaquim*; *Antonio* (7), *Lucio*, *Saturnina*, *Silvio*.

Pedroso (163) Spanish, Portuguese, and Galician: variant of PEDROSA.
GIVEN NAMES Spanish 50%. *Manuel* (6), *Armando* (4), *Gonzalo* (4), *Jose* (3), *Eduardo* (2), *Ernesto* (2), *Francisco* (2), *Octavio* (2), *Pedro* (2), *Rafael* (2), *Ramiro* (2), *Alberto*; *Antonio* (7), *Aldo* (2), *Clementina*, *Fausto*, *Heriberto*.

Pedrotti (192) Italian: patronymic from a pet form of the personal name PIETRO.
GIVEN NAMES Italian 5%. *Dario* (2), *Leno* (2), *Gino*, *Paride*.

Pedroza (898) Spanish: variant spelling of PEDROSA.
GIVEN NAMES Spanish 49%. *Jose* (22), *Juan* (15), *Jesus* (13), *Luis* (11), *Carlos* (10), *Francisco* (10), *Arturo* (8), *Manuel* (7), *Pedro* (7), *Roberto* (7), *Alberto* (5), *Enrique* (5).

Pedulla (160) Italian (**Pedullà**): of Greek origin, probably an occupational name from *petalas* 'farrier', 'blacksmith'.
GIVEN NAMES Italian 23%. *Carlo* (2), *Domenic* (2), *Antonio*, *Nicola*.

Peduto (142) Italian: nickname for someone with large or otherwise remarkable feet, from *piede* 'foot'.
GIVEN NAMES Italian 10%. *Carlo*, *Carmine*, *Pasquale*.

Peduzzi (142) Italian: nickname for someone with small feet, from a diminutive of *piedi* 'feet'.
GIVEN NAMES Italian 5%. *Aldo*, *Grazia*, *Remo*, *Reno*.

Pee (160) **1.** Dutch: from a short form of the personal name *Piet*, Dutch form of PETER. **2.** English (West Midlands): variant of PEA.

Peebler (115) **1.** Said to be an Americanized form of German BOEHLER. **2.** Variant of **Biebler**, from a Germanic personal name formed with a cognate of Old High German *bītan* 'to endure'.

FOREBEARS Bearers of this name are descended from Michael David Peebler, born in VA in about 1767.

Peebles (2997) Scottish: habitational name from Peebles on the river Tweed in southeastern Scotland, or from a smaller place of the same name in the parish of St. Vigeans, Angus. Both place names are cognate with Welsh *pebyll* 'tent', 'pavilion', to which the English plural *-s* has been added.

FOREBEARS This name has been made famous in upstate NY by Peebles Island, where the Mohawk River empties into the Hudson. The island was acquired by marriage by a Scots Peebles family in the late 18th century.

Peed (571) English: probably from the Middle English personal name *Pede* (Old English *Pēoda*).

Peedin (173) Scottish and northern Irish: from a Gaelic pet form of PATRICK. Compare PADEN.

Peek (3846) **1.** English: variant spelling of PEAK. **2.** Irish: variant of PEAK 2. **3.** North German: metonymic occupational name for a spearmaker, from Middle Low German *pēk* 'pike'. Compare PIKE 4. **4.** Dutch: variant of PECK 4 and 5.

Peeke (101) English and Irish: variant spelling of PEEK.

Peeks (228) **1.** North German: probably a variant of PEEK. **2.** Possibly an altered spelling of German **Pix** (see PEAKS).

Peel (2441) **1.** English (mainly northern): from Anglo-Norman French *pel* 'stake', 'pole' (Old French *piel*, from Latin *palus*), a nickname for a tall, thin man. It may also have been a topographic name for someone who lived by a stake fence or in a property defended by one, or a metonymic occupational name for a builder of such fences. Compare PALLISTER. **2.** Dutch: habitational name from places so called in North Brabant (where there is also a district called De Peel) and Dutch Limburg, from De Peel in Ravels, Antwerp province, or from Pedele in Kaggevinne and in Adorp, Brabant. **3.** German: possibly a habitational name from a lost or unidentified place name. **4.** German: perhaps an altered spelling of PIEL or PIEHL.

Peele (1533) English: variant of PEEL.

Peeler (2258) Probably in most cases an Americanized spelling of the German habitational name BIELER or of the topographic name PIEHLER, a variant of BIEHLER (of which this may also be an altered spelling) or of **Bühler** (see PEEL).

Peeling (122) **1.** English (East Anglia): perhaps a variant of **Pa(y)ling**, a variant of PALIN. **2.** Possibly also an Americanized form of German **Bühling**, a habitational name from any of several places so named.

Peelman (145) Probably an Americanized spelling of South German **Biehlmann** or

Bühlmann, variants of BIEHLER.

Peeper (103) **1.** Probably a variant of Dutch **Peper**, a metonymic occupational name for a spice merchant, from *peper* 'pepper'. **2.** Respelling of North German PIEPER 1, a Low German form of PFEIFFER.

Peeples (2369) Americanized spelling of Scottish PEEBLES.

Peer (1408) **1.** English: variant of PEAR. **2.** Dutch and North German: from a reduced form of the personal name PETER.

Peercy (121) Variant of English PERCY.

Peerenboom (115) Dutch: topographic name from *peerenboom* 'pear tree', or occupational name for someone who kept a pear orchard.

Peerman (135) Dutch: **1.** occupational name for a grower or seller or pears, from *peer* 'pear' + *man* 'man'. **2.** habitational name for someone from any of numerous places named Perre or Parre.

Peers (274) **1.** English: variant spelling of PEARCE. **2.** North German: patronymic from PEER.
GIVEN NAMES French 4%. *Gabrielle, Girard.*

Peerson (175) Scandinavian (Swedish **Peersson**): patronymic from the personal name *Pär, Per*, Scandinavian forms of PETER.

Peery (1661) Irish: variant of PERRY, taken to Ireland at the time of the Plantation of Ulster and in the Cromwellian period.

Peet (1251) **1.** English (Lancashire): from a pet form of the personal name PETER. **2.** Dutch: nickname from Middle Dutch *pete* 'godfather', 'godmother', or 'godchild'.

Peete (366) English: variant spelling of PEET 1.

Peeters (369) Dutch: patronymic from a vernacular form of the personal name *Petrus* (see PETER).
GIVEN NAMES French 7%; Dutch 4%. *Raoul* (3), *Jacques* (2), *Desire, Philippe; Adrianus, Flor, Frans, Henk, Martien, Piet.*

Peets (331) **1.** North German and Dutch: probably a patronymic from PEET 2. **2.** Possibly a short form of Dutch **Peetsvrouw**, literally 'Peet's wife', a name which occurred in New Netherland.
GIVEN NAMES French 5%. *Colette, Pierre, Rolande, Romain.*

Peetz (322) North German: **1.** from a pet form of the personal name *Petrus* (see PETER). **2.** possibly a habitational name from Peetz in Brandenburg or Peetzig in Pomerania.

Peevey (150) English: unexplained. Compare PEVEY, PEAVY, PEAVEY.

Peevy (303) English: unexplained. Compare PEVEY, PEAVY, PEAVEY.

Peffer (675) **1.** variant of German PFEFFER. **2.** English: metonymic occupational name or nickname from Anglo-Norman French *pivre* 'pepper' (see PEPPER).

Peffers (124) **1.** Scottish (East Lothian): probably a topographic name for someone who lived on from either of two burns so named in East Lothian. **2.** North German: variant of PFEFFER. **3.** German: altered spelling of PEFFER.

Peffley (214) Probably an Americanized spelling of German **Pfäffle**, a diminutive of PFAFF.

Pefley (111) Americanized spelling of German **Pfäffle** (see PEFFLEY).

Pegg (1009) English (chiefly Leicestershire): **1.** from Middle English *pegge* 'peg' (from Middle Dutch, of uncertain origin), applied as a metonymic occupational name for a maker or seller of wooden pegs, or perhaps a nickname for a person with a wooden leg. **2.** perhaps in some cases from the female personal name, a short form of *Margaret*.

Peggs (179) English: variant of PEGG.

Pegler (150) **1.** English: nickname for a fleet runner, from Old French *pie de lievre* 'hare's foot'. **2.** German: occupational name for a calibrator (someone who checked weights and measures), from an agent derivative of Middle Low German *pegel* 'mark or measure for gauging fluids', 'gauge'.

Peglow (150) German: habitational name from Pegelow near Stettin (now in Poland).

Pegram (1438) English (mainly Cambridgeshire): variant of PILGRIM.

Peguero (319) Spanish: occupational name from *peguero* 'dye producer'.
GIVEN NAMES Spanish 52%. *Jose* (7), *Juan* (6), *Rafael* (6), *Ana* (5), *Luis* (4), *Manuel* (4), *Altagracia* (3), *Jorge* (3), *Ramon* (3), *Andres* (2), *Francisco* (2), *Julio* (2).

Pegues (930) Catalan: probably from the plural of *pega* 'pitch', in various senses connected with pitch and dye.

Pehl (309) German: either from an Old Prussian name of uncertain origin, or a shortened form of **Pehlemann**, a habitational name from a place called Pehlen near Detmold. Alternatively, it could be a shortened form of North German **Pehlgrimm** 'pilgrim' (standard German PILGER).

Pehlke (114) **1.** Probably a variant or altered form of North German **Pahlke**, an occupational name for an overseer of pile driving. **2.** German: probably a variant of PEHL, of Slavic origin.

Pehrson (520) Swedish (**Pehrsson**): patronymic from the personal name *Pär, Pe(h)r* (see PETER).
GIVEN NAMES Scandinavian 5%. *Lennart* (2), *Nels, Nils.*

Pei (193) **1.** Chinese 裴: from the name of a village called Pei, which was granted to Bo Yi, a famous adviser to the model emperors Shun and Yao, in around 2200 BC. Some descendants adopted the village name as their surname. **2.** Chinese 貝: from a place name, Beiqiu, in Hebei province. This is the surname of the architect I. M. Pei. This name is currently spelled **Bei** in China. **3.** Chinese 皮: variant of PI 1.

GIVEN NAMES Chinese 33%. *Ting* (3), *Jin* (2), *Ming* (2), *Chih, Ching, Dehua, Ji, Kun, Lei, Pei, Shin, Shu*.

Peifer (638) German (Rhine-Franconian): variant of PFEIFFER.

Peiffer (1160) German: variant of PFEIFFER.

Peikert (113) German: probably an occupational name for a drummer, a variant of German PIKER.

GIVEN NAMES German 7%; Scandinavian 6%. *Johann* (2); *Detlev* (2).

Peil (471) **1.** Dutch: metonymic occupational name from Middle Dutch *pegel, peil,* a mark used in measuring liquids or a measure of the strength of beer. **2.** Dutch: variant of the habitational name PEEL 2. **3.** American spelling of Dutch **Pijl,** a metonymic occupational name for a maker of arrows or an archer, from *pijl* 'arrow'. **4.** German: variant of PFEIL, or an Americanized spelling of the same name. **5.** German: from a short form (*Bilo*) of a Germanic personal name related to Old Saxon *bīl* 'sword'.

Peinado (183) Spanish: from *peinado* 'combed' (past participle of *peinar* 'to comb'), hence a nickname for a well-groomed person or for someone with naturally smooth rather than curly hair.

GIVEN NAMES Spanish 42%. *Miguel* (4), *Francisco* (3), *Manuel* (3), *Salvador* (3), *Armando* (2), *Arnulfo* (2), *Ezequiel* (2), *Gerardo* (2), *Jesus* (2), *Marcelo* (2), *Raul* (2), *Ricardo* (2).

Peine (306) German: habitational name from Peine near Hannover.

GIVEN NAMES German 4%. *Alois, Hermann, Markus*.

Peirano (135) Italian: from a suffixed form of the personal name *Peiro,* a northern form of *Piero* (see PIETRO).

GIVEN NAMES Italian 5%; Spanish 4%. *Antonio, Dante, Silvio; Luis* (2), *Marta*.

Peirce (1368) English: variant spelling of PIERCE.

FOREBEARS The name Peirce first appears in colonial American records in 1623 with William Peirce, an English shipmaster who compiled the first almanac in English America.

Peirson (236) English: variant spelling of PIERSON.

Peiser (177) **1.** German (of Slavic origin): habitational name for someone from a place called Peise near Königsberg in former East Prussia (present name: Kaliningrad, an exclave of Russia). **2.** German (of Slavic origin): occupational name from a derivative of Polish *pisarz* 'scribe', 'clerk' or a cognate in some other Slavic language. **3.** German: variant of BEISER. **4.** English: variant spelling of PEYSER.

GIVEN NAME German 5%. *Otto* (2).

Peitz (263) German: habitational name from a place so named near Cottbus.

Peixoto (185) Portuguese and Galician: from *peixoto,* a diminutive of *peixe* 'fish' (Latin *piscis*); a metonymic occupational name for a fisherman or fish seller, or perhaps a nickname for someone thought to resemble a fish in some way.

GIVEN NAMES Spanish 30%; Portuguese 21%. *Jose* (11), *Manuel* (9), *Carlos* (3), *Julio* (2), *Mario* (2), *Pedro* (2), *Ricardo* (2), *Alvaro, Ana, Arnaldo, Elida, Enrique; Joao, Joaquim, Paulo; Antonio* (8), *Aldo, Angelo, Marcello*.

Pekala (181) Polish (**Pękala, Pękała**): nickname from the Polish dialect term *pękal* 'short, fat man', or possibly a nickname from a derivative of *pękać* 'to burst or explode'.

GIVEN NAMES Polish 10%. *Bogdan* (2), *Dariusz, Elzbieta, Krzysztof, Leszek, Walerian, Witold*.

Pekar (464) Czech (**Pekař**): occupational name from *pekař* 'baker'.

Pekarek (438) Czech (**Pekárek**): diminutive of PEKAR.

Pekrul (179) Romanian: unexplained.

GIVEN NAMES German 6%. *Erwin, Manfred*.

Pelaez (661) Spanish (**Peláez**): patronymic from the personal name PELAYO.

GIVEN NAMES Spanish 49%. *Jose* (28), *Carlos* (14), *Jorge* (9), *Juan* (9), *Luis* (8), *Pedro* (8), *Manuel* (7), *Raul* (6), *Roberto* (6), *Alberto* (5), *Fernando* (5), *Angel* (4).

Pelak (128) Polish (also **Pielak**): occupational name for an undergardener, someone who weeded the grounds of a great house, from a dialect derivative of Polish *pielić* 'weed'. Compare PIELA.

Pelan (126) Czech: **1.** from a derivative of the Old Czech personal name *Pelhřim.* **2.** nickname from *pela* 'cheerful', 'happy-go-lucky fellow'.

Pelayo (647) Spanish: from the medieval personal name *Pelayo,* from Greek *Pelagios* (a derivative of *pelagos* 'sea'). In the Middle Ages this was one of the most popular personal names in the northwestern Iberian peninsula, having been borne by the first king of the Reconquest, and by various martyrs, including a young boy in the 10th century who was, according to legend, tortured and killed by the Moors of Cordoba for refusing to renounce his faith.

GIVEN NAMES Spanish 55%. *Jose* (24), *Miguel* (12), *Carlos* (10), *Jesus* (10), *Manuel* (10), *Juan* (8), *Luis* (6), *Jorge* (5), *Sergio* (5), *Alfonso* (4), *Pedro* (4), *Raul* (4).

Pelc (438) Polish, Czech, Slovenian, and Jewish (Ashkenazic): Slavic spelling of German PELTZ 'fur', hence a metonymic occupational name for a furrier.

GIVEN NAMES Polish 6%. *Karol* (2), *Czeslawa, Jacek, Jozef, Ryszard, Stanislaw, Waclaw, Zofia*.

Pelchat (259) Possibly an Americanized form of French PELLETIER, common in

NH, MA, and ME. However, the name is found in French Canadian records in this form, and is said to be of Anglo-Norman French origin.

GIVEN NAMES French 16%. *Emile* (2), *Armand, Cyprien, Gilles, Herve, Hilaire, Jacques, Laurent, Laurette, Lucien, Remi, Renald*.

Pelcher (147) Americanized spelling of French PELLETIER, found in PA and NY.

Pelczar (168) Polish spelling of German *Pelzer* 'furrier'.

GIVEN NAMES Polish 9%. *Krzysztof, Mariusz, Stanislaw*.

Pelczynski (75) Polish (**Pełczyński**): habitational name for someone from places called Pełczyn or Pełczyce in northwest Poland, named with the Old Polish personal name *Pełka* (see PELKA).

Pelech (115) **1.** Czech and Ukrainian: from a derivative of the old Slavic personal name *Pelhřim.* **2.** Czech: nickname for someone who lived in a slum, Czech *pelech.* **3.** Ukrainian: nickname from Ukrainian *pelekh* 'tuft of hair', probably in the transferred sense 'old man'.

GIVEN NAMES German 5%; Slavic 4%. *Johann; Wolodymyr* (2).

Pelfrey (1301) English: variant of PALFREY.

Pelham (1197) English (mainly Sussex): habitational name from Pelham in Hertfordshire, so called from the Old English personal name *Pēotla* + Old English *hām* 'homestead'.

FOREBEARS The manor of Pelham in Hertfordshire, England, was held by Walter de Pelham in the reign of Edward I (1272–1307). His descendants became constables of Pevensey Castle, Sussex, and were so influential that their badge, the buckle, is seen in at least eleven of the county's churches, and as a decoration on iron chimney-backs in Sussex farmhouses. Various branches of the family were ennobled and their titles include earl of Chichester and earl of Yarborough. The family also once held the dukedom of Newcastle and the marquessate of Clare. Peter Pelham (b. *c.* 1695), an engraver, emigrated to Boston after 1728, and was stepfather to the artist John Singleton Copley.

Pelican (131) Southern French: from Occitan *pellican* 'pelican' (Latin *pelicanus,* classical Greek *pelekan,* medieval Greek *pelekas*), which was used to signify a beggar or destitute person. Compare also PELIKAN. This is also a habitational name from a place so named in Hérault.

GIVEN NAME German 7%. *Otto* (3).

Pelikan (197) Czech and Slovak (**Pelikán**), Hungarian, and German: habitational name for someone living at a house distinguished by the sign of a pelican (Czech and Hungarian *pelikán,* Middle High German *pellikān*). The pelican was regarded as a symbol of piety in Christian tradition: the female pelican was supposed, in medieval religious folklore, to feed her young with her own blood by plucking the feathers from her breast. Consequently, the family name might be a nickname for a selfless person.

GIVEN NAMES German 4%. *Otto, Wolfgang.*

Pelino (157) Italian: perhaps a variant of Italian PELLINO.

GIVEN NAMES Italian 17%. *Carmine* (2), *Donato, Francesco, Fulvio, Giuseppe, Marco, Marino, Pasco, Rocco, Severino.*

Pelissier (208) French (**Pélissier**): from Old French *pellice* 'fur cloak' (Late Latin *pellicia* from *pellis* 'skin', 'fur'), hence an occupational name for a maker of fur garments or a nickname for someone who wore furs. The surname was taken to Britain by Huguenot refugees; Reaney and Wilson mention a Huguenot, Abel Pelessier, who settled in Ireland.

FOREBEARS A Pelissier of uncertain origin in France, also known as Lafeuillade, is documented in Sorel, Quebec, in 1714.

GIVEN NAMES French 16%. *Georges* (2), *Marcel* (2), *Alain, Huguette, Leandre, Lydie, Normand, Pascal.*

Pelka (191) **1.** Polish (**Pełka**): from a reduced pet form of the Old Polish personal name *Świętopełk* or a similar name. **2.** Jewish (from Poland): habitational name for someone from Pełki in Poland.

GIVEN NAMES Polish 9%. *Andrzej, Jacek, Jozef, Lucjan, Wladyslaw, Zbigniew.*

Pelkey (1721) **1.** Americanized spelling of Polish or Jewish PELKA. **2.** Altered form of French PELLETIER; these are frequent in VT.

Pelky (178) **1.** Americanized form of Polish or Jewish PELKA. **2.** Altered form of French PELLETIER; these are frequent in VT.

Pell (1791) **1.** English: from the Middle English personal name *Pell*, a pet form of PETER. **2.** English: metonymic occupational name for a dealer in furs, from Middle English, Old French *pel* 'skin'. **3.** English: variant of PILL 1. **4.** German: variant of PELLE or, in some instances, a variant of **Pfell**, the South German form of this name, from Middle High German *phelle(e)* 'purple silk cloth'.

Pella (199) **1.** Italian: possibly a reduced form of *Iacopella*, a pet form of the personal name *Iacopa*, feminine form of *Iacopo* (see JACOB), or of *Filippella*, a pet form of *Filippa*, feminine form of FILIPPO. **2.** Italian: habitational name from Pella in Novara province. **3.** possibly Catalan: from old Catalan *pella* 'used clothes', perhaps a nickname for someone poorly dressed.

Pelland (427) French: possibly an altered spelling of the Breton family name **Pellant**, a topographic name, from *penn* + *lann* 'at the tip of the heath'.

GIVEN NAMES French 8%. *Alphonse, Camille, Donat, Gedeon, Herve, Huguette, Jean Marie, Jean Robert, Michelle Marie, Normand, Ovila.*

Pelle (252) **1.** Italian: from *pelle* 'skin', probably used as a nickname for someone with a peculiarity of the skin. **2.** French (**Pellé**): nickname for a bald man, from Old French *pelé*, Latin *depilatus* 'stripped (of hair)'. **3.** Danish and North German: from the personal name *Pelle*, a vernacular form of PETER. **4.** German: from Middle Low German *pelle* 'precious purple silk cloth', presumably a metonymic occupational name for a maker or seller of such cloth or for a maker of official and church vestments.

GIVEN NAMES Italian 8%. *Dino, Domenico, Natale, Pietro, Rocco, Romeo.*

Pellecchia (204) Italian: from *pellecchia* 'small skin or hide', from Latin *pellicula*.

GIVEN NAMES Italian 21%. *Carmine* (3), *Pasquale* (2), *Sal* (2), *Antonio, Carmel, Cesidio, Ciro, Gino, Nunzio, Settimio, Vincenzo.*

Pellegrin (700) **1.** French: southern variant of PELLERIN. **2.** Italian: northeastern variant of PELLEGRINO.

GIVEN NAMES French 5%. *Marcel* (2), *Andree, Camille, Ferrel, Gilles, Henri, Marie Anne, Mignonette, Monique, Oneil, Philippe, Pierre.*

Pellegrini (1486) Italian: patronymic or plural form of PELLEGRINO.

GIVEN NAMES Italian 25%. *Angelo* (9), *Mario* (8), *Aldo* (7), *Antonio* (6), *Luigi* (4), *Carlo* (3), *Claudio* (3), *Julio* (3), *Lucio* (3), *Nicola* (3), *Reno* (3), *Carmella* (2), *Delfino* (2), *Dino* (2), *Girolamo* (2), *Giulio* (2), *Lino* (2), *Guido* (2).

Pellegrino (2624) Italian: from *pellegrino* 'pilgrim', hence a nickname for a person who had been on a pilgrimage to the Holy Land or to a famous holy site elsewhere, such as Santiago de Compostella or Rome, or from the personal name *Pellegrino*, from the same word. See also PILGRIM.

GIVEN NAMES Italian 14%. *Angelo* (8), *Antonio* (8), *Carmine* (8), *Salvatore* (8), *Vito* (5), *Pasquale* (4), *Domenic* (3), *Alfio* (2), *Carlo* (2), *Domenico* (2), *Enrico* (2), *Giuseppe* (2).

Peller (320) **1.** English and German: occupational name from Middle English, Middle Low German *peller* 'maker (or seller) of expensive cloth', derived from Old English *pæll*, *pell* 'costly or purple cloth or cloak', Middle Low German *pelle* (see PELLE 2). **2.** Southern English: topographic name for someone living by an inlet of the sea, a derivative of Old English *pyll* 'inlet' (see PILL 1) + the *-er* suffix denoting an inhabitant. **3.** German: from a Germanic personal name formed with *bald* 'brave' + *heri* 'army'.

Pellerin (1227) French: from Old French *pel(l)erin*, *pelegrin* 'pilgrim'; a nickname for a person who had been on a pilgrimage to the Holy Land or to a famous holy site elsewhere. See also PILGRIM.

FOREBEARS A Pelerin of unknown regional background, who was also known as Saint-Amand, is recorded at Trois Rivières, Quebec, in 1655.

GIVEN NAMES French 12%. *Armand* (7), *Normand* (4), *Lucien* (3), *Norvin* (3), *Yvon* (3), *Alphonse* (2), *Andre* (2), *Cecile* (2), *Emile* (2), *Michel* (2), *Pierre* (2), *Alcide.*

Pellerito (266) Italian: habitational name for someone from Pèllaro in Reggio Calabria, from an adjectival form of the place name.

GIVEN NAMES Italian 18%. *Vito* (4), *Sal* (3), *Antonio* (2), *Pietro* (2), *Vita* (2), *Antonino, Benedetto, Concetta, Francesco, Gasper, Salvatore, Vincenzo.*

Pelletier (7169) French: occupational name for a fur trader, from Old French *pelletier* (a derivative of *pellet*, diminutive of *pel* 'skin', 'hide').

FOREBEARS Since the beaver fur trade was essential in the early development of Canada, by both the British and the French, the name Pelletier and its variants is, not surprisingly, quite common. The earliest documented arrival was at Quebec City in 1637, from the Beauce region of France.

GIVEN NAMES French 14%. *Armand* (27), *Lucien* (21), *Emile* (18), *Andre* (13), *Normand* (13), *Jacques* (11), *Marcel* (11), *Rosaire* (8), *Cecile* (6), *Laurent* (6), *Laurier* (6), *Adelard* (5).

Pellett (410) English (southeastern): either from a pet form of the personal name PELL, or a metonymic occupational name for a furrier, from Old French *pellet* 'fur', a diminutive of *pel* 'skin'. Compare PELLETIER.

Pelley (595) **1.** Variant spelling of PELLY. **2.** Hungarian: habitational name for someone from a place called Pele in Transylvania, now part of Romania.

Pellicane (139) Italian: **1.** variant of PELLICANO. **2.** in some cases, possibly a variant of **Pelacane**, an occupational name for a tanner, from *spellare* 'to skin' + *cane* 'dog'. However, since the term was also used to denote a rogue or villain, the respelling may have been deliberate.

GIVEN NAMES Italian 18%. *Salvatore* (2), *Antonino, Antonio, Rocco, Vito.*

Pellicano (238) Southern Italian: **1.** nickname from *pelecano*, *pelicano* 'woodpecker', from *pelyx* 'axe'. The Greek word was also used as an occupational nickname denoting a carpenter or 'axe wielder', and the surname may derive from this sense. **2.** occupational name for a tanner, *pelacani*, also used in a figurative sense, as a nickname for a rough, rude, or coarse person. In some cases it may have been a euphemistic alteration of *pellacane* 'rogue', 'pilferer'.

GIVEN NAMES Italian 22%. *Angelo* (4), *Saverio* (3), *Dino* (2), *Philomena* (2), *Sal* (2), *Ippolito, Luigi, Salvatore, Santo, Vicenzo.*

Pelliccia (125) Italian: from *pelliccia* 'fur (cloak)' (Late Latin *pellicia* from *pellis* 'skin', 'fur'), hence a metonymic occupational name for a furrier, or a nickname for someone habitually wore a fur cloak.
GIVEN NAMES Italian 27%. *Orlando* (3), *Rafael* (2), *Antonio, Carlo, Carmela, Domenico, Ettore, Franco, Marco, Sal, Salvatore, Santo.*

Pellicer (132) Catalan: occupational name for a furrier, from Catalan *pellisser*.
GIVEN NAMES Spanish 25%. *Manuel* (3), *Angel* (2), *Jose* (2), *Ramon* (2), *Alberto, Baldo, Eloisa, Fernando, Francisco, Gabriela, Jaime, Jose Manuel.*

Pellino (125) Italian: from a pet form of the personal name *Iacopo*, from Latin *Jacobus* (see JACOB), or a short form of the personal name *Ampellino*.
GIVEN NAMES Italian 11%. *Salvatore* (2), *Carmine, Giuseppe.*

Pellissier (158) French: variant spelling of PELISSIER.
GIVEN NAMES French 10%. *Francois* (2), *Andre, Henri.*

Pellitteri (105) Italian: occupational name from *pellettiere* 'furrier'.
GIVEN NAMES Italian 24%. *Angelo* (2), *Carmelo, Marcello, Orazio, Sal, Salvatore, Santo, Vincenzo, Vito.*

Pellman (285) English: derivative of PELL.

Pello (124) Catalan (**Pelló**): probably a nickname from *pelló* 'nutshell', the shuck or shell of certain nuts, especially chestnuts.
GIVEN NAMES Spanish 5%. *Florinda, Humberto, Jose, Pablo.*

Pellot (115) Catalan: apparently from a derivative of *pell* 'skin', 'fur'.
GIVEN NAMES Spanish 40%. *Carlos* (2), *Efrain* (2), *Juan* (2), *Luis* (2), *Raul* (2), *Alfredo, Alicia, Asuncion, Betzaida, Braulio, Eduardo, Graciela*; *Angelo, Manfredo.*

Pellow (247) **1.** English (Cornwall): from the medieval personal name PELL + the Middle English diminutive suffix *-oe*. **2.** English: variant of PEDLEY.

Pellowski (100) Polish: variant of PELOWSKI.

Pells (119) Variant spelling of Dutch PELS.
GIVEN NAME French 4%. *Andre.*

Pellum (166) Variant of English PELHAM.

Pelly (156) English (also established in Ireland): **1.** from a pet form of the personal name PELL. **2.** nickname from Old French *pele* 'bald'.

Pelo (122) **1.** Possibly a variant spelling of English PELLOW. **2.** Samoan: unexplained.

Pelon (132) Americanized spelling of French PILON.

Peloquin (1224) French: from a diminutive of Occitan *peloke* 'peel', Gascon *peloko* 'grain-husk', probably applied as a nickname for a miser or a poor wretch.
FOREBEARS A Peloquin, also called Crédit,

from the Poitou region of France is documented in Quebec City in 1690.
GIVEN NAMES French 14%. *Armand* (7), *Marcel* (6), *Normand* (5), *Andre* (3), *Fernand* (3), *Laurent* (3), *Pierre* (3), *Edouard* (2), *Lucien* (2), *Mathieu* (2), *Monique* (2), *Valmore* (2).

Pelosi (491) Italian: patronymic or plural form of PELOSO.
GIVEN NAMES Italian 19%. *Angelo* (6), *Marino* (2), *Vito* (2), *Agostino, Antonio, Carmine, Cosmo, Domenico, Gabriele, Geno, Gilda, Giovanni.*

Peloso (222) Italian (mainly southern): nickname for a man with long or unkempt hair and beard, from *peloso* 'hairy', 'shaggy'.
GIVEN NAMES Italian 10%. *Angelo, Antonio, Camillo, Carmelina, Dino, Domenic.*

Pelot (296) **1.** German: from *Pelloth*, a variant of the Germanic personal name *Baldhart*, composed of the elements *bald* 'bold', 'brave' + *hart* 'strong'. **2.** Americanized spelling of French PILOT.

Pelotte (103) French: from *pelote* 'pelote', 'ball', hence a metonymic occupational name for someone who was a ball maker or possibly a nickname for an inveterate player of ball games.
GIVEN NAMES French 9%. *Alphie* (2), *Emile.*

Pelowski (137) Polish: variant of **Pielowski**, habitational name from a place called Pielowce, in Lida province, now in Lithuania.

Pelphrey (209) Probably an altered spelling of PALFREY.

Pels (151) Dutch and North German: metonymic occupational name for a furrier, from Middle Dutch, Middle Low German *pels* 'fur'.
GIVEN NAMES German 5%. *Ernst, Siegfried.*

Pelster (178) German: variant of BALLESTER.

Pelt (563) Dutch: shortened form of VAN PELT.

Pelter (121) English (now rare): occupational name for a furrier, Middle English *pel(e)ter*.

Peltier (2356) French: variant of PELLETIER 'fur trader'.
GIVEN NAMES French 5%. *Pierre* (6), *Andre* (3), *Emile* (3), *Marcel* (2), *Aime, Alphonse, Armand, Clovis, Desire, Gilles, Jacques, Jean-Claude.*

Pelto (379) Finnish: from *pelto* 'field'. Originally a habitational name from a farm named for its location in a field, this surname was widely adopted as an ornamental name during the early 20th century; it is now also found throughout southern and central parts of the country.
GIVEN NAMES Finnish 5%; Scandinavian 4%. *Eino* (2), *Tyyne* (2), *Reino, Tauno, Veikko, Wilho.*

Peltola (119) Finnish: topographic name from *pelto* 'field' + the local suffix *-la*. This

name is found mainly in southern and western Finland.
GIVEN NAMES Finnish 23%. *Eino* (2), *Esa, Heikki, Irja, Jorma, Martti, Paavo, Sulo, Toivo, Torsti, Veikko.*

Pelton (2254) English: habitational name from Pelton, a place in County Durham, named from an unattested Old English personal name *Pēola* + *tūn* 'farmstead', 'settlement'.

Peltonen (148) Finnish: ornamental or topographic name from *pelto* 'field' + the common surname suffix *-nen*.
GIVEN NAMES Scandinavian 5%; Finnish 4%; German 4%. *Erik*; *Esko, Kimmo, Tapio*; *Fritz.*

Pelts (123) Jewish (eastern Ashkenazic): variant of PELTZ.
GIVEN NAMES Jewish 10%; Russian 10%. *Semen* (2), *Basya, Etya, Ilya*; *Mikhail* (2), *Arkady, Iosif, Leonid, Lev, Semyon.*

Peltz (943) German and Jewish (Ashkenazic): metonymic occupational name for a furrier, from Middle High German *bellez*, German *Pelz* 'fur', '(animal) skin'.

Peltzer (247) German and Jewish (Ashkenazic): variant spelling of PELZER.
GIVEN NAMES German 9%; French 4%. *Horst* (2), *Christl, Erwin, Kurt, Reinhold, Udo*; *Francois* (2), *Gilles.*

Peluso (1260) Italian (Neapolitan): southern variant of PELOSO.
GIVEN NAMES Italian 17%. *Salvatore* (5), *Carmine* (4), *Rocco* (4), *Angelo* (3), *Antonio* (3), *Domenic* (3), *Aniello* (2), *Cesare* (2), *Enrico* (2), *Gino* (2), *Giuseppe* (2).

Pelz (470) German and Jewish (Ashkenazic): variant spelling of PELTZ.
GIVEN NAMES German 7%. *Aloysius* (2), *Hans, Heinz, Hermann, Kurt, Mathias, Siegfried, Ulrich, Wenzel, Willi.*

Pelzel (295) German (Bavarian and Austrian) and Jewish (Ashkenazic): from a diminutive of PELTZ.

Pelzer (595) German: occupational name for a furrier, from an agent derivative Middle High German *bellez* 'fur'.
GIVEN NAMES German 6%. *Gerhard* (2), *Manfred* (2), *Frieda, Hannelore, Helmut, Hermann, Inge, Irmgard, Mathias.*

Pember (275) English: perhaps a variant of **Pamber**, a habitational name from a place in Hampshire named Pamber, from Old English *penn* 'fold', 'enclosure' + *beorg* 'hill'.

Pemberton (3856) English: habitational name from a place in Greater Manchester called Pemberton, from Celtic *penn* 'hill', 'head' + Old English *bere* 'barley' + *tūn* 'enclosure', 'settlement'.
FOREBEARS There seem to have been several families called de Pemberton in the Wigan area of Manchester, England, as early as the beginning of the 13th century, notably that of Adam de Pemberton, a substantial landowner Three Quaker brothers named Pemberton were born in Philadelphia:

Israel (b. 1715), James (b. 1723), and John (b. 1727); Israel and James became wealthy merchants and philanthropists.

Pemble (260) English (Kent): unexplained.

Pembleton (171) English (Nottinghamshire and Derbyshire): perhaps a variant of PEMBERTON.

Pembroke (330) Welsh: habitational name from Pembroke (Welsh *Penfro*) in South Wales. The surname has been established in Ireland since at least the 17th century.

Pen (198) **1.** English: variant of PENN. **2.** Dutch: metonymic occupational name for a clerk or penman, from Dutch *pen* 'pen'. **3.** Cambodian: unexplained.
GIVEN NAMES Cambodian 45%; Russian 5%. *Chhem* (2), *Chhum* (2), *Roeuth* (2), *Phal* (2), *Saroeun* (2), *Sokha* (2), *Boeun, Chan, Chhay, Chheng, Choung, Han, Heng, Hoeung, Kong, Lei, Leang, Leng, Nip, Nong, Noy, Phoeun, Samnang, Samoeun, Savath, Somaly, Sophath, Sopheap, Sheng, Soeun, Sophal, Tha, Yen; Iosif, Lev, Oleg*.

Pena (12859) Spanish (**Peña**), Catalan, Portuguese, and Galician: topographic name for someone who lived near a crag or cliff, Spanish *peña*, Catalan, Galician, and Portuguese *pena*, a common element of place names.
GIVEN NAMES Spanish 48%; Portuguese 9%. *Jose* (331), *Juan* (169), *Manuel* (125), *Carlos* (116), *Luis* (110), *Jesus* (84), *Pedro* (82), *Mario* (75), *Ramon* (75), *Francisco* (74), *Miguel* (62), *Rafael* (62); *Ligia* (6), *Marcio, Omero, Paulo*.

Penaloza (354) Spanish (**Peñaloza**): misspelling of **Peñalosa**, a habitational name from either of two places in Córdoba or one in Uesca named Peñalosa.
GIVEN NAMES Spanish 57%. *Jose* (10), *Juan* (6), *Francisco* (5), *Arturo* (3), *Gerardo* (3), *Gilberto* (3), *Jesus* (3), *Jorge* (3), *Manuel* (3), *Pablo* (3), *Roberto* (3), *Alfredo* (2); *Antonio* (3), *Marcello* (2), *Ceasar, Eliseo, Fausto, Filiberto, Marco, Marco Antonio*.

Penalver (110) Spanish (**Peñalver**): habitational name from Peñalver, a place so called in Guadalajara.
GIVEN NAMES Spanish 49%. *Rafael* (4), *Jose* (3), *Pedro* (3), *Francisco* (2), *Juan* (2), *Manuel* (2), *Mario* (2), *Ramon* (2), *Alberto, Arturo, Bienvenido, Carlos*.

Penaranda (134) Spanish (**Peñaranda**): habitational name from places in Burgos and Salamanca named Peñaranda.
GIVEN NAMES Spanish 53%. *Manuel* (5), *Luis* (4), *Jose* (3), *Alfonso* (2), *Eugenio* (2), *Francisco* (2), *Gonzalo* (2), *Juan* (2), *Liliana* (2), *Ramiro* (2), *Raul* (2), *Ruben* (2); *Guido* (3), *Antonio* (2), *Carlo, Federico*.

Penate (172) Spanish (**Peñate**): possibly a topographic name from *peña* 'cliff' + Basque *-ate* 'gate', 'ravine'.
GIVEN NAMES Spanish 54%. *Eduardo* (4), *Francisco* (4), *Manuel* (4), *Rolando* (4), *Carlos* (3), *Roberto* (3), *Aida* (2), *Alberto*

(2), *Ana* (2), *Armando* (2), *Jorge* (2), *Jose* (2); *Heriberto*.

Penberthy (279) English (Devon and Cornwall): habitational name from Penberthy Cross in Cornwall.

Pence (4729) Americanized spelling of German PENTZ or BENZ.

Pencek (119) Origin unidentified.

Pendarvis (493) English: habitational name from Pendarves or Pendarves Island in Cornwall.

Pendell (379) **1.** English: possibly from the hill name *Pendle* (composed of the Celtic element *penn* 'hill', 'head' + a tautologous Old English *hyll*). **2.** Probably an altered spelling of **Pendel**, a South German variant of BENDEL.

Pendelton (168) English: variant spelling of PENDLETON.
GIVEN NAMES French 4%. *Camille, Osborn*.

Pender (2101) English: occupational name for an official who was responsible for rounding up stray animals and placing them in a pound, from an agent derivative of Middle English *pind(en)* 'to shut up or enclose'. Black and MacLysaght quote Woulfe's opinion that in Ireland this is often a reduced form of PRENDERGAST.

Pendergast (1317) English: variant of Irish PRENDERGAST.

Pendergraft (968) Altered form of Irish PRENDERGAST.

Pendergraph (218) Altered form of Irish PRENDERGAST.

Pendergrass (2511) English: variant of Irish PRENDERGAST.

Pendergrast (294) English: variant of Irish PRENDERGAST.

Penders (153) Dutch and North German: occupational name from Middle Dutch *p(a)enre, paender* 'brewer', an agent derivative of *pan* '(brewing) pan'.

Pendexter (117) Variant of English and French POINDEXTER.

Pendlebury (136) English (Manchester and Lancashire): habitational name from a place in Greater Manchester called Pendlebury, from the hill name *Pendle* (composed of the Celtic element *penn* 'hill', 'head' + a tautologous Old English *hyll*) + Old English *burh* 'castle', 'fortified town'.

Pendleton (5705) English: habitational name from a place near Pendlebury, Greater Manchester, or another in Lancashire, both called Pendleton from the hill name *Pendle* + Old English *tūn* 'enclosure', 'settlement'.
FOREBEARS The Pendleton family were established in Caroline Co., VA, by Philip Pendleton, a schoolmaster of Norwich, England, who emigrated in 1682.

Pendley (1556) **1.** English: possibly a habitational name from a lost or unidentified place. **2.** Probably an altered spelling of German BENDELE or BENDLE, BENDLER.

Pendola (134) Italian: of uncertain origin; possibly from an old Germanic personal name *Pando, Bando*.
GIVEN NAMES Italian 13%; Spanish 6%. *Rocco* (2), *Gasper, Ignazio, Julieta, Santo; Arlita, Carlos, Eduardo, Humberto*.

Pendry (265) Welsh: variant of PENRY. Compare HENRY and HENDRY.

Penfield (627) English: habitational name from a place in Kent called Penfield.

Penfold (352) English (mainly Sussex and Kent): from Middle English *punfold* 'pound', Old English *pundfald*, applied as a topographic name for someone who lived by a pound for stray animals or a metonymic occupational name for someone in charge of such a pound; alternatively it may have been a habitational name from a minor place named with this word such as Poundfield in East Sussex.

Peng (1089) Chinese 彭: from the name of the fief of Peng, which was granted to a great-grandson of the legendary emperor Zhuan Xu, who then became known as Peng Zu. According to tradition, Peng Zu lived for over 800 years, and so came to be a symbol of long life. His descendants adopted Peng as their surname.
GIVEN NAMES Chinese 52%. *Wei* (8), *Liang* (6), *Ching* (5), *Ming* (5), *Hua* (4), *Song* (4), *Chen* (3), *Cheng* (3), *Gang* (3), *Hong* (3), *Jian* (3), *Mei* (3), *Hai* (2), *Tien* (2), *Chang, Chung, Da, Dat, Huan, Hung, Shen, Thy, Tui, Xuan, Yeh, Yen*.

Pengelly (134) Cornish: habitational name from any of the places (in thirteen parishes) named with Cornish *pen* 'head', 'top', 'end' + *kelly* (lenited form *gelly*) 'copse', 'grove'.

Pengra (121) Origin unidentified.

Penhollow (115) Cornish: habitational name from Penhallow in Roseland, Cornwall.
FOREBEARS Samuel Penhollow (1665–1726) of St. Mabyn, Cornwall, England, landed at Charlestown, MA, in 1686. He went on to become a leading figure in the colonial history of NH. In August 1699 he was appointed a Justice of the Peace in Portsmouth, NH; the following month he was elected speaker of the NH Assembly, and in December he was appointed treasurer of the Colony, a post which he held until his death.

Penick (1178) English: probably a variant of PINNOCK.

Peninger (199) German: variant of PENNINGER.

Penington (107) English: variant of PENNINGTON.
FOREBEARS Edward Penington, born in 1667 in Amersham, Buckinghamshire, England, was appointed surveyor-general of the province of PA in 1698 and accompanied William Penn to Philadelphia.

Peniston (153) English (Yorkshire): habitational name from Penistone near Sheffield,

South Yorkshire. The second element of the place name is Old English *tūn* 'enclosure', 'settlement'; the first is uncertain; it may be *Penning*, an Old English combination of Celtic *penn* 'hill' + Old English *-ing* 'place characterized by or belonging to'.

Penix (568) English: probably a variant of PINNOCK.

Penk (104) South German: variant of **Benk**: **1.** habitational name from any of various places so named in Bavaria. **2.** from a pet form of the baptismal name *Benignus*. **3.** German: diminutive of Sorbian *pien* 'tree trunk', 'stump', probably a nickname for a stocky person. **4.** German: from an Old Prussian personal name.
GIVEN NAME German 4%. *Heinz*.

Penka (119) Czech: probably a habitational name from places called Penk in Austria and Bavaria. unexplained.
GIVEN NAMES French 4%; German 4%. *Etienne*; *Erwin*, *Kurt*.

Penkala (155) Polish (also **Penkała**): variant of PEKALA.

Penland (1539) Of uncertain origin. Possibly an altered form of PENTLAND or a habitational name from Penlan Hall, Essex or Penlan Farm in Hereford and Worcester. There are also numerous places in Wales named Penlan, notably in Dyfed, and the name may have been adopted on arrival in the U.S. by immigrants from any of these places.

Penley (867) English: habitational name from Penleigh in Dilton, Wiltshire.

Penman (671) Scottish: **1.** occupational name for a scribe. **2.** habitational name from a lost place in the Border region, derived from the British elements *penn* 'hill', 'head' + *maen* 'stone'.

Penn (6309) **1.** English: habitational name from various places, for example Penn in Buckinghamshire and Staffordshire, named with the Celtic element *pen* 'hill', which was apparently adopted in Old English. **2.** English: metonymic occupational name for an impounder of stray animals, from Middle English, Old English *penn* '(sheep) pen'. **3.** English: pet form of PARNELL. **4.** German: from Sorbian *pien* 'tree stump', probably a nickname for a short stocky person. **5.** Americanized form of a like-sounding Jewish surname.
FOREBEARS The Commonwealth of PA was founded in 1681 by an English Quaker, William Penn (1644–1718), who was born in London into a family of Gloucestershire origin. His grandfather was a merchant and sea captain, and his father was an admiral on the Parliamentary side during the Civil War, who later served King Charles II after the Restoration. Because of his father's services to the crown, Penn the younger received a grant of a vast tract of land in North America, formerly part of New Netherland, which later became the state of PA.

Penna (832) **1.** Cornish: of uncertain origin; perhaps a habitational name from any of the places named Penare or Penarth, from Cornish *pen-arth* 'promontory', 'headland'. **2.** Italian (mainly southern): probably a topographic name for someone who lived on a hill or peak, or generally in an elevated location, *penna* (from Latin *pinnus* 'pointed'), a common element of place names. **3.** Greek: from the Greek vocabulary word *penna* 'quill', 'pen', hence a metonymic occupational name for a clerk or scribe (Greek **Pennas**, with the occupational suffix *-as*).
GIVEN NAMES Italian 14%; Spanish 7%. *Antonio* (3), *Enrico* (2), *Gennaro* (2), *Mario* (2), *Rocco* (2), *Amedeo*, *Angelo*, *Carmelo*, *Ferdinando*, *Gaetano*, *Giuseppe*, *Leonardo*, *Nicola*; *Angel* (2), *Juan* (2), *Camilo*, *Carlos*, *Diego*, *Esteban*, *Ines*.

Pennacchio (141) Italian: from *pennacchio* 'plume of feathers' (from Latin *pinnaculum*), hence a nickname for a tall thin person or possibly a metonymic occupational name for someone who wore a plume of feathers, perhaps a dignitary or knight.
GIVEN NAMES Italian 30%. *Vito* (3), *Nino* (2), *Pasquale* (2), *Rocco* (2), *Angelo*, *Salvatore*, *Sergio*.

Penne (125) **1.** Dutch: from Middle Dutch *penne* 'pen', 'quill', hence a metonymic occupational name for a scribe. **2.** Possibly Italian: habitational name from Penne in Pescara province.

Pennebaker (293) Americanized spelling of German **Pannebacker** or **Pfannebecker** (see PENNYPACKER).

Pennel (207) English: variant spelling of PENNELL (see PARNELL).
GIVEN NAME French 5%. *Vernice*.

Pennell (2323) English (mainly Shropshire and West Midlands): variant of PARNELL.

Pennella (229) Italian: from a derivative of PENNA.
GIVEN NAMES Italian 31%. *Angelo* (6), *Rocco* (5), *Carmine* (4), *Antonio* (2), *Camillo* (2), *Donato* (2), *Filippo* (2), *Pasquale* (2), *Amato*, *Antonietta*, *Gaetano*, *Salvatore*.

Penner (2184) **1.** English: occupational name, a variant of PENN 1, with the agent suffix *-er*. **2.** North German (including Lower Rhineland): variant of **Pfänner**, from *Pfann* 'pan'; according to Bahlow, a name denoting the owner of a salt-boiling pan. **3.** German: habitational name from Penna near Leipzig. **4.** Eastern German: in some cases a topographic name (of Salzburg emigrants) in East Prussia, equivalent of *Baintner*, *Paintner* (see BAINTER), from Middle High German *biunte* 'separate part of land or enclosure belonging to a village'.
GIVEN NAMES German 4%. *Kurt* (4), *Hans* (3), *Otto* (3), *Klaus* (2), *Bernhard*, *Dieter*, *Erna*, *Ernst*, *Franz*, *Gerhard*, *Gunther*, *Lothar*.

Pennewell (125) Variant of English PENNY-WELL.

Penney (2326) English and Scottish: variant spelling of PENNY.

Pennick (161) English: variant of PINNOCK.
GIVEN NAME German 4%. *Eldred*.

Pennie (208) Scottish: variant spelling of PENNY.
GIVEN NAME French 4%. *Monique*.

Penniman (307) English: occupational name for the servant (Middle English *man*) of someone called PENNY.

Penning (575) **1.** English, Dutch, and North German: from early Middle English *penning*, Low German *penning*, Middle Dutch *penninc* 'penny' (see PENNY), a topographic name (from a field name) or a nickname referring to tax dues of a penny. **2.** South German: from the short form, *Panno*, of a Germanic personal name derived from a word meaning 'ban', 'order', 'command'.

Penninger (241) **1.** Dutch: from an agent derivative of PENNING 1. **2.** German: habitational name from any of several places called Penning. **3.** Altered spelling of German PFENNINGER.

Pennings (230) English: patronymic from PENNING.

Pennington (14436) English (chiefly Lancashire and Cumbria): habitational name from places called Pennington, in Lancashire, Cumbria, and Hampshire. The latter two are so called from Old English *pening* 'penny' (PENNY) (used as a byname or from a tribute due on the land) + *tūn* 'enclosure', 'settlement'. The place of this name in the parish of Leigh in Lancashire is recorded in the 13th century as *Pinington* and *Pynington*, and may be from Old English *Pinningtūn* 'settlement (*tūn*) associated with a man named *Pinna*'.

Pennino (203) Italian: from a diminutive of PENNA.
GIVEN NAMES Italian 12%. *Sal* (2), *Agostino*, *Antonio*, *Carmela*, *Mario*, *Orlando*, *Salvatore*, *Santino*, *Valentino*.

Pennisi (281) Italian (mainly eastern Sicily): habitational name from Pennisi a district of Acireale in Catania province.
GIVEN NAMES Italian 28%. *Salvatore* (7), *Angelo* (3), *Giuseppe* (3), *Leonardo* (3), *Mario* (3), *Antonio* (2), *Carmelo* (2), *Rosario* (2), *Sal* (2), *Alfio*, *Carlo*, *Ettore*, *Isidoro*, *Marco*, *Martino*.

Pennison (139) Scottish or English: patronymic from PENNY. The name is established in France; it may have been taken there by Scottish Jacobite refugees in the 18th century.
GIVEN NAMES French 6%. *Elodie*, *Ulysse*.

Penniston (129) English (Yorkshire): variant spelling of PENISTON.

Pennix (169) English: probably a variant of PINNOCK.
GIVEN NAME French 5%. *Andre* (2).

Pennock (976) English (North Yorkshire): variant of PINNOCK.

Pennoyer (135) Welsh (Brecon): probably from Welsh *pen* 'head' + *aur* 'golden', 'yellow', denoting the head of the Golden Valley in Herefordshire.

Penny (3221) English (also present in Ireland): from Middle English *peni*, *peny* 'penny', applied as a nickname, possibly for a person of some substance or for a tenant who paid a rent of one penny. This was the common Germanic unit of value when money was still an unusual phenomenon. It was the only unit of coinage in England until the early 14th century, when the groat and the gold noble were introduced, and was a silver coin of considerable value. There is some evidence that the word was used in Old English times as a byname.

Pennycuff (123) Possibly an Americanized spelling of German *Pfannkuch*, an metonymic occupational name for a cook, meaning 'pancake'.

Pennypacker (334) Americanized form of German **Pfannebecker**, or more particularly the Low German form, **Pannebacker**, occupational names for a maker of roof tiles or a tiler, from Middle High German *pfanne* 'pan', 'tile' (Middle Low German *panne*) + *becker*, *backer* 'baker'.

Pennywell (129) English: habitational name from Pennywell in Tyne and Wear or from a similarly named lost place elsewhere.

Peno (132) Spanish (**Peño**): nickname for a foundling, from dialect *peño* 'abandoned'.

Penoyer (171) Variant of PENNOYER.

Penrod (2289) Origin unidentified. Possibly English, but the name is rare in England. It may equally well be an altered form of an unidentified German or Dutch habitational name.

Penrose (980) Cornish and Welsh: habitational name from any of the places called Penrose, in ten parishes of Cornwall, several in Wales, and in Herefordshire near the Welsh border. All are named with Celtic *pen* 'head', 'top', 'end' + *ros* 'heath', 'moor'.

Penry (337) Welsh: Anglicized form of Welsh *ap Henry* 'son of Henry' (see HENRY).

Pensabene (149) Italian: from a personal name, an omen name bestowed on child in the hope that he will be a deep and clear thinker, formed from *pensare* 'to think' + *bene* 'well'.

GIVEN NAMES Italian 21%; Spanish 4%. *Pietro* (2), *Antonio*, *Guiseppe*, *Mario*, *Natale*, *Pietrina*, *Santo*; *Jaime*, *Miguel Angel*.

Pense (259) German: perhaps a habitational name from a place called Pensau.

Pensiero (106) Italian: from the personal name *Pensiero* literally 'thinking', 'thought', or in some cases from a short

form of the personal name *Buonpensiero* 'good thought'.

GIVEN NAMES Italian 18%. *Mario* (4), *Angelo*, *Lorenzo*, *Orlando*, *Umberto*.

Pensinger (203) Probably an altered spelling of German **Benzinger**, a habitational name from Benzingen near Sigmaringen in southern Germany.

Penso (107) **1.** Italian: possibly from a short form of a personal name such as PENSABENE; otherwise a variant of *Penzo* (see PENZA). **2.** Portuguese: habitational name from any of several places of this name.

GIVEN NAMES Spanish 7%; Italian 6%. *Juan* (2), *Ana*, *Reinaldo*; *Elio*, *Gianfranco*, *Silvano*.

Penson (399) English: **1.** patronymic from PENN 3 'or PAINE 1. **2.** habitational name from Penson in Devon.

Pensyl (197) **1.** Possibly an altered spelling of South German **Penzel**, **Penzl**, or **Pensel**, short forms of the personal name BERTHOLD or sometimes BERNHARD. This name occurs chiefly in PA. **2.** (also **Pensel, Pinsel**), a metonymic occupational name for a painter or whitewasher, from Middle High German *pensel*, *pinsel* 'brush'.

Penta (404) Italian: of uncertain derivation; perhaps from Greek *pente* 'five'.

GIVEN NAMES Italian 9%. *Camillo* (2), *Salvatore* (2), *Antimo*, *Domenic*, *Domenico*, *Franco*, *Marcello*, *Rocco*, *Sal*.

Pentecost (1001) English: nickname for someone who was born at Whitsuntide or had some particular connection with that time of year, such as owing a feudal obligation then. The name is from Middle English, Old French *pentecost*, from Greek *pentēkostē (hēmera)* 'fiftieth (day)', i.e. the fiftieth day after Easter.

Pentico (122) Variant of PENTECOST.

Pentland (230) Scottish: habitational name from a place near Edinburgh, of uncertain etymology, perhaps from Middle English *pent* 'enclosed' + *land* 'land'.

Penton (1075) English: habitational name from Penton Mewsey, Hampshire, which is named with Old English *pening* 'penny' + *tūn* 'farmstead', 'settlement', i.e. a farmstead paying a penny rent.

Pentz (649) German: **1.** habitational name (of Slavic origin) from a place in Pomerania. **2.** variant of BENZ.

Penuel (201) Variant spelling of English PENWELL.

Penwell (557) English: probably a variant of PENNYWELL.

Penza (225) Italian (Apulia): from the medieval personal name *Penzo*, a short form of various Germanic compound names formed with *bandwo* 'banner', 'standard' (Lombard *bandu*).

GIVEN NAMES Italian 17%. *Angelo* (2), *Carmine* (2), *Domenic* (2), *Guido* (2), *Antonio*,

Giuseppe, Rinaldo, Sal, Salvatore, Saverio, Silvio, Vincenzo.

Peoples (4564) **1.** Irish (Ulster): adopted as an English equivalent of Gaelic **Ó Duibhne** 'descendant of *Dubhne*', a personal name meaning 'ill-going', 'disagreeable'. Compare DEENEY. *Peoples* is a pseudo-translation based on the phonetic resemblance of the Gaelic name to Gaelic *daoine* 'people'. **2.** English: patronymic from a pet form (in *-el*) of the Old French personal name *Pepis*, oblique case *Pepin* (see PEPIN).

Peot (168) Possibly an Americanized spelling of French **Piot**, **Piotte**. This surname is frequent in WI.

Peotter (119) Probably a variant spelling of English POTTER.

Pepe (1927) Northern Italian: from a pet form of *Giuseppe*, Italian form of JOSEPH.

GIVEN NAMES Italian 18%. *Angelo* (17), *Salvatore* (13), *Carmine* (6), *Vito* (5), *Enrico* (4), *Rocco* (4), *Vincenzo* (4), *Carlo* (3), *Sal* (3), *Antonio* (2), *Donato* (2), *Emidio* (2).

Peper (477) **1.** North German and Jewish (Ashkenazic): variant of PEPPER. **2.** Dutch: metonymic occupational name for a spicer, from Middle Dutch *pe(e)per* 'pepper'.

GIVEN NAMES German 5%. *Heinz* (2), *Bernhard*, *Ewald*, *Leonhard*, *Reinhold*, *Udo*.

Pepi (138) **1.** Italian: patronymic from *Pepe*, a pet form of *Giuseppe* (see JOSEPH), or from *pepe* 'pepper', as a nickname for a spirited or highly active person. **2.** Greek: patronymic from Albanian *Pepa*, a pet form of the personal name *Petros* (see PETER). **3.** Greek: alternatively, perhaps a metronymic from Aromanian *Pepa*, a pet form of the female personal name *Despina*. **4.** Greek: possibly also a patronymic from Italian *Pepi*, a pet form of *Giuseppe* (see 1 above).

GIVEN NAMES Italian 7%; Spanish 6%; French 6%. *Carmelo* (2), *Massimo*, *Rocco*; *Juan* (3), *Manuel*, *Salvador*; *Cecile*, *Constant*.

Pepin (1827) French (**Pépin**) and English: from the Old French personal name *Pepis*, oblique case *Pepin* (introduced to Britain by the Normans). Of uncertain origin, it was borne by several Frankish kings, most notably Pepin le Bref, father of Charlemagne, and remained popular throughout the early Middle Ages. Reaney and Wilson suggest that late-formed examples of the English surname may alternatively be from Old French *pepin*, *pipin* 'seed of a fruit', and thus a metonymic occupational name for a gardener or grower of fruit trees. This surname is also established in northwest Germany, around Cologne.

FOREBEARS The earliest Pépin in Canada, of unknown provenance, was documented in Trois-Rivières, Quebec, in 1645. Others originated in Normandy, France. Asso-

ciated secondary surnames include LA-
CHANCE, LAFORCE, Descardonnets, and
Cardonnet.
GIVEN NAMES French 11%. *Andre* (5),
Armand (5), *Camille* (5), *Emile* (4), *Pierre*
(4), *Gilles* (3), *Lucien* (3), *Normand* (3),
Alcide (2), *Fernand* (2), *Jacques* (2),
Marcel (2).

Pepitone (266) Italian (Sicily): variant of
PIPITONE.
GIVEN NAMES Italian 10%. *Salvatore* (4),
Angelo, Antonio, Vito.

Peplinski (581) Polish (**Pepliński**): habitational name for someone from Peplin in
Bydgoszcz voivodeship.

Peplow (138) **1.** English (chiefly Worcestershire and West Midlands): habitational name from Peplow in Shropshire,
recorded in Domesday Book as *Papelau*.
This may be from Old English *pyppel* 'pebble' + *hlāw* 'hill'. **2.** German: habitational
name from Peplow in Mecklenburg.
GIVEN NAMES Scandinavian 7%. *Hilmar* (2),
Thor.

Peppard (357) Irish: apparently a Norman
name, taken to Ireland in the 12th century
and associated particularly with County
Louth.

Peppe (143) **1.** Italian: from a short form of
the personal name *Giuseppe*. **2.** Dutch:
from *Peppo*, a pet form of a Germanic personal name.
GIVEN NAME Italian 5%. *Vincenzo.*

Peppel (228) German: from a Germanic
personal name, *Babo*, of uncertain origin,
possibly from a nursery word.
GIVEN NAMES German 6%; French 5%. *Otto*
(2), *Gerhart, Horst, Willi; Andre, Laurent,
Mihelle.*

Pepper (4554) **1.** English and North German: from Middle English *peper, piper*,
Middle Low German *peper* 'pepper', hence
a metonymic occupational name for a
spicer; alternatively, it may be a nickname
for a small man (as if the size of a peppercorn) or one with a fiery temper, or for a
dark-haired person (from the color of a
peppercorn) or anecdotal for someone who
paid a peppercorn rent. **2.** Americanized
form of the Ashkenazic Jewish ornamental
name PFEFFER, or Fef(f)er, a cognate, from
Yiddish *fefer* 'pepper'. **3.** Irish: variant of
PEPPARD.

Pepperman (191) Americanized form of
German **Pfeffermann**, occupational name
for a spicer (see PFEFFER).

Peppers (1361) Perhaps an altered spelling
of Dutch **Pepers**, a patronymic from
PEPER.

Peppin (170) English (Somerset): variant
spelling of PEPIN.

Pepple (526) Probably an altered spelling of
German PEPPEL or **Pöppel** (see POPPELL).

Peppler (364) South German: nickname
from an agent derivative of Middle High
German *pepelen* 'to feed or suckle (someone)'.

Pequeno (172) Spanish (**Pequeño**) and
Portuguese: nickname for a small person,
from Portuguese *pequeno*, Spanish *pequeño* 'small'.
GIVEN NAMES Spanish 54%; Portuguese 8%.
Jesus (4), *Domingo* (3), *Jose* (3), *Laureano*
(3), *Miguel* (3), *Ruben* (3), *Armando* (2),
Aurelio (2), *Enrique* (2), *Fermin* (2), *Juan*
(2), *Manuel* (2); *Joaquim.*

Pequignot (206) Eastern French (**Péqui-
gnot**): nickname for a weakling, from a
diminutive of Occitan *péquin* 'puny', 'sickly'.

Pera (457) **1.** Catalan and Portuguese:
habitational name from *La Pera*, a town in
Girona province, Catalonia, or from any of
various places called Pera in Portugal, from
Latin *Petra* 'stone'. **2.** Italian: metonymic
occupational name for a grower or seller of
pears, from *pera* 'pear'.
GIVEN NAMES Italian 16%; Spanish 8%.
Mario (4), *Alberto* (2), *Antonio* (3), *Angelo*
(2), *Sergio* (2), *Siro* (2), *Enzo, Franco,
Gino, Salvatore; Pedro* (2), *Gonzalo,
Gumercindo, Jaime, Margarita, Ruperto,
Socorro, Walfrido.*

Peragine (214) Italian (Puglia): variant of
PIRAINO.
GIVEN NAMES Italian 27%. *Salvatore* (4), *Vito*
(3), *Angelo* (2), *Francesco* (2), *Antonio,
Carmela, Donato, Filippo, Gianni, Nicola,
Onofrio, Pietro.*

Peraino (221) Italian: variant of PIRAINO.
GIVEN NAMES Italian 18%. *Vito* (6), *Sal* (4),
*Antonino, Baldassare, Giuseppe, Salva-
tore.*

Perala (208) Finnish (**Perälä**): habitational
name from a farm named for its location,
from *perä* 'end', 'back', 'remote' + the
local suffix *-la*. This name is common in
Western Finland, both as a surname and as
a farm name, especially in Ostrobothnia.
GIVEN NAMES Finnish 13%. *Toivo* (4), *Reino*
(2), *Sulo* (2), *Jukka, Olavi, Onni, Waino,
Wilho.*

Perales (1425) Spanish: habitational name
from any of the places named Perales, from
the plural of *peral* 'plantation of pear
trees', 'pear orchard', a derivative of *pera*
'pear'.
GIVEN NAMES Spanish 45%. *Jose* (42), *Juan*
(19), *Manuel* (19), *Jesus* (13), *Ruben* (13),
Carlos (9), *Miguel* (9), *Pedro* (9), *Raul* (8),
Sergio (8), *Luis* (7), *Francisco* (6).

Peralez (252) Spanish: misspelling of
PERALES.
GIVEN NAMES Spanish 41%. *Angel* (3),
Francisco (3), *Manuel* (3), *Ruben* (3),
Alfredo (2), *Arturo* (2), *Carlos* (2), *Efrain*
(2), *Lupe* (2), *Mario* (2), *Raul* (2), *Ricardo*
(2).

Peralta (2888) Aragonese, Catalan, and
Spanish: habitational name from any of the
places in Aragon, Catalonia, and Navarre
called Peralta, from Latin *petra alta* 'high
rock'. This name is also established in
Italy.

GIVEN NAMES Spanish 48%; Italian 9%. *Jose*
(64), *Juan* (49), *Carlos* (34), *Manuel* (30),
Rafael (21), *Miguel* (20), *Francisco* (19),
Ramon (18), *Jorge* (17), *Pedro* (16), *Luis*
(14), *Sergio* (13); *Antonio* (8), *Fausto* (4),
Girolamo (3), *Lucio* (3), *Dante* (2), *Eliseo*
(2), *Federico* (2), *Heriberto* (2), *Leonardo*
(2), *Marco* (2), *Rocco* (2), *Romeo* (2).

Perata (127) Southern Italian: according to
Caracausi, a variant of PERALTA.
GIVEN NAMES Italian 10%. *Aldo, Angelo,
Antonio, Filippo, Gino.*

Perault (108) French: variant of PER-
REAULT.

Peraza (483) Spanish: unexplained. Per-
haps a variant of PEDRAZA.
GIVEN NAMES Spanish 53%. *Jose* (17), *Carlos*
(11), *Luis* (8), *Jorge* (7), *Manuel* (7),
Roberto (6), *Pedro* (5), *Fernando* (4),
Orlando (4), *Ramon* (4), *Raul* (4), *Ana* (3);
Antonio (6), *Marco* (3), *Lucio* (2),
*Clemente, Donato, Eliseo, Franco,
Geronimo, Heriberto, Marco Antonio.*

Perazzo (163) Italian: from a pet form of
the personal name *Pero*, a north Italian
form of *Pietro* (see PETER).
GIVEN NAMES Italian 16%; Spanish 8%.
Albino (2), *Carlo, Dante, Dino, Virgilio;
Jorge, Jorge Alberto, Marta, Pascual,
Santiago.*

Percell (326) English: probably a variant
spelling of PURCELL, or alternatively of
Percil (from Old French *percer* 'to pierce'
+ *soel, suel* 'threshold').

Perch (133) Probably an Americanized
form of **Pertsch**, South German form of
BERTSCH, or possibly an altered spelling of
Bavarian **Pförtsch**, presumably a humorous nickname from Middle High German
verz, vorz 'fart'.

Percifield (207) English: altered form of
PERCIVAL 2.

Percival (1327) English: **1.** from the personal name *Perceval*, first found as the
name of the hero of an epic poem by the
12th-century French poet Crestien de
Troyes, describing the quest for the holy
grail. The origin of the name is uncertain; it
may be associated with the Gaulish personal name *Pritorīx* or it may be an alteration
of the Celtic name *Peredur* (see PRIDDY). It
seems to have been altered as the result of
folk etymological association with Old
French *perce(r)* 'to pierce or breach' + *val*
'valley'. **2.** Norman habitational name
from either of the two places in Calvados
named Perceval.

Percle (240) French: unexplained.
GIVEN NAMES French 10%. *Eves* (2), *Angelle,
Clovis, Emile, Fernand, Sylvian.*

Percoco (122) Southern Italian (mainly
Campania): from *percuoco* 'apricot tree',
hence a topographic name or possibly a
nickname.
GIVEN NAMES Italian 13%. *Enrico, Sal.*

Percy (1390) English (of Norman origin):
habitational name from any of various

places in northern France, so called from the Gallo-Roman personal name *Persius* + the locative suffix *-acum*. The suggestion has also been made that it is a nickname from Old French *perce(r)* 'to pierce or breach' + *haie* 'hedge', 'enclosure', referring either to a soldier remembered for his breach of a fortification, or in jest to a poacher who was in the habit of breaking into a private park.

FOREBEARS Percy is the name of a leading Northumbrian family, who were instrumental in holding the English border against the Scots from their stronghold at Alnwick. Their founder was a Norman, William de Percy (?1030–96), 1st Baron Percy, who accompanied William the Conqueror. Sir Henry Percy (1342–1408), 1st Earl of Northumberland, and his son Sir Henry Percy (1364–1403), known as Harry Hotspur, helped place Henry IV on the throne. The earldom, created in 1377, has continued, on two occasions through female members, in the same family to the present day. George Percy (1508–1632), son of the 8th Earl of Northumberland, was in VA from 1606 to 1612, serving briefly as governor.

Perdew (342) Variant of English PERDUE.

Perdomo (857) Spanish (Tenerife): apparently a derivative of the local place name La Perdoma, the seat of the town council of La Orotava, Santa Cruz de Tenerife (Canaries).
GIVEN NAMES Spanish 53%. *Jose* (36), *Luis* (16), *Juan* (12), *Manuel* (11), *Carlos* (10), *Jorge* (8), *Pedro* (8), *Ana* (7), *Julio* (7), *Rafael* (7), *Raul* (6), *Roberto* (6).

Perdue (5491) English and Irish: from Old French *par Dieu* 'by God', which was adopted in Middle English in a variety of more or less heavily altered forms. The surname represents a nickname from a favorite oath. According to MacLysaght, the surname in Ireland belonged to a French Protestant family who settled in County Cork.

Pere (146) **1.** Southern French (**Péré**): topographic name from a variant of **périer** 'pear tree'. **2.** Catalan: from the personal name *Pere*, Catalan equivalent of PETER. **3.** English: variant of PEAR 1. **4.** Hungarian: from the old secular personal name *Pere*, *Pöre*.
GIVEN NAMES Spanish 7%; French 5%. *Luis* (2), *Alejandro, Florinda, Jose Luis, Patria, Pedro, Roberto, Santiago*; *Camille, Etienne*.

Perea (1447) Spanish: habitational name from any of the places in southern Spain (Alacant, Ciudad Real, Jaen, Badajoz, and Cadiz) named Perea.
GIVEN NAMES Spanish 33%. *Carlos* (15), *Jose* (15), *Manuel* (14), *Juan* (7), *Ramon* (7), *Roberto* (7), *Ruben* (7), *Luis* (6), *Arturo* (5), *Jaime* (5), *Jesus* (5), *Raul* (5).

Pereda (260) Asturian-Leonese and Galician: habitational name from any of the places, mostly in Asturies, called Pereda, from *pereda* 'pear tree orchard'.
GIVEN NAMES Spanish 50%. *Jose* (7), *Carlos* (5), *Francisco* (5), *Ramon* (4), *Juan* (3), *Luis* (3), *Pedro* (3), *Roberto* (3), *Ana* (2), *Armando* (2), *Eduardo* (2), *Hipolito* (2).

Peredo (108) Galician: from any of the places in Galicia called Peredo ('pear tree orchard'; compare PEREDA).
GIVEN NAMES Spanish 45%. *Juan* (3), *Augusto* (2), *Carlos* (2), *Diosdado* (2), *Manuel* (2), *Alberto, Alphonso, Anicia, Armando, Arsenia, Casimiro, Edgardo*.

Peregoy (293) Americanized form of French **Périgord** (see PEDIGO).

Pereida (131) Spanish: possibly a variant of Portugese and Galician PEREIRA, or a confusion between PEREDA and PEREIRA. The name in this form is not found in Spain but only in Mexico and South America.
GIVEN NAMES Spanish 36%. *Juan* (2), *Julio* (2), *Manuel* (2), *Ernesto, Esteban, Eugenio, Felipe, Fermin, Hilario, Jose Luis, Leticia, Marina*; *Antonio, Eliseo, Lucio*.

Pereira (5243) Portuguese, Galician, and Jewish (Sephardic): topographic name from Portuguese *pereira* 'pear tree', or a habitational name from a place named with this word in Portugal and Galicia. The surname is also common in western India, having been taken there by Portuguese colonists.
GIVEN NAMES Spanish 31%; Portuguese 16%. *Jose* (165), *Manuel* (149), *Carlos* (58), *Luis* (43), *Mario* (40), *Fernando* (28), *Jorge* (27), *Francisco* (21), *Pedro* (21), *Juan* (17), *Julio* (16), *Armando* (15); *Joao* (31), *Paulo* (15), *Joaquim* (9), *Henrique* (5), *Ilidio* (5), *Agostinho* (4), *Duarte* (4), *Amadeu* (3), *Adao* (2), *Ademir* (2), *Ligia* (2), *Aderito*; *Antonio* (117), *Angelo* (4), *Luciano* (4), *Filomena* (3), *Leonardo* (3), *Mauro* (3), *Alessandro* (2), *Antonino* (2), *Dino* (2), *Enio* (2), *Flavio* (2), *Marco* (2).

Perel (156) **1.** Jewish (Ashkenazic): ornamental name from Yiddish *perl* 'pearl'. **2.** Jewish (Ashkenazic): from the Yiddish female personal name *Perl* 'pearl'. **3.** French (**Pérel**): from a pet form of the personal name *Pierre*, French form of PETER.
GIVEN NAMES Jewish 10%; Russian 6%; German 4%. *Aron, Shira, Yitzchok*; *Oleg* (2), *Yelena* (2), *Mikhail, Vladimir, Yuriy*; *Arno* (2), *Hannelore*.

Perella (229) **1.** Italian: from a female derivative of the personal name PERO. **2.** Catalan: habitational name from any of various places called Perella, in the Vallespir, Solsonè, and Ripollès areas (northern Catalonia) and also in Minorca. **3.** Italian: unexplained.

GIVEN NAMES Italian 12%. *Angelo, Enrico, Gino, Italo, Marco, Mauro, Nicola, Remo, Salvatore*.

Perelli (114) Italian: from a pet form of the personal name PERO.
GIVEN NAMES Italian 18%; Spanish 4%. *Dino* (3), *Giulio, Luigi, Nicola, Remo, Sergio, Silvana*; *Jorge* (2), *Getulio*, .

Perelman (316) Jewish (Ashkenazic): **1.** elaborated form of PEARL 2, with the addition of Yiddish *man* 'man'. **2.** from the Yiddish female personal name *Perl* (see PEREL) + *man* 'man', in the sense 'husband of Perl'.
GIVEN NAMES Jewish 19%; Russian 13%. *Gershon* (2), *Myer* (2), *Naum* (2), *Polina* (2), *Rakhil* (2), *Varda* (2), *Aron, Avigail, Bluma, Chaim, Genya, Haim*; *Lev* (4), *Leonid* (3), *Boris* (2), *Mikhail* (2), *Natalya* (2), *Aleksandr, Beyla, Efim, Grigoriy, Klavdiya, Liliya, Raisa*.

Perera (643) **1.** Catalan: topographic name from Catalan *perera* 'pear tree'. **2.** Galician and Portuguese: variant of PEREIRA. This name is also found in western India, where it was taken by Portuguese colonists.
GIVEN NAMES Spanish 20%; Indian 19%. *Jose* (5), *Emilio* (4), *Jorge* (4), *Orlando* (4), *Roberto* (4), *Armando* (3), *Carlos* (3), *Juan* (3), *Ana* (2), *Francisco* (2), *Hermino* (2), *Manuel* (2); *Nihal* (6), *Gamini* (3), *Rohan* (3), *Daya* (2), *Kusum* (2), *Mahesh* (2), *Manoj* (2), *Sonali* (2), *Swarna* (2), *Ananda, Anura, Ashok*.

Peres (422) **1.** Portuguese: patronymic from the personal name *Pedro* (see PETER). **2.** Spanish and Jewish (Sephardic): variant of PEREZ 2. **3.** English: variant of PIERCE. **4.** Possibly also Hungarian: occupational name from *peres* 'procurator', 'advocate' (from *per* 'trial').
GIVEN NAMES Spanish 26%. *Jose* (13), *Alejandro* (3), *Carlos* (3), *Manuel* (3), *Eloy* (2), *Gonzalo* (2), *Ramon* (2), *Agustin, Alfonso, Ana, Artemio, Bautista*.

Peretti (243) Italian: patronymic from a pet form of the personal name PERO.
GIVEN NAMES Italian 9%. *Angelo* (2), *Alessio, Dino, Enrico, Ettore, Lorenzo, Marcello, Marco*.

Peretz (266) Jewish: from a Biblical name, borne by a grandson of the patriarch Jacob, meaning 'burst forth' (Genesis 38:29).
GIVEN NAMES Jewish 27%. *Meir* (6), *Moshe* (3), *Shimon* (3), *Miriam* (2), *Zvi* (2), *Arie, Asher, Avital, Avner, Erez, Eyal, Hyman*.

Pereyra (403) Portuguese and Galician: variant spelling of PEREIRA.
GIVEN NAMES Spanish 48%. *Jose* (12), *Carlos* (9), *Luis* (7), *Manuel* (6), *Jorge* (5), *Ruben* (4), *Ana* (3), *Fernando* (3), *Juan* (3), *Julio* (3), *Pablo* (3), *Pedro* (3).

Perez (58404) **1.** Spanish (**Pérez**) and Jewish (Sephardic): patronymic from the personal name *Pedro*, Spanish equivalent of PETER. **2.** Jewish: variant of PERETZ.

GIVEN NAMES Spanish 49%. *Juan* (794), *Manuel* (597), *Carlos* (556), *Luis* (551), *Jesus* (441), *Francisco* (399), *Pedro* (350), *Miguel* (344), *Jorge* (322), *Ramon* (300), *Rafael* (282), *Mario* (264).

Perfect (156) English: variant of PARFITT.

Perfetti (319) Italian: patronymic or plural form of PERFETTO.

GIVEN NAMES Italian 25%. *Mario* (3), *Alfonso* (2), *Julio* (2), *Renato* (2), *Aldo, Angelo, Augusto, Cesare, Claudio, Cosimo, Dino, Elio, Gino, Guido, Gustavo, Italia, Marco, Marino.*

Perfetto (275) Italian: from *perfetto* 'perfect', applied either as a nickname or personal name.

GIVEN NAMES Italian 17%. *Antonio* (4), *Pasquale* (4), *Carlo* (3), *Enzo* (2), *Agostino, Aldo, Angelo, Damiano, Gino, Sal, Salvatore.*

Pergande (219) German (of Slavic origin): ethnic name, from *Burgund-* 'Burgundian', for a descendant of the Burgundians, a Germanic tribe, originally of northeastern Europe, around the Baltic Sea; later they migrated to the southwest and were for the most part wiped out in the middle Rhine area around AD 435.

Pergola (260) Italian: topographic name from *pergola* 'pergola' (particularly as a support for a grapevine), or a habitational name from any of various places named with this word, for example in Pesaro and Potenza.

GIVEN NAMES Italian 16%. *Rocco* (3), *Salvatore* (3), *Sal* (2), *Aldo, Angelo, Antonio, Concetta, Gerlando, Nicola, Saverio.*

Perhach (101) Origin unidentified.

Perham (459) English: habitational name from any of various places (for example those in Suffolk and Sussex now called Parham), originally named with the Old English elements *peru* 'pear' + *hām* 'homestead'.

Peri (271) **1.** Indian (Andhra Pradesh): Hindu name, derived from a place name. **2.** Italian: patronymic or plural form of PERO. **3.** Hungarian (**Péri**): habitational name for someone from a place called Pér. **4.** Greek: variant of PERRIS.

GIVEN NAMES Indian 12%; Italian 10%; Spanish 5%. *Diwakar* (2), *Aruna, Divakar, Janaki, Laxmi, Mani, Prasad, Rama, Ramesh, Satya, Shrinivas; Salvatore* (4), *Vito* (2), *Giovanni, Santo; Armando* (2), *Mario* (2), *Rosario* (2), *Alfonzo, Andres, Bernardo, Gabriela, Hernan.*

Perich (238) **1.** Croatian and Serbian (**Perić**): patronymic from the personal names *Pero* (Croatian) or *Pera* (Serbian), short forms of *Petar* (see PETER). **2.** Catalan: variant of **Peric**, derivative of the personal name PERE, Catalan equivalent of PETER.

Perigo (271) Americanized form of French **Périgord** (see PEDIGO).

Perilli (136) Italian: from a pet form of the personal name PERO.

GIVEN NAMES Italian 23%. *Angelo* (3), *Antonio* (2), *Silvio* (2), *Alessandro, Alfonse, Benedetta, Camillo, Corrado, Gaetano, Vito.*

Perillo (754) Italian: from either a pet form of the personal name PERO, or a nickname from Calabrian *pirillu* denoting a variety of small pear.

GIVEN NAMES Italian 16%. *Sal* (4), *Salvatore* (4), *Vito* (4), *Antonio* (3), *Angelo* (2), *Luigi* (2), *Pasquale* (2), *Alfonse, Carmela, Concetta, Donato, Filomena.*

Perilloux (148) French: nickname from a derivative of Occitan *perilh* 'misfortune' (from Latin *periculum* 'danger'). This name occurs chiefly in LA.

GIVEN NAME French 6%. *Emile.*

Periman (138) English: variant of PERRY 1.

Perin (395) **1.** Italian: from a pet form of the personal name PERO. **2.** French (**Périn**): variant of PERRIN.

Perine (389) French (**Périne**): feminine form of PERIN 2.

Perini (377) Italian: patronymic or plural form of PERINO. This is also found as a Greek family name.

GIVEN NAMES Italian 12%. *Gino* (3), *Remo* (3), *Amedeo, Angelo, Dario, Fiorello, Francesco, Fulvio, Giovanna, Giovanni, Lido, Luigi.*

Perino (457) Italian: from a pet form of the personal name PERO.

GIVEN NAMES Italian 8%. *Angelo* (2), *Aldo, Carmela, Concetta, Dante, Georgio, Guerino, Sal, Salvatore, Sisto.*

Peris (100) **1.** Catalan: patronymic from the Catalan personal name PERE, Catalan equivalent of PETER (compare PEREZ). **2.** Greek: variant of PERRIS.

GIVEN NAMES Spanish 8%. *Juan* (2), *Eduardo, Jose, Luis, Vicente.*

Perisho (134) Probably an Americanized form of French **Périgord** (see PEDIGO).

Perito (113) Italian: nickname from *perito* 'skilled', 'expert'.

GIVEN NAMES Italian 13%. *Domenic* (2), *Carmela, Romeo, Sal, Santo.*

Peritz (103) Jewish: variant of PERETZ.

GIVEN NAMES Jewish 7%; German 6%. *Isidor, Yardena; Guenter.*

Perk (111) **1.** English and Scottish: from a medieval pet form of the personal name PETER. Compare PERKIN. **2.** Jewish (from Lithuania): habitational name from Perki in Lithuania.

GIVEN NAME French 6%. *Jacques.*

Perkel (110) Jewish (from Ukraine): metonymic occupational name for a draper, from Yiddish *perkel* 'calico', 'muslin'.

GIVEN NAMES Russian 9%; Jewish 8%. *Fedor, Grigory, Mikhail, Oleg, Vladimir, Yefim; Fira.*

Perkes (157) **1.** English (West Midlands): variant spelling of PERKS. **2.** Jewish (from Ukraine): metronymic from the Yiddish name *Perke* (a pet form of the female personal name *Perl* 'pearl'; see PEREL 3) + the Yiddish possessive suffix *-s.*

Perkett (108) Origin unidentified.

GIVEN NAME French 4%. *Emile.*

Perkey (382) Probably an Americanized form of Swiss German **Bürgi**, **Bürgy** (see BURGY).

Perkin (184) **1.** English: variant of PARKIN. **2.** Probably an Americanized form of Swiss German **Bürgin** (see BURGY).

Perkins (43242) **1.** English: patronymic from PERKIN, also found throughout mid and south Wales. **2.** Dutch: patronymic from a pet form of *Peer*, a Dutch form of PETER.

Perkinson (902) English: variant of PARKINSON.

Perko (529) **1.** Slovenian and Croatian: from an old pet form of the personal name PETER (Slovenian) or *Petar* (Croatian). **2.** Slovenian: from an old pet form of the personal name BERNARD. Replacement of initial *B-* with *P-* is quite common in Slovenian names. **3.** Finnish: topographic name from *perkiö* 'meadow', 'cleared field'. This name is found mainly in southwestern Finland.

Perkoski (103) Polish: variant of PERKOWSKI.

Perkovich (207) **1.** Croatian (**Perković**) and Slovenian (**Perkovič**): patronymic from the personal name PERKO. **2.** Jewish (eastern Ashkenazic): metronymic from the Yiddish female personal name *Perke* (see PERKES).

Perkowski (500) Polish: habitational name for someone from Perkowo in Bydgoszcz voivodeship or Perkowice in Leszno voivodeship.

FOREBEARS This surname can be traced back to the 16th century.

GIVEN NAMES Polish 10%. *Bogdan* (3), *Tadeusz* (3), *Janusz* (2), *Casimir, Iwona, Jozef, Lucjan, Lucyna, Mariusz, Miroslaw, Piotr, Slawomir.*

Perks (464) English (West Midlands): patronymic from PARK 2.

Perl (757) **1.** Jewish (Ashkenazic): variant of PEREL. **2.** German: habitational name from any of several places named Perl, Berel, or Berl. **3.** German: metonymic occupational name for a jeweler, from Middle High German *perle* 'pearl'. **4.** German (Austria): from a pet form of BERNHARD.

GIVEN NAMES Jewish 11%; German 7%. *Asher* (3), *Chana* (3), *Gitty* (3), *Moshe* (3), *Mayer* (2), *Miriam* (2), *Moishe* (2), *Schlomo* (2), *Sholem* (2), *Alter, Aron, Chaim; Heinz* (2), *Otto* (2), *Wolf* (2), *Erna, Ernst, Erwin, Gerhard, Kurt, Manfred, Ursel, Wolfgang.*

Perla (447) **1.** Spanish: from *perla* 'pearl', possibly applied as a metonymic occupational name for a trader in pearls, which in the Middle Ages were fashionable among the rich for the ornamentation of clothes. **2.** Italian: generally, from the female personal name *Perla*, meaning 'pearl' (from Late Latin *Pern(u)la* ('little pearl'), whence Italian *perla* 'pearl'), but in some cases possibly a metonymic occupational name (see 1 above).

GIVEN NAMES Spanish 24%; Italian 7%. *Jose* (6), *Julio* (4), *Pedro* (3), *Roberto* (3), *Blanca* (2), *Carlos* (2), *Fabio* (2), *Jesus* (2), *Orlando* (2), *Adelina, Alba, Alfredo; Rocco* (2), *Attilio, Camillo, Carmino, Cesare, Ciro, Dario, Guido, Livio, Salvatore, Serafino, Silvano.*

Perlberg (161) Jewish (Ashkenazic): variant of PERLEBERG.

Perle (109) **1.** Variant of PEARL. **2.** German: from the French name **Perlet.**

GIVEN NAMES Jewish 5%; German 4%. *Miriam; Mathias.*

Perleberg (175) **1.** German: habitational name from a place in Brandenburg called Perleberg. **2.** Jewish (Ashkenazic): ornamental name from German *Perle* 'pearl' + *Berg* 'hill', 'mountain'.

GIVEN NAMES German 4%. *Kurt, Ulrich.*

Perley (337) **1.** Americanized form of some similar-sounding Eastern European or Jewish surname. **2.** Altered form of Swiss German **Berli** (see BERLEY).

Perlich (102) **1.** German: variant of PERLICK. **2.** Possibly also Serbian or Croatian (**Perlić**): perhaps from *perla* 'pearl', a nickname for a small or highly valued person.

GIVEN NAMES German 4%. *Hans, Ilse.*

Perlick (150) German: from a personal name formed with Old High German *bero* 'bear' + *līh* 'like'.

Perlin (321) **1.** Jewish (eastern Ashkenazic): metronymic from the Yiddish female personal name *Perle* (see PEREL) + the Slavic possessive suffix *-in*. **2.** German: from a pet form of BERNHARD or a habitational name from a place so named near Schwerin, Mecklenburg.

GIVEN NAMES Jewish 11%; Russian 4%. *Hyman* (2), *Haim, Inna, Iren, Isaak, Meyer, Moisey, Sol, Yetta; Boris* (3), *Arkadi, Igor, Mikhail, Yevgeniy.*

Perlinger (101) South German (Austria): variant of BERLINGER.

Perlis (113) Latvian: unexplained.

Perlman (2118) Jewish (Ashkenazic): variant of PERELMAN.

GIVEN NAMES Jewish 6%. *Gerson* (4), *Hyman* (4), *Isadore* (3), *Sol* (3), *Anshel* (2), *Aron* (2), *Meyer* (2), *Miriam* (2), *Ari, Ber, Herschel, Myer.*

Perlmutter (980) Jewish (Ashkenazic): ornamental name from German *Perlmutter* 'mother-of-pearl'.

GIVEN NAMES Jewish 7%. *Miriam* (3), *Dov* (2), *Hyman* (2), *Isadore* (2), *Shimon* (2), *Sol* (2), *Arye, Cheskel, Emanuel, Haia, Haya, Moshe.*

Perloff (150) Jewish (eastern Ashkenazic): alternative spelling of **Perlov** (see PERLOW).

GIVEN NAMES Jewish 9%. *Mayer* (3), *Miriam.*

Perlow (307) Jewish (from Belarus): Polish or German spelling of **Perlov**, a metronymic from the female personal name *Perl* 'pearl'.

GIVEN NAMES Jewish 7%. *Ari* (2), *Yaakov* (2), *Yisroel* (2), *Chaim, Zalman.*

Perlstein (508) Jewish (Ashkenazic): ornamental name composed of German *Perle* 'pearl' + *Stein* 'stone'.

GIVEN NAMES Jewish 15%. *Chaim* (4), *Hershel* (3), *Sol* (3), *Hyman* (2), *Meyer* (2), *Miriam* (2), *Mordechai* (2), *Mozes* (2), *Chana, Gitty, Haim, Meir.*

Perman (386) **1.** Dutch: from a short form the personal name *Perre*, a Dutch form of PETER. **2.** Dutch: occupational name for a seller or grower of pears, from *pere* 'pear'. **3.** German: southern variant of *Bermann*, from an old personal name formed with Old High German *bero* 'bear'. **4.** Jewish (Ashkenazic): variant of BERMAN and PERELMAN.

Permann (142) German: variant of BERMANN.

GIVEN NAMES German 5%. *Kurt, Otto.*

Permenter (616) German: occupational name for a preparer or seller of parchment, from an agent derivative of Middle High German *pergamente* 'parchment' (so called from the ancient city of *Pergamon* in Asia Minor, where the technique of producing the material originated). Parchment was in general use well into the 15th century.

Perna (1262) **1.** Italian: from the female personal name, Latin *Perna*. See also PERLA. **2.** Portuguese: habitational name from any of several places named Perna in Portugal. **3.** Catalan and Portuguese: from *perna* 'leg'; possibly a nickname for someone with long legs, or with a deformed or missing leg.

GIVEN NAMES Italian 16%. *Angelo* (12), *Rocco* (5), *Salvatore* (5), *Pasquale* (4), *Vito* (4), *Antonio* (3), *Carmine* (3), *Aniello* (2), *Gino* (2), *Giuseppi* (2), *Sabato* (2), *Sal* (2).

Pernell (628) English: variant of PARNELL.

Pernice (258) Southern Italian: nickname from *pernice* 'partridge'.

GIVEN NAMES Italian 21%. *Salvatore* (6), *Ciro* (4), *Sal* (2), *Sergio* (2), *Carmine, Concetta, Guglielmo.*

Perniciaro (188) Italian: occupational name for a rearer or hunter of partridges, from an agent derivative of *pernice* 'partridge'.

GIVEN NAMES Italian 5%. *Sal, Veto.*

Pernick (134) **1.** Jewish (from Belarus): nickname or metonymic occupational name from Belorussian *pernik* 'gingerbread'. **2.** German: variant of BERNICK in any of its various senses.

GIVEN NAME Jewish 7%. *Hyman* (2).

Perno (212) Italian: from the personal name *Perno*, either a masculine form of PERNA or from the old Germanic personal name *Berno*.

GIVEN NAMES Italian 12%. *Carlo* (2), *Angelo, Guerino, Matteo.*

Pero (808) **1.** Italian: from the personal name *Pero*, a variant of **Piero**, which is a French-influenced form of PIETRO. **2.** Galician: from the personal name *Pero*, Galician equivalent of PETER. **3.** Portuguese: habitational name from any of the places called Pero in Portugal. **4.** Catalan (**Peró**): pet form of the personal name PERE. **5.** In New England, probably an altered spelling of French PERRAULT.

Peron (190) **1.** Southern French: from a pet form of a personal name, a French form of PETER. **2.** Italian: from an augmentative of the personal name PERO. **3.** Spanish (**Perón**): possibly from a pet form of the personal name *Pedro* or a Castilianized form of Catalan **Peró** (see PERO).

GIVEN NAMES French 15%. *Andre* (3), *Cecile, Fernand, Herve, Michel, Philippe, Virginie.*

Perona (231) **1.** Catalan: from a feminine derivative of the personal name PERE. **2.** Italian: from a derivative of the personal name PERO.

Perone (393) Italian: variant of PERON.

GIVEN NAMES Italian 11%. *Pasquale* (3), *Angelo* (2), *Deno, Dino, Francesco, Orazio, Vito.*

Peroni (159) Italian: patronymic from PERON or PERONE.

GIVEN NAMES Italian 6%. *Silvio* (2), *Angelo, Vito.*

Perot (192) French (**Pérot**): from the personal name *P(i)errot*, a pet form of *Pierre* (see PETER).

GIVEN NAMES French 7%. *Alphonse, Antoine, Philippe, Remy.*

Perotti (345) Italian: from a pet form of the personal name PERO.

GIVEN NAMES Italian 9%. *Ugo* (2), *Aldo, Dante, Elio, Gaetano, Geno, Giacomo, Giovanni, Guido, Lorenzo, Luca, Piero.*

Peroutka (167) Czech: from *peroutka* 'feather', 'feather duster', 'quill', a nickname denoting either a small, light person, or possibly a clerk, on account of his use of a quill pen.

Perovich (146) Croatian (**Perović**): patronymic from the personal name *Pero*, pet form of *Petar* (see PETER).

Perper (103) Origin unidentified.

Perpich (174) Americanized spelling of Croatian and Serbian **Prpić**. *Prporuše* was a term denoting young girls who, in the dry season, would visit houses in the village and pray for rain.

Perr (116) **1.** English: probably a variant of PARR. **2.** Jewish (American): shortened form of some Ashkenazic surname such as PERELMAN and PERLSTEIN.

GIVEN NAMES Jewish 13%. *Jechiel* (2), *Aharon, Elchanan, Miriam, Yisroel, Yosef.*

Perra (220) Italian (Sardinia): **1.** nickname from *perra* 'stubbornness', 'pig-headedness', from Spanish. **2.** habitational name from a lost place named Perra, from *perra* 'leg', 'thigh' (perhaps from Latin *perna*).

Perras (354) French: topographic name for someone who lived in a stony place or near an obvious pile of stones, from a derivative of *pierre* 'rock', meaning 'pile of stones'. FOREBEARS A Perras from the Aunis region of France is documented in Montreal in 1660, with the secondary surname LAFONTAINE.
GIVEN NAMES French 13%. *Fernand* (3), *Armand* (2), *Alban*, *Cecile*, *Gaston*, *Jacques*, *Lucien*, *Oneil*, *Romain*, *Sylvie*, *Yoland*.

Perrault (1255) French: variant of PERREAULT.
GIVEN NAMES French 8%. *Armand* (3), *Gisele* (2), *Jacques* (2), *Marcel* (2), *Roch* (2), *Alphonse*, *Andre*, *Donat*, *Emile*, *Francoise*, *Gaston*, *Ghislaine*.

Perreault (1903) French: derivative of the Old French personal name *Perre*, variant of *Pierre*, French form of PETER.
FOREBEARS A Perrault from Brittany is documented in 1647 in Quebec City. A Perrot, also called Villedaigre and Vildaigre, from the Saintonge region of France, is recorded in Quebec City in 1654.
GIVEN NAMES French 15%. *Armand* (8), *Emile* (6), *Marcel* (6), *Andre* (5), *Gilles* (4), *Alain* (3), *Cecile* (3), *Fernand* (3), *Lucien* (3), *Oliva* (3), *Yvon* (3), *Celine* (2).

Perreira (471) Portuguese: unexplained; possibly a variant of PEREIRA.
GIVEN NAMES Spanish 11%; Portuguese 7%. *Manuel* (14), *Jose* (6), *Carlos* (2), *Alberto*, *Alfredo*, *Ana Lucia*, *Carmelita*, *Domingos*, *Gustavo*, *Lauriano*, *Luis*, *Orlando*; *Agostinho*.

Perrell (177) English: from a pet form of the medieval personal name *Perre*, an Old French form of PETER.

Perrella (289) Italian: from a pet form of the personal name PERRO.
GIVEN NAMES Italian 11%. *Angelo*, *Antonio*, *Carmine*, *Orfeo*, *Remo*, *Rocco*, *Silvio*, *Vito*.

Perrelli (228) Italian: patronymic from a pet form of the personal name PERRO.
GIVEN NAMES Italian 16%. *Pasquale* (3), *Carmine* (2), *Cosmo*, *Franca*, *Lorenzo*, *Sante*, *Vincenzo*.

Perren (129) English: variant spelling of PERRIN.

Perrenoud (135) French: from a pet form of the Old French personal name *Perre*, variant of *Pierre*, French form of PETER.
GIVEN NAMES French 5%. *Marcelle*, *Yves*.

Perret (461) **1.** French: from a pet form of the personal name *P(i)erre*, French form of PETER. **2.** English (Bristol): variant of PARROTT
GIVEN NAMES French 14%. *Pierre* (6), *Emile* (5), *Jacques* (2), *Michel* (2), *Andree*, *Dominique*, *Etienne*, *Fernand*, *Henri*, *Solange*.

Perrett (392) English (Bristol): variant of PARROTT 1.

Perretta (321) Italian: from a pet form of the personal name PERRO.

GIVEN NAMES Italian 22%. *Angelo* (3), *Antonio* (3), *Rocco* (3), *Amedeo*, *Assunta*, *Carmine*, *Cosmo*, *Donato*, *Elio*, *Fedele*, *Giuseppe*, *Leonardo*, *Mario*, *Sal*, *Simona*.

Perretti (157) Italian: patronymic from a pet form of the personal name PERRO.
GIVEN NAMES Italian 6%. *Ciro*, *Vito*.

Perri (1460) Italian: patronymic or plural form of PERRO. This is also found as a Greek family name.
GIVEN NAMES Italian 17%. *Angelo* (11), *Francesco* (6), *Antonio* (5), *Gaetano* (3), *Luigi* (3), *Salvatore* (3), *Santo* (3), *Agostino* (2), *Enrico* (2), *Ettore* (2), *Fiore* (2), *Gennaro* (2).

Perricone (422) Italian: of uncertain derivation; Caracausi proposes a variant of **Pernicone**, from a derivative of *pernice* 'partridge'.
GIVEN NAMES Italian 12%. *Antonio* (2), *Gasper* (2), *Luca* (2), *Carmine*, *Pino*, *Sal*, *Salvatore*, *Santo*, *Silvio*, *Vito*.

Perrie (118) Scottish: topographic name for someone who lived near a pear tree, Middle English *per(r)ie* (see English PERRY).

Perriello (189) Italian: from a pet form of the personal name PERRO.
GIVEN NAMES Italian 11%. *Angelo* (2), *Giuseppe* (2), *Vito* (2), *Antonio*, *Luigi*.

Perrien (109) Probably a variant of French or English PERRIN.

Perrier (452) **1.** French and English: occupational name for a quarryman, from Old French *perrier*, an agent derivative of *pierre* 'stone', 'rock'. **2.** English: topographic name for someone who lived by a pear tree, from Middle English *perie* 'pear tree' + the suffix *-er*, denoting an inhabitant.
FOREBEARS A Perrier, also called LAFLEUR, from the Béarn region of France, is documented in Quebec City in 1666. Another, from Brittany, bore the secondary surname OLIVIER.
GIVEN NAMES French 13%. *Armand* (5), *Alain* (2), *Antoine* (2), *Pierre* (2), *Adelard*, *Emanuelle*, *Jacques*, *Laurent*, *Lucien*, *Octavie*, *Serge*.

Perrigan (119) Irish: reduced Anglicized form of Gaelic **Mac Páraigín**. Compare PATRIQUIN.

Perrigo (610) Americanized form of French **Périgord** (see PERIGO, PEDIGO).

Perrill (120) Irish: variant of English PARRILL. This surname has been found in counties Clare and Wexford since the 16th century.

Perrin (4310) English and French: from the Middle English, Old French personal name *Perrin*, a pet form of French *Pierre* (see PETER).
FOREBEARS A Perrin from Brittany is documented in Montreal in 1661. Secondary surnames associated with Perrin are Garao, Duteau, and Languedoc.

Perrine (1926) Variant of French or English PERRIN.

Perrino (492) **1.** Italian: from a pet form of the personal name PERRO. **2.** Galician (**Perriño**): probably a variant of Portuguese **Perrinho**, habitational name from Vila Cova do Perrinho, in Portugal.
GIVEN NAMES Italian 18%. *Pasquale* (4), *Angelo* (3), *Cosmo* (2), *Giuseppe* (2), *Vito* (2), *Aldo*, *Antonio*, *Attilio*, *Domenico*, *Filippo*, *Francesco*, *Luigi*.

Perrins (108) English: patronymic from PERRIN.

Perris (128) Greek and Southern Italian: patronymic from the personal name *Perro*, a dialect form of Greek **Petros**, Italian *Pietro* (see PETER).
GIVEN NAMES Greek 4%. *Evangelos*, *Yiannis*.

Perritt (535) English: variant spelling of PERRETT.

Perrizo (115) Hispanic: unexplained.

Perro (177) **1.** Italian (Piemont): from the personal name *Perro*, a variant of PIERRO, influenced by French PIERRE. **2.** French: altered spelling of PERREAULT. **3.** Greek: from the Italian name, or from the Greek family name **Perros**, a variant of PERRIS.
GIVEN NAMES Italian 4%. *Angelo*, *Nunzio*, *Santo*.

Perrodin (186) French: from a pet form of PERRON 1. This name is concentrated in LA.
GIVEN NAMES French 5%. *Andrus*, *Berchman*.

Perron (1888) **1.** southern French: from a southern pet form of the personal name *Pierre*, French form of PETER. This name is also established in England, taken there by the Huguenots. **2.** French: habitational name from places in Côte d'Or, Manche, Jura, and Mayenne named Perron or Le Perron, from *pierre* 'stone', 'rock'. **3.** Spanish (**Perrón**): probably from an augmentative of *perro* 'dog'. **4.** Italian: shortened form of PERRONE.
FOREBEARS A Perron, also called SUIRE, from the Aunis region of France is documented at Château Richer, Quebec, in 1664.
GIVEN NAMES French 11%. *Andre* (5), *Armand* (5), *Normand* (4), *Laurent* (3), *Marcel* (3), *Aime* (2), *Cecile* (2), *Clovis* (2), *Emile* (2), *Fernand* (2), *Ferrel* (2), *Francois* (2).

Perrone (2093) Italian: from an augmentative of the personal name PERRO.
GIVEN NAMES Italian 13%. *Angelo* (14), *Salvatore* (11), *Antonio* (5), *Pasquale* (4), *Vito* (4), *Domenic* (3), *Cosmo* (2), *Gaetano* (2), *Pellegrino* (2), *Rocco* (2), *Sal* (2), *Aldo*.

Perrot (143) **1.** French: from a pet form of the personal name *Pierre*, French form of PETER. **2.** Irish: variant of PARROTT 1.
FOREBEARS The surname Perrot is recorded in Ireland from the 16th century.
GIVEN NAMES French 8%. *Emile*, *Gilles*, *Veronique*.

Perrott (321) **1.** French: variant of PERROT. **2.** English: variant of PARROTT 1.

Perrotta (963) Italian: from a feminine pet form of the personal name PERRO.
GIVEN NAMES Italian 15%. *Antonio* (5), *Carmine* (3), *Angelo* (2), *Cosmo* (2), *Nicola* (2), *Pasquale* (2), *Rocco* (2), *Salvatore* (2), *Alessandro, Attilio, Camillo, Clemente.*

Perrotte (110) French: variant of PERROT.
GIVEN NAMES French 9%. *Damien, Henri.*

Perrotti (553) Italian: patronymic or plural form of PERROTTO.
GIVEN NAMES Italian 13%. *Angelo* (3), *Carmine* (3), *Salvatore* (3), *Antimo, Caesar, Carlo, Domenic, Gaetano, Gennaro, Nunzio, Pasco, Pasquale.*

Perrotto (162) Italian: from a pet form of the personal name PERRO.
GIVEN NAMES Italian 18%. *Salvatore* (3), *Angelo* (2), *Antonio, Carmine, Pasquale, Sal, Saverio.*

Perrow (216) English: unexplained. Perhaps an Anglicized form of French PERREAULT.

Perrucci (129) Italian: patronymic from a pet form of the personal name PERRO.
GIVEN NAMES Italian 22%. *Angelo* (2), *Aldo, Carmine, Clemente, Cosmo, Dino, Oreste, Santino, Vincenzo, Vito.*

Perry (72800) **1.** Welsh: Anglicized form of Welsh *ap Herry* 'son of *Herry*', a variant of *Harry* (see HARRIS). **2.** English: topographic name for someone who lived near a pear tree, Middle English *per(r)ie* (Old English *pyrige*, a derivative of *pere* 'pear'). This surname and a number of variants have been established in Ireland since the 17th century.

Perryman (2849) English (mainly Devon): elaborated form of PERRY.

Persad (207) Name found among people of Indian origin in Guyana and Trinidad: variant of PERSAUD.
GIVEN NAMES Indian 44%. *Ganga* (3), *Anand* (2), *Mala* (2), *Ramesh* (2), *Vijay* (2), *Chandra, Chandrika, Davendra, Deodath, Gobin, Indrani, Kawall.*

Persall (146) English: variant of PEARSALL.
GIVEN NAME French 6%. *Laure.*

Persaud (1501) Name found among people of Indian origin in Guyana and Trinidad: altered form of Indian PRASAD.
GIVEN NAMES Indian 57%. *Ramesh* (15), *Rajendra* (13), *Ganga* (12), *Ganesh* (10), *Mahadeo* (8), *Vishnu* (8), *Mohan* (6), *Deonarine* (5), *Latchman* (5), *Narine* (5), *Savitri* (5), *Indira* (4).

Perschbacher (161) Eastern German: probably a habitational name for someone from a place named Perschbach, from Sorbian *pjersk* 'bass' + German *bach* 'stream'.

Perschke (105) **1.** German: from Slavic *persk* 'perch', hence a nickname for someone thought to resemble the fish in some way. **2.** German: from Sorbian *pjersk* 'bass' (fish), probably a nickname or an occupational name for a fish dealer.

GIVEN NAMES German 20%. *Kurt* (3), *Ewald, Gerhard, Gerhart, Helmut, Klaus, Uwe.*

Persell (154) English: variant spelling of PEARSALL or PURCELL.

Pershall (170) Americanized spelling of German **Perschall**, a variant of **Parschall** (see PARSHALL).

Pershing (508) Americanized spelling of German **Pfersching** (or the variants **Pfirsching, Pförsching**), a metonymic occupational name for a grower or seller of peaches, from Middle High German *pfersich* 'peach' (of Latin origin: see PERSICO).
FOREBEARS Gen. John Pershing (1860–1948), the commander of U.S. forces in World War I, was descended from Alsatian Huguenots whose name was originally *Pfoersching.*

Persichetti (175) Italian: patronymic from a diminutive of PERSICO.
GIVEN NAMES Italian 12%. *Carmine, Luigi, Orazio, Paolo.*

Persico (455) Italian: from *persico* 'peach tree' (from Late Latin *persica*, for classical Latin *persicum (malum)* 'Persian apple'). This was a topographic name for someone who lived near a peach tree or a habitational name from any of the numerous places named with this word in various parts Italy.
GIVEN NAMES Italian 12%. *Carmine* (2), *Luigi* (2), *Rocco* (2), *Salvatore* (2), *Dino, Marco, Nicola, Pasquale, Raffaele, Reno, Sal, Tullio.*

Persin (102) French: **1.** from a derivative of the medieval personal name *Perceval* (see PERCIVAL) or possibly from a derivative of *P(i)erre*, French form of PETER. **2.** habitational name from a shortened form of **Deplechin**, denoting someone from Espleschin near Doornik in Hainault, Belgium.

Persing (443) German: nickname or metonymic occupational name for a peach grower, from dialect *Persing* 'peach' (standard German *Pfirsich*). Compare PERSHING.

Persinger (1626) Variant spelling of the Swiss German family name **Bersinger**, a variant of **Pirsing**, from a Germanic personal name formed with *bero* 'bear' + the clan suffix *-ing(er)*.

Persky (352) Jewish (from Lithuania and Belarus): habitational name from Perki in Lithuania.
GIVEN NAMES Jewish 4%. *Avron, Mort.*

Persley (105) Scottish: habitational name from Persley in the Grampians.

Person (3935) **1.** Americanized spelling of Swedish PERSSON. **2.** German: patronymic from *Peer*, Low German variant of PETER. **3.** French (mainly northeastern): reduced form of **Per(r)esson**, from a pet form (with double diminutive suffix *-eçon, -esson*) of the personal name *Pierre*, French form of PETER. **4.** Jewish: origin uncertain; perhaps an Americanized form of one or more like-sounding Jewish names.

Personett (120) Variant of PERSONETTE.

Personette (152) North American French form of Belgian French **Personnet**, denoting a priest who had a benefice.

Personius (149) Swedish: Latinized form of PERSON.

Persons (1541) Perhaps an Americanized spelling of Dutch **Persoons, Persoens**, a patronymic from Middle Dutch *persoon* 'parson', probably denoting the servant of a parish priest, or possibly an altered spelling of English PARSONS.

Persson (901) Swedish: patronymic from the personal name *Pär, Per* (see PETER). The name is also found in Germany.
GIVEN NAMES Scandinavian 21%; German 5%. *Nils* (6), *Anders* (4), *Erik* (4), *Lars* (3), *Erland* (2), *Lennart* (2), *Agnar, Arnell, Bjorn, Helmer, Hilma, Joakim; Kurt* (4), *Darrold* (3), *Hans* (3), *Mathias* (2), *Frieda, Oskar.*

Persyn (129) Dutch: from a pet form of the personal name *Perceval* (see PERCIVAL), or from a French pet form (in *-ecin*) of the personal name *Pierre*, French form of PETER.

Pert (136) English and Scottish: nickname from Old French *apert* 'ready', 'skillful'.

Perteet (83) Americanized form of French PERTUIT.

Pertile (119) Northern Italian: from a derivative of a Lombardic variant of the personal name BERTO.
GIVEN NAMES Italian 7%. *Amedio, Paolo.*

Pertuit (161) French: of uncertain origin. It may be an altered form of **Pertuis**, a topographic name from Late Latin *pertusium* 'hole', 'tunnel'. Alternatively, it may be an altered form of **Perduit**, which according to Morlet is an occupational name for a guide, from the past participle of Occitan *perduire* 'to lead through', Late Latin *perducere.*

Peru (145) **1.** Basque: from the personal name *Peru*, Basque equivalent of PETER. **2.** Portuguese: nickname from *peru* 'turkey(cock)'.
GIVEN NAMES Spanish 18%. *Carlos* (2), *Francisco* (2), *Manuel* (2), *Amado, Angel, Enriqueta, Felipe, Imelda, Jose, Julio, Reyna, Roque.*

Perugini (383) Italian: patronymic from *perugino*, a habitational name denoting someone from the Umbrian city of Perugia, from an adjectival form of the place name.
GIVEN NAMES Italian 29%. *Rocco* (8), *Nicola* (6), *Angelo* (4), *Amedeo* (2), *Carlo* (2), *Pietro* (2), *Sal* (2), *Salvatore* (2), *Amedio, Amerigo, Antonio, Carmine.*

Perun (139) Ukrainian and Polish (**Pierun**): nickname from Ukrainian *perun*, Polish (Silesian dialect) *pierun* 'thunder'.
GIVEN NAMES Polish 8%. *Czeslaw, Izydor, Wasyl.*

Peruski (144) Origin unidentified. It is not a Polish name.

Perusse (227) French (**Pérusse**): from Occitan *perussa* 'wild pear tree', hence a topographic name, or a habitational name from La Pérusse in Alpes-de-Haute-Provence.
GIVEN NAMES French 8%. *Colette, Laurette, Marcel, Roch.*

Peruzzi (154) Italian: patronymic from a derivative of the personal name PERO.
GIVEN NAMES Italian 17%. *Albino, Aldo, Alicia, Alvaro, Carmela, Ceasar, Dario, Dino, Ezio, Francesca, Geno, Giovanni, Guido, Lino, Ottavio, Renzo.*

Peryea (103) Americanized spelling of French PERRIER.

Perz (259) German (also **Pertz**): from a southern German pet form of the personal name BERTHOLD.
GIVEN NAMES German 5%. *Franz* (2), *Erwin, Raimund, Reinhard.*

Perzan (105) Polish: from a derivative of *perz* 'quickgrass', 'couch grass'.
GIVEN NAMES Polish 5%. *Andrzej, Dorota.*

Pesa (115) Serbian and Croatian (Dalmatia) (**Peša**): from the personal name *Pešo*, pet form of *Petar* (see PETER).
GIVEN NAMES South Slavic 9%; German 4%. *Milenko, Nenad, Sinisa, Zivko.*

Pesavento (251) Italian: nickname from a compound of *pesa*, third person singular of *pesare* 'to weigh' + *vento* 'wind', denoting someone who engages in fatuous pursuits, an idler or waster.
GIVEN NAMES Italian 11%. *Domenic* (2), *Aldo, Attilio, Elio, Geno, Leno, Renzo, Rinaldo.*

Pescatore (295) Italian: occupational name for a fisherman, from an agent derivative of *pesce* 'fish'.
GIVEN NAMES Italian 22%. *Angelo* (4), *Pasquale* (3), *Carmine* (2), *Cosimo* (2), *Pellegrino* (2), *Attilio, Caesar, Guiseppe, Nino, Otello, Vincenzo.*

Pesce (989) Italian: from *pesce* 'fish' (Latin *piscis*), hence a metonymic occupational name for a fisherman or fish seller or a nickname for someone thought to resemble a fish in some way.
GIVEN NAMES Italian 26%; Spanish 6%. *Vito* (10), *Rocco* (7), *Carmine* (5), *Angelo* (4), *Gennaro* (3), *Mario* (3), *Vincenzo* (3), *Antonio* (2), *Armando* (2), *Carlo* (2), *Domenic* (2), *Giovan* (2), *Giovanni* (2), *Modesto* (2), *Oliviero* (2); *Maria Julia* (4), *Alejo, Carlos, Estela.*

Pesch (381) **1.** North German (Lower Rhine): from *pesch* 'pasture', 'meadow' (Latin *pascuum*), a topographic name for someone living by pastureland, or a habitational name from places so called in the Rhineland and Cologne. **2.** Eastern German: from *Peš*, a Slavic short form of the personal name PETER.
GIVEN NAMES German 5%. *Klaus* (2), *Dieter, Guenther, Wolfgang.*

Peschel (334) German (of Slavic origin): from a pet form (e.g. Czech *Pešl*) of the

Slavic personal name *Peš* (see PESCH 2), common in Lower Silesia, Upper Lausitz, Saxony.
GIVEN NAMES German 7%. *Erwin, Gottfried, Heinz, Inge, Klaus, Kurt, Monika.*

Peschke (199) German (Upper Silesia: of Slavic origin): from a Germanized form of Slavic *Peschek*, a pet form of a Slavic personal name equivalent to PETER.
GIVEN NAMES German 13%. *Kurt* (4), *Friedrich, Gerhard, Gunter, Hermann, Horst, Manfred.*

Pesci (178) Italian: patronymic or plural form of PESCE.
GIVEN NAMES Italian 13%. *Gino* (2), *Dante, Dino, Geno, Giancarlo, Giovanna, Livio.*

Pesek (596) **1.** Czech (**Pešek**): from a pet form of the personal name *Petr*, Czech form of PETER. **2.** Slovenian: probably a topographic name from *pesek* 'sand'.

Peshek (167) Americanized spelling of Czech **Pešek** (see PESEK).

Pesicka (134) Czech (**Pešička**): from a pet form of the personal name **Pešek** (see PESEK).
GIVEN NAME German 5%. *Philo* (2).

Pesina (248) Spanish (also **Pesiña**): variant of **Pecina** or **Peciña** (see PECINA).
GIVEN NAMES Spanish 47%. *Juan* (9), *Ruben* (4), *Pedro* (3), *Armando* (2), *Carlos* (2), *Esmeralda* (2), *Herminio* (2), *Jesus* (2), *Jose* (2), *Lupe* (2), *Alfredo, Ana.*

Peska (107) Czech (**Pešička**): from a pet form of the personal name **Pešek** (see PESEK).

Peskin (353) Jewish (eastern Ashkenazic): metronymic from the Yiddish female personal name *Peske*, a pet form of *Pesl*, which is of uncertain etymology.
GIVEN NAMES Jewish 4%. *Hyman, Semen.*

Pesko (101) See PESKA.

Pesnell (193) Altered spelling of French **Pesnel**, a topographic name for someone who lived by a fence or palisade, from a reduced form of *paissenel*, *pessenel*, a diminutive of *paisson*, *pesson* 'post', 'stake'.

Pesola (209) **1.** Italian: unexplained. This name is found mainly in Apulia, where many surnames have the ending *-ola*. **2.** Finnish: from the personal name *Peso*, a vernacular pet form of *Petrus* (see PETER) + the local suffix *-la*. The surname is recorded in central-western Finland from the 16th century onward.
GIVEN NAMES Italian 6%; Finnish 4%. *Rocco* (4); *Jarmo, Oiva, Taisto, Waino.*

Pesqueira (91) Portuguese and Galician: habitational name from any of the places called Pesqueira, named with from *pesqueira* 'fishpond'.
GIVEN NAMES Spanish 42%. *Francisco* (3), *Francisca* (2), *Jesus* (2), *Abelardo, Ana, Antonieta, Beatriz, Carolina, Concha, Elva, Gerardo, Ignacio*; *Claudina.*

Pessin (184) French: possibly a diminutive of **Pesse**, which may be a nickname either

from Old French *pesse* 'sorrow', or *passe*, *paisse* 'sparrow'.

Pessolano (131) Italian: of uncertain derivation; perhaps a habitational name from a place called Pessola; however, no link has been established.
GIVEN NAMES Italian 7%. *Angelo, Carlo.*

Pesta (356) Hungarian: from a pet form of the personal name *István*, Hungarian form of STEVEN.

Pestana (296) Portuguese and Spanish (**Pestaña**): from Portuguese *pestana*, Spanish *pestaña* 'eyelash', also in the Middle Ages 'eyebrow', hence a nickname for someone who had long eyelashes or bushy eyebrows.
GIVEN NAMES Spanish 22%; Portuguese 11%. *Jose* (4), *Luis* (3), *Alberto* (2), *Alfredo* (2), *Armando* (2), *Eduardo* (2), *Fernando* (2), *Francisco* (2), *Manuel* (2), *Pedro* (2), *Alfonso, Amado*; *Joao.*

Pester (341) **1.** English (Devon), Dutch, and German: occupational name for a baker, from Anglo-Norman French *pestour*, *pistour*, Middle Dutch *pester*, *pister* 'baker' (Old French *pestor*, *pesteur*, German *Pistor*, from Latin *pistor*). **2.** Jewish (Ashkenazic): unexplained. Possibly a habitational name from someone from Pest, the eastern half of the city of Budapest, Hungary.

Pestka (186) Polish: nickname for a small, hard person, from Polish *pestka* 'stone of a fruit'.
GIVEN NAMES Polish 4%. *Bogdan* (2), *Danuta, Iwona.*

Petak (136) Czech (**Peták**): derivative of the personal name *Petr*, Czech form of PETER.

Petch (124) **1.** English: variant of PEACH. **2.** Americanized spelling of German PETSCH.

Pete (902) **1.** Dutch: variant of PEET 2, or from a pet form of PETER. **2.** Hungarian: from a short form of the personal name *Péter* (see PETER). **3.** Altered spelling of PEET 1. **4.** Navajo: unexplained.

Petee (101) **1.** Variant of English PETTY or French PETIT. **2.** variant of Navajo PETE.

Petefish (130) Probably an Americanized spelling of North German **Bütefisch**, an occupational name for a fish seller, from Middle Low German *buten* 'to exchange, barter, or distribute', but also 'to take as booty', so that in some cases it may have been a derogatory nickname.

Petek (146) **1.** Slovenian and Croatian (northern Croatia): nickname from Slovenian (and Croatian dialect) *peti* 'fifth' or from *petek* 'Friday', perhaps denoting a child born as a fifth child or on a Friday, or (more probably) denoting an ill-fated person, because Friday was considered unlucky in the Middle Ages. This is a very frequent Slovenian surname. **2.** Hungarian: either a borrowing of the Slovenian name or from a pet form of the personal name *Péter*, Hungarian form of PETER.

Peter (3005) English, Scottish, German, Dutch, etc.: from the personal name *Peter* (Greek *Petros*, from *petra* 'rock', 'stone'). The name was popular throughout Christian Europe in the Middle Ages, having been bestowed by Christ as a byname on the apostle Simon bar Jonah, the brother of Andrew. The name was chosen by Christ for its symbolic significance (John 1:42, Matt. 16:18); St. Peter is regarded as the founding head of the Christian Church in view of Christ's saying, 'Thou art Peter and upon this rock I will build my Church'. In Christian Germany in the early Middle Ages this was the most frequent personal name of non-Germanic origin until the 14th century. This surname has also absorbed many cognates in other languages, for example Czech **Petr**, Hungarian **Péter**. It has also been adopted as a surname by Ashkenazic Jews.
GIVEN NAMES German 5%. *Hans* (4), *Kurt* (4), *Otto* (3), *Ernst* (2), *Fritz* (2), *Heinz* (2), *Helmut* (2), *Horst* (2), *Kaspar* (2), *Klaus* (2), *Siegfried* (2), *Wolfgang* (2).

Peterka (330) Slovenian: derivative of the personal name PETER, formed with the diminutive suffix *-ka*.

Peterkin (449) English: from a pet form of PETER.

Peterlin (139) German and Slovenian: from a pet form of PETER.

Peterman (3206) **1.** Dutch: elaborated form of PETER. **2.** Slovenian (Gorenjska): derivative of the personal name PETER, formed with the suffix *-man*, Slovenian form of German *-mann*.

Petermann (398) South German: derivative of PETER.
GIVEN NAMES German 7%. *Hans* (5), *Hermann* (2), *Claus*, *Edeltraud*, *Guenter*, *Kurt*, *Wolfgang*.

Peters (51189) **1.** English, Scottish, Dutch, and North German: patronymic from the personal name PETER. **2.** Irish: Anglicized form (translation) of Gaelic **Mac Pheadair** 'son of Peter'. **3.** Americanized form of cognate surnames in other languages, for example Dutch and North German **Pieters**.

Petersen (24388) Danish, Norwegian, Dutch, and North German: patronymic from PETER.
GIVEN NAMES Scandinavian 4%. *Erik* (32), *Nels* (17), *Lars* (10), *Niels* (9), *Jorgen* (8), *Holger* (7), *Anders* (6), *Einer* (6), *Aksel* (5), *Bent* (4), *Gunner* (3), *Knud* (3).

Petersheim (164) German: habitational name from a place so called.

Petersohn (115) German: patronymic from PETER.
GIVEN NAME German 6%. *Gernot*.

Peterson (110846) **1.** English, Scottish, and German: patronymic from PETER. **2.** Americanized form of similar surnames of non-English origin (such as PETERSEN, or Swedish **Pettersson**). **3.** In VT, there are Petersons who were originally called by the French name BEAUSOLEIL; in some documentation this was translated fairly literally as *Prettysun*, which was then assimilated to Peterson.

Petesch (102) Germanized form of **Peteš**, a Slavic pet form of PETER.

Peth (195) German: of uncertain origin; possibly from a short form of a personal name formed with Germanic *bad-* 'fight', 'battle' or *berht* 'bright'.

Pethel (206) Probably a variant of Welsh BETHEL.

Pethick (119) Cornish: variant of PEDRICK.

Pethtel (197) Probably a variant of German BECHTEL. This name is concentrated in the Ohio Valley.

Petillo (272) Italian: possibly from a derivative of an old Germanic personal name (*Peto, Beto, Bedo*, perhaps).
GIVEN NAMES Italian 16%; Spanish 5%. *Angelo* (4), *Antonio* (2), *Guillermo, Oreste, Sebastiano, Vito; Herlinda, Nestor*.

Petit (1931) French, Catalan, and English (mainly Leicestershire): from Old French or Catalan *petit* 'small', hence a nickname for a small person (or an ironic nickname for a big man), or for the younger of two bearers of the same personal name. This name was common among Catalan Jews. It is also established in Ireland.
FOREBEARS The earliest bearer of this name to appear in Canada was from Paris, France, documented in 1647 in Quebec. Other early settlers include Calvinists from La Rochelle, France, and people from Picardy, Normandy, and Lyon. One Jean Petit gave both names to his line, so they are known by the surname **Jeanpetit**, which has at times been transcribed as **Gentil** "nice".
GIVEN NAMES French 10%. *Alain* (5), *Michel* (4), *Normand* (4), *Mireille* (3), *Philippe* (3), *Pierre* (3), *Achille* (2), *Armand* (2), *Jean Claude* (2), *Jean Jacques* (2), *Ketly* (2), *Adrien*.

Petite (182) French: variant of PETIT.
GIVEN NAMES French 4%. *Celestine, Jacques*.

Petitjean (209) French: from a compound of Old French *petit* 'small' + the personal name *Jean* (see JOHN), hence a nickname for a small man called *Jean* (or an ironic nickname for a large man), or a distinguishing epithet for the younger of two bearers of the same name.
GIVEN NAMES French 7%. *Emile, Etienne, Jean-Pierre, Luc*.

Petito (341) Italian: nickname for a small man (or an ironic nickname for a one), from Sicilian *pititu* or some other dialect word derived from French *petit*.
GIVEN NAMES Italian 29%. *Angelo* (6), *Carmine* (5), *Pasquale* (5), *Antonio* (4), *Rocco* (3), *Alfonzo, Alphonso, Antimo, Emilio, Giovanni, Giuseppe, Orazio, Salvatore, Silvio, Tullio, Virginio*.

Petitt (848) English: variant spelling of PETIT.

Petitti (278) Italian: patronymic or plural form of PETITTO.
GIVEN NAMES Italian 16%. *Amedeo* (2), *Antonio* (2), *Cono* (2), *Domenic* (2), *Angelo, Donato, Gino, Giovanni, Mirella, Silvio*.

Petitto (188) Italian: variant of PETITO.
GIVEN NAMES Italian 18%; Spanish 5%. *Angelo* (5), *Rocco* (4), *Gilda, Sal; Juan, Salvador*.

Petko (207) Hungarian (**Petkó**): from a pet form of the personal name *Péter* (see PETER).

Petkovich (128) Croatian and Serbian (**Petković**): patronymic from *Petko*, a pet form of the personal name *Petar* (see PETER).
GIVEN NAMES South Slavic 7%. *Momir* (2), *Dejan, Goran*.

Petkovsek (127) Czech: probably a derivative (altered form) of **Petkovský**, a habitational name from Petkov, a place near Sobotka in Bohemia.

Petkus (218) Lithuanian: derivative of the personal name *Petjko*, of Slavic origin; compare Russian *Petr* (see PETER).

Peto (220) **1.** English: habitational name for someone from Poitou, Anglo-Norman French *Peitow*. **2.** Hungarian (**Pető**): from a pet form of the personal name *Péter*, Hungarian form of PETER.

Petosa (131) Italian: unexplained.
GIVEN NAMES Italian 16%. *Carmine* (4), *Angelo, Carlo, Martino*.

Petoskey (116) Probably an Americanized form of a Slavic derivative of PETER.

Petr (162) Czech: from the personal name *Petr* (see PETER).
GIVEN NAMES German 6%; Czech and Slovak 4%. *Otto* (2), *Erwin; Vilem*.

Petra (105) Aragonese and Catalan: habitational name from any of the place called Peralta, corresponding to old Aragonese *Petra Alta*; or possibly also from Petra in Mallorca, an important place during the 16th and 17th centuries.
GIVEN NAMES Spanish 9%. *Joaquin, Jorge, Juanita, Marta, Rubio, Teodora*.

Petracca (154) Italian and Greek (**Petrakas**): from a feminine form of *Petracco*, a derivative of the personal name Italian *P(i)etro*, Greek *Petros* (see PETER).
GIVEN NAMES Italian 28%. *Antonio* (3), *Carlo* (2), *Carmine* (2), *Carmino* (2), *Luca* (2), *Carmelo, Geno, Mario, Pasquale, Sabino*.

Petraglia (226) Italian: possibly from the personal name *P(i)etro* (see PETER), with the addition of the collective suffix *-aglia*.
GIVEN NAMES Italian 14%. *Angelo* (3), *Carmine* (3), *Salvatore* (2), *Carmello, Silvio*.

Petraitis (235) Lithuanian: patronymic from the personal name *Petras* (see PETER).

Petrak (242) Czech (**Petrák**): derivative of the personal name PETER.

Petrakis (211) Greek: patronymic from the personal name *Petros* (see PETER). The

-akis patronymic is particularly common in Crete, where it was adopted massively in the 19th century.

GIVEN NAMES Greek 9%. *Konstadinos, Loukas, Nikolaos, Panagiotis, Spiro, Stefanos.*

Petralia (258) **1.** Italian (Sicily): habitational name from Petralia Soprana or Petralia Sottana in Palermo. **2.** Greek (**Petralias**): topographic name from *petra leia* 'smooth stone'.

GIVEN NAMES Italian 16%. *Salvatore* (3), *Sal* (2), *Amadeo, Angelo, Gino, Giuseppe, Nino, Pietro, Vincenzo, Vito.*

Petranek (113) Czech (**Petránek**): from a pet form of the personal name *Petr* (see PETER).

Petrarca (522) Italian: probably a variant of PETRACCA, influenced by *arca* 'bow'.

GIVEN NAMES Italian 19%. *Domenic* (11), *Carmine* (7), *Angelo* (4), *Antonio* (3), *Eliseo* (2), *Dante, Domenico, Fausto, Gennaro, Gilda, Guido, Luca.*

Petras (716) **1.** Czech (also **Petraš**) and Slovak (**Petráš**): derivative of the personal name *Petr* (see PETER). **2.** Greek: occupational name for a quarryman, from *petra* 'stone', 'rock' + the occupational suffix *-as*.

Petrasek (179) Czech (**Petrásek, Petrášek**): from a pet form of PETRAS.

GIVEN NAMES German 4%. *Alois, Kurt, Otto.*

Petrash (146) Altered spelling of eastern German **Petrasch** or Czech and Slovak **Petráš**, Slavic derivatives of the personal name PETER.

Petrauskas (132) Lithuanian: patronymic from the personal name *Petras*, Lithuanian form of PETER.

GIVEN NAMES Lithuanian 7%. *Ignas, Rimas, Stasys.*

Petre (514) **1.** English: variant spelling of PETER. **2.** Swedish (**Petré**): shortened form of *Petrejus* or *Petraeus*, Latinized patronymics from the personal name *Per, Pär* (see PETER). **3.** Slovenian: derivative of the personal name PETER. **4.** French (**Pêtre**): metonymic occupational name for an apothecary or grocer, from Old French *pistel, pestel* 'pestle'.

Petrea (220) Romanian: from *Petrea*, Romanian form of the personal name PETER.

Petrecca (109) Italian: variant of PETRACCA.

GIVEN NAMES Italian 16%. *Silvio* (2), *Amerigo, Domenico, Erminio, Salvatore.*

Petree (1169) Variant of Scottish PETRIE.

Petrella (847) Italian: from a pet form of the personal name *P(i)etro*, an Italian form of PETER, or a habitational name from any of various places called Petrella, as for example Petrella Salto (Rieti, Lazio) and Petrella Tifernina (Campobasso, Molise).

GIVEN NAMES Italian 16%. *Angelo* (6), *Luciano* (4), *Salvatore* (4), *Carmine* (2), *Ennio* (2), *Gino* (2), *Giovanni* (2), *Giuseppe* (2), *Luigi* (2), *Rocco* (2), *Aldo, Antonio.*

Petrelli (258) Italian: **1.** patronymic from a pet form of the personal name *P(i)etro*, an Italian equivalent of PETER. This is also common as a surname in the Greek islands of the Aegean. **2.** from a pluralized form of a habitational name from PETRELLA.

GIVEN NAMES Italian 11%. *Vito* (2), *Antonietta, Enrico, Gaetano, Salvatore.*

Petrenko (102) Ukrainian: patronymic from the personal name *Petr* (see PETER).

GIVEN NAMES Russian 33%; Slovak 5%. *Mikhail* (4), *Igor* (3), *Galina* (2), *Leonid* (2), *Aleksey, Alexei, Anastasiya, Anatoly, Boris, Grigory, Jurij, Liliya.*

Petrey (708) Variant spelling of Scottish PETRIE.

Petri (1202) **1.** German and Dutch: Latinized patronymic from PETER. **2.** Hungarian: habitational name for someone from any of several places so named. **3.** Italian: patronymic from the personal names PETRO or PIETRO.

GIVEN NAMES German 5%. *Hans* (3), *Manfred* (3), *Gerhard* (2), *Otto* (2), *Ulrich* (2), *Arno, Eberhard, Ernst, Klaus, Wolfgang.*

Petric (124) Slovenian (**Petrič**); Croatian and Serbian (**Petrić**): patronymic from the personal name *Peter* (Slovenian) or *Petar* (Croatian and Serbian) (see PETER).

GIVEN NAMES South Slavic 13%. *Jerko, Marko, Rado, Radomir, Slavko, Slobodan.*

Petricca (130) Italian: probably a variant of PETRACCA.

GIVEN NAMES Italian 15%. *Angelo* (2), *Amadeo, Antonio, Arcangelo, Giulio, Livio.*

Petrich (648) **1.** Slovenian (**Petrič**); Croatian and Serbian (**Petrić**): see PETRIC. **2.** East German: enlarged form of PETER.

GIVEN NAMES German 5%. *Erwin* (2), *Gerd* (2), *Kurt* (2), *Bernhardt, Fritz, Gerhard, Horst, Reinhard.*

Petrick (1029) **1.** Germanized form of Czech **Petřík** (see PETRIK) or of a related pet form of PETER in some other Slavic language. **2.** Variant of Irish, Scottish, and English PATRICK.

Petrides (180) Greek: patronymic from the personal name *Petros* (see PETER). *-ides* is a classical patronymic suffix, revived in particular in the 19th century by Greeks from the Black Sea area.

GIVEN NAMES Greek 13%. *Demetrios* (2), *Anastasios, Andreas, Constantine, Georgios, Spiros, Thanos, Vasilios.*

Petrie (3299) Scottish: from a pet form of the personal names PETER or PATRICK.

Petriello (116) Italian: probably from a pet form of the personal name *Petro* (see PIETRO).

GIVEN NAMES Italian 33%. *Luigi* (2), *Orazio* (2), *Rocco* (2), *Sal* (2), *Salvatore* (2), *Angelo, Attilio, Gaetano, Italo, Raffaele, Silvio.*

Petrik (492) **1.** Czech (**Petřík**) and Slovak (**Petrík**): from a pet form of the personal name *Petr* (see PETER). **2.** Ukrainian: from

a pet form of *Petro*, Ukrainian form of PETER.

Petrilla (205) Italian: from a feminine form of the personal name PETRILLO.

Petrilli (337) Italian: patronymic or plural form of PETRILLO.

GIVEN NAMES Italian 23%. *Gaetano* (2), *Mario* (2), *Americo, Arnaldo, Arturo, Carlo, Carmine, Dino, Enrico, Gino, Guido, Lorenzo, Marco, Rocco, Sal, Salvatore, Renato, Roberto.*

Petrillo (1414) Italian: from *Petrillo*, a pet form of the personal name *P(i)etro*, Italian equivalent of PETER.

GIVEN NAMES Italian 10%. *Angelo* (5), *Carmine* (4), *Salvatore* (4), *Guido* (3), *Antonio* (2), *Ciro* (2), *Pasquale* (2), *Rocco* (2), *Sal* (2), *Umberto* (2), *Alberico, Aldo.*

Petrin (393) **1.** French: from *petrin* 'kneading trough'. The idiom *être dans le petrin* means to be in a difficult situation. **2.** Slovenian: patronymic from the personal name PETER.

GIVEN NAMES French 14%. *Adrien* (2), *Lucien* (2), *Andre, Armand, Cecile, Clovis, Emile, Fernand, Herve, Laurent, Normand, Origene.*

Petrina (125) **1.** Czech (**Petřina**): from a pet form of the personal name *Petr* (see PETER). **2.** Slovenian and Croatian: patronymic from the personal names *Peter* (Slovenian) or *Petar* (Croatian) (see PETER), formed with the augmentative suffix *-ina.*

GIVEN NAME Czech and Slovak 4%. *Bohdan* (3).

Petrini (377) Italian: patronymic or plural form of PETRINO.

GIVEN NAMES Italian 9%. *Angelo* (2), *Silvio* (2), *Amerigo, Arduino, Carlo, Dario, Enrico, Erminio, Geno, Giulio, Nevio, Spartaco.*

Petrino (263) Italian: from the personal name *Petrino*, a pet form of *P(i)etro*, Italian equivalents of PETER.

GIVEN NAMES Italian 8%. *Angelo* (2), *Donato* (2), *Sabastian.*

Petrizzi (102) Italian: **1.** patronymic or plural form of PETRIZZO 1. **2.** possibly a habitational name from Petrizzi in Catanzaro province.

GIVEN NAMES Italian 10%. *Luigi* (2), *Ercole.*

Petrizzo (198) Italian: **1.** from a pet form of the personal name *P(i)etro* (see PETER). **2.** see PETRIZZI 2.

GIVEN NAMES Italian 15%. *Angelo, Carmine, Dante, Domenico, Franco, Giuseppe, Pasquale, Stefano, Vito.*

Petro (2073) **1.** Italian: from a dialect form of the personal name PIETRO (from Latin *Petrus*). **2.** Greek: shortened form of PETROPOULOS or some other derivative of *Petros*, Greek form of PETER. **3.** Dutch: variant of PETRUS. **4.** Hungarian (**Petró**): from a pet form of the personal name **Péter** (see PETER).

Petrocelli (376) Italian: pluralized variant of **Petrosello**, itself a variant of PETRO-SINO.

GIVEN NAMES Italian 13%. *Angelo* (2), *Attilio, Domenic, Elio, Giovanni, Lucio, Marcello, Nichola, Nicola, Querino, Umberto.*

Petroff (723) Russian, Bulgarian, Macedonian, Serbian, and Croatian: alternative spelling of PETROV.

Petron (209) French (**Pétron**): diminutive of PETRE 3.

Petrone (1299) Italian: from an augmentative of the personal name PIETRO.

GIVEN NAMES Italian 12%. *Angelo* (11), *Rocco* (6), *Antonio* (4), *Carmine* (4), *Salvatore* (2), *Silvio* (2), *Vito* (2), *Aldo, Carlo, Dino, Ettore, Fausto.*

Petronella (143) Italian: from feminine pet form of PETRONE or PETRONIO.

GIVEN NAMES Italian 17%. *Rocco* (2), *Fedele, Francesco, Marco, Salvatore, Vito.*

Petroni (193) Italian: patronymic from PETRONE or PETRONIO.

GIVEN NAMES Italian 24%; Spanish 6%. *Gino* (3), *Angelo* (2), *Aldo, Attilio, Carlo, Carmela, Geno, Guido, Lido, Lorenzo, Mario, Nino, Rocco; Beatriz, Marcelo, Odulia, Silvia, Velia.*

Petronio (188) Italian: from the personal name *Petronio* (Latin *Petronius*), which is thought to be of Etruscan origin.

GIVEN NAMES Italian 17%. *Angelo* (2), *Adriano, Aldo, Carlo, Carmella, Eugenio, Fabiola, Francesca, Giorgio, Guido, Mario, Nicolo, Pasco, Rinaldo, Rosario, Sal, Salvatore, Sergio.*

Petronis (123) Lithuanian: patronymic from *Petras*, Lithuanian form of PETER.

Petropoulos (248) Greek: patronymic from the personal name *Petros* (see PETER) + the patronymic ending *-poulos*. This ending occurs chiefly in the Peloponnese; it is derived from Latin *pullus* 'nestling', 'chick'.

GIVEN NAMES Greek 17%. *Antonios* (2), *Dimitrios* (2), *Anastassios, Angelos, Demos, Evangelos, Ilias, Konstantinos, Kostas, Labros, Panagiota, Panayotis.*

Petros (385) **1.** Ethiopian: from the personal name *Petros* (see PETER). **2.** Greek: reduced form of PETROPOULOS or some other derivative of *Petros*, Greek form of PETER.

GIVEN NAMES Ethiopian 4%. *Berhane, Eyob, Haile, Mulugeta, Tsegaye, Yoseph.*

Petrosian (110) Armenian: patronymic from the classical Armenian personal name *Petros*, from Greek (see PETER). Compare BEDROSIAN.

GIVEN NAMES Armenian 48%. *Dikran* (2), *Anahid, Anahit, Anait, Antranik, Ara, Armen, Armine, Ashot, Gagik, Goar, Hagop.*

Petrosino (322) **1.** Italian: from *petrosino* 'parsley', a southern dialect variant of *prezzemolo*. The term had a figurative meaning, of an intrusive or meddling person, so this may have been a nickname for such an individual. **2.** Italian (Sicily):

possibly a habitational name from Petrosino in Trapani.

GIVEN NAMES Italian 20%; French 6%. *Angelo* (4), *Antonio* (2), *Carmine* (2), *Rocco* (2), *Benedetto, Carlo, Domenic, Gianluca, Luigi, Raffaele, Rinaldo, Sal; Andre* (2), *Alphonse, Armand.*

Petroske (135) Germanized form of Polish PETROWSKI.

Petroski (668) Polish: variant spelling of PETROWSKI.

Petrosky (866) Germanized form of Polish PETROWSKI.

Petrossian (145) Armenian: variant spelling of PETROSIAN.

GIVEN NAMES Armenian 38%; Scandinavian 5%; Russian 5%. *Tigran* (3), *Hasmik* (2), *Vahik* (2), *Zarik* (2), *Andranik, Ara, Ardavaz, Armen, Armik, Ashot, Avedis, Babken; Arkadi, Grisha, Gueorgui.*

Petrosyan (127) Armenian: variant spelling of PETROSIAN.

GIVEN NAMES Armenian 47%; Russian 12%. *Gayane* (3), *Sarkis* (3), *Akop* (2), *Samvel* (2), *Agavni, Anait, Andranik, Araks, Armen, Arpenik, Arshak, Artush; Aleksandr, Anatoly, Garri, Iosif, Mikhail, Natella, Sergey, Zhenya; Marat* (3), *Mariya.*

Petrou (160) Greek: patronymic from the genitive case of the personal name *Petros* (see PETER). Genitive patronymics are particularly associated with Cyprus.

GIVEN NAMES Greek 20%. *Demetrios* (3), *Evangelos* (2), *Argirios, Charalambos, Dimitris, Ioana, Isidoros, Pavlos, Takis, Vasilios.*

Petrov (250) Russian, Bulgarian, Macedonian, Serbian, and Croatian: patronymic from the personal names *Pyotr* (Russian), *Petr* (Bulgarian) and *Petar* (Macedonian, Serbian, and Croatian) (see PETER). It may also be a reduced form of Slovenian **Petrovič**, patronymic from the personal name *Peter*.

GIVEN NAMES Russian 31%; South Slavic 5%. *Vladimir* (8), *Oleg* (4), *Sergey* (4), *Andrei* (3), *Sergei* (3), *Boris* (2), *Dmitri* (2), *Konstantin* (2), *Mikhail* (2), *Valeri* (2), *Alexey, Anatolij; Slava; Dimitar* (3), *Aleksandar, Milorad, Mitko, Vasko.*

Petrovic (405) Croatian and Serbian (**Petrović**); Slovenian (**Petrovič**): patronymic from the personal names *Petar* (Croatian and Serbian) or *Peter* (Slovenian) (see PETER).

GIVEN NAMES South Slavic 35%. *Dragan* (4), *Petar* (3), *Rade* (3), *Vinko* (2), *Zivko* (2), *Aleksandar, Ankica, Biljana, Bojan, Bosko, Bozidar, Branimir; Milan* (3), *Alexandr* (2), *Branislav, Dusan, Milos, Radmila.*

Petrovich (847) **1.** Croatian and Serbian (**Petrović**); Slovenian (**Petrovič**): see PETROVIC. **2.** Ukrainian and Belorussian: patronymic from *Petro*, Ukrainian form of PETER.

GIVEN NAMES South Slavic 7%. *Bogoljub* (2), *Radosav* (2), *Vasko* (2), *Branka, Branko, Dragi, Milija, Milorad, Mladen, Radomir, Roko, Stojan.*

Petrow (182) Variant spelling, under Polish or German influence, of PETROV.

GIVEN NAMES Russian 4%. *Boris, Ksenia, Slavik, Vladmir.*

Petrowski (376) Polish, Ukrainian, and Belorussian: **1.** patronymic from eastern Slavic equivalents of the personal name PETER, as for example Ukrainian *Petro*, Russian *Petr*. **2.** habitational name for someone from a place named with this personal name. **3.** nickname for someone associated with a church dedicated to St. Peter.

Petrowsky (145) Germanized spelling of Polish PETROWSKI.

GIVEN NAME German 4%; Scandinavian 4%. *Erik.*

Petru (141) Czech (**Petrů**) and Rumanian: from a Czech and Rumanian form of the personal name PETER.

Petruccelli (206) Italian: patronymic from a double diminutive of the personal name PIETRO.

GIVEN NAMES Italian 20%. *Fedele* (2), *Pasquale* (2), *Angelo, Antonio, Biagio, Damiano, Dante, Donato, Franco, Gabriele, Guido, Nino.*

Petrucci (1085) Italian: patronymic from a pet form of the personal name PIETRO.

GIVEN NAMES Italian 17%. *Antonio* (5), *Dante* (5), *Dino* (4), *Lido* (4), *Angelo* (3), *Gino* (3), *Marco* (3), *Silvio* (3), *Aldo* (2), *Carlo* (2), *Carmine* (2), *Domenico* (2).

Petrucelli (363) Italian: variant of PETRUCCELLI.

GIVEN NAMES Italian 9%. *Ciro* (3), *Rocco* (3), *Domenic, Donato, Ornella, Salvator, Salvatore.*

Petrus (579) **1.** Dutch: from a Latinized form of the personal name *Pieter* (see PETER). **2.** Hungarian: from a pet form of the personal name **Péter** (see PETER). **3.** Ukrainian: from a pet form of the personal name *Petro*, the Ukrainian form of PETER.

Petruska (324) **1.** Czech (**Petruška**): from a pet form of the personal name *Petr* (see PETER). **2.** Czech (**Petruška**): nickname from Czech dialect *petruška* 'parsley'. **3.** Jewish (eastern Ashkenazic) (**Petrushka**): ornamental name from eastern Slavic *petrushka* 'parsley'.

Petrusky (101) Germanized spelling of Polish PETROWSKI.

Petruzzelli (244) Italian: patronymic from a double diminutive of the personal name PIETRO.

GIVEN NAMES Italian 27%. *Vito* (7), *Rocco* (3), *Dante* (2), *Angelo, Biagio, Corrado, Filomena, Franco, Luca, Pasquale, Sebastiano.*

Petruzzi (444) Italian: patronymic from a pet form of the personal name PIETRO.

GIVEN NAMES Italian 9%. *Rocco* (3), *Canio* (2), *Marco* (2), *Assunta*, *Conio*, *Guido*, *Roberto*, *Salvatore*.

Petruzziello (105) Italian: variant of PETRUZZELLI.

GIVEN NAMES Italian 42%. *Lorenzo* (4), *Alfonso* (2), *Gennaro* (2), *Luciano* (2), *Angelo*, *Armando*, *Carlo*, *Carmine*, *Fausto*, *Franco*, *Giuseppe*, *Guiseppe*, *Gustavo*, *Mario*, *Raffaele*, *Rosario*, *Vincenzo*.

Petry (1999) **1.** German and Dutch: from *Petri*, a Latinized patronymic from PETER. **2.** Probably also a variant of Scottish PETRIE.

FOREBEARS Johan Jacob Petry came to Philadelphia from the Palatinate in 1743 at the age of 21.

Petsch (329) German (of Slavic origin): from a pet form of a Slavic form of PETER.
GIVEN NAMES German 6%. *Ernst*, *Frederich*, *Otto*.

Petschauer (108) German: habitational name for someone from a place named Petschau (Czech Bečov) near Marienbad (Czech Mariánské Lázně) in the Czech Republic.
GIVEN NAMES German 14%. *Erwin* (4), *Ernst*.

Petsche (290) Variant of PETSCH.

Petska (149) Slavic-variant of **Petsch**.

Pett (389) **1.** English (southeast): variant of PITT. **2.** French: from a Germanic personal name, *Petto* or *Betto*, a short form of any of the various compound names formed with *berht* 'bright', 'famous' as the first element.

Petta (237) Italian: **1.** most probably of Albanian origin, from *petë* 'dented', 'battered'. **2.** possibly from a pet form of a female personal name such as *Filippa*, *Jacopa*, etc. **3.** from the Germanic personal name *Peta*, *Patta*.
GIVEN NAMES Italian 12%. *Angelo* (2), *Pasquale* (2), *Antonio*, *Benedetta*, *Domenic*, *Lorenzo*, *Rocci*, *Rocco*, *Sal*, *Vito*.

Pettaway (442) Altered spelling of English **Pittaway**, which is probably a habitational name from a lost or unidentified place named with Old English *pytt* 'pit', 'hollow' + *weg* 'path'.
GIVEN NAMES French 5%. *Andre*, *Chantel*, *Emile*, *Vernice*.

Pettay (128) Probably an Americanized form of English PETTY or French PETIT.

Pettee (189) Americanized form of English PETTY or French PETIT.

Pettegrew (108) Altered spelling of PETTIGREW.

Pettengill (727) English: medieval English name for someone from Portugal (see PORTUGAL) or who had connections with Portugal.

Petter (281) **1.** Dutch, German, and English: variant of PETER. **2.** German (southwest): from Middle High German *pfetter* 'godfather' or 'uncle' (from Late Latin *patrinus*, derivative of *pater* 'father'). **3.** Dutch: occupational name for someone who pumped water, from an agent deriva-

tive of Middle Dutch *putten*, *pitten*, *petten* 'to draw water'.

Petters (144) North German: patronymic from the personal name PETTER.
GIVEN NAME German 5%; Scandinavian 4%. *Rainer*.

Pettersen (615) Norwegian, Danish, and Dutch: patronymic from the personal name *Petter*. a vernacular form of PETER.
GIVEN NAMES Scandinavian 22%. *Erik* (3), *Johan* (3), *Per* (2), *Thor* (2), *Agnar*, *Arnt*, *Astrid*, *Audun*, *Bjorn*, *Gunner*, *Jarl*, *Ketil*.

Petterson (1093) Americanized spelling of Swedish PETTERSSON or Norwegian, Danish, and Dutch PETTERSEN.
GIVEN NAMES Scandinavian 7%. *Erik* (4), *Lars* (2), *Aksel*, *Arnt*, *Bernt*, *Lennart*, *Nels*, *Sig*, *Swen*.

Pettersson (150) Swedish: patronymic from the personal name *Petter*, a vernacular form of PETER.
GIVEN NAMES Scandinavian 45%; German 5%. *Berno* (2), *Bernt*, *Bjorn*, *Erik*, *Fredrik*, *Gudrun*, *Holger*, *Joakim*, *Karsten*, *Knut*, *Niklas*, *Per*; *Ilse*, *Kurt*, *Ulrika*.

Pettet (271) English: variant spelling of PETTIT.

Pettett (115) English: variant of PETIT.

Petteway (251) English: variant of PETTAWAY.

Pettey (568) Variant of English PETTY or French PETIT.

Petteys (179) English: patronymic from PETTEY.

Petti (589) Italian: shortened form of *Filippetti*, *Jacopetti*, etc., patronymics from pet names formed with the suffix *-petto*.
GIVEN NAMES Italian 12%. *Carmine* (3), *Ciro* (2), *Filippo* (2), *Gennaro* (2), *Alessandro*, *Angelo*, *Erminio*, *Gaetano*, *Guiseppe*, *Matteo*, *Natale*, *Pasquale*.

Pettibone (497) Probably an altered spelling of French **Petitbon**, a nickname composed of the elements *petit* 'small' + *bon* 'good'.

Petticrew (133) Scottish (of Norman origin): variant of PETTIGREW.

Pettie (357) Scottish: variant of PETIT.

Petties (129) Apparently a patronymic from PETTIE.

Pettiford (628) English (of Norman origin): nickname from Old French *pied de fer* 'iron foot', given perhaps to someone with an artificial foot or leg, or to a tireless walker or messenger.

Pettigrew (2425) Scottish (of Norman origin): probably a nickname for a small man, from Old French *petit* 'little', 'small' + *cru* 'growth' (past participle of *creistre* 'to grow, increase'). Another possible explanation is that it is a nickname for a man with long thin legs, from Old French *pie de grue* 'crane's foot'. The surname is also established in Ireland, having been taken there first by Scottish settlers, and then also by

Huguenots who went to County Tyrone in the 17th century.

Pettijohn (515) **1.** Americanized form of French PETITJEAN. **2.** English: variant spelling of PETTYJOHN.

Pettinato (354) Italian: nickname from *pettinato* 'combed', past participle of *pettinare* 'to comb'. Compare Spanish PEINADO.
GIVEN NAMES Italian 13%. *Carmino* (2), *Franco* (2), *Angelo*, *Nino*, *Nunzi*, *Nunzio*, *Salvatore*, *Vincenzo*.

Pettine (203) Italian: possibly a metonymic occupational name for a comb maker, from *pettine* 'comb'.
GIVEN NAMES French 4%; Italian 4%. *Biaggio*, *Carmine*, *Cosmo*, *Lucio*, *Pompeo*.

Pettinelli (153) Italian: possibly a patronymic from a diminutive of PETTINE or alternatively from a double diminutive of the personal name *Petto*, itself a reduced pet form of FILIPPO.
GIVEN NAMES Italian 15%; Spanish 4%. *Romeo* (2), *Antonio*, *Carlo*, *Domenica*, *Guido*, *Pietro*, *Remo*, *Silvio*; *Mario* (2), *Dalia*, *Elvira*.

Pettinger (273) **1.** English (mainly Lincolnshire): variant of POTTINGER. **2.** German: habitational name for someone from any of the places named Petting or Pötting in eastern Bavaria. **3.** German (**Böttinger**): habitational name for someone from any of four places in Württemberg called Böttingen.

Pettingill (367) English: variant of PETTENGILL.

Pettis (2076) English: From the possessive or plural form of Middle English *pytte*, *pitte* 'pit', 'hollow', hence a topographic name for someone who lived by a pit, or a habitational name from a place named with this word, as for example Pett in East Sussex.

Pettit (7263) English (especially southeastern): variant spelling of PETIT.

Pettitt (673) English (especially southeastern): variant spelling of PETIT.

Pettry (427) Scottish: variant of PETRIE.

Petts (125) English (Kent): variant of PETTIS.

Pettus (1628) English: variant of PETTIS.

Pettway (856) English: reduced form of PETTAWAY.

Petty (11722) English: variant of PETIT. The name is also found in Ireland, the main branch there having been established in County Kerry in the 17th century by Sir William Petty.

Pettyjohn (824) English: from Old French *petit* 'little' + the personal name JOHN, hence a nickname for a little man (or an ironic nickname for a big man; compare the character Little John in the legend of Robin Hood) named John.

Pettys (108) Variant of English and Irish PETTY.

Petway (258) Reduced form of English PETTAWAY.

Petz (501) German: from a pet form of a Slavic form of the personal name PETER, or from the personal names BERNHARD or BERTHOLD (in the southwest).

Petzel (150) German: from a pet form of PETZ.
GIVEN NAMES German 5%. *Detlef, Friedrich.*

Petzke (111) German: from a Slavic pet form of PETZ.
GIVEN NAMES German 7%. *Ernst, Kurt.*

Petzold (613) German: from a pet form of a Slavic form of the personal name PETER.
GIVEN NAMES German 11%. *Kurt* (4), *Detlef* (2), *Fritz* (2), *Gerhard* (2), *Otto* (2), *Erna, Ernst, Heinz, Hilde, Jochen, Joerg, Klaus.*

Petzoldt (220) German: variant of PETZOLD.

Peugh (461) Variant spelling of Welsh PUGH.

Peura (117) Finnish: ornamental name or nickname from *peura* 'deer' or 'reindeer'. This surname is found mainly in western Finland.
GIVEN NAMES Finnish 5%. *Lempi, Sulo, Waino.*

Peurifoy (116) Variant of French PURIFOY.
GIVEN NAME French 5%. *Reneau.*

Pevehouse (189) Probably an altered form of North German **Pevehaus**, a house name of uncertain origin.

Peveler (140) North German: from Middle Low German *peweler, pevler* (from *Paul*) 'Dominican (monk)', hence a nickname for a person connected with the order or serving in a Dominican friary.

Peveto (254) Americanized form of French **Pivoteau**, which is probably from a diminutive of *pivot* 'hinge', 'pivot', although the application as a surname is not clear.

Pevey (316) Scottish or English: unexplained. Compare PEAVEY.

Pevzner (103) Jewish (from Belarus): habitational name from Yiddish dialect *pevzner, peyzner* 'person from the city or province of *Poznań* (in west-central Poland)' (see POSNER).
GIVEN NAMES Russian 39%; Jewish 30%. *Boris* (7), *Mikhail* (3), *Aleksandr* (2), *Iosif* (2), *Leonid* (2), *Semyon* (2), *Valeriy* (2), *Alexei, Fruma, Gennady, Khasya, Lev; Irina* (3), *Mariya* (2), *Yakov* (2), *Bronya, Fira, Iakov, Igal, Khaim, Mendel, Polina, Rimma, Zinaida.*

Pew (599) **1.** Welsh: variant of PUGH. **2.** English: nickname from Old French *pi, pis, piu* 'pious'.

Pewitt (396) Welsh: patronymic from *ap* 'son of' + HEWITT.

Peyer (151) South German: variant of BEYER or BAYER.
GIVEN NAMES German 5%. *Otto* (2), *Hans.*

Peyser (280) **1.** English: from Anglo-Norman French *peiser, poiser* 'weigher' (Late Latin *pensarius*, a derivative of *pensare* 'to weigh'), hence an occupational name for an official in charge of weights and measures, especially one whose duty it was to weigh rent or tribute received. **2.** German: variant spelling of PEISER.

Peyton (3698) English and Irish (County Donegal): variant spelling of PAYTON.

Pezza (151) Italian: from *pezzo*, either in the sense 'plot of land', and hence a nickname for someone who owned a piece of land, or in the sense 'coin', 'money' (and hence possibly a metonymic occupational name for a moneyer or a nickname for a rich (or poor) man), as in various southern dialects.
GIVEN NAMES Italian 15%. *Antonio, Biagio, Carmine, Rocco, Salvatore, Vito.*

Pezzano (134) Italian: habitational name from a place named Pezzano.
GIVEN NAMES Italian 17%. *Rocco* (2), *Carmela, Enzo, Luigi, Salvatore.*

Pezzella (146) Italian: from a derivative of PEZZA.
GIVEN NAMES Italian 14%. *Alessandro, Carmine, Giro, Luigi, Salvatore, Silvio, Veto.*

Pezzi (123) Italian: variant (plural) of PEZZA, a habitational name from any of numerous places named with medieval Latin *pecia, petia* 'piece', 'fragment', or possibly from the same word as the name of an old silver coin.
GIVEN NAMES Italian 13%. *Aldo* (3), *Alberto, Antonio, Dino, Italo, Pio.*

Pezzino (117) Italian: diminutive of PEZZI.
GIVEN NAMES Italian 14%. *Antonio, Carmine, Cono, Gianfranco, Sal, Salvatore.*

Pezzullo (208) Italian: from a derivative of PEZZA.
GIVEN NAMES Italian 10%. *Angelo, Antimo, Antonio, Enrico, Giacomo, Lorenzo, Pasquale.*

Pezzuti (101) Italian: from a plural or patronymic form of PEZZUTO.
GIVEN NAME Italian 8%. *Carmine.*

Pezzuto (114) Italian: nickname for someone with a lot of money (see PEZZI).
GIVEN NAMES Italian 12%. *Pasquale* (2), *Angelo, Onofrio.*

Pfab (139) South German: from Middle High German *phāwe* (from Latin *pavo*) 'peacock', applied either as a nickname for someone who was proud or an ostentatious dresser, or as a habitational name for someone who lived at a house distinguished by the sign of a peacock (see *Pfau*).
GIVEN NAMES German 4%. *Hans, Helmut.*

Pfaff (2733) South German: nickname from Middle High German *pfaffe* 'cleric'. Compare PAPE.

Pfahl (225) German: from Middle High German *pfāl* 'post', 'stake', hence a nickname for a tall thin person, a topographic name for someone who lived by a palisade, or a metonymic occupational name for someone who made posts and stakes or erected them.
GIVEN NAMES German 8%. *Kurt* (3), *Otto.*

Pfahler (210) German (also **Pfähler**): variant of PFAHL with the addition of the agent suffix *-er*, hence an occupational name for someone who erected stakes in vineyards, for instance, or who built fencing.
GIVEN NAMES German 4%. *Eberhardt, Florian, Otto.*

Pfalzgraf (191) German: status name for the governor of a palace, or for someone in the service of such a dignitary, from Middle High German *phalenze* 'palace' (from Late Latin *palatia*) + *grāve* 'count', 'earl'.
GIVEN NAME French 6%. *Marcel* (2).

Pfander (124) German: variant of **Pfender** (see PFENDLER).
GIVEN NAMES German 9%. *Wilhelm* (2), *Ulrich.*

Pfannenstiel (546) South German: from Middle High German *pfannenstil* 'panhandle', hence a metonymic occupational name for a pansmith or tinker, or for a cook. Bahlow says the word is also recorded as a field name, which could have given rise to the surname.

Pfarr (310) South German: from Middle High German *pfarr* 'district' 'parish' or *pfarre(r)* 'parish priest', hence an occupational name for a parson, or perhaps a distinguishing nickname for a parishioner.
GIVEN NAMES French 4%. *Andree, Germaine.*

Pfau (893) German and Jewish (Ashkenazic): from Middle High German *pfā, pfāwe* 'peacock', modern German *Pfau*. Compare English PEACOCK. As a German name this is generally a nickname for a vain strutting person, or in some cases a habitational name for someone living at a house distinguished by the sign of a peacock. As a Jewish name, it is generally ornamental.

Pfautz (168) South German: nickname for a bloated, puffing person, from a noun derivative of Middle High German *phusen* 'to breathe hard', 'puff'.

Pfeffer (2002) German and Jewish (Ashkenazic): from Middle High German *pfeffer*, German *Pfeffer* 'pepper', a metonymic occupational name for a spicer; alternatively, it may be a nickname for a small man (as if the size of a peppercorn) or one with a fiery temper, or for a dark-haired person (from the color of a peppercorn) or anecdotal for someone who paid a peppercorn rent.

Pfefferkorn (206) German: variant of PFEFFER, from *pfefferkorn* 'peppercorn'.
GIVEN NAMES German 10%. *Otto* (2), *Bernhard, Egon, Gerhard, Kurt.*

Pfefferle (202) South German: diminutive of PFEFFER.
GIVEN NAME German 4%. *Bernhard.*

Pfeifer (4241) German and Jewish: variant spelling of PFEIFFER. This spelling of the surname is also found in Slovenia.

Pfeiffer (5929) German and Jewish (Ashkenazic): from an agent derivative of Middle High German *pfif(e)*, German *Pfeife* 'whistle', 'pipe', hence an occupational name for a pipe player.
GIVEN NAMES German 4%. *Kurt* (13), *Otto* (8), *Hans* (6), *Heinz* (4), *Ernst* (3), *Erwin* (2), *Franz* (2), *Fritz* (2), *Wilhelm* (2), *Wolfgang* (2), *Aloys, Aloysius.*

Pfeifle (349) South German: metonymic occupational name for a whistle player, from a diminutive of Middle High German *pfīf(e)* 'pipe', 'whistle'.

GIVEN NAMES German 5%. *Otto* (2), *Erna*, *Helmuth*, *Kurt*, *Milbert*.

Pfeil (1029) German: from Middle High German *pfīl* 'arrow' (from Latin *pilum* 'spike', 'javelin'), either a metonymic occupational name for an arrowsmith or possibly a nickname for a tall thin man.

GIVEN NAMES German 6%. *Hans* (3), *Otto* (2), *Arno*, *Eldor*, *Guenter*, *Helmut*, *Helmuth*, *Juergen*, *Kurt*, *Manfred*, *Theodor*.

Pfeiler (153) German: occupational name for an arrowsmith, from an agent derivative of Middle High German *pfīl* 'arrow'.

Pfender (125) South German: from Middle High German *pfender* 'court bailiff', an official who supervised collection of debts by legal officers.

Pfendler (117) German: from an agent derivative of Middle High German *pfanne* 'pan', hence an occupational name for a maker of pans.

Pfennig (173) German: variant of PFENNING.

GIVEN NAMES German 6%. *Armin*, *Arno*, *Helmuth*.

Pfenning (330) German: from Middle High German *pfenninc*, *pfennic* 'penny', a nickname applied with reference to tax obligations; later it may have been a metonymic occupational name for a merchant dealing in penny wares. Compare PENNY.

GIVEN NAMES German 4%. *Erhardt*, *Helmuth*, *Kurt*, *Otto*.

Pfenninger (194) Swiss and German: nickname for someone with tax obligations amounting to one Pfennig, or an occupational name for a toll collector on a turnpike, at a bridge, etc., from an agent derivative of Middle High German *pfenninc* 'penny' (see PFENNIG).

GIVEN NAMES German 5%. *Ernst*, *Otto*.

Pfeuffer (149) German (eastern Franconia) and Jewish (Ashkenazic): variant of PFEIFFER.

GIVEN NAMES German 7%. *Otto* (2), *Hans*.

Pfieffer (132) Variant of German PFEIFFER.

Pfiester (172) German: variant of PFISTER.

Pfiffner (205) German: occupational name for a maker of wind instruments, from an agent derivative of Middle High German *pfife* 'pipe', 'shawm' (from late Latin *pipa*) + the agent suffix *-(n)er*.

Pfingsten (302) German: from Middle High German *pfingeste(n)* 'Whitsun', 'Pentecost', probably a nickname for a person with tax or service obligations at that time of year. Compare PENTECOST.

GIVEN NAMES German 5%. *Fritz*, *Guenther*, *Hanns*, *Hans*, *Otto*.

Pfingston (100) Americanized spelling of German PFINGSTEN.

Pfister (2267) South German and Swiss German: occupational name for a baker, from Middle High German *pfister* 'baker' (from Latin *pistor*).

GIVEN NAMES German 4%. *Erwin* (3), *Willi* (3), *Hans* (2), *Heinz* (2), *Florian*, *Fritz*,

Gerhard, *Gottlieb*, *Guenter*, *Hans Peter*, *Irmgard*, *Klaus*.

Pfisterer (207) South German: variant of PFISTER.

Pfitzer (150) German: topographic name for someone who lived by a well or a pond, from Middle High German *pfütze* 'spring', 'well'.

Pflanz (158) South German: topographic name denoting someone who lived by or owned a plantation, from Middle High German *pflanze* 'plant'.

Pflaum (260) German and Jewish (Ashkenazic): metonymic occupational name for a grower or seller of plums, from Middle High German *pflūme*, German *Pflaume* 'plum'. As a Jewish surname, this is mainly ornamental.

Pflaumer (105) German: occupational name for a grower or seller of plums, from an agent noun derivative of Middle High German *pflūme* 'plum'.

Pfleger (354) German: status name for a legal guardian of a minor, from an agent derivative of Middle High German *pflegen* 'to supervise or administrate'.

GIVEN NAMES German 6%. *Kurt* (2), *Erwin*, *Hans Peter*, *Merwin*, *Otto*.

Pfleiderer (138) German (Swabian): perhaps a nickname for an unstable, indecisive person, from an agent derivative of a word related to Middle High German *vlöudern* 'to flutter'.

GIVEN NAMES German 6%. *Armin*, *Orlo*.

Pflieger (272) German: variant of PFLUEGER.

Pflueger (434) German (**Pflüger**): occupational name for a plowman or plowwright, from an agent derivative of Middle High German *pfluoc* 'plow'.

Pflug (480) German: metonymic occupational name for a plowman or plowwright, from Middle High German *pfluoc* 'plow'.

Pfluger (363) German (**Pflüger**): see PFLUEGER.

Pflugh (104) Variant spelling of German PFLUG.

Pflughoeft (102) German (**Pflughöft**): nickname for a plowman, literally 'plow head'.

Pflum (350) German: variant of PFLAUM.

Pfohl (381) German (Franconia): variant of PFAHL.

Pfost (236) German: from Middle High German *pfost* 'stake', 'post', hence a metonymic occupational name for a maker of stakes or posts or a topographic name for someone living near a prominent stake.

Pfotenhauer (127) South German: from Middle High German *phatte*, *vade*, *vate* 'fence post', 'roof beam', 'purlin' + an agent derivative of *houwen* 'to cut or hew', hence an occupational name for a maker of posts and beams, although the folk-etymological translation of the name would be 'paw slapper'.

Pfouts (114) Americanized spelling of German PFAUTZ.

Pfoutz (104) German: variant spelling of PFAUTZ.

GIVEN NAME German 5%. *Kurt*.

Pfrommer (112) German: variant of FROMMER.

Pfuhl (116) German: topographic name for someone who lived near a pool or pond, Middle High German *pfuol*.

GIVEN NAMES German 10%. *Arno*, *Erna*, *Heiner*, *Irmgard*, *Kurt*.

Pfund (324) German: metonymic occupational name for a sealer of weights, or for a wholesale merchant, from Middle High German *pfunt* 'pound' (as a measure of weight and a unit of currency).

GIVEN NAMES German 5%. *Kurt* (2), *Claus*, *Erwin*, *Gerhard*.

Phagan (175) Variant spelling of Irish FAGAN.

Phair (420) English and Irish: variant spelling of FAIR.

GIVEN NAME Irish 4%. *Brendan* (2).

Phalen (780) Variant of German **Vahlen**, from a tribal name, as in *Ostfalen* (Eastphalia) and *Westfalen* (Westphalia). Compare BAYER, HESS, SACHS, SCHWAB.

Phalin (100) German: see PHALEN.

Pham (8330) Vietnamese (**Phạm**): unexplained.

GIVEN NAMES Vietnamese 79%. *Hung* (158), *Thanh* (135), *Tuan* (98), *Minh* (82), *Hoa* (69), *Dung* (67), *Huong* (58), *Long* (58), *Anh* (56), *Duc* (55), *Hai* (54), *Hoang* (54); *Hong* (39), *Chi* (29), *Dong* (26), *Chien* (12), *Chan* (11), *Hang* (10), *Lai* (9), *Ho* (8), *Man* (8), *Sang* (8), *Han* (6), *Tong* (6); *Tam* (61), *Thai* (38), *Nam* (25), *Tinh* (25), *Phong* (21), *Thach* (11), *Sinh* (8), *Tuong* (8), *Chung* (7), *Manh* (6), *Sa* (5), *Tham* (4).

Phan (4293) Vietnamese: unexplained.

GIVEN NAMES Vietnamese 78%. *Thanh* (67), *Hung* (50), *Hoa* (49), *Minh* (42), *Tuan* (42), *Dung* (40), *Lan* (32), *Son* (30), *Long* (26), *Vinh* (26), *Chau* (24), *Huong* (24), *Hong* (19), *Dong* (14), *Sang* (10), *Hang* (9), *Chi* (8), *Chien* (5), *Ho* (5), *Man* (5), *Lai* (4), *Chan* (3), *Han* (3), *Ke* (3); *Tam* (38), *Nam* (21), *Thai* (14), *Phong* (11), *Tinh* (9), *Chung* (8), *Thach* (8), *Manh* (6), *Tuong* (4), *Chang* (3), *Sinh* (2), *Tham* (2).

Phaneuf (761) French Canadian: altered form of English FARNSWORTH.

FOREBEARS The first known bearer of this name was one Mathias Phaneuf, or **Fanef** or FARNSWORTH, son of Mathias Farnsworth, a weaver from Groton, MA, whose name was Frenchified.

GIVEN NAMES French 11%. *Armand* (6), *Normand* (5), *Emile* (3), *Jacques* (3), *Alphonse*, *Andre*, *Aurele*, *Camille*, *Marcel*, *Micheline*, *Monique*, *Philias*.

Phang (144) **1.** Vietnamese: unexplained. **2.** Cambodian: unexplained.

GIVEN NAMES Southeast Asian 23%; Vietnamese 9%. *Kok* (2), *Chyi*, *Heng*, *Hieng*, *Kin Wai*, *Kiu*, *Ming*, *Peng*, *Sang*,

Sarin, Song, Wai, Yan; Coong, Hinh, Tran Van, Tri, Trinh, Chung.

Phares (1312) Of uncertain origin. Perhaps a variant of English **Phare**, a variant spelling of FARE, or of English **Phair**, a variant spelling of FAIR.

Pharis (553) Irish: variant of FARRIS.

Phariss (171) Irish: variant of FARRIS.

Pharo (322) English: variant of FARRAR.

Pharr (1387) Perhaps an altered spelling of German PFARR or English **Farr**.

Pharris (483) Irish: variant spelling of FARRIS.

Phaup (145) Scottish: habitational name from Fawhope in Teviothead, Borders region (formerly Roxburghshire). The surname reflects the local pronunciation of the place name.

Pheasant (204) English (Wolverhampton): metonymic occupational name for a breeder of pheasants or a birdcatcher, or a nickname for someone thought to resemble the bird, from Middle English *fesaunt* 'pheasant'.

Phebus (290) Dutch and German: apparently a humanistic name, an adoption of the name of the sun god in Greek mythology, Phoebus Apollo. It is not clear whether this represents an underlying Germanic surname nor, if so, which.

Phegley (330) Probably an Americanized spelling of Swiss German VOGELE.

Pheifer (105) Altered spelling of German PFEIFFER.

Pheil (109) Altered spelling of German PFEIL.

Phelan (4369) Irish: **1.** variant of WHELAN. **2.** Anglicized form of Gaelic **Ó Fialáin** 'descendant of *Fialán*', a personal name representing a diminutive of *Fial*, meaning 'generous', 'modest', 'honorable'. This is the surname of a bardic family in northern Ireland.
GIVEN NAMES Irish 4%. *Kieran* (2), *Aine, Declan, Finbarr.*

Phelon (115) Variant of Irish PHELAN.

Phelps (19214) English (southwestern): patronymic from PHILIP.
FOREBEARS The brothers George and William Phelps emigrated from Gloucestershire, England, to Dorchester, MA, about 1630. Five years later they moved to Windsor, CT. George's sixth-generation descendant, Anson Greene Phelps (1781–1853), rose from being a penniless orphan to the status of a major industrialist and a prominent CT philanthropist.

Phemister (106) English and Scottish: variant of FEEMSTER 'senior herdsman'.

Phenicie (170) French (**Phénicie**, literally 'Phoenicia'): unexplained. This name occurs chiefly in PA, the southern states, and around the Great Lakes.

Phenis (100) French (**Phénis**): variant of PHENIX.

Phenix (354) **1.** Northern English and Scottish: variant of FENWICK. **2.** Canadian French (**Phénix**): from Old French *fénix* 'phoenix' (Latin *phœnix*), presumably a nickname, perhaps of anecdotal origin.
FOREBEARS A man of this name, known also as **Dauphiné**, from the Savoie region of France, is documented in Repentigny, Quebec, in 1721.
GIVEN NAMES French 6%. *Armand, Fabien, Gaston, Gilles, Marcel.*

Pherigo (175) Americanized form of French **Périgord** (see PERIGO, PEDIGO).

Pherson (143) Scottish: reduced form of MCPHERSON.

Phetteplace (194) English: variant spelling of **Fettiplace**.

Phibbs (285) English and Irish: variant of PHIPPS.

Phifer (1762) Altered form of German PFEIFFER.

Philbeck (338) Altered form of English PHILBRICK.

Philbert (110) Variant of French PHILIBERT or English FILBERT.
GIVEN NAMES French 5%; German 4%. *Monique; Kurt.*

Philbin (706) Irish: Anglicized form of Gaelic **Mac Philbín**, a patronymic from a Gaelic pet form of the personal name PHILIP.
GIVEN NAME Irish 6%. *Brendan.*

Philbrick (1288) English: possibly a habitational name from Felbrigg in Norfolk, named with Old Scandinavian *fjǫl* 'board', 'plank' + Old English *brycg* 'bridge'.

Philbrook (686) English: variant of PHILBRICK.

Philemon (110) French and Greek: from the personal name *Philemon*, Greek *Philēmon*, which was borne by an apostle and several martyrs.
GIVEN NAMES French 7%. *Gregoire, Jean-Claude, Serge.*

Philen (121) French: from a pet form of PHILIPPE or PHILIBERT.
GIVEN NAME French 5%. *Henri.*

Philhower (283) Classicized spelling of German **Vielhauer**, an occupational name for a file maker, from Middle High German *vīle* 'file' + an agent derivative of *houwen* 'to chop or cut'.

Philibert (172) French: from *Filibert*, a Germanic personal name composed of the elements *filu* 'very' + *berht* 'bright', 'famous', which was borne by a 7th-century saint, abbot of Jumièges. The spelling has been influenced by personal names of Greek origin containing the element *phil-* 'love', e.g. PHILIP.
GIVEN NAMES French 14%. *Armand* (2), *Fernand, Mirielle, Pascale, Pierrot.*

Philip (1151) Scottish, Dutch, English, South Indian, etc.: from the Greek name *Philippos* (from *philein* 'to love' + *hippos* 'horse'). In the New Testament this name is borne by one of the apostles; it was also borne by various other early Christian saints. It owes part of its popularity to the medieval romances about Alexander the Great, whose father was Philip of Macedon. As a Highland Scottish surname, it represents an Anglicized form of Gaelic **Mac Fhilib** 'son of Philip'. In North America, this surname has absorbed some cases of cognate names in other languages (e.g. French **Philippe**, Greek **Philippos**, Italian **Filippi**, Spanish **Felipe**, Catalan **Felip**, and their derivatives). As a Jewish name, it represents a borrowing of the personal name from Christians. It is found as a personal name among Christians in India, and in the U.S. is used as a family name among families from southern India.
GIVEN NAMES Indian 14%. *Varughese* (6), *Mathai* (4), *Babu* (3), *Reji* (3), *Anil* (2), *Binu* (2), *Neena* (2), *Prema* (2), *Raju* (2), *Reena* (2), *Susheela* (2), *Aleykutty.*

Philipp (842) German and Jewish (western Ashkenazic): from the personal name *Philipp* (see PHILIP).
GIVEN NAMES German 8%. *Kurt* (3), *Hans* (2), *Heinz* (2), *Manfred* (2), *Dieter, Erhard, Erhardt, Guenther, Gunther, Helmut, Hilde, Inge.*

Philippe (268) French: from the personal name *Philippe* (see PHILIP).
FOREBEARS Someone with the surname Philippe, with the secondary surname LAFONTAINE, from Chartres, France, is documented in 1669 in Beaupré, Quebec. Other bearers of this name came from Normandy; they bear the secondary surnames BEAULIEU, BELHUMEUR, and LEBEL.
GIVEN NAMES French 26%. *Jacques* (3), *Ghislaine* (2), *Alain, Andre, Camille, Dieuseul, Emile, Francois, Guerda, Henri, Jean Robert, Jean-Pierre.*

Philippi (543) German: Latinized patronymic from the personal name *Philipp* (see PHILIP).
GIVEN NAMES German 4%. *Florian, Hans, Klaus, Kurt, Udo.*

Philippon (102) French: from a pet form of the personal name PHILIPPE.
GIVEN NAMES French 28%. *Raoul* (2), *Andre, Carolle, Fernand, Fernande, Gabrielle, Gaetan, Gilles, Lucien, Michel, Normand.*

Philipps (499) English, Dutch, and North German: variant spelling of PHILLIPS.

Philips (1943) English, North German, Dutch, and Jewish (Ashkenazic): variant spelling of PHILLIPS.

Philipsen (105) Dutch, North German, and Danish: patronymic from PHILIP.
GIVEN NAMES German 5%; Dutch 4%. *Nikolaus; Dirk, Wim.*

Philipson (236) English, Swedish (**Philipsson**), and Jewish (western Ashkenazic): patronymic from the personal name PHILIP.
GIVEN NAMES Jewish 5%. *Aharon, Tali.*

Phillabaum (147) Americanized spelling of German **Vielbaum**, habitational name from a place so named in Altmark, from *vil* 'swamp' + *baum* 'tree'.

Philley (251) English and Scottish: from a pet form of the personal name PHILIP.

Phillip (1290) English and Scottish: variant spelling of PHILIP.
GIVEN NAMES French 4%. *Andre, Camille, Esme, Gaston, Monique.*

Phillipp (123) German and Dutch: variant spelling of PHILIP.
GIVEN NAMES German 8%. *Eldred, Gerhard, Oskar.*

Phillippe (547) French: variant spelling of PHILIPPE.

Phillippi (830) Altered spelling of Italian FILIPPI.

Phillipps (169) English and Dutch: variant spelling of PHILLIPS.

Phillips (126669) English, Dutch, North German, and Jewish (western Ashkenazic): patronymic from the personal name PHILIP. In North America this name has also absorbed cognate names from other European languages, for example Italian FILIPPI, Polish FILIPOWICZ.

Phillipson (303) English and Swedish (**Phillipsson**): variant of PHILIPSON.

Phillis (339) English (West Yorkshire): variant of PHILLIPS.

Philmon (121) Probably a variant of French or Greek PHILEMON.

Philo (351) Shortened form of any of various names based on Greek *philo-* 'friend' or 'loving', e.g. **Philopoemon** in Greek itself.

Philp (504) Scottish: reduced form of PHILIP.

Philpot (1680) English (chiefly southeastern): from the Middle English personal name *Phil(i)pot*, a pet form of PHILIP.

Philpott (1517) English: variant spelling of PHILPOT.

Philson (209) English: patronymic from *Phil*, a short form of the personal name PHILIP.

Philyaw (440) Americanized spelling of French FILIAULT; probably a Huguenot name.

Phinney (1479) English: altered spelling of FINNEY.

Phippen (318) English: from a pet form of the personal name PHILIP.

Phipps (8331) English: patronymic from a reduced form of PHILIP.
FOREBEARS The Phipps family, which holds the titles of marquess of Normanby and earl of Mulgrave, are descended from Constantine Phipps (1656–1723), who was lord chancellor of Ireland. A cousin with a different background, Sir William Phip(p)s (1651–95), was born in ME, where his parents had emigrated. Originally a ship's carpenter, he rose to become royal governor of MA.

Phlegar (144) Altered spelling of German PFLEGER (see also PFLUEGER).

Phlipot (106) English: variant spelling of PHILPOT.

Pho (162) **1.** Vietnamese: unexplained. **2.** Cambodian: unexplained.
GIVEN NAMES Vietnamese 51%; Other Southeast Asian 15%; Cambodian 12%. *Thanh* (5), *Hoa* (3), *Long* (3), *Phuc* (3), *Bic* (2), *Mai* (2), *Thoai* (2), *Thong* (2), *Vinh* (2), *Bach, Chau, Chieu; Tam* (3), *Hong, Kang, Sek, Sinh, Thai, Tham, Uyen; Phath, Pheap, Sophath, Sovann, Thoeun.*

Phoebus (178) See PHEBUS.

Phoenix (885) **1.** Northern English and Scottish: fanciful alteration of FENWICK, under the influence of classical mythology. **2.** Canadian French: variant of **Phénix** (see PHENIX).

Phong (109) **1.** Vietnamese: unexplained. **2.** Other Southeast Asian: unexplained.
GIVEN NAMES Vietnamese 36%; Other Southeast Asian 35%. *Duc* (3), *Nguyen* (3), *Pham* (3), *Anh, Chanh, Cong, Dao, Dau, Denh, Dieu, Dung, Dung My; Chan* (2), *Chee, Chung Ja, Hong, Keng, Mu, Sin; Kitti, Somchanh, Sunthorn.*

Phu (266) **1.** Vietnamese: unexplained. **2.** Cambodian: unexplained.
GIVEN NAMES Vietnamese 45%; Other Southeast Asian 25%. *Hoa* (4), *Minh* (4), *Mui* (4), *Long* (3), *Phat* (3), *Quang* (3), *Dieu* (2), *Hanh* (2), *Hung* (2), *Muoi* (2), *Phuoc* (2), *Quan* (2); *Hong* (2), *Sang* (2), *Chi, Chiu, Cun, Kiu, Kon, Lai, Tong; Chang, Manh, Pai, Sinh, Tam.*

Phung (849) Vietnamese (**Phùng**): unexplained.
GIVEN NAMES Vietnamese 73%. *Minh* (12), *Hoa* (10), *Thanh* (10), *Binh* (7), *Cuong* (7), *Hieu* (7), *Muoi* (7), *Anh* (6), *Hao* (6), *Hung* (6), *Lien* (6), *Trung* (6), *Tuong* (5), *Hong* (4), *Nam* (4), *Sinh* (3), *Sang* (3), *Chan* (2), *Chu* (2), *Dong* (2), *Thach* (2), *Tong* (2), *Bai, Chi, Han, Hang, Heng, Kan.*

Phuong (189) **1.** Vietnamese: unexplained. **2.** Other Southeast Asian: unexplained.
GIVEN NAMES Vietnamese 54%; Other Southeast Asian 24%. *Minh* (4), *Hoa* (4), *Hung* (3), *Quang* (3), *Ba* (2), *Hai* (2), *Hao* (2), *Lam* (2), *Lien* (2), *Mai* (2), *Muoi* (2), *Ngo* (2); *Chhay* (2), *Chia, Ho, Hong, Leng, Sen; Chang, Tam, Thach, Thai, Tuong, Uyen.*

Phy (171) Origin unidentified.

Pi (148) **1.** Catalan: topographic name from *pi* 'pine tree', or habitational name from any of the numerous places named with this word. **2.** Chinese 皮: from a character in the personal name of Fan Zhongpi, son of Wen Wang, the virtuous duke whose magnanimous rule led to the establishment of the Zhou dynasty in 1122 BC. Generations later, a branch of his descendants adopted the second character of his given name, Pi, as their surname. **3.** Chinese: see BI.
GIVEN NAMES Spanish 18%; Chinese 24%. *Esteban* (2), *Alberto, Alejandro, Aurelio,*

Carlos, Carlos Alberto, Eutimio, Mercedes, Ramon, Ramona, Santa, Zoraida; Chien (2), *Chun* (2), *Sun* (2), *Chen, Chien-Kuo, Ching Ming, Dong, Hong, Jong, Ming Yuan, Shang.*

Pia (226) **1.** Italian (Piedmont): from the female personal name *Pia*. **2.** Catalan (**Pià**): habitational name from a place so called in the Rosselló area, eastern Pyrenees, named with the Latin personal name *Appius* + suffix *-anum*.
GIVEN NAMES Italian 8%; Spanish 7%; French 6%. *Aldo* (2), *Gaetano* (2), *Alfonso, Amado, Emilio, Luciano, Luigi, Mario, Romildo; Felipe, Jaime, Manuel, Xavier; Alphonse, Leonie, Monique.*

Piacente (143) Italian: from the personal name *Piacente* (from *piacente* 'pleasing', 'comely'), or a nickname for a physically attractive from the same word.
GIVEN NAMES Italian 28%. *Angelo* (2), *Carmine* (2), *Saverio* (2), *Valerio* (2), *Antonio, Carmelo, Fiorino, Mario, Rocco, Sal.*

Piacentini (207) Italian: **1.** habitational name for someone from Piacenza, so called from Latin *Placentia* (neuter plural of the present participle of *placere* 'to please'). **2.** patronymic from the personal name *Piacentino*, a pet form of PIACENTE.
GIVEN NAMES Italian 12%. *Aldo, Angelo, Antonio, Carlo, Dante, Francesca, Geno, Graziella, Guido, Livio, Piero.*

Piacentino (121) Italian: **1.** from a pet form of the personal name PIACENTE. **2.** habitational name for someone from PIACENZA, from an adjectival form of the place name.
GIVEN NAMES Italian 7%. *Antonio, Carmelo.*

Piacenza (102) Italian: habitational name for someone from Piacenza in Emilia.
GIVEN NAMES Italian 14%. *Angelo, Carlo, Dante, Domenic, Romano.*

Piana (124) Italian: topographic name from *piana* 'plain', 'level ground', from Latin *planus*, or a habitational name from any of the places named with this word.
GIVEN NAMES Italian 19%. *Claudio* (2), *Marta* (2), *Dario, Fernando, Francisco, Julio, Quinto, Renato, Rocco.*

Pianalto (121) Italian: topographic name for someone who lived on a high plateau.

Pianka (170) Polish and Jewish (from Poland): nickname from Polish *pianka* 'foam', 'scum'; also 'mousse', 'meringue'.
GIVEN NAMES Polish 9%. *Genowefa* (2), *Krzysztof, Zigmund.*

Piano (173) Italian: **1.** topographic name for someone who lived on a plain or plateau, Italian *piano* (Latin *planum*, from the adjective *planus* 'flat', 'level'). **2.** nickname from the adjective *piano* in the sense 'unassuming'.
GIVEN NAMES Italian 12%; Spanish 6%. *Mario* (2), *Antonio, Carlo, Egidio, Heriberto, Salvatore; Elpidio, Juanito, Vicente.*

Piascik (172) Polish (**Piaścik**): **1.** nickname from Polish *piastować* 'to nurse'. **2.** from Old Polish *piasta* 'hub of a cartwheel'. **3.** derivative of the Old Polish personal name *Piast*, name of a mythological hero.

GIVEN NAMES Polish 13%. *Mieczyslaw* (2), *Czeslaw, Henryka, Janina, Karol, Leszek, Slawomir, Tomasz.*

Piasecki (808) Polish: topographic name for someone who lived in a sandy place, from Polish *piasek* 'sand', or a habitational name from any of the many places named with this element, for example Piasek and Piaski.

GIVEN NAMES Polish 7%. *Andrzej* (2), *Boguslaw* (2), *Wojciech* (2), *Bogdan, Czeslawa, Dariusz, Jacek, Jadwiga, Karol, Krzysztof, Piotr, Tadeusz.*

Piaskowski (128) Polish: habitational name for someone from places called Piaskowo in Poznań and Włocławek voivodeships, named with Polish *piasek* 'sand'.

GIVEN NAMES Polish 6%; German 4%. *Kazimierz, Stanislaw; Wolfgang.*

Piatek (301) Polish (**Piątek**): nickname *piątek* 'fifth', 'Friday'. This may have been from a given name for a fifth child, but more often it is from the name of the day of the week. Illegitimate children were often given the name of the day of the week on which they were baptized; also, converted Jews took as a surname the name of the day on which they were baptized.

GIVEN NAMES Polish 21%. *Bogdan* (2), *Elzbieta* (2), *Irena* (2), *Tadeusz* (2), *Boleslaw, Casimir, Danuta, Eugeniusz, Jadwiga, Janusz, Jolanta, Lucyna.*

Piatkowski (237) Polish (**Piątkowski**): habitational name for someone from any of various places called Piątkowo, Piątkowa, or Piątków.

GIVEN NAMES Polish 12%. *Jerzy* (2), *Bogdan, Halina, Leszek, Maciej, Pawel, Stanislaw, Tadeusz.*

Piatt (1525) Irish: Huguenot name, apparently from a French personal name, *Piat* (Latin *Piatus*).

Piatz (110) German: variant of the French Huguenot name PIATT.

GIVEN NAME German 6%. *Wendelin.*

Piazza (3089) Italian: **1.** topographic name from *piazza* 'town square'. **2.** in Sicily, where a third of the Italian bearers of this surname live, a habitational name from Piazza Armerina in Enna province.

GIVEN NAMES Italian 13%. *Salvatore* (28), *Sal* (18), *Angelo* (11), *Santo* (8), *Carmelo* (5), *Vito* (4), *Carlo* (3), *Francesco* (3), *Sebastiano* (3), *Cosmo* (2), *Dino* (2), *Gaspare* (2).

Pica (486) **1.** Italian: nickname for a gossipy or garrulous person, from the central-southern Italian word *pica* 'magpie'. Compare PICAZO. **2.** Catalan: habitational name from any of the numerous places

called Pica. **3.** Catalan: from either *pica* 'pointed object' (weapon, etc.) or a derivative of *picar* 'to prick'.

GIVEN NAMES Italian 20%; Spanish 7%. *Mario* (3), *Americo* (2), *Alessio, Arsenio, Carlo, Carmelina, Cosimo, Domiano, Emilio, Ferdinando, Francisco, Franco, Gregorio, Gino, Giuseppa, Luciana; Fernando, Jaime, Javier, Jorge, Marcos.*

Picado (108) Spanish: nickname from *picado*, literally 'pockmarked', figuratively 'peeved'.

GIVEN NAMES Spanish 53%. *Jose* (4), *Fernando* (3), *Sergio* (3), *Adolfo* (2), *Jorge* (2), *Jose Francisco* (2), *Luis* (2), *Rafael* (2), *Susana* (2), *Teodoro* (2), *Alberto, Ana.*

Picano (124) **1.** Italian: possibly related to PICA. **2.** Spanish (**Picaño**): nickname from *picaño* 'rogue', 'wag'.

GIVEN NAMES Italian 13%. *Antonio* (2), *Mario* (2), *Amedeo, Pasco, Silvio.*

Picard (3055) **1.** French, Scottish, and German: from Old French *Picard* 'Picard', a regional name for someone from Picardy in northern France. **2.** French: from a pejorative derivative of *pic* 'pick', 'pike', cognate of PIKE 3 and 4. **3.** Jewish (western Ashkenazic): Frenchification of the German name BICKHART.

FOREBEARS A Picard or Lepicard from Normandy, France, is documented in Quebec City in 1654. Another, from Brittany, was in Montreal in 1660, with the secondary surname LAFORTUNE. Others came from Grenoble and Poitou before 1700.

GIVEN NAMES French 12%. *Armand* (8), *Lucien* (6), *Andre* (5), *Marcel* (5), *Emile* (4), *Michel* (4), *Normand* (4), *Adrien* (3), *Antoine* (3), *Benoit* (3), *Elzear* (3), *Fernand* (3).

Picardi (304) Italian (Campania): patronymic from *Pic(c)ardo*, ethnic name for someone from the region of Picardy in northern France.

GIVEN NAMES Italian 23%. *Angelo* (2), *Amato, Antonio, Carmela, Carmine, Domenic, Domenico, Enrico, Gennaro, Gianna, Gino, Marino.*

Picarelli (123) Italian: patronymic or plural form of PICARELLO.

GIVEN NAMES Italian 19%. *Ciro* (2), *Americo, Angelo, Corrado, Domenic, Eduardo, Eugenio, Mario.*

Picarello (124) Italian: masculinized form of **Picarella**, a diminutive of PICA.

GIVEN NAME Italian 18%. *Carmine* (4).

Picariello (246) Italian (Campania): from a diminutive of PICA.

GIVEN NAMES Italian 16%. *Antonio* (3), *Carmine* (3), *Angelo, Carmela, Ciro, Dante, Gilda, Giuseppe, Marco, Nunzio, Pasquale, Sal.*

Picazo (191) Spanish: nickname from Spanish *picazo* 'magpie', applied perhaps to a talkative or thievish person, or someone who had a streak of white among black

hair. The word is probably derived from Latin *pica* 'magpie', although the suffix is obscure.

Picchi (207) Italian: patronymic from a personal name of Germanic origin (Latinized as *Picchius*), derived from a root meaning 'sharp', 'pointed'. According to De Felice, the Italian personal name represented by-names with various senses related to pointed or peaked objects or features, and even the green woodpecker (compare PIKE).

Picciano (435) Italian: habitational name from Picciano in Pescara province.

Piccini (137) Italian: nickname for a small person, from *piccino* 'little'.

Piccinini (169) Italian: from a derivative of *piccino* 'little'.

GIVEN NAMES Italian 26%. *Angelo* (5), *Gino* (2), *Mario* (2), *Pietro* (2), *Amedeo, Basilio, Enrico, Franco, Guido, Primo, Reno, Salvatore.*

Piccininni (151) Italian (Calabria and Sicily): nickname from Calabrian dialect *piccininnu* 'very little'.

GIVEN NAMES Italian 22%. *Rocco* (3), *Carlo, Damiano, Franco, Gianni, Mauro, Tommaso, Vita.*

Piccione (480) Italian: from *piccione* 'pigeon', hence a nickname for someone thought to resemble the bird or a metonymic occupational name for a keeper of pigeons.

GIVEN NAMES Italian 19%. *Salvatore* (4), *Angelo* (2), *Cosimo* (2), *Dino* (2), *Ezio* (2), *Rocco* (2), *Sal* (2), *Biagio, Calogero, Constantino, Costantino, Enzo.*

Piccioni (131) Italian: patronymic or plural form of PICCIONE.

GIVEN NAMES Italian 21%. *Angelo* (3), *Amedeo* (2), *Marcello, Oreste, Paolo, Remo, Sabatino.*

Piccirilli (347) Italian: patronymic or plural form of PICCIRILLO.

GIVEN NAMES Italian 21%. *Rocco* (3), *Alfonso* (2), *Angelo* (2), *Antonio, Cesare, Dante, Domenic, Erasmo, Florindo, Franco, Gianfranco, Gino, Giselda, Lino, Luciano, Pacifico, Rachele, Roberto, Sabino.*

Piccirillo (524) Southern Italian (Naples): nickname from southern dialect *piccerillë* 'little one', 'baby'.

GIVEN NAMES Italian 28%. *Angelo* (10), *Antonio* (3), *Mario* (3), *Ugo* (3), *Gennaro* (2), *Guido* (2), *Rocco* (2), *Vito* (2), *Carmine, Ciro, Emilio, Ersilia, Filomena, Generoso, Luciano, Lucio, Ninfa.*

Picco (220) Italian: possibly a topographic name from *picco* 'peak', 'summit', but more likely from *pikk*, the hypothetical etymon of *piccolo* 'small'.

GIVEN NAMES Italian 5%. *Antonio, Luigi, Pasquale, Pio.*

Piccola (190) Italian: nickname from a feminine form of PICCOLO.

GIVEN NAMES Italian 9%. *Carmine, Domenic, Italia, Salvatore.*

Piccoli (346) Italian: patronymic or plural form of PICCOLO.

GIVEN NAMES Italian 14%. *Dante* (2), *Geno* (2), *Antonio, Camillo, Evo, Gino, Guido, Luciano, Marco, Nino, Pina, Raffaello*.

Piccolo (929) Italian: nickname from *piccolo* 'small'.

GIVEN NAMES Italian 20%. *Salvatore* (14), *Sal* (5), *Angelo* (3), *Carlo* (3), *Antonio* (2), *Biagio* (2), *Carmine* (2), *Gaetano* (2), *Gaspare* (2), *Nunziata* (2), *Pasquale* (2), *Antonino*.

Piccone (264) Italian: probably from *piccone* '(pick)axe', hence a metonymic occupational name for someone who make or used a (pick)axe.

GIVEN NAMES Italian 18%. *Rocco* (5), *Angelo* (2), *Dante* (2), *Domenic* (2), *Antonio, Camillo, Carmine, Ettore, Nicola*.

Picerno (116) Italian: habitational name from Picerno in Potenza province.

GIVEN NAMES Italian 24%. *Rocco* (2), *Aldo, Amadeo, Carlo, Carmine, Luigi, Natale, Sal, Salvatore, Santino*.

Pich (183) **1.** German and Danish: variant of PECH. **2.** Polish: nickname for a pushy person, from Polish dialect *pichać* 'to push'. **3.** Catalan: variant of *pic*, a word of Celtic origin meaning '(mountain) peak', hence a topographic name for someone who lived by a hill with a pointed peak, or a habitational name from any place named with this word.

GIVEN NAMES German 4%. *Wilfried, Wilhelm*.

Picha (370) Czech (**Pícha, Pýcha**) and Slovak: **1.** nickname for a haughty person, from Czech *pýcha* 'pride'. **2.** from a pet form of the personal name *Petr* (see PETER).

Pichardo (802) Hispanic: unexplained.

GIVEN NAMES Spanish 55%. *Jose* (26), *Juan* (15), *Rafael* (13), *Ramon* (11), *Pedro* (9), *Ana* (8), *Manuel* (8), *Carlos* (7), *Jesus* (7), *Luis* (7), *Ramona* (7), *Francisco* (5).

Piche (678) **1.** German (of Slavic origin): from a pet form of a Slavic form of PETER. **2.** French (**Piché**): variant of **Pichet** (see PICHETTE).

FOREBEARS A Piché or Picher, also called Lamusette, is recorded in Quebec City in 1665. The secondary surname DUPRE is also known.

GIVEN NAMES French 12%. *Armand* (4), *Jacques* (3), *Marcel* (2), *Serge* (2), *Andre, Aurele, Camille, Charlemagne, Dominique, Edouard, Gaetan, Gilles*.

Pichette (404) Canadian spelling of French **Pichet**, from Old French *pichet* 'little pot', a measure for liquids or grain, hence a metonymic occupational name for a potter or a seller of foodstuffs, or nickname for a short person. The spelling reflects the Canadian practice of pronouncing the final *-t*, which is not done in metropolitan France.

FOREBEARS A Pichet, also called Pegin, from the Poitou region of France was documented in 1660 in Château Richer, Quebec.

GIVEN NAMES French 13%. *Fernand* (3), *Lucien* (3), *Andre* (2), *Marcel* (2), *Pierre* (2), *Antoine, Armand, Henri, Ovila, Viateur*.

Pichler (364) **1.** German (Bavaria, Austrian Tyrol): topographic name from *pichl, pühl* 'hill'; in Tyrol it tends to be a habitational name from a farm named with this word. **2.** North German: nickname for a drinker, from an agent derivative of Low German (Westphalian) *picheln* 'to drink'.

GIVEN NAMES German 10%. *Johann* (2), *Albrecht, Alfons, Ernst, Franz, Heinz, Jurgen, Monika, Raimund, Siegried*.

Pichon (302) **1.** French: southern variant of PIGEON. **2.** French: metonymic occupational name from a diminutive of Old French *pic* 'pick'. Compare PIKE 3. **3.** French: metonymic occupational name for a potter, from *pichon* 'jug', 'pitcher'. **4.** French: nickname from *pichon* 'little'. **5.** Spanish (**Pichón**): from a term of endearment, *pichón* 'little dove'.

FOREBEARS The name is rare in Canada; in the U.S. it is concentrated around the Great Lakes and in LA.

GIVEN NAMES French 11%. *Andre* (2), *Armand* (2), *Arnaud* (2), *Alphonse, Clotide, Germain, Jacques, Landry, Michel, Patrice*.

Picht (170) German: of uncertain origin; perhaps a nickname for an aggressive person, from Middle Low German *pichte* 'strife', 'fight', or a topographic name in the former Slavic Wendland region near Hannover.

Picinich (173) Italianized form of the Croatian surname **Pičinić**, probably from *picić* a dialect term for a small male child. This name originates from two islands (Susak and Lošinj) in the Kvarner Gulf of the Adriatic.

GIVEN NAMES Italian 19%. *Mario* (6), *Dino* (2), *Albino, Carmela, Domenica, Gildo, Matteo*.

Pick (1217) **1.** English (mainly East Midlands), Dutch, and German: from Middle English *pi(c)k*, Middle Dutch *picke*, Middle High German *bicke* 'pick', 'pickaxe', hence a metonymic occupational name for someone who made pickaxes or used them as an agricultural or excavating tool. **2.** North German: metonymic occupational name for a pitch-burner, from Low German *pick* 'pitch'. **3.** English: possibly from Middle English *pike* 'pike' (the fish), applied as a metonymic occupational name for a fisherman or seller of these fish, or as a descriptive nickname for someone thought to resemble a pike in some way. **4.** Jewish (eastern Ashkenazic): unexplained.

GIVEN NAMES Jewish 4%. *Aron* (3), *Dov* (2), *Yosef* (2), *Erez, Eytan, Isadore, Isidor, Moshe, Yael*.

Pickar (270) German: probably a variant, under Slavic influence, of PICKER 2.

Pickard (3424) **1.** English (mainly Yorkshire) and German: variant of PICARD. **2.** English: some early examples, such as Paganus filius Pichardi (Hampshire, 1160), seem to point to derivation from a Germanic personal name, probably composed of the elements *bic* 'sharp point', 'pointed weapon' + *hard* 'hardy', 'brave', 'strong'. **3.** Dutch: regional name for someone from Picardy in northern France. **4.** German: variant of PICKER 4.

Pickart (223) **1.** Dutch: variant of PICKARD. **2.** German: variant of PICKER 4 or of PICARD. This also occurs in Germany as a Huguenot name.

Pickel (991) **1.** Southern German: metonymic occupational name for someone who made or used pickaxes or a nickname for a gambler; a variant of BICKEL 1. **2.** Dutch: from Middle Dutch *pickel* 'leg', hence a nickname for someone with long or otherwise remarkable legs, or a metonymic occupational name for a carpenter. **3.** Jewish (eastern Ashkenazic): habitational name for someone from Pikeli in Lithuania.

Pickell (589) Altered spelling of German, Dutch, and Jewish PICKEL.

Pickelsimer (208) Variant spelling of PICKLESIMER, of German origin.

Picken (225) **1.** English (mainly West Midlands): from a diminutive of PICK. **2.** English and Scottish: from the Anglo-Norman French personal name *Picon, Pi(c)quin*, a pet form of *Pic*. The Scottish surname has been established in County Cavan, Ireland, since the 17th century. **3.** German: probably a variant of PICK 1 or 2.

Pickens (5222) Scottish and Irish: variant of PICKEN.

FOREBEARS Gen. Andrew Pickens (1739–1817) of the American Revolution was the son of a Scottish immigrant, whose forebears are reputed to have been French Protestants who left France after the beginning of religious persecution in 1685.

Picker (437) **1.** English: occupational name for someone who used a pick, from Middle English *pi(c)k* 'pick' (see PICK) + the agent suffix *-er*. **2.** English: occupational name for someone who caught or sold pike, from Middle English *pike* 'pike' + the agent suffix *-er*. **3.** English: topographic name for someone who lived on a pointed hill (see PIKE 1), the *-er* suffix denoting an inhabitant. **4.** German: occupational name for someone who used a pick or pickaxe, from an agent derivative of Middle High German *bicken* 'to prick or stab'. **5.** Dutch: occupational name for a stonemason or for a reaper or mower, from Middle Dutch *picker, pecker*. **6.** Jewish (eastern Ashkenazic): nickname for a big eater or a glutton, from Yiddish *pikn* 'to eat' with the noun suffix *-er*.

Pickeral (211) English: variant spelling of PICKERILL.

Pickerel (207) English: variant spelling of PICKERILL.

Pickerell (168) English: variant spelling of PICKERILL.

Pickerill (304) English: from Middle English *pykerell* 'young pike' (from Middle English *pike* 'pike' (a predatory fish) + the diminutive suffix *-erel*), applied as a nickname for a sharp and aggressive person, or possibly as a metonymic occupational name for a catcher or seller of these fish.

Pickering (5075) English: habitational name from Pickering in North Yorkshire, named with an Old English tribal name, *Piceringas*. However, Ekwall suggests that this was earlier *Pīcōringas* 'people on the ridge of the pointed hill' (see ORR 3 and PIKE 1).

FOREBEARS John Pickering of Newgate, Coventry, Warwickshire, England, came to MA in the early 1630s. He married Elizabeth Alderman in Ipswich, MA, in 1636 and moved a year later to Salem.

Pickert (266) German: variant of PICKER 4.

Pickett (10172) English: from the Middle English, Old French personal name *Picot*, *Pigot*, a pet form of *Pic* (see PIKE 6). In Middle English, the form *Piket* (Old French *Picquet*) was also common.

Pickford (389) English: habitational name, perhaps from Pickforde ('pig ford') in Ticehurst, Sussex. The surname is now most common in the Manchester region, but it does not seem to have reached there before the 17th century.

Pickhardt (133) German: probably a variant of **Pickert** (see PICKER 4) with a secondary element *-hardt*, or from French PICARD, a Huguenot name.

Picking (162) English: possibly from Middle English Old French personal name *Pic* (see PIKE 6) + the diminutive suffix *-in*.

Pickle (1182) **1.** English: topographic name from Middle English *pigh(t)el* 'small field', 'paddock' of obscure origin. **2.** Altered spelling of German PICKEL.

Pickler (297) **1.** German: occupational name for someone who made or used a pick or pickaxe, from PICKEL + the agent suffix *-er*. **2.** Altered form of German PICHLER.

Pickles (355) English (mainly Yorkshire): variant of PICKLE.

Picklesimer (452) Americanized spelling of a German habitational name of uncertain origin, perhaps from Bickelheim (now Gau-Bickelheim, in the Palatinate) or Peckelsheim near Paderborn, Westphalia.

Pickman (178) **1.** English: variant of PICKER. **2.** Jewish (Ashkenazic): nickname for a big eater or a glutton, from Yiddish *pikn* 'to eat' + *man* 'man'.

Pickney (274) English: variant of PINCKNEY.

Pickrel (244) English: variant of PICKERELL.

Pickrell (688) English: variant of PICKERELL.

Pickren (184) English: altered form of PICKERING.

Pickron (162) English: altered form of PICKERING.

Pickup (266) English (mainly Lancashire): habitational name from a place in Lancashire, so called from Old English *pīc* 'point' + *copp* 'top', i.e. a hill with a sharp peak.

Pickus (147) Jewish (eastern Ashkenazic): unexplained.

GIVEN NAMES German 6%; Jewish 5%. *Kurt* (3); *Miriam, Yitzchock*.

Pico (388) **1.** Spanish, Portuguese, Galician: from *pico* 'beak' or '(mountain) peak'; perhaps a nickname for someone who had a prominent pointed nose, a topographic name for someone who lived by a peak, or a habitational name from a place named with this word (Pico in Galicia, El Pico in Asturies). **2.** Catalan (**Picó**): probably a nickname from Catalan *picó* 'having a thick upper lip'. **3.** Italian: from *pico* 'woodpecker' or southern dialect *picu* '(pick)axe'.

GIVEN NAMES Spanish 29%. *Juan* (6), *Jose* (5), *Enrique* (4), *Alfonso* (3), *Carlos* (3), *Angel* (2), *Diego* (2), *Francisco* (2), *Gerardo* (2), *Manuel* (2), *Marcos* (2), *Pedro* (2); *Antonio, Eliseo, Marco, Pasquale, Salvatore, Silvio, Vito*.

Picon (177) **1.** French: from a diminutive of *pic* 'pick', hence probably a metonymic occupational name for someone who made or used such implements. **2.** Spanish and Galician (**Picón**): possibly a nickname from *picón* 'long in the tooth' (of a horse), or a habitational name from any of the places in Galicia so named.

GIVEN NAMES Spanish 39%; French 6%. *Juan* (5), *Jose* (4), *Rafael* (3), *Angel* (2), *Guadalupe* (2), *Leticia* (2), *Ana Maria*, *Antonio, Benito, Carlos, Concepcion, Cristina, Dominga, Filiberto; Dominique* (2), *Matilde*.

Picone (841) Italian: probably from an augmentative of PICO.

GIVEN NAMES Italian 13%. *Angelo* (4), *Sal* (4), *Salvatore* (4), *Carmela* (3), *Carmine* (2), *Vita* (2), *Ambrogio, Aniello, Carmelo, Domenico, Gaspare, Giacomo*.

Picot (128) **1.** French and English: from an Old French personal name *Picot*, *Pigot*, a diminutive of *Pic* (see PIKE 6). **2.** Catalan: nickname from Valencian dialect *picot* '(sheep or goat) bell'.

FOREBEARS A Picot with the secondary surname LABRIE is documented in 1653 in Quebec City.

GIVEN NAMES French 16%; Spanish 4%. *Pierre* (2), *Francois, Jacques, Jeanpaul, Luc, Pascal, Yves; Esperanza* (2), *Aida, Alicia, Ana, Felipe, Luis*.

Picotte (199) Variant spelling of French PICOT.

GIVEN NAMES French 10%. *Honore* (3), *Andre, Jacques, Serge*.

Picou (633) French: from Old French *picou* 'small cramp', 'clamp', hence probably a metonymic occupational name for someone made or used such items.

GIVEN NAMES French 7%. *Easton* (2), *Alphonse, Andre, Angelle, Armand, Cecile, Emile, Fernand, Jean Robert, Octave, Roussel*.

Picozzi (136) Italian: from a derivative of PICO.

GIVEN NAMES Italian 7%. *Giacomo, Salvatore*.

Picton (185) English: habitational name from any of various places, for example in Cheshire and North Yorkshire, so called from Old English *pīc* 'point', 'peak' (or the derived byname *Pīca*) + *tūn* 'enclosure', 'settlement'.

Pidcock (246) English (Leicestershire): from a Middle English pet form (with the diminutive suffix *-cok*) of an unattested Old English personal name, *Pydda*.

Pidgeon (741) **1.** English: from Middle English *pyion, peion* 'young bird', 'young pigeon' (from Old French *pijon*), a metonymic occupational name for a hunter of wood pigeons or a nickname for a foolish or gullible person, since the birds were easily taken. **2.** English: altered form of the nickname *Pet(y)jon* (see PETTYJOHN). **3.** Irish (County Monaghan): local form of McGUIGAN, from Gaelic **Mac Uiginn** 'son of the Viking'.

Piech (254) Polish, Czech, and German (of Slavic origin): from a vernacular pet form of PETER.

GIVEN NAMES Polish 11%. *Genowefa, Janina, Janusz, Kazimierz, Krzysztof, Stanislawa, Tadeusz, Teofil, Zbigniew*.

Piechocki (272) Polish: habitational name from Piechoty, in Tarnobrzeg voivodeship, or Piechota in Zamość voivodeship.

Piechota (180) Polish: **1.** nickname for someone who traveled about on foot, from Polish *na piechotę* 'on foot'. **2.** from a pet form of the personal name *Piotr* (see PETER).

GIVEN NAMES Polish 13%. *Casimir, Danuta, Grzegorz, Janusz, Jerzy, Stanislaw, Wladyslaw, Zygmunt*.

Piechowiak (96) Polish: patronymic from the personal name PIECH, a dialect pet form of *Piotr* (see PETER).

Piechowski (278) Polish: habitational name for someone from Piechów in Sieradz voivodeship, or Piechowice in Gdańsk voivodeship.

GIVEN NAMES Polish 5%. *Janusz, Jozef, Krystyna, Leszek, Tadeusz*.

Piecuch (268) Polish: unflattering nickname from *piecuch* 'idler', 'sluggard'.

GIVEN NAMES Polish 5%. *Zofia* (2), *Danuta, Mieczyslaw, Miroslawa*.

Pieczynski (232) Polish (**Pieczyński**): habitational name for someone from Pieczyn in Piła voivodeship.
GIVEN NAMES German 5%. *Kurt* (3), *Erwin*, *Hedwig*.

Piedmont (161) Americanized form of Italian **Piedimonte** or **Piemonte**, the former being a habitational name from places so called in the regions of Naples, Salerno, and Caserta, the latter being a regional name from the province of Piedmont, Italian Piemonte.
GIVEN NAME German 4%. *Otto* (2).

Piedra (421) Spanish: habitational name from any of the places named or named with Piedra (as for example La Piedra in Burgos province) or a topographic name from *piedra* 'rock'.
GIVEN NAMES Spanish 55%. *Jose* (22), *Juan* (10), *Alfredo* (6), *Armando* (6), *Angel* (5), *Francisco* (5), *Manuel* (5), *Alberto* (4), *Guillermo* (4), *Luis* (4), *Rafael* (4), *Aurelio* (3).

Piedrahita (104) Spanish: habitational name from any of the places named Piedrahita, in particular those in Ávila and Teruel.
GIVEN NAMES Spanish 52%. *Carlos* (4), *Jose* (3), *Luis* (3), *Cesar* (2), *Jorge* (2), *Mario* (2), *Alfredo*, *Amparo*, *Ana*, *Andres*, *Argemiro*, *Armando*.

Piehl (543) **1.** Swedish: variant of PIHL. **2.** German: Low German form of PFEIL, or a variant of PIEL 2.

Piehler (147) **1.** North German: occupational name for an arrowsmith, a Low German cognate of PFEILER. **2.** South German: variant of BIEHLER.
GIVEN NAMES German 7%. *Franz*, *Guenter*.

Piekarski (632) Polish: **1.** variant of PIEKARZ 'baker', with the addition of *-ski*, a common suffix of surnames. **2.** habitational name for someone from any of various places in Poland called Piekary.
GIVEN NAMES Polish 7%. *Waclaw* (2), *Andrzej*, *Bernadeta*, *Casimir*, *Irena*, *Janusz*, *Karol*, *Krystyna*, *Leszek*, *Slawomir*, *Zbigniew*.

Piekarz (130) Polish and Jewish (from Poland): occupational name for a baker, Polish *piekarz*.
GIVEN NAMES Polish 11%; Jewish 4%. *Henryk* (2), *Grazyna*, *Tadeusz*, *Tomasz*; *Jefim* (2).

Piekos (118) Polish: variant of **Piękoś**, a nickname meaning 'elegant' or 'foppish'.
GIVEN NAMES Polish 10%. *Jerzy*, *Zbigniew*.

Piel (613) **1.** North German: equivalent of PFEIL. **2.** East German (of Slavic origin): Sorbian short form of a personal name equivalent to PHILLIP.
GIVEN NAMES German 4%. *Armin* (2), *Erwin*, *Gerhardt*, *Hans*, *Kurt*, *Otto*.

Piela (199) Polish: **1.** from a local vernacular derivative of the personal name *Filip* (see PHILLIP). **2.** nickname either from Old

Polish *pielać* 'to hurry' or from *pielić* 'to weed'. Compare PELAK.
GIVEN NAMES Polish 5%. *Casimir*, *Janina*, *Jerzy*, *Tadeuz*.

Piemonte (116) Italian: regional name from Piedmont, Italian *Piemonte*, or a topographic name for someone living a the foot (*pie*) of a mountain (*monte*).
GIVEN NAMES Italian 16%. *Carmine* (2), *Antonio*, *Domenico*, *Gaetano*, *Silvio*, *Vito*.

Piening (128) German: nickname for a tormenter, or an occupational name for a torturer or executioner, from a derivative of Middle Low German, Middle High German *pīn* 'pain', 'torture', 'punishment'.
GIVEN NAMES German 4%. *Frieda*, *Guenter*.

Pienkowski (141) Polish (**Pieńkowski**): habitational name from any of several places, for example Pieńki and Pieńków, named with *pienkie* 'tree stump', or a topographic name for someone who lived where there were a lot of tree stumps.
GIVEN NAMES Polish 21%. *Stanislaw* (2), *Alojzy*, *Ireneusz*, *Jaroslaw*, *Kazimierz*, *Krzysztof*, *Radoslaw*, *Tadeusz*, *Tadeuz*.

Pienta (187) Polish (**Pięta**): nickname from *pięta* 'heel'.

Pientka (114) Polish: from a diminutive of PIENTA 'heel'.

Piepenbrink (134) North German: topographic name from Middle Low German *pīpe* 'water pipe', 'ditch' + *brink* 'edge', 'slope', 'raised grazing land surrounded by marshy ground'.
GIVEN NAMES German 7%. *Erwin* (3), *Kurt*.

Piepenburg (134) German: probably a partly standardized form of Low German **Piepenbrock**, a topographic or habitational name, from Middle Low German *pīpe* 'ditch' + *brōk*, *-brock* '(wooded) swamp'.
GIVEN NAMES German 9%. *Kurt* (3), *Eldor*.

Pieper (2922) **1.** Dutch and North German: occupational name for a piper, Middle Low German *piper*. Compare German PFEIFFER. **2.** In some cases it may derive from Sorbian *pipar* 'pepper' (see PFEFFER).
GIVEN NAMES German 4%. *Kurt* (4), *Otto* (4), *Erwin* (3), *Hans* (2), *Alois*, *Armin*, *Bernhard*, *Ernst*, *Fritz*, *Gerhard*, *Gunter*, *Heinz*.

Piepho (161) **1.** North German: topographic name composed of Middle Low German *pipe* 'pipe', 'narrow drainage channel' + *ho* 'elevation'. **2.** Eastern German (of Slavic origin): from a Sorbian form a of PHILLIP.

Piepmeier (104) German: distinguishing name for a tenant farmer (see MEYER), + Middle Low German *pipe* 'pipe', 'drainage channel'.

Pier (695) German: **1.** habitational name from a place so named near Düren (Lower Rhine). **2.** nickname from Middle Low German *pīr(-ās)* 'earthworm'.

Pieratt (278) Possibly an altered form of French **Piérat**, an augmentative form of the personal name *Pierre* (see PETER).

Pierce (49516) **1.** English, Welsh, and Irish: from the personal name *Piers*, the usual Norman vernacular form of PETER. In Wales this represents a patronymic *ap Piers*. In Ireland it represents a reduced Anglicized form of Gaelic **Mac Piarais** 'son of *Piaras*', a Gaelicized form of *Piers*. **2.** Americanized form of some similar-sounding Jewish surname.
FOREBEARS Franklin Pierce (1804–69), 14th president of the United States, was born in Hillsborough, NH, on the New England frontier. His English ancestor Thomas Pierce emigrated to Charlestown, MA, in 1633/34.

Pierceall (166) Variant spelling of English PEARSALL.

Piercefield (135) English: variant of PERCIVAL 2, altered by folk etymology.

Piercey (333) English: variant of PERCY. As English names, these are found chiefly in Reading, Berkshire.

Piercy (1452) English: variant of PERCY. As English names, these are found chiefly in Reading, Berkshire.

Pieretti (120) Italian: from the personal name *Pieretto*, a pet form of *Piero* (see PIERI).
GIVEN NAMES Italian 27%. *Luciano* (3), *Guido* (2), *Ananias*, *Augustino*, *Gino*, *Guglielmo*, *Mario*, *Tullio*.

Pieri (384) Italian: from the Tuscan personal name *Piero*, a variant of *Pietro* (see PETER).
GIVEN NAMES Italian 11%. *Dino* (2), *Franco* (2), *Pierino* (2), *Alessandro*, *Concetta*, *Dario*, *Giovanni*, *Guglielmo*, *Italo*, *Luigi*, *Luigia*, *Mauro*.

Pierini (171) Italian: from a pet form of the personal name *Piero* (see PIERI).
GIVEN NAMES Italian 23%. *Armando* (2), *Amedeo*, *Angelo*, *Antonio*, *Emilio*, *Francesca*, *Giorgio*, *Ivano*, *Mario*, *Mauro*, *Piero*, *Sabatino*, *Santi*.

Pierman (146) Altered spelling of German **Piermann**, a derivative of the medieval personal name *Pirminius*, possibly of Celtic origin, + *man* 'man'.

Piermarini (100) Italian: from a compound personal name, *Piermarino*, composed of *Piero* (see PIERI) + MARINO.
GIVEN NAMES Italian 29%. *Dino* (2), *Emidio* (2), *Lido* (2), *Angelo*, *Domenic*, *Domenico*, *Muzio*, *Pellegrino*, *Rocco*.

Pierog (121) Polish: occupational nickname for a cook, from *pieróg*, a kind of ravioli.

Pieroni (319) Italian: from a derivative of the personal name *Piero* (see PIERI).
GIVEN NAMES Italian 5%. *Angelo*, *Reno*, *Rino*, *Silvio*.

Pierotti (331) Italian: from a pet form of the personal name *Piero* (see PIERI).
GIVEN NAMES Italian 8%. *Aldino* (2), *Aldo* (2), *Duilio* (2), *Angelo*, *Dario*, *Giulio*, *Ivano*, *Silvio*.

Pierpoint (281) English: variant of PIERPONT.

Pierpont (427) English (of Norman origin): habitational name from any of various places, for example in Aisne and Calvados, so called from Old French *pierre* 'stone' + *pont* 'bridge'.

FOREBEARS All the New England Pierpont lines seem to be descended from James and his sons John and Robert, who came to America about 1640. James also may have had a brother Robert who was part of that group. The southern Pierpo(i)nt family are descended from Henry, who came to the VA–MD region in 1635.

Pierre (3912) French: **1.** from the French personal name *Pierre* (see PETER). **2.** from Old French *pierre* 'stone', 'rock' (Latin *petra*), a topographic name for someone who lived on a patch of stony soil or by a large outcrop of rock, or a metonymic occupational name for a quarryman or stonemason.

GIVEN NAMES French 26%. *Andre* (19), *Jacques* (14), *Antoine* (11), *Yves* (9), *Michel* (8), *Jean Claude* (7), *Mireille* (6), *Jean Robert* (5), *Francois* (4), *Monique* (4), *Raoul* (4), *Serge* (4).

Pierre-Louis (421) French: from a compound personal name consisting of *Pierre* (see PETER) + *Louis* (see LEWIS). According to Morlet, such compounds are found mainly in eastern France.

GIVEN NAMES French 45%. *Jacques* (4), *Francois* (3), *Magalie* (3), *Andre* (2), *Constant* (2), *Alide*, *Altagrace*, *Antoine*, *Carmelle*, *Celestin*, *Chantal*, *Fernand*.

Pierro (577) Italian: from the personal name *Pierro*, a variant of PIETRO, influenced by French *Pierre*.

GIVEN NAMES Italian 11%. *Carmine* (6), *Vito* (3), *Angelo* (2), *Salvatore* (2), *Donato*, *Nicola*, *Pasquale*, *Rocco*, *Sisto*.

Pierron (220) French: from a pet form of the personal name *Pierre*, French form of PETER.

GIVEN NAMES French 7%. *Firmin* (2), *Emile*, *Hyacinthe*.

Piers (115) English and Irish: from the personal name *Piers* (see PIERCE).

Piersall (285) English: variant spelling of PEARSALL.

Piersma (144) Frisian: from a pet form of the personal name *Pieter*, Frisian form of PETER.

Piersol (315) Variant of English PEARSALL.

Pierson (10539) **1.** English (London): patronymic from the personal name *Piers* (see PIERCE). **2.** North German: patronymic from the personal name *Pier*, a variant of *Peer*, reduced form of PETER.

FOREBEARS Born in Yorkshire, England, Abraham Pierson (1609–78) was the first pastor of the settlements at Southampton, Long Island, NY; Branford, CT, and Newark, NJ. He left his library of more than 400 books, one of the most extensive in the colonies, to his son Abraham, who was one of the first trustees of Yale College.

Pies (204) German: from a variant of the medieval personal name *Pius* (Latin *pius* 'the pious one').

Pieske (104) **1.** Eastern German (of Slavic origin): probably a habitational name from Pieski in Pomerania. **2.** German: from a pet form of the medieval personal name *Pius* (see PIES).

GIVEN NAMES German 8%. *Dieter*, *Gerhard*, *Siegfried*.

Piester (121) Probably an altered form or variant of German PFIESTER.

Piet (188) **1.** Dutch: from a very common short form of the personal name *Pieter* (see PETER). **2.** French: variant of PICOT.

FOREBEARS A Piet, also called Trempe, from the Saintonge region of France arrived at Sorel, Quebec, in 1665. The secondary surnames Fresnière and COURVILLE are also recorded.

GIVEN NAME French 5%. *Marcel* (2).

Pieters (317) Dutch and North German: patronymic from the personal name *Pieter* (see PETER).

GIVEN NAMES French 6%; Dutch 5%. *Raymonde* (2), *Laurent*, *Marcel*, *Pierre*, *Serge*; *Bernardus* (2), *Wim* (2), *Bram*, *Pieter*, *Willem*.

Pietig (102) German: **1.** unexplained; perhaps a shortened form of **Bietigheimer**, a habitational name for someone from Bietigheim in Württemberg. **2.** perhaps a nickname from Middle Low German *pit* 'strength', 'core' denoting a strong, resilient person.

Pietila (288) Finnish (**Pietilä**): habitational name from a farm named with the personal name *Pieti* (Finnish form of PETER) + the local ending *-la*. The surname occurs mainly in western and northern Finland, where it is first recorded in the 16th century.

GIVEN NAMES Finnish 5%. *Irja*, *Jukka*, *Onni*, *Osmo*, *Sulo*, *Waino*, *Wiljo*.

Pietrangelo (161) Italian: from a compound personal name formed from PIETRO and ANGELO.

GIVEN NAMES Italian 18%. *Antonio*, *Bruna*, *Carlo*, *Carmine*, *Cesare*, *Cosimo*, *Emidio*, *Giuseppe*, *Marco*, *Rocco*.

Pietrantonio (124) Italian: from a compound personal name formed from PIETRO and ANTONIO.

GIVEN NAMES Italian 18%. *Antonio* (3), *Angelo*, *Lucio*, *Marco*, *Mario*, *Tito*, *Ubaldo*.

Pietras (462) Polish: from an augmentative form of the personal name *Pietr*, dialect form of *Piotr* (see PETER).

GIVEN NAMES Polish 7%. *Stanislaw* (2), *Boleslaw*, *Dariusz*, *Dorota*, *Henryk*, *Ignacy*, *Jolanta*, *Kazimierz*.

Pietri (132) **1.** Italian: patronymic or plural form of PIETRO. **2.** Dutch: patronymic from the genitive of *Pietrus*, a Latinized form of *Pieter* (see PETER).

GIVEN NAMES Spanish 31%. *Miguel* (3), *Carlos* (2), *Eduardo* (2), *Jesus* (2), *Jose* (2), *Luz* (2), *Acosta*, *Cesar*, *Enrique*, *Francisco*, *Josefa*, *Juan*.

Pietro (318) Italian: from the personal name *Pietro*, an Italian equivalents of PETER.

GIVEN NAMES Italian 5%. *Angelo*, *Antonio*, *Sal*, *Salvatore*.

Pietropaolo (110) Italian: from a combination of the personal names *Pietro* (see PETER) and *Paolo* (see PAUL).

GIVEN NAMES Italian 28%. *Rocco* (3), *Americo* (2), *Antonietta*, *Damiano*, *Enrico*, *Giovanna*, *Nicola*, *Nicolo*, *Sal*.

Pietrowicz (140) Polish: patronymic from the personal name *Pietr*, a dialect form of *Piotr* (see PETER).

GIVEN NAMES Polish 10%. *Casimir* (2), *Mikolaj*, *Miroslaw*.

Pietrowski (490) Polish: habitational name for someone from places called Pietrowice in Katowice and Opole voivodeships.

GIVEN NAMES Polish 4%. *Bogdan*, *Casimir*, *Dariusz*, *Wojtek*.

Pietrucha (120) Polish: **1.** from a pet form of the personal name *Pietr*, dialect form of *Piotr* (see PETER). **2.** from an augmentative form of *pietruszka* 'parsley', a metonymic occupational name for someone who grew or sold this herb.

GIVEN NAMES Polish 12%. *Jozef* (2), *Ewa*, *Janina*, *Krzysztof*, *Stas*.

Pietruszewski (99) Polish: **1.** derivative of the personal name *Pietrusz*, a pet form of *Piotr* (see PETER), with the common surname ending *-ewski*. **2.** derivative of *pietruszka* 'parsley'.

GIVEN NAME Polish 4%. *Czeslaw*.

Pietruszka (144) Polish: **1.** from a pet form of the personal name *Pietr*, dialect form of *Piotr* (see PETER). **2.** from *pietruszka* 'parsley', a metonymic occupational name for someone who grew or sold this herb.

GIVEN NAMES Polish 13%. *Wieslaw* (3), *Jerzy*, *Malgorzata*, *Tomasz*, *Zbigniew*.

Pietrzak (743) Polish: patronymic from the personal name *Pietr*, dialect form of *Piotr* (see PETER).

GIVEN NAMES Polish 10%. *Janusz* (4), *Casimir* (3), *Boguslaw* (2), *Krystyna* (2), *Tadeusz* (2), *Andrzej*, *Bartosz*, *Elzbieta*, *Ewa*, *Gerzy*, *Ignacy*, *Irena*.

Pietrzyk (236) Polish: from a pet form of the personal name *Pietr*, dialect form of *Piotr* (see PETER).

GIVEN NAMES Polish 20%. *Zbigniew* (3), *Witold* (2), *Andrzej*, *Bronislawa*, *Casimir*, *Danuta*, *Halina*, *Henryk*, *Jadwiga*, *Jaroslaw*, *Kazimierz*, *Tadeusz*.

Pietrzykowski (92) Polish: habitational name for someone from places called Pietrzyków, Pietrzikowo, or Pietrzykowice.

GIVEN NAMES Polish 8%; German 4%. *Andrzej*, *Feliks*; *Wilhelm*.

Pietsch (660) German (of Slavic origin): from a pet form of a Slavic form of PETER.

GIVEN NAMES German 6%. *Hans* (2), *Christl*, *Claus*, *Erhard*, *Erna*, *Gerhart*, *Hannelore*, *Kurt*, *Lothar*, *Otto*, *Wilfried*, *Wolfgang*.

Piette (398) Canadian spelling of French PIET, reflecting the Canadian practice of pronouncing the final *-t*, which is not done in metropolitan France.
GIVEN NAMES French 10%. *Normand* (3), *Georges* (2), *Onesime* (2), *Adrien, Alain, Gaston, Marcel, Pierre.*

Piety (105) **1.** English: presumably a nickname for a pious person. **2.** It could also be an Americanized form of German PIETIG.

Pietz (495) German (of Slavic origin): from a pet form of a Slavic form of PETER.
GIVEN NAMES German 4%. *Milbert* (2), *Lothar.*

Pifer (1451) Americanized spelling of German PEIF(F)ER or similar variants of PFEIFFER.

Pigeon (545) **1.** French: from *pigeon* 'pigeon' (Old French *pijon* 'young bird'), hence a metonymic occupational name for a hunter of wood pigeons, or a nickname for a foolish or gullible person, since the birds are easily taken. **2.** In some cases, an altered form of French PETITJEAN. **3.** English: variant spelling of PIDGEON.
FOREBEARS A person from Paris with the name Pigeon is documented in Montreal in 1662. Another is recorded with the secondary surname **Petitjean**.
GIVEN NAMES French 10%. *Andre* (4), *Marcel* (3), *Florent* (2), *Andree, Armand, Calixte, Gaetan, Germain, Laurent, Lucien, Michel, Pierre.*

Pigford (336) English (Durham): possibly a variant of PICKFORD.

Pigg (1676) English (mainly Durham and Northumbria): from Middle English *pigge* 'young hog', hence a metonymic occupational name for a swineherd or nickname for someone supposedly resembling a hog.

Piggee (189) Origin unidentified.

Piggott (604) English and Irish (of Norman origin): from the Old French personal name *Picot, Pigot*, a pet form of *Pic* (see PIKE 6).

Pigman (357) Of uncertain origin; perhaps an altered spelling of English **Pickman**, a variant of PICKER 1–3.

Pignataro (308) Southern Italian: **1.** habitational name from Pignataro Interamna in Frosinone or Pignataro Maggiore in Caserta. **2.** occupational name for a potter, from an agent derivative of *pignat(t)a* 'pot'.
GIVEN NAMES Italian 20%. *Fiore* (4), *Angelo* (3), *Carmine* (2), *Franco* (2), *Rocco* (2), *Sal* (2), *Santo* (2), *Annamarie, Carlo, Dino, Gennaro, Gino.*

Pignatelli (172) Southern Italian: patronymic from **Pigntello**, from a diminutive of *pignat(t)a* 'pot', hence a metonymic occupational name for a potter, or a nickname for a rotund person.
GIVEN NAMES Italian 21%. *Antonio* (2), *Federico* (2), *Gerardo* (2), *Angelo, Fabio, Luigi, Marina, Mario, Ricardo, Sante.*

Pignato (152) Italian (Sicily): metonymic occupational name for a potter, from Sicilian *pignatu* 'pot'.

GIVEN NAMES Italian 6%. *Damiano, Salvatore.*

Pignone (148) Italian (Sicily): from a derivative of *pigna* 'pine cone'.
GIVEN NAMES Italian 7%. *Rocco* (2), *Gino.*

Pignotti (105) Italian: apparently a diminutive of an unrecorded family name **Pigno**, now found only as a place name. .
GIVEN NAMES Italian 14%. *Dante, Dino, Emidio, Ettore, Guido, Reno.*

Pigott (1128) English (mainly Yorkshire) and Irish: variant of PIGGOTT.

Pigue (154) French: from a Germanic personal name (derived from the root 'sharp', 'pointed'), found in Middle English and Old French as *Pic*. Compare English PIKE.

Pihl (338) **1.** Scandinavian: ornamental name from *pil* 'arrow'. **2.** North German: Low German form of PFEIL.
GIVEN NAMES Scandinavian 10%. *Erik* (4), *Niels.*

Pijanowski (153) Polish: habitational name for someone from places called Pijanowice in Leszno voivodeship or Pijanów in Kielce voivodeship. This surname is also established in German-speaking countries.
GIVEN NAME German 4%. *Kurt.*

Pike (10337) **1.** English: topographic name for someone who lived by a hill with a sharp point, from Old English *pīc* 'point', 'hill', which was a relatively common place name element. **2.** English: metonymic occupational name for a pike fisherman or nickname for a predatory individual, from Middle English *pike*. **3.** English: metonymic occupational name for a user of a pointed tool for breaking up the earth, Middle English *pike*. Compare PICK. **4.** English: metonymic occupational name for a medieval foot soldier who used a pike, a weapon consisting of a sharp pointed metal end on a long pole, Middle English *pic* (Old French *pique*, of Germanic origin). **5.** English: nickname for a tall, thin person, from a transferred sense of one of the above. **6.** English: from a Germanic personal name (derived from the root 'sharp', 'pointed'), found in Middle English and Old French as *Pic*. **7.** English: nickname from Old French *pic* 'woodpecker', Latin *picus*. Compare PYE and SPEIGHT. **8.** Irish: in the south, of English origin; in Ulster a variant Anglicization of Gaelic **Mac Péice** (see MCPEAKE). **9.** Americanized spelling of German **Peik**, from Middle Low German *pēk* 'sharp, pointed tool or weapon'. Compare 4 above or from a Germanic personal name (see 6 above).
FOREBEARS John Pike brought his family to Boston from England in 1635 and settled in Newbury, MA. His son Robert was a leading citizen and a vigorous defender of civil and religious liberty in colonial MA.

Piker (174) Americanized spelling of German **Pei(c)ker**, an occupational name for a

drummer, Middle Low German *pucker*, Middle High German *pūkære.*

Pikul (261) Polish: nickname from a derivative of *pikać* 'to squeak'.
GIVEN NAMES Polish 14%. *Stanislaw* (2), *Tadeusz* (2), *Andrzej, Czeslaw, Danuta, Hieronim, Piotr, Urszula, Wojciech, Zofia.*

Pikula (195) Polish (also **Pikuła**): nickname from a derivative of *pikać* 'to squeak'.
GIVEN NAMES Polish 8%. *Zbigniew* (2), *Gustaw, Ludwik, Mariusz, Teofil.*

Pikus (184) Lithuanian: **1.** probably a reduced form of the Lithuanian family name *Pikūnas* or *Pikutis*. **2.** perhaps from a family name of Germanic origin.
GIVEN NAMES Russian 13%. *Boris* (2), *Valeriy* (2), *Fedor, Iosif, Lev; Ilya, Semen.*

Piland (604) Altered spelling of German **Pieland** (of Slavic origin), a nickname for someone with white hair or a pale complexion, ultimately from Slavic *belu* 'white'.

Pilant (235) German: variant of PILAND.

Pilar (104) Spanish: metronymic from the Marian name *María del Pila*, associated with Zaragoza province.
GIVEN NAMES Spanish 39%. *Guillermo* (2), *Alvaro, Anastacio, Angelina, Arana, Arminda, Claudio, Diego, Dominador, Florencio, Jose, Luis.*

Pilarczyk (103) Polish: occupational name from Polish *pilarczyk*, diminutive of *pilarz* 'sawyer' or 'saw maker'.
GIVEN NAMES Polish 6%. *Ewa, Jozef, Pawel.*

Pilarski (531) Polish: occupational name for a sawyer, Polish *pilarz* (see PILARCZYK) + *-ski*, common ending of surnames.

Pilat (304) **1.** Polish (**Piłat**), Czech and Slovak (**Pilát**), and French: from Latin *Pilatus*, name of the Roman governor of Judea who interrogated Christ, then 'washed his hands' of responsibility for his crucifixion. This was used as a nickname for someone who would take no responsibility, or perhaps for someone who had played the role of Pontius Pilate in a pageant or passion play. **2.** French: habitational name from Pilat in Gironde, Le Mont Pilat in Loire, or Pilate in Cher.
GIVEN NAMES Polish 9%. *Jozef* (3), *Danuta* (2), *Iwan, Janina, Jerzy, Leszek, Slawomir.*

Pilato (298) Italian: **1.** from the Roman family name, Latin *Pilatus*. Pontius Pilatus was the Roman governor of Judea who interrogated Christ, then 'washed his hands' of responsibility for his crucifixion. This was used as a nickname for someone who would take no responsibility. **2.** perhaps also an altered form of **Pelato**, a nickname for a bald person, from *pelato*, past participle of *depilare* 'to remove hair'.
GIVEN NAMES Italian 17%. *Angelo* (4), *Salvatore* (3), *Antonio* (2), *Biagio, Damiano, Gasper, Nicola, Nino, Paolo, Pasquale.*

Pilch (442) **1.** English (Norfolk): from Middle English *pilch*, a metonymic occupational name for a maker or seller of

pilches or a nickname for a habitual wearer of these. A pilch (from Late Latin *pellicia*, a derivative of *pellis* 'skin', 'hide') was a kind of coarse leather garment with the hair or fur still on it. **2.** Polish: nickname from Old Polish *pilch* 'gray squirrel'. **3.** Jewish (from Ukraine): metonymic occupational name from Yiddish *piltsh* 'felt' (see 1).
GIVEN NAMES Polish 5%. *Jozef* (2), *Pawel* (2), *Beata, Jerzy, Krzysztof, Piotr, Ryszard.*

Pilcher (1996) English (Kentish): occupational name for a maker or seller of pilches, from an agent derivative of PILCH. In early 17th-century English, *pilcher* was a popular term of abuse, being confused or punningly associated with the unrelated verb *pilch* 'to steal' and with the unrelated noun *pilchard*, a kind of fish.

Pile (592) **1.** English (Devon): variant spelling of PYLE. **2.** French: of uncertain origin: perhaps from Old French *pile* 'trough', a topographic name for someone who lived in a hollow, or alternatively a habitational name from any of the minor places named with this word.

Pilecki (137) Polish: habitational name for someone from places called *Pilcza* (modern Pilica) in Katowice and Radom voivodeships.
GIVEN NAMES Polish 12%. *Andrzej* (2), *Zofia* (2), *Boleslaw, Brunon, Kazimierz.*

Pileggi (396) Italian: either a nickname from Calabrian *pileggiu* 'calm', 'tranquility', or possibly a topographic name or metonymic occupational name for a herb grower or seller from Calabrian *pileju* 'mint'.
GIVEN NAMES Italian 20%. *Salvatore* (4), *Antonio* (3), *Francesco* (3), *Vito* (2), *Aldo, Annamaria, Carlo, Giovanni, Giuseppe, Lorenzo, Luigi, Pasquale.*

Pilger (455) **1.** English: variant of PILCHER. **2.** German: shortened form (since the 15th century) of **Pilgerin** (see PILGRIM).

Pilgram (135) English and German: variant spelling of PILGRIM.
GIVEN NAME German 5%. *Kurt* (2).

Pilgreen (286) English: altered form of PILGRIM.

Pilgrim (2134) English (East Anglia) and German: from Middle English *pilegrim, pelgrim*, Middle High German *bilgerin, pilgerīn* 'pilgrim' (Latin *peregrinus, pelegrinus* 'traveler'), a nickname for a person who had been on a pilgrimage to the Holy Land or to some seat of devotion nearer home, such as Santiago de Compostella, Rome, or Canterbury. Such pilgrimages were often imposed as penances, graver sins requiring more arduous journeys. In both England and Germany *Pilgrim* was occasionally used as a personal name, from which the surname could also have arisen.

Pilkenton (271) Variant of English PILKINGTON.

Pilkerton (240) Variant of English PILKINGTON.

Pilkey (108) Origin unidentified. The surname is of Canadian origin and is said to be an Anglicized form of French PELTIER 'fur trader'.

Pilkington (1556) English (Lancashire): habitational name from a place in the parish of Prestwich, Lancashire, so named from Old English *Pīlecingtūn* 'settlement (Old English *tūn*) associated with *Pīleca*'. The surname is established in Ireland, where its presence was first recorded in the early 15th century.

Pilkinton (368) Variant of English PILKINGTON.

Pill (130) English (Devon and Cornwall): **1.** topographic name for someone who lived by a tidal creek or an inlet of the sea, Old English *pyll*, or a habitational name from Pylle in Somerset, which was named with this word. **2.** descriptive nickname for a small, rotund person, from Middle English, Old French *pil(l)e* 'ball'.
GIVEN NAMES German 5%. *Gerhard, Johann.*

Pilla (559) Italian: topographic name from *pilla* 'mud', 'mire', 'clayey ground', or a habitational name from a place named with this word.
GIVEN NAMES Italian 12%. *Angelo* (4), *Antonio* (3), *Nicola* (3), *Domenico* (2), *Amedeo, Carlo, Enrico, Enza, Erminio, Francesco, Giovanni, Giuseppe.*

Pillai (283) Indian (Tamil Nadu): Hindu name found in several communities of Tamil Nadu, from Tamil *piḷḷai* 'son', 'lad'.
GIVEN NAMES Indian 84%. *Radhakrishna* (5), *Raj* (5), *Krishna* (4), *Sivan* (4), *Vinod* (4), *Ammini* (2), *Anilkumar* (2), *Bala* (2), *Balakrishna* (2), *Kesava* (2), *Lata* (2), *Meena* (2).

Pillar (395) English (mainly Devon): **1.** from Old French *pilleur* 'plunderer', formerly used as a nickname for a bailiff. **2.** topographic name for someone who lived by a tidal creek (see PILL, PYLE). **3.** topographic name from Old French *piler* 'pillar'.

Pillard (190) Of uncertain origin. Pillard is a French surname, from a derivative of Old French *pilleur* 'plunderer'; however, the distribution of the name in the U.S. does not comply with the normal pattern for names of French origin. It could perhaps be an altered form of English POLLARD.

Pillars (141) Possibly an altered spelling of English **Pillers**, a variant of PILLAR 1.

Pillay (100) Indian: variant of PILLAI.
GIVEN NAMES Indian 66%. *Mohan* (2), *Rajeev* (2), *Sanjay* (2), *Sasi* (2), *Anand, Anil, Balakrishna, Dev, Gautam, Kavita, Narendra, Rajendra.*

Pille (180) **1.** North German, Danish, and Dutch: from a shortened form of the personal name *Billulf*, composed of the elements *bil* 'sword', 'axe' + *wulf* 'wolf', or some other name with *bil* as the first element. For German, however, the most likely source is **Pille**, a French Huguenot name

from the Dauphiné. **2.** English: variant spelling of PILL 2. **3.** French: habitational name from any of various minor places in northern France, so named from Old French *pile*, Latin *pila*, 'pillar', 'column'. In Middle French *pile* denoted a trough used for crushing or pounding various materials, such as lime, and in some cases the surname may have arisen as a metonymic occupational name for someone engaged in such work.

Pillen (100) **1.** North German: probably from a derivative of PILLE 1. **2.** Dutch: relationship name from Middle Dutch *pil(le)* 'godchild'. **3.** English: possibly a variant of PILLING.
GIVEN NAMES German 6%. *Klaus, Kurt.*

Piller (504) **1.** English: variant of PILLAR 1–3. **2.** German: variant of PILLE (from *Bilihar*, composed of *bil* 'sword' + *hari* 'army'). **3.** Jewish (Ashkenazic): unexplained.
GIVEN NAMES Jewish 4%. *Moshe* (2), *Chaim, Esti, Irina, Yakov.*

Pilley (174) English: habitational name from either of two places so named. One in southern Yorkshire is recorded as *Pillei* in Domesday Book and as *Pillay* in the late 12th century. It is probably from Old English *pīl* 'pile', 'post' + *lēah* 'wood', 'clearing', i.e. a wood where timber for piles could be obtained. The other, in Hampshire, appears in Domesday Book as *Piste(s)lei*, but has later spellings resembling those for *Pilley* in Yorkshire, and may have the same etymology.

Pilling (493) **1.** English (Lancashire): topographic name from Old English *pīling* 'dweller by the stake' or *pylling* 'dweller by the stream'. **2.** German: habitational name from a place so named near Straubing, Bavaria. Compare BILLING. **3.** German: patronymic derivative of PILLE 1.

Pillion (217) Irish: of uncertain origin. It was first recorded in the early 18th century in County Cork.

Pillman (105) **1.** English: probably from Middle English *pille* 'stake' or a homograph meaning 'stream', and so a topographic name for someone who lived by a stake (Old English *pīl*) or a stream (Old English *pyll*). **2.** German: from the personal name PILLE with the addition of *man* 'man'.
GIVEN NAME German 4%. *Franz.*

Pillot (105) French: unexplained.
GIVEN NAMES Spanish 18%. *Carlos* (4), *Ana, Emilia, Juan, Luis, Margarita, Marisol, Roberto; Giancarlo, Luciano.*

Pillow (1088) English: variant of PEDLEY 1.

Pillsbury (1006) English: habitational name from a place in Derbyshire, so named from the genitive of the Old English personal name *Pīl* + *burh* (dative *byrig*) 'fortified place'.
FOREBEARS William Pillsbury (or Pilsbury) came to MA from England as early as 1641, settling first in Dorchester and then

in Ipswich. His descendant John Sargent Pillsbury (1828–1901), who made the name famous for flour, was a miller and governor of MN.

Pilon (834) French: nickname for a quick-tempered or unpleasant person, from Old French *pelon* 'spiky outer case of a chestnut'.

FOREBEARS A Pilon, also called LAFORTUNE, from Paris is recorded in Repentigny, Quebec, in 1688. Another branch comes from Normandy, France.

GIVEN NAMES French 10%. *Andre* (3), *Henri* (2), *Jean-Paul* (2), *Marcel* (2), *Adelore*, *Aime*, *Alain*, *Anatole*, *Armand*, *Aurore*, *Elzear*, *Emile*.

Pilot (417) English: from the personal name *Pilot*, a Middle English pet form of the Old English personal name *Pīla*.

Pilotte (227) French: from Old French *pilot* 'stake', 'pile'.

FOREBEARS A Pilote from La Rochelle, France, is documented in Quebec City in 1659.

GIVEN NAMES French 10%. *Normand* (2), *Adrien*, *Andre*, *Germaine*, *Laurent*, *Ovila*, *Pierre*, *Yves*.

Pilotti (126) Italian: possibly related to Old Tuscan *Pilottus*, from *pilotto* 'pilot'.

GIVEN NAMES Italian 8%. *Angelo*, *Pasquale*, *Pierino*.

Pilson (313) English: unexplained.

Piltz (180) German and Jewish (Ashkenazic): variant spelling of PILZ.

GIVEN NAMES German 5%. *Hans*, *Kurt*.

Pilz (297) German and Jewish (Ashkenazic): metonymic occupational name for a gatherer of mushrooms, from Middle High German *bül(e)z*, German *Pilz* 'mushroom'.

GIVEN NAMES German 20%. *Gerhard* (5), *Horst* (2), *Otto* (2), *Dietmar*, *Erna*, *Franz*, *Gertraud*, *Guenter*, *Gunther*, *Hanns*, *Klaus*, *Kurt*.

Pimenta (126) Portuguese: nickname from *pimenta* 'red pepper' (Late Latin *pigmenta*, from classical Latin *pigmentum* 'paint', 'pigment'), originally perhaps a metonymic occupational name for someone who grew or sold peppers.

GIVEN NAMES Spanish 30%; Portuguese 19%. *Jose* (9), *Antonio* (6), *Carlos* (3), *Adriano* (2), *Acacio*, *Aurea*, *Avelino*, *Claudio*, *Fernando*, *Francisco*, *Jaime*, *Josue*, *Julio*; *Joao* (3).

Pimental (861) Portuguese: perhaps a topographic name from *pimental* 'pepper planting', a derivative of PIMENTA.

GIVEN NAMES Spanish 19%; Portuguese 8%. *Manuel* (30), *Jose* (12), *Carlos* (7), *Mariano* (4), *Ramon* (4), *Francisco* (3), *Luis* (3), *Alfredo* (2), *Emilio* (2), *Jeronimo* (2), *Jesus* (2), *Pedro* (2); *Joao* (2), *Albano*.

Pimentel (2220) Portuguese: from an irregular derivative, of uncertain significance, of PIMENTA.

GIVEN NAMES Spanish 38%; Portuguese 10%. *Jose* (45), *Manuel* (35), *Juan* (18), *Luis* (17), *Carlos* (16), *Francisco* (15), *Raul* (15), *Jesus* (13), *Mario* (12), *Rafael* (12), *Ramon* (12), *Miguel* (9); *Joao* (5), *Albano* (2), *Paulo* (2), *Godofredo*.

Pimienta (105) Spanish: from *pimienta* 'pepper' (the spice), probably a metonymic occupational name for a seller of spices.

GIVEN NAMES Spanish 52%. *Jose* (5), *Juan* (3), *Ana Maria* (2), *Francisco* (2), *Alfonso*, *Alfredo*, *Candido*, *Emilio*, *Enrique*, *Feliciano*, *Fernando*, *Geraldo*; *Antonio* (2), *Gabriella*, *Piero*, *Sal*.

Pimm (150) English: of uncertain origin. Bardsley believes it to be from the medieval female personal name *Pymme*, *Pimme*, vernacular short forms of *Euphemia*, which was popular in England in the Middle Ages. Reaney and Wilson, however, suggest that it is from a male name, presumably the Old English *Pymma*.

Pin (107) **1.** Variant spelling of English PINN. **2.** French and Dutch: from Old French *pin* 'pine', a topographic name for someone living by a pine tree or in a pine forest, or a habitational name from a place named with this word. **3.** Cambodian: unexplained.

GIVEN NAMES French 10%; Cambodian 15%. *Francois*, *Gisele*, *Jean Michel*, *Pierre*; *Sarin* (3), *Phorn*, *Saroeuth*, *Sophat*, *Chan*, *Pok*, *Soeun*, *Sou*, *Yoeum*, *Yong*.

Pina (2548) **1.** Spanish (from Portuguese) and Catalan: habitational name from a place called Pina (in Zaragoza or Castelló de la Plana). **2.** Spanish: possibly a habitational name from a place called Piña (in Palencia and Valladolid provinces), possibly from *piña* 'pinecone'.

GIVEN NAMES Spanish 43%; Portuguese 10%. *Jose* (41), *Juan* (30), *Carlos* (23), *Luis* (23), *Manuel* (22), *Domingo* (16), *Armando* (14), *Francisco* (13), *Miguel* (12), *Pedro* (12), *Raul* (12), *Roberto* (11); *Joao* (4), *Henrique*, *Ilidio*, *Ligia*, *Mateus*, *Paulo*.

Pinales (153) Spanish: topographic or habitational name, possibly a variant of **Pinares**, meaning 'pine forest'.

GIVEN NAMES Spanish 46%. *Jose* (7), *Manuel* (5), *Fidencio* (2), *Juan* (2), *Mario* (2), *Pablo* (2), *Rafael* (2), *Adelaida*, *Alfonso*, *Altagracia*, *Ana Maria*, *Armando*; *Giovanni* (2), *Antonio*, *Marco*.

Pinard (695) French: nickname from Old French *pinard*, a small medieval coin, so called because it bore the device of a pine cone. The name may have denoted someone who paid a rent of this amount; the term seems also to have been used as a derogatory term for a rich man or miser. This is a frequent name in New England.

FOREBEARS A Pinard from La Rochelle, France, is documented in Quebec City in 1647.

GIVEN NAMES French 18%. *Armand* (9), *Marcel* (4), *Normand* (4), *Emile* (3), *Antoine* (2), *Cecile* (2), *Jean-Paul* (2), *Renald* (2), *Adrien*, *Aime*, *Andre*, *Aurel*.

Pinault (135) French: variant of PINEAU.

FOREBEARS A Pineau, also known as LAPERLE, from the Maine region of France is documented in Trois-Rivières, Quebec, in 1648.

GIVEN NAMES French 16%. *Amedee*, *Emile*, *Gilles*, *Monique*.

Pinch (254) English (mainly Devon): **1.** nickname for a chirpy person, from Middle English *pinch*, *pink* '(chaf)finch'. Compare FINCH. **2.** possibly a metonymic occupational name from Middle English *pinche* 'pleated fabric', from Middle English *pinche(n)* 'to pinch (pastry)', 'to pleat (fabric)', 'to crimp (hair, etc.)', also 'to cavil', 'to be niggardly'.

Pinchback (121) English: habitational name from a place in Lincolnshire, apparently so called from Old English *pinc(a)* '(chaf)finch' + *bæc* 'back', 'ridge'.

GIVEN NAME French 4%. *Andre*.

Pinckard (400) See PINKARD.

Pinckley (103) English: variant of PINCKNEY.

Pinckney (1751) English (of Norman origin): habitational name from Picquigny in Somme, named with a Germanic personal name, *Pincino* (of obscure derivation) + the Latin locative suffix *-acum*.

FOREBEARS A prominent SC family of English ancestry, Pinckneys were living in Charleston by the 18th century, including Eliza Lucas Pinckney (1722–93), who introduced indigo to the colony in 1738. Her sons were prominent in politics, with Charles Pinckney, George Washington's aide and candidate for U.S. president in 1804 and 1808, and Thomas Pinckney, governor of SC.

Pincock (116) English (Lancashire): habitational name from Pincock in Lancashire.

Pincus (1020) Jewish (eastern Ashkenazic): from the Yiddish personal name *Pinkus*, derived from the Biblical Hebrew male personal name *Pinechas*, which is of ancient Egyptian origin.

GIVEN NAMES Jewish 6%. *Meyer* (3), *Hinda* (2), *Hyman* (2), *Sol* (2), *Aviva*, *Dov*, *Este*, *Gershon*, *Isidor*.

Pindar (114) Variant of PINTAR.

Pindell (254) Variant of German BINDEL.

Pinder (1213) **1.** English (mainly Yorkshire) and Irish: variant of PENDER. **2.** South German: variant of BINDER 'cooper'.

Pine (2567) **1.** English and French: from Middle English *pine*, Old French *pin*, a topographic name for someone who lived by a conspicuous pine tree or in a pine forest. It may also be a Norman habitational name from any of various places named with this word, such as Le Pin in Calvados; in other cases it may originally have been a nickname for a tall man, one thought to resemble a pine tree. **2.** German: variant spelling of PEINE.

Pineau (371) French: topographic name, from a diminutive of *pin* 'pine'. Compare PINE 2. This is found as a Huguenot name from the city of Lyon, France.

GIVEN NAMES French 11%. *Andre* (2), *Alcide, Alphonse, Andree, Armand, Chantal, Laurent, Lucien, Marcel, Marthe, Raoul, Yves.*

Pineault (133) Variant of PINEAU.

GIVEN NAMES French 15%. *Laurent* (2), *Benoit, Normand, Raoul, Sylvain.*

Pineda (4043) **1.** Spanish and Catalan: habitational name from any of the places in the provinces of Barcelona, Cuenca, and Burgos named Pineda, from Spanish and Catalan *pineda* 'pine forest'. **2.** in some instances possibly Asturian-Leonese **Piñeda**, from a town called Piñeda in Asturies.

GIVEN NAMES Spanish 52%. *Jose* (114), *Carlos* (52), *Manuel* (44), *Juan* (43), *Mario* (37), *Francisco* (34), *Jorge* (28), *Jesus* (27), *Luis* (27), *Pedro* (27), *Miguel* (25), *Javier* (22).

Pinedo (560) **1.** Basque: habitational name from Pinedo, a town in Araba province. **2.** Spanish (from Asturian-Leonese and Catalan): from any of the numerous places in Asturies and Valencia named Pinedo, a variant of *pineda* 'pine forest'.

GIVEN NAMES Spanish 53%. *Jose* (22), *Juan* (9), *Manuel* (7), *Roberto* (6), *Carlos* (5), *Mario* (5), *Pedro* (5), *Ruben* (5), *Armando* (4), *Cesar* (4), *Guadalupe* (4), *Jesus* (4).

Pinegar (406) Possibly an Americanized spelling of German **Peiniger**, an occupational name for a torturer or executioner, Middle High German, Middle Low German *pīneger*.

Pineiro (477) Galician (also **Piñeiro**): habitational name from any of numerous places in Galicia named Pineiro or Piñeiro, from *piñeiro* 'pine'.

GIVEN NAMES Spanish 50%. *Jose* (20), *Juan* (12), *Ana* (7), *Carlos* (7), *Angel* (5), *Manuel* (5), *Miguel* (4), *Armando* (3), *Efrain* (3), *Enrique* (3), *Francisco* (3), *Jaime* (3).

Pinel (102) Spanish (**Piñel**): habitational name from Piñel in Valladolid province.

GIVEN NAMES Spanish 7%. *Carlos, Guillermo, Javier, Marta, Raul.*

Pinell (131) Variant spelling of PINNELL.

GIVEN NAME German 4%. *Kurt.*

Pinelli (316) Italian: **1.** patronymic from a diminutive of PINO. **2.** patronymic from a reduced pet form of a personal name such as *Filippo, Giuseppe,* or *Iacopo.*

GIVEN NAMES Italian 6%; Spanish 7%. *Antonio* (2), *Cosmo, Dino, Emilio, Lino, Mario, Massimo, Orlando, Silvestro; Jose* (3), *Juan, Lourdes.*

Pineo (244) Americanized form of French PINEAU, name of a Huguenot family from Lyon, France.

Piner (567) Probably (in at least some cases) an altered form of German **Peiner**, a

habitational name for someone from a place called PEINE.

Pinero (321) **1.** Spanish (**Piñero**): Castilianized form of Galician PINEIRO. **2.** Jewish (Sephardic): Anglicized form of PINHEIRO.

GIVEN NAMES Spanish 36%. *Jose* (8), *Carlos* (5), *Jorge* (4), *Eugenio* (3), *Luis* (3), *Rafael* (3), *Ricardo* (3), *Angel* (2), *Jaime* (2), *Juana* (2), *Julio* (2), *Librado* (2); *Antonio* (4), *Heriberto* (3), *Leonardo, Salustiano.*

Pines (640) Jewish (eastern Ashkenazic): of uncertain origin. Most probably it is a derivative of the Yiddish personal name *Pinkhes.* Compare PINCUS.

Pinet (102) French: diminutive of PIN.

GIVEN NAMES French 16%. *Celine, Ghislain, Gillis, Herve, Martial, Sylvain.*

Pinette (421) Canadian spelling of French **Pinet**, from a diminutive of *pina* 'pine-cone'. The spelling reflects the Canadian practice of pronouncing the final *-t*, which is not done in metropolitan French.

FOREBEARS A Pinet of unknown origin in France is documented in Acadia in 1708.

GIVEN NAMES French 12%. *Adelard* (2), *Armand* (2), *Camille* (2), *Lucien* (2), *Raoul* (2), *Alphonse, Andre, Huguette, Jacques, Laurent, Laurier, Patrice.*

Ping (876) **1.** English: unexplained; perhaps a variant of PINK. **2.** Chinese 平: there are two sources of this name, which also means 'peace'. One is the name of a senior minister of the state of Qi during the Spring and Autumn period (722–481 BC), who was posthumously named Yan Pingzhong. The other source is a city called Ping in the state of Han during the Warring States period (403–221 BC). It was granted to a marquis whose descendants adopted the place name as their surname.

Pingel (823) **1.** German: nickname from Middle High German *pingel* 'little bell'. **2.** German: perhaps a spelling variant of BINGEL. **3.** North German: nickname for a fussy, petty person, from Low German *pingel.*

GIVEN NAMES German 4%. *Kurt* (2), *Armin, Erna, Hans, Heinz, Mathias, Otto, Uwe.*

Pinger (142) **1.** German: topographic name for someone who lived near a ditch or a crater-shaped depression, Geman *Binge.* **2.** variant of German BINGER.

Pingitore (171) Southern Italian: occupational name from *pittore* 'painter'.

GIVEN NAMES Italian 16%. *Dante* (2), *Angelo, Cesare, Vito.*

Pingle (115) **1.** German: variant of PINGER, or an Americanized spelling of German PINGEL. **2.** Indian (Maharashtra): pronounced as *ping-lay*: Hindu (Brahman, Maratha) name, from Marathi *pingḷa*, from Sanskrit *pingala* 'reddish brown (usually, of hair)' The Marathas have a clan called Pingle.

GIVEN NAMES Indian 13%. *Sanjay* (3), *Maneesh* (2), *Ajith, Vibha.*

Pingleton (235) English: probably a habitational name from a lost or unidentified place. This might be Pinglestone Farm in Hampshire.

Pingley (173) Apparently an English habitational name; there are places called Pingley Dyke in Nottinghamshire and Pingley Farm in Lincolnshire, which could perhaps have given rise to the surname. However, the surname, if it ever existed in the British Isles, now appears to be extinct.

Pingree (482) English (Worcestershire): unexplained.

Pingrey (101) English: variant of PINGREE.

Pinheiro (499) Portuguese and Jewish (Sephardic): topographic name for someone who lived by a conspicuous pine tree or by a pine forest, from *pinheiro* 'pine', or habitational name for any of the numerous places named Pinheiro.

GIVEN NAMES Spanish 27%; Portuguese 19%. *Jose* (20), *Manuel* (8), *Carlos* (4), *Francisco* (4), *Sergio* (4), *Alfredo* (3), *Mario* (3), *Orlando* (3), *Pedro* (3), *Ricardo* (3), *Ana* (2), *Augusto* (2); *Joao* (5), *Paulo* (3), *Goncalo* (2), *Joaquim* (2), *Duarte, Ilidio, Ligia, Marcio, Mateus, Sebastiao; Antonio* (17), *Angelo, Flavio, Lia, Luciano, Marcello, Rosangela.*

Pinho (243) Portuguese: habitational name from any of the numerous places named Pinho, from *pinho* 'pine', 'pine wood'.

GIVEN NAMES Spanish 30%; Portuguese 21%. *Antonio* (11), *Manuel* (10), *Jose* (6), *Carlos* (3), *Fernando* (3), *Abilio, Adolfo, Albino, Alfredo, Alvaro, Americo, Augusto, Cristina; Joao* (2), *Adao, Guilherme, Joaquim, Serafim.*

Pini (239) Italian: patronymic from PINO.

GIVEN NAMES Italian 11%. *Antonio* (2), *Geno* (2), *Aldo, Dario, Emidio, Giovanni, Giuseppe, Otello, Sante, Ugo, Vito.*

Pinion (783) English: unexplained; perhaps, as Reaney and Wilson propose, a variant of Welsh BEYNON. However, the modern surname in the UK is found mainly in Lincolnshire, on the other side of the country from Wales.

Pink (811) **1.** English: nickname, possibly for a small person, from Middle English *pink, penk* 'minnow' (Old English *pinc*). **2.** English (southeastern): variant of PINCH. **3.** Variant spelling of German **Pinck**, an indirect occupational name for a blacksmith, an onomatopoeic word imitating the sound of hammering which was perceived as *pink(e)pank*. **4.** German (of Slavic origin): from a diminutive of Sorbian *pien* 'log', 'tree stump', hence probably a nickname for a solid or stubby person.

Pinkard (668) Perhaps an altered spelling of German **Pinkhardt**, which may be a variant of PINKERT, formed in analogy to other personal names ending in *-hart*. Compare BURKHART.

Pinkas (109) Jewish (eastern Ashkenazic): variant of PINCUS.

GIVEN NAMES Jewish 27%. *Hershel* (3), *Yonatan* (2), *Aviva, Elchanan, Gadi, Haim, Moshe, Pnina, Shlomo; Ladislav.*

Pinkelman (168) **1.** North German: possibly a habitational name for someone from Pinkel in Westphalia. **2.** Dutch: unexplained. **3.** North German and Dutch: probably a variant of PINGEL 3.

GIVEN NAMES German 5%. *Alphons, Reinold.*

Pinkerman (202) English: unexplained.

Pinkert (188) **1.** German: metonymic occupational name for a blacksmith, from Low German *pinken* 'to strike sparks from a stone or metal'. **2.** German: from *Pinker*, a personal name of uncertain origin. **3.** Dutch: from a derivative of Middle Dutch *pinken* 'to twinkle', a nickname for someone who was in the habit of winking or blinking, or possibly had a squint. **4.** Jewish (Ashkenazic): ornamental adoption of the German surname, probably because of its similarity to the Yiddish personal name *Pinkhes* (see PINCUS).

Pinkerton (3190) Scottish and northern Irish: habitational name from a place near Dunbar, which is from an unexplained first element + Old English *tūn* 'enclosure', 'settlement'. This surname has been established in Ireland since the 17th century.

Pinkett (219) English (Nottinghamshire): diminutive of PINK 1.

GIVEN NAMES French 5%. *Napoleon, Patrice.*

Pinkham (1580) English (Devon): apparently a habitational name from a lost or unidentified place in or bordering on Devon.

Pinkins (110) English: probably a patronymic from a diminutive of PINK.

Pinkley (476) Americanized spelling of German **Pinkle**, which is of uncertain origin, perhaps a diminutive of PINK 2. Compare PINGLEY.

Pinkney (1282) English: variant spelling of PINCKNEY.

Pinkos (160) Polish: from the dialect word *pinka* 'hobnail', also a type of small pear, perhaps a nickname, or a metonymic occupational name for a grower of these pears.

GIVEN NAME Polish 4%. *Stanislaus.*

Pinkowski (371) Polish: variant of PIEN-KOWSKI.

GIVEN NAMES Polish 4%. *Casimir* (2), *Janusz, Zofia.*

Pinks (112) **1.** English: variant of or patronymic from PINK. **2.** Possibly a reduced form of German **Pinkus**, in the south a nickname for a short fat man, *Binkus*, but possibly also a Jewish name for a community scribe.

Pinkstaff (237) **1.** Possibly an Americanized form of German **Pinsdorf**, a habitational name from a place near Wels in Austria, so named from Middle High German *bin(e)z* 'reed' + *dorf* 'settlement', 'village', or from Bensdorf in Brandenburg.

2. Americanized form of German BIN-STOCK.

GIVEN NAME German 4%. *Wolf* (2).

Pinkston (2708) English: habitational name from Pinxton in Derbyshire. The second element is Old English *tūn* 'enclosure', 'settlement'; the first may be a personal name, *Penec.*

Pinkus (308) Jewish (eastern Ashkenazic): variant spelling of PINCUS.

GIVEN NAMES German 5%; Jewish 4%. *Ernst, Gerhard, Hermann; Haim, Irit, Mendel.*

Pinn (185) **1.** English and German: metonymic occupational name for a maker of pins or pegs, from Middle English *pin*, Middle Low German *pin(ne)* 'pin', 'peg'. In some cases the German name was an metonymic occupational name for a shoemaker. **2.** English (Devon): from Middle English *pinne* 'hill' (Old English *penn*), a topographic name or a habitational name from a place named with this word, e.g. Pinn, Pinn Court Farm, or Pin Hill Farm, all in Devon.

GIVEN NAMES German 4%. *Elke, Otto.*

Pinna (106) Italian (Sardinia): from *pinna* 'feather', also 'nostril'.

GIVEN NAMES Italian 19%. *Antonio* (2), *Salvatore* (2), *Angelo, Costantino, Emilia, Mario.*

Pinnell (684) English: diminutive of PINE 1.

Pinneo (146) Americanized form of French PINEAU, name of a Huguenot family from Lyon, France.

Pinner (655) **1.** English and North German: occupational name for a maker of pins or pegs (or alternatively, in the case of the German name, a metonymic occupational name for a shoemaker), a derivative of PINN, with the addition of the agent suffix *-er*. **2.** English: occupational name for a maker or user of combs, Anglo-Norman French *peigner*, an agent derivative of *peigne* 'comb'. **3.** English: habitational name from Pinner, now part of northwest London, which derives its name from Old English *pinn* 'pin', 'peg' + *ōra* 'slope', 'ridge', describing a projecting hill spur. **4.** Jewish (Ashkenazic): habitational name for someone from Pinne (Polish *Pniewy*) near Poznań. **5.** German: habitational name for someone from a place called Pinnan or Pinne.

Pinney (1290) English: possibly a variant of PENNY.

Pinnick (318) **1.** English: variant of PIN-NOCK. **2.** German (of Slavic origin): nickname from Slavic *piwnik* 'drinker'. **3.** Altered spelling of **Pinnecke**, a variant of PINNER 1.

Pinnix (436) English: variant of PINNOCK.

Pinnock (340) English: nickname from Middle English *pinnock* 'hedge sparrow'.

GIVEN NAME French 4%. *Odette.*

Pinnow (268) German: habitational name from any of three places so named, in Pomerania, Mecklenburg, and Brandenburg.

GIVEN NAMES German 5%. *Arno, Hans, Kurt.*

Pino (2123) **1.** Galician and Spanish: habitational name from any of the places in Galicia named Pino, from *pino* 'pine', or topographic name for somebody who lived by a remarkable pine tree. **2.** Italian: habitational name from Pino d'Asti in Asti province, Pino Torinese in Torino, or Pino Solitario in Taranto, all named with *pino* 'pine'. **3.** Italian: from the personal name *Pino*, a short form *Giuseppino* (from *Giuseppe*), *Filippino* (from FILIPPO), *Jacopino* (from *Jacopo*), or some other pet name formed with this suffix.

GIVEN NAMES Spanish 29%; Italian 7%. *Jose* (17), *Raul* (15), *Jorge* (13), *Juan* (13), *Manuel* (12), *Carlos* (11), *Luis* (11), *Mario* (11), *Ramon* (7), *Andres* (6), *Gustavo* (6), *Pedro* (6); *Antonio* (10), *Angelo* (8), *Lorenzo* (4), *Salvatore* (4), *Carmelo* (3), *Santo* (3), *Antonino* (2), *Carmela* (2), *Domenic* (2), *Giuseppe* (2), *Attilio, Caesar.*

Pinon (590) Galician and Spanish (**Piñón**): byname from Galician *piñón* 'pine kernel'.

GIVEN NAMES Spanish 51%. *Jose* (17), *Jesus* (13), *Manuel* (9), *Raul* (7), *Arturo* (6), *Carlos* (6), *Javier* (5), *Jorge* (5), *Francisco* (4), *Jaime* (4), *Pedro* (4), *Ramon* (4).

Pins (162) **1.** Possibly an altered spelling of southern German and Austrian **Pinz**, from a pet form of the personal name BERCHTOLD (see BERTHOLD). **2.** Dutch: from Middle Dutch *pin(ne)* 'wooden peg or pin', 'iron pin or point', hence presumably a metonymic occupational name for someone who made or used such items.

Pinsker (226) **1.** Jewish (eastern Ashkenazic): habitational name for someone from Pińsk in Polesia. **2.** German habitational name from any of several places named near Posen (Polish Poznań) and in West Prussia.

GIVEN NAMES Jewish 10%; German 4%. *Hyman* (2), *Avraham, Emanuel, Sol, Yakov; Frieda, Otto.*

Pinski (148) Variant of PINSKY.

GIVEN NAME German 6%. *Lorenz* (2).

Pinsky (509) Jewish (eastern Ashkenazic): variant of PINSKER.

GIVEN NAMES Jewish 6%; Russian 4%. *Anat, Baila, Hyman, Naum, Ronit, Shaindy, Yechiel; Lev* (3), *Vladmir* (2), *Shelya, Svetlana, Vladimir, Yury.*

Pinson (2555) **1.** English and French: from Old French *pinson* 'finch', perhaps a nickname applied to a bright and cheerful person. **2.** English and French: metonymic occupational name for someone who made pincers or forceps or who used them in their work, from Old French *pinson* 'pincers' (a derivative of *pincier* 'to pinch').

Pinsonneault (172) French: diminutive of PINSON.

FOREBEARS A Pinsonnault, also called **Lafleur**, from the Saintonge region of France is documented in St. Ours, Quebec, in 1673.

GIVEN NAMES French 8%. *Andre, Fernand, Laurier, Yves.*

Pint (255) Dutch: metonymic occupational name for an official who controlled measures, from Middle Dutch *pinte* 'pint'.

Pinta (108) **1.** Spanish, Portuguese, and Jewish (Sephardic): possibly a nickname from *pinta* 'shameless', 'outrageous', 'imprudent'. **2.** Italian: variant of PINTO. **3.** Galician and Spanish: nickname from *pinta* 'speck', possibly denoting someone with a blotchy complexion or a noticeable facial blemish.

GIVEN NAMES French 5%; German 4%. *Jean-Pierre*; *Otto.*

Pintado (123) Spanish: nickname from *pintado* 'spotted', 'dappled' (part participle of *pintar* 'to paint'), probably denoting someone with a blotchy complexion.

GIVEN NAMES Spanish 51%. *Enrique* (5), *Jose* (3), *Manuel* (3), *Miguel* (3), *Francisco* (2), *Julio* (2), *Luis* (2), *Raul* (2), *Agustin, Alfonso, Angel, Domingos*; *Fausto* (2), *Antonio, Giovani, Romeo.*

Pintar (294) Slovenian: occupational name for a cooper, from Bavarian dialect PINTER, variant of standard German BINDER 'cooper'. It may also be a reduced form of the patronymic **Pintarič**.

Pinter (1154) **1.** Variant of German PINDER or Slovenian PINTAR, variants of BINDER 'cooper'. **2.** Jewish: in England this is found as an Anglicized form of the Sephardic name PINTA. **3.** French and Hungarian (**Pintér**): occupational name for a maker of measures or for an official who controlled measures, from an agent derivative of Old French *pinte*, Hungarian *pint* 'pint', of uncertain origin. **4.** Pinter is also found as a Dutch surname, probably with the same meaning as in 3 (see PINT).

Pinto (4399) **1.** Spanish and Jewish (Sephardic): nickname from *pinto* 'colorful', 'painted'. **2.** Spanish: habitational name from Pinto in Madrid. **3.** Catalan (**Pintó**): Catalan variant of PINTOR 'painter'. **4.** Portuguese: from a nickname from *pinto* 'chick'. This name is also common in western India, where it was taken by Portuguese colonists. **5.** Italian: from *pinto* 'mottled', 'dotted' (Late Latin *pinctus*, for classical Latin *pictus* 'painted'), hence a nickname for a person with a blotchy or pock-marked complexion or pepper-and-salt hair, or in some parts of the south at least from the same word in the sense 'lively or restless person'.

GIVEN NAMES Spanish 18%; Italian 8%; Portuguese 7%. *Jose* (33), *Manuel* (33), *Carlos* (25), *Luis* (18), *Fernando* (16), *Mario* (14), *Ana* (9), *Juan* (8), *Ricardo* (8), *Alvaro* (7), *Cesar* (7), *Jorge* (7); *Antonio* (43), *Angelo* (10), *Vito* (9), *Carmine* (5), *Salvatore* (5), *Donato* (4), *Gaetano* (4), *Geno* (3), *Giovanni* (3), *Lucio* (3), *Marco* (3), *Rocco* (3); *Joao* (6), *Joaquim* (6), *Paulo* (3), *Armanda* (2), *Manoel* (2),

Ademir, Afonso, Agostinho, Albano, Anabela, Damiao, Henrique.

Pintor (168) Spanish, Catalan, Portuguese, Galician, and Italian (Sardinian): occupational name for a painter, from *pintor* 'painter'.

GIVEN NAMES Spanish 42%; Italian 5%. *Jose* (6), *Alfredo* (3), *Alberto* (2), *Juan* (2), *Julio* (2), *Manuel* (2), *Silvia* (2), *Adolfo, Ana, Andres, Arthuro, Ascencion*; *Antonio* (2), *Lorenzo, Tullio.*

Pinyan (187) Probably a variant spelling of English PINION.

Pinzon (341) Spanish (**Pinzón**): nickname from *pinzón* 'finch'.

GIVEN NAMES Spanish 52%. *Luis* (8), *Jorge* (6), *Carlos* (5), *Fernando* (4), *Jairo* (4), *Nydia* (4), *Francisco* (3), *Hernando* (3), *Jesus* (3), *Jose* (3), *Juan* (3), *Mauricio* (3).

Pio (295) **1.** Italian and Spanish (**Pío**): from the personal name, Italian *Pio*, Spanish *Pío*, meaning 'pious', 'devout' (Latin *Pius*), or from a nickname with the same meaning. **2.** Danish: from a French family name, *De Piou.*

GIVEN NAMES Italian 16%; Spanish 7%. *Jose* (2), *Leticia* (2), *Carlos, Fernando, Francisco, Joaquina, Manuel, Pedro*; *Antonio* (2), *Bartolomeo* (2), *Angelo, Arturo, Carlo, Caterina, Justo, Pasquale, Rafaela, Silva.*

Pioch (100) German: from the Slavic personal name *Pioch*, a pet form of *Piotr* (see PETER).

Pioli (111) Italian: most probably from a pet form of the personal name *Pio* 'Pius', or a pet form of *Olimpio*. Alternatively, it could be a metonymic occupational name for a peg or stake maker, from *piolo* 'peg', 'stake', or from a dialect word for celery, from *erba apiola* 'horehound', a medicinal herb, or from *melo apiolo* meaning 'apple'. Otherwise, it could be a Tuscanized form of Calabrian *piulu* 'screech owl', or from Piedmontese *piola* 'ax', 'hatchet'.

GIVEN NAMES Italian 10%. *Luigi* (2), *Angelo, Domenico, Giovanni.*

Pion (336) French: nickname for someone who traveled on foot, from an Old French variant of *peon* 'pedestrian'.

FOREBEARS A Pion, also called LAFONTAINE, from the Touraine region of France, is recorded in Quebec City in 1673.

GIVEN NAMES French 14%. *Armand* (3), *Andre* (2), *Pierre* (2), *Aime, Donat, Emile, Girard, Gisele, Jean Louis, Marcel, Rejean, Rosaire.*

Pionke (101) Germanized form of Slavic **Pionek**, nickname from *pionek* 'puppet'.

Piontek (503) Polish and Jewish (from Poland): nickname from the Polish vocabulary word *piątek* 'Friday' (see PIATEK). The surname is also borne by German speakers.

GIVEN NAMES German 4%. *Frieda, Heinz, Klaus, Wilhelm, Willi.*

Piontkowski (255) Polish: variant of **Piątkowski** (see PIATKOWSKI).

Piorkowski (304) Polish (**Piórkowski**): habitational name from places called Piórkowo in Toruń voivodeship or Piórków in Tarnobrzeg voivodeship.

GIVEN NAMES Polish 11%. *Andrzej, Casimir, Henryk, Kazimierz, Krystyna, Stanislaw, Wieslaw, Zigmond, Zyg.*

Piotrowicz (150) Polish: patronymic from the personal name *Piotr* (see PETER).

GIVEN NAMES Polish 11%; German 5%. *Andrzej, Janusz, Tadeusz, Witold, Zofia*; *Alfons, Aloysius, Matthias.*

Piotrowski (1999) Polish: habitational name for someone from any of various places called Piotrów, Piotrowo, or Piotrowice.

GIVEN NAMES Polish 9%. *Andrzej* (6), *Tadeusz* (5), *Casimir* (4), *Janusz* (4), *Zbigniew* (4), *Grazyna* (2), *Halina* (2), *Jerzy* (2), *Karol* (2), *Piotr* (2), *Wojciech* (2), *Zofia* (2).

Piotter (167) Germanized form of a Slavic form of the personal name PETER, e.g. Polish *Piotr*.

Pipe (173) English (East Anglia): **1.** metonymic occupational name for a piper, from Middle English *pipe* 'pipe' (Old English *pīpe*). In some cases it may have been a topographic name from the same word in the sense 'waterpipe', 'conduit', 'water channel', or a habitational name from Pipe in Herefordshire or Pipehill in Staffordshire, near Lichfield (earlier *Pipa*), both named from this word. **2.** occasionally from a personal name, *Pipe*, which is recorded in Domesday Book.

Piper (8480) **1.** English (mainly southern), Dutch, and North German: occupational name for a player on the pipes, Middle English *pipere*, Middle Dutch *pi(j)per*, Middle Low German *piper*. **2.** Translation of German PFEIFFER, or of the French secondary surname **Lefifre**.

Pipes (1181) **1.** English: variant of or patronymic from PIPE. **2.** Greek (**Pipēs**): from a pet form, *Pipis*, of the personal name *Spyridōn* (see SPIRO), borne by a bishop and saint venerated in the Eastern Church. He is the patron saint of Corfu.

Pipher (307) Altered form of German PFEIFFER.

GIVEN NAME French 4%. *Luce* (2).

Pipia (114) Italian (Sicily): from Sicilian *pipia* 'turkey hen', hence a metonymic occupational name for someone who raised poultry or possibly a nickname for someone thought to resemble a turkey hen in some way.

GIVEN NAMES Italian 25%. *Salvatore* (4), *Carmello, Francesco, Gaspare, Gildo, Gioacchino.*

Pipitone (371) Italian (Sicily): from Sicilian *pipitone* 'hoopoe', hence a nickname for someone thought to resemble the bird in some way. The term could also denote a stone-built figure used as a target by children, and so could have been a nickname for someone who was a regular victim of local children's taunts or persecution.

GIVEN NAMES Italian 22%; Spanish 5%. *Salvatore* (7), *Angelo* (2), *Nunzio* (2), *Sal* (2), *Vito* (2), *Adamo, Alberto, Antonio, Carlo, Gaspare, Guiseppe, Leonardo, Nino; Diego* (2), *Ana, Rosario.*

Pipkin (1901) English (Oxfordshire): from the personal name *Pipkin*, a pet form of PHILIP.

Pipkins (479) English: patronymic from PIPKIN.

Pipkorn (109) Variant of English PIPKIN.

Pipp (166) English: from a short form of PEPIN.

Pippen (475) Variant of English or German PIPPIN.

Pippenger (310) Probably an altered spelling of German **Pippinger**, a habitational name from either of two places named Pipping in Bavaria and Lower Saxony, near Brunswick.

Pippert (191) German: from the personal name *Bitbert*, of Germanic origin, derived from an equivalent to Old High German *bītan* 'to endure' or *bittan* 'to wish or ask for'.

Pippin (2528) **1.** English: from the old personal name *Pippin*, either a pet form of PHILIP or a variant of Old French PEPIN. **2.** German: from an Old Prussian personal name, *Pippin*.

Pippins (318) English: variant of PEPIN, with patronymic -*s*.

Pippitt (115) Origin unidentified.

Pique (102) **1.** Catalan (**Piqué**): variant of **Piquer**, an occupational name from Catalan *piquer* 'quarryman'. **2.** French: probably a metonymic occupational name for someone who wielded a pickaxe.

GIVEN NAMES French 11%; Spanish 9%. *Patrice* (2); *Roberto* (2), *Xavier* (2), *Adelaida, Fernando, Gonzalo, Guadalupe, Marta.*

Piquette (215) Canadian spelling of French **Piquet**, a metonymic occupational name for someone who worked with a pick, from a diminutive of *pic* 'pick'. The ending is not feminine, but reflects the Canadian practice of pronouncing the final -*t*, unlike metropolitan French.

FOREBEARS A Piquet, also called LAFLEUR, from the Maine region of France, is documented in Quebec City in 1706.

GIVEN NAMES French 6%. *Armand, Emile, Jacques.*

Piraino (466) Italian (Sicily): habitational name from Piraino in Messina province, or from other places named with Sicilian *pirainu* 'wild pear tree'.

GIVEN NAMES Italian 16%. *Salvatore* (3), *Giacomo* (2), *Aldo, Angelo, Antonio, Carlo, Concetta, Cosimo, Damiano, Dario, Enrico, Ettore.*

Pirani (124) **1.** Muslim: from Persian, a derivative of *Pūriyān*, a term denoting a

citizen of Kanoja. **2.** Italian: from **Pirano**, a variant of PIRAINO.

GIVEN NAMES Muslim 34%; Italian 6%. *Abdul* (2), *Abdul Karim* (2), *Amyn* (2), *Nasir* (2), *Salim* (2), *Ali, Altaf, Ameen, Ameena, Azeem, Bahram, Habib; Carlo* (3), *Attilio, Geno.*

Pirc (106) Slovenian: **1.** metonymic occupational name for someone who grew spelt (a type of grain), from *pira* 'spelt' (dialect *pir*). **2.** possibly from an unattested medieval respelled pet form of the personal name PETER.

GIVEN NAMES South Slavic 5%. *Boris, Dragica, Vladimir.*

Pires (1113) Portuguese: patronymic from the personal name *Pedro*, Portuguese equivalent of PETER.

GIVEN NAMES Spanish 25%; Portuguese 16%. *Manuel* (37), *Jose* (28), *Antonio* (23), *Luis* (9), *Sergio* (7), *Fernando* (6), *Alberto* (5), *Carlos* (5), *Domingos* (5), *Mario* (5), *Adelino* (3), *Albino* (3), *Armindo* (3); *Joao* (8), *Joaquim* (5), *Paulo* (3), *Vasco* (3), *Ilidio* (2), *Amadeu, Duarte, Lourenco.*

Pirie (402) Scottish: variant of PERRY 1.

Pirillo (124) Italian: probably a derivative of PIRO, or otherwise a variant of PERILLO.

GIVEN NAMES Italian 14%; French 8%. *Dante, Gianfranco, Salvatore; Armand* (5).

Pirkey (173) **1.** German: see BIRKEY. **2.** Americanized spelling of German BIRKE or of **Pirke**, a habitational name from Pirka in Bavaria.

Pirkl (200) South German (Bavaria, Tyrol): **1.** topographic name from a diminutive of Middle High German *birche* 'birch'. See BIRKE 2. **2.** from a short form of a personal name formed with Old High German *bero* 'bear'.

Pirkle (744) **1.** Americanized spelling of German PIRKL. **2.** Variant of German BIRKLE.

Pirner (104) German: variant of BIRNER.

GIVEN NAMES German 4%. *Hans, Kristen.*

Pirnie (138) Scottish: habitational name from Pirnie in the Borders or from Pairney (recorded in the 17th century as *Pirney, Pirnie*) near Auchterarder in Perthshire. The place names are related to Welsh *pren* 'tree'.

Piro (640) Italian: probably from Sicilian *piro* 'pear tree'.

GIVEN NAMES Italian 16%. *Salvatore* (8), *Angelo* (3), *Antonio* (3), *Rocco* (2), *Sal* (2), *Santo* (2), *Alessandra, Alessio, Edmondo, Gennaro, Giuseppe, Giuseppi.*

Pirog (257) Polish: variant of **Pieróg**, a nickname from *pieróg*, a dish resembling ravioli.

Pirolli (125) Italian: from a diminutive of PIRO.

GIVEN NAMES Italian 14%. *Carlo, Remo.*

Pirone (288) Italian: variant of PIRRONE.

GIVEN NAMES Italian 36%. *Mario* (3), *Carmine* (4), *Camillo* (2), *Angelo, Antonio, Basilio, Ciro, Cristina, Domenic, Elio,*

Luigi, Marco, Modestino, Olympia, Sebastiano, Sebastino, Vincenzo.

Pirozzi (285) Italian: patronymic from a pet form of *Pi(e)ro*, an Italian form of PETER.

GIVEN NAMES Italian 32%. *Mario* (3), *Rocco* (3), *Ciro* (2), *Pasquale* (2), *Angelo, Aniello, Antonio, Biagio, Dario, Mauro, Philomena.*

Pirrello (204) Italian: from a pet form of the personal name PIRRO.

GIVEN NAMES Italian 13%. *Pietro* (2), *Angelo, Antonio, Crispino, Gaspare, Gasper, Giovanna, Lorenzo, Nunzio.*

Pirri (146) Italian: patronymic or plural form of PIRRO.

GIVEN NAMES Italian 35%; Spanish 5%. *Angelo* (2), *Santo* (2), *Antonio, Carmela, Carmino, Domenic, Emidio, Enrico, Francesco, Franco, Giuseppe, Matteo; Carlos Manuel, Luis.*

Pirro (353) Italian: **1.** from a variant of the personal name *Pietro*, an Italian equivalent of PETER. **2.** from the personal name *Pirro*, Greek *Pyrrhos*, from *pyrrhos* 'red'. This was the name of a king of Epirus in classical times.

GIVEN NAMES Italian 11%; French 6%. *Salvatore* (5), *Rocco* (2), *Italia, Sal; Alphonse* (2), *Armand, Camille.*

Pirrone (272) Italian: from an augmentative of PIRRO.

GIVEN NAMES Italian 27%. *Cosmo* (2), *Filippo* (2), *Gaetano* (2), *Salvatore* (2), *Angelo, Antonino, Carlo, Caterina, Concetta, Gaspare, Giacomo, Giancarlo, Mario, Teodoro.*

Pirrung (101) German: probably a variant of PYRON.

Pirtle (1741) Americanized form of German BIRKLE.

Pisa (132) Italian: habitational name from the city of Pisa in Tuscany. The city was probably founded by Greek colonists, but before coming under Roman control it was in the hands of the Etruscans, who probably gave it its name. At any rate, the place name is of obscure origin and meaning.

GIVEN NAMES Italian 13%. *Angelo, Carlo, Marco, Sabastian.*

Pisani (1088) Italian: patronymic or plural form of PISANO.

GIVEN NAMES Italian 17%. *Salvatore* (6), *Angelo* (5), *Gino* (3), *Marino* (3), *Enzo* (2), *Fiorino* (2), *Natale* (2), *Rocco* (2), *Vincenzo* (2), *Aniello, Antonio, Biagio.*

Pisano (1460) Italian: habitational name for someone from Pisa in Tuscany (see PISA), from an adjectival form of the place name.

GIVEN NAMES Italian 17%. *Antonio* (7), *Salvatore* (7), *Mario* (6), *Carmine* (5), *Carmela* (4), *Vito* (4), *Angelo* (3), *Armando* (3), *Rocco* (3), *Sal* (3), *Aldo* (2), *Domenic* (2), *Paolo* (2), *Rosario* (2), *Stefano* (2).

Pisapia (110) Italian: unexplained; possibly from a compound nickname in which *pisa* corresponds with *pesa* 'weighing', from *pesare* 'to weigh'.

GIVEN NAMES Italian 21%. *Carmine* (3), *Guido, Luigi, Orazio, Salvatore, Silvio.*

Pisarcik (125) Czech and Slovak (**Pisarčík**) and Polish (**Pisarczyk**); from a diminutive of Czech *pisař* or Polish *pisarz* 'clerk', 'scribe'.

Pisarek (160) Polish: from a diminutive of *pisarz* 'clerk', 'scribe'.

GIVEN NAMES Polish 6%. *Boguslaw, Slawomir.*

Pisarski (259) Polish: **1.** habitational name from either of two places named Pisary, in Kraków and Tarnobrzeg voivodeships. **2.** derivative of **Pisarz**, occupational name for a clerk or scribe (from *pisać* 'to write') + the common surname suffix -*ski.*

GIVEN NAMES Polish 9%. *Andrzej, Casimir, Jerzy, Ryszard, Slawek, Witold, Zigmund.*

Pischel (115) Eastern German: from a pet form of the personal name PETER.

Pischke (236) Eastern German: from a pet form of the personal name *Pisch*, a Slavic derivative of PETER.

GIVEN NAMES German 5%. *Ernst, Florian, Gerhard, Otto.*

Pisciotta (603) Italian (mainly Sicily): perhaps from a derivative of *pisci* 'fish' (southern variant of *pesce*), hence a metonymic occupational name for a fisherman or fish seller, or a nickname for someone thought to resemble a fish. Alternatively, it could be a derivative of *pisciu* 'urine', and so a nickname from this, perhaps anecdotal. In Campania and surrounding areas it is also a habitational name from a place so called in Salerno province.

GIVEN NAMES Italian 18%. *Angelo* (4), *Salvatore* (4), *Antonio* (3), *Saverio* (3), *Francesca* (2), *Sal* (2), *Carlo, Cosmo, Filippo, Gasper, Giacomo, Giovanni.*

Piscitelli (718) Italian: patronymic or plural form of PISCITELLO.

GIVEN NAMES Italian 20%. *Vincenzo* (5), *Salvatore* (4), *Alessandro* (2), *Angelo* (2), *Antonio* (2), *Luigi* (2), *Tonino* (2), *Alfonse, Carmela, Carmine, Cosimo, Domenic.*

Piscitello (270) Italian: from a diminutive of southern Italian *pisci* 'fish'.

GIVEN NAMES Italian 16%. *Angelo* (2), *Vito* (2), *Agostino, Bartolo, Biagio, Calogero, Carmello, Domenico, Gaetano, Innocenzo, Rosario, Salvatore, Santo.*

Piscopo (354) Southern Italian (especially Campania and Apulia): from a reduced form of *episcopo* 'bishop' (Greek *episkopos* 'bishop', literally 'overseer'), hence a metonymic occupational name for someone in the service of a bishop, or perhaps a nickname for a pompous person.

GIVEN NAMES Italian 14%; French 6%. *Antonio* (3), *Carmine* (2), *Gennaro* (2), *Angelo, Carmel, Dino, Luigi, Salvatore, Vincenzo; Armand, Camille, Chantal, Monique.*

Piselli (127) Italian: from the plural of *pisello* 'pea', possibly applied as a topographic name, a metonymic occupational name, or a nickname.

GIVEN NAMES Italian 21%. *Donato* (2), *Carmela, Nunzio, Orazio, Pompeo, Rachele.*

Piske (127) German (of Slavic origin): topographic name for someone living or farming on sandy soil, from Sorbian *pesk* 'sand'.

GIVEN NAMES German 8%. *Heinz* (2), *Gerhardt, Otto.*

Piskor (103) Czech (**Piskoř**) and Polish (**Piskorz**): nickname from Czech *piskor*, Polish *piskorz* 'loach', 'mudfish'.

GIVEN NAME Polish 4%. *Halina.*

Pisoni (131) Italian: patronymic from **Pisone**, from a derivative of **Piso**, from Latin *pisum* 'pea'.

GIVEN NAMES Italian 6%. *Angelo, Salvatore, Umberto.*

Pistilli (203) Italian: from a derivative of **Pisto**, which may be from southern dialect *pistu* 'crushed', 'pounded', 'crushing', 'weighty', or from Calabrian *pistillu* 'dried chestnut'.

GIVEN NAMES Italian 16%. *Salvatore* (2), *Angelo, Carmine, Corrado, Dino, Filomena, Rocco, Umberto.*

Pistole (249) German: late formation from *Pistole* 'pistol', probably a nickname for a sharp and aggressive person. The vocabulary word is derived from Czech *píšt'ala* 'whistle'; early pistols, invented in Bohemia in the 16th century, were thought to resemble whistles.

Pistone (335) Italian: from a derivative of **Pisto** (see PISTILLI) or from Sicilian *pistuni* 'pestle', probably linked with the notion of pounding or crushing, and hence perhaps a metonymic occupational name for a spicer, grocer, or apothecary.

GIVEN NAMES Italian 20%. *Alfonso* (3), *Dante* (2), *Alfonse, Amando, Angelo, Antonio, Benedetta, Bernardo, Carmelo, Domenic, Enrico, Giuseppe, Guiseppe, Mario, Pietro, Roberto, Silvio.*

Pistorius (139) German, Dutch, and eastern French: Latinized variant of German PFISTER, Dutch PESTER, French **Pestre**, **Pestour**, occupational names for a baker.

Pisula (114) Lithuanian and Polish: informal nickname for a scribe or clerk, from a derivative of Polish *pisać* 'to write'.

GIVEN NAMES Lithuanian 4%. *Gertrudis, Hedvigis.*

Piszczek (122) Polish: nickname from a derivative of *piszcseć* 'squeal', 'squeak', also used as an occupational nickname for a fife player.

GIVEN NAMES Polish 4%. *Jozef, Wladyslaw.*

Pita (285) Spanish and Portuguese: from Spanish, Portuguese *pita* 'chicken' or in some cases possibly from the plant *pita* 'pita', 'American aloe', presumably a topographic name.

GIVEN NAMES Spanish 45%. *Jose* (12), *Carlos* (5), *Julio* (5), *Manuel* (5), *Armando* (4), *Eduardo* (4), *Enrique* (4), *Francisco* (4), *Ana* (3), *Jorge* (3), *Mario* (3), *Rafael* (3).

Pitcairn (136) Scottish: habitational name from the place so called in Fife, of Pictish-Gaelic origin.

FOREBEARS The first warring shot of the American Revolution was fired by Major John Pitcairn (1722–75) of the Royal Marines at the battle of Lexington and Concord (1775). His son, Robert Pitcairn (?1747–70), was the first to sight the South Pacific island of this name while serving in the Royal Navy, in 1767.

GIVEN NAME Russian 5%; Scottish 4%. *Feodor* (3).

Pitcher (2261) **1.** English (chiefly eastern and southern): from an agent derivative of Middle English *pich* 'pitch', hence an occupational name for a caulker, one who sealed the seams of ships or barrels with pitch. **2.** English: variant of PICKARD 2. **3.** Possibly from German *Pitscher*, from the short form of a personal name formed with Old High German *bītan* 'to endure', or *bittan* 'to wish or ask for'.

Pitchford (1277) English (West Midlands): habitational name from a place near Shrewsbury, where there was a bituminous well; the name is derived from Old English *pic* 'pitch' + *ford* 'ford'.

Pitcock (670) English: from a Middle English pet form of the Old English personal name *Pytta*.

Pitera (134) **1.** Polish: derivative of the personal name *Piter*, dialect variant of *Piotr* (see Peter). **2.** Polish: nickname from a derivative of *piter* 'purse', 'money bag'. **3.** Southern Italian (**Piterà**) and Greek (**Piteras**): occupational name from medieval Greek *piteras* 'bran merchant', or *pitaras*, 'maker of pita bread' or 'pie maker' from *pita* 'flat bread', 'pie' + the occupational suffix -*as.*

GIVEN NAMES Polish 13%; Italian 7%. *Andrzej, Casimir, Jozef, Krystyna, Marcin, Tadek, Wieslaw, Zigmund; Saverio* (2), *Domenic, Francesco, Vito.*

Pitkin (557) English (Bedfordshire): variant of PIPKIN.

FOREBEARS The Pitkin name was introduced by William Pitkin, a leading lawyer and judge in CT, who migrated from Marylebone, London, to Hartford, CT, in 1660. William was probably the largest landowner on the east side of the Connecticut River, where he owned part of a saw and grist mill.

Pitman (2720) **1.** English (mainly southwestern): variant of PITT, with the addition of *man.* **2.** German (**Pitmann**): variant of **Pittmann** (see PITTMAN). **3.** Dutch: variant of PUTMAN 2.

Pitmon (120) Variant spelling of English PITMAN.

Pitner (415) Variant spelling of German PITTNER.

Pitney (316) English: habitational name from a place in Somerset, named with the Old English personal name *Pytta* or *Pēota* (genitive *Pyttan*, *Pēotan*) + *ēg* 'island', 'dry ground in marsh'.

Pitoniak (143) Ukrainian: unexplained.

Pitre (1933) **1.** French: habitational name from Pîtres in Eure. **2.** French: variant of *pestre*, *pistre*, agent derivatives of Old French *pestel* 'pestle', hence a metonymic occupational name for an apothecary or grocer. **3.** Italian (**Pitrè**): unexplained.
FOREBEARS According to Canadian records, this surname is documented in Trois-Rivières, Quebec, in the 17th century, being described as English. There are VT records of a certain "Lajambe, also called Pitt or Pitre". Another Pitre is recorded in the Montreal area in 1661, said to be of Dutch origin. In the mid-18th century, there are Acadians bearing this name from the Belgian province of Hainault.
GIVEN NAMES French 7%. *Raoul* (4), *Emile* (3), *Armand* (2), *Monique* (2), *Alcid*, *Amedee*, *Anatole*, *Andrus*, *Aubert*, *Camille*, *Cecile*, *Clovis*.

Pitrone (100) Italian: variant of **Pietrone**, from the personal name *Pietro* (see PETER) + the augmentative suffix *-one*.

Pitsch (322) German: variant of PIETSCH.

Pitsenbarger (210) Probably an altered spelling of German **Bezzenberger**, habitational name from a place called Boizenburg in Mecklenburg.

Pitstick (197) Origin unidentified.

Pitt (2955) English: from Middle English *pytte*, *pitte* 'pit', 'hollow', hence a topographic name for someone who lived by a pit or hollow, or a habitational name from a place named with this word, as for example Pitt in Hampshire.

Pitta (172) **1.** Italian: from a feminine form of an old Germanic personal name, *Pitto* or *Bitto*. **2.** Italian: variant of **Pittà**, an occupational name from Greek *pitas* 'seller of pita bread (flat bread)', from *pita* 'flat bread' + the occupational suffix *-as*. **3.** Variant of Portuguese PITA.
GIVEN NAMES Spanish 8%; Italian 6%. *Manuel* (4), *Americo*, *Constanza*, *Jorge*, *Jose*, *Rosario*; *Annamaria*, *Carmine*, *Vito*.

Pittard (560) **1.** English: unexplained; probably of French origin (see 2). **2.** French: unflattering nickname from a derivative of Old French *pite* 'pitiful', 'lamentable', perhaps applied to a family living in extreme poverty.

Pittenger (1132) Altered spelling of German PITTINGER.

Pitter (147) **1.** English: topographic name for someone who lived by a pit or hollow (see PITT) + *-er*, suffix denoting an inhabitant. **2.** German: variant of PETER. **3.** Jewish (from Ukraine): metonymic occupational nanme from Yiddish dialect *piter* 'butter'. Compare PUTTERMAN.
GIVEN NAMES Jewish 6%. *Dalit* (2), *Hyman*, *Yetta*.

Pitti (104) Italian: from the personal name *Pitto*, a Lombard variant of BITTO.

GIVEN NAMES Italian 26%; Spanish 9%. *Salvatore* (5), *Ricardo* (2), *Francesca*, *Orlando*, *Rosario*; *Ana*, *Benedicto*, *Jorge*, *Jose*, *Mariela*.

Pittillo (138) Italian: from a derivative of PITTA.

Pittinger (213) German: perhaps a variant of **Pettinger**, a habitational name from any of several Bavarian places called Petting or Pötting, or possibly a variant of BUDINGER.

Pittman (16941) **1.** English: topographic name for someone who lived in a hollow (see PITT). **2.** German (**Pittmann**): probably from a compound personal name formed with *Pitt*, a short form of PETER + *Mann* 'man'.

Pittmon (123) English and German: variant of PITTMAN.

Pittner (179) German (Bavaria, Austria): variant of **Büttner** (see BUETTNER).
GIVEN NAMES German 7%. *Hans*, *Kurt*, *Otto*.

Pitts (15956) **1.** English: variant of PITT. **2.** Americanized spelling of German PITZ.

Pittsenbarger (120) German: variant spelling of PITSENBARGER.

Pittser (115) Americanized spelling of German PITZER or BITZER.

Pittsley (356) Possibly an altered spelling of German **Pitzler**, an occupational name for a mender of clothes or a cobbler, from an agent derivative of dialect *bizlen* 'to bite off a little'; or perhaps a nickname for an irascible man, from the same word in the sense 'to prickle'.

Pitz (451) **1.** North German: from a short form of the personal name *Petrus* (see PETER). **2.** South German: southern variant of *Butz*, a pet form of the personal name *Burkhard* (see BURKHARDT).

Pitzen (269) German: variant of PITZ 1.

Pitzer (1365) **1.** South German (Bavaria): probably from *pitz* 'corner', 'peak' + *-er*, suffix of habitation, hence a topographic name for someone living near such a feature in mountainous country. **2.** North German: perhaps a metonymic occupational name for a seal maker or die sinker, from Middle Low German *pitzēr* 'seal'.

Piva (157) Northern Italian: occupational name for a piper, from *piva* 'bagpipes' or 'player of bagpipes'.
GIVEN NAMES Italian 15%; Spanish 6%. *Piero* (2), *Aldo*, *Angelo*, *Fosco*, *Mario*, *Reno*, *Sergio*; *Diego*, *Esteban*, *Jorge*.

Pivarnik (114) Czech (**Pivarník**): reduced form of *pivovarník* 'brewer', an agent noun derived from *pivovar* 'brewery'.

Pivec (93) Czech: nickname for a drinker, from *pivo* 'beer'.

Piver (166) Origin uncertain. Most probably an altered spelling of French **Pivert**, a nickname meaning 'woodpecker'.

Pivirotto (127) Italian: unexplained; perhaps a derivative of PIVA.

Pivonka (227) Czech (**Pivoňka**): descriptive nickname for someone with rosy cheeks, from *pivoňka* 'peony'.
FOREBEARS In the 1840s five brothers called Piwonka jumped the draft in the Austro-Hungarian Empire and emigrated to America. One stayed in NY, another went on to the Cleveland, OH, area, another further west (probably to the coast), and another to Chile in South America; the descendants of the fifth brother live near Lubbock, TX. They all kept the Piwonka spelling of the name with the exception of the Cleveland branch.

Piwowar (147) Polish: occupational name for a brewer, Polish *piwowar*, from *piwo* 'beer' + *warzyć* 'to brew'.
GIVEN NAMES Polish 11%. *Czeslaw*, *Danuta*, *Grazyna*, *Jozef*, *Ryszard*, *Zbigniew*.

Piwowarski (131) Polish: **1.** habitational name for someone from Piwowary, in Łomża voivodeship. **2.** variant of PIWOWAR 'brewer', with the addition of the common surname suffix *-ski*.
GIVEN NAMES Polish 19%. *Casimir*, *Jacek*, *Jerzy*, *Krzystof*, *Krzysztof*, *Stanislaw*, *Witold*, *Zygmont*.

Pixler (312) German: variant of BIXLER.

Pixley (945) Probably an English habitational name from places so called in Herefordshire and Shropshire, the former being named in Old English with the personal name *Peoht* + *lēah* 'woodland', 'clearing in a wood'.

Pixton (180) English: possibly from an unrecorded Old English personal name, *Pīcstān*, from *pīc* 'point', 'pike' + *stān* 'stone'.

Pizana (153) Spanish (**Pizana**, **Pizaña**): unexplained; possibly from *pisana* literally 'from Pisa', denoting a type of cotton material. This name is mainly common in Mexico.
GIVEN NAMES Spanish 53%. *Juan* (4), *Manuel* (4), *Alfredo* (3), *Jaime* (3), *Jose* (3), *Ramon* (3), *Ruben* (3), *Arturo* (2), *Carlos* (2), *Jesus* (2), *Josefina* (2), *Miguel* (2).

Pizano (308) Hispanic (**Pizano**, **Pizaño**): unexplained; possibly from *pisano* literally 'from Pisa', or Castilianized form of PIZZANO. This name is extremely common in South America.
GIVEN NAMES Spanish 50%. *Jose* (12), *Jesus* (8), *Miguel* (7), *Arturo* (4), *Francisco* (4), *Juan* (4), *Pedro* (4), *Carlos* (3), *Guadalupe* (3), *Josefina* (3), *Manuel* (3), *Margarita* (3); *Antonio* (6), *Constantino*, *Eliseo*, *Federico*, *Marcellino*.

Pizarro (673) Spanish: from *pizarra* 'slate', hence a topographic name for someone who lived near a slate quarry or occupational name for someone who worked in one.
GIVEN NAMES Spanish 50%. *Jose* (18), *Luis* (18), *Carlos* (9), *Pedro* (8), *Ramon* (6), *Ricardo* (6), *Fernando* (5), *Juan* (5), *Raul* (5), *Ana* (4), *Angel* (4), *Edgardo* (4).

Pizer (262) **1.** English: variant of PEYSER. **2.** Jewish: unexplained.

GIVEN NAMES Jewish 4%. *Ari, Dvora, Yetta.*

Pizza (306) Possibly a variant of Italian PEZZA.

GIVEN NAMES Italian 13%. *Angelo* (2), *Antonio* (2), *Rocco* (2), *Dino, Gino, Giorgio, Lido, Pasquale, Pino, Salvatore.*

Pizzano (178) Italian: possibly a habitational name from a place called Pizzano.

GIVEN NAMES Italian 12%; Spanish 4%. *Pasquale* (2), *Saverio* (2), *Antonio, Roberto, Vito; Juan* (2), *Joaquin, Ricardo.*

Pizzi (537) Italian: patronymic or plural form of PIZZO.

GIVEN NAMES Italian 15%. *Mauro* (4), *Angelo* (3), *Antonio* (2), *Enzo* (2), *Paolo* (2), *Sal* (2), *Alberico, Alessandro, Antimo, Battista, Caesar, Carmine.*

Pizzimenti (149) Italian: patronymic from **Pizzimento**, a descriptive nickname from *pizzo* 'pointed beard' + *mento* 'chin'.

GIVEN NAMES Italian 19%. *Salvatore* (3), *Angelo, Giuseppe.*

Pizzini (157) Italian: **1.** (Venice): variant of PICCINI. **2.** see PIZZINO.

GIVEN NAMES Italian 7%; Spanish 4%. *Lucio* (3), *Angelo, Atilano, Giusto, Vittorio; Juan, Luis, Raul, Romualdo, Santiago.*

Pizzino (168) Italian: from a derivative of PIZZO.

GIVEN NAMES Italian 9%. *Angelo, Fiore, Nunzio, Salvatore.*

Pizzitola (148) Italian (western Sicily): possibly from a derivative of PIZZA or PEZZA.

GIVEN NAMES Italian 10%. *Neno, Vito.*

Pizzo (977) Italian: **1.** habitational name from Pizzo (Calabro) in Vibo Valentia province, or from other places named with *Pizzo* meaning 'peak', 'mountain summit', otherwise 'angle', 'head', 'point'. **2.** nickname from a variant of Old Italian *piccio* 'little' or from Southern Italian Greek *pitsos* with the same meaning. **3.** nickname from Old Tuscan *pizzo* 'beak', 'bill'. **4.** nickname from *pizzo* 'pointed beard'.

GIVEN NAMES Italian 20%. *Salvatore* (16), *Vito* (8), *Angelo* (6), *Carmine* (5), *Caesar* (3), *Sal* (3), *Marco* (2), *Rocco* (2), *Santo* (2), *Agostino, Carmela, Cesare.*

Pizzoferrato (107) Italian: habitational name from Pizzoferrato, a place in Chieti province.

GIVEN NAMES Italian 40%. *Aldo* (2), *Attilio* (2), *Emidio* (2), *Salvatore* (2), *Antonio, Dino, Domenic, Domenico, Francesco, Giovanni, Giuseppina, Italo.*

Pizzolato (268) Italian: from *pizzolato* 'pecked', hence a nickname for someone who was pockmarked.

GIVEN NAMES Italian 12%. *Carlo* (2), *Biagio, Ciro, Gaspare, Gasper, Giuseppe, Sal, Santo, Vincenza, Vito.*

Pizzurro (122) Italian: from a derivative of PIZZO.

GIVEN NAMES Italian 20%. *Salvatore* (2), *Angelo, Carmela, Vito.*

Pizzuti (296) Italian: patronymic or plural form of PIZZUTO.

GIVEN NAMES Italian 17%. *Angelo* (2), *Domenic* (2), *Pasquale* (2), *Salvatore* (2), *Dante, Donato, Egidio, Giovanna, Guido, Marco, Nino, Palma.*

Pizzuto (469) Italian: nickname from *pizzuto* 'elongated', 'pointed', also 'quarrelsome', 'spirited', 'malicious'.

GIVEN NAMES Italian 22%. *Carmelo* (3), *Alicia* (2), *Donato* (2), *Sal* (2), *Alfonso, Angelo, Antonio, Carmella, Domenico, Francesco, Gabriele, Giuseppe, Lauro, Mario, Pasquale, Rocco, Rosalia, Rosario.*

Pla (182) Catalan: topographic name from *pla* 'plain', 'plateau', denoting someone who lived on an area of flat ground, or habitational name from any of the numerous places named Pla, (from Latin *planum* 'plain', 'plateau').

GIVEN NAMES Spanish 45%; French 4%; Italian 4%. *Angel* (4), *Jaime* (4), *Luis* (4), *Bernardo* (3), *Mario* (3), *Carlos* (2), *Francisco* (2), *Javier* (2), *Jorge* (2), *Leandro* (2), *Miguel* (2), *Nestor* (2); *Jeanmarie, Philippe; Antonio, Lorenzo.*

Place (2918) French and English: **1.** topographic name for someone who lived in the main market square of a town or village, from Middle English, Old French *place* (Late Latin *platea (via)* 'broad street', 'free public open space in a town'). **2.** from Middle English, Old French *plaise* 'plaice', 'flatfish', hence a metonymic occupational name for a fisherman or a seller of these fish, or perhaps a nickname for someone thought to resemble a flatfish. **3.** topographic name for someone who lived near a quickset fence, from Middle English, Old French *pleis* (Latin *plexum*, past participle of *plectere* 'to plait or weave').

Placek (477) **1.** Polish: occupational name for a pastrycook, from *placek* 'cake'. **2.** Czech (**Plaček**): nickname from Czech *plaček* 'moaner', 'weeper', from *plář* 'to cry', 'bewail one's lot'.

GIVEN NAMES Polish 8%; German 4%. *Krzysztof* (2), *Wieslaw* (2), *Casimir, Mariusz, Zbigniew; Otto* (5).

Placencia (412) Spanish: habitational name from a Castilianized form of Basque *Plaentzia* a town in Gipuzkoa, Basque Country, also known as Soraluze.

GIVEN NAMES Spanish 51%. *Jose* (15), *Manuel* (8), *Jesus* (7), *Antonio* (5), *Pedro* (5), *Salvador* (5), *Eduardo* (4), *Juan* (4), *Marina* (4), *Miguel* (4), *Emilio* (3), *Felipe* (3), *Francisco* (3).

Plachta (131) Polish (**Płachta**), Czech, Slovak, and Jewish (from Poland): from *płachta* 'canvas', generally an occupational name for a sailmaker or tentmaker.

GIVEN NAMES Polish 7%; German 4%. *Ireneusz, Kazimierz, Malgorzata; Alfons.*

Plachy (105) Czech and Slovak (**Plachý**): nickname meaning 'shy'. This surname is also found in Poland.

GIVEN NAMES Polish 5%. *Jerzy, Jozef.*

Placido (200) Spanish (**Plácido**), Portuguese (**Plácido**), and Italian: nickname for a person with an equable temperament, from Spanish *plácido* and Italian *placido* 'calm', 'peaceful', 'placid' (Latin *placidus*), or from the personal name *Placido*, of the same origin.

GIVEN NAMES Spanish 26%; Portuguese 8%; Italian 6%. *Jose* (6), *Carlos* (2), *Orlando* (2), *Ramiro* (2), *Angel, Clarita, Donaciano, Enrique, Epifania, Florencio, Francisca, Jorge; Joao, Joaquim; Antonio* (2), *Aldo, Leonardo, Lorenzo, Luciano, Pasquale, Vito.*

Plack (170) German: from Middle Low German *plack*, Middle High German *placke, pflacke* 'scrap', 'patch (of material)', 'small plot (of land)'; probably a metonymic occupational name for a cobbler or a tailor who mended clothes, or a topographic name for someone living on a small piece of (flat) land.

Placke (247) **1.** Dutch: metonymic occupational name for a plasterer, from Middle Dutch *placke* 'plaster', 'whitewash'. **2.** German: variant of PLACK. **3.** German: habitational name from Placke or Placken in Westphalia.

GIVEN NAMES German 4%. *Lothar, Otto.*

Placko (134) Polish and Ukrainian: from a derivative of *placek* 'cake', hence a metonymic occupational name for a pastry chef.

Placzek (187) Polish (**Płaczek**): nickname for a moaner, from *płakać* 'to weep', 'complain'.

GIVEN NAMES Polish 10%. *Miroslawa* (2), *Zophia* (2), *Grzegorz, Wieslaw, Zigmund.*

Pladson (134) Possibly an Americanized form of the very common Norwegian farm name **Plassen**, from *plass* 'place', 'cotter's farm'.

Plageman (153) German (**Plagemann**): **1.** habitational name for someone from Plau or Plaue in eastern Germany. **2.** nickname for an unhappy or unfortunate person, from Middle Low German, Middle High German *pläge* 'misfortune', 'misery'. **3.** variant of PLAGER 1.

Plagens (167) German: variant of **Plage** (see PLAGEMAN 2).

GIVEN NAMES German 8%. *Erwin* (2), *Otto* (2), *Siegfried.*

Plager (141) **1.** Variant spelling of a Low German variant of PFLEGER; in particular, an occupational name for someone who tended dikes and ditches. **2.** Altered spelling of German **Pläger**, of uncertain origin.

Plagge (201) North German: from a term meaning 'sod', 'peat', hence a metonymic occupational name for a peat cutter or a topographic name for someone who lived by a peat bog.

GIVEN NAMES German 8%. *Kurt* (2), *Almut, Franz, Otto.*

Plagman (127) Variant of German **Plagemann** (see PLAGEMAN).

Plagmann (100) Variant of German **Plage-mann** (see PLAGEMAN).

Plahn (105) Swedish: ornamental spelling of Swedish *plan* 'open space', 'open piece of ground'.

GIVEN NAME Scandinavian 6%. *Lennart* (2).

Plaia (177) Southern Italian: habitational name from a place so named in southern Italy.

GIVEN NAMES Italian 15%. *Angelo, Antonio, Giacinto, Gino, Giuseppe, Rocco, Sal, Salvatore, Vito.*

Plain (376) English (of Norman origin): habitational name for someone from Plasnes in Eure.

Plair (210) English: probably a variant spelling of PLAYER.

Plaisance (1047) French: **1.** from the medieval female personal name *Plaisance*, meaning 'pleasantness', a feminine form of the much rarer personal name *Plaisant* (present participle of Old French *plaire* 'to please'), of common gender. **2.** habitational name from Piacenza in Italy, Latin name *Placentia* (see PIACENTINI). **3.** habitational name from any of a number of places so called in France. This name is found predominantly in LA.

GIVEN NAMES French 8%. *Eves* (3), *Armand* (2), *Autrey* (2), *Eloi* (2), *Emile* (2), *Julien* (2), *Lucien* (2), *Alcide, Amelie, Angelle, Antoine, Camille.*

Plaisted (523) English: topographic name for someone who lived by a piece of ground used for playing games, from Middle English *pleye* 'play' + *sted(e)* 'place', hence 'place for play or sport'. In some cases it may be a habitational name from Chapel Plaster in Box, Wiltshire. Compare PLASTER 2.

Plake (196) North German: probably a variant of PLACKE.

Plamann (195) German: variant of **Plaumann**, a habitational name from any of several places named Plau or Plaue in northern and eastern Germany.

Plambeck (282) German: habitational name from a place by a creek so named.

Plamondon (469) French: topographic name for someone who lived on or by an eminence with a flat top, from a diminutive of *plamont* 'flat-topped mountain'.

FOREBEARS A Plamondon, also called LAFLEUR, from the Auvergne region of France, is documented in Montreal in 1667.

GIVEN NAMES French 9%. *Andre* (2), *Marcel* (2), *Amedee, Benoit, Guylaine, Jacques, Laurier, Luc, Mignonne, Rejean.*

Planas (185) Aragonese and Catalan: topographic name from the plural of *plana* 'big plain', 'big plateau' for someone who lived in a plain area, or habitational name from any of the places called Planas, Catalan *Planes* (from Latin *plana* 'plane').

GIVEN NAMES Spanish 46%. *Luis* (9), *Jose* (7), *Carlos* (5), *Juan* (5), *Alberto* (4),

Ramon (4), *Jorge* (3), *Ana* (2), *Angel* (2), *Gonzalo* (2), *Luz* (2), *Roque* (2).

Planck (373) German: variant spelling of PLANK.

Plane (131) Variant of PLAIN.

Planer (175) **1.** South German and Jewish (Ashkenazic): habitational name for someone from Plan in Bohemia (Czech *Planá*). **2.** South German and Austrian (Tyrol): from Middle High German *plan* 'open space', 'plain'; a topographic name for someone living on a plateau, or a habitational name from a farm named with this word.

Plank (2454) **1.** English (chiefly Berkshire): from Middle English *planke* 'plank' (Late Latin *planca*). It is not clear how this word was applied as a surname: it may be a topographic name for someone who lived near a plank bridge over a stream, a metonymic occupational name for a carpenter, or a nickname for a thin person. **2.** North German: nickname for a cantankerous person, from Middle Low German *plank* 'quarrel', 'discord'. **3.** North German: metonymic occupational name from Middle Low German *plank* 'measure for liquids'. **4.** South German: topographic name from Middle High German *plank* 'plank', 'palisade'. **5.** South German: nickname for a fair-haired person, from a variant of Middle High German *blanc* 'light', 'shining'.

Plankenhorn (114) Variant of German **Blankenhorn**, a habitational name from a castle so named near Heilbronn in Baden.

GIVEN NAME German 4%. *Kurt.*

Plankey (131) Americanized spelling of French **Plantier**, a topographic name for someone who lived by a plantation, often of vines. Compare PELKEY.

Plano (116) Italian: variant of PIANO, from an older form.

GIVEN NAMES Italian 9%; Scandinavian 5%. *Salvatore* (2), *Italo*; *Anders.*

Plansky (106) Czech (**Plánský**): habitational name for someone from any of various places called Planá (four in Bohemia), Pláně (five in Bohemia), Planiny (two in Bohemia), or Plánice.

Plant (2250) **1.** English and French: metonymic occupational name for a gardener, in particular someone with a herb garden, from Middle English *plant* (Old English *plante*), Old French *plante* 'herb', 'shrub', 'young tree'. In English it may also be a nickname for a tender or delicate individual, from the same word in a transferred sense. **2.** French: topographic name for a planted area, in particular one planted with herbs or vines. Compare PLANTIER. **3.** Jewish (eastern Ashkenazic): unexplained.

Plante (2867) **1.** French (**Planté**): topographic name for someone living by an area of planted ground, a herb garden, shrub-

bery, or more specifically a vineyard. **2.** English: variant of PLANT.

GIVEN NAMES French 13%. *Normand* (13), *Marcel* (8), *Emile* (6), *Lucien* (6), *Andre* (4), *Gilles* (4), *Jacques* (4), *Armand* (3), *Fernand* (3), *Gaston* (3), *Pierre* (3), *Renald* (3).

Plantier (120) French: topographic name from *plantier* 'area with plants', 'shrubbery', more specifically 'vineyard'.

GIVEN NAMES French 12%. *Valmore* (2), *Jean-Marc, Marcel, Normand.*

Plants (386) Americanized form of German PFLANZ.

Planty (136) Americanized form of French **Planté** (see PLANTE) or PLANTIER.

Plantz (485) Americanized form of German PFLANZ.

Planz (110) **1.** South German (Swabian): nickname for a clumsy person, a variant of dialect *Plantsch*. **2.** German: variant of PFLANZ.

GIVEN NAMES German 6%. *Hans* (2), *Rainer.*

Plapp (109) **1.** South German and Swiss German: unexplained; perhaps a shortened form of **Plappert, Blappert, Blapphart**, from Middle High German *blaphart*, the name of a silver coin worth one-twentieth of a gulden. **2.** South German or Swiss German: from an onomatopoeic word referring to a clapping noise, hence a nickname for a blabbermouth.

GIVEN NAMES German 4%. *Merwin, Otto.*

Plas (145) **1.** Dutch (**Van den Plas**): from Middle Dutch *plas* 'puddle', 'pool', 'plash', hence a topographic name for someone who lived by a dip in a road, which filled up with water in wet weather. **2.** Possibly French: habitational name from places so called in the Ardèche and Corrèze.

GIVEN NAME French 4%. *Jean Francois.*

Plascencia (379) Variant of Spanish PLACENCIA or PLASENCIA.

GIVEN NAMES Spanish 58%. *Jose* (21), *Juan* (10), *Jesus* (9), *Manuel* (7), *Miguel* (5), *Roberto* (5), *Arturo* (4), *Francisco* (4), *Carlos* (3), *Javier* (3), *Luis* (3), *Pablo* (3).

Plasencia (413) Spanish: habitational name from Plasencia in Cácares province, or from a Castilianized form of Aragonese Plasenzia, towns in Zaragoza and Uesca.

GIVEN NAMES Spanish 48%. *Jose* (13), *Jesus* (8), *Juan* (7), *Jorge* (5), *Roberto* (5), *Carlos* (4), *Javier* (4), *Luis* (4), *Manuel* (4), *Miguel* (4), *Ana* (3), *Eusebio* (3).

Plaskett (208) English: topographic name from Old French *plasquet*, a diminutive of *plascq* 'damp meadow'.

Plaskon (119) Origin unidentified.

Plass (284) **1.** North German: topographic name from Middle Low German *plas* 'place', 'open square', 'street'. **2.** South German (also **Pläss**): from a short form of the medieval personal name BLASIUS. **3.** English: variant of PLACE 3.

GIVEN NAMES German 5%; French 4%. *Christoph, Mathias; Benoit, Michelene.*

Plasse (253) **1.** German: variant of PLASS 1. **2.** French: variant of PLACE 1, or a habitational name from a place so called in Loire.

GIVEN NAMES French 19%. *Herve* (4), *Emile* (2), *Alban, Aldor, Elzear, Gaston, Germain, Marcel, Napoleon, Normand, Phillippe.*

Plassmeyer (103) German: distinguishing name for a tenant farmer (see MEYER) whose farmhouse was by the main square of a village (see PLASS).

GIVEN NAME German 7%. *Gerhard* (2).

Plaster (935) **1.** English and North German: metonymic occupational name for a plasterer, from Middle English, Middle Low German *plaster* (from Latin *emplastrum* '(wound) plaster' (originally a paste), from Greek *emplastron*, a derivative of *emplassein* 'to shape or form'; the term was carried over into building terminology to mean 'bonding agent'). **2.** English: habitational name from any of various places called Plaistow (in East London, Derbyshire, Sussex, and elsewhere), from Old English *plegestōw* 'place where people gather for sport or play'. This can also be a variant of PLAISTED (through interchangeable use of the Old English elements *stōw* and *stede*, both meaning 'place', in earlier times). **3.** German and Ashkenazic Jewish (**Pflaster**): from Middle High German *pflaster* (German *Pflaster*, from Latin *plastrum*) 'street pavement', 'pavement', cognate with 1.

Plasterer (169) **1.** English: occupational name for a plasterer, from Old French *plastrier* or an agent derivative of Middle English *plaster* (see PLASTER 1). **2.** Americanized spelling of German **Pflasterer**, an occupational name for a paver or a *Pflästerer*, a manufacturer of plasters for wounds, from an agent derivative of Middle High German *pflaster* (see PLASTER).

Plasters (102) English: variant of PLASTER.

Plata (431) Spanish: **1.** habitational name from places in Toledo and Cáceres provinces named Plata, or various places named La Plata. **2.** byname from *plata* 'silver'.

GIVEN NAMES Spanish 44%. *Juan* (8), *Jose* (7), *Fernando* (6), *Raul* (6), *Armando* (5), *Carlos* (5), *Manuel* (5), *Julio* (4), *Pedro* (4), *Alfredo* (3), *Domingo* (3), *Gerardo* (3).

Platania (134) **1.** Italian (Sicily): habitational name from Platania in Catanzaro province. **2.** Southern Italian and Greek (**Platanias**) topographic name for someone living in the main square of a town, an open space where plane trees grow, from medieval Greek *platani* 'plane tree' (ancient Greek *platanos*).

GIVEN NAMES Italian 13%. *Giuseppe, Lorenzo, Mario, Sal.*

Plate (627) **1.** German and Dutch: metonymic occupational name for a maker of plate armor, from Middle High German *blate, plate*, Middle Dutch *plate* 'plate', 'armor plating'. **2.** German: habitational name from a place so named in Mecklenburg. **3.** Dutch: from West Flemish *plate* 'plaice', possibly a nickname for someone thought to resemble a flat fish, or a metonymic occupational name for a catcher or seller of these fish.

GIVEN NAMES German 5%. *Alfons, Gunther, Hans, Heinz, Otto, Reinold.*

Platek (253) Polish (**Płatek**) and Jewish (from Poland): nickname from Polish *płatek* 'little piece' in any of various senses, e.g. 'piece of cloth', 'snowflake', or 'petal'.

GIVEN NAMES Polish 5%. *Dorota, Ireneusz, Jozef.*

Plater (240) English: **1.** occupational name for a maker of plate-armor or armor-plates, from an agent derivative of Middle English *plate* 'armor-plate'. **2.** from an agent derivative of Old French *plait* 'plea' or *plaitier* 'to plead', hence an occupational name or nickname for an advocate.

Platero (125) Spanish: occupational name for a silversmith, *platero*.

GIVEN NAMES Spanish 35%. *Jose* (5), *Mario* (3), *Juan* (2), *Manuel* (2), *Milagro* (2), *Ana, Cesar, Edgardo, Graciela, Joaquin, Julio, Luis.*

Plath (636) German: **1.** habitational name from a place so named in Mecklenburg. **2.** topographic name from Slavic *błodo* 'swamp' and here probably from Sorbian *plot* 'woven fence'.

GIVEN NAMES German 4%. *Claus, Erna, Erwin, Wilhelm.*

Platko (128) Polish (**Płatko**) and Ukrainian: nickname from Polish *płatek* 'little piece'. Compare Polish **Płatek** (see PLATEK).

Platner (245) **1.** German, Jewish (Ashkenazic), and Czech (**Platnéř**): occupational name for an armorer (see BLATTNER). **2.** English: occupational name for a plate maker, from a Middle English agent derivative of Old French *platon* 'metal plate'. Compare PLATTEN.

Plato (364) Anglicized form of the Greek personal name **Platon**, the name of two early Christian martyrs, and as such found as a surname in Poland and elsewhere. However, it is much better known as the name of the great Greek philosopher (c.429–c.347 BC), in whose honor it was adopted as an English, Dutch, German, and Danish humanistic name during the Reformation.

Platt (8044) **1.** English: habitational name from Platt or Platt Bridge in Lancashire, named in Middle English with Old French *plat* 'flat', 'thin' (see PLATTE), in the dialect sense 'plank bridge'. **2.** English: topographic name from Middle English *plat* 'plot of land', 'piece of ground' (Old English *plætt*). **3.** Jewish (Ashkenazic): nick-

name from German *platt* 'flat'. **4.** German: variant of PLATTE 3.

Platte (460) **1.** French: from Old French *plat* 'flat' (Late Latin *plat(t)us*, from Greek *platys* 'broad', 'flat'). **2.** German: variant of PLATE 1. **3.** German: topographic name from Middle Low German, Middle High German *plate* 'plateau', 'rock wall'.

GIVEN NAMES German 4%. *Erna, Erwin, Franz, Hans, Kurt.*

Platten (195) English (Norfolk): **1.** diminutive of PLATT 1. **2.** metonymic occupational name for a platemaker, from Old French *platon* 'metal plate'.

Platter (328) **1.** English: variant of PLATT or PLATER. **2.** Scottish: habitational name from the Forest of Plater in Angus. **3.** German (Tyrol, Bavaria): variant of PLATTNER 1. **4.** German: variant of PLATNER.

Plattner (438) **1.** German (Tyrol, Bavaria): from *platte* 'ledge' (genitive *platten*) + *-er* suffix of habitation, hence a topographic name denoting someone who lived at a farm on a mountain ledge. **2.** German and Jewish (Ashkenazic): variant of PLATNER.

Platts (410) **1.** English (mainly South Yorkshire): variant of PLATT 1. **2.** Americanized form of German PLATZ.

Platz (1014) **1.** German and Jewish (Ashkenazic): topographic name for someone who lived in the main (market) square of a town or village, from (respectively) Middle High German *plaz*, German *Platz* 'town square'. As a Jewish name it may also be one of the names randomly selected by government officials when surnames were made compulsory. In Tyrol, where many farms are called *Platz(l)*, the name refers to an opening or suitable site for a dwelling. **2.** German: metonymic occupational name from *platz, plotz* 'wedge for splitting stone', or a nickname for a big, heavy man, from the same word in a transferred sense.

Platzer (255) South German and Jewish (Ashkenazic): variant of PLATZ 1, with *-er* suffix denoting an inhabitant.

Plauche (301) **1.** possibly a variant of German PLOCH. **2.** Possibly an altered spelling of German **Plache**, from Czech *plachý* 'shy' and cognate with Polish PLOCH 3.

Plaugher (200) Americanized form of German PLOCHER.

Plaut (257) North German: from Middle Low German *plaut* 'short and broad bayonet', or 'blunt knife', hence a nickname for a heavy, clumsy fellow or a lout.

GIVEN NAMES German 8%; French 4%; Jewish 4%. *Reinhard* (2), *Gerhard, Kurt, Manfred; Andre* (2); *Ari, Dovid, Tova, Yisroel.*

Plautz (461) **1.** Germanized spelling of Slovenian **Plavec** or **Plavc**, two different spellings of the archaic occupational name *plavec* 'raftsman', a derivative of *plaviti* 'to float', formed with the agent noun suffix *-ec*. **2.** German: variant of PLAUT.

Player (1045) English: from an agent derivative of Middle English *pleyen* 'to play', hence an occupational name for an actor or musician or a nickname for a successful competitor in contests of athletic or sporting prowess.

Playford (143) English (mainly Norfolk): habitational name from a place in Suffolk, so called from Old English *plæga, plega* 'sport', 'play' + *ford* 'ford'.

Plaza (801) Spanish: habitational name from any of various places called Plaza, from *plaza* 'town square'.
GIVEN NAMES Spanish 30%. *Jose* (16), *Carlos* (8), *Luis* (8), *Francisco* (7), *Juan* (6), *Jorge* (5), *Mario* (5), *Ruben* (4), *Alfredo* (3), *Angel* (3), *Jesus* (3), *Ramon* (3).

Pleas (145) English: variant of PLACE 3.

Pleasant (1791) English: from the medieval female personal name *Pleasant* (Old French *Plaisant*) (see PLAISANCE 1).

Pleasants (823) English (Norfolk): **1.** from the medieval female personal name *Plaisance* (see PLAISANCE) 1. **2.** habitational name for someone from Piacenza in Italy (earlier *Placentia*).

Pleau (141) French: variant of BELLEAU.
FOREBEARS A Pleau from Bourges, France, with the secondary surname LAFLEUR, is recorded in Quebec City in 1669.
GIVEN NAMES French 11%. *Andre, Emile, Gaetane.*

Pledger (924) **1.** English (Cambridgeshire): from Middle English *pleggere* 'one who stands surety in a lawsuit' (literally 'pledger'). **2.** Americanized form of German **Pletscher** (see PLETCHER).

Pleger (128) Americanized spelling of German PFLEGER or PFLUEGER.

Pleiman (158) Probably a variant of German **Bleimann**, an occupational name for the operator of a siege machine (ballista) (Middle High German *blīde*), with which stones were hurled at a castle or town ramparts.

Plein (161) **1.** Dutch: nickname for a plain, simple man (either unpretentious or simple-minded), from Old French *plain*, Latin *planus* 'plain', 'flat', 'straightforward'. **2.** German: habitational name from a place so named in Bohemia (Czech name *Planina*).

Pleines (105) Dutch and North German: variant of PLEIN.

Pleiss (139) German: habitational name from a place called Pleissa, near Chemnitz.

Plemmons (924) English, Irish, or possibly German: altered form of FLEMINGS, FLEMING, or FLEMMING.

Plemons (776) Variant spelling of PLEMMONS.

Plenge (119) German: **1.** Nickname from Old High German *blanc* 'bright', 'white'. **2.** From Middle Low German *plengen* 'to stir', 'bring about strife', 'deceive', hence an unflattering nickname for a troublemaker. **3.** German and Danish: unexplained.

GIVEN NAME German 6%. *Fritz.*

Plescia (223) Albanian: unexplained. This surname is established in the Albanian-speaking areas of Italy (in particular, Piana degli Albanesi in Sicily, and San Felice and Ururi in Molise).
GIVEN NAMES Italian 13%. *Carlo* (2), *Angelo, Constantino, Nicola, Rocco, Romeo, Sante, Santo, Vito.*

Plese (156) Origin unidentified.

Plesha (143) Probably an Americanized spelling of Italian-Albanian PLESCIA.

Plesko (128) Slovenian (**Pleško**): nickname for a bald person, from *pleša* 'bald patch' or *plešec* 'bald man'. **Plešec** is also found as a Slovenian surname.

Pless (832) East German (of Slavic origin): habitational name from any of various places named with the Slavic element *pleso* 'swamp', for example Pless in Upper Silesia.

Plessinger (199) Probably a variant spelling of German BLESSINGER.

Plessner (102) **1.** German: habitational name for someone from Plesse in Hesse or Plessen in Westphalia. **2.** East German: variant of PLESS.
GIVEN NAMES German 11%; Dutch 6%. *Kurt* (2), *Gerhardt, Hans; Dirk* (2).

Pletcher (1361) Americanized spelling of German **Pletscher**, a variant of PLETSCH 2–4, with the addition of the agent suffix *-er*.

Pletsch (119) South German: **1.** variant of PLETZ. **2.** habitational name from a place so named in the Rhineland. **3.** nickname for a person with a drooping lip. **4.** topographic name for someone who lived by a field where cattle fodder was grown, from the field name *Bletsch*.
GIVEN NAMES German 6%. *Heinz, Klaus.*

Plett (265) German: probably from a short form of a personal name formed with the root of modern *Blatt* 'leaf' or words with the sense of 'bloom'.

Pletz (230) South German: **1.** metonymic occupational name for a tailor who mended clothes, from Middle High German *bletz* 'scrap', 'patch'. **2.** altered spelling of PLOETZ.
GIVEN NAMES German 4%. *Ilse, Rudie.*

Pleva (261) Czech and Slovak: from *pleva* 'husk', 'shell', an unflattering nickname for someone regarded as lightweight or worthless.

Plew (279) Perhaps a variant of German **Plewe**, a habitational name from a place so named in Brandenburg.

Plewa (200) Polish: from *plewa* 'husk', 'shell', an unflattering nickname for a lightweight, worthless man, or possibly a metonymic occupational name for someone whose job was to winnow grain.
GIVEN NAMES Polish 14%. *Andrzej, Boleslaw, Grzegorz, Jozef, Katarzyna, Kazimierz, Krzysztof, Waclaw, Zdzislaw, Zofia.*

Plexico (111) Origin unidentified.

Plichta (234) Polish and Czech: unflattering or humorous nickname for a gambler or an idle or useless person, from Polish and Czech *plichta* 'card of low value'. This name is also found in Germany.
GIVEN NAMES Polish 6%. *Slawomir* (2), *Alojzy, Jozef, Ryszard.*

Plier (118) **1.** German: origin uncertain. Perhaps from Middle High German *blier* 'lead smelter', or of Slavic origin. **2.** Dutch: variant of **Pleyers**, a nickname from a derivative of Middle Dutch *pleien* 'to have fun', 'to cheer', 'to dance and jump with joy', or of **Plahiers**, which is possibly from Old French *pla(s)quier* 'marsh', 'bog', influenced by Old Dutch *plask* 'pool', or a Walloon variant of **Plaisir**, **Playsier**, from Walloon *plêhant, plêjant* 'pleasant'.

Pliler (140) Americanized spelling of German **Pleuler** (see PLYLER).

Plimpton (285) English: habitational name from Plympton in Devon, named in Old English with *plȳme* 'plum tree' + *tūn* 'settlement', 'farmstead'. It may also be a variant of **Plumpton**, from any of several places so named, which have the same etymology.
FOREBEARS John Plimpton emigrated from England to MA about 1636, becoming one of the original settlers of Deerfield. His descendants included manufacturers of agricultural implements at Plimptonville in the town of Walpole, near the family farm, and a prominent book publisher.

Pline (129) Americanized spelling of Dutch PLEIN.

Pliner (161) **1.** Jewish (from Belarus): habitational name for someone from Plino in Belarus. **2.** Altered spelling of German **Pleiner**, a variant of PLEIN 2.
GIVEN NAMES Jewish 7%; French 4%; Russian 4%. *Inna, Isser, Leyb, Myer; Edouard, Jacques; Genrikh, Mikhail, Yevgeniy.*

Pliska (312) Czech (**Pliška**) or Polish (**Pliszka**): nickname from Czech *pliška*, Polish *pliszka* 'wagtail'.

Pliskin (134) Jewish (from Belarus): habitational name from the village of Pliski, now in Belarus.
GIVEN NAMES German 5%; Jewish 4%. *Kurt* (2); *Aba.*

Plitt (340) German: of uncertain origin; in the south, perhaps a nickname for a cheerful, friendly person, from Middle High German *blīde* 'joyous'; in the north, perhaps a nickname for a short irascible individual, dialect Low German *plīte*.

Ploch (296) **1.** Southern and eastern German (of Slavic origin): variant of BLOCH. **2.** South German: nickname for a crude, clumsy, or short and fat individual, from Middle High German *bloch* 'block', 'stocks'. **3.** Polish: unflattering nickname from *płochy* 'timid' or 'sluttish'.
GIVEN NAMES German 5%. *Florian, Fritz, Kurt, Otto.*

Plocher (170) German: from an agent derivative of Middle High German *bloch* 'block', 'stocks'; either an occupational name for an official who put prisoners into stocks or a nickname for a clumsy or crude man. See also PLOCH.

GIVEN NAME German 4%. *Kurt.*

Plock (222) **1.** English: topographic name for someone who lived on a small plot of land, from Middle English *plocke* 'small piece of ground'. **2.** Americanized spelling of German PLOCH. **3.** Variant of German BLOCK.

Ploeger (388) Dutch and North German: occupational name for a plowman, from an agent derivative of Middle Low German *plōch* 'plow'.

GIVEN NAMES German 5%. *Kurt* (3), *Gunter, Markus.*

Ploen (101) German (also **Plön**): **1.** habitational name from Plön in Schleswig Holstein. **2.** From a short form of the medieval personal name *Apollonius.*

Ploetz (281) German (**Plötz**): **1.** from *plötz* 'roach', hence a nickname for someone thought to resemble the fish, or a metonymic occupational name for someone who caught or sold these fish. **2.** variant of PLOTZ. **3.** from an altered and shortened form for the Slavic personal name *Blogumil* (from *blogy* 'good', 'rich', 'happy').

GIVEN NAMES German 4%. *Ernst, Manfred, Wolfgang.*

Plog (193) Dutch and North German: metonymic occupational name for a plowright or plowman, from Middle Low German *plōch* 'plow'.

Plona (113) Polish (**Płona**): unflattering nickname derived from the adjective *płony* 'useless'.

GIVEN NAMES Polish 11%. *Arkadiusz, Bogdan, Kazimierz, Mieczyslaw.*

Plonka (165) Polish (**Płonka**): nickname from *płonka* 'ungrafted tree', from *płony* 'useless'.

GIVEN NAMES Polish 7%. *Andrzej, Boguslaw, Jacek, Janusz.*

Plonski (197) Polish (**Płoński**) and Jewish (from Poland): habitational name from Płońsk in Ciechanów voivodeship, or from Płonna, Płonne, or Płonnie in Krosno, Płock, and Siedlce voivodeships.

GIVEN NAMES Polish 18%. *Wieslaw* (2), *Andrzej, Boguslaw, Feliks, Jadwiga, Pawel, Ryszard, Slawomir, Witold, Wladyslaw, Zbigniew, Zygmunt.*

Plonsky (105) German or Jewish spelling of Polish PLONSKI.

GIVEN NAME German 4%. *Klaus.*

Ploof (577) American variant of Canadian French PLOUFFE. It is a frequent name in VT.

Ploog (109) Dutch and North German: variant of PLOG 'plow'.

GIVEN NAME German 6%. *Hans* (2).

Plooster (118) Dutch: occupational name for a plowman, from an agent derivative of Middle Low German *plōch* 'plow'.

Ploski (141) Polish (**Płoski**): habitational name from any of the places called Płosk in Leszno voivodeship, Płoskie in Zamość and Białystok voivodeships, or Płoska, now in Ukraine.

Ploss (235) German (Bavaria): nickname for someone who was destitute or who dressed inappropriately, from Middle High German *blōz* 'naked', 'wretched'.

GIVEN NAME French 4%. *Andree.*

Ploszaj (92) Polish (**Płoszaj**): from *płochliwy* 'shy', 'scared', a nickname for a timid person or an occupational name for a bird scarer.

GIVEN NAMES Polish 8%. *Elzbieta, Kazimierz.*

Plotkin (1192) Jewish (from Belarus): **1.** from Belorussian *plotka* 'roach', one of the many ornamental names based on fish names. **2.** habitational name for someone from Plotki in Belarus.

GIVEN NAMES Jewish 10%; Russian 5%. *Miriam* (3), *Levi* (2), *Shimshon* (2), *Yakov* (2), *Zalman* (2), *Arieh, Aron, Avrohom, Borukh, Chaim, Fridrikh, Ilya; Leonid* (5), *Boris* (3), *Lev* (2), *Mikhail* (2), *Vitaly* (2), *Vladimir* (2), *Yefim* (2), *Aleksandr, Anatoliy, Evgeny, Galena, Gennady.*

Plotner (438) South German: **1.** (**Plötner**): variant of PLATTNER 1. **2.** habitational name for someone from Plothen in Thuringia or Plotha near Merseburg.

Plotnick (304) Germanized or Americanized spelling of Jewish PLOTNIK.

GIVEN NAMES Jewish 6%. *Gerson, Isadore, Meyer, Yetta.*

Plotnik (134) Jewish (eastern Ashkenazic): occupational name from Russian *plotnik* 'carpenter' (originally a maker of wattles and wooden fences, from *plot* 'plaited or woven object').

GIVEN NAMES Jewish 10%. *Eyal, Itsik, Naftali, Ofer, Zvi.*

Plott (897) **1.** English: topographic name for someone who lived on a small plot of land, from late Old English *plot*. **2.** Jewish (eastern Ashkenazic): occupational name for a fence maker or carpenter, from Slavic 'fence' (Polish *plot*, Russian *plot*). Compare PLOTNIK.

Plotts (342) Americanized spelling of German PLOTZ or PLATZ.

Plotz (230) German: **1.** variant of **Plötz** (see PLOETZ). **2.** metonymic occupational name from *platz, plotz* 'wedge (for splitting stone)', or a nickname for a big, heavy man. **3.** variant of PLATZ 2. **4.** of Slavic origin: perhaps a nickname from a Slavic word meaning 'roach', e.g. Polish *płoć*.

GIVEN NAMES German 5%. *Alois, Arno, Eldred.*

Plouff (185) French: variant spelling of PLOUFFE.

GIVEN NAME French 4%. *Rosaire.*

Plouffe (532) French: probably an Alsatian French form of German PFLUG 'plow'.

FOREBEARS A bearer of this name from Paris is documented in 1666 in Montreal.

GIVEN NAMES French 19%. *Marcel* (6), *Normand* (5), *Andre* (4), *Armand* (3), *Aime* (2), *Ovila* (2), *Aldee, Aurel, Cecile, Lucien, Monique, Napoleon.*

Plough (249) English: from Middle English *plow* 'plow', metonymic occupational name for a plowwright or plowman. In some cases it may have been a topographic name for someone who lived at the edge of an area of plowed land.

Plourd (140) Variant of French PLOURDE.

GIVEN NAMES French 7%. *Armand, Colette, Rosaire.*

Plourde (1742) French: perhaps related to Old French *palorde*, a type of shellfish, and hence an occupational surname for a harvester of such comestibles.

FOREBEARS A Plourde from the Poitou region of France is documented in Rivière Ouelle, Quebec, in 1679.

GIVEN NAMES French 13%. *Normand* (8), *Marcel* (6), *Cecile* (5), *Lucien* (5), *Camille* (4), *Fernand* (3), *Adrien* (2), *Andre* (2), *Armand* (2), *Gaston* (2), *Julien* (2), *Aime.*

Plowden (362) English: habitational name from a place in Shropshire, so called from Old English *plæga, plega* 'play', 'sport' + *denu* 'valley'. Compare PLAYFORD. The vowel of the first syllable is not easy to explain, but it occurs as early as 1286, a single generation after the unambiguous *Plaueden, Pleweden* of 1252.

Plowman (1341) English and Scottish: occupational name for a plowwright or plowman, from late Old English *plōh* 'plow' + *mann* 'man'.

Pluchino (116) Italian: according to Caracausi a reduced metathesized form of **Pulichino**, from a diminutive of *pulica, pulice*, variants of *pulce* 'flea'.

GIVEN NAMES Italian 14%. *Carmelo* (2), *Angelo, Biagio, Giovanni, Sal, Salvatore.*

Plucinski (240) Polish (**Pluciński**): habitational name, possibly for someone from Plucice in Piotrków voivodeship, or any of various places called Pluty in other voivodeships.

GIVEN NAMES Polish 7%. *Janusz, Jozef, Wojtek, Zigmund, Zygmund.*

Plucker (207) North German (**Plücker**) and Dutch: occupational name for someone who gathered produce to sell, from an agent derivative of Middle Low German *plucken*, Dutch *plukken* 'to pick'.

Plude (232) Possibly of French origin, a respelling of **Palud**, a topographic name for someone who lived by a marsh (from Latin *palus*).

GIVEN NAME French 4%. *Emile* (2).

Plue (146) French: nickname from Old French *pelu* 'hairy'.

GIVEN NAMES French 4%. *Camille, Monique.*

Plueger (123) North German: **1.** variant of PLOEGER. **2.** variant of **Pflüger** (see PFLUEGER).

Pluemer (117) German: variant of BLUMER 3.

Pluff (196) **1.** German: probably an altered spelling of **Bluff**, perhaps from a Germanic personal name *Blotfrid*, composed of the elements *blōd*, *bluot* 'blood' or 'blossom' + *frid-* 'peace'. **2.** Perhaps an Americanized spelling of French PLOUFFE.

Plugge (135) Dutch and North German: from Middle Low German *plugge* 'dowel', 'tack', a nickname for a blockhead.

Pluhar (115) Czech: occupational name for a plowman, from Czech *pluhár*.

Pluim (112) German (Rhineland): variant of BLUM.

Plum (1033) **1.** English and North German: from Middle English *plum(b)e*, Middle Low German *plum(e)* 'plum', hence a topographic name for someone who lived by a plum tree, or a metonymic occupational name for a fruit grower. Reaney and Wilson, however, derive the English name from Old French *plomb* 'lead' (Latin *plumbum*), regarding it as a metonymic occupational name for a plumber. **2.** German and Jewish (Ashkenazic): variant of BLUM. **3.** Americanized form of PFLUM.

Plumadore (122) Probably an Americanized form of French **Plumardeau** or a similar name, based on *plume* 'feather', an occupational name for someone who sold feathers or quill pens, or a descriptive epithet for someone who wore a feather in his cap.

Plumb (1773) English: variant of PLUM.

Plume (214) **1.** English: metonymic occupational name for a dealer in feathers, from Middle English, Old French *plume* 'feather' (Latin *pluma*). **2.** English and North German: variant of PLUM. **3.** Catalan (**Plumé**): variant of *plomer*, occupational name for a worker in lead, from a derivative of *plom* 'lead'.

Plumer (475) **1.** North German (**Plümer**) and English: variant of PLUM, the suffix *-er* denoting habitation or occupation. **2.** Altered form of South German **Pflümer**, an occupational name for a grower or seller of plums, from an agent derivative of Middle High German *pflüme* 'plum'. **3.** English: variant of PLUMMER 1. **4.** English and Dutch: occupational name for a dealer in feathers and quills, from an agent derivative of Middle English *plume*, Middle Dutch *pluim* 'feather', 'plume'.

Plumhoff (112) German: habitational name from Plumhoff in Saxony or from various other places so named ('plum farm') (see PLUM 1 and HOFF).

GIVEN NAMES German 7%. *Helmut, Helmuth.*

Plumlee (965) **1.** Americanized spelling of German **Blümle**, from a pet form of BLUM. **2.** English: variant spelling of PLUMLEY.

Plumley (1448) English: habitational name from any of various places so called, the most likely source of the surname being the one in Cheshire near Knutsford. The place name is derived from Old English *plūme* 'plum' + *lēah* 'wood', 'clearing'.

Plummer (9014) English: **1.** occupational name for a worker in lead, especially a maker of lead pipes and conduits, from Anglo-Norman French *plom(m)er*, *plum(m)er* 'plumber', from *plom(b)*, *plum(b)* 'lead' (Latin *plumbum*). **2.** variant of PLUMER 1, 3. **3.** occasionally, a habitational name from a minor place name, such as Plummers in Kimpton, Hertfordshire, which was named with Old English *plum* 'plum(tree)' + *mere* 'pool'. The name is also established in Ireland, taken there from England in the 17th century.

Plump (149) North German: nickname for a heavy, clumsy, or tactless person, from Low German *plump* 'heavy', 'crude'.

Plunk (837) Possibly an altered spelling of German BLUNK.

Plunket (123) English and Irish: variant spelling of PLUNKETT.

Plunkett (3972) English and Irish: **1.** (of Norman origin): habitational name from a metathesized form of Plouquenet in Ille-et-Villaine, Brittany, so named from Breton *plou* 'parish' (from Latin *plebs* 'people') + *Guenec*, the personal name (a diminutive of *guen* 'white') of a somewhat obscure saint. As an Irish name, it has been Gaelicized as **Pluincéid**. **2.** alternatively, it may be a metonymic occupational name for a maker or seller of blankets, from Middle English *blaunket* (Anglo-Norman French *blanc-quet*, a diminutive of *blanc* 'white'), but replacement of *b* by *p* is not usual in English.

Plush (200) English: habitational name from Plush in Dorset, originally named with an Old English word *plysc* 'shallow pool'.

Plut (110) Slovenian: unexplained. It comes mainly from the southernmost part of central Slovenia.

Pluta (565) Polish: nickname from the Polish dialect term *pluta* 'bad weather', 'rain', 'sleet', or 'puddle', perhaps a nickname for someone of a gloomy disposition. This name also occurs in Germany.

GIVEN NAMES Polish 6%. *Danuta* (2), *Agnieszka, Bronislaw, Czeslaw, Jaroslaw, Jozef, Kinga, Lech, Stanislaw, Zdzislaw.*

Plute (145) Americanized spelling of German PLUTH.

Pluth (154) German (also **Plüth**): from Middle High German *bluot* 'blossom', perhaps a nickname for a thriving individual, or a habitational name from a house distinguished by a sign depicting a blossom.

Pluto (125) **1.** Polish: derivative of *pluta* 'bad weather', a nickname for a dissatisfied, complaining person. **2.** Apparently also French, an altered form of an unidentified French surname, possibly **Ploteau** or

Plotu, a nickname for someone with flat feet, from *plot*, southern French dialect variant of *plat* 'flat'.

GIVEN NAMES French 7%. *Patrice* (2), *Michel.*

Ply (103) French: habitational name from any of several places so called, named with Old French *ploi* 'hedge with interlaced branches'.

Plybon (203) Origin unidentified. The name is recorded in VA in the early 18th century; it is most probably of English or French Huguenot origin.

Plyler (1137) Americanized spelling of South German **Pleuler**, a variant of BLEILER (of which this could also be a respelling), an agent derivative from Middle High German *bliuwel* 'pounding mill'. Compare PLILER.

Plymale (519) Americanized spelling of German **Bleimöhl**, an occupational nickname for a tenant or owner of a pounding mill, from Middle High German *bliuwen* 'to beat or pound' + *moele* 'mill' (from Latin *molinae*).

Plymel (108) Origin unidentified.

Plymire (121) Americanized spelling of German **Bleimeier**, variant of **Bleimeister**, an occupational name for an operator of a siege machine (a ballista, Middle High German *blīde*), in which the second element *-meier* 'steward' has been substituted for *-meister* 'master' (a not uncommon exchange). Compare PLEIMAN.

GIVEN NAME German 4%. *Kurt.*

Pniewski (107) Polish and Jewish (from Poland): habitational name for someone from Pniewy in the district of Poznań, or from any of the many places in Poland named Pniewo.

GIVEN NAMES Polish 11%. *Andrzej, Krzysztof, Mieczyslaw, Waclaw.*

Po (144) **1.** Portuguese (**Pó**) and Spanish: habitational name from Pó, a town in Portugal, or probably a Spanish habitational name from any of several places called Poo, in northwest Spain. **2.** Italian: habitational name from any of the places called Po. **3.** Chinese: variant of BO. **4.** Chinese 蒲: variant of PU 1. **5.** Other Southeast Asian: unexplained.

GIVEN NAMES Spanish 15%; Chinese 11%; Other Southeast Asian 8%; Italian 4%. *Elvira* (2), *Fernando* (2), *Alfredo, Claudio, Edilberto, Guadalupe, Joaquin, Juanito, Ramon, Rosario, Silvia, Vicente; Chin* (2), *Ching* (2), *Eng, Hong, Hou, Lai Kuen, Pok, Sin, Wen, Wong; Hoi, Que, Sokhom, Tat, Than, Thy, Tuyet; Antonio, Carlo, Julieta.*

Poag (309) Northern Irish: variant of POGUE.

GIVEN NAMES French 4%. *Camille, Mathieu.*

Poage (572) Northern Irish: variant of POGUE.

Poague (125) Northern Irish: variant of POGUE.

Poarch (483) Perhaps an altered spelling of German BORSCH.

Pobanz (183) German: nickname for a braggart or bogeyman, of uncertain Slavic origin.

Poblete (191) Spanish: habitational name from Poblete in the province of Ciudad Real.
GIVEN NAMES Spanish 42%. *Jose* (4), *Luis* (4), *Carlos* (3), *Manuel* (3), *Pedro* (3), *Jaime* (2), *Lourdes* (2), *Ramon* (2), *Raul* (2), *Ricardo* (2), *Rodolfo* (2), *Adoracion*.

Pobst (144) German: variant of PABST (Middle High German and Middle Low German *ā* having been raised to *ō*).

Pobuda (101) Czech: nickname meaning 'vagabond', 'hobo'.
GIVEN NAMES German 4%. *Eckhard, Hans*.

Poccia (104) Italian: unexplained.
GIVEN NAMES Italian 26%. *Angelo* (3), *Alexandro, Amedeo, Claudio, Elia, Emilio, Ezio, Mario, Nicandro, Nicola, Pasquale, Salvatore*.

Poch (303) **1.** Catalan: nickname for a small man, from *poc* 'little', which in old Catalan meant also 'small' (Latin *paucus*). **2.** German (Bavarian): variant of BOCH (see BOCK). **3.** Respelling of Jewish (eastern Ashkenazic) **Pokh**; unexplained.
GIVEN NAMES German 5%. *Frieda, Gerhard, Gerhardt, Kurt, Oskar*.

Poche (767) French: from Old French *puche* 'purse', 'bag' (of Germanic origin), a metonymic occupational name for a maker of bags and purses, or a nickname for someone who was in the habit of carrying a distinctive bag or purse. In the Middle Ages this was a universal personal accessory, as clothing with pockets was unknown. In the U.S. this name occurs most frequently in LA.
GIVEN NAMES French 6%. *Emile* (2), *Henri* (2), *Camille, Curley, Gardy, Leonce, Odette, Simonne*.

Pochop (124) Czech: **1.** nickname meaning 'stooge' or 'dependent'. **2.** nickname for an understanding person.
GIVEN NAME German 4%. *Otto*.

Pociask (155) Polish: from *pociask*, a tool for drawing embers out of a stove, either a nickname or a metonymic occupational name for a servant whose job was to tend the stove.
GIVEN NAMES Polish 6%; German 4%. *Bogdan, Miroslaw; Johann, Otto*.

Pocius (219) Origin unidentified.

Pock (128) German: **1.** (Bavaria, Austria): variant of BOCK. **2.** (**Böck**; Bavaria): variant of BECK ('baker'). **3.** North German: probably nickname for a short man, from Low German *pōk* 'young child', 'dwarf'.

Pocklington (119) English: habitational name from a place in Humberside called Pocklington, named as 'the estate (Old English *tūn*) associated with (Old English *-ing-*) (a man called) *Pocela*'.

Pocock (463) English: variant of PEACOCK.

Podany (212) Czech (**Podaný**) and Slovak (**Poddaný**): **1.** nickname from the adjective *podaný* 'reaching out', 'offering a helping hand'. **2.** status name from Czech *poddaný* 'retainer', 'serf'.
GIVEN NAME Czech and Slovak 5%. *Vaclav*.

Podbielski (112) Polish: habitational name for someone from a place called Podbielsko in Konin voivodeship.
GIVEN NAMES Polish 10%; German 4%. *Czeslaw* (2), *Bogdan, Kazimierz; Kurt*.

Podd (101) English: nickname from Middle English *pode* 'toad'.

Podell (373) Origin unidentified.

Podesta (327) Italian (especially Genoa and Liguria; **Podestà**): occupational name for a mayor, administrator, or magistrate, *podestà*.
GIVEN NAMES Spanish 7%; Italian 5%. *Carlos* (3), *Julio* (2), *Armando, Augusto, Gabriela, Guillermo, Horacio, Juan, Justino, Mario, Nestor, Silvia; Guido* (2), *Giacomo, Giovanni, Olympia, Quinto*.

Podgorny (117) Polish (**Podgórny**), Ukrainian, and Jewish (from Ukraine): topographic name from *pod* 'under' + *góra* 'hill', 'mountain'. Compare PODGORSKI.
GIVEN NAMES Russian 10%; Polish 6%; Jewish 4%. *Jirina* (2), *Anatoly, Gennady, Leonid, Sergey, Vasily; Bogdan, Jacek, Zygmont; Rakhil*.

Podgorski (397) Polish (**Podgórski**) and Jewish (from Poland): habitational name for someone from places called Podgóra, Podgóry, Podgórki, or Podgorze, or topographic name for someone who lived at the foot of a hill, from *pod* 'under' + *góra* 'hill', 'mountain'.
GIVEN NAMES Polish 11%. *Jozef* (3), *Feliks* (2), *Stanislaw* (2), *Andrzej, Andrzey, Boguslaw, Boleslaw, Kazimierz, Miroslaw, Pawel, Zbigniew*.

Podgurski (165) **1.** Polish and Jewish (from Poland): variant of PODGORSKI. **2.** Jewish (from Belarus): habitational name for someone from Podgurye in Belarus.

Podlaski (71) Polish: habitational name for someone from the district of Podlasie (named with Polish *pod* 'under' + *las* 'wood').
GIVEN NAME Polish 7%. *Casimir*.

Podnar (110) Slovenian respelling of German BODNER.

Podolak (306) Polish: regional name from *podolak* 'Podolian'.

Podoll (190) Polish, Ukrainian and Jewish (American): shortened form of PODOLSKI.

Podolski (209) Polish, Ukrainian, and Jewish (eastern Ashkenazic): regional name for someone from Podolia in Ukraine (Polish *Podole*, Yiddish *podolye*; a region which had a large Jewish population from the Middle Ages up to the Second World War), or a habitational name for someone from any of numerous other regions named Podole.

Podolsky (393) Jewish (eastern Ashkenazic) and Ukrainian: variant spelling of PODOLSKI.
GIVEN NAMES Russian 6%; Jewish 6%. *Galima, Gennady, Grigory, Lubov, Mikhail, Milya, Nonna, Pasha, Svetlana,* *Yevgeny, Yevsey; Gerson, Hyman, Josif, Yakov*.

Podrasky (138) Czech (**Podraský**): topographic name for someone living downhill from a village pond or a dam, literally 'under the dike (or dam)'.

Podraza (271) Polish: nickname or metonymic occupational name from *podraza*, a wedge serving to raise the quern stone in a mill.
GIVEN NAMES Polish 4%. *Bronislaw, Jozef, Stanislawa, Tomasz*.

Podsiadlo (105) Polish: nickname from Polish *podsiadać* 'to supersede' or 'usurp', applied to someone who had engineered the dismissal of someone else from a post, in order to take his place.
GIVEN NAMES Polish 12%. *Andrzej, Feliks, Halina, Janina, Slawomir*.

Podvin (105) Variant of POTVIN.

Poe (7989) English: nickname from Old Norse *pá* 'peacock' (see PEACOCK). This surname is also established in Ireland.
FOREBEARS Poe is a common surname found in the 17th and 18th centuries in VA and SC. The ancestors of the poet Edgar Allan Poe (1809–49) were of Scotch-Irish descent, having emigrated from Ireland to Lancaster Co., PA, in about 1748.

Poehlein (104) German: probably a variant of **Pohley**, a habitational name in Silesia for someone from a place named Poley (also Pohley), from Slavic *polan* 'field dweller'. Misinterpretation of the etymology of the surname makes it sound like a German name ending with the diminutive suffix *-lein*.

Poehler (366) German (Westphalian) (also **Pöhler**): topographic name for someone who lived by a muddy pool, from an agent noun derived from Middle Low German *pōl* '(muddy) pool'.
GIVEN NAMES German 6%. *Alfons, Dieter, Horst, Juergen, Otto*.

Poehlman (220) German: see POEHLMANN.

Poehlmann (115) North German: topographic name for someone who lived by a muddy pool, from Middle Low German *pōl* '(muddy) pool' (see POEHLER).
GIVEN NAMES German 13%. *Kurt* (3), *Helmut, Otto*.

Poehls (153) North German (also **Pöhls**): patronymic from a Holstein form of the personal name PAUL.

Poel (132) **1.** Dutch: shortened form of VANDERPOEL, a topographic name for someone living by a muddy pool, from Middle Low German *pōl* '(muddy) pool'. **2.** English: variant of PAUL or POWELL.

Poelker (104) German (also **Pölker**): habitational name for someone from Polke or Polkau in Silesia.

Poellnitz (116) German (also **Pöllnitz**): habitational name from a place called Pöllnitz, in former West Prussia.

Poelman (118) Dutch and North German: habitational name for someone who lived by a pool, from Middle Low German *pōl* '(muddy) pool' + *man* 'man'.

Poelstra (104) Frisian: habitational name for someone living by a muddy pool, from an agent noun based on Middle Low German *pōl* '(muddy) pool'.

Poeppelman (136) German (**Pöppelmann**): from a pet form of the personal name *Poppo* (originally a nursery word) + *man* 'man'.
GIVEN NAMES German 5%. *Aloys* (2), *Kurt*.

Poepping (137) **1.** German (**Pöpping**): patronymic from BOPP. **2.** German (also **Pöpping**): derivative of *Poppo* (see POEPPELMAN).

Poer (253) Perhaps from Dutch **Van Poer**, which Debrabandere suggests is probably a hypercorrection of **Van Poeyer**, a habitational name for someone from Poederlee, the spelling being a reflection of the local pronunciation of the place name.

Poertner (149) North German (also **Pörtner**): occupational name for the gatekeeper of a walled town or city, or the doorkeeper in a great house, castle, or monastery, Middle Low German *portenere*. Compare FORTNER, PORTER.
GIVEN NAMES German 5%. *Erna, Siegfried*.

Poeschel (164) German (Bavarian) (also **Pöschel**): variant spelling of POESCHL.

Poeschl (195) German (Bavarian) (also **Pöschl**): from a pet form of the personal name PETER.
GIVEN NAMES French 4%; German 4%. *Andre; Alois* (2), *Hermann, Ilse*.

Poet (169) Scottish (formerly common in Fife): of uncertain origin, probably a variant of PATE.

Pofahl (178) German (of Slavic origin): variant of PUFAHL.

Poff (1823) Variant spelling of German **Paff** (see PFAFF).

Poffenbarger (169) Variant of German POFFENBERGER.

Poffenberger (459) Americanized form of German **Pfaffenberger**, a habitational name for someone from any of several places in southern Germany called Pfaffenberg (see PFAFF + BERG).

Pogany (120) Hungarian (**Pogány**): nickname for a non-Christian or a foreigner, from the vocabulary word *pogány* 'pagan'.
GIVEN NAMES Hungarian 13%. *Miklos* (2), *Andras, Arpad, Istvan, Lorant*.

Pogge (104) North German: nickname from Low German *pogge* 'frog'.
GIVEN NAMES German 7%. *Hans* (2), *Franz, Horst*.

Poggi (379) Italian (especially Liguria and Tuscany): habitational name from any of the numerous places named or named with Poggi, from *poggio* 'small hill'.
GIVEN NAMES Italian 12%; Spanish 7%. *Amleto* (2), *Edgardo* (2), *Mario* (2), *Alberto, Alvaro, Carlo, Libero, Oreste, Primo, Silvio, Stefano, Vito; Angel, Javier, Jorge, Jose, Juan, Julio, Luis*.

Poggioli (131) Italian: topographic name from a diminutive of *poggio* 'small hill' (see POGGI), or a habitational name from places named Poggiolo.
GIVEN NAMES Italian 9%. *Carlo, Gino, Livio, Sante*.

Pogoda (113) Polish: nickname from *pogoda* 'weather', 'good weather', also 'serenity', applied to a person with a serene temperament.
GIVEN NAMES Polish 14%. *Genowefa, Jerzy, Krzysztof, Wieslaw, Zuzanna*.

Pogorzelski (259) Polish: habitational name for someone from any of various places called Pogorzel, Pogorzela, or Pogorzele, named with *pogorzeć* 'to burn down'. This is also found as a nickname for someone who had lost his property in a fire.
GIVEN NAMES Polish 15%. *Krzysztof* (2), *Andrzej, Beata, Czeslaw, Eugeniusz, Grzegorz, Ireneusz, Jacek, Janusz, Jozef, Kazimierz, Walenty*.

Pogue (2781) Irish (northeastern Ulster): reduced form of Scottish POLLOCK.

Poh (164) German (Palatine): from a dialect word for standard German *Pfau* 'peacock', a nickname for a vain person or for someone with a strutting gait.

Pohl (2667) German: **1.** topographic name from Middle Low German *pōl* '(muddy) pool' (Low German *Pohl*). **2.** (**Pöhl**): habitational name for someone from the island of Poel, near Wismar. **3.** Variant of PAUL. **4.** Eastern German, Dutch, and Jewish (Ashkenazic): ethnic name for a Polish speaker or someone with some other connection with Poland, from German *Pole*, Dutch *Pool* 'Pole'.
GIVEN NAMES German 6%. *Kurt* (4), *Erwin* (3), *Otto* (3), *Wolfgang* (3), *Gerhard* (2), *Gunther* (2), *Hans* (2), *Horst* (2), *Manfred* (2), *Oskar* (2), *Claus, Dietrich*.

Pohle (344) **1.** Dutch and Jewish (Ashkenazic): variant of POHL 4. **2.** German: variant of POHL 1. **3.** Eastern German: habitational name from Pohla near Bautzen.
GIVEN NAMES German 8%. *Gunther, Hans, Heinz, Hellmut, Irmgard, Johannes, Reiner, Siegfried, Uwe*.

Pohler (131) North German (**Pöhler**): **1.** topographic name for someone living by a muddy pool, or habitational name for someone from Pohla near Bautzen (see POHL, POHLE). **2.** from a reduced and altered pet form of a personal name formed with Old High German *bald* 'bold', 'brave'.
GIVEN NAMES German 6%; Dutch 4%; French 4%. *Fritz; Gerrit* (3); *Vernice*.

Pohlman (1589) **1.** Jewish (Ashkenazic): variant of POHL 4. **2.** Altered spelling of POHLMANN.

Pohlmann (450) **1.** North German: variant of POHL. **2.** Altered spelling of **Pöhlmann** (see POEHLMANN).

GIVEN NAMES German 9%. *Hans* (3), *Aloysius, Erwin, Frieda, Fritz, Gerd, Gerhard, Guenter, Guenther, Horst, Juergen, Klaus*.

Poindexter (3485) English: nickname from Old French *poing destre* 'right fist'. This name is particularly associated with Huguenot refugees who fled from France to England, and from there to VA.

Poinsett (195) Altered spelling of French **Poinset**, from a derivative of Old French *poinson* 'pointed instrument', hence a metonymic occupational name for a maker or user of any pointed instrument.
FOREBEARS The *poinsettia* takes its name from an American diplomat, Joel Poinsett (1779–1851), who was a keen amateur botanist and who brought the flower back from Mexico, where he was the U.S. ambassador. He was born in Charleston, SC, and was descended from a Huguenot, Peter Poinset, who was born near La Rochelle, France, and settled in Charleston *c*.1700.

Point (236) English and French: probably an altered form of French **Pons**, a habitational name from places so named in Bourgogne and Franche-Comté.

Pointer (2035) **1.** English (Norfolk): occupational name from Middle English *pointer* 'point maker', an agent derivative of *point*, a term denoting a lace or cord used to fasten together doublet and hose (Old French *pointe* 'point', 'sharp end'). Reaney suggests that in some cases Pointer may have been an occupational name for a tiler or slater whose job was to point the tiles, i.e. render them with mortar where they overlapped. **2.** Possibly an altered form of German **Pointner**, a variant of BAINTER.

Pointon (153) English (Midlands): habitational name from Pointon in Lincolnshire, Poynton in Cheshire, or Poynton Green in Shropshire. The first is named from Old English *Pohhingtūn* 'settlement (Old English *tūn*) associated with *Pohha*', a byname apparently meaning 'bag'; the others have as the first element the Old English personal names *Pofa* and *Pēofa* respectively.

Points (380) English (of Norman origin): **1.** from the medieval personal name *Ponc(h)e, Pons* (see PONCE). **2.** habitational name from Ponts in La Manche and Seine-Maritime, Normandy, from Latin *pontes* 'bridges' (see PONT). **3.** nickname for a fop or dandy, from *points* 'laces for hose' (see POINTER 1).

Poire (103) French (**Poiré**): regional variant of **Poré**, a metonymic occupational name for a grower or seller of leeks, from Old French *porreau* 'leek' (Latin *porrum*).
GIVEN NAMES French 8%. *Gabrielle, Gilles, Laurent*.

Poirier (3807) French: topographic name for someone who lived by a pear tree, *poirier*, from Old French *perier*.
FOREBEARS A Poirier from Paris is recorded in Quebec City in 1655 with the secondary surname **Bellepoire**. Other associated sec-

ondary surnames include LAJEUNESSE, LANGEVIN, LAFLEUR.

GIVEN NAMES French 12%. *Armand* (14), *Marcel* (10), *Andre* (9), *Normand* (6), *Pierre* (6), *Emile* (5), *Laurent* (5), *Cecile* (4), *Jacques* (4), *Michel* (4), *Raoul* (4), *Gilles* (3).

Poirot (154) French: metonymic occupational name for a grower or seller of pears, from a diminutive of *poire* 'pear'.

GIVEN NAMES French 7%. *Andre, Hercule, Marcel.*

Poirrier (195) Variant of POIRIER.

GIVEN NAMES French 13%. *Cecile* (2), *Marcel* (2), *Remy* (2), *Achille, Maxime, Monique, Ulysse.*

Poissant (264) French: variant of **Poisant**, a nickname for a powerful robust individual, from Old French *poisant* 'strong', 'powerful', 'vigorous'.

FOREBEARS A Poissant from the Saintonge region of France is documented in Chambly, Quebec, around 1699, with the secondary surname *LaSaline.* PASCHAL is also recorded secondary surnames.

GIVEN NAMES French 8%. *Cecile, Gilles, Herve, Jacques, Laurent, Lilianne.*

Poisson (733) **1.** French: from *poisson* 'fish', a metonymic occupational name for a fisherman or fish seller or a nickname for someone supposedly resembling a fish. In North America this name is sometimes translated as Fisher. **2.** North American variant of POISSANT.

FOREBEARS A Poisson from the Perche region of France is documented in Quebec City in 1649. The secondary surname **Gentilly** is associated.

GIVEN NAMES French 18%. *Emile* (5), *Normand* (3), *Pierre* (3), *Alain* (2), *Andre* (2), *Armand* (2), *Fernand* (2), *Gilles* (2), *Michel* (2), *Alphonse, Arsene, Auguste.*

Poist (112) Origin unidentified.

Poitevint (114) Variant of POTVIN.

Poitier (108) Evidently an altered spelling of French POTHIER.

Poitra (179) Apparently an altered form of French POITRAS; it occurs chiefly in ND.

GIVEN NAME French 4%. *Pierre.*

Poitras (640) French: unexplained.

FOREBEARS Jean Poitras, born in Cugand, Brittany, came to Canada in about 1664. A Poitras from the Poitou region of France (possibly the same person) is documented in Quebec City in 1664, with the secondary surname Tourenne.

GIVEN NAMES French 11%. *Armand* (2), *Gilles* (2), *Jacques* (2), *Jean-Maurice* (2), *Lucien* (2), *Andre, Edouard, Emile, Etienne, Euclide, Gaston, Jean Pierre.*

Pojar (101) Americanized spelling of Slovenian **Požar**, a topographic name for someone who lived on a piece of ground that had recently been cleared by fire, from *požar* 'fire'.

Poje (129) **1.** German: variant spelling of **Boie** (see BOYE). **2.** Croatian and Slovenian: unexplained.

GIVEN NAMES German 4%. *Herta, Hertha.*

Pokora (110) Polish: nickname for a humble or self-effacing person, from *pokora* 'humility'.

GIVEN NAMES Polish 12%; German 5%. *Izabela* (2), *Fryderyk, Jadwiga, Maciej; Ilse.*

Pokorney (238) Altered spelling of POKORNY.

Pokorny (1148) Czech and Slovak (**Pokorný**), Polish, and Jewish (from Poland and Bohemia): from Czech *pokorný*, Polish *pokorny* 'humble', 'meek', a nickname for a humble or self-effacing person. This name is also found in eastern Germany.

Pokorski (226) Polish: **1.** nickname for a unassertive or humble man, from Polish *pokora* 'submission' + *-ski*, suffix of surnames. Compare POKORNY. **2.** habitational name from Pokorze in Skierniewice voivodeship.

Pokrywka (104) Polish: nickname from *pokrywka* 'cover', 'lid'.

GIVEN NAME Polish 6%. *Lucyna.*

Pol (264) **1.** Catalan and Occitan: from the personal name *Pol*, equivalent to PAUL. **2.** Dutch: topographic name for someone who lived by a grassy mound, from Middle Dutch *pol* 'tussock'. **3.** German and Jewish (Ashkenazic): variant of POHL. **4.** Polish: ethnic name or regional name meaning 'Pole' (see POLAK). **5.** Polish: from a shortened or reduced form of any of several personal name containing the syllable *-pol-*, e.g. *Polikarp, Hipolit,* or *Leopold.*

GIVEN NAMES Spanish 18%. *Guillermo* (3), *Manuel* (3), *Jose* (2), *Juan* (2), *Rafael* (2), *Abelardo, Adolfo, Ana, Angel, Beatriz, Fernando, Gilberto.*

Pola (125) **1.** Asturian-Leonese: habitational name from any of the places named Pola or La Pola in Asturies, from a variant of *puebla* 'settlement' (Latin *popula*). **2.** Catalan: habitational name from any of the places named Pola, La Pola, or Santa Pola in Catalonia, Valencia, and the Balearic Islands, or from the female personal name *Pola* (Latin *Paula*). **3.** Italian: habitational name from the city of Pola in Istria (Croatia), Croatian name *Pula.*

GIVEN NAMES Spanish 16%; Italian 12%. *Mario* (3), *Angel* (2), *Jorge* (2), *Juan* (2), *Orlando* (2), *Edgardo, Joaquin, Manuel, Natividad, Rosario, Ruben; Carlo* (3), *Dante, Ezio, Filippo, Nino.*

Polacek (462) Czech (**Poláček**) and Jewish (from Bohemia): from a diminutive of POLAK.

Polachek (168) **1.** Jewish (eastern Ashkenazic): altered spelling of Polish *polaczek,* a diminutive of POLAK. **2.** Americanized spelling of Czech **Poláček** (see POLACEK).

Polack (235) German and Jewish (Ashkenazic): altered spelling of POLAK.

GIVEN NAMES German 5%. *Helmuth, Otto.*

Polak (1073) Polish, Czech (**Polák**), and Jewish (Ashkenazic): ethnic name for someone from Poland. In the case of the Ashkenazic name, the reference is to a Jew from Poland. The name of the country (Polish *Polska*) derives from a Slavic element *pole* 'open country', 'cleared land'. This surname is found throughout central and eastern Europe.

GIVEN NAMES Polish 6%. *Miroslaw* (3), *Zbigniew* (3), *Boguslawa* (2), *Dorota* (2), *Jacek* (2), *Andrzej, Bogdan, Eugeniusz, Grzegorz, Irena, Jerzy, Jozef.*

Polakoff (177) Russian and Jewish (eastern Ashkenazic): alternative spelling of POLYAKOV.

GIVEN NAMES Jewish 8%. *Herschel* (3), *Hyman.*

Polakowski (251) **1.** Polish: habitational name for someone from Polaki in Sieradz voivodeship, or Polakowa in Belarus. **2.** Polish and Jewish (Ashkenazic): from POLAK 'Pole', with the addition of the Polish adjectival ending *-owski* (in this case with a patronymic function).

GIVEN NAMES Polish 5%. *Jerzy, Jozef, Ryszard, Tadeusz.*

Polan (389) **1.** Irish: variant of POLIN. **2.** Jewish (eastern Ashkenazic): habitational name from Polyany, in Belarus and Ukraine, named with Slavic *polyany* 'glad', 'clearing'.

Polanco (1528) Spanish: habitational name from Polanco in Santander province.

GIVEN NAMES Spanish 51%. *Jose* (54), *Juan* (28), *Ana* (17), *Carlos* (16), *Manuel* (16), *Luis* (14), *Pedro* (13), *Francisco* (12), *Juana* (12), *Ramon* (10), *Rafael* (9), *Mercedes* (7).

Poland (2964) **1.** German and English: from Middle High German *Polan* 'Poland' + inorganic *-d,* a name denoting a Pole or someone with Polish connections. **2.** Irish (County Offaly, also Armagh and Down): variant of POLIN. Compare POLAN. **3.** In New England, this is sometimes an Americanized spelling of French POULIN.

Polanski (267) **1.** Polish (**Polański**): ethnic name for a Pole, or more specifically for a descendant of the *Polanie,* one of the original Polish tribes. **2.** Polish, Jewish (eastern Ashkenazic), Ukrainian, and Belorussian: topographic name for someone who lived in a clearing, from *polana* 'glade', 'clearing' (a derivative of *pole* 'field'), or a habitational name for someone from placed called Polana, Polanka, Polany, or any of various other places named with *polana.*

GIVEN NAMES Polish 9%. *Stanislaw* (2), *Halina, Jurek, Kazimierz, Leszek, Wladyslaw.*

Polansky (843) **1.** Czech and Slovak (**Polanský**): ethnic or regional name for a

Pole (see POLANSKI). **2.** Jewish (Ashkenazic), Ukrainian, and Belorussian: variant spelling of POLANSKI.

Polasek (448) Czech and Slovak (**Polášek**): diminutive of **Polák** (see POLAK 'Pole').

Polaski (418) Polish: variant of PULASKI.

Polasky (152) German or Jewish spelling of Polish PULASKI.

Polcari (149) Italian (Campania): possibly a habitational name from a place called Policari.

GIVEN NAMES Italian 13%. *Angelo* (3), *Dante* (2), *Carmine*.

Polce (130) **1.** Italian: from a variant of *pulce* 'plea'. **2.** Perhaps an altered spelling of German **Polz**, a metonymic occupational name for a maker of bolts, from Middle High German *polz*, *bolz* 'bolt'. Compare POLZER.

GIVEN NAMES Italian 16%. *Agostino, Cesare, Delio, Enrico, Pietro, Rocco, Veto.*

Polcyn (248) Polish: variant of **Połczyn**, habitational name from Połczyn Zdrój in Koszalin voivodeship, named with Old Slavic *polk* 'regiment'.

Polczynski (128) Polish: habitational name from Polczyno in Gdańsk province or Połczyn Zdrój in Koszalin province.

Pole (215) **1.** English (Leicestershire): variant of PAUL or POOL. **2.** Americanized spelling of German POHLE or POHL.

Polega (105) Polish: nickname for a reliable person, from a derivative of *polegać* 'to depend upon' 'rely upon'.

Polek (154) Polish: from a pet form of the personal name *Pol* (see POL 5).

Polen (772) **1.** German and Dutch: ethnic name for a Pole or nickname for someone with some other connection with Poland, from *Polen* 'Poland'. **2.** Possibly also a variant of Irish POLIN.

Polenz (112) German: habitational name from any of three places in Saxony named Polenz, which may derive from Slavic *polje, poljana* 'plain'.

GIVEN NAMES German 8%. *Erwin, Hermann, Orlo.*

Poles (123) English: variant of POLE. It is not clear why there is a significant subset of Italian forenames with this surname.

GIVEN NAMES Italian 7%. *Angelo, Livio, Primo, Santo.*

Poleski (123) **1.** Polish, Jewish (eastern Ashkenazic), Ukrainian, and Belorussian: regional name for someone from Polesie, a region covering parts of modern Belarus, Poland, and Ukraine. **2.** Polish: habitational name for someone from any of various places called Polesie, named with a Slavic word meaning 'forest glade' or 'cleared forest land'.

Poletti (289) Italian: from a pet form of the personal name POLO.

GIVEN NAMES Italian 18%. *Mario* (5), *Alfredo* (2), *Adolfo, Aldo, Antonio, Elio, Gino, Giuseppe, Guido, Marcello, Olindo, Orlando, Silvio.*

Poley (432) **1.** French: variant of *Polet, Paulet*, pet forms of PAUL. **2.** German: variant of BOLEY. **3.** Jewish (from Belarus): variant of POLICH. **4.** East German: habitational name from a place so named near Frankfurt an der Oder.

Polgar (181) Hungarian (**Polgár**) and Jewish (from Hungary): **1.** status name for a freeman of a town, as a Hungarian name especially one who was a member of its governing council. Compare BURGER. **2.** status name for a free peasant or smallholder.

GIVEN NAMES Hungarian 7%. *Dezso, Geza, Jeno, Tibor, Zoltan.*

Polhamus (288) Dutch: variant of POLHEMUS.

Polhemus (478) Dutch: Latinized form of **Polheim**, a habitational name from a place in southern Germany or Switzerland.

FOREBEARS Johann Theodore Polheim, otherwise known as Johannes Theodorus Polhemus, was a 17th-century Lutheran minister, probably of German-Swiss origin. His earliest pastorates were probably in the Palatinate. In the early 1630s he was pastor at Meppel in the province of Overijssel, Netherlands, then from 1637 to 1654 he was a pastor in the Dutch settlement in Brazil. When that settlement failed in 1656, he came to Amersfoort, New Netherland, as its first Dominie.

Polhill (116) Origin uncertain. Probably English, from any of several places in England called Pole Hill.

Poli (533) **1.** Italian: patronymic or plural form of POLO. **2.** French: variant of POLLY. **3.** Hungarian (**Póli**): variant of *Pólyi*, habitational name for someone from a place called Póly in Abaúj county.

GIVEN NAMES Italian 17%. *Salvatore* (3), *Vito* (3), *Angelo* (2), *Antonio* (2), *Carlo* (2), *Guido* (2), *Aldo, Attilio, Corrado, Damiano, Dante, Domenic.*

Poliak (106) Jewish (eastern Ashkenazic): variant of POLAK.

GIVEN NAMES Jewish 6%; Russian 5%. *Inna, Jakov; Mikhail, Oleg, Sofiya, Vladimir.*

Policastro (394) Italian: habitational name from Petilia Policastro in Crotone province, Policastro Bussentino, a district of Santa Marina in Salerno, or Policastro del Golfo in Salerno province.

GIVEN NAMES Italian 12%. *Rocco* (3), *Antonio* (2), *Sal* (2), *Angelo, Attilio, Carmela, Cosimo, Filomena, Pasquale, Philomena, Vito.*

Police (125) Americanized form of Slovenian **Polič** or Croatian **Polić** (see POLICH).

Polich (452) **1.** Slovenian (**Polič**) and Croatian (**Polić**): from *pol* 'half', in any of various possible senses: most probably a status name for a peasant who held half the standard measure of land (i.e. half a 'grunt'), or for a tenant of a farm who had to pay half of its produce in rent. It may

also be from *polič*, a kind of jug-like drinking vessel containing half the standard measure of cubic capacity. **2.** Croatian (**Polić**): on the Dalmatian coast, a pet form of the personal name *Polo*, a pet form of PAUL under Venetian influence. **3.** Slovenian (**Polič**): perhaps a metronymic from a short form of the personal name *Polona*, vernacular form of *Apolonija*, Latin *Apollonia*. **4.** German and Jewish (Ashkenazic): occupational name for a distiller, from an eastern Slavic word meaning 'to burn' (Russian *palit*, Ukrainian *palyty*).

Polick (104) Americanized spelling of POLICH.

Policky (102) Jewish (from Bohemia) and Czech (**Polický**): habitational name from the town Police (German Politz) in Bohemia.

Polidori (151) Italian: patronymic or plural form of POLIDORO.

GIVEN NAMES Italian 25%. *Carlo* (2), *Quinto* (2), *Adamo, Domenico, Edo, Fausto, Gino, Giuseppe, Luigi, Maddalena, Nicola, Nino.*

Polidoro (176) Italian: from the personal name *Polidoro*, from Greek *Polydōros*, a compound of *polys* 'many' + *dōron* 'gift'.

GIVEN NAMES Italian 24%. *Mario* (4), *Carmine* (2), *Aladino, Angelo, Domenica, Gianni, Gino, Giuseppe, Guido, Marco, Pompeo, Rocco, Sal.*

Polifka (108) Czech (**Polífka**): variant of **Polívka** (see POLIVKA).

Polimeni (150) Italian: patronymic from the personal name *Polimeno*, from medieval Greek *polimenos*, variant of *poulimenos* 'sold' (classical Greek *pōlēmenos*). This may have denoted someone who had been sold into slavery as a child, or been given as an omen name intended to ward off such a fate.

GIVEN NAMES Italian 22%. *Rocco* (3), *Gino* (2), *Antonio, Cosimo, Enzo, Giulio, Lucrezia.*

Polin (369) **1.** French: from a pet form of the personal name PAUL. **2.** Irish (Counties Armagh and Down): Anglicized form of Gaelic **Mac Póilín**, patronymic from a personal name formed from a pet form of *Pól* (PAUL). **3.** Jewish (eastern Ashkenazic): regional name for someone from Poland, from a slavicized form of German *Polen* 'Poland'. **4.** Variant of German BOLLING.

GIVEN NAME Jewish 4%. *Hyman.*

Poling (2785) Altered form of BOLLING, possibly also of BOLLINGER or POLLINGER.

Polino (140) **1.** Italian: from a pet form of the personal name POLO. **2.** Spanish: respelling of PAULINO. This name is now well established in Mexico.

GIVEN NAMES Italian 16%; Spanish 9%. *Cosimo* (3), *Rocco* (3), *Amleto, Leonardo, Lucio; Jose* (2), *Angel, Asencion, Celso, Jesus, Vinicio.*

Polinski (291) Polish (**Poliński**): habitational name from Polinowo in Piła voivodeship or Polinów in Biała Podlaska voivodeship.

GIVEN NAMES Polish 4%. *Janusz, Jerzy, Slawek, Slawomir.*

Polinsky (383) Variant of Polish **Poliński** (see POLINSKI).

Poliquin (270) Variant of French PELOQUIN.

FOREBEARS A bearer of this name from Brittany is documented in Beaupré, Quebec, in 1667.

GIVEN NAMES French 20%. *Normand* (3), *Cecile* (2), *Andre, Armand, Camille, Colette, Edouard, Emilien, Jean-Pierre, Luc, Lucien, Marcel.*

Polis (302) Dutch and German: from an altered form of the personal name *Paulus* (see PAUL).

Polish (102) Jewish (American): English translation of Polish POLSKI, POLAK, or a similar name.

GIVEN NAME Jewish 4%. *Ari.*

Polit (119) **1.** Catalan and Polish: from a short form of the personal name *Hipolit* (see French HYPOLITE). **2.** English: variant of POLLITT.

GIVEN NAMES Spanish 23%. *Carlos* (5), *Jose* (3), *Mario* (2), *Andres, Gustavo, Jaime, Javier, Juan, Luis, Manuel, Marta, Oswaldo.*

Politano (254) Southern Italian: habitational name for someone from Polito in Cosenza province, from an adjectival derivative of the place name.

GIVEN NAMES Italian 18%. *Angelo* (3), *Vito* (3), *Cosmo* (2), *Domenic* (2), *Amedeo, Carmine, Guido, Remo.*

Polite (736) French: from a short form of the personal name *Hippolyte* (see HYPOLITE).

Polites (163) Greek: variant spelling of POLITIS.

Politi (263) **1.** Southern Italian (mainly Calabria and eastern Sicily) and Jewish (from Italy): **2.** variant of POLITO. This is also found as a Jewish surname. **3.** habitational name from Polito in Cosenza.

GIVEN NAMES Italian 12%. *Sal* (3), *Cosimo, Elio, Enzo, Gaetano, Mauro, Paolo, Vito.*

Politis (269) Greek: **1.** from a short form of the personal name *Hippolytos* (composed of the elements *hippos* 'horse' + *luein* 'loose'). This was the name of various minor early Christian saints as well as a figure in classical mythology (a young man who rejected the incestuous advances of his stepmother Phaedra). **2.** shortened form of medieval Greek **Konstantinopolitēs**, a habitational name for someone from Constantinople. Greek *politēs* literally means 'citizen', 'city dweller'; in the Levant the city in question was assumed (in the absence of any other specification) to be Constantinople.

GIVEN NAMES Greek 21%. *Christos* (3), *Constantine* (3), *Anastasios* (2), *Demetrios* (2), *Andreas, Apostolos, Demetre, Dimitrios, Dimitris, Ioannis, Kalliope, Konstantinos.*

Polito (1379) Southern Italian (especially Naples): **1.** reduced form of IPPOLITO. Compare French HYPOLITE, Greek POLITIS. **2.** from *Politēs*, a shortened form of medieval Greek *Konstantinopolitēs*, an ethnic name for someone from Constantinople.

GIVEN NAMES Italian 19%; Spanish 4%. *Angelo* (8), *Salvatore* (7), *Carmine* (6), *Antonio* (5), *Sal* (4), *Francisco* (3), *Carlo* (2), *Carmelo* (2), *Marco* (2), *Mariano* (2), *Natale* (2), *Santo* (2), *Emilio, Filippo, Gerardo; Alfonso, Diego, Elpidio, Felipe, Juanita, Luisa, Natividad, Osvaldo.*

Politte (415) Southern French: from a reduced form of the personal name *Hippolyte* (see POLITIS).

Politz (203) German: **1.** habitational name from any of several places so named, of Slavic origin. **2.** from a pet form of the personal name *Hippolitus*. Compare French HYPOLITE, Greek POLITIS.

Politzer (121) German: habitational name for someone from any of several places called POLITZ.

Polivka (336) Czech (**Polívka**): probably from *polevka* 'soup', 'broth', 'stock', perhaps a metonymic occupational name for a cook.

Polizzi (778) Sicilian: habitational name from Polizzi Generosa in Palermo, Sicily.

GIVEN NAMES Italian 17%. *Salvatore* (8), *Vito* (5), *Sal* (4), *Angelo* (3), *Antonino* (3), *Santo* (3), *Gasper* (2), *Giovanna* (2), *Giuseppe* (2), *Lorenzo* (2), *Umberto* (2), *Vincenzo* (2).

Polk (7607) **1.** Scottish: reduced form of POLLOCK. **2.** German (of Slavic origin): from an altered pet form of the Slavic personal name *Boleslav*, composed of the elements *bole* 'great', 'large' + *slav* 'glory'. This name was a favorite during the Middle Ages among the gentry class in Silesia. **3.** German: ethnic name for a Pole (see POLAK).

FOREBEARS The American president James Polk (1795–1849) was of Scots-Irish descent. His family reached America from Ireland, where their name had been contracted from Pollok to Polk. The first American bearer, Robert Bruce Polk, emigrated from Ireland to MD in the late 17th century.

Polka (244) **1.** German (of Slavic origin): variant of POLK 2 and 3. **2.** Czech, Slovak, and Polish: variant (feminine form) of POLAK. **3.** Perhaps also a derivative of *polka*, name of a lively dance that originated as a Polish folk dance. **4.** Polish: from a derivative of the female personal name *Apolonia*.

Polkinghorn (127) Cornish: habitational name from a place in the parish of Gwinear, recorded in 1316 as *Polkenhoern*, from Cornish *pol* 'pool', 'pond' + the Old Cornish personal name *Kenhoern* (composed of elements meaning 'hound' + 'iron').

Polkinghorne (135) Cornish: variant spelling of POLKINGHORN.

Polkowski (157) Polish and Jewish (from Poland): habitational name for someone from Polkowo in Siedlce and Suwałki voivodeships or Polków in Sieradz voivodeship.

GIVEN NAMES Polish 17%. *Casimir, Czeslaw, Henryk, Jaroslaw, Jerzy, Kazimierz, Malgorzata, Mieczyslaw, Ryszard, Waclaw.*

Poll (660) **1.** Dutch: variant spelling of POL. **2.** English (Norfolk): variant of PAUL or POOL. **3.** German (also **Pöll**): from a short form of a personal name composed with Old High German *bald* 'bold', 'brave'. **4.** North German: variant of POHL 2. **5.** South German form of BOLL.

GIVEN NAMES German 4%. *Ernst* (2), *Heinz* (2), *Gerda, Gerhard, Kurt, Otto.*

Pollack (4352) Jewish (Ashkenazic): variant of spelling of POLAK.

GIVEN NAMES Jewish 4%. *Hyman* (7), *Miriam* (4), *Chaya* (3), *Meyer* (3), *Moshe* (3), *Sol* (3), *Ari* (2), *Yaacov* (2), *Yoel* (2), *Avrohom, Dov, Faigy.*

Pollak (1433) Jewish (Ashkenazic): variant spelling of POLAK.

GIVEN NAMES Jewish 8%; German 4%. *Shmuel* (4), *Yaakov* (4), *Yehuda* (3), *Chaim* (2), *Moshe* (2), *Yitzchok* (2), *Arie, Aron, Avi, Avrom, Chaskel, Chavie; Kurt* (4), *Otto* (3), *Alois* (2), *Egon, Frieda, Hans, Heinz, Helmut, Ignatz, Ilse, Klaus, Manfred.*

Pollan (305) German (of Slavic origin): from *polan* 'dweller in a field' (from Slavic *polje* 'plain', 'field'), probably a nickname for a peasant as against a villager or townsman, which then came to denote someone from Poland.

Polland (143) **1.** German (of Slavic origin): variant of POLLAN, with excrescent -*d*. **2.** Scottish: unexplained.

Pollara (108) Italian: **1.** habitational name from a place named Pollara, possibly associated with poultry rearing. **2.** variant of **Pollarà**, a variant of **Pullarà**, an occupational name for a horse breeder, from modern Greek *poularas*, from Greek *poulari* 'colt'. **3.** from Sicilian *puddara* 'pimpernel'.

GIVEN NAMES Italian 12%. *Fabrizio, Luigi, Salvatore.*

Pollard (11580) English: **1.** nickname for a person with a large or unusually shaped head, from Middle English *poll* 'head' (Middle Low German *polle* '(top of the) head') + the pejorative suffix -*ard*. The term *pollard* in the sense denoting an animal that has had its horns lopped is not recorded before the 16th century, and as applied to a tree the word is not recorded until the 17th century; so both these senses are almost certainly too late to have contributed to the surname. **2.** pejorative derivative of the personal name PAUL. The surname has been established in Ireland since the 14th century.

Pollari (123) Finnish: probably from a place name or farm name of Germanic (Swedish or German) origin. This name is found chiefly in central–western Finland, where there are old place names like *Buldar* and *Pollarby* and old farm names like *Pollar* and *Pollare*, all thought to be of Germanic origin.
GIVEN NAMES Finnish 9%. *Arvo, Kaarlo, Tarja, Timo, Wiljo.*

Pollen (154) **1.** Norwegian: habitational name from any of several farmsteads, so named from Old Norse *pollr* 'small bay', 'pond'. **2.** English: possibly a respelling of Irish **Polan, Polin**, an Anglicized form of Gaelic **Mac Póilín** 'son of *Pólín*', from a pet form of *Pól*, Gaelic form of PAUL.

Poller (151) **1.** German (**Pöller**; Bavaria, Austria): variant of BOLLER. **2.** Dutch: from an agent derivative of Middle Dutch *polen, peulen* 'to peel', presumably an occupational name of some sort. **3.** Jewish (Ashkenazic): unexplained.
GIVEN NAMES Jewish 5%; German 4%. *Shmuel* (2), *Sol; Armin.*

Pollert (115) German: variant of POLLER.
GIVEN NAME German 4%. *Markus.*

Pollet (241) **1.** French: from a pet form of the personal name PAUL. **2.** Catalan: probably from a diminutive of *poll* 'chicken'.
GIVEN NAMES French 9%. *Guillaume* (3), *Clelie, Pierre.*

Pollett (208) Probably an altered spelling of POLLET or POLLITT.

Polletta (113) Italian: perhaps from a feminine form of the personal name *Poletto* (see POLETTI).
GIVEN NAMES Italian 32%. *Antonio* (2), *Vito* (2), *Amedeo, Angelo, Carmine, Donato, Gino, Luigi, Maddalena, Pasquale, Raffaele, Rocco.*

Polley (1737) **1.** English (Essex): variant spelling of POLLY. **2.** French: variant of POLLET. **3.** Altered spelling of French POLLY. **4.** Variant spelling of POLEY.

Polli (120) Italian: **1.** from *pollo* 'chicken', from Latin *pullus* 'young animal', applied perhaps as a nickname or a metonymic occupational name for a poultry keeper. **2.** variant of POLI (see POLO).
GIVEN NAMES Italian 13%. *Angelo* (2), *Attilio, Dario, Ettore.*

Pollick (394) Scottish: variant of POLLOCK.

Pollina (253) **1.** Italian: possibly a topographic from a diminutive of *polla* 'vein of water', 'spring'. **2.** Catalan: nickname from *pollina* 'young mare'.
GIVEN NAMES Italian 9%. *Salvatore* (2), *Vito* (2), *Annamarie, Antonino, Orazio.*

Pollinger (187) South German: **1.** habitational name for someone from any of several places named Polling in Bavaria and Austria. **2.** (**Pöllinger**): habitational name for someone from Pölling in Bavaria.
GIVEN NAMES German 7%. *Heinz, Johann, Nikolaus.*

Pollino (171) **1.** Italian: from a derivative of the personal name *Pollo*, a reduced form of *Apollo* or a variant of POLO. **2.** In some cases possibly Spanish: nickname from *pollino* 'young ass', hence 'fool', although this source appears not to have contributed greatly to the American surname.
GIVEN NAMES Italian 12%. *Angelo* (2), *Antonio* (2), *Francesco, Giuseppe, Salvatore.*

Pollins (105) English: patronymic from the medieval personal name *Pollin*, variant of PAULIN.

Pollio (191) Italian: probably from a variant of the personal name *Pollo* (see POLLINO).
GIVEN NAMES Italian 18%. *Guido* (2), *Salvatore* (2), *Antonio, Edoardo, Giuseppe, Vincenzo, Vito.*

Pollitt (836) English (Lancashire): from the personal name *Pollit*, an English vernacular form of the Greek personal name *Hippolytos*. Compare French HYPOLITE.

Pollman (315) **1.** German (**Pöllmann**): from a short form of a personal name formed with Old High German *bald* 'bold' + *man* 'man'. **2.** North German: variant of POHLMANN 1. **3.** South German variant of BOLLMANN. **4.** English: variant spelling of POLMAN.
GIVEN NAMES German 4%. *Erwin, Gunther, Kurt.*

Pollnow (132) German: unexplained.
GIVEN NAMES German 4%. *Fritz, Guenther.*

Pollock (9468) **1.** Scottish: habitational name from a place in Glasgow, apparently so named from a diminutive of a British cognate of Gaelic *poll* 'pool', 'pit'. The surname is also common in northeastern Ulster. **2.** German: ethnic name for someone from Poland. **3.** Americanized form of Jewish POLAK.

Pollok (172) Variant of Scottish POLLOCK.
GIVEN NAME French 5%. *Marcel.*

Pollom (100) English: variant of PULLUM.

Polly (757) **1.** French and English (of Norman origin): from Old French *poli* 'agreeable', 'polite' (literally 'polished', past participle of Old French *polir*), hence a nickname for a courteous or amiable person (perhaps also sometimes given ironically to a boor). **2.** Altered form of German **Polley**, a habitational name from any of several places so named in Anhalt and Brandenburg.

Polman (131) **1.** Dutch: topographic name for someone who lived by a pool, Dutch *poele*, or a habitational name for someone from a place named with this word. Compare POELMAN. **2.** Altered spelling of German **Pollmann**, a variant of POHL (cognate with 1), or a habitational name for someone from a place named Poll, two examples of which occur in North Rhine-Westphalia. **3.** English: topographic name for someone who lived by a pool, Middle English *pol(e)man*.
GIVEN NAMES German 4%. *Inge, Wolf.*

Polmanteer (111) Most probably a variant of English PARMENTER or French PARMENTIER. Compare PALMATEER.

Polo (692) **1.** Spanish: possibly of the same derivation as 2. **2.** Italian: from the personal name *Polo*, a variant of PAOLO (see PAUL).
GIVEN NAMES Spanish 21%; Italian 7%. *Luis* (7), *Jose* (5), *Ana* (4), *Jorge* (4), *Rafael* (4), *Carlos* (3), *Sergio* (3), *Alberto* (2), *Arturo* (2), *Cesar* (2), *Ernesto* (2), *Guillermo* (2); *Marco* (9), *Angelo* (2), *Guido* (2), *Antonio, Carmine, Cecilio, Delio, Franco, Fulvio, Gino, Gioacchino, Leonardo.*

Polon (105) Spanish (**Polón**) and Finnish: ethnic name for someone from Poland.
GIVEN NAMES French 5%. *Adrien, Camille.*

Polonsky (284) Jewish (from Ukraine and Belorussia): habitational name for someone from any of various places called Polonnoe, Polonka, and Polonsk, in Ukraine and Belarus.
GIVEN NAMES Jewish 12%; Russian 10%. *Hymen* (2), *Polina* (2), *Inna, Isadore, Khana, Sol, Yakov, Yenta; Boris* (2), *Leonid* (2), *Mikhail* (2), *Yury* (2), *Akim, Anatoly, Arkady, Konstantin, Nataliya, Sergey.*

Polosky (118) Jewish (from Ukraine and Belorussia): variant of POLONSKY.

Polselli (105) Italian: possibly from a suffixed form of *polse*, a northern form of *pulce* 'plea'.
GIVEN NAMES Italian 30%. *Amato* (2), *Rocco* (2), *Salvatore* (2), *Angelo, Dino, Elio, Pasquale, Pasqualino.*

Polsgrove (128) Americanized form of German PFALZGRAF. Compare PALSGROVE.

Polsinelli (170) Italian: patronymic form of **Polsinello**, possibly a northern variant of a *Pulcinello*, a derivative of *pulcino* 'young chicken' (see PULCINI).
GIVEN NAMES Italian 30%. *Angelo* (2), *Gino* (2), *Guido* (2), *Luigi* (2), *Vito* (2), *Antonio, Biagio, Biago, Carmine, Dino, Domenic, Donato.*

Polski (116) Polish and Jewish (Ashkenazic): ethnic name for a Pole, originating in areas of mixed population.
GIVEN NAMES Polish 6%. *Jacek* (2), *Bogdan.*

Polsky (420) Jewish (Ashkenazic), Ukrainian, and Belorussian: ethnic or regional name from eastern Slavic *polskij* 'Polish' (see POLAK).
GIVEN NAMES Jewish 6%. *Hyman* (2), *Meyer.*

Polson (1522) Scottish: patronymic from *Pole*, a Middle English variant of PAUL.

Polster (539) German: from Middle High German *polster* 'cushion', 'pillow', 'bolster' (Old High German *polstar*), hence a metonymic occupational name for a maker or seller of pillows, or a nickname for a plump man.

Polston (1023) Scottish: probably a variant of POLSON.

Polt (113) **1.** South German, Austrian, and Swiss German: from a short form of a Germanic compound personal name formed with *bald* 'bold', 'brave'. **2.** Possibly a variant of North German **Bolt**, a nickname from Middle Low German *bolt* 'quick', 'defiant', 'daring'. **3.** from a short form of the personal name *Hippolyt* (see HYPO-LITE). **4.** German: probably a variant spelling of **Pult** (see PULTE).

Polter (105) Jewish: unexplained.
GIVEN NAMES Jewish 15%. *Aviva, Dovid, Emanuel, Herschel, Mendel, Schneur, Shraga, Yehoshua, Yosef.*

Poltorak (133) Polish (**Półtorak**), Jewish (from Poland and Ukraine), and Ukrainian: nickname from Polish *półtorak* 'one and a half', denoting a coin of the value of one and half grosz. Alternatively, perhaps, a nickname for an exceptionally large person, from Polish *półtora*, Russian *poltora*, 'one and a half' + the Slavic noun suffix *-ak*, or from the same word in an expression meaning, roughly, 'he looks the very picture'.
GIVEN NAMES Polish 16%; Russian 7%; Jewish 5%. *Kazimierz* (2), *Augustyn, Leslaw, Maciej, Mariusz, Pawel, Piotr, Zygmunt; Aleksandr, Arkady, Nikolay, Raisa, Sosya; Naum, Polina.*

Polumbo (105) Italian: variant of PALOMBO.
GIVEN NAMES Italian 15%. *Angelo* (3), *Antonio, Biagio, Sal.*

Polus (178) **1.** Polish (**Poluś**): from a pet form of the personal name POL. **2.** French: variant of PAULHUS.
GIVEN NAME French 4%. *Francois.*

Polyak (245) Jewish (eastern Ashkenazic) and Hungarian (**Polyák**): variant of POLAK 'Pole'.
GIVEN NAMES Russian 20%; Jewish 16%; Hungarian 5%. *Leonid* (5), *Mikhail* (5), *Aleksandr* (3), *Boris* (3), *Yefim* (3), *Zhanna* (2), *Anatoly, Dmitry, Efim, Gelena, Gennadi, Iosif; Khana* (2), *Yakov* (2), *Aron, Blyuma, Genya, Ilya, Irina, Isaak, Isak, Khaim, Mariya, Naum; Andras, Bela, Erzsebet, Gabor, Istvan, Laszlo, Tibor.*

Polyakov (112) Russian and Jewish (eastern Ashkenazic): patronymic from the ethnic name POLAK 'Pole'.
GIVEN NAMES Russian 51%; Jewish 27%. *Leonid* (8), *Aleksandr* (5), *Mikhail* (5), *Boris* (4), *Vladimir* (3), *Aleksey* (2), *Galina* (2), *Igor* (2), *Yuriy* (2), *Zinoviy* (2), *Aleksei, Anatoly; Yakov* (6), *Irina, Khanan, Lenoid, Mikhael, Naum.*

Polzer (172) German: occupational name for a bolt maker, from Middle High German *polz, bolz* 'bolt' + *-er* agent suffix.
GIVEN NAMES German 4%. *Hans, Kurt.*

Polzin (1211) German: habitational name from a place so named in East Pomerania.

Poma (297) **1.** Italian: possibly a habitational name, but otherwise from a female personal name; the documentary evidence is not clear. **2.** Spanish: probably a byname from *poma* 'apple', 'fruit'. **3.** Catalan: nickname from Catalan *poma* 'apple', or variant of POMAR.

GIVEN NAMES Italian 20%; Spanish 14%. *Vito* (4), *Francesco* (2), *Giuseppe* (2), *Rocco* (2), *Aldo, Alfio, Antonino, Gaspare, Gioacchino, Giuseppa, Lorenzo, Marco; Rosario* (3), *Julio* (2), *Alejandro, Carlos, Cesar, Felipe, Hernan, Luis, Nestor.*

Pomales (129) Spanish: topographic name, from the plural of *pomar* (*pomal*) 'orchard'.
GIVEN NAMES Spanish 40%. *Angel* (2), *Manuel* (2), *Rafael* (2), *Adriana, Americo, Ana, Carlos, Carols, Elena, Eugenio, Gilberto, Gregorio; Antonio* (3).

Pomar (123) **1.** Spanish: habitational name from any of the towns called Pomar in Burgos, Palencia and Uesca provinces. **2.** Catalan: topographic name from *pomar* 'orchard', for someone who lived by an orchard or worked as apple grower, or habitational name from any of the many minor places named with this word.
GIVEN NAMES Spanish 36%. *Ana* (2), *Arturo* (2), *Facundo* (2), *Julio* (2), *Luis* (2), *Agustin, Aleida, Armondo, Arnulfo, Carlos, Catalino, Consuelo.*

Pomarico (127) Italian: habitational name from Pomarico in Matera province.
GIVEN NAMES Italian 12%. *Angelo* (2), *Salvatore.*

Pombo (185) Portuguese and Galician: nickname for a mild and inoffensive individual, from *pombo* 'dove'.
GIVEN NAMES Spanish 32%; Portuguese 12%. *Manuel* (7), *Carlos* (4), *Jose* (4), *Mirta* (3), *Alberto* (2), *Camilo* (2), *Luis* (2), *Raul* (2), *Sergio* (2), *Adolfo, Alfredo, Alicia; Joao.*

Pomerance (163) Americanized spelling of German and Jewish POMERANTZ.

Pomerantz (1061) **1.** German: metonymic occupational name for an importer or seller of bitter (Seville) oranges, Middle High German *pomeranz* (medieval Latin *pomarancia*, composed of the elements *arancia*, the name imported with the fruit. Compare NARANJO, with the explanatory Latin word *pomum* 'apple', 'fruit'). **2.** Jewish (Ashkenazic): from Yiddish *pomerants* 'orange' (German *Pomeranze*), one of the many ornamental names taken from plants.
GIVEN NAMES Jewish 8%. *Sol* (4), *Dorit* (2), *Gitty* (2), *Mendel* (2), *Mendy* (2), *Meyer* (2), *Moshe* (2), *Chavie, Hyman, Hymen, Menachem, Mort.*

Pomeranz (230) Variant of German and Jewish POMERANTZ.
GIVEN NAMES Jewish 4%. *Kuna, Shlomo.*

Pomerenke (162) German (**Pommerenke**): ethnic nickname for someone from Pomerania, from a derivative of Middle Low German *pomerene* 'Pomeranian' (see POMMERENING). There is a humorous connotation to this name and its many variants: people from Pomerania were considered somewhat slow and backward.
GIVEN NAME German 4%. *Kurt* (2).

Pomerleau (711) Probably a variant of French **Pommereau**, a diminutive of the topographic name POMMIER.

GIVEN NAMES French 18%. *Armand* (6), *Normand* (4), *Andre* (3), *Emile* (3), *Jacques* (2), *Julien* (2), *Laurent* (2), *Marcel* (2), *Ovide* (2), *Alphonse, Antoine, Collette.*

Pomeroy (3269) English (of Norman origin; associated mainly with Devon and Dorset): habitational name from any of the various places in northeastern France named with Old French *pommeroie, pommeraie* 'apple orchard' (collective of *pomme* 'apple').

Pomfret (152) English: habitational name from Pontefract in Yorkshire, formerly pronounced and sometimes spelled 'Pomfret'. The place name is from Latin *pons, pontis* 'bridge' + *fractus* 'broken'.

Pommer (215) **1.** German: ethnic name for a Pomeranian. **2.** South German: probably a nickname meaning 'blusterer' (see BOMMER).
GIVEN NAMES German 4%. *Alois, Kurt.*

Pommerening (136) German: ethnic name for someone from Pomerania, from a derivative of Middle Low German *pomerene* 'Pomeranian'.
GIVEN NAMES German 4%. *Kurt, Uwe.*

Pommier (223) French: topographic name for someone who lived by an apple tree or an apple orchard, from *pommier* 'apple tree'.

FOREBEARS A Pommier, also known as Pomier and Jolibois, from the Vendômois region of France, is documented in Quebec City in 1664.
GIVEN NAMES French 9%. *Andre, Henri, Laurent, Renald, Yves.*

Pomorski (92) Polish: **1.** habitational name for someone from a place called Pomorze in Ciechanów voivodeship. **2.** regional name for someone from Pomorze, a district of northwest Poland.
GIVEN NAMES Polish 7%. *Ignacy, Stanislaw.*

Pompa (615) **1.** Spanish: nickname from *pompa* 'pomp', 'splendor'. **2.** Italian: occupational or topographic name from *pompa* 'pump' or perhaps a nickname from 'pomp', 'pomposity'.
GIVEN NAMES Spanish 25%; Italian 8%. *Jose* (8), *Juan* (5), *Miguel* (4), *Ruben* (4), *Armando* (3), *Cruz* (3), *Manuel* (3), *Adolfo* (2), *Fernando* (2), *Margarita* (2), *Ramon* (2), *Roberto* (2), *Rocco* (2), *Romano* (2), *Vito* (2), *Angelo, Carmine, Cecilio, Domenico, Eliseo, Ermanno, Manfredo, Romeo, Sebastiano.*

Pompei (248) Italian: **1.** patronymic or plural form of POMPEO. **2.** habitational name from Pompei in Naples province.
GIVEN NAMES Italian 13%. *Romeo* (3), *Carlo* (2), *Angelo, Carmela, Gaetano, Gildo, Pierina, Rocco, Salvatore, Silvio.*

Pompeo (338) Italian: from the personal name *Pompeo*, Latin *Pompeius.*

Pomper (156) German: occupational name for someone, especially a miner, who worked a pump, from an agent derivative of

Middle Dutch *pompe* (ultimately from Spanish, Portuguese *bomba* 'ship's pump').

Pompey (468) Americanized form of Italian POMPEI.

Pompilio (131) Italian: from the personal name *Pompilio*.

Pomplun (184) German: habitational name for someone from Pamplona in Spain.

Pomponio (262) Italian: variant of POMPILIO.
GIVEN NAMES Italian 19%. *Angelo* (2), *Egidio* (2), *Gino* (2), *Giulio* (2), *Dino*, *Filomena*, *Francesco*, *Gabriele*, *Luigi*, *Nino*, *Pasquale*, *Rocco*.

Pomrenke (119) German: variant of POMERENKE.
GIVEN NAMES German 6%; French 4%. *Gernot*, *Kurt*; *Colette*, *Patrice*.

Pomroy (291) English: variant of POMEROY.

Pomykala (115) Polish: nickname from Polish *pomykać* 'to move forward'.
GIVEN NAMES Polish 15%. *Zbigniew* (2), *Dorota*, *Feliks*, *Irena*, *Krystyna*, *Tadeusz*, *Zdzislaw*.

Pon (342) **1.** English: unexplained. **2.** Chinese: see PAN.
GIVEN NAMES Chinese 5%. *Chan*, *Cheu*, *Cheuk*, *Chi*, *Chow*, *Chu*, *Guo Hui*, *Kim Hung*, *Sin*, *Sing*, *Wai*, *Wing*.

Ponath (101) German: variant of **Ponnath**, probably a Huguenot name from Vaud in French Switzerland.

Ponce (3984) Spanish and French: from the medieval personal name *Ponce*, ultimately from *Pontius*, a Roman family name of uncertain origin, perhaps an ethnic name for someone from *Pontus* (named with Greek *pontos* 'ocean') in Asia Minor, or an Italic cognate of Latin *Quintus* 'fifth' (i.e. 'fifthborn'). The name was borne by two 3rdcentury saints, a Carthaginian deacon and a martyr of Nice, but was not widely popular in the Middle Ages because of the inhibiting influence of the even more famous Pontius Pilate. In some cases, though, the surname may have been originally used for someone who had played the part of this character in a religious play.
GIVEN NAMES Spanish 50%. *Jose* (113), *Manuel* (55), *Juan* (48), *Luis* (47), *Jesus* (44), *Carlos* (38), *Francisco* (35), *Jorge* (21), *Miguel* (21), *Pedro* (20), *Raul* (20), *Roberto* (20).

Ponce de Leon (195) Spanish (**Ponce de León**): compound name composed of the family name PONCE + the habitational name *León* (see LEON).
FOREBEARS Juan Ponce De León, the Spanish explorer who discovered Florida, came from a noble Aragonese family. He is believed to have been on board for Columbus's second voyage to Hispaniola in 1493. After his death in Florida from a wound from an Indian arrow in 1521, Ponce De León's title and rights in Florida were passed on to his son.

GIVEN NAMES Spanish 49%. *Jose* (5), *Luis* (5), *Cesar* (3), *Mercedes* (3), *Alberto* (2), *Francisco* (2), *Javier* (2), *Juan* (2), *Lazaro* (2), *Leticia* (2), *Manuel* (2), *Ramon* (2).

Poncelet (118) French (Belgium): unexplained.
GIVEN NAMES French 5%; German 4%. *Alain*, *Benoit*; *Erwin*, *Fritz*.

Poncia (106) Origin unidentified.
GIVEN NAME French 4%. *Pierre*.

Ponciano (158) Spanish and Portuguese: from the personal name *Ponciano* (from Latin *Pontianus*).
GIVEN NAMES Spanish 39%. *Jose* (3), *Julio* (3), *Carlos* (2), *Isidoro* (2), *Luis* (2), *Mario* (2), *Alfaro*, *Andres*, *Aniceto*, *Claudio*, *Elia*, *Eloy*.

Pond (3496) **1.** Southern English: topographic name for someone who lived by a pond or lake, from Middle English *pond* 'enclosed expanse of water', in particular a man-made one (an altered form of POUND). **2.** Dutch: from *pond* 'pound' (a measure of weight and a coin), probably a metonymic occupational name for a controller of weights and measures or a minter.

Ponder (3782) Southern English: topographic name for someone who lived by a pond or man-made lake (see POND).

Ponds (361) English: variant of POND.

Pone (118) Americanized form of German **Pohn** or **Pöhn**, either from a personal name (*Pohn* (see BOHN) or a nickname (*Pöhn*) from early New High German *pön* (from Latin *poena* 'punishment') for someone who had to do penance.
GIVEN NAMES Italian 5%. *Remo*, *Sal*.

Pong (209) **1.** Chinese 庞: variant of PANG 3. **2.** Chinese 彭: variant of PENG. **3.** Korean: there are two Chinese characters for the surname Pong, but only one is common enough to warrant treatment here. Some records indicate that there are nineteen Pong clans, but only the clans of Kanghwa and Haŭm can be documented as legitimate clans. The majority of the Pong clan lives in either Hwanghae Province or Kyŏnggi Province. According to legends, an old woman walking along the beach in Haŭm district of Kwanghwa found a stone box floating on the water. Inside was an extraordinary baby boy, whom she presented to Koryŏ king Injong in 1107. The king named the baby *Pong-u* and raised him within the precincts of his court. Pong-u's descendants continued to live in the Haŭm area, and the clan came to be known as the Haŭm Pong clan. The founding ancestor of the Kanghwa Pong clan is unknown, and there is speculation that perhaps the Kanghwa Pong clan is in fact descended from the Haŭm Pong clan. **4.** German: unexplained.
GIVEN NAMES Chinese/Korean 10%. *Hing* (2), *Chu*, *Chun*, *Fong*, *Kil Yong*, *Kin*, *Ling*, *Mi Hwa*, *Sen*, *Sheng*, *Shing*, *Wai Fong*.

Pongracz (106) Hungarian (**Pongrácz**): from the ecclesiastical name *Pongrác*, Hungarian form of PANKRATZ.
GIVEN NAMES Hungarian 10%. *Gabor*, *Geza*, *Gyula*, *Sandor*.

Pongratz (200) Variant of German **Ponkratz** or Hungarian **Pongrác(z)** (see PANKRATZ).
GIVEN NAMES German 4%. *Florian*, *Fritz*.

Poniatowski (211) Polish: habitational name for someone from any of various places called Poniatowo, Poniatowa, or Poniatów, named with the personal name *Poniat*, from Old Slavic *poneteti* 'to set light to', 'to kindle'.
FOREBEARS This name, borne by Polish nobility, can be traced back to the 15th century. Stanisław August Poniatowski (1738–1798) was the last king of Poland. Józef Poniatowski (1763–1813), commander in chief of the Polish army, took part in Napoleon's campaigns and acquired the title marshal of France.
GIVEN NAMES Polish 9%. *Alicja*, *Grzegorz*, *Jaroslaw*, *Krzystof*, *Krzysztof*, *Zygmunt*.

Pons (727) French, Occitan, Catalan (variant of **Ponç**), and Dutch: from a medieval personal name (see PONCE).
GIVEN NAMES Spanish 23%; French 8%. *Jose* (6), *Juan* (6), *Pedro* (6), *Ramon* (5), *Guillermo* (4), *Roberto* (4), *Carlos* (3), *Francisco* (3), *Luis* (3), *Mario* (3), *Rafael* (3), *Apolonia* (2); *Adrien*, *Armand*, *Emile*, *Jacques*, *Marcel*, *Marcelle*, *Matilde*.

Ponsford (110) English (Devon): habitational name from Ponsford in Devon, recorded in Domesday Book as *Pontesfort* and in 1249 as *Pauncefort*.

Pont (187) **1.** English, Scottish, French, and Catalan: topographic name for someone who lived near a bridge, Middle English, Old French, Catalan *pont* (Latin *pons*, genitive *pontis*). **2.** Catalan: habitational name from any of the numerous places named with *Pont*. **3.** Dutch: variant of POND 2.
FOREBEARS A Pont from the Lorraine region of France is documented in Quebec City in 1640; Pont appears to be a secondary surname to ETIENNE and LAMONTAGNE.
GIVEN NAMES French 4%. *Marcel*, *Pierre*.

Pontarelli (192) Italian: of uncertain derivation. Possibly a patronymic linked with a lost place name.
GIVEN NAMES Italian 24%. *Antonio* (2), *Mario* (2), *Silvio* (2), *Vito* (2), *Alfonso*, *Elvira*, *Emilia*, *Emilio*, *Ennio*, *Germano*, *Guerino*, *Sabatino*, *Tiziana*, *Ugo*.

Pontbriand (143) French: habitational name from a place so named in the Loire Inférieure. There are bearers of this name also known as BRIAND and Sansregret.
GIVEN NAMES French 15%. *Marcel* (2), *Lucien*, *Normand*, *Serge*.

Ponte (748) **1.** Portuguese, Galician, Italian, and Jewish (Sephardic): habitational name from any of the many places in Portugal, Galicia, and Italy named or

named with Ponte, from *ponte* 'bridge'.
2. English: variant spelling of PONT.
GIVEN NAMES Spanish 15%; Portuguese 8%;
Italian 7%. *Manuel* (19), *Jose* (13), *Jorge*
(3), *Carlos* (2), *Enrique* (2), *Fernando* (2),
Graciela (2), *Mario* (2), *Miguel* (2),
Alberto, Alejandro, Alicia; Albano (4),
Joao (3); *Antonio* (6), *Alessandra, Angelo,
Cesare, Dino, Elio, Enrico, Ettore, Luigi,
Salvatore.*

Pontecorvo (147) Italian and Jewish (from
Italy): habitational name from Pontecorvo,
a place in Frosinone where a Jewish community was established following the expulsion of Jews from Rome in the 16th and
17th centuries.
GIVEN NAMES Italian 24%. *Angelina* (3),
Mario (2), *Carmine, Costantino, Giulio,
Emilia, Guilio, Mattia.*

Pontes (297) Portuguese and Galician:
habitational name from any of the numer-
ous places in Portugal named Pontes, from
the plural of *ponte* 'bridge'.
GIVEN NAMES Spanish 16%; Portuguese 9%.
Manuel (6), *Jose* (3), *Alvaro* (2), *Ana* (2),
Jorge (2), *Alberto, Amancio, Anselmo,
Avelino, Belmira, Carlos, Luis; Joao,
Serafim; Luigi, Romano, Vitorino.*

Ponthier (100) Variant of PONTIER.

Ponthieux (122) French: regional name
from an area of ancient Picardy between
the rivers Authie and Somme. In the U.S.
this name is heavily concentrated in LA.
GIVEN NAME Irish 5%. *Murphy.*

Ponti (184) Italian: **1.** patronymic or plural
form of PONTE. **2.** habitational name from
Ponti in Alessandria province.
GIVEN NAMES Italian 16%. *Ivano* (2), *Octavio*
(2), *Dulce, Elena, Elida, Franca, Marco,
Primo, Raffaele, Silvio.*

Ponticello (114) Italian: topographic name
meaning 'little bridge' or a habitational
name from Ponticelli in Naples.
GIVEN NAMES Italian 23%. *Salvatore* (2), *Vito*
(2), *Angelo, Carmela, Carmelo, Natale,
Santo.*

Pontier (136) French and Dutch: occupa-
tional name for a toll keeper on a bridge,
from an agent derivative of *pont* 'bridge'.
GIVEN NAMES Spanish 6%; French 5%.
*Francisco, Mercedes, Osvaldo, Ramon,
Roberto; Jean-Pierre, Pierre.*

Pontiff (215) English and French: from Old
French *pontife* 'pontiff', hence a nickname
for someone who had played the role of the
pope or a high priest in a medieval religious
play, or for a vain or pompous person.
GIVEN NAMES Irish 6%; French 4%. *Donovan*
(2), *Murphy; Evest, Octave.*

Pontillo (245) Italian: from a derivative of
PONTE.
GIVEN NAMES Italian 13%. *Gino* (2), *Salva-
tore* (2), *Alessandro, Angelo, Carmine, Sal,
Sylvio.*

Ponting (120) German: possibly a variant
spelling of **Bonting**, of uncertain origin.
GIVEN NAME German 7%. *Kurt* (3).

Pontious (452) Altered spelling of German
PONTIUS.

Pontius (957) German: from the medieval
personal name *Potentinus*, altered by association with *Pontius Pilatus* (see PILAT).
Potentinus was the name of a 4th-century
saint who lived in the valley of the Mosel,
and it was in that area and around
Schleiden, south of Aachen, that his cult
developed and the name became popular.

Ponto (314) German: variant of **Pontow**, of
unknown origin; perhaps a habitational
name from a lost or unidentified place of
this name. The family originated in the area
formerly known as the Netzekreis, a region
on the Netze River (Polish name *Notec*),
near Czarnków, Poland.
GIVEN NAMES German 5%. *Eldor, Elfriede,
Gerhardt, Gerhart, Orlo, Ralf.*

Ponton (687) Scottish and English: habitational name, probably from Great and Little
Ponton in Lincolnshire, named probably
with an obscure Old English word *pamp*
'hill' + *tūn* 'farmstead', 'enclosure'. The
surname is now found chiefly in Scotland.

Pontrelli (139) Italian: from a reduced
diminutive of **Pinturo**, an occupational
name from Old Italian *pintore* 'painter'.
GIVEN NAMES Italian 17%. *Vito* (5), *Francesco, Gaetano, Rocco, Saverio.*

Ponzi (119) Italian: patronymic or plural
form of PONZIO, PONZO.
GIVEN NAMES Italian 11%. *Angelo* (3), *Antonio, Emidio.*

Ponzio (300) Italian: from the personal
name *Ponzio*, from Latin *Pontius*, a Roman
family name. Compare French and Spanish
PONCE.
GIVEN NAMES Italian 11%. *Vito* (3), *Carlo,
Carmine, Leonardo, Pasquale, Rocco,
Salvatore, Silvio, Vincenzo.*

Ponzo (205) Italian: variant of PONZIO or
BONZO.
GIVEN NAMES Italian 11%. *Angelo, Carlo,
Elio, Nicolo, Santo.*

Poock (113) **1.** North German: habitational
name from a place so named near Stettin.
2. English: variant of PUCK.

Pool (5278) **1.** Southern English: topographic name for someone who lived near a
pool or pond, Middle English *pole* (Old
English *pōl*), or a habitational name from
any of the places named with this word, as
for example Poole in Dorset, South Pool in
Devon, and Poole Keynes in Gloucestershire. **2.** English: from a medieval variant
of the personal name PAUL. **3.** Jewish
(from the Netherlands) and Dutch: ethnic
name for someone from Poland.
4. Probably a variant of German POHL 1,
Puhl, or **Pfuhl**, all topographic names from
Middle Low German *pōl*, Middle High
German *pfuol*, 'pool', 'pond'.

Poole (19045) **1.** Southern English: variant
spelling of POOL 1. **2.** Possibly an Americanized form of German **Puhl** or **Pfuhl(e)**
(see POOL 4).

Pooler (1106) **1.** Southern English: topographic name for someone who lived near a
pool, or habitational name for someone
from a place named with this word (see
POOL). **2.** Possibly an Americanized form
of German **Pfuhler**, variant of PFUHL + *-er*,
suffix denoting an inhabitant.

Pooley (534) English: **1.** habitational name
from a place so called in Warwickshire. No
forms of the name are recorded before the
13th century, when *Povele, Poueleye,
Powelee, Pouelee,* and *Poleye* are all found.
The second element is Old English *lēah*
'wood', 'clearing'; the first is *pofel*, a word
found occasionally in place names (but not
attested independently), the meaning of
which has not been established. **2.** habitational name from Pooley Bridge in
Cumbria, so named from Old English *pōl*
'pool' + Old Norse *haugr* 'hill', 'mound'.
3. topographic name from Middle English
pole 'pool' + *ey* 'low-lying land' or *hey* 'enclosure', or a habitational name from minor
places originally named with these elements, such as Polly Shaw in Kent or the
former *Polleheye* (13th-century), later
Pooley (now named Hunt's Hall) in
Pebmarsh, Essex.

Poon (959) **1.** Chinese 潘: variant of PAN
2. **2.** Chinese: variant of PANG.
GIVEN NAMES Chinese 23%. *Kam* (6), *Wai*
(5), *Kwok* (4), *Cheuk* (3), *Sin* (3), *Chi Ming*
(2), *Ching* (2), *Chung Yin* (2), *Ho* (2), *Kam
Po* (2), *Keung* (2), *Lai Ping* (2).

Poor (1374) **1.** English (of Norman origin):
variant of POWER. **2.** Hungarian (**Poór**):
status name from *pór* 'peasant', 'lower
class'.

Poorbaugh (126) Altered spelling of German **Burbach**, a habitational name form a
place so named near Siegen.

Poore (3097) Southern English (of Norman
origin): variant of POWER.

Poorman (829) Possibly an altered spelling
of German **Porrmann**, a variant of PORR,
or **Purrmann**, from a variant of the personal name *Burgman*, from Old High German
burg 'castle', 'protection' + *man* 'man'.

Poos (119) Dutch: from Middle Dutch *pose*
'pause', 'resting-time', possibly a nickname for someone who was always ready
to take a rest or a nap.

Pooser (136) Probably an altered spelling
of German **Pfoser**, of uncertain origin, or
of POSER.

Poovey (305) Welsh: variant of POVEY.

Pop (209) Romanian: variant of POPA.
GIVEN NAMES Romanian 25%; French 5%;
Spanish 5%; German 4%. *Vasile* (5),
Cornel (2), *Estera* (2), *Florin* (2), *Mihai*
(2), *Sorin* (2), *Viorel* (2), *Alexandru, Anca,
Aurel, Corneliu, Dimitrie, Dumitru;
Andree, Marcel, Remy; Traian* (2),
*Alexandrina, Gabriela, Gustavo, Jorge,
Marcos Antonio, Mariana, Silvia, Terezia,
Tomas; Florian, Theodor, Viktor.*

Popa (574) **1.** Romanian: status name from Romanian *popa* 'priest' (in the case of Orthodox families, whose priests were allowed to marry), or (in the case of Roman Catholic families) a nickname for a pious individual. **2.** Hungarian (**Pópa**): nickname from *pópa* 'priest', in particular an Eastern Orthodox priest.

GIVEN NAMES Romanian 22%. *Gheorghe* (8), *Constantin* (5), *Mihai* (4), *Florica* (3), *Nicolae* (3), *Radu* (3), *Alexandru* (2), *Cornel* (2), *Dumitru* (2), *Horia* (2), *Neculai* (2), *Octavian* (2).

Popal (115) Muslim: unexplained.

GIVEN NAMES Muslim 89%. *Abdul* (12), *Mohammed* (4), *Abdullah* (3), *Mohammad* (3), *Enayatullah* (2), *Mohamad* (2), *Nooria* (2), *Roya* (2), *Zia* (2), *Abdul Majid*, *Amena*, *Aziz*.

Pope (21581) **1.** English: nickname from Middle English *pope* (derived via Old English from Late Latin *papa* 'bishop', 'pope', from Greek *pappas* 'father', in origin a nursery word.) In the early Christian Church, the Latin term was at first used as a title of respect for male clergy of every rank, but in the Western Church it gradually came to be restricted to bishops, and then only to the bishop of Rome; in the Eastern Church it continued to be used of all priests (see POPOV, PAPAS). The nickname would have been used for a vain or pompous man, or for someone who had played the part of the pope in a pageant or play. The surname is also present in Ireland and Scotland. **2.** North German: variant of POPPE.

FOREBEARS Nathaniel Pope, a "marriner" from London and Bristol, England, patented a property on Northern Neck, VA, in 1651 that later became known as "The Clifts".

Popejoy (519) English: nickname from Middle English *popinjay*, *papejai* 'parrot' (via Old French *papageai* from Arabic *bab(b)aghā*). The ending of the English word was altered by folk etymological association with the bird name *jay*. The nickname was probably acquired by a talkative person or by someone who habitually dressed in bright colors, but occasionally it may have denoted someone who was connected with or who excelled at the medieval sport of tilting or shooting at a wooden parrot (popinjay) on a pole.

Popek (307) Polish: nickname from a diminutive of *pop* 'priest', specifically an Eastern Orthodox priest. Formerly this also referred to Roman Catholic priests. Compare English POPE.

GIVEN NAMES Polish 8%. *Casimir*, *Elzbieta*, *Henryk*, *Janusz*, *Karol*, *Pawel*, *Teofil*, *Zbigniew*.

Popelka (328) Czech: nickname for someone thought of as 'gray', i.e. one who was neglected or overlooked, from a pet form of the word *popel* 'ashes'. Popelka is the Czech equivalent of Cinderella.

Poper (101) Probably a variant of German POPPER.

Popescu (256) Romanian: unexplained.

GIVEN NAMES Romanian 37%. *Nicolae* (8), *Radu* (7), *Bogdan* (4), *Dumitru* (3), *Florin* (3), *Gheorghe* (3), *Mihai* (3), *Mircea* (3), *Alexandru* (2), *Constantin* (2), *Petre* (2), *Sorin* (2), *Anca*, *Irena*, *Teofil*.

Popham (818) English: habitational name from a place in Hampshire, so called from an unexplained first element *pop* + Old English *hām* 'homestead'.

FOREBEARS The Popham Colony was the first organized attempt to establish an English colony on the shores of what is now known as New England, then called Northern Virginia. George Popham of Hunstworth, Somerset, England, helped establish the colony at the mouth of the Kennebec River in 1607. It lasted for little over a year until it was abandoned in 1608. Although George died that same year, he may have had descendants or relatives with him as there are Pophams in the U.S. who trace their family roots to the colony.

Popick (161) Jewish (from Ukraine): variant spelling of POPIK.

Popiel (249) Polish: from *popiół* 'ash', 'cinders'; the name of a legendary ruler of prehistoric Poland. This surname is also established in Germany.

Popik (166) Jewish (from Ukraine), Ukrainian, and Polish: nickname or a non-Jewish status name for an eastern Orthodox priest, from Ukrainian *popyk*, Polish *popik*, diminutives of *pop* 'priest'. See also POPEK and compare English POPE.

GIVEN NAMES French 4%; Russian 4%; Jewish 4%. *Camille*; *Mikhail* (2), *Vasily*, *Zinoviy*; *Isidor*.

Popish (100) English: nickname for a Roman Catholic, a comparatively late formation. Most surnames originated before the Reformation, with its schism between the Roman Catholic and Protestant Churches.

Popke (129) German **1.** (of Slavic origin): nickname from a diminutive of *pop* 'priest'. Compare Polish POPEK. **2.** from a pet form of the personal name *Poppo* (see POPP).

Popken (158) North German (also **Pöpken**): patronymic from a pet form of the personal name *Poppo* (see POPP).

GIVEN NAMES German 5%. *Erwin*, *Lorenz*.

Popkin (473) Welsh: Anglicized form of *ap Hopkin* 'son of Hopkin' (see HOPKIN).

Popko (188) Polish and Ukrainian: from a derivative of *pop* 'priest' (see POPEK).

GIVEN NAMES Polish 5%. *Irena*, *Krystyna*, *Wasyl*.

Poplar (148) English: topographic name for someone living by a poplar tree.

Poplaski (144) Variant of Polish **Popławski** (see POPLAWSKI).

GIVEN NAME Polish 4%. *Zigmunt*.

Poplawski (573) Polish (**Popławski**): habitational name for someone from any of

various places called Popławy, named with *popław* 'current', 'flowing water', or a topographic name for someone who lived near a river.

GIVEN NAMES Polish 9%. *Miroslaw* (2), *Stanislaw* (2), *Alojzy*, *Andrze*, *Bogdan*, *Dorota*, *Izydor*, *Krzysztof*, *Piotr*, *Slawomir*, *Waclaw*, *Weislaw*.

Poplin (901) English: at least in part, a variant of POPHAM.

Popma (135) Frisian: from the Germanic personal name *Poppo*, *Boppo* (see POPP).

Popoff (260) Russian and Bulgarian: alternative spelling of POPOV.

Popolizio (156) Italian (Bari): unexplained; perhaps from a derivative of *popolo* 'people', from Latin *populus*.

GIVEN NAMES Italian 17%. *Angelo*, *Attilio*, *Gaetano*, *Nicola*, *Pasquale*, *Sal*, *Ugo*.

Popov (244) **1.** Russian and Bulgarian: patronymic from *pop* 'priest', from Greek *pappas* (compare English POPE). The name may sometimes derive from a nickname, but celibacy was not enjoined on priests of the Orthodox Church and so the name can indeed mean 'son of the priest'. In many cases, however, the Russian name means no more than 'of the priest' and designates a servant of a priest. **2.** Jewish (American): most likely a shortened form of **Popovski**, a habitational name for someone from a place called Popovka, of which there are several examples in Ukraine.

GIVEN NAMES Russian 32%; South Slavic 12%; Jewish 8%. *Boris* (7), *Vladimir* (6), *Nikolay* (5), *Oleg* (4), *Grigoriy* (3), *Anatoly* (2), *Andrei* (2), *Arkadi* (2), *Dmitriy* (2), *Igor* (2), *Mikhail* (2), *Sergey* (2); *Atanas* (2), *Bosko*, *Bozidar*, *Branko*, *Dimitar*, *Lazar*, *Mladen*, *Stojan*, *Yordan*; *Ziva* (2), *Jakob*; *Pavel* (3), *Svetoslav*.

Popovic (242) Serbian (**Popović**): patronymic from *pop* 'priest'. Compare POPOV. Celibacy was not enjoined on priests of the Orthodox Church and so as a Serbian name it normally means literally 'son of the priest'.

GIVEN NAMES South Slavic 42%. *Milorad* (3), *Dejan* (2), *Marko* (2), *Predrag* (2), *Sanja* (2), *Bozidar*, *Cedo*, *Darko*, *Djordje*, *Dragan*, *Dragana*, *Dragisa*; *Milan* (5), *Dusan* (2), *Milos*.

Popovich (1515) **1.** Ukrainian and Belorussian: patronymic from *pop* 'priest' (see POPE). **2.** Americanized spelling of Serbian **Popović** 'son of the priest' (see POPOVIC).

GIVEN NAMES South Slavic 5%. *Marko* (5), *Miodrag* (4), *Branko*, *Drago*, *Dragomir*, *Ljubica*, *Ljubisa*, *Mihajlo*, *Milenko*, *Nenad*, *Rade*, *Ratko*.

Popowich (138) Germanized spelling of Ukrainian and Belorussian POPOVICH, Croatian and Serbian **Popović**, or Polish **Popowicz**, all patronymics from *pop* 'priest'. Compare POPOV.

Popowski (198) Polish: habitational name from any of the numerous places in Poland called Popowo or Popów.
GIVEN NAMES Polish 5%. *Andrzej, Irena, Wojciech, Zygmunt.*

Popp (3638) **1.** German: from a Germanic personal name *Poppo, Boppo,* of uncertain origin and meaning, perhaps originally a nursery word or a short form of for example *Bodobert,* a Germanic personal name meaning 'famous leader'. It was a hereditary personal name among the counts of Henneberg and Babenberg in East Franconia between the 9th and 14th centuries. **2.** English: from a Middle English continuation of an Old English personal name, *Poppa,* known only from occurrences in place names.

Poppa (125) **1.** German: variant of POPPE. **2.** Italian: possibly a variant of **Popa,** from a female personal name, *Popa, Pupa,* or *Bova,* of Germanic origin.

Poppe (1332) **1.** German: variant of POPP 1. **2.** English: variant spelling of POPP 2. **3.** Dutch: from the Germanic personal name *Poppo* (see POPP 1).

Poppel (118) South German (also **Pöppel**): from a pet form of the personal name POPP.
GIVEN NAMES German 4%. *Gerhard, Hans.*

Poppell (431) **1.** Altered spelling of South German **Poppel,** from a pet form of POPP. **2.** habitational name from any of several places called Pöppeln in Thuringia, Pomerania, East Prussia.

Poppen (362) North German: patronymic from POPP.
GIVEN NAMES German 4%. *Gerhard, Otto, Uwe, Wilhelmina.*

Popper (436) **1.** German: patronymic from POPP. **2.** German (**Pöpper**): variant of PEPPER. **3.** Jewish (Ashkenazic): origin uncertain; perhaps a habitational name from Poprad, now in Slovakia. Compare the Poprad river in the same region, called *Popper* in German.
GIVEN NAMES German 5%. *Fritz* (3), *Hans, Ilse, Otto, Wolf.*

Poppert (123) German: variant of POPPER.
GIVEN NAME French 5%. *Adrien.*

Popple (191) English (mainly East Midlands): habitational name from a lost minor place name, *Pophall* in Linchmere, Sussex, or from Pophills in Salford Priors, Warwickshire.

Poppler (101) German (also **Pöppler**): topographic name for someone who lived near poplars, from Middle Low German *poppele* 'poplar', or possibly a habitational name from a place named with this word.

Poppleton (200) English (West Yorkshire): habitational name from a place in West Yorkshire, so named from Old English *popel* 'pebble' + *tūn* 'enclosure', 'settlement'.

Popplewell (370) English (West Yorkshire): habitational name from any of several places so named in West Yorkshire, for example in the parish of Cleckheaton. The second element is Old English *well(a)* 'spring', 'stream'; the first may be *popel* 'pebble', or a word meaning 'bubbling spring'.

Poppy (174) English: from Middle English *popy* 'poppy', possibly applied as a nickname for someone with bright red hair or a ruddy complexion.

Popson (162) English: unexplained.

Popwell (209) English: probably a reduced form of POPPLEWELL.

Poquette (414) Altered spelling of French PAQUET.

Porada (146) Polish: nickname from *porada* 'advice', 'counsel'.
GIVEN NAMES Polish 12%. *Zygmunt* (2), *Jerzy, Jozef, Leszek, Ludwika.*

Porath (566) **1.** German (of Slavic origin): status or occupational name for a counselor, from Slavic *porada* 'advice', 'counseling', 'councilor'. **2.** Jewish (Israeli): from a Biblical personal name meaning 'fruitful' (an allusion to Joseph).

Porcaro (459) Italian: occupational name for a swineherd, *porcaro.*
GIVEN NAMES Italian 14%. *Salvatore* (4), *Angelo* (3), *Carmine* (3), *Antonio* (2), *Carlo, Dino, Gino, Giovanni, Leonardo, Luigi, Pasquale, Santo.*

Porcella (153) Italian: variant of PORCELLO, from the feminine.
GIVEN NAMES Italian 6%. *Guido, Leonardo, Mafalda, Rinaldo.*

Porcelli (542) Italian: patronymic from PORCELLO.
GIVEN NAMES Italian 16%. *Angelo* (2), *Carlo* (2), *Carmine* (2), *Pietro* (2), *Attilio, Carmelo, Concetta, Concetto, Franco, Giovanni, Lia, Lorenzo.*

Porcello (230) Italian: nickname from *porcello* 'piglet' (a diminutive of *porco* 'hog').
GIVEN NAMES Italian 10%. *Salvatore* (3), *Caesar, Carmine, Emelio, Pasquale, Santo.*

Porch (877) Variant of North German **Borch** (a variant of BURG) or of **Porsch** (see BORSCH 2).

Porche (642) **1.** French: topographic name for someone who lived at a house distinguished by a covered passage or walkway, *porche.* **2.** German: variant of BORSCH.
GIVEN NAMES French 5%. *Leonce* (2), *Alphonse, Antoine, Germaine, Jacques.*

Porcher (254) French and English: occupational name for a swineherd, from Old French, Middle English *porch(i)er,* an agent derivative of Old French *porc* 'pig'. This name is quite frequent in LA.

Porchia (131) Italian: from *porchia* 'female piglet', possibly applied as a nickname or as a metonymic occupational name for a swineherd.
GIVEN NAME Italian 4%. *Salvatore* (2).

Porco (354) Italian (Calabria): derogatory nickname from *porco* 'hog'. De Felice suggests it may also have been taken as a name by someone wishing to show Christian repentance and self-abasement.

GIVEN NAMES Italian 24%. *Angelo* (4), *Aldo* (2), *Antonio* (2), *Carmine* (2), *Domenico* (2), *Enrico* (2), *Francesco* (2), *Santo* (2), *Carlo, Fulvio, Gaetano, Gaspare.*

Pore (237) French (**Poré**): from a variant of *poireau, poreau* 'leek', hence a metonymic occupational name for someone who grew and sold leeks.

Poremba (317) Polish (**Poręba**) and Jewish (from Poland): habitational name from any of the many places in Poland called Poręba, from a word meaning 'clearing in a wood'.

Porges (135) Jewish (Ashkenazic from Central Europe): metronymic from the Yiddish female personal name *Porye,* a derivative of the Biblical Zipporah + the Yiddish or German possessive suffix *-s.*
GIVEN NAMES German 9%; Jewish 6%. *Armin* (2), *Inge, Kurt; Hillel, Mayer, Meir, Mendel.*

Porpora (139) Italian: variant of PURPURA (standard Italian *porpora*).
GIVEN NAMES Italian 16%. *Carmine* (2), *Gino, Orlando.*

Porr (161) German: **1.** metonymic occupational name for a grower or seller of leeks or other vegetables, from Middle High German *porre, pforre* 'leek' (from Latin *porrum*). **2.** Possibly an altered spelling of South German **Pforr,** a variant of 1.
GIVEN NAMES German 6%. *Ulrike* (2), *Gunther.*

Porras (1216) **1.** Spanish: habitational name from Porras, a town in Andalusia, or nickname from the plural of *porra* 'cudgel', 'club', nickname either for a stockily built person or for a tiresome person. '*Porras!*' is also used as an idiomatic expression meaning 'Go to the Devil'. **2.** Galician: habitational name from any of three places in Lugo province named Porras.
GIVEN NAMES Spanish 46%. *Jose* (27), *Manuel* (19), *Carlos* (15), *Juan* (13), *Jesus* (12), *Mario* (10), *Jorge* (9), *Enrique* (8), *Luis* (8), *Armando* (7), *Francisco* (7), *Jaime* (7).

Porrazzo (167) Italian: from a derivative of PORRO.
GIVEN NAMES Italian 12%. *Nicola* (3), *Carmine, Sal, Salvatore.*

Porreca (404) Italian: probably a variant of **Pirrecca,** a nickname from Greek *pyrrakios* 'man with red hair'.
GIVEN NAMES Italian 25%. *Antonio* (3), *Guido* (3), *Angelo* (2), *Carmine* (2), *Luigi* (2), *Camillo, Carmino, Claudio, Dino, Domenico, Emilio, Ettore, Lorenzo, Mario, Onofrio, Orlando, Renato, Silvana.*

Porretta (148) Italian: **1.** from a derivative of PORRO. **2.** habitational name from for example Porretta Terme in Bologna province.
GIVEN NAMES Italian 21%. *Emanuele* (2), *Costantino, Donato, Gino, Luigi, Remo, Rocco, Romano, Saverio, Silvio, Vincenzo, Vittoria.*

Porritt (216) English (West Yorkshire): variant of PARROTT 1.

Porro (210) **1.** Portuguese, Spanish, Catalan, and Italian: nickname from *porro* 'leek', 'allium'. In Spanish and Portuguese it denoted a stupid, coarse individual. In Italian, however, the term also means 'wart' and the nickname probably denoted someone with warts or boils. **2.** Catalan: possibly habitational name from *El Porró*, a place in Alacant, Valencia.

GIVEN NAMES Spanish 30%; Italian 6%. *Carlos* (6), *Manuel* (5), *Juan* (4), *Adolfo* (3), *Pedro* (3), *Rodolfo* (3), *Elia* (2), *Ines* (2), *Jorge* (2), *Jose* (2), *Juan Carlos* (2), *Julio* (2); *Cosmo, Edmondo, Emo, Franco, Santo*.

Porsch (103) German: variant of BORSCH.

GIVEN NAMES German 18%. *Dieter, Ernst, Hartmut, Klaus, Manfred, Ralf, Traude*.

Port (1125) **1.** English: from Middle English *port* 'gateway', 'entrance' (Old French *porte*, from Latin *porta*), hence a topographic name for someone who lived near the gates of a fortified town or city, typically, the man in charge of them. Compare PORTER 1. **2.** English: topographic name for someone who lived near a harbor or in a market town, from the homonymous Middle English *port* (Old English *port* 'harbor', 'market town', from Latin *portus* 'harbor', 'haven', reinforced in Middle English by Old French *port*, from the same source). **3.** German: topographic name for someone who lived near a (city) gate, from Middle Low German *porte* (modern German *Pforte*) (see sense 1). **4.** Jewish (from Lithuania and Belarus): unexplained.

Porta (549) Italian, Catalan, Galician, southern French (Occitan), and Jewish (Sephardic): topographic name for someone who lived near the gates of a fortified town, from Latin *porta* 'gate'. This is also found as a Polish name, with the same origin.

GIVEN NAMES Spanish 7%; Italian 4%. *Jorge* (4), *Carlos* (3), *Jose* (3), *Edmundo* (2), *Eduardo* (2), *Mario* (2), *Alfonso, Bolivar, Carols, Felino, Francisco, Ignacio*; *Aldo* (2), *Angelo* (2), *Pio* (2), *Vito* (2), *Cosmo, Giulio, Salvatore, Siena*.

Portal (195) **1.** Spanish, Catalan, Galician, Portuguese, and southern French (Occitan): topographic name for someone who lived near the gates of a fortified town, typically the gatekeeper, or a habitational name from any of the places in Portugal and Galicia named Portal. **2.** Jewish: unexplained.

GIVEN NAMES Spanish 43%; Portuguese 11%; Jewish 4%; French 4%. *Pedro* (7), *Carlos* (3), *Juan* (3), *Luis* (3), *Amado* (2), *Arnoldo* (2), *Caridad* (2), *Jose* (2), *Norberto* (2), *Ricardo* (2), *Rosa Elena* (2), *Tomas* (2); *Amadeu*; *Arie, Ber, Shlomo, Yael, Ziva*; *Marcelle* (2), *Andre, Jean Luc*.

Portalatin (126) probably of Spanish origin (**Portalatín**): topographic name for some-

one living 'by the Latin gate', a locality that has not been identified. This name is common mainly in Puerto Rico.

GIVEN NAMES Spanish 44%. *Luis* (3), *Manuel* (3), *Miguel* (3), *Ramon* (3), *Angel* (2), *Efrain* (2), *Felipe* (2), *Gerardo* (2), *Juan* (2), *Nestor* (2), *Rafael* (2), *Alfredo*; *Heriberto*.

Portales (159) Spanish, Galician and Portuguese: from the plural of *portal* 'gate' (see PORTAL), either as a topographic name or a habitational name from a place called Portales.

GIVEN NAMES Spanish 53%. *Carlos* (4), *Amando* (3), *Sergio* (3), *Alfredo* (2), *Andres* (2), *Arturo* (2), *Efrain* (2), *Feliberto* (2), *Juan* (2), *Lourdes* (2), *Mario* (2), *Rafael* (2); *Aldo, Bartolo, Marco*.

Portanova (191) Italian, Portuguese, and Galician: habitational name from a place or locality called Portanova 'new gate'.

GIVEN NAMES Italian 24%. *Rocco* (3), *Vito* (3), *Angelo* (2), *Carmine* (2), *Antonio, Concetta, Giovanni, Leonardo, Nicola, Ottavio, Sabato, Sal*.

Porte (243) **1.** English: variant spelling of PORT. **2.** French: from Old French *porte* 'gateway', 'entrance' (from Latin *porta*), hence a topographic name for someone who lived near the gates of a fortified town (typically, the man in charge of them). **3.** Jewish (Sephardic): variant of PORTA.

Portee (158) Origin uncertain; perhaps an Americanized form of French PORTIER.

Portela (258) Portuguese and Galician: habitational name from any of the numerous places named Portela, from *portela* 'passageway', 'gateway'.

GIVEN NAMES Spanish 49%; Portuguese 14%. *Jose* (11), *Manuel* (6), *Carlos* (5), *Luis* (5), *Rafael* (5), *Mercedes* (4), *Juan* (3), *Miguel* (3), *Raul* (3), *Alberto* (2), *Ana* (2), *Angel* (2); *Joao, Joaquim*.

Portell (332) Catalan: probably a habitational name from one of the places in Girona and Lleida provinces called Portell, from a diminutive of *porta* 'gate'.

Portella (103) **1.** Catalan: habitational name from Portella in Lleida or La Portella in Barcelona or Tarragona, so named from a diminutive of *porta* 'gate'. **2.** Italian: from Sicilian *purtedda* 'portal', 'door', 'pass', presumably applied as a topograhic name or as a habitational name from any of the numerous places named with this word.

GIVEN NAMES Spanish 25%. *Manuel* (4), *Albino* (2), *Bienvenido* (2), *Reinaldo* (2), *Blanca, Carlos, Consuelo, Javier, Jose, Mario, Roberto*.

Portelli (200) Italian: patronymic from **portello**, from a diminutive of PORTA. This is also found as a family name in Greece.

GIVEN NAMES Italian 13%. *Carmela* (2), *Lorenzo* (2), *Sal* (2), *Emilio, Giovanni, Remo, Salvatore*.

Porten (132) **1.** English: possibly a variant of **Porton**, a habitational name from Porton

in Wiltshire or Poorton in Dorset; both place names are formed with an obscure first element, perhaps the name of a river, + Old English *tūn* 'settlement'. **2.** Dutch: habitational name for someone from a place named with Dutch *poort* 'gate'.

Porteous (417) Scottish: probably a topographic name for someone who lived in the lodge at the entrance to a manor house, from Middle English *port* 'gateway', 'entrance' + *hous* 'house', or an occupational name with similar meaning, from Latin *portarius* 'porter'. Alternatively, as suggested by Reaney, it may be from Anglo-Norman French *porte-hors* 'portable prayerbook' (i.e. a book of hours), hence a metonymic occupational name for a scribe employed in writing such books. The surname is also established in Ireland, the earliest record of its presence there being dated 1563.

Porter (55056) **1.** English and Scottish: occupational name for the gatekeeper of a walled town or city, or the doorkeeper of a great house, castle, or monastery, from Middle English *porter* 'doorkeeper', 'gatekeeper' (Old French *portier*). The office often came with accommodation, lands, and other privileges for the bearer, and in some cases was hereditary, especially in the case of a royal castle. As an American surname, this has absorbed cognates and equivalents in other European languages, for example German **Pförtner** (see FORTNER) and North German POERTNER. **2.** English: occupational name for a man who carried loads for a living, especially one who used his own muscle power rather than a beast of burden or a wheeled vehicle. This sense is from Old French *porteo(u)r* (Late Latin *portator*, from *portare* 'to carry or convey'). **3.** Dutch: occupational name from Middle Dutch *portere* 'doorkeeper'. Compare 1. **4.** Dutch: status name for a freeman (burgher) of a seaport, Middle Dutch *portere*, modern Dutch *poorter*. **5.** Jewish (Ashkenazic): adoption of the English or Dutch name in place of some Ashkenazic name of similar sound or meaning.

Portera (238) **1.** Italian: occupational name for a female servant, from Spanish *portera*. **2.** In a few cases, possibly Catalan: habitational name from Portera in Valencia, so named from a derivative of *porta* 'gate'.

GIVEN NAMES Italian 19%; Spanish 5%. *Salvadore* (3), *Cosimo* (2), *Pasquale* (2), *Vito* (2), *Arturo, Mario, Rosaria, Salvatore, Vincenzo*; *Salvador* (2), *Ana*.

Porterfield (2563) Scottish (mainly Glasgow): topographic name from the hereditary lands owned by a porter (see PORTER 1), taken as a surname by the descendants of such an official. Black suggests that they would originally have been known as Porter but extended their name when 'territorial surnames' became fashionable.

Portes (100) Catalan: from the plural of *porta* 'door', 'gate' (see PORTA).

GIVEN NAMES Spanish 42%. *Rafael* (3), *Ana* (2), *Enrique* (2), *Luis* (2), *Manuel* (2), *Abdiel, Alejandro, Andres, Bernarda, Eduvigis, Emilia, Eulalia.*

Porteus (161) English: variant spelling of PORTEOUS.

GIVEN NAME French 6%. *Christophe* (2).

Porth (357) German: probably a variant of PORT 3.

GIVEN NAMES German 6%. *Manfred* (2), *Beate, Horst, Siegfried, Uwe, Volker.*

Portier (288) French: occupational name for the gatekeeper of a walled town or city, or the doorkeeper of a great house, Old French *portier* (Late Latin *portarius*). Compare English PORTER. The distribution of the name in the U.S., however, suggests it is either not of French origin or was brought in from another country, possibly Switzerland, where it is also established.

GIVEN NAMES French 5%. *Clovis, Leonce, Renauld.*

Portilla (148) Spanish: habitational name from any of the places named Portilla, from a diminutive of *porta* 'gate'.

GIVEN NAMES Spanish 42%. *Jose* (4), *Francisco* (3), *Juan* (3), *Manuel* (3), *Jesus* (2), *Sixto* (2), *Alfredo, Belgica, Blanca, Carlos, Eugenio, Gabriela.*

Portillo (2490) Spanish: habitational name from any of the places named Portillo, from the diminutive of *puerto* 'mountain pass', notably those in Valladolid, Soria, and Toledo.

GIVEN NAMES Spanish 52%. *Jose* (127), *Luis* (30), *Carlos* (29), *Juan* (24), *Francisco* (20), *Jesus* (19), *Mario* (19), *Manuel* (17), *Pedro* (16), *Jorge* (15), *Raul* (15), *Ana* (14).

Portis (664) Irish: variant of PORTEOUS.

Portlock (239) English (Gloucestershire): possibly a habitational name from Porlock in Somerset, recorded in Domesday Book as *Portloc*, being named with Old English *port* 'harbor' + *loca* 'enclosure'.

Portman (651) **1.** English (West Midlands): elaborated form of PORT. **2.** Dutch: from *poort* 'gate' + *man* 'man', an occupational name for a gatekeeper or a topographic name for someone who lived near the gates of a walled town (typically the man in charge of them). Compare PORTER. **3.** American spelling of German PORTMANN.

Portmann (152) North German: occupational name for a gatekeeper, from Middle Low German *port(e)* 'gate' (from Latin *porta*) + *man* 'man', or a topographic name for someone who lived near the gates of a fortified town. Compare PORTER.

GIVEN NAMES German 15%. *Otto* (3), *Helmut* (2), *Franz, Hansi, Kurt.*

Portner (477) North German (also **Pörtner**): occupational name for a doorkeeper or gatekeeper, from an agent derivative of Middle Low German *port(e)* 'gate'. Compare PORTER.

Portney (141) Origin uncertain. Perhaps an altered form of Jewish PORTNOY of North German PORTNER.

GIVEN NAME French 4%. *Jacques.*

Portnoy (969) Jewish (from Ukraine and Belarus): occupational name for a tailor from Russian *portnoj* (an adjective derivative of *port* 'uncut cloth').

GIVEN NAMES Jewish 14%; Russian 9%. *Sol* (4), *Moshe* (3), *Semen* (3), *Yakov* (3), *Boruch* (2), *Hershel* (2), *Isaak* (2), *Mendel* (2), *Aron, Chaim, Hyman, Isak; Boris* (12), *Aleksandr* (6), *Vladimir* (6), *Semyon* (4), *Dmitry* (2), *Yefim* (2), *Anatoly, Arkadiy, Evgeny, Galina, Gennady, Grigoriy.*

Porto (874) **1.** Portuguese: habitational name from Porto (Oporto). **2.** Spanish: habitational name from any of the numerous places, especially in Galicia, named Porto, usually in the sense 'mountain pass'. **3.** Italian: habitational name from any of numerous minor places named or named with Porto, from *porto* 'port', 'harbor'.

GIVEN NAMES Spanish 12%; Italian 10%; Portuguese 6%. *Mario* (11), *Jose* (8), *Manuel* (6), *Armando* (3), *Ana* (2), *Cesar* (2), *Emilio* (2), *Jorge* (2), *Miguel* (2), *Nestor* (2), *Raul* (2), *Roberto* (2); *Pasquale* (5), *Antonio* (3), *Salvatore* (3), *Enrico* (2), *Marcellino* (2), *Aldo, Angelo, Fabrizio, Fausto, Filomena, Gasper; Joao* (2), *Paulo* (2), *Ligia.*

Ports (178) Possibly an Americanized spelling of German PORTZ, variant of **Porz**, a habitational name from a town so named near Cologne.

Portugal (314) Spanish, Portuguese, Catalan, English, French, and Jewish: ethnic name or regional name for someone from Portugal or who had connections with Portugal. The name of the country derives from Late Latin *Portucale*, originally denoting the district around Oporto (*Portus Cales*, named with Latin *portus* 'port', 'harbor' + *Cales*, the ancient name of the city. In some cases the surname may be simply a nickname for someone who had business connections with Portugal.

GIVEN NAMES Spanish 33%; Portuguese 9%. *Jose* (6), *Carlos* (4), *Juan* (3), *Salvador* (3), *Alberto* (2), *Alejandra* (2), *Alejandro* (2), *Cesar* (2), *Fernando* (2), *Jesus* (2), *Luis* (2), *Manuel* (2); *Aderito.*

Portuondo (109) Basque: topographic name from *portuondo* 'close to the port', from Basque *portu* 'port', 'harbor' + *ondo* 'near to', or habitational for someone from Portuondo-Basaran, in Biscay.

GIVEN NAMES Spanish 62%. *Juan* (7), *Rafael* (6), *Jose* (5), *Angel* (2), *Erasmo* (2), *Graciela* (2), *Luis* (2), *Manuel* (2), *Mario* (2), *Miguel* (2), *Pablo* (2), *Salvador* (2).

Portwood (771) Apparently an English habitational name from a place so called in what is now Greater Manchester.

Portz (411) German (of Slavic origin): nickname for a quarrelsome person, from Old Slavic *boru* 'quarrel', 'fight', or from a Slavic personal name composed with this word.

Porzio (283) Southern Italian (especially Campania): from the personal name *Porzio*, from the Latin name *Porcius*, derived from *porcus* 'hog'.

GIVEN NAMES Italian 11%. *Constantino* (2), *Enrico* (2), *Gino* (2), *Angelo, Antonio, Gaetano, Guido.*

Posa (188) **1.** Italian: habitational name from Posa a locality of Treviso. **2.** Italian: nickname from *posa* 'attitude', 'air', also 'repose', 'stillness'. **3.** Spanish: probably a variant of **Poza**, topographic name for someone who lived by a well or pit, from Spanish *poza* (Latin *putea*; compare POZO), or variant of Spanish POSADA. **4.** Catalan: probably variant of old Catalan *possa* 'well' 'pit', common in some Catalan place names (Latin *putea*). **5.** Hungarian (**Pósa**): from a pet form of the personal name *Pál*, Hungarian form of PAUL.

GIVEN NAMES Italian 22%; Spanish 7%; French 6%. *Angelo* (2), *Antonio* (2), *Emilio* (2), *Alfredo, Arturo, Dino, Ennio, Ernesto, Franco, Mario, Rocco, Rodolfo, Sal, Serafino, Silvio, Vito; Consuelo, Javier, Juan; Andre* (2), *Monique.*

Posada (653) Spanish: habitational name from any of the numerous places named Posada, from *posada* 'halt', 'resting place'.

GIVEN NAMES Spanish 53%. *Jose* (15), *Luis* (12), *Juan* (11), *Carlos* (8), *Pedro* (8), *Roberto* (8), *Jorge* (7), *Mario* (6), *Fernando* (5), *Manuel* (5), *Miguel* (5), *Rafael* (5).

Posadas (246) Spanish: habitational name from *posadas*, plural of POSADA.

GIVEN NAMES Spanish 44%. *Jose* (7), *Manuel* (5), *Mario* (4), *Ana* (3), *Ernesto* (3), *Fernando* (3), *Pedro* (3), *Vicente* (3), *Augusto* (2), *Efrain* (2), *Felipe* (2), *Jorge* (2).

Posch (374) **1.** German (of Slavic origin): from a pet form of any of the many personal names composed with Slavic *bog* 'god'. **2.** South German (Austrian): nickname for a short, stocky person, from Middle High German *busch*, Bavarian and Austrian *bosch* 'shrubbery'. In Tyrol *Posch* denotes a flowering shrub and appears on house signs. **3.** Eastern German, of Slavic origin (also **Pösch**): from a short form of PETER or any of various other personal names beginning with *P-*.

GIVEN NAMES German 5%. *Alois* (2), *Heinz, Johann.*

Pose (102) Galician: unexplained.

GIVEN NAMES Spanish 16%; Portuguese 14%. *Manuel* (5), *Jose* (2), *Modesto* (2), *Rafael* (2), *Francisco, Javier, Marcelo, Orlando; Joaquim* (3).

Posen (160) **1.** Dutch: variant of PASCHEN. **2.** Jewish (Ashkenazic): habitational name from the city or province of Poznań in Poland (German *Posen*).

GIVEN NAMES Jewish 5%. *Chaim, Joachim, Yosef.*

Poser (216) **1.** German: habitational name for someone from Posa or Poserna, south of Merseburg, or a variant of **Pose** (see POSEY). **2.** English: variant of PEISER.

GIVEN NAMES German 9%. *Kurt* (2), *Otto* (2), *Alfons, Siegfried.*

Posey (6560) Possibly an altered spelling of German **Pose** (or POSER 2), a habitational name from Posa or Poserna, south of Merseburg, or a topographic name from Middle Low German *pōse* 'lump', 'pile' (from which the place names may also derive).

Posillico (135) Italian: unexplained. It occurs predominantly near Naples and for that reason it could be a habitational name, from Posillipo, the name of an important coastal quarter of the city of Naples.

GIVEN NAMES Italian 41%. *Carmine* (3), *Mario* (3), *Domenico* (2), *Vincenzo* (2), *Agostino, Angelo, Antonio, Costantino, Francesco, Gaetano, Lorenzo, Marco.*

Poskey (104) Probably an Americanized spelling of German **Poske** (also **Pöske**), perhaps from a short form of a Slavic personal name formed with *bog* 'god', for example *Bogumil.*

Posluszny (183) Polish (**Posłuszny**) and Jewish (from Poland): nickname from Polish *posłuszny* 'obedient', 'dutiful'.

GIVEN NAMES Polish 5%. *Krzysztof, Stanislaw.*

Posner (1696) German and Jewish (Ashkenazic): habitational name for someone from the city or province of Poznań (German *Posen*) in west-central Poland, the *-er* suffix indicating an inhabitant.

GIVEN NAMES Jewish 7%. *Hyman* (4), *Avrom* (3), *Chaim* (3), *Sol* (3), *Emanuel* (2), *Irina* (2), *Isak* (2), *Menachem* (2), *Yosef* (2), *Ari, Benzion, Chaya.*

Pospisil (639) Czech (**Pospíšil**): nickname for an impatient or active individual, from Czech *pospíšit* 'to be in a hurry'.

Poss (1167) German (of Slavic origin): from a pet form of a personal name, a Slavic form of PETER.

Possehl (155) German (of Slavic origin): from a pet form of a personal name formed with Slavic *bog* 'god', for example *Bogislaw.*

Possinger (113) **1.** altered form of German **Pösinger**, a habitational name for someone from Pösing in Bavaria, or **Bössinger**, a habitational name for someone from Bissingen near Ludwigsburg (earlier Bussingen) or from Baisingen (earlier Bössingen). **2.** German (**Pössinger**): habitational name for someone from Pösingen in the Upper Palatinate.

Posson (105) **1.** German: possibly a variant of BASON, which is likewise unexplained. **2.** French (Walloon): from Walloon *posson* 'beer jug', 'water jug', from Old French *poçon* 'jar', 'jug', applied as a

nickname, metonymic occupational name, or house name.

FOREBEARS Most if not all American bearers of this name are probably descended from Johann Nicolas Bason (1675–1728), who came to Somerville, NJ, from Nierstein, Germany, in about 1710–13.

Post (9721) **1.** North German, Danish, and Dutch: topographic name for someone who lived near a post or pole (Middle Low German, Middle Dutch *post*, from Latin *postis*), presumably one of some significance, e.g. serving as a landmark or boundary, or a habitational name from any of several places in northern Germany called Post, probably from this word. **2.** North German: occupational name for a mounted messenger or courier Middle Low German *post*. **3.** Jewish (Ashkenazic): metonymic occupational name for a mailman, from German POST 'mail'. **4.** Probably an altered spelling of German PFOST.

Postal (194) **1.** Northern French: occupational name from Old Walloon *postal(h)* 'mayor'. **2.** variant of German or Dutch POSTEL.

Postel (389) **1.** German (Bavaria, Austria): habitational name from any of various place names of Slavic origin, for example *Postelitz* and *Postlow.* **2.** German: nickname from Middle High German *possolt* 'handicraft'. **3.** German: from a Slavic pet form of SEBASTIAN. **4.** German: from *Apostel* 'apostle', a nickname for someone who played the part of an apostle in a medieval mystery play. Compare POSTLE. **5.** Dutch: habitational name from Postel in Antwerp province, Bavaria. **6.** Jewish (from Ukraine): metonymic occupational name for a shoemaker, from Yiddish *postele* 'leather shoe'.

GIVEN NAMES German 4%. *Heinz, Kurt, Otto.*

Postell (721) Variant POSTEL or **Postill**, a variant of POSTLE.

Postema (213) Frisian: variant of POSTHUMUS.

GIVEN NAMES Dutch 6%. *Gerrit* (2), *Dirk, Maarten, Marinus, Wiebe.*

Posten (317) German: probably a variant of POST 1 or 2; or alternatively from a (dialect) variant of the personal name SEBASTIAN.

Poster (388) **1.** Eastern German: habitational name for someone from any of various places called Post, Posta, or Postau. **2.** Eastern German: nickname for a person who regularly fasted, from Sorbian *postar* 'faster'. **3.** Jewish (Ashkenazic): occupational name for a mailman, from German *Post* 'mail' + the agent suffix *-er.*

Posthuma (149) Frisian: variant of POSTHUMUS.

Posthumus (177) Dutch and North German: from a personal name given to a child born after the death of his father, from Latin *postumus* 'after death', from *post* 'after' + *humus* 'grave'.

GIVEN NAMES French 4%; Dutch 4%; German 4%. *Dirk* (2), *Koos; Claus* (2).

Postier (121) Of German origin: unexplained.

Postiglione (127) Italian: habitational name from Postiglione in Salerno province, possibly named from Calabrian *pistiglionë* 'gecko'.

GIVEN NAMES Italian 13%. *Umberto* (2), *Antonio, Enrico, Rocco, Salvatore.*

Postle (268) English (Norfolk): nickname from a reduced form of Middle English *apostel* 'apostle' (Old English *apostol*, via Latin from Greek *apostolos* 'messenger', 'delegate', from *apostellein* 'to dispatch'). As a nickname, this may have been used for someone who had played the part of one of the twelve apostles in a play or pageant. However, the word was also used as a personal name. Compare POSTLETHWAIT.

Postler (103) German: **1.** Variant of POSTEL 2, 3. **2.** (of Slavic origin): habitational name for someone from Postel near Militsch in Silesia.

GIVEN NAMES German 9%. *Armin, Klaus.*

Postlethwait (272) English: habitational name from a minor place in the parish of Millom, Cumbria. The name is not recorded until the 13th century. The first element is probably from Middle English *apostel* 'apostle', used as a nickname or personal name (see POSTLE). Alternatively, it may represent a survival of an Old English personal name, *Possel.* The second element is northern Middle English *thwaite* 'clearing' (Old Norse *þveit*).

Postlethwaite (168) English: variant of POSTLETHWAIT. This is the more frequent spelling in the British Isles.

Postlewait (300) English: variant of POSTLETHWAIT.

Postlewaite (179) English: reduced form of POSTLETHWAIT.

Postma (823) Frisian: variant of POSTHUMUS.

Poston (3685) English: **1.** topographic name for someone who lived by a postern gate, from Old French *posterne*; in some cases it would have been a metonymic occupational name for a gatekeeper. **2.** habitational name from Poston in Herefordshire or Poston in Shropshire, which is named with an Old English personal name *Possa* + *þorn* 'thorn tree'.

Potash (418) Jewish (eastern Ashkenazic): metonymic occupational name for someone who extracted or used potash (in bleaching paper or material for example), from Yiddish *potash*, eastern Slavic *potash*, German *Pottasche*, 'potash'.

GIVEN NAMES Jewish 5%. *Hyman, Sol.*

Pote (317) **1.** English (Devon and Cornwall): unexplained. **2.** Possibly an altered spelling of German **Pothe**, a variant of POTH.

Poteat (1112) Variant of POTEET.

Poteet (1666) Said to be of French origin, this name is associated in the early 18th century with MD and subsequently with NC and SC. If it is French, it is probably a Huguenot name. It may be an altered form of French PETIT, or possibly of French **Pottet**, which is from a diminutive of *pot* 'pot', in any of several senses: a metonymic occupational name for a potter, a nickname for a market trader, or a nickname for a rotund individual.
FOREBEARS Francis Poteet, from England, is recorded in MD in 1667.

Poteete (317) Variant of POTEET.

Potempa (168) Polish (**Potępa**): nickname from a derivative of *potępić* 'to condemn', applied either to a very judgmental person or to someone who was condemned.

Potenza (388) Southern Italian: habitational name from Potenza in Basilicata.
GIVEN NAMES Italian 15%. *Carmine* (4), *Vito* (4), *Rocco* (3), *Angelo, Canio, Franco, Sal, Salvatore.*

Poth (427) North German: topographic name for someone who lived by a small pool, from Middle Low German *pōt* 'puddle', 'pool', or a habitational name from any of several places so named in northern Germany.
GIVEN NAMES German 4%. *Rudi* (2), *Detlef, Konrad, Kurt, Mathias.*

Pothast (113) German: variant of POTT-HAST.

Pothier (497) French: occupational name for a maker of drinking and storage vessels, from an agent derivative of Old French *pot* 'drinking vessel'.
FOREBEARS A Pothier from Paris is documented in Quebec City in 1670, with the secondary surname LAVERDURE.
GIVEN NAMES French 10%. *Armand* (2), *Andre, Andree, Chantal, Donat, Gaston, Josee, Lucien, Marcel, Narcisse, Raoul.*

Potier (220) Variant of POTHIER.
GIVEN NAMES French 6%; Irish 5%. *Marcel, Monique, Raoul; Murphy* (2).

Potocki (322) **1.** Polish and Jewish (from Poland): habitational name from any of various places called Potok. **2.** Polish: topographic name for someone who lived by a brook or stream, Polish *potok*.
FOREBEARS This name is borne by one of the most distinguished Polish noble families, among whose members have been many statesmen, military commanders, and writers. Forebears of the Potocki family were already prominent in Polish society in the 13th century.
GIVEN NAMES Polish 9%. *Czeslaw, Justyna, Kazimierz, Kinga, Krzysztof, Piotr, Witold, Zygmunt.*

Potocnik (113) **1.** Czech and Slovak (**Potočník**) and Slovenian (**Potočnik**): topographic name for someone who lived by a brook, from *potok* 'brook'. **2.** Slovenian (**Potočnik**): old habitational name for someone from any of various

places called Potok or Potoče, named with *potok* 'brook'.

Potosky (131) Germanized or Americanized form of Czech or Slovak **Potocký**, topographic name for someone who lived by a stream, Czech *potok*.

Potratz (429) Eastern German (of Slavic origin): habitational name from an unidentified place probably in eastern Germany.
GIVEN NAMES German 4%. *Kurt* (2), *Erhardt, Ernst.*

Potrykus (108) German: unexplained.
GIVEN NAMES German 6%. *Gerhardt, Wolfram.*

Pott (288) **1.** English: from a medieval personal name, a short form of PHILPOTT. **2.** English: topographic name for someone who lived by a depression in the ground, from Middle English *pot* 'drinking or storage vessel' used in this transferred sense, or a habitational name from one of the minor places deriving their name from this word, in the sense 'pit', 'hole'. **3.** English and North German (Lower Rhine-Westphalia): metonymic occupational name for a potter, from Middle English, Middle Low German *pot* 'pot'. See also POTTER. **4.** North German: topographic name for someone living on a low-lying plot, from Low German dialect *pōt* 'puddle'.
GIVEN NAMES German 4%. *Aloys, Christoph, Hans, Otto.*

Pottebaum (237) German: partly standardized form of North German **Pottböhm(er)**. The first part was misinterpreted as 'pot' (see POTT 4): In fact, it derives from dialect *pōt* 'puddle' + Middle Low German *bōm* 'tree' (standard German BAUM) and was probably a distinguishing name or a topographic name for someone who grew trees on a low-lying plot of land.

Potteiger (262) Probably an altered spelling of German **Pöttiger** (or possibly also of **Böttiger**), variants of **Böttcher** (see BOETTCHER).

Pottenger (246) English and Scottish: variant spelling of POTTINGER.

Potter (27402) English, Dutch, and North German (**Pötter**): occupational name for a maker of drinking and storage vessels, from an agent derivative of Middle English, Middle Low German *pot*. In the Middle Ages the term covered workers in metal as well as earthenware and clay.

Potterfield (101) English: probably a habitational name from a lost or unidentified place.

Potters (102) Dutch: patronymic for the son of a potter (see POTTER).

Potterton (118) English: habitational name from Potterton in West Yorkshire.

Potthast (204) North German (Lower Rhine-Westphalia): metonymic occupational name for a maker or seller of potage, from Middle Low German *potharst* (from *pot* 'pot' + *harst* 'roast'), a thick soup or

stew made with beef and root vegetables. The word was in common use until around 1850, when it was replaced by *Gulasch*.
GIVEN NAMES German 6%. *Berthold, Fritz, Kurt.*

Potthoff (422) North German: perhaps a habitational name from a place in Westphalia named as *Pothof* '(plant) nursery', from Middle Low German *pote* 'seedling', 'young plant' + *hof* 'farmstead', 'courtyard', or, more likely, a variant of PUTHOFF.
GIVEN NAMES German 5%. *Otto* (2), *Erwin, Henrich, Kurt, Sieglinde, Wilhelm.*

Pottinger (426) **1.** English and Scottish: occupational name for a maker or seller of pottage, from Middle English, Old French *potagier* (an agent noun from *potage* 'stew', 'thick soup'), with an intrusive -*n*-. **2.** English and Scottish: occupational name from Old French *potecaire* 'apothecary'. **3.** German: possibly a habitational name from a place called Potting in Bavaria.

Pottle (407) English: from a pet form of *Pott*, a short form of PHILPOTT.

Pottorf (139) Variant of German POTTORFF.

Pottorff (466) German: probably an altered form of PUTHOFF.

Pottratz (147) German: variant of POTRATZ.

Potts (13350) English and Scottish: patronymic from POTT 1, particularly common in northeastern England.

Potucek (148) Czech (**Potůček**): diminutive of Czech and Slovak **Potocký**, a topographic name for someone who lived by a brook or stream, *potok*.
GIVEN NAME Czech and Slovak 4%. *Zdenek.*

Potvin (1033) English and French: regional name from Old French *Poitevin*, denoting someone from Poitou in western France. The form Potvin has long been established in England and was brought to the U.S. from there. However, French bearers of the surname **Poitevin** also came to the New World, where their surname underwent a similar transformation on arrival in New England.
GIVEN NAMES French 12%. *Lucien* (5), *Armand* (4), *Gilles* (3), *Alphonse* (2), *Andre* (2), *Cecile* (2), *Michel* (2), *Pierre* (2), *Adelard, Adrien, Aime, Benoit.*

Potwin (113) Variant of French POTVIN.

Pou (308) Catalan: topographic name for someone who lived by a well, *pou* 'well' (Latin *puteus* 'well', 'pit').
GIVEN NAMES Spanish 15%. *Francisco* (3), *Jose* (3), *Alberto* (2), *Armando* (2), *Carlos* (2), *Andres, Angel, Fernando, Guillermo, Jose Rafael, Juan, Julio.*

Pouch (127) **1.** English: metonymic occupational name for a pouch maker (see POUCHER). **2.** Polish: possibly a nickname for a shirker, from a derivative of *pouchylać się* 'to avoid one's duties', 'shirk'.
GIVEN NAMES Polish 4%. *Aleksander, Ryszard.*

Poucher (276) English (Lincolnshire): occupational name for a maker of bags and purses, from an agent derivative of Middle English *pouche* 'purse', 'bag'. In the Middle Ages pouches were a universal personal accessory, as clothing with pockets was unknown.

Poudrier (186) French Canadian: secondary surname for LEMAY, first attested in 1717; it probably refers to a soldier charged with maintaining the supply of (gun)powder. It is sometimes translated as POWDERLY and is quite common in New England.
GIVEN NAMES French 11%. *Andre* (2), *Herve* (2), *Cecile, Normand, Veronique.*

Pough (251) Probably an English variant of Welsh PUGH.

Poulin (3027) French: metonymic occupational name for a breeder of poultry or nickname for a timorous person, from a diminutive of Old French *poule* 'chicken'. It is sometimes Americanized as POLAND.
GIVEN NAMES French 20%. *Marcel* (19), *Armand* (16), *Andre* (9), *Gaston* (9), *Lucien* (8), *Normand* (8), *Yvon* (8), *Emile* (7), *Fernand* (7), *Laurier* (6), *Pierre* (5), *Cecile* (4).

Pouliot (1051) French Canadian: probably from a derivative of *poule*, 'chicken'.
FOREBEARS A Pouliot from the Maine region of France is documented in Beaupré, Quebec, in 1667.
GIVEN NAMES French 18%. *Marcel* (9), *Andre* (5), *Normand* (4), *Armand* (3), *Adrien* (2), *Cecile* (2), *Colette* (2), *Emile* (2), *Fernand* (2), *Gilles* (2), *Julien* (2), *Lucien* (2).

Poullard (104) French: pejorative derivative of Old French *poule* 'chicken'.

Poulos (2007) Greek: short form of any of scores of Greek family names ending with the patronymic suffix *-poulos*, or from this form used independently as a term of endearment. It is derived from Latin *pullus* 'nestling', 'chick', and occurs mainly in the Peloponnese.
GIVEN NAMES Greek 6%. *Constantine* (4), *Spyros* (4), *Vasilios* (4), *Voula* (3), *Angelos* (2), *Evangelos* (2), *Kostas* (2), *Spiro* (2), *Spiros* (2), *Spyridon* (2), *Alexandros, Anastasios.*

Poulsen (1432) Danish and Norwegian: patronymic from the personal name *Poul* (see PAUL).
GIVEN NAMES Scandinavian 10%. *Erik* (5), *Jorgen* (3), *Bodil* (2), *Einer* (2), *Johan* (2), *Audun, Bent, Britt, Carsten, Gunner, Karsten, Kjeld.*

Poulson (1272) **1.** English: patronymic from Middle English *Pole* or *Poul*, vernacular forms of PAUL. **2.** Americanized spelling of Scandinavian POULSEN. .

Poulter (552) English: occupational name from Old French *po(u)letier* 'poultry dealer or breeder' (an agent derivative of *poule* 'chicken').

Poulton (617) English: habitational name from any of the various places, for example in Cheshire, Gloucestershire, Kent, and

Lancashire, so named from Old English *pōl* 'pool' + *tūn* 'enclosure', 'settlement'.

Pouncey (418) English (Dorset): unexplained. It may be a habitational name from a lost or unidentified place.
FOREBEARS The Pouncey family first came to America from Dorchester, England, in the 1630s, settling near Yorktown, VA.

Pouncy (260) English (Dorset): variant of POUNCEY.
GIVEN NAMES French 4%. *Albertine, Marcelle, Monique.*

Pound (1243) **1.** English: from Middle English *p(o)und* 'enclosure (especially for confining animals)'; a topographic name for someone who lived near an enclosure in which animals were kept, or a metonymic occupational name for an official responsible for rounding up stray animals and placing them in a pound. **2.** Probably a translation of German PFUND or the North German cognate PUND.

Pounder (146) **1.** English (Nottingham): variant of POUND, with the addition of the habitational or agent suffix *-er*. **2.** Probably a translation of South German **Pfunder**, **Pfünder**, occupational names for a weigh master or wholesaler, variants of PFUND with the addition of the agent suffix *-er*.

Pounders (731) Apparently a variant of POUNDER.

Pounds (2278) English: variant of POUND.

Poundstone (135) Literal translation of German **Pfundstein**, probably a metonymic occupational name for a weighing official or a merchant who used stones as weights (see PFUND).

Poupard (151) French: variant of POUPART.
FOREBEARS A Poupard from Brittany arrived in Montreal in 1665, with the secondary surname LAFLEUR, and another arrived from Paris in 1666. The secondary surname LAFORTUNE is also attested.
GIVEN NAME French 4%. *Marcel.*

Poupart (104) French: nickname from Old French *poupart* 'doll', 'puppet', 'coward'.
GIVEN NAMES French 17%. *Andre* (2), *Armand, Francois, Jean Louis, Yves.*

Poupore (162) Perhaps an Americanized spelling of French POUPARD, reflecting the characteristic Canadian rounding of the *-ard* ending. Compare *Picard* becoming *Pecor.*

Pour (121) **1.** Muslim: from Persian *pur(i)* 'son of', used like Arabic *ibn* or *bin*. For example, Mahmud of Ghaznah (971–1030), the founder of the Ghaznavid dynasty in Afghanistan and Khorasan, was known as Mahmud puri Sabuktagin 'Mahmud son of Sabuktagin'. **2.** Perhaps also an altered spelling of German **Pauer**, a Bavarian and Austrian variant of BAUER.
GIVEN NAMES Muslim 25%. *Bijan* (2), *Mohsen* (2), *Said* (2), *Hassan, Khalil, Shahriar, Taghi.*

Pourciau (267) French: from a variant spelling of *pourceau* 'piglet', presumably

an unflattering nickname for a dirty or disgusting man. This name is found chiefly in LA.
GIVEN NAMES French 6%. *Andre, Cecile, Emile.*

Pousson (270) French (Normandy): from Old French *pousson*, a spirit made from linseed oil or hemp, hence a metonymic occupational name for someone who made this. This name is found mostly in LA.
GIVEN NAMES French 5%. *Chantal, Curley, Gaston, Monique.*

Poust (194) Altered spelling of German **Pfaust**, a variant of PFAUTZ, or of German **Paust**, a variant of PABST.

Poutre (150) French: apparently from medieval French *poutre* 'young mare', 'filly', though the reasons for its adoption as a surname are unclear. It is found chiefly in VT.
FOREBEARS A Poutre from Valenciennes in France is documented in Quebec City in 1667, with the secondary surname LAVIGNE.
GIVEN NAMES French 13%. *Fernand* (2), *Andre, Fabien, Jean-Pierre, Solange.*

Poveda (119) Spanish (also **Póveda**): habitational name from any of the places called Poveda, in the provinces of Cuenca, Ávila, Salamanca, and Soria, or from Póveda de la Sierra in Guadalajara.
GIVEN NAMES Spanish 60%. *Carlos* (6), *Alberto* (3), *Galo* (3), *Gustavo* (3), *Humberto* (2), *Jorge* (2), *Jose* (2), *Rafael* (2), *Reinaldo* (2), *Renan* (2), *Alejandro, Alejo.*

Poveromo (145) Italian (Apulia and central Italy): nickname for a poor man, or an ironic nickname for a rich miser, from *povere* 'poor' + *uomo* 'man'.
GIVEN NAMES Italian 14%; French 7%. *Vito* (2), *Romolo, Sesto*; *Henri, Pascal, Patrice.*

Povey (136) Welsh: Anglicized form of Welsh *ap Hwfa* 'son of *Hwfa*' (see HOVEY).

Povich (116) Croatian and Serbian (**Povič**): unexplained.

Powanda (106) Polish (**Powęda**): occupational name for someone who smoked fish or meat, from *powędzić* 'to smoke', 'cure (meat)'.

Powderly (168) Irish: probably a habitational name from Powerlough in County Meath.
GIVEN NAME Irish 5%. *Caitlin.*

Powe (1008) **1.** English: nickname for a vain or proud man, from Middle English *po* 'peacock'. Compare PEACOCK. **2.** Welsh: variant of PUGH.

Powel (114) **1.** English: variant of POWELL. **2.** North German: from a form of the personal name PAUL.

Powell (74080) **1.** English (of Welsh origin): Anglicized form of Welsh *ap Hywel* 'son of *Hywel*', a personal name meaning 'eminent' (see HOWELL). **2.** Irish: mainly of Welsh origin as in 1 above, but sometimes a surname adopted as equivalent of

Gaelic **Mac Giolla Phóil** 'son of the servant of St. Paul' (see GUILFOYLE).

FOREBEARS This surname is extremely common in Wales and has also spread throughout England and Ireland. The first recorded occurrence of the surname in its modern form is Roger ap Howell, alias Powell, named in a lawsuit in 1563. He was the grandson of Howell ap John (d. 1535). Snelling Powell, born in Carmarthen, Wales, in 1758, came to America in 1793 and was a successful actor and theater manager in Boston. Later members of the family include the novelist Anthony Powell (b. 1905).

Powelson (389) Patronymic from North German or English POWEL.

Power (5975) **1.** Irish (Leinster and Munster) and English (of Norman origin): habitational name for someone from Pois, a place in Picardy (said to have been named with Old French *pois* 'fish' because of its well-stocked river), from Old French *Pohier* 'native of Pois'. **2.** English: nickname for a poor man, or ironically for a miser, from Middle English, Old French *povre*, *poure* 'poor' (Latin *pauper*). Woulfe gives this also as the meaning of the Norman Irish name, which in early records is found as *le Poer*, believing it to be a nickname for someone who has taken a vow of poverty.

Powers (35164) English: variant of POWER.

Powis (156) English (West Midlands): habitational name from the region of Powis in North Wales.

Powles (199) **1.** English (of Welsh origin): variant of POWELL, with redundant English patronymic *-s*. **2.** English: patronymic from *Poul*, a variant of the personal name PAUL.

Powless (274) Probably an altered spelling of PAULUS.

Powley (469) **1.** English (East Anglia): from a pet form of PAUL. **2.** Probably an altered spelling of German PAULI or PAULY.

Pownall (355) English: habitational name from a place in Cheshire, first recorded in the 12th century as *Pohenhale*, from the genitive case of the Old English personal name *Pohha* + Old English *halh* 'nook', 'recess'.

Pownell (149) English: variant of POWNALL.

Poyer (295) **1.** French: possibly a nickname from a variant of Old French *poier* 'power', 'powerful'. **2.** Possibly a variant of German BOYER.

FOREBEARS A Poyer of unknown regional origin in France is documented around 1706 in Chambly, Quebec, with the secondary surname Lapintade or Lapintarde.

Poyner (531) **1.** English (of Norman origin): nickname for someone who was handy with his fists, from Old French *poigneor* 'fighter' (Latin *pugnator*, from *pugnare* 'to fight', a derivative of *pugnus* 'fist'). **2.** Welsh: Anglicized form of Welsh

ab Ynyr 'son of *Ynyr*', a personal name from Latin *Honorius*.

Poynor (421) English: variant spelling of POYNER.

Poynter (1549) English: variant spelling of POINTER.

Poyser (170) English: variant of PEISER.

Poythress (402) English: unexplained. Perhaps a Huguenot name, an altered form of French POITRAS.

Poznanski (186) Polish (**Poznański**) and Jewish (eastern Ashkenazic): habitational name from the city of Poznań in west-central Poland, or possibly from other places of this name, in Katowice and Siedlce voivodeships.

GIVEN NAMES Polish 8%. *Halina, Krzysztof, Leszek, Tadeusz, Tomasz, Wladyslaw.*

Pozniak (192) Polish (**Późniak**), Jewish (from Poland and Belarus), and Belorussian: nickname from a noun derivative of *późny* 'late'. This was sometimes used for a person who habitually turned up late, but was more generally a nickname for someone who was born some days later than expected, or someone who was born when his parents were already rather old.

GIVEN NAMES Polish 11%. *Andrzej, Boguslaw, Bronislaw; Zvi.*

Pozo (308) Spanish and Galician: topographic name for someone who lived by a well, *pozo* (Latin *puteus* 'well', 'pit'), or habitational name from any of the many places named Pozo, in particular Pozo in Galicia or El Pozo in Asturies, named with *pozo* 'well' (from Latin *puteus*).

GIVEN NAMES Spanish 55%. *Jose* (9), *Carlos* (6), *Jaime* (6), *Luis* (6), *Rafael* (5), *Jorge* (4), *Juan* (4), *Pedro* (4), *Graciela* (3), *Roberto* (3), *Ernesto* (2), *Evangelina* (2).

Pozorski (147) Polish: of uncertain origin; perhaps a nickname for a dissimulator, from Polish *pozór* 'semblance', 'appearance'.

Pozos (104) Spanish and Galician: habitational name from any of several places named with the plural of *pozo* 'well'. See POZO.

GIVEN NAMES Spanish 52%. *Juan* (3), *Alejandro* (2), *Delfino* (2), *Javier* (2), *Rafael* (2), *Raul* (2), *Adolfo, Alfredo, Amalia, Armando, Arturo, Domingo; Antonio.*

Pozza (127) Italian (Venetian): habitational name from any of the numerous places named Pozza, especially in central Italy, as for example Pozza in Trento (since 1955, Pozza di Fassa). Compare POZZI.

GIVEN NAMES Italian 9%. *Aldo* (2), *Reno* (2), *Angelo, Luigi.*

Pozzi (509) Italian: habitational name from any of various places named Pozzi, for example in Calabria, or Pozzo, named with Italian *pozzo* 'well', or possibly a topographic name from the same word.

GIVEN NAMES Italian 15%; Spanish 6%. *Angelo* (3), *Emilio* (3), *Lucio* (3), *Mario*

(3), *Carlo* (2), *Dario* (2), *Piero* (2), *Ricci* (2), *Stefano* (2), *Alberto, Aldo, Cesare, Giancarlo, Gilberto, Gino, Livio; Ana, Armida, Carols, Diego, Julio, Rafael, Ramona.*

Prabhakar (111) Indian (southern states): Hindu name from Sanskrit *prabhākara* 'light maker' (from *prabhā* 'light' + *-kara* 'causing'), an epithet of the sun. This is found only as a male given name in India, but in the U.S. it has come to be used as a family name.

GIVEN NAMES Indian 85%. *Sunil* (6), *Ram* (2), *Satya* (2), *Anand, Anil, Aparna, Babu, Ganga, Giridhar, Jayanth, Kalyani, Prashant, Prem, Rajeev, Rajiv, Shyam; Ranjit; Arati, Diwakar.*

Prabhu (192) Indian (Goa, Karnataka): Hindu name found in several communities, from Sanskrit *prabhu* 'lord'.

GIVEN NAMES Indian 81%. *Satish* (5), *Pradeep* (3), *Santosh* (3), *Sunil* (3), *Vijay* (3), *Anil* (2), *Anjani* (2), *Ashok* (2), *Beena* (2), *Ganesh* (2), *Krishna* (2), *Manohar* (2), *Sameer* (2), *Vasant* (2), *Vikram* (2), *Ajay, Ajit, Devadas.*

Pracht (326) South German: **1.** nickname for a loud or boastful person, from Middle High German *braht* 'noise', 'boasting' or *brahten* 'to be noisy', 'to boast'. **2.** habitational name from a place so called, for example near Wissen or Koblenz.

Prada (242) **1.** Catalan and Galician: habitational name from Prada de Conflent, in northern Catalonia, or any other places in Catalonia and in Galicia named Prada, so named from Catalan *prada* or a variant of Galician *prado* 'meadow' (Latin *pratum*). **2.** Northern Italian: habitational name from any of numerous places in northern Italy called Prada, from a variant of PRATA, cognate with 1 above.

GIVEN NAMES Spanish 38%. *Jose* (7), *Juan* (5), *Guillermo* (4), *Hernando* (3), *Luis* (3), *Ana* (2), *Angel* (2), *Camilo* (2), *Enrique* (2), *Fernando* (2), *Francisco* (2), *Jorge* (2).

Pradhan (225) Indian (Bengal, Orissa, Maharashtra), Bangladeshi, and Nepali: Hindu name from Sanskrit *pradhāna* 'chief', originally a title, now widely used as a family name. In Maharashtra it is found in the Kayasth Prabhu community. In Bengal and Bangladesh it is used as a family name in both the Hindu and the Muslim communities.

GIVEN NAMES Indian 85%; Muslim 4%. *Ashok* (4), *Sanjay* (4), *Anil* (3), *Anup* (3), *Avinash* (3), *Kishore* (3), *Ramesh* (3), *Sachin* (3), *Shekhar* (3), *Suresh* (3), *Amit* (2), *Deepti* (2), *Amirali* (2), *Amal, Amin, Anis, Badruddin, Fateh, Inayat, Ismail, Jamila, Mahmood, Mohammed, Sadru.*

Prado (2247) Spanish, Galician, Portuguese, and Jewish (Sephardic): habitational name from any of the numerous places in Spain (especially in Galicia) and Portugal named or named with Prado, from *prado* 'meadow' (from Latin *pratum*).

GIVEN NAMES Spanish 48%. *Jose* (69), *Juan* (45), *Manuel* (29), *Luis* (27), *Carlos* (25), *Francisco* (21), *Jesus* (20), *Miguel* (20), *Rafael* (16), *Pedro* (15), *Jorge* (13), *Javier* (11).

Prados (118) Spanish, Galician, and Portuguese: habitational name from any of the places called Prados, from the plural of *prado* 'meadow' (see PRADO).

GIVEN NAMES Spanish 5%; French 4%. *Juan* (2), *Gonzalo*, *Miguel*, *Trino*; *Honore*, *Vernice*.

Praeger (148) **1.** German (also **Präger**) and Jewish (Ashkenazic): occupational name for a minter, from an agent derivative of Middle High German *præch(en)*, *bræchen*, German *prägen* 'to coin or mint'. **2.** Jewish: variant of PRAGER 1.

GIVEN NAMES German 5%. *Hans*, *Otto*.

Prager (983) **1.** German, Czech (**Práger**), and Jewish (Ashkenazic): habitational name for someone from the city of Prague (Czech *Praha*, German *Prag*), the capital of what is now the Czech Republic. The name may also have been applied to someone who came from elsewhere in Bohemia, the name of a major city being preferred to a more precise local designation. It is possible that in some cases the Jewish name may derive from a place called *Praga* on the Vistula opposite Warsaw, the Yiddish name of which is *Prage*. **2.** German (**Präger**) and Jewish (Ashkenazic): see PRAEGER 1.

GIVEN NAMES German 4%. *Erhard*, *Kurt*, *Lutz*, *Manfred*, *Uli*.

Prah (114) Slovenian: from *prah* 'dust', probably an occupational nickname for a miller.

Prahl (602) German: nickname for a loud, ostentatious, or boastful person, from Middle Low German *prāle* 'pomp', 'display', or 'noise', or from *prālen* 'to boast'.

Prairie (333) French: topographic name from *prairie* 'meadow', 'pasture'. In North America this is often a translation of French surnames such as LEPRE and DUPRE.

GIVEN NAMES French 4%. *Andre*, *Armand*, *Marcel*.

Prak (149) **1.** Dutch: unexplained. **2.** Probably also Slovak: unexplained. **3.** Cambodian: unexplained.

GIVEN NAMES Cambodian 34%. *Sareth* (2), *Sok* (4), *Yan* (2), *Chhem*, *Chhin*, *Chhoeuth*, *Chhon*, *Choeun*, *Chuon*, *Heang*, *Kin*, *Meng*, *Moeun*, *On*, *Pheap*, *Sai*, *Sambath*, *Sarin*, *Yam*, *Savoeun*, *Sokheng*, *Somaly*, *Voeun*, *Samnang* (2), *Sophal* (2), *Khon*, *Lap*, *Thy*, *To*.

Prakash (328) Indian (northern and southern states): Hindu name from Sanskrit *prakāśa* 'light'. In the northern states, it probably evolved into a family name from use as the final element of a compound name such as *Ramprakash*. In South India it is used only as a male given name, but

has come to be used as a family name in the U.S. among people from South India.

GIVEN NAMES Indian 89%. *Om* (10), *Raj* (9), *Chandra* (7), *Arun* (4), *Ravi* (4), *Surya* (4), *Amit* (3), *Divya* (3), *Rohit* (3), *Sanjay* (3), *Sanjeev* (3), *Sri* (3).

Prall (584) **1.** German: nickname for a noisy or boisterous person, from Middle High German *pral* 'noise'. **2.** English: habitational name from Prawle in Devon, probably named with Old English *prāw* 'lookout' + *hyll* 'hill'.

Pralle (231) German and English: variant spelling of PRALL.

Prange (912) **1.** North German: nickname for a brawler, from Middle Low German *prang(e)* 'fight', *prangen* 'to fight'. **2.** Altered form of German **Pfrange**, a topographic name for someone living in a narrow passageway or a gorge, from *Pfrange* 'narrows'.

Pranger (378) **1.** Dutch and North German: nickname for a brawler, from an agent derivative of Middle Dutch *prangen*, Middle Low German 'to fight'. **2.** German: nickname for an ostentatious or boastful person, from Middle High German *brangen* 'to flaunt', 'to brag'. **3.** Altered form of South German **Pfranger** or **Pfränger**, agent derivatives of **Pfrange** (see PRANGE 2) meaning 'narrows'. In some instances this may have been a nickname for a narrow-minded person, from the same word in an abstract sense.

Pranke (123) Southern German: from Middle High German *pranc*, *branc* 'show', 'display', hence a nickname for an ostentatious person.

GIVEN NAME Dutch 4%. *Dirk* (2).

Prante (110) German: variant of BRAND. This name was brought to Bergen, Norway, from Bielefeld in Westphalia around the beginning of the 19th century, and from there to the U.S.

Prasad (1122) Indian (northern and southern states): Hindu name from Sanskrit *prasāda* 'favor', 'grace', 'offering'. In the northern states, it probably evolved into a family name from use as the final element in a compound personal name such as *Deviprasad*, meaning 'gift of the god Hari', *Jagannathprasad* 'gift from the lord of the world (i.e. Shiva)'. In South India it is used only as a male given name, but has come to be used as a family name in the U.S. among people from South India.

GIVEN NAMES Indian 86%. *Rajendra* (17), *Ram* (17), *Krishna* (14), *Anil* (10), *Jagdish* (10), *Sanjay* (9), *Hari* (8), *Narendra* (8), *Raj* (8), *Ajay* (6), *Anand* (6), *Rama* (6).

Prasek (131) Czech (**Prášek**): occupational nickname for a miller's apprentice, from Czech *prášek* 'dust', 'flour' (a diminutive of *prach* 'powder').

Prashad (118) **1.** Indian: variant of PRASAD. **2.** variant of PERSAUD in Guyana and Trinidad.

GIVEN NAMES Indian 73%. *Ganga* (2), *Hari* (2), *Ravi* (2), *Rohan* (2), *Shanti* (2), *Anand*, *Arjun*, *Balram*, *Bharat*, *Chaitram*, *Chetram*, *Deonarine*.

Praska (137) Origin unidentified.

Prasse (113) German: nickname for a gourmet, from Middle High German *bras* 'feast'.

GIVEN NAMES German 11%. *Kurt* (2), *Erwin*, *Fritz*.

Prast (109) **1.** North German: occupational name from Middle Low German *pravest* 'provost'. See also PROVOST. **2.** German: nickname for an ostentatious person, from Middle High German *brast* 'pageantry', 'show', 'display'. **3.** Austrian: dialect form of PROPST.

Prata (152) **1.** Italian: habitational name from Prata di Principato Ultra in Avellino province, Prata Sannita (Caserta), Prata d'Ansidonia (Aquila), or Prata di Pordenone (Pordenone). **2.** Portuguese: metonymic occupational name for a worker in silver, from *prata* 'silver' (Late Latin *plata* 'sheet metal', apparently from *plat(t)us* 'flat').

GIVEN NAMES Italian 10%; Portuguese 9%; Spanish 8%. *Antonio* (3), *Dante*, *Gilda*, *Luigi*, *Marco*, *Pasquale*; *Guilherme*, *Joaquim*; *Ana* (2), *Jose* (2), *Alvaro*, *Armando*, *Jose Antonio*, *Manuel*, *Mario*, *Rogerio*.

Prater (5971) **1.** English: status name for a reeve, the chief magistrate or bailiff of a district, from Latin *praetor*. **2.** Dutch: occupational name for a warden of meadows or a gamekeeper, from Middle Dutch *prater*, *preter* (Latin *pratarius*, a derivative of *pratum* 'meadow'). **3.** Dutch and North German: nickname for an excessively talkative person, from Middle Low German *praten* 'to talk or prattle'. **4.** German: variant of **Brater** (see BRADER 2).

Prather (5620) German: **1.** variant of **Brather** (see BRADER 2). **2.** variant of PRATER. **3.** habitational name from Prath, Rhineland (near St. Goarshausen).

Pratico (128) Italian (**Praticò**): from medieval Greek *patrikos* 'paternal', presumably applied as a nickname. Alternatively, it may be from a reduced form of Greek *peratikos* 'foreigner'.

GIVEN NAMES Italian 13%. *Domenico*, *Pasco*, *Pasquale*, *Santo*.

Prato (344) Italian: habitational name from any of numerous places, large and small, named Prato (from *prato* 'meadow', Latin *pratum*), the most important of which is the administrative centre of Tuscany.

GIVEN NAMES Italian 11%. *Gioacchino* (2), *Angelo*, *Carmine*, *Domenic*, *Domenico*, *Fausto*, *Lucio*, *Nicola*, *Nunzio*, *Remo*, *Salvatore*, *Sandro*.

Prator (98) German (**Prätor**): Latinized humanistic form of any of various surnames meaning 'leader' or 'headman', for example MAYER, SCHULTZ, and VOGT. It is from Latin *praetor*, the title of various officials in Republican and Imperial Rome.

Prats (211) Catalan: habitational name from any of the numerous places in Catalonia called Prats, from the plural of *prat* 'meadow' (from Latin *pratum*). Compare Spanish PRADOS.
GIVEN NAMES Spanish 36%. *Jose* (5), *Armando* (3), *Francisco* (3), *Jorge* (3), *Juan* (3), *Luis* (3), *Mario* (3), *Benito* (2), *Consuelo* (2), *Enrique* (2), *Pedro* (2), *Ruben* (2); *Antonio* (3), *Aldo*, *Dario*.

Pratt (21792) English: nickname for a clever trickster, from Old English *prætt* 'trick', 'tricky', 'cunning' (which is found in use as a byname in the 11th century). This surname is quite common in southeastern Ireland.

Pratte (393) Canadian spelling of French **Prat**, a topographic name from *prat* 'meadow', a dialect form of standard French *prée*. The spelling reflects the Canadian practice of pronouncing the final -*t*, which is not the practice in metropolitan France. This name often represents French **Duprat**.
GIVEN NAMES French 10%. *Alain*, *Alphee*, *Alphonse*, *Gaston*, *Jacques*, *Lucien*, *Marcel*, *Michel*, *Normand*, *Pierre*, *Sylvie*, *Yvon*.

Pratts (112) **1.** Americanized spelling of Catalan PRATS. **2.** Americanized spelling of German **Prätz** (see PRATZ).
GIVEN NAMES Spanish 36%. *Carlos* (2), *Miguel* (2), *Alba*, *Alberto*, *Anabel*, *Aurelio*, *Belgica*, *Bienvenida*, *Dominga*, *Fernando*, *Juanita*, *Julio*.

Pratz (132) German (also **Prätz**): of uncertain origin. Possibly from Slavic *brat* 'brother'. See also BRATZ.

Praus (105) German: variant of PRAUSE.

Prause (192) German **1.** variant spelling of BRAUSE. **2.** variant of **Prauss**, habitational name from any of various eastern German places of Slavic origin, for example Prauss near Wrocław (Breslau).
GIVEN NAMES German 4%. *Guenther*, *Hans-Peter*.

Prawdzik (133) Polish: nickname for a truthful person, from *prawdziwki*, a derivative of *prawda* 'truth'.
GIVEN NAMES German 4%. *Horst*, *Wilfried*.

Pray (1363) **1.** Irish (chiefly County Down): variant of PREY. **2.** English: topographic name for someone who lived by a meadow, from Middle English *pre(y)*, Old French *pree* 'meadow', or a habitational name from any of the minor places deriving their name from this word, of which there are several examples in Surrey.

Praytor (295) Variant of German PRATOR.

Prazak (185) Czech (**Pražák**): habitational name for someone from the city of Prague, Czech *Praha*, or from the surrounding region.
GIVEN NAMES Czech and Slovak 5%. *Zdenek*, *Zdenka*.

Prchal (170) Czech: nickname from *prchal* 'fugitive' or 'deserter' (from *prchat* 'to run away').

Preacher (122) English: from Old French *precheor* 'preacher', perhaps a derogatory nickname for a moralizing person.

Preas (145) Americanized spelling of German PRIES.

Preast (136) **1.** Altered spelling of English PRIEST. **2.** Variant of PREAS with excrescent -*t*, an Americanized spelling of German PRIES.

Prebble (110) English: variant of PREBLE.

Prebish (105) Origin unidentified.

Preble (954) English: unexplained. It may be a variant of a medieval name, *Preville*, a habitational name from a Norman place named with the elements *pré* 'meadow' + *ville* 'settlement'. However, this theory is not supported by evidence of early forms.

Prechel (119) German: habitational name from either of two places so named in eastern Germany.

Precht (286) South German (Bavaria and Austria): variant of BRECHT.

Prechtel (121) South German: variant of PRECHTL.

Prechtl (151) South German (Bavarian and Austrian): from a pet form of PRECHT.

Preciado (989) Spanish and Jewish (Sephardic): ornamental name from Spanish *preciado* 'prized', 'valuable' (Late Latin *pretiosus*, a derivative of *pretium* 'price', 'prize').
GIVEN NAMES Spanish 53%. *Jose* (24), *Jesus* (19), *Juan* (16), *Manuel* (12), *Ramon* (12), *Carlos* (10), *Francisco* (10), *Jaime* (9), *Luis* (9), *Ruben* (9), *Miguel* (8), *Sergio* (8).

Precourt (215) French (**Précourt**): habitational name from a place so named in the Pas-de-Calais. It is found as secondary surname of **Degré** and **Vanasse**.
GIVEN NAMES French 5%. *Fernand*, *Normand*.

Preddy (281) Welsh: variant of PRIDDY.

Predmore (578) English: variant of PRIDMORE.

Pree (151) French (**Prée**): topographic name for someone who lived by a meadow, Old French *pred*.

Preece (1122) Welsh: Anglicized form of Welsh *ap Rhys* 'son of *Rhys*' (see REESE).

Prefontaine (185) French: topographic name for someone who lived by a meadow with a spring, from *pré de la fontaine*.
GIVEN NAMES French 17%. *Andre* (2), *Adelard*, *Armand*, *Henri*, *Marcel*, *Michel*, *Normand*, *Pierre*.

Pregler (180) German: nickname for a chatterer or grumbler, from an agent derivative of Middle High German *breglen* 'to chatter', 'complain', 'yell', 'roar'.

Preheim (212) German: habitational name from an unidentified place. This is one of the names that became established in Ukraine in the 19th century.

Prehm (104) North German: variant of PREHN.

Prehn (286) North German: metonymic occupational name for a cobbler, from Middle Low German *prēn* 'cobbler's awl'.
GIVEN NAMES German 6%; French 4%. *Hans* (2), *Detlef*, *Fritz*, *Gerhard*, *Guenther*, *Gunther*; *Yvon* (2), *Nicolle*.

Prehoda (108) Czech: unexplained.

Preis (403) **1.** German, Dutch, and Jewish (Ashkenazic): nickname for a laudable or celebrated person, from Middle High German *prīs*, Dutch *prijs*, German *Preis* 'praise', 'fame', 'worth'. **2.** Southern German and Jewish (Ashkenazic): regional name for someone from Prussia, from a southern German variant of PREUSS or from Yiddish *prays* 'Prussia'.
GIVEN NAMES German 4%. *Ernst*, *Helmut*, *Klaus*.

Preiser (173) **1.** South German: occupational name for a maker of shoelaces or braids from Middle High German *brīser*. **2.** Jewish (Ashkenazic): nickname from an agent derivative of German *preisen* 'to praize', 'to extol'.
GIVEN NAMES German 5%; Jewish 4%. *Dieter*, *Wolfgang*; *Moshe*.

Preisinger (107) German: habitational name for someone from Preising in Bavaria or Austria.

Preisler (249) German: variant of PREISER.

Preiss (585) **1.** German and Jewish (Ashkenazic): variant of PREIS 1. **2.** South German: regional name for someone from Prussia, Middle High German *Priuss(e)*. Compare PREUSS. **3.** Jewish (Ashkenazic): variant of PREIS 2.
GIVEN NAMES German 4%. *Heinrich*, *Heinz*, *Horst*, *Klaus*, *Kurt*, *Otto*.

Preister (117) North German: from Low German *pre(i)ster* 'priest', 'minister of the church', probably a nickname for someone in the service of a priest; occasionally an occupational name for the priest himself.

Prejean (1124) French: topographic name from *pré de Jean*, 'John's meadow'.
FOREBEARS Prejean is a frequent surname in LA, where bearers trace descent from four brothers who arrived from Acadia in 1765.
GIVEN NAMES French 5%. *Alcee*, *Alcide*, *Ambroise*, *Curley*, *Dupre*, *Easton*, *Emile*, *Fernest*, *Marcel*, *Matilde*, *Monique*.

Prell (436) South German: occupational name for a town crier, Middle High German *prelle* 'crier'.

Preller (117) **1.** German: nickname for a loud or noisy person, from an agent noun derived from Middle High German *brellen* 'to yell', 'to bawl'. **2.** South German: variant of PRELL.
GIVEN NAMES German 10%. *Alfons* (2), *Arno* (2).

Prellwitz (254) Variant of eastern German **Prillwitz**, a habitational name from places so named in Pomerania and Mecklenburg.

GIVEN NAMES French 4%. *Colette* (2), *Michel*.

Prem (165) **1.** Nepali: Hindu name, from Sanskrit *prema* 'love'. In India, it is quite common as a personal name. **2.** Slovenian: probably from a medieval short form of the personal name *Primož*, Latin *Primus* 'first'. GIVEN NAMES Indian 10%. *Ajit, Anil, Sunil, Sushil*.

Premer (102) German: probably a topographic name for someone living near a brier hedge or a thorny thicket, from dialect *breme* 'brier'.

Premo (646) Americanized spelling of French PRIMEAU.

Prenatt (149) Variant spelling of French **Prenat**, a reduced form of **Perrenat**, from a derivative of the personal name *Pierre*, French form of PETER.

Prendergast (2199) Irish: of Welsh origin and uncertain etymology. It is said by its bearers to have been the name of Flemish settlers in Normandy, who took their name from a lost place, Brontegeest, near Ghent in Flanders. GIVEN NAMES Irish 4%. *Assumpta, Brendan, Colm, Declan*.

Prenger (363) North German: variant of PRANGER 2.

Prentice (2952) Scottish and English: from a reduced form of Middle English, Old French *aprentis* 'apprentice' (from Old French *aprendre* 'to learn', 'to understand', Latin *appre(he)ndere* 'to understand, grasp'), denoting someone learning a craft or trade, but probably originating as a nickname in the case of the surname.

Prentis (111) Scottish and English: variant of PRENTICE.

Prentiss (921) Scottish and English: variant of PRENTICE.

Presby (177) Altered form of English **Pres(t)bury** from any of various places called Presbury (Devon) or Prestbury (Cheshire, Gloucestershire), all named in Old English as 'the manor house (*burh*) of the priests'.

Prescher (212) German: habitational name from someone from a place called Preschen (in particular one near Sorau) or Bresch. GIVEN NAME German 4%. *Kurt* (2).

Prescod (138) Variant of PRESCOTT.

Prescott (6212) English: habitational name from any of the places so called, in southwestern Lancashire (now Merseyside), Gloucestershire, Oxfordshire, Shropshire, and Devon, all of which are named from Old English *prēost* 'priest' + *cot* 'cottage', 'dwelling'. The surname is most common in Lancashire, and so it seems likely that the first of these places is the most frequent source. It is also present in Ireland, being recorded there first in the 15th century. FOREBEARS John Prescott of Standish, Lancaster, England, arrived in New England in 1640 and in 1643 was one of the first settlers of Lancaster, MA. His descendants include several prominent Americans of the revolutionary war, including Samuel Prescott, born in Concord, MA, in 1751, whose fame lies in completing the midnight ride of warning in 1775 after Paul Revere was captured.

Present (149) **1.** French (**Présent**): from Old French *présent* 'gift', presumably a nickname for a much-wanted child. **2.** Jewish (eastern Ashkenazic): ornamental name from Yiddish *presente* 'gift' (see 1). GIVEN NAME Jewish 5%. *Sol*.

Presgraves (131) English (Lincolnshire): unexplained; perhaps a habitational name from a lost or unidentified place.

President (133) Origin unidentified. Evidently from the English word *president* or a cognate in another language, but the circumstances under which this became a surname are unknown.

Preslar (463) Variant, under Slavic influence, of German PRESSLER.

Presler (288) **1.** German and Jewish (Ashkenazic): variant of PRESSLER 1. **2.** Jewish (Ashkenazic): occupational name for someone who ironed clothes, from Yiddish *pres* 'flat iron' + the agent suffix *-ler*. GIVEN NAMES Jewish 4%. *Ari* (2), *Amnon, Aron, Nechama*.

Presley (5553) **1.** English: variant of PRIESTLEY. **2.** Americanized form of German PRESSLER.

Presnall (184) English: variant of PRESNELL.

Presnell (1369) English (Kent): unexplained.

Press (1769) **1.** English: variant of PRIEST. **2.** Jewish (Ashkenazic): metonymic occupational name for someone who ironed clothes, from Yiddish *pres* 'flat iron'. GIVEN NAMES Jewish 4%. *Meyer* (4), *Myer* (3), *Miriam* (2), *Sol* (2), *Tova* (2), *Ari, Basya, Isak, Semen, Shalom, Shoshanna, Yakov*.

Pressel (223) German: habitational name from Pressel near Torgau, Saxony.

Presser (560) **1.** English: nickname from Old French *prestre* 'priest'. **2.** German: derogatory nickname for a bully or tyrant, from an agent noun derivative of *pressen* 'to oppress'. **3.** Jewish (Ashkenazic): occupational name for someone who did ironing, from Yiddish *pres* 'flat iron' + the agent noun suffix *-er*. GIVEN NAMES German 6%; Jewish 4%. *Detlef, Dieter, Helmut, Kurt, Lothar, Reinhold; Leiser* (3), *Bina* (2), *Hyman, Semen*.

Pressey (311) English: from Middle English *prest* 'priest' + *hay, hey* 'enclosure'; a topographic name for someone who lived by a piece of enclosed church land, or a habitational name from a minor place such as Priesthaywood Farm in Wappenham, Northamptonshire.

Pressler (868) **1.** German and Jewish (Ashkenazic): habitational name for some-one from the city of Breslau in Silesia (Polish name Wrocław), or from PRESSEL. **2.** Jewish (Ashkenazic): variant spelling of PRESLER.

Pressley (3376) **1.** English: variant of PRIESTLEY. **2.** Americanized form of German PRESSLER.

Pressly (273) **1.** English: variant of PRIESTLEY. **2.** Americanized form of German PRESSLER.

Pressman (712) **1.** English: occupational name for a priest's servant, from Middle English *pr(i)est* 'priest', 'minister' + *man* 'man'. **2.** Jewish (Ashkenazic): occupational name for someone who did ironing and pressing of clothes, from Yiddish *pres* 'flat iron' + *man* 'man'. GIVEN NAMES Jewish 4%. *Elchanan* (3), *Yaakov* (2), *Avrohom, Baila, Genya, Zev*.

Pressnall (135) English: variant spelling of PRESNELL.

Pressnell (256) English: variant spelling of PRESNELL.

Presson (905) **1.** English: patronymic from Middle English *prest* 'priest', i.e. 'son of the priest'. **2.** French: occupational name for a presser of wine or oil, from a derivative of *presser* 'to press'.

Presswood (374) English: variant of PRESTWOOD.

Prest (423) English (northern): variant of PRIEST.

Presta (206) Southern Italian: **1.** variant of PRESTO. **2.** possibly a habitational name from Presta, a locality of Sant'Agata dei Goti in Benevento province. GIVEN NAMES Italian 17%. *Aldo, Constantino, Ferdinando, Giovanni, Ignazio, Nicola, Oreste, Pasqualino, Remo, Robertino, Serafino, Vincenzo; Alfredo, Carlos, Mario, Palmira, Patria*.

Prestage (293) English: variant of PRESTWICH, reflecting the old local pronunciation of the place name.

Prestegard (103) Norwegian: habitational name from any of numerous places named as 'the priests' farm'.

Prestenbach (106) German: unexplained; probably a habitational name from a lost or unidentified place or creek so named.

Presti (439) Italian: patronymic or plural form of PRESTO. GIVEN NAMES Italian 17%. *Angelo* (5), *Salvatore* (4), *Sal* (3), *Pasquale* (2), *Biagio, Carmello, Carmelo, Francesco, Gasper, Giovanni, Nino, Rocco*.

Prestia (255) Southern Italian: variant of PRESTO, possibly connected with a place so named. GIVEN NAMES Italian 21%. *Mirella* (3), *Carmine* (2), *Gino* (2), *Giovanni* (2), *Rocco* (2), *Vincenzo* (2), *Domenic, Enzo, Luigi, Marco, Salvatore*.

Prestidge (255) English: variant of PRESTWICH, reflecting the old local pronunciation of the place name.

Prestigiacomo (196) Southern Italian: compound name meaning 'priest James' (see PRESTO, GIACOMO).
GIVEN NAMES Italian 20%; French 4%. *Angelo* (3), *Sal* (2), *Salvatore* (2), *Santo* (2), *Antonio*, *Concetta*, *Constantino*, *Francesco*, *Ignazio*, *Stefano*; *Colette* (2), *Monique*.

Prestipino (103) Southern Italian and Sicilian: from *preste*, *presto*, an old form of *prete* 'priest' derived from Old French *prestre* + the personal name PINO, i.e. 'Priest Pino'.
GIVEN NAMES Italian 17%. *Antonio* (2), *Julio* (2), *Antonino*, *Teresita*.

Presto (297) Southern Italian (mainly Calabria and Sicily): from southern Italian *preste*, *presto*, *pristo* 'priest' (see PRETE).
GIVEN NAMES Italian 18%; Spanish 6%. *Rocco* (3), *Salvatore* (3), *Liberato* (2), *Carmelo*, *Carmine*, *Domenic*, *Fiore*, *Mario*, *Ofelia*, *Orlando*, *Pietro*; *Juan* (2), *Agustin*, *Epifanio*, *Josefina*, *Ramon*.

Preston (16192) **1.** English: habitational name from any of the extremely numerous places (most notably one in Lancashire) so called from Old English *prēost* 'priest' + *tūn* 'enclosure', 'settlement'; the meaning may have been either 'village with a priest' or 'village held by the Church'. **2.** Scottish: habitational name from Presto(u)n, now Craigmillar, in Midlothian. This name has also been established in Ireland since the 13th century.

Prestridge (587) English: of uncertain origin; apparently a habitational name, perhaps an altered form of PRESTWICH.

Prestwich (192) English: habitational name from places in Lancashire (now Greater Manchester) and Northumbria, so called from Old English *prēost* 'priest' + *wīc* 'outlying settlement'. Compare PRESTON.

Prestwood (462) English: topographic name from Middle English *prest* 'priest' + *wode* 'wood', denoting someone who lived by a wood owned by the Church, or a habitational name from places so named in Buckinghamshire, Staffordshire, and Sussex.

Presutti (363) Italian: from *prosciutto* 'ham', hence a metonymic occupational name for someone who prepared or sold charcuterie or a nickname for someone with large thighs.
GIVEN NAMES Italian 22%. *Aldo* (3), *Antonio* (3), *Orlando* (3), *Mario* (2), *Nicola* (2), *Salvatore* (2), *Veto* (2), *Angelo*, *Claudio*, *Domenic*, *Germano*, *Marcello*, *Rocco*, *Tommaso*, *Valentino*.

Preszler (166) Variant spelling of German PRESSLER.
GIVEN NAMES German 5%. *Kurt*, *Milbert*.

Prete (412) Italian: from *prete* 'priest', derived from Old Italian *previte*, a nickname for a pious man or for someone in the service of a priest, or for someone suspected of being the son of a priest.

GIVEN NAMES Italian 10%. *Angelo*, *Aniello*, *Antonio*, *Carmela*, *Carmello*, *Cosmo*, *Federico*, *Gennaro*, *Giuseppe*, *Pasquale*, *Rocco*, *Santo*.

Pretlow (134) Origin unidentified.

Pretti (163) Italian: patronymic from the nickname PRETTO.

Pretto (126) Italian: a nickname from *pretto*, a reduced form of *puretto*, a derivative of *puro* 'pure'.
GIVEN NAMES Italian 12%; Spanish 8%; French 7%. *Lino* (2), *Paolo* (2), *Alessio*, *Attilio*, *Giosue*, *Mario*, *Rodolfo*, *Santo*; *Jose* (2), *Ana Maria*, *Raul*, *Rogelio*; *Amaury* (2), *Serge*.

Pretty (233) English (chiefly East Anglia): nickname for a fine or handsome fellow, from Middle English *prety*, *prity* 'fine', 'pleasing', 'excellent' (Old English *prættig* 'clever', 'artful', 'wily').

Prettyman (790) English (East Anglia): elaborated form of PRETTY, or an occupational name for a servant of someone called *Pretty*.

Pretz (123) **1.** Austrian: unexplained; perhaps a variant of **Protz**, from a short form of the personal name *Prokopius*, or a nickname from *Protz* 'toad'. **2.** German: habitational name from either of two places so named in Bavaria and Saxony, possibly also from Preetz in Schleswig-Holstein.

Pretzer (270) Eastern German (of Slavic origin): variant of **Pretzner**, a habitational name for someone from Pretzsch near Torgau, Saxony.

Preus (118) German: variant spelling of PREUSS.

Preuss (989) German and Jewish (Ashkenazic): regional name for someone from Prussia (German *Preussen*), a former state of northern Germany, so called from the ethnic name of the *Pruzzen*, a Baltic people displaced by the Germans during the 13th century, or an ethnic name for a member of this people.
GIVEN NAMES German 7%. *Kurt* (4), *Hans* (3), *Eckhard* (2), *Erwin* (2), *Gerda* (2), *Horst* (2), *Gunter*, *Ilse*, *Klaus*, *Lothar*, *Monika*, *Rainer*.

Preusser (207) German: variant of PREUSS.
GIVEN NAMES German 5%. *Egon*, *Helmuth*, *Hertha*.

Prevatt (581) French: variant of PRIVETT.

Prevatte (438) French: variant of PRIVETT.

Prevett (119) French: variant of PRIVETT.

Prevette (415) French: variant of PRIVETT.

Previte (287) Italian: from Old Italian or dialect *previte* 'priest' (see PRETE).
GIVEN NAMES Italian 16%. *Antonio* (2), *Carmela* (2), *Domenic* (2), *Angelo*, *Giorgio*, *Pietro*, *Rocco*, *Salvatore*.

Previti (172) Italian: patronymic or plural form of PREVITE.
GIVEN NAMES Italian 20%. *Angelo*, *Antonello*, *Carmelo*, *Giacomo*, *Marina*, *Mario*, *Nicolina*, *Rosario*, *Vito*.

Prevo (313) English: Anglicized spelling of French PREVOST.

Prevost (1431) French (also **Prévost**) and English: from Old French *prevost* 'provost' (from Latin *praepositus*, past participle of *praeponere* 'to place in charge'), a status name for any of various officials in a position of responsibility. Prevost is a Huguenot name in Britain, while Le Prevost is a Guernsey surname.
FOREBEARS A Prévost from Paris is recorded in Quebec City in 1644; other families came from the Guyenne and from Normandy. An associated secondary surname is LAVIOLETTE. The French surgeon François Marie Prevost (b. 1764) settled in Donaldsonville, LA, *c.* 1800.
GIVEN NAMES French 8%. *Andre* (3), *Adrien* (2), *Alphonse* (2), *Fernand* (2), *Jacques* (2), *Marcel* (2), *Pierre* (2), *Serge* (2), *Alban*, *Andree*, *Camille*, *Francois*.

Prevot (105) French (**Prévôt**) and English: variant of PREVOST.
GIVEN NAMES French 12%. *Andre*, *Damien*, *Monique*.

Prew (226) English: variant spelling of PRUE.

Prewett (643) English: diminutive of **Prew** (see PRUE).

Prewitt (2980) English: diminutive of **Prew** (see PRUE).

Prey (173) **1.** Irish (County Down): Anglicized form of Gaelic **Ó Préith**, from an ancient personal name of unknown etymology. **2.** French: variant of PREE. **3.** German (Austrian): metonymic occupational name for a brewer, from *preu*, *breu* 'brew'. Compare PREYER.

Preyer (193) German (Austrian): occupational name for a brewer, from an agent derivative of Middle High German *briuwen* 'to brew'.

Preziosi (217) Italian: patronymic or plural form of PREZIOSO.
GIVEN NAMES Italian 10%. *Aniello*, *Antonio*, *Dante*, *Luigi*, *Romolo*.

Prezioso (329) Italian: from the medieval personal name *Prezioso*, from the adjective *prezioso* 'valuable', 'precious', 'inestimable'.
GIVEN NAMES Italian 17%. *Angelo* (3), *Salvatore* (3), *Franco* (2), *Antonio*, *Canio*, *Carmine*, *Constantino*, *Domenica*, *Fausto*, *Giovanni*, *Luigi*, *Rocco*.

Pribbenow (116) German (of Slavic origin): habitational name from a place so named in Mecklenburg.

Pribble (575) English: variant of PREBLE.

Pribnow (117) German: variant of PRIBBENOW.
GIVEN NAMES German 7%. *Otto* (2), *Heinz*.

Pribula (165) Ukrainian: nickname from a derivative of *prybylyj* 'newcomer'.

Pribyl (496) Czech (**Přibyl**): **1.** nickname for someone who had recently arrived in a district, from *přibyl* 'newcomer'. **2.** from a reduced form of the personal name

Přibyslav, composed of elements meaning 'new' and 'glory'.

Price (80852) **1.** Welsh: Anglicized form of Welsh *ap Rhys* 'son of *Rhys*' (see REECE). This is one of the commonest of Welsh surnames. It has also been established in Ireland since the 14th century, where it is sometimes a variant of BRYSON. **2.** English: the name is also found very early in parts of England far removed from Welsh influence (e.g. Richard *Prys*, Essex 1320), and in such cases presumably derives from Middle English, Old French *pris* 'price', 'prize', perhaps as a metonymic occupational name for a fixer of prices. **3.** Americanized spelling of Jewish PREUSS or PREIS.

Pricer (182) Americanized spelling of German PREISER or PREUSSER.

Prichard (2473) Welsh: variant spelling of PRITCHARD.

Prichett (126) Welsh: variant spelling of PRITCHETT.

Prickett (1616) English: **1.** variant of PRITCHETT. **2.** nickname from Middle English *priket*, a buck in its second year.

Priddle (114) English (Somerset): possibly from the Welsh patronymic *ap Ridel* 'son of *Ridel*'.

Priddy (2016) **1.** Welsh: Anglicized form of Welsh *ap Rhiddid* 'son of *Rhiddid*', a personal name of unexplained etymology. **2.** Welsh: Anglicized form of *ap Redith* 'son of *Redith*', a short form of MEREDITH; the short form occurs only in this Anglicized spelling. **3.** Welsh: from the personal name *Predyr*, *Peredur* (perhaps from Old Welsh *peri* 'spears' + *dur* 'hard', 'steel'), which was borne, in Arthurian legend, by one of the knights of the Round Table. **4.** Welsh: occupational name, from Welsh *prydydd* 'bard'. **5.** English: habitational name from Priddy in Somerset, named probably with Celtic words meaning 'earth house'.

Pride (1928) Welsh and English: nickname from Welsh *prid* 'precious', 'dear' or Middle English *pride* 'pride'; in the case of the latter, applied to a vain or haughty or possibly on occasion to someone who had played the part of Pride in a pageant of the Seven Deadly Sins.

Prideaux (248) Cornish: habitational name from a place in the parish of Luxulyan, which is first recorded in the 12th and 13th centuries in the form *Pridias*, perhaps from Cornish *prȳ* 'clay' + an unknown word. Later forms of the place name, and hence the surname, show the results of folk etymological assimilation to French *près d'eaux* 'beside waters' or *pré d'eaux* 'meadow of waters'.

Pridemore (845) English: variant of PRIDMORE.

Pridgen (1869) English (mainly Lincolnshire): possibly from Old French *preux* 'wise', 'brave' + *Jean* 'John'.

Pridgeon (377) Variant of PRIDGEN.

Pridham (152) Americanized form of French PRUDHOMME.

Pridmore (417) English: unexplained; perhaps a habitational name from a lost or unidentified place.

Priebe (1494) Eastern German (Pomerania, Silesia): from a German pet form of the Slavic personal name *Pribislaw*, a name widely borne by members of the Slavic nobility.
GIVEN NAMES German 4%. *Erwin* (4), *Horst* (3), *Kurt* (2), *Egon*, *Eldred*, *Ewald*, *Fritzi*, *Hans*, *Heinrich*, *Heinz*, *Helmut*, *Sieg*.

Priem (314) **1.** Dutch and German: metonymic occupational name for a shoemaker, from Middle Dutch *priem(e)* 'awl', Middle Low German *prēme*. **2.** German: perhaps a habitational name from any of several places called Priemen in Pomerania and Bavaria.
GIVEN NAME French 5%. *Andre* (2).

Prien (194) **1.** North German: variant of PREHN. **2.** German (Bavaria): perhaps a habitational name from Prien in Bavaria.
GIVEN NAMES German 4%. *Hans* (2), *Detlef*.

Prier (323) English and German: variant spelling of PRIOR.
GIVEN NAMES German 4%. *Fritz*, *Monika*, *Otto*.

Pries (515) German: **1.** habitational name from places such as Priesen or Priessen in eastern Germany, probably named with the Slavic topographic element *bris-* 'birch'. **2.** perhaps a nickname from Middle High German *prīse* 'praiseworthy'.

Prieskorn (106) German: of uncertain origin; it may be a derisive nickname for a grain merchant, from *pries*, variant of Middle High German *brüsch* or Middle Low German *bross* 'brittle', 'crumbly' + *korn* 'grain', or alternatively an occupational nickname for a grain seller, from *prīsekorn* '(I) determine the price of grain'. Compare BRUSHABER.

Priesmeyer (113) German: distinguishing name for a tenant farmer (see MEYER) + an uncertain first element: it may be PRIES in either of its senses.

Priess (222) German: variant of PRIES.
GIVEN NAMES German 4%. *Joerg*, *Mathias*.

Priest (5454) English (mainly West Midlands): from Middle English *pr(i)est* 'minister of the Church' (Old English *prēost*, from Latin *presbyter*, Greek *presbyteros* 'elder', 'counselor', comparative of *presbys* 'old man'), used as a nickname, either for someone with a pious manner or possibly for someone who had played the part of a priest in a pageant. It may also have been an occupational name for someone in the service of a priest, and occasionally it may have been used to denote someone suspected of being the son of a priest.
FOREBEARS A John Priest is recorded as being in Woburn, MA, as early as 1675. The *Mayflower* Pilgrim Digory Priest of Holland died the first winter at Plymouth in 1620, leaving behind a widow who remarried and two daughters, who did not pass on the family name.

Priester (1086) Dutch and German: from Middle Dutch *priester*, *preester*, Middle High German *priester* 'priest', from Latin *presbyter*. Compare PRIEST.

Priestley (737) English (mainly Yorkshire): habitational name from any of the various minor places so named, especially the one in North Yorkshire. These are named from Old English *prēost* 'priest' + *lēah* 'wood', 'clearing', i.e. a wood or clearing belonging to the Church.

Priestly (192) English: variant of PRIESTLEY.

Prieto (2182) Spanish: nickname for a dark-haired or dark-skinned man, from Old Spanish *prieto* 'dark', 'black'. The adjective derives from the verb *apretar* 'to squeeze or compress', a metathesized form of *apetrar*, Late Latin *appectorare* 'to hold close to the chest' (from *pectus*, genitive *pectoris*, 'chest'). The use as a color term seems to have derived originally from its application to rain clouds and fog.
GIVEN NAMES Spanish 50%. *Jose* (66), *Luis* (30), *Carlos* (29), *Juan* (28), *Manuel* (26), *Jesus* (24), *Jorge* (23), *Francisco* (18), *Ramon* (15), *Guadalupe* (12), *Mario* (12), *Alberto* (11); *Antonio* (19), *Lorenzo* (3), *Marco* (3), *Aldo* (2), *Angelo* (2), *Dario* (2), *Enrico* (2), *Federico* (2), *Leonardo* (2), *Severino* (2), *Annalisa*, *Carmel*.

Prieur (225) French: from Old French *pri(o)ur* 'prior', a monastic official immediately subordinate to an abbot (from Latin *prior* 'superior'), hence a nickname or occupational name, which probably most often originated as an occupational name for a servant of a prior.
FOREBEARS A Prieur from the Poitou region of France is documented in 1688 in Quebec city. LAFLEUR is an associated secondary surname.
GIVEN NAMES French 6%. *Eugenie*, *Gaston*, *Jacques*.

Prieve (129) Respelling of German PRIEWE.

Priewe (109) German (of Slavic origin): variant of PRIEBE, from a short form of a personal name such as *Pribyslav*, from Old Slavic *pribyti* 'to increase'.

Prigge (536) **1.** North German and English: voiced variant of Low German, Middle English *prikke* 'piercing tool' (from Dutch *prikken* 'to pierce or prick'), hence a metonymic occupational name for someone who used such a tool (e.g. for cutting peat, catching eels, or indeed tattooing), or in the case of the English name possibly for a maker or user of pointed weapons. **2.** German: from an old personal name of uncertain origin.
GIVEN NAMES German 4%. *Armin*, *Detlef*, *Eldor*, *Frieda*, *Hans*, *Hermann*, *Kurt*, *Lorenz*, *Otto*.

Prigmore (296) English (Midlands): probably a variant of PRIDMORE.

Prihoda (208) Czech (**Příhoda**) and Slovak (**Príhoda**): nickname from *příhoda* 'adventure'. The application is not clear; it probably derives from some lost anecdote; alternatively, it may have been used as a nickname for an adventurous individual.

Prill (640) **1.** North German: habitational name, a variant of BRILL. **2.** nickname for someone thought to resemble a minnow, from dialect *Prill*, *Brüll*, *Prüll*.
GIVEN NAMES German 5%. *Helmut* (2), *Heinz*, *Kurt*, *Lothar*, *Otto*, *Siegfried*, *Willi*.

Prillaman (472) Altered spelling of German **Brillermann**, either an occupational name for an eyeglass maker, from Middle High German *berille* 'gemstone' or 'eyeglasses' (ultimately from Greek *beryllos*) + *man* 'man', or a habitational name (see BRILL).

Prim (596) **1.** German: of uncertain origin; possibly from the Latin personal name *Primus* ('the first'), borne by several saints; or one composed with a Germanic word meaning 'to prick or stab'; or from a personal name of Slavic origin *Primm*, from *prēmu* 'right'. **2.** French: from a personal name (from Latin *Primus*). **3.** French: nickname from Old French *prim* 'first', possibly given to the eldest child in a family, or alternatively a nickname from Old French and Occitan *prim* 'shrewd', 'clever', 'artful', 'sly'. **4.** Dutch: variant of PRIEM. **5.** English: variant of PRIME.
FOREBEARS Some of the Prim families in VT descend from a Simon Laval dit Printemps, who was known in English-speaking areas as Seymour Prim.

Primack (165) Jewish (eastern Ashkenazic), Belorussian, and Ukrainian: nickname from Belorussian *primak*, Ukrainian *pryjmak* 'one who lives in the house of his father-in-law'.
GIVEN NAME Jewish 5%. *Avram*.

Primas (134) German: variant of PRIMUS.

Primavera (401) Italian: from the female personal name *Primavera*, meaning 'Spring'.
GIVEN NAMES Italian 11%. *Angelo* (2), *Amadeo*, *Antonio*, *Cosmo*, *Dante*, *Dino*, *Elvio*, *Emidio*, *Fiore*, *Giacinto*, *Luigi*, *Marco*.

Prime (546) **1.** English: from a Middle English personal name or nickname. The personal name existed in Old English, and is probably derived from Old English *prim* 'early morning' (from Latin *primus* 'first', used as the name of one of the canonical hours). The surname may be derived from this word as a Middle English nickname in the sense 'fine', 'excellent'. **2.** French: feminine form of PRIM 3. **3.** Dutch: variant of PRIEM. **4.** Probably an Americanized spelling of German **Preim**, a topographic name (of Slavic origin), perhaps from a river near Hannover; or of **Preime**, a variant of PRIMUS.

Primeau (489) Variant of PRIMEAUX.
GIVEN NAMES French 6%. *Adelard*, *Andre*, *Gaston*, *Lucien*, *Marcel*, *Michel*, *Pierrette*.

Primeaux (587) French: nickname from a derivative, probably a pejorative, of Old French *prim* 'first', 'superior'.
FOREBEARS A bearer of the name from Normandy is recorded in Montreal in 1652.
GIVEN NAMES French 8%. *Armand* (3), *Emile* (2), *Alcide*, *Alphonse*, *Anite*, *Antoine*, *Christien*, *Eloi*, *Lamotte*, *Raywood*, *Susette*.

Primer (116) **1.** English: unexplained. **2.** Serbian: unexplained.
GIVEN NAMES South Slavic 5%. *Darko*, *Dubravko*.

Primerano (125) Italian: possibly from an Old Tuscan personal name *Primierano*, from *primerano* 'first'. Compare PRIMO.
GIVEN NAMES Italian 18%. *Antonio*, *Domenic*, *Fabio*, *Fernando*, *Sal*.

Primiano (188) Italian: unexplained.
GIVEN NAMES Italian 12%. *Carmine* (3), *Angelo*, *Cosmo*, *Dante*, *Vittorino*.

Primm (1035) Alsatian form of French PRIM 3.

Primmer (365) English: nickname from Old French *premier* 'first'.

Primo (240) **1.** Italian and Spanish: from the personal name *Primo*, meaning 'first' (Latin *Primus*), given to the eldest son in a family, or, in the case of the Italian name, a habitational name from a place named with this word. **2.** Portuguese and Spanish: relationship name, from *primo* 'cousin'. **3.** Greek (**Primos**): nickname for a sailor, from Greek *primos* in the sense 'favorable wind', a derivative of Italian *primo* 'first'.
GIVEN NAMES Spanish 10%; Italian 7%. *Juan* (3), *Carlos* (2), *Alfonso*, *Feliciano*, *Fernando*, *Gutierrez*, *Julio*, *Orlando*; *Angelo* (2), *Mauro* (2), *Carmelo*, *Dario*, *Enrico*, *Francesca*, *Sal*.

Primrose (470) Scottish: habitational name from a place in Fife, originally named *Prenrhos*, from Welsh *pren* 'tree' + *rhos* 'moor', later altered by folk etymological association with the name of the flower (Late Latin *prima rosa* 'first(-flowering)' rose).

Primus (584) German: **1.** nickname from Latin *primus* '(the) first', '(the) best'. Compare FURST. **2.** variant of PRIMM (of Slavic origin and perhaps ultimately from the same element as sense 1) (see PRIM 1).

Prince (15153) **1.** English and French: nickname from Middle English, Old French *prince* (Latin *princeps*), presumably denoting someone who behaved in a regal manner or who had won the title in some contest of skill. **2.** Translation of German and Ashkenazic Jewish PRINZ or of a word meaning 'prince' in some other language.

Principato (213) Italian: possibly from *principato* 'princedom', 'principality' (a derivative of *principe* 'prince'), but more likely a regional name from Principato Ultra or Principato Citra, old names for areas of southern Campania.
GIVEN NAMES Italian 26%. *Angelo* (4), *Salvatore* (4), *Enrico* (2), *Antonio*, *Carmine*, *Domenica*, *Elio*, *Giovani*, *Luigi*, *Santo*, *Saverio*.

Principe (657) **1.** Italian and Spanish (**Príncipe**): from *principe* 'prince', 'heir' (Latin *princeps*, genitive *principis*, from *prīmus* 'first' + *capere* 'to take'), applied probably as a nickname for someone who gave himself airs and graces or for someone in the service of a prince. **2.** Italian: from an old personal name of the same derivation and meaning as 1 above.
GIVEN NAMES Italian 10%; Spanish 5%. *Eduardo* (4), *Salvatore* (3), *Americo* (2), *Dante* (2), *Adriano*, *Aldo*, *Alfonso*, *Amedeo*, *Carmela*, *Concetta*, *Constantino*, *Evo*, *Francesco*, *Gennaro*, *Gino*, *Giovanni*, , *Mario*, *Orlando*, *Rodolfo*; *Jose* (4), *Jorge* (2), *Osvaldo* (2), *Juan*, *Luis*.

Prindiville (196) Perhaps a derivative of the French expression *prim de ville* 'first man in the town', a nickname for a citizen of the first importance.
GIVEN NAME French 5%. *Jacques* (2).

Prindle (908) Possibly an altered spelling of German **Bründel**, a habitational name from Bründeln near Peine in Lower Saxony, or of **Preindl**, a Bavarian diminutive of **Praun**, a variant of BRAUN.

Prine (1236) Americanized spelling of Dutch PRUYN.

Pring (208) English: variant of PRIME, or from an Old English personal name *Preng*.

Pringle (3887) Scottish and English (Northumbria): habitational name from a place near Stow Roxburghshire, formerly called *Hop(p)ringle*, from Middle English *hop* 'enclosed valley' + a name of Old Norse origin composed of the byname *Prjónn* 'pin', 'peg' + an unidentified second element.

Prinkey (196) Americanized spelling of Dutch and German **Prinke**, a variant of **Brinke** (see BRINK).

Prins (673) **1.** Dutch: from Middle Dutch *prince* 'prince', either an occupational name for someone in the service of a prince or a nickname for someone who behaved in a regal manner or who had won the title in some contest of skill. **2.** Jewish (from the Netherlands): ornamental adoption of Dutch *prins* 'prince'.
GIVEN NAMES Dutch 4%. *Gerrit* (3), *Tonnis* (2), *Cornie*, *Harm*, *Hendrik*, *Herm*, *Kees*, *Robertus*.

Prinsen (185) Dutch: derivative of PRINS.

Prinster (100) German: unexplained.
GIVEN NAME French 4%. *Antoine*.

Printup (179) English: unexplained.

Printy (220) Variant of Irish PRUNTY.

Printz (683) German: variant spelling of PRINZ.

Prinz (628) **1.** German: nickname from Middle High German *prinze* 'prince', presumably denoting someone who behaved in a regal manner or who had won the title in some contest of skill. **2.** Jewish (Ashkenazic): ornamental adoption of German *Prinz* 'prince'.
GIVEN NAMES German 8%. *Kurt* (3), *Matthias* (2), *Ulrich* (2), *Arno, Friedrich, Hans, Klaus, Mechthild*.

Prinzi (100) Italian: probably a variant of PRINCIPE, under the influence of French *prince*.
GIVEN NAME Italian 8%. *Carlo*.

Prinzing (128) German: of uncertain origin; perhaps from a Celtic personal name, *Brinno*, of unknown meaning, or a spelling variant of **Prinsing**, presumably an eastern German habitational name.

Priola (199) Italian: variant of PRIOLO 1.
GIVEN NAME Italian 5%. *Pietro*.

Prioleau (367) French: from a diminutive of *priou(l), priol* 'prior', a nickname or occupational name, which probably most often originated as an occupational name for a servant of a prior.

Priolo (272) **1.** Italian (southern Calabria and Sicily): from *priòlu, priùli*, southern Italian derivatives of Greek *priolos* 'prior', also 'lay authority'. The Greek word in turn is derived from Latin *prior*. This was a nickname for someone thought to resemble a prior or an occupational name for a servant of a prior or some important lay personage. **2.** Italian: habitational name from Priolo in Siracusa province, Sicily. **3.** Altered spelling of French PRIOLEAU.
GIVEN NAMES Italian 15%. *Salvatore* (4), *Liberato* (2), *Carmine, Domenic, Enzo, Nunzio, Sal, Stefano*.

Prior (2678) **1.** Southern English, Scottish, Dutch, and German: ultimately from Latin *prior* 'superior', used to denote a prior, a monastic official immediately subordinate to an abbot, hence a nickname for someone thought to resemble a prior or, more often, an occupational name for a servant of a prior. **2.** Irish: Anglicized form of Irish Gaelic **Mac an Phríora** 'son of the prior' (this is the usual origin in Counties Cavan and Leitrim). Some examples may be Anglo-Norman, the same name as in 1. **3.** Portuguese, Spanish, and Catalan: from *prior*, probably denoting someone in the service of a prior or a nickname for someone who behaved in a pompous way.

Priore (337) Italian: from *priore* 'prior', a nickname or occupational name, which probably most often originated as an occupational name for a servant of a prior or some important lay dignitary. Compare PRIOLO.
GIVEN NAMES Italian 17%. *Vito* (3), *Carmine* (2), *Benedetto, Carmela, Francesco, Gennaro, Gildo, Giulio, Luciano, Pasquale, Raffaele, Salvatore*.

Prisbrey (111) Altered form of English **Pres(t)bury** (see PRESBY).

Prisby (112) Altered form of English **Pres(t)bury** (see PRESBY).

Prisco (607) Italian, Portuguese, Spanish, and Greek (**Priskos**): from the personal name *Prisco*, from Latin *Priscus* meaning 'the old one'. There are three martyrs of this name, venerated in the Eastern Church.
GIVEN NAMES Italian 17%. *Salvatore* (6), *Angelo* (4), *Carmine* (4), *Pasquale* (2), *Rocco* (2), *Sal* (2), *Vincenzo* (2), *Aniello, Dino, Francesca, Gino, Leno*.

Prisk (208) English: habitational name from Priske in Cornwall.

Prisock (125) Variant of English **Prissick** or **Pressick**, a habitational name from any of several places called Prestwick, for example in Northumberland, so named from Old English *prēost* 'priest' + *wīc* 'outlying farm'. Compare PRYSOCK.

Pritchard (9167) Welsh: Anglicized form of Welsh *ap Rhisiart* 'son of Richard' (see RICHARD).

Pritchett (6243) **1.** Welsh: Anglicized form of Welsh *ap Rhisiart* 'son of Richard'. Compare PRITCHARD. **2.** English (Midlands): from a diminutive of Middle English *prik(e), prich* 'point', 'prick', hence a metonymic occupational name for a maker or user of any of various pointed instruments, or a nickname for a tall, thin man.

Pritt (891) English (Cumbria): variant of PRATT.

Pritts (570) **1.** Variant of English PRITT. **2.** Americanized spelling of German PRITZ.

Pritz (258) German: **1.** from a German short form of the Slavic personal name *Pribislaw* (Germanized as *Pritzlaff*). **2.** topographic name of Slavic origin for someone living near a birch wood (Sorbian *brjaza*), or a habitational name from any of several places named Pritz in Mecklenburg.

Pritzker (170) Jewish (from Ukraine): habitational name for someone from Pritski in Ukraine.
GIVEN NAMES Jewish 7%; Russian 5%. *Liat, Nachman, Raanan; Semyon* (2), *Yury*.

Pritzl (209) German: from a pet form of PRITZ 1.
GIVEN NAME French 4%. *Patrice*.

Pritzlaff (120) German: from a Slavic personal name such as *Pribislav*. Compare PRIEBE.

Prive (127) French (**Privé**): variant of PRIVETT.
GIVEN NAMES French 12%. *Marcel* (2), *Andre, Cecile, Gilles, Monique*.

Privett (1044) **1.** French: from the personal name *Privat*, Latin *Privatus* (from *privatus* 'private citizen', i.e. not a public official). This was the name of several early saints, including a bishop of Mende, martyred in the 3rd century. **2.** English: habitational name from a place in Hampshire, which probably gets its name from an unrecorded Old English word *pryfet* 'privet'. This word

is found from an early date in place names, for example Privett Farm in Standlynch, Wiltshire, which could be a source of the surname, but as a vocabulary element it is not recorded before the 16th century.

Privette (863) French: variant of PRIVETT.

Privitera (379) Southern Italian: from the feminine of *previtero* 'priest', denoting the wife of an Orthodox priest.
GIVEN NAMES Italian 20%. *Salvatore* (12), *Carmelo* (3), *Angelo* (2), *Giro* (2), *Rocco* (2), *Alfio, Antonio, Battista, Corrado, Dino, Paolo*.

Privitt (119) French or English: variant of PRIVETT.

Privott (154) French or English: variant of PRIVETT.

Privratsky (111) Czech: unexplained.

Prizzi (105) Italian (Sicily): habitational name from Prizzi in eastern Sicily.
GIVEN NAMES Italian 22%. *Salvatore* (3), *Ciro* (2), *Rosario* (2), *Carmine, Elio, Gasper*.

Pro (175) Hispanic: unexplained.
GIVEN NAMES Italian 12%; Spanish 11%. *Angelo* (2), *Antonio, Elio, Emiliano, Fernando, Francisco, Oresto; Miguel* (2), *Guillermo, Javier, Jorge, Julio, Maria Teresa, Pedro, Rogelio, Ruben*.

Proano (122) Spanish (**Proaño**): habitational name from Proaño in Santander province.
GIVEN NAMES Spanish 48%; Italian 7%; French 4%. *Juan* (5), *Luis* (4), *Jose* (3), *Alfredo* (2), *Carlos* (2), *Enrique* (2), *Julio* (2), *Augusto, Beatriz, Bolivar, Cesar, Diego; Marco* (4), *Leonardo* (2), *Fausto, Giovanni, Silvio; Gaston, Joffre*.

Probasco (451) This name was brought to North America from Amsterdam in the Netherlands; its ultimate origins are uncertain. It looks Spanish, but no such Spanish surname is recorded. If, as has been suggested, the original form of the name was **Probatski**, it is almost certainly of Polish origin, but this has not been identified as a Polish surname.
FOREBEARS Juriaen Probasco came to New Netherland in 1654, having previously lived in the Dutch colonies in South America. The files of the notary Hendrick Schaef for 17 June, 1654 (Amsterdam notarial archives) record that Jurrien Probatski from Breslau shipped to New Netherland as a midshipman on the West India Company's ship *Peartree*, having borrowed 130 guilders from the distiller Henrick Otten for his outfit, and undertaken to pay it back out of his wages.

Probert (536) Welsh: Anglicized form of Welsh *ap Roppert* 'son of Robert' (see ROBERT).

Probst (2469) **1.** German: from Middle High German *probest* 'superviser', 'provost' (from Latin *propositus*), an occupational name for the head of a religious chapter or educational establishment, or, since such officials were usually clergy and celibate, a nickname probably for a self-important person. **2.** Jewish (Ashkenazic): from German *Probst* 'provost'; the reason for its adoption is unknown.

GIVEN NAMES German 4%. *Kurt* (6), *Hans* (4), *Alois* (2), *Ewald* (2), *Franz* (2), *Manfred* (2), *Otto* (2), *Arno, Egon, Erwin, Florian, Fritz.*

Probus (208) German: variant of PROBST.

Proby (115) **1.** English: unexplained. **2.** French: habitational name from a place so named in Jura.

GIVEN NAME French 8%. *Lucien* (2).

Procaccini (265) Italian: from a diminutive of **Procaccio**, from Sicilian *prucacciu* 'proceeds', 'earnings', applied as an omen name.

GIVEN NAMES Italian 20%. *Antonio* (7), *Angelo* (3), *Carlo* (2), *Mario* (2), *Vito* (2), *Americo, Antonino, Camillo, Carmino, Constantino, Domenic, Federico, Guido, Luciano.*

Procell (297) Probably a metathesized variant of PURCELL.

Proch (163) Polish and German: from Polish *proch* 'dust', 'powder', 'gunpowder', probably a nickname for a miller.

Prochaska (1055) Germanized form of Czech PROCHAZKA.

Prochazka (335) Czech (**Procházka**): from an agent derivative of *procházíet* 'to walk or wander'; this was an occupational name for an itinerant tradesman, especially a traveling butcher. It could also be a nickname for an idle person, from the same word in the sense of one who sauntered around idly.

GIVEN NAMES Czech and Slovak 5%. *Vaclav* (2), *Jaroslav, Milos, Pavel.*

Prochnow (538) German: habitational name from places so named in former East Prussia (near Deutsch-Krone) and in Brandenburg.

Procida (119) Italian: habitational name from Procida, an island in the Gulf of Naples.

GIVEN NAMES Italian 26%. *Angelo, Carmelo, Carmine, Domenic, Florio, Gaspar, Orazio, Renato, Rocco, Salvatore, Valentino.*

Prock (671) **1.** German: of uncertain origin; it may be an altered form of North German BROCK or from **Pröck**, which is of unknown origin. **2.** Possibly an altered spelling of PROCH.

Procknow (104) Americanized form of German PROCHNOW.

Procopio (689) Italian (Calabria) and Greek (**Prokopios**): from the personal name *Procopio*, Greek *Prokopios*, from *pro* 'before', 'in front' + *kopē* 'cut', actually an omen name meaning 'success', 'prosperity' but as a Church name taken to mean 'pioneer' as it was the name of the first victim of Diocletian's persecutions in Palestine in AD 303. Compare Slavic PROKOP.

GIVEN NAMES Italian 24%; Spanish 7%. *Salvatore* (7), *Domenic* (3), *Adolfo* (2), *Angelo* (2), *Antonio* (2), *Vincenzo* (2), *Aida,*

Americo, Domenico, Francesco, Gino, Gregorio, Giuseppe, Mario, Oreste, Rocco, Sal; Jose (3), *Manuel* (2), *Cruz, Hermila, Vicente.*

Procter (592) English (Cumbria and West Yorkshire): variant spelling of PROCTOR.

Proctor (12497) English (northern): occupational name from Middle English *prok(e)tour* 'steward' (reduced from Old French *procurateour*, Latin *procurator* 'agent', from *procurare* 'to manage'). The term was used most commonly of an attorney in a spiritual court, but also of other officials such as collectors of taxes and agents licensed to collect alms on behalf of lepers and enclosed orders of monks.

FOREBEARS John Proctor (d. 1757) was a prominent citizen of Boston, MA, and is buried in the King's Chapel Burying Ground there.

Prodoehl (128) German: perhaps an altered form of **Prödel**, a habitational name from Predel in Saxony-Anhalt.

Proefrock (142) German (**Pröfrock**): metonymic occupational name for a quality-control official who operated in the marketplace, from Middle Low German *prœven* 'to test' + *rocke* 'rye'.

Proehl (349) German: **1.** (**Pröhl**) habitational name from any of several places so named in eastern Germany. **2.** from a nickname for a braggart, from Middle High German *progen, brogen* 'to boast or brag'.

GIVEN NAMES German 7%. *Arno, Darrold, Dieter, Erwin, Klaus, Otmar, Otto.*

Proell (111) German: **1.** (**Pröll**): variant of PROEHL. **2.** Perhaps a variant of PRELL.

Profeta (245) Italian and Jewish (Sephardic): nickname or occupational name for a seer, from Italian, Spanish *profeta* 'prophet'.

GIVEN NAMES Italian 13%. *Salvatore* (3), *Angelo, Attilio, Ermanno, Giuseppe, Pietro, Renzo, Umberto.*

Proffer (385) German: occupational name for a gardener or horticulturist, from Middle High German *proffer, pfropfer* 'grafter'.

Proffit (382) Scottish and English: variant spelling of PROFFITT.

Proffitt (3364) Scottish and English: nickname or occupational name for a soothsayer, someone gifted with the ability to foretell the future (see PROPHET).

Profit (296) Scottish and English: variant spelling of PROFFITT.

Profitt (625) Scottish and English: variant spelling of PROFFITT.

Proft (114) **1.** German: reduced form of **Profet**, a nickname for a soothsayer, from Middle High German, Middle Low German *prophēte, proft* 'prophet', 'seer'. **2.** Dutch: occupational name or nickname, from Middle Dutch *proofst* 'provost' (see PROVOST).

GIVEN NAME German 4%. *Hans* (2).

Progar (105) Slovenian: unexplained.

Prohaska (641) Germanized variant of Czech PROCHAZKA.

Proia (248) Italian: from a minor place in Calabria called Proia, possibly from Greek *prōia* 'morning'.

GIVEN NAMES Italian 16%. *Rocco* (4), *Angelo* (2), *Antonio* (2), *Attilio* (2), *Amerigo, Cataldo, Guido, Livio, Vito.*

Proietti (176) Italian (Lazio and Umbria): patronymic from *proietto* 'foundling', 'abandoned infant' (from Latin *proiectus* 'thrown, cast out').

GIVEN NAMES Italian 21%. *Angelo* (3), *Carlo* (2), *Mario* (2), *Sal* (2), *Antonio, Dario, Elio, Enrico, Fiorenzo, Gino, Giulio, Giuseppe, Silvio.*

Prokop (1233) Czech, Polish, Ukrainian, and Belorussian: from the personal name *Prokop*, Greek *Prokopios*, from *pro* 'before', 'in front' + *kopē* 'cut', originally an omen name meaning 'success', 'prosperity' but as a Church name taken to mean 'pioneer', as it was the name of the first victim of Diocletian's persecutions in Palestine in AD 303. He is venerated in the Orthodox Church, whence the popularity of the Russian personal name *Prokofi*. The popularity of the name in central Europe is largely due to a later St. Prokop, patron saint of Bohemia, who founded Sázava abbey in Prague in the 11th century.

Prokosch (117) German (of Slavic origin; compare Czech **Prokoš**): from a similar stem (Old Slavic *proku*) as the personal name PROKOP.

Proksch (105) German: variant of PROKOSCH.

GIVEN NAMES German 6%. *Gunther, Helmut.*

Prom (329) **1.** Danish: unexplained. **2.** Cambodian: unexplained.

GIVEN NAMES Cambodian 5%. *Phon* (2), *Da, Dang, Ky, Lap, Phen, Sophal, Sophea, Thy.*

Pronovost (182) French: variant of **Prénouveau**, a topographic name meaning 'new meadow', the form having been altered under the influence of PROVOST.

GIVEN NAMES French 17%. *Andre* (2), *Lucien* (2), *Marcelle* (2), *Armand, Julien, Marcel, Roch, Rollande, Solange.*

Pronschinske (154) Germanized spelling of Polish **Prądzyński**, a habitational name from a place called Prądzyna (now Prądzona) in Słupsk voivodeship.

Proper (949) Probably a respelling of PROPPER.

Propes (461) German and Jewish (Ashkenazic): probably an Americanized variant of PROPST.

Prophet (450) Scottish, English, French, and German: nickname from Middle English and Old French *prophete*, Middle High German *prophēt* 'prophet', 'seer', ultimately from Greek *prophētēs* 'predictor', from *pro* 'before' + a derivative of *phēmi* 'to speak'. As an American family name, this

name has absorbed some cases of Greek **Profitis** and **Profitidis**.
GIVEN NAMES French 6%. *Antoine, Ignace, Magalie, Pierre.*

Prophete (111) French: nickname from Old French *prophete*, Middle High German *prophēt* 'prophet', 'soothsayer', 'wise man'.
GIVEN NAMES French 50%. *Pierre* (3), *Solange* (3), *Antoine* (2), *Philomene* (2), *Andre, Etienne, Francois, Guerda, Huguette, Jacques, Lucien, Marie-Ange.*

Propp (473) **1.** North German: metonymic occupational name for a gardener and horticulturalist, from Middle Low German *prop* 'graft', or a reduced form of a Germanic personal name formed with a cognate of Old High German *proz* 'opening bud'. **2.** North German: nickname for a fat little man, from Middle Low German *proppe* 'stopper', 'plug'. **3.** Jewish (Ashkenazic): origin uncertain; possibly the same as 2 or 1 above.

Propper (205) North German (**Pröpper**): variant of PROFFER or PROPP, with the addition of the agent suffix -*er*.

Propps (221) Probably an altered form of German PROPST.

Propson (108) German: patronymic from a Germanic personal name formed with a cognate of *proz* 'opening bud' (see PROPP 1).

Propst (1901) German and Jewish (Ashkenazic): variant of PROBST.

Prorok (146) Polish: status name or nickname from Polish *prorok* 'prophet', 'seer'.
GIVEN NAMES Polish 6%; German 4%. *Czeslaw, Stanislaw; Kurt* (2).

Prosch (171) German (of Slavic origin): **1.** from a derivative of the personal name AMBROSE. **2.** in some instances from a pet form of a Slavic personal name with the first element *Prosi-*, for example *Prosimir* or *Prosislaw.*

Proscia (176) Italian (Puglia): unexplained.
GIVEN NAMES Italian 27%. *Angelo* (5), *Giovanni* (2), *Vito* (2), *Benedetto, Domenic, Nicola, Sebastiano, Tommaso.*

Prose (233) German (also **Pröse**): from a short form of the personal name AMBROSE.

Prosek (144) Czech (**Prošek**): from a short form of the old personal names *Prosimir, Prosislav*, PROKOP, or similar.

Prosen (130) **1.** Slovenian: nickname or topographic name from *proso* 'millet'. **2.** German (**Prösen**): habitational name for someone from a place named Prösen near Torgau.

Prosise (250) Origin unidentified.

Proske (148) German (of Slavic origin): from a pet form of PROSCH 1.
GIVEN NAMES German 11%. *Dietrich, Ernst, Gerhard, Hans, Heinz, Otto.*

Prosper (260) Dutch and French: from the personal name *Prosper* (Latin *Prosper(us)*, from *prosper(us)* 'prosperous', 'fortunate'), a name borne by three 5th-century saints.

GIVEN NAMES French 9%. *Benoit, Dieudonne, Dominique, Marie-France, Yves.*

Prosperi (202) Italian: patronymic or plural form of PROSPERO.
GIVEN NAMES Italian 11%; French 8%. *Aldo* (2), *Albo, Alessandra, Angelo, Carlo, Dante, Duilio, Gino, Silvio; Andre, Armand, Henri, Michel, Pierre.*

Prospero (114) Italian and Spanish (**Próspero**): from the personal name *Prospero*, Spanish *Próspero* (from Latin *Prosper(us)*, from *prosper(us)* 'prosperous', 'fortunate').
GIVEN NAMES Italian 16%; Spanish 12%. *Umberto* (2), *Alberto, Caesar, Guido, Pasquale; Ana, Carlos, Jose, Josefa, Pedro.*

Pross (259) German: **1.** from a pet form of the personal name AMBROSE. **2.** variant of PROSCH 2. **3.** habitational name from a place so named in Bavaria.
GIVEN NAMES German 4%. *Erwin, Heinz, Wilhelm.*

Prosser (3141) Welsh: Anglicized form of Welsh *ap Rhosier* 'son of Roger' (see ROGER).

Prost (335) **1.** Dutch: from Middle Dutch *proo(f)st* 'provost', an occupational name for the head of a religious chapter or educational establishment, or, since such officials were usually clergy and celibate, a nickname for a self-important person. **2.** German: reduced form of PROBST. **3.** German (of Slavic origin) and Jewish (from Poland): nickname from Polish *prosty* 'simple', 'common'.
GIVEN NAMES French 5%. *Constant* (2), *Alain, Francoise, Jean Pierre.*

Prothero (357) Welsh: Anglicized form of Welsh *ap Rhydderch* 'son of *Rhydderch*' (see RODERICK).

Protheroe (121) Welsh: variant spelling of PROTHERO.

Prothro (415) Welsh: reduced form of PROTHERO.

Proto (455) **1.** Italian: from Greek *prōtos* 'first', hence a name bestowed on the first born (male) child, or in some cases possibly a short form of an occupational or status name formed with this element, such as **Protonotaro**, literally 'first notary'. **2.** Altered spelling of French **Proteau** or **Protot**, from a pet form of *Protasius*.
FOREBEARS A Proteau from the Anjou region of France is documented in Quebec City in 1676; BLEAU is an associated secondary surname.
GIVEN NAMES Italian 19%. *Salvatore* (5), *Cosmo* (3), *Gaetano* (3), *Antonio* (2), *Pasquale* (2), *Vincenzo* (2), *Angelo, Biagio, Carlo, Carmela, Carmelo, Carmine.*

Protsman (124) Americanized spelling of German **Protzmann** (see BROTZMAN).

Protz (167) German: **1.** nickname from an old Bavarian word meaning 'toad' and, in a figurative sense, 'showy'. **2.** topographic name of Slavic origin, from *brjaza* 'birch', Sorbian *breza.*

Protzman (212) German: **1.** (**Protzmann**): variant of **Brotzmann** (see BROTZMAN). **2.** probably a habitational name for someone from any of various places in Lower Saxony, Brandenburg, and Luxembourg called Protz.

Proud (554) English (Northumberland and Durham): nickname for a vain or haughty man, from Middle English *prod, prud* 'proud' (late Old English *prūd*, from the oblique form of Old French *proz*).

Proudfit (146) Altered form of Scottish PROUDFOOT.

Proudfoot (441) English and Scottish: nickname for someone with strutting or swaggering gait, from Middle English *prod, prud* 'proud' + *fote* 'foot'. It now occurs mainly in Scotland.

Prough (487) Origin uncertain. Perhaps an Americanized spelling of German BRUCH, BRAUCH or French PROULX.

Proulx (2110) French (also **Prou**): from a western and southern French variant of French **Preux**, a nickname meaning 'wise', 'worthy', or 'valiant'. Compare PRUE.
FOREBEARS An immigrant from Normandy, France, documented as Prou, is recorded in Quebec City in 1667; other bearers came from Poitou (1666) and from Anjou (1667).
GIVEN NAMES French 13%. *Andre* (7), *Armand* (7), *Marcel* (7), *Normand* (5), *Jacques* (4), *Fernand* (3), *Michel* (3), *Yvon* (3), *Aime* (2), *Cecile* (2), *Francois* (2), *Gratien* (2).

Prouse (243) **1.** English (Devon): variant of PRUE. **2.** Americanized spelling of German and Jewish PREUSS.

Prout (1015) **1.** English (mainly Cornwall): variant of PROUD. **2.** French: from an eastern French regional word equivalent to *prévôt* 'provost' (see PROVOST).

Prouty (1711) Probably an altered form of Scottish **Proudy**, of unexplained origin. This is a distinguished family name in VT.

Provan (156) Scottish: habitational name from a place in Glasgow, so called from Middle English *provend, prebend* 'land providing revenue for a holder of religious office' (Old French *probende, prebende*, Late Latin *praebenda* 'supplies', 'things to be supplied'). The place was name for a prebendary of Barlanark, a canon of Glasgow cathedral.
GIVEN NAME French 4%. *Marielle* (2).

Provance (311) French and English: variant of PROVINCE.

Proveaux (133) French: variant spelling of PROVOST.

Provencal (308) French (**Provençal**) and Jewish (from southern France): regional name for someone from Provence in southern France, which was so called with Latin *provincia* 'province', 'sphere of office', because it was the first Roman province to be established outside Italy.
GIVEN NAMES French 13%. *Normand* (3), *Gaston* (2), *Achille, Adelard, Armand, Elphege, Jean-Paul, Monique.*

Provence (472) French and English: variant of PROVINCE.

Provencher (1317) French: perhaps derived from **Provenchère**, a habitational name from either of two places so called in Doubs and Haute-Saône; or from places called Provenchères in Orne, Aveyron, Vosges, and Haute-Marne.

FOREBEARS A Provencher, place of birth unknown, is recorded in Cap-de-la-Madeleine, Quebec, in 1667. DUCHARME is an associated secondary surname.

GIVEN NAMES French 13%. *Lucien* (6), *Andre* (5), *Armand* (5), *Emile* (4), *Cecile* (3), *Donat* (3), *Gilles* (3), *Laurent* (3), *Marcel* (3), *Normand* (3), *Alcide* (2), *Adelard*.

Provencio (316) Spanish: from the personal name *Provencio*, from a Latin derivative of *provincia* 'province'.

GIVEN NAMES Spanish 34%. *Manuel* (6), *Ignacio* (4), *Ramon* (4), *Francisco* (3), *Elena* (2), *Enrique* (2), *Ernestina* (2), *Jaime* (2), *Juan* (2), *Ricardo* (2), *Adelina*, *Adriana*.

Provenza (191) Italian: regional name for someone from Provence in southern France, the Italian name of which is *Provenza*. Compare PROVENCAL.

GIVEN NAMES Italian 11%. *Pietro* (2), *Angelo*, *Aniello*, *Concetta*, *Enzo*, *Salavatore*.

Provenzano (1289) Italian: regional name for someone from Provence in France, from an adjectival derivative of PROVENZA.

GIVEN NAMES Italian 15%. *Angelo* (8), *Salvatore* (6), *Rocco* (3), *Ciro* (2), *Gaetano* (2), *Santo* (2), *Aldo*, *Antonietta*, *Antonio*, *Calogero*, *Carmela*, *Carmelo*.

Province (476) English and French: regional name for someone from Provence in southern France.

Provine (218) Dutch: Americanized form of **Provijn**.

GIVEN NAME French 4%. *Andre* (2).

Provins (112) English: variant of PROVINCE.

Provo (538) Americanized spelling of French PROVOST.

Provost (3113) **1.** English: from Middle English *provost* 'provost', an occupational name for the head of a religious chapter or educational establishment, or, since such officials were usually clergy and celibate, a nickname for a self-important person. **2.** French: northern and western form of PREVOST.

FOREBEARS A Provost from Paris is documented in Quebec City in 1665. An Etienne Provost, a hunter and guide born in Canada *c.* 1782, is believed to be the first white man to visit the Great Salt Lake.

GIVEN NAMES French 7%. *Armand* (11), *Pierre* (9), *Andre* (5), *Emile* (4), *Camille* (3), *Lucien* (3), *Normand* (3), *Alphonse* (2), *Cecile* (2), *Gilles* (2), *Jacques* (2), *Oneil* (2).

Prow (249) English: variant of PRUE.

Prowant (173) Probably a variant of German **Probandt**, perhaps a metonymic occupational name for a provider of food, from Middle High German *profant*, *probande* 'provisions'.

Prowell (359) Welsh: variant of **Prowle**.

Prows (160) Probably a variant of English PROWSE.

GIVEN NAME French 4%. *Lucien*.

Prowse (298) **1.** English (Devon): variant of PRUE. **2.** In some cases probably an Americanized spelling of PRAUSE.

Prucha (293) Czech (also **Průcha**): from a pet form of the personal name PROKOP.

Prudden (104) English: Anglicized form of French PRUDHOMME.

Prude (244) English: perhaps a variant of PROUD.

Pruden (935) English: Anglicized form of French PRUDHOMME.

Prudencio (133) Spanish: from the personal name *Prudencio* (from Latin *Prudentius*).

GIVEN NAMES Spanish 47%. *Jose* (6), *Carlos* (3), *Manuel* (2), *Pablo* (2), *Raul* (2), *Arsenia*, *Beatriz*, *Dionicio*, *Fernando*, *Gilberto*, *Jesus*, *Jorge Alberto*.

Prudente (215) **1.** Italian: from the personal name *Prudente*, meaning 'prudent', 'careful'. **2.** Spanish and Portuguese: from *prudente* 'careful', 'prudent', applied mainly as a nickname, occasionally as a personal name.

GIVEN NAMES Italian 22%; Spanish 5%. *Amato* (3), *Natale* (3), *Antonio* (2), *Salvatore* (2), *Alfredo*, *Amedeo*, *Angelo*, *Carmela*, *Carmine*, *Ciro*, *Cosmo*, *Ernesto*, *Mario*, *Pasquale*; *Anacleto*, *Jose*, *Remigio*.

Prudhomme (1017) French (**Prud'homme**) and English (of Norman origin): nickname from Old French *prud'homme* 'wise', 'sensible man', a cliché term of approbation from the chivalric romances. It is a compound of Old French *proz*, *prod* 'good', with the vowel influenced by crossing with *prudent* 'wise' + *homme* 'man'.

GIVEN NAMES French 8%. *Lucien* (4), *Aime*, *Alcide*, *Alphonse*, *Andre*, *Armand*, *Dominique*, *Gilles*, *Henri*, *Hilaire*, *Jacques*, *Jean Pierre*.

Prue (594) **1.** English: nickname for a redoubtable warrior, from Middle English *prou(s)* 'brave', 'valiant' (Old French *proux*, *preux*). **2.** Americanized spelling of French **Prou** (see PROULX).

Prueitt (105) French and English: variant spelling of PRUITT.

GIVEN NAME French 7%. *Ravis* (2).

Pruess (173) North German (**Prüss**) form of PREUSS.

Pruet (122) French and English: variant spelling of PRUITT.

Prueter (128) North German (**Prüter**): **1.** perhaps from a personal name formed with a cognate of Old English *prūt* 'proud'. **2.** alternatively a nickname denoting a sloppy worker (used today in Schleswig-Holstein).

Pruett (4901) French and English: variant spelling of PRUITT.

Pruette (137) French: variant spelling of PRUITT.

Prugh (246) Probably an Americanized spelling of German BRUCH.

Pruiett (260) French and English: variant spelling of PRUITT.

Pruit (122) French and English: variant spelling of PRUITT.

GIVEN NAME French 4%. *Alain*.

Pruitt (13800) French and English: nickname from a pet form of Old French *proux* 'valiant', 'brave', or 'wise' (see PROULX, PRUE).

Pruneau (161) French: topographic name for someone who lived by a plum tree, or a metonymic occupational name for someone who sold plums, from a diminutive of *prune* 'plum'.

GIVEN NAMES French 17%. *Andre* (3), *Valmore* (2), *Cecile*, *Marjolaine*, *Nazaire*, *Normand*, *Rejean*.

Pruneda (297) Catalan: topographic name for someone who lived by a plantation of plum trees, *pruneda*, from Catalan *pruna* 'plum'.

GIVEN NAMES Spanish 59%. *Jose* (9), *Jesus* (8), *Guadalupe* (4), *Juan* (4), *Ramon* (4), *Arnulfo* (3), *Arturo* (3), *Ernesto* (3), *Tomas* (3), *Blanca* (2), *Carlos* (2), *Cosme* (2).

Pruner (305) Possibly an altered spelling of German *Prunner* (a variant of BRUNNER), or a variant of BRUNER.

Prunier (268) French: topographic name for someone who lived by a plum tree, Old French *prunier*.

FOREBEARS A Prunier or Preunier from Picardy, France, arrived in Quebec City in 1665. The secondary surname VADEBONCOEUR is recorded.

GIVEN NAMES French 6%. *Adrien*, *Armand*.

Prunty (889) Irish: Anglicized form of Gaelic **Ó Proinntigh** 'descendant of *Proinnteach*', a personal name, originally a byname denoting a generous person, literally 'banqueting hall', from *proinn* 'banquet' (from Latin *prandium* 'meal') + *teach* 'house', 'hall'.

Prus (226) **1.** Polish and Jewish (Ashkenazic): ethnic name for a Prussian, either a member of an ancient Baltic people related to the Lithuanians and Latvians or a member of the German people who displaced them in the 13th century. Compare PRUSAK, PREUSS. **2.** Slovenian (south-central Slovenia): altered reduced form of the personal name *Ambrož*, Latin *Ambrosius*. Compare BRUS 2.

GIVEN NAMES Polish 10%; Jewish 4%. *Arkadiusz*, *Danuta*, *Jacek*, *Jozef*, *Miroslaw*, *Tadeusz*, *Zdzislaw*; *Chaim* (2).

Prusa (134) Czech (**Průša**): **1.** from a pet form of PROKOP. **2.** possibly also an ethnic name for a Prussian.

Prusak (312) Polish, Jewish (eastern Ashkenazic), and Ukrainian: ethnic name from

Polish and Ukrainian *Prusak* 'Prussian'. Compare PRUS, PREUSS.

Prusha (112) Americanized spelling of Czech **Průša** (see PRUSA).

Prusinowski (117) Polish: habitational name for someone from any of various places called Prusinow, Prusinowo, or Prusinowice, named with the ethnic name *Prus* (see PRUS), meaning 'village of the Prussians'.

GIVEN NAMES Polish 8%. *Casimir, Jerzy*.

Prusinski (186) Polish (**Prusiński**): habitational name for someone from Prusina in Rzeszów voivodeship.

GIVEN NAME Polish 4%. *Waclaw*.

Pruski (213) Polish: regional name for someone from Prussia (Polish *Prusy*).

GIVEN NAMES Polish 6%. *Beata, Lukasz, Tadeusz, Zygmund*.

Pruss (431) North German (also **Prüss**): regional name for someone from Prussia (see PREUSS).

Prust (200) **1.** English: variant of PRIEST. **2.** German: variant of BRUST.

GIVEN NAMES German 5%. *Erwin* (2), *Joerg*.

Pruter (111) German: variant of **Prüter** (see PRUETER).

GIVEN NAMES German 5%. *Otto, Wilhelm*.

Prutsman (101) Americanized spelling of German **Protzmann** (see BROTZMAN) or **Prützmann** (see PRUTZMAN).

Prutzman (199) **1.** Americanized form of German **Protzmann** (see BROTZMAN). **2.** (**Prützmann**): habitational name for someone from Prützen in Pomerania or Prüzen in Mecklenburg.

Pruyn (208) Dutch: variant of **Pruim**, from Middle Dutch *prume* 'plum', a metonymic occupational name for someone who grew or sold plums, or possibly a nickname, for example for someone with a plum-colored birthmark. See also PRINE.

Pruyne (112) Variant of Dutch PRUYN.

Pry (457) **1.** Irish (chiefly County Down): variant of PREY. **2.** Perhaps also an Americanized spelling of German PREY.

Pryce (591) **1.** Welsh and English: variant spelling of PRICE. **2.** Americanized spelling of Jewish PREUSS or PREIS.

GIVEN NAMES French 4%. *Cecile, Odette, Olivier*.

Pryde (257) Scottish, English, and Welsh: variant spelling of PRIDE.

Pryer (218) **1.** English: variant spelling of PRIOR. **2.** Americanized form of some like-sounding Jewish surname.

Pryor (8891) English: variant spelling of PRIOR.

Pryse (123) Variant of Welsh or English PRICE.

Prysock (119) Variant of English **Prissick** (see PRISOCK).

Przybilla (113) Partly Germanized form of Polish **Przybyła** 'new arrival', 'foundling' (see PRZYBYLA).

GIVEN NAME German 4%. *Reinhart*.

Przybyl (137) Polish (**Przybył**): variant of **Przybyła** 'foundling' (see PRZYBYLA).

GIVEN NAMES Polish 5%. *Kazimierz, Miroslaw*.

Przybyla (342) Polish (**Przybyła**): nickname denoting a newcomer to a district or, in particular, a foundling, from a derivative of *przybysz* 'new arrival', a derivative of *przybyć* 'to arrive'.

GIVEN NAMES Polish 9%; German 4%. *Henryk, Ignatius, Janusz, Jaroslaw, Kazimierz, Kazimir, Krzysztof, Pawel, Wladyslaw, Wojtek, Zdzislaw*; *Florian* (2), *Alfons, Klaus, Kurt*.

Przybylinski (103) Polish (**Przybyliński**): habitational name from a place named with *przybyła* 'new arrival' or 'foundling' (see PRZYBYLA) + the common surname suffix *-iński*.

Przybylo (115) Polish (**Przybyło**): variant of **Przybyła** 'foundling' (see PRZYBYLA).

GIVEN NAMES Polish 10%. *Stanislaw* (2), *Krystyna, Malgorzata, Stanislawa*.

Przybylowicz (109) Polish (**Przybyłowicz**): patronymic from **Przybyła** 'foundling' (see PRZYBYLA).

GIVEN NAMES Polish 12%. *Beata, Casimir, Jerzy, Krysztof, Wojciech*.

Przybylowski (78) Polish (**Przybyłowski**): habitational name for someone from any of various places called Przybyłów or Przybyłowo, named with *przybyła*, probably in the original sense 'new arrival' rather than the derived sense 'foundling'.

GIVEN NAMES Polish 15%. *Leszek* (2), *Andrzej*.

Przybylski (802) Polish: derivative of **Przybyła** 'new arrival', 'foundling' (see PRZYBYLA), with the addition of the surname suffix *-ski*.

GIVEN NAMES Polish 6%. *Janusz* (3), *Andrzej* (2), *Boguslaw* (2), *Grzegorz, Jacek, Leszek, Malgorzata, Pawel, Piotr, Przemyslaw, Stanislaw, Zbigniew*.

Przybysz (203) Polish: nickname for someone who had recently arrived in a district, from *przybysz* 'newcomer'.

GIVEN NAMES Polish 13%. *Miroslaw* (2), *Zbigniew* (2), *Andrzej, Aniela, Bogumil, Irena, Jozef, Mieczyslaw, Witold*.

Przybyszewski (110) Polish: habitational name for someone from any of various places called Przybyszew or Przybyszewo.

GIVEN NAMES Polish 20%. *Zygmunt* (2), *Andrzej, Beata, Jozef, Miroslaw, Waclaw, Zbigniew*.

Przygocki (95) Polish: habitational name for someone from Przygody in Siedlce voivodeship or Przygodzice in Kalisz voivodeship.

GIVEN NAMES Polish 6%. *Boleslaw, Piotr*.

Przywara (144) Polish: unflattering nickname from Polish *przywara* 'defect', 'shortcoming'.

GIVEN NAMES Polish 8%; Czech and Slovak 5%. *Alicja, Stanislaw, Wojciech*; *Ladislav* (2).

Psencik (149) Czech (**Pšenčík**): nickname for a peasant, from an agent noun from *pšenka*, a diminutive of *pšenice* 'wheat'.

Psomas (110) Greek: occupational name meaning 'bread maker', from *psōmi* 'bread' + the occupational suffix *-as*.

GIVEN NAMES Greek 11%. *Tasos* (2), *Marios*.

Psota (105) Slovak: unexplained.

Ptacek (534) Czech (**Ptáček**): nickname for a small person or a smart individual, from a diminutive of PTAK 'bird'.

Ptak (662) Polish and Czech (**Pták**): nickname for a small, slight person or a smart individual, from Polish *ptak*, Czech *pták* 'bird'. This name is also found in German-speaking countries.

GIVEN NAMES Polish 8%. *Jerzy* (2), *Miroslaw* (2), *Aleksander, Bogdan, Bronislaus, Casimir, Ewa, Grazyna, Janusz, Jolanta, Jozef, Leszek*.

Ptaszynski (107) Polish (**Ptaszyński**): derivative of *ptaszek* 'little bird' + the common surname ending *-yński*.

GIVEN NAMES Polish 17%. *Ewa, Henryk, Ignacy, Irena, Tadeusz, Wieslaw, Wieslawa*.

Pu (179) **1.** Chinese 蒲: from a Chinese character meaning 'cattail', a long grass that grows in ponds. A family that owned ponds containing extraordinarily long cattails came to be called by this name. **2.** Chinese: see BU. **3.** Korean: there is only one Chinese character and one clan for the surname Pu. There is no historical information on the founder of this clan, but there is a legend which tells of three men who appeared from a cave on the north side of Cheju Island's Halla Mountain. These three men were the founders of the Yang, Ko, and Pu clans. The mythological founder of the Pu clan was Pu Ŭl-la. Shortly after the three men emerged from the cave, a box washed up on the shore of the island. Inside the box were three beautiful women, horses, cows, and agricultural seed. From these beginnings, the three established Cheju Island's T'amnaguk kingdom and ruled peacefully for centuries. Unlike the descendants of Yang and Ko, however, the descendants of Pu were for the most part content to remain on Cheju Island. A 1930 census revealed that 80% of bearers of the Pu surname were still located on Cheju Island. Pu is considered a rare surname in Korea today.

GIVEN NAMES Chinese/Korean 46%. *Xiao* (4), *Chung Suk* (2), *Jing* (2), *Li-Chun* (2), *Chuan, Feng, Hongbin, Hsiao, Hui Hua, Jian, Jiong, Lijun*; *Chung, Jeong, Min*.

Publicover (110) Americanized form of Swiss German **Puppikofer**, a habitational name from a place called Puppikon in Switzerland. This name is still strongly associated with Nova Scotia.

FOREBEARS Johann Peter Bubickhoffer or Bubickopfer (*c.*1718–89) came from Epfenbach in the Palatinate to Lunenburg, Nova Scotia, in 1752.

Puccetti (140) Italian: patronymic from a pet form of PUCCIO.
GIVEN NAMES Italian 6%. *Dante, Ermanno, Livio, Reno.*

Pucci (1013) Italian: patronymic from PUCCIO.
GIVEN NAMES Italian 12%. *Angelo* (7), *Dino* (2), *Gino* (2), *Sal* (2), *Salvatore* (2), *Silvio* (2), *Amato, Amleto, Attilio, Bruna, Enrico, Fiore.*

Puccia (115) Italian: variant (feminine form) of PUCCIO.
GIVEN NAMES Italian 20%. *Salvatore* (4), *Angelo* (2), *Carmine.*

Pucciarelli (149) Italian: patronymic from a pet form of PUCCIO.
GIVEN NAMES Italian 19%. *Domenic* (2), *Antonio, Donato, Fortunato, Lorenzo, Rocco, Sal, Ugo.*

Puccinelli (246) Italian: patronymic from a pet form of PUCCIO.
GIVEN NAMES Italian 10%. *Angelo* (3), *Reno* (3), *Dante, Dino, Gino, Giovanni, Primo.*

Puccini (197) Italian: patronymic from a pet form of PUCCIO.
GIVEN NAMES Italian 21%. *Aldo, Alvaro, Amparo, Carlo, Ezio, Francesca, Giacomo, Libero, Lido, Mario, Piero, Reno, Romeo, Sergio.*

Puccio (734) Italian: from a pet form of any of various personal names with *-p* as the final consonant, as for example FILIPPO (whence *(Filip)puccio*) and **Iacopo** *((Iaco)puccio)*.
GIVEN NAMES Italian 18%. *Salvatore* (7), *Antonio* (4), *Sal* (4), *Alfonso* (3), *Carmelo* (3), *Angelo* (2), *Caterina* (2), *Dino* (2), *Giuseppe* (2), *Remo* (2), *Rocco* (2), *Rosario* (2), *Vincenzo* (2), *Benedetto, Bernardo.*

Pucel (105) Slovenian (also **Pucelj**): unexplained.

Puch (102) **1.** Polish: nickname for someone who was 'as light as thistle down', from *puch* 'thistle down'. **2.** German: nickname for a stubborn person, from Middle Low German *puch* 'stubborness', 'defiance'.
GIVEN NAMES Polish 6%; German 4%; Spanish 4%. *Casimir, Ewa; Erwin; Juan* (2), *Eloina, Renato, Rolando.*

Puchalski (408) Polish: habitational name for someone from any of the various places called Puchały in Warszawa, Łomża, and Ostrołęka voivodeships.
GIVEN NAMES Polish 6%. *Andrzej* (2), *Bogdan, Eugeniusz, Ewa, Grzegorz, Jaroslaw, Wojciech.*

Pucillo (217) Italian: from a derivative of the personal name *Pucio*, which is probably a variant of *Puccio*.
GIVEN NAMES Italian 13%. *Angelo, Carmine, Ciriaco, Enrico, Fiore, Gaetano, Rocco.*

Puck (143) **1.** North German: probably from a nickname for someone who was spiteful or stubborn, from Middle Low German *puch* 'defiance'. **2.** German: from a short form of a medieval personal name such as BURKHART. **3.** Respelling of

Jewish (eastern Ashkenazic) **Puk**, a habitational name for someone from Puki, in Belarus. **4.** English: nickname from Middle English *puck, pook* 'goblin', 'mischievous sprite'.
GIVEN NAMES German 4%. *Armin, Hans.*

Puckett (9849) English (Dorset): of uncertain origin; perhaps a variant of **Pocket(t)**, from a diminutive of Anglo-Norman French *poque* 'small pouch', hence a metonymic occupational name for a maker of purses and pouches or a nickname. Alternatively it could be from a diminutive of Middle English *pouk(e)* 'evil spirit', 'puck', 'goblin'.

Pudenz (133) German: from a medieval personal name *Pudenz* (from Latin *pudens* 'modest'), a nickname for a shy, modest person.

Puder (164) **1.** German: from a short form of a personal name, *Botthar*, formed with Old High German *biutan* 'to bid or command' or *boto* 'messenger'. **2.** German: variant of BUDER. **3.** Jewish (Ashkenazic): from German *Puder* 'powder', most likely a nickname for miller or an apothecary.
GIVEN NAMES German 7%. *Markus, Otto.*

Puderbaugh (116) German: variant of PUTERBAUGH.

Pudlo (175) Polish (**Pudło**): from *pudło* 'box', presumably a metonymic occupational name for a carpenter or chest maker. However, it may be a nickname from the same word in the derogatory sense 'old frump'.
GIVEN NAMES Polish 11%. *Andrzej* (2), *Casimir, Ireneusz, Jerzy, Jozef, Stanislaw.*

Pudwill (178) German: of Slavic origin, habitational name from Podewils in Pomerania.

Pue (100) Probably a variant spelling of Welsh PUGH.

Puebla (147) Spanish: habitational name from any of the numerous places named Puebla, meaning 'settlement' (Latin *popula*).
GIVEN NAMES Spanish 51%. *Jose* (7), *Francisco* (4), *Carlos* (2), *Eulogio* (2), *Juan* (2), *Ramon* (2), *Raul* (2), *Ricardo* (2), *Adalberto, Alberto, Angel, Armando; Oreste* (2), *Marcello, Teodolo.*

Puente (1463) Spanish: habitational name from any of the numerous places named Puente, from *puente* 'bridge'.
GIVEN NAMES Spanish 48%. *Jose* (48), *Juan* (20), *Jesus* (19), *Manuel* (17), *Carlos* (12), *Ricardo* (11), *Ruben* (10), *Jaime* (9), *Luis* (9), *Raul* (9), *Guadalupe* (8), *Miguel* (8); *Antonio* (16), *Filiberto* (3), *Gabino* (2), *Angelo, Cesario, Clementina, Constantino, Dario, Eligio, Federico, Leonardo, Lorenzo.*

Puentes (650) Spanish: habitational name from any of various places named Puentes, from the plural of *puente* 'bridge'.
GIVEN NAMES Spanish 53%. *Jose* (17), *Jesus* (13), *Juan* (11), *Manuel* (10), *Carlos* (9),

Francisco (7), *Alicia* (5), *Julio* (5), *Luis* (5), *Roberto* (5), *Angel* (4), *Guadalupe* (4); *Antonio* (6), *Benigna, Ceasar, Flavio, Geronimo, Heriberto, Lorenzo, Marco.*

Puerta (154) Spanish: habitational name from any of various places named Puerta. Compare PORTA.
GIVEN NAMES Spanish 52%. *Jose* (4), *Luis* (4), *Carlos* (2), *Diego* (2), *Gustavo* (2), *Manuel* (2), *Ricardo* (2), *Alfonso, Alicia, Alvaro, Angel, Blanca.*

Puerto (130) Spanish: habitational name from any of the numerous places named Puerto, in most cases from *puerto* 'harbor' (from Latin *portus* 'harbor', 'haven').
GIVEN NAMES Spanish 57%. *Carlos* (3), *Jaime* (3), *Jose* (3), *Alfonso* (2), *Angel* (2), *Gerardo* (2), *Miguel* (2), *Ricardo* (2), *Sergio* (2), *Alba Luz, Alonso, Arturo; Antonio* (3).

Pueschel (130) Eastern German (Silesian): **1.** variant of PESCHEL, from a pet form of the personal name *Puscho*, from a Slavic form of PETER. **2.** from a pet form of a Slavic personal name formed with Slavic *bog* 'god'.
GIVEN NAME German 5%. *Klaus.*

Puett (434) North German (also **Pütt**): habitational name from any of several places so named in Rhineland, Westphalia, and Pomerania, but in most cases a topographic name from Middle Low German *putte* 'pit', 'well', 'puddle', 'pond'.

Puetz (521) German (**Pütz**): see PUTZ 2.
GIVEN NAMES German 4%. *Otto* (2), *Dietmar, Kurt.*

Pufahl (226) Eastern German (Mecklenburg, Pomerania): of uncertain origin. In northern Germany it may perhaps be from an onomatopoeic name of the hoopoe (Latin *upupa*), a variant of *Puvogel*; otherwise of Slavic origin.
GIVEN NAME German 4%. *Armin.*

Puff (318) German: **1.** nickname for a violent, aggressive person, from *buff* 'push', 'shove'. **2.** from a pet form of a personal name, *Bodefrit*, composed with Old High German *biutan* 'to bid or order' or *boto* 'messenger'. **3.** possibly an altered spelling of PFAFF.
GIVEN NAMES German 6%. *Kurt* (2), *Bernhardt, Erwin, Hans, Heinz.*

Puffenbarger (276) Americanized spelling of **Pfaffenberger** (see POFFENBERGER).

Puffenberger (103) Americanized spelling of **Pfaffenberger** (see POFFENBERGER).
GIVEN NAME Scandinavian 6%. *Erik* (2).

Puffer (702) German: variant of PUFF 2.

Puga (505) Galician: nickname from *puga* 'thorn', 'prickle', probably in the figurative sense 'sharp', 'clever'.
GIVEN NAMES Spanish 49%; Portuguese 11%. *Jose* (11), *Alfredo* (6), *Carlos* (5), *Francisco* (5), *Jesus* (5), *Jorge* (5), *Jose Luis* (4), *Juan* (4), *Luis* (4), *Manuel* (4), *Mario* (4), *Ricardo* (4); *Joao.*

Pugel (110) Americanized form of Slovenian **Pugelj**, a nickname from *pugelj*, an obsolete Slovenian word meaning 'wether', denoting someone with any of the characteristics attributed to a wether, e.g. a person with curly hair, or a fat person, or a roguish child.

Pugh (13739) Welsh: Anglicized form of Welsh *ap Hugh* or *ap Huw* 'son of Hugh' (see HUGHES).

Puglia (427) Italian: regional name for someone from Apulia (Italian *Puglia*) in southeastern Italy.
GIVEN NAMES Italian 16%; French 4%. *Salvatore* (4), *Gaetano* (3), *Guido* (2), *Marco* (2), *Angelo*, *Aniello*, *Dino*, *Edo*, *Giacomo*, *Gino*, *Giovanni*, *Pasquale*; *Armand*, *Francois*.

Pugliano (123) Italian: **1.** regional name for someone from Apulia (Italian *Puglia*) in southeastern Italy, from an adjectival form of the place name. **2.** habitational name from a place named Pugliano, in particular the locality so called in Montecorvino Pugliano, in Salerno province, but also one in Teano in Caserta province, named as inhabited by or belonging to people from Apulia.
GIVEN NAMES Italian 14%. *Fiore* (2), *Angelo*, *Lorenzo*.

Pugliese (1816) Italian and Jewish (from Italy): from an adjectival derivative of PUGLIA, hence a regional name for someone from Apulia.
GIVEN NAMES Italian 29%; Spanish 5%. *Antonio* (10), *Rocco* (10), *Mario* (8), *Salvatore* (8), *Angelo* (7), *Giuseppe* (5), *Carmine* (4), *Francesco* (4), *Gaetano* (4), *Lorenzo* (3), *Sal* (3), *Vincenzo* (3), *Alfonso* (2), *Attilio* (2); *Ramona* (2), *Rosario* (2), *Ana*, *Beatriz*, *Carlos*.

Puglise (118) Italian: southern variant of PUGLIESE.
GIVEN NAMES Italian 11%. *Angelo* (4), *Rosaria*.

Puglisi (971) Italian: southern variant of PUGLIESE.
GIVEN NAMES Italian 18%. *Salvatore* (14), *Angelo* (5), *Carmelo* (4), *Sal* (4), *Antonio* (3), *Santo* (3), *Franco* (2), *Giovanni* (2), *Orazio* (2), *Sebastiano* (2), *Amadeo*, *Attilio*.

Pugmire (286) English: habitational name from a lost place in Yardley, Birmingham, recorded in 1645 as Puggmyre Farm. This derives from the name of its 13th-century landlord, Robert Pugg, whose surname is of unknown etymology, + Middle English *myre* 'mire', 'bog'.

Pugsley (618) English (mainly Devon): habitational name from a place so called in Warkleigh, Devon.

Puhalla (102) Origin unidentified.

Puhl (461) North German: **1.** variant of POHL 2. **2.** German: variant of **Pfuhl**, a topographic name for someone who lived by a swamp or pond, Middle High German

phuol, or a habitational name from a place named with this word.
GIVEN NAMES German 4%. *Kurt* (3), *Gerhardt*, *Otto*.

Puhr (116) German: variant spelling of **Pur**, a variant of BAUER.
GIVEN NAME German 4%. *Alois*.

Puig (507) Catalan: from *puig* 'hill(ock)' (Latin *podium* 'platform'), hence a topographic name for someone who lived at a high place, or habitational name from any of the numerous places in Catalonia named with this word.
GIVEN NAMES Spanish 40%. *Jose* (12), *Luis* (10), *Miguel* (10), *Juan* (8), *Pedro* (8), *Carlos* (6), *Orlando* (6), *Alfredo* (5), *Manuel* (5), *Ramon* (5), *Alberto* (3), *Alejandro* (3).

Pujol (296) Catalan: topographic name for someone who lived at a high place, from *pujol*, a diminutive of *puig* 'hill', 'hillock' (Latin *podiolum*), or habitational name from any of the numerous places in Catalonia named with this word (see PUIG).
GIVEN NAMES Spanish 34%; French 9%. *Jose* (11), *Juan* (7), *Carlos* (4), *Armando* (3), *Jaime* (3), *Laureano* (3), *Fernando* (2), *Joaquin* (2), *Jose Luis* (2), *Lazaro* (2), *Ramon* (2), *Alfonso*; *Raoul* (3), *Pierre* (2), *Andre*, *Francois*, *Jean-Marc*, *Marcelle*, *Thierry*.

Pula (164) **1.** Polish (**Puła**): origin uncertain. It may be a nickname from Polish dialect *puła* 'shirttail', 'coattail' or from another dialect word, *poła* 'tasteless soup'. **2.** Italian: variant of POLA.
GIVEN NAMES Spanish 4%. *Balbina* (2), *Julio*, *Rafael*, *Ruperto*.

Pulaski (706) Polish (**Pułaski**): habitational name for someone from the Pułazie in Łomża voivodeship.
FOREBEARS This name, borne by a Polish noble family, is recorded from the 17th century. Kazimierz Pułaski (1747–79) was commander in chief of a legion that fought for American independence in the Revolution; he is regarded as a U.S. national hero.

Pulcini (170) Italian: either from *pulcino* 'young chicken', probably applied a nickname for someone thought to resemble a chicken in some way or perhaps as a metonymic occupatonal name for someone who raised fowl, or alternatively from a derivative of *pulce* 'flea', applied no doubt as a nickname.
GIVEN NAMES Italian 13%; Jewish 4%. *Camillo*, *Carmela*, *Dino*, *Domenic*, *Giovanni*, *Paolo*, *Primo*, *Valentino*; *Miriam*.

Puleo (1103) Italian (Sicilian): variant of **Puleio**, from Sicilian *puleiu*, *puleu* 'fleabane' (*Mentha pulegium*), a plant of the mint family, perhaps applied as an occupational name for a herbalist or seller of herbs.
GIVEN NAMES Italian 16%. *Salvatore* (9), *Angelo* (5), *Sal* (5), *Ignazio* (4), *Pasquale*

(3), *Carmelo* (2), *Carmine* (2), *Gaetano* (2), *Onofrio* (2), *Santo* (2), *Vincenzo* (2), *Antonino*.

Pulfer (127) Swiss German: variant spelling of PULVER.

Pulford (249) English: habitational name from a place in Cheshire, so called from Old English *pōl* 'pool' + *ford* 'ford'. However, the surname is now found predominantly in East Anglia.

Puliafico (109) Italian: from the medieval Greek personal name *Poliektos*, Greek *Polyefktos*, from *polyeuktos* 'much wanted'. This was borne by a Roman legionary who converted to Christianity and was martyred in Armenia in 259 AD.
GIVEN NAMES Italian 21%. *Domenic* (4), *Salvatore* (4), *Carmelo*.

Pulice (322) Italian: nickname from a dialect variant of *pulce* 'flea', denoting someone small and agile or perhaps an irritating individual.
GIVEN NAMES Italian 19%. *Salvatore* (3), *Fiore* (2), *Saverio* (2), *Bonaventura*, *Corrado*, *Dino*, *Domenico*, *Enrico*, *Francesco*, *Gaetano*, *Giacomino*, *Gino*.

Pulido (1609) Spanish, Portuguese, and Galician: nickname from *pulido* or *polido* 'smart', 'neat', 'handsome'.
GIVEN NAMES Spanish 53%; Portuguese 11%. *Jose* (37), *Jesus* (30), *Juan* (27), *Manuel* (22), *Salvador* (18), *Miguel* (15), *Pedro* (15), *Roberto* (15), *Carlos* (13), *Francisco* (13), *Jorge* (12), *Alfonso* (10); *Figueroa*, *Omero*; *Antonio* (13), *Angelo* (2), *Federico* (2), *Fructuoso* (2), *Leonardo* (2), *Carmela*, *Cecilio*, *Clemente*, *Delio*, *Edo*, *Elio*, *Eliseo*.

Pulis (347) Maltese: unexplained.

Pulito (104) Italian: nickname from *pulito* 'clean', 'nice'; also 'refined', 'courteous', from Latin *politus*.
GIVEN NAMES Italian 23%. *Vito* (2), *Aldo*, *Alfredo*, *Domenic*, *Gino*.

Pulizzi (103) Italian (Sicilian): variant of POLIZZI.
GIVEN NAMES Italian 15%. *Dino*, *Gasper*, *Maddalena*, *Matteo*, *Pietro*, *Salvatore*.

Pulk (116) **1.** Variant of German POLK. **2.** shortened form of Czech PULKRABEK.

Pulkkinen (103) Finnish: probably from the Germanic forename VOLK, meaning 'people' or 'troops', + the common surname suffix *-nen*. This name is found mainly in eastern Finland.
GIVEN NAMES Finnish 29%. *Antti* (2), *Lempi* (2), *Markku* (2), *Tauno* (2), *Eino*, *Jarmo*, *Reino*, *Sulo*, *Taisto*, *Teuvo*, *Waino*.

Pulkrabek (160) Czech (**Pulkrábek**): dissimilated derivative of the medieval status name *purkrabí* 'burgrave'.

Pullam (161) English: variant of PULLUM. There has also been some confusion with PULLIAM.

Pullan (162) English (Yorkshire): variant spelling of PULLEN.

Pullano (252) Italian (Calabria): habitational name, probably from Pullano in Sellia Marina, in Catanzaro province.
GIVEN NAMES Italian 16%. *Antonio* (2), *Concetta, Dante, Domenico, Giuseppe, Guido, Salvatore, Silvio.*

Pullar (145) Scottish: variant of PULLER.

Pullara (174) Italian (Sicily): **1.** from Sicilian *puddara* denoting a plant of the pimpernel family. **2.** (**Pullarà**): occupational name from Greek *poularas* 'horse breeder' (see POLLARA).
GIVEN NAMES Italian 15%. *Francesco* (2), *Salvatore* (2), *Santo* (2), *Angelo, Gioacchino, Luigi.*

Pullen (3645) English (southern): from Old French *poulain* 'colt'; a metonymic occupational name for a horse-breeder or nickname for a frisky person.

Puller (174) **1.** Scottish and English: topographic name for someone who lived on the bank of a creek, inlet, or pool, Old English *pyll* 'inlet' + the suffix -*er* denoting an inhabitant, or a reduced form of the Old Englsih word *ōra* 'bank'. **2.** Americanized form of German **Pfüller**, **Pfuller**, a variant of PFUHL.

Pulley (2605) **1.** English: from Middle English *Pulleis* 'man from Apulia' (in Italy) (Middle English *Poille, Poyle, Apuelle*). **2.** English: habitational name from Pulley in Shropshire. **3.** German (of Slavic origin): from a personal name formed with Old Slavic *bolij* 'more', or a variant of **Puley**, from the medieval name of a Christian martyr *Pelagius* (from Greek *pelagos* 'sea').

Pulli (100) **1.** Italian: probably from PULLO. **2.** Finnish: unexplained.
GIVEN NAMES Italian 15%. *Angelo* (3), *Aldo.*

Pulliam (3846) Anglicized form of Welsh *ap William* 'son of William' (see WILLIAMS).

Pullig (108) **1.** German: unexplained; perhaps a habitational name from Pillig in the Rhineland-Palatinate. **2.** German (of Slavic origin): variant of PULLEY 3.

Pullin (919) English (Bristol): variant spelling of PULLEN.

Pulling (306) English (Sussex): probably a variant of PULLEN.

Pullins (524) English: variant of PULLEN, with patronymic -*s*.

Pullis (152) Probably a variant of English PULLINS.

Pullman (697) **1.** English: derivative of the personal name PELL. **2.** German (**Pullmann**): variant of **Puhlmann**, itself a variant of PUHL. **3.** Jewish (Ashkenazic): occupational name for a bottle blower, from German *Pulle* 'bottle' + *Mann* 'man'.

Pullo (105) Italian: from Latin *pullus* 'young animal'; compare POLLI.
GIVEN NAMES Italian 21%. *Sergio* (2), *Angelo, Biagio, Gino, Saverio.*

Pullum (485) English: habitational name from any of the places called Pulham, in Dorset, Norfolk, or Devon. The first two are named with Old English *pōl* or *pull*

'pool' + *hām* 'homestead', 'settlement' or *hamm* 'river meadow', 'land surrounded by water'.

Pulos (153) Greek: variant transliteration of POULOS.
GIVEN NAMES Greek 7%; Dutch 5%. *Spiro* (2), *Constantine, Spero; Gust* (3).

Puls (925) **1.** North German and Dutch: from Middle Low German *puls, pulsstock*, Middle Dutch *puls, pols*, a wooden pole used to stir the water and drive fish into a net, hence a metonymic occupational name for someone who used this method of fishing. **2.** North German: habitational name from a place so named in Schleswig-Holstein. **3.** Dutch: from Middle Dutch *pulle* 'jug', 'pitcher', 'vase'; a nickname for a portly individual or a metonymic occupational name for a maker of earthenware or metal vessels. **4.** German (of Slavic origin): from a personal name formed with Old Slavic *bolij* 'more'.

Pulse (283) Probably an altered spelling of PULS.

Pulsifer (522) English: probably a variant of English PERCIVAL.

Pulsipher (284) English: variant of PULSIFER.

Pulte (103) German: **1.** variant of **Polte**, from a short form of the personal name *Hippolyt* (see HYPOLITE). **2.** (also **Pult**) from Middle Low German *pulpite, pult* 'desk for reading or writing', 'pulpit', also (as a field name) 'raised area'; probably a topographic name for someone living by a raised area of land, or possibly an occupational name for a manufacturer of desks.

Pultorak (133) Polish, Jewish, and Ukrainian: variant of **Półtorak** (see POLTORAK).

Pultz (332) **1.** Probably an Americanized spelling of German **Pfalz**, a regional name for someone from the Palatinate (German *Pfalz*), or an occupational or status name (see PFALZGRAF). **2.** German: (**Pülz**): variant of PILZ.

Pulver (1258) **1.** German and Jewish (Ashkenazic): from Middle High German *pulver* 'ash', 'dust' (of Latin origin), German *Pulver* 'powder'; a metonymic occupational name for an apothecary or herbalist who dispensed various types of medicinal powder. From the 15th century it may alternatively have denoted a manufacturer of gunpowder. **2.** Possibly a shortened form of Dutch **van Pulver**, a habitational name from a place named Pulver (meaning 'dust'; compare 1), for example in Wormhout in West Flanders.

Pulvermacher (224) German and Jewish (Ashkenazic): occupational name, a variant of PULVER 1, with the addition of Middle High German *macher*, German *Macher* 'maker'.

Puma (583) **1.** Italian (Sicily): from Sicilian *puma* 'apple', a variant of standard Italian *pomo*. **2.** Spanish: possibly from Spanish *puma* 'puma'.

GIVEN NAMES Italian 17%; Spanish 10%. *Angelo* (9), *Salvatore* (8), *Carmine* (3), *Sal* (3), *Vito* (3), *Carmelo* (2), *Carmello, Giacomo, Giuseppe, Ignazio, Santo, Saturnina; Luis* (5), *Jose* (3), *Manuel* (3), *Jacinto* (2), *Jorge* (2), *Angel, Baldo, Bolivar, Carmella, Cesar, Julio Cesar.*

Pumilia (151) Italian: variant of **Pomilia**, from Latin *pomilis* 'of or pertaining to apples'.
GIVEN NAMES Italian 12%. *Giuseppe, Lorenzo, Luca, Vito.*

Pummill (257) English: unexplained.

Pumper (112) Origin unidentified.

Pumphrey (1375) Welsh: Anglicized form of Welsh *ap Umffrey* 'son of Humphrey' (see HUMPHREY).

Pun (214) **1.** English: unexplained. **2.** Chinese 潘: see PAN 2.
GIVEN NAMES Chinese 30%. *Ching* (3), *Chi Keung* (2), *Hong* (2), *Kin* (2), *Cheung, Fu, Ho, Jung, Kam, Kam Cheung, Kee, Kin Chung.*

Punch (439) English: variant of POINTS 1. The surname now occurs chiefly in Ireland, having been taken there in the late 13th century.
GIVEN NAMES French 6%. *Andre, Antoine, Camile, Jacques, Lucien, Napoleon, Yoland.*

Punches (209) Americanized form of German PONTIUS.

Pund (149) **1.** English: variant of POUND. **2.** German (northern and central): variant of PUNDT. Alternatively it may be an altered spelling of PFUND.

Pundt (249) German: Low and Central German form of PFUND.
GIVEN NAMES German 4%. *Fritz, Hermann.*

Pung (408) Origin unidentified. Probably of German origin, but unexplained.

Punke (108) **1.** German: unexplained; possibly an altered form of **Bunke**, from a Middle Low German personal name. **2.** North German: from Middle Low German *punge* 'small sack', 'bag', which developed into an unflattering nickname in modern Low German dialects.

Punt (171) **1.** English (Norfolk): variant of PONT. **2.** German (also **Pünt**): variant of PUND.
GIVEN NAMES Dutch 4%. *Cornelis, Gerrit, Pieter.*

Punzel (113) **1.** German: variant of **Bunzel**, from a diminutive of *Bunze* 'officially stamped) wine barrel', possibly an occupational name, or a nickname for a short fat man. **2.** German: probably a metonymic occupational name for an engraver or a metal worker of similar activity, from Middle High German *punze* 'chisel', 'gouge' + excrescent -*l*.
GIVEN NAME German 4%. *Otto.*

Puopolo (279) Italian: possibly a diminutive of PUPO 2.
GIVEN NAMES Italian 17%. *Rocco* (5), *Angelo* (3), *Vito* (2), *Alfonse, Antonio, Carmine, Carmino, Vincenzo.*

Pupa (129) Italian: from the female personal name *Pupa*, a pet name from Latin *pupa* 'doll'.
GIVEN NAMES Italian 9%. *Angelo* (2), *Aldo*.

Pupillo (112) Italian: diminutive of PUPO.
GIVEN NAMES Italian 19%. *Angelo* (2), *Sal* (2), *Lorenzo*, *Neno*, *Salvatore*.

Pupo (271) **1.** Spanish and Portuguese: possibly of Italian origin (see 2 below). **2.** Italian: nickname from *pupo* 'child', 'baby', from Sicilian *pupu*, which can also mean 'puppet', 'doll', 'vain person'.
GIVEN NAMES Spanish 32%; Italian 8%. *Juan* (6), *Luis* (5), *Roberto* (5), *Jorge* (4), *Jose* (3), *Raul* (3), *Angel* (2), *Fidel* (2), *Pedro* (2), *Rafael* (2), *Tomas* (2), *Aida*; *Antonio* (2), *Franca*, *Francesco*, *Nicola*, *Nicolina*, *Pasquale*, *Reno*.

Puppe (125) German: **1.** variant of BUPP. **2.** habitational name for someone from Puppe in Pomerania or from any of several places called Puppen in East Prussia. **3.** nickname or a metonymic occupational name, from late Middle High German *puppe* 'doll' (from Latin *pupa* 'girl').
GIVEN NAMES German 5%. *Gerhart*, *Heinz*.

Purcell (8689) English, Welsh, and Irish (of Norman origin): from Old French *pourcel* 'piglet' (Latin *porcellus*, a diminutive of *porcus* 'pig'), hence a metonymic occupational name for a swineherd, or a nickname, perhaps affectionate in tone. This is a common surname in Ireland, having become established there in the 12th century.

Purcella (101) Origin unidentified.

Purchase (291) English: metonymic occupational name for an official responsible for obtaining the supplies required by a monastery or manor house, from Anglo-Norman French *purchacer* 'to acquire or buy' (Old French *pourchacier*, from *chacier* 'to chase or catch' + the intensive prefix *p(o)ur*, Latin *pro*).

Purdie (579) Scottish: variant spelling of PURDY.

Purdin (208) Probably of English origin, a variant spelling of **Purden**, a metathesized variant of French PRUDHOMME.

Purdom (501) English: metathesized variants of PRUDHOMME; the *-ru* reversal is a fairly common occurrence in words where *-r-* is preceded or followed by a vowel.

Purdon (297) English: metathesized variants of PRUDHOMME; the *-ru-* reversal is a fairly common occurrence in words where *-r-* is preceded or followed by a vowel.

Purdue (494) English: variant of PURDY.

Purdum (431) Variant spelling of English PURDOM.

Purdy (6167) English: from Anglo-Norman French *pur die* 'by God' (Old French *p(o)ur Dieu*), a nickname for someone who made frequent use of the oath. The surname was taken to northeastern Ireland during the 17th century, and is now to be found chiefly in northern Ireland and eastern and northern England.

Purgason (206) Americanized form of English PARKERSON (see PARKINSON).

Puri (363) Indian (Panjab): Hindu and Sikh name based on the name of a clan in the Khatri community. The word *purī* in Panjabi means 'small town', but it is unclear whether this word has anything to do with the name.
GIVEN NAMES Indian 87%. *Anil* (6), *Rakesh* (5), *Vijay* (5), *Vinod* (5), *Sanjeev* (4), *Satish* (4), *Anish* (3), *Raj* (3), *Sanjay* (3), *Sunil* (3), *Anuj* (2), *Anupam* (2).

Puricelli (151) Italian: patronymic from a derivative of PURO.
GIVEN NAMES Italian 15%. *Angelo* (3), *Carlo*, *Elio*, *Enzo*, *Ettore*, *Remo*, *Rinaldo*.

Purifoy (633) French and English: variant of **Purefoy**, which is from French *par foi* 'by (my) faith', Anglo-Norman French *par fei*, a nickname for someone who habitually used this expression.

Purington (364) English: variant of PURRINGTON.

Purinton (437) English: unexplained; probably a habitational name from a lost or unidentified place.

Purk (155) Altered spelling of German BURK 1.

Purkey (845) Altered spelling of Swiss German **Bürki** (see BURKEY).

Purkiss (122) English: variant of PURCHASE.

Purks (132) English: variant spelling of PERKS.

Purl (145) Origin unidentified.
GIVEN NAMES Southeast Asian 5%. *Rakesh*, *Renu*.

Purlee (101) English: habitational name from Purley in Surrey.

Purnell (2199) English (mainly southwest): variant of PARNELL.

Puro (121) **1.** Finnish: topographic name from *puro* 'creek', 'bog'. This name is found mainly in central-western Finland, but also occurs as an ornamental name in southwestern Finland. As an American family name it may also be a shortened form of a longer Finnish compound name such as **Hautapuro** 'pit creek'. **2.** Italian: from *puro* 'pure', 'honest', applied as a personal name, or occasionally a nickname.
GIVEN NAMES Finnish 10%. *Reino* (2), *Toivo*, *Wilho*.

Purohit (146) Indian (northern states): Hindu (Brahman) name meaning 'family priest', from Sanskrit *purohita* 'one placed foremost' (from *puras* 'front' + *hita* 'placed').
GIVEN NAMES Indian 91%. *Dilip* (4), *Chandrakant* (3), *Amul* (2), *Anand* (2), *Atul* (2), *Bharat* (2), *Devesh* (2), *Kishore* (2), *Manish* (2), *Naishadh* (2), *Parul* (2), *Prakash* (2).

Purple (146) Probably a translation of Italian PURPURA.

Purpura (543) Italian: from Latin or dialect *purpura* 'red', 'purple', in some cases probably a nickname for someone with a florid complexion. It could have denoted a bishop or cardinal, with reference to the color of their robes, but is perhaps less likely to have survived as a surname from this source, or it may have been a metonymic occupational name for someone who dyed cloth or made ecclesiastical robes.
GIVEN NAMES Italian 10%. *Salvatore* (6), *Giacomo* (2), *Agostino*, *Carmello*, *Gabriella*, *Gaetano*, *Lia*, *Santo*, *Vito*.

Purrington (263) English (Devon): evidently a habitational name from a lost or unidentified place, probably in Devon or neighboring counties.

Purse (143) **1.** English: metonymic occupational name for someone who made bags or purses or for an official in charge of expenditure, from Middle English *purse* (via Old English from Latin *bursa*). **2.** Scottish: variant of PURSER.
GIVEN NAME Scottish 5%. *Munro* (2).

Pursel (457) See PURSELL.

Pursell (946) **1.** Variant spelling of English PURCELL, a habitational name for someone from Purshull in Elmbridge, Worcestershire. **2.** Variant of German **Purschel**, **Burschel**, or **Bürschel**, diminutives of BURSCH. **3.** Altered spelling of **Burzel**, **Burzle**, or **Bürzel** (see BURTS).

Purser (1327) **1.** English: from an agent derivative of Middle English *purse* (see PURSE), hence an occupational name for someone who made or sold purses and bags, or for an official in charge of expenditure. **2.** Scottish: Anglicized form of Gaelic **Mac an Sparain** 'son of the purse', traditionally born by purse-bearers to the Lords of the Isles.

Pursifull (184) Variant of English PERCIVAL.

Pursley (1610) **1.** English: habitational name from Pursley Farm in Shenley, Hertfordshire. **2.** Probably an altered spelling of German **Bürschle**, a diminutive of BURSCH.

Purtee (255) Variant of PARTEE.

Purtell (659) English: variant spelling of PURTILL.

Purtill (147) English: from Old French *poutrel* 'colt' (Late Latin *pultrellus*), a metonymic occupational name for someone responsible for keeping horses, or a nickname for a frisky and high-spirited person. This surname is also found in Ireland, Mac Lysaght believing it to be a variant of PURCELL.

Purtle (307) Variant spelling of English PURTILL.

Purucker (108) German: variant of BUROKER.

Purves (329) Scottish: variant spelling of PURVIS.

Purviance (331) Perhaps an altered spelling of Scottish **Purveyance**, which seems likely to be a derivative of Middle English *purveyen* 'to provide'. Compare PURVIS.

Purvis (5893) Scottish and northern English (Northumberland and Durham): probably from Middle English *purveys* 'provisions', 'supplies' (from Middle English *purvey(en)*, Old French *porveoir* 'to provide, supply'), hence a metonymic occupational name for an official responsible for obtaining supplies for a monastery or manor house.

Puryear (1577) English: variant of PERRIER 1 and 2.
FOREBEARS American bearers of the surname include Bennet Puryear (1826–1914), born in Mecklenburg Co., VA, youngest son of Thomas and Elizabeth (Marshall) Puryear, who studied medicine and chemistry before the Civil War, after which he became a professor of chemistry; he did pioneering work in the application of chemistry to agriculture. He had 11 children by his two wives.

Pusateri (787) Italian (Sicily): patronymic from *pusatero*, an occupational name for an innkeeper or someone who worked at an inn, from Spanish *posadero* (a derivative of POSADA).
GIVEN NAMES Italian 21%; Spanish 6%. *Salvatore* (11), *Sal* (4), *Mario* (3), *Vita* (2), *Angelo, Baldassare, Carmelo, Casimiro, Cosmo, Lia, Luciano, Mariano, Mercurio, Natale, Nino, Orlando, Roberto*; *Salvador* (2), *Diego*.

Pusch (196) German (southern and eastern): possibly a variant of BUSCH, but probably in some instances of the same origin as PUESCHEL.
GIVEN NAMES German 13%. *Hans* (2), *Benno, Christoph, Fritz, Horst, Kurt, Otto, Siegfried, Wolfgang*.

Pusey (666) **1.** English: habitational name from Pusey in Oxfordshire (formerly in Berkshire), so called from Old English *peose, piosu* 'pea(s)' + *ēg* 'island', 'low-lying land', or from Pewsey in Wiltshire, recorded in Domesday Book as *Pevesie*, apparently from the genitive case of an Old English personal name *Pefe*, not independently attested + Old English *ēg* 'island'. **2.** French: habitational name form Pusey in Haute-Saône, so named from a Gallo-Roman personal name, *Pusius*, + the locative suffix *-acum*.

Pushard (110) Americanized form of German **Buschardt** (see BUSHART).

Puskar (349) Czech (**Puškař**) and Slovak (**Puškár**): occupational name for a rifle maker.

Puskarich (188) Croatian and Serbian (**Puškarić**): patronymic from *puškar* 'rifle maker'.
GIVEN NAMES South Slavic 4%. *Marko, Mile, Petar*.

Puskas (341) Hungarian (**Puskás**): occupational name for a gunner or possibly for a gunsmith, from Hungarian *puskás* 'shooter', from *puska* 'gun'.

GIVEN NAMES Hungarian 6%. *Tibor* (4), *Attila, Gabor, Imre, Kalman, Lajos, Zoltan*.

Pust (120) **1.** Slovenian: nickname from the name of a mythological being, *Pust*, folk patron of Shrovetide, hence probably denoting someone born between the end of Christmas and the start of Lent. The name *Pust* is a shortened form of the obsolete word *mesopust*, from *meso* 'meat' and *pust* 'abstain', meaning 'abstainer from meat', 'vegetarian'. **2.** German: variant of **Pfaus** (see PAUS), or a topographic name from Sorbian *pusty* 'wild', 'uncultivated' (land).
GIVEN NAMES German 7%. *Elfriede, Guenter*.

Pustejovsky (190) Czech (**Pustějovský**): habitational name from a place in Moravia.
GIVEN NAME German 5%. *Erwin* (2).

Puterbaugh (492) Altered spelling of German **Puderbach**, a habitational name from any of several places so named in Hesse, Westphalia, and Rhineland. Compare BUTTERBAUGH.

Puthoff (254) **1.** German (**Püthoff**): a habitational name from a farm in Westphalia, so named from Middle Low German *putte* 'puddle', 'pit', 'cistern', 'well' (from Latin *puteus* 'well') + *hof(f)* 'farmstead', 'manor farm'. **2.** Variant of POTTHOFF.

Putman (3367) **1.** English: variant of PITMAN 'dweller by the pit or hollow', formed with Middle English *putte*, a dialect form common in southern and southwestern England. **2.** Dutch: from *put* 'pit' or 'well' + *man* 'man', a topographic name for someone who lived by such a feature, or a habitational name derived from a minor place named with the term. **3.** Americanized spelling of North German **Püttmann**, a topographic name cognate with 2.

Putnam (7848) English: habitational name from either of two places, in Hertfordshire and Surrey, called Puttenham, from the genitive case of the Old English byname *Putta*, meaning 'kite' (the bird) + Old English *hām* 'homestead'.
FOREBEARS John Putnam emigrated from England to Salem, MA, before 1641, and established a family that was still prominent in Massachusetts four generations later, including the revolutionary war soldier Israel Putnam (1718–90) and his cousin Rufus Putnam (1738–1824), also a soldier, one of the first settlers in OH.

Putney (1144) English: habitational name from Putney in Surrey (now Greater London), named in Old English with the genitive of *Putta*, a personal name, or *putta* 'kite' + *hām* 'homestead' or *hamm* 'river meadow', 'land hemmed in by water or marsh'.

Putt (900) **1.** English (mainly Devon and Cornwall): variant of PITT. **2.** North German (**Pütt**): see PUETT.

Putter (101) North German **1.** (**Pütter**) topographic name for someone who lived by a pool, from Middle Low German *putte* 'pit', 'puddle', 'pool' (see PUETT) or habi-

tational name for someone from any of the various places named with this word. **2.** possibly also a variant of BUTTER.
GIVEN NAME German 7%. *Klaus* (2).

Putterman (179) **1.** North German (**Püttermann**): variant of **Püttmann** (see PUTMAN). **2.** Jewish (Ashkenazic): occupational name for a dairyman or seller of butter, from northeastern Yiddish *puter* 'butter' + *man* 'man'.
GIVEN NAMES Jewish 8%. *Chaim, Zev*.

Putty (113) Perhaps a Westphalian reduced form of **Putting**, **Pütting**, of uncertain origin.

Putz (885) South German: **1.** (Austria, Bavaria): topographic name for someone who lived by a well, *putz* (Latin *puteus*). **2.** (**Pütz**; Rhineland): from *pütz* 'well' (see 1), or a habitational name from a place so named in Luxembourg. **3.** (Austria): from a pet form of the personal name *Burghard*. **4.** nickname from a byname for the devil. See also BUTZ.
GIVEN NAMES German 4%. *Dieter, Frederika, Hans, Heinz, Kurt, Mathias, Matthias, Otto, Reiner, Viktor*.

Putzer (123) **1.** German (**Pützer**) topographic name for someone who lived by a pool (Latin *puteus* 'well', 'pool') or a habitational name for someone from a place named with this word, for example Pütz in North Rhine-Westphalia. **2.** Probably a habitational name from a place called Putz in the former West Prussia, or from Pütz in Luxembourg (see PUTZ 2). **3.** (in Austria) topographic name for someone who lived by a well (see PUTZ).

Putzier (183) German (of Slavic origin): habitational name, probably from a place named Pritzier in Mecklenburg.
GIVEN NAMES German 4%. *Erwin, Kurt*.

Puyear (123) English: much altered variant of PERRIER. Compare PURYEAR.

Puza (131) Polish: nickname from *pyza, puza* 'chubby-faced person'.

Puzio (319) **1.** Polish: nickname for a chubby-faced person (see PUZA). **2.** Italian: from a pet form the personal name of *Iacopo*, Italian form of JACOB.
GIVEN NAMES Polish 11%. *Jozef* (3), *Andrzej* (2), *Janina* (2), *Casimir, Marzena, Piotr, Zbigniew, Zdzislaw*.

Puzzo (199) Southern Italian and Sicilian: from *puzzo* 'well', hence a topographic name for someone who lived by a well or a habitational name from a place named with this word; compare POZZI.
GIVEN NAMES Italian 18%. *Salvatore* (4), *Rocco* (2), *Corrado, Dante, Dino, Giuseppe, Luigi*.

Pyatt (903) English (Midlands): nickname from a diminutive of Old French *pye* 'magpie' (see PYE 1), or possibly sometimes a late form of *pyard*, a pejorative form of *pye*.

Pyburn (398) English (Durham): apparently from some lost or minor place so named.

Pybus (117) English (Yorkshire): unexplained.

Pye (1197) **1.** English: from Middle English, Old French *pie*, *pye* 'magpie' (Latin *pica*), applied as a nickname for a talkative or thievish person. The modern English name of the bird, not found before the 17th century, is from the earlier dialect term *maggot-pie*, formed by the addition of *Mag*, *Maggot*, pet forms of the female personal name *Margaret*. **2.** Welsh: variant of PUGH.

Pyeatt (348) Variant spelling of English PYATT.

Pyers (111) Variant of English and Irish PIERCE.

Pyka (218) Polish: nickname from Polish dialect *pyka* 'face' or from a derivative of *pykać* 'to puff'.
GIVEN NAMES German 4%; Polish 6%. *Aloysius*; *Miroslaw*, *Stas*.

Pyke (412) English and Irish: variant spelling of PIKE.

Pyland (153) German (of Slavic origin): see PILANT.

Pylant (475) German (of Slavic origin): Altered spelling of **Pieland**, a nickname for someone with white hair or a pale complexion (see PILAND).

Pyle (6242) **1.** English: from Middle English *pile* 'stake', 'post' (via Old English from Latin *pilum* 'spike', 'javelin'), hence a topographic name for someone who lived near a stake or post serving as a landmark or a metonymic occupational name for a stake maker or a nickname for a tall strong man. **2.** Dutch: metonymic occupational name for a marksman or an arrowsmith, from *pijl* 'arrow'.

Pyles (2575) English: variant of PYLE.

Pylman (104) Dutch: unexplained.

Pyne (1115) English: variant spelling of PINE.

Pynes (158) English: variant of PINE.

Pynn (148) English: variant spelling of PINN.

Pyon (139) Korean (**Pyŏn**): there are two Chinese characters for this surname, born by two different groups of families. The larger of the two groups is composed of two closely related clans. The other group is said by some sources to be composed of 67 clans, but only three of them can be documented with certainty, and 90% of this second group are members of just one of those three clans.
GIVEN NAMES Korean 64%. *Yong* (6), *Young* (4), *Man* (3), *Song* (3), *Choong* (2), *Jung* (2), *Moo* (2), *Young Sook* (2), *Bok*, *Chang Kyu*, *Dok*, *Dong*; *Chang* (4), *Chong* (4), *Manho* (2), *Chung*, *Hae*, *Insoo*, *Ki Chul*, *Ki Man*, *Ki Yong*, *Myong*, *Sung Won*, *Taejin*.

Pyper (243) Scottish and English: variant spelling of PIPER.

Pyron (689) German: **1.** perhaps an altered spelling of French BIRON or PIERRON. **2.** variant of **Pyro**, of uncertain origin.

Pyrtle (142) Americanized form of German BIRKLE. Compare PIRTLE

Pysher (206) Possibly an altered spelling of German **Püscher** or **Büscher** (see BUSCHER). It also exists as a French name of German origin.

Pyszka (108) Polish: unflattering nickname for a self-satisfied or high-blown person, from a derivative of *pycha* 'conceit', 'overweening pride'.
GIVEN NAME Polish 4%. *Waclaw*.

Pytel (282) Polish: metonymic occupational name name for a flour bolter, from *pytel* 'bolting cloth', 'sieve'.
GIVEN NAMES Polish 14%. *Kazimierz* (3), *Casimir* (2), *Alojzy*, *Andrzej*, *Danuta*, *Genowefa*, *Grazyna*, *Leszek*, *Lucyna*, *Wladyslaw*, *Wlodzimierz*, *Zbigniew*.

Pytlak (100) Polish: patronymic from PYTEL.
GIVEN NAME Polish 5%. *Andrzej*.

Pytlik (125) Polish: from a diminutive of PYTEL.
GIVEN NAMES Polish 5%. *Bogdan*, *Wlodzimierz*, *Zbigniew*.

Pyun (134) Korean: variant of PYON.
GIVEN NAMES Korean 53%. *Byung* (2), *Chong* (2), *Eui* (2), *Jung* (2), *Minsoo* (2), *Young* (2), *Bok*, *Choon*, *Chun Cha*, *Chung*, *Duk*, *Hae*, *Heesoo*, *Hyonsuk*, *Hyewon*, *Hyun Ja*, *Hyung*, *Ik*, *Jin*, *Jung Hun*, *Moon*, *Sang-Hoon*, *Sung Dae*.

Pyzik (129) Polish, Jewish (from Belarus), and Belorussian (**Pyzhik**): nickname from Polish *pyzik*, Belorussian *pyzhik* 'chubby-faced person'. Compare PUZA.
GIVEN NAMES Polish 16%. *Casimir* (2), *Czeslaw*, *Janina*, *Krzysztof*, *Lucyna*, *Stanislaus*, *Zdzislaw*.

Q

Qadir (81) Muslim: see KADER.

Qasim (56) Muslim: see KASSEM.

Qazi (115) Muslim: status name for a judge, from a Persian form of Arabic *qāḍī*.
GIVEN NAMES Muslim 87%. *Abdul* (5), *Anjum* (4), *Mohammad* (4), *Haroon* (3), *Manzoor* (2), *Masood* (2), *Mohammed* (2), *Salim* (2), *Yousef* (2), *Aamir, Ahmed, Akhtar*.

Qi (223) **1.** Chinese 齐: a surname that originated during the Zhou dynasty (1122–221 BC) from the name of the state of Qi, an area located in parts of present-day Shandong and Hebei provinces. **2.** Chinese 祁: there are two sources of this name: the legendary emperor Huang Di (2697–2595 BC) gave one of his sons the name Qi, and there existed in the state of Jin during the Spring and Autumn period (722–481 BC) a fief named Qi. **3.** Chinese 戚: in the state of Wei during the Spring and Autumn period (722–481 BC) Sun Linfu, a high counselor, was granted the lordship of Qi. Sun Linfu became embroiled in power struggles within the state of Wei, however, and was defeated. His descendants fled to the state of Jin, where they adopted the name of their previous fiefdom, Qi, as their surname.
GIVEN NAMES Chinese 69%. *Ming* (6), *Min* (3), *Hong* (2), *Hui* (2), *Jian* (2), *Lei* (2), *Wang* (2), *Wei* (2), *Wenhua* (2), *Xiao* (2), *Xiaofeng* (2), *Yan* (2), *Yong* (2).

Qian (402) Chinese 钱: from a word meaning 'money'. In the early part of the Zhou dynasty (1122–256 BC) lived Peng Fu, a grandson of Peng Zu, the venerable man who represents longevity in Chinese culture. He himself was a great-grandson of the legendary emperor Zhuan Xu. Peng Fu became the chief financial official in an area of central China, now part of Jiangsu province. *Qian*, the Chinese character for 'money', was part of his title in this role, and was adopted by his descendants as their surname.
GIVEN NAMES Chinese 73%. *Ming* (5), *Yi* (5), *Bin* (4), *Gang* (4), *Wei* (4), *Fang* (3), *Feng* (3), *Jin* (3), *Yuan* (3), *Jian* (2), *Liang* (2), *Lihua* (2) *Chong, Hu, Min, Pao*.

Qiao (75) Chinese 乔: from the name of Qiao mountain. The ancient Chinese emperor Huang Di (2697–2595 BC), considered father of the Chinese people, is buried on Qiao mountain. In honor of this, some descendants later adopted the name of the mountain as their surname. Much later, during the Later Zhou dynasty (951–960 AD), the emperor ordered that the character

for this name (which also means 'bridge') be modified to another similar character of the same pronunciation, the current character for the surname Qiao.

Qin (227) **1.** Chinese 秦: from the name of Qin Valley, in present-day Gansu province. Gao Yao, a great-grandson of the legendary emperor Zhuan Xu, was a famous minister under the model emperors Yao and Shun in the 23rd century BC; he is said to have been the first to introduce laws for the repression of crime. 1300 years later a descendant of his was rewarded for his talents in animal husbandry by being granted the lordship of Qin Valley as a vassal state. Later descendants adopted the place name Qin as their surname. **2.** Chinese 覃: there are two branches of bearers of this character for the surname: one pronounced *Qin*, and the other *Tan* (see TAN), although both are represented with the same character.
GIVEN NAMES Chinese 59%. *Wei* (6), *Jian* (5), *Weiping* (3), *Chuan* (2), *Feng* (2), *Hong* (2), *Ning* (2), *Tao* (2), *Zhong* (2), *Bailin, Bin, Dong*.

Qiu (372) **1.** Chinese 邱: from a place called Yingqiu in the state of Qi, home of the ruling family of Qi during the Zhou dynasty (1122–221 BC). Descendants of this family adopted part of the placename as their surname, a situation that persisted until the reign of the Qing dynasty emperor Yongzheng (AD 1723–35), whose personal name contained the character for Qiu. He enforced a traditional prohibition upon others bearing the same name as the emperor. To comply, those with the surname Qiu, 丘, changed their name by adding an element to the character for Qiu which resulted in another character, 邱, with the identical pronunciation. This modified form of the surname Qiu is the one most commonly encountered today. **2.** Chinese 丘: there are two sources of this name. One is an area named Yingqiu, located in present-day Shandong province. This area was granted to a duke of the state of Qi, whose descendants adopted part of the place name as their surname. Another source is a man called Qiudun Shi, who was a member of the Hu minority during the Southern and Northern Dynasties (420–581 AD). **3.** Chinese 仇: from a character in the personal name of Qiu Mu, a senior adviser to Duke Min Gong of the state of Song during the Spring and Autumn period (722–481 BC). After Duke Min Gong was

killed by Wan of Song, Qiu Mu sent a punitive expedition against Wan of Song, which was, however, repulsed, with the result that Qiu Mu was killed as well. Coincidentally or not, the character for this name means 'revenge', and it was this character that was adopted by some of Qiu Mu's descendants as a surname. **4.** Chinese 裘: two sources are found for this name. One is a place called Qiu in the state of Wei during the Zhou dynasty (1122–221 BC). The other source is a family who originally used the character mentioned in 3 above, 仇. To avoid trouble, the family switched to a different character, 裘, which is also pronounced *Qiu*.
GIVEN NAMES Chinese 72%. *Ling* (5), *Bin* (3), *Chuan* (3), *Feng* (3), *Gang* (3), *Hong* (3), *Jian* (3), *Ping* (3), *Hai Yan* (2), *Jianping* (2), *Jing* (2), *Kang* (2), *Chang, Min*.

Qu (190) **1.** Chinese 曲: from the name of a place called Quwo, which existed in the state of Jin during the Zhou dynasty (1122–221 BC). A duke's son was granted this place as a fiefdom, and in due course his descendants adopted Qu as their surname. **2.** Chinese 瞿: from the name of one of the 'Three Gorges' of the Yangtze river, Qutang Gorge. The first character of the name of the gorge gave its name to residents of the area. **3.** Chinese 屈: from a city named Qu in the state of Chu during the Spring and Autumn period (722–481 BC). After it was granted to a member of the royal family, descendants adopted the name of the city as their surname.
GIVEN NAMES Chinese 74%. *Yi* (3), *Gang* (2), *Hong* (2), *Ming* (2), *Shu Min* (2), *Xinhua* (2), *Yuan* (2), *Zhi* (2), *Chang Sheng, Chun Sheng, Feng, Guang*; *Min* (2), *Chong, Long, Xuan*.

Quaas (124) German: nickname for a big eater, from Middle Low German *quās* 'guzzling', 'feasting'.
GIVEN NAMES German 9%. *Otto* (2), *Gerhard*.

Quach (1196) Vietnamese (**Quách**): unexplained.
GIVEN NAMES Vietnamese 72%. *Hung* (29), *Thanh* (27), *Minh* (18), *Cuong* (17), *Quang* (12), *Hoa* (11), *Huong* (9), *Long* (9), *Hai* (8), *Anh* (7), *Hong* (7), *Lan* (7), *Hue* (6), *Chi* (5), *Hon* (3), *Sen* (3), *Phong* (5), *Nam* (4), *Tam* (3), *Tinh* (3), *Tuong* (3).

Quackenbush (1704) Americanized spelling of Dutch **Quackenbosch**, a topographic name from Dutch *quaak* 'swamp' (cognate with the English word *quagmire*) + *bosch* 'woodland', 'wilderness'.

FOREBEARS Quackenbosch was the name of a prominent Dutch family in Beverwijck in New Netherland (Albany, NY) in the 17th century. The family was associated with the early brick-making industry in Fort Orange-Beverwijck. A house built by them in the early 1700s still stands; it is the oldest surviving house in Albany.

Quade (1296) **1.** German: nickname for an evil man, from Middle Low German *quāt* 'evil', 'malicious', 'false', or a topographic name from Middle High German, Middle Low German *quāt* 'dirt', 'refuse'. **2.** Irish: reduced and altered form of MCQUAID.

Quaderer (103) German: nickname for someone stocky, from Middle High German *quader* 'building stone'.
GIVEN NAME German 4%. *Otto*.

Quadri (136) Muslim: from Arabic *Qādiri* 'associated with Qādir', (see KADER). In particular this term denotes association with Qādiriyyah, a Sufi order established in Baghdad by 'Abd al-Qādir al-Jīlānī (died 1166), known as 'the Sultan of the saints'.
GIVEN NAMES Muslim 71%. *Syed* (27), *Mohammad* (2), *Abdul, Ashfaq, Atiq, Faisal, Habeeb, Hafeez, Hasan, Iqbal, Jamal, Jawaid*.

Quadros (140) Portuguese: from CUADROS, a Spanish habitational name which was taken to Portugal in the 15th century from Cuadros, a town in Lleón province.
GIVEN NAMES Spanish 22%; Portuguese 14%. *Jose* (3), *Manuel* (3), *Francisco* (2), *Raul* (2), *Alda, Ana, Carlos, Domingos, Eduardo, Herminio, Mario, Miguel; Albano, Joao, Paulo*.

Quaglia (251) Italian (Piedmont and Liguria): nickname from *quàglia* 'quail' (see QUAIL).
GIVEN NAMES Italian 21%. *Carlo* (3), *Rocco* (2), *Vito* (2), *Alessandro, Angelo, Antonio, Domenic, Gennaro, Gerlando, Graziano, Luigi, Nicola*.

Quagliata (102) Italian: possibly from QUAGLIA, with the addition of the Venetian suffix *-ato*.
GIVEN NAMES Italian 14%. *Salvatore* (4), *Sal*.

Quaid (299) Irish (County Limerick): reduced form of MCQUAID.
GIVEN NAMES Irish 5%. *Donal, Eoin*.

Quaife (104) Irish and Manx: Anglicized form of Gaelic **Ó Caoimh** (see O'KEEFE). Gaelic *c* followed by *a, o,* or *u* is often Anglicized as *q* in Manx.

Quail (445) **1.** Irish and Scottish: Anglicized form of Gaelic **Mac Phóil** (see MCFALL). **2.** Irish: variant of QUILL 1. **3.** English: from Middle English *quaille* 'quail', a nickname for a timorous, lecherous, or fat person, all qualities that were ascribed to the bird. **4.** In one family this is an Americanized form of the Ashkenazic Jewish ornamental surname **Kvalvaser**, meaning 'spring water' in Yiddish.

Quain (207) Irish (Cork, Limerick, Waterford): reduced Anglicized form of Gaelic **Ó Cuáin** 'descendant of *Cuán*' (see COYNE).

Quaintance (430) Variant spelling of **Quintance**, a Scottish name of unexplained origin.

Quakenbush (256) Dutch or North German: see QUACKENBUSH.

Quale (349) **1.** Variant spelling of QUAIL. **2.** Americanized spelling of Norwegian KVALE.

Qualey (305) **1.** Irish: variant of QUEALY. **2.** Americanized or variant spelling of Norwegian **Kvaløy**, a habitational name from any of some ten farmsteads so named, from *kval* 'whale' + *øy* 'island' (Old Norse *Hvaley*).

Quall (116) Origin unidentified.

Qualley (246) Variant spelling of Norwegian QUALEY.
GIVEN NAME Scandinavian 4%. *Britt*.

Qualls (3587) American variant of QUARLES.

Qualman (109) North German (**Qualmann**): habitational name for someone from a place near Segeberg called Quala.
GIVEN NAME German 5%. *Helmuth*.

Qualters (100) Irish: reduced form of **MacWalter**, an Anglicized form of Gaelic **Mac Ualtair, Mac Uaitear**, to which an English patronymic *-s* has been added.

Quam (1058) Americanized spelling of Norwegian KVAM.

Quamme (221) Americanized spelling of Norwegian KVAMME.

Quan (1285) **1.** Irish: reduced Anglicized form of Gaelic **Ó Cúain** 'descendant of *Cúan*' (see COYNE). **2.** Chinese 全: from a word that means 'coin'. During the Zhou dynasty (1122–221 BC) the coin official was an important functionary in charge of currency. Descendants of a coin official adopted the character 泉 as their surname. However, another character, 全, meaning 'all', pronounced identically, came to be used more often as a surname. **3.** Chinese 权: from the state of Quan, which existed during the Shang dynasty (1766–1122 BC). The name of the state is identical to a word meaning 'power'. The Shang king Wu Ding granted the state to his grandson, whose descendants adopted Quan as their surname.
GIVEN NAMES Chinese 26%. *Lan* (6), *Ha* (5), *Hoa* (5), *Hong* (5), *Thanh* (5), *Minh* (4), *Anh* (3), *Cuong* (3), *Hai* (3), *Hung* (3), *Luong* (3), *Toan* (3), *Toha* (3), *Chun* (2), *Fong* (2), *Hon* (2), *Kwong* (2), *Lai* (2), *Ming* (2), *Sang* (2), *Sheung* (2), *Wing* (2), *Chi*.

Quanbeck (115) Probably an altered form of Swedish **Quarnbäck**, an ornamental or topographic name composed of the elements *kvarn* 'millstone' + *bäck* 'stream'.

Quance (110) English (Devon): probably a variant of QUINCE.

Quandt (898) German: nickname from Middle Low German *quant* 'rogue', 'wag', 'prankster'. This surname is also established in the Netherlands and is a common name of Dutch origin in the Mohawk Valley.

Quang (169) Vietnamese (**Quảng**): unexplained.
GIVEN NAMES Vietnamese 77%. *Nguyen* (4), *Ha* (3), *Hoa* (3), *Thanh* (3), *Thinh Van* (3), *Tran* (3), *Vinh* (3), *Chanh* (2), *Chau* (2), *Hung* (2), *Minh* (2), *Muoi* (2).

Quann (147) Irish: variant of QUAN.
GIVEN NAME Irish 6%. *Brendan* (2).

Quant (150) **1.** English: nickname from Middle English *cointe, quointe* 'known' (via Old French, from Latin *cognitus* 'known'). The Middle English word was used in various senses, any of which could have given rise to the surname: 'cunning', 'crafty', 'knowledgeable' (especially about dress, hence 'elegant'), 'attractive'. The sense development continued with 'odd' or 'unusual', the normal meaning of the modern English word 'quaint'. **2.** German and Dutch: variant of QUANDT.
GIVEN NAMES Spanish 20%. *Javier* (2), *Jose* (2), *Mario* (2), *Roberto* (2), *Santiago* (2), *Andres, Angel, Azucena, Claudio, Eduardo, Elena, Emilia*.

Quante (100) Variant of German QUANDT.
GIVEN NAME German 6%. *Horst*.

Quantz (107) German: probably of Slavic origin, or a variant of QUANT.
GIVEN NAME French 5%. *Raoul* (2).

Quaranta (410) **1.** Southern Italian: etymology uncertain; possibly from an unexplained nickname from *quaranta* 'forty', or alternatively from a personal name *Quaranta*, as supported by the place name Santa Quaranta. **2.** French (Provence): habitational name from Quarante near Capestang in Hérault.
GIVEN NAMES Italian 20%. *Angelo* (6), *Vito* (5), *Rocco* (3), *Antonio* (2), *Salvatore* (2), *Silvio* (2), *Carmine, Ciro, Corrado, Dino, Filomena, Francesca*.

Quaranto (134) Italian: variant of QUARANTA.
GIVEN NAMES Italian 11%. *Rocco* (2), *Angelo, Vito*.

Quarles (2907) English: habitational name from a place in Norfolk, recorded in Domesday Book as *Huerueles*, named in Old English as *hwerflas* 'circles'.

Quarnstrom (150) Swedish (**Quarnström**): ornamental name composed of the elements *kvarn* 'mill' + *ström* 'stream', 'river'.
GIVEN NAMES German 5%; Scandinavian 5%. *Eldred; Dagny*.

Quarry (193) **1.** Irish and Manx: reduced Anglicized form of Gaelic **Mac Guaire** (see MCQUARRIE). **2.** English (of Norman origin): nickname for a thickset or portly man, from Anglo-Norman French *quaré* 'square'. Compare **Carré** (see CARRE).

3. English: from Middle English *quarey* 'quarry', a topographic name for someone who lived near a stone quarry, or a metonymic occupational name for someone who worked in one.

Quartararo (188) Italian: possibly from medieval Latin *quarta*, a land measurement (from which the place name and family name **Quartana** is derived), or else a dissimilated form of **Quartararo**, an occupational name for a maker or seller of jugs and bowls, which is particularly common in southern Sicily.
GIVEN NAMES Italian 10%. *Concetta, Matteo, Sal, Salvatore.*

Quarterman (439) English: nickname, possibly for someone who was very dextrous such as a juggler or conjuror, from Old French *quatremains* 'four hands'.
GIVEN NAMES French 5%. *Andre, Germaine, Marcel, Pascal.*

Quarto (110) Italian: **1.** from the personal name *Quarto*, from Latin *Quartus*, meaning 'fourth', a name given to a fourth son. **2.** habitational name from any of the numerous places so named throughout Italy.
GIVEN NAMES Italian 14%; Spanish 6%. *Alfredo, Angelo, Cosmo, Francesco, Pasquale; Alejandro, Jose, Orlino.*

Quartuccio (125) Italian (**Quartúccio**): from a pet form of the personal name QUARTO.
GIVEN NAMES Italian 14%. *Angelo, Nunzio, Rosario, Sal.*

Quast (899) German: **1.** habitational name from any of several places so named in northern Germany. **2.** metonymic occupational name for a barber or nickname for someone who wore a conspicuous tassel or feather, from Middle Low German, Middle High German *quast(e)* 'tuft', 'tassel', 'brush', also 'fool'.
GIVEN NAMES German 5%. *Johannes* (2), *Otto* (2), *Frieda, Hildegarde, Klaus, Lorenz, Manfred, Reinhardt, Ulrich.*

Quate (109) Mexican: variant of **Cuate** (or also COATE), Castilianized form of Nahuatl **Coatl**, nickname from *coatl* 'snake', also 'twin'.

Quattlebaum (1015) Altered spelling of German **Quattelbaum**, probably a topographic name from Middle Low German *quattele* 'quail' + *bōm* 'tree'.

Quattro (135) Italian: unexplained: possibly a shortened form of QUATTROCCHI or some other surname formed with *quattro* 'four', but more likely from the personal name *Quattro* ('four') a short form of *Santiquattro*, bestowed in honor of the four saints martyred under Diocletian (Severo, Severino, Carpoforo, and Vittorino), who are commemorated on November 8th.
GIVEN NAMES Italian 14%. *Rocco* (3), *Domenic, Guido, Romeo, Salvatore.*

Quattrocchi (371) Southern Italian (Calabria and Sicily): from *quattr'occhi* 'four eyes', applied as a nickname for someone

who wore glasses or for someone who was particularly diligent or shrewd.
GIVEN NAMES Italian 15%. *Rocco* (3), *Angelo* (2), *Sal* (2), *Salvatore* (2), *Antonio, Carmelo, Carmine, Ciro, Donato, Flavio, Guido, Guiseppe.*

Quattrochi (140) Respelling of Italian QUATTROCCHI.
GIVEN NAMES Italian 20%. *Angelo* (2), *Gaspare, Geno, Gino, Pasquale, Sal, Salvatore.*

Quattrone (249) Italian: probably from a derivative of *quattro* 'four', possibly applied as a personal name.
GIVEN NAMES Italian 15%. *Dante* (2), *Angelo, Antonio, Carmella, Cosmo, Emilio, Erminio, Mario, Nunzio, Pierluigi, Tiziana.*

Quattrucci (102) Italian: probably a respelling of QUATTROCCHI.
GIVEN NAMES Italian 10%. *Aldo, Gino, Rocco, Tommaso.*

Quave (210) Origin unidentified.

Quay (564) **1.** Scottish: reduced form of MCKAY. **2.** French: topographic name for someone who lived in a house on a quayside, from Old French *quai* 'quay'.
FOREBEARS A Quay of unknown specific origin is documented in Repentigny, Quebec, in 1694, with the secondary surname DRAGON.

Quayle (610) Variant spelling of QUAIL.

Que (110) **1.** Catalan (**Qué**): variant of **Quer**, a topographic name from *quer* 'rock', 'cliff'. **2.** Chinese 阙: from part of the name of a city named Quetang, in present-day Shandong province. Quetang is famous as the birthplace of the philosopher Confucius.
GIVEN NAMES Spanish 38%; Chinese 4%. *Leonardo* (3), *Marcos* (2), *Agustin, Alfonso, Ana, Benito, Ernestina, Fidel, Florentino, Juanito, Luis, Miguel, Nestor; Huong, Lam, Trinh.*

Quealy (154) Irish: reduced Anglicized form of Gaelic **Ó Caollaidhe** 'descendant of *Caollaidhe*' (see KEELEY).
GIVEN NAME Irish 11%. *Brendan* (3).

Quebedeaux (290) French (LA): the first recorded instance of this name is from a French post on the Mississippi, where there is a record of one *Quebedau dit l'espagnol* 'Quebedau called the Spaniard', from Paris. It is probably an altered form of Spanish QUEVEDO.
GIVEN NAMES French 5%. *Emile, Luce, Marcel.*

Quebodeaux (112) French: see QUEBEDEAUX.

Queen (5778) **1.** Scottish: reduced form of MCQUEEN. **2.** English: from a Middle English female personal name, *Quena*, from Old English *cwene* 'queen'.

Queenan (311) Irish (chiefly Counties Sligo and Roscommon): reduced Anglicized form of Gaelic **Ó Cuineáin**, from a diminutive of the personal name *Cú*, meaning 'hound'.

Queener (341) Origin uncertain. It is probably of German origin, perhaps an Americanized spelling of **Kühner** (see KUHNER).

Queeney (105) Irish: reduced form of MCQUEENEY.

Queer (107) Origin uncertain. Perhaps a variant of Scottish or Irish QUIRE (see MCQUIRE).

Quell (109) German: topographic name for someone living near a spring, Middle High German *quelle*. In some instances it may be a habitational name from Quelle near Bielefeld, Westphalia.

Quella (145) Catalan (**Quetllà**): probably a variant of **Catllà**, a habitational name from Catllà de Conflent, a town in northern Catalonia, or from **Catllar**, habitational name from any of the places named Catllar (from Latin *castellare* 'territory belonging to the castle').

Quenneville (231) French: habitational name from a place so called in Seine-Maritime.
FOREBEARS A Quenneville from Normandy, France, is documented in Montreal in 1674.
GIVEN NAMES French 11%. *Armand* (2), *Andre, Germaine, Jean Guy, Marcel, Yvon.*

Quenzer (257) South German: nickname for a cardplayer.
GIVEN NAMES German 4%. *Milbert* (2), *Hans.*

Quercia (110) Italian: topographic name for someone who lived by an oak wood or a conspicuous oak tree, from *quercia* 'oak'.
GIVEN NAMES Italian 25%. *Cosmo* (2), *Aldo, Cesare, Domenic, Emilio, Guiseppe, Orlando, Riccardo, Roberto, Vito.*

Querin (101) Italian: etymology uncertain; possibly related to the Latin personal name *Quirinus*.
GIVEN NAMES Italian 4%. *Angelo, Antonio, Dino.*

Querry (358) Manx, Irish, or Scottish: reduced form of MCQUARRIE.
GIVEN NAME Irish 4%. *Aileen* (3).

Quertermous (113) Altered form of English **Quatermass**, a habitational name of Norman origin, from Quatremares in Normandy.

Query (499) Irish: variant (under French influence) of QUERRY (see MCQUARRIE).
GIVEN NAMES French 4%. *Adrien, Armand, Jean-Paul, Normand.*

Quesada (1228) Spanish: habitational name from Quesada, a place in Jaén province. The place name is of uncertain derivation; there may be some connection with Old Spanish *requexada* 'corner', 'tight spot'.
GIVEN NAMES Spanish 45%. *Jose* (25), *Manuel* (20), *Juan* (14), *Carlos* (12), *Ramon* (12), *Raul* (11), *Jesus* (10), *Luis* (8), *Mario* (8), *Ruben* (8), *Francisco* (7), *Pedro* (7).

Quesenberry (1426) Probably a variant of English CHRISTENBERRY.

Quesinberry (242) Probably a variant of English CHRISTENBERRY.

Quesnel (387) French: topographic name from a diminutive of Norman, Picard *quesne* 'oak tree'.
FOREBEARS A Quesnel from Normandy is documented in Montreal in 1676.
GIVEN NAMES French 13%. *Andre* (3), *Aime* (2), *Alcide* (2), *Yves* (2), *Aurel*, *Aurele*, *Euclide*, *Jacques*, *Josee*, *Marcel*.

Quesnell (160) French: variant spelling of QUESNEL.
GIVEN NAMES French 5%. *Amie*, *Emile*.

Quest (265) German: variant of QUAST.

Quevedo (636) Spanish: habitational name from a place called Quevedo, such as Casa de Quevedo in Albacete province.
GIVEN NAMES Spanish 49%. *Jose* (19), *Luis* (11), *Carlos* (9), *Enrique* (7), *Fernando* (7), *Miguel* (7), *Jesus* (6), *Jorge* (6), *Manuel* (6), *Juan* (5), *Mario* (5), *Rafael* (5).

Quezada (1635) Spanish: probably a variant of QUESADA.
GIVEN NAMES Spanish 57%. *Jose* (51), *Juan* (23), *Jesus* (21), *Manuel* (21), *Carlos* (19), *Luis* (17), *Francisco* (16), *Jorge* (13), *Miguel* (12), *Ramon* (11), *Rafael* (10), *Mario* (9).

Quiambao (110) Hispanic (Philippines): unexplained.
GIVEN NAMES Spanish 43%; Italian 7%. *Renato* (4), *Alfredo* (2), *Felipe* (2), *Narciso* (2), *Rodolfo* (2), *Venancio* (2), *Adalia*, *Alberto*, *Arturo*, *Basilisa*, *Camila*, *Dominador*; *Antonio*, *Dante*.

Quick (8455) **1.** English, German, and Dutch: nickname for a lively or agile person, from Middle English *quik*, Middle High German *quick*, Middle Dutch *quic* 'alive', 'lively', 'fresh'. **2.** English: habitational name for someone who lived at a place called Cowick (notably one in Devon), denoting an outlying dairy farm, from Old English *cūwīc*, from *cū* 'cow' + *wīc* 'outlying settlement'. **3.** Cornish: habitational name from Gweek in the parish of Constantine, named from Cornish *gwyk*, which may have meant either 'village' or 'forest', or a topographic name from the same word. **4.** English: topographic name for someone who lived by a place overgrown with couch grass (Old English *cwice*).

Quickel (225) Dutch and North German: nickname from a diminutive of Middle Dutch *quic* 'vivacious', 'lively'.

Quickle (102) Altered spelling of Dutch and North German QUICKEL.

Quidley (105) Origin uncertain. Perhaps an altered form of Irish QUIGLEY.

Quier (106) Scottish or Irish: variant of QUIRE (see McQUIRE).

Quiett (158) English: nickname for a quiet, peaceable person.

Quigg (636) Irish (County Derry): reduced Anglicized form of Gaelic **Ó Cuaig**, from a personal name of unexplained origin. In County Down it is Anglicized as **Fivey**, as if from *cúig* 'five'.

Quiggins (112) Reduced and altered form of Irish McGUIGAN, with the addition of English patronymic *-s*.

Quiggle (360) Americanized form of Dutch and German QUICKEL.

Quigley (6806) Irish: reduced Anglicized form of Gaelic **Ó Coigligh** 'descendant of *Coigleach*', a byname apparently representing a simplified form of *coigealach* 'like a distaff', 'untidy person'. This was originally a Mayo name.
GIVEN NAMES Irish 6%. *Brendan* (4), *Declan* (3), *Eamonn* (3), *Cathal*, *Clancy*, *Colm*, *Fionnuala*, *James Patrick*, *John Patrick*, *Kiera*, *Kieran*.

Quijada (395) Spanish: possibly a nickname for a person with a prominent jaw, from *quijada* 'jaw', 'jawbone'.
GIVEN NAMES Spanish 49%. *Jose* (13), *Juan* (9), *Carlos* (6), *Jorge* (6), *Jesus* (4), *Manuel* (4), *Pedro* (4), *Rafael* (3), *Alberto* (2), *Armando* (2), *Graciela* (2), *Ignacio* (2).

Quijano (518) Spanish: habitational name from Quijano in Cantabria province.
GIVEN NAMES Spanish 44%. *Carlos* (10), *Luis* (9), *Jose* (8), *Francisco* (6), *Alfonso* (5), *Juan* (5), *Manuel* (5), *Armando* (4), *Pedro* (4), *Sergio* (4), *Alicia* (3), *Ana* (3).

Quijas (112) Spanish: probably a habitational name from Quijas in Cantabria province.
GIVEN NAMES Spanish 46%. *Jesus* (4), *Alfredo* (2), *Jose* (2), *Rodolfo* (2), *Salvador* (2), *Ventura* (2), *Armando*, *Brijido*, *Enrique*, *Eusebio*, *Felipe De Jesus*, *Fernando*.

Quiles (698) Spanish: variant of **Quilez**, which is perhaps a patronymic from the personal name *Aquileo*.
GIVEN NAMES Spanish 46%. *Jose* (20), *Juan* (17), *Luis* (16), *Carlos* (12), *Angel* (6), *Miguel* (6), *Ramon* (6), *Julio* (5), *Luz* (5), *Rafael* (5), *Ana* (3), *Blanca* (3).

Quilici (268) Italian: patronymic from the personal name *Quilico*, an altered form of *Quirico*, borne by a (probably fictitious) 4th-century infant saint, said to have been martyred at Tarsus with his mother Julitta, who was honored in the Middle Ages as a patron of children. The name is probably a blend of two other names, both borne by numerous early saints: Latin *Quirinus* (originally a title borne by Romulus, founding father of Rome, referring to the Sabine city of Cures) and Greek *Kyriakos* (a derivative of *kyrios* 'lord', 'master').
GIVEN NAMES Italian 11%. *Gino* (3), *Reno* (2), *Aldo*, *Angelo*, *Annunziata*, *Dino*, *Ermanno*, *Oreste*, *Paolo*, *Sal*.

Quill (546) Irish, Scottish, and Manx: reduced Anglicized form of Gaelic **Ó Cuill** 'descendant of *Coll*', or of **Mac Cuill** 'son of *Coll*', a personal name probably based on *coll* 'hazel tree'. In Ireland this is the name of a Munster family and is sometimes translated as WOODS.
GIVEN NAME Irish 6%. *Aileen*.

Quillan (108) Irish: reduced form of McQUILLAN.

Quillen (1983) Irish: reduced form of McQUILLAN.

Quiller (119) English: metonymic occupational name for a spoon maker, from Old French *cuiller* 'spoon', 'ladle'.

Quilliam (113) Scottish and Irish: reduced form of McWILLIAM.
GIVEN NAMES French 4%. *Alcide*, *Cecile*.

Quillian (190) Irish: variant of McWILLIAM or McQUILLAN.

Quillin (826) Irish: reduced variant spelling of McQUILLAN.

Quilling (167) German: patronymic from a Germanic personal name formed with *willio* 'will' as the first element. Compare QUILLMAN.

Quillman (143) German (**Quillmann**): variant of the Germanic personal name *Williman*, composed of the elements *willio* 'will' + *man* 'man'.

Quilter (196) English: occupational name for a maker of quilts and mattresses, and also of the quilted garments worn in battle by those who could not afford armor made of metal, from an agent derivative of Middle English, *cuilte*, *coilte* 'quilt', 'mattress' (from Old French, from Latin *culcita* 'mattress').

Quilty (283) Irish: Anglicized form of Gaelic **Ó Caoilte**, 'descendant of *Caoilte*' (see KIELTY).

Quimby (2028) English: of uncertain origin; perhaps a variant of **Quarmby**, a habitational name from a place so called in West Yorkshire.

Quin (507) **1.** Irish: variant spelling of QUINN. **2.** French: from a short form of the personal name *Jaquin*, itself a pet form of *Jacques*, French form of JACK.

Quinby (391) English: variant of QUIMBY.

Quince (151) English: probably a topographic name for someone who lived by a quince tree or a metonymic occupational name for a grower or seller of quinces, from Middle English, Old French *cooin* 'quince'.

Quincey (117) English: variant spelling of QUINCY.

Quincy (299) English (of Norman origin): habitational name from any of several places in France deriving their names from the Gallo-Roman personal name *Quintus*, meaning 'fifth(-born)' + the locative suffix *-acum*. The earliest bearers of the name in England were from Cuinchy in Pas-de-Calais, but other stocks may be from Quincy-sous-Sénard in Seine-et-Oise or Quincy-Voisins in Seine-et-Marne.
FOREBEARS The American Quincy family were established in MA by Edmund Quincy in 1633. Fifth in descent was Josiah Quincy (1744–75), a leading patriot, who was sent to England to argue the colonists' case in 1774. His son Josiah (1772–1864) was a powerful opponent of slavery, presi-

dent of Harvard, and mayor of Boston, a post also held by several of his descendants. The traditional pronunciation is "Quinzy".

Quine (202) **1.** Irish: variant of QUINN. **2.** French: from an aphetic form of the female personal name *Jacquine* (see QUIN).

Quinlan (4127) Irish: **1.** reduced Anglicized form of Gaelic **Ó Caoindealbháin** 'descendant of *Caoindealbhán*', a personal name composed of the elements *caoin* 'comely', 'fair' + *dealbh* 'form' + the diminutive suffix *-án*. **2.** reduced Anglicized form of Gaelic **Ó Conalláin** 'descendant of *Conallán*', a personal name representing a diminutive of *Conall* (see CONNELL).

GIVEN NAMES Irish 5%. *Brendan* (3), *Donal* (2), *Liam* (2), *Aileen, Caitlin, Cian, Conor, John Patrick, Kieran, Senan.*

Quinley (325) Apparently an altered form of Scottish MCKINLEY or a reduced form of Irish **(Mc)Quinnelly**, Anglicized form of Gaelic **Mac Coingheallaigh** or **Ó Coingheallaigh** 'son (or descendant) of *Coingheallach*', a personal name meaning 'faithful to pledges'.

Quinlin (169) Irish: variant spelling of QUINLAN.

Quinlivan (375) Irish: variant of QUINLAN 1, the *v* representing the pronunciation in certain dialects of the *bh* of *Ó Caoindealbháin*.

Quinn (29352) Irish: reduced Anglicized form of Gaelic **Ó Coinn** 'descendant of *Conn*' (see O'QUINN). This is the name of several families in Ulster and counties Clare, Longford, and Mayo.

GIVEN NAMES Irish 6%. *Brendan* (19), *Kieran* (6), *Conor* (4), *Declan* (4), *Dermot* (4), *Fionnuala* (3), *Aidan* (2), *Aileen* (2), *Brigid* (2), *Donovan* (2), *Eamon* (2), *Jarlath* (2).

Quinnell (220) **1.** English: metonymic from the Middle English female personal name *Quenilda*, Old English *Cwēnhild* 'woman-war'. **2.** In some instances, it may be an altered spelling of the French family name **Quinel**, which is from an aphetic pet form of the personal name *Jacques*, French form of JACK.

Quinney (368) Irish (Ulster): Anglicized form of Gaelic **Ó Coinne** 'descendant of *Coinne*', a derivative of the personal name *Coinneach*. Compare Scottish KENNETH and MCKENZIE.

Quinones (3578) Spanish and Asturian-Leonese (**Quiñones**): habitational name from any of the places named Quiñones, in Lleón, and Murcia provinces, so named from *quiñón* (Latin *quinio* 'group of five', genitive *quinionis*, a derivative of *quinque* 'five'), denoting a piece of land that was shared out among a group of five co-tenants for sowing.

GIVEN NAMES Spanish 44%. *Jose* (94), *Luis* (46), *Jesus* (35), *Manuel* (34), *Juan* (30), *Pedro* (28), *Carlos* (27), *Miguel* (27),

Rafael (27), *Angel* (26), *Jorge* (20), *Julio* (18).

Quinonez (782) Spanish (**Quiñónez**): variant of **Quiñones** (see QUINONES).

GIVEN NAMES Spanish 51%. *Jose* (13), *Carlos* (12), *Luis* (12), *Juan* (11), *Manuel* (10), *Jesus* (9), *Ramon* (9), *Mario* (6), *Pedro* (5), *Francisco* (4), *Javier* (4), *Lupe* (4).

Quint (1136) **1.** Catalan: from a personal name *Quint* (Latin *Quintus*) denoting the fifth-born child in a family. **2.** French: from Middle French *quint* 'fifth', a term used in western France to denote an administrative area consisting of five villages, presumably applied as a metonymic occupational name for the administrator of such an area. **3.** German: from the medieval personal name and saint's name *Quintinus*. Compare QUINTIN.

Quintal (468) **1.** Portuguese: habitational name from any of the numerous places named Quintal, or a topographic name from *quintal* 'small country house', 'vegetable garden'. This name is now common in Mexico. **2.** Southern French: from Old French *quintal* 'hundredweight', possibly applied as a nickname for a heavy man.

FOREBEARS A Quintal from La Rochelle, France, is recorded in Boucherville, Quebec, in 1668.

GIVEN NAMES Spanish 7%; French 6%; Portuguese 5%. *Manuel* (8), *Jose* (5), *Fabio* (2), *Roberto* (2), *Carlos, Diego, Jaime, Jorge, Luiz, Marina, Mario, Miguel; Armand* (2), *Adelard, Alain, Emile, Gilles, Henri, Marcel, Sylvain; Joao, Paulo.*

Quintana (4583) **1.** Spanish, Catalan, Asturian-Leonese, and Galician: habitational name from any of the numerous places, large and small, named Quintana, from *quintana* 'country house' (originally having a tax liability of one fifth of the annual produce). **2.** variant of French **Quintaine**, from an Old French term denoting a post for jousting practice, hence a nickname for one who was skilled at this.

GIVEN NAMES Spanish 40%. *Jose* (96), *Juan* (61), *Manuel* (60), *Jesus* (32), *Carlos* (31), *Luis* (31), *Francisco* (28), *Jorge* (23), *Miguel* (18), *Ramon* (18), *Pedro* (17), *Raul* (17).

Quintanar (201) Spanish: habitational name from any of the places in Toledo, Burgos, Cuenca, Soria, and Logroño called Quintanar, from a derivative of *quintana* 'country house' (see QUINTANA).

GIVEN NAMES Spanish 44%. *Jose* (5), *Manuel* (5), *Pedro* (5), *Ramon* (5), *Ruben* (5), *Guadalupe* (3), *Ernesto* (2), *Jaime* (2), *Javier* (2), *Joaquin* (2), *Julio* (2), *Luis* (2).

Quintanilla (1945) Spanish: habitational name from any of various places called Quintanilla, from a diminutive of *quintana* 'country house' (see QUINTANA).

GIVEN NAMES Spanish 50%. *Jose* (62), *Carlos* (32), *Luis* (21), *Juan* (18), *Manuel* (16), *Mario* (15), *Pedro* (15), *Francisco* (12),

Javier (12), *Ana* (11), *Jaime* (11), *Raul* (11).

Quintela (134) Portuguese and Galician: habitational name from any of the numerous places named Quintela, from a diminutive of *quinta* 'five', denoting a holding with dues amounting to one fifth of the produce. Compare QUINTANA.

GIVEN NAMES Spanish 46%. *Carlos* (5), *Alberto* (2), *Eduardo* (2), *Jose* (2), *Miguel* (2), *Ricardo* (2), *Alfredo, Amada, Cruz, Domingo, Eloisa, Emilio.*

Quinter (226) Probably a reduced form of Irish **Mac Quinter**, which MacLysaght believes to be a variant of MCWHERTER.

Quintero (3285) Spanish: variant of Galician **Quinteiro**, a habitational name from Quintero in Ourense province, Galicia, so named from *quinteiro* 'farmstead'.

GIVEN NAMES Spanish 53%. *Jose* (90), *Jesus* (43), *Luis* (40), *Manuel* (40), *Juan* (38), *Carlos* (35), *Francisco* (21), *Miguel* (21), *Fernando* (19), *Jorge* (18), *Pedro* (18), *Alfredo* (17).

Quinteros (232) Spanish: plural of QUINTERO, probably from a place name.

GIVEN NAMES Spanish 53%. *Jose* (9), *Carlos* (7), *Manuel* (4), *Eduardo* (3), *Ricardo* (3), *Ernesto* (2), *Francisco* (2), *Jaime* (2), *Juan* (2), *Luis* (2), *Mariana* (2), *Raul* (2).

Quintiliani (131) Italian: patronymic from the personal name *Quintiliano*, from Latin *Quintilianus*, a derivative of *Quintus* ('fifth').

GIVEN NAMES Italian 27%. *Donato* (5), *Gaetano* (3), *Domenic* (2), *Antonio, Carlo, Carmine, Egidio, Lucio, Reno.*

Quintin (267) French: from the Old French personal name *Quentin, Quintin*, Latin *Quintinus*, a derivative of *Quintus* 'fifth-born'.

FOREBEARS A Quintin from Normandy, France, is documented as Quentin in Quebec City in 1660, with the secondary surname LAFONTAINE.

GIVEN NAMES French 13%. *Armand* (2), *Yves* (2), *Andre, Dominique, Gilles, Lucien, Michel, Oliva, Roch.*

Quinto (399) **1.** Aragonese, Spanish, and Catalan: habitational name from a place called Quinto, for example in Zaragoza province. However, the high concentration of the surname in Alacant province suggests that in some cases at least it may derive from the personal name *Quinto* (from Latin *Quintus* denoting the fifth-born child) or Catalan *quinto* 'young soldier'. **2.** Italian: from the personal name *Quinto* (see 1 above). **3.** Italian: possibly a habitational name from any of the numerous places named with this word, as for example Quinto di Treviso (Treviso), Quinto Vicentino (Vicenza), Quinto Vercellese (Vercelli).

GIVEN NAMES Spanish 26%; Italian 8%. *Mario* (5), *Jose* (4), *Enrique* (2), *Juan* (2), *Roberto* (2), *Alberto, Alejandro, Amelita,*

Arsenio, Benigno, Carmelita, Cesar; Antonio (2), Aldo, Bonaventura, Leonardo, Marco, Nicola, Nunzi, Nunzio, Philomena, Romeo.

Quinton (1062) English: **1.** habitational name from any of the places, for example in Gloucestershire, Northamptonshire, and Birmingham, named in Old English as *cwēn tūn*, from Old English as 'the queen's settlement'. Compare KINGSTON. **2.** from the Old French personal name *Quentin*, *Quintin* (see QUINTIN). **3.** (of Norman origin): habitational name from any of the places in northern France named for St. Quentin of Amiens, a 3rd- century Roman missionary to Gaul, for example Saint-Quentin in La Manche or Saint-Quentin-en-Tourmont in Somme, the site of his martyrdom.

Quintrell (101) English (Cornwall): nickname from Old French *cointerel* 'beau', 'dandy', 'fop'.

Quiram (201) German: unexplained. Perhaps an altered form of an unidentified Slavic name, or of *Quirin*, from the Latin personal name *Quirinus*.

Quirarte (136) Hispanic (Mexico): unexplained.
GIVEN NAMES Spanish 49%. *Jose* (6), *Jesus* (4), *Juan* (4), *Raul* (3), *Francisco* (2), *Ramiro* (2), *Ramon* (2), *Roberto* (2), *Sergio* (2), *Alberto, Ana, Ana Isabel.*

Quire (234) Scottish or Irish: reduced form of McQUIRE (see McGUIRE).

Quirin (244) French: from the personal name *Quirin*, from Latin *Quirinus*, a Roman family name borne by no less than nine martyrs in the 11th–14th centuries.

Quiring (446) German: from the medieval personal name from *Quirin*, from Latin *Quirinus*. See also QUIRIN.
GIVEN NAMES German 4%. *Armin* (2), *Gerhard, Otto.*

Quirino (122) Spanish: from the personal name *Quirino* (from Latin *Quirinus*).
GIVEN NAMES Spanish 37%; French 6%. *Francisco* (2), *Sueli* (2), *Angel, Angelina, Bernardo, Carlos, Cristina, Domingo, Eduardo, Efren, Emilio, Erasmo; Alexandre, Antoine, Cecile, Idee.*

Quirion (294) Breton: of uncertain origin; perhaps based on the Breton root *ker* 'town', 'dwelling', which would often be followed by a personal name indicating the proprietor.
FOREBEARS A Quirion from Brittany is documented in Lauzon, Quebec, in 1686, with the secondary surname DANIEL.
GIVEN NAMES French 22%. *Benoit* (3), *Gilles* (3), *Luc* (2), *Aime, Cecile, Emile, Emilien, Gratien, Henri, Hercule, Josee, Julien.*

Quirk (2648) Irish (Munster) and Manx: Anglicized form of Gaelic **Ó Cuirc** 'descendant of *Corc*', a personal name from *corc* 'heart', or *curc* 'tuft (of hair)'. It is sometimes translated OATES, as if from *coirce* 'oats'.
GIVEN NAMES Irish 4%. *Brendan* (3), *Oona.*

Quirke (174) Irish and Manx: variant of QUIRK.
GIVEN NAME Irish 11%. *Declan.*

Quiroga (739) Galician: habitational name from Quiroga, a place in Lugo province, so named from the plant *queiroga*, *quiroga* 'erica'.
GIVEN NAMES Spanish 49%. *Jose* (19), *Carlos* (13), *Antonio* (11), *Luis* (10), *Jesus* (7), *Miguel* (7), *Jorge* (6), *Marcelo* (6), *Alberto* (5), *Francisco* (5), *Juan* (5), *Mario* (5), *Raul* (5).

Quiros (390) Asturian-Leonese (**Quirós**): habitational name from Quirós in Asturies.
GIVEN NAMES Spanish 47%. *Jose* (10), *Carlos* (6), *Mario* (6), *Alberto* (4), *Raul* (4), *Roberto* (4), *Efrain* (3), *Francisco* (3), *Javier* (3), *Jesus* (3), *Jorge* (3), *Manuel* (3); *Antonio* (2), *Manfredo* (2), *Constantino, Dario, Lucio, Marco, Romolo.*

Quiroz (2141) Spanish (mainly Mexico): variant of QUIROS.
GIVEN NAMES Spanish 50%. *Jose* (50), *Juan* (35), *Jesus* (21), *Manuel* (21), *Luis* (20), *Jorge* (19), *Francisco* (18), *Pedro* (14), *Carlos* (13), *Javier* (12), *Ramon* (12), *Fernando* (11).

Quisenberry (777) Probably a variant of English CHRISTENBERRY.

Quispe (111) Aymara (or possibly also Quechua): Castilianized variant of **Qhispi**, most probably a nickname from Aymara *qhispi* 'glass', 'precious stone' (or from Quechua *qhispi umiña* 'diamond'). This name is mainly found in Bolivia and Peru.
GIVEN NAMES Spanish 56%. *Eduardo* (3), *Juan* (3), *Angel* (2), *Carlos* (2), *Jesus* (2), *Juana* (2), *Julio* (2), *Luis* (2), *Aida, Alberto, Alejandro, Alicia; Amadeo, Antonio, Mauro.*

Quist (1288) **1.** Swedish: ornamental name from Swedish *quist*, an old or ornamental spelling of *kvist* 'twig'. When surnames were adopted on a large scale in the 19th century in Sweden, this was one of the elements that were widely used in combination with other words denoting natural features to form surnames such as **Lindqvist** and **Blomqvist**. **2.** Danish: nickname for a thin man, from *kvist* 'twig'.
GIVEN NAMES Scandinavian 4%. *Egil* (2), *Eyvind* (2), *Sig* (2), *Arnt, Erik.*

Quitter (107) Irish or Manx: probably a reduced and altered form of McQUITTY.

Quon (353) Korean: variant of KWON.

Quraishi (114) Arabic: variant of QURESHI.
GIVEN NAMES Muslim 86%. *Hamid* (5), *Mohammed* (4), *Abdul* (3), *Akhtar* (3), *Mohammad* (3), *Muhammad* (3), *Khalid* (2), *Nauman* (2), *Sabira* (2), *Shahid* (2), *Zia* (2), *Adnan.*

Qureshi (815) Arabic: name indicating descent from the Quraish, the leading tribe in Mecca at the time of the birth of the Prophet Muhammad (AD 570); the Prophet's mother was a member of it. The Quraish at first opposed Muhammad's teachings and persecuted him and his followers, but by the time of his death they had begun to accept the new faith and played an important role in bringing Arabia under the banner of Islam.
GIVEN NAMES Muslim 88%. *Mohammad* (30), *Abdul* (21), *Mohammed* (16), *Muhammad* (13), *Zahid* (12), *Shahid* (10), *Irfan* (9), *Saleem* (7), *Tariq* (7), *Abid* (6), *Bilal* (6), *Faisal* (6).

R

Ra (213) **1.** Scottish: variant of RAE. **2.** Korean: variant of NA.

GIVEN NAMES Korean 66%. *Sun* (4), *Young* (3), *Chang Soo* (2), *Jong* (2), *Joon* (2), *Jung* (2), *Myung* (2), *Seung* (2), *Sung* (2), *Anchi*, *Byong*, *Chan*; *Byung Ho*, *Byung Sun*, *Chong*, *Chul*, *Deok*, *Hyong*, *Jang*, *Jong Wook*, *Jung Hee*, *Ki Soo*, *Kum*, *Min*.

Raab (2160) German: variant of RABE.

GIVEN NAMES German 4%. *Kurt* (5), *Hans* (2), *Klaus* (2), *Otto* (2), *Ernst*, *Fritz*, *Gerhard*, *Hedwig*, *Heinz*, *Katharina*, *Konrad*, *Mathias*.

Raabe (833) German: variant of RABE.

GIVEN NAMES German 6%. *Otto* (3), *Volker* (3), *Erwin* (2), *Kurt* (2), *Ewald*, *Fritz*, *Gerhard*, *Guenter*, *Hans*, *Klaus*, *Willi*.

Raad (210) **1.** Muslim: from a personal name based on Arabic *rā'id* 'model', 'leader', 'pioneer'. **2.** Dutch: metonymic occupational name for an adviser, counselor, or member of a town council, from *raad* 'advice', 'counsel'.

GIVEN NAMES Muslim 24%; French 5%. *Nader* (3), *Naji* (3), *Ahmad* (2), *Ali* (2), *Amal* (2), *Hassan* (2), *Azim*, *Fadi*, *Fahed*, *Feryal*, *Ghassan*, *Hani*; *Camille*, *Dominique*, *Emile*, *Jean-Pierre*.

Raaf (105) Dutch (**de Raaf**): variant of RAVE.

Raak (117) **1.** Eastern German: from Sorbian, Polish, Czech, and Slovak *rak* 'crab', presumably applied as a nickname or possibly as a metonymic occupational name for someone who sold shellfish. **2.** German: nickname from Middle High German *rac* 'taut', 'stretched'; 'busy', 'free'. **3.** German: from a short form of any of various personal names beginning with *Rac-*. **4.** Shortened form of Dutch **van Raak**, a habitational name from any of various places named De Raak.

GIVEN NAME German 5%. *Egon*.

Raap (253) **1.** Dutch: from Middle Dutch *rape* 'turnip'; a metonymic occupational name for a turnip grower, or perhaps a derisory nickname. **2.** German: variant of RAAB (see RABE). **3.** North German: nickname from Middle Low German *rap* 'fast'.

Raasch (919) German: variant of RASCH.

Raatz (420) **1.** German: habitational name from a place so named in Silesia, near Wrocław (Breslau). **2.** German: from a short form of a Germanic personal name formed with *rād*, *rāt* 'advice', 'counsel'. **3.** Perhaps an altered spelling of the Dutch family name **Raats**, a variant of RAAD.

GIVEN NAMES German 5%. *Erwin*, *Ewald*, *Helmut*, *Kurt*, *Otto*, *Viktor*.

Raba (135) **1.** French: from a dialect variant of *rabe* 'turnip', 'oilseed rape' (itself a southern form of *rave*); a metonymic occupational name for a grower of turnips or rape, or perhaps a derisory nickname. **2.** Hungarian (**Rába**): habitational name from a place called Rába, or alternatively a topographic name for someone who lived by the river Rába, a tributary of the Danube in western Hungary. The name also occurs in Germany.

GIVEN NAME German 4%. *Manfred*.

Rabago (291) Spanish (**Rábago**): habitational name from Rábago in Cantabria province.

GIVEN NAMES Spanish 41%. *Jose* (6), *Juan* (5), *Manuel* (5), *Eduardo* (4), *Jesus* (4), *Arturo* (3), *Guadalupe* (3), *Roberto* (3), *Salvador* (3), *Angelita* (2), *Armando* (2), *Arnulfo* (2).

Rabalais (685) Southern French: variant spelling of **Rabelais**, from an adjectival form of **Rabel**, a derivative of RABA. This is a common name in LA, particularly Avoyelles parish.

FOREBEARS A Rabalais from the Poitou region of France was established in New Orleans, LA, around 1730, with the secondary surname Matelot.

GIVEN NAMES French 6%. *Gaston* (2), *Andre*, *Camille*, *Eraste*, *Francois*, *Henri*, *Marceline*, *Michel*, *Pierre*.

Rabas (111) Czech: unexplained.

Rabatin (151) Hungarian: from a Slavic variant of Hungarian *Robotos*, occupational name for a serf, a derivative of the Slavic loanword *robot* 'physical labor', 'compulsory work on a noble estate'.

Rabb (1019) Scottish: from a short form of ROBERT.

Rabbani (108) Muslim (common in Bangladesh, India, and Pakistan): from a personal name based on Arabic *rabbānī* 'divine', a derivative of Arabic *rabb* 'lord', 'master'. *Al-Rabb* 'the Lord' is an attribute of Allah. See the Qur'an 1:2: 'All praise belongs to Allah, the Lord of the universe.'

GIVEN NAMES Muslim 83%. *Golam* (3), *Jamal* (3), *Sayed* (3), *Tariq* (3), *Mohammad* (2), *Riaz* (2), *Shahram* (2), *Ahmad*, *Ahmed*, *Amir*, *Ayaz*, *Badr*.

Rabbitt (466) **1.** Scottish: from a pet form of RABB. **2.** English: from the Norman personal name *Radbode*, *Rabbode*, composed of the Germanic elements *rād* 'counsel', 'advice' + *bodo*, *boto* 'messenger', 'lord'. **3.** Irish: mistranslation of Gaelic **Ó Coinín**, which is actually a variant of **Ó Conáin** or

Ó Cuineáin (see CUNNEEN), as if it were from *coinín* 'rabbit', although in fact it is from a diminutive of *cano* 'hound', 'wolf'.

Rabe (1828) German: nickname from Middle High German *rab(e)*, *rapp(e)* 'raven'. Compare RAPP 2.

GIVEN NAMES German 4%. *Otto* (5), *Johann* (2), *Kurt* (2), *Armin*, *Arno*, *Fritz*, *Gunter*, *Heinz*, *Ignatz*, *Ingeborg*, *Klaus*, *Lutz*.

Rabel (338) German (also **Räbel**): **1.** diminutive of RABE. **2.** from a Germanic personal name formed with *rād*, *rāt* 'advice', 'counsel'. **3.** see ROUBAL.

GIVEN NAMES French 4%. *Alphonse*, *Andree*, *Marie Carmel*, *Yanick*.

Raben (199) **1.** German: from a Germanic personal name containing the element *hraban* 'raven'. **2.** Jewish (Ashkenazic): variant of RABIN.

GIVEN NAME Jewish 4%. *Hymen*.

Rabenberg (100) German: habitational name from any of several places called Rabenberg, as for example in Saxony or Lower Saxony.

Rabenold (154) German: from a Germanic personal name composed of the elements *hraban* 'raven' + *wald* 'rule'.

Rabenstein (124) German: habitational name from any of numerous places called Rabenstein.

Raber (1315) German and Swiss German: **1.** apparently an occupational name for a turnip grower, from an agent derivative of Middle High German *rabe* 'turnip'. **2.** (also **Räber**): from a Germanic personal name, *Radobert*, a compound of *rād*, *rāt* 'advice', 'counsel' + *berht* 'bright', 'famous'. **3.** variant of REBER.

Rabey (142) **1.** English: variant spelling of RABY. **2.** Hungarian (**Raby**): probably a pet form of the rare ecclesiastical name *Rabán*, from Latin *Rabanus*. **3.** Perhaps an Americanized spelling of German RABE.

Rabideau (881) North American spelling of French **Robideau**, a pet form of ROBERT.

Rabin (1095) **1.** Jewish (eastern Ashkenazic): status name for a rabbi, from Polish, Ukrainian, and Belorussian *rabin* 'rabbi' (ultimately from Hebrew *rav*). **2.** French: diminutive of RABA.

GIVEN NAMES Jewish 6%. *Sol* (4), *Hyman* (3), *Ephraim*, *Meyer*, *Morry*, *Moysey*, *Myer*, *Ofer*, *Rivkah*, *Shimon*, *Shira*, *Shoshanna*.

Rabine (186) Jewish: variant of RABIN.

GIVEN NAMES German 4%. *Kurt*, *Reinhardt*.

Rabinovich (499) Jewish (eastern Ashkenazic): Slavic patronymic from RABIN.

GIVEN NAMES Russian 32%; Jewish 31%. *Boris* (15), *Mikhail* (12), *Leonid* (11), *Vladimir* (8), *Yefim* (6), *Aleksandr* (5), *Igor* (4), *Iosif* (4), *Lev* (4), *Arkadiy* (3), *Arkady* (3), *Grigoriy* (3); *Yakov* (11), *Naum* (6), *Ilya* (5), *Aron* (4), *Isaak* (3), *Moisey* (3), *Inna* (2), *Isak* (2), *Marat* (2), *Moysey* (2), *Semen* (2), *Basya*.

Rabinovitz (237) Jewish (eastern Ashkenazic): variant of RABINOVICH.
GIVEN NAMES Jewish 9%. *Efrat, Hyman, Isadore, Mayer, Miriam, Mordechai, Nili*.

Rabinowitz (1699) Jewish (eastern Ashkenazic): Germanized variant of RABINOVICH.
GIVEN NAMES Jewish 13%. *Aryeh* (5), *Sol* (5), *Hyman* (4), *Dov* (3), *Meyer* (3), *Miriam* (3), *Shlomo* (3), *Yosef* (3), *Baruch* (2), *Lipman* (2), *Moshe* (2), *Yaakov* (2).

Rabito (108) Italian: reduced form of **Arabito**, an ethnic name from late or medieval Greek *Arabitēs* 'Arab'.
GIVEN NAMES Italian 16%. *Carina, Carmine, Dante, Giuseppe, Luciano, Salvatore, Vito*.

Rabkin (208) Jewish (from Belarus): habitational name from the village of Ryabki, now in Belarus, + the eastern Slavic possessive suffix *-in*.
GIVEN NAMES Jewish 18%; Russian 11%. *Sol* (2), *Aron, Chaya, Hyman, Isak, Meier, Meyer, Miriam, Naum*; *Boris* (4), *Vladimir* (3), *Igor* (2), *Mikhail* (2), *Dmitri, Galina, Leonid, Lev, Lidiya, Yevgeniy*.

Raboin (262) French: of disputed origin. Morlet describes it as a habitational name from a place so named in Loire; Dauzat, on the other hand, says it comes from an Old French word meaning 'devil' or 'small change', presumably applied as a nickname.
GIVEN NAMES French 10%. *Andre, Emile, Gilles, Lucien, Normand*.

Rabold (293) German: from a Germanic personal name composed of the elements *rād, rāt* 'counsel', 'advice' + *bald* 'bold', 'brave'.

Rabon (1316) Altered form of Scottish RAYBURN.

Raborn (510) Altered form of Scottish RAYBURN.

Rabourn (154) Altered form of Scottish RAYBURN.

Rabren (102) Altered form of Scottish RAYBURN.

Rabuck (212) Altered spelling of ROEBUCK, or perhaps a survival of an old spelling; Black cites the example of John Rabuk, bailie of Linlithgow, 1296.

Rabun (389) Variant of Scottish RAYBURN.

Raburn (415) Variant of Scottish RAYBURN.

Raby (1563) **1.** English: habitational name from places so named in Merseyside (formerly in Cheshire) and County Durham or from Roby in Merseyside (formerly in Lancashire). The first is named from Old Scandinavian *rá* 'pole' + *býr* 'farmstead', 'settlement'. **2.** French: variant of RABIN.

3. German: habitational name from Raby in Bohemia or perhaps from Rabingen in Lower Saxony.
FOREBEARS Probably from the Saintonge region of France, a Raby or Rabis was documented in Quebec City in 1689, with the secondary surname Saintonge.

Racanelli (190) Italian: either from a diminutive of **Racano**, which Caracausi derives from dialect *racana* 'knitted or woven material made of thick thread' (from Latin *racana* denoting a type of garment), or, perhaps more likely, a nickname from *raganella* denoting a species of green frog, also an old musical instrument.
GIVEN NAMES Italian 36%. *Vito* (13), *Saverio* (2), *Domenico, Gino, Giovanni, Luca, Luigi, Marco, Paolo, Pietro, Rocco*.

Racca (308) Italian: from the Germanic female personal name *Racca*. This name has been established in Louisiana since the beginning of the 19th century.
GIVEN NAMES French 8%. *Andre, Clovis, Dominique, Gaston, Marcel*.

Raccio (118) Italian: unexplained; possibly from a pet form of an unidentified personal name.
GIVEN NAMES Italian 23%. *Carmine* (3), *Angelo* (2), *Gaetano* (2), *Alfonse, Pasquale*.

Race (1829) **1.** English: of uncertain origin; Reaney suggests a nickname from Old French *ras* 'clean shaven', but he also cites documentary evidence of a personal name which probably also gave rise to the surname. **2.** Perhaps a variant of Dutch or German RASE. **3.** Slovenian (southwestern Slovenia): nickname from *raca* 'duck', formed with the suffix *-e*, used mainly of young people, possibly denoting someone who walked like a duck.

Racek (136) Czech: from a reduced form of a personal name such as *Radoslav* or *Radomir*, formed with the first element *rad-* 'joyful'.

Racer (287) Probably an Americanized spelling of German **Röser** (see ROSSER).

Racette (414) Possibly an altered spelling of the French family name **Rasset**, from a pet form of a Germanic personal name formed with *rād, rāt* 'counsel', 'advice'.
FOREBEARS A Rasset or Racet, from Normandy, France, is documented in Quebec City in 1678.
GIVEN NAMES French 7%. *Armand* (2), *Aurele, Gaetan, Normand, Odette, Rodolphe*.

Racey (295) English: unexplained. Compare RACY, RASEY, RAZEY.

Rach (292) German: **1.** from Middle High German *rach* 'rough', 'stiff', a nickname for someone affected by hard work, or a topographic name from the same word in the sense 'steep', 'rough'. **2.** perhaps in some instances from a Slavic personal name, such as a short form of *Radoslav*.

Rachal (941) Variant spelling of French RACHEL. This is a frequent surname in LA.

FOREBEARS Bearers of the name in LA claim descent from Pierre Rachal, a native of the Saintonge region of France, who appears to have been in Natchitoches Post around 1722. He bore the secondary surname St Denis.
GIVEN NAMES French 4%. *Jacques* (2), *Armelle, Chantel, Clotile, Colette, Eulice, Germaine, Numa*.

Rachel (569) **1.** German (mainly Bavaria): probably a topographic name from Middle High German *rach* 'rough', 'steep'. **2.** German: from a pet form of a Slavic personal name (see RACH). **3.** German: habitational name from a place called Rachel in Bohemia. **4.** French: metronymic from the female Biblical name *Rachel*, meaning 'ewe' in Hebrew. In the Bible (Genesis 28–35), Rachel is the wife of Jacob and the mother of Joseph and Benjamin.

Rachels (335) German: derivative of RACHEL.

Rachford (146) English: **1.** variant of ROCHFORD. **2.** variant of **Rackford**, a habitational name from Rackenford in Devon, recorded in Domesday Book as *Racheneforda*, which Mills interprets as 'ford suitable for riding, by a stretch of river'.

Rachlin (284) Jewish (eastern Ashkenazic): metronymic from the Yiddish female personal name *Rakhle*, a pet form of Biblical RACHEL + the eastern Slavic possessive suffix *-in*.
GIVEN NAMES Jewish 5%. *Hyman, Raanan*.

Rachow (106) German (of Slavic origin): habitational name from a place so named in Mecklenburg.

Rachwal (112) Polish: from the personal name *Rachwal*, a variant of *Rafal* (see RAPHAEL).
GIVEN NAMES Polish 13%. *Jurek, Lucyna, Tadeusz, Wojciech, Zygmunt*.

Racicot (490) French: unexplained. It is sometimes Americanized as ROSCOE or RASCO.
FOREBEARS A Racicot from the Anjou region of France is documented in Quebec City in 1715 with the secondary surname **Léveillé**.
GIVEN NAMES French 11%. *Armand* (2), *Gilles* (2), *Jacques* (2), *Normand* (2), *Adelard, Aime, Andre, Aurele, Fernand, Gaetan, Germaine, Ghislain*.

Racine (1692) French: from Old French *racine* 'root'; a metonymic occupational name for a grower or seller of root vegetables, or a nickname for a tenacious and stubborn man. It is frequently found translated as ROOT.
FOREBEARS A Racine from Normandy, France, was first documented in Quebec City in 1638; the secondary surnames Noyer and Ste-Marie are later attested.
GIVEN NAMES French 11%. *Marcel* (8), *Emile* (4), *Jacques* (4), *Andre* (3), *Normand* (3), *Camille* (2), *Fernand* (2), *Gaston* (2),

Napoleon (2), *Pierre* (2), *Yvon* (2), *Alphonse*.

Racioppi (146) Italian: from Sicilian *racioppu* 'cluster of grapes', hence presumably a metonymic occupational name for someone who sold or produced grapes.

GIVEN NAMES Italian 13%. *Pasquale* (2), *Biagio, Nicola, Sal*.

Raciti (136) Italian: from Greek *rakhitēs* 'mountain dweller'.

GIVEN NAMES Italian 26%. *Gregorio* (2), *Rosario* (2), *Salvatore* (2), *Angelo, Carmelo, Concetto, Dario, Grazio, Pasquale, Rocco, Sarino*.

Rack (300) German (also **Räck**): 1. from a short form of a Germanic personal name, formed with *rag-*, from *ragin* 'advice', 'counsel'. 2. nickname from the dialect word *Rack(e)* 'crow'.

GIVEN NAMES German 4%. *Hermann, Johann, Kaspar, Mathias*.

Rackers (235) German (**Räckers**): in the Lower Rhine-Westphalia area, from a reduced form of **Rädeker**, itself a reduced form of RADEMAKER.

Rackham (152) English: habitational name from a place in Sussex, so named from Old English *hrēac* 'mound', '(hay)rick' (probably the name of a nearby hill) + *hām* 'homestead'.

Racki (120) 1. Polish: habitational name for someone from places called Radzie in Białystok and Suwałki voivodeships. 2. Croatian (**Rački**) and south central Slovenian: unexplained.

Rackley (1876) English (mainly Berkshire): apparently a habitational name from a lost or unidentified place, which would derive its name from Old English *hrēac* 'mound' (compare RACKHAM) or *hraca* 'throat', 'gulley' + *lēah* 'woodland clearing'.

Rackliff (172) English: variant of RATCLIFF.

Rackliffe (150) English: variant of RATCLIFF.

Rackow (174) German (of Slavic origin): habitational name from places so named in Mecklenburg and Pomerania.

GIVEN NAMES German 7%. *Arno, Guenter, Helmut, Kurt*.

Raco (131) 1. Italian: possibly from an old Germanic personal name, *Rac(c)o*. 2. Possibly an altered spelling of the French family name **Racaud**, from a Germanic personal name composed of the elements *rac-*, short form of *ragin* 'counsel', 'advice' + *waldan* 'ruler', or a habitational name from places so named in Allier and Dordogne.

GIVEN NAMES Italian 15%. *Domenico, Giuseppina*.

Racy (109) English: unexplained. Compare RACEY, RASEY, RAZEY.

Racz (419) Hungarian (**Rácz**): ethnic name from *rác* 'Serbian', derived from the Serbian place name Ras, the capital of medieval Serbia.

GIVEN NAMES Hungarian 14%. *Zoltan* (4), *Dezso* (3), *Tibor* (3), *Gabor* (2), *Janos* (2), *Sandor* (2), *Andras, Endre, Eszter, Geza, Kalman, Karoly*.

Raczka (202) Polish: nickname from *raczek*, diminutive of *rak* 'crayfish'.

GIVEN NAMES Polish 10%. *Karol, Krystyna, Miroslaw, Stanislaw, Tadeusz, Wlodzimierz*.

Raczkowski (333) Polish: habitational name for someone from any of several places called Raczkowa, Raczkowo, or Raczków, named with *raczek*, diminutive of *rak* 'crayfish'.

GIVEN NAMES Polish 9%. *Faustyn* (2), *Andrzej, Bogdan, Boguslaw, Jadwiga, Stanislaw, Wojciech, Zbigniew, Zbyszek*.

Raczynski (168) Polish (**Raczyński**): habitational name for someone from any of several places, for example Raczyn in Piła and Sieradz voivodeships, or Raczyny in Ciechanów and Siedlce voivodeships.

GIVEN NAMES Polish 8%. *Casimir, Leszek, Slawomir, Zygmund*.

Rad (166) 1. Muslim: variant of RAAD. 2. German: from a short form of a Germanic personal name formed with *rād, rāt* 'advice', 'counsel'. 3. Hungarian (**Rád**): from the old secular personal name *Rád*, from Slavic *Rad* 'joyful' (see RADA).

GIVEN NAMES Muslim 48%. *Ali* (5), *Bijan* (3), *Abbas* (2), *Amad* (2), *Masoud* (2), *Nader* (2), *Nasser* (2), *Saeed* (2), *Ahmad, Alireza, Amir, Azin*.

Rada (580) 1. Spanish and Catalan: topographic name from *rada* 'natural bay'. 2. Spanish and Catalan: habitational name from places called Rada (Cantabria), Rada de Haro (Cuenca), La Rada (Albacete, Cuenca) or Rada de Moraira (Alacant), or from a Castilianized variant of Basque **Arrada**, habitational name from a place called Arrada in Navarre. 3. Czech: from a short form of any of several Slavic personal names containing the first element *rad-* 'glad', 'merry', in particular *Radoslav*, in which the second element means 'glory', and *Radomir*, in which the second element means 'great', 'famous'. 4. Hungarian: from the old secular personal name *Rada* or *Ráda*, of Slavic origin.

GIVEN NAMES Spanish 9%. *Carlos* (5), *Delfin* (2), *Ernesto* (2), *Jose* (2), *Lilia* (2), *Adelardo, Alipio, Arquimedes, Arturo, Cesar, Cruz, Eladia*.

Radabaugh (645) Probably an Americanized spelling of German **Reidenbach**.

Radach (108) German: from a short form of any of various Slavic personal names formed with *rad-* 'glad' as the first element, such as *Radomir* or *Radoslav* (see RADEK).

GIVEN NAMES German 7%. *Christoph, Otto, Waltraut*.

Radack (112) Germanized or Americanized spelling of Serbian **Radak**, a patronymic from the old personal name *Radak*, a pet form of *Rado*, a short form of any of vari-

ous compound Slavic personal names, such as *Radoslav* or *Radovan*, based on the Old Slavic element *rad* 'glad'.

Radaker (125) North German: altered spelling of **Rädeker**, a Westphalian occupational name for a wheelwright, a contraction of or a word formation parallel to RADEMAKER.

GIVEN NAME French 4%. *Camille*.

Radakovich (191) Serbian (**Radaković**): patronymic from the old personal name **Radak** (see RADACK).

Radant (153) German: probably from a Slavic personal name.

Radatz (144) German: variant spelling of RADDATZ.

GIVEN NAMES German 8%. *Erwin, Lutz, Reinhardt, Sigfried*.

Radcliff (1732) English: variant of RATCLIFF.

Radcliffe (2363) English: variant of RATCLIFF.

Raddatz (637) German: habitational name from a place in Brandenburg, originally so named from a secondary form of a Slavic personal name formed with *rad-* 'glad'.

GIVEN NAMES German 5%. *Otto* (3), *Bernhard, Erwin, Ewald, Guenter, Hans, Helmuth, Ruediger*.

Radde (175) German: 1. topographic name from any of several swamps so named. 2. from the Low German and Frisian personal name *Radde*, a short form of any of the various Germanic personal names formed with *rād, rāt* 'counsel', 'advice', for example *Radebert, Radebold*.

GIVEN NAMES German 9%. *Horst* (2), *Gerhardt, Kurt*.

Radden (137) German: patronymic from RADDE.

Radder (165) German: from a Germanic personal name, *Radheri*, composed of the elements *rād, rāt* 'advice', 'counsel' + *heri* 'army'.

Radebaugh (323) Americanized form of German **Radebach** (see RADABAUGH).

Radecki (376) 1. Polish: habitational name from Radecz, now called Redecz, in Włocławek voivodeship, or from the place once named Radecz or Redecz, now Recz. Both places are named with the personal name RADEK. 2. Czech: from any of five places in Bohemia called Radeč.

GIVEN NAMES Polish 9%. *Andrzej* (2), *Stanislaw* (2), *Boleslaw, Kazimierz, Krzysztof, Lucjan, Miroslaw, Tadeusz*.

Radek (119) Polish and Czech: from the personal name *Radek*, a pet form of any of various Slavic personal names formed with *rad-* 'glad' as the first element. The most common such names are *Radoslav* (Polish *Radosław*), in which the second element means 'glory', and *Radomir*, in which the second element means 'peace'.

GIVEN NAMES Polish 4%. *Leslaw, Piotr*.

Radeke (135) German: from a pet form of a Slavic compound name beginning with the element *rad-* 'glad' (compare RADEK), or from a short form of a Germanic personal name beginning with *rād-* 'counsel', 'advice'.

Radel (485) German: **1.** (also **Rädel**): from a pet form of any of the various Germanic personal names composed with *rād*, *rāt* 'advice', 'counsel', for example KONRAD. **2.** (**Rädel**): habitational name from Rädel near Potsdam.

Radell (186) Americanized spelling of German RADEL.

Rademacher (1546) North German: standardized spelling of RADEMAKER.
GIVEN NAMES German 4%. *Dieter* (4), *Kurt* (3), *Manfred* (2), *Aloys*, *Arno*, *Claus*, *Eldred*, *Franz*, *Fritz*, *Jurgen*, *Otto*, *Rudi*.

Rademaker (422) North German and Dutch: occupational name for a wheelwright or, by extension, a cartwright, from Middle Low German, Middle Dutch *rat* 'wheel' + *makære* 'maker'. Compare STELLMACHER, WAGNER.

Raden (175) German: habitational name from a place so named, as for example Raden near Rinteln and in Brandenburg, Saxony, and Silesia.

Rader (6315) German: **1.** occupational name for a wheelwright, from an agent derivative of Middle High German *rat* 'wheel'. **2.** (**Räder**): metonymic occupational name for a flour sifter or mill hand, from Middle High German *reder* 'sieve'. **3.** occasionally an occupational name from Middle Low German *rader* 'adviser'. **4.** from a Germanic personal name composed of the elements *rād*, *rāt* 'advice', 'counsel' + *heri* 'army'. **5.** Americanized spelling of German **Röder** (see ROEDER).

Radermacher (240) German: **1.** (**Rädermacher**): occupational name for a sieve maker, from archaic (16th century) *Räder*, *Rätter* 'sieve' (Middle High German *reden* 'to sift'). **2.** variant of RADEMACHER.
GIVEN NAMES German 6%. *Klaus*, *Kurt*, *Reiner*, *Reinhard*, *Wolfgang*.

Radford (4420) English: habitational name from any of the various places so named, for example in Devon, Nottinghamshire, Oxfordshire, Warwickshire, and Hereford and Worcester. Most are named from Old English *rēad* 'red' + *ford* 'ford', but it is possible that in some cases the first element may be a derivative of Old English *rīdan* 'to ride', with the meaning 'ford that can be crossed on horseback'.

Radhakrishnan (103) Indian (Kerala, Tamil Nadu): Hindu name from Sanskrit *rādhā* 'prosperity' (the name of Krishna's favorite gopi i.e. female cowherd) + *krṣṇa* (see KRISHNA), + the Tamil-Malayalam third-person masculine singular suffix *-n*. This is only a given name in India, but has come to be used as a family name in the U.S.
GIVEN NAMES Indian 92%. *Jayakumar* (2), *Jayant* (2), *Ravi* (2), *Suresh* (2), *Ananda*,

Anupama, *Asha*, *Bala*, *Ganesan*, *Indira*, *Ishwar*.

Radi (156) **1.** German: from a short form of a Germanic personal name formed either with *rād*, *rāt* 'advice', 'counsel' or in some cases with *hrād* 'quick'. **2.** Hungarian (**Rádi**): habitational name for someone from one of several places called Rád in Hungary. **3.** Muslim: from a personal name based on Arabic *raḍī* 'satisfied', 'pleased' (see the Qur'an 19:6).
GIVEN NAMES Muslim 6%. *Ahmed*, *Amin*, *Basem*, *Iyad*, *Kamel*, *Khalid*, *Mojtaba*, *Raouf*, *Said*.

Radican (141) Variant of Irish RATIGAN.

Radice (361) Italian: from *radice* 'root'; a metonymic occupational name for a grower or seller of root vegetables, or a nickname for a tenacious and stubborn man.
GIVEN NAMES Italian 7%. *Vito* (2), *Angelo*, *Annalisa*, *Fiore*, *Pasquale*, *Santo*.

Radich (231) Serbian and Croatian (**Radić**): patronymic from the personal name *Rado* or *Rade*, derivative of Old Slavic *rad* 'merry', 'joyful'.
GIVEN NAMES South Slavic 7%. *Zarko* (2), *Jozo*, *Miodrag*, *Nevenka*, *Velimir*.

Radick (182) Germanized or Americanized form of Czech **Radík**, a pet form of *Radoslav*, or of some other Slavic name containing the element *rad-* 'glad', 'merry' (see RADA).

Radigan (434) **1.** Irish (Connacht): variant of RATIGAN. **2.** Perhaps an altered spelling of the southern French family name **Radigon**, a diminutive of **Radigue**, which is of uncertain origin. It is largely confined to Gascony and is perhaps a derivative of Occitan *razigar* 'to tear out or uproot' (Latin *eradicare*, from *radix*, genitive *radicis*); if so, it is presumably a topographic name for someone who lived on a patch of cleared land.

Radil (100) Variant spelling of German RADEL.

Radin (531) **1.** Jewish (eastern Ashkenazic): habitational name from any of the places called Radzyń in Poland. **2.** Serbian, Croatian, and Slovenian: from the Old Slavic personal name *Radin*, which is derived from Old Slavic *rad* 'merry', 'joyful'.
GIVEN NAMES Jewish 4%. *Herschel*, *Myer*, *Sol*, *Yaakov*.

Radka (133) Czech: from a pet form of the personal name RADA. Compare RADEK.

Radke (2145) German: **1.** from a pet form of any of various Germanic personal names formed with *rād*, *rāt* 'advice', 'counsel', for example KONRAD. **2.** (of Slavic origin): variant of RADEK.
GIVEN NAMES German 5%. *Otto* (8), *Kurt* (6), *Reinhold* (2), *Claus*, *Erwin*, *Franz*, *Frieda*, *Klaus*, *Reinhart*, *Willi*.

Radl (104) South German: **1.** variant of RADEL 1. **2.** variant of RADLE 3.
GIVEN NAMES German 10%. *Otto* (2), *Frieda*.

Radle (318) **1.** Americanized spelling of German RADEL. **2.** German: from a Slavic personal name formed with *rad-* 'joyful'. **3.** German (**Rädle**): metonymic occupational name for a wheelwright, from a diminutive of Middle High German *rat* 'wheel'.

Radler (263) German (also **Rädler**): habitational name for someone from a place named Radel, Radelau, or Radlau, many examples of which are found in Bavaria and Austria.

Radley (752) English: habitational name from a place so named, from Old English *rēad* 'red' + *lēah* 'wood', 'clearing'. There are places so called in Berkshire and Devon.

Radliff (164) Apparently an altered form of **Radcliff** (see RATCLIFF).

Radloff (849) North German: from the personal name *Radolf*, composed of the Old Saxon elements *rād* 'counsel', 'advice' + *wolf* 'wolf'.

Radmacher (103) German: occupational name for a wheelwright, from Middle Low German *rademaker(e)*, Middle High German *rademecher*.
GIVEN NAME German 4%. *Gerhard*.

Radman (189) **1.** North German (**Radmann**): North German form of RATHMANN. **2.** German (**Radmann**) topographic name from either Middle High German *rode* 'forest clearing' or *rād* 'swamp' + *man* 'man'. **3.** Croatian and Serbian: from the old personal name *Radman*, which is composed with Old Slavic *rad* 'merry', 'joyful' + *-man*.
GIVEN NAMES South Slavic 5%. *Branko* (2), *Dejan*, *Marko*.

Radmer (146) German: from the Germanic personal name *Radmar*, composed of the elements *rād*, *rāt* 'advice' + *mar-* 'famous'.
GIVEN NAME German 4%. *Otto*.

Radner (124) **1.** German: perhaps a habitational name for someone from Raden near Güstrow in Mecklenburg. **2.** English: habitational name from Radnor in Cornwall or various other minor places so named.
GIVEN NAME French 6%. *Zoel* (2).

Radney (281) Of uncertain origin. Perhaps an altered spelling of Hungarian **Radnay**, a habitational name for someone from a place called Radna in Transylvania, or even of German **Radnick**, an occupational name for a councilman, from Sorbian. There are a few occurrences of the surname in England, and it could perhaps be a habitational name from Radnage in Buckinghamshire, named from Old English *rēad* 'red' + *āc*, dative of *āc* 'oak'. Early spellings of the place name include *Radeneghe* (1241, 1262) alongside the more usual *Radenache*.

Rado (348) **1.** Catalan (**Radó**): from the Germanic personal name *Rado*. **2.** Catalan (**Radó**): nickname for a fat person, variant of **Rodó**, from a derivative of Latin *rotundus* 'round'. **3.** Italian: from a Germanic

personal name, *Rato*, *Rado*, *Ratdo*.
4. Hungarian (**Radó**): from the old secular name *Radó*, from *Rád* (Slavic *Rad*).

Radomski (458) Polish: habitational name for someone from the city of Radom in central Poland, south of Warsaw. The place name is based on the Old Slavic personal name *Radomir*.
GIVEN NAMES Polish 6%. *Danuta* (2), *Jaroslaw* (2), *Bogdan*, *Jozef*, *Mieczyslaw*, *Miroslaw*, *Stanislaw*.

Rados (176) **1.** Hungarian: from the old secular personal name *Rados*. **2.** Serbian and Croatian (**Radoš**): from the personal name *Radoš*, a derivative of *Radoslav*, composed of the Old Slavic elements *rad* 'merry', 'joyful' + *slav* 'glory'.

Radosevich (399) Croatian (**Radošević**): patronymic from the personal name *Radoš*, a derivative of *Radoslav*, which is composed with the Old Slavic elements *rad* 'merry', 'joyful' + *slav* 'glory', 'fame'.

Radosta (124) Italian: from the medieval female personal name *Radosta*.
GIVEN NAMES Italian 13%. *Rocco* (2), *Angelo*, *Antonio*, *Dino*, *Emanuele*.

Radovich (407) Serbian and Croatian (**Radović**): patronymic from the personal name *Rado*, a derivative of Old Slavic *rad* 'merry', 'joyful'.
GIVEN NAMES South Slavic 5%. *Ratko* (2), *Dragomir*, *Rade*, *Slavko*.

Radtke (2685) North German: variant of RADEKE.
GIVEN NAMES German 6%. *Kurt* (13), *Erwin* (4), *Klaus* (4), *Otto* (4), *Dieter* (3), *Hans* (3), *Arno* (2), *Eldred* (2), *Gerhard* (2), *Heinz* (2), *Horst* (2), *Manfred* (2).

Radu (203) Romanian: from a short form of any of the various Slavic personal names beginning with the element *rad-* 'joyful'. Compare RADEK.
GIVEN NAMES Romanian 26%; German 4%; French 4%. *Gheorghe* (3), *Cornel* (2), *Nicolae* (2), *Petru* (2), *Aurelian*, *Cosmin*, *Danut*, *Doru*, *Dumitru*, *Georgeta*, *Ionel*, *Laurentiu*; *Ernst*, *Uwe*; *Aurel*, *Luc*, *Marcel*.

Radue (115) Eastern German (**Radü(g)e**): habitational name from a place called Radü(g)e, of Slavic origin.

Raduenz (132) German: unexplained.

Radunz (106) German (**Radünz**): see RADUENZ.
GIVEN NAMES German 7%. *Hans*, *Heinz*, *Otto*.

Radwan (178) **1.** Muslim: from a personal name based on Arabic *riḍwān* 'satisfaction', 'contentment' (see Qur'an 48:29). Compare Iranian REZA. **2.** German (under Slavic influence): nickname for a captivating person, from Old Slavic *radovati* 'to please or delight'.
GIVEN NAMES Muslim 47%. *Ibrahim* (3), *Mohammed* (3), *Farid* (2), *Ghassan* (2), *Khaled* (2), *Mohamad* (2), *Mohamed* (2), *Nabil* (2), *Salwa* (2), *Sami* (2), *Wadad* (2), *Abed*.

Radwanski (149) **1.** Polish (**Radwański**): habitational name for someone from places in Poland called Radwan in Piotrków, Tarnobrzeg, or Tarnów voivodeship or Radwany in Łomża voivodeship. **2.** German (of Slavic origin): habitational name from a place in Upper Saxony called Radwan.
GIVEN NAMES Polish 10%. *Wieslaw* (2), *Bogdan*, *Czeslawa*, *Leszek*, *Zbigniew*.

Radway (150) English: habitational name from various places, for example either of the places named Radway (in Devon and Warwickshire), Reddaway or Roadway (both in Devon), all named from Old English *rēad* 'red' + *waye* 'road', 'way', or from Rodway in Somerset, in which the first element is from Old English *rād* 'road', 'track'.

Rady (353) **1.** German: variant spelling of RADI. **2.** German: variant spelling of **Radey**, an occupational name from a Germanized form of Sorbian or Czech *rataj* 'plowman', 'servant'. **3.** English: variant of READY.

Radziewicz (186) Polish: patronymic from the personal name *Rad*, a pet form of a Old Slavic personal name such as *Radoslav* or *Radomir* (see RADEK).

Radzik (139) **1.** Polish: from a pet form of any of several Old Polish personal names beginning with *Rad-* (see RADEK). **2.** Jewish (from Poland): habitational name from a village called Radziki in Poland.
GIVEN NAMES Polish 8%; Jewish 4%. *Bronislaw*, *Lucjan*, *Slawomir*, *Stanislawa*; *Morty*, *Shlomo*.

Radzikowski (64) Polish: habitational name for someone from any of several places called Radzikowo or Radzików.
GIVEN NAMES Polish 15%; Italian 7%. *Andrzej*, *Jerzy*, *Piotr*, *Tomasz*; *Cosmo*.

Radzinski (127) Polish (**Radziński**, **Radzyński**): habitational name for someone from any of numerous places called Radzyń.

Radziwill (21) Polish (**Radziwiłł**): of Lithuanian origin, probably from Lithuanian *radvilà* 'foundling', from *ràsti* 'to find' + *viltis* 'hope'.
FOREBEARS This surname has enjoyed considerable prestige since the 16th century as the surname of one of the principal noble families of Poland; many military leaders and statesmen in Polish history have come from the ducal family of Radziwiłł.
GIVEN NAMES Polish 15%. *Andrzej*, *Jerzy*, *Piotr*, *Tomasz*.

Rae (2102) Scottish: reduced form of McRAE.

Raeburn (167) Scottish: variant spelling of RAYBURN.

Raeder (280) German (**Räder**): **1.** see RADER. **2.** variant of REDER.
GIVEN NAMES German 6%. *Lorenz* (2), *Willi* (2), *Ernst*, *Otto*.

Raef (121) English: probably a variant spelling of RALPH.

Rael (840) Hispanic: from northwestern Mexico, unexplained.
GIVEN NAMES Spanish 18%. *Jose* (9), *Juan* (5), *Arturo* (3), *Eloy* (3), *Juanita* (3), *Melecio* (2), *Orlando* (2), *Ramon* (2), *Seferino* (2), *Adelaido*, *Adolfo*, *Agustina*.

Raes (104) Dutch: variant of RASE.
GIVEN NAME French 5%. *Andre*.

Raether (384) German: **1.** from a Germanic personal name formed with *rād*, *rāt* 'advice', 'counsel'. **2.** habitational name from Rathen (Rhineland) or from any of several places called Rath.

Raetz (295) German (also **Rätz**): from a short form of any of various Germanic compound personal names formed with *rād*, *rāt* 'advice', 'counsel'.
GIVEN NAMES German 5%. *Fritz* (2), *Beate*, *Erna*, *Otto*.

Rafael (319) **1.** Spanish, Catalan, Portuguese, and Galician: from the personal name *Rafael* (see RAPHAEL). **2.** Jewish: variant spelling of RAPHAEL.
GIVEN NAMES Spanish 31%; Portuguese 9%. *Eduardo* (3), *Jose* (3), *Juan* (3), *Amado* (2), *Carlos* (2), *Gregorio* (2), *Jorge* (2), *Julio* (2), *Santiago* (2), *Ana*, *Basilio*, *Bernardo*; *Ilidio*, *Joao*.

Rafalko (122) Polish (**Rafałko**) and Ukrainian: from a pet form of the personal name *Rafal* (see RAPHAEL).
GIVEN NAMES Polish 9%. *Casimir*, *Kinga*, *Malgorzata*, *Zigmund*.

Rafalski (176) Polish: habitational name for someone from Rafały in Ciechanów voivodeship.
GIVEN NAMES Polish 5%. *Grzegorz*, *Irena*, *Pawel*.

Raff (699) **1.** German: nickname for a tall thin man, from Middle High German *rave* 'lath'. **2.** German: from a personal name, *Raffo*, as yet unexplained. **3.** English: variant of RALPH.

Raffa (466) Italian: **1.** from the old Germanic personal name *Raffo*, possibly a feminized form. **2.** habitational name from Raffa, a locality of Puegnano del Garda in Brescia province. This source is unlikely to have contributed greatly to the American surname, since it belongs to an area (Lombardy) outside the main sources of migration to the U.S.
GIVEN NAMES Italian 13%. *Angelo* (3), *Lorenzo* (2), *Nunzio* (2), *Carmelo*, *Carmine*, *Concetta*, *Guido*, *Luigi*, *Ricci*, *Romolo*, *Santo*, *Stefano*.

Raffaele (371) Italian: from the personal name *Raffaele*, an Italian equivalent of RAPHAEL.
GIVEN NAMES Italian 24%. *Angelo* (3), *Bartolo* (3), *Carmelo* (2), *Sal* (2), *Amedeo*, *Antonio*, *Armando*, *Carmine*, *Caterina*, *Francisco*, *Gino*, *Gustavo*, *Ippolito*, *Orlando*.

Raffaelli (142) Italian: patronymic from the personal name *Raffaello*, an Italian equivalent of RAPHAEL.

GIVEN NAMES Italian 14%. *Angelo, Chiara, Dino, Gino, Paolo, Pietro, Remo.*

Raffel (339) **1.** English: variant of RAPHAEL. **2.** German: nickname for someone who was loud or indiscreet, a blabbermouth, from Middle High German *raffeln* 'to be noisy', 'to scold'. **3.** German: from an unexplained personal name, *Raffo.* Compare RAFF.

GIVEN NAMES German 4%. *Erwin* (2), *Horst, Mathias.*

Raffensperger (194) German: altered spelling of **Ravensburger** or **Ravensberger**, a habitational name for someone from Ravensburg in Württemberg, but there are a number of similar surnames, for example **Raffenberg**, a farm name near Hamm, and **Raffsberger**.

Rafferty (3618) Irish (especially Ulster): reduced Anglicized form of Gaelic **Ó Rabhartaigh** or **Ó Robhartaigh** (often found as **Ó Raithbheartaigh**) 'descendant of *Rabhartach* or *Robhartach*', a personal name meaning 'flood tide', hence 'abundance', 'prosperity'.

GIVEN NAMES Irish 5%. *Brendan* (2), *Clodagh, Conor, Dermot, Donal, Eoin, Niall, Ronan.*

Raffetto (147) Italian: from a derivative of RAFFO.

Raffety (274) Variant spelling of RAFFERTY.

Raffield (190) English: variant of RAPHAEL.

Raffin (107) Italian (Venezia): from a pet form of the personal name RAFFO.

GIVEN NAMES Italian 8%. *Dante* (2), *Erminio, Gino.*

Raffo (231) Italian: **1.** from the old Germanic personal name *Raffo.* **2.** habitational name from Raffo in Petralia Soprana, Palermo province.

GIVEN NAMES Spanish 8%; Italian 5%. *Cesar* (2), *Jose* (2), *Adan, Alberto, Ana, Carlos, Julio, Luis, Raul; Geno, Giacomo, Romolo.*

Rafiq (102) Muslim: from a personal name based on Arabic *rafīq* 'intimate friend', 'companion' (see the Qur'an 4:69). The name is used in combinations such as *Rafiq ul-Islam* 'friend of Islam'.

GIVEN NAMES Muslim 85%. *Mohammad* (23), *Muhammad* (6), *Mohammed* (3), *Abdal, Abdul, Adnan, Agha, Ahmad, Amina, Amjad, Ashraf, Azhar.*

Rafter (688) Irish: variant of RAFTERY.

GIVEN NAMES Irish 4%. *Brendan, Malachy.*

Raftery (752) Irish: reduced Anglicized form of Gaelic **Ó Reachtabhra** 'descendant of *Reachtabhra*', from *reacht* 'decree'.

GIVEN NAMES Irish 8%. *Brendan* (2), *Dermot, Eamon, Mairead, Patrick James.*

Rafuse (209) Of uncertain origin; found mainly in Nova Scotia. Possibly an altered spelling of German **Rehfuss** 'deer foot', a nickname for someone who was fleet of foot, or **Raufuss**, a nickname for a crude man from Middle High German *rūh fuoz* 'hairy foot'.

Ragain (157) Of uncertain origin; possibly a Frenchified spelling of Irish REGAN.

GIVEN NAME French 6%. *Clovis* (3).

Ragains (142) Probably a variant of RAGAIN.

Ragan (4102) Probably a variant spelling of Irish REGAN.

Ragans (102) Probably a variant of Irish REGAN.

Ragar (132) Possibly an altered spelling of German REGER or RAGER.

Ragas (218) This is a LA name, perhaps a variant of RAGATZ.

GIVEN NAMES French 5%. *Emile, Euclide, Michel.*

Ragatz (142) Swiss German: habitational name from Ragaz in Grison canton.

GIVEN NAMES German 4%. *Fritz, Otto.*

Ragazzo (107) Italian: occupational name for a servant, from *ragazzo* 'boy', 'lad', 'servant', of Arabic origin.

GIVEN NAMES Italian 35%. *Rocco* (3), *Salvatore* (3), *Vito* (2), *Camillo, Corrado, Dino, Gino, Giuseppe, Pietro.*

Ragen (230) **1.** Probably a respelling of Irish REGAN. **2.** Alternatively, it could perhaps be a habitational name from Ragen in Tyrol, Austria.

Rager (1782) German: **1.** habitational name for someone from either of two places called Ragen: in Tyrol, Austria, and in East Prussia, Germany. **2.** (**Räger**): habitational name for someone from Rägen in Schleswig-Holstein. **3.** from a Germanic personal name composed of the elements *rag-* 'advice' + *hari, heri* 'army'. **4.** possibly an altered spelling of REGER or **Röger** (see ROEGER).

Raggio (343) Italian: possibly from an old Germanic personal name.

Raghavan (186) Indian (Kerala, Tamil Nadu): Hindu name from Sanskrit *rāghava* 'derived from Raghu', 'descendant of Raghu' (an epithet of the god Rama, incarnation of Vishnu) + the Tamil-Malayalam third-person masculine singular suffix *-n.* This is only a given name in India, but has come to be used as a family name in the U.S.

GIVEN NAMES Indian 96%. *Vijay* (11), *Ravi* (3), *Srikanth* (3), *Usha* (3), *Arun* (2), *Chitra* (2), *Dinesh* (2), *Hari* (2), *Murli* (2), *Padma* (2), *Prakash* (2), *Ragu* (2).

Ragin (470) Probably an altered spelling of REGAN.

Ragland (3964) English: topographic name from Middle English *ragge* 'stone' + *land* 'land', or a habitational name from a place named Ragland Coppice, in Corsley, Wiltshire, which is named with the local dialect word *rag* 'small piece of woodland'.

Ragle (486) German (**Rägle**): of uncertain origin; perhaps a variant of the Swiss family name **Regli**, which may derive from a Germanic personal name, *Ragilo*, formed with *rag-* 'advice', but more likely an altered spelling of REGEL.

Raglin (344) **1.** Of uncertain origin; perhaps an altered spelling of English RAGLAND. **2.** German: altered spelling of Reglin, a variant of Regelin, from a short form of a Germanic personal name (see RAGER 3).

Ragno (147) Italian: **1.** nickname from *ragno* 'spider'. **2.** from a Germanic personal name, *Ragino*, from the root *Ragin.*

GIVEN NAMES Italian 17%. *Antonio, Domenico, Pietro, Salvatore, Santo.*

Rago (800) Italian: probably from a Germanic personal name, *Rago*, from the root *Ragin.*

GIVEN NAMES Italian 13%. *Angelo* (8), *Rocco* (4), *Vito* (3), *Antonio* (2), *Pasquale* (2), *Calogero, Carlo, Carmine, Francesca, Gaetano, Giuseppe, Marco.*

Ragon (294) French: from the Germanic personal name *Rago* (from the oblique case), a short form of any of various names formed with with *rag-* 'advice'.

Ragona (154) Italian: **1.** ethnic name from a reduced form of *Aragona* 'Aragon', now part of Spain but an independent state up to 1479; the surname arrived in Italy in the wake of the Aragonese conquest and domination of southern Italy which began in 1282. **2.** habitational name from Aragona in Agrigento province, Sicily.

GIVEN NAMES Italian 7%. *Alfonse, Angelo, Gaetano, Sal, Silvio.*

Ragone (409) Italian: possibly from a derivative of the personal name RAGO.

GIVEN NAMES Italian 17%. *Angelo* (5), *Rocco* (2), *Vito* (2), *Carmine, Cono, Lorenzo, Luigi, Marino, Sabatino, Salvatore.*

Ragonese (237) Italian: variant of **Aragonese**, from an adjectival form of the place name ARAGON.

GIVEN NAMES Italian 22%. *Angelo* (6), *Salvatore* (4), *Domenic* (2), *Sal* (2), *Antonino, Bruna, Carmelo, Domenico, Duilio, Pietro.*

Ragosta (110) Italian: from a shortened form of *aragosta* 'lobster'; possibly a metonymic occupational name for a shell-fisherman or otherwise a nickname for someone thought to resemble a lobster in some way.

GIVEN NAMES Italian 17%. *Carmine* (2), *Angelo, Domenic, Luca, Nicola, Sal.*

Ragozzino (111) Italian (Sicily): probably a variant of **Raguzzino**, from a diminutive of **Raguzzi**, itself a Veneto variant of RAGUSA (in Croatia).

GIVEN NAMES Italian 18%. *Aldo* (2), *Alessandra, Carlo, Domenic, Giuseppe, Pasquale, Salvatore.*

Ragsdale (4622) Apparently an English habitational name from Ragdale in Leicestershire, which is probably named from Old English *hraca* 'gully', 'narrow pass' + *dæl* 'valley', 'dale'.

Ragucci (202) Italian: patronymic from *Raguccio*, a derivative of the personal name RAGO.

GIVEN NAMES Italian 24%. *Carlo* (2), *Carmine* (2), *Enzo* (2), *Angelo*, *Carmela*, *Cosimo*, *Dante*, *Gennaro*, *Rocco*.

Ragusa (882) Italian: habitational name from Ragusa in Sicily, or from the ancient city of Dubrovnik on the Dalmatian coast of Croatia (Italian name *Ragusa*).
GIVEN NAMES Italian 17%. *Salvatore* (12), *Angelo* (4), *Sal* (4), *Gaetano* (3), *Saverio* (3), *Antonio* (2), *Carmelo* (2), *Domenic* (2), *Giuseppe* (2), *Vito* (2), *Annalisa*, *Carlo*.

Raguse (120) German: unexplained.

Rahaim (147) Muslim: variant of RAHIM.

Rahal (174) Arabic: **1.** from a personal name based on *raḥāl* 'explorer', 'one who udertakes a journey'. **2.** alternatively, perhaps, from the female personal name *Rāḥīl* (Biblical RACHEL).
GIVEN NAMES Arabic 30%; French 5%. *Ahmad* (2), *Ahmed* (2), *Ali* (2), *Hussein* (2), *Abdul*, *Amira*, *Bilal*, *Ghassan*, *Haidar*, *Huda*, *Kamal*, *Malaki*; *Michel*, *Pierre*, *Verdun*.

Rahaman (126) Muslim: variant of RAHMAN.
GIVEN NAMES Muslim 67%. *Mohammed* (6), *Abdul* (5), *Bibi* (4), *Mohamed* (4), *Abdool* (2), *Abdulla* (2), *Abass*, *Ameena*, *Amzad*, *Arif*, *Azeez*, *Faizul*.

Rahe (666) German: nickname for a rough individual, from a North German variant of RAUH (see RAUCH).

Rahill (168) Irish: Anglicized form of Gaelic **Ó Raghaill** (see RAWL) or of **Ó Raghailligh** (see REILLY).
GIVEN NAME Irish 5%. *Seamus*.

Rahilly (187) Irish: reduced Anglicized form of Gaelic **Ó Raithile**.

Rahim (360) Muslim: from a personal name based on Arabic *raḥīm* 'merciful', 'compassionate'. *Ur-Raḥīm* 'the Merciful' is an attribute of Allah (see the Qur'an 2:173). The name is also found in combinations such as *'Abd ur-Raḥīm* 'servant of the Merciful'.
GIVEN NAMES Muslim 80%. *Abdul* (24), *Abdur* (14), *Mohamed* (5), *Hassan* (4), *Mohammad* (4), *Mohammed* (4), *Muhammad* (3), *Rafiq* (3), *Abdool* (2), *Ali* (2), *Aziz* (2), *Bibi* (2).

Rahimi (262) Muslim: from an Arabic name indicating descent from or association with someone called *Raḥīm* (see RAHIM).
GIVEN NAMES Muslim 77%. *Mohammad* (12), *Abdul* (10), *Ali* (5), *Abbas* (4), *Ahmad* (3), *Hamid* (3), *Mehdi* (3), *Abdullah* (2), *Amir* (2), *Farrokh* (2), *Fazal* (2), *Hakim* (2).

Rahl (202) German: from a short form of the Germanic personal name *Roloff*, Low German variant of RUDOLF.

Rahlf (123) German: from a reduced form of the personal name *Rahloff*, a variant of *Radolf* (see RADLOFF).

Rahm (694) German: **1.** topographic name from Middle High German, Middle Low German *rām(e)* 'end', 'target', 'mark', or a habitational name from any of several places in Westphalia and Rhineland named

with this word. **2.** from Middle High German, Middle Low German *rām* 'soot', possibly a metonymic occupational name for a blacksmith or charcoal burner, or a nickname for a dirty person. **3.** metonymic occupational name for a maker of frames (windows, looms, and the like), from Middle High German *rame* 'stand', 'rack', 'frame'. **4.** (**Rähm**): variant spelling of REHM.

Rahman (2019) **1.** Muslim: from a personal name based on Arabic *raḥmān* 'most gracious', usually forming part of a compound name such as *'Abd ur-Raḥmān* 'servant of the Most Gracious'. *ur-Raḥmān* (al-Rahman) 'the Most Gracious' is an attribute of Allah. *'Abd ur-Raḥmān ibn 'Awf* was one of the Companions to whom the Prophet Muhammad gave the good news of entering into paradise. This name is widespread throughout the Muslim world. **2.** German (**Rahmann**): variant of **Rademann**, topographic name from Low German *Rade* 'area cleared of forest', or a habitational name for someone from any of the places named Rade, from this word. Alternatively, it may be a habitational name for someone from Rahm (see RAHM 1).
GIVEN NAMES Muslim 78%. *Mohammed* (95), *Mohammad* (71), *Syed* (42), *Azizur* (20), *Abdul* (18), *Ataur* (17), *Mizanur* (17), *Muhammad* (17), *Abdur* (15), *Shafiqur* (15), *Habibur* (14), *Fazlur* (10).

Rahmani (171) Muslim: Arabic family name indicating descent from or association with someone called *Raḥmān* (see RAHMAN).
GIVEN NAMES Muslim 76%. *Abdul* (5), *Akbar* (4), *Aziz* (3), *Ali* (2), *Bahram* (2), *Bijan* (2), *Mohammad* (2), *Mohammed* (2), *Rachid* (2), *Abbas*, *Abolfazl*, *Ehsan*.

Rahming (142) German: nickname from Middle High German *rāmic* 'dirty', 'sooty'.

Rahn (2479) German: **1.** nickname from Middle High German *rān* 'slim', 'slight'. **2.** from a short form of the Slavic personal name *Ranislav*.

Rahner (130) German (Bavaria): habitational name for someone from Rahn in the Upper Palatinate or from Rahna near Merseburg.
GIVEN NAMES German 6%. *Erwin*, *Hans*, *Markus*.

Rahr (118) **1.** Swedish and Danish: nickname from *rar* 'rare'. **2.** German: East Prussian variant of ROHR.
GIVEN NAMES German 6%; Scandinavian 5%. *Fritz*, *Kurt*; *Knud*.

Rahrig (144) German: variant of **Röhrig** (see ROEHRIG).

Rai (364) **1.** Indian (northeastern states): Hindu name found among several communities, from Sanskrit *rājā* 'king'. **2.** Indian (Karnataka): name found in the Bunt community of coastal Karnataka, of unknown meaning.

GIVEN NAMES Indian 80%. *Arun* (3), *Arti* (2), *Ashok* (2), *Bharat* (2), *Jyoti* (2), *Kanti* (2), *Leela* (2), *Mani* (2), *Manish* (2), *Mukesh* (2), *Nisha* (2), *Pavan* (2).

Raia (542) Italian: **1.** topographic name from Sicilian *raia* 'smilax' (a climbing shrub). **2.** from Sicilian *raja* 'ray', 'skate' (the fish), presumably a nickname for someone thought to resemble the fish or a metonymic occupational name for a fisherman or fish seller. **3.** from Arabic *rāyah* 'flag'.
GIVEN NAMES Italian 15%. *Salvatore* (6), *Luigi* (2), *Vincenzo* (2), *Vito* (2), *Carmine*, *Domenico*, *Francesco*, *Gaetano*, *Gaspare*, *Genario*, *Gino*, *Giuseppe*.

Raible (280) **1.** South German (Swabia): variant diminutive form of a derogatory Swabian nickname from *Räuber* 'robber', 'bandit'. **2.** Variant of German **Reubal** or **Rübal** (see ROUBAL).
GIVEN NAMES German 6%. *Gerhard* (3), *Egon*, *Erwin*, *Kurt*.

Raich (162) Czech: nickname for a wealthy man or perhaps in some cases an ironic nickname for a pauper, from a Czech spelling of German *reich* 'rich'.

Raiche (320) French: unexplained. Perhaps a respelling of **Rèche**, a topographic name for someone who lived in a place characterized by ash trees, from *hrèche*, Gascon equivalent of standard French *frêne* (Latin *fraxinus*).
GIVEN NAMES French 13%. *Marcel* (3), *Adrien*, *Armand*, *Emile*, *Eugenie*, *Fernand*, *Gaston*, *Germaine*, *Lucien*, *Normand*, *Serge*.

Raichle (131) South German: from a diminutive of Middle High German *rouch* 'smoke', hence an occupational nickname for a blacksmith, metal smelter, or the like.
GIVEN NAMES German 14%. *Erwin* (5), *Kurt* (3).

Raider (218) Variant of German and Jewish REIDER.
GIVEN NAME Jewish 4%. *Avrohom*.

Raiford (719) See RAYFORD.

Raifsnider (130) German: old spelling of REIFSCHNEIDER ('cooper').

Raikes (242) English: variant of RAKE.

Rail (206) Apparently an altered spelling of RAILE.

Raile (156) **1.** South German: Swabian nickname for a nimble person, from a diminutive of Middle High German *rē* 'roe deer'. **2.** variant of REILE.
GIVEN NAMES German 5%. *Frieda*, *Gerhard*, *Hermann*.

Railey (796) **1.** Probably an Americanized spelling of Swiss German **Rölli** (see ROELLE). **2.** variant of RAILE or REILE.

Railing (159) Probably an Americanized spelling of the German habitational names REHLING and REILING.

Railsback (447) Altered spelling of German **Railsbach**, a habitational name of uncertain origin, probably a reduced form of

Raigelsbach, from Middle High German *reigel* 'heron' + *bach* 'stream', 'creek'; or an altered spelling of **Reulbach**, a habitational name from a place so named in the Rhön Mountains in Hesse.

Railton (122) Northern English: unexplained; probably a habitational name from a lost or unidentified place.

Raimer (189) German: variant of REIMER.

Raimo (286) Italian: from a reduced form of RAIMONDO, or possibly from an older Germanic form of this name.
GIVEN NAMES Italian 9%. *Ugo* (2), *Angelo, Domenic, Luigi, Philomena, Sal, Salvatore.*

Raimond (109) French: variant spelling of RAYMOND.

Raimondi (684) Italian: patronymic or plural form of RAIMONDO.
GIVEN NAMES Italian 17%. *Vito* (4), *Angelo* (3), *Cosmo* (3), *Carmine* (2), *Rocco* (2), *Sal* (2), *Salvatore* (2), *Benedetto, Carmello, Carmelo, Dante, Dino.*

Raimondo (452) Italian: from the personal name *Raimondo*, composed of the Germanic elements *rag-* 'advice' + *mund* 'protection'.
GIVEN NAMES Italian 24%; Spanish 4%. *Antonio* (6), *Angelo* (2), *Carlo* (2), *Natale* (2), *Rosario* (2), *Salvatore* (2), *Domenico, Filomena, Ignazio, Pasquale, Pietro, Silvio; Blanca, Juan, Ramona.*

Rain (299) **1.** English: variant of RAINE. **2.** German: topographic name from Middle High German *rein* 'margin', 'boundary', or a habitational name from a place in Bavaria named with this word.

Rainaldi (104) Italian: from the personal name *Rainaldo*, a variant of RENALDO.
GIVEN NAMES Italian 15%. *Nino* (2), *Angelo, Carmine, Ennio, Marino.*

Rainbolt (748) Variant of German **Rainbold** (see REINBOLD).

Rainbow (242) **1.** English: altered form of an Old French personal name, *Rainbaut*, composed of the Germanic elements *ragin* 'counsel' + *bald* 'bold', 'brave'. The form of the name has been affected by folk etymological association with the vocabulary word *rainbow*. Compare RAMMEL, RAYBOULD. **2.** Translation of the German and Ashkenazic Jewish surname **Regenbogen**. The German name is a habitational name for someone who lived at a house distinguished by the sign of a rainbow, Middle High German *regenboge*. The Jewish name is ornamental from German *Regenbogen*, one of the group of ornamental names based on natural phenomena.

Raine (719) **1.** English and French: from a short form of any of the various Germanic personal names formed with *ragin* 'counsel' as the first element (see, for example, RAYMOND, REYNOLD). **2.** English: from the medieval female personal name *Rayne* (from Old French *reine* 'queen', Latin *regina*). **3.** English and French: nickname from Old French *raine* 'frog' (Latin *rana*).

4. Scottish: habitational name from a place called Rayne in Aberdeenshire, so named from an English dialect term meaning 'strip of land'.

Rainer (1011) **1.** Variant spelling of the English family name RAYNER, or variant of the French cognate RAINIER. **2.** German: variant of REINER.

Raineri (217) Italian: from the Germanic personal name *Raineri*, composed of *ragin* 'advice' + *hari, heri* 'army'.
GIVEN NAMES Italian 15%. *Carlo* (3), *Angelo, Carmelo, Ciro, Gasper, Giovanni, Luciano, Milio, Nicola, Sal, Vincenzo.*

Raines (7087) **1.** English: habitational name for someone from Rayne in Essex, recorded in Domesday Book as *Raines*, possibly from an unattested Old English word, *hrægene* 'shelter', 'eminence'. **2.** English (of Norman origin): habitational name from Rennes in Brittany. **3.** English: patronymic from RAINE 1. **4.** Jewish (Ashkenazic): metronymic from the Yiddish female personal name *Rayne*, cognate with RAINE 2 and used as a translation of Hebrew *Malka* 'queen'.

Rainey (7394) Irish or Scottish: Anglicized form of Gaelic **Ó Raighne, Ó Ráighne**, from a personal name derived from the Old Norse name *Rǫgnvaldr* (see RONALD, REYNOLD).

Rainford (225) English: habitational name from a place in Lancashire, so named from an Old English personal name *Regna* or Old Scandinavian *rein* 'boundary' + Old English *ford*.

Rainier (263) French: from a personal name composed of the Germanic elements *ragin* 'advice' + *hari, heri* 'army'.
GIVEN NAME French 4%. *Patrice* (2).

Rainone (394) Altered spelling of French **Rainon**, from the oblique case of the personal name *Ragino*, from the Germanic element *ragin* 'counsel'.
GIVEN NAMES Italian 20%. *Carlo* (3), *Pasquale* (3), *Rocco* (3), *Salvatore* (3), *Angelo* (2), *Nicola* (2), *Antonietta, Carmelo, Carmine, Constantino, Cosimo, Domenic.*

Rains (4384) English: variant spelling of RAINES 1 and 2.

Rainsford (111) English: habitational name, perhaps a variant of RAINFORD.

Rainville (889) French: habitational name from a place so named in Vosges.
FOREBEARS A Rainville from Normandy, France, was first documented in Beauport, Quebec, in 1667.
GIVEN NAMES French 12%. *Gilles* (6), *Lucien* (6), *Armand* (3), *Andre* (2), *Fernand* (2), *Jacques* (2), *Alphonse, Antoine, Cecile, Gisele, Jean Guy, Laurent.*

Rainwater (2537) Americanized form of the German family name **Reinwasser**, possibly a topographic name for someone who lived by a source of fresh water, from Middle High German *reine* 'pure' + *wazzer* 'water'.

Raiola (101) Italian: of uncertain origin; possibly a topographic name from a diminutive of *raia* 'smilax' (the tree) or an occupational name or nickname from a diminutive of Sicilian *raja* (the fish).
GIVEN NAMES Italian 17%. *Domenic, Enrico, Filomena, Pasquale, Salvatore.*

Rairdon (100) Irish: variant of RIORDAN.

Rairigh (141) Americanized form of German **Röhrig** (see ROEHRIG).

Rais (130) **1.** Muslim: from a personal name based on Arabic *ra'īs* 'leader', also found in combinations such as *Ra'īs ud-Dīn* 'leader of religion'. **2.** German and Swiss German: from the personal name *Ragiso*, a pet form of any of the Germanic compound names beginning with the element *rag-*, a short form of *ragin* 'advice'. **3.** German and Czech: Slavic spelling of German REIS. **4.** German and Czech: from an altered short form of the Biblical personal name ZACHARIAS.
GIVEN NAMES Muslim 19%; German 5%; Czech and Slovak 5%. *Mohammed* (2), *Abdollah, Abdur, Ahmad, Amira, Fatima, Halim, Hamid, Jalal, Malik, Mohammad, Naushad; Otto, Theodor; Vaclav.*

Raisanen (188) Finnish (**Räisänen**): from an unexplained personal name (possibly of Russian Orthodox origin) + the common surname suffix *-nen*. It occurs chiefly in central and eastern Finland.
GIVEN NAMES Finnish 5%. *Arvo, Niilo, Reino, Toivo.*

Raisbeck (184) Northern English: habitational name from any of three small places so named in West Yorkshire.

Raisch (205) **1.** German and Swiss German: from Middle High German *rīsch, rūsch* 'reed', 'rush', hence a topographic name for someone who lived near a reed bed, or perhaps a metonymic occupational name for someone who used or harvested reeds. **2.** South German: variant of **Rösch** (see ROESCH).

Raiser (120) German: from Middle High German *reisære* 'warrior', 'traveler'.
GIVEN NAME German 12%. *Manfred* (4).

Raish (112) Americanized spelling of German RAISCH.

Raisner (101) Variant of German or Jewish REISNER.

Raison (115) English, Scottish, and French: nickname for an intelligent person, from Middle English, Old French *raison* 'reasoning', 'intellectual faculty' (Latin *ratio*, genitive *rationis*).

Raisor (353) Perhaps an altered spelling of English RASOR, or of German REISER or **Röser** (see ROSSER).

Raiter (100) German: occupational name for a taxman or accountant, from an agent derivative of Middle High German *reiten* 'to reckon', 'to calculate'.
GIVEN NAME German 4%. *Fritz.*

Raith (219) **1.** Scottish: habitational name from Raith near Monkton in Ayrshire.

2. German and Swiss German: topographic name from a common field name, probably related to Middle High German *reute* 'forest clearing' (see REUTER). **3.** German: nickname for someone with curly hair, from Middle High German *reit* 'frizzy', 'curly'.

GIVEN NAMES German 8%. *Erwin, Heinz, Helmuth, Johann, Nikolaus, Wolfgang.*

Raithel (178) South German: **1.** diminutive of RAITH 3. **2.** topographic name for someone living within the extent of a farm, *die Hofreite.* **3.** nickname for a rough individual, from Middle High German *reitel* 'pole', 'cudgel'.

GIVEN NAMES German 5%. *Erna, Otto, Wilhelm.*

Raitt (224) Scottish: **1.** habitational name from a place called Rait, of which there is one example in Perthshire. **2.** variant of RAITH.

Raitz (130) German: variant of REITZ.

Raj (316) Indian (northern and southern states): Hindu name from Sanskrit *rājā* 'king'. In the northern states, it probably evolved into a family name from use as the final element of a compound personal name such as *Prithviraj* 'king of the earth'. In South India it is used only as a male given name, but it has come to be used as a family name in the U.S. among people from South India. Among Tamil and Malayalam speakers who have migrated from their home states, it is a variant of RAJAN.

GIVEN NAMES Indian 73%. *Ashok* (4), *Dev* (4), *Hem* (4), *Mohan* (4), *Prithvi* (4), *Suresh* (4), *Anil* (3), *Dharam* (3), *Rishi* (3), *Alok* (2), *Atul* (2), *Bali* (2).

Raja (302) Indian: variant of RAJ in the southern states. Among Tamil and Malayalam speakers who have migrated from their home state, it is a variant of RAJAN.

GIVEN NAMES Muslim 55%; Indian 34%. *Mohammad* (9), *Abdul* (3), *Khalid* (3), *Mansoor* (3), *Mohammed* (3), *Azhar* (2), *Hafeez* (2), *Hayder* (2), *Munawar* (2), *Sajjad* (2), *Shahid* (2), *Abid; Geetha* (3), *Sekhar* (3), *Jitesh* (2), *Jogesh* (2), *Raj* (2), *Ravi* (2), *Sri* (2), *Vijay* (2), *Asim, Bose, Chander, Ganesan.*

Rajagopal (104) Indian (southern states): Hindu name from Sanskrit *rājagopāla* 'king of cowherds', from *rāja* 'king' + *gopāla* 'cowherd', an epithet of the god Krishna, who is said to have been brought up among cowherds. Among Tamil and Malayalam speakers who have migrated from their home states, it is a variant of RAJAGOPALAN. This is only a given name in India, but has come to be used as a family name in the U.S.

GIVEN NAMES Indian 95%. *Ramesh* (3), *Arun* (2), *Asha* (2), *Ganesh* (2), *Srinivasan* (2), *Sumanth* (2), *Usha* (2), *Vinayak* (2), *Ajay, Amu, Archana, Arjun.*

Rajagopalan (139) Indian (Kerala, Tamil Nadu): Hindu name from Sanskrit *rājago-*

pāla 'king of cowherds' (see RAJAGOPAL) + the Tamil-Malayalam third-person masculine singular suffix *-n.* This is only a given name in India, but has come to be used as a family name in the U.S.

GIVEN NAMES Indian 97%. *Narayanan* (3), *Ramesh* (3), *Ravi* (3), *Aruna* (2), *Bharath* (2), *Lalitha* (2), *Nandini* (2), *Raj* (2), *Ram* (2), *Sanjay* (2), *Sridharan* (2), *Srikanth* (2).

Rajala (265) Finnish: topographic name for someone living near a border, from *raja* 'boundary', 'border' + the local suffix *-la,* or an ornamental name from the same elements. The surname was first recorded in the 17th century, and was adopted during the name conversion movement of the 19th and early 20th centuries. It is common in central and western Finland.

GIVEN NAMES Finnish 9%; Scandinavian 4%. *Eino* (3), *Osmo, Paivi, Pekka, Reino, Teuvo, Waino.*

Rajan (297) Indian (Kerala, Tamil Nadu): Hindu name from Sanskrit *rājā* 'king' + the Tamil-Malayalam third-person masculine singular suffix *-n.* This is only a given name in India, but has come to be used as a family name in the U.S.

GIVEN NAMES Indian 83%. *Suresh* (6), *Raj* (5), *Sundar* (4), *Krishna* (3), *Ram* (3), *Ravi* (3), *Sanjay* (3), *Vijay* (3), *Arvind* (2), *Babu* (2), *Balaji* (2), *Gayatri* (2).

Rajchel (133) Polish spelling of the German personal name REICHEL.

GIVEN NAMES Polish 7%. *Jozef* (2), *Janusz, Ryszard.*

Rajewski (183) Polish: habitational name for someone from a place named with Polish dialect *raja* 'marsh', 'mud' or with Polish *raj* 'paradise'.

GIVEN NAME French 4%. *Albertine.*

Rajkowski (133) Polish: habitational name for someone from Rajki in Białystok voivodeship or Rajkowy in Gdańsk voivodeship.

GIVEN NAMES Polish 7%. *Janusz* (2), *Piotr.*

Rajotte (143) Variant of French **Rageot**, a Norman nickname meaning 'furious.'

GIVEN NAMES French 24%. *Lucien* (5), *Armand, Collette, Donat, Emile, Jacques, Marcel, Maxime, Ovide, Raoul.*

Rajski (118) Polish: habitational name for someone from any of the many places called Rajsko, named with the Polish dialect term *raja* 'marsh', 'muddy place' or with Polish *raj* 'paradise'.

GIVEN NAMES Polish 7%. *Andrzej, Tadeusz, Wlodzimierz.*

Raju (249) Indian (southern states): variant of RAJ.

GIVEN NAMES Indian 79%. *Seshadri* (3), *Padma* (2), *Ram* (2), *Ramesh* (2), *Sarwan* (2), *Srinivas* (2), *Surya* (2), *Anand, Balaji, Balakrishna, Bindu, Champak.*

Rak (474) Polish, Czech, Slovak, Slovenian, Hungarian (**Rák**), and Jewish (eastern Ashkenazic): from Slavic *rak* 'crab', 'lobster', or 'crayfish'. This was applied as an occu-

pational name for someone who caught and sold crayfish, crabs, or lobsters, or as a nickname to someone thought to resemble such a creature. In Polish, the word is found in several idioms, for example, *czerwony jak rak* 'red as a lobster'. In Slovenian, it only means 'crayfish'.

GIVEN NAMES Polish 9%. *Stanislaw* (3), *Danuta* (2), *Dariusz* (2), *Andrzey, Boleslaw, Janusz, Jerzy, Piotr, Slawek, Witold, Wlodzimierz, Zbigniew.*

Rake (558) **1.** English: topographic name for someone who lived by a pass or narrow valley, from Old English *hraca* 'throat', or a habitational name from any of the minor places deriving their name from this word, such as Rake in Devon or The Rake in Sussex. **2.** English and Dutch: from Middle English, Middle Dutch *rake* 'rake', applied as a metonymic occupational name for a maker of such implements or as a nickname for a tall thin man. (The expression 'lean as a rake' is found in Chaucer.)

Raker (650) **1.** German: from a Germanic personal name, *Raghar*, composed of *rag-* 'advice' + *hari, heri* 'army'. **2.** Germanized spelling of Slovenian **Rakar**, occupational name for someone who caught and sold crayfish (see RAK).

Rakers (216) Dutch: **1.** occupational name for a hangman or torturer, from a derivative of Middle Dutch *racke* 'rack'. **2.** from an agent derivative of Middle Dutch *raken* 'to rake', presumably an metonymic occupational name for a farmer.

Rakes (1091) English: variant of RAKE.

Rakestraw (1000) **1.** English: nickname for a scavenger, from Old English *racian* 'to rake' + *strēaw* 'straw'. **2.** Americanized spelling of German ROCKSTROH.

Rakich (114) Serbian and Croatian (**Rakić**): patronymic from the personal name *Rako,* a pet form of *Radoslav, Radomil,* etc., names formed with the Old Slavic element *rad* 'merry', 'joyful'.

GIVEN NAMES South Slavic 15%. *Milan* (5), *Dmitar, Drago, Radmila.*

Rakoczy (238) Hungarian (**Rákóczy**): habitational name for someone from any of four places called Rákóc in what was formerly part of Hungary, now in Slovakia and Ukraine. This surname is also well established in Poland and Austria.

GIVEN NAMES Polish 9%. *Tadeusz* (2), *Andrzej, Henryk, Ignatius, Ireneusz, Wieslaw.*

Rakow (361) Eastern German: habitational name from places so named near Grimmen in Pomerania and Doberan in Mecklenburg, or from some other similarly named place.

Rakowitz (112) Germanized form of Jewish (from Belarus) **Rakovich** and (from Poland) **Rakowicz**, habitational names from (respectively) the villages of Rakovichi in Belarus and Rakowo in Poland.

GIVEN NAMES German 8%. *Ewald, Otto.*

Rakowski (753) Polish, Ukrainian, Belorussian, and Jewish (from Poland): habitational name for someone from any of several places named Rakowo and Raków, including one south of Warsaw and another in Belarus, which was a frontier town between Poland and the Soviet Union from 1921 to 1939.
GIVEN NAMES Polish 6%. *Casimir* (4), *Lech* (2), *Andrzej*, *Henryk*, *Jozef*, *Karol*, *Stanislaw*, *Witold*, *Wlodzimierz*, *Zigmund*.

Rakowsky (107) Respelling of RAKOWSKI.
GIVEN NAME Ukrainian 10%. *Ihor* (4).

Raleigh (1381) English: habitational name from Raleigh in Devon, recorded in Domesday Book as *Radeleia*, from Old English *rēad* 'red' + *lēah* 'wood', 'clearing'.
FOREBEARS The English explorer Sir Walter Raleigh (1554–1618) was born in Hayes Barton, Devon, into a family of Devon gentry. He was related to most of the West Country's important families, including that of Sir Francis Drake. His half-brother was the explorer Sir Humphrey Gilbert. In 1578 Raleigh was granted a patent to explore and colonize "unknown lands" in America.

Raley (2487) English: variant of RALEIGH.

Rall (720) German: nickname for a raucous or noisy individual, from Swabian *rallen* 'to make noise', 'screech like a tomcat'.
GIVEN NAMES German 5%. *Kurt* (3), *Erwin* (2), *Bernhardt*, *Dieter*, *Fritz*, *Otto*, *Rainer*, *Reinhold*.

Rallis (235) Greek: patronymic from a derivative of the Germanic personal name *Raoul*, Greek and French form of RUDOLF. See also RALPH. *Raoul* is well attested as a personal name in the Byzantine Empire in the medieval period.
GIVEN NAMES Greek 11%. *Christos* (3), *Fotini*, *Fotios*, *Isidoros*, *Panos*, *Savvas*, *Sotirios*, *Stelios*.

Rallo (293) Italian: of uncertain derivation; possibly, as Caracausi suggests, from *rallo* 'pullet', 'woodcock', 'moorhen', or, less likely from Rallo, a district of Tassullo in Trento province.
GIVEN NAMES Italian 17%. *Angelo* (3), *Antonio* (3), *Vito* (3), *Biagio* (2), *Giancarlo*, *Ignazio*, *Sal*, *Salvatore*, *Vincenza*.

Ralls (943) English: patronymic from RALPH.

Ralph (3042) English: from a Middle English personal name composed of Germanic *rad* 'counsel', 'advice' + *wolf* 'wolf'. This was first introduced into England by Scandinavian settlers in the Old Norse form *Ráðulfr*, and was reinforced after the Conquest by the Norman form *Ra(d)ulf*. Compare German RUDOLF.

Ralphs (223) English: patronymic from RALPH.
GIVEN NAME French 6%. *Gabrielle*.

Ralstin (170) Variant spelling of Scottish RALSTON.

Ralston (4850) Scottish: habitational name from the lands or barony of Ralston near Paisley, in Renfrewshire.

Ram (592) **1.** Indian (northern and southern states): Hindu name from Sanskrit *rāma* 'pleasing', 'charming', name of an incarnation of Vishnu. In the northern states, it probably evolved into a family name from use as the final element of a compound personal names such as *Atmaram* (with Sanskrit *ātmā* 'soul') or *Sitaram* (with *Sita*, the name of Rama's wife). In South India it is used only as a male given name, but has come to be used as a family name in the U.S. among people from South India. Among Tamil and Malayalam speakers who have migrated from their home states, it is a variant of RAMAN. **2.** Dutch and English: from Middle Low German *ram*, Middle English *ram* 'ram', either in the sense 'male sheep' or in the sense 'battering ram' or 'pile driver'. **3.** Swedish: ornamental name from a place name element, either from Old Norse *hrafn* 'raven' (Swedish *ramm*) or from dialect *ramm* 'water meadow'. **4.** Jewish (Israeli): ornamental name from Hebrew *ram* 'lofty'. **5.** Jewish (eastern Ashkenazic): acronymic name of uncertain etymology. **6.** Southern French: topographic name meaning 'branch' and denoting someone who lived in a leafy wooded area.
GIVEN NAMES Indian 61%; Jewish 4%. *Raghu* (7), *Hari* (4), *Kewal* (4), *Mast* (4), *Mohan* (4), *Sadhu* (4), *Geetha* (3), *Paras* (3), *Satish* (3), *Vijay* (3), *Alka* (2), *Anil* (2); *Yossi* (2), *Amnon*, *Asher*, *Avi*, *Erez*, *Haim*, *Itzhak*, *Moshe*, *Shira*, *Yaron*, *Yosef*.

Rama (209) **1.** Indian (southern states): variant of RAM. **2.** Portuguese, Galician, and Catalan: habitational name from any of the places called Rama in Portugal (Guimarães), Galicia (A Coruña) and Catalonia (Girona). **3.** Spanish, Galician, and Portuguese: topographic name from *rama* 'branch'. **4.** Italian: topographic name from dialect *rama* 'branch' (see RAMO).
GIVEN NAMES Indian 17%; Spanish 13%. *Dharmendra* (2), *Arun*, *Bhola*, *Dinesh*, *Ganapathy*, *Krishna*, *Manhar*, *Natesan*, *Natvarlal*, *Sanjay*, *Satesh*; *Jose* (4), *Rodrigo* (2), *Adelino*, *Adriana*, *Amando*, *Angel*, *Isadora*, *Jorge*, *Luis*, *Manuel*, *Modesta*, *Nereida*.

Ramachandran (272) Indian (Kerala, Tamil Nadu): Hindu name from Sanskrit *rāma* 'pleasing', 'charming' (name of an incarnation of Vishnu; see RAM) + *čandra* 'shining', 'moon' (see CHANDRA), + the Tamil-Malayalam third-person masculine singular suffix *-n*. This is only a given name in India, but has come to be used as a family name in the U.S.
GIVEN NAMES Indian 96%. *Ravi* (5), *Anand* (4), *Bala* (4), *Subramanian* (4), *Narayanan* (3), *Ram* (3), *Sridhar* (3), *Vijay* (3), *Ajit* (2), *Anush* (2), *Dileep* (2), *Geetha* (2).

Ramadan (234) Muslim: from Arabic *Ramaḍān*, the ninth month of the Islamic calendar, a sacred month of fasting for Muslims. It is sometimes chosen by Muslim parents as a name for children born in this month. In this month the Qur'an, the Holy Book of Islam, was revealed to the Prophet Muhammad by the Angel Jibril (Gabriel). This name is widespread throughout the Muslim world.
GIVEN NAMES Muslim 81%. *Ahmed* (10), *Mohamad* (6), *Mohamed* (6), *Walid* (6), *Wafic* (5), *Ali* (4), *Hassan* (4), *Hussein* (3), *Osama* (3), *Sami* (3), *Akram* (2), *Ashraf* (2).

Ramaekers (120) Dutch: reduced form of RADEMAKER.

Ramage (1392) **1.** Scottish: nickname for a savage or unpredictable individual, from Middle English, Old French *rammage* 'wild' (applied to a bird of prey), Late Latin *ramaticus*, from *ramus* 'branch'. Compare SAVAGE. **2.** French: from a derivative of Old French *ramu* 'branch', with the sense 'forest', hence a topographic name for someone who lived by a forest. The term *ramage* also had a legal sense, denoting the right to cut branches within a manorial forest, and in some cases the surname may have arisen from a nickname for someone who had this feudal right.

Ramaglia (95) Italian: unexplained; probably a topographic name for someone who lived in a leafy or overgrown place, from *ramo* 'branch' + the collective suffix *-aglia*, denoting an abundance.
GIVEN NAMES Italian 9%. *Antonio*, *Concetta*, *Vito*.

Ramaker (195) Dutch: variant of RADEMAKER. This is a frequent name in New Netherland.

Ramakrishnan (174) Indian (Kerala, Tamil Nadu): Hindu name from Sanskrit *rāma* 'pleasing', 'charming' (name of an incarnation of the god Vishnu; see RAM) + *kṛṣṇa* 'black', 'Krishna' (see KRISHNA), + the Tamil-Malayalam third-person masculine singular suffix *-n*. This is only a given name in India, but has come to be used as a family name in the U.S.
GIVEN NAMES Indian 98%. *Anand* (4), *Ram* (4), *Anuradha* (2), *Kalpana* (2), *Prasad* (2), *Ramesh* (2), *Ravi* (2), *Sridhar* (2), *Srikanth* (2), *Sundar* (2), *Suresh* (2), *Usha* (2).

Ramaley (139) Of uncertain origin, a PA name. It may be a respelling of Swiss Italian **Ramelli** (see RAMELLA), Portuguese RAMALHO, or **Ramely** (an unexplained English name).

Ramalho (122) Portuguese: habitational name from any of the numerous places named Ramalho, from *ramalho* 'branch', 'brushwood'.
GIVEN NAMES Spanish 24%. *Manuel* (4), *Carlos* (2), *Fernando* (2), *Venancio* (2), *Herminia*, *Jose*, *Luis*, *Mario*, *Renaldo*, *Rogerio*.

Raman (370) Indian (Kerala, Tamil Nadu): Hindu name from Sanskrit *rāma* 'pleasing', 'charming' (see RAM) + the Tamil-Malayalam third-person masculine singular suffix *-n*. This is only a given name in India, but has come to be used as a family name in the U.S.

GIVEN NAMES Indian 78%. *Shankar* (6), *Krishna* (5), *Anand* (4), *Ravi* (4), *Usha* (4), *Natarajan* (3), *Sankar* (3), *Sudha* (3), *Vijay* (3), *Anil* (2), *Balu* (2), *Ganapathy* (2).

Ramanathan (166) Indian (Kerala, Tamil Nadu): Hindu name from Sanskrit *rāmanātha* 'lord Rama' (from *rāma* 'pleasing', 'charming' (name of an incarnation of the god Vishnu; see RAM) + *nātha* 'lord'), + the Tamil-Malayalam third-person masculine singular suffix *-n*. This is only a personal name in India, but has come to be used as a family name in the U.S.

GIVEN NAMES Indian 97%. *Ramesh* (5), *Mohan* (4), *Gopal* (3), *Ganesan* (2), *Janaki* (2), *Krishna* (2), *Kumar* (2), *Murali* (2), *Ram* (2), *Sriram* (2), *Swaminathan* (2), *Anuradha*.

Ramaswamy (179) Indian (Tamil Nadu, Karnataka): Hindu name meaning 'lord Rama' (from Sanskrit *rāma* 'pleasing', name of an incarnation of the god Vishnu, + *svāmī* 'lord'). This is only a personal name in India, but has come to be used as a family name in the U.S.

GIVEN NAMES Indian 91%. *Sridhar* (5), *Srinivasan* (5), *Suresh* (4), *Srinivas* (3), *Sunder* (3), *Arun* (2), *Ashok* (2), *Krishna* (2), *Kumar* (2), *Mahadevan* (2), *Raj* (2), *Ramesh* (2).

Rambeau (171) Altered spelling of the southern French family name **Rambaut**, from an Old French personal name, *Rainbaut*, composed of the Germanic elements *ragin* 'counsel' + *bald* 'bold', 'brave', or alternatively from the Germanic personal name *Hrambehrt* or *Hrambald*, composed of the elements *hramn* 'crow' + *berht* 'bright' or *bald* 'bold', 'brave'.

Ramberg (462) **1.** German: habitational name from a place so named in the Palatinate, near Landau. **2.** Norwegian: habitational name from any of some fifteen farmsteads named with *ramn* 'raven' (Old Norse *hrafn*) + *berg* 'mountain'.

GIVEN NAMES Scandinavian 5%. *Erik* (2), *Anders*, *Knute*, *Nels*, *Paal*, *Sven*.

Rambert (129) Southern French: variant of **Rambaud** (see RAMBEAU).

Rambin (252) French: unexplained.

Rambo (2412) **1.** French: variant of RAMBEAU. **2.** German: variant of RAMBOW.

Rambow (184) German (eastern): habitational name from either of two places near Perleberg, or others in northeastern Germany, called Rambow.

GIVEN NAMES German 4%. *Erwin*, *Ewald*.

Ramel (142) French: from Old French *ramel*, diminutive of *ra(i)m* 'branch' (Latin *ramus*), hence a topographic name for someone who lived in a thickly wooded area. It is possible that it was also used as a nickname for someone who had some particular connection with Palm Sunday, for which the French term is *(dimanche des) rameaux*.

Ramella (186) Italian: **1.** metathesized form of the female personal name *Armella*, from Latin *animula*, diminutive of *anima* 'soul'. **2.** possibly a habitational name from any of the many places in Piedmont (where the surname is most frequent) named Ramello, possibly from *ramo* 'branch'.

GIVEN NAMES Italian 7%. *Aldo*, *Amilcare*, *Concetta*, *Geno*, *Tullio*.

Ramer (1375) **1.** German: occupational name, perhaps for a dairy farmer, from Middle High German *rom* 'cream', or for a frame or loom-maker, from Middle High German *ram(e)* 'frame', 'loom'. **2.** Possibly and altered spelling of German *Römer* (see ROEMER).

Rameriz (180) Probably a respelling of RAMIREZ.

GIVEN NAMES Spanish 50%. *Jose* (5), *Juan* (4), *Luis* (4), *Alejandro* (2), *Felipe* (2), *Fermin* (2), *Lupe* (2), *Manuel* (2), *Margarita* (2), *Margarito* (2), *Miguel* (2), *Pedro* (2).

Rames (139) Origin unidentifed.

GIVEN NAMES French 5%. *Gervais*, *Patrice*.

Ramesh (159) Indian (southern states): Hindu name, from Sanskrit *rameša* 'lord (or husband) of Rama', an epithet of the god Vishnu. Rama is Vishnu's wife. This is only a given name in India, but has come to be used as a family name in the U.S.

GIVEN NAMES Indian 73%. *Radhika* (3), *Deepa* (2), *Mahadevan* (2), *Natarajan* (2), *Ram* (2), *Ramamoorthy* (2), *Rekha* (2), *Anand*, *Aravind*, *Asha*, *Ashok*.

Rametta (116) Italian: diminutive of RAMA.

GIVEN NAMES Italian 19%. *Angelo* (2), *Antonio*, *Francesco*, *Giuseppe*, *Nicola*, *Pasquale*, *Sebastino*.

Ramey (7226) French: eastern variant of RAM.

Ramig (109) German: variant spelling of **Rahnig**, a nickname from Middle High German *rāmic* 'dirty'.

GIVEN NAME German 6%. *Kurt* (2).

Ramin (164) Muslim: variant of RAHMAN.

GIVEN NAMES Muslim 11%. *Bahram* (2), *Aziza*, *Hafizullah*, *Mehrdad*, *Peyman*, *Pirooz*, *Rahim*, *Shokrollah*, *Taghi*.

Ramires (140) Portuguese: **1.** patronymic from the old personal name *Ramiro*, of Visigothic origin. **2.** in some cases, possibly a respelling of the Spanish cognate RAMIREZ.

GIVEN NAMES Spanish 55%. *Jose* (7), *Andres* (3), *Carlos* (3), *Juan* (2), *Luis Eduardo* (2), *Artemio*, *Beatris*, *Diego*, *Doroteo*, *Ebaristo*, *Elena*, *Ernestina*; *Antonio* (3), *Clemente*, *Federico*, *Flavio*, *Luciano*, *Marco*, *Umberto*.

Ramirez (41904) Spanish (**Ramírez**): patronymic from the personal name *Ramiro*, composed of the Germanic elements *ragin* 'counsel' + *mari*, *meri* 'fame'.

GIVEN NAMES Spanish 51%. *Juan* (662), *Manuel* (434), *Carlos* (408), *Jesus* (376), *Luis* (316), *Francisco* (289), *Miguel* (237), *Jorge* (233), *Raul* (221), *Roberto* (218), *Pedro* (214), *Ramon* (203).

Ramkissoon (125) Name found among people of Indian origin in Guyana and Trinidad: variant of Indian RAMAKRISHNAN.

GIVEN NAMES Indian 45%. *Gobin* (2), *Indra* (2), *Krishna* (2), *Anil*, *Ashok*, *Deokie*, *Dindial*, *Heeralall*, *Mahadeo*, *Parbhu*, *Radha*, *Ramesh*.

Ramler (166) German: nickname for a lusty man, from Middle High German *rammler* 'ram (in the breeding season)'.

Ramlow (179) Probably German, a habitational name from places called Ramelow in Mecklenburg and Pomerania.

GIVEN NAME German 4%. *Otto* (2).

Ramm (648) **1.** German and English: from Middle High German *ram*, Middle English *ram(m)* 'ram', 'male sheep', hence a nickname for a forceful or lusty individual (in the case of the English name, perhaps in part representing a continued use of an Old English byname). It may also occasionally have been a metonymic occupational name for a shepherd, or a habitational name for someone who lived at a house distinguished by the sign of a ram. The German term also denotes a pile-driver or battering ram, and the surname may have arisen as an occupational name for someone who operated either of these. **2.** German: habitational name from either of two places named Ramm, in Westphalia and Mecklenburg. **3.** Jewish: variant spelling of RAM.

GIVEN NAMES German 5%. *Hans* (2), *Eberhard*, *Hartmut*, *Kurt*, *Manfred*, *Otto*, *Reinold*, *Wilhelm*.

Rammel (190) **1.** German: from a pet form of a Germanic personal name based on Old High German *hraban* 'raven'. **2.** Altered spelling of the English family name **Rammell**, a variant of RAINBOW **3.** Variant of French **Ramel**, a derivative of RAM.

GIVEN NAMES German 4%. *Othmar*, *Otto*.

Rammer (181) German: habitational name for someone from Rammenau near Bautzen.

GIVEN NAMES French 4%. *Gisele* (2), *Patrice*.

Ramming (159) German: **1.** from a Slavic personal name, *Ramjenk*, meaning 'with strong shoulders' **2.** habitational name from Rammingen near Ulm or from any of several places called Raming.

Ramnarine (173) Name found among people of Indian origin in Guyana and Trinidad: from a variant of the Indian personal name *Ramnarayan*, from Sanskrit *rāma* 'pleasing', name of an incarnation of the god Vishnu + *nārāyana* (see NARAYAN).

GIVEN NAMES Indian 49%. *Kumar* (2), *Kumarie* (2), *Vishnu* (2), *Asha, Avinash, Basdeo, Chandroutie, Dharam, Ganga, Gangadai, Indar, Khemraj.*

Ramo (137) **1.** Finnish: unexplained. **2.** Galician and Portuguese: habitational name from O Ramo or Monte de Ramo, places in Galicia, or from Ramo in Portugal. **3.** Spanish: perhaps a topographic name from *ramo* 'branch' (compare RAMOS).

GIVEN NAMES Spanish 7%. *Carlos, Erasmo, Eulogio, Gerardo, Gonzalo, Santos.*

Ramon (1251) Spanish (**Ramón**), Portuguese, and Catalan: from the personal name *Ramón* or *Ramon*, of Germanic origin (see RAYMOND).

GIVEN NAMES Spanish 45%. *Jose* (21), *Juan* (19), *Jesus* (15), *Ruben* (13), *Carlos* (10), *Mario* (10), *Ricardo* (10), *Manuel* (8), *Pedro* (7), *Roberto* (7), *Francisco* (6), *Jaime* (6).

Ramos (23488) **1.** Portuguese and Spanish: habitational name from any of the towns called Ramos, in Portugal and Spain. **2.** Portuguese and Spanish: from the plural of *ramo* 'branch' (Latin *ramus*), a topographic name for someone who lived in a thickly wooded area.

GIVEN NAMES Spanish 47%; Portuguese 10%. *Jose* (625), *Juan* (306), *Manuel* (233), *Luis* (225), *Carlos* (184), *Jesus* (157), *Pedro* (129), *Francisco* (127), *Miguel* (125), *Ramon* (122), *Raul* (117), *Jorge* (115); *Joaquim* (7), *Paulo* (7), *Joao* (6), *Albano* (3), *Armanda* (2), *Catarina* (2), *Adao, Agostinho, Duarte, Heitor, Ilidio, Marcio.*

Ramp (297) German and Swiss German: variant of **Rampf**, from Middle High German *ramft, ranft* 'edge', 'wall', 'crust (of bread)'; applied as a topographic name for someone who lived at the limit or outer edge of some feature, for example a field, or possibly, in the sense 'crust', a nickname for a poor person.

Rampe (111) German and Danish: from a short form of a Germanic personal name composed with *rag-* 'counsel', 'advice', as in REIMOLD.

GIVEN NAME German 4%. *Kurt.*

Rampersad (224) Name found among people of Indian origin in Guyana and Trinidad: variant of RAMPERSAUD.

GIVEN NAMES Indian 38%. *Krishna* (2), *Radha* (2), *Anamika, Anil, Baskaran, Bharat, Bhola, Bisram, Deonarine, Gangaram, Hemraj, Indar.*

Rampersaud (156) Name found among people of Indian origin in Guyana and Trinidad: from the Indian personal name *Ramprasad*, from Sanskrit *rāma* 'pleasing', name of an incarnation of the god Vishnu, + *prasāda* 'favor', 'grace', 'gift', 'offering of food'.

GIVEN NAMES Indian 52%. *Indra* (3), *Deonarine* (2), *Hemwattie* (2), *Rookmin* (2),

Shakti (2), *Deokie, Devanand, Dianand, Heeralall, Khemraj, Krishna, Kumarie.*

Rampey (205) **1.** Probably an altered spelling of German **Rampe**: **2.** habitational name from a place so named near Schwerin. **3.** in the north, a metonymic occupational name for someone who looked after a warehouse or granary for example, from Middle Low German *rampe* 'storage', 'warehouse'.

Rampino (108) Italian: **1.** diminutive of **Rampa**, a nickname from Sicilian *rampa* 'claw', 'nail'. **2.** possibly from Salerno dialect *rampinu* 'grappling hook' (for retrieving a bucket from a well).

GIVEN NAMES Italian 22%. *Angelo* (2), *Rocco* (2), *Luigi.*

Rampley (220) English (mainly East Anglia): habitational name from an unidentified place, possibly in Suffolk.

Rampone (118) Italian: **1.** from an old Germanic personal name *Rampo*. **2.** habitational name from Rampone in Frinco, Asti province.

GIVEN NAMES Italian 6%. *Cosmo, Pasquale.*

Rampton (114) English: habitational name from either of two places named Rampton, in Cambridgeshire and Nottinghamshire; the first, and probably also the second, is named Old English *ramm* 'ram' + *tūn* 'settlement'. However, the modern surname is concentrated in Hampshire, suggesting perhaps that another, unidentified source could be involved.

Rampulla (115) Italian: possibly from a female personal name derived from *rampollo*, from *rampollare* 'to germinate', 'to spring up'.

GIVEN NAMES Italian 20%. *Vito* (3), *Salvatore* (2), *Angelo, Rocco, Sal.*

Rampy (250) See RAMPEY.

Ramroop (102) Name found among people of Indian origin in Guyana and Trinidad: from the Hindu personal name *Ramrup* 'manifestation of Rama', from Sanskrit *rāma* 'pleasing', name of an incarnation of the god Vishnu, + *rūpa* 'form', 'manifestation'.

GIVEN NAMES Indian 42%. *Gangaram* (2), *Ramnarine* (2), *Geetanjali, Hemchand, Ishwar, Kishore, Latchman, Leela, Motilal, Nish, Prem, Ramdeo.*

Ramsay (3229) Scottish: variant (the usual spelling in Scotland) of RAMSEY.

Ramsbottom (108) English: habitational name from a place so called in Lancashire (now part of Greater Manchester), named in Old English with *ramm* 'ram' (or possibly *hramsa* 'wild garlic') + *bothm* 'valley bottom'.

Ramsburg (251) German: probably a habitational name from a place so named near Gunzenhausen, Franconia. Alternatively it may be a variant of Swiss German **Ramsperger** or German **Ramsberger**, habitational names for someone from any of

several places in southern Germany called Ramsberg.

Ramsdell (1418) English: habitational name, possibly from Ramsdell in Hampshire, but more likely from Ramsdale, a place in North Yorkshire, named from Old English *hramsa* 'wild garlic' (or possibly the genitive case of the byname *Ram(m)* 'ram') + *dæl* 'valley', or from Ramsdale Farm in Arnold, Nottinghamshire. Compare RANSDELL.

Ramsden (693) Northern English: habitational name from any of various places so called from Old English *hramsa* 'wild garlic' (or possibly the genitive case of the Old English byname *Ram(m)* 'ram') + *denu* 'valley'. There are villages so named in Essex, Kent, Oxfordshire, and Warwickshire, but the surname is most common in Yorkshire, where there are several minor places so named, Ramsden in the parish of Kirkburton being a well-recorded instance.

Ramseier (121) Swiss German: variant spelling of RAMSEYER (see RAMSEUR).

GIVEN NAMES German 6%. *Dieter, Egon, Fritz.*

Ramsell (114) **1.** English: probably a habitational name from a lost or unidentified place. **2.** Probably an altered spelling of German **Rams(e)l**, Dutch **Ramsel**, a habitational name from Ramsel in Antwerp province, Belgium; a group of people migrated from there to Swabia in 1570. **3.** In some instances the German name may have derived from a nickname for a roguish person.

Ramser (198) German and Swiss German: habitational name for someone from any of several places in the Palatinate and in Switzerland called Ramsen, or from places in Austria and upper Bavaria called Ramsau. In the Bavarian dialect of German *Rams* means 'scree'.

Ramseur (440) Altered spelling of German **Ramsauer** (or of the variants RAMSEYER, **Ramseier**), a habitational name for someone from a place called Ramsau (see RAMSER).

Ramsey (26943) Scottish: habitational name from a place in Huntingdonshire (now part of Cambridgeshire), so called from Old English *hramsa* 'wild garlic' + *ēg* 'island', 'low-lying land'. There are other places in England called *Ramsey*, but the one in Huntingdonshire is almost certainly the source of the surname. The usual spelling of the surname in Scotland is RAMSAY.

Ramseyer (364) Swiss German: variant of **Ramsauer** (see RAMSEUR).

GIVEN NAMES German 4%. *Kurt* (2), *Lorenz, Siegfried.*

Ramshaw (116) English (Northumberland and Durham): either a variant of RENSHAW or of **Ravenshaw**, a habitational name from Ravenshaw in Warwickshire, or a topographic name for someone who lived by the 'raven wood'.

Ramsier (138) Altered spelling of Swiss German RAMSEUR.

Ramsland (105) Norwegian: habitational name from farmsteads in Agder and Rogaland named from *rams* 'ramson' (*Allium ursinum*) + *land* 'land', 'farmstead'.
GIVEN NAMES Scandinavian 20%. *Arnfinn, Erik, Thor.*

Ramson (100) **1.** English: presumably a patronymic from a Middle English survival of Old English *Ramm* 'ram' or *Hrafn* 'raven' as a personal name. **2.** Name found among people of Indian origin in Guyana and Trinidad: probably from the personal name RAM and the English suffix *-son*.
GIVEN NAMES Indian 4%. *Rabindranauth, Shanta.*

Ramsour (110) Altered spelling of German **Ramsauer** (see RAMSEUR).

Ramstad (262) **1.** Norwegian: habitational name from any of over twenty farmsteads named in Old Norse as *Hrafnsstaðir*, from the personal name *Hrafn*, meaning 'raven' + *staðir* 'farmstead', 'dwelling'. **2.** Swedish: ornamental name, probably of the same derivation as 1.
GIVEN NAME Scandinavian 6%. *Erik* (2).

Ramthun (239) German (Pomeranian): probably a habitational name from a place such as Ramten.
GIVEN NAMES German 5%. *Otto* (2), *Erwin, Kurt.*

Ramundo (133) **1.** Southern Italian: from a regional variant of the personal name RAIMONDO. **2.** Spanish: from a variant of the personal name RAYMUNDO, Spanish equivalent of RAYMOND.
GIVEN NAMES Italian 16%; Spanish 5%. *Marco* (2), *Vito* (2), *Alfredo, Gerardo, Gino, Romano, Sabato, Sal; Luis, Luis Alberto.*

Ramus (218) **1.** French: from Old French *ramu* 'branch', hence a nickname of similar application to RAMAGE 2, or a topographic name for someone who lived in a wooded place. **2.** Dutch: from a Germanic personal name composed of the elements *hraban* 'raven' + *wald* 'rule'.

Rana (654) **1.** Indian (Gujarat, Bombay city, and Rajasthan): Hindu and Parsi name meaning 'king' in modern Indian languages. *Rana* does not have a Sanskrit equivalent; it is probably a back-formation from *rāṇī* 'queen' (Sanskrit *rājñī*, based on the analogy that nouns ending in -*ī* and denoting females usually have masculine counterparts ending in -*ā*). The name Rana was used as a title by some Rajput kings. As a surname, it is now found among Rajputs as well as several other communities. It is cognate with the name **Rane**, which occurs in Maharashtra and Goa. **2.** Spanish and Italian: from *rana* 'frog', hence a nickname, perhaps for someone with bulging eyes. **3.** Galician (**Raña**): habitational name from a place so called in the province of A Coruña.

GIVEN NAMES Indian 50%; Muslim 27%. *Pravin* (6), *Bharat* (5), *Ashok* (4), *Ramesh* (4), *Jayanti* (3), *Rajendra* (3), *Vijay* (3), *Ajay* (2), *Ajit* (2), *Anil* (2), *Arvind* (2), *Atul* (2); *Mohammad* (7), *Muhammad* (6), *Khalid* (5), *Riaz* (4), *Tariq* (4), *Aslam* (3), *Naeem* (3), *Shahid* (3), *Aamer* (2), *Anwar* (2), *Jameela* (2), *Nasim* (2).

Ranalli (427) Italian: patronymic or plural form of RANALLO.
GIVEN NAMES Italian 12%. *Gino* (4), *Aldo, Deno, Eliseo, Fulvio, Lorenzo, Marcello, Marco, Massimo, Ottavio, Rocco.*

Ranallo (444) Italian (central and southern): from the personal name *Rinaldo*, Italian equivalent of REYNOLD.
GIVEN NAMES Italian 10%. *Rocco* (3), *Aldo* (2), *Angelo* (2), *Fiorino* (2), *Nunzio* (2), *Antonio, Carmine, Ennio, Filippo, Sabatino, Savino.*

Ranard (123) Variant spelling of an unexplained English name, **Rannard**, found chiefly in Lincolnshire and Lancashire.

Rance (348) English: patronymic from the personal name *Rand(e)* (see RAND 1).

Ranch (133) Origin unidentified. Possibly a respelling of German RENSCH or **Ränsch**, **Rantsch**, which are probably from a Germanic pet form of a Slavic personal name. The surname is found in English records, but appears to have been taken there from Germany and Switzerland.

Ranck (870) German: variant spelling of RANK.

Rancour (129) Altered spelling of RANCOURT.
GIVEN NAMES French 7%. *Jacques, Patrice.*

Rancourt (690) French: habitational name from places so called in Somme, Vosges, and Meuse.
FOREBEARS A Rancourt from Normandy, France, is documented in Quebec City in 1667.
GIVEN NAMES French 13%. *Andre* (5), *Laurent* (4), *Jean-Guy* (2), *Marcel* (2), *Antoine, Clemence, Emile, Gaston, Gilles, Jean Luc, Julien, Leontine.*

Rand (4241) **1.** English: from the Middle English personal name *Rand(e)*, a short form of any of the various Germanic compound personal names with the first element *rand* '(shield) rim', as for example RANDOLPH. **2.** English: topographic name for someone who lived on the margin of a settlement or on the bank of a river (from Old English *rand* 'rim', used in a topographical sense), or a habitational name from a place named with this word, as for example Rand in Lincolnshire and Rand Grange in North Yorkshire. **3.** German: from a short form of any of the various compound names formed with *rand-* 'rim'. Compare 1. **4.** German: topographic name from Middle High German, Middle Low German *rand, rant* 'edge', 'rim'.

Randa (244) **1.** Basque: reduced form of **Aranda**, a topographic name from *aran*

'blackthorn' + the locative suffix *-da*. **2.** French (eastern and southeastern): topographic name for someone who lived at the boundary of a territory or on the margin of a settlement.

Randal (183) English: variant spelling of RANDALL.
GIVEN NAME French 5%. *Collette.*

Randall (19118) English: from the Middle English personal name *Randel*, a diminutive of RAND with the Anglo-Norman French hypocoristic suffix *-el*.

Randazzo (2176) Italian (Sicily): **1.** habitational name from a place in Catania called Randazzo. **2.** possibly from a derivative of the personal name RANDO.
GIVEN NAMES Italian 21%. *Salvatore* (38), *Sal* (14), *Angelo* (9), *Vito* (8), *Pietro* (6), *Marco* (5), *Carlo* (4), *Nunzio* (4), *Santo* (4), *Antonino* (3), *Antonio* (3), *Gaspare* (3).

Randel (606) **1.** French: from a pet form of the Germanic personal name *Rando*, a short form of various compound names formed with *rand* '(shield) rim' as the first element. Compare RANDALL. **2.** South German: from a pet form of a compound name such as REINHARDT or *Randolf*.

Randell (758) **1.** English: variant spelling of RANDALL. **2.** German: variant spelling of German RANDEL.

Randels (129) Probably an altered form of RANDEL or a shortened form of compound names formed with this element, such as *Randelshofer, Randelz(h)ofer.*

Randerson (108) English (Yorkshire): patronymic from the personal name *Randel* (see RANDALL).

Randhawa (199) Indian (Panjab): Sikh name derived from the name of a Jat tribe.
GIVEN NAMES Indian 83%. *Preet* (3), *Balraj* (2), *Lakhbir* (2), *Adarsh, Ajeet, Ajit, Ajmer, Balwinder, Bindu, Dilawar, Gursewak, Jasvir.*

Randle (3344) **1.** English: variant spelling of RANDALL. **2.** Americanized spelling of RANDEL.

Randleman (270) Possibly an altered spelling of German **Rendelmann**, a habitational name for someone from Rendel near Frankfurt (Hesse).

Randles (808) English: patronymic from RANDALL. In Ireland, says MacLysaght, this is sometimes a variant of REYNOLDS.

Randlett (214) Origin unidentified. Compare RUNDLETT.

Rando (504) Italian (Sicily): from the Germanic personal name *Rando*, in part a short form of such names as *Bertrando* (see BERTRAM) or *Randolfo* (see RANDOLPH).
GIVEN NAMES Italian 12%. *Salvatore* (5), *Ignazio* (2), *Giuseppe, Marco, Philomena, Santo, Tommaso.*

Randol (515) Perhaps an altered spelling of RANDALL, RANDEL, or RANDOLPH.

Randolph (12714) English and German: classicized spelling of *Randolf*, a Germanic personal name composed of the elements *rand* 'rim' (of a shield), 'shield' + *wolf* 'wolf'. This was introduced into England by Scandinavian settlers in the Old Norse form *Rannúlfr*, and was reinforced after the Norman Conquest by the Norman form *Randolf*.

FOREBEARS An American family bearing the surname Randolph are descended from William Randolph (?1651–1711), a planter and merchant, a member of a family that originally came from Sussex, England, who emigrated from Warwickshire to VA *c*.1673. He was a forebear of Thomas Jefferson and Robert E. Lee. Randolph had seven sons, each of whom inherited an estate, the name of which was sometimes added to their own, such as Sir John Randolph of Tazewell. His great-grandsons included Edmund Randolph (1753–1813), first attorney general of the U.S. and one of the framers of the U.S. Constitution, and the diplomat and statesman John Randolph of Roanoke (1773–1833), who served as U.S. minister to Russia.

Randon (122) English: variant of RAND 1, from the Old French oblique case.
GIVEN NAME French 5%. *Marcel*.

Rands (302) English: patronymic from RAND 1.

Randt (107) German: variant of RAND 4.

Raneri (172) Italian (Sicily): patronymic from the personal name *Ranero*, an Italian equivalent of RAYNER.
GIVEN NAMES Italian 20%. *Alfio, Angelo, Carmel, Domenic, Francesco, Franco, Giuseppe, Salvatore*.

Ranes (391) Probably an altered spelling of English RAINES.

Raney (3379) Scottish and Irish: variant of RAINEY.

Ranft (227) German: nickname or topographic name, from Middle High German *ranft* 'edge', 'wall', 'crust (of bread)' (see RAMP).
GIVEN NAMES German 6%. *Gunter, Kurt, Otto, Wolfgang*.

Rang (286) German: **1.** variant of RANGE. **2.** topographic name for someone who lived by a bend or slope in a thoroughfare, from *rang* 'bend'. **3.** from a short form of a Germanic personal name based on *rang*, *rank* 'curved', 'bending'; 'slender'.

Ranganathan (104) Indian (Kerala, Tamil Nadu): Hindu name from Sanskrit *ranganātha* 'lord of mirth' (from *ranga* 'mirth' + *nātha* 'lord'), an epithet of the god Krishna, + the Tamil-Malayalam third-person masculine singular suffix *-n*. This is only a given name in India, but has come to be used as a family name in the U.S.
GIVEN NAMES Indian 98%. *Murali* (6), *Vijay* (4), *Indira* (3), *Srikanth* (3), *Ganesh* (2), *Giri* (2), *Kala* (2), *Madhavan* (2), *Sridhar* (2), *Anand, Chitra, Devika*.

Range (925) **1.** German: nickname for a ragamuffin, from Middle High German *range* 'naughty boy', 'urchin'. **2.** German:

variant of RANG 3. **3.** French: from Old French *renge* 'belt worn for battle', with a wider sense in Middle French of 'rein', 'strap', hence a metonymic occupational name for a maker of such articles.

Rangel (4547) Spanish: probably a variant of RENGEL. This name is also found in Portugal.
GIVEN NAMES Spanish 49%; Portuguese 9%. *Jose* (119), *Juan* (61), *Manuel* (55), *Carlos* (36), *Jesus* (35), *Pedro* (30), *Miguel* (29), *Luis* (28), *Ruben* (27), *Raul* (24), *Roberto* (24), *Francisco* (23); *Anatolio, Henrique, Marcio, Neuza*.

Ranger (819) **1.** English: occupational name for a gamekeeper or warden, from Middle English *ranger*, an agent derivative of *range(n)* 'to arrange or dispose'. **2.** German: variant of RANG 2, 3. **3.** German: habitational name for someone from any of the places named Rangen, in Alsace, Bavaria, and Hesse. **4.** French: from a Germanic personal name formed with *rang*, *rank* 'curved', 'bent'; 'slender'.
FOREBEARS A person called Ranger from La Rochelle, France, is documented in Quebec City in 1684 with the secondary surname LAVIOLETTE.

Ranieri (932) Italian: patronymic from the personal name *Raniero*, an Italian equivalent of RAYNER.
GIVEN NAMES Italian 26%. *Mario* (6), *Rocco* (4), *Dino* (3), *Romeo* (3), *Vito* (3), *Alfredo* (2), *Angelo* (2), *Emilio* (2), *Nino* (2), *Pasquale* (2), *Salvatore* (2), *Aida, Aldo, Amedeo, Antonietta, Armando, Gregorio, Orlando*.

Rank (1290) **1.** English: nickname for a powerfully built man or someone of violent emotions, from the Middle English adjective *rank* (Old English *ranc* 'proud', 'rebellious'). **2.** English: from a medieval personal name, a back-formation from the diminutive RANKIN. **3.** South German: variant of RANG 2. **4.** German: nickname either for an agile person, from Middle High German *ranc* 'quick turn', or in some instances for someone who was tall and thin, from Low German *rank*. In some cases the surname may have been from a personal name formed with this element. **5.** Czech: from a pet form of a personal name, which could be either Slavic *Ranožir* or Germanic *Randolf* (see RANDOLPH). **6.** Swedish and Danish: nickname from *rank* 'erect', 'upright', 'straight'.

Ranke (146) German: **1.** from a pet form of RAHN 2. **2.** habitational name from either of two places named Rankau, in Bohemia and Silesia.
GIVEN NAME Scandinavian 4%. *Erik* (2).

Ranker (211) German: **1.** topographic name from RANKE 2. **2.** variant of RANG 2.

Rankin (10815) Scottish and northern Irish: from the medieval personal name *Rankin*, a diminutive of RONALD or RAND, with the diminutive suffix *-kin*.

Rankine (164) Scottish and northern Irish: variant of RANKIN.

Rankins (759) Although not listed by Black, this may be presumed to be a patronymic from RANKIN, along with *Rankinson*, which Black does record.

Ranly (107) German: unexplained.

Rann (234) **1.** South German: topographic name for someone who lived by an area of wasteland in a forest or field, Middle High German *ranne*. **2.** Jewish (eastern Ashkenazic): acronymic name of uncertain derivation.
GIVEN NAMES French 4%; Jewish 4%. *Aviva, Mort*.

Rannells (125) English: patronymic from the Middle English personal name *Rannulf*, *Ranel*, of continental Germanic origin.

Ranney (1080) Variant of Scottish and northern Irish RAINEY.

Ranno (104) Italian: from a reduced form of the personal name *Arranno*.
GIVEN NAMES Italian 8%; German 4%. *Luigi, Santi*; *Kurt*.

Rannow (154) German: of uncertain origin; perhaps a habitational name from a Slavic form of Rammenau, a place near Bautzen, where Sorbian (a Slavic dialect) is still spoken.

Rans (116) English (Suffolk): variant spelling of RANCE.

Ransbottom (203) Variant of English RAMSBOTTOM.

Ransburg (102) Variant of German RAMSBURG.

Ransdell (668) Probably a variant form of English **Ransdale**, itself a variant of **Ramsdale** (see RAMSDELL).

Ransford (278) English: habitational name, probably from Ramsfold Farm in Lurgashall, Sussex. In a 14th-century record the name occurs as *de Rammesford*.

Ranshaw (103) English: variant of RENSHAW.
GIVEN NAME German 4%. *Kurt*.

Ransier (174) Probably an altered spelling of Swiss German **Ramseyer** (see RAMSEUR).

Ransom (5164) English (chiefly East Anglia): patronymic from the Middle English personal name *Rand(e)* (see RAND 1).

Ransome (420) English: variant of RANSOM.

Ranson (1044) **1.** English (chiefly East Anglia): patronymic from the Middle English personal name *Rand(e)* (see RAND 1). **2.** French: variant of **Renson**, a reduced form of **Rennesson**, a pet form (with the double diminutive suffix *-esson*) of a personal name derived from the Germanic name *Ragino* or a compound name with the first element *ragin-* 'counsel'.

Ransone (187) English (Lincolnshire): variant spelling of RANSON.

Ranstrom (108) Swedish (**Ranström**): ornamental name from a place name formed with *Ran-* (from Swedish *ramn* 'raven') + *ström* 'river'.

Ranta (477) Finnish: topographic name from Finnish *ranta* 'shore', or an ornamental name from the same word. First recorded in the 16th century, it was noted as the most frequently adopted ornamental surname at the celebrations in honor of the Finnish statesman Snellman on May 12, 1906. It occurs most frequently in western and southern coastal regions of Finland. In America, Ranta may be a shortened form of various other names formed with this element, such as **Hietaranta**.

GIVEN NAMES Finnish 11%; Scandinavian 7%. *Reino* (3), *Toivo* (3), *Jouko* (2), *Sulo* (2), *Wilhart* (2), *Ahti, Arvo, Eino, Helvi, Jyrki, Niilo, Osmo*; *Erik, Nels, Niklas*.

Rantala (189) Finnish: variant of RANTA 'shore', with the local suffix *-la*. Originally the surname was probably a habitational name, from a farm so called; later it was also adopted as an ornamental name during the name conversion movement in the 19th and early 20th centuries, often in place of Swedish surnames containing the element *strand* 'shore'. It is found chiefly in southwestern Finland.

GIVEN NAMES Finnish 22%. *Arvo* (2), *Seppo* (2), *Toivo* (2), *Wilho* (2), *Jaakko, Jorma, Martti, Olli, Pentti, Rauno, Reijo, Tauno*.

Rantanen (151) Finnish: variant of RANTA 'shore' + the common surname suffix *-nen*. This was widely adopted, often in place of Swedish surnames containing the element *strand* 'shore', during the name conversion movement of the 19th and early 20th centuries.

GIVEN NAMES Finnish 11%; Scandinavian 4%. *Pentti* (2), *Arvo, Eino, Esa, Mikko, Onni*.

Rantz (296) **1.** German: variant spelling of RANZ. **2.** Jewish (Ashkenazic): unexplained.

Ranucci (134) Italian: patronymic from a pet form of the personal name *Ragino, Raino*, which is from a short form of a Germanic personal name formed with *ra(g)in* 'counsel' as the first element.

GIVEN NAMES Italian 17%. *Sabatino* (2), *Lia, Marco, Rossano, Salvatore*.

Ranum (310) **1.** Norwegian: habitational name from any of several farmsteads named in Old Norse as either *Ranheimr* or *Randheimr*, the second element in each case being *heimr* 'home', 'farmstead', the first elements being respectively *rani* 'muzzle', 'nose' (with reference to a natural formation, such as a mountain or rocky outcrop so shaped), and *rand* 'edge', 'brink'. **2.** Danish: habitational name from a place name with the same derivation as *Randheimr* (see 1).

GIVEN NAMES Scandinavian 4%. *Iver, Juel, Nils*.

Ranz (182) **1.** German: from the Germanic personal name *Rando*, a short form of various names formed with *rand* '(shield) rim' as the first element, or from a Slavic name formed with *ranu* 'early'. **2.** German: from Middle High German *ranz* 'sow' or 'strife', or Middle High German *rans* 'paunch', a nickname from any of these senses. **3.** Jewish (Ashkenazic): variant of RANTZ.

GIVEN NAMES German 8%. *Gerhard, Helmut, Otto, Ulrich*.

Rao (2589) **1.** Italian: from a reduced form of the personal name *Radulfo*, composed of *hrōd* 'renown' + *wulf* 'wolf' (see ROLF). **2.** Indian (southern and western states and Orissa): Hindu name found among several communities, from Sanskrit *rājā* 'king'. It is freely added by men to their forename in several communities of Maharashtra, Goa, and Andhra Pradesh. **3.** Chinese 饶: from the name of an area called Rao, which existed in the state of Zhao during the Warring States period (403–221 BC).

GIVEN NAMES Indian 40%. *Mohan* (23), *Krishna* (15), *Srinivas* (15), *Prakash* (12), *Rama* (12), *Vijay* (12), *Madhu* (11), *Ramesh* (11), *Ravi* (11), *Arun* (10), *Bhaskar* (10), *Rajesh* (9).

Rapa (121) **1.** Italian: from *rapa* 'turnip'; a metonymic occupational name for a grower or seller of turnips, or a derogatory nickname for a stupid person, from the same word in a transferred sense. **2.** Portuguese and Galician: habitational name from any of the towns called Rapa, in Portugal and in A Coruña, Galicia.

GIVEN NAMES Italian 22%. *Renato* (2), *Americo, Angelo* (2), *Giuseppe, Margarita, Petrina*.

Rapacz (151) Polish: **1.** from a derivative of the personal name *Rapał*, a local variant of *Rafał* (see RAPHAEL). **2.** unflattering nickname from Polish dialect *rapacz* 'duffer', 'oaf'.

GIVEN NAMES Polish 8%. *Jacek, Jerzy, Slawomir, Stanislaw*.

Rapaport (455) **1.** Jewish (Ashkenazic): variant spelling of RAPPAPORT. **2.** Dutch: variant of RAPPORT.

GIVEN NAMES Jewish 9%. *Eliezer* (2), *Cyla, Ezriel, Irina, Mechel, Meir, Miriam, Moshe, Pinkhas, Pola, Yaakov, Zev*.

Rape (421) **1.** Irish: variant of REAP 2. **2.** German: probably an altered spelling of **Rappe** (see RAPP).

Raper (1860) **1.** English (Yorkshire): variant of ROPER. In southern dialects of English, Old English *-ā-* became Middle English *-ō-*, whereas in Yorkshire *-a-* was preserved and gave rise to this form of the surname. **2.** Possibly also an altered spelling of German **Röper** or **Röber** (see ROEBER).

Raphael (1364) Jewish, French, English, and German: from the Hebrew personal name *Refael* composed of the elements *rafa* 'to heal' + *el* 'God'. This is the name of one of the archangels, but for some reason it was less popular among Christians in the Middle Ages, except perhaps in Italy, than those of the archangels Michael and Gabriel.

GIVEN NAMES French 5%. *Antoine* (2), *Jacques* (2), *Micheline* (2), *Georges, Giraud, Huguette, Jean-Claude*.

Rapier (497) Dutch: of uncertain origin; it may be a derivative of *raap* 'turnip', and hence an occupational name for a grower of turnips or other root vegetables.

Rapin (123) Of uncertain origin. It is a French name, a nickname for a thief, from *rapin* 'rapine'. However, the distribution of the surname in North America does not really accord with a French origin.

Rapisarda (131) Italian: of uncertain derivation; probably a confusion of two distinct names derived respectively from Germanic and Latin.

GIVEN NAMES Italian 15%. *Salvatore* (2), *Gaetano, Mario, Marisa, Orazio, Sal, Sergio*.

Rapkin (164) Jewish (eastern Ashkenazic): variant of RABKIN .

GIVEN NAMES Jewish 5%. *Isadore* (2), *Asher*.

Rapley (159) **1.** English: probably connected with Rapley Farm in Berkshire, although it is not clear whether the surname is derived from the farm name or vice versa. **2.** Altered spelling of the Swiss family name **Räpple** (see RAPPLEYE).

Rapone (145) Italian: **1.** habitational name from Rapone in Potenza province. **2.** possibly from the Germanic personal name *Rapo, Rabo*.

GIVEN NAMES Italian 13%. *Guido* (2), *Angelo, Crescenzo, Geno, Pietro, Rocco*.

Rapoport (615) Jewish (Ashkenazic): variant of RAPPAPORT.

GIVEN NAMES Jewish 16%; Russian 12%. *Irina* (3), *Faina* (2), *Hyman* (2), *Ilya* (2), *Semen* (2), *Yakov* (2), *Yosef* (2), *Aron, Avrohom, Bentsion, Blyuma, Dov*; *Mikhail* (7), *Boris* (5), *Leonid* (4), *Aleksandr* (3), *Lev* (2), *Vladimir* (2), *Yefim* (2), *Yuriy* (2), *Arkady, Asya, Betya, Daniil*.

Raposa (559) Portuguese: **1.** habitational name from Raposa, a town in Portugal. **2.** nickname for a cunning person, or else for someone with reddish brown hair, from *raposa* 'fox'.

GIVEN NAMES Spanish 10%. *Manuel* (22), *Jose* (3), *Adelino* (2), *Julio* (2), *Raul* (2), *Aldina, Alicia, Alvarino, Ana, Carlos, Dionisio, Elvira*.

Raposo (445) Portuguese: variant of RAPOSA.

GIVEN NAMES Spanish 34%; Portuguese 20%. *Jose* (26), *Manuel* (15), *Antonio* (14), *Luis* (5), *Carlos* (4), *Jaime* (4), *Adriana* (2), *Alfonso* (2), *Americo* (2), *Ana* (2), *Eduardo* (2), *Fernando* (2), *Francisco* (2), *Joao* (9), *Duarte, Henrique, Paulo, Serafim, Vasco*.

Rapoza (589) Portuguese: variant of RAPOSA.

GIVEN NAMES Spanish 6%; Portuguese 4%. *Manuel* (16), *Adelino, Bento, Carlos,*

Celestino, Evaristo, Luiz, Margarito; Joao, Duarte, Vasco.

Rapozo (190) Portuguese: variant of RAPOSO.

GIVEN NAMES Portuguese 4%. *Duarte, Joao.*

Rapp (5996) **1.** Swedish: from *rapp* 'quick', 'prompt'; a soldier's name, one of the monothematic names adopted by soldiers in the 17th century, before surnames became general in Sweden. **2.** German: from Middle High German *rapp, rabe* 'raven' (German *Rabe*), hence a nickname for someone with black hair, or some other supposed resemblance to the bird. Compare RAVEN. In some cases the surname may have arisen from a house name, thus denoting someone who lived in a house distinguished by the sign of a raven.

Rappa (447) Italian: from Sicilian *rappa* 'bunch', 'cluster' or Italian *rappa* 'lock', 'quiff', presumably applied as a nickname with reference to someone's hair.

GIVEN NAMES Italian 17%. *Salvatore* (8), *Sal* (3), *Angelo* (2), *Antonio* (2), *Benedetto* (2), *Giovanni* (2), *Antonino, Carlo, Domenico, Emanuele, Franco, Guiseppe.*

Rappaport (1567) Jewish (Ashkenazic): most people bearing this name are descended from Avrom-Menakhem Ben-Yankev Hakoyen Rapa, who lived in Porto, Italy, at the beginning of the 16th century. The etymology of his name is uncertain but possibly from German *Rappe* 'raven'. Compare RAPP. According to one explanation his descendants added the name of their city, Porto, in order to distinguish themselves from unrelated Jews surnamed **Rapa**; according to another, there was a marriage between the Rapa and Porto families, and the issue of this union took the compound name.

GIVEN NAMES Jewish 5%. *Sol* (6), *Emanuel* (3), *Hyman* (2), *Moshe* (2), *Ber, Meyer, Miriam, Myer, Pinchus, Rivka, Tova, Yael.*

Rappe (355) **1.** German and Jewish (Ashkenazic): variant of RAPP 2. **2.** French: habitational name from La Rappe in the Vosges, so named from Middle French *raspe* 'wood cut from a copse', 'cut brushwood'.

Rappel (100) German: nickname from a diminutive of Middle High German *rapp, rabe* 'raven' (see RAPP).

Rappleye (162) **1.** Possibly an Americanized spelling of Swiss and South German **Räppli** or **Räpple**, diminutives of RAPP. **2.** Possibly a respelling of French **Rappelet**, which is most probably a derivative of Old French *rapel* 'occupation', 'profession'.

FOREBEARS This was the name of one of the first Walloon families to settle in New Netherland in the 17th century.

Rappleyea (141) Variant of RAPPLEYE.

Rappold (418) German: from a personal name composed of the Germanic elements *rād* 'counsel', 'advice' + *bald* 'bold', 'brave'.

GIVEN NAMES French 5%. *Marcel* (3), *Gabrielle.*

Rappoport (240) Jewish (Ashkenazic): variant of RAPPAPORT.

GIVEN NAMES Jewish 6%; Russian 5%. *Avi, Eyal, Nachum; Igor, Leonid, Lyubov, Vitaliy, Vlagimir, Yelena.*

Rapport (200) **1.** Dutch: possibly a nickname for some kind of official, from Middle Dutch *rappoort, rapport* 'report', 'statement', 'account', 'declaration'. **2.** Possibly an altered spelling of the Swiss family name **Rappard**, a habitational name from Rappertswyl, Switzerland, named from the Germanic personal name *Radobert*, a compound of *rād, rāt* 'advice', 'counsel' + *berht* 'bright'.

Rapps (105) Jewish: Americanized form of some like-sounding Ashkenazic name; see, for example, RAPPAPORT.

GIVEN NAMES Jewish 6%. *Ahron, Mandel.*

Rapson (278) English (Cornwall): patronymic from *Rab, Rap*, short forms of the personal name ROBERT.

Raptis (192) Greek: occupational name for a tailor, Greek *raptis* (colloquially *raftis*), a derivative of classical Greek *raptein* 'to sew'.

GIVEN NAMES Greek 22%. *Constantine* (3), *Anastasios* (2), *Demetrios* (2), *Dimitrios* (2), *Vasilios* (2), *Athanasios, Evangelos, Haralampos, Ilias, Konstantinos, Marianthi, Markos; Dino* (2).

Rapuano (173) Italian: unexplained.

GIVEN NAMES Italian 10%. *Domenic, Luigi, Pasquale, Salvatore.*

Raque (104) French: **1.** from a personal name of Germanic origin, a short form of compound names with the first element *ragin* 'counsel'. **2.** topographic name from Old Picard *raque* 'marsh', 'slough', 'fen'.

Raquet (148) French: diminutive of RAQUE.

GIVEN NAMES German 4%. *Fritz, Jutta.*

Rardin (508) Variant of Irish RIORDAN.

Rardon (162) Variant of Irish RIORDAN.

Rarey (121) **1.** Of German origin: possibly a nickname from Middle Low German *rāren* 'to roar'. **2.** Perhaps in some cases an altered spelling of the Walloon French surname **Rary**, which Debrabandere suggests may be from a French form of the Germanic personal name *Rairic*, composed of the elements *rād* 'counsel' + *rīc* 'power(ful)'. **3.** Possibly in some cases a shortened form of Irish MCCREARY.

Rarick (651) Americanized spelling of German **Röhrich** (see ROEHRIG).

Ras (179) **1.** Czech (**Raš**) and Polish (**Raś**): from a pet short form of any of various Slavic personal names with the first element *rad-* 'joyful' or *raci-* 'to fight'. **2.** Spanish: from *ras* 'level' (ultimately from Latin *radere* 'to scrape'); perhaps a topographic name for someone who lived on flat land. **3.** Catalan: topographic name for someone

who lived on bare, barren land, from *ras* 'shorn', 'bare', 'peeled'. **4.** French: from *ras* 'bare', 'shorn', 'close-shaven', hence a topographic name for someone who lived on bare or razed land, or a nickname for someone with closely cropped hair. **5.** Dutch: nickname for a nimble person, from *ras* 'quick', 'swift'. **6.** Altered spelling of German **Rass**, from a Germanic personal name *Rasso*, or of South German and Swiss **Räss**, a nickname for someone cheeky or sharp, from Middle High German *ræze* 'sharp', 'wild', 'caustic'.

Rasar (103) Origin unidentified. Perhaps a Slavic spelling of German RASER, or a variant spelling of RASOR.

Rasband (107) Of English origin: unexplained.

Rasberry (899) English: possibly a habitational name from Ratsbury in Lynton, Devon, although the modern English surname is concentrated in Norfolk.

Rasbury (140) English: variant spelling of RASBERRY.

Rasch (872) **1.** German and Jewish (Ashkenazic): nickname for a quick or rash person from Middle High German, German *rasch* 'quick', 'hot-headed', 'hasty'. **2.** German (of Slavic origin): from a pet form of any of various Slavic personal names formed with *rad-* 'joyful' or *rano* 'early' as the first element. **3.** German: habitational name from any of numerous places so named, for example in Franconia. **4.** English: variant of RASH.

GIVEN NAMES German 5%. *Erwin* (2), *Hans* (2), *Otto* (2), *Eldred, Gerd, Guenter, Gunther, Heinz, Ingo, Klaus, Ulrich, Wolfgang.*

Rasche (382) German: variant of RASCH 1 and 3.

GIVEN NAMES German 4%. *Gerhardt, Wolfgang.*

Rascher (128) German: **1.** variant of RASCH 1, from a noun derivative. **2.** habitational name for someone from places called Rasch (near Nuremberg) or Raschau (in Saxony).

GIVEN NAME German 6%. *Xaver* (2).

Raschke (550) German: from a pet form of RASCH 2.

GIVEN NAMES German 8%. *Erwin* (2), *Klaus* (2), *Alfons, Beate, Christoph, Fritz, Hans, Horst, Kurt, Manfred, Markus, Mathias.*

Rasco (642) **1.** English: variant of ROSCOE. **2.** Americanized spelling of French RACICOT.

Rascoe (589) Variant spelling of RASCO (see English ROSCOE, French RACICOT).

Rascon (543) Spanish (**Rascón**): **1.** probably a habitational name from either of the places called Rascón, in Cantabria and Badajoz provinces. **2.** possibly a nickname from *rascón* 'sour', 'sharp' or a homonym meaning 'rail' (the bird).

GIVEN NAMES Spanish 49%. *Jose* (16), *Manuel* (10), *Armando* (5), *Carlos* (5), *Jesus* (5), *Luis* (5), *Ruben* (5), *Francisco*

(4), *Guadalupe* (4), *Juan* (4), *Miguel* (4), *Pedro* (4).

Rase (200) **1.** Dutch: from the Germanic personal name *Razo*, a derivative of compound names with the first element *rād* 'counsel'. **2.** German: from an old field name, *ros*, *ras*, meaning 'swamp'. There is a stream called Rase near Göttingen, which may also be a source of the surname. **3.** German: from a short form of the personal name *Erasmus* (see RASMUS), or from a short form of a Slavic personal name with the first element *rad*. Compare RASCH 2. **4.** South German (**Räse**): variant of **Rass** or **Räss** (see RAS 6).

Raser (173) German: **1.** probably a nickname for a wild or volatile person, from an agent derivative of Middle High German *rāsen* 'to rage'. **2.** respelling of **Röser** (see ROESSER).

Rasey (218) **1.** English: unexplained. Compare RACY, RACEY. **2.** Possibly an altered spelling of Swiss German **Rasi** (see RASE 4) or of Dutch **Rasy**, a metonymic occupational name for someone who weighed out or measured corn, from Middle Dutch *razier* 'corn measure'.

Rash (2801) **1.** English: variant of ASH; the name arose as the result of misdivision of Middle English *atter ashe* 'at the ash tree' (Old English *æt þǣre æsce*). **2.** Jewish: of uncertain origin; the Guggenheimers consider it to be a variant of RASCH 1. **3.** Americanized spelling of German and Jewish RASCH.

Rashed (101) Muslim: variant of RASHID.
GIVEN NAMES Muslim 69%. *Abdul* (2), *Ahmad* (2), *Shakeel* (2), *Abdo*, *Abdul Karim*, *Abdulla*, *Ahmed*, *Atef*, *Ayesha*, *Aysha*, *Bilal*, *Fathi*.

Rasheed (343) Muslim: variant of RASHID.
GIVEN NAMES Muslim 72%. *Abdul* (17), *Ahmed* (6), *Abdool* (4), *Javed* (4), *Ahmad* (3), *Mohammed* (3), *Nasir* (3), *Shams* (3), *Abdullah* (2), *Aneesah* (2), *Atif* (2), *Bibi* (2).

Rashid (909) Muslim: from a personal name based on Arabic *rashīd* 'wise', 'judicious', 'rightly guided', 'right-minded'. *Al-Rashīd* 'the Right-Minded' is an epithet of Allah (see the Qur'an 11:87). *Rashīd* is used in combination with other words, e.g. *'Abd ur-Rashīd* 'servant of the Right-Minded'. Hārūn ur-Rashīd (786–809) was the most famous of the Abbasid khalifs. This name is widespread throughout the Muslim world.
GIVEN NAMES Muslim 65%. *Abdul* (31), *Mohammad* (19), *Mohammed* (19), *Faisal* (7), *Haroon* (7), *Imran* (7), *Khalid* (7), *Syed* (7), *Mian* (6), *Hassan* (5), *Rashid* (5), *Ali* (4).

Rasinski (121) Polish (**Raszyński**): habitational name for someone from a place called Raszyn in Warszawa voivodeship, named with *Rasz(a)*, pet form of the Old Polish personal name *Racibor*.
GIVEN NAME Polish 5%. *Zbigniew*.

Rask (516) Danish and Swedish: nickname from *rask* 'quick'; in Sweden, a soldier's name.
GIVEN NAMES Scandinavian 6%. *Niels* (2), *Ejnar*, *Knud*, *Lars*.

Raska (277) Czech (**Raška**): from a pet form of any of various Slavic personal names formed with *rad-* 'joyful' as the first element.
GIVEN NAMES German 4%. *Erwin*, *Irmgard*, *Otto*.

Raske (185) German: variant of **Raschke**, from a pet form of any of various Slavic personal names formed with *rad-* 'joyful' as the first element. Compare RASKA.

Raskin (1013) **1.** Jewish (eastern Ashkenazic): metronymic from the Yiddish female personal name *Raske*, a pet form of Biblical RACHEL + the eastern Slavic possessive suffix *-in*. **2.** Dutch: from a reduced pet form of the personal name *Erasmus* (see RASMUS).
GIVEN NAMES Jewish 7%; Russian 5%. *Hyman* (3), *Ilya* (2), *Sol* (2), *Zvi* (2), *Aviva*, *Emanuel*, *Hymie*, *Inna*, *Mort*, *Polina*, *Rivkah*, *Semen*; *Boris* (4), *Leonid* (4), *Seva* (2), *Anatoly*, *Arkadiy*, *Dmitriy*, *Galena*, *Iosif*, *Kuzma*, *Lev*, *Mikail*, *Natalya*.

Rasmus (335) Danish, North German, and Dutch: from a reduced form of the personal name *Erasmus*, Latin form of Greek *Erasmos*, a derivative of *erān* 'to love'. St. Erasmos (died 303) was a bishop of Formia in Campania, who was martyred under Diocletian. However, in northern Europe from the 16th century onwards, the name was more often selected in honor of the great Renaissance Dutch humanist scholar and teacher Erasmus Roterodamus (1469–1536).
GIVEN NAMES Scandinavian 5%. *Britt*, *Nelle*.

Rasmusen (108) Altered spelling of RASMUSSEN.
GIVEN NAME German 4%. *Hans*.

Rasmuson (175) Altered spelling of RASMUSSON.

Rasmussen (14805) Danish, Norwegian, German, and Dutch: patronymic from the personal name *Erasmus* (see RASMUS).
GIVEN NAMES Scandinavian 6%. *Erik* (29), *Nels* (17), *Lars* (7), *Jorgen* (6), *Niels* (6), *Bent* (4), *Holger* (4), *Thor* (4), *Borge* (3), *Knute* (3), *Per* (3), *Alf* (2).

Rasmusson (590) **1.** German and Swedish: patronymic from the personal name *Erasmus*. **2.** Americanized spelling of RASMUSSEN.
GIVEN NAMES Scandinavian 4%. *Britt*, *Hjalmer*, *Juel*, *Petter*.

Rasnake (482) Probably a respelling of German RASNICK.

Rasner (166) **1.** German, Austrian (Tyrol): probably a habitational name for someone from a farm called Rasen. **2.** Altered spelling of German **Rösner** (see ROSNER). **3.** Variant of RASER 1.

Rasnic (161) Origin unidentified. Perhaps a variant spelling of German RASNICK.

Rasnick (427) **1.** German: probably a nickname for an irascible man, from *rasen* 'to rage' + the Slavic suffix *-ni(c)k*. **2.** Perhaps an Americanized spelling of Slovenian RESNIK or of *Hrastnik*, a topographic name for someone who lived by an oak tree, from *hrast* 'oak', or a habitational name for someone from any of numerous places called Hrastje, named with this word.

Raso (401) **1.** Italian and Spanish: nickname for someone with close-cropped hair, from *raso* 'level', 'smooth', 'bare'; alternatively, the Italian name may correspond to the past participle *rasato*, meaning 'shaven'. *Raso* also means 'satin', and in some cases the name may have arisen from this sense of the word. **2.** Portuguese, Galician and Spanish: habitational name from any of the places called Raso, in Portugal, and in A Coruña (Galicia) and Ávila provinces.
GIVEN NAMES Italian 22%; Spanish 8%. *Angelo* (3), *Antonio* (3), *Guido* (3), *Vito* (3), *Salvatore* (2), *Alfonse*, *Dante*, *Dino*, *Ernesto*, *Francesca*, *Gennaro*, *Leno*, *Lia*, *Reginaldo*, *Silvana*; *Miguel* (2), *Alfonso*, *Asuncion*, *Jose*, *Manuel*.

Rasor (564) **1.** English: metonymic occupational name for a maker of razors or a barber, from Old French *rasor*, *rasur* 'razor'. **2.** Humanist Latinized form of the German occupational name **Bartscherer** 'barber' (literally 'beard cutter'), recorded as early as the 14th century.

Rasp (208) **1.** German: from Middle High German *raspen* 'to scrape together', 'amass', a nickname for a greedy person. **2.** North German: metonymic occupational name for someone who made rasps or used one in his work, from Middle Low German *raspe* 'file', 'rasp', 'grater'.

Raspa (101) Italian: from *raspa* 'rasp', 'file', hence probably a metonymic occupational name for a maker or user of files, or a nickname for a tiresome or irritating person.
GIVEN NAMES Italian 17%. *Gabriella*, *Guiseppe*, *Salvatore*, *Vincenzo*.

Raspberry (167) English: variant spelling of RASBERRY.

Rassel (108) **1.** English: probably a variant of **Ras(s)ell** or **Razzell** (unexplained). **2.** German: nickname for a hothead, from Middle High German *razzeln* 'to romp', 'rampage'. **3.** Dutch and Luxembourgois: perhaps from the Germanic personal name *Raas*, but more probably from French ROSSEL.

Rassi (131) **1.** Italian: perhaps a patronymic from the medieval personal name *Rasso*. **2.** Muslim: of uncertain origin; perhaps a variant of RAIS.
GIVEN NAMES Muslim 6%. *Abrahim*, *Bijan*, *Jafar*, *Jahan*.

Rassier (112) Possibly of German or Swiss origin: unexplained.

Rast (656) Swiss and German: habitational name from a place named Rast, for example near Messkirch, interpreted by Brechenmacher as meaning 'resting place', 'stopping place' (Middle High German *reste*), but by Bahlow as a term denoting water or marsh. In some cases the surname may be topographic in origin.
GIVEN NAMES German 4%. *Gunter, Helmut, Mechthild, Otto, Reinhold, Volker, Wolfgang.*

Rastelli (125) Italian: patronymic from the medieval personal name *Rastellus*, from *rastrello* 'rake'.
GIVEN NAMES Italian 21%. *Angelo, Cesar, Enzo, Ezio, Franco, Guillermo, Italo, Lorenzo, Roberto, Vincenzo.*

Rastetter (152) German: habitational name for someone from Rastatt in Baden.

Rastogi (135) Indian (northern and central states): Hindu (Bania) name of unknown origin and meaning.
GIVEN NAMES Indian 96%. *Jagat* (4), *Ravi* (4), *Sanjeev* (3), *Sharad* (3), *Vijay* (3), *Ajay* (2), *Alok* (2), *Alpana* (2), *Anupam* (2), *Harish* (2), *Laxmi* (2), *Mukul* (2).

Rasul (118) Muslim: from a personal name based on Arabic *rasūl* 'messenger'. The Prophet Muhammad is the messenger of Allah (see the Qur'an 48:29).
GIVEN NAMES Muslim 72%. *Ghulam* (4), *Golam* (3), *Ali* (2), *Amjad* (2), *Karim* (2), *Mohammad* (2), *Mujahid* (2), *Naeem* (2), *Abdul, Abrahim, Aminur, Aziz.*

Ratajczak (496) Polish: patronymic from the occupational term *rataj* 'plowman'.
GIVEN NAMES Polish 6%. *Andrzej* (2), *Bogdan* (2), *Janusz, Jerzy, Krzysztof, Marzanna, Tadeusz, Tomasz, Wojciech.*

Ratajczyk (122) Polish: from a diminutive of *rataj* 'plowman'.
GIVEN NAMES Polish 13%. *Andrzej* (2), *Jadwiga, Krystyna, Piotr, Wieslaw, Zbigniew.*

Ratay (170) **1.** Americanized spelling of Old Czech or Polish **Rataj**, an occupational term for a plowman. **2.** German: habitational name from a place called Ratay or Rattey, in Mecklenburg and near Posen (Polish Poznań).

Ratchford (706) Irish (Wexford) and English: variant of ROCHFORD.

Ratcliff (3596) English: habitational name from any of the places, in various parts of England, called Ratcliff(e), Radcliffe, Redcliff, or Radclive, all of which derive their names from Old English *rēad* 'red' + *clif* 'cliff', 'slope', 'riverbank'.

Ratcliffe (1715) English: variant of RATCLIFF.

Rater (153) German: **1.** occupational name meaning 'counselor', from an agent derivative of Middle High German *rāt*, modern German *Rat* 'counsel'. **2.** from a Germanic personal name based on *rād, rāt* 'advice',

'counsel'. **3.** habitational name for someone from places called Rath or Rathen.

Raterman (170) Americanized spelling of German RATERMANN.

Ratermann (130) German: variant of RATER or RATHMANN.

Rath (2544) **1.** German and Jewish (Ashkenazic): descriptive epithet for a wise person or counselor, from Middle High German *rāt* 'counsel', 'advice', German *Rat* 'counsel', 'advice', also 'stock', 'supply'. **2.** German (also Swiss **Räth**): from a short form of any of the various Germanic compound personal names formed with *rād, rāt* 'counsel', 'advice' as the first element. **3.** German (Rhineland): habitational name from any of various places called Rath, which derives from Middle Low German *roden, raden* 'to clear land for cultivation'. **4.** Irish: in some cases a habitational name from a place called Rath; in County Derry it is a reduced form of **McIlwraith** (see McILRATH).
GIVEN NAMES German 4%. *Otto* (7), *Hans* (5), *Kurt* (4), *Erna* (2), *Fritz* (2), *Lutz* (2), *Orlo* (2), *Reinhart* (2), *Arno, Bernd, Gerhardt, Hermann.*

Rathbone (835) English: probably a habitational name from Radbourn in Warwickshire or Radbourne in Derbyshire, both of which get their names from Old English *hrēod* 'reeds' (a collective singular) + *burna* 'stream'.

Rathbun (2780) English: variant of RATHBONE.

Rathburn (832) English: variant of RATHBONE.

Rathe (284) German: **1.** variant of RATH 1 and 2. **2.** habitational name from Rathe in Silesia or Rathen in Saxony, Silesia, and Rhineland. **3.** (**Räthe**): from a southern pet form of the personal name KONRAD.
GIVEN NAMES French 4%. *Camille, Fernand, Jacques.*

Rathel (153) German (**Räthel**): of uncertain origin; perhaps a pet form of RATH 2.

Rather (580) German: **1.** occupational name for a counselor or nickname for a wise person, from Middle High German *rāter* 'adviser'. **2.** variant of RATHERT. **3.** (**Räther**): habitational name for someone from a place called Rath (see RATH 3), or a habitational name from places named Räther and Räthern in northeastern Germany.

Rathert (236) German: **1.** from a Germanic personal name composed of the elements *rād, rāt* 'advice' + *hard* 'hardy', 'brave', 'strong'. **2.** variant of RATER 1.

Rathfon (126) German: probably a variant of **Rathvon**, of uncertain origin; possibly from a Germanic personal name formed with *rāt, rād* 'advice' + *-fons* (as in the Visigothic personal name *Alfons*; compare Old High German *funs* 'quick', 'active').

Rathgeb (123) Southern and Swiss German: variant of RATHGEBER.

GIVEN NAMES German 8%. *Erwin, Fritz, Otmar.*

Rathgeber (285) German: occupational name for an adviser or wise man, from Middle High German *rātgebe*, Middle Low German *rātgever* 'giver of advice', 'counselor', in Frisian also 'judge'.
GIVEN NAMES German 4%. *Fritz, Juergen, Kurt.*

Rathje (293) Frisian: from a pet form of RATH 2.
GIVEN NAMES German 4%. *Erwin, Frieda, Willi.*

Rathjen (549) Frisian: patronymic from a pet form of RATH 2.
GIVEN NAMES German 5%. *Kurt* (3), *Jurgen* (2), *Eldor, Ernst, Hans, Reinold.*

Rathke (596) North German: from a pet form of RATH 2.
GIVEN NAMES German 8%. *Armin* (2), *Dieter* (2), *Erwin* (2), *Klaus* (2), *Alois, Frieda, Fritz, Hans, Kurt, Lutz, Reinhold.*

Rathman (397) Altered spelling of RATHMANN.

Rathmann (280) German: occupational name for a counselor or arbitrator, or a nickname for a man respected for his opinions and advice, from Middle High German *rāt* 'counsel' + *man* 'man', in Hesse also 'executioner'.
GIVEN NAMES German 9%. *Aloysius, Detlef, Ernst, Fritz, Heinz, Horst, Joerg, Karlheinz, Otto, Wolfgang.*

Rathmell (173) English (Yorkshire): habitational name from Rathmell in North Yorkshire, so named from Old Norse *rauðr* 'red' + *melr* 'sandbank'.

Raths (114) Swiss German: variant of RATH 2.
GIVEN NAME German 5%. *Otto* (2).

Rathsack (175) German (of Slavic origin): from *Raczak*, a pet form of Slavic personal names with the first element *rad-* 'joyful', for example *Radoslav*; or, according to another opinion, a Germanized form of Slavic *radzak* 'adviser'.

Ratigan (291) Irish: reduced Americanized form of **Ó Reachtagáin** 'descendant of *Reachtagán*', a personal name from a diminutive of *reachtaire* 'steward', 'administrator', or *reacht* 'law'. This is the name of an ecclesiastical family in Connacht.
GIVEN NAMES Irish 6%. *Aidan, Brendan.*

Ratke (103) German: variant spelling of RATHKE.
GIVEN NAME German 5%. *Otto.*

Ratkovich (146) **1.** Serbian and Croatian (**Ratković**): patronymic from the personal name *Ratko*, pet form of *Rado*, derived from Old Slavic *rad* 'merry', 'joyful'. **2.** Jewish (from Lithuania): variant spelling of **Rotkovich**, a metronymic from the Yiddish female personal name *Rodke*, a pet form of *Rode*, of ultimate Czech origin.
GIVEN NAMES South Slavic 4%. *Drago, Marko.*

Ratkowski (155) Polish: variant of **Radkowski**, a habitational name for someone from any of many places called Radków, named with the personal name RADEK.

Ratledge (300) Variant of English RUTLEDGE.

Ratley (337) Perhaps an English habitational name from Ratley in Warwickshire, named with Old English *rōt* 'pleasant', or a personal name, *Rōta*, + *lēah* 'clearing in a wood'.

Ratliff (9548) English: variant of RATCLIFF.

Ratliffe (104) English: variant of RATCLIFF.

Ratner (1079) Jewish (eastern Ashkenazic): **1.** habitational name for someone from Ratno in Ukraine or Rathenau near Brandenburg. **2.** occupational name from Yiddish *rat* 'council' + the agent suffix *-ner*.

GIVEN NAMES Jewish 7%. *Sol* (2), *Aharon, Bina, Emanuel, Gershon, Hyman, Ilya, Isadore, Meyer, Miriam, Naum, Polina.*

Ratta (103) **1.** Indian (Panjab): Hindu name of unknown origin. **2.** Italian: variant of RATTO.

GIVEN NAMES Indian 8%; Italian 8%. *Annu, Ashwani, Avinash, Rajiv; Franco, Rocco, Salvatore, Saverio.*

Rattan (132) Indian (Panjab): Hindu and Sikh name from Sanskrit *ratna* 'jewel'. Among Sikhs, this name is found in the Ramgarhia subgroup.

GIVEN NAMES Indian 20%. *Asha, Deepak, Deodath, Pradeep, Sanjay, Sashi, Shashi, Vani, Vijay, Vinod.*

Ratte (210) **1.** German: from Middle German *ratte* 'rat', hence a nickname from the animal, perhaps for a sly and agile individual. **2.** Dutch: possibly a nickname from Middle Dutch *ratte* 'rat' (see 1).

GIVEN NAMES French 12%. *Armand, Chantal, Fernand, Gilles, Jean-Marc, Lucien, Marcel, Rosaire.*

Ratterman (212) Apparently an altered spelling of RATERMANN.

Ratterree (259) Probably an altered form of Scottish RATTRAY. This spelling is common in GA.

Ratti (268) **1.** Italian: patronymic or plural form of RATTO. **2.** Indian (Maharashtra): Hindu (Maratha) name of unknown meaning.

GIVEN NAMES Italian 9%; Indian 5%; French 4%. *Gino* (4), *Aldo, Alessandro, Enrico, Ermanno, Reno, Romano, Vito; Manohar, Rakesh, Ram, Ved, Vijay; Renald* (3).

Rattigan (219) Irish: variant spelling of RATIGAN.

GIVEN NAMES Irish 7%. *Brendan, Niall.*

Rattler (161) German: unexplained.

Rattner (264) Jewish (Ashkenazic): variant spelling of RATNER.

Ratto (430) Italian: **1.** nickname for an agile, opportunistic, or unprincipled person, from *ratto* 'rat'. **2.** occupational name from Greek *raptēs* 'tailor', in Southern Italy pronounced *raftis* or *rattis*.

Rattray (376) Scottish: habitational name from a feudal barony in the former county of Perthshire, named from a British cognate of Gaelic *ràth* 'fortress' + a Pictish term cognate with Welsh *tref* 'settlement'.

Ratts (174) Possibly an Americanized spelling of RATZ.

GIVEN NAME German 5%. *Hermann* (2).

Ratz (402) **1.** German and Jewish (Ashkenazic): nickname, probably for an agile or opportunistic individual, from Middle High German *ratz* 'rat', 'marten', 'polecat'. **2.** German (also **Rätz**): from a pet form of a compound personal name with the first element *rād* 'advice'. **3.** Jewish (Ashkenazic): acronym of uncertain derivation.

GIVEN NAMES German 8%. *Otto* (4), *Bernd, Gottlieb, Hans, Heinrich, Helmut, Hermann, Juergen, Kurt.*

Ratzel (122) German: **1.** habitational name from a place so named in Lower Saxony. **2.** from a short form of a Germanic personal name (see RATH 2).

GIVEN NAMES German 5%. *Gunther, Otto.*

Ratzlaff (1053) German (Pomeranian): from the Slavic personal name *Ratislav*, composed of the elements *rad-* 'joyful' + *slav* 'glory', 'fame', 'praise'.

GIVEN NAMES German 4%. *Kurt* (4), *Erwin* (2), *Erna, Fritz, Helmut, Konrad, Otto.*

Ratzloff (114) Variant of German RATZLAFF.

Rau (3483) **1.** German: nickname for a ruffian, earlier for a hairy person, from Middle High German *rūch, rūhe, rouch* 'hairy', 'shaggy', 'rough'. **2.** English: from a medieval personal name, a variant of RALPH. **3.** Italian (Sicily): from a local variant of the personal name *Rao*, an old form of *Ra(o)ul*, composed of the Germanic elements *rad* 'counsel', 'advice' + *wolf* 'wolf'. Compare RALPH. **4.** Indian: variant of RAO.

GIVEN NAMES German 4%. *Otto* (6), *Erwin* (4), *Ottmar* (3), *Bodo* (2), *Frieda* (2), *Hans* (2), *Reinold* (2), *Benno, Bernd, Bernhard, Berthel, Eberhard.*

Raub (736) German: nickname for a robber or plunderer, from Middle High German *roup* 'plunder', 'booty'.

Rauber (230) German (**Räuber**), Swiss German: derogatory nickname, from Middle High German *roubære* 'robber', 'bandit', 'highwayman' (from *roub, roup* 'booty', 'spoils').

GIVEN NAMES German 4%. *Florian, Hans, Otto.*

Raucci (257) Southern Italian: patronymic from a pet form of RAO, RAU.

GIVEN NAMES Italian 16%. *Carmine* (2), *Mauro* (2), *Salvatore* (2), *Aldo, Alfonse, Angelo, Concetta, Cosmo, Elio, Pasquale, Rocco, Sisto.*

Rauch (3732) German, Swiss German, and Jewish (Ashkenazic): **1.** variant of RAU. **2.** perhaps an occupational nickname for a blacksmith or charcoal burner, from Middle High German *rouch*, German

Rauch 'smoke', or, in the case of the German name, a status name or nickname relating to a hearth tax (i.e. a tax that was calculated according to the number of fireplaces in each individual home).

GIVEN NAMES German 4%. *Otto* (6), *Helmut* (5), *Kurt* (4), *Erwin* (2), *Franz* (2), *Hans* (2), *Heinz* (2), *Horst* (2), *Wilfried* (2), *Angelika, Dieter, Elke.*

Raudabaugh (133) Americanized spelling of German **Rautenbach**, a habitational name from a farm so named in Westphalia, or of **Rothenbach**, from a place in northern Hesse.

Raudenbush (232) Americanized spelling of German **Raudenbusch**, from Middle High German *rūte* 'rue' (also various other plants) + *busch* 'bush', hence a metonymic occupational name for a gardener or herbalist, or perhaps a habitational name derived from a house sign.

Raue (139) German: variant of RAU.

GIVEN NAMES German 7%. *Kurt, Siegfried.*

Rauen (366) German: **1.** variant of RAU 1. **2.** perhaps topographic name from a place named *die kalte Raue*, in northern Germany denoting a wild, wooded area.

GIVEN NAMES German 4%. *Kurt* (2), *Mathias, Matthias.*

Rauer (178) German: **1.** from Middle High German *rūh* 'rough', a nickname for an unkempt individual. **2.** in some instances a variant of RAUNER 1.

GIVEN NAMES German 10%. *Alfons, Hans, Hedwig, Heinz, Otto.*

Rauf (140) Muslim: from a personal name based on Arabic *ra'ūf* 'compassionate'. *Al-Ra'ūf* 'the Compassionate' is one of the attributes of Allah. This name is found in combinations such as *'Abd al-Ra'ūf* 'servant of the Compassionate'.

GIVEN NAMES Muslim 64%. *Abdul* (22), *Abdur* (2), *Ali* (2), *Azhar* (2), *Imran* (2), *Najam* (2), *Shaheena* (2), *Shahid* (2), *Tahir* (2), *Umar* (2), *Zahid* (2), *Abida.*

Raught (137) **1.** Americanized form of German RATH. **2.** Possibly also a respelling of English **Rought** (unexplained).

Rauh (653) German: variant of RAU.

GIVEN NAMES German 4%. *Helmut* (2), *Erwin, Fritz, Kurt, Maximilian, Wolf.*

Raulerson (878) **1.** Variant of English RAWLINSON. **2.** Perhaps also an altered spelling of English ROLLERSON.

Rauls (291) German: patronymic from a reduced form of the Germanic personal name *Radulf*, composed of *rāt* 'counsel' + *wolf* 'wolf'.

Raulston (470) Scottish: variant of RALSTON.

Raum (224) German: **1.** habitational name from any of the places so called, for example in Saxony. **2.** from a short form of a Germanic personal name formed with *hrōm, hruom* 'fame'.

Raun (160) **1.** Irish: variant of ROWAN. **2.** German and Danish: habitational name from a place so named near Plauen, eastern Germany. **3.** Danish: nickname from *ravn* 'raven'.

GIVEN NAMES German 4%. *Eldred, Frieda.*

Rauner (131) **1.** German: nickname for a gossipmonger or rumormonger, from Middle High German *rūner* 'whisperer', 'slanderer'. **2.** German: habitational name for someone from Raun near Plauen or from Hohenraunau (formerly Raun) in Allgäu.

Raup (281) German: **1.** of uncertain origin, possibly a nickname from *rūpe* 'uncouth'. **2.** variant of RAUPP 2.

Raupp (299) German: **1.** variant of RAUP 1. **2.** derogatory nickname for night watchmen and vintners, from a slang word of uncertain origin.

Raus (170) German: nickname for a noisy or raucous person, from Middle High German *rūz* 'noise'.

GIVEN NAME German 5%. *Harro.*

Rausch (3161) German: **1.** nickname for a noisy person, from a noun derivative of Middle High German *rūschen* 'to make a noise'. **2.** topographic name for someone who lived by a swamp, from Middle High German *rusch(e)* 'reed'.

Rauschenbach (115) German: probably a habitational name from any of several places so named in Saxony, Silesia, and Bohemia.

GIVEN NAMES German 14%. *Otto* (2), *Armin, Hans, Heinz, Kurt.*

Rauschenberg (110) German: habitational name from any of several places so named in Westphalia, Hesse, and Bavaria.

GIVEN NAMES German 10%. *Fritz, Kurt.*

Rauschenberger (122) German: habitational name for someone from a place called Rauschenberg (see RAUSCHENBERG).

GIVEN NAMES German 7%. *Dieter, Hans, Otto.*

Rauscher (933) German: **1.** habitational name for someone from Rausch in Bavaria or from Rauscha in Silesia or from Rausche in the former East Prussia. **2.** variant of RAUSCH with the addition of the agent suffix -*er*.

GIVEN NAMES German 6%. *Kurt* (5), *Alois* (2), *Dieter, Erna, Fritz, Gerhard, Guenter, Hans, Herta, Ignatz, Reinhold, Wolfgang.*

Rauseo (108) Italian: reduced form of **Raguseo**, a habitational name for someone from Ragusa (Dubrovnik) in Croatia. In many regions of Italy *raguseo* could also mean 'bad boy', or 'rough person', or 'stingy', and the surname may have arisen from a nickname from any of these senses.

GIVEN NAMES Italian 14%. *Angelo, Antonio, Salvatore, Savino, Vito.*

Rauser (192) German: nickname for a noisy person, from an agent derivative of Middle High German *rūsen* 'to make a noise', 'to move noisily' or from Early New High German *raussen* 'to snore'.

GIVEN NAMES German 9%. *Erhard, Gerhard, Gottlieb, Gunter, Gunther, Kurt.*

Rautenberg (164) German: habitational name from any of the places so called, for example in Thuringia.

GIVEN NAMES German 14%; Scandinavian 5%. *Kurt* (2), *Erwin, Hans, Helmuth, Ingo, Konrad, Rainer.*

Rauth (266) South German (Bavaria, Tyrol): **1.** from Middle High German *(ge)riute* 'clearing', hence a topographic name for someone who lived in a clearing or occupational name for a clearer of woodland, or a habitational name from a place so named in Bavaria. **2.** American spelling of RATH.

Rautio (246) Finnish: occupational name from *rautio* 'smith'. Found chiefly in central and western Finland.

GIVEN NAMES Finnish 8%; German 4%. *Ahti, Arvo, Olli, Tapio, Tyyne, Vilho, Waino, Weikko; Eldred, Ilse, Otto.*

Raval (183) Indian (Panjab): Hindu (Arora) and Sikh name meaning 'king' or 'commander', from *rāva* 'king' (Sanskrit *rājā*) + the suffix -*l*. It is based on the name of an Arora clan.

GIVEN NAMES Indian 83%. *Bharat* (4), *Pravin* (3), *Rajendra* (3), *Atul* (2), *Dinesh* (2), *Girish* (2), *Harshad* (2), *Kishor* (2), *Mahendra* (2), *Mahesh* (2), *Pankaj* (2), *Parag* (2).

Ravan (144) Variant of English, Scottish, or German RAVEN.

Rave (260) **1.** North German and Dutch: from Middle Low German *rave(n)*, Dutch *raaf* 'raven', applied as a nickname for a thievish or dark-haired person. **2.** Catalan or Spanish: unexplained; possibly from Catalan *rave* 'rape' (the plant), or a habitational name from Rabé in Burgos.

GIVEN NAMES Spanish 5%. *Jaime* (3), *Alejandro, Andres, Jose, Juan, Mario, Rodrigo, Valeria.*

Ravel (127) **1.** French: metonymic occupational name for a producer or seller of oilseed rape, from a diminutive of *rave* 'rape'. **2.** Indian: variant of RAVAL.

GIVEN NAMES Indian 8%; French 5%. *Kartik, Mihir, Murali, Rajendra; Jacques* (2), *Pierre.*

Raveling (150) German (Westphalia): nickname or patronymic from Middle Low German *rave(n)* 'raven' (see RAVE).

Ravelo (279) Galician and Spanish: habitational name from either of two places called Ravelo, in Pontevedra, Galicia, and Tenerife.

GIVEN NAMES Spanish 55%. *Jorge* (6), *Manuel* (6), *Raul* (6), *Carlos* (5), *Jose* (4), *Pedro* (4), *Rafael* (4), *Ramon* (4), *Francisco* (3), *Juan* (3), *Luis* (3), *Ricardo* (3).

Raven (993) **1.** English and Scottish: from Middle English *raven*, used as a nickname for a thievish or dark-haired person. In some cases it may be from a personal name derived from this word, a survival into Middle English of the Old Norse byname *Hrafn* or of an Old English cognate name

(Hræfn). A few early forms such as William *atte* Raven (London 1344) suggest that it may also in part be derived from a house sign. **2.** North German: from Middle Low German *rave(n)* 'raven', a nickname or an old personal name. Compare 1 above.

Ravencraft (112) Variant of English RAVENSCROFT.

Ravenel (183) French: **1.** habitational name from Ravenel in Oise. **2.** metonymic occupational name for a grower or seller of horseradish, from a diminutive of Old French *ravene* 'horseradish' (Latin *raphanus*). This name is also established in Switzerland, and may have been brought to the U.S. from there.

Ravenell (250) **1.** Variant spelling of French RAVENEL. **2.** Possibly English, a variant of **Ravenhall**, **Ravenhill**, or **Revnell**, either from an Old Norse female personal name *Hrafnhildr* (from elements meaning 'raven' + 'battle') or a habitational name from Ravenhill in North Yorkshire.

Ravenelle (126) French: variant (feminine form) of RAVENEL 1.

GIVEN NAMES French 12%. *Andre, Gaetan, Normand, Raoul.*

Ravens (120) English and Scottish: patronymic from RAVEN.

Ravenscraft (191) Variant of English RAVENSCROFT.

Ravenscroft (392) English: habitational name from Ravenscroft, a place in Cheshire, named from the genitive case of the Old English byname *Hræfn* 'raven' + Old English *croft* 'paddock', 'smallholding'.

Raver (535) Probably an Americanized spelling of German **Röver** (see ROEVER).

Ravert (130) German: variant of RAVER.

Ravi (128) Indian (southern states): Hindu name, from Sanskrit *ravi* 'sun'. This is only a given name in India, but has come to be used as a family name in the U.S.

GIVEN NAMES Indian 82%. *Prasad* (4), *Gayathri* (2), *Kumar* (2), *Natarajan* (2), *Naveen* (2), *Rajagopal* (2), *Raju* (2), *Bala, Geetha, Gopal, Hema, Hemanth.*

Ravin (141) Jewish (eastern Ashkenazic): status name, from Russian *ravvin* 'rabbi' (ultimately from Hebrew *rav*).

GIVEN NAMES Jewish 14%; Russian 5%. *Noach* (2), *Rakhil, Semen, Yael; Mikhail, Yefim, Yevgeny.*

Ravitz (195) Jewish (eastern Ashkenazic): habitational name from Rawicz (German *Rawitsch*) in the province of Poznań, Poland.

GIVEN NAMES Jewish 8%. *Dov, Eliezer, Shlomo, Sol, Tovah, Zelman.*

Raw (143) English: **1.** from a medieval personal name, a variant of RALPH. **2.** topographic name for someone who lived at a row (a hedgerow or a row of houses), from northern Middle English *raw* 'row', Old English *rāw*.

GIVEN NAME French 4%. *Andre.*

Rawding (173) English (East Midlands): possibly a variant of RAWDON.

Rawdon (251) English: habitational name from the place so called in West Yorkshire, named with Old Norse *rauðr* 'red' + *dūn* 'hill'.

Rawe (212) **1.** English: variant spelling of RAW. **2.** North German: variant of RAVE.
GIVEN NAME German 4%. *Otto*.

Rawl (218) Irish: reduced Anglicized form of Gaelic **Ó Raghaill** 'descendant of *Raghall*'.

Rawle (118) English: variant of RALPH.
FOREBEARS A Francis Rawle from the parish of St. Juliot in Cornwall, England, was recorded as living in Plymouth, MA, in 1660. Devout Quakers seeking to escape persecution, the family emigrated to PA in 1686, bringing with them a deed from William Penn for a tract of 2,500 acres of land, which was subsequently located in Plymouth township, Philadelphia (now Montgomery) Co. His son, who had six sons himself, was a political economist and one of the first people to write on the subject and its local applications in America.

Rawleigh (143) Altered spelling of English RALEIGH, reflecting a common pronunciation.
GIVEN NAMES German 5%. *Eldred, Erwin, Orlo*.

Rawles (341) English: variant of RAWLS.

Rawley (439) English: variant of RALEIGH.

Rawling (162) English: from the Middle English personal name *Rawlin*, Old French *Raulin*, a double diminutive of RAW 1, with the Anglo-Norman French suffixes *-el* and *-in*.

Rawlings (3394) English: patronymic from RAWLING.

Rawlins (2227) English: patronymic from RAWLING.

Rawlinson (790) English: patronymic from RAWLING.

Rawls (3701) English: patronymic from a medieval form of the personal name RALPH.

Rawn (178) Variant spelling of Irish ROWAN.

Rawnsley (119) English: habitational name from a place in Staffordshire called Rawnsley.

Rawski (159) Polish: habitational name for someone from places called Rawa in Lublin and Skierniewice voivodeships.
GIVEN NAMES Polish 6%. *Casimir, Teofil*.

Rawson (2476) English (chiefly Yorkshire): patronymic from RAW 1.

Raxter (130) Possibly of English origin: unexplained.

Ray (46185) **1.** English (of Norman origin): nickname denoting someone who behaved in a regal fashion or who had earned the title in some contest of skill or by presiding over festivities, from Old French *rey, roy* 'king'. Occasionally this was used as a personal name. **2.** English: nickname for a timid person, from Middle English *ray* 'female roe deer' or northern Middle English *ray* 'roebuck'. **3.** English: variant of RYE (1 and 2). **4.** English: habitational name, a variant spelling of WRAY. **5.** Scottish: reduced and altered form of MCRAE. **6.** French: from a noun derivative of Old French *raier* 'to gush, stream, or pour', hence a topographic name for someone who lived near a spring or rushing stream, or a habitational name from a place called Ray. **7.** Indian: variant of RAI.

Raya (553) **1.** Galician and Spanish: possibly a habitational name from Raya in Galicia or in Albacete and Murcia provinces. **2.** Spanish: possibly a topographic name from Spanish *raya* 'line', denoting the boundary between two countries or provinces.
GIVEN NAMES Spanish 50%. *Jose* (13), *Miguel* (8), *Jesus* (6), *Luis* (6), *Manuel* (6), *Roberto* (6), *Juan* (5), *Salvador* (4), *Armando* (3), *Guadalupe* (3), *Guillermo* (3), *Jose Luis* (3); *Antonio* (9), *Federico, Filiberto, Gasper, Leonardo*.

Rayas (120) Spanish: apparently from the plural of *raya*, which has numerous meanings, including 'boundary', 'strip', '(hair) parting', 'ray' (the fish) (compare RAYA).
GIVEN NAMES Spanish 53%. *Juan* (4), *Francisco* (2), *Gerardo* (2), *Jesus* (2), *Jose* (2), *Ladislao* (2), *Luis* (2), *Pedro* (2), *Ricardo* (2), *Roberto* (2), *Rodolfo* (2), *Angeles*.

Raybon (460) English: nickname for a swift runner, from northern Middle English *ray* 'roebuck' + *bane, bone* 'bone', 'leg'.

Rayborn (680) Altered spelling of Scottish RAYBURN or possibly of German **Rehborn**, a topographic name meaning 'deer spring or well'.

Raybould (136) English (of Norman origin): from an Old French personal name, *Rainbaut*, composed of the Germanic elements *ragin* 'counsel' + *bald* 'bold', 'brave'. Compare RAINBOW, RAMMEL.

Raybourn (186) English: see RAYBORN.

Raybuck (274) **1.** Americanized form of German **Rehbock** (see REBUCK) **2.** northern English: variant of ROEBUCK. See also RAY 2.

Rayburn (3108) Scottish: habitational name from Raeburn, a place in the Scottish Borders named from northern Middle English *ray* 'roebuck' + *burn* 'stream'.

Raycraft (149) English: variant of RYCROFT.

Rayder (116) Probaby an altered spelling of English RIDER or German **Räder** (see RADER, REDER).

Raye (521) English: variant spelling of RAY 1–4.

Rayer (156) **1.** English: from the Norman personal name *Raher*, composed of the Germanic elements *rad* 'counsel', 'advice' + *hari, heri* 'army'. **2.** French: occupational name for a barber, Old French *raier* (from *rère* 'to shave').

Rayes (158) **1.** English: unexplained. **2.** variant of Spanish RAYAS. **3.** Muslim: variant of RAIS.
GIVEN NAMES Spanish 14%; Muslim 11%; French 5%. *Jose* (3), *Ana, Asuncion, Carlos, Carolina, Genaro, Hermelo, Jose Natividad, Lilia, Luz, Mauricio, Modesto*; *Hassan* (2), *Ayman, Fouad, Kais, Khaldoun, Mohamed, Rania, Shamoon, Soha, Tamer, Wasim*; *Andre, Camille*.

Rayfield (925) English (Kent): origin unidentified; probably a habitational name from a lost or unidentified place, perhaps an altered form of RAYFORD.

Rayford (840) **1.** English (also **Wrayford**): topographic name for someone who lived by a ford on the Wray river. **2.** Probably an Americanized spelling of German **Reifarth, Raifarth**, or **Reifert**, from a Germanic personal name composed of the elements *rīc* 'power(ful)' + *frid-* 'peace'.

Raygor (126) Probably a respelling of German RAGER 1 or REGER.

Raygoza (246) Variant spelling of Galician **Reigosa**, a habitational name from either of two places called Reigosa, in Lugo and Pontevedra provinces.
GIVEN NAMES Spanish 60%. *Jose* (17), *Juan* (6), *Luis* (5), *Rafael* (4), *Ramon* (4), *Raul* (4), *Roberto* (4), *Arturo* (3), *Ignacio* (3), *Jesus* (3), *Manuel* (3), *Alicia* (2); *Antonio* (4), *Lucio, Marco, Vita*.

Rayhill (131) Irish: variant of RAHILL.

Rayl (680) Perhaps an Americanized spelling of German REHL.

Rayle (339) Perhaps an Americanized spelling of German REHL.

Rayman (506) **1.** English: topographic name, a variant of RYE 1 and 2, with the addition of 'man'. **2.** German (**Raymann**) and Dutch: from a Germanic personal name composed of the elements *rād* 'counsel' + *man* 'man'. **3.** Probably an Americanized spelling of German REHMANN. **4.** Jewish (eastern Ashkenazic): ornamental name from German *Reinmann* or central Yiddish *raynman* 'pure man'.

Rayment (142) English (eastern): variant of RAYMOND.

Raymer (1662) Probably an altered spelling of German **Römer** (see ROEMER), REHMER, or possibly REIMER.

Raymo (266) Altered spelling of southern Italian **Raimo**, a reduced form of the personal name *Raimondo*. Compare RAYMOND.

Raymon (102) French: variant of RAYMOND.

Raymond (14002) **1.** English and French: from the Norman personal name *Raimund*, composed of the Germanic elements *ragin* 'advice', 'counsel' + *mund* 'protection'. **2.** Americanized spelling of German **Raimund**, a cognate of 1.
FOREBEARS A Raymond, also called Passe-Campagne, from the Angoumois region of

France is documented in La Prairie, Quebec, in 1692.

GIVEN NAMES French 4%. *Normand* (9), *Andre* (8), *Camille* (5), *Jacques* (5), *Lucien* (5), *Armand* (4), *Francois* (4), *Emile* (3), *Fernand* (3), *Gilles* (3), *Laurier* (3), *Marcel* (3).

Raymundo (232) Spanish and Portuguese: from the personal name *Raymundo* (see RAYMOND).

GIVEN NAMES Spanish 47%; Portuguese 12%. *Jose* (9), *Fernando* (3), *Manuel* (3), *Carlos* (2), *Jaime* (2), *Jorge* (2), *Juan* (2), *Raul* (2), *Alberto*, *Alfredo*, *Ana*, *Anselma*; *Vasco*, *Wenceslao*.

Rayne (252) **1.** English: variant of RAINE 1 and 2. **2.** French: variant of RAINE 3.

Rayner (1475) **1.** English: from the Norman personal name *Rainer*, composed of the Germanic elements *ragin* 'counsel' + *hari*, *heri* 'army' **2.** Jewish (Ashkenazic): ornamental name from an inflected form of German *rein* or central Yiddish *rayn* 'pure'. **3.** Probably also an altered spelling of German REINER.

Raynes (665) English: **1.** habitational name from Rayne in Essex or Raines in Derbyshire. **2.** (of Norman origin): habitational name from Rennes in Normandy.

Rayno (151) Origin unidentified; possibly a respelling of French **Raineau**, a nickname from a diminutive of Old French *raine* 'frog' (Latin *rana*).

Raynolds (113) English: variant spelling of REYNOLDS.

Raynor (2783) English: variant spelling of RAYNER 1.

Rayo (170) **1.** Catalan (**Rayó**): variant of **Relló**, nickname from *relló*, a derivative of *rella* 'ploughshare'. **2.** Spanish (from Asturian-Leonese): Castilianized variant of **Rayu**, habitational name from El Rayu, a town in Asturies. **3.** Spanish: possibly from *rayo* 'flash of lightning', which may be a nickname in the sense 'lively'.

GIVEN NAMES Spanish 48%. *Francisco* (3), *Andres* (2), *Armando* (2), *Enrique* (2), *Felipe* (2), *Francisca* (2), *Adelaido*, *Adriana*, *Alvaro*, *Ascencion*, *Augusto*, *Bulmaro*; *Ciro*, *Fructuoso*, *Heriberto*, *Lorenzo*.

Rayon (128) **1.** Spanish (**Rayón**): augmentative of *rayo* 'ray', 'beam', 'shaft (of light)'; its application as a surname is unclear. **2.** French: topographic name for someone who lived by cultivated land, from a variant of *roion* 'furrow'. **3.** French: from a pet form of a personal name, either *Rahier* (see RAYER 1), or a Frenchified form of *Rado* (a short form of a compound Germanic personal name).

GIVEN NAMES Spanish 17%. *Jaime* (2), *Manuel* (2), *Alejandra*, *Armando*, *Blanca*, *Conrado*, *Eduardo*, *Enrique*, *Graciela*, *Guadalupe*, *Lurdes*.

Rayos (140) Spanish: from the plural of *rayo* 'ray (of light)' or 'lightning', hence

perhaps a nickname for a cheerful or quick person.

GIVEN NAMES Spanish 38%. *Jose* (3), *Efren* (2), *Francisco* (2), *Guadalupe* (2), *Juan* (2), *Luis* (2), *Alfonso*, *Andres*, *Armando*, *Carmelita*, *Cruz*, *Esperanza*, *Heriberto*, *Ireneo*, *Nino*.

Rayson (186) English: patronymic from the personal name RAY.

Raysor (206) Perhaps an altered spelling of English and German RASOR, or of German REISER or **Röser** (see ROESER).

Raz (223) Jewish: of uncertain origin; possibly a modern Hebrew name meaning 'secret'.

GIVEN NAMES Jewish 24%. *Avraham* (3), *Yael* (3), *Moshe* (2), *Anat*, *Avi*, *Avinoam*, *Avshalom*, *Mordechai*, *Naftali*, *Ofra*, *Ori*, *Rivka*.

Raza (316) Iranian: variant of REZA.

GIVEN NAMES Muslim 82%. *Syed* (55), *Ali* (10), *Mohammad* (7), *Asif* (5), *Mohammed* (5), *Abbas* (4), *Babar* (4), *Hassan* (4), *Abdul* (3), *Abid* (3), *Hashim* (3), *Saleem* (3).

Razavi (139) Iranian: variant of RIZVI.

GIVEN NAMES Muslim 77%. *Amir* (9), *Ali* (7), *Hossein* (5), *Mehdi* (3), *Abbas* (2), *Behzad* (2), *Masoud* (2), *Ramin* (2), *Ahmad*, *Asghar*, *Azam*, *Behnaz*.

Razey (101) English (Wiltshire): unexplained. Compare RACY, RACEY, RASEY.

Razo (910) Galician: perhaps a habitational name from Razo in A Coruña province, Galicia. However, the concentration of the surname in Andalusia suggests that another source should be sought.

GIVEN NAMES Spanish 47%. *Jose* (25), *Francisco* (10), *Juan* (10), *Manuel* (10), *Miguel* (10), *Carlos* (7), *Jorge* (7), *Ruben* (7), *Armando* (6), *Alfredo* (5), *Javier* (5), *Ramon* (5).

Razon (112) Spanish and Jewish (Sephardic): nickname from *razón* 'reason'.

GIVEN NAMES Spanish 35%; Jewish 4%. *Pedro* (2), *Ricardo* (2), *Ador*, *Adriano*, *Caridad*, *Carlito*, *Conrado*, *Domingo*, *Ernesto*, *Felipe*, *Fernando*, *Humberto*; *Benzion* (2).

Razor (269) Apparently an altered spelling of RASOR.

Razza (113) Italian: **1.** probably a metonymic occupational name for a herbalist, from a plant name which denoted different species in different dialects, for example charlock or rock cress (Sicily), rock rose (Modena), and the bramble, or the medicinal plant smilax, in certain other regions. **2.** in the Neapolitan region the word was used for certain kinds of fish, the weever, perch, or pike, and the surname probably arose from a nickname for someone with fish-like characteristics, or from a metonymic occupational name for a fisherman. **3.** possibly a habitational name from Razzà, a locality of Brancaleone in Reggio Calabria.

GIVEN NAMES Italian 26%. *Angelo* (2), *Carmine* (2), *Aldo*, *Carlo*, *Giacomino*, *Luca*, *Sal*, *Salvatore*, *Vito*.

Razzano (354) Italian: probably a habitational name from a place named Razzano.

GIVEN NAMES Italian 17%. *Pasquale* (9), *Angelo* (2), *Agostino*, *Carmine*, *Caterina*, *Sal*, *Vittorio*.

Re (664) **1.** Italian (**Ré**): from *re* 'king', possibly denoting someone who lived by or worked in a royal court, or someone who behaved in regal fashion, had played the part of a king in a pageant, or who had earned the title in some contest of skill. **2.** Northern Italian (**Re**): habitational name for someone from a place named with *ré* 'river', for example Re in Novara. **3.** French (**Ré**): habitational name from a place so named in Indre or from the Ile de Ré.

GIVEN NAMES Italian 12%. *Salvatore* (4), *Vito* (3), *Antonio* (2), *Gaspare* (2), *Gennaro* (2), *Aldo*, *Angelo*, *Antonella*, *Carlo*, *Enrico*, *Geno*.

Rea (4793) **1.** English: variant of RYE 1 and 2. **2.** reduced form of Scottish MCREA.

Reach (388) **1.** Scottish: nickname for someone with streaks of gray or white hair, from Gaelic *riabhach* 'brindled', 'grayish'. **2.** English: habitational name from either of two places called Reach, in Bedfordshire and Cambridgeshire, from Old English *rǣc* 'raised strip of land or other linear feature' (in the case of the Cambridgeshire name referring to Devil's Dyke, a post-Roman earthwork).

Read (7387) English: **1.** nickname for a person with red hair or a ruddy complexion, from Middle English *re(a)d* 'red'. **2.** topographic name for someone who lived in a clearing, from an unattested Old English *rīed*, *rȳd* 'woodland clearing'. **3.** habitational name from various places: Read in Lancashire, the name of which is a contracted form of Old English *rǣghēafod*, from *rǣge* 'female roe deer', 'she-goat' + *hēafod* 'head(land)'; Rede in Suffolk, so called from Old English *hrēod* 'reeds'; or Reed in Hertfordshire, so called from an Old English *ryhð* 'brushwood'.

FOREBEARS A family called Read were established in America in the early 18th century by John Read, who was born in Dublin, sixth in descent from Sir Thomas Read of Berkshire, England. His son, George Read (1733–98), was one of the signers of the Declaration of Independence, and as a lawyer helped frame the Constitution.

Reade (580) English: variant spelling of READ 1.

Readel (100) **1.** Probably an altered spelling of German RIEDEL or REIDEL. **2.** Alternatively, perhaps, an altered spelling of English **Reddell**, which is probably a variant of RIDDELL or RIDDLE.

Reader (1154) **1.** English: occupational name for someone who thatched cottages with reeds, from an agent derivative of Middle English *rēd(en)* 'to cover with reeds'. **2.** Americanized spelling of German RIEDER.

Reading (1209) English: **1.** habitational name from the county seat of Berkshire, which gets its name from Old English *Rēadingas* 'people of *Rēad(a)*', a byname meaning 'red'. **2.** topographic name for someone who lived in a clearing, an unattested Old English *ryding*.

Readinger (223) Americanized spelling of German RIEDINGER or REDINGER.

Readling (105) Of German origin: probably a respelling of **Riedling** (see RIDLING) or possibly of **Redling**, a habitational name from Redling in Bavaria.

Readus (118) Of uncertain origin. **1.** Possibly a reduced form of English **Redhouse** (see REDUS). **2.** Alternatively, perhaps, an altered form of an unidentified German name.

Ready (1868) **1.** English: nickname for a provident man, from Middle English *readi* 'prepared', 'prompt'. **2.** Irish: variant of REDDY. **3.** Scottish: variant of **Reedie**.

Reagan (6020) Irish: variant spelling of REGAN.

Reager (106) Altered spelling of German RIEGER or REGER.

Reagh (106) **1.** Irish: Anglicized form of Gaelic **Riabhach**, which MacLysaght describes as an adjectival surname (meaning 'gray' or 'brindled') that "took the place of an hereditary one". **2.** Possibly an altered spelling of German RECH.
GIVEN NAMES German 6%. *Kurt, Ute.*

Reagin (304) Irish: variant spelling of REGAN.

Reagle (364) Americanized spelling of German RIEGEL.

Reagor (263) Probably an Americanized spelling of German RIEGER or REGER.

Real (1131) **1.** Spanish, Catalan, Portuguese, and Galicia: habitational name from any of the numerous places called Real; those in Galicia and Portugal being named from *real* 'royal', while those in southern Spain and Catalonia are named in part from *real* meaning 'encampment', 'rural property' (Arabic *raḥāl* 'farmhouse', 'cabin'). **2.** French (**Réal**) and Spanish: from southern French *réal*, Spanish *real* 'royal', hence a nickname for someone who behaved in a regal manner or an occupational name for someone in the service of the king. **3.** French (**Réal**): habitational name from any of various places named for having been part of a royal domain (see REAU, REAUX). **4.** Probably an Americanized spelling of German RIEHL, RIEL, or **Rühl** (see RUEHL).
GIVEN NAMES Spanish 22%; Portuguese 4%. *Juan* (7), *Guillermo* (6), *Jose* (6), *Carlos* (4), *Francisco* (4), *Luis* (4), *Ricardo* (4), *Alberto* (3), *Armando* (3), *Blanca* (3), *Lourdes* (3), *Manuel* (3); *Joao, Joaquim.*

Reale (1117) Italian: from *reale* 'royal', either an occupational name for someone in the service of a king or a nickname for someone who behaved in a regal manner.
GIVEN NAMES Italian 15%. *Salvatore* (9), *Gaetano* (4), *Rocco* (3), *Antonio* (2), *Cosmo* (2), *Gino* (2), *Guiseppe* (2), *Pasquale* (2), *Agostino, Angelo, Carmela, Carmello.*

Reali (239) Italian: patronymic or plural form of REALE.
GIVEN NAMES Italian 15%. *Amedeo* (2), *Antonio* (2), *Amerigo, Angelo, Arcangelo, Arduino, Enio, Gino, Giovanni, Guido, Nino.*

Realmuto (145) Italian (Sicily): habitational name from Racalmuto in Agrigento. There has been confusion with a place called Regalbuto in Enna.
GIVEN NAMES Italian 22%. *Salvatore* (6), *Antonio, Carmela, Cesare, Leonardo, Vincenzo.*

Ream (2285) Perhaps an Americanized spelling of German RIEHM or **Röhm** (see ROEHM).

Reamer (827) Respelling of German and Jewish RIEMER.

Reames (1112) English (of Norman origin): habitational name from Rames in Seine-Inférieure.

Reams (1846) English: variant spelling of REAMES.

Reamy (274) English: unexplained.

Reaney (243) **1.** Scottish and Irish: variant of RAINEY. **2.** English (Sheffield): habitational name from Ranah Stones in Thurlstone, South Yorkshire, named with Old Norse *hrafn* 'raven' + *haugr* 'hill'.

Reap (264) **1.** English: variant spelling of REEP 2. **2.** Irish (County Mayo): reduced Anglicized form of Gaelic **Ó Réabaigh** 'descendant of *Réabach*', a personal name probably derived from *réabach* 'tearing'.

Reape (108) Variant of English and Irish REAP.

Rear (128) English: unexplained.

Rearden (316) Irish: see RIORDAN.

Reardon (5779) Irish: see RIORDAN.
GIVEN NAMES Irish 4%. *Brendan* (2), *Patrick Michael, Tighe.*

Rearick (722) Americanized spelling of German **Röhrich** (see ROEHRIG).

Reas (175) Altered spelling of German RIES, RIESS.

Rease (210) Welsh: variant spelling of REESE.

Reaser (357) Probably an Americanized spelling of German RIESER.

Reasner (168) Probably an Americanized spelling of German **Riesner**, a variant of REISNER.
GIVEN NAME French 4%. *Pierre.*

Reason (681) **1.** English: variant of RAISON. **2.** Probably also an Americanized spelling of German RIESEN.

Reasoner (782) **1.** Perhaps a translation of French **Raisonnier**, a derivative of RAISON. **2.** Possibly an Americanized spelling of German and **Riesener**, patronymic from the personal name *Riese, Rizo* meaning 'giant' or of German **Riesner** (see REASNER).

Reasonover (163) Altered spelling of REISENAUER.

Reasons (251) English (Somerset): probably a variant of RAISON.

Reasor (522) See REASER.

Reath (148) Probably an altered spelling of Scottish REITH or German RIETH.

Reau (102) French (**Réau**): variant of **Réal** 2 or 3, in the latter case probably referring specifically to Réau in Seine-et-Marne.

Reaume (404) French (**Réaume**): from Old French *réalme* 'kingdom'; a medieval regional name for someone who came from the Kingdom of France as opposed to the wider empire, for example on the other side of the Rhône.
FOREBEARS A Réaume from Paris is documented in Quebec City in 1665, with the secondary surname De Paris; another, from La Rochelle, France, was in Quebec City in 1665.
GIVEN NAMES French 4%. *Andre, Raoul, Vernice.*

Reaux (207) French (**Réaux**): French (**Réau**): variant of **Réal** 2 or 3, in the latter case probably referring specifically to Réaux in Charente-Maritime.
FOREBEARS The name is found in Canada as Rheault, Rault; an immigrant from La Rochelle, France, was in Trois-Rivières, Quebec, by 1664. Another line known as **Durault**, from the Saintonge region of France, was in Cap Madeleine by 1690, with the secondary surnames LAVERGNE and Saintongeais. Other associated secondary surnames include ALEXANDRE and Morinville.
GIVEN NAMES French 7%. *Camille, Curley.*

Reaver (182) English: occupational name for a robber, marauder, or pirate.

Reaves (4772) English: variant spelling of REEVES.

Reavey (131) **1.** Irish: reduced Anglicized form of Gaelic **Ó Riabhaigh** 'descendant of *Riabhach*', a byname meaning 'brindled', 'grizzled'. **2.** Possibly an altered spelling of German RIEWE.

Reavis (2051) English: variant of REEVES.

Reay (406) English: variant of RYE 1 and 2.

Reback (160) **1.** Variant spelling of Jewish and Slavic RYBAK. **2.** Variant spelling of German **Rehbock** (see REBUCK) 'roe deer' or of **Rehbach**, a topographic or habitational name meaning 'deer stream'.
GIVEN NAMES Jewish 4%. *Miriam, Nili.*

Rebar (214) Probably an altered spelling of German REBER or ROEBER.

Rebecca (101) Italian and Scottish: from the female personal name *Rebecca* (Hebrew *Ribqah*).

GIVEN NAMES Italian 9%. *Domenic, Gino, Vito.*

Rebeck (159) Dutch: metronymic from the female personal name REBECCA.

Rebel (231) **1.** German: from a Germanic personal name formed with *(h)rab-* 'raven'. **2.** French: from a variant of Old French *rebelle* 'rebel', hence a nickname for someone with little respect for authority or someone who had taken part in a rebellion.

Rebello (586) **1.** Variant of Portuguese REBELO. In this spelling, the name is also found in western India, where it was taken by Portuguese colonists. **2.** Catalan (**Rebelló**): variant of **Revelló** (see REVELLO).

GIVEN NAMES Spanish 9%; Portuguese 7%. *Manuel* (19), *Jose* (3), *Mario* (3), *Carlos* (2), *Arlita, Celso, Deodato, Ernesto, Fernanda, Gerardo, Horacio, Joaquin*; *Joaquim* (3), *Duarte, Marcio.*

Rebelo (236) Portuguese: habitational name from any of the places named Rebelo in Portugal.

GIVEN NAMES Spanish 29%; Portuguese 24%; Italian 10%. *Antonio* (12), *Jose* (11), *Manuel* (9), *Mario* (3), *Americo* (2), *Ana* (2), *Armindo* (2), *Luis* (2), *Altino, Carlos, Dionisio, Domingos, Edmundo*; *Joaquim* (3), *Amadeu* (2), *Vasco* (2), *Goncalo, Guilherme, Joao, Messias, Serafim.*

Reber (2098) **1.** German and Swiss German: occupational name for a vine-dresser or vintner, from Middle High German *rebe* 'vine' + *-er* agent suffix. **2.** German and Swiss German: from a Germanic personal name, *Radobert*, formed with *rād, rāt* 'counsel', 'advice' + *berht* 'bright'.

Rebert (255) **1.** French: variant of ROBERT. **2.** German: variant of REBER.

Rebhan (129) German: from Middle High German *rephān* 'partridge', a metonymic occupational name for a hunter of partridges or a nickname for someone supposedly resembling a partridge in some way.

GIVEN NAME German 5%. *Heinz.*

Rebholz (395) German: from Middle High German *rebe* 'vine' + *holz* 'wood', i.e. 'vine-plant', probably applied as a nickname or metonymic occupational name (compare REBER 1), or in some cases a habitational name for someone living at a house distinguished by a living vine or a sign depicting a vine.

Rebich (142) **1.** Americanized spelling of German **Rebisch**, a variant of **Rabitsch**, a nickname from Old Sorbian *rjabiš* 'spotted', 'speckled', 'freckled'. **2.** Serbian and Croatian (**Rebić**): unexplained.

Rebman (465) Altered spelling of REBMANN.

Rebmann (236) German: occupational name for a vine-dresser or vintner, from Middle High German *rebe* 'vine' + *man* 'man'.

GIVEN NAMES German 7%. *Kurt* (2), *Wilhelm* (2), *Erwin.*

Rebollar (159) Spanish: habitational name from any of the places named Rebollar, for example in Cáceres or Soria, named from the collective form of *rebollo* denoting a type of oak tree.

GIVEN NAMES Spanish 62%. *Miguel* (6), *Jose* (5), *Adolfo* (3), *Raul* (3), *Alfredo* (2), *Carlos* (2), *Mateo* (2), *Roberto* (2), *Rodolfo* (2), *Tomas* (2), *Adolfina, Alberto*; *Antonio, Enedino, Leonardo, Salustia.*

Rebolledo (118) Spanish: habitational name from any of various places named Rebolledo, for example Rebolledo de la Torre in Burgos, from *rebollo* denoting a species of oak.

GIVEN NAMES Spanish 52%. *Jose* (5), *Graciela* (2), *Pedro* (2), *Adolfo, Adriana, Alvaro, Amador, Andres, Angelina, Arturo, Carlos, Catalina*; *Antonio* (2), *Marco* (2), *Clemente, Gabino, Marino.*

Rebstock (301) German: from Middle High German *rebe* 'vine' + *stock* 'stick', 'cane', 'stem', i.e. 'vine', a metonymic occupational name for a vine-dresser or vintner, or a habitational name for someone living at a house distinguished by a living vine or a sign depicting a vine. Compare REBHOLZ.

GIVEN NAMES French 5%; German 4%. *Camille*; *Alfons, Juergen.*

Rebuck (294) Altered spelling of German **Rehbock**, probably a nickname for a hunter, from Middle High German *rēchboc* 'roebuck'.

GIVEN NAME French 4%. *Renald* (2).

Recchia (456) Italian: nickname from a reduced form of *orecchia* 'ear'.

GIVEN NAMES Italian 24%. *Vito* (6), *Domenic* (5), *Angelo* (4), *Antonio* (3), *Franco* (2), *Giovanni* (2), *Sante* (2), *Santo* (2), *Alessandro, Arduino, Carmino.*

Recchio (100) Italian: probably a shortened form of ORECCHIO or from the Salento dialect word *recchia*, also meaning 'ear'.

GIVEN NAME Italian 9%. *Rinaldo.*

Rech (649) German: **1.** from a Germanic personal name, *Recho*, a shortened form of a personal name composed with *rāhha* 'revenge'. **2.** nickname for someone who was timid or fleet of foot, from Middle High German *rēch* 'roe deer'. Compare REH. **3.** habitational name from a place near Koblenz called Rech.

Rechel (101) Variant of French RACHEL.

GIVEN NAME French 6%. *Camille.*

Recher (138) South German: **1.** occupational name for a rake maker, Middle High German *rechen*. **2.** habitational name for someone from Rech, near Remagen, Rhineland.

GIVEN NAME German 4%. *Otto.*

Rechner (143) German: **1.** occupational name from Middle High German *rechenære* 'reckoner', 'keeper of accounts'.

2. variant of RECHER 1. **3.** habitational name from a place so named near Bochum.

GIVEN NAME German 4%. *Kurt.*

Rechsteiner (118) Swiss German: probably a habitational name from Rechtenstein, near Ehingen, Swabia.

GIVEN NAMES German 19%. *Guenter* (4), *Fritz* (2), *Hans* (2).

Recht (278) **1.** German: probably a habitational name from a place so named in the Rhineland. **2.** German and Jewish (Ashkenazic): nickname for an upright person, from Middle High German *reht*, German *recht* 'straight'. As a Jewish name it is mainly of ornamental origin.

GIVEN NAMES Jewish 4%. *Emanuel, Mendel, Shoshi.*

Rechtin (107) Origin unidentified. It may be of German origin, possibly from a shortened form of a habitational name such as **Rechtenberg**, from a place so named in Baden-Württemberg.

Recine (184) Italian: probably a habitational name from Recina in Istria.

GIVEN NAMES Italian 42%. *Angelo* (3), *Carmine* (2), *Domenico* (2), *Enrico* (2), *Italo* (2), *Lorenzo* (2), *Sandro* (2), *Valentino* (2), *Alessio, Annunziato, Cesare, Domenic, Emilio, Lino, Renaldo, Ricardo, Silvana.*

Recinos (360) Hispanic: unexplained.

GIVEN NAMES Spanish 52%. *Jose* (14), *Juan* (5), *Mario* (5), *Manuel* (4), *Roberto* (4), *Alvaro* (3), *Jorge* (3), *Luis* (3), *Miguel* (3), *Blanca* (2), *Carlos* (2), *Cesar* (2); *Caesar, Elio, Eliseo, Italo, Leonardo, Marco, Romeo.*

Recio (409) **1.** Spanish: nickname for a strong or tough man, from *recio* 'strong', 'robust', 'tough'. **2.** Possibly Portuguese (**Récio**): possibly from the obsolete term *récio* 'strong', 'robust', 'tough', rather than from the personal name *Récio.*

GIVEN NAMES Spanish 47%. *Jose* (13), *Francisco* (7), *Juan* (7), *Alberto* (6), *Carlos* (5), *Luis* (4), *Altagracia* (3), *Homero* (3), *Orlando* (3), *Ricardo* (3), *Roel* (3), *Agustin* (2).

Reck (1111) **1.** German: nickname from Middle High German *recke* 'outlaw' or 'fighter'. **2.** North German and Westphalian: from Middle Low German *recke* 'marsh', 'waterlogged ground', hence a topographic name, or a habitational name from a place named with this term.

Reckard (168) Probably an altered spelling of German **Reckhard(t)**, from a Germanic personal name composed with *rag-* 'advice' + *hart* 'strong', 'brave'.

Reckart (145) Probably an altered spelling of German **Reckhard(t)**, from a Germanic personal name formed with *rag-* 'advice' + *hard* 'strong', 'brave'.

Recker (1135) **1.** North German, Frisian, and Dutch: from a form of the personal name RICHARD, or a variant of the Dutch name **Rijker**, composed of the Germanic elements *rīc* 'power(ful)' + *hari, heri* 'army'. **2.** North German: topographic name from Middle Low German *recke* 'stretch', 'route', 'hedge', or a habitational name for someone from Recke, near Osnabrück.

Reckers (142) North German, Frisian, Dutch: either a patronymic from RECKER or a Rhenish variant of the same name with an excrescent *-s*.

Reckley (106) **1.** Origin uncertain. Possibly an English habitational name from a lost or unidentifed place. **2.** Possibly a variant spelling of South German **Rechle**, a variant of the occupational name **Recher**, for someone who worked with a rake (Middle High German *reche*).

Reckling (154) North German: patronymic from the Germanic personal name *Rekolf* or *Reklef*, from *rīc* 'power(ful)' + *(w)olf* 'wolf' or *lef* 'life', 'heir'.

Recknagel (133) German (Thuringian): from Middle High German *recken* 'to raise or lift' (here in the imperative) + *nagel* 'nail', hence a metonymic occupational name for a blacksmith, or perhaps an obscene nickname (with a transferred sense for *nagel*, i.e. 'penis').
GIVEN NAMES German 8%. *Guenter, Otto.*

Reckner (299) Probably an altered spelling of RECHNER.

Recktenwald (218) German: habitational name from Recktenwald, near Saarbrücken.
GIVEN NAMES German 8%. *Diether* (3), *Jutta* (2), *Rudi.*

Recla (127) Italian: unexplained; in Italy the name occurs chiefly in Trentino-Alto Adige, near the border with Austria.

Recob (109) Possibly an altered spelling of German **Rekopp**, a variant of REHKOPF.

Recor (166) Probably an altered spelling of French RECORD.

Record (1243) **1.** English: from *Richward*, a Norman personal name composed of the Germanic elements *rīc* 'power(ful)' + *ward* 'guard'. **2.** French: from Old French *record*, *recort* 'recollection', 'account', 'testimony', and by extension 'witness', hence perhaps a nickname for someone who had given evidence in a court of law, or a metonymic occupational name for a clerk who recorded court proceedings. **3.** New England variant of French RICARD, reflecting an Americanized spelling of the Canadian pronunciation.

Records (376) English: patronymic from RECORD 1.

Recore (187) See RECOR.

Rectenwald (176) Altered spelling of German RECKTENWALD.

Rector (5298) **1.** German and Dutch: status name for the director of an institution, in particular the head of a religious house or a college. **2.** Americanized form of German RICHTER.

Recupero (197) Italian (southern, especially Sicily): from *ricupero* 'recovered', 'regained', bestowed as a personal name to a child born after the death of an elder brother.
GIVEN NAMES Italian 19%. *Salvatore* (5), *Angelo* (2), *Aldo, Emilio, Mario, Paolo, Sal, Vittorio.*

Reczek (158) Polish: nickname from *reczek* 'hamster'.
GIVEN NAMES Polish 10%. *Stanislaw* (2), *Andrzej, Tadeusz, Tomasz.*

Red (514) **1.** English (Durham): variant of READ 1. **2.** Translation of German ROTH.

Reda (821) Italian: **1.** from Old Italian relationship name *reda* 'heir'. **2.** from the feminine form of *Redo*, a reduced form of *Redolfo* or a short form of *Manfredo*, *Alfredo*, *Goffredo*, *Loffredo*, or directly from a reduced feminine form of any of these personal names.
GIVEN NAMES Italian 13%. *Antonio* (4), *Francesco* (3), *Angelo* (2), *Reno* (2), *Salvator* (2), *Salvatore* (2), *Damiano, Dante, Domenic, Domenico, Geno, Gino.*

Redburn (241) English: habitational name from Redbourn in Hertfordshire or Redbourne in Humberside (formerly Lincolnshire), named with Old English *hrēod* 'reeds' + *burna* 'stream'.

Redcay (216) Possibly an Americanized spelling of German and Polish RADKE.

Redd (3697) English: variant of READ 1.

Reddan (107) English: variant of REDDEN.
GIVEN NAME Irish 7%. *Donal.*

Reddell (423) English: **1.** from an Old English personal name, either *Rǣdweald* or *Rǣdwulf*. The first element in each is *rǣd* 'counsel', 'advice'; the final elements are *weald* 'rule' and *wulf* 'wolf'. **2.** topographic name, from Old English *(ge)ryd(d)* 'cleared' + *weald* 'woodland', 'high woodland subsequently cleared'.

Redden (3054) English: topographic name for someone who lived in a patch of cleared woodland, from Middle English *reden* 'clearing'.

Redder (257) North German: **1.** from a personal name composed of the Germanic elements *rād* 'counsel' + *heri, hari* 'army'. **2.** topographic name from Middle Low German *redder* 'path or space between two hedges', or a habitational name from a place near Schleswig named with this word.

Reddick (2721) **1.** Scottish and northern Irish: habitational name from Rerrick or Rerwick in Kirkcudbrightshire, named with an unknown first element + *wīc* 'outlying settlement'. It is also possible that the first element was originally Old Norse *rauðr* 'red'. **2.** English: habitational name from Redwick in Gloucestershire, named in Old English with *hrēod* 'reeds' + *wīc* 'outlying settlement'.

Reddig (203) North German: **1.** from Middle Low German *redik* 'radish', hence a metonymic occupational name for a grower or seller of radishes. Compare RETTIG. **2.** variant of REDDING 2.
GIVEN NAMES German 4%. *Otto, Volker.*

Reddin (446) **1.** English: variant of REDDEN. **2.** Irish: variant of RODEN. **3.** German and Dutch: variant of REDDING 2.

Redding (5159) **1.** English: variant spelling of READING. **2.** German and Dutch: patronymic from any of the Germanic personal names with the first element *rād* 'counsel', 'advice'.

Reddinger (207) **1.** habitational name for someone from Reddingen near Soltau. **2.** variant spelling of REDINGER.

Reddington (637) English: probably a variant of READING 1, from the place name + the Middle English suffix *-tune* 'settlement'. However, the surname is quite common in Lancashire and Yorkshire, and so perhaps a northern place named as the 'settlement (Old English *tūn*) associated with *Rēad(a)*' is to be sought.

Reddish (683) English: habitational name from Reddish in Lancashire or Redditch in Worcestershire, which are respectively 'reed ditch' (Old English *hrēod* + *dīc*) and 'red ditch' (from Old English *rēad*). The surname is now common in Nottinghamshire.

Redditt (279) Variant spelling of English **Reditt**, a topographic name for someone who lived by a reed-bed, from Middle English *redette* 'reed-bed', a derivative of *rede* 'reed' (Old English *hrēod*).
GIVEN NAMES French 5%. *Irby* (2), *Andre.*

Reddix (138) **1.** German: probably a variant of **Redix**, a patronymic from REDICK. **2.** German: possibly an altered spelling of **Radix**, a Latinized form of RETTIG. **3.** Perhaps also a variant of Scottish or English REDDICK.

Reddoch (173) Scottish: habitational name from Reddoch, earlier Redheuch, in Lanarkshire, or one of the other places similarly named.

Reddy (3045) **1.** Indian (Andhra Pradesh): Hindu name, from Telugu *reḍi* 'village headman'. The Kapus or Reddis are the largest caste in the former Madras Presidency (which included most of southern India before the reorganization of the Indian states on linguistic lines). **2.** Irish: reduced Anglicized form of Gaelic **Ó Roidigh**, a variant of **Ó Rodaigh** (see RODDY).
GIVEN NAMES Indian 56%. *Krishna* (27), *Ravi* (18), *Suresh* (15), *Srinivas* (14), *Ashok* (12), *Mohan* (12), *Ramesh* (11), *Chandra* (9), *Gopal* (9), *Ram* (9), *Uma* (9), *Madhavi* (8).

Redeker (364) North German: variant of RADEMAKER.
GIVEN NAMES German 5%. *Otto* (2), *Ernst, Kurt, Manfred.*

Redel (201) **1.** Jewish (eastern Ashkenazic): metonymic occupational name from Yiddish *redl* 'little wheel', 'tool for perforating matzoth'. **2.** German: from a short form of a Germanic personal name composed with *hrōd* 'fame', 'victory' as a first element. **3.** North German: occupational name for a cook, from Middle Low

German *rēdel* 'cooked food'. **4.** Possibly an altered spelling of German **Rödel** (see ROEDEL).

GIVEN NAMES German 5%. *Gunther, Otto.*

Redell (167) Probably an altered spelling of REDEL.

Redenbaugh (196) Altered spelling of German **Redenbach** or **Rettenbach**, habitational names from any of various places in Bavaria and Austria named Rettenbach.

Redenius (213) German: Latinized form of **Reden**, a habitational name from any of several places named Reden, Rehden, Rethen, or Rheden, all in Lower Saxony and East Prussia.

Redepenning (119) North German: from Middle Low German *rede* 'ready' + *penning* 'penny', together meaning 'cash', probably applied as an occupational nickname for a money changer.

Reder (546) **1.** English: variant spelling of READER. **2.** Dutch: variant of REEDER 2. **3.** North German and Dutch: from a Germanic personal name composed of the elements *rād* 'counsel' + *heri* 'army'. **4.** North German and Dutch: occupational name for a ship owner or outfitter, from an agent derivative of Middle Low German *rād* 'counsel'; 'provisions', 'stock'. **5.** North German: habitational name from any of various places named Rieder (earlier *Redere*) or Reher (earlier *Rethere*) in northern Germany. **6.** Possibly an altered spelling of German **Röder** (see ROEDER).

GIVEN NAMES German 4%. *Kurt* (2), *Helmut, Otto.*

Redetzke (111) Germanized form of Polish or Czech RADECKI.

Redfearn (643) English: variant spelling of REDFERN.

Redfern (1247) English: habitational name from Redfern near Rochdale, Greater Manchester, so called from Old English *rēad* 'red' + *fearn* 'fern', 'bracken'.

Redfield (1072) Apparently an English habitational name from any of several places so named in Scotland and England.

Redford (1070) English: variant of RADFORD.

Redgate (153) English (Nottinghamshire): habitational name from an unidentified place probably deriving its name from Old English *rēad* 'red' + Old Norse *gata* 'road'. There is a Redgate Wood in Kirklington, Nottinghamshire, but this place name may be of comparatively recent origin.

GIVEN NAME French 5%. *Patrice.*

Redhead (183) English and Scottish: nickname for someone with red hair, from Middle English *re(a)d* 'red' + *heved* 'head'. In some cases it is possibly also a topographic name with the sense 'red headland'. It occurs mainly in eastern and northern England.

Redic (183) Variant spelling of German REDICK or northern Irish and Scottish REDDICK.

Redican (124) Irish (Clare, Connacht): reduced Anglicized form of Gaelic **Ó Roideacháin** 'descendant of *Roideachán*', a personal name based on *rod* 'strong', 'spirited'.

Redick (602) **1.** German: variant of **Redecke**, from a pet form of a Germanic personal name formed with *rād* 'counsel'. **2.** Perhaps an altered spelling of REDDICK.

Redifer (199) Origin uncertain. Possibly a variant of English **Reddiford**, itself a variant of RADFORD.

Redig (145) Dutch and North German: variant of REDDING 2.

GIVEN NAME German 5%. *Kurt* (3).

Rediger (274) Dutch and German: from a Germanic personal name composed of the elements *rād* 'counsel' + *gār, gēr* 'spear', 'lance'.

Rediker (196) Dutch and North German: variant of REDIGER.

Redin (104) English: presumably a variant of REDDAN or READING.

Reding (1028) **1.** English: variant of READING. **2.** Dutch and German: variant of REDDING 2.

Redinger (626) German, Luxembourgeois, and Jewish (western Ashkenazic): habitational name for someone from Redingen in Luxembourg.

Redington (462) English: variant spelling of REDDINGTON.

Redish (121) **1.** English: variant spelling of REDDISH. **2.** Jewish (from Bohemia; also **Redisch**): from the Yiddish name for the town Hradišt in Bohemia.

GIVEN NAMES Jewish 4%. *Aaron David, Mendel.*

Rediske (155) German: variant of **Redieske**, an Eastphalian reduced form of **Redinges**, a patronymic form of REDING + -*ke* to make it a pet form.

Redler (204) German: **1.** variant of RADLER. **2.** habitational name for someone from Redl in Bavaria.

Redlich (289) German and Jewish (Ashkenazic): nickname for a responsible or honest person, from Middle High German *redelich* 'upright', 'honest' (an adjective derived from Old High German *reda* 'justification', 'account'), modern German *redlich*. As a Jewish surname it is mainly ornamental.

GIVEN NAMES German 7%; Jewish 5%. *Frieda* (2), *Otto* (2), *Fritz, Heinz, Raimund; Meyer* (3), *Nirit* (2), *Uri, Yaron.*

Redlin (405) German: habitational name from any of several places so named in Saxony, Brandenburg, and Pomerania.

Redline (129) Probably an Americanized form of German **Redlein**, from a pet form of the personal name *Konrad*.

Redling (139) German: from a short form of any of the Germanic personal names formed with the element *rād, rāt* 'advice', 'counsel' + -*ling*, suffix of affiliation.

Redlinger (235) German and Jewish (western Ashkenazic): habitational name for someone from Redling in Bavaria.

Redman (4549) **1.** English: variant of READ 1. **2.** English translation of Jewish ROTHMAN, ROT(T)MAN, ROITMAN, or REITMAN.

Redmann (294) **1.** North German: topographic name for someone who lived in a marshy place, from a term meaning 'boggy terrain' + *man* 'man'. **2.** German: from a Germanic personal name composed of the elements *rād* 'advice', 'counsel' + *man* 'man'.

GIVEN NAMES German 5%. *Erwin, Gunther, Heinz, Klaus, Otto.*

Redmer (137) North German: from the Frisian personal name, composed of the Germanic elements *rād* 'advice', 'counsel' + *mari, meri* 'fame'.

GIVEN NAMES German 10%. *Ewald* (3), *Eckert, Fritz.*

Redmon (2695) English: variant of REDMAN or REDMOND.

Redmond (7095) Irish: reduced Anglicized form of Gaelic **Mac Réamoinn**, a patronymic from the personal name *Réamonn* 'RAYMOND', introduced by Anglo-Norman settlers. Now widespread, this was the name of families in Connacht and Wexford.

Redner (364) German: possibly a variant of REDMER, or an occupational name for a spokesman, Middle High German *rednære*.

Rednour (332) Probably an altered spelling of German **Rittenauer** (see RIDENOUR).

Redondo (279) Spanish, Portuguese, and Galician: either a habitational name from any of the numerous places in Portugal and Galicia named Redondo, or a nickname for a plump person, also from *redondo* 'round' (Latin *rotundus*).

GIVEN NAMES Spanish 42%. *Jose* (5), *Luis* (5), *Andres* (4), *Carlos* (3), *Pedro* (3), *Francisco* (2), *Jacinto* (2), *Miguel* (2), *Octavio* (2), *Orlando* (2), *Ruben* (2), *Abelardo; Antonio, Dario, Filomena, Franco, Oreste.*

Redpath (331) Scottish: habitational name from a place in Berwickshire, probably so called from Old English *rēad* 'red' + *pæð* 'path'. This name is also common in northeastern England.

Redshaw (173) Northern English: habitational name, perhaps from Radshaw Gill in Fewston, West Yorkshire, named with Old English *rēad* 'red' + *sceaga* 'copse'.

Redstone (143) Jewish (American): English translation of the Ashkenazic family name ROTHSTEIN.

Redus (376) Of uncertain origin. Possibly a reduced form of English **Redhouse**, a habitational name from any of the numerous places named Redhouse, including over ninety farms.

Redwine (1213) Americanized form of South German **Rettwein**, from the personal name *Ratwin*.

Redwood (245) Southern English: habitational name from some minor place so called, probably from Old English *rēad* 'red' + *wudu* 'wood'. The reference is probably to birch trees as they appear in the spring.

FOREBEARS Abraham Redwood, a former English merchant ship captain, who had become owner through marriage of a valuable sugar plantation in Antigua and a large number of slaves, moved to America in 1712 when his son Abraham (1709–88) was three years old. Thirty years later, the son was one of the group of merchant princes whose prosperity and education was focused in Newport, RI. Intellectuals and people of culture flocked there, due in part to the Redwood Library, established in 1747 with a generous gift from Abraham the younger, who had three sons and a daughter who reached maturity.

Ree (270) **1.** English: variant of RYE 1 and 2. **2.** Norwegian: habitational name from any of six farmsteads named *Re*, the name being derived from an unattested Old Norse word meaning 'long narrow gravel ridge'. **3.** Korean: variant of YI.

Reeb (546) Dutch and German: from a Germanic pet name, *Ripo, Ribo*, derived from a compound name formed with *rīc* 'power' + *berht* 'bright'.
GIVEN NAMES German 4%. *Achim* (2), *Aloys*, *Hanni, Rudie*.

Reece (8378) Welsh: variant spelling of REESE.

Reecer (116) Origin uncertain. Perhaps a respelling of Swiss German RIESER. Compare REESER.

Reeck (166) **1.** German: habitational name from Reecke, near Lübeck or Reken, Westphalia. **2.** Dutch and Belgian (**van den Reeck**): habitational name for someone from places called Reek or Overreke, in Liège, Ghent, and North Brabant. It may also denote someone from Recq in Hainault.

Reed (92556) English: variant spelling of READ 1.
FOREBEARS An early American bearer of the common British name was George Reed who emigrated from England in 1635 with his son, William, and settled in Woburn, MA, several years later. His grandson James (1722–1807), a revolutionary war soldier who distinguished himself at the battle of Bunker Hill, moved to Fitzwilliam, NH, and was one of the original NH proprietors.

Reede (119) English: variant spelling of READ.

Reeder (7032) **1.** English: variant spelling of READER. **2.** Dutch: occupational name for someone who dressed new cloth, Middle Dutch *reder*. **3.** Dutch and German: variant of REDER 3.

Reeds (180) **1.** English: apparently a variant of REED. **2.** Possibly an Americanized spelling of German REETZ or RIETZ.

Reedus (105) Origin unidentified. Compare REDUS.
GIVEN NAME French 4%. *Chantel*.

Reedy (4269) **1.** Scottish and northern Irish: variant spelling of REEDIE. **2.** Irish: variant spelling of REIDY. **3.** Americanized form of German RIEDE.

Reef (192) North German: of disputed origin; either a metonymic occupational name for a maker or seller of rope, from Middle Low German *reep* 'rope', or alternatively, a nickname for a feeble or very thin person, from Middle Low German *ref, rif* 'body', 'skeleton'.

Reefer (113) Possibly a derivative of North German **Reef** 'rope', denoting a rope maker.

Reeg (229) German: habitational name from a place so named near Asbach, Westerwald.

Reeh (200) **1.** North German: nickname from Middle Low German *rē* 'roedeer'. Compare RAY 2. **2.** Korean: variant of YI.
GIVEN NAMES German 13%. *Ernst* (3), *Erwin* (3), *Arno, Friedrich, Klaus, Otto, Uwe*.

Reeher (133) Altered spelling of German REHER.

Reehl (121) Variant spelling of German RIEHL.

Reek (150) **1.** English: topographic name for someone who lived near a heap of some kind, from Middle English *reke* 'stack', 'heap'. **2.** German: from *Radeke*, a pet form of a Germanic personal name formed with *rād* 'advice', 'counsel'. **3.** Altered spelling of German REECK.

Reekie (127) Scottish: of uncertain origin, possibly a habitational name from Reikie in Aberdeenshire, or an altered spelling of *Rikie*, a diminutive of RICHARD. It is also possible that it originated from the nickname of Edinburgh, meaning 'smoky', from the Scottish dialect term *reek* 'smoke'.
GIVEN NAMES Scottish 6%. *Athol, Iain*.

Reeks (128) English: variant of REEK.

Reel (1811) Dutch: from a shortened form of the Germanic name *Radilo*, itself a short form of a compound name formed with *rād* 'counsel', 'advice' as the first element, for example *Radolf*. Compare RALPH.

Reels (140) Dutch: patronymic from REEL.

Reem (100) Of uncertain origin. Possibly a shortened form of an unidentified Ashkenazic Jewish surname.
GIVEN NAMES Jewish 5%. *Ido, Meir*.

Reen (169) Irish (western County Cork, Roscommon): reduced Anglicized form of Gaelic **Ó Rinn** 'descendant of *Rinn*' (see WREN).
GIVEN NAME Irish 6%. *Brendan*.

Reents (196) Frisian and North German: patronymic from a personal name formed with *Rein-* (from Germanic *ragin* 'advice', 'counsel').
GIVEN NAMES German 5%. *Heinz, Otto*.

Reep (727) **1.** Dutch: occupational name for a ropemaker (see ROPER). **2.** English: possibly a metonymic occupational name for a porter or a basket maker, from Middle English *(h)rip* 'basket'. Compare RIPPER.

Rees (5165) **1.** Welsh: variant spelling of REESE. **2.** German: habitational name from a place in the Rhineland called Rees **3.** German: short form of ANDREAS.

Reese (24188) **1.** Welsh: from one of the most common Welsh personal names, *Rhys*, Old Welsh *Rīs* 'ardor'. This was the name of the last ruler of an independent kingdom of Wales, Rhys ap Tewder, who died in 1093 unsuccessfully opposing the Norman advance. **2.** North German and Dutch: nickname for a very big man, from Middle Low German, Middle Dutch *rese* 'giant'. **3.** German: habitational name from places called Rees or Reese, in Rhineland and Lower Saxony.

Reeser (1177) Altered spelling of Swiss German RIESER.

Reesman (274) Probably an altered spelling of German **Reesemann**, a variant of REESE 3, or **Riesemann**, a variant of RIES.

Reesor (192) Altered spelling of Swiss German RIESER 3.

Reeter (135) German: from a Germanic personal name composed of the elements *rād, rāt* 'advice', 'counsel' + *heri* army.

Reetz (867) German: habitational name from places so named in the Prignitz region, Rhineland, and West Prussia, probably of Slavic origin, or alternatively from Reetze in Hannover district, the westernmost Slavic area in Germany.

Reeve (2170) English (most common in East Anglia): from Middle English *reeve*, an occupational name for a steward or bailiff, the precise character of whose duties varied from place to place and at different periods.

Reever (193) Possibly an altered form of German **Riefer**, a patronymic from the personal name *Rüef*, a reduced form of RUDOLF.

Reeves (28504) English: **1.** patronymic from REEVE. **2.** topographic name for someone who lived on the margin of a wood, from a misdivision of the Middle English phrase *atter eves* 'at the edge' (Old English *æt þære efese*).

Reff (254) **1.** Dutch: from a reduced form of a Germanic personal name composed of *ragin* 'counsel' + *fridu* 'peace'. **2.** German: metonymic occupational name for a carrier or peddler, from Middle High German *ref(f)* 'pannier', 'basket'. **3.** German: from a reduced form of a Germanic personal name composed of the elements *rīc* 'power(ful)' + *fridu* 'peace'.

Reffett (228) Altered spelling of any of various German surnames derived from the Germanic personal name *Ricfrid*, a compound of *rīc* 'power(ful)' + *frid-* 'peace', for example **Reffert**, **Refardt**, **Reifert**, **Reifarth**, and **Riffert**. Compare RAYFORD.

Reffitt (268) Altered spelling of any of various German surnames derived from the Germanic personal name *Ricfrid*, a compound of *rīc* 'power(ful)' + *frid-* 'peace', for example **Reffert**, **Refardt**, **Reifert**, **Reifarth**, and **Riffert**. Compare RAIFORD.

Reffner (224) German: of uncertain origin; perhaps an occupational name for a peddler, from an agent derivative of Middle High German *ref(f)* 'pannier', 'basket' (see REFF 2), or a nickname for a scold, from an agent derivative of Middle High German *reffen* 'to scold or chastise'.

Rega (351) **1.** Dutch: from a feminine personal name composed of the elements *ragin* 'counsel' + *gard* 'enclosure'. **2.** Dutch: from a masculine personal name composed of the elements *rīc* 'power(ful)' + *wald* 'rule'. The surname may also result from confusion with derivatives of the personal name RICHARD. **3.** Italian: unexplained.

GIVEN NAMES Italian 12%. *Angelo* (3), *Pasco* (3), *Aniello* (2), *Amato*, *Antonio*, *Carmine*, *Gennaro*, *Luciano*, *Rocco*, *Romeo*.

Regal (431) **1.** Spanish: topographic name for someone who lived by a pool formed by a stream. **2.** southern French (Occitan): nickname from the old Béarn dialect term *régal* 'royal'. Compare RAY 1. **3.** Southern French (Occitan): topographic name for someone who lived near a stream, from a derivative of *rega* (masculine form *rec*) 'stream', 'torrent'.

Regalado (1089) Portuguese, Spanish, and Galician: nickname from *regalado* 'gifted', 'pleasant', 'capable'.

GIVEN NAMES Spanish 46%; Portuguese 10%. *Jose* (34), *Juan* (17), *Raul* (14), *Manuel* (11), *Pedro* (9), *Ruben* (9), *Carlos* (8), *Guadalupe* (7), *Jesus* (7), *Roberto* (7), *Luis* (6), *Armando* (5); *Paulo* (2), *Agostinho*.

Regalia (146) Italian (Varese): apparently from *regalia* 'gift'.

GIVEN NAMES Italian 4%. *Angelo*, *Antonio*, *Immaculata*.

Regan (8889) Irish: reduced form of O'REGAN, an Anglicized form of Gaelic **Ó Ríagáin** 'descendant of *Riagán*', a personal name of uncertain origin, perhaps akin to *ríodhgach* 'impulsive', 'furious'. See also RYAN.

GIVEN NAMES Irish 8%. *Brendan* (6), *Eamon* (2), *Seamus* (2), *Bridie*, *Caitlin*, *Donovan*, *Dympna*, *Fintan*, *James Patrick*, *Kieran*, *Malachy*, *Michael Patrick*.

Regas (237) **1.** Greek: variant of RIGA. **2.** Catalan (**Regàs**): habitational name from any of numerous places called Regàs, derived from Catalan *rec* 'irrigation channel'. **3.** German (Frisian): unexplained.

GIVEN NAMES Greek 6%. *Constantine* (2), *Demetrios*, *Demosthenes*, *Stelios*.

Rege (104) Indian (Maharashtra, Goa); pronounced as *ray-gay*: Hindu name found among Saraswat Brahmans. It appears to be derived from Marathi *reg* 'line' (Sanskrit *rekhā*).

GIVEN NAMES Indian 49%. *Pramod* (2), *Subhash* (2), *Ajay*, *Amit*, *Anand*, *Aruna*, *Madhukar*, *Mahesh*, *Nakul*, *Prasad*, *Rajeev*, *Ratan*.

Regehr (214) German: see REGIER.

Regel (181) German: **1.** from Middle High German *regel* '(monastic) rule' (from Latin *regula*), perhaps a metonymic occupational name for someone who worked in a monastery. **2.** from a Germanic personal name composed with *rag-* 'advice', 'counsel'.

Regen (148) **1.** German: from a short form of a Germanic personal name with *ragin* 'advice', 'counsel'. **2.** German: habitational name from a place called Regen, for example in the Upper Palatinate. **3.** Jewish (Ashkenazic): ornamental name from German *Regen* 'rain'.

Regenold (138) German: archaic form of REINHOLD.

Reger (1128) **1.** German: from Middle High German *re(i)ger* 'heron', a nickname, no doubt bestowed on a tall, thin person with long spindly legs. **2.** German: nickname for a lively, restless, or passionate person, from an agent derivative of Middle High German *regen* 'to be excited or moved'.

Regester (276) English (Norfolk): see REGISTER.

Reggio (189) Italian and Jewish (from Italy): habitational name from Reggio Calabria or, to a lesser extent in the case of the American surname, from Reggio Emilia.

GIVEN NAMES Italian 7%. *Sal* (2), *Antonio*, *Enrico*, *Fulvio*, *Gino*.

Regier (677) German: from an Old Prussian name of uncertain origin; it was common in West Prussia.

GIVEN NAMES German 4%. *Ingo* (2), *Otto* (2).

Regimbal (105) French: learned spelling of **Raimbaud**, which is from the Germanic personal name *Raginbald*.

GIVEN NAME French 7%. *Andre*.

Regina (479) Italian: **1.** from *regina* 'queen' (Latin *regina*), applied either as a medieval female personal name alluding to the Virgin Mary, or, to a lesser extent as a nickname. Compare the masculine counterpart RE. **2.** habitational name from any of various places named or named with Regina, in particular Regina in Lattarico (Cosenza province) and Regina Elena in San Gregorio d'Ippona (Vibo Valentia province).

GIVEN NAMES Italian 18%. *Angelo* (5), *Rocco* (4), *Marino* (3), *Vito* (3), *Gennaro* (2), *Giovanni* (2), *Nicola* (2), *Salvatore* (2), *Carlo*, *Domenico*, *Francesco*, *Ilario*.

Reginato (109) Italian: from a Germanic personal name from *rag(in)* 'advice', 'counsel' + the suffix *-ato* which can be a diminutive or indicate belonging to a family.

GIVEN NAMES Italian 20%; French 6%. *Antonio* (2), *Adolfo*, *Alicia*, *Angelo*, *Armando*, *Carolina*, *Dino*, *Eugenio*, *Fabio*, *Humberto*, *Roberto*; *Andre*, *Jeanmarie*.

Regino (105) Spanish: possibly from a masculinized form of the female personal name *Regina* (Latin *regina* 'queen').

GIVEN NAMES Spanish 37%; Italian 7%. *Armando* (2), *Javier* (2), *Jesus* (2), *Jose* (2), *Adriana*, *Alvaro*, *Benito*, *Carlos*, *Cesar*, *Ernesto*, *Felipe*, *Gonzalo*; *Romeo* (2), *Ciro*, *Lorenzo*.

Regis (657) **1.** French (**Régis**): occupational name for a local dignitary, from a derivative of Old French *régir* 'to rule or manage'. **2.** French (**Régis**) and English: from Latin *regis*, genitive case of *rex* 'king', perhaps an occupational name for someone employed in the royal household, or a patronymic from a nickname. **3.** Italian: from RE, probably from an ablative form. **4.** German: habitational name from a place so named in Saxony.

GIVEN NAMES French 10%. *Clovis* (3), *Pierre* (2), *Yves* (2), *Andre*, *Antoine*, *Batiste*, *Camille*, *Carolle*, *Guillaume*, *Herard*, *Huguette*, *Jean Baptiste*.

Register (3259) English: perhaps from Middle English, Old French *registre* 'register', 'book for recording enactments', hence perhaps a metonymic occupational name for a scribe or clerk.

Regner (420) German: **1.** (Bavarian): habitational name for someone from Regen (a place on the Regen river, for which it is named). **2.** from a Germanic personal name composed of the elements *ragin* 'counsel' + *hari*, *heri* 'army'.

GIVEN NAMES German 4%. *Alois* (2), *Kurt* (2), *Erwin*, *Franz*, *Otto*.

Regnier (926) French (**Régnier**): from the personal name *Régnier*, of Germanic origin (see RAYNER 1).

FOREBEARS A Regnier from La Rochelle, France, is documented in Pointe-aux-Trembles, Quebec, in 1708, with the secondary surname BRION or Brillon.

GIVEN NAMES French 6%. *Lucien* (2), *Micheline* (2), *Pierre* (2), *Andre*, *Celestine*, *Felicie*, *Guilene*, *Marcel*, *Marcelle*, *Patrice*, *Romain*.

Rego (1493) **1.** Portuguese and Galician: habitational name from any of the numerous places in Portugal and Galicia called Rego, named with *rego* 'ditch', 'channel', 'furrow'. **2.** Dutch: from a Germanic personal name with the first element *ragin* 'counsel' + *guda* 'god', or *gōda* 'good', or *gauta* 'Goth'. **3.** Dutch: variant of REGA 2. **4.** Hungarian (**Regő**): occupational name for a musician or poet, from *rege* 'song', 'tale'.

GIVEN NAMES Spanish 15%; Portuguese 9%. *Manuel* (32), *Jose* (25), *Armando* (5), *Eduardo* (5), *Carlos* (4), *Fernando* (4),

Francisco (4), *Ramon* (4), *Humberto* (3), *Juan* (3), *Luis* (3), *Mario* (3); *Joao* (5), *Duarte* (2), *Adauto*, *Albano*, *Goncalo*, *Guilherme*, *Serafim*.

Regula (373) Polish (**Reguła**): from *reguła* 'rules', 'precepts', perhaps a nickname for an officious person or for the steward or butler in a great household.
GIVEN NAMES Polish 6%. *Jozef* (2), *Andrzej*, *Ludwik*, *Piotr*, *Tadeusz*, *Wasyl*.

Reh (320) **1.** German: variant of RECH. **2.** nickname for someone who was timid or fleet of foot, from Middle High German *rēch* 'roe deer'. Compare RECH. **3.** Jewish (western Ashkenazic): ornamental name from German *Reh* 'roe deer' (see 2).
GIVEN NAMES German 5%. *Eberhard*, *Gerd*, *Hans Peter*, *Klaus*, *Kurt*.

Reha (170) Czech (**Řeha**): from a pet form of the personal name *Řehoř*, the Czech form of GREGORY.

Rehagen (129) North German: habitational name from either of two places called Rehagen, one in Brandenburg, the other in Schleswig-Holstein.

Rehak (386) Czech (**Řehák**): pet form of the personal name *Řehoř*, the Czech form of GREGORY (see REHOR).

Rehard (101) Probably an Americanized form of Czech **Řehoř** (see REHOR).

Rehbein (460) German: **1.** nickname for someone who was fleet of foot or slender and graceful, from Middle Low German *rē* 'roe deer' + *been* 'bone', 'leg'. **2.** from the personal name *Rachwin*, a compound of *rahha* 'revenge' + *wini* 'friend'.
GIVEN NAMES German 4%. *Fritz*, *Gerhard*, *Hannelore*, *Hans*, *Irmgard*, *Volker*, *Willi*.

Rehberg (656) German: habitational name from any of the places so called throughout Germany.
GIVEN NAMES German 4%. *Erna*, *Ernst*, *Erwin*, *Frieda*, *Kurt*, *Udo*.

Rehberger (150) German and Jewish (Ashkenazic): habitational name for someone from a place called Rehberg, in particular one in Bohemia.
GIVEN NAMES German 5%. *Manfred*, *Monika*.

Rehder (433) North German: variant of REDER 3, 4.
GIVEN NAMES German 7%. *Erwin* (2), *Otto* (2), *Claus*, *Ernst*, *Helmut*, *Monika*.

Reher (194) **1.** North German: habitational name from places so called near Hamelin and Itzehoe, and in some cases perhaps from Rehe in Hesse or Rehau in Franconia. **2.** Altered spelling of Czech REHOR.

Rehfeld (227) German and Jewish (Ashkenazic): habitational name from any of the places, mainly in eastern Germany, so named from Middle German *rē* 'roe deer' + *feld* 'pasture', 'open country'. As a Jewish name, it can be ornamental name, with the same meaning.
GIVEN NAMES German 8%. *Kurt* (3), *Egon*, *Gunther*, *Heinz*.

Rehfeldt (207) German and Jewish (Ashkenazic): variant spelling of REHFELD.
GIVEN NAMES German 5%. *Ewald*, *Heinz*, *Udo*.

Rehill (113) Irish: variant of RAHILL.

Rehkop (131) North German or Dutch variant of REHKOPF.

Rehkopf (179) German: from Middle German *rē* 'roe deer' + *kopf* 'head', hence a nickname for someone thought to have a face like a deer's, perhaps with large soft eyes.

Rehl (163) German: **1.** (in the north) probably a habitational name from Rehl in Rhineland or Rehlen in East Prussia. **2.** see RIEHL.

Rehling (260) German: **1.** habitational name from Rehling in Bavaria or any of various places in western Germany called Rehlingen. **2.** nickname from the name of a fish, a type of bass.

Rehm (1643) **1.** German: from the medieval personal name *Rehm* (see REMY). The former name was borne by a 6th-century bishop of Rheims; the latter was borne by various minor saints of the 8th to 10th centuries. **2.** German: from Middle High German *reme* 'frame', 'loom', 'rack', hence a metonymic occupational name for someone who made or used such items. **3.** North German: metonymic occupational name for a maker of leather reins and similar articles (see RIEHM and RIEMER).
GIVEN NAMES German 4%. *Bernd* (3), *Otto* (3), *Armin* (2), *Hans* (2), *Gunter*, *Hermann*, *Lothar*, *Oskar*.

Rehman (424) **1.** Muslim: variant of RAHMAN. **2.** Variant of German REHMANN.
GIVEN NAMES Muslim 70%. *Abdul* (14), *Syed* (10), *Aziz* (9), *Habib* (7), *Fazal* (6), *Jamil* (5), *Zia* (5), *Hafeez* (4), *Mohammad* (4), *Mohammed* (4), *Obaid* (4), *Saif* (4).

Rehmann (168) **1.** North German: topographic name for someone who lived in a marshy place, from Middle Low German *red* 'bog' + *man* 'man'. **2.** North German: variant of REHM 2, with the addition of Middle Low German *man* 'man'. **3.** from a Germanic personal name formed with *ragin* 'advice', 'counsel' as a first element + *man* 'man'. **4.** Muslim: variant of RAHMAN.
GIVEN NAME German 4%. *Kurt*.

Rehmer (175) North German: **1.** variant of REMER 2. **2.** habitational name from any of various places called Rehm, Rehme, or Rehmen, mostly in the northern parts of Germany. The place names probably derive from a field name from Middle Low German *rēme* 'strap', 'ribbon', thus, by extension 'strip of land'.

Rehmert (134) German: variant of REHMER, with excrescent -t.
GIVEN NAMES German 5%. *Georg*, *Kurt*.

Rehn (435) North German: **1.** topographic name from a Low German form of standard German *Rain* 'edge of a field', 'ridge'.

2. from a Germanic personal name based on *ragin* 'advice', 'counsel'.

Rehnberg (114) German: probably a habitational name from a place called Reinberg, of which there are two in Mecklenburg-West Pomerania.
GIVEN NAMES German 6%. *Klaus*, *Klaus-Dieter*.

Rehor (161) Czech (**Řehoř**): from the personal name *Řehoř*, Czech form of Latin *Gregorius* (see GREGORY).

Rehr (125) North German: **1.** habitational name from either of the places called Rehren, both named with Middle Low German *red* 'bog'. **2.** topographic name from Middle Low German *red(d)er* 'space or way between two hedges'. **3.** contracted form of REHER, REHDER, or REDER.

Rehrer (117) German: probably a habitational name from a place named Rehren in Westphalia, or a topographic name (see REHR 2).
GIVEN NAME French 4%. *Raoul*.

Rehrig (296) German: of uncertain origin. Perhaps a variant of **Rehring** (also unexplained), or a habitational name from Rehrige in Brandenburg, or alternatively a variant of **Röhrig** (see ROEHRIG).

Reibel (188) **1.** German: from a Germanic personal name composed of the elements *rīc* 'power' + *bald* 'bold', 'brave'. **2.** Probably a variant of German **Reubel** (see ROUBAL).
GIVEN NAMES German 4%. *Erwin*, *Kurt*.

Reiber (706) **1.** German: occupational name for an assistant in a bathhouse or a barber's shop, from an agent derivative of Middle High German *riben* 'to rub'. **2.** Jewish (Ashkenazic): nickname from Yiddish *rayber* 'great eater', 'someone who rubs' (see 1).

Reich (5490) **1.** German and Jewish (Ashkenazic): nickname for a wealthy or powerful man, from Middle High German *rīch* 'of noble descent', 'powerful', 'rich', German *reich* 'rich'. **2.** German: from a short form of a personal name containing the Old High German element *rīhhi* 'power', 'might'.
GIVEN NAMES German 4%. *Hans* (7), *Kurt* (7), *Erwin* (5), *Gerhard* (4), *Alois* (3), *Otto* (3), *Volker* (3), *Erna* (2), *Udo* (2), *Wolfgang* (2), *Dieter*, *Egon*.

Reichard (1513) German: from a Germanic personal name (see RICHARD). This surname (and its variants) has also been adopted by Jews.

Reichardt (728) German: variant spelling of REICHARD.
GIVEN NAMES German 7%. *Otto* (5), *Kurt* (3), *Dieter*, *Elke*, *Fritz*, *Gerd*, *Hans*, *Horst*, *Juergen*, *Klaus*, *Manfred*, *Rudi*.

Reichart (570) German: variant spelling of REICHARD.

Reiche (223) German: variant of REICH.
GIVEN NAMES German 9%. *Gunter*, *Hans*, *Hermann*, *Juergen*, *Winfried*.

Reichel (1058) **1.** German: from a pet form of any of several Germanic personal names formed with the Germanic element *rīc* 'power'. **2.** Jewish (Ashkenazic): from the Yiddish female personal name *Raykhl*, a pet form of *Raykhe*, which in turn is derived from Yiddish *raykh* 'rich'.

GIVEN NAMES German 5%. *Kurt* (3), *Otto* (2), *Arno, Fritz, Gerhardt, Heinz, Helmut, Herwig, Rudi, Ulrich, Wolfgang.*

Reichelderfer (183) German: habitational name for someone from a place named Reicheldorf or Reichelsdorf (near Nuremberg).

Reichelt (401) German: variant of REICHEL 1.

GIVEN NAMES German 9%; Scandinavian 4%. *Kurt* (3), *Erna, Gerhard, Klaus, Lothar, Reiner, Wilhelm.*

Reichenbach (959) **1.** German and Jewish (Ashkenazic): habitational name from any of various minor places, particularly in Baden-Württemberg and Hesse, so named from Old High German *rīhhi* 'rich', 'powerful' (i.e. strongly flowing) + *bah* 'stream'. **2.** Jewish (Ashkenazic): ornamental name from German *reich* 'rich' + *Bach* 'stream' (see 1).

GIVEN NAMES German 5%. *Kurt* (3), *Gerhard* (2), *Inge* (2), *Bodo, Ernst, Franz, Fritz, Hans, Ullrich, Ulrich, Uwe.*

Reichenberg (218) **1.** German: habitational name from any of various places named Reichenberg, in several different areas of Germany. **2.** Jewish (Ashkenazic): ornamental name composed of German *reich(en)* 'rich' + *Berg* 'mountain', 'hill'.

Reichenberger (237) German: habitational name for someone from any of the several places in Germany called REICHENBERG.

Reicher (239) **1.** German and Jewish (Ashkenazic): from an inflected form of REICH. **2.** German: from a Germanic personal name (see RICHER). **3.** German: habitational name for someone from any of various places called Reich, Reichau, or Reichen in Bavaria and Bohemia.

GIVEN NAMES Jewish 5%. *Chana, Jacov, Shula, Sol.*

Reichert (4109) German: variant of REICHARD (see RICHARD).

GIVEN NAMES German 4%. *Kurt* (11), *Otto* (5), *Eldred* (3), *Arno* (2), *Erwin* (2), *Frieda* (2), *Gunter* (2), *Helmut* (2), *Horst* (2), *Rainer* (2), *Armin.*

Reichl (215) German (Bavaria): variant of REICHEL 1.

GIVEN NAMES German 6%. *Otto* (2), *Gunter, Hans.*

Reichle (522) German: **1.** variant of REICHEL 1. **2.** (in the south) metonymic occupational name for a blacksmith, from the unrounded diminutive of *Rauch* 'smoke'.

GIVEN NAMES German 5%. *Kurt* (2), *Albrecht, Claus, Fritz, Hans, Otto, Wieland.*

Reichley (173) Americanized form of REICHLE.

Reichlin (170) **1.** Swiss German and German: from a pet form of the medieval personal name *Richelin.* **2.** Jewish (from Belarus; **Raykhlin**): from the Yiddish female personal name *Raykhle*, a pet form of *Raykhe*, which in turn is derived from Yiddish *raykh* 'rich', + the eastern Slavic possessive suffix *-in.*

GIVEN NAME Jewish 5%. *Srul.*

Reichling (199) **1.** Swiss German and German: variant of the medieval personal name *Rīchelin.* **2.** German: habitational name from either of two places so named in Bavaria.

Reichman (705) German (**Reichmann**) and Jewish (Ashkenazic): nickname for a powerful or wealthy man, from Middle High German *rīch*, German *reich* 'noble', 'powerful', 'rich' + *man*, modern German *Mann* 'man'.

GIVEN NAMES Jewish 10%. *Avrom* (2), *Chaya* (2), *Eliezer* (2), *Itzhak* (2), *Leib* (2), *Pinchos* (2), *Hadassah, Hershel, Icek, Mandel, Meir, Merav.*

Reichmann (178) German and Jewish (Ashkenazic): see REICHMAN.

GIVEN NAMES German 11%. *Claus, Dieter, Eberhard, Egon, Erwin, Uwe.*

Reichmuth (199) Swiss and German: from the medieval personal name *Richmut*, from Middle High German *rīch* 'noble', 'powerful' + *muot* 'mind', 'sense'.

GIVEN NAMES German 5%. *Hans, Heinz.*

Reichner (135) German: habitational name for someone from any of various places called Reichenau, for example in Saxony and Baden-Württemberg.

Reichow (200) German: habitational name from places called Reichow, Reicho, or Reichau in Silesia, Pomerania, East Prussia, and Bavaria.

GIVEN NAMES German 6%. *Otto* (2), *Armin, Kurt.*

Reichstein (114) German: habitational name from places named Reichstein (in Saxony) or Reichenstein (in Rhineland, Schleswig-Holstein, and Württemberg).

GIVEN NAME German 8%. *Kurt.*

Reichwein (154) German: from the Germanic personal name *Rīchwin*, composed of *rīc* 'power(ful)' + *win* 'friend'.

GIVEN NAME German 5%. *Manfred.*

Reick (177) North German: **1.** from a medieval personal name, a short form of RICHARD, or less commonly of some other compound name with this first element. **2.** habitational name from a place so named near Dresden.

GIVEN NAMES German 7%. *Otto* (2), *Helmuth.*

Reicks (257) German: probably a patronymic from REICK 1.

Reid (36541) Scottish: **1.** nickname for a person with red hair or a ruddy complexion, from Older Scots *reid* 'red'. **2.** topographic name for someone who lived in a

clearing, from Old English *rȳd* 'woodland clearing'. Compare English READ.

FOREBEARS Samuel Chester Reid (1783–1861), the sea captain who designed the stars and stripes form of the present the American flag, was born at Norwich, CT. His father, Lt. John Reid, a former British naval officer of a distinguished Glasgow family, had resigned his commission and joined the cause of the American Revolution.

Reida (105) Of uncertain origin, perhaps Frisian.

Reidel (298) **1.** German: nickname for a rough person, from Middle High German *reitel* 'cudgel'. **2.** Jewish (eastern Ashkenazic): metonymic occupational name from southeastern Yiddish *reydl* 'little wheel', 'tool for perforating matzoth' (see REDEL). **3.** Altered spelling or variant of German RIEDEL.

Reidenbach (336) German: habitational name from any of various places so named in the Palatinate.

Reider (962) **1.** North German form of REITER 2. **2.** German: probably also an occupational name for a bookkeeper, from Middle High German *reiter* 'calculator'. **3.** Jewish (Ashkenazic): nickname from Yiddish dialect *reyder* 'chatterer'.

Reidhead (176) Northern English and Scottish: variant of REDHEAD.

Reidinger (219) **1.** German: perhaps a habitational name for someone from any of several places called Reiting in Bavaria and Austria, or from a Germanic personal name, a variant of REDIGER. **2.** Possibly a respelling of German RIEDINGER.

Reidt (175) **1.** South German: nickname for a curly-haired person, from Middle High German *reite* 'crisp', 'curly'. **2.** North German: habitational name from any of several places in Rhineland called Rheydt or Rheidt, so named Middle Low German *rēt*, *reit* 'reed', 'reedy terrain', or a topographic name from this word.

Reidy (1803) **1.** Irish: Anglicized form of Gaelic **Ó Riada** 'descendant of *Riada*' a personal name probably based on a word meaning 'drover'. **2.** Scottish: variant spelling of **Reedie.**

GIVEN NAMES Irish 6%. *Brendan* (4), *Conan, John Patrick, Mairead, Siobhan.*

Reier (243) German and Jewish (Ashkenazic): nickname for a long-legged person, from Middle High German *reiger*, German *Reiher* 'heron'.

Reierson (446) **1.** Swedish: patronymic from the personal name *Reier*, from Old Norse *Reiðarr*, from *reið* 'house', 'home' + *-arr*, representing a proto-Norse form *-har-jar* 'warrior', *-warjar* 'defender', or *-gairar* 'spear'. **2.** Respelling of Norwegian or Danish **Reiersen**, cognate with 1.

Reif (1362) Swiss German, German, and Jewish (Ashkenazic): variant spelling of REIFF.

GIVEN NAMES German 5%. *Udo* (3), *Willi* (3), *Guenter* (2), *Hans* (2), *Kurt* (2), *Alois, Dieter, Friedrich, Fritz, Helmut, Hilde, Horst.*

Reifel (192) South German: probably a diminutive of REIFF.

Reifer (164) **1.** South German: occupational name for a linen measurer, from Middle High German *reif*, a measure of length for linen. **2.** South German: occupational name for a maker of rope, **Reifschläger**, or for the owner of a tavern (see REIFF). **3.** South German (Tyrol): topographic name for someone living at a landing place, from Romansh *riva* 'riverbank'. **4.** Jewish (Ashkenazic): ornamental name or nickname from the inflected form of German *reif* 'mature'.

GIVEN NAMES Jewish 17%; German 5%. *Avrum* (5), *Chaim, Hyman, Jakob, Sol, Yaakov; Hans* (3), *Friedl.*

Reifert (113) German: variant of REIFER.

GIVEN NAMES German 5%. *Fritz, Hanni, Kurt.*

Reiff (1507) **1.** South German and German: from Middle High German *reif* '(barrel) hoop', 'ribbon', 'cord', hence a metonymic occupational name for a cooper or maker of ribbons, or from a house or tavern with the sign of a hoop. **2.** German: from the medieval personal name *Riff*, a short form of the Germanic name *Rīchfrit*, composed of the elements *rīc* 'power(ful)' + *frid* 'peace'. **3.** Jewish (Ashkenazic): ornamental name or nickname from German *reif* 'mature'.

Reifler (113) Swiss German: variant of **Reiffli**, a from a house name (see REIFF 1) with its sign announcing a commercial business or trade.

Reifschneider (332) German: occupational name for a cooper or hoop maker (see REIFF 1).

Reifsnyder (357) Altered spelling of REIF-SCHNEIDER.

Reifsteck (263) German: metonymic occupational name for a hoop maker or cooper, from Middle High German *reifsteck* 'bent or rounded wooden stick'.

Reigel (410) **1.** German: nickname for a long-legged person, from Middle High German *reigel* 'heron'. **2.** Altered spelling of German RIEGEL.

Reiger (261) German: variant of REIHER.

GIVEN NAMES German 4%. *Hans, Kurt.*

Reigh (130) Possibly a variant spelling of English RAY.

Reighard (447) Probably an altered spelling of German REICHARD.

Reigle (726) Variant of German REIGEL or RIEGEL.

Reigner (109) Northern French (Walloon): from the personal name *Rainier*. Compare RAYNER.

Reiher (189) German: nickname for someone with long legs, from Middle High

German, Middle Low German *reiger* 'heron'. Compare REIGEL.

GIVEN NAMES German 6%. *Franz, Fritz, Gunther.*

Reihl (182) German: variant of German **Reihle** (see REIL 2 and 3) or of RIEHL.

Reik (158) Jewish (from Belarus): unexplained.

GIVEN NAMES German 6%. *Angelika, Erwin.*

Reil (484) **1.** German: from a Germanic personal name composed with *rag-* 'advice', 'counsel', *rāh(ha)* 'revenge', or *rīc* 'power(ful)'. **2.** South German: nickname from a diminutive of Middle High German *rū* 'rough', derived from a base form *reule* 'coarse-haired (person)'. Compare German *rauh*. **3.** habitational name from a place in Rhineland called Reil.

Reiland (451) Dutch: possibly from a variant of the Germanic personal name *Ragiland.*

Reile (103) German: variant of REIL.

GIVEN NAMES German 7%. *Gerhard, Irmgard, Otto.*

Reiley (515) **1.** Irish: variant spelling of REILLY. **2.** Altered spelling of German REILE or of **Reihle**, a variant of REIL 2, 3.

Reiling (494) German: **1.** habitational name for someone from Reilingen in Baden. **2.** possibly from a derivative of REIL 1.

Reilley (584) Irish: variant of REILLY.

Reilly (17185) Irish: reduced form of O'REILLY, an Anglicized form of Gaelic **Ó Raghailligh** 'descendant of *Raghailleach*', Old Irish *Roghallach*, of unexplained origin.

GIVEN NAMES Irish 5%. *Brendan* (29), *Brennan* (2), *Brigid* (2), *Ciaran* (2), *Conor* (2), *Kieran* (2), *Aidan, Aileen, Caitlin, Clancy, Colm, Conn.*

Reily (316) Irish: variant of REILLY.

Reim (336) **1.** German: from a short form of the personal name *Reinmund* (see RAYMOND), *Reinmar*, or the female personal name *Reinburg(is)*. **2.** Jewish (Ashkenazic): unexplained.

GIVEN NAMES German 6%. *Kurt* (2), *Eldred, Heinz, Johannes.*

Reiman (1071) **1.** Jewish (Ashkenazic): variant spelling of RAYMAN. **2.** Respelling of German REIMANN.

Reimann (835) German: **1.** shortened form of *Rheinmann*, a regional name denoting someone from Rhineland. **2.** from French **Reimon** (see RAYMOND). **3.** from a pet form of a Germanic personal name formed with a first element from *ragin* 'advice', 'counsel' or *rīc* 'power(ful)', 'rich'.

GIVEN NAMES German 11%. *Hans* (5), *Kurt* (4), *Erwin* (3), *Gerhard* (3), *Frieda* (2), *Guenter* (2), *Heinz* (2), *Manfred* (2), *Oskar* (2), *Bernhard, Dieter, Eberhard.*

Reimel (131) German: variant of German **Reimelt**, a shortened form of the Germanic personal name *Reimbold*, composed of the

elements *ragin* 'advice', 'counsel' + *bald* 'bold', 'brave'.

GIVEN NAMES German 5%. *Alois* (2), *Monika.*

Reimer (3701) German: from a Germanic personal name, a reduced form of *Reinmar*, composed of the elements *ragin* 'counsel' + *māri, mēri* 'fame'.

GIVEN NAMES German 4%. *Kurt* (5), *Otto* (5), *Ernst* (4), *Erwin* (4), *Bernhard* (2), *Ewald* (2), *Gerhard* (2), *Hans* (2), *Eldred, Erna, Heinrich, Irmgard.*

Reimers (1252) North German: patronymic from REIMER.

GIVEN NAMES German 4%. *Berthold* (2), *Fritz* (2), *Kurt* (2), *Otto* (2), *Arno, Gerda, Gerhard, Hans, Hilde, Monika, Willi.*

Reimold (129) German: from a Germanic personal name composed of the elements *ragin* 'advice' + *bald* 'bold', 'brave'.

GIVEN NAMES German 5%. *Ekkehard, Erwin.*

Rein (1718) German: **1.** from a short form of any of the various personal names formed with the element *ragin* 'counsel', for example REINBOLD, *Reinhard* (see REINHARDT). **2.** variant of RAIN. **3.** perhaps a habitational name for someone who lived by the Rhine.

GIVEN NAMES German 4%. *Hans* (3), *Kurt* (3), *Otto* (2), *Dieter, Dietrich, Erna, Fritz, Gerda, Hedwig, Klaus, Manfred, Wolfgang.*

Reina (760) **1.** Spanish: habitational name from any of the places named Reina. **2.** Spanish and Portuguese: most likely from the female personal name *Reina* (from Latin *Regina*), otherwise a nickname from *reina* 'queen'. **3.** Italian: from a Sicilian variant of *regina* 'queen' (see REGINA).

GIVEN NAMES Spanish 23%; Italian 8%. *Francisco* (7), *Jorge* (5), *Gustavo* (4), *Jose* (4), *Alfonso* (3), *Luis* (3), *Miguel* (3), *Raul* (3), *Aida* (2), *Andres* (2), *Guillermo* (2), *Juan* (2); *Angelo* (7), *Salvatore* (5), *Antonio* (2), *Leno* (2), *Biagio, Ermanno, Rosaria, Sal, Silvio, Vitalia.*

Reinagel (104) French (Alsace): of German linguistic origin, but unexplained. Compare REINSCHMIDT.

Reinard (260) French: variant spelling of REYNARD.

Reinart (125) Probably a respelling of German **Reinert**, a variant of REINHARDT.

Reinauer (100) German: habitational name for someone from any of various places called Rheinau, for example one in Baden-Württemberg, Germany, or another in Zurich canton, Switzerland.

Reinbold (735) German: from a Germanic personal name composed of the elements *ragin* 'counsel' + *bald* 'bold', 'brave'.

GIVEN NAMES German 6%. *Fritz* (2), *Kurt* (2), *Erwin, Goetz, Hans, Ignatz, Johann, Markus, Otto.*

Reinbolt (189) Variant of German REIN-BOLD.

Reincke (196) North German: from a pet form of the personal name *Reinhard*, com-

posed of the Germanic elements *ragin* 'counsel' + *harð* 'hardy', 'brave', 'strong', or of other personal names with the same first element.
GIVEN NAMES German 8%. *Kurt* (2), *Ewald, Fritz, Ulrich.*

Reindel (141) **1.** German: from a pet form of the personal name *Reinhard.* Compare REINCKE above. **2.** Jewish (Ashkenazic): unexplained.
GIVEN NAMES German 6%. *Frieda, Hans, Kurt.*

Reinders (315) Dutch and North German (Frisian): patronymic from a reduced form of the personal name *Reinhard.* Compare REINCKE.
GIVEN NAMES German 4%. *Kurt* (2), *Fritz.*

Reindl (501) German (Bavarian): from a pet form of one of the Germanic compound names formed with *ragin* 'counsel' as the first element, for example *Reinhard.*

Reine (275) French: from Old French *reine* 'queen', used as a female personal name.

Reineck (241) German: **1.** variant of REINECKE. **2.** habitational name from any of the places in Germany and Switzerland called Reineck or Rheineck, for example one in Bavaria and another near Rorschach, Switzerland.

Reinecke (534) North German: from a pet form of any of the various Germanic personal names formed with *ragin* 'counsel' as the first element.
GIVEN NAMES German 8%. *Kurt* (3), *Erwin* (2), *Ernst, Fritz, Gunther, Hans, Manfred, Otto, Wilhelm.*

Reinecker (139) German: habitational name for someone from any of various places named Reineck or Rheineck (see REINECK).

Reineke (669) German: variant spelling of REINECKE.
GIVEN NAMES German 6%. *Kurt* (3), *Aloys* (2), *Alois, Arno, Bernd, Guenter, Hans, Hedwig, Herta, Johannes, Monika, Rudi.*

Reineking (129) North German: patronymic from REINECKE.
GIVEN NAME German 4%. *Kurt.*

Reinemann (134) German and Swiss German: **1.** habitational and topographic name (see REIN 2). **2.** elaborated form of REIN 1.

Reiner (2172) **1.** French, German, and Dutch: from a personal name formed with the Germanic elements *ragin* 'counsel' + *hari, heri* 'army'. **2.** German: topographic name for someone living at the edge of a field or wood, from Middle High German *rein* 'edge', 'embankment'.

Reiners (580) German and Dutch: patronymic from REINER 1.
GIVEN NAMES German 4%. *Otto* (2), *Frieda, Gernot, Kurt, Liesl.*

Reinert (1831) North German: from a Germanic personal name composed of the elements *ragin* 'counsel' + *hard* 'hardy', 'brave', 'strong', for example *Reinhard* (see REINHARDT).

Reinertsen (212) Norwegian: patronymic from the personal name REINERT.
GIVEN NAMES Scandinavian 14%. *Alf* (3).

Reinertson (257) Americanized spelling of REINERTSEN.
GIVEN NAMES Scandinavian 4%. *Erik, Lars, Nels.*

Reines (180) Jewish (Ashkenazic): variant spelling of RAINES.
GIVEN NAMES Jewish 4%. *Baruch, Meyer, Miriam, Sol.*

Reinfeld (108) German: habitational name from any of several places called Reinfeld, for example in Schleswig-Holstein, or from Rheinfeld in North Rhine-Westphalia.

Reingold (298) Jewish (Ashkenazic): ornamental name from German *rein* 'pure' + *Gold* 'gold'.
GIVEN NAMES Jewish 5%. *Haim, Herschel.*

Reinhard (1633) German and Jewish (Ashkenazic): variant spelling of REINHARDT.
GIVEN NAMES German 6%. *Gerd* (5), *Albrecht* (2), *Erwin* (2), *Gerda* (2), *Klaus* (2), *Kurt* (2), *Christoph, Dieter, Franz, Fritz, Georg, Gerhard.*

Reinhardt (4843) German and Jewish (Ashkenazic): from a Germanic personal name composed of the elements *ragin* 'counsel' + *hard* 'hardy', 'brave', 'strong'.
GIVEN NAMES German 4%. *Kurt* (9), *Otto* (8), *Hans* (5), *Heinz* (3), *Claus* (2), *Dieter* (2), *Ernst* (2), *Franz* (2), *Helmuth* (2), *Lothar* (2), *Bernd, Eldor.*

Reinhart (3519) German: variant spelling of REINHARDT.

Reinheimer (338) German: habitational name for someone from places called Reinheim, in Hesse and Saar, or from Rheinheim near Waldshut.
GIVEN NAMES German 5%. *Bernd* (3), *Kurt.*

Reinhold (1156) German: from a Germanic personal name composed of the elements *ragin* 'counsel' + *wald* 'rule', the second element having been reinterpreted as *hold* 'dear', 'beloved' in the 16th century. This is also Jewish, presumably an adoption of the German surname.
GIVEN NAMES German 5%. *Kurt* (3), *Manfred* (3), *Heinz* (2), *Armin, Arno, Bernd, Johannes, Oskar, Rudi.*

Reinholdt (127) German: variant spelling of REINHOLD.

Reinholt (166) Respelling of German REINHOLDT or REINHOLD.
GIVEN NAMES Scandinavian 6%; German 5%. *Erik; Hans* (2), *Kurt* (2).

Reinholtz (161) German (Austrian): variant spelling of REINHOLZ.
GIVEN NAME German 4%. *Erwin.*

Reinholz (205) German (Austrian): patronymic form (genitive case) from REINHOLD. The spelling shows some confusion with -*holz* 'wood', probably as a result of folk etymology.
GIVEN NAMES German 7%. *Ernst, Franz, Otto, Ute.*

Reinicke (122) North German: variant of REINECKE, or in some instances from an Old Prussian name.
GIVEN NAMES German 10%; Scandinavian 4%. *Gunther, Klaus, Kurt; Gudrun, Wulf.*

Reinier (159) French: from the personal name *Reinier*, of Germanic origin (see RAYNER 1).

Reinig (290) German: from a pet form of the various Germanic personal names formed with *ragin* 'counsel' as the first element, for example REINBOLD or *Reinhard* (see REINHARDT).

Reiniger (109) German: variant of REININGER.
GIVEN NAME German 4%. *Rudie.*

Reining (252) North German: patronymic from REIN 1.

Reininger (458) German: habitational name for someone from either of two places in Saxony called Reiningen, probably so named from the personal name REINIG.

Reinisch (125) Eastern German (East Prussia): from a pet form of any of the various Germanic personal names with the first element *ragin* 'counsel', for example REINHOLD or *Reinhard* (see REINHARDT).
GIVEN NAMES German 16%. *Bodo* (2), *Otto* (2), *Claus, Gerda, Hans, Ulrike.*

Reinitz (219) **1.** Jewish (Ashkenazic): variant of RAINES. **2.** German: variant of REINISCH (with a Slavic suffix added to REIN).
GIVEN NAMES Jewish 7%; German 4%. *Aharon, Chaim, Chaya, Emanuel, Miriam, Shmuel; Arno, Frieda, Hannelore.*

Reinke (2580) North German: from a pet form of the personal name *Reinhard* (see REINHARDT).

Reinkemeyer (103) German: distinguishing name for a tenant farmer (see MEYER) with the personal name REINKE.

Reinking (496) North German: patronymic from REINKE.
GIVEN NAMES German 4%. *Erwin* (2), *Lorenz, Otto.*

Reinmiller (115) Partly Americanized form of a German surname, a distinguishing name for a miller (see MUELLER) with REIN 1 as a first element.
GIVEN NAMES German 6%. *Aloysius, Kurt.*

Reinmuth (100) German: from a Germanic personal name composed of the elements *ragin* 'counsel' + *muot* 'mind', 'sense'.

Reino (135) Italian: possibly from a masculinized form of **Reina**, a southern form of REGINA.
GIVEN NAMES Italian 12%; Spanish 9%. *Antonio, Carlo, Carmela, Enrico, Matteo; Jose* (3), *Juan, Luis, Pilar.*

Reinoehl (284) German (**Reinöhl**): from an elaborated form of *Reinel*, a pet form of REIN 1.

Reinoso (244) Spanish and Portuguese: habitational name from either of the places called Reinoso, in Burgos and Palencia, apparently from a derivative of *reino* 'kingdom'.

GIVEN NAMES Spanish 51%. *Carlos* (8), *Jose* (6), *Luis* (6), *Juan* (5), *Ana* (3), *Francisco* (3), *Pedro* (3), *Ramon* (3), *Roberto* (3), *Eudaldo* (2), *Jaime* (2), *Lourdes* (2).

Reins (128) North German: patronymic from REIN 1.

GIVEN NAMES German 11%. *Alfons, Dieter, Gerhardt, Kurt.*

Reinsch (332) German: from a pet form of REIN 1. The *-sch* ending indicates a Slavic–Eastern German origin. Compare REINISCH.

Reinschmidt (147) **1.** German: distinguishing name for a smith called Reinbold or Reinhard (see REIN, SCHMIDT). **2.** Jewish (Ashkenazic): from German *rein* 'pure' + *Schmidt* 'smith', an occupational name with a qualifying or ornamental prefix.

Reinsel (170) Probably of German origin: unexplained.

Reinsmith (122) Americanization of German REINSCHMIDT.

Reinstein (322) Jewish (Ashkenazic): ornamental compound of German *rein* 'pure' + *Stein* 'stone'.

GIVEN NAMES Jewish 6%. *Sol* (5), *Arie, Jakob.*

Reints (156) North German (Frisian): patronymic from REINERT.

Reinwald (272) North German: from a Germanic personal name composed of the elements *ragin* 'counsel' + *wald* 'rule'.

GIVEN NAMES German 6%. *Fritz* (2), *Berthold, Hanns, Kurt, Udo.*

Reis (4042) **1.** German: from Middle High German *rīs* 'undergrowth', 'brushwood'; a topographic name for someone who lived in an overgrown area, or a habitational name from Reis or Reissen in Bavaria, named with this word. **2.** German: occupational name for a cobbler, Middle High German *riuze*. Compare REUSS. **3.** German: variant of REISS 2, or from the Huguenot name **Ris**. **4.** Altered spelling of German RIES. **5.** Portuguese and Galician: from a short form of *dos Reis* '(of) the (Three) Kings', a personal name popularly bestowed on someone born on the feast of the Epiphany, which celebrates the manifestation of Christ to the Gentiles as represented by the Magi. This is a frequent family name in southern Portugal. **6.** Jewish (Ashkenazic): metonymic occupational name for a dealer in rice or an ornamental name from German *Reis* 'rice'. **7.** Jewish (Ashkenazic): ornamental name from German *Reis* 'twig', 'branch'. **8.** Turkish: from *reis* 'boss', 'chief', 'head of a business enterprise'. A Greek derivative of this is also found as a surname, in the form **Reizis**.

GIVEN NAMES Spanish 5%; Portuguese 4%. *Manuel* (37), *Jose* (25), *Carlos* (10), *Luis* (10), *Jorge* (7), *Alberto* (4), *Julio* (4), *Luiz* (4), *Alvaro* (3), *Francisco* (3), *Geraldo* (3), *Juanita* (3); *Joao* (5), *Paulo* (3), *Guilherme*

(2), *Serafim* (2), *Afonso, Duarte, Henrique, Joaquim, Marcio.*

Reisberg (115) Jewish (Ashkenazic): ornamental name compound from German *Reis* 'rice' + *Berg* 'hill'.

GIVEN NAME Jewish 6%. *Aron.*

Reisch (449) German: from Middle High German *rīsch, rüsch* 'reed' or 'rush', a topographic name for someone who lived near a reedbed, or a habitational name from any of several places in Bavaria and Moravia named Reisch from the same word.

GIVEN NAMES German 5%. *Franz* (2), *Otto* (2), *Hans, Kurt.*

Reische (101) German: variant of REISCH.

Reischl (122) South German and Austrian: from a diminutive of Middle High German *rīsch, rüsch* 'reed' or 'rush' (see REISCH).

GIVEN NAMES German 9%. *Helmut, Manfred, Uwe.*

Reischman (163) Altered spelling of German **Reischmann**, a variant of REISCH.

Reisdorf (277) **1.** German: habitational name from any of various places called Reisdorf throughout Germany and in Austria. **2.** Dutch: habitational name from Reisdorf in the Grand Duchy of Luxembourg, or possibly from the places mentioned at 1.

Reise (195) **1.** German (Westphalia): topographic name, from Middle Low German *rīs, rēs* 'swamp'. **2.** German and Jewish (Ashkenazic): nickname for a well-traveled person, from Middle High German *reis(e)*, German *Reise* 'journey'.

Reisen (175) Jewish (Ashkenazic): origin uncertain; possibly an ornamental name from northeastern Yiddish *reyzn* 'roses' (standard Yiddish *royzn*) (see ROSE 3).

Reisenauer (245) German: probably a habitational name for someone from a minor place called Reisenau, or a topographic name for someone living by an overgrown water meadow, from Middle High German *rīs* 'undergrowth' + *ōwe* 'water meadow'.

Reiser (1852) South German: **1.** habitational name for someone from Reis or Reissen in Bavaria (see REIS 1). **2.** occupational name from Middle High German *reisære* 'warrior', 'traveler'. **3.** South German: topographic name for someone who lived near a thicket (see RIESER 1 and RISER 1). **4.** variant spelling of **Reisser**, an occupational name for a woodcutter, Middle High German *rīsser*.

GIVEN NAMES German 4%. *Hans* (4), *Erwin* (3), *Kurt* (3), *Otto* (2), *Hannelore, Heiner, Helmut, Markus, Siegfried, Willi.*

Reisert (180) variant of REISER 1, with the addition of an excrescent *-t*. **2.** variant of **Reissert**, a variant of the Germanic personal name *Ricohard* (see RICHARD).

GIVEN NAMES German 7%. *Hans* (2), *Kurt, Mathias.*

Reish (250) German: variant of REISCH.

Reishus (114) Norwegian: habitational name from the name of an an abandoned tenant farm called Reishus in Flatdal, Telemark. The first element is probably *røys*, Old Norse *hreysi* 'heap of stones', the second is *hus* 'house', 'small farm'.

Reisig (367) German: nickname from Middle High German *reisec*, Middle Low German *reisich* 'armed for war', later 'sprightly', 'tall'. See also REISER 2.

GIVEN NAMES German 4%. *Erna, Gerhard, Heinz.*

Reising (642) German: **1.** variant of REISINGER. **2.** from a Germanic personal name based on an unexplained stem, *riese.*

Reisinger (1527) German: **1.** habitational name for someone from any of several places called Reising or Reisingen in Bavaria. **2.** occupational name for a soldier, from Middle High German *reisinc* 'warrior', literally, 'traveler'. **3.** in the south a topographic name, from Middle High German *rīs* 'branch', 'shrubbery', denoting someone who lived near a thicket or underbrush.

Reisler (140) **1.** German: occupational name from Middle High German *reiseler* 'carter', 'carrier'. **2.** Respelling of German **Reissler**, a variant of REITZEL 2. **3.** Jewish (Ashkenazic): from REIS 4 + the agent suffix *-ler*.

GIVEN NAMES German 4%; Jewish 4%. *Kurt; Miriam* (2), *Gerson.*

Reisman (960) **1.** German (**Reismann**): occupational name for a woodcutter, Middle High German *rīsman*. Compare REISER. This name is also found in Slovenia. **2.** Jewish (Ashkenazic): elaborated variant of REIS 4.

GIVEN NAMES Jewish 7%. *Bernat* (2), *Chaim* (2), *Eyal* (2), *Moshe* (2), *Pinchas* (2), *Yisroel* (2), *Hinda, Isidor, Liat, Miriam, Sol.*

Reisner (785) **1.** German: probably a habitational name for someone from a place called Reisen (for example in Bavaria), Reissen in Thuringia, or Reussen on the Saale river. **2.** German: variant of REISNER 2. **3.** German: from an agent derivative of Middle High German, Middle Low German *rīse* 'veil'; perhaps an occupational name for someone who made veils. **4.** Jewish (Ashkenazic): nickname for a traveler, from an agent derivative of German *reisen* 'to travel' (see REISE 2). **5.** Jewish (Ashkenazic): variant of REIS 4 + the agent suffix *-ner*.

Reiss (3291) **1.** German: variant of REIS 1. **2.** German: from any of several Germanic personal names composed with *rīc* 'power(ful)'. **3.** Jewish (Ashkenazic): variant of REIS. **4.** German: from a French Huguenot name **Ris**, rendered as *Reis, Reiss.*

Reissig (201) German: **1.** variant of REISIG. **2.** nickname for an acquisitive person, from Middle High German *reizec*

'greedy', 'covetous'. **3.** topographic name from Middle High German *rīsach* 'undergrowth', 'brushwood'. Compare REIS 1.
GIVEN NAME German 4%. *Arnulf.*

Reissman (106) **1.** German (**Reissmann**): occupational name from Middle High German *reisman* 'warrior', 'mounted messenger'. **2.** Jewish (Ashkenazic): variant of REISMAN.
GIVEN NAMES Jewish 6%; German 4%. *Aviva, Yitzchak.*

Reist (302) Swiss German: unexplained.

Reistad (127) Norwegian: habitational name from any of several farmstead named from the Old Norse personal name *Reiðarr* + *staðir*, plural of *staðr* 'farmstead', 'dwelling'.
GIVEN NAMES Scandinavian 12%. *Knut* (2), *Egil, Erik.*

Reister (371) German: habitational name from someone from Reiste in Westphalia.
GIVEN NAMES German 4%. *Fritz, Guenter, Horst, Karlheinz.*

Reiswig (316) German: probably from a Germanic personal name composed of an unexplained element, *Ris* or *Reis*, + *wīg*, *wīc* 'battle', 'conflict'.

Reisz (211) **1.** Dutch: patronymic from a pet form of one of the Germanic compound names formed with *ragin* 'counsel' as the first element. **2.** Jewish (from Hungary): Hungarian spelling of REIS.
GIVEN NAMES Jewish 10%. *Moshe* (3), *Pincus* (3), *Zalmen* (2), *Hershel.*

Reitan (280) Norwegian: habitational name from any of numerous farmsteads in Trøndelag named with the definite plural form of *reit*, from Old Norse *reitr* 'small cultivated field'.
GIVEN NAMES Scandinavian 6%. *Arlys* (2), *Erik, Ketil.*

Reitano (307) Italian (Sicily): **1.** habitational name from a place so called in the Messina region. **2.** from *rizzitano, riitano*, dialect forms of Italian *reggino*, regional name for someone from Reggio Calabria.
GIVEN NAMES Italian 14%. *Salvatore* (5), *Domenic* (4), *Rocco* (2), *Carmelo, Gaetana, Guido, Luigi, Stefano.*

Reiten (179) **1.** German: topographic name for someone who lived in a clearing in woodland (see REITH 1). **2.** Norwegian: habitational name, a variant of REITAN, from the definite singular form of *reit*.
GIVEN NAME Scandinavian 5%. *Ardeen.*

Reiter (4497) German: **1.** occupational name for a mounted soldier or knight, from Middle Low German *rider*, Middle High German *rīter* 'rider'. **2.** variant of REUTER 1. **3.** habitational name for someone from any of various places in Germany and Austria called Reit or Reith (see REITH).

Reith (762) **1.** Scottish: of uncertain origin; possibly a reduced form of **McCreath** (see McRAE). **2.** German: habitational name from any of several places named with *riute* 'forest clearing'. Compare REITER, REUTER.

Reither (177) German: variant of REITER or REUTER.

Reitman (416) **1.** German (**Reitmann**): variant of REITMEIER or REITH 3. **2.** Jewish (from Belarus): from the northeastern Yiddish pronunciation of standard Yiddish *royt* 'red' + *man* 'man'; a nickname for a person with red hair, or an ornamental name. **3.** Jewish (Ashkenazic): from Yiddish *raytn* 'to ride' + *man* 'man', most probably an ornamental name.
GIVEN NAMES Jewish 4%. *Avram, Danit, Mort.*

Reitmeier (221) German: **1.** in southern Germany, a distinguishing nickname for a tenant farmer (see MEYER) who farmed in a forest clearing (Middle High German *riute*). **2.** in the north, a distinguishing nickname for a tenant farmer who farmed in a reedy location, from Middle Low German *rēt* 'reed'.
GIVEN NAMES German 4%. *Erwin, Franz, Johannes.*

Reitmeyer (246) German: variant of REITMEIER.

Reitnauer (103) Swiss German: habitational name for someone from a place called Reitnau in Aargau canton or possibly from Reitenau in Baden-Württemberg, Germany.
GIVEN NAMES German 9%. *Otto, Wilhelm.*

Reitsma (255) Frisian: variant spelling of **Reintsema**, from a short form of REINHART + patronymic *-s* + Frisian *-ma* 'man'.
GIVEN NAMES German 5%; Dutch 4%. *Erwin* (2), *Hans, Kurt*; *Dirk, Durk, Pim.*

Reitter (184) German: **1.** occupational name for a mounted soldier or knight, from Middle High German *rītære* 'horseman'. **2.** habitational name for someone from any of various places called Reit(t) 'clearing' (see REITH).
GIVEN NAMES German 11%. *Klaus* (2), *Otto* (2), *Erwin, Fritz, Waltraud.*

Reitz (3064) **1.** German (of Slavic origin): habitational name from a place near Stolpe in Pomerania called Reitz. **2.** German: from a late medieval short pet form of the personal name RICHARD or *Heinrich* (see HENRY). **3.** Jewish (Ashkenazic): from the Yiddish female personal name *Raytse*, of Germanic origin.

Reitzel (462) German: **1.** from a pet form of a Germanic name, *Ragizo*, derived from compound names formed with *rag-* 'advice' as the first element, or from a Slavic personal name. **2.** nickname from Middle High German *reiz(z)el* 'bait' (for fowling).

Reker (197) **1.** North German: reduced form of REDEKER. **2.** It may also be a respelled form of Slovenian **Rekar**, a topographic name for someone who lived by a river, from *reka* 'river', or a variant of **Rekar**, a habitational name for someone from any of numerous places called Reka, named with this element.

Rekow (144) German: probably a topographic name from Slavic *rēka* 'river'.

Rekowski (177) Polish: habitational name for someone from places called Rekowo in Płock and Gdańsk voivodeships.

Relaford (112) Origin unidentified. See RELIFORD.

Releford (202) Origin unidentified. See RELIFORD.

Relf (223) Southern English (of Norman origin): from the Old French personal name *Riulf*, composed of the Germanic elements *rīc* 'power' + *wulf* 'wolf'.

Relford (136) Origin unidentified. See RELIFORD.
GIVEN NAME French 4%. *Patrice.*

Reliford (395) Origin unidentified. This is a common LA surname; most bearers are African Americans. The surname has the form of an English habitational name, but no source has been identified and the surname is not found in Britain in present-day records. Compare RELAFORD, RELEFORD, RELFORD.

Relihan (125) Irish: reduced Anglicized form of Gaelic **Ó Roileacháin** 'descendant of *Roileachán*', probably a diminutive of the unexplained personal name *Roghallach*.

Rella (288) **1.** Italian: from a pet form (with the ending *-ella*) of a personal name ending in *-ro*, all other trace of which has been lost. **2.** Greek: reduced form of **Rellas** or **Rellakis**, an occupational name for an embroiderer, a derivative of Greek *reli* 'hem', 'border', from Italian *reglio*.
GIVEN NAMES Italian 29%. *Vito* (4), *Angelo* (3), *Giuseppe* (3), *Onofrio* (3), *Rocco* (3), *Orazio* (2), *Antonio, Carlo, Fedele, Lorenzo, Mauro.*

Reller (385) Swiss German: occupational name for a miller, from the dialect term *relle* 'grist mill'.

Relph (194) English: variant spelling of RELF.

Relyea (699) Altered spelling of South German **Rellier**, probably a regional variant of RELLER, especially in the western provinces of Austria.

Remaley (349) Probably an Americanized spelling of Swiss and German **Remele** or **Remmele** (see REMLEY).

Remaly (183) Probably an altered spelling of Swiss and German **Remele** or **Remmele** (see REMLEY).

Rembert (826) **1.** North German: from a personal name composed of the Germanic elements *ragin* 'counsel' + *berht* 'bright', 'famous'. **2.** French: from an Old French personal name, *Rainbert* (cognate with the name mentioned in 1).

Rembold (233) German: from a Germanic personal name composed of the elements *ragin* 'counsel' + *bald* 'bold', 'brave'.
GIVEN NAMES German 6%. *Manfred* (2), *Heinz.*

Remedies (110) Americanized form of Spanish and Portuguese REMEDIOS.

Remedios (125) Spanish: from a short form of the Marian name *Maria de los Remedios*, from *remedios*, plural of *remedio* 'cure'.

GIVEN NAMES Spanish 31%. *Fernando* (5), *Carlos* (3), *Jorge* (2), *Romulo* (2), *Aida*, *Alfonso*, *Armindo*, *Azucena*, *Benito*, *Candido*, *Enrique*, *Isidro*.

Rementer (128) Variant of German **Remter**, from Middle Low German *remeter*, *rēmter* 'refectory' (the dining hall in a convent or monastery), hence probably an occupational name for someone who worked there.

Remer (683) **1.** North German and Dutch: occupational name for a maker of leather reins and similar articles, from Middle Low German *remer* 'leather worker' (compare RIEMER). **2.** North German: from a Germanic personal name composed of the elements *ragin* 'counsel' + *māri*, *mēri* 'fame', as in REIMER. **3.** Jewish (Ashkenazic): ornamental name from German *Römer* 'Roman'.

Remes (134) **1.** Finnish: probably from a vernacular form of the personal name *Remigius* (see REMY). Found chiefly in eastern Finland. **2.** Greek, Dutch, and German: variant of REMIS 1 and 2. **3.** Jewish (from Belarus): habitational name for someone from Remezy, in Belarus.

GIVEN NAME Finnish 4%. *Waino* (2).

Remick (738) **1.** Variant of German **Remig**, a derivative of the medieval saint's name *Remigius* (see REMY). **2.** Americanized spelling of Slovenian **Remic**, nickname from the dialectal bird name *remec* 'penduline tit' (Latin *Parus pendulinus*).

Remigio (126) Spanish: from the personal name *Remigio*, Latin *Remigius* (see REMY).

GIVEN NAMES Spanish 37%. *Jose* (2), *Juan* (2), *Pedro* (2), *Andres*, *Angelito*, *Aurelio*, *Corazon*, *Cristino*, *Eduardo*, *Emilia*, *Eulalio*, *Francisco*.

Remillard (1010) French (**Rémillard**): probably a derivative of REMY.

FOREBEARS A Rémillard, apparently from the Limousin region of France, was recorded in Quebec City in 1678.

GIVEN NAMES French 12%. *Andre* (4), *Armand* (2), *Colette* (2), *Laurent* (2), *Lucien* (2), *Marcel* (2), *Michel* (2), *Pierre* (2), *Solange* (2), *Aime*, *Alain*, *Aldor*.

Remington (2299) English: habitational name from Rimington in Yorkshire, so called from the old name of the stream on which it stands (Old English *Riming* 'boundary stream') + Old English *tūn* 'enclosure', 'settlement'.

FOREBEARS The American painter Frederic Remington (1861–1909) was descended from John Remington, living in MA in 1639; his father, Eliphalet Remington, was born in Suffield, CT (1793), and was a noted firearms manufacturer.

Remis (150) **1.** Greek: from a medieval Greek personal name, *Remis*, a vernacular form of the personal name *Remigius* (see French REMY). **2.** Dutch and German: from a vernacular form of the personal name *Remigius* (see REMY). **3.** Asturian-Leonese (**Remís**): variant of the Latin personal name *Remigius*, from Asturian-Leonese *Remicio*.

GIVEN NAMES Spanish 6%. *Mario* (2), *Aleida*, *Carlos*, *Domingo*, *Ignacio*, *Luis*.

Remke (142) **1.** North German and Frisian: from the medieval personal name *Remko*, a pet form of REMBERT. **2.** Altered spelling of German **Römke**, a topographic name from a field in Altmark or a river in the Harz Mountains.

Remley (651) Americanized spelling of German and Swiss German **Remmele** (see REMMEL 1) or **Remmler**, a variant of **Rammler** (see RAMLER).

Remlinger (170) German: habitational name for someone from either of two places named Remlingen, one near Wolfenbüttel, the other near Würzburg.

Remme (173) North German: from a reduced form of the personal name REMBERT.

Remmel (302) German: **1.** from a pet form of the personal name *Rembold*, composed of the Germanic elements *ragin* 'counsel' + *bald* 'bold'. **2.** southern diminutive of RAMM 1.

Remmers (491) North German and Dutch: patronymic from a reduced form of the Germanic personal name REMBERT.

Remmert (292) North German: from the Germanic personal name REMBERT.

GIVEN NAMES German 4%. *Kurt* (2), *Erwin*.

Remmick (123) Of German origin: variant spelling of REMICK.

Remo (147) Hispanic: unexplained; possibly related to Spanish *remo* 'oar', 'paddle'.

GIVEN NAMES Spanish 13%. *Andres*, *Bernardo*, *Domingo*, *Efren*, *Ernesto*, *Eugenio*, *Jose*, *Manuel*, *Mariano*, *Marina*, *Raymundo*, *Remedios*.

Remp (136) German: **1.** (Swabian): from Middle German *remp* 'breeding bull'; a nickname for someone with a lecherous reputation, or for someone who owned a breeding bull. **2.** from a short form of the personal name *Rembold* or *Reimbert*. Compare REMMEL, REMMERT.

Rempe (398) German: **1.** variant of REMP 2. **2.** from a reduced and altered form of the female personal name *Reinburg*.

Rempel (475) German (eastern): from the medieval German personal name *Rempel*, a pet form of the Germanic personal name *Rambold*. Compare REMMEL 1.

GIVEN NAMES German 5%. *Florian* (2), *Wilhelm* (2), *Dietrich*, *Gerhard*, *Hans*, *Hertha*.

Rempfer (184) German: from a Germanic personal name, *Raganfrid*, composed of *ragin* 'advice' + *frid-* 'peace'.

Remsberg (156) Possibly an altered spelling of **Ramsberg**, a habitational name from any of several places so named in Bavaria.

Remsburg (186) Variant of German **Ramsberg** (see RAMSBURG).

Remsen (282) Possibly an altered spelling of **Ramsen**, a habitational name from any of two places so named in the Palatinate and Switzerland.

Remson (155) Walloon: from a Walloon pet form, with the double diminutive suffix *-eçon*, of a Germanic personal name formed with *ragin* 'counsel' as the first element.

GIVEN NAMES French 6%; German 4%. *Marcel* (2), *Susette*; *Eldred*, *Erna*.

Remund (163) Variant (especially Swiss) of French RAYMOND.

Remus (557) German: **1.** from a reduced form of the personal name *Remigius*; or *Remedius* (see REMY). **2.** from a reduced form of a Germanic personal name based on *ragin* 'advice', 'counsel' + *munt* 'protection'.

GIVEN NAMES German 6%. *Kurt* (3), *Dieter*, *Gerd*, *Hans*, *Heinz*, *Helmuth*, *Horst*, *Juergen*.

Remy (1030) French (**Rémy**) and Swiss German: from a medieval personal name which represents a falling together of two distinct Latin names: *Remigius* (a derivative of *remex*, genitive *remigis*, 'rower, oarsman'), and *Remedius* (from *remedium* 'cure', 'remedy'). The former name was borne by a 6th-century bishop of Rheims; the latter was borne by various minor saints of the 8th to 10th centuries.

FOREBEARS A Rémy is cited in 1663 in Trois-Rivières, Quebec, with the secondary surname CHAMPAGNE. **Lespérance** is also found as a secondary surname with this name.

GIVEN NAMES French 10%. *Andre* (3), *Jean-Claude* (2), *Evens*, *Germaine*, *Gisele*, *Henri*, *Hugues*, *Jacques*, *Jean Raymond*, *Jean-Daniel*, *Josee*, *Laurent*.

Ren (505) **1.** English: unexplained. Perhaps a variant of WREN. **2.** Dutch (**de Ren**): origin unexplained. **3.** Variant spelling of German RENN. **4.** Swedish: soldier's name, from *ren* 'reindeer'. **5.** Chinese 任: from the name of *Rencheng* 'Ren City', which was granted to Yu Yang, the 25th son of the Emperor Huang Di (2697–2595 BC). Some of his descendants later adopted the place name as their surname.

GIVEN NAMES Chinese 44%. *Wei* (4), *Yong* (4), *Hong* (3), *Hui* (3), *Chuan* (2), *Gang* (2), *Guang* (2), *Jian* (2), *Liang* (2), *Lihua* (2), *Ning* (2), *Qing* (2); *Chang* (2), *Min*, *Shen*, *Yiming*.

Renaker (122) Variant of German **Rennecker** (see RENNEKER).

Renaldi (141) Italian: patronymic or plural form of RENALDO.

GIVEN NAME Italian 5%. *Sarina*.

Renaldo (154) Italian: from the personal name *Renaldo*, Italian equivalent of REYNOLD.
GIVEN NAMES Italian 7%. *Angelo, Carmine, Chiara, Reno.*

Renard (718) French: variant of REYNARD.
FOREBEARS The name Renard is recorded in Quebec City in 1677, with the secondary surnames DESLAURIERS, CARDON or Cadron dit Saint Pierre.
GIVEN NAMES French 7%. *Andre* (2), *Henri* (2), *Armand, Emile, Jacques, Marielle, Michel, Monique, Olivier, Pierre, Remi, Serge.*

Renaud (2272) French: from a Germanic personal name composed of the elements *ragin* 'counsel' + *wald* 'rule' (equivalent to English REYNOLD).
FOREBEARS The North American Renaud families descend from settlers from Normandy, Poitou, the Languedcoc, and Anjou; they were first recorded in Quebec City in 1668. Secondary surnames associated with Renaud include: CANARD, Davenne, d'Avesne, DESLAURIERS, Desmoulins, LANGLOIS, Locat, Saint-Jean.
GIVEN NAMES French 12%. *Andre* (7), *Pierre* (6), *Armand* (5), *Normand* (5), *Gilles* (4), *Adelard* (3), *Gisele* (3), *Cecile* (2), *Chantal* (2), *Emile* (2), *Gaston* (2), *Germaine* (2).

Renault (214) French: variant spelling of RENAUD.
GIVEN NAMES French 15%. *Pierre* (3), *Jacques, Jean-Yves, Lucien, Marcel, Mireille, Pascal.*

Renbarger (177) Variant spelling of German **Renneberg** (see RENBERG).

Renberg (116) Swedish: ornamental name composed of the elements *ren* 'reindeer' or an element taken from a place name such as Renum + *berg* 'mountain'.
GIVEN NAME Scandinavian 4%. *Lennart.*

Rench (418) **1.** English: perhaps a variant spelling of **Wrench**, a nickname from Middle English *wrench* 'trick', 'artifice'. **2.** Probably an altered spelling of German RENSCH or RENTSCH.

Rencher (277) **1.** English: perhaps a variant of **Wrench** (see RENCH). **2.** probably also an Americanized spelling of German RENEGAR.

Renck (102) German: variant spelling of RENK.

Renda (666) **1.** Southern Italian: probably from a personal name, a derivative of *Lorenzo* or from a feminine form of the personal name *Rendo*, a variant of RANDO. **2.** Italian: habitational name from a place called Renda.
GIVEN NAMES Italian 15%. *Salvatore* (6), *Santo* (3), *Vito* (3), *Francesco* (2), *Angelo, Antonio, Carlo, Carmelo, Carmine, Corrado, Gilda, Italo.*

Rendahl (112) **1.** Swedish: ornamental name, the second element of which is *dahl* (ornamental spelling of *dal* 'valley'); the first element is unidentified, probably from a place name. **2.** Norwegian: habitational name from a farm name; the first element is either a river name or *rein* 'strip of grass at the margins of a field', 'headland'; the second element is *dal* 'valley'.

Rendall (289) **1.** English: variant of RANDALL. **2.** Scottish (Orkney): habitational name from Rendall in Orkney. **3.** Probably also an Americanization of Swedish RENDAHL.

Rende (309) Italian (Calabrian and Sicilian): habitational name from Rende in Cosenza province.
GIVEN NAMES Italian 15%. *Sal* (3), *Duilio* (2), *Carmela, Carmine, Emilio, Francesco, Luciano, Luigi, Rocco, Salvatore, Santo, Silvio.*

Rendel (122) **1.** German: habitational name from Rendel in Hesse. **2.** South German: variant of REINDL. **3.** Jewish (Ashkenazic): ornamental name from Yiddish *rendl* 'ducat (gold coin)'. **4.** Possibly also English: variant spelling of RENDALL.
GIVEN NAMES Jewish 8%. *Aryeh* (2), *Zvi.*

Rendell (199) English: **1.** variant of RANDALL. **2.** variant spelling of RENDALL 2.

Render (716) **1.** Northern English: of uncertain origin, perhaps from an agent derivative of Middle English *rend(en)* 'to divide or split', hence an occupational name for a woodcutter or a butcher. **2.** German: probably a habitational name for someone from Renda (or Rendel) in Hesse.

Renderos (113) Spanish: possibly a habitational name from a place named from *rendero* 'tenant', 'leaseholder'. The surname is not found in present-day Spain, but is recorded in El Salvador.
GIVEN NAMES Spanish 58%. *Jorge* (5), *Carlos* (3), *Elia* (3), *Juan* (2), *Luis* (2), *Mario* (2), *Roberto* (2), *Rosa Maria* (2), *Rosaura* (2), *Aida, Amada, Blanca; Antonio, Marco.*

Rendina (162) Italian: from a diminutive of RENDA.
GIVEN NAMES Italian 13%. *Cesare* (2), *Severino* (2), *Gaetano, Luigi.*

Rendine (109) Italian: from a diminutive of RENDA.
GIVEN NAME Italian 8%. *Luigi.*

Rendleman (294) Altered spelling of German **Rendelmann**, a habitational name for someone from Rendel in Hesse.

Rendon (2034) Spanish (**Rendón**): unexplained; possibly connected with the adverb *(de) rendón* 'bold', 'daring', old variant of Spanish *rondón* (see RONDON).
GIVEN NAMES Spanish 46%. *Manuel* (24), *Jose* (23), *Juan* (20), *Carlos* (19), *Jesus* (18), *Raul* (16), *Ruben* (16), *Jorge* (13), *Luis* (13), *Mario* (12), *Alfredo* (10), *Ramon* (10).

Rene (450) French (**René**): from a personal name (Latin *Renatus* 'reborn') borne by a 4th-century saint, and popular in France throughout the Middle Ages because of its transparent reference to Christian spiritual rebirth.

GIVEN NAMES French 17%. *Andre* (2), *Marcel* (2), *Pierre* (2), *Antoine, Collette, Emile, Fernand, Fernande, Frenel, Gaetan, Gisele, Jacques.*

Reneau (1078) French (Poitou): from Middle French *rein* 'limit', 'border', perhaps a topographic name for someone who lived at the edge of an estate.

Renee (170) Possibly a respelling of French **René** (see RENE).

Renegar (432) Altered spelling of German **Renger**, variant of RANG 3 or of RENKER.

Renehan (225) Irish (County Cork): reduced Anglicized form of Gaelic **Ó Reannacháin** 'descendant of *Reannachán*', from a diminutive of *reannach* 'sharppointed' or 'starry'.

Rener (101) French: probably a variant REINER.
GIVEN NAMES French 8%. *Pierre, Remy.*

Renew (126) Anglicized spelling of French RENEAU. This is the name of an influential Huguenot family in Cork, Ireland, in the 17th century.

Reney (107) Scottish and Irish: variant of RAINEY.

Renfer (139) German and Swiss German: from the German personal name *Reinfried*, composed of the Germanic elements *ragin* 'counsel' + *frid* 'peace'.
GIVEN NAME German 6%. *Kurt.*

Renfrew (295) Scottish: habitational name from Renfrew near Glasgow, named with a British term cognate with Welsh *rhyn frwd* 'point of current'.

Renfro (3531) Variant spelling of Scottish RENFREW.

Renfroe (1694) Variant spelling of Scottish RENFREW.

Renfrow (1456) Variant spelling of Scottish RENFREW.

Rengel (132) **1.** Swiss German: from a pet form of a Germanic personal name formed with *rang* 'curved', 'bending'; 'slender'. **2.** Spanish: habitational name from a place called Rengel in Málaga province.
GIVEN NAMES German 5%; Spanish 5%. *Urs* (2), *Mathias; Eduardo, Enrique, Jaime, Julio, Ramona, Roberto.*

Rengifo (104) Spanish: unexplained.
GIVEN NAMES Spanish 55%. *Luis* (6), *Jairo* (4), *Carlos* (3), *Jose* (3), *Francisco* (2), *Gustavo* (2), *Ricardo* (2), *Abelardo, Aida, Alcira, Ana, Andres.*

Renick (804) Possibly an altered form of Scottish RENWICK, or a variant spelling of **Renicke**, a variant of German REINECKE.

Renier (247) French: variant of RAINIER.

Reninger (101) Respelling of German RENNINGER.
GIVEN NAMES French 8%. *Normand, Patrice.*

Renk (353) **1.** North German: from a pet form of the personal name *Reinhard*, composed of the Germanic elements *ragin* 'advice' + *hard* 'hardy', 'brave', 'strong'. **2.** Southern German: habitational name from Rengg in the districts of Zurich and Lucerne.

Renken (845) German: derivative of RENK in either of its senses.

GIVEN NAMES German 4%. *Otto* (2), *Erhart, Erwin, Heinz, Konrad, Otmar, Uwe, Wolfgang.*

Renker (101) German: from a Germanic personal name *Reinger*, composed of the elements *ragin* 'advice', 'counsel' + *gār, gēr* 'spear', 'lance'.

GIVEN NAMES German 8%. *Horst* (2), *Dietmar.*

Renko (150) German: from a pet form of a Germanic personal name formed with the element *rang* 'curved', 'bending'; 'slender'.

Renn (1065) North German: Frisian RENNERT (see REINHART).

Renna (627) Southern Italian: variant of RENDA.

GIVEN NAMES Italian 11%. *Angelo* (3), *Salvatore* (3), *Antonio* (2), *Giovanni* (2), *Nicola* (2), *Carmela, Francesco, Franco, Gennaro, Graziella, Leonardo, Raffaela.*

Rennaker (160) German: see RENNEKER.

Rennard (141) English: variant of REYNARD.

Renne (366) North German: variant of RENN.

Renneker (122) Variant of German **Rennecker**, a habitational name for someone from Rieneck in Franconia, which was formerly written also as Reinekke and Renegge.

Rennels (193) English: patronymic from REYNOLD.

Renner (5521) English, German, and Swiss German: **1.** from an agent derivative of Middle English, Middle High German *rennen* 'to run', hence an occupational name for a messenger, normally a mounted and armed military servant. **2.** variant of RAYNER 1, REINER.

Rennert (265) **1.** North German: from the personal name *Reinhard* (see REINHARDT). **2.** Jewish (Ashkenazic): unexplained, possibly an adoption of the German name (see 1).

GIVEN NAMES Jewish 11%; German 4%. *Eliyohu* (2), *Meyer* (2), *Anshel, Chaim, Eliyahu, Menachem, Mordecai, Reuven, Shmuel; Hans, Klaus, Rudi.*

Rennhack (126) German: probably an occupational name for a fast-moving street trader or for one riding a horse, from Middle Low German *rennen* 'to run', 'ride (on horseback)' + *hake* 'huckster', 'street trader'.

GIVEN NAMES German 5%. *Dieter, Kurt.*

Rennick (467) **1.** Scottish and northern English: variant of RENWICK. **2.** Altered spelling of German **Rennich**, a variant of REINECKE.

Rennie (1518) Scottish: variant of RAINEY.

Renninger (842) German: habitational name for someone from Renningen in Württemberg. This name is concentrated in PA.

Rennison (116) English: patronymic from REYNOLD.

Renno (182) Southern Italian: **1.** variant of RENDA 1. **2.** variant of RANDO.

Reno (3284) Altered spelling of French RENAUD, RENAULT, or RENOUF.

Renouf (123) English (Channel Islands) and Norman French: from a Norman personal name, *Reginwulf*, composed of the Germanic elements *ragin* 'counsel' + *wulf* 'wolf'.

Rens (209) Dutch: from a reduced form of the personal name *Laurens* (see LAWRENCE).

Rensberger (161) Probably a Germanized form of Dutch **van Rensberg**, a habitational name for someone from Rensberg in Brabant, Belgium.

Rensch (267) German: **1.** from a reduced form of any of the Germanic compound personal names with the first element *ragin* 'counsel', for example REINHOLD or *Reinhard* (see REINHARDT). **2.** much altered reduced form of the personal name *Laurens* or *Lorenz* (see LAWRENCE). **3.** short form of a personal name of Slavic origin, formed with the element *ranu* 'early'. **4.** variant of RENSCHLER.

Renschler (131) German: variant of RENTSCHLER.

GIVEN NAMES German 8%. *Markus, Otto, Reinhold.*

Rensel (117) Americanized spelling of German **Renzel** (see RENTZEL).

Renshaw (1611) English: habitational name from Renishaw in Derbyshire, named from the Middle English personal name REYNOLD + *shawe* 'copse'. The name is still found chiefly in Derbyshire, South Yorkshire, and Lancashire.

Rensing (181) Dutch and North German: **1.** habitational name from a place so called near Itzehoe. **2.** (Frisian): patronymic from a short form of Germanic compound personal name formed with the initial element *ragin*.

Rensink (145) Variant of Dutch and North German RENSING.

GIVEN NAMES German 4%; Dutch 4%. *Kurt; Gerrit* (2), *Marinus.*

Renslow (135) Perhaps an altered spelling of German **Renzle**, from a pet form of RENTZ.

Renstrom (284) Swedish (**Renström**): ornamental name composed of the elements *ren* 'reindeer' or an element taken from a place name such as Renum + *ström* 'river'.

GIVEN NAME Scandinavian 7%. *Per.*

Renta (121) Spanish and Portuguese: most probably from *renta* 'income', 'rental'. This name is common mainly in the Caribbean; it is rare in Spain.

GIVEN NAMES Spanish 19%. *Jose* (3), *Angel* (2), *Alicia, Bolivar, Francisco, Jorge, Juan, Julio, Magda, Manuel, Nydia, Virgen.*

Rentas (198) Spanish and Portuguese: plural form of RENTA.

GIVEN NAMES Spanish 34%. *Carlos* (4), *Jose* (4), *Pedro* (3), *Ramonita* (3), *Angel* (2), *Juan* (2), *Manuel* (2), *Mario* (2), *Tomas* (2), *Aida, Armando, Blanca.*

Renter (118) German: probably a short form of a personal name composed with *rant* 'edge (of a shield)', 'shield'.

GIVEN NAMES German 5%. *Hans* (2), *Friedrich.*

Renteria (2140) Spanish (**Rentería**): Castilianized variant of Basque **Errenteria**, habitational name from either of the two Basque towns called Errenteria in Gipuzkoa and Biscay provinces, Basque Country.

GIVEN NAMES Spanish 51%. *Jose* (46), *Manuel* (28), *Carlos* (24), *Juan* (24), *Jesus* (21), *Luis* (15), *Pedro* (15), *Francisco* (14), *Roberto* (14), *Miguel* (13), *Javier* (12), *Ruben* (12).

Rentfro (243) Altered form of Scottish RENFREW.

Rentfrow (228) Altered form of Scottish RENFREW.

Rentmeester (225) Dutch: occupational or status name for a bailiff or steward, one whose job it was to receive rents, Middle Dutch *rentmeester.*

Renton (338) Scottish: habitational name from a place in Berwickshire, 'settlement (Old English *tūn*) associated with *Regna*' (a short form of the various compound personal names with the first element *regen* 'govern').

Rentsch (164) German (eastern) and Swiss German: variant of RENSCH.

GIVEN NAMES German 11%. *Hans* (3), *Lothar* (2), *Eberhard, Erwin.*

Rentschler (773) South German: nickname for a careless or carefree person, probably from an agent derivative of Middle High German *rensen* 'to stretch or swing one's limbs'.

Rentz (1457) German: **1.** from the personal name *Rentz*, a short form of *Reinhard* (see REINHARDT) or *Lorenz*, German form of LAWRENCE. **2.** habitational name from any of several places so named in Pomerania and the former East Prussia.

Rentzel (109) North German (**Renzel**): **1.** habitational name from Renzel in Hannover. **2.** from a pet form of the personal name RENTZ.

Renville (153) French: variant of RAINVILLE.

Renwick (825) Scottish and northern English (pronounced 'rennick'): habitational name from a place in Cumbria, so called from the Old English byname *Hræfn* (meaning 'raven') + *wīc* 'outlying settlement'.

Reny (220) **1.** Americanized form of French **René** (see RENE). **2.** Americanized

form of Hungarian **Rényi**, a habitational name for someone from a place called Rény in Pozsony county now in Slovakia.
GIVEN NAMES French 7%. *Armand, Cecile, Gilles, Laurier, Lucien.*

Renz (1330) German: variant spelling of RENTZ.
GIVEN NAMES German 4%. *Otto* (4), *Erwin* (2), *Horst* (2), *Fritz, Hans, Kurt.*

Renze (123) German: unexplained.
GIVEN NAMES Spanish 5%. *Rafael* (2), *Josefina, Mercedes.*

Renzetti (116) Italian: patronymic from a pet form of RENZO.
GIVEN NAMES Italian 12%. *Aladino, Reno, Roberto, Rocco.*

Renzi (702) Italian: patronymic or plural form of RENZO.
GIVEN NAMES Italian 12%. *Domenic* (4), *Pasquale* (3), *Angelo* (2), *Dino* (2), *Marco* (2), *Renzo* (2), *Aldo, Antonio, Benedetto, Biagio, Carlo, Cosimo.*

Renzo (140) Italian: from a short form of the personal name *Lorenzo*, Latin *Laurentius* (see LAWRENCE).
GIVEN NAMES Italian 18%. *Sal* (2), *Angelo, Antonio, Attilio, Nicola, Salvatore, Tommaso.*

Renzoni (108) Italian: from an augmentative form of RENZO.
GIVEN NAMES Italian 22%. *Dante* (2), *Reno* (2), *Aldo, Dino, Domenic, Renzo, Silvano.*

Renzulli (247) Italian: patronymic from a reduced pet form of the personal name *Lorenzo*, Latin *Laurentius* (see LAWRENCE).
GIVEN NAMES Italian 19%. *Angelo* (2), *Carlo* (2), *Dante* (2), *Elvio* (2), *Gennaro* (2), *Carmine, Donato, Flavio, Pellegrino.*

Reo (226) Italian: apparently a nickname from *reo* 'culprit', 'offender' but, more probably, from a short form of a personal name ending in *-reo.*
GIVEN NAMES Italian 13%. *Angelo* (4), *Cosmo, Sal, Ugo, Umberto.*

Reome (115) Canadian French: variant of **Réaume** (see REAUME).

Repa (108) **1.** Czech (**Řepa**) and Slovak (**Repaský**): nickname from the vocabulary word *řepa* 'turnip'. **2.** Hungarian (**Répa**): from Hungarian *répa* 'carrot', a derivative of the Slavic word in 1 above; a nickname for someone with carrot-colored hair or for a slow-witted person.

Repasky (309) Czech (**Řepaský**): probably a habitational name from an unidentified place named with *řepa* 'turnip'.

Repass (548) Origin unidentified. Perhaps an Americanized form of French **Repaissé**, **Repessé**, a nickname from Old French *repaissé, repessé* 'satisfied', 'replete' (past participles of *repaisser, repesser*). Compare RESPASS.

Repetti (174) Italian: patronymic or plural form of REPETTO.

Repetto (215) Italian (Liguria): possibly from an old Germanic personal name, *Rebi,*

Rabo, Rappo, which may have given rise to a hypothetical *Repo.*
GIVEN NAMES Spanish 16%; Italian 7%. *Carlos* (5), *Humberto* (2), *Mario* (2), *Armando, Arnoldo, Augusto, Eduardo, Educardo, Javier, Juan, Julio, Luis; Aldo, Angelo, Giovanni, Guido, Natale, Primo, Severino.*

Reph (116) Origin uncertain. Possibly a shortened form of **Rephael**, a variant of RAPHAEL.

Repine (139) Origin uncertain. Possibilities include: **1.** Reduced and altered form, under French influence, of Polish **Rzepiński** (see REPINSKI). **2.** altered spelling of German **Reppin**, a habitational name from a place named Reppin (of Slavic origin) in eastern Germany. **3.** altered spelling, under French influence, of Russian **Repin** or Slovenian **Repina**, both from nicknames based on the Slavic word *repa* 'turnip'.

Repinski (197) Polish: probably a variant of **Rzepiński**, habitational name for someone from a place called Rzepin in Kielce voivodeship.

Repka (314) Czech (**Řepka**) and Slovak: diminutive of Czech *Řepa* (see REPA). This name is also found in Germany.

Repke (140) German: nickname from a diminutive of Slavic (e.g., Sorbian) *řepa* 'turnip'.
GIVEN NAME German 4%. *Wolfgang* (2).

Repko (409) Of uncertain origin. It is found in the Netherlands; possibly a pet form of the Germanic personal name *Rippert* (see RIPP).

Replogle (885) German and French (Alsace): variant of German **Reploegel**, a compound of REPP 'rope' + Middle High German *lägel* 'keg', also a linear measure. The term probably denoted a rope of a particular length used for measuring wood and other bulky merchandise and the surname arose as a metonymic occupational name for someone who made such measures or for an official who used one.

Reposa (163) Portuguese: probably a variant of RAPOSA.

Repp (1095) **1.** Eastern German: from Slavic *repa* 'turnip', applied as a nickname for someone who was slow-witted or as a metonymic occupational name for a grower or seller of turnips. **2.** North German: metonymic occupational name for a ropemaker, from Middle Low German *rēp, rep* 'rope'.

Reppe (109) Eastern German: from Slavic *rep* 'turnip', 'beet', presumably applied for a grower or seller of root vegetables, or possibly as a nickname.
GIVEN NAMES Scandinavian 5%; German 4%. *Erik; Ingwald, Kurt.*

Reppert (800) German: from a Germanic personal name, *Ratbert*, composed of the elements *rād, rāt* 'counsel', 'advice' + *berht* 'bright'.

Reppond (182) Origin unidentified. Probably an altered spelling of **Repond**, an unexplained Swiss French name.

Reppucci (196) Italian: possibly from a derivative of *Reppo*, itself probably a derivative of a Germanic personal name (see REPETTO).
GIVEN NAMES Italian 16%. *Orlando* (2), *Alfonso, Alphonso, Angelo, Antonio, Eutimio, Oreste, Vittorio.*

Repsher (246) Probably an altered spelling of South German **Rebscher**, an occupational name for a vine dresser, from Middle High German *rebe* 'vine' + *scher(er)* 'cutter'.

Requa (207) German: variant of **Ricward**, from a Germanic personal name composed of the elements *rīc* 'power(ful)' + *ward* 'guardian'.
GIVEN NAME French 4%. *Chantelle.*

Requena (146) Catalan and Spanish: habitational name from Requena in Valencia or Requena de Campos in Palencia, apparently so called from a short form of the various Visigothic compound personal names with the first element *rīc* 'power(ful)', with the addition of the locative suffix *-ena.*
GIVEN NAMES Spanish 53%. *Pedro* (4), *Cesar* (3), *Jose* (3), *Alfredo* (2), *Andres* (2), *Berta* (2), *Carlos* (2), *Jorge* (2), *Juan* (2), *Reina* (2), *Ricardo* (2), *Angel; Antonio* (2), *Anastasio, Romeo.*

Rerucha (106) Czech: unexplained. The name is also established in Austria.

Resch (1431) Dutch and German: nickname for a quick, lively person, from Middle Low German *rasch* 'quick', 'strong'.

Reschke (443) German: **1.** nickname from Sorbian *rešk* 'shrew'. **2.** from a Sorbian short form of the personal name LORENZ, or a variant of RASCHKE (of Slavic origin). **3.** habitational name from a place so named in former West Prussia.
GIVEN NAMES German 10%. *Horst* (3), *Erwin* (2), *Ewald* (2), *Armin, Claus, Detlef, Gerhard, Heinz, Klaus, Kurt, Manfred, Merwin.*

Rescigno (239) Italian: habitational name for someone from Roscigno in Salerno province (Campania).
GIVEN NAMES Italian 18%. *Rocco* (2), *Aldo, Alfonso, Alfonzo, Americo, Carlo, Carmela, Carmine, Elvira, Federico, Gaetano, Marco, Mario, Saverio.*

Resendes (299) Portuguese: variant of **Resende**, a habitational name from any of several places so called in Portugal, for example in the province of Beira. The place name is from the genitive case of a Visigothic personal name composed of the elements *rēþs* 'counsel', 'advice' + *sinþs* 'way', 'path'.
GIVEN NAMES Spanish 31%; Portuguese 20%; Italian 9%. *Jose* (21), *Manuel* (17), *Carlos* (4), *Alberto* (3), *Alfredo* (2), *Eduardo* (2), *Fernando* (2), *Humberto* (2), *Rafael* (2), *Urbano* (2), *Alina, Antero; Joao* (4),

Agostinho, Guilherme; Antonio (22), *Angelo* (4), *Carmino, Franco, Leonardo.*

Resendez (978) Spanish (**Reséndez**): variant of Spanish **Reséndiz** (see RESENDIZ). GIVEN NAMES Spanish 49%. *Jose* (28), *Juan* (17), *Manuel* (12), *Ignacio* (9), *Jesus* (9), *Raul* (9), *Ruben* (6), *Gilberto* (5), *Miguel* (5), *Rafael* (5), *Ricardo* (5), *Alfredo* (4); *Antonio* (9), *Lorenzo* (3), *Angelo* (2), *Carmela, Cesario, Clemente, Eliseo, Federico, Geronimo, Luciano, Mauro.*

Resendiz (465) Spanish (**Reséndiz**): habitational name from any of various places in Portugal named Resende (see RESENDES). GIVEN NAMES Spanish 60%. *Jose* (16), *Juan* (11), *Francisco* (8), *Carlos* (7), *Jesus* (6), *Pedro* (6), *Alberto* (5), *Alejandro* (5), *Guadalupe* (5), *Roberto* (5), *Javier* (4), *Fernando* (3).

Reser (573) Perhaps an Americanized spelling of Swiss German RIESER.

Resetar (193) Croatian and Slovenian (**Rešetar**): occupational name for a sieve maker, from *rešeto* 'sieve'.

Resh (461) **1.** Americanized spelling of German RESCH. **2.** Americanized spelling of Slovenian **Reš**, of unexplained meaning.

Reske (150) German: variant of RESCHKE.

Resler (538) German: **1.** occupational name for a cobbler. **2.** Americanized spelling of RESSLER, **Rösler** (see ROESLER), or **Rössler** (see ROESSLER).

Resner (159) German: probably a variant of the occupational name RESLER, or an altered spelling of **Rösner** (see ROESNER) or **Rössner** (see ROESSNER).

Resnick (2593) Germanized or Americanized spelling of Jewish REZNIK. GIVEN NAMES Jewish 5%. *Sol* (7), *Miriam* (4), *Ephraim* (3), *Hyman* (3), *Isadore* (3), *Tova* (2), *Ber, Binyamin, Malca, Mayer, Meyer, Naum.*

Resnik (401) **1.** Variant spelling of Jewish REZNIK 'ritual slaughterer'. **2.** Slovenian: probably a topographic name from *resa* 'heather' (dialect *res*), or from *resnik* a type of barley. GIVEN NAMES Jewish 4%. *Sol* (3), *Ephraim, Hershel, Moysey, Rivka.*

Resnikoff (126) Jewish (eastern Ashkenazic): alternative spelling of **Resnikov**, patronymic from *Resnik* 'ritual slaughterer' (see REZNIK). GIVEN NAMES Jewish 8%. *Akiva, Sol.*

Resop (137) Origin unidentified.

Resor (190) Probably a variant spelling of German RASOR or RESER.

Respass (126) Origin unidentified. Compare REPASS.

Respess (234) Origin unidentified. Compare REPASS.

Respress (156) Origin unidentified. Compare REPASS.

Ress (339) German: **1.** nickname for an irascible or excitable man, from Middle High German *ræsse* 'wild', 'raging'.

2. (Bavaria): topographic name from *ress* 'slope' or 'drainage channel'. **3.** from a short form of a Germanic personal name formed with *rād, rāt* 'advice', 'counsel'.

Ressa (147) Italian and southern French: metonymic occupational name for a sawyer, from Italian *ressa* 'saw' (French *raisse*). GIVEN NAMES French 6%; Italian 5%; Spanish 4%. *Charlot, Jeanmarie; Angelo* (2), *Luigi; Orlando* (2), *Carmella, Ramon.*

Resseguie (183) French (Huguenot): variant of southern French **Resseguier**, an occupational name for a sawyer, from an agent derivative of *ressa* 'saw'.

Ressel (239) German: **1.** nickname from Middle High German *rössel*, diminutive of *ros* 'charger', 'draft horse'. **2.** topographic name from Low German *ressel* 'bitterling', 'fleabane', 'watercress'. **3.** from a short form of a Germanic personal name formed with *rāt* 'counsel', 'advice'. GIVEN NAMES German 6%. *Claus, Dieter, Franz.*

Resser (106) Origin unidentified. Perhaps an altered spelling of German **Riesser** (see RIESER 3) or **Rasser**, a nickname from Middle High German *rassen* 'to make an angry noise', 'to rage'.

Ressler (1529) German: **1.** topographic name for someone living by a slope or drainage channel, from RESS 2 + *-(l)er*, suffix denoting an inhabitant. **2.** variant of RESLER. **3.** variant of **Rössler** (see ROESSLER).

Rest (115) German: variant of RAST. GIVEN NAMES German 9%. *Friedrich, Johann, Monika.*

Resta (123) **1.** Italian and Greek (**Restas**): from the vocabulary word *resto* 'remainder', 'leftover'. **2.** Italian: possibly from a short form of the personal name *Oreste*. GIVEN NAMES Italian 17%. *Vito* (2), *Angelo, Cosimo, Francesco, Luigi.*

Restad (121) Swedish: habitational name from any of several places called Restad.

Restaino (253) Italian: possibly from a Germanic personal name composed of the elements *hrōd* 'fame' + *stain* 'stone', also the source of the French surname **Rostain**. GIVEN NAMES Italian 16%. *Angelo* (3), *Vito* (3), *Carmine, Donato, Gianni, Giovanni, Luciano, Nunzio, Pasquale, Silvio.*

Rester (423) German (Bavaria): from a derivative of Middle High German *reste* 'rest', 'resting place', originally a nickname for someone who took a rest on a military expedition.

Restifo (124) Italian: variant of RESTIVO. GIVEN NAMES Italian 18%. *Filippo* (2), *Salvatore* (2), *Agatino, Angelo, Carmelo.*

Restivo (741) Italian: nickname from Sicilian *restivu* 'stammering', 'wayward', 'contrary' (of animals 'obstinate'). GIVEN NAMES Italian 17%. *Angelo* (12), *Salvatore* (12), *Carlo* (2), *Carmine* (2), *Giuseppa* (2), *Rosaria* (2), *Sal* (2),

Alessandro, Calogero, Carmela, Enzo, Giuseppe.

Resto (294) Spanish (Puerto Rico): apparently from the vocabulary word *resto* 'remainder'. Compare RESTA. The surname is virtually unknown in present-day Spain. GIVEN NAMES Spanish 46%. *Jose* (7), *Luis* (7), *Angel* (6), *Manuel* (6), *Raul* (4), *Ana* (3), *Juan* (3), *Pedro* (3), *Ramon* (3), *Andres* (2), *Carlos* (2), *Ernesto* (2); *Angelo, Eliseo, Federico, Gabriella.*

Restrepo (849) Asturian-Leonese: habitational name from Restrepo in Asturies. GIVEN NAMES Spanish 57%. *Carlos* (30), *Jorge* (16), *Luis* (14), *Juan* (13), *Guillermo* (12), *Jairo* (11), *Jose* (11), *Luz* (10), *Francisco* (9), *Gustavo* (8), *Mario* (8), *Ricardo* (8).

Restuccia (129) Italian: **1.** (Sicily): nickname for a worthless person, from Sicilian *restuccia, ristuccia* 'stubble', 'stubble field'. **2.** from a pet form of RESTA. GIVEN NAMES Italian 15%. *Salvatore* (2), *Bartolo, Carmelo, Domenic, Enzo, Francesca, Giacomo.*

Reta (133) Spanish: Castilianized variant of Basque **Erreta**, a habitational name from a town called Erreta in Navarre, Basque Country. GIVEN NAMES Spanish 41%; Ethiopian 4%. *Jose* (6), *Cesar* (3), *Manuel* (3), *Blanca* (2), *Mario* (2), *Adolfo, Cipriano, Emeterio, Francisca, Francisco, Guadalupe, Jesus; Genet, Mehari, Melaku.*

Retallick (126) Cornish: unexplained. GIVEN NAME French 5%. *Gaston.*

Retana (198) Spanish: Castilianized variant of Basque **Erretana**, a habitational name from Erretana in Araba, Basque Country. GIVEN NAMES Spanish 58%. *Jose* (10), *Carlos* (4), *Guadalupe* (3), *Jesus* (3), *Juan* (3), *Juana* (3), *Pedro* (3), *Enrique* (2), *Eugenio* (2), *Francisco* (2), *Luis* (2), *Manuel* (2).

Reth (127) North German: from a dialect variant of RIED.

Retherford (668) Perhaps an altered spelling of the English family name RUTHERFORD.

Rethman (124) North German (**Rethmann**): topographic name for someone who lived where reeds grew, from Middle Low German *rēt* 'reed'.

Rettberg (164) German: habitational name from Rethberg in the Lippe district or from any of several places so named in northwestern Germany.

Retter (319) **1.** English: occupation name for a net-maker, from Old French *retier*. **2.** German: from a Germanic personal name composed with *rād, rāt* 'counsel' + *hari, heri* 'army'.

Retterath (132) German: habitational name from a place so named near Koblenz.

Retterer (136) German: probably from a Germanic personal name composed with *rād, rāt* 'advice', 'counsel' (see RETTER), or a variant of REDER 4.

Rettew (175) Possibly of German origin: unexplained. This name is concentrated in PA.

Rettig (1525) German: from Middle High German *retich*, Middle Low German *redig* 'radish'; a nickname for someone thought to resemble a radish in some way or a metonymic occupational name name for a grower or seller of radishes.

Rettinger (289) German: habitational name for someone from Retting or Rettingen in Bavaria.
GIVEN NAMES German 4%. *Nikolaus* (2), *Ernst*.

Rettke (203) German: **1.** from a pet form of a Germanic personal name formed with *rād*, *rāt* 'advice', 'counsel'. **2.** (in the east): habitational name from Rettkau near Glogau.
GIVEN NAMES German 6%. *Otto*, *Siegfried*, *Willi*.

Rettler (147) German: from a short form of a Germanic personal name formed with *rāt* 'counsel', 'advice'.

Retz (286) German: **1.** from a short form of the personal names *Rezo*, *Razo*. **2.** habitational name from any of several places named Retz or Retzen in northwestern Germany and Austria.

Retzer (404) German: **1.** habitational name for someone from Retz in Austria (see RETZ). **2.** nickname for a tease, from an agent derivative of Middle High German *ratzen* 'to scratch'. **3.** from a Slavic personal name based on the element *rat* 'glad' as in *Radoslav*.
GIVEN NAMES German 6%. *Otto* (4), *Helmut*, *Helmuth*, *Reinhold*.

Retzlaff (966) German: from the Slavic personal name *Radoslav* or *Ratislav*.
GIVEN NAMES German 4%. *Kurt* (2), *Erna*, *Erwin*, *Georg*, *Heinz*, *Horst*, *Klaus*, *Otto*, *Wolfgang*.

Retzloff (219) Variant of RETZLAFF.

Reuben (451) **1.** English and Welsh: from the Biblical personal name *Reuben* (see RUBIN), which was popular among Nonconformists from the 16th century onward. **2.** Jewish (Israeli): from the Hebrew form of the personal name RUBIN.
GIVEN NAMES Jewish 5%. *Ilan* (2), *Galit*, *Meyer*, *Miriam*, *Ziva*, *Zohar*.

Reuber (144) German: variant of **Räuber** (see RAUBER).

Reuer (146) German: nickname from Middle High German *riuwære* 'penitent'.
GIVEN NAMES German 10%. *Erna*, *Erwin*, *Gerhard*, *Gerhart*, *Milbert*, *Otto*.

Reukauf (114) German: nickname from Middle High German *riuwe kouf* 'compensation paid for backing out of a contract' (literally 'regret purchase').

Reul (151) German: **1.** (southern): from *reweli*, a diminutive of REH. **2.** from a Germanic personal name formed with *hrōd* 'renown'. **3.** variant of REIL 2.

GIVEN NAMES German 5%. *Eberhard*, *Hans*, *Heinz*.

Reuland (141) Dutch and German: from a personal name, the Dutch and German form of *Roland* (see ROWLAND).

Reule (158) South German: **1.** nickname from a diminutive of Middle High German *rū(he)*, *rūch* 'rough', 'hairy', 'tough'. **2.** variant of REUL 2.
GIVEN NAME German 4%. *Kurt*.

Reum (231) German: **1.** perhaps a habitational name from a place so named in Silesia. **2.** from a Germanic personal name formed with *hruom* 'fame' or *ragin* 'advice'.

Reus (134) **1.** Dutch: nickname for a big man, from Middle Dutch *reuse(n)* 'giant'. **2.** German: topographic name from Middle High German *riuse* 'fish trap' (Middle Low German *ruse*) or from a regional term *reuse* 'small stream', 'channel'. **3.** Catalan: habitational name from Reus in Tarragona province. However, this source seems not to have contributed greatly to the American name.
GIVEN NAME French 4%. *Georges*.

Reusch (440) German: habitational name from places in Bavaria called Reusch or Reisch.

Reuscher (124) German: **1.** habitational name for someone from Reusch or Reisch, both in Bavaria. **2.** a nickname from Sorbian *ryšar* 'knight', 'hero'. **3.** from a short form of a Germanic personal name formed with *(h)rōd* 'fame', 'victory'.

Reuss (647) German: **1.** occupational name for a cobbler, Middle High German *(alt)riusse*. **2.** ethnic name from Middle High German *riusse* 'Russian'; in some cases, a nickname for someone who had been in Russia or had connections there.
GIVEN NAMES German 5%. *Kurt* (3), *Otto* (2), *Detlef*, *Gerd*, *Willi*.

Reusser (213) South German: **1.** in Switzerland, an occupational name for a fisherman or maker of fish traps, from an agent derivative of Middle High German *riuse* 'fish trap', 'weir basket'. **2.** nickname from an agent noun based on Middle High German *riusen* 'to moan or complain'. **3.** occupational name for a castrator of farm animals, a derivative of *reussen* 'to castrate'.
GIVEN NAMES German 4%. *Fritz*, *Hans*.

Reust (182) Dutch (**van Reust**): topographic name, ultimately from French *(les) rues* 'streets'.

Reuter (3247) **1.** German: derivative of Middle High German *(ge)riute* 'clearing', hence a topographic name for someone who lived in a clearing or an occupational name for a clearer of woodland. *Reut(e)* and *Reit* are frequent elements of place names, indicating location in a forest or former forest. **2.** German: derogatory nickname from Middle High German *riutære* 'footpad', 'highwayman'; later, possibly an occupational name for a mounted soldier (see REITER).

GIVEN NAMES German 4%. *Fritz* (6), *Kurt* (4), *Otto* (4), *Gerd* (2), *Gunther* (2), *Horst* (2), *Annelies*, *Bernd*, *Franz*, *Frieda*, *Gerhard*, *Guenter*.

Reuther (655) German: variant spelling of REUTER.
GIVEN NAMES German 4%. *Hans* (3), *Otto* (2), *Arno*, *Erwin*, *Hermann*, *Willi*.

Reutlinger (135) German and Swiss German: habitational name for someone from either of two places called Reutlingen: in Baden-Württemberg, Germany, or Zürich canton, Switzerland.
GIVEN NAMES French 6%. *Andree*, *Jacques*.

Reutter (400) Variant spelling of German REUTER.

Reutzel (187) German: possibly an eastern variant of REITZEL or of **Räuzel**, **Reuz**, from short forms of a Germanic personal name formed with *hrōd* 'renown'.

Revak (281) Slovak (**Revák**): nickname from a derivative of *revat* 'to shout', 'cry out'.
GIVEN NAMES German 4%. *Kurt* (2), *Otto*.

Revard (154) Variant of French RIVARD.

Reveal (181) Probably an altered spelling of English REVELL.

Revel (293) **1.** English: variant spelling of REVELL. **2.** French: habitational name from any of the places so named, for example in Isère and Haute-Garonne. **3.** French and southern French: nickname from Old French, Occitan *reveau* 'rebel'.
GIVEN NAMES French 6%. *Andre*, *Gaston*, *Henri*, *Pascal*.

Reveles (323) Portuguese: habitational name from either of the towns called Reveles in Portugal.
GIVEN NAMES Spanish 53%. *Jose* (10), *Carlos* (4), *Ruben* (4), *Eduardo* (3), *Enrique* (3), *Humberto* (3), *Juan* (3), *Rafael* (3), *Raul* (3), *Salvador* (3), *Arturo* (2), *Francisco* (2); *Antonio* (2), *Lorenzo* (2), *Marco* (2), *Federico*, *Filiberto*, *Gino*, *Heriberto*, *Mauro*.

Revell (1033) English: nickname for a boisterous person, from Middle English, Old French *revel* 'festivity', 'tumult', 'riot' (from Old French *reveler* 'to revel').

Revelle (486) English: variant spelling of REVELL.

Revello (147) **1.** Italian: habitational name from Revello in Cuneo province. **2.** Catalan (**Revelló**): possibly nickname from the diminutive form *revell* 'wild olive tree'.
GIVEN NAMES Italian 12%; Spanish 5%. *Gennaro* (2), *Domenico*, *Ernesto*, *Rocco*; *Genaro*, *Jaime*, *Juan*, *Silvia*.

Revels (1320) English: variant of REVELL.

Revere (433) **1.** French: variant of **Rivière**, **Rivoire**, or **Rivier**, topographic name for someone living on the banks of a river, French *rivier* 'bank', or habitational name from any of the many places in France named with this word. **2.** English: nickname from Middle English *revere* 'reiver', 'robber'. **3.** English: topographic name for someone who lived on the brow of a hill, from a misdivision of the Middle English phrase *atter evere* 'at the brow or edge' (from Old English *yfer, efer* 'edge') or a habitational name from a place named with this phrase, as for example River in West Sussex or Rivar in Wiltshire. **4.** Jewish (from Italy): habitational name from a place in Mantua named Revere.

FOREBEARS The MA patriot Paul Revere (1734–1818), who in April 1775 undertook a famous ride from Boston to Lexington to warn of the approach of British troops, was a silversmith and instrument maker. He was descended from French Huguenots called Rivoire.

Reves (281) **1.** Americanized spelling of Hungarian **Révész**, occupational name for a ferryman, *révész*. **2.** Perhaps an altered spelling of REEVES.

Revette (178) Probably an altered spelling of English **Revett**, variant of RIVETT.
GIVEN NAME French 4%. *Alphonse*.

Revier (205) **1.** Dutch: topographic name for someone who lived by a river, a 17th century variant of *rivier*. **2.** Perhaps a variant of French **Reviers**, a habitational name from a place so named in Calvados.

Reviere (111) Dutch: variant of REVIER.

Revill (126) English: nickname for a rebel or reveler, from Old French *revel* 'rebellion', 'sport', or from an Old French, Middle English personal name, *Revel*, possibly derived from Latin *rebellus*.

Revilla (315) Spanish: habitational name from any of the numerous places, mainly in Castile, named Revilla, from Old Spanish *revilla* 'dependent settlement', a derivative of *villa* (see VILLA).
GIVEN NAMES Spanish 41%. *Luis* (4), *Ramon* (4), *Jose* (3), *Manuel* (3), *Pablo* (3), *Rodolfo* (3), *Alberto* (2), *Elva* (2), *Emilio* (2), *Enrique* (2), *Ernesto* (2), *Fernando* (2); *Antonio* (3), *Angelo*, *Franco*, *Marco*, *Marco Antonio*.

Reville (183) **1.** French: habitational name from either of two places named Reville, in Manche and Meuse. **2.** English: variant spelling of REVILL.

Revis (1038) English: **1.** habitational name for someone from Rievaulx in North Yorkshire. **2.** patronymic from REEVE.

Revoir (275) Variant of French **Rivoire** (see REVERE).

Revord (160) Variant of French RIVARD.
GIVEN NAME French 5%. *Raoul* (2).

Rew (485) **1.** English: variant of ROWE 1, from the Old English byform *rēw*, or a habitational name from places in Devon and Isle of Wight called Rew from this word. **2.** Americanized spelling of German RUH.

Rewerts (220) German (Frisian): patronymic from a short form of the Germanic personal name *Reinwarth*, composed of *ragin* 'counsel' + *wart* 'guard'.

Rewis (303) Americanized form of Dutch **Ruijs**, nickname for a noisy person.

Rex (2104) **1.** English: variant of RICKS. **2.** German: habitational name from a place so named near Fulda. **3.** Latinized form of German KOENIG.

Rexford (535) Americanized spelling of German **Rexforth**, a topographic name for someone living at a river crossing or ford near a place called Rex, perhaps the one near Fulda, Hesse.

Rexing (132) German: shortened form of **Rexinger**, a habitational name for someone from a place called Rexingen in Baden-Württemberg.

Rexroad (543) Americanized spelling of German **Rexrodt**, a variant of REXROTH.

Rexroat (481) Americanized spelling of German REXROTH.

Rexrode (736) Americanized spelling of German **Rexrodt**, a variant of REXROTH.

Rexroth (203) German: habitational name for someone from former places called Rexerode in Hesse and Thuringia, now abandoned.
GIVEN NAMES German 4%. *Gerhard, Klaus*.

Rey (1659) **1.** Spanish and southern French (Occitan): from Spanish and Old French *rey* 'king' (from Latin *rex*, genitive *regis*), which could have been applied any of in numerous ways: it may have denoted someone in the service of a king; it may have been from the title of someone in a brotherhood; or a nickname for someone who behaved in a regal fashion or who had earned the title in some contest of skill or by presiding over festivities. **2.** English: variant spelling of RAY 1, cognate with 1. **3.** German: from a short form of a Germanic personal name formed with *ragin* 'counsel'. **4.** German: nickname for a leader of dancing or singing, from Middle Low German *rei(e)* '(line) dance', '(satirical) song'.
GIVEN NAMES Spanish 31%. *Manuel* (28), *Jose* (27), *Luis* (25), *Juan* (10), *Alfredo* (9), *Roberto* (9), *Alfonso* (8), *Angel* (8), *Eduardo* (8), *Jesus* (7), *Mariano* (7), *Carlos* (6).

Reyburn (299) Scottish: variant spelling of RAYBURN.

Reyer (332) German: variant of REIHER.

Reyes (26007) Spanish: **1.** plural variant of REY. **2.** Castilianized form of the Galician habitational name REIS.
GIVEN NAMES Spanish 51%. *Jose* (737), *Juan* (365), *Carlos* (226), *Manuel* (221), *Luis* (210), *Jesus* (186), *Pedro* (159), *Ruben* (141), *Miguel* (136), *Roberto* (134), *Francisco* (133), *Ramon* (129).

Reyher (140) Perhaps an altered spelling of German REYER or REIHER.

Reyman (152) Americanized spelling of German REYMANN.

Reymann (155) German: variant spelling of REIMANN.
GIVEN NAME French 4%. *Marcel*.

Reymond (120) French: variant spelling of RAYMOND.

GIVEN NAMES French 8%; German 6%. *Briand, Jean-Louis, Noemie; Wendelin*.

Reyna (3482) Spanish: variant spelling of REINA.
GIVEN NAMES Spanish 47%. *Jose* (81), *Juan* (64), *Jesus* (30), *Manuel* (27), *Roberto* (27), *Raul* (26), *Ruben* (21), *Carlos* (20), *Miguel* (20), *Pedro* (20), *Armando* (17), *Guadalupe* (17).

Reynaga (213) Hispanic (Mexico): unexplained; possibly a habitational name from an unidentified place.
GIVEN NAMES Spanish 56%. *Jose* (11), *Carlos* (4), *Jesus* (4), *Luis* (3), *Miguel* (3), *Rafael* (3), *Enrique* (2), *Javier* (2), *Jose Luis* (2), *Juan* (2), *Leobardo* (2), *Pablo* (2); *Filiberto* (2), *Antonio*, *Constantino*, *Eliseo*, *Heriberto*, *Julieta*.

Reynard (424) English and French: from a Germanic personal name composed of the elements *ragin* 'counsel' + *hard* 'hardy', 'brave', 'strong', which was introduced into England by the Normans in the form *Re(i)nard*. This was the name borne by the cunning fox in the popular medieval cycle of beast tales, with the result that from the 13th century it began to replace the previous Old French word for the animal. Some French examples may be nicknames for crafty individuals, referring to the fox's reputation for cunning.

Reynaud (297) French: variant of RENAUD.
GIVEN NAMES French 11%; Spanish 4%. *Cecile* (2), *Andre, Jean-Louis, Marcel, Michel, Monique, Pierre, Serge; Berenice* (4), *Jesus* (2), *Alberto, Eduardo, Jose, Laureano, Marta, Patricio, Salvador, Suyapa*.

Reynders (102) Dutch: patronymic from a Germanic personal name composed of the elements *ragin* 'counsel', 'advice' + *heri, hari* 'army'. Compare French RAINIER.
GIVEN NAMES French 6%. *Benoit, Colette, Jean-Noel*.

Reynen (139) Dutch: from a short form of a Germanic personal name beginning with *ragin* 'counsel', 'advice'.

Reyner (115) English: variant spelling of RAYNER.

Reynold (242) English: from a Germanic personal name composed of the elements *ragin* 'counsel' + *wald* 'rule', which was first introduced to England by Scandinavian settlers in the Old Norse form *Rǫgnvaldr* (see RONALD), and greatly reinforced after the Conquest by the Norman forms *Reinald, Reynaud*. The surname is occasionally also borne by Jews, in which case it presumably represents an Americanized form of one or more like-sounding Jewish surnames.

Reynolds (72366) English: patronymic from REYNOLD.
FOREBEARS Christopher Reynolds of Gravesend, Kent, England, arrived in America sometime before his marriage in 1644 in Isle of Wight Co., VA.

Reynoldson (173) Northern English: patronymic from REYNOLD.

Reynosa (217) Spanish: variant spelling of **Reinosa**, a habitational name from Reinosa in Santander province.
GIVEN NAMES Spanish 44%. *Jose* (4), *Mario* (4), *Jesus* (3), *Manuel* (3), *Raul* (3), *Ana* (2), *Emilio* (2), *Felipe* (2), *Joaquin* (2), *Juanita* (2), *Maria Elena* (2), *Miguel* (2); *Antonio, Carmela, Lirio, Neri.*

Reynoso (1668) Spanish: habitational name from a place so named in Burgos or variant from Reinoso de Cerrata in the province of Palencia, *Reinoso* meaning 'place of fields'.
GIVEN NAMES Spanish 56%. *Jose* (65), *Juan* (23), *Manuel* (16), *Miguel* (15), *Francisco* (14), *Jesus* (14), *Ruben* (13), *Carlos* (12), *Jorge* (12), *Luis* (11), *Mario* (11), *Raul* (11).

Reza (573) **1.** Galician: habitational name from any of the three places in Ourense province, Galicia named Reza. **2.** Portuguese: from a derivative of *rezar* 'to pray'. **3.** Muslim (chiefly Iranian): from the Persian personal name *Reza*, from Arabic *riḍā* 'contentment', 'satisfaction'. *Riḍā* 'Ali ibn Musa (765–817) was the eighth imam of the Shiites. Reza Shah Pahlavi was the first Shah of the Pahlavi dynasty (1925–79) in Iran. *Reza* is used to form names in combination with other words, e.g. *Reza ul-Karim* (*Riḍā' al-Karīm*) 'satisfaction of The Most Generous', i.e. Allah.
GIVEN NAMES Spanish 39%; Muslim 13%. *Carlos* (8), *Jesus* (8), *Jose* (5), *Arturo* (4), *Cesar* (4), *Enrique* (4), *Manuel* (4), *Miguel* (4), *Alfredo* (3), *Fernando* (3), *Jaime* (3), *Javier* (3); *Syed* (6), *Ali* (5), *Mohammed* (5), *Hadi* (2), *Karim* (2), *Kazim* (2), *Shabana* (2), *Sultan* (2), *Abbas, Abdul, Ahmed, Amir.*

Rezabek (210) Czech (**Řeřábek**): nickname from Czech *řeřábek*, variant of *jeřábek* 'hazel colored hen'.

Rezac (580) Czech (**Řezáč**) and Slovak (**Rezáč**): occupational name for a woodcutter, an agent noun from the verb *řezat* 'to cut, trim, or lop'.

Rezek (247) **1.** Czech: nickname for someone with red hair, from a derivative of *rezarý* 'red', 'rusty'. **2.** Slovenian (**Režek**): probably a nickname for a person who was habitually smirking, from *režek*, from an agent noun derivative of *režati se* 'to smirk'.

Rezendes (494) Portuguese: variant of RESENDES.
GIVEN NAMES Spanish 13%; Portuguese 7%. *Manuel* (22), *Carlos* (3), *Jose* (2), *Armando, Arminda, Elvira, Francisco, Jacinto, Jorge, Luiz, Mario, Silvino; Duarte.*

Rezin (111) **1.** Scottish and English: variant of RAISON. **2.** Swiss French (**Rézin**): unexplained.

Reznicek (275) Czech (**Řesníček**): diminutive of **Řezník** 'butcher' (see REZNIK).

GIVEN NAMES German 5%. *Alfons, Gerhard, Viktor.*

Reznick (285) Jewish (Ashkenazic): Germanized or Americanized spelling of REZNIK.
GIVEN NAMES Jewish 8%. *Arie, Aron, Hyman, Leibel, Miriam, Sol.*

Reznik (469) **1.** Jewish (eastern Ashkenazic): occupational name for a Jewish ritual slaughterer, from Yiddish *reznik* (of Slavic origin). **2.** Czech (**Řezník**) and Slovak (**Rezník**): occupational name for a butcher.
GIVEN NAMES Russian 23%; Jewish 20%. *Boris* (6), *Mikhail* (6), *Yefim* (5), *Aleksandr* (4), *Igor* (4), *Leonid* (4), *Yelena* (4), *Anatoly* (2), *Arkady* (2), *Grigory* (2), *Lyudmila* (2), *Vladimir* (2); *Yakov* (6), *Ilya* (4), *Aron* (3), *Chaim* (2), *Isaak* (2), *Naum* (2), *Shaya* (2), *Akiva, Avraam, Blyuma, Faina, Filipp.*

Reznikov (100) Jewish (eastern Ashkenazic): patronymic form of REZNIK.
GIVEN NAMES Russian 38%; Jewish 30%. *Vladimir* (6), *Yefim* (4), *Galina* (3), *Aleksandr* (2), *Leonid* (2), *Lev* (2), *Oleg* (2), *Veniamin* (2), *Anatoliy, Asya, Boris, Dmitriy; Hanon* (2), *Ilya* (2), *Aron, Fira, Girsh, Inna, Naum, Yakov.*

Rhame (238) Perhaps an altered spelling of German **Rähme**, a variant of RAHM 3.

Rhames (170) Probably an altered spelling of German **Rahmes**, a habitational name from a place near Neuwied called Rahms.

Rhamy (108) Origin unidentified.

Rhatigan (186) Irish: variant spelling of RATIGAN.
GIVEN NAME Irish 9%. *Brendan* (3).

Rhea (3047) English: variant spelling of REA.

Rhead (148) English: variant spelling of READ.

Rheault (391) Apparently an altered spelling of French **Réault**, a variant of **Réau** (see REAU).
GIVEN NAMES French 12%. *Andre* (3), *Armand* (2), *Alphe, Alphonse, Dany, Emile, Florent, Jean Louis, Julien, Lucien, Ovila, Pierrette.*

Rheaume (698) Apparently an altered spelling of French *Réaume* (see REAUME).
GIVEN NAMES French 13%. *Normand* (4), *Armand* (3), *Andre* (2), *Alban, Alphonse, Amie, Camille, Donat, Fernand, Francois, Germaine, Herve.*

Rhee (960) **1.** Korean: variant of YI. **2.** German: habitational name from a place so named in Westphalia.
GIVEN NAMES Korean 52%. *Young* (13), *Sang* (12), *Chang* (7), *Chung* (6), *Dong* (6), *Kyung* (6), *Yong* (6), *Chong* (5), *Jae* (5), *Jin* (5), *Soo* (5), *Sung* (5), *Byung* (4), *Hyun* (4), *Joon* (4), *Jung* (4), *Moon Ja* (3), *Myong* (3), *Wook* (3), *Dae* (2), *Hae* (2), *Kwang Hyun* (2), *Kyung Sook* (2), *Pong* (2).

Rhees (126) Welsh: variant of REESE.

Rhein (653) German: **1.** topographic name for someone who lived by the Rhine river, which is first recorded in the Roman period in the form *Rhenus*; it may be derived from a Celtic element meaning 'to flow'. **2.** from a short form of a Germanic personal name formed with *ragin* 'advice', 'counsel'.
GIVEN NAMES German 4%. *Otto* (2), *Arno, Elke, Erna, Helmut, Horst, Kurt.*

Rheingans (151) German: nickname for a breeder or seller of geese, presumably one living near the Rhine river, from *Rhein* 'Rhine' + *Gans* 'goose'.
GIVEN NAME German 4%. *Kurt.*

Rheinheimer (128) German: variant spelling of REINHEIMER.
GIVEN NAMES German 5%. *Hans, Kurt.*

Rhem (171) Perhaps a metathesized spelling of German **Rehm**: **1.** nickname for a brawny man, from Middle High German *rem* 'pillar', 'post', 'frame', a topographic name from the same word, or a habitational name from places named Rehm, Rehme, or Rehmen. **2.** metonymic occupational name for a strap maker, from Middle Low German *reme* 'strap'.

Rhen (126) Possibly an altered spelling of German **Rehn**, a Low German variant of RAIN 2.

Rhett (279) Americanized form of Dutch **de Raedt**, from Middle Dutch *raet* 'advice'. This name occurs chiefly in SC.
FOREBEARS This name was brought to North America in 1694 by William Rhett (1666–1723). Robert Barnwell Rhett (1800–76) was a South Carolina congressman and senator, a noted secessionist.

Rhew (307) Perhaps an altered spelling of English **Rew** (a variant of ROW), French RUE, or German RUH.

Rhind (103) Scottish: variant spelling of RIND.

Rhine (1432) **1.** German: name from the common river name *Rhin*. **2.** Americanized form of German RHEIN.

Rhinehardt (142) Partly Americanized spelling of German and Jewish REINHARDT (see RHINEHART).

Rhinehart (1897) Partly Americanized spelling of German and Jewish REINHARDT, altered by folk etymology under the influence of the name of the river Rhine.

Rhiner (111) Americanized spelling of German REINER.

Rhines (493) Apparently an Americanized spelling of German REINS.

Rhinesmith (204) Anglicization of German REINSCHMIDT.

Rho (149) **1.** English (Devon): variant spelling of ROE. **2.** Korean: variant of NO.
GIVEN NAMES Korean 58%. *Sung* (5), *Young* (5), *Eul* (2), *Chi, Chun, Chung Nam, Hee, Hyun Ja, Jae, Jang Ho, Jong, Joon; Soo Kil* (2), *Chang Hyun, Chong Hun, Choon, Chul, Dae, Hyung Jin, Jong Ho, Jung Ho, Myong, Myung Sun, Sang Hyon.*

Rhoad (300) English: variant spelling of RHODE.

Rhoades (6858) English: variant spelling of RHODES.

Rhoads (5203) English: variant spelling of RHODES.

Rhoda (476) German: variant of ROHDE (see RODE).

Rhode (1365) **1.** English: variant of RHODES. **2.** German: variant spelling of ROHDE (see RODE), principally a habitational name from any of various places named Rohde or Rohden in Lower Saxony, Saxony, Westphalia, and Hesse.

FOREBEARS According to family tradition, a certain John Rhode (1752–1840) was a Quaker who came to SC from Germany in the 1770s and served as a baggageman or teamster during the American Revolution.

Rhoden (1805) **1.** English (West Midlands): unexplained. **2.** German: variant of RODEN.

Rhodenbaugh (100) Of German origin: see RODENBAUGH.

Rhoderick (139) Welsh: variant spelling of RODERICK.

Rhodes (31448) English (chiefly Yorkshire): topographic name for someone who lived in a clearing in woodland (see RODE 3). This, the most common form of the name, has been influenced in spelling by the English name of the Greek island of *Rhodes* (Greek *Rhodos*), with which there is no connection. There is no connection, either, with modern English *road* (Old English *rād* 'riding'), which was not used to denote a thoroughfare until the 16th century.

Rhodus (492) Perhaps an altered spelling of RHODES or Dutch or German **Rhodius**, a Latinized form of RODE, perhaps indicating the personal as opposed to the topographic name (see RODE 1).

Rhody (286) German: from a Germanic personal name formed with *hrōd* 'renown', or a respelling of ROHDE.

Rhomberg (125) German: variant of ROMBERG.
GIVEN NAMES German 7%. *Lorenz* (2), *Kurt*.

Rhome (153) Altered spelling of ROME.

Rhone (1150) **1.** French: habitational name for someone from Rhonne in Savoy, or topographic name for someone who lived by the Rhône river. **2.** English: apparently a variant spelling of RONE. **3.** German: variant spelling of **Rohne**, a variant of ROHN.

Rhoney (220) Possibly an altered spelling of German RHONE (see ROHN).

Rhorer (172) Probably an altered spelling of German ROHRER.

Rhoten (579) Altered spelling of ROTEN.

Rhoton (606) Altered spelling of French **Rodon**, a variant of RODE 1.

Rhude (171) Altered spelling of RUDE.

Rhudy (369) Probably an altered spelling of the Swiss family names RUDY or RHODY.

Rhue (252) Altered spelling of German RUHE.

Rhule (171) Probably an altered spelling of German **Rühl** (see RUHL) or **Rühle** (see RUHLE).

Rhyan (107) Irish: variant spelling of RYAN.
GIVEN NAME French 4%. *Michel*.

Rhymer (478) **1.** English: variant spelling of *Rymer*, a variant of RIMMER. **2.** Americanized spelling of German REIMER. **3.** Variant spelling of German RYMER.

Rhymes (430) English: unexplained.
GIVEN NAMES French 4%. *Andre* (2), *Patrice*.

Rhynard (114) Probably a respelling of German REINHARDT or French or English REYNARD.

Rhyne (1814) Respelling of Swiss German **Rhyn**, a topographic name for someone living on the Rhine river, Middle High German *Rīn*.

Rhyner (324) Swiss German: topographic name for someone living on the Rhine river (see RHYNE).

Rhynes (246) Possibly an Americanized spelling of German **Rheins**, from a short form of a Germanic personal name based on *ragin* 'advice', 'counsel'.
GIVEN NAMES French 4%. *Celestine, Chantal, Pierre*.

Riach (118) Scottish: variant of REACH.
GIVEN NAME Scottish 7%. *Alasdair* (2).

Rial (355) English: variant spelling of RYLE.

Rials (423) Probably a variant spelling of English **Ryalls**, itself a variant of RYLE.

Rian (106) Irish: variant of RYAN.

Riano (106) Spanish (**Riaño**): Castilianized form of Asturian-Leonese **Riañu**, habitational name from Riañu in Lleón and Asturies, or habitational name from one of the places so named in Santander or Galicia.
GIVEN NAMES Spanish 42%. *Carlos* (3), *Jose* (3), *Gustavo* (2), *Nestor* (2), *Aida, Alberto, Alfonso, Amparo, Angel, Armando, Blanca, Camilo; Antonio, Clementina*.

Riaz (124) Muslim: from a personal name based on Persian *Riaz*, from Arabic *riyāḍ*, plural of *rawḍah* 'garden'.
GIVEN NAMES Muslim 84%. *Mohammad* (17), *Muhammad* (7), *Mohammed* (6), *Mian* (3), *Tariq* (3), *Kashif* (2), *Khalid* (2), *Adil, Ahamad, Ahmad, Ahmed, Ali*.

Riba (157) **1.** Catalan: topographic name for someone who lived on the bank of a river or the shore of a lake, *riba* (Latin *ripa*), or a habitational name from La Riba, a town in Alt Camp, Tarragona, or any other place named with this word. **2.** Jewish (eastern Ashkenazic): variant spelling of RYBA 'fish'.
GIVEN NAMES Jewish 7%; German 6%; Spanish 5%. *Mendel* (2), *Yetta; Lothar* (2), *Erwin, Nikolaus; Jose* (2), *Alfredo, Carlos, Claudio, Fidel, Manuel, Ramon*.

Riback (158) Germanized or Americanized spelling of Jewish and Slavic RYBAK 'fisherman, angler, or fish seller'.
GIVEN NAME Jewish 4%. *Emanuel*.

Ribar (261) **1.** Slovak (**Rybár**), Serbian, Croatian, and Slovenian: occupational name for a fisherman or fish seller from an agent noun derivative of *riba* 'fish'. As a Slovenian surname, **Ribar** is an obsolete variant of **Ribič**, which is more frequent. **2.** Czech (**Ribář**): variant of **Rybář** 'fisherman', 'fish seller' (see RYBA).

Ribas (204) **1.** Catalan: variant of **Ribes**, habitational name from any of the places called with Ribes, from Catalan *ribes*, the plural of *riba* 'bank' (see RIBA). **2.** Spanish: habitational name from any of the places named with Ribas, from the plural of *riba* 'bank'.
GIVEN NAMES Spanish 39%; Portuguese 17%. *Jose* (10), *Manuel* (5), *Eduardo* (3), *Jorge* (3), *Julio* (3), *Alberto* (2), *Armando* (2), *Carlos* (2), *Francisco* (2), *Mario* (2), *Mirta* (2), *Rafael* (2); *Joao, Paulo; Antonio* (2), *Lorenzo*.

Ribaudo (363) Southern Italian (Piedmont and Sicily): nickname for a reprobate, *ribaldo*, originally a term denoting a soldier or servant who had to carry out the most arduous or distasteful tasks, and so perhaps in part an occupational name, or from a personal name of the same derivation.
GIVEN NAMES Italian 28%. *Salvatore* (5), *Carmine* (3), *Carmelo* (2), *Domenico* (2), *Mario* (2), *Rosario* (2), *Sal* (2), *Alfredo, Alonzo, Antonio, Bartolo, Benedetto, Ciro, Gaetano, Giuseppe, Giusto, Isidoro*.

Ribbens (100) **1.** Dutch: unexplained. **2.** English (Kent): unexplained. Perhaps of Dutch origin.
GIVEN NAMES Dutch 5%. *Dirk, Martinus*.

Ribble (549) English: from a Germanic personal name, *Ribald*.

Ribeiro (1115) Portuguese and Galician: habitational name from any of the numerous placed named Ribeiro, from *ribeiro* 'stream'.
GIVEN NAMES Spanish 30%; Portuguese 20%. *Jose* (33), *Manuel* (32), *Carlos* (15), *Fernando* (12), *Jorge* (9), *Americo* (5), *Mario* (5), *Armindo* (4), *Augusto* (4), *Julio* (4), *Luiz* (4), *Renato* (4); *Joao* (11), *Joaquim* (5), *Paulo* (5), *Albano* (2), *Vasco* (2), *Afonso, Agostinho, Almir, Amadeu, Guilherme, Henrique, Lidio; Antonio* (22), *Agostino, Alessandra, Angelo, Carmela, Ciro, Concetta, Emidio, Julieta, Leonardo, Marco, Mauro*.

Ribelin (115) German: origin uncertain; possibly an altered form of **Riebeling**, from a pet form of a Germanic personal name formed with *rīc* 'power(ful)', for example, *Richbert*.

Ribera (224) Catalan: habitational name from any of the numerous places named Ribera, from *ribera* 'bank', 'shore' (from Late Latin *riparia*). This is also found as a (southern) Italian surname, of the same derivation.
GIVEN NAMES Spanish 18%; Italian 7%. *Jose* (4), *Juan* (2), *Merced* (2), *Adolfo, Angel*,

Arnoldo, Belen, Carlos, Damaso, Domingo, Francisco, Joaquin; Angelo (4), Salvatore (2), Cesario, Heriberto, Sal.

Riberdy (122) Respelling of French **Riberty**, from the Germanic personal name *Ricbehrt*, composed of *rīc* 'powerful' + *berht* 'bright', 'famous'.
GIVEN NAMES French 6%. *Laurent, Normand.*

Riblet (110) French: nickname from a derivative of Old French *ribler* 'to roam', 'to wander'; also 'to pillage', 'to plunder'.
GIVEN NAME French 5%. *Raoul.*

Riblett (116) Apparently an altered spelling of French RIBLET.

Ribordy (107) Swiss French: unexplained.
GIVEN NAMES French 8%. *Armand (2), Euclide.*

Ricard (1033) English and French: variant of RICHARD.
FOREBEARS A Ricard is documented in Montreal in 1665, with the secondary surname Saint-Germain.
GIVEN NAMES French 10%. *Emile (4), Andre (2), Armand (2), Normand (2), Raoul (2), Adelard, Adrien, Amedee, Damien, Fernand, Francois, Germaine.*

Ricardo (476) Spanish and Jewish (Sephardic): from the personal name *Ricardo* (see RICHARD).
GIVEN NAMES Spanish 37%. *Jose (14), Manuel (7), Juan (6), Roberto (5), Carlos (4), Angel (3), Jorge (3), Ramon (3), Ediberto (2), Guillermo (2), Joaquin (2), Juana (2).*

Ricca (607) Italian: from the popular medieval personal name *Ricca*, from the feminine form of *ricco* 'rich', 'wealthy'.
GIVEN NAMES Italian 11%. *Sal (5), Angelo (4), Antonio (2), Cosimo (2), Salvatore (2), Aldo, Carlo, Carmelo, Carmine, Ciriaco, Domenic, Gaetano.*

Riccardi (938) Italian: patronymic or plural form of RICCARDO.
GIVEN NAMES Italian 14%. *Marino (3), Salvatore (3), Angelo (2), Domenic (2), Fiore (2), Giovanni (2), Agostino, Carlo, Carmela, Cinzia, Ciro, Dante.*

Riccardo (262) Italian: from the personal name *Riccardo*, Italian form of RICHARD.
GIVEN NAMES Italian 16%. *Rocco (3), Salvatore (3), Angelo (2), Vito (2), Antonio, Carmine, Domenico, Francesca.*

Riccelli (114) Italian: patronymic from a diminutive of RICCIO.
GIVEN NAMES Italian 19%. *Angelo, Cesare, Elio, Luigi, Nicola.*

Ricchio (130) Southern Italian: from a reduced form of **Oricchio**, a southern variant of ORECCHIO.
GIVEN NAMES Italian 8%. *Antonio, Attilio, Ferdinando, Giovanni.*

Ricci (4431) Italian: patronymic or plural form of RICCIO.
GIVEN NAMES Italian 13%. *Angelo (17), Dino (9), Antonio (8), Domenic (7), Gino (7), Rocco (7), Salvatore (6), Carmine (5),*

Carlo (4), Donato (4), Gaetano (4), Otello (4).

Ricciardelli (237) Italian: patronymic from the personal name *Ricciardello*, a pet form of *Ricciardo*, a variant of RICCARDO.
GIVEN NAMES Italian 13%; French 6%. *Domenic (2), Gino (2), Angelo, Ateo, Carmelo, Luigi, Marino; Armand (2), Camille, Marcel.*

Ricciardi (1336) Italian: patronymic from *Ricciardo*, a variant of the personal name RICCARDO.
GIVEN NAMES Italian 17%. *Rocco (12), Salvatore (6), Antonio (5), Pasquale (5), Carmine (4), Vito (4), Angelo (3), Filomena (3), Luigi (3), Caesar (2), Sal (2), Alessia.*

Riccio (1609) Italian: nickname for a person with curly hair, from *riccio* 'curly', or from a personal name of the same derivation.
GIVEN NAMES Italian 14%. *Angelo (8), Salvatore (7), Pasquale (5), Rocco (4), Antonio (3), Carmine (3), Donato (3), Nicola (3), Carlo (2), Gaetano (2), Gennaro (2), Silvio (2).*

Riccitelli (232) Italian: apparently a patronymic from *Riccitello*, a pet form of RICCO.
GIVEN NAMES Italian 20%. *Angelo (5), Carlo (2), Dino (2), Santo (2), Carmine, Dante, Enzo, Ettore, Luigi, Palma.*

Ricciuti (262) Italian: from a variant of *riccio* 'curly-haired' (see RICCIO).
GIVEN NAMES Italian 12%. *Rocco (2), Carmelo, Gaetano, Nunzio, Pompeo, Renzo, Silvio.*

Ricco (405) Italian: **1.** from the omen name *Ricco*, meaning 'rich', 'wealthy'. **2.** from a pet form of any of the various Lombardic personal names containing the Germanic element *rīc* 'power(ful)'.
GIVEN NAMES Italian 9%. *Angelo, Antonio, Carmela, Dino, Gilda, Luca, Marcello, Marco, Salvatore, Vito.*

Riccobono (217) Italian: from the medieval personal name *Riccobono*, a compound of RICCO + *buono* 'good'.
GIVEN NAMES Italian 29%. *Salvatore (4), Antonio (2), Carlo (2), Angelo, Arcangelo, Armando, Carmela, Carmelo, Domenic, Elena, Erasmo, Ettore, Francesca, Francesco, Gaetano, Xavier.*

Rice (54404) **1.** Welsh: variant of REESE. **2.** Americanized spelling of German REIS.

Rich (18489) **1.** English: nickname for a wealthy man (or perhaps in some cases an ironic nickname for a pauper), from Middle English, Old French *riche* 'rich', 'wealthy' (of Germanic origin, akin to Germanic *rīc* 'power(ful)'). **2.** English: from a medieval personal name, a short form of RICHARD, or less commonly of some other compound name with this first element. **3.** English: habitational name from the lost village of Riche in Lincolnshire, apparently so named from an Old English element *ric* 'stream' or, here, 'drainage channel'. Some early forms of the surname, such as Ricardus de la riche (Hampshire 1200) and Alexander

atte Riche (Sussex 1296) probably derive from minor places named with this element in southern counties, as for example Glynde Reach in Sussex. **4.** Americanized form of German REICH.

Richard (17226) English, French, German, and Dutch: from a Germanic personal name composed of the elements *rīc* 'power(ful)' + *hard* 'hardy', 'brave', 'strong'.
FOREBEARS A Richard from Normandy is documented in Quebec City in 1669, with the secondary surname LAVALLEE; other branches came from the Saintonge region and Poitou, France. Other secondary surnames include Des Sablons, DUSABLON, LAFLEUR, La Richardière, LAROSE, PETRUS. The LA Richard families are mainly descended from Acadian refugees in the second half of the 18th century.
GIVEN NAMES French 7%. *Armand (14), Emile (14), Jacques (14), Andre (11), Marcel (11), Pierre (11), Leonce (10), Normand (10), Camille (9), Lucien (9), Gilles (8), Henri (7).*

Richardi (134) Italian: variant spelling of RICCARDI.
GIVEN NAMES Italian 11%. *Donato (3), Rocco (2).*

Richards (45818) English and German: patronymic from the personal name RICHARD. Richards is a frequent name in Wales.

Richardson (81637) English: patronymic from the personal name RICHARD. This has undoubtedly also assimilated like-sounding cognates from other languages, such as Swedish **Richardsson**.
FOREBEARS An early English bearer of the common name Richardson, Francis Richardson emigrated to America in 1681 as a member of the Society of Friends. His grandson was a respected silversmith from Philadelphia, PA. The name was brought to North America independently by many other bearers from the 17th century onward.

Richardt (149) German: variant of RICHARD.
GIVEN NAMES German 7%. *Gerhard, Jurgen, Wendelin.*

Richarson (142) English: variant of RICHARDSON.

Richart (466) variant of German RICHARD or RICHARDT.

Richbourg (263) See RICHBURG.

Richburg (880) Perhaps an Americanized spelling of REICHENBERG.

Richcreek (187) Perhaps an Americanized form of German **Reichenbach**, a habitational name from any of numerous places so named ('(by the) richly flowing stream').

Riche (437) **1.** English: variant spelling of RICH. **2.** French: nickname for a rich man or perhaps an ironical name for a pauper, from Old French *riche* 'rich'.
GIVEN NAMES French 6%. *Pierre (2), Ghislaine, Philippe, Yanick, Yvon.*

Richel (122) German: from a pet form of a Germanic personal name (see REICH).

Richens (156) Probably an altered spelling of the German and Swiss German family name **Richen**, from a Germanic personal name (see REICH).

Richer (949) **1.** English and German: from a Germanic personal name composed of the elements *rīc* 'power(ful)' + *hari, heri* 'army'. The name was introduced into England by the Normans in the form *Richier*, but was largely absorbed by the much more common RICHARD. **2.** Americanized spelling of German **Ritscher**, a variant of RICHARD. **3.** German: nickname or status name from Sorbian *ryčer* 'knight'.
GIVEN NAMES French 10%. *Normand* (5), *Armand* (2), *Fernand* (2), *Herve* (2), *Laurent* (2), *Marcel* (2), *Aurele, Donat, Elphege, Emile, Flore, Gilles*.

Richerson (750) Apparently an altered spelling of RICHARDSON or perhaps a patronymic from RICHER.

Richert (1153) German: variant of RICHER or RICHARD.
GIVEN NAMES German 5%. *Otto* (2), *Willi* (2), *Alois, Alphons, Bernhard, Erhard, Erwin, Gerhard, Gerhardt, Hermann, Kurt, Monika*.

Riches (341) English: patronymic from RICH 2.

Richesin (141) See RICHESON.

Richeson (876) Apparently an altered form of RICHARDSON, but compare RICHERSON.

Richey (6666) **1.** German: from a short form of a Germanic personal name based on *rīc* 'power(ful)' (see REICH), or from the female personal name *Rikheit*, from *rīc* + suffix *-heit* 'way of being'. **2.** Possibly an Americanized spelling of German REICHE or **Ritsche** (see RITCHEY 2). **3.** English and northern Irish: variant spelling of RITCHIE.

Richgels (120) Origin unidentified.

Richhart (142) Americanized form of German **Reichhardt** (see RICHARD).
GIVEN NAMES German 7%. *Erwin, Georg, Kurt*.

Richichi (135) Italian: nickname from Arabic *raqīq* meaning 'slave', but also 'fine', 'soft', 'delicate'.
GIVEN NAMES Italian 18%. *Rocco* (3), *Pasquale, Sal*.

Richie (2204) **1.** English and Scottish: variant spelling of RITCHIE. **2.** Americanized spelling of the Swiss family names **Rütschi, Rütsche**, or **Rüetschi** (see RITCHEY).

Richins (692) English: patronymic from a pet form of *Ric*, a short form of RICHARD.

Richison (319) Apparently a patronymic from RICHIE or perhaps an altered form of RICHAR(D)SON.

Richley (109) **1.** English: probably a habitational name from an unidentified place, possibly in the Newcastle area of northeastern England, where the surname is now

most concentrated. **2.** Perhaps also an altered spelling of Swiss German **Richle** and **Richli**, from a short form of a Germanic personal name based on *rīc, rīh* 'power(ful)' (see REICH).

Richman (3236) **1.** English: nickname for a wealthy man (see RICH). **2.** English: occupational name for the servant of a man called RICH. **3.** English: variant of RICHMOND. **4.** German (**Richmann**): from a Germanic personal name composed of the elements *rīc* 'power(ful)' + *man* 'man'. **5.** German (**Richmann**): nickname for a rich man.

Richmeier (128) German: variant of **Richmann** (see RICHMAN 5), with *-meier* substituted for *-mann* 'man'.

Richmond (12518) English: habitational name from any of the numerous places so named, in northern France as well as in England. These are named with the Old French elements *riche* 'rich', 'splendid' + *mont* 'hill'. Richmond in North Yorkshire was named after a Richmont in France immediately after the Norman Conquest, and in many if not most cases the English surname can be derived from this place. Richmond in southwest London received this name only in the reign of Henry VII, in honor of the king, who had been Earl of Richmond until he came to the throne, and is unlikely to be the source of this surname.

Richner (275) German and Swiss German: habitational name for someone from Richen in Baden, or, in the case of the Swiss surname, from Riehen near Basel.

Richoux (202) French (Berry and Loiret): from the Germanic personal name *Ricwulf*, a compound of *rīc* 'power(ful)' + *wulf* 'wolf'.

Richter (12562) **1.** German: occupational name or status name for an arbiter or judge, Middle High German *rihtære* (from *rihten* 'to make right'). The term was used in the Middle Ages mostly to denote a part-time legal official. Such communal conciliators held a position of considerable esteem in rural communities; in eastern Germany the term came to denote a village headman, which was often a hereditary office. It is in this region that the surname is most frequent. **2.** Jewish (Ashkenazic): occupational name for a rabbinic judge, from modern German *Richter* 'judge' (see 1 above). See also DAYAN.
GIVEN NAMES German 6%. *Kurt* (43), *Otto* (19), *Hans* (15), *Fritz* (11), *Helmut* (11), *Horst* (11), *Erwin* (10), *Heinz* (10), *Juergen* (8), *Gerhard* (5), *Siegfried* (5), *Wolfgang* (5).

Richters (153) German (North Rhineland): patronymic form of RICHTER.
GIVEN NAMES German 7%; Scandinavian 4%. *Franz* (2), *Klaus; Johan* (2), *Lars*.

Richwine (473) From German **Reichwein**. *Richwine* is a literal translation of modern German *reich* 'rich' + *Wein* 'wine'. The

German name, however, is from an old personal name composed of the elements *rīc* 'power(ful)' + *win* 'friend'.

Ricigliano (149) Italian: habitational name from Ricigliano in Salerno province.
GIVEN NAME Italian 10%. *Sal*.

Rick (1636) **1.** English: variant of RICH 2. **2.** German: from a short form of any of the Germanic personal names formed with *rīc* 'power(ful)'.

Rickabaugh (311) Altered spelling of German RICKENBACH or REICHENBACH.

Rickard (3431) **1.** English (Devon and Cornwall) and German: variant of RICHARD. **2.** Americanized spelling of German REICHARDT.

Rickards (654) English: patronymic from RICKARD.

Ricke (512) **1.** German: variant of RICK. **2.** Dutch (**de Ricke**): nickname for a wealthy person, from *rijk* 'rich', 'wealthy'.

Rickel (472) German: **1.** habitational name from a place in Haspengau (near Lüttich) named Rickel. **2.** from a female Germanic personal name, *Riclind*. **3.** from a Germanic personal name composed of the elements *rīc* 'power(ful)' + *wald-* 'to rule'. **4.** altered spelling of RICHEL.

Rickelman (113) German (**Rickelmann**): elaborated form of RICKEL 3 + *man* 'man'.

Rickels (254) German: patronymic form of RICKEL 3 or possibly RICHEL.

Ricken (113) **1.** German: from a short form of any of the Germanic personal names composed with *rīc* 'power(ful)'. **2.** Dutch: perhaps a respelling of **Reichen**, a patronymic from a short form of a Germanic personal name formed with *rīc* 'powerful'.

Rickenbach (213) German and Swiss German: habitational name from any of several places so named, for example in Thurgau, near Überlingen, and Zürich.

Rickenbacker (131) Americanized spelling of German **Rickenbacher**, a habitational name for someone from RICKENBACH.

Rickenbaker (117) See RICKENBACKER.

Ricker (3582) **1.** English: variant of RICHER. **2.** German: variant of RICHER.

Rickerd (146) English: variant of RICHARD.

Rickers (138) North German and Frisian: patronymic from RICKER.

Rickerson (385) Possibly an altered spelling of German **Rickertsen**, a patronymic from RICHARD or RICKERT.

Rickert (2034) **1.** English: variant of RICHARD. **2.** North German and Frisian form of RICHARD. **3.** Probably an Americanized spelling of cognates in other languages, for example German REICHERT or Dutch **Rickaert**.

Ricketson (494) Altered spelling of German **Rickertsen**, a patronymic from RICKERT.

Rickett (869) English: from a pet form of RICH 2.

Ricketts (4125) English (chiefly West Midlands): patronymic from RICKETT.

Rickey (1012) **1.** English and northern Irish: probably a variant of **Richey** (see RICHIE). **2.** Possibly an altered spelling of German RICHEY.

Rickle (104) Americanized spelling of German RICKEL.

Ricklefs (250) North German: patronymic from a Frisian personal name composed of the elements *rīc* 'power(ful)' + *lef, leib* 'body', 'life'.

Rickles (236) Altered spelling of German RICKELS or English **Rickells**, probably derived from any of a number of Old German personal names including *Richild* (or the feminine form *Richeldis*) or *Richold*.

Rickman (2299) English: **1.** variant of RICHMAN 1. **2.** from an Old English personal name *Rīcmund*, composed of the elements *rīc* 'rich' + *mund* 'protection'. **3.** German: variant of **Richmann** (see RICHMAN).

Rickner (160) Americanized form of German RICHNER.

Ricks (5064) **1.** English and German: patronymic from a short form of RICHARD. **2.** English: topographic name for someone who lived where rushes grew, Middle English *rexe, rixe* (Old English *rix*).

Rickson (155) English: **1.** patronymic from a short form of RICHARD. **2.** topographic name for someone who lived where rushes grew, from West Saxon *ryxen* 'rushes', plural of *rixe* (see RICKS).

Rico (2204) Spanish (also Portuguese): nickname from *rico* 'rich'.
GIVEN NAMES Spanish 45%. *Jose* (53), *Juan* (35), *Manuel* (25), *Francisco* (16), *Luis* (14), *Jesus* (13), *Miguel* (13), *Carlos* (12), *Pedro* (12), *Ramon* (12), *Javier* (11), *Salvador* (11).

Ricord (106) French: variant of RECORD.
GIVEN NAMES French 9%. *Christophe, Colette, Fernande, Remi.*

Ricotta (322) Southern Italian: from *ricotta*, the name of a soft cheese, hence a metonymic occupational name for someone who made or sold cheese or a nickname for a man who was dominated by his womenfolk or thought to be 'soft in the head'.
GIVEN NAMES Italian 14%. *Salvatore* (3), *Sal* (2), *Santo* (2), *Albertina, Gesualdo, Giuseppe, Pasquale.*

Ridall (109) Scottish and northern English: variant spelling of RIDDELL.

Riddel (128) Scottish and northern English: variant spelling of RIDDELL.

Riddell (1891) Scottish and northern English: from a Norman personal name, *Ridel*. Reaney explains this as a nickname from Old French *ridel* 'small hill' (a diminutive of *ride* 'fold', of Germanic origin), but a more probable source is a Germanic personal name derived from the element *rīd* 'ride'.

Ridder (676) North German and Dutch form of RITTER.
GIVEN NAMES German 4%. *Hans* (2), *Kurt* (2), *Manfred, Otto.*

Riddick (2086) Scottish and northern Irish: variant of REDDICK.

Riddle (11839) Scottish and northern English: **1.** habitational name from Ryedale in North Yorkshire, being the valley of the river Rye (a name of Celtic origin). **2.** variant of RIDDELL.

Riddlebarger (102) Americanized form of a German habitational name, **Riedelberger** or **Riedelsberger**, from Riedelberg in Rhineland-Palatinate or Riedelsberg in the former East Prussia.

Riddles (221) English: variant of RIDDLE.

Rideau (203) French (Normandy): topographic name for someone who lived on ridged terrain, from an agent derivative of Old French *rider* 'to fold'.
GIVEN NAMES French 5%. *Francoise, Gilles.*

Rideaux (205) Apparently a variant of French RIDEAU.

Riden (326) English: unexplained. Compare RYDEN.

Ridener (207) Possibly an altered spelling of German **Reutener** or **Reitner**, variant forms of REUTER.

Ridenhour (637) Americanized form of **Rittenhauer**, an occupational name for a woodman living and working in a swampy area, from *Ritten* 'swamp' + *Hauer* 'woodcutter' (see HAUER).

Ridenour (3066) **1.** Americanized spelling of German **Rittenauer** or **Rettenauer**, a topographic name for someone living by a swampy water meadow (from *Retten* 'swamp' + *Au* 'water meadow' + *-er* suffix denoting an inhabitant), or a habitational name from a place named with these elements. **2.** Americanized spelling of South German **Rütt(e)nauer**, perhaps a topographic name from Middle High German *riute* 'clearing' + *ouwe* 'wet field', 'water meadow'. **3.** variant of RIDENHOUR.

Ridens (114) Origin unidentified.

Rideout (1460) English: occupational name for an outrider, from Middle English *rid(en)* 'to ride' + *out* 'out', 'forth'. An outrider (Middle English *outridere*) was an officer of a sheriff's court or of a monastery whose duties included riding out to collect dues and supervise manors.

Rider (6020) **1.** English: occupational name for a mounted warrior or messenger, late Old English *rīdere* (from *rīdan* 'to ride'), a term quickly displaced after the Conquest by the new sense of KNIGHT. **2.** English: topographic name for someone who lived in a clearing in woodland. Compare READ 2. **3.** Irish: part translation of Gaelic **Ó Marcaigh** 'descendant of *Marcach*', a byname meaning 'horseman'. The Gaelic name is also Anglicized as MARKEY. **4.** Americanized form of German REITER.

Ridge (2519) English: topographic name for someone who lived on or by a ridge, Middle English *rigge*, or a habitational name from any of the places named with this word, as for example Ridge in Hertfordshire. The surname is also fairly common in Ireland, in County Galway, having been taken to Connacht in the early 17th century. The name is sometimes Gaelicized as **Mac Iomaire**; *iomaire* is modern Irish for 'ridge'.

Ridgell (312) English (Yorkshire): unexplained.

Ridgely (470) English: variant spelling of RIDGLEY.

Ridgeway (3207) English: from Middle English *riggewey*, hence a topographic name for someone who lived by such a route or a habitational name from any of various places so named, for example in Cheshire, Derbyshire, Dorset, and Staffordshire.

Ridgley (674) English: probably a habitational name, perhaps from **Rugeley**, a habitational name from a place so named in Staffordshire.

Ridgway (2226) English: variant spelling of RIDGEWAY.

Riding (373) English: variant of READING 2.

Ridinger (406) German: **1.** habitational name for someone from any of several places in Bavaria named Riding or Rieding. **2.** possibly an altered spelling of **Reitinger**, a topographic name from dialect *Reit(e)* 'clearing' (Old High German *riuti*), which also gave rise to several place names in Bavaria and Austria.

Ridings (1230) English: variant of READING 2.

Ridl (110) Probably a respelling of German REIDEL or **Riedl**, a variant of RIEDEL.
GIVEN NAMES German 7%. *Otto* (2), *Kurt.*

Ridlehoover (100) Americanized form of an unidentified Dutch or German surname: **1.** possibly German **Reidelhuber**, a distinguishing name for a farmer (see HUBER) with an unexplained first element. **2.** alternatively, perhaps a habitational name for someone from Riedernhöfe near Singen, Württemberg.

Ridlen (129) Possibly from Swiss and South German **Riedlin** or **Rüdlin(g)**, from pet forms of RUDOLF.

Ridler (162) **1.** English: occupational name for a sifter of flour and meal, from an agent derivative of Middle English *rid(e)len* 'to sift' (from Old English *hriddel* 'sieve'). **2.** German: topographic name from Bavarian *Ridel* 'hill'. **3.** Perhaps an altered spelling of German **Riedler**, a variant of RIEDER or RIEDEL.

Ridley (3484) **1.** English: habitational name from any of various places in England so named, especially the one in Northumberland, which, like that in Cheshire, is derived from Old English *geryd* 'channel' + *lēah* 'wood', 'clearing'. Those in Essex and Kent appear in Domesday Book as *Retleia* and *Redlege* respectively, and get their names from Old English *hrēod* 'reed' + *lēah*. **2.** Possibly also an altered spelling of German RIEDEL or **Riedler** (see RIDLER).

Ridling (201) Possibly an altered spelling of German **Riedling**, a topographic name from Bavarian *Ridel* 'hill', or a habitational name from Riedling in Bavaria, named with this word.

Ridlon (341) Probably an altered spelling of German RIDLEN.

Ridner (203) Perhaps an altered spelling of German RITTNER or *Riedner*, a variant of RIEDER.

Ridnour (126) variant of RIDENOUR.

Ridolfi (211) Northern Italian: patronymic from the personal name *Rodolfo*, an old variant of *Rodolfo*, Italian equivalent of RUDOLF.

GIVEN NAMES Italian 12%. *Angelo* (2), *Italo* (2), *Carlo*, *Dante*, *Gino*, *Leno*.

Ridout (429) English: variant spelling of RIDEOUT.

Ridpath (220) Scottish: variant of REDPATH.

Rieb (104) French: from the Germanic personal name, *Ribo*.

GIVEN NAME Irish 5%. *Declan*.

Riebe (696) German: **1.** metonymic occupational name from Slavic *ryba* 'fish'. **2.** North German: from a short form of a personal name composed of the elements *rīc* 'power(ful)' + *bod* 'messenger'. **3.** metonymic occupational name for a turnip grower, from Middle High German *rüebe* 'turnip', 'beet'.

GIVEN NAMES German 4%. *Kurt* (3), *Fritz* (2), *Erwin*, *Ewald*, *Gerhard*.

Riebel (371) German: **1.** from the Germanic personal name *Riebold*, composed of the elements *rīc* 'power(ful)' + *bald* 'bold'. **2.** metonymic occupational name for a turnip grower (see RIEBE 3).

Riebeling (100) German: patronymic from the personal name RIEBE.

GIVEN NAMES German 9%. *Aloys* (2), *Elke*, *Hans*.

Rieben (155) German and Swiss German: **1.** variant of RIEBE 2. **2.** habitational name from any of several places so named in Brandenburg and Pomerania.

GIVEN NAMES German 7%. *Otto* (2), *Kurt*.

Rieber (265) German: **1.** from a reduced form of the Germanic personal name *Richberht*, composed of *rīc* 'power(ful)' + *berht* 'famous'. **2.** occupational name for a turnip grower, from a derivative of Middle High German *ruobe*, *rüebe* 'turnip'.

Riechers (252) German: patronymic from RICHARD.

GIVEN NAMES German 6%. *Heino*, *Heinz*, *Horst*, *Irmgard*, *Kurt*.

Riechmann (114) German: elaborated form of **Riech**, a variant of RIECK 2.

GIVEN NAMES German 8%. *Gunther*, *Otto*.

Rieck (1347) **1.** South German: from a pet form of the personal name *Ru(o)diger*, a compound of Old High German *hrōd* 'renown' + *gēr* 'spear', 'lance' (see

ROGER). **2.** North German: from a short form of a personal name containing the Middle Low German element *rīk(e)* 'rich', 'powerful'.

Riecke (209) South German: variant of RIECK 2.

GIVEN NAMES German 5%. *Erna*, *Hans*, *Hermann*, *Kurt*.

Riecken (111) North German: Low German variant of REICH or patronymic from RIECK 2.

GIVEN NAMES German 6%. *Hans-Peter*, *Kurt*.

Rieckhoff (114) German: habitational name from a farm so named in Westphalia, from either a local topographic term *rik* 'swamp water', or a distinguishing name from RIECK 2 + *hof(f)* 'farm(yard)'.

GIVEN NAMES German 8%. *Heinz*, *Juergen*.

Ried (307) German: **1.** topographic name from Middle High German *riet* 'damp, mossy area', 'wet land'. **2.** from a short form of a Germanic personal name based on *rīd* 'ride'.

GIVEN NAMES German 4%. *Friedrich* (2), *Johann*.

Riede (172) German: from a popular short form of the personal name RUDOLF, or from a Germanic personal name formed with *rītan*, *rīden* 'to ride'.

GIVEN NAMES German 7%. *Hermann*, *Johann*, *Kurt*.

Riedel (2743) South German: **1.** pet form of the personal name RIEDE. **2.** variant of the topographic name RIED 'mossy area'. **3.** pet form of a Germanic personal name formed with Middle Low German *rīden*, Middle High German *rītan* 'to ride'. Compare REIDEL 3.

GIVEN NAMES German 6%. *Hans* (6), *Kurt* (4), *Klaus* (3), *Manfred* (3), *Otto* (3), *Bernd* (2), *Fritz* (2), *Wilhelm* (2), *Wolfgang* (2), *Alfons*, *Armin*, *Beate*.

Riedell (149) Altered spelling of RIEDEL.

Riedeman (102) Respelling of German RIEDEMANN.

Riedemann (124) North German: topographic name from Low German *Riede* 'rivulet', or a habitational name from any of several places called Ried or Riede.

GIVEN NAME German 6%. *Siegfried* (2).

Rieder (971) German: topographic name from Middle High German *riet* 'damp, mossy ground', 'wet land' + -*er* suffix denoting an inhabitant, or habitational name from any of the numerous places named with this word.

GIVEN NAMES German 5%. *Kurt* (5), *Hans* (3), *Bernhard*, *Erwin*, *Florian*, *Franz*, *Georg*, *Guenther*, *Helmut*, *Irmgard*, *Orlo*, *Urs*.

Riederer (217) German: habitational name for someone from any of several places called Riedern, especially in Baden.

GIVEN NAMES German 5%. *Florian* (2), *Kurt*, *Maximilian*.

Riedesel (271) German: as yet unexplained. This is the name of a noble family of Hesse.

Riedinger (349) German: **1.** habitational name for someone from any of several places named Rieding or Riding in Bavaria. **2.** topographic name for someone who lived among reeds, from Middle High German *riet* 'reed' + -*er* suffix denoting an inhabitant.

Riedl (628) South German: variant of RIEDEL.

GIVEN NAMES German 7%. *Ernst* (2), *Heinz* (2), *Wilhelm* (2), *Erwin*, *Ewald*, *Gerhard*, *Helmut*, *Inge*, *Kurt*, *Lothar*, *Wenzel*.

Riedle (126) South German: variant of RIEDEL.

Riedlinger (236) South German: habitational name for someone from any of several places named Riedlingen, in Baden, Bavaria, and Württemberg.

GIVEN NAME French 4%. *Andre*.

Riedman (142) German (**Riedmann**): topographic name for a marsh dweller, from Middle High German *riet* 'bog', 'marsh'.

Riedy (426) Swiss German: variant of **Rüdi** (see RUEDY).

Rief (286) German: from a variant of the personal name *Rüef*, *Ruoff*, reduced forms of RUDOLF, or from a short form of the Germanic personal name *Ricfrid*, composed of *rīc* 'power(ful)', 'rich' + *frid* 'peace'.

Rieff (126) German: variant of RIEF.

Rieg (152) German: variant of RIECK 1.

GIVEN NAMES German 5%. *Bernhard*, *Dietmar*.

Riege (176) North German: **1.** topographic name from Middle Low German *rige* 'row (of houses)'. **2.** habitational name from any of several places so named in Westphalia, Brandenburg, and West Prussia.

Riegel (1609) German: from Middle High German *rigel* 'bar', 'crossbeam', 'mountain incline', hence a topographic name or a habitational name from any of numerous places named with this word in Baden, Brandenburg, and Silesia; in some instances it may have been a metonymic occupational name for a maker of crossbars, locks, etc.

Rieger (2345) German: **1.** from a reduced form of the personal name *Rüdiger* (see RUDIGER). **2.** nickname from Middle High German *rüegære*, *rüeger* 'complainer' (earlier 'prosecutor').

GIVEN NAMES German 5%. *Otto* (5), *Gerhard* (4), *Franz* (3), *Hans* (3), *Konrad* (3), *Kurt* (2), *Udo* (2), *Wolfram* (2), *Arno*, *Eckhard*, *Egon*, *Gebhard*.

Riegert (282) German: variant of RIEGER.

GIVEN NAMES German 4%. *Franz*, *Lutz*.

Riegle (324) Americanized spelling of German RIEGEL.

Riegler (434) German: variant of RIEGEL, with the addition of the agent suffix -*er*.

GIVEN NAMES German 5%. *Eugen*, *Guenter*, *Hans*, *Ingo*, *Kurt*, *Rudi*.

Riegsecker (123) Altered form of Swiss German **Rügsegger**, a habitational name from Rügsegg in Bern canton.

Riehl (1244) German: **1.** habitational name for someone from a place named Riehl or Rühle. **2.** altered form of the personal name *Rühle*, a pet form of RUDOLF.

Riehle (699) German: variant of RIEHL.

Riehm (242) German: from Middle High German *rieme* 'band', 'strap', hence a metonymic occupational name for a strap maker, a nickname for a wearer of such items, a topographic name from the same word in the sense 'narrow strip of land', or a habitational name from Riem near Munich.

Riek (274) German: variant spelling of RIECK.

GIVEN NAMES German 4%. *Edeltraud, Ute.*

Rieke (630) German: **1.** variant spelling of **Riecke**, itself a variant of RIECK. **2.** topographic name from Slavic *rēka* 'river'.

GIVEN NAMES German 4%. *Kurt* (4), *Ernst, Gerhard, Heinz, Otto.*

Rieken (299) German: patronymic from **Riek(e)** (see RIECK 2), or altered spelling of RIECKEN.

Rieker (365) **1.** North German: from the personal name *Rikher*, composed of the elements *rīc* 'power(ful)' + *heri* 'army' or *her* 'master', 'lord'. **2.** Eastern German: variant of RIEKE 2.

GIVEN NAMES German 4%. *Gerd* (2), *Otto* (2), *Erna.*

Riel (763) German: **1.** variant of RIEHL. **2.** habitational name from any of several places so named in Rhineland.

FOREBEARS The ancestor of the Riel families of Canada was an Irishman from Limerick, who was in Quebec in 1700; he was also called Lirlande. Variants of the name include Le Rell and Reel.

GIVEN NAMES French 4%. *Armand* (2), *Marcel* (2), *Emile, Normand, Rolande.*

Rieland (145) German: regional name from a locality named Rieland, presumably for someone from the Rhineland, from Middle High German, Middle Low German *Rīn* 'Rhine' + *land* 'land'.

Rielly (339) Scottish: perhaps a metathesized spelling of REILLY.

GIVEN NAMES Irish 6%. *Brendan, Bridie.*

Riels (102) German: probably a patronymic form of Riel, a variant of RIEHL.

Riely (103) Irish: variant of REILLY.

Rieman (537) Americanized spelling of RIEMANN.

Riemann (308) German: **1.** North German form of REIMANN. **2.** topographic name from Middle Low German *ri(d)e* 'stream', 'small watercourse' + *man* 'man'.

GIVEN NAMES German 5%; Scandinavian 5%. *Hans* (3), *Juergen, Kurt; Alf.*

Riemenschneider (421) German: occupational name for a maker of leather straps, belts, and reins (later a saddler), Middle High German *riemensnīder*, Middle Low German *remensnīder*.

GIVEN NAMES German 4%. *Fritz* (3), *Kurt.*

Riemer (1447) **1.** German and Jewish (Ashkenazic): occupational name for a maker of leather reins and similar articles, Middle High German *riemære*, German *Riemer*, Yiddish *rimer*. Compare RIEMENSCHNEIDER. **2.** Altered spelling of German REIMER.

GIVEN NAMES German 6%. *Otto* (5), *Dietrich* (2), *Elke* (2), *Erwin* (2), *Hans* (2), *Helmut* (2), *Kurt* (2), *Egon, Ernst, Heinrich, Lorenz, Reinhard.*

Riemersma (264) Frisian: patronymic from the personal name RIEMER.

GIVEN NAMES Dutch 4%. *Cornie, Dirk, Gerrit, Roelof.*

Riendeau (711) French: variant of REGUINDEAU.

FOREBEARS Reguindeau or Riendeau, also called JOACHIM, is documented in Pointe aux Trembles, Quebec, in 1671.

GIVEN NAMES French 17%. *Emile* (4), *Armand* (3), *Laurent* (3), *Camile* (2), *Gaston* (2), *Gilles* (2), *Lucien* (2), *Marcel* (2), *Adelard, Alban, Andre, Benoit.*

Rienstra (174) Frisian: habitational name from a place called Rien + the agent suffix -stra.

Rients (128) Dutch or Frisian: unexplained.

Rienzo (130) Italian: from a short form of the personal name *Laurienzo*, an Italian equivalent of LAWRENCE.

GIVEN NAME Italian 5%. *Salvatore.*

Riepe (248) German: **1.** from a short form of the Germanic personal name *Ribbert, Rippert* (a compound of *rīc* 'power(ful)' + *berht* 'bright'). **2.** habitational name from any of several places so named in northern Germany.

Riera (254) Catalan: habitational name from any of the numerous places named Riera or La Riera, from Catalan *riera* 'stream' (Late Latin *rivaria*). There are various places in northern Spain named with this word, for example in the province of Tarragona, and the surname may also be a habitational name from any of these.

GIVEN NAMES Spanish 44%. *Jose* (5), *Miguel* (5), *Luis* (4), *Fabio* (3), *Rafael* (3), *Ricardo* (3), *Rogelio* (3), *Abelardo* (2), *Alfonso* (2), *Arturo* (2), *Carlos* (2), *Fernando* (2); *Antonio* (4), *Giuseppe, Marco.*

Rierson (426) Variant spelling of Swedish REIERSON or Dutch **Ryersen** (see RYERSON).

Ries (3029) **1.** South German and Jewish (Ashkenazic): from a Germanic personal name, but mainly a nickname for an exceptionally tall or big man, Middle High German *rise*, German *Riese* 'giant'. In some cases the name may have been used to refer ironically to a particularly short man. **2.** South German: habitational name from any of several places named Ries. **3.** German: topographic name from Middle Low

German *rīs* 'branch', 'twig', 'brushwood'. **4.** Altered spelling of German RIESS or REIS.

Riesberg (192) Variant of German **Rieseberg**, a habitational name from a place so named near Helmstedt, Lower Saxony.

Riese (519) German and Jewish (Ashkenazic): variant of RIES 1.

GIVEN NAMES German 4%. *Kurt* (2), *Fritz, Horst, Willi.*

Riesen (252) German: **1.** habitational name from any of several places so named in Bavaria, Württemberg, and Tyrol. **2.** patronymic from RIESE.

GIVEN NAMES German 5%. *Armin, Kurt.*

Riesenberg (250) German: topographic name for someone who lived by a big mountain, from Middle High German *rise* 'giant' + *berc* 'mountain'.

GIVEN NAMES German 4%. *Kurt, Otto.*

Rieser (437) German: **1.** (Swiss): Alemannic form of REISER. **2.** habitational name for someone from Ries near Passau. **3.** Alemannic variant of **Rüs(s)er**, a variant of REUSSER 1. **4.** altered spelling of **Riesser**, a habitational name for someone from Ries(s), a region of Bavaria.

GIVEN NAMES German 5%; French 4%. *Aloys* (2), *Ernst, Fritz, Hannelore, Hans, Manfred, Ruedi, Volker; Norvin* (3), *Alain, Marcel.*

Riess (718) German: regional name from an area of Bavaria so named.

GIVEN NAMES German 10%. *Mathias* (3), *Kurt* (2), *Dietmar, Frieda, Fritz, Gerd, Gottfried, Guenther, Hans, Konrad, Otto, Reinhard.*

Riessen (125) **1.** German: possibly a habitational name from Riessen in Brandenburg. **2.** Dutch: habitational name for someone from Rijssen in Oberijssel. **3.** probably a variant spelling of RIESEN southern Germany or the U.S.

GIVEN NAMES German 6%. *Reinhard* (2), *Erwin.*

Riester (355) German: from Middle High German *riester* 'plow handle', 'leather patch', presumably applied as a metonymic occupational name for a maker of plow handles or, in north and central German, a metonymic occupational name for a cobbler.

Riesterer (239) South German: occupational name for a maker of plow handles or metonymic occupational name for a cobbler, from an agent derivative of Middle High German *riester* 'plow handle', 'leather patch' (see RIESTER).

GIVEN NAMES German 6%. *Alois, Jutta, Otto, Wilfried.*

Rieth (500) German: topographic name from Middle High German *riet* 'reed' or a habitational name from any of several places named with this word.

Rietman (121) Respelling of German RIETMANN.

GIVEN NAMES German 5%. *Alois* (2), *Erwin.*

Rietmann (101) German and Swiss German: elaborated form of RIED 1 or RIETH.
GIVEN NAMES German 6%. *Ewald, Kurt.*

Rietveld (207) Dutch: topographic name for someone living by a reedbed, from Dutch *riet* 'reed' (Old Saxon *hriod*) + *veld* 'uncultivated land'.
GIVEN NAMES Dutch 10%; German 4%. *Dirk* (3), *Gerrit* (3), *Willem* (2); *Hans, Natascha, Otto.*

Rietz (320) German: **1.** habitational name from any of various places so named in eastern Germany. **2.** altered spelling of REITZ.

Rieves (221) Origin uncertain. Perhaps an altered spelling of English REEVES, Hungarian **Révész** (see REVES), or a variant of German RIEWE.

Riewe (134) German: **1.** nickname from Middle Low German *rive* 'profligate', 'generous'. **2.** from a short form of a Germanic personal name formed with *rīc* 'power(ful)' + *frid* 'peace'.
GIVEN NAMES German 7%; Scandinavian 4%. *Arno, Hans, Ralf, Reinhold.*

Rife (2376) Americanized spelling of German REIFF.

Rifenburg (139) Altered spelling of German **Reifenberg**, a habitational name from any of various places so named.

Riff (186) **1.** German: variant of RIEWE 2. **2.** Americanized spelling of German REIFF. **3.** Jewish (eastern Ashkenazic): unexplained. It is most likely a Hebrew acronymic surname.
GIVEN NAMES Jewish 5%. *Mayer* (2), *Sol.*

Riffe (1114) Possibly an Americanized spelling of German REIFF.

Riffel (651) German: **1.** from a short form of a Germanic personal name formed with *hrōd* 'renown', 'victory', for example RUDOLF. **2.** metonymic occupational name for a flax or hemp worker, from late Middle High German *riffel* 'comb (for preparing flax)', a noun derivative of Middle High German *riffeln* 'to comb'.

Riffey (297) Possibly an altered spelling of German **Riffer**, from a Germanic personal name, *Ricfrid*, a compound of *rīc* 'power(ful)' + *frid* 'peace'.

Riffle (1859) Americanized spelling of German RIFFEL or of the Swiss German family names **Rüfle, Ruefli, Rüfli,** or **Rüeffli,** all from pet forms of RUDOLF.

Rifkin (840) Jewish (eastern Ashkenazic): metronymic from the Yiddish female personal name *Rifke* (from the Hebrew name *Rivka*; see REBECCA), with the addition of the Slavic metronymic suffix *-in*.
GIVEN NAMES Jewish 5%. *Hyman* (4), *Sol* (3), *Avron, Miriam, Mort, Yetta.*

Rifkind (112) Jewish (Ashkenazic): variant of RIFKIN. The final element was changed due to the influence of the Yiddish noun *kind* 'child'.
GIVEN NAMES Jewish 6%; French 5%. *Dovid, Miriam; Estelle, Jacques.*

Riga (178) Southern Italian and Greek: variant of Greek RIGAS.
GIVEN NAMES Italian 9%. *Carmelo, Carmine, Domenic, Emidio, Ennio.*

Rigali (156) Italian: possibly from a Sicilian variant of *regale* 'royal' (see REALE).

Rigano (127) Italian (Sicily): from Sicilian *riganu* 'marjoram', applied as a topographic name or as a metonymic occupational name for a grower or seller of herbs.
GIVEN NAMES Italian 19%. *Angelo* (2), *Luigi, Rocco, Sal, Salvatore, Vincenzo.*

Rigas (220) Greek: from a medieval Greek personal name, *Rēgas* 'king', a derivative of Latin *rex*, genitive *regis*.
GIVEN NAMES Greek 17%. *Stratos* (2), *Christos, Constantine, Emilios, Konstantinos, Konstantions, Lambros, Nikos, Spyros, Taso, Theodoros, Theofilos.*

Rigaud (129) French: from a derivative of the personal name *Ricard*, a variant of RICHARD.
FOREBEARS This name is documented in 1666 in Quebec City.
GIVEN NAMES French 35%; German 5%. *Andre* (2), *Jean-Philippe* (2), *Alexandre, Cassandre, Gesner, Gilberte, Jacques, Jean-Guy, Marie Ange, Marie Claude, Marie-Claude, Michel; Otto* (2).

Rigby (2261) English (chiefly Lancashire): habitational name from Rigby in Lancashire, named with Old Norse *hryggr* 'ridge' + *býr* 'farm', 'settlement'.

Rigdon (1877) Apparently an altered spelling of English **Rigden**, which Reaney believes to be from *Ricdun*, a reduced form of the personal name *Ricardun*, a pet form of RICHARD. There is no evidence for it as a habitational name: in medieval documents it is never found with a preposition and no relevant place name has been identified.

Rigel (229) Probably of German origin, an altered form of REIGEL or RIEGEL.

Riger (101) Jewish (eastern Ashkenazic): habitational name for someone from the city of Riga, the capital of Latvia.
GIVEN NAME Jewish 6%. *Semen.*

Rigg (1120) **1.** English: variant of RIDGE 1. **2.** German: from a short form of any of several Germanic personal names based on *rīc* 'power(ful)'. **3.** Possibly a variant of the Swiss family name **Rüegg** (see RUEGG).

Riggan (621) Perhaps an altered spelling of REGAN.

Riggen (195) Perhaps an altered spelling of REGAN.

Riggenbach (278) German: variant of RICKENBACH.

Riggers (123) North German: Frisian patronymic, a variant of RICKER.
GIVEN NAMES German 8%. *Manfred* (2), *Erwin, Monika.*

Riggert (130) North German and Frisian: variant of RICKERT 2.
GIVEN NAME German 4%. *Gerhard.*

Riggi (314) Italian: patronymic or plural form of RIGGIO.

GIVEN NAMES Italian 22%. *Salvatore* (4), *Vito* (3), *Angelo* (2), *Cataldo* (2), *Santo* (2), *Alfonse, Anastasio, Antonio, Domenic, Guido, Guilio, Pietro.*

Riggin (690) Perhaps an altered spelling of REAGAN.

Riggins (3309) English, Scottish, and Irish: unexplained. Possibly a variant of HIGGINS through misdivision of a name such as *Peter Higgins.*

Riggio (658) Italian: variant of REGGIO.
GIVEN NAMES Italian 17%. *Salvatore* (9), *Angelo* (4), *Sal* (4), *Vito* (3), *Carlo* (2), *Carmela* (2), *Nino* (2), *Aldo, Amedeo, Antonino, Gasper, Giuseppe.*

Riggle (1528) Perhaps an altered spelling of German RIEGEL or a variant of RICKEL 3.

Riggleman (741) Americanized spelling of German **Riegelmann** (see RIEGEL), a topographic name for a farmer owning a long strip of land or for someone who lived near a watershed or a mountain blocking a valley.

Riggles (111) English: possibly a variant of **Riggall,** which occurs chiefly in Lincolnshire, but is unexplained.

Riggs (12341) Northern English: topographic name for someone who lived on or by a ridge, Old Norse *hryggr*. Compare RIDGE.

Riggsbee (238) Altered spelling of English RIGSBY.

Riggsby (102) Altered spelling of English RIGSBY.

Righetti (169) Italian: patronymic from a pet form of the personal name *Rigo* (see RIGHI).
GIVEN NAMES Italian 9%. *Fulvio, Luigi, Plinio, Reno, Rino, Vincenzo.*

Righi (169) Italian: patronymic from the personal name *Rigo*, a short form of *Arrigo*, Italian equivalent of HENRY.
GIVEN NAMES Italian 15%. *Angelo* (3), *Amelio, Antonio, Dino, Evo, Flavio, Giuseppe, Guerino, Guido, Marino, Pietro, Vincenzo.*

Righter (514) Americanized spelling of German REITER or RICHTER.

Rightmire (217) Americanized form of German **Reitmeyer** (see REITMEIER).

Rightmyer (186) Americanized form of German **Reitmeyer** (see REITMEIER).

Rigler (352) German: variant of RIEGLER.

Rigley (120) English: variant spelling of WRIGLEY.

Rigney (1673) English: unexplained. It has been suggested that it may be a French Huguenot name, possibly an altered form of **Ruvigny**.

Rigo (269) **1.** Hungarian (**Rigó**): nickname from *rigó* 'blackbird'. **2.** Catalan and Italian: from the personal name *Rigo*, a short form of *Arrigo*, an Italian equivalent of HENRY, or of *Federigo*, a variant of *Federico*, Italian equivalent of FREDERICK.

GIVEN NAMES Hungarian 6%; French 5%; German 4%; Spanish 4%. *Tibor* (2), *Csaba, Dezso, Gyula, Laszlo, Zoltan, Zsolt; Andre, Henri, Hermas, Pascal, Serge; Ralf* (2), *Mathias; Raul* (3), *Ana, Elvira, Jose, Luiz, Manuel, Orlando.*

Rigoli (123) Italian: patronymic from a pet form of the personal name RIGO.
GIVEN NAMES Italian 10%. *Giuseppi, Riccardo, Salvatore.*

Rigoni (202) Italian: patronymic from an augmentative of the personal name RIGO.
GIVEN NAMES Italian 15%. *Oreste* (2), *Orlando* (2), *Reno* (2), *Albino, Aldo, Alfredo, Antonio, Carlo, Dino, Roberto.*

Rigor (117) Spanish (Philippines): possibly a nickname from *rigor* 'severity'.
GIVEN NAMES Spanish 18%. *Gavino* (2), *Alejandro, Amado, Angel, Armida, Avelino, Carlos, Carmelita, Conrado, Engracia, Jose, Maria Paz.*

Rigsbee (445) Altered spelling of English RIGSBY.

Rigsby (2446) English: habitational name from a place so named in Lincolnshire.

Riha (560) Czech (**Říha**): nickname from *říha* 'to reproach'.

Rihn (212) North German: variant of RHINE.

Riis (151) **1.** Scandinavian: nickname from *ris* 'twigs', 'scrub', or a habitational name from any of several places so named in Denmark. **2.** Norwegian: habitational name from any of five farmsteads named *Ris*, from Old Norse *hrís* 'brushwood'.
GIVEN NAMES Scandinavian 15%. *Holger, Johan.*

Rikard (508) Variant of German REICHARDT.

Rike (344) **1.** Norwegian: habitational name from a farmstead in Agder, so named from Old Norse *ríki* 'power', 'rule', 'kingdom'. **2.** Perhaps an Americanized spelling of German REICH.

Riker (1265) German: variant of RIECK 2.

Rilea (107) Origin unidentified. **1.** It could be a respelling of Irish RILEY. **2.** Alternatively, it may be of French origin, perhaps a respelling of **Rillieux**, a habitational name from Rillieux-la-Pape in Rhône.

Riles (583) English: variant spelling of RYLES.

Riley (44266) **1.** Irish: variant spelling of REILLY. **2.** English: habitational name from Ryley in Lancashire, so named from Old English *ryge* 'rye' + *lēah* 'wood', 'clearing'. There is a Riley with the same meaning in Devon, but it does not seem to have contributed to the surname, which is more common in northern England.

Riling (142) **1.** Americanized spelling of German REILING **2.** variant of Swiss German **Rilich**, a nickname for a rich and generous person, from Middle High German *rîchelich*.

Rill (384) German: from a short form of a Germanic personal name based on *rîd* 'ride' or *rîch* 'powerful', 'rich'.

Rilling (282) German and Swiss German: patronymic from RILL.

Rim (255) **1.** Swiss German: perhaps an altered form of **Riem**, a topographic name for someone who lived on a long narrow strip of land. **2.** Korean: unexplained.
GIVEN NAMES Korean 54%. *Jong* (4), *Chang Kyu* (2), *Hwa Young* (2), *Jeung* (2), *Jung* (2), *Young* (2), *Chan, Chang Ki, Chang Soo, Chin, Choy, Chu; Chong* (4), *Choon* (3), *Min* (2), *Byung, Chang, Chong Ho, Chung, Eun Hee, Hae, Insoo, Jaesik, Jeong.*

Rima (204) German: unexplained.

Rimbey (188) Origin unidentified. Possibly an altered form of **Ramby**, an unexplained English family name.

Rimel (324) English: from the Old English female personal name *Rimhild* composed of elements meaning 'border' + 'war'.

Rimer (633) **1.** English (Lancashire): occupational name for a poet, minstrel, or balladeer, from an agent derivative of Middle English *rime(n)* 'to compose or recite verses' (Old French *rimer*). **2.** Jewish (Ashkenazic): variant of RIEMER.

Rimes (355) English: unexplained.

Rimkus (255) Lithuanian: **1.** nickname for a calm, peaceful person, from a derivative of *rimti* 'to become calm or quiet'. **2.** reduced form of the Lithuanian family name **Rimkantas**.
GIVEN NAME French 4%. *Alain.*

Rimmel (118) **1.** English: probably a variant spelling of RIMEL. **2.** German: variant of **Rimmele**, from *Rümelin*, a pet form of the Germanic personal name *Ruombald*, a compound of *hruom* 'glory' + *balt* 'bold', 'brave'.

Rimmer (1184) English: variant of RIMER.

Rinaldi (2858) Italian: patronymic or plural form of RINALDO.
GIVEN NAMES Italian 19%. *Angelo* (26), *Rocco* (18), *Salvatore* (18), *Antonio* (12), *Domenic* (9), *Donato* (6), *Sal* (6), *Nicola* (5), *Vito* (5), *Carlo* (4), *Carmine* (4), *Aldo* (3).

Rinaldo (544) Italian: from the personal name *Rinaldo*, composed of the Germanic elements *ragin* 'advice', 'counsel' + *wald* 'rule'.
GIVEN NAMES Italian 6%. *Sal* (2), *Vito* (2), *Angelo, Carmine, Pasquale, Piero, Rocco.*

Rinard (415) Perhaps an altered spelling of French RENARD or an Americanized spelling of German REINHARDT.

Rinas (137) Polish: unexplained.
GIVEN NAMES German 13%. *Helmut, Kurt, Oskar, Otto, Rudi.*

Rinaudo (153) Italian: variant of RINALDO.
GIVEN NAMES Italian 18%. *Cosmo* (2), *Rocco* (2), *Salvatore* (2), *Vito* (2), *Paolo, Sal.*

Rinck (357) German and Dutch: variant of RING 1 and 3.

Rincon (1360) Spanish (**Rincón**): habitational name from any of the numerous places named Rincón or El Rincón, from *rincón* 'corner' (Old Spanish *re(n)cón*, from Arabic *rukún*).
GIVEN NAMES Spanish 49%. *Jose* (38), *Juan* (21), *Carlos* (19), *Miguel* (13), *Antonio* (12), *Francisco* (11), *Manuel* (11), *Jesus* (10), *Luis* (10), *Pedro* (9), *Jorge* (8), *Raul* (8), *Roberto* (8).

Rind (138) **1.** Scottish: habitational name from a small place in the former county of Perthshire called Rhynd, from Gaelic *rinn* 'point of land'. **2.** German: probably a metonymic occupational name for a cattle dealer or butcher, from Middle High German *rint* 'cow'. **3.** Jewish (Ashkenazic): from German *Rind*, Yiddish *rind* 'head of cattle', an ornamental name or otherwise from a house sign.
GIVEN NAMES Jewish 6%. *Emanuel* (2), *Mendel, Sol, Yael.*

Rindahl (179) Norwegian: habitational name from any of seven farms so named, probably from a river name derived from *rind* 'ridge' or *renna* 'to run', 'to flow' + Old Norse *dalr* 'valley'.

Rindal (172) Norwegian: variant spelling of RINDAHL.
GIVEN NAME Scandinavian 10%. *Bjorn.*

Rinde (138) Norwegian: habitational name from any of eight farms named with *rind* 'bank', 'ridge', or from one in Sogn originally named with this word + *vin* 'meadow'.
GIVEN NAMES Scandinavian 7%. *Erik, Knute.*

Rindels (112) North German: possibly from Middle Low German *rindele* 'cinnamon bark', an occupational name for a spicer.
GIVEN NAMES German 4%. *Erwin, Reiner.*

Rinder (113) German: derivative of *Rind* 'cow' as an occupational name for a cattle farmer (see RINDERER).
GIVEN NAMES Slavic 4%; German 4%. *Arron, Lilija; Ernst.*

Rinderer (122) German: occupational name for a dairy or cattle farmer, from an agent derivative of *rinder*, the plural of Middle High German *rint* 'cow'.
GIVEN NAMES German 8%. *Franz* (2), *Egon, Wilhelm.*

Rinderknecht (197) German: occupational name for a cowhand, from Middle High German *rint* 'cow' + *kneht* 'lad', 'farmhand'.
GIVEN NAMES German 5%. *Erna, Ernst, Heinrich, Otto.*

Rinderle (114) German: nickname for a dairy or cattle farmer, from a diminutive of Middle High German *rint* 'cow'. Compare RINDLER.

Rindfleisch (300) German: metonymic occupational name for a butcher, from Middle High German *rintvleisch* 'beef'.
GIVEN NAMES German 7%. *Otto* (3), *Hans, Oskar.*

Rindler (173) South German: from Middle High German *rinne* 'stream', 'spring'; 'drainpipe', 'channel', a topographic name for someone who lived by such a feature, or perhaps an occupational name for someone who built drainage channels and the like.
GIVEN NAMES German 5%. *Erwin, Heinz, Wolfgang.*

Rindone (138) Italian: **1.** from a variant of *rondone* 'swift', presumably a nickname for someone thought to resemble the bird in some way. **2.** from an augmentative of the personal name *Rindo*, which may be a reduced form of a personal name such as *Florindo* or *Clorindo*.
GIVEN NAMES Italian 22%. *Liborio* (2), *Salvatore* (2), *Vincenzo* (2), *Attilio, Carmelo, Emilio, Girolamo, Guido, Leopoldo, Rosario, Vincenza.*

Rindt (239) German: variant of RIND.
GIVEN NAMES German 4%. *Hans* (2), *Alois, Klaus.*

Rindy (105) Americanized form of Norwegian RINDE.

Rine (826) Probably an altered spelling of German REIN, RHINE, or RHEIN.

Rineer (371) Possibly an altered spelling of German **Reinehr**, a variant of REINER.

Rinehardt (180) Americanized spelling of German REINHARDT.

Rinehart (5106) Americanized spelling of German REINHARDT.

Rinehimer (179) Americanized spelling of German REINHEIMER.

Rinella (340) Italian: **1.** habitational name from Rinella in Leni, Messina province, Sicily. **2.** from a derivative of *Rina*, a female personal name derived from any of numerous names ending with *-ro* or *-ra*, or with the double suffix *-ino* + *-ella*, in either case showing complete loss of the root.
GIVEN NAMES Italian 18%; Spanish 4%. *Salvatore* (4), *Sal* (3), *Mariano* (2), *Agostino, Angelo, Liborio, Sergio; Salvador* (2), *Juanita.*

Riner (1059) Americanized spelling of German REINER.

Rines (570) **1.** Greek (also **Rinis**): nickname from classical Greek *rhis* 'nose', genitive *rhinos*. **2.** Americanized spelling of German REINS.

Riney (714) Perhaps an Americanized spelling of German REINE.

Ring (5916) **1.** English, German, and Dutch: metonymic occupational name for a maker of rings (from Middle English *ring*, Middle High German *rinc*, Middle Dutch *ring*), either to be worn as jewelry or as component parts of chain-mail, harnesses, and other objects. In part it may also have arisen as a nickname for a wearer of a ring. **2.** Scandinavian: from *ring* 'ring', probably an ornamental name but possibly applied in the same sense as 3 or 1. **3.** German: topographic name from Middle High German, Middle Low German *rink, rinc* 'circle'. **4.** Irish (eastern County Cork): reduced

Anglicized form of Gaelic **Ó Rinn** (see REEN).

Ringdahl (160) **1.** Norwegian: habitational name from any of several farmsteads named *Ringdal*, most from Old Norse *Ringdalr*, a compound of *ringr* 'ring', 'circle', 'bend' (referring to a meandering river) + *dalr* 'valley'. **2.** Swedish: ornamental name of the same meaning as 1.
GIVEN NAMES Scandinavian 7%. *Bjorn, Eskil.*

Ringe (149) German: **1.** from a Germanic personal name based on *hring* 'ring'. **2.** nickname from Middle High German *ringe* 'small', 'light', 'agile'.

Ringeisen (197) German: from a compound of Low German *ringen* 'to circle' + *Eisen* 'iron', probably a journeyman's nickname for a smith who made ring bolts, or perhaps an unflattering occupational name for a forger, from Middle High German *ringe* 'small', 'little' (in quality) + *īsan* 'iron'.

Ringel (593) German: **1.** from Middle High German *ringel*, diminutive of *rinc, ring* 'ring', hence a metonymic occupational name for a maker of bone, horn, or ivory rings (see RING). **2.** topographic name for someone who lived in or by a circular plot or settlement, from the same word. **3.** metonymic occupational name for a cooper, from Middle Low German *ringel* 'tub'.

Ringen (147) **1.** Dutch: patronymic from a short form of the Germanic personal names *Reingard* or *Reingoud*, based on *ragin* 'advice', 'counsel'. **2.** Norwegian: habitational name from Ringen, a common farm name in southeastern Norway, from Old Norse *ringr* 'ring', 'circle' describing a feature of the landscape, such as a lake.
GIVEN NAMES Scandinavian 8%. *Knut, Nels.*

Ringenberg (253) German: **1.** variant of RINGGENBERG. **2.** habitational name from any of various places in Germany so named.

Ringer (1907) **1.** English (of Norman origin): from the Old French personal name *Reinger, Rainger*, composed of the Germanic elements *ragin* 'advice', 'counsel' + *gār, gēr* 'spear', 'lance'. **2.** English: occupational name for a maker of rings (see RING 1) or for a bell ringer, from Middle English *ring(en)* 'to ring', Old English *hringan*. **3.** German: occupational name for a turner, someone who made objects by rotating them on a lathe or wheel.

Ringgenberg (218) German: habitational name from various places so named in Switzerland.

Ringger (120) German: variant of RINKER 2.

Ringgold (400) From German RINGOLD, altered by folk etymology.

Ringham (147) English: apparently a habitational name, from an unidentified place.

Ringhofer (119) German: ostensibly a habitational name but possibly an altered form of the Germanic personal name *Ringulf*,

composed of *ring* 'ring' (see RING) + *(w)ulf* 'wolf'.

Ringland (184) English: habitational name from a place so named in Norfolk. The place name is recorded in Domesday Book as *Remingaland*, probably 'cultivated land (Old English *land*) of the followers (*-inga-*) of Rȳmi'.

Ringle (538) **1.** English: from the Old English personal name *Hringwulf*. **2.** German: from a short form of a Germanic personal name based on *hring* 'ring'. **3.** German: metonymic occupational name for a ring maker (see RINGLER). **4.** German: altered spelling of **Ringel**, an Old Prussian personal name.

Ringler (1097) German: occupational name for a maker of bone, horn, or ivory rings, from an agent derivative of Middle High German *ringelen* 'to provide with rings'.

Ringley (248) Probably an altered spelling of RINGLE, or possibly RINGLER or **Ringele, Ringgeli**, or **Ringli**, which are Swiss variants of RINGLE.

Ringling (131) German: diminutive of the metonymic occupational name RING.

Ringo (706) Altered spelling of **Ringolt** (see RINGOLD).

Ringold (195) German: variant spelling of **Ringolt**, a Germanic personal name composed of the elements *hring* 'ring' or 'assembly' + *wald* 'rule'.

Ringquist (178) Swedish: ornamental compound of *ring* 'ring' + *quist*, an old or ornamental spelling of *kvist* 'twig'.

Ringrose (157) English: of uncertain origin. It is first attested in Norwich in 1259 as *Ringerose*, and later forms show no significant variation. Unless it had already been drastically altered by folk etymology at that early date, it is probably from Middle English *ring* 'ring' + *rose* 'rose', but if so the original meaning is far from clear.

Rings (168) **1.** English and German: variant of RING 1. **2.** Perhaps a Rhenish short form of the Latin personal name *Quirinus*.

Ringstad (207) Norwegian: habitational name from any of about twenty farmsteads named in Old Norse as *Ringsstaðir*, from the personal name *Ringr*, meaning 'ring', + *staðir* 'farmstead', 'dwelling'.
GIVEN NAME Scandinavian 4%. *Erik* (2).

Ringstaff (111) Origin unidentified. This has the form of an English surname but it does not appear in modern records.

Ringuette (207) Altered spelling of French **Ringuet**, from a pet form of the Germanic personal name *(H)ringhard*, composed of the elements *(h)rinc* 'ring' + *hard* 'hardy', 'strong'.
GIVEN NAMES French 14%. *Adrien* (2), *Armand, Arsene, Edmour, Emile, Jacques, Marcel, Rosaire.*

Ringwald (301) German: **1.** from the personal name *Ringolt, Ringwalt*. **2.** habitational name from Ringwalde in Silesia.

GIVEN NAMES German 5%. *Hans, Sigfried, Wessel, Wilhelm.*

Ringwelski (124) Polish: derivative of the Germanic personal name *Ringwelt* (see RINGWALD), + the Polish surname suffix *-ski*.

Ringwood (218) English: habitational name from a place so named in Hampshire. The place name, recorded in 955 as *Rimucwuda*, is probably from Old English *rimuc* 'boundary' + *wudu* 'wood'.

Rini (532) Italian: patronymic from the personal name *Rino*, probably a reduced form of any of numerous names ending with *-ro* or *-ra*, of which the root has been completely lost.

GIVEN NAMES Italian 7%. *Angelo* (3), *Domenica, Salvatore, Saverio, Sebastino.*

Rinier (103) Origin unidentified. Possibly a respelling of French **Renier**, from the Germanic personal name *Raginhari*, composed of *ragin* 'advice', 'counsel' + *hari* 'army'.

Riniker (162) Swiss German: variant of **Reinicker**, itself a variant of REINECKE.

Rininger (244) Americanized spelling of German REININGER.

Rink (1203) **1.** German and Dutch: variant of RING 1. **2.** German: metonymic occupational name for a buckle maker, from Middle High German *rinke* 'buckle', 'clasp'.

Rinke (431) German and Dutch: variant of RING 1.

GIVEN NAMES German 5%. *Kurt* (2), *Alois, Gerhard, Hartwig, Horst, Wolf.*

Rinkel (128) German: **1.** metonymic occupational name for a buckle maker, from a diminutive of Middle High German *rinke* 'buckle', 'clasp'. **2.** variant of RINGEL.

Rinkenberger (168) German: habitational name for someone from Rinkenberg in Carinthia, Austria, Ringenberg in Germany, or any of various places in Switzerland called Ringgenberg.

Rinker (1883) German: **1.** occupational name for a buckle maker, from an agent derivative of Middle High German *rinke* 'buckle'. **2.** from an old personal name based on *hring* 'ring'.

Rinks (192) German (Rhineland) and Dutch: variant of RINK.

Rinkus (100) German (Rhineland) and Dutch: variant of RINK.

Rinn (408) **1.** Irish (Leitrim): reduced Anglicized form of Gaelic **Mac Bhroin** 'son of *Bran*', a personal name from *bran* 'raven'. **2.** Altered spelling of German RINNE.

Rinne (421) **1.** Finnish: topographic name or ornamental name from *rinne* 'slope', or habitational name from a farm named with this word. Found chiefly in southwestern Finland. Mostly, this is an ornamental name adopted during the name conversion movement at the end of the 19th and the beginning of the 20th centuries. **2.** German: topographic name from Middle High

German *rinne* 'stream', 'spring'; 'channel', 'pipe'.

GIVEN NAMES Finnish 6%. *Eino* (3), *Oiva* (2), *Paavo, Pentti, Risto, Seppo, Wiljo.*

Rinner (133) German: **1.** variant of RENNER. **2.** topographic or occupational name from Middle High German *rinne* 'water pipe', 'water channel', for someone who lived near or built such things.

Rintala (142) Finnish: topographic name from *rinta* 'slope of a hill' + the local suffix *-la.* It originated in southern Karelia, where it dates back to the 16th century; it was also widely adopted as an ornamental name during the name conversion movement in the 19th and early 20th centuries.

GIVEN NAMES Finnish 11%. *Eino* (2), *Kaarlo* (2), *Reino, Toivo.*

Rintoul (127) Scottish: habitational name from a farm near Milnathort in Kinross-shire. The etymology of the place name is obscure.

Rio (478) **1.** Spanish (**Río**), Portuguese, and Italian: from *río* 'river', 'brook' (from Latin *rivus*), applied either as a topographic name or as a habitational name from a place named with this word. **2.** Southern French (Occitan): variant of RIOUX.

GIVEN NAMES Spanish 14%; Portuguese 4%. *Blanco* (4), *Jose* (4), *Carlos* (2), *Domingo* (2), *Manuel* (2), *Orlando* (2), *Rafael* (2), *Raul* (2), *Alberto, Alejandro, Ana, Argelio; Vito* (2), *Carmela, Concetta, Dino, Fiore, Mauro, Silvio; Joao, Joaquim.*

Riojas (764) Spanish: either a variant of a regional name from the province or region of La Rioja, or a habitational name from Rioja in Almeria province. The region is named for the Oja river, which flows through it; the Spanish word *río* 'river' has become fused with the river name, which is first recorded in the form *Ol(i)a*; it may possibly be derived from Latin *folia* 'leaves'.

GIVEN NAMES Spanish 43%. *Juan* (15), *Jose* (14), *Manuel* (12), *Carlos* (7), *Ruben* (7), *Jesus* (5), *Lupe* (5), *Roberto* (5), *Alfredo* (4), *Cesar* (4), *Javier* (4), *Luis* (4).

Riolo (245) Italian: **1.** possibly from a diminutive of *rio* 'river'. **2.** habitational name from a reduced form of Oriolo, the name of a place in Cosenza province.

GIVEN NAMES Italian 9%; French 4%. *Angelo, Caesar, Gaetano, Pasquale; Marcelle, Monique.*

Rion (252) French: habitational name from Rion-de-Landes in the canton of Tartas or from Rions in Gironde.

Riopel (168) French: variant of RIOPELLE.

GIVEN NAMES French 15%. *Andre, Armand, Jean-Guy, Lucien, Odile, Pierre, Yves.*

Riopelle (282) French: of uncertain origin; possibly linked to Occitan *riu* 'stream'.
FOREBEARS A bearer of the name (documented as Riopel and Riopelle) from the Saintonge region of France was in Ange-Gardien, Quebec, in 1687.

GIVEN NAMES French 4%. *Armand* (2), *Chanel.*

Riordan (3208) Irish: reduced form of O'RIORDAN, an Anglicized form of Gaelic **Ó Ríoghbhárdáin** 'descendant of *Ríogh-bhárdán*', a byname composed of the elements *ríogh-* 'royal' + a diminutive of *bárd* 'bard', 'poet'.

GIVEN NAMES Irish 6%. *Brendan* (3), *Liam* (3), *Aidan, John Patrick, Siobhan.*

Rios (11197) **1.** Galician and Spanish (**Ríos**): habitational name from any of the places called Ríos, predominantly in Galicia. **2.** Spanish (**Ríós**): habitational name from Ríós in Ourense, Galicia.

GIVEN NAMES Spanish 49%. *Jose* (332), *Juan* (153), *Jesus* (121), *Manuel* (106), *Carlos* (100), *Luis* (92), *Pedro* (65), *Francisco* (62), *Jorge* (62), *Roberto* (60), *Miguel* (58), *Raul* (58).

Riotto (107) Italian: **1.** habitational name from Riotto in Veneto. **2.** perhaps a nickname from Sicilian *riottu*, a diminutive of *re* 'king'.

GIVEN NAMES Italian 9%. *Rocco* (2), *Damiano.*

Rioux (998) **1.** French: habitational name from Rioux in Charente-Maritime or Rioux-Martin in Charente, or any of various minor places named with this word. **2.** Southern French: topographic name for someone who lived by a stream, from Old Provençal *rieu* (Latin *rivus*).
FOREBEARS A Rioux from Brittany is documented in Ste. Famille, Quebec, in 1673.

GIVEN NAMES French 14%. *Armand* (3), *Lucien* (3), *Pierre* (3), *Donat* (2), *Fernand* (2), *Jacques* (2), *Adrien, Alphonse, Andre, Antoine, Benoit, Berchman.*

Ripa (253) Italian: topographic name from *ripa* 'seashore', 'coast', a variant of RIVA.

GIVEN NAMES Italian 9%; Russian 4%. *Angelo* (2), *Santo* (2), *Carmelo, Carmine, Donato, Ennio, Giuseppe, Salvatore, Vito; Anatoly, Boris, Maksim, Oleg, Raisa, Vladimir.*

Ripberger (176) German: variant of RIPPERGER.

Ripka (330) Partly Germanized spelling of Czech and Slovak RYBKA 'fish' (see RYBA).

Ripke (152) German: **1.** Germanized form of Slavic RIPKA 'fish' (see Czech RYBA). **2.** from a pet form of the personal name RIEPE, *Ribbe* or *Rippert*, a compound of *ríc* 'power(ful)' + *berht* 'bright', 'famous'.

Ripley (3657) English: habitational name from any of various places in different parts of England, named in Old English with *ripel* 'strip of land' + *lēah* 'wood', 'clearing'.
FOREBEARS William Ripley (d. 1656) came from Wymondham, Norfolk, England, to Hingham, MA, in 1638.

Ripoll (127) Catalan: habitational name from a place in northern Catalonia, the site of a famous medieval monastery, originally named with the Latin elements *rivus* 'stream' + *pullus* 'dark gray'.

GIVEN NAMES Spanish 26%. *Julio* (3), *Luz* (3), *Emilia* (2), *Ignacio* (2), *Jose* (2), *Juan* (2), *Manuel* (2), *Agustin*, *Angel*, *Francisco*, *Javier*, *Jorge*.

Ripp (767) **1.** German and Dutch: from a short form of the personal name *Rippert*, composed of the elements *rīc* 'power' + *berht* 'bright', 'famous'. **2.** English: topographic name for someone who lived by a strip of woodland, an unattested Old English word *rip*, or a habitational name from Ripe in East Sussex, named with this word.

Rippe (472) North German and English: variant of RIPP.

Rippee (347) Probably an altered spelling of German RIPPE, written thus to preserve the second syllable.

Rippel (373) South German: **1.** variant of **Rüppel** (see RUPPEL), or a variant of **Rüpel** (see RUPEL). **2.** from a pet form of a Germanic personal name based on *rīc* 'power(ful)', 'rich'.

GIVEN NAMES German 5%. *Dieter*, *Frieda*, *Hans*, *Helmut*, *Hilde*, *Lorenz*.

Rippentrop (128) German: respelling of **Ribbentrop**, a habitational name from a place called Ribbentrup.

Rippeon (192) Origin uncertain; perhaps an altered form of English RIPPON.

Ripper (368) **1.** English: occupational name for someone who made or sold baskets, or else carried wares about in a basket, from an agent derivative of Middle English *(h)rip* 'basket' (Old Norse *hrip*). **2.** German: variant of RIPP.

Ripperger (352) German: habitational name for someone from Ripperg near Walldürn, Odenwald, earlier recorded as *Rietberg*, and *Ryperg*.

Rippetoe (373) English: unexplained. This is a predominantly southern name, found in TX, OK, and TN. It has died out in England. FOREBEARS John Rippetoe was in VA by 1711.

Rippey (455) This surname is found in small numbers in England, Ireland, and Scotland, but its exact origin and etymology have not been determined.

Ripple (995) Variant form or an altered spelling of RIPPEL or **Rüppel** (see RUPPEL).

Ripplinger (351) German: **1.** habitational name for someone from Ripp(o)lingen in the Rhineland. **2.** derivative of **Riepling**, a patronymic from pet form of the Germanic personal name *Riepl*, formed with *rīc* 'power(ful)' + *-ing*.

Rippon (182) English: habitational name from Ripon in North Yorkshire, so named from Old English *Hrypum*, dative plural (originally used after a preposition) of a tribal name of obscure etymology.

Ripps (144) **1.** German: variant of RIPP. **2.** Jewish (Ashkenazic): metonymic occu-

pational name from German *Rips* or Polish *ryps* 'ribbed silk'.

GIVEN NAMES Jewish 4%; German 4%. *Sol*; *Erwin*, *Hermann*.

Rippy (1010) Apparently a variant spelling of RIPPEY, or an altered spelling of German RIPPE.

Riquelme (131) Spanish: from a Germanic personal name composed of the elements *rīc* 'power(ful)' + *helm* 'helmet', 'protection'.

GIVEN NAMES Spanish 54%. *Juan* (3), *Luis* (3), *Adela* (2), *Jaime* (2), *Jorge* (2), *Jose* (2), *Marcial* (2), *Rafael* (2), *Adolfo*, *Alberto*, *Ana*, *Carlos*; *Antonio*, *Cecilio*, *Donato*, *Flavio*.

Ririe (139) Scottish: shortened form of **Macryrie** (unexplained), the name of a sept of McDONALD.

Ris (103) **1.** Swiss German: Alemannic variant of RIES 3 or REIS 1. **2.** Dutch: from a short form of a Germanic personal name formed with *Ris-*, variant of RIESA, or a patronymic from a short form of *Henri*, French equivalent of HENRY.

GIVEN NAME Dutch 4%. *Martinus*.

Risberg (240) **1.** Perhaps an altered spelling of German **Rissberg**, a habitational name from a place so named near Helmstedt, Lower Saxony, or from Risiberg in Württemberg. **2.** Scandinavian: habitational name from a farmstead or any of several other places named with *ris* 'brushwood' + *berg* 'hill', 'mountain'.

GIVEN NAMES Scandinavian 6%. *Sven* (2), *Hjalmer*, *Johan*, *Oivind*.

Risby (107) English: habitational name from any of various places, for example in Lincolnshire, Suffolk, and East Yorkshire, so named from Old Norse *hrís* 'brushwood' + *býr* 'farm', 'settlement'.

Risch (907) Swiss German and German: **1.** nickname from Middle High German *risch* 'fast', 'nimble', 'cheeky'. **2.** topographic name from a regional word meaning 'slope', 'incline'. **3.** from Middle Low German *rische* 'reed', a topographic name for someone who lived where reeds grew.

GIVEN NAMES German 4%. *Klaus* (2), *Kurt* (2), *Dieter*, *Hans*, *Rudi*, *Siegfried*, *Volkmar*, *Willi*.

Rische (119) German: variant of RISCH.

GIVEN NAME German 9%. *Gerhardt* (3).

Risden (135) English: variant spelling of RISDON.

Risdon (273) English (Devon): habitational name, primarily from Risdon in Devon; to a lesser extent possibly from Risden or Riseden, both in Kent.

Rise (246) **1.** English: topographic name from Old English *hrīs* 'brushwood', or a habitational name from Rise in East Yorkshire, named with this word. **2.** Norwegian: habitational name from any of over twenty farmsteads named Rise, from Old Norse *hrís* 'brushwood'. The name also occurs in Sweden and Denmark.

GIVEN NAMES Scandinavian 6%. *Aase*, *Lief*, *Sven*.

Risen (240) Of Swiss and German origin: possibly a respelling of RIESEN.

Risenhoover (245) Americanized spelling of **Riesenhuber**, a distinguishing nickname for a farmer (HUBER) who lived by a forest chute or track along which felled trees were transported, *Riese* (from Middle High German *rise* 'channel').

Riser (826) **1.** Swiss German: topographic name for someone who lived near a thicket or underbrush, from an agent noun based on Middle High German *rīs* 'branch', 'shrubbery'. **2.** Possibly an Americanized spelling of German REISER.

Rish (564) Americanized spelling of German RISCH or of South German (Swiss) **Rüsch**, a topographic name from Middle High German *rusch* 'reeds', or from a pet form of RUDOLF.

Rishel (676) Americanized spelling of German **Rischel**, from a pet form of a personal name beginning with the Old High German element *hrōd* 'renown' or *rihhi* 'power'.

Rishell (149) **1.** Perhaps an altered spelling of the English habitational name Rushall, from either of two places so named, in Norfolk and Wiltshire. In both cases the second element is *halh* 'nook of land'; the first element of the place in Norfolk, recorded in Domesday Book as *Riuessala*, is uncertain; that of the Wiltshire place is believed to be an Old English personal name, *Rust*. **2.** Altered spelling of German *Rischel* (see RISHEL).

Risher (863) **1.** English: variant of RUSHER. **2.** Americanized spelling of German **Rischer**, a nickname for a hasty or impetuous person, from an agent derivative of Middle High German *rischen* 'to rush'. **3.** Americanized spelling of Swiss German **Rüscher**, a topographic name for someone who lived on a mountainside, from southern dialect *risch* 'slope', 'mountainside' + *-er*, suffix denoting an inhabitant. **4.** Americanized spelling of North German **Rischer**, a topographic name from Middle Low German *risch* 'reed', a topographic name for someone who lived where reeds grew. **5.** Anglicized form of Eastern German **Rischar**, a nickname from Sorbian *rýsar* 'knight'.

Risi (234) **1.** Italian: patronymic or plural form of RISO. **2.** Some bearers of the name in the U.S. were originally from St. Gallen, a canton in the German-speaking part of Switzerland; in some cases, therefore, the surname may be an altered spelling of Swiss German **Rissi**, which is probably a variant of RISS or RISSE.

GIVEN NAMES Italian 12%. *Aldo* (2), *Guido* (2), *Nunzio* (2), *Angelo*, *Donato*, *Enrico*, *Silvio*.

Rising (811) **1.** Swiss and South German: variant of RISINGER. **2.** perhaps an Americanized spelling of German REISING, or from an unexplained stem *riese*.

FOREBEARS The last governor of New Sweden Colony (1638–55), on the Delaware River, was a man by the name of Johan Rising.

Risinger (1127) **1.** Swiss and South German: (Alemannic) variant of REISINGER 3. **2.** perhaps an Americanized spelling of German REISINGER.

Risk (664) Scottish: perhaps, as Black suggests, from Gaelic *riasg* 'morass with sedge', applied generally as a topographic name or specifically to someone who lived by the Risk of Drymen.

Riska (121) Czech (**Riška**): variant of **Ryška**, nickname for someone with red hair, a derivative of Old Czech *ryzí* 'red'.

Riske (315) German: variant of **Rieske**, of uncertain, probably Slavic origin.
GIVEN NAMES German 5%. *Ernst, Hedwig, Reinhold.*

Riskin (178) Jewish (eastern Ashkenazic): from the female personal name *Riske*, a Yiddish pet form derived from the full form *Rivke* (see REBECCA).
GIVEN NAME Jewish 5%. *Emanuel.*

Risko (322) Hungarian: unexplained.

Risler (166) **1.** South German and Swiss German: topographic name, a variant of RIS 1. **2.** German: probably a spelling variant of **Riessler**, a habitational name from a place called Riesel near Höxter. **3.** Americanized spelling of Swiss German REISLER or German RISSLER.

Risley (1601) English: habitational name from Risley in Derbyshire and Lancashire or Riseley in Bedfordshire and Berkshire, all so named from Old English *hrīs* 'brushwood' + *lēah* 'clearing'.

Rismiller (116) variant spelling of RISSMILLER.

Risner (1689) Variant of the German habitational name REISNER, or of German **Riesner**, an occupational name for a maker of veils and hoods, from an agent derivative of Middle High German, Middle Low German *rīse* 'veil'.

Riso (241) **1.** Italian: possibly a nickname from *riso* 'laugh', 'burst of laughter', but more likely from a Germanic personal name *Riso, Risi*, from an unattested root, *Risi.* **2.** Spanish and Portuguese: nickname from *riso* 'laughter'. Compare 1 above.
GIVEN NAMES Italian 13%; Spanish 4%. *Agatino, Antonio, Concetta, Neno, Pasquale, Pietro, Rocco, Sal, Salvatore; Juan, Manuel, Pedro, Rosario, Salvador.*

Rison (247) French: nickname for a jovial man, from a derivative of *ris* 'laugh' (Latin *risus*).

Rispoli (448) Italian: **1.** patronymic from a derivative of the personal name *Rispo*, which is probably of Germanic origin. **2.** alternatively, it could be a variant of **Ruspoli**, which is of unknown origin.

GIVEN NAMES Italian 20%. *Angelo* (5), *Alfonse* (2), *Mario* (2), *Pasquale* (2), *Alfonso, Aniello, Antonio, Carmella, Carmine, Ciro, Filomena, Sal, Salvatore, Tulio.*

Riss (227) German: **1.** topographic name from Middle High German *rise* 'channel', 'crevice', or a topographic name for someone living by a tributary of the Danube so named. **2.** from a short form of a Germanic personal name based on *rīc* 'power(ful)', 'rich'. **3.** altered spelling of RIESS.

Risse (352) German: **1.** variant of RISS. **2.** perhaps a habitational name for someone from Rissen, west of Hamburg. Bahlow identifies *riss* as a word meaning 'swamp', 'marsh'.

Risser (824) **1.** South German: variant of RISS 1,2. **2.** Americanized form of Swiss German **Rüsser** (see REUSSER).

Rissler (288) German and Swiss German: from a personal name based on *rīh* 'powerful', 'rich'.

Rissman (244) German (**Rissmann**): **1.** (in the north): topographic name from Middle Low German *risch* 'reed', or a habitational name for someone from a place called Risse (from *riss* 'swamp'), near Hamburg. **2.** (in the south): variant of RISS 2.
GIVEN NAMES German 5%. *Heinz, Jurgen, Klaus, Otto.*

Rissmiller (199) Americanized form of North German **Rissmüller** or South German **Reismüller**, a habitational name for someone from a place called **Reismühle**, literally 'mill in the bushes'.

Risso (204) Italian (Liguria): variant of RIZZO, itself a variant of RICCIO.
GIVEN NAMES Spanish 10%; Italian 7%. *Raul* (3), *Mario* (2), *Alfredo, Camila, Gustavo, Humberto, Lino, Rafael, Roberto; Aldo* (3), *Guglielmo* (2), *Guido* (2).

Rist (779) German: **1.** metonymic occupational name for a farmer, from *rist, riester* 'plow handle'. **2.** variant of RUEST.

Ristaino (110) Italian: variant of RESTAINO.
GIVEN NAMES Italian 17%. *Carmine* (2), *Amadeo, Carlo, Concetta, Francesco.*

Ristau (619) German: habitational name from any of several places in Pomerania called Ristau or Ristow.
GIVEN NAMES German 4%. *Erwin* (2), *Otto* (2), *Gerhart, Klaus.*

Rister (500) German (Silesia): unrounded form of **Rüster**, possibly from an Old High German personal name *Rusto* meaning 'strong', 'fat', or a variant of RIESTER.

Ristine (127) Americanized form of German **Ristein**, probably from Middle Low German *rīs* 'ream' (of paper or slate) + *stein* 'stone', a topographic name for someone who lived near an outcrop of slate.

Ristow (566) German: variant spelling of RISTAU.
GIVEN NAMES German 5%. *Kurt* (2), *Ernst, Frieda, Hans, Otto.*

Rita (296) Italian, Portuguese, Spanish, and Catalan: from the female personal name *Rita*, a reduced form of *Margharita* 'Margaret', chosen in particular in honor of a 15th-century Italian saint who bore the name in this form.
GIVEN NAMES Italian 11%; Spanish 10%. *Antonio* (4), *Angelo* (3), *Alfredo, Carmine, Donato, Italo, Pino, Vito; Carlos* (4), *Jose* (2), *Primitivo* (2), *Jaime, Josefina, Manuel, Norberto.*

Ritacco (302) Italian: probably a derivative of *Rito*, a masculinized form of the female personal name RITA.
GIVEN NAMES Italian 16%. *Angelo* (4), *Antonio* (2), *Natale* (2), *Salvatore* (2), *Giuseppe, Nicola, Nunziato, Pasquale, Santo, Vincenzo.*

Ritch (920) **1.** English: variant spelling of RICH. **2.** Altered spelling of German **Ritsch**, probably from a short form of a Germanic personal name based on *rīc* 'power(ful)' or *hrōd* 'renown'; or an altered spelling of Swiss German **Rütsch, Ruetsch**, from Alemannic short forms of RUDOLF.

Ritchey (3367) **1.** Scottish, northern Irish, or English: variant spelling of RITCHIE 1. **2.** Perhaps also an altered spelling of Swiss German **Rütsche, Rütschi, Ruetschi**, from pet forms of the personal name RUDOLF. .

Ritchhart (115) Altered spelling of **Ritschart**, a Swiss and South German variant of RICHARD.

Ritchie (10879) Scottish: from a pet form of the personal name *Rich*, a short form of RICHARD.

Ritchison (108) Scottish: patronymic from the personal name *Rich*, a short form of RICHARD.

Ritenour (932) See RIDENOUR.

Riter (428) Probably an altered spelling of German REITER or RITTER.

Ritger (133) Altered spelling of German and Dutch **Rutger** or **Rütger**, from the personal name *Rudiger* (see ROGER).

Ritland (139) Norwegian: habitational name from any of three farmsteads in Rogaland and Agder, named in Old Norse as *Rísland*, from *hrís* 'brushwood' + *land* 'land', 'farmstead'.

Ritner (151) Altered spelling of German RITTNER.

Ritschel (100) German: from a pet form of a personal name formed with Old High German *hruod* 'fame'.
GIVEN NAME German 4%. *Florian.*

Ritsema (274) Frisian: probably a variant of **Riddersma**.
GIVEN NAMES German 4%. *Gerhard* (2), *Kurt.*

Ritson (169) English (Northumberland and Yorkshire): patronymic from a short form of the personal name RICHARD.

Ritt (340) German: **1.** topographic name from Old High German *ritta* 'reeds' or a

habitational name from a place so named near Kassel. **2.** variant of RIED 2. **3.** from a short form of a Germanic personal name based on *rīd* 'ride'.
GIVEN NAMES German 4%. *Franz, Otto.*

Rittel (141) German: probably from Middle High German *riutili*, a diminutive of *riute* '(forest) clearing', hence a topographic name.

Rittenberg (210) Jewish (Ashkenazic): unexplained.

Rittenberry (324) Apparently a respelling of RITTENBERG.

Rittenhouse (2160) Americanized spelling of German **Rittinghaus**, a habitational name from a farm near Altena, Westphalia. FOREBEARS William Rittenhouse (1644–1708) was the first Mennonite preacher in North America. He was born in Rhenish, Prussia and worked as a papermaker in Amsterdam, emigrating to PA in 1688 and establishing the first paper mill in America. His great-grandson David Rittenhouse (1732–96) of Philadelphia was an astronomer and the first director of the U.S. Mint.

Rittenour (154) See RIDENOUR.

Ritter (13244) German: from Middle High German *rit(t)er* 'knight', 'mounted warrior', Middle Low German *ridder*, applied as a status name, occupational name, or nickname. Compare KNIGHT.

Ritterbusch (113) German: **1.** Rhenish-Westphalian topographic name from *Retten, Redden* 'swamp' + *Busch* 'woods' (regional). **2.** nickname for a highwayman, a compound of RITTER 'knight', 'mounted soldier' + BUSCH 'bush'.

Ritterbush (124) Americanized spelling of German RITTERBUSCH.

Rittgers (214) Perhaps an altered spelling of German **Röttgers** or **Rüttgers**, patronymics from a Low German form of the personal name *Rüdiger* (see RUDIGER).

Ritthaler (138) German: probably a topographic name from Middle High German *riet, (ritt)* 'reed', 'marsh' + *tal* 'valley', + the *-er* suffix denoting an inhabitant.
GIVEN NAMES German 4%. *Kurt, Rainer.*

Rittinger (119) South German: topographic name from the Bavarian word *Ritten* 'steep mountain slope' (see RITTNER 1).
GIVEN NAMES German 4%. *Bernd, Erwin.*

Rittle (151) Americanized spelling of German RITTEL.

Rittman (208) German (**Rittmann**): **1.** topographic name for someone who lived among reeds, from Middle High German *riet (ritt)* 'reed' + *man* 'man'. **2.** topographic name for someone who lived in a woodland clearing, Middle High German *riute*. **3.** from a Germanic personal name based on *rīd* 'ride'.
GIVEN NAMES German 4%. *Dieter, Otto.*

Rittner (153) **1.** German: habitational name for someone from Ritte near Kassel. **2.** South German (Bavarian): topographic

name for someone who lived by a steep incline, dialect *Ritten*. **3.** Probably also an altered spelling of Swiss German **Rütt(e)ner**, a variant of RITTMAN 3.
GIVEN NAMES German 8%. *Erwin (2), Heinz, Kurt.*

Ritts (256) Perhaps an altered spelling of RITZ.

Ritz (2445) **1.** German: from a short form of the personal name *Rizo*, itself derived in part from RICHARD and in part from *Heinrich* (see HENRY). **2.** probably an altered spelling of South German **Rütz** (see RUETZ).

Ritzel (191) German: from a pet form of any of the Germanic personal names formed with *rīc* 'power(ful)' (see for example RICHARD, HEINRICH, MORITZ).

Ritzenthaler (169) German and French (Alsace): habitational name for someone from a place in Alsace named Ritzenthal.

Ritzer (217) German: **1.** variant of **Ritscher** (see RICHER). **2.** habitational name for someone from Ritze near Salzwedel or in Lower Saxony.
GIVEN NAMES German 4%. *Ewald, Otto.*

Ritzert (152) German: variant of RICHERT.

Ritzinger (105) German: habitational name for someone from either of two places named Ritzing, in Bavaria, Germany and in Burgenland, Austria.
GIVEN NAMES German 9%. *Heimo, Kurt, Volker.*

Ritzler (105) German: **1.** from a short form of a Germanic personal name formed with *rīc* 'power(ful)'. **2.** variant spelling of **Riezler**, a Bavarian habitational name from Riezlern (formerly Riezler) in Austria.

Ritzman (353) German and Swiss German (**Ritzmann**): variant of RITZ, with the addition of *man* 'man' (see RICHARD).

Riva (449) **1.** Italian: topographic name for someone who lived by a wharf in a port or on the bank of a river, *riva* (Latin *ripa*). **2.** Catalan and Spanish: variant of RIBA, which has the same origin and meaning as 1.
GIVEN NAMES Spanish 10%; Italian 5%; French 4%. *Carlos (3), Digna (2), Mario (2), Ramon (2), Sergio (2), Alvaro, Angel, Armando, Benito, Cristina, Fernando, Guillermo; Angelo (2), Flavio (2), Agostino, Antonio, Italo, Sal, Santo, Sebastiano; Gaston, Jean-Paul.*

Rivadeneira (110) Galician: habitational name from Riva de Neira, in Lugo province.
GIVEN NAMES Spanish 51%. *Carlos (4), Manuel (3), Angel (2), Casimira (2), Cesar (2), Eduardo (2), Guillermo (2), Ignacio (2), Jorge (2), Juan (2), Pedro (2), Roberto (2); Flavio (2), Antonio, Fausto.*

Rivard (2231) French: topographic name for someone who lived on a riverbank, from a derivative of *rive* '(river) bank'.
FOREBEARS A Rivard from the Perche region of France is documented in Trois-Rivières, Quebec, in 1653, with the secondary

surname LAVIGNE. Other secondary surnames include Feuilleverte, LACOURSIERE, La Glanderie, LANOUETTE, LORANGER, Montendre, Préville.
GIVEN NAMES French 9%. *Armand (8), Normand (7), Andre (5), Marcel (5), Gilles (3), Fernand (2), Herve (2), Jacques (2), Adelard, Adrien, Alain, Alphee.*

Rivas (6205) **1.** Spanish: habitational name from any of the places named Rivas or Ribas, a variant of RIBAS. **2.** in some cases, variant of Catalan **Ribes** (see RIBAS).
GIVEN NAMES Spanish 49%. *Jose (199), Juan (81), Luis (79), Manuel (69), Carlos (58), Jesus (47), Francisco (45), Miguel (45), Rafael (38), Jorge (37), Ruben (37), Julio (30).*

Rivelli (131) Italian: habitational name for someone from Rivello in Potenza.
GIVEN NAMES Italian 10%; Irish 7%. *Salvatore (2), Carmine.*

Rivenbark (761) Americanized spelling of German *Reifenberg* (see RIFENBURG).

Rivenburg (182) Americanized spelling of German *Reifenberg* (see RIFENBURG).

Rivenburgh (174) Americanized spelling of German *Reifenberg* (see RIFENBURG).

River (215) Possibly English (see RIVERS), or an Americanized form of a like-sounding name in some other language, perhaps German **Riffer** (see RIFFEY).

Rivera (35425) **1.** Spanish: habitational name from any of the places named Rivera, a variant of RIBERA. **2.** Italian: northern variant of the southern (especially Sicily) topographic name RIBERA. **3.** Catalan: in some cases, variant of Catalan RIBERA.
GIVEN NAMES Spanish 45%. *Jose (1076), Juan (443), Luis (435), Carlos (363), Angel (278), Miguel (241), Manuel (232), Francisco (205), Jesus (200), Pedro (183), Jorge (166), Roberto (158).*

Rivere (161) Apparently of French origin; possibly an altered spelling of RIVIÈRE.
GIVEN NAME French 5%. *Honore.*

Riveria (161) possibly Italian: unexplained.
GIVEN NAMES Spanish 48%. *Jose (5), Carlos (3), Juan (3), Luis (3), Miguel (3), Julio (2), Adela, Alicia, Armondo, Carlosa, Domingo, Efrain.*

Rivero (1512) Spanish and Galician: habitational name from any of the places in Galicia, Santander, and Cáceres named Rivero, from *ribero* 'bank', 'shore' (Late Latin *riparium*, a derivative of *ripa* 'bank').
GIVEN NAMES Spanish 54%. *Jose (45), Manuel (29), Jorge (25), Juan (21), Roberto (17), Carlos (15), Luis (15), Raul (13), Pedro (12), Ramon (12), Ricardo (12), Armando (11).*

Riveron (123) **1.** Spanish (**Riverón**): topographic name for someone living by a riverbank, from an augmentative of *ribero, rivero* 'bank', 'shore'. **2.** French: unexplained.
GIVEN NAMES Spanish 52%. *Jorge (5), Alberto (4), Carlos (4), Roberto (4), Jose*

(3), *Pedro* (3), *Francisco* (2), *Gerardo* (2), *Luis* (2), *Manuel* (2), *Mario* (2), *Raul* (2); *Federico, Oreste.*

Rivers (10024) **1.** English (of Norman origin): habitational name from any of various places in northern France called Rivières, from the plural form of Old French *rivière* 'river' (originally meaning 'riverbank', from Latin *riparia*). The absence of English forms without the final *-s* makes it unlikely that it is ever from the borrowed Middle English vocabulary word *river*, but the French and other Romance cognates do normally have this sense. **2.** Common Americanized form of French LARIVIÈRE.

Rives (1395) **1.** Jewish (eastern Ashkenazic): from the Yiddish female personal name *Rive* a back-formation from *Rivke* (see RIFKIN). **2.** French: topographic name for someone who lived on the bank of a river or the shore of a lake, Old French *rive* (Latin *ripa*).

Rivest (238) French: variant of RIVET.
GIVEN NAMES French 10%. *Alain* (2), *Cecile, Michel, Napoleon, Ninon.*

Rivet (657) **1.** French: from a diminutive of Old French *rive* '(river) bank', 'shore' (see RIVES). **2.** Northern French and English: metonymic occupational name for a maker of bolts (see RIVETT).
GIVEN NAMES French 8%. *Marcel* (2), *Pierre* (2), *Aldor, Camille, Gilles, Gillis, Henri, Huguette, Landry, Laurent, Normand, Pierrette.*

Rivett (252) **1.** English (East Anglia): metonymic occupational name for a metalworker, from Middle English, Old French *rivet* 'small nail or bolt' (from Old French *river* 'to fix or secure', of unknown origin). **2.** French: variant of RIVET 1.

Rivette (266) French: variant of RIVET.
GIVEN NAMES French 9%. *Antoine* (4), *Emile, Octave.*

Riviello (187) Italian: variant, typical of Lucania, of the habitational name **Rivello**, from Rivello in Potenza province.
GIVEN NAMES Italian 17%. *Carmine, Cosmo, Dino, Domenico, Emidio, Filomena, Innocenzo, Nunzio, Romeo, Sal, Vito.*

Riviera (148) **1.** Italian: topographic name for someone who lived by the bank of a river (from Latin *riparia*). **2.** possibly also Spanish, from Italian RIVIERA. This name came to the U.S. mainly by way of Mexico.
GIVEN NAMES Spanish 31%. *Luis* (3), *Carlos* (2), *Jose* (2), *Juana* (2), *Ana, Arturo, Domingo, Eloisa, Eugenio, Germano, Guillermo, Gustavo.*

Riviere (417) French (**Rivière**): topographic name for someone who lived by the bank of a river or shore of a lake, from Old French *rivière* 'river', 'shore', or a habitational name from any of various places named (Le) Rivière, for example in Indre-et-Loire and Pas-de-Calais.
FOREBEARS A Rivière from the Poitou region of France is documented in Repentigny, Quebec in 1680.

GIVEN NAMES French 10%. *Pierre* (2), *Camille, Firmin, Hermite, Lucien, Monique, Stephane.*

Rivinius (103) German: humanistic name, an altered form of **Rivenich**, a habitational name from a village of this name.
FOREBEARS Johann Gregorius Rivinius (born 1657 in Trier, Germany) changed his name from Rivenich to Rivinius. In the early 19th century a branch of the family became established in Russia, and in 1900 a group of their descendants came to North America and settled in South Dakota.
GIVEN NAME German 5%. *Frieda.*

Rivkin (465) Jewish (eastern Ashkenazic): variant of RIFKIN.
GIVEN NAMES Jewish 15%; Russian 8%. *Mayer* (3), *Semen* (3), *Emanuel* (2), *Irina* (2), *Sholom* (2), *Zelig* (2), *Aron, Chana, Genya, Hyman, Isak, Miriam*; *Boris* (3), *Yefim* (3), *Leonid* (2), *Mikhail* (2), *Oleg* (2), *Aleksandr, Anatoliy, Arkady, Gol, Igor, Lev, Leya.*

Rivlin (142) Jewish (from Belarus): metronymic from the Yiddish female personal name *Rivle*, a pet form of *Rivke* (Yiddish form of Hebrew *Rivqah*; see REBECCA), with the addition of the Slavic possessive suffix *-in*.
GIVEN NAMES Jewish 11%. *Zeev* (2), *Emanuel, Hava, Smadar, Yael.*

Rix (915) English and German: variant spelling of RICKS.

Rixon (109) English: variant spelling of RICKSON.

Rizer (464) Americanized spelling of German REISER.

Rizk (416) Muslim: from a personal name based on Arabic *rizq* 'livelihood', 'subsistence' (see the Qur'an 34:15). The combination *Rizq Allah* means 'nourishment provided by Allah'.
GIVEN NAMES Muslim 43%; French 5%. *Nabil* (4), *Ashraf* (3), *Fouad* (3), *Medhat* (3), *Mohamad* (3), *Rizk* (3), *Youssef* (3), *Badie* (2), *Bassam* (2), *Hani* (2), *Issa* (2), *Latif* (2); *Alain, Andre, Antoine, Dany, Georges, Henri, Michel.*

Rizo (459) Spanish: nickname for someone with curly hair, from *rizo* 'curl'.
GIVEN NAMES Spanish 54%. *Jose* (21), *Jesus* (8), *Luis* (6), *Manuel* (6), *Carlos* (5), *Francisco* (5), *Juan* (4), *Miguel* (4), *Rafael* (4), *Ramon* (4), *Refugio* (4), *Ricardo* (4).

Rizor (219) Origin unidentified. Probably a respelling of German RIESER or REISER.

Rizvi (332) Iranian: from a Persian form of the Arabic name *Riḍāwī*, indicating descent from Riḍā 'Ali ibn Musa, eighth imam of the Shiites. See REZA.
GIVEN NAMES Muslim 91%. *Syed* (79), *Ali* (11), *Arshad* (5), *Hasan* (5), *Shakeel* (4), *Abbas* (3), *Akbar* (3), *Saiyid* (3), *Abid* (2), *Adnan* (2), *Anwar* (2), *Asif* (2).

Rizza (337) Italian: from *rizza*, a southern feminine form of *riccio* 'curly-headed'. Compare RICCI.

GIVEN NAMES Italian 27%. *Angelo* (6), *Salvatore* (5), *Antonio* (3), *Roberto* (2), *Alberto, Aldo, Alessandro, Benito, Concetta, Domenic, Enrico, Gaetano, Gino, Gulio, Luciana, Nino.*

Rizzardi (151) Southern Italian: southern form of RICCIARDI.
GIVEN NAMES Italian 11%. *Angelo* (2), *Florio, Guido, Rino, Savino.*

Rizzi (949) Italian: **1.** variant of RICCI. **2.** patronymic from RIZZO.
GIVEN NAMES Italian 26%; Spanish 5%. *Vito* (10), *Mario* (9), *Angelo* (3), *Mauro* (3), *Franco* (2), *Lorenzo* (2), *Nicola* (2), *Rocco* (2), *Aldo, Alessandro, Antonio, Caesar, Elvira* (2), *Lino* (2), *Aida, Claudio, Elida, Eusebio, Fortunato*; *Ramon* (2), *Ana, Carlos, Jose.*

Rizzio (100) Italian: variant of RICCIO.
GIVEN NAMES Italian 9%. *Carlo, Carmelo.*

Rizzo (6646) Italian: variant of RICCIO.
GIVEN NAMES Italian 14%. *Salvatore* (51), *Angelo* (36), *Sal* (19), *Antonio* (17), *Santo* (16), *Carmine* (15), *Carmelo* (7), *Giuseppe* (7), *Rocco* (7), *Gaetano* (6), *Vito* (6), *Carmela* (5).

Rizzolo (222) Italian: from a diminutive of RIZZO.
GIVEN NAMES Italian 15%. *Donato* (3), *Salvatore* (2), *Antonio, Filomena, Grazia, Primo, Rocco, Sal, Santo, Silvio.*

Rizzotti (125) Italian: patronymic or plural form of RIZZOTTO.
GIVEN NAMES Italian 12%. *Gaetano* (2), *Alfio, Antonio, Franco, Salvatore.*

Rizzotto (132) Italian: from a diminutive of RIZZO.
GIVEN NAMES Italian 10%; German 6%. *Antonio* (3), *Cosmo, Enza, Romeo, Sal*; *Otto* (2), *Erna.*

Rizzuti (154) Southern Italian: patronymic or plural form of RIZZUTO.
GIVEN NAMES Italian 15%. *Angelo, Dante, Francesca, Gaetana, Paolo, Rocco, Sal, Salvatore.*

Rizzuto (884) Southern Italian: southern variant of *Ricciuto* (see RICCIUTI).
GIVEN NAMES Italian 13%. *Salvatore* (7), *Angelo* (4), *Vito* (3), *Natale* (2), *Reno* (2), *Antonino, Baldassare, Camillo, Carmela, Concetta, Elio, Gabriele.*

Ro (392) **1.** Korean: variant of NO. **2.** Perhaps a shortened form of Dutch **de Ro**, a variant of RODE.
GIVEN NAMES Korean 55%. *Seung* (6), *Young* (6), *Sung* (5), *Jae* (4), *Kyung* (4), *Myung* (4), *Dong* (3), *Kwang* (3), *Chun* (2), *Joon* (2), *Sang* (2), *Sung Woo* (2); *Byung* (5), *Cheol* (2), *Myong* (2), *Young Kyun* (2), *Chong, Choon, Chul Soo, Dae, Eun Sook, Eunmi, Hae, Han Young.*

Roa (618) Spanish: habitational name from Roa in Burgos province.
GIVEN NAMES Spanish 41%. *Luis* (13), *Carlos* (11), *Jose* (10), *Jorge* (6), *Pedro* (6), *Roberto* (6), *Fernando* (5), *Jesus* (5), *Juan* (5), *Alfredo* (4), *Arturo* (4), *Manuel* (4).

Roach (15776) **1.** English: topographic name for someone who lived by a rocky crag or outcrop, from Old French *roche* (later replaced in England by *rock*, from the Norman byform *rocque*), or a habitational name from any of the places named with this word, such as Roach in Devon, or Roche in Cornwall and South Yorkshire. **2.** English and Irish (of Norman origin): habitational name from any of various places in Normandy, as for example Les Roches in Seine-Maritime, named with Old French *roche*, or from Roche Castle in Wales.

Roache (564) Irish: variant spelling of ROACH 2.
GIVEN NAMES Irish 4%. *Donovan, Sheelagh.*

Roadarmel (129) Americanized spelling of German **Rothärmel** (see ROTHERMEL).
GIVEN NAME German 4%. *Markus.*

Roadcap (216) Americanized form of German ROTHGEB.

Roaden (112) Altered spelling of Irish or German RODEN.

Roades (168) English: variant spelling of RHODES.

Roadman (160) Americanized spelling of German **Rod(e)mann** (see RODMAN), **Rot(h)mann** (see ROTHMAN), or **Rottmann** (see ROTTMAN).

Roads (178) English: variant spelling of RHODES.

Roady (231) Perhaps an Americanized spelling of German RODE.

Roake (98) English: variant of ROCK 2.

Roam (180) Perhaps an altered spelling of ROME.

Roan (1093) **1.** Irish: variant spelling of ROWAN. **2.** English (of Norman origin): habitational name from Rouen in Normandy. In Scotland the name is also derived in part from any of several places named Roan in the Borders and Strathclyde. There was also a medieval female personal name *Roana*, which may have given rise to some examples of the surname.

Roane (956) Irish: variant spelling of ROWAN or possibly a variant of RUANE.

Roark (4887) Irish: reduced variant spelling of O'ROURKE.

Roarty (182) Irish: reduced Anglicized form of Gaelic **Ó Robhartaigh** 'son of *Robhartach*', from *robharta* 'full tide'. There has been considerable confusion with **Ó Raithbheartaigh** (see RAFFERTY), which may well be a later variant.
GIVEN NAME Irish 9%. *Brigid.*

Roat (309) Probably an Americanized spelling of German ROTH.

Roath (329) Probably an Americanized spelling of German ROTH.

Roback (328) English: variant of ROEBUCK.

Robaina (129) Spanish: habitational name from Robaina in Seville province.
GIVEN NAMES Spanish 56%. *Jose* (6), *Julio* (5), *Juan* (4), *Ramon* (4), *Carlos* (3), *Cristina* (2), *Edmundo* (2), *Jorge* (2), *Manuel* (2), *Mario* (2), *Orlando* (2),

Roberto (2); *Antonio* (2), *Federico, Gervasio, Marcello, Marino, Silvio.*

Robak (380) Polish: unexplained.

Robar (229) Variant of French **Robard**, a variant of ROBERT.
GIVEN NAME French 4%. *Raoul* (2).

Robards (508) English: variant of ROBERTS.

Robare (300) Americanized spelling of French ROBERT.

Robarge (545) French: variant of ROBERGE.

Robart (215) English and French: variant of ROBERT.

Robarts (186) English: patronymic from ROBART.

Robb (5441) Scottish and northern Irish: from a short form of the personal name ROBERT.

Robbe (135) North German and Frisian: from the personal name *Robbe*, a short form of ROBERT.

Robben (448) North German: patronymic from the personal name ROBBE.

Robberson (224) Probably an altered spelling of English **Roberson**, a patronymic from ROBERT, which is particularly common in Scotland.

Robbert (112) Dutch and North German: variant spelling of ROBERT.

Robbie (151) Scottish: from a pet form of the personal name ROBERT.

Robbin (187) English: variant spelling of ROBIN 1.

Robbins (30645) English: patronymic from ROBIN.

Robbs (311) English: patronymic from the personal name ROBB.

Robe (153) French (**Robé**), English, and North German: from a short form of ROBERT.
GIVEN NAME French 4%. *Michel.*

Robeck (264) German: habitational name from a place so named in Rhineland or a reduced form of **Rodenbeck**, a habitational name from places so named in Hesse, Rhineland, the Palatinate, and Bavaria.

Robel (322) German: **1.** nickname from Sorbian *(w)robel* 'sparrow'. **2.** (**Röbel**): habitational name from a place so named in Mecklenburg. **3.** from a pet form of ROBERT or a Germanic personal name formed with *hrōd* 'renown' + *bald* 'bold', 'brave'.

Robello (194) Italian or Portuguese: unexplained.

Rober (123) German: variant of **Röber** (see ROEBER).
GIVEN NAMES German 5%. *Dieter, Hertha.*

Roberds (393) English: variant of ROBERTS.

Roberg (290) **1.** Norwegian: habitational name from a farmstead in Vestfold, named with Old Norse *rugr* 'rye' + *berg* 'hill', 'mountain'. **2.** Swedish: ornamental adoption of 1. **3.** German: perhaps a habitational name for someone from a place named Rodenberg, of which there are several examples in Saxony and Rhineland.

Roberge (1504) French: **1.** from a Germanic female personal name *Hrodberga*, composed of the elements *hrōd* 'renown' + *bergō* 'protection'. **2.** possibly a metonymic occupational name, from *roberge*, a term denoting a type of warship.
FOREBEARS A Roberge from Normandy, France, is documented in Château Richer, Quebec, in 1667. The secondary surnames LACROIX and LAPIERRE are also recorded.
GIVEN NAMES French 16%. *Lucien* (7), *Marcel* (5), *Andre* (4), *Jacques* (4), *Armand* (3), *Emile* (3), *Gaston* (3), *Normand* (3), *Urbain* (3), *Achille* (2), *Alphonse* (2), *Gilles* (2).

Robers (220) English: variant of ROBERTS.

Roberson (16453) Northern English: variant of ROBERTSON.

Robert (3818) English, French, German, Dutch, Hungarian (**Róbert**), etc: from a Germanic personal name composed of the elements *hrōd* 'renown' + *berht* 'bright', 'famous'. This is found occasionally in England before the Conquest, but in the main it was introduced into England by the Normans and quickly became popular among all classes of society. The surname is also occasionally borne by Jews, as an Americanized form of one or more likesounding Jewish surnames.
FOREBEARS A Robert from La Rochelle, France is documented in Trois-Rivières, Quebec, in 1666, with the secondary surname LAFONTAINE. A family from the Saintonge region of France are recorded in Contrecoeur in 1681, with the secondary surname DESLAURIERS. Other secondary surnames include Saint-Amand, BRETON and LEBRETON, WATSON, La Pomeray, Durandeau, and Dureau.
GIVEN NAMES French 11%. *Andre* (11), *Marcel* (9), *Gilles* (8), *Normand* (7), *Armand* (6), *Lucien* (6), *Pierre* (5), *Emile* (4), *Michel* (4), *Edouard* (3), *Gaston* (3), *Yves* (3).

Roberti (373) Italian: patronymic or plural form of ROBERTO.
GIVEN NAMES Italian 14%. *Angelo* (3), *Arcangelo* (2), *Gino* (2), *Carlo, Carmine, Guido, Marco, Pompeo, Remo.*

Roberto (934) Italian and Spanish: from the personal name *Roberto* (see ROBERT).
GIVEN NAMES Italian 18%; Spanish 9%. *Salvatore* (5), *Angelo* (4), *Antonio* (4), *Rosario* (3), *Vito* (3), *Armando* (2), *Gildo* (2), *Mario* (2), *Rocco* (2), *Alessandro, Americo, Arcangelo, Carmine, Domenic, Donato; Carlos* (2), *Jose* (2), *Manuel* (2), *Perez* (2), *Raul* (2), *Angel.*

Roberton (126) Scottish: unexplained; perhaps a variant of ROBERTSON.

Roberts (132659) English: patronymic from the personal name ROBERT. This surname is very frequent in Wales and west central England. It is also occasionally borne by Jews, presumably as an Americanized form of a like-sounding Jewish surname.

Robertshaw (298) **1.** English (West Yorkshire): habitational name from a lost place in Heptonstall, West Yorkshire, taking its name from an owner ROBERT + Middle English *shawe* 'copse' (Old English *sceaga*). **2.** Americanized spelling of French ROBICHAUD.

Robertson (53841) Scottish and northern English: patronymic from the personal name ROBERT. This surname is especially common in Scotland, where *Robert* was a popular personal name and the name of three kings of Scotland, including Robert the Bruce (1274–1329).

Robeson (1001) Northern English: patronymic from a short form of ROBERT.

Robey (1956) English and eastern French: from a pet form of the personal name ROBERT.

Robichaud (1327) French: probably an altered spelling of **Robichon** or **Roubichou**, pet forms of ROBERT.
FOREBEARS The name in its various spellings is frequent in LA, where bearers claim descent from one Louis Robichaux, of Laudun, France, who is found in Acadia, in Canada, in 1642. However, one 1752 mention concerns a native of England, perhaps a ROBERTSHAW.
GIVEN NAMES French 10%. *Andre* (3), *Yvon* (3), *Alphonse* (2), *Armand* (2), *Herve* (2), *Jacques* (2), *Raoul* (2), *Adelard, Adrien, Alyre, Aurore, Cecile*.

Robichaux (962) French: probably an altered spelling of **Robichon** or **Roubichou**, pet forms of ROBERT.
GIVEN NAMES French 5%. *Alcide, Camille, Emile, Fernand, Francois, Gillis, Jacques, Marcel, Monique, Octave, Pierre, Raoul*.

Robicheau (165) French: probably an altered spelling of **Robichon** or **Roubichou**, pet forms of ROBERT.
GIVEN NAMES French 4%. *Cecile, Lorette*.

Robicheaux (420) French: probably an altered spelling of **Robichon** or **Roubichou**, pet forms of ROBERT.
GIVEN NAMES French 4%. *Emile* (2), *Andre, Fernand*.

Robida (126) **1.** Slovenian: nickname or topographic name from *robida* 'bramble'. **2.** Perhaps also French: from a pet form of ROBERT.
GIVEN NAME French 4%. *Ovide*.

Robideau (283) French: probably from an altered form of the personal name *Robardeau*, a pet form of ROBERT.
FOREBEARS The first Robidoux recorded in Canada was from Burgos in Spain, and seems to have been in Canada from around 1664. He bore the secondary surname L'Espagnol.

Robideaux (144) French: probably from an altered form of the personal name *Robardeau*, a pet form of ROBERT.
GIVEN NAME French 4%. *Alain*.

Robidoux (641) French: probably from an altered form of the personal name *Robardeau*, a pet form of ROBERT.
FOREBEARS The first Robidoux recorded in Canada was from Burgos in Spain, and seems to have been in Canada from around 1664. He bore the secondary surname L'Espagnol.
GIVEN NAMES French 9%. *Lucien* (4), *Armand* (2), *Cecile* (2), *Normand* (2), *Alcide, Andre, Fernand, Jacques, Napoleon, Sebastien*.

Robie (587) English and Scottish: variant spelling of ROBEY.

Robillard (1400) French: from a pet form of ROBERT.
FOREBEARS A Robillard is documented in Champlain, Quebec, in 1672. His origins are unknown.
GIVEN NAMES French 9%. *Armand* (4), *Andre* (3), *Marcel* (3), *Emile* (2), *Luc* (2), *Normand* (2), *Aurore, Camille, Donat, Evens, Fernand, Henri*.

Robin (1833) **1.** Scottish, English, French, and German: from the personal name *Robin*, a pet form of ROBERT, composed of the short form *Rob* + the hypocoristic suffix *-in*. **2.** Slovenian: unexplained. **3.** Jewish (Ashkenazic): variant of RUBIN or RABIN.
FOREBEARS A Robin from the Burgundy region of France is documented in Quebec City in 1667, with the secondary surname LAPOINTE.
GIVEN NAMES French 5%. *Pierre* (3), *Andre* (2), *Curley* (2), *Emile* (2), *Marcel* (2), *Achille, Armand, Arnaud, Camille, Julien, Michel, Normand*.

Robinett (1369) French: see ROBINETTE.

Robinette (3228) Canadian spelling of French **Robinet**, a pet form of ROBIN. The spelling reflects the Canadian practice of pronouncing the final *-t*, a practice not followed in France.

Robino (107) Italian: from the personal name *Robino*, pet form of *Roberto* (see ROBERT).
GIVEN NAMES Italian 5%. *Carmela, Gasper*.

Robins (3688) Southern English: patronymic from the personal name ROBIN.

Robinson (153159) Northern English: patronymic from the personal name ROBIN.
FOREBEARS One of the most famous bearers of this widespread northern English name was the Puritan preacher John Robinson (*c.*1575–1625) of Sturton, Nottinghamshire, England. In 1604 he was removed from his fellowship of Corpus Christi College, Cambridge, for his religious views. He was the leader of the group of English Puritans who fled to Leiden in the Netherlands in 1608–9, among whom were many of the Pilgrims who sailed on the *Mayflower* in 1620. His son Isaac came to Plymouth, MA, in 1631, and eventually settled in Tisbury, Martha's Vineyard, in about 1670.

Robirds (120) Variant of English ROBARDS or ROBERTS.

Robishaw (150) English: variant of ROBERTSHAW.

Robison (9540) English: patronymic from the personal name ROBIN.

Robitaille (1008) Of French origin; unexplained. It is sometimes Americanized as **Robtoy**.
FOREBEARS A Robitaille from the Picard region of France is recorded in Quebec City in 1674.
GIVEN NAMES French 19%. *Andre* (5), *Jacques* (5), *Armand* (4), *Normand* (4), *Aime* (3), *Cecile* (3), *Alphee* (2), *Emile* (2), *Herve* (2), *Luc* (2), *Lucien* (2), *Pierre* (2).

Robl (218) **1.** South German: dialect form of **Rabl**, a diminutive of *Rabe* 'raven', presumably applied as a nickname for someone thought to resemble the bird. **2.** German: variant spelling of ROBEL.
GIVEN NAMES German 4%. *Erwin, Franz, Hermann*.

Roble (278) **1.** Spanish: topographic name for someone who lived by a conspicuous oak tree, from Spanish *roble* 'oak tree' (Latin *robur*). **2.** Altered spelling of German ROBEL.

Robledo (1331) Spanish: habitational name from any of the numerous places named Robledo, from *robledo* 'oak wood', a derivative of *roble* 'oak'.
GIVEN NAMES Spanish 50%. *Jose* (39), *Juan* (24), *Manuel* (18), *Jesus* (15), *Carlos* (13), *Francisco* (12), *Javier* (12), *Alfredo* (8), *Ruben* (8), *Felipe* (7), *Fernando* (7), *Jorge* (7).

Roblee (201) Apparently an altered spelling of Spanish ROBLE, no doubt to safeguard the second syllable.

Robles (7080) Spanish: topographic name from the plural of *roble* 'oak', or a habitational name from Los Robles in Lleón, named from the same word.
GIVEN NAMES Spanish 48%. *Jose* (180), *Juan* (91), *Manuel* (67), *Carlos* (60), *Luis* (58), *Jesus* (51), *Francisco* (47), *Pedro* (43), *Ruben* (43), *Miguel* (35), *Jorge* (34), *Roberto* (33).

Robleto (102) Hispanic (Nicaragua): apparently a variant of Spanish ROBLEDO.
GIVEN NAMES Spanish 36%. *Sergio* (3), *Adolfo* (2), *Carlos* (2), *Eduardo* (2), *Fernando* (2), *Francisco* (2), *Alberto, Alfonso, Ana, Helio, Jorge, Jose*; *Marco, Silvio*.

Robley (225) Possibly an Americanized spelling of Spanish ROBLE.

Roblin (153) English and French: from a pet form of *Rob*, short form of ROBERT.

Robling (240) German (**Röbling**): from a short form or pet form of a Germanic personal name formed with *hrōd* 'renown'.

Roblyer (128) Altered spelling of the North German derogatory nickname **Robelierer**, denoting a ruffian who bragged about his strength, probably from Dutch *rabbeln* 'to chatter' + the French suffix *-ierer*.
GIVEN NAME German 4%. *Kurt*.

Robnett (484) English and French: from **Robinet**, a pet form of the personal name ROBIN. Compare ROBINETTE.

Robotham (160) English: variant of ROW-BOTTOM.

Robson (3231) Northern English: patronymic from the personal name *Rob*, a short form of ROBERT.

Robuck (339) English: variant spelling of ROEBUCK.

Robustelli (112) Italian: patronymic from a pet form of the personal name *Robusto*, an omen name meaning 'robust'.
GIVEN NAMES Italian 15%. *Carmine, Ciro, Dante, Francesco, Gino.*

Roby (2903) English and Scottish: **1.** from a pet form of ROBERT. **2.** habitational name from Roby in Lancashire (now Merseyside), named with Old Norse *rá* 'pole', 'boundary mark' + *býr* 'farm', 'settlement'.

Robyn (119) Variant spelling of ROBIN.

Roca (623) Catalan: habitational name from any of the numerous places so named, from Catalan *roca* 'rock'. This name is also Occitan.
GIVEN NAMES Spanish 43%; Italian 7%. *Jose* (17), *Juan* (9), *Jorge* (7), *Luis* (7), *Carlos* (5), *Gustavo* (5), *Rafael* (5), *Alejandro* (4), *Alfonso* (4), *Francisco* (4), *Ruben* (4), *Sergio* (4); *Antonio* (7), *Vito* (4), *Carmine* (2), *Leonardo* (2), *Nicola* (2), *Amadeo, Carlo, Enio, Fiorella, Lorenzo, Marco, Matteo.*

Rocca (623) Italian: habitational name from any of the numerous places throughout Italy named or named with *rocca* 'fortress', 'stronghold'.
GIVEN NAMES Italian 13%. *Aldo* (2), *Pasquale* (2), *Saverio* (2), *Amedeo, Attilio, Baldassare, Bruna, Carlo, Carmine, Corrado, Elio, Filippo.*

Roccaforte (142) Italian: habitational name from Roccaforte del Greco in Reggio Calabria, Roccaforte Ligure in Alessandria, or Roccaforte Mondovì in Cuneo, all named with *roccaforte* 'stronghold', 'fort(ress)'.
GIVEN NAMES Italian 7%. *Carlo* (2), *Leonardo.*

Rocchi (171) Italian: **1.** patronymic from the personal name ROCCO. **2.** see ROCCA.
GIVEN NAMES Italian 15%. *Angelo, Antonio, Dante, Enzo, Ferruccio, Manlio, Marco, Nazzareno, Pasquale, Remo, Stefano.*

Rocchio (384) Italian: unexplained.
GIVEN NAMES Italian 16%. *Pasquale* (5), *Antonio* (3), *Domenico* (3), *Cosmo* (2), *Silvestro* (2), *Angelo, Giovanni, Mafalda, Pasco, Pasqualina, Pietro, Sante.*

Rocco (2120) Italian: from the Germanic personal name *Rocco*, which was borne by a 14th-century saint from Montpellier remembered for his miraculous healings during an outbreak of the plague in northern Italy. The etymology of the name is uncertain (see ROCH).

GIVEN NAMES Italian 14%. *Angelo* (9), *Salvatore* (6), *Carmine* (5), *Pasquale* (5), *Antonio* (4), *Dino* (4), *Carlo* (3), *Domenic* (3), *Gennaro* (3), *Giacomo* (3), *Vito* (3), *Aldo* (2).

Roch (304) **1.** German and French: from a Germanic personal name of uncertain origin. It may have been originally a byname meaning 'crow'. Compare Old High German *hruoh*, Old English *hrōc*, an imitative formation, but Dauzat derives it from a root *hroc* 'rest'. The name was fairly common in the Middle Ages and was sometimes bestowed in honor of a 14th-century saint (Latinized name *Rochus*) of Montpellier, remembered for his miraculous healings during an outbreak of the plague in northern Italy. **2.** Jewish (Ashkenazic): variant of RAUCH.
GIVEN NAMES French 14%. *Andre* (2), *Jacques* (2), *Emile, Gilles, Jean-Marc, Julien, Marcel, Michel, Pierre, Thierry, Yves.*

Rocha (5785) Portuguese and Galician: habitational name from any of the numerous places so named, from Portuguese and Galician *rocha* 'rock', 'cliff'.
GIVEN NAMES Spanish 41%; Portuguese 10%. *Jose* (148), *Manuel* (92), *Juan* (64), *Jesus* (46), *Carlos* (35), *Francisco* (29), *Raul* (27), *Luis* (26), *Guadalupe* (23), *Pedro* (23), *Mario* (22), *Jorge* (20); *Paulo* (6), *Joao* (3), *Ligia* (2), *Afonso, Caetano, Calixtro, Duarte, Henrique, Mateus, Zulmira.*

Rochat (158) French: from a diminutive of Old French *roche* 'rock' (see ROCHE).
GIVEN NAMES French 10%. *Andre, Monique, Philippe, Pierre.*

Roche (6912) **1.** Irish (of Norman origin): see ROACHE. This is the name of various important families in Munster (counties Cork, Wexford, and Limerick). **2.** French: topographic name for someone who lived by a rocky outcrop or crag, Old French *roche*. **3.** German: from a short form of a Germanic personal name, *Rocco*, based on *hrok*, of uncertain origin, or *hrōd* 'renown'.
FOREBEARS French bearers of the name were first documented in Château Richer, Quebec, in 1665; the secondary surname LAFONTAINE is also attested.
GIVEN NAMES Irish 4%. *Brendan* (4), *Aidan* (2), *Declan* (2), *Eamonn, Fergus, Fionnuala, Kevin Patrick, Liam.*

Rocheford (146) Respelling of French ROCHEFORT.
GIVEN NAMES French 4%. *Armand, Fernand.*

Rochefort (361) French: habitational name from any of numerous places named Rochefort, from Old French *roche* 'rocky outcrop'. This name is sometimes Americanized as RUSHFORD.
FOREBEARS Rochefort is recorded as a secondary surname for Audin or Odon, as well as Baudin, DUPRE, Hurette, JOY, Lairet,

Péreau, and YOU. It was first documented in Canada in 1690.
GIVEN NAMES French 15%. *Gaston* (2), *Adrien, Andre, Armand, Cecile, Celine, Dany, Gaetan, Herve, Jacques, Jean-Guy, Lucien.*

Rochel (124) Spanish: probably a name that was originally taken to Spain from France.
GIVEN NAMES Spanish 7%. *Fidel, Ignacio, Maria Luisa, Porfirio, Refugio, Salvador.*

Rocheleau (827) Perhaps a variant of French **Rochereau**, a diminutive of ROCHE, which is sometimes Americanized as RUSHLOW.
GIVEN NAMES French 9%. *Marcel* (5), *Armand* (4), *Alphonse* (2), *Andre* (2), *Normand* (2), *Aurore, Cecile, Elphege, Emile, Fernand, Gilles, Mathieu.*

Rochell (155) Altered spelling of French ROCHELLE, or **Rochel**, also a diminutive of ROCHE or of German **Rochel**, from a pet form of ROCH.

Rochelle (1246) French: diminutive of ROCHE.

Rochester (1221) English: habitational name from the city in Kent, which is recorded by Bede (*c.*730) under the names of both *Dorubrevi* and *Hrofæcæstre*. The former represents the original British name, composed of the elements *duro-* 'fortress' and *brīvā* 'bridge'. The second represents a contracted form of this (possibly affected by folk etymological connection with Old English *hrōf* 'roof') combined with an explanatory Old English *cæster* 'Roman fort' (from Latin *castra* 'military camp'). There is a much smaller place in Northumbria also called Rochester, which seems to have been named in imitation of the more important one, but which is a more than occasional source of the surname. In other cases there may also have been confusion with Wroxeter in Shropshire, recorded in Domesday Book as *Rochecestre*.

Rochette (290) French: diminutive of ROCHE.
GIVEN NAMES French 15%. *Marcel* (2), *Armand, Cecile, Coraline, Emilien, Gilles, Mathieu, Normand, Ovila, Patrice, Renald, Serge.*

Rochford (744) English: habitational name from either of two places so called: in Essex and Worcestershire. In both cases the name probably derives from the genitive case of Old English *ræcc* 'hunting dog' (perhaps a byname) + Old English *ford* 'ford', but its development has been influenced by the common French place name composed of the elements *roche* 'rock' + *fort* 'strong' (Latin *fortis*).
GIVEN NAMES Irish 5%. *Brendan* (2), *Niall.*

Rochin (110) Common in Mexico, this name is probably of French origin.
GIVEN NAMES Spanish 34%. *Mario* (4), *Carlos* (2), *Jose* (2), *Rafael* (2), *Eleazar, Juana, Leoncio, Leticia, Lupe, Maria Alejandra, Maria Juana, Pedro.*

Rochlin (181) Jewish (mainly from Belarus): metronymic from the Yiddish female personal name *Rokhle* (a pet form of the Biblical name RACHEL) + the Slavic metronymic suffix *-in*.

GIVEN NAMES Jewish 8%. *Mordecai* (2), *Miriam, Zalman*.

Rochman (138) **1.** German (**Rochmann**): variant of **Rückmann** (see RUCKMAN). **2.** Jewish (Ashkenazic): from **Rauchman**, elaborated form of RAUCH. **3.** Jewish (eastern Ashkenazic): metronymic name from the Yiddish female personal name *Rokhe*, a pet form of Biblical RACHEL + *man* 'man' in the sense of 'husband'.

GIVEN NAMES Jewish 13%; French 8%. *Mordechi* (2), *Aron, Dov, Hyman, Sol*; *Pierre* (2), *Piere*.

Rochon (803) French: diminutive of ROCHE.

GIVEN NAMES French 12%. *Pierre* (3), *Andre* (2), *Aurele* (2), *Gaston* (2), *Michel* (2), *Yves* (2), *Adrien, Antoine, Fernande, Gaetan, Germain, Gilles*.

Rochow (95) German: see ROCKOW.

GIVEN NAMES German 8%. *Otto* (2), *Hertha*.

Rock (6926) **1.** English: topographic name for someone who lived near a notable crag or outcrop, from Middle English *rokke* 'rock' (see ROACH), or a habitational name from a place named with this word, as for example Rock in Northumberland. **2.** English: variant of **Roke** (see ROKES 1). **3.** English: metronymic occupational name for a spinner or a maker of distaffs, from Middle English *rok* 'distaff' (from Old Norse *rokkr* or Middle Dutch *rocke* or an unattested Old English cognate). **4.** German: from a short form of the personal name *Rocco* (see ROCHE 3). **5.** German: metonymic occupational name for a tailor, from Middle High German *rok, roc* 'skirt', 'gown'. **6.** German (**Röck**): variant of ROCHE 3.

Rockafellow (320) Americanized spelling of German ROCKEFELLER.

Rocke (359) **1.** English: variant spelling of ROCK. **2.** German (**Röcke**): variant of ROCK 4.

Rockefeller (537) German: habitational name for someone from the village of Rockenfeld near Neuwied, Rhineland, named in Middle High German with *rocke* 'rye' (Old High German *rocko*) + *feld* 'open country'.

FOREBEARS The first immigrants to bring this name to America arrived in America in 1734. Their descendant, the millionaire industrialist John D. Rockefeller (1839–1937), founder of Standard Oil, was born in Richford, NY; his father was a commodities dealer and farm owner.

Rockel (157) German: **1.** habitational name from a place so named near Coesfeld, Westphalia, or Rockeln, East Prussia. **2.** (**Röckel, Röckl**): southern German nickname for a baker who sold rye rolls, Middle

High German *röckel*, a diminutive of *rocke* 'rye'.

GIVEN NAMES German 4%. *Hans, Monika*.

Rockenbach (163) German: habitational name from a place so named in Franconia.

Rocker (566) **1.** English: occupational name for a spinner or a maker of distaffs, from an agent derivative of Middle English *rok* 'distaff' (see ROCK). **2.** German: from a Germanic personal name based on *hrōd* 'renown'. **3.** habitational name from a farm named Rokken in Pustertal, south Tyrol (Italy). **4.** German (**Röcker**): from a topographic name or a place name Röcke (formerly Roke) near Bückeburg, Lower Saxony.

Rockers (190) German: **1.** patronymic from ROCKER 2. **2.** (**Röckers**) variant of ROCKER 4.

Rockey (974) English (Devon): unexplained.

Rockford (151) Apparently an altered spelling of English ROCHFORD; alternatively it may be an Americanized form of French ROCHEFORT or Italian ROCCAFORTE.

Rockhill (463) English: apparently a habitational name from a place in Shropshire or several farmsteads so named.

Rockhold (560) Variant of German **Rockolt**, a variant of **Rocholt**, or of **Rocholl**, thought by some to be from variants of a Germanic personal name composed of the elements *hrōk* 'prudence', 'care' + *wald* 'rule', and by others to be of Slavic origin.

Rockholt (159) See ROCKHOLD.

GIVEN NAME French 4%. *Philippe*.

Rocklin (155) **1.** Jewish: Americanized form of Ashkenazic ROCHLIN. **2.** Perhaps also an Americanized spelling of German **Röcklein**, a pet form of ROCK 4, or a variant of ROCKEL 2.

GIVEN NAMES Jewish 9%. *Avi* (2), *Hyman, Isadore, Sol*.

Rockman (275) **1.** German (**Rockmann**): possibly a habitational name for someone from Rockau in Thuringia. **2.** Possibly an altered spelling of German **Rochmann** (see ROCHMAN).

Rockmore (139) Origin unidentified. Probably English, possibly a habitational name from any of various minor places named Rockmoor or Rock Moor.

Rockoff (153) German: of Slavic origin (see ROCKOW).

Rockow (161) German: probably a habitational name from a place now called Rockau near Jena in Thuringia, or from Ruckoff near Chemnitz, Saxony.

Rocks (277) **1.** Scottish, northern Irish, and English: topographic name for someone living near a prominent outcrop of rocks (see ROCK 1). **2.** German: probably a variant of **Rochs**, a Lower Rhine variant of ROCH.

GIVEN NAME Irish 6%. *Brendan*.

Rockstroh (129) German: metonymic occupational name for a (cereal) farmer, from Middle High German *rocke* 'rye' + *strō* 'straw'.

GIVEN NAMES German 8%. *Kurt* (2), *Otto*.

Rockwell (4844) English: habitational name from places in Buckinghamshire and Somerset. The former was earlier *Rockholt*, and was so named from Old English *hrōc* 'rook' (perhaps a byname) + *holt* 'wood'. The second element of the Somerset place is probably (and more predictably) Old English *well(a)* 'spring', 'stream' (see WELL).

Rockwood (1067) English: apparently a habitational name, perhaps from Rockwood Park in West Sussex.

Rocque (206) Southern French: topographic name for someone who lived by a rocky crag or outcrop, a variant of ROCA.

GIVEN NAMES French 8%. *Emile* (2), *Andre*.

Rod (298) **1.** German: habitational name from any of several places named Rod, or a topographic name for someone who lived in a woodland clearing, from a derivative of Middle High German *roden* 'to clear land for cultivation'. Compare RHODES. **2.** Norwegian (**Rød**): habitational name from any of numerous farmsteads so named, from Old Norse *ruð* 'clearing'.

Roda (326) **1.** Catalan: habitational name from any of the various places named Roda, for example Roda de Ter, Roda de Berà, Roda de Ribagorça, from Catalan *roda* 'wheel' (Latin *rota*), possibly denoting a waterwheel. **2.** Greek: variant of **Rodias** (see RODIA). **3.** German: habitation name from any of numerous places, particularly in central eastern Germany, named Roda or Rhoda.

GIVEN NAMES Spanish 18%. *Arturo* (3), *Francisco* (3), *Domingos* (2), *Manuel* (2), *Mario* (2), *Alfredo, Amandio, Andres, Angel, Eduardo, Elia, Gustavo, Joaquim*.

Rodabaugh (323) See RODENBAUGH.

Rodak (301) Polish, Slovak, and Czech: nickname meaning 'fellow countryman', from Slavic *rod* 'origin', 'birth'.

GIVEN NAMES Polish 7%. *Zygmunt* (2), *Dorota, Justyna, Mariusz, Piotr, Wlodzimierz, Zbigniew*.

Rodarte (894) Portuguese: unexplained. This surname is also found in northern Mexico.

GIVEN NAMES Spanish 45%. *Jose* (23), *Jesus* (9), *Manuel* (9), *Juan* (8), *Jaime* (6), *Ruben* (6), *Salvador* (6), *Angel* (5), *Francisco* (5), *Guadalupe* (5), *Miguel* (5), *Arturo* (4).

Rodas (744) **1.** Catalan: variant of RODES 2. **2.** Galician and Portuguese: habitational name from any of three places in Galicia (in Lugo, Ourense, and Pontevedra), named Rodas, from the plural of *roda* 'wheel'. **3.** metonymic occupational name for a wheelwright, from *roda* 'wheel', cognate with 1.

GIVEN NAMES Spanish 48%. *Jose* (24), *Carlos* (13), *Luis* (11), *Jorge* (10), *Juan* (9), *Ana* (7), *Jaime* (6), *Rafael* (5), *Elvira* (4), *Manuel* (4), *Miguel* (4), *Raul* (4).

Rodberg (140) Norwegian (**Rødberg**): habitational name from any of four farmsteads so named from *rød* 'red' + *berg* 'mountain', 'hill'. The name is also found in Sweden.

Rodd (405) **1.** English: variant of RHODES. **2.** German: variant of RODE 1.

Rodda (566) Probably an altered spelling of RODA or RHODA.

Rodden (763) **1.** Irish, Scottish, and English: variant of RODEN. **2.** Altered spelling of German RODEN.

Roddenberry (197) Americanized spelling of Dutch and German RODENBERG.

Roddey (214) Altered spelling of RODDY or of German RODE.

Roddick (135) Scottish and northern Irish: probably a variant of REDDICK.
GIVEN NAME Scottish 4%. *Iain*.

Roddy (2427) Irish: reduced Anglicized form of Gaelic **Ó Rodaigh** 'descendant of *Rodach*', a personal name probably derived from *rod* 'spirited', 'furious'.

Rode (1388) **1.** German: from a short form of any of the various Germanic personal names with the first element *hrōd* 'renown'. Compare ROBERT, RUDIGER. **2.** North German, Danish, and English: topographic name for someone who lived on land cleared for cultivation or in a clearing in woodland, from Middle Low German *rode*, Danish *rothe*, Old English *rod*. Compare English RHODES. **3.** English: habitational name from any of the many places named with this word, as for example Rode in Cheshire. **4.** Slovenian: topographic name from the adjective *rod* 'barren', denoting someone who lived on a barren land. **5.** Slovenian: nickname from the Slovenian dialect word *rode* 'person with disheveled hair', a derivative of *rod* 'curly' or 'hairy'.
GIVEN NAMES German 6%. *Otto* (3), *Erwin* (2), *Ewald* (2), *Hans* (2), *Heinz* (2), *Oskar* (2), *Viktor* (2), *Claus*, *Frieda*, *Fritz*, *Gerhard*, *Horst*.

Rodebaugh (198) German: see RODENBAUGH.

Rodefer (155) German: see RODEHEAVER.

Rodeffer (171) German: see RODEHEAVER.

Rodeheaver (282) Americanized form of German **Rodenheber**: **1.** topographic name from Middle Low German *roden*, Middle High German *roten* 'to clear' + Middle High German *hou* 'assart', 'area of forest assigned for clearing'. **2.** Alternatively, the second element may be an agent derivative of Middle High German *houwen* 'to chop or cut down', in which case the name is of occupational origin.

Rodela (209) Galician: possibly habitational name from Rodel in A Coruña province, Galicia, so named from a diminutive of *roda* 'wheel'.

GIVEN NAMES Spanish 33%. *Eduardo* (3), *Andres* (2), *Jesus* (2), *Jose* (2), *Juan* (2), *Luis* (2), *Manuel* (2), *Margarita* (2), *Mario* (2), *Pedro* (2), *Rodolfo* (2), *Rogelio* (2).

Rodell (201) Altered spelling of German **Rödel**, from a pet form of any of the various Germanic compound names beginning with the element *hrōd* 'fame', or of **Rodel**, a chiefly Swiss variant of **Rödel** (see ROEDEL).

Rodeman (137) German (**Rodemann**): **1.** topographic name for someone who lived on woodland cleared for cultivation, a variant of RODE 2 with the addition of *man* 'man'. **2.** from a Germanic personal name, *Hrodman*, formed with *hrōd* 'renown', 'fame' + *man* 'man'.

Rodemeyer (105) German: distinguishing name for name a tenant farmer (see MEYER) whose farm was on a piece of woodland cleared for cultivation (see RODE 3).

Roden (2274) **1.** Irish: reduced Anglicized form of Gaelic **Ó Roideáin** 'descendant of *Rodán*', a personal name derived from a diminutive of *rod* 'strong', 'lively', 'spirited'. **2.** German: variant of RODE 3. **3.** Swedish (**Rodén**): ornamental name, probably from an unidentified place name element + the adjectival suffix *-én*, a derivative of Latin *-enius*.

Rodenbaugh (276) Americanized spelling of any of several German habitational names: **Rodenbach**, **Rothenbach**, or **Rottenbach**, though probably for the most part of the first, *Rodenbach*, which is from any of several places in Hesse, Bavaria, or the Palatinate, so named from Old High German *rōd* 'clearing' + *bach* 'creek'.

Rodenbeck (306) North German: habitational name from a place so named near Hannover.
GIVEN NAMES German 4%. *Egon*, *Erwin*, *Kurt*, *Otto*.

Rodenberg (401) Dutch or German: habitational name from any of various places named Rodenberg, from elements meaning 'red mountain'. One such place is in Hesse.
GIVEN NAMES German 5%. *Dieter*, *Kurt*, *Wolfgang*.

Rodenberger (181) German: habitational name for someone from any of the various places called RODENBERG.

Rodenburg (161) **1.** Dutch and Belgian: habitational name from places so named in West Flanders and the Grand Duchy of Luxembourg. **2.** German: variant of RODENBERG, from *Rotenburg*, an older form of the place name.
GIVEN NAME German 4%. *Erwin*.

Roder (550) **1.** Dutch and North German (also **Röder**): occupational name for someone whose job was to clear woodland for cultivation, from an agent derivative of Middle Dutch *roden* 'to grub up', 'to clear (undergrowth or woodland)'. **2.** German: habitational name from a place called Rod or Rode (see ROD). **3.** German (also

Röder): from the old personal name *Rodher* (a compound of the Germanic elements *hrōd* 'renown' + *hari* 'army'). **4.** German: occupational name in the Rhineland for someone who used a rod to gauge wine casks.
GIVEN NAMES German 4%. *Hans*, *Hartmann*, *Heinrich*, *Horst*, *Juergen*, *Kurt*.

Roderick (2551) **1.** English: from the personal name *Hrōdrīc*, composed of *hrōd* 'renown' + *rīc* 'power(ful)', Old Norse form *Hrøþrekr*. This name was in use among the Normans in the form *Rodric*, but was not frequent in the medieval period. **2.** Welsh: Anglicized form of the personal name *Rhydderch*, originally a byname meaning 'reddish brown'.

Rodes (340) **1.** Catalan and Southern French (**Rodés**): habitational name from any of several places named Rodés, mainly those in El Pallars and El Conflent districts, in northern Catalonia. This has the same origin as Occitan Rodés (Rodez in French), in Avairon department (southern France), which is first recorded in the 6th century in the Latin form *Rutensis*, apparently from the name of the Gaulish tribal name *Ruteni*. **2.** Catalan: variant of RODA, from Catalan *rodes*, the plural of *roda* 'wheel'. **3.** English: variant of RHODES.

Rodewald (442) German: **1.** habitational name from a place so named near Hannover or from places named Rodenwalde in Brandenburg, Mecklenburg, and East Prussia. **2.** from a Germanic personal name, *Hrodowald*, formed with *hrōd* 'renown', 'victory' + *wald* 'rule'.

Rodger (635) Scottish: variant spelling of ROGER 1.

Rodgers (24772) Scottish, northern Irish, and northern English: patronymic from the personal name ROGER 1.

Rodgerson (129) Northern English and Scottish: variant spelling of ROGERSON.

Rodi (257) **1.** Southern Italian: habitational name for someone from Rodi Garganico in Foggia, Rodì Milici in Messina, or from the Greek island of Rhodes. **2.** Greek: variant of **Rodis**.

Rodia (141) **1.** Italian: habitational name from Rodia, a locality in Messina, Sicily. **2.** Greek (**Rodias**): from *rodia* 'pomegranate tree', an occupational name for someone who grew pomegranates or lived by a prominent pomegranate tree.
GIVEN NAMES Italian 11%. *Carmela*, *Giovanni*, *Giuseppe*, *Lorenzo*, *Salvator*.

Rodich (118) **1.** Czech (**Rodič**) and German (of Slavic origin): probably from Old Czech *rodič* 'compatriot', 'fellow countryman'. **2.** German: perhaps a variant of **Rohdich**, from a Germanic personal name based on *hrōd* 'renown', 'victory'. **3.** Serbian and Croatian (**Rodić**); Slovenian (**Rodič**): patronymic from the personal name *Rodo*, a pet form of *Rodoslav*, which is from Slavic *rod* 'relative' + *slav* 'glory', 'fame', or from *Rodoljub*, a derivative of *roditi* 'to give birth'.

Rodick (182) Probably a variant of Scottish and northern Irish REDDICK. Compare RODDICK.

Rodie (104) Scottish: **1.** from a pet form of the personal name RODERICK. **2.** in some cases from Irish RODDY.

Rodier (269) Southern French: occupational name for a wheelwright or topographic name for someone who lived by a waterwheel, from an agent derivative of Occitan *rode* 'wheel' (Latin *rota*).
GIVEN NAMES French 7%. *Alphonse, Armand, Camille.*

Rodiguez (117) Spanish (**Rodíguez**): variant of RODRIGUEZ.
GIVEN NAMES Spanish 49%. *Luis* (4), *Jorge* (3), *Jose* (2), *Juan* (2), *Pedro* (2), *Raul* (2), *Adriana, Alvaro, Ana Luz, Angel, Armando, Arnulfo.*

Rodin (426) **1.** Swedish: variant of **Rodén** (see RODEN). **2.** English: unexplained. **3.** French: from a pet form of RODE. **4.** Russian: unexplained.
GIVEN NAMES Russian 7%. *Andrei* (2), *Yevgeniy* (2), *Alexei, Galina, Gennady, Gregori, Serguei, Vladimir, Yana, Yury.*

Rodine (132) Swedish: variant of **Rodén** (see RODEN).

Rodino (161) Italian (Calabria; **Rodinò**) and Greek (**Rodinos**): from a local personal name derived from medieval Greek *rodino* 'rosy', 'red' (ancient Greek *rhodinos*), which also had the sense 'auspicious', 'promising'.
GIVEN NAMES Italian 11%. *Salvatore* (3), *Antonio, Rocco, Vito.*

Rodio (115) Southern Italian (**Ròdio**): **1.** ethnic name for someone from the Greek island of Rhodes (Greek *Rodos*). **2.** habitational name from Ròdio in Salerno.
GIVEN NAMES Italian 10%. *Carmelo, Nicolo.*

Rodis (107) **1.** Greek: from *rodi* 'pomegranate', classical Greek *rhoidion*, diminutive of *rhoia*, hence an occupational name for someone who grew or sold pomegranates. **2.** Greek: alternatively, a nickname from the Greek dialect word *rodo* 'rose' (classical Greek *rhodon*). **3.** Galician (**Rodís**): habitational name from any of the places in Galicia called Rodis, in the provinces of Lugo, Pontevedra, and A Coruña.
GIVEN NAMES Greek 6%; Spanish 6%. *Antigoni, Costas; Hermilo, Ildefonso, Julio, Manuel, Rogelio.*

Rodkey (377) Probably an Americanized spelling of German RADKE.

Rodman (2245) German: variant of RODEMAN 1.

Rodney (926) English: habitational name from a minor place in Somerset, an area of land in the marshes near Markham. This is first recorded in the form *Rodenye*; it derives from the genitive case of the Old English personal name *Hroda* (a short form

of the various compound names with the first element *hrōð* 'renown') + Old English *ēg* 'island', 'dry land (in a fen)'.
GIVEN NAMES French 4%. *Andre* (2), *Camille* (2), *Evens, Jean Baptiste, Monique.*

Rodocker (194) Probably an altered spelling of German ROTHACKER.

Rodrick (309) English: variant of RODERICK.

Rodrigo (259) Spanish and Portuguese: from the personal name *Rodrigo*, from Germanic *Hrōdrīc* (a compound of *hrōd* 'renown' + *rīc* 'power(ful)'); it was borne by the last of the Visigoth kings and is one of the most important Spanish personal names of Germanic origin. This surname is also found in some former Portuguese territories of western India.
GIVEN NAMES Spanish 27%; Indian 6%. *Manuel* (4), *Elena* (2), *Rafael* (2), *Alfonso, Alicia, Angel, Araceli, Benardo, Carlos, Carlota, Cristina, Emilio; Devi, Dileep, Dilip, Gamini, Mahendra, Manoj, Sunil, Tilak.*

Rodrigue (1539) **1.** Jewish (Sephardic): shortened form of RODRIGUEZ. **2.** French: of Spanish or Portuguese origin (see RODRIGUEZ).
FOREBEARS Rodrigue is a frequent name in LA, where the present families claim descent from Jean-Baptiste Rodrigue, a French Canadian from Quebec, who settled in LA in the 1760s. However, the earliest documented Rodrigue (or Rodrigues) in Canada (1671) was of Portuguese descent.
GIVEN NAMES French 15%. *Normand* (6), *Armand* (4), *Marcel* (4), *Emile* (3), *Fernand* (3), *Jacques* (3), *Yvon* (3), *Andre* (2), *Andree* (2), *Benoit* (2), *Elzear* (2), *Gaetan* (2).

Rodrigues (4744) **1.** Portuguese: patronymic from the Germanic personal name RODRIGO. The surname is also common in the cities of the west coast of India, having been taken there by Portuguese colonists. **2.** Variant spelling of Spanish RODRIGUEZ.
GIVEN NAMES Spanish 27%; Portuguese 14%. *Manuel* (124), *Jose* (118), *Carlos* (47), *Luis* (32), *Mario* (22), *Fernando* (17), *Alberto* (13), *Juan* (13), *Julio* (11), *Armando* (9), *Eduardo* (9), *Francisco* (9); *Joao* (29), *Agostinho* (7), *Paulo* (7), *Joaquim* (6), *Guilherme* (3), *Ilidio* (2), *Serafim* (2), *Vasco* (2), *Albano, Albeiro, Amadeu, Anabela; Antonio* (101), *Mauro* (4), *Leonardo* (3), *Angelo* (2), *Carmelo* (2), *Elvio* (2), *Luciano* (2), *Lucio* (2), *Philomena* (2), *Agostino, Alberico, Aldino.*

Rodriguez (94100) Spanish (**Rodríguez**) and Portuguese: patronymic from the personal name RODRIGO.
GIVEN NAMES Spanish 49%; Portuguese 10%. *Manuel* (918), *Luis* (902), *Carlos* (873), *Jesus* (749), *Francisco* (597), *Jorge* (565), *Pedro* (561), *Raul* (561), *Miguel* (554), *Roberto* (507), *Ramon* (493), *Rafael* (454); *Wenceslao* (7), *Ligia* (6), *Catarina* (5),

Paulo (5), *Joaquim* (4), *Omero* (4), *Zaragoza* (4), *Joao* (2), *Wenseslao* (2), *Adauto, Albeiro, Godofredo.*

Rodriques (302) Portuguese: respelling of Portuguese RODRIGUES and possibly also of Spanish **Rodríguez** (see RODRIGUEZ).
GIVEN NAMES Spanish 29%; Portuguese 13%. *Jose* (5), *Manuel* (4), *Luis* (3), *Carlos* (2), *Fernando* (2), *Francisco* (2), *Gilberto* (2), *Juan* (2), *Adriano, Agusto, Alfredo, Alicia; Joao* (3), *Joaquim* (2), *Paulo.*

Rodriquez (5664) Spanish (**Rodríquez**; Spain and Philippines): variant spelling of Spanish RODRIGUEZ.

Rodway (116) English: habitational name from Rodway in Somerset, Radway in Warwickshire or Devon, or Reddaway or Roadway, both in Devon. The modern surname appears to relate principally to the Warwickshire place name, which is from Old English *rēad* 'red' (or possibly *rād* 'ride') + *weg* 'way'.

Rodwell (329) English (chiefly East Anglia): apparently a habitational name from an unidentified place, perhaps named with the Old English personal name *Hroda* (see RODNEY) + Old English *well(a)* 'spring', 'stream'.

Rody (209) **1.** German: variant of RODE 1. **2.** Variant spelling of Scottish **Rodie**, from a pet form of RODERICK.

Roe (9315) **1.** English: nickname for a timid person, from Middle English *ro* 'roe'; this is a midland and southern form of RAY 2. **2.** Norwegian: habitational name from any of several farmsteads named Roe or Røe, from Old Norse *ruð* 'clearing'. **3.** English name adopted by bearers of French BAILLARGEON. **4.** Korean: variant of NO.

Roeber (374) German (**Röber**): **1.** habitational name from a place named Roben, for example in Thuringia or Schleswig. **2.** from a Germanic personal name based on *hrōd* 'renown', 'victory'. **3.** Low German variant of **Räuber** (see RAUBER).
GIVEN NAMES German 4%. *Detlef, Frieda, Hans, Horst, Otto.*

Roebke (164) North German (**Röbke**): from a pet form of ROBERT.
GIVEN NAME German 4%. *Kurt.*

Roebuck (1782) English: from Middle English *robuc(k)* 'roebuck', applied as a nickname for someone thought to resemble the animal.

Roecker (341) German: variant of ROCKER 2.
GIVEN NAMES German 5%. *Berthold, Fritz, Gerhardt, Kurt, Otto.*

Roed (152) **1.** German: from a short form of the Germanic personal name *Hrodo*, from *hrōd* 'renown', 'fame'. **2.** Norwegian (**Røed**): variant of ROE. **3.** Danish: either from a byname, *Roth*, meaning 'root', or from a Danish place name.
GIVEN NAMES Scandinavian 16%; German 4%. *Bente, Berent, Egil, Jorgen, Karsten, Knute, Ludvig, Ove.*

Roedel (400) German (**Rödel**): **1.** metonymic occupational name for a scribe or registrar, from Middle High German *rodel* 'list', 'roll' (Latin *rotula* 'scroll'). **2.** habitational name from Rödel in Saxony and Rhineland. **3.** from a pet form of a Germanic personal name, *Rodilo*, formed with *hrōd* 'fame', 'renown'.
GIVEN NAMES German 4%. *Armin, Erwin, Gerhart, Otto.*

Roedell (109) Americanized form of German ROEDEL.

Roeder (2677) German (**Röder**): **1.** variant of RODER. **2.** habitational name for someone from any of the places named Rödern, in Alsace, Rhineland, and Saxony, or Röderau in Saxony, or from any of various places in Germany and Austria called Rode.
GIVEN NAMES German 4%. *Kurt* (3), *Otto* (3), *Heinrich* (2), *Merwin* (2), *Dieter, Dietrich, Eberhard, Erwin, Florian, Fritzy, Hans.*

Roederer (169) South German (**Röderer**): variant of ROEDER 2.
GIVEN NAME French 5%. *Philippe.*

Roediger (262) North German (**Rödiger**): variant of *Rüdiger* (see RUDIGER).

Roedl (180) South German: variant of ROEDEL.

Roeger (110) German (**Röger**): **1.** from a reduced form of the personal name *Rödiger*, Low German form of *Rüdiger* (see RUDIGER). **2.** habitational name of Slavic origin from Roga, Pomerania. **3.** Low German form of RUEGER 2.
GIVEN NAMES German 13%. *Otto* (2), *Armin, Theresia.*

Roeglin (105) German: habitational name, probably of Slavic origin, from an unidentified place in eastern Germany.

Roegner (177) German: **1.** occupational name from Middle High German *rokkener* 'baker of rye bread' (from Middle High German *rogge, rocke* 'rye'). **2.** habitational name for someone from Rögen near Coburg. **3.** possibly also a nickname from Middle High German *rogener* 'female fish'.
GIVEN NAME German 4%. *Kurt.*

Roehl (1015) German (**Röhle**): **1.** from a short form of the personal names RUDOLF or ROLAND. **2.** habitational name from a place so called near Trier.
GIVEN NAMES German 4%. *Kurt* (3), *Erwin* (2), *Hans* (2), *Benno, Frieda, Otto, Raimund, Wolfgang.*

Roehling (120) German (**Röhling**): see ROHLING.
GIVEN NAME German 4%. *Hertha.*

Roehm (594) German (**Röhm**): variant of REHM.
GIVEN NAMES German 5%. *Kurt* (4), *Klaus* (2), *Eberhard, Gerhard.*

Roehr (339) German (**Röhr**): **1.** variant of ROHR. **2.** North German: reduced form of **Röder** (see ROEDER 2). **3.** from a reduced form of a Germanic personal name, *Rothari*, based on *hrōd* 'renown', 'victory'.

GIVEN NAMES German 5%. *Alois, Claus, Horst, Kurt, Manfred.*

Roehrich (282) German and French (Alsace): variant of ROEHRIG.

Roehrig (511) German (**Röhrig**): **1.** topographic name from Middle High German *rōrach, rœrach* 'reed bed', or a habitational name from any of four places named with this word. **2.** from a Germanic personal name, *Hrodric*, from *hrōd* 'renown', 'victory'.
GIVEN NAMES German 4%. *Gerd* (2), *Hans* (2), *Frieda, Jutta, Manfred.*

Roehrs (204) North German (**Röhrs**): patronymic from a reduced form of **Röder** (see ROEDER 2).
GIVEN NAMES German 6%. *Ingo, Kurt, Otto.*

Roelfs (126) German: variant of ROHLFS.

Roelke (175) North German (**Rölke**): from a pet form of the personal names RUDOLF or ROLAND.

Roell (440) German and Swiss German (**Röll**): see ROLL.
GIVEN NAMES German 4%. *Otto* (2), *Eberhard, Hans.*

Roelle (159) **1.** French: from *roelle* 'disc' (Latin *rotella*, diminutive of *rota* 'wheel'). **2.** German: variant of **Röll** (see ROLL).

Roelofs (395) Dutch and North German: patronymic from the personal name *Roelof*, a Low German form of RUDOPH.
GIVEN NAMES Dutch 4%. *Gerrit, Harm, Hendrik, Henk, Jantje, Pieter.*

Roels (104) Dutch and Flemish: patronymic from a short form of the Germanic personal names *Roeland* (see ROLAND) or *Roelof* (see ROELOFS).
GIVEN NAME French 8%. *Romain.*

Roemer (1602) German (**Römer**): **1.** nickname for a pilgrim, Middle High German *Rœmer* (literally 'Roman'). **2.** habitational name for someone from Rom near Ludwigslust or Röhmen in Württemberg. **3.** nickname from Middle Low German *romer* 'braggart'. **4.** from a personal name composed of the Old High German elements *hrōd* 'renown' + *māri* 'outstanding', 'famous'. **5.** habitational name from a house so named because of its situation near Roman remains, as for example the Frankfurt city hall.
GIVEN NAMES German 5%. *Kurt* (5), *Hans* (3), *Otto* (3), *Erwin* (2), *Ingo* (2), *Armin, Gerhard, Gunther, Helmut, Horst.*

Roemhildt (118) German (**Römhild**): **1.** habitational name from Römhild in Thuringia. **2.** in some cases from a Germanic personal name composed of *ruom* 'fame' + *wald* 'rule', 'power'.
GIVEN NAMES German 6%. *Armin, Bernhardt, Erwin.*

Roemmich (213) German (**Römmich**): from a variant of the medieval personal name *Remigius*, which was particularly popular in the Palatinate.
GIVEN NAMES German 4%. *Otto, Reinhold.*

Roen (310) **1.** German: from a Germanic personal name derived from *rūn* 'rune', 'secret'. **2.** Norwegian (**Røen**): variant of ROE. **3.** Perhaps an altered spelling of German **Rönn**, a habitational name for someone from any of the places named Rönne, near Bielefeld, Kiel, and Winsen in northern Germany.

Roeper (188) German (also **Röper**): see ROEBER.
GIVEN NAMES German 9%; Scandinavian 4%. *Gerd* (4), *Hans* (2), *Inge, Jurgen, Kurt.*

Roepke (655) North German (also **Röpke**): from a pet form of the personal name *Rupprecht*, a variant of ROBERT.

Roerig (157) North German: variant of **Röhrig** (see ROEHRIG).

Roering (153) North German (also **Röring**): variant of **Röhrig** (see ROEHRIG).

Roers (143) **1.** Dutch: occupational name from Dutch *roer*, Middle Dutch *ro(e)der, rueder* 'gauger of wine casks'. **2.** North German (**Röers**): variant of **Röder** (see RODER 1).
GIVEN NAMES German 4%. *Florian, Matthias.*

Roes (171) Dutch and North German: **1.** habitational name for someone who lived at a house distinguished by the sign of a rose, Middle Dutch *roose*. **2.** from the female personal name *Rosa*.
GIVEN NAMES German 5%. *Heinz, Ursel.*

Roesch (1214) German and Swiss German (**Rösch**): nickname from Middle High German *rösch, rosch* 'quick', 'lively', 'brave'.
GIVEN NAMES German 5%. *Juergen* (4), *Kurt* (2), *Dieter, Guenter, Klaus, Otto, Rainer, Siegfried.*

Roese (272) German: **1.** variant of ROSE. **2.** (**Röse**) possibly a habitational name for someone from a place named Rösa near Bitterfeld.

Roesel (169) German (also **Rösel**): diminutive of ROSE.
GIVEN NAMES German 5%. *Erwin* (2), *Otto.*

Roeseler (121) German (also **Röseler**): variant of **Rösler** (see ROESLER).
GIVEN NAME German 6%. *Armin.*

Roesener (118) German (also **Rösener**): variant of ROSENER.
GIVEN NAME German 4%. *Kurt.*

Roeser (516) German (also **Röser**): **1.** variant of ROSSER. **2.** from a short form of any of the Germanic personal names formed with *hrōd* 'renown', for example RUDIGER.

Roeske (363) German (also **Röske**): from a pet form of ROSE.
GIVEN NAMES German 5%. *Erhardt, Ilse, Kurt, Otto, Siegfried.*

Roesler (1019) German (also **Rösler**): **1.** occupational name for a rose grower, from an agent derivative of Middle High German *röse* 'rose'. **2.** variant of **Rössler** (see ROESSLER). **3.** variant of RESLER in eastern German. **4.** from a short form of a

Germanic personal name formed with *hrōd* 'renown'.
GIVEN NAMES German 6%. *Ewald* (3), *Erwin* (2), *Helmut* (2), *Helmuth* (2), *Alois*, *Erhard*, *Hans*, *Juergen*, *Kurt*, *Manfred*, *Meggan*, *Otto*.

Roesner (379) German (also **Rösner**): variant of ROSNER.
GIVEN NAMES German 5%. *Achim*, *Franz*, *Gerd*, *Gerhard*, *Kurt*, *Ute*, *Wolfgang*.

Roessel (127) German (also **Rössel**): possibly in some cases an occupational name for a horse dealer, from a diminutive of Middle High German *röss* 'horse'; otherwise a habitational name from a house named with this word, for example *zum weissen Rössl* 'at (the sign of) the little white horse'.
GIVEN NAME Scandinavian 4%. *Hilmar* (2).

Roesser (102) German (**Rösser**): topographic name from Middle High German *ræsse* 'pool for retting flax'.

Roessler (985) German (also **Rössler**): occupational name for someone who bred, handled, worked, rode, or owned horses, from an agent derivative of Middle High German *ros*, *ors* 'horse', 'steed'.
GIVEN NAMES German 6%. *Fritz* (4), *Klaus* (2), *Wenzel* (2), *Erwin*, *Hans*, *Heinz*, *Helmut*, *Horst*, *Konrad*, *Kurt*, *Manfred*, *Ralf*.

Roessner (188) German (also **Rössner**): variant of ROSSNER.
GIVEN NAMES German 8%. *Reinhold* (2), *Klaus*, *Kurt*, *Wilhelm*.

Roeth (137) German: from a short form of a Germanic personal name formed with *hrōd* 'renown', as for example RUDOLF.

Roethel (161) German (also **Röthel**): diminutive of ROTH.
GIVEN NAMES German 15%. *Reinhold* (2), *Albrecht*, *Dieter*, *Gerhard*, *Guenther*, *Helmut*, *Wilhelm*.

Roether (155) German: from the Germanic personal name *Rodher* (see RODER 2).
GIVEN NAME German 4%. *Hermann*.

Roethle (107) German (**Röthle**): metonymic occupational name for a scribe or registrar, from Middle High German *rodel* 'list', 'roll'. See also ROETHLER.

Roethler (199) German (**Röthler**): 1. occupational name for a scribe or registrar, from an agent derivative of Middle High German *rodel* 'list', 'roll' (Latin *rotula* 'scroll'). 2. from a variant of *Rödler*, a pet form of the personal name RUDOLF.

Roethlisberger (110) Swiss German: habitational name for someone from a place called Röthlisberg or Rödlingsberg, so named from the personal name *Rödling*, a pet form of RUDOLF + Middle High German *berc* 'mountain'.

Roetman (137) Dutch: variant of ROTMAN.

Roets (176) Dutch: patronymic from a short form of any of the Germanic personal names beginning with the element *hrōd* 'fame'.

Roettger (486) North German (also **Röttger**): variant of RUDIGER or ROGER.

Roetzel (132) German (also **Rötzel**): probably a habitational name from Rotzel in Baden-Württemberg.

Roetzer (108) German (also **Rötzer**): habitational name for someone from a place in the Upper Palatinate called Rötz.
GIVEN NAMES German 12%. *Hans* (2), *Alois*, *Dieter*, *Florian*, *Gerhard*, *Helmut*.

Roever (198) North German (also **Röver**): derogatory nickname from Middle Low German *rover* 'robber'.
GIVEN NAMES German 6%. *Otto* (2), *Bernhard*, *Wilfried*.

Roewe (105) North German (**Röwe**): metonymic occupational name for a grower or seller of turnips, from Middle Low German *rove* 'turnip'.

Roff (554) 1. English: variant of ROLFE. 2. North German: variant of RUOFF.

Roffe (156) 1. English: variant of ROLF. 2. Jewish: occupational name from Hebrew *rofe* 'physician'.
GIVEN NAMES Jewish 4%. *Gady*, *Hyman*.

Roffers (137) German: patronymic from a Germanic personal name composed of *hrōd* 'renown' + *frid-* 'peace'.

Roffman (205) 1. German (**Roffmann**): from the personal name *Roff* + *man* 'man'. 2. Variant of Dutch **Rofman**, from Middle Dutch *roef* 'roof', 'ceiling' + *man* 'man', hence an occupational name for a roof builder. 3. Jewish (Ashkenazic): elaborated variant of ROFFE.
GIVEN NAME Jewish 4%. *Amiram*.

Rog (148) 1. Polish: nickname from *róg* 'horn', or occupational name for someone whose job was to blow a horn. 2. Dutch: from *rog* 'ray', hence perhaps a nickname for someone thought to resemble the fish or a habitational name for someone who lived at a house distinguished by the sign of a ray. 3. Dutch: variant of ROGGE.
GIVEN NAMES Polish 12%. *Bronislaw*, *Jacek*, *Janusz*, *Kazimierz*, *Ryszard*, *Zofia*.

Rogacki (156) Polish: habitational name from either of two places named Rogacz, in Rzeszów and Tarnobrzeg voivodeships, or from Rogacze in Białystok voivodeship. Both these place names are derived from Polish *rogacz* 'deer', 'stag'.
GIVEN NAMES Polish 8%. *Boleslaw*, *Casimir*, *Jerzy*, *Miroslaw*.

Rogal (150) 1. Polish and Jewish (eastern Ashkenazic): variant of ROGALA. 2. Jewish (eastern Ashkenazic): habitational name from the village Rogal(e), in Poland. 3. German variant of Polish ROGALA.
GIVEN NAME Jewish 4%. *Hyman*.

Rogala (416) Polish and Jewish (from Poland): nickname from Polish *rogala* 'roe deer'. This term also means 'croissant', and may be an occupational name for a baker. As a Jewish name it is generally of ornamental origin.
GIVEN NAMES Polish 7%. *Casimir* (2), *Krystyna* (2), *Bronislaw*, *Irena*, *Jacek*, *Miroslaw*, *Thadeus*.

Rogalla (184) 1. Germanized spelling of Polish ROGALA. 2. Eastern German: topographic name for someone who lived at the edge of a settlement, from Czech or Sorbian *roh* 'horn' or a habitational name for someone from a place named Rogallen.
GIVEN NAME French 4%. *Marcell*.

Rogalski (741) Polish and Jewish (from Poland): habitational name for someone from Rogal in Kalisz voivodeship, or from any of several places called Rogale. The place names are derived from *rogal* '(roe) deer', 'stag'.
GIVEN NAMES Polish 8%. *Andrzej* (4), *Casimir* (4), *Bogdan*, *Bronislaus*, *Czeslaw*, *Janina*, *Karol*, *Kazimierz*, *Lucja*, *Stanislaw*, *Tadeusz*, *Wieslaw*.

Rogalsky (120) Jewish (from Poland): variant spelling of ROGALSKI.

Rogan (1613) Irish: reduced Anglicized form of Gaelic **Ó Ruadhagáin** 'son of *Ruadhagán*', a personal name from a diminutive of *ruadh* 'red'.
GIVEN NAME Irish 5%. *Bridie*.

Rogel (259) 1. Spanish: from the personal name *Rogel*, Spanish form of French ROGER. 2. German: of uncertain origin; perhaps a nickname for a mischievous person, from Middle High German *rogel* 'loose'. 3. Slovenian: nickname or topographic name from *rogelj* 'horn', 'point', as a topographic name probably denoting someone who lived on a horn-shaped spur or ridge of a hill or on a pointed piece of land.
GIVEN NAMES Spanish 31%. *Jesus* (3), *Jose* (2), *Jose Luis* (2), *Juan* (2), *Marcos* (2), *Margarita* (2), *Wilfredo* (2), *Adilia*, *Alejandro*, *Ana Gladys*, *Ana Maria*, *Anacleto*.

Roger (1033) 1. Scottish, English, North German, French, and Catalan: from a Germanic personal name composed of the elements *hrōd* 'renown' + *gār*, *gēr* 'spear', 'lance', which was introduced into England by the Normans in the form *Rog(i)er*. The cognate Old Norse *Hróðgeirr* was a reinforcing influence in Normandy. 2. Irish: reduced Anglicized form of Gaelic **Mac Ruaidhrí** (see RORIE).
FOREBEARS In its French form, this name arrived in Quebec City in 1648 from Paris. LABRIE is an attested secondary surname.
GIVEN NAMES French 9%. *Philippe* (3), *Alcee* (2), *Armand* (2), *Laurent* (2), *Leonce* (2), *Marcel* (2), *Yves* (2), *Clovis*, *Fernand*, *Gilberte*, *Janvier*, *Jean Claude*.

Rogero (109) 1. Spanish and Italian: from the personal name *Rogero*, a variant of *Rogel*, *Roger* (see ROGER). 2. Catalan (**Rogeró**): possibly from a diminutive of the personal name ROGER, or nickname from Catalan *roger*, *rogeró* 'red mullet' (fish).
GIVEN NAMES Spanish 4%. *Cayetano*, *Jose*, *Silva*.

Rogers (106345) English: patronymic from the personal name ROGER.

FOREBEARS Thomas Rogers (*c.*1587–1621), born in London, England, was among the Pilgrim Fathers who sailed on the *Mayflower* in 1620. He died during the first winter at Plymouth Colony, but his son Joseph survived and married, and was later joined in MA by his brother John. This name was subsequently brought to North America independently by many different bearers.

Rogerson (1130) Northern English and Scottish: patronymic from the personal name ROGER.

Rogg (152) German: variant of ROGGE.
GIVEN NAME German 5%. *Oskar* (2).

Rogge (1103) **1.** German and Dutch: from a short form of the personal name ROGER. **2.** North German and Dutch: metonymic occupational name for a grower of rye or a baker of rye bread, from Low German, Dutch *rogge* 'rye'.
GIVEN NAMES German 4%. *Kurt* (2), *Otto* (2), *Bernd*, *Bernhard*, *Elke*, *Hans*, *Helmut*, *Wolfgang*.

Roggenbuck (258) German: Low German variant of **Roggenbauch**, a nickname for an obese man, from Middle High German *rogge* 'rye' + *būch* 'belly'.
GIVEN NAMES German 7%. *Achim* (2), *Jutta*, *Otto*, *Rudie*, *Wolf*.

Roggenkamp (252) North German and Dutch: topographic name for someone who lived by a rye field or a domain where rye was grown, from Middle Low German *rogge* 'rye' + *kamp* 'field', 'domain'.
GIVEN NAMES French 6%; German 4%. *Monique* (2), *Alphonse*, *Patrice*; *Klaus* (2), *Christoph*.

Roggie (100) Scottish: variant spelling of **Rogie**, which is probably a habitational name from Rogie in the parish of Fodderty, Ross-shire.

Roggow (247) German: habitational name from any of the places so named, in Brandenburg, Mecklenburg, and Pomerania.

Rogier (179) French: variant of ROGER.
GIVEN NAMES French 7%. *Herve* (2), *Alain*.

Rogillio (142) Origin unidentified. This is a LA name, apparently from a Germanic personal name cognate with ROGER.

Rogin (107) Jewish (from Belarus): habitational name from any of various villages named Rogi or from Rogin, all in Belarus.
GIVEN NAMES Jewish 4%. *Miriam*, *Tsvi*.

Rogina (121) Origin uncertain; probably Croatian.

Roginski (205) Polish (**Rogiński**): habitational name for someone from any of various places called Rogi, named with *róg* 'horn' (see ROG).
GIVEN NAMES Polish 6%. *Andrzej*, *Danuta*, *Jozef*, *Tadeusz*.

Rogne (154) Norwegian: habitational name from any of several farmsteads so named,

from Old Norse *hraun* 'rock-strewn ground' or *raunn* 'rowan tree', or from a word meaning 'long ridge'.

Rogness (309) Norwegian: habitational name from a farmstead named Rognes, from the name of a river or Old Norse *raunn* 'rowan tree' + *nes* 'headland', 'promontory'.
GIVEN NAME Scandinavian 4%. *Thor* (2).

Rogoff (424) Jewish (from Lithuania and Belarus): alternative spelling of **Rogov**, a habitational name from Raguva near Kaunas in Lithuania (Russian name *Rogovo*).
GIVEN NAMES Jewish 6%. *Irit* (2), *Chaim*, *Ilan*, *Isadore*, *Shoshanna*, *Sol*.

Rogovin (135) Jewish: variant of ROGOFF.
GIVEN NAME Jewish 7%. *Zvi*.

Rogow (151) Jewish (eastern Ashkenazic): variant spelling of ROGOFF.
GIVEN NAMES Jewish 6%. *Abbe*, *Asher*.

Rogowski (767) Polish and Jewish (from Poland): habitational name for someone from Rogów, Rogowa, or Rogowo, all named with the personal name *Róg*.
GIVEN NAMES Polish 6%. *Eugeniusz* (2), *Tadeusz* (2), *Casimir*, *Dariusz*, *Janina*, *Jaroslaw*, *Jerzy*, *Miroslaw*, *Thadeus*, *Witold*, *Zbigniew*, *Zygmund*.

Rogozinski (196) Polish (**Rogoziński**) and Jewish (from Poland): habitational name for someone from some place named with Polish *rogoża* 'bulrush', for example Rogoźnica, Rogoźnik, Rogoźno, or Rogożno.
GIVEN NAMES Polish 6%; German 4%. *Bronislaw*, *Casimir*; *Hans*.

Rogstad (220) Norwegian: habitational name from any of several farmsteads named Rogstad, Rokstad, or Rostad, from a personal name (for example Old Norse *Hrólfr*, a compound of *hróðolfr* 'fame', 'honor' + *ulfr* 'wolf', or *Hróarr*, of which the second element is *-arr* 'spear') + *staðir* 'farmstead', 'dwelling'.
GIVEN NAMES Scandinavian 5%; German 4%. *Erik*, *Lief*, *Selmer*; *Kurt* (2), *Ingwald*.

Rogus (223) German (of Slavic origin): topographic name for someone who lived where reeds grew, from Sorbian *rogoscha* 'rush'.

Roh (411) **1.** German: nickname for a crude person, from Middle Low German *rō* 'raw', 'rough'. This name is found in particular among Germans who settled in Russia in the 18th and early 19th centuries. **2.** Korean: variant of No.
GIVEN NAMES Korean 29%. *Young* (8), *Jae* (3), *Jin* (3), *Kun Soo* (2), *Won* (2), *Yong Sik* (2), *Chanho*, *Choong*, *Dong*, *Duk*, *Heung*, *Hong Shik*; *Byung* (2), *Chung*, *Dong Chul*, *Hak*, *Heewon*, *In Sup*, *Joo Hyun*, *Jung Ok*, *Junghoon*, *Ki Sung*, *Seong*.

Rohal (115) Hungarian (**Rohál**): variant of ROHALY.

Rohaly (110) Hungarian (**Rohály**): probably a derivative of *Roh*, nickname for some-

one with red hair or ruddy complexion, from *roh* 'red'.

Rohan (1081) **1.** French: habitational name from a place in Morbihan, in Brittany. There is also another place of the same name in Deux-Sèvres, which may have contributed to the surname. **2.** Irish: reduced Anglicized form of Gaelic **Ó Ruadháin** (see RUANE).
GIVEN NAMES Irish 5%. *Brendan*, *Brigid*, *Kieran*, *Oonagh*, *Padraig*, *Siobhan*.

Rohde (3086) German: variant of RODE 3.
GIVEN NAMES German 4%. *Erwin* (6), *Kurt* (5), *Otto* (3), *Bernd* (2), *Hans* (2), *Heino* (2), *Heinz* (2), *Ewald*, *Gerhard*, *Helmut*, *Hermann*, *Klaus*.

Rohe (580) North German (also **Röhe**): from a short form of a Germanic personal name formed with Middle High German *röhen* 'to roar' or Old High German *ruoh* 'care', 'intent' (see ROCH).

Roher (223) German (**Röher**): **1.** nickname for a rowdy or boisterous person, from an agent derivative of Middle High German *röhen* 'to make a noise'. **2.** reduced form of **Röder** (see ROEDER).

Rohl (367) German (**Röhl**): see ROEHL.

Rohland (241) German: **1.** variant spelling of ROLAND. **2.** habitational name from a place called Rohland in Westphalia, named as *Rodeland*, denoting a plot of land in a clearing.
GIVEN NAMES German 6%. *Gunter* (2), *Gerhard*, *Otto*.

Rohleder (353) German: metonymic occupational name for a tanner, from Middle High German *rō* 'raw' + *leder* 'leather'.
GIVEN NAMES German 4%. *Erwin* (2), *Otto* (2), *Detlef*, *Helmut*.

Rohlf (273) German: from a reduced form of the personal name *Rohloff*, a variant of RUDOLF.

Rohlfing (554) North German: patronymic from ROHLF.
GIVEN NAMES German 4%. *Liesl* (2), *Alois*, *Otto*.

Rohlfs (367) German: patronymic from ROHLF.
GIVEN NAMES German 6%. *Claus* (3), *Fritz*, *Heinz*, *Kurt*, *Otto*.

Rohling (338) German (**Röhling**): **1.** patronymic from ROEHL. **2.** nickname from Middle High German *rölich* 'raw', 'crude', 'ungodly'.
GIVEN NAMES German 6%. *Kurt* (2), *Gotthard*, *Othmar*, *Otto*.

Rohlman (211) German: from a short form of a Germanic personal name formed with *hrōd* 'renown' (for example RUDOLF) + *man* 'man'.

Rohloff (658) German: from the Germanic personal name *Hrodulf*, composed of *hrōd* 'renown' + *(w)ulf* 'wolf', for example RUDOLF.
GIVEN NAMES German 4%. *Horst* (2), *Florian*, *Franz*, *Fritz*, *Hans*, *Otto*.

Rohm (657) German: **1.** from the Germanic personal name *Ruom* (Old High German *hruom* 'fame'), a short form of *Ruombald* and similar personal names containing this element. **2. (Röhm):** see ROEHM.

Rohman (333) Respelling of North German ROHMANN.

Rohmann (108) North German: variant of **Rodemann** (see RODEMAN).
GIVEN NAMES German 10%. *Heinz, Helmut, Klaus.*

Rohmer (128) German: from a Germanic personal name composed of the elements *hruom* 'fame' + *heri* 'army' or *hrōd* 'renown' + *māri* 'famous', 'known'.
GIVEN NAME French 4%. *Patrice.*

Rohn (800) German: **1.** nickname for a coarse or uncouth person, from Middle High German *ron(e)* 'stump', 'block'. **2.** habitational name from places named Rohne, Rohna, or Ronau in Silesia, Thuringia, and Saxony. **3.** from a short form of the medieval personal name *Hieronymus* (see JEROME).

Rohner (543) Swiss German: **1.** habitational name for someone from any of various places named Rohne, Rohna, or Ronau (see ROHN 2). **2.** topographic name for someone living by an area of dead trees, from Middle High German *ron(e)* 'fallen tree', 'block of wood'. **3.** from a Germanic personal name formed with *rune* 'rune'.
GIVEN NAMES German 4%. *Ernst, Erwin, Fritz, Hans, Hedwig, Horst.*

Rohr (2484) **1.** German and Swiss German: topographic name for someone who lived in an area thickly grown with reeds, from Middle High German *rōr* (a collective singular) or near a well or channel *rōr*, or a habitational name from one of the several places named with this word. **2.** Jewish (Ashkenazic): ornamental from German *Rohr* 'reed' (see 1 above).

Rohrbach (1140) German and Swiss German: habitational name from any of numerous places called Rohrbach ('reed brook' or 'channel brook') in many parts of Germany, Switzerland, and Austria.
GIVEN NAMES German 4%. *Kurt* (3), *Milbert* (2), *Eldred, Erhart, Gerhard, Helmuth, Otto, Urs.*

Rohrbacher (369) German: habitational name for someone from any of the many places called ROHRBACH.
GIVEN NAMES German 4%. *Siegfried* (3), *Erwin, Kurt.*

Rohrback (203) Americanized spelling of German ROHRBACH.

Rohrbaugh (961) Americanized spelling of German ROHRBACH.

Rohrbeck (109) German: habitational name from any of numerous places named Rohrbeck, cognate with ROHRBACH.
GIVEN NAME German 4%. *Hartwig.*

Rohrbough (161) Americanized form of German ROHRBACH.

Rohrer (3114) German and Swiss German: habitational name for someone from any of the many places named with Middle High German *rōr* 'reed bed' or *rōr* 'well', 'channel' (see ROHR).

Rohrich (189) German (**Röhrich, Röhrig**): see ROEHRIG.
GIVEN NAME German 4%. *Manfred.*

Rohrig (309) German (**Röhrig**): see ROEHRIG.

Rohrman (184) German (**Rohrmann**): variant of ROHR, with the addition of *man* 'man'.
GIVEN NAME French 4%. *Andre.*

Rohrs (518) German (**Röhrs**): reduced form of **Röders**, variant of ROEDER.
GIVEN NAMES German 7%. *Kurt* (4), *Erna* (2), *Otto* (2), *Wetzel, Wolfgang.*

Rohs (143) German: variant spelling of ROSS.

Rohwedder (164) North German: nickname for a moody or cantankerous man, from Middle Low German *ro(u)w* 'rough', 'raw' + *weder* 'weather'.
GIVEN NAMES German 11%. *Otto* (2), *Arno, Ekkehard, Gerd, Heinz, Klaus.*

Rohweder (185) North German: nickname for a moody or cantankerous man, from Middle Low German *ro(u)w* 'rough', 'raw' + *weder* 'weather'.
GIVEN NAMES German 4%. *Erwin, Gitta, Hans.*

Rohwer (386) German: **1.** contracted form of ROHWEDDER. **2. (Röhwer)** variant spelling of **Röwer** (see ROEVER).
GIVEN NAMES German 5%. *Franz, Gunter, Ilse, Klaus, Lorenz, Otto.*

Roig (370) Catalan: nickname for someone with red hair or a ruddy complexion, from *roig* 'ruddy', 'red' (Latin *rubeus*).
GIVEN NAMES Spanish 40%. *Jose* (15), *Carlos* (7), *Juan* (6), *Ramon* (6), *Jorge* (5), *Francisco* (4), *Jaime* (3), *Aida* (2), *Armando* (2), *Aurelio* (2), *Cristina* (2), *Cristobal* (2).

Roiger (150) German: variant of REIGER.
GIVEN NAMES German 7%. *Gerhardt, Heinz, Kurt, Otto.*

Roisum (100) Norwegian: habitational name from the farmstead in Sogn named Røysum, from the dative plural of Old Norse *reysi* 'heap of stones'.
GIVEN NAME Scandinavian 4%. *Anders.*

Roitman (134) Jewish (eastern Ashkenazic): nickname for a red-headed man, from Yiddish *royt* 'red' + *man* 'man'. Compare ROTHMAN.
GIVEN NAMES Jewish 21%; Russian 13%. *Yakov* (2), *Avram, Iakov, Ilya, Khaim, Noach, Sol, Zvi; Mikhail* (3), *Efim* (2), *Boris, Liya, Semyon, Shelya, Simkha, Vladimir.*

Rojas (7792) Spanish: habitational name from places in Burgos or Lugo (Galicia) named Rojas, from a derivative of *rojo* 'red'.
GIVEN NAMES Spanish 52%. *Jose* (231), *Juan* (126), *Luis* (99), *Carlos* (93), *Manuel* (75),

Jorge (72), *Jesus* (70), *Francisco* (60), *Pedro* (59), *Ricardo* (46), *Rafael* (45), *Raul* (42).

Rojek (220) **1.** Polish: from a pet form of the Polish personal name *Rój.* **2.** Polish and Jewish (from Poland): from a diminutive of the vocabulary word *rój* 'hive', 'swarm'.
GIVEN NAMES Polish 16%; German 4%; French 4%. *Stanislaw* (2), *Alicja, Dorota, Elzbieta, Janusz, Krystyna, Leszek, Mariola, Miroslaw, Wladyslaw, Wojciech; Andreas, Hertha; Andre, Michelene.*

Rojewski (76) Polish: habitational name for someone from Rojew or Rojewo in Bydgoszcz voivodeship, both named with the personal name *Rój* or possibly the vocabulary word *rój* 'swarm', 'hive'.
GIVEN NAMES Polish 11%. *Andrzej, Janusz, Zdzislaw.*

Rojo (785) Spanish: **1.** nickname for someone with red hair, from *rojo* 'red' (Latin *rubeus*). **2.** habitational name from either of two places in Galicia called Rojo, in A Coruña and Lugo provinces.
GIVEN NAMES Spanish 51%. *Jesus* (13), *Jose* (12), *Manuel* (12), *Mario* (8), *Angel* (6), *Eduardo* (6), *Francisco* (5), *Gustavo* (5), *Juan* (5), *Miguel* (5), *Carlos* (4), *Fernando* (4).

Roker (110) German (also **Röker**): of uncertain origin. In the north, it may be from a short form of a Germanic personal name from *hrok* 'rook', or alternatively from an agent derivative of Middle Low German *rōk* 'smoke' and hence an occupational name for someone who smoked fish or meat or for a blacksmith or charcoal burner. In the east it could be an occupational name for a beekeeper, from Slavic *roj* 'swarm of bees'.

Rokes (133) English: **1.** variant of **Roke**, a topographic name for someone who lived near an oak tree (see OAK), from a misdivision of Middle English *atter oke* 'at the oak'. Roke in Oxfordshire and Rock in Worcestershire are named in this way, and so the surname may be habitational in some cases. **2.** possibly a variant of ROCK 1.

Rokicki (164) Polish: topographic name for someone living by a willow or osier, from *rokita* 'willow', 'osier'.
GIVEN NAMES Polish 13%. *Jaroslaw* (3), *Andrzej, Bronislaus, Henryk, Janusz, Kazimierz, Miroslawa.*

Rokita (117) Polish, Czech, and Slovak (**Rakyta**): from Slavic *rokita* 'osier', a topographic name for someone living where osiers grew, or a metonymic occupational name for a basket maker who made baskets out of osier branches.
GIVEN NAMES Polish 9%. *Mieczyslaw, Wladyslaw, Zbigniew.*

Rokos (141) **1.** Czech: from a dialect variant of Czech *rákos*, a topographic name for someone who lived by a reedbed, a nickname for a tall, slender person, or a metonymic occupational name for a basket-maker, from *rákos* in the sense of cane or wickerwork. **2.** Greek: from the personal name *Rok(k)os*, Greek form of Italian Rocco.

Rokosz (184) Polish: nickname from Polish *rokosz* 'rebellion'.
GIVEN NAMES Polish 9%. *Bogumil, Bronislawa, Eugeniusz, Janusz, Stanislaw.*

Rokusek (171) Czech (**Rokůsek**): from a diminutive of ROKOS 'reed'.
GIVEN NAME French 4%. *Laurier.*

Rolan (191) Spanish (**Rolán**): from the personal name *Rolán*, a variant of ROLANDO.
GIVEN NAMES Spanish 5%. *Jose* (2), *Francisco, Isidro, Manuel, Maria Lucia, Orlando, Roberto, Ruben.*

Roland (6081) **1.** French, German, English, and Scottish: from a Germanic personal name composed *hrōd* 'renown' + *-nand* 'bold', assimilated to *-lant* 'land'. Compare ROWLAND. **2.** Scottish: Anglicized form of Gaelic **Ó Ruadháin** (see RUANE, ROWAN).
FOREBEARS As a name of French origin this is attested in Quebec City in 1706, taken there from the Touraine region of France.

Rolando (349) Italian and Spanish: from the personal name *Rolando*, of Germanic origin (see ROLAND).
GIVEN NAMES Italian 4%. *Angelo, Antonio, Giovanni, Salvo, Valentino, Verino.*

Rold (119) Danish: unexplained.

Roldan (1371) Spanish (**Roldán**): **1.** variant of ROLANDO. **2.** habitational name from either of two towns named Roldán, in Murcia province.
GIVEN NAMES Spanish 47%. *Jose* (38), *Juan* (19), *Luis* (17), *Carlos* (16), *Manuel* (15), *Pedro* (10), *Angel* (8), *Mario* (8), *Ramon* (8), *Francisco* (7), *Gustavo* (7), *Rafael* (7).

Rolek (102) Polish: probably a derivative of *rola* 'soil', 'ploughed land' with the diminutive suffix *-ek*, and so a metonymic occupational name for a plowman.

Rolen (621) Dutch: from a variant of the personal names *Roeland* (Dutch form of ROLAND) or *Roelof* (Dutch form of RUDOLF).

Roles (535) English: patronymic from the personal name ROLLO or ROLF.

Roley (353) English: probably a variant spelling of ROWLEY. Compare ROLLEY.

Rolf (946) **1.** English: from the Middle English personal name *Rolf*, composed of the Germanic elements *hrōd* 'renown' + *wulf* 'wolf'. This name was especially popular among Nordic peoples in the contracted form *Hrólfr*, and seems to have reached England by two separate channels; partly through its use among pre-Conquest Scandinavian settlers, partly through its popularity among the Normans, who, however, generally used the form *Rou(l)* (see ROLLO). **2.** North German: from a personal name, a contracted form of *Rudolf*, cognate with 1.

Rolfe (1864) English: variant spelling of ROLF.

Rolfes (696) North German: patronymic from ROLF.

Rolfs (315) North German: patronymic from ROLF.

Rolfson (183) Respelling of Norwegian **Rolfsen**, a patronymic from the personal name *Rolf*, from Old Norse *Hrólfr*, a compound of *hróðolfr* 'fame', 'honor' + *ulfr* 'wolf'.

Rolin (244) Of uncertain origin. Rolin is a French surname, from a pet form of a Germanic personal name containing the element *hrōd* 'renown'. However, there is no evidence to support a French origin, and a different source should be sought.

Roling (466) English: from a pet form of the personal name ROLLO or ROLF.

Rolison (339) English: patronymic from a pet form of the personal name ROLLO or ROLF.

Roll (2090) **1.** German: from Middle High German *rolle, rulle* 'roll', 'list', possibly applied as a metonymic occupational name for a scribe. **2.** German: from a short form of the personal names RUDOLF or ROLAND. **3.** German: habitational name for someone from either of two places named Rolle, in Westphalia and Pomerania. **4.** English: variant of ROLLO or ROLF.

Rolla (229) **1.** Italian: origin uncertain; perhaps from a feminine form of an unattested male personal name *Rollo*, of Germanic origin. **2.** German: nickname for a farmer, from Sorbian *rola* 'cultivated field'.
GIVEN NAMES Italian 4%. *Nicolo* (2), *Caesar, Vincenzo.*

Rolland (936) Scottish, English, and French: variant spelling of ROLAND.
GIVEN NAMES French 5%. *Gaston* (2), *Joffre* (2), *Francois, Jean-Marc, Lucien, Mathieu, Pascal, Pierre.*

Rolle (889) **1.** German and English: variant of ROLL. **2.** German: variant of ROLLA.

Roller (3180) **1.** German: nickname from Swabian *roller* 'tom cat'. **2.** German: occupational name for a carter or driver of a wagon, early New High German *roller*. **3.** Scottish: probably a variant of ROLLO.

Rolleri (133) Italian: according to Caracausi, from a name of French origin, from medieval Latin *Rotularius* 'notary', 'scribe'.
GIVEN NAMES Italian 12%. *Aldo* (3), *Angelo, Concetta, Dante, Ennio, Italo.*

Rollerson (143) English: patronymic from a pet form of the personal name ROLLO or ROLF.

Rolley (305) English (West Midlands): variant spelling of ROWLEY.

Rolli (181) **1.** Italian: possibly a patronymic form of the personal name *Rollo* (see ROLLA). **2.** Swiss German: variant of ROLL 2.
GIVEN NAMES Italian 4%. *Aldo, Angelo, Raffaele.*

Rollie (114) English and northern Irish: variant spelling of ROWLEY.

Rollin (417) **1.** English: variant of ROLLING. **2.** German: of Slavic origin, a habitational name from an unidentified place.
GIVEN NAMES German 4%. *Otto* (2), *Kurt.*

Rolling (523) **1.** English: from a pet form of the personal name ROLLO or ROLF. **2.** German: patronymic from the personal name *Role*, a reduced form of RUDOLF. **3.** German: habitational name from any of several places called Rolling in Silesia. **4.** (**Rölling**): variant of 2 and 3, or a nickname for a lecher, from *Rölling* 'tom cat'.

Rollinger (206) **1.** Luxembourgeois: habitational name for someone from Rollingen in the Grand Duchy of Luxembourg. **2.** German: variant of ROLLING.

Rollings (765) English: variant of ROLLINS.

Rollins (11425) English: patronymic from a pet form of ROLLO or ROLF.

Rollinson (342) Northern English: patronymic from a pet form of ROLLO or ROLF.

Rollison (474) Northern English: patronymic from a pet form of ROLLO or ROLF.

Rollman (406) North German (**Rollmann**): from a short form of the personal name RUDOLF, with the addition of *man* 'man'.

Rollo (762) Scottish: from a Latinized form, common in early medieval documents, of the personal name *Rou(l)*, the usual Norman form of ROLF.

Rolls (408) English: patronymic from ROLLO or ROLF.

Rollyson (239) English: variant spelling of ROLLISON.

Rolnick (248) Jewish (Ashkenazic), Czech and Slovak (**Rolník**), and eastern German: occupational name from Polish and Belorussian *rolnik*, Czech *rolník* 'land worker', 'agricultural laborer'.
GIVEN NAMES Jewish 10%. *Aron* (3), *Mort* (2), *Isadore, Mordecai, Shamuel, Sol.*

Roloff (813) North German: variant of ROHLOFF.
GIVEN NAMES German 4%. *Dietrich, Erhard, Gottlieb, Hermann, Jurgen, Otto, Siegfried.*

Rolon (503) Spanish (**Rolón**): possibly from a derivative of *rol* 'roll', 'scroll', 'reel'. This is a rare surname in Spain, being associated chiefly with Mexico and Puerto Rico.
GIVEN NAMES Spanish 41%. *Angel* (8), *Jose* (8), *Luis* (8), *Ana* (6), *Juan* (5), *Julio* (5), *Francisco* (4), *Jorge* (4), *Manuel* (4), *Orlando* (4), *Miguel* (3), *Raul* (3); *Antonio* (3), *Eligio, Gildo, Heriberto.*

Roloson (155) Apparently an altered spelling of English ROLLISON.

Rolph (603) English: variant spelling of ROLF.

Rolstad (162) Norwegian: habitational name from ten farms mainly in the southeast of the country, so named from Old Norse *Róaldsstaðir*, from the personal name *Róaldr* (meaning 'fame', 'honor' +

valdr 'ruler', 'king') + *staðir* 'farmstead', 'dwelling'.

GIVEN NAME French 5%; Scandinavian 4%. *Honore*.

Rolston (667) English: habitational name from any of various places, such as Rowlston in Lincolnshire, Rolleston in Leicestershire, Nottinghamshire, and Staffordshire, or Rowlstone in Herefordshire, near the Welsh border. Most of these are named from the genitive case of the Old Norse personal name *Hrólfr* (see ROLF) or of the Old English cognate name *Hrōðwulf* + Old English *tūn* 'enclosure', 'settlement'. In the case of the Nottinghamshire place, however, the first element is from the genitive case of the Old Norse personal name *Hróaldr* (see ROWETT).

Rom (357) **1.** Dutch: variant of ROME. **2.** Jewish (eastern Ashkenazic): acronymic name of uncertain derivation. **3.** German: from a place name in Pomerania. **4.** German: ethnic name or epithet for someone who had a connection with Rome (see ROMAN).

GIVEN NAMES Jewish 8%; German 5%. *Carmit* (2), *Eran* (2), *Sol* (2), *Yonatan* (2), *Aviv*, *Dorit*, *Dror*, *Eitan*, *Hillel*, *Yakov*, *Zvia*; *Erhard* (2), *Bernhard*, *Ernst*, *Mathias*.

Roma (591) **1.** Italian: habitational name from the city of Rome (Italian *Roma*). **2.** Catalan (**Romà**): from the personal name *Romà* (from Latin *Romanus* ('from Rome'), borne by several saints). **3.** Catalan and Galician: habitational name from any of several places in Valencia and Galicia named Roma, of uncertain derivation.

GIVEN NAMES Italian 23%; Spanish 5%. *Angelo* (7), *Gino* (6), *Antonio* (3), *Armando* (3), *Eduardo* (3), *Americo* (2), *Gaetano* (2), *Gerardo* (2), *Pasquale* (2), *Renato* (2), *Vito* (2); *Jose* (3), *Fernando*, *Juan*, *Liduvina*.

Romack (263) Germanized or Americanized spelling of Czech **Romák**, a derivative of the personal name ROMAN.

Romagnoli (240) Italian: from an adjectival form of **Romagna**, a regional name for someone from the area so named.

GIVEN NAMES Italian 24%. *Edo* (3), *Adelmo* (2), *Dino* (2), *Guido* (2), *Marco* (2), *Mario* (2), *Mauro* (2), *Aldo*, *Carlo*, *Franco*, *Primo*, *Remo*, *Reno*, *Secondo*, *Tulio*.

Romain (679) French (also English): variant of ROMAN.

GIVEN NAMES French 13%. *Alain*, *Altagrace*, *Aurore*, *Camille*, *Dominique*, *Edele*, *Georges*, *Henri*, *Jacques*, *Jean-Marie*, *Jean-Michel*, *Jeanmarie*.

Romaine (703) French (also English): variant of ROMAN.

Roman (10171) **1.** Catalan, French, English, German (also **Romann**), Polish, Hungarian (**Román**), Romanian, Ukrainian, and Belorussian: from the Latin personal name *Romanus*, which originally meant 'Roman'. This name was borne by several

saints, including a 7th-century bishop of Rouen. **2.** English, French, and Catalan: regional or ethnic name for someone from Rome or from Italy in general, or a nickname for someone who had some connection with Rome, as for example having been there on a pilgrimage. Compare ROMERO.

GIVEN NAMES Spanish 27%. *Jose* (133), *Juan* (64), *Luis* (57), *Manuel* (53), *Carlos* (49), *Angel* (43), *Jorge* (41), *Miguel* (30), *Pedro* (28), *Francisco* (25), *Julio* (24), *Mario* (24).

Romanchuk (123) Ukrainian: patronymic from the personal name ROMAN.

GIVEN NAMES German 5%; Russian 4%. *Frieda* (2); *Gennadiy*, *Lyubov*.

Romanek (201) Czech (**Románek**): from a pet form of the personal name ROMAN.

Romanelli (628) Italian: patronymic or plural form of ROMANELLO.

GIVEN NAMES Italian 26%. *Angelo* (4), *Antonio* (4), *Mario* (3), *Nicola* (3), *Salvatore* (3), *Alfonso* (2), *Armando* (2), *Domenic* (2), *Eduardo* (2), *Aldo*, *Carlo*, *Cono*, *Cosimo*, *Cosmo*, *Dino*, *Gennaro*, *Gustavo*, *Mariano*.

Romanello (258) Italian: from a pet form of the personal name ROMANO.

GIVEN NAMES Italian 15%. *Angelo* (2), *Carmine* (2), *Vincenzo* (2), *Antonio*, *Domenic*, *Gennaro*, *Pasquale*, *Salvatore*, *Santo*, *Silvio*, *Tosca*.

Romani (417) **1.** Italian: patronymic or plural form of ROMANO. **2.** Catalan (**Romaní**): nickname from *romaní*, which is either from Arabic *romani* 'Christian' or Catalan *romaní* 'rosemary'. **3.** Catalan (**Romaní**): in some cases, possibly a habitational name from a place called Romaní in El Penedès, Barcelona province.

GIVEN NAMES Italian 21%; Spanish 12%. *Angelo* (3), *Romano* (3), *Antonio* (2), *Emedio* (2), *Vito* (2), *Carlo*, *Dino*, *Domenic*, *Guido*, *Guillermo*, *Marco*, *Massimo*, *Pasquale*; *Jose* (2), *Enedina*, *Enrique*, *Juan*, *Juan Jose*, *Julio*, *Pedro*, *Salvador*, *Vincente*.

Romanick (142) Americanized form of Czech **Romaník** (see ROMANIK).

Romaniello (200) Italian: southern variant of ROMANELLO.

GIVEN NAMES Italian 19%. *Rocco* (3), *Angelo* (2), *Canio* (2), *Antonio*, *Carlo*, *Carmine*, *Donato*, *Gino*, *Giovanni*, *Luciano*, *Pasquale*.

Romanik (197) Czech (**Romaník**): from a pet form of the personal name ROMAN.

Romanko (126) Ukrainian: from a pet form of the personal name ROMAN.

GIVEN NAMES Russian 4%. *Galina*, *Natalya*, *Tatjana*.

Romano (9584) **1.** Italian and Spanish: from the personal name *Romano*, Latin *Romanus*, borne by several saints and martyrs. This was originally a byname for someone from Rome or for a Roman citizen, from

Roma 'Rome'. See also ROMAN. **2.** Italian: (**Romanò**): in Calabria, a term for someone from *Nea Rhōmē* 'New Rome', a medieval Greek name for Constantinople.

GIVEN NAMES Italian 20%; Spanish 6%. *Salvatore* (59), *Angelo* (26), *Mario* (27), *Antonio* (24), *Carmine* (20), *Rocco* (18), *Sal* (15), *Vito* (14), *Pasquale* (13), *Gennaro* (9), *Alfonso* (8), *Gaetano* (7), *Santo* (7), *Vincenzo* (7); *Jose* (9), *Carlos* (6), *Rosario* (5), *Emilio* (4), *Juan* (4), *Miguel* (4).

Romanoff (327) **1.** Russian: alternative spelling of **Romanov**, a patronymic from the personal name ROMAN. **2.** Jewish (American): shortened form of ROMANOWSKI. **3.** Jewish (**Romanov**; from Belarus): habitational name from the town Romanovo, now in Belarus.

FOREBEARS The Romanov dynasty began its rule of Russia in 1613 with Michael Romanov (d. 1645), and ended with the execution of Nicholas II and his family at Yekaterinburg in July 1918. The family were descended from a Muscovite boyar, Andrei Kobyla, who had emigrated in the 14th century from Prussia. They took the name from Roman Yurievich (d. 1543), whose daughter Anastasia Romanovna was the first wife of Ivan the Terrible. Her brother Nikita was regent after Ivan's death, and after years of disorder Nikita's grandson Michael Romanov was elected czar in 1613.

GIVEN NAMES Jewish 4%. *Eliahu*, *Elihu*, *Hedva*.

Romanos (98) Greek: from the personal name *Romanos*, Latin *Romanus*, borne by several saints and martyrs, particularly Romanos Melodos (6th century), the major hymn writer of the Greek Orthodox Church. It was originally an ethnic byname from *Roma* 'Rome'.

Romanoski (202) Polish: variant of ROMANOWSKI.

Romanow (175) German spelling of Russian ROMANOFF.

Romanowicz (108) Polish: patronymic from the personal name ROMAN.

GIVEN NAMES Polish 14%. *Danuta* (2), *Ewa*, *Grzegorz*, *Halina*, *Jerzy*, *Krystyna*.

Romanowski (980) Polish, Ukrainian, Belorussian, and Jewish (eastern Ashkenazic): habitational name for someone from any of various places called Romanów, Romany, or Romanowo.

GIVEN NAMES Polish 6%. *Ryszard* (3), *Casimir* (2), *Ewa* (2), *Andrzej*, *Janusz*, *Jerzy*, *Jozef*, *Karol*, *Kazimier*, *Krzysztof*, *Stanislaw*, *Tadeusz*.

Romans (1326) English, Scottish, Dutch, German, and Catalan: patronymic from the personal name ROMAN.

Romanski (415) Polish (**Romański**): **1.** habitational name for someone from any of several places in Poland called Romany, named with the personal name *Roman*. **2.** in some cases perhaps a direct derivative

of the personal name *Roman*, with the addition of the common surname suffix *-ski*.
GIVEN NAMES Polish 6%. *Casimir* (2), *Feliks, Grazyna, Maciej, Ryszard, Tadeusz, Wojciech.*

Romansky (123) **1.** Czech (**Romanský**): habitational name from Romanov, a village in central Bohemia. **2.** Germanized spelling of Polish **Romański** (see ROMANSKI).

Romas (156) Spanish: **1.** possibly from Catalan *romàs* 'blackberry bush'. **2.** variant of ROMA.
GIVEN NAMES Spanish 7%. *Alberto, Andres, Jesus, Jose, Jose Antonio, Juana, Luis Alfonso, Violeta, Zayda.*

Rombach (273) German: habitational name from a place named Rombach (earlier *Ronnbach*).

Romberg (392) German, Dutch, and Scandinavian: habitational name from any of several places named Romberg.
GIVEN NAMES Scandinavian 6%. *Lars* (2), *Bjorn, Klas.*

Romberger (343) German: habitational name for someone from any of the various places called ROMBERG.

Rombough (102) Americanized form of German ROMBACH.

Rome (1756) French and English: habitational name for someone from Rome or a nickname for someone who had some connection with Rome, in particular having been there on a pilgrimage.
GIVEN NAMES French 4%. *Andre* (2), *Benoit* (2), *Oneil* (2), *Camile, Emile, Fernand, Gracien, Kearney, Ludger, Ulysse.*

Romel (108) Variant spelling of German ROMMEL.

Romenesko (175) Origin unidentified.

Romeo (2734) Italian: from the personal name *Romeo*, which derives ultimately from the classical Greek adjective *rhōmaios* (modern Greek *romeos*), originally denoting someone from the eastern Roman Empire, i.e. Byzantium, later someone from Rome itself, in particular someone who had been on a pilgrimage there, and finally someone who had made any pilgrimage, i.e. a pilgrim; from this last sense arose the personal name.
GIVEN NAMES Italian 16%. *Salvatore* (22), *Rocco* (19), *Angelo* (12), *Antonio* (4), *Domenic* (4), *Carlo* (3), *Carmine* (3), *Enrico* (3), *Santo* (3), *Silvano* (3), *Dante* (2).

Romer (1167) **1.** German and Swiss German (**Römer**): see ROEMER. **2.** English, Dutch, and German: regional or ethnic name for a Roman or more generally for an Italian. **3.** English and Dutch: nickname for a pilgrim, someone who has traveled to Rome (see ROMERO). **4.** German: from the Germanic personal name *Hrotmar*, composed of *hrōd* 'renown' + *māri* 'fame'.

Romero (21092) Spanish: nickname from *romero* 'pilgrim', originally 'pilgrim to Rome' (see ROMEO).

GIVEN NAMES Spanish 37%. *Jose* (433), *Juan* (213), *Manuel* (204), *Carlos* (157), *Luis* (129), *Jesus* (112), *Francisco* (102), *Pedro* (88), *Miguel* (84), *Ruben* (73), *Jorge* (71), *Mario* (69).

Romes (124) German: possibly a Rhineland variant of **Rohm** or an altered spelling of **Romeis**, both from a short form of a Germanic personal name formed with *hrōm* 'fame'.
GIVEN NAME German 4%. *Kurt.*

Romesburg (278) Possibly of German origin, perhaps an altered form of a habitational name (**Römersberg**) from a place so named in Hesse.

Romeu (110) **1.** Catalan and Portuguese: from Catalan and Portuguese *romeu* 'pilgrim' (originally 'pilgrim to Rome'). **2.** Catalan and Galician: in some cases, possibly a habitational name from any of the places called Romeu, especially in northern Catalonia and in Vigo, Galicia.
GIVEN NAMES Spanish 37%. *Carlos* (4), *Armando* (3), *Jorge* (3), *Jose* (3), *Alfredo* (2), *Aurelio* (2), *Ernesto* (2), *Agustin, Alberto, Diego, Enrique, Ersilia; Delio* (2), *Heriberto, Lorenzo.*

Romey (226) German: variant of ROMIG.

Romick (270) Variant of German ROMIG.

Romig (1089) German (**Römig**): from the personal name *Remigius.*

Romine (2718) Probably a respelling of French **Romain**, from a personal name (feminine *Romaine*) meaning 'Roman' (Latin *Romanus*), which was borne by two martyrs and a 7th century bishop of Rouen. The surname has been long established in French-speaking Belgium and England (also written **Romayn(e)**), whence it may also have been brought to the U.S.

Romines (605) Origin unidentified. Perhaps an altered form of Scottish **Romanes**, which Black derived form the manor of Rothmaneic (now called Romanno) in the parish of Newlands, Peebleshire. Compare ROMINE.

Rominger (638) German: patronymic from a personal name beginning with *hrōm* 'renown'.

Rominski (107) Polish (**Romiński**): probably a derivative of Old Polish *romień* 'chamomile'.

Romito (338) Italian: from *romito* 'hermit', presumably applied as a nickname for a solitary or reclusive person.
GIVEN NAMES Italian 10%. *Aldino, Angelo, Carmelo, Dante, Luigi, Marino, Palma, Paolo, Romeo, Vito.*

Romm (265) **1.** German: from a Germanic personal name formed with *hruom* 'fame'. **2.** Swedish: probably of German origin (see 1). **3.** Jewish (eastern Ashkenazic): variant of ROM.
GIVEN NAMES Jewish 5%. *Giora* (2), *Sol* (2).

Rommel (603) North German and Dutch: **1.** nickname for an obstreperous person, from Middle Low German, Middle Dutch

rummeln, rumpeln to make a noise, create a disturbance (of imitative origin). **2.** variant of RUMMEL 2.
GIVEN NAMES German 5%. *Kurt* (3), *Fritz* (2), *Erwin, Gerhart, Hans.*

Romney (496) English: habitational name from a place in Kent, so called from an obscure first element, *rumen*, + Old English *ēa* 'river' (see RYE).

Romo (2600) Spanish: nickname from *romo* 'snub-nosed', 'foreshortened' (of uncertain etymology, perhaps from Latin *rhombus*, itself a borrowing from Greek, with reference to the two obtuse angles of this figure).
GIVEN NAMES Spanish 44%. *Jose* (66), *Juan* (38), *Jesus* (34), *Manuel* (27), *Francisco* (19), *Ruben* (18), *Ramon* (16), *Raul* (16), *Carlos* (14), *Guadalupe* (13), *Javier* (13), *Jorge* (13).

Romoser (141) South German: habitational name for someone from Rohrmoos in Bavaria, so named from Middle High German *rō* 'reeds' + *mos* 'fen', 'marsh'.

Romp (100) **1.** English (East Anglia): unexplained. Perhaps a variant of RUMP. **2.** German: variant of RUMP 3.

Romrell (101) English: variant of RUMRILL.

Ron (210) **1.** Jewish (Israeli): ornamental name from Hebrew *ron* 'singing'. **2.** Galician: habitational name from Ron, a town in A Coruña, Galicia. **3.** Swedish: probably of German origin (see 2). **4.** Perhaps an altered spelling of German ROHN or **Rönn**, a variant of **Rönne** (see RONNE).
GIVEN NAMES Jewish 24%; Spanish 18%. *Avi* (3), *Eyal* (2), *Ori* (2), *Shlomo* (2), *Zvi* (2), *Ahuva, Aviv, Aviva, Erez, Gershon, Hagit, Nurit; Alberto* (2), *Arturo* (2), *Jorge* (2), *Manuel* (2), *Ruben* (2), *Azucena, Carlos, Cesar, Enrique, Gilberto, Graciela, Gustavo.*

Ronald (407) Scottish: Anglicized form of the Gaelic personal name *Raonull*, which is a borrowing from Old Norse *Rögnvaldr* (see REYNOLD).
GIVEN NAME Scottish 5%. *Gillespie.*

Ronan (1291) Irish: reduced Anglicized form of Gaelic **Ó Rónáin** 'descendant of *Rónán*', a personal name apparently representing a diminutive of *rón* 'seal'.
GIVEN NAMES Irish 5%. *Cormac, Nuala.*

Ronayne (334) Irish: variant of RONAN.
GIVEN NAME Irish 6%. *Brendan* (2).

Ronca (206) Italian: variant of RONCO.
GIVEN NAMES Italian 11%. *Amedeo, Dante, Gino, Guido, Luciano, Ottavio, Sandro, Stefano.*

Ronchetti (136) Italian: patronymic or plural form of RONCHETTO.
GIVEN NAMES Italian 6%. *Agatino, Carmel, Salvatore.*

Ronchetto (102) Italian: diminutive from a variant of RONCO.

Ronco (287) Italian (Naples and Puglia): topographic name from *ronco* 'cultivated land', 'terraced slope', 'hillside vineyard', or a habitational name from any of the numerous places named with this word, examples of which are found in Turin, Genoa, Milan, and Verona (Ronco); Bologna, Mantova, and Savona (Ronchi); Verona (Ronca).

GIVEN NAMES French 5%. *Gervais, Lucienne, Pierre.*

Roncone (121) Italian: habitational name from a place in Trento or another on the island of Pentelleria in Trapani province, Sicily, so named from an augmentative of RONCO.

GIVEN NAMES Italian 12%. *Angelo, Annamaria, Attilio, Raffaele, Rocco.*

Ronda (138) **1.** Spanish and Asturian-Leonese: habitational name from Ronda in Málaga or from any of the places, especially in Asturies, called Ronda or A Ronda, from *ronda* 'patrol', 'circuit round the parapet of a fort'. **2.** Greek (**Ronda**): from *ronda* 'curfew bell', metonymically associated with a night watchman.

GIVEN NAMES Spanish 16%. *Juan* (3), *Angel, Carlos, Efrain, Ernesto, Gustavo, Lilia, Mario, Nelida, Nilsa, Osvaldo, Ricardo.*

Rondeau (1440) French: nickname for a plump person, from a diminutive of Old French *rond* 'round' (Latin *rotundus*).

FOREBEARS The surname is attested around 1663 in Quebec; several families arrived slightly later from La Rochelle, France.

GIVEN NAMES French 10%. *Normand* (7), *Lucien* (5), *Armand* (3), *Emile* (3), *Laurent* (3), *Adelard* (2), *Andre* (2), *Marcel* (2), *Michel* (2), *Adrien, Andree, Gaston.*

Rondinelli (216) Italian: nickname from a diminutive of *rondine* 'swallow'.

GIVEN NAMES Italian 20%. *Mario* (4), *Aldo, Antonio, Federico, Gino, Giovanni, Giuseppe, Giuseppi, Guiseppe, Reno, Romeo, Vincenzo.*

Rondo (126) **1.** Greek: variant of RONDA. **2.** Perhaps also an altered spelling of French RONDEAU.

GIVEN NAMES Greek 4%. *Nicolaos, Pericles.*

Rondon (289) **1.** Spanish (**Rondón**): apparently linked with the idiomatic expression *de rondón* 'random', 'unexpected', 'surprising', or from a derivative of RONDA. **2.** Italian: possibly a topographic name denoting a place frequented by swifts, from a reduced form of *rondone* 'swift'.

GIVEN NAMES Spanish 42%. *Francisco* (7), *Jose* (7), *Juan* (5), *Luis* (5), *Carlos* (4), *Fernando* (4), *Pedro* (3), *Rafael* (3), *Angel* (2), *Juana* (2), *Orlando* (2), *Agustin*; *Antonio* (4), *Angelo, Carmela, Leonardo, Marco, Silvano.*

Rone (744) **1.** English: variant spelling of ROAN 2. **2.** Probably also an altered spelling of German ROHN.

Ronen (104) Jewish (Israeli): ornamental name derived from the Hebrew verb mean-

ing 'to sing', either directly or via a new Israeli male personal name *Ronen*.

GIVEN NAMES Jewish 34%. *Avner* (2), *Dafna, Dorit, Dov, Dror, Ephraim, Gili, Haim, Ilan, Miriam, Moshe, Ofer.*

Rones (111) Jewish (eastern Ashkenazic): metronymic from the Yiddish female personal name *Rone*, of uncertain origin, + the Yiddish possessive suffix *-s*.

GIVEN NAME Jewish 5%. *Shulamith.*

Roney (2165) Irish: variant of ROONEY.

Rong (161) **1.** Norwegian: habitational name from a farm name in Hordaland related to *rong* 'stern (of a boat)'. **2.** Chinese 容: there are two sources of this surname. One is Rong Cheng, a senior minister to Emperor Huang Di (2697–2595 BC), who is credited with the invention of the Chinese calendar. A second source is the title of an official who was in charge of ceremonial music, *rongguan*, during the Zhou dynasty (1122–221 BC). **3.** Chinese 荣: from the name of another senior minister to the Emperor Huang Di (2697–2595 BC), called Rong Yuan. A second source of the surname written with this character is a city called Rong, which was granted to a minister of the Zhou dynasty king Cheng Wang (1115–1078 BC). **4.** Chinese 戎: when the state of Zhou overthrew the corrupt and brutal last king of the Shang dynasty, Zhou Xin, to establish the Zhou dynasty in 1122 BC, the son of Zhou Xin was granted the area of the former Shang capital. The Zhou believed that, in order to obtain the mandate of heaven necessary to rule, they had to grant lands and titles to the principal descendants of the great emperors of the past, even if that meant granting lands to the progeny of their enemies. Zhou Xin's son rose in revolt against the new rulers and was killed. To replace him with another descendant of the Emperor Cheng Tang, the Zhou this time chose Zhou Xin's elder half-brother, who was regarded as a virtuous man and who had attempted to curb Zhou Xin's excesses; he was granted the title Duke of Song, but is usually known as Wei, Viscount of Song. Chinese sources state that the surname Rong was used by his ancestors, but do not indicate its origin. The Rong were a non-Chinese people living on the border of Chinese territories during the Shang and Zhou dynasties, and this may be the source.

GIVEN NAMES Chinese 54%. *Guang* (4), *Fang* (2), *Shuhong* (2), *Xiao* (2), *Zhao* (2), *Bai, Chen, Cheng, Ding, Guan, Guo, Han.*

Rongey (144) Probably an Americanized spelling of German RUNGE.

Rongstad (100) Norwegian: habitational name from a farmstead in Trøndelag, named with an uncertain first element + *stad* 'farmstead', 'dwelling'.

Ronis (120) **1.** Latvian: unexplained. **2.** Jewish (eastern Ashkenazic): variant of RONES.

GIVEN NAMES Latvian 9%; Jewish 7%; Russian 6%; German 6%. *Andris, Lucija, Valdis, Velta; Aivars; Josif, Rimma, Yakov; Iosif, Yefim, Yury; Erwin, Gerda, Kurt.*

Ronk (729) Of uncertain origin; possibly Dutch, a nickname from a noun derivative of *ronken* 'to snore or snort', or an altered spelling of German RUNK or RANK.

Ronne (165) **1.** German (**Rönne**): habitational name from any of the places so named, near Winsen, Kiel, and Bielefeld. **2.** Danish (**Rønne**): habitational name from a place named Rønne, of which at least one example has the meaning 'swamp'.

GIVEN NAMES Scandinavian 5%. *Erik, Sven.*

Ronnebaum (157) German (**Rönnebaum**): variant of **Rennebaum**, a topographic name from Middle High German *renneboum*, Middle Low German *rennebōm* 'barrier', 'boundary marker'.

Ronnie (102) Scottish: unexplained; perhaps a variant of Irish RONEY (see ROONEY).

Ronning (881) **1.** German: probably a variant of **Ronnig**, from a short form of a Germanic personal name based on *rūn* 'rune', 'secret', the suffix *-ing* denoting a descendant. **2.** Norwegian (**Rønning**): habitational name from any of over 100 farmsteads named Rønning or Rønningen, notably in eastern Norway and Trøndelag, from Old Norse *Ryðningr*, from *ruð* 'clearing'.

GIVEN NAMES Scandinavian 7%. *Dagny* (2), *Thor* (2), *Hilmer, Sig, Sven.*

Ronningen (135) Norwegian: variant of RONNING.

GIVEN NAMES Scandinavian 14%. *Nordeen* (2), *Erik, Johan, Oyvind, Thor.*

Ronquillo (521) Spanish: habitational name from El Ronquillo in Seville province.

GIVEN NAMES Spanish 42%. *Manuel* (7), *Jose* (6), *Raul* (6), *Francisco* (5), *Jesus* (4), *Miguel* (4), *Ruben* (4), *Carlos* (3), *Enrique* (3), *Juan* (3), *Adan* (2), *Aida* (2); *Antonio* (6), *Constantino* (2), *Carina, Eligio, Lorenzo, Sal, Severiano.*

Ronson (131) English: patronymic from a reduced form of ROWLAND.

Rood (2405) Dutch: nickname for someone with red hair, from Middle Dutch *ro(e)de* 'red'.

Roode (179) Dutch: variant of ROOD.

GIVEN NAME French 5%. *Andre.*

Roof (1606) **1.** English: variant of ROLFE. **2.** German: from *Ruffo*, a short form of a personal name formed with *hrōd* 'renown', 'victory'. **3.** Probably an Americanized spelling of German RUF(F).

Rook (1626) **1.** English: nickname from the bird (Old English *hrōc*), most likely given to a person with very dark hair or a dark complexion or to someone with a raucous voice. **2.** English: some early examples, such as Robert of ye Rook (London 1318) and Henry del Rook (Staffordshire 1332), point clearly to a local name of some kind.

The first of these could be from a house sign, the second may be a variant of ROCK 1. **3.** German: from a short form of a Germanic personal name formed with *hrok*, of uncertain origin; perhaps a cognate of 1 or from Middle High German *rōhen* 'to cry or yell (in battle)' or Old High German *ruoh* 'intent'. **4.** Perhaps an altered spelling of German RUCK.

Rookard (152) **1.** English (East Anglia): unexplained. **2.** Probably an Americanized spelling of German *Rückert* or RUCKERT.

Rooke (362) English: variant spelling of ROOK.

Rooker (1015) English: variant of ROCKER.

Rookey (125) English: unexplained.

Rooks (2319) English: patronymic from ROOK 1.

Rookstool (207) Americanized spelling of German **Ruckstuhl**, probably a contraction of Middle High German *ruck den stuol*, literally 'move the chair', perhaps the name of a game similar to musical chairs.

Roome (247) English: variant of ROME.

Roon (108) Irish: variant of RUANE.

Rooney (6667) Irish: **1.** reduced Anglicized form of Gaelic **Ó Ruanaidh** 'descendant of *Ruanadh*', a byname meaning 'champion'. **2.** reduced Anglicized form of Gaelic **Ó Ruadháin** (see RUANE).
GIVEN NAMES Irish 6%. *Brendan* (3), *Liam* (3), *Caitlin* (2), *Niall* (2), *Conor*, *Declan*, *Dermot*, *Eamonn*, *Fergus*, *Kieran*, *Roisin*, *Sean Patrick*.

Roop (1515) **1.** Dutch: from a short form of the Germanic personal name *Robrecht*. **2.** Altered spelling of German RUPP. **3.** English: variant spelling of ROOPE.

Roope (187) English: metonymic occupational name for a maker or seller of rope, Middle English *rop* (see ROPER 1).

Roorda (321) Frisian: from a personal name, *Rowertha*, a compound of the Germanic elements *hrōd* 'renown' + *warda* 'guardian'.
GIVEN NAMES Dutch 5%. *Hessel* (3), *Dirk*, *Wouter*.

Roos (2226) **1.** Dutch (also **de Roos**) and Swiss German: habitational name for someone living at a house distinguished by the sign of a rose. **2.** Dutch (also **de Roos**): metonymic occupational name for someone who grew roses, from *roos* 'rose'. **3.** Dutch: from the female personal name *Rosa* (Latin *rosa* 'rose'). **4.** Dutch: nickname from *roos* 'erysipelas', an infection which causes reddening of the skin and scalp, applied presumably to someone with a ruddy complexion. **5.** Swiss German: from a personal name formed with *hrōd* 'renown'. **6.** Swedish and Danish (of German origin): as 1. **7.** Swedish: variant of ROS. **8.** English and Scottish: variant of ROSS 2.

Roosa (664) Dutch: from a personal name *Rosart*, formed with *Rosa* 'rose' + the Germanic element *hard* 'hardy', 'brave'.

Roose (722) **1.** Dutch: variant of ROOS 1–3. **2.** English and Scottish: variant of ROSS 2.

Roosevelt (383) Dutch: topographic name for someone living by an area of uncultivated land overgrown with roses, from Dutch *roose* + *velt* 'open country'.
FOREBEARS The two U.S. presidents Theodore Roosevelt (1858–1919) and Franklin Delano Roosevelt (1882–1945) and the latter's wife Eleanor Roosevelt (1884–1962) were all descended from a common ancestor, Claes Martenzen van Rosenvelt or Roosevelt, who had settled in New Amsterdam (now NY) from the Netherlands in 1649. He was the son of Maertin Cornelissen Geldersman, who had bought the farm of Rosevelt in Tholen, Zeeland, from Pieter Jorissen op het Rosevelt and his son Joris Pietersen. The family became prosperous with the growth of Manhattan. Theodore Roosevelt was born in New York City; his mother was of Irish and Huguenot descent. Franklin Delano Roosevelt was his 5th cousin. His mother's family, the Delanos, were descended from Philippe de la Noye (1602–81), a young man who arrived at Plymouth Colony in 1621 in the 'Fortune', one year after the Pilgrims.

Root (8166) **1.** English: nickname for a cheerful person, from Middle English *rote* 'glad' (Old English *rōt*). **2.** English: metonymic occupational name for a player on the rote, an early medieval stringed instrument (Middle English, Old French *rote*, of uncertain origin but apparently ultimately akin to Welsh *crwth*). **3.** Dutch: topographic name for someone who lived by a retting place (Dutch *root*, a derivative of *ro(o)ten* 'to ret', akin to modern English *rot*), a place where flax is soaked in tubs of water until the stems rot to release the linen fibers.

Rootes (134) English: variant of ROOTS.

Rooth (129) Dutch: variant of ROOT 3.

Roots (316) English: patronymic from ROOT 1.

Roozen (101) Dutch: variant of ROOS 1–3.
GIVEN NAME French 4%. *Leonie*.

Roper (7005) **1.** English: occupational name for a maker or seller of rope, from an agent derivative of Old English *rāp* 'rope'. See also ROOP. **2.** Variant of French ROBERT. **3.** North German (**Röper**): occupational name for a town crier, from an agent derivative of Middle Low German *rōpen* 'to call'.

Ropp (808) German: **1.** from a short form of *Ruprecht*, one of the German forms of ROBERT. **2.** Altered spelling of RUPP.

Roppel (104) South German: **1.** from a short form of the personal name *Roppold*, a dialect variant of RAPPOLD. **2.** perhaps a variant spelling of RUPPEL.
GIVEN NAMES German 7%. *Guenther*, *Hans*, *Otto*.

Roppolo (220) Italian: perhaps a derivative of *Roppo*, a personal name of Germanic origin.
GIVEN NAMES Italian 8%. *Sal* (2), *Angelo*, *Gaspare*, *Luigi*.

Roque (1608) **1.** Spanish: habitational name from one of the places in A Coruña or Gran Canaria called Roque or from El Roque in Tenerife. **2.** Catalan (**Roqué**): from a variant of **Roquer**, habitational name from any of the places in Catalonia named Roquer or El Roquer, from a derivative of Catalan *roca* 'rock'. **3.** Possibly an altered spelling of French **Rocque**, a Picard and southern form of ROCHE.
GIVEN NAMES Spanish 46%. *Jose* (47), *Juan* (19), *Manuel* (19), *Pedro* (14), *Jesus* (13), *Francisco* (12), *Carlos* (10), *Mario* (10), *Luis* (9), *Ricardo* (9), *Jorge* (8), *Julio* (8).

Roquemore (463) Probably an altered form of French **Roquemaure**, a habitational name from either of two places so named, in Gard and Tarn. This name is concentrated in AL and GA.

Roques (131) Catalan: habitational name from any of the places called Roques, from the plural of ROCA. This name is also found in southern France, of Occitan origin.
GIVEN NAMES French 20%. *Andre* (2), *Emile* (2), *Achille*, *Alban*, *Pascal*, *Philippe*, *Raoul*, *Theophile*.

Roquet (130) French: topographic name from a diminutive of *roque* 'rock', a southern variant of *roche* (see ROCHE).
GIVEN NAMES French 4%. *Alain*, *Camille*.

Roraback (110) Respelling of German ROHRBACH.
GIVEN NAME French 4%. *Celina*.

Rorabaugh (326) Respelling of German ROHRBACH.

Rorer (238) Variant spelling of German ROHRER.

Rorex (211) Americanized form of German ROEHRIG.

Rorick (423) Americanized form of German ROEHRIG.

Rorie (663) Scottish and Irish (County Tyrone): Anglicized form of Gaelic **Mac Ruaidhrí** 'son of Rory' (see MCCRORY).

Rork (246) Irish: reduced and altered form of O'ROURKE.

Rorke (187) Irish: reduced and altered form of O'ROURKE.

Rorrer (341) Altered spelling of German ROHRER.

Ros (336) **1.** Catalan: nickname for someone with blond hair or a fair complexion, from Latin *russus*. **2.** Swedish: ornamental name from *ros* 'rose'. **3.** Slovenian: nickname from the dialect adjective *ros* 'russet', hence denoting a person with russet-colored hair. Compare RUS 2. **4.** Slovenian (**Roš**): probably also a nickname from *roš*, a reduced form of *rovaš* 'stick split lengthwise', which was used to keep accounts (by scoring or making notches in the wood).

5. Cambodian or other Southeast Asian: unexplained.

GIVEN NAMES Spanish 28%; Southeast Asian 6%. *Enrique* (6), *Luis* (6), *Jose* (4), *Alberto* (3), *Eduardo* (3), *Rafael* (3), *Elena* (2), *Fidel* (2), *Joaquin* (2), *Manuel* (2), *Pablo* (2), *Ramon* (2); *Leang* (2), *Phon* (2), *Lap*, *Phan*, *Pho*, *Saroeun*, *Sophal*, *Sophan*, *Sophea*, *Tha*, *Thang*, *Yen*.

Rosa (5219) **1.** Italian and Catalan: from *rosa* 'rose' (Latin *rosa*), applied in part as a topographic name for someone who lived where wild roses grew, in part as a habitational name for someone who lived at a house distinguished by the sign of a rose, and in part as a nickname for someone with a pink, rosy complexion. **2.** Portuguese and Spanish: in most cases a short form of a name such as *(de la) Rosa* (Spanish) or *(da) Rosa* (Portuguese), or occasionally from the female personal name *Rosa*. **3.** Polish and Czech: from the vocabulary word *rosa* 'dew', 'juice', 'sap', applied as a nickname.

GIVEN NAMES Spanish 24%; Portuguese 8%; Italian 6%. *Jose* (85), *Manuel* (70), *Luis* (45), *Carlos* (31), *Antonio* (30), *Juan* (26), *Angel* (19), *Mario* (19), *Pedro* (14), *Ana* (13), *Miguel* (13), *Rafael* (13), *Ramon* (13); *Joao* (4), *Joaquim* (4), *Adao*, *Guilherme*, *Henrique*, *Paulo*, *Zulmira*.

Rosacker (114) German: a reduced form of the topographic name **Rosenacker** 'rose field'.

Rosado (2649) Spanish: nickname for someone with a notably pink and white complexion, from Spanish *rosado* 'pink', Late Latin *rosatus*, a derivative of *rosa* (see ROSE).

GIVEN NAMES Spanish 44%. *Jose* (74), *Luis* (42), *Juan* (28), *Carlos* (26), *Rafael* (23), *Angel* (22), *Manuel* (21), *Francisco* (18), *Ramon* (18), *Miguel* (17), *Jorge* (15), *Pedro* (15).

Rosal (142) Galician, Spanish, and Portuguese: habitational name from any of the places named Rosal or El Rosal, for example in Pontevedra and Huelva provinces, from a collective of *rosa* 'rose', thus 'rose garden'.

GIVEN NAMES Spanish 42%. *Alberto* (2), *Concepcion* (2), *Felicitas* (2), *Jorge* (2), *Jose* (2), *Mario* (2), *Serafin* (2), *Ana*, *Arcenia*, *Armando*, *Arturo*, *Augusto*.

Rosales (5129) **1.** Spanish: habitational name from any of the places named Rosales, from the plural of *rosal*, collective of *rosa* 'rose' (see ROSAL). **2.** Galician (**Rosalés**): name for someone from Rosal, a town in Baixo Miñ district in Galicia.

GIVEN NAMES Spanish 52%. *Jose* (138), *Juan* (73), *Carlos* (60), *Manuel* (55), *Francisco* (42), *Luis* (41), *Pedro* (41), *Jesus* (39), *Mario* (33), *Ruben* (32), *Raul* (31), *Jorge* (28).

Rosalez (252) Spanish: variant of ROSALES.

GIVEN NAMES Spanish 44%. *Ruben* (5), *Jesus* (3), *Doroteo* (2), *Evaristo* (2), *Felipe* (2), *Francisco* (2), *Ignacio* (2), *Jaime* (2), *Javier* (2), *Jose* (2), *Juan* (2), *Miguel* (2).

Rosamilia (138) Italian (Avellino): unexplained.

GIVEN NAMES Italian 8%. *Alicia*, *Geraldo*, *Gerardo*, *Orlando*.

Rosamond (349) English: see ROSEMAN. It is of Huguenot origin in at least some cases.

Rosander (193) Swedish: ornamental name from *ros* 'rose' + the suffix *-ander* (from ancient Greek *anēr* 'man', genitive *andros*).

GIVEN NAMES Scandinavian 5%; German 4%. *Matts*; *Kurt*.

Rosania (143) Italian: perhaps from a derivative of ROSA.

GIVEN NAMES Italian 14%. *Gustavo* (2), *Antonio*, *Guido*, *Mario*, *Nichola*, *Salvatore*.

Rosano (265) Italian: habitational name from any of several places named Rosano, for example in Alessandria, Florence, and Reggio Emilia.

GIVEN NAMES Italian 16%; Spanish 10%. *Salvatore* (4), *Lorenzo* (3), *Antonio* (2), *Angelo*, *Carmelo*, *Filomena*, *Geno*, *Gino*, *Guido*, *Remo*, *Rocco*, *Romeo*; *Ricardo* (2), *Ambrosio*, *Carlos*, *Eduardo*, *Enrique*, *Lazaro*, *Luis*, *Mario*, *Mauricio*, *Ramon*, *Roberto*, *Rolando*.

Rosar (100) **1.** English: probably related to ROSER, which is also unexplained. **2.** Altered spelling of German **Roser** or **Röser** (see ROSER).

Rosario (4206) **1.** Spanish and Portuguese: mostly from a short form of Spanish *(del) Rosario*, Portuguese *(do) Rosá*, from *rosario* 'rosary'; or from the Marian name *María del Rosario*, given in particular to a girl who was born on the festival of Our Lady of the Rosary, celebrated on the first Sunday in October. The word derives from Late Latin *rosarium* 'rose garden', and was transferred to a set of devotions dedicated to the Virgin Mary as the result of the medieval symbolism which constantly compared her to a rose. **2.** Italian: from the male personal name *Rosario*, of the same origin as 1 above.

GIVEN NAMES Spanish 46%; Portuguese 10%; Italian 8%. *Jose* (104), *Juan* (62), *Luis* (61), *Angel* (47), *Carlos* (31), *Pedro* (31), *Manuel* (30), *Rafael* (28), *Luz* (26), *Ramon* (26), *Miguel* (25), *Julio* (23); *Batista*, *Joao*, *Vasco*; *Antonio* (28), *Angelo* (6), *Carmelo* (5), *Dario* (4), *Lorenzo* (4), *Saturnina* (3), *Cecilio* (2), *Clemente* (2), *Eliseo* (2), *Fausto* (2), *Federico* (2), *Luciano* (2).

Rosas (2862) **1.** Spanish and Portuguese: from the plural of *rosa* 'rose'. **2.** Catalan: variant of **Roses**, habitational name from Roses, a town in L'Alt Empordà, Catalonia (earlier *Rodas*). **3.** Spanish: habitational name from any of the numerous places named Las Rosas.

GIVEN NAMES Spanish 50%; Portuguese 10%. *Jose* (73), *Luis* (34), *Juan* (28), *Jesus* (27), *Carlos* (23), *Manuel* (23), *Ruben* (22), *Pedro* (21), *Miguel* (20), *Roberto* (19), *Francisco* (17), *Rafael* (17); *Agostinho*, *Gonsalo*, *Joaquim*; *Antonio* (28), *Marco* (6), *Leonardo* (4), *Lorenzo* (4), *Carmelo* (3), *Filiberto* (3), *Bartolo* (2), *Cecilio* (2), *Elbio* (2), *Fausto* (2), *Federico* (2), *Lucio* (2).

Rosasco (196) Italian: habitational name from any of several places in northwestern Italy named Rosasco.

Rosati (1020) Italian: **1.** patronymic or plural form of ROSATO. **2.** probably also a habitational name from a district named Rosate in Milan.

GIVEN NAMES Italian 19%. *Angelo* (11), *Rocco* (7), *Antonio* (4), *Guido* (4), *Dante* (3), *Gino* (3), *Italo* (3), *Agostino* (2), *Dino* (2), *Domenic* (2), *Salvatore* (2), *Silvio* (2).

Rosato (798) Italian: from the medieval personal name, ultimately derived from *rosa* 'rose'.

GIVEN NAMES Italian 19%. *Angelo* (6), *Rocco* (3), *Salvatore* (3), *Antonio* (2), *Caio* (2), *Carmin* (2), *Carmine* (2), *Francesco* (2), *Pietro* (2), *Sal* (2), *Alessandro*, *Attilio*.

Rosauer (130) German: reduced form of **Rosenauer**, a habitational name for someone from any of several places named ROSENAU.

GIVEN NAMES German 4%. *Bernhard*, *Kurt*.

Rosberg (173) **1.** Swedish: ornamental name composed of the elements *ros* 'rose' + *berg* 'mountain', 'hill'. **2.** Possibly also a variant spelling of German ROSSBERG.

Rosborough (414) **1.** English (now mainly northern Ireland): apparently a habitational name from an unidentified place. **2.** perhaps also an altered spelling of Swedish ROSBERG or German **Rossburg** (see ROSBURG).

Rosburg (144) Variant spelling of German **Rossburg**, a habitational name for someone from Rochsburg, Saxony, or from Roseburg near Lüneburg, Lower Saxony.

GIVEN NAMES German 5%. *Fritz*, *Klaus*.

Rosch (362) **1.** German: variant of **Rösch** (see ROESCH). **2.** Germanized spelling of Slovenian **Roš** (see ROS 4).

GIVEN NAMES German 5%. *Hans*, *Heinz*, *Jurgen*, *Reinhard*, *Wolfram*.

Rosche (151) German: **1.** variant of ROESCH. **2.** habitational name from a place named Rosche or Roschau. **3.** from a short form of the Slavic personal name *Rodoslav*. **4.** topographic name from Middle High German *rosche* 'cliff', 'mountainside'.

Roscher (182) South German: **1.** habitational name for someone from any of various places called Rosche, Roschau, Rascha, Rasch, or Raschau. **2.** variant of ROESCH.

GIVEN NAMES German 7%. *Heinz*, *Otto*, *Siegfried*.

Roscoe (1702) **1.** English: habitational name from a place in Lancashire called Roscoe, named in Old Norse with *rá* 'roebuck' + *scógr* 'copse'. **2.** Americanized spelling of French RACICOT.

Rosdahl (111) **1.** Norwegian: habitational name from a farm name, probably from Old Norse *ruð* 'clearing' + *dal* 'valley'. **2.** Danish: habitational name from a place so named. **3.** Swedish: ornamental name composed of the elements *ros* 'rose' + *dahl*, an old or ornamental spelling of *dal* 'valley'.

GIVEN NAMES Scandinavian 4%. *Erik, Nils.*

Rose (54636) **1.** English, Scottish, French, and German: from the name of the flower, Middle English, Old French, Middle High German *rose* (Latin *rosa*), in various applications. In part it is a topographic name for someone who lived at a place where wild roses grew, or a habitational name for someone living at a house bearing the sign of the rose. It is also found, especially in Europe, as a nickname for a man with a 'rosy' complexion. As an American surname, this name has absorbed cognates and similar-sounding names from other European languages. **2.** English: variant of ROYCE. **3.** Jewish (Ashkenazic): ornamental name from the word for the flower (German *Rose*, Yiddish *royz*), or a metronymic name from the Yiddish female personal name *Royze*, derived from the word for the flower.

FOREBEARS French families bearing the name Rose are descended from a native of Paris, documented in Quebec City in 1666.

Roseberry (1562) **1.** Scottish or English: habitational name from Rosebery in Midlothian. **2.** Americanized form of Swedish ROSBERG.

Roseboom (168) Dutch: variant of ROSEN-BOOM.

GIVEN NAME German 4%. *Kurt.*

Roseboro (315) See ROSEBOROUGH.

GIVEN NAME French 4%. *Amie.*

Roseborough (275) **1.** Northern Irish: variant of ROSBOROUGH. **2.** Probably also an altered spelling of Swedish ROSBERG or German **Rossburg** (see ROSBURG).

Rosebrock (263) North German: habitational name from Rosebruch, a district of Rotenburg, Lower Saxony, so named from Middle Low German *rose* 'rose' + *brōk*, *brūk* 'swamp'.

GIVEN NAMES German 7%. *Eldor, Fritz, Gunther, Hans, Otto.*

Rosebrook (214) Americanized form of German ROSEBROCK or possibly of ROSENBACH or ROSENBECK.

Rosebrough (152) Origin uncertain. Probably an altered spelling of ROSBERG or **Rossburg** (see ROSBURG).

Rosebush (124) Americanized form of French DESROSIERS or of **Rosenbusch**, which as a German name is topographic for someone who lived where roses grew; as an

Ashkenazic Jewish name it is ornamental ('rose bush').

Rosecrans (329) Dutch: see ROSENKRANZ.

Roseen (117) Swedish: ornamental name composed of the elements *ros* 'rose' + the common surname suffix *-en*, from Latin *-enius*.

GIVEN NAMES Scandinavian 8%; Dutch 4%. *Nels, Swen, Walfrid; Gust.*

Rosekrans (185) Dutch: see ROSENKRANZ.

Rosel (164) **1.** Catalan: possibly a variant of Catalan ROSSELL. **2.** German (**Rösel**): from a pet form of ROSE 1.

GIVEN NAMES Spanish 13%. *Felicitas* (2), *Araceli, Armando, Arturo, Cristina, Esequiel, Francisco, Margarita, Nestor, Paciano, Roberto, Rodelio.*

Roseland (271) **1.** English: Reaney identifies this as a habitational name from Roselands Farm in Ulcombe, Kent. However, he gives only one (late) citation, and the surname, if it exists at all in the United Kingdom, is now very rare. **2.** Americanized form of Norwegian **Røys(e)land**, a habitational name from about 30 farmsteads, many in Agder, named from Old Norse *reysi* 'heap of stones' + *land* 'land', 'farmstead'.

GIVEN NAMES Scandinavian 5%. *Nels* (3), *Vanja.*

Rosell (527) **1.** Catalan: variant of Catalan ROSSELL. **2.** Catalan: possibly also a habitational name from Rossell, a town in Castelló de la Plana. **3.** Swedish: ornamental name composed of the elements *ros* 'rose' + the common surname suffix *-ell*, from the Latin adjectival ending *-elius*. **4.** Probably an altered spelling of German **Rösel** (see ROESEL).

GIVEN NAMES Spanish 13%; Scandinavian 6%. *Luis* (7), *Teobaldo* (4), *Jorge* (3), *Pedro* (3), *Santiago* (3), *Ana* (2), *Carlos* (2), *Ernesto* (2), *Jose* (2), *Miguel* (2), *Modesto* (2), *Alberto; Erik, Nils.*

Roselle (335) Swedish: variant of ROSELL.

Roselli (606) Italian: **1.** patronymic from *Rosello*, a diminutive of ROSA. **2.** habitational name from Rosello in Chieti province.

GIVEN NAMES Italian 19%. *Antonio* (5), *Luigi* (4), *Marco* (3), *Carmine* (2), *Domenic* (2), *Giuseppe* (2), *Rinaldo* (2), *Angelo, Domenico, Enrico, Ercole, Francesco.*

Rosellini (137) Italian: diminutive of ROSELLI.

GIVEN NAMES Italian 19%. *Giovanni* (2), *Antonio, Gino, Ildo, Marino, Nilo, Pierluigi, Roberto, Romeo, Stefano.*

Rosello (152) Catalan (**Rosselló**): variant of ROSSELLO.

GIVEN NAMES Spanish 34%; Italian 7%. *Jose* (6), *Francisco* (4), *Carlos* (2), *Margarita* (2), *Mariano* (2), *Roberto* (2), *Alejandro, Alfredo, Argelio, Bernardo, Ernesto, Eulalia; Antonio, Elio, Enzo.*

Rosema (119) Frisian: unexplained.

Roseman (1494) **1.** English: from the medieval female personal name *Rosemunde*, a Norman name, actually a compound of the Germanic elements *hros* 'horse' + *mund* 'protection', but associated from an early date in the popular mind with the Latin phrase *rosa munda* 'pure rose', an epithet of the Virgin Mary. **2.** Jewish (Ashkenazic): ornamental name or name adopted by the husband of a woman bearing the Yiddish personal name *Royze* (see ROSE 3). **3.** Americanized spelling of German ROSEMANN.

Rosemann (142) **1.** German: occupational name for a merchant who sold raisins, from Middle High German *rosīn* 'raisin' (from Late Latin *rosina*) + *man* 'man'. **2.** German: from a Germanic personal name composed of the elements *hrōd* 'renown' + *man*. **3.** Jewish (Ashkenazic): variant of ROSEMAN 2.

GIVEN NAMES German 10%. *Otto* (2), *Wilhelm.*

Rosemeyer (229) German: nickname and distinguishing name for a farmer who grew or liked roses, from a compound of Middle High German *rose* 'rose' + *meier* '(tenant) farmer', 'steward'.

Rosemond (471) **1.** English and French: variant of **Rosamond** (see ROSEMAN), from the female personal name. **2.** German: probably from a Huguenot name **Rosemont** or its Germanized form **Rosemund**.

GIVEN NAMES French 4%. *Cecile, Francoise, Michel.*

Rosen (12584) **1.** Jewish (Ashkenazic): ornamental name from German *Rosen* 'roses'. **2.** German: from an inflected form of the personal name ROSE. **3.** German: habitational name from any of several places, in Westphalia, Silesia, and East Prussia, named Rosen, from *Rose* 'rose'. **4.** Swedish (**Rosén**): see ROSEEN.

GIVEN NAMES Jewish 5%. *Hyman* (23), *Meyer* (18), *Sol* (15), *Emanuel* (10), *Isadore* (6), *Chaim* (5), *Miriam* (5), *Yetta* (5), *Moshe* (4), *Velvel* (3), *Yosef* (3), *Chana* (2).

Rosenau (580) German: habitational name from any of numerous places so named, from Middle High German *rōse* 'rose' + *ouw(e)* 'water meadow'.

GIVEN NAMES German 7%. *Otto* (4), *Wolfgang* (2), *Dieter, Friedhelm, Horst, Kurt, Lorenz, Siegfried.*

Rosenbach (254) German: habitational name from any of numerous places so named (see ROSE and BACH).

GIVEN NAMES German 4%. *Kurt* (2), *Hans.*

Rosenbalm (372) Of uncertain origin; probably an Americanized spelling of German ROSENBAUM.

Rosenbauer (121) German: occupational name for a rose grower, from Middle High German *rōse* 'rose' + *gebūr* 'farmer' (see BAUER).

GIVEN NAMES German 7%. *Kurt, Rainer.*

Rosenbaum (4282) **1.** German: habitational name for someone who lived at a house distinguished by the sign of a rose-bush, Middle High German *rōsenboum*. **2.** Jewish (Ashkenazic): ornamental adoption of modern German *Rosenbaum* 'rose bush'.

GIVEN NAMES Jewish 5%. *Arie* (4), *Moshe* (4), *Sol* (4), *Avrohom* (3), *Baila* (3), *Baruch* (3), *Mayer* (3), *Akiva* (2), *Hyman* (2), *Isadore* (2), *Meyer* (2), *Miriam* (2).

Rosenbeck (132) German: habitational name from Rosenbeck in Brandenburg.

Rosenberg (13095) **1.** German and Jewish (Ashkenazic): habitational name from any of numerous places so named ('rose mountain'). **2.** Swedish, Danish, and Jewish (Ashkenazic): ornamental name composed of the elements *ros(e)* 'rose' + the affix *-en* (taken from German) + *berg* 'mountain'.

GIVEN NAMES Jewish 7%. *Sol* (24), *Hyman* (21), *Chaim* (19), *Miriam* (14), *Emanuel* (11), *Meyer* (11), *Aron* (10), *Isadore* (7), *Moshe* (7), *Mordechai* (6), *Mendel* (5), *Pinchas* (4).

Rosenberger (2581) German and Jewish (Ashkenazic): habitational name from any of the various places called ROSENBERG.

Rosenberry (665) Americanized form of ROSENBERG, in particular from this as a Swedish name.

Rosenblatt (1944) **1.** German: from Middle High German *rōsenblat* 'rose leaf', presumably applied as a nickname. **2.** Jewish (Ashkenazic): ornamental adoption of modern German *Rosenblatt* 'rose leaf'.

GIVEN NAMES Jewish 6%. *Sol* (4), *Hyman* (3), *Meyer* (3), *Ari* (2), *Elihu* (2), *Emanuel* (2), *Meir* (2), *Mort* (2), *Simcha* (2), *Zev* (2), *Aviva*, *Benyamin*.

Rosenbloom (833) Americanized spelling of Jewish ROSENBLUM.

GIVEN NAMES Jewish 4%. *Sol* (3), *Barak*, *Emanuel*, *Isador*, *Meir*, *Zalman*.

Rosenblum (2342) Jewish (Ashkenazic): ornamental name composed of modern German *Rosen-* 'rose' + *Blume* 'flower'.

GIVEN NAMES Jewish 9%. *Hyman* (5), *Sol* (4), *Moshe* (3), *Shimon* (3), *Avraham* (2), *Emanuel* (2), *Mendel* (2), *Meyer* (2), *Miriam* (2), *Shaul* (2), *Ahuva*, *Alter*.

Rosenbluth (274) Jewish (Ashkenazic) and German (**Rosenblüth**): from Middle High German *rōsenbluot*, German *Rosenblüt* 'rose (bloom)'. The Jewish name is of ornamental origin.

GIVEN NAMES Jewish 7%. *Sol* (2), *Avi*, *Emanuel*, *Hyman*, *Miriam*, *Yitzhak*.

Rosenboom (173) **1.** Dutch: habitational name from any of several places named Rozenboom. **2.** North German: variant of ROSENBAUM.

FOREBEARS The name **Roseboom** is recorded in Beverwijck in New Netherland (Albany, NY) in the 17th century.

Rosenbrock (99) North German or Dutch: habitational name from a place called Rosenbrock or (Dutch) Roosbroek, named with Middle Low German *rose* 'rose' + *brock* 'marsh'.

Rosenburg (368) German and Jewish (Ashkenazic): variant of ROSENBERG.

Rosencrance (122) Americanized spelling of ROSENKRANZ.

Rosencrans (345) Dutch, German, Scandinavian, and Jewish (Ashkenazic): variant spelling of ROSENKRANZ.

Rosencrantz (166) Dutch, German, Scandinavian, and Jewish (Ashkenazic): variant spelling of ROSENKRANZ.

Rosendahl (660) **1.** Swedish and Danish: either an ornamental name composed of the elements *rosen-* (combining form of *ros* 'rose') + *dahl*, an old or ornamental spelling of *dal* 'valley', or a habitational name from a widespread place name of comparatively recent origin. **2.** German: variant of ROSENTHAL.

GIVEN NAMES Scandinavian 4%; German 4%. *Anders*, *Eskil*, *Helmer*, *Nels*; *Kurt* (3), *Fritz*, *Gottfried*, *Gunter*, *Hans*.

Rosendale (340) Americanized form of Swedish ROSENDAHL.

Rosene (322) Variant of Swedish ROSEEN.

GIVEN NAME Scandinavian 4%. *Hilmer*.

Rosener (194) German: variant of ROSNER.

Rosenfeld (3196) **1.** German: habitational name from a place of this name, near Wittenberg. **2.** Jewish (Ashkenazic): ornamental name from German *Rosenfeld* 'rose field'.

GIVEN NAMES Jewish 9%. *Hyman* (6), *Meyer* (6), *Sol* (6), *Mendel* (4), *Hershel* (3), *Mort* (3), *Moshe* (3), *Myer* (3), *Shlomo* (3), *Arnon* (2), *Aron* (2), *Baruch* (2).

Rosenfeldt (141) German: variant spelling of ROSENFELD.

GIVEN NAMES German 6%. *Hans*, *Kurt*.

Rosenfield (801) Partly Americanized form of ROSENFELD.

Rosengard (125) Swedish and Jewish (from Sweden): ornamental name from *rosen-* (combining form of *ros* 'rose') + *gard* 'farm'.

Rosengarten (365) **1.** German: habitational name from any of numerous places so named, or from a house or an area of a town so named. *Rosengarten* was also used as a term for a red-light district. **2.** Jewish (Ashkenazic): ornamental name from German *Rosengarten* 'garden of roses'.

GIVEN NAMES Jewish 7%. *Avrohom* (2), *Sholom* (2), *Baruch*, *Miriam*, *Shimon*, *Shmuel*, *Zev*.

Rosengrant (181) Americanized form of ROSENKRANZ.

GIVEN NAME German 4%. *Kurt*.

Rosengren (344) Swedish: ornamental name composed of the elements *rosen-* (combining form of *ros* 'rose') + *gren* 'branch'.

GIVEN NAMES Scandinavian 8%. *Erik* (2), *Joakim*, *Lars*, *Lennart*.

Rosenheim (107) **1.** German: habitational name from any of various places so named. **2.** Jewish (Ashkenazic): ornamental name from *rosen-* 'rose' + *heim* 'home'.

Rosenkoetter (102) German: occupational name for a farm laborer (see KOETTER), with the distinguishing epithet *Rosen-* 'roses'.

Rosenkrans (182) Dutch: see ROSENKRANZ.

Rosenkrantz (254) Dutch, German, Scandinavian, and Jewish (Ashkenazic): variant spelling of ROSENKRANZ.

GIVEN NAMES Jewish 6%; German 5%. *Emanuel* (3), *Hyman*, *Meyer*, *Sol*, *Yetta*; *Ernst* (2), *Kurt*.

Rosenkranz (550) **1.** Dutch, German, and Scandinavian: from Middle Low German *rōsenkranz* 'wreath', 'rosary' (or a cognate in a related language), hence a metonymic occupational name for a wreath or rosary maker, or a habitational name for someone who lived at a house distinguished by the sign of a wreath or in a place named with this word. **2.** Jewish (Ashkenazic): ornamental adoption of the Dutch and German name, or of the German word *Rosenkranz* 'wreath'.

FOREBEARS The Rosenkranz family were powerful and influential throughout northern Europe in the medieval and Renaissance period. They originated in Denmark, but spread throughout the Baltic area and into the Netherlands, where they became well established. Harmon Hendrick Rosenkrans, a merchant of Dutch origin, came to New Amsterdam from Bergen in Norway before 1657, the year in which he was married. Bergen was a Hanseatic port in which there were many Dutch and German traders.

GIVEN NAMES German 6%. *Fritz* (2), *Kurt* (2), *Hans*, *Helmut*, *Otto*, *Wessel*.

Rosenlund (213) Swedish: ornamental name composed of the elements *rosen-* (inflected form of *ros* 'rose') + *lund* 'grove'.

GIVEN NAMES Scandinavian 15%. *Iver* (3), *Bertel* (2), *Alarik*, *Thor*.

Rosenman (221) **1.** Jewish (Ashkenazic): elaborated form of ROSEN. **2.** German (**Rosenmann**): variant of **Rosemann** (see ROSEMAN).

GIVEN NAMES Jewish 11%. *Avraham*, *Golda*, *Mandel*, *Moshe*, *Sol*, *Tova*, *Yehuda*.

Rosenow (697) German: habitational name from any of numerous places so named. Compare ROSENAU.

GIVEN NAMES German 4%. *Bernd*, *Dieter*, *Eldor*, *Fritz*, *Manfred*.

Rosenquist (665) Swedish: ornamental name composed of the elements *rosen-* (inflected form of *ros* 'rose') + *quist*, an old or ornamental spelling of *kvist* 'twig'.

GIVEN NAMES Scandinavian 8%. *Erik* (4), *Anders* (2), *Lars* (2), *Hakon*, *Swen*, *Thor*.

Rosenson (116) **1.** Jewish (Ashkenazic): metronymic from the Yiddish female

personal name *Royze* 'rose' + German *Sohn* 'son'. **2.** Swedish: patronymic from ROSEN.
GIVEN NAMES Jewish 7%; German 4%. *Hyman, Levi, Sol.*

Rosensteel (279) Americanized spelling of German ROSENSTIEL.

Rosenstein (1091) **1.** Jewish (Ashkenazic): ornamental name compound from German *Rosen-* 'rose' + *Stein* 'stone'. **2.** German: habitational name from a place so named. As a component of place names, *stein* 'rock', 'stone' typically signifies a stone structure such as a castle or house.
GIVEN NAMES Jewish 6%. *Hyman* (3), *Anat* (2), *Aviva* (2), *Sol* (2), *Zwi* (2), *Ari, Avram, Miriam, Mordechai, Rachmil, Yakob.*

Rosenstiel (138) German: from Middle High German *rōsenstil* 'rose stem'.

Rosenstock (333) **1.** German: habitational name for someone who lived at a house distinguished by the sign of a rose bush, Middle High German *rōsenstoc*. **2.** Jewish (Ashkenazic): ornamental name from the German compound *Rosenstock* 'rose bush'.
GIVEN NAMES Jewish 4%. *Hyman, Yechiel.*

Rosensweig (175) Respelling of Jewish ROSENZWEIG.
GIVEN NAMES Jewish 6%. *Meyer, Rebekah, Smadar.*

Rosenthal (8933) **1.** German: habitational name from any of numerous places named Rosenthal or Rosendahl ('rose valley'). **2.** Jewish (Ashkenazic): ornamental name from the German compound *Rosenthal* 'rose valley'.
GIVEN NAMES Jewish 4%. *Hyman* (8), *Miriam* (8), *Meyer* (6), *Isadore* (5), *Sol* (5), *Ari* (4), *Avi* (4), *Emanuel* (4), *Mort* (3), *Aron* (2), *Avram* (2), *Herschel* (2).

Rosentreter (220) German: from Middle High German *rose* 'rose' + an agent derivative of *treten* 'to step or tread', an occupational name for a rose grower or a topographic name for someone who lived by a path that was overgrown with roses.
GIVEN NAMES German 6%. *Egon, Erwin, Otto.*

Rosenwald (298) **1.** German: habitational name from any of several places so named, for example in East Prussia. **2.** Jewish (Ashkenazic): ornamental name from German compound *Rosenwald* 'rose wood'.
GIVEN NAMES French 4%. *Gisele, Remy.*

Rosenwasser (168) **1.** German: metonymic occupational name for a distiller or herbalist, from Middle High German *rōsenwazzer* 'rose water'. **2.** Jewish (Ashkenazic): ornamental adoption of modern German *Rosenwasser* 'rose water'.
GIVEN NAMES Jewish 14%. *Chaim* (2), *Hyman* (2), *Chaya, Devorah, Emanuel, Sol, Yaakov.*

Rosenwinkel (143) German: probably a topographic name for someone who lived in a secluded place (Middle High German *winkel* 'nook', 'corner') where roses grew.

GIVEN NAMES German 7%. *Erwin, Gerda, Hans, Kurt.*

Rosenzweig (1312) **1.** German: habitational name for someone who lived at a house distinguished by the sign of a rose spray, Middle High German *rōsenzwīc*. **2.** Jewish (Ashkenazic): ornamental name from German *Rosenzweig* 'rose twig'.
GIVEN NAMES Jewish 7%. *Meyer* (3), *Sol* (2), *Aron, Avrohom, Avrum, Eliahu, Eran, Gilad, Herschel, Hershel, Hyman, Hymen.*

Roser (813) **1.** German: topographic name for someone who lived at a place where wild roses grew (see ROSE 1), with the suffix *-er* denoting an inhabitant. **2.** German (**Röser**): habitational name from places called Rös, Roes, or Rösa in Bavaria, Rhineland, and Saxony, or a variant of ROSSER. **3.** Swiss German (**Röser**): from a short form of a Germanic personal name based on *hrōd* 'renown'. **4.** English: unexplained.

Rosero (133) Spanish: **1.** from a derivative of *rosa* 'rose'. **2.** possibly also from *rosero* 'gatherer of saffron crocus flowers'.
GIVEN NAMES Spanish 43%; Italian 7%. *Luis* (6), *Jaime* (3), *Carlos* (2), *Cesar* (2), *Manuel* (2), *Alfredo, Amparo, Ana, Angelina, Bernardo, Eduardo, Galo*; *Fausto* (4), *Eliseo, Marcello, Marco.*

Roses (134) Catalan: old form of ROSAS.
GIVEN NAMES Spanish 23%. *Luis* (3), *Francisco* (2), *Guillermo* (2), *Jose* (2), *Ana, Carlos, Enrique, Gerardo, Guilermo, Jesus, Juan, Marcelino.*

Rosete (154) Spanish: at all events, from a derivative of *rosa* 'rose'; possibly from the female personal name *Rosete* (from French *Rosette*).
GIVEN NAMES Spanish 46%. *Alfredo* (3), *Jose* (3), *Juan* (2), *Miguel* (2), *Adolfo, Alberto, Alfonso, Amador, Amaro, Arturo, Bartolome, Caridad*; *Antonio, Elio, Prisco, Romeo.*

Roseth (116) Norwegian: habitational name from any of several farmsteads named either Roset, probably from a personal name (Old Norse *Rói*, modern Norwegian *Roe*, + *set* 'farmstead', 'dwelling'), or Røset, Rødset, from Old Norse *ross* 'mare' or *rauðr* 'red' + *set*.

Rosett (106) **1.** English: probably an altered form of French ROSETTE. **2.** Norwegian: variant of ROSETH.

Rosetta (172) Italian: from a derivative of ROSA.
GIVEN NAMES Italian 4%. *Sal* (2), *Nicola.*

Rosette (216) Origin unidentified.
GIVEN NAMES Spanish 13%. *Carlos* (2), *Jose* (2), *Arturo, Cirilo, Consuelo, Cristina, Eloy, Eufrosina, Felipe, Jesus, Jorge, Manuel.*

Rosetti (339) Italian: patronymic from *Rosetto*, a masculine equivalent of ROSETTA.
GIVEN NAMES Italian 8%. *Antonio* (2), *Angelo, Attilio, Carlo, Carmine, Dino, Gennaro, Rocco.*

Rosevear (203) Cornish: habitational name from either of two places called Roseveare. The one in St. Austell is named from Cornish *ros* 'moor' + *mur* 'great', 'large'; the other, in St. Mawgan in Meneage, is from *res* 'ford' + *mur*. In both cases, the initial *m*- of the adjective has been lenited to *v*-.

Rosh (104) **1.** Dutch or German: Americanized spelling of ROSCH. **2.** Slovenian: nickname from *roš*, a reduced form of *rovaš* 'stick split lengthwise', used to keep accounts (by scoring or making notches in the wood). Compare ROS 4. **3.** Jewish: either a shortened form of some Ashkenazic surname, or from Hebrew *rosh* 'head'.
GIVEN NAMES Dutch 5%; Jewish 5%; German 4%. *Herm* (2), *Malene; Meyer* (2).

Roshak (109) Altered spelling of German **Roschack** or **Roschak**, probably a variant of **Raschack**, from *radzak* 'counselor', 'adviser'.

Rosholt (127) Norwegian: habitational name from either of two farms called Røsholt in southeastern Norway, named with Old Norse, either *ross* 'mare' or *ruð* 'clearing' + *holt* 'grove', 'wood'.

Roshon (134) Americanized form of German **Roschen**, variant of ROSCHE.

Roshto (141) Perhaps an Americanized spelling of French **Rocheteau**, a diminutive of ROCHE.

Rosi (171) **1.** Greek (**Rosis**): metronymic from the female personal name ROSA 1, or alternatively a variant of ROSSO. **2.** Italian: patronymic from the personal name *Roso*, which may be a masculinized form of ROSA or alternatively a derivative of a Germanic personal name.
GIVEN NAMES Italian 11%. *Reno* (3), *Angelo* (2), *Gianfranco, Gino, Luca, Paolo.*

Rosiak (168) Polish: patronymic from ROSA.
GIVEN NAMES Polish 4%. *Ignatius, Janina, Marcin.*

Rosica (114) Italian (Chieti): unexplained.
GIVEN NAMES Italian 9%. *Rocco* (2), *Antonietta, Giuseppe.*

Rosich (100) **1.** Croatian and Serbian (**Rosić**): metronymic from the female personal name *Rosa*, a pet form of *Rozalija*, Latin *Rosalia*. **2.** Slovenian (mainly westernmost Slovenia; **Rosič**): probably a nickname from the dialect adjective *ros* 'russet' (see ROS 3). **3.** Bosnian, Croatian, and Serbian (**Rošić**): unexplained.

Rosie (100) Scottish (Caithness): from a pet form of ROSE 1.

Rosiek (137) Polish: from a derivative of Polish *rosić* 'bedew', 'spatter', 'sprinkle', probably an occupational name for someone who sprayed a crop of flax during the fulling process.

Rosier (1158) French: topographic name from *rosier* 'rosebush'.

Rosin (812) **1.** German: habitational name from Rosien near Bentheim or Rosin in

Mecklenburg. **2.** French: pet form of the personal name ROSE 1.

GIVEN NAMES German 7%. *Ewald* (2), *Frieda* (2), *Helmut* (2), *Armin, Arno, Bodo, Dieter, Eberhard, Erwin, Gottieb, Gunter, Heinz.*

Rosine (136) Perhaps an altered spelling of German **Rosien**, a variant of ROSIN.

GIVEN NAMES French 5%. *Andre, Charlet.*

Rosing (197) **1.** German and Dutch: patronymic from a derivative of the medieval personal name *Rozinus*. **2.** German (also **Rösing**): from a short form of a Germanic personal name formed with *hrōd* 'renown'. **3.** Swedish: ornamental name from *ros* 'rose'.

Rosini (156) Italian: patronymic from the personal name *Rosino*, a pet form of *Roso* (see ROSI).

GIVEN NAMES Italian 7%. *Giuseppe* (2), *Pasquale.*

Rosinski (732) Polish (**Rosiński**) and Jewish (from Poland and Ukraine): habitational name from an unidentified place.

GIVEN NAMES Polish 5%. *Casimir* (2), *Eugeniusz, Ewa, Leszek, Piotr, Tadeusz, Waclaw, Zbigniew, Zigmund.*

Rosinsky (189) Jewish: variant spelling of ROSINSKI.

GIVEN NAMES German 4%; Jewish 4%. *Erwin* (2), *Armin*; *Meyer.*

Roskam (193) German and Dutch: metonymic occupational name for a horse dealer, from Middle High German *roskamp*, Middle Dutch *roscam* 'currycomb', 'horse comb'.

Roskamp (112) Dutch and German: variant of ROSKAM.

GIVEN NAME French 4%; German 4%. *Camille.*

Roske (191) German: from a pet form of a Slavic personal name beginning with the element *Rodo-*, from an Old Slavic word meaning 'race', 'line', or from a Slavic derivative of ROSE 1.

Roskelley (139) Cornish: habitational name from either of two places in Cornwall called Roskilly.

Rosko (415) Hungarian (**Roskó**): from a pet form of the personal name *Roska*, of Romanian origin.

Roskopf (123) German (**Rosskopf**): literally 'horse head'; a habitational name relating to the ancient custom of placing a horse head on house gabels or a nickname.

Roskos (234) Variant of Hungarian ROSKO.

Rosler (139) German (**Rösler**): **1.** occupational name for a rose grower. **2.** from an agent derivative of Middle High German *ræse* 'pool where hemp and flax were retted'. **3.** habitational name for someone who lived at a house named 'at the rose'.

GIVEN NAMES German 7%. *Hans* (2), *Ernst, Lieselotte.*

Roslund (100) Swedish: ornamental name composed of *ros* 'rose' + *lund* 'grove'.

GIVEN NAME Scandinavian 10%. *Iver.*

Rosman (457) **1.** Jewish (Ashkenazic): from South German *Ross* 'horse', hence an occupational name for a breeder or keeper of horses or perhaps a nickname for someone thought to resemble a horse or a habitational name for someone who lived at a house distinguished by the sign of a horse. **2.** Jewish (Ashkenazic): variant of ROSE 3 with the addition of *man* 'man'. **3.** German and Slovenian: variant spelling of German ROSSMANN or its Slovenian form **Rozman**.

GIVEN NAMES Jewish 6%. *Anat, Aron, Asher, Chana, Hyman, Lipot, Miriam, Rivka, Shalom, Shlomo, Tova.*

Rosmarin (137) German: metonymic occupational name for a herbalist, from *Rosmarin* 'rosemary' (from Latin *ros marinus*, literally 'sea dew').

Rosner (1705) **1.** German (**Rösner**): habitational name for someone from a place called Rosenau or Rosna, or for someone who lived at a house distinguished by the sign of a rose, from Middle High German *rōse* 'rose'. **2.** Jewish (Ashkenazic): variant of ROSE 3.

GIVEN NAMES Jewish 6%. *Moshe* (4), *Sol* (3), *Aron* (2), *Bernat* (2), *Chaim* (2), *Chana, Devorah, Dov, Eliezer, Elimelech, Herschel, Heshy.*

Roso (118) **1.** Italian: unexplained; perhaps a masculinized form of the personal name *Rosa* or a variant of ROSSO. **2.** Spanish: unexplained.

GIVEN NAME Italian 7%. *Carlo* (2).

Rosoff (332) Jewish: **1.** shortened form of eastern Ashkenazic **Rozovsky**, habitational name from the town of Grozov in Belarus. **2.** Germanized or Americanized form of eastern Ashkenazic (from Belarus) **Rozov**, most likely also derived from the town of Grozov.

GIVEN NAMES Jewish 4%. *Aviva, Hyman, Kalmen.*

Rosol (207) Polish (**Rosół, Rosoł**): from Polish *rosół* 'clear soup', 'beef tea'. This word is found in the idiomatic expression *rozebrany do rosółu* 'stripped to the skin', and this idiom may be the source of the surname as a nickname.

GIVEN NAMES Polish 6%. *Bronislaw, Casimir, Irena, Jozefa, Katarzyna, Stanislaw.*

Ross (81892) **1.** Scottish and English (of Norman origin): habitational name for someone from Rots near Caen in Normandy, probably named with the Germanic element *rod* 'clearing'. Compare RHODES. This was the original home of a family de Ros, who were established in Kent in 1130. **2.** Scottish and English: habitational name from any of various places called Ross or Roos(e), deriving the name from Welsh *rhós* 'upland' or moorland, or from a British ancestor of this word, which also had the sense 'promontory'. This is the sense of the cognate Gaelic word *ros*. Known sources of the surname include Roos in Humberside (formerly in East Yorkshire) and the region

of northern Scotland known as Ross. Other possible sources are Ross-on-Wye in Herefordshire, Ross in Northumbria (which is on a promontory), and Roose in Lancashire **3.** English and German: from the Germanic personal name *Rozzo*, a short form of the various compound names with the first element *hrōd* 'renown', introduced into England by the Normans in the form *Roce*. **4.** German and Jewish (Ashkenazic): metonymic occupational name for a breeder or keeper of horses, from Middle High German *ros*, German *Ross* 'horse'; perhaps also a nickname for someone thought to resemble a horse or a habitational name for someone who lived at a house distinguished by the sign of a horse. **5.** Jewish: Americanized form of ROSE 3.

Rossa (180) Italian: **1.** variant, feminine in form, of ROSSO. **2.** habitational name from a place called Rossa in Vercelli province.

Rossano (269) Italian: habitational name from Rossano in Cosenza province or, to a lesser extent, from Rossano Veneto in Vicenza province.

GIVEN NAMES Italian 12%. *Antonio* (2), *Sal* (2), *Enrico, Italo, Lorenzo, Rocco, Salvatore, Sandro.*

Rossbach (361) German: habitational name from any of numerous places named Rossbach or Rosbach.

GIVEN NAMES German 8%. *Kurt* (4), *Gerhard* (2), *Dietrich, Ingeburg, Otto, Uwe.*

Rossberg (143) German: habitational name from any of numerous places so named.

GIVEN NAMES German 7%. *Wolfgang* (2), *Erhard.*

Rosse (230) German: topographic name from Middle High German *ræsse* 'kiln', in particular one used for drying hemp and flax or for burning lime.

GIVEN NAMES Dutch 4%. *Dirk* (2), *Joris.*

Rossel (115) Spanish, Catalan, and French: nickname for a red-haired person, from a variant of *rosel(l)*, a diminutive of *ros* 'red'.

GIVEN NAMES Spanish 17%; French 5%; Dutch 4%. *Fernando* (2), *Juan* (2), *Alvaro, Ana, Carols, Catarino, Guillermo, Javier, Jose, Orlando, Pedro, Ruben*; *Philippe, Yves*; *Gerrit* (2), *Flor.*

Rossell (517) **1.** English: from the Anglo-Norman French personal name *Rocel*, a pet form of *Roce* (see ROSS 3). **2.** Catalan: nickname for someone with red hair, from a diminutive of *ros* 'red'.

Rosselle (108) French: variant spelling of ROSSEL.

Rosselli (325) Italian: patronymic or plural form of ROSSELLO.

GIVEN NAMES Italian 25%. *Salvatore* (9), *Angelo* (6), *Dante* (2), *Dino* (2), *Luigi* (2), *Antonio, Carmelo, Emelio, Francesco, Gaetana, Giuseppi, Lorenzo.*

Rossello (110) **1.** Italian: diminutive of ROSSO. **2.** Catalan (**Rosselló**): regional name from the Pyrenean district of El

Rosselló, or habitational name from a town named Rosselló, in Lleida. This name was common among Catalan Jews.
GIVEN NAMES Spanish 19%; Italian 6%. *Bernardo* (2), *Juan* (2), *Miguel* (2), *Pedro* (2), *Ana, Guillermo, Manuel, Rafael, Salvador, Zoilo; Carmelo, Dante.*

Rosselot (175) Apparently an altered spelling of French **Rousselot**, a diminutive of ROUSSEL or **Rocheleau**, of uncertain origin.
GIVEN NAME French 4%. *Andre.*

Rossen (235) **1.** German: habitational name from a place so named in East Prussia. **2.** English: possibly a variant spelling of ROSSON.

Rosser (2708) **1.** Welsh: variant of English ROGER. **2.** German (**Rösser**): occupational name for a horse dealer, a groom, or a carter.

Rossetti (1275) Italian: patronymic or plural form of ROSSETTO.
GIVEN NAMES Italian 15%. *Angelo* (9), *Rocco* (5), *Carmine* (4), *Domenic* (3), *Ettore* (3), *Gino* (3), *Salvatore* (3), *Antonio* (2), *Dante* (2), *Dino* (2), *Gilda* (2), *Luigi* (2).

Rossetto (182) Italian: from a pet form of the personal name ROSSO. This is also found as a family name in Greece.
GIVEN NAMES Italian 12%. *Domenic* (2), *Aldo, Annamaria, Carmel, Ciro, Dino, Paolo, Primo.*

Rossey (105) Probably an altered spelling of French **Rossé**, from a derivative of *ros* 'red', 'auburn', hence a nickname for someone with red hair, or **Rosset**, which has the same meaning.
GIVEN NAME French 5%. *Michel.*

Rossi (9787) Italian: patronymic from ROSSO. This is the commonest surname in Italy. It is also found as a family name in Greece.
GIVEN NAMES Italian 12%. *Angelo* (54), *Antonio* (20), *Rocco* (12), *Aldo* (11), *Gino* (11), *Luigi* (11), *Carlo* (10), *Carmine* (10), *Domenic* (10), *Pasquale* (9), *Salvatore* (9), *Dino* (7).

Rossie (160) See ROSSEY.

Rossier (129) French: probably a topographic name for someone who lived in marshy terrain, from a derivative of *ros* 'reed'.
GIVEN NAME French 4%. *Raoul.*

Rossignol (619) French: nickname for a person with a good singing voice, or ironically for a raucous person, from Old French *rossignol* 'nightingale' (Old Provençal *rossinhol*, from Late Latin *lusciniolus*).
GIVEN NAMES French 15%. *Andre* (3), *Lucien* (3), *Monique* (3), *Rosaire* (3), *Emile* (2), *Adelard, Alexina, Alphonse, Armand, Aurele, Camille, Cecile.*

Rossin (190) **1.** Italian: northern variant of ROSSINI, with loss of the final -*i*. **2.** French: diminutive of ROUX. **3.** German: habitational name from a place so named near Anklam in West Pomerania.

GIVEN NAMES German 8%. *Claus* (2), *Viktor* (2), *Ewald.*

Rossing (195) German (**Rössing**): habitational name from a place so named south of Hannover. This name is also established in Denmark and Sweden.
GIVEN NAMES Scandinavian 5%. *Bjorn, Erik.*

Rossini (488) Italian: **1.** patronymic from a pet form of the personal name ROSSO. **2.** habitational name from a place named Rossino in Bergamo.
GIVEN NAMES Italian 21%. *Aldo* (5), *Enrico* (5), *Luigi* (3), *Angelo* (2), *Ciro* (2), *Romolo* (2), *Salvadore* (2), *Antonio, Arnaldo, Arnoldo, Dario, Dino, Gino, Giovanni, Lorenzo, Mario, Orlando, Paulina.*

Rossiter (1331) English: variant of ROCHESTER.

Rossitto (139) Southern Italian: from the personal name *Rossitto*, a pet form of ROSSO.
GIVEN NAMES Italian 29%. *Carmelo* (2), *Sal* (2), *Sofio* (2), *Alessio, Cesario, Emilio, Luciano, Salvatore.*

Rossler (156) **1.** German (**Rössler**): see ROESSLER. **2.** Jewish (Ashkenazic): occupational name for someone who looked after horses, from German *Ross* 'horse' + the agent suffix -*ler*.
GIVEN NAME Jewish 5%. *Yehuda* (2).

Rossman (2173) **1.** Altered spelling of German ROSSMANN. **2.** Jewish (Ashkenazic): variant spelling of ROSMAN.

Rossmann (217) German: from Middle High German *ros* 'horse' + *man* 'man', applied as an occupational name for a horse breeder, handler or dealer, as a nickname for someone thought to resemble the horse in some way, or as a habitational name for someone who lived at a house distinguished by the sign of a horse.
GIVEN NAMES German 5%. *Gerhard, Nikolaus, Otto.*

Rossmiller (184) Altered spelling of German **Rossmüller**, a distinguishing nickname for the owner of a mill that was worked by horse power, or possibly a habitational name for someone living at a house named *Rossmühle*.

Rossner (182) German: **1.** variant of **Röesner** (see ROSLER), ROESLER, or ROESSLER. **2.** (**Rössner**): habitational name from any of several places called Rössen in Saxony and East Prussia. **3.** from a short form of a Germanic personal name formed with *hród* 'renown'.
GIVEN NAMES German 17%. *Otto* (3), *Gottlieb* (2), *Gernot, Heinz, Kurt, Reinhold, Ruediger.*

Rosso (1004) **1.** Italian: from the personal name *Rosso*, a nickname for someone with red hair, a red beard, or a ruddy complexion, from *rosso* 'red'. **2.** Greek (**Rossos**): ethnic name from *Rōssos* 'Russian'.
GIVEN NAMES Italian 4%. *Angelo* (3), *Nino* (2), *Dante, Dario, Enrico, Gino, Giovanna, Ignazio, Oreste, Salvatore, Silvio, Vittorio.*

Rosson (1231) **1.** English: habitational name from Rostherne in Cheshire, recorded in Domesday Book as *Rodestorne*, from the Old Scandinavian personal name *Rauthr* + Old English *thorn* or *thyrne* 'thorn tree'. **2.** Italian: from an augmentative of ROSSO.

Rossow (861) German (of Slavic origin): habitational name from any of several places so named in eastern Germany. **Rossau** may be a variant, from a place near Magdeburg.

Rossum (103) German and Dutch: habitational name from a place so named in the Dutch-German border area west of Nordhorn.

Rossy (110) Hispanic: unexplained; in form this is very unspanish.
GIVEN NAMES Spanish 16%. *Jose* (3), *Manuel* (2), *Miguel* (2), *Asencio, Edgardo, Estela, Francisco, Jaime, Jorge, Mercedes.*

Rost (1465) German: **1.** nickname for a red-haired person, from Middle High German *rost* 'rust'. **2.** metonymic occupational name for a limeburner or blacksmith, from Middle High German, Middle Low German *röst* 'grate', 'grill' or Middle High German *röst(e)* 'fire', 'embers', 'pyre', 'grate' (typically one for burning lime).
GIVEN NAMES German 4%. *Detlef* (2), *Manfred* (2), *Arno, Eldor, Heinrich, Heinz, Klaus, Kurt, Mathias, Otto, Ralf, Reinhart.*

Rostad (308) **1.** Norwegian: habitational name from any of over ten farmsteads so named from the Old Norse personal name *Hróarr* (see ROGSTAD) + *staðir* 'farmstead', 'dwelling'. The surname is also found in Sweden. **2.** Norwegian (**Røstad**): variant of RUSTAD.
GIVEN NAMES Scandinavian 13%. *Iver, Knut, Nels.*

Rostek (123) Probably a respelling of German **Rosteck**, a habitational name from a place so named in East Prussia.

Rosten (208) **1.** English: variant of ROSSON. **2.** Norwegian: habitational name from any of several farmsteads named Rosten or Røsten, from *rust* 'grove', 'ridge'. **3.** Americanized form of one or more likesounding Jewish surnames. Compare ROTHSTEIN.
GIVEN NAMES German 4%. *Bernhard, Bernhardt, Erna.*

Roster (158) German (also **Röster**): occupational name for a lime burner, smelter, or blacksmith, a variant of ROST, with the addition of the agent suffix -*er*.

Rostkowski (105) Polish: habitational name for someone from places called Rostków in Ciechanów and Płock voivodeships.
GIVEN NAMES Polish 8%. *Jadwiga, Wieslaw, Zbigniew.*

Roston (205) English: **1.** habitational name from a place in Derbyshire, recorded in Domesday Book as *Roschintone*, possibly 'estate (Old English *tūn*) associated with

Hrōthsige', an Old English personal name.
2. variant of ROSSON.

Rostron (209) English: variant of ROSSON.

Roswell (205) English: apparently a habitational name from an unidentified place.
GIVEN NAME French 5%. *Marcell*.

Roszak (167) Polish: from the personal name *Roszak*, a short form of *Rościsław*, which is composed of the Slavic elements *rosti* 'to grow' + *slav* 'glory'.
GIVEN NAMES Polish 6%. *Andrzej, Casimir, Irena*.

Roszel (108) Polish: from a pet form of the personal name *Rościsław* (see ROSZAK).

Roszell (188) Germanized or Americanized spelling of Polish ROSZEL.

Roszkowski (226) Polish: habitational name for someone from any of various places called Roszkowo, Roszków, or Roszkowice, named with the personal name *Roszek*.
GIVEN NAMES Polish 24%. *Jadwiga* (2), *Leszek* (2), *Casimir, Henryk, Ireneusz, Jacek, Janina, Jerzy, Krzysztof, Mieczyslaw, Miroslaw, Piotr*.

Rota (326) **1.** Northern Italian: habitational name from any of various places named with *rota* 'wheel', in particular Rota d'Imagna in Bergamo and Rota Greca in Cosenza. **2.** Italian: from a short form of *Buonarrota, Buonarroto*, an omen name meaning 'good addition'. **3.** Spanish: habitational name from a place in the province of Cádiz, so named from Latin *rota* 'wheel'. **4.** Greek (**Rotas**): from the vocabulary word *rota* 'course (of a ship)' (from Italian *rotta*, French *route*), hence perhaps an occupational nickname for a steersman.
GIVEN NAMES Italian 10%. *Sal* (3), *Angelo* (2), *Amedio, Antonio, Carmela, Gilda, Natale, Pasquale, Valentino*.

Rotan (164) Probably an altered spelling of German ROTHAN, a nickname meaning 'red John' for someone with red hair, from Middle High German *rōt* 'red' + *Han*, a short form of JOHANNES.

Rotar (126) Dutch: from the Germanic personal name *Rotard*, a compound of *hrōd* 'renown' + *hard* 'hardy', 'brave', 'strong'.
GIVEN NAMES Russian 5%. *Oksana, Vasiliy, Vladimir*.

Rotchford (161) Irish: variant spelling of English ROCHFORD.
GIVEN NAME Irish 5%. *Caitlin*.

Rote (543) Perhaps an Americanized spelling of German ROTH or ROTHE.

Rotella (662) Italian: **1.** from a derivative of ROTA. **2.** from a feminine pet form of the personal name *Roto* (see ROTI). **3.** habitational name from Rotella, in Scoli Piceno province.
GIVEN NAMES Italian 15%. *Salvatore* (4), *Saverio* (4), *Angelo* (2), *Antonio* (2), *Luigi* (2), *Carmel, Carmela, Filippo, Gennaro, Giacomo, Guido, Lorenzo*.

Rotelli (104) Italian: from the personal name *Rotello*, a pet form of ROTI.
GIVEN NAMES French 4%; Italian 4%. *Marcelle; Marco* (2), *Antonio*.

Roten (691) Swiss German: variant spelling of **Rothen**, recorded in 1832 as the surname of a Swiss Mennonite immigrant. It is probably topographic in origin, from a field or rocky slope so named due to the red color of the soil or rock.

Rotenberg (311) **1.** German (also found in Sweden): habitational name from any of numerous places named Rotenberg. **2.** Jewish (Ashkenazic): variant of ROTHEN-BERG.
GIVEN NAMES Jewish 19%; German 6%. *Mendel* (2), *Simcha* (2), *Aron, Dorith, Dov, Eliezer, Hershel, Ilya, Meir, Meyer, Moisey, Morry; Frieda* (2), *Wolfgang* (2), *Hilde, Wolf*.

Rotenberry (270) Probably an Americanized form of ROTENBERG.

Rotering (102) German: patronymic of ROTHER 2.
GIVEN NAME German 4%. *Mathias*.

Rotert (290) German: variant of ROTHERT.

Roth (25556) **1.** German and Jewish (Ashkenazic): nickname for a person with red hair, from Middle High German *rōt*, German *rot* 'red'. As a Jewish surname it is also at least partly ornamental: its frequency as a Jewish surname is disproportionate to the number of Jews who, one may reasonably assume, were red-headed during the period of surname adoption. **2.** German and English: topographic name for someone who lived on land that had been cleared, Old High German *rod*, Old English *rod, roð*. **3.** German: from a short form of any of the various Germanic personal names with the first element *hrōd* 'renown'. Compare RODE 1, ROSS 3.

Rothacker (136) German: **1.** habitational name based on a field name derived from Middle High German *riuten, roten* 'to clear land (for cultivation)' + *acker* 'field'. **2.** from a Germanic personal name, *Hrodachar*, formed with *hrōd* 'renown'. **3.** Altered spelling of Swiss German **Rothacher**, a habitational name for someone from any of several places named Rothach or Rottach.
GIVEN NAMES German 6%. *Eugen, Kurt*.

Rothbard (169) Altered spelling of German and Jewish ROTHBART.
GIVEN NAME Jewish 5%. *Mort*.

Rothbart (175) German and Jewish (Ashkenazic): nickname for someone with a red beard, from Middle High German *rōt* 'red' + *bart* 'beard', German *rot* + *Bart*.
GIVEN NAMES Jewish 6%. *Emanuel, Meyer, Shraga*.

Rothbauer (205) German: distinguishing nickname for a farmer whose land was in a clearing, from a noun derivative of Middle High German *riuten, roten* 'to clear land' + *gebūr(e)* 'farmer' (see BAUER).

Rothbaum (112) Jewish (Ashkenazic): ornamental name composed of German *rot* 'red' + *Baum* 'tree'.
GIVEN NAME German 4%. *Frieda*.

Rothberg (608) **1.** German: variant of ROTHENBERG. 1 **2.** Jewish (Ashkenazic): variant of ROTHENBERG 2.
GIVEN NAMES Jewish 5%. *Falk, Miriam, Myer, Sol*.

Rothchild (306) Jewish: variant of ROTHS-CHILD.
GIVEN NAMES Jewish 5%. *Eran, Herschel, Meyer, Moshe*.

Rothe (1128) German: **1.** variant of ROTH 1. **2.** habitational name from any of several places named Rothe, in Westphalia and Mecklenburg, or Rothau in Bavaria and Alsace.
GIVEN NAMES German 5%. *Kurt* (5), *Achim, Dietmar, Erhard, Franz, Friede, Heinrich, Helmut, Inge, Klaus, Siegfried, Wolfram*.

Rothell (122) Americanized spelling of German **Röthel**, a diminutive of ROTH 1, or a habitational name from a place so named in Switzerland.

Rothenbach (109) German (also **Röthenbach**): habitational name from any of numerous places named Rothenbach or Röthenbach.

Rothenberg (1521) **1.** German and Jewish (Ashkenazic): habitational name from any of numerous places named Rothenberg. **2.** Jewish (Ashkenazic): ornamental name from German *Rot(en)berg* 'red mountain'.
GIVEN NAMES Jewish 6%. *Hyman* (3), *Meyer* (3), *Chaim* (2), *Emanuel* (2), *Shlomo* (2), *Zvi* (2), *Arie, Hadassah, Isadore, Isak, Miriam, Mort*.

Rothenberger (716) German and Jewish (Ashkenazic): habitational name for someone from any of the various places called ROTHENBERG.

Rother (698) German: **1.** nickname for a person with red hair, from an inflected form of ROTH 1. **2.** from a Germanic personal name composed of the elements *hrōd* 'renown' + *hari, heri* 'army' or *hard* 'strong', 'hardy'. **3.** variant of RODER. **4.** habitational name from any of various places so named.
GIVEN NAMES German 5%. *Erwin* (3), *Hans* (2), *Heinz* (2), *Elke, Florian, Franz, Gerda, Konrad, Lotti, Reinhard*.

Rotherham (126) English: habitational name from Rotherham in South Yorkshire, named as 'homestead or village (Old English *hām*) on the river Rother', a Celtic river name meaning 'chief river'.

Rothermel (991) German: variant spelling of **Rothärmel**, literally 'red sleeve', a nickname referring to the medieval fashion for bicolored garments (e.g. a tunic consisting of a yellow bodice and red sleeves).
GIVEN NAMES German 4%. *Helmut* (2), *Otto* (2), *Arno, Gerhard, Kehl, Klaus, Kurt, Lieselotte*.

Rothermich (139) German: perhaps from *rot(er)* 'red' + the personal name *Michael*, i.e. a distinguishing nickname for a Michael with red hair.

Rothermund (102) German: **1.** literally a nickname for someone with a 'red mouth'. **2.** from a Germanic personal name composed of *hrōd* 'renown' + *mund* 'protection' with an added middle part *-er* to fit the form of 1.

Rothert (215) German: from a Germanic personal name composed of *hrōd* 'renown' + *hard* 'bold', 'brave'.

Rothery (160) English: perhaps a habitational name from an unidentified place.

Rothfeld (158) Jewish (Ashkenazic): ornamental name composed of German *rot* 'red' + *Feld* 'field'.
GIVEN NAMES Jewish 4%. *Emanuel, Mendel.*

Rothfus (123) Respelling of German ROTHFUSS.

Rothfuss (399) German: **1.** from Middle High German *rōt* 'red' + *vuoz* 'foot', a nickname for someone who followed the fashion for shoes made from a type of fine reddish leather. **2.** according to another opinion a variant of **Rotfuchs**, from the Middle Low German form *fos* 'fox', a nickname for a clever person.
GIVEN NAMES German 5%. *Hermann, Klaus, Kurt, Otto, Siebert.*

Rothgeb (339) German: variant of RATH-GEBER.

Rothkopf (164) German and Jewish (Ashkenazic): nickname for someone with red hair, from Middle High German *rōt* 'red' + *kopf* 'head', German *rot* + *Kopf*.
GIVEN NAMES Jewish 10%. *Moshe* (3), *Hyman* (2), *Ari, Sol.*

Rothlisberger (220) German (**Röthlisberger**): see ROETHLISBERGER.
GIVEN NAME German 5%. *Kurt* (2).

Rothman (2937) **1.** German (**Rothmann**) and Jewish (Ashkenazic): nickname for a person with red hair, from an elaborated form of ROTH 1. **2.** German: topographic name for someone who lived on land that had been cleared, from an elaborated form of ROTH 2. **3.** German (in Saxony and Silesia): occupational name for a counselor or nickname for a man respected for his opinions and advice, from a dialect variant of Middle High German *rāt* 'counsel' + *man* 'man'.
GIVEN NAMES Jewish 5%. *Emanuel* (5), *Sol* (4), *Meyer* (3), *Ari* (2), *Hyman* (2), *Miriam* (2), *Myer* (2), *Tovah* (2), *Arnon, Aviva, Binyomin, Chaya.*

Rothmann (117) German: see ROTHMAN.
GIVEN NAMES German 4%. *Heinrich, Heinz.*

Rothmeyer (122) German: distinguishing nickname for a red-haired tenant farmer (see ROTH 1, MEYER) or for one whose land had been cleared from forest or woodland (see ROTH 2, MEYER).

Rothrock (1340) German: from Middle High German *rōt* 'red' + *roc* 'skirt', 'tunic';

hence a nickname, probably for someone who habitually wore a red tunic.

Roths (159) German: patronymic form from ROTH.
GIVEN NAMES German 4%. *Aloysius, Math.*

Rothschild (1672) German and Jewish (Ashkenazic): habitational name from a house distinguished with a red sign (Middle High German *rōt* 'red' + *schilt* 'sign', 'shield'), the earliest recorded example dating from the 13th century. The famous banking family of this name took it from a house so marked in the Jewish quarter of Frankfurt-am-Main, but the name has also been adopted by many Ashkenazic Jews unrelated to the family. In Britain the surname is normally given the spelling pronunciation 'Roths-child'; the original pronunciation is 'Rote-shilt'.

FOREBEARS The Rothschild dynasty of bankers was founded by Meyer Amschel Rothschild (1744–1812). He abandoned his original intention to become a rabbi after his father's early death, and became a factor to the landgrave of Hesse-Kassel. His five sons established branches of the banking business, and of the family, in Vienna, London, Naples, and Paris. They were made barons of the Austrian Empire; successive generations in Britain produced the first practicing Jew to sit in Parliament and the first to be raised to the peerage.
GIVEN NAMES German 5%. *Kurt* (4), *Benno* (3), *Hans* (3), *Fritz* (2), *Herta* (2), *Erna, Ernst, Heinz, Hermann, Ilse, Klaus, Siegbert.*

Rothstein (2152) **1.** German: habitational name from a place so named near Merseburg. **2.** German: from a Germanic personal name, *Hrodstein* (*hrōd* 'renown'). **3.** Jewish (Ashkenazic): ornamental compound of German *rot* 'red' + *Stein* 'stone'.
GIVEN NAMES Jewish 5%. *Hyman* (4), *Chaim* (3), *Miriam* (3), *Mort* (3), *Emanuel* (2), *Meyer* (2), *Sol* (2), *Ari, Gershon, Isadore, Rebekah, Yaakov.*

Rothweiler (175) German: habitational name from either of two places called Rottweil, in Württemberg and Baden.

Rothwell (1742) English: habitational name from any of the places, in Lincolnshire, Northamptonshire, North Yorkshire, and elsewhere, so named from Old English *roð(u)* 'clearing' + *well(a)* 'spring', 'stream'.

Roti (144) Italian: probably a patronymic from the personal name *Roto*, from Germanic *Hrothi*.
GIVEN NAMES Italian 11%. *Salvatore* (3), *Vito* (2).

Rotman (419) **1.** Dutch: from a personal name composed of the elements *hroth* 'fame' + *man* 'man'. **2.** Jewish (Ashkenazic): variant of ROTHMAN.
GIVEN NAMES Jewish 5%. *Isadore, Morry, Moshe, Yetta, Yoel.*

Rotolo (502) Southern Italian (Sicily): **1.** from *rotolo*, a measure of weight roughly equivalent to 800 grams, which remained in use in southern Italy until the end of the 19th century. The surname presumably arose from a metonymic occupational name. **2.** from a derivative of the personal name *Roto* (see ROTI).
GIVEN NAMES Italian 14%; French 4%. *Salvatore* (4), *Antonio* (3), *Angelo* (2), *Rocco* (2), *Sal* (2), *Santo* (2), *Carlo, Carmine, Domenic, Elio, Gaspare, Giustino; Armand* (2), *Pascal* (2), *Bonaventure, Jacques.*

Roton (114) Origin unidentified. Perhaps an altered spelling of ROTEN.

Rotondi (347) Italian: patronymic or plural form of ROTONDO.
GIVEN NAMES Italian 25%. *Angelo* (4), *Vito* (4), *Pietro* (2), *Alberto, Antonio, Benito, Domenic, Emilio, Enzo, Francesco, Giovanni, Luigi, Marino, Natale, Paolo, Renato, Sergio, Valente.*

Rotondo (780) Italian: **1.** nickname for a rotund person, Italian *rotundo*. **2.** habitational name from any of the various places called Rotondo, as for example in Avellino and Potenza, or the district so named in Sassoferrato, Ancona.
GIVEN NAMES Italian 19%. *Angelo* (6), *Rocco* (4), *Salvatore* (4), *Dante* (3), *Pasquale* (3), *Pietro* (3), *Vito* (3), *Antonio* (2), *Francesco* (2), *Sal* (2), *Severino* (2), *Antonino.*

Rotramel (194) Metathesized form of German **Rothärmel**: see ROTHERMEL.

Rotruck (158) Variant of German ROTH-ROCK.
GIVEN NAME French 4%. *Amie.*

Rott (614) German: **1.** variant spelling of ROTH. **2.** habitational name from any of several places so named, for example in Bavaria.
GIVEN NAMES German 5%. *Helmut* (2), *Elfriede, Erwin, Heinz, Klaus, Manfred, Otto, Reinhard.*

Rotta (124) **1.** Italian: topographic name from *rotta* 'break', 'breach', probably denoting a pass through a range of mountains. **2.** Italian: from the vocabulary word *rotta* 'course (of a ship)', hence an occupational nickname for a steersman. Compare Greek ROTA.

Rottenberg (254) Jewish (Ashkenazic): variant spelling of ROTHENBERG.
GIVEN NAMES Jewish 32%; German 5%. *Meyer* (4), *Hyman* (3), *Moshe* (3), *Pincus* (3), *Chaim* (2), *Hagai* (2), *Leib* (2), *Mechel* (2), *Myer* (2), *Aharon, Aron, Benzion; Frieda, Fritz, Helmut, Lieb.*

Rotter (820) German: **1.** variant spelling of ROTHER. **2.** occupational name for the foreman or leader of a group or association of men, or a work gang, from an agent derivative of Middle High German *rotte* 'team', 'gang'. **3.** occupational name for a harp player, Middle High German *rottære*.

4. habitational name from any of the various places called ROTT.

GIVEN NAMES German 4%. *Kurt* (2), *Gerhard, Hans, Horst, Markus, Siegried.*

Rottier (153) French: **1.** habitational name from Rottier in Drôme. **2.** from the Germanic personal name *Hrothari* composed of the elements *hrōd* 'renown' + *hari* 'army'. **3.** occupational name for a player on the rote (a medieval stringed instrument), Old French *rote*.

Rottinghaus (236) German: habitational name from a place called Rottinghausen, near Osnabrück, Lower Saxony.

Rottler (153) German: **1.** variant of ROTTER. **2.** east Swabian occupational name for a carter or haulier.

GIVEN NAMES German 5%. *Juergen, Manfred.*

Rottman (515) **1.** Jewish (Ashkenazic): variant spelling of ROTHMAN. **2.** Altered spelling of German ROTTMANN or ROTHMANN.

Rottmann (202) **1.** German: habitational name, a variant of ROTT 2. **2.** Jewish (Ashkenazic): variant spelling of ROTHMAN.

GIVEN NAMES German 6%. *Erwin, Hans, Kurt, Maximilian.*

Rottner (111) German: of uncertain origin. Either a habitational name for someone from a place called in Rotten in Pomerania or a variant of ROTTER 2.

Rotunda (182) Italian: variant of **Rotonda**, from the adjective *rotonda*, feminine form of *rotundo* 'round'.

GIVEN NAMES Italian 5%. *Gilda, Marcello, Orlando.*

Rotundo (252) Italian: southern variant of ROTONDO.

GIVEN NAMES Italian 16%. *Cosmo* (2), *Luigi* (2), *Rocco* (2), *Antonio, Ceasar, Cesare, Fausto, Salvatore.*

Rotunno (330) Italian: southern variant of ROTONDO.

GIVEN NAMES Italian 12%. *Rocco* (3), *Angelo* (2), *Sal* (2), *Antonio, Giovanni, Salvatore, Saverio.*

Rotz (533) German (**Rötz**): habitational name from places so named in the Upper Palatinate, Bavaria, and Styria, Austria.

Roubal (187) **1.** Jewish (eastern Ashkenazic): pet form of REUBEN, or possibly an ornamental adoption of Russian *rubl* 'rouble', the Russian unit of currency. **2.** Americanized spelling of German **Rübal** (see RUBEL) or of Swiss German **Reubel** the latter being from a Germanic personal name formed with *hrōd* 'renown', for example ROBERT.

Rouch (340) **1.** Southern French: regional variant of **Rouge** (see ROUGEAU). **2.** Possibly an altered spelling of German RAUCH.

Roudabush (225) **1.** Americanized form of Dutch **Rondenbosch** (see ROUDEBUSH). **2.** Americanized spelling of German **Raudenbusch** (see RAUDENBUSH).

Roudebush (577) **1.** Americanized form of Dutch and Belgian **Ronderbosch** or

Rondenbosch, a habitational name for someone from Ronderbos in Dilbeek, Brabant, or Ronden Bos in Maldegen, East Flanders. **2.** Americanized spelling of German **Raudenbusch** (see RAUDENBUSH).

Roueche (105) French (**Rouèche**): possibly a topographic name for someone who lived by a woodland clearing, from *rudisca*, composed of Old High German *ruda* + the suffix *-isca*.

Roufs (133) Variant of German ROLFS.

Rougeau (321) French: diminutive of **Rouge**, a nickname for someone with a ruddy complexion.

GIVEN NAMES French 7%. *Andre, Aurore, Jacques, Napoleon, Raoul, Thierry.*

Rougeux (122) French: variant of ROUGEAU.

Rough (317) Scottish: from Older Scots *rughe, roghe* 'rough', a nickname for someone with a rough unkempt appearance or a topographic name for someone who lived by rough, uncultivated land.

Rought (185) **1.** variant of Scottish ROUGH. **2.** Americanized spelling of German **Rucht** (see RUCHTI).

Roughton (493) English: habitational name from any of various places named Roughton or Wroughton. Roughton, Lincolnshire, the most likely source of the surname according to its present-day distribution, and Roughton, Norfolk, are both named from Old English *rūh* 'rough' or Old Norse *rugr* 'rye' + *tūn* 'farm', 'settlement'. Roughton, Shropshire is named with Old English *rūh* + *tūn*, and Wroughton, Wiltshire (the least likely source of the surname) from *Worf*, a Celtic river name meaning 'winding stream', + Old English *tūn*.

Rouillard (354) French: diminutive of **Rouille**, apparently a nickname from Old French *rouiller* 'roll the eyes in anger'. However, in medieval slang the term denoted a type of barrel or cask, and the surname may have arisen, perhaps as a nickname or a metonymic occupational name, from this sense. The surname ROSS is associated with Rouillard, perhaps arising out of a confusion with *rouille* 'rust'.

FOREBEARS A Rouillard from the Maine region of France is documented in Quebec City in 1653, with the secondary surname LARIVIERE.

GIVEN NAMES French 9%. *Jacques* (2), *Andre, Emile, Jean-Guy, Marcel, Renald, Thierry.*

Rouland (114) French: southern variant of ROLAND.

Rouleau (941) French: diminutive of **Role**, a metonymic occupational name for a scribe, from Old French *role* 'scroll'.

GIVEN NAMES French 17%. *Lucien* (7), *Armand* (4), *Emile* (4), *Marcel* (3), *Pierre* (3), *Valmore* (3), *Fernand* (2), *Gilles* (2), *Serge* (2), *Adelore, Alcide, Andre.*

Roulette (139) Canadian French spelling of **Roulet**, from a pet form of the personal name *Roul* (see ROLF), or in some cases

possibly a habitational name for someone from Le Roulet in Puy-de-Dôme or Le Roullet in Allier.

Roulhac (164) French: habitational name from places in Charente and Côtes-d'Amor named Rouillac, or from Rouilhac in Lot.

Roulier (101) French: occupational name for a carrier or carter.

GIVEN NAMES French 8%. *Emile, Pierre.*

Roulston (247) English: variant of ROLSTON.

Round (508) English (chiefly West Midlands): nickname for a plump person, from Middle English, Old French *rond, rund* 'fat', 'round' (Latin *rotundus*).

Rounds (2275) English: patronymic from ROUND.

Roundtree (1547) English: variant of ROUNTREE.

Roundy (685) Possibly an altered spelling of German RUNDE.

Rounsavall (134) English (of French origin): variant of ROUNSAVILLE.

Rounsaville (354) English: French Huguenot name, probably a habitational name from the village of Roncesvalles in Navarra in the Basque country (French name *Roncevaux*).

FOREBEARS Philip Rounseville came from Honiton, Devon, England, to Bristol, MA, sometime before 1704.

Rounsville (105) English (of French origin): variant of ROUNSAVILLE.

Rountree (2437) English: topographic name for someone who lived by a rowan or mountain ash, from Middle English *rown* (Old Norse *rogn*) + *tree* (Old English *trēow*).

Roup (130) **1.** Dutch: from Middle Dutch *roep, roup* 'crying', 'shouting', hence perhaps a metonymic occupational name for a town crier. **2.** Altered spelling of German RAUP or RUPP.

Roupe (239) Altered spelling of German RUPP, RUPPE, or RUPE.

Roupp (142) Altered spelling of German RUPP, RUPPE, or RUPE.

Rourk (264) Irish: reduced form of O'ROURKE.

GIVEN NAMES Irish 4%. *Brendan, Delma.*

Rourke (1574) Irish: reduced form of O'ROURKE.

GIVEN NAMES Irish 4%. *Cian* (2), *Aileen.*

Rous (163) **1.** Americanized spelling of German RAUS. **2.** French: old southern form of ROUX, also found in Germany as a Huguenot name.

GIVEN NAMES German 5%. *Gunter, Kurt.*

Rouse (8907) **1.** English: nickname for a person with red hair, from Middle English, Old French *rous* 'red(-haired)' (Latin *russ(e)us*). **2.** Americanized spelling of German RAUS.

Rouser (211) Americanized spelling of RAUSER.

Rousey (386) Altered spelling of French **Roussy**, a southern derivative of ROUX, or **Roussée**, topographic name for someone who lived in an area prone to dew, *rosée*. Compare ROUSSEY, ROWSEY, ROWZEE.

Roush (4282) Americanized spelling of German RAUSCH or possibly of French **Rouch**.

Rousse (231) French: feminine form of ROUX.
GIVEN NAMES French 8%. *Pierre* (3), *Amie, Armand, Emile.*

Rousseau (3202) French: nickname for someone with red hair, from a diminutive of ROUX.
GIVEN NAMES French 11%. *Lucien* (7), *Pierre* (7), *Emile* (6), *Marcel* (6), *Armand* (5), *Andre* (4), *Jacques* (4), *Michel* (4), *Normand* (4), *Gilles* (3), *Philippe* (3), *Adrien* (2).

Roussel (923) French: variant of ROUSSEAU. Compare English RUSSELL.
GIVEN NAMES French 13%. *Michel* (5), *Normand* (3), *Andre* (2), *Emile* (2), *Fernand* (2), *Pierre* (2), *Serge* (2), *Adelard, Adrien, Alain, Anicet, Camille.*

Roussell (420) French: variant of ROUSSEL.
GIVEN NAMES French 5%. *Camille, Marcel, Patrice.*

Rousselle (258) French: from a feminine form of ROUSSEAU.
GIVEN NAMES French 14%. *Marcel* (2), *Adrien, Armand, Damien, Gaetan, Girard, Pierre, Rollande, Theophile, Yves.*

Roussey (137) French: variant of ROUSSEL or **Roussy** (see ROUSEY).
GIVEN NAME French 4%. *Camille.*

Roussin (227) French: diminutive of ROUX.
GIVEN NAMES French 11%. *Laurent* (2), *Fernand, Monique, Rudolphe.*

Rousso (149) **1.** Variant of Greek and Jewish (from Greece) ROUSSOS. **2.** Altered spelling of French ROUSSEAU.
GIVEN NAMES Jewish 10%; French 6%. *Abbe, Hyman; Gabrielle, Jacques, Michel, Sylvie.*

Roussos (182) Greek: nickname for a red-haired or blond person, from *roussos* 'red' (from Latin *russeus*).
GIVEN NAMES Greek 20%. *Andreas* (2), *Aristotle* (2), *Constantine* (2), *Argyrios, Efstratios, Georgios, Ioannis, Loucas, Nicos, Nikolaos, Odysseas, Stamatios.*

Rout (139) **1.** English (now chiefly East Anglia): probably a topographic name for someone who lived by a patch of rough ground, from a hypothetical Old English word *rū(we)t* or *rūhet*, derivatives of *rūh* 'rough', 'overgrown'. Compare RAUCH. There are places called Ruffet(t) in Surrey and Sussex which are thought to have this origin. **2.** German: Swabian variant of ROTH 1. **3.** Probably an Americanized spelling of German RAUTH. **4.** Indian (northern states): Hindu (Rajput, Jat, Maratha) and Sikh name meaning 'prince', from Sanskrit *rājaputra* (from *rāja* 'king' + *putra* 'son'). In India this is a variant of a name more commonly spelled **Ravat** or **Raut**. The Jats have a clan called **Ravat**.
GIVEN NAMES Indian 7%. *Biswa, Jyoti, Smruti.*

Route (165) **1.** French: topographic name for someone who lived by a road, French *route*. **2.** English: variant spelling of ROUT.
GIVEN NAME French 4%. *Michel.*

Routh (1446) English: habitational name from a place so named in Humberside. Recorded in Domesday Book as *Rutha*, the place name may derive from Old Norse *hrúedhr* 'rough shaly ground'.

Routhier (502) French: from Old French *rout(h)ier* 'itinerant soldier', 'vagabond'.
GIVEN NAMES French 15%. *Armand* (3), *Francois* (2), *Gaston* (2), *Valmore* (2), *Camile, Colette, Felicien, Germaine, Gilles, Jean Guy, Julien, Marcel.*

Routledge (155) English and Scottish: variant of RUTLEDGE. In Britain this is the usual spelling of the name.

Routon (300) English: probably a variant spelling of ROWTON.

Routson (312) Possibly an Americanized form of German RUTZEN. Compare ROUTZAHN.

Routt (599) English: variant spelling of ROUT.

Routzahn (200) German: probably an altered form of RUTZEN.

Roux (1140) French: nickname for someone with red hair, from Old French *rous* 'red' (Latin *russ(e)us*).
GIVEN NAMES French 13%. *Armand* (7), *Andre* (4), *Normand* (3), *Adrien* (2), *Emile* (2), *Jacques* (2), *Marcel* (2), *Michel* (2), *Pierre* (2), *Rejean* (2), *Cecile, Clovis.*

Rouzer (169) Perhaps an altered spelling of German RAUSER or French **Rouzé**, a nickname for someone with a pinkish complexion, from Old French *rose* 'pink'.

Rover (168) **1.** English: occupational name for someone who constructed or repaired roofs, from an agent derivative of Middle English *roof* (Old English *hróf*). In the Middle Ages roofs might be thatched with reeds or straw, or covered with tiles, slates, or wooden shingles. **2.** German and English: nickname for an unscrupulous individual, from Middle Low German *röver* 'pirate', 'robber', Middle English *rover*. The English verb *rove* 'to wander' is probably a back-formation from this, and is not attested before the 16th century, so it is unlikely to lie behind any examples of the surname. **3.** German: variant of *Röver* (see ROEVER).

Rovin (109) Origin uncertain. Possibly of Dutch origin, a variant of **Roven, Raven**, a patronymic from a short form of a Germanic personal name such as *Walrave*, formed with *hrafn* 'raven'.
GIVEN NAME French 4%. *Marcelle.*

Rovinsky (112) Jewish (eastern Ashkenazic): habitational name from Rovno in Ukraine.

GIVEN NAMES Russian 6%; Jewish 4%. *Serafima, Vladimir, Yury; Marat.*

Rovira (230) Catalan: **1.** habitational name from La Rovira in Barcelona province. **2.** topographic name for someone who lived by an oak wood, from Catalan *rovira*, collective form of *roure* 'oak' (from Latin *robur*).
GIVEN NAMES Spanish 40%; French 4%. *Jose* (11), *Luis* (8), *Juan* (5), *Margarita* (3), *Alberto* (2), *Carlos* (2), *Enrique* (2), *Gustavo* (2), *Marta* (2), *Miguel* (2), *Ramon* (2), *Roberto* (2); *Ivelisse, Marcel, Pierre.*

Rovito (172) Italian (Calabria): habitational name from Rovito in Cosenza province, so named from Latin *rubetum* 'thornbush', 'briar', 'bramble'.
GIVEN NAMES Italian 11%; Spanish 6%. *Gennaro* (2), *Mario, Nazzareno, Rafael; Carlos, Diego, Francisco, Mariela.*

Rovnak (100) Czech (**Rovnák**): habitational name from places called Rovné or Rovný.

Rovner (382) Jewish (eastern Ashkenazic): habitational name for someone from Rovno, formerly part of Poland, now in Ukraine.
GIVEN NAMES Jewish 8%; Russian 4%. *Hyman* (3), *Aron, Fridrikh, Izya, Uri, Yakov, Yetta; Galina* (2), *Yefim* (2), *Boris, Gennady, Igor, Misha.*

Row (907) English: variant spelling of ROWE.

Rowan (5269) Scottish and Irish: Anglicized form of Gaelic **Ó Ruadháin** (see RUANE). In Scotland, this name is sometimes Anglicized as ROLAND, while in Ireland it is often ROONEY.

Rowand (319) Scottish and Irish: variant of ROWAN.

Rowberry (108) English (Herefordshire and Worcestershire): habitational name from any of various places named from Old English *rūh* 'rough' + *beorg* 'hill', 'mound', notably Rubery in Hereford and Worcester.

Rowbotham (280) English: topographic name for someone living in an overgrown valley, from Old English *rūh* 'rough', 'overgrown' + *boðm* 'valley', or possibly a habitational name from an unidentified place so called. The surname is now most common in Lancashire, but does not seem to be found there before 1500.

Rowbottom (130) English: variant of ROWBOTHAM.

Rowden (1139) English: habitational name from a place near Hereford, so named from Old English *rūh* 'rough', 'overgrown' + *dūn* 'hill'.

Rowe (25391) English: **1.** topographic name for someone who lived by a hedgerow or in a row of houses built next to one another, from Middle English *row* (northern Middle English *raw*, from Old English *rāw*). **2.** from the medieval personal name *Row*, a variant of *Rou(l)* (see

ROLLO, ROLF) or a short form of ROW-LAND. **3.** English name adopted by bearers of French BAILLARGEON.

Rowekamp (118) German (**Röwekamp**): habitational name from any of several farms named Röwekamp.

Rowell (5673) English: **1.** habitational name, a variant of ROTHWELL (representing the local pronunciation of the place in Northamptonshire). **2.** habitational name from a place in Devon, so named from Old English *rūh* 'rough', 'overgrown' + *hyll* 'hill'. **3.** from a medieval personal name, a pet form of ROWE 2.

Rowen (728) English: topographic name for someone who lived by a rowan (see ROUNTREE).

GIVEN NAMES French 4%. *Chantelle, Laure, Marthe, Sylvie.*

Rowett (132) English: from a medieval personal name composed of the Germanic elements *hrōd* 'renown' + *wald* 'rule', which was introduced into England by Scandinavian settlers in the form *Róaldr*, and again later by the Normans in the form *Ro(h)ald*. This name has absorbed a much rarer one with the second element *hard* 'hardy', 'brave', 'strong', which was introduced into England by the Normans in the form *Ro(h)ard*. It has also sometimes been used as a pet form of ROWE 2, itself both a variant of ROLF and a short form of ROWLAND.

Rowin (154) Origin uncertain. **1.** Perhaps an Americanized form of Polish **Rowiński** (see ROWINSKI). **2.** Perhaps an altered spelling of English ROWAN.

Rowinski (185) Polish (**Rowiński**): habitational name for someone from Rowiny in Biała Podlaska voivodeship.

GIVEN NAMES Polish 11%. *Casimir* (2), *Jacek, Tadeusz, Tomasz, Wojciech.*

Rowland (13447) **1.** English: from *Rol(l)ant*, a Norman personal name composed of the Germanic elements *hrōd* 'renown' + *land* 'land', 'territory' (or + *-nand* 'bold', assimilated to *-lant* 'land'). This was popular throughout Europe in the Middle Ages as a result of the fame of Charlemagne's warrior of this name, who was killed at Roncesvalles in AD 778. **2.** English: habitational name from places in Derbyshire and Sussex, so named from Old Norse *rá* 'roebuck' + *lundr* 'wood', 'grove'. **3.** Variant of German and French ROLAND.

Rowlands (835) English: patronymic from ROWLAND 1.

Rowlee (116) Variant spelling of English ROWLEY.

Rowles (1121) English: patronymic from the personal name ROLLO or ROLF.

Rowlett (1241) English: from a pet form of the personal name ROLLO or ROLF.

Rowlette (275) Apparently an altered spelling of ROWLETT.

GIVEN NAMES French 4%. *Collette, Lucien.*

Rowley (5692) English: habitational name from any of the various places, in Devon, County Durham, Staffordshire, and Yorkshire, so named from Old English *rūh* 'rough', 'overgrown' + *lēah* 'wood', 'clearing'.

Rowling (152) English: from a pet form of the personal name ROLLO or ROLF.

Rowlison (128) English: patronymic from a pet form of the personal name ROLLO or ROLF.

Rowntree (137) English: variant spelling of ROUNTREE.

Rowse (362) English: variant spelling of ROUSE.

Rowsell (102) English: variant of RUSSELL.

Rowser (173) Americanized spelling of German RAUSER.

Rowsey (405) Origin unidentified. Possibly English, a variant of ROUSE, or alternatively a respelling of French **Roussy** (see ROUSEY).

Rowson (191) English: patronymic from ROWE 2.

Rowton (271) English: habitational name from places so named in Cheshire, East Yorkshire (now Humberside), and Shropshire. The first two are named from Old English *rūh* 'rough' + *tūn* 'hill'. The last, recorded in Domesday Book as *Routone*, is named from Old English *rūh* + *hyll* 'hill' + *tūn*.

Rowzee (130) Americanized spelling of French ROUSSEL or ROUSEY.

Roxas (182) Spanish: variant (old spelling) of ROJAS.

GIVEN NAMES Spanish 36%. *Jose* (5), *Nestor* (3), *Rodolfo* (3), *Francisco* (2), *Manuel* (2), *Ramon* (2), *Ana, Annaliza, Arsenio, Aureo, Beatriz, Cristina; Antonio* (2), *Primo.*

Roxburgh (113) Scottish: habitational name from Roxburgh near Kelso, Scotland, so named from the genitive case of the Old English byname *Hrōc*, meaning 'rook', + Old English *burh* 'fort', 'manor' (see BURY).

Roxbury (117) English (Kent): probably a variant of Scottish ROXBURGH.

Roxby (108) English (Durham): probably a variant of Scottish ROXBURGH.

Roy (18742) **1.** Scottish: nickname for a person with red hair, from Gaelic *ruadh* 'red'. **2.** English (of Norman origin): variant of RAY 1, cognate of 3. **3.** French: from Old French *rey, roy* 'king' (from Latin *rex*, genitive *regis*), a nickname for someone who lived in a regal fashion or who had earned the title in some contest of skill or by presiding over festivities. **4.** Indian (Bengal) and Bangladeshi: variant of RAI.

GIVEN NAMES French 10%; Indian 4%. *Armand* (36), *Lucien* (32), *Normand* (28), *Andre* (23), *Jacques* (16), *Marcel* (15), *Emile* (12), *Laurent* (12), *Pierre* (11), *Cecile* (10), *Donat* (10), *Gilles* (10); *Dipak* (9), *Sumit* (7), *Amit* (5), *Ajit* (4), *Dipankar* (4), *Partha* (4), *Ranjan* (4), *Shyamal* (4),

Aloke (3), *Amitava* (3), *Chitra* (3), *Gautam* (3).

Royal (4659) **1.** English: variant spelling of ROYLE. **2.** Americanized form of German REUL or REULE. **3.** Possibly also an Americanized form of Spanish and Portuguese REAL.

Royall (603) **1.** English: variant spelling of ROYLE. **2.** Altered spelling of German REUL or REULE.

Royals (441) **1.** Perhaps an Americanized form of Spanish **Reales**. **2.** Alternatively, perhaps a variant of English ROYLE.

Royalty (524) Origin unidentified. This is a Kentucky name; it is not found as a surname in the British Isles.

Roybal (1401) **1.** Galician: variant of **Ruibal** (Spanish **Rubial**), a habitational name from any of numerous places in Galicia, so named from a derivative of *ruivo* 'red' (Latin *rubeus*), denoting red earth. **2.** Perhaps an Americanized spelling of German **Rübal** (see RUEBEL).

GIVEN NAMES Spanish 18%. *Jose* (12), *Manuel* (12), *Eloy* (7), *Juan* (7), *Orlando* (6), *Alfredo* (4), *Ruben* (4), *Santiago* (3), *Vidal* (3), *Armando* (2), *Benito* (2), *Carlos* (2).

Royce (1969) **1.** English: from the medieval female personal name *Royse*, also found in the spelling *Rose* and popularly associated with the flower, but in fact originally from a Germanic personal name. This is recorded in Domesday Book in the form *Rothais* and is composed of the elements *hrōd* 'renown' + *haid(is)* 'kind', 'sort'. **2.** Americanized spelling of German REUSS.

Roycroft (200) English: variant of RYCROFT.

Roye (496) Variant spelling of ROY.

Royer (4335) **1.** English and French: occupational name for a wheelwright, from Old French *roier, rouwier, rouer, roer*. **2.** French: from a Germanic personal name composed of *hrōd* 'renown' + *hari, heri* 'army'. **3.** Respelling of German RAUER.

GIVEN NAMES French 4%. *Patrice* (3), *Alphonse* (2), *Andre* (2), *Emile* (2), *Fernand* (2), *Jacques* (2), *Rejean* (2), *Adelard, Clovis, Damien, Dominique, Elmire.*

Roylance (317) English (Lancashire and Cheshire): unexplained.

Royle (460) English (chiefly Lancashire): habitational name from a place in Lancashire, so named from Old English *rā* 'roe deer' + *hyll* 'hill'.

Roys (368) English and Norwegian (**Røys**): variant of ROYSE.

Roysden (110) Probably an altered form of English ROYSTON.

GIVEN NAME French 4%. *Clovis.*

Roysdon (110) Probably an altered form of English ROYSTON.

Royse (731) **1.** English: variant of ROYCE. **2.** Norwegian: habitational name from any of several farmsteads named *Røyse*, from

Old Norse *hreysi* 'heap of stones'.
3. Probably an Americanized spelling of German REUS (or the variant **Reuse**), REUSS (or the variant **Reusse**).

Royster (2135) English (Shropshire and Staffordshire): unexplained.

Royston (946) English: **1.** habitational name from a place in Hertfordshire, recorded in 1262 as *Croyroys*, from Old French *croiz* 'cross' (Latin *crux*, genitive *crucis*) + the female personal name *Royse* (see ROSE 2). Ekwall mentions forms from only twenty years later in which the place name first more or less assumes its modern form. It is not clear, however, whether this is to be interpreted as 'Royse's stone' (with the second element Middle English *stōn*, from Old English *stān*) or 'settlement at (Croiz) Royse' (with the second element Middle English *toun*, from Old English *tūn*). **2.** habitational name from a place in West Yorkshire, so called from the genitive case of the Old English byname *Hrōr*, meaning 'vigorous' (or its Old Norse cognate *Róarr*) + Old English *tūn* 'enclosure', 'settlement'. **3.** Americanized form of one or more like-sounding Jewish surnames.

Roytman (115) Jewish (eastern Ashkenazic): variant of ROITMAN.
GIVEN NAMES Jewish 37%; Russian 28%; Polish 4%. *Moisey* (3), *Yakov* (3), *Inna* (2), *Isaak* (2), *Tsilya* (2), *Faina, Genya, Gersh, Irina, Naum, Polina, Sarra; Leonid* (4), *Vladimir* (4), *Arkady* (3), *Boris* (3), *Mikhail* (2), *Mordko* (2), *Aleksandr, Anatoly, Arkadiy, Grigory, Iosif, Khuna; Feliks* (2).

Roza (249) Asturian-Leonese and Spanish: habitational name from any of the numerous places named Roza or La Roza, especially in Asturies, from Asturian-Leonese *roza* 'undergrowth', equivalent to Spanish *roza* 'cleared land' (from *rozar* 'to clear', 'to plow', from Late Latin *ruptiare*, from the past participle *ruptus* of classical Latin *rumpere* 'to break').
GIVEN NAMES Spanish 6%. *Francisco* (4), *Angel, Jorge, Manuel, Marina, Renato, Ronaldo.*

Rozak (182) Polish (**Rożak, Różak**): metronymic from the personal name *Róża*, a derivative of the vocabulary word *róża* 'rose' (see ROSE), or patronymic from the masculine form *Róg* (see ROG).
GIVEN NAMES Polish 5%; German 4%. *Casimir, Halina, Jadwiga; Kurt.*

Rozanski (573) Polish (**Różański**) and Jewish (eastern Ashkenazic): habitational name from any of various places called, in Polish, Różan(y), Różanna, and Różanka, in Poland and Belarus.
GIVEN NAMES Polish 7%. *Janusz* (2), *Stanislaw* (2), *Andrzej, Casimir, Jaroslaw, Jerzy, Jozef, Mieczyslaw, Tomasz.*

Rozansky (124) Jewish (Ashkenazic): variant spelling of ROZANSKI.
GIVEN NAMES Jewish 6%; Russian 4%. *Dror; Lev, Vladimir, Zoya.*

Rozar (200) Origin unidentified; possibly an Indian variant of Portuguese ROZARIO.

Rozario (103) Spanish and Portuguese: variant of ROSARIO. This spelling is also found among Christians in the former Portuguese colony of Goa and elsewhere in western India.
GIVEN NAMES Spanish 15%; Indian 12%. *Antonio, Consuelo, Maria Dominga; Jyoti* (2), *Asha, Babita, Shalu, Subodh, Swapan.*

Rozas (207) Galician and Spanish: habitational name from any of numerous places named Rozas, especially in Galicia, from the plural form of Galician and Spanish *roza* 'cleared land ready for plowing' (see ROZA).
GIVEN NAMES Spanish 7%. *Ramon* (2), *Santiago* (2), *Carlos, Emeterio, Fernando, Guillermo, Luis, Miguel, Rolando.*

Rozeboom (256) Dutch: variant of ROSENBOOM.
GIVEN NAMES Dutch 4%. *Gerrit* (4), *Marinus, Teunis.*

Rozek (493) **1.** Polish (**Rożek**): nickname from Polish *rożek* 'horn'. This word is found in the idiomatic expression *wystawić rożki* 'to become impertinent', which is a likely source of the nickname. **2.** Czech (**Rožek**): nickname from the vocabulary word *rožek*, a diminutive of *roh* 'horn'. In Czech dialect this word also means 'croissant'; as such, it may be a nickname for a baker or pastry chef.
GIVEN NAMES Polish 4%. *Henryk, Jacek, Janusz, Krzysztof, Stanislaw, Zbigniew, Zygmunt.*

Rozell (940) Apparently an altered spelling of ROSELL.

Rozelle (633) Swedish: see ROSELLE.

Rozema (271) Frisian: unexplained.

Rozen (285) **1.** Jewish: (eastern Ashkenazic): variant spelling of ROSEN. **2.** Jewish (Israeli): either an ornamental name from Hebrew *rozen* 'prince', or a Hebraicized form of any Ashkenazic name beginning with Rosen- or Rozen-.
GIVEN NAMES Jewish 14%. *Ari* (2), *Meyer* (2), *Shlomo* (2), *Chaya, Elihu, Hersh, Moshe, Shlomit, Sol, Tova, Uri, Zeev.*

Rozenberg (250) Jewish (eastern Ashkenazic): variant spelling of ROSENBERG.
GIVEN NAMES Russian 26%; Jewish 18%. *Boris* (5), *Leonid* (4), *Lev* (4), *Aleksandr* (3), *Mikhail* (3), *Dmitriy* (2), *Gennady* (2), *Grigory* (2), *Raisa* (2), *Semyon* (2), *Arkady, Daniil; Esfir* (2), *Isaak* (2), *Semen* (2), *Sima* (2), *Yakov* (2), *Aron, Genya, Inna, Irina, Menashe, Moshe, Rimma.*

Rozenfeld (123) Jewish (eastern Ashkenazic): variant spelling of ROSENFELD.
GIVEN NAMES Russian 35%; Jewish 26%. *Lev* (3), *Boris* (2), *Grigoriy* (2), *Leonid* (2), *Semyon* (2), *Yefim* (2), *Aleksandr, Arkady, Dmitry, Fanya, Galina, Genrikh; Naum* (2), *Aron, Feyga, Fira, Genya, Ilya, Itzhak; Moisey, Sarra, Semen, Yakov.*

Rozich (113) **1.** Croatian (**Rožić**) and Slovenian (**Rožič**): **2.** patronymic from *Rože* or *Rožo*, pet forms of the personal name *Erazmo* (Croatian), *Erazem* (Slovenian), Latin *Erasmus*. See RASMUS. **3.** nickname or topographic name from *rožič*, a diminutive of *rog* 'horn', as a topographic name possibly denoting someone who lived on a horn-shaped spur or ridge of a hill, or on a pointed piece of land.

Rozier (1132) Altered spelling of French ROSIER.

Rozman (393) **1.** Jewish (eastern Ashkenazic): variant of ROSMAN. **2.** Slovenian (also **Rožman**): occupational name for a carter or a horse breeder or dealer, from Middle High German *ros* 'horse' + *man* 'man'. Compare German ROSSMANN. **3.** Slovenian: from a medieval respelled form of the personal name *Erazem*, Latin *Erasmus*. See RASMUS.
GIVEN NAMES Russian 7%; Jewish 7%. *Mikhail* (3), *Aleksandr* (2), *Boris* (2), *Igor* (2), *Anatoly, Arkadiy, Lev, Nesya, Senya, Yefim, Yevgeny; Sol* (2), *Naum, Polina, Semen, Shlema.*

Rozmus (135) Polish and Dutch: variant of RASMUS.
GIVEN NAMES Polish 9%. *Aniela, Jaroslaw, Stanislaw, Zofia.*

Rozner (122) Jewish (eastern Ashkenazic): variant spelling of ROSNER.
GIVEN NAME Jewish 7%. *Miriam.*

Roznowski (200) Polish (**Rożnowski**): habitational name for someone from any of various places called Rożnów, Rożnowo, or Roznowa.

Rozsa (163) Hungarian (**Rózsa**): from the female personal name *Rózsa*, from the vocabulary word *rózsa* 'rose'. Compare ROSE. In some cases the family name might derive from an old secular male personal name of the same form.
GIVEN NAMES Hungarian 22%; German 4%. *Sandor* (4), *Tibor* (2), *Zoltan* (2), *Zsuzsanna* (2), *Balint, Gabor, Gyula, Imre, Istvan, Katalin, Laszlo, Miklos; Armin, Erwin, Theodor.*

Rozum (143) Polish: nickname for an intelligent person, from *rozum* 'mind', 'intelligence'.
GIVEN NAMES Polish 5%. *Ewa, Lech, Wladyslaw.*

Rozwadowski (58) Polish: habitational name for someone from Rozwady or Rozwadów in Biała Podlaska voivodeship.

Rozycki (323) Polish and Jewish (eastern Ashkenazic)(**Różycki**): habitational name for someone from places called Różyca or Różyce, named with *róża* 'rose'.
GIVEN NAMES Polish 14%. *Casimir* (2), *Janusz* (2), *Jerzy* (2), *Benedykt, Bogdan, Dariusz, Halina, Jozef, Jozef, Piotr, Radoslaw, Stanislawa.*

Rozzell (191) Probably a respelling of English or Catalan ROSSELL.

Rozzelle (113) Probably a respelling of English or Catalan ROSSELL.

Rozzi (296) Italian: **1.** from an old Germanic personal name. **2.** nickname from *rozzo* 'dirty', 'ill-natured', 'uncultivated'
GIVEN NAMES Italian 12%. *Camillo* (2), *Domenic* (2), *Olindo* (2), *Alfio, Gildo, Guido, Lorenzo, Lucio, Mauro, Nicola, Rocco, Romeo.*

Rua (284) **1.** Galician (**Rúa**): habitational name from any of the numerous places in Galicia so named, from *rua* 'street'. **2.** Italian: when not of Spanish origin, a topographic name from Sicilian *ruga* 'road', or a habitational name from any of various places named Rua, as for example the locality so named in San Pietro di Feletto in Teviso province. The form **Ruà**, typical of Piedmont, relates to a district of Pragelato in Torino province or to Ruà del Prato in Dronero, Cuneo province.
GIVEN NAMES Spanish 29%; Portuguese 11%. *Jose* (8), *Manuel* (5), *Domingos* (3), *Fernando* (3), *Ignacio* (2), *Jesus* (2), *Ricardo* (2), *Roberto* (2), *Aida, Alberto, Amandio, Amparo; Joaquim* (2), *Anabela.*

Ruan (319) **1.** Irish and Scottish: variant of RUANE. **2.** Spanish (**Ruán**): possibly from *ruán* 'roan' (a color of horses), a variant of RUANO 2. **3.** Chinese 阮: from the name of the state of Ruan, which existed during the later Shang dynasty (sometimes called the Yin dynasty, 1401–1122 BC). After this state was conquered by Wen Wang shortly before the Zhou dynasty displaced the Shang dynasty, the Ruan ruling class adopted the place name as their surname.
GIVEN NAMES Chinese 29%; Spanish 15%. *Ping* (2), *Xiu* (2), *Ying* (2), *Biao, Chao, Cheng, Guang, Guohua, Hua, Huiming, Jia, Jian Hua; Jorge* (2), *Arnulfo, Arturo, Blanca, Carlos, Eduardo, Gregorio, Guillermo, Javier, Jesus, Jose, Josefina.*

Ruane (936) Irish and Scottish: reduced Anglicized form of Gaelic **Ó Ruadháin** 'descendant of *Ruadhán*', a personal name from a diminutive of *ruadh* 'red'.
GIVEN NAMES Irish 6%. *Caitlin, Kieran.*

Ruano (419) Spanish: nickname from Spanish *ruano*, which denoted someone with reddish hair (compare RUAN), or alternatively a street dweller.
GIVEN NAMES Spanish 53%. *Jose* (14), *Carlos* (8), *Juan* (7), *Mario* (6), *Eduardo* (5), *Jorge* (5), *Juana* (5), *Luis* (5), *Rafael* (5), *Cesar* (4), *Blanca* (3), *Guadalupe* (3).

Ruark (1056) Irish: reduced and altered form of O'ROURKE.

Rub (108) Jewish (American): shortened form of some Ashkenazic surname, such as RUBIN or RUBINSTEIN.
GIVEN NAMES Jewish 15%. *Moshe* (3), *Eliezer* (2), *Arye, Faigy, Simcha.*

Rubach (140) German: Germanized variant of Slavic **Rubak** 'stonemason' (see RUBACK).

GIVEN NAMES German 7%. *Hermann, Kurt, Otto.*

Ruback (148) German: occupational name for a stonemason, from Slavic *rub-* 'to hew'.

Rubalcaba (375) Spanish: habitational name from a place called Rubalcaba in Santander province.
GIVEN NAMES Spanish 47%. *Jose* (12), *Manuel* (10), *Jesus* (6), *Juan* (4), *Raul* (4), *Francisco* (3), *Guadalupe* (3), *Miguel* (3), *Pedro* (3), *Ramon* (3), *Refugio* (3), *Alberto* (2).

Rubalcava (527) Variant of Spanish RUBALCABA.
GIVEN NAMES Spanish 49%. *Jose* (15), *Jesus* (9), *Manuel* (7), *Francisco* (6), *Juan* (6), *Guadalupe* (5), *Jose Luis* (4), *Mario* (4), *Ramon* (4), *Raul* (4), *Carlos* (3), *Juan Manuel* (3); *Antonio* (6), *Federico, Filiberto, Flavio, Gabino, Heriberto, Luciano.*

Rubano (173) Italian: habitational name from Rubano in Padova province.
GIVEN NAMES Italian 21%. *Carmine* (2), *Alberto, Aldo, Alfonso, Angelo, Arcangelo, Carmelo, Enrico, Decio, Isidro, Luciano, Mauro, Salvatore.*

Rubbelke (107) German (**Rübbelke**): pet form from a Germanic personal name formed with *hrōd* 'renown'.

Rubbo (225) Italian: from a personal name derived from Old German *Rupo, Rub(b)o.*
GIVEN NAMES Italian 22%. *Antonio* (2), *Giovanni* (2), *Rocco* (2), *Umberto* (2), *Angelo, Carmine, Domenic, Eligio, Emelio, Fiore, Guido, Mauro.*

Rube (118) **1.** German: from a short form of a Germanic personal name formed with *hrōd* 'renown'. **2.** German (**Rübe**): metonymic occupational name for someone who grew or sold turnips, from Middle High German *ruobe, rüebe* 'turnip'. **3.** Danish: unexplained.
GIVEN NAMES Scandinavian 5%. *Helle, Lars.*

Rubeck (262) German: variant of RUBACK.

Rubel (928) German: **1.** variant of RUBE 1, 2. **2.** (**Rübel**): metonymic occupational name from a diminutive of Middle High German *ruobe* (Latin *rapum*) 'turnip', 'beet', 'oilseed rape', grown for use as a fodder crop or in the case of rape for the oil obtained from its seeds. **3.** nickname for a big man, from a Slavic stem (Old Sorbian *gruby*, Czech *hrubý* 'big'). **4.** nickname from a Germanized form of Slavic *vrobl* 'sparrow'. Compare WROBEL.

Ruben (1066) **1.** Jewish (Ashkenazic): variant of RUBIN. **2.** German (of Slavic origin): habitational name from a place so named near Kottbus or from Rubyn. **3.** German (of Slavic origin): nickname for a big, heavy fellow (see RUBEL 2). **4.** German (**Rüben**): habitational name from a place so named near Leipzig.
GIVEN NAMES Jewish 4%. *Sol* (3), *Hymen* (2), *Moshe* (2), *Gershon, Hillel, Isadore, Maier, Miriam, Shlomo.*

Rubenacker (111) German (**Rübenacker**): topographic name for someone who lived by a field where turnips were grown, from Middle High German *ruobe, rüebe* 'turnip' + *acker* '(cultivated) field'.

Rubendall (215) Swedish: variant of **Rubbendal**, an ornamental name composed with *dal* 'valley' as the second element. The first element could be part of a place name.

Rubenfeld (134) Jewish: variant of RUBINFELD.
GIVEN NAMES Jewish 10%; German 6%. *Aharon, Aron; Viktor.*

Rubens (428) **1.** Dutch: patronymic from the Germanic personal name *Roprecht* (see RUPPRECHT). **2.** Jewish (Ashkenazic): patronymic from the personal name RUBEN.

Rubenstein (2671) Jewish (Ashkenazic): variant of RUBINSTEIN.
GIVEN NAMES Jewish 7%. *Hyman* (5), *Sol* (4), *Emanuel* (3), *Meyer* (3), *Miriam* (3), *Yetta* (3), *Zev* (2), *Arye, Avrohom, Chaim, Dov, Elihu.*

Rubenzer (137) German: of uncertain origin. Perhaps a nickname for a poor person who ate mostly turnips, a staple food in winter during the Middle Ages, from Middle High German *ruobe* 'turnip' + *zer(e)* 'meal'.

Ruberg (198) **1.** North German (also **Rüberg**): presumably a habitational name from a lost place in the vicinity of Rübergerbrücke in Westphalia. **2.** Swedish: variant of RUDBERG. **3.** Perhaps an altered spelling of Dutch **Rubberg**, a variant of **Robberecht**, itself a variant of ROBERT; alternatively perhaps, as Debrabandere suggests, a variant of RODBERG.

Rubert (219) German and Catalan: from *Rubert*, a variant of the personal name ROBERT.
GIVEN NAMES Spanish 4%. *Manuel* (2), *Andres, Herminio, Mercedes, Ruben.*

Ruberti (123) Italian: patronymic or plural form of RUBERTO.
GIVEN NAMES Italian 11%. *Angelo* (2), *Reno* (2), *Carmel, Nicola, Santina.*

Ruberto (210) Italian: from the personal name *Ruberto*, a southern variant of ROBERTO.
GIVEN NAMES Italian 24%. *Nicola* (3), *Raffaele* (2), *Angelo, Antonio, Carmela, Carmelo, Ciriaco, Domenico, Fedele, Francesco, Gustavo, Luciano, Mario, Pasquale.*

Rubey (202) **1.** English: Variant spelling of RUBY. **2.** German: variant of RUBIN 2.

Rubi (224) **1.** Catalan (**Rubí**): habitational name from Rubí in El Vallès, Catalonia, named with Latin *rubeus* 'red'. **2.** Spanish (**Rubí**): habitational name from Rubí de Bracamonte in Valladolid province. **3.** Spanish (**Rubí**): in some cases possibly from *rubi* 'ruby'. **4.** German: variant of RUBIN 2.

GIVEN NAMES Spanish 44%. *Jose* (4), *Juan* (3), *Manuel* (3), *Mario* (3), *Ruben* (3), *Carlos* (2), *Dagoberto* (2), *Delfin* (2), *Francisco* (2), *Isidro* (2), *Julio* (2), *Luis* (2); *Dario* (2), *Antonio*, *Lorenzo*.

Rubiano (122) Spanish: habitational name from the Castilianized variant of Asturian-Leonese *Rubianu*, name of a town in Asturies.

GIVEN NAMES Spanish 42%. *Alvaro* (3), *Eduardo* (3), *Carolina* (2), *Jose* (2), *Rodrigo* (2), *Alfonso*, *Andres*, *Cesar*, *Eliecer*, *Guillermo*, *Hernando*, *Ignacio*.

Rubin (11971) **1.** Jewish (Ashkenazic): from the Hebrew personal name *Reuven* (interpreted in Genesis 29:32 as *reu* 'behold' + *ben* 'a son'). This Biblical name influenced the selection of Ashkenazic surnames that are ostensibly derived from the German, Yiddish, Polish, Ukrainian, and Russian vocabulary word *rubin* 'ruby' (from Late Latin *rubinus (lapis)*, a derivative of *rubeus* 'red'). **2.** German and Swiss German: from a pet form of the personal name *Ruprecht* (see RUPPRECHT). **3.** Italian: variant of RUBINO. **4.** French: metonymic occupational name for a jeweler, from Old French *rubi* 'ruby'.

GIVEN NAMES Jewish 7%. *Sol* (27), *Hyman* (24), *Meyer* (15), *Miriam* (9), *Chaim* (8), *Emanuel* (8), *Isadore* (8), *Myer* (6), *Moshe* (5), *Yael* (5), *Dov* (4), *Ari* (3).

Rubinfeld (140) Jewish (Ashkenazic): ornamental compound of German *Rubin* 'ruby' (the selection of which was influenced by the personal name RUBIN) + *Feld* 'field'.

GIVEN NAMES Jewish 24%. *Yisroel* (3), *Chaim* (2), *Hyman*, *Meyer*, *Pinkus*, *Shloime*, *Simcha*.

Rubino (2252) Italian: from a personal name derived from *rubino* 'ruby', probably applied in the sense 'dear', 'precious'.

GIVEN NAMES Italian 16%. *Salvatore* (15), *Vito* (12), *Angelo* (9), *Carmine* (4), *Gaspare* (4), *Sal* (4), *Rocco* (3), *Antonio* (2), *Carlo* (2), *Ciro* (2), *Donato* (2), *Gaetano* (2).

Rubinoff (120) Jewish (eastern Ashkenazic): alternative spelling of **Rubinov**, a patronymic from the personal name RUBIN.

GIVEN NAMES Jewish 9%. *Aron*, *Ronit*.

Rubins (155) **1.** Jewish (Ashkenazic): patronymic from RUBIN. **2.** Possibly also a variant of Dutch RUBENS.

Rubinson (168) **1.** Jewish (Ashkenazic): patronymic from the personal name RUBIN + German *Sohn* 'son'. **2.** Perhaps also a variant of English ROBINSON.

GIVEN NAMES Jewish 22%. *Pinchos* (2), *Reuven* (2), *Aron*, *Benzion*, *Boruch*, *Gitty*, *Miriam*, *Mordechai*, *Mort*, *Sol*.

Rubinstein (1645) Jewish (Ashkenazic): ornamental name composed of German *Rubin* 'ruby' (the selection of which was influenced by the personal name RUBIN) + *Stein* 'stone'.

GIVEN NAMES Jewish 9%. *Meyer* (4), *Miriam* (3), *Moshe* (3), *Aron* (2), *Eytan* (2), *Kalmen* (2), *Myer* (2), *Sholom* (2), *Sol* (2), *Amnon*, *Arye*, *Blyuma*.

Rubio (4159) **1.** Spanish: nickname from *rubio* 'red' (Latin *rubeus*), probably denoting someone with red hair or a red beard. **2.** Catalan (**Rubió**): habitational name from any of the places named Rubió in Catalonia.

GIVEN NAMES Spanish 50%. *Jose* (126), *Juan* (64), *Manuel* (50), *Carlos* (45), *Jesus* (39), *Luis* (31), *Francisco* (28), *Jorge* (26), *Pedro* (25), *Rafael* (23), *Ramon* (23), *Armando* (21).

Rubis (200) **1.** Lithuanian: nickname for an unkempt person, from a derivative of *rubti* 'to become rough'. **2.** Greek (also **Roubis**): descriptive nickname from modern Greek *roubi* 'ruddy', 'ruby-colored', from Venetian *rubin*. **3.** Greek: alternatively it may be from *rombos* (classical Greek *rhombos*) 'knot', 'fist', or Peloponnesian dialect *roumbi* 'rag'.

Ruble (2383) **1.** South German: metonymic occupational name for a beet grower, from Middle High German *ruobe* 'beet' + the diminutive suffix *-le*. **2.** German (**Rüble**): from the personal name *Rubele*, *Rübele*, pet forms of *Ruprecht* (see RUPPRECHT). **3.** Americanized spelling of RUBEL.

Rubley (153) Probably an altered spelling of Swiss German **Rubli**, **Rübli**, or **Rubly**, from pet forms of *Ruprecht* (see RUPPRECHT), RUPERT, and ROBERT.

Rubner (152) German: **1.** habitational name for someone from a place called Ruben, Rubenau, Rüben or Rübenau. **2.** occupational name for a beet farmer, from an agent derivative of Middle High German *ruobe* 'beet'.

GIVEN NAMES German 4%. *Florian*, *Friederike*, *Willi*.

Rubottom (157) English: variant of ROWBOTTOM.

Rubright (342) Americanized form of German RUP(P)RECHT.

Rubsam (125) German (**Rübsam**): occupational nickname for a turnip grower, from Middle High German from Middle High German *ruobe*, *rüebe* 'turnip' + *sām(e)* 'seed'.

Ruby (3432) **1.** Americanized spelling of German RUBI. **2.** French: variant of RUBIN.

Rucci (312) Italian: patronymic from the personal name *Ruccio*, from a short form of various pet names formed with this suffix, as for example *Gasparuccio* (from GASPARI) or *Baldassaruccio* (from BALDASARE).

GIVEN NAMES Italian 14%. *Giuseppe* (2), *Amedeo*, *Angelo*, *Antonio*, *Domenic*, *Emidio*, *Gaetano*, *Gennaro*, *Natale*, *Nichola*, *Nunzio*, *Pasquale*.

Ruch (1506) **1.** Swiss and South German: nickname for a greedy person, from Middle High German *ruoch* 'eager', 'intent'. **2.** German: nickname for an unkempt or rough person, from Middle Low German *rū(ch)*, Middle High German *rūch* 'shaggy', 'rough', 'crude', 'hard'.

GIVEN NAMES German 4%. *Kurt* (3), *Willi* (2), *Erwin*, *Fritz*, *Gerlinda*, *Guenther*, *Wolfgang*.

Ruchti (177) Swiss German: probably a derivative of RUCH.

Rucinski (504) Polish (**Ruciński**): habitational name for someone from a place called Ruciany in Siedlce.

GIVEN NAMES Polish 5%. *Zygmunt* (3), *Andrzej* (2), *Janusz*, *Slawek*, *Slawomir*.

Ruck (730) **1.** German: nickname for someone with a peculiarity of the back, Middle High German *rucke*. **2.** German: topographic name from a southern field name denoting a slight dome-shaped elevation. **3.** German: from the personal names *Ruck*, *Rück*, short forms of *Rüdiger* (see RUDIGER). **4.** English: variant spelling of ROOK.

Ruckdeschel (134) German: nickname for a traveling journeyman, from Middle High German *rucke* 'back' + a diminutive of *tasche*, *tesche* 'bag', hence 'backpack', 'rucksack'.

GIVEN NAMES German 4%. *Klaus*, *Kurt*.

Ruckel (223) German (**Rückel**): from a pet form of RUCK 3.

Rucker (7426) **1.** German (also **Rücker**): nickname from Middle High German *rucken* 'to move or draw'. **2.** North German: nickname from Middle Low German *rucker* 'thief', 'greedy or acquisitive person'. **3.** German: from a reduced form of the Germanic personal name RUDIGER. **4.** English: variant of ROCKER.

Ruckert (229) German (**Rückert**): see RUECKERT.

GIVEN NAMES German 6%. *Fritz*, *Gretche*, *Horst*.

Rucki (158) Polish: **1.** variant of RUDZKI. **2.** possibly a habitational name from a place named with *ruta* 'rue' (see RUTA).

Ruckle (277) South German (**Rückle**): from a pet form of RUCK 3.

Ruckman (950) German (**Rückmann**): from a Germanic personal name based on *hrok* 'intent', 'eager' (Old High German *ruoh*).

Rucks (451) Americanized variant of Swiss German RUCK.

Rud (607) **1.** Norwegian: variant of RUUD. **2.** Hungarian (**Rúd**): from *rúd* 'stick', hence a metonymic occupational name for a soldier or a nickname for a fighter. **3.** Variant spelling of English RUDD.

Ruda (414) Polish: **1.** nickname for a man with red hair, from Polish *rudy* 'red-haired'. **2.** habitational name from a place called Ruda, named with *ruda* 'iron ore'.

Rudasill (163) Americanized spelling of Swiss German **Rüdisühli** or **Rüedisüli** (see RUDISILL).

Rudat (108) Eastern German: nickname from Lithuanian *rùdas* 'reddish brown', probably referring to someone's hair.
GIVEN NAMES German 12%; Scandinavian 5%. *Ernst, Erwin, Hans, Horst.*

Rudberg (112) Swedish: variant of RYD-BERG.

Rudd (5099) **1.** English: nickname for a person with red hair or a ruddy complexion, from Middle English *rudde*, Old English *rud* 'red', 'ruddy'. **2.** Americanized shortened form of any of various Jewish surnames beginning with *Rud-*.

Ruddell (549) **1.** English: unexplained. **2.** Probably also an altered spelling of German **Rüdel** (see RUDEL).

Rudden (247) Irish: see RODEN.

Rudder (955) **1.** German: variant of RUDER 2. **2.** Altered spelling of German RUDER 1 and 2.

Ruddick (431) English: variant of RUD-DOCK.

Ruddle (247) **1.** English: nickname from a diminutive of RUDD 'red'. **2.** English: habitational name from a place called Ruddle, near Newnham in Gloucestershire.

Ruddock (406) English: nickname for someone resembling a robin, Middle English *ruddock* (Old English *ruddoc, rudduc*, a diminutive of *rud(ig)* 'red').

Ruddy (1201) English: nickname for a person with red hair or a ruddy complexion, from Middle English *rudde*, Old English *rudig* 'red', 'ruddy' (see RUDD 1).

Rude (2001) German: **1.** from a pet form of a personal name formed with Old High German *hrōd* 'fame', for example RUDOLF or *Rüdiger* (see RUDIGER). **2.** from Middle High German *rude, rü(e)de* 'hound', probably applied as a nickname or as a metonymic occupational name for a keeper of hunting dogs.

Rudeen (190) Swedish (**Rudén**): variant of RUDEN.

Rudek (122) Polish: nickname for someone with red hair or a ruddy complexion, from a derivative of *rudy* 'red' (see RUDY).
GIVEN NAMES Polish 5%. *Cecylia, Dariusz, Irena.*

Rudel (156) German (also **Rüdel**): from a pet form of the personal names *Rüdiger* (see RUDIGER) or RUDOLF.
GIVEN NAMES German 6%; French 5%. *Heinz, Kurt; Jean Marc, Michel.*

Rudell (197) **1.** Altered spelling of RUDEL. **2.** Swedish: ornamental name composed of the place name element *rud-* 'woodland clearing' + the common suffix *-ell*, from the Latin adjectival ending *-elius*.

Ruden (322) **1.** German: habitational name from any of several places named Ruda, Rudau, Rude, Ruden or Rüde. **2.** German (**Rüden**): patronymic from the personal name *Rüde* (see RUDE 1). **3.** Swedish (**Rudén**): ornamental name composed of the place name element *rud-* 'woodland

clearing' + the common surname suffix *-én*, a derivative of Latin *-enius*.

Ruder (763) German: **1.** metonymic occupational name for a boatman or sailor, from Middle High German *ruoder, ruodel* 'rudder', 'oar'. **2.** from a personal name containing the Old High German element *hrōd* 'fame', 'renown'. **3.** variant of RUDE 3. **4.** (**Rüder**): variant of REUTER 1.

Ruderman (525) **1.** Jewish (Ashkenazic): metonymic occupational name from German *Ruder* 'rudder', 'oar' + *Mann* 'man'. **2.** German: from *Ruder* (pet form of the Germanic personal name *Rothari*, formed with *hrōd* 'renown') + *man* 'man'.
GIVEN NAMES Jewish 6%. *Aviva* (2), *Isaak, Mort, Slava, Sol.*

Rudes (101) Dutch: patronymic from a short form of the personal name RUDOLF.

Rudesill (169) Americanized spelling of Swiss German **Rüdisühli** or **Rüedisüli** (see RUDISILL).

Rudge (242) English (West Midlands): **1.** topographic name from West Midland Middle English *rugge*, a variant of *rigge* 'ridge', or a habitational name from the village of Rudge in Shropshire, which is named with this word. **2.** from a medieval personal name, a pet form of ROGER. **3.** nickname for a person with red hair or a ruddy complexion, from Old French *r(o)uge* 'red' (Latin *rubeus*).

Rudi (119) **1.** Swiss German and South German: from a short form, *Ruodo*, or a Germanic personal name formed with *hrōd* 'renown' (see RUDOLF). **2.** German (of Slavic origin): from Slavic *rudy* 'red', applied as a nickname for someone with red hair or a metonymic occupational name for a metalworker or miner (from *ruda* 'red earth'). **3.** Norwegian: habitational name from any of over fifteen farmsteads so named, from Old Norse *ruð* 'clearing'.
GIVEN NAMES Scandinavian 4%. *Iver, Nils.*

Rudich (166) **1.** German: from a pet form of the personal name RUDI. **2.** Jewish (eastern Ashkenazic): patronymic from RUDY 2.
GIVEN NAMES Jewish 7%. *Avi, Reuven, Yetta.*

Rudick (313) **1.** Variant spelling of English **Ruddick**, a variant of RUDDOCK. **2.** Americanized form of German RUDICH. **3.** Jewish (eastern Ashkenazic): variant of RUDY 2, with the eastern Slavic noun suffix *-ik*.
GIVEN NAME Jewish 4%. *Miriam.*

Rudie (232) Perhaps an Americanized spelling of German RUDE or RUDI.
GIVEN NAMES Scandinavian 7%. *Iver* (2).

Rudiger (205) German (**Rüdiger**): from the Germanic personal name *Rüdiger*, composed of the elements *hrōd* 'renown' + *gār, gēr* 'spear', 'lance' (see ROGER).
GIVEN NAME German 5%. *Kurt* (2).

Rudin (710) **1.** Swiss German: from a short form of any of the personal names formed with the Germanic element *hrōd* 'renown', for example RUDOLF. **2.** Swedish: variant

of RUDEN. **3.** Jewish (from Belarus): habitational name from a place in Belarus named Rudnya.
GIVEN NAMES Jewish 4%. *Sol* (2), *Doron, Hyman, Isaak, Yakov.*

Rudis (181) Perhaps a shortened form of any of various Swiss family names such as **Rudishauser, Rüdisüli** (see RUDISILL), or **Rüdisser**.

Rudisill (1276) Americanized spelling of Swiss German **Rüdisühli** or **Rüedisüli**, a compound of the personal names *Rüdi* (a short form of *Rüdiger* (see RUDIGER) or RUDOLF) + *Üli* (from ULRICH) with the connecting patronymic suffix *-s*.

Rudkin (232) English: diminutive of RUDD.

Rudloff (450) German: **1.** metathesized variant of RUDOLF. **2.** from a personal name composed of Old High German *hrōd* 'renown' + *leiba* 'rest'.
GIVEN NAMES German 5%. *Otto* (2), *Elke, Gerhard, Kurt, Winfried.*

Rudman (701) **1.** North German (**Rudmann**) and Dutch: variant of **Rothman(n)** (see ROTHMAN). **2.** English: nickname for a person with red hair or a ruddy complexion, from Middle English *rudde* 'red', 'ruddy' (see RUDD 1) + *man* 'man'. **3.** Jewish (eastern Ashkenazic): metronymic from the Yiddish female personal name *Rude* (variant of *Rode* used in Poland and Ukraine; compare RATKOVICH) + Yiddish *man* 'man', in the sense 'husband'.
GIVEN NAMES Jewish 4%. *Isaak* (2), *Herschel, Hyman, Hymen, Mendel, Mindel, Sima, Yakov.*

Rudner (183) German: unexplained.

Rudnick (1129) Eastern German: occupational name for a mine worker mining iron ore, from an agent noun based on Slavic *ruda* 'iron ore'. Compare Polish RUDNIK.

Rudnicki (409) Polish: habitational name from Rudnik in southeastern Poland, Rudniki, or some other place named with Slavic *ruda* 'iron ore'.
GIVEN NAMES Polish 12%. *Casimir* (2), *Danuta* (2), *Rafal* (2), *Zbigniew* (2), *Andrzej, Beata, Bogdan, Boguslaw, Bronislaw, Jozef, Ludwik, Stanislaw.*

Rudnik (211) Polish: occupational name for a worker in an iron-ore mine, from an agent noun based on Slavic *ruda* 'iron ore'.
GIVEN NAMES Polish 4%; Dutch 4%. *Alicja, Henryk, Tadeusz; Gust* (2), *Dirk.*

Rudnitsky (105) Jewish (eastern Ashkenazic), Belorussian, and Ukrainian: habitational name from any of the numerous places called Rudniki in Belarus, Ukraine, Poland, and Lithuania, all derived from Slavic *rudnik* 'mine'.
GIVEN NAMES Russian 14%; Jewish 14%. *Sergey* (2), *Vladimir* (2), *Anatoly, Semyon, Vasily, Yefim; Haim, Mariya, Miriam, Moisey.*

Rudo (110) Jewish (eastern Ashkenazic): variant of RUDY 2.
GIVEN NAME Jewish 4%. *Miriam.*

Rudolf (542) German: from a personal name composed of Old High German *hrōd* 'renown' + *wolf* 'wolf', equivalent to English RALPH. This name is also found in Slovenia.
GIVEN NAMES German 7%. *Heinz* (3), *Bernhard, Erna, Gottlieb, Helmuth, Johann, Manfred, Theodor, Uwe.*

Rudolph (7236) Variant spelling of RUDOLF, under Classicizing influence.

Rudow (149) Eastern German: habitational name from a place so named near Berlin, the name of which is of Slavic origin, based on *ruda* 'iron ore'.

Rudy (2891) **1.** Variant spelling of German RUDI. **2.** Ukrainian, Polish, and Jewish (eastern Ashkenazic): nickname for someone with red hair or a ruddy complexion, from Slavic *rudy* 'red'.

Rudzik (122) Polish: nickname for a red-haired man, from a derivative of *rudy* 'red'.
GIVEN NAMES Polish 5%. *Ewa, Jadwiga.*

Rudzinski (391) Polish (**Rudziński**): habitational name for someone from any of various places called Rudna or Rudno.
GIVEN NAMES Polish 8%; German 4%. *Maciej* (2), *Casimir, Franciszek, Grzegorz, Hieronim, Jacek, Mariola, Stanislaw, Witold; Florian* (2), *Fritz* (2), *Wilhelm.*

Rudzki (79) Polish: habitational name for someone from a place called Ruda or Rudka, named with Polish *ruda* 'iron ore'.
GIVEN NAMES Polish 10%. *Grazyna, Jerzy, Malgorzata; Marta.*

Rue (1637) **1.** French: topographic name for someone who lived on a track or pathway, Old French *rue* (Latin *ruga* 'crease', 'fold'). **2.** English: variant of ROWE 1, from the Old English byform *rǣw*, or a habitational name from places in Devon and Isle of Wight called Rew from this word. **3.** Norwegian: habitational name from any of over fifteen farmsteads so named, notably in Telemark, from Old Norse *ruð* 'clearing'.

Rueb (286) **1.** Dutch and German (southwest): from a short form of the Germanic personal name *Robrecht* (see ROBERT). **2.** German (**Rüb**): variant of RUPP.
GIVEN NAMES German 6%. *Konrad* (2), *Erwin, Gerhard, Helmut, Reinhold.*

Ruebel (161) German (**Rübel**): see RUBEL.
GIVEN NAME German 5%. *Viktor.*

Ruebush (131) Americanized spelling of German **Rubusch**, of Slavic origin, probably an occupational name for a stonemason, from a verb meaning 'to hew' (Czech *rubati*).

Ruecker (119) German (**Rücker**): see RUCKER.
GIVEN NAMES German 10%. *Christoph, Gunter, Kurt, Willi.*

Rueckert (357) German (**Rückert**): variant of RUCKER (1–3) or from a Germanic personal name composed of the elements *rīc* 'power(ful)' + *hard* 'hard', 'bold'.

Rueda (730) Spanish: habitational name from Rueda in Valladolid, Rueda de Jalón in Zamora, Rueda de la Sierra in Guadalajara, or any of the places called La Rueda, from Castilian *rueda* 'wheel', Latin *rota*. Compare Catalan RODA.
GIVEN NAMES Spanish 53%. *Jose* (21), *Luis* (12), *Fernando* (10), *Juan* (10), *Carlos* (9), *Francisco* (7), *Jaime* (5), *Jesus* (5), *Jorge* (5), *Miguel* (5), *Raul* (5), *Alfredo* (4).

Ruedas (127) Spanish: from the plural of *rueda* 'wheel', applied either as a topographic name or as a habitational name for someone from Ruedas in Logroño province.
GIVEN NAMES Spanish 45%. *Javier* (5), *Luis* (3), *Manuel* (3), *Pedro* (3), *Domingo* (2), *Estela* (2), *Mario* (2), *Agapito, Alfonso, Alfredo, Cleofas, Consuelo.*

Ruediger (193) German (**Rüdiger**): variant of RUDIGER.
GIVEN NAMES German 12%; Scandinavian 4%. *Heinz* (2), *Klaus* (2), *Hans, Kurt, Otto, Ralf; Bernt* (2).

Ruedinger (111) German (**Rüdinger**): from a variant of RUDIGER.
GIVEN NAMES German 12%. *Aloys, Frieda, Gerhard, Markus, Ralf.*

Ruedy (170) Variant spelling of Swiss German RUDI or **Rüedi** (see RUDE 1).

Ruef (173) South German and Swiss German: variant of RUEFF (see RUDOLF).
GIVEN NAMES German 4%. *Hanni, Helmut.*

Rueff (196) South German and Swiss German: from a reduced form of the personal name RUDOLF.
GIVEN NAMES French 4%. *Armand, Gaston, Marielle.*

Rueger (333) South German (**Rüger, Rüeger**): **1.** from a reduced form of the personal name *Rüdeger* (see RUDIGER). **2.** nickname or metonymic occupational name from Middle High German *rüegaere, rüeger* 'complainer', 'informant', 'plaintiff'.
GIVEN NAMES German 4%. *Otto, Raimund, Ute.*

Ruegg (281) German (**Rügg, Rüegg**): see RUGG.
GIVEN NAMES French 6%. *Marcel* (2), *Andre.*

Ruegsegger (204) Swiss German (**Rüegsegger**): compound name from the personal name *Rüeg* (see RUGG) + Middle High German *ecke, egge* 'corner', 'point', hence a habitational name for someone living at a place known as *Rüeg's corner*.
GIVEN NAMES German 4%. *Ernst, Fritz, Kurt.*

Ruehl (437) German (also **Rühle**): see RUHL.

Ruehle (362) German (also **Rühle**): see RUHL.
GIVEN NAMES German 5%. *Guenther, Gunter, Gunther, Horst, Jurgen, Wilhelm.*

Ruehling (117) German (also **Rüling**): from a pet form of the personal name RUDOLF.

GIVEN NAMES German 9%. *Kurt* (2), *Erwin, Lothar.*

Ruel (513) possibly Occitan, equivalent to French *roelle* 'disc' (Latin *rotella*, diminutive of *rota* 'wheel').
GIVEN NAMES French 15%. *Aime* (2), *Armand* (2), *Jacques* (2), *Monique* (2), *Valmore* (2), *Adrien, Alphonse, Andre, Antoine, Elzear, Gaetan, Germaine.*

Ruelas (833) Portuguese and Galician: habitational name from Ruelas in Lamego and Guimarãs or a topographic name from a plural diminutive of *rua* 'street'.
GIVEN NAMES Spanish 54%. *Jose* (35), *Jesus* (16), *Juan* (10), *Miguel* (9), *Salvador* (9), *Francisco* (8), *Raul* (8), *Manuel* (6), *Roberto* (6), *Andres* (5), *Jorge* (5), *Luis* (5).

Ruelle (209) French: topographic name for someone who lived in a narrow street, from a diminutive of *rue* 'road', 'street'.
GIVEN NAMES French 4%. *Patrice, Rodolphe.*

Ruen (120) **1.** German: variant of **Ruhn**, from a short form of a personal name such as *Ruomald*. **2.** altered spelling of **Rühen**, reduced form of German *Rüden* or RUDEN. **3.** Norwegian: unexplained. **4.** Possibly an altered spelling of Irish and Scottish RUANE.

Ruesch (504) **1.** German: variant of RUSCH. **2.** German and Swiss German: from a short form of any of the various personal names beginning with the Old High German element *hrōd* 'renown'. **3.** North German (**Rüsch**): nickname for a quick or unkempt, unrefined person, from Low German *rüsch* 'quick'; also 'shaggy', 'bristly'.
GIVEN NAMES German 4%. *Otto* (3), *Aloys, Hartwig, Jurgen, Kurt, Merwin.*

Ruesink (107) Dutch: variant spelling of **Roosingh**, a metronymic from the female personal name *Rosa*.

Ruess (169) German: **1.** from a short form of *Ruosso*, a derivative of RUDOLF. **2.** variant of RUSS.
GIVEN NAMES German 11%. *Manfred* (3), *Otto* (2), *Armin, Gerd.*

Ruest (163) German: variant of RUST.
GIVEN NAMES French 23%. *Fernand* (2), *Henri* (2), *Adrien, Antoine, Armand, Auguste, Cyrille, Donat, Gaston, Gilles, Monique, Normand.*

Rueter (533) German: variant of **Rüther** (see RUETHER) or of REUTER 1.
GIVEN NAMES German 4%. *Ilse, Monika, Siegfried.*

Rueth (196) German (also **Rüth**): northwestern topographic name, from a field name (see REUTER 1).

Ruether (197) German (**Rüther**): variant of REUTER 2.
GIVEN NAME German 6%. *Arno* (3).

Ruetten (111) German (**Rütten**): from a field name, here showing an inflected form from a full name like *aus den Rütten* 'from the clearing(s)' (see RUTTEN and REUTER 1).

Ruetz (184) German (also **Rütz**): variant of RUTZ.

Ruf (744) German: from a reduced form of the personal name RUDOLF.
GIVEN NAMES German 7%. *Egon* (3), *Dieter* (2), *Bernhard, Elke, Erwin, Fritz, Gerhard, Heinz, Hermann, Horst, Juerg, Jurgen.*

Rufe (114) German: variant of RUF.
GIVEN NAMES German 4%. *Aloysius, Elke.*

Rufenacht (179) German: habitational name from Rüfenacht in the Swiss canton of Bern or from Rüfenach in Aargau.

Rufener (271) Swiss German: topographic name for someone who lived by a scree slope or the site of a landslide, from Swiss dialect *Rufine* 'landslide', 'scree'.
GIVEN NAMES German 4%. *Armin, Erwin.*

Rufer (179) German: occupational name for a town crier or a nickname for a street vendor, from Middle High German *ruofære, rüefære* '(town) crier'.
GIVEN NAMES German 7%. *Ewald, Fritz, Hans, Heinz, Markus.*

Ruff (5371) **1.** English: variant of ROLFE. **2.** German: variant spelling of RUF.

Ruffalo (309) Apparently of Italian origin, but not found in present-day Italy.
GIVEN NAMES Italian 5%. *Carlo, Dante.*

Ruffcorn (150) Probably an Americanized spelling of German **Roffka(h)r**, a nickname for a simple or poor man, from Middle Low German *rove* 'beet' + *kar(e)* 'container', 'basket', but a play on words allows the interpretation 'rob the cart' (Middle Low German *roven* 'to rob' + *kare* 'cart').

Ruffer (154) **1.** German: variant of RUFER. **2.** German: variant of ROFFERS. **3.** English: variant of ROVER 1.

Ruffin (3513) English and French: from a personal name, Latin *Rufinus*, a derivative of *Rufus* (see RUFFO 1). This was popularized by various minor early saints, including a 3rd-century martyr of Soissons and a 4th-century Church Father.

Ruffing (712) German: patronymic or pet form of *Ruffo*, a short form of any of the personal names formed with Old High German *hrōd* 'renown', for example RUDOLF.

Ruffini (270) Italian: patronymic or plural form of RUFFINO.
GIVEN NAMES Italian 15%. *Gino* (2), *Nicola* (2), *Amelio, Dario, Domenic, Domenica, Domenico, Emidio, Franco, Gianfranco, Giulio, Giuseppe.*

Ruffino (613) Italian: from the personal name *Ruffino*, Latin *Rufinus*, cognate with *Rufus* (see RUFFO).
GIVEN NAMES Italian 22%. *Salvatore* (5), *Mariano* (3), *Santo* (3), *Vincenzo* (3), *Antonio* (2), *Mario* (2), *Rosario* (2), *Domenic, Filomena, Gasper, Italo, Sal, Vita.*

Ruffins (103) English: patronymic from RUFFIN.

Ruffner (1164) German: variant of RUFENER.

Ruffo (356) Southern Italian: **1.** from a personal name (Latin *Rufus*, originally a nickname for someone with red hair, from a dialect form of the standard Latin word *rubeus*). This name was borne by various minor early saints, and occasionally used as a personal name in the Middle Ages. **2.** from a personal name of Germanic origin but uncertain form and meaning. The Calabrian noble family of this name is said to be of Norman origin.
GIVEN NAMES Italian 19%; Spanish 5%. *Salvatore* (4), *Antonio, Arturo, Attilio, Attillo, Carmelo, Carmine, Eduardo, Elena, Gustavo, Mario, Ofelia, Rafael, Roberto, Rocco; Jose* (2), *Carmella, Juan, Raul.*

Ruffolo (342) Italian: from a pet form of the personal name RUFFO.
GIVEN NAMES Italian 24%. *Luigi* (3), *Aldo* (2), *Emilio* (2), *Fiorino* (2), *Mario* (2), *Natale* (2), *Serafino* (2), *Antonio, Aurelio, Carmine, Duilio, Enrico, Erminio, Ernesto, Filomena, Gaspare, Lilia, Rodolfo, Rosario, Sergio.*

Rufino (136) Spanish: from the personal name *Rufino* (Latin *Rufinus*, from *rufus* 'red').
GIVEN NAMES Spanish 47%. *Carlos* (2), *Jose* (2), *Manuel* (2), *Alberto, Alejandra, Ambrosio, Benito, Cesareo, Domingo, Edmundo, Enrique, Francisco; Angelo, Antonio.*

Rufo (414) Italian: nickname from *rufo*, denoting someone with red or frizzy hair, also (regionally) someone who was strong, robust, educated, or snooty.
GIVEN NAMES Italian 23%. *Antonio* (4), *Mario* (3), *Gino* (2), *Nino* (2), *Pompeo* (2), *Rogelio* (2), *Romeo* (2), *Aldo, Alfonse, Antonino, Benigno, Carmella, Dino, Donato, Emilio, Fortunato, Franco, Giulio, Isidra, Julio, Lauro, Liliana, Onofre.*

Rufty (132) Probably a derivative of German **Ruft**, a reduced form of the personal name *Hrotfrid*, formed with Old High German *hrōd* 'renown'.

Rufus (239) English: from a Latin nickname meaning 'red-haired' (see RUFFO). This is found in medieval English documents as a translation of various surnames with the same sense. (As a personal name it was not adopted until the 19th century.)
GIVEN NAMES French 5%. *Andre, Antoine, Vernice.*

Rugani (108) Italian (Sicily): unexplained.
GIVEN NAMES Italian 7%. *Angelo, Silvano, Silvio.*

Rugar (105) Variant spelling of German **Rüger** (see RUEGER).

Ruge (393) German: **1.** nickname from Middle High German *ruowe, rüge* 'quiet', 'calm' or Low German *rüg* 'rough', 'crude'. **2.** from the personal name *Rugo*, a reduced form of **Rüdiger** (see RUDIGER).

Rugen (160) German (also **Rügen**): patronymic from RUGE 2.
GIVEN NAMES German 4%. *Erwin, Gerhardt.*

Rugenstein (109) German: habitational name from a place so named, from Middle High German *rüge* 'rest' (a variant of *ruo*) + *stein* 'rock'.

Ruger (393) German (**Rüger**): see RUEGER.

Rugg (1147) South German: **1.** (**Rügg**): from the popular medieval personal name *Rüegg*, a reduced form of RUDIGER. **2.** variant of RUCK 1, 2.

Ruggeri (677) Italian: patronymic or plural form of RUGGERO.
GIVEN NAMES Italian 28%. *Mario* (9), *Angelo* (5), *Luigi* (3), *Salvatore* (3), *Antonino* (2), *Antonio* (2), *Arturo* (2), *Dino* (2), *Domenic* (2), *Francesco* (2), *Franco* (2), *Reno* (2), *Roberto* (2).

Ruggerio (195) Variant of Italian RUGGIERO.
GIVEN NAME Italian 9%. *Angelo* (2).

Ruggero (120) Italian: variant of RUGGIERO.
GIVEN NAMES Italian 12%. *Mario* (2), *Angelo, Antonio, Biagio, Vito.*

Ruggiano (122) Italian: habitational name from Roggiano Gravina in Cosenza province, or from either of two districts called Ruggiano, Monte Sant'Angelo in Foggia province or Salve in Lecce province.
GIVEN NAMES Italian 16%. *Pasco* (2), *Amerigo, Rachele, Rocco, Silvio.*

Ruggieri (822) Italian: patronymic or plural form of RUGGIERO.
GIVEN NAMES Italian 17%. *Antonio* (5), *Mauro* (5), *Salvatore* (4), *Luigi* (3), *Vito* (3), *Angelo* (2), *Ciro* (2), *Dante* (2), *Domenic* (2), *Giuseppe* (2), *Rocco* (2), *Sal* (2).

Ruggiero (3218) Italian: from *Ruggiero*, a personal name of Germanic origin, composed of the elements *hrōd* 'renown' + *gār, gēr* 'spear', 'lance'. Compare English ROGER.
GIVEN NAMES Italian 16%. *Angelo* (17), *Salvatore* (15), *Antonio* (12), *Carmine* (12), *Rocco* (7), *Vito* (6), *Donato* (4), *Pasquale* (4), *Sal* (4), *Vincenzo* (4), *Aniello* (3), *Carlo* (3).

Ruggirello (155) Italian: from a derivative of the personal name RUGGERO.
GIVEN NAMES Italian 18%. *Girolamo* (2), *Vito* (2), *Alfio, Angelo, Gaspare, Stefano.*

Ruggles (2070) English: patronymic from a pet form of RUDGE.
FOREBEARS The founder of this influential American family was Thomas Ruggles (1584–1644) of Sudbury, Suffolk, England, who settled in Roxbury, MA, in 1637.

Rugh (443) **1.** Apparently a variant spelling of English ROUGH. **2.** Probably an altered spelling of German RUCH.

Ruh (455) Swiss German: variant of RUCH.

Ruhe (390) North German: **1.** variant of RUGE 1. **2.** (**Rühe**): nickname from **Rüde** 'hound' (see RUDE 2). **3.** habitational name from places named Rühen, Rüden, Rhüden in northern Germany.

GIVEN NAMES German 4%. *Fritz* (2), *Heinz*, *Lutz*, *Manferd*.

Ruhl (1899) German (also **Rühl**): **1.** from a pet form of the personal name RUDOLF. **2.** habitational name from either of two places named Rühle in northern Germany.

Ruhland (628) German: from the personal name *Ruhland*, a common medieval form of ROLAND.

GIVEN NAMES German 4%. *Kurt* (4), *Erwin* (3), *Alfons*, *Reinhard*.

Ruhle (175) German (**Rühle**): variant of RUHL.

GIVEN NAME German 5%. *Wolfgang* (2).

Ruhlman (335) German (**Ruhlmann**): **1.** from a pet form of RUDOLPH + *man* 'man'. **2.** (**Rühlmann**) habitational name for someone from any of several places named Rühle in Lower Saxony.

Ruhmann (129) **1.** South German: vernacular form of the personal name ROMAN. **2.** North German (**Rühmann**): from a reduced form of **Rüdemann**, from **Rüde** (see RUDE 1); generally it may be from any of the compound personal names containing the Old High German element *hrōd* 'renown', for example *Ruombald*, *Rumold*.

GIVEN NAMES French 7%; Scandinavian 4%; German 4%. *Laure*; *Erik*; *Kurt*.

Ruhnke (328) German: from a short form of a Germanic personal name formed with *run-* 'rune', 'secret'.

GIVEN NAMES German 7%. *Hans* (2), *Kurt* (2), *Hertha*, *Irmgard*, *Lothar*.

Ruhr (100) German: perhaps a habitational name for someone who lived at a place named for the Ruhr river.

Ruhs (120) German: **1.** from Middle High German *ruoz* 'soot', 'dirt', hence a nickname for a blacksmith. **2.** nickname from Middle High German *rus* 'rascal', 'uncouth fellow'. **3.** from a short form of a personal name formed with Old High German *hruod* 'renown' + the suffix *-z*. **4.** see RUSS 5.

Ruis (279) **1.** Spanish: variant of RUIZ. **2.** Portuguese: variant of Portuguese **Rois** or **Roiz**.

GIVEN NAMES Spanish 12%. *Manuel* (2), *Arturo*, *Carlos*, *Conception*, *Elba*, *Fernando*, *Jose*, *Josue*, *Juan*, *Jubenal*, *Lazaro*, *Lupe*.

Ruisi (130) Italian: perhaps, as Caracausi proposes, an Italianized form of the Spanish surname RUIZ.

GIVEN NAMES Italian 27%. *Santo* (4), *Angelo* (3), *Matteo* (2), *Carmela*, *Lorenzo*, *Pasquale*, *Vittorio*.

Ruiter (281) Dutch: variant of RUTTER 3.

GIVEN NAMES Dutch 5%; German 4%. *Gerrit* (2), *Albertus*, *Cornie*, *Geert*, *Henk*, *Pieter*; *Hans*, *Kurt*.

Ruiz (21051) Spanish: patronymic from the personal name *Ruy*, a short form of RODRIGO.

GIVEN NAMES Spanish 49%. *Jose* (481), *Juan* (272), *Manuel* (227), *Carlos* (211), *Jesus*

(169), *Francisco* (150), *Luis* (146), *Miguel* (135), *Roberto* (120), *Pedro* (116), *Ramon* (116), *Jorge* (111).

Rukavina (256) Croatian and Serbian: nickname from an augmentative form of *ruka* 'hand', a nickname for someone with large hands.

GIVEN NAMES South Slavic 5%. *Branko*, *Darko*, *Davor*, *Mile*, *Nenad*.

Ruland (585) German (also **Rüland**): variant spelling of RUHLAND.

Rule (2314) **1.** English: from the medieval personal name *Roul* (see ROLLO, ROLF). **2.** Scottish: habitational name from a place in Roxburghshire, so named from the stream on which it stands. This name is of uncertain origin, possibly from Welsh *rhull* 'hasty', 'rash'. **3.** Probably an altered spelling of German RUHL.

Ruley (389) Perhaps an Americanized spelling of German RUHLE (or its Swiss German derivative **Rühli**), or of French **Roulet** (see ROULETTE).

Rulison (154) Probably an altered spelling of English ROLLISON.

Rull (100) Catalan: **1.** nickname from Catalan *rull*, either in its sense of mill roller, or hair curl. **2.** possibly also from a derivative of the Germanic personal name *Raülf*, composed of the elements *rad* 'counsel', 'advice' + *wolf* 'wolf'. Compare English RALPH.

GIVEN NAMES Spanish 15%. *Manuel* (2), *Rodolfo* (2), *Alejandro*, *Armando*, *Edmundo*, *Jaime*, *Juan*.

Rulli (279) Italian: patronymic from *Rullo*. Compare the Old Tuscan personal name *Rullus*, from a short form of names with this ending, such as *Barullus*.

GIVEN NAMES Italian 14%. *Pasquale* (2), *Angelo*, *Antonio*, *Dante*, *Dino*, *Donato*, *Franca*, *Francesco*, *Italo*, *Piera*, *Rocco*, *Valentino*.

Rullman (172) German (**Rullmann**): **1.** habitational name from a place called Rulle near Osnabrück. **2.** nickname for a fat person, from Middle Low German *rulle* 'roll', 'drum', 'roller'.

Rullo (332) Italian: from the old personal name *Rullo*, from a reduced pet form of various personal names formed with the suffix *-ullo*, as for example *Gasparullo* (from GASPARI), *Baldassarullo* (from BALDASSARE), or *Barullo* (from BARO).

GIVEN NAMES Italian 12%. *Angelo* (2), *Fiore* (2), *Amato*, *Antonio*, *Corrado*, *Donato*, *Modestino*, *Raffaele*, *Renzo*, *Romeo*.

Rulo (122) Origin unidentified; perhaps a variant of French RULON.

Rulon (226) Origin uncertain. Perhaps an altered spelling of French **Rouland** or **Rullan**, regional variants of ROLAND.

Rumage (138) Scottish: variant of RUMMAGE.

Ruman (136) **1.** South German: variant of ROMAN. **2.** Altered spelling of North German **Ruhmann**, **Rühmann**, reduced forms

of **Rudemann** and **Rüdemann**, derivatives of the personal name *Rude* or *Rüde* (see RUDE 1).

Rumbaugh (822) Americanized spelling of German ROMBACH or **Rumbach**, a habitational name from a place so named in the Palatinate.

Rumberger (205) German: perhaps a variant spelling of ROMBERGER, or a habitational name from a place named Rumburg on the German-Czech border, near Görlitz.

Rumble (651) **1.** English: variant of RUMBOLD. **2.** Altered spelling of German **Rumbel** or **Rumpel**, variants of RUMMEL 2.

Rumbley (160) **1.** English: see RUMLEY. **2.** Probably an Americanized spelling of Swiss German **Rümbeli**, from a pet form of a Germanic personal name formed with Old High German *hruom* 'fame', or of South German **Rümple**, **Rümpfle**, or **Rümpfli**, humorous nicknames for someone who was short and stocky, from Middle High German *rump(h)* 'bent', 'crooked'.

Rumbo (106) **1.** Galician: habitational name from Rumbo in A Coruña province. **2.** Spanish: nickname from Spanish *rumbo* 'splendor', 'magnificence'.

GIVEN NAMES Spanish 6%. *Cruz Maria*, *Emilio*, *Esperanza*, *Jorge*, *Marcelina*, *Procopio*.

Rumbold (143) **1.** English: from the Norman personal name *Rumbald*, composed of the Germanic elements *rūm* 'wide', 'spacious' (or, more plausibly, a by-form of *hrūm* 'renown') + *bald* 'bold', 'brave'. **2.** German: variant of **Rumpold**, **Rombold**, variants of RUMPEL 1.

Rumburg (100) Probably a variant of German ROMBERG.

GIVEN NAME German 4%. *Frieda*.

Rumer (286) **1.** Perhaps an altered spelling of English RUMMER. **2.** German: variant of **Ruhmer**, a nickname from Middle High German *ruomære* 'braggart'. **3.** German: from an old personal name formed with Old High German *hruom* 'fame'.

Rumery (282) English (Sussex): unexplained.

Rumfelt (325) **1.** Altered spelling of German **Romfeld**, from Middle Low German *rüm-* 'to clear (land)' + *feld* 'open country', 'field', a topographic name or possibly a metonymic occupational name for someone engaged in clearing woodland, or in some cases a habitational name for someone from Romfelt in the Ardennes. **2.** Perhaps an altered spelling of Dutch **Rumfels**, **Rundfeldt**, a habitational name from Romfelt (see 1).

Rumfield (132) See RUMFELT.

Rumford (222) English: habitational name for someone from Romford in Essex, probably so named from Old English *rūm* 'broad', 'spacious' + *ford* 'ford'.

Ruminski (184) Polish (**Rumiński**): habitational name for someone from Rumin in Konin voivodeship.
GIVEN NAMES Polish 6%. *Danuta, Ewa, Grazyna, Wladyslaw.*

Rumler (194) Probably an altered spelling of German **Rummler** or **Rümmler**, a nickname for a disruptive or noisy person, from an agent derivative of Middle High German *rummeln, rumpeln* 'to move impetuously', 'to make a noise', or occasionally from a short form of a personal name formed with Old High German *hrōd* 'renown'.

Rumley (662) **1.** English (Kent): origin uncertain; perhaps a habitational name from a lost or unidentified place. **2.** Altered spelling of German **Rümmelin** or **Rümmele**, variants of RUMMEL.

Rummage (286) **1.** Scottish: unexplained. **2.** Americanized form of German **Rometsch** or **Rumetsch**, which probably derives from a Germanic personal name formed with *hruom* 'fame', 'renown', via the saint's name *Romedius.*

Rummel (1555) **1.** North German and Dutch: variant of ROMMEL. **2.** German: perhaps a nickname for a noisemaker, from Middle High German *rummeln* 'to make noise', 'to move impetuously', which, however, is not recorded until the 15th century.

Rummell (328) Altered spelling of RUMMEL.

Rummer (121) English: variant of ROMER.

Rummler (123) German (also **Rümmler**): **1.** nickname for a noisy person, from a noun derivative of Middle High German *rumpeln, rummeln* 'to crash about', 'to make a noise'. **2.** in some cases, a patronymic from a personal name from Old High German *ruom* 'renown', 'glory'.
GIVEN NAMES German 10%. *Achim, Christoph, Erna, Kurt, Reinhold.*

Rumney (218) English: variant of ROMNEY.

Rumore (210) Altered spelling of the North German habitational name **Rumo(h)r**, from a place named Rumohr (earlier Rumor) in Schleswig-Holstein.
GIVEN NAMES Italian 12%. *Angelo* (2), *Antonio, Casimiro, Gaetano, Gasper, Sal, Salvatore.*

Rump (320) **1.** English: nickname for a person with a large behind, from Old English *rumpe* 'buttocks'. **2.** German: variant spelling of RUMPF. **3.** German: from a short form of RUMPEL.

Rumpel (195) German: **1.** from the personal name *Ruombald*, a compound of Old High German *hruom* 'fame' or *hrōd* 'renown' + *bald* 'bold'. **2.** variant of RUMMEL 2.
GIVEN NAME German 4%. *Manfred* (2).

Rumpf (549) German: nickname for a large man, from Middle High German *rumph, rump* 'trunk', 'body', or for someone who was bent or misshapen, from Middle High German *rumph* 'bent', 'crooked'.

Rumph (768) Altered spelling of RUMPF.

Rumple (395) Americanized or variant spelling of German RUMPEL (see also RUMBLEY).

Rumrill (239) English: unexplained. Compare ROMRELL.
FOREBEARS The name was brought to North America from Jersey in the Channel Islands by Simon Rumrill (*c.*1663–1705), who died in Enfield, CT.

Rumschlag (112) German: probably a nickname or topographic name in sentence form, '*raum den Schlag* ' 'clear the (tree-felling) area', from Middle Low German *rumen* 'to clear', 'leave' + *schlag* (standardized) 'cleared area'.

Rumsey (2024) English: habitational name from Romsey in Hampshire, so named from the genitive case of the Old English personal name *Rūm* (a short form of compound names with the first element *rūm*) + Old English *ēg* 'island', 'dry land in a fen'.

Runck (159) German: variant of RUNK.

Runco (207) Italian: variant of **Rungo**, apparently from an old German personal name *Rungus*, of uncertain origin and meaning.
GIVEN NAMES Italian 19%. *Aldo* (2), *Angelo* (2), *Casimiro* (2), *Gasper* (2), *Dino, Ettore, Franco, Mario, Orlando.*

Rund (414) German: variant of RUNTE.

Rundall (151) English: variant spelling of RUNDELL.

Rundberg (99) Swedish: ornamental name composed of the elements *rund* 'round' + *berg* 'mountain', 'hill'.
GIVEN NAMES Scandinavian 15%; German 14%. *Berger, Per, Sven; Franz* (2), *Kurt, Rudi.*

Runde (454) **1.** German: variant of RUNTE. **2.** Norwegian: habitational name from an island farmstead in Sunnmøre called Runde, probably derived from Old Norse *hrinda* 'thrust', 'push', with reference to a projecting island or promontory.

Rundel (113) German: from the personal name *Ru(o)nelin*.
GIVEN NAME German 5%. *Hermann* (2).

Rundell (736) **1.** English (mainly Devon and Cornwall): nickname from a diminutive of Middle English, Old French *rond, rund* 'fat', 'round'. Compare ROUND. **2.** English: habitational name from Rundale in the parish of Shoreham, Kent, named from Old English *rūm(ig)* 'roomy', 'spacious' + *dæl* 'valley'. **3.** Swedish: ornamental name composed of the elements *rund* 'round' + the common suffix *-ell*, from the Latin adjectival suffix *-elius*. **4.** Altered spelling of German **Rundel**, from a pet form of a Germanic personal name based on *rūn* 'secret', 'rune', 'cryptogram'.

Rundle (987) **1.** English: variant of RUNDELL. **2.** Respelling of German RUNDEL.

Rundlett (161) Origin unidentified. Compare RANDLETT.

Rundquist (383) Swedish: ornamental name composed of the elements *rund*

'round' + *quist*, an old or ornamental spelling of *kvist* 'twig'.

Runfola (129) Italian (Sicily): nickname from Sicilian *runfulari* 'to snore' (from French *ronfler*).
GIVEN NAMES Italian 12%. *Angelo* (2), *Onofrio, Sal, Salvatore.*

Rung (328) Probably an altered spelling of RUNGE.

Runge (2058) German: from Middle High German *runge* 'staff', 'stick' (Old High German *runga*). The precise sense of the surname is not clear, but the vocabulary word was used in particular of the support rung on the side of a (ladder) wagon; thus it is possibly a metonymic occupational name for a wheelwright.
GIVEN NAMES German 5%. *Kurt* (6), *Klaus* (3), *Otto* (3), *Erwin* (2), *Gerhard* (2), *Heinz* (2), *Siegfried* (2), *Arno, Bernd, Bismark, Ewald, Fritz.*

Runion (1013) Irish: variant of RUNYON.

Runions (308) Apparently a patronymic from RUNYON.

Runk (462) German: **1.** nickname for a lumbering person, from *Runke* 'big lump'. **2.** from a short form of a Germanic personal name formed with *rūn* 'secret', 'rune', 'cryptogram'.

Runke (109) German: nickname from Middle German *runge* 'big lump'.
GIVEN NAME German 4%. *Reinhold.*

Runkel (447) German: habitational name from a place so named in the Lahn area in Hesse.

Runkle (1235) Americanized spelling of German RUNKEL.

Runkles (163) Altered form of RUNKEL.

Runnells (336) English (Devon and Cornwall): probably a variant of RUNDELL.

Runnels (1595) English (Devon and Cornwall): probably a variant of RUNDELL.

Runner (556) Probably an altered spelling of German **Ronner**, an occupational name for a runner or messenger, a lightly armed mounted soldier. Compare RENNER.

Running (644) **1.** Scottish: perhaps a variant of Irish RUNYON. **2.** Probably also an altered spelling of German RONNING.

Runnion (294) Irish: variant of RUNYON.

Runquist (184) Swedish: ornamental name composed of the elements *run* 'rune', 'runic letter' or *rund* 'round' + *quist*, an old or ornamental spelling of *kvist* 'twig'.
GIVEN NAMES Scandinavian 10%. *Lars* (3), *Bjorn* (2).

Runser (130) South German and French (Alsace): from a topographic name **Runs** for a small creek + *-er* indicating habitation.

Runte (159) German: of uncertain origin; in the northwest of Germany it is most probably a topographic name from a field name based on *run* 'mud', which gave rise to several place names in the Rhine-Ruhr area, for example Runten, Runtenberg, Rünthe.
GIVEN NAMES German 9%. *Otto* (3), *Erhard.*

Runyan (2529) Irish: variant of RUNYON.

Runyon (3121) Irish: reduced Anglicized form of Gaelic Ó Rúnaidhin, from a diminutive of the personal name *Ruanaidh* (see ROONEY).

Ruocco (493) Italian: variant of ROCCO.
GIVEN NAMES Italian 17%. *Gennaro* (4), *Angelo* (2), *Giuseppe* (2), *Luigi* (2), *Vito* (2), *Alfonse, Antonio, Carmine, Fortunata, Franco, Luca, Pasquale.*

Ruoff (492) South German: from a reduced form of the personal name RUDOLF.
GIVEN NAMES German 5%. *Otto* (2), *Gerd, Heinz, Hermann, Kurt.*

Ruona (127) Finnish: topographic name from *ruona* 'creek' or 'alluvial land'. It is also found as an abbreviation of the surnames **Ruonakangas, Ruonakoski**, and **Ruonala**.
GIVEN NAMES French 5%; Finnish 4%. *Patrice; Martti* (2).

Ruopp (102) German: variant of RUPP.
GIVEN NAME German 5%. *Fritz.*

Ruotolo (297) Italian: variant of ROTOLO.
GIVEN NAMES Italian 17%. *Angelo* (5), *Pasquale* (3), *Salvatore* (2), *Augustino, Carmine, Enrico, Giuseppi, Lucio, Luigi.*

Rupar (121) Slovenian: habitational name for someone from any of numerous places called Rupe or Rupa, or a topographic name, all derived from *rupa* 'hole in a limestone karst', 'hollow', 'basin'.

Rupard (268) Variant spelling of German RUPERT.

Rupe (1206) **1.** German: from Middle Low German *rupe* 'caterpillar', hence a nickname for a gardener. **2.** Altered spelling of German RUPP or RUPPE.

Rupel (127) German (**Rüpel**) and Slovenian: from a pet form of RUPRECHT. From the 16th century, the name came to mean 'lout' and some late formations of the surname may have arisen from a nickname from this sense. It may also be an altered spelling of German RUPPEL.

Rupert (2943) Dutch, North German, and Slovenian: from a Germanic personal name composed of the elements *hrōd* 'renown' + *berht* 'bright'. Compare RUPPRECHT.

Rupinski (144) Polish (**Rupiński**): habitational name for someone from Rupin in Łomża or Ostrołęka voivodeships.
GIVEN NAMES Polish 7%. *Casimir, Grzegorz, Jozef.*

Rupiper (143) German: altered spelling of **Rupieper**, a variant of Low German **Rohrpieper**, nickname from the name of a bird, the marsh pipit (from *Rohr* 'reeds' + *Pieper* 'chirper'), or from an occupational name for a musician who played a reed pipe, from Middle Low German *rōr* 'reed' + *piper* 'piper'.

Ruple (329) **1.** German: variant of RUPP. **2.** Americanized spelling of German RUPPEL or **Rüpel** (see RUPEL).

Rupley (201) Americanized spelling of Swiss German **Rup(p)li**, from a short form of a Germanic personal name formed with *hrōd* 'renown', or of German RUPLE. Compare RUPRECHT, ROBERT.

Ruplinger (126) German: possibly a habitational name from Rüblingen in Baden-Württemberg.

Rupnow (223) German: habitational name from Rubenow near Anklam in West Pomerania.
GIVEN NAMES German 6%. *Frieda, Kurt, Ulrich, Wiltrud.*

Rupp (4675) German: from a short form of RUPPRECHT.

Ruppe (508) German: presumably a variant of RUPP, or possibly a habitational name from Ruppen in East Prussia.
GIVEN NAMES German 4%. *Helmuth* (3), *Alois, Erna, Kurt.*

Ruppel (964) South German: from a pet form of RUPPRECHT.

Ruppenthal (183) German: habitational name from a lost or unidentified place.
GIVEN NAMES German 5%. *Aloysius, Erwin, Markus.*

Ruppert (2077) German: variant spelling of RUPERT.

Rupple (149) Americanized spelling of German RUPPEL.

Rupprecht (629) German: from a Germanic personal name composed of the elements *hrōd* 'renown' + *berht* 'bright' (another form of which is ROBERT).
GIVEN NAMES German 8%. *Kurt* (3), *Bernhardt* (2), *Hans* (2), *Hermann* (2), *Reinhard* (2), *Alois, Erhardt, Georg, Otto, Wolfgang.*

Ruprecht (413) German: variant of RUPPRECHT.

Rupright (102) Americanized form of German RUPPRECHT.

Rury (103) Scottish: variant of RORIE.
GIVEN NAME German 4%. *Kurt.*

Rus (241) **1.** Czech, Slovak, Slovenian, Croatian, and Romanian (of Slavic origin): ethnic name for a Russian. **2.** Czech: descriptive nickname from the adjective *rusý* 'strawberry blond'. **3.** Slovenian and Croatian (northern Croatia): nickname from the adjective *rus* 'red-haired', or from the dialect word *rus* 'cockroach'. Compare ROS 3.
GIVEN NAMES Romanian 9%. *Simion* (3), *Grigore* (2), *Doina, Dorel, Ilie, Liviu, Petru, Vasile.*

Rusak (151) **1.** Polish, Ukrainian, Jewish (eastern Ashkenazic), and Belorussian: ethnic or regional name from Polish *rusak* 'Ukrainian', eastern Slavic *rusak* 'Russian'. The name derives ultimately from a Scandinavian term meaning 'rower', 'oarsman', the Russian state having been first established in the 9th century by Varangian (i.e. Norse) settlers who rowed up the rivers from the Baltic. **2.** Polish, Ukrainian, Jewish (eastern Ashkenazic), and Belorussian: nickname from an eastern Slavic word meaning 'light brown', with allusion to the coloring of hair or skin (compare Polish *rusy*, Ukrainian and Russian *rusyj*). **3.** Jewish (eastern Ashkenazic): habitational name from Rusaki, in Belarus.
GIVEN NAMES Polish 6%. *Andrzej, Henryk.*

Rusch (1959) German: **1.** topographic name from Middle High German, Middle Low German *rusch* 'rush', or a habitational name from a place named with this word. **2.** nickname from Middle Low German *rusch* 'quick', 'hasty'. **3.** (**Rüsch**): see RUESCH.
GIVEN NAMES German 5%. *Otto* (7), *Erwin* (2), *Helmuth* (2), *Kurt* (2), *Alfons, Claus, Ewald, Frieda, Fritz, Gerhardt, Hans, Heinz.*

Ruschak (112) Ukrainian: ethnic name for a Ruthenian. This surname is found in Hungarian in the form **Ruszcsák**.
GIVEN NAME Hungarian 5%. *Miklos* (2).

Rusche (295) German: **1.** variant of RUSCH. **2.** from Czech *růže* 'rose', probably a metonymic occupational name for a rose grower.
GIVEN NAMES German 4%. *Ernst, Erwin, Hans.*

Ruscher (107) Swiss German (**Rüscher**): probably a habitational name for someone from a place named with *rusch* 'rush' (see RUSCH).

Ruscio (142) Italian: southern variant of ROSSO.
GIVEN NAMES Italian 17%. *Domenic* (3), *Domenico, Romolo.*

Ruscitti (156) Italian: patronymic or plural form of RUSCITTO.
GIVEN NAMES Italian 20%. *Antonio* (2), *Dante* (2), *Angelo, Croce, Fabrizio, Gino, Nicola, Sal, Tullio.*

Ruscitto (104) Southern Italian: variant of ROSSITTO.
GIVEN NAMES Italian 20%. *Antonio* (2), *Angelo, Attilio, Gino, Guerino, Luciano, Pasquale, Umberto.*

Rusco (118) Italian: possibly a topographic name from *rusco* 'butcher's broom' (Latin *ruscus*), but the numerous derivatives of this name suggest that it more likely from a personal name, *Rusco*, of Germanic origin.

Ruscoe (123) English: variant spelling of ROSCOE.

Rusconi (188) Italian: patronymic from *Ruscone*, a derivative of RUSCO.
GIVEN NAMES Italian 10%; French 4%. *Angelo* (3), *Dino, Ettore, Giancarlo, Lorenzo, Nino, Rocco, Valentino; Andre, Pierre.*

Ruse (371) **1.** English: variant of ROUSE. **2.** German: variant of **Reusse** (see REUSS 1). **3.** Probably also an Americanized form of Czech RUS 'Russian'.

Rusek (139) Polish and Czech: from a diminutive of RUS 'Russian' or from the adjective *rusy* 'strawberry blond'.
GIVEN NAMES Polish 10%. *Casimir, Janusz, Jozef, Leszek, Wojiech.*

Rush (13544) **1.** English: topographic name for someone who lived among rushes, from Middle English *rush* (a collective singular, Old English *rysc*), or perhaps an occupational name for someone who wove mats, baskets, and other articles out of rushes. **2.** Irish: reduced Anglicized form of Gaelic **Ó Ruis** 'descendant of *Ros*', a personal name perhaps derived from *ros* 'wood'. In Connacht it has also been used as a translation of **Ó Luachra** (see LOUGHREY). **3.** Irish: Anglicized form (translation) of Gaelic **Ó Fuada**, 'descendant of *Fuada*' a personal name meaning 'hasty', 'rushing' (see FOODY). **4.** Altered spelling of German **Rüsch** or **Rusch** (see RUSCH) or ROSCH.

FOREBEARS Benjamin Rush (1745–1813), a physician and signer of the Declaration of Independence, was born in the PA farming community of Byberry. He was descended from John Rush, a yeoman from Oxfordshire, England, who came to Byberry in 1683.

Rusher (608) **1.** English: topographic name for someone who lived among rushes or occupational name for someone who made things out of rushes (see RUSH). **2.** Americanized spelling of German **Rüscher** (variant of RUSCH) or ROSCHER.

Rushford (415) English: apparently a habitational name from places named Rushford in Devon, Norfolk, and Warwickshire. However, in view of the present-day distribution of the surname, a more likely source is Ryshworth in Bingley, West Yorkshire, which was earlier called *Rushford* (from Old English *rysc* 'rushes' + *ford* 'ford').

Rushforth (130) English (Yorkshire): probably a habitational name from Ryshworth in Bingley, West Yorkshire (see RUSHFORD).

Rushin (409) See RUSHING.

Rushing (6593) Probably an altered spelling of the eastern German family name **Rusching**, a variant of RUSCHE 2.

Rushlow (302) **1.** Americanized spelling of German **Roschlau(b)**, a habitational name from Rosslau on the Elbe river perhaps, or from Röschlaub in Franconia. **2.** Americanized spelling of French ROCHELEAU.

Rushmore (140) **1.** English: perhaps a habitational name from Rushmere in Suffolk, near Lowestoft, so named from Old English *rysc* 'rushes' + *mere* 'pond', 'lake'. **2.** perhaps also an Americanized form of German **Ruschmeier**, a topographic name for a farmer who lived and farmed in an area where reeds grew (see RUSCH 1 and MEYER).

GIVEN NAMES German 6%. *Erna, Hilde, Kurt.*

Rushton (1607) English: habitational name from any of the various places so named, for example in Cheshire, Northamptonshire, and Staffordshire, from Old English *rysc* 'rushes' + *tūn* 'enclosure', 'settlement'.

Rushworth (148) English (West Yorkshire): habitational name from Rishworth in West Yorkshire, so named from Old English *rysc* 'rushes' + *worð* 'enclosure'.

Rusiecki (100) Polish: habitational name from Rusiec in Sieradz or Warszawa voivodeships.

GIVEN NAMES Polish 13%. *Lucjan, Miroslaw, Piotr, Tadeusz, Wieslaw.*

Rusin (537) **1.** Polish, Ukrainian, and Jewish (eastern Ashkenazic): ethnic or regional name from Polish and Ukrainian *rusin* 'Ruthenian'. **2.** Jewish (from Belarus): habitational name from Rusiny in Belarus.

GIVEN NAMES Polish 5%. *Irena* (2), *Stanislaw* (2), *Jacek, Jadwiga, Janina, Krystyna, Lucyna, Zygmund.*

Rusinko (222) Ukrainian: diminutive of RUSIN.

Rusk (1795) **1.** Scottish: probably a topographic name from Gaelic *riasg* 'marsh', 'bog'. Compare RISK. **2.** Probably also an altered form of German **Ruske**, **Roske**, diminutives of ROSE.

Ruskin (476) **1.** English: probably from a pet form of the medieval personal name *Rose* (see ROYCE). **2.** Scottish: from Gaelic *rusg(aire)an*, a reduced plural of *rusgaire* 'peeler (of bark)', hence an occupational name borne by family of tanners. **3.** Jewish: Americanized form of RASKIN or some other like-sounding Ashkenazic surname.

GIVEN NAMES Jewish 4%. *Sol* (2), *Tauba, Uzi.*

Ruskowski (100) Polish: habitational name for someone from Rusko in Kalisz voivodeship, Rusków in Biała Podlaska voivodeship.

Rusnak (1051) Polish and Slovak (**Rusnák**): ethnic nickname for a Russian or Ruthenian.

Rusnock (121) Germanized form of Polish and Slovak RUSNAK.

GIVEN NAME German 6%. *Matthias* (2).

Russ (5148) **1.** English: variant spelling of ROUSE. **2.** German: from a short form of a Germanic personal name formed with *hrōd* 'renown'. **3.** German (of Slavic origin): from Old Slavic *rusu* 'reddish', 'blond', hence a nickname or an ethnic name meaning 'Russian'. **4.** Swiss German: topographic name for someone who lived by a scree, Middle High German *ru(o)zze* 'scree'. **5.** In some instances the name referred to personal or business connections with Russia, the country of the *Reussen*, from Middle High German *Riusse*.

Russak (161) German, Ukrainian, Belorussian, and Jewish (eastern Ashkenazic): variant spelling of RUSAK.

GIVEN NAME Jewish 6%. *Hyman.*

Russaw (100) Americanized form of French ROUSSEAU.

GIVEN NAME French 5%. *Andre.*

Russeau (105) Variant spelling of French ROUSSEAU.

Russek (144) Jewish (from Poland): variant of RUSSAK.

GIVEN NAME German 4%. *Ignaz.*

Russel (572) English: variant spelling of RUSSELL.

Russelburg (126) Probably an Americanized form of Belgian **van Roeselberg**, a habitational name from Roeselberg in Brabant.

Russell (79186) **1.** English, Scottish, and Irish: from *Rousel*, a common Anglo-Norman French nickname for someone with red hair, a diminutive of ROUSE with the hypocoristic suffix *-el*. **2.** Americanized spelling of German **Rüssel**, from a pet form of any of the various personal names formed with the Old High German element *hrōd* 'renown'.

Russello (107) Southern Italian: from a diminutive of the nickname RUSSO.

GIVEN NAMES Italian 21%. *Angelo* (2), *Calogero, Nicola, Nicolo, Sal, Salvatore.*

Russett (184) English: nickname from Middle English *russet* 'reddish brown', (from Old French *rosset*, diminutive of *rous* 'red', from Latin *russus* 'red'). This may have been a nickname denoting hair coloring or complexion, but in Middle English *russet* denoted in particular a kind of coarse woolen cloth of a reddish brown or subdued color, typically worn by country people and the poor.

Russey (141) Americanized spelling of the Swiss family name RUSSI.

Russi (257) Italian and Spanish: **1.** possibly a southern variant of ROSSI. **2.** alternatively, perhaps, a habitational name from Russi in Ravenna province, Romagna, though this is not a major area of emigration to North America. The surname is also found in southern Spain and Switzerland, where it is most likely of Italian origin.

GIVEN NAMES Spanish 12%. *Alberto* (2), *Carlos* (2), *Humberto* (2), *Jose* (2), *Alicia, Americo, Elvira, Emilio, Francisco, Guillermo, Maria Elena, Mario.*

Russian (185) Jewish: Americanized form of a like-sounding Ashkenazic surname; possibly RUSIN, or a habitational name (**Rosseyn(y), Rossiensky**) derived from a place called Rossieny, now Raseiniai in Lithuania.

GIVEN NAME Jewish 4%. *Myer* (2).

Russillo (126) Variant of southern Italian RUSSELLO.

GIVEN NAMES Italian 16%. *Dante* (2), *Antonio, Cosmo, Domenico, Gennaro.*

Russin (327) Possibly of French origin, an altered spelling of ROUSSIN.

Russler (124) German (**Rüssler**): **1.** occupational name for a farmer, from an agent derivative of *rüsseln* 'to shallow plow'. **2.** variant of **Rüssel** (see RUSSELL 2).

Russman (220) German (**Russmann**): **1.** from *Ru(o)ss*, a derivative of the personal name RUDOLF + Middle High German *man* 'man'. **2.** nickname for someone who had traveled to Russia or had some connection with that country (see RUSS 2). **3.** (**Rüssmann**): perhaps a habitational name for someone from any of several places named Rüssen in Lower Saxony and Saxony.

Russo (17008) Italian: from the personal name *Russo*, southern variant of ROSSO, a nickname for someone with red hair, a red beard, or a ruddy complexion.

GIVEN NAMES Italian 15%. *Salvatore* (137), *Angelo* (78), *Rocco* (38), *Vito* (37), *Carmine* (36), *Sal* (32), *Antonio* (29), *Pasquale* (19), *Santo* (17), *Gaetano* (15), *Domenic* (13), *Gennaro* (12).

Russom (464) English: apparently a variant spelling of RUSSON.

Russomanno (143) Italian: compound name from *rosso* 'red (haired)' + the personal name *Manno*.

GIVEN NAMES Italian 12%. *Rocco, Salvatore, Vito.*

Russon (172) English: patronymic from ROSS or ROSE.

Russotto (100) Southern Italian: diminutive of RUSSO.

GIVEN NAMES Italian 10%. *Dario, Piera, Vita.*

Russow (160) German: habitational name from a place so named near Rostock.

Russum (345) English: apparently a variant spelling of RUSSON.

Rust (5017) **1.** Swiss German: topographic name for someone who lived by a prominent elm tree, *Rust* (Old High German *ruost*), or in northern Germany for someone who lived by a resting place or halt along a route, from Middle Low German *ruste* 'rest'. **2.** English (chiefly East Anglia) and Scottish: nickname for someone with red hair or a ruddy complexion, from Old English *rūst* 'rust' (from a Germanic root meaning 'red').

Rustad (654) Norwegian: habitational name from any of over thirty farmsteads in eastern Norway named Rustad, from Old Norse *Ruðstaðr*, a compound of *ruð* 'clearing' + *staðr* 'place', 'dwelling place'.

GIVEN NAMES Scandinavian 6%. *Alf, Bjorn.*

Rustan (104) English: variant spelling of RUSTON.

GIVEN NAME Welsh 4%. *Lewellyn.*

Rustemeyer (109) German: distinguishing name for a tenant farmer (see MEYER) whose land was marshy, from a word evidenced in the field name *Rust* 'reed'.

Rusten (100) **1.** English: variant spelling of RUSTON. **2.** Norwegian: habitational name from any of several farmsteads in eastern Norway named from *rust* 'slope with trees', 'hill', 'ridge'.

GIVEN NAME Scandinavian 12%. *Arnfinn.*

Rustin (457) English: variant spelling of RUSTON.

Ruston (304) English: habitational name from any of the various places so named, for example in Norfolk, North Yorkshire, and East Yorkshire. The two villages of this name in Norfolk are recorded in Domesday Book as *Ristuna*, and are from Old English *hrīs* 'brushwood' + *tūn* 'enclosure', 'settle-

ment'; Ruston Parva in East Yorkshire, recorded in Domesday Book as *Roreston*, is named from the genitive case of the Old Norse byname *Hrór* meaning 'vigorous' + Old English *tūn*. Ruston in North Yorkshire is *Rostune* in Domesday Book, apparently from Old English *hrōst* 'roost', 'roof' + *tūn*, referring to a building with an unusual roof.

Ruszala (124) Polish (**Ruszała**): nickname for someone who was constantly touching things or moving them from one place to another, from a derivative of the verb *ruszać* 'to touch or remove'.

GIVEN NAMES Polish 15%. *Alicja, Andrzej, Danuta, Fryderyk, Wiktor, Zigmond.*

Ruszczyk (143) Polish: ethnic name for a Ruthenian. Compare Ukrainian RUSCHAK.

GIVEN NAMES Polish 15%. *Jozef* (2), *Jerzy, Jolanta, Mieczyslaw, Ryszard, Wieslaw, Zdzislaw.*

Ruszkowski (247) Polish: habitational name for someone from Ruszkowo or Ruszków, a place name derived from the nickname *Ruszek*, a derivative of Polish *ruszać* 'to touch', 'to remove'.

GIVEN NAMES Polish 6%. *Bronislaw, Jaroslaw, Mariusz, Zygfryd.*

Ruta (270) **1.** Italian (Piedmont and Liguria): topographic name for someone who lived in an area where rue grew, *ruta*. **2.** Polish: topographic name for someone who lived by a patch of rue, Polish *ruta* (Latin *ruta*), or perhaps a nickname for someone thought to resemble the plant; the sap and foliage, for example, contain a strong irritant.

GIVEN NAMES Italian 23%; Polish 5%. *Angelo* (5), *Carmelo* (3), *Aldo* (2), *Mario* (2), *Amedeo, Attilio, Damiano, Enrico, Enzo, Giacomo, Giuseppe, Guiseppe, Raffaele; Casimir, Jadwiga, Jaroslaw, Jerzy.*

Rutan (840) **1.** French (Lorraine): unexplained. **2.** Polish: variant of RUTA.

Rutecki (117) Polish: habitational name from Rutka or Rutki, place names derived from *ruta* 'rue'.

Rutenberg (163) **1.** German: habitational name from a place near Neustrelitz named Rutenberg or from any of five places called Rautenberg (formerly Rutenberg). **2.** Jewish (Ashkenazic): variant of ROTHENBERG.

GIVEN NAMES Jewish 9%. *Yechezkel* (2), *Boruch, Yakov.*

Ruter (225) **1.** Dutch: variant spelling of RUTTER 3. **2.** German: see RUTHER.

Rutgers (139) Dutch: patronymic from the Germanic personal name *Rutger* (see ROGER).

Ruth (5454) **1.** English: from Middle English *reuthe* 'pity' (a derivative of *rewen* to pity, Old English *hrēowan*) nickname for a charitable person or for a pitiable one. The personal name *Ruth* was little used in England in the Middle Ages among non-Jews, and is unlikely to have had any influence on the surname. **2.** Swiss German:

from a short form of any of the Germanic personal names formed with *hrōd* 'renown' (see RODE).

Ruthenberg (161) **1.** German: habitational name from a place so named in Brandenburg or from various places called Rautenberg (earlier Ruthenberg). **2.** Jewish (Ashkenazic): variant of ROTHENBERG.

GIVEN NAMES German 6%. *Arno, Kurt.*

Ruther (284) **1.** German (also **Rüther**): habitational name for someone from Rüth or Rüthen in Westphalia. **2.** German: variant of REUTER, although in some cases *Ruther* and *Ruter* may represent dialect variants of Dutch RUITER. **3.** Dutch: variant of RUTTER 3.

Rutherford (10047) Scottish and northern English: habitational name from a place in the Scottish Borders near Roxburgh, probably named with an early British river name of unknown etymology + Old English *ford* 'ford'. There is another place of the same name in North Yorkshire, named with *hryðer* 'cattle' + Old English *ford* 'ford', but this does not seem to have contributed to the surname.

Ruthrauff (101) Of German origin, a variant of RUTHRUFF.

Ruthruff (116) Of German origin: probably an Americanized spelling of German **Rottorff** (or **Rotthoff**), a habitational name from any of several places so named.

Ruthven (225) Scottish: habitational name, traditionally pronounced 'Ri-ven', from any of various places in Scotland so named, especially one near Perth and one in Inverness-shire. The place is named either in Gaelic (*ruadh* 'red' + *mhaighin* 'place') or with a cognate of Welsh *rhudd faen* 'red stone'.

Rutigliano (355) Italian: habitational name from Rutigliano in Bari province.

GIVEN NAMES Italian 27%. *Donato* (5), *Rocco* (5), *Vito* (3), *Pasquale* (2), *Salvatore* (2), *Alessandro, Angelo, Carlo, Carmela, Cataldo, Domenic, Domenica.*

Rutka (131) **1.** Polish: topographic name or nickname from a diminutive of *ruta* 'rue' (see RUTA). **2.** Czech: metronymic from a pet form of the female personal name *Rut* (see RUTH). **3.** Czech: habitational name from Vroutek in north Bohemia.

GIVEN NAMES Polish 9%. *Andrzej, Boleslaw, Mieczyslaw, Tadeusz.*

Rutkoski (153) Polish: variant of RUTKOWSKI.

Rutkowski (2510) Polish: habitational name from any of various places called Rutki or Rutkowice, named with *rutak* 'rue' (see RUTKA).

GIVEN NAMES Polish 7%. *Stanislaw* (4), *Casimir* (3), *Ryszard* (3), *Andrzej* (2), *Janusz* (2), *Krystyna* (2), *Stas* (2), *Tadeusz* (2), *Wladyslaw* (2), *Aloisius, Andrzey, Boguslaw.*

Rutland (1462) English: regional name from the former English county of this name, so named from the Old English by-name *Rōta* (from *rōt* 'cheerful', 'glad') + *land* 'land', 'territory'.

Rutledge (9567) English: of uncertain origin. If it is a habitational name, the location and etymology of the place from which it derives are obscure. Routledge, the more common form in the British Isles, is found mainly on the English-Scottish borders. The place in Cumbria, now called Routledge Burn, seems to have received its name in the 16th century from a member of the family rather than vice versa.

Rutley (100) English: habitational name from Great Rutleigh in Northlew, Devon.

Rutman (265) **1.** Jewish (eastern Ashkenazic): origin uncertain; perhaps a variant of ROTHMAN. **2.** Variant and altered spelling of German **Rut(h)mann**, a habitational name for someone from Ruthe in Lower Saxony or Rutha in Thuringia.
GIVEN NAMES Jewish 10%; Russian 5%. *Hyman* (3), *Mayer* (2), *Ilya, Miriam, Shira, Tsilya; Boris, Ginda, Leonid, Leya, Mikhail, Nataly, Vyacheslav, Zyama.*

Rutstein (174) Jewish (Ashkenazic): variant of ROTHSTEIN.
GIVEN NAMES Jewish 5%. *Avi, Hyman.*

Rutt (792) **1.** English: variant of ROOT 1 and 2. **2.** German: variant of RUTH 2. **3.** German (**Rütt**): topographic name of uncertain meaning (see RUTTEN 3).

Ruttan (186) Probably a variant of Dutch RUTTEN.

Rutten (427) **1.** Dutch: patronymic from a short form of the Germanic personal name *Rutger* (see ROGER) or some other personal name formed with *hrōd* 'renown'. **2.** Dutch (**van Rutten**): habitational name for someone from Rutten in the Belgian province of Limburg. **3.** German (also **Rütten**): Westphalian and Rhenish topographic name from a field named *aus den Ruthen*; the element *Ruthen* is contained in numerous place names, for example Rüthen and Rütenbrock. It is most probably a variant of *Reute* 'clearing' (see REUTER).

Ruttenberg (334) Jewish (Ashkenazic): variant of ROTHENBERG.

Rutter (2610) **1.** English: occupational name for a player on the rote (see ROOT 2). **2.** English: nickname for an unscrupulous person, from Old French *ro(u)tier* 'robber', 'highwayman', 'footpad'. **3.** Dutch: nickname from Middle Dutch *rut(t)er* 'freebooter', 'footpad', cognate with 2. Compare REUTER 2.

Rutty (113) English: unexplained.
GIVEN NAME French 4%. *Yvon.*

Rutz (945) German and Swiss German: **1.** from a short form of any of the various personal names beginning with the Old High German element *hrōd* 'renown', for example RUDOLF. **2.** occupational name for a cobbler, Middle Low German *rütze, ruce.* **3.** habitational name from a place so named in Switzerland.

GIVEN NAMES German 5%. *Kurt* (3), *Alois* (2), *Erwin* (2), *Otto* (2), *Reinhard* (2), *Armin, Christoph, Lorenz.*

Rutzen (130) German: topographic name from an Austrian field name (as evident in the place name Rutzenmoos in Upper Austria), which probably denotes a wetland or marsh.

Ruud (773) Norwegian: habitational name from any of numerous farmsteads, in eastern Norway particularly, named Rud, from Old Norse *ruð* 'clearing'.
GIVEN NAMES Scandinavian 9%. *Erik* (5), *Knut* (2), *Nels* (2), *Nils* (2), *Alf, Egil, Lars, Ludvig, Ottar.*

Ruvalcaba (622) Spanish: variant of RUBALCABA.
GIVEN NAMES Spanish 61%. *Jose* (31), *Jesus* (12), *Juan* (12), *Salvador* (10), *Jaime* (8), *Miguel* (7), *Francisco* (5), *Guadalupe* (5), *Roberto* (5), *Alfredo* (4), *Carlos* (4), *Eduardo* (4).

Ruvolo (253) Italian (Sicily): from Sicilian *ruvolo* 'oak', hence possibly a topographic name for someone who lived by a particular oak or where oaks grew, a nickname, possibly for someone who was strong, or perhaps a metonymic occupational name for a wood worker.
GIVEN NAMES Italian 17%. *Vito* (5), *Salvatore* (3), *Antonio* (2), *Ignazio* (2), *Calogero, Ettore, Gaetano, Gasper, Sal, Silvio.*

Ruwe (218) Dutch (**de Ruwe**): nickname from Middle Dutch *ruwe* 'rough', 'coarse', 'crude'.

Rux (356) German: habitational name from a place so named near Breslau (now Wroclaw).

Ruxton (133) Scottish (Angus): unexplained. Perhaps a variant of English **Roxton**, a habitational name from Roxton in Bedfordshire, named from an Old English personal name, *Hrōc*, + *dūn* 'hill'.

Ruybal (209) Galician: see ROYBAL.
GIVEN NAMES Spanish 8%. *Ruben* (2), *Alfonso, Fermin, Jose, Juan, Rafael, Renaldo, Ubaldo.*

Ruyle (471) Probably an altered spelling of English RYLE or German REIL, REUL, or ROEHL.

Ruzek (155) Czech (**Růžek**): from the vocabulary word *růžek* 'little horn', a diminutive of *roh* 'horn'. In Czech this word also means 'croissant'; as such, it may be a nickname for a baker or pastry chef.

Ruzic (114) **1.** Croatian and Serbian (**Ružić**): probably a metronymic from the personal name *Ruža*, from *ruža* 'rose', 'flower'. **2.** Slovenian (**Ružič**): unexplained.
GIVEN NAMES South Slavic 9%. *Aco, Nebojsa, Predrag, Ranko, Snezana.*

Ruzich (207) Croatian and Serbian (**Ružić**); Slovenian (**Ružič**): see RUZIC.

Ruzicka (1081) Czech (**Růžička**): nickname meaning 'nice little rose', a diminutive of *růže* 'rose'.

Ruzzo (152) Italian: perhaps from the personal names *Hrozo, Rozzo, Ruozo*, diminutives of *Hrodo*, from Old High German *hruod* 'fame', 'renown'.
GIVEN NAMES Italian 15%. *Domenic* (3), *Angelo* (2), *Cosmo, Matteo, Pasquale, Sisto.*

Ryall (352) English: habitational name from any of several places in England named from Old English *ryge* 'rye' + *hyll* 'hill', e.g. Ryal and Ryle in Northumbria, Ryhill in West Yorkshire, or Ryehill in East Yorkshire. See also RYLE.

Ryals (1955) English: variant of RYALL.

Ryan (56499) **1.** Irish: simplified form of **Mulryan**. **2.** Irish: reduced form of O'RYAN, an Anglicized form of Gaelic **Ó Riagháin** (modern Irish **Ó Riain**) 'descendant of *Rian*'; **Ó Maoilriain** 'descendant of *Maoilriaghain*', or **Ó Ruaidhín** 'descendant of the little red one'. Ryan is one of the commonest surnames in Ireland; there has been considerable confusion with REGAN. **3.** Americanized spelling of German REIN.
GIVEN NAMES Irish 4%. *Brendan* (38), *John Patrick* (8), *Dermot* (4), *Liam* (4), *Paddy* (4), *Donovan* (3), *Eamon* (3), *Eamonn* (3), *Kieran* (3), *Parnell* (3), *Aileen* (2), *Brennan* (2).

Ryans (419) Variant of Irish RYAN, with English patronymic *-s.*

Ryant (100) Variant of Irish RYAN.

Ryba (610) Polish, Czech, Slovak, and Jewish (eastern Ashkenazic): metonymic occupational name, nickname, or an ornamental name from the common Slavic word *ryba* 'fish'. As an occupational name it may have denoted a fisherman or a seller of fish. As a nickname it may have been bestowed on account of some fancied physical resemblance to a fish.

Ryback (179) Germanized or Americanized spelling of Slavic RYBAK 'fisherman'.
GIVEN NAME German 4%. *Kurt* (2).

Rybacki (226) Polish: habitational name for someone from any of the many places in Poland called Rybaki, named with *ryba* 'fish'.
GIVEN NAMES Polish 6%. *Casimir, Tadeusz, Wieslaw, Zygmunt.*

Rybak (718) Polish, Ukrainian, German, and Jewish (eastern Ashkenazic): occupational name for a fisherman, an agent derivative of *ryba* 'fish' (see RYBA).
GIVEN NAMES Polish 5%; Jewish 4%; Russian 4%. *Casimir* (2), *Beata, Bogdan, Czeslaw, Halina, Irena, Janusz, Katarzyna, Miroslaw, Ryscard, Tadeusz, Wasyl; Pinkus* (2), *Iren, Miriam, Moshe, Semen; Mikhail* (4), *Boris* (3), *Lyudmila* (2), *Sergey* (2), *Konstantin, Luka, Nadezhda, Sofya, Yefim, Yelena, Yevgeniy, Yury.*

Rybarczyk (359) Polish: occupational name for a fisherman or a fish seller, a diminutive or patronymic derivative of **Rybarz**.

GIVEN NAMES Polish 4%. *Janusz, Kazimierz, Zygmont.*

Ryberg (491) Danish: habitational name from Rybjerg, a place name originally denoting a hill with young trees growing on it. The name is also found in Sweden.

GIVEN NAMES Scandinavian 6%. *Erik* (3), *Algot.*

Rybicki (670) Polish: habitational name from Rybice, now Rybitwy, in Płock voivodeship.

GIVEN NAMES Polish 5%. *Alojzy, Casimir, Janusz, Jaroslaw, Slawomir, Tadeusz, Witold, Zbig, Zbigniew, Zigmund, Zygmunt.*

Rybinski (175) Polish (**Rybiński**): habitational name for someone from any of several places called Rybno.

GIVEN NAMES Polish 7%. *Andrzej, Halina, Karol, Witold, Zygmunt.*

Rybka (226) Polish, Czech, and Slovak: from a diminutive of *ryba* 'fish'. In Czech the phrases *zdravý, čilý jako rybka* mean 'as healthy as a fish'; the surname may derive from these idiomatic uses.

GIVEN NAMES Polish 12%. *Stanislaw* (2), *Czeslawa, Henryk, Ryszard, Tadeusz, Waclaw, Wasyl, Witold, Zbigniew.*

Rybolt (252) Americanized spelling of German **Reibold**, a variant of REINBOLD.

Ryburn (304) Variant of Scottish RAYBURN.

Ryce (144) Variant spelling of RICE (Welsh REESE, German REISS).

Rychlik (212) Polish, Czech (**Rychlík**), and Slovak (**Rýchlik**): nickname from an agent noun derived from Polish *rychły* 'speedy', 'forthcoming', Czech *rychlý*, Slovak *rýchly* 'quick'.

GIVEN NAMES Polish 4%. *Ryszard, Wojciech.*

Ryckman (474) Dutch: nickname for a rich man, from Middle Dutch *rijc* 'rich' + *man* 'man'.

FOREBEARS This name is recorded in Beverwijck in New Netherland (Albany, NY) in the mid 17th century.

Rycroft (141) English: topographic name for someone who lived by a small enclosed field (Old English *croft*) where rye (Old English *ryge*) was grown, or a habitational name from any of various minor places so named, such as Ryecoft in Gloucestershire or Cheshire.

Ryczek (232) Polish: unflattering nickname from an agent noun meaning 'screamer', from the verb *ryczeć* 'to scream'.

GIVEN NAMES Polish 8%. *Casimir* (2), *Aniela, Boleslaw, Czeslaw.*

Rydalch (119) Origin unidentified. This is a Utah name; some 19th century U.S. bearers were from England, but the name is not found in contemporary British records.

Rydberg (506) Swedish: ornamental name composed of the place name element *ryd* 'woodland clearing' + *berg* 'mountain'.

GIVEN NAMES Scandinavian 7%. *Anders* (2), *Alf, Bjorn, Lennart, Nels.*

Rydeen (106) Swedish (**Rydén**): ornamental name composed of the place name element *ryd* 'woodland clearing' + the surname suffix *-én*, from the Latin adjectival ending *-enius*.

Rydel (136) Variant of Swedish RYDELL.

Rydell (443) 1. Swedish: ornamental name composed of the place name element *ryd* 'woodland clearing' + the common suffix *-ell*, from the Latin adjectival ending *-elius*. 2. English: perhaps a variant spelling of RIDDELL.

Ryden (469) 1. Swedish (**Rydén**): ornamental name composed of the place name element *ryd* 'woodland clearing' + the common surname suffix *-én*, from Latin *-enius*. 2. English: possibly a habitational name from a lost or unidentified place.

GIVEN NAMES Scandinavian 6%. *Anders* (2), *Lars, Per.*

Ryder (5695) 1. English and Irish: variant spelling of RIDER. 2. Dutch: occupational name for a mounted warrior or messenger, Middle Dutch *rider*.

Ryding (116) English: variant of READING.

Rydman (181) Swedish: ornamental name composed of the place name element *ryd* 'woodland clearing' + *man* 'man'.

Rydzewski (301) Polish: habitational name for someone from any of the many places called Rydzewo, named with *rydz*, an edible species of agaric.

GIVEN NAMES Polish 9%. *Janusz* (2), *Wieslaw* (2), *Bartosz, Boleslaw, Casimir, Thadeus.*

Rye (1497) 1. English: topographic name for someone who lived on an island or patch of firm ground surrounded by fens, from a misdivision of the Middle English phrase *atter ye* 'at the island' (from Old English *ēg, īeg* 'island'). 2. English: topographic name for someone who lived near a river or stream, from a misdivision of the Middle English phrase *atter eye* 'at the river' (from Old English *ēa* 'river'). 3. English: topographic name for someone living at a place where rye (Old English *ryge*) was grown, or perhaps a metonymic occupational name for someone who grew or sold it. 4. Norwegian: habitational name from a farmstead so named, most of them from Old Norse *rjóðr* 'clearing in a forest', but others from *ry* 'dry place with stones'. 5. Danish: habitational name from a place called Rye.

Ryel (115) Probably a variant spelling of English RYLE.

Ryen (166) 1. Probably an altered spelling of RYAN. 2. Norwegian: habitational name from any of more than ten farmsteads, originally named with Old Norse *rugr* 'rye' + *vin* 'meadow'.

GIVEN NAME Scandinavian 5%. *Erik.*

Ryer (320) Perhaps an Americanized spelling of REI(H)ER.

Ryerson (956) Americanized spelling of Swedish REIERSON or of any of its cognates, for example Dutch **Ryerse(n)** or Norwegian and Danish **Reiersen**.

FOREBEARS The name **Ryerse** is recorded in Beverwijck in New Netherland (Albany, NY) in the mid 17th century.

Rygg (151) 1. Norwegian: habitational name from any of fifteen farmsteads so named, from Old Norse *hryggr* 'backbone', 'spine', in allusion to a mountain ridge. 2. Perhaps an altered spelling of the English family name *Rigg*, a variant of RIDGE 1.

GIVEN NAMES Scandinavian 6%. *Alf, Bernt, Erik.*

Rygh (167) Norwegian: variant of RYGG.

GIVEN NAME Scandinavian 12%. *Alf* (2).

Rygiel (200) Polish: metonymic occupational name from Polish *rygiel* 'bolt', 'beam'.

GIVEN NAMES Polish 9%; German 4%. *Grzegorz, Halina, Karol, Pawel, Stanislaus, Zbigniew; Florian, Matthias.*

Ryherd (121) Possibly a respelling of German **Reihert** or **Reihard(t)**, variants of RICHARD.

Ryken (156) Dutch: from a pet form of the various Germanic personal names formed with *rīc* 'power(ful)'.

Ryker (347) Dutch (**de Ryker**): nickname from an agent derivative of Middle Dutch *riken* 'to become powerful or rich'.

Rykowski (155) Polish: habitational name for someone from places called Ryków in Płock and Radom voivodeships.

Ryks (116) Dutch: patronymic from a short form of a Germanic personal name formed with *rīc* 'power(ful)'.

Ryland (805) 1. English: topographic name for someone who lived near a piece of land where rye was grown, from Old English *ryge* 'rye' + *land* 'land'. 2. Norwegian: habitational name from any of three farmsteads in Vestlandet so named from an unexplained first element + *land* 'land', 'farm'. 3. Probably an altered spelling of Dutch REILAND.

Rylander (496) 1. Swedish: ornamental name possibly composed of the place name element *ryd* 'woodland clearing' + the suffix *-ander*, from Greek *anēr* 'man', genitive *andros*. 2. German: variant of REULAND.

GIVEN NAMES Scandinavian 5%. *Alf* (2), *Bergit, Erik, Erland, Thor.*

Rylant (128) Probably an altered spelling of Dutch REILAND.

Ryle (418) English: 1. habitational name from Royle in Lancashire (see ROYLE). 2. variant of RYALL.

Rylee (227) Perhaps an altered spelling of RILEY or German **Reile**, **Reihle**, variants of REIL.

Ryles (287) English: variant of RYLE.

Ryley (123) Variant spelling of English RILEY or Irish REILLY.

Ryll (114) German and Polish: of uncertain origin, perhaps a derivative of the personal name RIEDEL.

GIVEN NAMES German 10%; Polish 4%. *Ewald, Kurt, Viktor; Tadeusz.*

Ryman (842) **1.** English: topographic name, a variant of RYE 1 and 2, with the addition of *man* 'man'. **2.** Swedish: ornamental name composed of the place name element *ryd* 'woodland clearing' + *man* 'man'. **3.** Swiss German (**Rymann**): variant of REIMANN 1, 3.

Rymer (1069) **1.** English: variant spelling of RIMER 1. **2.** German: variant of RIEMER. **3.** German: habitational name for someone from Riem (now a suburb of Munich; formerly a separate town).

Rynard (107) English: variant spelling of REYNARD.

Rynd (101) Variant spelling of Scottish RIND.

Rynders (268) Dutch: variant spelling of REINDERS.

Rynearson (394) Origin unidentified. Compare RYNERSON.

Ryner (188) Americanized spelling of German REINER, or possibly of Swiss German **Rhyner**, a topographic name for someone living by or otherwise connected with the Rhine river.

Rynerson (100) Origin unidentified. Compare RYNEARSON.

Rynes (141) Perhaps an altered spelling of REINES.

Rynkiewicz (102) Polish: patronymic from the personal name *Rynko*, an east Slavic form of *Hrehor* (see GREGORY).
GIVEN NAMES Polish 15%. *Slawomir* (2), *Dorota, Halina, Mariusz, Urszula.*

Rynn (101) Irish: variant spelling of RINN.
GIVEN NAMES Irish 14%. *Brendan, Eamon.*

Rynne (112) Irish: Anglicized form of Gaelic **Ó Rinn** (see WREN).
GIVEN NAMES Irish 7%. *Ciaran, Niall.*

Ryno (206) English (Liverpool): unexplained.

Ryon (477) Perhaps a variant spelling of Irish RYAN.

Rypkema (105) Frisian: unexplained.

Rys (349) Czech, Slovak, and Polish: nickname for a nimble person, from Slavic *rys* (Polish *ryś*) 'lynx'.
GIVEN NAMES Polish 7%. *Stanislaw* (4), *Janusz* (2), *Andrzej, Beata.*

Rysavy (165) Czech and Slovak (**Ryšavý**): nickname meaning 'red-haired'.

Ryser (363) Swiss German: variant spelling of REISER 1.
GIVEN NAMES German 6%. *Hans* (2), *Armin, Klaus, Otto, Urs.*

Ryskamp (116) Dutch (**Ruyskamp**): unexplained.

Rystrom (100) Swedish (**Ryström**): ornamental name composed of the elements *ryd* 'woodland clearing' + *ström* 'river'.

Ryther (192) Perhaps an altered spelling of German **Reither**, a variant of REITER.

Rytlewski (95) Polish: habitational name for someone from Rytel in Bydgoszcz voivodeship or Rytele in Siedlce voivodeship.

Ryu (357) Korean: variant of YU.

GIVEN NAMES Korean 60%. *Seung* (5), *In* (4), *Jae* (4), *Ji* (3), *Young* (3), *Chi* (2), *Jung* (2), *Kwang* (2), *Sang* (2), *Sung* (2), *Won* (2), *Chang Soo*; *Chul* (2), *Jae Choon* (2), *Byung Soo, Chang, Choon, Chung, Eunsoon, Hae, Hee Young, Hye Kyung, Inhee, Jae In.*

Rzasa (165) Polish (**Rząsa**): topographic name for someone who lived near a pond where duckweed grew, from Polish *rząsa* 'duckweed'.
GIVEN NAMES Polish 5%. *Ignacy, Tomasz, Urszula.*

Rzepecki (114) Polish: habitational name from any of many places called Rzepki or Rzepedź, named with *rzepa* 'turnip'.
GIVEN NAME Polish 5%. *Janusz.*

Rzepka (316) Polish: from *rzepka*, diminutive of *rzepa* 'turnip', either a nickname or a metonymic occupational name for a peasant who grew root vegetables.
GIVEN NAMES Polish 11%. *Jozef* (3), *Danuta* (2), *Wojciech* (2), *Beata, Franciszek, Grazyna, Janina, Jaroslaw, Leszek, Wieslaw, Witold.*

Rzonca (115) Polish: nickname from Polish dialect *rzonca*, standard Polish *rzodca* 'land steward'.
GIVEN NAMES Polish 11%. *Henryk* (2), *Czeslawa, Mariola, Stanislaw.*

Rzucidlo (105) Polish: nickname for an eager or ebullient person from a derivative of *rzucić* 'to throw', 'to throw oneself at someone'.
GIVEN NAMES Polish 14%. *Andrzej* (2), *Jacek, Jozef, Stanislaw, Zbigniew.*

S

Sa (236) **1.** Portuguese (**Sá**): variant spelling of **Saa**, a habitational name from any of the numerous places named Saa, mainly in northern Portugal and Galicia. **2.** Korean: there are three Chinese characters associated with this surname. Two of these are extremely rare and are not treated here. The remaining Sa surname is also quite unusual. There are two distinct clans, one of Kyŏngsang South Province's Kŏch'ang County and the other originating with a refugee from Ming China who came to Korea near the end of the Koryŏ period (AD 918–1392).
GIVEN NAMES Spanish 15%; Portuguese 13%; Korean 11%. *Manuel* (4), *Arsenio* (3), *Francisco* (2), *Jose* (2), *Julio* (2), *Luis* (2), *Luiz* (2), *Acacio, Alfredo, Ana, Arnaldo, Geraldo; Joao* (3), *Messias; Kyung* (2), *Chen, Cheng Hua, Heang, Heng, Ho Jin, Hyang, Jaehoon, Jianjun, Myung, Sang Soon.*

Saab (296) Muslim: probably a variant of SABA. However, there is an Arabic word *ṣa'b* 'difficult', which may be the basis of a personal name.
GIVEN NAMES Muslim 29%. *Hassan* (6), *Abdulwahab* (2), *Ahmad* (2), *Salim* (2), *Samer* (2), *Abdo, Aiman, Ali, Bilal, Fida, Fouad, Ghassan.*

Saad (1036) **1.** Muslim: from a personal name based on Arabic *sa'd* 'good luck', 'good fortune', 'success'. *Sa'd* is often used to form names in combination with other words, for example *Sa'd Allāh* (*Sa'dullāh*) 'joy of Allah', an epithet of the Prophet Muhammad. *Sa'd ibn Abū Waqqās* was one of the ten Companions of the Prophet Muhammad. This name is prevalent in all Muslim countries. **2.** Jewish (Sephardic): a derivative of a personal name, either from Hebrew *saad* 'support' or from Arabic *sa'd* 'good luck' (see 1).
GIVEN NAMES Muslim 40%. *Mohamed* (9), *Ali* (7), *Hussein* (6), *Maher* (6), *Mohamad* (6), *Nabil* (6), *Samir* (6), *Hassan* (5), *Mahmoud* (5), *Ibrahim* (4), *Saad* (4), *Adnan* (3).

Saade (112) **1.** Muslim: variant of SAAD or **Sadeh**, especially in North Africa and other French-speaking areas. **2.** Portuguese: from Arabic *sa'ad* 'lucky', 'fortunate'.
GIVEN NAMES Muslim 18%; French 15%; Spanish 11%. *Saade* (2), *Bahia, Deeb, Fawzi, Habib, Karim, Muhamed, Nabila, Nouhad, Raja, Salim, Samir; Camille* (2), *Andre, Jacques, Marcel, Michel, Rodolphe;*

Alfredo, Javier, Juan, Mario, Mauricio, Pedro Luis, Raul, Silvia.

Saadeh (110) Muslim: probably from a personal name based on Arabic *sādāt* 'princes', 'lords', plural of *sayyid* 'lord', 'master' (see SAYED). This is a title of respect used in particular for descendants of the Prophet Muhammad.
GIVEN NAMES Muslim 59%; French 6%. *Ahmad* (4), *Ammar* (2), *Ibrahim* (2), *Youssef* (2), *Abdallah, Abir, Amer, Anwar, Azia, Emad, Farid, Fawzi; Antoine, Jean-Pierre, Michel.*

Saah (111) Muslim: variant of SHAH.
GIVEN NAMES Muslim 21%. *Nabih* (2), *Adib, Adla, Basem, Emad, Faraj, Ibrahim, Issa, Jamil, Mazen, Mousa, Nabil.*

Saal (290) German: **1.** from Middle High German *sal* 'hall', 'manorhouse', a metonymic occupational name for someone who worked at such a place. **2.** topographic name from Middle High German *sal* 'moist dirt', or a habitational name from a place named with this word.
GIVEN NAMES German 5%. *Elke, Heinz, Horst.*

Saalfeld (120) **1.** German: topographic name from Middle High German *sal* 'manor', 'hall' (or from a homonym meaning 'moist dirt') + *velt* 'field'. **2.** German and Jewish (Ashkenazic): habitational name from places so called in Thuringia and East Prussia. **3.** Jewish (Ashkenazic): compound ornamental name from *Sal* (a short form of SALOMON) + German *Feld* 'field', 'pasture'.

Saam (225) **1.** German (mostly southern): metonymic occupational name for a seed merchant, from Middle High German *sāme* 'seed'. **2.** Swedish: ethnic name from *same* 'Saami', a member of the indigenous people of northern Scandinavia.

Saar (490) **1.** German and Jewish (western Ashkenazic): habitational name from any of various places called Saar, in particular one in western Germany on the French border, which takes its name from the river on which it stands. This is found in Latin sources as *Saravus*, and ultimately goes back to an Indo-European root, *ser-, sar-* 'flow'. **2.** Dutch: from the Biblical female personal name SARA. **3.** Jewish: from Hebrew *saar* 'storm', a translation of German *Sturm*, perhaps a nickname or ornamental name.

Saarela (153) Finnish: variant of SAARI + the local suffix *-la*. Occurs mainly in west-

ern Finland. Mostly, this is an ornamental name adopted during the name conversion movement at the end of the 19th and the beginning of the 20th centuries.
GIVEN NAMES Finnish 9%. *Eero, Eino, Pekka, Sulo.*

Saari (1257) Finnish: from *saari* 'island'. Mostly, this is an ornamental name adopted during the name conversion movement at the end of the 19th and the beginning of the 20th centuries, but it may also be a topographic name for someone living on or near an island. It is found chiefly in central and southern Finland. In America, it is also found as an abbreviation of names containing this element, such as **Viitasaari**.
GIVEN NAMES Finnish 7%; Scandinavian 4%. *Arvo* (4), *Jorma* (3), *Reino* (3), *Toivo* (3), *Eino* (2), *Seppo* (2), *Waino* (2), *Wilho* (2), *Kaisa, Kauko, Lempi, Martti; Erik* (3), *Arni.*

Saarinen (138) Finnish: variant of SAARI + the common surname suffix *-nen*. Found chiefly in western Finland. Mostly, this is an ornamental name adopted during the name conversion movement at the end of the 19th and the beginning of the 20th centuries.
GIVEN NAMES Finnish 23%; Scandinavian 11%. *Waino* (2), *Alpo, Antti, Eero, Eija, Hannu, Jorma, Keijo, Pekka, Risto, Seppo, Timo; Erik, Olle, Sven.*

Saas (128) **1.** German: variant of SASSE. **2.** nickname for a settler, perhaps a newcomer, from Middle High German *sāze* 'seat', 'residence'.

Saathoff (859) North German (Westphalian): **1.** habitational name for someone working or living at a farm named with Middle Low German *sāt* 'seed' + *hof* 'farmstead'. **2.** status name for someone whose holding (Middle Low German *sate*, 'sāt' 'settlement', 'land') extended to one *Hufe*, an old measure of land.

Saavedra (1798) Galician: habitational name from any of the places in the Galician provinces of Ourense and Lugo named Saavedra, from *saa* 'hall' (from Gothic *sals* 'main house') + *vedro* 'old' (Latin *vetus*).
GIVEN NAMES Spanish 51%. *Jose* (38), *Carlos* (30), *Juan* (28), *Manuel* (15), *Pedro* (15), *Luis* (14), *Ramon* (13), *Jesus* (12), *Rafael* (12), *Mario* (11), *Pablo* (11), *Raul* (11).

Saba (977) **1.** Muslim: from an Arabic personal name *ṣabāḥ* meaning 'morning'. This is a popular name in Kuwait. **2.** Southern French: nickname from a variant of Occitan *sabe* 'tasty', 'flavorsome'. Compare SABOURIN.

GIVEN NAMES Muslim 15%; French 5%. *Salim* (4), *Issa* (3), *Jiries* (3), *Nabil* (3), *Ahmed* (2), *Fuad* (2), *Habib* (2), *Ibrahim* (2), *Jamil* (2), *Marwan* (2), *Mohammad* (2), *Sami* (2); *Pierre* (4), *Antoine* (3), *Michel* (3), *Camille* (2), *Emile* (2), *Briand, Chantal, Germaine, Nesly*.

Sabado (150) Spanish (**Sábadoz**) and Portuguese: from a nickname or personal name bestowed on someone born on a Saturday, which was considered a good omen (Late Latin *sabbatum*, Greek *sabbaton*, from Hebrew *shabat* 'Sabbath').

GIVEN NAMES Spanish 32%. *Jose* (3), *Artemio* (2), *Ernesto* (2), *Francisco* (2), *Mario* (2), *Agripina, Alejandro, Armando, Aurelio, Benito, Concepcion, Gregorio*.

Sabados (130) Hungarian (**Szabados**): status name for a freedman (an emancipated serf), from *szabados* 'liberated', from *szabad* 'free'.

Sabala (255) **1.** Spanish variant and Portuguese form of Basque ZABALA. **2.** Polish (**Sabała**) and Slovak: occupational name from Slovak *sabol* 'tailor', Hungarian *szabó*. **3.** Polish: possibly also from a pet form of the personal name SEBASTIAN.

GIVEN NAMES Spanish 18%. *Juan* (2), *Luis* (2), *Lupe* (2), *Luz* (2), *Alfonso, Ambrocio, Catalina, Domingo, Eduardo, Emilio, Fermin, Fernando*.

Saban (187) **1.** English: variant of SABIN 1. **2.** Jewish (Sephardic): occupational name from Arabic *ṣabbān* 'soap maker', 'soap merchant'.

GIVEN NAMES Jewish 5%; Spanish 5%. *Mertie, Nirit, Yosef; Pablo* (2), *Alberto, Apolinario, Francisco Javier, Ricardo, Salvador*.

Sabat (204) **1.** Catalan (**Sàbat**): from a nickname or personal name bestowed on someone born on a Saturday, which was considered a good omen (Late Latin *sabbatum*, Greek *sabbaton*, from Hebrew *shabat* 'Sabbath'). **2.** Jewish (Ashkenazic): ornamental name from German *Sabbat* 'Sabbath'. **3.** French: nickname for a noisy, rowdy person, from Middle French *sab(b)at* 'noise', 'racket'.

GIVEN NAMES Spanish 5%; French 4%. *Jose* (3), *Juanita* (2), *Eduardo, Jorge, Ofelia; Georges*.

Sabatelli (140) Italian: patronymic from *Sabatello*, a pet form of SABATO.

GIVEN NAMES Italian 10%. *Angelo, Antonio, Caesar, Dino, Ercole, Luigi*.

Sabater (136) Catalan: occupational name from *sabater* 'shoemaker'.

GIVEN NAMES Spanish 47%. *Juan* (5), *Carlos* (3), *Ernesto* (3), *Enrique* (2), *Jose* (2), *Julio* (2), *Pablo* (2), *Rolando* (2), *Ruben* (2), *Abelardo, Alberto, Alfonso; Antonio* (2).

Sabath (141) Jewish: variant of SABAT.

Sabatine (151) Italian and French: from a personal name bestowed on someone born on a Saturday (see SABATO).

GIVEN NAMES Italian 8%; French 4%. *Domenic, Onofrio, Vincenza; Antoine, Donat*.

Sabatini (823) Italian: patronymic or plural form of SABATINO.

GIVEN NAMES Italian 13%. *Angelo* (4), *Dario* (2), *Domenic* (2), *Marco* (2), *Primo* (2), *Reno* (2), *Aldo, Amerigo, Antonio, Domenico, Donato, Emidio*.

Sabatino (1141) Italian: from a pet form of the personal name SABATO.

GIVEN NAMES Italian 15%. *Salvatore* (9), *Gaetano* (4), *Angelo* (3), *Dante* (3), *Rocco* (3), *Alessandro* (2), *Carmelo* (2), *Aniello, Antonella, Antonio, Carlo, Cono*.

Sabatka (145) **1.** Czech (**Šabatka**): from a pet form of the personal name *Šebestián* (see SEBASTIAN). **2.** Altered spelling of Hungarian *Szabadkai* or **Szabatkai**, a habitational name for someone from Szabadka (Serbian name *Subotica*) in Vojvodina, Serbia, or from some place similarly named in Hungary.

Sabato (247) Southern Italian: from a nickname or personal name bestowed on someone born on a Saturday, which was considered a good omen, from Italian *sabbato* 'Saturday' (Late Latin *sabbatum*, Greek *sabbaton*, from Hebrew *shabat* 'Sabbath', a derivative of *shabat* 'rest').

GIVEN NAMES Italian 18%. *Angelo* (2), *Sal* (2), *Antonio, Carmelo, Claudio, Ernesto, Osvaldo, Ulises, Vito*.

Sabb (168) Probably of English origin: unexplained; the name is recorded in southern England the 16th and 17th centuries but since appears to have died out there.

GIVEN NAMES French 6%. *Camille, Celestine, Dominique*.

Sabbag (101) Arabic and Jewish (Sephardic): variant of SABBAGH.

Sabbagh (353) Arabic and Jewish (Sephardic): occupational name from Arabic *ṣabbāgh* 'dyer'.

GIVEN NAMES Muslim 35%; French 5%. *Karim* (3), *Sami* (3), *Ahmad* (2), *Amin* (2), *Beshara* (2), *Ghassan* (2), *Hani* (2), *Ibrahim* (2), *Issa* (2), *Nabil* (2), *Salim* (2), *Abdull; Michel* (2), *Andre, Antoine, Camille, Edouard, Pierre*.

Sabbatini (117) Italian: variant of SABATINI.

GIVEN NAMES Italian 14%. *Angelo, Attilio, Carlo, Enrico, Gino, Marco, Premo, Reno, Sandro*.

Sabean (112) Variant spelling of English SABINE.

Sabedra (115) Galician and Spanish: variant of SAAVEDRA.

GIVEN NAMES Spanish 28%. *Lupe* (2), *Adelina, Aida, Arcelia, Cruz, Demetrio, Elia, Enrique, Ernestina, Esmeralda, Eulalio, Guadalupe*.

Sabel (618) German (of Slavic origin): **1.** variant of SOBEL. **2.** habitational name from a place so called near Rostock.

Sabella (716) Italian: from the personal name *Sabello, Savello* (Latin *Sabellus*, originally derived from a tribal name).

GIVEN NAMES Italian 11%; French 5%. *Calogero* (4), *Angelo* (3), *Salvatore* (2), *Vito* (2), *Antonio, Biagio, Domenico, Filippo, Gaetano, Gasper, Guiseppe; Andre* (2), *Alphonse, Camille, Jean-Claude, Lucien*.

Saber (328) **1.** Muslim: variant of SABIR. **2.** English: variant of SEABERG. **3.** Southern French: nickname for a wise or knowledgeable man, from Occitan *saber* 'to know', which could also have the sense of 'knowledge'.

GIVEN NAMES Muslim 8%. *Mohammed* (2), *Ahmad, Ahmed, Ali, Jawad, Mahmoud, Mohammad, Nasser, Saber, Sadruddin, Said, Saleem*.

Sabers (138) Origin unidentified.

Sabet (126) **1.** Muslim: from a personal name based on Arabic *sābit, thābit* 'strong'. Thābit ibn Arqam was one of the ten Companions of the Prophet Muhammad. **2.** Jewish (Sephardic): adoption of the Arabic name.

GIVEN NAMES Muslim 65%; Jewish 4%. *Bijan* (3), *Hamid* (3), *Ali* (2), *Aly* (2), *Mojtaba* (2), *Abbas, Abdollah, Ahmed, Amr, Ata, Davoud, Farideh; Sima* (3).

Sabetta (116) Italian: from a shortened form of the personal name *Elisabetta* (see ELIZABETH), or a pet form of *Saba*, from a medieval Greek personal name *Sabas*.

GIVEN NAMES Italian 5%. *Ugo, Vito*.

Sabey (185) English: unexplained.

Sabharwal (101) Indian (Panjab): Hindu (Khatri) and Sikh name based on the name of a Khatri clan.

GIVEN NAMES Indian 86%. *Hemant* (3), *Rajiv* (3), *Amitabh* (2), *Atul* (2), *Harsh* (2), *Mohit* (2), *Pooja* (2), *Ravi* (2), *Subhash* (2), *Ajit, Anil, Arvind*.

Sabia (523) Southern Italian: from a feminine variant of SAVIO.

GIVEN NAMES Italian 19%. *Vito* (9), *Angelo* (6), *Salvatore* (4), *Carmine* (3), *Gennaro* (2), *Donato, Pasquale, Raffaele, Sal, Vita*.

Sabin (2034) **1.** English and French: from the medieval French form of the Latin personal name *Sabinus* or its feminine form *Sabina*, originally an ethnic name for a member of an ancient Italic people of central Italy, whose name is of uncertain origin. According to legend, in the 8th century BC the Romans slaughtered the Sabine menfolk and carried off the women. More influential as far as name-giving is concerned was the existence of several Christian saints bearing this name. The masculine name was borne by at least ten early saints (martyrs and bishops), but as a given name the feminine form was always more popular. **2.** Jewish: probably also an

Americanized form of some like-sounding Jewish name.

Sabina (128) Portuguese, Spanish, and Italian: from the personal name *Sabina*, feminine form of *Sabino*. This was the name of various saints.

GIVEN NAMES Spanish 19%. *Jose* (3), *Blanca* (2), *Humberto* (2), *Rolando* (2), *Cristina*, *Dalia*, *Lurdes*, *Manuel*, *Miguel Angel*, *Osvaldo*, *Ruben*.

Sabine (340) English and French: variant of SABIN 1 (in French, the feminine form of the personal name).

Sabino (567) Italian, Spanish and Portugal: from the personal name *Sabino*, Latin *Sabinus* (see SABIN).

GIVEN NAMES Spanish 15%; Italian 11%. *Mario* (6), *Manuel* (5), *Carlos* (3), *Pablo* (3), *Alipio* (2), *Ernesto* (2), *Adriana*, *Alfredo*, *Amaya*, *Angel*, *Azucena*, *Claudio*; *Antonio* (5), *Pasquale* (3), *Rocco* (3), *Angelo*, *Aniello*, *Carmine*, *Donato*, *Filomena*, *Franco*, *Gaetano*, *Giacomo*, *Leonardo*.

Sabins (170) English: patronymic from SABIN.

Sabio (111) Spanish and Portuguese: nickname from *sabio* 'clever', 'learned'. It was an epithet of the 13th-century King Alfonso X ('el Sabio').

GIVEN NAMES Spanish 29%. *Andres* (3), *Adonis*, *Alberto*, *Alejandro*, *Ana*, *Boanerges*, *Candido*, *Corina*, *Edgardo*, *Guillermo*, *Hernan*, *Jose*; *Dario*.

Sabir (127) Muslim: from a personal name based on Arabic *ṣābir* 'patient', 'tolerant', 'persevering', 'long-suffering'. See the Qur'an 2:153.

GIVEN NAMES Muslim 73%. *Mohammad* (5), *Mohammed* (3), *Muhammad* (3), *Altaf* (2), *Nadeem* (2), *Sultan* (2), *Abdullah*, *Abrahim*, *Adib*, *Adnan*, *Aisha*, *Azhar*.

Sabiston (108) Scottish: habitational name from the udal land of Sabistane in Birsay parish, Orkney.

Sablan (202) Perhaps an Americanized spelling of French **Sablon**, a topographic name for someone who lived in a sandy place, a derivative of SABLE.

GIVEN NAMES Spanish 19%. *Juan* (3), *Francisco* (2), *Jose* (2), *Theresita* (2), *Alberto*, *Artemio*, *Candido*, *Enrique*, *Guillermo*, *Joaquin*, *Luis*, *Manuel*.

Sable (652) **1.** French: topographic name for someone who lived in a sandy place, from *sable* 'sand'. **2.** French (**Sablé**): habitational name from a place so called in Sarthe. **3.** Dutch and North German: metonymic occupational name for a furrier, from *sabel* 'sable', 'black fur'.

Sablich (117) Croatian and Serbian (**Sablić** or **Sabljić**): nickname from *sablja* 'saber'. This surname is common in the islands of Cres and Lošinj, in the Kvarner Gulf of the Adriatic Sea.

GIVEN NAMES Italian 5%. *Matteo* (2), *Carmela*.

Sabo (3509) **1.** Norwegian: variant of SEBO. **2.** Americanized spelling of Hungarian **Szabó** (see SZABO).

Saboe (116) Hungarian: variant of SABO 2.

Sabol (1615) Czech and Slovak: variant of SOBOL.

Sabot (111) French: occupational name for a maker of clogs, French *sabots*, or nickname for someone who habitually wore clogs.

Sabourin (628) Southern French: nickname for a pleasant or amiable person, from a diminutive of *sabor* 'flavor', 'taste' (Old French *saveur*). The name Sabourin was introduced to England through Huguenot immigration, and from there it may have been brought to North America.

FOREBEARS An English family of this name trace their descent from a certain Pierre Sabourin, who arrived in England *c*.1750 from Saint-Maixent, France, and became a silk weaver in Bethnal Green, London. An earlier immigrant was Aaron Sabourin, recorded in 1682 in the archives of the French Protestant Church, London.

GIVEN NAMES French 11%. *Marcel* (4), *Aime* (3), *Armand* (3), *Lucien* (2), *Pierre* (2), *Alderic*, *Collette*, *Cyrille*, *Gilles*, *Laurier*, *Normand*, *Serge*.

Sacca (209) Southern Italian and Greek: **1.** occupational name for a maker or seller of sacks, from medieval Greek *sakkos* 'sack' + the occupational ending *-as*. **2.** occupational name from *saccà* 'water carrier', from Arabic *saqqā* 'water carrier', Turkish *saka*. **3.** Greek: nickname for a person thought to resemble a pelican, by reason of the 'sack' or pouch (Greek *sakkos*) underneath its bill.

GIVEN NAMES Italian 16%. *Mauro* (2), *Salvatore* (2), *Angelo*, *Antonio*, *Concetta*, *Gilda*, *Graziella*, *Massimo*, *Vincenzo*.

Saccente (145) Italian: nickname from medieval Italian *saccente* 'wise'.

GIVEN NAMES Italian 20%. *Angelo* (3), *Marco* (2), *Matteo*, *Onofrio*, *Vito*.

Sacchetti (351) Southern Italian: patronymic from *Sacchetto*, a derivative of SACCO.

GIVEN NAMES Italian 21%. *Antonio* (4), *Carlo* (3), *Domenic* (2), *Nicola* (2), *Nino* (2), *Vito* (2), *Angelo*, *Evo*, *Fiore*, *Francesca*, *Gaetano*, *Gennaro*.

Sacchi (128) Italian: patronymic or plural form of SACCO.

GIVEN NAMES Italian 13%. *Enrico* (3), *Dario*, *Guido*, *Luca*, *Luigi*.

Sacco (2627) Italian: **1.** from an old Tuscan personal name, *Saccus*, a reduced form of the Old Testament name *Isaccus* (see ISAAC). **2.** metonymic occupational name for a maker of sacks or bags, from *sacco* 'sack', or nickname for someone thought to resemble a sack. **3.** habitational name from Sacco in Salerno province.

GIVEN NAMES Italian 12%. *Angelo* (18), *Carmine* (6), *Antonio* (5), *Aldo* (4), *Gaetano* (3), *Italo* (3), *Pasquale* (3), *Severino* (3), *Vito* (3), *Gaeton* (2), *Rinaldo* (2), *Rocco* (2).

Saccoccio (177) Italian: from a derivative of SACCO.

GIVEN NAMES Italian 23%. *Salvatore* (5), *Angelo*, *Elio*, *Francesco*, *Gaetano*, *Gino*, *Ivano*, *Pasquale*, *Remo*, *Rocco*, *Silvio*.

Saccomanno (162) Italian: from the personal name *Saccomanno*, originally a status name for someone who was in charge of transporting an army's baggage and supplies, or the personal servant of a knight on campaign, a loanword from medieval German (see SACKMANN). Later it came to denote a marauder or plunderer.

GIVEN NAMES Italian 12%. *Sal* (2), *Geno*, *Giovanni*, *Mario*, *Rocco*.

Saccone (361) Italian: from an augmentative of SACCO. Theoretically this could also be a habitational name from one of the places in northeastern Italian called Saccone; however, the geographical concentration of the surname in Campania, Sicily, and northwestern Italy would suggest that this is not the source of the modern surname.

GIVEN NAMES Italian 11%. *Rocco* (4), *Angelo*, *Antonio*, *Carmine*, *Concetta*, *Gennaro*.

Sacha (123) Polish: from a pet form of a personal name beginning with *Sa*- (for example *Sambor*, *Salomon*, *Samson*, *Samuel*) or of *Aleksander* (see ALEXANDER).

GIVEN NAMES Polish 7%. *Jaroslaw*, *Stanislaw*, *Zygmunt*.

Sachar (124) Indian (Panjab, Gujarat): Hindu and Sikh name, probably from Sanskrit *satya* 'true, real'.

GIVEN NAMES Indian 20%. *Hardip* (3), *Ajay*, *Rajni*, *Supriya*, *Vijay*, *Vikas*.

Sachdev (131) Indian (Panjab): Hindu (Arora) and Sikh name, from Sanskrit *satya* 'true' + *deva* 'god', 'lord'. It is based on the name of a clan in the Arora community.

GIVEN NAMES Indian 96%. *Sunil* (5), *Vivek* (5), *Ravi* (4), *Rahul* (3), *Anupam* (2), *Aruna* (2), *Deepak* (2), *Sunita* (2), *Ameet*, *Amit*, *Anil*, *Arti*.

Sachdeva (128) Indian: variant of SACHDEV.

GIVEN NAMES Indian 91%. *Rajesh* (4), *Vinod* (4), *Ajit* (2), *Deepak* (2), *Dinesh* (2), *Meenu* (2), *Nand* (2), *Neeraj* (2), *Rajeev* (2), *Rakesh* (2), *Sanjay* (2), *Sunil* (2).

Sachen (111) German: probably a topographic name related to the family **Sachenbacher**, from Old High German *saher* 'reed grass', 'swamp grass'.

Sacher (325) **1.** German: from a vernacular form of the personal name *Zacharias*. Compare ZACHER. **2.** Jewish (Ashkenazic): unexplained.

GIVEN NAMES German 4%. *Kurt* (2), *Ernst*.

Sachs (3738) **1.** German and Jewish (Ashkenazic): regional name from (Lower) Saxony, German *(Nieder-)Sachsen* in northern Germany. The region is called after the Germanic tribe which settled there in Roman times and was named from a Germanic word which is preserved in Old Saxon, Old High German *sahs* 'knife', 'sword'. (The area in central Germany named *Sachsen* was named after the line of princes who had the title to the northern territories in 1422.) **2.** Jewish (eastern Ashkenazic): name adopted in memory of persecuted forebears, an acronym of the Hebrew phrase *Zera Qodesh SHemo* 'his name is of the seed of holiness'.

Sachse (431) Variant of SACHS.
GIVEN NAMES German 7%. *Hans* (2), *Rainer* (2), *Armin*, *Claus*, *Heinz*, *Hildegarde*, *Johannes*, *Kurt*, *Wolfgang*.

Sachtleben (113) North German: nickname for someone perceived to lead a carefree, easy life, from Middle Low German *sacht(e)* 'soft' + *leben* 'life'.
GIVEN NAMES German 5%. *Kurt*, *Otto*.

Sack (1628) **1.** English, German, and Jewish (Ashkenazic): metonymic occupational name for a maker of sacks or bags, from Old English *sacc*, Middle High German *sack*, German *Sack* 'sack'. Bahlow also suggests someone who carried sacks. **2.** German: topographic from Middle High German *sack* 'sack', 'end of a valley or area of cultivation'. **3.** Dutch: from a reduced form of the personal name *Zacharias*. **4.** Jewish (eastern Ashkenazic): from an acronym of the Hebrew phrase *Zera Keshodim* 'Seed of the Holy' (referring to martyred ancestors), or from a short form of the personal name *Isaac*.

Sackett (2265) English: diminutive of SACK 1.

Sackman (448) **1.** Jewish (Ashkenazic): elaborated form of SACK. **2.** Americanized spelling of German SACKMANN.

Sackmann (189) German: occupational name from Middle High German *sacman* 'baggage servant', one who was in charge of transporting and looking after a knight's baggage and supplies on campaign, or alternatively a nickname from the same word in the later sense 'plunderer'.
GIVEN NAMES German 4%. *Kurt*, *Lorenz*.

Sackrider (178) Americanized spelling of German **Sackreuter**, a nickname for a plunderer or cutpurse, from Middle High German *sack* 'sack', 'bag' + *riutære* 'one who tears out'.

Sacks (2468) **1.** Dutch: ethnic name from Middle Dutch *Sasse* 'Saxon' (see SACHS). **2.** Jewish (Ashkenazic): variant of SACHS 2. **3.** Anglicized and Americanized spelling of German and Ashkenazic Jewish SACHS.
GIVEN NAMES Jewish 5%. *Sol* (5), *Meyer* (3), *Hershel* (2), *Isadore* (2), *Arie*, *Aron*, *Avraham*, *Avram*, *Bracha*, *Emanuel*, *Hyman*, *Meir*.

Sacksteder (154) German (Alsace-Lorraine): habitational name for someone from a place called Sackstatt.
GIVEN NAME French 4%. *Colette*.

Sacra (209) Origin unidentified.

Sacre (125) French (**Sacré**): from the past participle of *sacrer* 'to consecrate', which

Morlet suggests denotes a bishop and De-brabandere describes as a personal name meaning 'consecrated', 'baptized'. Debra-bandere also derives it from the personal name *Sacreas*, *Zacharias*.

Sada (219) **1.** Spanish (of Basque origin): Castilianized variant of Basque **Zare**, a habitational name from Zare, a town in Navarre. **2.** Southern Italian: derivative of the Arabic personal name *Sa'ad*, meaning 'good fortune', 'prosperity' (see SAAD). **3.** Japanese: variously written, usually with characters meaning 'help' and 'rice paddy', and more usually pronounced 'sata'. It is a common place name throughout Japan. Some bearers of the surname have MINA-MOTO connections. **4.** Polish: occupational name for a fruit grower or topographic name for someone who lived by an orchard, from a derivative of Polish *sad* 'orchard' or *sadzić* 'to plant'. **5.** Polish (**Sąda**): occupational name for a court official, from Polish *sądzić* 'to judge' or *sąd* 'court of justice'.
GIVEN NAMES Spanish 33%; Japanese 5%. *Carlos* (4), *Andres* (3), *Fernando* (2), *Francisco* (2), *Hernan* (2), *Juan* (2), *Luis* (2), *Alberto*, *Alejandra*, *Alejandro*, *Ana Maria*, *Arturo*; *Toshio* (2), *Etsuko*, *Mayumi*, *Toshi*, *Yoshiro*.

Sadberry (148) Origin unidentified. Perhaps an English habitational name from Sadborow in Dorset or Sadbury Hill in Northumbria.

Sadd (140) English (East Anglia): nickname for a serious or solemn person, from Middle English *sad* 'serious', 'grave'. The modern English sense, 'unhappy', did not develop until the 15th century.

Saddler (1088) English and Scottish: variant spelling of SADLER.

Saddoris (134) Origin unidentified.

Sade (149) **1.** English: unexplained. Perhaps a variant of SADD. **2.** French: habitational name from a place in Hérault called Saddes. **3.** French: nickname from Latin *sapidus* 'prudent', 'wise'.

Sadeghi (196) Iranian: Persian form of the Arabic family name **Sadiqi**, an adjectival derivative of SADIQ.
GIVEN NAMES Muslim 78%. *Ali* (16), *Abbas* (6), *Hamid* (4), *Mohammad* (4), *Amir* (3), *Behzad* (3), *Seyed* (3), *Zahra* (3), *Ahmad* (2), *Hossein* (2), *Afsaneh*, *Afshin*.

Sadek (236) **1.** Muslim: variant of SADIQ. **2.** Polish: occupational name for a fruit grower or topographic name for someone who lived by an orchard, from a derivative of Polish *sad* 'orchard' or *sadzić* 'to plant' (see SADA).
GIVEN NAMES Muslim 40%. *Mohamed* (6), *Nabil* (4), *Azza* (2), *Fahim* (2), *Hisham* (2), *Mamdouh* (2), *Osama* (2), *Yasser* (2), *Abbas*, *Ahmad*, *Ahmed*, *Akram*.

Sader (214) **1.** English: unexplained. **2.** Muslim: from a personal name based on Arabic *ṣadr* 'breast', 'chest', 'forefront'. It

is also found in combinations such as *Ṣadr ud-Dīn* (**Sadruddin**) 'forefront of religion'.
GIVEN NAMES French 5%; Muslim 4%. *Antoine*, *Camil*, *Flore*, *Pierre*; *Naser* (3), *Habib* (2), *Ghassan*, *Hani*, *Jamel*, *Mahmoud*, *Osama*.

Sadiq (159) Muslim: from either of two Arabic personal names, based on *ṣadīq* 'friend', 'companion' (see the Qur'an 26:101) or *ṣiddīq* 'righteous', 'upright' (see the Qur'an 19:54).
GIVEN NAMES Muslim 81%. *Mohammad* (8), *Syed* (7), *Mohammed* (6), *Ahmad* (4), *Hamid* (3), *Suleman* (3), *Ahmed* (2), *Haji* (2), *Imran* (2), *Muhammad* (2), *Sheikh* (2), *Zahid* (2).

Sadler (7607) English and German: occupational name for a maker of saddles, from an agent derivative of Middle English, Middle High German, Middle Low German *sadel* 'saddle'.

Sadlier (167) German and English: variant of SADLER.
GIVEN NAMES German 6%. *Claus* (2), *Kurt*.

Sadlon (193) Czech (**Sádloň**) and Slovak (**Sadloň**): nickname for a fat man, from a derivative of *sádlo* 'fat', 'grease', 'dripping'.
GIVEN NAMES Czech and Slovak 4%. *Lubos*, *Milan*, *Zdenek*.

Sadlowski (266) Polish (**Sadłowski**): habitational name for someone from Sadłowo in Ciechanów or Włocławek voivodeships. There is possibly a connection with the vocabulary word *sadło* 'fat', 'lard'.
GIVEN NAMES Polish 7%; German 4%. *Zygmunt* (2), *Lech*, *Witold*, *Wlodek*; *Heintz*, *Heinz*.

Sadoff (189) **1.** Jewish (from Lithuania): alternative spelling of **Sadov**, a habitational name from a place called Shadovo. **2.** Shortened form of SADOWSKI.
GIVEN NAMES Jewish 8%. *Ari* (3), *Hyman*, *Isadore*, *Sol*.

Sadoski (157) Polish: variant of SADOWSKI.
GIVEN NAMES Polish 4%. *Jozef* (2), *Zigmund*.

Sadosky (109) Germanized spelling of Polish SADOWSKI.

Sadow (138) Japanese: see SATO.

Sadowski (2223) Polish, Jewish (eastern Ashkenazic), Ukrainian, and Belorussian: habitational name for someone from any of numerous places named with Polish *sad* 'orchard' or a cognate in a related Slavic language, for example Sadowa in northeastern Poland. This surname is also well established in German-speaking countries.
GIVEN NAMES Polish 7%. *Casimir* (5), *Zbigniew* (4), *Zigmund* (4), *Andrzej* (3), *Zygmunt* (3), *Tadeusz* (2), *Wieslaw* (2), *Beata*, *Boleslaw*, *Czeslaw*, *Genowefa*, *Henryk*.

Sadowsky (451) German and Jewish (eastern Ashkenazic): variant spelling of Polish SADOWSKI.
GIVEN NAMES Jewish 6%. *Gershon*, *Isidor*, *Mort*, *Shmuel*, *Sol*, *Yitzchak*.

Sadri (101) Muslim: adjectival derivative of SADER.

GIVEN NAMES Muslim 70%. *Ali* (3), *Saeid* (3), *Hamid* (2), *Mohamad* (2), *Shahram* (2), *Ahmad*, *Akbar*, *Alireza*, *Amir*, *Azita*, *Bahram*, *Fariba*.

Sadusky (133) Germanized form of Polish SADOWSKI.

Sady (102) Origin unidentified.

Saechao (521) Laotian: unexplained.

GIVEN NAMES Southeast Asian 61%. *Chan* (9), *Kao* (9), *Nai* (7), *Cheng* (4), *Fou* (4), *Yao* (4), *Yoon* (4), *Seng* (3), *Hun* (2), *Muang* (2), *Chieng*, *Choy*; *Meuy* (5), *Manh* (2), *Pao* (2), *Pak*; *Long* (3).

Saeed (353) Muslim: from a personal name based on the Arabic adjective *sa'īd* 'lucky', 'fortunate'. Compare SAAD.

GIVEN NAMES Muslim 88%. *Mohammad* (14), *Mohammed* (12), *Muhammad* (12), *Ahmed* (8), *Khalid* (8), *Tariq* (6), *Hamid* (4), *Mohamed* (4), *Abdulla* (3), *Ahmad* (3), *Ali* (3), *Anwar* (3).

Saeger (587) South German, Dutch (**de Saeger**), and Jewish (Ashkenazic): occupational name for a sawyer, from an agent derivative of Middle High German *segen*, *sagen* 'to saw', Middle Dutch *saghen*, German *sägen*.

Saeki (41) Japanese: written with characters denoting an assistant to an official such as a guard. The original pronunciation was *Saheki* or *Sahegi*. The word also denotes noisiness, and the Saeki were known for their loud ferocity in battle. They descended from the very ancient and warlike *Ōtomo* clan, which claimed descent from the hero Michi no Omi, a companion of the mythical Emperor Jinmu. Listed in the Shinsen shōjiroku, the name is found mostly in western Japan. Some families have taken the surname from their places of residence, which had been named after earlier residents of the original Saeki family. Owing to the similarity in pronunciation, it could be that the name is sometimes spelled SAIKI in America, but the two names are different originally.

Saelee (220) Southeast Asian: unexplained.

GIVEN NAMES Southeast Asian 66%. *Chan* (4), *Kao* (4), *Nai* (3), *Chai*, *Cheng*, *Chien*, *Foo*, *Hin*, *Muang*, *Pao*, *Seng*, *Song*, *Sou*.

Saelens (138) Dutch: patronymic from a derivative of the personal name SALOMON (see SOLOMON).

GIVEN NAME French 7%. *Marcel* (2).

Saeli (102) Italian: patronymic from the Jewish personal name *Asael*.

GIVEN NAMES Italian 10%. *Amadeo*, *Annamarie*, *Guido*, *Salvator*.

Saenger (229) German and Jewish (Ashkenazic): occupational name for a chorister or a nickname for someone who liked singing, from Middle High German *senger*, German *Sänger* 'singer'.

GIVEN NAME German 4%. *Fritz*.

Saenz (4188) Spanish (**Sáenz**): patronymic from an unidentified personal name.

GIVEN NAMES Spanish 46%. *Jose* (99), *Juan* (47), *Manuel* (41), *Raul* (37), *Carlos* (36), *Luis* (34), *Jesus* (33), *Mario* (24), *Francisco* (21), *Pedro* (21), *Ricardo* (21), *Alfredo* (18).

Saephan (141) Southeast Asian: unexplained.

GIVEN NAMES Southeast Asian 80%. *Muang* (3), *Seng* (3), *Chiew* (2), *Choy* (2), *Kao* (2), *Nai* (2), *Foo*, *Lai*, *On*, *Tsai*, *Tseng*, *Yao*; *Meuy* (2); *Thon*.

Saetern (165) 1. Cambodian or other Southeast Asian: variant of SAETEURN. 2. Norwegian: habitational name from any of numerous farmsteads named from the definite singular form of *saeter*, from Old Norse *sœtr*, *setr* 'farm'.

GIVEN NAMES Southeast Asian 75%. *Kao* (6), *Nai* (5), *Yao* (5), *Cheng* (4), *Chan* (3), *Lai* (3), *Chiew* (2), *Fou* (2), *Chien*, *Choy*, *Kong*, *Sou*; *Meuy* (2), *Pao* (2).

Saeteurn (127) Cambodian or other Southeast Asian: unexplained.

GIVEN NAMES Southeast Asian 77%. *Meng* (3), *Sou* (3), *Chan* (2), *Cheng* (2), *Choi* (2), *Kao* (2), *Lai* (2), *Nai* (2), *Chien*, *Ching*, *Foo*, *Han*; *Manh* (3), *Meuy* (2), *Cho*.

Saez (419) Spanish (**Sáez**): variant of SAENZ. In Spain this is the more frequent form.

GIVEN NAMES Spanish 49%. *Jose* (18), *Luis* (6), *Diego* (5), *Jorge* (5), *Juan* (5), *Carlos* (4), *Enrique* (4), *Miguel* (4), *Pedro* (4), *Rafael* (4), *Guillermo* (3), *Jaime* (3).

Safar (164) 1. Arabic and Jewish (Sephardic): occupational name from Arabic *şaffār* 'worker in copper or brass'. 2. Muslim: from Arabic *Şafar*, name of the second month of the Islamic calendar. This is sometimes chosen as a personal name for children born in this month. 3. Czech (**Šafář**); Slovak (**Šafár**), Croatian, and Slovenian (**Šafar**); and Hungarian (**Sáfár**): status name from Czech *šafář*, Hungarian *sáfár* 'steward', 'bailiff'. Compare German SCHAFFER.

GIVEN NAMES Muslim 23%; French 5%; Czech and Slovak 4%. *Fahim* (3), *Ammar* (2), *Mazin* (2), *Safar* (2), *Abdallah*, *Abdulrahman*, *Antoun*, *Fadel*, *Faisal*, *Farid*, *Fereydoun*, *Haitham*; *Gaston* (2), *Antoine*; *Ignac*, *Pavel*, *Zdenka*.

Safarik (175) Czech (**Šafařík**) and Slovak (**Šafárik**): from a diminutive of *šafář* 'steward' (see SAFAR).

GIVEN NAMES Czech and Slovak 6%. *Bohumil*, *Petr*, *Zdenek*.

Safe (107) English: unexplained.

Safer (236) Jewish: variant of SAFIR.

GIVEN NAMES Jewish 4%. *Hershel*, *Isadore*.

Saffel (106) Variant of English SAFFELL.

Saffell (461) English: from an Anglo-Scandinavian personal name, *Sæfugul*, from Old Norse *sæfogl* 'seabird', 'cormorant'. Though not recorded as a personal name in Scandinavia, it did become common in England after the Norman conquest.

Saffer (415) 1. English (of Norman origin): nickname for a greedy person, from Old French *saffre* 'glutton'. 2. South German: topographic name for someone living in a damp depression. 3. Jewish (Ashkenazic): variant of SAFIR.

Saffle (188) Variant of English SAFFELL.

Saffo (118) Origin uncertain. Perhaps a variant of English SAFFELL or SAFFORD.

Saffold (419) Probably English: perhaps a variant of SAFFELL or SAFFORD.

Safford (1216) English: habitational name from Seaford in East Sussex, named with Old English *sǣ* 'sea' + *ford* 'ford'. Until the 16th century, the Ouse river flowed into the sea at this point.

Saffran (177) German and Jewish (Ashkenazic): variant spelling of SAFRAN.

Safi (190) Muslim: from a personal name based on Arabic *şafī* 'honest friend', 'intercessor', from *şaffā* 'to make pure'.

GIVEN NAMES Muslim 73%. *Mohammad* (7), *Omar* (5), *Mohammed* (4), *Mohamed* (3), *Ehsan* (2), *Masoud* (2), *Safi* (2), *Samer* (2), *Wafa* (2), *Walid* (2), *Zahir* (2), *Abdul*.

Safian (120) Polish: metonymic occupational name for someone who cured goatskins and made things out of them, from Polish *safian* 'kind of goatskin'.

GIVEN NAME Polish 4%. *Jerzy*.

Safier (143) Jewish (Ashkenazic): variant of SAFIR.

GIVEN NAMES Jewish 7%; German 5%. *Isser*, *Jakob*, *Pinchus*; *Arno*.

Safir (143) Jewish (eastern Ashkenazic): ornamental name from northeastern Yiddish dialect *safir* and German *Saphir* 'sapphire'. Compare SAPIR.

GIVEN NAMES Jewish 16%; Russian 9%. *Dov* (3), *Igal*, *Ilya*, *Miriam*, *Polina*, *Ruvin*; *Lev* (3), *Boris*, *Galina*, *Raisa*, *Vladimir*.

Safko (162) Ukrainian: from a pet form of the personal name *Safa* (see SAVAS).

Safley (270) Scottish (Lanarkshire): unexplained.

Safran (496) 1. German, French, Hungarian (**Sáfrán**), and Jewish (Ashkenazic): from Middle High German *saffrān*, Old French *safran* 'saffron', Hungarian *sáfrány*, German *Safran* 'saffron', a bright yellow spice and colorant derived from the stigmas of a crocus, hence a metonymic occupational name for a spicer or a nickname for someone with reddish yellow hair. The word is ultimately derived from Arabic *za'farān*. The Jewish name is mainly ornamental. 2. Americanized spelling of Polish SZAFRAN, which has the same origin as 1.

GIVEN NAMES Jewish 5%. *Eliyahu*, *Hersh*, *Hyman*, *Mayer*, *Nadav*, *Sol*, *Zev*.

Safranek (251) Czech (**Šafránek**): from a diminutive of Czech *šafrán* 'saffron' (see SAFRAN), applied as nickname for someone with reddish yellow hair.

Safranski (115) Variant of Polish SZAFRAN-SKI.

Safrit (270) Origin unidentified.

Safstrom (102) Swedish (**Säfström**): ornamental name from Swedish *säf*, ornamental (old) spelling of *säv* 'rush' + *ström* 'river'.

Saft (146) Jewish (Ashkenazic): ornamental name from German *Saft* 'fruit juice'.
GIVEN NAME Jewish 6%. *Meyer* (2).

Sagan (492) **1.** Polish and Jewish (eastern Ashkenazic): from Polish *sagan* 'kettle', hence a metonymic occupational name for a maker of pots and pans, or a nickname from the same word in a less clear application. **2.** Jewish (Ashkenazic): habitational name from Sagan, a place in Lower Silesia. **3.** French (southeastern): nickname for a loud or noisy man, from a dialect word meaning 'noisy'.
GIVEN NAMES Polish 6%; German 4%. *Casimir, Elzbieta, Henryka, Jacek, Janusz, Jozef, Wladyslaw, Wojciech, Zdzislaw, Zygmunt; Hans* (2), *Guenther, Ilse, Kurt.*

Sagar (319) **1.** Indian (Panjab, Gujarat): Hindu and Sikh name from Sanskrit *sāgara* 'ocean'. **2.** English: variant of SEAGER.
GIVEN NAMES Indian 40%. *Vidya* (4), *Ajay* (2), *Ashok* (2), *Prem* (2), *Satya* (2), *Sushil* (2), *Vinod* (2), *Ajit, Alok, Amrit, Anand, Ananda.*

Sagastume (161) Basque: topographic name from Basque *sagasta* 'apple tree' + *-ume* 'young plant'.
GIVEN NAMES Spanish 55%. *Jose* (5), *Luis* (4), *Mario* (4), *Felipe* (3), *Ana* (2), *Carlos* (2), *Dagoberto* (2), *Jorge* (2), *Margarita* (2), *Pedro* (2), *Salvador* (2), *Sergio* (2).

Sage (4184) **1.** English and French: nickname for a wise man, from Middle English, Old French *sage* 'learned', 'sensible', from Latin *sagus* 'prophetic', akin to *sagax* 'sharp', 'perceptive'. **2.** Irish: variant of SAVAGE, via the Gaelicized form **Sabhaois**. **3.** German: habitational name from a place near Oldenburg, so named from an old word, *sege* 'sedge', 'reed'.

Sagebiel (107) North German: from a field name formed with *sage*, a variant of *sege* 'sedge', 'reed'.
GIVEN NAMES German 4%; Spanish 4%. *Erwin, Ewald; Ruben* (2), *Carlos.*

Sagehorn (125) German: habitational name from a place near Bremen, probably so named from *sege* 'sedge', 'reed' + Middle Low German *horn* 'corner', 'protruding area'.
GIVEN NAMES German 7%; French 4%. *Kurt* (2), *Eldor; Albertine, Camille.*

Sagel (105) South German: from a short form of a Germanic personal name formed with *sacha* 'legal action', litigation'.

Sagen (238) Norwegian: habitational name from any of numerous farmsteads so named, from the definite singular form of *sag* 'sawmill'.

Sagendorf (105) German (**Sägendorf**): habitational name from a place so called.

Sager (4271) **1.** English: variant of SEAGER. **2.** Dutch (**de Sager**), and North German: occupational name from Dutch, Low German *sager* 'sawyer'. **3.** French: from the Germanic personal name *Sagher*, composed of the elements *sag-* (an element related to Gothic and Old High German words meaning 'quarrel', 'law-suit') + *hari, heri* 'army'. **4.** Jewish (Ashkenazic): nickname from an agent derivative of German *sagen* 'to say'.

Sagers (255) Dutch: variant of SAGER 2.

Sagert (129) North German: variant of SAGER 2.

Sageser (121) An altered spelling of German **Sägesser, Segesser**, an occupational name for a scythe maker, from an agent derivative of Middle High German *sëgense* 'scythe'.

Saggese (205) Italian: perhaps a habitational name from a minor place in Foggia province named Saggese; however, the concentration of the modern surname in San Giuseppe Vesuviano in Naples province suggests that a different source is involved.
GIVEN NAMES Italian 21%. *Angelo* (3), *Mario* (3), *Vito* (2), *Alfonso, Francesco, Giuseppe, Sal, Salvatore, Umberto, Vincenza.*

Saggio (150) Italian: nickname from *saggio* 'wise', 'learned', from Latin *sagax* 'sharp', 'perceptive'. Compare English SAGE.
GIVEN NAMES Italian 15%. *Salvatore* (3), *Amelio, Carmela, Carmine, Giuseppe, Natale.*

Sago (197) Portuguese: habitational name from a place in Monção.

Sagona (179) **1.** Italian: habitational name from Sagona, the medieval name of Savona in northern Italy, before it became modified to its present form (*Sagona–Saona–Savona*; compare *Ligorno–Liorno–Livorno*). **2.** Greek (**Sagonas**): nickname for someone with a protruding jaw, from Greek *sagona* 'jaw' (Classical Greek *siagōn*).
GIVEN NAMES Italian 12%. *Salvatore* (2), *Angelo, Biagio, Santo.*

Sagraves (191) English: variant of SEAGRAVE.

Sagun (126) **1.** Spanish: variant of SAHAGUN. **2.** Aragonese: variant of **Sagunt**, a habitational name from Sagunt, a town in Aragon.
GIVEN NAMES Spanish 33%. *Macario* (2), *Rodrigo* (2), *Ruben* (2), *Arsenia, Conchita, Delfin, Dominador, Eleazar, Enedina, Faustino, Honorata, Jesus.*

Saha (326) Indian (Bengal) and Bangladeshi: Hindu (Baishya) name meaning 'merchant', from Sanskrit *sādhu* 'honest', 'good'.
GIVEN NAMES Indian 75%. *Amit* (4), *Arun* (4), *Krishna* (4), *Pradip* (4), *Ashok* (3), *Sankar* (3), *Ananda* (2), *Asis* (2), *Bijoy* (2), *Bikash* (2), *Gautam* (2), *Gour* (2).

Sahagian (271) Western Armenian: patronymic from the personal name *Sahak*, Armenian form of ISAAC. This was the name of the patriarch (*c.*345–439), who (with St. Mesrob) promoted the development of the Armenian alphabet and translation of the Bible into Armenian.
GIVEN NAMES Armenian 11%. *Armen* (2), *Nubar* (2), *Sahag* (2), *Ara, Aris, Avedis, Garen, Mesrob, Mesrop, Sarkis, Vahan, Vartan.*

Sahagun (300) Spanish (**Sahagún**): habitational name from Sahagùn in Lleón province (Latin name *Sanctus Facundus*).
GIVEN NAMES Spanish 46%. *Jose* (15), *Jesus* (6), *Francisco* (4), *Carlos* (3), *Luis* (3), *Miguel* (3), *Salvador* (3), *Armando* (2), *Guadalupe* (2), *Guillermo* (2), *Juan* (2), *Manuel* (2).

Sahakian (166) Eastern Armenian: variant of SAHAGIAN.
GIVEN NAMES Armenian 40%. *Ara* (3), *Armen* (3), *Garnik* (2), *Hasmik* (2), *Ohannes* (2), *Sahak* (2), *Vicken* (2), *Adik, Anoush, Antranik, Aram, Arax.*

Sahl (190) German: variant of SAAL.
GIVEN NAMES German 7%; Scandinavian 5%. *Guenter, Kurt; Nels.*

Sahlberg (120) **1.** German and Jewish (Ashkenazic): habitational name from any of several places named Saalberg, for example in Westphalia and Silesia. **2.** Swedish: ornamental name composed of the elements *sahl*, an ornamental name spelling of *sal* 'hall', or the same element taken from a place name + *berg* 'hill'. **3.** Jewish (Ashkenazic): variant of SALBERG 2. **4.** Norwegian: variant spelling of SALBERG.
GIVEN NAMES Scandinavian 8%; German 6%. *Hilmer, Sten; Gunther, Kurt.*

Sahli (299) Muslim: from an adjectival derivative of Arabic *saḥl* 'smooth', 'fluent', 'easy'. Abul Abbas Sahl ibn S'ad was a Companion of the Prophet Muhammad.

Sahlin (237) Swedish: ornamental name from *sahl*, an ornamental spelling of *sal* 'hall' (or the same element taken from a place name) + the adjectival suffix *-in* (from Latin *-inius*).
GIVEN NAMES Scandinavian 8%; German 8%. *Nels; Kurt* (4), *Hans* (2).

Sahlstrom (100) Swedish (**Sahlström**): ornamental name from *sahl* (variant of *sal* 'hall') + *ström* 'river'.

Sahm (286) **1.** Eastern German (of Slavic origin): from the Slavic personal name *Samo*, a short form of *Samobor*. **2.** German: metonymic occupational name for a seed merchant, from Middle High German *sām*.
GIVEN NAMES German 4%. *Kurt* (2), *Ruediger, Udo.*

Sahni (135) Indian: variant of SAWHNEY.
GIVEN NAMES Indian 89%. *Suresh* (3), *Kiran* (2), *Rakesh* (2), *Anirudh, Anuj, Arti, Ashok, Atam, Ganesh, Hardev, Ish, Jawahar.*

Sahota (116) Indian (Panjab): Sikh name meaning 'hare', derived from the name of a Jat clan.
GIVEN NAMES Indian 90%. *Darshan* (3), *Jarnail* (2), *Raghbir* (2), *Sohan* (2), *Ashwani*, *Bahadur*, *Hardev*, *Hari*, *Joga*, *Pradeep*, *Prem*, *Pritam*.

Sahr (427) German: habitational name from places called Sahr or Saar (for example Saar in Bohemia), or a topographic name from the same element (see SAAR).

Sahs (127) German: variant spelling of SASS.

Saia (710) Southern Italian: from a reduced form of the personal names *Isaia* (English *Isaiah*) or *Osaia* (English *Hosea*).
GIVEN NAMES Italian 13%. *Angelo* (5), *Salvatore* (5), *Carmelo* (2), *Domenic* (2), *Aldo*, *Antonino*, *Carmine*, *Concetta*, *Guido*, *Luigi*, *Nicolo*.

Said (641) Arabic and Jewish (Sephardic): variant of SAYED or SAEED.
GIVEN NAMES Muslim 57%. *Ali* (9), *Ahmed* (5), *Hasan* (5), *Mohamed* (5), *Mohammed* (5), *Aziz* (4), *Mohammad* (4), *Said* (4), *Abdul* (3), *Azhar* (3), *Hassan* (3), *Ibrahim* (3).

Saidi (128) Muslim: adjectival derivative of SAYED.
GIVEN NAMES Muslim 68%. *Ahmad* (6), *Mohammad* (3), *Ali* (2), *Parwin* (2), *Said* (2), *Abdo*, *Ahmed*, *Aisha*, *Amin*, *Ardavan*, *Ayad*, *Ayed*.

Saiki (254) Japanese: written with the characters for 'equal' and 'tree'. The family bearing this name descends from the TAKEDA branch of the MINAMOTO clan, and originated in Kai (now Yamanashi prefecture). However, in America this name more probably comes from a misspelling of, which is more common in Japan and has a similar pronunciation.
GIVEN NAMES Japanese 26%. *Kenji* (2), *Akio*, *Hideyo*, *Hiro*, *Hiroko*, *Hisao*, *Ikuo*, *Itsuo*, *Katsumi*, *Kazuo*, *Kazutaka*, *Kiichi*.

Saile (118) **1.** English (mostly Lancashire): probably a variant of SALE. **2.** German: older form of SEILER. **3.** Dutch: from Middle Dutch *salië*, *sailge* 'sage', hence a metonymic occupational name for someone who grew or sold herbs.
GIVEN NAMES German 6%. *Elke*, *Kurt*, *Volker*.

Sailer (991) **1.** English: variant spelling of SAYLOR. **2.** German: variant of SEILER.
GIVEN NAMES German 4%. *Bernhard* (2), *Eldor* (2), *Hans* (2), *Hermann*, *Klaus*, *Kurt*.

Sailor (692) English: variant of SAYLOR.

Sailors (601) English: variant of SAYLORS.

Sain (1510) French (**Saïn**): from Old French *saïn* 'grease', 'fat', 'dripping', hence a metonymic occupational name for a butcher, especially a pork butcher (charcutier).

Sainato (172) Southern Italian: of uncertain origin; possibly a nickname from old Sicilian *saynatu* 'white horse'; or from *sagginato* 'color of sorghum', presumably a nickname for someone with fair hair.

Alternatively, it may be a nickname for a fat man, from Latin *sagina* 'fattened'.
GIVEN NAMES Italian 17%. *Nicola* (4), *Aldo* (2), *Francesco*, *Giovanna*.

Saindon (384) French: from *Sandon*, an Old French oblique form of *Sando*, a personal name of Germanic origin.
GIVEN NAMES French 7%. *Viateur* (2), *Alban*, *Andre*, *Gaston*, *Lucien*, *Normand*.

Saine (358) Origin uncertain. **1.** In part, it may be French, a variant of SAIN. **2.** It could also be Finnish, a variant of **Sainio**, an ornamental name from a word meaning 'sleigh'. Found chiefly in south-western Finland. **3.** Spanish: unexplained.

Saini (334) Indian (Panjab): Hindu (Arora) and Sikh name derived from the name of an Arora clan.
GIVEN NAMES Indian 92%. *Avtar* (4), *Darshan* (3), *Raj* (3), *Sanjiv* (3), *Amar* (2), *Ashima* (2), *Ashok* (2), *Ashwani* (2), *Dyal* (2), *Hari* (2), *Jarnail* (2), *Mayuri* (2).

Sainsbury (281) English: habitational name from Saintbury in Gloucestershire, recorded in the 12th century as *Seynesbury*. The place name is probably from the genitive case of the Old English personal name *Sæwine* (composed of the elements *sæ* 'sea' + *wine* 'friend') + Old English *burh* 'castle', 'fortified town'.

Saint (695) English and French: nickname for a particularly pious individual, from Middle English, Old French *saint*, *seint* 'holy' (Latin *sanctus* 'blameless', 'holy'). The vocabulary word was occasionally used in the Middle Ages as a personal name, especially on the Continent, and this may have given rise to some instances of the surname.
GIVEN NAMES French 4%. *Andre* (2), *Cyr*, *Remy*.

St. Amand (611) French: variant of ST. AMANT.
GIVEN NAMES French 13%. *Gilles* (3), *Girard* (3), *Aurore* (2), *Emile* (2), *Lucien* (2), *Normand* (2), *Alyre*, *Andre*, *Armand*, *Camille*, *Clovis*, *Francois*.

St. Amant (428) French: habitational name from any of the various places dedicated to St. Amantius or St. Amand. It is a secondary surname associated with the French primary names André, Charrier, Huchereau, Lepage, and Robert, among others.
GIVEN NAMES French 7%. *Jacques* (2), *Andre*, *Angelle*, *Camile*, *Cecile*, *Michel*, *Pierre*, *Valmond*.

St. Amour (358) French: habitational surname from any of various places so named, for example in Jura and Saône-et-Loire. It is a secondary surname associated with the French primary names Bouchet, Nadal, Payet, and Roy, among others.
GIVEN NAMES French 10%. *Pierre* (5), *Andre* (2), *Armand*, *Luc*, *Raoul*, *Yvon*.

St. Andre (193) French (**St. André**): habitational name from any of the places so

called, named from a religious dedication to St. Andrew. In some cases the prefix may have been an ironic attachment to the family name ANDRE. St. Andre is a secondary surname associated with the French primary names Achin, André, Gilbert, Lafontaine, Landry, Martin, Raynard, Thomas, and others.
GIVEN NAMES French 9%. *Gisele* (2), *Cecile*, *Emile*, *Raoul*.

St. Ange (355) French (**Saint-Ange**): habitational name from any of the places so named, from a religious dedication to a St. Ange.

St. Angel (105) French (**Saint-Angel**): habitational name from any of the places so named, from a religious dedication to a St. Angelus.

St. Angelo (237) Partly Americanized form of southern Italian **Santàngelo**, a habitational name from any of the many places named Sant'Angelo from a religious dedication to a St. Angelus.
GIVEN NAMES Italian 4%. *Angelo* (2), *Rocco*.

St. Ann (171) French (**Saint-Ann(e)**): habitational name from any of the places so named, from a religious dedication to St. Anne.

St. Aubin (415) French: habitational name from any of many places so named, from a religious dedication to a St. Albinus. In some cases the prefix *St* may have been an iron attachment to the family name. St. Aubin is a secondary surname associated with the French primary names Aubin, Benjamin, Lafrance, and others.
GIVEN NAMES French 6%. *Marcel* (2), *Alcide*, *Andre*, *Armand*, *Normand*.

St. Charles (262) French: habitational name from either of two places so called, in Calvados and Mayenne, named from a religious dedication to a St. Charles.
GIVEN NAMES French 5%. *Antoine*, *Philippe*.

St. Clair (5354) **1.** French: habitational name from any of the places so called, for example in Normandy, named from a religious dedication to a (male) St. Clair. **2.** North American variant spelling of ST. CLAIRE.

St. Claire (241) **1.** French: habitational name from any of four places called Sainte Claire, in Aisne, Alpes-Maritime, Meurthe-et-Moselle, and Oise, named from a religious dedication to (the female) St. Claire. **2.** North American variant spelling of St. Clair.

St. Croix (113) French (**Saint-Croix**): habitational name from any of the places so named, from a religious dedication to the Holy Cross.
GIVEN NAMES French 11%. *Andre* (2), *Armand* (2), *Camille*.

St. Cyr (1065) French: habitational name from any of the places so called, named from a religious dedication to St. Cyrus. It is a secondary surname associated with the primary names Deshaies and Rouillard.

GIVEN NAMES French 10%. *Armand* (7), *Emile* (2), *Patrice* (2), *Alain, Alcide, Clemence, Cyr, Gabrielle, Germain, Jacques, Laurent, Laurette.*

St. Denis (392) French: habitational name from any of the many places so called, named from a religious dedication to St. Denis (Dionysios). In some cases the prefix *St* may simply have been an ironic addition to the surname DENIS. St. Denis is a secondary surname for the French primary names Denis, Folquier, and Quesnel.
GIVEN NAMES French 10%. *Marcel* (2), *Michel* (2), *Armand, Gabrielle, Henri, Jacques, Jean-Francois, Normand, Philippe.*

St. Dennis (151) Americanized spelling of French ST. DENIS.
GIVEN NAMES French 4%. *Armand, Emile.*

Ste. Marie (136) French (**Sainte-Marie**): habitational name from any of the numerous places so called, named with a religious dedication to the Virgin Mary.
GIVEN NAMES French 17%. *Andre* (2), *Adrien, Emile, Florent, Gaston, Jacques, Marcel.*

St. Fleur (118) French (**Saint-Fleur**): habitational name from any of the places so named, from a religious dedication to a St. Fleur (a personal name meaning 'flower').
GIVEN NAMES French 35%. *Aliette, Andre, Emile, Francois, Gislaine, Jean Claude, Marise, Martial, Michel, Pierre.*

St. Gelais (126) French (**Saint-Ann(e)**): habitational name from a place so named, from a religious dedication to a St. Gelais.
GIVEN NAMES French 20%. *Andre, Armand, Cecile, Constant, Gilles, Herve, Laurent, Marcel, Normand.*

St. George (1227) 1. English (of Norman origin): habitational name from any of the numerous places in France so called from the dedication of their churches to St. George (see GEORGE). 2. French: secondary surname to the primary surnames De la Porte, Godfroy, Lapointe, and Laporte.
GIVEN NAMES French 6%. *Lucien* (2), *Adlore, Andre, Calice, Celine, Donat, Lucienne, Monique, Normand, Philippe, Raoul, Roch.*

St. Germain (1671) French: habitational name from any of numerous places that take their name from a religious dedication to St. Germanus. It is a secondary surname associated with the primary surnames Chauvin, Diverny, Geoffroy, Lamoureux, Lemaire, Mignon, and others.
GIVEN NAMES French 11%. *Andre* (5), *Armand* (3), *Normand* (3), *Pierre* (3), *Adelard* (2), *Amie* (2), *Emile* (2), *Fernand* (2), *Lucien* (2), *Marcel* (2), *Michel* (2), *Monique* (2).

St. Germaine (253) French: variant spelling of ST. GERMAIN.
GIVEN NAMES French 5%. *Aime, Jean-Paul, Marcel.*

St. Hilaire (764) French: habitational name from any of the numerous places of this name in France and Belgium, which take

their name from a religious dedication to St. Hilarius (see HILAIRE). It is a secondary surname associated with the French surnames Frapier, GUERIN, ROBERT and others.
GIVEN NAMES French 14%. *Fernand* (3), *Marcel* (3), *Andre* (2), *Armand* (2), *Donat* (2), *Lucien* (2), *Normand* (2), *Serge* (2), *Alexandrine, Alphonse, Anselme, Antoine.*

St. Ives (104) 1. English: from a place so called, of which there is one in Cambridgeshire and another in Cornwall. 2. Americanized form of French **St. Yves**.

St. Jacques (241) French: habitational name from a place so named from a religious dedication to St. James (see JAMES). It is a secondary surname associated with LECOMTE, MARTEL, VIGNEAU, and others.
GIVEN NAMES French 15%. *Pierre* (2), *Armand, Benoit, Eudore, Fernand, Francois, Octave, Raoul, Yves.*

St. James (404) Translation of French ST. JACQUES.
GIVEN NAMES French 7%. *Fernand, Jean Marie, Lucien, Michel, Normand, Pierre.*

St. Jean (1039) French: habitational name from any of many places in France and Belgium named with a religious dedication to St. John (see JOHN). As a secondary surname St. Jean is associated with many primary surnames, such as Coulon, Delubac, Favre, Gervais, Hamelin, Langlois, Lefebvre, Martin, Renaud, Rousseau, and others.
GIVEN NAMES French 15%. *Armand* (4), *Adelard* (3), *Andre* (3), *Jacques* (3), *Marcel* (3), *Jean Claude* (2), *Micheline* (2), *Normand* (2), *Aldor, Antoine, Benoit, Chanel.*

St. John (6000) 1. English (of Norman origin): habitational name from any of the numerous places in France so called from the dedication of their churches to St. Jean (see JOHN). 2. Americanized form of French ST. JEAN.

St. Julian (107) Americanized form of French ST. JULIEN.

St. Julien (249) French: habitational name from any of the numerous places so called, named with a religious dedication to St. Julian. As a secondary surname, it is associated with Aubois, AUGER, GUYON, Hautbois, and JULIEN.
GIVEN NAMES French 7%. *Alphonse, Eusebe, Gaston, Luckner, Maxime, Monique.*

St. Laurent (969) French: habitational name from any of the numerous places so called, named with a religious dedication to St. Lawrence. In some instances the suffix *St* may have been an ironic attachment to the family name LAURENT. As a secondary surname, St. Laurent is associated with Charbonnier, JULIEN, LAURENT, LECLERC, and others.
GIVEN NAMES French 17%. *Normand* (8), *Andre* (7), *Armand* (5), *Marcel* (5), *Emile*

(3), *Jacques* (3), *Henri* (2), *Adrien, Benoit, Fernand, Fernande, Francois.*

St. Lawrence (306) Americanized form of French ST. LAURENT.

St. Louis (1287) French: habitational name from any of several places so called (in Aude, Dordogne, Gironde, Haut-Rhin, and Moselle), named with a religious dedication to a St. Louis (see LEWIS). In some instances the suffix *St* may have been an ironic attachment to the family name LOUIS. As a secondary surname, it is associated with many surnames, including DESPRES, DOUCET, GAUDET, JOURDAIN, LOUIS, ROY, and Supernant.
GIVEN NAMES French 12%. *Jacques* (4), *Pierre* (4), *Andre* (2), *Damien* (2), *Gaston* (2), *Monique* (2), *Antoine, Armand, Arsene, Astride, Carolle, Clovis.*

St. Marie (457) French (**Sainte-Marie**): habitational name from any of the numerous places so called, named with a religious dedication to the Virgin Mary. As a secondary surname, it is associated with the French surnames Lambert, Marie, and Racine.
GIVEN NAMES French 7%. *Andre* (2), *Normand* (2), *Adrien, Laurette, Pierre, Rosaire.*

St. Martin (892) French: habitational name from any of the numerous places so called in France and Belgium, named with a religious dedication to Saint Martin. As a secondary surname, it is associated with, amongst others, such French surnames as Boucher, Breton, Champagne, and Tavernier.
GIVEN NAMES French 6%. *Armand* (2), *Gaston* (2), *Edouard, Euclide, Francois, Lucien, Michel, Pierre, Romain.*

St. Mary (234) Americanized form of French **Sainte-Marie** (see ST. MARIE).
GIVEN NAMES French 5%. *Colette* (2), *Armand, Arsene.*

St. Michel (101) habitational name from any of the numerous places in France so called from the dedication of their churches to St. MICHAEL.
GIVEN NAMES French 7%. *Gabrielle, Ovila.*

St. Onge (1492) French: habitational name from any of several places in France so called from the dedication of their churches to St. Onge .
GIVEN NAMES French 11%. *Armand* (6), *Marcel* (4), *Andre* (3), *Laurier* (3), *Michel* (3), *Normand* (3), *Adelard* (2), *Camille* (2), *Ovila* (2), *Adrien, Alcide, Alphonse.*

St. Ores (119) French: habitational name from any of several places in France so called from the dedication of their churches to St. Ores .

St. Ours (125) French: habitational name from any of several places in France so called from the dedication of their churches to St. Onge .
GIVEN NAMES French 12%. *Cecile, Gilberte, Rejeanne, Renald, Rodolph.*

St. Peter (1063) Americanized form of French ST. PIERRE.
GIVEN NAMES French 5%. *Alphy, Aurele, Celestine, Euclide, Henri, Lucien.*

St. Pierre (3640) French (**Saint-Pierre**): habitational name from any of the places in northern France named Saint-Pierre, from the dedication of their churches to St. PETER. As a secondary surname, it is associated with BERNARD, BOUCHER, BRETON, DUPUIS, FRANCOIS, PERROT, Tranchemontagne, and others.
GIVEN NAMES French 14%. *Normand* (13), *Armand* (10), *Lucien* (9), *Marcel* (9), *Andre* (8), *Emile* (8), *Cecile* (4), *Laurent* (4), *Michel* (4), *Alphonse* (3), *Antoine* (3), *Camille* (3).

St. Rock (751) French: habitational name from any of several places in France so called from the dedication of their churches to a St. Roque.

St. Romain (429) French (**Saint Romain**): habitational name from any of the places so named for the dedication of their churches to a St. Romanus. It is a secondary surname associated with Chorel.
GIVEN NAMES French 5%. *Amie, Emile, Eusebe, Monique, Oneil.*

St. Roman (1014) Southern French: variant of ST. ROMAIN.

St. Sauveur (100) French: habitational name from any of several places in France so called from the dedication of their churches to *Saint Sauveur*, 'the Holy Savior', i.e Christ.
GIVEN NAMES French 13%. *Donat, Emile, Fernand, Germaine, Pierre.*

St. Thomas (208) habitational name from any of several places in France so called from the dedication of their churches to St. THOMAS.

St. Vincent (134) French: habitational name from any of several places in France so called from the dedication of their churches to St. Vincent (see VINCENT).
GIVEN NAMES French 4%. *Leandre, Monique.*

Sainz (510) Spanish (also **Sáinz**): variant of SAENZ.
GIVEN NAMES Spanish 40%. *Jose* (8), *Carlos* (7), *Miguel* (6), *Manuel* (5), *Andres* (4), *Francisco* (4), *Juan* (4), *Luis* (4), *Raul* (4), *Adriana* (3), *Alfredo* (3), *Armando* (3); *Antonio* (3), *Marco* (2), *Aureliano, Fausto, Lorenzo, Teodolo.*

Sais (196) Spanish: variant of **Sáez** (see SAEZ).
GIVEN NAMES Spanish 27%. *Fernando* (3), *Orlando* (2), *Angelita, Arturo, Delfina, Desiderio, Dionicio, Edgardo, Elva, Fidel, Isidoro, Jere.*

Saito (1175) Japanese (**Saitō**): variously written, this is one of the ten most common surnames, especially in northeastern Japan. The Saito descend from Fujiwara no Nobumochi, a 10th-century head of the Saigū Shrine; thus, *Saigū no Fujiwara* or *Saitō.*

GIVEN NAMES Japanese 68%. *Hiroshi* (11), *Takashi* (8), *Takeshi* (7), *Akira* (6), *Hiroyuki* (6), *Kenji* (6), *Mamoru* (6), *Takao* (6), *Atsushi* (5), *Makoto* (5), *Toshio* (5), *Fumio* (4).

Saitta (356) Italian (Sicily) and Greek (**Saitas**): metonymic occupational name for an archer or fletcher, or a nickname for one who was fleet of foot, from Sicilian *saitta* 'arrow' (Latin *sagitta*).
GIVEN NAMES Italian 17%. *Salvatore* (4), *Angelo* (3), *Cataldo* (2), *Vito* (2), *Antonio, Attilio, Biagio, Giuseppe, Maurizio, Nunzio, Philomena, Sal.*

Saiz (793) Spanish (also **Sáiz**): variant of **Sáez** (see SAEZ).
GIVEN NAMES Spanish 22%. *Manuel* (11), *Jose* (7), *Juan* (6), *Luis* (4), *Ramon* (4), *Felipe* (3), *Isidro* (3), *Amador* (2), *Camilo* (2), *Eloy* (2), *Florentino* (2), *Francisco* (2).

Sajdak (232) Polish: metonymic occupational name for a quiver maker, or perhaps for an archer or fletcher, from *sajdak* 'quiver'.
GIVEN NAMES Polish 11%. *Beata* (2), *Stanislaw* (2), *Boguslaw, Janusz, Krystyna, Tadeusc.*

Sak (308) **1.** Polish: from a reduced form of the personal name *Isaak* (see ISAAC). **2.** Polish and Hungarian (**Szák**): from Polish *sak*, Hungarian *szák*, 'fishing net', 'sack', hence a metonymic occupational name for a maker of nets or sacks. **3.** Dutch: variant of *Zack*, a short form of the personal name *Zacharias* or *Isaak*. **4.** Jewish (Ashkenazic): variant spelling of SACK.
GIVEN NAMES Polish 11%. *Darek* (2), *Jerzy* (2), *Casimir, Czeslaw, Grazyna, Jozef, Krzysztof, Leszek, Waclaw.*

Sakaguchi (221) Japanese: '(one who lives) at the mouth of the slope'; found mostly in western Japan.
GIVEN NAMES Japanese 53%. *Akira* (2), *Hiroko* (2), *Kenji* (2), *Makoto* (2), *Susumu* (2), *Yoichi* (2), *Yoshiko* (2), *Fumio, Goro, Hiroaki, Hirokazu, Hironori.*

Sakai (760) Japanese: variously written, most usually with the characters for 'rice wine (*sake*)' and 'well'. The latter family is descended from the Tokugawa family, and took its name from the village of Sakai in Izumi (now part of Ōsaka prefecture), though the name of the village is written with a character meaning 'boundary'. Another family's name, meaning 'well at the slope', is listed in the Shinsen shōjiroku, but written with yet another set of characters.
GIVEN NAMES Japanese 55%. *Hiroshi* (6), *Shoko* (5), *Kazuo* (3), *Kenji* (3), *Tomoko* (3), *Toshio* (3), *Yoshio* (3), *Akio* (2), *Atsushi* (2), *Ayako* (2), *Chie* (2), *Fumiyo* (2).

Sakal (148) **1.** Jewish (Sephardic): occupational name for someone who polished wood, gems, metals, or armor, from Arabic *ṣaqqāl* 'polisher'. **2.** Hungarian (**Szakál**):

descriptive nickname from Hungarian *szakál* 'beard', Turkish *sakal*.

Sakala (106) **1.** Finnish: unexplained. **2.** Samoan (Polynesian): unexplained.

Sakamoto (905) Japanese: written two ways, both meaning '(one who lives) at the bottom of the slope', this surname is common in all parts of Japan, but especially in the west and the Ryūkyū Islands. It is listed in the Shinsen shōjiroku, and so some bearers have connections with ancient nobility.
GIVEN NAMES Japanese 47%. *Koichi* (7), *Hiroshi* (5), *Masaru* (5), *Masao* (4), *Hiroki* (3), *Mitsuo* (3), *Shoji* (3), *Sueo* (3), *Susumu* (3), *Yoshimi* (3), *Gengo* (2), *Hidemi* (2).

Sakata (321) Japanese: variously written, mostly with characters meaning 'rice paddy at the slope', this name is found all over Japan and is listed in the Shinsen shōjiroku.
GIVEN NAMES Japanese 49%. *Naoki* (3), *Harumi* (2), *Hiro* (2), *Hiroshi* (2), *Keiichi* (2), *Kenji* (2), *Mitsuo* (2), *Seiji* (2), *Shigeru* (2), *Shinichi* (2), *Tsugio* (2), *Akihito.*

Saker (190) English: occupational name for a maker of sacks or bags, from an agent derivative of Old English *sacc* 'sack', 'bag'.

Sako (170) Japanese: written with characters meaning 'help' and 'ancient', the name is mostly found in western Japan, but it is not common.
GIVEN NAMES Japanese 30%. *Hiroshi* (2), *Toshio* (2), *Akihisa, Fumihiro, Hiroyuki, Isako, Itaru, Junichi, Kentaro, Masafumi, Masao, Momoko.*

Sakowicz (118) Polish: patronymic from the personal name SAK, a reduced form of *Isaak* (see ISAAC).
GIVEN NAMES Polish 14%. *Alicja* (2), *Janusz* (2), *Waclaw* (2), *Zygmont.*

Sakowski (342) Polish and Jewish (Ashkenazic): habitational name for someone from places called Sakowo or Saków in Poland.
GIVEN NAMES Polish 6%. *Jozef, Stanislaw, Zdzislaw, Zygmunt.*

Saks (583) Jewish (Ashkenazic) and German: variant of SACHS.
GIVEN NAMES Jewish 9%. *Miriam* (2), *Sol* (2), *Avi, Avinoam, Boruch, Chaim, Emanuel, Hyman, Moshe, Shaya, Yeshaya.*

Saksa (180) Finnish: ethnic name from Germanic *Sachs* 'Saxon'. In the 13th century, this term was used to denote German merchants from across the Baltic. It is found chiefly in southern Finland.

Sakuma (165) Japanese: habitational name from a village so named in Awa (now part of Chiba prefecture). Bearers are descended from the MIURA branch of the TAIRA clan.
GIVEN NAMES Japanese 53%. *Tadashi* (3), *Akira* (2), *Hitoshi* (2), *Minoru* (2), *Aki, Atsuo, Chizuko, Fumiko, Hiroshi, Izumi, Kaoru, Katsuji.*

Sakurai (200) Japanese: habitational name meaning 'cherry blossom well', from any of several places so named; the surname, however, is found mostly in eastern Japan. It is listed in the Shinsen shōjiroku. Cherry blossom is a favorite flower of the Japanese.

GIVEN NAMES Japanese 76%. *Hiroshi* (3), *Takashi* (3), *Yuichiro* (3), *Akio* (2), *Akira* (2), *Atsushi* (2), *Hirofumi* (2), *Hiroyuki* (2), *Koji* (2), *Makoto* (2), *Miwako* (2), *Sadao* (2).

Sala (1001) **1.** Italian, Catalan, Portuguese, southern French (Occitan), and Romanian: from *sala* 'hall', hence a topographic name or an occupational name for someone employed at a hall or manor house. Both the Italian and Catalan names may also be of habitational origin: in the case of Italian, from (amongst others) Sala Biellese (Biella province), Sala Consilina (Salerno province), and Sala Monferrato (Alessandria), and in the case of Catalan from places called Sala or La Sala. This name is very common in Catalonia. **2.** Spanish, Asturian-Leonese, and Aragonese: in some cases, habitational name from places called Sala (Asturies and Aragón) or La Sala (Asturies). **3.** Hungarian: from a short form of the Biblical name SALAMON (see SOLOMON). **4.** Muslim: variant of SALAH.

GIVEN NAMES Italian 11%; Spanish 9%. *Angelo* (5), *Salvatore* (4), *Arturo* (3), *Enrico* (2), *Alba, Alberto, Biagio, Carmine, Claudio, Dante, Erminio, Giovanni, Giuseppe, Guido, Livio, Lucio; Jose* (4), *Manuel* (3), *Luis* (2), *Marta* (2), *Andres, Annaliza, Carlos, Cesar.*

Salaam (204) Muslim: from a personal name based on Arabic *salām* 'peace', 'safety', 'security'. *As-Salām* 'the All-Peaceable' is an attribute of Allah. *As-salāmu 'alaikum* 'peace be upon you' is a universal greeting among Muslims. *Salām* is used in combination with other words to form names, e.g. **'Abdus Salām** 'servant of the All-Peaceable', i.e. Allah. This name is widespread throughout the Muslim world. It is a cognate of the Jewish and Christian Biblical name SOLOMON (Arabic form SULEIMAN).

GIVEN NAMES Muslim 65%. *Abdul* (6), *Ali* (3), *Khadijah* (3), *Rashad* (3), *Rashid* (3), *Bilal* (2), *Dawud* (2), *Maryam* (2), *Najla* (2), *Aaliyah, Abdel, Abdul Karim.*

Salada (134) Catalan: topographic name from *salada*, past participle of *salar* 'to salt' (water or soil), or a habitational name from Salada (Málaga) or La Salada (Seville), named from the same word.

Saladin (306) **1.** Muslim: from an Arabic personal name, *Ṭallāḥ ud-Dīn* 'righteousness of religion'. This was the title adopted by Yusuf ibn-Ayyub, sultan of Egypt (1138–93), known to the western world as *Saladin*, who opposed, for the most part successfully, the Crusades undertaken by Richard I of England and Philip II of France. This name is widespread throughout the Muslim world. **2.** French: nick-

name for a blustering or tyrannical individual, from the name of the medieval Egyptian sultan (see 1 above), who, because of his success in combating the Crusaders, became demonized in French and Italian folklore as a monster second only to Herod.

GIVEN NAMES French 4%. *Jacques, Pierre.*

Saladino (686) Italian: from the personal name *Saladino*, from Arabic (see SALADIN), or nickname from this word denoting a bully or tyrant.

GIVEN NAMES Italian 17%; Spanish 4%. *Angelo* (4), *Carmelo* (3), *Vito* (3), *Gasper* (2), *Onofrio* (2), *Salvatore* (2), *Alfonso, Antonio, Augustino, Aurelio, Crisanto, Dionisio, Gaspare, Nicola, Mario, Pino, Quirino; Gaspar, Jesus, Juan.*

Salafia (199) Southern Italian: from a nickname derived from Arabic *ṣalaf* 'arrogance'.

GIVEN NAMES Italian 18%. *Rosario* (2), *Salvatore* (2), *Angelo, Emanuele, Mirella, Nunzio, Sal, Santo.*

Salah (249) **1.** Muslim: from a personal name based on Arabic *ṣalāḥ* 'piety', 'righteousness', 'goodness'. *Ṭallāḥ* is used in combination with other words, for example **Ṭallāḥ ud-Dīn** (see SALADIN). The name is widespread in all Muslim countries. **2.** Jewish (Sephardic): adoption of the Arabic name.

GIVEN NAMES Muslim 52%. *Isam* (4), *Samir* (4), *Osama* (3), *Salah* (3), *Shamil* (3), *Abdo* (2), *Abdullah* (2), *Awad* (2), *Hashem* (2), *Hassan* (2), *Khaled* (2), *Maher* (2).

Salahuddin (132) Muslim: see SALADIN.

GIVEN NAMES Muslim 80%. *Sultan* (5), *Abu* (4), *Khalid* (4), *Kazi* (3), *Mohammed* (3), *Muhammad* (3), *Syed* (3), *Abdullah* (2), *Ahmad* (2), *Azhar* (2), *Nadirah* (2), *Wali* (2).

Salais (130) Hispanic: unexplained. This name is mainly found in northern Mexico.

GIVEN NAMES Spanish 48%. *Juan* (4), *Jesus* (2), *Jose* (2), *Raul* (2), *Alejos, Alfonso, Alicia, Armando, Armondo, Cesar, Delfino, Demetrio.*

Salaiz (108) Hispanic: variant of SALAIS.

GIVEN NAMES Spanish 26%. *Manuel* (3), *Jose* (2), *Rodolfo* (2), *Abelardo, Aida, Alfonso, Alonso, Bernardo, Elena, Faustino, Francisco, Jovita.*

Salak (193) **1.** Hungarian, Polish, Czech (**Salák**), and Slovak: from the personal name *Salak* (Czech *Salák*), a pet form of the Biblical name SALOMON or SALAMON (see SOLOMON). **2.** Czech: nickname or occupational name from *salák*, a Turkish soldier.

GIVEN NAMES Polish 4%. *Wasyl, Zofia.*

Salam (203) Muslim: variant of SALAAM.

GIVEN NAMES Muslim 78%. *Abdus* (15), *Abdul* (8), *Mohamed* (5), *Mohammed* (5), *Syed* (4), *Abdu* (2), *Gamil* (2), *Omar* (2), *Sami* (2), *Tanvir* (2), *Tareq* (2), *Yasser* (2).

Salama (273) **1.** Muslim: from a personal name based on Arabic *salamah* 'peace'. Salamah ibn 'Amr ibn al-Akwā was one of the ten Companions of the Prophet Muhammad. A related name is *Salāmah*, meaning 'safety', 'security', or 'integrity'. This name is found in combinations such as **Salāmat Allah** (**Salāmatullah**) meaning 'security of Allah'. **2.** Jewish (Sephardic): Arabic translation (see 1) of the Hebrew name *Shlomoh* (see SALOMON, SOLOMON).

GIVEN NAMES Muslim 41%; French 4%; Jewish 4%. *Mohamed* (5), *Mahmoud* (3), *Mostafa* (3), *Samir* (3), *Ahmed* (2), *Emad* (2), *Essam* (2), *Hany* (2), *Mamdouh* (2), *Nabil* (2), *Yousef* (2), *Amira; Andre* (2), *Jean-Pierre, Yves; Moises* (2), *Ovadia* (2), *Asaf, Mayer, Meir.*

Salamanca (276) Spanish: habitational name from the city of Salamanca in western Spain, which is of pre-Roman foundation and obscure etymology. During the Middle Ages it was one of the leading cultural centers of Europe, and the surname may in some cases have been been a respectful nickname for someone who had visited the city.

GIVEN NAMES Spanish 52%. *Jose* (10), *Carlos* (5), *Manuel* (5), *Miguel* (4), *Jesus* (3), *Jorge* (3), *Juan* (3), *Roberto* (3), *Adriana* (2), *Cesar* (2), *Eduardo* (2), *Esperanza* (2); *Federico, Leonardo, Pio, Salvator, Salvatore.*

Salame (106) Muslim: variant of SALAMA.

GIVEN NAMES Muslim 25%; Spanish 17%; French 5%. *Mohamad* (2), *Adnan, Ali, Bechara, Hassan, Hoda, Kamal, Kamil, Kareem, Mahmoud, Mansour, Mounir; Pablo* (3), *Jorge* (2), *Jose* (2), *Juan Carlos* (2), *Alfredo, Blanca, Guillermo, Jacobo, Melida; Andre, Antoine.*

Salameh (192) Muslim: variant of SALAMA.

GIVEN NAMES Muslim 62%. *Bassam* (4), *Ibrahim* (3), *Tamer* (3), *Yousef* (3), *Adnan* (2), *Ahmed* (2), *Jamal* (2), *Kamal* (2), *Khaled* (2), *Khodr* (2), *Mohammed* (2), *Mustafa* (2).

Salamon (790) Variant spelling of SOLOMON, the usual spelling in Hungarian and Slovenian (**Šalamon**) and a common variant in German, Dutch, Polish, English, and other languages. Compare SALOMON, SULEIMAN.

GIVEN NAMES Jewish 4%. *Emanuel* (2), *Akiva, Maier, Mayer, Moshe, Tali, Tziporah, Uzi, Yehuda.*

Salamone (1254) Italian: from the Biblical personal name *Salomone* (see SOLOMON).

GIVEN NAMES Italian 18%. *Salvatore* (13), *Angelo* (12), *Vito* (8), *Sal* (7), *Domenic* (4), *Santo* (3), *Attilio* (2), *Dante* (2), *Saverio* (2), *Antonio, Biagio, Carmel.*

Salamy (112) French: from a pet form of the personal name SALOMON (see SOLOMON).

GIVEN NAMES French 4%. *Andre, Pierre.*

Salant (123) Jewish (from Lithuania): habitational name from Salant, the Yiddish name for Salantai in Lithuania.
GIVEN NAMES Jewish 7%. *Ari, Hyman, Rakhil.*

Salas (5775) **1.** Spanish, Galician, Aragonese, and Portuguese: habitational name from any of the numerous places called with Salas, like Salas and Salas de los Barrios, (Galicia), Salas de los Infantes, (Burgos province), Salas Altas and Salas Baxas (Aragon), from the plural of SALA. **2.** Catalan and Asturian-Leonese: variant of SALES. **3.** Americanized spelling of Hungarian *Szálas*, a nickname from *szálas* 'tall'.
GIVEN NAMES Spanish 45%; Portuguese 9%. *Jose* (114), *Juan* (89), *Manuel* (55), *Jesus* (54), *Carlos* (50), *Luis* (46), *Pedro* (35), *Raul* (27), *Francisco* (26), *Miguel* (26), *Ruben* (26), *Ricardo* (24); *Duarte, Godofredo, Joaquim, Zaragoza.*

Salata (381) **1.** Italian: from a derivative of *salare* 'to salt' (from Latin *salire*), perhaps applied as a topographic name for someone living by brackish, salty water or a nickname or metonymic occupational name. **2.** Polish (**Sałata**) and Hungarian (**Saláta**): metonymic occupational name for a greengrocer, or possibly a nickname, from *saláta* 'lettuce'.
GIVEN NAMES Polish 5%. *Wieslaw* (2), *Bogdan, Edyta, Ewa, Ignacy, Janina, Jerzy.*

Salathe (109) Perhaps a variant or altered form of **Salat**, which Brechenmacher believes to be a shortened form of **Salatin**, **Saladin**, from the personal name *Salatin* or, in northwestern German, from a reduced form of the person name *Salentin*.
GIVEN NAMES German 9%. *Erwin* (2), *Leonhard, Matthias.*

Salatino (192) Italian: diminutive of **Salato**, the masculine form of SALATA.
GIVEN NAMES Italian 20%. *Vito* (5), *Rocco* (2), *Arcangelo, Domenic, Giovanni, Massimo, Raffaele, Renzo, Riccardo, Sal, Salvatore.*

Salava (102) Origin unidentified.

Salay (209) Hungarian (**Szalay**): regional name for someone from Zala county in western Hungary, or a habitational name from any of various villages called Szala.

Salaz (191) Spanish: unflattering nickname from *salaz* 'lecherous', 'lascivious'.
GIVEN NAMES Spanish 27%. *Jose* (3), *Catalina* (2), *Juan* (2), *Avelina, Beatriz, Carlos, Celestino, Domingo, Eloy, Eluteria, Ernesto, Esequiel.*

Salazar (14156) **1.** Spanish: habitational name from a place called Salazar in Burgos, probably named with *sala* 'hall' + Basque *za(h)ar* 'old', and thus a Basque equivalent of SAAVEDRA. **2.** Spanish: Castilianized variant of Basque **Zaraitzu**, a habitational name from a town so named in Navarre.
GIVEN NAMES Spanish 45%; Portuguese 9%. *Jose* (325), *Juan* (192), *Manuel* (132),

Carlos (117), *Luis* (107), *Jesus* (104), *Francisco* (90), *Jorge* (78), *Ruben* (77), *Pedro* (68), *Roberto* (65), *Mario* (60); *Goncalo, Ligia, Sil.*

Salb (116) German: **1.** metonymic occupational name for a maker or seller of ointments, from Middle High German *salbe* 'ointment', 'salve'. The name also came to mean 'flatterer', 'toady'. **2.** nickname from Midle High German *salwe* 'dark' 'sallow', 'dirty'. **3.** variant of **Salet(e)l**, probably Austrian, also found in the Gottschee area in Slovenia.
GIVEN NAME German 4%. *Wolfgang.*

Salber (122) French (Alsace): from German **Salber**, an occupational name or an ointment maker, from an agent noun derivative of Middle High German *salbe* 'ointment'.
GIVEN NAMES French 5%. *Henri, Michel.*

Salberg (249) **1.** Norwegian: habitational name from farmsteads in Trøndelag named *Soðulberg* in Old Norse, from *soðul* 'saddle' + *berg* 'mountain', with reference to the shape of the mountains. **2.** Jewish (Ashkenazic): ornamental name composed of a short form of the personal name SALOMON (see SOLOMON) + German *Berg* 'mountain', 'hill'.

Salce (156) Italian: topographic name from *salice* 'willow tree' (Latin *salix*, genitive *salicis*). This name is also found in Mexico.
GIVEN NAMES Spanish 13%; Italian 8%. *Agustin, Francisca, Juan, Juana, Luis, Paz, Rafael, Ricardo, Valerio; Antonio, Eustacchio, Pasquale, Smaraldo.*

Salcedo (1575) **1.** Spanish: habitational name from any of numerous places named Salcedo, so named from a collective form of *salce* 'willow tree'. Compare SALCE. **2.** Spanish: Castilianized variant of Basque **Saratsu**, a habitational name from a town so named, in Araba, Basque Country.
GIVEN NAMES Spanish 53%. *Jose* (54), *Juan* (29), *Luis* (18), *Francisco* (15), *Rafael* (15), *Ana* (13), *Jesus* (13), *Carlos* (12), *Manuel* (12), *Miguel* (12), *Pedro* (12), *Jorge* (11).

Salcido (1097) Spanish: variant spelling of SALCEDO.
GIVEN NAMES Spanish 42%. *Manuel* (27), *Jose* (18), *Jesus* (16), *Carlos* (12), *Juan* (10), *Ruben* (10), *Luis* (9), *Roberto* (9), *Raul* (8), *Francisco* (6), *Juana* (5), *Adelina* (4).

Saldana (2904) Spanish (**Saldaña**): habitational name from any of the places in the provinces of Palencia, Segovia, and Burgos named Saldaña.
GIVEN NAMES Spanish 48%. *Jose* (70), *Juan* (38), *Jesus* (27), *Francisco* (25), *Carlos* (23), *Guadalupe* (20), *Ruben* (17), *Luis* (16), *Manuel* (15), *Mario* (15), *Rafael* (15), *Miguel* (14).

Saldarriaga (108) Basque: variant of **Zaldarriaga**, a Basque topographic name of uncertain derivation; possibly from *zaldi* 'horse', but more likely *zaldu* 'wood', 'holt' + *arriaga* 'stoney'.

GIVEN NAMES Spanish 63%. *Juan* (5), *Carlos* (4), *Mauricio* (3), *Alvaro* (2), *Blanca* (2), *Diego* (2), *Gustavo* (2), *Jaime* (2), *Jairo* (2), *Adriana, Alejandro, Ana.*

Saldivar (1464) Spanish (**Saldívar**; from Basque): Castilianized variant of Basque **Zaldibar**, a habitational name from a place so named in Biscay province. The place name is of uncertain derivation: it may be from *zaldu* 'wood', 'copse' or from *zaldi* 'horse' + *ibar* 'water meadow', 'fertile plain'.
GIVEN NAMES Spanish 51%. *Jose* (43), *Juan* (29), *Jesus* (15), *Manuel* (14), *Enrique* (12), *Raul* (12), *Carlos* (11), *Roberto* (11), *Alfredo* (9), *Pedro* (9), *Ramon* (9), *Alfonso* (8).

Saldutti (120) Italian: from *Saldo* (a short form of the personal name *Ansaldo*) + the suffix *-utto.*
GIVEN NAMES Italian 9%. *Carmine, Pasquale, Salvator.*

Sale (1408) **1.** English: from Middle English *sale* 'hall', a topographic name for someone living at a hall or manor house, or a metonymic occupational name for someone employed at a hall or manor house. **2.** English: from Middle English *salwe* 'sallow' (a tree, a kind of willow), hence a topographic name for someone who lived by a sallow tree, or a habitational name from for example Sale in Greater Manchester, named from the old dative form of this word, in *atte sale*. **3.** French (**Salé**): from Old French *salé* 'salty', hence a topographic or occupational name for someone who lived by or worked in a salt marsh, or, in a figurative sense, a nickname for an amusing or witty person.

Saleeby (261) Origin unidentified.

Saleem (329) Muslim: variant of SALIM.
GIVEN NAMES Muslim 80%. *Mohammad* (30), *Muhammad* (16), *Mohammed* (11), *Abdul* (8), *Tariq* (5), *Ahmed* (4), *Khalid* (4), *Zahid* (4), *Ameer* (3), *Babar* (3), *Syed* (3), *Amer* (2).

Saleh (1016) Muslim: from a personal name based on Arabic *şāliḥ* 'pious', 'righteous', 'virtuous' (see the Qur'an 26: 83). Saleh is the name of a messenger of Allah (see the Qur'an 7:75). This name is widespread throughout the Muslim world.
GIVEN NAMES Muslim 73%. *Ali* (21), *Mohammed* (15), *Hassan* (12), *Abdul* (11), *Ahmed* (11), *Mohamed* (11), *Mahmoud* (10), *Khaled* (9), *Saleh* (9), *Mohammad* (8), *Jamal* (7), *Said* (7).

Salehi (173) Muslim: adjectival form meaning 'descendant of (or associated with) SALEH'.
GIVEN NAMES Muslim 75%. *Hamid* (5), *Abdollah* (3), *Mohsen* (3), *Nader* (3), *Amir* (2), *Azim* (2), *Fariba* (2), *Jahan* (2), *Mehdi* (2), *Mehrdad* (2), *Mohammad* (2), *Abdul.*

Salek (199) **1.** Czech (**Šálek**): from a pet form of the personal name *Šalamoun* (see SOLOMON). **2.** Muslim: variant of SALIK.

Salem (1902) **1.** Muslim: from a personal name based on Arabic *sālim* or *salīm* 'safe', 'secure', 'perfect', 'complete'. Sālim ibn 'Umayr was one of the Companions of the Prophet Muhammad. **2.** French (Alsace): habitational name from a place named Salem in Haut-Rhin, named for the holy city of Jerusalem.

GIVEN NAMES Muslim 23%. *Mohamed* (11), *Ahmed* (9), *Salem* (9), *Samir* (6), *Omar* (5), *Abdul* (4), *Ahmad* (4), *Mahmoud* (4), *Nabil* (4), *Tarek* (4), *Ali* (3), *Haitham* (3).

Salemi (492) Italian (Sicily): habitational name from a place so called in Trapani.

GIVEN NAMES Italian 12%. *Salvatore* (6), *Sal* (2), *Antonio*, *Biagio*, *Carmelo*, *Caterina*, *Cesario*, *Ciro*, *Matteo*, *Paolo*, *Pasquale*, *Santo*.

Salemme (183) Southern Italian: from an adjectival derivative of SALEMI.

GIVEN NAMES Italian 6%. *Antonio* (2), *Cosmo*, *Rino*, *Romeo*, *Sal*.

Salen (104) Origin unidentified.

Salentine (118) Origin unidentified.

Saler (131) **1.** English: unexplained. Probably a variant spelling of SAYLOR. **2.** German: variant of **Salmann**, an occupational name from Middle High German *sal(e)man* 'trustee', 'guardian'.

Salera (109) Italian: habitational name from a place so called.

GIVEN NAMES Italian 9%. *Angelo*, *Dante*, *Nino*, *Vitaliano*.

Salerno (3410) Southern Italian: habitational name from the city of Salerno in Campania.

GIVEN NAMES Italian 12%. *Angelo* (9), *Antonio* (9), *Sal* (9), *Salvatore* (9), *Pasquale* (7), *Carmine* (5), *Rocco* (5), *Aldo* (4), *Nunzio* (4), *Enrico* (3), *Francesco* (3), *Gaspare* (3).

Sales (2266) **1.** English: from Middle English *salwes* 'sallows', a topographic name for someone who lived by a group of sallow trees (see SALE 2). **2.** Catalan and Asturian-Leonese: a habitational name from any of the places called Sales, like Sales de Llierca (Catalonia) or Sales (Asturies), from the plural of SALA 1. This name is specially common in Catalonia. **3.** Portuguese: habitational name from a place that is probably so called from a Germanic personal name of uncertain form and derivation. **4.** Portuguese: religious byname adopted since the 17th century in honor of St. Francis of Sales (1567–1622), who was born at the Château de Sales in Savoy. **5.** French (**Salès**): habitational name from places named Salès in Cantal and Tarn.

GIVEN NAMES Spanish 4%. *Jose* (8), *Efren* (4), *Alberto* (3), *Francisco* (3), *Manuel* (3), *Camilo* (2), *Carlos* (2), *Fernando* (2), *Juan* (2), *Juanita* (2), *Mario* (2), *Ofelia* (2).

Salesky (114) Probably an Americanized spelling of Czech **Záleský** (see ZALESKY).

Saletta (107) Italian: diminutive of SALA.

GIVEN NAMES Italian 12%. *Marco*, *Rocco*, *Salvatore*.

Saley (113) English: unexplained.

Salgado (3241) Galician and Portuguese: nickname for a witty person, from *salgado* 'salty', figuratively 'witty', 'piquant' (from Late Latin *salicatus*, past participle of *salicare* 'to give salt to').

GIVEN NAMES Spanish 55%; Portuguese 11%. *Jose* (102), *Juan* (41), *Luis* (35), *Francisco* (32), *Manuel* (31), *Antonio* (28), *Jesus* (27), *Carlos* (25), *Javier* (21), *Miguel* (21), *Pedro* (19), *Mario* (18), *Roberto* (17); *Albano* (2), *Agostinho*.

Salge (117) **1.** North German: nickname for a person with a cheerful disposition, from Middle Low German *sālich* 'happy', 'fortunate'. **2.** from the short form of a Germanic personal name, from *sal* 'black', 'dirty'.

GIVEN NAMES German 6%; Scandinavian 4%. *Egon*, *Helmuth*, *Oskar*; *Hilmar*.

Salguero (394) Spanish: **1.** habitational name from Salguero in Burgos province, or a Castilianized form of the Galician habitational name **Salgueiro**, from any of numerous places so named from *salguero* meaning either 'willow tree' or 'place in which animals are given salt' (from *salgar* 'to salt'). **2.** possibly from a homonymous archaic term denoting a spot where salt was given to cattle (Late Latin *salicarium*, a derivative of *salicare* 'to give salt to', from *sal* 'salt').

GIVEN NAMES Spanish 51%. *Jose* (13), *Carlos* (9), *Jorge* (6), *Mario* (6), *Juan* (5), *Francisco* (4), *Julio* (4), *Manuel* (4), *Ricardo* (4), *Armando* (3), *Rafael* (3), *Alonso* (2).

Salib (104) Arabic: from the Arabic Christian name *salīb* 'cross', corresponding to Greek STAVROS.

GIVEN NAMES Arabic 52%. *Hany* (5), *Nader* (4), *Kamal* (2), *Samir* (2), *Amgad*, *Amir*, *Anis*, *Awni*, *Azmi*, *Bahig*, *Fadel*, *Gamil*.

Saliba (627) Arabic: variant of SALIB.

GIVEN NAMES Arabic 10%; French 6%. *Anis* (2), *Bassam* (2), *Beshara* (2), *Issam* (2), *Tammer* (2), *Assad*, *Charbel*, *Ghada*, *Ghassan*, *Issa*, *Jalal*, *Jamal*; *Georges* (2), *Pierre* (2), *Alcyone*, *Francois*, *Gisele*, *Hyacinthe*, *Jean-Claude*.

Salido (109) Spanish: **1.** nickname from *salido*, probably in the figurative sense 'ardent', 'lusty'. **2.** possibly a habitational name from places in Ciudad Real called El Salido, from *salido* in the sense 'projecting', 'prominent'.

GIVEN NAMES Spanish 42%. *Alfonso* (4), *Arnoldo* (2), *Carlos* (2), *Efrain* (2), *Fernando* (2), *Francisco* (2), *Prisciliano* (2), *Arturo*, *Blanca*, *Enrique*, *Epifanio*, *Erlinda*.

Saliga (101) Origin unidentified.

Salih (140) Muslim: variant of SALEH.

GIVEN NAMES Muslim 65%. *Hafid* (2), *Mohamed* (2), *Tarig* (2), *Abdul*, *Abdullah*, *Ahmad*, *Akram*, *Ali*, *Assad*, *Azem*, *Aziz*, *Driss*.

Salik (101) Muslim: from Arabic *sālik*, literally 'traveler', 'wayfarer'. This is a term used for members of a Sufi order whose intention is to actively seek the realization of God. This name is common in all Muslim countries.

GIVEN NAMES Muslim 12%. *Omar* (2), *Yasser* (2), *Abdul Majid*, *Farouk*, *Inaam*, *Noor*, *Rasheed*.

Salim (397) Muslim and Jewish (Sephardic): from a personal name based on Arabic *salīm* 'perfect', 'faultless', 'safe', 'secure'. Salīm bin Thabet was one of the Companions of the Prophet Muhammad. The Mughal emperor Jahangir (1605–1627) was also known as Prince *Salīm*. This is a widespread name in all Muslim countries.

GIVEN NAMES Muslim 57%. *Mohammad* (12), *Mohammed* (7), *Muhammad* (5), *Abdul* (4), *Ahmed* (4), *Ali* (4), *Mohamed* (3), *Salim* (3), *Syed* (3), *Abbas* (2), *Adnan* (2), *Bibi* (2).

Salin (157) **1.** French: habitational name from places so named in Cantal, Jura, Savoie, and Seine-et-Marne, from *salin* saltmarsh. **2.** Swedish (also common in Finland): variant of SAHLIN.

GIVEN NAMES Finnish 7%. *Eino*, *Jorma*, *Juha*, *Pentti*.

Salina (124) Spanish: habitational name from La Salina in Teruel province, or a topographic name from *salina* 'saltworks', 'salt marsh'.

GIVEN NAMES Spanish 17%; French 5%. *Jose* (2), *Alejandrina*, *Elida*, *Enrique*, *Francisco*, *Guilermo*, *Juan Jesus*, *Manuel*, *Miguel Angel*, *Pascasio*, *Porfirio*, *Rogelio*; *Jean-Paul*, *Marcel*.

Salinas (8108) Spanish: habitational name from any of the numerous places named Salinas, from the plural of *salina* 'saltworks' (Latin *salinae*, a derivative of *sal* 'salt').

GIVEN NAMES Spanish 50%. *Jose* (196), *Juan* (138), *Manuel* (80), *Jesus* (64), *Carlos* (63), *Mario* (55), *Luis* (52), *Raul* (52), *Guadalupe* (51), *Ricardo* (47), *Ruben* (47), *Roberto* (45).

Saline (197) French: from *saline* 'saltworks', hence a topographic name for someone who lived near a saltworks or an occupational nickname for someone who worked at one.

Saling (547) German: patronymic from a short form of the personal name SALOMON (see SOLOMON).

Salinger (378) **1.** English (of Norman origin): habitational name from Saint-Léger in La Manche or Saint-Léger-aux-Bois in Seine-Maritime, both so called from the dedication of their churches to St. Leger (see LEDGER), the martyred 7th-century bishop of Autun. **2.** German and Jewish (Ashkenazic): from a Germanized form of the personal name SALOMON.

Salins (100) **1.** Latvian (**Saliņš**): topographic name for someone living on an island, from a derivative of *sala* 'island'. **2.** Dutch: from a pet form of the personal name *Salomon* (see SOLOMON).
GIVEN NAME Latvian 5%. *Arturs.*

Salis (174) **1.** Southern French, Swiss French, and Catalan (**Salís**): unexplained. **2.** Greek: occupational name for a ferryman, from *sali* 'raft', 'ferry', classical Greek *issalion* (from *issos* 'equal' + *als* 'sea', 'water line').
GIVEN NAMES Spanish 4%. *Ruben* (2), *Amparo, Armando, Emilio, Juana, Rodolfo.*

Salisbury (4839) English: **1.** habitational name from the city in Wiltshire, the Roman name of which was *Sorviodunum* (of British origin). In the Old English period the second element (from Celtic *dūn* 'fortress') was dropped and *Sorvio-* (of unexplained meaning) became *Searo-* in Old English as the result of folk etymological association with Old English *searu* 'armor'; to this an explanatory *burh* 'fortress', 'manor', 'town' was added. The city is recorded in Domesday Book as *Sarisberie*; the change of *-r-* to *-l-* is the result of later dissimilation. **2.** habitational name from Salesbury in Lancashire, so named from Old English *salh* 'willow' + *burh* 'fortress', 'manor'.

Salk (202) Jewish (American): **1.** Respelling of **Zalk**, a Jewish name from Lithuania, of uncertain origin; most likely a pet form of the Yiddish personal name *Zalkind* (see SALKIN). **2.** Shortened form of some Ashkenazic surname.
GIVEN NAMES Jewish 5%. *Abbe, Hyman.*

Salkeld (223) English (Cumbria): habitational name from Salkeld in Cumbria, from Old English *salh* 'willow', 'sallow' + *hylte* 'wood'. This surname has been present (though never common) in Ireland for centuries.

Salkin (258) **1.** English: from a pet form (with the Middle English diminutive suffix *-kin*) of a personal name, possibly *Saul*, but more probably *Salomon* (see SOLOMON). **2.** Jewish (Ashkenazic): from the Yiddish personal name *Zalkind*, derived from SALOMON.

Salko (111) Polish: from a short form of the personal name SALOMON (see SOLOMON).

Salkowski (113) Polish (**Sałkowski**): habitational name from Sałków.

Sall (414) **1.** English: variant of SALE 1. **2.** English: from a short form of a personal name beginning with *Sal-*, for example SALOMON. **3.** Swedish (**Säll**): nickname from *säll* 'happy', 'fortunate', probably a soldier's name. **4.** African: unexplained.
GIVEN NAMES African 6%. *Cheikh* (3), *Amadou* (2), *Mamadou* (2), *Aliou, Babacar, Oumar, Serigne.*

Salladay (119) See SOLLIDAY.

Sallade (196) **1.** Probably an Americanized form of German SALATHE. **2.** Alternatively, perhaps an altered spelling of French **Salade**, a habitational name from a place in Haute-Garonne, which may have denoted a storage place for salt.

Sallas (182) Greek: nickname from Turkish *salli* 'broad', 'wide'.

Salle (194) **1.** French: occupational name for someone employed at a manor house, from Old French *salle* 'hall'. **2.** French (**Sallé**): variant of *Salé* 'salty' (see SALE) 3.
GIVEN NAMES French 4%. *Jacques, Pierre.*

Sallee (2297) Variant of French **Sallé(e)** (see SALLE) 2.

Saller (189) German: **1.** habitational name from Sallern in Bavaria. **2.** topographic name for someone who lived in an area where sallow willows grew, from Middle High German *salhe* 'sallow tree' + *-er*, suffix denoting an inhabitant.
GIVEN NAMES German 6%. *Aloysius, Bodo, Otto.*

Salles (209) **1.** French: variant of SALLE 1. **2.** Catalan (**Sallés**): possibly variant of **Sellés**, or variant of **Cellers**, two habitational names from the so named Catalan towns. **3.** Catalan: plural variant of **Salla**, unexplained. This name is common in the Lleida region.
GIVEN NAMES Spanish 10%; French 5%. *Carlos* (2), *Luiz* (2), *Ricardo* (2), *Ana, Armenia, Ernesto, Fabio, Francisco, Gustavo, Jaime, Luzia, Manuel; Andre, Emile, Jean-Luc.*

Salley (1700) Of uncertain origin. **1.** Possibly from the French personal name *Charlet* or *Sarlet*, pet forms of CHARLES. **2.** Alternatively a nickname based on French *sale* 'dirty'. **3.** Variant of SALLY.

Sallie (237) English (Lancashire): unexplained. Perhaps a variant of Irish **McSally** (an Anglicized form of Gaelic **Mac Salaigh**), which MacLysaght describes as an earlier form of SOLLY. Compare SALLEY.

Salling (168) Danish: regional name from Salling, a region of northeast Denmark that takes its name from Salling Fjord, around which it lies.

Sallis (278) **1.** English: topographic for someone who lived where sallows (a kind of willow) grew, from the plural of Middle English *salwe* 'sallow tree'. **2.** Greek: descriptive nickname from Turkish *salli* 'large and wide'.

Salloum (185) Muslim: variant of SALAAM, found especially in North Africa and other areas of former French influence.
GIVEN NAMES Muslim 37%; French 9%. *Bassel* (2), *Habib* (2), *Kaleel* (2), *Adnan, Ahmad, Anis, Bassam, Bishara, Eyad, Fadi, Farouk, Fayez; Antoine* (2), *Armand, Camille, Emile, Gabrielle, Michel.*

Salls (251) Americanized spelling of Dutch **Sals**, habitational name from a place in Limburg province, named for its salt deposits.

Sally (346) Irish: reduced Anglicized form of Gaelic **Mac Salaigh**.

Salm (437) **1.** German (southwest and Rhineland) and Dutch: from Middle High German *salm*, Dutch *zalm* 'salmon', probably in most cases a habitational name from a house distinguished by the sign of a salmon, but in some cases an occupational name for a salmon fisher. **2.** German: habitational name from Salm on the Mosel, or from Salm in Alsace. **3.** Dutch (**Van Salm**): habitational name from Zalm in Dutch Limburg or Vielsalm in the Belgian province of Luxembourg.
GIVEN NAMES German 7%. *Kurt* (3), *Erna, Ernst, Erwin, Gunther, Heinz, Johann, Otto, Rainer.*

Salman (412) **1.** Muslim: from a personal name based on Arabic *salmān* 'safe'. Salmān al-Farsi was one of the Companions of the Prophet Muhammad. This name is widespread throughout the Muslim world. **2.** Variant of SULEIMAN. **3.** Jewish (Ashkenazic): variant of SALMON 2. **4.** English, French, Dutch, and German: from a reduced form of SALOMON. Compare SALMON 1.
GIVEN NAMES Muslim 39%. *Mohammad* (4), *Salman* (4), *Faisal* (3), *Ahmad* (2), *Amira* (2), *Imad* (2), *Issam* (2), *Khalid* (2), *Mohamed* (2), *Mohammed* (2), *Moosa* (2), *Omar* (2).

Salmans (198) Patronymic from SALMAN 2 and 3.

Salmela (191) Finnish: topographic or ornamental name from *salmi* 'strait' + the local ending *-la*. It originated mainly as an ornamental name adopted during the names conversion movement at the end of the 19th century.
GIVEN NAMES Finnish 7%; Scandinavian 7%. *Juha, Reino, Senja, Sulo, Veikko; Erik* (3), *Jalmer.*

Salmen (253) Variant of English SALMON or German SALMAN.
GIVEN NAMES German 4%. *Wilhelm* (2), *Ilse.*

Salmeri (111) Italian (Sicily): occupational name for a muleteer, Sicilian *sarmeri, salmeri.*
GIVEN NAMES Italian 21%. *Carlo* (3), *Salvatore* (2), *Angelo, Sal.*

Salmeron (399) Spanish (**Salmerón**): habitational name from Salmerón in Guadalajara province, possibly also the one in Murcia.
GIVEN NAMES Spanish 57%. *Jose* (26), *Juan* (10), *Pedro* (6), *Miguel* (5), *Manuel* (4), *Alejandro* (3), *Francisco* (3), *Jesus* (3), *Julio* (3), *Carlos* (2), *Eduardo* (2), *Elvira* (2); *Eliseo* (2), *Alfonse, Antonio, Aureliano, Bartolo, Ceasar, Fausto, Federico, Filiberto, Marco, Rosaria, Sal.*

Salmi (372) Finnish: topographic name from Finnish *salmi* 'strait', a name adopted during the names conversion movement at the end of the 19th century. In America it is sometimes an abbreviation of SALMINEN.

GIVEN NAMES Finnish 15%. *Eino* (5), *Toivo* (4), *Waino* (3), *Reino* (2), *Jorma*, *Jussi*, *Kaino*, *Niilo*, *Pirjo*, *Raili*, *Seppo*, *Toimi*.

Salminen (258) Finnish: variant of SALMI + the common surname suffix *-nen*.

GIVEN NAMES Finnish 20%; German 4%; Scandinavian 4%. *Eino* (4), *Waino* (2), *Wilho* (2), *Antti*, *Armas*, *Ilmari*, *Jarmo*, *Jouko*, *Jyrki*, *Markku*, *Olavi*, *Outi*; *Otto*; *Nils*.

Salmon (4798) **1.** English and French: from the Middle English, Old French personal name *Salmon*, *Saumon*, a reduced form of *Salomon* (see SOLOMON). **2.** Jewish (Ashkenazic): from the Yiddish male personal name *Zalmen*, derived via a German form from Hebrew *Shelomo* (see SOLOMON). **3.** Irish: part translation of Gaelic **Ó Bradáin** 'descendant of *Bradán*', a personal name, probably from *bradach* 'spirited', but written the same as a word meaning 'salmon'; this name is also sometimes translated FISHER. The English surname is also present in Ireland (chiefly in counties Leix and Kilkenny).

Salmond (213) Scottish and French: variant of SALMON 1.

GIVEN NAMES French 5%. *Camille*, *Monique*.

Salmons (1095) English: patronymic from SALMON 1.

Salmonsen (137) Danish and Norwegian: patronymic from the personal name *Salomon* (see SOLOMON).

GIVEN NAMES Scandinavian 5%. *Nels*, *Oluf*.

Salmonson (232) Respelling of Swedish **Salmonsson**, a patronymic from the personal name *Sal(o)mon* (see SOLOMON), or the Danish and Norwegian cognate, SALMONSEN.

GIVEN NAMES Scandinavian 6%. *Einer*, *Erik*, *Sven*.

Salo (1201) Finnish: ornamental name from *salo* 'forested wilderness', perhaps chosen in some cases as a topographic name by someone who lived in such a place.

GIVEN NAMES Finnish 10%. *Eino* (6), *Reino* (6), *Toivo* (6), *Arvo* (4), *Reijo* (4), *Ahti* (3), *Waino* (3), *Sulo* (2), *Tauno* (2), *Veikko* (2), *Aimo*, *Alpo*.

Salois (324) French: of uncertain origin. The name is often Americanized in New England as SALTER or SALTUS.

FOREBEARS The originator of this line in Canada arrived from Flanders, and is documented in the Island of Orleans in 1666.

GIVEN NAMES French 7%. *Armand* (2), *Andre*, *Fabien*, *Normand*.

Salome (175) Spanish and Portuguese (**Salomé**): from the Marian personal name *Maria Salomé*, from the female Biblical name.

GIVEN NAMES Spanish 16%. *Angel*, *Angelina*, *Artemio*, *Domingo*, *Francisca*, *Guadalupe*, *Jaime*, *Jose*, *Juan*, *Manuel*, *Mario*, *Pedro*.

Salomon (1441) Jewish, German, Dutch, Danish, French, Spanish (**Salomón**), and

Polish: the usual spelling in these languages of SOLOMON and a variant in others.

GIVEN NAMES Spanish 10%; German 7%; French 6%; Jewish 5%. *Jose* (5), *Juan* (4), *Luis* (4), *Manuel* (4), *Miguel* (4), *Ramon* (4), *Alejandro* (3), *Osvaldo* (3), *Carlos* (2), *Felipe* (2), *Francisco* (2), *Jesus* (2); *Kurt* (8), *Erwin* (4), *Fritz* (3), *Gerhard* (3), *Hans* (3), *Heinz* (3), *Ilse* (3), *Dietrich* (2), *Lothar* (2), *Ernst*, *Gerhart*, *Gunther*; *Yves* (3), *Marcel* (2), *Pierre* (2), *Andre*, *Clovis*, *Franck*, *Jacques*, *Jean Claude*, *Jeremie*, *Marie Anne*, *Maxime*, *Nadege*; *Avraham* (3), *Chaim* (2), *Erez* (2), *Mayer* (2), *Shlomo* (2), *Sol* (2), *Yaakov* (2), *Batya*, *Gerson*, *Menachem*, *Meyer*, *Miriam*.

Salomone (417) Italian: from the personal name *Salomone*, Italian form of SOLOMON.

GIVEN NAMES Italian 16%. *Angelo* (2), *Gino* (2), *Italo* (2), *Rocco* (2), *Antonio*, *Carlo*, *Cesare*, *Cosimo*, *Franco*, *Geno*, *Leonardo*, *Livio*.

Salon (168) Southern French (Occitan): diminutive of SALLE 1.

GIVEN NAMES French 8%; Spanish 8%; Italian 5%. *Laurent*, *Marcel*, *Nicolle*, *Serge*; *Alberto*, *Aurelio*, *Dionisio*, *Elvira*, *Fernando*, *Florentino*, *Jose*, *Orlando*; *Aldo*, *Antonio*, *Francesca*, *Francesco*, *Gennaro*, *Mauro*.

Salone (193) **1.** French (**Saloné**): variant of SOLOMON. **2.** Italian (Sicily): augmentative of SALA.

GIVEN NAMES French 6%. *Blanchard* (2), *Pierre*.

Salonen (142) Finnish: variant of SALO + the common surname suffix *-nen*. Mostly, this is an ornamental name adopted during the name conversion movement in the late 19th and early 20th centuries.

GIVEN NAMES Scandinavian 9%; Finnish 7%. *Arvi*, *Jukka*, *Olavi*, *Reino*, *Riitta*.

Salopek (216) Serbian and Croatian: nickname from *salo* 'pork fat', 'lard' + a derivative of the verb *peći* 'to bake'.

Salow (167) German: habitational name from Salow in Mecklenburg-West Pomerania.

Salsberry (195) Variant spelling of English SALISBURY.

Salsbery (183) Variant spelling of English SALISBURY.

Salsbury (839) **1.** English: variant spelling of SALISBURY. **2.** Jewish (American): altered form of SALOMON or some other Jewish name beginning with *Sa-*.

Salser (196) Variant of German SALZER.

Salsgiver (210) Part-translation of southwestern German **Salzgeber**, an occupational name for a salt merchant, from Middle High German *salcz* 'salt' + an agent derivative of *geben* 'to give'.

Salsman (534) Altered spelling of German SALZMANN, or of Ashkenazic Jewish cognate **Salzman**.

Salstrom (109) Swedish (**Salström**): ornamental name from *sal* 'hall' + *ström* 'river'.

Salt (342) English: metonymic occupational name for a producer or seller of salt, from Middle English *salt*, or a habitational name from a place in Staffordshire, so called for a salt pit there.

Saltarelli (154) Southern Italian: **1.** patronymic from a pet form of **Salto**, from *Saltus*, an old Tuscan short form of the personal name *Bonassaltus*, meaning 'nice surprise'. **2.** nickname from *salterello* in any of its various meanings: 'maggot' or (in Tuscany) 'grasshopper'; it was also the name of a dance.

GIVEN NAMES Italian 19%. *Claudio* (2), *Mario* (2), *Aniceto*, *Arturo*, *Carmela*, *Guido*, *Luca*, *Olympio*, *Orlando*, *Primo*.

Salter (5077) **1.** English: occupational name for an extractor or seller of salt (a precious commodity in medieval times), from Middle English *salt* 'salt' + the agent suffix *-er*. **2.** English: occupational name for a player on the psaltery, a string instrument, Middle English, Old French *saltere* 'psaltery'. (The Middle English word is derived from Latin *psalterium*, Greek *psaltērion*, from *psallein* 'to sound'). **3.** North German form of SALZER.

Salters (559) English (chiefly northern Ireland): variant of the Lancashire surname **Salthouse**, an occupational name for a worker at a saltworks, a topographic name for someone who lived by a saltworks, or a habitational name from one of the minor places named from a saltworks. There are examples in Furness and Lytham St. Annes, among other places.

Saltiel (103) Jewish (Sephardic): from the male personal Biblical name *Shaltiel* (Haggai 1:1).

GIVEN NAMES Jewish 13%; Spanish 6%; French 5%. *Sol* (3), *Moises*; *Alberto* (2), *Jose*, *Luisa*; *Philippe*, *Serge*.

Saltis (112) Lithuanian (**Šaltis**): nickname from *šaltis* 'frost'.

Saltman (171) **1.** English: variant of SALT. **2.** Translation of German **Saltmann** or Jewish SALZMAN.

GIVEN NAMES French 4%. *Armand*, *Jean-marie*.

Saltmarsh (209) English: topographic name for someone who lived by a saltwater marsh, or a habitational name from places called Saltmarsh, in Gloucestershire and Herefordshire, or Saltmarshe, in East Yorkshire.

GIVEN NAME German 5%. *Kurt* (2).

Salto (101) **1.** Spanish: habitational name from any of the numerous places named Salto, from *salto* 'sloping'. **2.** Catalan (**Saltó**): variant of either **Saltor** or **Sautó**, both of them towns in northern Catalonia, in El Ripollès and El Conflent districts.

GIVEN NAMES Spanish 52%. *Jose* (3), *Marcos* (2), *Miguel* (2), *Raymundo* (2), *Reyna* (2), *Reynaldo* (2), *Adolfo*, *Alberto*, *Alejandro*, *Armando*, *Concepcion*, *Eladio*.

Salton (164) English and Scottish: habitational name from Salton in North Yorkshire, England, or Saltoun in East Lothian, Scotland. The first is named from Old English *salh* '(sallow) willow' + *tūn* 'farmstead', 'settlement'.

Saltonstall (122) English: habitational name from an unidentified place, probably a variant of SALTON.

Salts (238) Jewish (Ashkenazic): metonymic occupational name for a salt producer or seller, from German *Salz*, Yiddish *zalts* 'salt'.

Saltsman (613) **1.** Jewish (Ashkenazic): occupational name for an extractor or seller of salt, from German *Salz* 'salt' + *Mann* 'man'. **2.** Altered spelling of German SALZMANN.

Saltus (135) English: probably a variant of **Salthouse** (see SALTERS).

Saltz (578) German and Jewish (Ashkenazic): variant spelling of SALZ.
GIVEN NAMES Jewish 5%. *Hyman* (2), *Meir* (2), *Gerson, Hirsch, Meyer, Shimon*.

Saltzberg (159) Variant spelling of German SALZBERG.

Saltzer (140) German and Jewish (Ashkenazic): variant spelling of SALZER.

Saltzman (1997) **1.** Jewish (Ashkenazic): occupational name for a producer or seller of salt, from German *Salz* 'salt' + *Mann* 'man'. **2.** Altered spelling of German SALZMANN.

Salus (186) Origin unidentified.

Salva (345) **1.** Catalan (**Salvà**): from the personal name *Salvá*, Catalan form of Latin *Silvanus* (a derivative of *silva* 'wood'). **2.** Southern French (Occitan): from a variant of the personal name *Salvat*, Occitan equivalent of SALVATO.
GIVEN NAMES Spanish 8%. *Aida* (2), *Marina* (2), *Alfonso, Blanca, Carlos, Fernando, Gustavo, Jaime, Jose, Juan, Juana, Julio*.

Salvador (1454) **1.** Spanish, Catalan, and Portuguese: from the popular Christian personal name *Salvador*, meaning 'Savior' (Latin *Salvator*, a derivative of *salvare* 'to save'), bestowed in honor of Christ. **2.** In some cases, possibly a Spanish, Asturian-Leonese, or Galician habitational name from any of the places called Salvador, in Valladolid, Lugo, and Asturies.
GIVEN NAMES Spanish 32%; Portuguese 7%. *Jose* (19), *Manuel* (12), *Juan* (8), *Francisco* (6), *Jorge* (5), *Mario* (5), *Armando* (4), *Fernando* (4), *Julio* (4), *Ricardo* (4), *Alberto* (3), *Alfredo* (3), *Joao* (3), *Vasco; Antonio* (7), *Sal* (4), *Angelo* (3), *Carlo* (3), *Luciano* (3), *Fausto* (2), *Federico* (2), *Leonardo* (2), *Romeo* (2), *Amedeo, Carmela, Carmelo*.

Salvadore (200) Italian: variant of SALVATORE.
GIVEN NAMES Italian 8%. *Amleto* (2), *Guido* (2), *Angelo, Romeo, Vincenzo*.

Salvadori (103) Italian: patronymic or plural form of SALVADORE.

GIVEN NAMES Italian 16%. *Gino* (2), *Battista, Donatella, Giuseppina, Silvio*.

Salvage (180) **1.** French and English: nickname from Old French, Middle English *salvage* 'untamed' (see SAVAGE). **2.** Americanized form of some similar-sounding Jewish surname.
GIVEN NAMES French 4%. *Andre, Monique*.

Salvaggio (523) Italian: nickname for a wild or uncouth person, an older form of SELVAGGIO.
GIVEN NAMES Italian 14%. *Angelo* (5), *Antonio* (5), *Sal* (2), *Salvatore* (2), *Vito* (2), *Carlo, Gaetano, Gasper, Giuseppe, Grazia, Luigi, Nino*.

Salvant (105) French: variant of **Sauvan(t)**, from an older personal name derived from Latin *Silvanus*.
GIVEN NAMES French 10%. *Cyrille, Lucien, Michel*.

Salvas (235) possibly Spanish: origin uncertain; possibly from the plural of *salva* 'salvo', 'gun salute'. But it may be from a personal name. Compare SALVA.
GIVEN NAMES French 17%. *Adrien* (4), *Andre* (2), *Emile* (2), *Armand, Patrice, Raoul, Yves*.

Salvati (472) Italian: patronymic or plural form of SALVATO.
GIVEN NAMES Italian 17%. *Angelo* (4), *Domenic* (2), *Gildo* (2), *Luigi* (2), *Nicola* (2), *Nunzio* (2), *Salvatore* (2), *Berardino, Enza, Gilda, Gino, Guido*.

Salvatierra (169) Spanish: **1.** habitational name from any of the places named Salvatierra (literally 'save land'). This is a widespread place name, denoting a place of strategic importance. **2.** Castilianized form of Galician **Salvaterra** or Aragonese **Salbatierra**, habitational names from places in Galicia and Aragon.
GIVEN NAMES Spanish 49%. *Jose* (8), *Carlos* (3), *Juan* (3), *Rafael* (3), *Ana* (2), *Cesar* (2), *Jesus* (2), *Agustin, Beatriz, Bernabe, Carmelita, Cosme*.

Salvato (666) Italian: from the personal name *Salvato* (Latin *Salvatus*), which refers to Christian salvation.
GIVEN NAMES Italian 17%. *Salvatore* (7), *Carlo* (5), *Vito* (4), *Gaetano* (3), *Guido* (3), *Carmine* (2), *Agostino, Aldo, Angelo, Antonio, Fausto, Filippo*.

Salvatore (1820) Italian: from the personal name *Salvatore*, meaning 'Savior'. Compare SALVADOR.
GIVEN NAMES Italian 15%. *Angelo* (14), *Rocco* (8), *Carmine* (6), *Vito* (5), *Carlo* (4), *Domenico* (3), *Luigi* (3), *Pasquale* (3), *Gaetano* (2), *Giulio* (2), *Pietro* (2), *Alesio*.

Salvatori (195) Italian: patronymic or plural form of SALVATORE.
GIVEN NAMES Italian 12%; Spanish 5%. *Enrico, Fabio, Gino, Giulio, Lino, Lorenzo, Mario, Pio, Roberto; Carlos* (3), *Ana, Lupita*.

Salverson (110) Scandinavian: patronymic from the personal name *Salve(r)* (see SALVESEN).
GIVEN NAMES Scandinavian 7%; German 6%. *Nels, Selmer; Kurt*.

Salvesen (273) Norwegian: patronymic from the personal name *Salve* (Old Norse *Salvi*), probably formed with Old Norse *salr* 'house', 'hall' + *ve(r)* 'giant', 'hero'.
GIVEN NAMES Scandinavian 14%. *Britt, Fredrik, Nils*.

Salveson (244) Americanized spelling of Norwegian SALVESEN.
GIVEN NAMES Scandinavian 8%. *Erik* (2), *Jorgen, Juel, Knud, Sig*.

Salvetti (160) Italian: patronymic from the personal name *Salvetto*, a pet form of SALVO.
GIVEN NAMES French 6%; Italian 4%. *Celestine, Monique, Serge; Aldo, Antonio, Dario, Pio*.

Salvi (383) **1.** Italian: patronymic or plural form of SALVO. **2.** Italian: from a short form of the personal name *Diotisalvi* ('God save you'), which was widespread in the medieval period. **3.** Catalan: from a personal name *Salvi* (Latin *Salvius*, a derivative of *salvus* 'safe'), borne by various early saints, among them a 6th-century bishop of Albi and a 7th-century bishop of Amiens. **4.** Indian (Maharashtra): Hindu (Maratha) name of unknown meaning.
GIVEN NAMES Italian 13%; Indian 7%. *Angelo* (3), *Giovanni* (2), *Antonella, Carina, Carmela, Domenico, Enrico, Gasper, Gino, Guido, Luigi, Mafalda; Shantu* (2), *Anil, Dipali, Diwakar, Mahendra, Prakash, Rajesh, Ranjan, Rohan, Santosh, Satish, Sharad*.

Salvia (222) Southern Italian: **1.** from a variant of the personal name *Salvio* (see SALVI). **2.** habitational name from Savoia de Lucania in Potenza, earlier called *Salvia*. **3.** from *salvia* 'sage', presumably a metonymic occupational name for a herbalist or a grower or seller of herbs, or possibly a topographic name.
GIVEN NAMES Italian 15%. *Salvatore* (3), *Carmela, Gaspare, Onofrio, Pietro, Rocco, Vito*.

Salvini (107) Italian: patronymic or plural form of SALVINO.
GIVEN NAMES Italian 8%. *Angelo* (3), *Umberto*.

Salvino (262) Italian: from a pet form of the personal name SALVO.
GIVEN NAMES Italian 8%. *Angelo, Antonio, Gabriele, Luigi, Marco*.

Salvo (931) **1.** Italian: from the personal name *Salvo* ('safe'). **2.** Catalan (**Salvó**): possibly from a personal name, a pet form of the Latin personal name *Salvus*. **3.** Spanish and Portuguese: possibly a nickname from *salvo* 'saved'.
GIVEN NAMES Italian 15%. *Angelo* (9), *Salvatore* (7), *Antonio* (5), *Vito* (4), *Carlo*

(2), *Leonardo* (2), *Natale* (2), *Sal* (2), *Albertina, Biagio, Calogero, Carmelo.*

Salvucci (345) Italian: from a pet form of the personal name SALVO.

GIVEN NAMES Italian 22%. *Mario* (4), *Antonio* (3), *Carmine* (3), *Angelo* (2), *Cesidio* (2), *Gerardo* (2), *Guido* (2), *Dante, Dario, Donato, Luigi, Milio, Nazzareno, Nino.*

Salway (153) **1.** English: variant of SELWAY. **2.** Americanized form of French SALOIS.

Salyards (284) English: probably a variant of SAYLORS.

Salyer (2493) English: probably a variant of SAYLOR.

Salyers (1866) English: probably a variant of SAYLORS.

Salz (303) German and Jewish (Ashkenazic): metonymic occupational name for a salt producer or seller, from Middle High German *salz*, German *Salz* 'salt'.

GIVEN NAMES German 4%. *Berthold, Othmar.*

Salzano (298) Italian (mainly Campania): habitational name from a place in Venetia province named Salzano.

GIVEN NAMES Italian 17%. *Carmine* (2), *Gennaro* (2), *Nicolina* (2), *Antonio, Biagio, Carlo, Dario, Giuseppe, Guido, Lucio, Pasquale, Saverio.*

Salzberg (339) **1.** German: habitational name from any of various places named Salzberg, or a topographic name from Middle High German *salz* 'salt' + *berc* 'hill', 'mountain'. **2.** Jewish (Ashkenazic): ornamental name from German *Salz* 'salt' + *Berg* 'mountain', 'hill'.

GIVEN NAMES Jewish 9%. *Iser* (3), *Hyman* (2), *Miriam* (2), *Emanuel, Shira.*

Salzer (698) German: occupational name for an extractor or seller of salt, a precious commodity in medieval times, from an agent derivative of Middle High German *salz* 'salt'.

Salzillo (110) Italian: from a diminutive of **Salsa**, a topographic name for someone who lived by a volcanic spring, or possibly for someone who lived where the plants *Convolvulus soldanella* (known in Italian as *salsa di Catania*) or *Smilax aspera* (Italian common name *salsa paisana*) grew.

GIVEN NAMES Italian 21%. *Luigi* (2), *Agnese, Amato, Angelo, Camillo, Nichola, Sal, Salvatore, Sisto.*

Salzman (1663) **1.** Jewish (Ashkenazic): occupational name for a salt producer or seller, from German *Salz* 'salt' + *Mann* 'man'. Compare SALZER. **2.** Respelling of the German surname SALZMANN.

Salzmann (342) German: occupational name for an extractor or seller of salt, from Middle High German *salz* 'salt' + *man* 'man'.

GIVEN NAMES German 8%. *Klaus* (3), *Aloysius, Fritz, Horst.*

Salzwedel (307) North German: habitational name from any of several places so named, the largest being near Uelzen. The place name is a compound of SALZ 'salt' (Old Saxon *salt*) + Old Saxon *wedel* 'ford'.

GIVEN NAMES German 4%. *Hans, Horst, Otto.*

Sam (1619) **1.** English: from a pet form of the personal name *Samson* (see SAMSON). **2.** Dutch (**van Sam**): variant of **Van den Sand** (see SAND 2). **3.** Nigerian and Ghanaian: unexplained. **4.** Chinese 沈: variant of SHEN. **5.** Chinese 岑: variant of SHUM. **6.** Other Southeast Asian: unexplained.

GIVEN NAMES Southeast Asian 6%. *Saroeun* (4), *Phan* (3), *Dung* (2), *Hung* (2), *Lac* (2), *Mui* (2), *Cau, Dau, Ha, Ha To, Hinh, Hoa.*

Sama (188) **1.** Southern Italian (**Samá**): from the Biblical personal name. **2.** Catalan (**Samà**): habitational name from Samà, a place in Catalonia. **3.** Asturian-Leonese: in some cases, a habitational name from any of various places in Asturies named Sama. **4.** Indian (Gujarat): Hindu (Rajput) name of unknown meaning. The Samas are believed to be an offshoot of the Jadeja tribe. **5.** Japanese (not common in Japan): variously written, the name appears to be topographic, deriving from the word *semai* 'narrow'.

GIVEN NAMES Italian 21%; Indian 9%; Spanish 8%. *Antonio* (3), *Angelo* (2), *Carlo* (2), *Salvatore* (2), *Dante, Natale, Pasquale, Rocco, Romolo, Saverio; Madhukar, Murthy, Rahm, Sanjay, Shakti, Venugopal; Digna, Lourdes, Mario, Miguel, Modesta, Orlando, Roberto, Rolando, Serafina, Violeta.*

Samaan (130) Muslim: from a personal name based on Arabic *thaman* 'price', 'value'.

GIVEN NAMES Muslim 54%. *Kamel* (2), *Mousa* (2), *Nader* (2), *Adnan, Asaad, Ashraf, Ayoub, Azmi, Bahjat, Chawki, Ehsan, Fadel.*

Samad (157) Muslim: from a personal name based on Arabic *ṣamad* 'everlasting'. *As-Ṣamad* 'the Everlasting' is an epithet of Allah (Qur'an 112: 2). As a personal name, this is normally found in the combination *'Abd al-Ṣamad* (*Abdus-Ṣamad*) 'servant of the Lord'.

GIVEN NAMES Muslim 75%. *Abdul* (13), *Mohammed* (4), *Syed* (3), *Abdus* (2), *Anwar* (2), *Mohammad* (2), *Muhammad* (2), *Naeem* (2), *Tariq* (2), *Abdullah, Ahmed, Aisha.*

Samaha (277) Arabic: from a personal name based on Arabic *samāḥa* 'magnanimity'.

GIVEN NAMES Arabic 22%; French 10%. *Fadi* (3), *Fouad* (2), *Mohamed* (2), *Nabeel* (2), *Abdallah, Adib, Afif, Ahmad, Ahmed, Bassel, Chafic, Ehab; Jean-Paul* (3), *Antoine* (2), *Camil, Emile, Gaston, Georges, Huguette, Lucien.*

Samaniego (854) Basque: habitational name from Samaniego in Araba, Basque Country.

GIVEN NAMES Spanish 42%. *Jose* (18), *Manuel* (18), *Jesus* (11), *Ramon* (9), *Carlos* (7), *Pedro* (7), *Armando* (6), *Luis* (6), *Miguel* (6), *Francisco* (4), *Javier* (4), *Jorge* (4).

Samano (251) Spanish (**Sámano**): habitational name from Sámano, near Castro Urdiales, in Santander province, possibly of Basque origin.

GIVEN NAMES Spanish 53%. *Carlos* (5), *Jose* (5), *Armando* (4), *Silvia* (4), *Alejandro* (3), *Francisco* (3), *Guillermo* (3), *Javier* (3), *Jose Luis* (3), *Vicente* (3), *Angel* (2), *Enrique* (2).

Samara (201) Muslim: from a personal name based on Arabic *thamara* 'benefit', 'gain'.

GIVEN NAMES Muslim 25%. *Issam* (2), *Jawad* (2), *Jiries* (2), *Mohammad* (2), *Nimer* (2), *Afaf, Ahmad, Ali, Amal, Baha, Elham, Emad.*

Samaras (209) Greek: occupational name for a saddler, from *samari* 'pack saddle' (ancient Greek *sagmarion*) + the occupational ending -*as*.

GIVEN NAMES Greek 12%. *Dimitrios* (2), *Kostas* (2), *Andreas, Demetrios, Nikolaos, Yiannis.*

Samarin (121) **1.** Russian: habitational name for someone from the city of Samara. **2.** Jewish (from Belarus): etymology uncertain. **3.** possibly also a reduced form of the Greek family name **Samarinidis**, habitational name for someone from a place called Samarina.

Samaroo (165) Name of unknown etymology found among people of Indian origin in Guyana and Trinidad.

GIVEN NAMES Indian 31%. *Deonarine* (3), *Amar* (2), *Chaitram, Deo, Indra, Jewan, Nasib, Ragesh, Raj, Ramdeo, Ravin, Roopnarine.*

Samayoa (240) Basque: Latin American variant of **Zamalloa**, **Zamayoa**, a topographic name for someone who lived by a gorge or pass, from Basque *sama, zama* 'defile', 'pass', 'narrow ravine' + the locative suffix -*ola*.

GIVEN NAMES Spanish 49%. *Jose* (8), *Carlos* (7), *Roberto* (5), *Francisco* (3), *Mario* (3), *Adela* (2), *Juan* (2), *Manuel* (2), *Adelaida, Alba, Alberto, Alfredo; Marco* (3), *Albertina, Carmelina.*

Samberg (173) **1.** German and Jewish (Ashkenazic): habitational name from any of several places named Samberg. **2.** Swedish: probably of German origin.

GIVEN NAME Jewish 8%. *Aryeh* (3).

Sambol (111) Jewish: unexplained.

GIVEN NAMES Jewish 6%. *Moshe, Sima.*

Sambor (114) **1.** Polish: from the Old Slavic personal name *sambor*, composed of the elements *sam* 'alone' + *bor* 'fight'. **2.** Polish and Jewish (eastern Ashkenazic):

habitational name from Sambor, now Sambir in Ukraine.

GIVEN NAMES Polish 12%; German 5%. *Jadwiga, Janina, Jozef, Wladyslaw, Zygmunt; Monika.*

Samborski (178) Polish and Jewish (eastern Ashkenazic): habitational name for someone from Sambor, now Sambir in Ukraine, also (as a Polish name) from Sambor in Łomża voivodeship.

GIVEN NAMES Polish 7%. *Grzegorz, Henryk, Lucyna, Zdzislaw.*

Sambrano (278) Spanish: variant of the habitational name ZAMBRANO.

GIVEN NAMES Spanish 40%. *Jesus* (6), *Jose* (3), *Armando* (2), *Arturo* (2), *Carlos* (2), *Fernando* (2), *Guadalupe* (2), *Humberto* (2), *Juan* (2), *Manuel* (2), *Rodolfo* (2), *Alfredo.*

Samec (144) **1.** Czech and Slovak: from a pet form of the personal name SAMUEL. **2.** Slovenian: nickname from *samec* 'loner', 'solitary person', from the adjective *sam* 'alone'.

Samek (362) Czech and Slovak: from a pet form of the personal name SAMUEL.

Samel (123) German and Jewish (Ashkenazic): variant of SAMUEL.

GIVEN NAMES Jewish 4%. *Moshe, Yetta.*

Samelson (154) Dutch and Jewish (Ashkenazic): patronymic from the personal name SAMUEL.

GIVEN NAMES Jewish 7%. *Kalmen, Moty, Pinchas.*

Sames (208) **1.** English: unexplained. **2.** German: possibly from a Germanic stem *sam*, used of a personal name of unknown meaning.

Samet (398) German and Jewish (Ashkenazic): metonymic occupational name for a maker or seller of velvet, from Yiddish *samet* 'velvet' (German *Samt*, ultimately from Greek *hexamiton*, a compound of *hex* 'six' + *mitos* 'thread').

GIVEN NAMES Jewish 11%. *Mordechai* (2), *Aron, Aviva, Bracha, Chana, Chaya, Gittel, Isadore, Miriam, Moshe, Yair, Yardena.*

Samford (553) English: variant of SANDFORD, probably relating specifically to various minor places in Devon and Somerset, for example Sampford Arundel in Somerset or Sampford Courtenay in Devon.

Sami (135) **1.** Muslim: from a personal name based on Arabic *samī*' 'hearing', 'listening', or on *sāmī* 'august'. *As-Samī*' 'the All-Hearing' is an attribute of Allah. It is found in combinations such as '*Abd al-Samī*' (*Abdus-Sami*) 'servant of the All-Hearing'. **2.** Indian: variant of SWAMY.

GIVEN NAMES Muslim 66%; Indian 7%. *Ali* (2), *Hafez* (2), *Mohamad* (2), *Mohammad* (2), *Mohammed* (2), *Sami* (2), *Syed* (2), *Abdi, Abdul, Adly, Ahmad, Ahmed; Arvind, Kailash, Purnima, Usha.*

Samis (117) Dutch and North German: from a pet form of the personal name SAMUEL.

GIVEN NAMES Dutch 5%; German 4%. *Gust* (2); *Monika* (2).

Sammarco (329) Italian (mainly southern): habitational name from any place named with Italian *San Marco* or *Sammarco*, generally as the result of the dedication of a local church or shrine to St. Mark.

GIVEN NAMES Italian 22%. *Angelo* (5), *Vito* (3), *Carmine* (2), *Cono* (2), *Giuseppe* (2), *Carlo, Carmela, Carmino, Dino, Ermanno, Gennaro.*

Sammartino (280) Italian: habitational name from any place called San Martino, generally as the result of the dedication of a local church or shrine to St. Martin.

GIVEN NAMES Italian 22%; Spanish 4%. *Rocco* (4), *Sal* (3), *Salvatore* (3), *Angelo* (2), *Aldo, Camillo, Carlo, Mario, Nichola, Pasco, Pasquale, Vincenzo; Manuel* (2), *Pablo.*

Sammet (145) German and Jewish (Ashkenazic): variant spelling of SAMET.

GIVEN NAMES German 7%. *Gerhard* (2), *Aloysius.*

Sammis (352) Dutch and North German: from a pet form of the personal name SAMUEL.

Sammon (618) English and Irish: variant spelling of SALMON.

GIVEN NAME Irish 4%. *Brendan* (2).

Sammons (3031) English (West Midlands): patronymic from SALMON 1.

Samms (233) English: patronymic from a pet form of the personal name SAMUEL.

Sammut (130) Maltese: unexplained.

GIVEN NAMES French 8%. *Andre, Marcel, Patrice.*

Samons (264) English: variant of SAMMONS.

Samora (401) Spanish, Basque, and Catalan: variant of Spanish ZAMORA. In Spain this name is mainly found in the south, where there is no phonetic distinction between sounds *s* and *z*.

GIVEN NAMES Spanish 22%. *Manuel* (4), *Angel* (2), *Carlos* (2), *Eloy* (2), *Jose* (2), *Raul* (2), *Roberto* (2), *Ruben* (2), *Alfredo, Andres, Arturo, Benito.*

Samp (299) Probably English, from a pet form of the personal name SAMSON.

Sampaio (121) Portuguese and Galician: habitational name from any of the numerous places in Portugal and Galicia named Sampaio, generally as the result of the dedication of a local church or shrine to Saint St. Pelagius (*São Paio*).

GIVEN NAMES Spanish 38%; Portuguese 19%. *Jose* (3), *Carlos* (2), *Celso* (2), *Chico* (2), *Octavio* (2), *Ricardo* (2), *Alvino, Antero, Aurelio, Ernesto, Fernando, Frederico; Joao* (2), *Paulo, Vasco.*

Sampath (105) Indian (Karnataka): Hindu name from Sanskrit *sampat* 'prosperity', 'wealth'. This is used only as a male given name in India, but has come to be used as a family name in the U.S.

GIVEN NAMES Indian 83%. *Anand* (3), *Balaji* (2), *Kumar* (2), *Meera* (2), *Srikanth* (2), *Anupama, Ashwin, Deepak, Dhanraj, Dilip, Indira, Jagannathan.*

Samper (105) **1.** Aragonese: habitational name from any of the places called Samper, in Aragon. **2.** Catalan: habitational name from any of the places in Catalonia called Sant Pere, generally as the result of the dedication of a local church or shrine to St. Peter (*Sant Pere*).

GIVEN NAMES Spanish 44%. *Luis* (9), *Carlos* (5), *Edgardo* (2), *Juan* (2), *Amalia, Arturo, Camilo, Ernesto, Felipe, Joaquin, Jorge, Julio.*

Samperi (115) Southern Italian (especially eastern Sicily): habitational name from Sampieri in Ragusa, or from any of the places named San Piero, San Pier, or San Pietro, generally as the result of the dedication of a church or shrine to St. Peter. This is also found, in the form **Samperis**, as a Greek family name.

GIVEN NAMES Italian 27%. *Salvatore* (5), *Rosario* (2), *Ciro, Delphino, Giuseppe, Luigi, Raffaele, Santo, Vincenzo.*

Sampey (207) English (Midlands): unexplained.

Sample (4041) English (of Norman origin): habitational name from any of various places in Normandy called Saint-Paul or Saint-Pol, from the dedication of their churches to St. Paul (see PAUL).

Samples (2953) English (mainly Nottinghamshire): unexplained; probably a variant of SAMPLE.

Sampley (360) Origin unidentified.

Sampsel (231) Variant of German SAMSEL.

Sampsell (306) Variant of German SAMSEL.

Sampson (12173) English, Dutch, and Jewish: variant of SAMSON. The *-p-* was introduced in the Greek transliteration of the Hebrew name *Shimshon*. The English surname has also long been established in Ireland. In North America, this name has absorbed other European cognates, for example Greek *Sampsonakis, Sampsonides.*

Samra (229) **1.** Indian (Panjab): Sikh name derived from the name of a Jat tribe. **2.** Muslim: variant of SAMARA.

GIVEN NAMES Indian 41%; Muslim 6%. *Avtar* (2), *Gurdial* (2), *Nirmal* (2), *Balraj, Balwinder, Buta, Dev, Gurbax, Mahan, Mangal, Raj, Sadhu; Hisham* (2), *Abdul, Ahmad, Ajaib, Fouad, Iqbal, Issam, Kamil, Karim, Kemal, Munir.*

Sams (5094) English: patronymic from a short form of SAMUEL.

Samsa (118) **1.** Hungarian: from *Samsa, Sámsa*, pet forms of the personal name *Sámuel*, Hungarian form of SAMUEL. **2.** Czech: from a pet form of the personal name SAMUEL.

Samsel (649) German variant of Hungarian SAMSA.

Samson (3487) Scottish, English, Welsh, French, German, Dutch, Hungarian (**Sámson**), and Jewish: from the Biblical name *Samson* (Hebrew *Shimshon*, a diminutive of *shemesh* 'sun'). Among Christians it was sometimes chosen as a personal name or nickname with reference to the great strength of the Biblical hero (Judges 13–16). In Wales another association was with the 6th-century Welsh bishop Samson, who traveled to Brittany, where he died and was greatly venerated. His name, which is probably an altered form of an unknown Celtic original, was popularized in England by Breton followers of William the Conqueror, and to some extent independently from Wales.

FOREBEARS The first Canadian bearer of this name was from Normandy, France, and is documented in Quebec City in 1664; he was said to have been 100 years old when he died in 1724.
GIVEN NAMES French 5%. *Armand* (4), *Jacques* (4), *Andre* (3), *Alain* (2), *Herve* (2), *Pierre* (2), *Adelard, Arianne, Cecile, Dieudonne, Gedeon, Henri.*

Samudio (176) Southern Portuguese and Latin American: variant of Spanish **Zamudio**, a habitational name from Zamudio in Biscay province.
GIVEN NAMES Spanish 32%. *Jose* (5), *Manuel* (3), *Rafael* (3), *Carlos* (2), *Esperanza* (2), *Adolfo, Alberto, Alfredo, Basilio, Bulmaro, Cruz, Domingo.*

Samuel (4545) **1.** English, Scottish, Welsh, French, German, Dutch, Hungarian (**Sámuel**), Jewish, and South Indian: from the Biblical male personal name *Samuel* (Hebrew *Shemuel* 'Name of God'). This name is also well established in South India. In North America this has absorbed other European cognates such as Greek **Samouelidis**. **2.** It is found as a personal name among Christians in India, and in the U.S. is used as a family name among families from southern India.
GIVEN NAMES Indian 5%. *Raj* (3), *Varughese* (3), *Ashok* (2), *Babu* (2), *Eapen* (2), *Mathai* (2), *Saji* (2), *Aleykutty, Arul, Arun, Asha, Beena.*

Samuelian (106) Armenian: patronymic from the Armenian personal name *Samuēl* (see SAMUEL).
GIVEN NAMES Armenian 15%; French 5%. *Hagop, Haroutune, Hovsep, Kourken, Siranoush, Souren, Vartan, Vartkes; Arsene, Marielle.*

Samuels (6535) English and Jewish: patronymic from SAMUEL.

Samuelsen (212) Danish and Norwegian: patronymic from the personal name SAMUEL.
GIVEN NAMES Scandinavian 20%; German 4%. *Erik* (4), *Sig, Thor; Gunter.*

Samuelson (3573) English and Jewish (Ashkenazic): patronymic from SAMUEL. This form has also absorbed cognates in other languages, such as Danish and Norwegian SAMUELSEN, Swedish **Samuelsson**, and Jewish **Samuelsohn**.

San (327) **1.** Chinese 申: variant of SHEN 2. **2.** Chinese 山: variant of SHAN 2. **3.** Other Southeast Asian: unexplained.
GIVEN NAMES Southeast Asian 38%. *Khin* (2), *Pui* (2), *Sokhom* (2), *Heng, Kin, Kin Hong, Kun, Lai, Leong, Man, Ming, Ouk; Senh* (3), *Ly* (2), *Mui* (2), *Pha* (2), *Phal* (2), *Pham* (2), *Tha* (2), *Tran* (2), *Coong, Dam, Duy, Hanh; Noy* (2), *Hoeun, Noeun, Phath, Roeuth, Samoeun, Soeum, Sophat, Sovann, Yoeun; Pong, Savuth, Thai.*

Sanabria (820) Spanish: habitational name from Puebla de Sanabria in Zamora province.
GIVEN NAMES Spanish 45%. *Jose* (18), *Carlos* (10), *Luis* (10), *Manuel* (9), *Juan* (8), *Miguel* (8), *Rafael* (7), *Roberto* (7), *Angel* (6), *Francisco* (6), *Alberto* (5), *Ana* (5); *Antonio* (7), *Angelo* (2), *Leonardo* (2), *Silvio* (2), *Carmelo, Cecilio, Evangelio, Federico, Gervasio, Heriberto, Lorenzo, Marco.*

San Angelo (108) Spanish: habitational name from any of the numerous places so named for a local shrine or church dedicated to St. Angelo.

San Antonio (144) Spanish: habitational name from any of the numerous places so named for a local shrine or church dedicated to St. Anthony (*San Antonio*).
GIVEN NAMES Spanish 11%; Italian 10%. *Sergio* (2), *Alejandro, Candido, Dominador, Homero, Renato, Rey, Zosimo; Antonio* (2), *Amadeo, Amedeo, Pasco, Ugo.*

Sanborn (4181) Variant of English **Sandburn**, a habitational name from Sandburn House in North Yorkshire.

Sanburn (106) English: see SANBORN.

Sanches (425) **1.** Portuguese: patronymic from the personal name *Sancho* (see SANCHO). **2.** Spanish: variant of SANCHEZ.
GIVEN NAMES Spanish 37%; Portuguese 10%. *Jose* (8), *Carlos* (6), *Manuel* (6), *Juan* (5), *Jesus* (4), *Luis* (4), *Pedro* (4), *Adolfo* (2), *Alina* (2), *Arturo* (2), *Domingos* (2), *Guillermo* (2); *Joao* (2), *Amadeu, Marcio.*

Sanchez (52413) Spanish (**Sánchez**): patronymic from the personal name SANCHO.
GIVEN NAMES Spanish 47%. *Juan* (747), *Manuel* (484), *Carlos* (458), *Luis* (403), *Jesus* (401), *Francisco* (323), *Miguel* (272), *Jorge* (267), *Pedro* (249), *Ramon* (244), *Raul* (233), *Roberto* (228).

Sancho (208) Spanish and Portuguese: from *Sancho*, a popular medieval personal name, which is probably from a Latin form, *Sanc(t)ius*, a derivative of *sanctus* 'holy'. The personal name was borne by a 9th-century martyr of Cordova.
GIVEN NAMES Spanish 29%. *Jose* (5), *Elena* (3), *Carlos* (2), *Fernando* (2), *Jacinto* (2), *Mario* (2), *Agustin, Ana, Dulce, Emilio, Enrique, Eugenio.*

Sand (1968) **1.** English, Scottish, Danish, Norwegian, Swedish, German, and Jewish (Ashkenazic): topographic name for someone who lived on patch of sandy soil, from the vocabulary word *sand*. As a Swedish or Jewish name it was often purely ornamental. **2.** Dutch and Belgian: reduced form of **Van den Sand(e)**, **Van den Zande**, a habitational name from places such as Zande in West Flanders or various minor places named with *zand* 'sand'. **3.** English and Scottish: from a short form of ALEXANDER. **4.** French: from a Germanic personal name, *Sando*.
GIVEN NAMES Scandinavian 4%. *Erik* (2), *Bertel, Ejnar, Lars, Levinus, Nels, Niels, Thor.*

Sanda (185) **1.** Hungarian: nickname from *sandal* 'half-blind'. **2.** Hungarian: Americanized spelling of **Szanda**, a habitational name for someone from a place so called. **3.** Japanese: 'three rice paddies'; an alternative pronunciation of the name MITA.
GIVEN NAMES Japanese 5%. *Daisuke, Mayumi, Shigeo.*

Sandage (307) Probably an Americanized spelling of Polish **Sandacz**, a nickname from *sandacz* 'perch' (the fish).

Sandahl (405) **1.** Swedish: ornamental name composed of the elements *sand* 'sand' + *dahl*, an ornamental spelling of *dal* 'valley'. **2.** Norwegian: habitational name from any of several farmsteads on the west coast of Norway, named in Old Norse as *Sanddalr* 'sand valley'.
GIVEN NAMES Scandinavian 5%. *Jarl, Sven.*

Sandal (102) **1.** English: variant of SANDALL. **2.** Variant of Scandinavian SANDAHL. **3.** Indian (Panjab, Jammu and Kashmir): Hindu (Arora, Dogra) and Sikh name, from Arabic *şandal* 'sandal'. **4.** Jewish (eastern Ashkenazic): ornamental name from Polish *sandał*, Yiddish *sandal* 'sandalwood'.
GIVEN NAMES Scandinavian 16%; Indian 7%; Jewish 4%. *Selmer* (2), *Lars, Nels; Meena, Onkar, Raj, Rashmi.*

Sandall (250) English (Peterborough): **1.** habitational name from Sandal Magna in West Yorkshire, or Kirk Sandall and Long Sandall in South Yorkshire, named with Old English *sand* 'sand' + *halh* 'nook' (often referring to land in a riverbend or a hollow). **2.** from an otherwise unattested Old Norse personal name, *Sandúlfr*, composed of the elements *sandr* 'sand' + *úlfr* 'wolf'.

Sandau (184) **1.** German and Jewish (western Ashkenazic): habitational name from a place near Stendal called Sandau. **2.** Swedish: probably of German origin.
GIVEN NAMES German 6%. *Otto* (2), *Heinz, Udo.*

Sandbach (100) **1.** English: habitational name from Sandbach in Cheshire, named from Old English *sand* 'sand' + *bæce* 'valley stream'. **2.** German: habitational name from a place named with *sand* 'sand' + *bach* 'stream'.

Sandberg (3751) **1.** German: habitational name from any of various minor places so

called, named with Middle High German *sand* 'sand' + *berc* 'mountain'. **2.** Norwegian: habitational name from any of three farmsteads named with *sand* 'sand' + *berg* 'mountain'. **3.** Scandinavian and Jewish (Ashkenazic): ornamental name composed of *sand* 'sand' + *berg* 'mountain'.
GIVEN NAMES Scandinavian 5%. *Erik* (7), *Lars* (3), *Bjorn* (2), *Nels* (2), *Nils* (2), *Algot*, *Bertel*, *Evald*, *Fredrik*, *Joakim*, *Ove*, *Per*.

Sandborn (136) **1.** English: see SANBORN. **2.** Swedish: ornamental name from *sand* 'sand' + *born* 'well'.
GIVEN NAME German 4%. *Kurt* (2).

Sandbothe (138) Origin unidentified.

Sandburg (135) Swedish: ornamental name from *sand* 'sand' + *burg* 'castle'.

Sande (576) **1.** Norwegian: habitational name from any of forty or more farmsteads so named, especially on the west coast, from the dative case of Old Norse *sandr* 'sand', 'sandy plain', 'beach'. **2.** German: variant of SAND.
GIVEN NAMES Scandinavian 10%. *Thor* (3), *Lars*, *Sigvald*.

Sandeen (285) Swedish: variant of **Sandén** (see SANDEN).
GIVEN NAMES Scandinavian 7%. *Asmund* (2), *Erik*, *Erland*.

Sandefer (301) Variant of English SANDIFER.

Sandefur (1048) Variant of English SANDIFER.

Sandel (589) **1.** German: habitational name from a place near Jever called Sandel, or a reduced form of ALEXANDER. **2.** Swedish: ornamental name from *sandel* 'sandalwood' or 'sandal oil'. Alternatively, it may be an ornamental name from *sand* 'sand' + the adjectival suffix *-el*, a derivative of Latin *-elius*. **3.** Jewish (eastern Ashkenazic): ornamental name from German *Sandel* 'sandalwood' (see SANDAL 3). **4.** French: from a diminutive of SAND.
GIVEN NAMES Jewish 5%. *Aron* (2), *Simche* (2), *Ari*, *Dovid*, *Hyman*, *Isadore*, *Meyer*, *Pinchus*, *Sholem*, *Zalman*.

Sandelin (146) **1.** Dutch: from a pet form of SANDER, a reduced form of the personal name *Alexander* (see ALEXANDER). **2.** Swedish: ornamental name from *sand* 'sand' + the common surname suffix *-(e)lin*.
GIVEN NAMES French 6%; Scandinavian 5%. *Emile* (2); *Erik* (2).

Sandell (768) **1.** Swedish: probably a variant of SANDEL. **2.** English (Norfolk): topographic name for someone who lived by a sand-hill or sandy slope, from Middle English *sand* 'sand' + *hille* 'hill' or *helde*, *hilde* 'slope'.
GIVEN NAMES Scandinavian 4%. *Nils* (2), *Anders*, *Thor*.

Sanden (385) **1.** Swedish (**Sandén**): ornamental name composed of the elements *sand* 'sand' + the common surname suffix *-én*, derivative of Latin *-enius*. **2.** Norwe-

gian: habitational name from any of numerous farmsteads throughout Norway, so named from the definite singular form of *sand* 'sand', 'sandy plain', 'beach'.
GIVEN NAMES Scandinavian 8%. *Erik*, *Helmer*, *Lars*, *Mats*, *Selmer*, *Thor*.

Sander (3396) **1.** English, Scottish, Dutch, German, and Swedish: from the personal name *Sander*, a reduced form of ALEXANDER. **2.** German: topographic name for someone who lived on sandy soil, from SAND 1 + *-er*, suffix denoting an inhabitant. **3.** Norwegian: habitational name from any of seven farmsteads so named in southeastern Norway, from the indefinite plural form of Old Norse *sandr* 'sand', 'sandy plain', 'beach'.
GIVEN NAMES German 5%. *Hans* (6), *Kurt* (5), *Erna* (3), *Erwin* (3), *Fritz* (3), *Manfred* (3), *Bernhard* (2), *Dieter* (2), *Franz* (2), *Gerda* (2), *Klaus* (2), *Wolfgang* (2).

Sandercock (121) Scottish or English: from a pet form of the personal name *Sander* (see ALEXANDER).

Sanderfer (136) Variant of English SANDIFER.

Sanderford (302) English: probably a variant of SANDIFER, although it has been suggested that it may be a habitational name from Sandford Orcas in Dorset, named with Old English *sand* 'sand' + *ford* 'ford'.

Sanderlin (561) **1.** Jewish (Ashkenazic): from a pet form of the personal name ALEXANDER. **2.** Swedish: ornamental name composed of the personal name *Sander* (a short form of *Alexander*) + the surname suffix *-lin*.

Sanders (70393) English, Scottish, and North German: patronymic from SANDER 1.

Sandersfeld (114) German: perhaps a habitational name from a lost or minor place named 'Sander's field' (from a short form of the personal name ALEXANDER).

Sanderson (9318) Scottish and English: patronymic from the personal name SANDER (see ALEXANDER).

Sandford (880) **1.** English: habitational name from any of the various places, for example in Berkshire, Devon, Dorset, Oxfordshire, and Shropshire, so called from Old English *sand* 'sand' + *ford* 'ford'. **2.** Scottish: habitational name from a place in Fife, formerly called Sandford (see 1), now known as St. Fort.

Sandfort (121) North German: habitational name for someone from any of four places so named.
GIVEN NAME German 6%. *Gerhard* (2).

Sandgren (304) Swedish: ornamental name composed of the elements *sand* 'sand' + *gren* 'branch'.
GIVEN NAMES Scandinavian 7%; German 4%. *Algot*, *Erik*, *Thor*; *Hans*, *Kurt*.

Sandholm (100) Swedish: ornamental name from *sand* 'sand' + *holm* 'island'.
GIVEN NAME Scandinavian 4%. *Sven*.

Sandhu (633) Indian (Panjab): Sikh name which goes back to the tribal name *Sandhu* or *Sindhu*. The Sindhus are the second largest Jat tribe in the Panjab. Originally *sindhu* referred to the Indus river and to the region where it flows, a part of which is still called Sind. *Hindu* and the various names of India, *Hind*, *Hindustan*, and *India* are all derived from the Persian form of *sindhu*.
GIVEN NAMES Indian 84%. *Avtar* (5), *Raghbir* (4), *Raj* (4), *Balwinder* (3), *Nirmal* (3), *Beant* (2), *Gurdial* (2), *Gursewak* (2), *Hardev* (2), *Harjeet* (2), *Jarnail* (2), *Jeet* (2).

Sandidge (724) English: variant of SANDAGE.

Sandifer (1698) English: habitational name from a lost place named Sandiford (with the same etymology as SANDFORD 1), most probably in Lancashire or Yorkshire.

Sandiford (281) English: see SANDIFER.

Sandin (407) Swedish: ornamental name composed of the elements *sand* 'sand' + the surname suffix *-in*, from Latin *-in(i)us* meaning 'descendant of'.
GIVEN NAMES Scandinavian 9%. *Erik* (4), *Kerstin*, *Kjersten*, *Nels*, *Nils*, *Sig*.

Sandine (111) Variant of Swedish SANDIN.
GIVEN NAME Scandinavian 5%. *Nils*.

Sandino (137) **1.** Spanish: possibly a habitational name, e.g. from Villasandino in Burgos province or a similarly named place. **2.** Galician: (**Sandiño**) habitational name from Sandiño in Lugo province, Galicia.
GIVEN NAMES Spanish 43%. *Cayetano* (2), *Fabio* (2), *Francisco* (2), *Jose* (2), *Manuel* (2), *Mario* (2), *Rodrigo* (2), *Adan*, *Adelaida*, *Alberto*, *Alejandro*, *Alfonso*.

Sandison (134) Scottish: variant of SANDERSON.

Sandland (125) English: probably a topographic name for someone who lived in an area of sandy soil or a habitational name from a farmstead or other minor place so named.

Sandler (2501) **1.** English (of Norman origin): habitational name from Saint-Hilaire-du-Harcouët in La Manche, which gets its name from the dedication of its church to St. Hilary, or alternatively from either of the places, in La Manche and Somme, called Saint-Lô. Both of the latter are named from a 6th-century St. Lauto, bishop of Coutances; his name is of variable form in the sources and uncertain etymology. **2.** North German: habitational name for someone from SANDEL. **3.** Jewish (eastern Ashkenazic): occupational name for a cobbler or shoemaker, Yiddish *sandler* (from Hebrew *sandelar*, from Late Latin *sandalarius*, an agent derivative of *sandalium* 'shoe').
GIVEN NAMES Jewish 6%. *Sol* (6), *Hyman* (4), *Amnon* (2), *Faina* (2), *Feige* (2), *Herschel* (2), *Meyer* (2), *Semen* (2), *Avi*, *Fira*, *Ilya*, *Isack*.

Sandles (110) English (West Midlands): probably a variant spelling of **Sandels**, a variant of SANDELL, or possibly a variant of **Sandal(l)**, from the personal name *Sandolf*, from Old Norse *Sandúlfr*

GIVEN NAME German 6%. *Hedwig*.

Sandlin (2876) Swedish: ornamental name composed of the elements *sand* 'sand' + the common surname suffix *-lin*.

Sandman (702) **1.** Dutch: variant of **Van den Zande** (see SAND 2). **2.** Dutch: occupational name for someone who transported or sold sand, from *zand* 'sand' + *man* 'man'. **3.** Swedish: from *sand* 'sand' + *man* 'man'. **4.** Americanized spelling of German SANDMANN.

Sandmann (294) German: **1.** variant of SAND 1, with the addition of Middle High German *man* 'man'. **2.** variant of SANDER 1.

Sandmeier (113) German: variant of SANDMEYER.

GIVEN NAMES German 11%; Scandinavian 5%. *Otto* (2), *Helmuth*, *Ruedi*.

Sandmeyer (190) German: distinguishing name for a tenant farmer (see MEYER) whose farm was on sandy soil (Middle High German *sand*).

Sandner (214) German: **1.** topographic name, a variant of SAND 1, from the genitive case of Middle High German *sand* 'sand' + *-er*, suffix denoting an inhabitant. **2.** habitational name for someone from the city of Xanten on the Lower Rhine.

Sandness (185) Respelling of Norwegian **Sandnes**, a habitational name from any of fifty or more farmsteads all over Norway, so named from Old Norse *Sandnes*, a compound of *sand* 'sand', 'sandy plain', 'beach' + *nes* 'headland', 'promontory'.

Sando (346) **1.** Norwegian (**Sandø**): older form of **Sandøy**, a habitational name from any of about fifteen farmsteads so named, from Old Norse *Sandey*, a compound of *sand* 'sand' + *ey* 'island'. **2.** Swedish (**Sandö**): ornamental adoption of 1. **3.** Japanese: it is unclear whether instances of this name in America are *Sando*, usually written with characters meaning 'three doors', or *Sandō*, written with various characters, possible meanings being 'three wisteria' or 'east of the mountains'. None of these are common in Japan.

GIVEN NAMES Japanese 6%. *Susumu* (2), *Isamu, Musu, Setsuo, Shig, Takashi, Takayuki*.

Sandoe (139) Scandinavian (**Sandøe**): variant of SANDO.

Sandor (675) Hungarian (**Sándor**) and Jewish (from Hungary): from the personal name *Sándor*, Hungarian form of ALEXANDER.

GIVEN NAMES Hungarian 8%. *Bela* (6), *Laszlo* (5), *Andras* (2), *Attila, Erzsebet, Geza, Imre, Laszio, Sandor, Tamas, Tibor, Zsolt*.

Sandora (153) Origin unidentified.

GIVEN NAME Italian 4%. *Angelo*.

Sandoval (11374) Spanish: habitational name from any of the places named Sandoval, in particular the one in Burgos, also those in Murcia and Málaga, earlier called *Sannoval*, from Latin *saltus* 'grove', 'wood' + *novalis* 'newly cleared land'.

GIVEN NAMES Spanish 45%. *Jose* (287), *Juan* (156), *Jesus* (120), *Carlos* (107), *Manuel* (94), *Luis* (74), *Francisco* (67), *Ruben* (59), *Pedro* (58), *Miguel* (55), *Raul* (54), *Mario* (50).

Sandow (289) **1.** English (Cornwall): from a pet form of the personal name SANDER. **2.** Polish: variant of **Sędów**, a habitational name for someone from places called Sędów in Piotrków and Sieradz voivodeships.

Sandoz (341) French (Savoy) and Swiss French: from a Germanic personal name composed of the elements *sanths* 'true' + *wald* 'rule'.

GIVEN NAMES French 5%. *Edouard* (2), *Leonie, Marcel*.

Sandquist (593) Swedish: ornamental name composed of the elements *sand* 'sand' + *quist*, an old or ornamental spelling of *kvist* 'twig'.

GIVEN NAMES Scandinavian 5%. *Berger, Erik, Lennart*.

Sandretto (106) Italian: from a pet form of the personal name *Sandro*, a short form of *Alessandro* (see ALEXANDER).

Sandri (135) Italian: patronymic from *Sandro*, a short form of the personal name *Alessandro* (see ALEXANDER).

Sandridge (641) English: habitational name from places so named in Devon, Hertfordshire, and Wiltshire. The first two were named with Old English *sand* 'sand' + *hrycg* 'ridge'.

Sandrock (305) German: topographic name denoting either someone who lived in or owned a sandy place where rye was grown (Middle High German *sand* 'sand' + *rocke* 'rye') or where a weed known as *sandrocke* grew.

GIVEN NAMES German 4%. *Erwin, Rainer, Reinhard*.

Sandry (126) French, German, or English spelling of SANDRI.

Sands (6776) **1.** English, Scottish, and northern Irish: variant of SAND 1. **2.** Scottish: habitational name from Sands in Tulliallan in Fife.

FOREBEARS Comfort Sands, a revolutionary patriot born in 1748 at what is now Sands' Point, Long Island, NY, was descended from James (Sandys) Sands (1622–95), who emigrated from Reading, Berkshire, England, to Plymouth, MA, and followed Anne Hutchinson to Westchester Co., NY, and subsequently RI. In 1661 he settled on Block Island, RI.

Sandstedt (143) Swedish: ornamental name composed of the elements *sand* 'sand' + *stedt*, probably from North German *-stedt* (Middle Low German *stete*

'place', 'town'), compare German *Stadt* (plural *Städte*).

Sandstrom (1561) Swedish (**Sandström**): ornamental name composed of the elements *sand* 'sand' + *ström* 'river'.

GIVEN NAMES Scandinavian 8%. *Erik* (7), *Nils* (4), *Anders* (3), *Erland* (2), *Lars* (2), *Sven* (2), *Arnell, Astrid, Ejnar, Helmer, Hjalmer, Knute*.

Sandt (412) **1.** German: variant of SAND 1. **2.** Dutch (**Sandt**): variant of SAND 2.

GIVEN NAMES German 4%. *Bernd, Erna, Ingo, Kurt*.

Sandusky (987) Germanized spelling of Polish **Sandowski, Sędowski**, habitational name from places called Sędowice, Sędowo, Sędów, in Lublin, Bydgoszcz, Piotrków, and Sieradz voivodeships.

Sandvick (130) Americanized spelling of Norwegian SANDVIG.

Sandvig (392) Norwegian: habitational name from any of numerous farmsteads so named all over Norway, from Old Norse as *Sandvík*, a compound of *sand* 'sand', 'sandy plain', 'beach' + *vík* 'bay', 'inlet'.

Sandvik (308) **1.** Norwegian: variant of SANDVIG. **2.** Swedish: ornamental name composed of the elements *sand* 'sand' + *vik* 'bay', 'inlet'.

GIVEN NAMES Scandinavian 14%; German 5%. *Erik* (3), *Anders, Bente, Lars, Morten, Ottar, Thorleif; Wilhelm* (3), *Kurt*.

Sandwick (179) **1.** Americanized form of SANDVIG, SANDVIK. **2.** Probably a habitational name from any of the many places so called in Orkney and Shetland, or one in Cumbria, England.

GIVEN NAME Scandinavian 7%. *Thor*.

Sandy (1867) English: **1.** habitational name from a place in Bedfordshire, so named from Old English *sand* 'sand' + *ēg* 'island', 'dry land in a fen or marsh'. **2.** from the Old Norse personal name *Sand(i)*, a short form of the various compound names with the first element *sandr* 'sand'.

Sane (157) **1.** English: unexplained. **2.** Indian (Maharashtra); pronounced as two syllables: Hindu (Brahman) name found among Konkanasth Brahmans. It appears to be derived from Marathi *sana* 'small', a word of Kannada origin. **3.** African: unexplained.

GIVEN NAMES Indian 23%; African 4%. *Sachin* (2), *Shashikant* (2), *Suresh* (2), *Anand, Ashok, Deepak, Dhiraj, Jayant, Madhu, Purushottam, Sandeep, Shekhar; Amadou, Demba, Lamin, Mohamadou*.

Saner (451) English: unexplained; probably one of the many variants of SENIOR.

Sanes (107) **1.** Catalan (**Sanès**): variant of the Catalan habitational name **Senès** 'Sienese', 'from Siena (in Italy)'. **2.** Catalan (**Sanés**): variant of the Catalan habitational name **Seners**, a town in northern Catalonia.

GIVEN NAMES Spanish 7%; Jewish 4%. *Arnaldo, Elvira, Ernesto, Mercedes, Ramona, Santa, Yessenia; Miriam* (2).

Sanfelippo (105) Southern Italian: variant of SANFILIPPO.

GIVEN NAMES Italian 13%. *Sal, Salvatore, Santo.*

Sanfilippo (1367) Italian (mainly Sicily and southern Calabria): habitational name from any of several places so named for a local church or shrine dedicated to St. Philip, in particular San Filippo del Mela in Messina province.

Sanford (12755) English: variant of SAND-FORD.

Sanfratello (137) Italian (Sicily): habitational name from a place in Messina named San Fratello.

GIVEN NAMES Italian 13%. *Sal* (2), *Angelo, Ignazio, Matteo, Valentino.*

Sanft (109) German: nickname for a slow, easy-going person, from Middle High German *sanfte* 'easy'.

GIVEN NAME German 4%. *Helmut.*

Sang (426) **1.** Scottish: possibly a shortened form of **Sang(st)er** (see SANGER 2). **2.** German: habitational name from any of several places so named in the Rhineland. **3.** German and Jewish (Ashkenazic): occupational name or nickname for a singer (see SANGER 1). **4.** Chinese 桑: from a character in the name of Qiongsang, a place in present-day Shandong province. A son of the legendary emperor Huang Di (26th century BC), Shao Hao, also known as Jin Tianshi (see JIN) was enthroned at Qiongsang. Some descendants adopted the second character of the place name, Sang, as their surname. Another account of the source of the name in this form derives it from the legendary emperor Shen Nong, (2734–2697 BC), who was also referred to as Sangshui Shi.

GIVEN NAMES Chinese 13%; Vietnamese 6%. *Han* (2), *Jae* (2), *Yan* (2), *Chia Neng, Chor, Fong, Guo, Hong, Hua, Hun, Hyung, Jing; Ngai* (2), *Nguyen* (2), *Thy* (2), *Ahn, Dao, Diep, Hai, Lam, Le Thi, Nguyen Van, Phon, Tran.*

Sanger (1559) **1.** German (**Sänger**), Dutch, and Jewish (Ashkenazic): from Middle High German *senger*, Middle Dutch *sangher, sengher*, German *Sänger* 'singer', an occupational name for a singer or chorister, or in the case of the Jewish name for a cantor in a synagogue. **2.** English, from Old English *sangere* 'singer', occupational name for a singer or chorister, or nickname for a cheerful person who was always singing.

FOREBEARS The Sangers of MA are descended from Richard Sanger, who settled as a blacksmith in Sudbury, MA, in 1646.

Sangermano (104) Italian: habitational name from a place named San Germano.

GIVEN NAMES Italian 14%. *Armando, Carmela, Mario, Vinicio.*

Sangha (120) Indian (Panjab): Sikh name based on the name of a Jat tribe.

GIVEN NAMES Indian 89%. *Onkar* (2), *Raj* (2), *Susheel* (2), *Anoop, Atma, Avtar, Awtar, Darshan, Hardev, Jagdev, Jit, Karan.*

Sanghvi (129) Indian (Gujarat, Rajasthan): Jain name, from *sanghvi* 'one who offers hospitality to groups of Jain pilgrims', derived from Sanskrit *sangha* 'assembly', 'group'.

GIVEN NAMES Indian 95%. *Smita* (5), *Ashvin* (3), *Hemant* (3), *Sudhir* (3), *Vijay* (3), *Yogesh* (3), *Arun* (2), *Bharat* (2), *Chetan* (2), *Darshana* (2), *Girish* (2), *Jayesh* (2).

Sangiacomo (101) Italian: habitational name from a place so named for a local church or shrine dedicated to St. James (*San Giacomo*), as for example San Giacomo degli Schiavoni in Campobasso province or San Giacomo Vercellese in Vercelli.

GIVEN NAMES Italian 22%. *Angelo* (4), *Rocco* (2), *Antonio, Vito.*

Sangiovanni (135) Italian: habitational name from any of numerous places named for a local church or shrine dedicated to St. John (*San Giovanni*), as for example San Giovanni de Gerace in Reggio Calabria, San Giovanni a Piro in Salerno, San Giovanni Gemini in Agrigento, Sicily, or San Giovanni in Galdo in Campobasso.

GIVEN NAMES Italian 20%. *Antonio, Dante, Domenic, Domenico, Franca, Matteo, Pasquale, Sal.*

Sangrey (105) Origin unidentified.

Sangster (741) Scottish: variant of SANGER 2. The Old English ending *-ster* was originally a feminine agent suffix, contrasted with the masculine *-er*, but by the period of surname formation, the gender distinction had disappeared; the distinction is largely regional. Compare BAKER/BAXTER; WEBBER/WEBSTER, etc.

Sanguinetti (269) Italian and Jewish (from Italy): habitational name for someone any of various places named Sanguinet(t)o, as for example Sanguinetto in Verona province.

Sani (120) **1.** Muslim: from a personal name based on Arabic *sanī* 'majestic', 'brilliant'. **2.** Hindu name found among people from Sind, Pakistan. **3.** Indian (Panjab): Sikh name of unknown meaning. **4.** Italian: patronymic or plural form of SANO.

GIVEN NAMES Muslim 30%; Indian 11%; Italian 4%. *Mohammed* (2), *Sham* (2), *Abdul, Amir, Mehdi, Mohamed, Mohsen, Mustapha, Nasser, Othman, Rashid, Usman; Lal* (2), *Brahma, Sunil, Suresh; Giovanni, Paolo.*

San Jose (125) Spanish (**San José**): habitational name from any of the places named for a local church or shrine dedicated to St. Joseph (*San José*).

GIVEN NAMES Spanish 40%. *Manuel* (4), *Carlos* (3), *Angel* (2), *Luis* (2), *Pedro* (2),

Salvador (2), *Amelita, Arsenio, Augusto, Bonifacio, Delfin, Domingo; Antonio* (5), *Eliseo, Gilda, Liberato, Romeo.*

San Juan (364) Spanish (also **Sanjuan**): habitational name from any of the numerous places so named for a local shrine or church dedicated to St John (*San Juan*).

GIVEN NAMES Spanish 48%. *Jose* (10), *Pedro* (9), *Francisco* (6), *Juan* (6), *Jesus* (4), *Carmelita* (3), *Jaime* (3), *Luis* (3), *Miguel* (3), *Roberto* (3), *Alfredo* (2), *Armando* (2).

Sank (110) English: from a personal name, *Samke*, possibly from Old Norse *Sadúlfr*, or from *Sanni*, a pet form of Old Norse *Sandi.*

Sankar (177) Indian: see SHANKAR.

GIVEN NAMES Indian 57%. *Ravi* (3), *Subramanian* (3), *Kalpana* (2), *Krishna* (2), *Radha* (2), *Ananth, Aravind, Ashok, Balram, Bhavani, Chandra, Chetan.*

Sankaran (116) Indian (Kerala, Tamil Nadu): Hindu name from Sanskrit *śankara* 'bringer of happiness or prosperity' (an epithet of the god Shiva) + the Tamil-Malayalam third-person masculine singular suffix *-n*. This is only a given name in India, but has come to be used as a family name in the U.S.

GIVEN NAMES Indian 92%. *Nandakumar* (3), *Srini* (3), *Mahesh* (2), *Prakash* (2), *Ravindran* (2), *Sekhar* (2), *Siva* (2), *Sudhakar* (2), *Sumathi* (2), *Sundaram* (2), *Surya* (2), *Uma* (2).

Sanker (243) Probably a variant of English SANGER.

Sankey (1108) **1.** English: habitational name from a place in Lancashire, named with an ancient British river name, perhaps meaning 'sacred', 'holy'. **2.** Irish: when not of English origin (see 1 above), a rare reduced Anglicized form of Gaelic **Mac Seanchaidhe** 'son of the chronicler', a name found in Sligo and Leitrim, which is more commonly Anglicized as FOX, as the result of an erroneous association with *sionnach* 'fox'.

Sanko (281) Hungarian: from a pet form of *Sándor*, Hungarian form of ALEXANDER.

Sankovich (127) Serbian and Croatian (**Sanković**): patronymic from the personal name *Sanko*, a derivative of *san* 'dream'.

Sanks (233) Origin unidentified.

San Martin (240) Spanish (**San Martín**, also **Sanmartín**): habitational name from any of the numerous places so named for a local shrine or church dedicated to St. Martin.

GIVEN NAMES Spanish 46%. *Jose* (7), *Jorge* (5), *Juan* (5), *Luis* (5), *Carlos* (4), *Roberto* (4), *Francisco* (3), *Julio* (3), *Pedro* (3), *Alejandro* (2), *Ana* (2), *Arnaldo* (2).

San Miguel (696) Spanish (also **Sanmiguel**): habitational name from any of the numerous places so named for a local shrine or church dedicated to St. Michael (*San Miguel*).

GIVEN NAMES Spanish 44%. *Jose* (15), *Carlos* (11), *Luis* (10), *Juan* (9), *Manuel* (7), *Francisco* (6), *Guadalupe* (6), *Armando* (4), *Jorge* (4), *Juanita* (4), *Raul* (4), *Ruben* (4).

Sann (156) German: from a short form (*sano*, *sanno*) of a Germanic personal name from an unexplained stem *san*.

Sanna (253) **1.** Italian (Sardinian): nickname for someone with prominent front teeth, from *sanna* 'large, protruding tooth'. **2.** Dutch: metronymic from a reduced form of the Biblical female name *Susanna*. **3.** Greek (**Sannas**): occupational name for a seller of hay, from *sano* 'hay', from Slavic *seno*.

GIVEN NAMES Italian 9%. *Salvatore* (2), *Angelo, Antonio, Enrico, Pietro, Romeo, Sal, Vito*.

Sanner (1099) Swedish and Norwegian: variant of SANDER.

Sannes (341) **1.** Norwegian: variant of **Sandnes** (see SANDNESS). **2.**

GIVEN NAMES Scandinavian 5%. *Nels* (2), *Thor*.

San Nicolas (145) Spanish (**San Nicolás**; also **Sannicolás**): habitational name from any of the numerous places so named for a local shrine or church dedicated to St. Nicholas.

GIVEN NAMES Spanish 24%; Italian 5%. *Jose* (3), *Gregorio* (2), *Joaquin* (2), *Antolin, Carlos, Eduardo, Felipe, Florencio, Francisco, Juan, Mariano, Pedro*; *Antonio* (3), *Silbino*.

Sanning (121) Origin unidentified.

Sano (458) **1.** Japanese: variously written, it means 'small field' and is found throughout Japan. Some bearers have samurai connections. **2.** Italian: nickname from *sano* 'healthy', from Latin *sanus*, or from a short form of an adjectival habitational name formed with the suffix -*sano*, as for example FORMISANO.

GIVEN NAMES Japanese 38%; Italian 4%. *Hiroshi* (4), *Kazuhiko* (3), *Masaaki* (3), *Tomomi* (3), *Yumiko* (3), *Akira* (2), *Chiharu* (2), *Katsuhiko* (2), *Masashi* (2), *Takuya* (2), *Toru* (2), *Yuichi* (2); *Salvatore* (3), *Angelo* (2), *Pietro* (2), *Nunzio*.

Sanon (215) Perhaps an altered form of French **Sinon**, from a short form of the pet personal names *Massinon, Jossinon*, etc.

GIVEN NAMES French 47%; German 4%. *Ghislaine* (2), *Alain, Antoine, Bernadin, Berthe, Chantale, Emile, Ermite, Evens, Fernande, Fresnel, Georges*; *Fritz* (2).

Sanor (137) English (Yorkshire): unexplained. Perhaps one of the many variants of SENIOR.

Sanow (148) Polish: of uncertain origin; possibly a variant of **Sianów**, a habitational name from a place called Sianów in Gdańsk voivodeship.

San Pedro (173) Spanish (also **Sanpedro**): habitational name from any of the numer-

ous places named for a local church or shrine dedicated to St. Peter (*San Pedro*).

GIVEN NAMES Spanish 49%. *Jose* (4), *Juan* (4), *Jorge* (3), *Amalia* (2), *Benedicto* (2), *Cesar* (2), *Fernando* (2), *Jesus* (2), *Margarita* (2), *Reynaldo* (2), *Ricardo* (2), *Alejandro*; *Romeo* (2), *Aldo, Antonio, Dante, Luciano, Silvio*.

San Roman (153) Spanish: habitational name from any of the numerous places named for a local church or shrine dedicated to St. Roman (see ROMAN).

GIVEN NAMES Spanish 52%. *Manuel* (4), *Carlos* (3), *Jose* (3), *Elia* (2), *Enrique* (2), *Guillermo* (2), *Maximo* (2), *Orlando* (2), *Alejandro, Alfredo, Angel, Armando*.

Sans (194) Catalan and Southern French (Occitan): from the Occitan personal name *Sans*, or from the variant of the Catalan personal name *Sanç*, both of them equivalent to Spanish SANCHO.

GIVEN NAMES Spanish 15%; French 5%. *Rafael* (3), *Lourdes* (2), *Rolando* (2), *Agustin, Alfonso, Diego, Emilio, Enrique, Jorge, Jose, Luis, Maria Del*; *Henri* (2), *Marcel*.

Sansalone (115) Italian: from an augmentative of an old Italian occupational name, *sansale* 'agent', 'broker'. See also SANZARI.

GIVEN NAMES Italian 19%. *Aldo, Carmelo, Domenico, Giuseppe, Salvatore, Vincenzo*.

Sansbury (376) Variant of English SAINSBURY.

San Severino (123) Italian (mainly Naples): habitational name from San Severino in Potenza or Mercato San Severino in Salerno.

GIVEN NAMES Italian 22%. *Cono* (2), *Enrico* (2), *Rocco* (2), *Canio, Giuseppe, Vito*.

Sansing (397) Origin unidentified.

Sansom (1058) English: variant of SAMSON.

Sanson (709) Filipino: variant of **Samson**, probably from Tagalog *samson* meaning 'third grandson'.

GIVEN NAMES Spanish 4%. *Carlos* (3), *Adriana* (2), *Miguel* (2), *Serafin* (2), *Amado, Artemio, Dulce Maria, Elena, Francisco, Joaquin, Jose, Juana*.

Sansone (1798) Italian: from the personal name *Sansone*, Italian equivalent of SAMSON.

GIVEN NAMES Italian 11%. *Angelo* (10), *Salvatore* (7), *Rocco* (5), *Antonio* (4), *Sal* (3), *Vito* (3), *Carmela* (2), *Carmine* (2), *Cosmo* (2), *Amerigo, Cosimo, Dino*.

Sansouci (125) French: variant of SANSOUCIE.

GIVEN NAMES French 7%. *Aime, Normand*.

Sansoucie (237) French: nickname for a lighthearted, carefree person, from *sans souci* 'without care', 'without worry'.

Sansoucy (130) French: variant of SANSOUCIE.

GIVEN NAMES French 18%. *Armand* (4), *Andre* (2), *Monique, Reynald, Simonne*.

Sant (412) **1.** English and French: variant of SAINT. **2.** Italian (northeastern): variant of SANTO. **3.** Dutch (also **de Sant**): nickname from Middle Dutch *sant* 'saint'. **4.** Dutch: variant of VAN SANT. **5.** Jewish (Ashkenazic): variant of SAND. **6.** Indian (Maharashtra): Hindu (Brahman) name meaning 'saint', 'holy man'.

GIVEN NAMES Indian 7%. *Krishan* (2), *Anagha, Anjali, Arvind, Deepak, Milind, Nilima, Ravindra, Sanjeev, Sanjiv, Vasudev*.

Santa (467) **1.** Portuguese: habitational name from any of the places named Santa in Portugal, probably from *santa* '(female) saint'. **2.** Hungarian (**Sánta**): descriptive nickname for a disabled person, from *sánta* 'lame'.

GIVEN NAMES Spanish 15%. *Jose* (8), *Luis* (5), *Gerardo* (2), *Juan* (2), *Roberto* (2), *Aida, Alberto, Alicia, Angelina, Blanca, Carlos, Cesar*.

Santa Ana (149) Spanish and Portuguese: habitational name from any of the numerous places named for a local shrine or church dedicated to St. Anna (*Santa Ana*; compare SANTANA).

GIVEN NAMES Spanish 36%. *Gustavo* (3), *Alfonso* (2), *Jose* (2), *Rodrigo* (2), *Agustina, Alberto, Avelino, Blasa, Carlos, Cesar, Consuelo, Cruz*.

Santa Croce (356) Italian: habitational name from any of numerous places in all parts of Italy named with Santa Croce, in particular Santa Croce Camerina (Ragusa), Santa Croce del Sannia (Benevento), or Santa Croce di Maglicano (Campobasso). The place name is a religious dedication meaning 'holy cross'.

GIVEN NAMES Italian 17%. *Vito* (3), *Dino* (2), *Guido* (2), *Aldo, Angelo, Ciro, Cosmo, Dante, Guerino, Maurizio, Nunzio, Pasquale*.

Santa Cruz (711) Spanish (also **Santacruz**): habitational name from any of numerous places named with *Santa Cruz* 'holy cross', from the dedication of a local church or shrine.

GIVEN NAMES Spanish 42%. *Jose* (18), *Manuel* (11), *Carlos* (8), *Jorge* (8), *Alfredo* (7), *Ricardo* (7), *Jesus* (5), *Luis* (5), *Mario* (5), *Fernando* (4), *Juan* (4), *Julio* (4).

Santagata (222) Italian: habitational name from any of the many places named Sant'Agata for a religious dedication to St. Agatha (*Sant'Agata*), notably Sant'Agata del Bianco (Reggio Calabria), Sant'Agata de'Goti (Bologna), Sant'Agata di Esaro (Cosenza), Sant'Agata li Battiati (Catania, Sicily), or Sant'Agata Militello (Messina, Sicily).

GIVEN NAMES Italian 12%. *Luigi* (2), *Camillo, Pasquale, Sandro*.

Santa Lucia (156) Southern Italian: habitational name from a place so named for a local shrine or church dedicated to St. Lucy (*Santa Lucia*), notably Santa Lucia del

Mela (Messina, Sicily), Santa Lucia di Serino (Avellino), and Santa Lucia di Piave (Treviso).

GIVEN NAMES Italian 18%. *Salvatore* (3), *Gaetano* (2), *Pasquale* (2), *Antonio, Enzo.*

Santa Maria (1534) **1.** Italian, Spanish (**Santa María**), and Catalan (alongside the variants **Santamaria** in Italian and Catalan, and **Santamaría** in Spanish): **2.** habitational name from any of numerous places so named for the dedication of their churches to the Virgin Mary (or to some other St. Mary), of which there are over 150 examples in Italy alone. **3.** in some cases, possibly from a personal name of the same derivation. **4.** name often adopted by Catalan and Spanish Sephardic Jews who converted to Catholicism, often under duress, in the 14th and 15th centuries.

GIVEN NAMES Spanish 34%; Italian 8%. *Jose* (41), *Carlos* (20), *Luis* (14), *Jesus* (11), *Jorge* (8), *Juan* (7), *Manuel* (7), *Mario* (7), *Enrique* (6), *Francisco* (6), *Humberto* (6), *Pablo* (6); *Salvatore* (8), *Antonio* (7), *Angelo* (6), *Marco* (4), *Bartolo* (2), *Carmelo* (2), *Cosmo* (2), *Luciano* (2), *Vito* (2), *Alfonse, Bartolomeo, Carlo.*

Santana (5018) Spanish and Portuguese: habitational name from any of the numerous places named Santana, an assimilated form of SANTA ANA.

GIVEN NAMES Spanish 50%; Portuguese 10%. *Jose* (154), *Juan* (73), *Luis* (55), *Manuel* (45), *Carlos* (43), *Rafael* (43), *Ramon* (38), *Pedro* (37), *Miguel* (36), *Jesus* (33), *Jorge* (30), *Angel* (29); *Paulo* (2), *Conceicao.*

Santander (138) Spanish: habitational name from Santander, the regional capital of Cantabria, named in Latin as *Sanctus Emeterius.*

GIVEN NAMES Spanish 40%. *Jose* (7), *Mario* (6), *Arturo* (2), *Belisario* (2), *Jorge* (2), *Julio* (2), *Manuel* (2), *Adolfo, Alicia, Asela, Atanacio, Blanca*; *Antonio* (4), *Lucio, Silvano.*

Santangelo (1526) Southern Italian: **1.** habitational name from any of numerous places, especially in the south, named Sant'Angelo for a local shrine or church dedicated to St. Angelo, as for example Sant'Angelo a Cupolo (Benevento), Sant'Angelo a Fasanella (Salerno), Sant'Angelo all'Esca and Sant'Angelo a Scala (Avellino), Sant'Angelo d'Alife (Caserta), and Sant'Angelo del Pesco (Molise). **2.** in some cases, possibly a compound personal name composed of the elements SANTO + ANGELO.

GIVEN NAMES Italian 12%. *Salvatore* (7), *Angelo* (4), *Rocco* (3), *Carmine* (2), *Corrado* (2), *Cosmo* (2), *Geno* (2), *Sal* (2), *Vito* (2), *Carmelo, Cesare, Corradino.*

Santaniello (412) Italian (Naples): from a personal name adopted mainly in localities associated with St. Agnellus (*Sant'Aniello*) (see AGNELLO).

GIVEN NAMES Italian 22%. *Carmine* (5), *Pasquale* (4), *Salvatore* (4), *Antonio* (3),

Amedeo (2), *Luigi* (2), *Sal* (2), *Angelo, Carmela, Ferdinando, Fiore, Gaetano.*

Santarelli (330) Italian: patronymic from a double diminutive of SANTO.

GIVEN NAMES Italian 21%. *Carlo* (4), *Rocco* (4), *Angelo* (2), *Enrico* (2), *Marino* (2), *Sesto* (2), *Aldo, Alessandro, Carmin, Constantino, Domenic.*

Santarsiero (172) Italian: unexplained; perhaps a habitational name from Sant'Arsenio in Basilicata, where the surname is frequent.

GIVEN NAMES Italian 24%. *Vito* (5), *Angelo* (4), *Domenic, Rocco, Salvatore, Santina.*

Santavicca (118) Italian (Abruzzi): unexplained.

GIVEN NAMES Italian 21%. *Gino* (2), *Pietro* (2), *Constantino, Dante, Emedio, Fausto, Quirino.*

Sante (142) **1.** German and Dutch: from the female personal name *Sente* (Latin *Sancta*; compare SAINT). This may sometimes have been a reinterpreted derivative of a Germanic personal name ending in *-sind* (*-swind, -swinth*). **2.** Dutch (**Van Sante**): habitational name for someone from Xanten on the Lower Rhine.

GIVEN NAMES French 9%; Spanish 4%. *Luc* (2), *Camille, Lucien*; *Alejandro, Anselmo, Carlos, Emilio, Jesusa, Jorge.*

Santee (732) Probably an altered spelling of Dutch or German SANTE, written thus to preserve the pronunciation as two syllables.

Santel (140) Italian: Venetian (Balluno) variant of SANTELLI.

Santell (111) Italian: variant of SANTELLI.

GIVEN NAMES Italian 15%; Spanish 5%. *Saverio* (2), *Domenic, Orlando, Ricci, Roberto, Salvatore*; *Jose* (2), *Juan, Luis.*

Santella (329) Italian: from a feminine pet form of SANTO.

GIVEN NAMES Italian 13%. *Angelo* (4), *Carlo, Carmine, Dario, Dino, Gennaro, Gildo, Grazio, Guido, Lazzaro, Pasquale, Pietro.*

Santelli (317) Italian: patronymic from *Santello*, a pet form of SANTO.

GIVEN NAMES Italian 14%. *Angelo* (2), *Dino* (2), *Nunzio* (2), *Valentino* (2), *Domenico, Gaeton, Giovanni, Oreste, Pasquale, Rinaldo, Sal.*

Santer (122) **1.** German and Jewish (Ashkenazic): probably from a short form of the personal name ALEXANDER. Compare SANDER. **2.** English: variant of SENTER. **3.** French: variant of SANTERRE.

GIVEN NAMES Jewish 7%. *Mayer* (2), *Moshe.*

Santeramo (108) Italian: habitational name from a place called Santeramo in Colle, in Bari province.

GIVEN NAMES Italian 6%. *Gaetano, Vita.*

Santerre (274) French: habitational name from a place to the southeast of the Somme river, named with Latin *sana terra* 'healthy, wholesome land'.

GIVEN NAMES French 7%. *Emile, Ovila, Pierre.*

Santi (515) Italian: from the personal name *Santi*, plural form of SANTO, a short form of the devotional name *Ognisanti*, probably bestowed on a child born on All Saints' Day.

GIVEN NAMES Italian 11%; Spanish 6%. *Alfredo* (3), *Marco* (3), *Aldo* (2), *Dario* (2), *Gino* (2), *Giovanni* (2), *Mario* (2), *Antonio, Caesar, Carlo, Dante, Domenica, Donato, Enrico, Gustavo*; *Luis* (3), *Jesus* (2), *Adriana, Andreina, Angel, Carlos, Cesar, Jose.*

Santiago (9927) Galician, Portuguese, and Spanish: habitational name from any of the numerous places named for the dedication of their churches to St. James (*Sant Iago*). The apostle St. James the Greater is the patron saint of Spain; there is a medieval legend that, after the death of Christ, he did not meet a speedy end under Herod Agrippa, but visited and evangelized the Iberian peninsula. His alleged burial site at Compostela has been a place of pilgrimage from all over Europe for over a thousand years.

GIVEN NAMES Spanish 45%; Portuguese 10%. *Jose* (298), *Juan* (127), *Luis* (120), *Carlos* (110), *Angel* (89), *Miguel* (75), *Manuel* (69), *Pedro* (67), *Julio* (60), *Rafael* (60), *Ramon* (57), *Roberto* (44); *Joao* (2), *Paulo* (2), *Gonsalo, Joaquim, Ligia, Wenceslao.*

Santibanez (218) Spanish (**Santibáñez**): habitational name from any of the numerous places named for the dedication of a local church or shrine to St. John.

GIVEN NAMES Spanish 56%. *Juan* (6), *Jose* (5), *Manuel* (5), *Dalmacio* (2), *Francisco* (2), *Gonzalo* (2), *Guadalupe* (2), *Josefina* (2), *Mario* (2), *Miguel* (2), *Pablo* (2), *Ruben* (2).

Santiesteban (163) Spanish: variant of **Sant'Esteban**, a habitational name from any of various places named for St. Stephen, for example Santisteban del Puerto, in Jaén province. The spelling with medial *-i-* is probably due to the influence of the more common name SANTIAGO.

GIVEN NAMES Spanish 50%. *Jose* (6), *Carlos* (3), *Pedro* (3), *Arturo* (2), *Enrique* (2), *Jesus* (2), *Jorge* (2), *Mario* (2), *Raul* (2), *Ricardo* (2), *Roberto* (2), *Adan*; *Aldo, Antonio, Dario, Lorenzo, Vita.*

Santillan (808) Spanish (**Santillán**): habitational name from any of the places named for the dedication of a local church or shrine to a St. Julian (Latin *Sanctus Iulianus*).

GIVEN NAMES Spanish 56%. *Jose* (30), *Juan* (21), *Manuel* (11), *Jesus* (9), *Jaime* (8), *Javier* (7), *Carlos* (6), *Francisco* (6), *Miguel* (6), *Roberto* (6), *Ruben* (6), *Alberto* (5).

Santillanes (191) NM name of Spanish origin (not found in Spain): possibly a habitational name from a lost place. Compare SANTILLAN, to which this name is clearly related.

GIVEN NAMES Spanish 30%. *Jose* (4), *Jesus* (3), *Apolonio* (2), *Eloy* (2), *Manuel* (2), *Adelina, Alfredo, Ambrosio, Arnoldo, Consuelo, Emiliano, Fernando*.

Santilli (688) Italian: patronymic or plural form of SANTILLO.

GIVEN NAMES Italian 32%. *Mario* (9), *Angelo* (4), *Guido* (3), *Pasquale* (3), *Rocco* (3), *Salvatore* (3), *Antonio* (2), *Carlo* (2), *Domenic* (2), *Domenico* (2), *Donato* (2), *Emidio* (2), *Luigi* (2).

Santillo (508) Italian: from the personal name *Santillo*, a pet form of SANTO.

GIVEN NAMES Italian 14%. *Salvatore* (3), *Antonio* (2), *Carmine* (2), *Gennaro* (2), *Giulio* (2), *Livio* (2), *Luigi* (2), *Cosimo, Cosmo, Dario, Dino, Giuseppe*.

Santin (171) Spanish (**Santín**) and Italian (Venetian): from the personal name *Santin(o)*, a pet form of SANTO.

GIVEN NAMES Spanish 14%; Italian 5%. *Carlos* (3), *Jose* (2), *Alberto, Augusto, Beatriz, Carols, Gabriela, Lino, Lourdes, Luis, Manuel, Miguel; Alessandro* (2), *Antonio* (2), *Ceasar*.

Santini (900) Italian: patronymic form of SANTINO.

GIVEN NAMES Italian 21%; Spanish 5%. *Angelo* (3), *Antonio* (3), *Reno* (3), *Aldo* (2), *Claudio* (2), *Emilio* (2), *Giuseppe* (2), *Mario* (2), *Nicola* (2), *Oreste* (2), *Primo* (2), *Salvatore* (2), *Santino* (2), *Veto* (2); *Jose* (4), *Luis* (3), *Carlos* (2), *Manuel* (2), *Rafael* (2), *Ruben* (2), *Angel*.

Santino (264) Italian: from the personal name *Santino*, a pet form of SANTO.

GIVEN NAMES Italian 14%. *Angelo* (2), *Alphonso, Carmelo, Francisco, Gaspar, Giuseppe, Luciano, Mario, Sergio*.

Santistevan (449) Spanish: variant of SANTIESTEBAN.

GIVEN NAMES Spanish 21%. *Jose* (7), *Orlando* (4), *Carlos* (3), *Eloy* (2), *Juan* (2), *Manuel* (2), *Rosendo* (2), *Ruben* (2), *Adela, Agapita, Alfonso, Alfredo*.

Santizo (158) Galician: variant of **Santiso**, a habitational name from any of numerous places in Galicia, named for the dedication of a local church or shrine to a St. Tirso (Greek *Thyrsos*).

GIVEN NAMES Spanish 47%. *Luis* (6), *Carlos* (4), *Jorge* (4), *Juan* (3), *Mario* (3), *Pedro* (3), *Ana Maria* (2), *Guillermo* (2), *Jesus* (2), *Jose* (2), *Alba, Aracely*.

Santmyer (153) Variant spelling of German SANDMEYER.

Santner (109) South German and Austrian: topographic name for someone who lived on sandy soil, from a noun derivative of Middle High German *sant* 'sand'.

Santo (1209) **1.** Italian, Spanish, and Portuguese: from the personal name *Santo*, from *santo* 'holy'. In some instances the surname may have arisen from a nickname for a pious individual. **2.** Americanized spelling of Hungarian **Szántó** (see SZANTO).

GIVEN NAMES Italian 11%; Spanish 7%. *Antonio* (8), *Marino* (3), *Salvatore* (3), *Caesar* (2), *Pietro* (2), *Sal* (2), *Alfio, Angelo, Carmela, Ciro; Tomas* (5), *Juan* (4), *Manuel* (4), *Carlos* (2), *Jose* (2), *Justo* (2), *Raul* (2), *Abelino, Arnulso, Corrado*.

Santoli (149) Italian: from a patronymic form of *santolo* 'godfather'.

GIVEN NAMES Italian 22%. *Agnese, Angelo, Carmela, Domenic, Enza, Guiseppe, Massimo, Nunzio, Pietro, Sal, Vitaliano, Vito*.

Santomauro (123) Italian: habitational name from any of numerous places named for a local church or shrine dedicated to a Saint Mauro; there were several saints of this name. See MAURO and compare English MOORE 2.

GIVEN NAMES Italian 20%. *Angelo, Marco, Ornella, Pietro, Salvatore, Silvano, Vincenza*.

Santone (221) Italian: from an augmentative form of the personal name SANTO.

GIVEN NAMES Italian 10%. *Dante, Domenic, Donato, Philomena, Salvatore*.

Santoni (282) Italian: patronymic or plural form of SANTONE.

GIVEN NAMES Italian 22%; Spanish 6%. *Angelo* (2), *Dante* (2), *Alessandra, Claudio, Dino, Emidio, Enza, Ernesto, Evo, Flavio, Giampaolo, Gilberto, Gino, Gregorio, Livio, Rocco; Jose* (2), *Miguel* (2), *Elida, Gonzala, Juventino, Luis*.

Santo Pietro (215) Italian: **1.** habitational name from Santo Pietro, a district of Caltagirone in Catania province, Sicily, named for St. Peter (*Santo Pietro*). **2.** from a compound personal name composed of SANTO + PIETRO.

GIVEN NAMES Italian 15%. *Salvatore* (4), *Domenic* (2), *Donato, Guido, Libero, Nicola, Rocco, Saverio*.

Santor (205) Polish and eastern German: **1.** probably from an altered short form of the personal name ALEXANDER. Compare SANDER, SANTER. **2.** possibly a nickname based on Slavic *satori* 'to chatter idly', to wag one's tongue'.

Santora (927) Italian: variant (feminine in form) of SANTORO, the feminine form probably being due to the influence of the Italian word *famiglia* 'family'.

GIVEN NAMES Italian 12%. *Rocco* (5), *Carmine* (4), *Angelo* (3), *Sal* (2), *Salvatore* (2), *Antonio, Camillo, Carlo, Dante, Enrico, Natale*.

Santore (415) Italian: probably a variant of SANTORO.

GIVEN NAMES Italian 13%. *Carlo* (2), *Gennaro* (2), *Rocco* (2), *Angelo, Nunzio, Salvatore, Vito*.

Santorelli (186) Italian: patronymic from a pet form of SANTORO.

GIVEN NAMES Italian 26%. *Carmine* (6), *Angelo* (2), *Saverio* (2), *Alfonso, Angelina, Carmela, Ceasar, Fabio, Filomena, Gerardo, Mario, Pasquale, Sabato, Salvatore*.

Santori (152) Italian: patronymic or plural form of SANTORO.

GIVEN NAMES Italian 15%. *Emidio* (2), *Reno* (2), *Adalgisa, Aldo, Dino, Francesco, Gino, Guido, Rocco*.

Santoriello (117) Italian: from a pet form of the personal name SANTORO.

GIVEN NAMES Italian 13%; French 4%. *Angelo, Oreste, Santo; Germaine, Marie-Laure*.

Santoro (3159) Southern Italian: from a personal name, originally bestowed on someone who was born on All Saints' Day, Italian *santoro*, from Late Latin *sanctorum (omnium dies festus)* '(feast day of all) the saints'.

GIVEN NAMES Italian 17%. *Angelo* (17), *Vito* (15), *Rocco* (11), *Pasquale* (8), *Salvatore* (8), *Antonio* (7), *Carmine* (7), *Sal* (7), *Domenic* (4), *Giovanni* (4), *Nicola* (4), *Donato* (3).

Santos (15167) Spanish and Portuguese: **1.** from a personal name, byname, or nickname, *dos Santos* (from Spanish *Todos los Santos* 'All Saints', Portuguese *Todos os santos*), typically bestowed on a child born on All Saints' Day. **2.** in many cases, a habitational name from any of the places named Santos, from the dedication of a local church or shrine to all the saints. This is a very common Portuguese surname.

GIVEN NAMES Spanish 38%; Portuguese 11%; Italian 8%. *Jose* (357), *Manuel* (239), *Carlos* (141), *Juan* (91), *Francisco* (83), *Luis* (77), *Mario* (56), *Pedro* (55), *Roberto* (55), *Jesus* (51), *Ramon* (48), *Miguel* (46); *Joao* (39), *Paulo* (23), *Joaquim* (16), *Agostinho* (4), *Amadeu* (4), *Henrique* (4), *Marcio* (3), *Serafim* (3), *Ademir* (2), *Aderito* (2), *Albano* (2), *Ligia* (2); *Antonio* (198), *Romeo* (14), *Angelo* (12), *Carmelo* (8), *Leonardo* (7), *Marco* (7), *Mauro* (6), *Lorenzo* (5), *Luciano* (5), *Eliseo* (4), *Fausto* (4), *Federico* (4).

Santostefano (101) Italian: habitational name from a place so named for a local church or shrine dedicated to St. Steven (*San Stefano*; see STEVEN).

GIVEN NAMES Italian 28%. *Mario* (2), *Sal* (2), *Angelo, Domenic, Guido, Orlando, Romeo*.

Santosuosso (204) Italian (Campania): from a compound of *santo* 'holy', 'blessed' 'saint' + an unexplained second element, *s(u)osso*, possibly the name of an obscure local saint.

GIVEN NAMES Italian 5%. *Ceasar, Enza, Gilda, Saverio, Silvio*.

Santoyo (591) Spanish: habitational name from Santoyo in Palencia province.

GIVEN NAMES Spanish 55%. *Jose* (17), *Juan* (15), *Arturo* (9), *Jesus* (8), *Francisco* (7), *Manuel* (6), *Miguel* (6), *Carlos* (5), *Jorge* (5), *Luis* (5), *Alfredo* (4), *Armando* (4); *Lorenzo* (5), *Antonio* (3), *Federico* (2), *Ennio, Gabino, Sal, Salvator*.

Santry (255) English: from Middle English, Old French *seintuarie* 'sanctuary', 'shrine'

(Late Latin *sanctuarium*, a derivative of *sanctus* 'holy'); a topographic name for someone who lived near a shrine, or a nickname for someone who had had occasion to take sanctuary in a church or monastery, where he would have been afforded immunity from arrest or injury.

GIVEN NAMES French 4%. *Camille, Patrice.*

Santucci (1172) Italian: patronymic from the personal name *Santuccio*, a derivative of SANTO.

GIVEN NAMES Italian 18%. *Angelo* (6), *Carlo* (6), *Domenic* (5), *Pasquale* (5), *Ettore* (4), *Rocco* (3), *Silvio* (3), *Aldo* (2), *Antonio* (2), *Camillo* (2), *Carmelo* (2), *Domenico* (2).

Santulli (156) Southern Italian: patronymic from *Santullo*, a pet form of SANTO.

GIVEN NAME Italian 5%. *Domenic.*

Santy (253) Perhaps an altered spelling of SANTI.

Sanville (335) Origin unidentified.

Sanz (386) **1.** German: from a short form, *Sando*, of a Germanic personal name formed with *sand* 'true'. **2.** Spanish: variant of SANCHO.

GIVEN NAMES Spanish 42%. *Jose* (11), *Carlos* (9), *Ricardo* (6), *Juan* (5), *Luis* (5), *Enrique* (4), *Jaime* (4), *Armando* (3), *Ernesto* (3), *Francisco* (3), *Manuel* (3), *Miguel* (3).

Sanzari (101) Southern Italian: according to Caracausi an occupational name, a variant of Sicilian *sansali* 'broker', 'agent' (modern Italian *sensale*); this may represent a folk interpretation as if from *san Saro*, i.e. 'Saint Saro', *Saro* being a common personal name in Sicily.

GIVEN NAMES Italian 31%. *Adolfo, Aldo, Francesca, Gennaro, Lorenzo, Nicola, Orlando, Sergio.*

Sanzo (262) **1.** Italian: from a reduced form of the personal name *Sanson*, an old form of SANSONE (see SAMSON), or alternatively from an old personal name *Sanzo*, from Germanic *Santha-*. **2.** Asturian-Leonese and Spanish: habitational name from Sanzo in Asturies.

GIVEN NAMES Italian 16%. *Antonio* (2), *Salvatore* (2), *Adamo, Amerigo, Carmine, Domenic, Guiseppe, Rocco, Silvio, Vito.*

Sanzone (350) Italian: variant of SANSONE.

GIVEN NAMES Italian 17%. *Nicola* (3), *Salvatore* (3), *Antonio* (2), *Amadeo, Baldassare, Carmel, Gaetano, Gaspare, Giovan, Giulio, Rocco, Sal.*

Sao (169) **1.** Cambodian: unexplained. **2.** Filipino: unexplained.

GIVEN NAMES Southeast Asian 33%; Cambodian 6%. *Khon* (2), *Sophal* (2), *Nang, Phan, Phon, Tho, Thon, Thy, Yen; Deng, Heang, Kheng, Meng, Roeun, Seng, Yan, Yon; Savoeun* (2), *Chamroeun, Chheang, Chhom, Samoeun, Sophat, Yoeun; Chang, Ry, Savuth, Vang.*

Saper (124) Jewish (Ashkenazic): variant of SAPIR.

Saperstein (508) Jewish (Ashkenazic): ornamental name, a compound of Hebrew *sapir* 'sapphire' + German *Stein* 'stone'.

GIVEN NAMES Jewish 7%. *Haim, Herschel, Iren, Shira, Sol, Yisroel, Zalman.*

Sapia (207) Southern Italian (Sicily): from the feminine form of SAPIO.

GIVEN NAMES Italian 14%; French 6%. *Angelo* (4), *Salvatore* (2), *Antonio, Sabastian, Salvatrice, Santo; Pierre* (3), *Alcide.*

Sapien (225) **1.** Basque: variant of **Zapiain** (see ZAPIEN). **2.** Polish (**Sapień**): nickname for a wheezy person, derivative of *sapać* 'to wheeze'. **3.** Polish: possibly also a nickname derived from Latin *sapiens* 'clever', 'knowledgeable'.

GIVEN NAMES Spanish 32%. *Carlos* (5), *Alberto* (2), *Gabriela* (2), *Juan* (2), *Manuel* (2), *Pedro* (2), *Adriana, Angel, Armando, Benito, Demesio, Eduardo.*

Sapienza (738) Southern Italian (mainly Sicily): from the nickname or personal name *Sapienza*, meaning 'wisdom' (Latin *sapientia*).

GIVEN NAMES Italian 16%. *Salvatore* (9), *Vito* (5), *Rocco* (3), *Santo* (3), *Angelo* (2), *Antonio* (2), *Sal* (2), *Alfio, Antonino, Carmelo, Franco.*

Sapio (139) Southern Italian: from a personal name or nickname, *Sapio*, from Old Italian *sapio* 'wise'.

GIVEN NAMES Italian 12%. *Antonio, Francesco, Francisco, Renato, Rocco.*

Sapir (146) Jewish: **1.** ornamental name from Hebrew *sapir* 'sapphire'. **2.** reduced form of SAPIRO.

GIVEN NAMES Jewish 15%. *Akiva, Ari, Arie, Gidon, Moshe, Polina, Sima, Yael, Yehuda, Yonah.*

Sapiro (123) Jewish (Ashkenazic): variant of SHAPIRO.

GIVEN NAMES Jewish 7%; Russian 4%. *Irina, Isaak, Isadore, Itta; Galina, Vitaly.*

Saponaro (130) Italian: occupational name for a maker or seller of soap, from an agent derivative of *sapone* 'soap', Greek *sapōn*.

GIVEN NAMES Italian 18%. *Rocco* (2), *Angelo, Cesare, Donato, Erasmo, Marco, Savino.*

Sapone (128) Italian: metonymic occupational name for a maker or seller of soap, from *sapone* 'soap'.

GIVEN NAMES Italian 15%. *Angelo, Antonino, Carmella.*

Saporito (520) Italian (Sicily): nickname from Sicilian *sapuritu* 'witty', 'spirited'.

GIVEN NAMES Italian 26%. *Salvatore* (6), *Angelo* (4), *Arsenio* (2), *Carlo* (2), *Cosmo* (2), *Santo* (2), *Aldo, Annamaria, Basilio, Carmelo, Domenic, Donato, Franco, Gennaro, Mario, Orlando, Ramona, Sergio.*

Sapp (6611) **1.** German: from a short form (*Sabbe*) of a Germanic personal name with *sacha* 'legal case or action' as the first element. **2.** English: topographic name from Middle English *sap* 'spruce tree' (Old English *sæppe*).

Sappenfield (300) A part-translation of German **Sappenfeld**, a habitational name from a place so named in northern Bavaria.

Sapper (158) Southern German: probably from an agent derivative of Middle High German *sappen* 'to walk away awkwardly'; 'to gather or acquire', hence a nickname for someone with a slow, clumsy gait, or a greedy person.

Sappington (1036) Possibly an English habitational name from Sapperton in Gloucestershire or Lincolnshire, both named from an Old English *sapere* 'soapmakers', 'soap merchants' + *tūn* 'settlement', 'farmstead'. The surname, however, does not occur in present-day records.

Saputo (317) Italian: nickname for a wise man, or perhaps a know-all, from *saputo* 'wise', 'expert', 'conceited'.

GIVEN NAMES Italian 22%. *Vito* (5), *Sal* (3), *Benedetto* (2), *Onofrio* (2), *Pietro* (2), *Salvatore* (2), *Angelo, Cesare, Domenico, Gaetano, Gaspare, Gasper.*

Sar (123) **1.** Dutch: unexplained. **2.** Cambodian: unexplained. **3.** Other Southeast Asian: unexplained.

GIVEN NAMES Southeast Asian 24%; Cambodian 5%. *Hak, Pang, Ry, Thay; Leang* (2), *Hai; Him* (3), *Chan, Heang, Sarin; Chamroeun, Savoeun, Sokhom, Vuthy.*

Sara (242) French, English, Hungarian (**Sára**), and Jewish: from the female personal name *Sara*, borne in the Bible by the wife of Abraham, mother of Isaac. Compare SARAH.

Sarabia (726) Galician and Asturian-Leonese: habitational name from places in Asturies and Galicia (Pontevedra) called Sarabia, from Asturian and Galician *sarabia* 'hail'.

GIVEN NAMES Spanish 49%. *Jose* (16), *Juan* (9), *Carlos* (7), *Jesus* (6), *Ramiro* (6), *Ernesto* (5), *Jorge* (5), *Manuel* (5), *Ruben* (5), *Francisco* (4), *Miguel* (4), *Pedro* (4).

Saracco (205) Italian: **1.** from *saracchio*, a term denoting a type of grass used for matting, presumably a topographic name, or possibly a metonymic occupational name for someone who gathered the grass or wove it into mats. **2.** possibly a nickname from a derivative of Arabic *sarrāq* 'thief'. **3.** metonymic occupational name for a saw maker, from *saracco* 'hand saw' (from Latin *serra*).

GIVEN NAMES Italian 8%. *Angelo* (2), *Bruna, Dante.*

Saraceni (194) Southern Italian: **1.** plural or patronymic form of SARACENO. **2.** possibly also a habitational name from Saracena in Cosenza province.

GIVEN NAMES Italian 27%. *Antonio* (3), *Angelo* (2), *Fabrizio* (2), *Mario* (2), *Nicolo* (2), *Concetta, Domenico, Giovanni, Luigi, Nicola, Roberto, Rocco, Ulisse, Vincenzo.*

Saraceno (383) Italian: nickname from *saraceno* 'Saracen' (Late Latin *Saracenus*), denoting someone of swarthy appearance, an unruly person, or someone who had taken part in a Crusade.

GIVEN NAMES Italian 31%. *Domenic* (7), *Salvatore* (4), *Angelo* (3), *Carmella* (3), *Mario* (3), *Donato* (2), *Luigi* (2), *Aldo*, *Antonio*, *Cosmo*, *Domenico*, *Francesco*, *Gaetano*, *Liberto*, *Paola*, *Reginaldo*.

Saracino (359) Italian: variant of SARA-CENO.

GIVEN NAMES Italian 18%. *Vito* (4), *Angelo* (3), *Dino* (2), *Alessandro*, *Antonella*, *Antonio*, *Donato*, *Emanuele*, *Gennaro*, *Guiseppe*, *Nazareno*, *Orazio*.

Saraf (108) Indian: variant of SHROFF.

GIVEN NAMES Indian 43%. *Kishore* (2), *Rahul* (2), *Raj* (2), *Shreekant* (2), *Alok*, *Amitabh*, *Anil*, *Anupama*, *Aparna*, *Arvind*, *Krishna*, *Neeraj*.

Sarafian (155) Armenian: patronymic from Arabic *ṣaraf* 'money changer', 'banker'.

GIVEN NAMES Armenian 21%. *Osep* (2), *Ara*, *Aram*, *Armenag*, *Armenouhi*, *Dicran*, *Hagop*, *Karapet*, *Khatchik*, *Masis*, *Minas*, *Sarkis*.

Sarafin (149) Romanian: from a medieval personal name, Latin *Seraphinus* (see SERAFIN).

Saragosa (130) Catalan: variant of **Saragossa**, the Catalan form of the habitational name ZARAGOZA.

GIVEN NAMES Spanish 27%. *Jose* (4), *Ruben* (2), *Angelina*, *Artemio*, *Domingo*, *Felipe*, *Francisco*, *Guadalupe*, *Guillermina*, *Jacinto*, *Javier*, *Mario*; *Angelo*, *Marino*.

Sarah (106) **1.** metronymic from the personal name *Sara*. In the Bible this is the name of the wife of Abraham. According to the Book of Genesis she was originally called *Sarai* (said to mean 'contentious' in Hebrew), but had her name changed by God to the more auspicious *Sarah* 'princess' in token of a greater blessing (Genesis 17:15, 'And God said unto Abraham, As for Sarai thy wife, thou shalt not call her name Sarai, but Sarah shall her name be'). **2.** Muslim: from an Arabic personal name, *Sāra*, of Biblical origin, as in 1 above.

GIVEN NAMES Muslim 16%. *Farid* (2), *Abdel*, *Bachar*, *Jamal*, *Khaled*, *Laila*, *Munir*, *Said*.

Saraiva (142) Portuguese: unexplained.

GIVEN NAMES Spanish 29%; Portuguese 25%. *Jose* (7), *Manuel* (5), *Armenio* (2), *Francisco* (2), *Acacio*, *Adelino*, *Adilia*, *Aires*, *Alberto*, *Alvaro*, *Armando*, *Carlos*; *Joaquim* (4), *Agostinho*, *Joao*.

Saran (146) Indian (Panjab): Sikh name, from Sanskrit *śaraṇa* 'refuge', 'sanctuary', based on the name of a Jat tribe.

GIVEN NAMES Indian 40%. *Navin* (3), *Amitabh* (2), *Nihal* (2), *Yogesh* (2), *Ashish*, *Atul*, *Beant*, *Brij*, *Dayal*, *Madhukar*, *Neeta*, *Nisha*.

Sarantos (108) Greek: from the personal name *Sarantis*, bestowed in honor of the 'Holy Forty' (*Agii Saranda*, classical *Hagioi Tessarakonta*), forty Christians

martyred in the city of Sebastia, Armenia, around 320 AD.

GIVEN NAMES Greek 10%. *Christos*, *Constantine*, *Kostas*, *Takis*.

Sarasin (152) French and Dutch: variant of SARAZIN.

GIVEN NAMES French 4%. *Andre*, *Louis*.

Sarauer (109) German: probably a habitational name for someone from a place called Sarow in Pomerania, the Slavic suffix *-ow* (in place names) frequently being replaced by the German element *-au*.

Saravia (372) Galician and Asturian-Leonese: variant of SARABIA.

GIVEN NAMES Spanish 56%. *Jose* (18), *Carlos* (10), *Francisco* (6), *Luis* (6), *Mario* (6), *Ana* (5), *Jorge* (5), *Juan* (5), *Santos* (4), *Armando* (3), *Guadalupe* (3), *Manuel* (3).

Sarazen (101) French and Dutch: variant of SARAZIN.

Sarazin (163) French and Dutch: nickname for someone of swarthy appearance or for an unruly person, or for someone who had taken part in a Crusade, from Old French *sarrazin* 'Saracen' (compare Italian SARACENO). This word came into French via Latin and Greek from a Semitic term, perhaps akin to Arabic *sharq* 'sunrise', 'east', from *sharaqa* 'to rise'.

FOREBEARS A Sarrazin of Parisian origin is recorded in 1680 in Charlesbourg, Quebec.

GIVEN NAMES French 13%. *Alphonse*, *Benoit*, *Emile*, *Gilles*, *Jean Guy*, *Laurent*, *Laurier*, *Marcel*.

Sarber (263) Perhaps an altered spelling of German SAUBER.

Sarchet (220) French or English (Channel Islands): unexplained.

Sardella (264) Italian: from *sardella* 'sardine', a metonymic occupational name for a seller of sardines or a nickname for a skinny person (see SARDINA). This is also found, in the form **Sardellas**, as a Greek family name.

GIVEN NAMES Italian 12%. *Salvatore* (3), *Carmine* (2), *Angelo*, *Donato*, *Grazia*, *Levio*, *Luciano*, *Luigi*, *Mauro*, *Reno*.

Sardi (106) **1.** Italian: patronymic form of SARDO 'Sardinian'. **Sardis** is also found as a Greek family name. **2.** Hungarian (**Sárdi**): habitational name for someone from a place called Sárd in the counties of Zala and Somogy in western Hungary or from any of various places in Transylvania.

GIVEN NAMES Spanish 12%; Italian 11%; German 4%. *Armando* (3), *Leokadia* (2), *Adriana*, *Carmella*, *Elvira*, *Enrique*, *Liliana*; *Marco* (2), *Dino*, *Edvige*, *Sal*; *Otto*.

Sardina (357) Italian (southern and central), Spanish, and Galician (**Sardiña**): from *sardina* 'sardine'; either a metonymic occupational name for a catcher or seller of these fish or a nickname for a thin person.

GIVEN NAMES Spanish 31%; Italian 10%. *Jose* (6), *Luis* (4), *Carlos* (3), *Evelio* (3), *Ramon* (3), *Raul* (3), *Aida* (2), *Argentina*

(2), *Eduardo* (2), *Guillermo* (2), *Juan* (2), *Manuel* (2); *Angelo* (2), *Antonio* (2), *Concetta*, *Gaetano*, *Matteo*, *Pasquale*, *Sal*, *Salvatore*, *Santo*, *Stefano*.

Sardinas (191) Galician (**Sardiñas**): habitational name from Sardiñas in A Coruña province, so named from the plural of Galician *sardiña* 'sardine'.

GIVEN NAMES Spanish 52%. *Jorge* (7), *Julio* (5), *Alfredo* (3), *Carlos* (3), *Jose* (3), *Miguel* (3), *Pedro* (3), *Rolando* (3), *Alberto* (2), *Andres* (2), *Jesus* (2), *Juan* (2); *Antonio*, *Federico*.

Sardinha (164) Portuguese: from *sardinha* 'sardine', a metonymic occupational name for a sardine seller, or possibly a nickname.

GIVEN NAMES Spanish 20%; Portuguese 14%. *Manuel* (9), *Jose* (2), *Mario* (2), *Aurelio*, *Carlos*, *Casimiro*, *Domingos*, *Ferando*, *Jaime*, *Juan*, *Luiz*, *Palmira*; *Joao* (4).

Sardo (352) Italian and Catalan: ethnic name from *sardo* 'Sardinian'.

GIVEN NAMES Italian 20%; Spanish 5%. *Angelo* (5), *Antonio* (3), *Alfonso* (2), *Sal* (2), *Salvatore* (2), *Arnoldo*, *Damiano*, *Domenica*, *Francesco*, *Guido*, *Mario*, *Raimondo*, *Rocco*, *Santo*, *Vito*; *Manuel* (3), *Rosario* (2), *Carlos*, *Esmeralda*, *Ines*.

Sardone (118) Italian: **1.** variant of SARDINA. **2.** from an augmentative of SARDO, i.e. 'the big Sardinian'. **3.** from Sicilian *sarduni* 'archway', presumably a topographic name for someone who lived by such a feature. **4.** in the central and southern Adriatic region, from *sardone* 'anchovy'.

GIVEN NAMES Italian 22%. *Aldo*, *Carmelo*, *Francesco*, *Giuseppe*, *Luigi*, *Oronzo*, *Saverio*, *Vito*.

Sare (177) English and Welsh: variant of SAYER.

Sarfaty (113) Jewish (Sephardic): regional name from Hebrew *tsarfati* 'from France'.

GIVEN NAMES Jewish 16%. *Moshe* (3), *Chana*, *Eliahu*, *Emanuel*, *Shulamith*.

Sarff (277) Possibly English: unexplained.

Sarge (110) **1.** English: variant of SARK. **2.** German: unexplained.

Sargeant (922) English: variant spelling of SARGENT.

Sargent (10426) English and French: in medieval times this did not denote a rank in the army, but was an occupational name for a servant, Middle English, Old French *sergent* (Latin *serviens*, genitive *servientis*, present participle of *servire* 'to serve'). The surname probably originated for the most part in this sense, but the word also developed various more specialized meanings, being used for example as a technical term for a tenant by military service below the rank of a knight, and as the name for any of certain administrative and legal officials in different localities, which may also have contributed to the development of the surname. The sense 'non-commissioned officer' did not arise until the 16th century.

FOREBEARS William Sargent (1624–1717) came to Gloucester, MA, from Devon, England before 1678. Many of his descendants distinguished themselves in the civil and military affairs of the colonies and some in literary or artistic paths, notably the portrait painter John Singer Sargent (1856–1925).

Sargis (177) Reduced form of Armenian **Sargisian**, western Armenian form of SARKISIAN.

Sari (174) **1.** Turkish (*Sarı*): descriptive nickname meaning 'yellow', 'pale', or 'fair-haired'. This is also found as an element in Greek names, for example **Sarigiannis** 'fair-haired John'. **2.** Corsican: habitational name from Sari d'Orcino in southern Corsica or Sari di Porto Vecchio in the canton of Porte-Vecchio. **3.** Hungarian: from a pet form of the female personal name *Sára*, Hungarian form of SARAH.
GIVEN NAMES Muslim 16%. *Aziz, Bahia, Ibrahim, Idris, Kemal, Khaled, Mohamed, Musa, Nazmi, Nese, Raja, Yahya.*

Sarich (199) Serbian and Croatian (**Sarić**): **1.** metronymic from the Biblical female personal name *Sara*. **2.** (**Šarić**) perhaps a nickname from *šaren* 'motley', 'multicolored'.

Sarin (159) Indian (Panjab): Hindu (Khatri) and Sikh name based on the name of a subdivision of the Khatri community.
GIVEN NAMES Indian 59%. *Madhu* (3), *Ajay* (2), *Rani* (2), *Vinod* (2), *Vivek* (2), *Amrit, Apurva, Arun, Ashok, Dalip, Dhirendra, Harish.*

Sarinana (109) Spanish (**Sariñana**): habitational name from Sariñana in Zamora province.
GIVEN NAMES Spanish 58%. *Juan* (4), *Jesus* (3), *Jose* (3), *Carlos* (2), *Ignacio* (2), *Jaime* (2), *Pedro* (2), *Rosalio* (2), *Sergio* (2), *Adolfo, Armando, Arturo*; *Antonio* (3), *Lorenzo.*

Sarisky (108) Slovak: habitational name for someone from Šariš, a region in eastern Slovakia.

Sark (128) English: from the Middle English personal name *Saric, Seric* with loss of the unstressed vowel (see SURRIDGE 1).
GIVEN NAME Scandinavian 7%. *Erik* (3).

Sarka (162) **1.** Americanized form of Hungarian SZARKA 'magpie', a nickname for a thief. **2.** Czech (**Šárka**): topographic name for someone living by a bend in a river, from a derivative of the Old Czech adjective *šárový* 'curved'. **3.** Czech (**Šarka**): descriptive nickname from *šarý* 'gray'.

Sarkar (298) Indian (Bengal) and Bangladeshi: Hindu name found in several communities, from a title based on Persian *sarkār* 'chief', 'superintendent', 'lord'.
GIVEN NAMES Indian 82%. *Amit* (3), *Arindam* (3), *Purnendu* (3), *Salil* (3), *Shyamal* (3), *Somnath* (3), *Amitava* (2), *Anil* (2), *Aparna* (2), *Arun* (2), *Arup* (2), *Asis* (2).

Sarkis (352) Greek and Arabic: from a personal name borne by a 4th-century Christian saint martyred in Cappadocia under Diocletian, known in Latin as *Sergius* (see SERGIO) and in Russian as *Sergei.*
GIVEN NAMES Arabic 9%; French 4%. *Raafat* (3), *Fadia, Farid, Hashim, Jamal, Khalil, Nader, Nasri, Nazih, Nazli, Nouhad, Rafic*; *Antoine, Emile, Pierre.*

Sarkisian (576) Western Armenian: patronymic from the personal name *Sarkis*, classical Armenian *Sargis* (see SARKIS).
GIVEN NAMES Armenian 23%. *Sarkis* (17), *Aram* (3), *Anahid* (2), *Andranik* (2), *Ara* (2), *Armen* (2), *Dikran* (2), *Haig* (2), *Norair* (2), *Vartan* (2), *Vatche* (2), *Antranik.*

Sarkissian (379) Armenian: variant spelling of SARKISIAN.
GIVEN NAMES Armenian 49%. *Sarkis* (12), *Aram* (4), *Vahik* (4), *Vartan* (4), *Hrair* (3), *Anahid* (2), *Armen* (2), *Artin* (2), *Bedros* (2), *Haigh* (2), *Hrand* (2), *Krikor* (2).

Sarkisyan (116) Armenian: variant spelling of SARKISIAN.
GIVEN NAMES Armenian 59%; Russian 8%. *Sarkis* (5), *Anait* (3), *Gevork* (3), *Vardan* (3), *Armen* (2), *Grigor* (2), *Sako* (2), *Akop, Aram, Azatui, Gevorg, Grachik*; *Aleksandr, Asya, Igor, Lyudmila, Mayya, Oleg, Volodya.*

Sarles (365) French: from a Germanic personal name, *Sarilo*, a short form of compound names formed with *sar-*, related to Gothic *sarwa*, Old High German *saro* 'armor', 'coat of mail'.

Sarli (140) Italian: patronymic or plural form of SARLO.
GIVEN NAMES Italian 24%; Spanish 7%. *Rocco* (3), *Arnaldo, Enrico, Gennaro, Pasquale, Ricardo, Roberto, Rosalinda, Salvatore, Stefano, Vito*; *Carlos, Juan.*

Sarlo (237) **1.** Southern Italian: possibly from a reduced form of a Germanic personal name formed with *Sarva-* as the first element. **2.** Hungarian (**Sarló**): metonymic occupational name for a sickle maker, from *sarló* 'sickle'.
GIVEN NAMES Italian 13%. *Carmine* (2), *Rocco* (2), *Aldo, Angelo, Antonio, Ignazio, Nunzio.*

Sarma (146) Indian: variant of SHARMA.
GIVEN NAMES Indian 84%. *Radha* (4), *Ravi* (3), *Adarsh* (2), *Rajkumar* (2), *Satya* (2), *Seshu* (2), *Sudha* (2), *Ajit, Amit, Anant, Anjan, Arun.*

Sarmento (216) Portuguese: from *sarmento* 'vine shoot' (Latin *sarmentum* 'shoot', from *sarpere* 'to trim, prune'), presumably a nickname for a tall thin person.
GIVEN NAMES Spanish 12%. *Manuel* (5), *Jose* (2), *Roberto* (2), *Aurea, Carlos, Fernando, Ines, Juancarlos, Luisa, Mario, Nidia, Tomas*; *Antonio, Dino, Licinio, Luigi.*

Sarmiento (1146) Spanish: from *sarmiento* 'grape vine' (Latin *sarmentum* 'shoot', from *sarpere* 'to trim, prune'), apparently a nickname for a tall thin person. This is also found as an Italian surname, imported from Spain, which is present in the south, especially in Naples.
GIVEN NAMES Spanish 48%. *Jose* (23), *Carlos* (21), *Manuel* (19), *Luis* (17), *Jorge* (13), *Juan* (13), *Jesus* (12), *Pedro* (12), *Miguel* (7), *Ricardo* (7), *Fernando* (6), *Francisco* (6).

Sarna (345) **1.** Indian (Panjab): Hindu (Khatri) and Sikh name of unknown meaning. **2.** Polish and Jewish (from Poland): from Polish *sarna* 'roe deer', applied as a Polish nickname or Jewish ornamental surname.
GIVEN NAMES Indian 13%; Polish 4%. *Anupama, Arun, Chander, Gautam, Gursharan, Nand, Naveen, Sita, Sushil, Vandana, Vijay, Vikas*; *Mieczyslaw* (2), *Casimir, Karol, Tadeusz, Zofia.*

Sarnecki (117) Polish: derivative of *sarna* 'roe deer'. Compare SARNOWSKI.
GIVEN NAMES Polish 7%. *Boguslaw, Miroslaw.*

Sarner (136) Jewish (from Ukraine): habitational name for someone from Sarny in Ukraine.

Sarni (131) Italian: variant of SARNO.
GIVEN NAMES Italian 17%. *Angelo, Antonio, Carmine, Constantino, Gennaro, Guido, Mafalda, Marco, Pasquale, Vito.*

Sarno (1018) **1.** Italian (Naples and Campania): habitational name from Sarno in Salerno province. **2.** Jewish (from Ukraine): variant of SARNA or SARNER.
GIVEN NAMES Italian 16%. *Carmine* (11), *Rocco* (4), *Salvatore* (4), *Angelo* (3), *Sal* (3), *Primo* (2), *Silvio* (2), *Umberto* (2), *Amedio, Annamarie, Carmino, Clementina.*

Sarnoff (200) Jewish (from Ukraine): alternative spelling of **Sarnov**, a habitational name for someone from Sarny in Ukraine. Compare SARNER.

Sarnowski (341) Polish: habitational name for someone from any of the many places in Poland called Sarnowa, Sarnowo, or Sarnów, named with Polish *sarna* 'roe deer'.
GIVEN NAMES Polish 4%. *Casimir, Jozef, Stanislaw.*

Sarpy (100) Origin unidentified. Perhaps a respelling of the Italian surname **Sarpi**, a nickname from the goldline (a species of fish).

Sarr (160) **1.** English and Scottish: unexplained. Perhaps a variant of **Sarre**, itself a variant of SARA. **2.** African: unexplained.
GIVEN NAMES African 22%; Muslim 5%. *Aliou* (3), *Momodou* (3), *Amadou* (2), *Modou* (2), *Aboubacar, Isatu, Mamadou, Mohamadou*; *Abdoulaye* (3), *Ebrima, Essa, Moussa, Moustapha.*

Sarra (196) **1.** Italian: from a feminine form of SARRO. **2.** Catalan (**Sarrà**): respelling of **Serrà** (see SERRA 3). **3.** English: variant of SARA.

GIVEN NAMES Italian 5%. *Antonio, Carmine, Tullio.*

Sarracino (131) Italian (Naples): variant of SARACENO.

GIVEN NAMES Spanish 9%. *Enrique* (2), *Alfonso, Maximo, Orlando, Ramon.*

Sarraf (114) **1.** Arabic and Jewish (Sephardic): occupational name from Arabic *ṣarrāf* 'treasurer', 'paymaster'. **2.** Indian: variant of SHROFF.

GIVEN NAMES Muslim 44%; Indian 4%; Jewish 4%. *Gholam* (2), *Mehrdad* (2), *Pejman* (2), *Ramin* (2), *Afshin, Ali, Bishara, Fardin, Firouzeh, Fouad, Goli, Jamal; Doron, Reuven; Sangeeta* (2), *Madhav.*

Sarratt (357) English: from a pet form (with the diminutive suffix *-et, -ot*) of the female personal name *Sarre*, a variant of *Sara*, or possibly from a masculine name, *Saret.*

Sarrazin (193) French, Dutch, and German: variant of SARAZIN.

GIVEN NAMES French 16%; German 6%. *Emile* (2), *Yves* (2), *Etienne, Fernand, Gilles, Pierre, Serge, Yvon; Hubertus* (2), *Wolfgang* (2).

Sarrett (187) Variant of SARRATT.

Sarria (132) Catalan (**Sarrià** or **Sàrria**): habitational name from any of the places named Sarrià or Sàrria, in Catalonia.

GIVEN NAMES Spanish 47%; Italian 7%. *Manuel* (4), *Ricardo* (3), *Alberto* (2), *Carlos* (2), *Enrique* (2), *Jorge* (2), *Juan* (2), *Luis* (2), *Rodrigo* (2), *Adolfo, Alba, Alfredo; Federico* (2), *Angelo, Antonio, Flavio, Silvio.*

Sarris (376) **1.** Greek: nickname meaning 'fair-haired', 'pale', from a vocabulary word derived from Turkish *sarı* 'yellow'. **2.** Dutch: from a short form of the personal name *Sesaris*, derived from Latin *Caesarius*, a saint's name.

GIVEN NAMES Greek 8%. *Costas* (2), *Ilias* (2), *Andreas, Evangelos, Loukas, Panagiotis, Panayotis, Savvas, Stamatis, Stratos, Themis.*

Sarro (506) Italian: from the personal name *Sarro*, a short form of *Baldassarro* (see BALDASSARRE).

GIVEN NAMES Italian 12%; French 4%. *Salvatore* (3), *Angelo* (2), *Pietro* (2), *Rocco* (2), *Carmine, Corrado, Domenic, Domenico, Dominico; Armand, Camille, Emile.*

Sarsfield (333) Irish (of English origin): apparently a habitational name from an unidentified place in England. Bearers of this surname settled in Counties Dublin, Cork, and Limerick in Ireland from the 12th century onward.

GIVEN NAME Irish 4%. *Eamon.*

Sarson (107) English: **1.** nickname from Middle English, Old French *saracin, sarrazin* 'saracen' (see SARAZIN). **2.** possibly also a metronymic from the personal name *Sara.*

FOREBEARS Richard Sarson (b. 1607), tailor, came from London to MA in 1635. He and

his son (also called Richard) settled in Edgartown on Martha's Vineyard before 1656.

Sartain (1172) English: nickname from Old French *certeyn* 'self-assured', 'determined'. (The phonetic change of *-er-* to *-ar-* was a normal process in Middle English).

Sartell (111) English: unexplained.

Sarten (118) English: probably a variant of SARTAIN.

Sarti (198) Italian: patronymic form of *sarto* 'tailor'. Compare SARTOR.

GIVEN NAMES Italian 26%; Spanish 5%. *Mario* (3), *Antonio* (2), *Dino* (2), *Elio* (2), *Fernando* (2), *Renato* (2), *Adriana, Deno, Enza, Francesco, Leno, Marino, Paolo, Remo, Reno; Ana, Cesar, Maribel.*

Sartin (1294) **1.** English: variant of SARTAIN. **2.** French: topographic name from a diminutive of *sart*, a reduced form of Old French *essart* 'newly cleared and cultivated land'. **3.** Italian (Venetian): variant of SARTINI.

Sartini (125) Italian: patronymic from **Sartino**, from a diminutive of *sarto* 'tailor'.

GIVEN NAMES French 7%; Italian 7%. *Angelo, Francesca, Gino, Neno.*

Sarto (123) Italian: probably an occupational name for a tailor, from a reduced form of SARTORE.

GIVEN NAMES Italian 8%. *Antonio* (2), *Angelo, Giovan, Sandro.*

Sartor (877) **1.** French and Italian: occupational name from French, northern Italian *sartor* 'tailor' (Latin *sartor*). This was also adopted as a humanistic name in Germany and the Netherlands, a Latinized equivalent of vernacular names such as German SCHNEIDER. Compare SARTORIUS. **2.** English: topographic name denoting someone who lived on land which had been cleared for cultivation, Old French *assart, essart* 'woodland cleared for cultivation' + the habitational suffix *-er.*

Sartore (119) Italian: occupational name for a tailor, from *sartore*, an old and regional (central Italian) form of SARTOR.

GIVEN NAMES Italian 5%. *Gino* (2), *Aldo, Silvio.*

Sartori (764) **1.** Northern Italian: patronymic from SARTORE. This name is also established in Spain, taken there from Italy. **2.** German: variant of SARTORIUS.

GIVEN NAMES Italian 10%; Spanish 5%; French 4%. *Guido* (4), *Marco* (3), *Aldo* (2), *Romeo* (2), *Angelo, Antonio, Carlo, Dante, Dario, Delio, Dino, Domenic; Mario* (9), *Alberto, Alfonso, Carmella, Claudio, Diego, Fernando, Jorge, Lino, Luisa, Miguel, Osvaldo; Arnaud, Marcel, Raoul, Raymonde.*

Sartoris (116) Dutch: variant of SARTORIUS.

Sartorius (169) Humanistic name, a Latinized form of German SCHNEIDER, Dutch **Snijder**, occupational names for a tailor.

GIVEN NAMES German 5%. *Ernst, Matthias.*

Sartwell (214) English: apparently a habitational name from a lost or unidentified place.

Sarubbi (141) Italian (Basilicata): unexplained.

GIVEN NAMES Italian 15%. *Dante* (3), *Filippo, Gerardo, Nicola, Ovidio, Pasquale, Telmo.*

Sarver (2519) English and Jewish (eastern Ashkenazic): occupational name from Old French *serveur* (an agent derivative of *server* 'to serve'), Yiddish *sarver* 'servant'.

Sarvey (100) Origin unidentified.

Sarvis (595) English: variant of SERVICE.

Sarwar (143) Muslim: from a personal name based on Persian *sarwar* 'leader', 'chief', 'master'. *Sarwar Ambiya* is an epithet of the Prophet Muhammad.

GIVEN NAMES Muslim 89%. *Mohammad* (8), *Mohammed* (7), *Abu* (6), *Ghulam* (6), *Golam* (6), *Muhammad* (6), *Ishaq* (3), *Junaid* (3), *Shahid* (3), *Abul* (2), *Bilal* (2), *Hasan* (2).

Sas (229) **1.** Dutch, Polish, and Jewish (eastern Ashkenazic): ethnic and regional name from Middle Dutch *Sasse*, Polish *Sas* 'Saxon'. **2.** Dutch (**Van Sas**): habitational name denoting someone from places named Sas in North Brabant and Zeeland. **3.** Catalan: topographic name from a pre-Roman term meaning 'mound', 'hillock', or habitational name from any of the places named Sas in Catalonia. **4.** French: variant of SASSE 2. **5.** Hungarian: nickname from Hungarian *sas* 'eagle'. **6.** Americanized form of Hungarian **Szász**, an ethnic name for a Saxon.

Sasaki (1070) Japanese: **1.** variously written, the name, meaning 'wren', originated in Ōmi (now Shiga) prefecture and is found mostly in northeastern Japan. **2.** Alternatively, it may derive from *misasagi*, the term for the great tomb mounds dating from c. 250–710, which are found in clusters all over Japan.

GIVEN NAMES Japanese 54%. *Akira* (8), *Takashi* (8), *Shigeru* (6), *Takeshi* (6), *Hiroshi* (5), *Hitoshi* (5), *Yasuo* (5), *Hiroyuki* (4), *Kiyoshi* (4), *Masayuki* (4), *Shoji* (4), *Toshio* (4).

Sasala (129) Polish (**Sasała**): derogatory nickname meaning 'buffoon'.

Sasek (156) Czech and Slovak (**Šašek**): nickname from a word meaning 'fool' or 'buffoon'.

Saslow (170) Jewish: Americanized form of ZASLAVSKY (compare ZASLOW).

GIVEN NAMES Jewish 5%. *Emanuel, Meier.*

Sasnett (162) Origin unidentified.

Saso (137) Italian (Sicily): variant of SASSO.

Sass (2042) German and Dutch: variant of SASSE.

GIVEN NAMES German 4%. *Juergen* (3), *Claus* (2), *Erwin* (2), *Hans* (2), *Beate, Detlef, Eldor, Erna, Ernst, Gerhard, Gunther, Hertha.*

Sassaman (411) Altered form of German *Sass(e)mann* 'man from Saxony' (see SASSMAN).

Sassano (312) Italian: habitational name from Sassano in Salerno province.

GIVEN NAMES Italian 9%. *Carmine, Domenic, Donato, Francesca, Giovanni, Guido, Paolo, Salvatore.*

Sasse (721) **1.** Dutch and North German: ethnic name for a Saxon, from Middle Low German, Middle Dutch *sasse* 'Saxon'. **2.** French: from a Germanic personal name, *Sahso*, a reduced pet form of compound names formed with *sahs* 'Saxon' as the first element.

GIVEN NAMES German 4%. *Otto* (3), *Detlef, Erwin, Franz, Winfried.*

Sasseen (127) Dutch and North German: ethnic name for someone from Saxony. Compare SASSE.

GIVEN NAME German 6%. *Eldred* (2).

Sasser (2779) **1.** North German: derivative of SASSE 'Saxon', + *-er*, suffix of agent nouns. **2.** habitational name for someone from any of several places named Saasen in the Rhineland, Hesse, and Pomerania.

Sasseville (107) French: habitational name from a place so called.

GIVEN NAMES French 18%. *Andre* (2), *Armand, Laurette, Luc, Normand, Sarto.*

Sassi (213) Italian: patronymic or plural form of SASSO.

GIVEN NAMES Italian 16%. *Gino* (3), *Alessandro, Amedeo, Cesare, Dante, Enrico, Fabrizio, Marcello, Natale, Pietro.*

Sassin (102) Origin unidentified. Perhaps a variant of Jewish SASSON.

Sassman (197) German (**Sassmann**): regional name for someone from Lower Saxony (see SACHS).

Sasso (1075) Italian: **1.** from *sasso* 'rock' (Latin *saxum*), a topographic name or a habitational name from any of numerous places named or named with this word, as for example Sasso di Castalda in Potenza province. **2.** from an ethnic name, *Sasso* 'Saxon'.

GIVEN NAMES Italian 10%. *Angelo* (6), *Antonio* (2), *Gino* (2), *Giuseppe* (2), *Attilio, Augustino, Carlo, Cosmo, Damiano, Enrico, Erminio, Federico.*

Sasson (343) Jewish (Sephardic): from the Hebrew personal name *Sason*, meaning 'joy'.

GIVEN NAMES Jewish 22%; French 7%; Spanish 4%. *Moshe* (3), *Hyman* (2), *Mayer* (2), *Uzi* (2), *Avner, Baroukh, Benyamin, Chana, Drora, Haim, Ilan, Itshak*; *Alain* (2), *Gisele, Jacques, Marcelle, Michel, Pierre*; *Cristina* (2), *Jose* (2), *Carlos, Carolina, Cesar, Fernanda, Jaime, Marisa, Miguel, Salvador.*

Sassone (231) Italian: from an inflected form of SASSO 'Saxon'.

GIVEN NAMES Italian 18%; French 5%. *Rocco* (2), *Vito* (2), *Guido, Marco, Margherita,*

Neno, Pasquale, Serafino; *Alphonse* (3), *Pierre.*

Sassoon (121) Jewish (Sephardic): variant of SASSON.

GIVEN NAMES Jewish 20%; French 9%. *Moshe* (2), *Aharon, Benyamin, Gilad, Meir, Meyer, Shalom*; *Andre* (3), *Camille.*

Sastre (114) Catalan and Spanish: occupational name from *sastre* 'tailor' (from Latin *sartor*).

GIVEN NAMES Spanish 47%. *Luis* (5), *Cesar* (4), *Juan* (4), *Joaquin* (2), *Manuel* (2), *Alfonso, Anselmo, Armando, Carlos, Domingo, Enrique, Fernando.*

Sastry (109) Indian: Hindu (Brahman) name, from Sanskrit *šāstrī* 'versed in the Shastras' (from *šāstra* 'book of rules', 'religious treatise').

GIVEN NAMES Indian 87%. *Shankar* (4), *Anand* (3), *Suresh* (3), *Krishna* (2), *Prasad* (2), *Rama* (2), *Ravi* (2), *Santhosh* (2), *Suneel* (2), *Vasantha* (2), *Anitha, Arun.*

Satchell (622) English: metonymic occupational name for a maker of purses and bags, from Old French *sachel* 'little bag'.

Satcher (380) English (Sussex): unexplained.

Satchwell (122) English: variant of SATCHELL.

Sater (445) Respelling of Norwegian **Sæter**, a common habitational name from any of numerous farmsteads named Sæter, named with Old Norse *sætr, setr* 'farm'. In more recent formations it means 'mountain farm', 'summer dairy'.

Sathe (106) Indian (Maharashtra); pronounced as two syllables: Hindu (Brahman) name found among Konkanasth Brahmans. It is probably derived from Marathi *saṭha* 'store', 'stock'.

GIVEN NAMES Indian 57%. *Usha* (3), *Dilip* (2), *Shrikant* (2), *Abhay, Ajit, Anand, Aparna, Ashok, Chandra, Dinkar, Hemi, Jayant.*

Sather (1684) Respelling of Norwegian **Sæther**, a variant of **Sæter** (see SATER).

GIVEN NAMES Scandinavian 6%. *Erik* (3), *Hilmar* (2), *Torvald* (2), *Arnt, Bernt, Bjorn, Britt, Hedda, Hjalmer, Jalmer, Knute, Lars.*

Sathre (160) Respelling of Norwegian **Sæthre**, a variant (dative singular form) of **Sætre** (see SATER).

GIVEN NAMES Scandinavian 10%. *Selmer* (2), *Astrid, Nordeen, Sven.*

Satin (150) **1.** French: metonymic occupational name for a satin merchant or specialist satin weaver, from Middle French *satin* 'satin', a word of Arabic and (ultimately) Chinese origin, a derivative of the Chinese place name *Tsinkiang*, whence satin silk was brought to the Middle East and Europe in the Middle Ages. **2.** Jewish (Ashkenazic): probably a metonymic occupational name or ornamental name from Polish *satyna*, eastern Slavic *satin* 'satin'.

Satkowiak (98) Polish: variant of **Sadkowiak**, habitational name for someone from any of several places called Sadkowice, Sadkowo, or Sadków.

GIVEN NAMES French 6%; Jewish 5%. *Marcel, Pierre*; *Isadore* (2).

Satkowski (140) Polish: habitational name for someone from Sadkowo in Ciechnów province or Sadków in Kielce and Radom provinces.

GIVEN NAME Polish 4%. *Casimir.*

Sato (2192) Japanese (**Satō**): with SUZUKI, one of the two most common surnames in Japan. The Sato descend from the northern FUJIWARA through Fujiwara no Hidesato (10th century), who governed Shimotsuke (now Tochigi) prefecture from a place called Sano, hence *Sano no Fujiwara* or *Satō*. Another tradition takes the *sa* from the title *Saemon no jō*, an office held by a distinguished descendant of Hidesato's.

GIVEN NAMES Japanese 67%. *Hiroshi* (18), *Akira* (10), *Takao* (10), *Kenji* (9), *Tadashi* (9), *Takashi* (9), *Hideo* (8), *Makoto* (8), *Yutaka* (8), *Kazuo* (7), *Koji* (7), *Masao* (7).

Satow (129) Japanese: alternative Romanized spelling of **Satō** (see SATO).

GIVEN NAMES Japanese 11%. *Fumio, Hideo, Susumu, Tadao, Tomio.*

Satran (108) Probably a habitational name from either Satran in the Highland region of Scotland or Satron in North Yorkshire, England. The surname, however, is not found in UK records.

Satre (282) Variant spelling Norwegian **Sætre** (see SATER).

GIVEN NAMES Scandinavian 6%. *Astrid, Bernt, Helmer, Selmer.*

Satriano (120) Italian (southwestern): habitational name from Satriano in Catanzaro or Satriano di Lucania in Potenza.

GIVEN NAMES Italian 14%. *Salvatore* (2), *Gennaro, Giuseppe, Rocco.*

Satrom (135) Americanized spelling of Norwegian **Sætrom**, a habitational name from any of numerous farmsteads so named, from the dative plural of *sæter* 'farm', 'mountain farm', 'summer dairy' (see SATER).

Sattar (145) Muslim: from a personal name based on Arabic *sattār* 'veiler', As-Sattār 'the Veiler (of Sin)' is an attribute of Allah. The name is usually found in the combination *'Abd as-Sattār* (*Abdus-Sattar*) 'servant of the veiler'.

GIVEN NAMES Muslim 83%. *Abdul* (19), *Abdus* (6), *Mohammad* (5), *Mohammed* (3), *Ahmed* (2), *Asad* (2), *Bashir* (2), *Fouad* (2), *Wasif* (2), *Abrar, Adil, Akhtar.*

Satter (433) **1.** English and Scottish: unexplained; perhaps a variant of SETTER. **2.** German and Dutch: unexplained. **3.** Norwegian: unexplained. **4.** Muslim: variant of SATTAR.

Satterfield (4977) English: variant of SATTERTHWAITE.

Satterlee (1057) English: habitational name from Satterleigh in Devon, named in Old English with *sǣtere* 'robbers' + *lēah* 'clearing in a wood'.

Satterlund (103) Swedish (**Sätterlund**): ornamental name from *sät(t)er* 'mountain pasture' + *lund* 'grove'.
GIVEN NAMES Scandinavian 6%. *Nels, Sig.*

Satterly (404) Variant of SATTERLEE.

Satterthwaite (536) English: habitational name from a place in the Lake District, so named from Old English *sætr* 'shieling' + Old Norse *þveit* 'pasture'.

Satterwhite (1747) Altered form of SATTERTHWAITE.

Sattler (1906) German (also **Sättler**): occupational name for a saddler, from an agent derivative of Middle High German *sattel* 'saddle'.
GIVEN NAMES German 4%. *Otto* (3), *Erwin* (2), *Franz* (2), *Adelheid, Arno, Benno, Frieda, Hans, Horst, Johann, Klaus, Kurt.*

Saturday (126) English: probably a nickname for someone born on a Saturday (Middle English *Saterdai, Seterday*), or who had some other special connection with that day.

Satz (262) Jewish (Ashkenazic): acronym from the Hebrew phrase *Zera TSadikim* 'seed of the righteous', assumed in a spirit of pious respect for one's ancestors.
GIVEN NAMES Jewish 4%. *Chaim, Jakob.*

Sauber (410) German and Jewish (Ashkenazic): nickname for a tidy or well-groomed person, from Middle High German *sūber* 'smart', 'neat', German *sauber* 'clean'. The Jewish name was frequently ornamental.

Sauceda (1029) Spanish: habitational name from places in Cáceres and Málaga named Sauceda, or a topographic name from *salceda* 'willow grove'.
GIVEN NAMES Spanish 47%. *Jose* (19), *Juan* (13), *Francisco* (11), *Manuel* (11), *Guadalupe* (10), *Jesus* (10), *Carlos* (9), *Raul* (9), *Mario* (6), *Pedro* (6), *Ruben* (6), *Javier* (5).

Saucedo (2367) Spanish: from a variant of *salcedo* 'willow plantation', as a topographic or habitational name (see SALCEDO).
GIVEN NAMES Spanish 51%. *Jose* (61), *Juan* (44), *Jesus* (36), *Manuel* (28), *Carlos* (21), *Luis* (19), *Francisco* (18), *Raul* (16), *Miguel* (15), *Roberto* (15), *Alfredo* (14), *Guadalupe* (14).

Sauceman (105) English and Scottish: occupational name for a sauce maker (see SAUSER).

Saucer (174) English and Scottish: variant spelling of SAUSER.

Saucerman (133) English and Scottish: variant of SAUCEMAN.

Saucier (2400) French: occupational name for a cook who specialized in making sauces, Old French *saucier*.
FOREBEARS A Saussier from Paris is recorded in Quebec City in 1671. The name is frequent in LA and documented there from 1699.

GIVEN NAMES French 7%. *Camille* (3), *Normand* (3), *Alcide* (2), *Alphe* (2), *Armand* (2), *Oneil* (2), *Adelard, Adrien, Alberie, Alderic, Andre, Antoine.*

Sauder (956) German: variant of SAUTER.

Sauer (6438) German and Jewish (Ashkenazic): nickname for an embittered or cantankerous person, from Middle High German *sūr*, German *sauer* 'sour'.
GIVEN NAMES German 4%. *Kurt* (13), *Heinz* (6), *Otto* (5), *Achim* (4), *Dieter* (3), *Erwin* (3), *Hans* (3), *Helmut* (3), *Reinhold* (3), *Erna* (2), *Florian* (2), *Fritz* (2).

Sauerbrey (128) Americanized form of German **Sauerbr(a:)u**, an occupational name for someone who made vinegar, from Middle High German *sūrbriuwe*, Middle Low German *sūrbrouwe*.
GIVEN NAMES German 13%. *Heinz* (2), *Angelika, Fritz, Otto.*

Sauerland (101) German: regional name for someone from the area between Sieg and the Ruhr known as Sauerland.
GIVEN NAMES German 23%. *Erwin* (2), *Jurgen* (2), *Dieter, Franz, Heinz, Klaus, Otto, Ulrich.*

Sauers (1013) Variant of German SAUER.

Sauerwein (320) German: occupational nickname for someone who sold sour wine, or perhaps a nickname for someone with a sour disposition, from Middle High German *sūr* 'sour' + *wīn* 'wine', i.e. vinegar.

Saufley (119) Americanized form of German **Saufler**, a variant of *Sauf(f)*, nickname for a drinker, from Middle High German *sūfen, soufen* 'to slurp', 'drink'.

Saugstad (100) Norwegian: habitational name from a farmstead in eastern Norway named from *saug*, derived from Old Norse *sjóða* 'boil', 'seethe' (probably with reference to a spring) + *staðir*, plural of *staðr* 'farmstead', 'dwelling'.

Saul (2622) English, French, German, Italian, and Jewish: from the personal name Saul (Hebrew *Shaul* 'asked-for'), the name of the king of Israel whose story is recounted in the first book of Samuel. In spite of his success in uniting Israel and his military prowess, Saul had a troubled reign, not least because of his long conflict with the young David, who eventually succeeded him. Perhaps for this reason, the personal name was not particularly common in medieval times. A further disincentive to its popularity as a Christian name was the fact that it was the original name of St. Paul, borne by him while he was persecuting Christians, and rejected by him after his conversion to Christianity. It may in part have arisen as a nickname for someone who had played the part of the Biblical king in a religious play.

Saulino (128) Italian: from a pet form of the personal name *Saul* (see SAUL).
GIVEN NAMES French 6%; Italian 6%. *Alphonse* (2), *Armand*; *Marco, Rocco.*

Saulnier (645) French: occupational name for an extractor or seller of salt, from an agent derivative of Old French *sal, sel* (from Latin *salina*).
FOREBEARS A Saulnier is recorded in Acadia in 1738 with the secondary surnames Soumis and Beausoleil.
GIVEN NAMES French 6%. *Camille* (2), *Alcide, Alphonse, Anatole, Armand, Aurelie, Camile, Celine, Fernand.*

Sauls (2218) Patronymic from SAUL.

Saulsberry (456) American variant spelling of SALISBURY.

Saulsbury (486) American variant spelling of SALISBURY.

Sault (153) **1.** English: variant spelling of SALT. **2.** French: topographic name for someone who lived near a grove or small wood, Old French *saut* (Latin *saltus*).

Saulter (286) English: variant spelling of SALTER.

Saulters (193) Variant of SALTER.

Saum (444) South German: topographic for someone who lived close to a boundary, Middle High German *soum*. However, the word could also mean 'pack animal's load', and so may be a metonymic occupational name for a packer or carrier.

Saunders (24415) English and Scottish: patronymic from the medieval personal name **Saunder**, reduced vernacular form of ALEXANDER.

Saunderson (112) Scottish: patronymic from the medieval personal name **Saunder**, reduced vernacular form of ALEXANDER.
GIVEN NAME Scottish 7%. *Iain* (2).

Saunier (306) French: variant of SAULNIER.
GIVEN NAMES French 5%. *Guillaume, Philippe, Raynald.*

Saupe (152) Eastern German (of Slavic origin): occupational name, from Sorbian *sūpan* 'district administrator', 'governor', 'estate steward'.
GIVEN NAME German 4%. *Kurt.*

Saur (338) **1.** German: variant of German SAUER. **2.** French: nickname for a person with reddish hair, from Old French *sor* 'chestnut' (of Germanic origin, apparently referring originally to the color of dry leaves).
GIVEN NAMES German 5%. *Heinz* (2), *Gerhard, Kurt.*

Saurer (188) German: variant of SAUER, the ending *-er* reflecting the inflected form of the adjective.
GIVEN NAMES German 7%. *Hans, Kurt, Otto, Wolfgang.*

Saurman (140) Variant of Jewish (Ashkenazic) **Sauerman** or German **Sauermann**, nickname for an embittered person, literally 'sour man'.

Sauro (365) Italian: **1.** nickname for someone with light brown hair, from *sauro* 'sorrel color' (usually applied to a horse). **2.** Catalan (**Sauró**): possibly from a diminutive of SAUR.

GIVEN NAMES Italian 12%. *Angelo* (4), *Antonio, Dario, Donato, Gaetano, Matteo, Nicola, Rocco, Salvatore.*

Sause (157) Origin uncertain; in part possibly an altered spelling of French **Sauce**, a topographic name from an old form of *saule* 'willow tree'. The same name is found in England, etymology unexplained.

Sauseda (111) Spanish: variant of SAUCEDA.

GIVEN NAMES Spanish 23%. *Tiofilo* (2), *Armando, Benito, Concha, Felipe, Fidel, Hilaria, Javier, Jose, Juan, Lilia, Rafaela.*

Sauser (284) **1.** German: nickname for a clumsy person, from Middle High German *sūsen* 'to move noisily'. **2.** English and Scottish: occupational name from Middle English *sauser* 'sauce maker' (Old French *saucier, saussier*).

Sausser (129) Variant spelling of SAUSER.

Sausville (130) Probably an Americanized spelling of French **Sasseville**.

Sauter (1914) **1.** German: occupational name for a shoemaker or cobbler (one who sews leather), Middle High German *sūter* (from Latin *sutor*, an agent derivative of *suere* 'to sew'). **2.** English: variant of SALTER. **3.** Dutch: occupational name for a producer or seller of salt, from an agent derivative of *zout* 'salt'. Compare SALTER 1.

Sautner (177) German: variant of SAUTER 1.

Sautter (626) German: variant of SAUTER 1.

Sauvage (162) French and English: nickname for a wild or uncouth person, from Middle English, Old French *salvage, sauvage* 'untamed' (Late Latin *salvaticus*, a derivative of Latin *silva* 'wood', influenced by Latin *salvus* 'whole', i.e. natural).

FOREBEARS The surname Sauvage, documented in Champlain, Quebec, in 1690, with the secondary surname CHEVALIER, was taken there from Paris.

GIVEN NAMES French 11%. *Michel* (2), *Armand, Jean-Jacques.*

Sauvageau (370) French: diminutive of SAUVAGE.

FOREBEARS A Sauvageau (also spelled Sauvageot) from the Anjou region of France is documented in Lachenaie, Quebec, in 1678, with the secondary surname Maisonneuve.

GIVEN NAMES French 11%. *Aime, Aldor, Alphonse, Andre, Emile, Gaetan, Gilles, Joffre, Marcellin, Normand, Oliva, Pierre.*

Sauve (936) French (**Sauvé**): from Old French *sauvé* 'saved' (past participle of *sauver* 'to save'); a nickname for someone who had had a narrow escape, or from a personal name with a religious significance referring to Christian salvation.

FOREBEARS A Sauve from the Guyenne region of France is documented in Lachine, Quebec, in 1696, with the secondary surname LAPLANTE.

GIVEN NAMES French 8%. *Andre* (2), *Camille* (2), *Cecile* (2), *Henri* (2), *Adelard,*

Edouard, Emile, Gaetan, Germain, Gillis, Honore, Jacques.

Sava (218) **1.** Italian: habitational name from Sava in Taranto or the district so named in Baronissi, Salerno; the place name is probably from a pre-Latin element *saba, sava* 'ditch'. **2.** Romanian: from the personal name *Sava* (see SAVAS). Compare Serbian SAVICH, Polish SAWA, SAWICKI. **3.** Greek: see SAVAS.

GIVEN NAMES Italian 11%; Romanian 4%. *Saverio* (3), *Biaggio, Concetta, Filomena, Gaetano, Gino, Luigi, Pasquale, Salvatore; Dimitrie, Doina, Floarea, Vasile.*

Savacool (120) Origin unidentified.

Savage (17748) **1.** English and Scottish: nickname for a wild or uncouth person, from Middle English, Old French *salvage, sauvage* 'untamed' (Late Latin *salvaticus* literally 'man of the woods', a derivative of Latin *silva* 'wood', influenced by Latin *salvus* 'whole', i.e. natural). **2.** Irish: generally of English origin (it was taken to County Down in the 12th century), this name has also sometimes been adopted as equivalent of Gaelic **Ó Sabháin**, the name of a small south Munster sept, which was earlier Anglicized as **O'Savin** (see SAVIN). **3.** Americanized form of Ashkenazic Jewish SAVICH.

FOREBEARS A Jacob Savage, born in Exeter, Devon, England, in 1604, is recorded in Essex, NJ, by the early 1630s. Edward Savage, of Huguenot descent, emigrated from Ireland to Massachusetts in 1696. His grandson and namesake, who was born in Princeton, MA, in 1761 gained fame as an artist for his portrait of George Washington (1789–90).

Savageau (159) Variant of French SAUVAGE.

GIVEN NAMES French 5%. *Luc, Marcel, Normand.*

Savaglio (116) Southern Italian: unexplained; perhaps of Castilian or Catalan origin, but alternatively perhaps related to Savagli, the name of a district of Marano Principato in Cosenza province.

GIVEN NAMES Italian 30%. *Alessandro* (3), *Carlo* (2), *Italo* (2), *Aldo, Antonio, Carmine, Domenic, Enrico, Francesco, Gino, Luigi, Sante.*

Savala (310) Spanish: Castilianized variant of Basque ZABALA.

GIVEN NAMES Spanish 27%. *Jose* (4), *Pedro* (4), *Juan* (3), *Manuel* (3), *Alberto* (2), *Enrique* (2), *Gregorio* (2), *Jesus* (2), *Mariano* (2), *Ramon* (2), *Salvador* (2), *Santos* (2).

Savannah (116) Origin unidentified.

Savant (401) **1.** French: nickname from *savant* 'learned', a nickname for a university graduate or a particularly knowledgeable person. **2.** Indian (Maharashtra): Hindu (Maratha) name based on the name of a Maratha clan. It is derived from Sanskrit *sāmanta* 'feudatory prince'.

GIVEN NAMES Indian 5%. *Shrikant* (2), *Narayan, Paras, Rakesh, Sapna, Smita.*

Savard (694) French: **1.** topographic name, from Old French *savart* 'uncultivated land', 'waste land'. **2.** from a Germanic personal name composed of the elements *sab-, sav-*, of uncertain meaning + *hard* 'hardy', 'brave', 'strong'.

FOREBEARS The name is recorded in Quebec City in 1666, taken there from Paris.

GIVEN NAMES French 15%. *Gaston* (4), *Andre* (2), *Emile* (2), *Marcel* (2), *Normand* (2), *Serge* (2), *Aime, Alain, Albertine, Amedee, Armand, Francois.*

Savarese (796) Southern Italian: unexplained; it has the form of a habitational name for someone from a place called Savara, but no such place has been identified.

GIVEN NAMES Italian 9%. *Pasquale* (5), *Antonio* (4), *Marco* (2), *Sal* (2), *Carmine, Dario, Gabriella, Gaetano, Rocco, Salvatore, Vito.*

Savaria (136) Italian (also found in southern France): perhaps from a personal name *Saverio*, variant of *Severo* (see SEVERIN).

GIVEN NAMES French 16%. *Andre* (2), *Collette, Marcel, Normand, Raoul.*

Savarino (194) Italian (Sicily): variant of SEVERINO.

GIVEN NAMES Italian 14%. *Salvatore* (3), *Biagio, Carmela, Domenico, Gino, Giovani, Vincenzo.*

Savary (249) English and French: from a Germanic personal name composed of the elements *saba*, of uncertain meaning + *rīc* 'power', which was introduced into England by the Normans in the form *Savaric*.

FOREBEARS A Savary from the Limousin region of France is documented in Neuville, Quebec, in 1683.

GIVEN NAMES French 7%. *Fabien, Jacques, Normand, Philippe.*

Savas (276) Greek: from the personal name *Sav(v)as*, New Testament Greek *Sabbas*, a derivative of *Sabbaton* 'Sabbath', 'Saturday'. This name was borne by several saints and martyrs venerated in the Eastern Church, in particular a hermit (439–532) in Palestine, prominent in theological debates of his day.

GIVEN NAMES Greek 5%. *Constantine* (2), *Anastasios, Antonios, Orestis, Spyros.*

Savasta (137) Southern Italian: from Greek *Sebastia*, from medieval Greek *Sebastos*, a personal name meaning 'venerable', used in the Byzantine Empire as a title of respect, being the Greek equivalent of the Latin *Augustus* (see SEBASTIAN).

GIVEN NAMES Italian 10%. *Graziella, Salvatore, Umberto, Vito.*

Savastano (412) Italian (Sicily): from a dialect variant of the personal name SEBASTIANO.

GIVEN NAMES Italian 18%. *Carmine* (3), *Carmela* (2), *Giovanni* (2), *Saverio* (2),

Agostino, Alberico, Alfonse, Angelo, Aniello, Antonio, Dante, Florio.

Savedra (158) Galician and Portuguese: variant of SAAVEDRA.
GIVEN NAMES Spanish 40%. *Manuel* (2), *Ramon* (2), *Raul* (2), *Ricardo* (2), *Teofilo* (2), *Alberto, Ambrocio, Angel, Aurelio, Basilisa, Carlos, Del Carmen.*

Savel (145) **1.** French: habitational name from a place in Isère, originally named with Latin *sabellum*, a variant of *sabulum* 'sand'. **2.** Dutch: topographic name from *zavel, savel* 'sand', or a habitational name (**Van den Savel, Van de(r) Savel**) for someone from one of the places named with this word. **3.** Dutch: from Middle Dutch *sabel, savel* 'sable', 'black fur', a metonymic occupational name for a furrier, or nickname for a black-haired person.

Savela (140) Finnish: habitational name from a farm named with *savi* 'clay' + the local suffix *-la*. Farms with this name are common throughout Finland. The surname occurs mostly in western and northern Finland.
GIVEN NAMES Finnish 10%; German 4%. *Eino* (2), *Kaarlo, Mikko, Timo, Toivo; Kurt* (2).

Savell (596) English: variant of SAVILLE.

Savelle (123) English: variant of SAVILLE.

Savelli (120) Italian: **1.** patronymic from the personal name *Sabello, Savello* (Latin *Sabellius*). Sabellius (*fl.* 215) was an early Christian theologian who was excommunicated by Pope Calixtus I, but whose ideas enjoyed a considerable cult in the East. The name *Sabellius* is an ethnic term of uncertain origin. **2.** habitational name from Savelli in Crotone province.
GIVEN NAMES Italian 23%. *Enrico* (2), *Angelo, Gabriele, Gianni, Gino, Nicola, Paolo.*

Savely (169) Origin unidentified.

Saver (137) Probably an Americanized spelling of Portuguese and Catalan XAVIER.

Saverino (155) Italian: **1.** variant of SEVERINO. **2.** from a derivative of the personal name *Saverio*.
GIVEN NAMES Italian 30%. *Angelo* (3), *Alfonso* (2), *Mario* (2), *Salvatore* (2), *Santo* (2), *Ciro, Francesco, Gaetano, Giulio, Salvator, Umberto, Vittorio.*

Savery (349) English: variant spelling of SAVARY.

Saviano (337) Italian (mainly Campania): habitational name from a place in Naples province named Saviano.
GIVEN NAMES Italian 14%. *Luigi* (3), *Enrico* (2), *Angelo, Biagio, Concetta, Francesca, Gaetano, Ilario, Mafalda, Maurizio, Nunzio.*

Savic (103) Serbian (**Savić**): see SAVICH.
GIVEN NAMES South Slavic 53%; Russian 12%. *Branko* (2), *Milorad* (2), *Velimir* (2), *Dragutin, Jovo, Milica, Miodrag, Nebojsa, Petar, Predrag, Radomir, Slavica, Branislav, Dusan, Milan, Milos, Miroslav,*

Radoslav; Boris (3), *Milutin* (2), *Nicolai, Sava, Sofija.*

Savich (228) **1.** Serbian (**Savić**): patronymic from the personal name *Sava*, from Greek *Sabbas* (see SAVAS). **2.** Jewish (eastern Ashkenazic): habitational name for someone from a place called Savichi in Belarus. Compare SAVITSKY.
GIVEN NAMES South Slavic 15%. *Yaroslav* (2), *Branko, Mile, Rade, Savo; Milan* (4), *Milos, Milosh, Mirko, Radmila.*

Savickas (149) Lithuanian form of Polish SAWICKI, Belorussian *Savitsky.*

Savidge (467) Variant spelling of SAVAGE as an English (possibly also Jewish) surname.

Savignano (121) Italian: habitational name from a place named with Savignano, from the Latin personal name *Sabinius*: Savignano Irpino, in Avellino province, Savignano sul Panaro in Modena province, Savignano sul Rubicone in Forli province.
GIVEN NAME Italian 5%. *Angelo.*

Saville (1264) English (of Norman origin): habitational name from a place in northern France, of which the identity is not clear. It is probably Sainville in Eure-et-Loire, so called from Old French *saisne* 'Saxon' + *ville* 'settlement'.

Savin (430) **1.** Russian: from a personal name based on Latin *Sabinus* (see SABIN) or Greek *Sabbas* (see SAVAS). **2.** English and French: from the Middle English and Old French personal name *Savin*, a variant of SABIN. **3.** English and French: altered form of the Middle English and Old French personal name *Selvein*, Latin *Silvanus* (see SILVANO). **4.** Irish: reduced form of **O'Savin**, Anglicized form of Gaelic **Ó Sabháin** 'descendant of *Sabhán*', a personal name based on *sabh* 'cub'. The Irish surname has largely been absorbed into SAVAGE.
GIVEN NAMES Russian 4%. *Andrei* (2), *Anatoliy, Boris, Lev, Mikhail, Sergei, Sergey.*

Savini (255) Italian: patronymic or plural form of SAVINO.
GIVEN NAMES Italian 16%. *Amedio* (2), *Antonio* (2), *Gino* (2), *Amato, Angelo, Domenic, Dominico, Geno, Libero, Lorenzo, Luciano, Marco.*

Savino (1611) Italian: variant of SABINO. See also SABIN. **Savinos** is a Greek family name, a derivative of this Italian name.
GIVEN NAMES Italian 17%. *Vito* (12), *Rocco* (11), *Angelo* (6), *Carlo* (4), *Salvatore* (3), *Antonio* (2), *Carmela* (2), *Ciro* (2), *Cono* (2), *Domenic* (2), *Donato* (2), *Giovanni* (2).

Savio (310) Italian: nickname for a wise or knowledgeable man, from *savio* 'wise', 'learned', or from a personal name (*Savio*) derived from the same word.
GIVEN NAMES Italian 8%. *Giacomo* (2), *Aldo, Angelo, Dino, Gaetano, Gino, Luigi, Salvatore.*

Savitsky (215) Jewish (eastern Ashkenazic): habitational name for someone from a place called Savichi in Belarus, with the addition of the Slavic surname suffix *-sky*.
GIVEN NAMES Jewish 4%. *Avi, Mordecai, Yosef.*

Savitt (277) Origin unidentified; possibly a variant of English and Irish SAVAGE, or an Americanized form of Jewish SAVICH.

Savitz (288) Jewish: Americanized form of SAVICH.
GIVEN NAME Jewish 5%. *Reuven* (3).

Savko (144) Ukrainian: from a pet form of the personal name *Sava* (see SAVAS).

Savo (202) Italian: possibly a masculinized form of SAVA, or as **Savò**, of French origin, from *Sabau(t)*.
GIVEN NAMES Italian 28%. *Angelo* (2), *Antonio* (2), *Dante* (2), *Enrico* (2), *Gino* (2), *Pasquale* (2), *Aldo, Carlo, Francesco, Giuseppe, Marco, Natale.*

Savoca (263) Italian (Sicily): habitational name from Savoca in Messina, Sicily.
GIVEN NAMES Italian 16%. *Angelo* (2), *Salvatore* (2), *Vito* (2), *Annamaria, Antonio, Carmine, Guiseppe, Santo.*

Savoia (253) Italian: regional name for someone from Savoy, Italian *Savoia* (see SAVOIE).
GIVEN NAMES Italian 15%. *Aldo* (2), *Salvatore* (2), *Antonio, Dante, Enzo, Franco, Italo, Piero, Reno, Umberto, Vito.*

Savoie (2155) French: regional name from the region (former kingdom) of Savoy, French *Savoie*. This was consolidated in the 11th century by Count Humbert the White-handed, feudal lord of the kingdom of Arles. His descendants formed the great European noble house of Savoy, with large holdings in France, Switzerland, and Italy. Piedmont was closely connected with Savoy as early as the 11th century, since Humbert acquired a number of possessions there through marriage.
GIVEN NAMES French 9%. *Andre* (5), *Pierre* (5), *Marcel* (4), *Damien* (3), *Jacques* (3), *Normand* (3), *Raoul* (3), *Alphonse* (2), *Antoine* (2), *Armand* (2), *Julien* (2), *Alcee.*

Savona (200) Southern Italian: habitational name from the city of Savona in Liguria.
GIVEN NAMES Italian 15%. *Giuseppe* (2), *Luigi* (2), *Marco* (2), *Antonio, Francesca, Gaspare, Gasper, Gerardo, Natale, Nicasio.*

Savory (288) English: variant spelling of SAVARY.

Savoy (2092) English form of French SAVOIE.

Sawa (165) **1.** Japanese (mostly found in eastern Japan): meaning 'swamp', it is sometimes written with characters used phonetically. A few bearers have samurai connections. The name is not very common in Japan, but is a very common element in many other names; so some instances in America could have been shortened from names either beginning or ending with *sawa.* **2.** Polish: from the personal name *Sawa*, from Greek *Sabbas* (see SAVAS).

GIVEN NAMES Japanese 21%; Polish 5%. *Koji* (2), *Ayako, Fumio, Hitoshi, Iwao, Joji, Kazuto, Kiyo, Masato, Noriko, Shintaro, Shozo; Halina, Stanislawa, Wojtek.*

Sawada (154) Japanese: common topographical name, meaning 'rice paddy in the swamp'. It is found throughout Japan. Some bearers, especially from Ise, Kai, and Musashi (Mie, Yamanashi, and Tōkyō-Saitama prefectures) are descended from ancient Shintō priestly families.

GIVEN NAMES Japanese 77%. *Toshio* (3), *Haruko* (2), *Kenji* (2), *Minoru* (2), *Miyuki* (2), *Tomohiro* (2), *Toshinori* (2), *Akemi, Akira, Akiyoshi, Asao, Atsushi.*

Sawall (166) **1.** Variant of English SEWELL. **2.** German: unexplained.

GIVEN NAMES German 9%. *Helmut* (2), *Erwin, Ewald, Gerhard, Wilhelm.*

Sawatzki (104) Germanized form of Polish ZAWADZKI.

GIVEN NAMES German 7%. *Heinz, Otto.*

Sawatzky (278) Germanized form of Polish ZAWADZKI.

GIVEN NAMES German 4%. *Gerhart* (2), *Erna, Hans.*

Sawaya (324) **1.** Muslim: from a personal name probably based on Arabic *sawīya* 'equality', a derivative of *sawī* 'well-proportioned', 'shapely', 'harmonious'. **2.** Japanese: topographic name meaning 'swamp valley'.

GIVEN NAMES Muslim 7%; French 7%. *Sami* (2), *Anwar, Fuad, Hiam, Jabir, Khaled, Nabil, Nadim, Nasri, Ramzi, Ramzy, Riad; Emile* (2), *Andre, Antoine, Pierre.*

Sawchuk (195) Polish spelling of Ukrainian **Savchuk**, a patronymic from the personal name *Savka*, pet form of *Sava* (see SAVAS).

Sawdey (190) English: unexplained.

Sawdon (124) English: habitational name from a place so called in North Yorkshire, from Old English *salh* 'sallow tree' + *denu* 'valley'.

Sawdy (144) English (Devon and Cornwall): unexplained.

Sawhill (165) Origin unidentified.

Sawhney (197) Indian (Panjab): Hindu (Khatri) and Sikh name, said to mean 'commander' and 'companion', based on the name of a Khatri clan.

GIVEN NAMES Indian 90%. *Sanjeev* (5), *Deepak* (3), *Rajiv* (3), *Ramesh* (3), *Satish* (3), *Vijay* (3), *Anil* (2), *Ashit* (2), *Gopal* (2), *Harish* (2), *Navin* (2), *Niraj* (2).

Sawicki (1504) Polish and Jewish (from Poland): habitational name for someone from Sawica in Olsztyn voivodeship or Sawice in Siedlce voivodeship, both place names being derived from the saint's name *Sawa*, from Greek *Sabbas* (see SAVAS).

GIVEN NAMES Polish 9%. *Casimir* (3), *Krzysztof* (3), *Czeslaw* (2), *Jacek* (2),

Janusz (2), *Jerzy* (2), *Lech* (2), *Pawel* (2), *Ryszard* (2), *Bogdan, Danuta, Elzbieta.*

Sawin (405) English: unexplained.

FOREBEARS The name was brought to Watertown, MA, by John Sawin (b. about 1620 in Boxford, Suffolk, England).

Sawka (222) Polish: from a pet form of the personal name SAWA.

GIVEN NAMES Polish 6%. *Casimir* (2), *Bogdan, Danuta, Janusz.*

Sawmiller (122) Americanized form of German **Sägemüller**, an occupational name for someone who worked in a sawmill, from Middle High German *sege* 'saw' + *müller* 'miller'.

Sawtell (204) Possibly reduced Americanized form of French DESAUTELS.

Sawtelle (555) Possibly reduced Americanized form of French DESAUTELS.

Sawvel (108) Origin unidentified. Compare SAWVELL. It could perhaps be a respelling of French **Sauval(le)**, which, according to Morlet, may be a topographic name from *saus*, an old form of *saul* 'willow' + *val* 'valley', or perhaps of French **Sauville**, a habitational name from places so named in Ardennes and Vosges.

Sawvell (102) Origin unidentified. See SAWVEL.

Sawyer (18288) **1.** English: occupational name for someone who earned his living by sawing wood, Middle English *saghier*, an agent derivative of *sagh(en)* 'to saw'. **2.** Americanized form of some like-sounding Jewish surname or a translation of SEGER.

Sawyers (1498) English: patronymic from SAWYER.

Sax (829) **1.** South German: variant of SACHS 1. **2.** Dutch: variant of SAS 1 and 3. **3.** English: from an Old Norse personal name, *Saxi* meaning 'sword'. **4.** Jewish (Ashkenazic): variant spelling of SACHS.

Saxby (308) English: **1.** habitational name from places in Leicestershire and Lincolnshire called Saxby, from the Old Norse personal name *Saxi* meaning 'sword', or the genitive of the Old English folk name *Seaxe*, Old Norse *Saksar* 'Saxons' + Old Norse *býr* 'farm', 'settlement'. **2.** nickname for someone quick to take offense and draw his sword, from Middle English *sakespey*, Old French *sacquespee*, from Old French *sacque(r)* 'to draw or extract' (from *sac* 'sack') + *espee* 'sword' (Latin *spatha*).

Saxe (866) **1.** German: variant spelling of SACHSE. **2.** Dutch: variant of SAS 1 and 3. **3.** English: variant spelling of SAX 3. **4.** Jewish (Ashkenazic): variant of SACHS 1.

Saxena (295) Indian (northern states): Hindu (Kayasth) name from one of the subgroups of the Kayasth community. According to Saxena tradition, their name is from Sanskrit *sakhisenā* 'friend of the army', a title awarded to them by the kings of Srinagar.

GIVEN NAMES Indian 93%. *Sanjay* (9), *Arvind* (5), *Manoj* (5), *Sunil* (5), *Atul* (4), *Naveen* (4), *Ravi* (4), *Sandeep* (4), *Vivek* (4), *Anil* (3), *Praveen* (3), *Rakesh* (3).

Saxer (199) **1.** Dutch and German: ethnic name for someone from Saxony. **2.** Swiss German (Swiss): habitational name for someone from a place called Sax or Saxe.

Saxman (235) Origin unidentified.

Saxon (2628) English (Lancashire): **1.** variant of SAXTON. **2.** from the medieval personal name *Saxon*, originally an ethnic byname for someone from Saxony.

Saxton (3159) English: **1.** habitational name from a place in West Yorkshire, possibly also one in Cambridgeshire, both so named from Old English *Seaxe* 'Saxons' + *tūn* 'enclosure', 'settlement'. **2.** variant of SEXTON 1.

Say (495) **1.** English (of Norman origin): habitational name from Sai in Orne or Say in Indre, perhaps so called from a Gaulish personal name *Saius* + the Latin locative suffix *-acum*. **2.** English: metonymic occupational name for a maker or seller of *say*, a kind of finely textured cloth, Middle English *say* (from Old French *saie*, Latin *saga*, plural of *sagum* 'military cloak'). In some instances the surname may have arisen from a nickname for an habitual wearer of clothes made of this material. **3.** Southern French: topographic name from *saix* 'rock' (Latin *saxum*), or a habitational name from a place named with this word, for example, Say in Loire, Saix in Tarn and Vienne, Le Saix in Hautes-Alpes, or Les Saix in Isère.

FOREBEARS William Say of Bristol, England, was a member of the Society of Friends who settled in America toward the close of the 17th century. His descendant Thomas Say (1787–1834) of Philadelphia is known as the father of descriptive entomology in America.

Saya (100) Italian: variant spelling of SAIA.

GIVEN NAMES Italian 13%. *Rocco* (2), *Concetto, Santo.*

Sayavong (110) Cambodian or other Southeast Asian: unexplained.

GIVEN NAMES Southeast Asian 48%; Cambodian 18%. *Kong* (2), *Chan, Seng; Dao, My, Phat, Pho, Thanh; Somvang* (3), *Bouavanh, Chay; Kham* (2), *Khambay.*

Saye (456) English: variant spelling of SAY 1 and 2.

Sayed (201) Muslim: from a personal name based on Arabic *sayyid* 'lord', 'master', 'chief'. This is a title of respect used for the descendants of Fatima, daughter of the Prophet Muhammad.

GIVEN NAMES Muslim 71%. *Abu* (4), *Waseem* (4), *Abdul* (3), *Ahmed* (3), *Ibrahim* (3), *Mohamed* (3), *Ahmad* (2), *Ali* (2), *Daud* (2), *Khalil* (2), *Luay* (2), *Mohamad* (2).

Sayegh (395) Arabic and Jewish (Sephardic): occupational name for a goldsmith, from Arabic *ṣā'igh.*

GIVEN NAMES Muslim 42%; French 5%. *Hani* (5), *Fouad* (3), *Jamil* (3), *Munir* (3), *Nader* (3), *Samir* (3), *Abdullah* (2), *Bassam* (2), *Ghassan* (2), *Hassan* (2), *Ibrahim* (2), *Issa* (2); *Emile* (3), *Antoine* (2), *Georges*, *Henri*, *Jean-Pierre*, *Marcelle*.

Sayen (126) Of French origin: unexplained.

Sayer (1199) **1.** English: from the Middle English personal name *Saher* or *Seir*. This is probably a Norman introduction of the Continental Germanic personal name *Sigiheri*, composed of the elements *sigi* 'victory' + *heri* 'army'. However, it could also represent a Middle English survival of an unrecorded Old English name, *Sǣhere*, composed of the elements *sǣ* 'sea' + *here* 'army'. **2.** English: occupational name, from Middle English *saghier* (see SAWYER) or Old French *seieor*. **3.** English: occupational name for a professional reciter, from an agent derivative of Middle English *say(en)*, *sey(en)* 'to say'. **4.** English: from a reduced form of Middle English *assayer*, an agent derivative of *assay* 'trial', 'test', Old French *essay* (from Late Latin *exagium*, a derivative of *exagmināre* 'to weigh'), hence an occupational name for an assayer of metals or a taster of food. **5.** English: occupational name for a maker or seller of *say*, a type of cloth, from Middle English *say* + the agent suffix *-er*. See also SAY. **6.** Welsh: occupational name from Welsh *saer* 'carpenter' or from *saer maen* 'stonecutter', i.e. mason. **7.** French: occupational name for a reaper or mower, from an agent derivative of Old French *seer* 'to cut' (Latin *secare*). **8.** Dutch: occupational name for a weaver of serge, from an agent derivative of *saai* 'serge'. **9.** Dutch: occupational name from *zaaier* 'sower'.

Sayers (2701) **1.** English: patronymic from SAYER 1. This English name is also well established in Ireland. **2.** Irish: Anglicization of Gaelic **Mac Saoghair** (see SEARS).

Sayle (159) **1.** Manx: unexplained. **2.** Possibly a variant or Americanized spelling of German SAILE.
GIVEN NAME Scandinavian 5%. *Erik* (3).

Sayler (1095) English: probably a variant SAYLOR.

Sayles (1847) English: habitational name from Sales in Lancashire.

Saylor (5482) English: occupational name for a dancer or acrobat, from Old French *sailleor* 'dancer', 'leaper'.

Saylors (565) English: variant of SAYLOR, with patronymic *-s*.

Sayne (123) **1.** English: unexplained; possibly the same as 2. **2.** Probably an Americanized spelling of French **Sain**, a metonymic occupational name for a charcutier, someone who prepared cooked meats, from Old French *sain* 'fat'.

Sayre (3260) English: variant spelling of SAYER.

Sayres (160) English: variant spelling of SAYERS.

Sayward (157) English: variant of SEWARD 1 and 2.

Sazama (226) Japanese: written with a character meaning 'help' used twice, plus the character for 'space', the name may actually mean '(one who lives) amid the bamboo grass'. The name is not common in Japan.

Sbarra (132) Italian: topographic name from *sbarra* 'fence', 'partition'.
GIVEN NAMES Italian 17%. *Carmine*, *Enrico*, *Giuseppe*, *Tommaso*, *Vita*.

Sberna (105) Italian (Sicilian): topographic name for someone who lived where alders grew, from Sicilian *sberna* 'alder'.
GIVEN NAMES Italian 14%. *Salvatore* (4), *Antonio*, *Carmelo*.

Scaccia (274) Italian: **1.** from a short form of a nickname derived from Italian *scacciare* 'to drive or chase away'. **2.** from Sicilian *scacciari* 'to squash', 'to crush', applied as a metonymic occupational name for someone who crushed grapes or pressed olives, or possibly as a nickname for a bully.
GIVEN NAMES Italian 19%. *Angelo* (3), *Salvatore* (2), *Carlo*, *Carmelo*, *Cosmo*, *Dante*, *Dino*, *Ermenegildo*, *Francesco*, *Franco*, *Giacomo*, *Sandro*.

Scacco (108) Italian: probably from the personal name *Isacco* via Arabic *Isḥāq*, or alternatively perhaps a nickname for an inveterate dice or chess player, from *scacco* 'chess'.
GIVEN NAMES Italian 14%. *Guido* (2), *Angelo*, *Biagio*, *Domenic*, *Santo*.

Scadden (180) Irish: of uncertain origin. It is possibly a reduced form of the Scottish surname **Garscadden**, a habitational name from a place east of Glasgow; alternatively it may be from Gaelic *scadán* 'herring', a word probably borrowed from Norse. There have been Scaddans in Tipperary since the 12th century.

Scaduto (248) Southern Italian: nickname for someone who was impoverished or in difficult circumstances, from *scaduto* 'finished', 'run down'.
GIVEN NAMES Italian 23%. *Gasper* (2), *Mario* (2), *Sal* (2), *Salvatore* (2), *Alvaro*, *Antonio*, *Carmela*, *Cosmo*, *Giuseppe*, *Lucio*, *Massimo*, *Rosaria*.

Scafe (116) Northern English: variant of SCAIFE.

Scaff (223) **1.** English: unexplained; possibly a variant of SCAIFE. **2.** Dutch (Belgium): from German *schaf*, hence a metonymic occupational name for a shepherd or a nickname for someone thought to resemble a sheep in some way.

Scaffidi (258) Southern Italian: variant of SCAFIDI.
GIVEN NAMES Italian 13%. *Attilio*, *Carmello*, *Carmelo*, *Concetta*, *Cono*, *Costantino*, *Nino*, *Pietro*, *Salvatore*, *Siro*, *Vincenzo*.

Scafidi (364) Southern Italian and Greek (**Skafidis**): **1.** habitational name for someone from any of the many place in Greece, Southern Italy, and Sicily named with medieval Greek *skafidion* 'trough', 'tub', 'kneading trough', 'drinking trough for animals'. **2.** *skaphidion* also means 'skiff', 'light boat', and in some cases this may be an occupational name for a boatman. **3.** possibly a habitational name for someone from a place named Scafa, in particular a district so named in Capo d'Orlando in Messina, Sicily.
GIVEN NAMES Italian 16%. *Gaetano* (2), *Nicola* (2), *Sal* (2), *Salvatore* (2), *Santo* (2), *Biagio*, *Carlo*, *Dario*, *Giuseppe*, *Nicolo*, *Rosaria*.

Scaggs (902) English: unexplained. Clearly a variant of SKAGGS, also unexplained.

Scaglione (724) Southern Italian: perhaps from *scaglione* 'stallion's canine tooth' (an augmentative form of *scaglie* 'canine tooth', from Old French *escaillon* 'horse's tooth'), presumably a nickname for someone with exceptionally large teeth. According to family tradition, this is the name of a family of Norman origin.
GIVEN NAMES Italian 17%. *Angelo* (5), *Sal* (5), *Salvatore* (3), *Vito* (3), *Aldo* (2), *Francesco* (2), *Silvio* (2), *Bartolomeo*, *Carmelo*, *Carmine*, *Carmino*, *Dino*.

Scagnelli (127) Italian: possibly a habitational name from Scagnello in Cuneo province, although Caracausi derives the surname from *scagno* 'seat', 'bank'.
GIVEN NAMES Italian 18%. *Angelo*, *Bartolomeo*, *Carlo*, *Domenica*, *Domenico*, *Giacomo*, *Giovanni*, *Guiseppe*, *Luigi*.

Scahill (190) Irish: reduced Anglicized form of Gaelic **Mac Scaithghil**, a Connacht name, a patronymic from a personal name probably composed of the elements *scaith* 'flower' + *geal* 'bright'. (Later, the surname sometimes had the prefix Ó 'descendant of').
GIVEN NAME Irish 5%. *Brendan*.

Scaife (489) Northern English (Yorkshire): nickname from the northern English dialect word *scafe* 'crooked', 'awry', 'awkward', 'wild' (Old Norse *skeifr*).

Scala (1107) **1.** Italian and Greek (**Skalas**): habitational or topographic name from any of various places named with *scala* 'ladder', 'steps', 'wharf'. In Greece this is especially common as the name of a settlement by the seashore, often with the main settlement on higher ground above. Elsewhere, especially in Italy, it also denotes a stepped or terraced landscape, as for example Scala in Salerno province, Scala Coeli in Cosenza, or the district so named in Torregrotta, in Messina province, Sicily. **2.** Jewish: variant spelling of SKALA.
GIVEN NAMES Italian 12%. *Luigi* (3), *Sal* (3), *Antonio* (2), *Carmine* (2), *Corrado* (2), *Orazio* (2), *Tiziana* (2), *Aldo*, *Angelo*, *Carlo*, *Carmela*, *Concetta*.

Scalera (247) Italian: **1.** habitational name from a district so named in Filiano in Potenza province. **2.** otherwise, from *scalera*, either a topographic name from the sense 'ladder' (see SCALA), or, in Salento, a metonymic occupational name from the sense 'artichoke'.

GIVEN NAMES Italian 17%. *Domenic* (2), *Vito* (2), *Angelo, Carmine, Ciro, Gilda, Lorenzo, Luciano, Pasquale.*

Scales (3716) Northern English: topographic name for someone who lived in a rough hut or shed, northern Middle English *scale* 'hut' (from Old Norse *skáli*), later also *sc(h)ole*, or a habitational name from one of the various places named with this word, as for example Scales in Lancashire and Cumbria. The surname has been established in southern Ireland since the 14th century.

Scalese (169) Southern Italian: probably a habitational name for someone from Scala in Salerno province (see SCALA).

GIVEN NAMES Italian 14%. *Salvatore* (3), *Angelo, Gennaro, Guido, Pasquale, Vincenzo.*

Scaletta (192) Italian: habitational name from Scaletta Zanclea in Messina, Sicily.

GIVEN NAMES Italian 12%. *Sal* (2), *Salvatore* (2), *Angelo, Ciro, Paolo, Santo.*

Scalf (1014) Possibly an altered form of English SCARFF.

Scali (261) Southern Italian: **1.** habitational name from Scali in Piedimonte Etneo, Sicily, named with Greek *skali* 'step', 'terrace', or from some other similarly named place. **2.** variant of SCALA.

GIVEN NAMES Italian 28%. *Salvatore* (5), *Domenic* (3), *Antonio* (2), *Geraldo* (2), *Orlando* (2), *Pasquale* (2), *Rocco* (2), *Carmela, Cesare, Fortunato, Giuseppe, Mauro, Pasqualina, Piero, Rosario, Saverio.*

Scalia (619) Southern Italian: habitational name from Scalea in Cosenza province, named with medieval Greek *skaleia* 'hoeing'. See also SCALA.

GIVEN NAMES Italian 22%; Spanish 4%. *Sal* (6), *Salvatore* (6), *Angelo* (3), *Alfio* (2), *Rocco* (2), *Vito* (2), *Annamarie, Antonino, Antonio, Carmelo, Cosimo, Dino, Osvaldo, Rosario; Diego* (2), *Rosalia* (2), *Luisa.*

Scalice (117) Southern Italian: probably a variant of SCALESE.

GIVEN NAMES Italian 16%; German 4%. *Salvatore* (4), *Giacomo* (2); *Otto* (2).

Scalici (125) Southern Italian: probably a variant of SCALESE.

GIVEN NAMES Italian 30%. *Salvatore* (5), *Angelo* (2), *Francesco* (2), *Emanuele, Giovanni, Nicola, Rocco, Santino, Vito.*

Scalise (1148) Southern Italian: dialect variant of SCALESE.

GIVEN NAMES Italian 13%. *Domenic* (4), *Aldo* (3), *Fiore* (3), *Luigi* (3), *Salvatore* (3), *Angelo* (2), *Antonio* (2), *Saverio* (2), *Camillo, Carmela, Carmine.*

Scalisi (200) Southern Italian: variant of SCALESE.

GIVEN NAMES Italian 24%. *Mario* (4), *Angelo* (3), *Gino* (2), *Salvatore* (2), *Adamo, Alberto, Carmella, Claudio, Cosmo, Domenic, Elvira, Sal, Vicenzo.*

Scallan (350) Irish: reduced Anglicized form of Gaelic **Ó Scealláin** 'descendant of *Sceallán*', a personal name derived from a word meaning 'kernel'.

GIVEN NAMES French 5%. *Benoit, Camille, Pierre.*

Scalley (138) Irish: variant of SCALLY.

Scallion (175) Irish: variant of SCULLION.

Scallon (273) Irish: variant of SCALLAN.

Scally (492) Irish (counties Roscommon and Westmeath): reduced Anglicized form of Gaelic **Mac Scalaidhe** (Midlands **Ó Scalaidhe**), a patronymic probably from a variant of Gaelic *scolaidhe* 'scholar' (see SCULLY).

GIVEN NAMES Irish 5%. *Ciaran, Niall.*

Scalone (117) Italian (Sicilian): from Sicilian *scaluni* 'step', perhaps a topographic name for someone who lived on terraced land.

GIVEN NAMES Italian 19%. *Aldo, Amedeo, Gasper, Giorgio, Ovidio, Rocco, Sabastian, Salvatore.*

Scalzi (218) Italian: patronymic form of SCALZO.

GIVEN NAMES Italian 13%. *Domenic* (2), *Saverio* (2), *Angelo, Antonio, Dante, Giancarlo, Guido, Sal.*

Scalzitti (132) Italian: patronymic from a diminutive of SCALZO.

GIVEN NAMES Italian 10%. *Amato, Attilio, Carmine, Nicola.*

Scalzo (937) Italian: from *scalzo* 'barefoot', a nickname for someone too poor to have shoes or for a member of an order of mendicant friars who were customarily unshod.

GIVEN NAMES Italian 14%. *Salvatore* (7), *Angelo* (4), *Antonio* (4), *Rocco* (3), *Gino* (2), *Pasquale* (2), *Santo* (2), *Alfonse, Amadeo, Carmine, Cataldo.*

Scamardo (101) Italian (Sicily): possibly related to Calabrian *scamardatu* 'lazy', 'slightly unbalanced'.

GIVEN NAMES Italian 5%. *Alessandra, Antonio, Salvatore.*

Scammell (181) English: **1.** metonymic occupational name for someone who worked in a meat or fish market, from Old English *scamol* 'bench (on which meat was laid out for sale)'. **2.** possibly from an unattested Middle English personal name, *Skammel*, a diminutive of an Old Norse byname from *skammr* 'short'.

Scammon (153) Of English origin: unexplained. The name does not appear in modern English records.

Scandrett (122) English (Hereford and Worcester): unexplained.

Scanga (128) Italian: variant of **Sganga**, possibly from a short form of a compound name formed with Sicilian *sgangari* ' to glean', 'to pick', 'to pull out'.

GIVEN NAMES Italian 8%. *Antonio, Giuseppe, Ugo.*

Scanio (128) Italian (Sicily): from a reduced form of the personal name *Ascanio* (Latin *Ascanius*). In Roman legend, Ascanius was the son of Aeneas and founder of Alba Longa.

GIVEN NAMES Italian 15%. *Salvatore* (3), *Sal* (2), *Francesco, Vito.*

Scanlan (2231) Irish: variant spelling of SCANLON. The surname occasionally occurs with the patronymic prefix *Mac*.

GIVEN NAMES Irish 5%. *Liam* (2), *Bridgid, Cliona, Conan, Siobhan.*

Scanland (106) Variant of Irish SCANLON.

GIVEN NAME Irish 4%. *Conan.*

Scanlin (233) Variant of SCANLON.

Scanlon (5002) Irish: reduced Anglicized form of Gaelic **Ó Scannláin**, 'descendant of *Scannlán*', a personal name formed from a diminutive of *Scannal* (see SCANNELL).

GIVEN NAMES Irish 5%. *Brendan* (2), *Siobhan* (2), *Caitlin, Clancy, Colm, Dympna, James Patrick, Loman, Mairead, Seamus, Sioban.*

Scannapieco (121) Italian (Naples): occupational name for an itinerant butcher, *scannapiecure*, a compound of *scanna* 'to butcher' + *piecuro* 'sheep', 'lamb'.

GIVEN NAMES Italian 11%. *Angelo, Carmine, Dario, Gildo.*

Scannell (1256) Irish: reduced Anglicized form of Gaelic **Ó Scannail** 'descendant of *Scannal*', a byname meaning 'contention'.

GIVEN NAMES Irish 4%. *Brendan, Patrick Joseph.*

Scantland (119) Variant of Irish SCANLON.

Scantlebury (143) English (Cornwall and Devon): unexplained.

GIVEN NAMES Irish 5%. *Aileen, Fitz.*

Scantlin (234) Variant of Irish SCANLON.

Scantling (125) Irish: variant of SCANLON.

Scaramella (110) Italian: possibly a topographic name from medieval Latin *scaravellus* 'stepped street', or alternatively from Old Italian *scaramella, scaramilla* 'sword fight', 'skirmish', presumably applied as a nickname for a swordsman or perhaps for someone given to brawling.

GIVEN NAMES Italian 8%. *Cesare, Donato.*

Scarangella (103) Italian: variant of **Scaringella**, a female pet form of **Scaringi**, a patronymic from a Germanic personal name *Ans(i)gar, Anscar.*

GIVEN NAMES Italian 18%. *Antonio* (2), *Vito* (2), *Antonietta.*

Scarano (439) Southern Italian (Sicily): derogatory nickname from medieval Latin *scaranus* 'marauder' (of Gothic origin).

GIVEN NAMES Italian 14%. *Domenic* (2), *Pasquale* (2), *Pio* (2), *Amerigo, Biaggio, Carmel, Enrico, Rocco, Sal, Silvio.*

Scarantino (151) Italian: topographic name from a diminutive of Old Italian *scaranto* 'steep and stoney mountain tract', or from Italian (also Venetian) *caranto* 'tuff'.

GIVEN NAMES Italian 17%. *Angelo* (2), *Sal* (2), *Cataldo, Dino, Pasquale, Salvatore.*

Scarber (130) **1.** Possibly an altered form of Northern French **Scarbert**, from the Germanic personal name *Skarberht*, composed of an element related to Old High German *skara* 'band', 'troop' + *berht* 'bright'. **2.** Possibly an altered form of SCARBOROUGH.

Scarberry (1022) Variant of SCARBOROUGH.

Scarboro (543) Variant of SCARBOROUGH.

Scarborough (4682) English: habitational name from Scarborough on the coast of North Yorkshire, so named from the Old Norse byname *Skarði* + Old Norse *borg* 'fortress', 'fortified town'.

Scarbro (253) English: variant of SCARBOROUGH.

Scarbrough (2973) English: variant of SCARBOROUGH.

Scarce (122) English (Suffolk): unexplained.

Scarcella (278) Southern Italian: variant of SCARSELLA.
GIVEN NAMES Italian 25%. *Salvatore* (3), *Angelo* (2), *Gaetano* (2), *Sal* (2), *Agatino, Antonino, Camillo, Carlo, Chiara, Domenic, Nunzio, Oronzo.*

Scarcelli (125) Italian: variant of SCARSELLA.
GIVEN NAMES Italian 14%. *Dino, Francesco, Guido, Salvatore.*

Scarcello (108) Italian: variant of SCARSELLA.
GIVEN NAME Italian 5%. *Rocco.*

Scardina (374) Italian: of uncertain derivation; possibly from a diminutive of southern Italian *scarda* 'splinter', 'chip' (from Germanic *skard-*, probably of Lombardic origin), perhaps a metonymic occupational name for a carpenter or woodcutter.
GIVEN NAMES Italian 10%. *Marco* (4), *Angelo* (2), *Santo* (2), *Ciro, Giovanni, Giuseppina, Vito.*

Scardino (419) Italian: probably a masculinized form of SCARDINA.
GIVEN NAMES Italian 11%. *Sal* (2), *Salvatore* (2), *Aldo, Carlo, Cosmo, Dino, Gasper, Guiseppe, Piero, Pietro, Vito.*

Scarff (265) English: from northern Middle English *scarfe* 'cormorant' (Old Norse *skarfr*), either a nickname for someone bearing some supposed resemblance to a cormorant, or else a survival into Middle English of the Old Norse byname *Scarfi*, from the same source.

Scarfo (217) Italian (Calabria): habitational name from Scarfó in Pizzo, in Vibo Valentia province.
GIVEN NAMES Italian 18%. *Carmine* (2), *Carmela, Domenic, Filippo, Rocco, Salvatore.*

Scarfone (133) Southern Italian: unflattering nickname from Calabrian *scarfune* 'scorpion'.

GIVEN NAMES Italian 18%. *Antonio, Carmine, Eufemia, Francesco, Saverio, Tiberio.*

Scarlata (229) Italian (mainly Sicily): **1.** from the old female personal name *Scarlata*. **2.** feminine form of SCARLATO.
GIVEN NAMES Italian 12%. *Romeo* (2), *Salvatore* (2), *Angelo, Giuseppe, Luigi, Paolo.*

Scarlato (127) Italian: from Sicilian *scarlatu* 'scarlet' (Italian *scarlatto*), applied as a metonymic occupational name for a dyer, or as a nickname for someone who habitually wore scarlet or who had bright red hair.
GIVEN NAMES Italian 16%. *Angelo* (4), *Aldo, Antonio, Cesare, Damiano, Gilda.*

Scarlett (1303) English (mainly East Anglia): metonymic occupational name for a dyer or for a seller of rich, bright fabrics, from Old French *escarlate* 'scarlet cloth' (Late Latin *scarlata*).

Scarola (287) Italian: metonymic occupational name for a grower or seller of endives, Calabrian *scarola*.
GIVEN NAMES Italian 22%. *Vito* (11), *Angelo* (5), *Antonio* (3), *Gilda* (2), *Carlo, Giacoma, Nicola, Rocco, Sal.*

Scarpa (558) Italian and Jewish (from Italy): from Italian *scarpa* 'shoe', a metonymic occupational name for a shoemaker or perhaps a nickname for someone with large or otherwise remarkable feet.
GIVEN NAMES Italian 19%; Spanish 5%. *Mario* (2), *Rodolfo* (2), *Salvatore* (4), *Aldo, Amerigo, Angelo, Annamarie, Antonio, Benito, Carmine, Domenic, Gino, Pasquale, Riccardo, Sal; Angel, Jose, Rafael, Tomas, Victorio.*

Scarpace (107) Italian: patronymic or plural form of SCARPACI.
GIVEN NAME Italian 9%. *Sal* (2).

Scarpaci (116) Southern Italian: probably from the Greek personal name *Skarpakēs*, a diminutive of *Skarpas*.
GIVEN NAMES Italian 10%. *Domenica, Salvatore.*

Scarpati (179) Italian: patronymic or plural form of SCARPATO.
GIVEN NAMES Italian 21%. *Salvatore* (3), *Antonino* (2), *Gennaro* (2), *Emilio, Marina, Philomena, Rito, Salvatore.*

Scarpato (101) Italian: from a derivative of SCARPA, probably in the sense 'having shoes', i.e. denoting in particular a friar who wore shoes, as opposed to one who wore clogs or went barefoot (see SCALZO).
GIVEN NAMES Italian 13%. *Sal* (2), *Domenico, Salvatore, Stefano.*

Scarpelli (432) Italian: patronymic or plural form of SCARPELLO.
GIVEN NAMES Italian 15%. *Vito* (3), *Antonio* (2), *Salvatore* (2), *Aldo, Carmel, Carmela, Dante, Enrico, Gennaro, Gino, Giulio, Goffredo.*

Scarpello (143) Southern Italian: **1.** from a diminutive of SCARPA. **2.** metonymic occupational name for a carpenter or stone-

mason, from a regional variant of *scalpello* 'chisel'.
GIVEN NAMES Italian 15%. *Pasquale* (3), *Angelo, Bartolomeo, Nunziata, Sal, Salvatore.*

Scarpinato (109) Italian: **1.** from a derivative of SCARPA. **2.** possibly a nickname derived from Sicilian *scarpinari* 'to walk in haste'.
GIVEN NAMES Italian 17%. *Rocco* (2), *Carmello, Mario, Vita.*

Scarpino (252) Italian: from a diminutive of SCARPA.
GIVEN NAMES Italian 13%. *Salvatore* (2), *Emedio, Gino, Giuseppe, Luigi, Pasquale, Sal.*

Scarpitti (124) Southern Italian: from a derivative of SCARPA.
GIVEN NAMES Italian 15%. *Angelo* (2), *Giovanna, Pasquale, Romeo, Ugo, Vito.*

Scarpone (157) Italian: from an augmentative form of SCARPA.
GIVEN NAMES Italian 14%. *Pasquale* (2), *Aldo, Ezio, Fiorella, Marino, Paolo, Santina.*

Scarpulla (183) Southern Italian: from a diminutive of SCARPA.
GIVEN NAMES Italian 19%. *Angelo* (5), *Ciro* (3), *Carmelo, Carmine, Domenic, Francesco, Giuseppe, Rosaria.*

Scarr (139) English: topographic name from Old Norse *sker* 'rock', later dialect *scar* 'rocky cliff'.

Scarrow (108) English: unexplained.

Scarry (184) Irish: shortened Anglicized form of Gaelic **Ó Scurra** 'descendant of *Scurra*', a personal name of uncertain origin. See also SCURRY.
GIVEN NAME Irish 5%. *Nuala.*

Scarsella (158) Italian: from *scarsella* 'purse or satchel for carrying money, letters, or documents', either a nickname or a metonymic occupational name for a messenger.
GIVEN NAMES Italian 14%. *Angelo* (2), *Carlo, Dino, Luciano, Luigi, Marcello, Silvano, Ugo, Umberto, Vittorio.*

Scatena (178) Italian (Sicily): nickname for a troublemaker, from a derivative of *scatenare* 'to provoke', 'to stir up'.
GIVEN NAMES Italian 9%; French 6%. *Gino, Piero, Rocco; Armand, Girard.*

Scates (785) English: unexplained.

Scattergood (171) English: from Middle English *skater(en)* 'to squander, dissipate' (a byform, under Scandinavian influence, of *shatter*) + *gode* 'property', 'goods', 'wealth'; a nickname for a man who was careless and free with money, perhaps a philanthropist who gave his goods to the poor.

Scaturro (271) Italian: habitational name from any of several minor places in Sicily named Scaturro.
GIVEN NAMES Italian 21%; Spanish 5%. *Gasper* (5), *Salvatore* (3), *Saverio* (2), *Alessio, Angelo, Antonio, Gaspare,*

Girolamo, Giuliano, Grazia, Martino, Romano; Jaime, Luis, Magda, Marta, Rosario.

Scavo (316) Italian (Sicily): status name for a serf, from Old Sicilian *scavu* 'slave', 'bondsman'.
GIVEN NAMES Italian 17%. *Vito* (4), *Angelo* (2), *Giuseppe* (2), *Carmine, Cataldo, Domenic, Palma, Salvatore, Santo.*

Scavone (419) Italian: **1.** ethnic name for a Slav, *Schiavone* (Old Sicilian *Scavonia* 'Illyria'). **2.** from an augmentative form of SCAVO.
GIVEN NAMES Italian 18%. *Rocco* (7), *Salvatore* (6), *Rosaria* (3), *Angelo* (2), *Cirino* (2), *Vito* (2), *Vittorio* (2), *Concetta, Domenic, Donato, Filomena, Gaetano.*

Scavuzzo (173) Italian: from a diminutive of SCAVO.
GIVEN NAMES Italian 15%. *Santo* (3), *Cosmo* (2), *Vito* (2), *Pasquale.*

Scearce (588) English: unexplained. Compare SCARCE.

Scelfo (129) Italian (Sicily): possibly a variant of **Gelfo**, a nickname from Sicilian *cerfu, gerfu* 'unripe', 'immature'. Compare SCERBO.
GIVEN NAME Italian 9%. *Salvatore* (2).

Scelsi (100) Southern Italian: perhaps from the personal name *Scelsus*, from Latin *excelsus* 'high', 'lofty'.
GIVEN NAMES Italian 12%. *Rocci* (2), *Carmella, Orlando, Salvatore.*

Scelza (101) Italian: probably a variant of SCELSI.
GIVEN NAMES Italian 13%. *Sebastiano* (2), *Angelo, Sebastino.*

Scenna (113) Italian: probably a variant of SCIANNA.
GIVEN NAMES Italian 28%. *Rocco* (3), *Antonio* (2), *Mario* (2), *Amadio, Colomba, Ennio, Marco, Pasquale, Salvatore, Tito.*

Scerbo (312) Italian (Sicily): nickname from Sicilian *cerbu* 'unripe', 'immature'. Compare SCELFO.
GIVEN NAMES Italian 22%. *Ezio* (2), *Erminio, Fortunato, Italo, Luigi, Mario, Romeo, Salvatore.*

Schaab (296) **1.** South German: metonymic occupational name for a carpenter, from Middle High German *schabe* 'plane', 'scraper'. **2.** South German: habitational name from a place so called in Bohemia. **3.** Dutch: variant of SCHAAP.
GIVEN NAMES German 7%. *Hans, Helmut, Klaus, Kurt, Otto.*

Schaack (197) North German and Dutch: **1.** reduced form of the medieval personal name *Godschack* (see GOTTSCHALK). **2.** from *schaak* 'checkerboard'; either a nickname for a good chess player, or (in the form **Van Schaack**) a habitational name for someone living at a house distinguished by the sign of a checkerboard.
FOREBEARS A Dutch American family called **Van Schaack** are descended from Elias van Schaack, a fur trader in New Netherland in the 17th century.
 Claes Schaack was born in Amersfoort, Utrecht, Netherlands, in about 1635, and was in New Netherland by 1660.

Schaad (489) German and Dutch: variant of SCHADE.

Schaadt (191) German: variant of SCHADE.
GIVEN NAMES German 4%. *Waltraut, Wolfgang.*

Schaaf (2126) German: metonymic occupational name for a shepherd, from Middle High German *schāf* 'sheep'. In some cases it may have been a nickname for someone thought to resemble a sheep, or a habitational name for someone living at a house distinguished by the sign of a sheep. Compare SCHAAP.

Schaafsma (210) Frisian: patronymic meaning 'son of (the) shepherd'.

Schaak (149) Dutch and German: variant of SCHAACK.
GIVEN NAME German 4%. *Kurt.*

Schaake (118) Dutch and North German: variant of SCHAACK.
GIVEN NAMES German 5%. *Erna, Kurt.*

Schaal (858) **1.** German: habitational name from Schaala in Thuringia (so named from *scalaha* 'dirty water') or Lake Schaal on the Schaale river near Ratzeburg. **2.** German and Dutch: metonymic occupational name for someone who made dishes (for scales), vessels for drinking, etc., from Middle Low German, Dutch *schale* 'dish'.

Schaan (166) West German: Germanized form of French **Jean**, variant of **Schan**.

Schaap (512) Dutch and North German: from Middle Low German, Dutch *schāp* 'sheep', hence a metonymic occupational name for a shepherd, a nickname for someone thought to resemble a sheep in some way, or a habitational name for someone living at a house distinguished by the sign of a sheep. Compare SCHAAF.

Schaar (473) **1.** German: from *Scarius*, from a short form of a Germanic compound name formed with *skar-* 'army', 'cutting weapon' as the first element, which in the Middle Ages provided a nickname for someone working on a team due to a feudal obligation and also a metonymic occupational name for someone working with plowshares. **2.** Dutch: metonymic occupational name for a shearer, knife grinder, or tailor, from *schaar*, plural *scharen* 'shears'. **3.** Dutch (**Van der Schaar**): topographic name from *schare, schaar* 'bank', 'dike'.
GIVEN NAMES German 4%. *Alois, Gerhard, Hermann, Kurt, Otto, Rudi.*

Schab (231) Dutch: variant of SCHAAP.
GIVEN NAMES German 5%. *Gerhard, Heinz.*

Schabacker (175) German: of uncertain origin; possibly a topographic name from Middle Low German *schāp* 'sheep' + *acker* 'field', 'pasture', or an altered spelling of **Schapbacher**, reduced to **Schabacher**, from a place named Schapbach near Freudenstadt in Baden.

Schabel (273) South German: nickname from Middle High German *schaben* 'to scratch', 'shave', 'strain', for someone who worked hard, or an occupational nickname for a barber or carpenter (see SCHABER).
GIVEN NAMES German 4%. *Hans* (2), *Armin, Dietrich.*

Schaben (182) German (**Schäben**): unexplained.

Schaber (416) German: from an agent derivative of *schaben* 'to shave', an occupational name for a barber.

Schaberg (215) German: probably a topographic name composed of an unexplained first element + Middle High German *berc* 'hill', 'mountain'.

Schach (146) **1.** German: topographic name for someone who lived by or owned an area of woodland, Middle High German *schache*. **2.** Jewish (eastern Ashkenazic): from an acronym of Hebrew *śiftē kōhēn* 'lips of the priest'. This is the title of a religious commentary by Rabbi Schabtai Cohen.
GIVEN NAMES German 7%. *Horst, Matthias.*

Schacher (343) **1.** German (also **Schächer**): derogatory nickname from Middle High German *schāchære* 'robber', 'swindler'. **2.** German: variant of SCHACH 1. **3.** Jewish (Ashkenazic): derogatory nickname from Yiddish *shakher* 'petty traffic', 'bartering', or 'cheating'; or from the Polish word *szacher* 'swindler'.

Schachner (212) **1.** South German: variant of SCHACHER 2. **2.** Jewish (Ashkenazic): patronymic from the Yiddish personal name *Shakhne*, of uncertain (probably Slavic) origin.
GIVEN NAMES Jewish 9%; German 7%. *Faige* (2), *Chaim, Chana, Jechiel, Shulem, Sol; Kurt* (3), *Erwin, Konrad.*

Schacht (1074) North German and Dutch: metonymic occupational name for someone who prepared shafts for tools or weapons, a turner, from Middle Low German *schacht*, Middle Dutch *scacht* 'shaft'.
GIVEN NAMES German 4%. *Otto* (4), *Fritz* (2), *Hans* (2), *Detlef, Ernst, Jochen, Kurt.*

Schachter (808) Jewish (Ashkenazic): variant of SCHECHTER.
GIVEN NAMES Jewish 10%. *Isidor* (3), *Sol* (3), *Isadore* (2), *Yael* (2), *Ahron, Aviva, Avram, Avrohom, Basya, Benzion, Gitty, Hershel.*

Schack (593) **1.** German and Dutch: variant of SCHAACK. **2.** Jewish (eastern Ashkenazic): origin uncertain; perhaps a habitational name for someone from Shaki (Šakiai) in Lithuania, or Szaki in northeastern Poland.

Schacter (112) Variant of Jewish SCHECHTER.

Schad (1084) South German: variant of SCHADE.

Schade (1667) **1.** German and Dutch: from *schade* 'damage', a derivative of *schaden* 'to do damage', generally a nickname for a thug or clumsy person, or, more particularly, a robber knight, who raided others' lands. **2.** Scottish and English: variant spelling of SHADE.

GIVEN NAMES German 6%. *Gerhard* (5), *Kurt* (4), *Erwin* (2), *Merwin* (2), *Dieter, Erhard, Frieda, Fritz, Helmut, Jochen, Johannes, Juergen.*

Schadegg (130) German: habitational name from a place called Schadeck in Hesse.

Schadel (143) South German (**Schädel**): nickname for someone with some peculiarity of the head, from Middle High German *schedel* 'skull'.

Schader (181) German (**Schäder**): from an agent derivative of Middle High German *schade* 'damage' (see SCHADE 1), denoting a robber knight or someone who caused damage.

Schadle (134) Americanized spelling of German SCHADEL.

Schadler (341) German (**Schädler**): occupational name for a tub- and bucketmaker, from an agent derivative of Middle Low German, Middle High German *schedel* 'small wooden tub', 'bucket'.

GIVEN NAMES German 5%. *Alfons, Ernst, Otto, Reinhold.*

Schadt (394) German: variant of SCHADE 1.

GIVEN NAMES German 6%. *Arno, Ewald, Helmut, Wilfried.*

Schaecher (175) German (**Schächer**): see SCHACHER.

Schaedel (161) German (**Schädel**): see SCHADEL 1.

Schaedler (186) German (**Schädler**): see SCHADLER.

Schaefbauer (104) German (**Schäfbauer**): occupational name for a farmer who grew peas and other legumes, from South German *schefe* 'pod', 'peas' + *bauer* 'grower'.

Schaefer (17323) German (**Schäfer**) and Jewish (Ashkenazic): occupational name for a shepherd, from an agent derivative of German *Schaf*, Middle High German *schâf* 'sheep'. This name is widespread throughout central and eastern Europe.

GIVEN NAMES German 4%. *Kurt* (24), *Otto* (23), *Erwin* (12), *Ernst* (8), *Hans* (7), *Gerhard* (6), *Helmut* (6), *Dieter* (5), *Wolfgang* (4), *Hermann* (3), *Horst* (3), *Manfred* (3).

Schaefers (235) North German and Dutch: patronymic from SCHAEFER 1, i.e. 'son of the shepherd'.

GIVEN NAMES German 21%. *Bernd* (20), *Kurt.*

Schaeffer (6511) German: **1.** variant of SCHAFFER 1. **2.** variant of SCHAEFER.

FOREBEARS The Schaeffer line of Lutheran clergyman was brought over from Frankfurt-am-Main and Hanau, Germany, in 1774 by Frederick David Schaeffer (1760–1836), who accompanied one of his uncles to PA. Four of his sons, including

the organizer of the Maryland Synod, and at least one of his grandsons became Lutheran clergymen.

Schaeffler (144) South German (mostly **Schäffler**): occupational name for a cooper, from an agent derivative of Middle High German *scheffel* 'bushel'.

GIVEN NAMES German 6%. *Kurt, Otto, Wilhelm.*

Schaer (340) South German (also **Schär**): variant of SCHERER.

GIVEN NAMES German 4%. *Juerg, Kurt, Wolfgang.*

Schaerer (100) Variant of German SCHERER, found in this spelling especially in Alsace-Lorraine.

GIVEN NAMES French 10%; German 5%. *Marcel* (2), *Jacques*; *Ueli.*

Schaf (100) German: variant of SCHAAF.

Schafer (10089) German (**Schäfer**) and Jewish (Ashkenazic): see SCHAEFER.

Schaff (1205) **1.** German: variant of SCHAAF. **2.** Jewish (Ashkenazic): ornamental or occupational name from German *Schaf* 'sheep'. **3.** German: metonymic occupational name for a tubmaker, from Middle High German *schaff(e)* 'wooden vessel', 'scoop' (see SCHEFFEL).

Schaffer (7980) **1.** German: occupational name for a steward or bailiff, from an agent derivative of Middle High German *schaffen* 'to manage'. **2.** South German (**Schäffer**) and Jewish (Ashkenazic): variant of SCHAEFER.

Schaffert (167) **1.** German, Swiss German: habitational name from a place so named in Switzerland. **2.** German (Silesia): from a reduced form of **Schaffroth**, a nickname composed of the imperative of Middle High German *schaffen* 'to create', 'to bring about' + *rât* 'advice'.

GIVEN NAMES German 6%. *Kurt* (2), *Horst.*

Schaffhauser (117) Swiss German: habitational name for someone from Schaffhausen, on the Rhine river.

GIVEN NAME German 5%. *Otto.*

Schaffler (100) German (**Schäffler**) and Jewish: variant of SCHEFFLER.

GIVEN NAMES German 14%; Jewish 4%. *Bernhard, Frieda, Gunter, Helmut, Hermann, Otto; Getzel.*

Schaffner (1641) German: occupational name for a steward or bailiff, variant of SCHAFFER 1.

Schaffran (112) German: unexplained.

Schaffter (117) German (**Schäffter**): occupational name for a maker of wooden shafts for tools and weapons, from an agent derivative of Middle High German, Middle Low German *schaft* 'weapon'.

Schager (151) German (Rhineland) and Austrian: occupational name for a sawyer, variant of SAGER 2. This form is typical of the Gottschee area, an Austrian settlement in Slovenia.

GIVEN NAMES German 7%. *Franz, Gerhardt, Helmut.*

Schaible (795) German: variant of **Schäuble** (see SCHAUBLE).

GIVEN NAMES German 5%. *Gerhardt* (2), *Armin, Eldred, Erna, Fritz, Irmgard, Kurt, Milbert, Otto, Reinhold, Siegfried.*

Schaich (115) South German (Württemberg): variant of SCHEU.

GIVEN NAME German 5%. *Jurgen.*

Schain (158) German: unexplained.

GIVEN NAME German 4%. *Fritz.*

Schairer (171) South German (Württemberg): dialect variant of SCHEURER.

GIVEN NAME German 4%. *Franz.*

Schake (176) North German: variant of SCHAACK.

Schakel (136) German (**Schäkel**): habitational name from a place called Schäkeln in Lower Saxony.

GIVEN NAMES German 5%. *Hans* (2), *Kurt.*

Schalk (997) **1.** German: from Middle High German *schalk* 'servant', hence an occupational name for a servant or, more specifically, a jester. Later the word came to be used as a term of reproach, 'knave', and some cases of the surname may reflect this use. **2.** Dutch: from the Germanic personal name *Scalco*, a pet form of compound names formed with *-schalc* (see 1).

GIVEN NAMES German 4%. *Otto* (3), *Alois, Gerhardt, Hans, Horst, Kurt, Manfred, Willi.*

Schall (1546) **1.** German: nickname for a braggart or for a market crier, from Middle High German *schal* 'noise' 'bragging'. **2.** Jewish (Ashkenazic): ornamental name from German *Schall* 'sound'.

Schaller (2405) **1.** German: nickname from Middle High German *schallære* 'braggart', 'orator', 'babbler'. **2.** Jewish (Ashkenazic): occupational name for a trumpeter or a shofar player, from an agent derivative of Yiddish *shaln* 'to sound'.

GIVEN NAMES German 4%. *Gunther* (3), *Kurt* (3), *Eldred, Franz, Gerda, Heinz, Hermann, Horst, Lorenz, Markus, Otto, Ulrich.*

Schallert (149) Variant of SCHALLER.

Schallhorn (114) German: possibly a nickname for a person with a loud voice, from Middle High German *schal* 'sound' + *horn* 'horn', 'bugle', or a variant of SCHELLHORN.

Schallock (151) partly Americanized spelling of North German **Schalloch**, a habitational name from Schaloch in Westphalia.

GIVEN NAMES German 5%. *Eldor, Erwin, Frieda.*

Schalow (192) German: Pomeranian name of Slavic origin.

GIVEN NAMES German 5%. *Otto, Reinhard.*

Schambach (154) German: habitational name from any of several places so named.

Schamber (289) German: nickname for a shy, bashful person, from Middle High German *schambære* 'modest', 'bashful'.

GIVEN NAMES German 6%. *Rudi* (2), *Erwin, Florian, Gerhard, Hildegarde, Otto.*

Schamberger (228) German and Jewish (Ashkenazic): habitational name for someone from any of several places named Schamberg, in particular in Westphalia and the Rhineland.
GIVEN NAMES German 7%. *Hermann* (2), *Ernst, Heinz, Otto*.

Schamel (153) South German: nickname for a shy person, from Middle High German *schamel* 'modest', 'bashful'.
GIVEN NAME German 4%. *Kurt*.

Schamp (250) **1.** Dutch and German: nickname for someone with a sardonic or derisive sense of humor, from Middle Low German, Dutch *schamp, schimp* 'play', 'fun', 'mockery'. **2.** Dutch: respelling of French CHAMP.

Schanbacher (171) German: habitational name for someone from Schanbach near Stuttgart.

Schanck (229) Dutch: variant of SCHENK.

Schane (115) Americanized form of German **Schön** (see SCHOEN).

Schanen (105) German: unexplained.
GIVEN NAME German 4%. *Kurt*.

Schaner (294) Americanized form of German *Schöner* (see SCHOENER).

Schang (112) Germanized dialect form of French JEAN (compare SCHAAN).

Schank (624) **1.** German and Dutch: variant of SCHENK. **2.** Dutch (**de Schanck**): spelling of French DESCHAMPS.

Schanke (134) North German and Norwegian: variant of SCHENK.
GIVEN NAME Scandinavian 4%. *Nils* (2).

Schantz (1353) German: **1.** from Middle High German *schanz* 'peasant jacket', probably applied as a nickname for a peasant. **2.** topographic name from Middle High German *schanze* . **3.** nickname for a gambler, from Middle High German *schanz(e)* 'game of dice', 'hazard'.
FOREBEARS Johnstown (earlier Shantztown) in PA was founded in 1800 by Johann Schantz, an immigrant from Switzerland.

Schanz (453) Variant of SCHANTZ.
GIVEN NAMES German 6%. *Kurt* (3), *Heinz, Horst, Siegmund*.

Schanzenbach (119) German: habitational name from a farm near Offenburg (Baden) called Schanzbach.
GIVEN NAMES German 7%. *Hans, Kurt*.

Schanzer (130) German: **1.** (also **Schänzer**): occupational name for someone working on an earthwork or a (city) wall. **2.** habitational name for someone from a place called Schanz.

Schaper (1010) North German form of SCHAEFER.
GIVEN NAMES German 5%. *Otto* (3), *Armin* (2), *Hans* (2), *Juergen* (2), *Bernhardt, Erhardt, Horst, Jurgen, Klaus, Uwe*.

Schapira (126) Jewish (Ashkenazic): variant of SHAPIRO.
GIVEN NAMES Jewish 5%; German 5%. *Arieh, Joachim, Mendel; Hans*.

Schapiro (548) Jewish (Ashkenazic): variant spelling of SHAPIRO.
GIVEN NAMES Jewish 9%. *Isadore* (2), *Miriam* (2), *Anat, Chaya, Dorit, Emanuel, Leib, Meyer, Nochum, Pinkas, Sol, Yael*.

Schappell (229) Altered spelling of South German **Schappel**, an occupational name for a maker of headdresses, from an agent derivative of Middle High German *schapel* 'headdress' (from Old French *chapel* 'wreath of leaves or flowers'; compare modern French *chapeau* 'hat').

Schappert (221) North German: from a reduced form of *Schafhirt* 'shepherd', 'sheep herder', from Middle Low German *schāp* 'sheep' + *herde* 'herder'.

Schar (165) **1.** German: from a Germanic personal name with *scar(a)* 'army' or 'cutting weapon' as the first element. **2.** South German (**Schär**): see SCHAER. **3.** German: variant of SCHAAR 1.
GIVEN NAMES German 7%. *Kurt* (2), *Ernst, Markus*.

Schara (228) German: probably an altered spelling of SCHARER or SCHERER.

Scharber (135) German: habitational name for someone from Scharben in Württemberg.

Schardt (396) German: **1.** topographic name from Middle High German *schart* '(small) pass', 'gap in a mountain ridge'. **2.** nickname for someone with a noticeable bodily injury or malformation, from Middle High German *schart* 'notched', 'damaged'.
GIVEN NAMES German 5%. *Fritz, Hans, Helmut, Horst, Kurt, Margarethe*.

Scharer (258) German (**Schärer**): variant of SCHERER.
GIVEN NAMES German 4%. *Fritz* (2), *Hans*.

Schares (131) German: unexplained.

Scharf (2166) South German: nickname for an energetic, active person, from Middle High German *scharf, scharpf* 'sharp-cutting'.
GIVEN NAMES German 5%. *Otto* (7), *Erwin* (3), *Gerhardt* (2), *Kurt* (2), *Uwe* (2), *Frieda, Fritz, Grete, Helmuth, Horst, Juergen, Klaus*.

Scharfenberg (204) German: habitational name from any of a number of places so named, for example in Moravia and near Meissen.
GIVEN NAMES German 5%. *Georg, Horst, Udo*.

Scharff (697) Variant of SCHARF.
GIVEN NAMES German 4%. *Kurt* (2), *Gerhard, Gunter, Hanns, Hans, Otto*.

Scharlau (167) German (eastern): habitational name from a place so named.

Scharmer (146) North German and Dutch: variant of SCHERMER.
GIVEN NAMES German 6%. *Klaus, Otto*.

Scharnhorst (217) North German: habitational name from any of various places, for example near Dortmund and near Celle, apparently so named from the Germanic

elements *skarn* 'damp', 'dirty' + *horst* 'wooded hill'.

Scharp (169) North German form of SCHARF.

Scharpf (197) South German: variant of SCHARF.
GIVEN NAMES German 8%. *Jurgen* (2), *Eberhard, Niklaus, Otto*.

Scharping (122) North German (also **Schärping**): derivative of SCHARF.
GIVEN NAMES German 7%. *Erwin* (2), *Kurt*.

Scharr (162) South German: variant of SCHARRER 2.

Scharrer (229) South German: **1.** from an agent derivative of Middle High German *scharren* 'to scrape or scratch'; an occupational name for a wool carder, or a nickname for a miser. **2.** habitational name for someone from any of various places, such as Scharr in Switzerland, Bavaria, and the Upper Palatinate, or Scharre in Saxony, named with Old High German *scara* 'wooded area'.
GIVEN NAMES German 8%. *Fritz* (2), *Ernst, Klaus, Kurt*.

Schartner (136) German: variant of SCHARDT 1.

Schartz (274) **1.** German: nickname for a juggler, from Middle High German *scharz* 'move (of a chess piece)'. **2.** German and Dutch: habitational name from a place so called near Trier.

Schatte (125) German: of uncertain origin. Possibly from a nickname or personal name derived from Middle High German *schate* 'shadow' or *schade* 'damage(r)'.
GIVEN NAME German 4%. *Aloys*.

Schattner (144) German and Jewish (western Ashkenazic): habitational name for someone from any of several places named Schaten or Schatten, or a topographic name for someone living in a shady location, from Middle High German *schate* 'shade', 'protection'.
GIVEN NAMES German 8%. *Detlef, Gerd, Gerhardt*.

Schatz (2831) **1.** German and Jewish (Ashkenazic): metonymic occupational name for a treasurer, from German *Schatz* 'treasure', Middle High German *scha(t)z*. It may also have been a nickname for a rich man (or ironically for a miser), or else for a well-liked person or a ladies' favorite, from the use of the vocabulary word as a term of endearment. As a Jewish name it is mainly of ornamental origin. **2.** Jewish (Ashkenazic): occupational name from an acronym of the Hebrew phrase *SHeliach-TSibur* 'emissary of the congregation', an epithet of the cantor.
GIVEN NAMES German 4%. *Alois* (4), *Otto* (4), *Kurt* (3), *Manfred* (3), *Erwin* (2), *Friedrich* (2), *Siegfried* (2), *Bernd, Gerhard, Hans, Johann, Klaus*.

Schatzberg (158) **1.** German: habitational name from a place so named in East Prussia. **2.** Jewish (Ashkenazic): ornamental name composed of German *Schatz* 'treasure' + *Berg* 'mountain', 'hill'.

Schatzel (144) German (**Schätzel, Schätzle**): diminutives of SCHATZ 1, or a nickname for a lover (from the same word used as a term of endearment).

Schatzle (149) German (**Schätzel, Schätzle**): diminutives of SCHATZ 1, or a nickname for a lover (from the same word used as a term of endearment).

Schatzman (307) **1.** German (**Schatzmann**): variant of SCHATZ 1. **2.** Jewish (Ashkenazic): ornamental name from German *Schatz* 'treasure' + *Mann* 'man', or an elaboration of SCHATZ 2.

Schau (336) **1.** North German form of SCHUH. **2.** Norwegian: habitational name from any of several farmsteads in southeastern Norway named Skau, from Old Norse *skógr* 'wood', 'forest'.
GIVEN NAMES Scandinavian 4%; German 4%. *Gudrun, Per; Hans* (2), *Eldred, Kurt.*

Schaub (2428) German: from Middle High German *schoup* 'sheaf or wisp of straw', hence a habitational name from a house distinguished by the sign of a sheaf of grain for a licensed brewer, or perhaps a nickname for a scrawny person or someone with straw-colored hair.

Schaubert (110) German: variant of SCHUBERT.

Schauble (167) German (**Schäuble**): diminutive of SCHAUB.
GIVEN NAMES German 4%. *Otto, Reinhardt.*

Schauder (129) German and Jewish (Ashkenazic): from a noun derivative of Middle High German *schudern* 'to shudder', German *Schauder* 'shudder', hence probably a nickname for a sick- or ghoulish-looking person.
GIVEN NAME German 4%. *Theodor.*

Schauer (2219) German and Austrian: occupational name for an official inspector, for example the official overseer of a market, from Middle High German *schouwer*, an agent derivative of *schouwen* 'to inspect'.

Schauf (294) German: **1.** metonymic occupational name for a shepherd, from a Swabian dialect word meaning 'sheep'. **2.** variant of SCHAUB.

Schaufele (122) German (**Schäufele**): metonymic occupational name for someone who made shovels or used one in his work, from Middle High German *schüfel* 'shovel'.
GIVEN NAMES German 5%. *Johannes, Markus, Otto.*

Schaufler (164) German: occupational name for someone who made shovels or used one in his work, from an agent derivative of Middle High German *schüfel* 'shovel'.

Schaul (169) **1.** Dutch and German: from Middle Dutch *scholle, schulle*, Middle Low German *schulle*, Middle High German *schülle* 'plaice', either a metonymic occu-

pational name for a fisherman or seller of these fish, or a nickname for someone thought to resemble a plaice. Compare SCHOLL 2. **2.** Dutch and German: nickname for a short, thickset person, from Middle Dutch, Middle High German *scholle* 'clod of earth'. **3.** Jewish (Ashkenazic): from the personal name *Schaul* (see SAUL).

Schaum (325) German: nickname either for a cook or an empty talker, from Middle High German, Middle Low German *schūm* 'froth', 'foam'.

Schauman (130) Respelling of German SCHAUMANN.

Schaumann (126) German: **1.** in central Germany, a variant of SCHUMANN. **2.** habitational name from any of several places named Schaum, for example near Wernigerode.
GIVEN NAMES Scandinavian 7%; German 7%. *Erik, Niels; Ilse, Waltraud.*

Schaumberg (163) **1.** German and Jewish (Ashkenazic): habitational name from Schaumburg in Lower Saxony or from Schömberg in Württemberg. **2.** German: topographic name from Middle High German *schūm* 'slag', 'cinder' + *berc* 'mountain'.
GIVEN NAMES German 4%. *Erwin, Kurt.*

Schaumburg (315) German, Dutch, and Belgian: habitational name from any of the places called Schaumburg or Schauenburg in Germany, or Schauwberg in Brabant, Belgium.
GIVEN NAMES French 4%. *Camille, Rodolph.*

Schaupp (136) South German: variant of SCHAUB.
GIVEN NAMES German 11%. *Ulrich* (2), *Dietrich, Gerhardt, Hans.*

Schaus (384) German: nickname for a simpleton, from a Rhenish Franconian and Lower Rhine dialect word, *Schaus.*

Schauss (140) German: variant of SCHAUS.
GIVEN NAMES German 10%. *Dietmar, Guenther, Heinz, Manfred.*

Schaut (254) Dutch: status name for a village headman, Middle Dutch *schoute, scholte.*

Schauwecker (157) German: habitational name for someone from Schaubeck near Marbach (Württemberg).
GIVEN NAMES German 6%. *Kurt, Ulrike.*

Schave (223) **1.** Dutch: derivative of Dutch *schouwen* 'to inspect', hence an occupational name for an inspector of weights and measures in a market. Compare SHAVER. **2.** North German variant of SCHAAB 1.

Scheaffer (155) Altered spelling of German SCHAEFFER.

Schear (228) Altered spelling of German SCHAER.

Schearer (151) Altered spelling of German **Schärer**, a variant of SCHERER.

Schechinger (104) German: habitational name for someone from Schechingen near Schwäbisch-Gmünd (Württemberg).

Schechner (103) German: variant of SCHACHER 2.
GIVEN NAME German 6%. *Fritz.*

Schechter (1557) Jewish (Ashkenazic): occupational name, from Yiddish *shekhter* 'ritual slaughterer' (an agent derivative of *shekhtn*, of which the stem is from Hebrew *shachat* 'to slaughter').
GIVEN NAMES Jewish 8%. *Emanuel* (3), *Hyman* (3), *Aryeh* (2), *Avraham* (2), *Avrohom* (2), *Dov* (2), *Mendel* (2), *Sol* (2), *Yakov* (2), *Boruch, Chaya, Leib.*

Schechtman (195) Jewish (Ashkenazic): occupational name for a ritual slaughterer, a variant of SCHECHTER, with the agent suffix *-er* replaced by Yiddish *man* 'man'.
GIVEN NAMES Jewish 5%. *Sura* (2), *Emanuel, Hyman.*

Scheck (735) **1.** German: metonymic occupational name for a jacket maker and also for an armorer, from Middle High German *schecke* 'quilted jacket', 'coat of mail'. **2.** Jewish (Ashkenazic): ornamental name from German *Schecke* 'dappled horse' or 'spotted ox or bull'.

Scheckel (170) German: diminutive of SCHECK.

Schecter (530) Altered spelling of Jewish SCHECHTER.
GIVEN NAMES Jewish 7%. *Sol* (3), *Meir* (2), *Anat, Chaim, Emanuel, Isadore, Miriam, Myer, Pnina, Shira, Sima.*

Schectman (109) Jewish: variant of SCHECHTMAN.
GIVEN NAME Jewish 7%. *Sol.*

Schedler (207) German (southwestern): variant of **Schädler** (see SCHADLER).
GIVEN NAMES German 6%. *Erwin, Kurt.*

Scheel (1420) North German and Dutch: nickname from Middle Low German *schele*, Dutch *sche(e)le* 'squinting', 'with a squint'.
GIVEN NAMES German 5%. *Klaus* (4), *Erwin* (3), *Hans* (3), *Dieter, Dietmar, Egon, Erna, Gerhardt, Guenter, Hellmut, Horst, Konrad.*

Scheele (692) North German and Dutch: variant of SCHEEL.
GIVEN NAMES German 4%. *Frieda, Gerhardt, Joerg, Juergen, Jurgen, Klaus, Orlo.*

Scheeler (411) German: variant of SCHEEL.

Scheer (2514) **1.** German and Dutch: metonymic occupational name for a maker of shears and scissors, or a metonymic occupational name for a cutter (of cloth, hair, etc.), from Middle High German *schere*, Middle Dutch *sc(h)erre* 'shears'. **2.** Jewish: variant of SCHER.
GIVEN NAMES German 4%. *Kurt* (3), *Achim, Claus, Dietmar, Gerhard, Gunter, Heinz, Helmuth, Ilse, Manfred, Otmar, Otto.*

Scheerer (421) German and Dutch: occupational name for a cutter (of hair, cloth, etc.), Middle High German *scherer*, Middle Dutch *sc(h)errer*.
GIVEN NAMES German 4%. *Kurt* (2), *Dieter, Otto.*

Scheets (139) Perhaps an Americanized form of Dutch and North German SCHUTTE 'archer', otherwise see SCHEETZ.

Scheetz (1067) Americanized form of German **Schütz** (see SCHUETZ).

Scheff (423) North German: descriptive nickname for someone with a physical deformity, from Middle Low German *schēf* 'crooked'.

Scheffel (415) South German: metonymic occupational name for a cooper, from southern dialect *Schäffl*, diminutive of *Schaff* 'tub', 'barrel'.
GIVEN NAMES German 7%. *Fritz* (3), *Hannes* (2), *Arno, Konrad, Kurt, Mathias*.

Scheffer (666) **1.** German: variant of **Schäffer** (see SCHAFFER 1). **2.** Jewish (Ashkenazic): variant of SCHAEFER.

Scheffert (124) German and Dutch: variant of German SCHAEFER.

Scheffler (1440) South German (Bavaria): occupational name for a cooper, from an agent derivative of *Schäffl*, a diminutive of the southern dialect term *Schaff* 'tub', 'barrel'.
GIVEN NAMES German 5%. *Kurt* (5), *Erwin* (2), *Gunter* (2), *Egon, Ernst, Fritzy, Gerhard, Guenther, Gunther, Hans, Hartmut, Ilse*.

Schehr (169) German: variant of SCHEER.

Schei (116) **1.** Norwegian: habitational name from any of twenty or more farmsteads so named, from Old Norse as *skeið* 'horse race', 'race', 'run'. **2.** Dutch: nickname for someone of sturdy build or a clumsy person, from Middle Dutch *scheye* 'wedge', 'piece of split wood'. **3.** Dutch: from Middle Dutch *scheiden, scheien* 'to divide or split', presumably a topographic name for someone who lived by a fork in a road, river, or the like.
GIVEN NAME Scandinavian 5%. *Ansgar*.

Scheib (696) German: **1.** variant of SCHEIBE. **2.** nickname for a person afflicted with some deformity, from Middle High German *schief* 'crooked', 'awry'. Compare SCHEFF.
GIVEN NAMES German 4%. *Erwin, Helmut, Juergen, Kurt, Otto*.

Scheibe (546) German: topographic name from Middle High German *schībe* 'disk', 'sphere', 'wheel', commonly used as a field name.
GIVEN NAMES German 4%. *Hans* (2), *Egon, Erwin, Hilde, Inge, Otto*.

Scheibel (326) German (southern and eastern): **1.** diminutive of SCHEIBE. **2.** (Silesia and Bohemia): from a German pet form of the Slavic personal name *Schiban*.

Scheiber (373) **1.** German (Tyrol): variant of SCHEIBE, the *-er* suffix denoting an inhabitant. **2.** Jewish (Ashkenazic): occupational name for a glazier, from German *Scheibe* 'window pane' + the agent suffix *-er*.

Scheible (386) South German: variant of **Schäuble** (see SCHAUBLE).

GIVEN NAMES German 5%. *Fritz* (2), *Otto* (2), *Kurt*.

Scheibner (167) **1.** German (eastern): habitational name for someone from Scheiben in Bohemia. The place name is related to SCHEIBE. **2.** German: occupational name for a maker of window panes, especially the so-called 'bull's eyes', from Middle High German *schībe* 'disk' + the agent suffix *-(n)er*.
GIVEN NAMES German 11%. *Ewald* (2), *Hans, Heinz, Kurt*.

Scheid (1316) **1.** German: variant of SCHEIDT. **2.** German and Jewish (Ashkenazic): from Middle High German *scheide*, German *Scheide* 'sheath (of a sword)', applied as a German metonymic occupational name for someone who made scabbards or a Jewish ornamental name.

Scheidecker (145) South German: habitational name for someone from any of various places named Scheideck, in Bavaria, Tyrol, and Switzerland.

Scheidegger (315) South German: variant of SCHEIDECKER.
GIVEN NAMES German 4%. *Benno, Eugen, Otto, Theodor*.

Scheidel (292) German: **1.** habitational name from a place so named, of which there is one in Luxembourg. **2.** diminutive of SCHEID(T).

Scheideler (101) German: habitational name for someone living in Scheidel in Luxemburg.
GIVEN NAME German 4%. *Hans* (2).

Scheideman (133) **1.** German (**Scheidemann**) and Jewish (Ashkenazic): occupational name for an arbitrator or judge, Middle High German *scheideman*. **2.** German: habitational name from any of several places called Scheide(n), Scheidt.

Scheider (384) German: **1.** occupational name for an arbitrator or judge, from Middle High German *scheiden* 'to decide' (see SCHEIDEMAN). **2.** variant of SCHEIDT, the *-er* suffix denoting an inhabitant.
GIVEN NAMES German 4%. *Kurt, Merwin, Ulrich*.

Scheiderer (230) German: occupational name for an arbitrator or judge. Compare SCHEIDEMAN.

Scheidler (363) German: **1.** occupational name from Middle High German *scheid-(l)er* 'mediator', 'arbitrator'. Compare SCHEIDEMAN. **2.** variant of SCHEIDT, the *-ler* suffix denoting an inhabitant. **3.** occupational name for a blade maker, from Middle High German *scheide* '(sword) blade'.

Scheidt (988) German: topographic name for someone who lived near a boundary or crossroads, Middle High German *scheit*, or a habitational name from any of the numerous places named with this word.
GIVEN NAMES German 4%. *Johann* (2), *Kurt* (2), *Rudi* (2), *Otto, Udo*.

Scheier (278) **1.** German: variant of SCHEUER. **2.** Jewish (Ashkenazic): from Yiddish *shayer* 'barn' (see SCHEUER).

GIVEN NAMES German 4%. *Wendelin* (2), *Kurt*.

Scheihing (110) German: unrounded form of *Scheuhing*, a nickname for a specter or a person who inspires fear, from Middle High German *schiuhe, schiuhinc* 'specter'.

Scheiman (150) **1.** German (**Scheimann**): variant of SCHEIDEMAN. **2.** Jewish (Ashkenazic): variant of SCHEINMAN.
GIVEN NAMES Jewish 4%. *Binyomin, Hinda*.

Schein (656) **1.** German and Jewish (Ashkenazic): from Middle High German *schīn*, German *Schein* 'a shining', 'brightness', hence a German nickname for someone with a radiant personality or possibly for someone living in a sunny location, or a Jewish ornamental name. **2.** Jewish (Ashkenazic): variant of SCHOEN 2, from Yiddish *sheyn*, central Yiddish *shayn*.

Scheinberg (213) Jewish (Ashkenazic): ornamental name composed of Yiddish *sheyn* 'beautiful' or German *Schein* 'shining' (noun) + German *Berg* 'mountain', 'hill'.
GIVEN NAMES Jewish 9%. *Meyer* (2), *Hyman, Isadore, Reuven*.

Scheiner (557) **1.** German: nickname for someone with a radiant face or personality, from an agent derivative of Middle High German *schīnan* 'to shine or radiate'. **2.** German: occupational name for a surveyor, from Middle High German *schīner* 'person who issues a document (modern German *Schein*) or a certificate'. **3.** Jewish (Ashkenazic): from an inflected form of SCHEIN 2.
GIVEN NAMES Jewish 9%; German 5%. *Aryeh* (2), *Sol* (2), *Aviva, Avram, Chaim, Chanie, Eliezer, Faige, Leib, Menachem, Mendel, Meyer; Otto* (3), *Siegfried* (2), *Erwin, Georg*.

Scheinman (139) Jewish (Ashkenazic): elaborated form of SCHEIN 2.

Scheirer (301) German: variant of SCHEURER.

Schelb (113) German: nickname for a cross-eyed (or sometimes one-eyed) person, from Middle High German *schelw(e)* 'one-eyed', 'squinting'.
GIVEN NAME German 7%. *Ernst* (3).

Scheler (136) German: from an agent derivative of Middle High German *scheln* 'to peel', probably an occupational name for someone who peeled bark from trees for use in the tanning process.
GIVEN NAMES German 7%. *Erwin, Kurt, Otto*.

Schelin (165) **1.** Swedish: ornamental name, probably from an unidentified place name element + the Swedish adjectival suffix *-in*, based on Latin *-inius*. **2.** German: variant spelling of SCHELLIN.
GIVEN NAMES Scandinavian 6%. *Jorgen, Lennart*.

Schell (5123) German: nickname for a loud or obstreperous person, from Middle High German *schel* 'noisy', 'loud'.

Schelle (122) **1.** German: variant of SCHELL. **2.** Dutch: habitational name from places called Schelle, in Antwerp and Overijssel. **3.** Dutch: from Middle Dutch *schelle*, *schille* '(small) bell', perhaps a metonymic occupational name for a town crier.

GIVEN NAMES German 6%. *Dietrich, Kurt, Maximilian*.

Schellenberg (401) German and Swiss German: habitational name from any of various places in Germany and Switzerland called Schellenberg.

GIVEN NAMES German 4%. *Erwin* (2), *Hans* (2), *Fritz*.

Schellenberger (152) German: habitational name for someone from any of the places called SCHELLENBERG.

GIVEN NAMES German 8%. *Hans, Klaus, Kurt, Volker*.

Schellenger (168) German: variant of SCHILLINGER.

Scheller (1227) German and Jewish (Ashkenazic): nickname for a noisy person or one with a loud voice, from an inflected form of Middle High German *schel* 'noisy', 'loud'.

GIVEN NAMES German 5%. *Otto* (3), *Bernhard* (2), *Hans* (2), *Horst* (2), *Manfred* (2), *Arno, Bernd, Ernst, Friedrich, Fritz, Gerd, Heinz*.

Schellhaas (101) German: variant of SCHELLHASE.

Schellhammer (165) German: metonymic occupational name for someone who worked in a quarry, from Middle High German *schelhamer* 'sledgehammer'.

Schellhase (213) German: nickname for a nervous, easily frightened person, from Middle High German *schel* 'startled', 'nervous', 'wild' + *hase* 'hare'.

GIVEN NAMES German 4%. *Ernst, Otto*.

Schellhorn (206) German (Franconia): **1.** from Middle High German *schelle-horn* 'horn', a nickname for a hunter or a night-watchman who blew a horn, or perhaps for someone with a penetrating voice like a horn. **2.** topographic or habitational name from either of two places, in Schleswig and on Rügen Island, named Schellhorn, the second element of which is Middle High German *horn*, 'corner', 'nook'.

GIVEN NAMES German 6%. *Arno, Erwin, Franz, Hans, Lorenz*.

Schellin (146) German: habitational name from any of several places so named in Pomerania.

GIVEN NAMES German 13%. *Otto* (3), *Detlef* (2).

Schelling (529) **1.** German and Jewish (Ashkenazic): variant of SCHILLING. **2.** Dutch: nickname from *scellinc* 'shilling', perhaps for someone who owed a shilling in feudal dues. **3.** Swiss German: nickname for a farmer known for his stud horse, from Middle High German *schel* 'stallion'.

Schellinger (342) German: possibly a variant of SCHILLINGER.

Schelp (100) North German: topographic name for someone living near or working with reeds, from Middle Low German *schelp* 'reed(s)' (modern German *Schilf*).

GIVEN NAMES German 6%. *Eldred, Rainer*.

Schelske (150) German (of Slavic origin): nickname from a Slavic word meaning 'rustic' or 'boorish'. Compare Czech *selský* 'peasant'.

Schember (126) Perhaps a variant of Maltese SCHEMBRI.

Schembri (224) Maltese: from Maltese *xkembri*, denoting a kind of lemon, or perhaps from Italian *schembro* 'mackerel'.

GIVEN NAMES Italian 15%; Spanish 4%. *Angelo* (4), *Cosmo* (2), *Carmel, Carmela, Carmelo, Carmine, Lorenzo, Salvatore, Saverio; Salvador* (3), *Serafin*.

Schemel (141) **1.** German: variant spelling of SCHEMMEL. **2.** Jewish (Ashkenazic): from German *Schemel* 'stool'.

Schemenauer (163) German: habitational name for someone from an unidentified place named Schemenau.

Schemm (208) German: from Middle High German *scheme, schem* 'mask', 'shadow', perhaps a nickname for someone who was considered mysterious.

Schemmel (340) German: nickname for a disabled person, from Middle High German *schemel* 'stool', which was used as a crutch by invalids.

GIVEN NAMES German 5%. *Franz* (3), *Kurt, Otto*.

Schemmer (113) German: habitational name for someone from any of several places named Schemm in Westphalia and the Rhineland.

Schempp (312) German: variant of SCHIMPF.

GIVEN NAMES German 7%. *Ewald, Gerhard, Karlheinz, Kurt, Reinhold, Uli*.

Schena (260) Italian: unexplained.

GIVEN NAMES Italian 9%. *Luigi* (2), *Antonio, Domenico, Fiore, Gino, Lorenzo, Pasquale, Rino*.

Schenck (2581) German: variant of SCHENK.

Schendel (653) German: from Middle High German *schendelīch* 'shameful', 'disgraceful', presumably applied as a derogatory nickname.

GIVEN NAMES German 4%. *Franz* (2), *Kurt* (2), *Alois, Erwin, Gerhard, Rinehart, Winfried*.

Schenk (3236) **1.** German and Dutch: from Middle High German, Middle Dutch *schenke*, 'cupbearer', 'wine server' (from Old High German *scenko*, from *scenken* 'to pour out or serve'), hence an occupational name for a cupbearer or server of wine. As a German name it also denotes a tavern-keeper. In another development, similar to English BUTLER, the word came to be used as an honorary title for a high court official, and some cases of the surname may have arisen from this use. **2.** Jewish (Ashkenaz-

ic): metonymic occupational name for an innkeeper, from German *Schenke* 'inn', 'tavern'. At one time only Jews were allowed to sell alcohol in the Russian empire, which is why *Shenk* and its related surnames are very common.

GIVEN NAMES German 4%. *Kurt* (10), *Otto* (6), *Arno* (2), *Erwin* (2), *Gerhard* (2), *Hans* (2), *Lothar* (2), *Armin, Florian, Frieda, Fritz, Gottlieb*.

Schenke (126) German and Dutch: variant of SCHENK.

GIVEN NAMES German 7%. *Reiner, Wolfgang*.

Schenkel (750) German, Dutch, and Jewish (Ashkenazic): nickname for someone with long or otherwise notable legs, from Middle High German *schenkel*, Middle Dutch *schenkel, schinkel* 'thigh', 'lower leg', German *Schenkel* 'thigh'.

Schenkelberg (113) German: habitational name from a place so called in the Westerwald area.

GIVEN NAME German 6%. *Fritz*.

Schenker (534) South German and Jewish (Ashkenazic): occupational name for a tavernkeeper, Middle High German *schenker*, German *Schenker* 'tavernkeeper'.

GIVEN NAMES German 7%; Jewish 4%. *Heinz* (3), *Kurt* (3), *Frieda, Ulrika; Aron, Eran, Gerson, Hillel, Hyman, Shmuel*.

Schenkman (111) South German (**Schenkmann**) and Jewish (Ashkenazic): occupational name for a tavernkeeper. Compare SCHENKER.

Schenone (143) Italian: unexplained.

GIVEN NAMES Italian 4%. *Ettore, Ezio, Mino*.

Scheper (268) **1.** North German and Dutch: occupational name from Middle Dutch, Middle Low German *schēper* 'shepherd'. **2.** Dutch: occupational name for a tailor, from Middle Dutch *scheper* 'maker'.

Schepers (434) Dutch and North German: patronymic from SCHEPER.

Schepis (278) Southern Italian: from the medieval Greek personal name *Skepis*, a derivative of the vocabulary word *skepē* 'cover', 'protection', commemorating the legend of Our Lady of the Protecting Veil (*Hagia Skepē*), according to which the Virgin Mary appeared to St. Andrew the Fool extending a veil over the cathedral of St. Sophia in Constantinople.

GIVEN NAMES Italian 19%. *Antonino* (2), *Nunzio* (2), *Antonio, Carmine, Nicola, Nino, Rocco, Rosaria*.

Schepker (100) Dutch: unexplained.

Schepman (102) Dutch: occupational name for a shepherd (see SCHEPER 1) or a ship's captain, mariner.

Schepp (341) North German: occupational name from Middle Low German *schepp(e)* 'lay assessor (in court)'.

Schepper (123) **1.** North German: variant of SCHIPPER 1. **2.** Dutch: variant of SCHEPER 2.

GIVEN NAME German 4%. *Heinz*.

Schepps (144) Jewish (Ashkenazic): ornamental name from Yiddish *sheps* 'ram', 'sheep'.
GIVEN NAMES Jewish 8%. *Chaim, Elihu, Morry.*

Scher (1346) German, Dutch, and Jewish (Ashkenazic): from Middle High German *schere*, Middle Low German *schēre*, Middle Dutch *sceere*, Yiddish *sher* 'scissors', 'shears', hence a metonymic occupational name for a maker of scissors or shears, or for a barber, cloth cutter or possibly a sheep shearer.
GIVEN NAMES Jewish 6%. *Meyer* (6), *Anshel* (3), *Isadore* (3), *Emanuel* (2), *Hyman* (2), *Aron, Ezriel, Herschel, Isidor, Mayer, Menachem, Miriam.*

Scherb (152) Southern German: metonymic occupational name for a potter, from *scherbe* 'pot', 'potsherd'.

Scherbarth (181) German: occupational name for a barber, from Middle High German *scheren* 'to shear or cut' + *bart* 'beard'.

Scherber (161) German and Jewish (Ashkenazic): from an agent derivative of Middle High German, German *scherben* 'to cut into small pieces', 'to shave off', hence a metonymic occupational name for a carpenter, tailor, or the like.
GIVEN NAMES German 6%. *Erna* (2), *Georg, Hans.*

Scherer (5397) German and Jewish (Ashkenazic): occupational name for a sheep-shearer or someone who used scissors to trim the surface of finished cloth and remove excessive nap, from German *Scherer*, Yiddish *sherer*, agent derivatives of Middle High German *scheren* 'to shear'.

Scherf (444) **1.** German and Jewish (Ashkenazic): from Middle High German, Middle Low German *scherf*, a coin worth half a penny, possibly applied as a nickname for a poor person. **2.** German: nickname from Middle High German *scharpf*, *scherf* 'sharp', 'rough', 'eager'. **3.** German: habitational name from places in the Rhineland named Scherf, or from Scherfede near Warburg.
GIVEN NAMES German 5%. *Otto* (2), *Friedrich, Heinz, Kurt, Uwe.*

Scherff (258) Variant spelling of German and Jewish SCHERF.

Scherger (187) Possibly a variant of German **Scherge**, an occupational name for a (court) messenger, Middle High German *scherge*.

Scherich (112) German: variant of SCHEURICH.

Scherle (104) German: from a Germanic personal name with *scar(a)* 'army' or 'cutting weapon' as the first element.
GIVEN NAMES German 8%. *Helmut, Ottmar, Uwe.*

Scherling (109) German: nickname for someone with a short haircut or a hairstyle like a monk's, from regional *Scherling* 'shearling', 'shorn sheep'.

Scherman (264) **1.** German (**Schermann**) and Jewish (Ashkenazic): variant of SCHERER. **2.** Dutch: occupational name for a barber, shearer, or the like, from *scheren* 'to shear', 'to clip or cut' + *man* 'man'.
GIVEN NAMES Jewish 5%. *Aviva, Avraham, Emanuel, Mendy, Nosson, Sol, Yitzchok.*

Schermer (397) **1.** Dutch and North German: occupational name from Middle Low German *schermere* 'fencer', 'street player'. **2.** Jewish (western Ashkenazic): origin uncertain; most likely, a variant of SCHIRMER.
GIVEN NAMES German 6%. *Friedrich* (2), *Gerhard, Manfred, Nicolaus, Reinhold.*

Schermerhorn (1252) Dutch: habitational name from a place so named in the area of the Schermermeer of northern Holland.
FOREBEARS This was a prominent family name in Schenectady, NY, from the 17th century onward; Ryer Schermerhoorn made a celebrated ride from Schenectady to Albany in 1690 to warn of an impending Indian attack.

Scherr (1107) German and Jewish (Ashkenazic): variant spelling of SCHERER.
GIVEN NAMES German 4%. *Otto* (3), *Wendelin* (3), *Balzer, Erwin.*

Scherrer (854) German: variant spelling of SCHERER.

Scherschel (129) German: probably a diminutive of SCHORSCH, which is a variant of *Georges*, French form of the personal name GEORGE, which is common in the Rhine area.

Schertz (495) German and Jewish (Ashkenazic): metonymic occupational name for a jester or a nickname for a facetious person, from Middle High German *scherz*, German *Scherz* 'amusement', 'game', 'jest'.

Schertzer (175) German and Jewish: variant spelling of SCHERZER.

Scherz (164) German and Jewish: variant spelling of SCHERTZ.
GIVEN NAME German 5%. *Otto.*

Scherzer (441) **1.** German, Austrian, and Jewish (Ashkenazic): occupational name for a jester or a nickname for a facetious person, from an agent derivative of Middle High German *scherz*, German *Scherz* 'amusement', 'game', 'jest'. **2.** German (Swiss): habitational name for someone from a place called Scherz in Switzerland.
GIVEN NAMES German 6%; Jewish 4%. *Lorenz* (3), *Fritz, Heinz, Otto, Wolfgang; Dov* (2), *Shimon* (2), *Baruch.*

Scherzinger (162) Swiss German: habitational name for someone from Scherzingen on Lake Constance.

Schessler (109) **1.** German: variant of SCHUESSLER. **2.** North German: probably a habitational name for someone from Schesselberge, a hilly area near Gifhorn (Lower Saxony).
GIVEN NAME German 5%. *Hans Peter.*

Schetter (206) **1.** South German: metonymic occupational name for someone who sold fine fabric, from Middle High German *scheter* 'fine, shiny linen'. In some cases it may have been a nickname for an extravagant dresser. **2.** North German: occupational name for an appraiser, from Middle Low German *scheten* 'to gauge', 'appraise' + the agent suffix *-er*.

Schettini (123) Italian: patronymic or plural form of SCHETTINO.
GIVEN NAMES Italian 19%; Spanish 11%. *Carmela, Carmelo, Crescenzo, Domenic, Francesco, Luciano, Rocco, Salvatore; Alfonso, Ana Maria, Carlos, Ines, Marcela, Mario, Nelida.*

Schettino (226) Italian: of uncertain derivation; possibly from a reduced pet form of *Franceschetto*, itself a pet form of the personal name *Francesco* (see FRANCIS). Caracausi proposes a derivation from the old French personal name *Ansketil*, ultimately from Old Norse *Ásketill* (see ANCTIL).
GIVEN NAMES Italian 14%. *Salvatore* (2), *Angelo, Elio, Enrico, Giovanni, Luigi.*

Schettler (386) German: **1.** variant of **Schüttler** (see SCHUTTLER). **2.** variant of **Schöttler** (see SCHOETTLER).
GIVEN NAMES German 4%. *Heinrich* (2), *Fritz.*

Scheu (398) South German: nickname for a modest or shy person, from Middle High German *schiuhe, schiuwe* 'shyness' or 'aversion'.
GIVEN NAMES German 8%. *Otto* (3), *Johann* (2), *Eberhard, Erwin, Ulrike, Viktor.*

Scheuer (718) **1.** German: from Middle High German *schiur(e)*, German *Scheuer* 'barn', 'granary', a topographic name for someone who lived near a tithe-barn. As a German name it could also be a metonymic occupational name for an official responsible for receiving the tithes of agricultural produce rendered. **2.** Jewish (Ashkenazic): topographic name from German *Scheuer* 'barn'.

Scheuerman (608) **1.** Jewish (Ashkenazic): variant of SCHEUER. **2.** Altered spelling of SCHEUERMANN.

Scheuermann (550) German and Jewish (Ashkenazic): variant of SCHEUER.
GIVEN NAMES German 7%. *Kurt* (5), *Otto* (2), *Aloysius, Friedrich.*

Scheufler (145) German: variant of **Schäufler** (see SCHAUFLER).
GIVEN NAMES German 5%. *Kurt, Otto.*

Scheumann (148) German: nickname or occupational name for someone who had an elaborate fence on his property or who manufactured picket fences or lattice fences, from Middle High German *schīge, schie* 'paling'.

Scheuneman (120) Altered spelling of SCHEUNEMANN.

Scheunemann (199) North German: from Middle Low German *schüne* 'barn' + *man* 'man'; either a topographic name for some-

one who lived near a tithe-barn, or a metonymic occupational name for an official responsible for receiving the tithes of agricultural produce. Compare SCHEUER.
GIVEN NAMES German 7%. *Erwin* (3), *Gerhard*, *Hasso*, *Heinz*.

Scheurer (395) German: **1.** topographic or occupational name, from Middle High German *schiur(e)* 'barn', 'granary' + the agent suffix *-er* (see SCHEUER). **2.** habitational name for someone from Scheuren near Euskirchen.

Scheurich (228) German: from a Germanic personal name (*Scuro*) of uncertain meaning. The name is found in various old place names (compare SCHEURING).

Scheuring (203) German: habitational name from any of several places so named in Bavaria, notably one near Augsburg.
GIVEN NAMES German 4%. *Alois*, *Egon*, *Wolfgang*.

Scheve (228) German: variant of SCHEFF.

Schewe (439) North German: variant of SCHEFF.
GIVEN NAMES German 5%. *Erwin* (3), *Heinz* (2), *Frieda*, *Kurt*.

Schexnayder (866) LA surname, of German origin under French influence. It is probably a German occupational name for a maker of jackets and jerkins, from Middle High German *schecke*, Middle Low German *scheke* 'jacket', 'jerkin' + Middle High German, Middle Low German *snīder* 'tailor'. The name is not found in Germany.
GIVEN NAMES French 7%. *Desire* (2), *Emile* (2), *Marcel* (2), *Alcee*, *Alphonse*, *Andrus*, *Camille*, *Curley*, *Damien*, *Felicien*, *Francois*, *Gaston*.

Schexnaydre (138) See SCHEXNAYDER.
GIVEN NAMES French 11%. *Alcee*, *Amedee*, *Benoit*.

Schexnider (194) See SCHEXNAYDER.
GIVEN NAMES French 12%; Irish 5%. *Andrus* (2), *Calice*, *Cecile*, *Fernest*, *Nolton*, *Odilon*, *Pierre*; *Murphy* (3).

Schey (269) **1.** South German: variant of SCHEU. **2.** Jewish (Ashkenazic): from the Yiddish personal name *Shay(e)*, a pet form of *Yeshaye* 'Isaiah'.
GIVEN NAME German 4%. *Lorenz*.

Scheyer (106) German: **1.** variant of SCHEUER. **2.** habitational name for someone from Scheyern, Bavaria.

Schiano (386) Italian: from a short form of *Ischiano* (standard Italian **Ischitano**), a habitational name for someone from the island of Ischia.
GIVEN NAMES Italian 22%. *Ciro* (3), *Sal* (3), *Salvatore* (3), *Angelo* (2), *Biagio* (2), *Giosue* (2), *Carmela*, *Domenic*, *Dominico*, *Edmondo*, *Fortunata*, *Gennaro*.

Schiappa (164) Italian: probably a reduced form of **Schiappapietra** (an occupational name for a stone mason or cutter) or **Schiappacasse** (an occupational name for a docker), formed with Ligurian *schiapa* 'to break', 'to split' (standardized to *schiappa*).

GIVEN NAMES Italian 26%. *Marco* (3), *Salvatore* (3), *Antonio* (2), *Dario* (2), *Albino*, *Amedeo*, *Angelo*, *Calisto*, *Carlo*, *Domenic*, *Egidio*, *Elio*, *Ennio*, *Franco*, *Mario*, *Orlando*, *Ricardo*.

Schiavi (205) Italian: **1.** patronymic or plural form of SCHIAVO. **2.** habitational name from Schiavi d'Abruzzo in Chieti province or from Schiavi (now called *Liberi*) in Caserta.
GIVEN NAMES Italian 19%. *Aldo* (2), *Ennio* (2), *Guido* (2), *Americo*, *Mario*, *Medardo*, *Romeo*, *Vincenzo*.

Schiavo (600) Italian: **1.** ethnic name from *schiavo* 'Slav'. **2.** habitational name from Schiavo in Ardore, Reggio Calabria.
GIVEN NAMES Italian 13%. *Angelo* (2), *Salvatore* (2), *Biagio*, *Carmel*, *Carmine*, *Ceasar*, *Elio*, *Gennaro*, *Giuseppe*, *Lorenzo*, *Nino*, *Pasco*.

Schiavone (1136) Italian: ethnic name from *schiavone*, *slavone* 'Slav', specifically a south Slav from the eastern Adriatic.
GIVEN NAMES Italian 17%. *Salvatore* (8), *Rocco* (7), *Pasquale* (4), *Vito* (4), *Attilio* (3), *Carmela* (3), *Gino* (3), *Antonio* (2), *Carmine* (2), *Domenic* (2), *Francesco* (2), *Dante*.

Schiavoni (216) Italian: patronymic or plural form of SCHIAVONE.
GIVEN NAMES Italian 12%. *Angelo*, *Dante*, *Dino*, *Ercole*, *Evo*, *Geno*, *Guido*, *Reno*.

Schibi (104) probably a variant spelling of Swiss German **Schiebi**, Alemannic form of *schiebe* 'dowel', 'board', hence a nickname for a short, plump person.

Schichtel (139) German: from a diminutive of Middle High German *schuoch* 'shoe' (see SCHUH).

Schick (2571) **1.** German: nickname for a well-mannered and experienced person, from Middle High German *schic* 'orderly', 'skillful'. **2.** Jewish (Ashkenazic): of uncertain origin; perhaps from a pet form of the Yiddish personal name *Shimen* 'Simon', but compare SIK.
GIVEN NAMES German 5%. *Otto* (8), *Kurt* (4), *Bernd* (2), *Dieter* (2), *Erwin* (2), *Hans* (2), *Milbert* (2), *Uwe* (2), *Frieda*, *Helmut*, *Helmuth*, *Klaus*.

Schickel (175) South German: metonymic occupational name for a trader, from a noun derivative of *schickelen* 'to deal or trade'.

Schicker (197) German: variant of SCHICK 1, or from Middle High German *schicken* 'to make (something) happen', 'arrange', 'prepare'.

Schickler (165) **1.** German: occupational name for a trader, from an agent derivative of Alemannic *schickelen* 'to deal or trade'. **2.** Jewish (Ashkenazic): possibly from a derivative of German *schicken* 'to send', with the agent suffix *-ler*.

Schickling (186) German: occupational name for a trader, from a diminutive of SCHICKLER.

Schiebel (291) South German: possibly from Middle High German *schübel* 'bung', 'stopper', 'bolt', 'something used to stop a gap', hence a nickname for a short, fat fellow.

Schieber (579) German: **1.** habitational name for someone from any of several places named Schieben. **2.** occupational name for someone who used a tool that is pushed, from an agent derivative of Middle High German *schieben* 'to push or shove'.

Schieck (136) **1.** South German: nickname for someone with a deformity, from Middle High German *schiec* 'crooked', 'twisted'. **2.** German: metonymic occupational name for someone who worked with palings, from Middle High German *schīge*, *schie* 'paling' (for building fences).
GIVEN NAMES German 4%. *Lorenz*, *Oskar*.

Schied (142) German: **1.** topographic name for someone living near a border or boundary, Middle High German *schide*. **2.** habitational name from Schied, near Salzburg, Austria.
GIVEN NAMES German 5%. *Detlef*, *Kurt*.

Schiedel (136) German: habitational name from any of several places so named, for example near Bautzen.

Schiefelbein (545) German: habitational name from Schievelbein in Pomerania.

Schiefen (101) German: probably a topographic name from a place called Schiefenbusch or Schiefendorf, denoting an irregular plot or field (German *schief*, Low German *scheef* 'slanted', 'bent', 'crooked').

Schiefer (502) German and Jewish (Ashkenazic): metonymic occupational name for a roofer, from Middle High German, Middle Low German *schiver* 'slate', 'shingle', German *Schiefer* 'slate'.
GIVEN NAMES German 7%. *Manfred* (4), *Bernhard* (2), *Eberhard*, *Konrad*, *Otto*, *Ulrich*, *Wolfgang*.

Schieferstein (132) German: habitational name from a place near Wrocław (Breslau), Silesia, or a metonymic occupational name for a worker in a slate quarry, from Middle High German *schiver* 'slate' + *stein* 'stone'.

Schieffer (424) German: variant of SCHIFFER or SCHIEFER.

Schiek (136) German: variant spelling of SCHIECK.
GIVEN NAMES German 5%. *Kurt*, *Ulrich*.

Schiel (319) North German: variant of SCHEEL.
GIVEN NAMES German 7%. *Ewald* (2), *Bernhard*, *Dietmar*, *Erna*, *Erwin*, *Gunther*, *Kurt*, *Reinhold*.

Schield (219) Of German or Swiss German origin: possibly a variant or an Americanized form of SCHILD.

Schiele (532) **1.** North German: variant of SCHEEL. **2.** German (Swabian): unrounded form of **Schühle**, a diminutive of SCHUH.
GIVEN NAMES German 5%. *Bernhard* (2), *Gerhard*, *Kurt*, *Markus*, *Otto*, *Ute*.

Schielke (159) German: variant of **Schülke** (see SCHUELKE).

GIVEN NAMES German 9%. *Erwin, Gerhard, Gunther, Reinhart.*

Schieman (124) Altered spelling of German SCHIEMANN.

GIVEN NAMES German 6%. *Egon, Erwin.*

Schiemann (157) **1.** German: of uncertain origin. **2.** East German: form of the personal name SIMON. **3.** Northwest German: occupational name for a helmsman (of a boat), from Middle Low German *sē* 'sea' + *man* 'man'.

GIVEN NAMES German 11%. *Christoph, Fritz, Gerhard, Heinz, Hilde, Lothar, Otto.*

Schier (366) **1.** North German: topographic name from *scir* 'muddy water', or a habitational name from places named with this word, for example Schier near Uelzen. **2.** South German: from a short form of a Germanic personal name formed with *skīr-* 'clear', 'clean'.

GIVEN NAMES German 5%. *Guenter* (2), *Gernot, Hermann.*

Schierer (149) **1.** South German: variant of SCHEURER. **2.** North German: topographic name from a regional word *schiere* 'boundary', hence for someone who lived near a dividing line. **3.** Dutch: variant of SCHEERER 1.

Schierling (112) German: **1.** habitational name from a place of that name in Bavaria. **2.** variant of SCHERLING.

GIVEN NAME German 4%. *Hartmut.*

Schierman (149) German (**Schiermann**): variant of SCHIER 1.

Schiermeyer (106) North German: variant of SCHIERER 2 + MEYER, which in Westphalia took on the function of -*man* 'man' in a compound name.

GIVEN NAMES German 4%. *Erwin, Hans.*

Schiess (259) German: probably a variant of SCHIESSER.

GIVEN NAMES German 4%. *Erwin, Klaus, Otto, Ulrich.*

Schiesser (252) German: **1.** nickname for a hunter or shooting enthusiast, from an agent derivative of Middle High German *schiezzen* 'to shoot'. **2.** topographic name from a dialect word meaning 'pointed nook'.

GIVEN NAMES German 5%. *Hans* (2), *Gunter, Kurt.*

Schiessl (131) South German: variant of SCHIESSER 2.

GIVEN NAMES German 9%. *Hans* (3), *Alois* (2), *Hannelore, Konrad.*

Schieve (115) Possibly a variant or altered form of German **Schiewe**, a nickname from Middle Low German *schēf* 'crooked', 'slanting', 'twisted' or from Middle Low German *scheve* denoting the waste from processing flax, i.e. a nickname for a worthless person.

GIVEN NAMES German 6%. *Erwin, Gerhardt.*

Schievelbein (102) Variant of SCHIEFELBEIN.

Schiewe (138) German: variant of SCHIEVE. Compare SCHEVE.

GIVEN NAME German 4%. *Kurt.*

Schifano (286) Southern Italian: habitational name from any of various minor places in Sicily named Schifano.

GIVEN NAMES Italian 18%. *Salvatore* (6), *Angelo* (5), *Carmelo, Francesco, Vito.*

Schiferl (147) South German: probably a variant of **Schifferl**, Bavarian form of SCHIFFER.

Schiff (2091) **1.** German: from Middle High German *schif* 'ship', applied as a metonymic occupational name for a sailor, or a habitational name for someone who lived at a house distinguished by the sign of a ship. **2.** Jewish (Ashkenazic): ornamental name or habitational name (see 1 above), from German *Schiff* 'ship'.

GIVEN NAMES Jewish 6%. *Sol* (3), *Isadore* (2), *Meyer* (2), *Miriam* (2), *Moshe* (2), *Yaakov* (2), *Yehuda* (2), *Akiva, Anshel, Arieh, Emanuel, Hadassah.*

Schiffbauer (161) German: occupational name for a shipbuilder, from Middle High German *schif* 'ship' + an agent derivative of *būwen* 'to build'.

Schiffer (885) **1.** German: occupational name for a mariner or boatman, from an agent derivative of Middle High German *schif* 'ship'. **2.** Jewish (Ashkenazic): ornamental name from German *Schiffer* 'boatman', 'skipper'. **3.** Jewish (Ashkenazic): from the Yiddish female personal name *Shifre*, derived from a Hebrew word meaning 'beautiful'.

GIVEN NAMES German 4%. *Franz* (2), *Bernhard, Fritzi, Hans, Rudi, Wilhelm, Wolfgang.*

Schiffhauer (124) German: **1.** occupational name for a shipbuilder, from Middle High German *schif* 'ship' + an agent derivative of *hauen* 'to cut or hew'. **2.** variant of **Scheffauer**, a habitational name for someone from any of several places named Scheffau.

Schiffler (135) **1.** Dutch: occupational name for a piper, from an agent derivative of Middle Dutch *schufelen* 'to whistle', 'to play the flute'. **2.** German: probably a variant of Low German **Schüffler**, an occupational name, a variant of SCHAUFLER.

GIVEN NAMES German 7%. *Hans* (2), *Klaus, Phares.*

Schiffman (1016) **1.** German (**Schiffmann**): occupational name for a shipman (see SCHIFFER). **2.** Jewish (Ashkenazic): from German *Schiff* 'ship' + *Mann* 'man', an ornamental name or possibly denoting someone who lived at a house distinguished by the sign of a ship.

GIVEN NAMES German 4%. *Wolf* (2), *Franz, Inge, Kurt, Theodor.*

Schiffner (218) German: variant of SCHIFFER 1.

Schilb (118) German: variant of SCHELB.

Schild (672) **1.** German and Dutch: metonymic occupational name for a maker or painter of shields, from Middle High German, Middle Dutch *schilt* 'shield'.

2. Jewish (Ashkenazic): from German *Schild* 'shield', '(house) sign', applied either as an ornamental name or as a habitational name for someone who lived in a house distinguished by a sign. Compare ROTHSCHILD and **Schwarzschild**.

GIVEN NAMES German 7%. *Fritz* (3), *Kurt* (3), *Manfred* (3), *Johannes* (2), *Otto* (2), *Ewald, Gerda, Hans, Helmuth, Ilse.*

Schilder (203) **1.** German: occupational name for a shield maker or painter, from Middle High German *schilt* 'shield' + the agent suffix -*er*. Compare SCHILD. **2.** Dutch (**de Schilder**): occupational name for a painter of shields, a decorative painter, or a gilder, Middle Dutch *schildere*.

GIVEN NAMES German 4%. *Inge, Kurt.*

Schildgen (113) German: **1.** from a Germanic personal name based on *scild* 'disk', 'shield' + Rhenish diminutive suffix of endearment -*gen*. **2.** Variant of SCHILD.

Schildknecht (175) German: occupational name for the page or squire of a knight, who was responsible for his armor and his horse, from Middle High German *schilt* 'shield' + *knecht* 'boy', 'servant'.

Schildkraut (120) Jewish (Ashkenazic): ornamental name from a Germanized form of Yiddish *shildkroyt* 'tortoise', 'turtle'.

GIVEN NAME German 5%; Jewish 4%. *Monika.*

Schildt (327) German and Jewish (Ashkenazic): variant spelling of SCHILD.

Schilke (291) Eastern German: variant of SCHUELKE.

GIVEN NAMES German 5%. *Reinhold, Waltraud.*

Schill (1091) German: habitational name from Schill, a place in Silesia. See also SCHILLE.

Schillaci (356) Southern Italian: variant of SQUILLACE.

GIVEN NAMES Italian 14%. *Salvatore* (6), *Angelo, Biagio, Carmelo, Francesco, Giovanna, Marino, Rocco, Sal.*

Schille (129) German: probably a habitational name from Schille near the river Leine or Schillau Creek in the Harz Mountains.

GIVEN NAME German 5%. *Wolfram.*

Schiller (3972) **1.** German and Jewish (southern Ashkenazic): dialect variant of SCHULER. **2.** German: nickname for someone with a squint, from an agent derivative of Middle High German *schilhen, schiln* 'to squint'.

GIVEN NAMES German 4%. *Kurt* (10), *Otto* (4), *Ulrich* (4), *Ernst* (3), *Erwin* (3), *Heinz* (2), *Ilse* (2), *Ingo* (2), *Alois, Berthold, Eugen, Friedrich.*

Schillig (153) German: **1.** habitational name from a place so named near Wilhelmshaven. **2.** variant of SCHILLING 1.

Schilling (6596) **1.** German and Jewish (Ashkenazic): nickname from Middle High German *schillinc*, Middle Low German *schillink*, German *Schilling* 'shilling'. The

German surname may have referred originally to a rent or fee owed, or have some other anecdotal origin, now irrecoverable. The Jewish surname is mainly ornamental. **2.** German: habitational name from Schilling in Bavaria or from places called Schillingen in the Rhineland and East Prussia.

Schillinger (952) German and Jewish (Ashkenazic): habitational name for someone from a place called Schilling or Schillingen (see SCHILLING 2).

Schillo (158) German (of Slavic origin): metonymic occupational name for a cobbler, from Sorbian *šylo* 'awl', or for someone who used that instrument in his trade.
GIVEN NAMES German 4%. *Klaus, Kurt.*

Schilly (103) probably a variant of Swiss German **Schilli** or **Schieli**, nickname for a cross-eyed (sometimes one-eyed) person, Middle High German *schiel.*

Schilt (154) German and Dutch: variant of SCHILD 1.

Schiltz (860) German (Palatinate and Mosel region): from a pet form of the personal and saint's name *Ägilius*, a variant of *Ägidius.* The German name developed via the French variant *Gilles.*

Schilz (277) German: variant of SCHILTZ.

Schimanski (127) Germanized spelling of Polish **Szymański** (see SZYMANSKI).
GIVEN NAMES German 10%. *Erwin* (2), *Fritz, Hans, Manfred.*

Schimek (170) Germanized spelling of a Slavic pet form of the personal name SIMON (e.g. Czech **Šimek**).
GIVEN NAMES German 4%; French 4%. *Ottmar* (2), *Alois*; *Amie, Pierre.*

Schimel (133) **1.** Jewish (Ashkenazic): variant of SCHIMMEL. **2.** Respelling of German SCHIMMEL.
GIVEN NAMES Jewish 8%. *Isak, Shaya.*

Schimke (431) German (of Slavic origin): from a pet form of the personal name SIMON.
GIVEN NAMES German 4%. *Otto* (3), *Friedrich.*

Schimmel (1233) **1.** German and Dutch: nickname for a man with gray or white hair, from Middle High German, Middle Dutch *schimel*, a term used to denote both mildew and a white horse. Old High German forms are not found, and the semantic development is not entirely clear. **2.** Jewish (Ashkenazic): from German *Schimmel* 'mildew', imposed by a non-Jewish government official. **3.** Jewish (Ashkenazic): from a pet form of the personal name *Shimon* (see SIMON).
GIVEN NAMES German 4%. *Kurt* (6), *Beate, Egon, Erwin, Hermann, Horst, Otto, Wilhelm, Willi.*

Schimmelpfennig (106) German: nickname for a miser who lets his pennies become moldy, from *schimmeln* 'to become moldy, mildewy' (Middle High German *schimel* 'mildew') + *Pfennig* 'penny' (Middle High German *phenninc*).

GIVEN NAMES German 11%. *Otto* (2), *Dieter.*

Schimmer (126) **1.** German: probably a topographic name; it is found as the first element in compound topographic names, but its meaning is unclear. There are several places called Schimm, for example near Wismar and near Osnabrück, and in some instances the surname may be habitational. **2.** Jewish (Ashkenazic): ornamental from German *Schimmer* 'glimmer', 'shimmer'.
GIVEN NAME Scandinavian 5%. *Erik* (2).

Schimming (208) North German: nickname for a person with gray or white hair, from Middle Low German *schimmink* 'gray or white horse'.

Schimmoeller (107) German: from *Möller* (a variant of *Müller* 'miller'), with an unexplained first element. Compare SCHIMMER.

Schimp (104) North German: variant of SCHIMPF.

Schimpf (601) German: nickname for a humorous or playful person, from Middle High German *schimpf* 'sport', 'play', 'amusement'.

Schinasi (36) Variant of ASHKENAZI.
GIVEN NAME French 8%. *Alain.*

Schindel (364) **1.** German (southern and eastern) and Jewish (Ashkenazic): metonymic occupational name for someone who made or laid roof tiles, from Middle High German *schindel*, German *Schindel* 'shingle', 'wooden tile'. **2.** South German: habitational name from places named Schindel or Schindeln in Baden.
GIVEN NAMES German 4%. *Egon, Erwin, Horst, Otto.*

Schindele (164) German: variant of SCHINDEL 2.

Schindler (4041) **1.** German (southern and eastern) and Jewish (Ashkenazic): occupational name for someone who made or laid wooden roof tiles, from an agent derivative of Middle High German *schindel*, German *Schindel* 'shingle'. **2.** South German: habitational name from places named Schindel or Schindeln (see SCHINDEL).
GIVEN NAMES German 4%. *Hans* (5), *Kurt* (5), *Otto* (5), *Guenter* (3), *Reinhardt* (3), *Frieda* (2), *Horst* (2), *Rainer* (2), *Bernhard, Florian, Fritz, Gerd.*

Schink (163) **1.** Southern German: nickname for someone with long or otherwise remarkable legs, from Middle High German *schinke* 'thigh', 'leg'. Compare SCHENKEL. **2.** Dutch: variant of SCHENK 1.
GIVEN NAME German 5%. *Hans.*

Schinke (174) German: variant of SCHINK.

Schinkel (168) German (mainly North German) and Dutch: variant of SCHENKEL.
GIVEN NAMES German 5%. *Helmut, Otto.*

Schinker (104) German: unexplained.

Schipani (179) Southern Italian (Calabria and Sicily): perhaps a habitational name from Schipani, a minor place in Catanzaro, but more probably, a surname of Albanian origin.

GIVEN NAMES Italian 24%. *Alfonso, Angelo, Carmela, Carmine, Costantino, Dante, Domenic, Franco, Mario, Salvatore, Saturnina.*

Schipp (110) North German and Dutch: metonymic occupational name for a shipman or a shipbuilder, from *schip* 'ship'.
GIVEN NAME German 4%. *Fritz.*

Schipper (1105) **1.** Dutch and North German: occupational name for a shipman or (in German) a shipbuilder, from an agent derivative of *schip* 'ship'. **2.** Jewish (Ashkenazic): occupational name for a shovel maker or a digger, from German *Schippe* 'shovel', 'spade' + the agent suffix *-er.*

Schippers (369) Dutch: patronymic for the son of a shipman, from SCHIPPER 1.

Schira (124) Italian: variant of SCHIRO.

Schiraldi (151) Italian: from any of various Germanic personal names ending with *-valda.*
GIVEN NAMES Italian 18%. *Angelo* (4), *Domenic* (2), *Caesar, Donato, Gennaro, Orazio, Vito.*

Schirm (213) German: from Middle High German *schirm* 'shield', 'defense', hence a metonymic form of SCHIRMER 1.
GIVEN NAMES German 4%. *Inge, Kurt.*

Schirmacher (106) German: occupational name for someone who makes harnesses and bridles for horses, from Middle High German *(ge)schirre* 'harness' + *macher* 'maker'.
GIVEN NAMES German 9%. *Wolfgang* (2), *Eberhard, Hans.*

Schirmer (1351) German: **1.** occupational name, from Middle High German *schirmer* 'fencing master', 'street player' (see SCHERMER 1). **2.** (Saxony): habitational name for someone from Schirma near Freiberg.
GIVEN NAMES German 5%. *Kurt* (6), *Hans* (3), *Horst* (3), *Ernst* (2), *Otto* (2), *Dietmar, Guenther, Liselotte, Merwin, Milbert, Reinhold.*

Schiro (735) Italianized form of Albanian **Skiro**, of unexplained etymology. This surname is found among Italians of Albanian descent in Sicily and southern Italy.
GIVEN NAMES Italian 6%. *Angelo* (2), *Gasper* (2), *Carmela, Sal, Salvatore, Vincenzo, Vito.*

Schirra (111) Italian (of Albanian origin): variant of SCHIRO.

Schirripa (146) Italian (Calabria): unexplained.
GIVEN NAMES Italian 31%. *Rocco* (9), *Carlo* (2), *Domenico, Dominico, Franco, Julio, Mario, Osvaldo, Paola, Salvatore, Virgilio.*

Schirtzinger (152) German: probably a topograhic name related to **Schürzinger**, from Middle High German *schürritze* 'scree'.

Schisel (106) Variant of German and Jewish SCHISSEL.

Schisler (632) Variant of German SCHUESSLER.

Schissel (226) German and Jewish (Ashkenazic): metonymic occupational name for a maker of dishes, probably of wood and hence a turner, from Middle High German *schüssel*, Yiddish *shisl* 'dish'.

Schissler (363) German: variant of **Schüssler** (see SCHUESSLER).

Schkade (104) German: local, possibly Westphalian, variant of SCHADE.

Schlabach (733) German (Siegen area): topographic name with an unidentified first element + Middle High German *bach* 'creek'. This is a frequent Amish name.

Schlachter (563) North German and Jewish (Ashkenazic): occupational name for a slaughterer of animals, from Middle Low German *slachtere*, German *Schlachter* 'slaughterer'.

Schlack (212) North German: nickname for a weak or listless person, from Middle Low German *slak* 'weak', 'slack'.
GIVEN NAMES German 5%. *Alois, Heinz.*

Schlader (133) North German: habitational name for someone from any of various places in northern Germany and the Rhineland named Schlade.

Schladweiler (105) German: evidently a habitational name from an unidentified place.
GIVEN NAMES German 6%. *Aloys, Erwin, Otto.*

Schlaefer (143) German (**Schläfer**): see SCHLAFER.
GIVEN NAME German 5%. *Kurt* (2).

Schlafer (193) German (**Schläfer**) and Jewish (Ashkenazic): nickname for a lazy or indolent person, from Middle High German *släfer*, German *Schläfer* 'sleeper'.

Schlaff (112) German: from Middle High German *slaf* 'limp', 'listless' (a cognate of English *sleep*), a nickname for a lazy or indolent person (see SCHLAFER).

Schlag (257) South German: topographic name from Middle High German *slac* 'clearing in a wood', or a habitational name from a place named with this word.

Schlagel (489) German (**Schlägel**): variant of SCHLEGEL.

Schlager (437) German (**Schläger**) and Jewish (Ashkenazic): from an agent derivative of Middle High German, German *schlagen* 'to strike', hence an occupational nickname for a craftsman whose work involved striking or beating something, such as metal.
GIVEN NAMES German 4%. *Wolfgang* (2), *Ernst, Gunther.*

Schlageter (226) German: habitational name for someone from a place called Schlageten in the Black Forest.

Schlaht (155) Variant of German **Schlacht** (see SCHLACHTER).

Schlais (107) German: variant spelling of **Schlaiß, Schlaiss**, a metonymic occupational name for someone who made pinewood chips for lighting candles, etc., from Middle High German *sleisse*.

Schlake (147) North German: variant of SCHLACK.

Schlamp (102) German: nickname from Middle High German *slamp* 'feast', 'banquet', hence a nickname for a big eater.
GIVEN NAMES French 4%. *Odette, Solange.*

Schlangen (200) German: habitational name from Schlangen, a place between Detmold and Paderborn.

Schlanger (339) Jewish (Ashkenazic): ornamental name from German *Schlange* 'snake' + the agent suffix *-er*.
GIVEN NAMES Jewish 5%. *Emanuel, Mordechai, Moric, Moshe.*

Schlapkohl (102) North German: nickname for someone with a dangling, pointed cap or hood, from Middle Low German *slap* 'limp' + *kogel* 'hood', 'cowl' (attached to a coat) (from Late Latin *cuculla*).

Schlappi (119) Swiss German (**Schläppi**): nickname for someone with a dangling, baggy cap or hood, from Middle High German *slappe* 'baggy, hanging headdress'.
GIVEN NAMES German 4%. *Oskar.*

Schlarb (241) South German: **1.** probably related to the Swabian dialect word *schlarpen* 'to shuffle along' and Middle High German *slarfe* 'slipper', hence a nickname for a negligent, sloppy person. **2.** habitational name from Schlarpe in Solling Forest.

Schlarman (115) German (**Schlärmann**): variant of **Schläger** (see SCHLAGER).

Schlater (215) German: variant of SCHLATTER.

Schlatter (564) South German: topographic name from Middle High German *slâte* 'reedy place', or a habitational name from any of several places named Schlatt, from the same word.
GIVEN NAMES German 5%. *Kurt* (4), *Otto* (3), *Bernhard, Hans, Konrad.*

Schlau (107) German: nickname meaning 'shrewd', 'cunning', or 'crafty', from Middle Low German *slû*.
GIVEN NAMES German 4%. *Kurt.*

Schlauch (206) **1.** German: nickname for a heavy drinker, from Middle High German *slûch* 'throat', 'gullet'. **2.** variant of SCHLAU in Bavaria.
GIVEN NAMES German 4%. *Kurt, Otto.*

Schlecht (689) **1.** nickname for a straightforward person, from Middle High German, Old High German *sleht* 'direct', 'natural' (though it later came to mean 'defective', 'bad'). **2.** habitational name from any of various minor places so named, for example in Mecklenburg and the Upper Palatinate, from Old High German *sleht* in the sense 'flat'.
GIVEN NAMES German 4%. *Bernhard, Frieda, Gerhard, Kurt, Otto, Reinhold, Wolfgang.*

Schlechter (207) German and Jewish (Ashkenazic): variant of *Schlächter* (see SCHLACHTER).
GIVEN NAMES German 4%. *Mathias, Matthias.*

Schleder (130) German: occupational name for a sled maker or a driver of one, from German *schlede*, Low German for 'sled'.
GIVEN NAMES German 4%. *Matthias, Otto.*

Schlee (332) German: topographic name for someone who lived near a sloe bush, or an occupational name for someone who sold sloes, from Middle High German *slêhe* 'sloe'.
GIVEN NAMES German 5%. *Kurt* (2), *Otto* (2).

Schleef (103) North German: nickname from Middle Low German *slef* 'large wooden spoon (made and used by peasants)', which later came to mean 'coarse fellow', 'rube'.
GIVEN NAME German 6%. *Dietrich* (2).

Schleeter (120) Americanized form of German **Schlüter** (see SCHLUETER).

Schlegel (2958) German: from Middle High German *slegel* 'hammer', 'tool for striking' (Old High German *slegil*, a derivative of *slahan* 'to strike'), hence a metonymic occupational name for a smith or mason, or a nickname for a forceful person.
GIVEN NAMES German 4%. *Kurt* (10), *Hans* (9), *Ernst* (2), *Erwin* (2), *Ulrich* (2), *Fritz, Gerhard, Heinrich, Heinz, Ilse, Ingeborg, Otto.*

Schlegelmilch (163) German: metonymic occupational name for a dairyman, from Middle High German *schlegelmilch* 'buttermilk'.
GIVEN NAMES German 5%. *Juergen* (2), *Otto.*

Schlehuber (149) South German: from Middle High German *slêhe* 'sloe' + *huober* 'peasant', 'farmer', hence a nickname for someone who worked or owned land identified by the blackthorn (sloe) bushes growing on or around it.

Schlei (122) German: occupational nickname from *Schleie* 'tench' (Middle Low German, Middle High German *slî, slie*) (see SCHLEY).
GIVEN NAMES German 4%. *Dietmar.*

Schleich (321) German: nickname for a furtive or stealthy person, from Middle High German *slîchen* 'to creep silently'.
GIVEN NAMES German 6%. *Horst, Kurt, Markus, Otto.*

Schleicher (1471) German and Jewish (Ashkenazic): nickname for a furtive or stealthy person, from an agent derivative of Middle High German *slîchen*, German *schleichen* 'to creep silently'.
GIVEN NAMES German 4%. *Kurt* (7), *Hans* (3), *Erwin* (2), *Hannelore, Helmut, Horst, Juergen, Jurgen, Mathias, Volkmar, Wenzel.*

Schleider (128) **1.** German: habitational name for someone from Schleid (near Fulda) or Schleiden (near Aachen). **2.** Jewish (Ashkenazic): unexplained.
GIVEN NAME German 4%. *Fritz.*

Schleif (365) German and Jewish (Ashkenazic): occupational name for a (knife) grinder, from Middle High German *slîfen*, German *schleifen* 'to grind'.

Schleifer (508) **1.** German and Jewish (Ashkenazic): occupational name for a grinder (of knives, scissors, and the like), from an agent derivative of Middle High German *slīfen*, German *schleifen* 'to grind'. **2.** German: habitational name for someone from *Schleife* in Silesia.

Schleiger (160) German: metonymic occupational name for a maker or seller of scarves and veils, from Middle Low German *sleiger*, *sleier* '(head)scarf'.

Schleigh (101) Americanized spelling of German SCHLEICH.

Schleimer (137) South German and Austrian: occupational name for a maker of glue or bird lime, from an agent derivative of Middle High German *slīm* 'glue', 'bird lime'.

GIVEN NAMES German 8%. *Ernst* (2), *Alois*, *Gunther*, *Hans*.

Schlein (238) **1.** German: metonymic occupational name for a maker or seller of glue or seller of bird lime, from Middle High German *slīn*, a variant of *slīm* (see SCHLEIMER). **2.** Jewish (Ashkenazic): ornamental name from Yiddish *shlayn* 'tench' (German *Schleie*). This is one of the many Ashkenazic ornamental names taken from words denoting fishes.

Schleis (293) German: metonymic occupational name for a carpenter or woodcutter, in particular one whose job was to split wood, from Middle High German *sleiss* 'wood shaving' or *sleissen* 'to split'.

Schleisman (116) German (**Schleissmann**): variant of SCHLEIS with the addition of *Mann* 'man'.

Schlemmer (746) German: from an agent derivative of Middle High German *slamp* 'feast', 'banquet', hence a nickname for a gourmet or a glutton.

GIVEN NAMES German 4%. *Armin*, *Dieter*, *Erhard*, *Ernst*, *Kurt*, *Wolfgang*.

Schlender (279) North German: nickname from an agent derivative either of Middle Low German *slinderen* 'to dawdle', 'to go about aimlessly', or of Middle Low German *slinden* 'to swallow or devour'.

GIVEN NAMES German 9%. *Heinz* (2), *Ernst*, *Erwin*, *Fritz*, *Jurgen*, *Otto*, *Wilhelm*, *Wolfgang*.

Schlenk (120) German: nickname for a person with a swinging or dragging gait, from Middle High German *slenken* 'to swing'.

GIVEN NAMES German 8%. *Hermann* (2), *Fritz*, *Kurt*.

Schlenker (884) German: **1.** from Middle High German *slenger*, *slenker* 'slingshot', an occupational name or a nickname for someone who used a sling to hurl stones. **2.** nickname for someone with a dragging or swinging gait, from an agent noun based on Middle High German *slenken* 'to swing'.

GIVEN NAMES German 4%. *Erna*, *Helmut*, *Helmuth*, *Juergen*, *Manfred*, *Otto*, *Ralf*.

Schlenz (115) German: **1.** habitational name from a place so named near Wrocław (Breslau), Silesia. **2.** nickname from Swabian *Schlanz*, *Schlänz* 'go-getter'.

Schleper (134) North German: nickname for a lazy person, from Middle Low German *slēper* 'sleeper'. Compare SCHLAEFER.

Schlepp (183) German: probably a nickname or occupational name for a laborer or carrier, especially in a mine, from Middle Low German *slepen*, Middle High German *slēpen* 'to drag or carry (a load)' (modern German *schleppen*, *schleifen*).

GIVEN NAMES German 4%. *Erna*, *Reinhold*.

Schlereth (222) German (Franconia): habitational name from a place called Schleerieth.

Schlesener (112) German and Jewish: variant of SCHLESINGER.

Schlesinger (1961) German and Jewish (Ashkenazic): regional name for someone from Silesia, German *Schlesien*, *Schlesing* 'Silesia' (Polish *Śląsk*). The area was named for the *Silingae*, a Germanic people who occupied the region before being displaced by Slavs in the 8th century AD. It has been governed at different times by Prussia and by Poland. Since 1945 it has been part of Poland. Other places named with the same element include Schleusingen in Saxony, Schlenzig in Pomerania, and Schlenz in Silesia itself, and it is possible that in some instances the surname derives from one of these.

GIVEN NAMES Jewish 5%; German 4%. *Moshe* (3), *Avram* (2), *Chaim* (2), *Sol* (2), *Tovia* (2), *Aron*, *Avi*, *Baruch*, *Chana*, *Cohen*, *Eran*, *Gitty*; *Hans* (4), *Otto* (3), *Heinz* (2), *Kurt* (2), *Bernd*, *Erna*, *Erwin*, *Eugen*, *Gerhard*, *Hilde*, *Ingeborg*, *Manfred*.

Schlesselman (136) German (**Schlesselmann**): habitational name for someone from Schleessel on the river Wümme (with the addition of Middle Low German *man* 'man').

GIVEN NAMES German 5%. *Helmuth*, *Kurt*.

Schlesser (155) **1.** German: variant of **Schlösser** (see SCHLOESSER). **2.** Jewish (Ashkenazic): derivative of SCHLOSS 3.

Schlessinger (179) German and Jewish (Ashkenazic): variant of SCHLESINGER.

GIVEN NAME German 5%. *Gunther* (2).

Schleusner (147) German: habitational name for someone from Schleusingen in Thuringia.

GIVEN NAMES German 5%. *Erwin*, *Heinz*, *Otto*.

Schley (919) German: **1.** from Middle Low German *slīc* 'tench', a nickname for someone thought to resemble a tench or a metonymic occupational name for a fisherman or seller of these fish. **2.** possibly a topographic name for someone living by the Schlei river.

Schleyer (185) German: metonymic occupational name for a maker or seller of veils, from Middle High German *sleier* 'veil', 'headscarf'.

GIVEN NAMES German 5%. *Ilse*, *Reiner*, *Wilhelm*.

Schlicher (315) German: habitational name for someone from any of several places in the Rhineland named Schlich.

Schlicht (498) German: variant of SCHLECHT.

GIVEN NAMES German 6%. *Gunter* (4), *Otto* (2), *Heinz*, *Kurt*.

Schlichte (158) German: variant of SCHLECHT.

Schlichter (326) German: **1.** occupational name for someone who smoothes out cloth. **2.** occupational name for an arbitrator. Both senses are from Middle High German *slecht* 'straight', 'smooth', 'plane', 'even'.

GIVEN NAMES German 7%. *Wolfgang* (2), *Claus*, *Klaus*, *Kurt*.

Schlichting (881) North German: nickname for someone who arbitrates or one who meddles in other people's affairs, from Middle High German *slihtinc* 'arbitrator', 'intervener'.

GIVEN NAMES German 6%. *Kurt* (6), *Fritz* (4), *Hans* (4), *Otto* (2), *Erwin*, *Frieda*, *Heinz*, *Helmuth*, *Wolfgang*.

Schlick (376) **1.** German: nickname for a glutton, from a derivative of Middle High German *slicken* 'to gulp or swallow'. **2.** North German: topographic name for someone who lived in a marshy area, from Middle Low German *slik* 'slime', 'bog'. **3.** Jewish (Ashkenazic): of uncertain origin, probably an unflattering name from German *Schlick* 'slime', 'mud', imposed by a non-Jewish government official.

GIVEN NAMES German 6%. *Kurt* (3), *Hertha*, *Otto*, *Wilfried*.

Schlicker (149) **1.** German: nickname for a glutton, from an agent derivative of Middle High German *slicken* 'to gulp or swallow'. **2.** North German: topographic name for someone living in a marshy area, from SCHLICK 2 + -*er*, suffix denoting an inhabitant.

GIVEN NAMES German 10%. *Fritzy*, *Hans*, *Inge*, *Jurgen*, *Kurt*.

Schlie (165) North German: metonymic occupational name for a seller of freshwater fish, from Middle Low German *slī* 'tench'.

GIVEN NAME German 4%. *Gunther*.

Schlief (154) North German: from Middle Low German *slef* 'wooden spoon', hence a metonymic occupational name for a spoon maker. The word also had a figurative sense of 'ruffian', so it could be a nickname from this.

Schliep (196) North German: occupational name for a grinder of knives, scissors, and the like, from Middle Low German *slipen* 'to grind or sharpen'. Compare SCHLEIFER 1.

Schlieper (140) North German: occupational name for a grinder of knives, scissors, and the like, Middle Low German *sliper*.

GIVEN NAMES German 7%. *Detlef, Otto, Reinhold*.

Schlies (116) German: **1.** habitational name from Schliess in Westphalia or from Schliessa in Silesia. **2.** possibly also a spelling variant of SCHLEIS.

Schliesman (116) German (**Schliessmann**): spelling variant of SCHLEISMAN, or a variant of **Schliesser**, South German form of **Schlüter** (see SCHLUETER, from Middle High German *sliezen* 'to shut, lock').

Schlimgen (168) German (Rhineland): nickname for someone with a physical deformity, from Middle Low German *slim* 'crooked', 'bent' + *-gen*, local form of the diminutive suffix *-ken*.

Schlinger (112) German: **1.** topographic name for someone living by the winding course of a shoreline, river, fence, etc., from *schlingen* 'to wind' or perhaps a habitational name for someone from a place called Schlingen, although this has not been identified. **2.** nickname or occupational name for someone who used a sling, Middle High German *slinger*.

Schlink (262) German: **1.** topographic name from an element meaning 'sling' or 'style (in a fence)', or from Middle Low German *slink* 'fence', 'border', 'shore'. **2.** nickname for a glutton or a drunkard, from Middle High German *slinc* 'throat'.

Schlipf (132) South German: topographic name for someone who lived in an area of slippery ground or in an area prone to landslides, from Middle High German *slipfe* 'landslide'.

GIVEN NAMES German 7%. *Erwin, Gerhard, Heinz*.

Schlissel (107) Jewish (eastern Ashkenazic): variant of SCHLUSSEL.

GIVEN NAMES Jewish 6%. *Miriam, Sol*.

Schlitt (355) German: **1.** (South German) topographic name for someone who lived in an area of slippery ground, from *slid, slit* 'smooth', 'slippery'. **2.** German: habitational name from a place so named in East Prussia. **3.** In some cases a variant of SCHLITTER 2.

Schlitter (154) **1.** German: habitational name from SCHLITT in East Prussia. **2.** occupational name for a maker of sleds, from an agent derivative of Middle High German *slite*.

GIVEN NAMES German 10%. *Arno, Eldred, Elke, Fritz, Karl-Heinz*.

Schlitz (176) German: topographic name for someone living by the Schlitz river or habitational name from the town of Schlitz, near Fulda.

Schlobohm (283) North German: topographic name for someone who lived in an area where blackthorns (sloe bushes) grew, from Middle Low German *slē* 'sloe' + *bōm* 'tree'.

GIVEN NAMES German 9%. *Hartwig* (2), *Otto* (2), *Bernhard, Dietrich, Hans, Helmut*.

Schloegel (124) German: variant of SCHLEGEL.

GIVEN NAME German 6%. *Hermann* (2).

Schloemer (305) **1.** North German (**Schlömer**): nickname from Middle Low German *slōmer* 'feaster', 'glutton'. Compare SCHLEMMER. **2.** habitational name from Schlöhm near Cologne or from Schlömen near Kulmbach.

Schloesser (270) German (**Schlösser**): occupational name for a locksmith, from an agent derivative of Middle High German *sloz* 'lock'.

GIVEN NAMES German 5%. *Aloysius, Erwin, Hannes, Hans, Wolfgang*.

Schlomer (130) Dutch: nickname for a gourmandizer, a loan word from Middle High German *slemmer*.

GIVEN NAME Dutch 4%. *Harm* (2).

Schlosberg (201) Jewish (Ashkenazic): variant of SCHLOSSBERG.

Schloss (951) German and Jewish (Ashkenazic): **1.** metonymic occupational name for a locksmith, from Middle High German *sloz* 'lock'. **2.** from *Schloss* 'castle' (originally the same word as in 1), a topographic name for someone who lived in or near a castle or was employed at one. The Jewish name is generally ornamental.

GIVEN NAMES German 4%. *Kurt* (4), *Eldred, Erwin, Gerd, Gerhard, Gunther, Hans, Herta, Konrad, Manfred*.

Schlossberg (487) Jewish (Ashkenazic): **1.** ornamental name composed of German *Schloss* 'castle' + *Berg* 'mountain', 'hill'. **2.** habitational name from any of various places in Germany so named, because they were the sites of castles (see SCHLOSS 2) on hills (see BERG).

GIVEN NAMES Jewish 7%. *Golda, Hirsch, Hyman, Rivka, Rivky, Yehuda*.

Schlosser (2965) **1.** German and Jewish (Ashkenazic): occupational name from German *Schlosser* 'locksmith'. **2.** German (also **Schlösser**): topographic or occupational name for someone who worked at a castle, from SCHLOSS with the addition of the agent or habitational suffix *-er*.

Schlossman (149) German (**Schlossmann**) and Jewish (Ashkenazic): variant of SCHLOSSER.

Schlote (108) North German and Dutch: **1.** variant of SCHLOSS 1 'locksmith'. **2.** variant of SCHLOTT.

Schlotfeldt (152) German: habitational name from Schlotfeld near Itzehoe.

Schlotman (156) North German and Dutch: **1.** (**Schlotmann**) topographic name for someone who lived on marshy land, from Middle Low German *slōt* 'ditch', 'swamp' + *man* 'man'. **2.** occupational name for a locksmith, from Middle Low German *slot* 'lock' + *man* 'man'.

Schlott (243) North German: **1.** metonymic occupational name for a locksmith, from

Middle Low German *slot* 'lock'. Compare SCHLOSS 1. **2.** topographic name for someone who lived on wet or marshy land, from Middle Low German *slōt* 'ditch', 'swamp'.

GIVEN NAMES German 6%. *Dieter* (2), *Eldred, Friedrich, Johannes*.

Schlotter (203) **1.** South German: topographic name for someone living in an area of loamy soil, from Middle High German *slōte* 'loam'. **2.** North German: occupational name for a locksmith, from an agent derivative of Middle Low German *slot* 'lock'.

GIVEN NAMES German 7%. *Kurt* (2), *Bernd*.

Schlotterback (107) Variant of German **Schlotterbach** (see SCHLOTTERBECK).

Schlotterbeck (234) Variant of German **Schlotterbach**, habitational name from some minor place named as 'muddy stream'.

GIVEN NAMES German 6%. *Kurt* (2), *Horst*.

Schlotthauer (157) German: **1.** occupational name for a reed cutter, from *slot* 'reed' + an agent derivative of Middle High German *houwen* 'to hew or cut'. **2.** occupational name for a locksmith, from Middle Low German *slot* 'lock' + *houwer* 'maker', 'striker'.

GIVEN NAME German 4%. *Kurt*.

Schlottman (217) North German (**Schlottmann**): see SCHLOTMAN.

Schlotzhauer (198) German: **1.** variant of SCHLOTTHAUER 2 (formed with *slotz*, the Middle High German equivalent of *slot*). **2.** habitational name from Schlotzau near Fulda.

Schlough (184) Altered spelling of German SCHLAUCH.

Schluckebier (109) German: nickname for a heavy drinker or for someone who slurped his beer.

Schlueter (1936) North German: from Middle Low German *sluter* (an agent derivative of *sluten* 'to shut or lock'), an occupational name for a jailer or for a chatelain or steward in charge of the keys to the pantry and storerooms in a large household.

GIVEN NAMES German 4%. *Kurt* (3), *Eberhard* (2), *Erwin* (2), *Juergen* (2), *Otto* (2), *Uwe* (2), *Wolfgang* (2), *Alfons, Alois, Arno, Dietrich, Fritz*.

Schlund (130) German: nickname for a glutton or drunkard, from Middle High German *slunt* 'feaster', 'carouser'.

Schlundt (137) German: variant of SCHLUND.

Schlup (163) **1.** German (**Schlupp**): probably a nickname from a Slavic word akin to Polish *słup* 'pole', 'column', applied as a nickname for a tall person. **2.** Perhaps also an altered spelling of South German **Schlupf**, a topographic name for someone living near a hole in a hedge or a fence, used as a shortcut, from Middle High German *slupf*, equivalant to Middle Low German *slup*, with the same meaning.

Schlussel (135) German and Jewish (Ashkenazic): occupational name for a locksmith, from German *Schlüssel* 'key'. The Jewish name may also be an ornamental name.
GIVEN NAMES Jewish 8%. *Chaim, Gershon.*

Schluter (671) North German (**Schlüter**): see SCHLUETER.
GIVEN NAMES German 6%. *Kurt* (3), *Hans* (2), *Dietmar, Georg, Heinz, Hermann.*

Schmadeke (129) German (**Schmädecke**): **1.** Low German variant of SCHMIED + the diminutive suffix *-ke.* **2.** alternatively, perhpas, from a Czech personal name **Smědek**, from *smědý* 'dark brown'.

Schmader (220) German: see SCHMAUDER.

Schmahl (297) German: variant of SCHMAL.
GIVEN NAMES German 4%. *Heinz, Kurt.*

Schmal (163) German: nickname from Middle High German, Middle Low German *smal* 'small', 'slight', 'thin'.
GIVEN NAMES German 10%. *Kurt* (4), *Ingeborg* (2), *Hans, Katharina.*

Schmale (287) Probably a variant of SCHMAL.
GIVEN NAMES German 4%. *Otto* (2), *Helmut.*

Schmaling (128) North German (**Schmäling**): from a derivative of SCHMAL.

Schmall (273) German: variant spelling of SCHMAL.

Schmaltz (881) German and Jewish: variant spelling of SCHMALZ.

Schmalz (900) **1.** German and Austrian: from Middle High German *smalz* 'tallow', 'grease', 'fat', hence a metonymic occupational name for a chandler. **2.** Jewish (Ashkenazic): nickname from German *Schmalz* or Yiddish *shmalts* 'animal fat'.
GIVEN NAMES German 5%. *Otto* (2), *Alois, Armin, Bernhard, Erwin, Gerhard, Gertraud, Guenter, Heinz, Ignatz, Kurt, Lothar.*

Schmalzried (141) German: topographic name for a 'fat' pasture (i.e., one especially suitable for fattening dairy cattle), from Middle High German *smalz* 'grease' + *ried* 'meadow'.

Schmauch (101) German: variant of SCHMOCK, from Middle High German *smouch* 'smoke'.
GIVEN NAME German 4%. *Christoph.*

Schmauder (102) German (Swabian): of uncertain origin, perhaps a variant of SCHMUDE. The name occurs mostly in Württemberg.
GIVEN NAMES German 8%. *Erwin* (2), *Theodor.*

Schmaus (187) German: nickname for a Jew.
GIVEN NAMES German 4%. *Jutta, Siegfried.*

Schmechel (154) **1.** German: probably a nickname for a small person, related to Old High German *smāhi* 'small', 'negligible'. **2.** Jewish (Ashkenazic): unexplained.
GIVEN NAMES German 6%. *Kurt* (2), *Fritz.*

Schmeck (181) German: **1.** nickname for a gourmet, from Middle High German *smecken* 'to taste'. **2.** from a Sorbian personal name *Smějk*, meaning 'smiler'.
GIVEN NAME German 4%. *Kurt.*

Schmeckpeper (119) German: nickname for someone with a taste for pepper or for a lover of food, from Middle High German *smecken* 'to taste' + *peper* 'pepper'.

Schmeer (142) German: metonymic occupational name for someone who sold fat, from Middle High German, Middle Low German *smer* 'grease', 'fat'.
GIVEN NAME German 5%. *Kurt.*

Schmehl (256) North German: **1.** from a Sorbian personal name based on *smel* 'bold'. **2.** perhaps a metonymic occupational name for a fisherman, related to *Schmel*, a kind of fish.
GIVEN NAMES German 4%. *Hermann, Otto.*

Schmeichel (257) German: nickname for a flatterer, from Middle High German *smeichlen* 'to flatter'.
GIVEN NAMES German 5%. *Erwin, Helmut, Kurt, Rainer.*

Schmeiser (170) Altered spelling of SCHMEISSER.
GIVEN NAME German 4%. *Marliese.*

Schmeisser (126) German (**Schmeisser**): from an agent derivative of Middle High German *smīzen* 'to spread or smear', 'to strike', hence an occupational name for a painter or plasterer, or for a miner using a pickaxe.
GIVEN NAMES German 12%; Scandinavian 5%. *Fritz, Gerhard, Heinz, Kurt.*

Schmeling (651) North German: nickname from Middle Low German *smal* 'narrow', 'slight', 'thin'.
GIVEN NAMES German 4%. *Fritz, Hertha, Horst, Kurt, Udo.*

Schmelter (167) North German: occupational name for a smelter, from an agent derivative of Middle Low German *smelten* 'to smelt metal'.
GIVEN NAMES German 6%. *Kurt* (2), *Arno.*

Schmeltz (267) **1.** German (Bavaria, Franconia, Hesse): occupational name for a smelter, from Middle High German *smelzen* 'to smelt metal'. **2.** German: habitational name from Schmelz in the Saarland or Schmöltz in Bavaria. **3.** Jewish (Ashkenazic): metonymic occupational name for a smelter, from German *Schmelze* 'smelting' (see 1 above).

Schmeltzer (284) German and Jewish (Ashkenazic): variant spelling of SCHMELZER.

Schmelz (296) German and Jewish (Ashkenazic): variant spelling of SCHMELTZ.
GIVEN NAMES German 4%. *Bernd, Guenter.*

Schmelzer (928) German and Jewish (Ashkenazic): occupational name for a smelter, from an agent derivative of Middle High German *smelzen*, German *schmelzen* 'to smelt metal'.
GIVEN NAMES German 5%. *Kurt* (5), *Hans* (3), *Otto* (3), *Franz, Fritz, Jurgen.*

Schmelzle (232) German (Württemberg): diminutive of SCHMALZ.
GIVEN NAMES German 4%. *Ernst, Ulrich.*

Schmenk (127) German: unexplained.

Schmer (140) German: variant of SCHMEER.
GIVEN NAME German 4%. *Gottfried.*

Schmick (463) North German: metonymic occupational name for a maker of whips, or a nickname for a harsh person, from Middle Low German *smicke* 'whip'.

Schmid (5042) South German: variant of SCHMIDT.
GIVEN NAMES German 8%. *Kurt* (10), *Otto* (9), *Erwin* (7), *Hans* (7), *Heinz* (4), *Merwin* (4), *Alois* (3), *Franz* (3), *Fritz* (3), *Guenter* (3), *Hermann* (3), *Johann* (3).

Schmidbauer (149) South German: occupational name for a farmer who was also a blacksmith, from Middle High German *smit* 'smith' + *būr* 'farmer'.
GIVEN NAMES German 8%. *Kurt, Markus.*

Schmidgall (301) German (Württemberg): distinguishing nickname composed of Middle High German *smit* 'blacksmith' + the personal name *Gall* (see GALL 2).

Schmidlin (284) South German: from a diminutive of Middle High German *smit* 'blacksmith', probably denoting a blacksmith who was the son of a blacksmith.

Schmidlkofer (114) German (Bavaria, Austria): occupational name for a farmer who was also a blacksmith, from a diminutive of Middle High German *smit* 'smith' + the suffix *-kofer*, a variant of *-hofer* (see HOFF).

Schmidt (62346) German and Jewish (Ashkenazic): occupational name from Middle High German *smit*, German *Schmied* 'blacksmith'. The German surname is found in many other parts of Europe, from Slovenia to Sweden.
GIVEN NAMES German 5%. *Kurt* (121), *Otto* (64), *Hans* (62), *Erwin* (44), *Gerhard* (24), *Klaus* (24), *Helmut* (23), *Fritz* (19), *Manfred* (17), *Wolfgang* (16), *Ewald* (12), *Gunter* (12).

Schmidtberger (121) German: a distinguishing name for someone named BERGER who was a blacksmith by occupation, or a habitational name for someone from any of several places called Schmidtberg in Bavaria and Switzerland.

Schmidtke (592) German: diminutive of SCHMIDT.
GIVEN NAMES German 8%. *Dieter* (3), *Otto* (2), *Wilhelm* (2), *Dietmar, Erwin, Fritz, Gerhard, Hans, Klaus, Kurt, Manfred.*

Schmied (208) German: variant of SCHMIDT; this is the form of the modern German vocabulary word for blacksmith.
GIVEN NAMES German 9%; French 6%. *Bernhard, Gerhard, Hans, Heinz, Hildegarde, Ingo; Jacques, Michel.*

Schmiedel (155) South German: diminutive of Middle High German *smit* 'blacksmith'. Compare SCHMIDLIN.
GIVEN NAMES German 4%. *Dietmar, Kurt.*

Schmieder (457) German and Jewish (Ashkenazic): variant of SCHMIED, with the addition of the agent suffix *-er*.
GIVEN NAMES German 5%. *Otto* (3), *Claus, Georg, Hans*.

Schmieding (149) North German: variant of SCHMIDT.
GIVEN NAME German 4%. *Juergen*.

Schmieg (224) Variant of SCHMIEGE.

Schmiege (109) German: **1.** topographic name from a word meaning 'bend', 'turn' (in a road or river). **2.** from a Sorbian personal name *Smĕjk*, meaning 'smiler'.

Schmier (129) German: variant of SCHMIEDER.

Schmierer (256) German: nickname from Middle High German *smirer* 'flatterer'.
GIVEN NAMES German 6%. *Gottlieb* (2), *Erna, Frieda, Otto*.

Schmiesing (201) North German: a derivative of **Schmies**, which is a reduced genitive or patronymic form of SCHMIED.

Schminke (102) German: of uncertain origin, perhaps a metonymic occupational name for a maker of cosmetics and ointments, from Middle High German *smicke, sminke* 'make-up'.
GIVEN NAMES German 4%. *Inge, Konrad*.

Schmit (2045) Variant of German SCHMIDT or Dutch SMIT.

Schmith (125) German: variant spelling of SCHMIDT.
GIVEN NAME Scandinavian 5%. *Erik* (2).

Schmits (105) Dutch: variant of SMITS.

Schmitt (14668) South German: variant spelling of SCHMIDT.
GIVEN NAMES German 4%. *Kurt* (15), *Erwin* (13), *Hans* (9), *Dieter* (7), *Gerhard* (5), *Alfons* (4), *Bernhard* (4), *Franz* (4), *Heinz* (4), *Helmut* (4), *Otto* (4), *Bernd* (3).

Schmitter (222) German: occupational name for someone who owned or worked at a forge, from Middle High German *smitte* 'forge' + agent suffix *-er*.
GIVEN NAMES German 9%. *Otto* (2), *Ernst, Kurt, Markus, Monika*.

Schmittou (153) Origin unidentified.

Schmitz (9564) German (Rhineland): variant or patronymic form of SCHMIDT.
GIVEN NAMES German 4%. *Kurt* (16), *Hans* (6), *Dieter* (4), *Erwin* (4), *Heinrich* (4), *Helmut* (4), *Johann* (3), *Manfred* (3), *Alois* (2), *Florian* (2), *Fritz* (2), *Gerhard* (2).

Schmitzer (194) German: **1.** occupational name from the dialect word *smitzen* 'to dye hides'. **2.** nickname for an impatient person, from Middle High German *smitzen* 'to go fast'.
GIVEN NAMES German 4%. *Alois* (2), *Kurt*.

Schmock (116) North German: variant of SCHMAUCH, from Middle Low German *smōk* 'smoke', 'haze', a metonymic occupational name for a charcoal burner or a coal miner.

Schmoker (199) North German (**Schmöker**): from Low German *smöker* 'smoker', a metonymic occupational name for a charcoal burner.

Schmoldt (210) North German: from Middle Low German *smolt* 'tallow', 'fat', 'grease', hence a metonymic occupational name for a chandler.
GIVEN NAMES German 5%. *Hans* (2), *Gunter, Ingo, Kurt*.

Schmoll (593) German: of uncertain origin. It may be a nickname from a South German dialect word meaning 'lump of lard'. In eastern Germany, it could be a metonymic occupational name for a pitch boiler, from a Slavic word akin to Polish *smoła* 'pitch'.
GIVEN NAMES German 4%. *Fritz* (2), *Gerhard, Helmuth, Kurt, Rudi*.

Schmotzer (147) South German (also **Schmötzer**): either a nickname for a dirty person, from Middle High German *smotzen* 'to make greasy', or from the noun *smotz* 'grease', an occupational name for a dealer in grease.

Schmoyer (404) Origin unidentified.

Schmuck (554) **1.** German and Austrian: from Middle High German *smuc* 'jewel', 'finery', hence a metonymic occupational name for a jeweler, or a nickname for someone who wore a prominent jewel or ornament. **2.** North German: nickname from Middle Low German *smuck* 'neat', 'dainty'.
GIVEN NAMES German 7%. *Erwin, Hans, Heinz, Helmut, Hermann, Jurgen, Kurt, Mathias, Nikolaus, Reinhard*.

Schmucker (743) South German: nickname from an agent derivative of Middle High German *smucken* 'to cuddle', 'to kiss'.

Schmude (174) North German: from Middle Low German *smūden* 'to roast', a nickname either for a cook or for someone feeling hot.
GIVEN NAMES German 5%. *Ewald, Kurt, Otto*.

Schmuhl (198) German: **1.** metonymic occupational name for a pitch boiler, from a Slavic word akin to Polish *smoła* 'pitch'. Compare SCHMOLL. **2.** from the Hebrew personal name SAMUEL, which in some instances was used as a generic term for a Jew.

Schmunk (220) German: unexplained.

Schmutz (376) **1.** South German and Jewish (Ashkenazic): nickname for a dirty or slovenly person, from German *Schmutz* 'dirt', Middle High German *smuz*. **2.** South German: nickname for a cheerful person, from a noun derivative of Middle High German *smutzen* 'to smile'.
GIVEN NAMES German 7%. *Fritz* (3), *Gerhard* (2), *Hans*.

Schmutzler (194) South German: nickname for a cheerful person, from an agent derivative of Middle High German *smutzen* 'to smile in amusement'.
GIVEN NAMES German 5%. *Kurt* (2), *Erwin*.

Schnabel (1336) German and Jewish (Ashkenazic): nickname for a gossip or a glutton, from Middle High German *snabel*, German *Schnabel* 'beak', 'mouth'.
GIVEN NAMES German 6%. *Otto* (3), *Florian* (2), *Frieda* (2), *Kurt* (2), *Bodo, Claus, Dieter, Fritz, Hans, Hermann, Juergen, Markus*.

Schnable (131) Americanized spelling of SCHNABEL.
GIVEN NAMES German 5%. *Kurt, Trud*.

Schnack (221) North German: nickname for a talkative person, from Middle Low German *snacken* 'to chatter'.
GIVEN NAMES German 9%. *Franz, Fritz, Guenther, Helmut, Inge, Klaus, Otto*.

Schnackenberg (209) German: variant of SCHNAKENBERG.
GIVEN NAMES German 4%. *Fritz, Hermann*.

Schnaible (124) German (Württemberg): from a diminutive of an agent derivative of Middle High German *snouwen* 'to breathe heavily', hence a nickname for someone who easily became breathless, or for a snorer.
GIVEN NAMES German 6%. *Ernst, Otto*.

Schnaidt (143) South German: variant of SCHNEID.
GIVEN NAMES German 6%. *Otto* (2), *Kurt*.

Schnake (205) **1.** South German: nickname for a small or annoying person, from Middle High German *snāke* 'midge', 'gnat'. **2.** North German: nickname for a sly, stealthy, or malicious person, from Middle Low German *snake* 'snake'.

Schnakenberg (236) German: habitational name from places so named, in southern Germany from Middle High German *snāke* 'gnat'; in northern Germany from Middle Low German *snake* 'snake' + Middle Low German *berg* 'hill', 'mountain'.
GIVEN NAMES German 10%. *Kurt* (3), *Eldor, Juergen, Wilhelm*.

Schnall (252) German and Jewish (Ashkenazic): metonymic occupational name for a maker of buckles, Middle High German *snalle*, German *Schnalle*.
GIVEN NAMES Jewish 8%. *Avrohom* (2), *Emanuel, Leser, Meyer, Ra zel, Yael*.

Schnapp (281) German: nickname for a chatterer, from Middle High German *snappen* 'to chatter'.

Schnare (108) Altered spelling of German SCHNARR.

Schnarr (315) German: metonymic occupational name for a rope maker, from Middle Low German, Middle High German *snar* 'string', 'cord'.

Schnaufer (144) German: nickname for someone who has difficulty breathing, from Middle High German *snūfer* 'someone who pants or puffs'.
GIVEN NAME German 5%. *Theodor*.

Schnautz (123) Jewish (Ashkenazic): from German *Schnauze* 'muzzle', one of unflattering names selected from vocabulary

words by non-Jewish government officials when surnames were made compulsory.
GIVEN NAME Jewish 4%. *Isadore*.

Schneberger (180) Variant spelling of German SCHNEEBERGER.

Schnebly (167) **1.** Americanized spelling of South German **Schnäbele**, **Schnäbeli(n)**, a diminutive of SCHNABEL. **2.** Possibly an altered form of Swiss German **Schneebeli** or **Schnebli**, a nickname for a white-haired person, from derivative of Middle High German *snē, snēw* 'snow'.

Schneck (1057) German and Jewish (Ashkenazic): affectionate nickname for a slow person or for a slow or indolent worker, from Middle High German *snecke*, German *Schneck(e)*, Yiddish *shnek* 'snail'.

Schneckloth (155) Altered spelling of German SCHNEEKLOTH.

Schnee (414) **1.** German and Jewish (Ashkenazic): from German *Schnee* 'snow', Middle High German *snē, snēw*, a nickname for someone with white hair or an exceptionally pale complexion. The Jewish name is mainly of ornamental origin. **2.** German: habitational name from any of several places in Lower Saxony and Westphalia named Schnee.
GIVEN NAMES German 4%. *Otto* (3), *Florian*, *Frieda, Udo*.

Schneeberg (102) **1.** German and Jewish (Ashkenazic): habitational name from any of several places in Germany, Bohemia, and Austria named Schneeberg. **2.** Jewish (Ashkenazic): ornamental name composed of German *Schnee* 'snow' + *Berg* 'mountain'.
GIVEN NAME German 5%. *Kurt*.

Schneeberger (412) German: habitational name for someone from any of the places called SCHNEEBERG.

Schneekloth (154) North German: from Middle Low German *snē* 'snow' + *klōt* 'lump', 'clod', perhaps a nickname for a fat, pale person. Compare SNOWBALL.
GIVEN NAMES German 4%. *Heinz, Kurt*.

Schneeman (163) German (**Schneemann**): habitational name for someone from Schneen near Göttingen or Schnee (see SCHNEE 2), with the addition of Middle High German *man* 'man'.
GIVEN NAMES German 8%. *Kurt, Otto*.

Schneid (156) **1.** South German: topographic name from Middle High German *sneite* 'boundary path in a forest', or a habitational name from a place named with this word. **2.** Jewish (Ashkenazic): metonymic occupational name from German *Schneide* 'blade'.
GIVEN NAMES German 8%; Jewish 4%. *Helmut* (2), *Hans, Kurt*; *Emanuel, Haim, Sol*.

Schneider (44215) German and Jewish (Ashkenazic): occupational name for a tailor, literally 'cutter', from Middle High German *snīder*, German *Schneider*, Yiddish *shnayder*. The same term was sometimes used to denote a woodcutter. This name is widespread throughout central and eastern Europe.
GIVEN NAMES German 4%. *Kurt* (98), *Hans* (32), *Otto* (31), *Franz* (23), *Erwin* (19), *Fritz* (13), *Dieter* (10), *Manfred* (10), *Heinz* (9), *Alois* (8), *Ewald* (8), *Helmut* (7).

Schneiderhan (108) German: occupational name meaning 'Tailor John', from SCHNEIDER + *Han*, a reduced form of JOHANN.
GIVEN NAMES German 7%. *Kurt, Markus*.

Schneiderman (825) German and Jewish (Ashkenazic): variant of SCHNEIDER, with the addition of Middle High German, Middle Low German, Yiddish *man* 'man'.
GIVEN NAMES Jewish 5%. *Sol* (3), *Hyman* (2), *Ari, Meyer, Miriam, Rochel, Yael, Yudel*.

Schneiders (117) North German: patronymic from SCHNEIDER.
GIVEN NAME German 4%. *Wolfgang*.

Schneidewind (148) German: from Middle High German *snīden* 'to cut' + *wind* 'wind', probably a nickname for a vagrant or itinerant worker.
GIVEN NAMES German 7%. *Erwin, Frieda, Gerda*.

Schneidman (102) German: occupational name for a tailor, literally 'cut man' (see SCHNEIDER).

Schneier (221) **1.** German: habitational name for someone from a place called Schney, to the south of Coburg. **2.** Jewish (Ashkenazic): from the Yiddish male personal name *Shneyer*, ultimately derived from Latin *senior*.
GIVEN NAMES Jewish 4%. *Avi, Ephraim, Hyman*.

Schneiter (271) German: variant of SCHNEID.

Schnell (2899) German and Jewish (Ashkenazic): nickname for a brisk or active person, from Middle High German *snell*, German *schnell* 'quick'.
GIVEN NAMES German 4%. *Fritz* (4), *Hans* (4), *Erwin* (2), *Kurt* (2), *Othmar* (2), *Ernst, Franz, Frieda, Friedrich, Hanspeter, Hartmut, Helmuth*.

Schnelle (425) German: variant of SCHNELL.

Schneller (572) **1.** German: nickname for a swift runner, from an agent derivative of Middle High German *snellen* 'to hurry'. The word in Middle High German also had other meanings, including 'penis', so there is also the possibility of an obscene nickname. **2.** Jewish (Ashkenazic): nickname for a brisk or active man, from an inflected of German *schnell* 'quick'. Compare SCHNELL.

Schnepf (322) **1.** German: from Middle High German *snepfe* 'snipe', perhaps a metonymic occupational name for a birdcatcher, or a nickname from some characteristic of the bird. **2.** Jewish (Ashkenazic): ornamental name from German *Schnepf* 'snipe'.
GIVEN NAMES German 4%. *Elfriede, Fritz, Kurt*.

Schnepp (375) North German form of SCHNEPF 1.

Schnepper (113) South German: nickname for a chatterer, from an agent derivative of Middle High German *snappen* 'to chatter'.
GIVEN NAME German 4%. *Willi*.

Schnettler (164) German (Westphalia): variant of SCHNEIDER.
GIVEN NAMES German 4%. *Hans, Helmut, Kurt*.

Schnetzer (176) German: variant of SCHNITZER.
GIVEN NAMES German 7%. *Erwin, Manfred, Otto*.

Schnetzler (115) German: variant of SCHNITZER.

Schneyer (120) Variant of SCHNEIER.

Schnick (183) German: either from Middle Low German *snicke* 'small ship', presumably a metonymic occupational name for a sailor, or from Middle High German *sneck* 'snail', a nickname for a slow person.
GIVEN NAMES German 4%. *Ernst, Otto*.

Schnider (215) German: variant of SCHNEIDER.
GIVEN NAMES German 4%. *Erwin, Otto*.

Schnieder (262) North German and American variant of SCHNEIDER.
GIVEN NAMES German 6%. *Bernd* (2), *Franz* (2), *Helmut*.

Schnieders (323) North German: patronymic from SCHNIEDER.

Schnier (146) **1.** North German: variant of SCHNEIDER. **2.** Jewish (Ashkenazic): from southern Yiddish *shnir* 'cord', 'rope' (see SCHNUR).
GIVEN NAMES French 7%. *Jacques* (2), *Camille*.

Schnipke (152) probably an altered form of German SCHNITTKER, or a nickname for someone with a conspicuous cap, from Low German *snip* 'tip (on a cap)'.

Schnitker (274) Variant of German SCHNITTKER.
GIVEN NAMES German 4%. *Bernd* (2), *Detmar*.

Schnittker (142) North German: occupational name from Middle Low German *sniddeker* 'joiner' or 'woodcarver'.
GIVEN NAME German 4%. *Klaus*.

Schnitz (125) German: variant of SCHNITZER.

Schnitzer (781) German and Jewish (Ashkenazic): occupational name for a woodworker, from an agent derivative of Middle High German *snitzen*, German *schnitzen* 'to cut or carve'.
GIVEN NAMES Jewish 5%; German 4%. *Hillel* (3), *Chaim* (2), *Avraham, Leib, Meyer, Myer, Shraga, Sol, Zev*; *Wolf* (2), *Ernst, Kurt, Math, Willi*.

Schnitzius (113) German: occupational name for a woodworker, from a Latinized form of SCHNITZER.

Schnitzler (459) German and Jewish (Ashkenazic): variant of SCHNITZER 'woodworker'.
GIVEN NAMES German 5%; Jewish 4%. *Hans* (2), *Kurt* (2), *Manfred* (2), *Helmut*; *Aharon*,

Aron, Chaim, Hershy, Meyer, Moshe, Sholom.

Schnobrich (158) South German: from a Germanic personal name composed of the elements *snot* 'wise' + *berht* 'bright'.
GIVEN NAMES German 5%. *Erwin* (2), *Eldor, Florian.*

Schnoebelen (207) German (**Schnöbelen**): Swabian variant of **Schneble** (see SCHNEBLY).

Schnoll (124) Jewish (eastern Ashkenazic): ornamental name from Yiddish *shnol* 'buckle'.
GIVEN NAMES Jewish 6%. *Hyman, Sol.*

Schnoor (611) North German: metonymic occupational name for a rope maker, from Middle Low German *snōr* 'string', 'cord' (see SCHNUR).
GIVEN NAMES German 5%. *Hans* (2), *Egon, Joerg, Kurt, Otto, Ulrich.*

Schnorr (296) German: variant of SCHNURR.

Schnupp (132) German: nickname from a derivative of Middle High German *snouwen* 'to breathe heavily'. Compare SCHNAIBLE.

Schnur (820) German and Jewish (Ashkenazic): metonymic occupational name for a maker of cords and rope, from Middle High German *snuor*, German *Schnur*, Yiddish *shnur* 'cord', 'rope'.
GIVEN NAMES German 4%. *Elke* (2), *Frieda, Horst, Manfred, Mathias, Reiner.*

Schnurbusch (162) German: nickname for a hunter, from Middle High German *snurren* (of hounds) 'to pick up the quarry's scent' + *busch* 'bush', 'thicket'.

Schnurr (484) German: of uncertain origin, possibly: **1.** occupational name for a jester or a nickname for a prankster, from Middle High German *snurrære* 'jester'. **2.** occupational name for a busker, one who begged by playing the *Schnurrpfeife*, an instrument similar to a penny whistle. **3.** metonymic occupational name for a night-watchman, from Middle High German *snurre* 'rattle'; night-watchmen carried rattles.
GIVEN NAMES German 4%. *Bernhard, Klaus, Otto, Uwe, Wolfgang.*

Schnyder (172) Americanized or Dutch spelling of SCHNEIDER.
GIVEN NAMES German 4%. *Kurt, Manfred.*

Schobel (162) German (also **Schöbel**; Württemberg): variant of SCHAUBLE.
GIVEN NAME German 4%. *Hans.*

Schober (900) German and Austrian: topographic name for someone who lived near or worked in a barn, from Middle High German *schober* 'barn', 'haystack'.
GIVEN NAMES German 5%. *Horst* (2), *Kurt* (2), *Otto* (2), *Dietrich, Erhard, Erwin, Hans, Helmut, Johann, Manfred.*

Schobert (243) German: **1.** (**Schöbert**): variant of SCHOBER. **2.** variant of SCHUBERT.

Schoch (1148) **1.** South German: topographic name from Middle High German *schoche* 'barn', 'haystack' (compare

SCHOBER). **2.** Dutch and German: variant of SCHOCK.
GIVEN NAMES German 6%. *Otto* (4), *Kurt* (3), *Hans* (2), *Arno, Erwin, Franz, Fritz, Gerhard, Wieland, Wilhelm.*

Schochet (113) Jewish (eastern Ashkenazic): occupational name for a ritual slaughterer, Yiddish *shoykhet* (of Hebrew origin).
GIVEN NAMES Jewish 11%. *Sol* (2), *Ari, Chaim, Chana.*

Schock (1637) **1.** German (**Schöck**): variant of SCHECK 1. **2.** Dutch and German: from Middle Dutch *schoc*, Middle High German *schoc* 'pile', 'heap', 'stack'. Compare SCHOCH 1.
GIVEN NAMES German 4%. *Gottlieb* (2), *Woldemar* (2), *Arno, Erhard, Erwin, Ewald, Frieda, Friedrich, Gerhard, Gottfried, Kurt, Oskar.*

Schoeberl (111) South German: diminutive of SCHOBER.

Schoeck (163) German (**Schöck**): see SCHECK 1.

Schoedel (169) German (**Schödel**): Bavarian variant of **Schädel** (see SCHADEL).

Schoeder (111) German (**Schöder**): habitational name for someone from a place called Schoden near Trier in the Palatinate, or a variant of SCHEIDER 1, possibly also denoting a gold-washer.

Schoeff (131) German (**Schöff**): in most cases a variant of SCHIFF; in some cases an occupational name from Middle High German *scheffe* 'lay assessor at a court, juror' (Modern German *Schiffe*).

Schoeffel (108) German: variant of SCHAEFFLER.
GIVEN NAMES German 5%. *Dietmar, Erwin.*

Schoeffler (212) South German (**Schöffler**): variant of SCHAEFFLER.
GIVEN NAMES German 6%; French 4%. *Klaus* (2), *Franz, Otto; Andre, Edmound.*

Schoeler (103) North German (**Schöler**): variant of SCHOLER 1.

Schoell (119) German: a variant or altered form of SCHOLL or a shortened form of a name formed with this element (see for example SCHOELLKOPF), or of SCHELL.

Schoeller (254) **1.** North German: variant of SCHOELER. **2.** South German (**Schöller**): nickname for a loud or noisy person, from an agent derivative of Middle High German *schel* 'loud'.
GIVEN NAMES German 4%. *Hans, Kurt, Otto.*

Schoellkopf (124) German (**Schöllkopf**): variant of SCHOELLER, or a nickname for a nitwit, from Middle High German dialect *schol* 'shallow', 'flat' + *kopf* (standardized form) 'head'.
GIVEN NAMES German 11%. *Jochem* (2), *Elke, Juergen, Otto.*

Schoemaker (131) Dutch: occupational name for a shoemaker, Middle Dutch *scoemaker(e).*

Schoemann (114) German: **1.** variant of SCHUMANN 'shoemaker'. **2.** North Ger-

man (**Schömann**) and Dutch: variant of SCHUENEMANN.

Schoemer (104) German (**Schömer**): of uncertain origin; probably in Bavaria a nickname for someone given to insulting, from Middle High German *schemen* 'to shame or abuse'.
GIVEN NAMES German 6%. *Grete, Hans.*

Schoen (3429) **1.** German (**Schön**): nickname for a handsome or pleasant man, from Middle High German *schoene* 'fine', 'beautiful'; 'refined', 'friendly', 'nice'. **2.** Jewish (Ashkenazic): ornamental name from the same vocabulary word as in 1, in any of its senses. **3.** Dutch: metonymic occupational name for a shoemaker, from *schoen* 'shoe'.
GIVEN NAMES German 5%. *Kurt* (12), *Otto* (7), *Erwin* (3), *Manfred* (3), *Fritz* (2), *Gerhard* (2), *Arno, Bernhard, Elke, Erdmann, Ewald, Heinz.*

Schoenbachler (111) German (**Schönbächler**): topographic name for someone who lived by a 'pretty stream' (German *schön bächlein*).
GIVEN NAMES German 8%. *Alfons, Meinrad.*

Schoenbauer (109) German: apparently a nickname from a compound of Middle High German *schœn(e)* 'beautiful' + BAUER, perhaps in the sense 'neighbor' rather than 'farmer'.

Schoenbaum (141) Jewish (Ashkenazic): ornamental name composed of German *schön* 'beautiful' + *Baum* 'tree'.
GIVEN NAMES Jewish 6%. *Miriam* (2), *Aron.*

Schoenbeck (322) **1.** North German (**Schönbeck**): topographic name from Middle Low German *schōne* 'beautiful' + *beke* 'creek', or a habitational name from any of numerous places named Schönbeck or Schönebeck. It is also found as a Jewish name, in some cases ornamental rather than habitational. **2.** Belgian: habitational name from places in Belgium named Schoenbeek in Limburg, or Schoonbeek in West Flanders.
GIVEN NAMES German 5%. *Otto* (2), *Guenter, Lorenz.*

Schoenberg (892) **1.** German (**Schönberg**) and Jewish (Ashkenazic): habitational name from any of several places named Schönberg. **2.** Jewish (Ashkenazic): ornamental name from German *schön* 'beautiful' + *Berg* 'mountain', 'hill'.
GIVEN NAMES German 4%; Jewish 4%. *Kurt* (3), *Dieter, Erna, Otto; Meyer* (2), *Hyman, Mendel, Shira, Sol, Zalman.*

Schoenberger (908) German (**Schönberger**) and Jewish (Ashkenazic): habitational name for someone from any of the places named Schönberg (see SCHOENBERG).
GIVEN NAMES German 5%. *Otto* (5), *Hans* (2), *Kurt* (2), *Gunther, Konrad, Ulrich.*

Schoenborn (495) German (**Schönborn**): habitational name from any of numerous places so called in Saxony, Silesia, and the Rhineland.

GIVEN NAMES German 4%. *Aloys, Benno, Gerd, Hans, Kurt.*

Schoendorf (131) **1.** German (**Schöndorf**) and Jewish (Ashkenazic): habitational name from any of numerous places called Schöndorf, named as 'beautiful village'. **2.** Jewish (Ashkenazic): ornamental name from German *schön* 'beautiful' + *Dorf* 'village'.

Schoene (222) German (**Schöne**): variant of SCHOEN 1.

GIVEN NAMES German 14%. *Bodo, Franziska, Gunter, Heinz, Hermann, Horst, Juergen, Kaethe, Rainer, Reiner.*

Schoeneberg (103) German (**Schöneberg**): variant of **Schönberg** (see SCHOENBERG).

GIVEN NAMES German 5%. *Johann, Otto.*

Schoeneck (193) German (**Schöneck**): habitational name from any of various places so named, from Middle High German *schœn* 'beautiful' + *ecke* 'corner'.

GIVEN NAMES German 6%. *Otto (3), Johann.*

Schoenecker (352) German (**Schönecker**): habitational name for someone from any of the various places called Schöneck (see SCHOENECK).

Schoeneman (301) German: variant spelling of SCHOENEMANN.

GIVEN NAMES German 4%. *Erwin (2), Kurt (2).*

Schoenemann (156) German (**Schönemann**): derivative of SCHOEN 1, with the addition of Middle High German *man* 'man'.

GIVEN NAMES German 9%. *Kurt (2), Otto, Theodor.*

Schoenenberger (114) German (**Schönenberger**): habitational name for someone from any of several places in Germany and Switzerland named Schönenberg.

GIVEN NAME German 5%. *Alfons.*

Schoener (508) German (**Schöner**): variant of SCHOEN 1.

Schoenfeld (1670) **1.** German (**Schönfeld**): habitational name from any of numerous places named Schönfeld, from Middle High German *schoen* 'beautiful' + *velt* 'open country', 'field'. **2.** Jewish (Ashkenazic): ornamental name composed of German *schön* 'beautiful' + *Feld* 'field'.

GIVEN NAMES German 5%. *Kurt (3), Otto (3), Ernst (2), Erwin (2), Franz (2), Klaus (2), Adelheid, Eugen, Frieda, Fritz, Gerhard, Hanns.*

Schoenfelder (440) German (**Schönfelder**): habitational name for someone from any of numerous places named Schönfeld.

Schoenfeldt (228) German: variant spelling of SCHOENFELD.

GIVEN NAMES German 6%. *Otto (2), Arno, Kurt.*

Schoenhals (192) German: nickname from Middle High German *schœn* 'beautiful' + *hals* 'neck'.

Schoenherr (573) German (**Schönherr**): nickname for someone who gave himself airs and graces, from Middle High German *schœn* 'fine' (see SCHOEN 1) + *herre* 'lord', 'gentleman'.

GIVEN NAMES German 7%. *Klaus (3), Ernst (2), Kurt (2), Dieter, Ewald, Helmut, Ulrich.*

Schoenig (145) German (**Schönig**): probably a habitational name from any of several places named Schöning or Schöningen.

Schoenike (127) German: nickname from a pet form of SCHOEN 'handsome'.

Schoening (797) **1.** North German: patronymic from SCHOEN 1. **2.** habitational name (see SCHOENIG).

GIVEN NAMES German 7%. *Kurt (5), Klaus (4), Heinz (3), Alois, Frieda, Gunther, Hans, Hertha.*

Schoenleber (139) South German (**Schönleber**): nickname for someone who led a comfortable or luxurious life, from Middle High German *schœn* 'fine' (see SCHOEN 1) + an agent derivative of *leben* 'to liver'.

Schoenly (106) Swiss German: nickname from a pet form of SCHOEN 'handsome'.

Schoenrock (358) **1.** German (**Schönrock**): metonymic occupational name for a baker, from Middle High German *schœn* 'fine' (see SCHOEN 1) + *rogge* 'rye'. **2.** German: nickname for a wearer of fine clothes, from Middle High German *schœn* + *rock* 'coat'. **3.** Jewish (Ashkenazic): nickname or ornamental name composed of German *schön* 'beautiful' + *Rock* 'jacket', 'frock coat'.

GIVEN NAMES German 5%. *Erwin (2), Kurt (2), Irmgard.*

Schoenstein (142) **1.** German (**Schönstein**): locational or habitational name, from any of numerous places named Schönstein, from Middle High German *schœn* + *stein* 'stone', 'rock'. **2.** Jewish (Ashkenazic): ornamental name composed of German *schön* 'beautiful' + *Stein* 'stone'; in some cases it may be habitational (see 1).

GIVEN NAMES German 4%. *Erwin, Otto.*

Schoenthal (146) **1.** German (**Schönthal**) and Jewish (Ashkenazic): topographic name from Middle High German *schœn* 'beautiful' + *tal* 'valley', or a habitational name from any of several places called Schönthal or Schöntal. **2.** Jewish (Ashkenazic): ornamental name composed of German *schön* 'beautiful' + *Tal* 'valley', or a habitational name for someone from a place named with these elements (see 1 above).

GIVEN NAME German 5%. *Gerhard (2).*

Schoenthaler (149) German (**Schönthaler**) and Jewish (Ashkenazic): habitational name for someone from a place called Schoenthal or topographic name for

someone living in a beautiful valley (see SCHOENTHAL).

Schoenwald (207) **1.** German (**Schönwald**) and Jewish (Ashkenazic): habitational name from any of several places named Schönwald. **2.** Jewish (Ashkenazic): ornamental name composed of German *schön* 'beautiful' + *Wald* 'forest'.

Schoenwetter (156) German (**Schönwetter**): nickname for someone with a happy disposition, from Middle High German *schœn* 'beautiful', 'fine', 'nice' + *wetter* 'weather'.

Schoepf (197) German: variant of **Schöpf** (see SCHOPF) 2.

Schoepflin (132) South German (**Schöpflin**): diminutive of **Schöpf** (see SCHOPF 1).

GIVEN NAMES German 7%. *Erwin, Hans, Otto.*

Schoepke (219) German (Silesian): from a pet form of the personal name *Stepan, Czepan*, Slavic vernacular forms of Latin *Stephanus* (see STEVEN).

GIVEN NAMES German 4%. *Ewald, Ilse, Otto.*

Schoepp (171) **1.** Dutch: nickname or a metonymic occupational name for a shepherd, from the Limburg dialect word *shoepp* 'sheep'. **2.** North German (**Schöpp**): occupational name for a juryman, Middle Low German *schepe, schepen(e)*.

GIVEN NAME French 4%. *Vernice (2).*

Schoeppner (178) **1.** South German: from an agent noun derived from Middle High German *schope* (from Italian *giubba*, Modern German *Joppe*), denoting a kind of overcoat, hence a metonymic occupational name for a maker of such coats. **2.** North German (**Schöppner**): occupational name for a juryman (see SCHOEPP 2).

GIVEN NAME German 5%. *Otto (2).*

Schoer (101) North German (**Schöer**): occupational name for a shoemaker, from Middle Low German *schō* 'shoe' + agent suffix *-er*.

GIVEN NAME German 4%. *Karl-Heinz.*

Schoessler (123) North German: variant of SCHUESSLER.

GIVEN NAME German 4%. *Kurt.*

Schoessow (140) Eastern German (**Schössow**): variant of SCHOSSOW. The Schössows come from the Kammin area; in the U.S. they are located mainly in WI.

GIVEN NAMES German 9%. *Eldor, Gerhard, Kurt.*

Schoettle (205) German (**Schöttle**): from a diminutive of *schotte* 'peddler', originally 'Scotsman', which acquired the additional meaning 'peddler' in German because many so peddlers were from Scotland (see SCHOTT 1).

GIVEN NAMES German 9%. *Kurt (2), Ekkehard, Manfred, Ulrich.*

Schoettler (129) North German (**Schöttler**): occupational name for a wood turner, Middle Low German *scoteler* (an agent derivative of *scotel* 'wooden bowl').

GIVEN NAME French 4%. *Patrice.*

Schoettmer (114) German (**Schöttmer**): habitational name for someone from Schötmar in the Lippe area.

Schoewe (101) North German (**Schöwe**): from a nickname for a tall, thin person, *Schowe*, the current form of which is *Schaub*, derived from or related to Middle Low German *schōf* 'sheaf of straw'.

Schofer (113) German: of uncertain origin; as a variant of **Schoffer**, see SCHAFFER; for **Schöfer**, a variant of **Schäfer**, see SCHAEFER.

Schoff (429) German: **1.** variant of SCHAUB. **2.** Occupational name for a juryman (see SCHOEFF). **3.** Possibly a variant spelling of **Schaf** (see SCHAAF).

Schoffstall (245) Altered spelling of German **Schafstall**, probably a metonymic occupational name for a shepherd or a maker of hurdles, from Middle High German *schāf* 'sheep' + *stall* 'stall', 'pen'.

Schofield (4736) English (mainly northern): habitational name from any of various minor places, in Lancashire and elsewhere, named from Middle English *sc(h)ole* 'hut' (see SCALES) + *feld* 'pasture', 'open country'.

Scholar (137) English and Scottish: **1.** nickname for a person who could read and write, at a time when education was the exception rather than the rule. **2.** According to Reaney, a local name from Old Norse *skáli* 'hut' + *erg* 'shieling'.

Scholer (271) **1.** German: status name from Middle Low German *schōler* 'scholar', 'pupil' (especially one studying to be a clergyman). **2.** German: nickname for someone with money, Middle High German *scholære*. **3.** English: variant spelling of SCHOLAR.

GIVEN NAMES Scandinavian 5%. *Knud, Niels.*

Scholes (638) Northern English: topographic name from northern Middle English *sc(h)ole* 'hut', 'shed' (see SCALES), or a habitational name from one of the various places named with this word, as for example Scholes in South Yorkshire.

Scholfield (216) English: variant of SCHOFIELD.

Scholl (3833) **1.** German and Dutch: nickname for a lumpish person or a farmer, from Middle High German, Middle Dutch *scholle* 'clod of earth'. **2.** Dutch and North German: from Middle Dutch *scholle*, *schulle* 'flounder', 'plaice', hence a metonymic occupational name for a fisherman or a fish seller, or a nickname for someone thought to resemble a flouder. **3.** German (**Schöll**): variant of SCHELL.

Scholle (306) Dutch and North German: variant of SCHOLL 1 and 2.

GIVEN NAMES German 5%. *Ilse* (2), *Bernhard, Kurt, Manfred.*

Schollenberger (108) South German: habitational name for someone from a place called Schollenberg, a compound of Middle High German *scholle* 'clod' + *berg* 'mountain'.

Scholler (208) **1.** German: variant of SCHOLL 1 or 2, with the addition of the agent suffix -*er*. **2.** South German (**Schöller**): variant of SCHELLER.

GIVEN NAMES German 5%. *Kurt, Lorenz, Markus.*

Schollmeyer (171) German: nickname for a farmer, from Middle High German *scholle* 'clod of earth' + *meier* '(tenant) farmer'.

GIVEN NAMES German 8%. *Arno* (2), *Kurt* (2).

Scholnick (125) Jewish: variant spelling of SKOLNICK.

GIVEN NAMES Jewish 10%; German 4%. *Meyer* (2), *Sol.*

Scholten (973) Dutch: from the genitive form of the Middle Dutch status name *scholte*, *schulte* 'village headman'.

GIVEN NAMES Dutch 4%. *Gerrit* (8), *Dirk* (2), *Bastian, Berend, Gradus, Harmen, Hendrick, Jacobus, Willem, Wim.*

Scholtens (126) Dutch: variant of SCHOLTEN.

Scholtes (262) Dutch and North German: status name from Middle High German *schultheize* 'village headman' (see SCHULTZ).

Scholtz (516) Eastern German: variant of SCHULTZ 1.

GIVEN NAMES German 5%. *Erwin* (2), *Annelies, Eberhard, Ewald, Wilhelm.*

Scholz (2224) Eastern German: variant of SCHULTZ 1.

GIVEN NAMES German 11%. *Dieter* (7), *Kurt* (6), *Gerhard* (4), *Klaus* (4), *Wolfgang* (4), *Erwin* (3), *Gerd* (3), *Heinz* (3), *Helmut* (3), *Horst* (3), *Otto* (3), *Alfons* (2).

Scholze (217) German: variant of SCHULTZ 1.

GIVEN NAMES German 8%. *Erwin, Hans, Rainer, Uwe, Volker.*

Schomaker (469) North German: occupational name for a shoemaker, from Middle Low German *scho* 'shoe' + an agent derivative of *maken* 'to make'.

GIVEN NAMES German 5%. *Guenter* (2), *Guenther.*

Schomberg (168) German (also **Schömberg**): and Jewish (Ashkenazic): habitational name from places in Thuringia, Württemberg, and Silesia called Schomberg or Schömberg.

Schomburg (359) German: habitational name from Schomberg in Württemberg, or from any of the places called Schaumburg, near Hameln, in Hesse, and in Brandenburg.

GIVEN NAMES German 6%. *Fritz* (3), *Armin, Guenther, Reinhard.*

Schomer (383) **1.** German (mostly **Schömer**; Bavarian): nickname for an offensive person, from an agent derivative of Middle High German *schemen* 'to insult'. **2.** Jewish (Ashkenazic): occupational name from Hebrew *shomer* 'watchman'.

Schommer (846) German (Saar area) and Belgian (Walloon) form of a North German surname, **Schummer**, a nickname for a vagabond or rascal.

Schomp (104) German: probably a variant of SCHAMP 1.

Schon (526) German (**Schön**) and Jewish (Ashkenazic): see SCHOEN.

GIVEN NAMES German 8%. *Kurt* (2), *Mathias* (2), *Otto* (2), *Wilhelm* (2), *Armin, Franz, Gunter, Jurgen, Manfred.*

Schonauer (141) German (**Schönauer**): habitational name for someone from any of several places called Schönau.

GIVEN NAMES German 5%. *Katharina, Manfred.*

Schonberg (243) German (**Schönberg**) and Jewish (Ashkenazic): see SCHOENBERG.

GIVEN NAMES Scandinavian 8%; German 5%. *Erik* (3), *Bent* (2); *Ernst.*

Schonberger (227) German (**Schönberger**) and Jewish (Ashkenazic): see SCHOENBERGER.

GIVEN NAMES Jewish 7%. *Chaim, Emanuel, Isidor.*

Schonbrun (101) Jewish (Ashkenazic): ornamental name from German *schön* 'pretty', 'beautiful' + *Brun(nen)* 'well', 'spring'.

GIVEN NAMES Jewish 16%. *Ari, Aron, Chaim, Hillel, Mendy, Mordechai, Rebekah, Yanky, Yidel, Zev.*

Schone (263) German (**Schöne**): variant of **Schön** (see SCHOEN 1).

Schoneman (218) German (**Schönemann**): see SCHOENEMANN.

Schoner (164) German (**Schöner**): see SCHOENER.

Schonert (120) German (**Schönert**): variant of **Schöner** (see SCHONER), with excrescent -*t*.

Schonfeld (422) German (**Schönfeld**) and Jewish (Ashkenazic): see SCHOENFELD.

GIVEN NAMES Jewish 8%; Jewish Biblical 4%; German 4%. *Chaim* (2), *Yoel* (2), *Aron, Elihu, Hyman, Mordechi, Naftula, Sholom, Sol, Tovia, Zalman*; *Klaus* (2), *Erwin, Gunter, Kurt.*

Schons (219) Perhaps an altered form of German SCHANTZ.

GIVEN NAMES German 4%. *Claus, Mathias.*

Schoo (140) Possibly an altered spelling of German SCHUH.

Schoof (358) **1.** German and Dutch: from Middle Low German *schōf*, Middle Dutch *scoof* 'sheaf', possibly a metonymic occupational name for a sheaf-binder. **2.** Variant of SCHAAF.

Schook (143) Altered spelling of SCHUCK.

School (191) Dutch: topographic name for someone who lived by a school or perhaps someone who taught in one.

Schoolcraft (854) English: topographic name for someone who lived on a plot of land with a hut, from northern Middle

English *sc(h)ole* 'hut', 'shed' (see SCALES) + *croft* 'small enclosed field'.

Schooler (845) Partly Americanized form of German SCHULER.

Schooley (1580) English: of uncertain origin; perhaps a topographic name for someone living on low-lying land (Old English *ēg*) with a hut or temporary shelter (Old Norse *skáli*) on it.

Schoolfield (330) Variant of English SCHOFIELD.

Schooling (141) **1.** English: unexplained; perhaps of the same origin as 2. **2.** Possibly an Americanized form of Dutch **Schoeling**, **Schuiling**, an occupational name for a shoe maker, from Middle Dutch *scoe* + the diminutive suffix *-lin*.

Schoolman (125) Dutch: occupational name for a school teacher.
GIVEN NAMES German 5%. *Kurt, Wolfram.*

Schools (337) Dutch: patronymic from a variant of SCHOLL 1 or 2.

Schoon (619) North German and Dutch: nickname from Middle Low German *schōne*, Middle Dutch *scoon* 'beautiful'. Compare SCHOEN.

Schoonhoven (133) Dutch (**van Schoonhoven**): habitational name for someone from Schoonhoven in South Holland or another place of the same name in Kampenhout in Brabant province, Belgium.
FOREBEARS This name is recorded in Beverwijck in New Netherland (Albany, NY) in the mid 17th century. Geurt Hendrickse van Schoonhoven was a carpenter who came to New Netherland in about 1650.
GIVEN NAMES Dutch 10%. *Andries* (2), *Cornelis, Pieter, Teunis, Wim.*

Schoonmaker (1155) Variant of Dutch SCHOEMAKER.

Schoonover (2966) Dutch: unexplained. Perhaps an altered form of SCHOONHOVEN?

Schoop (116) Dutch: metonymic occupational name for a maker of shovels, spades, and the like, from Middle Dutch *schoepe*, *schope* 'shovel', 'scoop'.

Schoor (102) North German: **1.** from a topographic name for someone who lived on the coast or shore of a body of water, from Middle Low German *schor(e)* 'shore', 'coast', 'coastal land'. **2.** Variant of **Schohr**, from Low German *schōr* 'sheared wool', hence perhaps an occupational name for a sheep shearer or a seller of raw wool.

Schopf (232) **1.** South German: nickname for someone with a wild shock of hair, from Middle High German *schopf* 'tuft (of hair)'. **2.** German (**Schöpf**; Bavarian): status name from Middle High German *schepfe* 'juryman'.

Schopfer (139) South German: topographic name for someone who lived by or in a shed, from Middle High German *schopf* 'shed'.

Schopp (536) **1.** North German: metonymic occupational name for a maker of ladles

and clippers or scoops, from Middle Low German *schōpe* 'ladle'. **2.** German: habitational name from a place so named near Kaiserslautern.

Schoppe (397) **1.** North German: variant of SCHOPP. **2.** Eastern German: from the personal name *Czepan*, a Slavic vernacular form of Latin *Stephanus* (see STEVEN).
GIVEN NAMES German 7%. *Kurt* (4), *Erna, Manfred, Otto.*

Schopper (122) Southern German (Württemberg, Bavaria): **1.** from an agent derivative of Middle High German *schoppen* 'to stuff', possibly an occupational name for someone who stuffed cushions or mattresses. **2.** topographic name for someone who lived by a reed-grown bank, from the dialect word *Schoppen* 'reedbank'. **3.** habitational name for someone from SCHOPP near Kaiserslautern.

Schoppert (135) German (Rhineland): unexplained.

Schor (507) **1.** South German: of uncertain origin; possibly a topographic name related to dialect words meaning either 'rock outcrop' or 'spade'. **2.** Jewish (Ashkenazic): variant of SHOR.
GIVEN NAMES Jewish 5%. *Moshe* (2), *Avraham, Isidor, Jakob, Yisroel.*

Schorer (126) German: **1.** variant of SCHOR. **2.** Habitational name for someone from Schora near Dessau. **3.** (**Schörer**) variant of SCHERER.
GIVEN NAMES German 9%. *Hilde, Manfred, Otto, Wolfgang.*

Schork (205) South German (Baden; also **Schörk**): occupational name for a shoemaker, a much-altered dialect variant of SCHUBERT.

Schorn (270) South German: habitational name from a place so called in Bavaria, or an occupational name for someone who worked with a shovel, from Middle High German *schor* 'shovel'.
GIVEN NAMES German 6%. *Dieter* (2), *Arno, Eldor, Manfred.*

Schornack (100) East German (of Slavic origin): nickname for a black-haired person (compare CZARNY).

Schorr (1197) **1.** German: of uncertain origin; possibly related to Middle Low German *schurren* 'to slide'. **2.** German: in the south a topographic name from Middle High German *schor(re)* 'steep rock', 'rocky shore'. **3.** German (of Slavic origin): nickname for a skillful person, from Slavic *skory* 'quick'. **4.** Jewish (Ashkenazic): variant of SHOR.
GIVEN NAMES Jewish 5%. *Joachim* (2), *Mort* (2), *Moshe* (2), *Pinkus* (2), *Simcha* (2), *Sol* (2), *Avrohom, Chana, Isadore, Menashe, Miriam, Peretz.*

Schorsch (212) German: from a local spelling of the personal name *George* (see GEORGE).

Schorzman (105) German (**Schorzmann**): of uncertain origin, perhaps a habitational

name from an area near Säckingen or from *Skořc*, a Sorbian name.

Schossow (141) Eastern German: habitational name from Schossow in Pomerania, a place name of Slavic origin.

Schott (4054) **1.** German: occupational name for a peddler or a nickname for someone who always had something to sell, from Middle High German *schotte* 'peddler'. **2.** German (**Schött**): metonymic occupational name for a tax collector, from Middle Low German *schot* 'tax'. **3.** Jewish (Ashkenazic): ornamental name from either German *Schotte* 'Scotsman' or German *Schote* 'pod'.

Schou (196) **1.** Danish: topographic name for someone who lived by a small wood, from a Germanized form of Danish *skov* 'wood', 'forest', 'copse'. **2.** Norwegian: see SCHAU.
GIVEN NAMES Scandinavian 18%; German 6%. *Bertel* (2), *Bjorn, Kjeld, Per; Kurt* (2), *Hans.*

Schouest (167) Origin unidentified.

Schoultz (138) Chiefly Danish form of the German surname SCHULTZ.
GIVEN NAMES Scandinavian 6%; German 4%. *Lars, Nils; Kurt.*

Schouten (634) Dutch: variant of SCHOLTEN.
GIVEN NAMES Dutch 5%. *Willem* (4), *Cor, Gerrit, Henk, Kees, Marten, Peiter.*

Schouweiler (138) Luxembourgeois: habitational name from a place called Schouweiler in the Grand Duchy of Luxembourg.

Schow (421) Americanized spelling of German SCHAU.

Schowalter (306) German (Rhineland, Bavaria): unexplained.

Schowengerdt (138) Dutch: unexplained.

Schrack (337) Possibly a variant of German SCHRAG.

Schrad (103) North German: variant of SCHRADE.

Schrade (251) North German: nickname for a skinny person, from Middle Low German *schrade* 'thin', 'wretched', 'scrawny' (see also SCHRAGE).
GIVEN NAMES German 5%; French 4%. *Frieda, Hans, Katharina; Honore* (2), *Frederique.*

Schrader (6685) North German: occupational name for a tailor, Middle Low German *schrāder*. Compare German SCHROEDER.

Schraeder (461) German: variant of **Schräder** (see SCHRADER).

Schraer (122) German: variant of **Schräder** (see SCHRADER).

Schrag (645) **1.** German: variant of SCHRAGE 1. **2.** Jewish (Ashkenazic): variant of SCHRAGE 3.
GIVEN NAMES German 4%. *Erwin* (4), *Frieda* (2), *Horst, Minne.*

Schrage (696) **1.** German: nickname for a tall, thin person, from Middle High German *schrage* 'rack', 'stand', or from the same word in Middle Low German meaning 'scrawny'. **2.** German: from Middle High German, Middle Low German *schrage* 'slanting', by extension used to refer to a market stall with crossed legs, hence an occupational name for a carpenter or a stallholder. **3.** Jewish (Ashkenazic): from the Yiddish personal name *Shrage*, meaning 'candle' in Aramaic.

Schrager (409) **1.** German: from a derivative of SCHRAGE 1 and 2. **2.** Jewish (Ashkenazic): variant of SCHRAGE 3.
GIVEN NAMES Jewish 7%. *Aron, Avrum, Mandel.*

Schram (1898) Variant of German and Jewish SCHRAMM.

Schramek (146) Jewish (Ashkenazic): Germanized spelling of a nickname from Polish *szramek*, a diminutive of *szram* 'scar' (see SCHRAMM).
GIVEN NAME German 4%. *Kurt.*

Schramel (111) German: nickname for someone with a scar, from a pet form SCHRAMM.

Schramer (114) German: variant spelling of **Schrammer**, an occupational name for a miner, from Middle High German *schram* 'crevice in a rock' + agent suffix *-er*.

Schramm (3227) German and Jewish (Ashkenazic): metonymic nickname for a person with a scar, from Middle High German *schram(me)*, German *Schramme*, Yiddish *shram* 'scar'.
GIVEN NAMES German 5%. *Kurt* (9), *Otto* (5), *Gunter* (3), *Ernst* (2), *Erwin* (2), *Gerhard* (2), *Hans* (2), *Heinrich* (2), *Horst* (2), *Armin, Dieter, Elke.*

Schrand (182) North German: variant of SCHRANDT.

Schrandt (197) North German: probably a variant of SCHRAGE, an occupational name for a butcher or baker selling at a stall in a market, from Middle High German *schrande, schrange* 'market stall, table, counter'.
GIVEN NAMES German 4%. *Kurt, Siegfried.*

Schrank (769) **1.** South German: topographic name for someone who lived by a gate or fence, from Middle High German *schranc* 'gate', 'barrier'. **2.** Jewish (Ashkenazic): occupational name from German *Schrank* 'wardrobe', 'closet'.
GIVEN NAMES German 5%. *Kurt* (2), *Erhardt, Erwin, Heinz, Helmut, Horst, Reimund, Wilhelm.*

Schrantz (333) German: nickname for a dandy, from Middle High German *schranz* 'slit', 'crack', 'young man wearing a slit cloak (*schranze*)'.

Schranz (203) German: variant spelling of SCHRANTZ.
GIVEN NAMES German 9%. *Ernst* (2), *Kurt* (2), *Erwin, Monika, Rudi.*

Schratz (112) German (also **Schrätz**): **1.** nickname for someone with a strange appearance, a bogeyman, from Middle High German *schrat* 'goblin', 'specter'. **2.** topographic name from Alemannic *schratt* 'gorge'. **3.** Possibly also a nickname for a greedy person, from Czech *žrac* 'devourer', or a Sorbian cognate.

Schraub (113) German and Jewish (Ashkenazic): from Middle High German *schrūbe*, Middle Low German *schrūve* 'screw', 'nail', 'peg', 'rivet'; German *Schraube* 'screw'; probably a metonymic occupational name for someone who made and sold this hardware or for a carpenter.
GIVEN NAMES German 7%. *Arno, Lorenz.*

Schrauben (123) German: probably a variant of SCHRAUB.

Schraufnagel (249) South German: from a southern variant, *Schrauf*, of standard German *Schraube* 'screw' + Middle High German *nagel* 'nail'; perhaps a metonymic occupational name for a maker of screws and nails.

Schraut (123) German: variant of SCHROTH.
GIVEN NAME German 4%. *Kurt.*

Schrauth (124) German (mainly Franconia): variant of SCHROTH.
GIVEN NAME Russian 4%. *Valeri* (2).

Schray (138) South German (Württemberg): variant of SCHREY.
GIVEN NAMES German 6%. *Kurt, Volker.*

Schrecengost (408) German: see SCHRECKENGOST.

Schreck (1656) German: nickname from Middle High German *schrecken* 'to jump' or 'to frighten'.

Schreckengost (335) Altered form of German **Schreckengast**, a nickname from Middle High German *schreck* (imperative of *schrecken* 'to frighten') + *den gast* 'the guest', presumably a nickname for an unfriendly innkeeper.

Schrecongost (112) Variant spelling of German SCHRECKENGOST.

Schreder (149) North German: variant of **Schräder** (see SCHRADER).
GIVEN NAMES German 4%. *Kurt, Ludwina.*

Schreffler (547) German: topographic name for someone who lived by a split crag, Middle High German *schreffe*.

Schreiber (7248) **1.** German: occupational name for a clerk, from an agent derivative of Middle High German *schrīben* 'to write' (via Old High German from Latin *scribere*). **2.** Jewish (Ashkenazic): from German *Schreiber*, Yiddish *shrayber* 'writer', adopted as a translation of Hebrew SOFFER 'scribe'.
GIVEN NAMES German 4%. *Kurt* (14), *Otto* (11), *Klaus* (8), *Erwin* (4), *Hans* (4), *Ernst* (3), *Gerhard* (3), *Gerhardt* (3), *Bernhard* (2), *Egon* (2), *Eugen* (2), *Franz* (2).

Schreibman (193) Jewish (Ashkenazic): variant of SCHREIBER.
GIVEN NAMES Jewish 4%. *Hyman, Yetta.*

Schreier (969) **1.** German: occupational name for a town crier, or nickname for a noisy individual, from an agent derivative of Middle High German *schrī(e)n* 'to shout'. **2.** Jewish (Ashkenazic): from German *Schreier*, Yiddish *shrayer* 'shouter'; a nickname for a noisy person, or, possibly, an occupational name for a person whose duty it was to summon Jews to public worship.

Schreifels (249) German: topographic name for someone living near a crag or precipice, from *Schreif*, dialect variant of German *Schroff* 'precipice' + *fels* 'rock'.
GIVEN NAMES German 5%. *Eldred* (2), *Aloys, Hans.*

Schreiner (3406) German: occupational name for a joiner, from Middle High German *schrīnære, schrīner*, an agent derivative of *schrīn* 'chest', 'box'. This word and surname are found mainly in southern and southwestern parts of Germany.
GIVEN NAMES German 4%. *Kurt* (11), *Rudi* (4), *Ernst* (2), *Mathias* (2), *Wolfgang* (2), *Aloysius, Christoph, Egon, Gebhard, Georg, Gunter, Gunther.*

Schreiter (195) German: nickname for someone with a striding walk, from an agent derivative of *schreiten* 'to stride'. The element *Schreit* also appears in place names.
GIVEN NAMES German 8%. *Otto* (2), *Eberhard, Heinz, Kurt.*

Schremmer (135) German: variant of **Schrammer**, an occupational name for a miner (see SCHRAMM).
GIVEN NAMES German 12%. *Gerhard* (2), *Kurt, Lutz, Matthias.*

Schremp (217) German: variant of SCHRIMPF.

Schrempp (140) German: variant of SCHRIMPF.

Schrenk (297) German: from Middle High German *schrenk* 'slanting', 'crossed' (from *schrenken* 'to put across', 'to lay diagonally'), possibly a metonymic occupational name for someone who did wickerwork or made fences.
GIVEN NAMES German 5%. *Alois, Juergen, Lorenz.*

Schrepfer (123) German: from Middle High German *schrepfer* 'barber-surgeon's assistant', an agent derivative of *schrepfen* 'to bleed someone'.
GIVEN NAMES German 8%. *Kurt, Reiner, Willi.*

Schreuder (106) Dutch: occupational name for a tailor. Compare German SCHROEDER.
GIVEN NAMES Dutch 8%; German 5%; French 5%. *Harm* (2), *Willem; Hans, Hermann; Normand* (2), *Marc.*

Schreur (213) Dutch: occupational name for a tailor, from a reduced form of SCHREUDER.
GIVEN NAMES Dutch 4%; German 4%. *Gerrit* (2), *Cornelis, Harm.*

Schreurs (196) Dutch: variant of SCHREUR.

Schrey (118) North German and Dutch: occupational name for a town crier, or nickname for a noisy individual, from a noun derivative of Middle Dutch *schreien* 'to cry'.
GIVEN NAMES German 10%. *Wolf* (3), *Erwin*, *Joerg*.

Schreyer (322) **1.** German: variant spelling of SCHREIER. **2.** Dutch (**de Schreyer**): occupational name for a town crier, or nickname for a noisy individual, from an agent derivative of Middle Dutch *schreien* 'to cry'. **3.** Jewish (Ashkenazic): variant spelling of SCHREIER.
GIVEN NAMES German 7%. *Kurt* (2), *Gerd*, *Gerlinde*, *Gunter*, *Heinz*, *Ralf*, *Willibald*.

Schriber (347) Variant of German SCHREIBER.

Schrick (212) **1.** German: nickname from Middle High German *schric* 'fright'. **2.** Dutch: either a nickname, cognate with 1, from a noun derivative of Middle Dutch *schricken* 'to frighten', or a reduced form of **van Schrieck**, a habitational name from Schriek in the Belgian province of Antwerp or various minor places so named (from a word meaning 'nook', 'corner', 'bend').
GIVEN NAMES German 5%. *Fritz*, *Gerd*, *Otto*.

Schricker (170) German: from the agent derivative of Middle High German *schricken* 'to hunt', hence an occupational name for a driver in a hunt.
GIVEN NAMES German 7%. *Kurt* (2), *Otto*.

Schrider (143) German: probably an altered spelling of **Schridder**, a variant of **Schridde**, a nickname for a beggar or vagrant, from Middle Low German *schridde*.

Schrieber (333) North German: occupational name for a scribe or clerk, from an agent derivative of Middle Low German *schrīven* 'to write'. Compare SCHREIBER.

Schriefer (305) **1.** North German: variant of SCHRIEBER. **2.** South German: topographic name for someone living near a crag, related to Middle High German *schreffen* 'to split'.
GIVEN NAMES German 6%. *Arno*, *Hans*, *Kurt*, *Otto*, *Volker*.

Schrier (602) Dutch: variant of SCHREYER.

Schriever (346) Dutch and North German: occupational name for a scribe or clerk, from an agent derivative of Middle Dutch, Middle Low German *schrīven* 'to write'. Compare German SCHREIBER.

Schrimpf (245) German: nickname for someone with a conspicuous scar, from Middle High German *schrimpf* 'scratch', 'cut', or possibly for a small person, from a noun derivative of *schrimpfen* 'to shrink or diminish'.

Schrimsher (395) Variant of English **Scrimshaw**, an occupational name for a fencer or fencing-master, from Old French *eskermisseo(u)r* 'fencer', 'skirmisher'. Fencing-masters always found plentiful employment in medieval England, although they were officially banned from the City of London because of their dangerous influence.

Schriner (580) Variant of German SCHREINER.

Schriver (665) Probably an altered spelling of German **Schriever**, a variant spelling of SCHRIEFER 1.

Schroader (227) Americanized spelling of German SCHROEDER.

Schrock (2840) German: **1.** (**Schröck**): variant of SCHRECK or SCHRAGE. **2.** (**Schröck**): habitational name from Schröck near Marburg. **3.** possibly a habitational name from a place called Schrocko in eastern Germany, of Slavic origin. **4.** of Slavic origin, from Sorbia *sroka* 'magpie' (bird), a nickname for someone who had some fancied similarity with the bird.

Schroder (2021) **1.** North German and Scandinavian (**Schröder**): see SCHROEDER. **2.** Dutch: from Middle Dutch *schroder* 'cutter', denoting various occupations, including tailor, minter or finisher of coins (see also SCHROEDER).
GIVEN NAMES German 4%. *Erwin* (4), *Kurt* (4), *Hans* (3), *Klaus* (2), *Darrold*, *Dietrich*, *Erna*, *Frieda*, *Gunther*, *Horst*, *Juergen*, *Otto*.

Schrodt (201) German: variant of SCHROTH.

Schroeck (207) German (**Schröck**): see SCHROCK 1.
GIVEN NAMES German 8%. *Hans* (2), *Kurt* (2), *Fritz*, *Maximilian*.

Schroedel (129) German (**Schrödel**): from a pet form of a short form of a Germanic personal name formed with *skrotan* 'to strike or cut' as the first element.
GIVEN NAMES German 9%. *Guenter*, *Heinz*.

Schroeder (28652) North German (**Schröder**): occupational name for a cloth cutter or tailor, from an agent derivative of Middle Low German *schrōden*, *schrāden* 'to cut'. The same term was occasionally used to denote a gristmiller as well as a shoemaker, whose work included cutting leather, and also a drayman, one who delivered beer and wine in bulk to customers; in some instances the surname may have been acquired in either of these senses. This name is widespread throughout central and eastern Europe.
GIVEN NAMES German 4%. *Kurt* (74), *Otto* (38), *Hans* (32), *Erwin* (20), *Fritz* (9), *Helmut* (6), *Horst* (6), *Alois* (5), *Ernst* (5), *Ewald* (5), *Gerhard* (5), *Klaus* (5).

Schroedl (195) German (**Schrödl**): variant of **Schrödel** (see SCHROEDEL).
GIVEN NAMES German 4%. *Fritz*, *Vogel*.

Schroen (106) Northwest German and Dutch: occupational name for a variety of activities, the same as SCHROEDER, from an agent derivative of *schröen*, a reduced form of *schröden* 'to cut'.
GIVEN NAME German 6%. *Wolfgang*.

Schroepfer (353) German: variant of SCHREPFER.

Schroer (1221) North German: variant of SCHROEDER.

Schroeter (668) North German: variant of SCHROEDER.
GIVEN NAMES German 10%; Scandinavian 4%. *Hans* (2), *Juergen* (2), *Otto* (2), *Elke*, *Ernst*, *Erwin*, *Gerd*, *Gertraud*, *Hermann*, *Ingeborg*, *Klaus*, *Kurt*; *Sven* (2), *Birgit*, *Gorm*, *Niels*.

Schroff (224) South German (Baden): topographic name from Middle High German *schroffe* 'rough rock', 'wall of rock'.
GIVEN NAMES German 6%. *Frieda*, *Kurt*, *Udo*.

Schroll (526) South German: nickname for an ungainly or uncouth person, from Middle High German *schrolle* 'lump', 'clod'.

Schrom (269) German (Silesian): habitational name from a place so named in the area of Frankenstein.
GIVEN NAMES German 5%. *Herta*, *Kurt*, *Otto*.

Schronce (192) Probably an altered spelling of German SCHRAN(T)Z.

Schropp (212) South German: possibly a nickname (of uncertain application) from the Bavarian dialect word *Schropp*, meaning 'pile of earth'.
GIVEN NAMES German 5%. *Kurt* (2), *Manfred*, *Otto*.

Schrotenboer (143) Dutch: a distinguishing nickname meaning 'ammunition farmer' from Dutch *schroten* 'small pieces of metal', i.e. shot, ammunition for use in firearms + *boer* 'farmer' (see BOER).

Schroth (728) German: from Middle High German *schrōt* 'cut', 'blow', 'scrap', possibly applied as a nickname for a rude or rough man from its secondary meaning 'lump', 'block'.
GIVEN NAMES German 4%. *Gerd* (2), *Wolfgang* (2), *Beate*, *Fritz*, *Gertraud*, *Kurt*, *Lorenz*.

Schrott (135) South German: variant of SCHROTH.
GIVEN NAMES German 7%; Scandinavian 4%. *Hans*, *Helmut*, *Hermann*; *Alf*.

Schroyer (569) Pennsylvania German variant of SCHREIER.

Schrum (688) Perhaps an altered spelling of German **Schromm**, a variant of SCHRAMM, or, in eastern Germany, a habitational name from a place named Schrom, near Breslau.

Schrumpf (180) South German: of uncertain origin; perhaps related to German *schrumpfen* 'to shrink' and hence a nickname for a small person.

Schrunk (142) Perhaps an altered form of German SCHRANK.
GIVEN NAME German 4%. *Otto* (2).

Schrupp (300) Northern and central German: variant of SCHROPP.

Schryer (179) Variant spelling of German SCHREIER.
GIVEN NAMES French 4%. *Andre*, *Aurel*.

Schryver (336) Dutch: occupational name for a clerk or scribe, from Middle Dutch *scrivere* 'scribe', 'clerk' (see SCHREIBER).

Schu (112) Variant of German SCHUH.

Schub (103) Jewish (Ashkenazic): see SHUB.

GIVEN NAMES Jewish 5%. *Drora, Zeva*.

Schubach (172) German: probably a variant of SCHUPBACH.

GIVEN NAMES German 16%. *Kurt* (3), *Ernst, Erwin, Franz, Manfred, Rudi*.

Schubbe (115) German (also **Schübbe**): probably a variant of SCHUPPE.

Schubel (146) German: from Middle High German *schubel, schübel* 'bunch', 'clump', 'tuft'; of uncertain application. In Bavaria it seems also to have been a nickname for a plump little fellow, from the same vocabulary word used in a transferred sense.

GIVEN NAME German 6%. *Otto* (2).

Schuber (112) Altered form of German SCHUBERT.

Schubert (5166) German and Jewish (Ashkenazic): occupational name for a shoemaker or cobbler, from Middle High German *schuoch* 'shoe' + *würhte* 'maker'. The sound *b* was often substituted for *v* in eastern dialects of German.

GIVEN NAMES German 6%. *Franz* (12), *Otto* (7), *Hans* (6), *Kurt* (6), *Erwin* (5), *Arno* (4), *Fritz* (3), *Gerhard* (3), *Horst* (3), *Alois* (2), *Angelika* (2), *Guenter* (2).

Schubring (213) German (Sudetenland): a derivative of *Schubrich*, an occupational name for a shoemaker (see SCHUBERT).

Schuch (580) German: variant of SCHUH.

GIVEN NAMES German 4%. *Hans* (2), *Arno, Gerd, Lorenz, Markus, Otto, Rudi*.

Schuchard (242) Variant of German SCHUCHARDT.

Schuchardt (320) German (Hesse and Thuringia): from a regional form of Middle High German *schuochwürhte* 'shoemaker' (see SCHUBERT).

GIVEN NAMES German 5%. *Kurt* (2), *Bernd, Ernst*.

Schuchart (190) German: variant of SCHUCHARDT.

Schuchert (111) German: variant of SCHUCHARDT.

Schuchman (305) **1.** Jewish (Ashkenazic): variant spelling of SCHUCHMANN. **2.** Altered spelling of German SCHUCHMANN.

Schuchmann (136) German and Jewish (Ashkenazic): occupational name for a shoemaker, from Middle High German *schuoch* 'shoe' + *man* 'man', German *Schuh* + *Mann*.

GIVEN NAME German 5%. *Kurt*.

Schuck (1558) **1.** Variant of German SCHUH. **2.** Variant spelling of Jewish **Shuk**, a habitational name for someone from Shuki, a place in Lithuania.

Schucker (223) **1.** South German (Baden): occupational name for a shoemaker, from SCHUCK + the agent suffix *-er*. **2.** Jewish (Ashkenazic): patronymic from SCHUCK.

Schuckman (218) Altered spelling of German **Schuckmann**, a variant of SCHUCHMANN.

GIVEN NAMES German 4%. *Berthold, Frieda*.

Schudel (148) Swiss German: nickname for someone with locks of thick, touseled hair, from an Alemannic dialect word.

Schuder (135) **1.** German: habitational name from a place so called near Köthen (now called Scheuder). **2.** North German (**Schüder**): occupational name for a worker in a mill, from an agent derivative of Middle Low German *schudden* 'to tip or pour (grain)'.

GIVEN NAMES French 5%; German 4%. *Celine, Monique; Fritz, Hans*.

Schue (217) Variant of German SCHUH.

Schuele (169) German (**Schüle**): from a diminutive of Middle High German *schuoch* 'shoe' (see SCHUH).

GIVEN NAME German 10%. *Hans-Peter*.

Schueler (1010) German (**Schüler**): variant of SCHULER 1.

GIVEN NAMES German 7%. *Kurt* (8), *Heinz* (4), *Eldor, Erna, Erwin, Ewald, Gerd, Gerhard, Gunter, Helmut, Hertha, Joerg*.

Schuelke (676) North German (**Schülke**): **1.** probably a nickame from a Slavic word meaning 'tender' or 'lively'. Compare Polish *czuły* 'tender'. **2.** alternatively, a pet form of a Slavic personal name such as *Sulimir*. Compare the Polish pet form of this name, *Sułek*.

GIVEN NAMES German 4%. *Eldor* (2), *Kurt* (2), *Armin, Ewald*.

Schueller (787) South German (**Schüller**): variant of SCHULLER.

Schueneman (201) German: variant of **Schünemann** (see SCHUENEMANN).

Schuenemann (172) North German (**Schünemann**): from Middle Low German *schune* 'barn' + *man* 'man'; a topographic name for someone who lived near a barn, or an occupational name for someone who worked in one. Compare SCHEUER.

GIVEN NAMES German 11%. *Helmut* (2), *Erwin, Guenter, Helmuth, Ilse*.

Schuenke (134) German (**Schünke**): variant of SCHUNK.

Schuerger (127) South German and Swiss German (**Schürger**): nickname for a harsh master (a 'slave driver'), from an agent derivative of Middle High German *schürgen* 'to push or drive'.

GIVEN NAMES German 5%. *Kurt, Otto, Wilhelmina*.

Schuerman (485) Variant of German SCHUERMANN.

Schuermann (289) North German (**Schürmann**): habitational name for someone from a place called Schüre(n), or a topographic name for someone who lived by a barn, from Middle Low German *schüre* 'barn'.

GIVEN NAMES German 8%. *Franz, Guenter, Hans, Heiner, Klaus, Kurt, Udo*.

Schuessler (966) German (**Schüssler**): occupational name for a maker of dishes and bowls, for example a turner, from an agent derivative of Middle High German *schüssel(e)* 'bowl', 'dish'.

GIVEN NAMES German 5%. *Kurt* (2), *Erwin, Heinrich, Irmgard, Juergen, Klaus, Wolfgang*.

Schuett (703) North German: variant of **Schütt** (see SCHUTTE).

GIVEN NAMES German 6%. *Guenter* (3), *Egon* (2), *Erwin* (2), *Gerhard* (2), *Hans* (2), *Hannes, Heinz, Helmut*.

Schuette (1693) North German: variant of **Schütte** (see SCHUTTE).

GIVEN NAMES German 4%. *Erwin* (2), *Gerhardt* (2), *Klaus* (2), *Kurt* (2), *Markus* (2), *Otto* (2), *Angelika, Armin, Eldor, Eldred, Gerhart, Hans*.

Schuetter (117) North German: see SCHUTTER.

Schuettpelz (129) North German: literally 'shake the fur or hide', from Middle High German *schütten*, a nickname probably for a bold, unconcerned person.

GIVEN NAMES German 4%. *Erwin, Hildegarde, Konrad*.

Schuetz (1358) **1.** German (**Schütz**): occupational name for an archer, Middle High German *schütze* (from Middle High German *schützen* 'to guard or protect'), or alternatively an occupational name for a watchman, from the same word in its original sense, 'guard', i.e. the warden of a piece of common land or a night watchman in a town. **2.** Jewish (Ashkenazic): ornamental name from German *Schütze* 'archer', 'rifleman'. Compare 1.

GIVEN NAMES German 6%. *Hans* (3), *Kurt* (3), *Franz* (2), *Reiner* (2), *Eberhard, Egon, Florian, Gerd, Gerda, Heinz, Helmuth, Juergen*.

Schuetze (258) German (**Schütze**): variant of **Schütz** (see SCHUETZ).

GIVEN NAMES German 14%. *Armin, Dietrich, Frieda, Gerhard, Heinz, Helmuth, Juergen, Klaus, Otto, Siegfried, Willi, Wolfram*.

Schuff (171) German: metonymic occupational name for a maker or user of scoops and ladles, from Middle High German *schuofe* 'ladle'.

Schug (580) German: variant of SCHUH.

GIVEN NAMES German 6%. *Erwin* (2), *Mathias* (2), *Alois, Ewald, Gunther, Klaus, Lorenz, Otto*.

Schuh (2093) German and Jewish (Ashkenazic): metonymic occupational name for a maker or repairer of shoes, from Middle High German *schuoch*, German *Schuh* 'shoe'; sometimes from a house name.

Schuhmacher (206) German and Jewish (Ashkenazic): variant of SCHUMACHER.

GIVEN NAMES German 4%. *Inge, Juergen*.

Schuhmann (165) German and Jewish (Ashkenazic): variant of SCHUMANN.

GIVEN NAMES German 6%. *Otto, Ralf*.

Schuitema (153) Frisian: patronymic name for the son of a bargemaster, from *schuiter* 'bargemaster', derivative of *schuit* 'barge'.

Schuknecht (213) German: occupational name for a shoemaker's assistant, from Middle High German *schuoch* 'shoe' + *knecht* 'journeyman', 'assistant'.

GIVEN NAMES German 4%. *Eldred, Ingo, Konrad.*

Schul (201) **1.** German: variant of SCHULE. **2.** Jewish (Ashkenazic): metonymic occupational name for a Talmudic scholar or the sexton of a synagogue, from Yiddish *shul* 'synagogue'. Compare SCHULER.

GIVEN NAMES German 5%. *Georg, Kurt.*

Schulberg (109) Jewish (Ashkenazic): ornamental name from German *Schule* 'school' or Yiddish *shul* 'synagogue' + *Berg* 'hill'.

Schuld (304) German: variant of SCHULTE.

Schuldt (943) German: variant of SCHULTE.

GIVEN NAMES German 4%. *Kurt* (3), *Gerhard* (2), *Hans* (2), *Egon, Erna, Fritz, Hermann, Otto.*

Schule (109) German (**Schüle**): **1.** occupational name for a maker or repairer of shoes, from a diminutive of Middle High German *schuoch* 'shoe' (see SCHUH). **2.** variant of SCHIELE 'cross-eyed', altered by folk etymology in such a way that it conforms to the German word *Schule* 'school'.

Schulenberg (315) German: habitational name from any of several places so named, for example near Rostock and near Goslar. There has probably been some confusion with SCHULENBURG.

Schulenburg (241) North German: habitational name from any of several places so named, for example near Lübeck and near Hildesheim.

GIVEN NAMES German 5%. *Guenter, Kurt, Otto.*

Schuler (5826) **1.** South German (also **Schüler**): occupational name for a scholar or a student training to be a priest, from an agent derivative of Middle High German *schuol(e)* 'school'. **2.** Jewish (Ashkenazic): occupational name for a Talmudic scholar or the sexton of a synagogue, from an agent derivative of Yiddish *shul* 'synagogue'.

Schulist (121) Origin unidentified.

Schulke (336) German (**Schülke**): see SCHUELKE.

GIVEN NAMES German 4%. *Gerhard, Gunter, Gunther.*

Schull (330) German: of uncertain origin: **1.** possibly a variant of SCHOLL or SCHUL. **2.** alternatively, perhaps a derogatory nickname from **Schüll** 'lout', Middle High German *schülle*.

GIVEN NAMES German 4%. *Armin, Arno, Ilse.*

Schuller (1379) **1.** South German: variant of SCHULER 1. **2.** South German (**Schüller**): possibly a habitational name

from Schüller in the Eifel. **3.** Jewish (Ashkenazic): variant of SCHULER.

GIVEN NAMES German 5%. *Friedrich* (3), *Kurt* (2), *Manfred* (2), *Reinhold* (2), *Dieter, Erna, Franz, Gerhard, Gunther, Hans, Heinz, Katharina.*

Schullo (101) probably an altered spelling of German SCHOLLER.

Schulman (2660) **1.** German (**Schulmann**): probably an occupational name for a teacher in a school or seminary, from Middle High German *schuol(e)* + *man* 'man'. **2.** Jewish (Ashkenazic): variant of SCHULER.

GIVEN NAMES Jewish 6%. *Sol* (10), *Miriam* (3), *Chaim* (2), *Hyman* (2), *Ari, Avi, Batya, Chana, Ephraim, Gershon, Isidor, Mandel.*

Schulmeister (122) **1.** German: occupational name for a teacher in a school or seminary, from Middle High German *schuol(e)* + *meister* 'master'. **2.** Jewish (Ashkenazic): occupational name for a teacher in a Jewish school, from German *Schulmeister* 'schoolmaster'.

Schult (535) North German and Dutch: variant of SCHULTE.

GIVEN NAMES German 6%. *Hans* (2), *Rudi* (2), *Eldor, Erna, Erwin, Kurt, Lorenz.*

Schulte (6786) North German and Dutch: status name from Middle Low German *schulthete*, Middle Dutch *schulte* 'village headman'. Compare SCHULTZ, SCHULTHEIS.

GIVEN NAMES German 4%. *Kurt* (9), *Otto* (6), *Erwin* (4), *Dieter* (3), *Heinz* (3), *Rainer* (3), *Alois* (2), *Dietmar* (2), *Franz* (2), *Fritz* (2), *Gerhard* (2), *Hans* (2).

Schulteis (132) North German and Dutch: variant of SCHULTHEISS.

Schulten (145) North German (Rhineland): patronymic from SCHULTE.

GIVEN NAMES German 9%. *Juergen, Klaus, Kurt.*

Schultes (279) Dutch and North German: variant of SCHULTE or SCHULTHEIS.

GIVEN NAMES German 6%. *Kurt* (2), *Franz, Otto.*

Schultheis (1002) German (**Schultheiss**) and Dutch: status name from Middle High German *schultheize* 'village headman'. The term originally denoted a man responsible for collecting dues and paying them to the lord of the manor. See also SCHULTZ 1.

Schultheiss (252) German: see SCHULTHEIS.

GIVEN NAMES German 4%. *Fritz, Helmut.*

Schultz (43814) **1.** German: status name for a village headman, from a contracted form of Middle High German *schultheize*. The term originally denoted a man responsible for collecting dues and paying them to the lord of the manor; it is a compound of *sculd(a)* 'debt', 'due' + a derivative of *heiz(z)an* 'to command'. The surname is also established in Scandinavia. **2.** Jewish (Ashkenazic): from German **Schulze** (see 1 above). The reason for adoption are

uncertain, but may perhaps have referred to a rabbi, seen as the head of a Jewish community, or to a trustee of a synagogue.

Schultze (1008) German: variant of SCHULTZ 1.

GIVEN NAMES German 5%. *Dietrich* (2), *Benno, Erwin, Hans, Heinz, Helmuth, Ilse, Reinhold, Siegfried.*

Schulz (10425) German and Jewish (Ashkenazic): variant spelling of SCHULTZ. In this spelling, it is also found as a surname in Slovenia and elsewhere.

GIVEN NAMES German 8%. *Kurt* (31), *Otto* (25), *Hans* (17), *Gerhard* (14), *Erwin* (11), *Ewald* (9), *Gunter* (8), *Manfred* (8), *Heinz* (7), *Helmut* (6), *Horst* (6), *Jurgen* (6).

Schulze (3765) German: variant of SCHULTZ 1.

GIVEN NAMES German 8%. *Erwin* (15), *Otto* (11), *Kurt* (7), *Manfred* (7), *Hans* (4), *Heinz* (3), *Helmut* (3), *Horst* (3), *Wolfgang* (3), *Albrecht* (2), *Christoph* (2), *Dieter* (2).

Schum (354) **1.** Jewish (Ashkenazic): unexplained. **2.** Respelling of German SCHUMM.

Schumacher (10678) German and Jewish (Ashkenazic): occupational name for a shoemaker, from Middle High German *schuoch* 'shoe', German *Schuh* + an agent derivative of *machen* 'to make'.

GIVEN NAMES German 4%. *Kurt* (23), *Hans* (8), *Otto* (6), *Bernd* (4), *Klaus* (4), *Alois* (3), *Erwin* (3), *Fritz* (3), *Horst* (3), *Juergen* (3), *Bernhard* (2), *Ewald* (2).

Schumacker (199) Dutch: variant of SCHOEMAKER.

Schumaker (1216) Dutch: variant of SCHOEMAKER.

Schuman (2531) Altered spelling of German and Jewish SCHUMANN.

Schumann (2894) German and Jewish (Ashkenazic): occupational name for a shoemaker, from Middle High German *schuoch* 'shoe' + *man* 'man', German *Schuh* + *Mann*.

GIVEN NAMES German 6%. *Kurt* (7), *Otto* (4), *Gerhard* (3), *Hans* (3), *Juergen* (3), *Reinhard* (3), *Wolfgang* (3), *Arno* (2), *Heinz* (2), *Helmut* (2), *Klaus* (2), *Benno.*

Schumer (438) **1.** German: unexplained. **2.** North German (**Schümer**): nickname from Middle Low German *schumer* 'good-for-nothing', 'vagabond'.

Schumm (508) **1.** Eastern German: habitational name from Schumm, a place in Upper Saxony , or in some cases a shortened form of SCHUMANN. **2.** Jewish (Ashkenazic): variant of SCHUM.

Schummer (146) North German (**Schümmer**): variant of **Schümer** (see SCHUMER).

Schumpert (236) German: probably a nickname for a good-for-nothing, derived from Swabian *Schump* 'a young cow'. Compare SCHUMER.

Schuneman (220) Altered spelling of North German **Schünemann** (see SCHUENEMANN).

Schunk (563) **1.** South German (Bavarian, Austrian): nickname for someone with long legs, from Middle High German *schinke* 'leg bone'. **2.** German (of Slavic origin): nickname from a Slavic word meaning 'piglet', for example Czech *čunka*.

Schunke (120) German: variant of SCHUNK.

Schupbach (383) German: habitational name from a place so named near Limburg.

Schupp (758) **1.** Dutch: metonymic occupational name for someone who made or used shovels or scoops, from Middle Dutch *schoepe, schope, schuep* 'shovel', 'scoop'. **2.** German: variant of SCHUPPE.

Schuppe (135) German: metonymic occupational name for a fish seller or fisherman, from Middle High German *schuope* '(fish)-scale'.

GIVEN NAME German 5%. *Viktor.*

Schuppert (121) German: **1.** variant of SCHUBERT. **2.** From the name of a fish, a kind of carp, hence probably an occupational name for a seller of such fish.

Schur (501) **1.** North German: from Middle Low German *schūr* 'shower of rain' or 'bad storm', in any of several possible senses. It may be a nickname for an easily excitable person, an occupational name for the warden of a park or piece of common land (from the same word in the sense 'protection'; compare SCHUETZ), or a nickname from the same word in the sense 'clever'. **2.** German (**Schür**): see SCHEUER. **3.** Jewish (Ashkenazic): variant of SHOR.

Schurig (127) Eastern German: from the personal name *Schurek*, Sorbian form of GEORGE.

GIVEN NAMES German 9%. *Gerhard, Gerhardt.*

Schuring (254) Dutch: from a derivative of SCHUUR.

GIVEN NAMES German 4%. *Claus, Dieter, Kurt.*

Schurman (672) Americanized spelling of German **Schürmann** (see SCHUERMANN).

Schurmann (115) German (**Schürmann**) (see SCHUERMANN).

GIVEN NAME German 5%. *Franz.*

Schurr (694) **1.** South German: from a dialect word meaning 'scree', hence a topographic name for someone who lived near an area of scree. **2.** Nickname for a hot-tempered person (see SCHUR).

Schurter (115) Swiss German: occupational name for a bill collector, from Alemannic *schurten* 'to collect debts'.

Schurtz (130) German: variant spelling of SCHURZ.

Schurz (105) German: metonymic nickname for a craftsman, one who wore an apron at work, from Middle High German *schurz* 'apron'.

GIVEN NAMES German 9%. *Albrecht, Kurt.*

Schussler (346) German (**Schüssler**): see SCHUESSLER.

Schuster (7507) German and Jewish (Ashkenazic): occupational name for a maker or repairer of shoes, Middle High German *schuochsūtœre* (a compound of *schuoch* 'shoe' + *sūtœre* 'one who sews'), German *Schuster*, Yiddish *shuster*.

GIVEN NAMES German 5%. *Kurt* (21), *Otto* (8), *Hans* (7), *Erwin* (6), *Helmut* (4), *Alois* (3), *Ernst* (3), *Manfred* (3), *Arno* (2), *Franz* (2), *Fritz* (2), *Gerhard* (2).

Schut (366) **1.** Dutch: occupational name for an archer, Middle Dutch *scutte*. **2.** Jewish (Ashkenazic): occupational name from eastern Slavic and Yiddish *shut* 'jester', 'joker'.

Schuth (164) North German: metonymic occupational name for an owner, builder, or sailor of a small, flat-bottomed cargo boat, Middle Low German *schute*.

GIVEN NAMES German 5%. *Math, Otto.*

Schutt (1815) Dutch and North German: variant of SCHUTTE.

Schutte (2099) Dutch and North German (**Schütte**): occupational name for an archer, from Middle Low German *schutten* 'to shoot'. Compare German SCHUETZ.

Schutter (419) **1.** North German (**Schütter**): occupational name for a guard, watchman or warden, from an agent derivative of Middle Low German *schutten* 'to protect'. See also SCHUETZ. **2.** Dutch: occupational name for a bowman, subsequently a status name for a member of a marksman's guild, Middle Dutch *scut(t)ere*. This was also an occupational name for an official who impounded stray cattle.

Schuttler (152) **1.** East German (**Schüttler**; Lower Silesia): habitational name for someone from Schüttlau in Guhrau district. **2.** North German (**Schüttler**): variant of SCHUESSLER.

GIVEN NAME German 4%. *Bernd* (2).

Schutts (103) North German and Dutch: occupational name for an archer, Middle Low German, Middle Dutch *schuts*, or for a watchman or guard. Compare German SCHUETZ.

Schutz (2260) **1.** German (**Schütz**) and Jewish (Ashkenazic): see SCHUETZ. **2.** German: habitational name from Schutz, a place near Trier. **3.** Jewish (Ashkenazic): ornamental name from German *Schutz* 'protection'.

Schutze (123) German and Jewish (Ashkenazic): see SCHUETZ.

GIVEN NAMES German 10%. *Gunter, Markus, Otto, Wolfgang.*

Schutzman (177) **1.** German (**Schütz-mann**): occupational name for an archer (see SCHUETZ). **2.** Jewish (Ashkenazic): ornamental name from German *Schu(e)tz* 'protection' + Yiddish *man* 'man'.

Schuur (199) North German and Dutch: topographic name from Middle Low German *schure*, Middle Dutch *schuur, schuer* 'barn'.

Schuyler (1483) Dutch: status name for a scholar or school teacher.

FOREBEARS Schuyler is the name of one of the oldest and wealthiest Dutch families of NY, established there by Philip Pieterse Schuyler from Amsterdam; his marriage is recorded in North America in 1650. He was a merchant and colonial administrator. Four generations later one of his best-known descendants was Philip Schuyler (1733–1804), a member of Congress and a leading figure in the American Revolution; he was in command of the American army at Saratoga before being replaced by Horatio Gates.

Schwaab (118) German: variant of SCHWAB.

Schwab (6837) German and Jewish (Ashkenazic): regional name for someone from Swabia (German *Schwaben*), from Middle High German *Swāp*, German *Schwabe* 'Swabian'. The region takes its name from a Germanic tribe recorded from the 1st century BC in the Latin form *Suebi* or *Suevi*, of uncertain origin; it was an independent duchy from the 10th century until 1313, when the territory was broken up.

Schwabauer (136) German: habitational name for someone from Swabau in Styria, Austria.

GIVEN NAME German 5%. *Kurt* (2).

Schwabe (617) German and Jewish (Ashkenazic): variant of SCHWAB.

GIVEN NAMES German 9%. *Klaus* (4), *Erwin* (2), *Ewald* (2), *Wolfgang* (2), *Erna, Gottfried, Heinz, Kurt, Manfred, Urs, Ute, Wilfried.*

Schwaderer (154) South German: **1.** nickname for a voluble person, from Middle High German *swaderer* 'chatterer'. **2.** topographic name from the dialect term *Schwader* 'marshes' (a collective form of *schwad* 'marshy place'), + the suffix *-er* denoting an inhabitant.

Schwadron (102) Jewish (Ashkenazic): ornamental name from German *Schwadron* 'squadron'.

GIVEN NAMES Jewish 9%. *Gershon, Zev.*

Schwager (670) German and Jewish (Ashkenazic): relationship name from Middle High German *swāger* 'brother-, son-, or father-in-law'; German *Schwager* 'brother-in-law'.

GIVEN NAMES German 6%. *Kurt* (4), *Fritz* (2), *Alois, Egon, Erwin, Franz, Hermann, Lorenz.*

Schwahn (162) German: variant of SCHWAN.

GIVEN NAMES German 5%. *Gunther, Heinz.*

Schwaiger (160) German (mainly Bavaria): **1.** occupational name for a cheesemaker, from an agent derivative of Middle High German *sweigen* 'to make cheese'. **2.** habitational name for someone from any of several places named Schwaig or Schwaigern.

GIVEN NAMES German 14%. *Hans* (3), *Herta* (2), *Hermann, Kurt, Nikolaus, Otto, Sieglinde, Wolfgang.*

Schwake (210) North German: status name for someone of low social standing or inadequate means, from Middle Low German *swak* 'poor', 'humble'.
GIVEN NAMES German 4%. *Dieter, Lorenz.*

Schwalb (287) Variant of SCHWALBE.
GIVEN NAMES German 5%. *Erwin, Fritz, Markus, Otto.*

Schwalbach (276) German and Jewish (Ashkenazic): habitational name from any of several places named Schwalbach, of which there are examples near Wetzlar, Saarlouis, and Wiesbaden (now Bad Schwalbach).

Schwalbe (438) **1.** German: nickname from Middle High German *schwalbe*, 'swallow'. **2.** Jewish (Ashkenazic): ornamental name from German *Schwalbe*, Yiddish *shvalb* 'swallow'.
GIVEN NAMES German 7%; French 4%. *Kurt* (4), *Alfons, Dieter, Gerd, Gerhard, Lothar, Manfred; Armand* (2), *Jacques* (2), *Laure.*

Schwalenberg (124) German and Jewish (Ashkenazic): habitational name from Schwalenberg, a place near Höxter.
GIVEN NAME German 4%. *Manfred.*

Schwall (290) South German: habitational name from places so named in Nassau and the Rhineland.

Schwaller (249) South German: habitational name for someone from a place called SCHWALL.

Schwallie (138) perhaps Swiss German: an Americanized form of **Schwalle**, a topographic name from Middle High German *swal* 'lock', 'sluice', 'place where water collects'.

Schwalm (652) German: **1.** habitational name from Schwalm in Hesse, the name of a district and of a river. **2.** alternatively, the Middle High German word *swalm* 'swarm of bees' might lie behind the surname, possibly denoting a beekeeper.

Schwam (150) **1.** Jewish (Ashkenazic): ornamental name from German *Schwamm* 'sponge' or 'mushroom'. **2.** Variant of German **Schwamm**, a metonymic occupational name for a gatherer of edible fungi (see SCHWAMB).
GIVEN NAMES Jewish 4%. *Emanuel, Limor, Yitzchok.*

Schwamb (140) German: metonymic occupational name for a gatherer of mushrooms and other edible fungi, from Middle High German *swamp* 'mushroom' (inflected *swamb*).

Schwamberger (130) German: altered spelling of German **Schwammberger**, a habitational name for someone from a place called Schweinberg, formerly Schwamberg, near Buchen (Baden); otherwise the name occurs as a field name in Württemberg.
GIVEN NAMES German 5%. *Kurt, Otto.*

Schwan (825) **1.** German: from Middle High German, Middle Low German *swan* 'swan'; a nickname derived for a very clean person or for someone with a long neck, or alternatively a habitational name for someone living at a house distinguished by the sign of a swan. **2.** Jewish (Ashkenazic): ornamental name from German *Schwan* 'swan'.
GIVEN NAMES German 5%. *Kurt* (5), *Manfred* (3), *Bernhard, Ernst, Gerhart.*

Schwanbeck (113) German: habitational name from any of several places so named, for example near Lübeck and near Anklam.

Schwander (132) South German: habitational name for someone from a place called Schwand or Schwanden (see SCHWANDT).
GIVEN NAMES German 7%. *Hans, Helmut.*

Schwandt (644) South German: topographic name for someone who lived in a forest clearing, from Middle High German *swant* (from *swenden* 'to thin out', 'make disappear', causative from *swinden* 'to disappear'), or a habitational name from any of the various places called Schwand or Schwanden, named with this element, all in southern Germany.
GIVEN NAMES German 6%. *Otto* (3), *Kurt* (2), *Siegfried* (2), *Gerhardt, Gernot, Horst, Monika, Willi.*

Schwaner (144) German: from a Germanic personal name composed of the elements *swana* 'swan' + *hard* 'hard', 'strong'.

Schwaninger (104) German: habitational name for someone from a place called Schwaningen, near Eichstädt.
GIVEN NAMES German 7%. *Kurt* (2), *Bernhard.*

Schwank (126) North German: variant of SCHWANKE.
GIVEN NAMES German 8%. *Fritz* (2), *Bernd, Johannes, Urs.*

Schwanke (700) North German: from a short form of the personal name *Swaneke*, a pet form of *Swane*, from a Germanic compound name formed with *swana* 'swan' as the first element.
GIVEN NAMES German 5%. *Otto* (3), *Eldred, Erwin, Ewald, Frederich, Hans, Helmuth, Jurgen, Konrad.*

Schwantes (377) German: **1.** from a pet form of the Slavic personal name *Sviatoslav*, composed of the Slavic elements *swia(n)t* 'holy' + *slav* 'glory', 'fame', 'praise'. **2.** possibly a habitational name from a place called Schwantus near Wollin.

Schwantz (122) German: variant of SCHWANZ.

Schwanz (319) German: nickname for a dandy, from Middle High German *swanz* 'train of a dress', literally 'tail', but also used to mean 'decoration' or 'finery'.
GIVEN NAMES German 6%. *Armin, Eldred, Fritz, Kurt, Otto.*

Schwarck (100) Variant of German SCHWARK.
GIVEN NAME German 4%. *Kurt.*

Schwarcz (120) Jewish (from Hungary): variant spelling of SCHWARTZ.
GIVEN NAMES Jewish 12%; Hungarian 8%. *Zalmon* (2), *Dov, Moises, Moishe, Sol, Zev; Jeno, Laszlo, Sandor, Zoltan.*

Schwark (365) North German: from Middle Low German *swark* 'dark clouds', 'sorrow', a nickname for a gloomy person.

Schwarm (195) **1.** North German: habitational name from Schwarme, a place south of Bremen. **2.** German: from Middle High German *swarm* 'swarm (of bees)', possibly a nickname for a beekeeper.
GIVEN NAMES German 5%. *Franz, Heinz.*

Schwarte (105) Dutch and North German: nickname for someone with black hair or a dark complexion. Compare German SCHWARTZ.
GIVEN NAMES German 7%. *Erwin, Heribert, Horst.*

Schwarting (353) Dutch and North German: patronymic from a nickname from Middle Low German *schwart* 'black'. Compare German SCHWARTZ.
GIVEN NAMES German 4%. *Kurt* (2), *Fritz.*

Schwartz (39069) German and Jewish (Ashkenazic): nickname for someone with black hair or a dark complexion, from Middle High German *swarz*, German *schwarz*, Yiddish *shvarts* 'dark', 'black'. This name is widespread throughout central and eastern Europe.
GIVEN NAMES Jewish 4%. *Sol* (58), *Hyman* (40), *Emanuel* (30), *Miriam* (28), *Meyer* (20), *Chaim* (18), *Isadore* (13), *Moshe* (13), *Aron* (10), *Ari* (8), *Mayer* (6), *Hershel* (5).

Schwartzbauer (125) German: distinguishing name for a farmer with dark hair, from Middle High German *swarz* 'black' + BAUER.

Schwartzberg (428) **1.** Jewish (Ashkenazic): ornamental name composed of German *schwarz* 'black' + *Berg* 'mountain', 'hill'. **2.** Altered spelling of German **Schwarzberg**, a habitational name from any of several places so named in Bavaria.
GIVEN NAMES Jewish 9%. *Sol* (2), *Avraham, Hyman, Leib, Mayer, Moshe, Shimon, Yett, Yosef.*

Schwartze (148) German and Jewish (Ashkenazic): variant of SCHWARTZ.

Schwartzenberger (108) German: habitational name for someone from any of several places called Schwarzenberg, literally 'black mountain'.

Schwartzkopf (451) German and Jewish (Ashkenazic): nickname for someone with dark hair, from Middle High German *swarz* 'black', 'dark' + *kopf* 'head', German *schwarz* + *Kopf*.

Schwartzman (717) German (**Schwartzmann**) and Jewish (Ashkenazic): descriptive nickname for a dark-skinned or black-haired man, from German *schwartz* 'black' + *Mann* 'man'.

Schwarz

GIVEN NAMES Jewish 5%. *Hayim* (2), *Naum* (2), *Arie, Emanuel, Ilya, Miriam, Sol, Yakov.*

Schwarz (7184) German and Jewish (Ashkenazic): variant spelling of SCHWARTZ.
GIVEN NAMES German 9%. *Kurt* (27), *Hans* (18), *Otto* (15), *Erwin* (8), *Gunter* (8), *Heinz* (8), *Wolfgang* (8), *Gerhard* (7), *Manfred* (7), *Klaus* (6), *Bernhard* (5), *Ernst* (5).

Schwarzbach (118) German: habitational name from any of several places so named, literally the 'dark stream'.

Schwarze (425) German and Jewish (Ashkenazic): variant spelling of SCHWARTZ.
GIVEN NAMES German 10%. *Fritz* (3), *Kurt* (3), *Erhard, Helmut, Hermann, Joerg, Jurgen, Reiner, Wilfried.*

Schwarzenbach (110) German: habitational name from any of several places so named, literally 'dark stream'. It is also established as a French name, probably from a place in Alsace.

Schwarzer (190) German and Jewish (Ashkenazic): nickname from an inflected form of Middle High German *swarz*, German *schwarz*, meaning 'the black one or the dark one'.
GIVEN NAMES German 17%. *Dieter* (4), *Angelika, Bernd, Fritz, Hedwig, Helmut, Horst, Joerg, Kurt, Otto.*

Schwarzkopf (319) German and Jewish (Ashkenazic): variant spelling of SCHWARTZKOPF.
GIVEN NAMES German 7%. *Claus, Erwin, Florian, Gerd, Hans, Kurt.*

Schwarzman (129) Jewish (Ashkenazic): descriptive nickname for a dark-skinned or black-haired man, from German *schwarz* 'black' + *Mann* 'man'.
GIVEN NAMES Jewish 10%. *Zvi* (2), *Rivka, Shulem.*

Schwarzmann (100) Jewish (Ashkenazic): variant spelling of SCHWARZMAN.

Schwass (103) Eastern German: habitational name from a place called Schwass, near Rostock.

Schwebach (180) German: probably an altered spelling of German **Schwebbach**, a topographic name denoting a river or stream, from Middle High German *sweben* 'to move in a winding way, meander' + *bach* 'stream'.

Schwebel (276) German and Jewish (Ashkenazic): 1. regional name from a diminutive of SCHWAB 'Swabian'. 2. possibly also from Middle High German *swebel*, Yiddish *shvebl* 'sulfur'. Its application as a German surname is obscure. The Jewish name is mainly of ornamental origin.
GIVEN NAMES Jewish 4%. *Avrohom, Heshy, Nechama.*

Schwebke (191) German: regional name for someone from Swabia (see SCHWAB) + diminutive suffix *-ke*, or a nickname for someone with a swaying gait (see SCHWEBACH).
GIVEN NAMES German 4%. *Fritz, Kurt.*

Schwed (176) 1. German and Jewish (Ashkenazic): habitational name from Schwedt in Brandenburg. 2. German: ethnic name for someone of Swedish origin. 3. Jewish (Ashkenazic): ornamental name from German *Schwede*, Polish *Szwed* 'Swede'.
GIVEN NAME French 4%. *Andre* (2).

Schweda (140) German: ethnic name for a Swede, from a Germanized spelling of Polish **Szweda**, from *Szwed* 'Swede', or a cognate in some other Slavic language.

Schwede (188) German: variant of SCHWED.
GIVEN NAMES German 4%. *Fritz, Otto.*

Schweder (173) 1. German: ethnic name for a Swede. 2. North German: from the medieval personal name *Swider, Sweder*, from a Germanic personal name composed with *swi(n)d* 'strong', 'fast' + *heri* 'army'.

Schweer (298) 1. North German: variant of SCHWEDER 2. 2. Variant of SCHWEHR.
GIVEN NAMES German 4%. *Helmuth* (2), *Erwin, Kurt.*

Schweers (342) North German: patronymic from SCHWEER 1.
GIVEN NAMES German 4%. *Dietrich, Hermann, Lisl.*

Schwegel (226) German (Rhineland): nickname for a pipe or flute player, from Middle High German *swegel* 'pipe', 'flute'.
GIVEN NAMES German 4%. *Ernst* (2), *Alois, Otto.*

Schwegler (229) Southern German: from an agent derivative of Middle High German *swegele* 'pipe', 'flute', hence nickname for someone who played such an instrument.
GIVEN NAMES German 7%. *Erwin* (2), *Armin, Gunter, Kurt.*

Schwegman (197) North German (**Schwegmann**): habitational name for someone from any of several places named Schwege or Schwegen, for example near Bremen.

Schwehr (129) German: relationship name, a variant of *Schwäher*, a variant of SCHWAGER.
GIVEN NAME German 4%. *Willi.*

Schweich (118) German: habitational name from a place so named in Luxembourg near Trier.

Schweickert (223) German (chiefly Württemberg and Bavaria): from a Germanic personal name composed of the elements *swind* 'strong', 'skillful' + *gār, gēr* 'spear'; the *-t* is epenthetic.
GIVEN NAMES German 4%. *Ewald, Hans.*

Schweiger (964) 1. German and Jewish (Ashkenazic): nickname for a somewhat taciturn or 'deep' person, from an agent derivative of Middle High German *schwīgen*, German *schweigen*, Yiddish *shvaygn* 'to be silent'. 2. German: variant of SCHWAIGER.
GIVEN NAMES German 5%. *Helmut* (3), *Hans* (2), *Ernst, Erwin, Franz, Heinz, Hertha, Konrad, Kurt, Maximilian, Wolfgang.*

Schweigert (568) German: variant of SCHWEICKERT.

Schweighardt (126) German: variant of SCHWEICKERT.

Schweikart (147) Variant of German SCHWEICKERT.
GIVEN NAME German 4%. *Helmut.*

Schweiker (115) Variant of German SCHWEICKERT.
GIVEN NAMES German 8%. *Kurt, Matthias.*

Schweikert (526) Variant of German SCHWEICKERT.
GIVEN NAMES German 5%. *Otto* (2), *Juergen.*

Schwein (132) German: occupational name for a swineherd, from Middle High German *swīn* 'hog'.

Schweinfurth (103) German: habitational name from any of several places so named in Bavaria and Saxony.

Schweinsberg (144) German: habitational name from any of several places so named in Saxony, Westphalia, Hesse, and Bavaria.

Schweiss (257) German (Rhineland): apparently a nickname for someone who worked very hard or sweated excessively, from Middle High German *sweiz* 'sweat'. However, it is possible that this may be no more than a folk-etymological alteration of SCHWEITZ '(person from) Switzerland'.
GIVEN NAMES German 4%. *Dieter, Helmut, Kurt.*

Schweitz (103) German: ethnic name for a Swiss, from German *Schweitz* 'Swiss'.

Schweitzer (4494) German and Jewish (Ashkenazic): ethnic name for a native or inhabitant of Switzerland, from Middle High German *swīzer*, German *Schweizer*.
GIVEN NAMES German 4%. *Kurt* (11), *Erwin* (3), *Franz* (3), *Arnulf* (2), *Fritz* (2), *Helmut* (2), *Ulrich* (2), *Alois, Christoph, Darrold, Dieter, Guenter.*

Schweizer (1307) German and Jewish (Ashkenazic): variant spelling of SCHWEITZER.
GIVEN NAMES German 7%. *Hans* (6), *Kurt* (6), *Erwin* (5), *Otto* (2), *Alois, Berthold, Christoph, Ingeborg, Jochen, Joerg, Manfred, Ulrich.*

Schwemmer (150) German: 1. occupational name for someone who floated logs downstream from the forests where they were felled, from an agent derivative of Middle High German *swemmen*, causative of *swimmen* 'to float or swim'. 2. topographic name from Middle High German *swem(me)*, denoting a deep ford where horses had to swim across (from the same word as in 1).
GIVEN NAMES German 8%. *Heinz* (2), *Ewald, Ute.*

Schwend (151) German: variant of SCHWANDT.

Schwendeman (289) German (**Schwendemann**): topographic or habitational name from places called Schwende, denoting cleared areas in the forest, for instance in Switzerland (Appenzell canton).

Schwendemann (117) German: see SCHWENDEMAN.

Schwender (101) German: topographic name, see SCHWENDEMAN.
GIVEN NAMES German 6%. *Kurt, Wolfgang.*

Schwendiman (125) German: Swiss variant of SCHWENDEMAN.

Schwendinger (119) German: variant of SCHWEND.

Schwenger (101) South German: habitational name from a place called Schweningen in Baden, or from a Germanic personal name *Swaniger*, composed with *swana* 'swan' as the first element.
GIVEN NAMES German 9%. *Rudi* (2), *Hans, Wolfgang.*

Schwenk (1008) **1.** North German: variant of SCHWANKE. **2.** South German (mainly Württemberg, Silesia, and Bavaria): from Middle High German *swenken* 'to swing or sling', apparently a nickname, of which the original application cannot now be established.
GIVEN NAMES German 5%. *Kurt* (3), *Reinhold* (2), *Alfons, Alois, Deiter, Dieter, Franz, Frieda, Fritz, Helmut.*

Schwenke (362) German: variant of SCHWENK.
GIVEN NAMES German 8%. *Kurt* (2), *Fritz, Gerhard, Otto, Rainer, Reinhold, Wolfang.*

Schwenker (218) **1.** North German: patronymic form of SCHWENKE 1. **2.** Variant of SCHWENK 2.
GIVEN NAME German 5%. *Wolfgang.*

Schwenn (308) North German: from the dialect word *swen* 'boy', 'servant', used as a personal name.

Schwent (164) Probably an altered spelling of German **Schwendt**, a variant of SCHWANDT.
GIVEN NAME German 4%. *Georg.*

Schweppe (271) North German: metonymic occupational name for a maker of whips, from Middle Low German *swep(p)e* 'whip'. In some cases the surname may have arisen as a nickname for a harsh master.
GIVEN NAMES German 4%. *Armin, Egon.*

Schwer (237) **1.** South German: relationship name from Middle High German *sweher* 'father-in-law'. **2.** German: variant of SCHWEDER 2. **3.** Jewish (Ashkenazic): nickname from German *schwer* 'heavy'.

Schwerdt (191) German (Bavarian): metonymic occupational name for a sword maker, from Middle High German *swert* 'sword'.
GIVEN NAMES German 10%. *Kurt* (4), *Erwin, Heinz.*

Schwerdtfeger (283) German: occupational name for an armorer or specifically for a servant whose job was to polish swords, Middle High German, Middle Low German *swertfeger* (from *swert* 'sword' + an agent derivative of *fegen* 'to polish or clean').
GIVEN NAMES German 8%. *Erwin* (2), *Hans* (2), *Dietrich, Horst, Konrad, Kurt.*

Schwerin (463) German and Jewish (Ashkenazic): habitational name from any of the places named Schwerin, in Mecklenburg, Brandenburg, and Pomerania.

Schwering (163) German (Westphalian): patronymic from SCHWEDER 2.

Schwerman (104) variant of North German **Schwiermann**, from a reduced form of the personal name *Schwider, Schweder*, from Middle Low German *swide*, Frisian *swide*, Old Saxon *swīd-* 'strong', 'fast'.

Schwertfeger (236) German: variant of SCHWERDTFEGER.
GIVEN NAMES German 5%. *Horst, Otto.*

Schwertner (186) German: **1.** habitational name for someone from Schwerta in Silesia. **2.** occupational name for a sword maker (see SCHWERDT).

Schwery (108) German: probably a kinship name, from Middle High German *sweher*, *swēr* 'father-in-law'.

Schwetz (102) German: German form of Czech *švec* 'shoemaker', hence an occupational name, or a habitational name from either of two places so called in Bohemia or West Prussia (now Poland). In some instances it may be from a Slavic personal name based on Old Slavic *švetu* 'strong'

Schwichtenberg (243) German: habitational name from any of several places so named, for example those near Demmin and Anklam.
GIVEN NAMES German 6%. *Ewald, Heinz, Helmuth, Kurt.*

Schwickerath (137) German: habitational name for someone who lived on a farmstead so called near Wittlich, near the Mosel river.

Schwiebert (140) German: from the Germanic personal name *Swītbert*, composed of the elements *swinth* 'strong' + *berht* 'bright', 'illustrious'.
GIVEN NAMES German 4%. *Erwin* (2), *Leonhard.*

Schwieger (309) North German: from the Middle Low German personal name *Swideger*, from a Germanic personal name composed of the elements *swind* 'strong' + *gār, gēr* 'spear'. Compare SCHWEICKERT.

Schwier (263) North German: reduced form of the personal name *Schwieder*, a variant of SCHWEDER 2.

Schwiesow (159) Eastern German: habitational name from places named Schwiesow or Schwiesau, for example one near Gardelegen.

Schwieterman (264) (North?) German (**Schwietermann**): probably a patronymic from the medieval personal name *Swider* (see SCHWEDER 2) + Middle Low German *man* 'man'. If the surname exists at all in present-day Germany, it is very rare.

Schwimmer (388) German and Jewish (Ashkenazic): nickname for a good swimmer, from an agent derivative of German *schwimmen*, Yiddish *shvimen* 'to swim', Middle High German *swimmen*.
GIVEN NAMES Jewish 11%. *Chaim* (2), *Leiser* (2), *Mendel* (2), *Naftali* (2), *Cheskel, Mayer, Meyer, Moise, Moishe, Nosson, Yetta, Yitzchak.*

Schwind (660) South German: nickname from Middle High German *swinde* 'impetuous', 'violent'.

Schwindt (738) Variant of SCHWIND.

Schwing (436) **1.** German: occupational name for someone whose job was to swingle flax, i.e. to beat the flax with a swingle in order to remove the woody parts of the plant prior to spinning, from Middle German *swingen* 'to swing' or *swing* 'swingle'. **2.** German: habitational name from any of the places called Schwinge (near Stade and in Pomerania) or Schwingen (Bavaria).

Schwinger (140) German and Jewish (Ashkenazic): habitational name for someone from places called Schwinge or Schwingen (see SCHWING 2).
GIVEN NAME German 5%. *Kurt.*

Schwinghammer (130) German: occupational name for a blacksmith, from the sentence *Schwing den Hammer* 'Swing the hammer'.
GIVEN NAMES German 4%. *Ingeborg, Kurt.*

Schwinn (502) German: of uncertain origin; possibly a reduced form of SCHWINDT.

Schwisow (182) Eastern German: variant of SCHIWESOW.

Schwitters (113) German: patronymic of a Germanic personal name *Swindheri*, formed with *swi(n)d* 'strong', 'fast' (Old Saxon *swīdh*) + *heri* 'army'.

Schwitzer (122) **1.** German: variant of SCHWEITZER. **2.** German: habitational name for someone from Schwitz in Bohemia. **3.** Jewish (Ashkenazic): nickname from Yiddish *shvitser* 'one who perspires' or 'dandy' (one who dressed in fine clothes even if they made him perspire).
GIVEN NAMES German 6%. *Eldor* (2), *Fritz.*

Schwoch (119) German: of uncertain origin. Either an altered spelling or a variant of *Schwach*, a nickname for a weak, feeble person (from Middle High German *swach*), or, if of Slavic origin, from the reflexive adjective *svoj* 'own'.
GIVEN NAMES German 10%. *Kurt, Manfred, Matthias.*

Schwoerer (231) South German (Baden) and Swiss German (**Schwörer**): nickname for a conspirator, from an agent derivative of Middle High German *swern* 'to swear an oath'.

Schworm (107) German: of uncertain origin. Perhaps a nickname for a noisy person, from the verb stem of Middle Low German *schwormen* 'to make noise', 'rage'.

Sciacca (559) Italian (Sicily): habitational name from Sciacca in Agrigento.
GIVEN NAMES Italian 24%. *Angelo* (4), *Salvatore* (4), *Vito* (2), *Antonio, Attilio, Baldassare, Biagio, Bruna, Carmine, Francesco, Gasper, Geno, Mariano, Mario, Ricardo, Rosario.*

Scialabba (190) Italian (Sicily): most probably an unflattering nickname from a variant of *sciarabba*, *sciarrabba* 'imbiber', 'drunkard'.

GIVEN NAMES Italian 11%. *Angelo* (3), *Salvatore*.

Scialdone (181) Italian (Sicily): from a personal name of Arabic origin, an altered form of *Khaldūn*.

GIVEN NAMES Italian 14%. *Gino* (2), *Pasquale* (2), *Antimo, Antonio, Luigi, Salvatore, Vittorio*.

Sciandra (254) Italian (Sicily): from a feminine reduced form of the personal name *Lisciandro* (*Lysander*).

GIVEN NAMES Italian 22%. *Angelo* (9), *Salvatore* (9), *Luigi* (2), *Sal* (2), *Calogero, Carmela, Carmelo, Gaetano*.

Scianna (235) Italian (Sicily): **1.** assimilated form of SCIANDRA. **2.** from Arabic *shann* 'leather bag', 'bottle', presumably a metonymic occupational name for a maker of such items.

GIVEN NAMES Italian 17%. *Salvatore* (4), *Cosmo* (3), *Luciano* (2), *Carlo, Domenic, Francesco, Petrina, Sal*.

Sciara (182) Italian (Sicily): habitational name from any of various places so named, notably one near Palermo, named with Sicilian *sciara* 'lava (flow)', 'sandy plain', or 'scrubland'.

GIVEN NAMES Italian 17%. *Carlo* (2), *Sal* (2), *Angelo, Gaspare, Giuseppe, Salvatore, Sebastino, Vita*.

Sciarappa (114) Variant spelling of Italian **Sciarabba**, from Sicilian *sciarabba* 'wine', from Arabic *šarāb* 'potion', 'wine', applied as a nickname for a heavy drinker.

GIVEN NAMES Italian 11%; French 6%. *Angelo* (2), *Domenic, Domenico; Camille* (2).

Sciarra (316) Italian (Sicily and Campania): **1.** nickname for a quarrelsome or litigious person, from Sicilian, Calabrian *sciarra* 'quarrel', 'dispute', 'lawsuit'. **2.** habitational name from Sciarra in Palermo province, Sicily, named with a word denoting a volcanic area. Compare SCIARA.

GIVEN NAMES Italian 28%. *Mario* (4), *Antonio* (2), *Carmin* (2), *Nicola* (2), *Salvatore* (2), *Americo, Angelo, Carmella, Emilia, Enrico, Enzo, Federico, Gerardo, Gino, Giuseppe, Italo, Livio, Marisa, Temo*.

Sciarretta (107) Italian: diminutive of SCIARRA.

GIVEN NAMES Italian 20%. *Silvio* (2), *Antonio, Emidio, Gildo, Palma, Remo, Salvatore*.

Sciarrino (228) Italian (Sicily and Campania): nickname for a litigious person, from Sicilian, Calabrese *sciarrinu* 'one who readily goes to law', a derivative of *sciarra* (see SCIARRA 1).

GIVEN NAMES Italian 23%. *Sal* (4), *Antonino* (2), *Salvatore* (2), *Santo* (2), *Aldo, Angelo, Carmela, Domenico, Filippo, Marcello, Nunzio, Vicenzo*.

Sciascia (206) Southern Italian (Calabrian and Sicilian): **1.** from the female personal name *Sciascia*, a regional pet form of *Rosaria*. **2.** otherwise, possibly from Arabic *shāsha* 'length of muslin or silk for a turban'.

GIVEN NAMES Italian 18%. *Angelo* (4), *Salvatore* (4), *Vito* (2), *Carmelo, Dino, Leonardo, Marco, Rocco*.

Sciba (101) of Polish or German origin: possibly a variant of **Skibba**, a nickname from Sorbian *skiba* 'slice of bread'.

Scibelli (253) Italian (Campania): variant of *Sibelli*, itself a variant of the female personal name SIBILIA, *Sibilla*. Compare SCIBILIA.

GIVEN NAMES Italian 14%. *Salvatore* (6), *Gennaro* (2), *Filomena, Marco, Paolo, Salvator*.

Scibetta (226) Italian (Sicily): habitational name from Calascibetta in Enna, originally named in Arabic as *Qal'at-ṣibet*.

GIVEN NAMES Italian 15%. *Salvatore* (6), *Angelo, Carmelo, Gaetano, Stefano*.

Scibilia (200) Italian: from a variant of the female personal name SIBILIA.

GIVEN NAMES Italian 37%. *Giuseppe* (3), *Rosario* (2), *Angelo, Antonio, Carmela, Fabio, Fortunato, Gaspare, Girolamo, Rocco, Sal, Salvatore, Santo*.

Scicchitano (191) Southern Italian (Sicily, Calabria): habitational name for someone from Scicli in Ragusa.

GIVEN NAMES Italian 25%. *Agostino, Aldo, Angelo, Carmine, Caterina, Cosimo, Cosmo, Geno, Giancarlo, Pasquale, Salvatore, Saverio*.

Scifres (251) Origin unidentified.

Scigliano (132) Italian (northern Calabria): habitational name from Scigliano in Cosenza.

GIVEN NAMES Italian 8%. *Domenic, Mauro, Rocco, Sal*.

Scime (134) Italian (Sicily): from a reduced form of a personal name, *Scimen*, derived from an archaic form of the Spanish personal name *Jimeno* (see SIMON).

GIVEN NAMES Italian 16%. *Salvatore* (2), *Angelo, Luigi, Pasquale, Santo*.

Scimeca (355) Italian (Sicily): **1.** from a derivative of SCIME. **2.** habitational name from a place so named.

GIVEN NAMES Italian 13%. *Salvatore* (5), *Sal* (2), *Vito* (2), *Antonio, Santo*.

Scimone (143) Southern Italian (Sicily and southern Calabria): from the personal name *Scimone*, a palatalized variant of *Simone*, Italian form of SIMON.

GIVEN NAMES Italian 17%. *Angelo* (2), *Antonino, Antonio, Bartolo, Gaspar, Mario, Matteo, Santo*.

Scinta (136) Italian: unexplained; presumably a variant of SCINTO. This is a rare name in Italy, occurring mainly in the north, in Liguria and Piedmont.

GIVEN NAMES Italian 7%; French 5%. *Marco, Salvatore; Alphonse, Pierre*.

Scinto (242) Southern Italian (Campania and Apulia): of uncertain derivation; possibly from a variant of the personal name *Cinto*, probably a short form of GIACINTO.

GIVEN NAMES Italian 7%. *Angelo* (2), *Antonio, Leonardo, Nicola*.

Scioli (157) Italian: patronymic from a derivative of *Scio*, a palatalized reduced form of the personal name DESIO.

GIVEN NAME Italian 5%. *Filomena*.

Scioneaux (159) LA name from French **Sionneau**, a diminutive of **Sion**, a habitational name from a place so named; or perhaps a patronymic from a nickname from *scion* 'twig', 'shoot'.

GIVEN NAMES French 6%. *Antoine, Germaine, Monique*.

Scionti (117) Southern Italian (Calabria, Sicily): perhaps a variant of **Cionti** and so a variant of GIUNTA.

GIVEN NAMES Italian 22%. *Salvatore* (2), *Angelo, Guido, Mario, Ricardo, Santo, Sebastiano, Vittorio*.

Sciortino (747) Italian (Sicily): **1.** occupational name from a diminutive of *sciorta*, *sciurta* 'city guard', 'watchman', 'policeman' (Arabic *shurṭī*). **2.** habitational name from Sortino in Siracusa.

GIVEN NAMES Italian 27%; Spanish 5%. *Salvatore* (12), *Rosario* (5), *Sal* (5), *Vito* (4), *Antonio* (3), *Lorenzo* (3), *Alfonso* (2), *Gino* (2), *Luigi* (2), *Pietro* (2), *Saverio* (2), *Angelo, Carmine, Ciro; Salvador* (2), *Carlos, Ines, Raul*.

Scioscia (127) Italian: from a Neapolitan dialect word meaning 'to wash out', 'to rinse'; *Sciosciammocca* is a character of Neapolitan folk theatre representing idle words.

GIVEN NAMES Italian 17%. *Oreste* (2), *Angelo, Dante, Domenico, Gaetano*.

Scipio (220) Italian (Sicily): **1.** from the ancient Roman personal name, Latin *Scipio*, originally a nickname meaning 'stick', 'sceptre'. **2.** habitational name from a place so named.

GIVEN NAME French 5%. *Dominique* (2).

Scipione (239) Italian: from the personal name, a derivative of SCIPIO.

GIVEN NAMES Italian 16%. *Angelo* (2), *Umberto* (2), *Aldo, Giuseppe, Guerino, Libero, Paolo, Rocco, Salvatore, Vittorio*.

Scipioni (114) Italian: patronymic or plural form of SCIPIONE.

GIVEN NAMES Italian 16%; French 6%. *Gino* (3), *Dario, Francesco, Gesualdo, Mauro, Renzo, Sylvio; Aristide, Camille*.

Scire (222) Italian (Sicily): from a shortened form of **Scirea**, an occupational name for a barber, from Greek *xyréas*, composed of *xyron* 'razor' + the occupational suffix *-éas*.

GIVEN NAMES Italian 11%. *Salvatore* (3), *Antonio* (2), *Bartolo, Luigi, Pino, Sal*.

Scism (373) Origin unidentified.

Scites (125) Origin unidentified.

Sciulli (259) Italian: patronymic or plural form of SCIULLO.

GIVEN NAMES Italian 41%. *Enrico* (6), *Domenico* (4), *Carmine* (3), *Lorenzo* (3), *Angelo* (2), *Antonio* (2), *Carlo* (2), *Dino* (2), *Domenic* (2), *Mario* (2), *Nicola* (2), *Nicoletta* (2), *Nunzio* (2), *Orlando* (2).

Sciullo (212) Italian: palatalized variant of SULLO.

GIVEN NAMES Italian 15%. *Angelo* (5), *Donato, Italo, Nevio, Nicola, Oreste*.

Sciuto (201) Italian: Ligurian variant (from Sicilian *sciutu*) of **Sciutto**, a nickname for a thin person, from Old Italian *sciutto*, a reduced form of *asciutto* 'skinny', 'thin' (from Latin *exsuctus* 'sucked out', 'dried up').

GIVEN NAMES Italian 21%. *Alfio* (3), *Carmelo* (2), *Salvatore* (2), *Agatino, Angelo, Antonio, Cesare, Gaetano, Gaspare, Ignazio, Leonardo, Sebastino*.

Scivally (108) Origin unidentified.

Sclafani (694) Italian (Sicily): habitational name from a place so called in the Palermo region, probably from Latin *scaphula* 'little boat', 'skiff'.

GIVEN NAMES Italian 19%. *Salvatore* (8), *Mario* (5), *Sal* (5), *Gasper* (4), *Angelo* (2), *Antonio* (2), *Damiano* (2), *Francesco* (2), *Luciano* (2), *Santo* (2), *Amadeo, Amedio, Carmello*.

Sclar (108) Variant spelling of Jewish and Slavic SKLAR.

GIVEN NAMES Jewish 7%. *Arieh, Hyman*.

Scobee (321) Altered spelling of SCOBIE.

Scobey (268) Variant of SCOBIE.

Scobie (215) Scottish: habitational name from a lost place in Perthshire, named with Gaelic *sgolbach* 'thorny place'.

Scoble (141) English (Devon and Cornwall): habitational name from Scoble in Devon.

Scoby (211) Northern Irish variant of Scottish SCOBIE.

Scofield (2592) English: variant spelling of SCHOFIELD.

Scoggin (784) English: unexplained.

Scoggins (2942) English: unexplained.

Scogin (499) Variant of English SCOGGIN.

Scola (526) Italian (Sicily): topographic name from *scola*, Sicilian form of *scuola* 'school', 'retreat'; also 'synagogue'.

GIVEN NAMES Italian 10%. *Angelo* (5), *Ercole* (2), *Gino, Luigi, Pasquale, Pietro, Rocco, Salvatore, Silvio*.

Scolari (144) Italian: patronymic or plural form of SCOLARO.

GIVEN NAMES Italian 18%. *Marco* (3), *Giacomo, Lino, Rafael, Sergio, Ulisse*.

Scolaro (366) Italian: occupational name or nickname from *scolaro* 'scholar', 'pupil', 'follower' (from Late Latin *scholaris* 'of or belonging to a school'). The Greek word *skholarios* also denoted a member of the imperial guard in Byzantium.

GIVEN NAMES Italian 21%; Spanish 5%. *Salvatore* (3), *Carmelo* (2), *Domenic* (2), *Mario* (2), *Antonio, Attilio, Carmello, Cono, Sal, Salvator, Santino, Santo, Teodoro*; *Placido, Ramona, Rosalia, Salvador*.

Scoles (570) Northern English: variant spelling of SCHOLES.

Scollard (179) English and Scottish: variant of SCHOLAR 1. The surname is also established in Ireland.

Scollon (105) Irish: Leinster variant of SCULLLIN (see SCULLION).

Scolnick (124) Respelling of Jewish SKOLNICK.

GIVEN NAME Jewish 7%. *Meyer*.

Scoma (162) Italian (Sicily): variant of **Scuma**, a nickname from *scuma*, a Sicilian variant of *schiuma* 'thick froth or foam'; also 'peasant', 'rustic'.

GIVEN NAMES Italian 13%. *Salvatore* (4), *Carmelo, Petrina, Sal, Vito*.

Sconce (139) Scottish and English: of uncertain origin: **1.** perhaps a topographic name from Middle English *sconce* 'defensive earthwork' or 'protective screen of brushwood', from Dutch *schans*. **2.** alternatively, perhaps a nickname for someone who carried a lantern with a screen to protect the flame from the wind, Middle English *skonse*, Old French *esconse*.

Sconiers (135) Variant of English CONYERS.

Sconyers (250) Variant of English CONYERS.

Scopel (108) Italian: reduced form of the Sicilian family name **Scopello**, a habitational name from any of various places named with this word, for example in Trapani, from Latin *scopellus*, from Greek *skopelos* 'watch tower'. The Greek word also means 'reef' and 'obstacle'. Skopelos is the name of an island in the Aegean.

GIVEN NAMES Italian 11%. *Attilio, Elio, Ennio, Siro*.

Scopelliti (107) Italian: from a diminutive of **Scopello** (see SCOPEL).

GIVEN NAMES Italian 23%. *Pasquale* (2), *Rocco* (2), *Franca, Francesca, Francesco, Orlando*.

Scordato (136) Italian (Sicily): from *scurdatu* 'forgotten', 'left behind', presumably a nickname of anecdotal origin.

GIVEN NAMES Italian 23%. *Angelo* (6), *Alicia* (2), *Rosario* (2), *Alessandro, Concetta, Sal, Salvatore*.

Scordo (137) Southern Italian (Calabria and Sicily): metonymic occupational name for someone who grew or sold garlic, from a regional word derived from medieval Greek *skordon* 'garlic' (Classical Greek *skorodon*).

GIVEN NAMES Italian 22%. *Angelo* (2), *Francesco, Nunzio, Pasquale, Rosario, Sal, Vincenzo*.

Score (219) English: topographic name from Middle English *score* 'steep place'

(Old English *scoru*), or a habitational name from Score in Ilfracombe or Scur Farm in Braunton, Devon.

Scorsone (156) Italian (Sicily): nickname from *scursuni*, Sicilian form of Italian *scorzone*, denoting a type of snake.

GIVEN NAMES Italian 16%. *Domenica, Ernesto, Francesco, Hermina, Santo, Vito*.

Scorza (149) Italian: metonymic occupational name for a tanner or for someone who removed or worked the bark from the cork oak, from *scorza* 'bark', 'peel', 'skin', a derivative of *scorzare* 'to skin or flay' (Latin *excoriare*, from *corium* 'skin', 'hide').

GIVEN NAMES Italian 12%. *Mario* (2), *Raul* (2), *Aldo, Enzo, Salvatore, Vito*.

Scotch (124) English and Irish: ethnic name for someone from Scotland.

Scotland (228) **1.** English: ethnic name for someone from Scotland. **2.** English: from the rare Norman personal name *Escotland*, composed of the ethnic name *Scot* + *land* 'territory'. **3.** Scottish: habitational name from a place called Scotland(well) near Loch Leven in Kinross.

Scott (137971) **1.** English: ethnic name for someone with Scottish connections. **2.** Scottish and Irish: ethnic name for a Gaelic speaker.

Scotten (217) English: variant spelling of SCOTTON.

Scotti (744) Italian: patronymic or plural form of SCOTTO.

GIVEN NAMES Italian 16%. *Carmine* (5), *Salvatore* (5), *Antonio* (3), *Ciro* (2), *Rocco* (2), *Silvio* (2), *Angelo, Domenic, Elio, Gaetano, Giacomo, Gino*.

Scotto (684) Italian: **1.** ethnic name for someone from Scotland or Ireland, from medieval Italian *scot(t)o* 'Scot'. **2.** from a reduced form of personal names such as *Marescotto*, a pet form of MARESCO, or *Francescotto*, a pet form of FRANCESCO.

GIVEN NAMES Italian 32%. *Salvatore* (10), *Sal* (7), *Aniello* (4), *Biagio* (3), *Ciro* (3), *Alessio* (2), *Antonio* (2), *Elvira* (2), *Gennaro* (2), *Mario* (2), *Marta* (2), *Angelo, Arturo, Biaggio, Biago, Geraldo, Gerardo, Liberta, Mariano*.

Scotton (255) English: habitational name from places so named in Lincolnshire and North Yorkshire, from Old English *scot* 'Scot' (influenced by Scandinavian *sk-*) + *tūn* 'enclosure', 'settlement'.

Scouten (289) Possibly of Dutch origin: unexplained.

Scovel (310) English: variant of SCOVILLE.

Scovell (179) English: variant of SCOVILLE.

Scovil (233) English: variant of SCOVILLE

Scovill (347) English: variant of SCOVILLE.

Scoville (1174) English (of Norman origin) and French: habitational name from Escoville in Calvados, Normandy, or in some cases perhaps from a place so called in Mohiville, in the Belgian province of Namur.

Scow (175) **1.** Americanized spelling of Norwegian SKAU. **2.** Perhaps English, a habitational name from Scow in Cumbria. There is also a Scow Brook in Derbyshire, and Scow Hall in North Yorkshire.

Scowden (161) English: unexplained.

Scozzafava (155) Italian: phrasal nickname or occupational name for someone who removed beans from their pods, from *scozzare* 'to shell' + *fava* 'bean'.
GIVEN NAMES Italian 15%. *Angelo* (3), *Luigi*, *Saverio*.

Scozzari (154) Italian (western Sicily): from **Scozzaro**, probably an occupational name for someone who lopped trees; compare Calabrian *scuzzari* 'to pollard'.
GIVEN NAMES Italian 16%. *Gaetano* (3), *Salvatore* (2).

Scragg (149) English: from an Old Norse personal name or byname, *Skragg*, related to Norwegian dialect *skragg* 'a shriveled, wretched person', and English *scraggy* 'lean', 'skinny'.

Scranton (930) Apparently English: unexplained.

Screen (199) English (West Midlands): unexplained.

Screws (320) Origin unidentified.

Scriber (190) Americanized form of SCHREIBER.

Scribner (2552) English: variant of SCRIVENER.
FOREBEARS The Scribner family that founded the American publishing house was established in America by one Benjamin Scrivener, who settled in Norwalk, CT in 1680. The present form of the name was adopted after 1742. The firm was established in 1846 by Charles Scribner (1821–71), who was born in NY, where his father was established as a prosperous merchant.

Scrima (140) Italian (Sicily): **1.** from an old Sicilian word *scrima* 'fencing', a derivative of *scrimire* 'to fence', presumably a nickname for a skilled swordsman or perhaps for a quarrelsome person. **2.** alternatively, it may be a descriptive nickname from Sicilian *scrima* 'parting (of the hair)'.
GIVEN NAMES Italian 7%. *Lorenzo*, *Salvatore*.

Scripps (112) Origin unidentified; perhaps a variant of CRIPPS with excrescent initial *S-*.

Scripter (160) Probably English (see SCRIPTURE).

Scripture (174) English and Scottish: occupational name for a clerk or scribe, from Latin *scriptor* 'writer', 'clerk'. The name has been altered from its original Latin form through association with the more familiar English word *scripture* 'Bible'.

Scritchfield (260) English: habitational name from a lost or unidentified place.

Scrivani (131) Italian: patronymic form of **Scrivano**, an occupational name for a clerk, secretary, or scribe, *scrivano* (from medieval Latin *scribanus*, from Late Latin *scriba*, *scribanis*). Compare English

SCRIVEN. In the form **Skrivanos** this also occurs as a Greek family name.
GIVEN NAMES Italian 6%. *Angelo*, *Tullio*.

Scriven (631) English: occupational name for a clerk or copyist, from Old French *escrivein*, *escrivain* 'writer', 'scribe' (medieval Latin *scribanus*).

Scrivener (327) English and Scottish: occupational name for a clerk or copyist (see SCRIVEN).

Scrivens (266) English: patronymic from SCRIVEN.

Scriver (148) Americanized form of Dutch **de Scrijver** 'the scribe', from Middle Dutch *scrivere* 'scribe', 'clerk'. Compare English SCRIVEN, German SCHREIBER.

Scrivner (995) English: variant of SCRIVENER.

Scroggie (100) Scottish: habitational name from a place in Perthshire called Scroggie.

Scroggin (387) Scottish or English: unexplained. Compare SCOGGIN.

Scroggins (2780) Scottish or English: unexplained.

Scroggs (765) **1.** English: topographic name from Middle English *scrogge* 'brushwood'. **2.** Scottish: habitational name from Scrogges in Peeblesshire.

Scrogham (191) English: possibly a habitational name from a lost or unidentified place.

Scronce (241) Origin unidentified.

Scruggs (5152) Probably an altered form of SCROGGS.

Scruton (226) English: habitational name from a place in North Yorkshire, so called from the Old Norse byname *Skurfa* 'scurf' + Old English *tūn* 'enclosure', 'settlement'.

Scudder (1634) English: variant of SCUTT 1, with the addition of the Middle English agent suffix *-er*.

Scuderi (502) Italian (Sicily): patronymic form of **Scudero**, a status name equivalent to SQUIRE, from *scudero* 'shieldbearer', Latin *scutarius*, an agent derivative of *scutum* 'shield'. In Byzantium, the Greek word *skoutarios*, a derivative of this, denoted a member of the imperial guard.
GIVEN NAMES Italian 26%. *Carmelo* (6), *Salvatore* (5), *Angelo* (4), *Carlo* (3), *Gaetano* (3), *Vito* (3), *Antonio* (2), *Dante* (2), *Mario* (2), *Rocco* (2), *Rosario* (2), *Antonino*, *Biaggio*, *Eduardo*, *Ermelinda*, *Margarita*.

Scull (789) English: nickname for a bald-headed man or someone of cadaverous appearance, from Middle English *sc(h)olle*, *sc(h)ulle* 'skull' (probably of Scandinavian origin).
FOREBEARS Nicholas Scull emigrated from Bristol, England, to Philadelphia, PA, with his brother John in 1685. He founded a wealthy Quaker family whose descendants have been prominent in western PA, in law, newspaper publication, and banking.

Sculley (281) Irish: variant spelling of SCULLY.

Scullin (366) Irish: variant of SCULLION.
GIVEN NAMES Irish 5%. *Brendan*, *Brigid*.

Scullion (349) Irish (Ulster): reduced form of **O'Scullion**, probably an Anglicized form of Gaelic **Ó Scoláidhín**, from a diminutive of *scolaidhe* 'scholar'. Compare SCULLY.

Scully (3596) Irish: reduced Anglicized form of Gaelic **Ó Scolaidhe** 'descendant of the scholar', from *scolaidhe* 'scholar'.
GIVEN NAMES Irish 5%. *Dermot* (2), *Aidan*, *Aileen*, *Brendan*, *Bridie*, *Declan*, *Donal*, *Eamon*, *Liam*, *Niall*, *Ronan*.

Sculthorpe (102) English: habitational name from an place in Norfolk, named with the Old Norse personal name *Skúli* + *thorp* 'outlying settlement', 'hamlet'.

Scungio (121) Italian: unexplained. In Italy this surname is found chiefly in Campania, in Avellino and Caserta.
GIVEN NAMES Italian 14%. *Pasco* (2), *Angelo*, *Antonio*, *Carmine*, *Silvio*.

Scurlock (928) Welsh and Irish: probably from a personal name formed with Welsh *ysgor* 'fort', 'camp', 'defense' + the adjectival suffix *-og*. The family name is strongly associated from an early date (1184 and 1250) with two fortified manors in South Wales, Scurlage in the Gower Peninsula and Scurla, now known as Trecastell, near Llantrisant, in mid Glamorgan. However, it is not clear whether the family name is derived from the place name or vice versa.

Scurry (513) Irish: reduced Anglicized form of Gaelic **Ó Scoireadh** 'descendant of *Scoireadh*'. Woulfe believes Ó Scoireadh and Ó Scurra (see SCARRY) to be localized variants of the same name, while Mac-Lysaght regards them as two different names.

Scutt (297) **1.** Americanized spelling of Dutch SCHUTTE 'archer'. **2.** English: occupational name for a scout or spy, or a nickname for someone who behaved like one, from Middle English *scut* 'scout' (Old French *escoute*, from *escouter* 'to listen'). **3.** English: nickname for a swift runner, from Middle English *scut* 'hare'.
GIVEN NAMES French 4%. *Camille*, *Pierre*.

Sczepanski (129) Variant spelling of Polish **Szczepański** (see SZCZEPANSKI).
GIVEN NAMES German 4%. *Aloysius*, *Otto*.

Sea (261) English: variant spelling of SEE.

Seabaugh (530) Altered spelling of German SEEBACH.

Seaberg (475) **1.** Partial translation of Swedish **Sjöberg**, an ornamental name composed of the elements *sjö* 'sea' + *berg* 'mountain', 'hill'. **2.** English: from a Middle English form of an Old English feminine personal name, *Sǣburh*, composed of the elements *sǣ* 'sea' + *burh* 'fortified place'. **3.** Possibly also English: habitational name from Seaborough in Dorset (from Old English *seofon* 'seven' +

beorg 'hill', 'burial mound') or possibly from Seaborough Hall in Essex.

GIVEN NAMES Scandinavian 8%; German 4%. *Einer, Erik, Gunner, Hilmer, Iver; Kurt* (2), *Gerhard*.

Seaberry (153) Variant of Swedish SEABERG.

Seabold (183) See SEABOLT.

Seabolt (1249) Americanized spelling of German **Se(e)bold(t)** or **Siebold** (see SEBALD).

Seaborn (569) English: from an Old English personal name, *Sǣbeorn*, composed of the elements *sǣ* 'sea' + *beorn* 'warrior', which survived into Middle English.

Seaborne (102) English: variant of SEABORN.

Seabourn (123) English: variant of SEABORN.

Seabright (147) English: from a medieval continuation of an Old English personal name, *Sǣbeorht*, composed of the elements *sǣ* 'sea' + *beorht* 'bright'. The Middle English name was probably reinforced by the more common Old English name *Sigebeorht*, whose first element is *sige* 'victory'.

Seabrook (799) English: habitational name from a place in Buckinghamshire, so called from the Old English river name *Sǣge*, which probably meant 'trickling', 'slow-moving', + Old English *brōc* 'stream'.

Seabrooks (226) English: variant of SEABROOK.

Seaburg (202) Variant Americanized form of Swedish **Sjöberg** (see SEABERG).

GIVEN NAMES Scandinavian 5%; German 4%. *Erik; Kurt*.

Seaburn (101) Variant of SEABORN.

Seabury (372) English: variant of SEABERG.

FOREBEARS The first bishop of the Episcopal Church in America, Samuel Seabury (1729–96), was born at Groton, CT, and was a descendant of John Seabury who had emigrated from England to Boston, MA, in 1639.

Seacat (137) Origin unidentified.

Seachrist (128) Altered form of German SIEGRIST.

Seacrist (139) Altered spelling of German SIEGRIST.

Seader (165) English: occupational name for a farm laborer, from Middle English *sedere* 'sower' (agent derivative of *sed* 'seed').

Seaford (156) English: habitational name from Seaford in East Sussex, named in Old English with *sǣ* 'sea' + *ford* 'ford'; until the 16th century the Ouse river flowed into the sea here.

Seager (780) **1.** English: from the Middle English personal name *Segar*, Old English *Sǣgar*, composed of the elements *sǣ* 'sea' + *gār* 'spear'. **2.** Americanized spelling of German SEEGER.

Seagle (696) Americanized form of Jewish SEGAL or German SIEGEL.

Seago (609) English (Norfolk): unexplained.

Seagrave (253) English: habitational name from a place in Leicestershire, recorded in Domesday Book as *Satgrave* and *Setgrave*; probably named from Old English *(ge)set* 'fold', 'pen' (or *sēað* 'pit', 'pool') + *grāf* 'grove' or *grǣf* 'ditch'.

Seagraves (1003) English: variant of SEAGRAVE.

Seagren (291) Part translation of the common Swedish ornamental name **Sjögren** (see SJOGREN).

Seagroves (291) English: variant of SEAGRAVE.

Seaholm (172) Part-translation of the Swedish ornamental name **Sjöholm**, composed of the elements *sjö* 'sea' + *holm* 'islet'.

GIVEN NAMES Scandinavian 10%. *Nils, Ove*.

Seahorn (109) Origin unidentified.

Seal (3258) **1.** English: variant of SALE 1. **2.** English: metonymic occupational name for a maker of seals or signet rings, from Middle English, Old French *seel* 'seal' (Latin *sigillum*). **3.** English: metonymic occupational name for a maker of saddles, from Old French *seele* 'saddle'. **4.** English: nickname for a plump or ungainly person, from Middle English *sele* 'seal' (the aquatic mammal). **5.** Americanized form (translation) of Jewish SIEGEL.

Sealander (117) **1.** German: altered spelling of German **Seeländer**, a status name from Middle High German *sellant, sallant* 'manor' for the person upon whom the manor was bestowed. Compare SAAL 1. **2.** German: habitational and topographic name for a person from a place named Seeland in Schleswig-Holstein or from the Danish island so named. **3.** Americanized spelling of Swedish **Sjölander**, an ornamental name from *sjö* 'sea' + the common surname suffix *-ander*.

Seale (2413) English: variant of SEAL 1–4; it is also established as a surname in Ireland.

Seales (520) English: patronymic from SEAL 4.

Sealey (994) English: variant spelling of SEELEY.

Sealock (263) Origin unidentified.

Seals (4329) English: patronymic from SEAL 4.

Sealy (1121) **1.** English: variant spelling of SEALEY. **2.** Welsh: from the personal name *Selyf* or *Selau*, medieval Welsh vernacular forms of SOLOMON. **3.** Irish: probably a variant of SHEALY (in counties Kerry and Cork); in other areas it is of English or Welsh origin, as in 1 and 2.

Seaman (5612) **1.** English (Norfolk): from a medieval continuation of the Old English personal name *Sǣmann*, composed of the elements *sǣ* 'sea' + *mann* 'man'. **2.** English: occupational name for a sailor.

3. Americanized spelling of German and Jewish SEEMANN.

Seamans (861) Variant of English SEAMONS.

Seamon (859) Variant of English SEAMAN.

Seamons (300) English: patronymic from SEAMAN.

Seamster (390) English: occupational name for someone who sewed for a living.

Seaney (119) Variant of English and Irish SEENEY.

Seanor (136) English: variant of SENIOR, mainly of 1.

Seaquist (171) Americanized form of Swedish SJOQUIST.

GIVEN NAMES German 4%; Scandinavian 4%. *Klaus; Maren*.

Sear (224) English and Welsh: variant of SAYER.

Searcey (131) English or Irish: variant of SEARCY.

Search (299) English: variant of SURRIDGE 1.

Searcy (3359) English: unexplained. It may be a variant of SEARS or SAYERS.

Searer (149) English: unexplained.

Searfoss (535) Origin unidentified.

Searight (263) English: variant of SURRIDGE 1.

Searing (314) English: unexplained.

Searl (429) English: variant of SEARLE.

Searle (1700) English: from the Norman personal name *Serlo*, Germanic *Sarilo, Serilo*. This was probably originally a byname cognate with Old Norse *Sorli*, and akin to Old English *searu* 'armor', meaning perhaps 'defender', 'protector'.

Searles (2277) English: patronymic from SEARLE.

Searls (554) English: variant spelling of SEARLES.

Sears (11763) **1.** Irish (Kerry): Anglicized form of Gaelic **Mac Saoghair**, which in turn may be a patronymic from a Gaelicized form of the Old English personal name *Saeger* (see 2 below). **2.** English: patronymic from a Middle English personal name *Saher* or *Seir* (see SAYER 1). **3.** Americanized form of French CYR.

FOREBEARS Richard Sears came to Plymouth, MA, from England about 1630.

Searson (175) English: patronymic from a Middle English personal name, *Saher* or *Seir* (see SAYER 1).

Sease (625) Origin unidentified. In part, possibly a respelling of German **Siess**, a variant of **Süss** (see SUSS).

Seasholtz (102) Partly altered spelling of German **Süssholz**, literally 'sweet wood', of uncertain origin.

Seastrand (103) Americanized form of an unidentified German name.

GIVEN NAME German 11%. *Kurt* (4).

Seastrom (157) Part-translation of Swedish **Sjöström** (see SJOSTROM).

Seat (259) English: perhaps a variant of **Sait**, from the Old English personal name *Sǣgēat* ('sea Geat').

Seaton (3327) Scottish and English: habitational name from any of the various places so called. A Scottish place of this name near Longniddry is so named because it was held from the 12th century by a Norman family *de Sey*, from Say in Indre. Other places of this name, for example those in Cumbria, Devon, County Durham, Northumbria, and Yorkshire, are mostly named with Old English *sǣ* 'sea', 'lake' + *tūn* 'enclosure', 'settlement'. One in Rutland seems to have as its first element a stream name, *Sǣge* (see SEABROOK), or a personal name *Sǣga*. One in Kent is named with Old English *seten* 'plantation', 'cultivated land'.

Seats (261) English (Gloucestershire): unexplained.

Seaver (1407) English: from the medieval personal name *Sefare*. a continuation of an unattested Old English female name, *Sǣfaru*, composed of the elements *sǣ* 'sea' + *faru* 'journey'. This name has also been established in Ireland since the early 17th century.

Seavers (282) **1.** English (Yorkshire): patronymic from SEAVER. **2.** Altered spelling of German SIEVERS.

Seavey (1063) Possibly English: unexplained. Compare SEAVY

Seavy (114) Possibly English: unexplained. Compare SEAVEY.

Seaward (210) English: variant of SEWARD.

Seawell (464) Variant of English SEWELL.

Seawright (548) English: see SURRIDGE 1.

Seay (4768) Scottish or Irish:

Seba (119) German (of Slavic origin): from Sorbian *zeba* 'finch', hence a nickname. Compare ADLER, FINK, SCHWALBE.
GIVEN NAMES German 6%. *Franz, Heinz, Kurt.*

Sebald (212) German (chiefly Bavaria) and French (**Sébald**): from the Germanic personal name *Sebald*, composed of the elements *sigi* 'victory' + *bald* 'courageous', 'bold'. This was popular in Nuremburg, being the name of the city's patron saint. Compare SEIBOLD.
GIVEN NAMES German 7%. *Erwin, Hans, Johann, Otto, Reinhold.*

Sebastian (3139) German, Spanish (**Sebastián**), and southern French (**Sébastian**): from the personal name *Sebastian*, Latin *Sebastianus*. This was originally an ethnic name meaning 'man from *Sebastia*', a city in Pontus named from Greek *sebastos* 'revered' (the Greek equivalent of *Augustus*). This surname is also sometimes born by Jews, presumably as an adoption of the German surname.

Sebastiani (146) Italian: patronymic or plural form of SEBASTIANO.
GIVEN NAMES Italian 25%; Spanish 14%. *Angelo* (2), *Pasquale* (2), *Agnese, Antonio,* *Berardino, Dino, Franca, Guelfo, Luigi, Marco, Piero, Salvatore*; *Luis* (4), *Jose* (2), *Mario* (2), *Americo, Elesio, Eraldo, Frederico, Gabriela, Lino, Tito.*

Sebastiano (127) Italian: from the personal name *Sebastiano*, from Latin *Sebastianus* (see SEBASTIAN).
GIVEN NAMES Italian 24%. *Angelo* (3), *Americo, Carmine, Pasquale, Rinaldo, Sal, Serafina, Vito.*

Sebben (135) Dutch: patronymic from a pet form of a Germanic compound personal name formed with *sigi* 'victory' + an element beginning with *b-* (for example, *bald, brand, berht*).
GIVEN NAMES Italian 13%. *Angelo* (3), *Mauro* (3), *Aldo* (2), *Guido* (2), *Gildo, Reno.*

Sebby (142) English: unexplained.

Sebek (284) Czech and Slovak (**Šebek**): from a pet form of the personal name *Šebestián*, Czech form of SEBASTIAN.
GIVEN NAMES Czech and Slovak 5%; German 4%. *Milan* (2), *Jaroslav, Ladislav, Pavel*; *Kurt* (2), *Fritz.*

Sebens (111) Variant of Dutch **Sibbens**, **Siebens**, a patronymic from *Sibbe, Siebe,* a short form of a Germanic personal name such as *Sebrecht, Sibrand.*

Seber (187) Probably an altered spelling of French SEBERT.

Sebert (233) German and French: from a German personal name composed of the elements *sigi* 'victory' + *berht* 'bright', 'famous'.

Sebesta (542) Czech and Slovak (**Šebesta**): from a short form of the personal name *Šebestián* (see SEBASTIAN).

Sebestyen (139) Hungarian (**Sebestyén**): from the personal name *Sebestyén*, Hungarian form of SEBASTIAN.
GIVEN NAMES Hungarian 18%. *Geza* (2), *Zoltan* (2), *Bela, Denes, Elek, Laszlo, Mihaly, Tamas, Tibor.*

Sebo (188) **1.** Americanized form of Norwegian **Sæbø**, a habitational name from any of over fifteen farmsteads on the west coast of Norway, named in Old Norse as *Sæbær* or *Sævarbýr*, from *sær* 'sea' + *býr* 'farm'. **2.** Hungarian (**Sebő**): from a pet form of the personal name *Sebestyén*, Hungarian form of SEBASTIAN.

Sebok (136) Hungarian (**Sebők**): from a pet form of the personal name **Sebestyén**, Hungarian form of SEBASTIAN.

Sebold (226) Variant of German or French SEBALD.

Sebolt (131) Variant of German or French SEBALD.

Sebourn (107) Variant of English SEABORN.

Sebranek (117) Czech (**Sebránek**): descriptive name for a foundling, from a derivative of the adjective *sebraný* 'picked up'.

Sebree (333) English: probably a variant of English **Sebry**, a variant of SEABERG.

Sebren (144) Origin unidentified. Perhaps a metathesized variant of **Siburn**, itself a variant of SEABORN.

Sebright (102) English: variant of SEABRIGHT.

Sebring (951) Possibly an Americanized form of Swedish **Sjöbring**, an ornamental name formed with *sjö* 'sea' + a second element of uncertain etymology, perhaps the place name element *bring*, denoting a protrusion in the landscape.

Seccombe (101) English (Devon): habitational name from either of two places in Devon, both so named from the Old English personal name *Secca* + Old English *cumb* 'valley'.

Sechler (645) Perhaps a variant of German SECKLER.

Sechrest (483) Variant of German SIEGRIST.

Sechrist (1035) Variant of German SIEGRIST.

Seck (261) **1.** North German: topographic name for someone who lived in a damp place, from Low German *seck* 'wet land', or a habitational name from Seck near Limburg. **2.** Dutch: nickname from a Dutch spelling of French *sec* 'dry'.
GIVEN NAMES African 11%. *Mamadou* (4), *Cheikh* (2), *Aissatou, Babacar, Fatou, Mame, Mohamadou, Oumar, Serigne, Thierno.*

Seckel (238) **1.** German: metonymic occupational name for a maker of purses from Middle High German *seckel* 'purse'. **2.** North German: metonymic occupational name for a sickle maker, from Middle Low German *sekele* 'sickle'. **3.** South German: nickname from a diminutive of Middle High German *sack* 'sack'.
GIVEN NAMES German 5%. *Gunter* (2), *Heinz.*

Secker (142) **1.** English: variant of SAKER. **2.** North German: habitational name for someone who lived in a damp place, a derivative of SECK 1. **3.** Jewish (Ashkenazic): from SACK 1, with the agent suffix *-er*.
GIVEN NAMES Jewish 5%. *Nachum* (2), *Zehava.*

Seckinger (353) German: habitational name for someone from Säckingen, on the Rhine near Basel.

Seckler (204) **1.** German and Jewish (Ashkenazic): occupational name for a purser, or for a purse-maker, from an agent derivative of Middle High German *seckel*, Yiddish *zekl* 'purse', 'pouch'. **2.** English: from Old French *seculier* 'secular', hence a status name for a member of the secular clergy, or a nickname for someone without religious inclination.

Seckman (283) Origin unidentified.

Secor (1229) **1.** Altered form of Dutch SEGER. **2.** Altered spelling of French Canadian SICARD.

Secora (146) Polish and Jewish (from Poland): variant of SIKORA.

Secord (706) Origin unidentified. Possibly an altered spelling of French Canadian SICARD.

Secore (109) Origin unidentified. Possibly an altered spelling of French Canadian SICARD.

Secoy (129) Origin unidentified. Perhaps an altered spelling of French Canadian SICARD.

Secrease (102) Variant of German SIEGRIST.

Secrest (1317) Variant of German SIEGRIST.

Secrist (796) Variant of German SIEGRIST.

Secunda (101) Origin unidentified. Perhaps a respelling of French **Secondat**, from the personal name *Second* 'second' (from Latin *Secundus*), bestowed on the second child.

Seda (483) **1.** Jewish (Sephardic) and Catalan: metonymic occupational name for a silk merchant, from *seda* 'silk'. **2.** Portuguese: habitational name from a place so called in the Portuguese region of Alentejo. **3.** Czech (**Šeda**): nickname from the adjective *šedý* 'gray(-haired)'. **4.** Polish (**Sęda**): from *Sęda*, a pet form of the Polish personal names *Sędzimir*, composed of the elements *sądzić* 'to judge' + *mir* 'peace', or *Sędziwoj*, from *sądzić* 'to judge' + *woj* 'warrior'.
GIVEN NAMES Spanish 32%. *Jose* (7), *Eduardo* (5), *Juan* (5), *Julio* (5), *Miguel* (5), *Carlos* (3), *Eugenio* (3), *Jorge* (3), *Ramon* (3), *Wilfredo* (3), *Aida* (2), *Ana* (2).

Sedam (263) Origin unidentified.

Sedano (216) Spanish: habitational name from Sedano in Burgos province.
GIVEN NAMES Spanish 55%. *Jose* (9), *Juan* (6), *Guadalupe* (4), *Jesus* (4), *Jorge* (4), *Javier* (3), *Manuel* (3), *Pedro* (3), *Sergio* (3), *Andres* (2), *Cesar* (2), *Ernesto* (2); *Antonio* (4), *Primo* (2), *Angelo*, *Clementina*, *Fausto*, *Lorenzo*, *Marco*, *Marino*, *Romeo*.

Sedar (123) Origin unidentified.

Sedberry (306) Perhaps an Americanized form of an unidentified original.

Seddon (571) English: perhaps a habitational name from an unidentified place, the last element of which could be Old English *dūn* 'hill'. Without early forms, it is impossible even to speculate what the first element might be. The surname is extremely common in Lancashire, especially in the Manchester area, where it was first recorded in the 14th century.

Seder (393) Hungarian (**Szeder**): topographic name from *szeder* 'cranberry'.

Sederstrom (133) Swedish (**Söderström**): ornamental name composed of the elements *ceder* 'cedar' + *ström* 'stream', 'river'.

Sedgwick (1068) English: habitational name from Sedgwick in Cumbria, so named from the Middle English personal name *Sigg(e)* (from Old Norse *Siggi* or Old English *Sicg*, short forms of the various compound names with the first element 'victory') + Old English *wīc* 'outlying settlement', 'dairy farm'; or from Sedgewick in Sussex, named with Old English *secg* 'sedge' + *wīc*.

Sedillo (668) Spanish: Latin American variant of CEDILLO.
GIVEN NAMES Spanish 20%. *Manuel* (6), *Lupe* (3), *Carlos* (2), *Cruz* (2), *Diego* (2), *Fidel* (2), *Francisco* (2), *Marcos* (2), *Rafael* (2), *Adelaido*, *Adelina*, *Agapito*.

Sedita (207) Southern Italian: from *sei* 'six' + *dita*, plural of *dito* 'finger', hence a nickname either for someone having six fingers or metaphorically for someone who was very dextrous.
GIVEN NAMES Italian 13%. *Sergio* (3), *Luigi* (2), *Alfonso*, *Angelo*, *Sal*, *Salvatore*.

Sedivy (265) Czech (**Šedivý**): nickname from *šedivý* 'gray(-haired)', 'hoary'.

Sedlacek (1091) Czech (**Sedláček**): from a diminutive of **Sedlák** (see SEDLAK), either an affectionate form of a status name for a Sedlák, or a status name for a farmer who owned a smaller piece of land than a Sedlák in the same village, or else for a young farmer.

Sedlack (196) Americanized spelling of Czech **Sedlák** (see SEDLAK).

Sedlak (800) Czech (**Sedlák**): status name from Czech *sedlák* 'peasant', 'farmer'. A *sedlák* was a comparatively rich farmer, with more land than a *zahradník* 'smallholder', 'truck farmer' (see ZAHRADNIK) or a *chalupník* 'cottager' (see CHALUPA).

Sedlar (201) Slavic spelling of German SADLER.

Sedler (188) **1.** German: variant of SADLER. **2.** Jewish (from Ukraine): variant of SIDLER.
GIVEN NAMES German 5%. *Wilhelm* (2), *Kurt*.

Sedlock (449) **1.** English: variant of **Sidlock**, from a Middle English survival of an Old English personal name, *Sidlāc*. **2.** Americanized form of Czech SEDLAK.

Sedmak (110) Slovenian and Croatian (northern and eastern Croatia): from a personal name from *sedmi* 'seventh', with the noun suffix *-ak*, typically given to a seventh son.

Sedor (347) Galician: habitational name from Sedor in A Coruña province, Galicia.

Sedore (166) Origin uncertain.

Sedwick (280) English: variant of SEDGWICK.

See (2836) English and German: topographic name for someone who lived by the sea-shore or beside a lake, from Middle English *see* 'sea', 'lake' (Old English *sǣ*), Middle High German *sē*. Alternatively, the English name may denote someone who lived by a watercourse, from an Old English *sēoh* 'watercourse', 'drain'.

Seeba (107) Origin uncertain. Perhaps an Americanized form of German SEEBACH.
GIVEN NAME German 5%. *Jochen*.

Seebach (242) German: habitational name from any of numerous places so named.
GIVEN NAMES German 4%. *Guenter*, *Joerg*, *Juergen*.

Seebeck (218) North German: habitational name from any of several places so named from Middle Low German *sē* 'lake' + *beke* 'creek'.
GIVEN NAMES German 7%. *Claus*, *Hans*, *Horst*, *Jurgen*, *Ralf*.

Seeber (632) South German: habitational name for someone from places called Seeba, Seeben, or Seeb, named with Middle High German *sē*, *sēwes* 'lake'.

Seeberger (231) German and Jewish (Ashkenazic): habitational name for someone from any of several places named Seeberg or Seebergen.
GIVEN NAMES German 4%. *Erhart*, *Hans*, *Otto*.

Seebold (156) Variant of German or French SEBALD.

Seeburger (134) German: habitational name for someone from any of the numerous places called Seeburg, named as 'fortress on the lake'.
GIVEN NAMES German 6%. *Gerhard*, *Kurt*.

Seed (378) English (chiefly Lancashire): **1.** from Middle English *sede* 'seed'; a metonymic occupational name for a gardener or husbandman, or a nickname for a small person. **2.** from a late Old English personal name, *Sida*, a post-Conquest short form of compound names formed with *sidu* 'custom', 'manner'; 'morality', 'purity' as the first element.

Seeders (104) Origin unidentified.

Seedorf (180) German: habitational name from any of numerous places so named, from *See* 'lake' + *Dorf* 'village'.
GIVEN NAMES German 6%. *Helmuth*, *Matthias*.

Seeds (406) English: variant of SEED.

Seefeld (325) North German variant or Americanized form of German SEEFELDT.

Seefeldt (821) German: habitational name from any of numerous places named Seefeld, from Middle High German *sē* 'lake' + *velt* 'open country'.

Seefried (143) German: variant of SIEGFRIED.
GIVEN NAMES German 5%. *Gerda*, *Monika*, *Wilhelm*.

Seegars (115) Variant of SEAGER or, possibly, SEEGERS.

Seeger (1674) **1.** German and Dutch: from the Germanic personal name *Sigiheri*, composed of the elements *sigi* 'victory' + *heri* 'army'. **2.** South German: variant of SAGER. **3.** English: variant spelling of SEAGER.
GIVEN NAMES German 4%. *Kurt* (3), *Heinz* (2), *Willi* (2), *Aloys*, *Fritz*, *Guenter*, *Gunter*, *Hans*, *Hildegarde*, *Horst*, *Konrad*, *Otto*.

Seegers (391) North German and Dutch: patronymic from SEEGER 1.

Seegert (157) German: variant of SEEGER 1.

Seegmiller (273) Part-translation of German **Seegmüller**, an occupational name for the owner of a sawmill, from Middle High German *sege* 'saw' + *mülnære* 'miller'.

Seehafer (277) German: topographic name for someone who lived close to a stand of lakeside grasses, such as marram, from Middle High German *sē* 'lake' + *haver* 'oats', or a metonymic occupational name for someone who collected them.

Seehusen (177) North German: habitational name from any of several places named Seehausen or Seehusen.

Seek (195) Altered spelling of North German **Seeck**, from a short form of a compound name formed with *sigi* 'victory' as the first element, or a nickname from *siech* 'sick', 'ill'.

Seekamp (149) North German: topographic name for someone living by an enclosed field or domain (Middle Low German *kamp*) beside a lake or by the sea (Middle Low German *sē*).

Seekford (128) Possibly of English origin, a habitational name from Seckford Hall in Suffolk. However, the surname is not found in current English records.

Seekins (374) Probably a variant of English **Seekings**, a Cambridgeshire name of unexplained etymology.

Seel (464) **1.** English: variant of SEAL. **2.** North German: metonymic occupational name for a rope maker, from Middle Low German *sēl* 'rope'.
GIVEN NAMES German 4%. *Erwin* (2), *Heinz*, *Kurt*.

Seelbach (217) German: habitational name from any of numerous places so named.
GIVEN NAMES German 5%. *Heinz*, *Kurt*.

Seele (132) North German: **1.** topographic name from Middle Low German *sele* 'meadow', 'bog'. **2.** metonymic occupational name for a harness maker, from Middle Low German *sele* 'harness'.
GIVEN NAMES German 7%. *Frederika*, *Horst*, *Wolfgang*.

Seelen (107) German: habitational name from any of several places named Sehlem in Lower Saxony and the Rhineland or from any of several places named Sehlen in Hesse and Pomerania.

Seeley (4334) **1.** English: nickname for a person with a cheerful disposition, from Middle English *seely* 'happy', 'fortunate' (Old English *sælig*, from *sæl* 'happiness', 'good fortune'). The word was also occasionally used as a female personal name during the Middle Ages. The sense 'pitiable', which developed into modern English *silly*, is not attested before the 15th century. **2.** Altered form of German SEELE, respelled to preserve the bisyllabic pronunciation of the German name.

Seelig (622) **1.** German: habitational name from Seelig near Bamberg. **2.** German and Jewish (Ashkenazic): nickname for a cheerful person, variant of SELIG.
GIVEN NAMES German 7%. *Dieter* (3), *Kurt* (2), *Gunther*, *Hans*, *Klaus*, *Reinhold*, *Siegfried*, *Uwe*, *Winfried*.

Seeliger (176) **1.** German: habitational name for someone from SEELIG near Bamberg. **2.** German and Jewish (Ashkenazic): nickname for a cheerful person, variant of SELIG.
GIVEN NAMES German 12%. *Kurt* (3), *Arno*, *Hans*, *Horst*, *Ilse*.

Seeling (199) German: habitational name from Sehlingen in Lower Saxony.
GIVEN NAME German 4%. *Fritz* (2).

Seelinger (168) German: habitational name for someone from Sehlingen in Lower Saxony (see SEELING).

Seelman (197) North German (**Seelmann**): topographic name from Middle Low German *sele* 'bog' + *man* 'man'.
GIVEN NAMES German 5%. *Erwin*, *Kurt*.

Seely (2228) English: variant of SEELEY.

Seelye (513) English: variant of SEELEY.

Seem (106) German: possibly an altered spelling of SIEM.
GIVEN NAMES German 7%. *Gerda*, *Otto*, *Udo*.

Seeman (1102) **1.** English: variant spelling of SEAMAN. **2.** Jewish (Ashkenazic): variant of SEEMANN. **3.** Americanized spelling of German SEEMANN.

Seemann (450) **1.** German: topographic name for someone who lived by a lake, from Middle High German *sē* + *man* 'man'. **2.** Jewish (Ashkenazic): ornamental name from German *See* 'lake' + *Mann* 'man'.
GIVEN NAMES German 8%. *Erwin* (2), *Kurt* (2), *Ernst*, *Heinz*, *Juergen*, *Jurgen*, *Reinhold*, *Siegfried*, *Udo*.

Seeney (136) **1.** English: variant of SENIOR. **2.** Irish: variant of SWEENEY.

Seering (114) North German: patronymic from a Germanic personal name formed with Old High German *saro* 'armor'.

Seery (583) Irish (Westmeath): reduced Anglicized form of Gaelic **Ó Saoraidhe** 'descendant of *Saoraidhe*', a personal name derived from *saordha* 'noble'. It has been Anglicized ('translated') as FREEMAN. Woulfe, however, believes the original Gaelic form was **Ó Síoghraidh**, from a borrowing of the Norse personal name *Sigefrith*.

Sees (282) German: variant of SEESE.

Seese (854) German: from a Germanic personal name, *Sigizo*, from a compound name formed with *sigi* 'victory' as the first element.

Seeton (133) Scottish or English: variant of SEATON.

Seever (219) North German and Dutch: **1.** variant of SIEVER. **2.** possibly a topographic name for someone living by the Seeve river (near Hamburg).

Seevers (605) North German: variant of SIEVERS.

Seewald (313) **1.** German: habitational name from a place so called in Bavaria, from Middle High German *sē* 'lake' + *wald* 'forest'. **2.** German: from the German personal name *Siegbald*, composed of the Germanic elements *sigi* 'victory' + *bald* 'bold', 'courageous'. **3.** Jewish (Ashkenazic): ornamental name composed of German *See* 'lake' + *Wald* 'forest'.
GIVEN NAMES German 5%; Jewish 5%. *Bernhard* (4), *Fritz* (2); *Mordechai*, *Tzvi*.

Sefcik (438) Czech (**Šefčík**): variant of **Ševčík** 'shoemaker' (see SEVCIK).

Seff (117) Welsh (Monmouthshire): unexplained.

Sefton (472) English: habitational name from a place in Lancashire, so called from Old Norse *sef* 'rush' + Old English *tūn* 'enclosure', 'settlement'.

Segal (3963) Jewish (Ashkenazic): acronym from the Hebrew phrase *SeGan Levia* 'assistant Levite'.
GIVEN NAMES Jewish 10%. *Meyer* (7), *Moshe* (7), *Hyman* (5), *Miriam* (5), *Zalman* (4), *Doron* (3), *Gershon* (3), *Mayer* (3), *Yakov* (3), *Zipporah* (3), *Chaim* (2), *Getzel* (2).

Segale (149) **1.** Catalan (**Segalé**): respelling of **Segaler**, metonymic occupational name for a grower or seller of rye, from *segaler*, a derivative of Catalan *sègol* 'rye', or topographic name from a field where rye is cultivated, *segaler*. **2.** Jewish: variant spelling of SEGAL.
GIVEN NAMES Italian 8%. *Angelo*, *Attilio*, *Dino*, *Enrico*.

Segall (660) Jewish: variant spelling of SEGAL.
GIVEN NAMES Jewish 6%. *Herschel* (2), *Shlomo* (2), *Sol* (2), *Ascher*, *Aviva*, *Avram*, *Chaim*, *Maier*, *Miriam*, *Shai*.

Segalla (143) Northern Italian: unexplained.
GIVEN NAMES Italian 11%; French 4%. *Angelo* (3), *Domenic*, *Francesco*, *Valentino*, *Vita*; *Colette*.

Segan (119) **1.** Jewish: unexplained, possibly a variant of SAGAN. **2.** Serbian (**Šegan**): unexplained.
GIVEN NAMES Jewish 7%; South Slavic 5%. *Meyer* (2); *Simo*, *Zarko*.

Segar (413) **1.** English: variant spelling of SEAGER. **2.** Dutch: from a Germanic personal name composed of the elements *sigi* 'victory' + *hard* 'hardy', 'brave', 'strong'.

Segarra (484) Catalan: regional name from the district of La Segarra, or habitational name from any of the places named with Segarra or La Segarra in Catalonia and Valencia.
GIVEN NAMES Spanish 36%. *Jose* (17), *Jorge* (7), *Luis* (7), *Ana* (6), *Carlos* (5), *Pedro* (4), *Rafael* (4), *Angel* (3), *Orlando* (3), *Ramon* (3), *Aida* (2), *Alicia* (2); *Angelo* (5), *Antonio*, *Concetta*, *Ennio*, *Federico*, *Flavio*, *Gilda*.

Segars (793) Variant of SEAGER or, possibly, SEEGERS.

Segel (376) **1.** North German: metonymic occupational name for a sail maker, from Middle Low German *segel* 'sail'. **2.** Jewish (Ashkenazic): variant of SEGAL.
GIVEN NAMES Jewish 4%. *Baruch, Isadore, Shoshana, Yakov.*

Seger (1552) **1.** Dutch: from the Germanic personal name *Sigiheri*, a compound of *sigi* 'victory' + *heri* 'army'. **2.** English: variant spelling of SEAGER. **3.** Jewish (Ashkenazic): occupational name from Yiddish *zeger* 'sawyer' (see SAGER).

Segers (415) North German and Dutch: patronymic from SEGER.

Segerson (122) Swedish: patronymic from *Siger*, a personal name formed with Old Norse *sigr* 'victory' + *-ar* 'warrior'.

Segerstrom (170) Swedish: ornamental name composed of the elements *seger* 'victory' + *ström* 'river'.

Seggerman (130) North German (**Seggermann**): possibly a variant of North German **Segger**, an occupational name for a sawyer, Middle Low German *segger*, or a spokesman for or the head of a corporation such as a guild, from Middle Low German *segen* 'to tell', 'speak'.

Seghers (128) Dutch: patronymic from SEEGER 1.
GIVEN NAMES French 7%. *Andre, Dreux.*

Segler (300) **1.** North German form of SIGLER. **2.** occupational name for a sailor or a sail maker, from Middle Low German *segeler*.

Segner (247) South German: nickname from Middle High German *segener* 'magician' (agent derivative of *sēgen* 'magical blessing', 'charm').

Sego (479) Hungarian (**Szegő**): **1.** occupational name for a stonecutter or woodcutter, from *szegő* 'cutter'. **2.** possibly a nickname for an unreliable person, from *megszegni* 'to break a promise'.

Segovia (1182) Spanish: habitational name from the city of this name in central Spain. The place name is of uncertain origin (possibly based on a Celtic element *sego* 'victory').
GIVEN NAMES Spanish 49%. *Jose* (29), *Juan* (20), *Manuel* (17), *Francisco* (15), *Carlos* (14), *Miguel* (12), *Roberto* (10), *Jesus* (9), *Ana* (7), *Pedro* (7), *Fernando* (6), *Mario* (6).

Segraves (461) Variant of English SEA-GRAVE.

Segrest (513) Altered spelling of German SIEGRIST.

Segreti (121) Italian: patronymic or plural form of SEGRETO.
GIVEN NAMES Italian 22%. *Fabio* (2), *Mario* (2), *Angelo, Francesco, Pasquale, Raffaele, Salvatore.*

Segreto (136) Italian: **1.** nickname from Old Italian *segreto* 'confidant' (from Latin *secretum* literally 'hidden place', hence

'personal business', 'secret'). **2.** occupational name from medieval Greek *ek sekretōn*, literally 'from the hidden place', i.e. 'financial administrator', likewise a derivative of Latin *secretum*.
GIVEN NAMES Italian 17%. *Angelo, Luigi, Pio, Rocco, Salvatore.*

Segrist (127) Variant of German SIEGRIST.

Segroves (108) English: variant of SEA-GRAVE.

Segui (156) Catalan form (**Seguí**) of Occitan SEGUIN.
GIVEN NAMES Spanish 40%. *Juan* (4), *Diego* (2), *Gerardo* (2), *Jesus* (2), *Luis* (2), *Agustin, Aracelia, Aura, Bibiana, Cesar, Efrain, Elva.*

Seguin (1219) Southern French (**Séguin**): from a Germanic personal name composed of the elements *sigi* 'victory' + *wine* 'friend'.
FOREBEARS A Séguin from the Poitou region of France is documented in Ste. Famille, Quebec, in 1669. Another, with the secondary surname Ladéroute, from Picardy, France, was in Boucherville in 1672.
GIVEN NAMES French 10%. *Gilles* (4), *Pierre* (4), *Andre* (3), *Marcel* (3), *Normand* (3), *Armand* (2), *Fernand* (2), *Germain* (2), *Adelard, Aime, Alban, Alcee.*

Seguine (112) Probably an altered spelling of SEGUIN.

Segundo (165) Spanish: from a variant of *secundo* 'second', applied as a personal name for the second son of a family.
GIVEN NAMES Spanish 47%. *Guadalupe* (2), *Jose* (2), *Luis* (2), *Mario* (2), *Alfonso, Andres, Antolina, Benito, Carlos, Diego, Domingo, Edilberto.*

Segur (142) Southern French (**Ségur**) and Catalan: habitational name from any of various minor places so called, from Catalan *segur* or from Provençal (a dialect of Occitan) *ségur* 'safe', 'well-defended'.

Segura (3021) Spanish and Catalan: habitational name from any of various places called Segura, named with *segura* 'safe', 'secure'.
GIVEN NAMES Spanish 39%. *Jose* (70), *Juan* (43), *Manuel* (28), *Jesus* (24), *Pedro* (21), *Jorge* (17), *Mario* (14), *Francisco* (13), *Luis* (13), *Arturo* (11), *Carlos* (11), *Roberto* (11).

Seher (172) **1.** South German: topographic name for someone who lived by a lake, from a derivative of Middle High German *sē* 'lake'. **2.** Jewish (Ashkenazic): nickname for a visionary, from German *Seher* 'seer'.

Sehgal (218) Indian (Panjab): Hindu (Khatri) and Sikh name of unexplained origin, based on the name of a clan in the Khatri community.
GIVEN NAMES Indian 89%. *Krishan* (5), *Rajesh* (5), *Vijay* (5), *Ajay* (3), *Amolak* (3), *Anil* (3), *Pravin* (3), *Alka* (2), *Ashok* (2), *Chander* (2), *Lakshman* (2), *Mukesh* (2).

Sehl (156) North German: variant of SEELE.

Sehnert (158) German: from the Germanic personal name *Senhart*, of unexplained etymology.

Sehon (133) Origin unidentified.

Sehorn (158) Origin unidentified.

Sehr (173) South German: variant of SEHER 1.

Seib (527) South German: from a pet form of SEIBOLD.

Seibel (1825) **1.** South German: from a pet form of the personal name *Seibold* (see SEIBOLD) or SEIBERT. **2.** Jewish (Ashkenazic): unexplained.

Seiber (657) North German: variant of SEIBERT.

Seiberlich (165) German: variant of SAUBER, with the addition of the adjectival suffix *-lich*.

Seiberling (134) German: patronymic or clan name for a member of a clan led by someone called SEIBERT.
GIVEN NAME German 4%. *Kurt.*

Seibert (4486) **1.** German: from a Germanic personal name composed of the elements *sigi* 'victory' + *berht* 'bright', 'famous'. **2.** Jewish (Ashkenazic): adoption of the German personal name *Seibert* as a surname.

Seibold (687) German: from a Germanic personal name composed of the Germanic elements *sigi* 'victory' + *bald* 'courageous', 'daring'. Compare SEBALD.
GIVEN NAMES German 5%. *Otto* (3), *Hans Peter* (2), *Kurt* (2), *Dieter, Gerhard, Hans, Horst, Ralf, Wenzel.*

Seid (441) **1.** German: from the Germanic personal name *Sito*, a short form of a compound name formed with *sigi* 'victory' as the first element. **2.** Jewish (Ashkenazic): metonymic occupational name from German *Seide* and Yiddish *zayd* 'silk' (see SEIDE).

Seide (182) German and Jewish (Ashkenazic): from Middle High German *sīde*, German *Seide* 'silk' (from Late Latin *seta*, originally denoting animal hair), hence a metonymic occupational name for a manufacturer or seller of silk.
GIVEN NAMES French 11%; Jewish 7%; German 5%. *Claudel, Dominique, Lucien, Pierre, Serge; Yosef* (2), *Sol; Egon, Heinz, Rinehart.*

Seidel (3622) **1.** South German: from the medieval name *Sidel*, a pet form of *Sīfrit* (see SIEGFRIED). **2.** Jewish (Ashkenazic): nickname or ornamental name from German *Seidel* 'beer mug', 'pint'.
GIVEN NAMES German 6%. *Kurt* (11), *Gerhard* (6), *Dieter* (4), *Erwin* (4), *Otto* (4), *Gunther* (3), *Fritz* (2), *Hans* (2), *Horst* (2), *Klaus* (2), *Arno, Dietrich.*

Seidell (159) Americanized spelling of German SEIDEL.

Seidelman (125) **1.** German (**Seidelmann**): variant of SEIDEL. **2.** Jewish (Ashkenazic): elaborated form of SEIDEL.
GIVEN NAME German 5%. *Otto.*

Seideman (149) German (**Seidemann**) and Jewish (Ashkenazic): **1.** occupational name for a silk merchant, from German *Seide* 'silk', Middle High German *sīde*, + *man* 'man'. **2.** Variant of SEID.

Seiden (646) **1.** German and Jewish (Ashkenazic): variant of SEIDE. **2.** Jewish (eastern Ashkenazic): nickname from German *seiden*, *zaydn* 'of silk'; 'kind-hearted', 'gentle'.
GIVEN NAMES Jewish 4%. *Emanuel, Hyman, Isadore, Mascha, Miriam, Morry, Sol.*

Seidenberg (305) **1.** German: habitational name from any of several places named Seidenberg. **2.** Jewish (Ashkenazic): ornamental name from German *Seide* 'silk' + *Berg* 'mountain'.
GIVEN NAMES German 7%. *Otto* (3), *Eberhard, Fritz, Gerhard, Irmgard.*

Seidenfeld (109) Jewish (Ashkenazic): ornamental name from German *Seide* 'silk' + *Feld* 'field'.
GIVEN NAMES Jewish 26%. *Mendy* (2), *Amrom, Aron, Avrohom, Levi, Mendel, Moshe, Naftali, Shalom, Shulem, Yehoshua, Yeshaye.*

Seidensticker (157) German: occupational name for a silk embroiderer, from Middle High German *sīde* 'silk' + *sticken* 'to stitch'.
GIVEN NAMES German 7%. *Gerd* (2), *Kurt* (2).

Seider (291) **1.** South German and Jewish (Ashkenazic): occupational name for a silk merchant, from an agent derivative of German *Seide* 'silk', Middle High German *sīde*. **2.** South German: habitational name for someone from Seyde in Saxony or Seiderau in Bavaria.

Seiders (355) Variant of German SEIDER.

Seidl (1335) Southern German: from a pet form of the personal name SIEGFRIED. Compare SIEGEL.
GIVEN NAMES German 5%. *Alois* (4), *Erwin* (2), *Manfred* (2), *Otto* (2), *Bernhard, Eugen, Gottfried, Gunter, Kurt, Ursel, Wendelin.*

Seidle (136) Variant of German SEIDEL.
GIVEN NAME German 4%. *Wendelin.*

Seidler (970) German and Jewish (Ashkenazic): occupational name for a silk weaver, from an agent derivative of Middle High German *sīde*, German *Seide* 'silk'.
GIVEN NAMES German 8%. *Hans* (6), *Kurt* (5), *Helmut* (2), *Alois, Dieter, Erna, Erwin, Gerhard, Gernot, Gottlieb, Ingo, Manfred.*

Seidlitz (169) German: habitational name from a place so named in eastern Germany.
GIVEN NAMES German 7%. *Otto* (2), *Dieter, Klaus.*

Seidman (1183) Jewish (Ashkenazic): variant of SEID.
GIVEN NAMES Jewish 8%. *Isadore* (5), *Sol* (5), *Hyman* (2), *Myer* (2), *Abbe, Ari, Avrohom, Dov, Ephraim, Hershel, Hirsch, Meyer.*

Seidner (400) German and Jewish (Ashkenazic): variant of SEIDLER.

Seier (204) South German: **1.** probably a variant of SEIGER. **2.** Variant of SEEGER 1.

Seif (314) **1.** German and Jewish (Ashkenazic): metonymic occupational name for a soap maker, from Middle High German *seife*, German *Seife* 'soap'. **2.** Arabic: from a personal name based on *sayf* 'sword'. *Saifullah* 'sword of Allah' was a title of honor bestowed by the Prophet Muhammad on the military leader Khālid ibn-al-Walīd (see KHALID).
GIVEN NAMES Muslim 6%; Jewish 4%; German 4%. *Medhat* (2), *Rahmat* (2), *Ali, Essam, Ezzat, Fayez, Huda, Kamal, Khaled, Mohamed, Nabil, Nahid; Emanuel, Gershon, Meyer, Yehuda; Ulrich* (2).

Seifer (276) **1.** German and Jewish (Ashkenazic): variant of SIEGFRIED. **2.** Jewish (Ashkenazic): occupational name for a soap maker, from an agent derivative of German *Seife*, Yiddish *zeyf* 'soap'.

Seifert (4282) German: from a local variant of the personal name SIEGFRIED.
GIVEN NAMES German 4%. *Kurt* (9), *Otto* (4), *Erwin* (3), *Franz* (3), *Gunter* (2), *Heinz* (2), *Horst* (2), *Juergen* (2), *Achim, Alfons, Arno, Bernhardt.*

Seiferth (102) German: variant of SEIFERT.
GIVEN NAME German 5%. *Kurt.*

Seiffert (375) German: variant of SEIFERT.
GIVEN NAMES German 6%. *Kurt* (3), *Armin, Ingeborg, Jurgen, Siegrid.*

Seifried (401) German: variant of SIEGFRIED.

Seigal (130) Variant of German SIEGEL.

Seigel (677) Americanized spelling of German SIEGEL.

Seiger (233) **1.** German: from Middle High German *seiger* 'scales', hence a metonymic occupational name for a tester of weights. The word later developed the meaning 'clock', 'watch', and some examples of the surname may have arisen from a metonymic occupational name for a maker of timepieces. **2.** Jewish (Ashkenazic): metonymic occupational name for a watchmaker, from Yiddish *zeyger* 'watch', 'clock' (see 1 above).

Seigfried (116) Americanized spelling of German SIEGFRIED.

Seigle (337) Americanized spelling of German SIEGEL.

Seigler (751) Americanized spelling of German SIGLER.

Seikel (110) Variant of German SIEGEL.
GIVEN NAMES German 4%. *Hans, Kurt.*

Seil (142) German: **1.** metonymic occupational name for a rope maker, from Middle High German *seil* 'rope'. **2.** From a short form of a Germanic personal name (*Segilo*) formed with *sigi* 'victory' as the first element.
GIVEN NAMES German 7%. *Alfons, Friedrich.*

Seiler (3419) **1.** German and Jewish (Ashkenazic): occupational name for a rope maker, from an agent derivative of German

Seil 'rope', Middle High German *seil*. **2.** English: variant of SAYLOR.

Seiling (103) German: variant of SEIL 2, with the suffix *-ing* indicating affiliation.
GIVEN NAME German 6%. *Otto.*

Seils (171) German: patronymic of SEIL 2.
GIVEN NAME German 5%. *Gunter.*

Seim (623) **1.** German: metonymic occupational name for a beekeeper, from Middle High German *seim* 'honey'. **2.** Norwegian: habitational name from any of ten or more farms so named, notably on the west coast of Norway, named with Old Norse *Sæheimr*, a compound of *sær* 'sea' + *heimr* 'home', 'farmstead'.
GIVEN NAMES Scandinavian 5%. *Arlis, Erik.*

Sein (115) Basque: nickname from Basque *sein* 'child'.
GIVEN NAMES Spanish 9%. *Blanca, Jorge, Juan, Manuel, Ramona.*

Seiner (112) **1.** South German: nickname from Middle High German *seinen* 'to hesitate', 'to tarry'. **2.** North German: occupational name from an agent derivative of Middle Low German *seine*, *segene* 'trawl net'.

Seinfeld (108) Jewish (Ashkenazic): ornamental name from an unexplained first element + *Feld* 'field'.
GIVEN NAMES Jewish 13%; German 5%. *Eyal* (2), *Shoshana* (2); *Kurt.*

Seip (495) South German: from a short form of the personal names *Seipold* (see SEIBOLD) or *Seiprecht* (see SEIBERT). This name is also established in the Netherlands.

Seipel (478) South German (Bavaria, Austria): from a pet form of SEIP.
GIVEN NAMES German 5%. *Aloysius, Bernhard, Erna, Heinz, Horst, Kurt, Winfried.*

Seiple (407) Altered spelling of SEIPEL.

Seipp (354) Variant of SEIP.
GIVEN NAMES German 4%. *Otto, Reinhard, Ulrich.*

Seiser (164) German: habitational name for someone from Seis, Tyrol.

Seiss (126) German: **1.** habitational name from Seis, Tyrol. **2.** variant of SEITZ. **3.** variant of SEITH.

Seiter (688) German (Swabian): occupational name for a cobbler (see SAUTER 1).
GIVEN NAMES German 4%. *Frieda* (2), *Kurt* (2), *Aloys, Erwin, Franz, Irmgard.*

Seith (171) German: from a pet form (*Sito*) of a Germanic personal name, for instance *Sigbert*, formed with *Sigi* 'victory' as the first element.

Seither (159) **1.** German: variant of SEITH. **2.** Topographic name for someone living at the side of a settlement, from Middle High German *sīte* 'side'.

Seitter (160) German: variant of SEITER.
GIVEN NAMES German 5%; French 5%. *Egon* (2), *Hedwig; Girard* (2).

Seitz (5188) **1.** South German (mainly Bavaria): from a reduced form of the personal name *Seifried*, a variant of SIEG-

FRIED. **2.** Germanized spelling of Slovenian **Zajc**, nickname from *zajec* 'hare'.

Seitzer (160) German: variant of SEITZ.

Seitzinger (301) South German: habitational name from a place called Seitzingen.

Seiver (130) Variant of German SIEVER.

Seivers (116) Variant of German SIEVERS.

Seivert (227) Dutch: from the Germanic personal name *Ziveerd*, *Sivert*, Dutch form of SIEGFRIED.

Seiwert (170) Dutch or German: variant of SEIVERT.

Seiz (108) German and Jewish (Ashkenazic): variant of SEITZ.

Sek (110) **1.** Polish (**Sęk**): see SENK. **2.** Slovenian (eastern Slovenia; **Šek**): unexplained. **3.** Cambodian: unexplained.
GIVEN NAMES Polish 17%; Cambodian 18%. *Krzysztof* (2), *Dariusz*, *Ewa*, *Jozefa*, *Katarzyna*, *Urszula*; *Chamroeun*, *Hoeun*, *Koeun*, *Moeun*, *Soeung*, *Sophal*, *Sophan*, *Sopheap*, *Soun*, *Vuthy*, *Yen*.

Sekel (110) Germanized or Slavicized form of Hungarian SZEKELY. The Slovenian form is **Sekelj**.

Sekelsky (127) Slavic: probably a variant of SEKEL, with the common Slavic surname ending -*sky*.

Sekerak (239) Czech (**Sekerák**): occupational name for an axeman, from a derivative of Czech *sekera* 'axe'.

Sekhon (122) Indian (Panjab): Sikh name based on the name of a Jat tribe.
GIVEN NAMES Indian 91%. *Balwinder* (2), *Amrit*, *Avtar*, *Balraj*, *Dilbag*, *Jagbir*, *Jagdish*, *Mani*, *Mohan*, *Mukhtiar*, *Partap*, *Preet*.

Seki (170) Japanese (variously written): topographic name meaning 'barrier', apparently taken from the many checkpoints set up throughout Japan by the Shogunate for the purpose of checking travelers' passes. The surname occurs mostly in the Tōkyō area and the Ryūkyūan island of Amami.
GIVEN NAMES Japanese 76%. *Tomoaki* (3), *Hajime* (2), *Koji* (2), *Kotaro* (2), *Takahiro* (2), *Yukio* (2), *Akihiko*, *Ayako*, *Fumio*, *Fusae*, *Hanako*, *Hideki*.

Sekiguchi (108) Japanese: meaning 'barrier opening', referring to barriers set up by the Shogunate at highway checkpoints. This name is found mostly in eastern Japan.
GIVEN NAMES Japanese 74%. *Hiroshi* (3), *Hiroki* (2), *Koichi* (2), *Masaaki* (2), *Masami* (2), *Noboru* (2), *Tomoko* (2), *Akihisa*, *Akira*, *Emiko*, *Fujiko*, *Fumiko*; *Juri* (2), *Yori*.

Sekula (352) **1.** Jewish (from Poland): habitational name from the village of Sekuła in eastern Poland. **2.** Polish (**Sekuła**): apparently from Latin *saecula* 'centuries', 'ages', perhaps a nickname for someone who constantly repeated the Latin religious incantation *saecula saeculorum* 'for ever and ever' (literally 'for centuries of centuries').

GIVEN NAMES Jewish 5%; Polish 4%. *Avrohom*, *Chaim*, *Mayer*, *Menachem*, *Shimon*, *Yecheskel*, *Yosef*; *Jerzy*, *Kazimierz*, *Zbigniew*.

Selak (104) Croatian, Serbian, and Slovenian: nickname from *selo* 'hamlet', 'village'. It may also be a simplified form of **Seljak**, of similar origin, denoting a peasant or a villager.
GIVEN NAMES South Slavic 5%. *Dragica*, *Radosav*.

Selan (116) Slovenian: habitational name for a person from any of the many places in Slovenia called Sela, Sele or Selo, named with the archaic Slovenian word *selo* 'hamlet', 'village' (plural *sela*, *sele*), or an archaic nickname for a villager (of the same origin). Compare SELAK.
GIVEN NAMES Spanish 5%; South Slavic 4%. *Andres*, *Luis*, *Marta*, *Sixto*; *Franjo* (2).

Selander (432) Swedish: ornamental name composed of the place name element *sel* 'stretch of smooth water' + the suffix -*ander*, from Greek *anēr* 'man', genitive *andros*.
GIVEN NAMES Scandinavian 7%. *Erik*, *Helmer*, *Lars*.

Selbach (106) German: habitational name from any of several places so named.
GIVEN NAME German 4%. *Kurt*.

Selbe (161) German: habitational name, from Selb near Hof.
GIVEN NAMES French 6%. *Jeanne Marie*, *Serge*.

Selberg (219) **1.** North German: habitational name from a place so named in Westphalia and one, now lost, in Pomerania. **2.** Norwegian: habitational name from a farmstead, probably so named from Old Norse *selja* 'willow' + *berg* 'mountain'. **3.** Swedish: ornamental name composed of the place name element *sel* 'stretch of smooth water' + *berg* 'mountain', 'hill'.

Selby (4590) **1.** English: habitational name from a place in West Yorkshire, so named from Old Norse *selja* 'willow' + *býr* 'farm', 'settlement'. The surname is now very common in Nottinghamshire. **2.** Americanized form of some like-sounding Jewish surname.

Selcer (110) Slavic spelling of German SELTZER.

Selden (801) English: habitational name from Selden Farm in the parish of Patching, Sussex, probably so called from Old English *s(e)alh* 'willow' + *denu* 'valley'.

Selders (368) German: topographic or status name, from Middle High German *selder* 'dweller in a hut or peasant's cottage'.

Seldin (217) Jewish (Ashkenazic): variant of ZELDIN.
GIVEN NAMES Jewish 6%. *Chana*, *Gerson*, *Naum*, *Sol*.

Seldomridge (168) Americanized form of German **Seltenreich**, a nickname for

someone of limited means, from Middle High German *selten* 'seldom' + *rīch* 'rich'.

Seldon (387) English: variant spelling of SELDEN 1.

Selensky (108) Americanized spelling of Jewish and Ukrainian **Zelinsky** (see SELINSKY).

Selesky (112) Jewish (from Ukraine): habitational name from any of a number of places called Selishche.

Seley (200) Variant spelling of English SEELEY.

Self (8204) English (East Anglia): from the Middle English personal name *Saulf*, Old English *Sǣwulf*, composed of the elements *sǣ* 'sea' + *wulf* 'wolf'.

Selfe (142) Variant of SELF.

Selfridge (594) English: of uncertain origin; it may be a habitational name from an unidentified minor place, possibly so called from Old English *scelf* 'shelf' + *hrycg* 'ridge'.

Selhorst (115) North German: from a topographic (field) name, Seelhorst, near Hannover.

Selig (1007) **1.** South German: nickname for a person with a cheerful disposition, from Middle High German *selig* 'happy', 'fortunate', or a variant of SALGE 2. **2.** Jewish (Ashkenazic): from the Yiddish male personal name *Zelik* 'fortunate', 'blessed'.
GIVEN NAMES German 4%. *Ernst* (3), *Bernd*, *Franz*, *Fritz*, *Guenther*, *Heinz*, *Hildegarde*, *Kurt*, *Manfred*, *Otto*, *Reinhold*.

Seliga (271) Variant of German SEELIGER.

Seliger (194) German: variant of SEELIGER.

Seligman (967) **1.** German (**Seligmann**): variant of SELIG. **2.** Jewish (Ashkenazic): from the Yiddish male personal *Zelikman*, a variant of *Zelik* (see SELIG).
GIVEN NAMES German 5%. *Erwin* (2), *Gunther* (2), *Kurt* (2), *Benno*, *Bernhardt*, *Ernst*, *Hans*, *Heinz*, *Hilde*, *Otto*, *Siegfried*.

Seligmann (115) German: see SELIGMAN.
GIVEN NAMES German 12%; Scandinavian 5%. *Otto* (2), *Gunther*, *Hans*, *Kurt*.

Seligson (253) Jewish (Ashkenazic): patronymic from the personal name *Zelik* (see SELIG).
GIVEN NAMES German 4%. *Gerda*, *Kurt*.

Selim (149) Muslim: variant of SALIM.
GIVEN NAMES Muslim 50%. *Mohamed* (4), *Elsayed* (2), *Ibrahim* (2), *Mohammed* (2), *Nabil* (2), *Sami* (2), *Ahmed*, *Ali*, *Ashraf*, *Assaad*, *Ezzat*, *Fayek*.

Selin (281) **1.** Swedish: variant of SELLIN. **2.** French and German (Liechtenstein): from a Germanic personal name, *Sigilin*, a pet form of any of the compound names formed with *sigi* 'victory'.
GIVEN NAMES Scandinavian 6%; German 5%. *Borge*; *Alfons*, *Hans*, *Kurt*.

Selinger (350) **1.** German: probably a variant of **Söllinger**, a habitational name from any of several places named Söllingen, particularly one near Karlsruhe. **2.** Jewish (Ashkenazic): variant of SALINGER.

GIVEN NAMES German 5%. *Helmut, Kurt.*

Selinsky (116) Americanized spelling of Jewish and Ukrainian **Zelinsky**, a habitational name for someone from Zelenki or Zelenka in Ukraine.

Selix (145) Probably a variant of English **Sellick, Sellex**, a habitational name from Sellick in Clawton or Sellake in Halberton, both in Devon, or in some cases from Sellack in Herefordshire.

Selk (348) **1.** German: habitational name from a place so named near Schleswig. **2.** Belgian: habitational name from Zelk in Diest, Brabant, Belgium.

GIVEN NAMES German 4%. *Otto* (2), *Juergen.*

Selke (356) German: habitational name from Selk near Schleswig or Selke near Altenburg.

Selkirk (199) Scottish: habitational name from Selkirk in the Scottish Borders, named from Middle English *sale, sele* 'hall', 'manor' + *kirk* 'church'.

FOREBEARS Alexander Selkirk (1676–1721), the Scottish sailor who was the model for the fictional Robinson Crusoe, was also known as *Selcraig.* He was born in Largo, Fife, the son of a shoemaker.

GIVEN NAME Scottish 4%. *Alastair.*

Sell (4343) **1.** English: from Middle English *selle*, a rough hut of the type normally occupied by animals, hence a topographic name for someone who lived in a hut like this. In many cases the name may have been in effect a metonymic occupational name for a herdsman. **2.** Americanized spelling of Hungarian and Hungarian Jewish **Széll**, a topographic name for someone who lived in a spot exposed to the wind, from Hungarian *szél* 'wind'. **3.** German: variant of SELLE.

Sella (185) Italian: metonymic occupational name for a saddler, from Italian, Latin *sella* 'saddle'. The term is also used in a topographic sense for a mountain pass, and in some cases the surname may have arisen from this meaning. **Sellas** is found as a Greek family name, derived from the Latin word in the occupational sense.

GIVEN NAMES Italian 13%. *Enzo* (2), *Antonio, Dante, Geno, Giovanni, Libero, Marco, Piero, Salvatore, Silvio.*

Selland (176) Norwegian: habitational name from any of four farmsteads in Rogaland and Hordaland, named in Old Norse as *Seljuland*, from *selja* 'willow' + *land* 'land', 'farm'.

Sellar (107) Scottish: variant of SELLER.

Sellards (208) Scottish: variant of SELLARS.

Sellars (2085) Scottish: patronymic from **Sellar** (see SELLER).

Selle (665) **1.** English: variant of SELL 1. **2.** German: from Middle High German, Middle Low German *selle* 'friend', 'companion'. **3.** French: habitational name from any of the various places called Selle, Selles, or La Selle, named with Latin *cella*

'cell', 'cot', 'hut', 'stall'. **4.** Dutch (**Van Selle**): habitational name for someone from Zelle in Herenthout, Antwerp.

FOREBEARS A Selle (or De Selle) from the Burgundy region of France was documented in Montreal in 1729.

GIVEN NAMES German 4%. *Otto* (2), *Dietrich, Gerhard, Hans, Hedwig, Hermann, Kurt, Wolfgang.*

Selleck (601) Variant of English SELLICK.

Sellen (176) **1.** German: possibly a habitational name from a place so called in Westphalia. **2.** Swedish (**Sellén**): ornamental name probably formed with the place name element *sel* 'stretch of smooth water' + the common surname suffix *-én*, a derivative of Latin *-enius.*

Seller (300) **1.** English and Scottish: topographic name, a variant of SELL 1. **2.** English and Scottish: occupational name for a saddler, from Anglo-Norman French *seller* (Old French *sellier*, Latin *sellarius*, a derivative of *sella* 'seat', 'saddle'). **3.** English and Scottish: metonymic occupational name for someone employed in the cellars of a great house or monastery, from Anglo-Norman French *celler* 'cellar' (Old French *cellier*), or a reduction of the Middle English agent derivative *cellerer*. **4.** English and Scottish: occupational name for a tradesman or merchant, from an agent derivative of Middle English *sell(en)* 'to sell' (Old English *sellan* 'to hand over, deliver'). **5.** German: probably a habitational name from a place named Sella near Hoyerswerda.

Sellers (14645) English (mainly Yorkshire): patronymic from SELLER 1–4.

Selley (180) English: **1.** (chiefly Devon) variant spelling of SEALEY. **2.** habitational name from Selly Oak in Birmingham, named, like SHELLEY, from Old English *scylf* 'shelf' + *lēah* 'wood', 'clearing'.

Sellick (183) English: habitational name from either of two minor places in Devon, Sellake and Sellick, or from Sellack in Herefordshire, recorded *c.*1130 as *Lann Suluc* 'church (Old Welsh *lann*) of *Suluc*', a personal name, a pet form of *Suliau.*

Sellier (105) French: occupational name for a seller of saddles and packsaddles.

GIVEN NAMES German 7%; French 6%. *Claus, Ulrich; Marc, Philippe.*

Sellin (224) **1.** North German: habitational name from any of several places so named, for example on the island of Rügen. **2.** Swedish: ornamental name, perhaps from a place-name element *sel-* 'stretch of smooth water' + the Swedish adjectival suffix *-in*, based on Latin *-inius.*

Selling (104) **1.** English: unexplained. **2.** Swedish: variant of SELLIN.

GIVEN NAME Scandinavian 11%. *Holger* (4).

Sellinger (258) **1.** English: variant of SALINGER 1. **2.** South German: habitational name from Selling in Bavaria.

GIVEN NAMES German 4%. *Otto, Wolfgang.*

Sellitti (108) Italian: patronymic or plural form of SELLITTO.

GIVEN NAMES Italian 14%. *Dante, Domenic, Gaetano, Rocco.*

Sellitto (168) Italian: from the Late Latin personal name *Sellictus*, from the adjective *selectus* 'select', 'choice', a name favored by early Chirstians who regarded themselves as members of the chosen few.

GIVEN NAMES Italian 19%. *Gennaro* (2), *Antonio, Ciriaco, Fiore, Francesco, Gaetano, Guido, Matteo, Rocco, Salvatore.*

Sellman (682) **1.** English: variant of SELMAN. **2.** North German (**Sellmann**): topographic name from Middle Low German *sele* 'meadow', 'bog' + *man* 'man'. **3.** South German: occupational name for a middleman in a land or property sale or for a guardian, from Middle High German *sale* 'property transfer'. **4.** Jewish (Ashkenazic): variant of SELMAN.

Sellmeyer (124) German: occupational name for the steward of a hall or manor house, from Middle High German *sal* 'hall', 'residence' + *meier* 'steward' (see MEYER 1).

Sellner (521) South German: from Middle High German *seldener* 'inhabitant of a *selde*', i.e. a hut with a small kitchen-garden, but no agricultural land attached.

GIVEN NAMES German 4%. *Aloysius, Dietrich, Erna, Florian, Frieda, Otto, Wendelin.*

Sellnow (131) North German: habitational name from any of several places so named.

Sellon (167) English (Kent and Sussex): unexplained.

Sells (2932) English: variant of SELL 1.

Selman (1425) **1.** English: nickname for a happy or fortunate man, from Middle English *seely* 'happy', 'fortunate' + *man*, German *Mann* 'man'. **2.** English: from the Middle English female personal name *Seely* (see SEELEY 1), or of the nickname *Sele* (see SEAL 4) + *man* 'servant', hence an occupational name for a servant employed by a bearer of either of these names. **3.** Jewish (Ashkenazic): from the Yiddish personal name *Zelman*, a pet form of *Zalmen* (see SALMON).

Selmer (179) South German: variant of SELLMEYER.

Selmon (279) Variant of English or Jewish SELMAN.

Selner (234) Variant of German SELLNER.

Selover (269) Probably Dutch: unexplained.

Selph (965) Variant spelling of SELF.

Selser (106) Possibly a Dutch or Americanized variant of German and Jewish SELTZER.

Selsor (296) Origin unidentified; possibly an Americanized variant of German and Jewish SELTZER.

Selter (117) Probably an Americanized variant of German and Jewish SELTZER.

Seltz (223) German: habitational name from a place so named in Pomerania.

Seltzer (2079) German and Jewish (Ashkenazic): occupational name for an extractor or seller of salt, from an agent derivative of Middle High German *salz*, German *Salz* 'salt'.

Selva (236) Catalan and Italian: from any of various places in Catalonia, the Balearic Islands, or northern Italy named Selva, as for instance the Catalan district La Selva, from *selva* 'wood', Latin *silva*.
GIVEN NAMES Spanish 18%; Italian 8%; French 4%. *Adolfo* (2), *Carlos* (2), *Ricardo* (2), *Ana, Argentina, Armando, Bayardo, Domingos, Eleazar, Florencio, Gustavo, Idalia; Aldo* (2), *Angelo* (2), *Erminio, Giuseppe, Riccardo; Eloi, Renaud.*

Selvage (333) English: unexplained. Perhaps from the Old English personal name *Sǣlwīg* (see SELWAY).

Selvaggi (157) Italian: patronymic or plural form of SELVAGGIO.
GIVEN NAMES Italian 27%. *Rocco* (4), *Vito* (3), *Agostino* (2), *Nicola* (2), *Antonio, Camillo, Dante, Domenico, Libero, Salvatore.*

Selvaggio (284) Italian: nickname for an unruly or uncouth person, from *selvaggio*, earlier *salvaggio*, 'wild', 'savage', or an occupational or status name for someone who lived and worked in the woods, isolated from urban or village life, from a Late Latin derivative of Latin *silva* 'wood', influenced by Latin *salvus* 'whole', i.e. 'natural'.
GIVEN NAMES Italian 19%. *Dino* (2), *Vito* (2), *Carlo, Domenico, Elio, Gaetano, Giuseppe, Ignazio, Marco, Nicola, Rocco, Sal.*

Selvey (369) English (mainly Staffordshire): probably from a variant of the medieval personal name *Selwei* (see SELWAY).

Selvidge (471) English: variant of SELVAGE.

Selvig (266) Norwegian: habitational name from any of ten or more farmsteads named Selvik, notably on the west coast of Norway, probably so named from Old Norse *selja* 'willow' or *selr* 'seal' + *vík* 'inlet'.
GIVEN NAMES Scandinavian 7%. *Bjorn, Erik, Thor.*

Selvy (111) Variant spelling of English SELVEY.

Selway (167) English: from a Middle English personal name, *Salewi*, probably from an unattested Old English personal name, *Sǣlwīg*, composed of the elements *sǣl* 'good fortune' + *wīg* 'war'.

Selwyn (180) English: from a Middle English personal name, *Selewyne*, from the Old English personal name *Selewine*, composed of the elements *sele* 'hall' + *wine* 'friend'.

Selz (177) South German: habitational name from any of several places so named.
GIVEN NAME German 4%. *Manfred.*

Selzer (795) **1.** German and Jewish (Ashkenazic): variant spelling of SELTZER. **2.** German: habitational name for someone from any of several places named Selz or Seltz.

Selzler (170) German: occupational name, from an agent derivative of a diminutive of Middle High German *salz* 'salt' (see SALZ).
GIVEN NAMES German 4%. *Aloys.*

Sem (186) **1.** Norwegian: habitational name from any of about fifteen farms so named, a variant of SEIM. **2.** Slovenian: from the medieval personal name *Sem*, a shortened form of SIMON. **3.** Cambodian: unexplained. **4.** Indian (Panjab): Hindu (Saraswat Brahman) name of unknown meaning.
GIVEN NAMES Cambodian 14%; Indian 7%. *Chamroeun* (2), *Sophal* (2), *Kim Seng, Kosal, Lam, Phan, Phat, Soeum, Tan; Arup, Chander, Harish, Suman.*

Semaan (107) Muslim: variant of SAMAAN.
GIVEN NAMES Muslim 32%. *Rami* (2), *Aiman, Akram, Amal, Assaf, Aziz, Emad, Fadi, Fadia, Fady, Gihan, Khalil.*

Seman (690) **1.** Czech and Slovak: variant of ZEMAN 'yeoman farmer'. **2.** Jewish (Ashkenazic) variant of SEEMANN. **3.** English: variant spelling of SEAMAN.

Semancik (138) Czech and Slovak (**Semančík**): variant spelling of **Zemančík** 'yeoman farmer', a pet form of ZEMAN.

Semans (187) **1.** variant of SEMAN in any of its senses, with excrescent or patronymic -*s*. **2.** Americanized spelling of German SIEMENS.

Semar (123) **1.** German: a Germanized form of French **Saint Marc**, the name of a Huguenot family that migrated to the Palatinate. **2.** English: variant of SEYMOUR.

Sember (141) English: variant of SEMPER.

Semel (253) Jewish (Ashkenazic): variant spelling of SEMMEL.
GIVEN NAMES Jewish 5%. *Gitel, Moshe, Shmuel.*

Semelsberger (102) Jewish (Ashkenazic): ornamental-occupational name for a baker, from Yiddish *zeml* (German *Semmel*) 'white bread roll' + *berg* 'mountain'.

Semenza (155) Italian: apparently from *semenza* 'seeds', hence perhaps an occupational name for a seed merchant.
GIVEN NAMES Italian 8%. *Amato, Angelo, Lorenzo, Nunzi.*

Semer (133) German: variant of SIEMER.

Semerad (127) Czech (**Semerád**): from the old Czech personal name, *Sěmirad*, composed of *sěmi* 'person' + *rad* 'nimble', 'swift'.

Semeraro (175) South Italian (Apulia): occupational name for someone who led pack animals, southern Italian *semeraro*, a derivative of *soma* 'pack', 'load'.
GIVEN NAMES Italian 19%. *Angelo* (3), *Carmelo* (2), *Domenic* (2), *Cosimo, Cosmo, Giovanni, Grazio, Lorenzo, Rocco.*

Semien (224) Americanized spelling of Hungarian *Semjén*, from the ecclesiastical name *Semjén*, from SIMEON.
GIVEN NAMES French 9%. *Adrien, Andrus, Antoine, Elodie, Elrick, Nolton.*

Seminara (257) South Italian (most common in Calabria and Sicily): habitational name from any of the places in Reggio Calabria called Seminara.
GIVEN NAMES Italian 20%. *Sal* (4), *Rocco* (2), *Salvatore* (2), *Santo* (2), *Angelo, Biagio, Carmel, Carmelo, Concetta, Domenico, Pasquale.*

Semler (748) German and Jewish (Ashkenazic): occupational name for a baker of white rolls, from an agent derivative of Middle High German *semel*, German *Semmel*, Yiddish *zeml* 'white bread roll' (from Middle High German *semel(e)*, *simel* 'fine wheat flour'). Such rolls were in contrast to the coarse rye bread that was and is the norm in many households.

Semmel (229) German and Jewish (Ashkenazic): metonymic occupational name for a baker of white bread rolls (see SEMLER). The German surname may also be a metonymic occupational name for a dealer in fine wheat flour.

Semmens (201) English (Devon and Cornwall): **1.** patronymic from SEAMAN. **2.** variant of SIMMONS.

Semmes (187) Origin unidentified.

Semmler (310) German: variant of SEMLER.
GIVEN NAMES German 8%. *Alfons* (2), *Dieter, Hans, Juergen, Klaus, Willi.*

Semo (134) Origin unidentified. Possibly Spanish, but unexplained.

Semon (653) English, Dutch, and French (Swiss): variant of SIMON.

Semones (413) Variant spelling of English SIMONS.

Semper (142) **1.** English (of Norman origin): habitational name from any of the various places in northern France called Saint-Pierre, from the dedication of their churches to St. Peter (see PETER). **2.** Eastern German: from a medieval personal name *Sindperht*, from *sind* 'journey' + *berht* 'shining'. **3.** possibly variant of Catalan or Aragonese SAMPER.
GIVEN NAMES German 5%; Spanish 4%. *Heinz, Horst; Felipe, Fidel, Jose, Luis.*

Semple (946) Scottish and northern Irish: nickname from Middle English, Old French *simple* 'simple', 'straightforward', 'humble' (Latin *simplus*).

Semrad (245) Czech (**Semrád**): variant of **Semerád** (see SEMERAD).

Semrau (350) German: standardized spelling of SEMROW.
GIVEN NAMES German 5%. *Gerda, Konrad, Otto, Siegfried, Sigismund, Ulrich.*

Semrow (161) Eastern German: habitational name from any of several places so named, all in Pomerania.
GIVEN NAMES German 5%. *Otto* (2), *Ewald.*

Sen (540) Indian (Bengal) and Bangladeshi: Hindu (Baidya, Kayasth) name, from Sanskrit *sena* 'army', 'armament'. It occurs frequently in Sanskrit literature as the final element of compound names.
GIVEN NAMES Indian 71%. *Amitava* (4), *Arun* (4), *Ashok* (4), *Chandra* (4), *Dipankar* (4), *Amit* (3), *Amitabha* (3), *Dev* (3), *Harsha* (3), *Santanu* (3), *Somnath* (3), *Tapan* (3).

Sena (1645) Portuguese: religious byname adopted in honor of St. Catherine of Siena (Portuguese *Sena*). This saint was born in 1347 at Siena in Tuscany, the daughter of a wool-dyer with the surname Benincasa, and combined her work among the poor of the city with an influential role in ecclesiastical politics.
GIVEN NAMES Spanish 14%; Italian 5%. *Manuel* (15), *Jose* (10), *Carlos* (6), *Arturo* (3), *Diego* (3), *Jesus* (3), *Juan* (3), *Orlando* (3), *Alfonso* (2), *Angelina* (2), *Armando* (2), *Ignacio* (2); *Antonio* (8), *Angelo* (6), *Giuseppe* (3), *Salvatore* (3), *Carmel* (2), *Carmelo* (2), *Cecilio* (2), *Sal* (2), *Agostino*, *Carlo*, *Cosmo*, *Dante*.

Senatore (306) Italian: status name from *senatore* 'senator' (Latin *senator*), or nickname for a stately man.
GIVEN NAMES Italian 10%. *Carmine*, *Enrico*, *Ignazio*, *Massimo*, *Ottavio*, *Pasquale*, *Sal*.

Senay (127) Possibly a respelling of French **Sené**, a nickname from Old French *sené* 'wise'.
GIVEN NAMES French 10%. *Adelard*, *Armand*, *Marcel*, *Origene*.

Sendek (111) Slovak: unexplained.

Sendelbach (209) German: habitational name from places so called near Lohr on the Main river and near Oberkirch in Baden.
GIVEN NAMES German 6%. *Frieda* (2), *Juergen*.

Sender (302) Jewish (eastern Ashkenazic): from the Yiddish personal name *Sender*, a pet form of ALEXANDER.
GIVEN NAMES German 8%; Jewish 6%. *Ernst*, *Ewald*, *Horst*, *Kurt*, *Wilfried*, *Wolf*; *Mordechai*, *Shraga*, *Yaakov*.

Sendra (111) Catalan: either respelling of **Cendra**, a nickname from *cendra* 'ash(es)' or from the old personal name *Sendra*, medieval Latin *Senderedus*.
GIVEN NAMES Spanish 15%. *Fidel* (2), *Jose* (2), *Amaro*, *Angel*, *Digna*, *Luis*, *Richardo*; *Sal*, *Salvatore*.

Seneca (301) Italian (chiefly Naples): from the ancient Roman family name *Seneca*.
GIVEN NAMES Italian 4%. *Carlo*, *Giocondo*, *Orazio*, *Rocco*.

Senecal (1043) French (**Sénécal**): status name for a seneschal, an official in a large household who was responsible for overseeing day-to-day domestic arrangements, from Old French *seneschal* (of Germanic origin, composed of the elements *sini* 'old' + *scalc* 'servant'). The seneschal of a royal or ducal household in the Middle Ages was a very powerful man indeed, often having control over the administration of justice, among other things. In some cases the surname may have originated as nickname for an officious man.
FOREBEARS A Senécal from Rouen, Normandy, France, was in Boucherville, Quebec, around 1648, with the secondary surname LAFRAMBOISE.
GIVEN NAMES French 7%. *Andre* (3), *Adrien* (2), *Gilles* (2), *Jacques* (2), *Edmour*, *Elzear*, *Emile*, *Fernand*, *Gabrielle*, *Germain*, *Jean-Claude*, *Philippe*.

Senechal (274) French (**Sénéchal**): variant of **Sénécal** (see SENECAL).
GIVEN NAMES French 9%. *Aldea*, *Cecile*, *Georges*, *Lucien*, *Pierre*.

Senegal (205) French (**Sénégal**): variant of **Sénécal** (see SENECAL).

Senerchia (119) Italian: habitational name from Senerchia in Avellino province.
GIVEN NAMES Italian 18%. *Angelo* (3), *Antonio* (2), *Concetta*, *Generoso*, *Nicola*, *Tobia*, *Ulisse*.

Senesac (244) French: unexplained.
GIVEN NAMES French 6%. *Armand*, *Emile*, *Girard*, *Laure*.

Senese (282) Italian: habitational name for someone from Siena, a reduced form of *Sienese* 'inhabitant of Siena'.
GIVEN NAMES Italian 14%. *Antonio* (2), *Vito* (2), *Angelo*, *Carmine*, *Dante*, *Dino*, *Filomena*, *Francesca*, *Giuliano*, *Maurizio*, *Rocco*.

Seney (301) Possibly a variant of SEENEY.

Senf (191) German: from Middle High German *sen(e)f* 'mustard', hence a metonymic occupational name for a dealer in or producer of mustard or a nickname for someone with a fiery temper.
GIVEN NAMES German 5%. *Dieter*, *Wolfgang*.

Senff (150) Variant of SENF.
GIVEN NAMES German 7%. *Annice*, *Christoph*, *Frieda*, *Kurt*.

Senft (652) German: **1.** nickname for a helpful or friendly person, from Middle High German *senfte* 'soft', 'accommodating'. **2.** variant of SENF.
GIVEN NAMES German 4%. *Eldred*, *Gunther*, *Jodel*, *Kurt*, *Otto*.

Seng (912) South German: **1.** topographic name for someone who lived by land cleared by fire, from Middle High German *sengen* 'to singe or burn'. **2.** habitational name from a place so named in Bavaria.

Senger (1059) **1.** German, Jewish (Ashkenazic), and Dutch: variant of German **Sänger**, Jewish and Dutch **Sanger** (see SANGER 1). **2.** German: habitational name for someone from Seng in Bavaria.

Sengstock (144) German: metonymic occupational name for a stoker or blacksmith, from Middle High German *sengen* 'to singe or burn' + *stock* 'rod', 'bar'.

Sengupta (201) Indian (Bengal) and Bangladeshi: Hindu (Baidya) name, a compound of SEN + GUPTA.
GIVEN NAMES Indian 89%. *Chandan* (3), *Dipak* (3), *Nandini* (3), *Tapan* (3), *Amitava* (2), *Bhaskar* (2), *Dipankar* (2), *Kaushik* (2), *Pradip* (2), *Somnath* (2), *Sumedha* (2), *Alok*.

Senick (139) Origin unidentified. Possibly a variant of English **Senneck**, apparently a habitational name from Sevenoaks in Kent, reflecting the local pronunciation of the place name. Alternatively, it could be a respelling of Dutch **Senik**, according to Debrabandere either from *Seneca*, the name of the Roman writer, or an occupational name from Middle Dutch *seneschael* 'seneschal'.

Senior (1145) **1.** English (mainly Yorkshire): nickname for a peasant who gave himself airs and graces, from Anglo-Norman French *segneur* 'lord' (Latin *senior* 'elder'). **2.** English and Dutch: distinguishing nickname for the elder of two bearers of the same personal name (for example, a father and son or two brothers), from Latin *senior* 'elder'.

Senk (208) **1.** Polish (**Sęk**): topographic name or nickname from Polish *sęk* 'knag', or a Ukrainian cognate of this. **2.** German: variant of SCHENK or SENG. **3.** Slovenian (north central Slovenia; **Šenk**): Slovenian spelling of German SCHENK.
GIVEN NAMES Polish 6%. *Lech*, *Stanislaus*, *Zigmont*.

Senkbeil (217) German: metonymic occupational name for an archer, or possibly a crude sexual nickname, from Middle Low German *senken* 'to sink' + *pīl* 'arrow'.
GIVEN NAMES German 5%. *Gerhard*, *Horst*, *Kurt*.

Senko (356) **1.** Ukrainian: patronymic from the Ukrainian personal name *Siemion* (see SIMON). **2.** Slovak: occupational name for a seller of hay, from *seno*, 'hay'.

Senkowski (104) Polish (**Sękowski**): habitational name for someone from places called Sękowo in Ciechanów, Płock, and Poznań voivodeships, or Sęków in Chełm voivodeship, all named with *sęk* 'knag' (see SENK).

Senn (2150) South German: occupational name for a dairy farmer, from Middle High German *senne* 'dairy farmer', 'cheese maker'.

Senna (251) Italian: **1.** habitational name from Senna Comasco or Senna Lodigiana in Lombardy, possibly taking their names from an Etruscan personal name, *Semna*. **2.** possibly a topographic name for someone who lived by a cassia plant, *senna*, or perhaps a metonymic occupational name for a herbalist. **3.** possibly from a feminine form of the male personal name *Senno*, a short form of a personal name formed with this suffix, such as *Bonsenno*.
GIVEN NAMES Italian 4%. *Angelo*, *Pasquale*, *Salvatore*.

Senne (359) **1.** German: variant of SENN. **2.** German: habitational name from a place so named, for example near Bielefeld. **3.** Dutch: from the Frisian personal name

Senne. **4.** French: from Old French *senne* 'assembly', 'gathering', or from the word in northern Middle French, which referred to a fine imposed on someone who worked on a Sunday, so this could be a nickname for someone who had had to pay such a fine. **5.** French (**Senné**): nickname for a wise person, from Old French *sené* 'wise', 'sensible'. **6.** Italian: variant (plural) of SENNA 2.

Senner (266) South German: occupational name, from Middle High German *sennære* 'alpine herdsman', 'milker', 'cheesemaker'.

Sennett (749) Irish and English: variant of SINNOTT.

Sennott (185) Irish and English: variant of SINNOTT.
GIVEN NAME Irish 5%. *Siobhan*.

Seno (139) **1.** Japanese (**Senoo**): habitational name from Senoo-mura in Bitchū (now part of Okayama prefecture). It is pronounced SEO farther west in Japan. **2.** Filipino: unexplained. **3.** Italian: nickname from *seno* 'sense', Venetian dialect form of standard Italian *senno*. **4.** Catalan (also **Senó**): habitational name from any of the places named Seno or Senó.
GIVEN NAMES Japanese 8%; Italian 6%; Spanish 5%. *Haruo, Kaoru, Kenso, Koji, Toshio; Salvatore* (2), *Angelo, Ireneo; Artemio, Elvira, Eugenio, Purita, Salvador, Serapio*.

Senor (113) Spanish (**Señor**): nickname from the title *señor* 'mister'.
GIVEN NAMES Spanish 8%. *Andres, Blanca, Don Juan, Felipe, Valeria*.

Sens (211) **1.** French: habitational name from places so called in Cher, Ille-et-Vilaine, and Saône-et-Loire, derived from an adjectival form of the Latin personal name *Sancius*, or Sens in Yonne, which takes its name from the Gaulish tribe of the *Senones*. **2.** French (Gascon): from a variant of the personal name SAINT. **3.** North German and Dutch: from a short form of the personal name *Vincens* (see VINCENT).
GIVEN NAME French 4%. *Jean-Marc*.

Sensabaugh (404) Americanized form of German **Sensenbach**, a topographic name formed with an unexplained first element + Middle High German *bach* 'creek'.

Sensat (108) Origin unidentified.

Sensel (122) **1.** South German: probably from a pet form of the Latin personal name *Vincens* (see VINCENT). **2.** perhaps a variant of Swiss German **Sensal** or **Zensel**, an occupational name for a stockbroker, probably derived from Latin *census* 'census'.

Senseman (123) German: possibly a variant of SENSEL 1.

Senseney (189) Origin unidentified. Perhaps a respelling of French **Sansonnet**, from a pet form *Sanson*, either a variant of the biblical name *Samson* or a pet form of a Gascon personal name derived from Latin *Sanctius*.

Sensenig (694) German: altered spelling of German **Sinzenich**, a habitational name from a place so named near Cologne.

Sensibaugh (104) Americanized form of German **Sensenbach** (see SENSABAUGH).

Sensing (193) German: unexplained.

Senske (184) North German and Dutch: from a pet form of SENS 3.

Sentell (381) English: unexplained.

Senter (1403) **1.** English: occupational name, from Old French *saintier* 'bell-founder'. **2.** English: metonymic occupational name for a maker of belts and girdles, from Middle English *ceinture, ceintere* 'girdle'.

Senters (278) Probably a variant of English SENTER.

Sentman (158) Origin unidentified.

Sentner (131) German: unexplained. Possibly a variant of ZENTNER.

Sentz (280) German: variant of SENS 3.

Seo (746) **1.** Korean: variant of SO. **2.** Japanese: written with characters meaning 'younger sister' and 'tail'. This name is not common in Japan.
GIVEN NAMES Korean 65%; Japanese 7%. *Young* (17), *Jung* (8), *Dong* (7), *Myung* (5), *Sang* (5), *Kwang* (4), *Kyung* (4), *Young Soo* (4), *Hyun* (3), *Soon* (3), *Sung* (3), *Yong* (3); *Jeong* (5), *Byung* (4), *Chang* (3), *Jung Ho* (3), *Chul* (2), *Jung Soo* (2), *Jung Woo* (2), *Kyong Hee* (2), *Seong* (2), *Seoung* (2), *Yeon* (2), *Chang Hyun; Akio* (2), *Sumio* (2), *Toru* (2), *Kaoru, Kazuo, Kenji, Kenzo, Masaya, Miho, Osamu, Saichi, Tadao*.

Seoane (131) Galician: habitational name from any of the numerous places in Galicia named Seoane, for Saint John (*San Xoan*).
GIVEN NAMES Spanish 49%. *Luis* (6), *Manuel* (5), *Jose* (4), *Carlos* (3), *Cesar* (3), *Julio* (3), *Juan* (2), *Abelino, Andres, Argentina, Armando, Candelario*.

Sepanski (134) Americanized or Germanized spelling of Polish SZCZEPANSKI.

Sepe (421) **1.** Italian (Salento): topographic name from the dialect word *sepe* 'hedge', 'fence' (Latin *saepes*). **2.** Americanized spelling of Hungarian *Szépe*, from the old Hungarian secular name *Szépe*, or *Szípe*.
GIVEN NAMES Italian 21%. *Angelo* (4), *Manuel* (3), *Gennaro* (2), *Gino* (2), *Nicola* (2), *Aldo, Alfonso, Amante, Carlo, Concetta, Donato, Elvira, Gaetano, Gabriela, Gerardo, Guido, Luigi, Mario, Rito, Salvatore*.

Sepeda (249) Spanish: (Latin American) variant of the habitational name CEPEDA.
GIVEN NAMES Spanish 30%. *Lupe* (4), *Elida* (3), *Santos* (3), *Alberto* (2), *Fidel* (2), *Manuel* (2), *Orlando* (2), *Raul* (2), *Rumaldo* (2), *Alfonso, Amador, Angelina*.

Seper (106) Origin unidentified.

Sepich (162) Croatian (**Šepić**): patronymic from a nickname *šepa* 'lame man', derived from *šepati* 'to limp'. It may also be an Italianized form of this surname, originating from Istria and the city of Rijeka.

Sepp (135) German (Bavarian) and Dutch: from a short form of the personal name *Joseph*.
GIVEN NAME German 6%. *Ingeborg* (4).

Seppala (324) Finnish (**Seppälä**): topographic name, found chiefly in western Finland, for someone who was a smith or lived at the house of a smith, from *seppä* 'blacksmith' + the local suffix *-la*.
GIVEN NAMES Finnish 10%. *Pentti* (2), *Armas, Arvo, Eino, Jouni, Juha, Runo*.

Seppanen (164) Finnish (**Seppänen**): patronymic from the occupational name *seppä* 'blacksmith' + the common surname suffix *-nen*. This name is found chiefly in central and eastern Finland.
GIVEN NAMES Finnish 14%; Scandinavian 4%. *Erkki* (2), *Markku* (2), *Toivo* (2), *Jukka, Raimo, Reijo, Waino; Jarl*.

Seppi (158) Italian: from a short form of the personal name *Giuseppe*, Italian form of JOSEPH.
GIVEN NAMES Italian 4%. *Aldo, Carlo, Leno, Martino*.

Septer (156) Of Dutch origin: unexplained.

Sepulvado (378) Origin uncertain; probably an American variant of Spanish SEPULVEDA.

Sepulveda (2159) Spanish (**Sepúlveda**): habitational name principally from Sepúlveda in Segovia, although there are other places so named which could also have given rise to the surname in some cases.
GIVEN NAMES Spanish 45%. *Jose* (65), *Juan* (43), *Carlos* (29), *Luis* (19), *Jesus* (18), *Roberto* (15), *Ramon* (14), *Manuel* (12), *Pedro* (12), *Raul* (9), *Angel* (8), *Armando* (8).

Sequeira (671) Portuguese and Galician: habitational name from any of the numerous places in Portugal named Sequeira, or (in Galicia) a topographic name from *sequeira* 'arid land', from Late Latin *siccaria*, a derivative of *siccus* 'dry'. This name is also found in western India, where it was taken by Portuguese colonists.
GIVEN NAMES Spanish 27%; Portuguese 12%. *Jose* (23), *Manuel* (17), *Carlos* (7), *Francisco* (6), *Rafael* (5), *Luis* (4), *Mario* (4), *Alejandro* (3), *Alvaro* (3), *Jorge* (3), *Mauricio* (3), *Ricardo* (3); *Agostinho, Caetano, Damiao, Joao, Ligia, Margarida*.

Sequin (141) **1.** French: unexplained. **2.** Americanized spelling of French CHICOINE.
GIVEN NAMES French 4%. *Alcide, Cecile*.

Sera (298) **1.** Catalan: most probably a mispelling of Catalan SERRA. **2.** Italian: from a short form of a personal name with this ending, such as *Baldisera, B(u)onasera*. **3.** Hungarian: unexplained. **4.** Japanese: written with characters meaning either 'good' and 'world' or 'west' and 'silk gauze'. This name is not common in Japan and may be Ryūkyūan in origin.
GIVEN NAMES Spanish 12%; Japanese 11%. *Carlos* (5), *Armando* (2), *Fernando* (2),

Jose (2), *Alberto, Alvaro, Ana, Assunta, Elia, Enrique, Ernesto, Evelio*; *Yoshio* (2), *Hideo, Hitomi, Katsumi, Kenji, Kimihiro, Masao, Mikio, Nobuhiro, Sadao, Takeo, Tsuneo.*

Serafin (1145) Polish, Spanish (**Serafín**), Portuguese, and Italian (Venetian): from a medieval personal name, Latin *Seraphinus*, from Hebrew *serafim*. In the Bible this term is applied to the class of six-winged creatures described in Isaiah 6, which came to be regarded in the Middle Ages as a class of angels; it is the plural form of Hebrew *saraf*, probably a derivative of *saraf* 'to burn'. In part the Portuguese surname may represent a religious byname adopted in honor of the Capuchin monk St. Seraphinus (1540–1604, formally canonized in 1767).
GIVEN NAMES Polish 5%; Spanish 4%. *Jerzy* (2), *Jozef* (2), *Stanislaw* (2), *Boguslawa, Boleslaw, Elzbieta, Irena, Iwona, Jacek, Janusz, Jolanta, Karol*; *Jesus* (4), *Jose* (2), *Jose Luis* (2), *Luis* (2), *Mario* (2), *Adela, Angel, Angeles, Angelina, Armando, Avila, Cruz.*

Serafine (147) Italian: variant of SERAFINO.
GIVEN NAMES Italian 7%. *Gino, Guido.*

Serafini (579) Italian: patronymic or plural form of SERAFINO.
GIVEN NAMES Italian 16%. *Angelo* (7), *Aldo* (3), *Luigi* (3), *Dante* (2), *Egidio* (2), *Guido* (2), *Leno* (2), *Anello, Carmine, Dino, Francesco.*

Serafino (247) Italian: from the personal name *Serafino* (see SERAFIN).
GIVEN NAMES Italian 14%. *Pasquale* (2), *Carmino, Ercole, Francesco, Orazio, Rocco, Sal, Silvio.*

Seraphin (128) German and French: from a Classicized variant spelling of the personal name SERAFIN.
GIVEN NAMES French 14%; German 11%. *Andre, Dominique, Jacques, Yanick*; *Dietrich* (2), *Otto* (2), *Klebert.*

Seratt (153) Variant of English SARRATT or SYRETT.

Serban (114) Romanian: ethnic name for someone from Serbia, from *Serb* 'Serb'.
GIVEN NAMES Romanian 19%; Russian 6%; Hungarian 4%. *Liviu* (2), *Andreea, Danut, Gheorghe, Ionel, Mihai, Mircea, Radu, Toader, Valeriu*; *Andrei* (3); *Zsolt* (2).

Serber (100) German: ethnic name for a Serb or a Sorb (a Slavic tribe in eastern Germany), from an inflected form of the adjective *Serbe*.

Serbin (254) **1.** Spanish: variant of SERVIN. **2.** Polish: ethnic name for someone from Serbia.
GIVEN NAMES Spanish 4%. *Benito, Guillermina, Isidro, Jorge, Juan, Oralia, Salvador.*

Serbousek (113) Czech: occupational name for a servant, or an ironic nickname for an obsequious man, from *serbus*, altered form of Latin *servus* 'servant'.

Serbus (117) Latinized form of an ethnic name for a Serb.

Serda (129) **1.** Catalan (**Serdà**): variant of the regional name CERDA. **2.** Catalan: habitational name from a place called La Serda, in Valencia.
GIVEN NAMES Spanish 39%. *Agustin* (2), *Angel* (2), *Humberto* (2), *Juan* (2), *Lupe* (2), *Manuel* (2), *Reynaldo* (2), *Santos* (2), *Adela, Ana, Angelina, Bacilio.*

Sereda (128) Hungarian (**Szereda**): from the old secular personal name *Szereda*. The Hungarian name was also well established in Russia.
GIVEN NAMES Russian 11%; Polish 4%. *Yury* (2), *Boris, Kirill, Sofiya, Vladimir, Zhanna*; *Arkadiusz.*

Serena (262) Italian and Catalan: from the female personal name *Serena* (from Latin *serenus, serena* 'clear', 'calm').
GIVEN NAMES Italian 7%. *Ottavio* (2), *Attilio, Domenic, Egidio, Giancarlo, Rocco.*

Serene (131) **1.** French: from a female personal name, from Latin *serena* 'clear', 'calm'. Compare Italian and Catalan SERENA. **2.** Perhaps also an Americanized form of Hungarian *Serény*, or *Serényi*, from *serény* 'quick'.

Sereno (332) **1.** Italian: from the personal name *Sereno* (from Latin *serenus, serena* 'clear', 'calm'). **2.** Portuguese and Spanish: nickname from *sereno* 'serene', 'calm'.
GIVEN NAMES Italian 18%; Spanish 9%. *Salvatore* (3), *Angelo, Antonio, Corrado, Gilberto, Roberto, Tommaso*; *Guadalupe, Jose, Luis, Manuel, Maria Del Carmen, Marta, Pedro.*

Seres (146) Hungarian and Jewish (from Hungary): occupational name from *seres* 'brewer', a derivative of *ser* or *sör* 'beer'.
GIVEN NAMES Hungarian 8%. *Akos, Gabor, Laszlo, Tamas, Zoltan.*

Serfass (444) North German: from the Low German personal name **Servas, Servaes, Servatz**, Dutch **Servaas**, from Latin SERVATIUS.

Serfling (119) German: nickname for a sickly person, from Middle High German *serben, serwen* 'to be sick'.
GIVEN NAME German 5%. *Hermann* (2).

Serge (156) French: **1.** metonymic occupational name for a maker or seller of serge, a type of woolen fabric, from Old French *sarge*. **2.** from the personal name *Serge* (Latin *Sergius*, of obscure origin). The name was borne by several early martyrs and a pope.
GIVEN NAMES Italian 9%; Spanish 6%. *Emilia, Rocco, Santo*; *Diego* (2), *Carmel, Hernando, Luz, Melida.*

Sergeant (571) English and Irish: variant spelling of SARGENT.

Sergent (987) **1.** English and French: variant of SARGENT. **2.** Americanized form of the Polish Jewish ornamental name **Sierżant** 'sergeant' (senior noncommissioned officer in the Polish infantry).

Sergi (422) Italian: patronymic or plural form of SERGIO.

GIVEN NAMES Italian 16%. *Salvatore* (5), *Angelo* (4), *Antonio* (2), *Gaetano* (2), *Nunzio* (2), *Rocco* (2), *Antonino, Enrico, Giovanni.*

Sergio (255) Italian, Portuguese (**Sérgio**), and Spanish: from the personal name, from Latin *Sergius* (originally a family name, of uncertain, possibly Etruscan, origin). This was borne by a 4th-century Christian saint martyred in Cappadocia under Diocletian. The personal name was hereditary in the ducal houses of Amalfi and Naples between the 11th and 13th centuries.
GIVEN NAMES Italian 15%; Spanish 13%. *Alessandro, Dino, Gaetana, Giuseppe, Luca, Palma, Paolo, Roberto, Rocco*; *Jose* (2), *Garcia, Gonzalez, Gutierrez, Jose Luis, Juarez, Laureano, Manuel, Molina, Reyes.*

Serianni (129) Southern Italian: from a compound of the title *sere* 'sir' + the personal name *Ianni*, a variant of *Giovanni* (see JOHN).
GIVEN NAME Italian 5%. *Caesar.*

Serie (109) French (**Serié**): variant of **Cerier**, a southern form of **Cerisier**, a topographic name for someone who lived by a cherry tree or in an area characterized by cherry trees.

Seright (123) Variant of English SEARIGHT.

Serino (526) Italian: **1.** habitational name from Serino in Avellino province. **2.** from a diminutive of SERIO.
GIVEN NAMES Italian 14%. *Carmine* (4), *Antonio* (2), *Angelo, Attilio, Carmelo, Gaetano, Giuliano, Guiseppe, Lorenzo, Nunzio, Palma.*

Serio (1131) **1.** Italian and Portuguese (**Sério**): nickname for a grave, sober person, from *serio* 'serious', 'sober'. **2.** Italian: from a variant of the personal name SERGIO, influenced by the Greek pronunciation *Seryios*.
GIVEN NAMES Italian 12%. *Salvatore* (11), *Sal* (7), *Antonio* (4), *Carmelo* (3), *Cosimo* (2), *Salvator* (2), *Vito* (2), *Antonino, Ciriaco, Domenic, Gennaro, Luigi.*

Serlin (178) **1.** Jewish (eastern Ashkenazic): metronymic from a pet form of the Yiddish female personal name *Sere*, variant of *Sore* 'Sarah' (see SORIN) + the eastern Slavic possessive suffix *-in*. **2.** French: from a vernacular form of the personal name *Saturnin* (from the Roman family name *Saturninus*, a derivative of *Saturnus*, the name of a Roman god).
GIVEN NAME Jewish 5%. *Omri.*

Sermersheim (189) German (Baden area): habitational name from a place so named in Alsace.

Sermon (158) **1.** English: from Middle English *serm(o)un* 'sermon', a metonymic occupational name for a preacher, or perhaps a nickname for a long-winded and pompous person. **2.** Dutch: variant of SIMON, with epenthetic *-r-*.

Sermons (141) English: variant of SERMON.

Serna (2542) Spanish: habitational name from any of various places named La Serna, from *serna* 'grainfield' (of Celtic origin).
GIVEN NAMES Spanish 47%. *Jose* (64), *Juan* (36), *Jesus* (34), *Carlos* (20), *Manuel* (18), *Ruben* (16), *Guadalupe* (15), *Luis* (14), *Javier* (13), *Mario* (12), *Pedro* (12), *Ramon* (12).

Seroka (153) Jewish (eastern Ashkenazic): variant of SOROKA.

Serota (239) Polish (**Sierota**) and Jewish (eastern Ashkenazic): from Polish *sierota* 'orphan'.
GIVEN NAMES Jewish 4%. *Meyer, Tali.*

Serpa (718) Portuguese: habitational name from a place so named near Beja.
GIVEN NAMES Spanish 18%. *Manuel* (19), *Jose* (9), *Andres* (4), *Francisco* (4), *Alberto* (2), *Ambrosio* (2), *Ana* (2), *Carlos* (2), *Cristina* (2), *Fernando* (2), *Jorge* (2), *Juan* (2).

Serpas (291) Hispanic: unexplained. In the U.S. this surname occurs chiefly in LA; elsewhere it is found mainly in El Salvador.
GIVEN NAMES Spanish 13%. *Ana* (3), *Francisco* (2), *Jose* (2), *Ana Cecilia, Carlos, Cristina, Efrin, Guillermo, Ivette, Jorge, Jose Felix, Jose Manuel.*

Serpe (195) **1.** Italian and Portuguese: nickname from *serpe* 'serpent', 'reptile'. **2.** French: metonymic occupational name for a maker or seller of scythes and similar implements, from Old French *sarpe* (hypercorrected to *serpe*) 'scythe', 'sickle'.
GIVEN NAMES Italian 18%. *Angelo* (3), *Carmelo* (2), *Carmine* (2), *Gaetano* (2), *Luciano* (2), *Salvatore* (2), *Annamaria, Fausto, Ferdinando, Sal.*

Serpico (249) Italian: origin uncertain; perhaps from a derivative of SERPE.
GIVEN NAMES Italian 11%; French 4%. *Biagio, Carmine, Gennaro, Giuseppe, Raffaele; Alphonse* (2), *Camille.*

Serr (319) German (Baden): probably related to a dialect word meaning 'fence', 'bolt', hence a metonymic occupational name for a locksmith.

Serra (1718) **1.** Italian, Portuguese, and Catalan: topographic name from Italian, Portuguese, Catalan *serra* 'ridge or chain of hills' (Latin *serra* 'saw'). **2.** Italian: habitational name from any of various places named with *serra* 'ridge' (see 1 above), as for example Serra d'Aniello and Serra Pedace (Cosenza), Serra San Bruno (Vibo Valentia), Serracapriola (Foggia). **3.** Catalan: habitational name from any of various places, in Valencia and Catalonia, named Serra or with Serra, as for example Serra d'Almos or Serra d'en Galceran. **4.** Catalan (**Serrà**): topographic name for somebody who lived by a sierra, from Catalan *serrà*, an adjective derived from *serra* 'mountain range'.
GIVEN NAMES Spanish 12%; Italian 9%; Portuguese 5%. *Jose* (16), *Juan* (6),

Eduardo (5), *Francisco* (5), *Jorge* (5), *Mario* (5), *Enrique* (4), *Jaime* (4), *Luis* (4), *Manuel* (4), *Miguel* (4), *Ramon* (3); *Antonio* (11), *Angelo* (6), *Enrico* (3), *Guido* (3), *Salvatore* (3), *Amedeo* (2), *Elio* (2), *Marco* (2), *Nicolo* (2), *Sandro* (2), *Caesar, Carlo; Henrique, Joaquim.*

Serrano (6235) Spanish (also found in Portugal and Brazil): topographic name for someone who lived by a mountain ridge or chain of hills, from an adjectival derivative of *serra*.
GIVEN NAMES Spanish 47%; Portuguese 10%. *Jose* (183), *Juan* (83), *Luis* (61), *Manuel* (56), *Pedro* (52), *Carlos* (47), *Miguel* (42), *Francisco* (36), *Jesus* (33), *Jorge* (32), *Ricardo* (32), *Rafael* (31); *Joao, Joaquim, Wenseslao.*

Serrao (283) Portuguese (**Serrão**): topographic name from Latin *serranus* 'mountain dweller'.
GIVEN NAMES Portuguese 19%. *Manuel* (3), *Mario* (3), *Ana, Carlos, Francisco, Jaime, Rafael; Aldo, Antonio, Francesco, Gilda, Pina, Romano.*

Serrata (104) Italian: habitational name from a place in Reggio Calabria named Serrata, possibly from *serrata* 'enclosure', 'sluice'.
GIVEN NAMES Spanish 42%. *Jose* (3), *Raul* (3), *Juan* (2), *Baldo, Carlos, Corina, Franscisco, Gonzalo, Gregorio, Leonida, Lucrecia, Luis.*

Serrato (737) **1.** Spanish: apparently a variant of the habitational name CERRATO or a habitational name from Serrato in Málaga. **2.** Catalan (**Serrató**): topographic name for someone who lived by a low hill, from a diminutive of *serrat*. **3.** Southern Italian: apparently from *serrato* 'closed', 'shut', but more likely a topographic name related to SERRA or SERRATA.
GIVEN NAMES Spanish 51%. *Jose* (17), *Juan* (10), *Manuel* (10), *Jesus* (9), *Pedro* (8), *Carlos* (7), *Jaime* (7), *Roberto* (7), *Fernando* (6), *Francisco* (6), *Miguel* (6), *Arturo* (5).

Serratore (183) Italian: occupational name for a sawyer, from an agent derivative of *serra* 'saw'.
GIVEN NAMES Italian 18%. *Giuseppe* (2), *Francesco, Giacomo, Vincenza, Vito.*

Serres (230) **1.** Catalan and southern French (Occitan): habitational name from any of the places so named in Catalonia and southern and eastern France. **2.** Catalan and Occitan: topographic name from *serres*, the plural of Catalan *serra* and Occitan *serre* 'ridge', 'chain of hills'.
GIVEN NAMES French 4%. *Edouard, Philippe.*

Serritella (159) Italian: of uncertain derivation; possibly a topographic name related to SERRA.
GIVEN NAMES Italian 10%. *Amelio, Angelo, Carmela, Rocco, Romeo, Santa.*

Sertich (150) Croatian and Serbian (**Sertić**): unexplained. It may be a deriva-

tive of the adjective *sert* 'severe', 'hard', a word of Turkish origin.

Servais (384) **1.** French: from the personal name *Servais*, Latin *Servatius* (see SERVATIUS). **2.** English: variant of SERVICE.
GIVEN NAMES French 4%. *Francois, Jean-Louis, Marcel.*

Servant (130) French: occupational name for a servant, Old French *servant* (from Latin *serviens*).
GIVEN NAMES French 9%. *Clovis, Germain, Pierre.*

Servatius (131) German and Dutch: from the Latin personal name *Servatius* (a derivative of the Roman family name *Servatus*, meaning 'protected'). This was the name of the patron saint of Maastricht.
GIVEN NAME German 6%. *Fritz.*

Servedio (129) Italian: variant of SERVIDIO.
GIVEN NAMES Italian 24%. *Giovanna* (2), *Rocco* (2), *Vito* (2), *Damiano, Giovanni.*

Servello (192) Italian (mainly Campania): from a pet form of the personal name *Servo*, from *servo* 'servant', 'slave', bestowed with devotional reference to the service of God.
GIVEN NAMES Italian 13%; Spanish 4%. *Agostino, Aldo, Angelo, Antonio, Orlando, Pasquale, Sergio; Carlos, Jorge.*

Serven (134) Catalan (**Servén**) and Occitan: variant of **Servent**, an occupational name from *servent* 'servant' (from Latin *serviens*).

Server (168) English: status name for a servant.

Servi (127) Italian: from the personal name *Servo* 'servant', 'slave', used by early Christians with devotional reference to the service of God.
GIVEN NAMES Italian 6%. *Franco* (2), *Domenica, Elio, Italo, Tullio.*

Service (607) Scottish and English: metonymic occupational name for a brewer or a tavern-keeper, from Anglo-Norman French *cerveise* 'ale' (Old French *cervoise*, a word of Gaulish origin).

Servidio (226) Italian: from the personal name *Servidio*, representing the injunction *servo di dio* '(be a) servant of God' (Latin *Servusdei*).
GIVEN NAMES Italian 19%. *Angelo* (6), *Vito* (2), *Antonella, Antonio, Damiano, Salvatore.*

Servin (481) **1.** Hispanic (not found in present-day Spain but common in Mexico): it may derive from *cervin* 'deer' (Latin *cervus*). **2.** French: habitational name from a place in Doubs, recorded in the 14th century as *Cervins*.
GIVEN NAMES Spanish 48%. *Jose* (12), *Jose Luis* (9), *Francisco* (7), *Manuel* (6), *Jorge* (5), *Luis* (5), *Alejandro* (4), *Miguel* (4), *Alfonso* (3), *Alfredo* (3), *Ernesto* (3), *Jaime* (3).

Servis (373) English: variant spelling of SERVICE.

Serviss (271) English: variant spelling of SERVICE.

Servoss (108) Variant of English SERVICE.

Sesay (172) **1.** Muslim: unexplained. **2.** African: unexplained.
GIVEN NAMES Muslim 43%; African 16%. *Mohamed* (10), *Ibrahim* (4), *Abdul* (3), *Ahmed* (2), *Abdulai, Abu, Alusine, Amina, Idris, Ishmail, Kaba, Mohammed; Kadiatu* (3), *Alimamy* (2), *Foday* (2), *Aminata, Fatmata, Idrissa, Isatu, Kadijatu, Mariama.*

Seshadri (121) Indian (southern states): Hindu name, from a personal name based on the name of a hill in Andhra Pradesh, where there is a well-known temple of Vishnu. It is from Sanskrit *śeṣādri* 'Shesha's hill' (from *śeṣa* 'Shesha, the king of serpents' + *adri* 'hill'). This is found only as a male given name in India, but has come to be used as a family name in the U.S. among South Indians.
GIVEN NAMES Indian 95%. *Sridhar* (5), *Anand* (3), *Prasad* (3), *Ramesh* (3), *Ashok* (2), *Krishna* (2), *Prakash* (2), *Ram* (2), *Aravind, Balaji, Chandrika, Gayatri.*

Sesler (191) Variant spelling of SESSLER.

Sesma (101) Basque: habitational name from Sesma in Navarre province, Basque Country.
GIVEN NAMES Spanish 23%. *Carlos* (2), *Adolfo, Angel, Delfina, Dulce, Ernesto, Fernando, Graciela, Leticia, Luis, Mario, Petrona; Antonio* (2).

Sessa (630) Southern Italian (Sicily): habitational name from Sessa Aurunca in the province of Caserta, or from Sessa Cilento in Salerno.
GIVEN NAMES Italian 18%. *Carmine* (7), *Angelo* (6), *Antonio* (3), *Sal* (3), *Vito* (3), *Alberico* (2), *Giro* (2), *Pasquale* (2), *Salvatore* (2), *Alfonse, Carlo, Ezio.*

Session (550) English: variant of SESSIONS.

Sessions (2528) English (of Norman origin): habitational name from Soissons in northern France, named for the Gaulish tribe who once inhabited the area, and whose name is recorded in Latin documents in the form *Suessiones*, of uncertain derivation.

Sessler (468) German: **1.** habitational name for someone from a place called Sessel in Bavaria. **2.** Occupational name for a chair maker, from Middle High German *sezzel* 'chair'.

Sessom (106) Altered form of English SESSIONS.

Sessoms (1228) Altered form of English SESSIONS.

Sessum (105) Altered form of English SESSIONS.

Sessums (353) Altered form of English SESSIONS.

Sestak (244) Czech and Slovak (**Šesták**), and Hungarian (**Sesznták**): from Czech *šesták*, the name of an old coin (literally 'sixer'; it was at one time worth six kreuzers). The surname would have been acquired by someone who had to pay rent of this amount or for some other anecdotal reason.

Sester (119) South German (Baden): metonymic occupational name for a cooper who made measures, from Middle High German *sehster*, a dry or liquid measure (Latin *sextarius*).
GIVEN NAMES German 5%. *Kurt, Matthias.*

Sestito (223) Southern Italian: from a pet form of SESTO.
GIVEN NAMES Italian 23%. *Sal* (3), *Antonio* (2), *Carlo, Caterina, Domenic, Domenico, Enrico, Francesco, Gino, Rocco, Salvatore.*

Sesto (105) Italian: from the personal name *Sisto*, Latin *Sextus*, which was often conferred on a sixth son, or perhaps a topographic or habitational name for someone living six miles from a major settlement.
GIVEN NAMES Italian 15%. *Francesco, Giampaolo, Guido, Vincenzo, Vito.*

Seta (126) **1.** Italian: metonymic occupational name for a silk weaver or merchant, from *seta* 'silk'. **2.** Spanish: from *seta* 'fungus' or 'pig bristle'. **3.** Japanese: variously written, the meaning is probably 'rice paddy located on the strait'. This name is not common in Japan.
GIVEN NAMES Italian 13%; Japanese 9%. *Mario* (2), *Carlo, Guillermo, Marco, Pasquale, Salvatore; Joji, Kazuo, Shigeru, Yoshio.*

Setaro (161) Italian: occupational name for a silk weaver or merchant, from an agent derivative of *seta* 'silk'.
GIVEN NAMES Italian 9%. *Antonio* (6), *Angelo, Domenic, Gaetano, Pasquale.*

Setchell (115) Variant of English SATCHELL.

Seth (718) **1.** Indian (northern states): Hindu, Jain, and Parsi name found among several mercantile communities, from *seth* 'merchant', 'banker' in Hindi and neighboring languages (from Sanskrit *śreṣṭhī*, a term denoting the head of a mercantile or other guild). The Khatris of the Panjab have a clan called Seth. **2.** Scottish and Irish: reduced Anglicized form of Gaelic **Mac Sithigh** or **Ó Síthigh** (see SHEEHY).
GIVEN NAMES Indian 39%. *Deepak* (5), *Sanjay* (4), *Shiv* (4), *Ajay* (3), *Anand* (3), *Arvind* (3), *Nikhil* (3), *Rahul* (3), *Rajeev* (3), *Rajendra* (3), *Suresh* (3), *Vijay* (3).

Sether (165) Norwegian (**Sæther**): habitational name from any of numerous farmsteads named Seter or Sæter (see SATHER).

Sethi (445) Indian (Panjab): Hindu (Arora, Khatri) and Sikh name, based on the name of clans in the Arora and Khatri communities. It is derived from Sanskrit *śreṣṭhī*, which denotes the head of a mercantile or other guild. Compare SETH.
GIVEN NAMES Indian 91%. *Ashok* (8), *Anil* (6), *Sanjeev* (6), *Amrit* (4), *Rajesh* (4), *Ravi* (4), *Sanjay* (4), *Satish* (4), *Sunil* (4), *Ajay* (3), *Ashwani* (3), *Deepak* (3).

Setliff (483) Variant of English SUTCLIFFE.

Setlock (145) Variant of English SEDLOCK.

Seto (681) **1.** Japanese: written with characters meaning 'strait' and 'door'. The name is probably connected with the Seto Naikai, called the 'Inland Sea' in English. The name is found mostly in the island of Kyūshū, which bounds the Inland Sea on the west. **2.** Chinese 司徒: variant of SITU.
GIVEN NAMES Chinese 18%; Japanese 11%. *Wai* (5), *Kin* (4), *Chiu* (3), *Fung* (3), *Kam* (3), *Ming* (3), *Chun* (2), *Fong* (2), *Foon* (2), *Kuen* (2), *Kwing* (2), *Kyong* (2); *Hiroshi* (2), *Masao* (2), *Takeshi* (2), *Akira, Fujio, Haruo, Hideaki, Hidenori, Hideto, Kazunori, Kazuto, Kenichiro.*

Seton (124) Scottish or English: variant of SEATON.

Setser (676) Probably an altered spelling of SETZER.

Sette (231) French: metonymic occupational name for an otter hunter, from Old French *set(t)e* 'otter'.
GIVEN NAMES Italian 18%. *Domenic* (2), *Primo* (2), *Angelo, Camillo, Cosimo, Donato, Leonardo, Nicola, Orazio, Vincenzo, Vito.*

Setter (428) **1.** English: occupational name for a stone or bricklayer, from Middle English *setter* 'one who lays stones or bricks in building' (agent derivative of *setten* 'to set'). **2.** English: occupational name from Old French *saietier* 'silk weaver' (an agent derivative of *sayete*, a kind of silk). **3.** English: from an agent derivative of Middle English *setten* 'to place (decoration, on a garment or metal surface)', probably an occupational name for an embroiderer. **4.** German: unexplained. **5.** Norwegian: unexplained.

Setterberg (106) Swedish: ornamental name composed of the place-name element *säter* 'mountain pasture' + *berg* 'mountain', 'hill'.
GIVEN NAMES Scandinavian 6%; German 5%. *Nils; Kurt.*

Settergren (104) Swedish: ornamental name composed of the place-name element *säter* 'mountain pasture' + *gren* 'branch'.

Setterlund (224) Swedish: ornamental name composed of the place-name element *säter* 'mountain pasture' + *lund* 'grove'.

Setters (268) English: patronymic from SETTER.

Settle (3012) English: habitational name from a place in North Yorkshire, so named from Old English *setl* 'seat', 'dwelling'.

Settlemire (170) Americanized form of German **Settelmeier**: **1.** North German (Oldenburg; **Settelmeier**): distinguishing nickname for the tenant farmer (see MEYER) of a principal farm or estate (Middle Low German *sadel(hof)*). **2.** South German (**Sedlmair, Sedlmayr** in Bavaria): distinguishing nickname for the tenant farmer (see MEYER) of an estate that was required to furnish a saddled horse (Middle High German *satel*, *sadel* 'saddle') in time of war.

Settlemyer (141) Of German origin: see SETTLEMIRE.

Settlemyre (196) Of German origin: see SETTLEMIRE.

Settles (1769) Of uncertain origin; presumably a variant of English SETTLE.

Setton (122) **1.** Scottish or English: variant of SEATON. **2.** French: of uncertain origin. Possibly a Frenchified form of Scottish SEATON. **3.** Jewish (Sephardic): unexplained.

FOREBEARS The name **Settoon** was established in the 18th century in LA, for example with Daniel Settoon (born 1782 in St. Helena, LA) and Samuel Lanier Settoon (1790–c.1849, of Livingston, LA).

GIVEN NAMES Jewish 9%; French 7%. *Avi* (2), *Ronit*, *Yossef*; *Andree*, *Henri*, *Jacques*, *Maryse*.

Setty (227) Indian (Andhra Pradesh, Karnataka): Hindu name found in various mercantile communities, from Sanskrit *śreṣṭhī*, which refers to the head of a mercantile or other guild. *Chetty* in Tamil Nadu is a cognate name. Compare SETHI.

GIVEN NAMES Indian 30%. *Ashok* (2), *Dinesh* (2), *Kumar* (2), *Raj* (2), *Srinivas* (2), *Amar*, *Anup*, *Asha*, *Lata*, *Madhava*, *Meera*, *Mohan*.

Setzer (1954) **1.** German: occupational name for a market inspector or possibly a tax official, Middle High German *setzer*, an agent derivative of Middle High German *setzen* 'to set (prices)'. **2.** Jewish (Ashkenazic): occupational name from German *Setzer*, Yiddish *zetser* 'typesetter', 'compositor of typography'.

Setzler (209) German (Baden): variant of SETZER.

Seubert (522) German: East Franconian variant of SEIBERT.

GIVEN NAMES German 4%. *Egon* (2), *Kurt* (2), *Gunther*, *Helmut*, *Johann*.

Seufert (401) German: from an East Franconian personal name, a variant of SIEGFRIED.

GIVEN NAMES German 6%. *Helmut* (3), *Arno*, *Kurt*.

Seurer (135) Probably a variant of Swiss German **Saurer**, nickname for a grumpy person, from Middle High German *sūr* 'sour'.

Sevcik (351) Czech and Slovak (**Ševčík**): from a diminutive of the occupational name *švec* 'shoemaker'.

Sever (701) **1.** Slovenian and Croatian: topographic name from *sever* 'north', denoting someone who lived in the northern part of a village or estate. **2.** Croatian: from the personal name *Sever*, a pet form of SEVERIN. **3.** Dutch: variant of SIEVERT.

Severa (200) Czech: from the Latin personal name *Severus* (see SEVERE).

Severance (1405) Alteration by folk etymology of German **Severens**, a derivative of the Latin personal name *Severinus* (see SEVERIN).

Severe (421) French (**Sévère**): from the personal name *Sévère*, Latin *Severus*, meaning 'harsh, austere'. *Severus* was the name of several Roman Emperors, including Alexander Severus (died 235), born in Syria, who was noted for his virtuous and studious character and his tolerance towards Christians. The personal name enjoyed some popularity among early Christians.

GIVEN NAMES French 10%. *Michel* (2), *Pierre* (2), *Clovis*, *Elodie*, *Fanchon*, *Gabrielle*, *Lucien*, *Monique*, *Regine*, *Rigaud*.

Severin (888) **1.** French (**Séverin**), Italian (Venice), German, Swedish, etc.: from a personal name, Latin *Severinus*, from the same root as *Severus* (see SEVERE). This was borne by several early Christian saints, including bishops of Trier (2nd century), Cologne (4th century), Bordeaux (5th century), and Santempeda (6th century), and hermits of Paris (6th century) and Tivoli (8th century), as well as a 5th-century apostle of Austria. **2.** Reduced form of Ashkenazic Jewish **Severinovsky**, a habitational name for someone from Severinovka in Ukraine.

GIVEN NAMES French 5%. *Christophe*, *Florien*, *Francois*, *Marcel*, *Monique*, *Olivier*, *Patrice*.

Severini (152) Italian: patronymic or plural form of SEVERINO.

GIVEN NAMES Italian 24%. *Valentino* (2), *Aldo*, *Armando*, *Camillo*, *Egidio*, *Reno*, *Mario*, *Sal*, *Salvatore*.

Severino (808) Italian and Spanish: from the personal name *Severino* (see SEVERIN).

GIVEN NAMES Spanish 14%; Italian 10%. *Mario* (3), *Alfonso* (2), *Eusebia* (2), *Juan* (2), *Luz* (2), *Orlando* (2), *Rafael* (2), *Ramon* (2), *Adriana*, *Agueda*, *Agustina*, *Alba*; *Angelo* (5), *Antonio* (2), *Alfio*, *Amato*, *Bruna*, *Domenica*, *Elvio*, *Enrico*, *Filomena*, *Francesco*, *Gerlando*, *Manlio*.

Severn (452) English: **1.** from a personal name equivalent to SEVERIN. **2.** topographic name from the river Severn, which flows from Wales through much of western England to the Bristol Channel. The river name is recorded as early as the 2nd century AD in the form *Sabrina*. This is one of Britain's most ancient river names; the original meaning is uncertain, but it may have been 'slow-moving'.

Severns (701) English: variant of SEVERN.

Severo (100) Italian, Spanish, and Portuguese: from the personal name *Severo* (Latin *Severus*, meaning 'harsh, austere'). *Severus* was the name of several Roman Emperors, including Alexander Severus (died 235), born in Syria, who was noted for his virtuous and studious character and his tolerance towards Christians. The personal name enjoyed some popularity among early Christians.

GIVEN NAMES Italian 16%; Spanish 16%. *Carlo* (4), *Antonio* (2), *Angelo*, *Antonella*; *Miguel* (3), *Alfredo*, *Armando*, *Fernando*, *Gaspar*, *Jimenez*, *Luis*, *Orlando*, *Osvaldo*.

Severs (618) **1.** English: metronymic from *Sever*. **2.** Dutch: variant of SIEVERS.

Severson (4516) Probably an Americanized form of Scandinavian SIVERTSEN or SIVERTSON or of German **Sievertsen**, patronymic of SIEVERT.

Severt (461) North German: variant of SIEVERT.

Severtson (263) Americanized form of Scandinavian SIVERTSEN or SIVERTSON.

Severy (140) English: variant of SAVARY.

Sevey (212) Hispanic (Mexican): unexplained.

Sevick (142) English: unexplained.

Sevier (1074) English: occupational name for a sieve-maker, Middle English *siviere* (from an agent derivative of Old English *sife* 'sieve').

Sevigny (698) Altered spelling of French **Sévigné**, a habitational name from a place in Ille-et-Vilaine, so called from the Gallo-Roman personal name *Sabinius*, a derivative of Latin *Sabinus* (see SABIN) + the locative suffix *-acum*.

FOREBEARS A Sévigny from Brittany is documented in Neuville, Quebec, in 1695; he bore the secondary surname LAFLEUR.

GIVEN NAMES French 12%. *Armand* (3), *Lucien* (3), *Andre* (2), *Normand* (2), *Adrien*, *Aime*, *Alphonse*, *Amedee*, *Camille*, *Cecile*, *Fabien*, *Fernand*.

Sevilla (844) Spanish: habitational name from the city of this name, the capital of Andalusia, in southwestern Spain. The city is extremely ancient, having reputedly been founded by the Phoenicians. The origin of the name is obscure, presumably Phoenician. It is first recorded in the Latin form *Hispalis*, which was adopted in Arabic as *Isbilia*, and thence into early Spanish as *Sibilia*, now *Sevilla*.

GIVEN NAMES Spanish 47%. *Jose* (23), *Carlos* (12), *Jesus* (9), *Miguel* (9), *Rafael* (9), *Jorge* (7), *Juan* (7), *Luis* (6), *Manuel* (5), *Mario* (5), *Pedro* (5), *Ramon* (5).

Seville (309) English: variant of SAVILLE.

Sevin (324) German: topographic name from a dialect term for a kind of juniper (*Juniperus sabina*).

GIVEN NAMES French 6%. *Eves*, *Lucien*, *Monique*, *Oneil*, *Philippe*.

Sevy (361) French (**Sévy**): habitational name from a place so named in Yonne.

Sewald (125) German: variant of SEEWALD 1.

GIVEN NAMES German 8%. *Otto* (2), *Alois*.

Sewall (597) English: variant of SEWELL.

FOREBEARS Samuel Sewall (1652–1730) came with his parents from Bishop Stoke, Hampshire, England, to Newbury, MA, as a nine-year-old boy. In 1676 he married Hannah Hull, a wealthy heiress, and in 1681 he was appointed printer to the

Council in Boston. He served as a judge in the infamous Salem witchcraft trials of 1692—the only one of the judges to admit publicly that he had been wrong. In 1700 he published *The Selling of Joseph*, which argues that all men are created equal and presents theological arguments against slavery.

Seward (3720) **1.** English: from a Middle English personal name representing two originally distinct personal names, *Siward* and *Seward*, Old English *Sigeweard* and *Sǣweard*, composed of the elements *sige* 'victory' and *sǣ* 'sea' + *weard* 'guard', 'protect'. They became confused in the late Old English period. **2.** English: occupational name for a swineherd, from Old English *sū* 'pig' + *hierde* 'herdsman'. **3.** Irish: when not of English origin (see 1 above) a reduced Anglicized form of Gaelic **Ó Suaird**, **Ó Suairt**, usually Anglicized as SWORD.

Sewell (7748) **1.** English: from the Middle English personal names *Siwal(d)* and *Sewal(d)*, Old English *Sigeweald* and *Sǣweald*, composed of the elements *sige* 'victory' and *sǣ* 'sea' + *weald* 'rule'. **2.** English: habitational name from Sewell in Bedfordshire, Showell in Oxfordshire, or Seawell or Sywell in Northamptonshire, all of which are named from Old English *seofon* 'seven' + *wella* 'spring'.

Sexauer (265) German: habitational name for someone from Sexau in the Black Forest.

GIVEN NAME German 4%. *Kurt* (2).

Sexson (253) Probably a variant of SEXTON.

Sexton (14363) **1.** English: occupational name for a sexton or churchwarden, from Middle English *sexteyn* 'sexton' (Old French *secrestein*, from Latin *sacristanus*). **2.** Irish (Munster and midlands): reduced Anglicized form of Gaelic **Ó Seastnáin** 'descendant of *Seastnán, Seasnán*', a personal name meaning 'bodyguard', from *seasuighim* 'to resist', 'to defend'.

Seybert (471) German: variant spelling of SEIBERT.

Seybold (686) German: variant spelling of SEIBOLD.

Seydel (198) German: variant spelling of SEIDEL.

GIVEN NAMES German 5%. *Gunter, Kaethe, Uwe.*

Seyer (287) **1.** North German: occupational name for a farm laborer, from an agent derivative of Middle Low German *seien* 'to sow'. **2.** Dutch: variant of **de Sayer** 'the serge weaver' or 'the sower' (see SAYER 8 and 9).

Seyfarth (140) German: variant of SEIFERT.

GIVEN NAMES German 9%. *Fritz, Hans, Kurt, Lothar, Otto.*

Seyfert (365) German: variant of SEIFERT.

Seyferth (115) German: variant of SEIFERT.

GIVEN NAMES German 20%. *Fritz* (2), *Dieter, Dietmar, Gerhard, Hans, Horst, Johann, Kurt.*

Seyfried (390) German: variant of SIEG-FRIED.

GIVEN NAMES German 5%. *Jurgen* (2), *Hans, Ingeborg, Kurt.*

Seykora (114) Americanized spelling of Jewish and Polish SIKORA.

Seyler (736) **1.** English: variant spelling of SAYLOR. **2.** German: variant spelling of SEILER.

Seyller (189) German: variant spelling of SEILER.

Seymore (1156) English: variant of SEY-MOUR.

Seymour (9279) English (of Norman origin): habitational name from Saint-Maur-des-Fossées in Seine, northern France, or possibly from Saint-Maur-sur-Loire in Touraine. Both places are named from the dedication of the church there to St. Maur (see MOORE 3).

Sferra (155) Italian (Sicily): probably an altered spelling of **Sfera**, a habitational name from a locality in Biancavilla, named from Sicilian *spera* 'subterranean aqueduct'.

GIVEN NAMES Italian 23%. *Giorgio* (2), *Mario* (2), *Stefano* (2), *Antonio, Ascanio, Guido, Guiseppe, Luigi, Oreste, Pietro, Sal, Umberto, Vincenzo.*

Sferrazza (144) Italian: **1.** occupational name for a scrap-metal merchant, from a derivative of **Sferro** in the sense 'old and broken iron'. **2.** habitational name from the district of Paternò in Catania, Sicily.

GIVEN NAMES Italian 38%. *Angelo* (5), *Sal* (5), *Salvatore* (5), *Costantino* (3), *Calogero* (2), *Giuseppe* (2), *Carmelo, Concetta, Grazia, Lorenzo, Matteo, Sabatino.*

Sforza (336) Italian: nickname from a variant of *forza* 'force', 'strength'.

GIVEN NAMES Italian 16%. *Saverio* (4), *Pasquale* (2), *Rocco* (2), *Aldo, Angelo, Donato, Egidio, Enrico, Leonardo, Marco, Nicolina, Tillio.*

Sgambati (158) Italian: patronymic form of **Sgambato**, a nickname for a one-legged or lame person, from a derivative of *gamba* 'leg'.

GIVEN NAMES Italian 18%. *Alfonse* (2), *Elio* (2), *Salvatore* (2), *Alessandro, Angelo, Guerino.*

Sgarlata (143) Italian (Sicily): occupational name for a dyer, from the dialect word *sgarlatu* 'scarlet', a variant of SCARLATA. There is also a place of this name, but the place name is probably derived from the surname rather than vice versa.

GIVEN NAMES Italian 19%. *Domenico, Giovanna, Giuseppe, Sal, Salvatore.*

Sgro (472) Southern Italian (**Sgrò**): nickname for someone with curly hair, from medieval Greek *sgouros* 'curly'.

GIVEN NAMES Italian 22%. *Rocco* (7), *Vito* (4), *Angelo* (3), *Antonio* (2), *Gino* (2),

Nicola (2), *Salvatore* (2), *Attilio, Carmelo, Carmine, Maddalena, Nunzio.*

Sgroi (441) Southern Italian (Sicily): variant of SGRO.

GIVEN NAMES Italian 15%. *Salvatore* (6), *Vito* (4), *Angelo* (2), *Francesco* (2), *Sal* (2), *Carlo, Carmela, Federico, Ferdinando, Santo.*

Sha (166) **1.** Chinese 沙: there are different accounts of the origin of Sha as a surname. Two accounts derive it from the Yi and Hu Chinese minorities around the time of the Tang dynasty (618–907). Two other accounts trace it back to individuals who had Sha as a part of their name. **2.** Indian: variant of SHAH.

GIVEN NAMES Chinese 20%; Indian 5%. *Fei* (2), *Ching, Ding, Feng, Hongjian, Jian, Ke, Lei, Ling, Weijian, Xin, Xue; Deven, Gaurang, Suresh.*

Shaak (194) Variant of North German and Dutch SCHAACK.

Shaban (136) Muslim: from a personal name based on Arabic *Sha'bān*, the eighth month of the Muslim year, regarded by Muslims as a sacred month. Muslim parents sometimes name their children *Shā'bān* if they are born in this month.

GIVEN NAMES Muslim 48%. *Mohtaram* (3), *Ali* (2), *Abdul, Abdullah, Ahmad, Aly, Amad, Bassam, Fakhri, Feras, Haifa, Hasan.*

Shabazz (414) Muslim (mainly Iranian): from the Persian personal name *Shāhbāz*, meaning 'royal falcon'. The word generally means 'royal, generous, noble'.

GIVEN NAMES Muslim 60%. *Abdul* (6), *Ali* (6), *Malik* (6), *Maryam* (4), *Omar* (4), *Ahmad* (3), *Ayesha* (3), *Muhammad* (3), *Yahya* (3), *Bilal* (2), *Hakim* (2).

Shack (394) Americanized spelling of Dutch and North German SCHAACK.

Shackelford (3985) English: habitational name of uncertain origin, possibly from Shackleford Heath in Surrey.

Shackelton (145) English: variant of SHACKLETON.

Shackett (172) Americanized spelling of French CHOQUETTE.

Shackford (132) English: probably a reduced form of SHACKELFORD.

Shackleford (1150) English: variant spelling of SHACKELFORD.

Shackleton (367) English: habitational name from a place in the parish of Halifax, West Yorkshire, so named from an unattested Old English word, *scacol* 'tongue of land' + *tūn* 'enclosure', 'settlement'.

FOREBEARS The British Antarctic explorer Sir Ernest Shackleton (1874–1922) was born in Kilkee, Ireland; his father's Quaker family came from Yorkshire, England.

Shacklett (244) English: unexplained.

Shackley (150) English: habitational name from Shackerley or Shakerley in Lancashire, so named from Old English *scēacere*

'robber' + *lēah* 'clearing in a wood', 'glade' + *tūn* 'enclosure', 'settlement'.

Shad (136) **1.** Muslim: from a personal name based on Arabic *shād* 'happy'. **2.** English: metonymic occupational name for a fisherman or fish seller, from Old English *sceadd* 'shad', a kind of fish. Reaney and Wilson note that during the Old English period there was a 'shad season', so it must have been of some economic importance. **3.** Americanized spelling of German SCHADE.
GIVEN NAMES Muslim 21%. *Mohammad* (2), *Tahir* (2), *Abdul, Jaffer, Javaid, Mahmood, Mohsin, Muhammad, Rana, Zahir.*

Shada (140) German: Americanized spelling of SCHADE.

Shadbolt (140) English: of uncertain origin. Possibly topographic, from Old English *scēad* 'boundary' + *bōþl* 'building', 'dwelling house', 'hall'.
GIVEN NAME German 4%. *Kurt.*

Shadburn (151) Possibly English, a habitational name from a lost or unidentified place. The surname, however, does not occur in current English records.

Shadd (143) English: variant of SHAD 2.

Shadden (336) Scottish: variant of SHEDDEN.

Shaddix (380) English: derivative **Shaddick**, an altered form of CHADWICK.

Shaddock (250) English: variant of CHADWICK.

Shaddox (238) English: from **Shaddick**, a variant of CHADWICK.

Shadduck (262) English: from **Shaddick**, a variant of CHADWICK.

Shaddy (117) Origin unidentified. Perhaps a variant of Irish SHEEDY?

Shade (2478) Scottish and English: **1.** topographic name for someone who lived near a boundary, from Old English *scēad* 'boundary'. **2.** nickname for a very thin man, from Middle English *schade* 'shadow', 'wraith'. **3.** Americanized spelling of German and Dutch SCHADE.

Shadel (179) Americanized spelling of German SCHADEL.

Shader (231) Americanized spelling of German SCHADER.

Shadid (235) Arabic: from a personal name based on Arabic *shadīd* 'strong'.
GIVEN NAMES Muslim 7%. *Bassam* (2), *Belal, Esam, Eyad, Fadia, Hend, Kamel, Khalid, Mamoon, Mousa, Reem, Saleem.*

Shadix (211) Much altered variant of English CHADWICK.

Shadle (770) Americanized spelling of German SCHADEL.

Shadley (312) Americanized spelling of German SCHADEL.

Shadoan (226) Origin unidentified.

Shadow (133) Origin unidentified. The name **Shadue**, **Schadewe** is recorded in England in the 12th and 13th centuries, from Middle English *shadwe* 'shadow',

Old English *sceadu* (see SHADE). However, there is no evidence of its continuation into modern times in this form.

Shadowens (197) Origin unidentified.

Shadrick (433) English (Devon): from a vernacular form of the Old Testament personal name *Shadrach*, name of one of the 'three holy children', Shadrach, Meshach, and Abednego, who were cast into a fiery furnace and not harmed.

Shadwell (149) English: habitational name from any of the places so called, in London, Norfolk, and West Yorkshire. The first is named from Old English *sceald* 'shallow' + *well(a)* 'spring', 'stream', the latter two from *scēad* 'boundary' + *well(a)*.

Shadwick (384) English: variant of CHADWICK.

Shady (334) Origin unidentified. Possibly Irish or English: unexplained.

Shaefer (188) Americanized spelling of German and Jewish SCHAEFER 'shepherd'.

Shaeffer (919) Americanized spelling of German SCHAFFER.

Shaer (109) **1.** Muslim: probably from a personal name based on Persian *sher* 'lion'. Sher Shah 'king of the lions' was a Delhi sultan (1540–45). **2.** Jewish (eastern Ashkenazic): ornamental name from Yiddish *shayer* 'barn'.
GIVEN NAMES Muslim 10%; Jewish 5%. *Amin, Bassam, Hassan, Issa, Nadeem, Nasser, Saliba; Ari, Haim.*

Shafer (10163) Americanized spelling of German SCHAEFER 'shepherd' or SCHAFFER 'steward'.

Shaff (361) Americanized spelling of German SCHAAF and Jewish SCHAFF.

Shaffer (22271) Americanized spelling of German SCHAFFER 'steward' or of SCHAEFER 'shepherd'.

Shaffner (550) Americanized spelling of German SCHAFFNER.

Shafi (129) Muslim: from a personal name based on Arabic *shāfiʿ* or *shafī* 'intercessor', 'mediator' (see the Qurʾan 10:3). Muhammad ibn Idris ash-Shāfiʿ (767–820) was the founder of a school of Islamic law.
GIVEN NAMES Muslim 83%. *Mohammad* (13), *Mohammed* (4), *Tariq* (4), *Mohamed* (3), *Muhammad* (3), *Abdul, Adil, Adli, Ahamed, Ahmad, Akbar, Ali.*

Shafir (118) Jewish (eastern Ashkenazic): ornamental name from Yiddish *shafir*, Polish *szafir* 'sapphire'.
GIVEN NAMES Jewish 36%; Russian 27%; Jewish Biblical 4%; West Slavic 4%. *Shlomi* (3), *Yakov* (3), *Haim* (2), *Naum* (2), *Aron, Faina, Gershon, Igal, Ilan, Ilya, Khana, Polina; Boris* (8), *Leonid* (2), *Mikhail* (2), *Anatoly, Ayzik, Gennady, Iosif, Nelya, Raisa, Semyon, Shura, Valeriy.*

Shafran (250) Jewish (eastern Ashkenazic): mainly ornamental name, cognate with SAFRAN, from eastern Yiddish *shafran*, Polish *szafran* 'saffron'.

GIVEN NAMES Jewish 10%; Russian 4%. *Simcha* (2), *Avi, Meyer, Shoshana, Sol, Tsilya, Uri; Anatoly, Mikhail, Natalya, Oleg, Semyon, Yuriy.*

Shaft (165) German (**Schaft**): metonymic occupational name for a maker of wooden shafts for tools or weapons, from Middle High German, Middle Low German *schaft*.

Shafter (124) **1.** German: altered spelling of SCHAFFTER. **2.** German and Jewish (Ashkenazic): variant of SCHAFFTER.
GIVEN NAMES Jewish 4%. *Ber, Mort.*

Shafto (121) Northern English: from a place of this name in Northumbria.

Shah (8518) **1.** Muslim: from the Persian royal title *Shāh* 'king', 'emperor'. This was the title adopted by the kings of the Pahlavi dynasty (1925–79). *Shāh* is found in combination with other words, e.g. *Shāh Jahan* (name of a Mughal emperor, ruled 1628–57) and *Shāh ʾĀlam* 'king of the world' (name of a Mughal emperor, ruled 1707–12). This name is widespread in Iran and the subcontinent. **2.** Indian (Gujarat, Rajasthan): Hindu (Bania, Vania) and Jain name, from Gujarati *sah* 'merchant' (from Sanskrit *sādhu* 'honest', 'good'). This name was originally *Sah*; it appears to have been altered under the influence of the Persian word for 'king' (see 1).
GIVEN NAMES Indian 85%; Muslim 4%. *Bharat* (104), *Dinesh* (75), *Ramesh* (74), *Ashok* (73), *Dilip* (71), *Rajesh* (67), *Mahendra* (62), *Sanjay* (57), *Dipak* (56), *Pravin* (56), *Pankaj* (55), *Mahesh* (54); *Syed* (91), *Samir* (41), *Mehul* (20), *Tushar* (19), *Chirag* (14), *Sayed* (12), *Kamal* (9), *Mohammad* (9), *Ali* (8), *Hina* (8), *Khalid* (8), *Mohammed* (8).

Shahan (1217) **1.** Irish: variant of SHEEHAN. **2.** Muslim: from the Persian word *shāhān* 'kings', the plural of SHAH. *Shāhān Shāh* 'King of Kings' was a title used by royalty in Iran before the revolution of 1979. *Shahan* is a widespread name in Iran and the Indian subcontinent.

Shaheed (125) Muslim: variant of SHAHID.
GIVEN NAMES Muslim 73%. *Abdul* (3), *Abdullah* (3), *Khalid* (3), *Nadirah* (3), *Adib* (2), *Ahmad* (2), *Ali* (2), *Bayyinah* (2), *Dawud* (2), *Wali* (2), *Yusuf* (2), *Ahmed.*

Shaheen (1110) Muslim: from the Persian personal name *Shahīn*, meaning 'royal white falcon'. This name is widespread in Iran and throughout the Indian subcontinent.
GIVEN NAMES Muslim 11%; French 4%. *Shaheen* (4), *Layla* (3), *Salem* (3), *Jamal* (2), *Kaleel* (2), *Milad* (2), *Mohammad* (2), *Osama* (2), *Said* (2), *Abdullah, Adeel, Adib; Emile* (2), *Odette* (2), *Antoine, Cecile, Michel, Patrice.*

Shahid (237) Muslim: from a personal name based on Arabic *shahīd* 'martyr' (see the Qurʾan 57:19) It is a title of honor accorded to those who have embraced death in the cause of Islam. The associated word *shāfid* means 'witness'. *Ash-Shāfid* 'the witness' is an epithet of the Prophet Muhammad.

GIVEN NAMES Muslim 65%. *Mohammad* (6), *Abdul* (4), *Sheikh* (4), *Mohammed* (3), *Muhammad* (3), *Abdus* (2), *Ali* (2), *Hasan* (2), *Kamal* (2), *Mian* (2), *Saleem* (2), *Syed* (2).

Shahidi (101) Muslim: from Arabic *Shāhidi* 'descended from (or associated with) a Shahīd' (see SHAHID).

GIVEN NAMES Muslim 74%; Indian 5%. *Masoud* (4), *Massoud* (3), *Afshin* (2), *Ahmad* (2), *Amin* (2), *Behzad* (2), *Hooman* (2), *Anoosh, Ata, Azra, Camran, Firouzeh*; *Mani* (2), *Shahnam*.

Shahin (200) Muslim: variant of SHAHEEN.

GIVEN NAMES Muslim 55%. *Emad* (3), *Amir* (2), *Hosein* (2), *Issa* (2), *Mahmoud* (2), *Marwan* (2), *Omar* (2), *Abdu, Abolfazl, Ali, Amr, Asghar*.

Shahinian (147) Armenian: patronymic from the Persian personal name *Shahin* (see SHAHEEN).

GIVEN NAMES Armenian 25%. *Armen* (2), *Vasken* (2), *Andranik, Ara, Aram, Arra, Edick, Garen, Haig, Kaloust, Masis, Ohannes*.

Shaia (103) Jewish (eastern Ashkenazic): from the Yiddish male personal name *Shaye*, a pet form of *Ishaye* 'Isaiah'.

Shaikh (595) Muslim: variant of SHEIKH.

GIVEN NAMES Muslim 88%. *Abdul* (12), *Mohammad* (10), *Mohammed* (8), *Muhammad* (8), *Haroon* (6), *Iqbal* (6), *Salim* (6), *Hamid* (5), *Khalid* (5), *Moin* (5), *Ali* (4), *Arif* (4).

Shain (832) Jewish (eastern Ashkenazic): **1.** patronymic form of SHAIA, with the eastern Slavic possessive suffix *-in*. **2.** variant spelling of SCHEIN.

GIVEN NAMES Jewish 8%. *Dovid* (2), *Eliyahu* (2), *Hyman* (2), *Shimon* (2), *Yehuda* (2), *Zorach* (2), *Avrom, Basya, Eliyohu, Ephraim, Isadore, Miriam*.

Shake (394) Americanized form of Dutch and North German SCHAACK.

Shaker (356) **1.** Muslim: variant of SHAKIR. **2.** English: unexplained.

GIVEN NAMES Muslim 16%. *Batool* (2), *Shaker* (2), *Abdul, Ahmad, Ahmed, Amin, Ayman, Erfan, Fouad, Fuad, Hassan, Iman*.

Shakespeare (318) English: from Middle English *schak(k)en* 'to brandish' + *speer* 'spear', nickname for a belligerent person or perhaps a bawdy nickname for an exhibitionist or womanizer.

Shakir (225) Muslim: from a personal name based on Arabic *shākir* 'grateful', 'thankful'. *Al-Shākir* (*Ash-Shakir*) 'the All-Thankful' is an attribute of Allah (see the Qur'an 2:158).

GIVEN NAMES Muslim 63%. *Mohammad* (4), *Abdul* (3), *Fareed* (3), *Jamilah* (2), *Saleem* (2), *Sultan* (2), *Yusuf* (2), *Abdullah, Abid, Adib, Aisha, Amin*.

Shaklee (138) Variant spelling of English SHACKLEY.

Shakoor (113) Muslim: from a personal name based on Arabic *shakūr* 'grateful', 'thankful'. *Al-Shakūr* (*Ash-Shakir*) 'the All-Thankful' is an attribute of Allah (see the Qur'an 64:17). The name is found in combinations such as *Abdus Shakoor* 'servant of the All-Thankful'.

GIVEN NAMES Muslim 71%. *Tariq* (7), *Abdul* (4), *Arif* (2), *Afroz, Aftab, Akm, Akmal, Ali, Amir, Aslam, Bibi, Dawud*.

Shaler (165) Altered spelling of English **Shailer**, a nickname for someone who walked in a slow, clumsy, aimless way, from Middle English *shailer* 'shambler'.

Shales (114) English: nickname for a shambler, from Middle English *sheyl* 'shambling gait'.

Shalhoub (125) Arabic (Lebanon): from a personal name based on *shalhūb* 'generous'.

GIVEN NAMES Arabic 5%; French 5%. *Hadi, Hisham, Kalil, Samir, Wadia, Wael*; *Andre, Philippe*.

Shall (133) **1.** Jewish (Ashkenazic): variant spelling of SCHALL. **2.** Americanized spelling of German SCHALL.

Shallcross (299) English: habitational name from a place named after an ancient stone cross in the High Peak forest of Derbyshire, in the parish of Chapel en le Frith, known as the *Shackelcross*. The first element in this name appears to be from Old English *sceacol* 'chain', 'bond', perhaps denoting a cross to which penitents could be fettered.

Shallenberger (403) Americanized spelling of German **Schellenberger**, a habitational name from any of numerous places named Schellenberg, for example near Chemnitz and Limburg.

Shaller (128) French (Alsace): variant of German SCHALLER.

Shallow (272) Irish: Anglicized form of Gaelic **Ó Sealbhaigh** (see SHEALY).

Shalom (208) Jewish (Israeli): from Hebrew *shalom* 'peace'.

GIVEN NAMES Jewish 19%. *Sol* (3), *Shalom* (2), *Aharon, Avinoam, Chaim, Dafna, Eitan, Isaak, Itzhak, Izhak, Kaplan, Yosi*.

Sham (126) **1.** Chinese 岑: variant of SHUM. **2.** Chinese 沈: variant of SHEN 1. **3.** Muslim: variant of CHAM. This name is found mainly in northwest India (Gujarat). **4.** Southeast Asian: unexplained. **5.** Perhaps also an altered spelling of French **Cham**, a habitational name from any of several places called La Champ, named with *champ* 'meadow'.

GIVEN NAMES Chinese 12%; Indian 7%. *Foon* (2), *Lai* (2), *Ming* (2), *Chuen, Gan, Hing, Kwong, Mei Yee, Teng, Ting, Wai Ming, Yuk*; *Alka, Ghan, Krishna, Radhey*.

Shamah (125) Jewish: variant of SAMA.

GIVEN NAMES Jewish 16%. *Haim* (2), *Isadore* (2), *Hymie, Menashe, Yaron*.

Shambach (103) Americanized spelling of German SCHAMBACH.

Shambaugh (569) Americanized form of German SCHAMBACH.

Shamberger (147) Americanized spelling of SCHAMBERGER.

Shamblen (121) Variant of SHAMBLIN, an Americanized form of French CHAMBERLIN.

Shambley (147) Possibly a variant of SHAMBLIN, or Americanized form of French **Chamblay**, a habitational name from a place so called in the Jura.

Shamblin (1103) Americanized form of French CHAMBERLIN.

Shambo (224) Americanized spelling of French ARCHAMBAULT with loss of the unstressed first syllable.

Shamburg (160) Variant of Jewish **Schamberg**, a habitational name from any of several places named Schamberg (see SCHAMBERGER).

Shamburger (350) Altered spelling of German and Jewish SCHAMBERGER.

Shamel (189) Americanized spelling of German SCHAMEL.

Shames (285) Jewish (eastern Ashkenazic): status name from Yiddish *shames* 'sexton (in a synagogue)' (Hebrew *shammash*).

GIVEN NAMES Jewish 8%; Russian 4%. *Miriam* (2), *Raanan*; *Igor, Mikhail, Semyon, Valeriy, Yuriy, Zyama*.

Shamis (144) Jewish (eastern Ashkenazic): variant of SHAMES.

GIVEN NAMES Jewish 25%; Russian 18%. *Aron* (2), *Faina* (2), *Itta* (2), *Bentsion, Ilya, Irina, Izya, Moisey, Moysey, Yosef*; *Mikhail* (5), *Yefim* (3), *Arkadi, Arkady, Asya, Boris, Dmitry, Igor, Ikhil, Iosif, Nicolai, Sofya*.

Shammas (118) Arabic: status name in the Christian community from *shammās* 'deacon', 'sexton'.

GIVEN NAMES Arabic 38%. *Fahmi* (2), *Issa* (2), *Nabil* (2), *Namir* (2), *Sameer* (2), *Abdallah, Amer, Amir, Aziz, Bahjat, Basem, Basma*.

Shamon (108) Arabic: variant of SHAMOON.

GIVEN NAMES Arabic 9%. *Younan* (2), *Namir, Sami, Samir, Yacoub, Zaia*.

Shamoon (131) Arabic: from the personal name *Sham'ūn*, Arabic form of SIMON, used mainly among Christian Arabs.

GIVEN NAMES Arabic 35%. *Talal* (3), *Aziz* (2), *Emad* (2), *Mohamed* (2), *Adnan, Bassam, Fawzia, Jamal, Kausar, Majid, Mehri, Mohammad*.

Shamoun (107) **1.** Arabic: variant of SHAMOON. **2.** Jewish (Sephardic): adoption of the Arabic name.

GIVEN NAMES Muslim 30%; French 5%; Jewish 4%. *Hani* (2), *Malek* (2), *Sabri* (2), *Samir* (2), *Amer, Bassim, Bushra, Haithem, Kais, Kamal, Layla, Najma*; *Michel* (2), *Henri*; *Nisan, Nissan*.

Shamp (359) Americanized spelling of Dutch and German SCHAMP.

Shampine (208) Probably an altered spelling of CHAMPAGNE.

Shamrock (139) English and Irish: according to MacLysaght, a habitational name from an unidentified place in England. There is a current English habitational surname **Shambrook**, which may be the source.

Shams (151) Muslim: from a personal name based on Arabic *shams* 'sun'. Al-Shams (Ash-Shams) 'the Sun' is the title of the 91st sura of the Qur'an. It is found as a personal name in combinations such as *Shams ud-Dīn* 'sun of religion'. This was the name borne by a famous Persian poet (died 1319).
GIVEN NAMES Muslim 72%. *Ahmad* (3), *Zia* (3), *Ali* (2), *Habib* (2), *Hamid* (2), *Jila* (2), *Khalid* (2), *Majid* (2), *Rashid* (2), *Samir* (2), *Abdollah*, *Abdul*.

Shan (268) **1.** Chinese 单: from the place name Shan. Cheng Wang, the second king (1115–1079 BC) of the Zhou dynasty, granted to a son the area of Shan, and the son's descendants adopted the place name as their surname. **2.** Chinese 山: from a word meaning 'mountain'. The legendary emperor Shen Nong (2734–2697 BC) was supposedly born on Lie Mountain, the name of which he gave to one of his sons. One of the descendants of that son adopted the word for 'mountain', *shan*, as his surname. Another source of the name was an official post that existed during the Zhou dynasty (1122–221 BC) called the Mountain Master, which carried the responsibilities of overseeing mountains and forests. Again, the word for 'mountain', *shan*, was adopted as a surname. **3.** Indian (Gujarat): Hindu (Vania) name of unknown meaning. **4.** Reduced form of northern Irish and Scottish MCSHANE. **5.** Variant of English SHANN.
GIVEN NAMES Indian 18%; Chinese 17%. *Ajit*, *Amrat*, *Bhanu*, *Bharat*, *Bhupendra*, *Harshad*, *Jagdish*, *Kamlesh*, *Kesavan*, *Kiran*, *Mayur*, *Nikhil*; *Jing* (2), *Wen* (2), *Chanho*, *Chao*, *Chen*, *Daming*, *Guo Hui*, *Hua*, *Jia*, *Li*, *Li Xin*, *Ling*.

Shanafelt (254) Americanized spelling of German **Schönefeldt** (see SHANEYFELT).

Shanahan (3387) Irish (Munster): reduced Anglicized form of Gaelic **Ó Seanacháin** 'descendant of *Seanachán*', a diminutive of *Seanach*, a personal name from *sean* 'ancient', 'old'.
GIVEN NAMES Irish 6%. *Brendan* (3), *Eamonn* (2), *Aidan*, *Donovan*, *Kieran*, *Liam*, *Marypat*, *Siobhan*.

Shanaman (107) Americanized form of German **Schönemann** (see SCHOENEMANN).

Shand (546) Scottish and northern Irish: reduced and altered form of MCSHANE, an Anglicized form of Gaelic **Mac Seáin** 'son of *Seán*'.

Shandor (134) Americanized spelling of Hungarian SANDOR.

Shands (472) **1.** Variant of Scottish SHAND, formed with the English patronymic ending *-s*. **2.** Perhaps an Anglicized spelling of German SCHANTZ.

Shandy (128) Probably English: unexplained.

Shane (2618) **1.** Northern Irish: shortened form of MCSHANE, an Anglicized form of Gaelic **Mac Seáin** 'son of John'. **2.** Americanized spelling of Jewish SCHEIN or SHAIN. **3.** Americanized spelling of German **Schön** (see SCHOEN).

Shaner (1890) **1.** Americanized spelling of Jewish SCHEINER. **2.** Americanized spelling of German **Schöner** (see SCHOENER) or **Schönherr** (see SCHOENHERR).

Shanes (107) English: unexplained; possibly a variant of Irish SHANE.

Shaneyfelt (284) Americanized spelling of German **Schönefeldt**, a habitational name from any of several places so named, or a topographic name from Middle High German *schöne* 'beautiful' + *felt* 'open country'.

Shang (185) **1.** Chinese 尚: from the name of an ancestor, Lü Shang, who lived around the beginning of the Zhou dynasty (1122–221 BC). **2.** Chinese 商: from the name of the Shang dynasty (1766–1122 BC).
GIVEN NAMES Chinese 33%; Vietnamese 6%. *Yi* (2), *Ding*, *Fu*, *Guihua*, *Hua*, *Jian*, *Jianguo*, *Jin*, *Jing*, *Kung*, *Ping*, *Sung*; *Hai* (5), *Quan*.

Shangraw (126) Americanized form of a French name, probably **Champgrand**, a topographic name for someone who lived by a large, open expanse of flat land, from Old French *champ* 'open country' + *grand* 'big'.
GIVEN NAMES French 4%. *Cecile*, *Christien*.

Shanholtz (319) Americanized spelling of German **Schönholtz**, a topographic name from Middle High German *schoen* 'beautiful' + *holz* 'wood', 'forest'.

Shanholtzer (166) Americanized spelling of German **Schönhol(t)zer**, a variant of **Schönholtz** (see SHANHOLTZ).

Shank (5064) **1.** Americanized spelling of SCHANK. **2.** Northern English and Scottish: variant of SHANKS.

Shankar (261) Indian (southern states): Hindu name from Sanskrit *śankara* 'one who brings about happiness or prosperity' (from Sanskrit *śam* 'happiness', 'prosperity' + *-kara* 'causing'). This is an epithet of the god Shiva. It is a variant of SANKARAN among people who have migrated from Kerala and Tamil Nadu. In India it is found only as a male personal name, but has come to be used as a family name in the U.S. among South Indians.
GIVEN NAMES Indian 89%. *Ravi* (26), *Uday* (6), *Vijay* (5), *Hari* (4), *Vidya* (4), *Raj* (3), *Amitabh* (2), *Arun* (2), *Gowri* (2), *Manoj* (2), *Natarajan* (2), *Rama* (2).

Shankel (167) Americanized spelling of German, Dutch, and Jewish SCHENKEL.

Shanker (268) Indian: variant of SHANKAR.
GIVEN NAMES Indian 30%. *Ajay* (3), *Ravi* (3), *Ganapathy* (2), *Naresh* (2), *Deo*, *Gauri*, *Gayatri*, *Geetha*, *Gopal*, *Gowri*, *Hari*, *Manoj*.

Shankland (273) Scottish: habitational name from a lost or unidentified place.

Shankle (962) Perhaps an altered spelling of German, Dutch, and Jewish SCHENKEL.

Shankles (249) Origin unidentified.

Shanklin (1269) Scottish: variant of SHANKLAND.

Shankman (261) Americanized spelling of Jewish SHENKMAN.
GIVEN NAMES Jewish 5%. *Herzl*, *Meyer*.

Shanks (4212) Scottish and northern Irish: nickname for someone with long legs or some peculiarity of gait, from Old English *sceanca* 'shin bone', 'leg'. This vocabulary word was preserved in Scotland, whereas in England it was replaced by Old Norse *leggr*.

Shanley (1602) Irish (Connacht): reduced Anglicized form of Gaelic **Mac Seanlaoich** 'son of *Seanlaoch*', a personal name composed of the elements *sean* 'old' + *laoch* 'hero'.
GIVEN NAMES Irish 5%. *Brendan* (4), *Padraic*.

Shann (121) English: habitational name from a minor place so named near Keighley in West Yorkshire.

Shannahan (260) Irish: variant spelling of SHANAHAN.

Shannon (16233) Irish: **1.** reduced form of SHANAHAN. **2.** reduced Anglicized form of Gaelic **Ó Seanáin** 'descendant of *Seanán*', a personal name based on a pet form of *seán* 'old'. **3.** in County Clare, a reduced Anglicized form of **Mac Giolla tSeanáin** 'son of the servant of St. Seanán'. In the Irish midlands LEONARD and NUGENT have been adopted as equivalents of this name.

Shanor (152) Origin unidentified.

Shantz (403) Americanized spelling of German SCHANTZ.

Shao (526) Chinese 邵: from an altered form of the place name Zhao. Zhao Gongshi was the senior statesman of the Zhou under four successive kings; he played an important role in administration of the kingdom and the establishment of the Zhou dynasty (1122–221 BC). He was granted the area of Zhao (召); his descendants added to the character for Zhao a component which meant city or county, thus creating the character for Shao, 邵, which they adopted as their surname.
GIVEN NAMES Chinese 55%. *Ming* (5), *Bin* (4), *Chi* (4), *Wei* (4), *Hui* (3), *Li* (3), *Ping* (3), *Qing* (3), *Jianzhong* (2), *Liming* (2), *Ning* (2), *Rong* (2); *Min* (3), *Chung*, *Hu*, *Kok*, *Shiu*, *Yiping*.

Shapard (155) Variant of English SHEP-HERD.

Shapero (218) Jewish (eastern Ashkenazic): variant of SHAPIRO.

Shapira (169) Jewish (eastern Ashkenazic): variant of SHAPIRO.
GIVEN NAMES Jewish 28%. *Avi* (2), *Meir* (2), *Shmuel* (2), *Arie*, *Doron*, *Dov*, *Erez*, *Eyal*, *Itzhak*, *Kolman*, *Menahem*, *Reuven*.

Shapiro (14123) Jewish (eastern Ashkenazic): habitational name among Eastern European Jews from the Yiddish name of the German city of Speyer (see SPEYER and compare SPIRO).
GIVEN NAMES Jewish 7%. *Hyman* (24), *Sol* (23), *Meyer* (12), *Isadore* (10), *Emanuel* (9), *Miriam* (9), *Myer* (8), *Ari* (6), *Yaakov* (5), *Yakov* (5), *Moshe* (4), *Semen* (4).

Shapland (144) English (mainly Devon): habitational name from a lost or unidentified place.

Shapleigh (117) English: variant of SHAPLEY.
FOREBEARS Thomas Shapleigh (1765–1800), born in Kittery MA, was librarian of Harvard College in the 1790s.

Shapley (317) English: habitational name from Shapley in Chagford, Devon.

Shappell (312) Americanized spelling of German SCHAPPELL.

Sharaf (118) **1.** Muslim: from a personal name based on Arabic *sharaf* 'honor', 'nobility', 'dignity'. It is used in combination with other words in names such as *Sharaf-ud-Din* 'honor of religion' and *Sharaf-ud-Dawlah* 'honor of the state', the latter being the name of a Buwayhid sultan (ruled 983–989). **2.** Indian: variant of SHROFF.
GIVEN NAMES Muslim 35%; Indian 8%. *Abdul*, *Ahmed*, *Ali*, *Aly*, *Atef*, *Farouk*, *Hamid*, *Huda*, *Hussein*, *Idris*, *Mohamed*, *Moneer*; *Narain* (2), *Savita* (2), *Renu*.

Sharar (169) Origin unidentified; perhaps an altered form of Scottish SHEARER. Compare SHARRAR.

Sharbaugh (161) Americanized form of German **Scharbach** or **Schorbach**, a habitational name from a place so named, from Middle High German *schor* 'dirt' + *bach* 'creek'.

Sharber (302) Americanized spelling of German SCHARBER.

Sharbono (185) Americanized spelling of French CHARBONNEAU.

Share (476) English: unexplained.

Shareef (130) Muslim: variant spelling of SHARIF.
GIVEN NAMES Muslim 76%. *Mohammed* (4), *Iqbal* (3), *Omar* (3), *Rashad* (3), *Tahseen* (3), *Abdullah* (2), *Ali* (2), *Ibrahim* (2), *Karim* (2), *Abdul Hakim*, *Abdul Rahman*, *Akhter*.

Sharek (113) Americanized form of Czech **Šarek**.

Sharer (662) Scottish and northern English: variant of SHEARER.

Sharf (167) Jewish (Ashkenazic): nickname for an energetic or quick-minded person, Yiddish *sharf*. Compare German SCHARF.
GIVEN NAMES Jewish 20%; Russian 7%. *Noam* (3), *Arie* (2), *Avrohom*, *Hirsh*, *Mayer*, *Mikhael*, *Sarra*, *Schlomo*, *Shimon*; *Lev* (2), *Boris*, *Igor*, *Mikhail*, *Semyon*, *Zinovy*.

Sharff (144) Jewish: variant of SHARF.
GIVEN NAMES Jewish 6%. *Aharon*, *Hyman*.

Sharick (139) English: variant of SHARROCK.

Sharif (401) Muslim: from a personal name from Arabic *sharīf* 'noble', 'honorable', 'highborn'. *Sharīf* is used as an honorific title for descendants of the Prophet Muhammad through his daughter Fāṭima. This name is widespread in all Muslim countries.
GIVEN NAMES Muslim 78%. *Mohammad* (17), *Mohammed* (9), *Muhammad* (9), *Omar* (6), *Sami* (6), *Hassan* (5), *Ali* (4), *Mohamed* (4), *Abdul* (3), *Ahmad* (3), *Ahmed* (3), *Rahman* (3).

Shariff (166) Muslim: variant of SHARIF.
GIVEN NAMES Muslim 81%. *Mohammed* (9), *Abdul* (3), *Mohamed* (3), *Sameera* (3), *Shiraz* (3), *Amin* (2), *Karim* (2), *Nuzhat* (2), *Sadrudin* (2), *Yasmeen* (2), *Abbas*, *Abu*.

Sharifi (194) **1.** Muslim: Arabic name meaning 'associated with (or descended from) someone called SHARIF'. **2.** Jewish (Sephardic): adoption of the Arabic name.
GIVEN NAMES Muslim 74%; Jewish 4%. *Mohammad* (8), *Hassan* (5), *Bahram* (3), *Massoud* (2), *Mehdi* (2), *Mohammed* (2), *Mohsen* (2), *Nosrat* (2), *Abbas*, *Afshin*, *Ahmad*, *Ali*; *Avi* (2), *Moshen*, *Sasson*.

Shark (125) English: possibly a variant of **Chark**, a metonymic occupational name for a porter or carrier, from Old French *charche* 'load'.

Sharkey (3093) Irish (Ulster and Connacht): reduced Anglicized form of Gaelic **Ó Searcaigh** 'descendant of *Searcach*', a byname meaning 'beloved'.
GIVEN NAMES Irish 6%. *Brendan*, *Colum*, *Declan*, *Mairead*.

Sharlow (271) Probably an altered form of English **Shardlow**, a habitational name from Shardlow in Derbyshire, so named from Old English *sceard* 'notch', 'indentation' + *hlāw* 'mound'.

Sharma (2840) Indian: Hindu (Brahman) name from Sanskrit *šarmā* 'joy', 'shelter'. It is regarded as a prestigious name and as such has been adopted in recent times in various non-Brahman communities.
GIVEN NAMES Indian 92%. *Anil* (38), *Raj* (31), *Ramesh* (30), *Vijay* (27), *Ashok* (26), *Sanjay* (26), *Vinod* (26), *Rajesh* (25), *Ram* (23), *Satish* (22), *Ajay* (20), *Arun* (20).

Sharman (493) English: variant of SHERMAN.

Sharon (1085) Jewish (Israeli): modern Hebrew name from a Biblical place name.

GIVEN NAMES Jewish 6%. *Arie* (3), *Zeev* (3), *Chaim* (2), *Miriam* (2), *Shimon* (2), *Aharon*, *Aryeh*, *Asher*, *Batia*, *Eti*, *Gershon*, *Giora*.

Sharp (28169) **1.** English: nickname from Middle English *scharp* 'keen', 'active', 'quick'. **2.** Irish (County Donegal): Anglicized (part translated) form of Gaelic **Ó Géaráin** 'descendant of *Géarán*', a byname from a diminutive of *géar* 'sharp'. **3.** Americanized form of any of several European names with similar meaning, for example German SCHARF.

Sharpe (10271) Mainly Irish: variant of SHARP.

Sharper (174) Northern English and Scottish: unexplained.

Sharples (494) English (common in Lancashire): habitational name from Sharples Hall near Bolton, probably so called from Old English *scearp* 'sharp', i.e. 'steep' + *lǣs* 'pasture'.

Sharpless (645) Variant of SHARPLES.

Sharpley (238) English: habitational name from any of various places so called, for example in Northumberland.

Sharpnack (175) Americanized spelling of German **Scharpenack**, a habitational name from Scharpenacken in Rhineland.

Sharps (255) English: patronymic from SHARP.

Sharpsteen (125) Americanized form of Ashkenazic Jewish **Scharfstein**, an ornamental name from German *scharff* 'sharp' + *Stein* 'stone'.

Sharpton (397) English: habitational name from Sharperton in Northumberland, possibly so named from Old English *scearp* 'steep' + *beorg* 'hill', 'mound' + *tūn* 'settlement'.

Sharr (145) Americanized spelling of German SCHARR.

Sharrah (105) Variant of English SHARROW.

Sharrar (149) Origin unidentified; perhaps a variant of Scottish and English SHEARER or English SHARROW, or an Americanized spelling of German SCHARRER.

Sharrard (149) English: variant of SHERRARD.
GIVEN NAMES Scandinavian 5%. *Tor* (2), *Erik*.

Sharratt (163) Scottish or English: variant of SHERRATT.

Sharrer (233) Americanized spelling of German SCHARRER.

Sharrett (222) Probably an Americanized spelling of French CHARETTE, or a variant spelling of English SHERRATT.

Sharrock (421) English (Lancashire): habitational name from Shorrock Green in Lancashire, probably so named from Old English *scora* 'bank' + *āc* 'oak'.

Sharron (273) **1.** Americanized spelling of French **Charron**, a metonymic occupational name for a wagonmaker. **2.** Variant spelling of SHARON.

Sharrow (528) **1.** English: habitational name from Sharrow in Sheffield or Sharow in North Yorkshire, both named with Old English *scearu* 'boundary' + *hōh* 'hill-spur'. **2.** Americanized spelling of French CHARRON.

Sharry (107) Reduced and altered form of Irish McSHERRY.

Shartle (129) Americanized spelling of German **Schartl**, from a diminutive of Middle High German *schart* 'notched', 'damaged', hence probably a nickname for someone who had some deformity or mutilation.

Shartzer (252) Americanized spelling of SCHERTZER.

Sharum (167) Americanized spelling of French **Charron**, a metonymic occupational name for a wagonmaker.

Shasky (102) Slovak (**Šášky**): unexplained.

Shasteen (258) Origin unidentified.

Shatkin (101) Jewish (from Ukraine): occupational name, Russified form of Yiddish *shatkhn* 'matchmaker' (a word of Hebrew origin).
GIVEN NAMES Russian 8%. *Valeriy* (2), *Boris*, *Misha*.

Shatley (220) Possibly of English origin, a variant of English **Shotley**, a habitational name from places in Northamptonshire and Suffolk named Shotley or various other places named with this word. Compare SHETLEY.

Shatney (118) Origin unidentified.

Shatswell (122) English: unexplained; possibly a habitational name from a lost or unidentified place.

Shatto (551) Variant of Scottish CATTO.

Shattuck (2097) English: variant of CHADWICK.

Shatz (287) Jewish (Ashkenazic): variant of SCHATZ, or Americanized spelling of this as a German name.
GIVEN NAMES Jewish 7%. *Ephraim, Ilan, Kopel, Meyer, Yael, Yakov.*

Shatzer (404) Altered spelling of German **Schatzer** or **Schätzer**, an occupational name for a tax collector. Compare SCHATZ.

Shaub (479) Americanized spelling of German SCHAUB.

Shauger (154) Origin unidentified.

Shaughnessy (2537) Irish: reduced form of O'SHAUGHNESSY.
GIVEN NAMES Irish 5%. *Brid, Egan, Paddy.*

Shaul (579) Jewish: from the Hebrew form of the Biblical name SAUL.
GIVEN NAMES Jewish 5%. *Shaul* (2), *Shlomo* (2), *Avi, Mordechai, Morry.*

Shaulis (461) Lithuanian (**Šaulis, Šaulys**): occupational name from Lithuanian *šaulys* 'rifleman'.

Shaull (334) Variant of Jewish SHAUL or an Americanized spelling of German SCHAUL or SCHOLL.

Shaum (128) Americanized spelling of German SCHAUM.

Shaut (126) Americanized spelling of Dutch SCHAUT.
GIVEN NAME German 6%. *Otto.*

Shave (176) Americanized spelling of North German SCHAVE.

Shaver (6458) **1.** Americanized form of Dutch **Schouwer**, an occupational name for an inspector of market weights and measures, Dutch *schouwer* 'inspector'. **2.** Altered form of German SCHAEFER.

Shavers (657) Dutch: patronymic from SHAVER.

Shaw (56401) **1.** English: topographic name for someone who lived by a copse or thicket, Middle English *s(c)hage, s(c)hawe* (Old English *sceaga*), or a habitational name from any of the numerous minor places named with this word. The English surname was also established in Ireland in the 17th century. **2.** Scottish and Irish: adopted as an English form of any of various Gaelic surnames derived from the personal name *Sitheach* 'wolf'. **3.** Americanized form of some like-sounding Ashkenazic Jewish surname. **4.** Chinese 邵: variant of SHAO.
FOREBEARS Early American merchants and revolutionary patriots were Nathaniel Shaw (b. 1735 in New London, CT) and Samuel Shaw (b. 1754 in Boston).

Shawgo (204) Origin unidentified.

Shawhan (232) Variant of Irish SHEEHAN.

Shawl (184) Altered spelling of SHAUL or SCHAUL.

Shawler (147) English: unexplained.

Shawley (387) Irish or English: probably a variant of SHEALY.

Shawn (343) Scottish or Irish: possibly a variant of SHANE.

Shawver (1059) Variant of Dutch **Schouwer** 'inspector (of market weights and measures)' (see SHAVER).

Shay (3572) Irish: variant spelling of SHEA.

Shayne (199) Irish: variant spelling of SHANE.

Shea (14291) Irish: reduced form of O'SHEA, Anglicized form of Gaelic **Ó Séaghdha** 'descendant of *Séaghdha*', a byname meaning 'fine' or 'fortunate'.
GIVEN NAMES Irish 5%. *Brendan* (12), *Brigid* (3), *Dermot* (2), *Kieran* (2), *Aidan, Cian, Conor, Donal, James Patrick, Michael Patrick, Murphy, Paddy.*

Shead (347) **1.** English: variant spelling of SHEDD. **2.** Irish: reduced variant of SHEEDY.

Sheaff (103) English (Kent): from Middle English *shefe* 'sheaf', 'bundle' (Old English *scēaf*), hence possibly a metonymic occupational name for a harvest worker, or for someone who paid or collected tithes, from the same term in the sense 'tenth' (or other proportion of produce paid as a tithe).
FOREBEARS Jacob Sheafe (d. 1658) was one of the founders of Boston, MA. He is buried in the King's Chapel Burying Ground there.

Sheaffer (1617) Americanized spelling of German **Schäffer** (see SCHAFFER).

Sheahan (1088) Irish: variant of SHEEHAN.
GIVEN NAMES Irish 5%. *Brendan, Clancy, Eamonn, Niall.*

Sheaks (106) Origin unidentified. Compare SHEEKS.

Shealey (344) Irish: variant of SHEALY.

Shealy (1938) Irish (County Clare): reduced form of **O'Shealy**, an Anglicized form of Gaelic **Ó Sealbhaigh** 'descendant of *Sealbhach*', a byname from the adjective *sealbhach* 'having possessions', 'wealthy'.

Shean (358) **1.** Irish: reduced form of SHEEHAN. **2.** English: nickname for an attractive person, from Middle English *schene* 'fair', 'comely', 'handsome'. **3.** English: habitational name from Sheen in Surrey and Staffordshire, both named in Old English with the plural of *scēo* 'shed', 'shelter'.

Shear (1411) English: nickname for a beautiful or radiant person, or one with fair hair, from Middle English *scher, schir* 'bright', 'fair'.

Sheard (567) English (West Yorkshire): topographic name for someone who lived by a gap between hills, from Middle English *sherd, sharde* (Old English *sceard*, a derivative of *sceran* 'to cut or shear').

Shearer (6941) Scottish and northern English: from an agent derivative of Middle English *schere(n)* 'to shear'; an occupational name for a sheep shearer or someone who used scissors to trim the surface of finished cloth and remove excessive nap. Middle English *schere* denoted shears and scissors of all sizes.

Shearin (1066) Irish: variant spelling of SHEERAN.

Shearman (357) English: variant of SHERMAN 1. The surname is also well established in Ireland.

Shearn (262) English (Bath): unexplained.

Shearon (448) Irish: variant spelling of SHEERAN.

Shearouse (204) Origin unidentified. Compare SHEROUSE.

Shears (958) English: patronymic from SHEAR 1.

Sheasley (141) Origin unidentified; probably English. Compare SHEESLEY.

Sheats (519) Probably an Americanized spelling of German **Schütz** (see SCHUETZ).

Shebesta (104) Americanized spelling of Czech and Slovak **Šebesta** (see SEBESTA, SEBASTIAN).

Shechter (133) Jewish: variant of SCHECHTER 'slaughterer'.
GIVEN NAMES Jewish 14%. *Ben-Zion, Benyamin, Itamar, Motti, Yaakov, Yosef, Zvi.*

Shechtman (133) Jewish: occupational name for a slaughterer (see SCHECHTER).
GIVEN NAMES Jewish 7%; Irish 5%. *Zev; Keane.*

Sheck (156) Americanized spelling of SCHECK 'armorer'.

Sheckells (132) Variant of English **Shackles**, from *Schakel*, an Anglicized form of Anglo-Scandinavian *Skakel*, from the Old Norse by *Skǫkull*, Old Swedish *Skakli*.

Sheckler (343) German (usually **Scheckeler**): Americanized spelling of German **Scheckler** or **Scheckeler**, an occupational name for a maker of jackets, especially of heavy jackets or coats, from Middle High German 'quilted (house)coat'.

Sheckles (103) Of English origin: see SHECKELLS.

Shecter (111) probably an Americanized spelling of Dutch and German **Schechter**, an occupational name for someone who made shafts for spears and lances, from Middle Low German *schacht* 'shaft'.
GIVEN NAME German 4%. *Markus*.

Shed (149) English: variant of SHEDD.

Shedd (1494) English: topographic name for someone who lived in a hovel, Middle English *sched(d)e*.

Shedden (204) Scottish: perhaps a habitational name from Sheddens in the former county of Renfrewshire, which derives its name from an unidentified first element + Middle English *den* 'hollow', 'valley'.

Shedlock (290) Possibly a variant of English **Shadlock**, from Middle English *schaken* 'to shake' + *loc* 'lock' (found in the plural in one early example, *Schakelokes*). If this is right, it was either a nickname for someone with the habit of shaking back his or her long hair, or a metonymic occupational name for a jailer. Alternatively, it could be from Middle English *schaklock* 'fetter', 'shackle', again an occupational name for a jailer.

Shedrick (223) English: variant of SHADRICK.

Sheeder (249) Americanized spelling of German SCHEIDER 'judge', or a variant of **Schieder**.

Sheedy (977) Irish: reduced form of **O'Sheedy**, an Anglicized form of Gaelic Ó **Síoda** 'descendant of *Síoda*', a byname meaning 'silk'.
GIVEN NAMES Irish 6%. *Declan* (2), *Brendan*, *Brigid*.

Sheehan (11205) Irish: reduced form of **O'Sheehan**, an Anglicized form of Gaelic Ó **Síodhacháin** 'descendant of *Síodhacháin*', a personal name representing a diminutive of *síodhach* 'peaceful', the same word as *sítheach*. Compare SHEEHY.
GIVEN NAMES Irish 5%. *Brendan* (12), *Aileen* (3), *Rourke* (3), *Ciaran* (2), *Kiera* (2), *Kieran* (2), *Siobhan* (2), *Brigid*, *Donal*, *Eamonn*, *Ethna*, *Finbarr*.

Sheehe (103) Irish: variant spelling of SHEEHY.

Sheehy (2015) Irish (Munster): reduced form of **McSheehy**, an Anglicized form of Gaelic **Mac Síthigh** 'son of *Sítheach*', a personal name from the adjective *sítheach* 'peaceful' or 'otherworldly'. (The noun *síth*,

from which this adjective derives, means basically 'settlement', hence both 'peace' and 'place inhabited by otherworld beings'.) In some cases the name may be a reduced Anglicized form of Ó **Síthigh**, 'descendant of *Sítheach*', a later form of the Irish name.
GIVEN NAMES Irish 7%. *Brendan* (5), *Aileen*, *Aisling*, *Brigid*, *Declan*, *Egan*, *Eoin*, *Finbar*, *Ronan*.

Sheek (180) Americanized spelling of German SCHIECK.

Sheeks (261) Variant of SHEEK.

Sheeler (494) Americanized form of German **Schüler** (see SCHULER).

Sheeley (746) Irish: variant spelling of SHEALY.

Sheely (789) Irish: variant spelling of SHEALY.

Sheen (532) **1.** Irish: reduced form of SHEEHAN. **2.** Korean: variant of SHIN.

Sheer (352) English: variant spelling of SHEAR.

Sheeran (631) Irish: reduced form of **O'Sheeran**, an Anglicized form of Gaelic Ó **Sírín** 'descendant of *Sírín*', a variant of the personal name *Síorán*, from a diminutive of *síor* 'long-lasting'.
GIVEN NAMES Irish 6%. *Eilis*, *Eoin*, *Fintan*.

Sheerer (151) **1.** English: variant spelling of SHEARER. **2.** Possibly an Americanized form of German **Schürer**, a southern variant of SCHEURER.

Sheerin (457) Irish: variant spelling of SHEERAN.
GIVEN NAMES Irish 6%. *Brendan*, *Bridie*.

Sheesley (370) Origin unidentified. Compare SHEASLEY.

Sheets (7850) Americanized spelling of German **Schütz** (see SCHUTZ).

Sheetz (1046) Americanized spelling of German **Schütz** (see SCHUETZ).

Shefchik (107) Americanized form of Czech and Slovak **Ševčík** 'shoemaker' (see SEVCIK).

Sheff (319) **1.** Americanized spelling of Slovenian *Šef*, Slovenized form of German *Scheffe*, which was used as a translation of the Slovenian surnames **Sodja**, **Sodin**, or **Sodnik**, status names for a judge. **2.** Variant spelling of Jewish (eastern Ashkenazic) **Schef**, of unexplained origin.
GIVEN NAMES Jewish 4%. *Hyman*, *Sol*.

Sheffer (1483) **1.** Jewish (Ashkenazic): variant of SCHAEFER. **2.** Americanized spelling of German SCHEFFER.

Sheffey (248) Origin unidentified. Probably an Americanized spelling of SCHEFFE.

Sheffield (6811) English: habitational name from the city in South Yorkshire, so called from the river name *Sheaf* (from Old English *sceað* 'boundary') + Old English *feld* 'pasture', 'open country'. There are also minor places of the same name in Sussex (from Old English *sceap*, *scīp* 'sheep' + *feld*) and Berkshire (from Old English *sceo* 'shelter', 'shed' + *feld*), which may have contributed to the surname.

Sheffler (527) **1.** Jewish (Ashkenazic): perhaps an occupational name for a shepherd, from Yiddish *shof*, German *Schaf* 'sheep' + the agent suffix *-ler*. **2.** Americanized spelling of German SCHEFFLER.

Sheftel (112) Jewish (Ashkenazic): from the Yiddish personal name *Sheftl*, derived from Biblical *Sabbetai*.
GIVEN NAME Jewish 12%. *Miriam* (2).

Shehadeh (121) Muslim: from a personal name based on Arabic *shahādah* 'testimony', 'belief in Islam'. The *shahādah* is the declaration of faith by Muslims, 'I testify that there is no god but Allah and that Muhammad is the messenger of Allah.' New converts recite the *shahādah* when they become Muslims.
GIVEN NAMES Muslim 77%. *Ahmad* (3), *Hani* (3), *Abdullah* (2), *Iyad* (2), *Mahmoud* (2), *Mohammad* (2), *Nazmi* (2), *Walid* (2), *Abbas*, *Adnan*, *Arafat*, *Assad*.

Shehan (648) Irish: variant spelling of SHEEHAN.

Shehane (187) Irish: variant spelling of SHEEHAN.

Shehata (125) Muslim: variant of SHEHADEH.
GIVEN NAMES Muslim 72%. *Mahmoud* (3), *Selim* (3), *Sherif* (3), *Ahmed* (2), *Ashraf* (2), *Hany* (2), *Ibrahim* (2), *Kamal* (2), *Medhat* (2), *Nabil* (2), *Wagih* (2), *Abdelhamid*.

Shehee (119) Variant spelling of Irish SHEEHY.

Shehorn (200) Origin unidentified.

Sheikh (662) Muslim: from Arabic *shaikh*, a title denoting a political or spiritual leader of a community. *Shaikh ul-Islam* 'leader of Islam', was the title of the highest religious office in Ottoman Turkey. *Shaikh* also means 'chief' or 'head' (Qur'an 28:23). This name is found throughout the Muslim world.
GIVEN NAMES Muslim 88%. *Mohammad* (14), *Mohammed* (11), *Shahid* (10), *Abdul* (8), *Khalid* (7), *Tariq* (7), *Arshad* (6), *Iqbal* (6), *Mahmood* (6), *Zahid* (6), *Ali* (5), *Muhammad* (5).

Sheil (284) Irish: variant of SHIELD 3.
GIVEN NAMES Irish 8%. *Brendan*, *Eamonn*.

Sheilds (268) Irish, English, and Scottish: variant spelling of SHIELDS.

Sheils (223) Scottish and Irish: variant of SHIELDS.

Shein (250) **1.** Jewish (Ashkenazic): nickname or ornamental name from Yiddish *sheyn* 'fine', 'beautiful'. Compare SCHOEN. **2.** Americanized spelling of German and Jewish (Ashkenazic) SCHEIN.
GIVEN NAMES Jewish 7%. *Miriam*, *Nurit*, *Sol*.

Sheinberg (136) Variant spelling of Ashkenazic Jewish SCHEINBERG.
GIVEN NAMES Jewish 6%. *Nurit*, *Sol*.

Shek (152) Chinese 石: Cantonese variant of SHI 1.
GIVEN NAMES Chinese 20%. *Chi Fai* (2), *Kam* (2), *Kwong* (2), *Ting* (2), *Kuan*, *Kwai*, *Kwok Hung*, *Man*, *Ming*, *On*, *Rui Hua*, *Sou*.

Shelander (110) Altered spelling of Dutch **Schellander**, itself an adaptation of the French surname **Chalandre**, a nickname for a lively, cheerful person or someone fond of singing, from Old French *c(h)alandre* 'lark', 'skylark'.

Shelburn (124) English: variant of SHELBURNE.

Shelburne (538) English: habitational name from a lost or unidentified place, probably in Devon.

Shelby (3732) English: of uncertain origin; perhaps a variant of SELBY, or a habitational name from an unidentified place named with the northern Middle English elements *schēle* 'hut' + *by* 'settlement', 'farm' (Old Norse *býr*).

Sheldahl (129) Origin unidentified.

Shelden (501) **1.** Variant of English SHELDON. **2.** Altered form of Dutch **van de(r) Schelden**, a topographic name for someone who lived by the Schelde river.

Sheldon (7882) English: habitational name from any of the various places so called. The main source is probably the one in Derbyshire, recorded in Domesday Book as *Scelhadun*, formed by the addition of the Old English distinguishing term *scylf* 'shelf' to the place name *Haddon* (from Old English *hǣð* 'heath(er)' + *dūn* 'hill'). There are also places called Sheldon in Devon (from Old English *scylf* 'shelf' + *denu* 'valley') and Birmingham (from Old English *scylf* + *dūn* 'hill').

Sheldrake (121) Variant of SHELDRICK.

Sheldrick (136) English (chiefly East Anglia): nickname for a vain or showy person, from Middle English *scheldrake*, a type of brightly colored duck (from the East Anglian dialect term *scheld* 'variegated' + *drake* 'male duck').

Sheler (100) German or Jewish: Americanized spelling of SCHELLER or **Schüler** (see SCHULER).

Sheley (556) Irish: variant spelling of SHEALY.

Shelfer (136) English: unexplained.

Shelhamer (216) Americanized spelling of German SCHELLHAMMER.

Sheline (229) Probably an Americanized spelling of German **Schielein**, a variant of **Schühlein**, a metonymic occupational name for a shoemaker, from Middle High German *scuoch* 'shoe' + the diminutive suffix *līn*.

Shell (4394) **1.** English: habitational name from Shell, a place in Worcestershire, so named from Old English *scylf* 'bank', 'shelf'. **2.** Jewish (Ashkenazic): ornamental name from German SCHELLE 'bell'. **3.** Americanized spelling of German SCHAL or SCHILL.

Shellabarger (309) Americanized form of German SCHELLENBERGER.

Shellenbarger (272) Americanized form of German SCHELLENBERGER.

Shellenberger (787) Americanized form of German SCHELLENBERGER.

Sheller (388) Americanized spelling of SCHELLER.

Shelley (5119) English: habitational name from any of various places, for example in Sussex, Suffolk, Essex, and West Yorkshire, all so named from Old English *scylf* 'shelf' + *lēah* 'wood', 'clearing'.

Shellhamer (102) Americanized spelling of German SCHELLHAMMER.

GIVEN NAMES German 6%. *Kurt, Otto.*

Shellhammer (332) Americanized spelling of SCHELLHAMMER.

Shellhorn (141) Americanized spelling of German SCHELLHORN.

Shellito (170) English: variant of SHILLITO.

Shellman (358) Americanized spelling of German **Schellmann**, a variant of SCHELL.

Shellnut (108) Origin unidentified. See SHELNUTT.

Shelly (1789) English: variant of SHELLEY.

Shelman (248) Americanized spelling of German **Schellmann**, a variant of SCHELL.

Shelnut (153) Variant of SHELNUTT.

Shelnutt (502) Origin unidentified. This name appears to have originated in North America, probably in SC in the 18th century.

Shelor (427) Origin unidentified. Perhaps an Americanized spelling of German SCHELLER or **Schüler** (see SCHULER).

Shelp (220) Possibly an Americanized spelling of North German SCHELP.

Shelstad (197) Probably an Americanized form of Norwegian **Skjelstad**, a habitational name from any of six farmsteads so named. The first element is probably a river name or a personal name (for example, Old Norse *Skjalgr*); the second element is from Old Norse *staðir* 'farmstead', 'dwelling'.

Shelton (29881) English (mainly Nottinghamshire): habitational name from any of various places, for example in Nottinghamshire, Bedfordshire, Norfolk, Shropshire, and Staffordshire, which are named from Old English *scylf* 'shelf' + *tūn* 'enclosure', 'settlement'.

Sheltra (152) Origin unidentified.

Shely (113) Variant of Irish SHEALY.

Shema (111) Origin unidentified.

Shemanski (188) Variant spelling of Jewish (eastern Ashkenazic) **Shimanski**, from the personal name *Shiman* (see SHIMON). Compare Polish SZYMANSKI.

Shemwell (362) English (Derbyshire): unexplained; possibly a habitational name from a lost or unidentified place.

Shen (2159) **1.** Chinese 沈: from the name of the state of Shen, in present-day Henan province. During the reign of the second Zhou dynasty king Cheng Wang (1115–1079 BC), Dan Shuji, the tenth son of Wen Wang, was granted the state of Shen, and his descendants subsequently adopted the name of the state as their surname. **2.** Chinese 申: two accounts of the source of Shen both deal with states named Shen; one was established early in the Zhou dynasty (1122–221 BC) while the other was established later in the Zhou dynasty. Descendants of the ruling classes adopted the state name Shen as their surname. **3.** Jewish (Ashkenazic): variant spelling of SCHOEN.

GIVEN NAMES Chinese 42%. *Hong* (12), *Ming* (9), *Wen* (9), *You Qin* (9), *Ning* (8), *Jian* (7), *Ying* (7), *Li* (6), *Wei* (6), *Yi* (6), *Fei* (5), *Hui* (5); *Min* (6), *Chang* (3), *Chung* (3), *Tian* (2), *You* (2), *Sa, Yiping, Yu-Min.*

Shenberger (245) Americanized form of German **Schönberger** (see SCHOENBERGER).

Shenefield (182) Americanized form of German **Schönefeld** (see SHANEYFELT).

Sheneman (255) Americanized form of German SCHOENEMANN.

Sheng (331) Chinese 盛: from the name of an area named Sheng. Mu Wang, fifth king (1001–947 BC) of the Zhou dynasty, granted this area to a follower, whose descendants adopted the place name as their surname. There also is an account of a man surnamed Shi who, to escape persecution by an emperor of the Yuan dynasty (1271–1368), changed his name to Sheng.

GIVEN NAMES Chinese 43%. *Chen* (4), *Jia* (3), *Shan Shan* (3), *Tao* (3), *Ji* (2), *Li* (2), *Lihong* (2), *Wen Ching* (2), *Xiaoming* (2), *Chi, Chien-Hung, Chuan, Hu.*

Shenk (1419) **1.** Jewish (Ashkenazic): variant spelling of SCHENK 2. **2.** Americanized spelling of German SCHENK or Slovenian **Šenk** (see SENK).

Shenker (249) Jewish (Ashkenazic): variant of SHENK, with the addition of the German or Yiddish agent suffix *-er*.

GIVEN NAMES Jewish 10%; Russian 9%. *Yoram* (3), *Rivka* (2), *Benzion, Ilya, Moisey, Sarra, Semen, Sol; Boris* (2), *Dmitriy* (2), *Betya, Gennadiy, Maksim, Sofiya, Vladimir, Yefim, Yelena.*

Shenkman (217) Jewish (Ashkenazic): variant of SHENK, with the addition of Yiddish *man* 'man'.

GIVEN NAMES Jewish 12%; Russian 5%. *Meyer* (2), *Dov, Hyman, Marat, Zeev; Anatoly, Arkady, Boris, Dmitry, Igor, Yelena.*

Shenoy (181) Indian (Goa): Hindu (Brahman) name found among the Konkani-speaking Saraswat Brahmans, who are originally from Goa but are now found in larger numbers in coastal Karnataka. The name is from Konkani *šeṇəy* 'accountant', 'clerk', from Sanskrit *senāpati* 'commander of an army' (from *senā* 'army' + *pati* 'lord').

GIVEN NAMES Indian 96%. *Suresh* (8), *Gopal* (4), *Mohan* (3), *Prakash* (3), *Vittal* (3), *Vivek* (3), *Ajit* (2), *Arvind* (2), *Ashok* (2), *Deepak* (2), *Ganesh* (2), *Krishna* (2).

Shenton (247) English: habitational name from a place in Leicestershire, originally named as the settlement (Old English *tūn*) on the river *Sence*. This river name is a Normanized form of Old English *Scenc* 'drinking-cup', referring to its abundance of potable water.

Shepard (13600) **1.** English: variant spelling of SHEPHERD. **2.** Americanized form of some Jewish surname sounding like or meaning 'shepherd'.

Shepardson (644) English: patronymic from SHEPHERD.

Sheperd (406) English: variant spelling of SHEPHERD.

Shephard (2084) English: variant spelling of SHEPHERD.

Shepheard (137) English: variant spelling of SHEPHERD.

Shepherd (20686) English: from Middle English *schepherde* 'shepherd' (composed of words meaning 'sheep' + 'herdsman' or 'guardian'), hence an occupational name for a shepherd. This English form of the name has absorbed cognates and equivalents from several other languages (for forms, see Hanks and Hodges 1988).

Shepler (830) Americanized spelling of **Schepler**, a North German form of SCHEFFLER.

Shepley (466) English: habitational name from a place in West Yorkshire, so named from Old English *scēap* 'sheep' + *lēah* 'woodland clearing'.

Shepp (185) Americanized spelling of German SCHEPP.

Sheppard (12096) English: variant spelling of SHEPHERD.

Shepperd (572) English: variant spelling of SHEPHERD.

Shepperson (246) English: patronymic from SHEPHERD.

Sher (1159) **1.** English: variant of SHEAR 1. **2.** Jewish (eastern Ashkenazic): variant spelling of SCHER.
GIVEN NAMES Jewish 6%. *Hyman* (3), *Emanuel* (2), *Ilya* (2), *Izy* (2), *Abbe*, *Avrohom*, *Filipp*, *Irina*, *Isadore*, *Mandel*, *Mendel*, *Meyer*.

Shera (128) **1.** Irish: reduced Anglicized form of Gaelic **Mac Séartha** 'son of *Séartha*', a personal name equivalent to English GEOFFREY. Compare MCSHERRY. **2.** Scottish and Northern English: variant of SHEARER.

Sherard (430) English: variant spelling of SHERRARD.

Sherba (96) Americanized form of Polish SZCZERBA.

Sherbert (368) Perhaps an altered form of German SCHERBARTH.

Sherbon (101) Variant of English SHERBURNE.

Sherbondy (214) Origin unidentified; possibly an Americanized form of French CHARBONNEAU.

Sherburn (172) English: variant of SHERBURNE.

Sherburne (683) **1.** English (mainly Yorkshire): habitational name from any of various places, for example in Durham and Yorkshire, so called from Old English *scīr* 'bright' + *burna* 'stream'. (In southern English dialects, *burna* became modern *bourne*, and Sherborne in Dorset is one of several places so called.) **2.** Americanized form of French **Charbon** (see JARBOE) or CHARBONNEAU.

Shere (189) **1.** English: variant spelling of SHEAR 1. **2.** Indian (Maharashtra); pronounced as two syllables: Hindu (Vani) name, probably from Marathi *šera* 'rate'.
GIVEN NAMES Indian 9%. *Kalpana* (2), *Aniruddha*, *Ashok*, *Laxman*, *Mitesh*, *Pratish*, *Sunil*.

Sheren (134) English: variant of SHERRIN.

Sherer (1857) **1.** Scottish and northern English: variant spelling of SHEARER. **2.** Jewish (Ashkenazic): occupational name from Yiddish *sherer* 'barber'.

Sherfey (222) Origin unidentified. Compare SHERFY.

Sherfield (249) English: habitational name from a place so named in Hampshire, named from Old English *scīr* 'bright' + *feld* 'open country'.

Sherfy (114) Origin unidentified; compare SHERFEY.

Sherick (152) **1.** English: variant of SHARROCK. **2.** Americanized form of German SCHERICH, a variant of SCHEURICH.
GIVEN NAME German 4%. *Kurt* (2).

Sheridan (8700) Irish: reduced Anglicized form of Gaelic **Ó Sirideáin** 'descendant of *Sirideán*', a personal name of uncertain origin, possibly akin to *sirim* 'to seek'.

Sheriff (925) English and Scottish: variant of SHREVE.

Sherin (219) English: variant of SHERRIN.

Sherk (424) Origin unidentified. Possibly a variant of English SHARK.

Sherley (201) **1.** Variant spelling of English SHIRLEY. **2.** Americanized form of Norwegian **Sjøli**, **Sjølie**, a habitational name from a farmstead named with *sjø* 'sea', 'lake' + *li* 'hillside'.

Sherlin (260) Possibly of Irish or English origin; unexplained.

Sherling (119) English: unexplained.

Sherlock (1827) English: nickname for someone with fair hair or a lock of fair hair, from Middle English *schirloc*, composed of words meaning 'bright', 'fair' + 'lock (of hair)'. This surname has also been established in Ireland since the 13th century.
GIVEN NAMES Irish 4%. *Kieran* (2), *Liam* (2), *Brendan*.

Sherman (28370) **1.** English: occupational name for a sheepshearer or someone who used shears to trim the surface of finished cloth and remove excess nap, from Middle English *shereman* 'shearer'. **2.** Americanized spelling of German SCHUERMANN. **3.** Jewish (Ashkenazic): occupational name for a tailor, from Yiddish *sher* 'scissors' + *man* 'man'.

FOREBEARS Roger Sherman (1722–93), the only man to sign all three documents at the foundation of the American republic (the Declaration of Independence, the Articles of Confederation, and the U.S. Constitution), was born in Newton, MA, a descendant of Capt. John Sherman, who had emigrated in about 1636 to MA from Dedham, Essex, England, where his father was a farmer, following his brother Edmund, who had emigrated two years earlier. A descendant of Edmund Sherman was the U.S. general William Tecumseh Sherman (1820–91), who led the Union march through GA. He was born in Lancaster, OH, the son of a judge; his middle name was bestowed in honor of a Shawnee chieftain.

Shermer (338) Americanized spelling of German SCHERMER, or variant spelling of this as a Jewish name.

Shern (120) Perhaps an Americanized spelling of a Slavic nickname meaning 'black', e.g. Czech **Černý** (see CERNY).

Shero (149) Americanized form of French **Cherot**, an occupational name from a diminutive of *char* 'wagon', 'cart'.

Sherod (158) **1.** English: variant spelling of SHERROD. **2.** Probably also an Americanized form of French **Cherot**. Compare SHERO.

Sheron (116) English and Scottish: variant spelling of SHERRON.

Sherouse (108) Origin unidentified. Compare SHEAROUSE.

Sherr (398) English: variant of SHEAR.

Sherrard (812) English and Irish: of uncertain origin; probably a derivative of Middle English *shere* 'bright', 'fair', with the addition of the Anglo-Norman French pejorative suffix *-ard*. It has been established in County Derry, Ireland, since the 17th century.

Sherratt (142) English and Scottish: of uncertain origin; probably a variant of SHERRARD or of SYRETT. However, According to Black, in Scotland Sherratt and its variants are forms of SHERWOOD.

Sherrell (867) English (Devon): unexplained. There is a farm called Sherrell Farm near Ivybridge in Devon. Compare SHERRILL.

Sherrer (709) Americanized spelling of German SCHERER.

Sherrick (593) English: variant of SHARROCK.

Sherriff (183) English and Scottish: status name for a sheriff, from Middle English *schiref* 'sheriff', 'administrative officer of an English shire', from Old English *scīr* 'shire' + *(ge)rēfa* 'reeve' (see REEVE). Compare SHREVE.

Sherrill (5183) English (Devon): unexplained. Compare SHERRELL.

Sherrin (178) English: habitational name from Sheering in Essex, probably so called from an unattested Old English personal name, *Scear(a)*, + the suffix *-ingas*, meaning 'people, family, or followers of'.

Sherritt (108) English: variant of SHERRARD.

Sherrod (2352) **1.** English: variant of SHERRARD. **2.** Americanized form of French **Cherot** 'wagoner' (see SHERO).

Sherron (469) Probably a variant of English SHERRIN.

Sherrow (294) **1.** Irish: variant of SHERRY. **2.** Perhaps an Americanized form of French **Cherot** 'wagoner' (see SHERO).

Sherry (2949) **1.** Irish: reduced form of MCSHERRY, Anglicized form of Gaelic **Mac Searraigh** 'son of *Searrach*', a personal name based on *searrach* 'foal'. It is sometimes 'translated' as FOLEY. **2.** reduced Anglicized form of Gaelic **Mac Séartha** 'son of GEOFFREY' (see MCSHERRY).

Shertzer (266) Americanized spelling of SCHERTZER.

Sherwin (1453) English: nickname for a swift runner, from Middle English *schere(n)* 'to shear' + *wind* 'wind'.

Sherwood (8426) **1.** English: habitational name from a place in Nottinghamshire, around which once stood the famous Sherwood Forest. The place is so called from Old English *scīr* 'shire' or *scīr* 'bright' + *wudu* 'wood'. **2.** Americanized form of some Jewish name.

Sheth (671) Indian: variant of SETH.

GIVEN NAMES Indian 92%. *Dilip* (8), *Ashvin* (7), *Dinesh* (7), *Amit* (6), *Jagdish* (6), *Kiran* (6), *Kirit* (6), *Pankaj* (6), *Pravin* (6), *Ramesh* (6), *Vijay* (6), *Anish* (5).

Shetler (768) Americanized spelling of SCHETTLER.

Shetley (193) Possibly of English origin: compare SHATLEY and SHETTERLY.

Shetter (239) Americanized spelling of German SCHETTER.

Shetterly (250) Origin unidentified.

Shetty (242) Indian (Karnataka): Hindu and Jain name found among the people of the Bunt or Nadava community in coastal Karnataka; it derives from Sanskrit *śreṣṭhī*, which refers to the head of a mercantile or other guild. Unlike bearers of the cognate names SETH and SETTY, however, the Bunts are not a mercantile community; they are a land-owning and farming class in South Kanara, a coastal district of Karnataka. This name is also found among the Jains of this region.

GIVEN NAMES Indian 92%. *Navin* (6), *Satish* (6), *Ajay* (2), *Anand* (2), *Anil* (2), *Ashok* (2), *Ashwin* (2), *Bhaskar* (2), *Deepak* (2), *Dinesh* (2), *Rajiv* (2), *Ram* (2).

Sheu (177) Chinese 许: variant of XU 2.

GIVEN NAMES Chinese 14%. *Chih* (2), *Chimin*, *Dong*, *Jong*, *Ling*, *Ning*, *Rong*, *Ting-Ting*, *Tsai*, *Weiming*.

Shevchenko (122) Ukrainian: from the occupational name *shevts* 'shoemaker' + the diminutive suffix *-enko*, whose role in Ukrainian surnames is generally patronymic.

GIVEN NAMES Russian 41%; Jewish 10%. *Boris* (3), *Aleksandr* (2), *Igor* (2), *Nikolay* (2), *Sergey* (2), *Svetlana* (2), *Alexei*, *Arkady*, *Dmytro*, *Ekaterina*, *Gennadiy*, *Grigoriy*; *Irina*.

Shevchuk (118) Ukrainian and Jewish (eastern Ashkenazic): from *shevchuk* 'son (or assistant) of the shoemaker', from *shevts* 'shoemaker' + the diminutive or patronymic suffix *-(ch)uk*.

GIVEN NAMES Russian 20%; Jewish 6%; Czech and Slovak 4%. *Anatoly* (3), *Aleksey*, *Boris*, *Leonid*, *Nadezhda*, *Valeriy*, *Vasily*, *Vitaliy*, *Vitaly*, *Vladmir*, *Yevgeniy*; *Ilya*; *Pavel* (2), *Miroslav*.

Shevlin (651) Irish: reduced Anglicized form of Gaelic **Ó Seibhleáin** 'descendant of *Seibhleán*', a personal name possibly derived from a diminutive of *siabhal* 'moving'.

GIVEN NAME Irish 5%. *Aidan*.

Shew (874) **1.** English: unexplained. **2.** Probably also an Americanized spelling of German and Jewish SCHUH.

Sheward (165) English (West Midlands): probably a variant of SEWARD.

Shewbridge (118) English (Kent): apparently a habitational name from a lost or unidentified place.

Shewchuk (167) Polish or German spelling of Ukrainian **Shevchuk**.

Shewell (178) English: perhaps a variant form of SEWELL.

Shewey (138) Origin unidentified.

Shewmake (367) Americanized form of Dutch SCHOEMAKER or German SCHUMACHER.

Shewmaker (588) Americanized form of Dutch SCHOEMAKER or German SCHUMACHER.

Shewman (105) Americanized spelling of German SCHUMANN.

Shey (100) Probably a variant of Irish SHEA.

Shi (887) **1.** Chinese 石: from a character in the personal name *Shi Que*, name of a high adviser in the state of Wei during the Spring and Autumn period (722–481 BC). This character also means 'stone'. **2.** Chinese 史: from a word meaning 'history'. During the Zhou dynasty (1122–221 BC) a man named Yin Yi held the title of 'High Historian'; he came to be regarded as setting a model for subsequent historians, and his descendants adopted *Shi* as their surname. **3.** Chinese 施: The earliest records of this surname go back 4000 years to a prince during the Xia dynasty who was granted an area named Shi. Although his

descendants adopted the name, historical records do not show a continuation of the clan to the present. Another branch of the name started later, during the Zhou dynasty (1122–221 BC), when a prince of the state of Lu bore the given name Shi Fu, and his descendants adopted the character for Shi as their surname. **4.** Chinese 师: from a word that also means 'master' or 'teacher' and is derived from *Shiyin*, an official title during the Zhou dynasty (1122–221 BC). Descendants of various Shiyin adopted the first character of the title as their surname. **5.** Chinese 时: this name, which also means 'time', is derived from a character in the given name of Shenshu Shi, a senior minister in the state of Chu during the Zhou dynasty (1122–221 BC).

GIVEN NAMES Chinese 66%. *Wei* (12), *Jian* (11), *Hong* (8), *Ming* (7), *Yi* (7), *Yuan* (7), *Lei* (6), *Li* (6), *Hao* (4), *Jing* (4), *Ping* (4), *Ting* (4), *Yan* (4), *Hai* (3), *Chang* (2), *Lan* (2), *Min* (2), *Mai*, *Quan*, *Quang*.

Shia (108) Origin unidentified.

Shiau (100) Chinese: see XIAO.

GIVEN NAMES Chinese 18%. *Ying* (2), *Chin*, *Hwang*, *Jeng*, *Mei-Lin*, *Wen*, *Yih*.

Shiba (119) Japanese: there are two names with this pronunciation; the first, meaning 'turf', is found mainly in western Japan; the other, meaning 'brushwood', occurs chiefly in eastern Japan.

GIVEN NAMES Japanese 45%. *Katsumi* (2), *Tosh* (2), *Haru*, *Hideshi*, *Hisa*, *Izumi*, *Keiichi*, *Masao*, *Mikio*, *Noriyuki*, *Seiji*, *Shig*.

Shibata (367) Japanese: there are two names with this pronunciation, written with different characters. The one written with characters meaning 'turf' and 'rice paddy' is found mainly in eastern Japan and is from the Tachibana family. The other, written with characters meaning 'brushwood' and 'rice paddy', is found chiefly on the island of Kyūshū and along the southeastern seaboard, and is from the Seiwa-Genji. Both forms occur in the Ryūkyū islands.

GIVEN NAMES Japanese 65%. *Kenji* (5), *Kenichi* (3), *Masaaki* (3), *Chiaki* (2), *Hiroshi* (2), *Hiroyuki* (2), *Hitoshi* (2), *Kaoru* (2), *Kazu* (2), *Masao* (2), *Masaru* (2), *Minoru* (2).

Shibley (384) English (Norfolk): probably a variant of SIBLEY.

Shibuya (152) Japanese: the character *shibu* has several widely different meanings; in this case, the name probably means 'tan valley' or possibly 'quiet valley'. It is found mostly in eastern Japan. One noble family bearing this name claims descent from the FUJIWARA clan.

GIVEN NAMES Japanese 55%. *Kenichi* (2), *Kinji* (2), *Kumiko* (2), *Tomoko* (2), *Toshifumi* (2), *Akio*, *Akira*, *Hideo*, *Hiro*, *Hiroo*, *Hisashi*, *Kana*.

Shick (933) Jewish (Ashkenazic): variant spelling of SCHICK.

Shideler (384) Americanized spelling of German SCHEIDLER.

Shidler (364) Americanized spelling of German SCHEIDLER.

Shie (100) altered spelling of German *Schie*, a nickname from Middle High German *schie* 'shy'.

Shieh (360) Chinese: see XIE.
GIVEN NAMES Chinese 22%. *Wen* (4), *Chi-Chang* (2), *Ching* (2), *Kuo* (2), *Ming* (2), *Rong* (2), *Chan, Chao, Chih, Ching- Yao, Chyi, Gwo*.

Shiel (250) **1.** Scottish: variant of SHIELD 2. **2.** Irish: variant of SHIELDS.
GIVEN NAMES Irish 8%. *Fergus* (2), *Brendan, Conor*.

Shield (468) **1.** English: metonymic occupational name for an armorer, from Middle English *scheld* 'shield' (Old English *scild, sceld*). **2.** English: topographic name for someone who lived near the shallow part of a river, from Middle English *scheld* 'shallow place' (Old English *sceldu, scieldu*). **3.** Irish: Anglicized form of Gaelic **Ó Siadhail** 'descendant of *Siadhal*' (see SHIELDS).

Shields (17959) **1.** Irish: reduced form of O'SHIELDS, an alternative Anglicized form of Gaelic **Ó Siadhail** 'descendant of *Siadhal*'. **2.** Northern English and Scottish: habitational name from a pair of places in Northumberland and County Durham (now both in Tyne and Wear) called North and South Shields, named with Middle English *schele* 'shed', 'hut', 'shelter'. There has been much confusion between **Shields** and SHIELD and their variants.

Shiell (115) Irish: variant of SHIELD 3.

Shiels (331) Scottish and Irish: variant of SHIELDS.
GIVEN NAMES Irish 4%. *Aidan, Dermot*.

Shier (477) **1.** English and Irish (County Limerick): variant of SHIRE. **2.** Jewish (eastern Ashkenazic): metonymic occupational name for a Talmudic teacher, from Yiddish *shier* 'lesson of the Talmud'. **3.** Americanized spelling of German SCHIER.

Shiers (153) English: variant spelling of SHEARS or possibly a variant of SHIRES.

Shiff (203) **1.** Jewish (Ashkenazic): from German *Schiff*, Yiddish *shif* 'ship' (see SCHIFF). **2.** Americanized spelling of German SCHIFF.
GIVEN NAMES Jewish 8%. *Miriam* (3), *Hyman, Zeev, Zohar*.

Shiffer (440) Americanized spelling of German and Jewish SCHIFFER.

Shiffler (212) Americanized spelling of SCHIFFLER.

Shifflet (291) Of French origin: see SHIFFLETT.

Shifflett (2628) Americanized form of French **Chifflet**, nickname for someone given to scoffing or mocking, from a diminutive of *chifle* 'whistle', 'mockery'.

Shifflette (114) North American spelling of French **Chifflet** (see SHIFFLETT). The spelling *-ette* is not a feminine form, but a spelling prompted by the continuing pronunciation of final *-t* in Canadian French surnames after it had become silent in ordinary French vocabulary words.

Shiffman (326) German and Jewish (Ashkenazic): Americanized spelling of SCHIFFMAN.
GIVEN NAMES Jewish 7%. *Isadore, Miriam, Ronit, Slava*.

Shiflet (650) Americanized spelling of French **Chifflet** (see SHIFFLETT).

Shiflett (1262) Americanized spelling of French **Chifflet** (see SHIFFLETT).

Shifman (150) Jewish (Ashkenazic): variant spelling of SCHIFFMAN.
GIVEN NAMES Russian 12%; Jewish 12%. *Anatoly* (2), *Fanya, Lyubov, Mikail, Mikhail, Sofiya, Yelena; Baruch, Ilya, Isak, Osher, Sol, Yehuda*.

Shifrin (318) Jewish (from Belarus): metronymic from Yiddish female personal name *Shifre*, from the Hebrew for 'beautiful' + the eastern Slavic possessive suffix *-in*.
GIVEN NAMES Russian 12%; Jewish 12%. *Lev* (3), *Boris* (2), *Dmitry* (2), *Grigoriy* (2), *Leonid* (2), *Vladimir* (2), *Zinovy* (2), *Arkady, Lilya, Mikhail, Semyon, Yefim; Hirsh, Hymen, Isaak, Isak, Izya, Sarra, Yitzchok*.

Shigley (217) Americanized form of a German name, probably SCHICKLER 'trader', or a related form.

Shih (1253) Chinese: see SHI.
GIVEN NAMES Chinese 21%. *Ching* (5), *Wei* (4), *Chi* (3), *Hsiao* (3), *Ling* (3), *Wen* (3), *Chen* (2), *Cheng* (2), *Chiou* (2), *Fu* (2), *Fung* (2), *Jung* (2).

Shiley (311) Perhaps a variant of Irish SHEALY.

Shill (263) **1.** English (Gloucestershire): unexplained. **2.** Americanized spelling of SCHILL.

Shiller (239) **1.** Jewish (southern Ashkenazic): variant spelling of SCHILLER (see SCHULER). **2.** Americanized spelling of SCHILLER.
GIVEN NAMES Jewish 5%. *Abbe, Dror, Zvi*.

Shilling (1829) **1.** English: from the Middle English coin name *schilling*, probably a nickname referring to a fee or rent owed. **2.** Jewish (Ashkenazic): variant spelling of SCHILLING. **3.** Americanized spelling of German SCHILLING.

Shillingburg (186) Americanized form of German SCHELLENBERG.

Shillingford (113) English: habitational name from Shillingford in Oxfordshire, probably named with an Old English personal name *Sciell(a)* + Old English *-inga-* denoting 'family or followers of' + *ford* 'ford'.

Shillinglaw (178) Scottish: habitational name from Shillinglaw in Peeblesshire. The first element is unexplained; the second element is presumably Northern Middle English *law* 'hill'.

Shillings (185) Probably an Americanized spelling of the German surname **Schillings**, a Rhineland variant of SCHILLING.

Shillington (146) English: habitational name from a place in Bedfordshire, so named from an unattested Old English personal name, *Scyttel* + *-inga-* (genitive plural) 'belonging to the people of' + *dūn* 'hill'.

Shillito (138) English: unexplained. This surname seems to have a unique origin, in the parish of Featherstone, West Yorkshire.

Shilt (101) Americanized spelling of German **Schild(t)** (see SCHILD).

Shilts (340) **1.** Jewish (eastern Ashkenazic): origin uncertain; perhaps a variant of SCHULZ, with the transition from *u* to *i* peculiar to southern Yiddish. **2.** Americanized spelling of German SCHILTZ.

Shim (864) Korean: there is only one Chinese character for the surname Shim. Some sources indicate that there are 63 different Shim clans, but only six can be documented. Each of these clans claims a different founding ancestor. The founding ancestor of at least one of them, the P'ungsan Shim clan, originated in China. Most of the other Shim clans came into being during the Koryŏ period (918–1392). Members of the Shim clans can be found throughout the Korean peninsula.
GIVEN NAMES Korean 55%. *Jae* (25), *Jung* (9), *Sang* (9), *Young* (9), *Eun* (4), *Hyun* (4), *Sung* (4), *Chae* (3), *Joon* (3), *Kwang* (3), *Kyung* (3), *Wan* (3); *Chang* (5), *Chul* (3), *Chung* (3), *Dong Sup* (3), *Yeon* (3), *Chong* (2), *Dae* (2), *Hae* (2), *Jae Bong* (2), *Jae Chul* (2), *Jae Won* (2), *Min* (2).

Shima (270) Japanese: meaning 'island'; it is often written with characters used phonetically. The word does not necessarily denote an island surrounded by water, but can also mean a field separated from its village and surrounded by someone else's property (see SHIMADA, NAKASHIMA, etc.). The surname is listed in the Shinsen shōjiroku. It is found mostly in the Kyōto–Ōsaka area and in the Ryūkyū Islands. Some instances in America may be the result of shortening other names containing the *shima* component.
GIVEN NAMES Japanese 24%. *Hiroshi* (3), *Osamu* (3), *Takemi* (2), *Akihiko, Akira, Chikako, Ichiro, Iwao, Jiro, Kaori, Katsunori, Koji*.

Shimabukuro (411) Japanese (Ryūkyū Islands): written with characters meaning 'island' and 'bag'.
GIVEN NAMES Japanese 36%. *Takeo* (4), *Sadao* (3), *Kazuo* (2), *Kenichi* (2), *Kuni* (2), *Mitsuo* (2), *Seiko* (2), *Akira, Hajime, Hatsumi, Hideo, Hiroko*.

Shimada (362) Japanese: meaning 'island rice paddy', but not necessarily denoting an

island surrounded by water (see SHIMA). The surname is listed in the Shinsen shōjiroku and is found mostly in eastern Japan and the Ryūkyū Islands.
GIVEN NAMES Japanese 65%. *Akira* (4), *Junko* (3), *Koji* (3), *Masa* (3), *Takeo* (3), *Aki* (2), *Akiko* (2), *Hiroshi* (2), *Kenichi* (2), *Kiyoshi* (2), *Kyoko* (2), *Masao* (2).

Shimamoto (147) Japanese: meaning '(one who is) from the island'; it is found mostly in western Japan and the Ryūkyū Islands.
GIVEN NAMES Japanese 42%. *Tadao* (2), *Aiko*, *Eiji*, *Hanako*, *Hiko*, *Iwao*, *Keiji*, *Kenta*, *Kiyomi*, *Kosei*, *Maiko*, *Mamoru*.

Shimanek (113) Americanized spelling of Czech **Šimánek** (see SIMANEK).

Shimek (719) Americanized spelling of Czech and Croatian **Šimek** (see SIMEK), or perhaps of Polish **Szymek**, from a pet form of the personal name *Szymon* (see SIMON).

Shimel (187) **1.** Jewish (Ashkenazic): variant spelling of SCHIMMEL. **2.** Americanized spelling of German SCHIMMEL.

Shimer (600) **1.** Jewish (Ashkenazic): variant spelling of SCHIMMER. **2.** Respelling of German SCHIMMER.

Shimizu (855) Japanese: variously written; the characters are also read *Kiyomizu*, and both words mean 'pure water'. It is found throughout Japan, especially in the east. One family bearing this name is descended from Tokugawa Shigeyoshi (1745–1795), a son of the 9th Tokugawa Shōgun, Ieshige.
GIVEN NAMES Japanese 63%. *Hiroshi* (9), *Akira* (7), *Kenji* (5), *Yuji* (5), *Hiroyuki* (4), *Kiyoshi* (4), *Koichi* (4), *Koji* (4), *Takahiro* (4), *Hiro* (3), *Hiroko* (3), *Kazuko* (3).

Shimko (513) Belorussian and Jewish (eastern Ashkenazic): from a pet form of a personal name equivalent to SIMON (Yiddish *Shimen*).

Shimkus (429) Lithuanian (**Šimkus**): patronymic from Polish *Szimko* or Belorussian *Shimko*, pet forms of a personal name equivalent to SIMON.

Shimmel (249) **1.** Jewish (Ashkenazic): variant spelling of SCHIMMEL. **2.** Americanized spelling of German SCHIMMEL.

Shimmin (236) Irish: reduced Anglicized form of Gaelic **Mac Símín**, a patronymic from a Gaelic pet form of SIMON.

Shimoda (149) Japanese: meaning 'lower rice paddy'; it is found as a place name and surname throughout Japan.
GIVEN NAMES Japanese 53%. *Emiko* (2), *Masaharu* (2), *Osamu* (2), *Hideto*, *Hiroshi*, *Isamu*, *Jiro*, *Kaname*, *Kazuaki*, *Kazuya*, *Keiko*, *Kenji*.

Shimomura (133) Japanese: 'lower village'; the name is not common in Japan and is found mostly in the western part of the country. Some bearers pronounce it *Shitamura*.
GIVEN NAMES Japanese 47%. *Akihiro* (2), *Masaki* (2), *Takashi* (2), *Hiromu*, *Jiro*, *Kayo*, *Kazuhiro*, *Kei*, *Kenichi*, *Kenji*, *Kiyoko*, *Kumiko*.

Shimon (261) Jewish (Ashkenazic): variant of SIMON. Compare the Yiddish form *Shimen* and Polish form *Szymon*.
GIVEN NAMES Jewish 8%. *Baruch* (2), *Ilan* (2), *Aron*, *Itzchak*, *Menashe*, *Musya*, *Shimon*, *Shlomo*, *Ziva*.

Shimp (698) Perhaps an Americanized form of German **Schimpp**, a variant of SCHIMPF.

Shin (3453) Korean: there are three Chinese characters for the Shin surname. Between these three characters, there are five different clans. Each Shin clan descends from a different founding ancestor. One of the Shin clans traces its origins to China. Members of the various Shin clans can be found throughout the Korean peninsula.
GIVEN NAMES Korean 64%. *Young* (69), *Hyun* (51), *Yong* (39), *Dong* (35), *Sang* (33), *Jae* (25), *Kwang* (22), *Jung* (21), *Kyung* (18), *Sung* (18), *Jong* (15), *Chang* (13), *Myung* (12), *Chong* (11), *Chung* (7), *Min* (7), *Moon* (6), *Chul* (5), *Dae* (5), *Dong Hoon* (5), *Myong* (5), *Sook* (5), *Byung* (4), *Dong Soo* (4).

Shinabarger (129) Probably an altered form of German **Schöneberger** (see SCHOENENBERGER).

Shinaberry (144) Possibly an Americanized spelling of Jewish SCHEINBERG or German **Schöneberg**, a habitational name from any of several places so named in Germany and also in Switzerland.

Shinabery (102) See SHINABERRY.

Shinall (228) Origin unidentified. Perhaps an Americanized spelling of French CHENAULT.

Shinault (461) Americanized spelling of French CHENAULT.

Shindel (119) Variant of SCHINDEL.
GIVEN NAMES Russian 7%; Jewish 5%. *Matvey* (2), *Dmitry*, *Yevgenia*; *Yakov* (2).

Shinder (123) Jewish (eastern Ashkenazic): occupational name from Yiddish *shinder* 'skinner', 'flayer'.
GIVEN NAMES Jewish 14%; Russian 10%; Jewish Biblical 4%. *Aron*, *Genya*, *Ilya*, *Irina*, *Sol*, *Yakov*, *Zakhary*; *Anatoliy*, *Boris*, *Grigoriy*, *Igor*, *Iosif*, *Leya*.

Shindle (155) Americanized spelling of SCHINDEL.

Shindledecker (145) Americanized spelling of German **Schindeldecker**, an occupational name for a roofer, composed of Middle High German *schindel* 'shingle', 'wooden tile' + an agent derivative of *decken* 'to cover (a building)', 'to roof'.

Shindler (391) **1.** Jewish (Ashkenazic): variant of SCHINDLER. **2.** Americanized spelling of German SCHINDLER.
GIVEN NAMES Jewish 7%; German 4%. *Shmuel* (3), *Yitzchok* (2), *Bezalel*, *Ilanit*, *Isadore*, *Miriam*; *Kurt* (3), *Gerd* (2).

Shine (2014) **1.** Irish: reduced Anglicized form of Gaelic **Ó Seighin** 'descendant of *Seighin*', possibly a derivative of *séaghainn* 'accomplished'. **2.** English: nickname from Middle English *schene* 'beautiful' (Old

English *scīene*). **3.** Americanized form of Ashkenazic Jewish or German SCHEIN.

Shiner (774) **1.** English: unexplained. **2.** Americanized spelling of SCHEINER.

Shing (106) **1.** Chinese 盛: variant of SHENG. **2.** Chinese 成: variant of CHENG 3.
GIVEN NAMES Chinese 20%. *Chin*, *Chuen*, *Chun*, *Chung Yee*, *Ho*, *Shih*, *Yon*, *Yuen*.

Shingle (127) Possibly a translation of SCHINDEL 1.

Shingledecker (216) Americanized form of German **Schindeldecker** (see SHINDLEDECKER).
GIVEN NAME German 4%. *Kurt* (3).

Shingler (456) English: occupational name for someone who laid wooden tiles (shingles) on roofs, from an agent derivative of Middle English *schingle* 'shingle'.

Shingleton (620) English: probably a late medieval variant of SINGLETON.

Shinholster (119) an Americanized form of German **Schönholzer**, a habitational name from a place called Schönholz near Eberswalde, also one near Berlin.

Shinkle (695) Americanized spelling of SCHINKEL.

Shinn (3179) English: metonymic occupational name for a SKINNER, from Old English *scinn*, Middle English *shin* 'hide', 'pelt'. In Middle English this word was replaced by the Norse equivalent, *skinn*.

Shinneman (128) Possibly an Americanized spelling of German **Schienemann**, a variant of **Schönemann** (see SCHOENEMANN).

Shinners (248) Irish (of English origin): probably an altered form of SKINNER.
GIVEN NAME Irish 4%. *Seamus*.

Shinnick (283) Irish (Cork): **1.** reduced Anglicized form of Gaelic **Mac an tSionnaigh** 'son of the fox', from *sionnach*, presumably applied as a nickname. This name is often translated as FOX. **2.** according to Woulfe, a reduced Anglicized form of **Ó Sionaigh**, a variant of **Ó Seanaigh** (whence **Shanny**) 'descendant of *Seanach*', from a personal name meaning 'old', 'wise'. However, it was understood as **Ó Sionnaigh** 'descendant of fox' and often translated as FOX in Connacht.

Shinohara (102) Japanese: 'plain of bamboo grass'; the name is not common in Japan and is found mostly in the eastern part of the country and in the Ryūkyū Islands.
GIVEN NAMES Japanese 80%. *Yutaka* (4), *Noriyuki* (2), *Takumi* (2), *Yoshio* (2), *Atsuko*, *Chiharu*, *Eiji*, *Fusae*, *Haruki*, *Hidetoshi*, *Hisao*, *Kazuhiko*.

Shinpaugh (103) Perhaps a much altered form of German **Schönbach**, a habitational name from any of at least 13 places so named in Germany and Austria.

Shinsato (112) Japanese (Ryūkyū Islands): meaning 'new village'.
GIVEN NAMES Japanese 39%. *Minoru* (2), *Yoshio* (2), *Fusako*, *Haruo*, *Hisao*, *Isao*,

Kame, Katsumi, Kenzo, Kiyoshi, Kosei, Masao.

Shinsky (196) Jewish (eastern Ashkenazic): unexplained.

Shintani (104) Japanese: an alternative pronunciation of the name ARAYA or **Aratani**, meaning 'new valley', found mostly in western Japan, where it is also pronounced *Niitani* by some bearers.
GIVEN NAMES Japanese 52%. *Koji* (2), *Akira, Hajime, Hidekazu, Hiroyuki, Iwao, Kazumi, Kazuo, Keiko, Kiyoshi, Masaichi, Masanobu.*

Shipe (988) Possibly an Americanized spelling of German SCHEIB.

Shipes (225) American variant of German SHIPE.

Shipler (110) Possibly English: unexplained.

Shiplett (183) Origin unidentified.

Shipley (7330) English: habitational name from any of the various places, for example in Derbyshire, County Durham, Northumberland, Shropshire, Sussex, and West Yorkshire, so called from Old English *scēap, scīp* 'sheep' + *lēah* 'wood', 'clearing'.

Shipman (5371) English: **1.** occupational name for a shepherd, Middle English *schepman* (literally 'sheep man'). **2.** occupational name for a mariner, or occasionally perhaps for a boatbuilder, Middle English *schipman* (literally 'ship man').

Shipp (3839) English (mainly East Anglia): metonymic occupational name for a boatbuilder or a mariner, from Middle English *ship* 'ship'.

Shippee (522) Variant of English SHIPPEY.

Shippen (175) English: habitational name from any of various places named from Old English *scypen, scipen* 'cattleshed', such as Shippen in West Yorkshire and Shippon in Berkshire, or a topographic name derived directly from the vocabulary word. In some cases it may originally have been acquired as a metonymic occupational name for a cowman, who in medieval times would often have lived in the same building as his animals.
FOREBEARS Born in Methley, Yorkshire, England, in 1639, Edward Shippen emigrated to Boston, MA, in 1668. He joined the Society of Friends and moved his family and business to Philadelphia in about 1694 to avoid religious persecution, eventually becoming mayor of Philadelphia, where his sons and grandsons continued to be prominent.

Shipper (200) Jewish (Ashkenazic): variant spelling of SCHIPPER.

Shippey (366) English: from Old English *scēap, scīp* 'sheep' + *ēg* 'island' or *(ge)hæg* 'enclosure'; a topographic name for an island with sheep on it (which might be no more than a piece of raised dry ground surrounded by wet, low-lying land), or an enclosure where sheep were kept.

Shipps (234) English: metonymic name for a shipbuilder (see SHIPP).

Shippy (553) English: variant spelling of SHIPPEY.

Shipton (331) English: habitational name from any of the various places, for example in Dorset, Glloucestershire, Hampshire, Oxfordshire, and Shropshire, so called from Old English *scēap, scīp* 'sheep' + *tūn* 'enclosure', 'settlement'.

Shipwash (121) English: topographic name for someone who lived close to a sheepwash, Middle English *shepewassh* (Old English *scēapwæsce*), or a habitational name from a place named with this word, for example Sheepwash in Devon and Northumberland, or Sheepwash Farm in Nuthurst, Sussex.

Shira (276) **1.** Scottish and northern English: Americanized spelling of SHEARER. **2.** Jewish (Israeli): modern Hebrew name from a Hebrew word meaning 'song'.

Shirah (502) **1.** English and Scottish: Americanized spelling of SHEARER. **2.** Jewish (Israeli): variant of SHIRA.

Shirai (116) Japanese: 'white well', found mostly in eastern Japan.
GIVEN NAMES Japanese 64%. *Eiji* (2), *Takeshi* (2), *Akira, Atsuo, Atsushi, Hiro, Hiroko, Hiromi, Hiromichi, Isami, Junji, Junko.*

Shiraishi (186) Japanese: meaning 'white rock'; the surname is found mostly in west-central Japan and the island of Shikoku. It is also a habitational name from a place in Rikuchū (now Iwate prefecture).
GIVEN NAMES Japanese 62%. *Atsushi* (2), *Hiroshi* (2), *Kenichi* (2), *Minoru* (2), *Ryoichi* (2), *Seiji* (2), *Toru* (2), *Yoko* (2), *Yuji* (2), *Akio, Goro, Hayato.*

Shiraki (109) Japanese: meaning 'white tree'; the surname is found mostly in western Japan. It is listed in the Shinsen shōjiroku.
GIVEN NAMES Japanese 43%. *Mitsuru* (2), *Satoshi* (2), *Takeo* (2), *Akiko, Eriko, Itsuo, Katsuyuki, Kenichi, Masaki, Mikako, Ryoji, Shoji.*

Shirar (120) Scottish and northern English: variant of SHEARER.

Shirazi (230) Iranian: from the Persian family name *Shirāzī*, denoting a descendant of someone from the Iranian city of Shiraz.
GIVEN NAMES Muslim 76%. *Mehdi* (5), *Ahmad* (4), *Ali* (4), *Masoud* (4), *Syed* (4), *Bijan* (3), *Hadi* (3), *Haider* (3), *Mehrdad* (3), *Bahram* (2), *Elham* (2), *Hamid* (2).

Shircliff (161) English: habitational name from Shirecliff in Sheffield, South Yorkshire.

Shire (375) English and Irish (County Limerick; of English origin): from Old English *scīr*, Middle English *s(c)hire* 'shire', perhaps a topographic name for someone who lived by the meeting place of a shire.

Shireman (504) English: from Middle English *schireman*, Old English *scīrman*,

literally 'shire man'. This was a name for a sherriff or other administrative official of a county; later it came to mean 'bailiff' or 'steward'.

Shirer (300) **1.** Scottish and northern English: variant of SHEARER. **2.** Jewish (eastern Ashkenazic): occupational name for a barber, a Yiddish dialect variant of SHERER 2.

Shires (774) English (Yorkshire): patronymic from SHEAR.

Shirey (2204) Irish: **1.** variant of **Shirra**, a reduced Anglicized form of **Mac Séartha** 'son of Geoffrey' (see SHERRY). **2.** in the midlands and north, possibly an Anglicized form of Gaelic **Ó Siochfhradha** (see SUGRUE).

Shirilla (102) Origin unidentified. Perhaps an altered form of Italian CHIRILLO.

Shiring (111) Probably a variant of English **Shearing**, a Norfolk name, itself a variant of SHERRIN.

Shirk (2337) Possibly an Americanized spelling of German **Scherk**, probably of eastern German or Slavic origin.

Shirkey (460) Irish: variant of SHARKEY.

Shirley (9602) English: habitational name from any of various places, for example in Derbyshire, Hampshire, Surrey, and the West Midlands, all so called from Old English *scīr* 'bright' + *lēah* 'wood', 'clearing'.
FOREBEARS William Shirley (1694–1771) was born in Sussex, England, and came to MA in 1731. He rose in the colonial service, was appointed governor in 1741, and was responsible for the British capture of the French fortress of Louisburg, Cape Breton Island, in 1745.

Shiro (102) Japanese: 'castle'; another pronunciation of the character for the surname **Jō** (see JO).
GIVEN NAMES Japanese 11%. *Joji, Kiyo, Mamoru, Naoki, Setsuko.*

Shiroma (327) Japanese: apparently a Japanized version of the Okinawan names **Gushikuma** and **Gusukuma**, which have the same meaning, '(one who lives) between the castles'. It is rare in Japan but more common in the Ryūkyū islands.
GIVEN NAMES Japanese 27%. *Shigeru* (2), *Sumie* (2), *Takeo* (2), *Akira, Ayumi, Hideki, Hideo, Isamu, Jiro, Kiyoko, Koichi, Kosei.*

Shirrell (151) English: variant of SHERRELL.

Shirts (120) **1.** Americanized spelling of German SCHERTZ. **2.** Possibly a variant of English **Shirt**, a topographic name for someone who lived on a detached piece of land, Middle English *shurte*, from Old English *scyrte* 'skirt', 'cut off piece'.

Shishido (188) Japanese: habitational name taken from a district in Hitachi (now Ibaraki prefecture), written with a variant character for 'flesh' and 'door'. It is found mostly in northeastern Japan.
GIVEN NAMES Japanese 41%. *Hiroshi* (3), *Yoshio* (3), *Mamoru* (2), *Rikio* (2), *Akira,*

Fujie, Hakaru, Haruo, Hidehiro, Hiroaki, Ichio, Ichiro.

Shisler (522) Americanized spelling of SCHISSLER.

Shissler (140) Americanized spelling of SCHISSLER.

Shiu (184) **1.** Chinese 邵: variant of SHAO. **2.** Chinese 蕭: variant of XIAO 2.
GIVEN NAMES Chinese 25%. *Chan, Chi, Chih, Guo Jun, Hing, Hok, Hon, Kuan, Kwai, Leung, Mei, Ming; Cho, Kwok Fai, Nam, Pak, Tun, Yuet.*

Shivar (121) Probably an American variant of English and Irish CHIVERS.

Shive (641) Possibly an Americanized spelling of Dutch **Schive**, unexplained.

Shiveley (203) Variant of SHIVELY.

Shively (2871) Americanized spelling of Swiss German **Schäublin** or **Scheublein**, nicknames for a thin or skinny person, from Middle High German *shoup* '(straw) bundle' + the diminutive suffix *-lein, -lin*.

Shiver (1517) American variant of English and Irish CHIVERS.

Shiverdecker (174) Americanized form of German **Schieferdecker**, an occupational name for a slater, from Middle High German *schīver* 'piece of wood or stone', 'slate' + the agent derivative of *decken* 'to lay a roof'.

Shivers (2053) Irish (County Tyrone): variant of CHIVERS.

Shives (539) Scottish (Aberdeen): variant of **Shivas**, a habitational name from the barony of Shivas in the parish of Tarves, Aberdeenshire.

Shivley (204) Variant of SHIVELY.

Shkolnik (153) Jewish (eastern Ashkenazic): occupational name from Polish *szkolnik*, Belorussian *shkolnik* 'sexton in a synagogue'.
GIVEN NAMES Russian 30%; Jewish 25%; Jewish Biblical 4%. *Boris* (5), *Raisa* (3), *Aleksandr* (2), *Dmitry* (2), *Grigory* (2), *Leonid* (2), *Mikhail* (2), *Oleg* (2), *Yefim* (2), *Ayzik, Betya, Daniil; Isaak* (2), *Naum* (2), *Rina* (2), *Elik, Esfir, Faina, Fishel, Genya, Inna, Irina, Isadore, Moisey.*

Shnayder (118) Jewish (eastern Ashkenazic): variant spelling, transliterated from Russian, of SCHNEIDER.
GIVEN NAMES Russian 40%; Jewish 34%; Czech and Slovak 6%. *Mikhail* (9), *Boris* (6), *Igor* (5), *Vladimir* (4), *Anatoly* (2), *Lev* (2), *Zhanna* (2), *Aleksandr, Anatoliy, Dmitry, Fanya, Foma; Aron* (3), *Faina* (2), *Syoma* (2), *Bentsion, Bronya, Elik, Ilya, Irina, Josif, Liba, Molka, Shmuel; Pavel* (2), *Petr* (2).

Shoaf (1331) Possibly an Americanized form of German **Schauf(f)**, from the Swabian for 'sheep', hence probably a metonymic occupational name for a shepherd or a nickname for someone thought to resemble a sheep in some way. Compare SHOAFF.

Shoaff (238) See SHOAF.

Shobe (627) Americanized spelling of German and Swiss German SCHAUB or of its variant spelling **Schöbe**.

Shober (309) Americanized spelling of German SCHOBER or Slovenian **Šober** (see SOBER 2).

Shoberg (200) Probably an Americanized spelling of Swedish **Sjöberg**, an ornamental name composed of the elements *sjö* 'sea' + *berg* 'hill'.
GIVEN NAMES Scandinavian 6%. *Iver* (2), *Erik, Kerstin.*

Shobert (153) Americanized spelling of German SCHOBERT.

Shock (1143) **1.** English: from Middle English *schock*, 'shock', 'group of sheaves (of grain)', either a metonymic occupational name for someone who arranged sheaves in a shock, or a descriptive nickname for someone whose hair stood up on end, thus resembling a shock of sheaves. **2.** Americanized spelling of German SCHOCK.

Shockey (1587) Americanized form of Dutch and North German SCHAAKE.

Shocklee (150) Variant of SHOCKLEY.

Shockley (4455) **1.** English: of uncertain origin. Most probably a habitational name from Shocklach in Cheshire, named in Old English with *sceocca* 'goblin', 'evil spirit' + *lœcc* 'boggy stream'. In the 17th century, the name was most common in Buckinghamshire, England. **2.** Perhaps also an Americanized form of Swiss German **Schoechli**, a topographic name meaning 'barn', from a diminutive of SCHOCH.
FOREBEARS Richard Shockley (b. about 1634, probably in Buckinghamshire, England) arrived in MD in 1671.

Shockney (108) Origin unidentified.

Shoda (143) Japanese (**Shōda**): 'small rice paddy'; an alternative pronunciation of the name ODA. It is not common in Japan.
GIVEN NAMES Japanese 25%. *Akira, Hiromi, Hitoshi, Keiji, Keiko, Kenji, Kojiro, Masafumi, Masanobu, Masao, Mitsuru, Naohiro.*

Shoe (349) **1.** English: from Middle English *shoe* 'shoe' (Old English *scōh*), applied as a metonymic occupational name for a shoemaker or possibly a topographic name for someone who lived on a shoe-shaped piece of land. **2.** Translation of SCHUH.

Shoemake (1410) Americanized variant of Dutch SCHOEMAKER or German **Schumach**, the latter a variant of SCHUMACHER.

Shoemaker (11832) Translation of Dutch SCHOEMAKER or German and Jewish SCHUMACHER.

Shoemate (154) Americanized form of southern French **de la Chaumette** (see SHUMATE).

Shoen (247) Americanized spelling of German or Ashkenazic Jewish *Schön* or SCHOEN.

Shoenberger (119) Americanized spelling of *Schönberger* or SCHOENBERGER.

Shoener (131) Americanized spelling of German **Schöner** or SCHOENER.

Shoenfelt (117) Americanized spelling of German **Schönfeld** (see SCHOENFELD).

Shoesmith (123) English (Yorkshire): occupational name for a blacksmith who specialized in shoeing horses, from Middle English *schosmith* 'farrier' (composed of words meaning 'shoe' and 'smith').

Shoff (609) Americanized spelling of German SCHOFF.

Shoffner (997) Americanized form of German SCHAFFNER.

Shoffstall (107) Americanized spelling of German **Schafstall**, an occupational name for a sheep breeder, from Middle High German *schāf* 'sheep' + *stal* 'stable'.

Shofner (736) Americanized spelling of German SCHAFFNER.

Shogren (470) Americanized spelling of Swedish **Sjögren**, an ornamental name composed of the elements *sjö* 'sea' + *gren* 'branch'.
GIVEN NAMES Scandinavian 4%. *Arlys, Bjorn.*

Shoji (147) Japanese (**Shōji**): '(one who lives near a) small road'. The name is not common in Japan.
GIVEN NAMES Japanese 60%. *Akio* (2), *Eriko* (2), *Hiromu* (2), *Aoi, Chizuko, Daisuke, Etsuko, Fujio, Hiroshi, Hiroto, Hitoshi, Isao.*

Sholar (578) Anglicized spelling of Slovenian **Šolar**, status name for an educated person or a teacher, someone in charge of a school, from an agent derivative of *šola* 'school'.

Sholes (448) Possibly a form representing an altered pronunciation of SCHOLES.

Sholl (427) **1.** Cornish: of uncertain origin. It may be a topographic name from Cornish *is* 'under' + *hall* 'moor'. **2.** Americanized spelling of German SCHOLL.

Shollenberger (339) Americanized spelling of German SCHOLLENBERGER.

Sholley (137) Americanized spelling of German SCHOLLE.

Sholly (256) Americanized spelling of German SCHOLLE.

Sholtis (268) **1.** Americanized spelling of Dutch and German SCHOLTES (see SCHULTZ). **2.** Americanized spelling of Hungarian **Soltész** (see SOLTESZ).

Sholty (120) Americanized spelling of North German **Scholte**, an occupational name for someone who gave out obligations or duties, Middle Low German *schulte, schulthête*.

Sholtz (125) Americanized spelling of SCHOLZ.

Shomaker (240) Americanized spelling of Dutch SCHOEMAKER and German and Jewish SCHUMACHER.

Shomo (301) Origin unidentified.

Shomper (116) Origin unidentified.

Shon (241) **1.** English: unexplained. **2.** Jewish (Ashkenazic): variant of SCHOEN. **3.** Korean: variant of SON.
GIVEN NAMES Korean 43%. *Chang* (7), *Chan* (4), *Young* (4), *Moo* (3), *Kwang* (2), *Sung* (2), *Won* (2), *Young Kyu* (2), *Boon, Chang Hee, Chang Suk, Chang Young, Chin, Eunjung*; *Byung, Chang Sik, Gyeong, Hae, In Sung, Jinwoo, Jung Ho, Kyunghee, Namsik, Seong*.

Shone (246) Welsh: from the personal name *Siôn* (see JOHN), a later formation than EVAN, which is likewise from Latin *Johannes*.

Shong (122) Origin unidentified.

Shonk (494) **1.** Americanized spelling of Czech **Šonk**, a variant of **Šonka** (see SHONKA). **2.** Variant of German SCHANK.

Shonka (181) Americanized spelling of Czech **Šonka**, a nickname for a thrifty or parsimonious person, from a derivative of the Old Czech adjective *šonit* 'frugal', 'tightfisted'.

Shonkwiler (260) Americanized spelling of German **Schankweiler**, probably a habitational name, of unidentified origin.

Shontz (243) Variant of German SCHANTZ.

Shook (6017) Variant of German SCHUCK.

Shoop (1560) Americanized spelling of North German and Dutch **Schoop**, a metonymic occupational name for a maker of ladles, from Middle Low German *schope*, Middle Dutch *schoepe, schope, schuep* 'ladle'; in numerous cases, however, for German SCHUPP.

Shoopman (351) Dutch: occupational name for a shopkeeper.

Shooter (103) Variant of SHUTTER.

Shoots (111) Probably an Americanized spelling of German and Jewish SCHUTZ.

Shope (1537) Americanized form of North German or Dutch SCHOEPP.

Shoptaw (160) Origin unidentified.

Shoquist (117) Americanized form of Swedish SJOQUIST.

Shor (439) Jewish (Ashkenazic): from Hebrew *shor* 'ox', perhaps taken by bearers of the personal name JOSEPH because the Biblical character of this name is compared to an ox in Deuteronomy 33:17: 'His glory is like the firstling of his bullock'.
GIVEN NAMES Jewish 16%; Russian 10%. *Ilya* (3), *Pinchas* (3), *Yakov* (3), *Amnon, Arie, Chaya, Feige, Garik, Itzhak, Josif, Mariya, Mort*; *Boris* (4), *Aleksandr* (2), *Igor* (2), *Mikhail* (2), *Yefim* (2), *Anatoliy, Fanya, Ikhil, Iosif, Oleg, Raisa, Semyon*.

Shorb (354) Possibly an altered spelling of German **Schorp**, a nickname from Middle High German *schorp(e)*, Middle Low German *schorpie* 'scorpion', 'tortoise'.

Shore (4473) **1.** English: topographic name for someone who lived by the seashore, Middle English *schore*. **2.** English: topographic name for someone who lived on or by a bank or steep slope, Old English *scora*. There are minor places named with this word in Lancashire and West Yorkshire, and the surname may also be a habitational name from these. **3.** Americanized spelling of Ashkenazic Jewish S(c)hor(r) or Szor, variants of SCHAUER.

Shores (2728) English: variant of SHORE 1 and 2.

Shorette (128) Variant of French CHARETTE.

Shorey (811) English: topographic name for someone who lived on an island lying close to shore, from Middle English *schore* 'shore' + *eye* 'island'.

Shorkey (165) Americanized spelling of French Canadian CHARTIER.
FOREBEARS The Shorkey-Chartier (Pominville) family in Canada and the U.S. can trace their ancestry back to the 14th-century poet and diplomat Alain Chartier and beyond.

Shorr (373) Jewish (Ashkenazic): variant of SHOR.
GIVEN NAMES Jewish 4%; German 4%. *Eran*; *Udi* (2), *Erwin*.

Shorrock (122) English: variant of SHARROCK.

Short (20128) **1.** English: nickname from Middle English *schort* 'short'. **2.** Scottish and northern Irish: reduced Anglicized form of Gaelic **Mac an Gheairr, Mac an Ghirr** 'son of the short man' (see McGIRR).

Shortall (242) Anglo-Irish: possibly a nickname from Old English *scort hals* 'short neck'. The name was taken to Ireland in the 13th century, where it has been Gaelicized as **Soirtéil**.
GIVEN NAMES Irish 5%. *Aileen, Liam*.

Shortell (283) Irish: re-Anglicized form of Gaelic **Seartal, Soirtéil**, Gaelicized forms of the English surname **Shorthals**. This was taken to Ireland in the reign of King Edward I. It was originally a nickname from Middle English *schort* 'short' + *halse* 'neck'.

Shorten (307) Irish: Anglicized form of Gaelic **Seartáin**, a variant of **Soirtéil** (see SHORTELL).

Shorter (2025) English: from the comparative form of Middle English *schort* 'short', hence a distinguishing nickname for the shorter of two closely associated people with the same personal name (for example, members of the same household).

Shortino (113) Americanized spelling of Italian (Sicily) SCIORTINO, a habitational name from Sortino in Siracusa, or from a diminutive of Sicilian *sciorta, sciurta* 'watchman', 'city guard' (a word of Arabic origin).
GIVEN NAMES Italian 16%. *Cosimo* (2), *Mario* (2), *Cosmo, Sal*.

Shortridge (783) English (Devon): habitational name from either of two places so named in Devon.

Shorts (602) Variant of English SHORT.

Shortsleeve (143) Literal translation of French COURTEMANCHE.

Shortt (1009) English and Scottish (now mainly found in Ireland): variant spelling of SHORT.

Shorty (116) Origin unidentified. Possibly a variant of English SHORT or SHORTER.

Shortz (106) German: Americanized spelling of SCHARTZ or SCHURZ.
GIVEN NAME German 7%. *Otto* (2).

Shostak (185) Jewish (eastern Ashkenazic), Ukrainian, and Belorussian: nickname from Ukrainian *shostak*, Belorussian *shastak* 'someone with a six-fingered hand'. Compare Polish SZOSTAK.
GIVEN NAMES Jewish 4%; Russian 4%. *Irina, Moisey*; *Aleksandr, Kirill, Vasiliy*.

Shott (444) English: topographic name for someone who lived by a projecting piece of land, from Old English *scēat*, or a steep slope, from an unattested Old English *scēot*.

Shotton (126) English (mainly northeastern): habitational name from places so called in County Durham and Northumberland. The former is named with an unattested Old English *scēot* 'steep slope' + Old English *tūn* 'enclosure', 'settlement', the latter with Old English *scota*, genitive plural of *scot* 'Scot' + *dūn* 'hill'. The surname may also have been a topographic name for someone who lived by an enclosure on a slope.

Shotts (610) Probably a variant of SHOTT.

Shotwell (1297) Possibly of English origin, a habitational name from a lost or unidentified place.

Shough (218) Possibly an Americanized spelling of SCHAU or SCHOCH.

Shoulders (754) **1.** English (mainly Sussex): from Middle English *schulder* 'shoulder'; a nickname for someone with exceptionally broad shoulders or some deformity or other peculiarity of the shoulders. **2.** Americanized form of Slovenian **Šolar** (see SHOLAR).

Shoults (465) Americanized spelling of Dutch or German SCHULZ.

Shoultz (402) Americanized spelling of Dutch or German SCHULZ.

Shoun (330) perhaps an Americanized spelling of German **Schön** (see SCHOEN), or of **Schaun**, probably a habitational name for somone living at a place called Schauen near Wernigerode in the Harz mountains.

Shoup (2045) Americanized spelling of Dutch **Schoup**, a metonymic occupational name for a maker of ladles, from Middle Dutch *schoepe, schope, schuep* 'ladle'.

Shoupe (198) Probably an Americanized spelling of Dutch **Schouppe**, a variant of **Schoup** (see SHOUP).

Shouse (1545) Americanized spelling of German SCHAUSS.

Shovan (110) Origin unidentified. Perhaps an Americanized spelling of French CHAUVIN.

Shove (218) **1.** Variant of Dutch SCHAVE. **2.** English: nickname from Middle English *schove*, probably from Old English *scufa*, a derivative of *scūfan* 'to thrust or push'.

Shover (499) Americanized form of Dutch **de Schouwer**, an occupational name from *schouwer* 'inspector (of weights and measures)'.

Shovlin (237) Irish: variant of SHEVLIN.

Show (305) **1.** English (Lancashire): unexplained. **2.** Perhaps an Americanized spelling of SCHAU.

Showalter (3268) Americanized spelling of German SCHOWALTER.

Showell (274) English (West Midlands): from Middle English *schovel* 'shovel', hence a metonymic occupational name for a maker or seller of shovels, or for someone who regularly used a shovel in his work.

Showen (129) Possibly an altered form of Dutch **van Schouwen**, a habitational name for someone from Schouwen in Zeeland.

Showerman (102) Americanized spelling of German **Schauerman**, an occupational name for an officially designated assayer (of coins, etc.), from Middle High German *schouwer*.

Showers (1629) English: nickname from Middle English *shouere* 'pusher', an agent derivative of Old English *scūfan* 'to thrust or push'.

Showman (368) **1.** English: unexplained. **2.** Possibly an Americanized spelling of German **Schaumann** (see SCHAUMAN).

Shown (321) probably an altered spelling of German **Schön** or **Schaun** (see SCHOEN).

Shows (1075) Perhaps an Americanized spelling of German SCHAUS.

Shrader (2561) Americanized spelling of German SCHRADER.

Shrager (128) Jewish (Ashkenazic): variant spelling of SCHRAGER.
GIVEN NAMES Jewish 10%. *Ari* (2), *Hyman*, *Isadore*.

Shrake (220) Perhaps an Americanized form of German SCHRECK.

Shramek (169) Americanized spelling of Jewish SCHRAMEK.

Shrauger (101) Americanized spelling of German SCHRAGER.

Shrawder (134) Americanized spelling of North German SCHRADER (see SCHROEDER).

Shreck (174) Americanized spelling of German SCHRECK.
GIVEN NAMES French 4%. *Collette*, *Laure*.

Shreckengost (116) Variant spelling of German SCHRECKENGOST.

Shreeve (291) English (mainly East Anglia): variant of SHREVE.

Shreeves (113) English (Bedfordshire): patronymic from SHREEVE.

Shreffler (484) Americanized spelling of German SCHREFFLER.

Shreiner (256) Altered spelling of German SCHREINER.

Shrestha (201) Hindu name from Sanskrit *śreṣṭha* 'greatest', found among people from Nepal.
GIVEN NAMES Indian 86%. *Ganesh* (4), *Ganga* (4), *Rajendra* (4), *Rajesh* (4), *Sanjay* (4), *Arun* (3), *Suman* (3), *Anil* (2), *Anjali* (2), *Chandra* (2), *Indira* (2), *Kishore* (2).

Shreve (2354) English: occupational name for a sheriff, from Middle English *schiref*, *shreeve*, *shryve* 'sheriff', from Old English *scīr* 'shire', 'administrative district' + *(ge)rēfa* 'reeve' (see REEVE). In some cases it may have arisen from a nickname.

Shreves (413) English: variant of SHREEVES.

Shrewsberry (224) English: variant spelling of SHREWSBURY.

Shrewsbury (1020) English: habitational name from Shrewsbury in Shropshire, which is named from an ancient district name derived from Old English *scrobb* 'scrub', 'brushwood', + Old English *byrig*, dative case of *burh* 'fortified place'.

Shriber (172) Americanized spelling of German and Jewish SCHREIBER.

Shrider (192) Americanized form of Dutch **de Schreider**, a variant of SCHREYER.

Shrier (149) Americanized form of German SCHREIER.

Shrieves (139) English: variant of SHREEVES.

Shrimplin (118) English: unexplained.

Shriner (756) Americanized spelling of German and Jewish SCHREINER.

Shriver (2361) Americanized spelling of Dutch SCHRIEVER.

Shrock (536) Americanized spelling of German SCHROCK.

Shrode (283) Americanized form of German **Schrode**, a nickname for a loutish person, from Middle High German *schrōt(e)* 'stick', 'block', 'log'.

Shroff (243) **1.** Indian (Gujarat and Bombay city): Hindu (Vania) and Parsi name from Gujarati *sǝraf* 'banker', 'money-changer', from Arabic *ṣarrāf*. There has probably been some confusion with Arabic *sharīf* 'noble' and *sharāfat* 'nobility', which have also been borrowed into Hindi and other modern Indian languages. *Shroff* is used as a vocabulary word in Indian English to denote a banker or money changer. **2.** English: although this is for the most part an Indian name (see 1 above), it was already well established in England in the 19th century (see below), and may also be of English origin. If it is not Indian, the etymology is unknown.
GIVEN NAMES Indian 68%. *Vijay* (4), *Ashwin* (3), *Mahesh* (3), *Nilesh* (3), *Anil* (2), *Ashish* (2), *Girish* (2), *Hitesh* (2), *Manish* (2), *Zubin* (2), *Ajay*, *Aparna*.

Shroll (103) English: unexplained; possibly an Anglicized form of the German name **Schroll**, a nickname for a coarse person,

from Middle High German *schrolle* 'lump', 'clod'

Shropshire (1479) English: regional name from the county of Shropshire, on the western border of England with Wales.

Shrout (729) Probably an Americanized form of German SCHRAUTH.

Shroyer (1525) Pennsylvania German variant of SCHREIER. Compare SCHROYER.

Shrum (1787) Americanized spelling of German SCHRUM.

Shryock (606) Possibly an Americanized form of German **Schrei(j)äck**, **Schreijöck**, a nickname for a noisy person, from a dialect word for a jay, which began as a compound of Middle High German *schrien* 'to cry' + a pet form of the personal name JACOB.

Shu (510) **1.** Chinese 舒: from this character used as part of a personal name. Gao Yao, a great-grandson of the legendary emperor Zhuan Xu, was a minister under the model emperors Yao and Shun in the 23rd century BC. He is famous for being the first to introduce laws for the repression of crime. A descendant of his had Shu as part of one of his names; this character was adopted by some later descendants as their surname. **2.** Chinese: see XU.
GIVEN NAMES Chinese 26%. *Xin* (3), *Chi Ming* (2), *Chi-Man* (2), *Li Li* (2), *Li Min* (2), *Wei* (2), *Yee* (2), *Yonghui* (2), *Baolin*, *Bin*, *Chi*, *Chih-Cheng*.

Shuart (219) **1.** Apparently an English habitational name from a place so called in Kent. **2.** Possibly an altered spelling of French **Chuart**, from *choe*, *choue* 'jackdaw' + the pejorative suffix -*ard*.
GIVEN NAME German 4%. *Kurt*.

Shub (152) Jewish (eastern Ashkenazic): occupational name from an acronym of Hebrew *šoḥēṭ ubōdēq* 'approved ritual slaughterer'.
GIVEN NAMES Jewish 15%; Russian 14%. *Gersh*, *Inna*, *Zelik*; *Galina* (3), *Igor* (2), *Mikhail* (2), *Boris*, *Grigori*, *Leonid*, *Lev*, *Vladimir*, *Yelena*, *Yevgeniy*, *Zhanna*.

Shuba (135) Jewish (Ashkenazic): metonymic occupational name for a furrier, from Ukrainian and Belorussian *shuba* 'fur coat'.

Shubert (1475) **1.** Jewish (Ashkenazic): variant of SCHUBERT. **2.** Americanized spelling of German SCHUBERT.

Shubin (369) **1.** Russian and Jewish (from Belarus): from a derivative of SHUBA. **2.** Jewish (from Belarus): habitational name from Shubino in Belarus.
GIVEN NAMES Russian 4%. *Mikhail* (2), *Oleg* (2), *Boris*, *Fenya*, *Sergei*, *Valeriy*.

Shuck (1523) **1.** English (Worcestershire): of uncertain origin; perhaps a nickname from Middle English *schucke* 'devil', 'fiend'. **2.** Jewish (Ashkenazic): variant of SCHUCK. **3.** Americanized spelling of German SCHUCK.

Shuda (168) German: unexplained; possibly of Slavic origin.

Shue (1090) Americanized spelling of German SCHUH or SCHUE.

Shuey (1303) Perhaps an altered spelling of Dutch **Schuy** (see SHY).

Shufeldt (103) Americanized form of German SCHOENFELD.

Shufelt (515) Americanized form of German SCHOENFELD.

Shuff (672) Americanized spelling of German SCHUFF or SCHAFF.

Shuffield (348) Variant of English SHEFFIELD.

Shufflebarger (110) Americanized spelling of German (Rhineland) **Schaufelberger**, probably a habitational name for someone from any of several places called Schaufenberg.

Shuffler (194) Possibly an Americanized form of German SCHAUFLER.

Shuford (1073) Origin unidentified. Perhaps an altered form of **Shefford**, an English habitational name from Shefford in Bedfordshire, or Great or East Shefford in Berkshire, all named with Old English *scēap* 'sheep' + *ford* 'ford'. Alternatively, it could be an Americanized form of French **Chuffard**, probably derived from the dialect word *chuffer* 'to call', and hence a nickname for a (town) crier.

Shugar (141) English (Dorset): variant spelling of SUGAR.

Shugars (277) Variant of English SUGAR.

Shugart (955) Americanized form of German **Schugard**, a variant of SCHUCHARDT.

Shugarts (124) Americanized form of German **Schugard**, a variant of SCHUCHARDT.

Shughart (205) Americanized form of German **Schugard**, a variant of SCHUCHARDT.

Shugrue (277) Irish: variant of SUGRUE.

Shuker (109) English (Shropshire): unexplained. Origin unidentified.

Shukis (112) Lithuanian (**Šukis**): of uncertain origin, perhaps from a derivative of *šuke* 'judgement' or *šukoti* 'comb'.

Shukla (377) Indian (northern states): Hindu (Brahman) name, from Sanskrit *šukla* 'white', 'bright', 'pure'. A *shukla* Brahman was supposed to take up only *shuklavritti* 'pure employment', i.e. maintenance derived from serving or begging from Brahmans only.

GIVEN NAMES Indian 93%. *Sanjay* (8), *Vinay* (5), *Amit* (4), *Pankaj* (4), *Rajiv* (4), *Ashish* (3), *Deepak* (3), *Dilip* (3), *Harshad* (3), *Jyoti* (3), *Ram* (3), *Shyam* (3).

Shular (218) Variant spelling of SHOLAR or (under Slavic influence) of Jewish SHULER.

Shuler (3715) **1.** Jewish (Ashkenazic): variant of SCHULER. **2.** Americanized spelling of German SCHULER. **3.** Americanized spelling of Slovenian **Šuler**, archaic spelling of **Šolar** (see SHOLAR).

Shulkin (139) Jewish (from Belarus): metronymic from the Yiddish female personal name *Shulke*, a pet form of the biblical Hebrew name *Shulamith*.

GIVEN NAMES Jewish 10%; Russian 9%. *Irina, Semen, Yakov, Yuzik; Mikhail* (2), *Aleksandr, Arkadiy, Boris, Leonid, Yefim.*

Shull (3762) Americanized spelling of German SCHULL.

Shulman (2320) Jewish (Ashkenazic): variant of SCHULMAN.

GIVEN NAMES Jewish 9%; Russian 4%. *Sol* (7), *Hyman* (6), *Yakov* (4), *Miriam* (3), *Ephraim* (2), *Golda* (2), *Moisey* (2), *Motti* (2), *Naum* (2), *Shmuel* (2), *Ari, Avi; Boris* (6), *Mikhail* (6), *Igor* (4), *Semyon* (4), *Leonid* (3), *Lev* (3), *Aleksandr* (2), *Vladimir* (2), *Yelena* (2), *Yury* (2), *Arkady, Dmitry.*

Shult (115) Americanized spelling of North German and Dutch SCHULTE.

Shultis (449) **1.** Americanized spelling of Dutch and German SCHOLTES (see SCHULTZ). **2.** Lithuanian spelling of German SCHOLTES (see SCHULTZ).

Shults (1618) Americanized spelling of German SCHULTZ, or a variant spelling of the Jewish name.

Shultz (6633) Americanized spelling of German SCHULTZ, or a variant spelling of the Jewish name.

Shum (515) **1.** English: unexplained. **2.** Jewish (Ashkenazic): variant spelling of SCHUM. **3.** Chinese 岑: (Pinyin *Cen*) this surname was derived from an area so named during the Zhou dynasty (1122–221 BC).

GIVEN NAMES Chinese 22%. *Wing* (9), *Kwok* (3), *Man* (3), *Shek* (3), *Chun* (2), *Kam Yin* (2), *Shu* (2), *Suet* (2), *Wing Kwong* (2), *Yuk* (2), *Cheng Hua, Chi Ming.*

Shumake (524) Altered form of German **Schumach**, a variant of SCHUMACHER.

Shumaker (3314) Americanized spelling of Dutch SCHOEMAKER or German SCHUMACHER.

Shuman (3527) **1.** Jewish (Ashkenazic): variant of SCHUMANN. **2.** Americanized spelling of German SCHUMANN.

Shumar (125) Origin unidentified. Compare SHUMARD.

Shumard (326) Origin unidentified. Possibly an Anglicized or Americanized form of French **Chaumard**, a nickname for a lazy person, from a derivative of Old French *caume* 'great heat'.

Shumate (3250) Americanized form of southern French **De la Chaumette**, a topographic name for someone who lived on a *chaumette*, a high, arid plateau with very little vegetation, derived from a diminutive of *chaume* 'bare land' (a specialized sense of Latin *calmus* 'calm', 'unruffled').

FOREBEARS Jean de la Chaumette, from Rochouard, France, became a wealthy colonist in Martinique and subsequently (1722) a tobacco planter in VA. In North America the name was changed to Shumate. See also DELASHMIT.

Shumpert (589) Americanized form of German SCHUMPERT.

Shumski (111) Jewish (eastern Ashkenazic): variant of SHUMSKY.

Shumsky (174) Jewish (eastern Ashkenazic): habitational name for someone from Shumsk in Ukraine or Shumskas in Lithuania.

GIVEN NAMES Jewish 5%; Russian 4%. *Shmul; Arkady, Grigory, Leonid, Yefim.*

Shumway (1896) English and Scottish: unexplained; possibly of French origin.

Shunk (511) Americanized spelling of German SCHUNK or SCHANK.

Shupe (2113) Possibly an Americanized spelling of SCHUPP or SCHUPPE.

Shupert (217) Americanized spelling of German **Schupert**, a variant of SCHUBERT.

Shuping (282) Americanized form of North German **Schüpping**, from Middle Low German *schuppinge* 'push', 'shove', hence a nickname for an aggressive person or a pusher.

Shupp (585) Americanized spelling of SCHUPP.

Shur (228) Jewish (Ashkenazic): variant of SCHOR.

GIVEN NAMES Jewish 15%; Russian 14%. *Ilya* (2), *Moisey* (2), *Avi, Blyuma, Esfir, Herzl, Isak, Moishe, Naum, Ophir, Sol; Boris* (3), *Leonid* (2), *Aleksandr, Dmitri, Grigoriy, Iosif, Lyuba, Lyudmila, Mikhail, Nicolai, Nikolay, Vasily.*

Shurden (142) Irish: reduced form of SHERIDAN.

Shure (264) Jewish (Ashkenazic): variant of SCHOR.

Shurley (271) English: variant spelling of SHIRLEY.

Shurman (109) **1.** Americanized spelling of German SCHUERMANN. **2.** Variant of English SHERMAN.

GIVEN NAMES German 5%. *Hans* (2), *Markus.*

Shurr (126) Jewish (Ashkenazic): variant of SHUR.

Shurtleff (813) English: variant of SHIRCLIFF.

Shurtliff (171) English: variant of SHIRCLIFF.

Shurts (137) Americanized spelling of German SCHURZ.

Shurtz (526) Partly Americanized spelling of German SCHURZ.

Shuster (1882) **1.** Americanized spelling of German SCHUSTER or variant spelling of this as a Jewish surname. **2.** Americanized spelling of Slovenian **Šuster**, archaic occupational name, of German origin, for a shoemaker (see SCHUSTER).

GIVEN NAMES Russian 4%; Jewish 4%. *Boris* (5), *Vladimir* (3), *Aleksandr* (2), *Gennadiy* (2), *Mikhail* (2), *Svetlana* (2), *Aleks, Arkady, Dmitriy, Dmitry, Galina, Gennady, Aron* (2), *Izya* (2), *Moises* (2), *Shlomo* (2), *Yakov* (2), *Genya, Hyman, Ilya, Irina, Khaim, Miriam, Shmul.*

Shusterman (245) **1.** Jewish (Ashkenazic): elaborated form of SCHUSTER, with the addition of Yiddish *man* 'man'. **2.** Americanized spelling of German **Schustermann**, a variant of SCHUSTER, with the addition of Middle High German *man* 'man'. GIVEN NAMES Russian 17%; Jewish 16%. *Boris* (6), *Leonid* (3), *Mikhail* (3), *Aleksandr* (2), *Dmitry* (2), *Arkadiy, Arkady, Efim, Galina, Gennadiy, Lev, Lyubov; Azriel* (2), *Blyuma, Chana, Eliezer, Genya, Ilya, Inna, Meir, Meyer, Moysey, Polina, Shlema.*

Shute (1213) English (Devon): habitational name from Shute or Shewte in Devon, or possibly Shute in Wiltshire, named with Old English *scīete* 'corner of land'.

Shuter (111) German and Jewish: variant of SCHUTTER.
GIVEN NAME Jewish 4%. *Aryeh.*

Shutes (204) English: variant of SHUTE.

Shutler (117) Americanized spelling of German **Schüttler** (see SCHUTTLER).

Shutt (1395) **1.** English (mainly Yorkshire): occupational name for an archer, Middle English *schut(te), schit(te)* (from Old English *scytta,* a primary derivative of *scēotan* 'to shoot'). **2.** Americanized spelling of German SCHUTT.

Shutter (276) **1.** English: occupational name for a marksman, from an agent derivative of Middle English *schoot(en)* 'to shoot'. **2.** Americanized spelling of German and Dutch SCHUTTER.

Shutters (148) **1.** Variant of English SHUTTER. **2.** Possibly an Americanized spelling of Dutch **Schutters**, a patronymic from **de Schutter** (see SCHUTTER).

Shuttlesworth (250) English: variant of SHUTTLEWORTH.

Shuttleworth (671) English: habitational name from any of several places so called (in Lancashire, Derbyshire, and West Yorkshire), which are named from Old English *scyttel(s)* 'bar', 'bolt' + *worð* 'enclosure'. Reaney and Wilson give also Shuttlewood in Bolsover, Derbyshire, as a source of the surname.

Shutts (501) English: patronymic from SHUTT.

Shvarts (148) Jewish (eastern Ashkenazic): variant spelling, transliterated from Russian, of SCHWARTZ.
GIVEN NAMES Russian 38%; Jewish 31%. *Boris* (6), *Vladimir* (3), *Yury* (3), *Anatoly* (2), *Betya* (2), *Grigoriy* (2), *Igor* (2), *Iosif* (2), *Leonid* (2), *Lev* (2), *Mikhail* (2), *Yefim* (2); *Yakov* (5), *Alter, Ber, Golda, Ilya, Inna, Irina, Itsik, Mikhael, Moisey, Sarra, Semen.*

Shvartsman (192) Jewish (eastern Ashkenazic): variant spelling, transliterated from Russian, of SCHWARZMAN.
GIVEN NAMES Russian 37%; Jewish 33%. *Mikhail* (10), *Vladimir* (6), *Boris* (5), *Yefim* (5), *Igor* (3), *Leonid* (3), *Yuriy* (3), *Aleksandr* (2), *Arkady* (2), *Grigoriy* (2), *Semyon* (2), *Yevgeny* (2); *Isaak* (4), *Polina* (4), *Yakov* (3), *Blima, Faina, Filipp, Fira, Ilya, Josif, Khaim, Khana, Mariya.*

Shwartz (120) Jewish: variant of SCHWARTZ 'dark'.
GIVEN NAMES Jewish 9%. *Eliyahu, Meyer, Sol, Tali.*

Shy (603) **1.** Americanized form of Dutch **Schuy**, an occupational name for a shoemaker, from Middle Dutch *schoeyen* 'to shoe'. **2.** Americanized spelling of Norwegian and Dutch SCHEI. **3.** Chinese: see SHI.

Shyne (149) Variant spelling of Irish SHINE.

Shytle (115) Dutch: occupational name for a bargemaster, from a diminutive of *schuit* 'barge'.
GIVEN NAME German 4%. *Eldred.*

Shyu (112) Chinese 徐: see XU 1.
GIVEN NAMES Chinese 33%. *Ching* (2), *Ching-Mei, Liching, Ling, Mei-Fang, Ming, Rong, Shih, Wei.*

Si (116) **1.** Chinese 司: from the name of a city called Si, which existed in the State of Wei during the Spring and Autumn period (722–481 BC). **2.** Chinese 施: variant of SHI 3. **3.** Dutch: unexplained.
GIVEN NAMES Chinese 43%; Vietnamese 8%. *Jing Sheng* (2), *Yang* (2), *Chu, Guojun, Hui Fang, Huifang, Kiu, Lai Wah, Lixing, Mei Lan, Shuyi, Suh; Yiu* (2), *Phong; Hum, Kieu, Kinh, Tha, Thin.*

Sia (165) Spanish (mainly Latin America): variant of **Cía**, a habitational name from either of two places so named in Navarra province.
GIVEN NAMES Spanish 22%; French 4%. *Lourdes* (3), *Bernardo* (2), *Esteban* (2), *Aurelio, Concepcion, Dominador, Generosa, Julio, Manuel, Maria Cristina, Rey, Roque; Dominique, Stephane.*

Sian (104) Filipino: unexplained.
GIVEN NAMES Spanish 11%. *Delfin* (2), *Catalino, Jose, Narciso, Ricardo, Rogaciano, Salomon, Tita.*

Siani (101) Southern Italian: patronymic or plural form of SIANO.

Siano (421) **1.** Southern Italian: habitational name from Siano in Salerno province. **2.** Southern Italian: from the Latin personal name *Seius* with the addition of the suffix *-anu.* **3.** Polish and Jewish (from Poland): metonymic occupational name or ornamental name from Polish *siano* 'hay'.
GIVEN NAMES Italian 13%. *Salvatore* (3), *Sal* (2), *Antonio, Carmine, Clementina, Fabrizio, Franca, Luigi, Matteo, Sabato.*

Sias (704) **1.** English: unexplained; possibly a variant of SEARS. The name was already well established both in New England and in MD by the mid 18th century. It is believed to have been brought to NH in or before 1677. **2.** Spanish (**Sías**): unexplained. In Spain this name occurs chiefly in Extremadura.
GIVEN NAMES Spanish 5%. *Domingo* (2), *Francisco* (2), *Manuel* (2), *Abran, Adela, Alfredo, Alonzo, Blasa, Delfino, Eugenio, Gustavia, Hernan.*

Sibal (105) **1.** Spanish: variant of **Siabal**, a habitational name from Siabal in Ourense

province. **2.** Indian (Panjab): Hindu (Khatri) and Sikh name of unknown meaning.
GIVEN NAMES Spanish 21%; Indian 9%. *Abelardo, Benedicto, Benito, Conception, Erlinda, Ernesto, Francisco, Juan, Marcelina, Marcial, Natalio, Nenita; Amrit, Arun, Sandeep, Shiv.*

Sibbald (144) Scottish and northern English: from the Middle English personal name *Sybald,* Old English *Sigebeald,* composed of the elements *sige* 'victory' + *beald* 'bold', 'brave', reinforced in the early Middle Ages by the Norman introduction of a Continental cognate.

Sibbett (103) Scottish and English: from the early modern English personal name *Sebode,* probably from an unattested Old English personal name *Sigeboda,* composed of the elements *sige* 'victory' + *boda* 'messenger'. However, there has been some confusion with SIBBALD.

Sibert (1119) **1.** English: variant of SEABERG. **2.** German: variant of SIEBERT.

Sibila (100) Spanish and Catalan (variant of **Sibil.la**): from the medieval female personal name *Sibila.* Compare English SIBLEY.
GIVEN NAMES Spanish 20%. *Jose* (4), *Jorge* (2), *Mercedes* (2), *Raul* (2), *Benito, Evilio, Juan, Manuel, Marta, Pedro.*

Sibilia (214) Italian (especially southern): from the female personal name *Sibilla, Sibilia* (common in 12th-century Italy), from Latin *Sibylla.* Compare English SIBLEY.
GIVEN NAMES Italian 15%; Spanish 5%. *Emilio* (6), *Angelo, Antonio, Rocco, Sal, Salvatore, Silvio; Jose* (2), *Juan, Zoraida.*

Sibille (118) French: from the medieval female personal name *Sibil(i)a.* Compare English SIBLEY.
GIVEN NAMES French 15%. *Philippe* (2), *Alain, Etienne, Jean-Michael.*

Sible (163) Possibly a variant of English **Sibble**, which is from the French female personal name *Sibille* (see SIBLEY).

Sibley (3562) English: from the popular medieval female personal name *Sibley,* a vernacular form of Latin *Sibilla,* from Greek *Sibylla,* a title of obscure origin borne by various oracular priestesses in classical times. In Christian mythology the sibyls came to be classed as pagan prophets (who had prophesied the coming of Christ), and hence the name was an acceptable one that could be bestowed on a Christian child.

Sibold (106) **1.** Variant of English SIBBALD. **2.** Variant of German or French SEBALD.

Sibole (146) Variant of English SIBBALD.

Sibson (120) English: **1.** habitational name from places in Leicestershire and Cambridgeshire so called. The former, *Sibetesdone* in Domesday Book, is named with the Old English personal name *Sigebed + dūn* 'hill'; the latter (*Sibestune* in Domesday Book) is named with the Old

English personal name *Sibbi* or *Sibba* + *tūn* 'settlement'. **2.** patronymic from the personal name *Sib(be)*, which is a short form either of the female name *Sibilla* (see SIBLEY) or of the Middle English male name *Sybald* (see SIBBALD).

Sica (669) **1.** Italian: from the medieval personal name *Sica*, a short form of any of various Germanic compound personal names formed with *sigi* 'victory' as the first element. **2.** Greek (**Sykas**): occupational name for a grower or seller of figs, from Greek *siko* 'fig' (classical Greek *sykon*) + the occupational suffix *-as*.

GIVEN NAMES Italian 15%. *Angelo* (6), *Carmine* (6), *Domenic* (6), *Salvatore* (3), *Vito* (3), *Antonio, Egidio, Fiore, Gaetano, Valentino.*

Sicard (672) French, Catalan, and Occitan: from the personal name *Sicard*, from Germanic *Sigihard* (see SIEGERT).

FOREBEARS A Sicard or Sicart from the Saintonge region of France was documented in Montreal in 1680.

GIVEN NAMES French 8%. *Adrien, Albertine, Aude, Benoit, Camille, Elzear, Francois, Jacques, Jean-Paul, Marcel, Monique, Numa.*

Sicari (126) Southern Italian: from Italian *sicario* 'hired assassin', 'killer'.

GIVEN NAMES Italian 24%. *Salvatore* (3), *Alberto, Amedeo, Domenico, Gennaro, Giosue, Margarita, Pasquale, Rosaria, Sal.*

Sichel (212) German and Jewish (Ashkenazic): from Middle High German *sickel*, German *Sichel* 'sickle', a metonymic occupational name for a sicklesmith or for someone who used a sickle, or possibly a nickname for someone bent like a sickle.

GIVEN NAMES German 5%; French 4%. *Erna, Manfred; Lucien, Pierre.*

Sicher (131) German: **1.** nickname for a carefree person, from Middle High German *sicher* 'without worry', 'assured'. **2.** from a Germanic personal name (*Sigiheri*) composed of *sigi* 'victory' + *heri* 'army'.

GIVEN NAMES German 5%. *Erwin, Horst.*

Sicignano (109) Italian: habitational name from Sicignano degli Alburni in Salerno province (Campania).

GIVEN NAMES Italian 11%. *Antonio* (2), *Carmela, Ciro, Luigi.*

Sicilia (292) Italian, Catalan (**Sicília**), Aragonese, and Spanish: habitational name for someone from the island of Sicily (the Latin, Italian, Aragonese, and Spanish name of which is *Sicilia*, Catalan *Sicília*). From 1282 to 1713 Sicily was part of the kingdom of Aragon.

GIVEN NAMES Italian 17%; Spanish 12%. *Angelo* (2), *Franco* (2), *Antonio, Attilio, Carmine, Cesare, Dante, Domenico, Giovanni, Matteo, Ornella, Pasquale; Miguel* (2), *Pedro* (2), *Abramo, Carlos, Jose, Mercedes, Seferina.*

Siciliano (1134) Italian: from *Siciliano* 'Sicilian', an adjectival derivative of SICILIA.

GIVEN NAMES Italian 17%. *Angelo* (9), *Carmine* (6), *Rocco* (4), *Giovanni* (3), *Sal* (3), *Domenico* (2), *Francesco* (2), *Luciano* (2), *Nicola* (2), *Salvatore* (2), *Vito* (2), *Amedeo.*

Sick (319) North German: **1.** from a medieval personal name, a short form of any of the various Germanic personal names formed with *sigi* 'victory' as the first element. **2.** variant of SIECK.

Sickafoose (106) **1.** Probably an Americanized form of German **Ziegenfuss**: **2.** Nickname meaning 'goat's foot', presumably a nickname for a nimble man. **3.** Alternatively, it may be an altered form (by folk etymology) of the Germanic personal name *Sigifuns*, composed of elements meaning 'victory' + 'quick'.

Sickel (176) **1.** German: variant of SIEGEL 2. **2.** North German: nickname from Middle Low German *sickel* 'kid', 'young goat'. **3.** Dutch and Belgian (**van der Sickel**): habitational name for someone from a place called Sikkel, for example in Asse, Brabant; or a habitational name from a house sign denoting the shop of a sicklesmith (from *sikkel* 'sickle').

Sickels (660) Of German origin; see SICKEL.

Sicking (138) North German (Westphalia): from a pet form or patronymic of SICK.

Sickinger (245) South German: habitational name for someone from Sickingen in Baden or Sicking in Bavaria.

GIVEN NAMES German 4%. *Erwin, Gerhard, Kurt.*

Sickle (217) Americanized spelling of SICKEL.

Sickler (1112) German (Rhineland, Westphalia): of uncertain origin. Possibly an altered spelling of SIEGLER.

Sickles (1173) Possibly an altered form of German SICKEL (compare SICKELS).

Sickman (168) Possibly an Americanized spelling of German SIEGMANN.

Siclari (102) Southern Italian: **1.** occupational name for a maker of buckets, from an agent derivative of Latin *sicla* 'bucket'. **2.** occupational name for a money coiner, from medieval Latin *siclarius*.

GIVEN NAMES Italian 25%. *Pasquale* (2), *Aida, Carmela, Domenic, Emilia, Placido, Rocco.*

Sico (123) Italian: from a Germanic personal name.

GIVEN NAMES Italian 21%. *Gaetano* (2), *Digna, Julieta, Marco, Mariano, Raul, Vito.*

Siconolfi (156) Italian (Neapolitan): from a medieval personal name derived from a Germanic personal name composed of the elements *sigi* 'victory' + *wulf* 'wolf'.

GIVEN NAMES Italian 25%. *Angelo* (3), *Rocco* (3), *Carmine* (2), *Luigi* (2), *Antonio, Carlo, Gaetano, Lorenzo, Pasquale.*

Sicotte (184) French: from pet form of a Germanic personal name such as *Sicard* or *Sicault*.

GIVEN NAMES French 14%. *Lucien* (2), *Francois, Hugues, Marcel, Sylvain.*

Sicurella (120) Italian: diminutive of **Sicuro**, from Latin *securus* 'secure', 'safe'.

GIVEN NAMES Italian 19%. *Angelo* (2), *Salvatore* (2), *Liborio, Sal.*

Sida (104) Hispanic, but not found in present-day Spain: unexplained.

GIVEN NAMES Spanish 42%. *Jose* (8), *Jesus* (2), *Miguel* (2), *Rodrigo* (2), *Arturo, Domitila, Emilio, Felipe, Hermenegildo, Jaime, Leticia, Manuel.*

Sidbury (117) English: probably a variant of SUDBURY.

GIVEN NAME French 7%. *Andre.*

Siddall (457) English (northern): habitational name from places in Lancashire (in the parish of Middleton) and West Yorkshire (part of Halifax) called Siddal, from Old English *sīd* 'wide' + *halh* 'nook', 'recess', and possibly also from Siddle in East Harsley, North Yorkshire.

Siddell (126) English: variant of SIDDALL.

Sidden (143) English: variant of SIDDONS.

Siddens (239) English: variant spelling of SIDDONS.

Sidders (105) English (Kent): unexplained.

Siddiqi (345) Muslim: Arabic family name (**Ṭiddīqī**) meaning 'descended from or associated with Ṭiddīq'. *Ṭiddīq* is a personal name meaning 'truthful' or 'righteous'; it was an epithet of the first 'rightly guided' caliph, Abu Bakr, who ruled 632–634 (see ABU). This name is also found in combinations such as *Ṭiddīq-ullah* 'truthful to Allah', an epithet of the prophet Yusuf.

GIVEN NAMES Muslim 87%. *Khalid* (6), *Mohammed* (6), *Mohammad* (5), *Faisal* (4), *Imran* (4), *Iqbal* (4), *Muhammad* (4), *Nasir* (4), *Imtiyaz* (3), *Jamal* (3), *Nadeem* (3), *Sultan* (3).

Siddique (171) Muslim: variant of *Ṣiddiq* 'truthful' (see SIDDIQI).

GIVEN NAMES Muslim 87%; Indian 5%. *Mohammad* (13), *Mohammed* (9), *Abu* (6), *Mohamed* (5), *Muhammad* (5), *Asif* (4), *Arif* (2), *Iqbal* (2), *Mahboob* (2), *Mumtaz* (2), *Nayyar* (2), *Ullah* (2); *Asim* (2), *Manju.*

Siddiqui (820) Muslim: variant of SIDDIQI.

GIVEN NAMES Muslim 90%. *Mohammed* (33), *Mohammad* (30), *Muhammad* (17), *Khalid* (13), *Abdul* (9), *Tariq* (9), *Ahmed* (7), *Farrukh* (7), *Ahmad* (6), *Nadeem* (6), *Naeem* (6), *Shahid* (6).

Siddle (165) English (northern): variant of SIDDALL.

Siddons (332) English: unexplained.

Siddoway (156) English: variant of **Sidway**, a habitational name from Sidway in Staffordshire.

Sidebotham (111) English: variant of SIDEBOTTOM.

Sidebottom (528) Northern English (mainly Yorkshire): habitational name from a place in Cheshire, so called from Old English *sīd* 'wide' + *boðm* 'valley bottom'.

Sidel (151) German: **1.** metonymic occupational name for an upholsterer, from Middle High German *sidel* 'piece of upholstered furniture'. **2.** variant of SEIDEL.

Sidelinger (127) Americanized form of German **Seitlinger**, a habitational name from a place called Seitlingen.

Sidell (322) **1.** English (Norfolk): variant of SIDDALL. **2.** Possibly a respelling of German SEIDEL.

Sidener (235) Americanized spelling of German SEIDNER.

Sider (210) **1.** Americanized spelling of German and Jewish SEIDER. **2.** Jewish (eastern Ashkenazic): nickname from Yiddish *sider* (Hebrew *sidur*) 'prayer book'.

Sideris (241) Greek: reduced and altered form of the personal name *Isidōros* (see ISADORE), altered by folk etymology as if derived from *sidero* 'iron' (classical Greek *sidēron*), and hence regarded as an omen name: 'may the child grow up to be as strong as iron'.
GIVEN NAMES Greek 18%. *Constantine* (4), *Antonios* (2), *Spiro* (2), *Christos, Eleni, Evangelos, Georgios, Ioannis, Isidoros, Konstantions, Lambros, Panagiotis.*

Siders (737) Americanized spelling of German SEIDERS.

Sides (3069) English: topographic name for someone who lived on a slope, from Middle English *side* 'slope' (Old English *sīde*), or a habitational name from Syde in Gloucestershire, named with this word. This name is also established in Ireland.

Sidhu (444) Indian (Panjab): Sikh name (from Sanskrit *siddha* 'accomplished') derived from the name of a major Jat tribe. The Sidhu trace their origin to Jaisal, a Bhatti Rajput who was founder of Jaisalmer. Among his descendants was Khiwa, who married a Jat woman and had by her Sidhu, the ancestor of the Sidhu tribe.
GIVEN NAMES Indian 84%. *Darshan* (3), *Sandeep* (3), *Amrita* (2), *Anup* (2), *Avtar* (2), *Bahadur* (2), *Hardev* (2), *Nirmal* (2), *Rajindar* (2), *Sukhbir* (2), *Ajit, Amol.*

Sidle (242) English: variant of SIDDALL.

Sidler (191) Jewish (from Ukraine): occupational name, the Yiddishized form of Ukrainian *sidlyar* 'saddler'.

Sidley (160) English: habitational name from Sidley Green in Bexley Hill, Sussex.

Sidlo (101) Czech and Slovak (**Šídlo**): **1.** metonymic occupational name for a shoemaker, from *šídlo* 'awl'. **2.** nickname for a restless or hyperactive person, a fidget, from a different sense of the same word.

Sidman (281) **1.** English: unexplained. **2.** Swedish: unexplained.

Sidney (559) English: **1.** habitational name from Sidney in Surrey and Lincolnshire, so named from Old English *sīd* 'wide' + *ēg* 'island', 'dry island in a fen', with the adjective retaining traces of the weak dative ending, originally used after a preposition and definite article. Two places in Cheshire called Sydney are from Old English *sīd* + *halh* 'nook', 'recess' and may also be sources of the surname. **2.** possibly a habitational name from a place in Normandy called Saint-Denis, from the dedication of its church to St. Dionysius (see DENNIS). There is, however, no evidence to support this derivation beyond occasional early modern English forms such as *Seyndenys*, which may equally well be the result of folk etymology.
GIVEN NAMES French 5%. *Andree, Batiste, Curley, Heloise, Phillippe, Yves.*

Sidor (330) Polish: from an eastern Slavic form of the personal name *Izydor*, Greek *Isidōros* (see ISADORE).
GIVEN NAMES Polish 5%; German 4%. *Janusz, Katarzyna, Kazimierz, Zbigniew; Gerhard, Reinhard, Wolfgang.*

Sidoti (372) Italian: variant of **Scidoti**, a habitational name for someone from Scido in Reggio Calabria.
GIVEN NAMES Italian 22%. *Sal* (5), *Antonino* (3), *Salvatore* (3), *Aldo, Alfio, Antonio, Biagio, Cono, Filippo, Gino, Giuseppe, Pasquale, Rosario, Santa.*

Sidwell (1009) English: of uncertain origin. It appears to be a habitational name from an unidentified place with a second element from Old English *well(a)* 'spring', 'stream', but on the other hand early forms are found without prepositions. It may be a phrasal nickname.

Sieb (100) Dutch and North German: from a pet form of the personal name *Siebert* (see SIEBERT), or an altered spelling of SEIB.

Siebe (141) North German: from a pet form of the personal name *Siebert* (see SIEBERT).
GIVEN NAME Dutch 4%. *Adrianus* (2).

Siebel (269) North German: from a Germanic personal name (see SIEBOLD), or an altered spelling of SEIBEL.
GIVEN NAMES German 5%. *Hedwig, Mathias.*

Siebels (179) North German: patronymic from SIEBEL.

Sieben (407) North German: patronymic from a pet form of a personal name, formed with the element Sieb-, for example SIEBERT.

Siebenaler (278) German (Rhineland): from Middle High German *siben* 'seven' + *aller* 'alder', hence a topographic name for someone who lived by a group of seven alder trees, or a habitational name from Siebenaler in Luxembourg.

Siebeneck (117) North German: from a standardized form of Low German *Seveneken*, the original form of the place and topographic name *Siebeneichen* ('seven oaks')

near Lauenburg, from Middle Low German *seven* + *eke*, plural *eken* .

Sieber (1112) German: **1.** occupational name for a sieve maker, from an agent derivative of Middle High German *sib* 'sieve'. **2.** possibly a variant of SIEBERT.
GIVEN NAMES German 6%. *Otto* (5), *Hans* (3), *Konrad* (2), *Kurt* (2), *Franz, Fritz, Gerhard, Gunter, Heinz, Helmuth, Joerg, Oskar.*

Sieberg (102) German: habitational name from Siberch (modern Siegburg) in the Rhineland and Westphalia, from the river Sieg + *Berg*.
GIVEN NAMES German 7%. *Otto, Woldemar.*

Siebers (262) North German: patronymic from the personal name SIEBERT.

Siebert (2958) German: from a Germanic personal name composed of the elements *sigi* 'victory' + *berht* 'bright', 'famous'.
GIVEN NAMES German 4%. *Kurt* (4), *Klaus* (3), *Wenzel* (3), *Frieda* (2), *Hans* (2), *Horst* (2), *Otto* (2), *Eldor, Erhart, Gerd, Gunter, Gunther.*

Siebler (105) South German: variant of the occupational name name SIEBER 'sieve maker'.
GIVEN NAMES German 10%. *Arno, Erwin, Klaus, Markus.*

Siebold (406) Variant of German SEIBOLD.

Siebrecht (125) German: variant of SIEBERT.
GIVEN NAMES German 7%. *Heinz, Otto, Rainer.*

Sieck (396) North German: variant of SICK.
GIVEN NAMES German 5%. *Arno, Erna, Frieda, Gerhardt, Gunter, Kurt.*

Sieczkowski (133) Polish: habitational name for someone from a place called Sieczków in Kielce voivodeship, named with Polish *sieczka* 'chaff'.
GIVEN NAMES Polish 8%; German 4%. *Stanislaw, Wlodzimierz; Florian, Manfred.*

Siedlecki (309) Polish and Jewish (from Poland): habitational name from a place named Siedlce or Siedlec, of which there are many in different parts of Poland. The most important of them is in Siedlce voivodeship in eastern Poland. The place name is derived from *siodło*, meaning 'abode' or 'dwelling place' in Old Polish.
GIVEN NAMES Polish 11%. *Bogdan, Boleslaw, Janusz, Jozef, Karol, Krystyna, Krzysztof, Leszek, Stanislaw, Tadeusz, Wojciech, Zygmunt.*

Siedler (95) German: **1.** nickname for a settler or incomer, from an agent derivative of Middle High German *sidelen* 'to establish residence'. **2.** occupational name for an upholsterer, from an agent derivative of Middle High German *sidel* 'piece of upholstered furniture'.
GIVEN NAMES German 23%. *Gerhard* (2), *Manfred* (2), *Beate, Elfriede, Franz, Gerd, Gunter, Rainer.*

Siedschlag (204) Eastern German: from a Slavic personal name formed with *-slav* 'fame' as the second element.

Siefer (119) **1.** North German and Dutch: variant of SIEFERT. **2.** altered spelling of SEIFER.

Siefert (777) **1.** North German and Dutch: from a personal name, a local form of SIEGFRIED. **2.** altered spelling of SEIFERT.

Sieffert (143) North German and Dutch: variant of SIEFERT.

Siefke (129) North German: from a pet form of the personal name SIEFERT (see SIEGFRIED).

Siefken (358) North German: patronymic from a pet form of the personal name SIEFERT (see SIEGFRIED).

Siefker (306) North German: patronymic from a pet form of the personal name *Siefert, Siegfried* (see SIEGFRIED).

Siefkes (128) North German: patronymic from a pet form of the personal name SIEFERT (see SIEGFRIED).

GIVEN NAMES German 4%. *Erwin, Hermann.*

Siefring (144) German: of uncertain origin. Either a variant of **Siffring**, a Rhenish form of SEVERIN, or a variant of SIEVERDING, a Westphalian patronymic of SIEFERT or its spelling variant SIEVERT.

Sieg (817) **1.** German: from a short form of a Germanic personal name formed with *sigi* 'victory' as the first element. **2.** North German: variant of SIEK.

GIVEN NAMES German 4%. *Bernd, Elfriede, Erwin, Ewald, Fritz, Guenter, Helmut, Klaus, Kurt, Manfred, Reinhold, Wilfried.*

Siegal (667) Jewish: variant of SEGAL.

GIVEN NAMES Jewish 6%. *Hyman* (2), *Arieh, Asher, Bluma, Elkan, Isadore, Shira, Sol, Yakir, Yosef.*

Siegel (11605) **1.** German and Jewish (Ashkenazic): metonymic occupational name for a maker of seals or signet rings, or for an official in charge of a seal, from Middle High German *sigel* 'seal'. The Jewish name can also be ornamental. **2.** German: from a medieval personal name, a pet form of the various Germanic personal names formed with *sigi* 'victory' as the first element, for example SIEGFRIED. **3.** Jewish (Ashkenazic): variant of SEGAL.

GIVEN NAMES Jewish 4%. *Sol* (28), *Hyman* (11), *Meyer* (9), *Miriam* (8), *Emanuel* (4), *Yetta* (4), *Aron* (2), *Avrom* (2), *Chaim* (2), *Hyam* (2), *Isadore* (2), *Isidor* (2).

Siegelman (161) **1.** Jewish (Ashkenazic): variant of SIEGEL 1 and 3. **2.** German (**Siegelmann**): variant of SIEGEL, with the addition of Middle High German *man* 'man'.

GIVEN NAME Jewish 5%. *Miriam.*

Siegenthaler (331) German: habitational name for someone from a place named Siegent(h)al ('Siegen Valley') in Switzerland.

GIVEN NAMES German 11%. *Fritz* (4), *Manfred* (2), *Ernst, Erwin, Hans, Kurt, Uli.*

Sieger (501) German: from the Germanic personal name *Sigiheri*, a compound of *sigi* 'victory' + *heri* 'army'.

Siegert (517) German: from the Germanic personal name *Sigihart*, a compound of *sigi* 'victory' + *hart* 'hard'.

GIVEN NAMES German 6%. *Ewald, Gunter, Johann, Klaus, Kurt, Manfred, Otto.*

Siegfried (1505) German: from a Germanic personal name composed of the elements *sigi* 'victory' + *fridu* 'peace'. The German surname has also occasionally been adopted by Ashkenazic Jews.

Siegl (106) Variant of German and Jewish SIEGEL.

GIVEN NAMES German 9%; Jewish 5%. *Hermann, Ludwing; Zev* (2).

Siegle (563) Americanized spelling of German and Jewish SIEGEL.

GIVEN NAMES German 5%. *Wilhelm* (2), *Florian, Hermann, Horst, Manfred.*

Siegler (743) German: variant of SIGLER.

Siegman (266) **1.** Jewish (Ashkenazic): ornamental name from German *Sieg* 'victory' + *Mann* 'man'. **2.** Respelling of German SIEGMANN.

GIVEN NAMES Jewish 6%. *Anchel, Aron, Elihu, Isak.*

Siegmann (219) North German form of SIEGEL 2.

GIVEN NAMES German 4%. *Bernhard, Guenter, Heinz.*

Siegmund (427) German: from a Germanic personal name composed of the elements *sigi* 'victory' + *mund* 'protection'.

GIVEN NAMES German 7%. *Otto* (3), *Erwin* (2), *Alois, Dieter, Ernst, Ewald, Kurt.*

Siegner (105) South German: topographic name for someone who lived on wet ground, from a dilaect word *Seigen* 'low, wet spot'.

Siegrist (1084) German: occupational name for a sexton or churchwarden, Middle High German *sigriste*.

Sieh (214) Chinese: possibly a variant spelling of XIE.

Sieja (155) Polish: nickname from *sieja*, a kind of fish.

GIVEN NAMES Polish 7%. *Henryk, Tadeusz, Zygmund.*

Siek (177) **1.** Polish: nickname from a derivative of *siekać* 'to hack', ' to chop'. **2.** North German: topographic name for someone who lived in a marshy place, from Middle Low German *sīk* 'wet ground'.

GIVEN NAMES Polish 6%; German 4%. *Andrzej, Ryszard, Stanislaw; Rainer.*

Sieker (134) North German: topographic name for someone who lived in a marshy place, variant of SIEK 2 + the suffix *-er* denoting an inhabitant.

Siekierski (122) Polish: habitational name for someone from any of various places called Siekierki or Siekierka, named with *siekierka* 'hatchet'.

GIVEN NAMES Polish 11%. *Mieczyslaw* (2), *Maciej, Marzanna, Tadeusz.*

Siekman (171) Altered spelling of SIEKMANN.

Siekmann (107) North German: variant of SIEK 1, with the addition of Middle High German *man* 'man'.

GIVEN NAME German 5%. *Ilse.*

Sielaff (276) German: possibly from a Germanic personal name composed of the elements *sigi* 'victory' + *wolf* 'wolf'.

GIVEN NAMES German 5%. *Ernst, Ulrich.*

Sieler (285) German: occupational name for a harness maker, from an agent derivative of Middle High German *sil* 'harness for draught animals'.

Sieling (200) North German: patronymic from a short form of the Germanic personal name *Sigilo*, of which the first element is *sigi* 'victory'.

Sieloff (222) German: variant of SIELAFF.

GIVEN NAMES German 5%. *Kurt, Otto.*

Sielski (179) Polish: habitational name, probably for someone from a place called Sioło (from *sioło* 'village'), now in Ukraine.

GIVEN NAMES Polish 5%. *Casimir, Ireneusz, Mariusz.*

Siem (160) **1.** North German: from a reduced form of the Germanic personal name *Siegmar* (see SIEMER). **2.** Norwegian: variant of SEIM.

GIVEN NAME German 4%. *Kurt* (2).

Siemen (155) German: variant of SIEMENS.

Siemens (644) North German: patronymic from the personal name SIEM.

Siemer (535) German: from the Germanic personal name *Siegmar*, composed of the elements *sigi* 'victory' + *mari, meri* 'famous'.

GIVEN NAMES German 4%. *Helmut, Helmuth, Otto, Theresia.*

Siemers (536) North German: patronymic from SIEMER.

GIVEN NAMES German 4%. *Hans* (4), *Eldor, Eldred, Konrad, Otto.*

Sieminski (229) Polish (**Siemieński**): habitational name for someone from any of various places called Siemień, in Bielsk, Podlaski, and Łomża voivodeships, or Siemienie in Nowy Sącz and Płock voivodeships. The place names are from a short form of any of various Old Polish personal names such as *Siemisław, Siemomyśl,* and *Siemirad* (see SEMERAD), having Old Slavic *sěmi* 'person' or *sěmja* 'family' as the first element.

GIVEN NAMES Polish 6%. *Aleksander, Andrzej, Jacek, Tadeusz.*

Siemion (126) Polish, Ukrainian, and Jewish (from Poland): from the eastern Polish and Ukrainian form of the personal name SIMON.

GIVEN NAMES Polish 5%. *Elzbieta, Piotr.*

Siemon (307) From a form of the personal name SIMON in German, Ukrainian, and other languages.

Siems (563) North German: patronymic from SIEM.

GIVEN NAMES German 4%. *Kurt* (2), *Erwin, Gunther, Orlo, Otto, Volker.*

Siemsen (250) North German, Dutch, and Danish: patronymic from *Siem* (see SIEM 1). GIVEN NAMES German 5%. *Franz, Gunter, Hans, Manfred.*

Sien (100) North German: from a short form of a Germanic personal name composed with *sind* 'journey'.

Siena (114) Italian (mainly Tuscany): habitational name from the city of Siena. GIVEN NAMES Italian 10%. *Angelo, Carmelo, Giuseppe, Salvatore.*

Siener (135) Probably an altered form of German SEINER.

Sienicki (110) Polish: habitational name from a place called Sienickie in Łomża voivodeship or Sieniec in Sieradz voivodeship, both named with *siano* 'hay' (see SIANO). GIVEN NAMES Polish 9%. *Jerzy, Krzysztof, Slawomir.*

Sienkiewicz (646) Polish: patronymic from *Sieńko*, a pet form of the eastern Slavic personal name *Siemion* (see SIMON). GIVEN NAMES Polish 9%. *Andrzej* (6), *Henryk* (3), *Dorota* (2), *Zdzislaw* (2), *Casimir, Dariusz, Grazyna, Irena, Miroslawa, Slawomir, Tadeusz, Zigmond.*

Sienko (253) Polish (**Sieńko**) and Ukrainian: from a pet form of the eastern Polish personal name *Siemion*, Ukrainian *Semen* (see SIMON). GIVEN NAMES Polish 6%. *Feliks, Izabela, Lucyna, Stanislaw, Waclaw, Zofia.*

Sieracki (307) Polish: variant of SIERADZKI.

Sieradzki (118) Polish and Jewish (from Poland): habitational name for someone from places called Sieradz in Sieradz and Piotrków voivodeships, or from Sieradza in Tarnów voivodeship. GIVEN NAMES Polish 14%; German 4%. *Ireneusz, Krzysztof, Mariusz, Ryszard, Waclaw, Zigmont; Kurt.*

Sierakowski (111) Polish: habitational name for someone from any of various places called Sieraków or Sierakowo, named with the personal name *Sierak*, pet form of the Old Slavic name *Siroslav*. GIVEN NAMES Polish 5%. *Halina, Jacek.*

Sieren (146) Dutch: patronymic from a short form of the personal name *Zierik*, composed of the Germanic elements *sigi* 'victory' + *rīk* 'rule', 'governance', or from a personal name composed of *sigi* + *harja* 'army'.

Sierer (100) probably an altered form of German **Seirer**, which derives from the Germanic personal name *Sigiheri*, composed of *sig-* 'victory' + *heri* 'army'. GIVEN NAME German 4%. *Grete.*

Sierra (3432) Spanish and Jewish (Sephardic): habitational name from any of the numerous places named Sierra or La Sierra, from *sierra* 'ridge or chain of hills' (from Latin *serra* 'saw'). GIVEN NAMES Spanish 46%. *Jose* (71), *Juan* (43), *Luis* (37), *Carlos* (35), *Manuel* (24),

Pedro (24), *Jesus* (23), *Ana* (19), *Rafael* (19), *Roberto* (18), *Angel* (17), *Mario* (17).

Siers (351) **1.** English: variant of SEARS. **2.** Dutch: variant of SIEREN.

Sierzega (109) Polish (**Sierzęga**): from *sierzęga* 'bent grass', 'grass with sharp blades', topographic name for someone living in a spot where such grass was growing.

Sies (153) German: variant of SIESS.

Siess (204) South German: **1.** from the Germanic personal name *Sigizo*, formed with *sigi* 'victory' as the first element. **2.** nickname from Middle High German *süeze* 'sweet', 'pleasant', 'agreeable'. GIVEN NAMES French 7%; German 4%. *Germain, Girard, Pierre; Erwin, Kurt.*

Sietsema (178) North German: patronymic from the Frisian personal name *Sito* (suffixed by Frisian *-ma* 'man').

Sieve (263) North German (Oldenburg): from a short form of a Germanic personal name formed with *sigi* 'victory' as the first element. GIVEN NAME German 5%. *Kurt* (4).

Siever (195) Dutch and North German: from a local form of the German personal name *Siegfried* (see SIEGFRIED).

Sieverding (144) North German: patronymic from a form of the personal name *Siegfried* (see SIEGFRIED).

Sievers (2298) North German and Dutch: patronymic from SIEVER. GIVEN NAMES German 4%. *Hans* (3), *Kurt* (3), *Erna* (2), *Ulli* (2), *Eckhart, Eldred, Ernst, Erwin, Fritz, Gerd, Gerhard, Heinz.*

Sievert (1068) North German and Dutch: from a form of the German personal name *Siegfried* (see SIEGFRIED). GIVEN NAMES German 4%. *Kurt* (2), *Claus, Hertha, Otto, Reinhard, Ute, Wolfgang.*

Siewert (1034) North German and Dutch: variant of SIEVERT. GIVEN NAMES German 4%. *Helmut* (2), *Horst* (2), *Otto* (2), *Bernhard, Egon, Gotthilf, Heinz.*

Sifers (153) Possibly a Dutch variant of SIEVERS.

Siff (145) Respelling of Jewish (eastern Ashkenazic), **Zif**, an ornamental name from Hebrew *ziv* 'brilliance', 'charm'.

Sifford (666) Probably an Americanized spelling of German SEIFFERT. The surname is found in the British Isles, where it could well be of German origin; alternatively, it may be a habitational name from a lost or unidentified place.

Siford (108) Irish (of English origin): unexplained. GIVEN NAME Irish 5%. *Donal.*

Sifuentes (972) Southern Spanish and Latin American variant of CIFUENTES. GIVEN NAMES Spanish 51%. *Jose* (27), *Jesus* (16), *Carlos* (13), *Juan* (12), *Manuel* (10), *Pedro* (7), *Ramon* (6), *Ricardo* (6), *Alberto* (5), *Javier* (5), *Jorge* (5), *Luis* (5).

Sigafoos (201) See SICKAFOOSE.

Sigal (375) Jewish (eastern Ashkenazic): variant of SEGAL.

GIVEN NAMES Jewish 14%; Russian 9%. *Meyer* (2), *Myer* (2), *Ari, Bronia, Faina, Feyga, Gersh, Hyman, Hymen, Iakov, Isidor, Rakhil; Boris* (2), *Leonid* (2), *Mikhail* (2), *Yefim* (2), *Aleksandr, Arkagy, Dmitriy, Fima, Grigory, Igor, Illya, Liliya.*

Sigala (402) probably Spanish: variant of **Cigala**, nickname from Spanish *cigala* 'crayfish'. GIVEN NAMES Spanish 50%. *Juan* (10), *Jose* (9), *Jesus* (6), *Pedro* (4), *Roberto* (4), *Ruben* (4), *Carlos* (3), *Fernando* (3), *Manuel* (3), *Pablo* (3), *Ramon* (3), *Salvador* (3).

Sigel (513) Jewish (Ashkenazic): variant of SIEGEL 1 and 3. GIVEN NAMES Jewish 6%. *Hyman, Isadore, Mort, Naum, Sol.*

Sigg (253) South German: variant of SICK 1. GIVEN NAME German 4%. *Hans* (2).

Siggers (206) English: patronymic from an old personal name, either Old English *Sigegār*, Old Norse *Sigarr*, Old Danish and Swedish *Sighar*, or the Continental Germanic *Sigger*, all composed of related elements meaning 'victory' + 'spear'.

Siggins (175) Irish (Sligo): of English origin but unexplained etymology. This surname was established in Ireland in the Middle Ages, but is now rare.

Sightler (122) Americanized form of German **Seitler**, perhaps a variant of SEITER 'cobbler'. Compare SEITER, SAUTER.

Sigl (251) German (Bavaria): variant of SIEGEL 2.

Sigle (211) South German: variant of SIEGEL 2. GIVEN NAMES German 7%. *Gerhard, Gunther, Helmut.*

Sigler (3191) German: **1.** occupational name for a maker of seals and signet rings, or for an official keeper of a seal, from an agent derivative of Middle High German *sigel* 'seal'. **2.** Possibly an Americanized form of ZIEGLER.

Sigley (216) Possibly an altered spelling of German SIGLE, written thus to preserve the second syllable.

Siglin (242) altered spelling of German **Seiglin**, from a short form of the Germanic personal name *Sigilo*, which is a short form of SIEGFRIED.

Sigman (1405) **1.** Jewish (Ashkenazic): variant of SIEGMAN. **2.** Possibly an altered form of German SIEGMANN.

Sigmon (2319) **1.** Variant of Scandinavian and German SIGMOND. **2.** Variant of German SIEGMANN.

Sigmond (111) Scandinavian and German: variant of SIGMUND. GIVEN NAME Scandinavian 9%. *Erik.*

Sigmund (644) German and Dutch: from the Germanic personal name *Sigmund*, composed of the elements *sigi* 'victory' + *mund* 'protection'.

Signer (192) South German and Swiss German: habitational name for someone from Signau near Bern, Switzerland.

Signor (354) Italian: variant of SIGNORE.

Signore (302) Southern Italian: **1.** from the medieval personal name *Signore* (from Latin *senior* 'senior', 'elder', genitive *senioris*). **2.** from *signore* 'lord', hence a derisive nickname for a peasant who gave himself airs and graces, or occupational name for someone in the service of a great lord. This also came to be used as a title of respect for professional men such as notaries.

GIVEN NAMES Italian 12%. *Antonio* (3), *Pasquale* (3), *Dino, Enzo, Gennaro, Luigi, Marco, Vincenzo.*

Signorelli (610) Italian: patronymic or plural form of SIGNORELLO.

GIVEN NAMES Italian 20%. *Mario* (5), *Salvatore* (4), *Carmelo* (2), *Mauro* (2), *Vito* (2), *Angelo, Antonio, Carmine, Cosmo, Eduardo, Emilio, Francesca, Gaspare, Guido, Marco.*

Signorello (114) Italian: diminutive of SIGNORE.

GIVEN NAMES Italian 24%. *Antonio* (3), *Aldo, Benito, Carmelo, Dino, Gaetano, Gino, Marcello, Marco, Pietro, Rinaldo, Sal, Salvatore.*

Signorile (121) Southern Italian (most common in Apulia): nickname from the adjective *signorile* 'gentlemanly', 'refined'.

GIVEN NAMES Italian 23%. *Vito* (3), *Cosmo, Giuseppe, Pasquale.*

Signorino (137) Italian (Naples): from a diminutive of SIGNORE.

GIVEN NAMES Italian 14%. *Angelo* (2), *Gasper* (2), *Aldo, Antonio, Gaetano, Salvatore, Santo, Vincenzo.*

Signs (162) Origin unidentified; possibly English (unexplained). Compare SINE.

Sigona (110) Italian: nickname from an augmentative of Greek *siagon* 'jaw'.

GIVEN NAMES Italian 23%. *Angelo, Carlo, Orazio, Rocco, Sal, Salvatore.*

Sigrist (404) German: variant of SIEGRIST.

GIVEN NAMES German 4%. *Hans* (2), *Erwin, Gerhard, Ulrich.*

Siguenza (145) Spanish (**Sigüenza**): habitational name from Sigüenza in Castile.

GIVEN NAMES Spanish 46%. *Jose* (6), *Carlos* (3), *Mario* (3), *Rafael* (3), *Angel* (2), *Miguel* (2), *Alberto, Blanca, Carolina, Consuelo, Diego, Eduardo.*

Sigur (131) **1.** French: variant of **Ségur** (see SEGUR). **2.** reduced form of Greek **Sigouros**, a Greek adaptation of the French surname.

GIVEN NAMES French 7%. *Gaston, Monique.*

Sigurdson (297) Americanized form of a Scandinavian patronymic from the personal name Sigurd, Old Norse *Sigurðr*, composed of the elements *sig* 'victory' + *varðr* 'guardian'.

GIVEN NAMES Scandinavian 9%. *Erik* (2), *Arni, Bjorn, Sig.*

Siino (133) Italian: **1.** from a diminutive of *Sio*, an unattested pet form of the personal name *Desio*. **2.** variant of **Ziino**, which is

probably a nickname for a good singer, from Sicilian *ziinu* 'linnet'.

GIVEN NAMES Italian 16%. *Sal* (5), *Sebastiano, Vincenzo.*

Sik (126) **1.** Dutch: from the personal name *Sik*, a short form of *Siegfried, Siegmund*, or some other name formed with *sieg-* 'victory'. **2.** Czech: from the German adjective *schick* 'orderly', 'useful', 'skillful'. **3.** Jewish (from Bohemia): from the acronym *Šme Jehudim Kadoším* 'Jewish names are sacred'.

Sikes (3947) Northern English: variant spelling of SYKES.

Sikich (108) Croatian and Serbian (**Šikić**): unexplained. Perhaps a nickname from *šikati* 'to hiss', 'to fizz'.

Sikkema (280) Frisian: patronymic from the personal name element *Sik*, short form of any of the Germanic personal names containing the element *sigi-* 'victory'.

Sikkenga (108) Dutch: patronymic from the personal name element *Sik*, short form of any of the Germanic personal names containing the element *sigi-* 'victory'.

Sikkink (149) Dutch: patronymic from the personal name element *Sik*, short form of any of the Germanic personal names containing the element *sigi-* 'victory'.

Siko (103) Hungarian (**Sikó**): from a pet form of the ecclesiastical name *Szixtusz*, Latin *Sixtus* 'sixth'. Compare Italian SESTO.

GIVEN NAME Hungarian 5%. *Rezso* (2).

Sikora (2098) **1.** Polish and Jewish (from Poland): from Polish *sikora* 'titmouse', 'coalmouse', hence a nickname for a small, dark person, or, in the case of the Jewish name, an ornamental name. Compare Czech and Slovak **Sýkora** (see SYKORA). **2.** Jewish (from Poland): habitational name from any of the villages called Sikory.

GIVEN NAMES Polish 6%. *Jozef* (3), *Zbigniew* (3), *Zdzislaw* (3), *Andrzej* (2), *Casimir* (2), *Jadwiga* (2), *Janina* (2), *Janusz* (2), *Katarzyna* (2), *Kazimierz* (2), *Miroslaw* (2), *Piotr* (2).

Sikorski (1601) Polish and Jewish (from Poland): habitational name for someone from any of several places called Sikora, Sikory, or Sikorzyce, named with *sikora* 'titmouse'.

FOREBEARS This name, borne by many Polish noble families, has been recorded since the 15th century. The statesman and general Władysław Sikorski (1881–1943) was prime minister of the Polish government in exile and commander in chief of the Polish army during World War II.

GIVEN NAMES Polish 7%. *Andrzej* (3), *Ewa* (2), *Janusz* (2), *Jerzy* (2), *Krzysztof* (2), *Casimir, Elzbieta, Eugeniusz, Grazyna, Iwona, Jacek, Jolanta.*

Sikorsky (113) Variant spelling of Polish SIKORSKI, chiefly as a Russian name.

GIVEN NAMES Russian 8%. *Sergei* (2), *Igor, Nickolai, Sergey.*

Silano (154) Italian and Portuguese: from a variant of the Latin personal name *Silvanus* (see SILVANO).

GIVEN NAMES Italian 11%. *Antonio, Carmela, Carmine, Giovanni, Italo, Pietro.*

Silas (852) **1.** English: from the personal name *Silas*, a vernacular form of Latin *Silvanus* (see SILVANO). **2.** Hungarian (**Szilas**): from the old Hungarian personal name *Szilas*, or from a pet form of the ecclasiastical names *Szilveszter* or *Szilvánusz* (see SILVESTER, SILVANO).

Silbaugh (332) Altered form of German **Silbach**, habitational name from Silbach in the Sauerland, from a dialect word *sil*, *sel*, *sal* 'moist dirt' + Middle High German *bach* 'creek'.

Silber (1088) German and Jewish (Ashkenazic): from Middle High German *silber*, German *Silber* 'silver'; a metonymic occupational name for a silversmith, or often, in the case of the Jewish surname, an ornamental name.

GIVEN NAMES Jewish 8%; German 4%. *Mendel* (3), *Arye* (2), *Chaim* (2), *Meyer* (2), *Moishe* (2), *Moshe* (2), *Asher, Chanie, Charna, Cyla, Faina, Hinda*; *Kurt* (4), *Wilhelm* (2), *Jurgen, Klaus, Siegmar.*

Silberberg (385) **1.** German: habitational name from any of numerous places named Silberberg. **2.** Jewish (Ashkenazic): ornamental name composed of German *Silber* 'silver' + *Berg* 'mountain', 'hill'.

GIVEN NAMES Jewish 12%. *Ephraim* (2), *Leib* (2), *Aron, Chaim, Dov, Gadi, Hyman, Mayer, Meilech, Meir, Moshe, Naftali.*

Silberg (164) **1.** Swedish: ornamental name from the place-name element *sil* 'stretch of smooth water' + *berg* 'mountain'. **2.** Danish: habitational name from a place named Silberg. **3.** German: habitational name from a place so named in Hesse, or possibly a variant of SILBERBERG. **4.** Jewish (Ashkenazic): variant of SILBER, the last syllable being replaced with German *Berg* 'mountain', 'hill'.

Silberman (1330) German (**Silbermann**) and Jewish (Ashkenazic): variant of SILBER, with the addition of Middle High German *man*, Yiddish *man* 'man'.

GIVEN NAMES Jewish 7%. *Chaim* (3), *Miriam* (3), *Sol* (3), *Emanuel* (2), *Ari, Aviva, Chana, Chaskel, Dov, Henia, Hyman, Meyer.*

Silbernagel (425) German: metonymic occupational name for a silversmith, from Middle High German *silber* 'silver' + *nagel* 'nail'.

Silberstein (650) **1.** German: from Middle High German *silber* 'silver' + *stein* 'stone'; a habitational name from a place so named in Bavaria, or a topographic name. **2.** Jewish (Ashkenazic): ornamental name from German *Silber* 'silver' + *Stein* 'stone'.

GIVEN NAMES Jewish 13%; German 5%. *Uri* (5), *Aron* (3), *Chaim* (3), *Miriam* (2), *Shaya* (2), *Avi, Chana, Devorah, Ehud, Ilan,*

Jascha, Lazer; Kurt (4), *Armin, Fritz, Otmar.*

Silbert (396) German: variant of SILBER.

Silcott (266) English: apparently a habitational name, from a lost or unidentified place, possibly in the Surrey or Kent area, where the name is most frequent.

Silcox (1082) English: patronymic from a pet form of SILL.

Silence (111) English (Hampshire): unexplained.

Sileo (322) Italian: unexplained.
GIVEN NAMES Italian 13%. *Rocco* (3), *Vito* (2), *Angelo, Carmela, Carmine, Salvatore.*

Siler (2790) **1.** German: of uncertain origin; a variant of SIELER and SILLER. **2.** Possibly an Americanized spelling of German SEILER.

Siles (118) Spanish: habitational name from Siles in Jaén province.
GIVEN NAMES Spanish 28%; French 6%. *Alba, Alfredo, Bernardo, Digna, Fernando, Francisco, Hernan, Jose, Juan Antonio, Luis, Marcelo, Mauricio; Gaston* (2).

Silfies (244) Origin unidentified.

Silguero (141) Spanish: from *silguero, jilguero* 'goldfinch' (Latin *sericarium*), hence a nickname, perhaps for someone who liked wearing bright colors.
GIVEN NAMES Spanish 46%. *Jose* (3), *Ricardo* (3), *Arturo* (2), *Manual* (2), *Marina* (2), *Pedro* (2), *Adolfo, Armando, Carlos, Chelo, Cristina, Efigenia.*

Silk (1138) **1.** English: metonymic occupational name for a silk merchant, from Middle English *selk(e), silk(e)* 'silk'. **2.** English: from a medieval personal name, a back-formation from *Silkin* (see SILL). **3.** Irish (Galway): Anglicized form (part translation) of Gaelic **Ó Síoda** (see SHEEDY). **4.** Americanized form (translation) of German and Jewish SEIDE or SEID.

Silke (102) Irish: variant spelling of SILK.

Silkey (208) Irish: variant of SILK.

Silkwood (228) Probably an English habitational name from a place so named, for example Silk Wood in Gloucestershire or Silkwood Top in Devon. However, the surname does not appear in present-day English records.

Silkworth (120) Possibly an English habitational name from Silksworth in Tyne and Wear (formerly in County Durham), named in Old English with the personal name *Sigelāc* + *worð* 'enclosure'. However, the surname does not appear in present-day English records.

Sill (1296) English: from a medieval personal name, a short form of *Silvester* (see SILVESTER) or *Silvanus* (see SILVANO).

Silla (110) Italian: possibly a hypercorrected spelling of **Scilla**, a habitational name from a place so called in Reggio Calabria.

GIVEN NAMES Italian 14%. *Angelo, Antonio, Dino, Donato, Ugo.*

Sillars (122) Scottish: variant of SILLERS.

Siller (471) **1.** Hispanic (Mexico): unexplained. **2.** South German: habitational name for someone from a place called Sill, in particular one on the Salzach river, or from a farm so named in the Tyrol, the suffix *-er* denoting an inhabitant.
GIVEN NAMES Spanish 17%; German 4%. *Juan* (6), *Jose* (4), *Luis* (3), *Mario* (3), *Santiago* (3), *Alfonso* (2), *Guadalupe* (2), *Javier* (2), *Miguel* (2), *Prisciliano* (2), *Raul* (2), *Ruben* (2); *Gerd* (2), *Kurt* (2), *Konrad, Manfred, Otto.*

Sillers (138) Scottish: Anglicized form of Gaelic **Mac an Airgid** 'son of the silver', possibly a metonymic occupational name for a silversmith. The more usual spelling in the U.K. is Sillars.

Sillery (107) Irish: unexplained.

Silliman (742) According to family tradition, this is an Americanization of an Italian name, *Sillimandi*; however, the latter is not identified as a family name in Italian sources. The form *Sillivant* suggests possible derivation from Irish SULLIVAN.
FOREBEARS Benjamin Silliman, one of the most influential scientists of his time in America, was born in Trumbull, CT, in 1779 and came from a prominent CT family of Yale graduates whose paternal ancestors were Italians named Sillimandi. They lived in Switzerland and emigrated to America through Holland with the great Puritan migration, eventually settling in Fairfield, CT, with a Daniel Sillivant showing in Fairfield Co. records in the mid 1600s. By 1690 the family name had been changed to Silliman.

Sillman (254) **1.** English: variant of SELMAN. **2.** German (**Sillmann**): possibly a variant of SIELER, or a topographic name for someone living on a ridge, from Low German *süll, sill* 'sill', 'threshold', 'ramp'.

Silloway (114) Origin unidentified. Possibly related to SILLERY.

Sills (2456) English: patronymic from SILL.

Silman (229) English: variant of SELMAN.

Silmon (163) Variant spelling of SILLMAN.

Silsbee (114) Variant of SILSBY.
FOREBEARS Henry Silsbee (1613–1700), a prominent and prosperous English sea captain, is mentioned as being in Salem, MA, in 1639. Four generations later, there were still Silsbee descendants in Salem who were noted merchants, seamen, and politicians.

Silsby (312) English: habitational name from a lost or unidentified place; perhaps a variant of SALISBURY.

Silva (23427) Portuguese, Galician, and Jewish (Sephardic): habitational name from any of the many places called Silva, or a topographic name from *silva* 'thicket', 'bramble'.

GIVEN NAMES Spanish 29%; Portuguese 10%. *Jose* (426), *Manuel* (426), *Carlos* (171), *Juan* (134), *Luis* (103), *Jesus* (76), *Mario* (69), *Fernando* (67), *Francisco* (67), *Pedro* (63), *Roberto* (62), *Miguel* (61); *Joao* (41), *Paulo* (28), *Joaquim* (22), *Agostinho* (6), *Duarte* (6), *Henrique* (4), *Serafim* (4), *Vasco* (4), *Ilidio* (3), *Adao* (2), *Afonso* (2), *Altair* (2).

Silvani (102) Italian: patronymic or plural form of SILVANO.
GIVEN NAMES Italian 6%; German 5%. *Agostino, Bruna, Deno, Rocco; Siegmund.*

Silvano (101) Italian: from a personal name (Latin *Silvanus*, a derivative of *silva* 'wood'), bestowed in honor of various minor early Christian saints. This name is now well established in Mexico.
GIVEN NAMES Italian 18%; Spanish 14%. *Nino* (2), *Antonio, Luigi, Romeo, Salvatore, Tarcisio, Vito; Francisco* (2), *Ignacio, Joaquin, Leoncio, Toribio, Violeta.*

Silvas (608) **1.** Portuguese and Galician: topographic name from *silvas*, plural of *silva* 'thicket', 'bramble'. See SILVA. **2.** Hungarian (**Szilvás**): occupational name for a grower or seller of soft fruits, from *szilva* 'plum'.
GIVEN NAMES Spanish 32%. *Ruben* (7), *Carlos* (5), *Juan* (5), *Manuel* (5), *Raul* (5), *Jose* (3), *Lupe* (3), *Roberto* (3), *Alfredo* (2), *Armando* (2), *Domingo* (2), *Emilio* (2).

Silveira (1619) Galician and Portuguese: habitational name from places called Silveira in Lugo and Pontevedra provinces or a topographic name from *silveira* 'woodland', a collective derivative of *silva*.
GIVEN NAMES Spanish 22%; Portuguese 13%. *Manuel* (77), *Jose* (36), *Luis* (9), *Fernando* (8), *Carlos* (7), *Pedro* (5), *Francisco* (4), *Mario* (4), *Ana* (3), *Joaquin* (3), *Jorge* (3), *Adolfo* (2); *Joao* (12), *Paulo* (3), *Altair, Duarte, Henrique, Joaquim, Serafim.*

Silver (9796) **1.** English: from Middle English *silver* 'silver', hence a nickname for a rich man or for someone with silvery gray hair, or a metonymic occupational name for a silversmith. **2.** English: topographic name from any of the various streams in different parts of England named with this word, probably from the silvery appearance of the water. **3.** Translation of German and Ashkenazic Jewish SILBER.
GIVEN NAMES Jewish 4%. *Sol* (16), *Hyman* (10), *Meyer* (5), *Miriam* (4), *Emanuel* (3), *Myer* (3), *Hymen* (2), *Isadore* (2), *Yetta* (2), *Avrum, Dorit, Dov.*

Silvera (417) Spanish: Castilianized form of SILVEIRA.
GIVEN NAMES Spanish 13%. *Ricardo* (3), *Jorge* (2), *Juan* (2), *Manuel* (2), *Narciso* (2), *Orlando* (2), *Roberto* (2), *Adelina, Adolfo, Adriano, Alfredo, Alicia.*

Silverberg (1064) **1.** Partly Americanized form of German and Ashkenazic Jewish SILBERBERG. **2.** Swedish: ornamental name composed of the elements *silver* + *berg* 'mountain'.

GIVEN NAMES Jewish 6%. *Hyman* (3), *Miriam* (2), *Aron, Aryeh, Avi, Falk, Isadore, Yael.*

Silverblatt (95) Partly Americanized form of Ashkenazic Jewish **Silberblatt**, an ornamental name composed of German *Silber* 'silver' + *Blatt* 'leaf'.

Silveri (196) Italian: patronymic from the personal name SILVERIO.

GIVEN NAMES Italian 17%. *Angelo* (3), *Dante* (2), *Gino* (2), *Donato, Marco, Nicoletta, Romeo, Vincenzo.*

Silveria (356) Italian: from a feminine form of the personal name SILVERIO.

Silverio (445) Spanish, Portuguese, and southern Italian: from the medieval personal name (Latin *Silverius*, a derivative of *silva* 'wood'), borne in honor of a 6th-century pope, who met a premature end as the result of the enmity of the Empress Theodora, but was subsequently revered as a saint.

GIVEN NAMES Spanish 35%; Portuguese 8%; Italian 7%. *Jose* (9), *Ana* (3), *Carlos* (3), *Juan* (3), *Mario* (3), *Miguel* (3), *Ramon* (3), *Rogelio* (3), *Andres* (2), *Ines* (2), *Jorge* (2), *Josefina* (2); *Joaquim*; *Antonio* (4), *Nichola* (2), *Pietro, Salvato, Silvio, Vincenzo.*

Silverman (8639) Translation of German and Ashkenazic Jewish SILBERMAN.

GIVEN NAMES Jewish 6%. *Sol* (14), *Hyman* (13), *Miriam* (12), *Isadore* (9), *Meyer* (7), *Emanuel* (5), *Mendel* (5), *Shalom* (4), *Shmuel* (3), *Ari* (2), *Devorah* (2), *Mort* (2).

Silvernail (593) Translation of German SILBERNAGEL.

Silvernale (169) See SILVERNAIL.

Silvers (2572) English: patronymic from SILVER.

Silversmith (116) English: occupational name for a silversmith.

Silverstein (3122) Part-translation of German and Ashkenazic Jewish SILBERSTEIN.

GIVEN NAMES Jewish 6%. *Sol* (7), *Hyman* (6), *Meyer* (5), *Emanuel* (2), *Gershon* (2), *Miriam* (2), *Myer* (2), *Yetta* (2), *Ari, Chayim, Esti, Hava.*

Silverstone (226) **1.** English: habitational name from a place in Northamptonshire, recorded in Domesday Book as *Silvetone* and *Selvestone*, from the genitive case of an Old English personal name, either *Sæwulf* (see SELF) or *Sigewulf* ('victory wolf') + Old English *tūn* 'enclosure', 'settlement'. **2.** Translation of German and Ashkenazic Jewish SILBERSTEIN.

GIVEN NAMES Jewish 4%. *Aron, Emanuel, Herschel.*

Silverthorn (399) English (mainly Bristol and Gwent): of uncertain origin, apparently a habitational name from some lost or unidentified place deriving its name from Old English *seolfor* 'silver' + *þorn* 'thorn bush'.

Silverthorne (253) Variant of SILVERTHORN.

Silverwood (109) English (West Yorkshire): apparently a habitational name, perhaps from Silver Wood in Ravenfield, West Yorkshire (although that is not recorded until 1764). The place name may refer to a wood of silver birches.

Silvester (401) English and German: variant spelling of SYLVESTER. This is also found as an Americanized form of the Greek family name **Silvestriadis**.

Silvestre (327) **1.** Galician and Spanish: habitational name from any of the places named Silvestre in Pontevedra and Badajoz. **2.** Catalan, Occitan, French, and Spanish: from the personal name *Silvestre* (see SYLVESTER). **3.** Spanish and Portuguese: byname from *silvestre* 'wild', 'rustic'.

GIVEN NAMES Spanish 41%; Portuguese 15%. *Jose* (9), *Manuel* (6), *Fernando* (5), *Juan* (4), *Miguel* (4), *Carlos* (3), *Ramon* (3), *Raul* (3), *Efren* (2), *Josefina* (2), *Mario* (2), *Pedro* (2); *Joao* (8), *Joaquim.*

Silvestri (1660) Italian: patronymic or plural form of SILVESTRO.

GIVEN NAMES Italian 27%. *Mario* (13), *Angelo* (10), *Antonio* (8), *Rocco* (8), *Gino* (6), *Carlo* (5), *Giovanni* (4), *Marco* (4), *Pasquale* (4), *Salvatore* (4), *Dante* (3), *Delio* (3), *Domenic* (3).

Silvestro (425) Italian: from the personal name *Silvestro*, Latin *Silvester* (see SYLVESTER).

GIVEN NAMES Italian 16%. *Domenic* (4), *Angelo* (3), *Sal* (3), *Caesar* (2), *Agostino, Antonio, Camillo, Carmelo, Dino, Ennio, Gaetano, Giovanni.*

Silveus (125) Variant of SILVIUS.

Silvey (1505) **1.** English: unexplained; perhaps a metronymic from the female personal name SILVIA. **2.** Possibly a variant spelling of French **Silvy**: from the personal name *Silvy* (Latin *Silvius*; compare SILVIO).

Silvi (102) Italian: patronymic or plural form of SILVIO.

GIVEN NAMES Italian 14%. *Domenic* (3), *Sesto, Silvio.*

Silvia (1923) Southern Italian and Portuguese: from the female personal name *Silvia*. According to classical legend, this was the name of the mother of the twins Romulus and Remus, founders of Rome. It was a very popular personal name among Christians throughout Europe, having been borne by the mother of Pope Gregory the Great, a saint in her own right.

GIVEN NAMES Spanish 6%; Portuguese 4%. *Manuel* (65), *Jose* (4), *Ana* (2), *Perez* (2), *Alcina, Alfonso, Alicia, Almerinda, Alvarez, Angelina, Belmira, Carlos*; *Agostinho, Joaquim.*

Silvio (212) southern Italian: from the personal name *Silvio* (Latin *Silvius*, a derivative of *silva* 'wood'), a masculine form of the more common female name SILVIA.

GIVEN NAMES Italian 15%. *Angelo* (2), *Antimo, Carlo, Ciro, Gaspare, Salvatore.*

Silvis (647) Variant of the humanistic name SILVIUS.

Silvius (222) Humanistic name adopted as a Latin equivalent, meaning 'wood', of vernacular names such as Dutch VANDENBOSCH, German BUSCH, FORSTER, etc.

Sim (1352) **1.** Scottish and Dutch: from the personal name *Sim*, a short form of SIMON. **2.** Korean: variant of SHIM. **3.** Indonesian: unexplained.

GIVEN NAMES Korean 28%. *Sang* (14), *Jae* (11), *Young* (5), *Jong* (4), *Kyong* (4), *Yong* (4), *Chang* (3), *Chong* (3), *Dong* (3), *Song* (3), *Won* (3), *Chae* (2), *Chul* (2), *Hyun* (2), *Jae Bong* (2), *Jae Hoon* (2), *Myong* (2), *Nam* (2), *Pyong* (2), *Byung, Chong Ho, Chong Su, Dae, Hae.*

Sima (297) **1.** Czech and Slovak (**Šíma**): from a pet form of the personal name *Šimon* (see SIMON). **2.** Hungarian: from a pet form of the personal name SIMON. **3.** Jewish (from Ukraine): from the Yiddish female name *Sime*, derived from Hebrew *Simcha* 'joy'.

Simak (111) Czech (**Šimák**): from a pet form of the personal name *Šimon* (see SIMON).

Siman (129) **1.** Spanish (Andalusia): unexplained. **2.** Czech and Slovak (**Šiman**): from a pet form of the personal name *Šimon* (see SIMON). **3.** Jewish: variant of SIMON.

GIVEN NAMES Spanish 10%; Jewish 6%. *Jose* (2), *Ana Patricia, Gerardo, Guillermo, Humberto, Jaime, Juan, Sergio, Wilfredo*; *Myer, Sol, Yael.*

Simanek (110) Czech and Slovak (**Šimánek**): from a pet form of **Šiman** (see SIMAN).

Simao (174) Portuguese (**Simão**): from the personal name *Simão*, Portuguese form of SIMON.

GIVEN NAMES Spanish 27%; Portuguese 15%; Italian 8%. *Manuel* (7), *Carlos* (4), *Fernando* (2), *Luis* (2), *Salvador* (2), *Adelino, Aguinaldo, Arlindo, Celso, Edmundo, Eugenio, Julio*; *Joaquim* (2), *Amadeu, Guilherme*; *Antonio* (7), *Angelo* (2), *Aureliano, Filomena, Gilda.*

Simar (180) **1.** French: variant of SIMARD. **2.** Czech (**Šimář**): from a pet form of the personal name *Šimon* (see SIMON).

Simard (990) French: from a Germanic personal name composed of the elements *sigi* 'victory' + *mari, meri* 'famous'.

FOREBEARS A Simard or Simart from the Angoumois region of France was documented in 1661 at Château-Richer, Quebec, with the secondary surname Lombrette.

GIVEN NAMES French 22%. *Marcel* (7), *Lucien* (5), *Andre* (4), *Alphonse* (3), *Armand* (3), *Fernand* (3), *Gaston* (3), *Jacques* (3), *Emile* (2), *Germain* (2), *Gilles* (2), *Gisele* (2).

Simas (578) Portuguese: from the personal name *Simas*, of unexplained origin.

GIVEN NAMES Spanish 15%; Portuguese 9%. *Manuel* (26), *Jose* (8), *Mario* (3), *Carlos* (2), *Luis* (2), *Adelino*, *Ana*, *Dalia*, *Domingos*, *Fernando*, *Filomeno*, *Gabriela*; *Joao* (2), *Albano*, *Duarte*.

Simbeck (124) German: habitational name from any of several places in Bavaria named Simbach.

Simcik (145) Czech and Slovak (**Šimčík**): from a pet form of the personal name *Šimon*, Czech form of SIMON.

Simco (144) English (and possibly Hungarian): see SIMCOE.

Simcoe (265) **1.** English: variant of **Simcock** (see SIMCOX). **2.** Possibly also an Americanized spelling of **Simko**, from a Hungarian or Slavic pet form of the personal name SIMON.

Simcox (848) English: patronymic from *Simcock*, a medieval pet form of SIM + the diminutive suffix -*cok*.

Sime (520) **1.** Scottish: variant of SIM. **2.** Respelling of Norwegian SEIM.

Simecek (105) Czech and Slovak (**Šimeček**): from a pet form of the personal name *Šimon*, Czech form of SIMON.

Simek (581) Czech and Croatian (**Šimek**): from a pet form of the personal name *Šimon* (Czech) or *Šime* (Croatian) (see SIMON).

Simensen (103) Norwegian: patronymic from *Simen*, Norwegian form of SIMON.
GIVEN NAME Scandinavian 6%. *Erik*.

Simenson (237) **1.** Dutch: variant of SIMONSON. **2.** Respelling of Norwegian SIMENSEN.

Simental (259) Hispanic (Mexican): unexplained; probably a topographic name from a variant of Spanish *semental* 'seedbed'. The surname is not found in Spain.
GIVEN NAMES Spanish 55%. *Jose* (6), *Juan* (4), *Arturo* (3), *Jesus* (3), *Luis* (3), *Manuel* (3), *Mario* (3), *Miguel* (3), *Ruben* (3), *Alfonso* (2), *Ernesto* (2), *Estela* (2); *Antonio*, *Caesar*, *Constantino*, *Eliseo*, *Leonardo*, *Sal*.

Simeon (365) French, Spanish (**Simeón**), and English: from the personal name *Simeon*, a variant of SIMON. This was chosen in honor of any of many saints so named, venerated especially in the Eastern Church, including Simeon Theodochos, who recognized the infant Christ as the Messiah during the presentation in the temple, and St. Simeon Stylites, an ascetic 5th-century Syrian monk who lived for 40 years on top of a pillar. It is also found as a Greek surname, a reduced form of patronymics such as **Simeonides**, **Simeonakis**, or **Simeonoglou**.
GIVEN NAMES French 12%; Spanish 7%. *Gabrielle*, *Jean-Claude*, *Laurent*, *Laurette*, *Marcel*, *Marie Carmel*, *Marielle*, *Michel*, *Micheline*, *Reynald*, *Serge*, *Wilner*; *Eduardo* (4), *Ricardo* (2), *Roberto* (2), *Aida*, *Alfredo*, *Efren*, *Francisco*, *Guillermo*, *Juan Cruz*, *Mario*, *Maximo*, *Miguel*.

Simeone (889) Southern Italian: from the personal name *Sim(e)one*, Italian equivalents of SIMON.

GIVEN NAMES Italian 15%. *Salvatore* (8), *Antonio* (3), *Carlo* (3), *Aldo* (2), *Alfonse* (2), *Angelo* (2), *Carmine* (2), *Rocco* (2), *Amerigo*, *Cosmo*, *Gildo*, *Giorgio*.

Simer (186) English: occupational name for a roper or a loader, from an agent derivative of Middle English *sime* 'cord', 'rope' (Old English *sīma*), or of Middle English *simen* 'to load' (Old English *sīman*).

Simerly (475) Americanized form of German ZIMMERLE.

Simerson (214) English: patronymic from the personal name SIMON.

Simes (370) **1.** English: patronymic from SIM. **2.** Jewish (Ashkenazic): metronymic from the Yiddish female personal name *Sime* (see SIMA).

Simi (240) Southern Italian: variant of **Simio**, from a personal name based on Latin *eximius* 'excellent'.
GIVEN NAMES Italian 5%; French 4%. *Aldo*, *Dante*, *Florio*, *Gabriella*, *Giovanni*, *Silvio*; *Alain*, *Celina*, *Laure*.

Simic (133) **1.** Serbian (**Simić**): patronymic from the personal names *Sima* or *Simo*, short forms of SIMEON. **2.** Croatian (**Šimić**): patronymic from the personal name *Šime*, short form of *Šimun* (see SIMON).
GIVEN NAMES South Slavic 50%. *Dragana* (2), *Dusan* (2), *Marko* (2), *Miodrag* (2), *Miroslav* (2), *Slobodan* (2), *Srecko* (2), *Biljana*, *Bosko*, *Branislav*, *Darko*, *Dragan*, *Dragisa*, *Dragutin*, *Dusanka*, *Milan*.

Simich (146) Serbian (**Simić**) and Croatian (**Šimić**): see SIMIC.
GIVEN NAMES South Slavic 8%. *Bozidar*, *Jovo*, *Slavko*, *Zika*.

Simiele (104) Italian (Molise): unexplained.
GIVEN NAMES Italian 10%. *Angelo*, *Carmela*, *Gino*.

Simien (290) French: variant spelling of SIMEON.
GIVEN NAMES French 6%. *Curley* (2), *Michel*, *Thierry*.

Simington (348) Irish spelling of Scottish SYMINGTON, taken to Ulster from Scotland in the early 17th century.

Siminski (157) Polish (**Simiński**): variant of **Siemiński** (see SIEMINSKI).

Simione (178) Italian: from the personal name *Simione*, Italian equivalent of SIMON.
GIVEN NAMES Italian 18%. *Angelo* (3), *Carmela*, *Carmine*, *Paride*, *Rocco*, *Salvatore*, *Saverio*.

Simison (178) English: patronymic from SIMON.

Simkin (265) **1.** English (Midlands): from the Middle English personal name, a pet form of SIM. **2.** Jewish (from Belarus): metronymic from *Simke*, a pet form of the Yiddish female personal name *Sime* (see SIMA) with the eastern Slavic possessive suffix -*in*.
GIVEN NAMES Jewish 12%; Russian 8%. *Aharon*, *Aron*, *Boruch*, *Doron*, *Leib*, *Sol*, *Volf*, *Yakov*; *Leonid* (3), *Boris* (2), *Galina*,

Gennadiy, *Gennady*, *Grigori*, *Inessa*, *Semion*, *Yasha*.

Simkins (1052) English (West Midlands): patronymic from SIMKIN.

Simko (850) Hungarian (**Simkó**): from a pet form of the personal name SIMON.

Simkus (111) Lithuanian (**Šimkus**): see SHIMKUS.
GIVEN NAME Lithuanian 5%. *Algimantas* (2).

Simler (227) German: **1.** from an agent derivative of Middle High German *similen* 'to explain', probably a nickname for a capable adviser. **2.** variant of SEMLER.

Simm (191) **1.** Northern English (Lancashire and Northumberland): variant spelling of SIM. **2.** German: from a short form of the personal name *Simon* (see SIMON).

Simmelink (105) Dutch: unexplained.

Simmen (123) German, Swiss German, and Danish: variant of SIMON.

Simmer (386) **1.** Scottish form of SUMMER. **2.** Americanized form of German ZIMMER 'carpenter'. **3.** German: habitational name from any of various places named Simmern, in Hesse, near Koblenz, and near Bingen. **4.** Jewish (eastern Ashkenazic): ornamental name from southern Yiddish *zimer* 'summer'.

Simmering (191) Dutch and North German: patronymic from the personal name *Sigmar*, composed of the elements *sigi* 'victory' + *mari* 'famous'.

Simmerman (664) Americanized form of German ZIMMERMANN.

Simmermon (110) Americanized form of German ZIMMERMANN.

Simmers (788) English: patronymic from SUMMER 1.

Simmet (107) Americanized spelling of Jewish ZIMET or its German cognate **Zimmet**.

Simmon (338) German: variant of SIMON.

Simmonds (1375) Variant of SIMMONS.

Simmons (63923) English (southern): patronymic either from the personal name *Simon* (see SIMON) or, as Reaney and Wilson suggest, from the medieval personal name *Simund* (composed of Old Norse *sig* 'victory' + *mundr* 'protection'), which after the Norman Conquest was taken as an equivalent *Simon*, with the result that the two names became confused.

Simms (7841) English: patronymic from SIM.

Simo (213) **1.** Catalan (**Simó**): from a personal name, the Catalan form of SIMON. **2.** Hungarian (**Simó**): from a pet form of SIMON.
GIVEN NAMES Spanish 18%. *Fernando* (3), *Juan* (2), *Luisa* (2), *Miguel* (2), *Alberto*, *Amable*, *Bernarda*, *Consuelo*, *Diosdado*, *Eduardo*, *Lourdes*, *Luis*.

Simoes (515) Portuguese (**Simões**): patronymic from the personal name *Simão*, Portuguese equivalent of SIMON.

GIVEN NAMES Spanish 32%; Portuguese 22%. *Jose* (26), *Manuel* (26), *Carlos* (10), *Luis* (5), *Avelino* (3), *Mario* (3), *Raul* (3), *Adelino* (2), *Adriana* (2), *Alberto* (2), *Ana* (2), *Armando* (2); *Joao* (10), *Joaquim* (3), *Paulo* (2), *Amadeu, Guilherme; Antonio* (15), *Fausto* (2), *Carmela, Leonardo, Marino, Sal.*

Simon (27027) English, French, German, Dutch, Spanish (**Simón**), Czech and Slovak (**Šimon**), Slovenian, Hungarian, and Jewish (Ashkenazic): from the personal name, Hebrew *Shim'on*, which is probably derived from the verb *sham'a* 'to hearken'. In the Vulgate and in many vernacular versions of the Old Testament, this is usually rendered *Simeon*. In the Greek New Testament, however, the name occurs as *Simōn*, as a result of assimilation to the pre-existing Greek byname *Sīmōn* (from *sīmos* 'snub-nosed'). Both *Simon* and *Simeon* were in use as personal names in western Europe from the Middle Ages onward. In Christendom the former was always more popular, at least in part because of its associations with the apostle Simon Peter, the brother of Andrew. In Britain there was also confusion from an early date with Anglo-Scandinavian forms of *Sigmund* (see SIEGMUND), a name whose popularity was reinforced at the Conquest by the Norman form *Simund*.

FOREBEARS The earliest documented bearer of the surname Simon in New France came from the Saintonge region of France and was in Montreal by 1655. Another, from Paris, is recorded in Quebec City in 1659 with the secondary surname Lapointe.

Simoncini (125) Italian: patronymic from the personal name *Simoncino*, a pet form of *Simone*, Italian equivalent of SIMON.

GIVEN NAMES Italian 24%; French 4%. *Vincente* (3), *Albino, Amedeo, Americo, Angelo, Dante, Gabriele, Gaspare, Mario, Salvatore, Stefano; Antoine, Serge.*

Simonds (2042) English: variant (with excrescent -*d*) of SIMMONS.

Simone (2447) Italian: from the personal name *Simone*, Italian equivalent of SIMON.

GIVEN NAMES Italian 11%. *Angelo* (7), *Rocco* (7), *Vito* (7), *Antonio* (5), *Salvatore* (5), *Carlo* (4), *Guido* (4), *Dante* (3), *Mauro* (3), *Saverio* (3), *Domenic* (2), *Domenica* (2).

Simoneau (823) French: from a pet form of the personal name *Simon* (see SIMON).

FOREBEARS A Simoneau from Brittany is documented in La Pérade, Quebec, in 1694, with the secondary surname Dumoulin.

GIVEN NAMES French 13%. *Marcel* (4), *Andre* (3), *Emile* (3), *Armand* (2), *Fernand* (2), *Laurent* (2), *Normand* (2), *Ovide* (2), *Adrien, Aime, Alain, Alcide.*

Simoneaux (836) French (LA): variant of SIMONEAU.

GIVEN NAMES French 6%. *Camille* (2), *Mignonne* (2), *Amie, Emile, Gaston, Monique, Pierre, Ulysse.*

Simonelli (696) Italian: patronymic from the personal name *Simonello*, a pet form of SIMONE.

GIVEN NAMES Italian 15%. *Angelo* (3), *Salvatore* (3), *Carlo* (2), *Carmine* (2), *Donato* (2), *Italo* (2), *Rocco* (2), *Aldo, Antonio, Carmela, Carmin, Cesare.*

Simones (107) English: variant of SIMONS.

Simonet (208) **1.** Italian: reduced form of Italian SIMONETTI or SIMONETTA. **2.** French: from a pet form of the personal name *Simon* (see SIMON).

Simonetta (184) Italian: from a feminine pet form of the personal name *Simone*, Italian form of SIMON.

GIVEN NAMES Italian 22%. *Salvatore* (3), *Aurelio* (2), *Rocco* (2), *Santo* (2), *Cosimo, Domenic, Erminio, Francesca, Nicolo.*

Simonette (129) Italian and French: from a pet form of the personal name *Simone* (see SIMON).

GIVEN NAMES Italian 9%. *Salvatore* (3), *Benedetto.*

Simonetti (948) Italian: patronymic from a pet form of the personal name *Simone*, Italian form of SIMON.

GIVEN NAMES Italian 14%. *Sal* (4), *Geno* (3), *Gaetano* (2), *Marco* (2), *Marino* (2), *Pietro* (2), *Salvatore* (2), *Agostino, Amerigo, Angelo, Camillo, Carlo.*

Simoni (430) Italian: patronymic or plural form of SIMONE.

GIVEN NAMES Italian 14%. *Gino* (5), *Carlo* (3), *Angelo* (2), *Guido* (2), *Luigi* (2), *Adamo, Dante, Dino, Domenic, Francesca, Franco, Lucio.*

Simonian (537) Armenian: patronymic from the personal name *Simon* (see SIMON).

GIVEN NAMES Armenian 25%. *Armen* (3), *Avedis* (3), *Raffi* (3), *Sarkis* (3), *Vazgen* (3), *Ara* (2), *Berge* (2), *Haig* (2), *Hovsep* (2), *Krikor* (2), *Anait, Andranik.*

Simonich (174) Slovenian (**Simonič**) and Belorussian: patronymic from the personal name *Simon* (see SIMON).

Simonin (166) French: from a pet form of the personal name *Simon* (see SIMON).

Simonini (132) Italian: patronymic from the personal name *Simonino*, a pet form of SIMONE.

GIVEN NAMES French 7%; Italian 5%. *Marcel, Phillippe; Reno* (3), *Aldo, Angelo.*

Simonis (509) **1.** Dutch: variant of SIMONS. **2.** Lithuanian (**Šimonis**): patronymic from the personal name *Šimas*, a variant of *Simonas* (see SIMON).

Simons (10040) English, North German, and Dutch: patronymic from SIMON.

Simonsen (1459) North German, Danish, and Norwegian: patronymic from SIMON.

GIVEN NAMES Scandinavian 12%. *Erik* (9), *Sven* (5), *Nils* (2), *Bent, Bente, Egil, Einer, Erlend, Eyvind, Hedvig, Helmer, Knud.*

Simonson (3595) **1.** English and Jewish (Ashkenazic): patronymic from SIMON.

2. Respelling of SIMONSEN or the Swedish cognate, **Simonsson**.

Simonton (998) Irish: variant of SIMINGTON (see SYMINGTON).

Simos (126) Greek: **1.** from the personal name *Simos*, a pet form of the personal name SIMON. **2.** nickname from Greek *simos* 'snub-nosed'. **3.** from a reduced form of the personal name *Gerasimos*, a derivative of *geras* 'old age', or of the homonymous *geras* 'honor'. This was borne by a 5th-century saint, venerated in the Eastern Church, who was chiefly famous for extracting a thorn from a lion's paw. Compare GRASMICK.

GIVEN NAMES Greek 17%. *Evangelos* (2), *Athanasios, Costas, Efstathios, Nikolaos, Panagiotis.*

Simper (190) English and German: variant of SEMPER.

Simpers (110) Variant of English **Semper** (see SIMPER).

Simpkin (121) English: variant of SIMKIN 1.

Simpkins (3566) English: patronymic from SIMKIN 1.

Simpler (212) probably an altered form of German **Simperl** or **Semperl**, from a short form of the Germanic personal name *Sintperht*, composed of *sind* 'journey' + *berht* 'bright'.

Simpson (54544) **1.** Scottish and northern English: patronymic from SIM. **2.** English: habitational name from any of three places in Devon, so named from Old English personal name *Sigewine* + *tūn* 'enclosure', 'settlement'.

Simrell (126) Scottish: unexplained; perhaps related to the Ulster name **Sumeril**, a variant of SOMERVILLE.

Sims (33883) English: patronymic from SIM.

Simson (265) **1.** English: patronymic from SIM. **2.** German and Jewish (Ashkenazic): variant of SAMSON.

GIVEN NAMES German 5%. *Frieda, Guenther, Otto.*

Simunek (127) Czech (**Šimůnek**): from a pet form of the personal name *Šimon*, Czech form of SIMON.

GIVEN NAMES Czech and Slovak 7%. *Kveta, Miroslava.*

Sin (608) **1.** Chinese: probably a variant of SHEN or XIN. **2.** Korean: variant of SHIN. **3.** Indonesian and Malaysian: unexplained.

GIVEN NAMES Chinese/Korean 54%; Vietnamese 9%. *Yong* (7), *Chae* (4), *Hyun* (4), *Sung* (4), *Dong* (3), *Hyon* (3), *Jae* (3), *Sun* (3), *Yang* (3), *Young* (3), *Bok* (2), *Chan* (2); *Chong* (8), *Myong* (5), *Chang* (2), *Dong Sup* (2), *In Soo* (2), *Nam* (2), *Yiu* (2), *Boyoung, Byung Ho, Byung Sun, Chol, Chong Ho; Dam* (2), *Hau* (2), *Senh* (2), *Son* (2), *Bau, Can, Dui, Hung, Lan, Ly, Mui, Nga.*

Sinacore (106) Italian: **1.** variant of **Sanacore**, a nickname meaning 'cure the heart'. **2.** variant of **Senacore**, which, when not also a variant of Sanacore, may

be from the Campania dialect word *senacoli* 'black mustard' (*Brassica nigra*), or even an adaptation of the Greek personal name *Senagoras*, via Latin.
GIVEN NAMES Italian 19%. *Salvatore* (4), *Gaetano*.

Sinagra (180) Italian (Sicily): **1.** from a personal name, ultimately from Greek *Xenagoras*, a derivative of *xenos* 'strange' + *geras* 'honor'. **2.** habitational name from a place so called in the region of Messina.
GIVEN NAMES Italian 19%. *Ciro* (4), *Angelo* (3), *Salvatore* (2), *Antonino*, *Gianfranco*, *Sal*.

Sinai (118) **1.** Jewish: name bestowed with reference to Mount Sinai, where Moses received the Ten Commandments from God (Exodus 20). It can be either ornamental name, or derived from the identical male personal name which in turn is derived from the name of the Mount. **2.** Muslim: this is also found as an Arabic personal name. In the Qur'an, Mount Sinai is mentioned as *saynā'* and *sīnīn*.
GIVEN NAMES Arabic 10%; Jewish 4%. *Farrokh, Massoud, Mehran, Parisa, Parto, Rafik, Said, Simin; Irit, Zvi*.

Sinatra (381) Italian: from a personal name borne by both men and women in Sicily and southern Calabria. The name was apparently in origin a nickname from Latin *senator* member of the Roman senate (Latin *senatus*, a derivative of *senex* 'old'), which later came to be used as a title of magistrates in various Italian states.
GIVEN NAMES Italian 12%. *Salvatore* (5), *Angelo* (3), *Enrico, Nino, Rocco, Santina, Santo, Vincenzo*.

Sinay (116) Jewish: variant of SINAI.
GIVEN NAMES Jewish 15%; Spanish 4%. *Hanon, Hershel, Ilan, Naum, Shmuel, Yacov, Yehuda; Diosdado, Isabelo, Jose, Rey*.

Sincavage (218) Origin unidentified.

Sinchak (108) Origin unidentified.

Sinclair (9612) **1.** Scottish (of Norman origin): name of a powerful Scottish clan, originally a habitational name from Saint-Clair-sur-Elle in La Manche or Saint-Clair-l'Évêque in Calvados, so called from the dedication of their churches to St. Clarus (see CLARE 3). **2.** Jewish: Americanized form of some like-sounding Ashkenazic Jewish surname.

Sincock (105) English: variant of **Simcock** (see SIMCOX).

Sindel (128) **1.** German: nickname for a useless person, from Middle High German *sinder, sindel* 'slag', 'cinder'. **2.** German: from a pet form of the medieval personal name *Sind* (see SINDT). **3.** Jewish (Ashkenazic): from the Yiddish personal name *Zindl*. **4.** Hungarian (**Sindely**): metonymic occupational name for a roofer, from *zsindely* 'shingle', 'wooden roof tile'.

Sindelar (588) Czech (**Šindelář**): occupational name for a shingler (someone who laid shingles (wooden tiles) on roofs).

Sinden (135) English (Sussex): unexplained.

Sinder (120) **1.** German: variant of ZINDLER. **2.** From a Germanic personal name composed with *sind* 'journey' as the first element.

Sindler (110) German: variant of ZINDLER.

Sindlinger (164) German: habitational name for someone from Sindlingen near Böblingen.

Sindoni (176) Italian (Sicily): from a medieval Greek personal name, *Sindonē*, based on Greek *sindōn* 'winding sheet', 'shroud', and adopted as a Christian name with reference to Christ's shroud.
GIVEN NAMES Italian 16%; French 6%. *Vito* (2), *Marcello, Martino, Orazio, Rocco, Sal, Vittorio; Armand* (3), *Andre, Gisele*.

Sindt (277) German: from *Sindo*, a short form of a Germanic personal name formed with *sind* 'journey' as the first element.

Sine (785) Origin unidentified.

Sineath (194) Origin unidentified.

Sinegal (138) Possibly a variant of French **Sénégal** (see SENEGAL).

Siner (226) English: unexplained.

Sines (1118) Hispanic: unexplained; possibly a habitational name from *sinés*, denoting someone from Sin in Uesca province.

Sinex (121) Origin unidentified.

Sing (586) **1.** German: probably a variant of SENG. **2.** Name found among people of Indian origin in Guyana and Trinidad: altered spelling of Indian SINGH. **3.** Chinese 成: Cantonese variant of CHENG 3.
GIVEN NAMES Indian 8%. *Nirmal* (2), *Bhola, Dev, Harsh, Jainarine, Kashmira, Parbattie, Prem, Rookmin, Shalini, Sree*.

Singel (124) Dutch (**van Singel**): habitational name for someone from any of various minor places in Belgium named Singel, for example in Brugge (West Flanders), Lombeek (Brabant), and Sleidinge (East Flanders), or a topographic name for someone who lived by a wall or way encircling a town.

Singer (12026) **1.** Jewish (Ashkenazic): occupational name for a cantor in a synagogue, from Yiddish *zinger* 'singer'. **2.** English: variant of SANGER 2, in fact a Middle English recoinage from the verb *sing(en)* 'to sing'. **3.** German: variant of **Sänger** (see SANGER 1) in the sense of 'poet'.
GIVEN NAMES Jewish 4%. *Sol* (17), *Miriam* (9), *Hyman* (8), *Isadore* (7), *Emanuel* (5), *Meyer* (4), *Yisrael* (4), *Mort* (3), *Yetta* (3), *Yosef* (3), *Aron* (2), *Chaim* (2).

FOREBEARS Isaac Merrit Singer, inventor of the eponymous sewing machine, was born in 1811 in Pittstown, NY, the son of German immigrant Adam Reisinger. He had five wives and fathered 24 children. Singer, who incorporated his company as the Singer Manufacturing Company in 1864,

left a fortune worth $13 million to his various heirs.

Singerman (193) Jewish (Ashkenazic): occupational name for a cantor (see SINGER).
GIVEN NAMES Jewish 5%. *Hyman, Mayer*.

Singh (12875) Indian (northern states): originally a Hindu Kshatriya name but now adopted by many different communities, from Sanskrit *simha* 'lion', hence 'hero' or 'eminent person'. It is freely added to Rajput and Sikh male personal names and in the U.S. often serves as a Sikh surname.
GIVEN NAMES Indian 86%. *Avtar* (85), *Balwinder* (58), *Nirmal* (56), *Mohan* (54), *Darshan* (49), *Ram* (49), *Jarnail* (39), *Ajit* (35), *Karnail* (35), *Raj* (34), *Kewal* (32), *Sohan* (32).

Singhal (159) Indian (northern states): Hindu (Bania) and Jain name based on the name of a clan in the Agarwal Bania community meaning 'leonine', from Sanskrit *simha* 'lion'.
GIVEN NAMES Indian 95%. *Anil* (4), *Arun* (4), *Arvind* (4), *Gopal* (4), *Raj* (4), *Vipul* (4), *Ashok* (3), *Pravin* (3), *Vijay* (3), *Vinod* (3), *Ajay* (2), *Amit* (2).

Single (245) **1.** English: topographic name for someone who lived in a place cleared of woods by fire, from Middle English *sengle* 'burnt clearing'. **2.** German: from a pet form of a short form of a Germanic person name formed with *sing* 'sing' as the first element.

Singler (343) **1.** English: from Middle English *sengler, syngler* 'singular' (Old French *se(i)ngler*), perhaps a nickname for a solitary person. **2.** German: topographic name for a valley dweller, from a diminutive of Middle High German *senke* 'valley' + the suffix *-er*, denoting an inhabitant. **3.** German: habitational name for someone from Singeln near Waldshut. **4.** German: variant of SING 1.

Singletary (3513) English (Cambridgeshire): unexplained.

Singleterry (247) English: variant of SINGLETARY.
GIVEN NAMES Spanish 10%. *Guillermo* (2), *Luis* (2), *Raul* (2), *Baldomero, Carlos, Eduardo, Jorge, Mario, Marquita, Pilar, Rafaela, Roberto*.

Singleton (14945) English: habitational name from places in Lancashire and Sussex. The former seems from the present-day distribution of the surname to be the major source, and is named from Old English *scingel* 'shingle(s)' + *tūn* 'enclosure', 'settlement'; the latter gets its name from Old English *sengel* 'burnt clearing' + *tūn*.

Singley (1126) English: unexplained.

Singson (106) Filipino: unexplained. Compare SANSON and SISON.
GIVEN NAMES Spanish 35%. *Jose* (2), *Adelina, Ana, Augusto, Conchita, Domingo, Eduardo, Emilio, Fernando, Filomeno, Florentino, Gregoria*.

Sinha (597) Indian: variant of SINGH.

GIVEN NAMES Indian 91%. *Arun* (7), *Ashok* (7), *Sanjay* (7), *Sunil* (7), *Alok* (5), *Amit* (5), *Gautam* (5), *Ranjan* (5), *Ravi* (5), *Vikas* (5), *Arvind* (4), *Krishna* (4).

Siniard (230) Probably English, a variant of SENIOR.

GIVEN NAMES French 6%. *Gaston* (3), *Andre*.

Sinibaldi (152) Italian (northern and Tuscan): patronymic from the medieval personal name *Sinibaldo*, composed of the Germanic elements *sigin*, *sin* (secondary forms of *sigi* 'victory') + *bald* 'bold', 'brave'.

GIVEN NAMES Italian 7%; French 5%. *Sal*, *Serafino*; *Armand* (2), *Monique*.

Sinicki (125) **1.** Polish (**Siniecki**) and Jewish (from Poland): habitational name for someone from a place called Siniec in Zamość voivodeship. **2.** Polish: nickname from *siny* 'blue in the face', 'purple (with cold)', or perhaps from *siniec* 'bruise'.

GIVEN NAME Polish 5%. *Tadeusz* (2).

Sinicropi (110) Southern Italian: unexplained.

GIVEN NAMES Italian 22%. *Armando* (2), *Rosario* (2), *Gianpaolo*, *Giovanni*, *Giuseppe*, *Pietro*, *Rocco*, *Vito*.

Siniscalchi (146) Southern Italian (Naples): status name for a seneschal, *siniscalco*, or a nickname for someone with an officious manner (see SENECAL).

GIVEN NAMES Italian 22%. *Aldo*, *Carlo*, *Carmela*, *Carmine*, *Dino*, *Rocco*, *Salvatore*, *Silvio*, *Tillio*.

Sinisgalli (109) Variant of Italian SINISCALCHI.

GIVEN NAMES Italian 16%. *Rocco* (3), *Vito* (2), *Nichola*.

Sinisi (200) Southern Italian: **1.** from the Latin personal name *Synesius*, borne by a saint martyred in about 258 AD. The personal name is of Greek origin, based on *synesis* 'intelligence', 'conscience'. **2.** perhaps also a habitational name from Senise in Potenza.

GIVEN NAMES Italian 17%. *Rocco* (4), *Vito* (2), *Angelo*, *Dino*, *Donato*, *Marino*, *Pasquale*.

Sink (2282) **1.** Dutch, from Middle Dutch *sinke*, Middle High German *zinke* 'trumpet', 'horn', hence a metonymic occupational name for a musician. **2.** Slovenian (central Slovenia; **Šink**): unexplained.

Sinkey (136) English (Lancashire): perhaps an altered form of SANKEY.

Sinkfield (178) Americanized form of French **Cinquevilles** (see SINQUEFIELD).

Sinkhorn (160) German: unexplained.

GIVEN NAME German 4%. *Kurt*.

Sinkler (373) Possibly an altered spelling of SINGLER.

Sinko (266) Hungarian (**Sinkó**): from a pet form of the personal name SIMON. It is also found in eastern Slovenia, where it is spelled **Šinko**.

Sinks (450) Origin unidentified.

Sinn (799) German: **1.** habitational name from any of several places named Sinn or Sinne, or a topographic name from a river so called. **2.** From a Slavic personal name. **3.** Variant of SINNER 2.

GIVEN NAMES German 5%. *Kurt* (2), *Otto* (2), *Baerbel*, *Friedrich*, *Gunter*, *Herta*, *Ulrich*, *Wolfgang*.

Sinner (468) **1.** South German: occupational name an inspector and sealer of weights and measures, Middle High German *sinner*. **2.** Habitational name from any of several places named Sinn.

GIVEN NAMES German 4%. *Frieda*, *Gunter*, *Heinz*, *Kurt*.

Sinnett (528) Irish: variant of SINNOTT, now mostly found in South Wales.

Sinning (203) North German: habitational name from places named Sinning or Sinningen in northern Germany. There is also a place called Sinning in Bavaria, but this does not seem to have contributed to the surname to any significant extent.

Sinnott (1191) English and Irish: from the Middle English personal name *Sinod*, Old English *Sigenōð*, composed of the elements *sige* 'victory' + *nōð* 'brave' Although of English origin, the surname is now far more common in Ireland than in England; it has been prominent in Wexford since the 13th century.

Sinon (145) Irish: variant of SYNAN.

Sinopoli (330) Italian (Calabria): habitational name from Sinopoli in Reggio Calabria.

GIVEN NAMES Italian 19%. *Vito* (5), *Antonio* (3), *Salvatore* (3), *Angelo* (2), *Annunziata*, *Francesco*, *Italo*, *Vincenza*.

Sinor (312) English: unexplained. Possibly a reduced form of SENIOR.

Sinquefield (200) Proably an Americanized form of French **Cinquevilles**, a habitational name from an unidentified place named as 'five towns'.

Sinsabaugh (112) Americanized form of a German name (see SENSABAUGH).

Sinsel (146) Possibly an altered form of German **Sinzel**, from the Germanic personal name *Sinzilo*, a pet form from a short form of a compound name formed with the first element *sin*, related to words meaning either 'old' or 'judgment', 'opinion'.

Sinton (187) Scottish: habitational name from a place near Selkirk, also spelled Synton. In the 12th and 13th centuries it is recorded several times as *Sintun*, from an unexplained first element + Old English *tūn* 'enclosure', 'settlement'. In the British Isles, the surname is now found mainly in northern Ireland.

Sinyard (230) English: variant of SENIOR, with excrescent *-d*.

Sinz (144) South German: **1.** habitational name from Sinz near Saarburg, a place name of Celtic origin. **2.** from a pet form of the medieval personal name *Sindo*, from a Germanic compound personal name

formed with *sind* 'journey' as the first element.

GIVEN NAMES German 6%. *Kurt* (2), *Siegfried*.

Siok (117) Polish: nickname from *sio* 'shoo', a cry to drive away animals.

GIVEN NAMES Polish 9%. *Andrzej*, *Kazimierz*, *Wieslaw*.

Sion (177) **1.** Galician (**Sió**): habitational name from Sión in Pontevedra province. **2.** French and Dutch: from a variant of the French personal name *Chon*, a reduced form of French names such as *Michon*, a pet form of *Michel* (see MICHAEL).

GIVEN NAMES French 8%; Spanish 6%. *Jacques* (2), *Gilles*, *Martial*, *Romain*; *Americo*, *Corazon*, *Jacobo*, *Jorge*, *Jose*, *Manuel*, *Rafael*, *Rogelio*, *Salomon*.

Siordia (101) Variant of Basque **Ziordia**, a habitational name from Ziordia in Navarre province, named with Basque *zi(d)or* 'path', 'track'.

GIVEN NAMES Spanish 42%. *Jose* (5), *Alfonso* (3), *Maria Eugenia* (2), *Roberto* (2), *Alejandro*, *Carlos*, *Consuelo*, *Demetrio*, *Elvira*, *Graciela*, *Guillermo*, *Gustavo*; *Dante*, *Marco*.

Sipe (2403) Americanized spelling of German SEIP.

Sipes (2496) Probably an altered form of German SEIP.

Siple (408) Possibly an Americanized spelling of SEIPEL.

Sipos (599) Hungarian and Jewish (from Hungary): occupational name for a musician, from Hungarian *sípos* 'piper', a derivative of *síp* 'whistle'.

GIVEN NAMES Hungarian 8%. *Bela* (3), *Sandor* (3), *Attila* (2), *Laszlo* (2), *Miklos* (2), *Tibor* (2), *Balint*, *Elek*, *Endre*, *Ferenc*, *Gabor*, *Imre*.

Sipp (346) North German: from a short form of the personal name *Sibbert* (see SIEBERT).

Sippel (923) South German (Württemberg): variant of **Süpple** (see SUPPLE).

Sipper (114) German: origin uncertain; possibly an altered spelling of SIEBER.

Sipple (833) South German (Württemberg): variant of **Süpple** (see SUPPLE).

Sippola (118) Finnish: habitational name from a farm named with the personal name *Sippi*, a derivative of Swedish *Sigfrid*, + the local suffix *-la*, i.e. 'Sippi's place'. This name is found chiefly in western Finland.

Sippy (121) Hindu name found among people from Sind, Pakistan, which goes back to *Sipahimalani* '(descendant) of *Sipahimall*', presumably the name of an ancestor, derived from Persian *sipāhī* 'soldier' + *məll* (Sanskrit *malla* 'wrestler'). The element *məll* is frequently added to the given name in Sindhi names.

GIVEN NAMES Indian 9%. *Anil*, *Arvind*, *Dilip*, *Vishal*.

Siqueiros (140) Galician: habitational name from any of various places in Galicia

called Sequeiros, named with *sequeiro* 'arid land' or 'drying place (for fruit, etc.)', a derivative of *seco* 'dry'.
GIVEN NAMES Spanish 35%. *Manuel* (3), *Armando* (2), *Jesus* (2), *Alfonso, Alicia, Carlos, Cesar, Eduardo, Elva, Elvira, Epigmenio, Erlinda.*

Sir (114) Variant of French CYR.

Siracusa (387) Italian (Sicily): habitational name from the city of Siracusa (Syracuse) in southeastern Sicily.
GIVEN NAMES Italian 16%. *Nino* (2), *Angelo, Antonio, Carmelo, Carmine, Domenic, Fabrizio, Gerlando, Gianni, Giuseppe, Luciano, Philomena.*

Siracuse (128) Americanized form of SIRACUSA.
GIVEN NAME Italian 5%. *Angelo.*

Siragusa (390) Italian (Sicily, mostly Palermo): variant of SIRACUSA.
GIVEN NAMES Italian 14%. *Angelo* (3), *Salvatore* (2), *Santo* (2), *Antonino, Bartolo, Franco, Gaeton, Gino, Giuseppe, Matteo, Nino, Sebastiano.*

Sirak (152) Polish: from a pet form of any of several Old Polish personal names, such as *Sirobąd* or *Sirosław*, formed with the first element *sir-* 'deprived', 'destitute'.

Siravo (183) Italian (Abruzzo and Molise): unexplained.
GIVEN NAMES Italian 27%. *Antonio* (2), *Donato* (2), *Enrico* (2), *Mario* (2), *Rocco* (2), *Alfredo, Giustino, Gustavo, Leonardo, Pasco, Pasquale, Romeo.*

Sirbaugh (125) This has the form of a German topographic or habitational name, *-baugh* being a characteristic respelling of German *-bach* 'creek' in North America. However, no source place name in Germany has been identified.

Sircy (230) See SEARCY.

Sirek (201) Polish: see SIRAK.

Siren (107) Swedish (**Sirén**; also common in Finland): ornamental name, probably from an unidentified place-name element + the adjectival suffix *-én*, a derivative of Latin *-enius*.
GIVEN NAMES Finnish 14%; Scandinavian 5%. *Pentti* (2), *Heikki, Risto, Runo; Helmer, Nils.*

Sires (398) **1.** Catalan (**Sirés**): variant of Cirés, a habitational name from a town in l'Alt Berguedà district, Catalonia. **2.** Catalan (**Sirès**): variant of Cirès, a habitational name from a town in l'Alta Ribagorça district. **3.** English: probably a variant spelling of SYERS.

Siri (225) Italian (mainly Liguria): patronymic from the personal name *Siro*, a continuation of the Roman family name *Syrus*, meaning 'Syrian'. The name was borne by two 4th-century bishops, of Pavia and Genoa.
GIVEN NAMES Spanish 10%; French 5%. *Jose* (2), *Adolpho, Ana, Herminia, Horacio, Margarita, Miguel, Olinto, Rafael, Ramon, Santiago; Elodie, Honore.*

Sirianni (620) Italian (Calabria): from the Calabrian title of respect *sir* 'lord', 'master' (Old French *sire*) + the personal name *Ianni*, a short form of *Gianni* (see JOHN). This was the kind of title often given to a cleric. Compare MASTRIANNI.
GIVEN NAMES Italian 12%. *Sal* (3), *Carmine* (2), *Ottavio* (2), *Salvatore* (2), *Vincenzo* (2), *Antonio, Attilio, Carmel, Dino, Nicola, Pasquale, Quinto.*

Sirico (170) Italian (Naples): from Latin *sericus* 'silk(en)', applied as a nickname or occasionally as a personal name.
GIVEN NAMES Italian 23%. *Angelo* (4), *Carmine* (3), *Salvatore* (2), *Aniello, Enrico, Sal, Santo.*

Sirignano (117) Southern Italian: habitational name from Sirignano in Avellino province, so called from the Latin personal name *Serenius* + the suffix *-anu*.
GIVEN NAMES Italian 16%. *Carmine* (2), *Orazio* (2), *Luigi, Pasquale, Vito.*

Sirk (241) Slovenian: topographic name from *sirek* 'sorghum' (dialect *sirk*), also in some dialects meaning 'grain'.

Sirkin (237) Jewish (eastern Ashkenazic): metronymic from the Yiddish female personal name *Sirke* (see SIRKO) + the Slavic metronymic suffix *-in*.

Sirko (146) Jewish (from Ukraine): from the Yiddish personal name *Sirke*, a pet form of *Sore* 'Sarah' (from the Hebrew female personal name *Sara* 'princess').

Sirles (144) Origin unidentified; in part, perhaps an altered spelling of SEARLES.

Sirls (103) Origin unidentified; perhaps an altered spelling of SEARLES.

Sirman (148) English: variant of SERMON.

Sirmans (411) English: variant of SERMON.

Sirmon (211) English: variant of SERMON.

Sirmons (289) English: variant of SERMON.

Sirna (170) Italian (Sicily): from the Greek place name *Súrna*.
GIVEN NAMES Italian 11%. *Salvatore* (2), *Calogero, Elvira, Marisam Sal.*

Sirois (1579) French: perhaps from *sire* + *roi* 'king', a form of address, comparable to an ironic 'your majesty'.
FOREBEARS A Sirois, also called DUPLESSIS, from Paris is documented in Rivière-Ouelle, Quebec, in 1714.
GIVEN NAMES French 15%. *Armand* (6), *Fernand* (6), *Normand* (4), *Adrien* (3), *Andre* (3), *Marcel* (3), *Emilien* (2), *Herve* (2), *Rosaire* (2), *Yvon* (2), *Alain, Alban.*

Siroky (160) **1.** Czech and Slovak (**Široký**): descriptive nickname from the adjective *široký* 'broad'. **2.** Hungarian: habitational name for someone from places in Hungary called Sirok or Siroka.

Siron (190) French: derisive nickname for someone who gave himself airs and graces, or an occupational name for someone in the service of a great lord, from a diminutive of Old French *sire* 'lord' (from Latin *senior* 'elder').

Sirota (574) **1.** Polish: dialect and archaic form of **Sierota** (see SEROTA). **2.** Jewish (from Ukraine): nickname from Ukrainian *syrota* 'orphan'.
GIVEN NAMES Jewish 14%; Russian 10%. *Golda* (2), *Mariya* (2), *Reuven* (2), *Aharon, Ahron, Aron, Esfir, Hyman, Ilya, Isadore, Itzchak, Izhak; Mikhail* (4), *Vladimir* (3), *Boris* (2), *Fedor* (2), *Leonid* (2), *Anatoly, Arkadiy, Egor, Galina, Grigoriy, Igor, Iosif.*

Sirrine (161) Origin unidentified.

Sis (104) Czech: nickname from an altered form of the German adjective *süss* 'sweet', 'sweet-natured' (see SUESS).

Sisak (126) Polish (**Sisiak**) and Slovak (**Sisák**): nickname from Polish dialect *sisiak* 'little horse' or a related word in another Slavic language.

Sischo (136) Variant spelling of Italian SISCO.

Sisco (2603) Italian: from the personal name *Cisco*, a southern variant of *Cesco*, a short form of FRANCESCO.

Siscoe (128) Americanized spelling of SISCO.

Sise (136) English: unexplained.

Sisemore (390) English: from Old French *sis* 'six' + *mars*, plural of *mar* 'mark' (a coin), a nickname probably of anecdotal origin.

Sisk (4397) Irish: of uncertain origin, found in County Cork since the 18th century.

Siska (326) **1.** Czech and Slovak (**Šiška**): nickname from Old Czech *šiška* 'cone-shaped dumpling', 'cone', applied to someone with a cone-shaped head. **2.** Slovenian (south central Slovenia; **Šiška**): nickname from *šiška* 'gallnut'. **3.** Greek (**Siskas**): descriptive nickname from Turkish *siska* 'rickety', 'crippled'.

Siskin (160) Jewish (Ashkenazic): variant of SUSSKIND.
GIVEN NAMES Jewish 5%. *Meyer, Miriam.*

Siskind (268) Jewish (Ashkenazic): variant of SUSSKIND.
GIVEN NAME Jewish 4%. *Sol* (2).

Sisko (267) **1.** Slovenian (**Šiško**): reduced form of the personal name *Fransisko* (see FRANCIS). **2.** Greek (**Siskos**): nickname from Turkish *sişko* 'fat', 'overweight'.

Sisler (938) variant of Swiss German **Zisler**, an occupational name for a grower of chickpeas (from Late Latin *cisser*), or an obscene nickname from Middle High German *zisel* 'penis'.

Sisley (233) English: from the medieval female personal name *Sisley, Cecilie* (Latin *Caecilia*, feminine form of the Roman family name *Caecilius*, originally a derivative of *caecus* 'blind'). This was the name of a Roman virgin martyr of the 2nd or 3rd century, who came to be regarded as the patron saint of music.

Sisneros (891) Variant spelling of Spanish CISNEROS.
GIVEN NAMES Spanish 21%. *Jose* (12), *Manuel* (10), *Carlos* (5), *Luis* (5), *Arturo* (3), *Fran-*

cisco (3), *Juanita* (3), *Orlando* (3), *Ruben* (3), *Armando* (2), *Cosme* (2), *Diego* (2).

Sisney (257) Possibly of English origin, a variant of **Sismey**, a Cambridgeshire name of unexplained etymology.

Sison (467) **1.** Filipino: from Tagalog *sison* 'fourth grandson'. **2.** Spanish (**Sisón**): derogatory nickname from *sisón* 'cheat', 'petty swindler'. **3.** Spanish (**Sisón**): alternatively perhaps a nickname from the homonym *sisón* meaning 'sandpiper'. This is also found as a Sephardic Jewish surname.
GIVEN NAMES Spanish 37%. *Luis* (6), *Jose* (5), *Alberto* (2), *Alfredo* (2), *Carlito* (2), *Eduardo* (2), *Erlinda* (2), *Joselito* (2), *Juanito* (2), *Mario* (2), *Orlando* (2), *Perfecto* (2); *Antonio* (5), *Amadeo* (2), *Angelo*, *Gilda*.

Sissel (262) German: unexplained.

Sissom (330) Variant of English SISSON.

Sisson (4486) English: **1.** metronymic from the medieval female personal name *Siss*, *Ciss*, short for *Sisley*, *Cecilie* (see SISLEY), or possibly from a pet form of *Sisley* (with the old French diminutive suffix *-on*). **2.** variant of SESSIONS.

Sissons (112) Variant of English SESSIONS.

Sistare (161) Origin unidentified.

Sistek (146) Czech (**Šístek**): from a noun derivative of the vocabulary word *šest* 'six'. This is sometimes a house name, from a house on which the number 6 was prominently displayed. In addition, it is a nickname for someone with long hair that hung down and curled at the bottom, resembling the figure 6.

Sisti (312) Italian (mainly central and northern): patronymic or plural form of SISTO.
GIVEN NAMES Italian 12%. *Angelo* (2), *Marco* (2), *Antonio*, *Gaetano*, *Gino*, *Lido*, *Vito*.

Sisto (385) **1.** Italian (mainly southern): from the personal name *Sisto*, a variant of SESTO (Latin *Sixtus*, *Sextus* 'sixth(-born)'). **2.** Galician: habitational name from any of various places in Galicia named Sisto or Sixto.
GIVEN NAMES Italian 11%; Spanish 10%. *Elvira* (3), *Rocco* (3), *Vito* (3), *Angelo*, *Armando*, *Arturo*, *Aurelio*, *Carmino*, *Mario*, *Nicola*, *Nunzio*, *Salvatore*; *Juan* (3), *Jesus* (2), *Javier*, *Manuel*, *Miguel*, *Pedro*, *Salvador*.

Sistrunk (973) Of Swiss German origin: unexplained.

Sit (193) Chinese 薛: Cantonese variant of XUE.
GIVEN NAMES Chinese 29%. *Chun* (4), *Hin* (3), *Kwan* (3), *Fung* (2), *Wai* (2), *Yau* (2), *Chi*, *Chi Shing*, *Chow*, *Hon*, *Hong*, *Kit Man*; *Chung*, *Pak*.

Sita (141) **1.** Southern Italian and Greek (**Sitas**): probably an occupational name for a sieve maker, from Greek *sēta* 'sieve'. **2.** Hungarian (**Szita**): metonymic occupational name for a sieve maker, from *szita* 'sieve'.

GIVEN NAMES Italian 16%. *Gino* (2), *Angelo*, *Carlo*, *Constantino*, *Francesco*, *Sal*.

Sitar (236) Czech (**Sítař**), Slovak (**Sitár**), and Slovenian: occupational name for a maker of sieves, from an agent noun derivative of Czech *sít'*, Slovenian *sito* 'sieve'.

Sitarski (110) Polish: **1.** habitational name for someone from a place called Sitarze in Siedlce voivodeship. **2.** variant of SITARZ, with the addition of the surname suffix *-ski*.
GIVEN NAMES Polish 15%. *Ewa*, *Jacek*, *Marzena*, *Mieczyslaw*, *Thadeus*, *Wojtek*.

Sitarz (135) Polish: occupational name for a maker or seller of sieves, *sitarz*, an agent derivative of *sito* 'sieve'.
GIVEN NAMES Polish 17%. *Andrzej* (2), *Irena*, *Katarzyna*, *Kazimierz*, *Krystyna*, *Miroslawa*, *Stanislaw*, *Tadeusz*.

Sitek (212) Polish: from *sitek*, metonymic occupational name for a sieve maker, a derivative of *sito* 'sieve'.
GIVEN NAMES Polish 4%. *Andrzej*, *Ewa*.

Sites (1744) Perhaps an Americanized spelling of SEITZ.

Sitko (396) Polish: from *sitko*, diminutive of *sito* 'sieve'.
GIVEN NAMES Polish 7%. *Andrzej*, *Casimir*, *Elzbieta*, *Irena*, *Karol*, *Kazimierz*, *Krystyna*, *Piotr*, *Wieslaw*, *Zbigniew*.

Sitkowski (100) Polish: habitational name from a place called Sitkowo in Białystok voivodeship, named with *sitek* (see SITEK).
GIVEN NAME Polish 4%. *Wojciech*.

Sitler (443) German: variant spelling of SITTLER.

Sitter (431) German: possibly a variant of SITTIG.

Sitterly (156) Americanized spelling of South German **Sitterli**, **Sitterle**, occupational name for a shoemaker or tailor, from a diminutive of Middle High German *sūter* 'sewer'.

Sittig (364) German: **1.** nickname from Middle High German *sitic* 'well-mannered'. **2.** nickname for a loud or talkative person, from Middle High German *sitich* 'parrot'. **3.** from the personal name *Sitto*, a short form of a Germanic personal name formed with *sigi* 'victory' as the first element.
GIVEN NAMES German 4%. *Kurt* (3), *Otto*.

Sittler (221) German: topographic name for someone who lived in a place where water collected, from *sütte(l)* 'puddle', 'pool' + the suffix *-er* denoting an inhabitant.

Sittner (180) German: **1.** variant of SITTLER. **2.** habitational name for someone from either of two places named Sitten.

Sitton (1275) English (London): unexplained.

Sitts (174) Americanized spelling of German SITZ.

Situ (240) Chinese 司徒: unusual for a Chinese surname, this name is composed of two characters. Situ was the title of an official post, the minister of education, during

the Zhou dynasty (1122–221 BC). Descendants of an important situ of this period adopted his official title as their surname.
GIVEN NAMES Chinese 61%; Vietnamese 6%. *Ming* (5), *Yan* (4), *Chao* (3), *Jian* (3), *Wen* (3), *Chi* (2), *Guo* (2), *Jian Min* (2), *Sumei* (2), *Geng*, *Guo Hui*, *Guo Qiang*; *Hao* (2), *Bao*, *Can*, *Cong*, *Hai*, *Hoi*, *Long*, *Mai*, *Xuan*.

Sitz (465) German: **1.** from *Sizzo*, a short form of a Germanic compound personal name formed with *sigi* 'victory' as the first element. **2.** nickname for someone who owned a house, from Middle High German *siz* 'seat', 'domicile'.

Sitze (140) German: variant of SITZ.

Sitzer (154) **1.** German: from an agent derivative of Middle High German *siz* 'seat', 'domicile' (see SITZ). **2.** Jewish (Ashkenazic): from Yiddish *zitsn* 'to sit', possibly applied as a nickname for a stallholder in a marketplace, or else for someone who spent most of his time in study.

Sitzes (199) German: variant of SITZ.

Sitzler (105) German: variant of SITZER.

Sitzman (382) **1.** Jewish (Ashkenazic): variant of SITZER. **2.** Respelling of German SITZMANN.

Sitzmann (221) South German: elaborated form of SITZ, with the addition of Middle High German *man* 'man'.

Siu (856) **1.** Chinese 萧: see XIAO. **2.** Chinese 邵: Cantonese variant of SHAO.
GIVEN NAMES Chinese 19%. *Ming* (6), *Kin* (5), *Kam* (3), *Wai* (3), *Chan* (2), *Chi* (2), *Kam Hung* (2), *Kwok* (2), *Kwong* (2), *Man* (2), *Wing* (2), *Bik*.

Siuda (137) Polish: nickname from the dialect word *siuda*, denoting grain of poor quality, containing grains of weeds and other impurities.
GIVEN NAMES Polish 5%. *Jerzy*, *Zdzislaw*.

Sivak (343) Czech and Slovak (**Sivák**), Ukrainian, and Jewish (from Ukraine): nickname for a gray-haired man, from a noun derivative of Slavic *sivy* 'gray'.
GIVEN NAMES Russian 5%; Jewish 4%. *Anatoly*, *Ginda*, *Grigoriy*, *Igor*, *Mikhail*, *Semyon*, *Svetlana*, *Vladimir*, *Yury*; *Ilya*.

Siver (264) Variant of Dutch SIEVER.

Siverling (164) Probably an Americanized spelling of South German **Seiferling**, a derivative of the personal name *Seifer(t)*, a variant of SIEGFRIED.

Siverly (120) Americanized form of German **Sifferle**, from a pet form of the personal name *Seifer(t)*, a variant of SIEGFRIED.

Sivers (140) German: variant of SIEVERS.

Siverson (177) Americanized form of Scandinavian **Syversen** (see SYVERSON), SIVERTSEN, SIVERTSON, or SYVERTSEN.
GIVEN NAMES Scandinavian 4%. *Erik*, *Nels*.

Sivert (108) Dutch, Danish, and Norwegian: from the personal name *Sivert* (see SIVERTSEN).

Sivertsen (301) Dutch, Danish, and Norwegian: patronymic from the personal name *Sivert*. In Norwegian and Danish the name is from *Sigvard*, a form of Old Norse *Sigurðr*, from *sigr* 'victory' + *varðr* 'guardian'; in Dutch it may have been an equivalent of SIEGFRIED.
GIVEN NAMES Scandinavian 12%. *Sigvard* (2), *Bodil, Erik, Nanna, Per, Selmer, Sig, Tor.*

Sivertson (289) Americanized spelling of SIVERTSEN or of the Swedish cognate **Sivertsson**.
GIVEN NAMES Scandinavian 9%. *Alf* (3), *Sig* (3), *Lars.*

Sivils (307) Catalan: variant of **Civils**, **Civils**, and **Sibils**, topographic name from old French *sevil* 'fence', 'enclosure'. See CIVIL.

Sivley (312) Americanized form of German **Sifferle** (see SIVERLY).

Siwek (255) Polish and Jewish (from Poland): nickname for a gray-haired man, from Polish *siwy* 'gray'.
GIVEN NAMES Polish 12%. *Zygmunt* (2), *Alicja, Andrzej, Casimir, Dariusz, Grzegorz, Janusz, Jerzy, Krzysztof, Maciej, Pawel, Urszula.*

Siwicki (104) Polish: from a derivative of *siwy* 'gray'.
GIVEN NAMES Polish 12%. *Jacek, Krzysztof, Mariusz, Stanislaw, Zygmunt.*

Siwik (150) Polish: variant of SIWEK.
GIVEN NAMES Polish 16%. *Slawomir* (2), *Andrzej, Jozef, Mariola, Miroslaw, Witold, Zdzislaw, Zofia.*

Siwinski (138) Polish (**Siwiński**): habitational name from a placed named with a derivative of *siwy* 'gray'.
GIVEN NAMES Polish 9%. *Jerzy* (2), *Thadeus.*

Six (1185) **1.** French and German: from a personal name (Latin *Sixtus*, a variant of *Sextus* 'sixth(-born)'), borne by various saints and popes in the early centuries of the Christian era, and subsequently adopted in their honor. **2.** French: nickname from Old French *six* 'six' (Latin *sex*), given for some anecdotal reason now lost; the surnames **Deux** ('two'), **Huit** ('eight'), and **Dix** ('ten') also exist, but all are rare.

Sixkiller (102) Origin unidentified. Perhaps a much altered form of German **Sechsheller**, a habitational name for someone from Sechshelden in Hesse.

Sizelove (212) Origin unidentified.

Sizemore (6041) English: variant of SISEMORE.

Sizer (580) English: status name or occupational name from Middle English *sysour* 'assizer', i.e. a member of the court of assize.

Sjoberg (555) Swedish (**Sjöberg**): ornamental name composed of the elements *sjö* 'sea' + *berg* 'mountain', 'hill'.
GIVEN NAMES Scandinavian 10%. *Gothard* (2), *Lennart* (2), *Britt, Erik, Hjalmer, Mats, Nils, Sten, Sven.*

Sjoblom (240) Swedish (**Sjöblom**): ornamental name composed of the elements *sjö* 'sea' + *blom* 'flower'.
GIVEN NAMES Scandinavian 10%. *Erik* (3), *Astrid, Eskil, Sven.*

Sjodin (188) Swedish (**Sjödin**): ornamental name composed of the elements *sjö* 'sea' + -*din*, a common suffix of surnames.
GIVEN NAMES Scandinavian 7%. *Alf, Anders, Berent, Mats, Nils.*

Sjogren (442) Swedish (**Sjögren**): ornamental name composed of the elements *sjö* 'sea' + *gren* 'branch'.
GIVEN NAMES Scandinavian 14%. *Astrid, Erik, Hedda, Hedvig, Johan, Per.*

Sjolander (191) Swedish (**Sjölander**): ornamental name composed of the elements *sjö* 'sea' + *land* 'land' + the suffix -*er*. The coinage may have been influenced by the common surname suffix -*ander*, derived from Greek *anēr* 'man', genitive *andros*.
GIVEN NAMES German 4%; Scandinavian 4%. *Kurt; Matts.*

Sjoquist (176) Swedish (**Sjöqvist**): ornamental name composed of the elements *sjö* 'sea' + *quist*, an old or ornamental spelling of *kvist* 'twig'.
GIVEN NAMES Scandinavian 6%. *Kerstin, Swen.*

Sjostrand (101) Swedish (**Sjöstrand**): ornamental name composed of *sjö* 'sea' + *strand* 'shore'.
GIVEN NAMES Scandinavian 11%; German 4%. *Mats, Nels; Kurt.*

Sjostrom (403) Swedish (**Sjöström**): ornamental name composed of the elements *sjö* 'sea' + *ström* 'river'.
GIVEN NAMES Scandinavian 9%. *Erik* (2), *Nils* (2), *Anders, Berger, Lars, Lasse, Lennart.*

Skaar (461) Norwegian: habitational name from any of numerous farmsteads, notably on the west coast of Norway, named Skår or Skor, from Old Norse *skor* 'ledge', 'cleft in a mountain'.
GIVEN NAMES Scandinavian 10%; German 4%. *Anders* (2), *Espen, Karsten, Nels, Sig; Kurt* (2), *Gerhard, Gerlinda.*

Skaer (133) Altered form of Norwegian **Skjær**, a habitational name, meaning 'skerry', 'rock', from any of several farmsteads so named.

Skaff (370) Origin unidentified.

Skagen (104) Norwegian: habitational name from any of several farmsteads named from the definite singular of *skage*, Old Norse *skagi* 'headland', 'promontory', 'cape'.

Skaggs (6025) English: probably a variant of **Skegg**, which Reaney and Wilson describe as a nickname from Old Norse *skegg* 'beard'; curiously, though, the modern surname occurs chiefly in Hertfordshire, with very little evidence of it in the north, where it might be expected to be concentrated.

Skahan (138) Variant of Irish SKEHAN.

Skahill (158) Irish: variant spelling of SCAHILL.
GIVEN NAME Irish 5%. *Tierney.*

Skaife (119) Variant of SCAIFE.

Skains (176) English (also **Skeins**): see SKEENS.

Skaja (130) Origin unidentified.

Skala (706) Czech (**Skála**), Slovak, Polish (**Skała**), and Jewish (from Poland): topographic name for someone who lived by a rock or crag, Czech *skála*, Polish *skała*. As a Jewish surname this is often ornamental.

Skalecki (88) Polish: habitational name from places called Skałka or Skałki, named with Polish *skałka* 'rock', 'flint'.

Skalicky (265) Czech and Slovak (**Skalický**): habitational name from places called Skalice or Skalička, named with *skála* 'rock', 'crag'.

Skalitzky (128) Germanized spelling of Czech SKALICKY.

Skalka (135) Polish and Jewish (from Poland): topographic name, nickname, or ornamental name from Polish *skałka* 'flint' (see SKALA).

Skalla (173) Americanized spelling of Czech, Slovak, Polish, or Jewish SKALA.

Skalski (338) Polish: habitational name from any of several places named Skała and Skały, named with *skała* 'rock', 'flint'.
GIVEN NAMES Polish 9%. *Jacek* (2), *Andrzej, Czeslaw, Janusz, Jerzy, Krzysztof, Tadeusz, Zygmunt.*

Skalsky (217) Czech and Slovak (**Skalský**): habitational name from any of several places named with *skála* 'rock', 'flint'.

Skanes (110) English: see SKEENS.

Skar (128) Norwegian: habitational name from any of numerous farmsteads in every part of Norway called Skar(d), from Old Norse *skarð* 'cleft', 'mountain pass'.
GIVEN NAME Scandinavian 6%. *Alf* (2).

Skarbek (149) Polish: nickname for a miser or a rich individual, from a derivative of *skarb* 'treasure', 'wealth'. Compare *skarbnik* 'treasurer'.
GIVEN NAMES Polish 12%. *Tadeusz* (3), *Krzysztof, Slawomir, Zigmund.*

Skarda (328) Czech (**Škarda**): nickname from Czech *škaredý* 'sullen', 'sour-faced'.

Skare (188) Norwegian: habitational name from any of numerous farmsteads named with the dative case (*skarði*) or the definite singular form (*skardet*) of Old Norse *skarð* 'cleft', 'mountain pass'.

Skarin (108) Swedish: ornamental or topographic name from *skar* 'edge', 'precipice' + the surname suffix -*in*, based on Latin -*in(i)us*.

Skarzynski (130) Polish (**Skarżyński**): habitational name for someone from places called Skarżyn in Konin, Ostrołęka, Siedlce, and Płock voivodeships, or Skarzyń in Leszno voivodeship. The place names are derived from *skarga* 'complaint'.
GIVEN NAMES Polish 14%. *Czeslaw, Dariusz, Kazimierz, Wladyslaw, Zofia.*

Skates (280) Northern English: patronymic from SKEETE.

Skau (135) Scandinavian: habitational name from a common farm name or place name, a form of Old Norse *skógr* 'wood', 'forest'.
GIVEN NAMES Scandinavian 6%. *Carsten, Evald, Thor.*

Skaug (102) Norwegian: variant of SKAU.
GIVEN NAMES Scandinavian 6%. *Jorgen, Viggo.*

Skawinski (100) Polish: habitational name for someone from Skawina in Kraków province.
GIVEN NAMES Polish 9%. *Boleslaw, Bronislaw.*

Skeans (164) Irish: variant of SKEHAN, with the addition of English patronymic -*s*.

Skeel (181) English: metonymic occupational name for a maker or seller of buckets, from Middle English *skele, skeyll* 'wooden bucket'.

Skeels (488) English (Cambridgeshire): variant of SKEEL.

Skeen (1960) **1.** Scottish: habitational name from Skene in Aberdeenshire, named with Gaelic *sceathan* 'thorn bush'. **2.** variant of Irish SKEHAN.

Skeens (1031) English (Hampshire): possibly a variant of the Scottish name SKEEN.

Skees (297) Dutch: perhaps a variant of KEES.

Skeete (224) Northern English: from the Old Norse byname *Skjótr* 'swift'.

Skeeter (117) This has the form of an English or Scottish surname, but if it originated from the British Isles it is not known there now.
GIVEN NAMES German 5%. *Fritz, Lorenz.*

Skeeters (173) Origin unidentified. Compare SKEETER.

Skeffington (187) English: habitational name from a place in Leicestershire, so called from Old English *Scēaftingtūn* 'settlement (Old English *tūn*) associated with *Scēaft*', a byname meaning 'shaft', 'spear'. The initial consonant was modified from 'sh' to 'sk' under Scandinavian influence.
GIVEN NAME Irish 7%. *Fitzpatrick.*

Skehan (258) Irish: reduced Anglicized form of Gaelic **Mac Sceacháin** or **Ó Sceacháin** 'son (or 'descendant') of *Sceachán*', a personal name which appears to be derived from a diminutive of *sceach* 'briar', 'thorn bush'. The Gaelic name has sometimes been 'translated' as THORNTON.

Skeie (139) Norwegian: habitational name from any of about twenty farmsteads so named, notably in southwestern Norway, from Old Norse *skeiði*, the dative case of *skeið* 'horse race', 'race', 'run'.
GIVEN NAMES Scandinavian 14%. *Thor (2), Lars.*

Skelding (110) English: habitational name from a place in West Yorkshire, near Ripon, also known as Skelden. It is so called from

the river name *Skell* (Old Norse *Skjallr* 'resounding') + Old English *denu* 'valley'.

Skeldon (125) Scottish and northern English: habitational name from a place in Ayrshire, probably so named from Old English *scylf* 'shelf', 'ledge' + *dūn* 'hill', with a later change of 's' to 'sk' under Scandinavian influence.

Skellenger (171) English?

Skelley (613) Irish: variant of SCALLY.

Skellie (101) Irish: variant of SCALLY.

Skelly (1708) Irish: variant of SCALLY.

Skelton (5792) Northern English: habitational name from places in Cumbria and Yorkshire, originally named with the same elements as SHELTON, but with a later change of 's' to 'sk' under Scandinavian influence. The surname has also been established in Ireland for four or five centuries.

Skemp (142) English: variant of KEMP.

Skenandore (177) Origin unidentified.

Skender (137) From the personal name *Iskender*, Arabic, Turkish, Albanian, etc., form of ALEXANDER.

Skene (194) Scottish: variant spelling of SKEEN.

Skerl (110) Slovenian (**Škerl**): probably a metonymic occupational name for a slater, from the dialect word *škrl* 'slate'.

Skerrett (113) English: variant of SKERRITT.

Skerritt (154) English: **1.** habitational name from Skirwith in Cumbria, formerly pronounced *Skerritt*, which was named with Old Norse *skjallr* 'resounding' (a river name or a waterfall) + *vath* 'ford'. **2.** metonymic occupational name for someone who grew or sold caraway, from Middle English *skirwhit(e)* 'caraway', 'water parsnip' (apparently an alteration of Old French *escheris*), a plant cultivated for its tubers, which were used in sauces and medicine.

Skerry (164) Irish: variant of SCARRY or SCURRY.

Skewes (174) Cornish: habitational name from any of various minor places named with Cornish *skaw* 'elder bush' + the locative suffix -*es*.

Skiba (983) Polish: from *skiba* 'thin strip of land between two furrows'; perhaps a metonymic occupational name for a peasant or a plowman.
GIVEN NAMES Polish 7%. *Krystyna (3), Zbigniew (3), Tadeusz (2), Andrzej, Beata, Bogumil, Casimir, Dariusz, Ignatius, Jadwiga, Jerzy, Malgorzata.*

Skibba (145) Variant of German SKIBBE.
GIVEN NAMES German 4%. *Gerhardt, Horst.*

Skibbe (163) North German: from Sorbian *skiba* 'slice of bread', perhaps a nickname for a poor person.
GIVEN NAMES German 4%. *Erwin, Hertha, Volker.*

Skibicki (147) Polish: habitational name for someone from places called Skibice in Włocławek and Zamość voivodeships.
GIVEN NAME Polish 5%. *Iwan.*

Skibinski (369) Polish (**Skibiński**): habitational name for someone from Skibin in Włocławek voivodeship, named with *skiba* 'strip of raised land between two furrows'.
GIVEN NAMES Polish 7%. *Ewa (2), Casimir, Eugeniusz, Jacek, Karol, Krzysztof, Wojciech, Zdzislaw, Zygmund.*

Skibo (181) Origin unidentified.

Skidgel (155) English (Devon): unexplained.

Skidmore (4121) English (West Country): of uncertain origin, perhaps a habitational name from an unidentified place named in Old English with *scīte* 'shit', 'dung' + *mōr* 'moor', 'fen'.

Skiff (372) English: unexplained. Possibly a metonymic occupational name for a waterman on the Thames. The name is found in the 16th and 17th centuries in and around London.
FOREBEARS James Skiffe came from London, England, to Lynn, MA, in about 1635. Subsequently the family settled in Sandwich, MA.

Skiffington (161) English: variant of SKEFFINGTON.
GIVEN NAME Irish 5%. *Aidan.*

Skiles (1861) English: perhaps a variant of **Skoyles**, a Norfolk name of unexplained etymology.

Skillen (187) **1.** Irish and Scottish: variant of SKILLING. **2.** English: variant of SKILLERN.

Skillern (331) English: habitational name from Skeleron in Rimington, Lancashire (formerly in West Yorkshire), earlier known as Skelhorn.

Skillin (211) Probably a reduced form of Scottish SKILLING.

Skilling (238) Scottish: patronymic from an Old English personal name *Scilling*, which is possibly related to Old English *scyl* 'sonorous'.

Skillings (415) English (Norfolk): perhaps a patronymic from the Old English personal name *Scilling* (see SKILLING).

Skillman (1040) English: nickname from Old Norse *skilamaður* 'trustworthy man'.

Skilton (200) English (Sussex): variant of SKELTON.

Skinner (19283) English: occupational name for someone who stripped the hide from animals, to be used in the production of fur garments or to be tanned for leather, from an agent derivative of Middle English *skin* 'hide', 'pelt' (Old Norse *skinn*).

Skipper (3333) English (chiefly Norfolk): **1.** occupational name for the master of a ship, Middle English *skipper* (from Middle Low German, Middle Dutch *schipper*). **2.** from an agent derivative of Middle English *skip(en)* 'to jump or spring' (apparently of Scandinavian origin), hence an occupational name for an acrobat or professional tumbler, or nickname for a high-spirited person. **3.** occupational name for a basket-maker, from an agent derivative of Middle English *skipp(e)*, *skepp(e)* 'basket', 'hamper' (Old Norse *skeppa*).

Skipton (172) English: habitational name from Skipton or Skipton-on-Swale in North Yorkshire. Both places are named with Old English *scīp* 'sheep' (with later change of 's' to 'sk' under Scandinavian influence) + *tūn* 'enclosure', 'settlement'.

Skipwith (128) English (Yorkshire): habitational name from a place in Yorkshire, recorded in Domesday Book as *Schipwic*, from Old English *scēap*, *scīp* 'sheep' + *wīc* 'outlying settlement'. Under later Scandinavian influence the initial 's' became 'sk' and the second element was changed to *-with* (Old Norse *viðr* 'wood').
FOREBEARS The main Skipwith family held the manor of Skipwith in England in the early Middle Ages, and direct descendants can be traced to the present day. In the 13th century they moved from Yorkshire to Lincolnshire, where their principal seat was at southern Ormsby. In the early 17th century there was further migration, to Leicestershire, Warwickshire, and across the Atlantic to VA. Other bearers of the name seem to have been tenants of Lincolnshire manors held by the Skipworth family, and to have taken the surname of their overlords.

Skipworth (525) English: variant of SKIPWITH.

Skirvin (364) Scottish: unexplained.

Skiver (340) **1.** Dutch: occupational name for someone who ground and polished diamonds on a rotating wheel, Dutch *schijf*. **2.** English or Scottish: occupational name for a leatherworker whose job was to pare thin strips off a skin, for use as laces, ties, etc.

Sklar (1461) Czech (**Sklář**), Slovak (**Sklár**), Ukrainian, and Jewish (from Ukraine): occupational name from Czech *sklář*, Ukrainian *sklyar* 'glazier', from *sklo* 'glass'.
GIVEN NAMES Jewish 6%. *Meyer* (3), *Sol* (3), *Ari* (2), *Batya* (2), *Emanuel* (2), *Hyman* (2), *Herschel*, *Hinda*, *Isadore*, *Izia*, *Morty*, *Moshe*.

Sklenar (217) Czech (**Sklenář**) and Slovak (**Sklenár**): occupational name for a glazier, Czech *sklenář*.

Skluzacek (196) Czech (**Skluzáček**): from a derivative of *skluz* 'to slide', 'to slip', hence probably an occupational name for someone who carried wood or other things on a sledge during winter.
GIVEN NAMES French 4%. *Laure*, *Marcel*.

Skoczylas (203) **1.** Polish: from *skoczyć* 'to leap' + *las* 'forest', a nickname for someone who often went into the forest. **2.** Jewish (from Poland): habitational name for someone from a place called Skoczylas in Poland.

GIVEN NAMES Polish 16%. *Andrzej* (2), *Jerzy* (2), *Beata*, *Grazyna*, *Iwan*, *Kazimierz*, *Krzysztof*, *Ryszard*, *Wlodzimierz*, *Wojciech*.

Skoda (251) Czech, Slovak, and Slovenian (**Škoda**): from *škoda* 'damage', 'loss'; apparently a nickname denoting someone who was accident-prone or a bungler.

Skoff (173) **1.** Americanized or Germanized spelling of Slovenian **Škof**, nickname from *škof* 'bishop', derived from Old High German *biscof*. Compare BISCHOFF. **2.** Americanized spelling of Danish SKOV.

Skog (319) Swedish and Norwegian: from the vocabulary word *skog* 'wood', 'copse'. In Norwegian, this is often a topographic name for someone who lived by a wood or copse, but as a Swedish surname it is generally ornamental.
GIVEN NAMES Scandinavian 7%. *Alf*, *Erik*, *Lars*, *Mauritz*, *Nils*.

Skogen (392) Norwegian: habitational name from any of numerous farmsteads, notably in eastern Norway, named with *skogen*, the definite singular form of *skog*, from Old Norse *skógr* 'wood', 'forest'.
GIVEN NAMES Scandinavian 4%. *Arnt*, *Ordell*, *Selmer*.

Skoglund (918) Swedish and Norwegian: ornamental or topographic name composed of the elements *skog* 'copse', 'wood' + *lund* 'grove'.
GIVEN NAMES Scandinavian 6%. *Erik*, *Lars*, *Nils*, *Sten*, *Swen*.

Skogman (127) Swedish: ornamental name composed of *skog* 'copse', 'wood' + *man* 'man'.

Skogstad (136) Norwegian: habitational name from any of eight farmsteads so named, probably from the Old Norse personal name *Skógr* + Old Norse *staðir*, plural of *staðr* 'farmstead', 'dwelling'.
GIVEN NAMES Scandinavian 12%. *Alf*, *Britt*, *Obert*, *Tor*.

Skok (266) **1.** Slovenian: nickname for a refugee from the Turks in the 15th and 16th century, from a derivative of *uskočiti* 'to flee'. Slovenian territory was a refuge for Christians from Bosnia when it was conquered by the Ottoman Empire and from the parts of Croatia which were a war zone. **2.** Dutch: variant of SCHOCK 2.

Skokan (136) Polish and Slovak: nickname for someone who tended to dash about, or an occupational name for an acrobat, from a derivative of *skok* 'spring', 'bound', 'leap', or of *skoczyć* 'to jump or spring'.
GIVEN NAMES Czech and Slovak 4%. *Ladislav*, *Zdenek*.

Skold (154) Swedish (**Sköld**): from *sköld* 'shield', either as a soldier's name or from a place name.

Skolnick (676) Americanized spelling of Jewish SHKOLNIK.
GIVEN NAMES Jewish 6%. *Isadore* (3), *Emanuel*, *Meyer*, *Sol*, *Zelig*, *Zev*.

Skolnik (448) Americanized spelling of Jewish SHKOLNIK.

GIVEN NAMES Jewish 7%. *Arie*, *Ehud*, *Hyman*, *Ilan*, *Isadore*, *Miriam*, *Sol*, *Yaacov*, *Yitzchok*.

Skonieczny (181) Polish: variant of KONIECZNY, from an inflected form of the phrase *z konica* 'from the end', in this case someone who came from the end of a village.
GIVEN NAMES Polish 6%. *Boleslaw*, *Henryk*, *Zbigniew*.

Skoog (718) Swedish: variant of SKOG.
GIVEN NAMES Scandinavian 8%. *Erik* (5), *Birgit*, *Nels*, *Per*.

Skop (185) Polish, Czech, and Jewish (Ashkenazic): nickname from Slavic *skop* 'wether', 'castrated ram'. The Polish word has other meanings, denoting for example a pail and a kind of tax; the surname could also have originated with one of these senses, i.e. as an occupational name either for a maker of pails or for a tax collector.
GIVEN NAMES Jewish 5%; Polish 4%. *Syma*; *Jadwiga*, *Katarzyna*, *Piotr*.

Skora (234) **1.** Polish (**Skóra**) and Jewish (from Poland): metonymic occupational name for a leather worker or tanner, from *skóra* 'leather'. **2.** Norwegian: habitational name from any of numerous farmsteads named Skora, from Old Norse *skor* 'ledge', 'cleft in a mountain'.
GIVEN NAMES Polish 10%. *Casimir*, *Henryka*, *Katarzyna*, *Kazimierz*, *Stanislawa*, *Sylwester*, *Wieslawa*, *Zygmunt*.

Skorich (116) Serbian or Croatian (**Skorić**, **Škorić**): unexplained.

Skorski (94) Polish: habitational name for someone from Skórka in Łódź voivodeship or Skórki in Piła and Bydgoszcz voivodeships.
GIVEN NAMES Polish 12%. *Alfons* (2), *Mariusz*, *Tomasz*, *Zdzislaw*.

Skorupa (226) Polish and Jewish (from Poland): from *skorupa* 'shell', hence a nickname for a secretive individual.
GIVEN NAMES Polish 8%. *Stanislaw* (2), *Andrzej*, *Elzbieta*, *Ireneusz*, *Jerzy*, *Leszek*.

Skorupski (254) Polish: habitational name for someone from Skorupy in Siedlce voivodeship.
GIVEN NAMES Polish 7%. *Jacek*, *Witold*, *Zigmund*.

Skotnicki (131) Polish: habitational name for someone from any of various place called Skotniki, named with *skotnik* 'herdsman'.
GIVEN NAMES Polish 10%; French 5%. *Andrzej*, *Kazimierz*, *Ludwik*; *Andre*, *Camille*.

Skousen (184) Danish: patronymic from **Skou**, a variant of SKOV.

Skov (246) Danish: topographic name from *skov* 'forest'.
GIVEN NAMES Scandinavian 13%; German 5%. *Erik* (5), *Carsten*, *Niels*, *Thor*; *Hans* (2), *Kurt*.

Skow (529) Danish: variant spelling of SKOV.

GIVEN NAMES Scandinavian 4%. *Erik* (4), *Einer, Thora.*

Skowron (399) Polish and Jewish (from Poland): variant of SKOWRONEK.

GIVEN NAMES Polish 14%. *Andrzej* (2), *Kazimierz* (2), *Tadeusz* (2), *Wladyslaw* (2), *Alicja, Casimir, Eugeniusz, Grazyna, Halina, Krystyna, Krzysztof.*

Skowronek (303) Polish and Jewish (from Poland): from Polish *skowronek* 'skylark', applied as a nickname for a happy, cheerful person, or, in the case of the Jewish surname, as an ornamental name. This surname is also established in Germany, where it is usually written **Skowronnek.**

GIVEN NAMES Polish 7%; German 7%. *Dorota, Henryk, Ignacy, Janina, Ludwik, Tadeusz; Kurt* (2), *Bernd, Hans, Reinhard, Sieglinde.*

Skowronski (736) Polish (**Skowroński**): habitational name for someone from a place called Skowronów, Skowronna, or Skowronki, all named with Polish *skowronek* 'skylark'.

GIVEN NAMES Polish 7%. *Casimir* (2), *Jerzy* (2), *Krzysztof* (2), *Grazyna, Ignacy, Mariusz, Piotr, Wieslaw, Wladyslawa, Zbigniew, Zigmund, Zygmund.*

Skramstad (166) Norwegian: habitational name from any of five farmsteads so named, notably in Hedmark. The first element is probably a river name derived from Old Norse *skráma* 'shine'; the second, *stad*, is from Old Norse *staðir* 'farmstead', 'dwelling'.

GIVEN NAMES Scandinavian 13%. *Erik* (3), *Thorvald.*

Skrivanek (108) Czech (**Skřivánek**): nickname from *skřivánek* 'lark'.

Skroch (190) German (of Slavic origin): topographic name from Sorbian *šrok* 'pine tree'. Compare SCHROCK 3, a variant with the same origin.

Skrocki (223) Polish: habitational name from a place called Skrodzkie in Łomża voivodeship, named for the Skroda river, on which it stands.

GIVEN NAMES Polish 4%. *Boleslaw, Casimir, Czeslaw.*

Skrypek (102) Variant of Polish **Skrzypek** 'fiddle player'.

Skrzypczak (103) Polish: variant of SKRZYPEK.

GIVEN NAMES Polish 18%; German 4%. *Bogdan* (2), *Andrzej, Irena, Janina; Florian, Franz.*

Skrzypek (181) Polish and Jewish (from Poland): occupational name from *skrzypek* 'fiddle player' (from *skrzypieć* 'to creak or groan', ultimately cognate with English *scrape*).

GIVEN NAMES Polish 10%; Jewish 4%. *Casimir, Danuta, Jozef, Katarzyna, Leszek, Tadeusz, Zosia; Mayer* (2).

Skubal (178) Czech (**Škubal**): anecdotal nickname from a derivative of *škubat* 'to tear up'.

Skube (108) **1.** Americanized form of Czech **Škub**, an unflattering nickname for a ragged, ill-dressed person. **2.** Slovenian: perhaps a nickname from *skubsti* 'to pluck' (feathers from poultry).

Skubic (118) **1.** Slovenian: probably an occupational name for someone whose job was to pluck poultry or a seller of feathers, from an agent noun derivative of *skubsti* 'to pluck'. **2.** Croatian (**Skubić**): unexplained.

Skudlarek (114) Czech (**Škudlárek**): nickname for a stingy person, from a derivative Czech *škudil* 'stingy', 'tight-fisted'.

Skufca (173) Slovenian (**Škufca**): from the archaic word *škufica*, denoting a kind of small coin, probably a nickname for a poor man.

Skultety (107) Hungarian (**Skultéty**) and Slovak (**Škultéty**): origin uncertain; possibly a habitational name from an unidentified place.

Skupien (153) Polish (**Skupień**): nickname for someone noted for great powers of concentration, from Polish *skupić* 'to concentrate'.

Skura (146) Polish and Jewish (from Poland): variant of SKORA.

GIVEN NAMES Polish 6%. *Andrzej, Urszula.*

Skurka (168) Jewish (Ashkenazic): metonymic occupational name for a furrier or tanner, from Polish *skórka* 'skin', 'fur'. Compare SKORA.

Skuse (105) Cornish: variant spelling of SKEWES. The surname is now found mainly in Gloucestershire and Avon, though it was also taken to southwestern Ireland in the 17th century.

Skutt (184) Variant spelling of English SCUTT.

Skuza (109) Polish (also **Skudza**): nickname from Polish dialect *skuza* 'miser', 'niggard'.

GIVEN NAMES Polish 11%. *Andrzej* (2), *Krystna* (2), *Urszula, Zygmunt.*

Skwarek (115) Polish: nickname for a slight, tiny person, from *skwarek* 'crackling'.

GIVEN NAMES Polish 9%. *Boleslaw, Casimir, Eugeniusz.*

Sky (184) Jewish (American): **1.** English translation of HIMMEL. **2.** Shortened form of any eastern Ashkenazic surname ending in Slavic suffix *-sky*.

GIVEN NAMES Jewish 4%. *Asher, Chana, Hyman.*

Skyberg (142) Norwegian and Swedish: habitational name from any of four farms in eastern Norway and at least two places in Sweden, named with *sky* (of uncertain origin; apparently the word *sky* 'sky') + *berg* 'mountain'.

GIVEN NAME Scandinavian 6%. *Bjorn.*

Skye (111) **1.** English: unexplained. **2.** Perhaps a respelling of the Orcadian name **Skae, Skea**, from the lands of Skea in Deerness.

Skyles (311) See SKILES.

Slabach (131) German: variant of SCHLABACH.

Slabaugh (612) Americanized spelling of German SCHLABACH.

Slaby (413) Polish (**Słaby**) and Czech and Slovak (**Slabý**): unflattering nickname for a feeble individual, from Polish *słaby*, Czech *slabý* 'weak'.

GIVEN NAMES Polish 4%. *Kazimierz, Stanislaw, Waclaw, Wasil, Witold.*

Slack (5014) **1.** English and Dutch: nickname for an idle person, from Middle Dutch *slac*, Middle English *slack*, 'lazy', 'careless'. **2.** English: topographic name from northern Middle English *slack* 'shallow valley' (Old Norse *slakki*), or a habitational name from one of the places named with this word, for example near Stainland and near Hebden Bridge in West Yorkshire. **3.** Scottish (Dumfriesshire): habitational name, maybe from Slake or Slack in Roberton, Roxburghshire (now part of Borders region). **4.** It may also be an Americanized spelling of Slovenian **Slak**, a nickname from *slak* 'bindweed'.

Slacum (117) Variant of English SLOCUM.

Slade (4231) English (southern): topographic name from Middle English *slade* 'small valley', or a habitational name from any of the places named with this word (Old English *slæd*), for example in Devon and Somerset, or Slad in Gloucestershire.

Sladek (614) **1.** Czech (**Sládek**): occupational name for a brewer, from Czech *slad* 'malt'. **2.** Polish (**Śladek**): nickname from *śladek* 'ambush', 'trap'.

Slader (102) English (Devon): unexplained.

Sladky (197) Czech and Slovak (**Sladký**) and Jewish (Ashkenazic): nickname for someone with an appealing personality, from Czech *sladký* 'sweet', 'lovely' or a related word in another Slavic language.

GIVEN NAMES German 4%. *Math* (2), *Kurt.*

Slaga (101) Origin unidentified.

Slagel (300) Altered spelling of German SCHLEGEL.

Slager (499) **1.** Dutch: occupational name for a butcher, *slager*. **2.** Possibly an altered form of SCHLAGER.

Slaght (263) Dutch: of uncertain origin, possibly from *slagt* 'slaughtering (of animals)', hence an occupational name for a slaughterer, or a derogatory nickname from a variant of *sleght, slecht* 'bad', 'evil', 'wicked'

Slagle (3419) Americanized form of German SCHLEGEL.

Slagter (220) **1.** English: variant of SLAUGHTER. **2.** Dutch: occupational name for a butcher, *slagter*, a variant of SLAGER.

Slaight (133) Scottish: variant spelling of SLIGHT.

Slama (565) Slovak and Czech (**Sláma**): from *sláma* 'straw', a nickname for someone with straw-colored hair. Compare STRAW.

Slane (627) Irish (County Meath): reduced form of **de Slane**, a Norman habitational name.

Slaney (305) Irish: variant of SLANE.

Slanina (118) Czech and Slovak: nickname from a vocabulary word meaning 'bacon'.

Slankard (217) Origin unidentified.

Slanker (113) Dutch: identifying nickname for the thinner of two bearers of the same surname, from *slanker* 'thinner', the comparative of *slank* 'slender', 'slim'

Slansky (140) Czech and Slovak (**Slánský**): habitational name from Slaný in Bohemia.

Slape (269) English: topographic name from Middle English *slape* 'slippery, miry place', or a habitational name from any of the places named with this word (Old English *slæp*), as for example Slape in Dorset or Sleap in Shropshire.

Slappey (222) Probably an Americanized form of Czech **Slepý** 'blind' (see SLEPPY).

Slappy (125) See SLAPPEY.

Slaski (85) Polish: **1.** (**Śląski**): regional name for someone from Silesia (Polish *Śląsk* 'Silesia'). **2.** (**Ślaski**) habitational name from a lost place in Kielce voivodeship, or from any of various places called Szlasy, in various different voivodeships.

Slate (2146) English: metonymic occupational name for a slater, from Middle English *slate* 'slate'.

Slaten (531) English: unexplained. Compare SLATON.

Slater (11659) English and Scottish: occupational name for a slater, from an agent derivative of Middle English *s(c)late* 'slate'.

Slates (245) English: variant of SLATE.

Slatkin (149) Jewish (from Belarus): metronymic from the Yiddish female personal name *Zlatke*, a pet form of *Zlate* (from Slavic *zlata* 'golden'), with the eastern Slavic possessive suffix *-in*.
GIVEN NAME Jewish 4%. *Meyer*.

Slaton (1782) English (Midlands): unexplained. Compare SLATEN.

Slatten (241) Possibly an Americanized form of any of a number of related Norwegian names such as **Slåtten**, **Slaatten**, or **Slotten**, from the definite singular form of *slåttr*, *slátta* 'hay field'.

Slatter (233) English and Scottish: variant of SLATER.

Slattery (3482) Irish (Munster): reduced form of **O'Slattery**, an Anglicized form of Gaelic **Ó Slat(ar)ra** 'descendant of *Slatra*', a byname meaning 'robust', 'strong', 'bold'.
GIVEN NAMES Irish 5%. *Brendan* (2), *Jarlath*, *Liam*.

Slatton (429) English (Gloucestershire): possibly habitational name from a lost or unidentified place.

Slaubaugh (133) Americanized form of German SCHLABACH.

Slaugh (228) Altered spelling of English SLOUGH or German SCHLAUCH.

Slaughter (8609) English: **1.** occupational name for a slaughterer of animals, from Middle English *slahter* (an agent derivative of *slaht* 'killing'). **2.** topographic name from Middle English *sloghtre* 'boggy place', or a habitational name from a place named with this term (Old English *slōhtre*), for example Upper and Lower Slaughter in Gloucestershire. **3.** topographic name for someone who lived by a blackthorn or sloe, Old English *slāhtrēow*.

Slauson (297) English: variant spelling of SLAWSON.

Slauter (106) **1.** Possibly an altered form of German **Schlaut(t)er**, a Swabian variant of SCHLATTER. **2.** Altered spelling of English SLAUGHTER. Compare SLAWTER.

Slaven (1067) Irish: variant of SLAVIN.

Slavens (567) Irish: variant of SLAVIN, with the superfluous English patronymic ending *-s*.

Slavich (131) **1.** Slovenian (**Slavič**): nickname from *slavič*, an archaic form of *slavec* 'nightingale', probably denoting someone with a good voice. **2.** Croatian (**Slavić**): patronymic from the personal name *Slavo*, short form of any of various personal names with the suffix *-slav*, or a nickname from *slavić* 'nightingale'.

Slavick (191) Germanized or Americanized spelling of Czech and Jewish SLAVIK.

Slavik (685) Czech and Slovak (**Slavík**) and Jewish (from Czech-speaking lands): from Czech *slavík* 'nightingale', a nickname for a good singer. As a Jewish surname, it may have been adopted by a cantor in a synagogue.

Slavin (1795) **1.** Irish: reduced form of O'Slavin, an Anglicized form of Gaelic **Ó Sléibhín** 'descendant of *Sléibhín*', a name probably derived from *sliabh* 'mountain' (perhaps originally a short form of *Donnshléibhe*; see DUNLEAVY). **2.** Jewish (from Belarus): metronymic from the Yiddish female personal name *Slave* (from the Slavic word *slava* 'glory', 'fame', 'praise') + the eastern Slavic possessive suffix *-in*.

Slavinski (134) Variant spelling of Polish SLAWINSKI.

Slavinsky (110) Variant spelling of Polish SLAWINSKI, chiefly as a Russian name.
GIVEN NAMES Russian 6%. *Leonid, Nikolay, Vladimir*.

Slawinski (272) Polish: **1.** (**Sławiński**) habitational name for someone from Sławin, or Sławiny in Siedlce voivodeship, the place names being derived from *sławny* 'glorious' or *sława* 'glory', 'fame'. **2.** possibly also a variant of **Sławienski**, a habitational name from a place called Sławno.
GIVEN NAMES Polish 6%. *Bogumil, Casimir, Henryk, Janusz*.

Slawson (833) English (Midlands): unexplained.

Slawter (142) English: variant of SLAUGHTER.

Slay (1316) English: **1.** from Middle English *slaye* (Old English *slege*, from *slēan* 'to strike'), a metonymic occupational name for a slay maker, an implement used in weaving to push the weft thread tightly against the thread of the preceding pass of the shuttle. **2.** topographic name from Middle English *slay* 'grassy slope'.

Slayback (156) Americanized spelling of German SCHLABACH.

Slaybaugh (429) Americanized spelling of German SCHLABACH.

Slayden (396) Variant of SLAYDON.

Slaydon (212) English: apparently a habitational name from a lost or unidentified place.

Slaymaker (429) **1.** English: occupational name for a maker of slays (see SLAY 1). **2.** Altered form of German **Schleiermacher**, an occupational name for a maker or shawls or scarves, from Middle High German *sleier* 'scarf', 'shawl', 'veil' + *macher* 'maker'.

Slayman (129) Possibly an altered form of Dutch SLIMAN.

Slayter (190) English: variant of SLAUGHTER 1.

Slayton (2431) This has the appearance of an English habitational name, but its origin is unknown. Compare SLAYDON, SLAYDEN.

Slazak (23) Polish (**Ślązak**): regional name for someone from Silesia (see SLASKI).

Sleasman (144) Origin unidentified.

Slechta (273) Czech (**Šlechta**): from *šlechta* 'nobility', generally an ironic nickname for someone who gave himself airs and graces.

Sledd (332) English: variant of SLADE.

Sledge (2377) English: from Middle English *slech* 'sledgehammer' (Old English *slecg*); a metonymic occupational name for someone who made sledgehammers or used one at work.

Sledz (115) Polish (**Śledź**): from *śledź* 'herring', hence a metonymic occupational name for a catcher or seller of herrings, or a nickname for someone with a wan complexion.
GIVEN NAMES Polish 8%. *Bronislaw, Tadeusz, Zygmunt*.

Slee (309) English: variant of SLY.

Sleeman (368) English: variant of SLY, with the addition of Middle English *man* 'man'.

Sleep (211) English (mainly Devon): variant of SLAPE.

Sleeper (1015) English: nickname for an indolent person, from Middle English *sleper* 'sleeper'.

Sleet (116) English: unexplained.

Sleeter (156) Possibly a variant spelling of **Sleator**, a variant of SLAUGHTER 1.

Sleeth (397) Irish: thought by different authorities to be a variant of SLY or of SLADE.

Sleezer (144) Origin unidentified.

Sleigh (141) **1.** English (Midlands): variant of SLY. **2.** Scottish: either of English origin, as in 1, or a habitational name from a place such as Sliach in Glengairn, Sleach in Strathdon, Slioch in Drumblade, Sleich in former Perthshire, or Slioch in former Ross-shire.

Sleight (520) English: **1.** nickname from Middle English *sleght, sleight, slyght* 'cunning', 'artfulness'. **2.** topographic name from Middle English *sleyte* 'level field' (Old Norse *slétta*) or from Middle English *sleyte* 'sheep pasture'.

Sleiman (101) Arabic: variant of SULEIMAN. GIVEN NAMES Muslim 56%; French 8%. *Ahmad* (3), *Ali* (3), *Nabil* (3), *Mahmoud* (2), *Riad* (2), *Wajih* (2), *Antoun, Atallah, Ayad, Haytham, Hussam, Ismail*; *Francois* (2), *Antoine, Jacques.*

Slemmer (193) Americanized form of German SCHLEMMER.

Slemmons (125) English: patronymic from SLEEMAN.

Slemp (388) Americanized form of German SCHLAMP.

Slenker (129) Americanized form of German SCHLENKER.

Slentz (273) Possibly an Americanized form of German (Sorbian) **Schlenz**, a habitational name from a place so called in Silesia.

Slepian (117) Jewish (from Belarus): habitational name from the village Slepnya, now in Belarus.

Slepicka (111) Polish: unexplained.

Sleppy (132) Americanized form of a descriptive nickname from Czech *slepý* or Polish *ślepy* 'blind'.

Slesinski (121) Polish (**Ślesiński** or **Śleszyński**): habitational name for someone from Ślesin in Bydgoszcz and Konin voivodeships, or Śleszyn in Płock voivodeship. GIVEN NAMES Polish 7%. *Casimir, Ireneusz.*

Slette (102) Norwegian: see SLETTEN. GIVEN NAME Scandinavian 12%. *Obert* (2).

Sletten (676) Norwegian: habitational name from any of numerous farmsteads all over Norway, most of which are named with the definite singular form of *slette* 'plain'. GIVEN NAMES Scandinavian 6%. *Erik* (2), *Selmer* (2), *Knute, Nils.*

Slevin (506) Irish: variant of SLAVIN. GIVEN NAMES Irish 6%. *Kieran* (2), *Colum, Sinead.*

Slezak (820) Czech and Slovak (**Slezák**) and Jewish (Ashkenazic): ethnic or regional name for someone from Silesia, the Czech name of which is *Slezsko*. Compare Polish SLAZAK.

Slice (159) Americanized form of German **Schleiss** (see SCHLEIS).

Slicer (134) Probably an Americanized form of German **Schleisser**, an occupational name for someone whose job was to split wood (see SCHLEIS).

Slick (677) Possibly an Americanized form of German SCHLICK.

Slicker (196) Possibly an Americanized form of German SCHLICKER.

Slider (422) Possibly an Americanized form of German and Jewish SCHLEIDER.

Slife (215) Americanized form of German SCHLEIF.

Slifer (521) Americanized form of German SCHLEIFER.

Slifka (261) Variant of SLIVKA,

Slifko (155) Ukrainian: from a pet form of SLIVA 'plum'.

Sligar (281) Probably an altered spelling of German SCHLEIGER.

Sliger (805) Americanized spelling of German SCHLEIGER.

Sligh (595) Scottish: nickname for a crafty person, from Middle English *sligh* 'sly' (from Old Norse *slǽgr*). GIVEN NAMES French 4%. *Andre* (2), *Chanel, Napoleon.*

Slight (182) Scottish: **1.** nickname from northern Middle English *sleght, slyght* 'smooth', 'sleek', 'slender', 'slim' (probably of Old Norse origin). **2.** nickname from Middle English *sleghth* 'craft', 'cunning', 'dexterity', 'adroitness' (Old Norse *slǽgð*, a derivative of *slǽgr* 'sly').

Sliker (310) Dutch: **1.** nickname for a furtive or stealthy person, from an agent derivative of *slijken* 'to creep about'. Compare German SCHLEICHER. **2.** topographic name from *slijk* 'mud', 'slime' + *-er*, suffix denoting an inhabitant.

Slimak (143) Polish (**Ślimak**): nickname for a slow-moving person, from *ślimak* 'snail', 'slug'.

Sliman (137) **1.** English: variant of SLY, with the addition of Middle English *man* 'man'. **2.** Dutch: from Middle Dutch *slie, sly* 'tench' + *man* 'man', occupational name for a catcher or seller of these fish.

Slimmer (156) Dutch: nickname from the comparative of *slim* 'smart', 'clever'

Slimp (175) altered spelling of German **Schlimp**, nickname for a bent or bad person, from Middle High German *slimp* 'crooked', 'wrong', 'bad'.

Slinde (120) Norwegian: habitational name from a farmstead in Sogn, most likely named from *slind* 'beam', 'crossbeam' (probably relating to the shape of a field). GIVEN NAMES Scandinavian 6%; German 5%. *Gunhild, Jarl, Johan*; *Frieda, Gerhart.*

Sliney (207) Irish: reduced Anglicized form of Gaelic **Mac Sleimhne** 'son of *Sleimhne*', a personal name meaning 'smoothness', 'sleekness', 'polish'.

Slinger (297) **1.** Northern English and Dutch: from an agent derivative of Middle English *sling*, Dutch *slinge* 'strap for hurling stones' (of Low German origin), hence an occupational name for a soldier or hunter armed with a sling, or nickname for someone who was a particularly good shot with this weapon. The word was also used of the ropes and pulleys used for lifting blocks of stone during building work, and the surname would also have denoted a worker who operated these slings. **2.** German: see SCHLINGER.

Slingerland (417) Dutch (**van Slinger-**

land): habitational name from a place so called in Overijssel.

FOREBEARS This was the name of a prominent Dutch family in the Albany area from the 17th century onwards.

Slingluff (145) altered spelling of German **Schlingloff**, perhaps a nickname for a great eater, from Middle Low German *slingen* 'to gobble up' + *Loff*, short form of a personal name *Liutfried.*

Slingsby (116) English: from a place so named in North Yorkshire, named with the Old Norse personal name *Slengr* + *býr* 'farmstead', 'settlement'.

Slinkard (472) Possibly an altered spelling of Dutch **Slinkaert**, a nickname for a clumsy person, from Middle Dutch *slinc* 'left', 'left-handed'.

Slinker (264) Dutch: nickname for a left-handed person, from Dutch *'s linker*, literally 'of the left (hand)'.

Slisz (109) Polish (**Słysz**) nickname for an eavesdropper, from *słyszeć* 'to hear', 'to listen'. GIVEN NAME Polish 4%. *Ferdynand.*

Sliter (301) Americanized spelling of Dutch **Sluyter**, an occupational name from Middle Dutch *sluter* 'porter', 'doorkeeper'.

Sliva (471) **1.** Czech (**Slíva**), Belorussian, and Ukrainian: occupational name for a grower or seller of plums, or nickname for a short, round person, from Czech and Belorussian *slíva*, Ukrainian *slyva* 'plum'. **2.** In Czech it is also a nickname for a drunken man, from the idiom *opilý jaho slíva* 'drunk as a plum', the word *slíva* having been connected by folk etymology with *slívat* 'to spill'.

Slivinski (227) Variant spelling of Polish **Śliwiński** (see SLIWINSKI).

Slivka (400) **1.** Ukrainian and Belorussian: from a diminutive of SLIVA. **2.** Jewish (from Ukraine, Poland, and Bohemia): ornamental name or occupational name for a grower or seller of plums, from Polish *śliwka* 'plum' (see SLIWA). **3.** Jewish (from Belarus): habitational name from a village called Slivka or for someone who lived by the Slivka river in Belarus.

Sliwa (384) Polish (**Śliwa**): metonymic occupational name for a grower or seller of plums, from *śliwa* 'plum'. In some cases the surname may have arisen as a nickname from this word. GIVEN NAMES Polish 13%. *Andrzej* (2), *Jolanta* (2), *Wojciech* (2), *Arkadiusz, Casimir, Czeslaw, Danuta, Elzbieta, Janina, Krystyna, Krzysztof, Mieczyslaw.*

Sliwinski (472) Polish: **1.** (**Śliwiński**) habitational name for someone from places called Śliwin or Śliwiny, named with *śliwa* 'plum'. **2.** (also **Śliwieński**) habitational name from a place called Śliwno. GIVEN NAMES Polish 9%. *Jurek* (2), *Bronislaw, Ewa, Iwona, Jozef, Krzysztof, Krzysztof, Malgorzata, Michalina, Wieslaw, Zbigniew, Zosia.*

Sloan (15999) Irish: reduced Anglicized form of **Ó Sluaghadháin** 'descendant of *Sluaghadhán*', a diminutive the Gaelic personal name *Sluaghadh* (see SLOWEY).

Sloane (1593) Irish: variant spelling of SLOAN.

Sloas (136) Scottish: possibly a variant of SLOSS.

Sloat (886) Americanized form of Dutch **Sloot**, a topographic name from *sloot* 'drainage ditch', 'channel' (compare VANDERSLOOT), or of SLOTT 'lock'.

FOREBEARS Early Sloats in America were Dutch, emigrating from Holland in the mid 17th century. A Jan Pieterson Sloat or Slott (c. 1613–1703), is recorded as an immigrant in New Amsterdam in 1650.

Sloboda (233) Polish (**Słoboda**), Czech, Slovak, and Jewish (Ashkenazic): habitational name from any of various places named with Slavic *sloboda* 'freedom', denoting an estate or village that was exempt from paying tribute or taxes. In Poland there are several places so called, in particular in Białystok, Rzeszów, and Suwałki voivodeships.

GIVEN NAMES Slavic 4%. *Nadezhda, Nicolai, Vasily, Vladimir.*

Slobodnik (106) Slovak (**Slobodník**): status name for a freedman (a serf who had been freed).

Slocomb (139) English: variant spelling of SLOCUM.

Slocombe (100) English: variant spelling of SLOCUM.

Slocum (3524) English (West Country): habitational name from a place named with the Old English elements *slāh* 'sloe' + *cumb* 'valley', in particular Slocum on the Isle of Wight and in Devon.

FOREBEARS Anthony Slocombe or Slocum (1590–1674/75) came from Taunton, Somerset, England, to Taunton, MA, in 1637.

Slocumb (282) English: variant spelling of SLOCUM.

Sloma (226) **1.** Polish (**Słoma**) and Jewish (from Poland): from Polish *słoma* 'straw', most probably a nickname for an inconstant person, a 'straw in the wind'. **2.** Jewish (from Poland): from the Yiddish personal name *Shloyme*, Yiddish form of SOLOMON.

GIVEN NAMES Polish 7%. *Henryk* (2), *Andrzej, Janina, Krystyna, Ludwik.*

Sloman (256) **1.** English: topographic name for someone who lived near a swamp or bog, from Old English *slōh* 'slough', or a habitational name from one of the various places, for example Slough in Berkshire, named with this word. **2.** English: nickname for a sluggish or stupid person, from Middle English *slou* 'slow'. **3.** English: topographic name for someone who lived by a blackthorn or sloe, from Middle English *sloh*. Compare SLAUGHTER 3. **4.** Americanized form of Polish and Jewish SLOMA.

Slominski (342) Polish (**Słomiński**): habitational name for someone from Słomin in Warszawa and Płock voivodeships, named with *słoma* 'straw'.

Slomka (110) **1.** Polish (**Słomka**): nickname for a thin or insignificant person, from *słomka* 'blade of straw', 'straw stalk'. **2.** Jewish (from Poland): from a pet form of the Yiddish personal name *Shloyme*, Yiddish form of SOLOMON.

GIVEN NAMES Polish 6%. *Jerzy, Mariusz.*

Slomkowski (74) Polish (**Słomkowski**): habitational name for someone from places called Słomków, Słomkowa, or Słomkowo, all named with *słomka* 'little straw'.

Slomski (172) Polish (**Słomski**): from *słoma* 'straw' plus the suffix -*ski*, used commonly in forming surnames. It may be a nickname, or more probably a habitational or topographic name from an unidentified place.

Slonaker (433) Origin unidentified. Probably an altered form of an unidentified German topographic or habitational name. Compare SLONEKER.

Slone (3337) Scottish and northern Irish: variant spelling of SLOAN.

Slonecker (131) Origin unidentified. Compare SLONAKER.

Sloneker (124) See SLONAKER.

Sloniker (162) See SLONAKER.

Slonim (146) Jewish (from Belarus): habitational name from Slonim in Belarus.

GIVEN NAMES Jewish 12%. *Moshe, Reuven, Rivkah, Yigal, Zvi.*

Sloop (690) Possibly an altered spelling of Dutch **Sloep**, an occupatonal nickname for the owner or sailer of a *schloup*, a type of sailing boat.

Sloper (166) English: occupational name for a maker of overalls, from an agent derivative of Middle English *slop(e)* 'overall' (apparently of Old English origin, akin to *slūpan* 'to slip', reinforced by a Middle Low German cognate).

Slosberg (142) Jewish (Ashkenazic): variant of SCHLOSSBERG.

GIVEN NAMES Jewish 4%; Scandinavian 4%. *Sheva; Bjoern, Carsten.*

Sloss (557) **1.** Scottish: shortened form of **Auchincloss**, a habitational name from a place so called in the parish of Kilmarnock. **2.** altered form of German or Jewish SCHLOSS.

Slosser (123) Variant of German or Jewish SCHLOSSER.

Slosson (120) Origin unidentified.

Slota (245) Polish (**Słota**): nickname for a gloomy person, from *słota* 'rain', 'period of rainy weather'.

GIVEN NAMES Polish 6%. *Dorota, Jacek, Krzysztof, Zofia, Zygmunt.*

Slote (147) **1.** Dutch and North German: occupational name for a locksmith, from Middle Low German *slot* 'lock'. **2.** Dutch: topographic name for someone who lived

by a drainage ditch (see VANDERSLOOT). **3.** German: variant of SCHLOTT 2.

Slothower (186) Americanized form of German SCHLOTTHAUER.

Slotkin (145) **1.** Respelling of Jewish (eastern Ashkenazic) **Zlotkin**: **2.** metronymic from the Yiddish female personal name *Zlotke*, a pet form of *Zlote*, derived from Polish *złota* 'golden' (see SLATKIN). **3.** from a derivative of SLOTNICK.

GIVEN NAMES Jewish 12%. *Meyer* (3), *Sol, Zevi.*

Slotnick (358) Jewish (eastern Ashkenazic): occupational name for a goldsmith, from Belorussian *zlotnik*, Polish *złotnik*.

GIVEN NAMES Jewish 5%. *Sol* (2), *Emanuel, Isadore, Meyer, Rebekah.*

Slott (172) **1.** English: topographic name for someone who lived in a muddy place, from Middle English *slott* 'mud', 'slime'. **2.** Swedish and Danish: ornamental name from *slot(t)* 'palace'. **3.** Variant spelling of Dutch **Slot**, a metonymic occupational name for a locksmith, from Middle Dutch *slo(e)t* 'lock', 'clasp'. **4.** Americanized form of Czech and Slovak *slota* 'bad weather', 'evil person', 'witch'.

Slotten (112) Dutch: variant of SLOTT 3, from the plural form *Slotten* 'locks'.

GIVEN NAME German 5%. *Kurt* (2).

Slotter (115) Dutch: metonymic occupational name for a locksmith, from Middle Dutch *slo(e)t* 'lock', 'clasp', + -*er*, suffix of agent nouns.

Slough (621) English: topographic name for someone who lived near a swamp or bog, from Old English *slōh* 'slough', or a habitational name from one of the various places named with this word, for example Slough in Berkshire.

Sloup (126) Dutch: see SLOOP.

Slovacek (194) Czech (**Slováček**): from a diminutive of *Slovák* (see SLOVAK).

Slovak (410) Czech and Slovak (**Slovák**): ethnic name for a Slovak, someone from Slovakia or one whose native language was Slovak.

Slovensky (108) Czech: ethnic name for someone from Slovakia or who had connections with Slovakia.

Slover (902) Dutch (**de Slover**): occupational name for an apron maker.

Slovick (135) Jewish (Ashkenazic): Americanized form of Polish **Słowik** (see SLOWIK).

Slovin (124) Jewish (eastern Ashkenazic): metronymic from the Yiddish female personal name *Slove*, a variant of *Slave* (see SLAVIN).

GIVEN NAME Jewish 6%. *Sol* (2).

Slowey (310) Irish: reduced form of **O'Slowey**, an Anglicized form of Gaelic **Ó Sluaghadhaigh** 'descendant of *Sluaghadhach*', a personal name meaning 'raider', derived from *sluaghadh* 'expedition', 'raid'. In Ulster there was also **Mac**

Sluaghaigh, which was Anglicized as **(Mc)Slowey** or sometimes MOLLOY.
GIVEN NAMES Irish 6%. *Dermot, Niall.*

Slowiak (103) German (of Slavic origin): nickname for a singer or a night-time reveler, literally meaning 'nightingale' (see SLOVICK).
GIVEN NAMES German 7%. *Florian* (3), *Wilhelm.*

Slowik (493) Polish (**Słowik**) and Jewish (from Poland): nickname for someone with a mellifluous voice or a night-time reveler, from Polish *słowik* 'nightingale'. As a Jewish name, this was sometimes adopted by a cantor in a synagogue (see SLAVIK).
GIVEN NAMES Polish 5%. *Jozef* (2), *Grzegorz, Halina, Leszek, Malgorzata, Ryszard, Zygmunt.*

Slowikowski (110) Polish (**Słowikowski**): habitational name from a place called Słowikowoa in Nowy Sącz voivodeship, Słowików in Częstochowa and Radom voivodeships, or Słowikowo in Konin voivodeship, all named with *słowik* 'nightingale'.
GIVEN NAMES Polish 17%. *Jerzy* (2), *Danuta, Jacek, Jadwiga, Jozef, Tadeusz, Zigmund.*

Slowinski (350) Polish (**Słowiński**): **1.** habitational name for someone from Słowin in Gorzów voivodeship. **2.** from the adjective *słowiński*, denoting a member of the Słowińcy, a Slavic people living in Pomerania.
GIVEN NAMES Polish 5%. *Jacek, Jozef, Maciej, Piotr, Wladyslaw.*

Sloyer (132) Possibly an altered form of German **Schleier**, a metonymic occupational name for a maker or shawls, scarves, and the like, from Middle High German *sleier* 'scarf', 'shawl', 'veil'. Compare SLAYMAKER.

Sluder (1099) **1.** Americanized form of German **Schlüter** (see SCHLUTER). **2.** Altered spelling of South German **Schluder**, a nickname from Middle High German *slūdern* 'to dangle one's legs', the source of the dialect word *schluderig* 'slovenly', 'untidy'.

Sluga (172) Polish (**Sługa**): occupational name from *sługa* 'servant'.

Sluis (138) Dutch: topographic name for someone who lived by a lock or weir, Middle Dutch *sluis*. In some cases, it may be a habitational name from a place in the province of Zeeland, founded in the 13th century and named with this word.
GIVEN NAMES Dutch 8%. *Joost* (2), *Pieter, Siebe, Willem.*

Sluiter (170) Dutch: occupational name for a porter or gatekeeper, Middle Dutch *sluter*. Compare English PORTER.

Sluka (193) Czech: from *sluka* 'woodcock', a nickname for a shy, nervous person, or perhaps a metonymic occupational name for a fowler.

Slusar (105) Ukrainian and Jewish (from Ukraine): occupational name from Ukrain-

ian *slyusar* 'locksmith'. Compare Polish SLUSARZ.

Slusarczyk (116) Polish (**Ślusarczyk**): occupational name for a metal smith, from a diminutive of *ślusarz* (see SLUSARZ).
GIVEN NAMES Polish 13%. *Jacek, Jerzy, Krzysztof, Miroslaw, Urszula, Wieslaw.*

Slusarski (123) Polish (**Ślusarski**): derivative of *ślusarz* 'metal smith' (see SLUSARZ), with the common surname ending -*ski*.
GIVEN NAMES Polish 6%; German 4%. *Jolanta, Zygmunt; Aloysius.*

Slusarz (110) Polish (**Ślusarz**): occupational name for an ironworker or locksmith, from *ślusarz* 'metal smith'.
GIVEN NAMES Polish 13%. *Andrze, Augustyn, Jadwiga, Katarzyna, Zbigniew.*

Slusher (1627) Americanized spelling of Polish SLUSARZ.

Sluss (540) Possibly an altered form of Scottish SLOSS or German SCHLOSS.

Slusser (1221) Germanized spelling of a Slavic name meaning 'metalsmith'. Compare Polish SLUSARZ.

Slutsky (460) Jewish (eastern Ashkenazic) and Belorussian: habitational name for someone from Slutsk, a city in Belarus.
GIVEN NAMES Jewish 13%; Russian 7%. *Avron* (2), *Naum* (2), *Sima* (2), *Sol* (2), *Aron, Etya, Hyman, Irina, Isadore, Khana, Revekka, Semen; Boris* (7), *Leonid* (3), *Arkady, Efim, Fanya, Gennady, Igor, Mikhail, Raisa, Semyon, Yana, Yefim.*

Slutz (171) Possibly an altered form of German **Schlutz**, of unexplained origin.

Slutzky (160) Jewish (eastern Ashkenazic) and Belorussian: variant of SLUTSKY.

Sluyter (139) Dutch: variant spelling of SLUITER.

Sly (1039) English (chiefly West Midlands): nickname for a cunning or crafty individual, from Middle English *sligh* 'sly' (earlier *slegh*, from Old Norse *slægr*).

Slye (432) English: variant spelling of SLY.

Slyman (129) English: elaborated form of SLY, with the addition of Middle English *man* 'man'.

Slyter (183) Probably an altered form of SLUYTER.

Smack (183) Possibly an Americanized form of German **Schmack**, a nickname for a glutton, from Middle High German *smac* 'appetite'.

Smaha (130) Czech (also **Šmaha**): nickname from Old Czech *smaha* 'juice', 'sap'.

Smail (695) **1.** Scottish and northern English: variant of SMALL. **2.** English: habitational name from a lost place in eastern Sussex named *Smeghel*, from Old English *smēagel* 'burrow', or from Brooksmarle (now Broxmead) in Sussex (named with Old English *brocc* 'badger' + *smēagel*).

Smailes (102) Scottish and northern English: variant of SMAIL.

Smaldone (184) **1.** Italian: unexplained. **2.** Variant spelling of English **Smaldon**, a

habitational name from any of several places named with Old English *smæl* + *dene* 'valley', for example Smalldene in Buckinghamshire and Northumberland, or Smalldane in Ospringe parish, Kent.
GIVEN NAMES Italian 6%. *Carmine, Luigi, Marco, Rocco.*

Smale (461) English (Devon): variant of SMALL.

Smales (105) English: patronymic from SMALL.

Small (16114) **1.** English: nickname for a person of slender build or diminutive stature, from Middle English *smal* 'thin', 'narrow'. **2.** Translation of equivalents in other European languages, such as German KLEIN and SCHMAL, French PETIT.

Smallen (170) Irish: variant of SMULLEN 2.

Smalley (4252) English: habitational name from places in Derbyshire and Lancashire, so called from Old English *smæl* 'narrow' + *lēah* 'wood', 'clearing'.

Smallidge (115) English: unexplained. Perhaps from *smallage*, a kind of celery or parsley.

Smalling (538) Possibly an Americanized spelling of German *Schmäling* (see SCHMALING).

Smallman (297) English: ostensibly a nickname for a small man, but the vocabulary word was also a feudal term denoting a subtenant, and the surname is more probably a status name with this origin.

Smallridge (152) English: habitational name from either of two places in Devon, so called from Old English *smæl* 'narrow' + *hrycg* 'ridge', or a topographic name from Middle English *smal* 'narrow' + *rugge, rigge* 'ridge'.

Smalls (2032) English: patronymic from SMALL.

Smallwood (5468) English (chiefly West Midlands): habitational name from a place in Cheshire, so called from Old English *smæl* 'narrow' + *wudu* 'wood'.

Smaltz (179) Americanized form of German or Jewish SCHMALZ.

Smarr (376) Dutch (**Smar**): perhaps from a reduced form of *Sigmar*, a Germanic personal name composed of the elements *sigi* 'victory' + *meri, mari* 'famous'.

Smarsh (141) Perhaps an Americanized form of Polish **Smarz, Smardz**, from *smarz, smardz* 'morel', a type of mushroom, probably applied as a nickname.

Smart (8494) English: nickname for a brisk or active person, from Middle English *smart* 'quick', 'prompt' (Old English *smeart* 'stinging', 'painful', from *smeortan* 'to sting'). This name is common and widespread throughout England, Wales, and Scotland.

Smartt (594) English: variant spelling of SMART.

Smathers (786) English: variant of SMITHERS.

Smay (253) English: unexplained; possibly a variant of SMEE (see SMEAD).

Smead (551) English: possibly from Middle English *smethe* 'smooth', hence a topographic name for someone who lived on a piece of smooth, level ground, or a nickname from the same word used in a transferred sense for someone of an amiable disposition. Alternatively, it could be a topographic or metonymic occupational name from Old English *smiðða*, *smeðe* 'smithy', or a habitational name from a place named with this word, as for example Smeeth in Kent.

Smeal (421) English: variant of SMALL.

Smeaton (138) Scottish and English: habitational name from any of various places, notably Smeaton near Edinburgh, Great, Little, and Kirk Smeaton in North Yorkshire, or Smeeton in Leicestershire, all named with Old English *Smiðatūn* 'settlement (Old English *tūn*) of the smiths'.

Smeby (154) Norwegian: habitational name from any of three farmsteads in southeastern Norway, named in Old Norse as *Smiðabýr*, from *smiðr* 'smith' + *býr* 'farm', 'settlement'.

GIVEN NAME Scandinavian 8%. *Carsten*.

Smedberg (178) **1.** Swedish: ornamental name composed of the elements *smed* 'smith' + *berg* 'mountain'. **2.** Norwegian: habitational name from a farm name of the same meaning as 1.

GIVEN NAME Scandinavian 10%. *Astrid*.

Smedley (1591) English (mainly Nottinghamshire): apparently a habitational name from a lost or unidentified place, perhaps so called from Old English *smeðe* 'smooth' + *lēah* 'wood', 'clearing'.

Smee (199) **1.** English: variant of SMEAD. **2.** Dutch: variant of SMET.

Smeed (104) Variant of SMEAD.

Smejkal (249) Czech (**Šmajkal**, **Šmejkal**): from a derivative of *smýkat* 'to drag', hence a nickname for someone with a bad limp.

GIVEN NAMES German 4%. *Wenzel* (2), *Erwin*.

Smelcer (392) Slavic spelling of German SCHMELZER.

Smelko (114) Origin unidentified.

Smelley (409) Altered spelling of Scottish **Smellie**, a variant of SMILLIE.

Smelser (962) Americanized form of German SCHMELZER.

Smeltz (319) Respelling of German or Jewish SCHMELTZ.

Smeltzer (1529) Respelling of German or Jewish SCHMELTZER.

Smerdon (129) English (Devon): habitational name from Smeardon Down in the parish of Petertavy, so named from Old English *smeoru* 'butter' + *dūn* 'hill'.

Smeriglio (101) Italian: probably a topographic name from *smeriglio* 'corundum', from medieval Latin *smeriglum*.

GIVEN NAMES Italian 12%. *Rocco* (3), *Carmela*.

Smestad (177) Norwegian: habitational name from any of ten or more farmsteads, notably in southeastern Norway, mostly named from the Old Norse personal name *Smiðr*, literally 'smith' + Old Norse *staðir* 'farmstead', 'dwelling'.

GIVEN NAMES Scandinavian 6%. *Erik*, *Nils*.

Smet (259) Dutch: occupational name for a smith, Middle Dutch *smet*, *smit*.

Smetak (114) Czech (**Smeták**): from Czech *smeták* 'brush', a nickname for someone with hair or a moustache thought to resemble a brush.

Smetana (672) Czech and Jewish (from Ukraine): from Czech and Ukrainian *smetana* 'cream', a nickname, perhaps ironic, for a 'delicious' person or for someone who liked cream, or a metonymic occupational name for a trader in dairy products.

Smethers (233) Altered form of SMITHERS.

Smethurst (206) English (Lancashire): habitational name from a minor place near Manchester, so named from Old English *smeðe* 'smooth' + *hyrst* '(wooded) hill'.

Smetzer (168) Possibly an Americanized form of German **Schmetzer**, a nickname for a garrulous person, from an agent derivative of Middle High German *smetzen* 'to chatter'.

Smialek (157) Polish (**Śmiałek**): nickname from *śmiałek* 'bold'.

GIVEN NAMES Polish 8%; German 4%. *Mariusz* (2), *Grazyna*, *Jaroslaw*, *Mariola*; *Kurt*.

Smick (266) Probably an Americanized form of German SCHMICK.

Smid (297) **1.** Dutch and North German: variant of SMET. **2.** Czech (**Šmíd**): altered spelling of German SCHMIDT. **3.** Slovenian (**Šmid**): variant spelling of German SCHMIDT.

GIVEN NAMES Dutch 4%. *Derk* (3), *Dirk*.

Smiddy (374) Variant spelling of Scottish **Smiddie**, a habitational name from a place so called on the island of South Ronaldsay.

Smidt (644) **1.** Dutch: variant of SMET. **2.** Altered spelling of German SCHMIDT.

Smieja (148) Polish (**Śmieja**): nickname for a jolly person, from Old Polish *śmiejać się* 'to laugh'.

Smietana (106) Polish (**Śmietana**): from *śmietana* 'soured cream', probably applied as a nickname or as a metonymic occupational name for a producer or supplier of dairy products.

GIVEN NAMES Polish 5%; German 4%. *Stanislaw*; *Franz*.

Smigel (212) Polish (**Śmigel**): variant of SMIGIEL.

Smigelski (211) Variant of Polish SMIGIELSKI.

Smigiel (200) Polish (**Śmigiel**): nickname from *śmigiel* 'rung of a ladder', or perhaps a derivative of *śmigać* 'to swish or crack (a whip)'.

Smigielski (194) Polish (**Śmigielski**): habitational name for someone from Smigiel in Leszno voivodeship.

GIVEN NAMES Polish 13%. *Arkadiusz* (3), *Janina*, *Jerzy*, *Leszek*, *Ludwik*, *Ryszard*, *Tadeusz*, *Wieslaw*.

Smiles (191) **1.** Scottish: patronymic from SMALL. **2.** English: possibly a topographic name for someone who lived by a rabbit warren, from the plural of Middle English *smyle* 'burrow' (Old English *smygels*).

Smiley (6319) Scottish and northern Irish: of uncertain origin; probably a variant spelling of SMILLIE, but perhaps a habitational name, a variant of SMALLEY, or a nickname from Middle English *smile* 'smile', 'grin'.

Smilie (129) Scottish and northern Irish: variant spelling of SMILEY.

Smillie (287) Scottish: **1.** variant of SMILEY. **2.** from a derivative of Middle English *smil*, *smel* 'odor', hence a nickname for someone notorious for giving off a smell that was obnoxious even by medieval standards, or for someone who made great use of perfumes and pomanders to counteract this trait.

Smilowitz (140) Jewish: **1.** respelling of **Shmilovich** (from Ukraine) or **Szmilowicz** (from Poland), patronymics from the Yiddish personal name *Shmil*, Hebrew *Shemuel* (see SAMUEL). **2.** habitational name for someone from Smilovichi, in Belarus.

GIVEN NAMES Jewish 10%; German 4%. *Aron* (3), *Moshe*; *Otto*.

Smink (169) Possibly an Americanized form of German **Schminke**, a metonymic occupational name for a maker of cosmetic potions and ointments, from Middle High German *smincke* 'make up' (see SCHMINKE).

Smirl (110) Probably an Americanized form of German *Schmirl* (see SMYRL).

Smisek (201) Czech (**Smíšek**): nickname for a cheerful person, from *smíšek* 'laughter', from *smích* 'to laugh'.

Smit (1074) **1.** Dutch: variant of SMET. **2.** Americanized form of German SCHMIDT. **3.** Slovenian (**Šmit**): variant spelling of German SCHMIDT.

GIVEN NAMES Dutch 8%. *Dirk* (3), *Hendrik* (3), *Maarten* (3), *Willem* (3), *Jacobus* (2), *Jeroen* (2), *Marinus* (2), *Pieter* (2), *Bernardus*, *Egbert*, *Gerrit*, *Harm*.

Smith (831783) English: occupational name for a worker in metal, from Middle English *smith* (Old English *smið*, probably a derivative of *smītan* 'to strike, hammer'). Metalworking was one of the earliest occupations for which specialist skills were required, and its importance ensured that this term and its equivalents were perhaps the most widespread of all occupational surnames in Europe. Medieval smiths were important not only in making horseshoes, plowshares, and other domestic articles, but above all for their skill in forging swords, other weapons, and armor. This is the most frequent of all American surnames; it has also absorbed, by assimilation and translation, cognates and equivalents from many other languages (for forms, see Hanks and Hodges 1988).

Smitha (127) Apparently an English habitational name from Smitha in Devon, which is named from Old English *smiththe* 'smithy'. The surname, however, does not occur in current English records.

Smithart (121) Americanized form of German **Schmitthardt** (older form, **Smidhart**). See SMITHHART.

Smithberger (124) Americanized form of German **Schmiedberger**, a habitational name from a place named Schmiedberg.

Smithe (115) English: variant of SMITH.

Smithee (233) English: variant spelling of SMITHEY.

Smither (545) English: occupational name from Middle English *smith* + the agent suffix *-er*.

Smitherman (1269) English: occupational name for a smith's servant, from SMITHER + Middle English *man* 'servant'.

Smithers (1157) English: patronymic from SMITHER.

Smithey (797) English: topographic name for someone living by a smithy, from Middle English *smithe*, *smythy* 'smithy', or a habitational name from a place named with this word, as for example Smitha in Devon. It could also be a metonymic occupational name for the smith himself.

Smithhart (235) Origin unidentified. Compare SMITHART.

Smithson (2530) Northern English: patronymic from SMITH.

FOREBEARS The Smithsonian Institution in Washington, DC was founded (1846) with a bequest from the English chemist and mineralogist James Smithson (1765–1829). He was born James Lewes Macie, the illegitimate son of Hugh Smithson Percy, Duke of Northumberland. His mother, Elizabeth Macie, a widow, was a direct descendant of Henry VIII; through her family James Smithson inherited a fortune.

Smithwick (656) English: habitational name from Smethwick in the West Midlands, or a lost Smithwick in the parish of Southover, Sussex (last recorded in 1608). Smethwick is named with the genitive plural of Old English *smith* 'smith' + *wīc* (see WICK). The surname has been established in southern Ireland since the 17th century.

Smitley (478) Possibly a variant of English **Smithley**, a habitational name from Smithley in the parish of Darfield, South Yorkshire, presumably named with Old English *smith* + *lēah* 'clearing in a wood'.

Smits (1027) Dutch: patronymic from SMIT.

GIVEN NAMES Dutch 4%. *Dirk* (6), *Cornelis* (2), *Pieter* (2), *Gerrit*, *Gerritt*, *Hendrik*, *Willem*.

Smittle (192) Possibly an Americanized form of German **Schmittel**, a diminutive of SCHMITT.

Smoak (1084) English: possibly a variant of SMOCK.

Smock (1533) English: from Middle English *smoc*, *smok* 'smock', 'shift', hence a metonymic occupational name for someone who made or sold such garments, or a nickname for someone who habitually wore a smock (the usual everyday working garment of a peasant).

Smoke (405) Possibly a variant of English SMOCK or an altered form of German SCHMUCK.

Smoker (560) Dutch: from an agent derivative of *smoken* 'to smoke', hence a nickname for someone who used coal as fuel, or a punning nickname for a brothelkeeper.

Smola (396) Czech and Slovak, Polish (**Smoła**), and Jewish (eastern Ashkenazic): metonymic occupational name for a distiller of pitch, from Czech *smola*, *smůla*, Polish *smoła*, eastern Slavic *smola* 'pitch'. In Czech this is also a nickname for someone with dark hair and for an unlucky person.

GIVEN NAMES Polish 4%. *Halina*, *Ludwik*, *Mieczyslaw*, *Thadeus*.

Smolak (143) Polish and Czech (**Smolák**): patronymic or pet form from SMOLA.

GIVEN NAMES Polish 5%. *Bogdan*, *Jadwiga*.

Smolar (120) **1.** Slovenian: occupational name for someone who gathered natural resins from pines and firs, from *smola* 'resin'. **2.** Jewish (from Ukraine) and Ukrainian: altered spelling of Ukrainian *smolyar*, an occupational name for a distiller of pitch.

GIVEN NAMES Jewish 4%. *Sol*, *Yehuda*.

Smolarek (115) Polish: occupational name from a diminutive of *smolarz* 'pitch burner', from *smoła* 'pitch'.

Smolek (100) Czech and Polish (**Smołek**): nickname for a dirty person or an occupational name for a pitch burner (see SMOLA).

Smolen (619) Polish (**Smoleń**): **1.** unflattering nickname for a dirty person, from Polish *smolić się* 'to soil', 'make dirty'. **2.** perhaps also a habitational name from places called Smoleń, in Ciechanów and Katowice voivodeships.

Smolenski (294) **1.** Polish (**Smoleński**): habitational name for someone from a place called Smoleń, in Ciechanów and Katowice voivodeships. **2.** Jewish (from Belarus): habitational name from the city of Smolensk in western Russia. **3.** Jewish (eastern Ashkeanzic): variant of SMOLINSKI.

GIVEN NAMES Polish 5%. *Janusz*, *Zdzislaw*.

Smolensky (114) Jewish (Ashkenazic): variant spelling of SMOLENSKI.

GIVEN NAMES Jewish 7%. *Avron*, *Yakov*.

Smoley (161) Americanized form of Slovenian **Smolej** or **Smole**, a nickname derived from *smola* 'resin', 'pitch', figuratively 'bad luck'. is another surname of the same origin. Compare SMOLAR 1.

Smolik (328) Czech (**Smolík**) and Slovak: metonymic occupational name for a distiller of pitch, from Slavic *smola* 'pitch'.

Smolin (138) Jewish (eastern Ashkenazic) and Russian: metonymic occupational name for a pitch burner, from eastern Slavic *smola* 'pitch'.

GIVEN NAMES Jewish 7%; Russian 7%. *Anatoly*, *Michail*, *Natalya*, *Yevgeniy*.

Smolinski (786) Polish (**Smoliński**) and Jewish (eastern Ashkenazic): habitational name for someone from a place named with eastern Slavic *smola*, Polish *smoła* 'pitch'.

GIVEN NAMES Polish 5%. *Jadwiga* (2), *Bogdan*, *Jacek*, *Janusz*, *Jaroslaw*, *Kazimierz*, *Lucyna*, *Maciej*, *Szczepan*, *Wieslaw*, *Wieslawa*, *Zbigniew*.

Smolinsky (194) Jewish (eastern Ashkenazic): variant spelling of SMOLINSKI.

Smolka (221) Polish (also **Smołka**): metonymic occupational name for a distiller of pitch, or perhaps a nickname for someone with black hair, from a derivative of *smoła* 'pitch'.

GIVEN NAMES German 6%. *Horst* (2), *Gerda*, *Matthias*.

Smolko (148) Polish: variant of SMOLEK or SMOLKA.

Smollen (107) Irish: Anglicized form of Gaelic **Ó Smealláin**.

Smoller (145) Jewish (eastern Ashkenazic): occupational name from Yiddish *smoler* 'pitch burner' (see SMOLAR).

GIVEN NAME Jewish 4%. *Meyer*.

Smoot (3068) Americanized spelling of Dutch **Smout**, a metonymic occupational name for someone who sold fat or lard, Dutch *smout*, or a nickname for someone who had a taste for, and could afford, rich foods.

Smoots (187) Possibly an Americanized spelling of Dutch **Smouts**, a variant of **Smout** (see SMOOT).

Smotherman (767) Variant of English SMITHERMAN.

Smothermon (214) Variant of English SMITHERMAN.

Smothers (2273) Variant of English SMITHERS.

Smouse (348) **1.** Dutch: from Middle Dutch *moes* 'food', 'stew', 'porridge', hence a nickname for a greedy person, or metonymic occupational name for a cook. **2.** Americanized form of German SCHMAUS.

Smoyer (303) Origin unidentified. Compare SCHMOYER.

Smrekar (159) **1.** Czech (**Smrekář**) and Slovak (**Smrek**): occupational or topographic name for someone who worked or lived in a spruce forest, from an agent noun derivative of the dialect word *smrek*

'spruce' (standard Czech *smrk*).
2. Slovenian: topographic name derived from *smreka* 'spruce fir', probably denoting someone who lived in a place where spruces grew.

Smuck (156) Americanized spelling of German SCHMUCK.

Smucker (392) Americanized form of German SCHMUCKER.

Smuda (127) Czech: nickname for a sour-faced person, a derivative of Czech *smudit (se)* 'to look sour'.
GIVEN NAMES Slavic 4%. *Bogdan, Casimir.*

Smuin (110) English (Oxford): unexplained.

Smull (158) Americanized form of Dutch **de Smul**, a nickname for a glutton, toper, or lecher, from the definite article *de* + Middle Dutch *smul* 'person of large appetites'.

Smullen (337) Irish: reduced Anglicized form of Gaelic **Ó Smolláin**, according to Woulfe, a variant of **Ó Spealáin** (see SPILLANE).

Smulski (72) Polish: habitational name, probably for someone from Smoła in Warszawa voivodeship or from Smólsk.

Smutny (123) Czech and Slovak (**Smutný**): nickname for a person with a gloomy disposition, from *smutný* 'sad'.
GIVEN NAME German 4%. *Alois.*

Smutz (126) Americanized form of German and Jewish SCHMUTZ.

Smyer (140) Probably a variant of Dutch SMYERS.

Smyers (356) Dutch: variant of MEYER 1.

Smykowski (103) Polish: habitational name from any of various places called Smyków, named with *smyk* 'folk musician'.
GIVEN NAMES Polish 8%. *Agnieszka, Jadwiga, Krzysztof.*

Smylie (248) Northern Irish and Scottish: variant spelling of SMILEY.

Smyly (177) Variant spelling of SMYLIE.

Smyre (176) See SMYER.

Smyrl (142) **1.** Probably a Slavic or Americanized form of German **Schmirl**: **2.** from Middle High German *smerl* 'gudgeon' (a small freshwater fish), hence a metonymic occupational name for a fisherman or a seller of these fish. The gudgeon was considered gullible, so it may be a nickname for a gullible person. **3.** metonymic occupational name for a falconer, from Middle High German *smire* 'falcon'.

Smyser (391) Possibly an altered form of German SCHMEISSER.

Smyth (4030) Variant spelling, especially in Ireland, of SMITH.
GIVEN NAMES Irish 8%. *Brendan* (8), *Ronan* (2), *Aidan, Brigid, Conor, Eoin, Malachy, Paddy.*

Smythe (1837) English: **1.** topographic name for someone who lived by a forge, or a metonymic occupational name for someone employed at a one, from Middle English *smithe, smythy* 'smithy'. **2.** variant of SMITH.

Smythers (123) English: variant of SMITHERS.

Snader (339) Respelling of Dutch SNIDER or Jewish SCHNEIDER.

Snape (192) English and Scottish: habitational name from any of various places in England and southern Scotland, for example in North Yorkshire near Bedale, in the Lowlands near Biggar, and in Suffolk, so named with Old English *snæp* 'area of boggy land'. In Sussex the dialect term *snape* is still used of boggy, uncultivable land.

Snapp (1680) Americanized form of German SCHNAPP or of the Dutch cognate **Snap(pe)**.

Snare (336) Norwegian: habitational name from any of several farms named Snare, from *snar* 'brushwood', 'thicket'.

Snarr (288) Americanized form of German SCHNARR.

Snarski (189) Polish: habitational name for someone from a place called Snarki, in Radom voivodeship.
GIVEN NAMES Polish 6%. *Miroslaw* (2), *Jadwiga, Ludwik.*

Snavely (1382) Possibly an altered form of South German **Schnäbele** or **Schnäbeli(n)**, or of Swiss German **Schneebeli** or **Schnebli** (see SCHNEBLY).

Snawder (94) Americanized form of Dutch SNIDER.

Snay (301) Possibly an Americanized form of SCHNEE.
GIVEN NAMES French 5%. *Armand, Joffre.*

Snaza (101) Origin unidentified.
GIVEN NAME German 4%. *Kurt.*

Snead (3534) English: variant spelling of SNEED.

Sneary (159) Possibly English: unexplained.

Sneath (240) English: habitational name from Snaith in East Yorkshire, near Goole, so called from Old Norse *sneið* 'cut off piece of land', or from the same word used in other minor place names. Compare SNEED.

Snedaker (148) Probably Dutch: unexplained. Compare SNEDEKER.
GIVEN NAME German 4%. *Otto.*

Snedden (449) **1.** Scottish: variant of SNEDDON. **2.** Dutch: occupational name for a cloth cutter or tailor, from Middle Dutch *snede* 'cut'.

Sneddon (577) Scottish: habitational name from a place near Dumfries, so called from Old English *snāw* 'snow' + *dūn* 'hill'.

Snedecor (133) Dutch: variant of SNEDEKER.

Snedegar (193) Dutch: variant of SNEDEKER.

Snedeker (821) Dutch: unexplained. This is the name of a prominent Dutch family name in New Netherland.

Sneden (117) Scottish: variant of SNEDDON.

Snee (361) **1.** English: variant of SNEED. **2.** Irish (Connacht): reduced Anglicized form of Gaelic **Ó Sniadhaigh** 'descendant of *Sniadhach*', a personal name, apparently meaning 'nitty', from *sneadh*.

Sneed (5271) English: topographic name for someone who lived by a detached piece of land or woodland, from Middle English *snede*, or a habitational name from a place named with this word (Old English *snǣd*), as for example Snead in Worcestershire or The Sneyd in Staffordshire.

Sneeringer (206) Dutch: unexplained.

Sneider (315) **1.** Dutch: occupational name for a tailor, from an agent derivative of Middle Dutch *sneden* 'to cut'. **2.** Jewish (Ashkenazic): variant of SCHNEIDER.

Snelgrove (412) English: variant spelling of SNELLGROVE.

Snell (8001) English: nickname for a brisk or active person, from Middle English *snell* 'quick', 'lively', in part also representing a survival of the Old English personal name *Snell* or the cognate Old Norse *Snjallr*.

Snellen (143) Dutch: **1.** nickname for a brisk or active person, from *snel* 'speedy', 'swift'. **2.** perhaps a patronymic from the Germanic personal name *Snello*, presumably of the same meaning as 1.

Snellenberger (136) Americanized form of German **Schnellenberger**, of unexplained origin.

Sneller (316) English: nickname from Middle English *snell* 'quick', 'lively' + the French pejorative suffix *-ard*.

Snellgrove (412) English: apparently a habitational name from a lost or unidentified place, perhaps so called from Old English *snæg(e)l* 'snail' + *grāf* 'grove'.

Snelling (1480) English: patronymic from SNELL.

Snellings (472) Dutch: patronymic from a derivative of a Germanic personal name, either *Snello* or a compound name such as *Snellaert* (composed of the elements *snell* 'quick', 'lively' + *hard* 'hardy', 'brave', 'strong') or *Snellegeer* (with the second element *gār, gēr* 'spear').

Snelson (909) English: patronymic from SNELL.

Snethen (255) Origin unidentified.

Snide (164) Probably an Americanized form of German SCHNEID.

Snider (12470) **1.** Dutch: variant of SNEIDER 'tailor'. **2.** Americanized form of German SCHNEIDER. **3.** Respelling of Slovenian **Žnider**, from *žnidar*, an occupational name for a tailor of German origin (see SCHNEIDER).

Snidow (134) Origin unidentified.

Sniegowski (165) Polish (**Śniegowski**): derivative (probably a habitational name from an unidentified place), from *śnieg* 'snow' + the common surname suffix *-owski*.

Sniezek (136) Polish (**Śniezek**): nickname for a white-haired person, from a diminutive of *śnieg* 'snow'.
GIVEN NAMES Polish 10%. *Bogdan, Czeslaw, Kazimierz, Leszek, Tadeusz.*

Sniff (133) Origin unidentified.

Sniffen (258) Of uncertain origin. According to family historians it is a variant of KNIFFEN.

Sniffin (112) See SNIFFEN.

Snipe (166) English: **1.** from a personal name, Old English *Snīp* or Old Norse *Snípr*. **2.** habitational name from a place so called in former Northumberland.

Snipes (2595) English: variant of or patronymic from SNIPE.

Snitker (203) German (northwestern): occupational name for a woodworker, from Middle Low German *snitker* 'joiner', 'woodcarver'.

Snitzer (167) Probably an Americanized form of German or Jewish SCHNITZER.

Snively (702) Americanized form of South German, Swiss **Schnaible, Schneebeli,** or **Schnewli,** a nickname for someone with white or very fair hair, from a derivative of Middle High German *snē* 'snow'.

Snodderly (177) Of uncertain origin; perhaps an English habitational name from a lost or unidentified place. The surname, however, is not found in present-day U.K. records.

Snoddy (930) Northern Irish and Scottish: nickname from northern Middle English *snod* 'neat', 'trim', 'smart' + a diminutive suffix.

Snoderly (118) Of uncertain origin; perhaps an English habitational name from a lost or unidentified place. The surname, however, is not found in present-day U.K. records.

Snodgrass (5190) Scottish: habitational name from a place near Irvine in the former county of Ayrshire, named with northern Middle English *snod* 'smooth', 'sleek', 'even' + *grass* 'grass'.

Snoke (370) **1.** variant of English SNOOK. **2.** Americanized form of Dutch **Snoek,** a nickname meaning 'pike' (the carnivorous fish), or (particularly in Zeeland) from a personal name.

Snook (2732) English: topographic name for someone who lived on a projecting piece of land, from Middle English *snoke* 'projection'. It is possible that this term was also used as a nickname for someone with a long nose.

Snooks (134) English: patronymic from SNOOK.

Snoots (103) Origin unidentified.

Snopek (121) Polish: nickname for someone thought to resemble a small sheaf, from Polish *snopek* 'little sheaf'.
GIVEN NAMES Polish 5%. *Casimir, Merek.*

Snouffer (184) Americanized form of German **Schnauffer,** a nickname for someone with noticeably noisy breathing, from Middle High German *snūfen* 'to breathe heavily', 'to pant'.

Snover (362) Americanized form of German **Schnauffer** (see SNOUFFER).

Snow (17174) **1.** English: nickname denoting someone with very white hair or an exceptionally pale complexion, from Old English *snāw* 'snow'. **2.** Americanized and shortened form of any of the Jewish ornamental names composed with German *Schnee, Schnei, Schneu* 'snow' as the first element.

Snowball (129) English (northeastern): from Middle English *snow* 'snow' + *ball*. The second element may refer to a streak or lock of hair, or it may mean a bald patch. The surname therefore originated as a nickname for someone with a patch of white hair or a pale bald patch, amid dark hair.

Snowbarger (111) Part-translation of German SCHNEEBERGER.

Snowberger (297) Part-translation of German SCHNEEBERGER.

Snowden (3514) English: habitational name from Snowden, a place in West Yorkshire named from Old English *snāw* 'snow' + *dūn* 'hill', i.e. a hill where snow lies long.

Snowdon (262) English: habitational name from places named with the same elements as in SNOWDEN, for example Snowdon in Devon. This was the earlier name of Snow End in Hertfordshire and Snow Hill in Windsor, Berkshire.

Snowman (195) American translated form of any of various European names meaning 'snow', for example Polish SNIEZEK, or of the Jewish ornamental name **Schneemann** (German spelling), **Sznejman, Sznajman** (Polish forms), derived from Yiddish *shney* 'snow' + *man* 'man'.

Snuffer (232) Americanized form of German **Schnauffer** (see SNOUFFER).

Snuggs (260) English: unexplained.

Snyder (63835) **1.** Dutch: occupational name for a tailor, from an agent derivative of Middle Dutch *sniden* 'to cut'. **2.** Americanized form of German SCHNEIDER.

Snyderman (176) **1.** Americanized respelling of Jewish and German SCHNEIDERMAN. **2.** Dutch: occupational name for a tailor, from SNYDER + *man* 'man'.
GIVEN NAMES Jewish 7%. *Reuven* (2), *Meyer.*

Snyders (178) Dutch: patronymic from SNYDER 1.
GIVEN NAMES French 4%. *Jacques, Pierre.*

So (1277) **1.** Korean (**Sŏ**): although there are two Chinese characters for the Sŏ surname, one of these is extremely rare and can be discounted (there are only about two hundred people in Korea who use this rare character). Some records indicate that the more common character for Sŏ has as many as 165 clans, but only eleven of them can be

documented. The first recorded ancestor of the Sŏ clans seems to be a Shilla figure named Sŏ Shin-il. According to some legends, the rulers of the Old Chosŏn kingdom (died 194 BC) were driven from power by the Wiman Chosŏn and settled in the Ich'ŏn area. The Sŏ clans are among the descendants of these ancient rulers. About fifty percent of modern members of the Sŏ clans live in the Kyŏngsang provinces or in Chŏlla South province. **2.** Chinese 苏: a Cantonese form of **Su** 1. **3.** Hungarian (**Só**): metonymic occupational name for a salt seller or producer, from *só* 'salt'.
GIVEN NAMES Chinese/Korean 40%. *Jin* (6), *Sang* (6), *Young* (6), *Jung* (5), *Yong* (5), *Song* (4), *Wai* (4), *Ying* (4), *Chun* (3), *Jae* (3), *Sun* (3), *Tong* (3); *Chong* (11), *Chang* (4), *Byung* (3), *Myong* (3), *Chong Hun* (2), *Kum* (2), *Yiu* (2), *Cho, Chong Ha, Chong Kil, Chong Sok, Chong Soon.*

Soard (174) English: variant spelling of SWORD.

Soares (2599) **1.** Portuguese: occupational name from *soeiro* 'swineherd', Latin *suerius*. **2.** English: patronymic from a nickname for someone with reddish hair, from Anglo-Norman French *sor* 'chestnut (color)'.
GIVEN NAMES Spanish 18%; Portuguese 12%. *Manuel* (72), *Jose* (49), *Carlos* (16), *Luis* (11), *Francisco* (8), *Luiz* (6), *Jorge* (5), *Mario* (5), *Miguel* (5), *Pedro* (5), *Joaquin* (4), *Sergio* (4); *Joao* (18), *Joaquim* (3), *Paulo* (3), *Anabela* (2), *Henrique* (2), *Vasco* (2), *Agostinho, Duarte, Goncalo, Marcio, Serafim, Seraphine.*

Soave (205) Italian and Jewish (from Italy): **1.** regional name for a Swabian, from *Soave* 'Swabia'. **2.** habitational name from any of several places in northern Italy called Soave, especially the one in Verona province.
GIVEN NAMES Italian 28%. *Angelo* (6), *Antonio* (5), *Giuliano* (2), *Marco* (2), *Attilio, Clemente, Emanuele, Enrico, Fiore, Luigi, Mario, Remo, Rocco, Sergio.*

Sobania (102) German: unexplained; possibly from a Slavic name, for example SOBANSKI or SOBCZAK.

Sobanski (91) Polish: habitational name for someone from a place called Sobanice, in Ciechanów voivodeship.
GIVEN NAMES Polish 8%; German 4%. *Henryk, Krzysztof, Zbigniew; Kurt.*

Sobczak (1066) Polish: patronymic from the personal name *Sobek,* a pet form of *Sobiesław,* composed of the elements *sobie* 'take for oneself' + *sław* 'glory'.
GIVEN NAMES Polish 5%. *Jerzy* (3), *Janusz* (2), *Zbigniew* (2), *Andrzej, Casimir, Halina, Janina, Kazimierz, Krystyna, Krzysztof, Lech, Piotr.*

Sobczyk (226) Polish: from a diminutive form of the personal name *Sobek,* a pet form of *Sobiesław* (see SOBCZAK).

GIVEN NAMES Polish 12%. *Aniela, Elzbieta, Halina, Janina, Jerzy, Krystyna, Lech, Stanislaw, Tadeusz, Wladyslawa, Wlodzimierz.*

Sobczynski (74) Polish (**Sobczyński**): habitational name for someone from a place called Sobczyna.

Sobeck (332) Germanized form of Polish SOBEK.

Sobecki (156) Polish: habitational name for someone from Sobki in Piotrków voivodeship.
GIVEN NAME Polish 4%. *Janusz.*

Sobek (249) Polish: from a pet form of the personal name *Sobiesław* (see SOBCZAK). This surname is also established in German-speaking countries.
GIVEN NAMES German 4%. *Manfred, Otto.*

Sobel (1812) Eastern German and Jewish (eastern Ashkenazic): from Slavic *sobol* 'sable', Yiddish *soybl*, a type of marten with handsome black fur. As a German name this is either a nickname for someone thought to resemble a sable (for example, someone with sleek black hair), or an occupational name for a fur trader; as a Jewish name it is generally ornamental.
GIVEN NAMES Jewish 5%. *Sol* (5), *Avner, Chanina, Gerson, Herschel, Hershel, Heshy, Isadore, Meyer, Miriam, Mort, Pesach.*

Sobelman (165) Jewish (eastern Ashkenazic): elaborated form of SOBEL, with the addition of Yiddish *man* 'man'.
GIVEN NAMES Jewish 5%. *Meyer, Sol.*

Sober (419) **1.** Northeastern English: nickname for a person of moderate habits, or a teetotaler. **2.** Slovenian (**Šober**): Slovenian spelling of German SCHOBER. **3.** Jewish (Ashkenazic): variant of SAUBER.

Soberg (141) Variant of Swedish **Sjöberg** (see SJOBERG).
GIVEN NAMES Scandinavian 5%; German 5%. *Einer; Kurt* (2).

Sobers (251) English (Newcastle and Durham): variant of SOBER.

Sobey (169) English (Devon): unexplained.

Sobie (136) **1.** English: variant of SOBEY. **2.** Jewish (Ashkenazic): shortened form of some Ashkenazic surname such as SOBIECH.
GIVEN NAMES Jewish 4%. *Pincus, Sol.*

Sobiech (164) Polish: from a derivative of the personal name *Sobiesław* (see SOBCZAK).
GIVEN NAMES Polish 7%. *Casimir, Janina, Tadeusz.*

Sobieck (107) Americanized spelling of Polish SOBIECH.

Sobieraj (107) Polish: nickname from Polish *sobie* 'take for oneself' + *raj* 'paradise'.
GIVEN NAMES Polish 23%. *Zygmunt* (2), *Casimir, Krzysztof, Slawomir, Wieslawa, Wojciech.*

Sobieski (508) Polish: habitational name for someone from Sobieszyn, or Sobieska Wola, in Lublin voivodeship.
GIVEN NAMES Polish 4%. *Jaroslaw, Stanislaw, Tadeusz, Zigmunt.*

Sobin (184) Polish: from the personal name *Sobin*, a pet form of *Sobiesław* (see SOBCZAK).

Sobkowiak (134) Polish: patronymic from the personal name SOBEK, a pet form of *Sobiesław* (see SOBCZAK).

Soble (192) Americanized spelling of North German and Jewish SOBEL.

Sobocinski (294) Polish (**Sobociński**): habitational name for someone from a place called Sobocin in Kalisz voivodeship.
GIVEN NAMES Polish 7%. *Augustyn, Boleslaw, Elzbieta, Karol, Wojciech.*

Sobol (595) **1.** Polish and Czech: from *sobol* 'sable', a type of marten with handsome black fur; possibly a nickname but more often an occupational name for a fur trader. **2.** Jewish (eastern Ashkenazic): variant of SOBEL.
GIVEN NAMES Jewish 6%; Russian 5%; Polish 4%. *Aron, Inna, Meyer, Moisey, Nechama, Rochel, Shai, Srul, Sura, Zelman; Alexei* (2), *Igor* (2), *Iosif* (2), *Leonid* (2), *Asya, Boris, Iouri, Konstantin, Oleg, Sofiya, Yefim, Yevsey; Janusz, Jozef, Rostyslaw, Slawomir, Stanislaw, Stanislawa, Zdzislaw, Zygmunt.*

Soboleski (220) Polish: variant of SOBOLEWSKI.

Sobolewski (598) Polish: habitational name for someone from Sobolew in Lublin voivodeship, or Sobolewo in Białystok, Łomża, and Suwałki voivodeships, all named with Polish *sobol* 'sable' (see SOBOL).
GIVEN NAMES Polish 10%. *Stanislaw* (3), *Zigmund* (3), *Grzegorz, Jacek, Jerzy, Jozef, Karol, Krzysztof, Maciej, Mariusz, Miroslawa, Slawomir.*

Sobolik (195) Czech (**Sobolík**): from a pet form of SOBOL or a nickname from the Czech vocabulary word *sobolík* 'crested lark'.

Sobon (197) Polish (**Soboń**): from the personal name *Soboń*, a pet form of *Sobiesław* (see SOBCZAK).
GIVEN NAMES Polish 8%. *Casimir, Jerzy, Thadeus, Zdzislawa.*

Sobota (403) Polish, Czech, and Slovak (also established in German-speaking countries): **1.** from Polish and Czech *Sobota* 'Saturday', a name bestowed on or taken by someone who was born, baptized, or registered on a Saturday, especially an adult convert to Christianity. **2.** derivative of the personal name *Sobiesław* (see SOBCZAK).
GIVEN NAMES Polish 6%. *Andrzej, Boleslaw, Janusz, Jozef, Piotr, Tadeusz, Wladyslaw, Zdzislaw.*

Sobotka (511) Polish and Czech: from a pet form of SOBOTA as a personal name.

GIVEN NAMES Polish 7%; German 4%. *Wieslaw* (2), *Arkadiusz, Jadwiga, Jerzy, Jolanta, Klaudia, Ludwik, Piotr, Tadeusz, Wladyslaw; Aloysius, Erwin, Florian, Manfred, Monika, Rudie.*

Sobotta (203) Eastern German (Upper Silesia): variant of Polish and Czech SOBOTA.

Sobus (115) Polish (**Sobuś**): from a pet form of the personal name *Sobiesław* (see SOBCZAK).
GIVEN NAME Polish 5%. *Casimir.*

Socarras (137) Spanish: from a derivative of *socarrar* 'to burn', 'to toast', possibly applied in a figurative sense as a nickname for a person given making sarcastic remarks.
GIVEN NAMES Spanish 59%. *Jose* (5), *Angel* (4), *Miguel* (4), *Carlos* (3), *Horacio* (3), *Jorge* (3), *Cruz* (2), *Francisco* (2), *Gustavo* (2), *Joaquin* (2), *Lourdes* (2), *Luis* (2).

Socci (205) Italian: patronymic or plural form of SOCCIO.
GIVEN NAMES Italian 29%. *Antonio* (4), *Carmine* (4), *Mario* (4), *Angelo* (3), *Armando, Donato, Emilio, Enrico, Gerardo, Geremia, Luciano, Rocco, Sal, Salvatore.*

Soccio (105) Italian: from a short form of a pet name formed with the suffix *-occio* of a personal name ending in *-so*, as for example *Tommasoccio* from *Tommaso*.
GIVEN NAMES Italian 12%. *Antonio* (2), *Rocco* (2), *Angelo, Gilda.*

Socha (1116) **1.** Polish, Czech, and Slovak: metonymic occupational name for a plowman, from Polish, Czech *socha* 'plow'. **2.** Czech: nickname for a strong man, from *socha* 'bar', 'column'.
GIVEN NAMES Polish 5%. *Andrzej, Boguslaw, Boleslaw, Bronislaus, Bronislaw, Franciszek, Ignatius, Irena, Janina, Janusz, Jerzy, Jozef.*

Sochacki (184) Polish: habitational name for someone from Sochacz in Krosno voivodeship.
GIVEN NAMES Polish 12%. *Andrzej* (2), *Janusz, Pawel, Tadeusz, Zbigniew, Zygmunt.*

Socher (100) Germanized variant of Czech SOCHOR.
GIVEN NAMES German 5% *Aloys, Otto, Raoul.*

Sochor (158) Czech and Slovak: from a metaphorical use of the vocabulary word *sochor* 'crowbar', hence a nickname for a man of exceptional strength.

Socia (270) Portuguese: habitational name from Soza, near Vagos, recorded in 1088 as *Socia*.

Sock (108) German: of uncertain origin. Perhaps a metonymic occupational name for a shoemaker (of light, slipperlike shoes), from Middle High German *socke* 'sock'; East German from a Slavic personal name *Sock*. Compare SOKOL.
GIVEN NAMES German 6%. *Bernhard, Florian, Kurt.*

Socks (116) **1.** Possibly an Anglicized or Americanized form of German and Jewish SACHS. **2.** Possibly a variant of or patronymic from English **Sock**, from an Old English personal name *Socca*, or a metonymic occupational name for a maker of slippers, from Middle English *sock* 'light shoe', 'slipper' (Old English *socc*).

Sockwell (389) Origin unidentified. Possibly an English habitational name from a lost or unidentified place.

Socorro (112) Spanish and Portuguese: from a personal name derived from the Marian epithet *socorro* 'help', 'aid', 'succor' (Portuguese *Maria do Socorro*, Spanish *María del Socorro*).
GIVEN NAMES Spanish 56%. *Jose* (5), *Alberto* (3), *Alfredo* (3), *Juan* (3), *Rafael* (3), *Ana* (2), *Caridad* (2), *Carlos* (2), *Gustavo* (2), *Raul* (2), *Adalberto, Adelaida*.

Soda (194) Japanese (**Sōda**): written with characters meaning 'mutual' or 'councilor' and 'rice paddy'; it is sometimes pronounced *Aida*. It occurs mostly in northeastern Japan.
GIVEN NAMES Japanese 5%. *Kazuhiro, Kikuko, Osamu, Taisuke, Takatoshi.*

Sodano (280) Southern Italian: **1.** nickname or ethnic name from Arabic *sawdān* 'black', 'Negro'. **2.** nickname from Old Sicilian *sudanu* 'sultan'.
GIVEN NAMES Italian 12%. *Antonio* (3), *Salvatore* (2), *Carmela, Carmine, Gino, Philomena.*

Sodaro (132) Italian: from a shortened and altered from of the personal name *Isadoro* (modern Italian *Isidoro*).

Sodders (139) Probably English, a variant of an unexplained Lancashire name **Sudders**.

Soden (783) English: from Middle English, Old French *soudan*, from Arabic *sulṭān* 'ruler', specifically the ruler of the Ottoman Empire. In medieval England this was used as a nickname, either for someone who behaved in an outlandish and autocratic manner or for someone who had played the part of a sultan in a pageant.

Soder (308) **1.** German (also **Söder**): topographic name from Middle High German *sōt* 'puddle', 'wet ground', Middle Low German *sod* 'turf', the suffix *-er* denoting an inhabitant, or a habitational name for someone from Söder near Hildesheim. **2.** Swedish (**Söder**): ornamental name from *söder* 'south'.
GIVEN NAMES Scandinavian 7%; German 5%. *Thor* (3), *Erik, Hilmer, Sig; Erna, Ewald, Hans, Viktor.*

Soderberg (1237) Swedish (**Söderberg**): ornamental name composed of the elements *söder* 'south' + *berg* 'mountain', 'hill'.
GIVEN NAMES Scandinavian 9%. *Erik* (6), *Lars* (3), *Elof* (2), *Iver* (2), *Nels* (2), *Peer* (2), *Algot, Anders, Astrid, Bjorn, Hilmer, Sven.*

Sodergren (272) Swedish (**Södergren**): ornamental name composed of the elements *söder* 'south' + *gren* 'branch'.
GIVEN NAME Scandinavian 5%. *Erik.*

Soderholm (327) Swedish (**Söderholm**): ornamental name composed of the elements *söder* 'south' + *holm* 'island'.
GIVEN NAMES Scandinavian 7%. *Erik* (2), *Lars* (2), *Thor* (2), *Nils.*

Soderlind (122) Swedish (**Söderlind**): ornamental name composed of the elements *söder* 'south' + *lind* 'lime', 'linden tree'.
GIVEN NAMES Scandinavian 7%. *Erik, Per.*

Soderlund (505) Swedish (**Söderlund**): ornamental name composed of the elements *söder* 'south' + *lund* 'grove'.
GIVEN NAMES Scandinavian 11%; German 4%. *Erik* (3), *Thor* (2), *Alf, Algot; Hans* (3), *Kurt.*

Soderman (305) Swedish (**Söderman**): from *söder* 'south' + *man* 'man', probably an ornamental name but possibly a regional name for someone who had migrated from the south.
GIVEN NAMES Scandinavian 9%; German 4%. *Helmer, Lennart, Nils; Ernst, Hans, Kurt.*

Soderquist (557) Swedish (**Söderqvist**): ornamental name composed of the elements *söder* 'southern' + *quist*, an old or ornamental spelling of *kvist* 'twig'.
GIVEN NAMES Scandinavian 5%. *Helmer, Nils, Sven.*

Soderstrom (722) Swedish (**Söderström**): ornamental name composed of the elements *söder* 'south' + *ström* 'river'.
GIVEN NAMES Scandinavian 10%; German 4%. *Bjorn* (2), *Nels* (2), *Anders, Erik, Holger, Lars, Lennart, Nils, Sven, Swen; Georg, Gerhard, Kurt.*

Sodhi (108) Indian (Panjab): Sikh name based on the name of a clan in the Khatri community, from Sanskrit *soḍhī* 'one who has endured'. Some of the Sikh gurus came from this clan. The Sodhis claim descent from an ancestor called Sodhi Rai.
GIVEN NAMES Indian 93%. *Deepak* (2), *Karan* (2), *Raj* (2), *Vimal* (2), *Ajit, Amit, Anil, Avtar, Brij, Gursewak, Hardev, Harleen.*

Soeder (267) North German (**Söder**): see SODER.

Soehner (103) German (**Söhner**): kinship name, from Middle High German *sun, son* 'son' + *-er* suffix of affiliation meaning 'son-in-law'.

Soelberg (106) Scandinavian: variant spelling of SOLBERG.

Soellner (139) South German: variant of SELLNER.

Soenksen (123) Danish and North German: variant of SONNICHSEN.
GIVEN NAMES German 4%. *Friede, Uwe.*

Soens (149) Dutch: patronymic from a variant of *zoon* 'son'. Compare SOHN.
GIVEN NAMES French 6%; German 4%. *Leonie, Prosper; Aloys, Kurt.*

Soergel (110) German (**Sörgel**): nickname for a sorrowful person, from a derivative of

Middle High German *sorge* 'sorrow', 'trouble'.

Soetaert (122) Dutch: patronymic from a Germanic personal name composed of the elements *sote* 'sweet' + *hard* 'bold', 'brave', 'hardy'.

Sofer (173) Jewish: variant of SOFFER 'scribe'.
GIVEN NAMES Jewish 23%; French 5%. *Uri* (3), *Chaim* (2), *Moshe* (2), *Zalmen* (2), *Gitty, Hyman, Irit, Lipot, Nurit, Ori, Shlomo, Yeshaya; Sylvain* (2), *Raoul.*

Soffa (106) Origin unidentified.

Soffer (358) Jewish: occupational name for a scribe, Hebrew *sofer*, Yiddish *soyfer*.
GIVEN NAMES Jewish 13%. *Haskel* (3), *Avi* (2), *Sasson* (2), *Avraham, Avrohom, Efi, Emanuel, Heskel, Miriam, Moishe, Rinat, Rivka.*

Sofia (348) Southern Italian: metronymic from a female personal name *Sofia*, based on Greek *sophia* 'wisdom', or a nickname with this meaning.
GIVEN NAMES Italian 21%. *Salvatore* (6), *Santo* (5), *Pasquale* (3), *Cono* (2), *Saverio* (2), *Angelo, Antonio, Carmela, Margherita, Sal, Vito.*

Sofield (146) Possibly an English habitational name from a lost or unidentified place.

Sofka (105) Slavic: unexplained. Perhaps a Serbian form of the female personal name *Sofija* (see SOFIA).

Sofranko (195) Czech or Slovak (**Šfranko**): patronymic from the personal name *Sofron*, a derivative of Greek *sophrosunē* 'wisdom'.

Soga (77) Japanese: meaning 'sedge', the word for which is nowadays pronounced *suge* or *suga*. The surname is written variously, with characters used phonetically. It is a habitational name, taken from a village in the ancient region of Asuka (now part of Nara Prefecture).

FOREBEARS The name is no longer common, but it is important in Japanese history. According to the Shinsen shōjiroku, the family descended from the mythical Emperor Kōgen through the legendary hero-statesman Takenouchi no Sukune. Actually of Korean origin, the Soga had close ties with Korean immigrant families and enthusiastically supported the importation of Buddhism from Korea. Prince Regent Shōtoku (574–622), the "father of Japanese civilization", was half Soga and married to a Soga princess. Heads of this family, beginning with Soga no Iname (d. 570), were leading scholars and all-powerful in Japanese politics for over a hundered years. They became too overbearing and violent, and finally the main branch of the family was crushed in the coup of 645, engineered by Nakatomi no Kamatari and the future Emperor Tenji (who was himself partly of Soga descent and was the husband of several Soga princesses). Several locales throughout Japan were named for resident Soga families; later, unrelated families took these habitational names as their own surnames.

Sogard (107) Danish and Norwegian (**Søgaard**, **Søgård**): habitational name from any of several places named with Danish *sø* 'sea', 'lake' + *gård* 'farm' or Norwegian *sø* 'south' + *gård* 'farm'.

Sogge (149) Norwegian: habitational name from either of two farmsteads in central Norway, named in Old Norse as *Soðgar*, from *sjóða* 'to boil or seethe', with reference to a fast-flowing river.

GIVEN NAME Scandinavian 4%. *Norvald.*

Soh (161) **1.** Chinese 苏: variant of **Su** 1. **2.** Korean: variant of **Sŏ** (see SO).

GIVEN NAMES Chinese/Korean 42%. *Won* (3), *Jin* (2), *Cheng, Eng, Hongjun, Hyun, Jae, Jung, Kwang, Man, Mun, Myung; Byung* (3), *Byung Joon, Eui Young, Jin Young, Siew.*

Soha (126) Origin unidentified.

Sohl (457) German: topographic name for someone who lived in a marshy place, from Middle High German, Middle Low German *sol* 'puddle of dung', 'muddy pool'.

Sohler (109) German: variant of SOHL.

Sohm (223) South German: **1.** variant of SAHM 2. **2.** topographic name from Middle High German *soum* 'edge', 'border', 'grassy place marking the edge of cultivated land'.

Sohmer (165) **1.** German: topographic name for someone living by the grassy border of an area of cultivation (see SOHM 2). **2.** Jewish (Ashkenazic): variant of SOMMER.

GIVEN NAMES Jewish 5%. *Anchel, Hyman, Yetta.*

Sohn (1501) **1.** German and Jewish (Ashkenazic): from Middle High German *sun, son*, German *Sohn* 'son', hence a distinguishing epithet for a son who shared the same personal name as his father. **2.** Korean: variant of SON.

GIVEN NAMES Korean 13%. *Young* (16), *Jung* (5), *Hyung* (4), *Kyung* (4), *Dong* (3), *Sang* (3), *Suk* (3), *Sung* (3), *Yong* (3), *Han* (2), *Hee* (2), *Jin* (2); *Byung* (3), *Chul* (3), *Chang* (2), *Dongwon* (2), *Hye Kyung* (2), *Byung Jin, Chang Sik, Chong, Choon, Chung, Daewon, Hak.*

Sohns (176) German (also **Söhns**): **1.** patronymic from SOHN. **2.** (northwestern): habitational name from Zons, a place near Düsseldorf.

GIVEN NAMES German 6%. *Armin, Klaus, Kurt.*

Sohr (105) German: topographic name from *sor* 'swamp water' or a habitational name from a place named with this word.

Soifer (208) Jewish (from Ukraine and Poland): variant of SOFFER.

GIVEN NAMES Jewish 13%. *Gershon* (2), *Mendel* (2), *Amiram, Avrom, Baruch, Moishe, Zelman.*

Soileau (1494) Variant spelling of French **Soileux**, an occupational name for a grower or seller of rye, from a derivative of Artois and Picard *soille* 'rye' (standard French *seigle*). This name is frequent in LA.

FOREBEARS American bearers of the name are said to be descended from one Noël Soileau, from Mézières, France, who settled in North America in 1719.

Soine (135) Variant spelling of French **Soin, Soinne**: **1.** nickname for an unfortunate or unhappy person, from Old French *soigne, soing* 'sorrow', 'care'. **2.** habitational name from Soinne in Celles, in the province of Namur.

GIVEN NAMES German 5%. *Gerhard, Wolfgang.*

Soisson (156) French: from a variant of medieval French *soçon, sosson* 'companion', 'partner', 'workmate' (from Latin *socius*), hence a nickname for a laborer, perhaps one who usually worked alongside a horse or ox. This name is sometimes Americanized as SESSIONS.

Soja (254) Polish: nickname for someone with a raucous voice or who liked to dress brightly, from *soja* 'jay'.

GIVEN NAMES Polish 13%. *Bronislawa, Henryka, Janina, Jozef, Krzysztof, Lech, Mariusz, Stanislaw, Tadeusz.*

Sojka (426) Polish and Jewish (from Poland): from Polish *sojka, sójka* 'jay', applied as a nickname, or, among Jews, as an ornamental surname.

GIVEN NAMES Polish 9%. *Stanislaw* (2), *Zofia* (2), *Bogdan, Bronislaw, Bronislawa, Casimir, Ewa, Grazyna, Maciej, Wieslaw, Wladyslaw, Zygmund.*

Sojourner (164) Americanized form of French **Séjourné** or **Séjournant**, derivatives of *séjourner* 'to stay (at a place)'.

Sok (516) **1.** Korean (**Sŏk**): there are three Chinese characters for this surname. One of these is so rare that it does not warrant treatment here. One of the remaining two characters is used by the Wŏlsŏng (or Kyŏngju) Sŏk clan, which provided the Shilla kingdom with eight of its 56 kings. Nowadays most members of this clan live in South Korea's Ch'ungch'ŏng South province, Chŏlla North province, and in the old Shilla capital, Kyŏngju, located in Kyŏngsang North province. There are two clans which use the remaining Sŏk character. The Haeju Sŏk clan's founding ancestor, Sŏk Sŏng, was of Chinese extraction and held an important government post in Ming China. When Hideyoshi led the Japanese in an attack against Korea in 1592, Sŏk Sŏng was part of the Ming forces sent to help defend Korea. Sŏng distinguished himself on the battlefield, and his son, Sŏk Tam, later migrated to Korea and was given a royal land grant in the Haeju area. The Ch'ungju Sŏk clan's founding ancestor was Sŏk In, an important Koryŏ

general, who lived in the late 10th century. Sŏk is a fairly common surname and can be found throughout the Korean peninsula. **2.** Cambodian: unexplained.

GIVEN NAMES Korean 38%; Cambodian 18%. *Chea* (4), *Sang* (3), *Sarin* (3), *Eng* (2), *Han* (2), *Kun* (2), *Leng* (2), *Lim* (2), *Yong* (2), *Chang Hun, Chean, Hak* (2), *Ry* (2), *Chang, Chong, Chong Sun, Min, Pak, Pheng, Young Kyu; Sophal* (6), *Saroeun* (5), *Sokhom* (3), *Sopheap* (3), *Chamroeun* (2), *Noy* (2), *Pheap* (2), *Savoeun* (2), *Bunthoeun, Chay, Chhoeun, Chhom, Huon, Kosal, Oeum, Ly* (4), *Kha* (3), *Khen* (3), *Phal* (3), *Phan* (3), *Da* (2), *Khon* (2), *Son* (2), *Diep, Duong.*

Sokal (104) Polish: nickname for a just or fair-minded man, a derivative of *sok* 'justice'.

GIVEN NAMES Polish 6%. *Kazimier, Tadeusz.*

Sokalski (104) Polish: habitational name for someone from Sokale in Tarnobrzeg voivodeship or Sokal, now in Ukraine.

GIVEN NAMES Polish 13%; German 5%. *Mieczyslaw, Ryszard, Tadeusz.*

Sokol (2450) Polish (**Sokół**), Czech, Slovak, Belorussian, and Jewish (eastern Ashkenazic): from Belorussian and Czech *sokol*, Polish *sokół* 'falcon', hence a metonymic occupational name for a falconer, or a nickname for someone thought to resemble a falcon in some way. As a Jewish name it is generally ornamental.

Sokolik (247) Polish (**Sokół**) and Jewish (eastern Ashkenazic): from a diminutive of SOKOL 'falcon'.

Sokoloff (529) Russian, Belorussian, and Jewish (eastern Ashkenazic): alternative spelling of SOKOLOV.

GIVEN NAMES Jewish 7%; Russian 4%. *Miriam* (2), *Hyman, Meyer, Shoshana, Sol; Boris* (4), *Kiril* (4), *Igor, Vladimir.*

Sokoloski (403) Variant of Polish SOKOLOWSKI.

Sokolosky (109) Germanized variant of Polish SOKOLOWSKI.

Sokolov (146) Russian, Belorussian, and Jewish (eastern Ashkenazic): patronymic from Russian *sokol* 'falcon'. In some cases the Russian surname arose from a nickname. In other cases it represents an ornamental name assigned to pupils in ecclesiastical schools. As a Jewish name, it is generally a patronymic from an ornamental nickname meaning 'falcon'.

GIVEN NAMES Russian 29%; Jewish 16%; French 4%. *Mikhail* (3), *Vladimir* (3), *Andrei* (2), *Igor* (2), *Leonid* (2), *Oleg* (2), *Sergey* (2), *Aleksandr, Aleksey, Boris, Grigory, Iliya; Naum* (2), *Yakov* (2), *Hyman; Serge* (2), *Marcel.*

Sokolow (280) **1.** Variant spelling (under Polish influence) of Russian, Belorussian, and Jewish SOKOLOV. **2.** Jewish (from Poland): habitational name for someone from a place called Sokołów in Poland (see SOKOLOWSKI).

GIVEN NAMES Jewish 7%. *Hinda, Isadore, Meyer, Moshe, Noam.*

Sokolowski (1458) Polish (**Sokołowski**) and Jewish (eastern Ashkenazic): habitational name for someone from any of numerous places called Sokołów or Sokołowo, named with *sokół* 'falcon'.

GIVEN NAMES Polish 10%. *Stanislaw* (5), *Zygmunt* (3), *Andrzej* (2), *Casimir* (2), *Czeslaw* (2), *Janusz* (2), *Jaroslaw* (2), *Jerzy* (2), *Krzysztof* (2), *Mieczyslaw* (2), *Piotr* (2), *Wladyslaw* (2).

Sokolski (147) Polish, Ukrainian, Belorussian, and Jewish (eastern Ashkenazic): habitational name for someone from any of several places named Sokola or Sokole, Sokoły, or Sokółka, named with *sokół* 'falcon'.

GIVEN NAMES Polish 6%; German 4%. *Andrzej, Piotr; Kurt.*

Sokolsky (120) Variant spelling of eastern Slavic and Jewish SOKOLSKI.

GIVEN NAMES Jewish 16%; Russian 12%; French 5%. *Sol* (2), *Avram, Hayim, Hyman, Ilya, Isaak, Semen; Leonid* (2), *Boris, Dmitry, Gennady, Lev, Raisa, Vladimir, Zhanna; Anatole, Pierre.*

Sol (178) **1.** Spanish and Portuguese: nickname ((*del*) *Sol*) for someone with a cheerful disposition, from *sol* 'sun' (Latin *sol*), but more likely from the female personal name *Sol*, of the same meaning and derivation or possibly in some cases from the Marian epithet (*María del Sol*). This name was frequent among Jews in Spain. **2.** Catalan and southern French (Occitan): nickname from Catalan, Occitan *sol* 'calm'. **3.** Catalan (**Sòl**) and southern French (Occitan): habitational name from any of the places called Sòl in Catalonia, or Sol in southern France, as for example Le Sol in Cantal and Lot. **4.** Jewish: when not of Spanish origin (see 1 above), from Poland: metonymic occupational name for a salt merchant, from Polish *sól* 'salt'.

GIVEN NAMES Spanish 19%; Portuguese 7%. *Jose* (2), *Margarita* (2), *Mauricio* (2), *Miguel* (2), *Aida, Carlos, Elena, Ernesto, Fernando, Javier, Jose Ricardo, Manuel; Joao.*

Sola (494) **1.** Catalan (**Solà**): habitational name from any of the minor places called Solà in Catalonia, or topographic name from Catalan *solà*, 'place exposed to the sun'. This is a very common Catalan name. **2.** Portuguese and Catalan: possibly an occupational nickname for a shoemaker, from *sola* 'sole (of a shoe)'.

GIVEN NAMES Spanish 16%; Portuguese 7%. *Jose* (9), *Francisco* (4), *Juan* (4), *Marcos* (4), *Javier* (3), *Manuel* (3), *Mario* (2), *Miguel* (2), *Orlando* (2), *Alfonso, Ana, Berta; Valentim.*

Solak (238) Polish: **1.** metonymic occupational name for a salt producer or seller, from *sól* 'salt'. Compare SOLARZ. **2.** possi-

bly also a patronymic from the forename *Sól*, literally 'salt'.

Solan (335) Irish (mainly County Mayo): reduced Anglicized form of Gaelic **Ó Sochlacháin** 'descendant of *Sochlachán*', a personal name formed with a diminutive of *sochlach* 'renowned'.

GIVEN NAMES Irish 4%. *Dermot, Pat.*

Solana (183) Catalan, Aragonese, and Spanish: habitational name from any of the numerous places named Solana or La Solana, derived from Catalan *solà* or Aragonese and Spanish *solano* 'sun-facing place' (see SOLA and SOLANO).

GIVEN NAMES Spanish 27%. *Jose* (4), *Alberto* (2), *Blanca* (2), *Eugenio* (2), *Francisco* (2), *Gustavo* (2), *Juan* (2), *Luis* (2), *Manuel* (2), *Alfonso, Carlos, Eduardo.*

Soland (199) Norwegian: habitational name from either of two farmsteads in southwestern Norway, probably so named from the Old Norse personal name *Sóli* + *land* 'farm'.

GIVEN NAMES Scandinavian 7%; German 4%. *Knute* (2), *Gunner; Orlo, Wenzel.*

Solanki (161) Indian (northern states): Hindu (Rajput) name of unknown origin. The Solankis, earlier known as Chalukyas, are a Rajput clan that ruled in Rajasthan, Gujarat, and Uttar Pradesh. They consider themselves one of the Agnikulas or Fire Tribes. See CHAUHAN for the Agnikula legend.

GIVEN NAMES Indian 92%. *Dilip* (3), *Rajendra* (3), *Rajesh* (3), *Surendra* (3), *Anand* (2), *Anil* (2), *Balvant* (2), *Bhadresh* (2), *Bharat* (2), *Gopal* (2), *Kishor* (2), *Madhu* (2).

Solano (2078) **1.** Spanish, Aragonese, Asturian-Leonese: habitational name from any of the places named Solano (Burgos and Málaga provinces) or El Solano (Asturies, and Uesca, Aragon), named with *solano* 'place exposed to the sun' (Late Latin *solanum*, a derivative of *sōl* 'sun'). **2.** Spanish and Portuguese: from a personal name adopted in honor of Francisco Solano, a 17th-century missionary to South America. **3.** Italian: possibly also from the personal name adopted in honor of Francisco Solano.

GIVEN NAMES Spanish 42%. *Jose* (48), *Luis* (18), *Juan* (17), *Francisco* (15), *Manuel* (15), *Carlos* (14), *Jorge* (13), *Pedro* (11), *Julio* (9), *Miguel* (9), *Fernando* (8), *Jaime* (8).

Solar (479) **1.** Spanish, Catalan, Aragonese, and Asturian-Leonese: topographic name from Latin *solarius* 'ancestral home' (a derivative of *solum* 'ground', 'floor'), perhaps denoting someone who lived near or at the house of an important family. **2.** Galician: habitational name from any of the places named Solar (Lugo, Logroño). **3.** Jewish (from Ukraine): occupational name from Ukrainian *solyar* 'salt merchant'. Compare Polish SOLARZ.

GIVEN NAMES Spanish 6%. *Manuel* (4), *Ana* (2), *Armando* (2), *Francisco* (2), *Luis* (2), *Alfonso, Alfredo, Artemio, Bienvenido, Carlos, Fermin, Gerardo.*

Solares (274) Spanish and Asturian-Leonese: habitational name from any of the places named Solares, in Asturies and Santander provinces.

GIVEN NAMES Spanish 50%. *Jose* (8), *Luis* (8), *Juan* (5), *Manuel* (5), *Ana* (4), *Enrique* (4), *Julio* (4), *Mario* (4), *Cesar* (3), *Emilio* (3), *Ramon* (3), *Alberto* (2); *Dario* (2), *Antonio, Emiliana, Guido, Marco, Mauro.*

Solari (669) Northern Italian: habitational name from any of various places called Solaro or Solara, from *solaro* 'site', 'plot', 'meadow', literally 'land exposed to the sun'.

GIVEN NAMES Italian 17%; Spanish 7%. *Mario* (6), *Angelo* (2), *Dario* (2), *Gustavo* (2), *Aldo, Attilio, Benito, Cesare, Chiara, Dante, Dino, Enrico, Franco, Gianna, Libero; Fernando* (2), *Miguel* (2), *Pedro* (2), *Ana Cristina, Benicio, Blanca.*

Solarz (188) Polish and Jewish (from Poland): occupational name for an extractor and seller of salt, from *solarz* 'salter', 'salt merchant' (from *sól* 'salt').

GIVEN NAMES Polish 7%. *Andrzej, Boguslawa, Czeslaw, Mariusz, Zbigniew.*

Solazzo (181) Italian: nickname from *solazzo* 'solace', 'consolation' (from Latin *solacium*), probably reduced from *buonsolazzo* 'good solace'.

GIVEN NAMES Italian 12%. *Angelo* (2), *Santo, Vito.*

Solberg (2285) **1.** German: habitational name from the common place name So(h)lberg. **2.** Norwegian: habitational name from any of numerous farmsteads (especially in southeastern Norway) named Solberg, from *sol* 'sun' + *berg* 'mountain'. **3.** Swedish: ornamental name composed of the same elements as 2.

GIVEN NAMES Scandinavian 6%. *Erik* (3), *Selmer* (3), *Alf, Bjorn, Gunard, Karsten, Knud, Lars, Morten, Nels, Nordahl, Petter.*

Soldan (181) **1.** English: variant of SODEN. **2.** Italian (Venetian): variant of SOLDANO.

Soldano (286) Italian: nickname for someone who behaved in an outlandish or autocratic manner, from *soldano* 'sultan' (earlier *sultano*, from Arabic *sulṭān* 'ruler').

GIVEN NAMES Italian 13%. *Angelo* (2), *Calogero, Carmine, Domenico, Gennaro, Giuseppe, Sal, Salvatore.*

Soldner (198) South German (**Söldner**): variant of SELLNER.

Soldo (175) **1.** Italian: from the old Tuscan personal name *Soldus*, from *soldo* 'pay', 'wage' (from Latin *solidus*). **2.** Italian: from a short form of a compound personal name ending with -*soldus* in Latin. **3.** Croatian: nickname for a soldier, from a reduced form of Italian *soldato* 'soldier'.

GIVEN NAMES Italian 13%; South Slavic 4%. *Nino* (2), *Saverio* (2), *Dino, Rocco, Salvatore*; *Gordana, Ivica, Slavko, Stojan.*

Sole (495) English: **1.** topographic name from Old English *sol* 'muddy place', or a habitational name from one of the places named with this word, as for example Soles in Kent. **2.** nickname for an unmarried man or woman, from Middle English, Old French *soul* 'single', 'unmarried' (Latin *solus* 'alone'). **3.** Catalan (**Solé**): variant of SOLER.

Solecki (217) Polish: habitational name for someone from any of a number of places called Solec, named with *sól* 'salt'.
GIVEN NAMES Polish 12%. *Lech* (3), *Zbigniew* (2), *Janina, Janusz, Jozefa.*

Solem (616) Norwegian: habitational name from thirty or more farmsteads, notably in Trøndelag, so named from Old Norse *Sólheimr* (see SOLHEIM).
GIVEN NAMES Scandinavian 5%. *Anders, Selmer, Sigfred.*

Soler (890) Catalan: **1.** habitational name from El Soler, a town in El Rosselló district, northern Catalonia, or form any other place named El Soler or with Soler, from *soler* 'ground', 'floor' (Late Latin *solarium*, a derivative of *solum* 'bottom', 'ground'). **2.** occupational name from Catalan *soler*, the person who makes or sells soles (of canvas sandals or shoes). This is a very common Catalan name.
GIVEN NAMES Spanish 42%. *Jose* (27), *Juan* (16), *Rafael* (14), *Carlos* (12), *Ana* (9), *Eduardo* (8), *Luis* (8), *Pedro* (8), *Jorge* (7), *Miguel* (6), *Emilio* (5), *Fernando* (5).

Soles (1206) English: variant of SOLE.

Solesbee (250) American variant spelling of English SOULSBY.

Soley (287) **1.** English: unexplained. **2.** Catalan: variant of **Solell**, topographic name from Catalan *solell* 'sunny side', 'southern slope', from a derived of *sol*, 'sun'. Compare SOL 2.

Solheim (458) Norwegian: habitational name from any of thirty or more farmsteads, notably in Hordaland and Sogn og Fjordane, so named from Old Norse *Sólheimr*, a compound of *sól* 'sun' + *heimr* 'home', 'farmstead'.
GIVEN NAMES Scandinavian 9%. *Karsten* (2), *Aagot, Erik, Oystein, Thor, Toralf.*

Soli (189) Italian: of uncertain derivation; it corresponds in form to the plural of *solo* 'only', 'alone', but it could be from a shortened pet form of a personal name ending in *-so*, as for example *Ambrosolo* from *Ambroso, Tommasolo* from *Tommaso*, etc.

Soliday (435) Americanized form of German SALATHE.

Solie (364) Norwegian: variant spelling of SOLLIE.
GIVEN NAMES Scandinavian 4%. *Erik* (2), *Lars.*

Soliman (487) Muslim: variant of SULEIMAN.

GIVEN NAMES Muslim 67%. *Mohamed* (12), *Samir* (11), *Nabil* (9), *Ahmed* (7), *Soliman* (6), *Mahmoud* (5), *Mostafa* (5), *Nader* (5), *Said* (5), *Amr* (4), *Hesham* (4), *Ibrahim* (4).

Solimine (177) Italian: from an Italianized form of the Arabic personal name SULEIMAN.
GIVEN NAMES Italian 16%. *Amedeo* (2), *Antonio* (2), *Carmine* (2), *Alessandro, Angelo, Enrico, Lorenzo, Sal.*

Solin (167) Swedish: ornamental name composed of the elements *sol* 'sun' + the common surname suffix *-in*, derived from Latin *-in(i)us* 'descendant of'.

Solinger (214) German and Jewish (Ashkenazic): habitational name for someone from Solingen in the Rhineland.

Solinski (142) Polish (**Soliński**) and Jewish (Ashkenazic): habitational name for someone from Solina in Krosno voivodeship or Soliny in Suwałki voivodeship (both named from *sól* 'salt'). This surname is also established in German-speaking countries.
GIVEN NAMES Polish 6%; French 5%. *Lucyna, Zdzislaw*; *Camile, Jean Marie.*

Solinsky (145) Variant spelling of Polish and Jewish SOLINSKI.
GIVEN NAMES Jewish 4%. *Asher, Chaim, Moshe.*

Solis (6710) **1.** Spanish and Asturian-Leonese (**Solís**): habitational name from Solís in Asturies or a similarly named place elsewhere. **2.** English: from a medieval personal name bestowed on a child born after the death of a sibling, from Middle English *solace* 'comfort', 'consolation'. The word also came to have the sense 'delight', 'amusement', and in some cases the surname may have arisen from a nickname for a playful or entertaining person.
GIVEN NAMES Spanish 51%; Portuguese 9%. *Jose* (162), *Juan* (98), *Jesus* (63), *Carlos* (62), *Manuel* (61), *Javier* (58), *Ruben* (50), *Francisco* (49), *Luis* (39), *Mario* (35), *Ramon* (35), *Jorge* (34); *Conceicao, Lidio, Ligia, Omero, Zaragoza.*

Soliz (1197) Spanish: variant of **Solís** (see SOLIS).
GIVEN NAMES Spanish 40%. *Jose* (21), *Manuel* (18), *Juan* (16), *Pedro* (8), *Francisco* (6), *Jesus* (6), *Mario* (6), *Roberto* (6), *Alfredo* (5), *Guadalupe* (5), *Juanita* (5), *Rafael* (5).

Soll (377) **1.** German: topographic name for someone who lived in a marshy place, a variant of SOHL, or a habitational name from a place named with this word. **2.** South German (**Söll**): habitational name from a place so called in Bavaria. **3.** German: variant of SELLE 2. **4.** Jewish: variant spelling of SOL.

Sollami (44) Italian (Sicily, Villa Rosa): variant of **Sollima**, from *Solyma* (*Hierosolyma*), which is found as a medieval personal name, although the surname is most probably a habitational name derived from

a place called Casa Sollima, presumably named with the old personal name.

Sollars (540) English (Gloucestershire): from Middle English *soler* 'solar', 'upper floor of a house' (Old English *solor*), probably an occupational name for a servant whose duties were centered in the upper part of a house.

Sollberger (118) German and Swiss German: habitational name for someone from any of various minor places in Germany named Solberg or Sohlberg.
GIVEN NAMES French 7%; German 4%. *Jacques, Julien, Marcel*; *Hans, Kurt.*

Sollecito (150) Italian: nickname from *sollecito* 'quick', 'attentive'.
GIVEN NAMES Italian 23%. *Rocco* (3), *Carmelo* (2), *Salvatore* (2), *Vito* (2), *Francesca, Sal, Santo.*

Sollenberger (522) Dutch and Belgian: habitational name for someone from Sollenberg in Huizingen, in the Belgian province of Brabant.
GIVEN NAME German 4%. *Kurt* (3).

Soller (313) **1.** English: variant of SOLLARS. **2.** German: topographic name for someone who lived in a marshy place, from *Soll* (variant of SOHL 1), the suffix *-er* denoting an inhabitant. **3.** South German (**Söller**): nickname for someone whose house had a characteristic arbor or sunroom attached or a loggia in the upper story, from Latin *solarium* 'sun room'.
GIVEN NAME German 4%. *Kurt* (2).

Sollers (165) Possibly a variant spelling of SOLLARS.

Solley (359) English (Kent): unexplained. Compare SOLLY.

Solliday (135) See SOLIDAY.

Sollie (189) Norwegian: habitational name from any of numerous farmsteads all over Norway, so named from *sol* 'sun' + *li* 'hillside', 'mountainside' (hence 'the sunny side').

Sollinger (138) English: **1.** variant of SALINGER. **2.** habitational name from Solinger in Kimble, Buckinghamshire.

Sollitto (130) Southern Italian: unexplained.
GIVEN NAMES Italian 15%. *Domenic, Gaetano, Sal.*

Sollman (157) German (**Sollmann**): elaborated form of SOLL or SOHL with the addition of Middle High German *man* 'man'.

Solloway (148) English and Jewish (American): variant spelling of SOLOWAY.

Solly (186) **1.** English (Kent): unexplained. Compare SOLLEY. **2.** Irish: reduced Anglicized form of Gaelic **Mac Soilligh** 'son of *Soilleach*', possibly derived from *soilghe* 'ease', 'agreeableness'.

Solmonson (109) Variant of Swedish and Jewish SOLOMONSON.

Solo (268) Basque: from *solo* 'rural estate', hence a topographic or occupational name for someone who lived or worked on a country estate.

Soloff (167) Jewish (Ashkenazic): alternative spelling of **Solov** (see SOLOW).
GIVEN NAMES Jewish 10%. *Mordecai* (3), *Sol* (2), *Miriam, Rivki, Shimon, Zorach.*

Soloman (520) Variant spelling of SOLOMON.

Solomon (15712) Jewish, English, Scottish, Dutch, French, Swedish, Italian, Portuguese, and Spanish (**Solomón**): vernacular form of the Biblical Hebrew male personal name *Shelomo* (a derivative of *shalom* 'peace'). This was fairly widespread in the Middle Ages among Christians; it has for generations been a popular Jewish name. In the Bible it is the name of King David's successor, noted for his wisdom. Among Christians it was also used as a nickname for a man who was considered wise. In North America it is also found as an Anglicized form of SALOMON and SALAMON.

Solomons (144) Jewish (Ashkenazic) and English: patronymic from the personal name SOLOMON.

Solomonson (143) Swedish (**Solomonsson**) and Jewish (Ashkenazic): patronymic from the personal name SOLOMON.

Solon (443) **1.** Irish: variant of SOLAN. **2.** French: habitational name from Les Solons in Oise, named with a regional variant of *sablon* 'sand'.

Solorio (854) Portuguese (**Solório**): unexplained.
GIVEN NAMES Spanish 53%. *Jose* (21), *Jesus* (12), *Juan* (11), *Francisco* (10), *Roberto* (10), *Miguel* (9), *Mario* (8), *Luis* (7), *Manuel* (7), *Carlos* (6), *Javier* (6), *Ricardo* (6).

Solorzano (1030) Spanish (**Solórzano**): habitational name from Solórzano in Santander province.
GIVEN NAMES Spanish 54%. *Jose* (31), *Carlos* (17), *Juan* (14), *Jorge* (13), *Luis* (12), *Jesus* (11), *Francisco* (10), *Manuel* (10), *Pedro* (8), *Miguel* (7), *Rafael* (7), *Alfonso* (6); *Antonio* (2), *Leonardo* (2), *Sal* (2), *Ceasar, Clementina, Flavio, Franco, Gabino, Galileo, Giovanni, Marco, Mario Roberto.*

Solow (281) Jewish (eastern Ashkenazic): Polish or German spelling of **Solov**, probably a reduced form of the personal name *Solovei* (see SOLOWAY).
GIVEN NAME Jewish 4%. *Zalman.*

Soloway (360) **1.** English: unexplained. **2.** Americanized form of Jewish (eastern Ashkenazic) **Solovei**, ornamental name or occupational nickname for a cantor in a synagogue, from Russian *solovei* 'nightingale'.

Solt (692) English: perhaps a respelling of SALT.

Soltani (134) Muslim: from the Arabic adjectival form *Sulṭānī*, meaning 'pertaining to (or descended from) a sultan or someone called SULTAN'.
GIVEN NAMES Muslim 75%. *Ali* (3), *Roya* (3), *Abbas* (2), *Amir* (2), *Bahram* (2), *Ebrahim*

(2), *Hassan* (2), *Mohammed* (2), *Nader* (2), *Rahim* (2), *Sepehr* (2), *Ahmad.*

Soltau (179) German: habitational name from a place so called near Hannover or Soldau in East Prussia, named with *solt* 'boggy or dirty water'.
GIVEN NAMES German 5%; French 5%. *Dietrich, Gerd, Hans, Kurt; Camille* (2), *Emile.*

Solter (108) Catalan: nickname from *solter* 'journeyman', 'bachelor'.

Soltero (325) Spanish: nickname from *soltero* 'journeyman', 'bachelor'.
GIVEN NAMES Spanish 47%. *Jose* (13), *Felipe* (4), *Luis* (4), *Ramon* (4), *Alfredo* (3), *Francisco* (3), *Andres* (2), *Carlos* (2), *Cruz* (2), *Esperanza* (2), *Genaro* (2), *Gerardo* (2).

Soltes (179) Origin uncertain. Perhaps a variant spelling of Polish and Jewish (from Poland) **Sołtys**, a status name meaning 'village administrator'. As a Jewish name it can designate a specific Jewish occupation (see SCHULTZ.)

Soltesz (271) Hungarian (**Soltész**): status name from *soltész* (*soltísz*) 'village headman', earlier 'emancipated serf'.
GIVEN NAMES Hungarian 9%. *Balint* (2), *Laszlo* (2), *Attila, Bela, Gaza, Istvan, Kalman, Sandor.*

Soltis (1297) **1.** Altered spelling of Polish **Sołtys**, Czech **Šoltys**, or Slovak **Šoltýs** (see SOLTYS). **2.** Americanized spelling of Hungarian **Soltész** (see SOLTESZ).

Soltow (102) East German: variant of SOLTAU.

Soltys (498) Polish (**Sołtys**), Czech (**Šoltys**), and Slovak **Šoltýs**: of German origin, a status name for a village headman (see SCHULTZ, SCHULTHEIS).
GIVEN NAMES Polish 7%. *Andrzej, Bronislaw, Bronislawa, Danuta, Irena, Janina, Jozef, Malgorzata, Stanislaw, Tadeusz, Wojciech.*

Soltysiak (135) Polish (**Sołtysiak**): derivative or patronymic from **Sołtys** (see SOLTYS).
GIVEN NAMES Polish 8%. *Zbigniew* (2), *Kazimierz, Stanislaw.*

Soltz (121) Jewish (from Lithuania and Belarus): habitational name for someone who lived near the river Solcha in Belarus.
GIVEN NAMES Jewish 6%. *Meyer* (2), *Geula.*

Solum (368) Norwegian: habitational name from any of ten or more farmsteads, mostly in southeastern Norway, named in Old Norse as *Sólheimr* (see SOLHEIM).
GIVEN NAME Scandinavian 4%. *Anders.*

Soluri (116) Perhaps a variant of Italian SOLARI.
GIVEN NAMES Italian 9%. *Luciano* (2), *Angelo, Leonardo.*

Solverson (105) Norwegian: patronymic from the personal name *Sølver*, Old Norse *Sǫlvir*, a compound of *sol* 'house' + *vir* 'giant'.
GIVEN NAMES Scandinavian 7%. *Selmer, Thor.*

Solway (105) **1.** English: unexplained. **2.** Jewish (American): variant spelling of SOLOWAY.
GIVEN NAME Jewish 5%. *Chana.*

Som (258) **1.** Indian (Bengal and southern states) and Bangladeshi: Hindu name from Sanskrit *soma* 'moon'. It is usually a Kayasth name in Bengal. It is a variant of SOMAN among people from Kerala and Tamil Nadi who have migrated from their home state. It is only a given name in southern India, but has come to be used as a family name in the U.S. by families from southern India. **2.** Cambodian: unexplained. **3.** Hungarian: probably a nickname for someone with a sour disposition, from *som*, a sour-tasting forest fruit.
GIVEN NAMES Indian 18%; Cambodian 17%; Other Southeast Asian 12%. *Dilip* (2), *Amitabh, Ananda, Anup, Kushal, Mrinal, Pradip, Ranjan; Roeun* (3), *Oeun* (2), *Sarin* (2), *Sambath, Sarath, Sareth, Savuth, Sophan; Chay, Chham, Chhom, Doeun, Oeurn, Saroeun, Savath, Sokunthea, Sophat, Soun, Sovann, Voeun; Lim* (2), *Phon* (2), *Son* (2), *Yom* (2), *Bok, Chen, Ching, Hau, Hoa, Khon, Heng, Ling, Phan, Rin, Sen, Seng, Long, Ly, Neng, Ry, Than, Thanh, Youn.*

Soma (277) Japanese (**Sōma**): habitational name taken from a village in Shimōsa (now part of Chiba prefecture). It is found mostly in eastern Japan. Bearers are of TAIRA lineage, some being descended from the famous 10th-century rebel Masakado.
GIVEN NAMES Japanese 9%. *Daisuke, Hiroshi, Izumi, Keigo, Kuniko, Nobuo, Osamu, Seiichi, Tadashi, Yasuhiro, Yoshiro.*

Soman (120) Indian (Kerala, Tamil Nadu): Hindu name from Sanskrit *soma* 'moon' + the Tamil-Malayalam third-person masculine singular suffix *-n*. This is only a given name in India, but has come to be used as a family name in the U.S.
GIVEN NAMES Indian 39%. *Ramdass* (2), *Satish* (2), *Anagha, Anjali, Bharat, Dilip, Gopal, Narendra, Narine, Nikhil, Pravin, Ram.*

Somer (198) **1.** English and Irish: variant of SUMMER. **2.** Irish: variant of SUMMER or SUMMERS. **3.** Jewish (Ashkenazic): variant of SOMMER.
GIVEN NAME German 4%. *Fritz.*

Somera (131) Spanish: habitational name from La Somera in Cuenca province.
GIVEN NAMES Spanish 37%; Italian 7%. *Abelino, Adela, Alberto, Alfredo, Ana, Angel, Asuncion, Domingo, Elena, Emiliano, Emilio, Eusebio; Eliseo* (2), *Antonio, Constantino, Geronimo, Romeo.*

Somero (168) Spanish: topographic name from *somero* 'close to the surface'.

Somers (4409) **1.** Irish: variant of SUMMER or SUMMERS. **2.** English (northern): patronymic from SUMMER.

Somerset (192) English: regional name from the county of this name, so called from

Old English *Sumor(tūn)sǣte* 'dwellers at the summer settlement'.

Somerville (2440) **1.** Scottish (of Norman origin): habitational name, probably from Graveron Sémerville in Nord, named with the Germanic personal name *Sigimar* (see SIEMER) + Old French *ville* 'settlement'. **2.** Irish: reduced Anglicized form of Gaelic **Ó Somacháin** (see SUMMERS).

Somes (244) English: habitational name from places in Cambridgeshire and Suffolk called Soham, from Old English *sā* 'sea', 'lake' (a byform of *sǣ*) + *hām* 'homestead'.

Somma (539) Italian: **1.** habitational name from any of various places named Somma, notably Somma Vesuviana in Naples province, from *somma*, *sommo* 'high point', 'place above'. **2.** in some instances possibly from a female personal name, *Somma*.

GIVEN NAMES Italian 21%. *Carmine* (6), *Salvatore* (6), *Pasquale* (5), *Sal* (3), *Angelo* (2), *Antonio* (2), *Attilio* (2), *Carmela* (2), *Dante* (2), *Aldo*, *Aniello*, *Gildo*.

Sommer (4974) **1.** English and Irish: variant of SUMMER. **2.** German and Danish: from Middle German *sumer*, Danish, Norwegian *sommer* 'summer', a nickname for someone of a warm disposition, or for someone associated with the season in some other way or from living in a sunny place, in some instances a metonymic occupational name for a basketweaver or a drummer, from Middle High German *sum(b)er*, *sum(m)er* 'basket', 'basketry', 'drum'. **3.** Jewish (Ashkenazic): ornamental name from German *Sommer* 'summer'. Like the other seasonal names, this was also one of the group of names that were bestowed on Jews more or less at random by government officials in 18th- and 19th-century central Europe.

GIVEN NAMES German 6%. *Kurt* (8), *Otto* (8), *Hans* (7), *Fritz* (4), *Aloys* (3), *Helmut* (3), *Wolfram* (3), *Armin* (2), *Eldor* (2), *Erwin* (2), *Gerhard* (2), *Guenther* (2).

Sommerer (117) German (Austria): variant of SOMMER, a nickname for a summer tenant or a worker hired for the summer.

GIVEN NAMES German 6%. *Erhardt*, *Otto*.

Sommerfeld (781) **1.** German: habitational name from any of several places so named. **2.** German: topographic name from fields so named because they were cultivated only in the summer, from Middle High German *sumer*, Middle Low German *somer* 'summer' + Middle High German, Middle Low German *velt* 'open country'. **3.** Jewish (Ashkenazic): ornamental name composed of German *Sommer* 'summer' + *Feld* 'field'. Compare SOMMER. **4.** English: variant of SUMMERFIELD.

GIVEN NAMES German 6%. *Kurt* (4), *Otto* (4), *Detlef*, *Gerhard*, *Gunther*, *Helmut*, *Johannes*, *Reinhold*, *Wolfgang*.

Sommerfeldt (245) German and Jewish (Ashkenazic): variant of SOMMERFELD.

Sommerfield (330) English: variant spelling of SUMMERFIELD.

GIVEN NAMES German 4%. *Ewald*, *Otto*.

Sommers (4561) English: patronymic from SUMMER 1.

Sommerville (817) Scottish: variant spelling of SOMERVILLE 1.

Somogyi (263) Hungarian: habitational name for someone from Somogy county or one of several places so called.

GIVEN NAMES Hungarian 23%. *Laszlo* (6), *Zoltan* (5), *Andras* (2), *Bela* (2), *Gabor* (2), *Janos* (2), *Arpad*, *Ferenc*, *Istvan*, *Jozsef*, *Karoly*, *Sandor*.

Somoza (157) Galician: habitational name from any of the numerous places in Galicia called Somoza, named as being situated 'below the mountain' (Latin *sub montia*).

GIVEN NAMES Spanish 45%. *Jose* (6), *Julio* (4), *Carlos* (3), *Francisco* (3), *Luis* (3), *Juan* (2), *Miguel* (2), *Orlando* (2), *Ramon* (2), *Alfredo*, *Alvaro*, *Ana*.

Somsen (106) Variant of Dutch, German, English, etc. SAMSON.

Son (1527) **1.** Korean: there is one Chinese character for the Son surname. Some sources mention as many as 118 clans for the Son family, but only seven can be documented. According to legend, the Son clan's founding ancestor was named Kuryema and was one of the six pre-Shilla elders who made Pak Hyŏkkŏse the first king of Shilla. The first documented ancestor, however, was called Sun. Sun is said to have lived a poverty-stricken existence in the Shilla period. His son was a voracious eater and ate Sun's old mother's food as well as his own. Sun, feeling that he could always get another son but that his mother was irreplaceable, decided to go into the mountains to bury his son. When he dug into the ground, however, he found a bell. He hung the bell on a nearby tree and rang it. So loud and clear was the cry of the bell that the king heard it in the palace below and came to investigate. The king was amazed at the bell and gave Sun a house and food. Later, a Buddhist temple was built on that spot. The founding ancestor of the Iljik (or Andong) Son clan originally bore the surname Sun, but during the reign of Koryŏ king Hyŏnjong (1009–1031), Sun was changed to Son. **2.** English: from Middle English *sone* 'son', hence a distinguishing epithet for a son who shared the same personal name as his father. **3.** Jewish (Ashkenazic): variant of SOHN, or SONN.

GIVEN NAMES Korean 46%. *Young* (27), *Jong* (7), *Sang* (7), *Jung* (6), *Kwang* (6), *Dong* (5), *Jin* (5), *Yong* (5), *Joon* (4), *Seung* (4), *Sung* (4), *Chan* (3); *Chong* (9), *Chang* (8), *Byung* (4), *Chung* (3), *Jung Hyun* (3), *Young Chul* (3), *Young Seok* (3), *Chul* (2), *Myong* (2), *Sang Wook* (2), *Sookja* (2), *Thai* (2); *Minh* (5), *Ha* (4), *Lam* (4), *Hien* (3),

Hoa (3), *Hoang* (3), *Banh* (2), *Cao* (2), *Duc* (2), *Dung* (2), *Son* (2), *Suong* (2).

Soncrant (121) Origin unidentified.

Sondag (213) Dutch: from *zondag* 'Sunday', probably applied as a nickname or personal name for someone borne on a Sunday or otherwise associated with the day.

Sonday (131) Americanized form of Dutch SONDAG.

Sonderegger (153) South German: topographic name from Middle High German *sunder* 'separate' or 'southern' + (dialect) *egg* 'corner' + *-er*, suffix denoting an inhabitant.

GIVEN NAME German 6%. *Kurt* (2).

Sondergaard (136) Danish (**Søndergaard**): habitational name from a place named with *sønder* 'southern' + *gård* 'enclosure', 'farm'.

Sonderman (223) German (**Sondermann**): **1.** (North German): from Middle Low German *sunderman* 'bondsman'. **2.** topographic name denoting someone who lived to the south of a settlement, from Middle High German *sunder* 'southern' + *man* 'man'.

Sondgeroth (165) Origin unidentified.

GIVEN NAMES French 4%. *Collette*, *Jacques*.

Sondrol (108) Norwegian: habitational name from farmsteads named Søndrål or Søndrol: in Hallingdal, from *Sondre*, either a personal name (from Old Norse *Sundri*) or 'southern' + *hol* 'rise', 'hillock'; in Valdres, from *sund* 'sound', 'inlet' + *ro* 'corner', 'nook'.

GIVEN NAMES Scandinavian 8%. *Iver* (2), *Knute*.

Sone (117) **1.** Japanese: written with characters meaning 'former' or 'ancestor' and 'root'. This name is found mostly in eastern Japan and in the Ryūkyū Islands. One family were samurai of Suō province (now part of Yamaguchi prefecture). **2.** Variant of English SON or Jewish SOHN or SONNE.

GIVEN NAMES Japanese 24%. *Koji* (2), *Fujio*, *Hiroyoshi*, *Ichiro*, *Kaori*, *Masahito*, *Minako*, *Nobuhiro*, *Sachi*, *Saya*, *Shinichi*, *Yoko*.

Sones (516) English: patronymic from SON 1.

Song (3733) **1.** Korean: there are two Chinese characters for this surname, covering sixteen clans. The smaller clan is the only clan to use one of the two Chinese characters, and it has only one or two households. The remaining clans all descend from a common ancestor, Song Chuŭn, who seems to have migrated from Tang China to Korea sometime during the Shilla period. Sixty percent of the Songs live in southern Korea. **2.** Korean (**Sŏng**): there are two Chinese characters for the surname Sŏng, but one of them is registered for just a single household. Only the common Sŏng clan, the Ch'angnyŏng clan, is treated here. This was founded by Sŏng In-bo just prior to the establishment of the Koryŏ kingdom

in 918. According to legend, Sŏng In-bo died in Seoul. His son set out to transport his father's body back to Ch'angnyŏng, but, the weather being poor, he decided to stop for the night and finish the journey in the morning. When he awoke, he discovered that his father's body was missing. Upon investigation, he found that a tiger had dragged the body to a secluded grave site in the mountains near Ch'angnyŏng. It was there that the son buried his father and established his home. Many of the members of the Sŏng clan today live in the Ch'angnyŏng area of Kyŏngsang province. **3.** Chinese 宋: from a place name, the state of Song. After the Zhou overthrew the corrupt king of the Shang dynasty, Zhou Xin, in 1122 BC, the new Zhou dynasty granted the state of Song to the overthrown king's half-brother, Wei Ziqi. His descendants eventually adopted the place name Song as their surname. This name was that of the Song dynasty, (960–1279), and in more recent times was borne by the powerful Soong siblings: T.V. Soong, once one of the richest men in the world; Soong Ch'ingling, wife of Sun Yat-Sen; and Soong Meiling, wife of Chiang Kai-shek.
GIVEN NAMES Korean 46%; Chinese 16%. *Young* (79), *Yong* (28), *Jae* (22), *Sung* (19), *Chang* (18), *Kyung* (15), *Chae* (14), *Jin* (14), *Chong* (12), *Jong* (12), *Joon* (12), *Jung* (12), *Myung* (12), *Byung* (11), *Chan* (11), *Chung* (11), *Dae* (10), *Min* (10), *Moon* (8), *Myong* (6), *Nam* (6), *Chul* (5), *Sook* (5), *Jae Hong* (4).

Songer (1090) English: variant of SANGER 2.

Songy (202) French: unexplained.
GIVEN NAMES French 6%. *Angelle, Antoine, Etienne.*

Soni (400) Indian (Panjab, Rajasthan, Gujarat): Hindu (Khatri, Bania, Vania) and Sikh name meaning 'goldsmith' in the languages of the region, derived from *son-* 'gold', from Sanskrit *svarṇa*. Banias and also the Panjabi Khatris have clans called Soni.
GIVEN NAMES Indian 90%. *Ashok* (6), *Bharat* (6), *Ajay* (5), *Mukesh* (5), *Ramesh* (5), *Amrit* (4), *Dilip* (4), *Vijay* (4), *Deepak* (3), *Girish* (3), *Manish* (3), *Nalin* (3).

Sonia (135) French: metronymic from the female personal name *Sonia*.
GIVEN NAMES French 4%. *Amedee, Monique.*

Soniat (115) Origin unidentified. This is a Louisiana name.
GIVEN NAMES French 5%. *Angelle, Jean-Claude.*

Sonier (208) Probably an altered spelling of French SONNIER or SAULNIER.

Sonkin (137) Jewish (from Belarus): metronymic from the Yiddish female personal name *Sonke*, derived from an eastern Slavic pet form of *Sofiya*, equivalent of *Sophie*, with the eastern Slavic possessive suffix *-in.*

GIVEN NAMES Russian 13%; Jewish 10%. *Boris* (2), *Dmitriy* (2), *Leonid, Mikhail, Nikolai, Vitaly, Yury; Golda, Inna, Isadore.*

Sonn (209) **1.** English: variant spelling of SON. **2.** Jewish (Ashkenazic): variant of SONNE.

Sonnabend (160) German: from Middle Low German *sunnavent* 'Saturday' (literally 'Sun(day) eve'), hence a nickname for someone who was born or paid rent or compulsory feudal service on a Saturday.
GIVEN NAMES German 5%. *Otto, Volker.*

Sonne (253) **1.** German: from Middle German *sonne, sunne* 'sun', either a habitational name for someone living at a house distinguished by the sign of a sun, or from a field name. **2.** Jewish (Ashkenazic): ornamental name from German *Sonne* 'sun'.
GIVEN NAMES German 5%; Scandinavian 4%. *Rudi, Uwe; Erik, Niels.*

Sonneborn (200) German and Jewish (Ashkenazic): habitational name from any of the places called Sonneborn. In some cases, the Jewish name may be ornamental.

Sonnek (170) German: possibly a topographic name from Middle High German *sunne, sonne* 'sun' + *ecke* 'corner', 'ridge'. However, the final element may be the Slavic diminutive suffix *-ek*.

Sonneman (100) German (**Sonnemann**): occupational name from Middle Low German *soneman* 'arbitrator' in the north; in the south perhaps an elaborate compound of SONNE + *mann* 'man'.

Sonnen (194) **1.** German: habitational name from any of several places so named in Bavaria. **2.** German: variant of SONNE 1. **3.** Dutch: from Middle Dutch *sonne* 'sun', applied as a term of endearment for a loved one, or a habitational name for someone living at a house distinguished by the sign of a sun.

Sonnenberg (1210) **1.** German: habitational name from any of the places called Sonnenberg. **2.** Jewish (Ashkenazic): ornamental name formed with German *Sonne* 'sun' + *Berg* 'mountain', 'hill'.
GIVEN NAMES German 5%. *Otto* (5), *Hans* (2), *Kurt* (2), *Arno, Dieter, Eldor, Eldred, Heinz, Ilse, Ingo, Reinhart, Reinhold.*

Sonnenburg (244) German: habitational name from any of the places called Sonnenburg.
GIVEN NAMES German 8%. *Dieter, Erwin, Helmut, Helmuth, Kurt, Lothar, Reinhart.*

Sonnenfeld (191) German: topographic name for someone who lived by or farmed a south-facing area of land, from Middle High German, Middle Low German *sunne, sonne* 'sun' + Middle High German, Middle Low German *velt* 'field', 'open country'.
GIVEN NAMES German 12%. *Erwin* (3), *Heinz* (2), *Kurt* (2), *Erna, Otto, Rainer.*

Sonnenschein (181) **1.** German: nickname for someone with a cheerful or warm disposition, from Middle High German *sunne* 'sun' + genitive *-n* + *schîn* 'shine'. In

part it may be a topographic name for someone who lived at a place which caught the sun, or a habitational name from a house marked with the sign of the sun. **2.** Jewish (Ashkenazic): ornamental name from German *Sonnenschein* 'sunshine'.
GIVEN NAMES German 6%; Jewish 5%. *Hans* (2), *Helmut* (2); *Ezriel, Gershon, Nurit.*

Sonnentag (138) German: from an older form of SONNTAG, especially long-established in Swabia.

Sonner (375) South German (Bavarian): **1.** occupational name for someone who bleached cloth, from an agent derivative of Middle High German *sunnen* 'to bleach'. **2.** habitational name for someone from a place named Sonne.

Sonnichsen (122) Danish and North German (**Sönnichsen**): patronymic from a pet form of Middle Low German *sone* 'son'.
GIVEN NAME German 4%. *Fritz.*

Sonnier (1901) French: occupational name for a bell ringer, Old French *sonnier* (Late Latin *sonarius*, an agent derivative of *sonare* 'to ring').
GIVEN NAMES French 6%. *Alcee* (2), *Antoine* (2), *Minos* (2), *Remy* (2), *Alcide, Amie, Armand, Calice, Clovis, Curley, Donat, Emile.*

Sonntag (768) German and Jewish (Ashkenazic): from Middle High German *sun(nen)tac*, German *Sonntag* 'Sunday', a nickname for someone who had some particular connection with Sunday. The German surname may have arisen from a personal name for a child born on a Sunday, for this was considered a lucky day. Among Jews, it seems to have been one of the group of names referring to days of the week that were distributed at random by government officials.
GIVEN NAMES German 5%. *Hans* (2), *Otto* (2), *Volker* (2), *Erwin, Fritz, Guenter, Heinz, Markus.*

Sonoda (146) Japanese: 'garden rice paddy'; it is found mostly in the island of Kyūshū, where bearers are descended from the KIKUCHI family. A priestly family of Ise (now part of Mie prefecture) is descended from Fujiwara no Hidesato (10th century), of the northern FUJIWARA, through the Arakida family. They take their name from a village in Kōzuke (now Gunma prefecture).
GIVEN NAMES Japanese 45%. *Koji* (2), *Tadashi* (2), *Takeshi* (2), *Aiko, Ayako, Eiko, Emiko, Fujio, Hidenori, Hideyo, Hiromi, Kazumi.*

Sons (637) Dutch form of North German **Sohns**, a patronymic from SOHN.

Sonsalla (156) German: unexplained.

Sontag (841) German and Jewish (Ashkenazic): variant spelling of SONNTAG.

Sontheimer (137) German: habitational name for someone from any of several places named Sontheim.
GIVEN NAME German 4%. *Kurt.*

Soo (302) Chinese: see SU.

GIVEN NAMES Chinese 9%. *Kwang* (2), *Suk* (2), *Chan, Chia, Chin, Chyi, Han, Keng, Kwan, Kyung, Leong, Liang.*

Sood (343) Indian (Panjab): name of a Hindu mercantile community of the Panjab, believed to be derived from Persian *sūd* 'benefit', 'gain', 'interest'.

GIVEN NAMES Indian 87%. *Satish* (10), *Rajiv* (7), *Anil* (6), *Sanjay* (5), *Arun* (4), *Virendra* (4), *Ajay* (3), *Harish* (3), *Rajesh* (3), *Rakesh* (3), *Ravi* (3), *Rohit* (3).

Soo Hoo (397) Chinese 司徒: variant of SITU. An unusual name, both for containing two Chinese characters and for its spelling. Many early Chinese immigrants came from Taishan, only about a hundred miles from Canton but speaking a different dialect. *Soo Hoo* is a Taishan form of SITU.

GIVEN NAMES Chinese 10%. *Ming* (2), *Foo, Hoon, Lim, Moo, Mow, Sek, Tsui, Wah, Wan Ying, Yee.*

Soon (198) Chinese 孙: variant of SUN.

GIVEN NAMES Chinese/Korean 14%. *Choi, Duck, Eng, Fook, Jae, Jeon, Joon, Keum, Kim Hung, Shih-Chung, Shin Young, Wong.*

Soong (262) Chinese 宋: variant of SONG.

GIVEN NAMES Chinese 8%. *Yang* (2), *Cheng, Cheng-Yi, Chi Hung, Hsia, Kee, Meng, Tsai, Wen, Yee Man, Yong, Yuan.*

Soos (345) Hungarian (**Soós**): occupational name for someone who mined or sold salt, from *só* 'salt'. See SO 3.

GIVEN NAMES Hungarian 12%. *Geza* (3), *Lajos* (3), *Arpad* (2), *Imre* (2), *Zoltan* (2), *Emese, Endre, Gaza, Gyula, Karoly, Laszlo.*

Sooter (312) Probably an altered spelling of English SOUTER.

Soots (250) Possibly an altered spelling of Dutch **Soodts**, of uncertain origin.

Sooy (266) Origin unidentified. Possibly a variant of Dutch **Soy**, a short form of **Soyer**, from a Germanic personal name composed of *sigi* 'victory' + *hari, heri* 'army'.

Soper (2663) English (chiefly Devon): occupational name for a soapmaker, from an agent derivative of Middle English *sōpe* 'soap' (apparently of Celtic origin). The process involved boiling oil or fat together with potash or soda.

Sopha (108) Origin unidentified.

Sopher (378) French: unexplained; possibly in some cases a variant spelling of Jewish SOFFER.

Sopko (701) Polish: nickname for an emotional person, from a derivative of the Polish dialect verb *sopkać* 'to breathe heavily', 'to wheeze'.

Sopp (216) **1.** English: metonymic occupational name for a soap maker, from Middle English *sōpe* 'soap'. **2.** English: from the Old English personal name *Soppa*. **3.** German: metonymic occupational name for a cook, from Middle High German *soppe, suppe* 'soup', 'stock', 'meal'.

GIVEN NAMES German 4%. *Eberhard, Kurt.*

Soppe (152) English: variant of SOPP.

Soprano (162) Italian: from *soprano* 'higher', 'situated above', a topographic name for someone who lived at the top end of a place on a hillside.

GIVEN NAMES Italian 13%. *Angelo* (3), *Nicola, Pasquale, Vito.*

Soracco (129) Italian: perhaps a derivative of *Sorace* (see SURACE).

Sorace (122) Italian: variant of SURACE.

GIVEN NAMES Italian 16%. *Ricardo* (2), *Salvatore* (2), *Antonio, Carlo, Domenic, Isidoro, Rocco.*

Sorah (124) English (Lancashire): unexplained. Perhaps a variant of SARAH.

Soranno (144) Italian: perhaps a masculinized form of **Soranna** 'signora Anna'.

GIVEN NAMES Italian 27%. *Vito* (4), *Carlo* (3), *Angelo, Canio, Carmine, Nicolo, Nunzio, Rocco.*

Sorbello (236) Italian: **1.** diminutive of SORBO. **2.** nickname from Old Italian *sorbello* 'extremely handsome'.

GIVEN NAMES Italian 23%. *Salvatore* (6), *Angelo* (2), *Sal* (2), *Santo* (2), *Alfio, Amelio, Dino, Nicolo, Sebastiano, Vito.*

Sorber (367) German: topographic name from a Bavarian dialect word *sorbe, surbe* 'marsh', the suffix *-er* denoting an inhabitant.

Sorbo (161) **1.** Italian: from *sorbo* 'sorb apple', the fruit of the true service tree, *Sorbus domestica*, edible when very ripe; hence an occupational name for a grower or seller of these fruits, a topographic name for someone who lived where service trees grew, or a habitational name from a place named with this word, such as Sorbo Serpico (Avellino) or Sobro San Basile (Catazaro). **2.** Norwegian (**Sørbø**): habitational name from any of ten or more farms, mostly in southwestern Norway, named in Old Norse as *Saurbér*, from *saurr* 'mire', 'mud' + *bér* 'farm', 'settlement'.

Sorby (140) **1.** Norwegian (**Sørby**): habitational name from any of fifteen or more farmsteads in southeastern Norway, most of them variants of **Sørbø** (see SORBO), with Old Norse *býr* 'farm', 'settlement' as the final element. In some cases the first element may be *sør* 'south'. **2.** English: variant of SOWERBY.

GIVEN NAMES Scandinavian 6%. *Selmer, Thor.*

Sorce (365) Southern Italian: nickname for someone thought to resemble a mouse, from *sorce* 'mouse', from Latin *surix* 'mouse', accusative *suricem*.

GIVEN NAMES Italian 13%. *Angelo* (4), *Sal* (3), *Carmelo* (2), *Gerlando* (2), *Filippo, Gino, Nicolo, Nunzio, Salvatore.*

Sorci (175) Italian: patronymic or plural form of SORCE.

GIVEN NAMES Italian 16%. *Carmine* (2), *Angelo, Gaeton, Giusto, Nino, Sal, Salvatore, Vito.*

Sorden (120) Scottish and Irish: unexplained.

Sordillo (100) Italian: from a diminutive of **Sordo**; the suffix *-illo* is a southern variant of *-ello*.

GIVEN NAMES Italian 10%. *Antonio, Carmelina, Gilda, Salvatore.*

Sorel (261) French: nickname for a person with reddish hair, from a diminutive of Old French *sor* 'chestnut' (of Germanic origin, apparently referring originally to the color of dry leaves).

GIVEN NAMES French 8%. *Armand* (2), *Fernand* (2), *Monique, Pierre.*

Sorell (187) Variant spelling of French SOREL or English SORRELL.

GIVEN NAMES French 4%. *Armand, Laurent.*

Sorelle (108) French: variant of SOREL.

Sorem (137) Norwegian: variant spelling of **Sørum** (see SORUM).

Soren (104) Danish and Norwegian (**Søren**): from the personal name *Søren*, Danish form of Latin *Severinus* (see SEVERIN).

Sorensen (10994) Danish and Norwegian (**Sørensen**): patronymic from the personal name *Søren* (see SOREN).

GIVEN NAMES Scandinavian 7%. *Erik* (21), *Nels* (7), *Niels* (7), *Per* (6), *Viggo* (6), *Einer* (5), *Lars* (5), *Morten* (5), *Bent* (4), *Holger* (3), *Jorgen* (3), *Knud* (3).

Sorenson (6730) **1.** Americanized spelling of Danish and Norwegian *Sørensen* (see SORENSEN) or the Swedish cognate **Sörensson**. **2.** Jewish (northeastern Ashkenazic): metronymic from the Yiddish female personal name *Sore* (from the Hebrew female personal name *Sara* 'princess') + German *Sohn* 'son'.

GIVEN NAMES Scandinavian 4%. *Erik* (5), *Nels* (4), *Niels* (3), *Nils* (3), *Helmer* (2), *Sig* (2), *Thor* (2), *Iver, Kerstin, Kjeld, Knute, Ove.*

Sorey (250) Probably a respelling English or Irish **Sawrey**, unexplained.

Sorg (1046) German and Dutch: variant of SORGE 1.

Sorge (631) **1.** German and Dutch: nickname for a careworn individual or for a guardian or caregiver, from Middle High German, Middle Low German *sorge*, Middle Dutch *zorghe* 'care', 'concern', 'worry', 'anxiety'. **2.** German: habitational name from any of several places named Sorge or Sorga. **3.** Italian (Sicily): dialectal variant of SORCE.

Sorgen (166) German: variant of SORGE.

GIVEN NAMES German 4%. *Merwin* (2).

Sorgenfrei (112) German: nickname for a carefree individual.

GIVEN NAMES German 6%; Dutch 4%. *Erhardt, Hans; Michiel.*

Sorger (117) German: variant of SORGE.

GIVEN NAMES German 6%. *Gunther, Wolfgang.*

Sorgi (120) Italian: patronymic or plural form of SORGE.

GIVEN NAMES Italian 13%. *Angelo* (4), *Ezio, Sandro.*

Soria (1255) Spanish and Jewish (Sephardic): habitational name from the city of Soria in Castile.

GIVEN NAMES Spanish 47%. *Jose* (30), *Manuel* (21), *Juan* (16), *Carlos* (14), *Javier* (11), *Luis* (10), *Miguel* (9), *Pedro* (9), *Jesus* (8), *Ramon* (8), *Ricardo* (8), *Armando* (7); *Antonio* (10), *Lorenzo* (4), *Aureliano* (3), *Marco* (3), *Bartolo, Caesar, Cecilio, Constantino, Dario, Deno, Dino, Eligio.*

Soriano (2208) **1.** Spanish and Jewish (Sephardic): habitational name for an inhabitant of Soria in Castile, from the adjective *soriano* 'from Soria'. **2.** Southern Italian: habitational name from Soriano Calabro in Vibo Valentia province or Soriano nel Cimino in Viterbo, or of the same derivation as 1.

GIVEN NAMES Spanish 43%; Italian 9%. *Jose* (47), *Juan* (29), *Carlos* (20), *Manuel* (16), *Luis* (14), *Ramon* (12), *Francisco* (11), *Jesus* (10), *Pedro* (10), *Cesar* (9), *Alfredo* (8), *Angel* (8); *Antonio* (14), *Lucio* (3), *Romeo* (3), *Albertina* (2), *Filiberto* (2), *Julieta* (2), *Marco* (2), *Salvatore* (2), *Angelo, Caesar, Ceasar, Cecilio.*

Sorice (145) Italian (Campania): nickname for someone thought to resemble a mouse, Italian *sorce* (see SORCE).

GIVEN NAMES Italian 15%. *Salvatore* (2), *Angelo, Antonio, Guiseppe, Italo, Lorenzo, Sal.*

Sorich (132) Croatian and Serbian (**Sorić**): unexplained.

Sorin (158) **1.** Jewish (from Belarus): metronymic from the Yiddish female personal name *Sore* (from the Hebrew female personal name *Sara* 'Princess'), with the Slavic possessive suffix *-in*. **2.** French: from a diminutive of *sor* (see SOREL).

GIVEN NAMES Russian 13%; Jewish 9%. *Mikhail* (3), *Aleksandr, Arkady, Boris, Leonid, Lev, Pinya, Raisa, Vitaly; Irina.*

Sorkin (563) Jewish (from Belarus): metronymic from the Yiddish female personal name *Sorke*, a pet form of *Sore* (see SORIN).

GIVEN NAMES Jewish 9%; Russian 4%. *Isadore* (2), *Naum* (2), *Sol* (2), *Emanuel, Faina, Girsh, Hyman, Meyer, Moisey, Nachum, Shlema, Yankel; Aleksandr* (2), *Oleg* (2), *Grigoriy, Leonid, Lev, Mikhail, Valenti, Vitaly, Vladimir, Zoya.*

Sorlie (202) **1.** Norwegian: habitational name from a common farm name, Sørli, composed of the elements *sør* 'south' + *li* 'slope', 'hillside'. **2.** Scottish: reduced Anglicized form of Gaelic **Mac Somhairle** (see MCSORLEY).

GIVEN NAME Scandinavian 9%. *Knute.*

Sorn (103) Slovenian (central Slovenia; **Šorn**): Slovenian spelling of German SCHORN.

Sornberger (129) German (Palatinate): habitational name from an unidentified place.

Sornson (108) Probably an American reduced form of SORENSON.

Soroka (574) Ukrainian and Jewish (eastern Ashkenazic): from the nickname *Soroka* 'magpie', denoting a garrulous or thievish person, or someone with a streak of white among black hair. In the case of the Jewish surname it is normally an ornamental name, one of the many taken from bird names.

GIVEN NAMES Russian 7%; Polish 5%. *Boris* (3), *Leonid* (2), *Lev* (2), *Lyudmila* (2), *Anatoly, Arkadiy, Galina, Igor, Lyubov, Maks, Mikhail, Nikolaj; Wasyl* (3), *Jozef* (2), *Waclaw* (2), *Casimir, Czeslaw, Halina, Janusz.*

Sorokin (148) Russian and Jewish (from Belarus): patronymic from the nickname *soroka* 'magpie', denoting a garrulous or thievish person, or someone with a streak of white among black hair. In the case of the Jewish surname it is normally an ornamental name, one of the many taken from the names of birds.

GIVEN NAMES Russian 31%; Jewish 13%. *Vladimir* (6), *Grigory* (2), *Igor* (2), *Mikhail* (2), *Oleg* (2), *Aleksandr, Aleksey, Anatoliy, Boris, Dmitri, Fima, Lev; Ilya, Sol, Yoram, Zeev.*

Soroko (107) Jewish and Ukrainian: variant of SOROKA.

GIVEN NAMES Jewish 9%. *Sol* (2), *Haim, Meyer.*

Sorrell (2826) English (southeastern): nickname for someone with reddish hair, from a diminutive of Anglo-Norman French *sor* 'chestnut (color)'.

Sorrells (2083) English: patronymic from SORRELL.

Sorrels (677) English: patronymic from SORRELL.

Sorrenti (154) Southern Italian: patronymic or plural form of SORRENTO.

GIVEN NAMES Italian 23%. *Mario* (2), *Salvatore* (2), *Sabino* (2), *Angelo, Ferdinando, Francesca, Nicola, Rocco, Savino.*

Sorrentino (1673) Southern Italian: habitational name for someone from Sorrento, from an adjectival derivative of the place name.

GIVEN NAMES Italian 22%. *Sal* (13), *Angelo* (8), *Antonio* (8), *Mario* (7), *Salvatore* (6), *Ciro* (4), *Pasquale* (4), *Alfonse* (3), *Angelina* (3), *Carmine* (3), *Luigi* (3), *Vincenzo* (3), *Vito* (3), *Amedeo* (2).

Sorrento (118) Italian: habitational name for someone from Sorrento on the Bay of Naples.

GIVEN NAMES Italian 23%. *Salvatore* (3), *Vito* (2), *Angelo, Gaetana, Orlando, Valentino.*

Sorrick (117) Origin unidentified.

Sorrow (379) Probably a translation of German SORGE.

Sorsby (120) English (South Yorkshire): habitational name from an unidentified place; perhaps a variant of SALISBURY or SOWERBY.

Sorter (181) Origin unidentified. In part English, a variant of **Sarter**, a topographic name for someone who lived in a woodland clearing, from Old English *assart, essart* 'clearing in woodland'.

Sortino (318) Italian (Sicily): variant of SCIORTINO.

GIVEN NAMES Italian 13%. *Angelo* (2), *Vito* (2), *Caesar, Concetta, Giorgio, Graziano, Lido, Sal.*

Sorto (369) Hispanic (El Salvador and Honduras): unexplained. This name is not found in Spain.

GIVEN NAMES Spanish 60%. *Jose* (28), *Juan* (10), *Miguel* (6), *Carlos* (5), *Francisco* (5), *Santos* (5), *Mario* (4), *Angel* (3), *Luis* (3), *Adela* (2), *Agustin* (2), *Ana* (2).

Sortor (159) See SORTER.

GIVEN NAME German 4%. *Kurt.*

Sorum (385) Norwegian (**Sørum**): habitational name from any of fifteen or more farmsteads in southeastern Norway, named in Old Norse as *Suðrheimr*, from *suðr* 'south' + *heimr* 'homestead', 'farm'.

GIVEN NAMES Scandinavian 6%. *Erik* (2), *Arndt, Jorgen, Ordell, Per, Syvert.*

Sosa (4332) Spanish: probably a Castilianized or Americanized form of SOUSA, or (less likely) from *sosa* 'seaweed'.

GIVEN NAMES Spanish 51%. *Jose* (128), *Juan* (65), *Manuel* (61), *Carlos* (53), *Luis* (44), *Pedro* (32), *Jesus* (28), *Guadalupe* (26), *Miguel* (26), *Jorge* (25), *Alberto* (20), *Arturo* (20).

Sosby (128) Probably an altered form of English SOULSBY.

GIVEN NAMES French 6%. *Marise, Vernice.*

Soscia (112) Italian (Latina): unexplained.

GIVEN NAMES Italian 12%. *Dino, Domenic, Lia; Alphonse.*

Sosebee (795) Origin unidentified.

Sosh (122) Origin unidentified.

Sosin (151) Jewish (from Belarus): metronymic from the Yiddish female personal name *Sosye*, a pet form of *Sore* (see SORIN).

GIVEN NAMES Jewish 5%; Russian 4%. *Gershon; Nikolay, Pyotr.*

Sosinski (209) Polish (**Sosiński**): **1.** habitational name for someone from Sosina in Katowice voivodeship. **2.** variant of **Sosieński**, habitational name for someone from places called Sosna or Sosno. The places are named with Polish *sosna* 'pine tree'.

Soskin (141) Jewish (from Belarus): metronymic from the Yiddish female personal name *Soske*, a pet form of *Sore* (see SORIN).

GIVEN NAMES Jewish 5%; Russian 4%. *Yakov, Yetta; Osip, Semyon.*

Sosna (176) Polish, Ukrainian, and Jewish (eastern Ashkenazic): from Ukrainian and Polish *sosna* 'pine'. As a Jewish name it is mainly of ornamental origin, while the Ukrainian and Polish names probably originated as nickname for a tall person.

Sosnoski (135) Variant of Polish SOSNOWSKI.

Sosnowski (692) Polish and Jewish (eastern Ashkenazic): habitational name for someone from any of a number of places called Sosnowa, Sosnów, or Sosnowo, named with *sosna* 'pine tree'.
GIVEN NAMES Polish 7%. *Jacek* (2), *Krystyna* (2), *Leszek* (2), *Andrzej, Danuta, Ewa, Halina, Jerzy, Krzysztof, Mariusz, Tadeusz, Witold.*

Soss (136) Possibly a respelling of Ashkenazic Jewish **Sos**, a nickname from Hungarian *sós* 'of salt', 'salty'.

Sossaman (138) Variant of German **Sassemann** (see SASSAMAN).

Sossamon (178) Variant of German **Sassemann** (see SASSAMAN).

Sotak (264) Slovak: habitational name from Soták, an eastern Slovak region near Humenné.

Sotello (128) Spanish or Asturian-Leonese: possibly variant of Spanish SOTELO or Asturian-Leonese **Sotiel.lo**, a habitational name from Sotiel.lo, a town in Asturies. This variant is found mainly in the Philippines.

Sotelo (1644) Spanish: Castilianized form of Galician **Soutelo**, a habitational name from any of numerous places so called in Galicia, from a diminutive of *souto*, Spanish *soto* 'grove', 'small wood'.
GIVEN NAMES Spanish 52%. *Jose* (33), *Jesus* (21), *Juan* (19), *Manuel* (18), *Francisco* (13), *Mario* (12), *Carlos* (11), *Javier* (11), *Miguel* (11), *Pedro* (11), *Arturo* (10), *Enrique* (10).

Soter (260) Greek: from the Greek personal name *Sōtērios*, an adjectival form meaning 'redeeming', 'saving', based on the vocabulary word *sōtēr* 'savior', 'redeemer' (compare Italian SALVATORE), or a reduced form of a patronymic surname based on this (**Soterakis, Soteriadis, Soteropoulos**, etc.). **Soter** is also found as an Albanian name.

Soth (165) **1.** North German (**Söth**) and Danish: nickname from Middle Low German *sote* 'sweet'. **2.** Southeast Asian: unexplained.
GIVEN NAMES Southeast Asian 4%. *Him* (2), *Chan, Hin, Pok, Roeun, Sarin, Sin, Song.*

Sotir (117) Greek and Albanian: see SOTER.

Sotiropoulos (112) Greek: from the personal name *Sōtērios* (see SOTER) + the patronymic ending *-poulos*. This ending occurs chiefly in the Peloponnese; it is derived from Latin *pullus* 'nestling', 'chick'.
GIVEN NAMES Greek 18%; Italian 5%. *Dimitrios* (2), *Fotis* (2), *Damianos, Evangelos, Ilias, Spiro, Stamatis; Angelo* (2), *Carlo, Dino.*

Soto (12087) Spanish: **1.** habitational name from any of numerous places named Soto or El Soto, from *soto* 'grove', 'small wood' (Latin *saltus*). **2.** Castilianized spelling of Asturian-Leonese **Sotu**, a habitational name from a town so named in Asturies. **3.** Castilianized spelling of the Galician equivalent, SOUTO.

GIVEN NAMES Spanish 48%. *Jose* (326), *Juan* (156), *Manuel* (128), *Luis* (120), *Jesus* (117), *Carlos* (106), *Francisco* (77), *Angel* (71), *Miguel* (71), *Pedro* (69), *Jorge* (64), *Armando* (54).

Sotolongo (294) Galician: habitational name from Sotolongo in Pontevedra province, Galicia, named with *soto* 'grove', 'small wood' + *longo* 'long'.
GIVEN NAMES Spanish 53%. *Pedro* (8), *Ignacio* (7), *Jesus* (6), *Jose* (6), *Carlos* (5), *Jorge* (5), *Manuel* (5), *Roberto* (5), *Armando* (4), *Luis* (4), *Alberto* (3), *Froilan* (3); *Elio, Federico, Filiberto, Leonardo, Lorenzo.*

Sotomayor (526) Spanish: Castilianized form of **Soutomaior**, a habitational name from the name of two places in Pontevedra and Ourense provinces, Galicia, so named from *souto* 'grove', 'small wood' + *maior* 'larger', 'main'.
GIVEN NAMES Spanish 46%. *Carlos* (15), *Juan* (12), *Luis* (8), *Miguel* (7), *Manuel* (6), *Jorge* (5), *Jose* (5), *Orlando* (5), *Rafael* (5), *Raul* (5), *Javier* (4), *Lourdes* (4).

Sottile (533) Southern Italian: nickname from *sottile* 'delicate', 'refined', also 'lean', 'thin' (from Latin *subtilis* 'small', 'slender').
GIVEN NAMES Italian 14%. *Angelo* (5), *Santo* (3), *Antonio, Francesco, Giuseppi, Luigi, Orazio, Osualdo, Sal, Santina.*

Sottosanti (118) Italian: topographical name from *sotto Santi* 'below Santi'.
GIVEN NAMES Italian 21%. *Salvatore* (2), *Angelo, Antonio, Guido, Guiseppe, Nicolo, Sal, Santo.*

Soucek (292) Czech (**Souček**): nickname for a strong, awkward, or stubborn man, from a pet form of SUK.

Soucie (550) Variant spelling of French SOUCY.
GIVEN NAMES French 4%. *Laurent, Ludger, Pierre.*

Soucy (1872) French: habitational name from either of two places, in Aisne and Yonne, so called from the Latin estate name *S(a)uciacum*.
GIVEN NAMES French 17%. *Armand* (11), *Andre* (7), *Cecile* (7), *Lucien* (6), *Gilles* (5), *Normand* (5), *Marcel* (4), *Adelard* (3), *Jacques* (3), *Jean-Paul* (3), *Laurent* (3), *Alphonse* (2).

Souder (1526) French (Breton): occupational name for a mercenary soldier, Old French *soldoier*.

Souders (1537) Origin unidentified.

Souers (197) Variant of German SAUER; compare SAUERS.

Souhrada (127) Czech: topographic name from Czech *souhrada* 'turnpike', 'road between fences'.

Soukup (1497) Czech: occupational name for a merchant or dealer, Czech *soukup* (from Slavic *sou-* 'with' + *kup* 'buy'). The vocabulary word later acquired the sense 'fence', i.e. 'one who receives stolen prop-

erty or abets a thief', but this is probably irrelevant to the surname, which was formed before this sense was established.

Soule (2520) **1.** English: of uncertain origin; perhaps derived from the vocabulary word *soul* as a term of affection. **2.** French (**Soulé**): variant of SOULIER 1.
FOREBEARS George Soule (1600–80), one of the passengers on the *Mayflower* in 1620, was one of the founders of Duxbury, MA, where he became comparatively wealthy. He left eight children.

Soules (581) French (**Soulès**): plural form of *Soulé* (see SOULIER 1, of which it is a variant).

Soulia (108) Origin unidentified. Perhaps an Americanized form of French SOULIER.

Soulier (219) French: **1.** metonymic occupational name for a shoemaker, from Old French *soulier* 'shoe', 'sandal'. **2.** from a derivative of Old French *soule* 'platform', 'storey', a topographic name for someone who lived in a house with more than one storey, something of a rarity in the Middle Ages.
GIVEN NAMES French 9%. *Emile* (2), *Aime, Jean-Michel, Pierre, Solange.*

Souliere (151) French: variant of SOULIER.
GIVEN NAMES French 10%. *Armand, Colette, Laurette, Raynald.*

Soulis (105) **1.** Scottish: unexplained. **2.** Greek: unexplained. **3.** Lithuanian: variant of SHAULIS.

Soulliere (181) French: variant of SOULIER.

Soulsby (122) English (Northumbria): of uncertain origin, perhaps a habitational name from either of two places called Soulby, one near Penrith and the other near Kirkby Stephen. These are probably named from Old Norse *súl* 'post' + *býr* 'farm', 'settlement'. If this is right, it is hard to explain why the place name should have developed a form with an *-s-* in it. However, this alternation is found in other surnames (for example BOWLBY/BOWLSBY).

Sours (704) English: patronymic from Middle English *sour* 'sour', 'tart', used as a nickname for a sour-tempered, sharp-tongued person.

Sousa (4017) Portuguese and Galician: habitational name from any of the numerous places in Portugal named Sousa. The place name is of pre-Roman origin.
FOREBEARS John Philip Sousa (1854–1932), the American composer, was born in Washington, DC, the son of a U.S. Marine Corps bandmaster. His father was born in Spain, the son of a Portuguese refugee, and had emigrated to America in the 1840s.
GIVEN NAMES Spanish 21%; Portuguese 14%. *Manuel* (146), *Jose* (107), *Carlos* (24), *Fernando* (17), *Luis* (17), *Francisco* (15), *Mario* (13), *Alfredo* (10), *Jorge* (10), *Ana* (8), *Armando* (7), *Geraldo* (6); *Joao* (27), *Joaquim* (10), *Duarte* (3), *Mateus* (2), *Paulo* (2), *Serafim* (2), *Agostinho, Albano, Anabela, Armanda, Braz, Goncalo.*

Sousley (169) Perhaps an English habitational name from a lost or unidentified place.

Soutar (214) Scottish: variant of SOUTER.

Souter (470) **1.** Scottish and English: occupational name for a cobbler or shoemaker, Middle English *soutere*, *sutere* (from Latin *sutor*, an agent derivative of *suere* 'to sew'). **2.** Altered spelling of the German cognate SAUTER, or of SUTER.

South (3919) English: from Middle English *south*, hence a topographic name for someone who lived to the south of a settlement or a regional name for someone who had migrated from the south.

Southall (1072) English (chiefly West Midlands): habitational name from any of the various places so called, from Old English *sūð* 'south' + *halh* 'nook', 'recess'. The distribution of the surname in Britain makes a Midlands origin likely: places called Southall in Doverdale, Worcestershire, and Billingsley, Shropshire, are possible sources.

Southam (219) English: habitational name from places in Gloucestershire and Warwickshire, so named from Old English *sūð* 'south' + *hām* 'homestead' or *hamm* 'land in a river bend'.

Southard (3511) English: unexplained.

Southards (142) Variant of English SOUTHARD.

Souther (1045) Probably an altered form of German **Sauther**, a variant of SAUTER.

Southerland (2749) Scottish: variant of SUTHERLAND.

Southerly (101) English: topographic name for someone living in the 'south clearing', from Middle English *suther(n)* 'southern' + *leye* 'clearing (in a wood)'.

Southern (2684) English: topographic name, from an adjectival derivative of SOUTH.

Southers (438) English: apparently a variant of SOUTHER.

Southgate (179) English (East Anglia): **1.** habitational name from a place in Norfolk, so named from Old English *sūð* 'south' + *geat* 'gate'; the village was situated near the southern entrance to a large enclosed medieval forest. The place of this name formerly in Middlesex, now part of Greater London, may also have contributed to the surname. **2.** topographic name for someone who lived near the south gate of a medieval walled city or other enclosed place.

Southmayd (109) Origin unidentified. Possibly English: unexplained.

Southward (409) English: variant of SOUTHWORTH.

Southwell (826) English: habitational name from a place in Nottinghamshire, so called from Old English *sūð* 'south' + *well(a)* 'spring', 'stream', or a topographic name with the same meaning.

Southwick (1499) English: habitational name from any of a number of places so called, for example in Tyne and Wear, Northamptonshire, and Hampshire, named in Old English with *sūþ* 'south' + *wīc* 'dwelling', 'dairy farm'.

Southwood (336) English: habitational name from a place in Norfolk, so named from Old English *sūð* 'south' + *wudu* 'wood', or a topographic name with the same meaning.

Southworth (1970) English (Lancashire): habitational name from a place in Cheshire (formerly in Lancashire), so named from Old English *sūð* 'south' + *worð* 'enclosure'.

Souto (220) **1.** Portuguese: topographic name from *souto* 'grove', 'small wood'. **2.** Galician: topographic name from *souto* 'grove' or, more specificaly, 'chestnut grove'.
GIVEN NAMES Spanish 35%; Portuguese 13%. *Manuel* (6), *Carlos* (4), *Jose* (4), *Francisco* (3), *Salvador* (3), *Ana* (2), *Fernando* (2), *Javier* (2), *Ramiro* (2), *Aires, Alejandro, Alfonso; Ademir, Amadeu, Joaquim, Vasco*.

Soutter (122) Scottish and English: variant of SOUTER.

Souva (112) Portuguese: unexplained.

Souza (6390) Portuguese and Galician: variant of SOUSA.
GIVEN NAMES Spanish 8%; Portuguese 5%. *Manuel* (138), *Jose* (26), *Sergio* (10), *Marcos* (9), *Mario* (9), *Carlos* (8), *Geraldo* (6), *Luiz* (6), *Ricardo* (6), *Fernando* (5), *Claudio* (4), *Jaime* (4); *Paulo* (10), *Joao* (6), *Marcio* (3), *Henrique* (2), *Joaquim* (2), *Mateus* (2), *Ademir, Altair, Heitor, Manoel, Sebastiao, Terezinha*.

Sova (802) Czech, Slovak, Croatian, and Slovenian: nickname from *sova* 'owl'.

Sovereign (209) Translation of French **Souverain**, a topographic name from Old French *souverain* 'high place', or an occupational name for a leader or supervisor or a nickname for a domineering person, from the same word in the sense 'superior', 'director', 'chief'.

Sovern (110) Possibly of English origin; unexplained.

Sovey (141) Origin unidentified. Possibly an Anglicized or Americanized spelling of French **Sauvé** (see SAUVE) or a Slavic name meaning 'owl' (see SOVA).

Sovich (136) Slovenian (**Sovič**); Croatian or Serbian (**Sović**): patronymic from a nickname from *sova* 'owl'.

Sovine (212) Origin unidentified.

Sow (121) African: unexplained.
GIVEN NAMES African 55%; Muslim 20%. *Mamadou* (6), *Fatou* (5), *Amadou* (4), *Boubacar* (2), *Cheikh* (2), *Mariama* (2), *Mouhamadou* (2), *Oumar* (2), *Aissatou, Aliou, Demba, Mahamadou; Lamine* (3), *Abou* (2), *Abdoul, Abdoulaye, Elhadji, Ibrahima, Ismail, Karim, Mohammed, Moustapha, Souleymane*.

Sowa (1084) Polish: nickname from *sowa* 'owl'.
GIVEN NAMES Polish 8%; German 4%. *Kazimierz* (3), *Andrzej* (2), *Aleksander, Aniela, Czeslawa, Eugeniusz, Franciszek, Grzegorz, Irena, Janina, Janusz, Jozef; Kurt* (4), *Hans* (2), *Otto* (2), *Aloysius, Gunter, Konrad*.

Sowada (124) Polish: unexplained.

Soward (331) English: unexplained; possibly a variant SEWARD.

Sowards (1143) Probably a variant of English or Irish SEWARD.

Sowash (170) altered spelling of German **Sowatsch**, probably of Slavic origin.

Sowden (324) English: variant of SODEN.

Sowder (964) Probably an Americanized spelling of German SAUDER or SAUTER.

Sowders (523) Probably an altered form of German SAUDER or SAUTER.

Sowell (3051) English (Cornwall): variant of SEWELL.

Sower (202) Americanized spelling of German or Jewish SAUER.
FOREBEARS The PA printer and publisher Christopher Sower was born 1693 in Laasphe on the Lahn, Germany, in 1693. Seeking greater economic and religious freedom, he emigrated in 1724 to Germantown, PA, with his wife and son, and later settled in the Leacock township in Lancaster Co., PA.

Sowerby (133) English: habitational name from any of various places in northern England named with the Old Norse elements *saurr* 'mud', 'excrement' + *býr* 'farm', 'settlement'.

Sowers (3765) Americanized form of German SAUERS.

Sowersby (105) English: variant of SOWERBY.

Sowinski (682) Polish (**Sowiński**): habitational name for someone from places called Sowin, Sowina, or Sowiniec, all named with *sowa* 'owl'. This surname is also established in Germany.
GIVEN NAMES Polish 8%. *Casimir* (2), *Zbigniew* (2), *Zdzislaw* (2), *Andrzej, Dariusz, Grzegorz, Ignatius, Karol, Leszek, Ludwik, Miroslaw, Pawel*.

Sowl (123) English: probably a variant of SOULE.

Sowle (354) English: probably a variant of SOULE.

Sowles (258) Variant of SOULES.

Sox (275) See SOCKS.

Soyars (221) Origin unidentified. Perhaps an Americanized form of Dutch **Soyer** (see SOOY).

Soyka (153) Americanized spelling of Polish and Jewish SOJKA.

Soza (268) Spanish and Portuguese: probably an altered form of SOSA.
GIVEN NAMES Spanish 37%. *Carlos* (4), *Arturo* (2), *Cornelio* (2), *Felipe* (2),

Humberto (2), *Jaime* (2), *Jesus* (2), *Jose* (2), *Juan* (2), *Rafael* (2), *Raul* (2), *Amalia*.

Sozio (156) Southern Italian: nickname from *socio* 'companion', 'ally'.

GIVEN NAMES Italian 15%. *Carlo, Fiore, Francesco, Marcello, Pellegrino, Vittorio.*

Spaar (127) German: **1.** habitational name from a place so named near Meissen. **2.** variant of SPARK 2.

Space (368) English or Scottish: unexplained.

Spacek (334) Czech (**Špaček**): nickname from a word meaning 'starling'.

Spach (157) German: from Middle High German *spach* 'dry', 'bone-dry', 'a stick'; perhaps a topographic name for someone who lived in a very dry place, or a nickname for a thin person.

Spack (180) **1.** English: from the Old Norse personal name *Spakr*. **2.** Respelling of Jewish, Ukrainian, and Belorussian **Shpak**, a nickname from Ukrainian and Belorussian *shpak* 'starling'. In the case of Jewish bearers, it is generally an ornamental name.

GIVEN NAMES German 4%. *Kurt, Walburga.*

Spackman (458) English: variant of SPEAK-MAN.

Spada (704) Italian: from *spada* 'sword' (Late Latin *spatha*), hence a metonymic occupational name for an armorer or swordsman, or possibly a nickname for someone thought to resemble a sword in some way.

GIVEN NAMES Italian 18%. *Salvatore* (9), *Vito* (7), *Angelo* (3), *Sal* (3), *Cosimo* (2), *Ennio* (2), *Gino* (2), *Aldo, Carmine, Chiara, Cosmo, Elio.*

Spadaccini (173) Italian: nickname for an accomplished swordsman, from a diminutive of SPADA.

GIVEN NAME Italian 7%. *Angelo.*

Spadafora (467) Southern Italian (Calabria and Sicily): habitational name from Spadafora in Messina province, Sicily.

GIVEN NAMES Italian 13%. *Angelo* (2), *Salvatore* (2), *Amedeo, Antonio, Duilio, Francesco, Franco, Gennaro, Gino, Giovanna, Giovanni, Luigi.*

Spadafore (241) Italian: variant of SPADA-FORA.

GIVEN NAMES Italian 10%. *Orlando* (2), *Carmelo, Carmine, Fedele, Gennaro, Salvatore.*

Spadaro (669) Southern Italian: occupational name for a swordsman, sword bearer, or armorer, from medieval Latin *spatharius*.

GIVEN NAMES Italian 17%. *Salvatore* (6), *Angelo* (4), *Carmelo* (3), *Agatino* (2), *Giorgio* (2), *Santo* (2), *Antonella, Antonino, Antonio, Concetto, Gasper, Giovanna.*

Spade (819) **1.** German: variant of **Späthe**, itself a variant of SPATH. **2.** Scottish: unexplained.

Spadea (112) Italian: from Greek *spadéas* 'swordsmith'.

GIVEN NAMES Italian 20%. *Domenic, Giuseppe, Raffaele, Salvatore, Vito.*

Spader (250) German: occupational name for a spade maker or for someone who used a spade in his work, from an agent derivative of Middle High German, Middle Low German *spade* 'spade'.

Spadoni (261) Italian: from an augmentative of SPADA.

GIVEN NAMES Italian 15%. *Gildo* (4), *Dante* (2), *Stefano* (2), *Aldo, Dario, Dino, Gino, Leonardo, Marco, Nicolo, Reno, Umberto.*

Spady (449) American variant of German SPADE, spelled thus to preserve the second syllable in pronunciation.

Spaeth (1462) German (**Späth**): see SPATH.

GIVEN NAMES German 5%. *Otto* (5), *Kurt* (4), *Alois* (2), *Horst* (2), *Erwin, Franz, Hans, Lorenz, Wolfgang.*

Spafford (651) English (South Yorkshire): habitational name from Spofford in the former West Riding of Yorkshire or possibly in some instances from Spofforth in North Yorkshire (formerly also in the West Riding).

Spagna (191) Italian: from *Spagna* 'Spain', hence an ethnic name for a Spaniard or a nickname for someone who had trading connections with Spain or who had been there on a pilgrimage.

GIVEN NAMES Italian 13%. *Rocco* (4), *Francesca, Fulvio, Mauro, Neno, Santina, Stefano.*

Spagnola (503) Sicily: habitational name from a place so named in Marsala, Sicily.

GIVEN NAMES Italian 12%. *Vito* (3), *Domenic* (2), *Sal* (2), *Angelo, Antimo, Concetta, Gildo, Remo, Rocco, Salvatore.*

Spagnoletti (111) Italian (Sicily): from SPAGNOLO with the addition of the suffix *-etto*.

GIVEN NAMES Italian 15%. *Amato* (3), *Carmelo, Giovanni.*

Spagnoli (254) Italian: patronymic or plural form of SPAGNOLO.

GIVEN NAMES Italian 16%. *Aldo* (5), *Ivano* (2), *Remo* (2), *Angelo, Berardino, Carmino, Dante, Francesco, Gino, Marino, Reno, Rinaldo.*

Spagnolo (392) Italian: ethnic name for someone from Spain, from *spagnolo* 'Spaniard'.

GIVEN NAMES Italian 22%; Spanish 4%. *Angelo* (6), *Luigi* (3), *Dante* (2), *Mario* (2), *Salvatore* (2), *Aldo, Antonio, Carlo, Domenico, Enio, Gianfranco, Giuseppe, Lucrezia, Sabino*; *Juan, Justina, Liborio, Marcelo, Rosario.*

Spagnuolo (455) Italian: from Neapolitan *spagnuolo* 'Spaniard', a variant of SPAGNOLO.

GIVEN NAMES Italian 28%. *Antonio* (4), *Salvatore* (4), *Emilio* (3), *Carmine* (2), *Francesco* (2), *Pasquale* (2), *Orlando* (2), *Angelo, Caesar, Carmela, Cesare, Ciro, Constantino, Dino, Emerico, Gerardo, Mario, Renato.*

Spahn (955) German: **1.** metonymic occupational name for a carpenter or for a roofer who applied wooden shingles, from Middle German *spān* 'chip', 'shaving', 'splinter'. **2.** nickname for a skinny person.

Spahr (1247) North German: nickname for someone thought to resemble a sparrow in some way, Middle High German *spar*.

Spaid (459) American variant of German SPADE.

Spaide (107) American variant of German SPADE.

Spain (4010) English and Irish: **1.** (of Norman origin): habitational name from Épaignes in Eure, recorded in the Latin form *Hispania* in the 12th century. It seems to have been so called because it was established by colonists from Spain during the Roman Empire. **2.** (of Norman origin): habitational name from Espinay in Ille-et-Vilaine, Brittany, so called from a collective of Old French *espine* 'thorn bush'. **3.** ethnic name for a Spaniard or, in the case of the Irish name, for someone returning from Spain (from Gaelic *Spainneach* 'Spanish'); many Irish took refuge in Spain during the 17th century wars.

Spainhour (494) Americanized form of German **Spanhauer**, an occupational name for a lath cutter or for a carpenter, from Middle High German *spān* 'wood chip' + *-hauer*, an agent derivative of *hauen* 'to cut or hew', or 'to knock'.

Spainhower (244) See SPAINHOUR.

Spak (294) Variant of Jewish, Ukrainian, and Belorussian **Shpak** 'starling' (see SPACK).

Spake (319) English: variant of SPEAKE.

Spakes (100) English: variant of SPEAKE.

Spalding (3351) English and Scottish: habitational name from a place in Lincolnshire, so called from the Old English tribal name *Spaldingas* 'people of the district called *Spald*'. The district name probably means 'ditches', referring to drainage channels in the fenland.

FOREBEARS The surname was taken to Scotland in the 13th century by Radulphus de Spalding. His descendants prospered, and the name is still common in Scotland. Early American Spaldings include Thomas Spalding, born in Frederica, GA, in 1774, who introduced sea-island cotton in GA, and the physician Lyman Spalding, born in Cornish, NH, in 1775, who founded U.S. Pharmacopoeia.

Spall (242) English (East Anglia): unexplained.

Spalla (189) Southern Italian: from *spalla* 'shoulder(blade)', hence a nickname for someone with a deformity or peculiarity of the shoulder, or in some cases a topographic name for someone living by a hillock named with this word in this transferred sense.

GIVEN NAMES Italian 15%. *Nunzio* (2), *Sal* (2), *Salvatore* (2), *Antonino, Marco, Pietro.*

Spallino (124) Italian: from a diminutive of SPALLA.

GIVEN NAMES Italian 15%. *Pasquale* (2), *Pietro* (2), *Antonio, Giuseppe, Maurizio*.

Spallone (230) Italian: from an augmentative of SPALLA.

GIVEN NAMES Italian 10%. *Pasquale* (2), *Marco, Salvatore, Silvio, Umberto*.

Spampinato (211) Southern Italian: from *spampinato* 'chopped off', 'lopped', (from *spampinare, spapanare* 'to prune'), presumably a nickname for a short person.

GIVEN NAMES Italian 25%. *Angelo* (3), *Mario* (3), *Onofrio* (3), *Rosario* (2), *Alfonso, Angelina, Antonio, Carmelo, Clemente, Fabrizio, Fabio, Gaetano, Natale, Salvatore, Vincenzo*.

Span (227) **1.** Slovenian (**Špan**): from *špan*, a feudal status name for a serf chosen by an overlord to oversee other serfs and villeins working on the overlord's estate. This was also a status name for a village headman. The word in both senses is derived from Slovenian *župan* (see ZUPAN). **2.** German: occupational name for a carpenter, a variant of SPAHN. **3.** German: nickname for a quarrelsome person, a variant of SPANN. **4.** Jewish (Ashkenazic): nickname or ornamental name from *Span* 'chip'.

Spanbauer (277) South German: occupational name for someone who was responsible for a team of draft animals, from Middle High German *spannen* 'to hitch up' (horses, oxen, etc.)' + *būr* 'peasant'.

Spanel (118) South German: **1.** altered spelling of **Spänle, Spähnle**, or **Spähnel**, diminutives of SPAHN, hence a nickname for a skinny person or an occupational name for a woodworker. **2.** Possibly a variant of **Spanne(h)l** (see SPANIER 1).

GIVEN NAME German 4%. *Kurt*.

Spang (592) **1.** German: metonymic occupational name for a maker of buckles, from Middle High German *spange* 'clasp', 'buckle', 'ornamental fastening'. **2.** Scottish: unexplained.

Spangenberg (791) German: habitational name from a place so called in the region of Nassau.

GIVEN NAMES German 4%. *Otto* (4), *Ernst, Hans, Horst, Kurt*.

Spangle (315) Possibly an Americanized spelling of German **Spangel**, from a diminutive of Middle High German *spange* 'buckle' (see SPANG).

Spangler (7452) German (Bavarian): originally an occupational name for a maker of buckles, from an agent derivative of a diminutive form of Middle High German *spange* 'clasp', 'buckle', 'ornamental fastening', later coming to mean 'tinsmith', 'plumber'.

Spaniel (106) Altered form of Romanian SPANIOL.

Spanier (554) German and Jewish (Ashkenazic): **1.** regional name for someone from

Spain, from German *Spanier*, Yiddish *shpanyer* 'Spaniard'. **2.** possibly a metonymic occupational name for a maker of brocade or a cloth merchant, from Yiddish *shpanyer* 'brocade'.

Spaniol (158) Romanian: ethnic name for a Spaniard (from Latin *Hispaniolus*, from *Hispania* 'Spain').

Spanjer (127) Variant spelling of Jewish SPANIER.

Spann (3410) German: nickname for a quarrelsome person, from Middle High German *span*, Middle Low German *spenne* 'disagreement', 'dispute', 'quarrel'.

Spannagel (137) German: from Middle High German *span-nagel* 'connecting bolt' (that joined the front part of a wagon or plow with the back), an occupational nickname for a nailsmith.

Spano (1556) Italian (mainly Sicily): descriptive nickname from *spanu* 'having thinning hair', medieval Greek *spanos*, probably from Classical Greek *spanios* 'scarce' (see SPANOS).

GIVEN NAMES Italian 15%. *Angelo* (11), *Vito* (8), *Salvatore* (6), *Domenic* (4), *Rocco* (4), *Sal* (4), *Bartolo* (2), *Carlo* (2), *Carmelo* (2), *Domenico* (2), *Gaspare* (2), *Antonio*.

Spanos (515) Greek: descriptive nickname from Greek *spanos* 'clean shaven', 'hairless'. In Greek this term is often compounded with a personal name, e.g. *Spanovassilis* 'Basil the hairless', *Spanomanolis* 'Emanuel the hairless', etc.

GIVEN NAMES Greek 11%. *Spyros* (3), *Christos* (2), *Isidoros* (2), *Stergios* (2), *Anastasios, Angeliki, Argyrios, Costas, Dimitrios, Eleftherios, Gerasimos, Konstantinos*.

Spanton (143) English (Norfolk): habitational name from Spaunton in North Yorkshire, so named from Old Norse *spánn* 'shingle', 'wooden tile' + Old English *tūn* 'settlement', i.e. 'settlement with shingled roofs'.

Spar (166) German: variant spelling of SPAHR.

Sparacino (498) Southern Italian: nickname from a diminutive of SPARACIO ('asparagus'), or from Sicilian *sparacinu* 'thin', 'spindly', from a transferred sense of the same word.

GIVEN NAMES Italian 16%. *Angelo* (5), *Salvatore* (5), *Sal* (4), *Filippo* (2), *Vito* (2), *Carlo, Domenic, Ignazio, Nicolo, Pietro*.

Sparacio (298) Southern Italian: from southern Italian *sparacio*, Sicilian *sparaciu* 'asparagus' (standard Italian *asparago*), hence a metonymic occupational name for a grower or seller of asparagus, a nickname for a tall thin person, or a topographic name.

GIVEN NAMES Italian 21%. *Vito* (5), *Salvatore* (3), *Gasper* (2), *Giovanni* (2), *Rosario* (2), *Antonio, Carlo, Girolamo, Olympia, Sal*.

Sparaco (143) Southern Italian: variant of SPARACIO, from Calabrian *sparacu* 'asparagus'.

GIVEN NAMES Italian 10%. *Filippo, Pasquale, Vito*.

Sparano (212) Southern Italian: from a personal name, probably a variant of *Sparaino*, a nickname meaning 'mean', 'niggardly'.

GIVEN NAMES Italian 13%. *Alfonse* (2), *Carlo, Gaetano, Ugo*.

Sparber (131) **1.** German: variant of SPERBER. **2.** Jewish (Ashkenazic): ornamental from Yiddish *shparber* 'sparrowhawk' (see SPERBER).

GIVEN NAMES French 5%. *Andre, Gabrielle*.

Sparby (130) Probably English: habitational name from a lost or unidentified minor place.

Spare (184) English: nickname for a frugal person, from Middle English *spare* 'sparing', 'frugal'.

Sparer (107) Jewish (Ashkenazic): nickname for a frugal person, from German *sparen* 'to save', 'to economize' + the agent suffix *-er*.

GIVEN NAMES Jewish 7%. *Meyer* (2), *Gerson*.

Sparger (171) German: variant of *Spargel* 'asparagus' (Middle High German *spargel, sparger*, from Latin *asparagus*), probably for a grower of the vegetable or a nickname for a tall, thin person.

Spargo (447) Cornish: habitational name from Higher or Lower Spargo, in the parish of Mabe, so named from Cornish *spern* 'thorn bushes' + *cor* 'enclosure'.

Spargur (208) German: variant of SPARGER.

Sparhawk (163) English: from Middle English *sparhauk* 'sparrowhawk', originating either in the Old English *Spearh(e)afoc*, used as a personal name, or as a medieval nickname for someone thought to resemble the bird.

Spark (199) **1.** Northern English: from the Old Norse byname or personal name *Sparkr* 'sprightly', 'vivacious'. **2.** German: nickname either from Middle High German *spar* 'sparrow' (see SPARROW) or from Middle Low German *sparke* 'spark'. Compare 1 above.

Sparkes (258) English: variant of SPARKS.

Sparkman (2463) Northern English: nickname for a lively individual, a derivative of SPARK.

Sparks (21834) English: patronymic from SPARK 1.

Sparlin (246) Possibly an altered form of SPARLING.

Sparling (983) **1.** English: nickname from a diminutive of Middle English *sparewe* 'sparrow' (see SPARROW). **2.** Altered form of German SPERLING.

Sparr (433) **1.** English: topographic name for someone who lived by an enclosure, Middle English *sparre*. **2.** German: metonymic occupational name for a carpenter, from Middle Low German *spar* 'beam', 'rafter'.

Sparrow (2583) English: nickname from Middle English *sparewe* 'sparrow', perhaps for a small, chirpy person, or else for someone bearing some fancied physical resemblance to a sparrow.

Spartz (226) German (Rhineland): unexplained.

Spata (110) **1.** Italian: southern variant of SPADA. **2.** Albanian: unexplained.

GIVEN NAMES Italian 14%. *Carmela, Gianni, Salvatore, Santo.*

Spatafora (181) Italian (Sicily): variant of SPADAFORA.

GIVEN NAMES Italian 21%. *Salvatore (5), Carmine (3), Domenico, Matteo, Nicolo, Pietro, Sal, Vito.*

Spatafore (166) Italian (Sicily): variant of SPADAFORA.

GIVEN NAMES Italian 7%. *Geno, Salvatore.*

Spataro (487) Italian (Sicily): variant of SPADARO.

GIVEN NAMES Italian 18%. *Salvatore (9), Angelo (5), Domenic (3), Sal (2), Aldo, Carlo, Carmel, Carmelo, Carmine, Chiara, Gaetano, Rocco.*

Spates (613) Possibly an Americanized variant of German SPATH.

Spath (675) German (**Späth**): nickname for a tardy person, from Middle High German *spæte* 'late'.

GIVEN NAMES German 6%. *Otto (5), Christoph, Hans, Rainer, Wolfgang.*

Spatola (266) Italian: **1.** from a diminutive of SPATA. **2.** from old Sicilian *spatula* 'grass', 'iris' (or other plant with lanceolate leaves), used as a topographic name. **3.** nickname from *spatola*, a species of wading bird, so named for the shape of its beak. **4.** from Sicilian *spàtula*, a kind of fish, presumably applied as a nickname for someone thought to resemble this fish or as a metonymic occupational name for a fisherman.

GIVEN NAMES Italian 20%. *Carmelo (3), Giuseppe (3), Carmine (2), Salvatore (2), Francesca, Giacomo, Giovanni, Massimo, Pasqualina, Raffaele, Rocco, Sal.*

Spatz (902) South German: nickname for someone thought to resemble a sparrow in some way, from a diminutive of Old High German *sparo*.

Spaude (129) German: probably an altered spelling of German SPADE.

Spaugh (276) Americanized form of German SPACH.

Spaulding (6966) Scottish: variant of SPALDING.

Spaur (234) Variant of German SPOHR.

Spaw (270) English: variant of SPOOR.

Spawn (144) Americanized spelling of Slavic SUPAN.

Spayd (257) Origin unidentified. In part possibly a variant of English SPEED.

Spayde (147) See SPAYD.

Spaziani (180) Italian: patronymic or plural form of SPAZIANO.

GIVEN NAMES Italian 12%. *Angelo (2), Achille, Fulvio, Giuseppe, Leonardo, Ulisse, Vita.*

Spaziano (119) Italian: origin uncertain; possibly a habitational name from a lost place in Lazio, or a habitational name for someone from the naval port of La Spezia.

GIVEN NAMES Italian 15%. *Antonio, Carmine, Domenic, Leonardo, Orazio, Rocco.*

Speagle (151) Americanized spelling of German and Jewish SPIEGEL.

Speak (247) Variant of SPEAKE.

Speake (369) English: nickname for someone thought to resemble a woodpecker in some way, Middle English *spek(e)* (a reduced form of Old French *espeche(e)*, of Germanic origin).

Speaker (593) Perhaps an Americanized form of North German SPIEKER.

Speakes (149) English: variant of SPEAKS.

Speakman (1141) English (chiefly Lancashire): nickname or occupational name for someone who acted as a spokesman, from Middle English *spekeman* 'advocate', 'spokesman' (from Old English *specan* to speak + *mann* 'man').

Speaks (970) English: patronymic from SPEAK.

Spear (5268) English: from Middle English *spere* 'spear', hence a nickname for a tall, thin person, or else for a skilled user of the hunting spear. In part it may also have been a metonymic occupational name for a maker of spears

Speare (153) English: variant of SPEAR.

Spearin (153) Probably an altered spelling of SPEARING.

Spearing (269) English: patronymic from SPEAR.

Spearman (2118) English: **1.** occupational name for a soldier armed with a spear, from Middle English *spere* 'spear' + *man*. **2.** from the Middle English, Old English personal name *Spereman*, of the same origin as the occupational name above.

Spears (12473) English: patronymic from SPEAR.

Speas (476) Americanized spelling of German **Spiess** (see SPIES).

Spease (198) Americanized spelling of German **Spiess** (see SPIES).

Specht (2391) German: from Middle High German *speht* 'woodpecker' (from *spehten* 'to chatter'), hence a nickname derived from some characteristic of the bird, or a habitational name for someone living at a house distinguished by the sign of a woodpecker.

GIVEN NAMES German 4%. *Kurt (4), Erwin (3), Hans (2), Heinz (2), Otto (2), Willi (2), Dieter, Eldred, Fritz, Helmut, Karl Heinz, Klaus.*

Speciale (362) Southern Italian: variant spelling of SPEZIALE.

GIVEN NAMES Italian 9%. *Serafino (2), Carmela, Cesare, Giuseppe, Sal, Salvatore, Vicenzo, Vito.*

Speck (2514) **1.** German: from Middle High German *spec* 'bacon', hence a metonymic occupational name for a seller of bacon or a pork butcher, or a nickname for a bacon eater. **2.** German: topographic name from Middle High German *speck(e)* 'log bridge'. **3.** English: variant of SPEAK.

Specker (159) German: topographic name for someone who lived by a log bridge, from Middle High German *specke* 'log bridge', or a habitational name for someone from a place called Speck, named with this word.

Speckman (356) North German (**Speckmann**): **1.** topographic name for someone who lived by a path through a swampy area, Middle Low German *specke*. In some cases, it may have been a metonymic occupational name for someone who constructed such paths, usually from brush, soil, or the like. **2.** habitational name for someone from places named Specke or Specken in northern Germany and Holland. **3.** variant of SPECK 1, with the addition of Middle High German *man* 'man'.

Speckmann (122) North German: see SPECKMAN.

Specter (169) Jewish (Ashkenazic): variant of SPECTOR.

GIVEN NAME Jewish 6%. *Herschel (2).*

Spector (2673) Jewish (eastern Ashkenazic): occupational name from *szpektor* 'teacher's assistant in a Jewish school', a derivative of Polish *inspecktor* 'supervisor'.

GIVEN NAMES Jewish 7%. *Sol (6), Myer (5), Asher (2), Avron (2), Isadore (2), Miriam (2), Shira (2), Yaakov (2), Ari, Chaim, Gershon, Ilan.*

Spedale (102) Italian: from *spedale* 'lodging house', 'infirmary'; compare SPITALE.

GIVEN NAMES Italian 15%. *Angelo (4), Carlo, Salvatore.*

Spedden (143) Scottish and northern Irish: reduced form of MCSPADDEN. Compare SPEDDING.

Spedding (132) **1.** Northern English and Scottish: of uncertain origin, possibly a patronymic from the Old English byname *Spēd*, meaning 'success', 'prosperity'. **2.** Scottish and northern Irish: reduced and altered variant of MCSPADDEN. (**McSpedding** is attested as an Irish name with this origin.)

Speece (431) See SPEAS.

Speed (2303) **1.** English: nickname for a fortunate person, from Middle English *sped* 'success', 'good fortune', 'smooth progress' (hence the modern meaning 'swiftness'). **2.** English: from the derived sense of Middle English *sped* mentioned above, hence a nickname for a swift runner. **3.** Irish: Anglicization (part translation) of Gaelic *Ó Fuada*, from *fuad* 'haste' (see FOODY). **4.** Translation of German and Ashkenazic Jewish SCHNELL.

Speedy (221) Scottish: from an adjectival or diminutive form of SPEED 2.

Speegle (613) Americanized spelling of German SPIEGEL.

Speelman (515) Variant spelling of Dutch and Jewish SPIELMAN or German SPIELMANN.

Speer (4850) **1.** German and Dutch: from Middle High German, Middle Dutch *sper* 'spear', hence a nickname for a tall, thin person, or else for a skilled user of the hunting spear. In part it may also have been a metonymic occupational name for a maker of spears. **2.** German: nickname for someone thought to resemble a sparrow, Middle High German *spar(e)* 'sparrow'. **3.** Jewish (Ashkenazic): variant of SPEYER. **4.** Northern Irish: variant spelling of SPEIR.

Speers (710) Northern Irish: variant or patronymic form of SPEER.

Spees (320) Dutch: probably from a reduced form of **Peterszoon**, a patronymic from the personal name PETER, with an anticipatory initial *s-*.

Speese (110) Dutch: variant of SPEES.

Spegal (176) Variant spelling, in Slavic-speaking regions, of German SPIEGEL.

Spehar (348) **1.** Czech (**Špehař**): from an Old Czech vocabulary word meaning 'spy'. **2.** Slovenian (**Špehar**): occupational name for a seller of bacon, from *špeh* 'bacon' + the agent noun suffix *-ar*.

Speich (209) German: **1.** metonymic occupational name for a spoke maker, from Middle High German *speiche* 'spoke'. **2.** from Middle High German *speich* 'spittle', perhaps a nickname for someone who tended to produce a spray of spittle when speaking.

Speicher (1141) German: from Middle High German *spīcher* 'grain store', hence a metonymic occupational name for someone in charge of a granary, or a topographic name for someone who lived near one.

Speidel (704) German: from Middle High German *spidel* 'wooden wedge', 'peg', probably used in a figurative sense as a nickname for a uncouth or rough and ready person.

Speier (301) German: habitational name from Speyer.

GIVEN NAMES German 11%. *Claus* (2), *Heinz* (2), *Kurt* (2), *Siegbert* (2), *Berthold, Erna, Hans, Manfred.*

Speigel (123) **1.** South German: variant of SPIEGEL. **2.** (Swabian) variant of SPEIDEL.

Speight (1655) English (now chiefly Yorkshire): nickname from Middle English *speght* 'woodpecker', probably from an unrecorded Old English word akin to *specan* 'to speak, talk, chatter'. Compare SPEAK.

Speights (835) English: patronymic from SPEIGHT.

Speigle (113) Americanized spelling of German SPIEGEL.

Speigner (147) Of German origin, but unexplained etymology.

Speir (682) Scottish and northern Irish: possibly, as Black suggests, an occupational name for a watchman from Old French *espier* 'to watch'.

Speirs (445) Scottish and northern Irish: patronymic from SPEIR.

Speiser (532) **1.** German: occupational name for a steward in charge of the supply and distribution of provisions in a great house or monastery, from an agent derivative of Middle High German *spīse* 'food', 'supplies', (via Old High German from a reduced form of Late Latin *expe(n)sa (pecunia)* '(money) expended'). **2.** Jewish (Ashkenazic): occupational name for a grocer, from a later semantic development of the same word as in 1.

Spektor (199) Variant of SPECTOR.

GIVEN NAMES Russian 43%; Jewish 23%. *Boris* (9), *Mikhail* (7), *Leonid* (6), *Yefim* (4), *Igor* (3), *Vladimir* (3), *Aleksandr* (2), *Grigory* (2), *Nikolay* (2), *Semyon* (2), *Svetlana* (2), *Vitaly* (2); *Ilya* (2), *Naum* (2), *Boruch, Bronya, Faina, Feyga, Inna, Meyer, Mordecai, Sarra, Sheva, Slava.*

Spell (1795) German: of uncertain origin; perhaps a habitational name from Spelle (see SPELLER).

Spellacy (167) Variant spelling of Irish **(O) Spellissey**, an Anglicized form of Gaelic **Ó Spealghusa** 'descendant of *Spealghusa*', a personal name probably composed of a compound of *speal* 'scythe' + *gus* 'vigor'.

Speller (544) **1.** English and South German: occupational name for a reciter, from an agent derivative of Middle English *spell(en)*, Middle High German *spellen* 'to tell or relate'. In the case of the English surname there has probably been some confusion with SPILLER. **2.** German: habitational name for someone from Spelle near Rheine. **3.** Variant of SPILLER 1.

Spellman (2557) **1.** German: occupational name for a musician or minstrel, from Middle Low German *spel* 'play' + *man* 'man'. **2.** German (**Spellmann**): habitational name for someone from Spelle near Rheine or Spellen near Wesel. **3.** English: variant of SPELLER.

Spellmeyer (160) North German (Westphalia): distinguishing name from MEYER 'tenant farmer' + an unexplained first element.

GIVEN NAMES German 6%. *Ernst, Kurt.*

Spells (414) Origin uncertain; perhaps a variant of SPELL.

Spelman (429) English: variant of SPELLER.

Spelts (136) Americanized spelling of German **Spelz** (see SPELTZ).

Speltz (272) German: variant **Spelz**, a metonymic occupational name for a grower of spelt (a type of grain), Middle High German *spëlze*.

Spenard (143) French: unexplained.

GIVEN NAMES French 17%. *Fernand* (2), *Andre, Cecile, Gaston, Jacques, Laurier, Lucien.*

Spence (12160) English and Scottish: metonymic occupational name for a servant employed in the pantry of a great house or monastery, from Middle English *spense* 'larder', 'storeroom' (a reduced form of Old French *despense*, from a Late Latin derivative of *dispendere*, past participle *dispensus*, 'to weigh out or dispense').

Spencer (45592) English: occupational name for someone employed in the pantry of a great house or monastery, from Middle English *spense* 'larder' + the agent suffix *-er*.

Spendlove (236) English: nickname for someone who was free with his affections, from Middle English *spend(en)* 'to spend or squander' + *love* 'love'.

Spengler (930) German: variant of SPANGLER.

Spenner (193) **1.** English: habitational name for someone from places so named in West Yorkshire and Lancashire, or from High Spen in County Durham. **2.** German: from Middle High German *spanner*, an occupational name for someone whose work involved pulling, tensioning, or tightening, for example a carter.

Speno (150) Possibly of Italian origin, although the name is not found in present-day Italy.

GIVEN NAMES Italian 9%. *Angelo* (3), *Nunzio.*

Spens (101) Scottish: variant of SPENCE.

Spensley (111) English (Yorkshire): apparently a habitational name from a lost or unidentified place.

Spera (645) **1.** Southern Italian: nickname from *spera* 'ray of light'. **2.** Jewish (Ashkenazic): variant of SPIRO.

GIVEN NAMES Italian 11%. *Salvatore* (4), *Angelo* (3), *Antonio* (2), *Vittorio* (2), *Attilio, Carina, Carlo, Carmine, Costantino, Francesca, Giuseppe, Lorenzo.*

Sperandeo (118) Italian: from a personal name or religious name formed from the phrase *spera in Dio* 'put your hope in God' (Latin *spera in deo*).

GIVEN NAMES Italian 22%. *Dino, Francesca, Francisco, Gino, Marco, Mario, Renato, Rodolfo, Salvatore.*

Sperandio (120) Italian: variant of SPERANDEO.

GIVEN NAMES Italian 9%. *Filippo* (2), *Dante.*

Speranza (540) Italian: from a male or female personal name derived from *speranza* 'hope'.

GIVEN NAMES Italian 14%. *Antonio* (2), *Santo* (2), *Arcangelo, Attilio, Camillo, Carmine, Domenica, Enrico, Giovanni, Luigi, Maurizio, Pasqualina.*

Sperbeck (175) South German: occupational nickname for a poor baker, from Middle High German *spör* 'dry', 'meager' + *beck* 'baker'.

Sperber (767) **1.** German: nickname for a small but belligerent person, from Middle High German *sperwære* 'sparrowhawk' (Old High German *sparwāri*, a compound of *sparw* 'sparrow' + *āri* 'eagle'). **2.** Jewish (Ashkenazic): ornamental name from German *Sperber* 'sparrowhawk'.
GIVEN NAMES German 6%. *Otto* (3), *Kurt* (2), *Dieter, Hans, Hertha, Horst, Ignatz, Leonhard, Lothar, Siegfried.*

Sperberg (106) German: topographic name for someone who lived or farmed on a dry hill, from Middle High German *spör* 'dry', 'poor', 'meager' + *berg* 'hill', 'mountain'.

Sperduti (118) Italian: patronymic or plural form of SPERDUTO.
GIVEN NAMES Italian 24%. *Adolfo, Antonio, Augusto, Carmin, Caterina, Domenico, Geno, Gilda, Giulio, Luigi, Natale, Paolo.*

Sperduto (182) Italian: nickname for a foundling, from *sperduto* 'lost', past participle of *sperdere* 'to scatter or disperse'.
GIVEN NAMES Italian 20%. *Angelo* (3), *Pasquale* (3), *Vito* (2), *Antonio, Elvio, Rocco, Salvatore, Sylvio.*

Sperl (362) German: nickname from a diminutive of Middle High German *spar(e)* 'sparrow'.
GIVEN NAMES German 5%. *Bernhard, Gerhard, Gottlieb, Irmgard, Reinhard, Wenzel.*

Sperle (195) Variant of SPERL.
GIVEN NAMES German 7%. *Otto* (2), *Gottlieb, Hans.*

Sperling (1992) **1.** English and German: nickname from a diminutive of Middle English *sparewe*, Middle High German *spar(e)* 'sparrow'. **2.** Jewish (Ashkenazic): ornamental name from German *Sperling* 'sparrow'.

Spero (763) Jewish (Ashkenazic): variant of SPIRO.

Speroni (110) Italian: **1.** from the plural of *sperone* 'spur', hence a metonymic occupational name for a spurrier. **2.** reduced form of *Gasperoni*, an augmentative form of the personal name *Gaspare*, Italian form of CASPER.
GIVEN NAMES Italian 17%. *Luigi* (5), *Enrico, Vito.*

Speros (173) Greek: variant of SPIROS.
GIVEN NAMES Greek 4%. *Demetrios, Despina, Spyro.*

Sperr (141) South German: perhaps a metonymic occupational name for a jailer, from Middle High German *sperre* 'bolt', 'clip', *sperren* 'to lock or shut'.
GIVEN NAME German 4%. *Horst.*

Sperrazza (183) Italian: probably a variant of SFERRAZZA.
GIVEN NAMES Italian 12%. *Angelo* (3), *Salvatore* (3), *Rocco.*

Sperring (115) English (Somerset): metonymic occupational name for a spurrier (a maker of spurs), from Old French *esporon*, *esperun* 'spur'.

Sperry (3155) English (Leicestershire): unexplained.

Spessard (150) Variant of German **Spessart**, a common topographic name, earlier *Spechtshart* 'woodpecker forest', as for example the Spessart mountains southeast of Frankfurt am Main.
GIVEN NAME German 4%. *Kurt.*

Speth (539) German: variant of **Späth** (see SPATH).

Spetz (106) German: variant of **Specke** (see SPECKER), a topographic name from Middle High German *specke* 'corduroy road', 'wooden bridge', for someone who lived near one; or a habitational name from the river Spetze, a tributary of the Aller.

Spevak (230) Jewish (eastern Ashkenazic): variant of SPIEWAK or SPIVAK.
GIVEN NAMES Russian 5%; Jewish 4%. *Arkady, Leonid, Lev, Nikolay, Vladimir, Yefim; Ruvin.*

Speyer (303) German and Jewish (Ashkenazic): habitational name from the German city of Speyer, which had a large Jewish population in the Middle Ages.

Speyrer (132) **1.** German (Bavaria): habitational name for someone from Speyer on the Rhine. **2.** perhaps also Jewish, as the original form of SHAPIRO.
GIVEN NAMES French 8%. *Chantel, Dominique, Emile.*

Spezia (146) Italian: metonymic occupational name for a spicer or apothecary, from old Italian *spezia* 'spice', 'drug', or from the same word used as a personal name.
GIVEN NAMES Italian 10%. *Domenic* (3), *Angelo, Bartolo.*

Speziale (260) Southern Italian: occupational name for a spicer or apothecary, *speziale* (Late Latin *speciarius*, an agent derivative of *species* 'spice', 'groceries', 'merchandise').
GIVEN NAMES Italian 16%. *Vito* (4), *Angelo* (2), *Salvatore* (2), *Alfonse, Carlo, Croce.*

Spezzano (132) Southern Italian: habitational name from any of several places in Calabria named with the personal name *Spedius*, in particular Spezzano Albanese, Spezzano della Sila, and Spezzano Piccolo.
GIVEN NAMES Italian 13%. *Angelo* (2), *Gaetano* (2), *Carmine, Francesco.*

Sphar (237) Origin unidentified.

Spice (335) English: metonymic occupational name for a spicer (see SPICER).

Spicer (6187) **1.** English: occupational name for a seller of spices, Middle English *spic(i)er* (a reduced form of Old French *espicier*, Late Latin *speciarius*, an agent derivative of *species* 'spice', 'groceries', 'merchandise'). **2.** Jewish (from Poland): variant of SPITZER.

Spicher (428) German (Rhineland): habitational name for someone from any of various places named Spicher (Rhineland), Spichern (Lorraine), or Spich (Rhineland).

Spickard (271) probably an Americanized form of German **Spickert, Speckar(d)t**, or **Speckhardt**, a topographic name for someone who lived by or worked on a plank road,

from Middle Low German, Middle High German *specke, spicke* 'raised dam through swampy terrain', 'plank road'.

Spickerman (123) North German (**Spickermann**): **1.** occupational name for someone in charge of a granary, from Middle Low German *spiker* 'granary' + *man* 'man'. **2.** habitational name for someone from Spicker or Spieckern in the Rhineland. **3.** metonymic occupational name for a nailsmith, from Middle Low German *spiker* 'nail', 'bolt' + *man* 'man'.

Spickler (335) German: topographic name for someone living near or working on a corduroy road or wooden bridge (across a swamp), from (Middle Low German) Middle High German *specke* + agent suffix *-er*.

Spicola (100) Italian (Sicily): diminutive of **Spica** (see SPICUZZA).
GIVEN NAMES Italian 23%. *Angelo* (3), *Carlo, Salvatore.*

Spicuzza (208) Italian (Sicily): from a dimunitive of Old Italian and Sicilian *spica* 'spike' (Latin *spica*), possibly applied as a nickname; the Sicilian term also denotes 'lavender', and may have been applied as a topographic name.
GIVEN NAMES Italian 6%; French 4%. *Salvatore* (3), *Ciro, Marino; Cecile, Pascal.*

Spidel (147) Possibly Americanized forms of German SPEIDEL.

Spidell (246) Americanized form of German SPEIDEL.

Spidle (303) Americanized form of German SPEIDEL.

Spiegel (2962) German and Jewish (Ashkenazic): metonymic occupational name for a maker or seller of mirrors, from Middle High German *spiegel*, German *Spiegel* 'mirror' (via Old High German from Latin *speculum*, a derivative of *specere* 'to look').
GIVEN NAMES Jewish 4%. *Sol* (4), *Chaim* (3), *Miriam* (3), *Naftali* (3), *Chana* (2), *Shmuel* (2), *Aron, Baruch, Binyomin, Boruch, Elchonon, Gershon.*

Spiegelberg (204) **1.** German: habitational name from any of the places so called, from Middle High German *spiegel* 'lookout point' + *berg* 'hill'. **2.** Jewish (Ashkenazic): ornamental name, from German *Spiegel* 'mirror' + *Berg* 'mountain', 'hill'.
GIVEN NAMES German 7%. *Erna, Hans, Wilhelm.*

Spiegelman (257) Jewish (Ashkenazic): variant of SPIEGEL.
GIVEN NAMES Jewish 5%. *Emanuel, Isadore, Meyer, Sol.*

Spiegler (216) German and Jewish (Ashkenazic): occupational name for a maker or seller of mirrors, from Middle High German *spiegel*, German *Spiegel* 'mirror' + the agent suffix *-er*.

Spieker (423) North German: from Middle Low German *spiker* 'granary', hence a metonymic occupational name for someone in charge of a granary, or topographic name for someone who lived near one.

GIVEN NAMES German 4%. *Erwin* (2), *Kurt* (2), *Eldor, Fritz, Otto*.

Spiekermann (124) German (**Spiekermann**): variant of SPIEKER.
GIVEN NAMES German 10%. *Kurt* (2), *Otto*.

Spielberg (222) **1.** German and Jewish (Ashkenazic): habitational name from any of the various places so called, from a contracted form of Middle High German *spiegel* 'lookout point' + *berg* 'mountain', 'hill'. **2.** Jewish: ornamental name from German *Spiel* 'play', 'game' + *Berg* 'mountain', 'hill'.
GIVEN NAMES Jewish 6%; German 4%. *Sol* (3), *Mayer; Erna, Helmut, Horst*.

Spielberger (152) South German and Jewish (Ashkenazic): habitational name for someone from any of the various places called SPIELBERG.
GIVEN NAME Slavic 4%. *Ladislaus* (2).

Spieler (282) German and Jewish (Ashkenazic): occupational name for a tumbler or jester, German *Spieler* 'player', Middle High German *spilære*, an agent derivative of *spiln* 'to play, jest, or sport'.
GIVEN NAMES German 6%; Jewish 4%. *Gerhard, Helmuth, Kurt, Otto; Yaffa* (2), *Meyer*.

Spielman (1340) **1.** Dutch: occupational name for a musician, tumbler or jester, from *spelen* 'to play' + *man* 'man'. **2.** Jewish (Ashkenazic): occupational name for a musician, from German *Spielmann* 'minstrel', 'musician'. **3.** Altered spelling of German SPIELMANN.
GIVEN NAMES Jewish 4%. *Chaim* (3), *Sol* (3), *Shmuel* (2), *Zev* (2), *Aron, Chaya, Ephraim, Golda, Hershel, Rivka, Yael, Yitzchok*.

Spielmann (200) German: variant of SPIELER.
GIVEN NAMES German 14%. *Hans* (2), *Franz, Gerhard, Heinz, Irmgard, Kurt, Liesl, Reinhold, Siegfried, Woldemar*.

Spielvogel (196) **1.** German: nickname from Middle High German *spilvogel* 'pet bird' (literally 'play bird'), used in a transferred sense as an affectionate term for a lover. **2.** Jewish (Ashkenazic): ornamental name from German *Spielvogel* 'pet bird' (see 1 above).
GIVEN NAME German 4%. *Kurt*.

Spier (755) **1.** English: from an agent derivative of Middle English *(e)spi(en)* 'to watch', hence an occupational name for a lookout or watchman, or a nickname for a nosy person. **2.** Scottish: variant spelling of SPEAR. **3.** German: nickname for a small person, from Middle Low German *spīr* 'trifle', 'small piece'. **4.** German: habitational name from any of several places named Spier, notably the city in the Palatinate, now spelled Speyer (see SPEYER, SPIERING). **5.** Jewish (Ashkenazic): variant of SPIRO.
GIVEN NAMES German 4%. *Erhardt* (2), *Gerd* (2), *Ewald, Ilse, Kurt, Monika, Otto*.

Spiering (371) German: **1.** habitational name for someone from any of several places called Spier (named with the old

element *spir* '(muddy) water'), notably Speyer (see SPIER 4). **2.** metonymic occupational name for a fisherman, from Middle Low German *spiring* denoting a small salt-water fish; in some instances the surname may have arisen as a nickname for someone thought to resemble the fish.

Spiers (1100) **1.** Scottish: patronymic from **Spier**, a variant spelling of SPEIR. **2.** German: unexplained.

Spies (1487) German: **1.** metonymic occupational name for a spear maker, from Middle High German *spiez* 'spear', 'pike', or an occupational name from the same word in the sense 'soldier armed with a spear'. **2.** habitational name from any of several places named Spies, in particular one near Nuremberg.

Spiess (829) German: variant of SPIES.
GIVEN NAMES German 4%. *Ernst, Erwin, Franz, Kurt, Monika, Reinhold*.

Spieth (291) German: **1.** nickname from Middle High German *spuot* 'successful', 'speedy'. Compare SPEED. **2.** metonymic occupational name for a peat-cutter, from Middle Low German *spit* 'peat'.
GIVEN NAMES German 7%. *Dieter, Erwin, Hannes, Helmut, Kurt, Manfred, Otto*.

Spiewak (313) Polish (**Śpiewak**) and Jewish (from Poland): from *śpiewak* 'singer', hence a nickname for someone with a good voice, or an occupational name for a chorister or ballad singer, or, in the case of the Jewish name, a cantor in a synagogue. This is also a frequent name in Germany, where it is also written **Spiewack, Spiewok**.
GIVEN NAMES Polish 7%. *Tadeusz* (2), *Andrzej, Eugeniusz, Ewa, Jarek*.

Spiezio (112) Italian (Campania): unexplained.
GIVEN NAMES Italian 10%. *Geno, Sal*.

Spigarelli (110) Northern Italian: from a diminutive of *spiga* 'spike', 'ear (of a cereal plant)', possibly applied as a nickname for a thin person.
GIVEN NAMES Italian 12%. *Angelo* (2), *Domenic, Geno, Remo, Rinaldo*.

Spigel (110) Jewish (Ashkenazic): variant of SPIEGEL.

Spigelmyer (113) altered spelling of German **Spiegelmeyer**, a distinguishing name for a tenant farmer (see MEYER) who farmed land named with *Spiegel* 'glass', 'mirror' (probably in the sense 'lookout point').

Spight (205) Probably an altered spelling of English SPEIGHT.

Spigner (385) German: perhaps a nickname from Middle Low German *spigen* 'to spit', denoting someone who was known for this habit.

Spike (204) English: from Middle English *spike* 'spike'; perhaps a nickname for a tall, thin person.

Spiker (1185) Americanized spelling of Dutch **Spijker** (see SPYKER).

Spikes (1117) English: patronymic from SPIKE.

Spilde (233) Norwegian: habitational name

from either of two farmsteads in Hordaland, named probably from Old Norse *spildr*, denoting a natural formation forming a right angle.
GIVEN NAME Scandinavian 4%. *Iver*.

Spilka (103) Czech: occupational name for a brewer, from *spilka*, denoting a part of a brewery. It is also found as a nickname for a beer drinker.

Spilker (470) North German: occupational name for a maker of spindles, from an agent derivative of Middle Low German *spille* 'spindle'.

Spillane (1175) Irish: reduced form O'Spillane, an Anglicized form of Gaelic Ó Spealáin or 'descendant of *Spealán*', a personal name representing a diminutive of *speal* 'scythe'. Compare SMULLEN. In some cases the name may be a reduced Anglicized form of **Mac Spealáin** 'son of *Spealán*'.
GIVEN NAMES Irish 7%. *Brendan* (2), *Kieran* (2), *Ciaran, Donal*.

Spillar (137) Presumably an altered spelling of English SPILLER.

Spille (132) German and Dutch: metonymic occupational name for a spindle maker, from Middle High German *spinnel, spindel, spille*, Middle Low German *spinele, spille*; Middle Dutch *spille* 'spindle'. In some cases, the surname may have arisen from a nickname for a very thin person or someone with spindly legs.
GIVEN NAME German 4%. *Erwin*.

Spiller (1860) **1.** English: occupational name for a tumbler or jester, from an agent derivative of Middle English *spill(en)* 'to play, jest, or sport' (Old English *spilian*). **2.** English: nickname for a destructive or wasteful person, from an agent derivative of the homonymous Middle English *spill(en)* 'to spoil, waste, or squander' (Old English *spillan*). **3.** German and Dutch: occupational name for a spindle maker, a variant of SPILLE with the addition of the agent suffix *-er*. **4.** In some cases a variant of German SPIELER.

Spillers (883) English: patronymic from SPILLER.

Spillman (1790) **1.** English: from a Middle English personal name *Spileman*, which was originally an Old English byname meaning 'juggler', 'tumbler', 'actor'. Compare SPILLER. **2.** German (**Spillmann**): variant of SPIELMANN.

Spilman (586) **1.** Jewish (Ashkenazic): variant of SPIELMAN. **2.** Variant spelling of German **Spillmann** (see SPILLMANN).

Spilsbury (100) English: habitational name from Spelsbury in Oxfordshire, named in Old English with the personal name *Spēol* + *burh* 'stronghold'.

Spina (1445) Italian: topographic name from *spina* 'thorn', 'thorn bush', or a habitational name from any of the numerous places named with this word. De Felice believes there may also have been a religious byname involved (probably as the subject of the dedication of a shrine), referring to Christ's crown of thorns.

GIVEN NAMES Italian 14%. *Salvatore* (10), *Ciro* (5), *Antonio* (4), *Carmine* (4), *Angelo* (3), *Rocco* (3), *Vito* (3), *Carlo* (2), *Carmela* (2), *Santo* (2), *Vincenza* (2), *Vincenzo* (2).

Spinale (272) Southern Italian: probably from Sicilian *spinali* 'spiny', 'prickly', applied as a nickname, although some authorities believed that it is of Iberian origin. It may actually be a variant of Catalan **Espinaler**, a derivative from ESPINAL, that most probably arrived at the area during the rule of Napoli and Sicily by the Catalano-Aragonese king, in the Medieval Age.

GIVEN NAMES Italian 22%. *Salvatore* (7), *Angelo*, *Carmela*, *Carmello*, *Domenico*, *Giuseppe*, *Santo*, *Umberto*, *Vincenza*, *Vito*.

Spinazzola (122) Italian: habitational name from a place called Spinazzola in Bari province.

Spindel (263) German and Jewish (Ashkenazic): metonymic occupational name for a spindle maker, from Middle High German *spindel*, Yiddish *shpindl* 'spindle', 'distaff'.

GIVEN NAMES German 4%. *Manfred*, *Monika*, *Wolf*.

Spindle (214) **1.** English: perhaps a metonymic occupational name for a spindle maker, from Middle English *spindle*, *spindel* (Old English *spinel*). **2.** Americanized spelling of German and Jewish SPINDEL.

Spindler (1521) English, German, and Jewish (Ashkenazic): occupational name for a spindle maker, from an agent derivative of Middle English *spindle*, Middle High German *spindel*, German *Spindel*, Yiddish *shpindl* 'spindle', 'distaff'.

GIVEN NAMES German 5%. *Kurt* (6), *Erwin* (2), *Otto* (2), *Arno*, *Dieter*, *Dietmar*, *Gerhard*, *Hanns*, *Herta*, *Inge*, *Juergen*, *Manfred*.

Spinella (506) Southern Italian: **1.** diminutive of SPINA. **2.** topographic name from Sicilian *spinedda* 'butcher's broom' (*Ruscus aculeatus*), untimately of the same etymology as 1.

GIVEN NAMES Italian 14%. *Salvatore* (5), *Carmelo* (3), *Orlando* (3), *Constantino* (2), *Gasper* (2), *Agostino*, *Angelo*, *Carmela*, *Carmine*, *Domenico*, *Eliseo*, *Giovanna*, *Marcello*, *Mario*.

Spinelli (1875) Southern Italian: patronymic or plural form of SPINELLO.

GIVEN NAMES Italian 16%. *Angelo* (15), *Salvatore* (11), *Rocco* (9), *Vito* (9), *Carmine* (6), *Sal* (4), *Antonio* (2), *Domenic* (2), *Ercole* (2), *Gaetano* (2), *Gino* (2).

Spinello (168) Italian: **1.** possibly from the personal name *Spinellus*, which is most probably a pet form of *Crispinus* (see CRISPIN). **2.** from a diminutive of SPINA or SPINO. **3.** from a reduced form of *Ospinello*, a personal name derived from French *(H)ospinel*, the name of a character in French medieval romances.

GIVEN NAMES Italian 15%. *Angelo* (2), *Elio*, *Gaspare*, *Raffaela*, *Santo*.

Spingler (110) Americanized form of German SPENGLER (see SPANGLER).

Spingola (146) Southern Italian: **1.** from *spingola*, denoting a type of brooch or pin, hence an occupational name for a jeweler or a nickname for someone who wore such a brooch. **2.** from Sicilian *spingula* 'musky storksbill' (*Erodium moschatum*), presumably a topographic name for someone who lived where there was an abundance of this plant.

GIVEN NAMES Italian 9%. *Guido*, *Pietro*, *Sal*.

Spink (911) English: from Middle English *spink* 'chaffinch' (probably of imitative origin), hence a nickname bestowed on account of some fancied resemblance to the bird.

Spinks (1974) English: patronymic from SPINK.

Spinler (152) English, German, or Jewish: variant of SPINDLER.

Spinnato (141) Italian: perhaps a nickname for a bald-headed man, from *spennato* 'plucked'.

GIVEN NAMES Italian 16%. *Salvatore* (4), *Angelo*, *Carmelo*, *Francesco*, *Franco*, *Sal*.

Spinner (1158) English and South German: occupational name for a spinner of yarn, from the agent derivative of Middle English, Middle High German *spinnen* 'to spin'.

Spinney (739) English: topographic name from Middle English *spyn(n)eye*, 'spinney', i.e. a small patch of woodland, clump of trees (Old French *espinei*).

Spino (407) Italian and Greek (**Spinos**): nickname from Greek *spinos* 'thin', 'spindly' or the noun *spinos* 'linnet'.

GIVEN NAMES Italian 13%. *Angelo* (2), *Pasquale* (2), *Rocco* (2), *Sebastiano* (2), *Antonio*, *Carmine*, *Carmino*, *Emidio*, *Nichola*, *Nicola*, *Sando*.

Spinola (178) **1.** Italian (Liguria): diminutive of SPINA. **2.** Italian: topographic name for someone living by Monte Spinola in the province of Pavia. **3.** Portuguese (**Spínola**): topographic name from a diminutive of *espinha* 'thorn', 'thorn bush'.

GIVEN NAMES Italian 24%. *Salvatore* (2), *Alvaro*, *Camilo*, *Carmine*, *Domenic*, *Emilio*, *Gabriella*, *Rafael*, *Remo*, *Roberto*, *Sal*, *Sergio*, *Sylvio*.

Spinosa (345) Italian: from the feminine form of *spinoso* 'thorny', used as a nickname in the figurative sense of 'contrary', 'difficult', 'intractable'. In some cases it may be an Italianization of Spanish ESPINOSA.

GIVEN NAMES Italian 15%. *Salvatore* (4), *Angelo*, *Elio*, *Ercole*, *Ettore*, *Gaetano*, *Nicola*, *Pasquale*, *Sal*, *Vito*.

Spira (340) Jewish (Ashkenazic): variant of SPIRO.

GIVEN NAMES Jewish 19%. *Binyomin* (3), *Eliezer* (2), *Moshe* (2), *Shimon* (2), *Zorach*

(2), *Aryeh*, *Avi*, *Avrohom*, *Chaya*, *Gershon*, *Gitty*, *Hirsch*.

Spire (166) **1.** English: nickname for a tall, thin man, from Middle English *spir* 'stalk', 'stem'. This was apparently used as a personal name or byname, in view of the fact that there are patronymic derivatives. In some Middle English dialects this word also denoted reeds, and the surname may in part have been originally a topographic name for someone who lived in a marshy area. The application to a church steeple is not attested before the 16th century, and is not a likely source of the surname. **2.** Jewish (Ashkenazic): variant of SPIRO.

Spires (2243) English: patronymic from SPIRE 1.

Spirito (240) Italian: from the personal name *Spirito*, a devotional name alluding to the *Spirito Santo* 'Holy Spirit'. This name was bestowed on children born on the religious festival of Pentecost, the day when the Holy Spirit descended on Christ's apostles.

GIVEN NAMES Italian 19%. *Angelo* (2), *Carlo* (2), *Domenic* (2), *Biagio*, *Camillo*, *Domenico*, *Gino*, *Mafalda*, *Nicola*, *Rocco*, *Sal*, *Saverio*.

Spirk (129) South German: nickname from Alemannic dialect word meaning 'sparrow'.

GIVEN NAMES German 6%. *Konrad* (3), *Hans*, *Irmgard*.

Spirko (115) Altered spelling of Jewish (from Poland) **Szpirko**, a nickname (or unflattering name to Jews assigned by Polish Christian officials), from Polish *szperka* 'bacon', 'lard', 'pork fat'.

Spiro (791) Jewish (Ashkenazic): habitational name from *Shpire*, the Yiddish name of the German city of SPEYER. This surname appears in central Europe in the 16th century.

GIVEN NAMES Jewish 5%. *Ari* (2), *Binyomin* (2), *Emanuel* (2), *Meyer* (2), *Avron*, *Miriam*, *Pinchas*, *Tova*.

Spiros (106) Greek: from the personal name *Spiros* or a patronymic derived from it. This is a vernacular form of *Spyridōn*, the name of the patron saint of Corfu, who died in 348 AD; it is ultimately derived from classical Greek *spyris* 'large basket'.

Spisak (589) Polish and Slovak (**Spišák**): regional name for someone from Spisz, an area of the West Carpathians partly in Poland and partly in Slovakia.

Spitale (149) Southern Italian: topographic name from Sicilian *spitale* 'lodging house', 'infirmary'. Compare English SPITTLE.

GIVEN NAMES Italian 15%. *Angelo* (2), *Leonardo* (2), *Cono*, *Mauro*, *Salvatore*, *Santo*.

Spiteri (178) Southern Italian and Greek (**Spiteris**): occupational name from a derivative of medieval Latin *hospitarius*, denoting someone who was employed at a lodging house.

GIVEN NAMES Italian 10%; Greek 4%; Spanish 4%. *Angelo, Antonio, Carmel, Vincenza*; *Spiro, Spiros, Spyros*; *Mario* (3), *Alicia, Manuel*.

Spitler (1270) Variant spelling of German SPITTLER.

Spittle (247) **1.** English: occupational name for someone who was employed at a lodging house, from Middle English *spital* 'lodging house' (a reduced form of Old French *hospital*, Late Latin *hospitale*, from *hostis*, genitive *hospitis*, guest). **2.** Americanized spelling of eastern German **Spittel**, metonymic occupational name for someone who worked in an infirmary, from Middle High German *spital, spittel* 'hospital'.

Spittler (359) English and eastern German: occupational name for someone who was employed at a lodging house or infirmary, from agent derivatives of Middle English *spital*, Middle High German *spital, spittel* 'lodging house', 'infirmary'.

Spitz (1639) German and Jewish (Ashkenazic): from German *Spitz* 'point', a topographic name for someone who lived by a pointed hill or by a field with an acute angle, or a habitational name from any of the numerous minor places throughout Germany named with this word. As a Jewish name it is mainly ornamental.
GIVEN NAMES German 4%. *Kurt* (3), *Otto* (3), *Erwin* (2), *Angelika, Ilse, Johann, Mathias, Siegfried, Volker, Willi, Willibald*.

Spitzer (2781) **1.** German: derivative of SPITZ, the suffix *-er* denoting an inhabitant. **2.** Jewish (Ashkenazic): origin uncertain; possibly from SPITZ.
GIVEN NAMES Jewish 4%; German 4%. *Chaim* (3), *Miriam* (3), *Aron* (2), *Eliezer* (2), *Hershel* (2), *Toba* (2), *Arnon, Bracha, Chaya, Etti, Gitty, Moishe*; *Kurt* (6), *Hellmut* (2), *Berthold, Erwin, Frieda, Friedrich, Hans, Helmuth, Hertha, Hilde, Katharina*.

Spitzley (194) Americanized spelling of Bavarian **Spitzli**, a diminutive of SPITZ 1.
GIVEN NAMES German 4%. *Kurt, Mathias*.

Spitzmiller (102) Partly Americanized form of German **Spitzmüller**, a compound of the topographic (field) name SPITZ + MUELLER.

Spitznagel (169) German: metonymic occupational name for a nailsmith, from Middle High German *spitz* 'pointed' + *nagel* 'nail'.

Spitzner (108) German: topographic name from an agent noun based on *Spitz* 'point' (see SPITZ).
GIVEN NAMES German 13%. *Kurt* (3), *Alois, Erna, Fritz*.

Spiva (387) Slavic: unexplained.

Spivack (418) Germanized or Americanized spelling of Jewish and Ukrainian SPIVAK.
GIVEN NAMES Jewish 6%. *Gershon, Mayer, Miriam, Sol*.

Spivak (705) Jewish (eastern Ashkenazic) and Ukrainian: from Ukrainian *spivak* 'singer'. As a Jewish name it is an occupational name for a cantor in a synagogue.
GIVEN NAMES Jewish 13%; Russian 13%. *Yakov* (4), *Ilya* (3), *Sol* (2), *Aron, Baruch, Basya, Bronya, Golda, Hadar, Inna, Iren, Irina*; *Boris* (11), *Lev* (6), *Grigoriy* (4), *Igor* (4), *Leonid* (4), *Mikhail* (4), *Vladimir* (4), *Aleksandr* (3), *Arkady* (2), *Iosif* (2), *Tuba* (2), *Aleksey*.

Spivey (6578) English (Yorkshire): from a medieval personal name, *Spivey*.

Spiwak (142) Jewish (eastern Ashkenazic): variant of SPIEWAK or SPIVAK.

Spizzirri (178) Italian: unexplained.
GIVEN NAMES Italian 15%. *Achille, Angelo, Antonio, Carlo, Dante, Fausto, Giovanni, Vito*.

Splain (221) Irish: reduced form of SPILLANE.

Splaine (177) Irish: reduced form of SPILLANE.
GIVEN NAMES Irish 7%. *Brendan, Teague*.

Splan (163) English or Irish: unexplained.

Splane (127) Reduced form of Irish SPILLANE.

Splawn (458) Probably an altered form of Irish SPILLANE.

Splichal (154) Czech: nickname from a derivative of *šplíchat* 'to splash'.

Splinter (283) North German: from Low German *splinter* 'splinter'; probably a metonymic occupational name for a woodworker.

Splitt (171) North German: metonymic occupational name for someone who split wood, for example for shingles, from Middle Low German *split* 'split piece of wood', 'shingle'.

Splittgerber (126) North German: occupational name for someone who crushed stone, split wood, or tanned leather, from Middle Low German *spliten* 'to split' + an agent derivative of *gerben* 'to prepare'.
GIVEN NAME German 4%. *Erwin* (2).

Spock (137) Americanized form of Dutch **Spaak**, a metonymic occupational name for someone who made spokes for wheels, from Middle Dutch *spaak* 'spoke'.
FOREBEARS The American pediatrician Dr. Benjamin Spock (1903–98) was of Dutch descent; his ancestors, whose name was *Spaak*, were early settlers in the Hudson River valley of NY.

Spoden (195) **1.** Dutch: habitational name from *aan 's boden huis*, *'s Boden* 'at the house of the messenger', the name of a house in Amel in Deidenberg, in the Belgian province of Liège. **2.** Dutch: habitational name from Spaden. There is a place so called in Schiffdorf, Lower Saxony, and it was the former name of Spouwen in the Belgian province of Limburg. **3.** Dutch: metonymic occupational name for a laborer who used a spade, from Low German *Spaden* 'spade'. **4.** German: probably of the same origin as 2 and 3.

Spoelstra (192) Frisian: probably a topographic name meaning 'from the pool', from an agent noun based on Middle Low German *pōl* '(muddy) pool', with excrescent initial *-s*. Compare POELSTRA.

Spoerl (272) **1.** South German (**Spörl**): nickname from a diminutive of Middle High German *spar(e)* 'sparrow'. **2.** Nickname for a poor, lowly person, from Middle High German *spör* 'poor', 'meager', 'destitut'.

Spofford (431) English: habitational name from Spofforth in North Yorkshire, recorded in Domesday Book as *Spoford* and perhaps so named from Old English *splott* 'spot', 'plot' of land + *ford* 'ford'.

Spohn (1220) German: variant of SPAHN.

Spohr (284) German: **1.** metonymic occupational name for a maker of spurs, from Middle High German *spor* 'spur'. **2.** topographic name, from Middle High German *spor* 'spoor', 'track (of an animal)'.
GIVEN NAMES German 4%. *Hans* (3), *Irmgard, Ulrike*.

Spohrer (106) Variant of SPORER.

Spolar (121) Americanized spelling of Croatian and Serbian **Špoljar**, of unexplained origin.

Spolarich (104) Americanized spelling of the Croatian and Serbian patronymic **Špoljar**, of unexplained origin. Compare SPOLAR.

Spomer (258) Possibly an altered form of German **Spamer**, a habitational name from *Spanemer*, the old name of Schotten in the Vogelsberg district; the first element is *span* 'dampness'.

Sponaugle (437) Americanized form of German SPANNAGEL.

Spong (297) **1.** English: topographic name from Middle English *spong* 'narrow strip of land', or a habitational name from Spong Farm in Elmstead, Kent, which is named with this word. **2.** Swedish: topographic or ornamental name from *spång* 'footbridge', 'plank'.

Spongberg (117) Swedish (**Spångberg**): ornamental name from *spång*- 'footbridge', 'plank' + *berg* 'mountain'.

Sponholz (100) German: metonymic occupational name for someone who split wood (for shingles, for example) or cut or sold wood for splitting, from Middle High German *spān* '(wood) chip', 'shaving', 'splinter' + *holz* 'wood'; alternatively a habitational name from a place so named (Spohnholz) in Mecklenburg.
GIVEN NAME German 4%. *Otto*.

Sponsel (187) German: contracted form of **Spannseil**, a metonymic occupational name for a rope maker, from Middle High German *spān* 'wood chip' or *spannen* 'to pull', 'tighten' + *seil* 'rope'.

Sponseller (463) Americanized form of German **Spannseiler**, an occupational name for a ropemaker or a farmer who was hired out as a carter or teamster (of horses), an agent derivative of SPANNSEIL.

Sponsler (489) See SPONSELLER.

Spoo (138) French (Walloon): habitational name for someone from Spa in Liège province, Belgium (Walloon Spô).

Spoon (1004) **1.** Dutch: unexplained. **2.** English: apparently a metonymic occupational name either for a maker of roofing shingles or spoons, from Old English *spōn* 'chip', 'splinter' (see also SPOONER). **3.** Possibly an Anglicized or Americanized form of German SPOHN (see SPAHN).

Spoonemore (180) Origin unidentified.

Spooner (2825) English: occupational name for someone who covered roofs with wooden shingles, from an agent derivative of Middle English *spoon* 'chip', 'splinter'. However, from the 14th century, under Scandinavian influence, the word had also begun to acquire its modern sense denoting the eating utensil, and in some cases the surname may have been acquired by someone who made spoons, typically from wood or horn.

Spoor (669) Dutch and English (Northumbria): metonymic occupational name for a maker of spurs, a lorimer, from Middle Dutch *spore*, Middle English *spore*, *spure* 'spur'.

Spor (150) South German: variant spelling of SPOHR.
GIVEN NAME Scandinavian 5%; German 5%. *Otto* (2).

Spore (349) English (Northumbria): variant of SPOOR.

Sporer (294) South German: occupational name for a maker of spurs, Middle High German *sporer*.
GIVEN NAMES German 4%. *Erna*, *Maximilian*, *Otto*.

Spores (101) German: variant of SPORS.

Sporleder (302) North German: metonymic occupational name for a maker of leather straps for spurs, from Middle Low German *spore* 'spur' + *led(d)er* 'leather'.

Sporn (201) **1.** German: possibly from Middle High German *sporn* 'to spur'; of uncertain application. **2.** Jewish (Ashkenazic): ornamental name from German *Sporn* 'spur'.
GIVEN NAMES Jewish 10%; German 4%. *Ephraim*, *Faina*, *Hershy*, *Moshe*, *Shimon*, *Sol*; *Jurgen*.

Sporrer (175) South German: variant of SPORER.
GIVEN NAMES German 6%. *Kurt* (2), *Gottlieb*.

Spors (103) German: genitive form (patronymic) of SPOHR.
GIVEN NAMES German 5%. *Heinz*, *Irmgard*.

Sport (114) English and German: unexplained.

Sportsman (207) **1.** Possibly an altered form of Dutch **Sportmans**: **2.** habitational name for someone from any of several

places called Spork. **3.** variant of PORTMAN.

Sposato (511) Italian: from *sposato* 'married' (past participle of *sposare* 'to wed'). perhaps used as a nickname for someone who had married the daughter of the chief family in a village.
GIVEN NAMES Italian 14%. *Angelo* (7), *Fiore* (3), *Dino* (2), *Antonio*, *Carmela*, *Carmine*, *Enrico*, *Gaetana*, *Gaetano*, *Gennaro*, *Giuseppe*, *Maurizio*.

Sposito (252) Italian: nickname for a foundling, a reduced form of ESPOSITO.
GIVEN NAMES Italian 14%. *Luigi* (3), *Gennaro* (2), *Salvatore* (2), *Angelo*, *Antonio*, *Carlo*, *Carmine*, *Giuseppe*, *Natale*, *Pasquale*, *Vincenzo*.

Spoto (406) Southern Italian: status name from a reduced form of the Greco-Calabrian word *codespoto* 'head of a household', from Greek *oikos* 'house' + *despotēs* 'master'.
GIVEN NAMES Italian 17%. *Angelo* (11), *Salvatore* (3), *Carmelo*, *Erminio*, *Franco*, *Gaetano*, *Gino*, *Giuseppe*, *Sal*, *Sebastiano*, *Vincenza*.

Spotswood (114) Scottish: habitational name from a place in the parish of Gordon, Berwickshire, first recorded in 1249 as *Spottiswode*. The second element is Middle English *wode* 'wood'; the first appears to derive from a personal name.
FOREBEARS All bearers of this surname are probably descended from Robert de Spotswood (fl. *c.*1300). Alexander Spotswood, a British army officer born in Tangiers in 1676, was appointed lieutenant governor of VA in 1710, was removed from office in 1722 for his support of VA colonists, and died in Annapolis, MD, while raising a colonial regiment to fight the Spanish.

Spott (143) German: nickname for someone who likes to ridicule, from Middle High German *spot* 'mockery', 'jest', 'joke'.
GIVEN NAME German 6%. *Bernd*.

Spotts (1263) Probably a variant of English **Spott**, from Middle English *spot* 'spot', 'blemish', perhaps a nickname for someone with a spotty complexion; or of Scottish **Spott**, a habitational name from a place so called near Dunbar.

Spottswood (110) Variant spelling of SPOTSWOOD.

Spracklen (160) Southern English: possibly a variant of **Sprackling**, itself a variant of SPRATLING.

Spracklin (121) Southern English: possibly a variant of **Sprackling**, itself a variant of SPRATLING.

Spradley (1105) Variant of English SPRATLEY.

Spradlin (2514) Variant of English SPRATLING.

Spradling (1243) Variant of English SPRATLING.

Spragg (424) English: variant of SPRAGUE.

Spraggins (634) English (Suffolk): patronymic from a diminutive of SPRAGG.

Spraggs (115) English: variant of SPRAGG.

Spragins (134) Apparently a variant of English SPRAGGINS.

Sprague (9033) English: from northern Middle English *Spragge*, either a personal name or a byname meaning 'lively', a metathesized and voiced form of SPARK 1.
FOREBEARS William Sprague came from England to Salem, MA, in 1628 with his brothers Ralph and Richard. He was one of the founders of Charlestown, MA, and later of Hingham, MA. His descendants include Peleg Sprague, a jurist and MA legislator, who was born in 1793 in Duxbury, MA; William Sprague a textile manufacturer born in 1773 in Cranston, RI; and Yale College educator Homer Baxter Sprague, who was born in 1829 in South Sutton, MA, and whose legacy lives on in Yale's Sprague concert hall.

Sprain (108) Origin unidentified.

Spraker (412) Variant of Dutch **Spreker** 'speaker', an occupational name for someone who acted as the speaker on behalf of a community, or for a poet. Compare *Sprakers*, name of a place east of Canajoharie in the Mohawk Valley.

Sprandel (119) South German: nickname from a dialect word meaning 'conceited or haughty person'.

Sprang (270) **1.** German: related to Old High German *spranc* 'spring', hence a topographic name for someone who lived by a spring or well. **2.** Dutch (**van Sprang**): habitational name from Sprang in North Brabant.

Spranger (283) German: **1.** topographic name for someone who lived by a spring or well (see SPRANG). **2.** variant of SPRINGER 1.
GIVEN NAMES German 4%. *Hermann*, *Lothar*, *Manfred*.

Sprangers (132) German: variant of SPRANGER.

Sprankle (440) Altered spelling of German **Sprankel**, a nickname for a lively, athletic person, from a diminutive of Middle High German *spranke* 'grasshopper', or from Middle Low German *sprenkel*.

Spratley (406) English: apparently a habitational name, from a lost or unidentified place.

Spratlin (271) Variant of English SPRATLING.

Spratling (217) English: nickname for an old or infirm man, from Middle English *sprakeling* 'one with creaking legs' (Old Norse *sprakaleggr*).

Spratt (1581) English: nickname for a small or insignificant person, from Middle English *sprat* 'sprat' (of uncertain origin).

Sprau (131) German (Palatinate): see SPRAUER.

Sprauer (132) East German: dialect variant of **Spreuer**, from Middle High German *spriu(w)e* 'chaff', a derisive nickname for a useless person.

Spray (1011) English (Nottinghamshire): nickname for a thin person, from Middle English *spray* 'slender branch' (of uncertain origin).

Sprayberry (755) Americanized form of German **Spreeberg**, of unexplained origin. The German name occurs chiefly in the Rhineland.

Sprecher (835) German and Jewish (Ashkenazic): from an agent derivative of German and Middle High German *sprechen* 'to speak', an occupational name for a poet, a reciter, or a public announcer.

Spreemann (140) Americanized spelling of German **Spreemann**, a habitational name for someone from a place named Spree (for example, near Görlitz), or a topographic name from the river so called.

Spreen (269) North German: nickname for someone thought to resemble a starling in some way, Middle Low German *sprēn*.

GIVEN NAMES German 5%. *Johannes* (2), *Gerhart, Otto.*

Sprehe (177) North German: probably a variant of SPREEN, from *sprēi*, a variant form of Middle Low German *sprēn* 'starling'.

GIVEN NAMES German 4%. *Erwin* (2), *Reinhold.*

Spreitzer (220) German: a Sorbian family name of uncertain origin, perhaps a habitational name from a place called Spreewitz near Hoyerswerda, Lausitz

GIVEN NAME German 4%. *Fritz.*

Spreng (232) 1. South German: topographic name from a dialect word, *Spreng* 'steep area'. 2. North German: habitational name from any of several places called Sprenge, for example near Otterndorf and near Kiel.

Sprengel (116) German: 1. habitational name from a place so called, north of Soltau. 2. hence a nickname for a lively, athletic person, from Middle Low German *sprengel* 'grasshopper'. 3. from Middle High German *sprengel* 'aspergill', 'sprinkler for holy water'; of uncertain application.

Sprenger (852) 1. North German form of SPRINGER 1. 2. Occupational name for a stoneworker, from Middle High German *sprengen* (causative of *springen*) 'to break up', 'blast'.

GIVEN NAMES German 7%. *Kurt* (3), *Eldor* (2), *Florian* (2), *Siegfried* (2), *Erwin, Franz, Frieda, Gerhardt, Helmut, Johann, Klaus, Manfred.*

Sprenkle (410) Americanized spelling of North German **Sprenkel**, from Middle Low German *sprenkel* 'grasshopper' (see SPRENGEL) 2.

Sprick (240) North German: from Middle Low German *sprik* 'dry, fragile twig', hence a nickname for a slightly built person.

GIVEN NAMES German 5%. *Erwin, Hermann, Lorenz.*

Sprigg (209) English: nickname for a tall, thin person, from Middle English *sprigge* 'twig', 'branch' (apparently of Old Norse or Low German origin, first recorded as a vocabulary word in English in the 15th century).

Spriggs (2105) English: patronymic from SPRIGG.

Sprik (111) Dutch: unexplained.

Spring (3268) 1. English: of uncertain origin. Early examples, as for example William Spring (Yorkshire 1280), all point to a personal name or nickname, perhaps going back to an Old English byname derived from the verb *springan* 'to jump or leap' (see SPRINGER 1). Alternatively, it could be a topographic name from Middle English *spring* 'young wood', 'spring'. Compare SPRINGER. Reaney derives the surname from the word denoting the season, although the word is not attested in this sense until the 16th century, the usual Middle English word being *lenten*. Compare LENZ. The surname has also been established in Ireland (County Kerry) for several centuries. 2. German: from Middle High German *sprinc*, Middle Low German *sprink* 'spring', 'well', hence a topographic name for someone who lived by a spring or well, or habitational name from Springe near Hannover. 3. Jewish (Ashkenazic): variant of SPRINGER.

FOREBEARS John Spring emigrated from England and settled in Watertown, MA, in 1634.

Springborn (241) German: from Middle Low German *sprinkborn* 'spring' (*born* means 'well'), hence a topographic name for someone who lived by a spring, or a habitational name from any of several places named Springborn.

GIVEN NAMES German 5%. *Heinz* (2), *Otto.*

Springer (12024) 1. English, German, Dutch, and Jewish (Ashkenazic): nickname for a lively person or for a traveling entertainer, from an agent derivative of Middle English, Middle High German *springen*, Middle Dutch *springhen*, Yiddish *shpringen* 'to jump or leap'. 2. English: topographic name for someone who lived by a fountain or the source of a stream, Middle English *spring* 'spring' + the habitational suffix *-er*. The same word was also used of a plantation of young trees, and in some cases this may be the source of the surname.

Springett (104) English (Essex and Kent): from a diminutive of SPRING.

Springfield (1094) English: habitational name from a place in Essex, recorded in Domesday Book as *Springinghefelda* and as *Springafelda*, probably from Old English *Springingafeld* 'pasture (*feld*) of the people who live by a spring'.

Springle (104) English: in part probably a metonymic occupational name for a soldier in charge of a catapult- or bow-like machine used for throwing heavy missiles, Old French *espringalle*, Anglo-French *springalde*. However, Reaney and Wilson, believe the Middle English word *springal(d)* (which appears to have contributed to the surname), to have a different derivation, perhaps a nickname for a young man, a stripling, from *spring* (see SPRING).

Springman (601) 1. South German: habitational name for someone from any of the places named Spring, Springe, Springen, or Sprink. 2. Dutch: occupational name for an acrobat or tumbler, from Middle Dutch *springen, sprengen* 'to jump or leap' + *man* 'man'. 3. Jewish (Ashkenazic): variant of SPRINGER, from Yiddish *shpringen* 'to jump' + *man* 'man'.

Springmeyer (155) German: distinguishing name for a tenant farmer (see MEYER) whose farm was situated by a spring (Middle High German *sprinc* 'spring', 'wellhead').

Springs (997) English: variant of SPRING.

GIVEN NAMES French 4%. *Andre* (2), *Camille, Gabrielle, Julien.*

Springstead (342) Possibly of English origin, a habitational name from a lost or unidentified place.

Springsteen (405) Dutch or North German: topographic name from *springsteen*, a kind of stone used as a stepping stone in unpaved streets or between two houses.

Springston (311) Probably an Americanized form of Dutch SPRINGSTEEN.

Sprinkel (230) Dutch: nickname for an athletic, lively person, from Middle Dutch *sprinkel* 'grasshopper'.

Sprinkle (2251) Americanized spelling of SPRINKEL.

Sprinkles (165) Possibly an Americanized form of Dutch **Sprenkels**, a variant of SPRINKEL.

Spritzer (146) Jewish (Ashkenazic): occupational nickname for a medical doctor, from German *Spritze* 'syringe' + agent suffix *-er*.

GIVEN NAMES Jewish 8%. *Sol, Yaakov, Yakov.*

Sproat (404) Scottish and northern English: variant of SPROTT.

Sprock (173) Dutch: 1. metathesized form of **Spork**, a habitational name from any of several places so named. 2. nickname for a spokesman, a storyteller, or a good speaker, from Middle Dutch *sproke, sprooc* 'utterance', 'speech', 'story'.

Sproles (504) Possibly an altered form of English **Sprules**, of unexplained origin.

Sprong (188) Dutch: nickname from Middle Dutch *spronc* 'jumper'.

Spross (109) German: probably a nickname (or earlier a personal name also) from

Middle High German *spross* 'scion', 'descendant'.

GIVEN NAME German 4%. *Johann*.

Sprott (358) **1.** Scottish and northern English: from the Old English personal name *Sprot*, of uncertain origin. It may be derived from Old English *sprot* 'sprout', 'young shoot'. **2.** Northern Irish (County Down): variant of SPRATT. **3.** German: probably a habitational name from places named Sprotte (Westphalia, Saxony-Anhalt), Sprotta (Silesia).

Sproul (1171) Scottish: unexplained. The derivative ending in *-s* may be patronymic, in which case this is from an otherwise unrecorded medieval personal name.

Sproule (347) Scottish: variant spelling of SPROUL.

Sproull (310) Scottish: variant spelling of SPROUL.

Sprouls (148) Derivative of Scottish SPROUL, found mainly in northern Ireland.

Sprouse (2793) English or Scottish: unexplained. Posslbly a variant of SPROULS.

Sprout (477) **1.** Dutch: from Middle Dutch *sprute* 'sprout', 'shoot', either a nickname for a young or delicate person, or possibly, in the sense of 'offshoot', 'descendant', a nickname for someone linked by birth to a distinguished local family. **2.** Scottish: variant of SPROTT.

Sprow (295) Americanized spelling of German SPRAU.

Sprowl (384) Variant spelling of Scottish SPROUL, found mainly in northern Ireland.

Sprowles (115) See SPROWLS.

Sprowls (413) Derivative (possibly patronymic) of Scottish SPROUL, found mainly in northern Ireland.

Spruce (289) English: ethnic name for someone from Prussia, Middle English *Spruce*, *Sprewse*. Compare German PREUSS. The adjective *spruce* 'neat', 'dapper', which probably derives from an attributive use of the name of the country, is not recorded until the late 16th century, too late for it to be a likely source of the surname. The tree (earlier called *spruce fir*) has likewise only come to be known by this name in the last couple of centuries.

GIVEN NAME Scandinavian 7%; German 6%. *Jutta*.

Spruell (496) Variant of Scottish or northern Irish SPROUL.

Spruiell (298) Variant of Scottish or northern Irish SPROUL.

Spruill (2243) Variant of Scottish or northern Irish SPROUL.

Sprung (473) **1.** German: from Middle High German *sprunc* 'spring', topographic name for someone who lived by a spring or well (see also SPRING 2, SPRANG). **2.** Dutch: variant of SPRONG. **3.** Jewish (Ashkenazic): nickname or ornamental name from German *Sprung* 'jump', 'leap', 'crack'.

GIVEN NAMES German 4%. *Achim, Gerhard*.

Sprunger (515) Swiss German: topographic name for someone who lived by a spring or well, a variant of SPRUNG, the suffix *-er* denoting an inhabitant.

Sprunk (129) Dutch: variant of SPRONG.

Spry (1394) English: apparently a nickname for an active, brisk, or smart person. Although *spry* is not recorded in OED until the 18th century, it was probably in colloquial use in the West Country dialect and in Scots much earlier. The word is of obscure origin. The surname is found mainly in Devon, but there is also a modest concentration of bearers in northeastern England.

Spuhler (225) German: **1.** from Middle High German *spuole* 'bobbin', 'shuttle', hence a metonymic occupational name for a wood turner who made spools. **2.** metonymic occupational name for a scribe, from Middle High German *spuol* 'quill'.

GIVEN NAME German 4%. *Hanspeter* (2).

Spurbeck (102) altered spelling of South German SPERBECK.

Spurgeon (2669) English (mainly East Anglia): unexplained.

Spurgin (481) Variant of English SPURGEON.

Spurlin (994) Variant of English SPURLING.

Spurling (944) English (mainly East Anglia): nickname from a diminutive of Middle English *sparewe* 'sparrow'. Compare SPARROW.

Spurlock (3896) English (Somerset): unexplained.

Spurr (618) English (now chiefly Yorkshire): metonymic occupational name for a maker of spurs, from Middle English *spore*, *spure* 'spur'.

Spurrell (108) English: habitational name from Spirewell in Devon or some other similarly named place.

Spurrier (732) English: occupational name for a maker of spurs, from an agent derivative of Middle English *spore*, *spure* 'spur'.

Spychalski (188) Polish: probably from a nickname, **Spychała**, for an idle worker, a variant of Polish dialect *spychacz* 'shirker', 'ducker' (from *spychać* 'to push down').

Spyker (178) Dutch: **1.** metonymic occupational name for a nailsmith, from *spijker* 'nail'. **2.** topographic name from *spijker* 'granary'. Compare SPICKERMAN.

GIVEN NAMES Dutch 4%. *Dirk* (2), *Kryn*.

Squadrito (125) Southern Italian: probably a nickname from an altered form of *scaltrito* 'shrewd', 'pragmatic'.

GIVEN NAMES Italian 31%. *Angelo* (3), *Salvatore* (3), *Biagio, Cirino, Gino, Giuseppe, Sal, Salvo, Sandro, Santi*.

Square (272) Respelling of Scottish **Squair**, a variant of SQUIRE.

Squeo (127) Southern Italian: unexplained.

GIVEN NAMES Italian 28%. *Angelo* (2), *Giovanni* (2), *Sergio* (2), *Alessandro, Ettore, Lorenzo, Rocco, Mario*.

Squibb (404) English: perhaps a nickname for a sarcastic, witty, or spiteful person,

from early modern English *squibbe* 'lampoon', 'satirical attack'. The word, which is probably of imitative origin, is not recorded until the 16th century; the original sense was 'firework'.

Squicciarini (110) Italian (Puglia): unexplained.

GIVEN NAMES Italian 22%. *Carlo* (3), *Vito* (2), *Angelo, Domenico, Mauro, Palma*.

Squier (847) English: variant of SQUIRE.

Squiers (240) English: patronymic from SQUIRE.

Squillace (299) Southern Italian: habitational name from Squallace, a place in Catanzaro province.

GIVEN NAMES Italian 10%. *Sabatino* (2), *Angelo, Giuseppe, Luigi, Salvatore*.

Squillante (267) Italian: nickname for someone with a high-pitched or penetrating voice, from *squillante* 'sharp', 'shrill' (a derivative of *squillare* 'to ring').

GIVEN NAMES Italian 23%. *Alfonso* (4), *Camilo* (3), *Emilio* (3), *Nunzio* (2), *Pasquale* (2), *Angelo, Domenic, Gennaro, Luigi, Matteo, Raffaela*.

Squire (1858) English: status name from Middle English *squyer* 'esquire', 'a man belonging to the feudal rank immediately below that of knight' (from Old French *esquier* 'shield bearer'). At first it denoted a young man of good birth attendant on a knight, or by extension any attendant or servant, but by the 14th century the meaning had been generalized, and referred to social status rather than age. By the 17th century, the term denoted any member of the landed gentry, but this is unlikely to have influenced the development of the surname.

Squires (5338) English: patronymic from SQUIRE.

Squitieri (230) Italian (Sicily): probably a status name from an altered form of *scudiero* 'squire'.

GIVEN NAMES Italian 14%. *Aniello* (2), *Carmine* (2), *Gennaro, Giancarlo, Immaculata, Rocco, Umberto*.

Squyres (409) Variant spelling of English SQUIRES.

Srader (164) Variant of German SCHRADER.

Sramek (213) Czech (**Šrámek**): nickname for a person with a prominent scar, from a diminutive of *šrám* 'scar'.

Srey (107) Cambodian: unexplained.

GIVEN NAMES Cambodian 31%; Other Southeast Asian 5%. *Hoeun* (2), *Lanh* (2), *Sareth* (2), *Bunthoeun, Chhay, Kosal, Nhep, Pheap, Phoeun, Roeuth, Saroeun, Soeuth, Sokhom, Sokunthea, Thavy; Leang, Tha, Yen; Dong, Eng, Leng, Sarin*.

Sridhar (102) Indian (southern states): Hindu name from Sanskrit *śrīdhara* 'possessor of Lakshmi' or 'possessor of good fortune', from *śrī*, a byname of Lakshmi, wife of Vishnu, also meaning 'good fortune' + *dhara* 'holding', 'possessing'. It is an epithet of Vishnu. In South India it is used only as a male given name, but it has come to be used as a family name in the U.S. among people from South India.

GIVEN NAMES Indian 95%. *Srinivasan* (3), *Ashwin* (2), *Kasi* (2), *Srinivas* (2), *Anusha*, *Bala*, *Jayaraman*, *Jayasree*, *Kala*, *Kumar*, *Lalitha*.

Srinivas (114) Indian (southern states): Hindu name from Sanskrit *śrīnivāsa* 'abode of Lakshmi' or 'abode of good fortune', from *śrī* (a byname of Lakshmi, wife of Vishnu, also meaning 'good fortune') + *nivāsa* 'abode'. This name is an epithet of the god Vishnu. In South India this is used only as a male given name, but it has come to be used as a family name in the U.S. among people from South India. Among Tamil and Malayalam speakers who have migrated from their home states, it is a variant of SRINIVASAN.

GIVEN NAMES Indian 91%. *Vijay* (4), *Geeta* (2), *Lakshmi* (2), *Naveen* (2), *Ratna* (2), *Ravi* (2), *Usha* (2), *Ajay*, *Chitra*, *Ganga*, *Girish*, *Jayashree*.

Srinivasan (649) Indian (Kerala, Tamil Nadu): Hindu name from Sanskrit *śrīnivāsa* 'abode of good fortune or prosperity' (see SRINIVAS) + the Tamil-Malayalam third-person masculine singular suffix *-n*. This is only a given name in India, but has come to be used as a family name in the U.S.

GIVEN NAMES Indian 93%. *Ram* (11), *Balaji* (10), *Ravi* (10), *Ramesh* (7), *Anand* (6), *Murali* (6), *Ashok* (5), *Kumar* (5), *Ranganathan* (4), *Sanjay* (4), *Sriram* (4), *Suresh* (4).

Srivastava (422) Indian (northern states): Hindu (Kayasth) name, from Hindi *śrīvāstəv* 'from Srivasta', based on the name of a subgroup of the Kayasth community. Srivasta is the name of an ancient city of northern India (from Sanskrit *śrīvasta* 'abode of wealth').

GIVEN NAMES Indian 95%. *Alok* (10), *Sunil* (8), *Rajesh* (7), *Amit* (6), *Pradeep* (6), *Vinod* (6), *Ashok* (5), *Atul* (5), *Ravi* (5), *Sanjay* (5), *Suresh* (5), *Anil* (4).

Srock (207) Probably an Americanized or Germanized form of a Slavic nickname meaning 'magpie' (see Polish SROKA).

Sroczynski (125) Polish (**Sroczyński**): habitational name for someone from Sroczyn in Poznan voivodeship, named with Polish *sroka* 'magpie'.

GIVEN NAMES Polish 9%. *Jerzy*, *Piotr*, *Zbigniew*, *Zygmunt*.

Sroka (773) Polish: nickname from Polish *sroka* 'magpie'.

GIVEN NAMES Polish 5%. *Jerzy* (2), *Mieczyslaw* (2), *Casimir*, *Elzbieta*, *Jadwiga*, *Kazimierz*, *Stanislaw*, *Wieslaw*, *Wlodzimierz*, *Zbig*.

Sroufe (266) Origin unidentified.

Srour (142) **1.** Muslim (common in Arabic-speaking countries): from a personal name based on Arabic *surūr* 'joy', 'happiness'.

2. Jewish (Sephardic): adoption of the Arabic name.

GIVEN NAMES Arabic 34%; French 5%; Jewish 4%. *Ahmad* (2), *Mohamad* (2), *Moussa* (2), *Ali*, *Alia*, *Amjad*, *Aref*, *Aslan*, *Bassem*, *Chafic*, *Farag*, *Farid*; *Marcel* (2), *Jacques*; *Shlomo* (2).

Staab (1418) German: from Middle High German *stap* 'rod', 'staff', a metonymic occupational name for anyone who carried a staff as a symbol of office.

Staack (180) North German: from Middle Low German *stake* 'rod', 'stake'. Compare STAPLE and STAAB.

GIVEN NAMES German 7%. *Fritz*, *Georg*, *Hans*, *Otto*.

Staal (232) **1.** North German: nickname or metonymic occupational name, from Middle Low German *stāl* 'steel'. Compare English STEELE. **2.** Dutch (**van Staal**,**van der Staal**): habitational name for someone from any of various places called De Staal, for example, one in Izenberge, West Flanders.

GIVEN NAMES German 8%. *Kurt* (2), *Ursel*.

Staas (163) North German and Dutch: from a male personal name, a reduced vernacular form of Latin *Eustacius* (see STACEY).

Staat (207) North German and Dutch: variant of STAAS.

Staats (1795) North German and Dutch: patronymic from *Staat* (see STAAS).

FOREBEARS This was the name of a prominent Dutch family in New Netherland, where it was often spelled **Staets**.

Stabenow (223) German: habitational name from a place so called near Stettin (Szczecin).

GIVEN NAMES German 5%. *Erwin*, *Gerhard*, *Rainer*.

Staber (126) South German: unexplained.

Stabile (1022) Italian (mainly southern): from the medieval personal name *Stabile*, from Latin *stabilis* 'firm', 'constant', 'steadfast'.

GIVEN NAMES Italian 13%. *Angelo* (4), *Antonio* (3), *Vito* (3), *Carmine* (2), *Guiseppe* (2), *Natale* (2), *Pasquale* (2), *Amadeo*, *Benedetto*, *Carmela*, *Dante*, *Domenico*.

Stablein (146) German (**Stäblein**): diminutive of STAAB.

GIVEN NAME German 5%. *Otto* (2).

Stabler (968) **1.** English: occupational name for someone who looked after horses or cattle, from an agent derivative of Middle English *stable* 'stable'. **2.** German (**Stäbler**): occupational name for an official who carried a staff as a symbol of office, Middle High German *stebelære*.

Stables (249) English: topographic name for someone who lived by a stable, or an occupational name for someone employed in one, from Middle English *stable*, plural *stables* (via Old French from Latin *stabulum*, a derivative of *stare* 'to stand'). In Middle English the term was used of the

quarters occupied by cattle as well as those reserved for horses.

Stabley (199) English (Durham): unexplained

Stace (119) English and Irish: variant of STACEY.

Stacer (111) English: unexplained.

Stacey (3188) English and Irish: from a pet form of the medieval male personal name *Stace*, a reduced vernacular form of EUSTACE.

Stach (464) **1.** Polish and Czech: from the personal name *Stach*, a pet form of Polish *Stanisław* or Czech *Stanislav* (see STANISLAW). **2.** German: from a male personal name, a reduced vernacular form of Latin *Eustatius* or *Eustachius* (see STACEY, EUSTACE).

Stache (113) German: variant of STACH 2.

GIVEN NAME German 4%. *Armin*.

Stachel (127) German: from a pet form of STACH 2, coincidentally having the same form as a word meaning 'bristle'.

GIVEN NAME German 6%. *Wolfgang*.

Stachler (132) German: derivative of Middle High German *stachel* 'sting', 'bristle', either a variant of STECHER in any of its many senses, or a nickname for an aggressive person.

Stachnik (202) Polish: derivative of *Stach*, a pet form of the personal name *Stanisław* (see STANISLAW).

GIVEN NAMES Polish 6%. *Grzegorz*, *Jerzy*, *Krzysztof*, *Tadeusz*.

Stachowiak (552) Polish: patronymic from the personal name STACH. This surname is also well established in German-speaking countries.

Stachowicz (249) Polish: patronymic from the personal name STACH.

GIVEN NAMES Polish 9%. *Bogdan* (2), *Lucyna* (2), *Zofia* (2), *Jozef*, *Mariusz*, *Stanislaw*.

Stachowski (352) Polish: habitational name for someone from places named Stachów, one of which is in Warszawa voivodeship, another in what is now Ukraine, or from Stachowo in Warszawa and Ciechanów voivodeships. The place name is from the personal name STACH. This surname is also found in German-speaking lands.

Stachura (377) Polish, Czech, and Slovak (**Štachura**): derivative of the personal name *Stach*, a pet form of *Stanislav*, Polish *Stanisław* (see STANISLAW).

GIVEN NAMES Polish 7%. *Stanislaw* (2), *Agnieszka*, *Bogdan*, *Malgorzata*, *Marcin*, *Slawomir*, *Waclaw*, *Witold*.

Stachurski (149) Polish: habitational name for someone from Stachura in Kielce voivodeship, or another place of this name, now in Belarus.

GIVEN NAMES Polish 10%. *Henryka*, *Ignatius*, *Jerzy*, *Wieslaw*, *Witold*, *Zygmunt*.

Stack (4693) **1.** English: nickname for a large, well-built man, from Middle English *stack* 'haystack' (from Old Norse *stakkr*).

The surname is now less common in England than in Ireland (especially County Kerry), where it was first taken in the 13th century; it has been Gaelicized **Stac**. **2.** German: variant of STAACK. **3.** Americanized form of Polish or Czech STACH.

Stacker (191) North German (**Stäcker**): from an agent derivative of Middle Low German *steken* 'to stab or cut', probably an occupational name for someone who castrated or slaughtered farm animals.

Stackhouse (1906) English (mainly West Midlands): probably a habitational name from a place so named in North Yorkshire.

Stackpole (550) Irish (of Welsh origin): habitational name from a place in Pembrokeshire called Stackpole from a stack of rocks on the coast at the entrance to Broadhaven, from which settlers of Norman descent made their way into Ireland; probably derived from Old Norse *stakkr* 'stack' + *polr* 'pool'. The name is recorded in Dublin as early as 1200, and has been Gaelicized as **de Stacapúl**; bearers were also known as **Galldubh** 'black stranger'.

Stackpoole (102) Irish (of Welsh origin): variant of STACKPOLE.

Stacks (696) English: variant or patronymic form of STACK.

Stacy (6097) English and Irish: variant spelling of STACEY.

Stade (279) German: habitational name from any of various places so named, for example on the River Elbe.
GIVEN NAMES German 9%. *Bernhard, Bertel, Erhardt, Erna, Hannelore, Kurt, Wolfgang.*

Stadel (243) German: topographic name for someone who lived near a barn or granary, Middle High German *stadel*.

Stadelman (295) German (**Stadelmann**): variant of STADLER.

Stader (208) South German: topographic name for someone who lived by a riverbank or lakeside, from Middle High German *stade* 'bank', 'shore' + *-er* suffix denoting an inhabitant.

Stadick (125) German: unexplained; compare STADIG.

Stadig (106) German: unexplained; compare STADICK.
GIVEN NAMES German 5%. *Fritz, Otto.*

Stading (113) German (**Städing**): variant of STEDING.

Stadler (2027) German: from a derivative of Middle High German *stadel* 'barn', 'granary', hence a topographic name for someone who lived near a barn or granary, or occupational name for an official who was responsible for receiving tithes into the manorial storehouse. The surname is also occasionally borne by Ashkenazic Jews, apparently as an adoption of the German surname. It is also found in Slovenia, where it is commonly spelled **Štadler**.
GIVEN NAMES German 4%. *Alois (3), Gerhard (3), Hans (2), Otto (2), Alfons, Ernst, Erwin, Franz, Fritz, Heiner, Johann, Kurt.*

Stadnik (192) Ukrainian: occupational name from *stadnyk* 'chief shepherd'.
GIVEN NAMES Russian 9%; Polish 5%. *Vladimir (2), Gennadiy, Igor, Leonid, Mikhail, Nikolay, Oksana, Oleg; Beata, Danuta, Halina, Katarzyna.*

Stadt (165) German and Dutch (**van de(r) Stadt**): from Middle High German, Middle Dutch *stat* 'town', 'city', hence a nickname for someone who had come from a city to the country.

Stadtlander (173) North German (**Stadtländer**): topographic name for someone who lived on or rented land belonging to a nearby town.

Stadtler (120) German: **1.** variant of STADLER. **2.** habitational name from a place named Stadtl, in Bohemia.

Stadtmiller (171) Partly Americanized form of German STADTMUELLER.

Stadtmueller (127) German (**Stadtmüller**): from Middle High German *stet* 'place', 'town' + *müller* 'miller', hence an occupational name for a miller who ground the grain for a town.
GIVEN NAMES German 8%. *Aloys, Franz, Kurt.*

Staebell (197) Dutch: from French *stable*, Dutch *stabiel* 'stable', 'steady', 'firm', hence a nickname for someone of reliable character.

Staebler (220) German (**Stäbler**): see STABLER 2.

Staehle (232) German (**Stähle**) and Dutch: variant of STAAL.

Staff (629) English (mainly Norfolk): from Middle English *staf* 'rod', 'staff'; a nickname for a tall, thin person, or a metonymic occupational name for anyone who carried a staff of office, a reminder of his right to inflict physical discipline.

Staffa (169) Italian: metonymic occupational name for a maker of stirrups, from *staffa* 'stirrup'.
GIVEN NAMES Italian 11%. *Gaetano (2), Enrico, Francesco, Pasqualino, Raffaele.*

Staffen (122) Dutch or German: variant of STEFFAN.

Staffieri (203) Italian: patronymic from **Staffiero**, an occupational name for a manservant.
GIVEN NAMES Italian 15%. *Angelo, Dino, Domenic, Ezio, Pasquale, Vittorio.*

Stafford (16226) English: habitational name from any of the various places in England so called, which do not all share the same etymology. The county seat of Staffordshire (which is probably the main source of the surname) is named from Old English *stæð* 'landing place' + *ford* 'ford'. Examples in Devon seem to have as their first element Old English *stān* 'stone', and one in Sussex is probably named with Old English *stēor* 'steer', 'bullock'.

Stage (857) **1.** North German: from Middle Low German *stake* 'rod'. Compare STAPLE, STAAB. **2.** Dutch: apparently a metonymic

occupational name for a scaffolder, from Middle Dutch *stage, staedge, staetge* 'scaffolding'.

Stager (699) Swiss German (**Stäger**): variant of STEGER.

Stagg (1282) English: nickname from Old English *stagga* 'male deer', 'stag'. In northern dialects of Middle English the term was also used of a young horse, perhaps under Scandinavian influence, and in some cases this meaning may lie behind the original application of the name.

Staggers (412) English: unexplained.
GIVEN NAMES French 4%. *Clovis, Veronique.*

Staggs (3123) English: patronymic from STAGG.

Stagliano (246) Southern Italian: probably a derivative of **Staglio**, probably a topographic or status name from Calabrian *stagliu, stagghiu* 'rented land' (from medieval Latin *extallium*).
GIVEN NAMES Italian 13%. *Carmine, Gino, Guiseppe, Salvatore, Vito.*

Stagnaro (180) Italian: occupational name for a pewterer or tinker, from a derivative of *stagnare* 'to plate or solder'.
GIVEN NAMES Italian 18%; Spanish 5%. *Angelo (7), Leopoldo (2), Alida, Erasmo, Mario Alberto; Florido, Ines, Luis.*

Stagner (899) Origin uncertain; perhaps an altered spelling of German STEGNER.

Stagnitta (116) Italian: topographic name from a diminitive of STAGNO 'pool'.
GIVEN NAMES Italian 20%. *Rosario (2), Salvatore (2), Carmelo, Concetta, Natale, Rocco.*

Stagno (103) Italian: topographic name from *stagno* 'pond', 'pool', from Latin *stagnum*, or a habitational name from a place named with this word, such as Stagno Lombardo in Cremona.
GIVEN NAMES Italian 36%. *Domenic (3), Angelo (2), Orlando (2), Arcangelo, Arturo, Pietro, Sergio, Tino.*

Staheli (166) **1.** Swiss German: occupational name for an armorer, from a diminutive of STAHL. **2.** nickname for someone with a firm personality.
GIVEN NAME German 6%. *Otto (3).*

Stahl (8941) German: metonymic occupational name for a smith or armorer, from Middle High German *stāl* 'steel', 'armor'.

Stahlberg (182) **1.** German: habitational name from any of several places so named in Rhineland, the Palatinate, and Saxony. **2.** Swedish (**Ståhlberg**): ornamental name composed of the elements *stáhl*, an ornamental spelling of *stål* 'steel' + *berg* 'mountain', 'hill'.
GIVEN NAMES German 7%. *Kurt, Lothar, Rainer.*

Stahle (280) **1.** German (**Stähle**): variant of STAHL. **2.** Swedish (**Ståhle**): soldier's name from *ståhl*, an ornamental spelling of *stål* 'steel'.

Stahlecker (223) German: habitational name for someone from any of several places called Stahleck or Stahlegg, with the first part derived from Old High German *stal* 'seat', 'place'.

GIVEN NAMES German 5%. *Helmuth, Otto, Rinehart.*

Stahler (523) German (also **Stähler**): metonymic occupational name for a foundry worker, from an agent derivative of Middle High German *stal* 'steel'.

Stahley (399) Americanized form of South German and Swiss **Stäheli** or **Stähli**, from a diminutive of Middle High German *stal* 'steel', 'armor' (see STAHL).

Stahlhut (181) German: nickname for a soldier who wore a metal helmet, from Middle High German *stālhuot* 'steel helmet'.

GIVEN NAMES German 4%. *Heinz, Kurt.*

Stahlman (619) German (**Stahlmann**): variant of STAHL.

Stahlnecker (122) Apparently of German origin (see STALNAKER).

Stahly (314) See STAHLEY.

Stahmer (164) North German: variant of STAMER.

GIVEN NAMES German 17%; Scandinavian 4%. *Fritz* (3), *Gerhard* (2), *Kurt* (2), *Albrecht; Karsten* (2), *Carsten.*

Stahnke (233) Eastern German: from a German pet form of the Slavic personal name *Stanislav* (see STANISLAW).

GIVEN NAMES German 6%. *Dietmar, Gerhard, Helmut.*

Stahr (449) German: **1.** nickname from a word meaning 'starling'. Compare STARLING. **2.** nickname from the Slavic word *stary* 'old', either an identifying name for the older of two bearers of the same name or, in some cases, an identifying name for an 'old' inhabitant, as distinct from a newcomer.

GIVEN NAMES German 4%. *Bernd, Fritz, Helmuth, Kurt.*

Stahura (115) Czech and Slovak: variant of STACHURA.

Stai (236) Norwegian: habitational name from either of two farmsteads in Hedmark, so named from Old Norse *staðr* 'riverbank'.

Staiano (141) Southern Italian: habitational name from some minor place named with the Latin personal name *Staius.*

GIVEN NAMES Italian 18%. *Mario* (2), *Claudio, Giulio, Sal, Salvatore.*

Staib (375) German (Swabia): variant of STEIB.

GIVEN NAMES German 4%. *Hans, Kurt.*

Staiger (512) South German: topographic name for someone living on or at a steep path, from Middle High German *steige* + *(e)r* suffix denoting an inhabitant.

GIVEN NAMES German 8%. *Kurt* (7), *Gerhard* (2), *Alois, Dieter, Egon, Hans, Horst, Reinhardt, Walther.*

Stailey (190) Probably a variant form of English STALEY.

Stain (103) English: habitational name from Stain in Lincolnshire, named with Old Norse *steinn* 'stone', 'rock'.

Stainback (359) Perhaps an Americanized spelling of German **Steinbäck** (see STEINBACK).

Stainbrook (500) Apparently English, from a lost place, probably named with Old English *stān* or Old Norse *steinn* 'stone' + *brōc* 'brook', 'creek'.

Staines (257) English: habitational name from a place on the Thames west of London, apparently named with the plural of Old English *stān* 'stone'. The reference may be to milestones on the Roman road that ran through the town.

Stains (162) Variant spelling of English STAINES.

Stainton (117) English: habitational name from any of many places in northern England called Stainton, named with Old Norse *steinn* 'stone', 'rock', + Old English *tūn* 'settlement'.

Stair (964) English: from Middle English *stegher* 'stair' (Old English *stæger*). In Kent and Sussex this was a topographic name denoting someone who lived on rising ground.

Stairs (408) English: variant of STAIR.

Stake (412) Irish: variant of STACK.

Stakem (111) Possibly Irish or English: unexplained.

Staker (470) English: occupational name for someone who made and drove in stakes, or a topographic name for someone who lived near a boundary post for example, from a derivative of Middle English *stake* 'post', 'stake'.

Stakes (163) English: topographic name for someone who lived by a prominent post or stake, for example a boundary marker, from Middle English *stake* 'post', 'stake', or from the same word used as a nickname for a tall, thin person.

GIVEN NAMES French 7%. *Camille* (2), *Kearney.*

Stalbaum (114) South German (**Württemberg**): topographic name from Middle High German *stalboum* 'mature tree'. Compare STALLBAUMER.

Stalcup (941) Possibly of English origin, a habitational name from a lost or unidentified place.

Stalder (669) South German: from Middle High German *stalde* 'steep path', 'steep slope', hence a topographic name for someone who lived on a steep slope, or a habitational name for someone from a place named with this word, as for example Stalden in Switzerland.

Staley (6522) **1.** English: byname from Middle English *staley* 'resolute', 'reliable', a reduced form of STALLARD. **2.** Belgian French: from Old French *estalee* 'fish trap', hence possibly a metonymic occupational name for a fisherman, or topographic name

for someone who lived near where fish traps were set.

Stalford (112) Scottish: apparently a habitational name from a lost or unidentified place.

Stalker (1225) Scottish and northwestern English: occupational name or nickname for a stealthy person, from an agent derivative of Middle English *stalk(en)* 'to stalk or approach stealthily, for example in hunting deer'.

Stall (700) North German: from Middle Low German *stal* 'stable'; a topographic name for someone who lived by a stable or possibly an metonymic occupational name for a stable lad.

Stallard (1495) English: byname for a valiant or resolute person, from a reduced pronunciation of Middle English *stalward, stalworth* 'stalwart' (an Old English compound of *stæl* 'place' + *wierðe* 'worthy').

Stallbaumer (172) South German (**Württemberg**): topographic or occupational name from Middle High German *stalboum* 'mature tree', 'framing post'. Bearers of the surname in Germany are found predominantly in the area of Biberach an der Riss.

Stallcup (337) See STALCUP.

Staller (330) **1.** South German: topographic name from Middle High German *stal* 'seat', 'place' + *-er* suffix denoting an inhabitant, or a habitational name for someone from any of several places named Stall, for example in the Rhineland and in Carinthia. **2.** occupational name for a worker in a cattle or sheep shelter or fold, from Middle High German *stal* 'place', 'stall', 'barn'.

GIVEN NAMES German 5%. *Erwin* (3), *Kurt, Nikolaus, Wolfram.*

Stalling (329) North German: unexplained.

Stallings (6013) Probably an altered form of German STALLING.

Stallins (115) Probably an altered form of German STALLING.

Stallman (707) **1.** German (**Stallmann**): variant of STALLER. **2.** German: topographic name for someone who lived in a muddy place, from the dialect word *stal.* **3.** English: habitational name from Stalmine in Lancashire, named probably with Old English *stæll* 'creek', 'pool' + Old Norse *mynni* 'mouth'. **4.** English: possibly an occupational name for a stockman, from Middle English *stall* 'stall' + *man* 'man', or a topographic name for someone who lived by some cattle stalls.

Stallone (436) Italian: from *stallone* 'stallion', applied either as a nickname for someone thought to resemble a stallion, or as a metonymic occupational name for someone who bred horses.

GIVEN NAMES Italian 20%. *Vito* (8), *Angelo* (3), *Antonella, Cosmo, Dino, Filomena, Gasper, Gaspere, Giovanni, Luigi, Nunzio, Premo.*

Stallons (114) Origin unidentified.

Stalls (254) Perhaps an Americanized spelling of Dutch **Stals**: **1.** variant of STAAL. **2.** hence a metonymic occupational name for a cowhand, from *stal* 'cattle-stall', 'byre'.

Stallsmith (201) Partly Americanized form of German **Stahlschmidt**, **Stahlschmitt**, an occupational name for a smith, from Middle High German *stāl* 'steel' + *smit* 'smith'.

Stallsworth (125) English: variant of STALLARD.

Stallworth (1759) English: variant of STALLARD.

Stalnaker (1480) Altered spelling of German **Stallecker** or **Stahlecker**, a topographic name, from Middle High German *stal* 'seat', 'place', 'corral', 'stall' + *ecke* 'corner' or *äcker* (from *äckerer*) 'owner (of a field)', 'farmer'.

Staloch (138) Origin unidentified.

Stalsberg (111) Probably an Americanized form of German STOLZENBERG.

GIVEN NAMES German 7%. *Gerhard, Kurt, Otto.*

Stalter (770) South German: variant of STALDER.

Stalvey (522) Metathesized variant of English STAVELY.

Stalzer (373) South German: of uncertain origin, possibly a variant of STELZER.

GIVEN NAMES German 12%. *Helmuth* (3), *Bernhard* (2), *Franziska* (2), *Kurt* (2), *Ernst, Erwin, Helmut, Mathias, Reinhold, Siegfried.*

Stam (498) **1.** Dutch: nickname for a heavily built man, from *stam* 'stem', '(tree)-trunk'. **2.** Jewish (Ashkenazic): variant spelling of STAMM. **3.** Altered spelling of German STAMM.

GIVEN NAMES Dutch 4%. *Gerrit* (2), *Bernardus, Dirk, Marinus, Pieter, Roelof.*

Staman (101) probably a reduced form of German **Stammann**, a variant of STAMM 2.

Stamas (203) Greek: from a pet form of the personal name STAMATIS.

Stamatis (147) Greek: from a personal name based on medieval Greek *stamatō* 'stop' (a derivative of classical Greek *histēmi*), an omen name expressing the wish of parents to stop giving birth to girls, or given to a boy after the death of older siblings and meaning 'stop dying'. *Stamatios* is the name of two saints venerated in the Eastern Church.

GIVEN NAMES Greek 5%. *Anastasios, Despina, Lazaros.*

Stambaugh (1982) Americanized spelling of German **Stambach**, a habitational name from a place so named near Zweibrücken in the Palatinate.

Stamer (210) English and North German: nickname for someone who stammered, from Middle English, Middle Low German *stamer* 'stammerer'.

GIVEN NAMES German 6%. *Almut, Frieda, Kurt.*

Stamets (150) Possibly a respelling of German **Stamitz**, a variant of STEINMETZ in the Sudeten region.

Stamey (1302) Possibly of English origin: unexplained.

Stamler (196) Jewish (Ashkenazic): nickname for a stammerer, Yiddish *shtamler.*

Stamm (2414) **1.** North German: habitational name from any of various places in East Prussia named Stamm. **2.** German and Swiss German: from Middle High German, Middle Low German *stam* 'family tree', 'descent', 'stock', hence 'son and heir', possibly applied as a nickname for the eldest son of a family. **3.** Jewish (Ashkenazic): ornamental name from German *Stamm* 'stem', 'stock', or perhaps in some cases a short form of names such as *Aronstam* 'stock of AARON' (the first high priest), **Kohenstam** 'stock of the kohenim' (see COHEN), and **Löwenstam** 'stock of the Levites' (see LEVI and LOWE 2).

Stammen (192) Dutch: derivative of STAM 1.

Stammer (321) **1.** English: from the Old English personal name *Stānmǣr*, composed of the elements *stān* 'stone' + *mǣr* 'famous'. **2.** English: habitational name from Stanmer in Sussex, so called from Old English *stān* 'stone' + *mere* 'lake'. **3.** North German: variant of STAMER.

GIVEN NAMES German 4%. *Detlef, Dieter, Kurt.*

Stamos (385) Greek: from a pet form of the personal name STAMATIS, also short for composite names such as **Stamokostas** 'Constantine, son of Stamatis'.

GIVEN NAMES Greek 6%. *Spiro* (2), *Antonios, Aristotle, Despina, Dimitrios, Kosta, Lambros, Spyros, Stamos.*

Stamp (1120) **1.** German: metonymic occupational name for someone who worked at a crushing mill, from Middle Low German *stamp* 'pestle', 'crusher'. **2.** English: variant of STAMPS.

Stampe (103) German: habitational name from a place so named near Kiel.

GIVEN NAMES German 4%. *Hans, Kurt.*

Stamper (4055) English: from the agent derivative of Middle English *stampen* 'to stamp'; probably an occupational name for a worker at a mint, someone who stamped coins.

Stampfli (158) South German: altered spelling of **Stempfli**, a metonymic occupational name for someone who worked at a crushing mill, from a diminutive of Middle High German *stampf* 'pestle', 'crusher', 'crushing mill'. In some instances it may have been applied as a nickname for a small, fat person.

GIVEN NAMES German 8%. *Fritz, Hans, Markus, Otto.*

Stampley (337) Variant of STAMPFLI.

Stamps (2114) English (of Norman origin): habitational name from Étampes in Seine-et-Oise; the place name is of Celtic origin.

Stan (292) Romanian: unexplained. Possibly from a shortened form of the Slavic personal name *Stanislav* (see STANISLAW).

GIVEN NAMES Romanian 16%. *Alexandru* (3), *Florea* (2), *Gheorghe* (2), *Mihai* (2), *Anca, Dumitru, Floare, Matei, Nicolae, Nicoleta, Niculae, Petre.*

Stanage (114) English: habitational name from Stanage in Derbyshire.

Stanaland (310) Variant of **Staniland**, an English topographic name for someone who lived on stony ground, from Middle English *stany* 'stony' + *lond* 'land', or of Norwegian origin. Compare STANGELAND.

Stanard (365) English: variant spelling of STANNARD.

Stanaway (219) Possibly a variant form of English **Stanway**, a habitational name from any of the places called Stanaway, in Essex, Gloucestershire, Herefordshire, and Shropshire, all named with Old English *stān* 'stone' + *weg* 'track', 'road'.

Stanback (289) Perhaps an altered form of German **Stam(m)bach** (see STAMBAUGH) (see also STAINBACK).

GIVEN NAMES French 5%. *Cecile, Monique, Vernice.*

Stanberry (470) Variant of STANBROUGH.

Stanbery (241) Variant of STANBROUGH.

Stanbro (159) Variant of STANBROUGH.

Stanbrough (167) English: habitational name from Stanborough in Devon, so named from Old English *stān* 'stone' + *beorg* 'hill', 'tumulus'. There is a place called Stanbury in West Yorkshire near Haworth, but it does not seem to have given rise to the surname.

Stanbury (123) English: variant spelling of STANBROUGH.

Stancato (123) Southern Italian: from *stancato* 'tired', an informal equivalent (especially southern) of STANCO 1.

GIVEN NAMES Italian 13%. *Antonio, Francesco, Pasquale.*

Stancel (112) Probably an altered spelling of STANCIL or possibly of German STENZEL.

Stancell (119) See STANCEL.

Stanchfield (264) English: unexplained; probably a habitational name from a lost or unidentified place. Neither the place name nor the surname are found in current British records. Compare STINCHFIELD.

Stancik (157) Czech and Slovak (**Stančík**): from a pet form of the personal name *Stanislav* (see STANISLAW).

Stancil (1651) English: habitational name from a place so named in South Yorkshire.

Stancill (202) English: variant spelling of STANCIL.

Stancliff (212) English (West Yorkshire): habitational name, probably from a minor place such as Stonecliff or Stancliffe in

Agbrigg, West Yorkshire, so called from Old English *stān* 'stone' + *clif* 'slope'.

Stanco (304) Italian: **1.** nickname from *stanco* 'tired', 'exhausted', 'fading'. **2.** (Venetia-Giulia): from a pet form of the Slavic personal name *Stanislav* (see STANISLAWSKI).

GIVEN NAMES Italian 27%. *Angelo* (10), *Pasquale* (3), *Rocco* (3), *Amerigo* (2), *Carmine* (2), *Vito* (2), *Alessandra, Aniello, Antonio, Carmela, Concetta, Donato.*

Stanczak (331) Polish (**Stańczak**): patronymic from *Staniek*, a pet form of the personal name *Stanisław* (see STANISLAW).

GIVEN NAMES Polish 6%. *Eugeniusz, Ignacy, Krzysztof, Mariusz, Stanislaw, Zigmund.*

Stanczyk (309) Polish (**Stańczyk**): derivative of *Staniek*, a pet form of the personal name *Stanisław* (see STANISLAW).

GIVEN NAMES Polish 8%. *Tadeusz* (3), *Zbigniew* (2), *Jaroslaw, Zdzislaw.*

Standaert (125) Dutch: metonymic occupational name for the standard bearer of a regiment.

Standafer (106) See STANDIFER.

Standage (160) English: variant of STANDISH.

Standard (690) English: habitational name from Standard Hill in Ninfield, Sussex.

Standefer (347) See STANDIFER.

Standen (274) English: habitational name from any of various places, for example in Berkshire, Lancashire, and Wiltshire, so called from Old English *stān* 'stone' + *denu* 'valley', or from another on the Isle of Wight, the second element of which is Old English *dūn* 'hill'.

Stander (411) English: unexplained.

Standerfer (195) Variant of STANDIFER.

Standfield (122) Altered form of English STANFIELD.

Standifer (978) Americanized form of German **Steindörfer**, a habitational name for someone from a place called Steindorf. Compare STANDEFER, STANDERFER.

Standiford (461) Probably an Americanized form of German **Steindörfer** (see STANDIFER).

Standing (282) English (chiefly Sussex): variant of STANDEN, or a habitational name from a place in Lancashire with the same etymology.

Standish (1288) English: habitational name from a place in Lancashire (now part of Greater Manchester), so named from Old English *stān* 'stone' + *edisc* 'pasture'. There is another place so named in Gloucestershire, but it does not seem to be the source of the surname.

FOREBEARS Myles Standish (?1584–1656) was a soldier of fortune, from 1620 captain of the *Mayflower* Pilgrims at Plymouth Colony. Little is known of his origins and early life, but in his will he claimed to be descended from a leading Catholic family, the Standishes of Standish, Lancashire,

England. He also claimed to have been deprived of his inheritance, a claim not confirmed.

Standlee (268) Altered spelling of STANDLEY.

Standley (1652) Variant of English STANLEY.

Standridge (1678) English: habitational name from a place so called in Lancashire.

Standring (160) English (Lancashire): unexplained.

Stanek (1994) Czech (**Staněk**) and Polish: from a pet form of the personal name *Stanislav* (Czech), *Stanisław* (Polish) (see STANISLAW).

Stanfield (4114) English (Leicestershire): habitational name from either of two places called Stanfield, in Norfolk and Staffordshire, or a topographic name from Middle English *stan(e)* 'stone' + *feld* 'field'.

Stanfill (1291) Altered form of English STANFIELD.

Stanford (7151) English: habitational name from any of various places named Stanford, for example in Bedfordshire, Kent, and Norfolk, or Stanford Dingley in Berkshire, Stanford in the Vale in Oxfordshire, or Stanford le Hope in Essex, etc., all named from Old English *stān* 'stone' + *ford* 'ford'.

FOREBEARS An early bearer, Thomas Stanford of England, settled in Charlestown, MA, in the mid 17th century and started a family line that includes Leland Stanford (1824–93), the railroad developer who was governor of CA, a U.S. senator, and the founding benefactor of Stanford University.

Stanforth (178) English: variant of STANFORD.

Stang (1230) German and Jewish (Ashkenazic): from Middle High German *stang*, German *Stange* 'pole', 'shaft', hence a nickname for a tall, thin person, a metonymic occupational name for a maker of wooden shafts for spears and the like, or a metonymic occupational name for a soldier.

Stanga (164) Altered spelling of German STANGE or STANGER.

Stange (800) German: variant of STANG.

GIVEN NAMES German 6%. *Kurt* (4), *Otto* (3), *Arno, Detlef, Dieter, Erwin, Fritz, Heinrich, Horst, Ingo, Klaus, Manfred.*

Stangel (345) German and Jewish (Ashkenazic): from a diminutive of STANG.

Stangeland (295) Norwegian: habitational name from any of six farmsteads in Rogaland and Hordaland named in Old Norse as *Stangaland*, from *stǫng* 'pole', 'bar' + *land* 'land', 'farm'; the significance of this is not clear.

GIVEN NAMES Scandinavian 13%. *Alf* (2), *Sig* (2), *Lars, Nils, Thoralf.*

Stanger (1262) **1.** English (mainly Newcastle and Durham): of uncertain origin, probably a derivative of northern Middle English *stang* 'pole' (of Old Norse

origin). Possible meanings include a topographic name for someone who lived by a pole or stake (compare STAKES) or an occupational name for someone armed with one. Alternatively, it may be a nickname for someone who had 'ridden the stang', i.e. been carried on a pole through the streets as an object of derision, in punishment for some misdemeanor. However, this custom is of uncertain antiquity. **2.** Orcadian: probably a habitational name from a minor place called Stanagar in the parish of Stromness. **3.** German: occupational name for a maker of shafts for spears and the like, from an agent derivative of Middle High German *stange* 'pole', 'shaft'.

Stangl (590) South German (Austria): diminutive of STANG 2.

GIVEN NAMES German 5%. *Franz* (2), *Otto* (2), *Gertraud, Jochen, Kurt, Wilhelm.*

Stangland (145) Probably an altered form of STANGELAND.

Stangle (348) Possibly an Americanized spelling of STANGEL.

Stangler (279) South German: variant of STANGER 3.

Stango (232) Reduced form of southern Italian SANTANGELO.

GIVEN NAMES Italian 19%. *Rocco* (4), *Carmine* (2), *Dino, Domenic, Gennaro, Santo, Ugo.*

Stanhope (776) English: habitational name from a place in County Durham, so called from Old English *stān* 'stone' + *hop* 'enclosed valley'.

Stanich (332) **1.** Serbian or Croatian (**Stanić**): a patronymic or metronymic from a short form of the personal names *Stanislav* (see STANISLAW), or its female cognate **Stanislava**, or any other personal name beginning with *Stani-*. The female short form *Stana* was sometimes given to a girl in a family where only girls were being born, because it was understood as a derivative of *stati* 'stop'. **2.** Slovenian (**Stanič**): patronymic from the personal name *Stane*, short form of *Stanislav* (see STANISLAW).

Stanick (110) Americanized spelling of **Staník**, a Czech and Slovak pet form of *Stanislav* (see STANISLAW), or of a related Polish, Serbian, Croatian, or Slovenian name (see STANEK, STANICH).

Staniec (123) Polish: from a derivative of the personal name *Stanisław* (see STANISLAW).

GIVEN NAMES Polish 8%. *Andrzej, Arkadiusz, Casimir, Irena.*

Stanifer (256) See STANDIFER.

Stanis (214) **1.** Americanized form of Polish **Stanisz** (see STANISH). **2.** Greek: probably a derivative of the Slavic personal name STANISLAW, although it has also been associated with the Greek vocabulary word *stani* 'sheepfold', 'pen'.

Stanish (326) Americanized form of Polish **Stanisz**, a pet form of the personal name *Stanisław* (see STANISLAW).

Stanislaus (120) From a Latinized form of the Slavic personal name Stanislav (see STANISLAW).

Stanislaw (253) Polish (**Stanisław**): from the personal name *Stanisław*, composed of the Slavic elements *stani* 'become' + *slav* 'glory', 'fame', 'praise'. This surname is well established in German-speaking lands.

Stanislawski (343) Polish (**Stanisławski**): habitational name for someone from any of various places called Stanisław, Stanisławów, or Stanisławice, named with the personal name *Stanisław* (see STANISLAW).

Staniszewski (351) Polish: habitational name for someone from Staniszewo in Gdańsk and Poznań voivodeships, or Staniszów or Staniszewice in Radom voivodeship.
GIVEN NAMES Polish 10%. *Krzysztof* (2), *Elzbieta, Jerzy, Krystyna, Mieczyslaw, Sylwester, Wieslaw, Zdzislaw, Zygmunt.*

Stank (167) Variant of German STANKE.

Stanke (453) German: from a German pet form of the Slavic personal name *Stanislav* (see STANISLAW).
GIVEN NAMES German 5%. *Erhart, Fritz, Gerhard, Guenter, Rainer, Rudi, Siegfried.*

Stankevich (143) Belorussian: patronymic from *Stanek* or *Stanko*, pet forms of the personal name *Stanislav* (see STANISLAW).

Stankewicz (102) Variant of Polish STAN-KIEWICZ.

Stankey (171) **1.** Americanized form of German STANKE. **2.** Shortened Americanized form of Polish STANKIEWICZ or Belorussian STANKEVICH.

Stankiewicz (910) Polish: patronymic from *Stanek* or *Stanko*, pet forms of the personal name *Stanisław* (see STANISLAW).
GIVEN NAMES Polish 11%. *Pawel* (3), *Andrzej* (2), *Irena* (2), *Jaroslaw* (2), *Tadeusz* (2), *Zbigniew* (2), *Bogdan, Boguslaw, Casimir, Czeslaw, Halina.*

Stanko (941) **1.** Polish: from a pet form of the personal name *Stanisław* (see STANISLAW). **2.** Slovenian and Slovak: from the personal name *Stanko*, pet form of *Stanislav* (see STANISLAW).

Stankovic (101) Serbian and Croatian (**Stanković**): patronymic from the personal name *Stanko*, pet form of *Stanislav* (see STANISLAW) or any other personal name beginning with *Stani-*.
GIVEN NAMES South Slavic 44%. *Dragan* (2), *Goran* (2), *Ljubisa* (2), *Biljana, Blagoje, Branko, Drago, Milivoje, Miodrag, Mladen, Novica, Predrag, Vladislav.*

Stankovich (182) Serbian (**Stanković**): see STANKOVIC.

Stankowski (204) Polish: habitational name for someone from either of two places named Stankowo, in Leszno and Olsztyn voivodeships. The place name is derived from *Stanek*, a pet form of the personal name *Stanisław* (see STANISLAW).
GIVEN NAMES Polish 11%. *Jerzy* (3), *Bogdan* (2), *Janusz* (2), *Zbigniew, Zigmund.*

Stankus (444) Polish: from a pet form of the personal name *Stanisław* (see STANISLAW).

Stanley (32463) **1.** English: habitational name from any of the various places, for example in Derbyshire, County Durham, Gloucestershire, Staffordshire, Wiltshire, and West Yorkshire, so named from Old English *stān* 'stone' + *lēah* 'wood', 'clearing'. **2.** Americanized form of any of various like-sounding names in other European languages, for example Polish STANISLAW-SKI and Greek **Anastasiou**.
FOREBEARS The explorer and journalist Sir Henry Morton Stanley (1841–1904) was born John Rowlands in Denbigh, Wales, but traveled as a cabin boy in 1858 from Liverpool, England, to New Orleans, LA, where he was adopted by a merchant surnamed Stanley. From the late 1860s he worked as a correspondent for the *New York Herald*, and traveled extensively in Africa.

Stannard (822) English (East Anglia): from the Middle English personal name *Stanhard* (Old English *Stānheard*), composed of the elements *stān* 'stone' + *heard* 'hardy', 'brave', 'strong'.

Stano (286) **1.** Italian (Sicily): from a reduced form of the Slavic personal name *Stanislao* (see STANISLAW). **2.** Italian (**Stanò**): habitational name from either of two places so named in Cosenza and Reggio di Calabria. **3.** Czech and Slovak: from a pet form of the personal name *Stanislav* (see STANISLAW).

Stanovich (133) Serbian and Croatian (**Stanović**): patronymic from a shortened form of the Slavic personal name *Stanislav* (see STANISLAW).
GIVEN NAME South Slavic 5%. *Milan* (3).

Stanphill (224) English: variant of STAN-FILL, itself a variant of STANFIELD.

Stansberry (1229) English: variant of STANBROUGH.

Stansbery (249) English: variant of STAN-BROUGH.

Stansbury (1916) English: probably a variant of STANBROUGH.

Stansel (283) Variant of English STANCIL or possibly an Americanized spelling of German STANZEL or STENZEL.

Stansell (1109) **1.** English: possibly a variant spelling of STANCIL. **2.** Possibly an Anglicized or Americanized spelling of German STANZEL or STENZEL.

Stansfield (611) English: **1.** habitational name from a place in West Yorkshire, probably named with the genitive case of the Old English personal name *Stān* 'stone', a byname or short form of any of various compound names with this as the first element (compare, for example, STAMMER, STANNARD) + Old English *feld* 'pasture', 'open country'. **2.** alternatively, it may be a topographic name from Middle English *stanesfeld* 'open country of the (standing) stone', with reference to a prominent

monolith. There are other places so called, for example in Suffolk, but the distribution suggests that the one in Yorkshire is the source of the surname.

Stant (201) English and Welsh: unexplained.

Stanton (13313) English: habitational name from any of the extremely numerous places throughout England so called from Old English *stān* 'stone' + *tūn* 'enclosure', 'settlement'. Most of them are named for their situation on stony ground, but in the case of Stanton Harcourt in Oxfordshire and Stanton Drew in Avon the reference is to the proximity of prehistoric stone monuments. The name has also sometimes been chosen by Ashkenazic Jews as an Americanized form of various like-sounding Jewish surnames. This surname has long been established in Ireland also.

Stantz (132) Possibly an altered spelling of German **Stanz**, a habitation name from places called Stans or Stanz in Austria and Switzerland (see also STENTZ).

Stanwick (111) English: habitational name from a place so called in Northamptonshire, named in Old English with *stān* 'stone' + *wīc* 'outlying dairy farm'.

Stanwood (296) English: evidently a habitational name from an unidentified or lost place.

Stanzel (134) German: **1.** from a pet form of the Slavic personal name *Stanislav* (see STANISLAW). **2.** from a pet form of a short form of the personal name *Constantinus* (see CONSTANTINE).
GIVEN NAMES German 8%. *Reinhart* (2), *Arno, Otto.*

Stanzione (267) Italian (Sicily): from an augmentative of *stanza* 'dwelling', 'lodging', 'room'.
GIVEN NAMES Italian 17%. *Rocco* (3), *Gaetano* (2), *Salvatore* (2), *Angelo, Carmela, Carmine, Domenic, Franca, Franco, Pasquale, Raffaela, Sabato.*

Stapel (220) North German: **1.** from Middle Low German *stapel* 'column', 'signpost', 'warehouse', perhaps applied as a nickname for a tall thin man. **2.** topographic from a diminutive of the old dialect term *stap* 'marsh'.

Stapert (105) Dutch (**Stappaert**): from the verb *stappen* 'to step or stride out'.

Stapf (263) German: topographic name from Middle High German *stapfe* 'path' or 'ford'.

Staple (181) **1.** English: from Middle English *stapel* 'post', hence a topographic name for someone who lived near a boundary post, or a habitational name from some place named with this word (Old English *stapel*), as for example Staple in Kent or Staple Fitzpaine in Somerset. **2.** Americanized spelling of German STAPEL.

Stapleford (170) English: habitational name from any of a number of places, in Cambridgeshire, Cheshire, Essex, Hertfordshire, Leicestershire, Lincolnshire, Nottinghamshire, and Wiltshire, so named from Old English *stapol* 'post' + *ford* 'ford'.

Stapler (280) English: topographic name for someone who lived near a boundary post, from Middle English *stapel* 'post' + the suffix *-er*, denoting an inhabitant.

Staples (5913) English: variant of STAPLE.

Stapleton (6215) Irish, of English origin: habitational name from any of various places in England, for example in Cumbria, Gloucestershire, Herefordshire, Leicestershire, Shropshire, Somerset, and North Yorkshire, so named from Old English *stapol* 'post' + *tūn* 'enclosure', 'settlement'.

Stapley (332) English: habitational name from Stapeley in Cheshire or Stapely in Hampshire, so named from Old English *stapol* 'post' + *lēah* 'wood', 'clearing'. The reference may have been to a place where timber was got for posts.

Stapp (1425) English: topographic name from Middle English *stappe* 'step', probably denoting someone who lived by a ford with stepping stones.

Star (716) **1.** German and Jewish (Ashkenazic): nickname from German *Star*, Middle High German *star*, 'starling', probably denoting a talkative or perhaps a voracious person. **2.** Dutch: nickname either for a gloomy person or for someone who was rigid and inflexible, from Middle Dutch *staer* 'having a troubled or gloomy expression'; 'tight', 'stiff'. **3.** English translation of German and Jewish STERN. **4.** Slovenian: from the adjective *star* 'old' (see STARE).

Starace (211) Southern Italian: from Greek *Stavrakis*, a medieval derivative of the personal name STAVROS. The Greek diminutive and patronymic ending *-akis* was taken into Italian as *-ace*.

GIVEN NAMES Italian 13%. *Salvatore* (2), *Carmela, Cinzia, Giorgio, Marino.*

Starbird (319) English: unexplained.

Starbuck (889) English (mainly Leicestershire): habitational name from Starbeck in Harrogate, North Yorkshire.

Starcevich (193) Serbian and Croatian (**Starčević**): patronymic from *starac* 'old man' or 'elder' (i.e. 'chief', 'headman').

Starcher (1125) perhaps English or Scottish, an occupational name for someone who used starch to stiffen fabric when ironing.

Starck (529) German (also **Stärck**): variant of STARK 2.

Starczewski (78) Polish: habitational name for someone from any of three places named Starczewo, in Bydgoszcz, Gorzów, and Ciechanów voivodeships.

GIVEN NAMES Polish 8%. *Jacek, Jozef.*

Stare (182) **1.** Slovenian: from *star* 'old', either an identifying name for the older of two bearers of the same name or, in some

cases, an identifying name for an 'old' inhabitant, as distinct from a newcomer. **2.** perhaps also a variant of English STAIR.

Starek (134) Czech (**Stárek**) and Polish: nickname meaning 'old man', from a derivative of Czech *stáry*, Polish *stary* 'old'. In Czech, this is a status name for the foreman ('the old man') in a mill, brewery, etc.

Stargel (151) Origin unidentified. Compare STARGELL, STURGELL, STURGILL.

Stargell (113) Origin unidentified. Possibly English: unexplained. Compare STURGELL, STURGILL.

Stariha (112) Slovenian: from a noun derivative of *star* 'old', either an identifying name for the older of two bearers of the same name or, in some cases, an identifying name for an 'old' inhabitant, as distinct from a newcomer.

Starin (163) Slovenian: from a noun derivative of *star* 'old', either an identifying name for the older of two bearers of the same name or, in some cases, an identifying name for an 'old' inhabitant, as distinct from a newcomer.

Staring (121) English: unexplained.

Stark (16694) **1.** Scottish and English: from Middle English *stark* 'firm', 'unyielding', hence a nickname for a stern, determined, or physically strong person. **2.** German and Jewish (Ashkenazic): nickname for a strong, bold person, from Middle High German *stark(e)*, German *stark* 'strong', 'brave'.

Starke (1215) German and Dutch: nickname for a strong, bold person, from Middle High German *stark(e)*, Middle Dutch *starck(e)*, *staerk(e)*, 'strong', 'brave'.

Starkel (167) German (**Stärkel**): diminutive of STARK.

Starker (152) German and Jewish (Ashkenazic): nickname for a strong, bold person, from an inflected form of Middle High German *stark(e)*, German *stark* 'strong', 'brave'.

Starkes (222) English: patronymic from STARK.

Starkey (5424) **1.** English: from a diminutive of STARK 1. **2.** Altered spelling of German STARKE, written thus to preserve the second syllable.

Starkie (113) English: variant spelling of STARKEY.

Starkman (301) English, German (**Starkmann**), and Jewish (Ashkenazic): elaborated form of STARK.

GIVEN NAME Jewish 4%. *Sol* (2).

Starkovich (168) Ukrainian: patronymic from a noun based on the adjective *stary* 'old'. Compare Polish STAREK.

Starks (4678) English: patronymic from STARK.

Starkweather (748) English: unexplained. Perhaps a nickname for a stormy-tempered person. Compare STARK.

Starley (142) English (Sussex): unexplained.

Starlin (189) English: altered form of STARLING.

Starling (3141) English: from Middle English *starling* 'starling' (Old English *stærling*), probably a nickname for a raucous or voracious person.

Starliper (193) Origin unidentified.

Starman (254) English: **1.** variant of STARR 1. **2.** from the medieval nickname *Starre* (see STARR 1) + *man* 'servant', hence an occupational name for the servant of a man known as 'Star'.

Starmer (200) English (Northamptonshire): unexplained.

Starn (240) English: unexplained (STARNS).

Starner (809) German or English: unexplained.

Starnes (5051) English (Sussex): unexplained.

Starns (360) English: unexplained. Compare STARNES.

Staron (266) Polish (**Staroń**): nickname from a derivative of *stary* 'old'.

GIVEN NAMES Polish 9%. *Czeslawa, Jozef, Kazimierz, Kazmierz, Stanislaw, Urszula, Zbigniew, Zigmunt.*

Starosta (111) Jewish (eastern Ashkenazic): occupational name from Russian *starosta* 'elected authority'.

GIVEN NAMES Jewish 7%; Russian 4%. *Rakhmil, Yaron; Anatoly, Asya, Boris, Fanya, Mikhail.*

Starr (11364) **1.** English: nickname from Middle English *sterre, starre* 'star'. The word was also used in a transferred sense of a patch of white hair on the forehead of a horse, and so perhaps the name denoted someone with a streak of white hair. It is possibly also a habitational name, for someone who lived at a house distinguished by the sign of a star. **2.** Jewish (Ashkenazic): variant of STAR 1 and 3.

Starratt (145) Scottish and northern Irish: variant of STARRETT.

Starrett (1245) Scottish and northern Irish: habitational name from Stairaird (now Stirie) in the parish of Dalry, Ayrshire.

Starritt (104) Scottish and northern Irish: habitational name from Stairaird (now Stirie) in the parish of Dalry, Ayrshire.

Starrs (136) Variant of English STARR or STORRS.

Starry (374) **1.** English: unexplained. **2.** Perhaps an Americanized spelling of Czech and Slovak **Starý** 'old' (see STARY).

Start (323) English: habitational name from any of the various minor places, for example Start Point in Devon, named from Old English *steort* 'tail', in the transferred sense of a promontory or spur of a hill.

Startup (119) English (Kent): apparently a nickname from Middle English *sterten* 'to leap or jump' + *up*. Reaney and Wilson note that *startup* was the original form of 'upstart' and also the name of a kind of rustic boot and believe these senses may have contributed to the surname, although neither is recorded beofe the 16th century.

Startz (128) South German: **1.** possibly a habitational name from Starzen in Bavaria, Starsen in Brandenburg, or Starz in Bohemia; also a topographic name for someone who owned an odd-shaped field. **2.** variant of STERTZ.

Starwalt (167) Origin unidentified.

Stary (208) Czech and Slovak (**Starý**): nickname from *starý* 'old'.

Starzec (105) Polish: nickname meaning 'old man', Polish *starzec*.

GIVEN NAMES Polish 7%. *Halina, Zbigniew.*

Starzyk (210) Polish: nickname from Silesian dialect *starzyk* 'old man', a derivative of *stary* 'old'.

GIVEN NAMES Polish 11%. *Bronislaus, Bronislaw, Elzbieta, Jozef, Wieslaw, Zbigniew, Zigmund, Zofia.*

Starzynski (125) Polish (**Starzyński**): habitational name for someone from Starzyna in Białystok voivodeship, Starzyno in Gdańsk and Płock voivodeships, or Starzyny in Częstochowa, Poznań, and Sierad voivodeships.

GIVEN NAMES Polish 11%; French 4%. *Jacek, Lucyna, Pawel, Wladyslaw, Wojciech; Camille, Lucien.*

Stas (107) Dutch: from a reduced form of the personal name *Eustaes*, a vernacular form of Latin *Eustacius* (see STACEY).

GIVEN NAME German 4%. *Aloys.*

Stasch (107) German: from the Slavic personal name *Staš*, a pet form of *Stanislav* (see STANISLAW).

Staser (148) North German: probably a variant of STASSEN.

Stash (177) Americanized spelling of German STASCH.

Stasi (194) Southern Italian: patronymic or plural form of STASIO.

GIVEN NAMES Italian 17%. *Luigi* (2), *Rocco* (2), *Luca, Luciano, Mafalda, Nicola, Romano, Santo.*

Stasiak (422) Polish: patronymic from a reduced form of the personal name *Stanisław* (see STANISLAW).

GIVEN NAMES Polish 11%. *Andrzej* (2), *Janina* (2), *Alicja, Bogumil, Bronislaw, Casimir, Dariusz, Jadwiga, Jerzy, Kazimierz, Leszek, Piotr.*

Stasik (266) Polish: from a pet form of the personal name *Stanisław* (see STANISLAW).

GIVEN NAMES Polish 8%. *Andrzej, Grzegorz, Janina, Jozef, Stanislaw, Tadeusz.*

Stasio (206) Italian (southern): from a short form of the personal names *Ostasio*, from Greek *Eustathios* (see EUSTACE).

GIVEN NAME Italian 6%. *Antonio* (3).

Stasiowski (119) Polish: derivative (perhaps a habitational name from an unidentified place) from *Staś*, a pet form of the personal name *Stanisław* (see STANISLAW).

GIVEN NAMES Polish 8%; German 4%. *Andrzej, Tadeusz.*

Stasiuk (102) Ukrainian: from a pet form of the personal name *Stanislav* (see STANISLAW).

GIVEN NAMES Polish 15%; Ukrainian 5%. *Andrze, Eugeniusz, Iwan, Pawel, Wasyl; Halyna, Markian, Olha.*

Staskiewicz (129) Polish (**Staśkiewicz** or **Staszkiewicz**): patronymic from a pet form of the personal name *Stanisław* (see STANISLAW).

GIVEN NAMES Polish 9%. *Mariusz, Miroslawa, Stanislawa, Zdzislaw.*

Stasko (421) Polish (**Staśko** or **Staszko**): from a pet form of the personal name *Stanisław* (see STANISLAW).

Stasney (145) Americanized spelling of Czech and Slovak **Šťastný** (see STASTNY).

Stasny (162) Americanized spelling of Czech and Slovak **Šťastný** (see STASTNY).

Stassen (168) **1.** German and Dutch: patronymic from a reduced form of the personal name *Anastasius* **2.** Dutch: from the medieval personal name *Stassin*, a pet form of *Eustaes* (see STACEY).

GIVEN NAMES French 4%. *Fabienne* (2), *Eloi.*

Stassi (197) Southern Italian: patronymic from *Stassio*, a short form of the personal name ANASTASIO. This is also found as a Greek family name in the form **Stassis**.

GIVEN NAMES Italian 8%. *Nino* (2), *Antonio, Enrico, Margherita, Vito.*

Stastny (427) Czech (**Šťastný, Šťastnej**) and Slovak (**Šťastný**): from a personal name derived from the adjective *Šťastný* 'happy', 'fortunate', 'lucky', used as a translation of Latin FELIX.

Staszak (369) Polish: patronymic from a reduced form of the personal name *Stanisław* (see STANISLAW).

GIVEN NAMES Polish 7%. *Casimir* (2), *Zigmond* (2), *Iwona, Janusz, Jerzy, Walenty, Zygmunt.*

Staszewski (173) Polish: habitational name for someone from either of two places, in Radom and Tarnobrzeg, named Staszów, named with a reduced form of the personal name *Stanisław* (see STANISLAW).

GIVEN NAMES Polish 13%. *Zygmunt* (4), *Franciszek, Jerzy, Jozef, Witold.*

State (210) German (**Stät(e)**): nickname from Middle High German *stæt(e)* 'firm', 'steadfast', 'constant'.

Stateler (115) Americanized form of German STADLER.

Staten (1941) Dutch: unexplained.

Stater (134) **1.** Scottish: unexplained; early forms with the definite article suggest it may have been an occupational name. **2.** German (**Stäter**): variant of **Stäte** (see STATE).

States (930) English: unexplained.

Stathakis (116) Greek: patronymic from STATHIS. The -akis patronymic suffix is particularly associated with Crete.

GIVEN NAME Greek 4%. *Argirios.*

Statham (739) English: habitational name from Statham in Cheshire, named with the dative plural *stæðum* of Old English *stæð* 'landing stage', i.e. 'at the landing stages'.

Stathis (288) Greek: from a Greek personal name, a reduced form of *Efstathios*, classical Greek *Eustathios* 'well-grounded', 'firm', 'steadfast' (from *eu* 'well' + *stathēs* 'standing', a derivative of *histēmi* 'to stand'). In the early Middle Ages this name became confused with *Eustakhios* 'fruitful' (see EUSTACE). *Eustathios* was the name of several saints and patriarchs of the Eastern Church.

GIVEN NAMES Greek 8%. *Demetrios* (2), *Angelos, Constantine, Eleni, Fotini, Haralambos, Konstantinos, Stathis.*

Stathopoulos (173) Greek: from the personal name STATHIS + the patronymic ending -*poulos* . This ending occurs chiefly in the Peloponnese; it is derived from Latin *pullus* 'nestling', 'chick'.

GIVEN NAMES Greek 31%. *Christos* (3), *Marios* (3), *Panagiotis* (2), *Andreas, Demetre, Dimitrios, Eleftherios, Georgios, Joannis, Nikos, Pavlos, Sotirios.*

Stathos (118) Greek: from a pet form of the personal name *Efstathios* (see STATHIS), or a reduced form of patronymics based on *Stathis*, such as STATHOPOULOS.

Statler (996) Variant of German STADLER.

Statom (104) Variant of English STATHAM.

GIVEN NAME Irish 5%. *Brendan.*

Staton (4414) English (South Yorkshire and East Midlands): apparently a habitational name, possibly a variant of STATHAM.

Statton (202) English (mainly Cornwall): variant of STATHAM or from a lost or unidentified place, possibly in southwestern England, where the surname is most frequent.

Statum (195) Variant of English STATHAM.

Statz (512) **1.** German: probably from Middle High German *statzen* 'to stammer', hence a nickname for someone who suffered from a stammer. **2.** from a vernacular form of the medieval personal name *Eustacius*.

GIVEN NAMES German 4%. *Eldred, Hans, Hermann, Kurt, Matthias.*

Statzer (297) German: nickname for a stammerer, from the agent derivative of Middle High German *statzen* 'to stammer'.

Staub (1872) German and Jewish (Ashkenazic): occupational nickname for a miller, from Middle High German *stoup*, German *Staub* 'dust'. The Jewish surname may also be ornamental.

Staubach (113) German: possibly a Swiss topographic name from Middle High German *stouwen* 'to dam' + *bach* 'creek'.

GIVEN NAMES German 7%. *Ernst, Otto.*

Stauber (652) German (also **Stäuber**) and Jewish (Ashkenazic): occupational name from STAUB, with the addition of the German agent suffix -*er*.

GIVEN NAMES Jewish 4%; German 4%. *Chaim* (3), *Baruch, Berish, Hersh, Nachman, Yidel, Zalmen*; *Horst* (2), *Wolf* (2), *Erwin, Markus, Ulrich, Wolfgang.*

Stauble (127) South German (**Stäuble**): diminutive of STAUB.

Staubs (176) Possibly an altered form of STAUB.

Stauch (299) German: **1.** from Middle High German *stūche*, a term used to denote both a type of wide sleeve and a headcovering, hence a nickname for someone who was distinguished by some peculiarity of dress. **2.** habitational name form a place named Staucha, near Dresden.
GIVEN NAMES German 8%. *Hans* (2), *Benno, Gottlieb, Helmut, Ilse, Johann, Manfred, Siegfried.*

Staudacher (192) German (Austria): topographic name for someone who lived in an overgrown place, from Middle High German *stūdach* (a collective form of *stūde* 'thicket', 'wilderness'), or a habitational name for someone from any of various places named with this word.

Staude (162) German: topographic name for someone who lived by a patch of uncleared dense undergrowth, a thicket, from Middle High German *stūde* 'thicket', 'wilderness'.
GIVEN NAMES German 7%. *Juergen* (2), *Gunther, Reinhart.*

Staudenmaier (169) German: distinguishing name for a tenant farmer (see MEYER) whose farm was situated by a thicket (see STAUDE).
GIVEN NAMES German 7%. *Bernd* (2), *Erhard, Kurt.*

Stauder (336) German (also **Stäuder**): topographic name for someone who lived by a thicket, from STAUDE + the suffix *-er* denoting an inhabitant.
GIVEN NAMES German 4%. *Kurt* (3), *Alois.*

Staudinger (308) **1.** South German: Tyrolean form of STAUDER. **2.** habitational name from a place named Stauding in the Sudeten region.
GIVEN NAMES French 4%. *Alphonse* (2), *Pierre.*

Staudt (713) German: variant of STAUDE.
GIVEN NAMES German 4%. *Alois* (2), *Ernst* (2), *Otto* (2), *Bernhard, Volker.*

Stauff (156) German: metonymic occupational name for a maker of beakers, from Middle High German *stouf* 'beaker', or a topographic name from the same word used with refence to a beaker-shaped hill, or a habitational name from a place named with this word (see STAUFFER).

Stauffacher (317) German: topographic name for someone who lived by a river named *Stoufahe*, from Middle High German *stouf* 'beaker', 'stoup' + *ahe* 'river'.
GIVEN NAMES German 4%. *Fritz, Kurt, Otto.*

Stauffer (5949) South German: **1.** occupational name for a maker or seller of beakers or mugs, from an agent derivative of

Middle High German *stouf* 'beaker', 'stoup'. **2.** habitational name for someone from any of the various minor places named with this word, for example Stauf, Staufen; the reference is to hills thought to resemble a beaker in shape.

Staunton (336) Irish (of English origin): habitational name from any of the places so called in Gloucestershire, Herefordshire, Leicestershire, Nottinghamshire, Somerset, and Worcestershire, which have the same etymology as STANTON. This name has been established in Ireland (Mayo, Connacht) from medieval times. See also MCEVILLY.
GIVEN NAMES Irish 7%. *Caitlin, Ciaran, Cormac.*

Staup (175) German and Jewish (Ashkenazic): variant of STAUB.

Staus (125) German: variant of STAUSS.

Stauss (416) South German: nickname from Middle High German *stūz* 'buttocks'.

Stauter (173) South German and Palatinate: variant of STAUDER.

Stava (118) Norwegian: habitational name from a farmstead in Rogaland, named with Old Norse *stafr* 'staff', 'pole', denoting a natural formation such as a steep mountain peak.
GIVEN NAMES German 4%. *Elke, Otto.*

Stave (279) **1.** North German: occupational name for an official, for example a judge or church official, from Middle Low German *staf* 'staff', a symbol of office. **2.** Americanized spelling of Jewish (eastern Ashkenazic) **Staw**, either an ornamental name from Polish *staw* 'pond' or a habitational name for someone from a place called Stawy (see STAWSKI). **3.** Norwegian: habitational name from any of several farmsteads named Stave, a variant of STAVA.
GIVEN NAMES German 5%; Scandinavian 5%. *Gunter, Otto, Uwe*; *Holger.*

Stavely (208) English: habitational name from any of several places named Staveley, in Cumbria, Derbyshire, and North Yorkshire.

Staver (312) English: variant of **Stavers**, an occupational name for a stave maker (see STAVES), found predominantly in the northeast of England.

Staves (213) English (East Midlands and South Yorkshire): possibly a metonymic occupational name for a stave maker, from the plural of Middle English *staf* 'rod', 'staff'.

Stavig (140) Norwegian: habitational name from a farmstead named Stavik, from Old Norse *stafr* 'staff', 'pole' (see STAVA) + *vik* 'bay', 'inlet'.

Stavinoha (231) German: of Slavic origin; unexplained.

Stavis (120) Variant of Jewish STAVISH.
GIVEN NAMES Jewish 4%. *Hillel, Sol.*

Stavish (175) Jewish (from Ukraine): habitational name for someone from Stavishche in Ukraine.

Stavola (199) Italian and French: unexplained.

GIVEN NAMES Italian 8%; French 4%. *Antonio, Mafalda*; *Jacques* (2), *Nicolette.*

Stavropoulos (269) Greek: patronymic from the personal name STAVROS + the patronymic ending *-poulos*. This ending occurs chiefly in the Peloponnese; it is derived from Latin *pullus* 'nestling', 'chick'.
GIVEN NAMES Greek 24%. *Spiros* (4), *Athanasios* (2), *Demetrios* (2), *Eleni* (2), *Ioannis* (2), *Panagiotis* (2), *Stavros* (2), *Andreas, Aphrodite, Christos, Costas, Dimitris.*

Stavros (357) Greek: from a Christian personal name based on the vocabulary word *stavros* 'cross' (classical Greek *stauros*), originally meaning 'stake'. The adoption of the word as a personal name is associated with the Feast of the Exaltation of the Holy Cross (September 14) in the Eastern Church, commemorating Emperor Heraclius' recovery of the Holy Cross from the Persians in 630.

Stavrou (127) Greek: patronymic from the genitive form of the personal name STAVROS. Genitive patronymics are typical of Cyprus.
GIVEN NAMES Greek 33%. *Stavros* (5), *Christos* (3), *Afroditi, Costas, Demetrios, Evangelos, Marios, Nicos, Socratis, Soterios.*

Stawarz (119) Polish: occupational name for a digger of ponds, from an agent derivative of *staw* 'pond'.
GIVEN NAMES Polish 24%. *Casimir* (2), *Andrzej, Boguslaw, Ignacy, Karol, Krystyna, Teofil, Waclaw, Zbigniew.*

Stawicki (299) Polish: habitational name for someone from Stawik, the name of settlements in Kielce, Kraków, and Lublin voivodeships and of a place now in Ukraine.

Stawski (144) Polish and Jewish (Ashkenazic): habitational name for someone from any of several places called Staw or Stawy, named with Polish *staw* 'pond'.
GIVEN NAMES Polish 7%. *Casimir, Mariusz, Tadeusz.*

Stay (275) Irish: reduced form of MCSTAY.

Stayer (271) German: variant of STEYER.

Stayner (190) Variant spelling of English **Stainer**, a variant of STEINER.

Stayton (668) Possibly of English origin, a habitational name from a lost of unidentified place.

Stead (1099) English (chiefly West Yorkshire): **1.** habitational name from Stead in West Yorkshire, or from some other place taking its name from Old English *stede* 'estate', 'farm', 'place'. **2.** from Middle English *steed* 'stud horse', 'stallion', applied as a nickname to a lusty person or as an occupational name to someone responsible for looking after stallions.

Steadham (354) Possibly of English origin, a habitational name from a lost or unidentified place.

Steadman (2568) English: occupational name for someone responsible for looking after stallions, from Middle English *steed*

'stud horse', 'stallion' + *man* 'man', 'servant'.

Steady (132) English: nickname for a resolute person, from Middle English *stedy* 'firm', 'steadfast'.

Steagall (402) Variant spelling of English STEGALL.

Steakley (266) Origin unidentified. Perhaps an Americanized form of Swiss German **Steckli** (see STECKLEY).

Stealey (160) English and Welsh (also **Steeley**): unexplained.

Stear (229) English: variant spelling of STEER.

Stearley (127) Origin unidentified. Possibly a variant of English **Sturley**, **Sterley**, which has the form of a habitational name, though its source has not been identified.

Stearman (409) English: occupational name for someone who was responsible for tending cattle, from Middle English *steer* 'bullock' + *man* 'man'.

Stearn (330) English: variant spelling of STERN 2.

Stearns (6252) English: patronymic from STERN 2.

FOREBEARS In 1646 Charles Stearns was admitted as a freeman of Watertown, MA.

Stears (192) English: patronymic from STEER.

GIVEN NAME Scandinavian 4%. *Juel* (2).

Stebbins (2616) English: **1.** topographic name from Middle English *stebbing, stubbing* 'clearing' (from an unattested Old English *stybbing*, a derivative of *stubb* 'tree stump'). **2.** habitational name from Stebbing in Essex, which is named in Old English either as 'the family or followers (Old English *-ingas*) of a man called *Stybba*', an unattested Old English personal name, or 'the dwellers among the tree stumps (Old English *stybb*)'.

FOREBEARS Edward Stebbins was one of the founders of Hartford, CT (coming from Cambridge, MA, with Thomas Hooker) in 1635.

Stebelton (114) Origin unidentified. Perhaps an English habitational name from a lost or unidentified place.

Steber (318) German: occupational name for an official before whom oaths were taken, from Middle High German *stebaere* (see STABLER 2).

Stebleton (109) Possibly a habitational name from a lost or unidentified place.

Stebner (201) **1.** North German: occupational name from Middle Low German *stevener, stavener* 'person before whom an oath is taken'. **2.** South German: habitational name for someone from Steben, near Hof in Bavaria.

GIVEN NAMES German 9%. *Otto* (2), *Reinhard* (2), *Johann*.

Stec (756) Polish: from a pet form of the personal name *Stefan*, Polish vernacular form of Latin *Stephanus* (see STEVEN).

GIVEN NAMES Polish 8%. *Stanislaw* (3), *Jacek* (2), *Aniela, Augustyn, Boguslaw, Boleslaw, Casimir, Genowefa, Halina, Janina, Jerzy, Myroslaw*.

Stech (320) **1.** Czech and Slovak (**Štěch, Štech**): from a pet form of the personal name **Štěpán, Štefan**, Czech and Slovak forms of Latin *Stephanus* (see STEVEN). **2.** Eastern German: from a pet form of STEFFEN.

Stecher (705) German: occupational name for someone who castrated farm livestock, Middle High German *stechære*.

Stechschulte (216) North German: compound of the Germanic personal name *Stecho* + Middle Low German *schulthete* 'village headman' (see SCHULTE).

Steck (1338) German: **1.** from Middle High German *stecke* 'stick, rod, cudgel', hence a nickname for a tall thin man, or a topographic name from a posted area. **2.** variant of STECH 2.

GIVEN NAMES German 4%. *Hans* (3), *Kurt* (3), *Armin, Dieter, Ernst, Fritz, Gunther, Otto, Reinhard, Siebert, Urs*.

Steckbauer (115) German: from Middle High German *steck(e)* 'steep hill', hence a nickname for a farmer in such a place.

Steckbeck (101) German: **1.** probably a topographic name from a compound of *steg* 'path', 'narrow bridge' + *beck* 'creek', or a habitational name from a place named with this word. **2.** occupational nickname from *steg* 'path', 'narrow bridge' + South German *beck* 'baker', denoting a baker who lived by a path or bridge.

Steckel (663) **1.** North German: nickname from Middle Low German *stekel* 'easily affronted'. **2.** German and Jewish (Ashkenazic): from Middle High German *steckel* and Yiddish *shtekl* 'little stick', hence perhaps a nickname for a thin person. **3.** Jewish (Ashkenazic): from German *Stöckel* 'outhouse'.

Steckelberg (188) North German: topographic name for someone living on a steep hill, from Middle High German *stechel* 'steep' + *berg* 'hill', 'mountain'.

Stecker (806) North German: variant of STECHER.

Stecklein (237) South German: from a pet form of the personal name *Stecho*.

Steckler (773) **1.** North German: nickname for a person known for making snide remarks, from Middle Low German *stekeln*, compare STECKEL 1. **2.** Jewish (eastern Ashkenazic): occupational name for a glass worker or glazier, from Russian *steklo* 'glass' + the Yiddish agent suffix *-er*.

Steckley (162) Americanized spelling of Swiss German **Steckli** or **Stächeli**, from Middle High German *steckel(in)* 'small stick, cudgel' (see STECK).

GIVEN NAMES German 6%. *Kurt, Markus*.

Steckman (231) **1.** German (**Steckmann**): topographic name for someone who lived by a steep, narrow path, or by a plank bridge, from Middle Low German *stège* 'steep path', 'plank bridge' + *man* 'man'. **2.** Jewish (Ashkenazic): probably a nickname for a thin man, from German *Stecken* 'stick' + *Mann* 'man' (Yiddish *man*).

GIVEN NAMES Jewish 4%. *Sol* (2), *Hyman*.

Steding (115) North German: habitational name from the region of Stedingen near Oldenburg (Lower Weser). The place name is composed of Old Saxon *stath* 'shore, bank' + the suffix *-ing(en)* denoting affiliation. This name is also found in Sweden, where it is of Pomeranian origin.

GIVEN NAMES German 8%; Scandinavian 5%. *Bernhard, Gerhard, Juergen, Otto; Erik.*

Stedman (1812) English: variant spelling of STEADMAN.

Steeb (156) South German: nickname from Middle High German *steb(e)* 'dust', probably denoting a miller. Compare STAUB.

GIVEN NAMES German 4%. *Erna, Heinz.*

Steeber (181) Perhaps an Americanized spelling of German STIEBER or Swiss German **Stüber**, probably a nickname for a restless person, from Middle High German *stueben* 'to fly about (of dust)', 'move in a fidgety manner'.

Steeby (157) Perhaps an Americanized spelling of Swiss German **Stübi**, a topographic name from Middle High German *stubich* 'brushwood'. Compare HAGY.

Steed (3260) English: variant of STEAD.

Steede (116) Variant of STEAD.

Steedley (249) Perhaps an Americanized spelling of Swiss German **Stüdle, Stüdli**, diminutives of STUDE.

Steedman (193) Scottish and English: variant of STEADMAN.

Steeg (177) North German and Dutch: topographic name from Middle Low German *stège*, Middle Dutch *stege, steeg* 'alley', 'steep path or track', also 'plank bridge'.

GIVEN NAMES French 4%; German 4%. *Gerard, Murielle; Frederika, Monika.*

Steege (399) German: variant of STEEG.

GIVEN NAMES German 7%. *Lorenz* (3), *Armin, Kurt, Reinhart.*

Steel (2402) **1.** English and Scottish: variant spelling of STEELE. **2.** Americanization of German STAHL.

Steele (30690) English and Scottish: from Middle English *stele* 'steel', hence a nickname for someone considered as hard and durable as steel, or metonymic occupational name for a foundry worker.

FOREBEARS This name was brought independently to New England by several different bearers from the 17th century onward. John Steele was one of the founders of Hartford, CT, (coming from Cambridge, MA, with Thomas Hooker) in 1635.

Steeley (320) Americanized form of Swiss German **Stühle**, a variant of STUHL (see STEELY).

Steelman (1781) Perhaps a translation of German **Stahlmann**, a variant of STAHL with the addition of Middle High German *man* 'man'.

Steely (672) Americanized form of Swiss German **Stühle**, a variant of STUHL.

Steen (4926) **1.** Scottish: from a reduced form of the personal name STEVEN. **2.** North German, Dutch, and Scandinavian: from *sten* 'stone', hence a topographic name for someone who lived on stony ground, or a metonymic occupational name for someone who worked with stone: a quarryman, stonecutter, or stonemason. The Swedish surname probably originated as a soldier's name. **3.** Swedish: from the personal name *Sten*.

Steenberg (131) **1.** Dutch and North German: habitational name from any of several places so called, named with Middle Low German *stēn* 'stone' + *berc* 'mountain', 'hill'. **2.** Scandinavian: variant of STENBERG.
GIVEN NAME Scandinavian 4%; German 4%. *Carsten* (3).

Steenbergen (253) German (Rhineland) and Dutch: habitational name from any of the places so called.

Steenbock (109) Dutch: nickname from Dutch *steenbock* 'ibex'.

Steenburgh (103) Americanized form of STEINBERG, **Steinburg** (see STONEBERG), or STEENBERG.
GIVEN NAME German 7%. *Kurt* (2).

Steenhoek (155) Dutch: habitational name from a place name meaning 'stone corner'.

Steeno (141) Belgian: variant of **Steenhout**, habitational name from a place in East Flanders, so named from Middle Dutch *steen* 'rock' + *hout* 'wood'.

Steenrod (140) **1.** Dutch: unexplained. **2.** Possibly Norwegian: from a farmstead named Stenrød, from *sten* 'stone' + *rød* 'clearing'.

Steensen (103) Scandinavian: patronymic from *Sten*, a personal name derived from Old Norse *steinn* 'stone'.
GIVEN NAMES Scandinavian 13%; German 6%. *Erik; Helmut*.

Steensma (184) Frisian: occupational name for someone who worked with stone: a quarryman, stonecutter, or stonemason, from *stēn* 'stone' + *ma* 'man'.

Steenson (272) **1.** Scottish and northern Irish: patronymic from STEEN (reduced form of Steven). **2.** Americanized spelling of **Steensen**, **Stensen**, Norwegian and Danish patronymics from *Sten*, a personal name derived from Old Norse *steinn* 'stone'.

Steenstra (119) Frisian: occupational name for a mason or quarryman, from an agent derivative of *steen* 'stone', 'rock'.

Steenwyk (111) Dutch: habitational name from a place so called, named with Dutch *steen* 'stone' + *wijk* 'village'.

Steer (476) **1.** English (mainly Devon) and German: from Middle English *steer*, Middle Low German *stēr* 'bullock', hence a nickname for a truculent person or a metonymic occupational name for someone who was responsible for tending cattle. **2.** South German: from Middle High German *ster* 'ram', probably a nickname for a hard-nosed, stubborn person.

Steere (695) Variant of STEER.

Steerman (135) **1.** North German (**Steermann**): occupational name for someone who looked after steers (see STEER). **2.** South German: occupational name for someone who raised rams (see STEER 2).

Steers (421) English: patronymic from STEER.

Stees (139) Dutch: unexplained.
GIVEN NAME Irish 5%. *Gearold*.

Steever (198) Origin unidentified.

Steeves (1080) Origin unidentified.

Stefan (979) Slovenian and Slovak (**Štefan**), Polish, and Romanian: from the personal names *Štefan* (Slovenian and Slovak) or *Stefan*, Latin *Stephanus* (see STEVEN).
GIVEN NAMES German 5%; Romanian 4%. *Franz* (3), *Kurt* (3), *Helmut* (2), *Darrold*, *Erwin*, *Gerhard*, *Heinrich*, *Heinz*, *Otto*; *Constantin* (2), *Gheorghe* (2), *Ilie* (2), *Nicolae* (2), *Gelu*, *Mihai*, *Mircea*, *Radu*, *Todor*, *Vasile*, *Viorel*.

Stefanek (124) Polish: from a pet form of the personal name STEFAN.
GIVEN NAMES Polish 7%; German 4%. *Lucjan*, *Marcin*, *Stanislawa*.

Stefanelli (351) Italian: patronymic from the personal name *Stefanello*, a pet form of STEFANO.
GIVEN NAMES Italian 14%. *Angelo*, *Carmel*, *Enrico*, *Enzo*, *Gaetano*, *Gilda*, *Primo*, *Sal*, *Salvatore*, *Sandro*, *Sesto*, *Stefano*.

Stefani (705) Italian: patronymic or plural form of STEFANO.
GIVEN NAMES Italian 10%. *Dino* (3), *Gino* (3), *Aldo* (2), *Angelo* (2), *Marco* (2), *Amedeo*, *Antonio*, *Concetta*, *Dario*, *Fausto*, *Francesco*, *Franco*.

Stefaniak (387) Polish: patronymic from the personal name STEFAN.
GIVEN NAMES Polish 7%. *Andrzej* (2), *Jozefa*, *Kazimierz*, *Krzystof*, *Malgorzata*, *Slawomir*, *Stanislaw*, *Waclawa*.

Stefanic (146) Slovenian (**Štefanič**); Croatian and Serbian (**Stefanić**, **Štefanić**): patronymic from the personal name *Štefan* (Slovenian and Croatian) or *Stefan* (Croatian and Serbian), Latin *Stephanus* (see STEVEN).

Stefanich (154) Slovenian (**Štefanič**); Croatian and Serbian (**Stefanić**, **Štefanić**): see STEFANIC.

Stefanick (258) Americanized spelling of Polish STEFANIK.

Stefanik (622) Polish: from a pet form of the personal name STEFAN.

Stefanini (116) Italian: from a pet form of the personal name STEFANO.

GIVEN NAMES Italian 24%. *Mario* (4), *Gino* (3), *Stefano* (2), *Americo*, *Augusto*, *Duilio*, *Nino*, *Osvaldo*, *Raffaello*, *Ruggero*.

Stefanko (252) Slovak and Croatian (mainly northern Croatia; **Štefanko**): from a pet form of the personal name *Štefan* (see STEVEN).

Stefano (446) Italian: from the personal name *Stefano*, Italian form of Latin *Stephanus* (see STEVEN).
GIVEN NAMES Italian 8%. *Rocco* (3), *Ciro*, *Domenic*, *Enzo*, *Filippo*, *Nicola*, *Pasquale*, *Salvatore*, *Vito*.

Stefanovich (115) Serbian and Croatian (**Stefanović**, **Štefanović**): patronymic from *Stefan* or *Štefan*, Latin *Stephanus* (see STEVEN).
GIVEN NAMES South Slavic 11%. *Dragan*, *Milorad*, *Radomir*, *Slave*, *Trifun*.

Stefanowicz (224) Polish: patronymic from the personal name STEFAN.
GIVEN NAMES Polish 9%. *Bogdan*, *Bronislaw*, *Iwona*, *Jozef*, *Krzystof*, *Tadeusz*, *Zdzislaw*.

Stefanski (835) Polish (**Stefański**): habitational name for someone from Stefanów or Stefanowo, named with the personal name *Stefan*.
GIVEN NAMES Polish 8%. *Ignatius* (3), *Casimir* (2), *Jacek* (2), *Janusz* (2), *Jerzy* (2), *Bogdan*, *Dariusz*, *Ewa*, *Jolanta*, *Jozef*, *Karol*, *Kazimierz*.

Steff (110) **1.** German: from a short form of the personal name *Steffen*, a German form of Latin *Stephanus* (see STEVEN). **2.** English: nickname for a resolute or obstinate person, from Middle English *stef* 'stiff', 'unyielding'.

Steffan (760) Dutch or German: variant of STEFFEN.

Steffe (177) South German: variant of STEFF 1.

Steffee (138) Variant of STEFFEY.

Steffek (223) German (Sorbian): from a pet form of the personal name *Stefan*, vernacular form of Latin *Stephanus* (see STEVEN).

Steffel (251) Variant spelling of German STEFFL.

Steffen (4652) Dutch, North German, and English: from the personal name *Steffen*, a vernacular form of Latin *Stephanus* (see STEVEN).

Steffenhagen (221) North German: probably a habitational name from a minor place named with the personal name STEFFEN + Middle Low German *hagen* 'enclosure'.

Steffens (2048) Dutch, North German, and English: patronymic from STEFFEN.

Steffensen (427) Danish, Norwegian, and North German: patronymic from the personal name STEFFEN.
GIVEN NAMES Scandinavian 7%. *Erik* (3), *Aksel*, *Kresten*, *Nils*.

Steffensmeier (220) North German: distinguishing name for a tenant farmer (see MEYER) whose personal name was

STEFFEN (or, if the middle -*s*- is possessive, one whose landlord's name was STEFFEN).

Steffenson (193) Americanized form of Danish or Norwegian **Steffensen**, a patronymic from the personal name *Steffen* (see STEVEN).
GIVEN NAMES Scandinavian 5%. *Hilmer, Thora.*

Steffes (994) Dutch: patronymic from a reduced form of the personal name *Steffen*.

Steffey (847) Americanized spelling of South German **Steffi**, from a pet form of the personal name *Steffen*, a German vernacular form of Latin *Stephanus* (see STEVEN).

Steffl (152) South German: from a pet form of the personal name *Steffen*, a German vernacular form of Latin *Stephanus* (see STEVEN).

Steffler (206) South German: patronymic from STEFFL.

Steffy (669) Variant of STEFFEY.

Stefka (121) Slavic: variant of STEFKO.

Stefko (150) Slovenian (**Štefko**): from a pet form of personal name *Štefan*, Latin *Stephanus* (see STEVEN).

Stefl (166) **1.** German: variant spelling of STEFFL. **2.** Slovenian (**Štefl**): from a pet form, with the southern Germanic suffix -*l*, of the personal name *Štef*, a short form of *Štefan* (see STEVEN).

Steg (123) German: topographic name from Middle High German *stec*, Middle Low German *steg* 'narrow or uphill path' or 'plank bridge'. Compare STEEG.

Stegall (2704) English: topographic name for someone who lived by a steep uphill path, Middle English *stegele*, Old English *stigol*.

Stege (237) German or Dutch: variant of STEG.
GIVEN NAMES German 5%. *Kurt, Reinhold.*

Stegeman (576) **1.** Dutch: variant of STEEG, with the addition of *man* 'man'. **2.** Variant of German STEGEMANN.

Stegemann (194) German: topographic name for someone who lived by a narrow uphill path or a bridge, from STEG + *man* 'man'.
GIVEN NAMES German 17%. *Fritz* (3), *Gerhard* (2), *Elfriede, Franz, Hermann, Horst, Kurt, Otto, Rainer.*

Stegemoller (115) German (**Stegemöller**): topographic name for a miller whose mill was by a narrow path or bridge, from STEG + MOLLER 'miller'.

Stegen (127) North German and Dutch: variant of STEGE.

Stegenga (155) Frisian: unexplained.

Steger (1928) German: topographic name for someone who lived by a path or by a plank bridge, from an agent derivative of Middle High German *stec* 'steep path or track', 'narrow bridge'.

Steggall (102) English: variant spelling of STEGALL.

Stegmaier (187) German (Bavaria, Württemberg): distinguishing name for a tenant farmer (see MEYER) whose land was either by a plank bridge or a steep narrow path (Middle High German *stec* 'plank bridge' or 'steep narrow path').
GIVEN NAMES German 8%. *Otto* (4), *Arnulf, Erwin.*

Stegman (980) German: see STEGMANN.

Stegmann (211) German: topographic name for someone who lived by a narrow or uphill path or by a plank bridge, from Middle High German *stec* 'steep path or track', 'plank bridge' + *man* 'man'.
GIVEN NAMES German 15%. *Claus* (2), *Helmut* (2), *Johann* (2), *Gottfried, Hans, Matthias, Otto, Ralf, Wilfried.*

Stegmeier (100) German: variant spelling of STEGMAIER.
GIVEN NAMES German 12%. *Eberhard, Gunther, Helmut, Manfred.*

Stegner (598) German: variant of STEGER.

Stehl (125) German: variant of **Stähle** (see STAHL).

Stehle (581) German: variant of **Stähle** (see STAHL).

Stehlik (356) Czech and Slovak (**Stehlík**): nickname for a person with bright yellow hair, from *stehlík* 'goldfinch'.
GIVEN NAMES Czech and Slovak 4%. *Jaroslav, Ladislav, Milos, Vaclav.*

Stehlin (186) German (Baden, Alsace): from an Alemannic diminutive of Middle High German *stāl* 'steel' (see STAHL).

Stehling (246) Eastern German: perhaps from an altered form of Sorbian or Czech *stehlík* 'goldfinch' (see STEHLIK).
GIVEN NAMES German 4%. *Hermann* (2), *Kurt.*

Stehman (238) North German (**Stehmann**): **1.** variant of STEEN 2, with the addition of Middle Low German *man* 'man'. **2.** habitational name (originally *Stedemann*) for someone from Steden near Bremen.

Stehr (477) German: from Middle High German *stēr* 'ram', hence probably a nickname for a lusty person, or possibly a metonymic occupational name for a shepherd.
GIVEN NAMES German 5%. *Kurt* (2), *Franz, Fritz, Gerhard, Gunter.*

Steib (307) German: dialect variant of STAUB.
GIVEN NAMES French 13%. *Clovis* (3), *Lucien* (2), *Celestine, Firmin, Jacques, Julien, Pierre, Prudent, Vernice.*

Steiber (120) German (Swabian): metonymic occupational name for a miller, from an agent derivative of Middle High German *stouben* 'to whip up dust'.

Steichen (409) German: variant of STAUCH.

Steidel (160) German: topographic name from *stiūdelīn*, a diminutive of *stūde*, 'thicket', 'wilderness'.

Steidinger (166) South German (Württemberg, Baden): topographic name formed like STAUDINGER, from the collective noun *Steiding* 'wilderness', 'thicket'; compare STEIDLE.

Steidl (388) German: Bavarian variant of STEIDLE.
GIVEN NAMES German 4%. *Kurt* (2), *Hans, Liesl, Mathias.*

Steidle (172) German: topographic name from a diminutive of Middle High German *stūde* 'thicket'. Compare STEIDEL.

Steidley (143) Possibly an Americanized form of STEIDLE.

Steier (402) **1.** German: variant of STEIGER 2. **2.** Jewish (Ashkenazic): from Yiddish *shtayer* 'impost', 'duty'.
GIVEN NAMES Jewish 5%. *Meyer* (2), *Anshel, Golda, Herschel, Leib, Moshe, Shmuel.*

Steiert (149) South German: possibly a variant of STEIER.
GIVEN NAMES German 5%. *Kurt, Markus.*

Steig (176) German and Jewish (Ashkenazic): topographic name for someone who lived by a steep track or path, from Middle High German *steige*, German *Steig* 'steep path or track'.
GIVEN NAMES German 4%. *Kurt, Otto.*

Steiger (1667) German: **1.** variant of STEGER. **2.** occupational name from Middle High German *stīger* 'foreman', 'mine inspector'. **3.** habitational name for someone from Steige in Alsace.
GIVEN NAMES German 4%. *Kurt* (4), *Fritz* (3), *Horst* (3), *Hans* (2), *Ueli* (2), *Volker* (2), *Bernhard, Hildegarde, Johann, Nikolaus, Reinhard.*

Steigerwald (737) German: topographic name from any of the ranges of wooded hills in Franconia so named, from a derivative of Old High German *stīc* 'steep path or track' + *wald* 'forest'.

Steigerwalt (337) Altered spelling of German STEIGERWALD.

Steighner (100) Possibly an alltered spelling of German **Stegner**, a topographic name for someone who lived by a steep uphill path, from a derivative of STEG.

Steigman (137) **1.** German (**Steigmann**): variant of STEGMANN. **2.** Jewish (Ashkenazic): nickname or ornamental name from a derivative of German *steigen*, Yiddish *shtaygn* 'to climb' + German *Mann*, Yiddish *man* 'man'.
GIVEN NAMES French 5%; Jewish 4%. *Josette, Michel; Mendel, Miriam.*

Steil (490) German: topographic name for someone who lived on steep ground, from Middle High German *steil* 'steep'.

Steiman (132) **1.** German (**Steimann**): probably a variant of STEINMANN. **2.** Jewish (Ashkenazic): variant of STEINMAN.
GIVEN NAMES Jewish 13%. *Aron, Hyman, Yehuda.*

Steimel (299) German: variant of STEIMLE.

Steimer (221) German: from the Germanic compound personal name *Steinmar*, composed of the elements *stein* 'stone' + *mari*, *meri* 'famous'.

Steimle (301) German: from a pet form of the personal name *Steinmar* (see STEIMER).

Stein (20872) **1.** German and Jewish (Ashkenazic): from German *Stein* 'rock', Middle High German *stein*, hence a topographic name either for someone who lived on stony ground or for someone who lived by a notable outcrop of rock or by a stone boundary marker or monument. It could also be a metonymic occupational name for a mason or stonecutter, or, among Jews, an ornamental name. This name is widespread throughout central and eastern Europe. **2.** Dutch: from a reduced form of the personal name *Augustijn* (see AUSTIN). **3.** Norwegian: habitational name from any of ten or more farmsteads, notably in southeastern Norway, so named from Old Norse *steinn* 'stone'. **4.** Scottish: from a reduced form of the personal name *Steven* (see STEEN, STEVEN). **5.** Northern English and Scottish: from the Old Norse personal name *Steinn* meaning 'stone'. **6.** Southern English: habitational name from a place named with Old English *stæne* 'stony place', for example Stein in Sussex or Steane in Northamptonshire.

Steinacker (149) German: from Middle High German *stein* 'stone' + *acker* '(cultivated) field', hence a topographic name for someone who lived near a stony field, or a habitational name from a place so called.

Steinauer (109) German: habitational name for someone from any of various places named Steinau.

Steinbach (1699) **1.** German: habitational name from any of the many places named Steinbach, named with Middle High German *stein* 'stone' + *bach* 'stream', 'creek'. **2.** Jewish (Ashkenazic): ornamental name composed of German *Stein* 'stone' + *Bach* 'stream', or a habitational name (see 1 above).
GIVEN NAMES German 6%. *Kurt* (7), *Otto* (5), *Fritz* (3), *Klaus* (2), *Lorenz* (2), *Alois*, *Bernhard*, *Deiter*, *Hans*, *Heinz*, *Irmgard*, *Lothar*.

Steinbacher (377) German: habitational name for someone from any of the many places named STEINBACH.
GIVEN NAMES German 6%. *Gerhard* (3), *Kurt* (2), *Friedrich*, *Lorenz*.

Steinback (182) **1.** Norwegian: habitational name from any of several farmsteads, mainly in northern Norway, named *Steinbakk*, from *stein* 'stone' + *bakke* 'hill'. **2.** Altered spelling of German STEINBACH.

Steinbauer (205) South German: from Middle High German *stein* 'stone' + an agent derivative of *bauen* 'to build', 'to farm', hence an occupational name for a stonemason, or a farmer with stony land or whose farm was by a conspicuous rock formation.

Steinbaugh (131) Altered spelling of STEINBACH.

Steinbeck (451) **1.** German: habitational name from any of various places called Steinbeck or Steinbach. **2.** South German: occupational name for a mason.
GIVEN NAMES German 4%. *Dieter, Fritz, Klaus.*

Steinberg (6650) **1.** German, Jewish (Ashkenazic), and Swedish (of German origin): habitational name from any of the many places named Steinberg, from Old High German *stein* 'stone' + *berg* 'mountain', 'hill'. **2.** Jewish (Ashkenazic): ornamental name composed of German *Stein* 'stone' + *Berg* 'mountain', 'hill'.
GIVEN NAMES Jewish 6%. *Meyer* (10), *Sol* (7), *Hyman* (6), *Moshe* (6), *Emanuel* (5), *Miriam* (5), *Yehuda* (4), *Chaim* (3), *Isadore* (3), *Ari* (2), *Aron* (2), *Aviva* (2).

Steinberger (783) German and Jewish (Ashkenazic): habitational name for someone from any of the places called STEINBERG.

Steinbock (227) **1.** German: probably a variant of STEINBECK. **2.** Jewish (Ashkenazic): ornamental name from German *Steinbock* 'ibex'.
GIVEN NAMES German 6%. *Gunter, Kurt, Reinhold.*

Steinborn (282) German: topographic name from Middle High German *stein* 'stone' + *born* 'well', 'creek', or a habitational name from a place so called.
GIVEN NAMES German 10%. *Frieda* (2), *Udo* (2), *Benno, Dieter, Lothar, Mathias, Wolfgang.*

Steinbrecher (430) German: occupational name for someone who worked in a stone quarry, from Middle High German *stein* 'stone' + an agent derivative of *brechen* 'to break'.
GIVEN NAMES German 4%. *Bernd, Ernst, Kurt.*

Steinbrenner (247) German: occupational name for a lime burner, from Middle High German *stein* 'stone' (in this case limestone) + an agent derivative of *brennen* 'to burn'. Compare KALKBRENNER.
GIVEN NAMES German 12%. *Erwin* (2), *Kurt* (2), *Otto* (2), *Gerhard, Gerhart, Horst, Juergen.*

Steinbrink (210) German: habitational name from either of the places, in Hannover and the Rhineland, named with Old German *stein* 'rock' + *brink* 'edge', 'slope', 'grazing land'.

Steinbrunner (129) German: topographic name for someone who lived near a stone-edged well, from Middle High German *stein* 'stone' + *brunne* 'spring', 'well', or habitational name for someone from a place called Steinbrunn or Steinbronn.
GIVEN NAME German 6%. *Helmut.*

Steindl (119) South German: diminutive of STEIN with intrusive -d-.

Steindorf (136) German: habitational name from any of several places so called, named with German *Stein* 'stone' + *Dorf* 'village'.

Steiner (9940) **1.** German and Jewish (Ashkenazic): occupational name for someone who worked with stone: a quarryman, stonecutter, or stonemason; an agent derivative of STEIN. **2.** Topographic name for someone who lived on stony ground or near a prominent outcrop of rock.
GIVEN NAMES German 4%. *Kurt* (18), *Erwin* (13), *Hans* (9), *Otto* (6), *Armin* (3), *Heinz* (3), *Markus* (3), *Dieter* (2), *Fritz* (2), *Helmut* (2), *Konrad* (2), *Manfred* (2).

Steinert (891) German: variant of STEINER.
GIVEN NAMES German 5%. *Kurt* (5), *Eberhardt* (2), *Erna, Heinz, Otto, Reinhold, Ulrike.*

Steines (222) Possibly a variant of STAINES.
GIVEN NAMES German 4%. *Reinold* (2), *Gerhard.*

Steinfeld (529) **1.** German: habitational name from any of the places named Steinfeld, from Old German *stein* 'stone' + *feld* 'open country'. **2.** Jewish (Ashkenazic): ornamental name composed of German *Stein* 'stone' + *Feld* 'field'.
GIVEN NAMES Jewish 4%. *Alter, Ari, Chaim, Chavie, Moishe, Yehuda.*

Steinfeldt (242) German and Jewish (Ashkenazic): variant of STEINFELD.
GIVEN NAMES German 5%. *Kurt* (2), *Otto.*

Steingart (101) Jewish (eastern Ashkenazic): variant of STEINHART. The change from *h* to *g* is due to the Russian influence, as the sound *h* is lacking in Russian.
GIVEN NAMES Jewish 7%; French 5%. *Meyer, Nathan; Cecile* (2), *Matilde.*

Steingraber (135) German: occupational name for a quarry worker, from Middle High German *stein* 'stone' + agent derivative of Middle High German *graben* 'to dig'.

Steinhagen (200) German: habitational name from any of the places so named, from Old High German with *stein* 'stone' + *hagen* 'enclosure'.
GIVEN NAMES German 7%. *Erwin, Ewald, Gerhard, Horst.*

Steinhardt (448) **1.** German: from the Germanic personal name *Steinhart*, composed of the elements *stein* 'stone' + *hart* 'hardy', 'brave', 'strong'. **2.** Jewish (Ashkenazic): ornamental name composed of German *Stein* 'stone' + *hart* 'hard'.
GIVEN NAMES German 4%; Jewish 4%. *Otto* (3), *Hans* (2), *Gunther, Kurt; Ber, Eliyahu, Mayer, Nechama, Shmuel, Zev.*

Steinhart (378) Variant of German and Jewish STEINHARDT.
GIVEN NAMES German 5%; Jewish 4%. *Erwin, Horst, Juergen, Kurt; Arnon, Isidor, Shmuel, Sol.*

Steinhauer (850) German: occupational name for a quarryman or stonemason, from Middle High German *stein* 'stone' + an agent derivative of *houwen* 'to cut'.
GIVEN NAMES German 4%. *Kurt* (3), *Heinz.*

Steinhaus (386) German and Jewish (Ashkenazic): topographic name for someone living in a stone-built house, from Middle High German *stein* 'stone' + *hūs* 'house', German *Stein* + *Haus*, or a habitational name from any of the many places named Steinhaus, for example near Fulda and near Wels in Austria. In some cases the Jewish name is of ornamental origin.

GIVEN NAMES German 4%. *Armin, Kurt, Otto.*

Steinhauser (598) German (Austria): habitational name for someone from any of the many places called STEINHAUS, or topographic name for someone living in a stone-built house.

GIVEN NAMES German 4%. *Armin, Hans, Kurt, Otto.*

Steinhilber (277) German (Württemberg): habitational name for someone from Steinhilben, named with Old High German *stein* 'stone' + *hülwe, hülbe* 'puddle', 'muddy or marshy ground'.

GIVEN NAMES German 8%. *Theodor* (2), *Wilhelm* (2), *Bernhard, Otto, Reinhold, Udo.*

Steinhofer (106) German: habitational name for someone living at a farm named Steinhof (see STEINHOFF).

GIVEN NAMES German 5%. *Hans* (2), *Kurt.*

Steinhoff (826) **1.** North German (standardized from **Steenhoff**): from Middle Low German *stēn* 'stone' + *hof* 'farmstead', 'manor farm'; a topographic name for someone whose farm had stony soil or was distinguished by some conspicuous boulder or rocky outcrop. **2.** Jewish (Ashkenazic): ornamental name from German *Stein* 'stone' + *Hof* 'farmstead', 'manor farm', 'court'.

Steinhorst (200) North German: habitational name from any of the places so called, in Lower Saxony, North Rhine-Westphalia, and Schleswig-Holstein.

GIVEN NAMES Scandinavian 4%. *Ansgar* (2), *Bjorg.*

Steiniger (128) **1.** German: variant of STEININGER. **2.** Jewish (Ashkenazic): ornamental name from a noun derivative of German *steinig* 'stony'.

GIVEN NAMES German 8%; Scandinavian 4%. *Hans, Kurt; Fredrik, Karsten.*

Steininger (479) German: habitational name for someone from Steiningen in the Rhineland or Steining in Bavaria.

GIVEN NAMES German 5%. *Alois, Fritz, Johann, Juergen, Maximilian, Otto, Uwe.*

Steinkamp (664) North German (standardized from **Steenkamp**): topographic name for someone living by a field with a prominent rocky outcrop or boulder in it, from Middle Low German *stēn* 'rock', 'stone' + *kamp* ' enclosed field'.

Steinke (2348) German: from a diminutive of Middle Low German *stēn* 'stone'. Compare STEIN 1.

GIVEN NAMES German 5%. *Klaus* (4), *Erwin* (3), *Guenter* (3), *Kurt* (3), *Armin* (2), *Bodo* (2), *Ewald* (2), *Arno, Detlef, Ernst, Fritz, Gerhard.*

Steinkirchner (101) German: topographic name for someone living near a church

built of stone, or a habitational name for someone from any various places in Germany and Austria named Steinkirchen.

Steinkraus (188) North German and Jewish (Ashkenazic): from Middle Low German *stēn* 'stone(ware)' + *krōs, krūs* 'jug', German *Stein* + *Krauss*, hence a metonymic occupational name for a potter or an occupational name for an innkeeper.

GIVEN NAMES German 6%. *Erwin, Frieda.*

Steinlage (166) North German: probably a topographic name composed of Middle Low German *stēn* 'stone' + *lage* 'open space between wooded areas'.

GIVEN NAMES German 5%. *Aloysius, Florian, Guenter.*

Steinle (554) German: diminutive of STEIN 1.

GIVEN NAMES German 4%. *Dieter, Gerhard, Hans, Kurt, Siegfried.*

Steinman (1843) **1.** Jewish (Ashkenazic): from STEIN, with the addition of Yiddish *man* 'man'. **2.** Respelling of German STEINMANN.

Steinmann (551) German: elaborated form of STEIN, with the addition of Middle High German *man* 'man'.

GIVEN NAMES German 8%. *Heinz* (4), *Hans* (2), *Horst* (2), *Kurt* (2), *Otto* (2), *Dieter.*

Steinmetz (3154) German and Jewish (Ashkenazic): occupational name from Middle High German *steinmetze*, German *Steinmetz* 'stonemason', 'worker in stone'.

Steinmeyer (403) German: distinguishing name for a tenant farmer (see MEYER) whose farm was on stony ground or was distinguished by a conspicuous rock formation (Middle High German *stein* 'rock').

GIVEN NAMES German 5%. *Erwin* (2), *Klaus* (2), *Kurt* (2).

Steinmiller (170) **1.** Americanized spelling of German **Steinmüller**. **2.** distinguishing name for a miller whose mill was built of stone or located by a distinctive rock formation, from Middle High German *stein* 'stone' + *müller* 'miller'. **3.** habitational name for someone from a place called Steinmühle (literally 'stone mill').

Steinruck (164) German: topographic name for someone who lived close to a stony ridge, from Middle High German *stein* 'stone' + *ruck, rück* 'ridge'.

Steinwand (148) German: habitational name from a place so called near Fulda.

GIVEN NAMES German 6%. *Gottlieb, Kurt, Otto.*

Steinway (128) Americanized form of German **Steinweg**, a topographic name for someone living at a stone (not dirt) road, from Middle High German *stein* 'stone' + *weg* 'path'.

FOREBEARS The well-known firm of piano makers called Steinway was founded by Heinrich Steinweg (1797–1871) in Brunswick, Germany, in 1835. He was born in Wolfshagen, Germany, and in 1851 moved with his three sons to NY, changing his name to Steinway. The firm expanded

with new designs by Christian Steinway (1825–89) and remained in family ownership until 1972.

Steitz (380) German: **1.** habitational name from a place so named in Sachsen-Anhalt. **2.** from Middle High German *stiussen* 'to push', probably a nickname for a fuller in the cloth trade.

GIVEN NAMES German 7%. *Klaus* (3), *Wolfgang* (2), *Ewald, Konrad.*

Stejskal (280) Czech: nickname for a miserable, unhappy, or complaining person, from a derivative of *stejskat, stýskat* 'to be unhappy, lonely, or grumpy'.

GIVEN NAMES Czech and Slovak 7%. *Antonin* (2), *Lubor, Petr, Vaclav, Zuzana.*

Steketee (163) Dutch: from *steken* 'to wound', 'to stub' + Middle Dutch *tee* 'toe', hence a nickname probably for someone with corns.

Stell (1030) **1.** North German: topographic name for someone who lived near a marsh, from an old dialect word *stel* 'bog', where the land was built up on mudflats (behind the dyke) for cattle grazing. The word later assumed the meaning 'small farm'. **2.** English (West Yorkshire): variant of STILL 2, possibly also of STEELE.

Stella (1475) **1.** Italian: from *stella* 'star'. In most cases it probably derives from a medieval female personal name or nickname, but it may also have been a habitational name for someone who lived at a house distinguished by the sign of a star or from any of the places so named (for example in Savona and Salerno), or a topographic name for someone who lived at a place from which roads radiated out in various different directions. **2.** Dutch: from a Latin translation of Dutch *Ster*, meaning 'star', a habitational name derived from a house sign.

GIVEN NAMES Italian 11%. *Angelo* (6), *Salvatore* (3), *Umberto* (3), *Vito* (3), *Cosimo* (2), *Domenic* (2), *Ettore* (2), *Luigi* (2), *Amerigo, Annamaria, Carmine, Cono.*

Stellato (306) Italian (Campania): from a derivative of STELLA.

GIVEN NAMES Italian 14%. *Antonio* (2), *Amato, Amedeo, Angelo, Domenic, Dominico, Gennaro, Luigi, Rocco, Vito.*

Stelle (293) North German: **1.** variant of STELL. **2.** habitational name from any of several places so named, all in northern Germany. **3.** Topographic name from STELL 1 + the suffix *-er* denoting an inhabitant.

Steller (394) German: variant of STILLER.

Stellhorn (161) North German: topographic name from *stel* 'bog' (see STELL) + *horn* 'horn (of land)' (see HORN), or a habitational name from any of several places so named.

GIVEN NAMES German 4%. *Erna, Kurt.*

Stelling (566) **1.** English: habitational name from places in Northumberland and Kent. The former is probbly from an Old

English *stelling* 'shelter or fold for cattle'; the latter may be named with an unattested Old English male personal name, *Stealla*, + *-ingas*, a suffix denoting 'family or followers of'. **2.** Dutch: topographic name from a derivative of Middle Dutch *stelle* 'land built up on mudflats behind a dike'. **3.** German: derivative of STELL 1, for a small cattle farmer.

GIVEN NAMES German 7%. *Otto* (3), *Konrad* (2), *Claus, Eldor, Hannelore, Hans, Helmut, Ilse, Kurt, Rudi*.

Stelljes (161) Dutch: topographic name for someone who lived in an area contained by dikes, from a diminutive of Middle Dutch *stel(le)* (see STELLING 2).

GIVEN NAMES German 16%. *Gunther* (2), *Fritz, Otto, Wilfried*.

Stellmach (194) **1.** German (Upper Silesia): variant of STELLMACHER. **2.** Jewish (Ashkenazic) and Ukrainian: variant of STELMACH.

Stellmacher (195) German: occupational name for a cartwright, from late Middle High German *stelle* 'carriage' (originally 'frame', 'chassis') + *macher* 'maker'. The term originated in Silesia and spread across northern Germany during the Middle Ages.

GIVEN NAMES German 8%. *Johann* (2), *Heinz, Merwin, Ruediger*.

Stellman (170) **1.** North German (**Stellmann**): topographic name for someone who owned a small cattle farm, originally from land in by a marsh, from the old dialect word *stel* 'bog' + Middle Low German *man* 'man'. **2.** Jewish (Ashkenazic): unexplained.

Stello (137) Italian: unexplained.

GIVEN NAMES Italian 7%. *Dino, Geno, Quido, Sante*.

Stellrecht (124) German: occupational name for a cartwright, from Middle High German *stel* 'framework' + *reht* (from Old High German *wurht-*) 'maker'. Compare English *-wright*.

GIVEN NAMES German 13%. *Ewald* (2), *Kurt* (2), *Gerhard, Hans, Rainer*.

Stellwagen (124) German: metonymic occupational name for a carter or a cartwright, from Middle High German *stelle* 'cart' + *wagen* 'wagon'.

Stelly (1251) **1.** Americanized spelling of South German **Stelli**, a nickname for a robust person, from Middle High German *stehelin* 'made of hardened iron'. **2.** North German: probably a derivative of STELLING, which may go back to an Old Saxon personal name also reflected in other family names.

GIVEN NAMES French 6%. *Easton* (3), *Andre* (2), *Ravis* (2), *Aurelie, Euclide, Fernand, Gaston, Germaine, Julien*.

Stelma (137) Dutch: unexplained.

Stelmach (353) Ukrainian, Polish, and Jewish (eastern Ashkenazic): occupational name from Ukrainian *stelmakh* and Polish *stelmach* 'wheelwright', 'cartwright' (a

word of German origin; compare STELL-MACHER).

GIVEN NAMES Polish 10%. *Tadeusz* (2), *Alicja, Bogdan, Elzbieta, Henryk, Irek, Jacek, Krzysztof, Stanislaus, Stanislaw, Zbigniew, Zdzislaw*.

Stelmack (173) Americanized spelling of STELMACH.

Steltenpohl (129) North German: distinguishing name or nickname, literally 'stilt Paul', for a person of that name who used stilts or a wooden leg (see STELTER), or perhaps an occupational name for a manufacturer of stilts or wooden legs, from Middle Low German *stelte* + Low German *Pohl*.

GIVEN NAME German 7%. *Kurt* (3).

Stelter (940) North German: nickname for a disabled person, from Middle Low German *stelte, stilt* 'wooden leg'.

GIVEN NAMES German 5%. *Kurt* (2), *Otto* (2), *Erhardt, Ewald, Gerhardt, Lothar, Manfred*.

Steltz (191) German: nickname for a disabled person, from Middle High German *stelze, stilt* 'wooden leg'.

Stelzer (917) German: **1.** nickname from Middle High German *stelzære* 'person with a wooden leg'. **2.** habitational name for someone from any of various places named Stelzen.

Stelzner (179) German: **1.** variant of STELZER, but probably an occupational name for a stilt-maker. **2.** habitational name for someone from any of the places named Stelzen.

GIVEN NAMES German 10%. *Otto* (2), *Eldred, Hans, Hermann, Kurt, Lorenz*.

Stem (582) Respelling of German STEMM.

Stember (105) **1.** North German (Westphalia): variant of STEMMER. **2.** Jewish (Ashkenazic): variant of STEINBERG.

GIVEN NAMES Jewish 4%. *Doron, Sol*.

Stembridge (423) English: topographic name for someone who lived near a stone bridge, from Middle English *stenen* 'made of stone' + *brigge*, 'bridge'.

Stemen (452) Origin unidentified.

Stemler (273) Variant spelling of German STEMMLER.

GIVEN NAME German 4%. *Otto* (2).

Stemm (321) North German: habitational name from any of several places, all in northern Germany, called Stemmen, from an Old Low German element meaning 'marsh'.

Stemmer (229) North German: habitational name from places called Stemmen, Stemmer, or Stemmern.

GIVEN NAMES German 6%. *Klaus* (2), *Guenter, Wilhelmina*.

Stemmler (234) German (also **Stämmler**): nickname from Middle High German *stameler* 'stammerer'.

GIVEN NAMES German 10%. *Klaus* (2), *Kurt* (2), *Heinz, Horst, Lorenz*.

Stempel (313) German and Jewish (Ashkenazic): from Middle High German *stempel*, German *Stempel* '(coin) stamp', hence a metonymic occupational name for a worker in a mint or someone who made seals.

Stemper (355) German: from an agent derivative of Middle Low German *stempen* 'to stamp', hence an occupational name for anyone whose work involved a stamping process, for example a worker in a mint or in a mill where grain was crushed rather than ground.

Stempien (244) Polish (**Stempień**): variant of **Stępien** (see STEPIEN).

GIVEN NAMES Polish 5%. *Jacek, Jerzy, Thadeus*.

Stemple (714) Americanized spelling of German STEMPEL.

Stempler (104) German: variant of STEMPER.

Sten (142) Swedish: see STEEN.

GIVEN NAMES Scandinavian 15%; German 5%. *Erik* (2), *Lars*; *Alfons, Johannes*.

Stenberg (1066) **1.** Swedish: ornamental name composed of the elements *sten* 'stone' + *berg* 'mountain', 'hill'. **2.** Norwegian and Danish: habitational name from any of several farmsteads; the etymology is as 1.

GIVEN NAMES Scandinavian 5%. *Holger* (2), *Erik, Erland, Knute, Per*.

Stencel (282) Polish and Jewish (from Poland): from a pet form of the Slavic personal name *Stanislav*, Polish *Stanisław* (see STANISLAW) + the Germanic diminutive suffix *-il*.

Stencil (213) Polish and Jewish (from Poland): variant of STENCEL.

Stendahl (124) Swedish: ornamantal name from *sten* 'stone' + *dahl*, ornamental (old) spelling of *dal* 'valley'.

Stender (793) North and central German: metonymic occupational name for a carpenter, from Middle Low German *stender* 'post (of a timber-framed building)'.

Stene (316) Norwegian: habitational name from any of thirty or more farmsteads, so named from Old Norse from *steini*, dative singular of *steinn* 'stone'.

GIVEN NAMES Scandinavian 9%. *Lars* (3), *Sig* (2), *Astrid, Norvald, Thor*.

Stenehjem (101) Probably Norwegian, a habitational name from a farm named from *sten* 'stone' + *hjem* 'homestead', 'farm'.

GIVEN NAMES Scandinavian 8%; German 4%. *Erik, Ove*; *Kurt*.

Stenerson (326) Americanized spelling of Norwegian **Stenersen**, a patronymic from *Stener*, itself from the Old Norse personal name *Steinarr*, derived from *steinn* 'stone' + *-ar* 'warrior', 'spear', or 'patron'.

GIVEN NAMES German 4%. *Kurt* (2), *Gerhard*.

Stengel (1184) German: nickname for a thin, lanky person, from Middle High German *stengel* 'stalk', 'stem'.

GIVEN NAMES German 4%. *Otto* (3), *Heinz* (2), *Erwin, Frieda, Fritz, Gerhard, Kurt*.

Stenger (1757) German: occupational name for a post maker or a carpenter, from Middle High German *stange* 'pole'. Compare STENDER.

Stengle (127) Americanized spelling of German STENGEL.

Stenglein (201) South German: diminutive of STENGEL.
GIVEN NAME German 4%. *Otto*.

Stenhouse (179) Scottish: habitational name from a former barony near Falkirk, whose name has the same origin as STONEHOUSE.

Stenlund (118) Swedish: ornamental name composed of *sten* 'stone', 'rock' + *lund* 'grove'.
GIVEN NAME Scandinavian 12%. *Sig*.

Stenner (158) English: occupational name for a stonemason or stonecutter, or a topographic name for someone who lived on stony ground, from a derivative of Middle English *stene* 'stony place'. Compare STONE.
GIVEN NAMES German 4%. *Hans, Kurt*.

Stennes (176) Norwegian: habitational name from any of several farmsteads, mainly in western Norway, named Steinnes, from Old Norse *steinn* 'stone' + *nes* 'headland', 'promontory'.

Stennett (526) English: from a pet form of *Sten*, a reduced form of STEVEN.

Stennis (223) Scottish: unexplained.

Stenquist (191) Swedish: ornamental name composed of the elements *sten* 'stone' + *quist*, an old or ornamental spelling of *kvist* 'twig'.
GIVEN NAMES Scandinavian 8%. *Majken, Nils, Sven*.

Stensby (104) Norwegian: habitational name from any of about ten farmsteads in eastern Norway named from *sten* 'stone' + *by* 'farmstead', 'settlement'.
GIVEN NAMES Scandinavian 7%. *Birgit, Per*.

Stenseth (174) Norwegian: habitational name from any of numerous farmsteads, notably in eastern Norway, named Steinset, from either the noun *stein* 'stone' or the same word as a personal name + *set* 'farmstead'.

Stensland (429) Norwegian: habitational name from any of twenty-five or more farmsteads, notably in Agder, Rogaland, and Hordaland, so named from *stein* 'stone' (or the same word as a personal name) + *land* 'land'.
GIVEN NAMES Scandinavian 5%. *Lars* (2), *Erik, Knut, Per*.

Stenson (1099) **1.** English: patronymic from a reduced form of the personal name STEVEN. **2.** English: habitational name from a place in Derbyshire, recorded in Domesday Book as *Steintune*, later as *Steineston*, from the Old Norse personal name *Steinn* (meaning 'stone') + Old English *tūn* 'enclosure', 'settlement'. **3.** Variant of STEENSON 2.

Stensrud (401) Norwegian: habitational name from any of numerous farmsteads, notably in Oppland and Buskerud, named in Old Norse as *Steinsrud*, formed generally with the personal name *Steinn* (meaning 'stone') but sometimes with the common noun *steinn* + *ruð* 'clearing'.
GIVEN NAME Scandinavian 4%. *Thor* (2).

Stenstrom (356) Swedish (**Stenström**): ornamental name composed of the elements *sten* 'stone' + *ström* 'river'.
GIVEN NAMES Scandinavian 5%; German 4%. *Anders, Oddvar; Kurt* (3).

Stentz (210) **1.** Eastern German: from a reduced pet form of the Slavic personal name *Stanisław* (see STANISLAW). **2.** South German: unexplained. In Germany the spelling **Stenz** (pronounced 'stents') is more common than **Stentz**, and it is likely that some immigrant families with that name may have added the *-t-* in order to preserve the original pronunciation.

Stenz (182) German: see STENTZ.

Stenzel (1014) German: from a reduced pet form of the Slavic personal name *Stanisław* (see STENCEL, STANISLAW).
GIVEN NAMES German 5%. *Kurt* (5), *Franz* (2), *Eldred, Erna, Erwin, Florian, Hans, Hans George, Helmut, Klaus, Reiner, Ulrich*.

Stepan (379) Czech (**Štěpán**): from the personal name **Štěpán**, Czech form of Latin *Stephanus* (see STEVEN).

Stepanek (549) Czech (**Štěpánek**): from a pet form of the personal name *Štěpán*, Czech form of Latin *Stephanus* (see STEVEN).

Stepaniak (131) Ukrainian: patronymic from the personal name *Stepan*, a vernacular form of Latin *Stephanus* (see STEVEN).

Stepanian (284) Armenian: patronymic from the personal name *Step'an*, Armenian form of Greek *Stephanos* (see STEVEN).
GIVEN NAMES Armenian 27%. *Stepan* (5), *Aram* (4), *Ara* (2), *Sarkis* (2), *Antranig, Armen, Avetis, Berch, Berdj, Dikran, Gagik, Garbis*.

Stepanovich (122) Serbian (**Stepanović**) and Ukrainian: patronymic from the personal name *Stepan*, vernacular form of Latin *Stephanus* (see STEVEN).
GIVEN NAMES South Slavic 5%. *Marko* (2), *Zivota*.

Stepanski (206) Jewish (from Ukraine) and Ukrainian: habitational name for someone from Stepan or Stepantsy in Ukraine. The place names are derived from the personal name *Stepan*, eastern Slavic form of *Stephen* (see STEFFEN).

Stephan (3200) German: from the German personal name *Stephan*, a vernacular form of Latin *Stephanus* (see STEVEN).

Stephani (233) **1.** German: Latinized patronymic from the personal name *Stephanus* (see STEVEN). **2.** Italian: variant spelling of STEFANI.

Stephano (105) Classicized spelling of Italian STEFANO.
GIVEN NAMES Italian 6%. *Angelo, Carmel, Gilda, Reno*.

Stephans (261) **1.** English: variant spelling of STEPHENS. **2.** Reduced form of German **Stephanhans**, from a compound of the personal names *Stephan* (see STEVEN) + HANS.
GIVEN NAMES French 4%. *Gabrielle, Patrice*.

Stephanus (107) German, Dutch, etc.: humanistic adoption of the Latin form of the vernacular personal name STEFFEN, STEVEN, or a cognate.

Stephany (384) Variant spelling of German STEPHANI.

Stephen (2797) Scottish and English: from the personal name *Stephen*, variant spelling of STEVEN.

Stephens (49773) English: patronymic from the personal name *Stephen* (see STEVEN).

Stephensen (106) Danish, Norwegian, and North German: patronymic from the personal name *Stephen* (see STEVEN).
GIVEN NAMES German 7%. *Erna, Kurt*.

Stephenson (18290) Northern English and Scottish: patronymic from the personal name *Stephen* (see STEVEN).

Stepherson (110) Variant of Northern English and Scottish STEPHENSON.

Stepien (338) Polish (**Stępień**): nickname for a plodder, someone with a slow gait, from *stąpać*, Old Polish *stępać* 'to plod'.
GIVEN NAMES Polish 17%. *Stanislaw* (3), *Grzegorz* (2), *Krzysztof* (2), *Wladyslaw* (2), *Beata, Boguslaw, Dariusz, Henryk, Jacek, Jadwiga, Jerzy, Piotr*.

Stepka (159) Of Slavic origin, possibly Ukrainian: from a pet form of the personal name *Stepan*, a vernacular form of Latin *Stephanus* (see STEVEN).

Stepler (115) Americanized spelling of German **Steppler**, of uncertain origin.

Stepney (253) English (mainly Sussex): habitational name from Stepney in London, named probably with an unattested Old English personal name, *Stybba* (genitive *Stybban*) + *hȳþ* 'hythe', 'landing place'.

Stepnowski (105) Polish (**Stępnowski**): habitational name for someone from Stępno in Kalisz voivodeship, named with *stępać* 'to plod' (see STEPIEN), or from a place called Stepnów, now in Ukraine.
GIVEN NAME Polish 5%. *Krystyna*.

Stepp (3424) German and Dutch: from a short form of the personal name *Stephan*, a vernacular form of Latin *Stephanus* (see STEVEN).

Steppe (392) North German and Dutch: variant of STEPP.

Stepper (101) German: **1.** topographic name for someone who lived near a path or ford, from Middle High German *stapf* 'step', 'path'. **2.** occupational name for an embroiderer or stitcher, from Middle High German *steppen* 'to stitch', 'embroider'.

Stepter (109) Origin unidentified.

Steptoe (330) English: nickname from Middle English *step* 'step' + *toe* 'toe', perhaps for someone who treads lightly.

Sterba (363) Czech (**Štěrba**): from Czech *štěrba* 'gap', probably a nickname for someone with a front tooth missing.
GIVEN NAMES German 5%. *Otto* (2), *Wilhelm* (2), *Reinhold*.

Sterbenz (239) German: unexplained.
GIVEN NAMES German 6%. *Bernhard, Erna, Franz, Kurt*.

Sterchi (187) Swiss German: from the word for 'breeding bull', probably for who owned or raised one, or a nickname for a 'superman'.

Sterett (105) Scottish and northern Irish: variant spelling of STARRETT.

Sterk (455) **1.** Dutch: nickname from Middle Dutch *sterke, star(c)ke, staerke* 'strong', 'brave'. **2.** Jewish (Ashkenazic): ornamental name or nickname from German *Stärke* 'strength' (see 1 above).

Sterkel (270) German (**Störkel**): from a diminutive of *storch, storke* 'stork', hence a nickname for someone thought to resemble the bird.

Sterken (128) **1.** Dutch: unexplained. Perhaps a shortened form of **(van) Sterkenburg**, a habitational name from a place so named in Utrecht. **2.** South German (Bavaria): nickname for a short person, from a dialect word for stalk, stub, stump.

Sterle (162) South German (Austrian): **1.** habitational name for someone who lived at a house distinguished by the sign of a star, from a diminutive of Middle High German *sterre*, a variant of *stern* 'star'. **2.** diminutive of STEHR.

Sterling (8176) **1.** Scottish: variant spelling of STIRLING. **2.** English: perhaps a variant of STARLING. **3.** German: from Middle High German *sterlinc*, the name of a coin, hence probably a nickname for someone who paid that amount in rent.
FOREBEARS William Sterling settled in Haverhill, MA, in 1662.

Sterman (198) **1.** English: variant of STEARMAN. **2.** Jewish (Ashkenazic): from **Sternman**, elaborated form of STERN.
GIVEN NAMES Jewish 8%. *Avrom* (2), *Sol* (2), *Baruch, Dalit*.

Stermer (412) Americanized spelling of North German **Störmer** (see STORMER).

Stern (12591) **1.** German and Jewish (Ashkenazic): from Middle High German *stern*, German *Stern* 'star', a habitational name for someone living at a house distinguished by the sign of a star, or a Jewish ornamental name. This name is widespread throughout central and eastern Europe. In Slovenia it is commonly spelled **Štern**. **2.** English: nickname for a severe person, from Middle English *stern(e)* 'strict', 'austere'.
GIVEN NAMES Jewish 5%. *Sol* (19), *Emanuel* (13), *Miriam* (10), *Moshe* (7), *Aviva* (5),

Chaim (5), *Meyer* (5), *Hyman* (4), *Pinkas* (4), *Zvi* (4), *Devorah* (3), *Dov* (3).

Sternbach (144) Jewish (Ashkenazic): ornamental name composed of German *Stern* 'star' + *Bach* 'stream'.
GIVEN NAMES Jewish 11%. *Bernath, Dov, Emanuel, Isidor, Yaron*.

Sternberg (1882) **1.** German and Jewish (Ashkenazic): habitational name from any of various places so named all over Germany. **2.** Jewish (Ashkenazic): ornamental name from German *Stern* 'star' + *Berg* 'mountain', 'hill'.
GIVEN NAMES Jewish 5%; German 4%. *Aizik* (2), *Chaim* (2), *Emanuel* (2), *Shlomo* (2), *Ari, Aron, Eytan, Faina, Hyman, Isadore, Menachem, Meyer; Armin* (3), *Hans* (3), *Bernhard, Claus, Helmut, Herwig, Hilde, Kurt, Manfred, Oskar, Otto, Siegfried*.

Sternberger (160) German and Jewish (Ashkenazic): habitational name for someone from any of the many places called STERNBERG.
GIVEN NAMES Jewish 7%; German 6%. *Moshe* (2), *Yitzchok; Ilse, Lutz*.

Sterne (346) English: variant spelling of STERN 2.

Sterner (2062) German: habitational name for someone from a place or house called STERN.

Sternfeld (144) **1.** German: habitational name from any of various places called Sternfeld, in most cases composed of Middle High German *ster* 'ram' + *feld* 'fiels'. **2.** Jewish (Ashkenazic): ornamental name from German *Stern* 'star' + *Feld* 'field'.
GIVEN NAME Jewish 5%. *Chaim*.

Sternhagen (214) **1.** German: topographic name from Middle High German *ster* 'ram' + *-n-* (either the plural ending or a folk etymological insert by association with Middle High German *stern* 'star') *hagen* 'enclosed field or pasture'. **2.** Swedish: probably an ornamental name composed of German *Stern* 'star' + *Hagen* 'enclosure'.

Sterns (480) English: patronymic from STERN 2.

Sterr (218) German: variant of STEHR.
GIVEN NAMES German 7%. *Alois, Gerd, Kurt, Otto, Wolfgang*.

Sterrett (966) Northern Irish: variant of START.

Sterritt (158) Northern Irish: variant of START.

Sterry (214) English (Suffolk, Gloucestershire): unexplained.

Stertz (137) German: from Middle High German *sterz* 'tail', possibly a nickname for a short, stocky, and clever man.

Sterzinger (102) German: habitational name for someone from Sterzing in Tyrol, Austria.

Stetler (818) Altered spelling of German STETTLER.

Stetser (122) Americanized spelling of German **Stezer** (see STETZER).

Stetson (1688) Possibly English: unexplained.

Stetter (327) **1.** German: variant of STETTNER. **2.** Nickname for someone who lives in a town as opposed to a village or in the country, from Middle High German *stat* 'place', 'settlement', 'town'.

Stettler (601) German: habitational name for someone from Stetlen in the district of Bern, or Stödtlen in the district of Ellwangen.
GIVEN NAMES German 4%. *Kurt* (2), *Alfons, Franz, Hans, Urs*.

Stettner (275) German: habitational name for someone from any of numerous places named Stetten.
GIVEN NAMES German 5%. *Heinz, Reinhard*.

Stetz (460) German: nickname for a stockily built man, from Middle High German *stotze* 'clod', 'lump', 'log'.

Stetzel (154) Altered spelling of South German **Stötzel**, a nickname for a stockily built man, from a diminutive of Middle High German *stotze* 'log', 'clod', 'lump'.

Stetzer (212) German (**Stezer**): from Middle High German *stotze* 'clod', 'lump', hence a nickname for a stockily built man.

Steuart (258) Scottish: variant spelling of STEWART.

Steuber (284) German: variant of STEIBER.
GIVEN NAMES German 7%. *Kurt* (3), *Armin, Fritz, Hans*.

Steubing (136) German: variant of STEUBER.

Steuck (211) North German: unexplained.
GIVEN NAMES German 5%. *Hans* (2), *Armin, Kurt*.

Steuer (498) **1.** German: variant of STEURER. **2.** German: occupational name for a helmsman, from Middle High German *stiur* 'steer'. **3.** Jewish (Ashkenazic): metonymic occupational name for a tax collector, from German *Steuer* 'tax', 'impost'.
GIVEN NAMES German 7%. *Franz* (2), *Gebhard* (2), *Jurgen* (2), *Benno, Egon, Guenter, Klaus, Kurt*.

Steuerwald (169) German: habitational name from a place so called in the Hannover area.

Steurer (224) German: occupational name, from Middle High German *stiurære* 'tax collector', 'helmsman'.

Steury (175) Probably an altered spelling of Swiss German **Steuri**, from Middle High German *stiur(i)* 'big', 'brave', a nickname for a strong person .

Steve (415) **1.** English: from a short form of STEVEN. **2.** French (**Stève**): from the personal name *Estève*, an Old French vernacular form of Latin *Stephanus* (see STEVEN).

Steven (781) Scottish, English, Dutch, and North German: from the personal name *Steven*, a vernacular form of Latin *Stephanus*, Greek *Stephanos* 'crown'. This was a popular name throughout Christendom in the Middle Ages, having been borne by the first Christian martyr, stoned to death at Jerusalem three years after the death of Christ. In English the variant spelling *Stephen* is almost equally common.

Stevener (117) North German: unexplained.

Stevens (65676) English: patronymic from the personal name STEVEN. It is also found in this spelling as a Dutch and North German name, and as an Americanized form of some like-sounding Jewish name, as well as cognate names in other European languages such as STEFAN and STEFFEN and their derivatives.

Stevenson (24321) Scottish and northern English: patronymic from the personal name STEVEN. As a North American surname, it has assimilated some European cognates such as STEFAN and STEFFEN and their derivatives.

Stever (686) German: habitational name from Stevern near Münster or topographic name from the Stever river (named with a prehistoric word denoting a marsh).

Stevers (105) English: variant of STEVENS.

Steverson (660) English: variant of STEVENSON.

Steves (533) English: reduced form of STEVENS.

Steveson (241) English: patronymic from a reduced form of the personal name STEVEN.

Stevick (226) Origin unidentified.

Stevison (215) English or Scottish: patronymic from a reduced form of the personal name STEVEN.

Steward (6502) English: variant of STEWART.

Stewardson (101) English: patronymic meaning 'son the of steward' (see STEWART).

Stewart (109121) Scottish: originally an occupational name for an administrative official of an estate, from Middle English *stiward*, Old English *stigweard*, *stīweard*, a compound of *stig* 'house(hold)' + *weard* 'guardian'. In Old English times this title was used of an officer controlling the domestic affairs of a household, especially of the royal household; after the Conquest it was also used more widely as the native equivalent of **Seneschal** for the steward of a manor or manager of an estate.

FOREBEARS Stuart or Stewart is the surname of one of the great families of Scotland, the royal family of Scotland from the 14th century, and of England from 1603, when James VI of Scotland acceded to the English throne as James I. There were many minor branches of the family left in Britain after the flight of James II in 1688, but not every bearer of the surname can claim relationship with the royal house, even in Scotland. Every great house in medieval England and Scotland had its steward, and in many cases the office gave rise to a hereditary surname. The fall of the house of

Stuart in Britain, conversely, led to the establishment of several highly placed branches bearing this surname in continental Europe, which are in most cases related to the old Scottish royal family.

Stewman (103) Origin unidentified. Possibly English: unexplained.

Steyer (401) German: probably a regional name for someone from Steiermark (Styria) in Austria.

Stibbe (123) North German: habitational name from a place so named in West Prussia.
GIVEN NAMES German 12%. *Egon, Erwin, Fritz, Manfred, Otto.*

Stice (892) Possibly an Americanized spelling of German **Steiss**, a nickname from Middle High German *stiuz* 'buttocks'.

Stich (760) **1.** German and Jewish (Ashkenazic): occupational nickname for a tailor or cobbler, from Middle High German *stich*, German *Stich* 'stitch'. **2.** German: habitational name from two manors so named near Düsseldorf and Mülheim. **3.** Czech: variant of **Štícha** (see STICHA).

Sticha (213) Czech (**Štícha**): from a pet form of the personal name *Štěpán*, Czech forms of Latin *Stephanus* (see STEVEN).

Sticht (116) North German: from Middle Low German *sticht(e)* 'religious foundation', 'chapter' (modern German *Stift*), hence a status name for the founder or a member of such a community, or an occupational name for a worker at one. Compare STIFTER.
GIVEN NAMES German 10%. *Lorenz* (2), *Otto.*

Stichter (198) North German: from Middle Low German *stichter* 'founder', 'creator', hence perhaps a status name for the founder or a member of some institution.

Stick (208) Jewish (Ashkenazic): variant of STUECK.
GIVEN NAMES German 6%. *Fritz, Hannelore, Klaus, Kurt.*

Sticka (165) Americanized form of Czech **Štička**, a diminutive of **Štika** (see STIKA), or **Štícha** (see STICHA).

Stickel (890) **1.** English: variant of STYLES. **2.** German: topographic name for someone who lived on or by a hill, from Middle High German *stickel* 'hill', 'slope'. **3.** German: nickname from Middle High German *stickel* 'prickle', 'spine', 'pointed object'.

Stickels (212) English: variant of STYLES.

Stickland (161) English: topographic name for someone who lived by a steep slope, from Middle English *stickel* 'steep' (Old English *sticol*) + *land* 'land'.

Stickle (581) Americanized spelling of German STICKEL.

Stickler (1008) **1.** English: nickname for a person who insisted on a strict code of social behavior. **2.** German: topographic name for someone who lived on or by a hill, from Middle High German *stickel* 'hill', 'slope' + the suffix *-er* denoting an inhabitant; in the south an occupational name for

someone who shapes and sets stakes in vineyards.

Stickles (570) English: variant of STYLES.

Stickley (829) English: habitational name from a place so called in Northumberland.

Stickney (1821) English: habitational name from a place in Lincolnshire, so named from the genitive case of Old English *sticca* 'long strip of land' + *ēg* 'island', i.e. a strip of land between streams.

Stickrod (101) Origin unidentified.

Stidd (200) Origin unidentified. Perhaps a variant of an unexplained English name, STODD.

Stidham (2336) Apparently an English habitational name from a lost or unidentified place. However, the surname does not occur in current English records.

Stidman (110) English: probably a variant of STEADMAN.

Stieb (115) **1.** German: variant of STEIB (see STAUB). **2.** North German: from the short form of a Germanic personal name composed with *stūde* 'stiff', 'hard'.

Stiebel (104) **1.** German: variant of STIEFEL. **2.** Jewish (Ashkenazic): nickname from Yiddish *shtibl* 'small house', 'Hasidic house of prayer'.
GIVEN NAMES German 5%; Jewish 5%. *Gerhard; Este, Mayer.*

Stieben (105) German: unexplained.

Stieber (518) **1.** German: nickname, possibly for a coward, from an agent derivative of Middle High German *stiuben* 'to run away'. **2.** Variant of STUBER 1.
GIVEN NAMES German 5%. *Otto* (4), *Dietrich, Helmut, Kurt.*

Stief (269) **1.** German (Sorbian): from a pet form of the personal name *Stefan*, vernacular form of Latin *Stephanus* (see STEVEN). **2.** North German: nickname from Middle Low German *stīf* 'stiff', 'rigid'.

Stiefel (816) **1.** German and Jewish (Ashkenazic): metonymic occupational name for a bootmaker, from German *Stiefel* 'boot', Middle High German *stivel*. **2.** German: from a pet form of the personal name *Stefan*, German form of Latin *Stephanus* (see STEVEN).
GIVEN NAMES German 4%. *Otto* (3), *Kurt* (2), *Arnd, Erna, Erwin, Frieda, Hertha, Ilse.*

Stiefvater (177) German: from Middle Low German *stēfvader* 'stepfather', hence a relationship name.
GIVEN NAMES German 4%. *Gerhard, Kurt.*

Stieg (262) German: topographic name for someone who lived by a path or track, from Middle High German *stīc* 'path'.
GIVEN NAMES French 4%. *Mechelle, Nerine.*

Stiegler (327) German: topographic name for someone who lived near a stile, from Middle High German *stigele* 'stile'.
GIVEN NAMES German 6%. *Friedrich* (2), *Guenther, Kurt, Siegfried.*

Stieglitz (318) Eastern German and Jewish (Ashkenazic): from Middle High German *stiglitz*, German *Stieglitz* 'goldfinch', a nickname for someone thought to resemble the bird, or in the case of the Jewish name an ornamental name.

Stiegman (103) South German (**Stiegmann**): topographic name from Middle High German *stieg(e)* 'stairs', 'stile' (across a fence), denoting someone who lived by such a feature. See also STEGMANN.
GIVEN NAME German 5%. *Kurt.*

Stiehl (300) German: metonymic occupational name for someone who made tool handles, from Middle High German *stil* 'stalk', 'handle'.
GIVEN NAMES German 4%. *Kurt* (2), *Hans.*

Stiel (100) **1.** German: variant of STIEHL, or in some cases from a Germanic personal name, from *stilli* 'quiet', 'gentle'. **2.** Jewish (Ashkenazic): from German *Stiel* 'handle', 'stem', 'stalk', most likely one of the names selected at random from vocabulary words by government officials when surnames were made compulsory.
GIVEN NAMES German 8%; Jewish 7%. *Hans, Heinrich, Wolf; Fishel* (2), *Miriam.*

Stieler (126) German: variant of **Stühler** (see STUHLER).
GIVEN NAME German 4%. *Fritz.*

Stielow (124) German: probably a variant of **Stilow**, a habitational name from a place so named in Pomerania.
GIVEN NAMES German 7%. *Erwin, Horst, Jurgen, Kurt.*

Stien (116) **1.** Norwegian: habitational name from any of numerous farmsteads, notably in Hordaland and Nordland, named with the definite singular form of *stig* 'path', 'trail'; this often denotes a steep mountain path. **2.** German and Dutch: from a reduced form of the personal name *Augustin*, Dutch *Augustijn* (see AUSTIN).

Stiens (157) Dutch: patronymic from STIEN.

Stier (1150) German, Dutch, and Jewish (Ashkenazic): from Middle High German, Middle Dutch *stier*, German *Stier* 'bull', 'bullock', hence a nickname for someone thought to resemble the animal in some way or a metonymic occupational name for someone who tended cattle.
GIVEN NAMES German 4%. *Kurt* (2), *Alois, Erwin, Frieda, Gerhard, Hans, Siegfried, Ulrich, Willi.*

Stierle (112) South German: pet form of STIER.
GIVEN NAMES German 14%. *Hans* (3), *Erwin* (2), *Otto, Rudi.*

Stiers (413) German and Dutch: variant of STIER.

Stierwalt (248) Altered spelling of German **Stierwald**, **Stierwaldt**, a habitational name from a place called Steuerwald, near Hildesheim.

Stieve (158) North German: nickname from Middle Low German *stīf* 'stiff', 'rigid'.

Stifel (143) South German: variant of STIEFEL.

Stiff (788) English: nickname from Middle English *stif* 'rigid', 'inflexible', hence a nickname for someone who had difficulty in bending. The term was also used in a transferred sense of character (generally in the approving sense 'resolute', 'steadfast') from the 12th century, and this use may lie behind many examples of the surname.

Stiffler (1412) German: unexplained.

Stifter (218) German and Dutch: from a derivative of Middle High German, Middle Dutch *stift*, a non-monastic religious community, hence a status name for a member of such a brotherhood.

Stigall (726) Variant spelling of English **Stygall**, a variant of STILES.

Stigen (150) Norwegian: habitational name from several farmsteads named from the definite singular of *stig*, Old Norse *stígr* 'path', 'trail', frequently denoting a position high on a hillside.

Stiger (342) Possibly an altered form of STEIGER.

Stigers (229) Altered form of Dutch **Steygers**, **Stygers**, which may be a metonymic occupational name for a scaffolder, from Middle Dutch *ste(i)ger* 'step', 'stairs', 'scaffold', or alternatively a habitational name from Stegers (French Estaires) in French Flanders. In Limburg this is a topographic name for someone who lived by an ascending track, from a derivative of *stege*, *steeg* '(steep) path'.

Stigger (100) English (Kent): unexplained.

Stiggers (115) Dutch: See STIGERS.

Stigler (361) German: variant of STIEGLER.

Stigliano (134) Italian: habitational name from Stigliano in Matera province.
GIVEN NAMES Italian 10%. *Giovanna, Rocco.*

Stiglich (145) Variant of German STIEGLITZ.

Stiglitz (160) German and Jewish (Ashkenazic): variant of STIEGLITZ.
GIVEN NAME German 6%; Jewish 4%. *Dieter* (2).

Stika (143) Czech (**Štika**) and Slovak (**Štuka**): from the vocabulary word *štika* 'pike', nickname for a quick, sharp, or agile person.

Stikeleather (215) Americanized form of German **Steigleder**, probably a metonymic occupational name for a stirrup maker, from Middle High German *stīcleder* 'stirrup' (from a derivative of Middle High German *stīgan* 'to climb' + *leder* 'leather').

Stile (170) **1.** English: variant of STILES, or a habitational name from a place named with this word, for example in Cumbria. **2.** Americanized spelling of German STEIL.
GIVEN NAMES Italian 7%. *Angelo, Carlo, Sabato.*

Stiles (8258) English: topographic name from Old English *stigel*, *stigol* 'steep uphill path' (a derivative of *stīgan* 'to climb').

Still (4323) **1.** Scottish, English, and German: nickname for a calm man, from Middle English, Middle High German *stille* 'calm', 'still'. The German name may also have denoted a (deaf) mute, from the same word in the sense 'silent'. **2.** English:

topographic name for someone who lived by a fish trap in a river, from Middle English *still*, *stell* 'fish trap'. **3.** German: habitational name from a place so named, in Alsace, near Strasbourg.

Stillabower (109) Americanized form of **Stillebauer**, a nickname from Middle High German *stille* 'quiet', 'secretive' + *-bauer* (see BAUER). The first element may derive from a topographic name denoting a quiet place.

Stille (408) English and German: variant of STILL.

Stiller (1012) **1.** German: nickname for a calm individual, variant of STILL 1. **2.** English: topographic name for someone who lived by a fish trap in a river (see STILL 2). **3.** German: habitational name from STILL in Alsace.
GIVEN NAMES German 5%. *Hans* (2), *Helmut* (2), *Bernd, Dieter, Frieda, Gerda, Helmuth, Manfred, Rudi, Ulrich, Uwe, Wolfgang.*

Stilley (651) **1.** Scottish: of uncertain origin; possibly a derivative of STILL. **2.** Altered spelling of German **Stille** (see STILL), written thus to preserve the second syllable of the German pronunciation.

Stilling (110) English: unexplained. Possibly a variant of STELLING.

Stillinger (185) South German: inflected adjectival or pseudo-habitational form of **Stilling** (see STILLING).

Stillings (541) **1.** German (Westphalia): patronymic from a short form of *Stillo*, from a Germanic personal name formed with *stille* 'calm', 'quiet', 'mute' as the first element. **2.** Possibly English, an altered form of **Stilling**, a Cumbrian surname of unexplained etymology.

Stillion (174) Origin unidentified. Perhaps a variant of English **Stallion**, a nickname for a lusty or lascivious man from Old French *estalon* 'stallion'.

Stillions (128) Origin unidentified. See STALLION.

Stillman (2355) **1.** English and German (**Stillmann**): variant of STILL. **2.** Jewish (Ashkenazic): nickname or ornamental name, from German *still* 'calm', 'quiet' + *Mann* 'man' (Yiddish *shtil* + *man*).

Stills (553) Probably a variant of STILL.

Stillson (314) Perhaps an English patronymic from STILL 1.

Stillwagon (467) Americanized form of German STELLWAGEN.

Stillwell (2610) English: topographic name from Middle English *stille* 'calm', 'quiet', + *welle* 'spring', 'stream', or possibly a habitational name from a minor place, now lost, of which the first element may have been Old English *stigel*, *stigol* 'stile', 'steep place'.

Stilp (134) German: unexplained.

Stilson (624) Origin unidentified. Compare STILLSON.

Stiltner (970) Origin unidentified.

Stilts (143) Americanized spelling of German STILTZ.

Stiltz (128) German: variant of **Stülz** (see STULTZ).

Stilwell (2366) English: variant spelling of STILLWELL.

Stimac (594) Croatian and Serbian (**Štimac**): unexplained.

Stimmel (515) German: variant of **Stümmel**, a nickname for a short person, from Middle Low German *stumpel* 'stub', 'butt end'.

Stimmell (102) German: Americanized spelling of **Stümmel** (see STIMMEL).

Stimpert (153) South German: variant or dialect pronunciation of **Stümpert**, a nickname for a weak, wretched, or maimed person, from Middle High German *stümper* 'weakling' + excrescent *-t*. Compare STUMP 2 . In Germany this name is most frequent around Frankfurt-am-Main.

Stimpson (1043) English: variant of STENSON 1.

Stimson (1163) English: variant of STENSON 1.

Stinar (132) **1.** Scandinavian: unexplained. **2.** Americanized spelling of STEINER.

Stinchcomb (541) English: habitational name from Stinchcombe in Gloucestershire, recorded in the 12th century as *Stintescombe*, from the dialect term *stint* 'sandpiper' + *cumb* 'narrow valley'.

Stinchfield (255) English: unexplained; probably a habitational name from a lost or unidentified place. Neither the place name nor the surname are found in current British records. Compare STANCHFIELD, STINCHCOMB.
FOREBEARS John Stinchfield immigrated from England to Gloucester, MA, in 1735.

Stine (4034) **1.** Dutch: Americanized spelling of **Stijn**, a reduced form of the personal name *Augustijn* (see AUSTIN). **2.** Americanized spelling of German STEIN. **3.** Northern English and Scottish: variant of STEIN.

Stinebaugh (236) Americanized form of German STEINBACH.

Stineman (226) Americanized spelling of STEINMANN or STEINMAN.

Stiner (842) Altered spelling and variant of German and Jewish STEINER.

Stines (716) Patronymic from STINE, as a Dutch, northern English, and Scottish name.

Stinger (397) **1.** English: unexplained. **2.** possibly an altered form of German STENGER.

Stingle (154) German: variant of STENGEL.

Stingley (402) Americanized spelling of German STINGLE.

Stinner (107) from a short form of a Germanic personal name composed with *stīde* 'stiff', 'hard'
GIVEN NAME German 4%. *Helmut.*

Stinnett (2850) Probably a variant of English STENNETT.

Stinnette (261) Variant spelling, under French influence, of English STENNETT.

Stinson (8658) English (mainly northern Ireland): variant of STENSON 1.

Stinton (114) English: habitational name from Market Stainton in Lincolnshire, recorded in Domesday Book as *Staintone*, from Old English *stān* 'stone' (replaced by Old Norse *steinn*) + *tūn* 'farmstead', 'settlement'.

Stipanovich (116) Croatian (Dalmatia and Bosnia; **Stipanović**): patronymic from the personal name *Stipan*, vernacular form of Latin *Stephanus* (see STEVEN).

Stipe (579) English: perhaps a habitational name from a minor place in Wiltshire named Stype.

Stipek (121) Czech (**Štípek**): from a pet form of the personal name **Štěpán**, Czech form of Latin *Stephanus* (see STEVEN).

Stipes (179) Origin unidentified.

Stipp (375) **1.** German: from a short form of a Germanic personal name formed with *stid* 'stiff', 'hard' as the first element. **2.** Dutch: nickname from *stip* 'dot', 'mark', perhaps for someone who had a conspicuous birthmark. **3.** Dutch: from the personal name *Stippe*, a short form of *Stephan* (see STEVEN).

Stippich (146) German: unexplained. Compare STIPP.
GIVEN NAME German 4%. *Gunther.*

Stires (305) Origin unidentified. Perhaps a variant of English STEERS.

Stirewalt (358) Americanized spelling of German STEUERWALD.

Stirk (137) English: from Middle English *stirk* 'bullock', hence a nickname for someone thought to resemble a bullock or metonymic occupational name for someone who had charge of bullocks.

Stirling (1174) Scottish: habitational name from the city in central Scotland, the name of which is of uncertain etymology. It is recorded in the 12th century as *Strevelin*, and is perhaps from a river name.

Stirn (207) German: **1.** nickname for someone with a distinctive forehead, from Middle High German *stirn* 'forehead'. **2.** habitational name from a place so called in Franconia.

Stirrat (125) Scottish: habitational name from a place called Stirie, formerly called Stairaird, near Stair in Ayrshire.

Stirton (107) Scottish and English: habitational name from places in Tayside and North Yorkshire named Stirton.

Stitcher (110) English: probably a status name for someone who owned or cultivated a piece of land, from Middle English *stiche* 'piece of land', Old English *stycce*.

Stiteler (276) probably an Americanized form of **Steidler**, a variant of STEIDLE.

Stitely (223) Americanized form of South German **Steidle**.

Stites (1605) Possibly an Americanized form of STEITZ.

Stith (1676) Of English origin: unexplained. The name is not found in modern English records.

Stithem (107) Variant of English STATHAM.

Stitt (2150) Scottish, northern English, and northern Irish: unexplained. Possibly a variant of STOTT.

Stitts (110) Americanized form of German STUTZ.

Stitz (223) German: variant of STUTZ.

Stitzel (299) German: from a diminutive of STUTZ.

Stitzer (221) Jewish (Ashkenazic): occupational name from an agent derivative of Yiddish *shtitsn* 'to assist', 'to aid'.

Stiver (674) English: occupational name for a plowman, from Old French *estivur* (Latin *stivarius*).

Stivers (1588) Possibly an Americanized spelling of Dutch **Stijvers**, occupational name from an agent derivative of Middle Dutch *stiven* 'to play the flute or shawm' (from Middle Dutch *stive* 'flute').

Stiverson (218) English: variant of STEVERSON.

Stoa (101) Norwegian: habitational name from any of several farmsteads in eastern Norway named Støa, from Old Norse *stoð* 'landing place', 'enclosure'.

Stoakes (145) English: variant of STOKES.

Stob (130) German (**Stöb**): variant of STEIB.

Stobart (112) English (Northumberland and Durham): from a late Old English personal name *Stubheard*.

Stobaugh (392) Americanized spelling of German STAUBACH.

Stobbe (309) English, Dutch, North German, and Danish: variant of STUBBE.
GIVEN NAMES German 7%; Scandinavian 4%. *Erwin* (3), *Goetz, Klaus, Kurt, Lothar, Manfred; Knud* (2), *Tor.*

Stobbs (128) Northern English (Northumberland): variant of STUBBS.

Stober (460) **1.** North German (**Stöber**): variant of **Stöver** (see STOEVER). **2.** German: nickname from Slavic *stobor* 'fighter'. **3.** German (**Stöber**): from Middle High German *stöuber* 'hunting dog', possibly a metonymic occupational name for someone who bred or cared for hunting dogs or a nickname for someone who resembled one.

Stobie (177) Scottish: habitational name from Stobo near Peebles in southern Scotland, so called from Old English *stubb* 'tree stump' + *holh* 'hollow' or *halh* 'nook', 'recess'.

Stock (5017) **1.** English: probably for the most part a topographic name for someone who lived near the trunk or stump of a large tree, Middle English *stocke* (Old English *stocc*). In some cases the reference may be to a primitive foot-bridge over a stream consisting of a felled tree trunk. Some early examples without prepositions may point to a nickname for a stout, stocky man or a metonymic occupational name for a keeper of punishment stocks. **2.** German: from Middle German *stoc* 'tree', 'tree stump', hence a topographic name equivalent to 1, but sometimes also a nickname for an impolite or obstinate person. **3.** Jewish (Ashkenazic): ornamental name from German *Stock* 'stick', 'pole'.

Stockard (546) **1.** Scottish: occupational name for a trumpeter, Gaelic *stocaire*, an agent derivative of *stoc* 'Gaelic trumpet'. The name is borne by a sept of the McFarlanes. **2.** Dutch: nickname from a derivative of Middle Dutch *stoken*, *stocken* 'to attack or knock with a stick'.

Stockberger (140) Possibly an altered spelling or variant of German STOCK-BURGER.

Stockbridge (357) English: habitational name from places called Stockbridge, in Hampshire and a lost place in Spofforth in North Yorkshire, or Stock Bridge in Owston, South Yorkshire, and in Brantingham in Humberside. The place name is derived from Old English *stocc* 'tree trunk', 'log' + *brycg* 'bridge'. FOREBEARS John Stockbridge emigrated from England in about 1635 and settled in Scituate, MA. He had many prominent descendants.

Stockburger (208) South German: habitational name for someone from any of several places named Stockburg.

GIVEN NAMES German 5%. *Bernd, Elke, Juergen, Otto.*

Stockdale (1682) English: habitational name from a place in Cumbria and North Yorkshire, so called from Old English *stocc* 'tree trunk' + *dæl* 'valley'.

Stockdill (139) English: variant of STOCK-DALE.

Stocke (199) **1.** English and German: variant of STOCK. **2.** Probably an Americanized form of STOKKE.

Stockel (164) South German (**Stöckel**): see STOECKEL.

GIVEN NAME German 5%. *Ernst.*

Stocker (2613) German (also **Stöcker**): **1.** topographic name for someone living by a tree stump (see STOCK 2) or an occupational name for a tree cutter, from Middle High German *stocken* 'to clear land'. **2.** from Middle High German *stocker* 'jailer'.

Stockert (323) German and Dutch: from Middle Dutch, Middle High German *stocker* 'jailer'.

Stockett (244) English: topographic name from Middle English *stoket*, 'clearing containing tree stumps' (from a derivative of Old English *stocc*).

Stockford (165) English: **1.** topographic name for someone who lived by a ford marked by a stump, from Middle English *stocke* 'treestump' + *ford* 'ford'. **2.** habitational name from some minor place, as for example Stokeford in Dorset (earlier *Stockford*) 'ford near to East Stoke' (so named from Old English *stoc* 'outlying farmstead', 'secondary settlement').

Stockham (400) English (Avon and Gwent): habitational name from any of various places so called, for example in Devon and Somerset.

Stockhausen (219) German: habitational name from any of several places so called.

Stockholm (156) **1.** Americanized form of Norwegian **Stokholm**, a habitational name from a farmstead in Hordaland named Skotholmen, from *skot* (related to *skyta* 'shoot', denoting a land formation that juts out) + *holme* 'islet'. **2.** In some cases possibly a habitational name for someone from Stockholm, Sweden, presumably adopted on arrival in the U.S., since this name is not used in Scandinavia.

Stocki (111) Polish and Jewish (from Poland): habitational name for someone from places called Stok or Stoki, named with *stok* 'hillside', 'slope'.

GIVEN NAME Polish 7%. *Jerzy* (2).

Stocking (830) **1.** English: topographic name from Middle English *stocking* 'ground cleared of stumps'. **2.** South German: habitational name from any of several places in Bavaria and Styria named Stocking.

Stockinger (294) South German: habitational name for someone from any of several places in Bavaria and Styria named Stocking.

GIVEN NAMES German 5%. *Erwin, Hans, Kurt, Mathias.*

Stockley (256) English: habitational name from any of various places, for example in Devon, County Durham, and Staffordshire, called Stockleigh or Stockley, from Old English *stocc* 'tree trunk' + *lēah* 'clearing'.

Stocklin (113) German (**Stöcklin**) and Swiss (**Stoecklin**): topographic name or nickname from a diminutive of Middle German *stoc* 'tree', 'tree stump' (see STOCK 2).

GIVEN NAMES German 6%. *Inge, Johann, Mathias.*

Stockman (2263) **1.** Dutch and English: from Middle Dutch *stock* 'stump', 'stick', Middle English *stock* 'stump', 'stick' (see STOCK) + *man* 'man'. **2.** German (**Stockmann**): variant of STOCKER 1 and 2.

Stockmann (119) German (also **Stöckmann**): see STOCKMAN 2.

GIVEN NAMES German 13%; Scandinavian 4%. *Bernd, Bernhard, Erwin, Franz, Reinhard, Siegfried; Holger.*

Stockner (109) German: **1.** nickname for a stupid person (see STOCK). **2.** (**Stöckner**) habitational name from any of the many places named Stöcken, in all parts of Germany.

Stocks (1610) English and German: variant of STOCK.

Stocksdale (165) Presumably a variant of STOCKDALE.

Stockslager (188) Americanized spelling of German **Stockschläger**, probably an occupational name for a lumberman, from Middle High German *stoc* 'tree' + an agent derivative of *slān*, *slagen* 'to hit or cut'.

Stockstill (662) Perhaps a variant of STOCKSDALE.

Stockton (4971) English: habitational name from any of the places, for example in Cheshire, County Durham, Hertfordshire, Norfolk, Shropshire, Warwickshire, Wiltshire, Worcestershire, and North and West Yorkshire, so called from Old English *stocc* 'tree trunk' or *stoc* 'dependent settlement' + *tūn* 'enclosure', 'settlement'. It is not possible to distinguish between the two first elements on the basis of early forms. FOREBEARS A family of this name were established in America by an English Quaker, Richard Stockton, in 1656. He bought large tracts of land around Princeton, NJ, and founded an estate on which his great-grandson, Richard Stockton (1730–81), a leading colonial lawyer and one of the signers of the Declaration of Independence, was born.

Stockwell (2594) English: habitational name from a place now in Greater London, so called from Old English *stocc* 'tree trunk', 'plank bridge' + *well(a)* 'spring', 'stream'.

Stocum (139) Origin unidentified. Possibly a variant of English STOCKHAM.

Stoddard (5390) English (Northumbria): occupational name for a breeder or keeper of horses, from Old English *stōd* 'stud' or *stott* 'inferior kind of horse' + *hierde* 'herdsman', 'keeper'. There is a difficulty in deriving this name from Old English *stōd* in that *stud* is not recorded in the sense 'collection of horses bred by one person' until the 17th century; before that it denoted a place where horses were kept for breeding, but that sense does not combine naturally with 'herdsman'. FOREBEARS The Stoddard family of Boston, MA, was introduced by Anthony Stoddard (1600–1686), who settled there in 1639. Solomon Stoddard (1643–1728/9) was a prominent Congregational clergyman in MA, the grandfather of Jonathan Edwards, and progenitor of many noted descendants.

Stoddart (537) English (Northumbria) and Scottish: variant of STODDARD.

Stodden (143) English: habitational name from a minor place called Studding's Farm in Herstmonceaux, Sussex, or possibly from an unidentified place in Devon.

Stodghill (322) Probably an English habitational name from a lost or unidentified place. The surname does not occur in England now.

Stodola (464) Polish (**Stodoła**): topographic name for someone who lived by a barn, Polish *stodoła*.

Stoebe (104) German (**Stöbe**): from Middle Low German *stove* 'heated room', especially '(public) bathhouse' (modern German *Stube*), hence a metonymic occupational name for an owner or operator of a public bath, or a topographic name for someone living near one.

GIVEN NAMES German 7%. *Kurt, Wolfgang.*

Stoeber (143) North German (**Stöber**): variant of STOEVER.

GIVEN NAMES German 7%. *Kurt (2), Willi.*

Stoebner (146) German (also **Stöbner**): occupational name for a bathhouse operator or owner; see STOVER.

GIVEN NAMES German 6%. *Darrold (2), Helmuth.*

Stoeckel (355) South German (**Stöckel**): diminutive of STOCK 2.

GIVEN NAMES German 10%. *Kurt (4), Gerhard (2), Klaus (2), Dieter, Franz, Fritz.*

Stoecker (504) German (**Stöcker**): see STOCKER.

GIVEN NAMES German 4%. *Erwin (3), Kurt, Reinhold.*

Stoeckle (165) German (**Stöckle, Stöcklein**): diminutives of STOCK 2.

Stoecklein (172) German (**Stöckle, Stöcklein**): diminutives of STOCK 2.

Stoecklin (109) Swiss German and German (**Stöcklin**): see STOCKLIN.

Stoeffler (133) German (**Stöffler**): variant of STEFFLER.

Stoeger (179) German (**Stöger**): Bavarian variant of STEGER.

GIVEN NAMES German 7%. *Bernd, Edelgard, Franz, Gerhard.*

Stoehr (817) North German (**Stöhr**): 1. from Middle Low German *store* 'sturgeon', hence a metonymic occupational name for someone who caught or sold sturgeon, or a nickname for someone with some supposed resemblance to the fish. 2. occasionally, a topographic name for someone who lived by the Stör river in Holstein (See STOHR).

GIVEN NAMES German 4%. *Heinrich, Helmut, Horst, Ingeborg, Ingo, Karl Heinz, Klaus, Klaus-Dieter, Konrad, Raimund.*

Stoel (104) German: probably a variant of STOHL.

GIVEN NAME German 7%. *Kurt (2).*

Stoelting (169) North German (**Stölting**): patronymic from STOLDT.

Stoen (149) Norwegian: habitational name from any of several farmsteads named Støen, from Old Notse *støð* 'landing place', 'enclosure'.

GIVEN NAMES Scandinavian 7%. *Erik, Sophus, Thorvald.*

Stoermer (192) North German (**Störmer**): nickname for a hot-tempered person, from a derivative of Middle Low German *storm* 'storm'.

GIVEN NAMES German 10%. *Arno, Horst, Klaus, Manfred, Otto.*

Stoessel (158) German (**Stössel**): metonymic occupational name for someone who used a pestle, an apothecary or spicer, from Middle High German *stœzel* 'pestle'.

GIVEN NAMES German 7%. *Achim, Johann, Otto.*

Stoesz (111) German: variant spelling of **Stöss**, from Middle High German *stōz(en)* 'to push', 'hit', an early form of a derivative agent noun equivalent to modern German **Stösser**, an occupational name for a worker in a warehouse or in a vineyard.

Stoetzel (128) South German (**Stötzel**): nickname for a stockily built man, from a diminutive of Middle High German *stotz* 'clod', 'lump', 'log'.

Stoever (160) North German (**Stöver**): from Middle Low German *(bad)stover* 'bather' or 'worker at a public bathhouse', mainly an occupational name, but occasionally perhaps a nickname for a dedicated bather.

GIVEN NAMES German 6%. *Hans (2), Harro, Lorenz.*

Stofan (123) North German: variant of STEFFEN.

Stofer (262) South German: of uncertain origin; perhaps in part a variant of STOFFER.

Stoff (152) 1. North German: metonymic occupational nickname for a miller, from Middle Low German *stof* 'dust'. Compare STAUB 1. 2. Jewish (Ashkenazic): metonymic occupational name for a cloth merchant, from German *Stoff* 'material', 'cloth'.

GIVEN NAMES German 4%. *Erwin, Otto.*

Stoffel (1406) South German: from a pet form of a reduced form of the personal name *Christoffer* (see CHRISTOPHER).

Stoffels (143) German (Rhineland) and Dutch: patronymic from the personal name STOFFEL.

GIVEN NAMES German 7%. *Mathias, Meinrad, Otto.*

Stoffer (526) English and German: from a reduced form of CHRISTOPHER.

Stofferahn (101) variant of North German **Stofferan**, of unexplained origin. Compare SCHAFFRAN.

Stoffers (171) North German: patronymic from STOFFER.

GIVEN NAMES German 8%. *Erwin (2), Gunther, Hans, Kurt.*

Stoffle (101) Americanized spelling of German STOFFEL.

Stofflet (133) North German (also **Stoffleth**): topographic name for someone living near a channel or an outlet from a lake, from Middle Low German *stof* 'something that flows fast', 'dust' + *flet* 'running water', 'channel'.

Stoffregen (261) North German: from Middle Low German *stofregen*, literally 'dust rain', possibly 'downpour', of uncertain application; possibly a nickname for either a long-suffering or a hot-tempered person.

Stofko (251) Slovak (also **Štofko**): unexplained.

Stoflet (114) Variant of German STOFFLET.

Stogdill (199) Probably an altered form of STOCKDALE.

Stogner (924) South German (**Stögner, Stoegner**): variant of STEGNER.

Stogsdill (721) Origin unidentified. Perhaps a further variant of English STOCKDALE (compare STOGDILL).

Stohl (273) 1. North German: metonymic occupational name for a chair maker, from Middle Low German *stōl* 'chair'. 2. Norwegian: habitational name from a farmstead in Rogaland named Stol meaning 'chair', probably from the name of a hill.

GIVEN NAMES Scandinavian 5%. *Johan (2), Lasse, Nils.*

Stohler (262) German: occupational name for a chair maker, from Middle Low German *stōl* 'chair' + the agent suffix *-er.*

Stohlman (135) North German (**Stohlmann**): variant of STOHL with the addition of *man* 'man'.

Stohr (312) 1. North German (**Stöhr**): see STOEHR. 2. South German (**Stöhr**): nickname from Middle High German *stœraere, stœrer* 'disturber', 'unregistered craftsman (in a guild)' (who worked in homes for pay and meals), or a variant of STEHR.

GIVEN NAMES German 7%. *Otto (3), Christl, Elfriede, Gunter, Hermann.*

Stohs (107) German: variant of STOSS.

GIVEN NAMES German 5%. *Leonhard (2), Gerhard.*

Stoia (149) Romanian: from a personal name of Slavic origin (*Stoja*), a derivative of *stojan* 'to stand'.

GIVEN NAMES Romanian 7%; French 5%. *Cornel, Corneliu, Liviu, Viorel; Alphonse, Aurel.*

Stoiber (231) German (Bavarian): variant of STEIBER.

GIVEN NAMES German 7%. *Claus, Egon, Inge, Kurt.*

Stoick (114) German: of Slavic origin, from Old Slavonic *stojati* 'to stand'.

GIVEN NAME Dutch 5%. *Gust (2).*

Stoke (134) English: habitational name from any of the numerous places throughout England named from Middle English *stoke*. The exact sense in individual cases is not clear; it seems to have meant originally merely 'place', and to have been used mainly for an outlying hamlet or dependent settlement.

Stokely (448) English: variant of STOCKLEY.

Stoken (119) English: unexplained; possibly a variant of **Stocken**, a topographic name for someone who lived by '(the) stumps', from the weak plural of *stocc* 'stump'.

Stoker (2109) 1. English: habitational name for someone from any of the numerous places called STOKE. 2. Dutch: occupational name for a stoker, Middle Dutch *stokere*, or from the same word in the sense 'fire raiser', 'arsonist'. 3. Scottish: occupational name for a trumpeter, Gaelic *stocaire*, an agent derivative of *stoc* 'Gaelic trumpet'. The name is borne by a sept of the McFarlanes.

Stokes (18887) English: variant of STOKE.

Stokesberry (120) Origin unidentified. Possibly an English habitational name from a lost or unidentified place.

Stokey (110) English: habitational name from a minor place such as Stockey in Meeth, Devon, named from Old English *stocc* 'stump' + *(ge)hæg* 'enclosure', or a topographic name with the same meaning.

Stokke (340) Norwegian: habitational name from any of thirty or more farmsteads, notably in Møre og Romsdal, so named from Old Norse *stokkr* 'log', 'trunk', 'beam', denoting either growing timber or a natural formation shaped like a log, for example a straight-sided inlet.
GIVEN NAMES Scandinavian 5%. *Knute* (2), *Nels, Nils.*

Stokley (676) English: variant of STOCKLEY.

Stoklosa (202) Polish (**Stokłosa**): topographic name from *stokłosa* 'brome grass'.
GIVEN NAMES Polish 8%; German 4%. *Bogdan, Leszek, Stanislaw, Zdzislaw; Florian, Otto.*

Stokoe (128) English: habitational name from Stockhow in Cumbria, first attested in 1581 as *Stackay*.

Stokowski (91) Polish: habitational name for someone from a place called Stoki or Stokowo, both named from *stok* 'hillside', 'slope'.

Stolar (231) Jewish (from Ukraine): occupational name from Ukrainian *stolyar* 'joiner'. Compare Polish STOLARZ.

Stolarczyk (135) Polish: occupational name from a diminutive of *stolarz* 'joiner' (see STOLARZ).
GIVEN NAMES Polish 10%. *Janusz, Jerzy, Stanislaw, Wieslaw, Wladyslaw.*

Stolarski (247) Polish: derivative of STOLARZ 'joiner', with the addition of the common suffix of surnames *-ski*.
GIVEN NAMES Polish 12%. *Casimir* (2), *Elzbieta, Henryk, Ignacy, Kazimierz, Malgorzata, Tadeusz, Thadeus, Waclaw, Wojciech.*

Stolarz (200) Polish and Jewish (from Poland): occupational name from *stolarz* 'joiner'.
GIVEN NAMES Polish 5%. *Beata, Kazimierz.*

Stolba (118) Origin unidentified.
GIVEN NAMES German 5%. *Kurt, Otto.*

Stolberg (296) German: habitational name from any of several places so called. The name also occurs in Sweden, where it probably originates from Germany.
GIVEN NAMES Jewish 6%. *Ilya, Irina, Meyer, Yaakov.*

Stoldt (163) North German: variant of STOLTE.
GIVEN NAMES German 7%. *Erwin, Guenter, Juergen.*

Stolen (140) **1.** Norwegian: habitational name from any of numerous farmsteads, chiefly in western Norway, named Stølen, from the definite singular form of *støl* (Old Norse *stoðull*), denoting a mountain dairy for summer milking. **2.** Dutch: from a personal name, *Stoelin*, derived from the Germanic personal name *Stodilo*.
GIVEN NAME Scandinavian 7%. *Ingman.*

Stoler (284) Jewish (eastern Ashkenazic): occupational name from eastern Yiddish *stolyer* 'joiner'. Compare Polish STOLARZ.
GIVEN NAMES Jewish 7%. *Alter, Emanuel, Meyer, Moshe, Myer, Slava.*

Stolfi (173) Northern Italian: patronymic from *Stolfo*, a reduced form of a Germanic personal name, *Astolfo*, formed with *haist(i)* 'force', 'valor' + *wulf* 'wolf'.
GIVEN NAMES Italian 10%. *Domenic* (2), *Aldo, Gaetano.*

Stoliker (118) German: unexplained.
GIVEN NAME German 4%. *Kurt.*

Stolk (125) Dutch: unexplained.
GIVEN NAMES Dutch 6%. *Dirk* (2), *Marinus.*

Stoll (4658) **1.** German: from Middle High German, Middle Low German *stolle* 'prop', 'support', 'frame', hence a metonymic occupational name for a carpenter, or a nickname for a rigid person. **2.** Jewish (Ashkenazic): unexplained.
GIVEN NAMES German 4%. *Hans* (8), *Gerhard* (5), *Klaus* (4), *Nikolaus* (3), *Alois* (2), *Kurt* (2), *Otto* (2), *Ulrich* (2), *Alfons, Bernd, Dieter, Dietrich.*

Stollar (179) **1.** Jewish: variant of STOLAR. **2.** Hungarian (**Stollár**): occupational name for a joiner, from Slavic *stoler* (compare Polish STOLARZ).

Stolle (485) German: variant of STOLL.
GIVEN NAMES German 7%. *Erwin* (5), *Otto* (2), *Reinhard* (2), *Ernst, Hans, Kurt, Manfred.*

Stollenwerk (162) German (Rhineland): **1.** metonymic occupational name for a furrier, from Middle Low German *stōlwerk* 'furriery'. **2.** from Middle High German *stolle* 'prop', 'support' + *werk* 'work', hence a metonymic occupational name for a carpenter, especially one who made pit props.
GIVEN NAMES German 6%. *Berthold, Erwin, Otto.*

Stoller (1432) **1.** German and Jewish (Ashkenazic): occupational name for a joiner, from a word of Slavic origin. Compare Polish STOLARZ. **2.** German (Switzerland and Upper Rhine): habitational name for someone from a place called Stolle, near Zurich (now called Stollen). **3.** English: occupational name for a stole maker, from an agent derivative of Middle English *stole* 'stole'.

Stolley (148) Perhaps an Americanized spelling of South German **Stölli**, a dialect diminutive of Middle High German *stolle* (see STOLL).
GIVEN NAMES German 5%. *Otto, Sieg.*

Stollings (307) Origin unidentified. Possibly an altered spelling of STALLINGS.

Stoloff (145) Jewish (eastern Ashkenazic): alternative spelling of **Stolov**, from Slavic *stól* 'table', most probably a metonymic occupational name for a carpenter who made tables, but possibly also for a servant at table, which is the meaning of the cognate Polish surname **Stołowy**.
GIVEN NAME Jewish 4%. *Avi.*

Stolp (436) Eastern German: habitational name from places called Stolp or Stolpe in Pomerania, Mecklenburg, and Brandenburg.
GIVEN NAMES German 6%. *Armin* (2), *Dieter, Horst, Theresia, Uwe, Volker.*

Stolpe (159) Eastern German: variant of STOLP.
GIVEN NAMES Scandinavian 6%; German 4%. *Johan, Nils.*

Stolper (172) **1.** Eastern German: habitational name for someone from Stolpen in Saxony, or a variant of STOLP. **2.** Jewish (eastern Ashkenazic): habitational name for someone from Stolp in Pomerania or Stolpy in Belarus.
GIVEN NAME German 7%. *Arno* (2).

Stolt (281) North German and Danish: variant of STOLTE.
GIVEN NAMES Scandinavian 5%; German 4%. *Hjalmer; Johannes, Juergen, Kurt.*

Stolte (733) North German: nickname from Middle Low German *stolt* 'proud', 'magnificent'.

Stoltenberg (646) German: habitational name from places so called in Pomerania and Rhineland.

Stoltenburg (108) Variant of German STOLTENBERG.

Stoltman (230) German (**Stoltmann**): variant of STOLT.

Stoltz (2359) German and Jewish (Ashkenazic): nickname from Middle High German, German *stolz* 'magnificent', 'proud', Yiddish *shtolts* 'proud'. The Jewish name is often ornamental.

Stoltzfus (1434) Altered form of German **Stolzfuss**, from Middle Low German **Stoltefoth**, a nickname composed of the elements *stolt* 'proud' + *vōt* 'foot', denoting someone of haughty gait; alternatively, from Middle High German *stolzen* 'to limp' + *fuos* 'leg', a nickname for someone who walked with a limp.

Stolz (1427) German and Jewish (Ashkenazic): nickname from Middle High German, German *stolz* 'magnificent', 'proud', Yiddish *shtolts* 'proud'.
GIVEN NAMES German 4%. *Otto* (3), *Heinz* (2), *Erwin, Gunter, Hans, Helmut, Helmuth, Mathias, Reinhard, Seigfried.*

Stolze (258) German: variant of STOLZ.
GIVEN NAMES German 6%. *Erwin, Gunther, Heinz, Horst, Kurt.*

Stolzenberg (135) **1.** German: habitational name from any of the places so called. **2.** Jewish (Ashkenazic): ornamental name from German *stolz* 'proud' + *Berg* 'mountain', 'hill'.
GIVEN NAMES German 7%; Jewish 4%. *Dieter, Kurt; Eliezer, Sol.*

Stolzenburg (124) German: variant of STOLZENBERG.

GIVEN NAMES German 10%. *Kurt* (3), *Theodor*.

Stolzer (162) German (also **Stölzer**): nickname from an agent derivative of Middle High German *stolzen* 'to limp'.

Stolzman (125) German (**Stolzmann**): variant of STOLZ with the addition of Middle High German *man* 'man'.

Stombaugh (284) Altered form of German *Stambach* (see STAMBAUGH).

Stomberg (139) 1. Swedish: ornamental name probably composed of the place name element *Stom-* (denoting church ownership) + *berg* 'mountain'. 2. North German (East Friesland): unexplained.

GIVEN NAMES Scandinavian 4%; German 4%. *Dagny*; *Eldor*.

Stommel (148) German (Rhineland) and Dutch: nickname for a short, stout person, from Middle Low German, Middle Dutch *stommel* 'stump', 'something cut off short'.

Stonaker (102) Americanized form of German STEINACKER or of **Steinacher**, a habitational name from any of six places in Germany and one in Switzerland named Steinach.

Stone (58496) 1. English: from Old English *stān* 'stone', in any of several uses. It is most commonly a topographic name, for someone who lived either on stony ground or by a notable outcrop of rock or a stone boundary-marker or monument, but it is also found as a metonymic occupational name for someone who worked in stone, a mason or stonecutter. There are various places in southern and western England named with this word, for example in Buckinghamshire, Gloucestershire, Hampshire, Kent, Somerset, Staffordshire, and Worcestershire, and the surname may also be a habitational name from any of these. 2. Translation of various surnames in other languages, including Jewish STEIN, Norwegian **Steine**, and compound names formed with this word.

FOREBEARS This name was brought independently to New England by many bearers from the 17th century onward. Thomas Scott was one of the founders of Hartford, CT, (coming from Cambridge, MA, with Thomas Hooker) in 1635.

Gregory Stone (1590–1672) came to North America in 1635, and is buried in the old burial ground at Cambridge MA.

Thomas Stone (1743–87), one of the signers of the Declaration of Independence, was born into a prosperous family at Poynton Manor, MD. He was a descendant of William Stone (born c.1603), who had emigrated to VA from Northamptonshire in England around 1628 and who later became governor of MD.

Stoneback (217) Americanized form of German **Steinbäck** (see STEINBECK) or Swedish **Steinback** or **Stenbäck**, an ornamental name composed of the elements *sten* 'stone' + *bäck* 'stream'.

Stonebarger (118) Anglicized or Americanized form of German and Jewish STEINBARGER.

Stoneberg (199) Partly Americanized form of STEINBERG.

Stoneberger (165) Partly Americanized form of STEINBERGER.

Stonebraker (775) Variant spelling of STONEBREAKER.

Stonebreaker (105) 1. English: occupational name for a worker in a quarry, from Middle English *stone* 'stone' + an agent derivative of *breken* 'to break'. . 2. Translation of German STEINBRECHER or the Dutch equivalent, **Steenbreker**.

Stoneburg (103) Americanized spelling of German **Steinburg**, a habitational name from any of numerous places so named, or of STEINBERG.

Stoneburner (705) Americanized form of German STEINBRENNER.

Stonecipher (722) Americanized form of German **Steinseifer**, a topographic name composed of Middle High German *stein* 'stone', 'rock' + *sīfe* 'swampy creek'. In Germany the surname occurs chiefly in the Siegen area.

Stonecypher (223) Americanized form of German **Steinseifer** (see STONECIPHER).

Stoneham (257) English: habitational name from either of a pair of villages in Hampshire, so called from Old English *stān* 'stone' + *hām* 'homestead'.

Stonehill (154) English: 1. from an unattested Old English female personal name, *Stānhild*, composed of the elements *stān* 'stone' + *hild* 'strife', 'battle'. 2. possibly a habitational name from Stone Hill in Kent, named in Old English with *stānig* 'stony' + *helde* 'slope'.

Stonehocker (202) Most probably, an Americanized form of Jewish (Ashkenazic) **Steinhacker**, an occupational name, from German *Steinhacker* 'stone cutter'.

Stonehouse (296) 1. English: topographic name (from Middle English *stone* 'stone' + *hous* 'house') for someone who lived in a house built of stone, something of a rarity in the Middle Ages, or a habitational name from a place so named, for example in Devon and Gloucestershire. 2. Americanized form of Ashkenazic Jewish **Steinhaus** 'stone house', a topographic name for someone who lived in or by such a house.

Stoneking (810) Translation of German **Steinkönig**, composed of Middle High German *stein* 'stone' + *kūnic* 'king', perhaps a nickname of anecdotal origin.

Stoneman (737) 1. English (Devon): variant of STONE, with the addition of *man* 'man'. 2. Translation of German STEINMANN.

Stoner (6216) 1. English (Sussex): topographic name for someone who lived in a stone-built house (see STONE), with the habitational or agent suffix *-er*. 2. Translation of German STEINER.

Stonerock (257) Americanized form of German STEINRUCK.

Stones (276) English: variant of STONE.

Stonesifer (382) Americanized spelling of German **Steinseifer** (see STONECIPHER).

Stonestreet (410) English: topographic name for someone who lived by a paved road, in most cases a Roman road, from Middle English *stane*, *stone* 'stone' + *strete* 'paved highway', 'Roman road', or a habitational name from either of two places called Stone Street in Kent and Suffolk, which have this origin.

Stoney (428) English: habitational name from Stanney in Cheshire, named with Old English *stān* 'stone', 'rock' + *ēg* 'island'.

Stong (313) Altered form of German STANG.

Stonier (124) English: occupational name for someone who cut and dressed stone, Middle English *stanyer*, *stonier* 'stonecutter' (from *stan*, *ston* 'stone' + a reduced form of *hewer*, agent derivative of *hew(en)* 'to cut, chop', assimilated to the agent suffix *-(i)er*).

Stonum (120) Probably a respelling of English STONEHAM.

Stoodley (118) English: variant spelling of STUDLEY.

Stookey (392) Altered spelling of English STUCKEY or German STUCKI.

Stooksberry (100) Variant of STOOKSBURY.

Stooksbury (341) Possibly an English habitational name from a lost or unidentified place.

Stoop (156) 1. Dutch and North German: from Middle Dutch *stoop*, Middle Low German *stōp* 'pitcher', 'stone bottle', hence a nickname for a heavy drinker or a metonymic occupational name for a wine seller or innkeeper. 2. English: of uncertain origin, perhaps from Middle English *stulpe*, *stolpe* 'post' or 'boundary marker' (Old Norse *stolpi*), or from Middle English *stoppe* 'bucket' (Old English *stoppa*), hence a topographic name for someone who lived either by a boundary post or in a deep hollow. Alternatively, it could be a habitational name from a place so named, most probably Stop in Fonthill Giffard in Wiltshire, named with Old English *stoppa* 'bucket'.

GIVEN NAMES German 6%. *Jurgen* (2), *Christoph*.

Stoops (1477) Dutch: variant of STOOP 1.

Stoos (134) German: nickname for a quarrelsome person, from Middle High German *stoz* 'quarrel', 'dispute'.

Stoots (361) German (Rhineland): Americanized spelling of STUTZ.

Stopa (216) Polish: nickname for someone with some peculiarity or deformity of the foot, from *stopa* 'foot'.

GIVEN NAMES Polish 12%. *Janusc* (2), *Arkadiusz, Danuta, Krystyna, Krzysztof, Stanislaw, Tadeusz, Weislaw.*

Stophel (109) German: variant spelling of STOFFEL.

Stopher (202) German and English: from a reduced form of CHRISTOPHER.

Stopka (181) Polish: nickname for someone with a peculiarity of the foot, from *stopka*, diminutive of *stopa* 'foot' (see STOPA).

GIVEN NAMES Polish 13%; German 6%. *Zofia* (2), *Andrzej, Bronislawa, Krystyna, Mieczyslaw, Tadeusz, Wladyslaw, Zosia; Eldred* (2), *Christoph.*

Stopp (125) **1.** North German and Danish: from Middle Low German *stōp* 'pitcher', 'stone bottle', hence a nickname for a heavy drinker or a metonymic occupational name for a wine seller or innkeeper. **2.** Variant of STOLP.

GIVEN NAME Scandinavian 5%; German 4%. *Erhardt.*

Stoppel (175) **1.** North German: from Middle Low German *stoppel* 'thorn', hence a nickname for someone with a prickly personality, or for someone with a stubbly beard. **2.** North German: habitational name from a place in Westphalia named Stöppel.

GIVEN NAMES German 6%. *Johann, Manfred, Otto.*

Stopper (226) **1.** English: habitational name from Stockport in Greater Manchester, formerly known as *Stopford*. The place name is recorded in the 12th century as *Stokeport*, probably from Old English *stoc* 'hamlet', 'dependent settlement' + *port* 'marketplace' (see PORT). The confusion of the second element with *ford* appears in 1288, and the form *Stopford* is recorded in 1347. **2.** German: occupational name from an agent derivative of Middle High German *stoppen* 'to repair'. **3.** German: Sorbian short form of CHRISTOPHER.

GIVEN NAME German 4%. *Matthias.*

Stopyra (103) Polish: nickname from a derivative of *stopa* 'foot', or possibly from Polish dialect *stopyrczyć* 'to protrude'.

GIVEN NAMES Polish 16%. *Bronislaw* (2), *Andrzej, Ludwik, Zofia.*

Storbeck (196) North German: habitational name from any of the places so called, from a word meaning 'foul' + *beck* 'stream'.

Storch (1090) **1.** German: from Middle High German *storch* 'stork', hence a nickname for someone thought to resemble the bird. **2.** Jewish (Ashkenazic): ornamental name from German *Storch* 'stork', one of the many Jewish surnames taken from bird names.

GIVEN NAMES German 4%. *Kurt* (4), *Otto* (2), *Bernd, Eldor, Gitta.*

Storck (695) German: variant of STORK 2, 3.

GIVEN NAMES German 6%. *Kurt* (5), *Otto* (2), *Erwin, Grete, Lisel, Reimund, Udo.*

Stordahl (278) Norwegian: habitational name from any of fifteen or more farmsteads so named, generally from *stor* 'big' + *-dal* 'valley'.

GIVEN NAMES Scandinavian 4%. *Erik, Helmer.*

Storer (1354) **1.** English and Scottish: from an agent derivative of Middle English *stor* 'provisions', 'supplies', hence an occupational name for an official in charge of dispensing provisions in a great house or monastery, or who collected rents paid in kind. The word *stor* was also used in the Middle Ages for livestock, and the surname may sometimes have denoted a keeper of animals. **2.** South German: from a Bavarian dialect word, *storer*, denoting an unskilled workman, i.e. someone who was not a member of a craft guild.

Storey (5129) Northern English: from the Old Norse byname *Stóri* (from *stórr* 'big'), also used as a personal name in northern England in the early Middle Ages.

Storie (778) Scottish: variant spelling of STOREY.

Storino (142) Italian (Calabria): unexplained.

GIVEN NAMES Italian 18%. *Antonio* (3), *Aldo, Angelo, Armando, Carlo, Franco, Mario.*

Storjohann (124) Danish and North German (Holstein): distinguishing nickname composed of the adjective *stor* 'big' + the personal name *Johann* 'John'.

GIVEN NAMES German 10%. *Erwin, Guenter, Gunter, Helmut.*

Stork (1282) **1.** English: from Middle English *stork* 'stork', hence a nickname for a thin man with long legs, or perhaps occasionally a habitational name for someone living at a house distinguished by the sign of a stork. In Yorkshire, where the name is most frequent, it may be a habitational name from a place so named (now known as Storkhill), near Beverley. **2.** North German: nickname for someone thought to resemble a stork, Middle Low German *stork*. **3.** German: habitational name from a place so named in Hesse.

GIVEN NAMES German 4%. *Erwin* (2), *Otto* (2), *Aloysius, Elke, Erna, Fritz, Georg, Guenter, Gunther, Hans, Irmgard, Juergen.*

Storlie (330) Norwegian: habitational name from any of numerous farmsteads named Storli, from *stor* 'big' + *-li* 'hillside'.

GIVEN NAMES Scandinavian 5%. *Selmer* (2), *Erik, Knute.*

Storm (3821) **1.** English, North German, Dutch, and Scandinavian: nickname for a man of blustery temperament, from Middle English, Middle Low German, *storm*, Old Norse *stormr* 'storm'. **2.** Dutch: name given to a child born at sea during a storm.

FOREBEARS The Dutch name first appeared when the son of Albert Andriessen Bradt was born at sea in 1636 during a storm on the family's voyage to New Netherland; he was christened *Storm van der Zee* ("Storm from the sea"). Both **Storm** and VANDERZEE are found as American family names.

Storment (247) Probably a variant spelling of STORMONT.

Stormer (424) North German (**Störmer**): variant of STORM.

Stormes (178) English: patronymic from STORM.

Stormo (170) Norwegian: habitational name from any of numerous farmsteads, notably in northern Norway, so named from *stor* 'big' + *mo* 'moor', 'heath'.

Stormont (167) Scottish: from a place so called near Perth.

Storms (1928) German (Rhineland) and Dutch: patronymic from STORM.

Storr (228) **1.** Northern English: nickname from Old Norse *stórr* 'big'. **2.** South German: nickname for a crude man, from Middle High German *storr* 'tree stump', 'clod'.

GIVEN NAMES German 5%. *Hans* (3), *Otto.*

Storrer (147) German: variant of STORER 2.

Storrs (665) English: topographic name from Old Norse *storð* 'brushwood' or 'young plantation'. There is a place so named in Cumbria (formerly in Lancashire), as well as a High Storrs in Sheffield, South Yorkshire, both named from this word.

Storti (293) Italian: patronymic or plural form of STORTO.

GIVEN NAMES Italian 6%. *Evo, Franco, Gaetano, Marcello, Oresto, Quinto.*

Storto (112) Italian: nickname for a man with a twisted back, from *storto, torto* 'twisted', 'crooked'.

GIVEN NAMES Italian 18%. *Luciana* (2), *Lucio, Mario, Pasquale, Rocco, Valerio.*

Storts (372) Probably an Americanized spelling of German STORZ.

Stortz (485) German: variant of STORZ.

Story (7134) Northern English: variant spelling of STOREY.

Storz (364) German: from the dialect word *storz* 'stalk', 'stump', presumably a nickname for a short person.

GIVEN NAMES German 12%. *Kurt* (2), *Otto* (2), *Ulrich* (2), *Erwin, Gerhardt, Matthias, Sigfried, Wolfgang.*

Stoskopf (150) German (Alsace): nickname from an agent derivative of Middle High German *stōzen* 'to push or thrust', 'to clink (glasses)' + *kopf* 'head', 'mug', hence a nickname for a drinker or an obstinate or dashing man.

Stoss (130) **1.** German: nickname for a quarrelsome person, from Middle High German *stōz* 'quarrel', 'fight'. **2.** Jewish (Ashkenazic): from German *Stoss* 'push', 'shove', probably one of the names selected at random from vocabulary words by government officials when surnames were made compulsory.

Stossel (125) Jewish (Ashkenazic): unexplained; apparently a diminutive form of STOSS.

GIVEN NAMES Jewish 7%. *Hyman, Lazer, Tova, Yechiel.*

Stotler (1069) Perhaps an altered form of German STADTLER.

Stott (2281) English: metonymic occupational name for a cattleman, from Middle English *stott* 'steer', 'bullock'. The term was also occasionally used in Middle English of a horse or of a heifer (and so as a term of abuse for a woman), and these senses may also lie behind some examples of the surname.

Stottlemyer (403) Americanized form of German **Stadelmayer**, a distinguishing name for a tenant farmer (see MEYER) who stuttered (from the dialect word *stotteln* 'to stutter').

Stottlemyre (144) Americanized form of German **Stottelmeyer** (see STOTTLEMYER).

Stotts (1596) Origin unidentified; probably a variant of STOTT, or possibly an Americanized form of STOTZ.

Stotz (534) German: nickname for a rough or heavily built person, from Middle High German *stotze* 'block (of wood)', 'lump'.

GIVEN NAMES German 5%. *Egon, Erhard, Ewald, Friedrich, Otto, Reinhold, Willi.*

Stoudemire (281) Americanized form of German STAUDENMAIER.

Stoudenmire (153) Americanized form of German STAUDENMAIER.

Stouder (388) Americanized spelling of German STAUDER.

Stoudt (984) Americanized spelling of German STAUDT.

Stoufer (110) Probably an Americanized spelling of German STAUFFER.

Stouffer (1439) Probably an Americanized spelling of German STAUFFER.

Stough (1173) **1.** Possibly an Americanized spelling of German **Stauch**. **2.** metonymic occupational name for a maker of scarves. **3.** habitational name from places named Stauch in the Rhineland and Saxony.

Stoughton (791) English: habitational name from places in Leicestershire, Surrey, and Sussex, so named from Old English *stoc* 'dependent settlement' + *tūn* 'enclosure', 'settlement'.

FOREBEARS Israel Stoughton, who came to New England from England in about 1630, was one of the founders of Dorchester, MA, and became one of the largest landowners in the Massachusetts Bay Colony.

Stoup (136) **1.** Americanized spelling of German and Jewish STAUP. **2.** Dutch: variant of STOOP 2.

Stout (16056) Irish and English: **1.** nickname for a brave or powerfully built man, from Middle English *stout* 'steadfast'. **2.** from the Old Norse byname *Stútr* 'gnat', denoting a small and insignificant person. **3.** possibly also a habitational name from a

minor place named with the Old English element *stūt* 'stumpy hillock', which is found as a component in various Devon place names.

Stoutamire (116) Americanized form of German STAUDENMAIER.

Stoute (272) Irish: variant of STOUT.

GIVEN NAMES French 6%. *Clovis, Irby, Marcelle.*

Stoutenburg (214) Americanized form of German STOLTENBERG.

Stovall (5435) English: unexplained.

Stover (9055) North German (**Stöver**): from Middle Low German *stover, badstover* 'bather', 'worker at a public bathhouse'.

Stow (573) English: variant of STOWE.

Stowe (4060) **1.** English: habitational name from any of the numerous places, for example in Cambridgeshire, Essex, Gloucestershire, Lincolnshire, Norfolk, Shropshire, and Suffolk, so called from Old English *stōw*, a word akin to *stoc* (see STOKE), with the specialized meaning 'meeting place', frequently referring to a holy place or church. Places in Buckinghamshire, Cambridgeshire, Lincolnshire, Northamptonshire, and Staffordshire having this origin use the spelling *Stowe*, but the spelling difference cannot be relied on as an indication of locality of origin. The final *-e* in part represents a trace of the Old English dative inflection. **2.** Americanized form of various like-sounding Jewish surnames.

FOREBEARS A John Stowe settled in Roxbury, MA, and took the freeman's oath in 1634.

Stowell (2401) English: habitational name from places in Gloucestershire, Somerset, and Wiltshire, so named from Old English *stān* 'stone' + *wella* 'spring', 'stream'.

Stowers (2154) English: **1.** patronymic from an Old Swedish personal name, *Sture*. **2.** topographic name for someone who lived by the Stour river in Essex.

Stoy (453) German (of Slavic origin): from Old Slavic *stojati* 'stand'.

Stoyanoff (104) Bulgarian: alternative spelling of **Stoyanov**, a patronymic from the personal name *Stoyan*.

Stoyer (171) North German: unexplained.

Straatmann (110) North German: topographic name for someone who lived by a road outside a village or town, from Middle Low German *strate* 'road', 'street', orginally from Latin *(via) strata* 'paved road' (for military use). Compare STRASSMAN.

Strabala (129) Origin unidentified.

Stracener (485) Possibly an altered form, under Slavic influence, of German **Strässner** (see STRASSNER).

Strach (105) Germanized or Americanized spelling of Slovenian **Strah**, a nickname for a timid or easily frightened person, from *strah* 'fear'.

Strachan (1461) Scottish: habitational name from a place in the parish of Ban-

chory, Kincardineshire, which is first recorded in 1153 in the form *Strateyhan*, and is perhaps named from Gaelic *srath* 'valley' + *eachain*, genitive case of *eachan* 'foal'. The pronunciation is traditionally 'Strawn'.

Strachota (118) Polish: nickname for a timid or fearful person, derivative of Old Polish *strachać sié* 'to be afraid'.

Strack (1237) North German: from Middle Low German *strak* 'stiff', hence a nickname for an upright and highly principled person or alternatively for someone who was obstinate.

Strackbein (135) North German: nickname from Middle Low German *strak* 'stiff' + *bein* 'leg'.

GIVEN NAMES German 7%. *Erwin (2), Johann.*

Stracke (202) North German: variant of STRACK.

GIVEN NAMES German 6%. *Gerhard (2), Lothar, Reiner.*

Strada (170) Italian (northern and Tuscan): topographic name from *strada* 'street', or a habitational name from any of various places named with this word.

GIVEN NAMES Italian 9%. *Luigi, Remo, Vito.*

Strader (2191) Origin unidentified.

Stradford (190) English: variant of STRATFORD.

Stradley (481) Possibly of English origin, a habitational name from a lost or unidentified place.

Stradling (253) English: habitational name from Strättlingen near Thun in Germany. A William Stradlinge is recorded in the Protestation Returns for Devon for 1642.

Stradtman (107) German: variant of STRAATMANN.

Strahan (1223) Scottish: variant of STRACHAN.

Strahl (516) **1.** German: from Middle High German *strāle* 'flash of lightning', 'strip of land'; it may have been a nickname from the first sense, but appears more generally to have derived from the second sense, as a topographic name or from a field name. **2.** German (**Strähl**): metonymic occupational name for a comb maker, from Middle High German *stæl* 'comb'. **3.** Jewish (Ashkenazic): ornamental name from Yiddish *shtral* or German *Strahl* 'ray of light', 'sunbeam'.

GIVEN NAMES German 5%. *Erwin, Gunther, Hanni, Manfred, Matthias, Siegfried, Ulrich, Wolfgang.*

Strahle (195) German and Jewish: variant of STRAHL.

Strahler (158) **1.** German: variant of STRAHL 1. **2.** South German (**Strähler**): occupational name for a comb maker, from an agent derivative of Middle High German *stræl* 'comb'. **3.** Jewish (Ashkenazic): variant of STRAHL.

Strahm (394) German: topographic name from Middle High German *strām* 'strip of land'.

Straight (1557) English: nickname from Middle English *streȜt* 'straight', 'upright', presumably applied in either a literal or figurative sense.

Strain (3385) Northern Irish: reduced and altered spelling of STRACHAN.

Strait (2393) English: variant of STRAIGHT.

Straka (1021) **1.** Czech and Slovak: nickname from *straka* 'magpie', probably for a thievish or insolent person. **2.** possibly also from Greek **Strakas**: nickname for a dandy, from Greek *straka*, literally 'crack of the whip', used metaphorically to denote someone concerned to impress with his appearance.

Straker (288) English: variant of STRIKER (from the Old English byform *strācian*).
GIVEN NAMES French 4%. *Gervais* (2), *Marcel*.

Straley (943) Perhaps an Americanized spelling of German **Strahle**, a variant of STRAHL, or of STREHLE.

Stram (197) **1.** German: variant of STRAHM. **2.** Jewish (Ashkenazic): ornamental name and nickname from German *stramm* 'upright'.

Strama (115) Polish: occupational name for a maker of runners for sleds, from Polish dialect *strama* 'sled runner'.
GIVEN NAMES Polish 7%; German 4%. *Aniela*, *Genowefa*, *Jozef*, *Wojciech*; *Franz*, *Inge*.

Stramel (160) Jewish (from Ukraine): metonymic occupational name or nickname, from Yiddish *shtrayml* '(Jewish) cap edged with fur'.

Stranahan (310) Irish (County Down): reduced Anglicized form of Gaelic **Ó Sranacháin** 'descendant of *Sranachán*', a personal name apparently derived from *srann* 'snoring'.

Strand (4662) **1.** North German, Danish, and Swedish: topographic name for someone who lived by the seashore, from Middle Low German, Danish, Swedish *strand* 'shore' . In some cases the Swedish name may have been ornamental. **2.** Norwegian: habitational name from any of numerous farmsteads so named, from *strand* 'shore'.
GIVEN NAMES Scandinavian 5%. *Erik* (5), *Nels* (4), *Selmer* (4), *Johan* (2), *Lars* (2), *Aase*, *Berger*, *Bjorn*, *Iver*, *Knute*, *Ludvig*, *Morten*.

Strandberg (731) Swedish: ornamental name composed of the elements *strand* 'shore' + *berg* 'mountain', 'hill'.
GIVEN NAMES Scandinavian 8%. *Nels* (3), *Sigvald* (2), *Anders*, *Erik*, *Fritjof*, *Lars*, *Sten*, *Sven*.

Strande (164) Norwegian: habitational name from any of several farmsteads named with either the dative singular *strǫndu* or the plural *strandir* of Old Norse *strǫnd* 'shore'.
GIVEN NAMES Scandinavian 6%. *Iver*, *Nels*.

Strandell (102) Swedish: unexplained.

Strane (109) Variant spelling of Irish **Strain**, an Anglicized form of Gaelic **Ó Sruitheáin**, from *sruth* 'stream'.

Straney (112) Scottish or Irish: unexplained.

Strang (1890) **1.** Scottish: variant of STRONG, or possibly, as Black suggests, of STRANGE. **2.** German: topographic name from Middle High German *stranc* 'strip of land', or a habitational name from any of the places so called. **3.** German and Jewish (Ashkenazic): metonymic occupational name for a rope maker, from Middle High German *stranc*, German *Strang* 'cord', 'rope'.

Strange (5203) English: nickname for an incomer, a newcomer to an area, from Middle English *strange* 'foreign' (a reduced form of Old French *estrange*, Latin *extraneus*, from *extra* 'outside').

Stranger (151) English: nickname for an incomer, a newcomer to an area, from Middle English *stran(u)gere* 'stranger', 'foreigner'.

Strano (339) Southern Italian: nickname for a stranger or incomer, from Sicilian *stranu* or Calabrian *stranio* 'stranger'.
GIVEN NAMES Italian 19%. *Angelo* (5), *Sal* (4), *Salvatore* (3), *Antonio* (2), *Orazio* (2), *Agatino*, *Alessandro*, *Carmela*, *Carmelo*, *Corrado*, *Domenica*, *Sebastiano*.

Stransky (407) Czech (**Stránský**): topographic name from *stráň* 'hillside', or a habitational name from a place named with this element, for example Strán, Strana, or Stránka.

Strantz (123) German: nickname from Middle High German *stranz* 'bragging'.

Stranz (114) German: variant spelling of STRANTZ.

Strapp (105) English: unexplained.

Strasburg (437) German and Jewish (Ashkenazic): variant of STRASSBURG.

Strasburger (215) Alsatian: variant of STRASSBURGER.

Strasheim (104) Americanized spelling of German **Strassheim(er)**, a habitational name for someone from any of several places in Bavaria called Strassham or possibly from Strassenheim in Baden-Württemberg.

Strassberg (139) Jewish (Ashkenazic): **1.** ornamental name composed of German *Strasse* 'street' + *Berg* 'mountain', 'hill'. **2.** variant of STRASSBURG.
GIVEN NAMES Jewish 10%. *Emanuel*, *Shmuel*, *Shulamith*, *Sol*, *Yosef*.

Strassburg (333) German and Jewish (Ashkenazic): habitational name from any of the various places named Strassburg, in Brandenburg, or Uckermark, or from Strasbourg, Alsace (France).

Strassburger (165) German and Jewish (Ashkenazic): habitational name for someone from Strasbourg in Alsace or any place called STRASSBURG in German.
GIVEN NAMES French 6%; German 5%; Jewish 4%. *Francois*, *Julien*; *Fritz*, *Lothar*; *Aron*.

Strassel (126) South German: pet form from a personal name derived from Old Slavic **strēgu** 'protection', Germanized as **Stross** + the diminutive suffix *-el*.

Strasser (1685) **1.** German and Jewish (Ashkenazic): topographic name for someone living by a main street or highway, from Middle High German *strasse*, German *Strasse* 'street', 'road'. **2.** Slovenian: phonetically Germanized spelling of Slovenian **Stražar**, occupational name for a sentinel, from an agent derivative of *straža* 'watch', 'guard', 'sentry'.
GIVEN NAMES German 4%. *Hans* (4), *Kurt* (3), *Mathias* (2), *Alois*, *Arno*, *Christoph*, *Franz*, *Gerhard*, *Gunter*, *Jurgen*, *Klaus*, *Otto*.

Strassman (205) German (**Strassmann**) and Jewish (Ashkenazic): topographic name for someone living on a main street, from Middle High German *strasse*, German *Strasse* 'street', 'road' + *man* 'man'.

Strassner (251) German: variant of STRASSER.
GIVEN NAMES German 7%. *Heinz* (2), *Hertha*, *Horst*, *Kurt*.

Strate (441) North German and Dutch (**van de Strate**, **van der Strate**): habitational name for someone from any of the places called Strate or Ter Strate 'at the road'.

Strater (198) North German (**Sträter**) and Dutch: topographic name for someone who lived in a street, from Middle Low German *strāte* 'street', 'road' + the agent suffix *-(e)r*. Compare STRASSER.
GIVEN NAME German 6%. *Kurt* (2).

Stratford (646) English: habitational name from any of various places, for example in Greater London, Bedfordshire, Buckinghamshire, Northamptonshire, Suffolk, Wiltshire, and Warwickshire, named in Old English with *strǣt* 'paved highway', 'Roman road' (see STREET) + *ford* 'ford'.

Strathman (205) North German (**Strathmann**): variant of STRATMANN.

Stratis (131) Greek: from a pet form of the personal name *Efstratios*, classical Greek *Eustratios*, literally 'good soldier'. This was a popular given name among early Christians, and was borne by several saints venerated in the Greek Orthodox Church.
GIVEN NAMES Greek 15%. *Antonios*, *Constantine*, *Demetrios*, *Dimitrios*, *Eleni*, *Nicos*, *Nikolaos*, *Spiro*.

Stratman (875) Americanized spelling of STRATMANN.

Stratmann (195) North German: variant of STRATER.
GIVEN NAMES German 8%. *Horst* (3), *Johannes*, *Reinhardt*.

Stratos (118) Greek: variant of STRATIS.
GIVEN NAMES Greek 5%. *Stratos* (2), *Constantine*.

Stratton (8559) English: habitational name from any of various places, in Bedfordshire, Dorset, Hampshire, Norfolk, Oxfordshire, Somerset, Suffolk, Surrey, and Wiltshire, so named from Old English *strǣt* 'paved highway', 'Roman road' (see STREET) + *tūn* 'enclosure', 'settlement'. A place of the same name in Cornwall, which may also be a partial source of the surname, probably has as its first element Cornish *stras* 'valley'.

Straub (3913) German (Austria): nickname from Middle High German *strūp* 'rough', 'unkempt'.

Straube (375) German: variant of STRAUB.
GIVEN NAMES German 10%. *Kurt* (3), *Hans* (2), *Florian, Heinz, Helmut, Lothar, Manfred, Otto, Reinhard, Siegfried.*

Strauch (1095) German: topographic name from Middle High German *strūch* 'bush', 'brush', or a habitational name from places so called in Saxony and Bohemia.
GIVEN NAMES German 5%. *Fritz* (2), *Kurt* (2), *Otto* (2), *Erwin, Ewald, Franz, Hans, Helmuth, Reiner, Reinhart.*

Straughan (401) Northern English (Northumbria and the Northeast): variant of Scottish STRACHAN.

Straughn (593) Variant of northern English STRAUGHAN.

Straughter (244) Origin unidentified.

Straus (1312) German, Dutch, and Jewish (Ashkenazic): variant of STRAUSS.

Strausbaugh (680) Americanized form of German **Strassenbach**, a topographic name from Middle High German *strasse* 'street', 'road' + Middle High German *bach* 'creek', or perhaps a habitational name from a place named with these elements.

Strause (287) German: altered spelling of STRAUSS.
GIVEN NAME German 4%. *Kurt.*

Strauser (487) German: variant of STRASSER.

Strauss (6783) **1.** German: nickname for an awkward or belligerent person, from Middle High German *strūz* 'quarrel', 'complaint'. **2.** German and Jewish (Ashkenazic): from Middle High German *strūze*, German *Strauss* 'ostrich', hence a habitational name for someone who lived at a house distinguished by the sign of an ostrich, or (among the German nobility) a nickname for someone whose coat-of-arms featured an ostrich, or a nickname for someone thought to resemble the bird. In some cases the Jewish surname was ornamental. **3.** Dutch: from a Germanic personal name, *Strūsso*.
GIVEN NAMES German 4%. *Kurt* (11), *Manfred* (7), *Otto* (7), *Erwin* (3), *Inge* (3), *Gerda* (2), *Gerhard* (2), *Hannelore* (2), *Heinrich* (2), *Helmut* (2), *Wolfgang* (2), *Albrecht.*

Strausser (472) Southern German: variant of STRASSER.

Straut (107) German: variant spelling of **Strauth**, a topograpic name for someone who lived near a thicket, from Middle High German *strūt* 'scrub', 'thicket'.

Straw (1561) English (chiefly Nottinghamshire): from Old English *strēaw*, hence a metonymic occupational name for a dealer in straw, or a nickname for an exceptionally thin man or someone with straw-colored hair.

Strawbridge (631) English (Devon): habitational name from a place so called in Hatherleigh, Devon.
FOREBEARS The Methodist Robert Strawbridge was born in Drummersnave (now Drumsna), near Carrick-on-Shannon, Co. Leitrim, Ireland. Some time between 1759 and 1766 he emigrated to MD and settled on Sam's Creek, Frederick Co.

Strawder (307) Origin unidentified. Possibly English: unexplained.

Strawderman (258) **1.** Probably an Americanized form of North German STRAATMANN. **2.** Also possibly an Americanized form of **Strodmann** 'robber', from Middle Low German *stroder* 'highwayman', robber'. **3.** Another possibility is derivation from **Strademann**, a cognate of Old Norse *stredha* 'to throw down', hence a nickname for a fighter.

Strawn (2158) Probably an altered form of STRACHAN or STRAUGHAN, reflecting the pronunciation.

Strawser (795) Possibly an altered form of STRAUSSER or STRASSER.

Strawther (100) Origin unidentified. Probably a variant of Scottish and northern English STROTHER.

Stray (108) **1.** English: unexplained. **2.** Norwegian: habitational name from a farmstead in Agder named Strai, of uncertain derivation.

Strayer (1438) Origin unidentified.

Strayhorn (455) Origin unidentified. Possibly an Americanized form of STRACHAN, STRAUGHAN, reflecting the pronunciation, or of **Strawhorn**, a Scottish name found in Ayrshire and Dumfries, which Black believes to be of local origin, from the lands of Strowarrane or Strawarrane, recorded in Ayr in the 17th century.

Strazza (115) Italian: from a shortened pet form of a compound name formed with *strazza*, from Sicilian *strazzari* 'to rip', 'to tear'.
GIVEN NAMES Italian 22%. *Rocco* (5), *Angelo, Arturo, Emilio, Nicola, Umberto.*

Stream (281) **1.** English: topographic name for someone who lived beside a stream, Middle English *streme*. **2.** Americanized form of Swedish **Ström** or Danish **Strøm** (see STROM).
GIVEN NAME Scandinavian 4%. *Viljo.*

Streat (145) English: variant spelling of STREET.

Streater (381) English: variant of STREETER.

Streb (398) German: variant of STREBE, related to Dutch *streber* 'striver', from German *streben*.

Strebe (196) German: nickname for a person with drive or ambition, from Middle High German *strebe* 'one who strives'.

Strebeck (167) Origin unidentified.

Strebel (359) German: diminutive of STREBE.
GIVEN NAMES German 4%. *Kurt* (2), *Johann.*

Streblow (124) East German: habitational name from a place ao called in Pomerania.
GIVEN NAMES German 5%. *Eldor, Horst.*

Streck (376) German: variant of STRACK 1.

Strecker (878) German: **1.** from an agent derivative of Middle High German *strecken* 'to stretch', hence perhaps an occupational name for someone who stretched cloth out on tenterhooks. **2.** from an agent derivative of Middle Low German *strecken* 'to plow (a piece of land) for the first time', hence a nickname for someone who owned or worked a plot of land that had been newly taken into cultivation. **3.** (eastern): possibly a habitational name for someone from Streckau near Zeitz. **4.** occupational name for a torturer or executioner.
GIVEN NAMES German 6%. *Otto* (3), *Erwin* (2), *Armin, Arno, Franz, Frieda, Heinz, Helmut, Konrad, Kurt, Lothar, Reiner.*

Streed (233) Origin unidentified.
GIVEN NAMES Scandinavian 6%; German 4%. *Elof, Erik, Evald; Bernhard, Jutta.*

Streeper (208) possibly an Americanized form of German **Strüber**, a variant of STRAUB, or an altered form of **Streber**, a variant of STREB.

Street (6733) **1.** English: habitational name from any of the various places, for example in Hertfordshire, Kent, and Somerset, so named from Old English *strǣt* 'paved highway', 'Roman road' (Latin *strata (via)*). In the Middle Ages the word at first denoted a Roman road but later also came to denote the main street in a town or village, and so the surname may also have been a topographic name for someone who lived on a main street. **2.** Jewish: Americanized form of the Sephardic surname **Chetrit**, of uncertain origin. **3.** Americanized form of Ashkenazic Jewish STRASSER and a number of other similar surnames.
FOREBEARS The Rev. Nicholas Street (1603–74) came from England to Taunton, MA, between 1630 and 1638, and later moved to New Haven, CT, where his descendant Augustus Russell Street, a leader in art education, was born in 1791 and went on to become one of the most important early benefactors of Yale College.

Streeter (3904) English (Sussex): topographic name for someone living by a highway, in particular a Roman road (see STREET).

Streetman (652) American translation of German STRASSMAN.

Streets (602) English (South Yorkshire): variant of STREET.

Streett (355) Variant spelling of STREET.

Streety (113) Origin unidentified.

Streff (312) North German: nickname for a stiff or unbending person, from Middle Low German *stref* 'stiff', 'rigid', 'taut'.

Strege (332) German (Sorbian): habitational name from Strega in Lausitz.

Strehl (164) German: **1.** variant of STRAHL 2. **2.** variant of STREHLE.
GIVEN NAMES German 6%. *Kurt* (2), *Gunther.*

Strehle (264) German: habitational name from Strehla on the Elbe river in Saxony, or Strehlen in Silesia.
GIVEN NAMES German 5%. *Ernst* (2), *Alois*, *Gerhard*, *Siegfried*.

Strehlow (463) German: habitational name from either of two places named Strehlow, in Pomerania and Brandenburg.
GIVEN NAMES German 4%. *Fritz* (2), *Otto* (2), *Wolfgang*.

Streib (235) German: perhaps a variant of STRAUB (compare STRUB), of from a Germanic personal name (*Stribo*) whose first element is cognate with Old High German, Middle High German *strīt* 'quarrel', 'fight'.
GIVEN NAMES German 4%. *Hans* (2), *Fritz*, *Kurt*.

Streich (805) German: **1.** standardized form of North German **Streek**, topographic name from Middle Low German *streke* 'strip of land'. **2.** from Middle High German *strīch* 'stroke', 'blow', hence probably a nickname for a strong fighter.
GIVEN NAMES German 5%. *Erwin* (2), *Hans* (2), *Otto* (2), *Wolfgang* (2), *Gerhardt*, *Gunter*, *Heinz*, *Inge*, *Klaus*, *Markus*, *Reinold*.

Streicher (593) German: **1.** occupational name for someone who measured grain or inspected cloth, from Middle High German *strīcher*. Compare STRIKER. **2.** habitational name for someone from places named Streich or Streichen in Württemberg.

Streif (120) German: variant of STREIFF.

Streifel (168) German: probably a variant of **Streibel**, **Streubel** (see STRAUB).

Streiff (428) German: **1.** from Middle High German *streif* 'raid', hence a nickname for an aggressive warrior, someone who had led war-raids. **2.** topographic name from late Middle High German *streif* 'narrow strip of land'.
GIVEN NAMES German 4%. *Erwin*, *Fritz*, *Kurt*, *Wolfram*.

Streight (195) Probably an altered spelling of STRAIGHT or STREIT.

Streit (1186) **1.** English: nickname from Middle English *streit* 'narrow', 'strict' (Anglo-Norman French *estreit*). **2.** German and Jewish (Ashkenazic): nickname for a quarrelsome person, from Middle High German *strīt*, German *Streit* 'strife', 'argument'.
GIVEN NAMES German 4%. *Kurt* (3), *Otto* (3), *Wolfgang* (3), *Arno* (2), *Dieter* (2), *Markus*, *Oskar*, *Rainer*, *Urs*.

Streitmatter (163) South German: variant of STRITTMATTER.

Streitz (147) German: habitational name from any of several places so named in Pomerania and East Prussia.
GIVEN NAMES German 4%. *Kurt*, *Matthias*.

Strelecki (116) Polish: variant of STRZELECKI.
GIVEN NAMES Polish 5%. *Karol*, *Thadeus*.

Strelow (309) German: variant of STREHLOW.

GIVEN NAMES German 4%. *Ernst*, *Erwin*, *Helmut*, *Kurt*.

Stremel (153) North German: topographic name from Middle Low German *stremel* 'narrow strip (of land or cloth)', hence a nickname for a thin person. Compare STRAHM.
GIVEN NAMES French 4%. *Andre*, *Celestin*.

Stremmel (129) North German: variant of STREMEL.

Streng (314) **1.** German: variant of STRANG 2. **2.** German: from Middle High German, Middle Low German *strenge* 'strong', 'brave'; 'hard', 'pitiless', hence a nickname for a strong or tough person. **3.** Dutch: metonymic occupational name for a rope maker, from Middle Dutch *strenc*, *stringe* 'rope', 'cord'. **4.** Jewish (Ashkenazic): nickname from German *streng* 'strict', 'severe'.
GIVEN NAMES German 5%. *Erwin*, *Heinz*, *Kurt*.

Strenge (136) German: **1.** nickname from Middle High German, Middle Low German *strenge* 'strong', 'brave', 'hardy'.
GIVEN NAME German 4%. *Kurt*. **2.** from Old Slavonic *strēgu*, 'guardianship', 'protection'.

Strenger (114) **1.** German: topographic name from Middle High German *stranc* 'strip of land', or habitational name from any of several places called Strang, named with this word. **2.** Jewish (Ashkenazic): nickname for a strict or severe person from an inflected form of German *streng* (see STRENG).
GIVEN NAMES Jewish 11%; German 4%. *Miriam* (2), *Aron*, *Menashe*; *Kurt*.

Strength (282) Possibly Scottish. Black lists the surname **Strengthie**, also giving an example of *Strength* used as a byname in the 18th or 19th century: a James Stuart known as Jamie Strength.

Strenk (137) German (Westphalia): probably a variant of STRENG.

Stretch (440) English: nickname from Middle English *strech*, *strecche* 'strong', 'violent'.

Stretton (142) English: habitational name from places so named in Cheshire, Derbyshire, Herefordshire, Leicestershire, Shropshire, Staffordshire, and Warwickshire. Compare STRATTON.

Stretz (106) German: of Slavic origin, unexplained.
GIVEN NAMES German 4%. *Fritz*, *Hans*.

Streu (121) German: **1.** habitational name from any of the places so called, for example in Franconia. **2.** (of Slavic origin): from a Slavic word meaning 'order', 'honor'.
GIVEN NAME German 6%. *Horst*.

Streufert (110) German: probably a habitational name from a lost or unidentified place.
GIVEN NAMES German 7%. *Gerhardt*, *Siegfried*.

Strevel (102) Of German origin: unexplained; perhaps an Americanized spelling

of **Streubel** or **Steibel**, diminutive forms of STRAUB.

Strever (105) Origin unidentified.

Strey (292) German: **1.** variant of STREU. **2.** variant of STREGE.
GIVEN NAMES German 5%. *Erna*, *Hans*, *Kurt*, *Otto*.

Striano (128) Italian (Naples): habitational name from Striano in the region of Naples.
GIVEN NAMES Italian 13%. *Antonio*, *Carmine*, *Enrico*, *Luigi*, *Riccardo*.

Stribling (1136) English (Devon): variant of STRIPLING.

Strick (431) German: **1.** metonymic occupational name for a rope maker, from Middle High German *stric*, Middle Low German *strik* 'cord', 'rope'. **2.** nickname for a rogue or prankster.

Stricker (2094) **1.** German: occupational name for a rope maker or knitter (of hose, for example), from an agent derivative of Middle High German, Middle Low German *stricken* 'to tie'. **2.** German: occupational name for someone who snared animals, from an agent derivative of Middle High German *stric*, Middle Low German *strik* 'cord', 'rope'. **3.** Dutch: occupational name for someone whose job was to fill level measures of grain by passing a flat stick over the brim of the measure, thus removing any heaped excess, Middle Dutch *strijker*. Compare STREICHER.

Strickfaden (132) German: occupational nickname meaning 'knit (or tie) the thread'.

Stricklan (130) English: variant of STRICKLAND.

Strickland (22938) English: habitational name from a place in Cumbria, so called from Old English *styr(i)c*, *steorc* 'bullock' + *land* 'land', 'pasture'.

Stricklen (308) English: variant of STRICKLAND.

Strickler (2469) German (Rhineland): variant of STRICKER.

Stricklin (1837) Probably a variant of German STRICKLING, or a diminutive of STRICK 2.

Strickling (221) German (Westphalia): derivative of STREICH 2, a nickname for someone who deals heavy blows, a fighter.

Strid (135) Swedish: soldier's name from *strid* 'combat', 'fighting', 'war'.
GIVEN NAME Scandinavian 6%. *Erik*.

Stride (122) English: from Middle English *stride* '(long) pace' (from *stride(n)* 'to walk with long steps'), presumably a nickname for someone with long legs or whose gait had a purposeful air, although Reaney and Wilson suggest it may also have been a topographic name for someone who lived by a crossing point over a stream, presumably no wider than a stride. They cite as an example a place known as The Strid, in North Yorkshire.

Strider (343) Probably an Americanized form of Dutch **Strijder** or German **Streiter**, a nickname for an aggressive person, an agent noun derived from Middle Low German *strīden*, Middle High German *strīten* 'to fight', or perhaps an altered spelling of German **Strieder**, from a Germanic personal name formed with *strīt*, originally 'striving', 'contest', 'quarrel' + the agent suffix *-er*.

Striebel (140) German: variant of STRUBEL.
GIVEN NAMES German 11%. *Otto* (3), *Erna*, *Frieda*, *Hans*.

Strieby (128) Swiss German or an altered form of German **Striebe**, a variant of **Strübe** (see STRUBE).

Striegel (500) South German: from Middle High German *strigel* 'curry comb', possibly applied as a nickname for a rough person, but the term also meant 'penis' and may well have been an obscene nickname.
GIVEN NAMES German 4%. *Kurt* (2), *Hannelore*, *Othmar*, *Otto*.

Strieter (198) South German: topographic name from Middle High German *struot* 'swamp', 'bush', 'thicket' + *-er*, suffix denoting an inhabitant.

Striffler (117) South German: unexplained.

Strike (310) English: metonymic occupational name from Middle English *strike*, the stick used by a STRIKER.

Striker (433) English: from an agent derivative of Middle English *strike(n)* 'to stroke, smooth', applied as an occupational name for someone whose job was to fill level measures of grain by passing a flat stick over the brim of the measure, thus removing any heaped excess.

Strimple (188) Americanized form of North German **Strümpel**, a nickname for a dejected person, from Low German *strümpel*; or perhaps from Middle Low German *strumpelen* 'to falter', hence a nickname for a disabled person.

Strine (541) Possibly an Americanized spelling of German (Austrian) **Strein**, a nickname from Middle High German *streun* 'roamer'.

String (114) English: metonymic occupational name for a maker of strings or bow strings, from Middle English *streng* 'string', 'cord'.

Stringer (6170) English: occupational name for a maker of string or bow strings, from an agent derivative of Middle English *streng* 'string'. In Yorkshire, where it is still particularly common, Redmonds argues that the surname may have been connected with iron working, a stringer having operated some form of specialist hearth.

Stringfellow (1657) English (Lancashire): nickname for a powerful man, Middle English *streng* 'mighty', 'strong' + *felaw* 'fellow' (see FELLOWS).

Stringfield (690) English: of uncertain origin. It is argued by Redmonds that this surname may have developed as a variant of STRINGFELLOW, through a process, attested in various parish records, in which the original name is first shortened and then expanded into a form different from the orig-

inal; thus *Stringfellow* becomes *Stringfell*, which becomes reinterpreted as *Stringfield*.

Stringham (760) English: apparently a habitational name from a lost or unidentified place.

Stripe (123) English: topographic name for someone who lived on or by a strip of land, Old English *strip*.

Striplin (296) English: variant of STRIPLING.

Stripling (960) English: nickname from Middle English *stripling* 'youth'.

Strite (264) Possibly an Americanized spelling of German STREIT 2.

Strittmatter (379) South German: habitational name for someone from Strittmatt, near Waldshut.
GIVEN NAMES German 4%. *Armin*, *Fritz*, *Guenther*, *Kurt*.

Stritzel (112) German (Austrian): variant of **Strützel**, a metonymic occupational name for a baker, from Middle High German *strützel* 'bread from fine flour'.
GIVEN NAME German 7%. *Ernst*.

Stritzinger (109) German: derivative of a short form of a Germanic personal name composed with *strīt* 'strife', 'feud', originally perhaps meaning 'striving'.

Strnad (465) Czech, Slovak, and Slovenian: from *strnad* 'bunting', hence a nickname for someone thought to resemble the bird.

Strobbe (119) Dutch (Netherlands and Belgium): variant of STRUBBE.
GIVEN NAMES French 7%. *Andre*, *Monique*.

Strobeck (132) North German (also **Ströbeck**): habitational or topographic name from a place so named in Saxony-Anhalt, from *strö(te)beke* 'a stream flowing through swampy underbrush'. Compare STRODTMAN.

Strobel (2476) **1.** German: nickname from a diminutive of Middle High German *strūp* 'rough', 'unkempt'. **2.** Dutch: nickname for a short, thickset person, from Middle Dutch *strobbel*, *strubbel*, diminutives of *strobbe*, *strubbe* 'tree stump'.
GIVEN NAMES German 5%. *Otto* (5), *Kurt* (3), *Fritz* (2), *Guenter* (2), *Hans* (2), *Manfred* (2), *Reinhold* (2), *Wolfgang* (2), *Erwin*, *Franz*, *Gottfried*, *Gottlieb*.

Strober (107) German (**Ströber**): variant of STROBEL 1.

Strobl (328) South German: variant of STROBEL.
GIVEN NAMES German 14%. *Helmut* (2), *Franz*, *Frederich*, *Georg*, *Heinz*, *Ignatz*, *Johann*, *Karlheinz*, *Kurt*, *Markus*, *Mathias*, *Reinhard*.

Stroble (478) Either an altered spelling of STROB(E)L or a reduced form of South German **Ströbele**, another variant.

Strobridge (132) English: variant of STRAWBRIDGE.

Strode (1105) **1.** English: variant of STROUD. **2.** German (**Ströde**): topographic name from a dialect word meaning 'thicket'.

Stroder (173) German (**Ströder**): topographic name for someone living by a thicket, variant of **Ströde** (see STRODE 2).

Strodtman (115) German: **1.** altered spelling of North German **Strodtmann**, a topographic name, from Middle Low German *strōt* 'damp thicket' + *man* 'man'. **2.** from Middle Low German *stroden* 'to rob', 'plunder'.
GIVEN NAME German 5%. *Fritz* (2).

Stroebel (236) German (**Ströbel**): **1.** variant of German STROBEL. **2.** habitational name from any of the places named Ströbel.
GIVEN NAMES German 7%. *Ernst* (2), *Kurt* (2), *Mathias*.

Stroede (107) North German (also **Ströde**): topographic name for someone who lived by a thicket; compare STROTHMAN.

Stroh (1974) German: from Middle High German *strō* 'straw', hence a metonymic occupational name for a dealer in straw, or a nickname for an exceptionally thin man or someone with straw-colored hair.

Strohecker (383) German: occupational name for a chaff cutter, from Middle High German *strō* 'straw', 'chaff' + *hecker* 'chopper'.

Strohl (913) South German: diminutive of STROH, hence a nickname for a skinny person or a slight, fair-haired one, or a pet name for a farmer.

Strohm (956) German: **1.** probably a variant of STRAHM. **2.** habitational name for someone from Strohm near Bremen.

Strohmaier (163) Variant of German STROHMEYER.
GIVEN NAMES German 12%. *Dietrich*, *Erwin*, *Gottlieb*, *Hanni*, *Kurt*, *Otto*.

Strohman (238) **1.** German (**Strohmann**): equivalent of STROHMEYER. **2.** German (**Strohmann**): from Middle High German *strō* 'straw' + *man* 'man', hence a nickname for a farmer or for a stupid person. **3.** Jewish (Ashkenazic): nickname or occupational name from German *Stroh* 'straw' + *Mann* 'man'.

Strohmeier (173) German: variant of STROHMEYER.
GIVEN NAMES German 7%. *Elfriede*, *Erna*, *Wilhelm*.

Strohmeyer (442) German: occupational name for a collector of straw taxes, i.e. taxes in kind from the grain harvest, from Middle High German *strō* 'straw' + *meier* 'bailiff', 'steward' (see MEYER).

Strohschein (140) German: nickname from Middle High German *strō* 'straw' + *schīn* (modern German *Schein*) 'glow', 'visible proof', for a brewer who hung out his 'license' in the form of a sheaf of straw (the clientele being largely illiterate in the Middle Ages).
GIVEN NAMES German 10%. *Manfred* (2), *Kurt*.

Stroik (192) Polish: from *stroik* 'headdress', hence a metonymic occupational name for a maker of headgear, or a nickname for someone noted for his headgear.

Strojny (205) Polish: nickname for a dandy, from *strojny* 'elegant', 'well-dressed'.
GIVEN NAMES Polish 10%. *Wojciech* (2), *Gejza, Mariusz, Piotr, Tadeusz, Thadeus.*

Stroker (110) **1.** English: unexplained. **2.** North German (**Ströker**): from an agent derivative of STRUCK.

Strole (229) South German: (**Ströle**) a variant of **Ströhle** (see STROHL).

Strollo (235) Italian: unexplained.
GIVEN NAMES Italian 12%. *Angelo* (3), *Rocco* (2), *Giacomo, Oreste.*

Strom (3871) **1.** Swedish (**Ström**) and Danish (**Strøm**): from *ström* 'current', probably an arbitrarily adopted ornamental name but possibly a topographic name for someone who lived by a river. **2.** Norwegian: habitational name from any of numerous farmsteads so named from Old Norse *straumr* 'current', 'stream'. **3.** German: variant of STRAHM. **4.** Dutch: from Middle Dutch *stroom*, of uncertain meaning. **5.** Polish: topographic name for someone who lived on a steep slope, from *strom* 'slope' or *stromy* 'precipitous'. **6.** Czech: topographic name or nickname from *strom* 'tree'. **7.** Jewish (Ashkenazic): topographic or ornamental name, from German *Strom* 'stream', 'river'.
GIVEN NAMES Scandinavian 6%. *Erik* (10), *Lars* (2), *Nils* (2), *Sven* (2), *Alvar, Anders, Aslaug, Astrid, Helmer, Jarl, Knut, Sigfrid.*

Stroman (1014) Southern French (**Saint Roman**): habitational name from any of the places so named from the dedication of their churches to a St Romanus.

Strombeck (169) North German: possibly a habitational name from any of various places named Strombach, in Westphalia and Rhineland.

Stromberg (1550) **1.** German: habitational name from any of the various places so named, in Westphalia, Rhineland, and Hesse. **2.** Swedish (**Strömberg**): ornamental name composed of the elements *ström* 'river' + *berg* 'mountain', 'hill'.
GIVEN NAMES Scandinavian 6%. *Erik* (5), *Lennart* (2), *Arndt, Gunn, Knute, Lisen, Maija, Mats, Nels, Olle, Thor.*

Strome (225) Americanized spelling of STROM, especially STROM 6 (Czech: 'tree').

Stromer (258) **1.** South German: from Middle High German *strömer*, a reduced form of *strömeier* (see STROHMEIER). **2.** German: (also **Strömer**): nickname from Middle High German *strömer* 'tramp', 'vagrant' (agent derivative of *strömen* 'to pull one way and another').

Stromgren (163) Swedish (**Strömgren**): ornamental name composed of the elements *ström* 'river' + *gren* 'branch'.

Stromme (255) Norwegian (**Strømme**): habitational name from any of fifteen or more farmsteads, notably in western Norway, so named from Old Norse *Straume*, the dative singular of *straumr* 'current', 'stream'.

GIVEN NAMES Scandinavian 7%. *Erik, Lars, Obert, Peer.*

Strommen (258) Norwegian: habitational name from any of numerous farmsteads named Strømmen or Straumen, from the definite singular of Old Norse *straumr* 'current'.
GIVEN NAME Scandinavian 5%. *Erik.*

Strommer (120) German: variant of STROM 3.
GIVEN NAME German 4%. *Mathias.*

Stromquist (218) Swedish (**Strömqvist**): ornamental name composed of the elements *ström* 'river' + *quist*, an old or ornamental spelling of *kvist* 'twig'.

Stronach (164) Scottish: nickname from Gaelic *srònach* 'nosy'.

Strong (14941) **1.** English: from Middle English *strong, strang* 'strong', generally a nickname for a strong man but perhaps sometimes applied ironically to a weakling. **2.** French: translation of **Trahand**, a metonymic occupational name for a silkworker who drew out the thread from the cocoons (see TRAHAN). **3.** Translation of Ashkenazic Jewish STARK.

Strongin (169) Jewish (from Belarus): unexplained.
GIVEN NAMES Jewish 9%. *Isaak, Yaakov, Yakov.*

Stroop (287) Dutch and North German: from Middle Dutch, Middle Low German *stropen* 'to plunder' or 'to flay', a nickname for a raider or looter, or an occupational name for a skinner.

Stroope (201) Variant of Dutch STROOP.

Stroot (176) Dutch: from Middle Dutch *strote* 'throat', nickname for someone with some peculiarity of the throat or neck, perhaps a goiter.
GIVEN NAMES French 6%. *Francois, Pierre.*

Strop (106) **1.** North German: variant of **Stropp**, either a metonymic occupational name for a rope maker, from the Low German word for rope, or a nickname for a rascal, the sense it has today. **2.** possibly an Americanized form of Dutch **Stroop**, a nickname for a poacher, from a derivative of the verb *stropen* 'to raid', 'to plunder'.
GIVEN NAMES German 4%. *Hans, Kurt.*

Strope (629) Origin unidentified.

Stropes (132) Origin unidentified. Possibly English: unexplained.

Stroschein (185) German: variant of STROHSCHEIN.

Strosnider (331) Americanized spelling of German **Strohschneider**, an occupational name for a chaff cutter, from Middle German *strō* 'straw' + an agent derivative of *sniden* 'to cut'.

Stross (116) German: of Slavic origin, from Old Slavonic *strēgu*, 'guardianship', 'protection'.

Stroth (107) **1.** German: variant of **Strothmann** (see STROTHMAN). **2.** Probably a variant of Scottish **Strath** (unexplained).

Strother (2450) Northern English and Scottish: topographic name from northern Middle English *strother* 'damp land overgrown with brushwood', or a habitational name from any of the various places named with this word, as for example Strother in Tyne and Wear, or Struthers in Fife and Strathclyde.
FOREBEARS A William Strother is recorded in VA in 1673, probably the same man who, as William Strouder, was granted land in 1658.

Strothers (242) English and Scottish: variant of STROTHER.

Strothman (207) Altered spelling of North German **Strothmann**, a topographic name from Middle Low German *strōt* 'damp thicket' + *man* 'man'.

Strotman (152) Variant of North German **Strothmann** (see STROTHMAN).

Strott (115) variant of German **Struth** (see STROTH 1).

Stroub (124) Probably an altered spelling of STRAUB.

Stroud (8585) English (southern): habitational name from places in Gloucestershire and Middlesex, so named from Old English *strōd* 'marshy ground overgrown with brushwood'. Strood in Kent is named with the same word, and some examples of the surname are no doubt derived from this term in independent use.

Strouf (113) Americanized form of German **Strauf**, an occupational name for a skinner or knacker, from Middle High German *stroufen* 'to flay'.

Strough (210) Origin unidentified.

Stroup (3009) Perhaps an altered spelling of STROOP.

Stroupe (919) Perhaps an altered spelling of STROOP.

Strouse (1472) Perhaps an Americanized spelling of German, Dutch, and Jewish STRAUSS.

Strouss (142) Perhaps an Americanized spelling of German, Dutch, and Jewish STRAUSS.

Strout (1207) English (Cornwall): perhaps, as Reaney suggests, a variant of STRUTT.

Strouth (263) Origin unidentified. Compare STROUGH.

Strow (138) Origin unidentified. It could be an Americanized spelling of German STROH; on the other hand, there is a handful of bearers recorded in southwestern England in the 19th century, suggesting it could be of English origin, perhaps a variant of STRAW.

Strowbridge (144) English: variant of STRAWBRIDGE.

Strozewski (124) Polish (**Stróżewski**): habitational name for someone from any of various places named with *stróż* 'gatekeeper', for example Stróżewo in Piła voivodeship.
GIVEN NAMES Polish 4%; German 4%. *Bronislaus; Alois, Florian.*

Strozier (473) Origin unidentified.

Strozyk (110) Polish (**Strózyk**): occupational name from a diminutive of Polish *stróź* 'gatekeeper'.

GIVEN NAMES Polish 5%. *Brunon, Tomasz.*

Strub (539) German: nickname for someone with stiff, bristly hair, from Middle Low German *strūf*, Middle High German *strūp* 'unkempt', 'rough'. Compare STRUVE.

Strubbe (171) Dutch and North German: nickname for a short, thickset man, from Middle Low German, Middle Dutch *struppe* 'stump', 'treetrunk'.

Strube (594) Variant of Dutch and North German STRUB.

Strubel (211) German (also **Strübel**): **1.** from a diminutive of Middle High German *strūp* (see STRUB). **2.** from a pet form of the personal name *Strubo*, possibly originally *Strudbald*, a compound of the Germanic elements *strud* 'lay waste', 'destroy' + *bald* 'bold', 'daring'.

Struble (1756) Americanized spelling of German STRUBEL.

Struchen (159) Swiss German: unexplained.

Struck (1347) North German and Dutch: topographic name from Middle Low German *strūk*, Middle Dutch *struuc* 'bush'.

Struckhoff (163) North German: habitational name for someone who lived on a farm so named, from Middle Low German *struck* 'bush', 'brush' + *hof* 'farmstead', 'manor farm' (see HOFF).

Struckman (220) North German (**Struckmann**): variant of STRUCK with the addition of Middle Low German *man* 'man'.

Struckmeyer (100) German: variant of STRUCKMAN.

GIVEN NAMES German 11%. *Horst, Ingo, Kurt.*

Strudwick (118) English: habitational name from Strudgwick in Kirdford, Sussex.

Struebing (206) North German (**Strübing**): patronymic from STRUBE.

Strum (645) Dutch: variant of STROM 4.

Strumpf (120) **1.** German: nickname for a short, stout person, from Middle High German *strumpf* 'stump'. **2.** Jewish (Ashkenazic): metonymic occupational name for a maker of socks or stockings, from German *Strumpf* 'sock', 'stocking'.

GIVEN NAMES German 9%; Jewish 4%. *Gunter* (2), *Kurt.*

Strunk (2667) North German: from Middle Low German *strunk* 'stalk', 'stump', hence a nickname for a short, stout, ungainly person, or a topographic name for someone who lived in an area with tree trunks.

Strupp (272) Possibly a variant of German **Strub**, a nickname for someone with unkempt or unruly hair, from Middle High German *strūben* 'to stand on end'.

GIVEN NAMES German 4%. *Armin, Hans, Reinhard.*

Struss (311) North German form of STRAUSS.

GIVEN NAMES German 5%. *Eberhard, Kurt.*

Struthers (814) Scottish: variant of STROTHER.

Strutt (138) **1.** English: of uncertain origin, probably from the Old Norse byname *Strútr* (from a vocabulary word referring to a cone-like ornament on a headdress or cap). Alternatively it may be a nickname for an argumentative person, from Middle English *strut(t)* 'quarrel'. **2.** German: topographic name from Middle High German *struot*, *strūt* 'brush', 'thicket', 'swamp', or a habitational name from any of several places named Struth with this word.

Strutton (133) English: variant of STRATTON.

Strutz (415) **1.** North German: nickname from Middle Low German *strūs* 'ostrich'. Compare German STRAUSS. **2.** German: from a short form of a Germanic personal name formed with *strud* 'lay waste', 'destroy', as the first element. **3.** Swedish: ornamental name from *struts* 'ostrich'.

GIVEN NAMES German 4%. *Kurt* (2), *Hans, Manfred.*

Struve (503) Dutch and North German: nickname for someone with stiff, bristly hair (see STRUB).

GIVEN NAMES German 4%. *Arno, Fritz, Kurt, Otto, Willi.*

Struzik (106) Polish: metonymic occupational name for a carpenter, someone who used a plane, from a diminutive agent noun from *strug* 'plane'.

GIVEN NAMES Polish 6%. *Ewa, Zbigniew.*

Strycharz (184) Polish: occupational name from Polish *strycharz* 'bricklayer'.

GIVEN NAMES Polish 9%. *Casimir, Cazimir, Grzegorz, Jozef, Tadeusz.*

Strycker (104) Dutch (**de Strycker**): occupational name for someone responsible for measuring out cloth or grain.

Stryjewski (110) Polish: habitational name for someone from a place called Stryjów in Zamość voivodeship, named with *stryj* 'paternal uncle', 'father's brother'.

GIVEN NAMES Polish 10%. *Casimir, Stanislaus, Wieslaw.*

Stryker (1305) **1.** Dutch (**Strijker**): occupational name for someone whose job was to fill level measures of grain by passing a flat stick over the brim of the measure, thus removing any heaped excess. **2.** Possibly an altered spelling of English STRIKER, or even an Americanized spelling of German STREICHER.

Strzalkowski (80) Polish (**Strzałkowski**): habitational name for someone from any of the places called Strzałki, Strzałkowo, Strzałków, all named with *strzałka* 'arrow'.

GIVEN NAMES Polish 27%. *Andrzej* (2), *Henryk* (2), *Cecylia, Kazimierz, Mikolaj, Zbigniew.*

Strzelczyk (120) Polish: nickname from Polish *strzelczyk*, diminutive of *strzelec* 'bowman'.

GIVEN NAMES Polish 10%. *Dariusz, Pawel, Witold, Zbigniew.*

Strzelecki (321) Polish: habitational name for someone from any of several places called Strzelce, named with *strzelec* 'bowman'.

GIVEN NAMES Polish 11%. *Andrzej, Arkadiusz, Jacek, Jerzy, Krystyna, Leszek, Piotr, Stanislaw, Tadeusz, Tadusz, Thadeus, Wlodzimierz.*

Strzyzewski (111) Polish (**Strzyżewski**): habitational name for someone from places called Strzyżew in Kalisz and Siedlce voivodeships, named with *stryż* 'wren'.

Stuard (378) Variant spelling of STEWARD.

Stuart (14359) Scottish: variant of STEWART. FOREBEARS Stuart or Stewart is the surname of one of the great families of Scotland (see note at STEWART).

Stubbe (455) English, North German, and Dutch: from Old English *stub(b)*, Middle Low German, Middle Dutch *stubbe* 'tree stump' or 'tree trunk', hence a topographic name for someone who lived on newly cleared land, or a nickname for a short, stout man.

Stubbins (179) English: **1.** variant of STEBBINS 1. **2.** from an unattested Old English nickname *Stybbing* 'stumpy one'.

Stubblebine (116) Americanized form of German **Stoppelbein**, either for a person with one shorter leg (from Middle Low German *stoppel* 'stump' + *bein* 'leg'), or a topographic name from the same first element + *bein(t)* 'communal land' (outside the village).

Stubblefield (3190) English (Cambridgeshire): topographic name or a habitational name, perhaps from Stubblefield Farm in Kent or some other place similarly named.

Stubbs (6380) English: patronymic from the Middle English nickname *Stubb* (see STUBBE).

Stubenrauch (134) German: occupational nickname for a boilerman or stoker employed in a public establishment or bathhouse, from Middle High German *stube* 'heatable room' + *rauch* 'smoke'.

GIVEN NAMES German 6%. *Fritz, Winfried.*

Stuber (1156) **1.** North German (**Stüber**): variant of STOEVER. **2.** German: habitational name for someone from a place called Stuben in Württemberg. **3.** German: occupational name for the owner/operator of a public gathering place or room, such as a guild room, tavern, or inn, from Middle High German *stube* 'heatable room' + the agent suffix *-er*.

GIVEN NAMES German 4%. *Kurt* (3), *Florian* (2), *Horst* (2), *Otto* (2), *Elfriede.*

Stubler (152) German (**Stübler**): variant of STUBER.

Stuchell (163) Origin unidentified.

Stuchlik (130) Of Czech origin: unexplained.

Stuck (1477) German: **1.** (also **Stück**), from Middle High German *stuck(e)*, **stück(e)**, a topographic name, from the sense 'subdivision of a piece of land'.

2. topographic name from Low German *Stuck* 'tree stump'.

Stucke (219) German: variant of STUCK 2.

Stucker (923) **1.** German: derivative of STUCK, the suffix *-er* denoting an inhabitant or agent. **2.** (**Stücker**): occupational name for an embroiderer, from Middle High German *sticken* 'to stitch', 'embroider' + the agent suffix *-er*.

Stuckert (247) German: variant of STUCKER 1.

Stuckey (3798) **1.** English: habitational name from Stiffkey in Norfolk (pronounced *Stuckey*), so named from Old English *styfic* 'tree stumps' + *ēg* 'island' or 'higher ground in a marsh'. **2.** Americanized spelling of German STUCKI.

Stucki (456) German: variant of STUCK.

GIVEN NAMES German 5%. *Hans* (2), *Ernst, Franz, Manfried, Otto.*

Stuckman (175) German (**Stuckmann**): variant of STUCK 2, with the addition of Middle High German *man* 'man'.

GIVEN NAME German 5%. *Kurt* (3).

Stuckwisch (132) German (Westphalia): topographic name from Low German *stuck* 'tree stump' + *wisch*, Westphalian dialect for *Wiese* 'meadow', for a farmer living near such land.

Stucky (1116) **1.** German: variant spelling of STUCKI. **2.** Probably a variant spelling of English STUCKEY.

Stuczynski (131) Polish (**Stuczyński**): derivative (possibly a habitational name from an unidentified place) from *stuka* 'bit', 'fragment', 'piece of something'.

Studdard (696) English: variant of STODDARD.

Stude (140) German: topographic name for someone who lived by a thicket, variant of STAUDE.

GIVEN NAMES German 7%. *Armin, Fritz, Otto.*

Studebaker (1002) Altered spelling of German **Studebacker, Stutenbecker**, an occupational name for a baker, from Middle Low German *stute* 'fine white bread' + *becker* 'baker'.

FOREBEARS The wagon maker who made the name famous, Clement Studebaker (1831–1901) was a fourth-generation descendant of Clement and Anna Catherine Studebecker, who arrived in Philadelphia in the ship *Harle* from Rotterdam in 1736. They settled with other Germans in what is now Adams Co., PA.

Student (107) German (Rhine area, Westphalia): nickname for a studious person or a cleric, from Middle High German *student* 'student', 'scholar'.

GIVEN NAMES German 6%. *Hans, Kurt, Otto.*

Studer (2071) German: topographic name for someone who lived by a thicket, variant of STAUDER.

Studio (120) Origin unidentified.

GIVEN NAMES Italian 13%. *Arno, Paolino.*

Studley (706) English: habitational name from any of various places, in Oxfordshire, Warwickshire, Wiltshire, and North York-

shire, so called from Old English *stōd* 'stud farm' + *lēah* 'wood', 'clearing', 'pasture'.

Studnicka (188) Slovak (**Studnička**) and Polish (**Studniczka**): habitational name for someone from any of various places called Studnica, named with *studnica* 'spring'.

GIVEN NAMES Czech and Slovak 5%. *Petr, Vojtech, Zdenek.*

Studstill (252) Origin unidentified.

Studt (356) North German: metonymic occupational name for a baker, from Middle Low German *stute*, a particular kind of loaf made with white flour.

GIVEN NAMES German 4%. *Kurt* (3), *Erwin.*

Studwell (140) English.

Study (187) English: probably a variant spelling of **Studdy**, a habitational name from Studdah in Yorkshire, Stodday in Lancashire (both named with Old English *stōd* 'stud' + *haga* 'hedged enclosure'), or Stody in Norfolk (from the same first element + *(ge)hæg* 'enclosure'), or a topographic name from Middle English *stode* 'stud' + *hey* 'enclosure'.

Studzinski (134) Polish (**Studzieński**): habitational name for someone from places called Studzień or Studzieniec, named with Polish *studnia* 'well' (dialect *studzień*).

GIVEN NAMES Polish 10%. *Bogumil, Casimir, Mieczyslaw, Zygmunt.*

Stuebe (135) North German (**Stübe**): variant of **Stüve** (see STUVE).

Stueber (414) German (**Stüber**): see STUBER.

GIVEN NAMES German 6%. *Otto* (2), *Ernst, Erwin, Ewald, Fritz, Hans.*

Stuebs (103) German (**Stübs**): patronymic form from an unexplained personal name *Stubo*.

GIVEN NAMES German 8%. *Gerhard, Kurt, Rainer.*

Stueck (208) German (**Stück**) and Jewish (Ashkenazic): topographic name from Middle High German *stück*, German *Stück* 'piece', 'part of a whole'. The Jewish surname is mainly ornamental.

GIVEN NAMES German 5%. *Kurt* (2), *Otto.*

Stuedemann (117) German (**Stüdemann**): habitational name from a place named Stüde near Bifhorn in Lower Saxony.

GIVEN NAMES German 5%. *Franz, Kurt.*

Stuenkel (132) North German (**Stünkel**): nickname for a malodorous person, from Middle Low German *stinken* 'to stink', 'smell'.

GIVEN NAME German 5%. *Otto* (2).

Stuermer (102) German (**Stürmer**): nickname for a tumultuous person, an agent noun derived from Middle High German *stürmen* 'to make a noise', 'rage', 'fight'.

GIVEN NAMES German 11%. *Hans, Udo, Wolfgang.*

Stuessy (103) Swiss German (**Stüssy, Stüssi**): nickname for a gumpy person, agent derivative from Alemannic dialect *stüssen* 'to be angry'.

Stueve (499) North German (**Stüve**): from Middle German *stuve* 'stump', hence a topographic name for someone who lived on newly cleared land, or nickname for a short, stout man.

Stueven (119) German: variant of STUEVE.

GIVEN NAMES German 8%. *Hans* (2), *Kurt* (2).

Stuewe (197) North German (**Stüwe**): variant of **Stüve** (see STUEVE).

Stuff (139) German: from a short form of the personal name *Christoph* (see CHRISTOPHER).

Stuffle (105) Americanized form of German STOFFEL.

Stufflebeam (317) See STUFFLEBEAN.

Stufflebean (156) Americanized form of German **Stoppelbein** or its variant **Stupfelbein**, probably a nickname for a person a stump leg, from Middle High German *stupfe(l)* 'stubble', 'stump', + *bein* 'leg', 'bone'.

Stuhl (123) **1.** German: metonymic occupational name for a maker of chairs or looms, from Middle High German *stuol* 'chair', 'loom'. **2.** Jewish (Ashkenazic): metonymic occupational name from German *Stuhl* 'chair'.

GIVEN NAMES Jewish 5%; German 4%. *Lazar* (3), *Mordechai, Raizel, Shloma; Aloysius, Guenter.*

Stuhler (131) German (also **Stühler**): occupational name for a chair maker, from an agent derivative of Middle High German *stuol* 'chair', or a topographic name for someone who lived in a place known as a *Stuhl*, from the same word in the transferred sense 'area of raised land'.

GIVEN NAMES German 7%. *Kurt* (2), *Gerhard.*

Stuhlman (126) German (**Stuhlmann**): occupational name for a chair maker (see STUHLER).

Stuhr (659) North German: nickname for an inflexible, obstinate person, from Middle Low German *stūr(e)* 'rigid', 'unbending'.

Stuit (101) Of Dutch origin: possibly an Americanized spelling of **Stuut, Stuijt**, a metonymic occupational name for a baker of fancy breads, from Middle Dutch *stute, stuyt* 'white bread', 'cake'.

Stukel (155) Slovenian (**Štukelj**): unexplained.

Stukes (292) English: variant of STOKES.

Stukey (256) English: variant of STUCKEY.

Stull (3507) German: possibly a variant of **Stuhl**, a metonymic occupational name for a furniture maker, Middle High German *stuol* 'chair', or a topographic name from the same word in the transferred sense 'area of raised land'.

Stuller (294) German: possibly a variant of STUHLER.

Stults (1070) Dutch or Americanized spelling of STULTZ.

Stultz (1841) German: nickname for someone with long legs or a crutch, from a variant of Middle High German *stelze* 'stilt', 'leg'. (On the insertion of *t* [see STENTZ].)

Stulz (121) German: variant spelling of STULTZ.

Stum (238) Dutch: descriptive nickname for a mute person, from Middle Low German *stum* 'mute'.

Stumbaugh (366) Americanized form of German *Stambach* (see STAMBAUGH).

Stumbo (585) Americanized form of German *Stambach* (see STAMBAUGH).

Stumm (232) German: descriptive nickname for a mute person, from Middle High German, Middle Low German *stum* 'mute'.

Stumme (104) German: variant of STUMM.

Stump (5118) **1.** English and German: from Middle Low German *stump* 'tree stump' (borrowed into Middle English), hence a topographic name for someone who lived by a conspicuous tree stump, or a nickname for a short, stout man. **2.** German (mainly northern and central): variant of STUMM.

Stumpe (183) German: variant of STUMP.

Stumpf (2580) German: cognate of STUMP, from Middle High German *stumpf* 'stump', hence a topographic name for someone who lived on newly cleared land, or a nickname for a short, stout man.
GIVEN NAMES German 4%. *Kurt* (6), *Erwin* (4), *Otto* (3), *Hans* (2), *Alois*, *Armin*, *Bernhard*, *Heinrich*, *Manfred*, *Wolfram*.

Stumpff (244) German: variant spelling of STUMPF.

Stumph (273) German: variant spelling of STUMPF.

Stumpo (188) Italian: from Salento dialect *stumpu* 'millstone', from Greek *stoympos* 'large stone', perhaps applied as a metonymic occupational name for a miller.
GIVEN NAMES Italian 15%. *Dante* (2), *Rocco* (2), *Angelo*, *Gaetano*, *Santo*, *Silvio*.

Stumpp (165) German: variant spelling of STUMP.

Stunkard (136) Variant of English and Irish **Stankard**, which MacLysaght believes to have been originally Stangford, an English habitational name.
GIVEN NAME German 4%. *Fritz*.

Stunkel (145) German: variant spelling of STUENKEL.

Stuntz (182) German: nickname from Middle High German *stunz* 'short', 'blunt'.

Stup (159) Variant of German STUPP.

Stupak (191) Jewish (eastern Ashkenazic) and Ukrainian: metonymic occupational name for someone who worked at a mill using horse power, from Ukrainian *stupak* 'horse mill'.
GIVEN NAMES Russian 5%. *Lyubov*, *Nadezhda*, *Vasili*, *Vasily*.

Stupar (166) Croatian: occupational name for a person who shelled groats, from the name of the wooden device used for this

purpose, from *stupa* 'stamp mill' + the agent noun suffix *-ar*.
GIVEN NAMES South Slavic 9%. *Branko* (4), *Blagoje*, *Mladen*, *Petar*.

Stupka (176) Czech and Slovak: from Old Czech *stupka* 'robber', 'bandit'. This name is also frequent in German-speaking lands.
GIVEN NAMES German 5%; Czech and Slovak 4%. *Otto* (3); *Milan*, *Petr*.

Stupp (157) German: from a Germanic personal name, *Stubo*, of uncertain meaning.
GIVEN NAMES Jewish 4%. *Izaak*, *Mort*.

Stuppy (115) German: possibly a variant of STUPP; it occurs chiefly in southwestern Germany and the Palatinate.

Sturch (122) English (Oxfordshire): habitational name from Stirch in Warwickshire.

Sturdevant (1070) English: variant of STURTEVANT.

Sturdivant (1894) English: variant of STURTEVANT.

Sturdy (251) English: nickname for an impetuous or hot-headed man, from Middle English *st(o)urdi* 'reckless', 'rash' (a reduced form of Old French *est(o)urdi*, past participle of *estourdir* 'to daze or stupefy').

Sturgell (261) Origin unidentified. Compare STURGILL, STARGELL.

Sturgeon (3187) English: from Middle English *sturgeon* 'sturgeon' (a reduced form of Old French *estourgeon*), hence a metonymic occupational name for a fisherman or seller of these fish, or possibly a nickname for someone thought to resemble a sturgeon.

Sturges (1190) English: variant of STURGIS.

Sturgess (302) English: variant of STURGIS.

Sturgill (2417) Origin unidentified. Compare STURGELL, STARGELL.

Sturgis (1950) English: from the Old Norse personal name *Þorgils*, composed of the name of the Norse god of thunder, *Þorr* + *gils* 'hostage', 'pledge'. However, the inorganic initial *s-* is not easily explained; it may be the result of Old French influence.
FOREBEARS Edward Sturgis of England settled in Charlestown in 1634 and moved to Yarmouth, MA, in 1638. His descendants included a revolutionary war soldier and Cape Cod shipmaster, and a Massachusetts legislator.

Sturkey (126) English: possibly a variant of STARKEY.

Sturkie (267) Possibly a variant of English STARKEY.

Sturm (4036) **1.** German: nickname for a man of blustery temperament, from Middle High German *sturm* 'storm'. It is also found in Slovenia, where it is commonly spelled **Šturm**. **2.** Dutch: variant of STORM. **3.** Dutch: from the Germanic personal name *Sturm*, *Sturmi*. **4.** Jewish (Ashkenazic): ornamental name from German *Sturm* 'storm'.

Sturman (539) **1.** English: occupational name for a navigator, from Old Norse *stýri-*

maðr 'steersman' (a compound of *stýra* 'to steer' + *maðr* 'man'). **2.** English: from an Old French diminutive form *Esturmin* of a Germanic byname meaning 'storm'. Compare STORM. **3.** North German (**Sturmann**): altered spelling of **Stuhrmann**, an occupational name for a helmsman, from Middle Low German *stüren* 'to steer' + *mann* 'man'. **4.** Jewish (eastern Ashkenazic): origin uncertain; possibly an ornamental name from Polish *szturman* 'mate (of a ship)'.

Sturmer (174) **1.** English: habitational name from Sturmer in Essex, named from the Stour river (of Celtic or Old English origin) + Old English *mere* 'pool'. **2.** German (**Stürmer**): see STUERMER.

Sturms (140) Dutch: patronymic from STURM 2.

Sturn (143) German (of Slavic origin): according to Gottschald, probably related to Czech *studnice* 'well', 'spring'.
GIVEN NAMES German 6%. *Hans*, *Kurt*, *Ralf*.

Sturniolo (125) Italian: variant of **Storniolo**, from *storno* 'starling', Latin *sturnus*, possibly applied as a nickname for someone who was garrulous.
GIVEN NAMES Italian 14%. *Carmine* (2), *Sal*.

Sturrock (255) Scottish: occupational name for a sheep farmer or a store master. The connection, if any, with Middle English *stor*, Old French *estor* (see STORER) is by no means clear.

Sturtevant (1253) English: apparently a nickname for a hasty individual, from Middle English *stert(en)* 'to start or leap' + Anglo-Norman French *avaunt* 'forward'.

Sturtz (714) German: topographic name from Middle High German *sturz* 'slope', 'precipice'.

Sturz (100) (also **Stürz**): variant of German STURTZ.

Stute (147) **1.** North German: variant of STUDT. **2.** Scottish: unexplained.
GIVEN NAMES German 8%. *Hartwig*, *Kurt*.

Stutes (442) Americanized form of German STUTZ, or an altered spelling of Dutch **Stuijts**, **Steuts**, a metonymic occupational name for a baker of fine bread, from Middle Dutch *stute*, *stuyt* 'white bread', 'cookie'.
GIVEN NAMES French 4%. *Andre*, *Andrus*, *Mechelle*, *Pierre*.

Stutesman (200) Americanized form of German **Stutzmann** (see STUTZMAN).

Stuteville (226) English (of Norman origin): habitational name from Estouteville or Etouteville in Seine-Inferieure.

Stutheit (164) German: possibly a topographic name composed of *stut(e)* 'horse (farm)', from Middle High German *stuote* + a variant spelling of *heide* 'heath', 'open land'.

Stutler (573) Origin unidentified. Possibly an Anglicized form of German STATLER (see STADLER).

Stutman (128) Jewish (from Ukraine and Poland): nickname for a town or city dweller, from central and southeastern Yiddish *shtut* 'town', 'city' + *man* 'man'.

Stutsman (482) Dutch or Americanized spelling of German STUTZMAN.

Stutts (1389) Americanized spelling of German STUTZ.

Stutz (1366) **1.** South German (also **Stütz**): topographic name from the dialect word *stutz* 'steep slope'. **2.** German: metonymic occupational name for a wood turner who made a particular type of wooden vessel, Middle High German *stutze*.

Stutzman (2326) German (**Stutzmann**): variant of STUTZ 1.

Stuve (155) North German (**Stüve**): from Middle Low German *stuve* 'stump', 'treetrunk', hence a nickname for a short, stout man.

Stuver (146) North German (**Stüver**): **1.** variant of STUVE. **2.** from Middle Low German *stuver*, the name of a coin, hence perhaps a nickname for someone who owed this amount in rent or taxes.

Stuyvesant (74) Dutch: unexplained.
FOREBEARS Petrus (Peter) Stuyvesant (1592–1672) was director general of New Netherland in 1647–64. He was in the service of the Dutch West India Company from 1635 or earlier, and served as governor of Curaçao in 1643–47. He was famous for his silver leg, the original having been amputated after he was shot in the leg during a siege in 1644. In 1664 he was compelled to surrender New Netherland to the British, and thereafter he lived quietly until his death on his farm (Dutch *bouwerij*) on the East River in what is now the Bowery in New York City.

Styczynski (124) Polish (**Styczyński**): habitational name for someone from an unidentified place. There may be some connection with Polish *styczeń* 'January'.
GIVEN NAMES Polish 7%; German 5%. *Ludwik* (2), *Piotr*; *Fritz*.

Styer (770) English: **1.** occupational name for someone who worked at a pigsty, a swineherd, from an agent derivative of Middle English *stye* 'sty' (Old English *stig(u)*). **2.** topographic from Middle English *stye* 'path' (Old English *stīg*) + the suffix *-er* denoting an inhabitant.

Styers (580) English: variant of STYER.

Stygar (109) Polish (**Sztygar**): occupational name from *sztygar* 'pitman'.
GIVEN NAMES Polish 5%. *Boleslaw*, *Janina*.

Style (108) English: variant spelling of STILE.

Styler (110) English (Worcestershire): topographic name for someone living by a steep uphill path, from a derivative of Old English *stigel*, *stigol* 'steep uphill path'. Compare STILES.

Styles (1917) English: variant spelling of STILES.

Styron (627) Variant of English **Styring**, of unexplained origin.
FOREBEARS Bearers of this surname are almost certainly all descended from George

Styring, who is recorded in VA in the early 1700s and who moved to NC around 1720. The family are said to come from Yorkshire, England.

Stys (159) Polish: nickname for someone who was constantly complaining or grumbling, from a derivative of Old Polish *styskać* 'to complain'.
GIVEN NAME Polish 5%. *Andrzej*.

Su (1874) **1.** Chinese 苏: from the place name *Su*. A descendant of the emperor Zhuan Xu, who lived in the 26th century BC, was granted a fiefdom called Su, and his descendants eventually adopted the place name as their surname. **2.** Chinese 粟: from part of an official title, Zhisu Duwei, of the Western Han dynasty (206 BC–24 AD). This title was borne by the official in charge of granaries, an important role as granaries could be strategic military targets. A descendant of one such official adopted the character Su from the title as his surname. **3.** Chinese 宿: from the name of an ancient kingdom called Su, which existed during the reign of the first of the three legendary emperors, Fu Xi (2852–2734 BC). **4.** Vietnamese: unexplained.
GIVEN NAMES Chinese 47%; Vietnamese 19%. *Ming* (11), *Hong* (6), *Jing* (6), *Bin* (5), *Yi* (5), *Yuan* (5), *Chan* (4), *Chao* (4), *Chen* (4), *Hua* (4), *Hui* (4), *Qi* (4), *Min* (3), *Tam* (2), *Ti* (2), *Chang*, *Hyun Ho*, *Hyun Sun*, *Jang*, *Jeong*, *Jung Ho*, *Kwang Sook*, *Thanh* (6), *Hoa* (3), *Hung* (3), *Nam* (3), *Lan* (2), *Minh* (2), *Nu* (2), *Phong* (2), *Quang* (2), *Tuan* (2), *Anh*, *Binh*, *Buu*, *Chau*.

Suarez (7563) Spanish (**Suárez**): occupational name for a swineherd, Latin *Suerius*. Compare Portuguese SOARES.
GIVEN NAMES Spanish 49%. *Jose* (225), *Juan* (95), *Carlos* (93), *Manuel* (93), *Luis* (88), *Jorge* (64), *Miguel* (54), *Jesus* (53), *Mario* (47), *Roberto* (47), *Pedro* (44), *Raul* (42).

Suazo (601) Castilianized form of Basque **Zuhatzu**, habitational name from places in Araba and Navarre named Zuhatzu, from Basque *zu(h)aitz* 'tree' + the collective suffix *-zu*, *tsu*.
GIVEN NAMES Spanish 36%. *Jose* (19), *Jorge* (7), *Luis* (7), *Manuel* (5), *Juana* (4), *Rafael* (4), *Javier* (3), *Jesus* (3), *Julio* (3), *Mario* (3), *Alberto* (2), *Arturo* (2).

Suba (162) **1.** Hungarian: nickname (or metonymic occupational name for a furrier) from *suba* 'fur', 'long sheepskin coat'. This name is also found in Germany. **2.** Hispanic (Philippines and Mexico): unexplained; not found in present-day Spain.
GIVEN NAMES Spanish 5%. *Carmencita*, *Catalino*, *Jose*, *Leticia*, *Roque*, *Vicente*.

Subbert (112) German (Frisian): Frisian variant of **Sibbert**, itself a variant of SIEBERT.

Suber (1185) German (also **Süber**): nickname for a clean, decent person, from Middle Low German *sūber* 'clean'.

Subia (252) **1.** Spanish: Castilianized form of Basque ZUBIA, or variant of Spanish

ZUBIA. This surname is found mostly in Mexico. **2.** Italian (Sicily): possibly from *subbia* 'chisel', 'awl', presumably a metonymic occupational name for a carpenter, or a metonymic occupational name for a maker of such tools.
GIVEN NAMES Spanish 33%; Italian 5%. *Alfredo* (3), *Felipe* (3), *Manuel* (3), *Carlos* (2), *Cruz* (2), *Eloy* (2), *Jose* (2), *Ramona* (2), *Alfonso*, *Alicia*, *Alida*, *Alvaro*; *Angelo* (2), *Lorenzo* (2), *Donato*, *Fausto*, *Sisto*.

Subler (129) Origin unidentified; possibly a variant of SUBLETTE.

Sublett (1004) Variant of French SUBLETTE.

Sublette (289) French: the usual spelling in North America of **Sublet** 'whistler', from Old French *sublet* 'whistle', 'hiss' (from the verb *subler*, *sibler*), hence a nickname for someone who was able to whistle in imitation of birdsong, to attract and catch birds. The spelling *-ette* is not a feminine form, but a spelling prompted by the continuing pronunciation of final *-t* in American French surnames after it had become silent in European French.

Subramaniam (207) Indian (Tamil Nadu, Andhra Pradesh): variant of SUBRAMANIAN.
GIVEN NAMES Indian 95%. *Suresh* (6), *Ram* (5), *Ravi* (4), *Bala* (3), *Ramesh* (3), *Srinivasan* (3), *Anand* (2), *Arun* (2), *Balaji* (2), *Bhavani* (2), *Hari* (2), *Kumar* (2).

Subramanian (438) Indian (Kerala, Tamil Nadu): Hindu name from Sanskrit *subrahmaṇya* 'dear to Brahmans' (an epithet of the god Kartikeya, son of Shiva) + the Tamil-Malayalam third-person masculine singular suffix *-n*. This is only a given name in India, but has come to be used as a family name in the U.S.
GIVEN NAMES Indian 96%. *Shankar* (9), *Ravi* (8), *Mani* (7), *Bala* (6), *Suresh* (6), *Uma* (5), *Ashok* (4), *Murali* (4), *Ram* (4), *Vijay* (4), *Gopal* (3), *Rajesh* (3).

Such (489) **1.** English: of uncertain origin; perhaps a habitational name of Norman origin from some minor place in France called La Souche, from Old French *s(o)uche* 'tree stump'. **2.** Polish, Czech, Slovak, and German (of Slavic origin): from Polish *suchy*, Czech and Slovak *suchý* 'dry' (perhaps a topographic name) or, when applied to people, 'thin'.

Suchan (261) Czech, Slovak (also **Suchán**), and Polish: nickname for a thin or boring man, from the adjective *suchý* (Czech), *suchy* (Polish) 'dry', 'thin'.

Suchanek (201) Czech (**Suchánek**): diminutive of SUCHAN.
GIVEN NAME German 4%. *Juergen* (2).

Sucharski (179) Polish: habitational name for someone from Suchary in Bydgoszcz, Konin, and Rzeszów voivodeships, named with *suchy* 'dry'.

Suchecki (164) Polish: habitational name, probably from a place called Suchcice in Ostrołęka voivodeship, named with *suchta*, derivative of *suchy* 'dry'.

GIVEN NAMES Polish 5%. *Grzegorz, Jozef, Tadeusz.*

Sucher (388) **1.** German: from Middle High German *suocher* 'searcher', 'investigator', 'pursuer', an agent derivative of *suochen* 'to seek (out)', probably an occupational nickname for a huntsman. **2.** Respelling of Jewish (from Lithuania) **Zukher**, a nickname from a derivative of Yiddish *zukhn* 'to seek'.

Suchman (135) German (**Suchmann**) and Jewish (Ashkenazic): derivative of SUCH 2.
GIVEN NAMES Jewish 7%. *Sol* (2), *Hyman, Isadore.*

Suchocki (226) Polish: habitational name from Suchocin in Warszawa and Siedlce voivodeships.
GIVEN NAMES Polish 9%. *Andrzej, Jerzy, Krzysztof, Miroslaw, Ryszard, Zigmund.*

Suchodolski (118) Polish: habitational name for someone from a place called Suchodoły in Lublin voivodeship.
GIVEN NAMES Polish 11%. *Andrej, Bronislaw, Janusz, Kazimierz, Zygmunt.*

Suchomel (240) Czech and Slovak: status name for the owner of a windmill (literally 'dry mill'). This name is also established in German-speaking countries.
GIVEN NAMES German 5%. *Kurt* (2), *Matthias, Reinold, Ute.*

Suchy (746) Czech and Slovak (**Suchý**) and Polish: nickname for a thin man, from *suchý* (Czech), *suchy* (Polish), the basic meaning of which is 'dry'.

Suckow (405) German: habitational name from places so called in Brandenburg, Mecklenburg (near Parchim and on Usedom island), and Pomerania.
GIVEN NAMES German 4%. *Eldred, Helmuth, Otto.*

Suda (548) Japanese: variously written and found mostly in northeastern and west-central Japan, and on Okinawa Island. For the majority of bearers it is a habitational name from a village in Shinano (now Nagano prefecture). These bearers descend from the MINAMOTO clan through the INOUE family.
GIVEN NAMES Japanese 13%. *Tatsuya* (2), *Yuichi* (2), *Asano, Atsushi, Chieko, Eriko, Hiroshi, Hiroto, Junichi, Kanae, Katsutoshi, Kenji.*

Sudak (100) Origin unidentified. Possibly a variant of German **Sudeck**, an Old Prussian personal name or a habitational name from a place so named in Hesse.

Sudano (179) Southern Italian: variant of SODANO.
GIVEN NAMES Italian 14%. *Salvatore* (2), *Alessio, Angelo, Carmine, Giuseppe, Orazio.*

Sudar (105) Croatian and Serbian: probably an occupational name for a cooper, from *sud* 'barrel' + the agent noun suffix *-ar.*
GIVEN NAMES South Slavic 4%. *Branko, Dragan.*

Sudbeck (203) German (**Südbeck**): Apparently a habitational name from a lost or unidentified place, perhaps in Germany.
GIVEN NAMES French 5%. *Marcel* (2), *Veronique.*

Sudberry (162) Variant of English SUDBURY.

Sudbury (181) English: habitational name from places in Derbyshire, Middlesex (Greater London), and Suffolk, so named from Old English *sūð* 'south' + *byrig*, dative of *burh* 'fortified place'.

Suddarth (381) Much altered form of English SOUTHWORTH.

Suddath (195) Much altered form of English SOUTHWORTH.

Sudderth (416) Much altered form of English SOUTHWORTH.

Suddeth (453) Much altered form of English SOUTHWORTH.

Suddith (114) Much altered form of English SOUTHWORTH.

Suddreth (275) Much altered form of English SOUTHWORTH.

Sudduth (1350) Much altered form of English SOUTHWORTH.

Suder (340) Variant of German **Söder** (see SODER).
FOREBEARS Philip Suder (b. 1822) immigrated to Marietta, OH, from Germany in 1857.

Suderman (208) German (**Sudermann**): topographic name for someone living to the south of a settlement or for an incomer from the south, from Middle Low German *sūder* 'south' + *man* 'man'. Compare SOUTH.

Sudhoff (104) German: habitational name for someone living at 'the south farm'.
GIVEN NAMES German 6%. *Alfons, Hans.*

Sudler (205) South German: from an agent derivative of Middle High German *sudelen* 'to soil', probably applied as a nickname for someone with a neglected or dirty appearance.

Sudlow (170) English (Shropshire): apparently a habitational name from an unidentified place, perhaps Sudlow Farm in Cheshire.

Sudman (123) North German (**Sudmann**): nickname for someone who lived to the south of a settlement, from Middle Low German *sud(en)* 'south' + *man* 'man'. Compare SUDERMAN.

Sudol (568) Polish (**Sudół**): habitational name from places called Sudół in Kielce voivodeship or Sudoły in Sieradz and Tarnobrzeg voivodeships.
GIVEN NAMES Polish 13%. *Stanislaw* (4), *Dorota* (2), *Janina* (2), *Mariusz* (2), *Zbigniew* (2), *Jozef, Jozefa, Krystyna, Marzena, Mieczyslaw, Piotr, Stanislawa.*

Sudweeks (146) English (Kent): unexplained.

Sue (405) Origin unidentified.

Suell (105) Variant spelling of English SEWELL.

Suen (238) **1.** Dutch: from a dialect variant of *zoon* 'son', hence a distinguishing nickname for a son who had the same personal name as his father. **2.** Chinese 孙: variant of **Sun**.
GIVEN NAMES Chinese 28%. *Fan* (2), *Kai Ming* (2), *Kam* (2), *Kin* (2), *Wai* (2), *Wing* (2), *Ching-Yun, Fong, Kan, Kin Wing, Kong, Kwok Leung.*

Suer (118) German: nickname for a bitter or unpleasant person, from Middle High German, Middle Low German *sūr* 'sour', 'bitter'.

Suero (221) Spanish: from a medieval personal name of Germanic origin, attested in the Latinized form *Suerius*. The first element is of obscure origin; the second is *heri, hari* 'army'.
GIVEN NAMES Spanish 52%. *Jose* (7), *Carlos* (4), *Manuel* (4), *Fernando* (3), *Ramon* (3), *Ana* (2), *Jesus* (2), *Jorge* (2), *Julio* (2), *Luis* (2), *Orlando* (2), *Rafael* (2); *Licinio* (2), *Angelo, Aniello, Antonio, Dario, Heriberto, Pasquale, Pasqualina.*

Suess (973) German (**Süss**) and Jewish (Ashkenazic): nickname or Jewish ornamental name from Middle High German, German *süss* 'sweet', 'pleasant', 'agreeable'.
GIVEN NAMES German 5%. *Erwin* (2), *Manfred* (2), *Bernd, Bernhard, Florian, Gerhard, Hans, Hartmut, Hedwig, Hermann, Otto.*

Suffern (110) Irish or English: unexplained.

Suffridge (112) Origin unidentified.

Sugai (124) Japanese (mostly found in northeastern Japan): 'sedge well'. An alternate pronunciation is *Sugei.*
GIVEN NAMES Japanese 45%. *Fusao* (2), *Saburo* (2), *Ayame, Chihiro, Hideaki, Hirofumi, Iwao, Jiro, Kiyoko, Kyoko, Masako, Masami.*

Sugalski (103) Polish: of uncertain origin; possibly a habitational name from a place called Sugajno in Toruń voivodeship.

Sugar (640) **1.** Hungarian (**Sugár**): nickname for a well-built person, from *sugár* 'tall', 'slim'. **2.** Translation of German and Jewish ZUCKER 'sugar'. **3.** English: nickname from the vocabulary word *sugar* as a term of affection, or possibly an occupational name for a confectioner or dealer in sugar, although there is no evidence for this in English sources.
GIVEN NAMES Jewish 4%. *Charna, Emanuel, Mandel, Mordechai, Moshe.*

Sugarman (874) Jewish: Americanized form of Ashkenazic ZUCKERMAN, occupational name for a confectioner or dealer in sugar.
GIVEN NAMES Jewish 4%. *Hyman* (2), *Dov, Eytan, Isidor, Meyer, Rina.*

Sugawara (119) Japanese: 'sedge plain', found mostly in northeastern Japan; listed in the Shinsen shōjiroku as *Sugahara.* The family was prominent at court throughout the ninth century. Their most noted son, Sugawara no Michizane (845–903), was a famous scholar and poet who is now revered as the patron saint of scholarship. Some bearers of the name pronounce it *Kanbara*.

GIVEN NAMES Japanese 73%. *Eriko* (2), *Katsuya* (2), *Seiji* (2), *Takeshi* (2), *Yutaka* (2), *Etsuko, Fujio, Fumio, Hajime, Hiroki, Hisao, Isao.*

Sugden (547) English: habitational name from a place in West Yorkshire, so called from Old English *sucga* 'sparrow' (or other small bird) + *denu* 'valley'.

Sugerman (182) Jewish (American): see SUGARMAN.

Sugg (1130) English: nickname for a small, birdlike person, from Middle English *sugge* '(small) bird', 'sparrow'.

Suggett (127) English: variant of SOUTH-GATE.

Suggs (3941) Probably an English patronymic from SUGG.

Sughrue (165) Irish: variant spelling of SUGRUE.

Sugihara (140) Japanese: 'cedar plain'. The name is found mostly in western Japan and in the Ryūkyū Islands. A noble family of TAIRA origin bore the name but became extinct in the 17th century.

GIVEN NAMES Japanese 38%. *Atsushi, Hideo, Hiroshi, Itsuo, Katsuo, Kazuhiro, Kazuo, Kenichiro, Kosuke, Masaaki, Masanobu, Masao.*

Sugimoto (317) Japanese (found mostly in eastern Japan and the Ryūkyū Islands): habitational name from a village so called ('(one who lives) beneath the cedars') near Kamakura. Many bearers are of MIURA or ISHII family descent.

GIVEN NAMES Japanese 51%. *Hiroshi* (4), *Atsushi* (2), *Kazuto* (2), *Keiji* (2), *Michiharu* (2), *Osamu* (2), *Shinji* (2), *Tomoko* (2), *Aiko, Akio, Akira, Asako.*

Sugita (104) Japanese (mostly found in western Japan): habitational name from a village so named ('cedar rice paddy') in Iwashiro (now Fukushima prefecture). Bearers are descended from the MINAMOTO clan.

GIVEN NAMES Japanese 67%. *Hideo* (2), *Motomi* (2), *Yoshio* (2), *Akira, Ayako, Etsuko, Gengo, Hiroki, Hisako, Kaoru, Katsuhiro, Kenichi.*

Sugiyama (283) Japanese (mostly found along the coast between Tōkyō and Kyōto): from *sugi* 'cedar' + *yama* 'mountain'; in some cases it is a habitational name from a village so called in Mikawa (now part of Aichi prefecture). These bearers of the name are descended from the FUJIWARA clan, while others are of TAIRA origin.

GIVEN NAMES Japanese 67%. *Takashi* (4), *Aki* (2), *Kazuko* (2), *Mineo* (2), *Sakae* (2), *Shigeru* (2), *Susumu* (2), *Tetsuro* (2),

Tomoko (2), *Yosh* (2), *Yoshiko* (2), *Yuichi* (2).

Sugrue (452) Irish: reduced Anglicized form of Gaelic **Ó Siochfhradha** 'descendant of *Siochfhradh*', a personal name representing a Gaelicized form of an Old Norse cognate of Germanic SIEGFRIED. The surname is largely confined to County Kerry.

GIVEN NAMES Irish 9%. *Bridie, Donal, Liam, Niall.*

Suh (1344) **1.** Korean: variant of **Sŏ** (see SO). **2.** North German: from Middle Low German *sū* 'sow', either a metonymic occupational name for a swineherd or an offensive nickname.

GIVEN NAMES Korean 66%. *Jung* (38), *Young* (27), *Kwang* (13), *Byung* (12), *Chung* (12), *Sang* (12), *Jae* (11), *Sung* (10), *Jin* (9), *Kyung* (8), *Myung* (6), *Chang* (6), *Chong* (4), *Hyun* (4), *In* (4), *Joon* (4), *Jung Sun* (4), *Moon* (4), *Sook* (3), *Choon* (2), *Chul* (2), *Dae* (2), *Daewon* (2), *Hee Jung* (2).

Suhl (113) German: topographic name from *Suhle* 'muddy pool', 'mudbath', or a habitational name from Suhl in Thuringia.

Suhr (1195) North German: **1.** nickname for a bitter or cantankerous person, from Middle Low German *sūr* 'sour'. **2.** German: habitation name from a place so named in Schleswig-Holstein. The surname is also found in Sweden and Denmark, probably taken there from Germany.

GIVEN NAMES German 5%. *Kurt* (3), *Horst* (2), *Jurgen* (2), *Monika* (2), *Wolfgang* (2), *Claus, Eberhard, Gerhard, Manfred.*

Suhre (213) **1.** North German and Swedish: variant of SUHR. **2.** German: nickname for a spotty person, from Middle Low German *sure* 'pimple', 'pustule'.

Suhy (106) Origin unidentified.

Sui (110) Chinese 隋: from the name of the state of Sui (随) that existed during the Zhou dynasty (1122–221 BC). Descendants of a ruler of this state adopted its name as their surname. However, the current form of the name is in most cases the character 隋, which was used to represent the name of the Sui dynasty (581–618 AD). An emperor of that dynasty, Wen Di, commanded the change in form.

GIVEN NAMES Chinese 45%. *Ping* (2), *Aiping, Chi Wai, Dexin, Dong, Fen, Gang, Kuang, Kwok, Kwong, Leung, Li-Hua*; *Binh, Da, Tung*; *Chong, Yu-Min.*

Suing (108) Origin unidentified. The name is found in Belgium, an adaptation of **Cho(u)in, Chuin**, a metonymic occupational name for a baker of white bread.

Suire (404) French: occupational name for a shoemaker or cobbler, Old French *sueur*, (from Latin *sutor*, an agent derivative of *suere* to sew).

GIVEN NAMES French 7%. *Ambroise, Clemile, Emile, Evest, Marcel, Raywood.*

Suit (374) English and Scottish: probably a variant of **Sewatt**, which is from the common Old Norse personal name *Sigvarðr*, composed of *sigr* 'victory' + *varðr* 'guardian'. The International Genealogical Index records several UK ancestors called **Suit(t)**, though the name is hardly found in Britain today.

Suite (100) English and Scottish: variant of SUIT.

Suiter (1027) South German: occupational name for a shoemaker, from a metathesized form of Middle High German *siuter*, compare SAUTER.

Suitor (226) Variant of German SUITER.

Suits (720) Probably an ethnic name for someone from Switzerland. This is a common surname in the Mohawk Valley and may be of Dutch or Palatine German origin, derived for example from Dutch **Switser**.

Suitt (261) Probably a variant of English and Scottish SUIT.

Suitter (106) Variant of German SUITER.

Suk (276) **1.** Czech: from *suk* 'knot', 'knar', a nickname for a powerful, unyielding man or a stubborn, awkward one. **2.** Korean: variant of **Sŏk** (see SOK).

GIVEN NAMES Korean 38%. *Sang* (5), *Jin* (4), *Jae* (2), *Jung* (2), *Sun* (2), *Chang Won, Chin, Choong, Choy, Chung Hyun, Dong, Eui*; *Chang* (2), *Chul* (2), *Chun Ho* (2), *Eui Young, Jeong, Jin Ok, Jinsoo, Jong Hwan, Jong Kyu, Jung Hoon, Jung Woo, Kum.*

Sukenik (105) Jewish (eastern Ashkenazic): occupational name from Polish *sukiennik* 'clothier', 'draper'.

GIVEN NAMES Jewish 12%; Russian 6%. *Avrohom* (2), *Chaim, Hillel, Moshe*; *Boris, Dmitry, Galina, Grigory.*

Suko (110) Japanese: written apparently phonetically with characters meaning 'necessary' and 'child'. The meaning is uncertain. The name is not common in Japan.

GIVEN NAMES Japanese 6%. *Mitsuru, Shoji, Yoshi.*

Sukow (113) German: habitational name from a place so called in Mecklenburg-West Pomerania, of Slavic origin.

Sukup (155) North German: nickname for a stubborn man, from Middle Low German *sū* 'sow' + *kop* 'head'.

Sukut (120) Ukrainian: unexplained.

Sula (118) Origin uncertain; perhaps a variant of Hungarian **Süle** (see SULE).

Sulaiman (110) Muslim: variant of SULEIMAN.

GIVEN NAMES Muslim 66%. *Abdallah* (2), *Ibrahim* (2), *Laila* (2), *Mohamed* (2), *Abdul, Abed, Afifa, Afzal, Ahmed, Altaf, Ayman, Faisal.*

Sulak (318) Czech (**Šulák**): nickname from the vocabulary word *šulák* 'swindler'.

Sulc (108) Slovenian, Czech, and Slovak (**Šulc**): Slavicized form of German SCHULTZ.

GIVEN NAMES South Slavic 9%. *Jaroslav, Milan, Zdenko.*

Sulcer (136) Slavic spelling of German SULZER.

Sule (111) **1.** Indian (Maharashtra); pronounced as two syllables: Hindu (Maratha) name, from Marathi *suḷa* 'pointed tooth', from Sanskrit *šūla* 'spike', 'spear'. **2.** Hungarian: from a pet form of the personal name *Szilveszter* (see SYLVESTER).
GIVEN NAMES Indian 13%; Hungarian 5%. *Aparna, Dileep, Geeta, Harsh, Pushkar, Sangeeta, Vikram; Mihaly, Sandor.*

Suleiman (199) Muslim: from the Arabic personal name *Suleiman* (see SOLOMON). Suleiman (Solomon) is regarded in Islam as a prophet (Qur'an 27:17). Suleiman the Magnificent (1498–1566) was a renowned khalif of the Ottoman Empire. This name is widespread throughout the Muslim world.
GIVEN NAMES Muslim 78%. *Ahmad* (4), *Abdullahi* (3), *Anver* (3), *Hussein* (3), *Raed* (3), *Talat* (3), *Abdul* (2), *Adnan* (2), *Ali* (2), *Fayez* (2), *Khaled* (2), *Khalid* (2).

Sulek (176) **1.** Polish (also **Sułek**): from a pet form of the Slavic personal name *Sulimir*, composed of the elements *suli-* 'promise' + *mir* 'peace'. **2.** Slovenian (**Šulek**): unexplained.
GIVEN NAMES Polish 6%. *Alicja, Jerzy, Zbigniew, Zofia.*

Sulentic (103) Serbian and Croatian (**Šulentić**): unexplained.

Suleski (145) Variant of Polish SULEWSKI.

Sulewski (216) Polish: habitational name from Sulewo in Łomża voivodeship. Perhaps also an altered form of **Sulejewski**, from Sulejewo in Leszno and Poznań voivodeships.
GIVEN NAMES Polish 10%. *Andrzej, Bogdan, Boleslaw, Halina, Kazimierz, Krzysztof, Ludwik, Zigmund.*

Sulfridge (133) English: variant of SELFRIDGE.

Sulik (214) Czech (**Šulík**): nickname meaning 'swindler', from a diminutive form of **Šulák** (see SULAK).

Sulkin (102) Jewish (eastern Ashknazic): variant of SHULKIN.

Sulkowski (284) Polish (**Sułkowski**) and Jewish (from Poland): habitational name for someone from any of several Polish villages called Sułków or Sułkowo.
GIVEN NAMES Polish 9%; German 4%. *Alicja, Jerzy, Kazimierz, Leszek, Stanislaw, Waclaw, Witold, Wladyslaw; Viktor* (2), *Hedwig.*

Sulla (102) **1.** Italian: from *sulla* 'sainfoin' (Latin *sulla*), probably applied as a topographic name for someone who lived where the plant grew or possibly a habitational name from a place named with this word. **2.** Jewish (from Ukraine): ornamental name from Ukrainian *sula* 'pike-perch'.
GIVEN NAMES Italian 7%; Jewish 5%. *Salvatore* (2), *Angelo, Antonio, Sal; Moisey.*

Sullen (102) English: probably a nickname for someone with a gloomy disposition, from the vocabuarly word *sullen*.

Sullenberger (313) German; habitational name from a lost or unidentified place called Sullenberg or from Schallenberg in Baden.

Sullender (120) Origin unidentified.

Sullenger (348) German: habitational name for someone from any of the places called Sulingen, Suligen (in Switzerland), or Solingen in the Rhineland.

Sullens (502) English (Essex): variant of SULLEN.

Sullinger (202) See SULLENGER.

Sullins (1291) English (Essex): variant spelling of SULLENS.

Sullivan (86937) Irish: reduced form of **O'Sullivan**, an Anglicized form of Gaelic **Ó Súileabháin** 'descendant of *Súileabhán*', a personal name composed of the elements *súil* 'eye' + *dubh* 'black', 'dark' + the diminutive suffix *-án*.
GIVEN NAMES Irish 8%. *Brendan* (51), *Liam* (11), *Donal* (7), *James Patrick* (5), *Michael Patrick* (5), *Aileen* (4), *Brigid* (4), *Paddy* (4), *Siobhan* (4), *John Patrick* (3), *Kevin Patrick* (3), *Parnell* (3).

Sullivant (206) Irish: variant of SULLIVAN.

Sullo (245) Southern Italian: **1.** probably from a short form of a personal name such as *Tommasullo*, a pet form of *Tommaso* (see THOMAS). **2.** possibly a topographic name, from Calabrian *sulla*, denoting a variety of trefoil or clover.
GIVEN NAMES Italian 10%. *Alfonse, Angelo, Ennio, Palma, Sal, Salvatore, Santo.*

Sully (246) **1.** French: habitational name from any of various places, for example in Calvados, Loiret, and Oise. The first of these is recorded in 1180 as *Silleium*, from the Gallo-Roman personal name *Silius* or *Cilius* + the Latin locative suffix *-acum*. The others are from a personal name *Sol(l)ius* + *-acum*. **2.** Southern English: of uncertain origin; possibly a habitational name imported from France and so identical with 1, or alternatively a variant of **Sulley**. It may also be from the parish of Sully in Glamorgan, Wales, so called either from Old Norse *sul* 'cleft' + *ey* 'island' or from the Norman family name *de Sulley* (as in 1), which is recorded in Glamorgan in the 12th century.
GIVEN NAMES French 8%. *Armelle, Christophe, Geralde, Luce, Pierre, Reynald.*

Sulpizio (127) Italian: from the personal name *Sulpizio* (Latin *Sulpicius*, the name of a famous and powerful family in ancient Rome). The name was borne by various saints, including St. Sulpicius Severus (d. 591), bishop of Borges in France, not to be confused with the writer and ascetic Sulpicius Severus (*c.* 363–*c.* 420) of Aquitaine, the biographer of St. Martin of Tours.
GIVEN NAMES Italian 15%. *Domenic* (2), *Alicia, Amalia, Americo, Dante, Lorenzo, Orlando, Sal.*

Sulser (262) Altered spelling of German SULZER.

Sult (389) North German: topographic name from Middle Low German *sulte* 'salty spring', 'salt works', or possibly an occupational name for someone engaged in the salt trade.

Sultan (694) **1.** Muslim: from a personal name based on Arabic *sulṭān* 'ruler'. This was the title of rulers in many parts of the Muslim world, including the monarch of the Ottoman Empire. **2.** English: see SODEN. **3.** Spanish (**Sultán**), Polish (**Sułtan**): nickname for someone who behaved in an outlandish or autocratic manner, from Arabic *sulṭān* 'sultan'.
GIVEN NAMES Muslim 38%; French 4%. *Mohammad* (8), *Ahmed* (5), *Omar* (5), *Ali* (4), *Mohammed* (4), *Iqbal* (3), *Jalal* (3), *Mohamed* (3), *Syed* (3), *Tariq* (3), *Ahmad* (2), *Amer* (2); *Jacques* (3), *Michel* (3), *Jean-Michael, Mireille, Olivier.*

Sultana (156) **1.** Maltese and Italian: nickname for someone who behaved in an outlandish and autocratic manner, from Arabic *sulṭāna* 'wife of a sultan'. Compare English SODEN. **2.** Muslim: from the feminine form of SULTAN.
GIVEN NAMES Muslim 37%; Italian 5%. *Razia* (3), *Salma* (2), *Sayeeda* (2), *Zehra* (2), *Akhtar, Azra, Fareeda, Farida, Jameel, Khawar, Kishwar, Mahmuda; Angelo, Carmela, Constantino, Grazio.*

Sultemeier (111) German: probably an altered spelling of German **Schultemeier**, a status name for a village headman who was also a tenant farmer (see SCHULTE and MEIER).
GIVEN NAMES German 7%. *Erwin, Kurt, Otto.*

Sulton (124) English: perhaps a variant of SALTON.

Sultzer (110) German: variant spelling of SULZER.

Sulzbach (166) German and Jewish (western Ashkenazic): habitational name from any of the many places named Sulzbach.
GIVEN NAMES German 6%. *Kurt* (2), *Horst.*

Sulzberger (114) German: habitational name from a place called Sulzberg.
GIVEN NAME German 5%. *Otto.*

Sulzer (351) **1.** German: occupational name for someone who made prepared meats, from Middle High German *sulzer* 'butcher', 'charcutier'. **2.** German: from a derivative of Middle High German *sulze* 'brine', hence a topographic name for someone who lived near a source of salty water, or a habitational name for someone from a place called Sulz.
GIVEN NAMES German 5%. *Hans* (3), *Otto* (2), *Bernhard, Fritz.*

Sum (240) **1.** Jewish (eastern Ashkenazic): ornamental occupational name from Polish *sum* 'wels', 'sheatfish', a species of catfish. **2.** Chinese 岑: variant of SHUM. **3.** Chinese 沈: variant of SHEN 1. **4.** Cambodian: unexplained.

GIVEN NAMES Southeast Asian 9%. *Chak, Chi, Chun, Eng, Heng, Ho, Kin Wai, Kong, Kwok, Kwok Leung, Kwok Ying, Lun.*

Suman (278) Dutch: unexplained.

Sumerel (108) Origin unidentified.

Sumerlin (209) Variant of SUMMERLIN.

Sumey (130) Origin unidentified. Possibly English: unexplained.

Sumida (308) Japanese: variously written, the name appears to have originated in Buzen (now part of Fukuoka prefecture) as a habitational name meaning 'corner rice paddy'. Families bearing this name are found throughout Japan and may or may not be related.
GIVEN NAMES Japanese 36%. *Hideo* (3), *Kazuo* (3), *Etsuo* (2), *Haruo* (2), *Minoru* (2), *Tadao* (2), *Akira, Chiyeko, Hajime, Hiroshi, Hisao, Iwao.*

Suminski (210) Polish (**Sumiński**): habitational name for someone from any of various places called Sumin, named with *sum* 'wels' (see SUM).
GIVEN NAMES French 4%. *Colette* (2), *Germain.*

Sumler (360) English: unexplained.

Sumlin (386) Possibly English, a reduced form of SUMMERLIN.

Summa (551) Southern Italian: most probably a habitational name, a variant of SOMMA.
GIVEN NAMES Italian 17%. *Rocco* (8), *Donato* (6), *Angelo* (4), *Vito* (4), *Alfonse, Antonio, Attilio, Canio, Domenic, Domenica, Gasper, Giovanni.*

Summar (189) Variant spelling of English SUMMER.

Summer (1140) **1.** English and German: from Middle English *sum(m)er*, Middle High German *sumer* 'summer', hence a nickname for someone of a warm or sunny disposition, or for someone associated with the season of summer in some other way. **2.** English: assimilated variant of SUMNER. **3.** English: assimilated variant of SUMPTER. **4.** Irish (Leinster and Munster): Anglicization (part translation) of Gaelic Ó Samhraidh 'descendant of *Samhradh*', a byname meaning 'summer'. The Gaelic name is also Anglicized as **O'Sawrie, O'Sawra. 5.** German: from Middle High German *summer* 'woven basket' and, by extension, a measure of grain; also 'drum', hence a metonymic occupational name or nickname from any of these senses.

Summerall (356) English (Somerset and Gloucestershire): probably a variant of SUMMERHILL.

Summerfield (940) **1.** English: habitational name from Summerfield in Wiltshire. **2.** Scottish: variant of SOMERVILLE. **3.** Americanized form of Ashkenazic Jewish **Sommerfeld(t)** (see SOMMERFELD).

Summerford (465) English: habitational name from Somerford in Cheshire, Somerford Keynes in Gloucestershire, or Great and Little Somerford in Wiltshire, named

with Old English *sumor* 'summer' + *ford* 'ford', i.e. a place where a river could be forded in the summer.

Summerhays (195) Southern English: probably a topographic name referring to an enclosure (on upland pasture), where animals were kept in summer, from Middle English *sumer, somer* 'summer' + *hay* 'enclosure' (Old English *(ge)hæg*).

Summerhill (298) Scottish and English: habitational name from any of various minor places named with Old English *somer* 'summer' + *hyll* 'hill', i.e. hill used for summer grazing. In Scotland there is one such place in the parish of New Machar in Aberdeenshire, and another in Ayton, Berwickshire.

Summerlin (1639) **1.** German: diminutive of SUMMER 5. **2.** English (Bedfordshire): unexplained.

Summerour (256) Origin unidentified.

Summers (19385) **1.** English: patronymic from SUMMER 1. **2.** Irish (Sligo): adopted as an English equivalent of Gaelic Ó Somacháin 'descendant of *Somachán*', a nickname meaning 'gentle', 'innocent'. **3.** Americanized form of some like-sounding Ashkenazic Jewish name.

Summersett (115) English: variant spelling of SOMERSET.

Summerson (206) English: patronymic from SUMMER 1.

Summerton (117) English: habitational name from a place named Somerton, usually from Old English *sumor* 'summer' + *tūn* 'farmstead', notably Somerton in Oxfordshire, where the surname is still relatively common. There are also places so named in Somerset and Norfolk which may also have contributed to the surname.

Summerville (1400) Scottish: variant spelling of SOMERVILLE.

Summey (820) Origin unidentified. In part perhaps an Americanized spelling of the Swiss family name **Sumi** (unexplained) or of southern French **Soumet**, a topographic name from a diminutive of Occitan *soum* 'summit', 'peak'.

Summit (205) Origin unidentified.

Summitt (546) Origin unidentified.

Summy (305) See SUMMEY.

Sumner (7020) English: occupational name for a summoner, an official who was responsible for ensuring the appearance of witnesses in court, Middle English *sumner, sumnor.*
FOREBEARS William Sumner came to Dorchester, MA, from England in about 1635. His descendants include U.S. Senator Charles Sumner, a major force in the struggle to end slavery, who was born in 1811 in Boston.

Sumners (475) English: variant or patronymic form of SUMNER.

Sump (185) North German: topographic name for someone who lived in a marshy

place, from Middle Low German *sump* 'swamp', or a habitational name from a place named with this word.
GIVEN NAMES German 4%. *Eldor, Kurt.*

Sumpter (2118) English: occupational name for a carrier, from Middle English *sum(p)ter* '(driver of a) pack animal'.

Sumption (162) English: unexplained.
GIVEN NAMES German 4%. *Frieda, Kurt.*

Sumrall (1516) Origin unidentified; perhaps a variant of English SUMMERHILL. Compare SUMMERALL.

Sumrell (183) Origin unidentified; perhaps a variant of English SUMMERHILL. Compare SUMMERALL.

Sumrow (150) Origin unidentified.

Sumsion (120) English (Somerset and Wiltshire): unexplained.

Sumter (406) English: variant of SUMPTER.
FOREBEARS Fort Sumter, SC, was named in honor of Thomas Sumter, known as the 'Gamecock of the Revolution' for the fear he inspired in the British and Tory forces and the pivotal role he played in key American victories. Born in 1734 near Charlottesville, VA, he was of Welsh heritage; his ancestors probably emigrated to America in the late 17th century.

Sumwalt (109) Americanized form of German ZUMWALT.

Sun (3469) **1.** Chinese 孙: from the name of Hui Sun, a high official of the state of Wei, which existed during the Zhou dynasty (1122–221 BC), located in present-day Shanxi province in north-central China. Wen Wang, the virtuous duke whose magnanimous rule led to the establishment of the Zhou dynasty in 1122 BC, had an eighth son named Kang Shu, who was enfeoffed the state of Wei. The ruling line continued through Wu Gong, whose son Hui Sun became a high official of Wei; his descendants adopted the given name Sun as their surname. Sun Tzu was author of *The Art of War*, written during the Spring and Autumn period (770–476 BC) and still much quoted today. Sun Yat-Sen (1866–1925) was the revolutionary leader instrumental in the overthrow of the Chinese dynastic system early in the twentieth century. **2.** Korean: variant of SON.
GIVEN NAMES Chinese 38%; Korean 6%. *Wei* (22), *Li* (17), *Hong* (11), *Jian* (10), *Qi* (10), *Yi* (10), *Jing* (9), *Hui* (8), *Ming* (8), *Tong* (7), *Weimin* (7), *Xin* (7); *Chang* (6), *Chung* (5), *Min* (3), *Tian* (2), *Yiping* (2), *Youn* (2); *Byung, Byung Soo, Chong, Chong Kil, Dae, Dong Chul.*

Sunada (102) Japanese: 'sandy rice paddy'. The name is not common in Japan.
GIVEN NAMES Japanese 36%. *Kayo* (2), *Hideo, Hiromitsu, Hisao, Ichiro, Kaoru, Katsuki, Kazuo, Masaji, Masao, Masaru, Satoshi.*

Sund (634) **1.** Swedish and Danish: from *sund* 'strait', 'sound', probably an arbitrarily adopted or ornamental surname, but

possibly a topographic name adopted by someone who lived near the shore by a strait. **2.** Norwegian: habitational name from any of twenty-five or more farmsteads, mainly in Nordland, so named from Old Norse *sund* 'strait', 'sound'. **3.** English: nickname for a healthy or prosperous man, from Middle English *sund*, *sound* 'sound', 'healthy'. **4.** English: topographic name from Middle English *sund*, *sound* 'water', 'strait', 'sound'.
GIVEN NAMES Scandinavian 5%. *Erik* (2), *Morten*, *Sven*.

Sundahl (182) **1.** Swedish: ornamental name composed of the elements *sund* 'strait', 'sound' + *dahl*, an ornamental spelling of *dal* 'valley'. **2.** Norwegian: habitational name from any of several farmsteads, most of them named with *sunn* 'south' + *dal* 'valley'.

Sundaram (189) Indian (Tamil Nadu, Andhra Pradesh): Hindu name from Sanskrit *sundara* 'beautiful'. This is only a given name in India, but has come to be used as a family name in the U.S.
GIVEN NAMES Indian 89%. *Meenakshi* (5), *Shankar* (4), *Bala* (3), *Kalyana* (3), *Anand* (2), *Lakshmi* (2), *Mohan* (2), *Raj* (2), *Ram* (2), *Sekhar* (2), *Sridhar* (2), *Vijay* (2).

Sunday (1170) English: nickname for someone born on a Sunday, from Middle English *Sunday*.

Sundberg (1846) Swedish: ornamental name composed of the elements *sund* 'strait', 'sound' + *berg* 'mountain', 'hill'.
GIVEN NAMES Scandinavian 5%. *Nils* (4), *Lars* (3), *Erik* (2), *Sven* (2), *Bernt*, *Bjorn*, *Gunhild*, *Kerstin*, *Sig*, *Stellan*, *Thor*.

Sundblad (124) Swedish: ornamental name composed of the elements *sund* 'strait', 'sound' + *blad* 'leaf'.
GIVEN NAMES Scandinavian 6%. *Birgit*, *Helmer*.

Sundby (348) Norwegian: habitational name from any of twenty-five or more farmsteads, notably in southeastern Norway, named in Old Norse as *Sunnbýr*, from *sunn* 'south' + *býr* 'farm', 'settlement'.
GIVEN NAMES Scandinavian 6%. *Bertel*, *Dagny*.

Sunde (525) Norwegian: habitational name from any of twenty-five or more farmsteads, notably in western Norway, named with the dative singular of Old Norse *sund* 'strait', 'sound'.
GIVEN NAMES Scandinavian 13%. *Carsten*, *Erik*, *Johan*, *Lars*, *Morten*, *Per*.

Sundeen (454) Perhaps an altered spelling of Swedish **Sundén**, a variant of SUND 1.
GIVEN NAMES German 4%. *Kurt* (3), *Reinhold*.

Sundell (409) Swedish: ornamental name composed of the elements *sund* 'strait', 'sound' + the ornamental suffix *-ell*, taken from the Latin adjectival ending *-elius*.
GIVEN NAMES Scandinavian 6%; German 4%. *Erik*, *Kerstin*; *Kurt* (2).

Sunder (149) Indian (southern states): Hindu name from Sanskrit *sundara* 'beautiful'. This is only a given name in India, but has come to be used as a family name in the U.S. Among Tamil and Telugu speakers who have migrated away from their home state, it is a variant of SUNDARAM.
GIVEN NAMES Indian 15%; German 5%. *Shyam* (4), *Jayanthi*, *Mohini*, *Sanjay*, *Sankar*, *Srinivas*; *Klaus* (2), *Hans*, *Orlo*.

Sunderhaus (134) German: topographic name from Middle High German *sunder* 'southern' or *sunder* 'separate', 'apart', in either case denoting a place of residence in relation to a village or settlement.

Sunderland (1767) English: habitational name from any of various places so called, especially the city at the mouth of the river Wear. This, like other places so called in Cumbria, Lancashire, and southern Scotland, derives its name from Old English *sundor* 'separate' + *land* 'land'; a further example in Northumbria has the same origin as SUTHERLAND.

Sunderlin (238) Swedish: unexplained.

Sunderman (770) North German (**Sundermann**): **1.** habitational name for someone from any of the places called Sundern, Sonder, or Sondern, for example in Westphalia. **2.** variant of **Sudermann** (see SUDERMAN). **3.** variant of SONDERMAN.

Sundermann (112) German: see SUNDERMEYER.
GIVEN NAMES German 10%. *Arno* (2), *Erwin*, *Kurt*.

Sundermeyer (153) **1.** North German: distinguishing name from Middle Low German *sunder* 'wooded area of common land' + *meier* 'tenant farmer'. **2.** variant of SUNDERMAN 2.

Sundet (126) Norwegian: habitational name from any of several farmsteads named with the definite singular form of *sund* 'strait', 'sound'.
GIVEN NAMES Scandinavian 7%; German 4%. *Erik*; *Hans* (2).

Sundgren (121) Swedish: ornamental name composed of *sund* 'strait', 'sound' + *gren* 'branch'.
GIVEN NAME Scandinavian 7%. *Swen*.

Sundheim (180) **1.** Norwegian: habitational name from any of several farmsteads so named, or more recently formed as a compound of *sund* 'strait', 'sound' + *heim* 'home', 'farmstead'. **2.** German: habitation name from any of various places so named.

Sundholm (127) Swedish: from *sund* 'strait', 'sound' + *holm* 'island', mainly an ornamental name, but in some cases a topographic name for someone who lived on an island.
GIVEN NAMES Scandinavian 8%. *Erik*, *Helmer*, *Sigfred*.

Sundin (445) Swedish: ornamental name composed of the elements *sund* 'strait',

'sound' + the ornamental suffix *-in*, taken from Latin *-in(i)us* 'descendant of'.
GIVEN NAMES Scandinavian 11%. *Nils* (2), *Alvar*, *Lennart*, *Per*, *Sigfrid*, *Sten*.

Sundling (148) Swedish: ornamental name composed of the elements *sund* 'strait', 'sound' + the ornamental suffix *-ling* denoting a member of a family or household.

Sundman (111) Swedish (also in Finland): ornamental name composed of the elements *sund* 'strait', 'sound' + *man* 'man'.

Sundquist (1142) Swedish: ornamental name composed of the elements *sund* 'strait', 'sound' + *quist*, an old or ornamental spelling of *kvist* 'twig'.
GIVEN NAMES Scandinavian 6%. *Nils* (4), *Erik* (2), *Lennart*, *Niels*, *Selmer*.

Sundstrom (1071) Swedish (**Sundström**): from *sund* 'strait', 'sound' + *ström* 'river', mostly an ornamental name, but in some cases a topographic name for someone who lived by a river running into a strait.
GIVEN NAMES Scandinavian 8%. *Gunvor* (2), *Lennart* (2), *Helmer*, *Hilmer*, *Jarl*, *Johan*, *Lars*, *Sven*, *Thord*.

Sundt (195) **1.** Norwegian and Swedish: variant of SUND. **2.** North German: habitational name from places named Stralsund or Sunden. **3.** North German: topographic name from Middle Low German *sunt* 'narrows'. **4.** North German: nickname from Middle Low German *sunt* 'healthy', 'unhurt'.
GIVEN NAMES Scandinavian 7%. *Ingard*, *Lars*, *Thoralf*.

Sundy (131) English and Welsh: perhaps a variant spelling of SUNDAY.

Sung (1282) **1.** Chinese 宋: variant of SONG 1. **2.** Korean: variant of SONG 2.
GIVEN NAMES Chinese/Korean 42%. *Nak* (5), *Young* (5), *Jung* (4), *Sun* (4), *Eun* (3), *Jin* (3), *Kwang* (3), *Myung* (3), *Ying* (3), *Yoon* (3), *Ching* (2), *Chun* (2); *Chang* (6), *Chong* (2), *Mi Kyung* (2), *Min* (2), *Moon* (2), *Myong* (2), *Baek*, *Bok Soon*, *Byung Joon*, *Chang Hyun*, *Chol*, *Dae*.

Sunga (109) : perhaps a variant of Spanish **Zúñiga** (see ZUNIGA).
GIVEN NAMES Spanish 53%; Italian 8%. *Ramon* (3), *Jose* (2), *Luis* (2), *Orlando* (2), *Roberto* (2), *Amado*, *Augusto*, *Eduardo*, *Eloisa*, *Elvira*, *Erlinda*, *Ernesto*; *Enrico*, *Fausto*, *Francesco*, *Marco*.

Suniga (230) Basque (**Súñiga**): variant of **Zúñiga** (see ZUNIGA).
GIVEN NAMES Spanish 29%. *Juan* (5), *Jose* (3), *Raul* (2), *Ruben* (2), *Xavier* (2), *Abelardo*, *Agapito*, *Alberto*, *Ana*, *Anselma*, *Benito*, *Domingo*; *Antonio* (2), *Savino* (2), *Heriberto*, *Romeo*, *Sal*, *Salvatore*.

Sunkel (99) German: possibly a habitational name from Sunkeln in East Prussia.

Sunseri (382) Italian (Sicily): occupational name for a pork butcher or renderer of lard, from *sunza* 'pork fat' (medieval Latin *sungia*) + the occupational suffix *-eri*.

GIVEN NAMES Italian 14%. *Sal* (7), *Salvatore* (4), *Antonio* (2), *Elvira* (2), *Domenic*, *Matteo*.

Sunshine (505) Translation of German and Jewish SONNENSCHEIN.

GIVEN NAMES Jewish 7%. *Ari, Chaim, Golde, Hyman, Meyer, Miriam, Sol*.

Suntken (119) North German: probably a nickname for a healthy-looking person, from Middle Low German *sunt* (German *gesund*) + the diminutive suffix *-ke(n)*.

Suomi (108) Finnish: ethnic name from Finnish *Suomi* 'Finland'. At one time this term denoted only southwestern Finland, but nowadays it is the national name for the whole of Finland. As a surname it is mostly an adopted name during the names conversion movement at the beginning of the 20th century.

GIVEN NAMES Finnish 12%. *Eino* (2), *Antti, Arvo, Martti, Niilo*.

Suozzo (117) Southern Italian: nickname from a southern variant of *sozzo* 'dirty'.

GIVEN NAME Italian 8%. *Rocco* (2).

Supak (186) Czech (**Šupák**): unflattering nickname from the vocabulary word **šupák** 'bum', 'layabout'.

Supan (180) **1.** German (Austrian): status name for a mayor or district administrator in a Slavic-speaking region, from Middle High German *sūpān*, from Slavic *župan* (see ZUPAN). **2.** Slovenian: Germanized spelling of Slovenian ZUPAN.

Super (860) **1.** English: from a personal name, Latin *Superius*. **2.** Jewish (from Latvia): probably a much altered variant of SHAPIRO.

Supernaw (129) Origin unidentified.

Supinger (113) Variant spelling of German **Suppinger**, a habitational name for someone from Suppingen.

Supino (107) Italian: habitational name from Supino in Frosinone province.

GIVEN NAMES Italian 10%; French 7%. *Angelo, Concetta, Elio, Ruggero*; *Andre* (2).

Supinski (178) Polish (**Supiński**) and Jewish (from Poland): habitational name from Supienie near Suwalki.

GIVEN NAMES Polish 7%. *Janina, Jozef, Zbigniew*.

Supko (103) Polish: possibly a derivative of *supa* 'soup', perhaps a nickname for someone who liked soup.

Suplee (135) Perhaps an altered spelling of French **Suply** (see SUPPLEE).

Suppa (345) Southern Italian: probably from a Germanic personal name, *Sup(p)o*.

GIVEN NAMES Italian 18%. *Salvatore* (3), *Angelo* (2), *Domenico* (2), *Francesco* (2), *Carlo, Enrico, Giuseppe, Luigi, Pio*.

Suppes (289) German: unexplained.

Supple (574) **1.** Irish (Munster): from a Norman topographic name, *de la Chapelle*, which was taken to Ireland in the 12th century, where it became well established in the counties of Limerick and Cork. **2.** German (**Süpple**): metonymic occupational name for a cook, from Middle High German *suppe(līn)* 'soup', 'stock', 'meal'.

Supplee (389) Perhaps from the French personal name *Supplie*, an altered and metathesized variant of *Sulpice* (Latin *Sulpicius*).

Suprenant (202) Canadian variant of French **Supernant** (see SURPRENANT).

GIVEN NAMES French 5%. *Andre, Normand*.

Suprise (113) Origin unidentified. Possibly French: unexplained.

Sur (163) **1.** German: variant of SAUER. **2.** Indian (Bengal) and Bangladeshi: Hindu name, a nickname from Sanskrit *šūra* 'brave'. **3.** Korean: variant of **Sŏ** (see SO).

GIVEN NAMES Indian 19%; Korean 14%. *Abha, Amit, Gopa, Partha, Prabhat, Sandip, Sanjiv, Shakti, Shyama, Sonali, Sumana, Sumit*; *Chae, Jin, Jong, Kheng, Ki Suk, Soon, Sun Kyu, Wan*.

Sura (309) **1.** Americanized spelling of Polish **Szura**, a nickname from *szurać* 'to shuffle' or from Old Polish *szura* 'brother-in-law'. **2.** Indian (Gujarat): Hindu (Vania) and Muslim name of unknown meaning.

GIVEN NAMES Indian 15%. *Anjana* (2), *Chandrakant* (2), *Kiritkumar* (2), *Suresh* (2), *Amish, Aruna, Ashvin, Ashwin, Gautam, Hemant, Jayshree, Kirit*.

Surabian (121) Armenian: from the personal name *Surab*, a variant of Persian *Zohrab*.

GIVEN NAMES Armenian 6%. *Herach, Karekin, Sarkis, Vahan*.

Surace (349) Southern Italian: from the Greek personal name *Surakēs*, of unexplained etymology.

GIVEN NAMES Italian 26%. *Rocco* (6), *Alessandro* (4), *Leandro* (2), *Santo* (2), *Angelo, Carmella, Clemente, Domenic, Donato, Fortunato, Francesca, Francesco, Pasquale, Sal*.

Suraci (162) Southern Italian: variant of SURACE.

GIVEN NAMES Italian 14%. *Mauro* (2), *Emilio* (2), *Giuseppe, Mario, Vito*.

Suratt (136) Probably a variant of English SYRETT.

Surbaugh (170) Altered form of German **Surbach**, a habitational name from a minor place named with Middle Low German *sūr* 'sour' (or *sure* 'sorrel') + *beke* 'creek'. In Germany this surname occurs chiefly in the Ruhr.

Surbeck (100) Swiss German: habitational name of unexplained etymology.

Surber (1495) South German: from Bavarian dialect *surbe, sorbe* 'grass', 'turf', 'swamp', 'reedy soil', a topographic name for someone who lived on such ground.

Surdam (138) Origin unidentified.

Suresh (114) Indian (southern states): Hindu name from Sanskrit *sureša* 'lord of the gods' (from *sura* 'god' + *īša* 'lord'), which is an epithet of the god Indra. It is only a given name in India but has come to be used as a family name in the U.S.

GIVEN NAMES Indian 91%. *Ram* (3), *Srinivasan* (3), *Bala* (2), *Chetan* (2), *Dev* (2), *Nallan* (2), *Pushpa* (2), *Suri* (2), *Archana*.

Surette (609) French Canadian: variant of French **Suret**, an occupational name from a diminutive of *sûr* 'shoemaker'. The spelling *-ette* is not a feminine form, but a spelling prompted by the continuing pronunciation of final *-t* in Canadian French surnames after it had become silent in ordinary French vocabulary words.

GIVEN NAMES French 4%. *Alphee, Alyre, Andree, Elphege, Emile, Odile*.

Surface (904) Origin unidentified. Compare SURFUS.

Surfus (111) Origin unidentified. Compare SURFACE.

Surgener (101) English: occupational name from a late, extended form of Anglo-Norman French *surgien* 'surgeon'.

Surgent (102) English: variant of SARGENT.

GIVEN NAMES French 6%. *Anatole, Emile* (2).

Surgeon (204) **1.** English: from Middle English, Old French *sur(ri)gien* (from a derivative of Late Latin *chirurgia* 'handiwork'), hence an occupational name for a person who performed operations, mostly amputations. Before the advent of anaesthetics, only crude surgery was possible, and the calling was often combined with that of the barber or bathhouse attendant. **2.** French: topographic name for someone who lived close to a gushing spring.

Surges (163) German: possibly a Rhenish form of **Surke**, nickname for a grumpy person, from Middle High German, Low German *sūr* 'sour' + the diminutive suffix *-ke*.

Suri (257) **1.** Indian (Panjab): Hindu (Khatri) and Sikh name, based on the name of a clan in the Khatri community, from Sanskrit *sūri* 'sun', 'priest', 'sage'. It is also an epithet of Krishna. **2.** Hungarian (**Súri**): habitational name for someone from any of several places called Sur, in Komárom and Veszprém counties and in former Pozsony county in Hungary, now in Slovakia.

GIVEN NAMES Indian 71%. *Anil* (4), *Darshan* (3), *Ramesh* (3), *Sanjay* (3), *Subhash* (3), *Amita* (2), *Ashish* (2), *Ashu* (2), *Atul* (2), *Pramod* (2), *Promila* (2), *Seema* (2).

Suriano (303) Southern Italian: variant of SORIANO.

GIVEN NAMES Italian 22%; Spanish 4%. *Angelo* (3), *Crescenzo* (2), *Rocco* (2), *Antonio, Carmelo, Corradino, Domenic, Enzo, Giacomo, Mario, Nino, Orazio, Orlando, Philomena, Rodolfo*; *Miguel* (2), *Julio, Luis, Santos*.

Suriel (106) Hispanic (Mexico): unexplained.

GIVEN NAMES Spanish 55%. *Jose* (4), *Juan* (4), *Luis* (3), *Pedro* (3), *Mercedes* (2), *Ramona* (2), *Abad, Aleida, Alfonsa, Aura, Carolina, Francisca*.

Surina (106) Origin unidentified.

Surles (745) English: probably a variant spelling of SEARLES.

Surls (122) English: probably a variant spelling of SEARLES.

Surma (324) Polish: metonymic occupational name for a trumpet or horn player, from *surma* 'trumpet', 'horn'.
GIVEN NAMES Polish 4%. *Malgorzata, Stanislaw*.

Surman (338) English: variant spelling of SERMON 1.

Surowiec (238) Polish: nickname for a serious, grim, or unrefined person, from a derivative of *surowy* 'raw', 'serious'. The word *surowiec* also means 'raw material'.
GIVEN NAMES Polish 7%. *Ignacy, Janina, Jozef, Krystyna, Leszek, Zofia*.

Surprenant (734) French: variant of **Supernant**, a topographic name denoting a dwelling above the town of Nant, altered by folk etymology to conform to the French vocabulary word *surprenant* 'surprising'.
FOREBEARS A Surprenant from the Perche region of France is documented in Laprairie, Quebec, in 1678 with the secondary surname Sanssoucy.
GIVEN NAMES French 10%. *Marcel* (3), *Raoul* (3), *Andre* (2), *Armand* (2), *Monique* (2), *Normand* (2), *Adelard, Aldor, Cecile, Dieudonne, Gaston, Germain*.

Surprise (166) Origin unidentified; perhaps a mistranslation of French SURPRENANT.

Surratt (1514) Probably a variant of English SYRETT.

Surrell (147) English (of Norman origin): habitational name from either of the places called Sourdeval, in Calvados and La Manche.

Surrency (278) Origin unidentified.

Surrett (417) Origin uncertain: **1.** perhaps a variant of English SYRETT. **2.** possibly an Americanized spelling of French **Suret** (see SURETTE).

Surrette (181) French Canadian: see SURETTE.

Surrey (112) English: regional name for someone from the county of Surrey, so named from Old English *sūther* 'southerly' + *gē* 'district', possibly a reference to its position south of the Thames.

Surridge (133) English: **1.** from a Middle English personal name, *Seric*, which represents a coalescence of two Old English personal names, *Sǣrīc* (composed of *sǣ* 'sea' + *rīc* 'power') and *Sigerīc* (composed *sige* 'victory' + *rīc* 'power'). This would normally have given modern English *Serrich*, but the form has been altered under the influence of Old French *surreis* 'southerner' (see 2 below). **2.** regional name for someone who had migrated from the South, from Old French *surreis* 'southerner'. **3.** habitational name from a place in the parish of Morebath, Devon, so named from Old English *sūð* 'south' + *hrycg* 'ridge'.

Susa (219) **1.** Hungarian: metronymic from an archaic spelling of the female personal name *Zsuzsa*, a short form of *Zsuzsanna*, Hungarian form of *Susanna*.

2. Slovenian (**Suša, Šuša**): unflattering nickname from *suša*, (dialect *šuša*) 'scraggy or scrawny fellow'.

Susalla (102) Polish (**Susała**): nickname from a derivative of *sus* 'leap', 'jump'.

Susan (231) **1.** English and Dutch: from the female personal name *Susanna, Susanne* (Middle English), *Susanna* (Dutch), from Hebrew *Shushannah* 'lily', 'lily of the valley'. **2.** Southern French: from Occitan *susan* 'above', 'higher', hence a topographic name for someone living at the top end of a village or on the side of a valley. **3.** Jewish (Sephardic): from the male personal name *Susan*, a derivative of Arabic *susan* 'lily'.

Susco (117) Italian (Puglia): unexplained.
GIVEN NAMES Italian 11%. *Dante, Nunzio, Vito*.

Susi (412) Italian: of uncertain origin; it could be Greek, compare modern Greek *Soyses*, or alternatively, Caracausi suggests, of Arabic or Hebrew origin.
GIVEN NAMES Italian 22%; Spanish 7%. *Angelo* (3), *Dante* (2), *Mario* (2), *Salvino* (2), *Silvio* (2), *Aldo, Antonio, Artemio, Assunta, Claudio, Clementina, Concezio, Dino, Enio, Enrico, Orlando, Panfilo; Bienvenido* (2), *Jose* (2), *Andres, Ines, Juanita, Salvador*.

Suski (292) Polish: habitational name from any of numerous places called Sucha (see SUCHY).
GIVEN NAMES Polish 5%. *Lech, Piotr, Wojciech*.

Suskin (118) Jewish (Ashkenazic): variant of SUSSKIND.

Susko (284) Slavic

Susman (392) Altered spelling of German **Süssmann** or a variant spelling of Jewish **Sussman** (see SUSSMAN). This is also found as a Slovenian name.
GIVEN NAMES Jewish 7%. *Ari* (4), *Avram* (2), *Beril, Devorah*.

Susong (182) Of French origin: unexplained.
FOREBEARS Andrew Susong and his family came from Alsace-Lorraine, France, arriving at Georgetown, SC, in 1777, aboard the ship *Victoire*, with the Marquis de Lafayette.

Suss (202) **1.** German (**Süss**) and Jewish (Ashkenazic): see SUESS. **2.** Jewish (Ashkenazic): from the Yiddish personal name *Zus*, a pet form of SUSSMAN.
GIVEN NAMES Jewish 6%; German 4%. *Ari, Asher, Ilissa, Miriam, Zahava; Hermann* (2).

Susser (182) German (**Süsser**) and Jewish: variant of SUSS.
GIVEN NAMES Jewish 8%. *Moshe* (2), *Isak, Levi, Reuven*.

Sussex (114) English: regional name for someone from the county of Sussex, named '(territory of) the South Saxons', from Old English *sūth* + *Seaxe*.

Susskind (173) Jewish (Ashkenazic): from

the Yiddish personal name *Ziskind*, German *Süsskind*, literally 'sweet child'.
GIVEN NAMES German 8%. *Horst* (3), *Kurt*.

Sussman (2534) **1.** German (**Süssmann**): elaborated form of SUESS, literally 'sweet man'. **2.** Jewish (Ashkenazic): from the Yiddish personal name *Zusman*, literally 'sweet man'.
GIVEN NAMES Jewish 5%. *Emanuel* (4), *Meyer* (3), *Miriam* (3), *Isadore* (2), *Isidor* (2), *Este, Hinda, Hyman, Moshe, Pola, Shira, Sholom*.

Sustaita (303) **1.** Castilianized variant (common in Mexico) of Basque **Suztaeta**, which has two origins. **2.** topographic name denoting someone who lived where broom grew, from a reduced form of *isutz* 'broom' + the suffix *-ta* + the locative suffix *-eta*. **3.** topographic name for someone who lived in a grassy field, from *usa* 'grass' + the locative suffix *-eta*.
GIVEN NAMES Spanish 47%. *Jose* (8), *Juan* (4), *Carlos* (3), *Francisco* (3), *Jesus* (3), *Luis* (3), *Raul* (3), *Ricardo* (3), *Agapito* (2), *Alicia* (2), *Cruz* (2), *Fernando* (2).

Suszek (116) German: of Slavic origin, unexplained.

Sutch (337) English: variant spelling of SUCH 1.

Sutcliffe (988) English: habitational name from any of the three places in West Yorkshire, so named from Old English *sūð* 'south' + *clif* 'riverbank', 'slope', 'cliff', or a topographic name with the same meaning.

Suter (2252) **1.** English and Dutch: occupational name from Middle English *suter, souter*, Middle Dutch *sutter* 'shoemaker' (Latin *sutor*). **2.** German: variant of SAUTER.

Sutera (381) Italian (Sicily): habitational name from a place so called in Caltanisetta.
GIVEN NAMES Italian 16%. *Salvatore* (6), *Sal* (3), *Vito* (3), *Angelo, Ciro, Emanuele, Gaspare, Ignazio, Saverio*.

Sutfin (351) Dutch: see SUTPHIN.

Suthard (148) Possibly of English origin, a variant of **Suddard**, a Yorkshire habitational name from a variant spelling of Southworth in Lancashire.

Suther (222) German: variant spelling of SUTER.

Sutherby (118) English: topographic name for someone who lived to the south or on the south side of a settlement, from Old Norse *suðr í bý*.

Sutherland (11072) Scottish: regional name from the former county of this name, so named from Old Norse *suðr* 'south' + *land* 'land' because the territory lay south of Scandinavia and the Norse colonies in the Orkney and Shetland Islands.

Sutherlin (750) **1.** German: variant of *Sütterlin* (see SUTTERLIN). **2.** Probably Scottish: Black lists the surname **Sutherline**, apparently a variant of *Suthern* (see SOUTHERN).

Suthers (162) Variant of German **Suther** (see SUTER).

Sutkowski (132) Polish: habitational name for someone from a place called Sutków in Tarnów voivodeship, or from Sutków or Sutkowce, both now in Ukraine.
GIVEN NAMES Polish 12%. *Tadeusz* (2), *Andrej, Krystyna, Przemyslaw.*

Sutley (208) English: unexplained; possibly a habitational name from a lost or unidentified place.

Sutliff (804) English: variant of SUTCLIFFE.

Suto (229) **1.** Hungarian (**Sütő**): occupational name for a baker, *sütő*, from *sütni* 'to bake'. **2.** Japanese: written apparently phonetically with characters meaning 'necessary' and 'door'; the meaning is uncertain. The name is not common in Japan.
GIVEN NAMES Hungarian 11%; Japanese 10%. *Gabor* (3), *Istvan* (2), *Laszlo* (2), *Elek, Ferenc, Ildiko; Ichiro, Kiyoshi, Masaru, Sachiko, Shinichi, Shoji, Takashi, Yasuko, Yugo, Yukio.*

Sutor (316) **1.** English: variant spelling of SUTER. **2.** German and Polish: occupational name for a tailor or shoemaker, from Latin *sutor*.
GIVEN NAMES German 5%. *Claus* (2), *Frieda, Otto.*

Sutphen (416) See SUTPHIN.

Sutphin (1633) Americanized spelling of Dutch **van Zutphen**, a habitational name for someone from Zutphen in the province of Gelderland.

Sutt (113) English: unexplained.
GIVEN NAMES Russian 4%. *Juri, Konstantin.*

Sutter (3849) English and South German: occupational name for a shoemaker or cobbler (rarely a tailor), from Middle English *suter, souter*, Middle High German *sūter, sūtære* (from Latin *sutor*, an agent derivative of *suere* 'to sew').

Sutterer (104) German: variant of SUTTER.
GIVEN NAME German 4%. *Kurt.*

Sutterfield (779) English: possibly a habitational name from a lost or unidentified place.

Sutterlin (122) South German (**Sütterlin**): diminutive of SUTTER.
GIVEN NAME German 8%. *Armin.*

Suttie (118) Scottish: probably a habitational name from a place called Suthie, in Perthshire, or possibly from Suddy (or Suddie) in Knockbain.

Suttle (1157) English (East Anglia): **1.** nickname for a clever person, from Anglo-Norman French *sotil* 'subtle', 'clever', 'cunning'. **2.** habitational name from Soothill in West Yorkshire.

Suttles (1455) Altered form of English SUTTLE.

Suttner (148) South German (also **Süttner**): topographic name for someone who lived in a wet, boggy place, from the genitive of Middle High German *sutte* 'puddle', 'marsh' + -*er* suffix denoting an inhabitant, or a habitational name for someone from a place called Sutten, named with this word.
GIVEN NAMES German 5%. *Erwin* (2), *Erhard.*

Sutton (30717) English: habitational name from any of the extremely numerous places called Sutton, from Old English *sūð* 'south' + *tūn* 'enclosure', 'settlement'.

Sutula (102) Polish: nickname for someone with a hump back, from dialect *sutuł* 'hump'.
GIVEN NAMES Polish 9%. *Andrzej, Tadeusz, Zbigniew.*

Suver (134) German: **1.** Americanized form of **Süwer**, nickname from the Low German equivalent of standard German *sauber* 'clean'. **2.** (**Süver**) from a reduced form of the Germanic personal name *Siegwart*, composed of *sig* 'victory' + *wart* 'guardian'.

Suydam (534) Dutch

Suzuki (1836) Japanese: variously written, usually with characters meaning 'bell tree', the name is probably taken from Japan's lovely pampas grass, *susuki*. An alternate pronunciation is *Susuki*. This is one of the two most common surnames in Japan, the other being SATO. Legend says that one Suzuki family descended from a priestly line named Hozumi, of Kumano in present-day Mie prefecture. The Hozumi, in turn, are listed in the Shinsen shōjiroku and claim descent from the Mononobe clan.
GIVEN NAMES Japanese 74%. *Hiroshi* (18), *Hiroyuki* (12), *Toshio* (12), *Akira* (11), *Kenji* (11), *Toru* (10), *Minoru* (8), *Yoko* (8), *Takashi* (7), *Yasuo* (7), *Hideo* (6), *Hiroko* (6).

Svatek (144) Czech (**Svátek**): from a pet form of any of various traditional Slavic personal names containing the Old Slavic element *svat* 'holy', e.g. *Svatoslav, Svatopluk, Svatomir.*

Svatos (119) Czech (**Svatoš**): from a pet form of a personal name such as *Svatoslav* (see SVATEK).
GIVEN NAME German 4%. *Kurt.*

Svec (559) Czech (**Švec**): occupational name for a shoemaker, Czech *švec*, a derivative of *šíti* 'to sew'.
GIVEN NAMES Czech and Slovak 4%. *Milan* (3), *Frantisek, Jaroslav, Lubos, Vaclav, Zdenek.*

Sveda (108) Czech (**Švéda, Švejda**): ethnic name for someone of Swedish origin, in particular a descendant of the Swedish soldiers who invaded Bohemia during the Thirty Years War (1618–48).

Sveen (164) Norwegian: habitational name from any of numerous farmsteads in eastern Norway, named Sveen, from Old Norse *svið* 'land cleared by burning', from *sviða* 'to burn'.
GIVEN NAMES Scandinavian 14%. *Arnfinn* (2), *Erik* (2), *Knut, Lars, Sven.*

Svehla (218) **1.** Czech (**Švehla**): nickname from a derivative of Old Czech *švehlat* 'to twitter'. **2.** Norwegian: habitational name from any of several farmsteads in Rogaland named Svela (unexplained).

Svendsen (938) Danish and Norwegian: patronymic from the personal name *Sven*, from Old Norse *Sveinn*, originally a byname meaning 'boy', 'servant'.
GIVEN NAMES Scandinavian 14%; German 4%. *Bjorn* (2), *Erik* (2), *Knut* (2), *Lars* (2), *Niels* (2), *Per* (2), *Thor* (2), *Astrid, Britt, Carsten, Einer, Evald; Kurt* (3), *Arnulf, Claus, Ernst, Lorenz, Otto.*

Svenningsen (103) Danish and Norwegian: patronymic from the personal name *Svenning*, a variant of *Sveinung*, from Old Norse *Sveinn* (see SVENDSEN) + the suffix -*ung* 'son of'.

Svenson (469) Americanized spelling of Swedish SVENSSON or Danish and Norwegian **Svensen** (see SVENDSEN).
GIVEN NAMES Scandinavian 15%; German 6%. *Sven* (6), *Erik* (2), *Bjorn, Dagny; Kurt* (2), *Gerhard, Irmgard.*

Svensson (349) Swedish: patronymic from the personal name *Sven*, from Old Norse *Sveinn*, originally a byname meaning 'boy', 'servant'.
GIVEN NAMES Scandinavian 42%; German 6%. *Lars* (9), *Anders* (3), *Erik* (3), *Lennart* (3), *Sven* (3), *Ejnar* (2), *Johan* (2), *Bent, Bjorn, Gunn, Holger, Mats; Ernst* (2), *Kurt, Markus, Otto.*

Svetlik (155) **1.** Czech (**Světlík**), Slovak (**Svetlík**), and Slovenian: nickname from Czech *světlý*, Slovak *svetlý*, Slovenian *svetel* 'bright'. **2.** Czech (**Světlík**) and Slovak: perhaps from a pet form of any of various traditional personal names containing the Old Slavic element *svat* 'holy', e.g. *Svatoslav, Svatopluk, Svatomir* (see SVATEK).

Sveum (176) Norwegian: habitational name from any of numerous farmsteads in Oppland and Hedmark, so named from the dative plural of SVEEN.

Svitak (187) Czech and Slovak (**Sviták**): **1.** from a pet form of any of various traditional Slavic personal names containing the Old Slavic element *svat* 'holy', e.g. *Svatoslav, Svatopluk, Svatomir* (see SVATEK). **2.** habitational name for someone from Svitavy.

Svoboda (2466) Czech: from a noun literally meaning 'freedom'. This was a technical term in the feudal system for a freeman, i.e. a peasant farmer as opposed to a serf.

Svrcek (119) Czech and Slovak (**Svrček**): from an old variant spelling of *cvrček* 'cricket', used as a nickname for a small, chirpy person.

Swab (286) **1.** Altered spelling of Dutch **Swaab**, a regional name for someone from Swabia, or the German cognate SCHWAB. **2.** American form of Slovenian **Švab**, ethnic name for a colonist from Swabia, or any German speaker (see German **Schwab**). In the Balkans, this was a generic term for a German speaker.

Swaby (257) **1.** English: habitational name from a place in Lincolnshire, so called from the Old Norse ethnic byname *Sváfi* 'Swabian' (see SCHWAB) + Old Norse *býr* 'farm', 'settlement'. **2.** Americanized spelling of German SCHWABE.

Swackhamer (191) Possibly an altered spelling of German **Schwaikheimer**, a habitational name for someone from Schwaikheim near Ludwigsburg (Württemberg).

Swackhammer (136) Probably of German origin (see SWACKHAMER).

Swader (220) Possibly an altered spelling of German **Schwader**, a variant of SCHWADERER.

Swadley (260) Possibly of English origin, a habitational name from a lost or unidentified place.

Swaffar (133) Origin unidentified.

Swafford (3156) English: of uncertain origin, probably a habitational name from a lost or unidentified place. Compare SWOFFORD.

Swager (372) Variant spelling of Dutch **Swaager**, from Middle Dutch *zwager* 'son-' or 'father-in-law', used to distinguish between two bearers of the same personal name related by marriage.

Swagerty (219) Americanized form of German SCHWEIGERT.

Swagger (107) Variant spelling of Dutch **Swaager** (see SWAGER).

Swaggerty (237) Americanized form of German SCHWEIGERT.

Swagler (135) Americanized form of German **Schwägler**, an occupational name for a musician who played the fife, from Middle High German *swegel*.

Swahn (107) Swedish and German: variant of German SCHWAN.

GIVEN NAME Scandinavian 11%. *Lennart.*

Swailes (186) English (West Yorkshire): variant spelling of SWALES.

Swails (414) English: variant spelling of SWALES.

Swaim (2273) Origin unidentified.

Swain (8371) **1.** Northern English: occupational name for a servant or attendant, from the Middle English word *swein* 'servant' or Old Norse *sveinn* 'boy', 'servant'. In Old Norse this word is also found as a personal name in the form *Sveinn*; so in some cases the origin may be patronymic. **2.** Scottish and Irish: reduced form of MCSWAIN.

Swaine (223) Northern English and Irish: variant of SWAIN.

Swainston (183) English: habitational name from an unidentified place. There is a place so named on the Isle of Wight (and one called Swainstone in Devon). However, in England the surname is concentrated in County Durham, suggesting that it could be a variant of the habitational name SWANSTON.

GIVEN NAMES German 5%. *Kurt* (2), *Erwin.*

Swales (302) English (Yorkshire): in all probability from the Swale river in Yorkshire. (Reaney and Wilson list a 17th-century example, **Swayles**, with this origin.) Alternatively, it may be a metronymic from the Old Norse female personal name *Svala.*

Swalley (258) Origin unidentified. Possibly English: unexplained.

Swallow (1081) English (Yorkshire): **1.** from Middle English *swal(e)we*, *swalu* 'swallow', hence a nickname for someone thought to resemble the bird, perhaps in swiftness and grace. **2.** habitational name from a place in Lincolnshire, so called from the Swallow river on which it stands. The river name is probably ultimately akin to that of the bird, with some transferred meaning such as 'swirling' or 'rushing'.

Swallows (300) English: variant of SWALLOW.

Swalve (125) Possibly an Americanized form of Dutch **Swalue**, nickname from Middle Dutch *swaluwe*, *swaluë* 'swallow'.

Swalwell (105) English (County Durham): habitational name from a place so named in Tyne and Wear.

Swaminathan (113) Indian (Kerala, Tamil Nadu): Hindu name composed of the Sanskrit elements *svāmi* 'lord' (see SWAMY) + *nātha* 'lord', + the Tamil-Malayalam third-person masculine singular suffix *-n*. This is only a given name in India, but has come to be used as a family name in the U.S.

GIVEN NAMES Indian 96%. *Anand* (2), *Bala* (2), *Hari* (2), *Krishna* (2), *Murali* (2), *Ramesh* (2), *Sriram* (2), *Sundar* (2), *Aravind, Arun, Ashok, Balaji.*

Swamy (135) Indian (Karnataka): Hindu name from Sanskrit *svāmī* 'lord', 'master'. It also refers to a learned Brahman or religious man. As a personal name, it appears to have evolved from use as the final element in compound personal names such as *Ramaswamy* 'lord Rama' and *Krishnaswamy* 'lord Krishna'. It is found only as a given name in India, but has come to be used as a family name in the U.S.

GIVEN NAMES Indian 81%. *Ravi* (4), *Kumar* (3), *Narayana* (3), *Ananth* (2), *Bhaskar* (2), *Chandra* (2), *Deepak* (2), *Krishna* (2), *Mahesh* (2), *Narasimha* (2), *Anand, Arun.*

Swan (8447) **1.** Scottish and English: from Middle English *swan* 'swan', hence a nickname for a person noted for purity or excellence (which were taken to be attributes of the swan), or resembling a swan in some other way. This was also an Old Norse and Old English personal name, from which the surname may be derived. In some cases it may be a habitational name for someone who lived at a house with the sign of a swan. **2.** variant of English SWAIN. **3.** Americanized form of German SCHWAN. **4.** Americanized form of Norwegian SVEEN or Swedish SWAHN.

Swanberg (684) Swedish: ornamental name composed of the elements *svan* 'swan' + *berg* 'mountain'.

GIVEN NAMES Scandinavian 5%. *Erik, Sigvard, Sven.*

Swanda (178) Polish (**Swenda** or **Szwenda**): nickname for an idle layabout, from a

derivative of *szwędać* 'to hang about', 'to loiter'.

Swander (274) Altered spelling of German SCHWANDER.

Swaner (211) Altered spelling of German SCHWANER.

Swaney (1497) Scottish: probably an occupational name for a servant or retainer. Compare SWAIN 1.

Swanger (1076) **1.** Perhaps an altered form of German **Schwanger**, from *Swano*, a short form of a Germanic compound personal name formed with *swan* 'swan', or directly from this word. **2.** Perhaps an Americanized form of German **Zwanger**, from Middle High German *zwange* 'pliers', hence an occupational name for a maker or user of pliers, or maybe a nickname for someone with very strong hands.

Swango (304) possibly an Americanized form of South German (Bavarian) **Schwankl**, nickname for a limber person, from Middle High German *swankel* 'slender', 'flexible'.

Swanick (144) English: habitational name from Swanwick in Derbyshire, possibly also Swanwick in Hampshire. Both are named from Old English *swān* 'herdsman' + *wīc* 'outlying (dairy) farm'.

Swanigan (237) Irish: of uncertain origin; perhaps an Anglicized form of a Gaelic **Ó Suibhneacháin**, which is not recorded in Ireland, but is possibly a pet form of **Ó Suibhne** (see SWEENEY).

Swank (3010) Americanized form of German SCHWANK or SCHWENK.

Swanke (179) Altered spelling of German SCHWANKE.

GIVEN NAME German 4%. *Kurt.*

Swanlund (122) Origin unidentified. Possibly Swedish: unexplained.

Swann (4281) English: variant spelling of SWAN.

Swanner (839) Perhaps an altered form of German SCHWANER.

Swansen (115) Americanized spelling of Danish and Norwegian **Svensen** (see SVENDSEN).

GIVEN NAME Scandinavian 4%. *Nils.*

Swanson (32636) **1.** Americanized spelling of Swedish SVENSSON or Danish and Norwegian **Svensen** (see SVENDSEN). **2.** Scottish and northern English: patronymic from the personal name SWAN.

GIVEN NAMES Scandinavian 6%. *Erik* (42), *Nils* (12), *Nels* (11), *Sven* (9), *Lars* (8), *Thor* (7), *Helmer* (4), *Iver* (4), *Alf* (3), *Astrid* (3), *Eskil* (3), *Hilmer* (3).

Swanston (157) Scottish: habitational name from a place near Edinburgh, probably named with the genitive case of the Old English byname *Swān* 'swain' (or the personal name SWAN) + Old English *tūn* 'enclosure', 'settlement'.

Swanstrom (394) Swedish (**Svanström**): ornamental name composed of the elements *svan* 'swan' + *ström* 'river'.
GIVEN NAMES Scandinavian 5%. *Erik, Nord.*

Swantek (292) Americanized form of Polish **Świątek** (see SWIATEK).

Swanton (369) English: habitational name from any of the places, in Kent and Norfolk, so called from Old English *Swānatūn* 'settlement (Old English *tūn*) of the retainers' (see SWAN 2).

Swanzy (138) English and Irish: unexplained.

Swapp (210) Scottish (Aberdeen): unexplained.

Swarbrick (118) English (Lancashire): habitational name from a place in the parish of Kirkham, Lancashire, named from Old Norse byname *Svartr* 'black' + Old Norse *brekka* 'slope'.

Sward (442) Americanized spelling of Swedish **Svärd** or **Swärd**, a soldier's name or ornamental name from *svärd* 'sword'.
GIVEN NAMES Scandinavian 5%. *Nels, Nils.*

Swaringen (237) Perhaps an Americanized form of German **Schweringen**, a habitational name from Schweringen in Lower Saxony.

Swarm (169) Probably an Americanized spelling of German SCHWARM.

Swarner (156) Origin unidentified.

Swarr (109) possibly an altered form of German **Schwar**, from Sorbian *šwar* 'brother-in-law', 'male relative', or from **Schwär**, reduced form of **Schwäher**, from Middle High German *swe(he)r* of the same meaning.

Swart (1722) Dutch and English: nickname for a dark-haired or dark-skinned person, from Middle Dutch *zwart*, *swert*, Middle English *swart* 'dark', 'swarthy'.

Swarthout (722) Dutch: apparently from *swart* 'black' + *hout* 'wood'.

Swartley (283) Origin unidentified.

Swartout (495) See SWARTHOUT.

Swarts (710) **1.** Dutch: variant of SWART. **2.** Variant of German and Jewish SCHWARTZ.

Swartwood (464) Americanized form of Dutch SWARTHOUT.

Swartwout (222) Dutch: variant of SWARTHOUT 'black skin'.

Swartz (10199) **1.** Dutch: variant of SWART. **2.** Variant of German and Jewish SCHWARTZ.

Swartzbaugh (197) Americanized spelling of German **Schwarzbach**, a habitational name from any of several places so named, or a topographic name from Middle High German *swarz* 'black' + *bach* 'creek'.

Swartzel (124) Americanized spelling of southern German **Schwärzel**, a diminutive of SCHWARZ.

Swartzell (112) Of German origin: variant of SWARTZEL.

Swartzendruber (372) Of Swiss German origin: variant of SWARTZENTRUBER.

Swartzentruber (366) Variant of Swiss German **Schwarzentruber**, **Schwartzentrauber**, an occupational name for a grower of black wine grapes, from Middle High German *swarz* 'black' + *trūbe* 'grape', or from the name of a house or tavern with a sign a dark grapes.

Swartzfager (101) German: Americanized form of **Schwarzfeger**, probably a nickname for a black-haired armorer or for a ruffian or for a vagrant, from Middle High German **swarz** 'black' + **feger** 'armorer', 'tramp'.

Swartzlander (268) Americanized form of German **Schwarzländer**, a habitational name for someone from an area of Bavaria known as *Schwarzland* 'the black land', from Middle High German *swarz* 'black' + *land* 'land'.

Swartzmiller (110) Americanized form of German **Schwarzmüller** 'black miller'.
GIVEN NAME German 5%. *Kurt.*

Swartzwelder (158) Americanized form of German **Schwarzwälder**, topographic name for someone from the Black Forest in southwest Germany, from Middle High German *swartz* 'black' + *walt* 'forest', or a habitational name from any of several places named Schwarzwald, for example near Gotha.

Swasey (345) English: unexplained. Possibly an Anglicized form of Dutch **Swijse(n)**, variant of **Wijs** 'wise' (see WISE).
FOREBEARS The name was brought to North America by John Swasey, a Quaker who came from England to Salem, MA, with two sons, John and Joseph, in or before 1640. Banished from Salem because of his religious beliefs, he moved first to Setauket, Long Island, NY, and subsequently to Southold, Long Island. His son Joseph remained in MA and inherited his estate at Salem.

Swatek (226) Polish: occupational name for someone who helped families to arrange marriages, from *swat* 'matchmaker'.

Swatzell (212) perhaps an Americanized form of German **Schwärzel**, **Schwerzel**, a nickname from a diminutive of SCHWARZ, or of German **Schwetzel**, of uncertain origin.

Swauger (254) Possibly an altered spelling of German SCHWAGER.

Swavely (250) Possibly Welsh: unexplained.

Swayne (597) English: variant spelling of SWAIN.

Swayze (778) Variant of English SWASEY.

Sweaney (228) Variant of Irish SWEENEY.

Sweany (275) Variant of Irish SWEENEY.

Swearengen (148) Variant of Dutch SWEARINGEN.

Swearengin (567) Variant of Dutch SWEARINGEN.

Swearingen (3110) Dutch: altered form of a habitational name, almost certainly from one of two places in Germany named Schweringen: one in the Hannover region and the other near Bremen.
FOREBEARS A 17th-century law-enforcement officer by the name of Gerrit van Sweeringen is recorded at New Amstel on the Delaware River.

Swearinger (114) Dutch: variant of SWEARINGEN, the suffix -*er* denoting an inhabitant.

Swearingin (171) Variant of Dutch SWEARINGEN.

Sweat (2742) Probably a variant of English SWEET.

Sweatman (515) English: variant of SWEET.

Sweatt (1313) Probably a variant of English SWEET.

Sweazey (131) Variant of English SWASEY.

Sweazy (197) Variant of English SWASEY.

Swecker (402) Possibly an Americanized form of southern German **Zwecker**, an occupational name for a nail maker, from Middle High German *zweck* 'tack', 'nail' + the agent suffix -*er*.

Sweda (192) Variant of Polish SZWEDA, an ethnic name for a Swede.

Swedberg (520) Swedish: from *sved* '(burnt) clearing' + *berg* 'mountain', 'hill', mostly an ornamental name, but in some cases perhaps a topographic name for someone who lived by a hillside clearing.

Swedlund (199) Swedish: ornamental name composed *sved* '(burnt) clearing' + *lund* 'grove'.

Swee (139) Americanized form of Norwegian **Sve** (see SVEEN).
GIVEN NAMES Scandinavian 12%. *Knut* (2), *Erik, Obert, Ragner.*

Sweeden (260) Dutch: ethnic name for a Swede, someone from Sweden.

Sweeley (132) Perhaps a variant of Irish SWEENEY.

Sween (241) **1.** Scottish: reduced form of McSWEEN. **2.** Norwegian: variant of SVEEN.

Sweeney (20601) **1.** Irish: reduced form of McSWEENEY, an Anglicized form of Gaelic **Mac Suibhne** 'son of *Suibhne*', a byname meaning 'pleasant'. **2.** Americanized form of French **Choinière** (see CHOINIERE).
GIVEN NAMES Irish 8%. *Brendan* (7), *Donal* (3), *Kieran* (3), *Eamonn* (2), *Paddy* (2), *Senan* (2), *Tadhg* (2), *Aileen, Assumpta, Brennan, Caitlin, Colm.*

Sweeny (764) Irish: variant spelling of SWEENEY.

Sweere (114) Dutch: **1.** relationship name, from Middle Dutch *swere* 'father-in-law'. **2.** from the Germanic personal name *Sweer, Swier*.

Sweers (151) Dutch: from Middle Dutch *swere* 'father-in-law', 'son-in-law', hence a nickname to distinguish between bearers of the same personal name related by marriage.

Sweet (11094) **1.** English (most common in the West Country): nickname from Middle English *swete* 'sweet', 'pleasant', 'agreeable'. The Old English bynames *Swēt(a)* (masculine) and *Swēte* (feminine) derived from this word survived into the early Middle English period, and may also be sources of the surname. **2.** Translation of German and Jewish (Ashkenazic) SUESS. **3.** In New England, a translation of French LEDOUX.

Sweeten (678) Variant of English SWEETING.

Sweetin (146) Variant of English SWEETING.

Sweeting (614) English: **1.** from a medieval personal name, originally an Old English patronymic from *Swēt(a)* (see SWEET). **2.** from Middle English *sweting* 'darling', 'sweetheart', hence a nickname for a popular and attractive person, or for somebody who habitually addressed people with the term.

Sweetland (544) English (Devon): habitational name from Sweetlands in Upottery, Devon, so named from Old English *swēte* 'sweet', 'pleasant', 'fertile' + *land* 'cultivated land', 'estate', or possibly a topographic name with the same meaning.

Sweetman (773) English and Irish: variant of SWETNAM.

Sweetnam (105) Irish: variant of SWETNAM.

Sweeton (219) Irish: variant of SWEETMAN.
GIVEN NAME Irish 4%. *Conley.*

Sweetser (521) **1.** English: nickname for a kindly master, from Middle English *swete* 'sweet', 'pleasant', 'agreeable' + *sire, sier* 'master' (often used to address an older man). **2.** Possibly an Americanized spelling of German and Jewish SCHWEITZER.

Sweetwood (150) Origin unidentified.

Sweezey (188) Variant of English SWASEY.

Sweezy (225) Variant of English SWASEY.

Sweger (222) Dutch: **1.** occupational name for an official in charge of weights and measures, from *weger* 'weigher' **2.** from Middle Dutch *sweger*, a term denoting a relative by marriage. Compare German SCHWAGER. **3.** from the Germanic personal name *Swidger* (see SCHWEICKERT).

Swegle (118) Origin unidentified.

Swehla (166) Altered spelling of SVEHLA.

Sweigard (190) Variant of German SCHWEICKERT.

Sweigart (1045) **1.** Variant of German SCHWEICKERT. **2.** possibly an altered spelling of German **Zweigart**, a metonymic occupational name for the owner of a tree nursery, from Middle High German *zwīggart* (*zwīg* 'twig' + *gart* 'enclosure').

Sweigert (191) Variant of German SCHWEICKERT.

Sweitzer (1628) Variant of German and Jewish SCHWEITZER 'Swiss'.

Swem (165) German: Americanized form of **Schwemm**, a topographic name from Middle High German *swem(me)*, denoting a deep ford where horses had to swim across, from the Middle High German verb *swemmen*, causative of *swimmen* 'to float or swim'.

Swendsen (215) Variant of Danish and Norwegian SVENDSEN.

Sweney (214) Irish: variant spelling of SWEENEY.

Swenor (128) Origin unidentified.
GIVEN NAMES French 4%; German 4%. *Alphonse, Colette; Elke, Kurt.*

Swensen (904) Altered spelling of Norwegian and Danish **Svensen**, a variant of SVENDSEN.
GIVEN NAMES Scandinavian 5%. *Alf, Erik, Helmer, Knud, Lars, Sven, Swen, Tor, Viggo.*

Swenson (10296) **1.** Swedish or Americanized spelling of Danish and Norwegian **Svensen**, or Americanized spelling of Swedish **Sven(s)son** (see SVENDSEN). **2.** English: patronymic from SWAIN.
GIVEN NAMES Scandinavian 4%. *Erik* (17), *Swen* (12), *Nels* (6), *Selmer* (4), *Britt* (3), *Helmer* (3), *Lars* (3), *Eskil* (2), *Lennart* (2), *Nils* (2), *Ordell* (2), *Sten* (2).

Swensson (120) Americanized spelling of Swedish **Sven(s)son** (see SVENDSEN) or a German name of the same derivation.
GIVEN NAMES Scandinavian 21%; German 8%. *Erik* (6); *Kurt* (2), *Gerda.*

Swepston (128) English: habitational name from Swepstone in Leicestershire, so named from an unattested Old English personal name, *Sweppi + tūn* 'enclosure', 'settlement'.

Swerdloff (130) Jewish (from Belarus): Respelling, under German influence, of **Sverdlov**, a habitational name for someone from Sverdly, in Belarus.
GIVEN NAMES Jewish 8%. *Avrum, Bluma.*

Swerdlow (178) Variant of Jewish **Sverdlov** (see SWERDLOFF).
GIVEN NAME Jewish 4%. *Moisey.*

Swetland (263) Probably a variant of English SWEETLAND.

Swetman (126) English and Irish: variant of SWETNAM.

Swetnam (287) Reduced form of English **Swetenham**, **Swettenham**, or **Sweetnam**, a habitational name from Swettenham in Cheshire, named from the genitive of the Old English personal name *Swēta + hām* 'homestead' or *hamm* 'enclosure hemmed in by water', 'water meadow', 'land in a riverbend'.

Swets (153) Dutch: patronymic from a nickname for someone with dark hair or a dark complexion, from Dutch (Brabantine dialect) *zwet* 'black'. Compare SWART.
GIVEN NAMES Dutch 7%. *Gerrit, Marinus.*

Swett (1346) **1.** Dutch: nickname for a dark-haired or swarthy person (see SWETS). **2.** Americanized spelling of

Slovenian *Svet*, a nickname from the adjective *svet* 'holy' (most likely), or possibly from the noun *svet*, which has various meanings, including 'world', 'advice'.

Swetz (198) Dutch: variant spelling of SWETS.

Swezey (338) Variant of English SWASEY.

Swiatek (481) Polish (**Świątek**): from a pet form of any of various Old Polish personal names such as *Świętosław, Świętobor*, or *Świętopełk*, with *święt-* 'holy' as the first element.
GIVEN NAMES Polish 7%. *Dorota, Ewa, Jacek, Jerzy, Jozef, Kazimierz, Piotr, Ryszard, Stanislaw, Tadeusz.*

Swiatkowski (169) Polish (**Świątkowski**): habitational name for someone from Świątkowo in Bydgoszcz voivodeship, Świątkowa in Krosno voivodeship, or Świątkowice in Sieradz and Włocławek voivodeships.
GIVEN NAMES Polish 11%. *Janusz* (2), *Aniela, Dariusz, Jerzy, Piotr, Urszula.*

Swicegood (488) Americanized form of Swiss German **Schweissgut**, **Schweisgut**, literally 'sweat well', occupational nickname for a blacksmith.

Swick (1643) **1.** Dutch: nickname for a weak or malleable person, from Middle Dutch *swike, swick* 'one who yields', from *swiken* 'to yield or give way'. **2.** Dutch: from a pet form of the Germanic personal name *Swidger* (see SCHWEICKERT). **3.** Altered spelling of German ZWICK.

Swickard (262) Americanized spelling of German **Schwickardt**, from the medieval personal name *Swidger* or SCHWEICKERT.

Swider (555) Polish (**Świder**): nickname from *świder* 'drill'. Compare SWIDERSKI.
GIVEN NAMES Polish 4%. *Jacek, Jerzy, Jozefa, Krzysztof, Zygmund.*

Swiderski (660) Polish (**Świderski**): habitational name for someone from any of the many places in Poland called Świdry, or from Świder in Siedlce voivodeship, named with *świder* 'drill', 'gimlet'.
GIVEN NAMES Polish 6%. *Miroslaw* (2), *Czeslaw, Janusz, Jozef, Marcin, Piotr, Slawomir, Wieslaw, Witold, Zygmunt.*

Swidler (149) Jewish (from Belarus): nickname from northeastern Yiddish *svindler* 'swindler'.
GIVEN NAMES Jewish 6%. *Hyman, Meyer.*

Swiech (179) Polish (**Święch**): from a pet form of the Old Polish personal names *Świętosław, Świętobor*, or *Świętopełk*.
GIVEN NAMES Polish 11%. *Dorota, Jaroslaw, Jerzy, Jozef, Kazimierz, Krzysztof, Ludwik.*

Swiecicki (123) Polish (**Święcicki**): habitational name from either of two places named Święcica, in Chełm and Tarnobrzeg voivodeships, or either of two places named Święcice, in Kielce and Warszawa voivodeships.
GIVEN NAMES Polish 8%. *Ignacy, Jozef, Marcin.*

Swier (232) Dutch and North German: from a Germanic personal name, *Sweder*, *Sweer*, *Swier*, composed of the elements *swind* 'strong' + *hari*, *heri* 'army'. Compare SCHWEDER 2.

Swierczek (136) Polish (**Świerczek**):
1. nickname for a small, chirpy person, from a diminutive of *świercz* 'cricket'.
2. topographic name or nickname from *świerk* 'spruce'.
GIVEN NAMES Polish 12%. *Eugeniusz, Kazimierz, Krzysztof, Miroslaw, Wieslawa, Zbigniew.*

Swierczynski (104) Polish (**Świerczyński**): habitational name for someone from places called Świerczyn (in Płock and Włocławek voivodeships) or Świerczyna (of which there are many). The places are named with either *świerk* 'spruce' or *świercz* 'cricket'.
GIVEN NAMES Polish 7%. *Boguslawa, Mariusz, Pawel.*

Swift (8975) 1. English: nickname for a rapid runner, from Middle English *swift* 'fleet'. 2. Irish: Anglicization (part translation) of Gaelic **Ó Fuada** (see FOODY). 3. Americanized form of some likesounding Jewish name.

Swigart (722) Perhaps an Americanized spelling of German SCHWEIGHARDT or **Zweigert** (see SWIGERT).

Swiger (1189) Possibly a respelling of German and Jewish SCHWEIGER.

Swigert (453) Americanized form of German SCHWEIGERT or **Zweigert**, an occupational name for a gardener or tender of fruit trees or vines, from an agent derivative of Middle High German *zwīgen* 'to graft', 'to plant'. Compare SWEIGART.

Swiggett (118) Possibly an Americanized form of German SCHWEIGERT or **Zweigert** (see SWIGERT), or of **Schwigat**, of Slavic origin.

Swiggum (222) Respelling of Norwegian **Sviggum**, a habitational name from a farmstead in Sogn named Sviggum, from Old Norse *Sviðgum*, denoting a place where the grass easily dries.
GIVEN NAMES Scandinavian 4%. *Lars, Nordahl.*

Swihart (964) Perhaps a reduced Americanized form of SCHWEIGHARDT or **Zweichard** (see SWIGERT).

Swilley (683) Origin unidentified. Possibly English: unexplained.

Swilling (192) Possibly an Americanized form of German ZWILLING.

Swim (635) English: unexplained. Perhaps an Anglicized form of German SCHWAM.

Swimm (134) Origin unidentified. Perhaps an Anglicized form of German SCHWAM.
GIVEN NAME Scandinavian 4%. *Erik.*

Swimmer (164) Translation of German and Jewish SCHWIMMER.
GIVEN NAMES Jewish 5%. *Mendel, Rebekah.*

Swims (175) English: variant of SWIM.

Swinburne (106) English: habitational name from Swinburne in Northumberland, named from Old English *swīn* 'swine', 'wild boar' + *burna* 'stream'.

Swindall (328) English: variant spelling of **Swindell**.

Swindell (1600) English: of uncertain origin; probably a habitational name from Swindale in Skelton, North Yorkshire, so named from Old English *swīn* 'pig', 'wild boar' + *dæl* 'valley'.

Swindells (133) English: variant of SWINDELL.

Swinderman (115) Origin unidentified.

Swindle (1655) 1. English: variant spelling SWINDELL. 2. Perhaps an Americanized spelling of German **Schwind(e)l**, a nickname from a diminutive of Middle High German *swinde* 'wild', 'impetuous'.

Swindlehurst (150) English (Lancashire and Cumbria): probably a habitational name from Swinglehurst in Bowland Forest, West Yorkshire, so named from Old English *swīn* 'hog', 'wild boar' + *hyll* 'hill' + *hyrst* 'wooded ridge'.

Swindler (582) Translation of South German **Schwindler**, a nickname from an agent derivative of Middle High German *swindeln* 'to swindle'.

Swindoll (114) Respelling of English SWINDELL.

Swinea (120) Origin unidentified.

Swineford (180) Scottish: habitational name from one of the English places that gave rise to SWINFORD.

Swinehart (1046) 1. Americanized spelling of German **Schweinhardt**, an occupational name for a swineherd, from Middle High German *swīn* 'hog', 'swine' + *hertære* 'herder'. 2. from a Germanic personal name meaning 'boy' (in Old High German *swein*, Scandinavian *sven*, Middle Low German *sven*) + *hart* 'strong'.

Swiney (706) Irish: variant of SWEENEY.

Swinford (1192) English: habitational name from places called Swinford in Oxfordshire and Leicestershire, from Kingswinford in Staffordshire, or Old Swinford in Worcestershire, named with Old English *swīn* 'swine', 'hog' + *ford* 'ford'.

Swing (697) Probably an Americanized spelling of German SCHWING or **Zwing**, from Middle High German *zwinc* 'legal district', hence possibly a metonymic occupational name for a district administrator.

Swinger (220) 1. English (Norfolk): unexplained. 2. In some instances probably an Americanized form of German and Jewish SCHWINGER, or German **Zwinger**, a nickname from Middle High German *zwinger* 'oppressor'.

Swingle (1137) 1. English: metonymic occupational name for a worker in the linen or hemp industry, from Middle English *swingle* 'swingle', a wooden implement used for beating flax or hemp (Middle

Dutch *swinghel*, from the verb 'to swing'). 2. Possibly an Americanized spelling of German **Zwingel**, a topographic name from Middle High German *zwingel* 'citadel'.

Swingler (166) English (West Midlands): occupational name for a worker in the linen or hemp industry, from an agent derivative of Middle English *swingle* 'swingle' (see SWINGLE).

Swingley (152) Americanized form of South German **Zwingly**, a nickname from Middle High German *zwinelinc* 'twin'.

Swink (1378) Possibly an altered spelling of German **Zwink**, from Sorbian *wink* 'wreath', probably from a house name given because of the sign of a wreath.

Swinney (1686) English (Northumberland and Durham): 1. possibly a habitational name from Swinnie in Borders region, Swinney Beck in North Yorkshire, or Swinny Knoll in West Yorkshire, or some other similarly named place. 2. alternatively, perhaps an Americanized form of Irish SWEENEY.

Swinson (1085) Perhaps an Americanized form of SVENSSON.

Swint (867) Origin unidentified. Perhaps an Anglicized or Americanized spelling of German **Schwind(t)** (see SCHWIND).

Swinton (707) English and Scottish: habitational name from any of various places, for example in Lancashire and North and South Yorkshire, so named from Old English *swīn* 'pig', 'wild boar' + *tūn* 'enclosure', 'settlement'.

Swiontek (175) Polish (**Świątek**, **Świontek**): nickname from *święty* 'holy' or occupational name for a carver of icons, from *świątek* 'icon', 'holy image'.
GIVEN NAMES Polish 4%. *Halina, Teofil.*

Swire (171) English: variant of SQUIRE, from a northern form of the word.

Swires (115) English (Yorkshire): variant of SWIRE.

Swirsky (197) Jewish (from Lithuania and Belarus): habitational name for someone from Svir, a town now in Belarus.
GIVEN NAMES Jewish 9%. *Hyman (2), Avram, Limor, Lipman.*

Swisher (3627) Americanized form of German SCHWEITZER 'Swiss'.

Swiss (208) Americanized form of German SCHWEISS or SCHWEITZ.

Swisshelm (122) Americanized form of German **Schweisshelm**, literally 'sweat helmet', but a wrongly standardized form of the Germanic personal name *Schwethelm*, from *swind*, *swīd* 'strong', 'fast' + *helm* 'helmet'.

Swist (124) Polish (**Świst**): nickname for a whistler, from *świstać* 'to whistle'.

Swistak (133) Polish (**Świstak**): nickname for a whistler, variant of SWIST, with the agent suffix *-ak*.
GIVEN NAMES Polish 8%. *Andrzej, Dariusz, Piotr, Zofia.*

Switala (169) Polish (**Świtała**): nickname for an early riser, from *świt* 'dawn' (or *świtać* 'to dawn').

Switalski (342) Polish (**Świtalski**): variant of SWITALA + *-ski* suffix of surnames.

Switzer (4481) **1.** English: variant of SWEETSER. **2.** Americanized spelling of SCHWEITZER.

Swoboda (932) Polish: from *swoboda* 'freedom', a technical term in the feudal system for a freeman, i.e. a peasant farmer as opposed to a serf. The name in this form is also found in German-speaking countries, as a German form of both the Polish name and Czech SVOBODA.
GIVEN NAMES German 4%. *Otto* (2), *Ralf* (2), *Bernhard, Dieter, Franz, Friedrich, Hilde, Jutta, Kurt, Wendelin.*

Swofford (793) English: variant of SWAFFORD.

Swoger (101) Americanized form of Dutch SWEGER or German SCHWAGER.

Swogger (262) Americanized form of Dutch SWEGER or German SCHWAGER.
GIVEN NAMES German 6%. *Kurt* (3), *Otto, Ralf.*

Swonger (277) Perhaps an altered form of German **Schwanger** (see SWANGER 1) or **Zwanger** (see SWANGER 2).

Swoope (193) Possibly an altered form of German SCHWAB.
GIVEN NAMES French 4%. *Andre, Monique.*

Swope (3316) Possibly an altered form of German SCHWAB.

Swopes (248) Possibly an altered form of German SCHWAB, with the addition of an inorganic *-s.*

Swor (212) Variant spelling of German **Schwör**, itself a variant of SCHWEHR. Compare SCHWER, SCHWEER

Sword (1104) **1.** Scottish and English: metonymic occupational name for a swordsman or armorer, from Middle English *swerd, sword* 'sword'. **2.** Irish: reduced Anglicized form of Gaelic **Ó Suaird, Ó Suairt** 'descendant of *Suart*', a personal name derived from Old Norse *Sigvarðr* 'victory keeper', a cognate of Old English *Sigeweard*. Compare SEWARD 1.

Swords (969) Irish: **1.** (Counties Leix and Offaly) variant of SWORD 2, with superfluous English patronymic *-s.* **2.** habitational name from a place of this name in County Dublin. **3.** Anglicized form of Gaelic **Ó Claimhín**, a translation as though from *claidheamh* 'sword' (see CLAVIN).

Swoveland (142) Americanized form of German **Schwabeland**, a regional name for someone from Swabia (German *Schwaben*; see SCHWAB).
FOREBEARS Peter Swoveland or Schwabeland, born about 1720 in Germany, came to PA in 1774 aboard the *Union*, sailing from Portsmouth, England, together with his children Ludwig, Christian, Catherine, and Peter.

Swoyer (289) Origin unidentified. Perhaps a variant of English SWIRE.

Swyers (328) English (Dorset): variant of SWIRE.

Swygert (270) Dutch: see SWIGERT.

Sy (542) **1.** Hispanic (Philippines): unexplained. **2.** African: unexplained.
GIVEN NAMES Spanish 16%; African 4%. *Jose* (4), *Teresita* (4), *Alfredo* (3), *Roberto* (3), *Edgardo* (2), *Erlinda* (2), *Lourdes* (2), *Ruben* (2), *Angelito, Armando, Benito, Carlos; Hamidou* (2), *Cheikh, Mamadou, Modou, Oumar, Ousmane, Thierno.*

Sybert (296) Variant of German SIEBERT.

Sybesma (136) Frisian: patronymic from a short form of the personal name SYBERT.

Sybrant (124) Dutch: from the Germanic personal *Siebrand*, composed of *sigi* 'victory' + *brand* 'sword'.

Sydenstricker (118) Americanized spelling of **Seidenstricker** (see SEIDENSTICKER).

Sydney (192) English: variant spelling of SIDNEY.
GIVEN NAMES French 5%. *Andre, Sylviane.*

Sydnor (811) Origin unidentified.

Sydor (137) Polish: from an eastern Slavic personal name, *Sydor*, from a medieval personal name based on Greek *Isidōros* (see ISADORE).
GIVEN NAME Polish 4%. *Wasyl.*

Sydow (429) North German: habitational name from any of several places so named, for example near Berlin, in Pomerania, and Anhalt. The surname is also established in Sweden, presumably having been taken there from Germany.
GIVEN NAMES German 4%. *Benno, Erwin, Florian, Hans, Kurt, Wolfgang.*

Syed (878) Muslim: variant of SAYED.
GIVEN NAMES Muslim 88%. *Ali* (19), *Ahmed* (10), *Mohammed* (10), *Asif* (8), *Hassan* (7), *Mahmood* (6), *Nadeem* (6), *Shahid* (6), *Akbar* (5), *Hasan* (5), *Iqbal* (5), *Mohammad* (5).

Syers (183) English: from Middle English *sire, sier* 'master' (Old French *sire*), hence a status name for the master of a household or group of apprentices, or a nickname for an elderly man or perhaps a pompous or domineering person.

Syfert (155) Americanized spelling of German and Dutch SIEFERT.

Syfrett (118) Origin unidentified. Perhaps a metathesized form of SYFERT.

Sykes (8226) English (mainly Yorkshire): topographic name for someone who lived by a stream in a marsh or in a hollow, from Middle English *syke* 'marshy stream', 'damp gully', or a habitational name from one of the places named with this word, in Lancashire and West Yorkshire.

Sykora (788) Czech and Slovak (**Sýkora**): nickname for a small, agile person, from *sýkora* 'titmouse', 'coalmouse'.

Syler (291) Altered spelling of German SEILER.

Sylla (190) North African and Muslim: unexplained. Perhaps a variant of SALAH.
GIVEN NAMES African 25%; Muslim 14%; French 8%. *Mamadou* (9), *Serigne* (3), *Aboubacar* (2), *Bakary* (2), *Balla, Cheikh, Demba, Djibril, Dou, Idrissa, Lassana, Mame; Abdoulaye* (2), *Mohamed* (2), *Moussa* (2), *Abdoul, Daouda, Ibrahima, Karim, Lamine, Mustapha, Omar, Souleymane; Prosper* (2), *Jean Baptiste, Jean-Marie, Monique.*

Sylte (139) Norwegian: habitational name from any of seven farmsteads, notably in Møre og Romsdal, named in Old Norse as *Sultar*, denoting a low-lying, marshy place.
GIVEN NAME Scandinavian 4%. *Agnar.*

Sylva (357) Variant spelling of SILVA.
GIVEN NAMES French 4%. *Alain, Fernande, Mathieu.*

Sylvain (482) French: from the Old French personal name *Seluein* (Latin *Silvanus*, a derivative of *silva* 'wood'), bestowed in honor of various minor early Christian saints.
FOREBEARS A Sylvain from the Saintonge region of France is documented in Montreal in 1720, with the secondary surname Larosée.
GIVEN NAMES French 21%. *Emile* (2), *Fernand* (2), *Jacques* (2), *Michel* (2), *Pierre* (2), *Andre, Armand, Benoit, Fernande, Francois, Gardy, Germain.*

Sylvan (195) **1.** Altered spelling of French SYLVAIN. **2.** Swedish: derivative of the Latin adjective *sylvanus* 'of or pertaining to forest', used as a translation of Swedish *skog* 'forest', for any of several Swedish vernacular names of which this word was a component.

Sylve (150) Origin unidentified.

Sylvest (169) Danish: from a personal name, a reduced form of Latin *Silvester* (see SYLVESTER).

Sylvester (6411) English and German: from a personal name (Latin *Silvester*, a derivative of *silva* 'wood'). This was borne by three popes, including a contemporary of Constantine the Great.

Sylvestre (347) French: from the personal name *Sylvestre* (see SYLVESTER).
FOREBEARS A Sylvestre from the Champagne region of France is documented in Quebec City in 1677, with the secondary surname Champagne.
GIVEN NAMES French 21%. *Andre* (2), *Armand* (2), *Normand* (2), *Pierre* (2), *Adelard, Aime, Alphonse, Carmelle, Donat, Gilles, Jean Claude, Marcel.*

Sylvia (2017) Apparently an altered spelling of Italian SILVIA.

Sylvis (100) Variant spelling of SILVIS.

Symanski (222) Americanized spelling of Polish **Szymański** (see SZYMANSKI).

Syme (377) Scottish and English: from a variant of the medieval personal name *Sim*, a short form of SIMON.

Symes (512) English: patronymic from the medieval personal name *Sim*, a short form of SIMON.

Symington (373) Scottish: habitational name from any of various places in southern Scotland named with the personal name *Simon* (see SIMON) + northern Middle English *toun* 'settlement'. The two places in Ayrshire of this name were both held in the late 12th century by a certain Simon Loccard or Lockhart, from whom they presumably derive their name.

Symmes (237) Respelling of English SYMES.

Symmonds (205) English: variant spelling of SYMONDS.

Symon (181) Scottish and English: variant spelling of SIMON.

Symonds (1175) English: patronymic from SIMON, with an excrescent *-d*.

Symons (1264) English (Devon): patronymic from SIMON.

Sympson (148) English: variant spelling of SIMPSON.

Syms (174) **1.** English: patronymic from a short form of the personal name SIMON. **2.** Jewish (from Ukraine; **Symes, Symis**): metronymic from the Yiddish female personal name *Sime* (see SIMA).

FOREBEARS Benjamin Syms was a planter and philanthropist, probably the earliest inhabitant of any North American colony to bequeath property for the establishment of a free school. His name was spelled variously as *Sims*, *Simes*, *Sym*, *Symms*, *Syms*, and *Symes*. He was probably born in England, but was reported in the VA census of 1624/25 as age 33 and living at Basse's Choice in what was later known as Isle of Wight County.

Synan (174) Irish (County Cork): according to Woulfe, a reduced Anglicized form of Gaelic **Ó Sionáin**, a variant of **Ó Seanáin** (see SHANNON).

Synder (308) German: **1.** from Middle Low German *sunder* 'wooded area of common land'. **2.** altered spelling of **Sünder**, a topographic name from Middle High German *sunder* 'separate'.

Synnott (174) English and Irish: variant spelling of SINNOTT.
GIVEN NAMES Irish 8%. *Aidan, Cormac, Declan.*

Sypek (135) Polish and Czech (**Sýpek**): occupational name for someone who worked in a granary, a derivative of Polish *sypać*, Czech *sypat* 'to sprinkle'.
GIVEN NAMES Polish 4%. *Danuta, Czeslaw.*

Sypher (226) Dutch: variant spelling of **Syfer**, a variant of SIEVERT.

Syphers (132) Dutch: variant spelling of **Siffers** or **Seyffers**, a patronymic from *Syfer* (see SYPHER).
GIVEN NAMES German 4%. *Erwin, Kurt.*

Sypniewski (207) Polish: habitational name for someone from places named Sypniewo in Bydgoszcz, Ostrołęka, and

Piła voivodeships, named from *sypać*, *sypnąć* 'to heap up or build (an embankment or dike)' or 'to pour or spill'.

Sypolt (209) Americanized spelling of German SEIBOLD, **Seipolt**, **Seipold**, from the Germanic personal name *Sigibald*, composed of the elements *sigi* 'victory' + *bald* 'brave'.

Syracuse (232) Americanized form of Italian SIRACUSA.
GIVEN NAMES Italian 5%. *Carmelo, Nino.*

Syrek (157) Polish: metonymic occupational name for a maker or seller of cheese, from Old Polish (or dialect) *syr* 'cheese'.

Syrett (140) English: **1.** from the Middle English male personal name *Syred*, Old English *Sigerǣd*, composed of the elements *sige* 'victory' + *rǣd* 'counsel'. **2.** from the Middle English female personal name *Sigerith*, Old Norse *Sigríðr*, a contraction of *Sigfríðr*, composed of the elements *sige* 'victory' + *fríðr* 'lovely'.

Syring (357) North German: patronymic from a Germanic personal name composed of the elements *sigi* 'victory' + *heri* 'army'.

Syron (163) Irish: reduced Anglicized form of Gaelic **Ó Sírín** (see SHEERAN).

Syslo (136) Polish (**Sysło**): nickname from a derivative of *sysać* 'to smack'.

Sytsma (389) Frisian: unexplained.

Syverson (1023) Respelling of Norwegian **Syversen**, a variant of SIVERTSEN, or of the Swedish cognate **Syversson**.

Syvertsen (181) Dutch, Danish, and Norwegian: variant of SIVERTSEN.
GIVEN NAMES Scandinavian 18%; German 6%. *Alf, Erik, Jorgen, Per; Georg, Hans, Kurt, Otto.*

Syvertson (123) Variant of Dutch, Danish, and Norwegian SIVERTSEN.

Syzdek (116) Polish: probably a topographic name from *syzd*, a dialect form of *szyst* 'schist'.

Szablewski (145) Polish: habitational name for someone from Szablewo in Gdańsk voivodeship or Szabły in Łomża voivodeship, named with *szabla* 'sabre'. The place name was probably applied either to a sabre-shaped piece of land or to a place where a noted swordsman lived.

Szabo (2782) Hungarian (**Szabó**): occupational name for a tailor, Hungarian *szabó*.
GIVEN NAMES Hungarian 18%. *Zoltan (26), Laszlo (20), Bela (14), Imre (11), Sandor (11), Tibor (10), Istvan (9), Lajos (9), Andras (8), Gabor (8), Jozsef (8), Antal (6).*

Szafran (185) Polish and Jewish (from Poland): from *szafran* 'saffron', a topographic name for someone who lived where the saffron crocus grew, a metonymic occupational name for a spicer, or possibly a nickname for someone with yellow hair. See SAFRAN.
GIVEN NAME Polish 4%. *Karol.*

Szafranski (437) Polish (**Szafrański**): habitational name for someone from either

of two places called Szafranki in Łomża or Ostrołęka voivodeships, or Szafranów, in Płock and Rzeszów voivodeships, all named with *szafran* 'saffron' (see SAFRAN 1).
GIVEN NAMES Polish 7%. *Andrzej (2), Bogdan (2), Halina, Krzysztof, Miroslaw, Stanislaw, Tadeuz, Wieslaw.*

Szakacs (136) Hungarian (**Szakács**): occupational name from *szakács* 'cook'.
GIVEN NAMES Hungarian 14%. *Geza (2), Antal, Bela, Ferenc, Gyula, Jeno, Tibor.*

Szala (107) **1.** Polish: nickname for a short-tempered person, from *szaleć* 'to rage'. **2.** Polish: metonymic occupational name for a merchant, from *szala* 'scales'. **3.** Hungarian: from the old secular personal name *Szala* or *Zala*.
GIVEN NAMES Polish 11%. *Jacek, Jozef, Malgorzata, Wieslaw, Wojciech.*

Szalay (322) Hungarian: regional name for someone from Zala county in Hungary, or a habitational name from a place called Szala.
GIVEN NAMES Hungarian 16%; Jewish 4%. *Laszlo (4), Bela (3), Kalman (2), Tibor (2), Aladar, Attila, Dezso, Ferenc, Gabor, Gaza, Imre, Janos; Kalmen.*

Szalkowski (158) Polish (also **Szałkowski**): habitational name for someone from places called Szałkowo or Szalkowsk.

Szanto (172) Hungarian (**Szántó**) and Jewish (from Hungary): occupational name for a plowman, from Hungarian *szántó* 'plowman' (from *szánt* 'to plow').
GIVEN NAMES Hungarian 18%; German 4%. *Istvan (2), Mihaly (2), Andras, Arpad, Katalin, Lajos, Laszlo, Lazlo, Miklos, Rezso, Sandor, Tibor; Erwin, Otto.*

Szarek (202) Polish: **1.** nickname for someone with gray hair or a grayish complexion, from a derivative of *szary* 'gray'. **2.** possibly also a derogatory nickname from Old Polish *szarek* 'whipper-snapper'.
GIVEN NAMES Polish 13%. *Andrzej, Eugeniusz, Ireneusz, Janusz, Jozef, Krystyna, Ludwika, Malgorzata, Zofia.*

Szarka (132) Hungarian: from *szarka* 'magpie', hence a nickname for a thief.
GIVEN NAMES Hungarian 13%. *Laszlo (3), Bela, Geza, Sandor, Zoltan.*

Szasz (145) Hungarian (**Szász**) and Jewish (from Hungary): ethnic or regional name for a German speaker from Transylvania or Szepes, etymologically a derivative of German SACHS.
GIVEN NAMES Hungarian 10%. *Csaba, Ferenc, Laszlo, Levente, Tamas, Tibor.*

Szatkowski (443) Polish and Jewish (from Poland): variant of **Szadkowski**, habitational name for someone from places called Szadek in Kalisz and Sieradz voivodeships, or Szadki in Warszawa voivodeship, or from Szadkowice in Piotrków and Sieradz voivodeships.

GIVEN NAMES Polish 6%. *Casimir* (3), *Krystyna* (2), *Janusz, Mariusz, Stanislaw, Waclawa.*

Szczech (224) Polish (**Szczęch**): nickname for a cheerful person (or, ironically, for a miserable person), from *szczęsny* 'happy' (see SZCZESNY).

GIVEN NAMES Polish 18%. *Tadeusz* (3), *Aniela* (2), *Kazimier* (2), *Andrzej, Arkadiusz, Bernadeta, Mariola, Mariusz, Mieczyslaw, Wladyslaw, Zuzanna.*

Szczepanek (137) Polish: from a pet form of the personal name *Szczepan,* Polish form of Latin *Stephanus* (see STEVEN).

GIVEN NAMES Polish 12%. *Dariusz, Henryk, Mieczyslaw, Thadeus.*

Szczepaniak (245) Polish: patronymic from the personal name *Szczepan,* Polish form of Latin *Stephanus* (see STEVEN).

GIVEN NAMES Polish 11%. *Dorota* (2), *Elzbieta, Grazyna, Iwona, Jacek, Jaroslaw, Karol, Lucjan, Mariusz, Tadeusz, Witold, Zbigniew.*

Szczepanik (209) Polish: from a pet form of the personal name *Szczepan,* Polish form of Latin *Stephanus* (see STEVEN).

GIVEN NAMES Polish 9%. *Andrzej, Dorota, Jaroslaw, Ludwik, Slawomir, Sylwester.*

Szczepanski (724) Polish (**Szczepański**): habitational name for someone from places called Szczepany in Białystok and Sieradz voivodeships, named with the personal name *Szczepan,* Polish form of Latin *Stephanus* (see STEVEN), + *-ski,* suffix of surnames.

GIVEN NAMES Polish 8%. *Andrzej* (2), *Casimir* (2), *Jacek* (2), *Miroslaw* (2), *Dariusz, Grzegorz, Janusz, Kazimierz, Krzysztof, Ryszard, Tadeusz, Urszula.*

Szczepkowski (123) Polish: habitational name for someone from a place named Szczepków, from the personal name *Szczepek,* a pet form of *Szczepan,* Polish form of Latin *Stephanus* (see STEVEN).

GIVEN NAMES Polish 13%. *Jerzy* (2), *Leszek, Piotr, Stanislaw.*

Szczerba (178) Polish: from *szczerba* 'gap', probably a nickname for someone with a front tooth missing.

GIVEN NAMES Polish 14%. *Stanislaw* (2), *Wasyl* (2), *Bogdan, Kazimierz, Mikolaj, Tadeusz, Zigmund.*

Szczesniak (222) **1.** Polish (**Szcześniak, Szczęśniak**): **2.** patronymic from the personal name *Szczęsny* (see SZCZESNY). **3.** from a nickname meaning 'lucky fellow'.

GIVEN NAMES Polish 8%. *Boleslaw, Ewa, Marzena, Tadeusz, Waclaw.*

Szczesny (291) Polish (**Szczęsny**): from the personal name **Szczęsny,** from *szczęsny* 'happy', 'fortunate', 'lucky', adopted as a vernacular equivalent of Latin FELIX.

GIVEN NAMES Polish 7%. *Czeslaw* (2), *Tadeusz* (2), *Janusz, Wladyslaw.*

Szczygiel (197) Polish (**Szczygieł**) and Jewish (from Poland): nickname for some-

one with a positive, joyful temperament, from *szczygiel* 'goldfinch'. The Jewish name is mainly ornamental.

GIVEN NAMES Polish 13%. *Zbigniew* (2), *Boguslaw, Jacek, Janusz, Kazimierz, Stanislaw, Tadeusz.*

Sze (316) **1.** Chinese 施: variant of SHI 3. **2.** Chinese 司: variant of SI 1.

GIVEN NAMES Chinese 16%. *Chun* (2), *Wing* (2), *Chia, Chien, Chikeung, Chung Ching, Chung Yee, Fung, Heung, Hua, Kwong, Man.*

Szekely (366) Hungarian (**Székely**): ethnic name for a Szekler (Hungarian *székely*), a member of a large and culturally distinct Hungarian community in Transylvania, now part of Romania.

GIVEN NAMES Hungarian 16%. *Bela* (5), *Laszlo* (4), *Ildiko* (2), *Akos, Arpad, Attila, Balint, Csaba, Emese, Gabor, Istvan, Janos.*

Szekeres (113) Hungarian: occupational name for a cartwright or carter, from *szekér* 'cart'.

GIVEN NAMES Hungarian 19%. *Janos* (3), *Karoly* (2), *Andras, Arpad, Bela, Gaza, Sandor.*

Szeliga (225) Polish: habitational name from places called Szeliga or Szeligi. It is not clear whether there is any connection with the Polish vocabulary word *szeliga* 'coat-of-arms'.

GIVEN NAMES Polish 8%. *Casimier, Jerzy, Jozef, Karol, Kazimierz, Maciej, Miroslaw.*

Szeto (578) Chinese 司徒: variant of SITU.

GIVEN NAMES Chinese 37%. *Hung* (6), *Chun* (5), *Wai* (5), *Wing* (4), *Chiu* (3), *Kan* (3), *Kin* (3), *Man* (3), *Yuen* (3), *Chau* (2), *Cheung* (2), *Chi* (2), *Chung* (2), *Kuen* (2), *Kwok* (2), *Chong, Koo, Min, Pang, Sik, Woon, Yuet.*

Szewczyk (593) Polish: patronymic or diminutive from *szewc* 'shoemaker' (a derivative of *szew* 'seam').

GIVEN NAMES Polish 17%. *Kazimierz* (4), *Bogdan* (3), *Zdzislaw* (3), *Andrzej* (2), *Halina* (2), *Janina* (2), *Alicja, Andrej, Beata, Casimir, Czeslaw.*

Szilagyi (403) Hungarian (**Szilágyi**): regional name for someone from the Szilágyság, now part of Romania, or a habitational name from any of several places called Szilágy in Hungary.

GIVEN NAMES Hungarian 17%. *Laszlo* (5), *Zoltan* (5), *Bela* (4), *Attila* (2), *Imre* (2), *Antal, Arpad, Balint, Dezso, Gyula, Istvan, Jozsef.*

Szoke (296) Hungarian (**Szőke**): descriptive nickname from Hungarian *szőke* 'fair-haired'.

GIVEN NAMES Hungarian 10%. *Istvan* (3), *Laszlo* (3), *Lajos* (2), *Balazs, Ferenc, Ildiko, Kalman, Sandor, Tibor.*

Szopinski (128) Polish (**Szopiński**): habitational name for someone from places

called Szopa, Szopinek, or Szopy, named with *szopa* 'shed', 'booth'.

GIVEN NAMES Polish 6%. *Casimir, Ryszard.*

Szostak (286) Polish (**Szóstak**) and Jewish (eastern Ashkenazic): nickname from Polish *szóstak* 'six-fingered person', also the name of an old Polish coin, both derived from *szósty* 'sixth'.

GIVEN NAMES Polish 8%. *Piotr* (2), *Henryk, Jadwiga, Kazimierz, Leszek, Tadeusz, Wojciech, Zofia.*

Szostek (149) Polish: nickname from a derivative of *szosty* 'sixth' in any of various senses. Compare SZOSTAK.

GIVEN NAMES Polish 12%. *Bogdan, Ewa, Grazyna, Irena, Janusz, Jozef, Mieczyslaw, Stanislaw, Zofia.*

Szot (318) Polish: **1.** ethnic name for a Scot, Polish *Szot.* **2.** nickname for a fish seller with a bad reputation, from *szot* 'bad herring'.

GIVEN NAMES Polish 13%. *Krystyna* (2), *Agnieszka, Aleksander, Andrzej, Dariusz, Elzbieta, Ignacy, Jerzy, Karol, Michalina, Ryszard, Tadeusz.*

Szott (135) Variant spelling of Polish SZOT.

Szpak (149) Polish and Jewish (from Poland): **1.** nickname for someone with some fancied resemblance to a starling, Polish *szpak.* Compare SPACK. **2.** nickname from *szpakowaty* 'grayish', 'tinged with gray'.

GIVEN NAMES Polish 16%. *Basia, Casimir, Eugeniusz, Jolanta, Kazimierz, Piotr, Stanislaw, Stanislawa, Waclawa.*

Szpara (106) Polish: nickname from *szpara* 'cleft', 'crevice', or 'flaw'.

GIVEN NAMES Polish 14%. *Casimir* (2), *Andrzej, Bogdan, Krystyna, Wieslaw.*

Szuba (194) Polish: nickname for someone who habitually wore a fur-lined coat (*szuba*), or a metonymic occupational name for a maker of or dealer in such coats. Compare SUBA.

GIVEN NAMES Polish 15%. *Bronislaw, Jacek, Janina, Krystyna, Krzysztof, Stanislawa, Tadeusz, Tadeuz, Waclaw, Wieslaw.*

Szuch (203) Polish spelling of German SCHUH 'shoe', a metonymic occupational name for a shoemaker.

Szucs (318) Hungarian (**Szűcs**): occupational name from *szűcs* 'furrier'.

GIVEN NAMES Hungarian 14%. *Andras* (3), *Laszlo* (3), *Bela* (2), *Ferenc* (2), *Sandor* (2), *Zoltan* (2), *Antal, Arpad, Csaba, Istvan, Janos, Tibor.*

Szulc (114) Polish spelling of German SCHULTZ.

GIVEN NAMES Polish 22%. *Boguslaw, Bronislaw, Danuta, Grzegorz, Halina, Irena, Jozef, Jurek, Ludwik, Zdzislaw.*

Szumski (157) Polish and Jewish (from Poland): habitational name for someone from Szumsk in Ciechanów voivodeship or Szumsko in Kielce voivodeship.

GIVEN NAMES Polish 6%. *Karol, Krzysztof, Miroslaw.*

Szurgot (72) Polish: nickname from *szurgot* 'shuffling sound'.

Szwarc (102) Polish spelling of German SCHWARTZ.

GIVEN NAMES Polish 24%. *Zofia* (3), *Brunon, Dariusz, Janina, Janusz, Mariusz, Pawel, Waclaw, Zbigniew.*

Szwed (157) Polish and Jewish (from Poland): ethnic or regional name for someone from Sweden, Polish *Szwed* 'Swede'. As a Jewish name it is in some cases of ornamental origin.

GIVEN NAMES Polish 13%. *Stanislaw* (2), *Franciszek, Jozef, Slawomir, Tomasz.*

Szweda (114) Polish: derivative of SZWED.

GIVEN NAME Polish 4%. *Mariusz.*

Szydlo (122) Polish (**Szydło**) and Jewish (from Poland): metonymic occupational name for a cobbler, from *szydło* 'awl'.

GIVEN NAMES Polish 7%. *Darek, Janina, Urszula.*

Szydlowski (340) Polish (**Szydłowski**) and Jewish (from Poland): habitational name for someone from Szydłów, Szydłowo, or Szydłowiec, all named with a nickname, *Szydło,* from *szydło* 'awl'.

GIVEN NAMES Polish 7%. *Wieslaw* (2), *Dariusz, Janusz, Kazimierz, Miroslaw, Stanislaw, Teofil.*

Szymanowski (182) Polish: habitational name for someone from Szymanów, Szymanowo, or Szymanowice.

GIVEN NAMES Polish 9%. *Franciszek, Halina, Jadwiga, Jozef, Krzysztof, Ryszard.*

Szymanski (3263) Polish (**Szymański**): habitational name for someone from Szymany in Konin or Łomża voivodeships.

GIVEN NAMES Polish 6%. *Jolanta* (4), *Jozef* (3), *Kazimierz* (3), *Ludwik* (3), *Stanislaw* (3), *Wieslaw* (3), *Wojciech* (3), *Andrzej* (2), *Casimir* (2), *Danuta* (2), *Halina* (2), *Janusz* (2).

Szymborski (166) Polish: habitational name for someone from places called Szymbory Łomża voivodeship and Szymoborze in Bydgoszcz voivideship.

GIVEN NAMES Polish 6%. *Casimir, Lech.*

Szymczak (542) Polish: patronymic from *Szymek,* a pet form of the personal name *Szymon,* Polish form of SIMON.

GIVEN NAMES Polish 7%. *Aleksander, Alicja, Casimir, Henryk, Kazimierz, Krzysztof, Ludwik, Mariusz, Rafal, Stanislaw, Zbigniew, Zdzislaw.*

Szymczyk (140) Polish: from *Szymek,* pet form of the personal name *Szymon,* Polish form of SIMON.

GIVEN NAMES Polish 20%. *Jerzy* (2), *Danuta, Halina, Irena, Jozef, Kazimierz, Krystyna, Krzysztof, Wieslaw, Zygmunt.*

Szymkowiak (124) Polish: patronymic from the personal name *Szymek,* pet form of *Szymon,* Polish form of SIMON.

GIVEN NAMES Polish 6%. *Jolanta, Krzysztof, Wojtek.*

Szymkowski (101) Polish: habitational name for someone from a place called Szymkowo, named with Polish *Szymek,* pet form of the personal name *Szymon,* Polish form of SIMON.

T

Ta (892) Vietnamese (**Tạ**): unexplained.
GIVEN NAMES Vietnamese 73%. *Thanh* (19), *Hung* (13), *Minh* (13), *Anh* (7), *Cuong* (7), *Dung* (7), *Hai* (7), *Hoa* (7), *Hao* (6), *Huy* (6), *Hong* (5), *Hue* (5), *Phoung*, *Quang* (5), *Dong* (3), *Man* (3), *Thai* (3), *Tuong* (3), *Chang* (2), *Chi* (2), *Chung* (2), *Min* (2), *Phong* (2), *Sieu* (2), *Tam* (2), *Tham* (2).

Taaffe (265) Irish (of Welsh origin): this has generally been assumed to be a derivative of the personal name *Dafydd*, Welsh form of DAVID. However, Morgan and Morgan think the etymology is more likely to be from *Taf(f)*, the name of two rivers in Wales, one flowing through Cardiff, the other in Pembrokeshire.
GIVEN NAMES Irish 8%. *Declan* (3), *Padraic*.

Taake (105) German (Frisian): probably a variant of **Taacks**, from a short form of a Germanic personal name formed with *theod* 'people'.
GIVEN NAMES German 6%. *Erwin*, *Otto*.

Tabacchi (118) Italian: from an old Ligurian name *Tabacus*, probably from Arabic *ṭabbāh* '(ship's) cook'.
GIVEN NAMES Italian 12%. *Dante*, *Ferruccio*, *Gildo*, *Gino*, *Leno*.

Tabachnick (134) Jewish (eastern Ashkenazic): from eastern Slavic and Yiddish *tabachnik* 'tobacco seller'. Compare TABAK.
GIVEN NAMES Jewish 6%. *Emanuel* (2), *Naum* (2).

Taback (104) Jewish (Ashkenazic): variant spelling of TABAK.
GIVEN NAME Jewish 7%. *Este*.

Tabak (387) **1.** Jewish (Ashkenazic): metonymic occupational name for a seller of tobacco, from German *Tabak*, Yiddish and Ukrainian *tabik* (all ultimately from Spanish *tabaco*, a word of Caribbean origin). Tobacco was introduced to Europe in the 16th century. **2.** Turkish: occupational name for a tanner, Turkish *tabak*. **3.** Dutch: occupational name for a butcher or hog breeder, from Middle Dutch *tucbake*, from *tucken* 'to pull, push, or strike' + *bake* 'hog'.
GIVEN NAMES Jewish 17%; Russian 4%. *Baruch* (2), *Miriam* (2), *Arie*, *Chaim*, *Chana*, *Eitan*, *Gershon*, *Haim*, *Hyman*, *Isak*, *Leiba*, *Maier*; *Lyubov* (2), *Anatoly*, *Arkady*, *Boris*, *Igor*, *Mikhail*, *Natalya*, *Pinya*, *Svetlana*, *Yevgeny*.

Tabaka (266) Polish: metonymic occupational name for a tobacco merchant, from *tabaka* 'tobacco'.

Tabar (165) Basque: habitational name from Tabar in Navarre province, Basque Country.
GIVEN NAMES Spanish 4%. *Jose* (2), *Francisco*, *Marta*, *Miguel*, *Miguelina*, *Pedro*, *Salomon*.

Tabares (260) Spanish (**Tabarés**): habitational name from someone from Tábara, a town in Zamora province.
GIVEN NAMES Spanish 48%. *Carlos* (8), *Jose* (5), *Francisco* (4), *Humberto* (3), *Jesus* (3), *Juan* (3), *Alicia* (2), *Gilberto* (2), *Luis* (2), *Marcos* (2), *Miguel* (2), *Orlando* (2).

Tabata (131) Japanese: meaning 'edge of the rice paddy'; it is found in eastern Japan and the Ryūkyū Islands.
GIVEN NAMES Japanese 51%. *Akira* (2), *Noriko* (2), *Takashi* (2), *Takeshi* (2), *Yasutaka* (2), *Yumi* (2), *Akiko*, *Atsuko*, *Chiaki*, *Hiroshi*, *Hirotsugu*, *Kenzo*.

Tabatabai (121) Muslim: Arabic family name (**Tabātabā'ī**), an adjectival form denoting descent from someone called *Tabātabā*, in particular Ismā'īl bin Ibrahim Tabātabā, a great-grandson of Khalif 'Alī, fourth and last of the 'rightly guided' khalifs (see ALI).
GIVEN NAMES Muslim 83%. *Ali* (10), *Hamid* (5), *Kasim* (3), *Mohammad* (3), *Simin* (3), *Fareed* (2), *Farrokh* (2), *Habib* (2), *Hossein* (2), *Jafar* (2), *Masoud* (2), *Mostafa* (2).

Tabb (1319) English: according to Reaney and Wilson, this is from a Middle English personal name derived from an unattested Old English one, *Tæbba*. The surname is found mainly in Cornwall, so it could be from a Cornish personal name.

Tabbert (468) German and Dutch: **1.** from Middle Low German *tabbert*, Middle Dutch *tabbaert* 'tabard', a sleeveless overgarment worn by men in the Middle Ages, (ultimately from French *tabard*, from Late Latin *tabardum*). The surname may be derived from a house sign, from a garment of livery, perhaps worn by a herald, or from a metonymic occupational name for a tailor. **2.** from a reduced form of the Germanic personal name *Dagobert* (from Old High German *tac* 'day' + *berht* 'bright'); or in some instances possibly from a Frisian personal name, *Tjabbert*, composed of an unattested Germanic element *theudō-* 'people', 'race' + *berht* 'bright'; though the form Tabbert is not recorded except as a surname.

Taber (3073) **1.** English: variant spelling of TABOR. **2.** Polish: altered form of the Germanic personal name *Dagobert* (see TABBERT 2).

Tabert (118) German: variant of TABBERT 2.
GIVEN NAMES German 12%. *Kurt* (2), *Otto* (2), *Gottfried*, *Matthias*.

Tabet (164) Muslim: from a personal name based on Arabic *thābit* 'strong', 'well established'. Thabit ibn Arqam was one of the ten Companions of the Prophet Muhammad.
GIVEN NAMES Muslim 21%; French 7%. *Ibrahim* (3), *Maroun* (2), *Abdullah*, *Amine*, *Atef*, *Bechara*, *Fadi*, *Haifa*, *Kareem*, *Khaled*, *Milad*, *Nagi*; *Georges* (2), *Alexandre*, *Aude*.

Tabler (633) English (of Norman origin): occupational name from Old French *tablier* 'joiner'.

Taboada (225) Galician: habitational name from any of the places in Galicia named Taboada.
GIVEN NAMES Spanish 45%. *Jose* (7), *Luis* (7), *Carlos* (4), *Javier* (3), *Juan* (3), *Ana* (2), *Emilio* (2), *Jose Luis* (2), *Justo* (2), *Miguel* (2), *Rosario* (2), *Alberto*; *Antonio*, *Enrico*, *Marco*, *Savino*.

Tabone (334) Italian (Sicily): **1.** probably an occupational name from Arabic *ṭābūna*, denoting a kind of hollowed-out hearth in which a fire was kept alight. **2.** nickname from Sicilian *tabbuni* 'silly', 'foolish'.
GIVEN NAMES Italian 15%. *Angelo* (3), *Salvatore* (3), *Carmine* (2), *Carmel*, *Carmello*, *Carmelo*, *Concetta*, *Gaspare*, *Nicolina*, *Pietro*, *Reno*, *Rocco*.

Tabor (5428) **1.** English: metonymic occupational name for a drummer, from Middle English, Old French *tabo(u)r* 'drum'. **2.** Hungarian: from the old secular personal name *Tábor*. **3.** Czech and Slovak (**Tábor**) and Jewish (from Bohemia): habitational name from the city of Tábor in southern Bohemia. This was a center of the Hussite movement; in Czech it came to denote a member of the radical wing of the Hussite movement.

Tabora (111) Spanish (**Tábora**): Spanish spelling of the Portuguese habitational name **Távora**, from a place so named.
GIVEN NAMES Spanish 45%. *Jose* (3), *Benigno* (2), *Guillermo* (2), *Javier* (2), *Jorge* (2), *Maria Luisa* (2), *Raul* (2), *Rolando* (2), *Ana*, *Armando*, *Bernardo*, *Blanca*.

Taborn (157) English: probably a variant of **Tabern**, a metonymic form of **Taverner** (see TAVENNER).

Tabrizi (144) Iranian and Azerbaijani: habitational name for someone from the city of Tabriz in northwest Iran.
GIVEN NAMES Muslim 69%. *Ali* (7), *Hamid* (7), *Masoud* (3), *Majid* (2), *Mohammad* (2), *Nasrin* (2), *Peyman* (2), *Abdi, Afsaneh, Amir, Ata, Azam.*

Tabron (248) Possibly English: unexplained.

Tacey (212) **1.** English (mainly East Midlands): from a pet form of the personal name STACEY. **2.** Possibly an Americanized form of French TESSIER.

Tache (119) **1.** French: either from Old French *tache* 'hook', 'buckle', 'loop'; 'distinctive mark', possibly applied as a nickname for someone with a deformity or distinctive mark. (**Taché** is an adjectival form of this name.) Alternatively, it may be a habitational name from any of various places named Tâche or La Tâche, for example in Charente-Maritime and Vienne. **2.** Romanian: unexplained.
GIVEN NAMES French 7%; Romanian 6%. *Yvan* (2), *Monique; Constantin, Danut, Georgeta, Valeriu.*

Tacheny (118) Origin unidentified.

Tachibana (109) Japanese: 'wild orange'; the name is listed in the Shinsen shōjiroku. It was first taken as a surname by the distinguished statesman Katsuragi Moroe (684–757), a son of imperial prince Minu and Tachibana no Michiyo (d. 733), a court lady of great renown. Several poems by Moroe and one of his mother's are included in the eighth-century anthology Manyōshū. Few bearers today are likely to be descended from this family however, due to the practice followed long ago of taking one's master's name as one's own. The name is found mostly in eastern Japan.
GIVEN NAMES Japanese 60%. *Hiroko* (4), *Kazuko* (3), *Hideki* (2), *Hideo* (2), *Mieko* (2), *Shinichi* (2), *Eiichi, Eiki, Fumiko, Hiro, Hisayoshi, Kokichi.*

Tack (601) North German and Dutch: **1.** from a reduced form of Frisian *Tjadeke*, a pet form of any of several compound personal names with the first element *thiod-* (from Germanic *theudo-* 'people', 'race'; compare TABBERT 2). **2.** alternatively from a short form of a personal name formed with Old High German *tac* 'day' + *berht* 'bright'. **3.** alternatively, perhaps from *tak* 'twig', 'sprout', 'branch', Middle Low German *tack(e)* 'twig'. This may have been an ironic nickname for a big man, or a nickname for a hard worker.

Tacke (209) North German and Dutch: variant of TACK.
GIVEN NAMES German 4%. *Mathias, Wilhelm.*

Tacker (418) **1.** German (Frisian): variant of TACK. **2.** South German (**Täcker**): occupational name for a weaver of mats, from an agent derivative of Middle High German *tacke.*

Tackett (5714) Scottish: probably a habitational name from a place called Tecket in North Tyndale.

Tackitt (310) Variant of Scottish TACKETT.

Tackman (120) North German: **1.** elaborated variant of TACK. **2.** nickname from Low German *tacke* 'bough', 'limb', denoting a hard worker.

Tacy (304) English: variant spelling of TACEY.

Tada (144) Japanese: from a common place name meaning 'many rice paddies'. Some bearers descend from the MINAMOTO, FUJIWARA, and other important clans. The surname is listed in the Shinsen shōjiroku.
GIVEN NAMES Japanese 68%. *Minoru* (4), *Mitsuru* (3), *Osamu* (3), *Takeshi* (3), *Akiko* (2), *Hiroshi* (2), *Keiko* (2), *Asuka, Ayumi, Chieko, Chisato, Fumio.*

Taddei (252) Italian: patronymic or plural form of TADDEO.
GIVEN NAMES Italian 15%. *Valentino* (3), *Angelo* (2), *Giuseppi* (2), *Amelio, Carlo, Dante, Domenic, Gabriele, Geno, Luigi, Pasquale, Riccardo.*

Taddeo (531) Italian: **1.** from a vernacular form of the personal name *Thaddeus*. This is the name ascribed in St. Mark's Gospel to one of Christ's disciples, referred to elsewhere as Judas son of James. It represents an Aramaic form *Thaddai*, which is probably of Hebrew origin, meaning 'beloved'. **2.** altered form of the personal name *Teodoro*, Greek *Theodōros* (see THEODORE).
GIVEN NAMES Italian 15%. *Angelo* (6), *Rocco* (3), *Antonio* (2), *Gabriele* (2), *Verino* (2), *Amato, Carmine, Ciro, Dante, Domenica, Donatella, Fiore.*

Taddonio (102) Italian: unexplained; perhaps from a derivative of the personal name *Taddeo.*
GIVEN NAMES Italian 10%; Jewish 4%. *Nicolo, Pasquale, Salvatore; Miriam* (2), *Emanuel.*

Tade (133) Origin unidentified: **1.** possibly an altered spelling of English **Tadde**, a nickname from Old English *tadde* 'toad'. **2.** alternatively perhaps an altered spelling of North German **Thade**, from a reduced form of a Frisian personal name (see TACK), or of THEDE.

Tadeo (161) Spanish: from a vernacular form of the personal name *Thaddeus*. This is the name ascribed in St. Mark's Gospel to one of Christ's disciples, referred to elsewhere as Judas son of James. It represents an Aramaic form *Thaddai*, which is probably of Hebrew origin, meaning 'beloved'.
GIVEN NAMES Spanish 47%. *Juan* (5), *Jose* (3), *Alberto* (2), *Anselmo* (2), *Armando* (2), *Eusebio* (2), *Javier* (2), *Mario* (2), *Raul* (2), *Adriana, Agustina, Angel; Angelo, Narcisso.*

Tadesse (154) Ethiopian: unexplained.

GIVEN NAMES Ethiopian 71%; Jewish 5%. *Getachew* (3), *Belay* (2), *Benyam* (2), *Berhane* (2), *Bruke* (2), *Girma* (2), *Tesfaye* (2), *Yeshi* (2), *Zewditu* (2), *Aklilu, Alemu, Amare; Aron.*

Tadlock (1219) Apparently an altered or variant spelling of TATLOCK.

Tadros (223) Arabic form of Greek *Theodōros* (see THEODORE).
GIVEN NAMES Arabic 64%. *Samir* (9), *Hany* (5), *Ashraf* (3), *Maher* (3), *Fakhry* (2), *Maged* (2), *Nader* (2), *Youssef* (2), *Adly, Adnan, Amani, Anwar.*

Tadych (232) Polish: from a pet form of the personal name *Tadeusz*, equivalent of English Thaddeus (see TADDEO).

Tafel (200) **1.** German: from Middle High German *tafel* 'table', 'gameboard', or 'panel painting', a metonymic occupational name for a maker of wooden panels (for tables, carvings, paintings, or room paneling), or alternatively a topographic name for someone who lived by a roadside shrine or other religious motif; such depictions were (and still are common) in Bavaria and Austria. In some instances this may be a reduced form of **Tafelmacher**, literally 'panel maker'. In this sense the name is also established as a Polish surname. **2.** German: from a field name, Middle High German *tavel*, for a field in a slightly elevated position.
GIVEN NAMES German 5%. *Dieter, Heinz, Kurt.*

Tafelski (152) Polish: derivative of TAFEL 1, with the addition of the suffix *-ski*, commonly used in forming surnames.

Taff (765) English: probably a respelling of Irish TAAFFE. In England this name now occurs mainly in South Yorkshire.

Taffe (245) **1.** Irish: variant spelling of TAAFFE. **2.** Dutch and North German: probably from a pet nursery form of a Germanic personal name with the first element *dag-, tag-* 'day'.

Taffet (103) Origin uncertain. It may be the French surname **Taffet**, a nickname for a coward, from an onomatopaeic root *taff*, now preserved only in dialects in the sense 'fear'.

Taflinger (141) German: unexplained; perhaps a habitational name, for example for someone from Thalfingen in Bavaria.

Tafolla (217) Possibly Spanish (Mexico): unexplained. Perhaps a derivative of southern Spanish *tafulla, tahulla*, a term denoting a measure of land. The surname is not found in present-day Spain.
GIVEN NAMES Spanish 45%. *Jose* (8), *Juan* (4), *Manuel* (3), *Andres* (2), *Enrique* (2), *Guadalupe* (2), *Guillermo* (2), *Jaime* (2), *Jesus* (2), *Pablo* (2), *Ramon* (2), *Roberto* (2); *Antonio* (2), *Eliseo* (2), *Fausto, Heriberto, Marco.*

Tafoya (1717) possibly Spanish: variant of TAFOLLA.

GIVEN NAMES Spanish 20%. *Manuel* (19), *Jose* (18), *Juan* (7), *Rafael* (5), *Alfredo* (4), *Arturo* (4), *Carlos* (4), *Eloy* (4), *Ramona* (4), *Alfonso* (3), *Florentino* (3), *Jesus* (3).

Taft (3402) English: topographic name or habitational name from a dialect variant of Old and Middle English *toft* 'curtilage', 'site', 'homestead', also applied to a low hillock where a homestead used to be. Compare TOFT.
FOREBEARS Robert Taft (b. about 1640), lived in Braintree, MA, and subsequently Mendon, MA. Alphonso Taft (1810–91), jurist and politician born in Townshend, VT, was the father of William Howard Taft (1857–1930), 27th president of the U.S. and chief justice of the U.S. Supreme Court.

Tafuri (125) Italian (mainly southern): probably from an Arabic personal name, based on either *ṭafūr* 'jumper' or *ṭayfūr*, a species of small bird.
GIVEN NAMES Italian 24%. *Angelo* (2), *Mario* (2), *Achille, Assunta, Emilio, Giovanni, Sabino, Sebastiano.*

Tag (101) 1. English: variant of TAGG. 2. Anglicized form of Irish TIGHE. 3. German: from a short form of the personal name *Taggo* or *Tacco*, itself a pet form of DAGOBERT.

Tagawa (126) Japanese: from a common place name in Japan and the Ryūkyū Islands, meaning 'rice paddy river'; bearers are therefore not necessarily related.
GIVEN NAMES Japanese 49%. *Yoshi* (4), *Akio, Hideo, Hiroshi, Ikuyo, Kanae, Kayoko, Kenji, Kiyoshi, Koichi, Koshi, Kunihiko.*

Tager (216) 1. German (**Täger**): from a Germanic personal name formed with *tac* 'day' as the first element. 2. Jewish (Ashkenazic): occupational name, a Yiddishized form of Hebrew *tagar* 'merchant'.
GIVEN NAMES Jewish 6%. *Mikhael, Revekka.*

Tagert (110) 1. Scottish and northern Irish: variant spelling of TAGGART. 2. German (**Tägert**): variant of TAGER 1.

Tagg (316) 1. English (East Midlands): probably from a personal name based on Old English *tacca* 'lamb', 'young sheep'. 2. Anglicized form of Irish TIGHE.

Taggart (3607) Scottish and northern Irish: reduced form of MCTAGGART, an Anglicized form of Gaelic **Mac an t-Sagairt** 'son of the priest', from *sagart* 'priest'. Marriage by members of the clergy was prohibited after the 12th century, but was frequently practised nevertheless.

Tagge (138) 1. German: from a short form of a Germanic personal name similar to DIETRICH. 2. English: variant spelling of TAGG.
GIVEN NAME German 5%. *Arno.*

Taggert (128) Scottish and northern Irish: variant spelling of TAGGART.

Tagle (248) Spanish: habitational name from a place in Santander province called Tagle.

GIVEN NAMES Spanish 43%. *Jose* (5), *Juan* (4), *Raul* (3), *Alfredo* (2), *Alonzo* (2), *Edilberto* (2), *Francisco* (2), *Gerardo* (2), *Jesus* (2), *Jorge* (2), *Luis* (2), *Pablo* (2); *Antonio, Dario, Lorenzo, Nolasco.*

Tagliaferri (190) Italian: patronymic or plural form of TAGLIAFERRO. This surname is widespread in Italy, being most common in Lombardy, Tuscany, and Campania.
GIVEN NAMES Italian 11%. *Aldo* (2), *Carlo, Enrico, Olindo, Vincenzo.*

Tagliaferro (137) Italian: from *tagliare* 'to cut' + *ferro* 'iron', an occupational name for an ironworker or a nickname for a strong or ferocious fighter, one who was adept at cutting through the cuirass of the enemy with his sword. Compare TELFER.
GIVEN NAMES Italian 12%. *Salvatore* (2), *Gino, Sal.*

Taglieri (184) Italian: occupational name from French *tailleur* 'cutter' (of cloth, stones, etc.).
GIVEN NAMES Italian 14%. *Angelo* (2), *Carmine* (2), *Cosimo, Dante, Domenic, Franco, Guido.*

Taguchi (182) Japanese: 'entrance to the rice paddies'; it is found mainly in northeastern Japan and is the surname of an ancient family descended from the SOGA family. Other bearers are descended from the Ōtomo clan or the ASHIKAGA branch of the FUJIWARA clan.
GIVEN NAMES Japanese 68%. *Kenji* (3), *Minoru* (3), *Hiro* (2), *Masa* (2), *Takashi* (2), *Tooru* (2), *Aki, Akiko, Akira, Atsushi, Chie, Chizuko.*

Tague (1103) Irish: variant of TIGHE.

Taha (205) Muslim: from the mystic letters *Ṭā Hā* mentioned at the start of sura 20 of the Qur'an. *Ṭā Hā* is an epithet of the Prophet Muhammad.
GIVEN NAMES Muslim 77%. *Ahmed* (6), *Mohammed* (5), *Mahmoud* (4), *Hassan* (3), *Jamal* (3), *Safi* (3), *Ali* (2), *Ayman* (2), *Fawzi* (2), *Ibrahim* (2), *Khalid* (2).

Tahan (159) Arabic and Jewish (Sephardic): occupational name from Arabic *ṭaḥḥān* 'miller'.
GIVEN NAMES Muslim 13%; French 8%. *Fadi* (2), *Samir* (2), *Fouad, Hussein, Issam, Karem, Naguib, Saliba, Tahereh, Tarek; Antoine* (2), *Georges, Michel.*

Tahara (109) Japanese: 'plain of rice paddies'; the name is found mostly in western Japan. An alternative pronunciation is *Tawara* and in the Ryūkyū Islands it is pronounced *Tabaru*.
GIVEN NAMES Japanese 49%. *Setsuko* (2), *Akihiro, Goro, Hajime, Hideaki, Hidetaka, Hiroyuki, Hisami, Hitomi, Isamu, Keiko, Kumiko.*

Taheri (156) Muslim: Arabic family name meaning 'descended from or associated with TAHIR'.
GIVEN NAMES Muslim 73%. *Ali* (8), *Gholam* (2), *Hassan* (2), *Mohammad* (2), *Nahid* (2),

Shahram (2), *Abbas, Akhtar, Ashraf, Bahram, Bejan, Farid.*

Tahir (156) Muslim: from a personal name based on Arabic *ṭāhir* 'pure', 'virtuous'.
GIVEN NAMES Muslim 78%. *Mohammad* (11), *Mohammed* (7), *Syed* (5), *Nadeem* (4), *Abdul* (2), *Ali* (2), *Asghar* (2), *Irfan* (2), *Mohamed* (2), *Naeem* (2), *Rashid* (2), *Saghir* (2).

Tahtinen (101) From Finnish *tähti* 'star' + the common surname suffix *-nen*. This name was commonly adopted in the early 20th century as an ornamental name. It occurs chiefly in central Finland.

Tai (944) 1. Chinese 傣: variant of DAI. 2. Chinese 邰: supposedly from a territory named Tai that was granted to Hou Ji, a legendary personage who lived over 4,000 years ago and was responsible for early developments in agriculture.
GIVEN NAMES Chinese/Korean 31%. *Chi* (3), *Kam* (3), *Ming* (3), *Cheung* (2), *Chi Sing* (2), *Han* (2), *Hong* (2), *Hsing* (2), *Man* (2), *On* (2), *Pin* (2), *Ping* (2); *Hak* (2), *Nam* (2), *Woon* (2), *Cho, Chong, Chung, Heeyoung, Kok, Min, Pang, Tam, Wook.*

Taibi (149) Italian (Sicily): nickname for a robust person, from Arabic *ṭayyib* 'good', 'in good health'.
GIVEN NAMES Italian 21%; French 7%; Spanish 4%. *Salvatore* (4), *Carmela* (3), *Antonio, Concetta, Franco, Pasquale; Pascale, Patrice; Alfonso* (2), *Rosario* (2), *Eduardo.*

Taillon (260) French: topographic name from Old French *taillon* 'coppice', 'copse'.
FOREBEARS The name Taillon is documented in Château-Richer, Quebec, as early as 1671. It is associated with the secondary surnames LeTardif, MICHEL, OLIVIER.
GIVEN NAMES French 13%. *Alcide* (2), *Normand* (2), *Aime, Alphonse, Colette, Napoleon, Pierre, Raoul, Sebastien.*

Tailor (170) 1. English: variant spelling of TAYLOR. 2. Indian (Gujarat and Bombay city): Hindu and Parsi occupational name from the English word *tailor*.
GIVEN NAMES Indian 76%. *Pravin* (4), *Dilip* (3), *Mahesh* (3), *Sanjay* (3), *Kanchan* (2), *Kaushik* (2), *Manilal* (2), *Mohanlal* (2), *Navnit* (2), *Shailesh* (2), *Ajay, Alpana.*

Taing (245) Cambodian or other Southeast Asian: unexplained.
GIVEN NAMES Southeast Asian 58%. *Hong* (5), *Seng* (4), *Huy* (4), *Cheng* (2), *Eng* (2), *Haing* (2), *Heng* (2), *Hoang* (2), *Hu* (2), *Song* (2), *Suy* (2), *Chan, Chhay, Chin, Choa, Chuang, Fou, Hao, Hoat, Ky, Leang, Nguon, Pang, Saroeun, Son, Tay, Vay.*

Tainter (224) English (of Norman origin): occupational name from Old French *teinturier* 'dyer'.

Taira (236) Japanese: 'peace'. Together with the FUJIWARA and MINAMOTO, this is one of the most prominent clans in Japanese history. It is listed in the Shinsen shōjiroku. The name appears to have been taken from

Taira no Miyako ('Capital of Peace'), an ancient name for the city of Kyōto, and was created in 825 by the ex-Emperor Kanmu when his son Takamune (804–867) became a commoner. Later emperors bestowed the name on some of their children, so the various branches of the clan were distinguished by the names of their parent-emperors. The Taira are also commonly called *Heike* or *Heishi*, from the Sino-Japanese pronunciation of *taira* plus the words for family or clan

GIVEN NAMES Japanese 47%. *Isamu* (2), *Kenji* (2), *Minoru* (2), *Tsutomu* (2), *Yoshinori* (2), *Aiko, Fumiko, Haruo, Hatsu, Hiromi, Hiromitsu, Hiroshi.*

Tait (2378) Scottish and northern English: nickname for a cheerful person, from Old Norse *teitr* 'cheerful', 'gay'. This surname is quite distinct in origin from TATE.

Taitano (107) Hispanic: unexplained.

GIVEN NAMES Spanish 16%. *Jose* (2), *Francisco, Jesus, Juan, Lourdes, Manuel, Miguel, Tomas.*

Taite (161) Scottish and northern English: variant of TAIT.

Taitt (204) Scottish and northern English: variant of TAIT.

GIVEN NAMES Irish 6%. *Fitzroy* (2), *Declan.*

Tajima (115) Japanese: 'island of rice paddies'; the name is found mostly in western Japan and in the Ryūkyū Islands.

GIVEN NAMES Japanese 76%. *Hiroshi* (4), *Shoichi* (3), *Eriko* (2), *Kenji* (2), *Makoto* (2), *Noriko* (2), *Aki, Gaku, Hideki, Hiro, Hiromi, Kayo.*

Tak (147) **1.** Korean (**T'ak**): there is one Chinese character and one clan associated with this surname. The founding ancestor, T'ak Chi-yŏp, was a Koryŏ Kingdom scholar who settled in the Kwangju area of Chŏlla South Province. **2.** Indian (northern states): Hindu (Rajput) name of unknown meaning based on the name of a Rajput clan.

GIVEN NAMES Korean 41%; Indian 8%. *Hyun* (3), *Young* (3), *Gong* (2), *Jung* (2), *Seung* (2), *Byeong, Byong, Chin, Eng, Hae Young, Heekyung, Ho; Byung Kook, Eun Ju, Jae Hong, Jang, Jeong, Moon, Soo Hyun, Soon Ja; Ram, Ravi, Ravindra, Sanjeev, Sharad.*

Takach (366) Occupational name for a weaver, an altered form of Hungarian TAKACS, Ukrainian TKACH, or Polish TKACZ.

Takacs (1254) Hungarian (**Takács**): occupational name from *takács* 'weaver'. Compare Polish TKACZ.

GIVEN NAMES Hungarian 10%. *Imre* (7), *Laszlo* (7), *Zoltan* (6), *Zsolt* (5), *Kalman* (3), *Sandor* (3), *Gabor* (2), *Gyula* (2), *Karoly* (2), *Lajos* (2), *Tibor* (2), *Aladar.*

Takagi (266) Japanese: 'tall tree', especially denoting a sacred tree; it is mostly found in eastern Japan. The name originated in Kii province (presently Wakayama prefecture), location of the famous and ancient Ise

shrine. The name is also written by some as 'tall castle', and is pronounced *Takaki* in the Ryūkyū Islands.

GIVEN NAMES Japanese 71%. *Akira* (3), *Osamu* (3), *Shinichi* (3), *Akiko* (2), *Kanji* (2), *Keiji* (2), *Reiko* (2), *Shinji* (2), *Tetsuya* (2), *Tomoko* (2), *Toshimitsu* (2), *Yoshio* (2).

Takahashi (1603) Japanese: variously written, usually with characters meaning 'high bridge', it is one of the ten most common surnames and is particularly frequent in eastern Japan. It is the name of an ancient family of Kyūshū island. Various legends concerning origin suggest several unrelated families. The name is also found in the Ryūkyū Islands.

GIVEN NAMES Japanese 68%. *Hiroshi* (16), *Akira* (9), *Junichi* (8), *Kenichi* (7), *Kenji* (7), *Kiyoshi* (7), *Toru* (7), *Toshio* (7), *Hideo* (6), *Ichiro* (6), *Koji* (6), *Makoto* (6).

Takai (100) Japanese: 'high well'; the name is listed in the Shinsen shōjiroku and is found mostly in central and western Honshū.

GIVEN NAMES Japanese 41%. *Masaki* (2), *Shigeru* (2), *Yoshio* (2), *Eiji, Hideya, Hiroyuki, Hisao, Kaname, Kenji, Masahiko, Nobuko, Shozo.*

Takaki (195) Japanese: 'tall tree'; pronounced thus in the Ryūkyū Islands, but elsewhere generally pronounced TAKAGI.

GIVEN NAMES Japanese 45%. *Chizuru* (2), *Masaru* (2), *Minoru* (2), *Mitsuo* (2), *Satoshi* (2), *Asayo, Fujio, Fumiko, Hideaki, Hideo, Hirokazu, Hiroshi.*

Takala (114) Finnish: topographic name referring the remote location of a farm, from *taka* 'back', 'behind' + the local suffix *-la*. Found throughout Finland but especially in western Finland.

GIVEN NAMES Finnish 12%. *Reino* (2), *Toivo* (2), *Aimo, Erkki.*

Takamoto (100) Japanese: 'one who lives high (up the slope or hill)'; found mostly in the Ryūkyū Islands.

GIVEN NAMES Japanese 34%. *Takenori* (2), *Chiyoko, Eiji, Fusae, Hiroshi, Kenso, Kiyoshi, Michie, Mitsutoshi, Naoto, Norio, Sachie.*

Takano (161) Japanese: from a common place name meaning 'high field'. The surname is found mostly in eastern Japan and is listed in the Shinsen shōjiroku. Alternate readings found in western Japan are **Kōno** and **Kōya**, the latter being taken from the name of the famed mountain in Kii (now Wakayama prefecture), where the monk Kūkai (774–835) built a monastery, the Buddhist teachings of which had a profound effect on Japanese civilization.

GIVEN NAMES Japanese 75%. *Koji* (3), *Haruka* (2), *Ikuko* (2), *Junichi* (2), *Kentaro* (2), *Shigeru* (2), *Shinichi* (2), *Toshio* (2), *Toshiyuki* (2), *Akiyoshi, Atsushi, Eiji.*

Takara (184) Japanese: 'treasure', variously written; it is found mostly in the Ryūkyū Islands.

GIVEN NAMES Japanese 31%. *Seiichi* (3), *Takeo* (2), *Tamotsu* (2), *Yoshio* (2), *Emiko, Isami, Isamu, Junko, Kame, Kazuko, Koichi, Masao.*

Takashima (147) Japanese: from a common place name meaning 'tall island'. The surname is found mostly in western Japan and the island of Okinawa.

GIVEN NAMES Japanese 65%. *Toshio* (6), *Minoru* (2), *Momo* (2), *Yoko* (2), *Yuji* (2), *Yuta* (2), *Akira, Akitoshi, Chisako, Emiko, Harumi, Hideo.*

Takata (319) Japanese: 'high rice paddy'; also pronounced *Takada*. The most ancient family to bear the name originated in the Kyōto region and is listed in the Shinsen shōjiroku. Other families have taken the name from various places so named.

GIVEN NAMES Japanese 43%. *Toshio* (3), *Hiro* (2), *Isamu* (2), *Michio* (2), *Toshiki* (2), *Akio, Chieko, Chikako, Fujie, Fumiko, Hajime, Haruyoshi.*

Takayama (215) Japanese: 'high mountains'; habitational name from the city so named in mountainous Hida (now part of Gifu prefecture). The name is found mostly in western Japan, as well as on Okinawa Island.

GIVEN NAMES Japanese 62%. *Akira* (2), *Hiroshi* (2), *Kenji* (2), *Makoto* (2), *Masami* (2), *Soichi* (2), *Yasuo* (2), *Yoshimi* (2), *Chihiro, Eiko, Hanako, Hideki.*

Takeda (396) Japanese: 'bamboo rice paddy', also written with characters meaning 'warrior rice paddy'. The most famous Takeda family was descended from Minamoto Yoshimitsu (1056–1127) and ruled several provinces, most notably Kai (present-day Yamanashi prefecture). Other families, such as OGASAWARA, AKIYAMA, Matsumae, Nishina, and IWASAKI, are of Takeda descent. An alternate pronunciation is *Taketa*. It is listed in the Shinsen shōjiroku.

GIVEN NAMES Japanese 70%. *Hiroshi* (7), *Atsushi* (4), *Toyoko* (4), *Akira* (3), *Masato* (3), *Yoichi* (3), *Yukihiro* (3), *Akiko* (2), *Atsuko* (2), *Ichiro* (2), *Kenichi* (2), *Koji* (2).

Takei (102) Japanese: though usually written with characters meaning 'warrior' and 'well', the original meaning is probably 'bamboo well'. The name is found mostly in the Tōkyō region.

GIVEN NAMES Japanese 62%. *Hiroki* (2), *Koji* (2), *Akira, Hideaki, Hideo, Hideyuki, Hisae, Isao, Junji, Kaori, Kuni, Makoto.*

Takemoto (332) Japanese: '(one who lives) near the bamboo'. This name is found mostly in western Japan and the Ryūkyū Islands.

GIVEN NAMES Japanese 46%. *Akira* (3), *Isamu* (2), *Kiyoshi* (2), *Masashi* (2), *Noboru* (2), *Shigemi* (2), *Shigeo* (2), *Susumu* (2), *Takeshi* (2), *Tamotsu* (2), *Yoshio* (2), *Aiko.*

Takenaka (120) Japanese: '(one who lives) in the midst of the bamboo'. This name is found mostly in the Ōsaka region and in the Ryūkyū Islands.

GIVEN NAMES Japanese 50%. *Akiko* (2), *Hideaki, Hideko, Hideyuki, Hiroshi, Hisato, Ikuo, Kenichi, Kiyoshi, Makoto, Masao, Masaya.*

Takes (109) Greek: reduced form of any surname ending in *-takis*, such as **Anagnostakis** or **Kostantakis**. Such a surname would involve a proper name stem ending in *-t* and the patronymic suffix *-akis*. This patronymic is particularly common in Crete, where it was adopted massively in the 19th century.

GIVEN NAME Greek 4%. *Spiro* (2).

Takeshita (159) Japanese: '(one who lives) beneath the bamboo'; it was originally pronounced *Takenoshita* and taken from a village of that name in Suruga (now part of Shizuoka prefecture). The original bearers were descended from the northern FUJIWARA through the Kuzuyama family. The name is found mainly in western Japan and the Ryūkyū Islands.

GIVEN NAMES Japanese 49%. *Hitoshi* (2), *Keiko* (2), *Masaru* (2), *Akira, Asano, Eiji, Eiko, Fumio, Hideo, Hiro, Isami, Kenichi.*

Taketa (181) Japanese: 'bamboo rice paddy'; alternate pronunciation of TAKEDA.

GIVEN NAMES Japanese 30%. *Haruo* (2), *Akio, Fujio, Fumiko, Hideo, Kiyomi, Kiyono, Masao, Masaru, Masayoshi, Midori, Shigeru.*

Takeuchi (496) Japanese: 'within the bamboos'. This name is found mostly in west-central Japan, and pronounced *Takenouchi* by some bearers. The family claims descent from the legendary hero-statesman Takenouchi no Sukune, himself supposedly a descendant of the mythical Emperor Kōgen and a counselor to several other emperors, including Ōjin (late 4th century). Other families, such as the SOGA, also claim Takenouchi no Sukune as an ancestor.

GIVEN NAMES Japanese 65%. *Hiroshi* (6), *Kenji* (6), *Akira* (3), *Kazuhiro* (3), *Koji* (3), *Minoru* (3), *Seiji* (3), *Shinji* (3), *Yoshiko* (3), *Eriko* (2), *Hideo* (2), *Hisashi* (2).

Tal (152) Jewish: **1.** Ashkenazic: ornamental name from German *Tal* 'valley'. **2.** Israeli: ornamental name from Hebrew *tal* 'dew'.

GIVEN NAMES Jewish 45%. *Aharon* (3), *Doron* (2), *Gilad* (2), *Moshe* (2), *Tomer* (2), *Arieh, Avi, Avinoam, Aviva, Avner, Bruria, Chaim.*

Talaga (186) Polish: nickname from Old Polish *talaga* 'rickety wagon'.

GIVEN NAMES Polish 8%. *Casimir* (2), *Mieczyslaw, Zdzislaw.*

Talamantes (475) Spanish: habitational name from Talamantes in Zaragoza province.

GIVEN NAMES Spanish 50%. *Jose* (13), *Manuel* (13), *Jesus* (9), *Francisco* (6), *Guadalupe* (5), *Juan* (5), *Armando* (4), *Pedro* (4), *Alfonso* (3), *Arturo* (3), *Gonzalo* (3), *Leticia* (3).

Talamantez (243) Spanish: variant spelling of TALAMANTES.

GIVEN NAMES Spanish 29%. *Cruz* (2), *Esequiel* (2), *Guadalupe* (2), *Jose* (2), *Juan* (2), *Leandro* (2), *Rodolfo* (2), *Alfonso, Alfredo, Aracely, Arturo, Benito.*

Talamo (208) Southern Italian: possibly an unflattering nickname from Calabrian *talamu* 'stupid'.

GIVEN NAMES Italian 26%; Spanish 9%. *Salvatore* (4), *Angelo* (2), *Gennaro* (2), *Corrado, Elena, Giampaolo, Giuseppi, Nicola, Pasquale, Sal; Enrique, Francisco, Javier, Jose, Salvador, Sevilla.*

Talarico (938) Italian: of uncertain origin; probably from the Germanic personal name *Athalaric* 'noble power'.

GIVEN NAMES Italian 10%. *Angelo* (5), *Pasquale* (3), *Nicola* (2), *Salvatore* (2), *Antonio, Caesar, Carmine, Deno, Ezio, Fiore, Guido, Luigi.*

Talaska (106) Origin unidentified.

Talavera (677) Spanish: habitational name from any of several places named Talavera, especially Talavera de la Reina in Toledo province.

GIVEN NAMES Spanish 49%. *Jose* (28), *Manuel* (14), *Juan* (11), *Jorge* (8), *Luis* (7), *Carlos* (6), *Miguel* (6), *Pedro* (6), *Jesus* (5), *Julio* (5), *Mario* (5), *Roberto* (5); *Antonio* (2), *Federico* (2), *Lorenzo* (2), *Clemente, Dino, Eligio, Flavio, Julieta, Marco, Quirino.*

Talbert (3910) French and English: from a continental Germanic personal name composed of the elements *tal* 'valley' + *berht* 'bright'.

Talbot (6092) English (of Norman origin): of much disputed origin, but probably from a Germanic personal name composed of the elements *tal* 'destroy' + *bod* 'message', 'tidings', i.e. 'messenger of destruction'. In this form the name is also found in France, taken there apparently by English immigrants; the usual French form is TALBERT.
FOREBEARS Talbot is the name of an ancient Irish family of Norman origin, which have held the earldoms of Shrewsbury and Waterford since the 15th century. They were granted the baronial estate of Malahide, near Dublin, by Henry II (1154–89), an estate that they held for over 850 years. They trace their descent from Richard de Talbott, mentioned in the Domesday Book. His son, Hugh de Talbot or Talebot'h, became governor of Plessis Castle, Normandy, France, in 1118.

A Talbot, also known as GERVAIS, from Rouen, Normandy, is recorded in Pointe-aux-Trembles, Quebec, in 1689.

GIVEN NAMES French 4%. *Emile* (6), *Marcel* (4), *Anatole* (2), *Armand* (2), *Aubert* (2), *Camille* (2), *Gilles* (2), *Normand* (2), *Adrien, Alcide, Andre, Auguste.*

Talbott (3016) Variant of TALBOT.

Talburt (134) Probably an altered spelling of French TALBERT.

Talcott (692) **1.** English: unexplained. The name has all but died out in Britain, but thrives in North America. Possible origins that have been proposed include: **2.** Norman habitational name from Taillecourt in France. **3.** topographic name from Middle English *tile* 'tile' + *cot* 'cottage'.
FOREBEARS John Talcott was one of the founders of Hartford, CT, (coming from Cambridge, MA, with Thomas Hooker) in 1635.

Talent (146) English: variant spelling of TALLENT or possibly TALLANT.

Talerico (429) Italian: variant of TALARICO.

GIVEN NAMES Italian 10%. *Angelo, Dario, Fiore, Sal, Salvatore, Santo, Tommaso, Vito.*

Talford (117) English (South Yorkshire): variant of TELFORD.

Taliaferro (1444) Altered spelling of TAGLIAFERRO.

Taliercio (122) Italian (Campania): unexplained.

GIVEN NAMES Italian 20%; Spanish 4%. *Antonio, Gaetano, Giovanni, Guglielmo, Luigi, Pasquale, Rocco, Sal, Salvatore; Jorge Luis* (3), *Salvador.*

Talkington (850) English: habitational name from Torkington in Greater Manchester (formerly in Cheshire), named in Old English as 'settlement (*tūn*) associated with *Turec*'.

Tall (424) English: nickname for a respectable or decent person, or else a good-looking one, both these senses belonging to Middle English *tall* (Old English *getæl* 'swift', 'prompt'). The modern sense 'of high stature' did not develop until the end of the 16th century; the usual Middle English equivalents were LONG and HIGH.

Tallant (799) **1.** English (of Norman origin): occupational name for a tailor or nickname for a good swordsman, from *taillant* 'cutting', present participle of Old French *tailler* 'to cut' (Late Latin *taliare*, from *talea* '(plant) cutting'). **2.** English: variant spelling of TALLENT. **3.** Irish: of English origin, recorded in Ireland from the 16th century; also a variant form of TALLON.

Tallarico (275) Italian: variant of TALARICO.

GIVEN NAMES Italian 22%. *Angelo* (3), *Antonio* (2), *Gennaro* (2), *Sal* (2), *Adolfo, Franco, Liborio, Mario, Salvatore.*

Tallent (1826) English: habitational name from Talland in Cornwall, which is thought to be named as 'hill-brow church site', from Cornish *tal* + *lann*.

Tallerico (188) Variant spelling of Italian TALARICO.

GIVEN NAMES Italian 10%. *Franca, Giuseppe, Luigi, Salvatore.*

Talley (9801) **1.** Irish: reduced Anglicized form of Gaelic **Ó Taithligh** 'descendant of *Taithleach*', a byname or personal name meaning 'peaceable'. **2.** Possibly an altered spelling of German *Tallig*, from a short form of a Germanic personal name similar to DIETRICH.

Tallmadge (281) Variant spelling of English and Jewish TALMADGE.

Tallman (2836) Possibly an altered form of German DALLMANN.

Tallo (145) **1.** Catalan (**Talló**): Catalan habitational name from Talló in La Cerdanya district, Catalonia. **2.** in some cases possibly also Galician, a habitational name from Tallo, a place so named in A Coruña, Galicia. **3.** Italian: from *tallo* 'stem', 'stalk (of a plant)' (Latin *thallus*), a nickname for a tall, thin person.
GIVEN NAMES Spanish 4%. *Juanita, Mercedes, Ramon, Uriel*.

Tallon (657) **1.** English and Irish (of Norman origin), and French: from a Germanic personal name derived from *tal* 'destroy', either as a short form of a compound name with this first element (compare TALBOT) or as an independent byname. **2.** English and Irish (of Norman origin), and French: metonymic nickname for a swift runner or for someone with a deformed heel, from Old French *talon* 'heel' (a diminutive of *tal*, Latin *talus*). **3.** Spanish (**Tallón**): either a Spanish variant of Catalan **Talló** (see TALLO) or a habitational name from any of the places in A Coruña, Ourense, and Pontevedra provinces called Tallón.
FOREBEARS A native of the Champagne region of France, Jean Talon was intendant for New France in 1665–68, and again in 1669–72. A Talon from the Picardy region of France is documented in Quebec City in 1666. Another, from Guyenne, is recorded in Rivière Ouelle, Quebec, in 1698, with the secondary surname Le Bourdelais.

Talluto (120) Sicilian and Southern Italian: nickname from Sicilian *taddutu* 'big and robust'.
GIVEN NAMES Italian 24%. *Angelo* (2), *Salvatore* (2), *Antonio, Calogero, Gaetano, Marco, Mariano* (3), *Mario, Matteo, Nunzio*.

Tally (820) **1.** Irish: variant spelling of TALLEY. **2.** Irish (County Longford): occasionally a variant of TULLY. **3.** French: occupational name from a variant of Old French *tailleur*, an agent derivative of *tailler* 'to cut', hence an occupational name for a tailor or stonecutter.

Talmadge (840) **1.** English: metonymic occupational name for an itinerant merchant, from Old French *talemasche* 'knapsack' (a word of uncertain origin). **2.** Americanized form of one or more like-sounding Jewish surnames. Compare TALMAGE.

Talmage (492) **1.** English: variant spelling of TALMADGE. **2.** Americanized form of one or more like-sounding Jewish surnames, most likely from eastern Ashkenazic **Tolmach**, either an occupational name from Russian *tolmach* 'interpreter' or a habitational name from a village called Tolmach in Ukraine.

Talman (144) **1.** Dutch: occupational name from *taelman, taleman* 'lawyer', 'orator'. **2.** Jewish (Ashkenazic) and German (**Thalmann**): topographic name for someone who lived in a valley, composed of the elements *tal* 'valley' + *man* 'man'. Compare DALLMANN.
GIVEN NAMES Jewish 5%. *Ilya, Yigal*.

Talone (94) Italian: from a personal name of Germanic origin, a short form of a compound name such as *Talabert*.
GIVEN NAMES Italian 11%. *Donato, Salvatore, Santo*.

Talsma (311) cf. TOLSMA.

Talton (864) English: habitational name, possibly from Talton in Worcestershire, named in Old English as 'settlement (*tūn*) associated with *Tǣtel*', but more likely from Tallington in Lincolnshire, 'settlement associated with *Talla*', an unattested Old English personal name.

Talty (310) Irish (County Clare): reduced Anglicized form of Gaelic **Ó Tailtigh** 'descendant of *Tailteach*', a personal name which Woulfe believes to be a variant of *Taithleach* (see TALLEY).
GIVEN NAME Irish 10%. *Brendan* (4).

Talwar (125) Indian (Panjab): Hindu (Khatri) and Sikh name based on the name of a clan in the Khatri community, derived from Panjabi *təlwār* 'sword' (Sanskrit *taravāri*).
GIVEN NAMES Indian 90%. *Ajay* (3), *Anil* (3), *Deepak* (3), *Rajeev* (3), *Rakesh* (3), *Akshay* (2), *Jagdish* (2), *Naresh* (2), *Rajesh* (2), *Ravi* (2), *Sandeep* (2), *Vijay* (2).

Tam (2945) Chinese: see TAN.
GIVEN NAMES Chinese 31%. *Wing* (31), *Kwok* (18), *Kam* (15), *Kin* (14), *Chun* (11), *Wai* (11), *Yuk* (10), *Siu* (9), *Chung* (8), *Man* (8), *Chi* (7), *Ding* (7), *Kwong* (7), *Pak* (6), *Shiu* (3), *Hak* (2), *Yeung* (2), *You* (2), *Choon, Chun Ho, Kok, Kum, Kun Ho, Sa*.

Tamaki (112) Japanese: though more commonly written with characters meaning 'jewel tree', the original meaning of the name is probably 'rice paddy planter'. It is found mostly in the Ōsaka region. In the Ryūkyū Islands the name is pronounced *Tamagusuku* and means 'jeweled castle'.
GIVEN NAMES Japanese 59%. *Isao* (2), *Mayumi* (2), *Akihiro, Akiko, Asami, Eiki, Hakaru, Haruhiko, Hideo, Hitoshi, Jiro, Junko*.

Tamanaha (150) Japanese: written with the characters for 'ball' and 'Naha' (the name of the main city on the island of Okinawa). The surname is found in the Ryūkyū islands.
GIVEN NAMES Japanese 34%. *Masaru* (2), *Shigeo* (2), *Hitoshi, Keichi, Kiyoshi, Masao, Matsuo, Mitsue, Satoru, Seichi, Shigemasa, Shigeru*.

Tamargo (140) Asturian-Leonese: habitational name from a place in Asturies.
GIVEN NAMES Spanish 40%. *Manuel* (5), *Francisco* (4), *Armando* (3), *Jorge* (3), *Alejandro* (2), *Angel* (2), *Jose* (2), *Julio* (2), *Mauricio* (2), *Caridad, Celestino, Domingo*.

Tamas (151) Hungarian (**Tamás**): from the personal name *Tamás*, Hungarian form of THOMAS.
GIVEN NAMES Hungarian 24%. *Imre* (3), *Istvan* (2), *Arpad, Attila, Denes, Endre, Gabor, Janos, Jeno, Jolan, Karoly, Sandor*.

Tamashiro (308) Japanese: 'ball castle'; it is not a common name, but is found in western Japan and the Ryūkyū Islands, where it is also pronounced **Tamagushiku**.
GIVEN NAMES Japanese 41%. *Masao* (4), *Hideo* (3), *Minoru* (3), *Shigeo* (3), *Kenji* (2), *Masayuki* (2), *Seichi* (2), *Shigeru* (2), *Akira, Fusako, Hajime, Hatsuko*.

Tamasi (116) **1.** Italian: variant of TOMASSI. **2.** Hungarian (**Tamási**): patronymic from the personal name *Tamás*, Hungarian form of THOMAS.
GIVEN NAMES Italian 8%; Hungarian 6%. *Angelo* (2), *Nicola*; *Gabor* (3).

Tamayo (1473) Spanish: habitational name from places called Tamayo in the provinces of Burgos and Albacete.
GIVEN NAMES Spanish 51%; Italian 10%. *Jose* (44), *Juan* (19), *Carlos* (18), *Manuel* (17), *Pedro* (12), *Fernando* (11), *Jorge* (11), *Jesus* (10), *Alberto* (9), *Angel* (8), *Luis* (8), *Rafael* (8); *Antonio* (11), *Federico* (4), *Lorenzo* (4), *Marco* (3), *Clemente, Clementina, Delio, Dino, Eligio, Geronimo, Heriberto, Marcello*.

Tambasco (132) Italian: unexplained.
GIVEN NAMES Italian 16%. *Matteo* (2), *Vito* (2), *Aldo, Antonio, Natale, Vincenzo*.

Tambellini (119) Italian: unexplained; perhaps from a derivative of **Tambello**, a reduced compound of *tantum* + *bellus* 'very beautiful'.
GIVEN NAMES Italian 12%. *Angelo* (2), *Dante* (2), *Gino*.

Tamblyn (304) English (chiefly Devon and Cornwall): from the Middle English personal name *Tamlin*, a double diminutive, with the Anglo-Norman French suffixes *-el* and *-in*, of *Tam, Tom*, a short form of THOMAS.

Tamborello (106) Italian (Sicily): variant of TAMBURELLO.

Tamburello (294) Italian: metonymic occupational names for a drummer, from a diminutive of *tamburo* 'drum'.
GIVEN NAMES Italian 25%. *Ignazio* (3), *Sal* (2), *Salvatore* (2), *Casimiro, Dario, Ezio, Gaetano, Gaspare, Gerlando, Giovanni, Giuseppe, Luigi, Mario, Rocco, Rosario*.

Tamburino (137) Italian: metonymic occupational names for a drummer, from a diminutive of *tamburo* 'drum'.
GIVEN NAMES Italian 14%. *Armando, Gaetano, Orlando, Salvatore, Savino*.

Tamburo (183) Italian: metonymic occupational name for a drummer, from *tamburo* 'drum'.

GIVEN NAMES Italian 18%. *Carmine* (2), *Nicolo* (2), *Salvatore* (2), *Concetta*, *Silvio*.

Tamburri (166) Italian: from a plural or patronymic form of **Tamburro**, a variant of TAMBURO.

GIVEN NAMES Italian 13%. *Angelo* (3), *Luigia*, *Sandro*.

Tamburrino (186) Italian: from a diminutive of TAMBURO, or from Sicilian *tammurinu* 'drum'.

GIVEN NAMES Italian 21%. *Angelo* (2), *Pasquale* (2), *Antonio*, *Epifanio*, *Florinda*, *Humberto*, *Marcello*, *Nicola*, *Rocco*, *Sal*.

Tamburro (290) Italian: variant of TAMBURO.

GIVEN NAMES Italian 19%. *Angelo* (4), *Carlo* (2), *Nicola* (2), *Rocco* (2), *Domenic*, *Fulvio*, *Giuseppe*, *Lucio*, *Luigi*, *Pasquale*, *Romeo*.

Tamer (180) Muslim: from a personal name based on Arabic *tāmir* 'rich in dates'.

GIVEN NAMES Muslim 14%; French 5%. *Akram* (2), *Tamer* (2), *Coskun*, *Faisal*, *Fuad*, *Ilhan*, *Issam*, *Mahmoud*, *Nabil*, *Nadim*, *Omar*, *Salem*; *Lucien*, *Phillippe*, *Pierre*.

Tamez (900) Spanish (**Támez**): perhaps a derivative of the Arabic personal name *tamīz* 'distinction', 'perception', 'awareness'.

GIVEN NAMES Spanish 47%. *Jose* (20), *Manuel* (15), *Juan* (11), *Jesus* (9), *Luis* (8), *Ramiro* (8), *Ruben* (8), *Carlos* (7), *Jaime* (7), *Armando* (6), *Javier* (6), *Raul* (6).

Tamm (325) North German: **1.** from a short form of the personal name *Tancmar*, composed of the Germanic *thank* 'thought' + *māri*, *mēri* 'famous'. **2.** habitational name from Tamm in southern Germany or Thamm, Damm(e) in northern Germany. The place names may derive from the personal name (see 1) or from Middle High German *tam* 'dam', 'dike'.

GIVEN NAMES German 8%. *Arno*, *Ernst*, *Karlheinz*, *Manfred*, *Meinhard*, *Oskar*, *Otto*.

Tammaro (387) Italian: from the personal name *Tammaro* (ecclesiastical Latin *Tammarus*), of obscure origin. This name was borne by one of twelve African priests who, persecuted by the Vandals, came to Campania to preach Christianity. San Tammaro in Caserta province is named for him.

GIVEN NAMES Italian 22%. *Angelo* (6), *Salvatore* (4), *Aldo* (2), *Antonio* (2), *Gaetano* (2), *Lucio* (2), *Annalisa*, *Antimo*, *Carmine*, *Domenico*, *Fiore*, *Gabriele*.

Tammen (252) North German: patronymic from TAMM 1.

GIVEN NAMES German 6%. *Hermann* (2), *Lorenz*, *Meinhard*, *Reinhold*.

Tamminga (167) Frisian: patronymic from a pet form of the personal name *Tammo*, formed with the Germanic stem *thank* 'thought'.

Tamplin (307) English (mainly southeastern Wales): variant of TAMBLYN.

Tams (138) **1.** North German: from a short form of THOMAS. **2.** English (Staffordshire): apparently from a patronymic of *Tam*, a variant of *Tom*, a short form of THOMAS.

Tamura (657) Japanese: usually written with characters meaning 'rice paddy village'; it is especially common in the Kyōto–Ōsaka region and the northeast. Most bearers descend from Date Muneyoshi (17th century). His mother was a descendant of Shōgun Sakanoue Tamuramaro (758–811), who was a descendant of Sino-Korean prince Achi no Omi, who settled in Japan in the late 4th century.

GIVEN NAMES Japanese 54%. *Hiroshi* (5), *Akira* (4), *Kaz* (4), *Taichi* (4), *Hideo* (3), *Toshiko* (3), *Aki* (2), *Hitoshi* (2), *Kaoru* (2), *Kazumi* (2), *Kazuyuki* (2), *Kenji* (2).

Tan (4674) **1.** Chinese 譚: from the name of the state of Tan during the Zhou dynasty. After Wu Wang established the Zhou dynasty in 1122 BC, he enfeoffed the state of Tan to a descendant of the model emperor Yu (2205–2198 BC), with the status of Viscount. Descendants adopted the name of the state Tan as their surname. **2.** Chinese 談: said to be from the name of a certain King Tan of the state of Song, a 36th-generation descendant of its founder (see SONG). **3.** Chinese 陈: variant of CHEN. **4.** Chinese 覃: there are two groups of bearers of the character for this surname: one pronounced Tan, and the other Qin (see QIN), although both are represented with the same character. **5.** Korean: there are three Chinese characters for this surname; two of them are used by clans that now have only one surviving family each, according to a recent census. Some records indicate that there are 10 clans that use the third character for their surname, but only two can be documented: the Kangüm clan and the Yönan clan. Neither of these clans is very large. **6.** Filipino: unexplained.

GIVEN NAMES Chinese/Korean 20%; Spanish 7%. *Jian* (12), *Ming* (12), *Hong* (11), *Wei* (11), *Jin* (8), *Eng* (7), *Li* (7), *Lian* (7), *Seng* (7), *Chin* (6), *Heng* (6), *Mei* (6); *Jose* (9), *Manuel* (9), *Carlos* (7), *Luis* (7), *Cristina* (6), *Ricardo* (5), *Teresita* (5), *Armando* (4), *Elena* (4), *Mario* (4), *Reynaldo* (4), *Alfredo* (3).

Tanabe (416) Japanese: usually written with characters meaning 'side of the rice paddy'; it is found mostly in western Japan. The ancient pronunciation was *Tanobe* and meant 'rice paddy guild', denoting a group charged with care of the emperor's fields. The ancient Tanabe of Kawachi (presently part of Nara prefecture) claimed descent from emperors of the Chinese Han dynasty (206 BC–AD 220). The surname is listed in the Shinsen shōjiroku.

GIVEN NAMES Japanese 47%. *Kaori* (3), *Yasuhiro* (3), *Yoshio* (3), *Hiroko* (2), *Hiroyuki* (2), *Jiro* (2), *Junji* (2), *Keiichi* (2), *Masao* (2), *Takeshi* (2), *Toru* (2), *Toshiaki* (2).

Tanaka (2571) Japanese: usually written with characters meaning 'center of the rice paddy'. One of the ten most common surnames, it is particularly frequent around the city of Ōsaka, and is also found in the Ryūkyū Islands. It is listed in the Shinsen shōjiroku, but the surname is borne by many unrelated families.

GIVEN NAMES Japanese 57%. *Akira* (18), *Hiroshi* (16), *Kenji* (13), *Koji* (11), *Satoru* (9), *Yoshio* (9), *Shigeru* (8), *Yukio* (8), *Kiyoshi* (7), *Yuji* (7), *Hideo* (6), *Koichi* (6).

Tanberg (119) Norwegian: habitational name from any of six farmsteads in eastern Norway named from Old Norse *þorn* 'thorn bush' + *berg* 'mountain'.

Tanck (105) Norwegian and North German: from a short form of a personal name such as *Thankmar*.

GIVEN NAMES Scandinavian 5%. *Erik* (2).

Tancredi (477) Italian: from the personal name *Tancredi*, composed of the Germanic elements *thank* 'thought' + *rēd* 'counsel', 'advice'.

GIVEN NAMES Italian 14%. *Angelo* (3), *Rocco* (2), *Salvatore* (2), *Silvio* (2), *Aniello*, *Carmino*, *Gaetano*, *Giovanni*, *Guido*, *Italo*, *Luigi*, *Pasquale*.

Tandberg (100) **1.** German: unexplained; apparently a habitational name from a lost or unidentified place. **2.** Norwegian: variant of TANBERG.

GIVEN NAMES German 7%; Scandinavian 6%. *Eldor*, *Otto*.

Tande (132) **1.** Dutch (**de Tande**): nickname for someone with prominent or otherwise remarkable teeth, from *tand* 'tooth'. **2.** Norwegian: habitational name from any of three farmsteads in eastern Norway, named in Old Norse as *Tandar*; the etymology of the name is uncertain, but it may be derived from Old Norse *tǫnn* 'tooth'.

GIVEN NAME German 7%. *Kurt* (3).

Tandon (213) Indian (Panjab): Hindu (Khatri) and Sikh name of unknown meaning; it is based on the name of a clan in the Khatri community (see KHATRI).

GIVEN NAMES Indian 90%. *Manish* (5), *Rajiv* (5), *Jagdish* (4), *Pankaj* (4), *Ashok* (3), *Atul* (3), *Dinesh* (3), *Kishan* (3), *Raj* (3), *Rajesh* (3), *Som* (3), *Arun* (2).

Tandy (783) English and Irish: from a pet form of the personal name ANDREW. The surname has been in Ireland since the 14th century, especially in County Meath.

Taneja (115) Indian (Panjab): Hindu (Arora) and Sikh name based on the name of a clan in the Arora community, apparently derived from *tən* 'blade of grass' (from Sanskrit *trṇa*).

GIVEN NAMES Indian 90%. *Jugal* (3), *Krishan* (3), *Sanjeev* (3), *Ajay* (2), *Dinesh* (2), *Kapil* (2), *Rajesh* (2), *Rajiv* (2), *Rakesh* (2), *Ramesh* (2), *Sanjay* (2), *Seema* (2).

Tanenbaum (522) German and Jewish (Ashkenazic): variant spelling of TANNEN-BAUM.

GIVEN NAMES Jewish 6%. *Sol* (3), *Miriam* (2), *Meyer*, *Moshe*.

Taney (197) English: variant of TAWNEY.

Tang (5203) **1.** Chinese 邓: variant spelling of DENG. **2.** Chinese 唐: from the name of the region of Tang, in present-day Shanxi province. The legendary emperor Huang Di (2697–2595 BC) granted this region to his son Dan Zhu, whose descendants eventually adopted it as their surname. They held power in the region until they were conquered by Cheng Wang, second king (1115–1079 BC) of the Zhou dynasty. Cheng Wang granted the region to his brother Shu Yu, whose descendants also adopted the place name Tang as a surname. This character is also that used for the Tang dynasty (618–907). **3.** Chinese 汤: from the given name of Cheng Tang, Prince of Shang, a model of virtue and humanity, who overthrew the corrupt last king of the Xia Dynasty and became first emperor of the Shang Dynasty, in 1766 BC. Some of his descendants adopted Tang as their surname. **4.** Chinese 滕: Cantonese variant of TENG. 1. **5.** Vietnamese: unexplained. **6.** Korean: only one Chinese character is used in Korean for the surname Tang, and the Miryang is the only Tang clan. Its founding ancestor, Tang Sŏng, migrated from Yüan China some time during the latter part of the 14th century. This is a comparatively rare surname in Korea.

GIVEN NAMES Chinese 31%; Vietnamese 18%. *Wei* (14), *Chung* (13), *Hong* (13), *Li* (12), *Chi* (11), *Hua* (10), *Ming* (10), *Wing* (10), *Cheng* (9), *Kwan* (9), *Ying* (9), *Ching* (8), *Kwok* (8), *Chang* (5); *Minh* (24), *Hung* (15), *Hoa* (13), *Thanh* (13), *Hai* (12), *Muoi* (12), *Phat* (11), *Quan* (10), *Hue* (9), *Duc* (8), *Ha* (8), *Khanh* (8), *Tam* (7), *Yiu* (6), *Min* (5), *Chong* (4), *Nam* (4), *Manh* (2), *Pak* (2), *Phong* (2), *Sinh* (2), *Ti* (2).

Tangeman (407) North German (**Tangemann**): probably a habitational name for someone from Tange in Oldenburg, or a topographic name for someone living on a sandy ridge between swamps or moors, Middle Low German *tange*.

Tangen (599) Norwegian: habitational name from any of numerous farmsteads, named with the definite singular form of *tange*, from Old Norse *tangi* 'tongue (of land)'.

GIVEN NAMES Scandinavian 9%. *Erik* (3), *Audun* (2), *Erland*, *Iver*, *Kristoffer*, *Nels*, *Selmer*, *Svein*.

Tanger (116) **1.** Northern German: from the Tanger river or a habitational name from any of several places so named in Brandenburg and Pomerania. **2.** North German: nickname for a waspish person, from Middle Low German *tanger* 'strong', 'fresh', 'biting', 'sharp'.

Tangney (317) Irish form of TANGUAY. The name was introduced to England at the time of the Norman Conquest, and later taken to Kerry in Ireland.

GIVEN NAME Irish 6%. *Brennan*.

Tango (150) Italian: probably from a personal name of Germanic origin composed with the element *thank* 'thought'.

GIVEN NAMES Italian 10%. *Antonio*, *Domenic*, *Gioia*, *Raffaela*, *Rocco*, *Vito*.

Tangredi (165) Italian (Naples): variant of TANCREDI.

GIVEN NAMES Italian 17%. *Rocco* (2), *Salvatore* (2), *Amedeo*, *Aniello*, *Dino*.

Tanguay (990) French (Breton) and English (of Norman origin): from a personal name, a contraction of *Tanneguy*, from Breton *tan* 'fire', and *ki*, 'dog', which was borne by a 6th-century Christian saint associated with Paul Aurelian. The name was introduced to England at the time of the Norman Conquest.

FOREBEARS A bearer of the name from Brittany in France is documented in Saint-Jean, Island of Orleans, Quebec province, in 1692, with the secondary surname LaNavette.

GIVEN NAMES French 18%. *Adrien* (5), *Marcel* (5), *Andre* (4), *Normand* (4), *Armand* (3), *Gaston* (3), *Gilles* (3), *Pierre* (3), *Alphonse* (2), *Herve* (2), *Lucien* (2), *Michel* (2).

Tanguma (121) probably from a native American language (Mexico): unexplained.

GIVEN NAMES Spanish 52%. *Guadalupe* (2), *Javier* (2), *Jesus* (2), *Jose* (2), *Leandro* (2), *Pedro* (2), *Ramon* (2), *Teodoro* (2), *Alfredo*, *Alicia*, *Elva*, *Emiliano*.

Tani (260) **1.** Italian: from a pet form of the personal names *Gaetano* or *Ottaviano*. **2.** Japanese: topographic name meaning 'valley', taken by many families. It is found chiefly in western Japan. The most ancient bearers are listed in the Shinsen shōjiroku. *Tani* is also a common element in many other surnames.

GIVEN NAMES Japanese 37%. *Yukiko* (3), *Eiji* (2), *Keiko* (2), *Shiro* (2), *Yohei* (2), *Yuichi* (2), *Yusuke* (2), *Akihiro*, *Atsuko*, *Chiyoko*, *Fumiko*, *Fusae*.

Tanielian (42) Armenian: western Armenian form of DANIELIAN.

Tanigawa (121) Japanese: 'valley river'. Some families pronounce the name **Tanikawa**. It is found mostly in western Honshū.

GIVEN NAMES Japanese 46%. *Toru* (2), *Chieko*, *Fumio*, *Hajime*, *Hidehiro*, *Hiromichi*, *Hiroshi*, *Ikuko*, *Kanichi*, *Katsuki*, *Katsumi*, *Kenji*.

Taniguchi (421) Japanese: 'mouth of the valley'. This name is found mostly in northern Japan. Some bearers descend from the SASAKI family, others from the Kuga branch of the MINAMOTO clan.

GIVEN NAMES Japanese 56%. *Seiji* (4), *Makoto* (3), *Noboru* (3), *Hiroshi* (2), *Katsumi* (2), *Masao* (2), *Matsue* (2), *Miyuki* (2), *Shigeki* (2), *Shinji* (2), *Sumio* (2), *Toru* (2).

Tanimoto (153) Japanese: topographic name meaning '(one who is) from the valley'. This name is found mostly in western Japan.

GIVEN NAMES Japanese 48%. *Toshio* (2), *Goro*, *Hajime*, *Hidenori*, *Hiroshi*, *Isao*, *Itaru*, *Katsushi*, *Kazumi*, *Kenji*, *Kentaro*, *Kiyomi*.

Tanis (789) Dutch: probably a variant of DANIS.

Tanji (103) Japanese: rare in Japan, the name is written with characters meaning 'red' and 'govern'. The actual meaning is unclear.

GIVEN NAMES Japanese 42%. *Hisao* (2), *Toru* (2), *Goro*, *Hideo*, *Kazuko*, *Kazunari*, *Misao*, *Mitsuru*, *Norio*, *Satoru*, *Shigeo*, *Takao*.

Tank (888) **1.** North German and Frisian: from a pet form of the personal name *Thankmar* (see TAMM). **2.** Indian (Gujarat): Hindu name of unknown meaning.

GIVEN NAMES Indian 4%. *Ajay* (2), *Hasmukh* (2), *Shekhar* (2), *Bhupendra*, *Girish*, *Harsh*, *Himat*, *Mahesh*, *Mandar*, *Nayana*, *Pinakin*, *Shantanu*.

Tankard (149) English (mainly Yorkshire): **1.** from a Norman personal name, *Tancard*, composed of the Germanic words *þank* 'thought' + *hard* 'hardy', 'brave', 'strong'. **2.** metonymic occupational name for a maker of barrels and drinking vessels, or a nickname for a hardened drinker, from Middle English *tankard* 'tub', 'cup' (apparently a borrowing from Middle Dutch).

Tanke (157) Dutch and North German: from a short form of a Germanic compound name with the first element *þank* 'thought'. Compare TANK.

GIVEN NAMES German 5%. *Erna*, *Helmut*, *Reinhold*.

Tankersley (2264) English: habitational name from Tankersley in South Yorkshire (formerly in the West Riding), named in Old English as 'Tancred's clearing (*lēah*)'. Compare Italian TANCREDI.

Tanksley (840) Apparently a reduced form of TANKERSLEY.

Tann (368) **1.** German: topographic name for someone who lived in a forest, Middle High German *tan*. This was originally a distinct word from *tanne* 'pine tree', and denoted a forest of any kind. Inevitably, however, the two became confused, with the result that *Tann* now denotes only coniferous forests; it is a rather rare and literary word. **2.** English (East Anglia): variant of TANNER 1.

Tannahill (243) Scottish: habitational name from Tannahill in Ayrshire.

Tannehill (767) Scottish: variant of TANNA-HILL.

Tannen (200) **1.** German and Jewish (Ashkenazic): habitational name from any of several places in Lower Saxony or Baden named with German *Tannen* 'pine', or from a short form of any of the many compound names formed with this element. **2.** Jewish (American): shortened form of TANNENBAUM.

GIVEN NAMES Jewish 8%. *Hyman, Meyer, Rebekah.*

Tannenbaum (1147) German and Jewish (Ashkenazic): German topographic name or Jewish ornamental name from German *Tannenbaum* 'fir tree', 'pine tree'.

GIVEN NAMES Jewish 8%. *Sol* (4), *Dov* (3), *Meyer* (3), *Hyman* (2), *Mayer* (2), *Amron, Aron, Ber, Chaim, Emanuel, Gershon, Isadore.*

Tanner (16579) **1.** English and Dutch: occupational name for a tanner of skins, Middle English *tanner*, Middle Dutch *taenre*. (The Middle English form derives from Old English *tannere*, from Late Latin *tannarius*, reinforced by Old French *taneor*, from Late Latin *tannator*; both Late Latin forms derive from a verb *tannare*, possibly from a Celtic word for the oak, whose bark was used in the process.) **2.** Swiss and German: habitational name for someone from any of several places called Tanne (in the Harz Mountains and Silesia) or Tann (southern Germany). **3.** Finnish: topographic or ornamental name from Finnish *tanner* 'open field'.

Tannery (123) Origin unidentified.

Tanney (181) **1.** English: unexplained. **2.** Northern Irish: unexplained; it could perhaps be from Gaelic *tanaidh* 'thin'.

Tannous (141) Arabic: ethnic name for a Tunisian.

GIVEN NAMES Muslim 38%; Indian 5%. *Bechara* (2), *Issa* (2), *Afif, Dib, Farid, Fayez, Fouad, Fuad, Houssam, Ibrahim, Izzat, Jeries; Ranga.*

Tano (132) **1.** Italian: from a short form of the personal name GAETANO, or from pet forms thereof. **2.** Spanish (**Taño**): possibly nickname from *taño* 'sucker', 'shoot'. **3.** Japanese: it is unclear whether instances of this name in America are *Tano*, meaning 'many fields', or *Tanō*, meaning 'many offerings'. Neither is common in Japan.

GIVEN NAMES Spanish 18%; Japanese 11%. *Jose* (3), *Mario* (3), *Raul* (2), *Roberto* (2), *Alejandro, Cesar, Lourdes, Nelida, Rey, Ricardo, Venancio; Kunio* (2), *Yoshiko* (2), *Shigeko, Sumio, Yoshinori.*

Tanous (119) Origin unidentified.

Tanquary (108) Origin unidentified.

Tansey (741) Irish (Connacht) and Scottish: reduced Anglicized form of Gaelic **Mac an Tánaiste** 'son of the tanist'. The word *tanist* denoted a senior and respected member of a clan who was heir presumptive to its chief. Clan leadership was not hereditary, but depended on ability.

GIVEN NAME Irish 5%. *Aileen.*

Tansill (101) English (Worcestershire): unexplained.

Tanski (367) Polish (**Tański**): habitational name for someone from Tańsk in Ciechanów voivodeship.

GIVEN NAMES Polish 5%. *Eugeniusz* (2), *Casimir, Dorota, Thadeus.*

Tansley (107) English: habitational name from Tansley in Derbyshire, named from an Old English *Tan* or Old English *tān* 'branch' + *lēah* 'woodland clearing'.

Tant (736) English: unexplained. In the U.S., this is a predominantly a southern name, with large concentrations in NC, SC, and GA.

Tantalo (109) Italian and Greek (**Tantalos, Tandalos**): from a nickname or humanistic name based on classical Greek *Tantalos*, name of a mythological king of Sipylos, who offended the gods and was punished in the underworld by being forced to stand up to his neck in water, which sank down whenever he tried to drink it. It may be a nickname for someone who was tantalized.

GIVEN NAMES Italian 24%. *Lazzaro* (2), *Angelo, Carmine, Domenic.*

Tantillo (451) Italian: from a pet form of the personal name *Tanto*, perhaps a short form of *Tantobene* or possibly from *Antillo*, a pet form of ANTONIO.

GIVEN NAMES Italian 15%; Spanish 4%. *Salvatore* (7), *Sal* (3), *Mario* (2), *Ciro, Domenic, Domenica, Enrico, Franca, Gasper, Giovanni, Matteo, Santo, Vito; Salvador* (2), *Jose.*

Tanton (307) English (mainly Devon): variant of TAUNTON.

Tanzer (341) German and Jewish (Ashkenazic): nickname for a skilled or enthusiastic dancer, or, as a German name, an occupational name for a professional acrobat, from an agent derivative of Middle High German, German *tanzen* 'to dance' (from Old French *danser*; the initial *t-* is the result of hypercorrection of a presumed Low German form). Among Jews, the name may have been taken by Chasidim, since members of this branch of Jewry (which arose in the 18th century) place great emphasis on dancing, and in some cases the name may have been ornamental.

Tanzi (198) Italian: patronymic or plural form of a reduced form of the personal names *Costanzo* or *Lattanzio*.

GIVEN NAMES Italian 37%. *Carlo* (8), *Luigi* (3), *Vito* (3), *Angelo* (2), *Gino* (2), *Nicola* (2), *Onofrio* (2), *Sal* (2), *Domenico, Donato, Franco, Matteo.*

Tanzman (102) Jewish (Ashkenazic): nickname from German *Tanz*, Yiddish *tants* 'dance' + German MANN, Yiddish *man* 'man'.

GIVEN NAME Jewish 5%. *Dov.*

Tao (720) **1.** Chinese 陶: according to tradition, from *Tao Tangshi*, the name of the emperor Yao (2357–2257 BC), first of the three model emperors, before he came to power. A branch of his descendants retained the surname Tao. Another source of this surname is the word for 'pottery'; this is traced back to a descendant of the second of the three model emperors, Shun (2257–2205 BC). During the Zhou dynasty (1122–221 BC), this descendant was in charge of the manufacture of pottery. As the character for Tao also means 'pottery' and was part of his official title, his descendants adopted Tao as their surname. **2.** Japanese: unexplained.

GIVEN NAMES Chinese 41%; Vietnamese 6%; Japanese 5%. *Wei* (9), *Yun* (5), *Li* (4), *Ying* (4), *Jing* (3), *Lian* (3), *Qing* (3), *Xiao* (3), *Yung* (3), *Anping* (2), *Feng* (2), *Foo* (2); *Chung* (2), *Nam* (2), *Weng* (2), *Chang, Ki Hong, Shen; Dinh* (2), *Anh, Can, Cau, Chuong, Dao, Hai, Hung, Huong, Khoa, Khue, Mai; Yuki* (2), *Fumiyo, Harumi, Haruyuki, Katsumi, Kota, Midori, Minoru, Nao, Ryutaro, Shuichi, Yu.*

Taormina (699) Italian (Sicily): habitational name from Taormina in the region of Messina.

GIVEN NAMES Italian 28%. *Salvatore* (8), *Sal* (6), *Angelo* (4), *Rosario* (3), *Mario* (2), *Ciro* (2), *Francesco* (2), *Gasper* (2), *Santo* (2), *Annamarie, Battista, Caesar, Carlo, Concetta, Epifanio, Manuel, Marcela, Mariano, Susana.*

Tapanes (120) Hispanic: unexplained.

GIVEN NAMES Spanish 51%; Italian 9%. *Luis* (6), *Mario* (6), *Armando* (4), *Rolando* (4), *Francisco* (3), *Jorge* (3), *Aida* (2), *Alina* (2), *Ernesto* (2), *Orlando* (2), *Pedro* (2), *Reinaldo* (2); *Elio, Heriberto.*

Tape (108) **1.** French (**Tapé**): unexplained. **2.** German: possibly an altered spelling of TAPPE.

GIVEN NAMES German 5%; French 4%. *Kurt* (2), *Johann Heinrich; Amelie, Rolande.*

Taphorn (123) German: variant of TAPPHORN, unexplained.

Tapia (3902) Galician, Asturian-Leonese, Spanish, and Jewish (Sephardic): habitational name from any of the places in Galicia, Asturies, and Burgos so named from *tapia* 'mud wall'.

GIVEN NAMES Spanish 47%. *Jose* (87), *Juan* (42), *Jorge* (35), *Manuel* (34), *Carlos* (32), *Miguel* (31), *Francisco* (28), *Jesus* (22), *Luis* (22), *Mario* (22), *Ramon* (22), *Ruben* (19).

Tapley (1204) English (Devon): habitational name from Tapeley in Devon, which Ekwall derives from Old English *tæppa* 'peg' + *lēah* 'wood', 'clearing', i.e. 'wood where pegs are obtained'.

Taplin (699) English: from a pet form of the personal name *Tæppa* (see TAPP).

Tapp (2185) **1.** English: from an Old English personal name *Tæppa*, of uncertain origin and meaning. **2.** German: from a short form of the Germanic name *Theudobrand*, composed of the elements *theodo-* 'people' + *brand* 'sword'. **3.** North German: nickname for a clumsy person or a simpleton, from Middle Low German *tappe* 'oaf'.

Tappan (630) Possibly an altered spelling of TAPPEN.

Tappe (319) **1.** German: metonymic occupational name for the owner of a tavern or a nickname for a drinker, from Low German *tappe* 'tap'. **2.** German: variant of TAPP. **3.** English: variant spelling of TAPP.

Tappen (215) North German: **1.** variant of TAPPE 1. **2.** nickname for a clumsy person, from Middle Low German *tappe* 'oaf'.

Tapper (821) **1.** English and German: occupational name for a wine merchant or tavernkeeper, Middle English *tapper* (an agent derivative of *tappen* 'to draw off'), Low German *tappe* 'tap'. **2.** North German: nickname from Middle Low German *tapper* 'capable', 'eager', 'courageous'. **3.** Swedish: soldier's name from *tapper* 'brave'.

Tappin (151) English: from Old English *Tæpping*, an unattested patronymic from *Tæppa*. Compare TAPP.
FOREBEARS Joseph Tapping (d. 1678) is buried in King's Chapel Burying Ground, Boston, MA.

Tappy (108) Probably a variant of English TAPPIN.

Tapscott (565) English (Devon): habitational name probably from Tascott in North Petherwin, Devon. There are no early spellings of this place name, but could perhaps be 'Tapp's cottage(s)', from the Middle English surname TAPP.

Tara (126) **1.** Polish: nickname from dialect *tarać się* 'to roll or welter'. **2.** Indian (Panjab): Sikh name, probably from Panjabi *tārā* 'star' (Sanskrit *tāraka*). It is based on the name of a Jat tribe.
GIVEN NAMES Indian 7%; Polish 6%. *Kamla, Nirmala, Sandeep; Jozef* (2).

Tarallo (236) Southern Italian: nickname from the southern term *tarallo*, a kind of sweet biscuit.
GIVEN NAMES Italian 19%. *Angelo* (3), *Vito* (2), *Antonio, Carmela, Carmine, Edoardo, Giovanni, Giuseppe, Luigi, Ottavio, Sal.*

Taran (154) **1.** Polish and Ukrainian: nickname for a man of powerful build, from Polish and Ukrainian *taran* 'battering ram'. **2.** Jewish (eastern Ashkenazic) and Ukrainian: either a nickname from Ukrainian *taran* 'pock', or a metonymic occupational name from another meaning of the same word, 'tool used in a churn for butter making'.
GIVEN NAMES Russian 12%; Jewish 7%. *Boris* (4), *Lev* (2), *Gleb, Igor, Leonid, Leya, Mikhail, Vladimir; Ilya.*

Tarango (560) probably from a native American language (Mexico): possibly habitational name from Tarango, a mountain range called Tarango in Mexico. The name is commonly found in the Chihuahua region, but not in current Spain.
GIVEN NAMES Spanish 49%. *Jose* (16), *Raul* (10), *Jesus* (8), *Manuel* (7), *Ramon* (6),

Carlos (4), *Eduardo* (4), *Jose Luis* (4), *Juan* (4), *Juana* (4), *Miguel* (4), *Alberto* (3).

Tarantino (1399) Italian: habitational name for someone from the city of Taranto, from an adjectival form of the place name. See also TARANTO.
GIVEN NAMES Italian 14%. *Sal* (10), *Salvatore* (6), *Angelo* (5), *Antonio* (3), *Carmine* (3), *Giuseppe* (3), *Pietro* (3), *Rocco* (3), *Cosimo* (2), *Florio* (2), *Gilda* (2), *Marco* (2).

Taranto (711) Italian and Jewish (Sephardic): habitational name from the southern Italian city and provincial capital of this name (Latin name *Tarentum*, from Greek *Taras*).
GIVEN NAMES Italian 14%. *Angelo* (15), *Gaetano* (4), *Sal* (3), *Salvatore* (3), *Gasper* (2), *Bartolomeo, Carmela, Domenica, Giuseppe, Luciano, Vincenza, Vincenzo.*

Tarantola (128) Southern Italian: **1.** habitational name from a diminutive of TARANTO. **2.** nickname from Calabrian and Sicilian *tarantula* 'spider'.
GIVEN NAMES Italian 21%. *Angelo* (3), *Sal* (2), *Carlo, Girolamo, Mario, Renato.*

Taras (254) Ukrainian and Belorussian: from the personal name *Taras* (Greek *Tarasios* 'native of Taras', Greek name of the city of Taranto in southern Italy). This name was borne by an 8th-century patriarch of Constantinople, venerated in the Eastern Church.

Taravella (177) Italian: possibly a nickname for someone who was crippled or deformed, from dialect *taravella* 'crooked or deformed limb (or other part)'.
GIVEN NAMES Italian 15%. *Angelo* (2), *Carlo, Gaetano, Gandolfo, Giovanni, Salvatore, Santo.*

Tarbell (654) Possibly English: unexplained.

Tarbert (163) Scottish: variant of TARBET.

Tarbet (326) Scottish: habitational name from a place named with Gaelic *tairbeart* 'narrow isthmus', 'portage', as for example, Tarbert on Loch Fyne in Argyll or Tarbat in Easter Ross.

Tarbox (868) English (now mainly Bedfordshire): habitational name from Tarbock Green, formerly in Lancashire, now in Merseyside, named in Old English with *þorn* 'thorn tree' + *brōc* 'brook', 'stream'.

Tarbutton (208) English (Yorkshire and Northumberland): unexplained. Probably a habitational name from an unidentified or lost place in northern England, or possibly from Tarbolton in Ayrshire, Scotland.

Tarby (124) English (Sussex and Essex): unexplained; perhaps a variant of Irish TARPEY.

Tardie (139) Possibly French, a variant of TARDIF.
GIVEN NAMES French 7%. *Armand, Laurette, Rosaire.*

Tardif (733) English and French (Channel Islands): nickname for a sluggish person, from Middle English, Old French *tardif* 'slow' (Late Latin *tardivus*, for classical Latin *tardus*).
FOREBEARS A Tardif from the Brittany region of France is documented in Quebec City in 1637.
GIVEN NAMES French 26%. *Armand* (7), *Andre* (5), *Marcel* (5), *Rosaire* (4), *Gaetan* (3), *Lucien* (3), *Renald* (3), *Alderic* (2), *Camille* (2), *Cecile* (2), *Elphege* (2), *Gaston* (2).

Tardiff (794) English: variant spelling of TARDIF.
GIVEN NAMES French 8%. *Armand* (4), *Lucien* (3), *Cecile* (2), *Alban, Fleurette, Gabrielle, Girard, Laurier, Valere, Yvan, Yves.*

Tardio (107) Spanish (**Tardío**) and Italian: nickname from Spanish *tardío*, Italian *tardio* 'belated', 'sluggish', 'tardy' (from Latin *tardus*).
GIVEN NAMES Italian 18%; Spanish 14%. *Salvatore* (3), *Angelo* (2), *Antonio* (2), *Vincenzo; Juan* (2), *Carlos, Elba, Fernando, Humberto, Julio, Roberto.*

Tardy (491) **1.** French: variant of TARDIF. **2.** Hungarian: habitational name for someone from either of two places called Tard in Borsod and Somogy counties.

Targett (118) **1.** English: variant of TAGGART. **2.** Possibly an altered spelling of French **Target**, a nickname for someone who carried a square buckler, Old French *targe*.

Targonski (100) Polish: habitational name from places called Targonie in Ciechanów voivodeship and Targoń in Łomża voivodeship, named with *targ* 'market'.
GIVEN NAMES Polish 27%. *Arkadiusz, Bogdan, Boleslaw, Dariusz, Franciszek, Janusz, Miroslaw, Tadeusz, Witold, Wladyslaw.*

Tarin (401) **1.** Spanish (**Tarín**) and French: metonymic occupational name for a moneyer, from *tarin*, a medieval coin, from Late Latin *tarinus*, probably a derivative of *Tarentum* (see TARANTO), where the coins were first minted. **2.** Spanish: habitational name from places in the provinces of Uviéu and Teruel named Tarín. **3.** French: nickname from *tarin* 'siskin' (a small songbird similar to the goldfinch).
GIVEN NAMES Spanish 40%. *Manuel* (8), *Jose* (7), *Jesus* (6), *Ramon* (5), *Armando* (4), *Juan* (4), *Mario* (4), *Raul* (4), *Guadalupe* (3), *Amada* (2), *Andres* (2), *Arturo* (2).

Tariq (123) Muslim: from a personal name based on Arabic *ṭāriq* 'morning star'. Al-Tāriq is the title of the 86th sura of the Qur'an. Tarīq Ibn Ziyad (d. 720) was the leader of the Moors who brought Spain under Muslim rule and who gave his name to *Gibraltar* (*Jabal Tariq* 'mountain of Tariq' in Arabic).

GIVEN NAMES Muslim 88%. *Mohammad* (21), *Mohammed* (9), *Syed* (6), *Muhammad* (4), *Saeed* (3), *Mian* (2), *Muhammed* (2), *Shakir* (2), *Sheikh* (2), *Abida, Arshad, Asghar.*

Tarka (112) Polish: nickname for a sarcastic, sharp-tongued person, from Polish *tarka* 'grater', 'rasper'.
GIVEN NAMES Polish 12%. *Bronislaw, Elzbieta, Janusz, Thadeus.*

Tarkington (583) English: variant of TALKINGTON.

Tarkowski (163) Polish: habitational name for someone from Tarkowo in Bydgoszsz voivodeship or Tarków in Siedlce voivodeship, so named from *tarka* 'grater', 'rasper'.
GIVEN NAMES Polish 7%. *Jacek, Maciej, Valeska, Zbigniew.*

Tarleton (656) English: variant spelling of TARLTON.

Tarlow (194) Polish and Jewish (eastern Ashkenazic): habitational name for someone from Tarłów, in Poland.
GIVEN NAMES Jewish 8%. *Emanuel* (2), *Isidor, Myer, Nechama, Sol.*

Tarlton (805) English: **1.** habitational name from Tarleton in Lancashire, near Croston, named with the Old Norse personal name *Þóraldr* (composed of the elements *Þórr*, name of the Norse god of thunder (see THOR) + *valdr* 'rule') + Old English *tūn* 'enclosure', 'settlement'. **2.** habitational name from Tarlton in Gloucestershire, recorded in Domesday Book as *Torentune* and in 1204 as *Torleton*, probably from Old English *thorn* 'thorn tree' + *lēah* '(forest) clearing' + *tūn* 'enclosure', 'settlement'.

Tarman (220) English: unexplained.

Tarner (107) Americanized form of TARNOWSKI.

Tarnoff (137) Jewish (American): shortened form of eastern Ashkenazic **Tarnowski** or **Tarnovski**, habitational name for someone either from Tarnów in southern Poland or from the village of Tarnovo in Belarus.

Tarnow (241) German: habitational name from a place so called near Güstrow (Mecklenburg). The place name is of Slavic origin.
GIVEN NAMES German 4%. *Erwin, Eugen.*

Tarnowski (564) Polish and Jewish (eastern Ashkenazic): habitational name for someone from any of the places called Tarnów, Tarnowa, Tarnowiec, and Tarnowo (named with Polish *tarn* 'blackthorn' + *-ów* suffix). In the case of the Jewish surname, the source is usually, if not exclusively, Tarnów in southern Poland.
FOREBEARS This name, borne by a very illustrious Polish aristocratic line, has been recorded since the 14th century. From this line have sprung many famous individuals, including Jan Tarnowski (1488–1561), commander in chief of the Polish royal army; Jan Feliks Tarnowski (1777–1842), senator and castellan; and Stanisław

Tarnowski (1837–1917), critic and professor of literary history at the Jagellonian University in Kraków.
GIVEN NAMES Polish 4%. *Andrzej* (2), *Casimir, Ludwik, Tomasz, Zbigniew.*

Tarolli (102) Italian (Trento): unexplained.

Tarpey (383) Irish (Connacht and Munster): reduced Anglicized form of Gaelic **Ó Tarpaigh** 'descendant of *Tarpach*', a byname originally denoting a sturdy person.

Tarpinian (145) Armenian: patronymic from the personal name *Tarpin*, of unexplained origin.
GIVEN NAMES Armenian 17%. *Aram* (2), *Agop, Ara, Arax, Hasmig, Missak, Raffi, Sarkis, Vahe, Vartan.*

Tarpley (1343) Possibly a habitational name from Tarporley in Cheshire, recorded in Domesday Book (1086) as *Torpelei* and in 1281 as *Thorperlegh*, possibly from an unattested Old English word *thorpere* 'peasant', 'cottager' + *lēah* '(woodland) clearing'.

Tarpy (110) Possibly a variant of Irish TARPEY.

Tarquinio (272) Italian: from the personal name *Tarquinio*, from Latin *Tarquinius* (of Etruscan origin), borne by two early kings of Rome in the 7th and 6th centuries BC.
GIVEN NAMES Italian 17%. *Gino* (3), *Domenic* (2), *Salvatore* (2), *Amedeo, Angelo, Pasquale, Remo, Reno, Siro.*

Tarr (2864) **1.** English (southwestern England and South Wales): apparently from *tar* (Old English *te(o)ru*), and applied perhaps to someone who worked with tar or bitumen in waterproofing ships. **2.** Possibly an altered spelling of German **Tharr**, of uncertain origin.

Tarrance (222) Variant of Scottish and northern Irish TORRENCE.

Tarrant (1522) **1.** English (southern): topographic name for someone living on the banks of the Tarrant river in Dorset, of which the name is of the same origin as TRENT. **2.** Irish: reduced Anglicized form of Gaelic **Ó Toráin** (see TORRENS).

Tarrence (166) Variant of Scottish and northern Irish TORRENCE.
GIVEN NAMES Irish 6%. *Aidan, Brennan.*

Tarro (121) Southern Italian: apparently from a Germanic personal name, *Tarro, Terro.*
GIVEN NAME Italian 4%. *Angelo* (2).

Tarry (289) English: variant of TERRY 1.

Tarshis (128) Jewish (eastern Ashkenazic): **1.** ornamental from Hebrew *tarshish* 'chrysolite'. **2.** from the Biblical personal name Tarshish (Esther 1:14, 1 Chronicles 7:10), also a Biblical place name (Genesis 10:4).
GIVEN NAME Jewish 6%. *Izrael.*

Tarsi (116) Italian: unexplained.
GIVEN NAMES Italian 14%. *Aldo* (2), *Angelo* (2), *Giacomo* (2), *Elio, Evo, Geno.*

Tart (1119) **1.** English (West Midlands): from Old English *teart* 'sharp', 'rough',

used as a nickname and sometimes a personal name. **2.** Americanized spelling of French TARTE.

Tartaglia (805) Italian: nickname for a stammerer, from Italian *tartagliare* 'to stutter'. This is the name of a stock character in the Commedia del'Arte.
GIVEN NAMES Italian 11%. *Antonio* (3), *Nunzio* (3), *Angelo* (2), *Dante* (2), *Guido* (2), *Salvatore* (2), *Carmine, Cesidio, Domenico, Enrico, Erminio, Gino.*

Tartaglione (179) Italian: nickname from *tartaglione* 'stutterer'.
GIVEN NAMES Italian 17%. *Angelo* (3), *Antonio, Donato, Gaetano, Nichola, Sal.*

Tarte (225) **1.** English: variant spelling of TART. **2.** French: metonymic occupational name for a maker and seller of fine pastries, from Old French *tarte* 'tart', 'pastry'. **3.** Possibly an altered form of **Tartre**, a regional variant of **Tertre**, a habitational name from a common place name meaning 'height', 'hill'.
FOREBEARS A Tartre with the secondary surname LARIVIERE, from the Saintonge region of France, is documented in Montreal in 1697.
GIVEN NAMES French 10%. *Fernand* (2), *Marcel* (2), *Normand, Octavie.*

Tarter (1260) German: unexplained.

Tartt (242) English: variant spelling of TART.

Tarulli (101) Italian: from a diminutive of **Taro**, which Caracausi relates to a Germanic personal name *Tarro, Terro.*
GIVEN NAMES Italian 22%. *Vito* (3), *Rocco* (2), *Donato, Raffaele, Rosolino.*

Tarver (2630) English: unexplained.

Tarvin (770) English: habitational name from Tarvin in Cheshire, which takes its name from the earlier (Celtic) name of the Gowy river, meaning 'boundary (stream)'.

Tarwater (465) Americanized form of German **Turwachter** 'door (or gate) watchman'. Compare DEERWESTER, WACHTER.

Tarzia (117) Variant spelling of Italian **Tarsia**, either from a personal name derived from Greek *Tharsias*, or a habitational name from Tarsia in Cosenza province. *Tharsia* may have gained popularity as the name of the daughter of Apollonius of Tyre, in an eponymous romance that was popular in Europe in the Middle Ages.
GIVEN NAMES Italian 26%. *Cosimo* (2), *Angelo, Arturo, Domenic, Gilda, Gustavo, Nicola, Raffaela, Rocco.*

Tasca (166) Italian: possibly from a feminine form of the personal name *Tasco*, but more likely a metonymic occupational name for a maker of bags and pouches, from *tasca* 'bag', 'pouch'. Compare Old High German *tasca*.
GIVEN NAMES Italian 17%. *Angelo* (4), *Antonio* (2), *Amedeo, Carmelo, Domenic, Gino, Pasquale.*

Tasch (189) German (also **Täsch**): **1.** German: metonymic occupational name for a bagmaker, from Middle High German *tasche*, *tesche* 'pouch', 'bag', 'purse'; in some instances the surname may be topographical, from the same word in the sense 'pocket of land'. **2.** variant of TESCH.

GIVEN NAME German 4%. *Helmuth* (2).

Taschner (154) German (**Taschner**, **Täschner**): from an agent derivative of Middle High German *tasche* 'purse', 'pouch', 'bag' (genitive *taschen*), an occupational name for a maker of these, which were hung from the belt or carried on the back in the Middle Ages as garments had no pockets then.

GIVEN NAMES German 8%. *Hedwig*, *Helmut*, *Horst*, *Manfred*.

Tash (473) **1.** English: topographic name for someone who lived by an ash tree, from the Middle English phrase *at(te) asche* 'at (the) ash'. **2.** Jewish (Ashkenazic): metonymic occupational name for a maker or seller of bags and purses, from German *Tasche* 'bag', 'purse'. Compare TASCHNER.

Tashiro (194) Japanese: habitational name, written with characters for 'rice paddy' and 'generation', from villages in Izu (now part of Shizuoka prefecture), Ōsumi (now part of Kagoshima prefecture), and elsewhere.

GIVEN NAMES Japanese 49%. *Akira* (3), *Kazuo* (3), *Masaaki* (2), *Noriko* (2), *Satoru* (2), *Yosuke* (2), *Yukio* (2), *Aiko*, *Akihiko*, *Chieko*, *Chiyo*, *Chizuko*.

Tashjian (469) Armenian: patronymic from Turkish *taşçı* 'stonemason', from *taş* 'stone' + the occupational suffix *-ci*.

GIVEN NAMES Armenian 26%. *Arsen* (4), *Haig* (4), *Aram* (3), *Armen* (3), *Berj* (3), *Vahram* (3), *Berge* (2), *Deran* (2), *Kevork* (2), *Mesrob* (2), *Souren* (2), *Ara*.

Tashman (154) Jewish: occupational name for a maker or seller of bags and purses (see TASH).

GIVEN NAME German 4%. *Monika*.

Tasker (1093) **1.** English: occupational name for someone who did piece-work (especially someone who threshed grain), from an agent derivative of Anglo-Norman French *tasque* 'task' (Old French *tasche*, Late Latin *taxa*, of uncertain origin). **2.** Slovenian (**Tašker**): unexplained.

Taskey (115) Altered spelling of German **Taske** or **Taski**, of Slavic origin, from a personal name from the Slavic stem meaning 'to give'.

GIVEN NAME German 4%. *Kurt*.

Tasler (150) **1.** German: nickname for a womanizer or philanderer, from an agent derivative of Middle High German *taselen* 'to pat', 'to dally or flirt'. **2.** occupational name for a clasp maker, from Middle High German, Middle Low German *tassel* 'clasp', 'fastening'. **3.** Slovenian (**Tašler**): from a German occupational name for a bag maker, derived from Middle High German *tasche* 'purse', 'pouch', 'bag' (see TASCHNER).

Tassell (103) English: **1.** probably a habitational name from Tessel in Calvados. **2.** nickname for someone thought to resemble a hawk in some way, from Middle English *tassel* 'tercel', 'male hawk' (Old French *tiercel*).

Tassey (121) Variant spelling of Scottish TASSIE.

Tassi (141) **1.** Italian: patronymic or plural form of TASSO. **2.** Greek (**Tassis**): from a reduced form of the personal name *Anastasios* (see ANASTAS).

GIVEN NAMES Italian 12%; Spanish 4%. *Aldo*, *Angelo*, *Egidio*, *Guido*, *Mario*, *Nino*, *Veto*; *Alejandra*, *Carlos*.

Tassie (118) Scottish: according to Black, probably a nickname from a diminutive of French *taisson* 'badger'.

Tassin (550) French: from a diminutive of Old French *tasse* 'purse' (apparently of Arabic origin), hence a metonymic occupational name for a maker or seller of purses and bags, or nickname for a rich man or a miser.

GIVEN NAMES French 6%. *Anatole*, *Andre*, *Antoine*, *Aubert*, *Germaine*, *Heloise*, *Lucien*, *Marcel*, *Orelia*, *Sylvian*.

Tassinari (302) Italian (mainly Liguria): from a derivative of TASSO.

GIVEN NAMES Italian 11%. *Amedeo* (2), *Enrico* (2), *Remo* (2), *Arrigo*, *Dante*, *Dario*, *Dino*, *Leno*, *Silvio*, *Ugo*.

Tasso (161) **1.** Italian: topographic name for someone who lived near a prominent yew tree, Italian *tasso* (Latin *taxus*, genitive *taxi*). **2.** Italian: from a Germanic personal name derived from the obscure element *tāt*, possibly akin to Old High German *tāt* 'deed'. Compare English TATE. **3.** nickname for a person thought to resemble a badger, for example in his nocturnal habits, from Italian *tasso* 'badger' (Late Latin *taxo*, genitive *taxonis*, of Germanic origin). **4.** Greek (**Tassos**): from a reduced form of the personal name *Anastasios* (see ANASTAS) or a patronymic derived from it, such as **Anastasopoulos**.

GIVEN NAMES Italian 6%; German 4%. *Carmine*, *Giancarlo*, *Gianpaolo*, *Lorenzo*; *Dieter* (2).

Tassone (531) Italian: from an augmentative form of TASSO.

GIVEN NAMES Italian 20%. *Vito* (5), *Rocco* (4), *Sal* (3), *Angelo* (2), *Cosimo* (2), *Cosmo* (2), *Ettore* (2), *Giovanni* (2), *Guerino* (2), *Domenico*, *Fiore*, *Francesco*.

Tastad (106) Norwegian: habitational name from a farmstead in Rogland named Tasta.

GIVEN NAMES Scandinavian 7%. *Jalmer*, *Selmer*.

Tat (201) Vietnamese: unexplained.

GIVEN NAMES Vietnamese 40%; Chinese 24%. *Ha* (6), *Muoi* (6), *Ha To* (3), *Nguu* (3), *Thang* (3), *Vinh* (3), *Chau* (2), *Cuong* (2), *Dao* (2), *Minh* (2), *Mui* (2), *Trinh* (2); *Dong* (2), *Han*, *Hon*, *Kin*, *Lung*, *Man*, *Tang*, *Tong*; *Chang*, *Nam*, *Sieu*, *Tuong*.

Tata (305) **1.** Italian: from the Germanic personal name *Tata*, *Tada*. **2.** Indian (Gujarat and Bombay city): Parsi name, probably from Gujarati *tat* 'father' (Sanskrit *tāta*). **3.** Albanian and Greek (**Tatas**): nickname from Albanian *tatë* 'father', 'daddy'. **4.** Turkish and Greek: nickname for a stammerer, from Turkish and Arabic *ta'ta* 'stammer'. **5.** Polish: nickname from Polish *tata* 'papa', 'daddy'.

GIVEN NAMES Italian 16%; Indian 9%. *Angelo* (4), *Rocco* (2), *Salvatore* (2), *Antonio*, *Giovanni*, *Giulio*, *Luca*, *Manfredo*, *Pasquale*, *Rinaldo*, *Vincenzo*; *Madhukar* (2), *Anjali*, *Bhavani*, *Prasad*, *Rajiv*, *Ratan*, *Sundari*, *Suresh*, *Vijay*.

Tatar (368) Czech, Slovak, Polish, Hungarian (**Tatár**), and Jewish (eastern Ashkenazic): ethnic name or nickname from *tatar* 'Tatar'. In some languages, e.g. Czech, the word came to be used as a nickname for a wild or uncontrolled man, while in 18th-century Hungary it became a nickname for a godless person. In some cases the name was given to people who had been captured by the Tatars. The surname is also found in Greek in the form **Tataris** and patronymic derivatives such as **Tatarakis**, **Tataridis**, and **Tataroglou**.

GIVEN NAMES German 4%. *Otto* (2), *Theodor*, *Wilhelm*.

Tate (21264) English: from the Old English personal name *Tāta*, possibly a short form of various compound names with the obscure first element *tāt*, or else a nursery formation. This surname is common and widespread in Britain; the chief area of concentration is northeastern England, followed by northern Ireland.

Tatem (364) English: variant of TATHAM.

Tates (149) English: patronymic from the Old English personal name *Tāt*, an unrecorded variant of *Tāta* (see TATE).

GIVEN NAME French 7%. *Andre* (2).

Tatge (232) Frisian and North German: variant of Low German **Thiedeke**, a personal name based on Old Saxon *thiod-*, Germanic *theudo-* 'people' (see TACK).

Tatham (419) English: habitational name from a place in northern Lancashire, so named from the Old English personal name *Tāta* (see TATE) + Old English *hām* 'homestead'.

Tatlock (185) English: probably a habitational name from a lost or unidentified place in Lancashire or Cheshire, where the surname occurs most frequently.

Tatman (971) English: either a name denoting the servant (Middle English *man*) of a man called TATE, or from an unattested Old English personal name, *Tātmann*.

Tatom (472) Probably a variant of English TATHAM.

Taton (114) English: probably a variant spelling of TATTON.

Tator (114) Origin unidentified. Possibly an altered spelling of German **Tatter**, from

Middle High German *Tater* 'goblin', 'puppet', a nickname for a puppeteer.

Tatro (1767) Americanized form of French TÉTR(E)AULT.

Tatsch (194) German: perhaps from Low German *tatsche* 'paw', hence a nickname for someone with large hands.

Tattersall (270) English (mainly Lancashire): habitational name from Tattershall in Lincolnshire, named from the genitive of the Old English personal name *Tāthere* (composed of an obscure element *tāt* + *here* 'army') + Old English *halh* 'nook', 'recess'. The surname has been common in Lancashire from an early period.

Tatton (131) English: habitational name from places in Cheshire and Dorset named Tatton, from the Old English personal name *Tāta* (see TATE) + Old English *tūn* 'enclosure', 'settlement'.

Tatum (7465) English (Essex): variant of TATHAM.

Taub (1265) German and Jewish (Ashkenazic): 1. variant of TAUBE 1. 2. nickname for a deaf person, from Middle High German *toup*, German *taub* 'deaf'. The adjective also had the sense 'dull', 'stupid', and this may lie behind some examples of the German name.
GIVEN NAMES Jewish 12%. *Hyman* (4), *Aron* (3), *Moshe* (3), *Shmuel* (3), *Asher* (2), *Chaim* (2), *Mayer* (2), *Meyer* (2), *Shaul* (2), *Sol* (2), *Tova* (2), *Yerachmiel* (2).

Taube (658) 1. German and Jewish (Ashkenazic): from German *Taube* 'pigeon', 'dove' (Middle High German *tūbe*). The German name is either a metonymic occupational name for a keeper of doves or pigeons or a nickname for a mild and gentle person; the Jewish surname is ornamental. 2. Jewish (Ashkenazic): from the Yiddish female personal name *Toybe* (from Yiddish *toyb* 'dove').
GIVEN NAMES German 5%. *Fritz, Gerhard, Gunter, Heinrich, Kurt, Otto, Wolfram.*

Tauber (1029) 1. German: variant of TAUBE 1 'pigeon', 'dove'. The *-er* inflection denotes the male bird, but in most cases this is an occupational name for a pigeon breeder, from an agent noun derivative ending in *-er(t)*. 2. German and Jewish (Ashkenazic): variant of TAUB 2, with the strong inflectional ending *-er*, originally used before a male personal name. 3. German: occupational name for a player of the horn or a similar musical instrument, Middle High German *toubære*.
GIVEN NAMES Jewish 9%; German 4%. *Chaim* (4), *Hillel* (3), *Yitzchok* (3), *Aron* (2), *Elchonon* (2), *Ezriel* (2), *Moshe* (2), *Shachar* (2), *Shlomy* (2), *Aba, Ben Zion, Benzion; Kurt* (2), *Otto* (2), *Aloysius, Armin, Frieda, Ilse, Katharina, Konrad, Manfred, Uwe.*

Taubert (263) German (**Taubert, Täubert**): 1. variant of TAUBE 1, from Middle High German *tūber, tiuber*, Middle Low German

duver 'male dove or pigeon'. 2. occupational name from Middle High German *toeber, toiber* 'wind player'.
GIVEN NAMES German 7%. *Frieda, Fritz, Gunter, Heinz, Helmut, Wilfried.*

Taubman (306) Jewish (Ashkenazic): 1. variant of TAUBE 1 and 2. 2. variant of TAUB 2.
GIVEN NAMES Jewish 8%. *Gershon* (2), *Miriam, Yael.*

Taucher (198) 1. German: habitational name for someone from Taucha near Leipzig or from Tauche on the Spree river, derived from a Slavic place-name element, *Tuch-*. 2. South German: topographic name from dialect *Dauch* 'wetland', 'swamp'. 3. Americanized spelling of Slovenian **Tavčer**, an old Slovenian dialect spelling of the German ethnic name DEUTSCHER 'German'.

Tauer (376) 1. German (Silesian): habitational name from the fairly common Silesian place name Tauer. 2. North German: occupational name for a tanner. 3. South German: variant of TAUCHER 2.
GIVEN NAMES German 4%. *Otto* (3), *Alois, Erwin.*

Taugher (127) Americanized spelling of German TAUCHER.

Taul (283) Danish: short form of the habitational name Taulov.

Taulbee (911) Origin unidentified. Perhaps a variant of DALBY.

Taulman (108) Americanized spelling of Dutch TALMAN.

Taunton (564) English: habitational name from Taunton in Somerset, Taunton Farm in Coulsdon, Surrey, or Tanton in North Yorkshire. The Somerset place name was originally a combination of a Celtic river name (now the Tone, possibly meaning 'roaring stream') + Old English *tūn* 'enclosure', 'settlement'. The Surrey name is possibly from Old English *tān* 'branch', 'stalk' + *tūn*, while Tanton was named in Old English as 'settlement (*tūn*) on the Tame', another Celtic river name.

Tauriello (151) Italian: unexplained. In Italy the surname is associated chiefly with San Fele in Potenza province.
GIVEN NAME Italian 7%. *Rocco.*

Tauro (101) Italian: most probably a nickname from Sicilian and southern Italian *tauro* 'bull', 'ox' (Latin *taurus*).
GIVEN NAMES Italian 13%. *Benito, Raniero, Romeo, Saverio.*

Taus (146) Jewish (Ashkenazic) and German (also **Tauss**): habitational name from Taus in Bohemia (Czech Domažlice, Yiddish Toysk).
GIVEN NAME Jewish 4%. *Naum.*

Tausch (223) German: nickname or metonymic occupational name from Middle High German *tūsch* 'trick' or 'barter'. This is a common surname in Munich.
GIVEN NAMES German 7%. *Egon, Gerda, Hans, Johannes, Kurt.*

Tauscher (417) German (also **Täuscher**): 1. occupational name for a barterer, market trader, from Middle High German *tūscher*. 2. nickname from the alternative sense 'cheat', 'deceiver' (see TAUSCH).
GIVEN NAMES German 5%. *Hans, Kurt, Wenzel, Wilhelm.*

Taussig (252) Jewish (from Bohemia): Germanized form of *Toysk*, the Yiddish name for the Czech town of Domažlice (see TAUS).

Taute (119) German: 1. from a short form of the personal name DIETRICH or possibly, as Bahlow proposes, from the old personal name *Tuto*. 2. from an Old Prussian name.

Tautges (108) German: from a short form of any of the many Germanic personal names formed with *theod* 'people', 'tribe'. Compare DAUT.

Tauzin (236) French (southwestern): topographic name denoting someone who lived by a dwarf oak.
GIVEN NAMES French 9%. *Lucien* (2), *Dominique, Elmire, Emile, Leonce.*

Tavakoli (119) Iranian: from a personal name based on Arabic *tawakkul* 'trust in Allah'.
GIVEN NAMES Muslim 76%. *Ahmad* (3), *Ali* (2), *Assad* (2), *Ghassem* (2), *Hamid* (2), *Mohammad* (2), *Nader* (2), *Nassrin* (2), *Abbas, Abolfazl, Ali Reza, Ameer.*

Tavani (109) Italian: patronymic or plural form of TAVANO.
GIVEN NAMES Italian 16%. *Domenic* (2), *Filiberto, Gaetano.*

Tavano (186) Southern Italian: unflattering nickname for an irritating person, from *tavano* 'horsefly'.
GIVEN NAMES Italian 21%. *Carlo, Cataldo, Donato, Eduardo, Elvira, Fabrizio, Fiore, Marcello, Mario, Sal, Salvatore, Sergio, Vito.*

Tavares (2418) 1. Portuguese: habitational name from any of at least seven minor places so called. 2. Tavarés: variant of **Tabarés** (see TABARES).
GIVEN NAMES Spanish 26%; Portuguese 13%. *Manuel* (65), *Jose* (48), *Carlos* (23), *Fernando* (12), *Juan* (12), *Luis* (8), *Pedro* (8), *Jorge* (7), *Humberto* (6), *Julio* (6), *Ana* (5), *Dulce* (5); *Joao* (18), *Paulo* (6), *Duarte* (5), *Joaquim* (5), *Henrique* (2), *Armanda, Goncalo, Guilherme, Ligia, Margarida.*

Tavarez (687) Variant spelling of Portuguese TAVARES.
GIVEN NAMES Spanish 54%. *Jose* (40), *Juan* (12), *Rafael* (10), *Manuel* (9), *Pedro* (8), *Ana* (7), *Francisco* (7), *Luis* (7), *Carlos* (6), *Luz* (6), *Ramon* (6), *Jesus* (5).

Tavel (170) French: 1. from Old French *tavel* 'braid', 'ribbon', hence a metonymic occupational name for a maker or seller of such items. 2. habitational name from a place so called in Gard.

Tavella (157) Italian: from Neapolitan or Old Italian *tavella* 'board', 'plank', 'slab' (from Latin *tabella*), presumably a nickname for someone who was tall and thin, or perhaps a metonymic occupational name for a woodworker.

GIVEN NAMES Italian 31%. *Antonio* (2), *Domenico* (2), *Angelo, Antonino, Carmelo, Concetta, Cosmo, Domenic, Fernando, Nino, Paolo, Pasquale, Rocco.*

Tavenner (335) English: occupational name for an innkeeper, Anglo-Norman French *taverner* (Old French *tavernier*, Late Latin *tabernarius* from *taberna* 'shop', 'inn').

Tavera (200) Spanish: variant of **Tabera**, a habitational name from Tabera in Salamanca province, or variant of **Tabeira**, a Galician habitational name from Tabeira in A Coruña, Galicia.

GIVEN NAMES Spanish 56%. *Jose* (9), *Francisca* (3), *Andres* (2), *Arturo* (2), *Carlos* (2), *Carolina* (2), *Delfino* (2), *Enriqueta* (2), *Evelia* (2), *Mario* (2), *Ramon* (2), *Abelino.*

Taveras (681) Probably Spanish, though not found in present-day Spain: a plural form of TAVERA.

GIVEN NAMES Spanish 55%. *Rafael* (17), *Jose* (16), *Ana* (15), *Luis* (11), *Miguel* (10), *Juan* (9), *Francisco* (8), *Juana* (8), *Carlos* (7), *Luz* (7), *Altagracia* (6), *Ramon* (6).

Taverna (276) Italian: **1.** metonymic occupational name for an innkeeper, from *taverna* 'inn', 'tavern'. **2.** habitational name from any of the many places in southern Italy named with this word, in particular one in Catanzaro province. **3.** Possibly also a shortened form of Greek **Tavernakis, Tavern(i)aris** 'tavernkeeper'.

GIVEN NAMES Italian 17%. *Vito* (5), *Angelo* (2), *Carmine* (2), *Caesar, Carmelo, Domenic, Giuseppe, Raffaele, Rocco.*

Tavernier (306) French: occupational name from Old French *tavernier* 'innkeeper' (Late Latin *tabernarius* from *taberna* 'shop', 'inn').

FOREBEARS A Tavernier from the Perche region of France is documented in Beaupré, Quebec in 1666 with the variant **Letavernier.**

GIVEN NAMES French 6%. *Edouard, Patrice, Rodolphe.*

Taves (202) Americanized form of German TEWES.

GIVEN NAME German 6%. *Kurt* (2).

Tavis (185) Americanized form of German TEWES.

Tavitian (75) Armenian: western Armenian form of DAVIDIAN.

Tavolacci (106) Italian: unexplained; possibly from medieval Greek *tavoularios* 'archivist', from Latin *tabula* (see TAVOULARIS).

GIVEN NAMES Italian 16%. *Salvatore* (2), *Antonino.*

Tavoularis (42) Greek: from medieval Greek *tavoularis* 'amanuensis', 'secretary', 'literary assistant', an agent noun derived from *tavoula*, Latin *tabula* 'writing tablet'.

Tawes (122) **1.** Probably a variant of English, Scottish, and German DAWES. **2.** Altered spelling of German TEWES.

Tawil (404) Muslim and Jewish (Sephardic): from a personal name or nickname based on Arabic *ṭawīl* 'tall'.

GIVEN NAMES Muslim 16%; Jewish 6%. *Mohamad* (3), *Hani* (2), *Imad* (2), *Jamal* (2), *Nabil* (2), *Nadir* (2), *Ramzi* (2), *Ahmad, Amin, Asad, Ayoub, Bassam; Hyman* (2), *Meyer* (2), *Nissim* (2), *Arye, Hillel, Sol, Yigal.*

Tawney (570) English (of Norman origin): habitational name from either of two places, Saint-Aubin-du-Thennay or Saint-Jean-du-Thennay, in Eure, Normandy, both so named from an uncertain first element (possibly a Gallo-Roman personal name or the Gaulish word *tann* 'oak', 'holly') + the locative suffix *-acum*.

Tax (119) **1.** Spanish: perhaps a topographic name from Portuguese and Galician *teixo* 'yew tree' (Latin *taxus*). **2.** German: nickname from Middle High German *dahs* 'badger', also perhaps an occupational name for a breeder of dachshunds or for a hunter who used them.

GIVEN NAMES Spanish 9%; German 4%. *Alberto* (2), *Agustin, Alfonso, Elena, Feliciano, Josue, Luisa, Rosario.*

Tay (286) **1.** English: possibly a variant of TYE. **2.** Jewish (from Poland): metonymic occupational name for a tea merchant, from central Yiddish *tay* 'tea'. **3.** Chinese 郑: variant of ZHENG.

GIVEN NAMES Chinese 8%; Vietnamese 4%. *Soo* (2), *Chhay, Chin, Choo, Eng, Han, Heng, Khin, Li-Mei, Meng, Ming, Sang; Dung, Loi, Thang, Thong, Tu.*

Tayler (204) English: variant spelling of TAYLOR.

Tayloe (258) Possibly a variant of English TAYLOR.

Taylor (241254) English and Scottish: occupational name for a tailor, from Old French *tailleur* (Late Latin *taliator*, from *taliare* 'to cut'). The surname is extremely common in Britain and Ireland, and its numbers have been swelled by its adoption as an Americanized form of the numerous equivalent European names, most of which are also very common among Ashkenazic Jews, for example SCHNEIDER, SZABÓ, and PORTNOV.

Tayman (226) **1.** Possibly an altered spelling of German **Dehmann** (see DEMANN). **2.** English (Surrey): unexplained.

Taynor (100) Possibly an Americanized form of German DEHNER.

Tays (240) Probably an altered form of TAY.

Tazelaar (138) Dutch (Zeeland): variant of *'t Hazelaar*, topographic name for someone living by hazel bushes.

GIVEN NAMES Dutch 4%. *Egbert, Willem.*

Te (139) **1.** Chinese: possibly a variant of DAI. **2.** Filipino: unexplained.

GIVEN NAMES Chinese 21%; Vietnamese 7%; Spanish 7%. *Heang* (2), *Heng* (2), *Chheng, Eng, Kheng, Khun, Sang, Seng, Sung; Anh, Hoa, Huong, Mang, Thao, Thong; Angelita, Arturo, Enrique, Guillermo, Renato, Rosario.*

Tea (194) **1.** English (Gloucestershire): probably a variant of TYE. Compare TEE. **2.** Perhaps also an Americanized spelling of German THIE. **3.** Cambodian: unexplained.

GIVEN NAMES Southeast Asian 11%; Vietnamese 4%. *Yin* (2), *Bak, Boon, Chak, Heng, Him, Hing, Tong; Huy, Ngo, Nguon, Thy, Tien.*

Teach (271) **1.** Americanized spelling of South German and Swiss DIETSCH. **2.** Americanized spelling of Swiss German **Dütsch** or **Tütsch**, Alemannic forms of DEUTSCH.

Teachey (373) **1.** Americanized spelling of Swiss **Dietschi** or South German **Dietsche** (see DIETSCH). **2.** Americanized spelling of German TIETJE.

Teachman (113) Perhaps an Americanization of German **Lehrmann**, which was construed as deriving from *lehren* 'to teach', in fact a habitational name for someone from Lehre in Lower Saxony.

GIVEN NAME German 4%. *Kurt.*

Teachout (550) Altered form of Dutch **Ti(e)tsoort**; unexplained.

FOREBEARS A family of this name from Schenectady, NY, moved to Port Jervis, NY on the Delaware River after the massacre during Leisler's Rebellion of Schenectady in 1690.

Teaff (145) Probably an Americanized spelling of German **Tief**: **1.** from the Germanic personal name *Theudofrid* (from *þeudo-* 'people' + *fridu* 'peace'). **2.** topographic name for someone who lived in low-lying terrain, from Middle High German *tief* 'low', or a habitational name from Tiefen in Baden.

Teaford (241) Americanized spelling of German **Tiefert** or **Tiffert**, variants of **Tief** (see TEAFF), or possibly an Americanized spelling of **Differt**, a habitational name from Differeden, Saarland.

Teagarden (269) Dutch and North German: see TEEGARDEN.

Teagle (348) **1.** English (Wiltshire and Gloucestershire): unexplained. **2.** Possibly an Americanized spelling of German **Diegel** or Swiss **Digel**, from a short form of a Germanic personal name formed with *þeudo-* 'people', 'tribe'.

Teague (8557) **1.** Irish: variant of TIGHE. **2.** Cornish and Welsh: descriptive nickname for a handsome person, from Cornish *tek*, Welsh *teg* 'fair', 'beautiful'. There has been considerable confusion between the Welsh and Irish names, both in Wales and Ireland.

Teahan (175) Irish (Kerry): reduced Anglicized form of Gaelic **Ó Téacháin** 'descen-

dant of *Téachán*', a personal name proba-
bly derived from *teitheachán* 'fugitive'.
GIVEN NAMES Irish 9%. *Dermot, Donal,
Siobhan.*

Teakell (108) See TEAGLE.

Teal (2962) **1.** English (mainly Yorkshire):
from Middle English *tele* 'teal' (of uncertain origin), hence a nickname for a person
considered to resemble this duck. **2.** Americanized spelling of German DIEHL or
THIEL.

Teale (230) Variant of TEAL.

Teall (206) Variant of TEAL.

Teamer (161) Possibly an Americanized
spelling of German DIEMER.

Teaney (140) **1.** Irish: variant of **O'Taheny**,
O'Teheny, Anglicized forms of Gaelic **Ó
Teitheanaigh**, from the same root as
TEAHAN. **2.** Possibly an Americanized
spelling of German and Swiss DIENER.

Tear (104) **1.** Scottish: variant of MCIN-
TYRE. **2.** Possibly an altered spelling of
German THIER.

Teare (233) Scottish: reduced variant of
MCINTYRE.

Teas (248) Probably an Americanized spelling of German THIES(S).

Teasdale (540) northern English: variant
spelling of TEESDALE.

Tease (135) English: unexplained.

Teasley (1123) Possibly an Americanized
form of Swiss and South German **Düssli**,
unexplained.

Teaster (225) English: unexplained.

Teat (227) Probably an Americanized
spelling of German **Thiet**, a variant of
THIEDE.

Teate (128) Probably an Americanized
spelling of German **Thiet** (see TEAT) or
THIEDE.

Teater (385) Probably an altered spelling of
German DIETER.

Teats (185) Americanized spelling of South
German TIETZ or DIETZ.

Tebay (130) **1.** English: habitational name
from Tebay in Cumbria. **2.** Respelling
of German **Tiebe**, from a short form of
several names formed with *theod* 'people'
as the first element. Compare DIEBEL,
TEBBE.

Tebbe (500) North German and Frisian:
from a pet form of any of the masculine or
feminine compound personal names with
the first element *Det-, Diet-* (Germanic
theudo- 'people', 'race') and a second element beginning with *b-* (e.g. *-bern* 'bear',
-brand 'sword', or *-burg* 'castle', 'fortified
town').

Tebben (194) North German and Frisian:
patronymic (or metronymic) from TEBBE.

Tebbetts (237) English: variant of TIB-
BETTS.

Tebbs (198) English: variant of TIBBS.

Tebeau (224) French: variant of THIBAULT.

Tebo (635) New England spelling of French
THIBAULT.

Tebow (114) Origin unidentified.

Tech (169) German (of Slavic origin) and
Czech: variant of TESCH.
GIVEN NAMES German 7%. *Kurt* (2), *Dietmar,
Jutta.*

Tecklenburg (114) German: habitational
name from a place so called in North
Rhine-Westphalia.

Tedder (1913) English: possibly from an
Old English personal name, *þeodhere,*
composed of elements meaning 'people',
'folk', 'nation' and 'army'.

Teddy (122) English: unexplained.

Tedeschi (891) Italian and Jewish (from
Italy): patronymic from TEDESCO.
GIVEN NAMES Italian 13%. *Angelo* (5), *Vito*
(4), *Marino* (3), *Aldo* (2), *Cosmo* (2),
Domenic (2), *Rocco* (2), *Vittorio* (2),
Antonio, Dante, Dino, Erminio.

Tedesco (2228) Italian and Jewish (from
Italy): ethnic name denoting someone of
German origin, from Italian *tedesco* 'Ger-
man', Old High German *diutisc* (see
DEUTSCH). As a Jewish name, it was given
to or taken by Ashkenazic Jews in Italy.
GIVEN NAMES Italian 14%. *Angelo* (16),
Salvatore (6), *Luigi* (4), *Pasquale* (4),
Rocco (4), *Vito* (4), *Guiseppe* (3), *Aldo* (2),
Antonio (2), *Sal* (2), *Santo* (2).

Tedford (1275) Scottish and northern Irish:
unexplained. Sean de Bhulbh believes it to
be an English habitational name, but no
likely source has been identified.

Tedone (101) Italian: **1.** from a personal
name of Germanic origin formed with the
element *þeudō-* 'people', 'race'. **2.** from a
derivative of Sicilian *teda* 'pine' (the wood).
GIVEN NAMES Italian 18%. *Gaetano* (2),
Cosmo, Natale.

Tedrick (403) German: variant spelling of
DEDRICK.

Tedrow (713) Americanized form of Ger-
man DOTTERER.
FOREBEARS Family historians report that
Reuben Tedrow (b. September 1759) is
recorded as such in the family Bible, and in
Lutheran church records in New Hanover,
Montgomery Co., PA, as the son of
Michael and Catharina Dotterer. The fami-
ly are believed to have originated in
Stebbach, Baden, Germany.

Tee (275) English (Yorkshire): variant of
TYE.

Teed (602) English: unexplained.

Teegarden (696) Americanized spelling of
Dutch and North German **Theegarten**, a
topographic name from Low German *te
garden* 'at the garden or enclosed plot'.

Teegardin (177) Americanized spelling of
Dutch and German **Theegarten** (see
TEEGARDEN).

Teehan (227) Irish (south midlands): variant spelling of TEAHAN.
GIVEN NAME Irish 7%. *Brendan* (2).

Teel (3001) **1.** Probably an Americanized
spelling of German THIEL. **2.** Possibly also

English or Scottish: variant spelling of
TEAL.

Teele (276) See TEEL.

Teeling (162) **1.** English and Irish: unexplained; most probably a habitational name
from a lost or unidentified place somewhere in South Wales or southern England.
This name was established in County
Meath, Ireland, soon after the Anglo-
Norman invasion of the 12th century.
2. Dutch: unexplained. **3.** Probably a
respelling of German **Tiling**, a patronymic
form of THIEL.

Teem (138) Americanized spelling of Dutch
and German THIEM, possibly of THIEME
and also of German DIEHM or DIEM.

Teems (381) Probably an Americanized
spelling of German **Thiems**, a patronymic
from THIEM(E).

Teeple (725) Probably an Americanized
spelling of German DIEBEL.

Teeples (285) Variant of TEEPLE.

Teer (703) **1.** English: probably a variant
spelling of TEAR. **2.** Perhaps also a reduced form of Irish MCTEER. **3.** Americanized spelling of German THIER or DIER.

Teesdale (139) Northern English: regional
name from Teesdale in northeastern
England, which is named for the river *Tees*
(named with Old English *(ge)twis* 'forking', 'river fork') + Old English *dæl* 'valley'.

Teeter (2194) Americanized form of German DIETER.

Teeters (1079) Variant of TEETER, with the
addition of *-s*, a common feature of adapted
German surnames in the U.S.

Teetor (129) Americanized form of German
DIETER.

Teets (1020) Americanized form of German
DIETZ or DIEZ.

Teffeteller (214) Americanized form of
German **Diefenthäler**, a habitational name
for someone from Diefenthal in Alsace or
from any of three places in southern Germany called Tiefenthal, all named with
Middle High German *tief* 'deep' + *tal* 'valley'.

Tefft (795) Variant of English TAFT. This
surname was already well established in
CT and RI by 1715.

Tegarden (109) See TEEGARDEN.

Tegeler (385) North German: occupational
name for a tiler, from an agent derivative of
Low German *tegel* 'tile'. Compare TYLER.

Tegen (142) German: from Low German
teege 'tithe', presumably denoting a tithe
collector.
GIVEN NAMES French 6%. *Colette, Collette,
Thierry.*

Tegethoff (198) North German: from
Middle Low German *teget, teigent* 'tithe' +
hof 'farmstead', 'manor farm', hence a
habitational name for someone who lived at
a farmstead where tithes were collected.

Tegge (172) North German: **1.** from Middle Low German *tege* 'tithe', hence a metonymic occupational name for someone who collected tithes. **2.** from a Germanic personal name (see TACK).
GIVEN NAMES German 5%. *Hans, Lothar, Rudi.*

Tegtmeier (341) German: status name for a steward (see MEYER) who collected tithes (Middle Low German *teget, teigent* 'tithe').

Tegtmeyer (223) Variant of German TEGTMEIER.
GIVEN NAMES German 9%. *Egon, Gunther, Herta, Kurt, Otto, Rainer, Volker.*

Teh (127) **1.** Chinese 郑: variant of ZHENG. **2.** Filipino: unexplained.
GIVEN NAMES Chinese 39%. *Eng* (3), *Guan* (3), *Kan* (2), *Yin* (2), *Cheng, Chin, Hin, Jin, Lim, Pek, Pin, Poh; Chong, Kok, Siew.*

Tehan (253) Irish (Counties Tipperary, Leix, and Kilkenny): variant of TEAHAN.

Tehrani (255) Iranian and Jewish (from Iran): habitational name for someone from the city of Tehran, capital of Iran.
GIVEN NAMES Muslim 71%. *Ali* (5), *Amir* (5), *Ahmad* (3), *Majid* (3), *Masoud* (3), *Mehdi* (3), *Mohammad* (3), *Nasser* (3), *Abbas* (2), *Bahram* (2), *Farideh* (2), *Fereidoon* (2).

Teich (577) German and Jewish (Ashkenazic): topographic name from Middle High German *tīch* 'dike', 'dam', or '(fish)pond', German *Teich* 'pond'. In some cases the Jewish surname was topographic, from Yiddish *taykh* 'river'; otherwise it was ornamental.

Teicher (244) German and Jewish (Ashkenazic): topographic name for someone who lived by a fishpond, from TEICH + the suffix *-er*, denoting an inhabitant.
GIVEN NAMES Jewish 8%. *Avrohom* (2), *Rifka* (2), *Aron, Chaya, Miriam.*

Teichert (232) German: variant of TEICHER.
GIVEN NAMES German 12%. *Egon* (2), *Franz, Gerhart, Helmut, Horst, Kurt, Otto, Ulrich.*

Teichman (513) Variant spelling of Jewish or respelling of German TEICHMANN.
GIVEN NAMES Jewish 12%; German 4%. *Moshe* (3), *Sol* (2), *Aron, Avraham, Avrohom, Gerson, Haim, Hyman, Mayer, Miriam, Moishe, Mordechai; Erhard, Franz, Jutta.*

Teichmann (153) German and Jewish (Ashkenazic): variant of TEICH.
GIVEN NAMES German 22%. *Eberhard* (2), *Gerhard* (2), *Heinz* (2), *Erwin, Friedrich, Fritz, Hans, Horst, Kurt, Otto, Reiner, Rudi.*

Teig (178) **1.** German and Jewish (Ashkenazic): metonymic occupational name for a baker, from Middle High German *teic* (modern German *Teig*) 'dough', Yiddish *teyg*. **2.** Norwegian: habitational name from any of three farmsteads, so named from Old Norse *teigr* 'strip of land'.
GIVEN NAMES French 5%. *Andre, Lucien.*

Teigen (472) Norwegian: habitational name from any of numerous farmsteads all over Norway, named with the definite singular of *teig*, from Old Norse *teigr* 'strip of land'.
GIVEN NAMES Scandinavian 7%. *Helmer, Obert, Selmer.*

Teigland (145) Norwegian: habitational name from any of several farmsteads in Hordaland, named in Old Norse as either *Telgland* or *Teigland*. In each case, the second element is *land* 'piece of land'; the first elements are respectively *telg* 'bracken', 'fern' and *teigr* 'strip of land'.
GIVEN NAME Scandinavian 11%. *Hjordis.*

Teinert (143) Altered or variant spelling of German **Theinert**, from a Germanic personal name, composed of Old High German *degan* 'warrior', 'vassel' + *hart* 'strong'.
GIVEN NAMES German 11%. *Otto, Reinhold, Traugott.*

Teitel (183) Jewish (Ashkenazic): **1.** ornamental from Yiddish *teytl* 'date' (the fruit). **2.** occupational nickname for a teacher, from Yiddish *taytl* 'pointer'.
GIVEN NAMES Jewish 4%. *Emanuel, Shosh.*

Teitelbaum (1024) Jewish (eastern Ashkenazic): ornamental name from Yiddish *teytlboym* 'date palm' (from Middle High German *tahtel* 'date' + *boum* 'tree').
GIVEN NAMES Jewish 22%. *Chaim* (9), *Boruch* (5), *Meyer* (5), *Sol* (5), *Menashe* (4), *Sholem* (4), *Hyman* (3), *Leibish* (3), *Miriam* (3), *Hershel* (2), *Mendel* (2), *Moishe* (2).

Teitelman (128) Jewish: ornamental name, a variant of TEITELBAUM.
GIVEN NAMES Jewish 9%; Russian 5%. *Emanuel* (3), *Herzl, Jakov; Boris* (2), *Betya, Efim, Mordko.*

Teitler (161) Jewish (Ashkenazic): from TEITEL with the addition of the agent suffix *-er*.
GIVEN NAMES Jewish 10%; German 5%. *Hyman, Limor, Morty, Nir; Theodor.*

Teixeira (1893) Portuguese and Galician: habitational name from any of the places in Portugal and Galicia named Teixeira (written *Teijeira* in Castilian Spanish), from a derivative of Portuguese and Galician *teixo* 'yew tree' (Latin *taxus*).
GIVEN NAMES Spanish 22%; Portuguese 16%. *Manuel* (61), *Jose* (41), *Carlos* (17), *Mario* (17), *Fernando* (9), *Luis* (8), *Jorge* (6), *Adelino* (5), *Alvaro* (5), *Pedro* (5), *Aida* (4), *Augusto* (3); *Joao* (23), *Paulo* (8), *Henrique* (5), *Marcio* (3), *Joaquim* (2), *Manoel* (2), *Albano, Duarte, Guilherme, Ilidio, Vasco; Antonio* (49), *Albertina, Angelo, Augustino, Fabiano, Firmino, Flavio, Francesco, Luciano, Ludovina, Rosangela, Silvio.*

Tejada (1125) Spanish: probably a habitational name from a place named Tejada, most likely the one in Burgos province but possibly the one in Huelva province, so named from a derivative of *teja* '(roof) tile'.
GIVEN NAMES Spanish 51%. *Jose* (34), *Carlos* (22), *Juan* (19), *Luis* (12), *Miguel* (12), *Ana* (11), *Rafael* (10), *Ramon* (10), *Francisco* (7), *Manuel* (7), *Roberto* (7), *Jesus* (6).

Tejeda (1038) Spanish: habitational name from any of the numerous places (in Cáceres, Gran Canaria, and Toledo) named Tejeda, from a collective form of *tejo* 'yew tree' (Latin *taxus*).
GIVEN NAMES Spanish 56%. *Jose* (32), *Juan* (19), *Manuel* (19), *Ramon* (13), *Jesus* (12), *Luis* (11), *Carlos* (10), *Sergio* (10), *Ana* (9), *Francisco* (9), *Miguel* (9), *Roberto* (8).

Tejera (149) Spanish: habitational name from any of the numerous places named Tejera, from a derivative of *tejo* 'yew tree' (Latin *taxus*).
GIVEN NAMES Spanish 56%. *Jose* (7), *Luis* (7), *Carlos* (6), *Juan* (6), *Julio* (4), *Pedro* (4), *Diego* (3), *Lazaro* (3), *Ricardo* (3), *Angel* (2), *Felipe* (2), *Manuel* (2).

Tekle (108) Ethiopian: unexplained.
GIVEN NAMES Ethiopian 76%; African 6%. *Haile* (4), *Kidane* (3), *Alem* (2), *Berhane* (2), *Genet* (2), *Hagos* (2), *Lemlem* (2), *Tsegai* (2), *Abeba, Abiy, Alemayehu, Berhanu; Almaz* (2), *Lishan.*

Tekulve (107) Origin unidentified. Probably an altered spelling of North German (and possibly also Dutch) **Tehülwe** (from dialect *hülwe* 'swamp puddle', 'swamp hole') 'at the swamp hole', a topographic name for someone who lived near such terrain.
GIVEN NAME German 5%. *Kurt* (2).

Telander (141) Swedish: unexplained.

Telep (112) Slavic: unexplained.

Telesca (119) Italian: variant of TELESCO.
GIVEN NAMES Italian 22%. *Donato* (3), *Vito* (3), *Angelo, Caesar, Luigi, Rocco.*

Telesco (229) Italian (Naples): most probably a variant of TEDESCO.
GIVEN NAMES Italian 18%. *Angelo* (3), *Carlo* (2), *Canio, Rocco, Salvatore, Vito.*

Telfair (147) Scottish and northern English: variant of TELFER.
GIVEN NAME German 5%. *Kurt* (2).

Telfer (528) Scottish and northern English: from a personal name based on a byname for a strong man or ferocious warrior, from Old French *taille(r)* 'to cut' + *fer* 'iron' (Latin *ferrum*).

Telford (1151) Scottish and English (Northumbria): not, as its form would imply, a habitational name, even though there is a place in Shropshire so called, but a variant of TELFER, assimilated to the pattern of habitational names in *-ford*. The Shropshire place is a new town, named after the celebrated Scottish civil engineer Thomas Telford (1757–1834).

Telkamp (102) German: topographic name from Middle Low German *tel* 'young tree' + *kamp* ' enclosed field', 'domain', for someone who lived near a tree nursery.
GIVEN NAME German 7%. *Mathias* (2).

Tell (526) **1.** North German: from a pet form of DIETRICH. **2.** South German: topographic name from Middle High German *telle* 'gorge', 'depression'. The name of the

Swiss hero Wilhelm Tell has not been explained. **3.** North German (mainly Westphalia): topographic name from Middle Low German *telg(e)* 'branch', 'twig', 'undergrowth'. **4.** Catalan: topographic name from *tila* 'linden' (Latin *tilia*), denoting someone who lived near a conspicuous linden.

Tella (106) **1.** Indian (Andhra Pradesh): Hindu name meaning 'white' in Telugu. **2.** Aragonese and Galician: probably a habitational name from places in Uesca (Aragon) or A Coruña (Galicia) called Tella, possibly from *tella* '(roof) tile' (Latin *tegula*). **3.** Italian: from *Tella*, a feminine form of TELLO (see also LA TELLA).
GIVEN NAMES Indian 11%; Italian 7%; Spanish 5%. *Vijayakumar* (2), *Manjula, Nalini, Rao; Amadeo, Antonio, Nicola, Nino; Eduardo, Emilio, Gustavo, Jose, Manuel, Mariano.*

Telle (127) **1.** North German: variant of TELL 2 or 3. **2.** Belgian French: topographic name from Old French *teil* 'lime tree', 'linden' (Latin *tilia*).

Tellefsen (183) Norwegian: patronymic from *Tellef*, a form of the Old Norse personal name *þorleifr*, composed of the name of the god *þórr* + *leifr* 'heir', 'descendant'.
GIVEN NAMES Scandinavian 14% *Tellef* (2), *Aane, Ingeborg, Toralf, Torleif.*

Teller (1199) **1.** English: occupational name from Old French *telier* 'weaver', 'linen-weaver'. **2.** German: variant of TELL 2 and 3. **3.** Dutch: occupational name for a *teller*, a marketplace official. **4.** Jewish (Ashkenazic): either a metonymic occupational name for a dish maker or a nickname, from German *Teller*, Yiddish *teler* 'plate'. **5.** Catalan: from a derivative of TELL 4.
FOREBEARS This name is recorded in Beverwijck in New Netherland (Albany, NY) in the mid 17th century.
GIVEN NAMES Jewish 5%. *Moshe* (4), *Dov* (3), *Hyman* (2), *Aron, Avrum, Hershel, Menachem, Meyer, Nuchem, Yitzchock, Zalman, Zvi.*

Telleria (109) **1.** Basque: habitational name from Telleria in Navarre, Basque Country. **2.** possibly also Spanish (**Tellería**): topographic name from *tellería* 'brickworks'.
GIVEN NAMES Spanish 40%. *Carlos* (5), *Roberto* (4), *Juan* (2), *Mario* (2), *Nestor* (2), *Violeta* (2), *Alida, Angel, Blanca, Eduardo, Fernando, Francisco.*

Telles (813) Portuguese (**Teles**): patronymic from the medieval personal name *Tellus*, probably of Germanic origin.
GIVEN NAMES Spanish 27%. *Manuel* (11), *Jose* (7), *Luis* (5), *Adolpho* (3), *Alfonso* (3), *Armando* (3), *Francisco* (3), *Jorge* (3), *Pablo* (3), *Ramon* (3), *Ruben* (3), *Alberto* (2).

Tellez (1668) Spanish (**Téllez**): patronymic from the medieval personal name *Tellus*, probably of Germanic origin.
GIVEN NAMES Spanish 49%. *Jose* (37), *Juan* (16), *Ramon* (16), *Manuel* (14), *Ruben* (14), *Carlos* (12), *Jesus* (12), *Luis* (12), *Javier* (11), *Roberto* (11), *Jorge* (10), *Mario* (10).

Tellier (673) French (Normandy, Picardy): occupational name from Old French *tel(l)ier* 'weaver'.
FOREBEARS A Tellier from the Normandy region of France is documented in Quebec City in 1659, with the variant LETELLIER. Another, also from Normandy, is documented in Quebec City in 1665 with the secondary surname LAFORTUNE.
GIVEN NAMES French 13%. *Herve* (4), *Armand* (3), *Normand* (3), *Andre* (2), *Marcel* (2), *Benoit, Francois, Gilles, Jean-Guy, Josee, Laurent, Leonide.*

Telling (121) **1.** Dutch and North German: patronymic from a Middle Dutch pet form of *Theudilo*, a short form of Germanic compound names formed with an unattested element, *theudo-* 'people', 'tribe'. **2.** English (Wiltshire and Gloucestershire): unexplained.

Tellinghuisen (134) Dutch: unexplained; possibly a habitational name from a lost or unidentified place.

Tellis (300) Probably a variant of Scottish TULLIS.

Tellman (142) German (**Tellmann**): variant of TELL 3 or of **Tillmann** (see TILLEMAN).

Tello (791) **1.** Spanish and Aragonese: from the personal name *Tello* (see TELLEZ). **2.** Italian: from a short form of a personal name formed with this suffix, as for example *Donatello*, MOSCATELLO, *Otello*.
GIVEN NAMES Spanish 50%. *Jose* (16), *Juan* (13), *Luis* (11), *Jorge* (10), *Fernando* (9), *Pedro* (9), *Francisco* (8), *Arturo* (7), *Miguel* (7), *Carlos* (6), *Manuel* (6), *Pablo* (6).

Tellock (105) **1.** variant spelling of Scottish TULLOCH. **2.** Perhaps also German, of Slavic origin.

Telschow (134) Eastern German: habitational name from Telschow in Brandenburg.

Teman (108) Jewish: unexplained.
GIVEN NAMES Jewish 5%. *Hyman, Isadore.*

Temby (116) English (Cornwall): unexplained.

Temkin (337) Jewish (from Belarus): metronymic from the Yiddish female personal name *Temke* (a pet form of TOMER) + the eastern Slavic possessive suffix *-in.*
GIVEN NAMES Jewish 10%. *Meyer* (3), *Ilya, Isaak, Isadore, Miriam, Myer, Ruvim, Varda, Yakov.*

Temme (311) North German and Frisian: from a Low German and Frisian pet form of *Thetmar* (standard German *Dietmar*), a personal name composed of the Germanic elements *þeudo-* 'people', 'nation' (unattested) + *meri, mari* 'renowned'.

GIVEN NAMES German 6%. *Ernst, Franz, Juergen, Klaus, Otto, Siegfried.*

Tempel (462) **1.** North German: topographic name from Westphalian *tempel* 'knoll', 'round hill' or a habitational name from any of fifteen places so named. **2.** Dutch (**van den Tempel, van der Tempel**): habitational name from any of various places named De Tempel.
GIVEN NAMES German 6%. *Kurt* (2), *Baerbel, Dieter, Guenter, Horst, Juergen, Otto.*

Tempest (242) English (Yorkshire): nickname for someone with a blustery temperament, from Middle English, Old French *tempest(e)* 'storm' (Latin *tempestas* 'weather', 'season', a derivative of *tempus* 'time').

Tempesta (274) Italian: nickname for someone with a blustery temperament, from *tempesta* 'storm', 'tempest' (see TEMPEST).
GIVEN NAMES Italian 17%. *Antonio* (2), *Carlo* (2), *Raffaele* (2), *Agostino, Angelo, Carmelo, Cesare, Cesidio, Dante, Elio, Ezio, Gino.*

Templar (114) English: occupational name for a servant of the Knights Templar (see TEMPLE).

Temple (8184) **1.** English and French: occupational name or habitational name for someone who was employed at or lived near one of the houses ('temples') maintained by the Knights Templar, a crusading order so named because they claimed to occupy in Jerusalem the site of the old temple (Middle English, Old French *temple*, Latin *templum*). The order was founded in 1118 and flourished for 200 years, but was suppressed as heretical in 1312. **2.** English: name given to foundlings baptized at the Temple Church, London, so called because it was originally built on land belonging to the Templars. **3.** Scottish: habitational name from the parish of Temple in Edinburgh, likewise named because it was the site of the local headquarters of the Knights Templar.

Templeman (626) **1.** English: variant of TEMPLE. **2.** German (**Tempelmann**): variant of TEMPEL 1.

Templer (234) English: occupational name for a servant of the Knights Templar (see TEMPLE).

Temples (514) Altered form of TEMPLE.

Templet (479) French: from a diminutive of TEMPLE 1.
GIVEN NAMES French 7%. *Lucien* (2), *Aldes, Ancil, Felicie, Ovide, Pierre, Ulysse.*

Templeton (5377) Scottish: habitational name from a place near Dundonald in Ayrshire, so called from Middle English *temple* 'house of the Knights Templar' + *toun* 'settlement'. There are also places called Templeton in Wales, Berkshire and Devon, but these do not seem to have contributed to the surname.

Templin (1642) **1.** French: possibly from a diminutive of TEMPLE. **2.** German: habitational name from a place so named in Brandenburg, of Slavic origin.

Tena (257) Catalan: habitational name from any of the places called Tena or with Tena, or metonymic occupational name from Catalan *tena* 'tent', 'booth', 'stall' (Spanish *tienda*).

GIVEN NAMES Spanish 56%. *Manuel* (7), *Jose* (5), *Ramon* (5), *Juan* (4), *Luis* (4), *Miguel* (4), *Roberto* (4), *Servando* (3), *Jaime* (2), *Jesus* (2), *Jesus Manuel* (2), *Jorge* (2).

Tenaglia (397) Italian: from *tenaglia* 'pincers', 'pliers' (from Provencal *tenalba*, French *tenaille*, from Latin *tenaclum* 'tie'), hence probably a metonymic occupational name for a blacksmith, or possibly a nickname for an incisive person.

GIVEN NAMES Italian 30%. *Rocco* (8), *Mario* (7), *Aldo* (6), *Alfredo* (3), *Antonio* (2), *Ciro* (2), *Guido* (2), *Umberto* (2), *Vittorio* (2), *Amadeo, Caterina, Conrado, Domenic, Domenico, Francesco.*

Ten Barge (121) Variant of Dutch **Ten Berge** 'at the hill' (see BERG).

Ten Brink (310) Dutch (**Ten Brink**) and North German: topographic name for someone who lived by a pasture (*to den brink* 'at the pasture'), from Middle Dutch, Middle Low German *brinc* 'edge', 'slope', 'grazing land', in particular a raised meadow in low-lying marshland.

Ten Broeck (140) Dutch (**Ten Broek**) and North German: topographic name for someone who lived by a marsh or swamp (*to den broek* 'at the creek'), from Dutch, Low German *broek*.

FOREBEARS This name is recorded in Beverwijck in New Netherland (Albany, NY) in the mid 17th century. See also WESSELS.

Tench (414) English: nickname from Old French *tenche* 'tench', a kind of freshwater fish; a 'fat and sleek fish' according to Reaney and Wilson.

Tencza (229) Polish (**Tęcza**): nickname from *tęcza* 'rainbow'.

GIVEN NAME Polish 4%. *Thadeus.*

Tendick (103) German: compound topographic name meaning 'at the dike' or 'at the pond', from Middle Low German *te* 'at' + *-n* (inflected definite article) + *dīk*.

Tendler (215) German and Jewish (Ashkenazic): occupational name for a dealer in secondhand goods, Middle High German *tendelære*, Yiddish *tendler*, an agent derivative of *tändeln* 'to deal', 'to trade', ultimately from Late Latin *tantum* 'price' (originally meaning 'so much'). The German surname, like the vocabulary word, is restricted largely to Bavaria, Austria, and the Sudetenland.

GIVEN NAMES Jewish 12%. *Hillel* (3), *Meyer* (2), *Sholom* (2), *Aron, Eliyahu, Mayer, Miriam, Shmuel.*

Tenenbaum (655) Jewish (Ashkenazic): variant of TANNENBAUM.

GIVEN NAMES Jewish 15%. *Emanuel* (4), *Meyer* (3), *Sol* (3), *Avraham* (2), *Shlomie* (2), *Alter, Ari, Bezalel, Devorah, Herschel, Hersh, Hinda.*

Tener (269) Jewish (Ashkenazic): unexplained, probably from an unidentified personal name.

Tenerowicz (113) Jewish (Ashkenazic): patronymic from TENER.

Ten Eyck (769) Dutch (**Ten Eyck**): topographic name for someone who lived by a prominent oak tree, Middle Dutch *eyk*. This has been a prominent family name in Albany, NY, area since the 1630s.

Teng (624) **1.** Chinese 滕: from the name of a fiefdom called Teng in present-day Shandong province, which existed during the Zhou dynasty (1122–221 BC). Accounts of the name Teng in fact go back much further, to the legendary emperor Huang Di (2697–2595 BC), who had a son called Teng. The Zhou dynasty name is documented from 1122 BC, when the fourteenth son of Wen Wang, the founder of the dynasty, was granted a fief named Teng in present-day Shandong province. His descendants eventually adopted the place name as their surname. **2.** Chinese 邓: variant spelling of DENG.

GIVEN NAMES Chinese 26%. *Cheng* (4), *Chia* (2), *Chia-Chi* (2), *Chunyan* (2), *Kam* (2), *Ming* (2), *Ming Yi* (2), *Wei* (2), *Yu Ming* (2), *Yung* (2), *Beng, Bin.*

Tengan (172) Japanese: meaning 'heavenly prayer' and possibly taken from a river and nearby village so named on the island of Okinawa. This surname occurs chiefly in the Ryūkyū islands.

GIVEN NAMES Japanese 34%. *Shigeo* (2), *Yoshio* (2), *Eizo, Goro, Haruo, Katsuko, Kenjiro, Masanori, Mitsue, Nobuo, Sadako, Sakaye.*

Tengler (117) German: occupational name for a knife-sharpener, a variant of DENGLER.

Ten Hagen (103) Dutch: variant of HAGEN 1.

GIVEN NAME German 4%. *Alfons.*

Ten Haken (125) Dutch: topographic name for someone who lived 'at the (Dutch *ten*) hook (*haak*)', denoting a hook-shaped parcel of land.

GIVEN NAMES German 5%. *Erna, Kurt.*

Tenison (136) English: variant of TENNYSON.

Tenley (117) English: habitational name, possibly from Tineley in Northumberland, thought to be named with Old English *tind* 'tine', 'spike' + *lēah* 'forest clearing', or possibly from Teenley, in West Yorkshire, which is recorded in 1538 as *Tyndeley* and may be named as 'burnt (Middle English *tend*) clearing'.

Tenn (100) Origin uncertain. The 1881 British census records some thirty bearers of the surname **Ten(n)**, in some cases in compounds such as *Ten Brocke, Ten Bruggenkate,* and *Ten Meer,* which are

clearly of Dutch origin; whether the other examples are a residual element of such names is a possibility that can be verified only by genealogical research.

Tennant (3223) Scottish and English: status name for a farmer who held his land from an overlord by obligations of rent or service, from Old French, Middle English *tenant* (present participle of Old French *tenir* 'to hold', Latin *tenere*). This was the normal situation for landholders in the Middle Ages, since in the feudal system all land belonged ultimately to the king and use of it was granted in return for financial or military support.

Tennell (147) Possibly an Americanized spelling of German **Dähnel**, from a short form of a Germanic personal name formed with *dan-* (also contained in the ethnic name DANE); alternatively, *Dannehl* is a short form of DANIEL.

Tennenbaum (145) German and Jewish (Ashkenazic): variant of TANNENBAUM.

GIVEN NAMES Jewish 10%. *Avrum, Emanuel, Moshe, Reuven.*

Tennent (227) Scottish and English: variant spelling of TENNANT.

Tenner (323) **1.** German: variant of TANNER 2. **2.** English: from Old French *teneor, teneur, tenor,* 'holder of a tenement', hence an equivalent of TENNANT.

Tenneson (139) English: variant spelling of TENNYSON.

Tennessen (188) Probably an Americanized spelling of Norwegian **Tønnessen** (see TONNESSEN), or possibly of German **Thönissen**, a patronymic from a short form of the personal name *Antonius* (see ANTHONY), or a respelling of English TENNISON.

Tenney (2593) English (Yorkshire): from a medieval personal name, a diminutive of DENNIS 1.

FOREBEARS This name was brought to America in 1638 by Thomas Tenney, a member of a party led by the Rev. Ezekiel Rogers from Rowley, Yorkshire, England, to found Rowley, MA. Most (probably all) modern American families with this name are descended from him.

Tennies (123) **1.** English: perhaps from a pet form of DENNIS 1. **2.** variant of German TENNIS.

Tennis (622) **1.** Possibly an altered spelling of North German or Dutch **Tönnis**, a short form of the personal name *Antonius* (see ANTHONY). **2.** English (Welsh borders): origin uncertain; perhaps a variant of DENNIS 1.

Tennison (1011) English: variant spelling of TENNYSON.

Tenny (264) Possibly an Americanized form of Jewish TENNENBAUM.

Tennyson (1460) English: patronymic from TENEY.

Tenold (158) Norwegian: habitational name from a farmstead in Sogn so named, from

Old Norse *Túnhváll*, a compound of *tún* 'enclosure' + *hváll* 'small hill', 'rise'.
GIVEN NAMES Scandinavian 7%. *Bjorn, Magnar, Obert.*

Tenore (199) Southern Italian (Apulia): possibly from a nickname for a singer (tenor), or alternatively from a reduced form of the personal name *Antenore*.
GIVEN NAMES Italian 17%. *Antonio* (3), *Mario* (3), *Angelo, Carmine, Donato, Luigi, Rocco, Salvatore.*

Tenorio (803) Galician: probably a habitational name from Tenorio in Pontevedra province, Galicia.
GIVEN NAMES Spanish 40%. *Juan* (12), *Carlos* (10), *Jose* (10), *Luis* (8), *Jesus* (6), *Mario* (6), *Manuel* (5), *Jorge* (4), *Ana* (3), *Andres* (3), *Angelina* (3), *Francisco* (3).

Ten Pas (218) Dutch: unexplained.

Tenpenny (260) English: metonymic occupational name for a player on the timpani, Middle English *timpan(e)*, a kind of drum or tambourine.

Tenuta (186) Italian: possibly from *tenuta* 'estate', 'land holding', medieval Latin *tenuta* (from *tenere* 'to hold'), applied as a nickname for the owner of a large property or for someone who worked on one.
GIVEN NAMES Italian 28%. *Aldo* (2), *Antonio* (2), *Emilio* (2), *Eugenio* (2), *Angelo, Annunziato, Caesar, Carmelo, Cesare, Dino, Domenico, Fedele, Fernando, Franco, Giampiero, Mariana, Mariano, Sergio.*

Tenzer (186) German and Jewish (Ashkenazic): variant of TANZER.
GIVEN NAMES Jewish 6%; German 4%. *Sol* (2); *Inge, Otto.*

Teo (178) Chinese 张: variant of ZHANG.
GIVEN NAMES Chinese 14%. *Boon, Chiew, Chin, Eng, Hai, Liang, Ming, Peng, Seng, Sing, Siong, Soo, Ting, Tua.*

Teodoro (155) Spanish and Italian: from the personal name *Teodoro* (see THEODORE).
GIVEN NAMES Spanish 32%; Italian 12%; Portuguese 6%. *Manuel* (4), *Jose* (3), *Jorge* (2), *Rodrigo* (2), *Arturo, Carlos, Domingo, Elvira, Erlinda, Gavino, Gustavo, Jacinto; Antonio* (2), *Donato, Nunzio, Umberto; Duarte, Joao.*

Tepe (408) North German and Frisian: variant of TEBBE.

Tepedino (124) Italian (Salerno): nickname from a diminutive of *Tiepidi* 'lukewarm', 'tepid' (Latin *tepidus*).
GIVEN NAMES Italian 14%; Spanish 5%. *Salvatore* (2), *Angelo, Carmine, Silvio; Jose, Carlos, Trinidad.*

Teper (177) Jewish (eastern Ashkenazic): occupational name from Yiddish *teper* 'potter'.
GIVEN NAMES Jewish 17%; Russian 5%; Polish 4%. *Meir* (2), *Aron, Hershel, Isaak, Israil, Meyer, Miriam; Boris* (2), *Anatoly, Arkady, Dmitriy, Leoned, Mikhail; Czeslawa, Stanislaw, Zygmunt.*

Tepfer (161) Variant of German and Jewish TOEPFER.
GIVEN NAMES Jewish 5%. *Avi, Miriam.*

Tepley (153) Americanized spelling of Czech and Slovak TEPLY.

Teplitz (116) German: habitational name from Teplice in northern Bohemia.

Teply (178) Czech and Slovak (**Teplý**): nickname for an eager or enthusiastic person, from Czech *teplý* 'warm'.

Tepp (105) North German: variant of **Tebbe**, from a Frisian short form of the personal name *Detbern, Thetbern*, or possibly in some cases from a female personal name, recorded in old documents.

Tepper (1459) **1.** North German: occupational name for a wine or beer merchant or tavern owner, Middle Low German *tepper*. **2.** German: variant of **Töpfer** (see TOEPFER). **3.** Jewish (Ashkenazic): variant of TEPER.
GIVEN NAMES Jewish 4%. *Sol* (7), *Emanuel, Haim, Hyman, Isadore, Itzhak, Ofra, Yitzchok.*

Terada (221) Japanese: meaning 'temple rice paddy'; bearers are said to be descended from the FUJIWARA clan. The surname is found chiefly in western Honshū and the Kyōto–Ōsaka area.
GIVEN NAMES Japanese 57%. *Minoru* (3), *Akira* (2), *Fumio* (2), *Hideo* (2), *Keisuke* (2), *Kenji* (2), *Masami* (2), *Mitsuji* (2), *Takefumi* (2), *Tomomi* (2), *Akihiro, Akiko.*

Teramoto (111) Japanese: '(one who lives) near the Buddhist temple', found mostly in western Japan.
GIVEN NAMES Japanese 53%. *Atsuko* (2), *Nami* (2), *Takashi* (2), *Akihiko, Akio, Akira, Hidemi, Kazuo, Keiko, Kenso, Masato, Masayo.*

Teran (774) Spanish (**Terán**): habitational name from Terán in Santander province.
GIVEN NAMES Spanish 48%. *Jose* (17), *Carlos* (15), *Luis* (12), *Juan* (11), *Manuel* (7), *Francisco* (6), *Ramon* (6), *Ricardo* (6), *Alfredo* (5), *Javier* (5), *Julio* (5), *Raul* (5).

Ter Bush (183) Dutch: Americanized form of **Ter Boes**, a topographic name for someone who lived in uncultivated woodland.

Tercero (190) Spanish: from *tercero* 'third' (Latin *tertiarius* 'third part').
GIVEN NAMES Spanish 45%. *Miguel* (5), *Carlos* (3), *Jose* (3), *Alejandro* (2), *Francisco* (2), *Jesus* (2), *Juan* (2), *Leticia* (2), *Manuel* (2), *Roberto* (2), *Ruben* (2), *Santiago* (2).

Terek (142) **1.** Hungarian (**Terék**): metonymic occupational name for a herbalist or healer, from *terék, terjék* 'drug used against poisons'. **2.** Possibly a topographic name from Low German or Dutch *ter Ek*, meaning 'at the oak', from Middle Low German *to* 'at' + *der* (inflected definite article) + *ēk* 'oak'.

Terenzi (144) Italian: **1.** patronymic form of the personal name *Terenzio*, from Latin *Terentius*, of uncertain etymology. **2.** pos-

sibly a habitational name for someone from the city of Taranto, from Latin *Tarentum*.
GIVEN NAMES Italian 20%. *Marino* (4), *Antonio* (3), *Aldo* (2), *Armando* (2), *Alipio, Americo, Dante, Enio, Guido, Italo, Primo, Saverio.*

Teresi (337) **1.** Italian and Greek (**Terezis**): metronymic from the female personal name *Teresa*, a derivative of Greek *Thēresia* 'hunting', originally a name associated with the goddess of the hunt, Artemis. **2.** Greek (**Terezis**): variant of **Terzis** (see TERZI).
GIVEN NAMES Italian 12%. *Mario* (4), *Cosmo* (3), *Carmela, Giovanna, Nino, Sal, Salvatore, Vito.*

Ter Haar (425) North German and Dutch (**Ter Haar**): topographic name for someone who lived on a moor, from Middle High German *haar* 'marsh', 'moor'.

Ter Hark (144) Perhaps a respelling of Dutch **Ter Haak**, a variant of TEN HAKEN.

Ter Horst (199) North German and Dutch: topographic name from a reduced form of *to der horst* 'at the bushy knoll'.
GIVEN NAMES German 5%. *Hans* (3), *Heinrich, Otto.*

Terhune (1185) Dutch: unexplained. This has been a prominent family name in the Albany area since the 17th century.

Terlecki (157) Polish: habitational name for someone from a place called Terło, now in Ukraine.
GIVEN NAMES Polish 11%. *Janusz, Jozef, Krzysztof, Mieczyslaw, Mikolaj, Piotr, Stanislawa.*

Terlizzi (216) Southern Italian: habitational name from Terlizzi in Bari province, probably so named from Latin *inter iliceas* 'among the holm oaks'.
GIVEN NAMES Italian 11%. *Angelo* (2), *Antonio, Carmine, Cosmo, Guido, Silvio.*

Ter Maat (126) Dutch: unexplained.
GIVEN NAMES Dutch 5%. *Gerrit, Michiel.*

Terman (216) See DERMAN.

Termine (167) Southern Italian: **1.** variant of TERMINI. **2.** from a personal name from *termine* 'end', bestowed on a child in the expectation or hope that he would be the last.
GIVEN NAMES Italian 21%. *Sal* (3), *Rosario* (2), *Angelo, Carmella, Emilio, Ettore, Gaspare, Giuseppa, Marco, Mario, Roberto, Salvatore, Vito.*

Termini (348) Southern Italian: habitational name from any of three places named Termini, in the provinces of Palermo, Messina, and Naples.
GIVEN NAMES Italian 26%. *Salvatore* (11), *Rosario* (4), *Angelo* (3), *Mario* (2), *Antonino, Antonio, Concetta, Emilio, Fortunato, Margherita, Remo, Sal, Santina, Saverio.*

Ternes (525) German: from a short form of the personal name *Maternus*, from Latin, 'the maternal (i.e. motherly) one'. Compare MATTERN.

GIVEN NAMES German 4%. *Aloys, Balzer, Hans, Kurt, Mathias, Otto.*

Ternus (126) German: variant of TERNES.

Terp (137) German: **1.** possibly a habitational name from a place in Brandenburg or Schleswig-Holstein. **2.** perhaps a nickname for a patient person, from Czech *trepeti* 'to tolerate'.

Terpening (526) Dutch: habitational name for someone who lived at a house distinguished by the sign of a coin, Middle Dutch *penninc* (cognate with English *penny*, German *Pfennig*).

Terpenning (124) Dutch: variant of TERPENING.

Terpstra (957) Frisian: topographic name denoting someone who lived on a *terp*, a prehistoric man-made mound built on low-lying land as a habitation site.

Terra (341) Catalan and Portuguese: habitational name from any of the places called Terra either in Portugal or Catalonia, or topographic name from *terra* 'earth', 'homeland' (Latin *terra*); among immigrants from Madeira, possibly a translation of Dutch **Aard**.
GIVEN NAMES Spanish 13%; Portuguese 6%. *Jose* (7), *Carlos* (3), *Manuel* (3), *Fernando* (2), *Florencio* (2), *Laurentino* (2), *Sergio* (2), *Alberto, Esperanca, Jorge, Juan Pablo, Julio; Aloisio, Duarte, Joao.*

Terracciano (176) Italian: topographic name from an altered form of Sicilian *tirrazzanu* 'terrace'.
GIVEN NAMES Italian 29%. *Carmine* (4), *Angelo* (3), *Salvatore* (2), *Giovanna, Giovanni, Orazio, Rocco, Umberto.*

Terrace (101) Scottish: variant of TERRIS.

Terracina (112) Italian and Jewish (Sephardic): habitational name from a place called Terracina in Latina province, Italy, where there was a substantial medieval Jewish community that was dispersed in the 16th and 17th centuries.
GIVEN NAMES Italian 18%. *Roberto* (2), *Ambrogio, Angelo, Orlando, Rosaria, Stefano.*

Terral (281) Altered spelling of TYRRELL.

Terrana (215) Southern Italian: from a feminine form of TERRANO.
GIVEN NAMES Italian 12%. *Antonio* (2), *Dante* (2), *Angelo, Gaspare, Guiseppe, Sal.*

Terrance (160) Irish: Anglicized ('translated') form of Gaelic **Mac Toirdhealbhaigh** (see TURLEY). *Terence* was sometimes used as an English equivalent of the Gaelic personal name *Toirdhealbach*.

Terrano (135) Italian: topographic name from an unattested Latin word *terranus*; compare Sicilian *tirranu* '(place on) flat land'.
GIVEN NAMES Italian 18%. *Salvatore* (4), *Angelo, Carmelo, Nunzio, Sal, Tosca.*

Terranova (1145) Southern Italian: habitational name from any of numerous places named with *terra* 'land' + *nuova* 'new'.

GIVEN NAMES Italian 17%. *Salvatore* (12), *Sal* (7), *Angelo* (6), *Vito* (5), *Domenic* (3), *Gino* (3), *Rocco* (3), *Carmela* (2), *Carmine* (2), *Gandolfo* (2), *Gasper* (2), *Giuseppe* (2).

Terrasi (161) Southern Italian: occupational name from Arabic *ṭarrāz* 'upholsterer', 'embroiderer'.
GIVEN NAMES Italian 22%. *Antonio* (3), *Salvatore* (3), *Carmelo* (2), *Elva* (2), *Julio* (2), *Sal* (2), *Vincenzo* (2), *Alfonso, Angelo, Carlo, Paolo, Salvator.*

Terrazas (1094) Spanish: habitational name from Terrazas in Burgos, so named from the plural of *terraza* 'terrace' (Latin *terraceus*).
GIVEN NAMES Spanish 46%. *Jose* (19), *Manuel* (18), *Jesus* (17), *Juan* (14), *Carlos* (12), *Luis* (8), *Mario* (8), *Alfredo* (7), *Armando* (7), *Enrique* (7), *Ruben* (7), *Alberto* (6).

Terrebonne (366) Apparently a French topographic name, from *terre* 'land' + *bonne* 'good'. However, the surname is not found in French sources; moreover, the adjective is in the wrong position for French, and the distribution of the name in the U.S. does not comply with the normal French pattern. It would seem to be a Frenchification of some other surname.
GIVEN NAMES French 5%. *Alphonse, Evest, Noemie.*

Terrel (265) English and Irish: variant of TYRRELL.

Terrell (10701) English and Irish: variant of TYRRELL.

Terreri (121) Italian: unexplained.

Terrero (135) Asturian-Leonese: habitational name from Terrero in Asturies, so named from *terrero* 'mound of earth', or a topographic name with the same meaning. This name is particularly common in the Dominican Republic and Mexico.
GIVEN NAMES Spanish 46%; Italian 6%. *Jose* (5), *Luis* (4), *Carlos* (3), *Altagracia* (2), *Ana* (2), *Josefa* (2), *Julio* (2), *Tomas* (2), *Amado, Ana Maria, Anselmo, Argentina; Fausto, Santo, Silvio.*

Terres (120) **1.** French: unexplained; possibly a habitational name from a place named with this word. **2.** German: unexplained. **3.** Scottish: variant of TERRIS. **4.** Catalan: plural variant of Catalan TERRA. **5.** Catalan (**Terrés**): variant of **Terrers**, a habitational name from a derivative of Catalan *terra*, or possibly also variant of **Tarrés**, a habitational name from a town in Les Garrigues district, of the same origin as *Terrers*.

Terrian (132) Variant of TERRIEN.

Terrien (286) French: topographic name from an adjectival derivative of *terre* 'land', denoting someone who lived and worked on the land, i.e. a peasant. It is Americanized frequently as LANDERS, and occasionally as FARMER.
FOREBEARS A Therrien or Terrian from Normandy, France, also called DUHAIME,

is recorded in Trois-Rivières, Quebec, in 1667.
GIVEN NAMES French 4%. *Normand, Rene.*

Terrill (2262) English and Irish: variant of TYRRELL.

Terrio (409) Origin unidentified.

Terris (201) **1.** Scottish (Fife): habitational name from Tarras in Morayshire. **2.** Catalan: from a personal name derived from the Germanic name *Theodoric*, composed of the elements *þeudo-* 'people', 'race' + *rīc*. See also TERRY 1.

Territo (265) Southern Italian: nickname for a timid person, from Calabrian *territu* 'frightened', 'terrified'.
GIVEN NAMES Italian 9%. *Ciro, Onofrio, Rosolino, Sal, Salvatore.*

Terrizzi (113) Southern Italian: variant of TERLIZZI.
GIVEN NAMES Italian 31%. *Angelo* (3), *Rocco* (3), *Carmela, Giovanna, Natale, Pietro, Salvatore, Vittorio.*

Terrones (322) Spanish: habitational name from places in Salamanca and Málaga named Terrones, from *terrón*, probably in the sense 'small estate', or a topographic name from the same word.
GIVEN NAMES Spanish 38%. *Jose* (5), *Carlos* (4), *Alicia* (3), *Manuel* (3), *Delfino* (2), *Eduardo* (2), *Francisco* (2), *Jesus* (2), *Jorge* (2), *Juan* (2), *Luis* (2), *Margarito* (2).

Terronez (112) Spanish: variant of TERRONES.
GIVEN NAMES Spanish 17%. *Rosendo* (2), *Abad, Alvino, Armondo, Carlos, Erlinda, Felipe, Manuel, Mario, Pedro, Ramon.*

Terry (27333) **1.** English and Irish: from the common Norman personal name, *T(h)erry* (Old French *Thierri*), composed of the unattested Germanic element *þeudo-* 'people', 'race' + *rīc* 'power'. *Theodoric* was the name of the Ostrogothic leader (*c.* 454–526) who invaded Italy in 488 and established his capital at Ravenna in 493. His name was often taken as a derivative of Greek *Theodōros* (see THEODORE). There was an Anglo-Norman family of this name in County Cork. **2.** Irish: Anglicized ('translated') form of Gaelic **Mac Toirdhealbhaigh** (see TURLEY). **3.** Southern French: occupational name for a potter, from Occitan *terrin* 'earthenware vase' (a diminutive of *terre* 'earth', Latin *terra*).

Tersigni (145) Southern Italian: unexplained. There is a place in Naples province called Terzigno, but there is no certain link between the place name and the surname.
GIVEN NAMES Italian 20%. *Aldo* (3), *Geno* (2), *Adriana* (2), *Adriano, Antonio, Arduino, Emilio, Fausto, Fulvio, Guilio, Nicola.*

Teruya (220) Japanese: 'shining house'; it is found in western Japan and the Ryūkyū Islands.
GIVEN NAMES Japanese 34%. *Fumio* (3), *Shizue* (2), *Yukichi* (2), *Haruo, Hiroaki,*

Hiroyasu, Hisako, Ichiro, Isamu, Kazuko, Kazuo, Keiji.

Ter Veer (107) Dutch: unexplained; perhaps a topographic name for someone who lived 'at the (Dutch *ter*) ferry (*veer*)'.

Tervo (163) Finnish: from *terva* 'tar', a topographic or habitational name for someone living at place a called *Terva* or possibly a nickname for a tar burner. This name is common throughout Finland, especially in the north.

GIVEN NAMES Finnish 10%; Scandinavian 5%. *Reino* (2), *Eino, Esa, Lempi, Olavi, Olli; Erik, Hjalmer, Swen.*

Terwilleger (122) Dutch: possibly a habitational name meaning 'at William's'.

Terwilliger (1606) Of Dutch origin: possibly a habitational name meaning 'at William's'.

Terzi (115) **1.** Italian: patronymic or plural form of TERZO. **2.** Greek (**Terzis**): occupational name from *terzis* 'tailor', specifically a tailor of Greek traditional costume as opposed to European-style suits, from Turkish *terzi*.

GIVEN NAMES Italian 15%. *Ezio* (2), *Cesare, Dante, Gianna, Giulio, Guido.*

Terzian (337) Armenian: patronymic from *terzi* 'tailor', a word of Persian origin.

GIVEN NAMES Armenian 34%. *Aram* (3), *Armen* (3), *Seta* (3), *Berj* (2), *Hagop* (2), *Hrayr* (2), *Krikor* (2), *Mihran* (2), *Sebouh* (2), *Seda* (2), *Agavni, Antranik.*

Terzo (120) Southern Italian: from the personal name *Terzo* 'third', given to the third son in a family.

GIVEN NAMES Italian 29%. *Guido* (4), *Alfonso, Carlo, Dante, Lorenzo, Nunzio, Rino, Rosario, Sal, Vito.*

Tesar (432) Czech (**Tesař**) and Slovak (**Tesár**): occupational name meaning 'carpenter'.

Tesauro (137) Italian: variant of TESORO.

GIVEN NAMES Italian 5%. *Massimino, Vita.*

Tesch (1427) German: from a short form of the various Slavic personal names with a first element *teš* 'comfort', 'consolation', for example *Tešimir* (with a second element meaning 'great', 'famous'), *Tešislav* (where the second element means 'glory').

GIVEN NAMES German 4%. *Otto* (5), *Eldor* (2), *Armin, Dieter, Erwin, Guenter, Guenther, Kurt, Reinhard.*

Teschendorf (143) German: habitational name for someone from any of several places so named, for example in Brandenburg.

GIVEN NAMES German 7%. *Arno, Kurt, Otto.*

Tescher (102) North German and Danish: occupational name for a joiner (see TISCHLER) or a variant of TASCH.

GIVEN NAME Scandinavian 4%; German 4%. *Erwin.*

Teschke (102) German: from a pet form of the personal name TESCH.

GIVEN NAMES German 14%; Scandinavian 5%. *Gerd* (2), *Ernst, Herta, Inge, Juergen, Klaus; Astrid.*

Teschner (272) **1.** German: variant of TASCHNER. **2.** Jewish (Ashkenazic): habitational name for someone from Teschen (Polish Cieszyn) in Silesia.

GIVEN NAMES German 7%. *Wolfgang* (2), *Gerhard, Kurt, Otto, Willi.*

Teselle (103) Origin unidentified. Possibly a respelling of French **Tesel**, probably a variant of **Taissel**, a nickname for someone thought to resemble a badger in some way.

Tesfaye (115) Ethiopian: unexplained.

GIVEN NAMES Ethiopian 74%. *Amanuel* (4), *Getachew* (2), *Henok* (2), *Mesfin* (2), *Saba* (2), *Abrehet, Anteneh, Berhane, Binyam, Dereje, Ermias, Fesseha.*

Tesh (346) **1.** English: topographic name for someone who lived by an ash tree, from the Middle English phrase *at(te) asche* 'at (the) ash', often *at(te) esche* in some dialects, especially in southeastern England. **2.** Probably an altered spelling of TESCH.

Teshima (104) Japanese: though sometimes written with characters meaning 'hand' (*te*) and 'island', the original name as listed in the Shinsen shōjiroku means 'abundant island'. The first character has other pronunciations, so other versions of the name are *Toshima* and *Toyoshima*. All are found mostly in eastern Japan.

GIVEN NAMES Japanese 34%. *Haruko, Hideo, Hidetaka, Isamu, Kazumi, Kiyoshi, Mami, Masaki, Masao, Mitsuyo, Miyuki, Nami.*

Teska (267) German (of Slavic origin): from the personal name *Teska*, variant of TESKE.

GIVEN NAMES German 4%. *Heinz* (2), *Wolfgang.*

Teske (1318) German (of Slavic origin): from *Teska*, a pet form of any of several Slavic personal names formed with the first element *Teš-* 'consolation', for example *Tešimir* (see TESSMER).

Teskey (122) Americanized spelling of German TESKE.

Tesler (185) **1.** Jewish (eastern Ashkenazic): occupational name from Yiddish *tesler* 'carpenter'. **2.** English: variant of TESSLER. **3.** German: variant of TESCHER.

GIVEN NAMES Jewish 12%; Russian 8%. *Semen* (2), *Ilya, Inna, Isidor, Naum, Sol, Yosef, Zhana; Arkady, Asya, Boris, Dmitri, Grigoriy, Iosif, Lev, Svetlana.*

Teslow (108) Norwegian: habitational name from a farmstead in Oppland so named.

Tesmer (324) German (of Slavic origin): variant of TESSMER.

Tesnow (100) German (Mecklenburg-Schwerin): habitational name from either of two places in Mecklenburg-West Pomerania named Tessenow.

Teson (114) Origin unidentified. Perhaps a respelling of French **Tesson**, meaning 'badger' in the Normandy dialect and hence a nickname for someone thought to resemble the animal in some way.

Tesoriero (352) Italian: occupational name for a treasurer or purser, Italian *tesoriere*, from French *trésorier*, from medieval Latin *thesaurarius*.

GIVEN NAMES Italian 24%. *Bartolo* (4), *Angelo* (3), *Salvatore* (3), *Orlando* (2), *Armando, Bartolomeo, Concetta, Domenic, Julio, Maddalena, Marino, Mario, Natale, Ricardo, Rosario, Sal, Umberto.*

Tesoro (198) **1.** Italian: metonymic occupational name for a treasurer or person in charge of financial administration, from Old Italian *tesoro* 'treasure', 'treasury' (Latin *thesaurus* 'hoard'). **2.** Spanish: from *tesoro* 'treasure' (Latin *thesaurus*), possibly applied as a metonymic occupational name for a treasurer or in some cases as a habitational name from El Tesoro in southern Spain.

GIVEN NAMES Spanish 11%; Italian 6%. *Ernesto* (2), *Pedro* (2), *Alejandra, Angel, Augusto, Cesar, Conrado, Estrella, Francisco, Jesus, Lamberto, Marcela; Angelo, Ciro, Francesco, Pietro, Sal, Salvatore.*

Tess (241) German (of Slavic origin): variant of TESCH.

Tessaro (118) Italian: variant of TESSITORE found in the Veneto region.

GIVEN NAMES Italian 8%. *Gino* (2), *Attilio, Dino, Primo.*

Tessendorf (124) Variant of German TESCHENDORF.

Tesser (144) **1.** Dutch and North German: occupational name for a joiner, from an agent derivative of Middle Dutch *tesch* 'table' (compare German TESCHER, TISCHLER). **2.** Dutch and North German: from an agent derivative of Middle Low German *tasche* 'purse' (compare German TASCHNER). **3.** Dutch: occupational name for a weaver, from French TESSIER. **4.** Jewish: unexplained.

GIVEN NAMES Jewish 11%. *Chaim, Chanie, Eliezer, Shaya, Yitzchok, Yossi.*

Tessier (1633) French: occupational name for a weaver, Old French *tissier* (Late Latin *texarius*, a derivative of *texere* 'to weave').

FOREBEARS A Tessier or Tixier, also called Lavigne, from the Touraine region of France, is documented in Quebec City in 1648. Another, from the Poitou region of France, is documented in Lachine in 1679 with the secondary surname Le Marquis. Another, from the Limousin region of France, known as Tixier and Éringué, was documented in Beauport, Quebec, in 1687, with the secondary surname LAPLANTE.

GIVEN NAMES French 11%. *Andre* (5), *Pierre* (4), *Fernand* (3), *Jacques* (3), *Lucien* (3), *Armand* (2), *Emile* (2), *Gaston* (2), *Marcel* (2), *Yannick* (2), *Yvan* (2), *Yvon* (2).

Tessin (133) **1.** German: habitational name from any of several places so named in Mecklenburg. **2.** Possibly an altered form of French **Tassin**, from a reduced pet form of the personal name *Eustasse*, vernacular form of the saint's name *Eustachius*.

Tessitore (288) Italian: occupational name for a weaver, *tessitore*, an agent derivative of *tessere* 'to weave' (from Latin *texere*).
GIVEN NAMES Italian 8%. *Antonio* (2), *Amadeo*, *Emanuele*, *Gaetano*.

Tessler (523) **1.** Jewish (Ashkenazic): occupational name from Yiddish *tesler* 'carpenter'. Compare TESLER. **2.** German: variant of TESCHNER. **3.** English: from an agent derivative of Old English *tæsel* 'teasel', hence an occupational name for someone whose job was to brush the surface of newly-woven cloth or to card wood preparatory to spinning, using the dry seedheads of teasels (a kind of thistle).
GIVEN NAMES Jewish 12%. *Mendel* (3), *Aron*, *Aviva*, *Boruch*, *Chaim*, *Gitty*, *Meir*, *Menachem*, *Meyer*, *Miriam*, *Mordechai*, *Ofra*.

Tessman (359) Variant of German TESSMANN.

Tessmann (149) German (of Slavic origin): from a personal name derived from Slavic TESS (from a Slavic element meaning 'consolation') + German *Mann* 'man'.
GIVEN NAMES German 12%. *Armin*, *Gerhard*, *Gerhardt*, *Hans*, *Kurt*, *Otto*, *Winfried*.

Tessmer (679) German: from the Lower Sorbian personal name *Tešimir*, composed of the Slavic elements *tešiti* 'to console' + *mir* 'peace'.

Tesson (110) French: from a dialect word meaning 'badger', applied as a nickname for someone thought to resemble the animal in some way.
GIVEN NAMES French 10%. *Arnaud*, *Elmire*, *Gaston*, *Pierre*.

Test (399) **1.** Jewish (Ashkenazic): metonymic occupational name for a refiner, from Yiddish *test* 'crucible', 'melting pot'. **2.** English: nickname for someone with a large or otherwise remarkable head, from Old French *teste* 'head'.

Testa (2994) **1.** Italian: from *testa* 'head' (Late Latin *testa*, originally used to denote an earthenware pot); hence a nickname for someone who was exceptionally learned or intelligent or for someone who had a large or otherwise remarkable head. **2.** Galician and Portuguese: possibly a nickname from Galician and Portuguese *testa* 'forehead', 'brow'.
GIVEN NAMES Italian 12%. *Salvatore* (13), *Angelo* (11), *Carmine* (8), *Antonio* (7), *Cosmo* (5), *Enrico* (5), *Rocco* (5), *Marco* (4), *Pasquale* (4), *Nunzio* (3), *Sal* (3), *Aldo* (2).

Testani (162) Italian: perhaps from a derivative of TESTA.
GIVEN NAMES Italian 35%. *Rocco* (4), *Amerigo* (2), *Angelo* (2), *Domenic* (2), *Enrico* (2), *Gino* (2), *Antonio*, *Egidio*, *Fausto*, *Gabriele*, *Ignazio*, *Orazio*.

Tester (1292) **1.** English: nickname from Old French *testard*, a pejorative derivative of *teste* 'head' (see TESTA). **2.** German: from Latin *testa* 'head', hence a nickname

for someone with a large or otherwise remarkable head, or, especially in Bavaria, a topographic name for someone who lived at one end of a village or a row of fields, from the same word. **3.** German: metonymic occupational name for a silver smelter, from Bavarian *test* 'furnace for refining silver'.

Testerman (1053) Belgian or Dutch: probably a habitational name for someone from Testelt in Brabant.

Testo (101) Italian: unexplained.
GIVEN NAMES Italian 11%. *Rocco* (2), *Angelo*.

Teston (313) **1.** Asturian-Leonese (**Testón**): nickname from Asturian-Leonese *testón* 'headstrong', 'stubborn', 'obstinate'. **2.** French and Occitan: nickname from a diminutive of Old French *teste* 'head' (see TESTA).

Teta (219) Southern Italian: variant of TETI.
GIVEN NAMES Italian 21%. *Rocco* (4), *Salvatore* (3), *Stefano* (2), *Amato*, *Dante*, *Giuseppe*.

Teten (113) North German: variant of and patronymic from THEDE.
GIVEN NAMES German 9%. *Johann* (2), *Kurt*, *Reinhold*.

Teter (1490) Altered spelling of German DETER.

Teters (230) Altered spelling of German DETER.

Teti (461) **1.** Italian: of uncertain origin; possibly a habitational name from Teti in Sardinia. **2.** Italianized form of an Albanian habitational name, from a place called Thethi in northern Albania.
GIVEN NAMES Italian 16%. *Antonio* (2), *Salvatore* (2), *Vito* (2), *Angelo*, *Domenic*, *Domenico*, *Ezio*, *Falco*, *Francesco*, *Franco*, *Giuseppina*, *Guido*.

Tetley (204) English (Yorkshire): apparently a habitational name from an unidentified place, perhaps named from the Old English byname *Tæta* or its Old Norse cognate *Teitr* meaning 'cheerful', 'gay' + Old English *lēah* 'wood', 'clearing'.

Tetlow (236) English (northern): habitational name from Tetlow in Lancashire.

Tetrault (683) Variant of TETREAULT.
GIVEN NAMES French 8%. *Jacques* (2), *Leopaul* (2), *Michel* (2), *Adhemar*, *Aime*, *Gaston*, *Lucien*, *Napoleon*, *Raoul*, *Rodolph*, *Valmore*, *Yvon*.

Tetreau (102) Variant of TETREAULT.
GIVEN NAMES French 10%. *Fernand*, *Jacques*.

Tetreault (1573) French: perhaps an occupational name, derived from *testre*, *tétre*, variants of *tistre* 'to weave'. This name has been Americanized as ROE or ROWE.
FOREBEARS A Tetreault from the Poitou region of France is documented as Tétreau or Tétrault in Trois-Rivières, Quebec, in 1663. A secondary surname DUCHARME is documented in 1700.
GIVEN NAMES French 14%. *Andre* (7), *Armand* (6), *Marcel* (6), *Emile* (4), *Jacques*

(4), *Normand* (4), *Donat* (3), *Gaston* (3), *Adrien* (2), *Laurent* (2), *Lucien* (2), *Napoleon* (2).

Tetrick (389) Variant of North German and Dutch DEDRICK. Compare DIEDRICH.

Tetro (220) Respelling of French **Tétreau** (see TETREAULT).
GIVEN NAMES Italian 7%. *Rocco* (2), *Concetta*, *Mauro*.

Tetterton (215) English (Yorkshire): apparently a habitational name from a lost or unidentified place.

Tetu (119) French (**Tétu**): nickname from *têtu* 'stubborn', a derivative of *tête* 'head' (Old French *teste*).
GIVEN NAMES French 7%. *Emile*, *Gaston*.

Tetz (105) German: **1.** in northeastern Germany, from a short form of the Slavic personal name *Tetzlaff*. **2.** in northwestern Germany, a habitational name from Tetz in North Rhine-Westphalia. **3.** otherwise, from a short form of a personal name formed with *Diet-* (see for example DIETRICH).
GIVEN NAMES German 6%. *Guenther*, *Otto*.

Tetzlaff (743) Eastern German (of Slavic origin): from a personal name formed with the Slavic stem *tech-* 'consolation'.
GIVEN NAMES German 7%. *Gerhardt* (3), *Erwin* (2), *Heinrich* (2), *Kurt* (2), *Eckhard*, *Frederick*, *Frieda*, *Helmut*, *Konrad*, *Manfred*, *Otto*, *Ralf*.

Tetzloff (185) Eastern German: variant of TETZLAFF.

Teuber (188) German: variant of TAUBE 1.
GIVEN NAMES German 17%. *Hans* (4), *Hartmut* (2), *Kurt* (2), *Aloysius*, *Dieter*, *Erwin*, *Gerhard*, *Hans-Peter*, *Klaus*, *Wolfgang*.

Teubert (168) German: variant of TAUBE 1.

Teubner (194) German: variant of TAUBE 1.
GIVEN NAMES German 9%. *Ewald*, *Hans*, *Helmut*, *Horst*, *Otto*, *Willi*.

Teufel (386) German: nickname for an intrepid or aggressive person, from Middle High German *tiufel*, *tiuvel*, *tievel* 'devil'.
GIVEN NAMES German 4%. *Gerhardt*, *Johann*, *Rainer*.

Teunissen (136) Dutch: patronymic from the personal name *Teunis*, a vernacular form of *Antonius* (see ANTHONY).
FOREBEARS The surname **Teunisse** is recorded in Beverwijck in New Netherland (Albany, NY) in the mid 17th century.
GIVEN NAMES Dutch 9%. *Joost* (2), *Cornie*, *Gerritt*.

Teuscher (355) German: variant of TAUSCHER.

Teuton (130) Origin unidentified. The name is recorded in England in the 19th century but its origin and meaning are unclear.

Teutsch (231) Jewish (Ashkenazic): variant of DEUTSCH, influenced by the Yiddish form *taytsh* 'German'.
GIVEN NAMES German 6%. *Dieter*, *Fritz*, *Grete*, *Hans*, *Kurt*.

Tevebaugh (152) Altered spelling of German **Tiefenbach** or **Diefenbach** (see Dieffenbach), reflecting a dialect pronunciation of the surname.

Teves (338) **1.** Portuguese: unexplained. **2.** variant of German Tewes.

GIVEN NAMES Spanish 16%. *Jose* (7), *Manuel* (6), *Carlos* (3), *Luis* (2), *Alfonso, Ana, Augusto, Avelino, Belen, Eduardo, Elena, Elenita.*

Tevis (520) Altered spelling of German Tewes.

Tevlin (140) Irish (Counties Cavan and Meath): reduced form of **O'Tevlin**, an Anglicized form of Gaelic **Ó Teibhlin** 'descendant of *Teibhlin*', a personal name of unknown origin (possibly related to Shevlin).

GIVEN NAME Irish 6%; Russian 4%. *Yuriy* (2).

Tew (1927) **1.** Welsh: nickname for a fat man, from *tew* 'plump'. **2.** English: habitational name from a place in Oxfordshire (Great, Little and Duns Tew), named with an Old English *tīewe* 'row', 'ridge'. The surname has been established in Ireland since the 16th century.

Tewalt (116) Probably an altered spelling of German Dewald.

Tewell (428) Probably an Americanized spelling of North German **Düwel**, a nickname from Middle Low German *duvel* 'devil' (see Teufel).

Tewes (293) German: from a personal name, a reduced short form of *Matthäus* (see Matthew).

GIVEN NAMES German 5%. *Hermann, Kurt, Wolf.*

Tewksbury (520) English: habitational name from Tewkesbury in Gloucestershire, named in Old English with the (otherwise unattested) personal name *Tēodec* + *byrig*, dative case of *burh* 'fortified place'.

Tews (704) North German: from a reduced short form of the personal name *Matthäus* (see Matthew).

Texeira (364) Portuguese and Galician: variant of Teixeira.

GIVEN NAMES Spanish 12%; French 5%. *Manuel* (6), *Jose* (3), *Americo* (2), *Armindo, Benilda, Bernardo, Carlos, Francisco, Graciela, Joaquin, Juanita, Luisa*; *Damien* (2), *Dany, Edouard, Marcel.*

Texidor (130) Catalan: variant of **Teixidor**, an occupational name for a weaver, Catalan *texidor*.

GIVEN NAMES Spanish 41%. *Roberto* (3), *Andres* (2), *Blanca* (2), *Carlos* (2), *Cesar* (2), *Julio* (2), *Manuel* (2), *Alfonso, Angel, Arnaldo, Asuncion, Belen*; *Rinaldo.*

Texter (230) Dutch and German: variant of Textor.

Textor (204) German and Dutch: occupational name from Latin *textor* 'weaver'; a humanistic name, equivalent to the vernacular form Weber or variants.

Tezak (218) Slovenian (**Težak**) and Croatian (northern Croatia; **Težak**): from *težak*, an occupational name for a farmhand or laborer. This surname is also established in Germany, chiefly Bavaria.

Tezeno (151) Origin unidentified. This is a Louisiana name.

Thach (685) **1.** English: variant of Thatch. **2.** Vietnamese (**Thạch**): unexplained. **3.** Cambodian: unexplained.

GIVEN NAMES Vietnamese 51%; Cambodian 8%. *Thanh* (7), *Cuong* (4), *Dung* (4), *Hai* (4), *Huong* (4), *Chinh* (3), *Ha* (3), *Hon* (3), *Hung* (3), *Lan* (3), *Minh* (3), *My* (3), *Sau* (3), *Hong* (2), *Lai* (2), *Manh* (2), *Nam* (2), *Pich* (2), *Song* (2), *Chen, Chi, Chien, Choi, Fu, Gan, Phong, Thai, Then, Tuong, Vang*; *Chea* (2), *Pom, Ry, Savuth, Sieu.*

Thacher (318) English: variant of Thatcher.

Thacker (6811) English: occupational name for a thatcher, from an agent derivative of northern Middle English *thack* 'thatch' (Old Norse *þak*). Compare Thatcher.

Thackeray (244) English (Yorkshire): habitational name from *Thackray* in the parish of Great Timble, West Yorkshire, now submerged in Fewston reservoir. It was named with Old Norse *þak* 'thatching', 'reeds' + *(v)rá* 'nook', 'corner'.

Thackery (153) English: variant of Thackeray.

Thackston (413) English: variant spelling of Thaxton.

Thaden (180) North German: from a personal name *Diet-* (from Germanic *þeudo-* 'people', 'tribe').

Thaemert (119) Dutch or North German: probably from a variant of the Germanic personal name *Dämert* (see Dehmel) or *Dankmar* (see Dankert).

GIVEN NAMES German 7%; French 5%. *Ewald, Kurt, Lorenz*; *Jacques, Verdun.*

Thagard (158) Danish (**Thagaard**): habitational name from a place so named.

Thaggard (244) Variant of Danish Thagard.

Thai (1321) **1.** Vietnamese: unexplained. **2.** Cambodian: unexplained.

GIVEN NAMES Vietnamese 54%; Cambodian 12%; Other Southeast Asian 8%. *Thanh* (28), *Hung* (25), *Minh* (18), *Hoa* (16), *Binh* (12), *Hoang* (12), *Vinh* (12), *Huong* (10), *Quang* (10), *Dung* (9), *Long* (9), *Duc* (8); *Hong* (9), *Chi* (4), *Ho* (3), *Sang* (3), *Chu* (2), *Lai* (2), *On* (2), *Kheng, Ku, Kwan, Lim, Lung*; *Tam* (6), *Nam* (3), *Tay* (2), *Thai* (2), *Tham* (2), *Manh, Pai, Sieu, Sinh, Tau, Tea, Ti.*

Thain (194) Scottish: status name for a noble retainer or attendant, Middle English *thayn* (Old English *þegn*). In Scotland in the later Middle Ages the term was used to denote someone who held land directly from the king.

Thaker (151) Indian: variant of Thakkar.

GIVEN NAMES Indian 91%. *Ashok* (4), *Devang* (3), *Gautam* (3), *Jayant* (3), *Bharat* (2), *Deven* (2), *Gaurang* (2), *Harsh* (2), *Jagdish* (2), *Mahesh* (2), *Mukesh* (2), *Pankaj* (2).

Thakkar (319) Indian (Gujarat): Hindu (Lohana) name, from Sanskrit or Middle Indo-Aryan *ṭhakkura* 'deity', 'god', 'lord' (see Thakur).

GIVEN NAMES Indian 95%. *Bharat* (6), *Mukesh* (6), *Anil* (5), *Ashok* (4), *Deepak* (4), *Harish* (4), *Paresh* (4), *Raj* (4), *Yogesh* (4), *Arvind* (3), *Dilip* (3), *Dinesh* (3).

Thakur (196) Indian (northern states): Hindu name meaning 'deity', 'god', 'lord' in modern Indian languages, from Sanskrit or Middle Indo-Aryan *ṭhakkura*. Compare Thakkar. Although this name is commonly associated with Kshatriyas, it is also found among Brahmans and other communities.

GIVEN NAMES Indian 87%. *Anil* (5), *Ajit* (4), *Asha* (3), *Rajeev* (3), *Ravi* (3), *Ajay* (2), *Anand* (2), *Arun* (2), *Ashok* (2), *Deepak* (2), *Ganesh* (2), *Rakesh* (2).

Thal (279) **1.** German: topographic name for someone who lived in a valley, from Middle High German *tal* 'valley'. **2.** Jewish (Ashkenazic): ornamental name from German *Tal* 'valley'.

Thalacker (198) German: topographic name from Middle High German *tal* 'valley' + *acker* 'field', 'open country'.

Thaler (1050) **1.** South German: topographic name from Middle High German *tal* 'valley' + the suffix *-er* denoting an inhabitant. **2.** Germanized form of Slovenian surname **Dolar**, a topographic name for someone who lived in a valley, from *dol* 'valley', a word of German origin.

Thalheimer (197) German and Jewish (Ashkenazic): habitational name for someone from Thalheim in Saxony.

GIVEN NAMES German 5%. *Hans* (2), *Gerda.*

Thalken (108) Origin unidentified. Probably from a patronymic form of **Talig** or a similar short form of a Germanic personal name formed with *theod* 'people', 'tribe'.

Thall (199) Probably an altered spelling of German and Jewish Thal.

GIVEN NAMES Jewish 5%. *Aron, Hyman, Isadore.*

Thaller (151) South German: variant of Thaler.

GIVEN NAMES German 6%. *Gerhard, Kurt.*

Thalman (284) Partly Americanized spelling of German Thalmann or **Thälmann**.

Thalmann (196) German: **1.** variant of Thal with the addition of Middle High German *man* 'man'. **2.** (**Thälmann**): from a personal name from Old High German *diot* 'people', 'tribe' (Germanic *þeudo-*) + *man* 'man'.

GIVEN NAMES German 10%. *Ruediger* (2), *Erwin, Hans, Heinz, Kurt, Manfred, Rudi.*

Tham (264) **1.** Vietnamese: unexplained. **2.** Variant spelling of German **Thamm**, from a short form of the personal name

Thankmar, from Germanic *þank* 'thought' + *mári* 'famous'.

GIVEN NAMES Vietnamese 48%. *Thanh* (4), *Binh* (3), *Khai* (2), *Min* (2), *Nga* (2), *Quang* (2), *Cang, Chau, Chinh, Dung Tien, Hoa Ngoc, Hoang, Hung, Bai, Chen, Cheng, Chia-Wei, Chin, Choon, Choy, Dong, Fong, Fook, Fu, Joon, Kah, Thach, Thai, Tuoi, Tuong, Vong*.

Thaman (109) Indian (Panjab): Hindu name meaning 'support' in Panjabi (Sanskrit *stambha-* 'to support').

GIVEN NAMES Indian 7%. *Ash* (2), *Shalu*.

Thames (2328) English: apparently a topographic name for someone who lived by the river so named in southeastern England.

Thamm (109) German: variant spelling of TAMM.

GIVEN NAMES German 17%. *Gerhard* (3), *Reinhard* (2), *Dieter, Erwin, Hans*.

Thammavongsa (101) Laotian: unexplained.

GIVEN NAMES Southeast Asian 55%. *Bang, Bouachanh, Bounkhong, Bounleua, Bounlieng, Chanh, Ketsana, Khamtanh, Khanh, Narong, Ngon, Ouane, Phan, Phonekeo, Somphou, Tieng, Vanh Soukanh, Thavone*; *Deng, Nong*.

Than (214) Vietnamese: unexplained.

GIVEN NAMES Vietnamese 56%; Other Southeast Asian 10%. *Thanh* (9), *Hung* (3), *Than* (3), *Anh* (2), *Ha* (2), *Hao* (2), *Hoa* (2), *Lien* (2), *Thu* (2), *Thuan* (2), *Tran* (2), *Tuan* (2); *Eung, Hong, Khin, Kyaw, Nou, Sang, Tao*.

Thane (164) English: apparently a variant spelling of THAIN.

GIVEN NAMES German 6%. *Fritz* (2), *Klaus*.

Thang (121) **1.** Danish: unexplained. **2.** Vietnamese: unexplained. **3.** Cambodian: unexplained.

GIVEN NAMES Vietnamese 40%; Cambodian 23%. *Nu* (3), *Bui* (2), *Hoa* (2), *Loi* (2), *Muoi* (2), *Nguyen* (2), *Thuong* (2), *Cuong, Dinh, Ha, Hoang, Hung*; *Chin, Heang, Ho, Lai, Peng*; *Kok* (2), *Chung, Tam*; *Chamroeun, Loeum, Yoeun*.

Thanh (100) Vietnamese: unexplained.

GIVEN NAMES Vietnamese 81%. *Tran* (8), *Pham* (5), *Nguyen* (4), *Phan* (3), *Vo* (3), *Duong* (2), *Hoang* (2), *Muoi* (2), *Truong* (2), *Bui, Chinh, Chuc, Ho, Theng, Wen*.

Thanos (139) Greek: from a short form of the personal name *Athanasios*, literally 'immortal', the name of several saints venerated in the Greek Orthodox Church, the most important of them being Athanasios the Great (293–373), theologian and patriarch of Alexandria in Egypt.

GIVEN NAMES Greek 15%. *Andreas, Christos, Costas, Demos, Dimitrois, Panayotis, Spero, Stamatios, Voula*.

Thao (1303) Laotian: unexplained.

GIVEN NAMES Southeast Asian 77%. *Chao* (19), *Ying* (17), *Yang* (15), *Chai* (14), *Chia* (14), *Chou* (14), *Yee* (14), *Chue* (13), *Kao* (13), *Nhia* (12), *Seng* (12), *Mee* (10); *Neng*

(27), *Pao* (23), *Vang* (22), *Yer* (13), *Chong* (12), *Thai* (12), *Shoua* (9), *Blong* (8), *Moua* (8), *Pang* (8), *Toua* (8), *Yeng* (8); *Mai* (13), *Dang* (8), *Long* (8), *Hue* (4), *Bao* (3), *Dao* (2), *Kha* (2), *Ly* (2), *Mang* (2), *Thong* (2), *Cao, Khue*.

Tharaldson (156) Norwegian: patronymic from *Tarald*, from the Old Norse personal name *þóraldr* (*þórvaldr*), formed with the name of the god *þórr* (see THOR) + *valdr* 'ruler'.

Tharp (5092) Variants of English THORPE.

Tharpe (1398) Variants of English THORPE.

Tharrington (303) English: variant of THORINGTON.

Thatch (184) English: perhaps from a metonymic occupational name for a THATCHER, or a nickname for someone with thick blond hair.

Thatcher (3449) English: occupational name for a thatcher, someone who covered roofs in straw, from an agent derivative of Middle English *thach(en)* 'to thatch' (Old English *þæccan* 'to cover or roof').

Thate (148) North German and Dutch: from the Frisian personal name *Tjade* (see THADEN).

Thau (224) Jewish (Ashkenazic): ornamental name from German *Tau* 'dew', or possibly from the Hebrew letter *tau*, from a personal name beginning with this letter.

GIVEN NAMES Jewish 5%. *Dovid* (2), *Ephraim, Iren*.

Thaut (121) North German: from a short form of a Germanic personal name formed with Old High German *diot* 'people', 'tribe' (see, for example, DIETRICH).

GIVEN NAME German 6%. *Reinold*.

Thaw (178) **1.** English and Scottish: unexplained. In some instances at least, perhaps a variant spelling of THOR. **2.** Jewish (American): Americanized spelling of THAU.

GIVEN NAME Jewish 5%. *Mort*.

Thawley (103) English (South Yorkshire): probably a variant of THORLEY.

Thaxter (100) English: variant of THATCHER.

Thaxton (1568) English (Norfolk): habitational name from Theakston in North Yorkshire, named with an Old English personal name *Thēodes* + *tūn* 'farmstead', 'settlement'.

Thayer (6917) Variant of French **Taillier**, derived from Old French *taillere*, an oblique case of *tailleur* 'tailor' (see TAYLOR).

Thayne (212) Scottish and English: variant spelling of THAIN.

Theall (250) English: topographic name from Old English *þel* 'footbridge', or possibly a habitational name from a place named with this word, such as Theale in Berkshire or Somerset.

Theard (139) French (**Théard**): from a Germanic personal name composed of *þeudo-* 'people', 'nation' + *hard* 'hardy', 'brave', 'strong'.

GIVEN NAMES French 22%; German 4%. *Emile* (3), *Jacques* (2), *Antoine, Geralde, Maxime, Olivier, Theophile*; *Franz* (2).

Thebeau (268) French: variant of THIBAULT.

GIVEN NAMES French 5%. *Fernand, Jacques, Jean Guy, Monique*.

Theberge (431) French: variant of THIBERT.

GIVEN NAMES French 21%. *Emile* (3), *Andre* (2), *Jacques* (2), *Marcel* (2), *Normand* (2), *Raynald* (2), *Aime, Alphonse, Antoine, Aurele, Dominique, Fernand*.

Thede (357) North German: from a Low German pet form, *Thiede*, of the personal name DIETRICH.

Thedford (423) English: variant of THETFORD.

Thee (140) North German: variant of THEDE.

Theel (320) **1.** North German: from a Low German pet form of the personal name DIETRICH. **2.** Possibly an altered spelling of German THIEL.

Theesfeld (121) German: habitational name from a place named with the personal name *Thees* (a short form *Matthäus*; see MATTHEW) + *feld* 'open country'.

Theil (227) **1.** French: topographic name from a central and western form for *tilleul* 'lime tree', more frequently seen as **Dutheil, Deltheil** (with the fused preposition). **2.** North German: variant of THEEL. **3.** Altered spelling of German THIEL.

GIVEN NAMES German 4%. *Hellmut, Reinhold*.

Theile (166) German: **1.** North German: variant of THEEL. **2.** altered spelling of THIELE.

GIVEN NAMES German 5%. *Horst, Klaus*.

Theilen (165) German: **1.** North German: patronymic from THEILE. **2.** variant spelling of THIELEN.

Theiler (285) Swiss and German: from an agent derivative of *Teilen* 'division', 'dividing', an occupational name for someone responsible for supervising the cutting up of cloth in a merchant's chambers, an activity known as the *Teilen*.

GIVEN NAMES German 5%. *Hans* (2), *Kurt* (2).

Theimer (158) Eastern German: occupational name for a pigeon breeder, from a reduced form of TEUBNER (see TAUBE 1).

GIVEN NAMES German 4%. *Ernst, Franz, Ingeborg*.

Thein (415) **1.** German: from a short form of a Germanic personal name formed with *thegan* 'young warrior', 'vassal'. **2.** German and Jewish (from Bohemia): habitational name from Thein, a place in Bohemia.

Theis (2508) North German: variant spelling of THEISS.

Theisen (2147) German, Danish, and Norwegian: patronymic from a reduced form of the personal name *Matthias* or *Mathies* (see MATTHEW).

Theiss (1037) North German: from a reduced form of the personal name *Matthias*
(see MATTHEW).
GIVEN NAMES German 4%. *Frieda, Helmut,
Ingo, Johann, Klaus, Viktor.*

Theissen (178) North German: patronymic
from THEISS.

Thelander (215) Swedish: from an unexplained first element (perhaps derived from
a place name element such as *Täll* from *tall*
'pine tree') + the common suffix *-ander*,
from Greek *anēr* 'man', genitive *andros*.
GIVEN NAMES Scandinavian 6%. *Anders,
Fredrik.*

Thelen (2029) **1.** Dutch and North German:
patronymic from a pet form of the personal
name *Thietilo*, of Germanic origin, derived
from a short form of *Theodoric* (see TERRY
1). **2.** Swedish: from an unexplained first
element (see THELANDER) + the common
ornamental suffix *-en.*

Thelin (203) **1.** Swedish: variant of
THELEN. **2.** French Swiss (Vaud): unex-
plained.
GIVEN NAMES Scandinavian 6%; French 4%.
Anders, Bjorn; Olivier (2), *Ghyslaine,
Jacques.*

Thell (128) German: variant of TELL 2.

Then (310) **1.** Hispanic: unexplained.
2. German: of uncertain origin. From a
short form of *Antonius* (see ANTHONY) or a
humanist form of **Ten**, perhaps a metonymic occupational name for a mintmaster,
from Middle Low German *tēn(e)* 'blank'
(metal piece from which coins were
struck).
GIVEN NAMES Spanish 18%. *Luis* (5), *Jose*
(3), *Manuel* (3), *Ana* (2), *Alejandro,
Bibiana, Bolivar, Domingo, Emilia,
Esmeralda, Fernando, Fiordaliza.*

Theobald (1742) English and German:
from a Germanic personal name composed
of the unattested element *þeudo-* 'people',
'race' + *bald* 'bold', 'brave'. The English
surname represents a learned form, re-cre-
ated from French *Théobald*; the common
medieval form of the name was *Tebald,
Tibalt* (Old French *Teobaud, Tibaut*).

Theodore (1205) French (**Théodore**) and
English: from the personal name *Théodore*
(Greek *Theodōros*, a compound of *theos*
'God' + *dōron* 'gift'), which was relatively
popular in the Middle Ages because of its
auspicious meaning. There was considerable confusion with the Germanic personal
name *Theodoric* (see TERRY). As an
American family name, it has also absorbed various other European cognates,
e.g. Greek **Theodorakis, Theodoropou-
los.**
GIVEN NAMES French 8%. *Serge* (5), *Henri*
(2), *Pierre* (2), *Alide, Andre, Antoine,
Benoit, Berthony, Chantal, Daphnee,
Edouard, Guilene.*

Theodorou (162) Greek: patronymic from
the genitive case of the personal name
Theodōros (see THEODORE). Patronymics

formed with the genitive case are typical of
Cyprus in particular.
GIVEN NAMES Greek 32%. *Andreas* (2),
Stavros (2), *Stelios* (2), *Anastasios,
Christos, Demetrios, Dimitrios, Dimitris,
Dimitrois, Evangelos, Kostas, Nicolaos.*

Theriault (2510) French: from a derivative
of THIERRY.
FOREBEARS A bearer of the surname from
the Angoumois region of France was docu-
mented as Thériault or **Terriot** in Sainte-
Famille, Quebec, in 1713, with the second-
ary surname Granmaison.
GIVEN NAMES French 10%. *Armand* (9),
Lucien (7), *Marcel* (5), *Normand* (4),
Camille (3), *Fernand* (3), *Ghislaine* (3),
Pierre (3), *Adrien* (2), *Alphonse* (2), *Cecile*
(2), *Euclide* (2).

Therien (181) French: variant spelling of
TERRIEN.
GIVEN NAMES French 14%. *Andre, Armand,
Chantal, Jean Claude, Michel, Rodolphe,
Yvon.*

Thering (126) German: probably a variant
of **Therig**, from a Germanic personal name
(see DIETRICH).

Theriot (2197) LA spelling of French
THERIAULT.
FOREBEARS The LA Theriot families trace
their descent from a Jean **Terriau**, who ar-
rived in Acadia in the late 1630s from
west–central France.
GIVEN NAMES French 6%. *Emile* (4), *Pierre*
(4), *Leonce* (3), *Ovide* (2), *Ulysse* (2),
*Amie, Andre, Antoine, Camille, Clovis,
Jacques, Leonie.*

Theroux (768) Southern French (**Théroux**):
of uncertain origin; perhaps a topographic
name for someone living by 'the wells',
from a plural variant of Occitan *théron*
'well'.
FOREBEARS A Theroux from Toulouse,
France, is documented in Montreal in 1706
with the secondary surname Laferté.
GIVEN NAMES French 12%. *Armand* (3),
Manon (3), *Andre* (2), *Emile* (2), *Herve* (2),
Marcel (2), *Normand* (2), *Aime, Amie,
Cecile, Donat, Dreux.*

Therrell (296) Apparently an altered or variant spelling of TERRELL.

Therrian (120) French: variant spelling of
TERRIEN.

Therriault (385) Altered or variant spelling
of French THERIAULT.
GIVEN NAMES French 9%. *Emile* (2), *Andre,
Camille, Cecile, Fernand, Lucien, Marcel,
Normand, Rudolphe.*

Therrien (1931) French: variant spelling of
TERRIEN.
GIVEN NAMES French 12%. *Armand* (9),
Andre (7), *Emile* (7), *Lucien* (5), *Marcel*
(5), *Cecile* (4), *Normand* (3), *Camille* (2),
Fernand (2), *Gilles* (2), *Adelard, Adrien.*

Thesing (317) North German: patronymic
from the personal name *Thees*, a reduced
form of *Matthäus* (see MATTHEW).

Thetford (498) English (Norfolk): habitational name from a place in Norfolk, named
in Old English with *þeodo-* 'people' + *ford*
'ford'.

Theune (125) German: variant of **Thöne**,
from **Thönissen** (see THEUNISSEN).
GIVEN NAMES German 8%. *Hans* (2),
Ehrhardt.

Theunissen (102) Dutch and German:
Rhenish short form of *Antonius* (see
ANTHONY).

Theurer (440) South German: **1.** from an
agent derivative of Middle High German
tiuren 'to assess', hence an occupational
name for a tax assessor. **2.** perhaps a habitational name from any of the places called
Theuern, in Bavaria, Thuringia, and Silesia,
or from the Silesian place name Taurer,
Thauraw.
GIVEN NAMES German 4%. *Otto* (2), *Gerd,
Gunther, Hans, Kurt.*

Theus (379) Dutch and North German:
from a short form of the personal name
Matheus or *Matthäus* (see MATTHEW).

Thevenin (109) French (**Thévenin**): from a
pet form of *Thève*, a short form of the personal name *Estèvene* (see ESTEVE).
GIVEN NAMES French 13%. *Dominique,
Pierre, Yves.*

Thevenot (120) French (**Thévenet**): from a
pet form of *Thève*, a short form of the personal name *Estèvene* (see ESTEVE).
GIVEN NAMES French 13%. *Edouard,
Guylaine, Martial, Philippe.*

Thew (222) English: status name from
Middle English *thewe* 'thrall', 'slave' (Old
English *þeow*).

Thewes (104) **1.** English: variant of THEW.
2. German: variant of THIES.

Theys (174) Dutch: from a short form of the
personal name *Mathijs*, Dutch form of
MATTHEW.
GIVEN NAMES French 9%. *Alphonse, Camille,
Denys, Emile, Philippe.*

Thi (154) Vietnamese: unexplained.
GIVEN NAMES Vietnamese 69%. *Anh* (3), *Hoa*
(2), *Hoang* (2), *Ly* (2), *Minh* (2), *Binh,
Cung, Cuu, Dau, Dinh, Doan, Dung, Kiu,
Liping, Man.*

Thibadeau (109) French: pet form of
THIBAULT.

Thibaudeau (152) French: pet form of
THIBAULT.
GIVEN NAMES French 16%. *Armand, Benoit,
Gilles, Henri, Jacques, Yves.*

Thibault (2314) French: from the Old
French personal name *Teobaud, Tibaut* (see
THEOBALD).
FOREBEARS A bearer of the surname from
Normandy, France, is documented in
Quebec City in 1655.
GIVEN NAMES French 15%. *Lucien* (8), *Andre*
(7), *Emile* (7), *Normand* (6), *Armand* (4),
Cecile (4), *Jacques* (4), *Laurent* (4), *Michel*
(4), *Adrien* (3), *Gilles* (3), *Henri* (3).

Thibaut (152) French: variant of THIBAULT.

GIVEN NAMES French 8%. *Germaine, Jean Claude, Marie Jean, Pierre.*

Thibeau (305) French: variant of THIBAULT.

Thibeault (1317) French: variant of THIBAULT.

GIVEN NAMES French 13%. *Marcel* (5), *Normand* (5), *Armand* (4), *Emile* (4), *Jacques* (3), *Adrien* (2), *Alban* (2), *Alphonse* (2), *Andre* (2), *Cecile* (2), *Lucien* (2), *Rejean* (2).

Thibeaux (205) French: variant of THIBAULT.

GIVEN NAMES French 4%. *Minos, Raoul, Ravis.*

Thibedeau (158) Variant form of French **Thibaudeau**, a pet form of THIBAULT.

Thibert (232) French: from a Germanic personal name composed of the unattested element *þeodo-* 'people', 'nation' + *berht* 'bright', 'famous'.

GIVEN NAMES French 12%. *Marcel* (2), *Pierre* (2), *Aime, Armand, Girard, Laurent.*

Thibodaux (653) French: see THIBODEAUX.

GIVEN NAMES French 5%. *Agathe, Alcide, Alphonse, Andre, Armand, Gillis, Leonce, Lucien, Noemie, Odette, Oneil, Timothee.*

Thibodeau (3225) French: see THIBODEAUX.

GIVEN NAMES French 9%. *Armand* (7), *Marcel* (5), *Andre* (4), *Pierre* (4), *Rejean* (4), *Fernand* (3), *Normand* (3), *Raynald* (3), *Alban* (2), *Alcide* (2), *Alphee* (2), *Alphonse* (2).

Thibodeaux (4425) French: from a pet form of THIBAULT.

FOREBEARS A bearer of the surname from the Poitou region of France was documented in Quebec City in 1666. In LA, the Thibodeaux trace their descent from Acadians from the Poitou, France, who settled in Acadia in the late 17th century. After the British expelled the French from that province in 1755, many resettled in LA.

GIVEN NAMES French 6%. *Leonce* (4), *Pierre* (4), *Andrus* (3), *Armand* (3), *Emile* (3), *Laurent* (3), *Lucien* (3), *Oneil* (3), *Irby* (2), *Monique* (2), *Alcee.*

Thiboutot (111) French: see THIBODEAUX.

GIVEN NAMES French 22%. *Armand* (3), *Henri* (2), *Cecile, Herve, Normand, Octave.*

Thick (103) English: nickname from Middle English *thikke* 'thick-set', 'sturdy', 'stout'.

Thie (164) North German: from the personal name, a reduced form of THIEDE, with characteristic Low German loss of the dental consonant between vowels.

GIVEN NAMES German 7%. *Heinz* (2), *Manfred, Wilhelm.*

Thiebaud (170) French (**Thiébaud**): variant of THIBAULT.

Thiede (805) North German: from a pet form of the personal name DIETRICH.

GIVEN NAMES German 5%. *Gerhard* (2), *Erwin, Frieda, Helmut, Herta, Klaus, Kurt, Ralf.*

Thiel (3995) **1.** North German and Dutch: reduced form of the personal name *Thietilo*, an early medieval pet form of DIETRICH (German), **Diederik** (Dutch), or from some other compound name with the same first element. **2.** Eastern German: from a short form of Sorbian *Bartyl*, from the personal name *Bartholomäus* (see BARTHOLOMEW).

GIVEN NAMES German 4%. *Kurt* (8), *Otto* (6), *Hans* (5), *Erwin* (3), *Egon* (2), *Franz* (2), *Reinhard* (2), *Wolfgang* (2), *Angelika, Arno, Bernhard, Eldred.*

Thielbar (178) German: from Middle Low German *tile bere* 'honey bear', a nickname for a clumsy person.

Thiele (1863) North German and Dutch: variant of THIEL 1.

GIVEN NAMES German 7%. *Otto* (9), *Hans* (4), *Horst* (2), *Kurt* (2), *Reinhold* (2), *Wilhelm* (2), *Albrecht, Eberhard, Edelgard, Eldred, Erna, Erwin.*

Thielemann (163) North German: elaborated form of THIELE (see THIEL 1), with the addition of *man* 'man'.

GIVEN NAMES German 9%. *Helmut* (2), *Erna, Hans, Otto, Uwe.*

Thielen (1138) North German and Dutch: patronymic from THIELE.

Thielges (104) Possibly an altered form of German **Theilkes**, a nickname for someone who owed feudal service to several people.

Thielke (325) **1.** North German: from a pet form of THIEL 1. **2.** Eastern German: variant of THIEL 2.

Thielman (405) Altered spelling of THIELMANN.

Thielmann (140) North German: patronymic of THIELE.

GIVEN NAMES German 4%. *Klaus, Nikolaus.*

Thiem (417) **1.** Dutch: from a pet form of a Germanic name formed with the unattested element *þeodo-* 'people', 'tribe' + a second element beginning with m-, as in *Dietmar* (*māri, mēri* 'famous'). **2.** Possibly an altered spelling of German THIEME.

GIVEN NAMES German 4%. *Gerhard* (3), *Kurt, Reinhardt.*

Thieman (512) Altered spelling of THIEMANN.

Thiemann (407) **1.** North German: from a short form of a variant of the personal name DIEDERICH + *man* 'man'. **2.** North German: topographic name for someone who lived by a meeting place, Low German *Tie*. **3.** German: from a vernacular form of the Latin personal name *Timotheus*, from Greek *Timotheos* (see TIMOTHY).

GIVEN NAMES German 6%. *Hans* (2), *Heinz* (2), *Dieter, Eberhardt, Elke, Helmut, Otto, Uwe.*

Thieme (768) German: from a pet form of the personal name *Dietmar* (see DITTMAR).

GIVEN NAMES German 5%. *Otto* (2), *Arno, Beate, Benno, Gerhard, Gunther, Hans, Hertha, Horst, Juergen, Klaus, Lorenz.*

Thien (289) German (**von Thien**): habitational name from Thiene near Bramsche, named from *tin* 'mud', 'bog'.

Thier (264) German: from Middle High German *thier* 'wild animal', 'deer', hence a nickname either for a wild or timid person, or a nickname for a hunter.

Thierer (102) German: habitational name for someone from a place named Thier near Waldbröe, near Siegburg.

GIVEN NAME Dutch 5%. *Dirk* (2).

Thierry (428) French (also **Thiéry**): from the Old French personal name *Thierri* (see TERRY 1).

FOREBEARS A Thierry from Luxembourg, also known as Noland and St Claude, is documented in Montreal in 1716.

GIVEN NAMES French 9%. *Leonce* (4), *Olivier* (2), *Alain, Armand, Fernand.*

Thiers (104) French: habitational name from Thiers in Puy-de-Dôme, Thiers-sur-Thève in Oise, or Thiers-la-Grange in Nord.

GIVEN NAMES French 4%; German 4%. *Dominique, Francois; Erwin, Wolfgang.*

Thiery (153) French: variant of THIERRY.

GIVEN NAMES French 7%. *Alban, Francois, Michel.*

Thies (1728) North German and Dutch: from a reduced form of the personal name *Matthias* (see MATTHEW).

Thiesen (286) North German and Danish: variant of THIESSEN.

GIVEN NAMES German 4%. *Claus, Otto, Ulrich.*

Thiess (142) North German: from a reduced form of the personal name *Matthias* (see MATTHEW).

GIVEN NAMES German 11%. *Dietrich, Helmut, Hermann, Reinhold, Wilhelm.*

Thiesse (139) North German: variant of THIESSEN.

GIVEN NAMES German 4%. *Ernst, Erwin.*

Thiessen (1277) North German and Danish: reduced form of the personal name *Matthias* or *Mathies(s)* (see MATTHEW).

Thigpen (3038) Origin unidentified.

Thilges (171) Dutch: patronymic from *Til, Tijl*, a pet form of the Germanic personal name *Diederik, Theodoric* (see TERRY).

Thill (1071) French: from Old French *teil* 'lime tree', 'linden' (Latin *tilia*), hence a topographic name for someone who lived near a lime tree, or a habitational name from a place named Thil or Le Thil (of the same origin), in northern France.

Thimm (141) North German: variant spelling of TIMM 2.

GIVEN NAMES German 6%. *Dieter, Erwin, Horst.*

Thimmesch (131) Luxembourgois and Belgian: from a short pet form of a Germanic personal name formed with *Diet* + a second element beginning with m, as for example *Dietmar* (see DITTMAR).

GIVEN NAME German 4%. *Mathias.*

Thinnes (201) North German: from a pet form of the personal name *Antonius* (see ANTHONY) or from a pet form of MARTIN.

Thirion (102) French: from a pet form of *Thiry*, a variant of THIERRY.
GIVEN NAMES French 5%. *Jean-Marie, Pierre*.

Thiry (417) French: variant of THIERRY.

Thissell (113) German and Danish (of German origin): from a pet form based on *Thias*, a reduced form of the personal name *Mathias* (see MATTHEW).

Thissen (171) German and Danish (of German origin): patronymic from *Thias*, a reduced form of the personal name *Mathias* (see MATTHEW).

Thistle (427) **1.** English: apparently a topographic name for someone who lived where there was an abundance of thistles, from Middle English *thistle*. **2.** Probably an Americanized form of German DISTEL.

Thistlethwaite (133) English (Lancashire): habitational name from a minor place in the parish of Lancaster called Thistlethwaite, from Middle English *thistle* + *thwaite* 'meadow' (see THWAITES), i.e. a meadow overgrown with thistles.

Thivierge (229) Altered form of French **Thibierge**, itself a derivative of THIBERT.
FOREBEARS An immigrant from the Orléan region of France is documented as Thibierge or **Tibierge** in Island of Orleans, Quebec, in 1666.
GIVEN NAMES French 18%. *Andre* (2), *Armand* (2), *Henri* (2), *Hermel* (2), *Lucien* (2), *Herve, Renald, Rosaire*.

Thobe (187) Americanized form of German **Thöby**: **1.** from a reduced pet form of the personal name *Matthäus* (see MATTHEW). **2.** from a pet form of any of the Germanic personal names formed of *Diet* 'people' + *bald* 'bold', *bert* 'shining', or *brand* 'sword'.
GIVEN NAMES German 5%. *Aloysius* (2), *Erwin*.

Thoburn (134) Northern English: variant of THORBURN.

Thode (473) North German, Frisian: from a pet form of a Germanic personal name formed with Old High German *diot* 'people', 'tribe' as the first element (see for example DIETRICH).
GIVEN NAMES German 4%. *Frieda, Gunter, Heinz, Manfred*.

Thoe (144) Norwegian: unexplained.

Thoele (341) Frisian (**Thöle**): see THOLE.

Thoemke (118) Dutch and North German: from a pet form of the personal name THOMAS.

Thoen (207) **1.** Dutch: from a short form of the personal name *Anton(ius)* (see ANTHONY). **2.** Norwegian: habitational name from any of several farmsteads in southeastern Norway so named, most from Old Norse *Tónni*, the dative singular definite form of *tó* 'patch of grass'; a few from *tún* 'enclosure', 'yard'.

Thoene (143) Dutch and North German: variant of THOEN.
GIVEN NAMES German 9%; French 4%. *Ernst* (2), *Bernhard, Wolfgang*; *Alphonse, Marcel*.

Thoennes (295) Dutch and North German: patronymic form from THOEN.

Thoeny (100) Swiss German: from a pet form of the medieval personal name *Anton* (see ANTHONY).

Thole (567) Frisian (**Thöle**): from a pet form of the personal name *Thöle*, a derivative of the Germanic name *Theodoric* (see DIETRICH).

Tholen (392) Frisian (**Thölen, Tholen**): patronymic from personal name *Thöle* (see THOLE).

Tholl (186) **1.** South German: topographic name for someone living in or above a forest, from South German *dold* 'tree tops', 'branches'. **2.** Swedish: probably from German *toll* 'mad', 'crazy'.

Thom (2071) Scottish and French: from a short form of THOMAS.

Thoma (1546) **1.** German and Swiss German: variant of THOMAS. **2.** Greek: genitive patronymic from THOMAS. Genitive patronymics are particularly associated with Cyprus.
GIVEN NAMES German 4%. *Hans* (5), *Klaus* (3), *Georg* (2), *Kurt* (2), *Armin, Ernst, Florian, Franz, Gerhart, Gunter, Lorenz, Otto*.

Thomae (149) German: from a pet form of THOMAS.
GIVEN NAMES German 5%. *Helmut, Kurt*.

Thoman (940) **1.** South German: variant of THOMAS. **2.** Altered spelling of THOMANN.

Thomann (465) South German and Swiss German: from a pet form of THOMAS.
GIVEN NAMES German 4%. *Hans* (3), *Dieter, Erna, Ernst*.

Thomas (219271) English, French, German, Dutch, Danish, and South Indian: from the medieval personal name, of Biblical origin, from Aramaic *t'ōm'a*, a byname meaning 'twin'. It was borne by one of the disciples of Christ, best known for his scepticism about Christ's resurrection (John 20:24–29). The *th-* spelling is organic, the initial letter of the name in the Greek New Testament being a theta. The English pronunciation as *t* rather than *th-* is the result of French influence from an early date. In Britain the surname is widely distributed throughout the country, but especially common in Wales and Cornwall. The Ukrainian form is *Choma*. It is found as a personal name among Christians in India, and in the U.S. is used as a family name among families from southern India.

Thomason (7753) **1.** Northern English and Scottish: patronymic form from the personal name THOMAS. **2.** Scandinavian and Dutch: Americanized form of THOMASSEN or THOMASSON.

Thomassen (230) Danish, Norwegian, Dutch, and North German: patronymic form from THOMAS.
GIVEN NAMES Scandinavian 15%; Dutch 5%. *Tor* (2), *Jorgen, Lars, Oddmund, Per*; *Pieter* (4), *Frans*.

Thomassie (100) French: from a pet form of the personal name THOMAS.
GIVEN NAMES French 8%. *Antoine, Emile*.

Thomasson (1887) **1.** Swedish, North German, and English: patronymic from THOMAS. **2.** Variant of THOMASSEN.

Thomaston (184) Scottish: habitational name from a place so named in Strathclyde region. The surname is no longer found in Britain.

Thombs (139) Variant of Scottish THOMS.

Thome (1128) **1.** German: variant of THOMAS. **2.** French (**Thomé**): from a pet form of THOMAS.

Thomen (120) North German: patronymic from a short form of the personal name THOMAS.

Thomerson (127) English: patronymic from the personal name THOMAS.

Thomes (275) German: from a pet form of the personal name THOMAS.

Thometz (127) German: variant of THOMES.
GIVEN NAME German 5%. *Kurt* (2).

Thomey (141) Variant of a French name derived from a pet form of THOMAS, such as **Thomet, Thomez**, or **Thomé**.
GIVEN NAME French 6%. *Pierre* (2).

Thomison (283) Variant of THOMASON.

Thomley (291) English: habitational name from Thomley in Oxfordshire, so named from Old English *þūma* 'thumb' (used either as a nickname or in a transferred sense such as 'dwarf') + *lēah* 'wood', 'clearing'.

Thomlinson (130) English: variant spelling of TOMLINSON.

Thommen (167) Dutch, Swiss, and German: patronymic from a short form of THOMAS.
GIVEN NAMES German 8%. *Lorenz* (2), *Fritz, Hans, Markus*.

Thommes (101) Variant of THOMES.

Thompkins (1255) Altered spelling of TOMPKINS.

Thompsen (302) Variant of Danish and Norewegian THOMSEN.
GIVEN NAMES Scandinavian 9%. *Per, Tellef*.

Thompson (226220) **1.** English: patronymic from THOMAS. Thompson is widely distributed throughout Britain, but is most common in northern England and northern Ireland. **2.** Americanized form of THOMSEN.

Thoms (1154) North German, Scottish, and English: patronymic from a short form of THOMAS.

Thomsen (3472) Dutch, North German, Danish, and Norwegian: patronymic form from a short form of THOMAS.
GIVEN NAMES Scandinavian 8%. *Erik* (16), *Niels* (6), *Bent* (4), *Carsten* (3), *Einer* (2),

Nels (2), *Sven* (2), *Viggo* (2), *Aksel*, *Anders*, *Astrid*, *Bjorn*.

Thomson (10144) Scottish spelling of THOMPSON.

Thomure (268) French: variant of **Thomire**, **Thomyre**, which is probably derived from a female personal name of classical antiquity, borne, in the form *Tomyris*, by a queen of the Scythians who defeated the Persian king Cyrus.

Thon (451) **1.** German: from a reduced form of the personal name *Ant(h)on* (see ANTHONY). **2.** Jewish (eastern Ashkenazic): metonymic occupational name for a potter from German *Ton*, Polish *ton* 'clay', 'potter's earth'. **3.** Norwegian: variant of THOEN.

Thone (204) **1.** German (**Thöne**): variant of THON 1. **2.** Dutch: variant of THOEN.

Thong (217) **1.** Vietnamese (**Thông**): unexplained. **2.** Cambodian or other Southeast Asian: unexplained.
GIVEN NAMES Vietnamese 29%; Cambodian 24%. *Tran* (4), *Mui* (2), *Nguyen* (2), *Than* (2), *Vieng* (2), *Cong*, *Dinh Van*, *Doa*, *Duong*, *Hiem*, *Hoa*, *Hoi*; *Siong* (2), *Chai*, *Chee*, *Chia*, *Chun*, *Fong*, *Heang*, *Heng*, *Hieng*, *Hong*, *Kong*, *Peng*; *Hoeun*, *Kosal*, *Phet*, *Savath*.

Thor (488) **1.** Scandinavian (mainly Swedish): from a personal name, a short form of any of the various Scandinavian personal names containing the first element *Thor* (Old Norse *þórr*), the name of the god of thunder in Scandinavian mythology. **2.** English: from the Anglo-Scandinavian name *þōr*, *þūr*, probably short forms of Old Norse compound names in *þór-*, *þúr-* (see 1). **3.** German: habitational name for someone who lived by the gates of a town or a metonymic occupational name for someone responsible for guarding them, from Middle High German *tor* 'gate' (modern German *Tor*). Compare PORTMANN. **4.** German: nickname from Middle Low German *dor*, Middle High German *tor* 'fool'; also 'deaf person'. **5.** Southeast Asian: unexplained.
GIVEN NAMES Scandinavian 17%; Southeast Asian 13%. *Erik* (2), *Erland* (2), *Eyvind*, *Nels*; *Chor* (3), *Tong* (3), *Chia* (2), *Chu* (2), *Kong* (2), *Seng* (2), *Tou* (2), *Chee*, *Ching*, *Chou*, *Chue*, *Eng*; *Thai* (3), *Moua* (2), *Neng* (2), *Pao* (2), *Yeng* (2), *Yer* (2), *Blong*, *Chong*, *Choua*, *Houa*, *Shoua*, *Soua*.

Thorburn (434) Scottish: from a northern Middle English personal name, Old Norse *þórbjörn*, composed of the elements *þórr* (see THOR) + *bjórn* 'bear', 'warrior'.
GIVEN NAME Scottish 4%. *Iain*.

Thore (126) **1.** English and Scandinavian: variant of THOR. **2.** French (**Thoré**): nickname for a strong or violent individual, from Old French *t(h)or(el)* 'bull'. Compare Spanish TORO. **3.** French (**Thoré**): from a reduced pet form of the personal name MATURIN.

Thorell (183) **1.** Swedish: compound name from the personal name THOR + the common surname ending -*ell*, which is from the Latin adjectival ending -*elius*. **2.** French (Huguenot): variant spelling of French **Thorel**, a pet form of THORE 3.
GIVEN NAMES Scandinavian 11%. *Lennart* (2), *Nils* (2), *Algot*, *Bjorn*, *Erik*.

Thoren (460) Swedish (**Thorén**): ornamental name composed of the personal name THOR + the adjectival suffix -*én*, from Latin -*enius*.
GIVEN NAMES Scandinavian 5%. *Erik*, *Hilmer*, *Lennart*.

Thoresen (356) Danish and Norwegian: patronymic from the personal name THOR.
GIVEN NAMES Scandinavian 20%; German 4%. *Erik* (3), *Birgit*, *Borge*, *Britt*, *Lars*, *Nils*, *Paal*, *Thoralf*; *Kurt* (3).

Thoreson (1049) Americanized spelling of THORESEN or of the Swedish cognate **Thoresson**. Compare THORSON.
GIVEN NAMES Scandinavian 4%. *Nels* (2), *Erik*, *Kjersti*, *Nils*, *Sten*.

Thorington (228) English: habitational name from Thorrington in Essex or Thorington in Suffolk, both probably named from Old English *thorn* or *thyrne* 'thorn tree' + *tūn* 'settlement', 'enclosure'.

Thorkelson (120) Norwegian and Swedish: variant of TORKELSON.

Thorley (205) Northern English: habitational name, in most cases probably a variant of THORNLEY, although there are places called Thorley (in Hertfordshire (near Bishop's Stortford) and in the Isle of Wight), which could have contributed to the surname; these are also named from Old English *þorn* 'thorn bush' + *lēah* 'wood', 'clearing'.

Thormahlen (144) North German (**T(h)ormählen**): topographic name from Low German *tor* (*to der*) 'at the' + *Mähl*, a variant of *Möhl* 'mill' (standard German *Mühle*).
GIVEN NAME German 5%. *Erwin*.

Thorman (436) **1.** English: variant of THURMAN. **2.** Danish and North German (**Thormann**): elaborated form of the personal name THOR + *Mann* 'man'.

Thorn (3642) **1.** English and Danish: topographic name for someone who lived by a thorn bush or hedge (Old English, Old Norse *þorn*). The name is also found in Sweden. **2.** English: habitational name from a place named with Old English, Old Norse *þorn* 'thorn bush' (see 1), for example Thorne in Kent, Somerset, and South Yorkshire. **3.** North German and Danish: topographic name for someone who lived near a tower, from Middle Low German *torn* 'tower'. **4.** German: habitational name from the city of Thorn (*Toruń* in Poland), which was named with Middle High German *torn* 'tower'.

Thornberg (233) Swedish: ornamental name from *t(h)orn* 'thorn bush' + *berg* 'mountain', 'hill'.

Thornberry (911) **1.** English: habitational name from Thornborough in North Yorkshire (*Thornebergh* in 12th-century records) or Thornbrough in Northumberland and North Yorkshire (*T(h)orneburg* in 13th-century records). The former is probably so named from Old English *þorn* 'thorn bush' + *beorg* 'hill'; the latter from *þorn* + *burh* 'fort'. Other possible though less likely sources are Thornbury in Devon, Gloucestershire, or Herefordshire, which are all named from Old English *þorn* + *byrig*, dative of *burh* 'fortified place'. **2.** Possibly an Americanized spelling of Swedish THORNBERG.

Thornbrough (107) Variant spelling of English THORNBERRY.

Thornbrugh (144) English: variant of THORNBERRY.

Thornburg (2696) Variant of English THORNBERRY or Swedish THORNBERG.

Thornburgh (475) English: variant of THORNBERRY.

Thornbury (348) English: variant of THORNBERRY.

Thorndike (310) English: topographic name for someone who lived by a defense consisting of a thorn hedge and a ditch, or a habitational name from some minor place named with Old English *þorn* 'thorn bush' + *dīc* 'ditch', 'dike'.

Thorndyke (116) English: variant spelling of THORNDIKE.

Thorne (6800) **1.** English (mainly southern): variant spelling of THORN 1. **2.** Swedish: ornamental name from *thorn*, an ornamental spelling of *torn* 'thorn bush'.

Thornell (406) **1.** Swedish: ornamental name composed of the elements *thorn*, an ornamental spelling of *torn* 'thorn bush' + the common adjectival suffix -*ell*, from Latin -*elius*. **2.** English: variant of THORNHILL.

Thorner (211) **1.** German (**Thörner**): topographic name for someone who lived by a thorn bush, or habitational name for someone from a place called Thorn (see THORN 3 and 4). **2.** German: occupational name for a watchman on a tower. **3.** Swedish: ornamental name composed of the elements *torn*, *törne* 'thorn bush' + the suffix -*er*, from German.
GIVEN NAMES German 5%. *Hans* (3), *Fritzi*, *Ilse*.

Thornes (129) **1.** English: variant (plural) of THORN 1. **2.** Norwegian: habitational name from any of five farmsteads named Tornes, from an unexplained first element + *nes* 'headland', 'promontory'.

Thorngren (117) Swedish: ornamental name from *t(h)orn* 'thorn' + *gren* 'branch'.
GIVEN NAME Scandinavian 10%. *Erik*.

Thornhill (2548) English: habitational name from any of various places named

Thornhill, for example in Derbyshire, West Yorkshire, Dorset, and Wiltshire, from Old English *þorn* 'thorn bush' + *hyll* 'hill'.

Thornley (685) English (mainly Lancashire): habitational name from Thornley in Lancashire, so named from Old English *þorn* 'thorn bush' + *lēah* 'woodland clearing'.

Thornock (247) English: unexplained.

Thornquist (107) Swedish: ornamental name from *thorn* 'thorn bush' + *quist*, an old or ornamental spelling of *kvist* 'twig'. GIVEN NAMES Scandinavian 10%; German 5%. *Dagny, Lennart, Owe; Hannes.*

Thornsberry (606) Irish: variant of English THORNBERRY.

Thornsbury (201) English (Worcestershire): variant of THORNBERRY.

Thornton (27083) **1.** English and Scottish: habitational name from any of the numerous places throughout England and Scotland so called, from Old English *þorn* 'thorn bush' + *tūn* 'enclosure', 'settlement'. **2.** Irish: Anglicized (translated) form of Gaelic **Mac Sceacháin** 'son of *Sceachán*' (see SKEHAN). **3.** Irish: reduced Anglicized form of Gaelic **Ó Draighneáin** 'descendant of *Draighneán*' (see DRENNAN). **4.** Irish: possibly a translated form of Gaelic **Ó Muineacháin** (see MONAHAN).

Thorogood (106) English: variant of THURGOOD.

Thoroughman (114) Origin unidentified.

Thorp (2514) **1.** English: variant spelling of THORPE. **2.** Scandinavian: variant of TORP.

Thorpe (7192) English: habitational name from any of the numerous places in England named with Old Norse *þorp* 'hamlet', 'village' or the Old English cognate *þrop*.

Thorsell (147) Swedish: ornamental name composed of the elements *Thor*, name of the Norse god of thunder (see THOR) + possessive *-s-* + the common adjectival suffix *-ell*, from Latin *-elius* 'descendant of'. Alternatively, *Thors* may represent a place name formed with *Tors-*, as for example Torshälla. GIVEN NAMES Scandinavian 9%. *Anders, Erik.*

Thorsen (1368) Danish and Norwegian: patronymic from the personal name THOR. GIVEN NAMES Scandinavian 10%. *Thor* (8), *Niels* (3), *Lars* (2), *Anders, Arnt, Erik, Iver, Jarl, Knute, Magnar, Oystein, Viggo.*

Thorson (2995) Respelling of Swedish **Thorsson**, or of Danish and Norwegian THORSEN, patronymics from the personal name THOR. GIVEN NAMES Scandinavian 4%. *Thor* (10), *Erik* (6), *Monrad* (2), *Obert* (2), *Johan, Knute, Lars, Maren, Nels, Nordahl, Selmer.*

Thorstad (286) Norwegian: habitational name from any of six farmsteads, named in Old Norse as *þórisstaðir* 'Thor's farm', from *þórir* (see THOR) + *staðir*, plural of *staðr* 'farmstead', 'dwelling'.

GIVEN NAMES French 4%. *Andre, Gaile, Marise, Mechelle.*

Thorstenson (268) Respelling of Swedish **Thorstensson** or Norwegian **Thorstensen**, both patronymics from the personal name *Thorstein* (see THURSTON 1). GIVEN NAME German 4%. *Otto.*

Thorton (465) English: probably a reduced form of THORNTON, or a habitational name from Thorton in Marnhull, Dorset, which has the same origin.

Thorup (169) Danish and Swedish: habitational name from a place so named in Denmark or various places called Torup. GIVEN NAME Scandinavian 5%. *Kresten.*

Thostenson (102) Scandinavian: variant of THORSTENSON.

Thousand (126) Possibly a translation of Italian **Mille**, ostensibly from the vocabulary word meaning 'thousand', but more probably derived from a reduced form of a personal name such as *Camilla* or *Emilia*.

Thraen (100) Variant of THRANE.

Thrailkill (453) Variant spelling of English THRELKELD.

Thrall (714) English: status name from Old English *þræl* 'thrall', 'serf' (from Old Norse *þræll*).

Thran (123) German (**Thrän**): of uncertain origin; probably a variant of **Thraene**, a habitational name from any of several places so named in Thuringia and Silesia, or a nickname from Middle Low German *träne* 'tear', 'drop'. GIVEN NAME German 4%. *Udo.*

Thrane (108) Danish: nickname from *trane* 'crane'. GIVEN NAMES Scandinavian 6%. *Ingeborg, Ole.*

Thrapp (149) English: perhaps a variant of THROOP.

Thrash (1640) **1.** English: unexplained; possibly an altered form of THRUSH. **2.** Possibly an Americanized form of German DRESCH.

Thrasher (4553) **1.** English: occupational name from Middle English *thressher* 'thresher', a derivative of Old English *þerscan, þrescan, þryscan* 'to thresh'. **2.** Translated form of German DRESCHER.

Threadgill (1005) English: metonymic occupational name for someone who embroidered fine clothes with gold thread, from Middle English *thred(en)* 'to thread' (from Old English *þræd* 'thread') + *gold* 'gold'.

Threat (172) Americanized spelling of German TRITT.

Threats (145) Derivative of THREAT.

Threatt (926) Americanized spelling of German TRITT.

Threet (517) Americanized spelling of German TRITT.

Threlfall (161) English (Lancashire): habitational name from a place near Kirkham, named with Middle English *thrall* 'serf'

(Old Norse *þræll*) + *fall* 'clearing', 'place where the trees have been felled'.

Threlkeld (889) English (Cumbria): habitational name from Threlkeld in Cumbria, so named from Old Norse *þræll* 'thrall', 'serf' + *kelda* 'spring'.

Thresher (367) **1.** English: variant of THRASHER. **2.** Translated form of German DRESCHER.

Thress (126) German: **1.** metronymic from *Theresa*. **2.** habitational name from a town so named in Lower Franconia.

Thrift (1246) English and Scottish: **1.** nickname for a thrifty person, from Middle English *thrift*. **2.** possibly also a much altered form of FIRTH.

Throckmorton (1234) English: habitational name from Throckmorton in Worcestershire, possibly named from Old English *þroc* 'beam bridge' + *mere* 'pool' + *tūn* 'enclosure', 'settlement'. FOREBEARS Bearers of the name Throckmorton in the U.S. trace their descent from a John Throckmorton (1601–1684) of New England or a Robert Throckmorton (1609–1663) of VA.

Throgmorton (280) English: variant of THROCKMORTON.

Throm (162) South German: nickname for a crude person, from Upper German *trum* 'block of wood', 'clod' 'rafter', 'log'. GIVEN NAMES German 4%. *Hedwig, Rainer.*

Thron (139) **1.** German: habitational name from any of several places so named, in Hesse, Westphalia, and near Bernkastel (Mosel). **2.** Swedish: probably from the personal name *Thron* (see THRONSON). GIVEN NAMES German 8%. *Kurt* (2), *Wolfgang* (2).

Throne (416) Americanized spelling of German or Swedish THRON.

Throneberry (210) Probably an Americanized form of German THRONEBURG.

Throneburg (109) Variant of THRONEBERRY.

Thronson (247) Americanized form of Norwegian **Thron(d)sen, Tron(d)sen**, patronymics from *Trond*, Old Norse *þróndr* 'person from Trøndelag'.

Throop (571) English: habitational name from Throop in Hampshire, Throope in Wiltshire, Thrup in Oxfordshire, or places called Thrupp in Berkshire, Gloucestershire, and Northamptonshire, probably named from Old English *þrop* 'hamlet', 'village', or the Old Norse cognate *þorp*. Compare THORPE.

Thrower (1525) English (mainly East Anglia): occupational name for someone who made silk thread from raw silk, from an agent derivative of Middle English *thrōw(en)* (Old English *þrāwan* 'to twist'). From the 13th century the verb began to be used in its modern sense, including throwing clay in pottery, and so in some cases the surname may have originated as an occupational name for a potter.

Thrun (229) German: variant of THRON.

Thrush (806) English: nickname from Middle English *thruss(h)e*, *thrusche* 'thrush' (Old English *þrysce*), given probably to a cheerful person, the bird being noted for its cheerful song.

Thruston (109) English: metathesized variant of THURSTON 1.

Thue (147) Norwegian: habitational name from any of several farmsteads named Tue, from Old Norse *þúfr* 'hillock', 'mound'.
GIVEN NAME Scandinavian 4%. *Baard*.

Thuesen (136) Danish and Norwegian: patronymic from *Tue*, a short form of names beginning with *Thor-* (in Old Norse *þórr*).
GIVEN NAMES Scandinavian 11%. *Bjorn, Erik, Viggo*.

Thueson (158) Americanized spelling of THUESEN.

Thul (270) German: **1.** habitational name from Thule in Silesia, or Thüle or Thülen in Westphalia. **2.** nickname for someone with an unusual style or growth of hair, from Middle Low German *túl* 'tuft'.

Thulin (321) Swedish and Danish: perhaps from Latin *Thulinius*, from *Thule* denoting the Nordic countries.
GIVEN NAMES Scandinavian 5%. *Erik, Sven*.

Thull (283) **1.** German: from a short form, *Thietilo*, of a Germanic personal name related to DIETRICH. **2.** Swedish: possibly a variant of THOLL.

Thum (308) **1.** English: nickname from Middle English *thum* 'thumb', for someone with a missing or deformed thumb, or for someone of very small size. Compare the folk tale of 'Tom Thumb'. **2.** German: from a short form (of Slavic origin) of the personal name THOMAS. **3.** German: habitational name from places called Thum in Rhineland and Saxony, or Thumen in Bavaria, or a topographic name from Middle High German *tuom* 'episcopal church' (*Dom*).
GIVEN NAMES German 7%. *Kurt* (2), *Dieter, Guenther, Gunter, Heinrich, Reinhard*.

Thuma (176) German: from a short form (of Slavic origin) of the personal name THOMAS. This surname is also found in Slovenia.

Thuman (158) Altered spelling of German THUMANN.

Thumann (173) South German: from a pet form of the personal name THOMAS. Compare THOMANN.

Thumm (200) German: nickname for a foolish person, from Middle High German *tump* 'ignorant', 'stupid' (Old High German *tumb* 'mute').
GIVEN NAMES German 11%. *Hans, Manfred, Ulrich, Uwe, Wilhelm, Wolfgang*.

Thumma (149) Variant of German THUMM.

Thummel (200) German (**Thümmel**): nickname for a loud or boisterous person, from Middle High German *tumel* 'loud noise' or *tumelen* 'to play around boisterously'.

Thums (127) German: from a reduced form of the personal name THOMAS.

Thun (165) **1.** German: variant of THUNE. **2.** German: from a short form of the personal name *Anton(ius)* (see ANTHONY). **3.** Swedish: from an ornamental spelling of *tun* 'fence' or 'yard', a common element of place names (from Old Norse *tún*), mostly an ornamental adoption, but possibly in some instances a topographic name taken by someone who lived by an enclosure or yard.
GIVEN NAMES German 11%. *Egon, Ewald, Hans, Kurt*.

Thunberg (131) Swedish: ornamental name from *thun*, an ornamental (old) spelling of *tun* 'fence', 'yard' + *berg*.

Thune (261) **1.** Norwegian: habitational name from any of six farmsteads, mostly in southeastern Norway, so named from Old Norse *tún* 'enclosure', 'yard'. **2.** German: habitational name from Thune near Braunschweig or Thune on the river Thune, or from Thun near Hannover, all named with Middle Low German *tún* '(woven) fence', 'hedge', 'enclosure'.
GIVEN NAMES German 5%; Scandinavian 5%. *Gerhard* (2), *Dieter; Lars* (2), *Erik, Knut*.

Thunstrom (104) Swedish (**Thunström**): ornamental name from *thun*, an ornamental (old) spelling of *tun* 'fence', 'yard' + *ström* 'river'.

Thur (166) **1.** German (also **Thür**): habitational name from Thür, a place named near Koblenz, or from Thur in Brandenburg and Pomerania. **2.** Swedish: variant of THOR.

Thurber (1683) English (Lincolnshire): unexplained.
FOREBEARS This name is recorded in Rehoboth, MA, from the mid 17th century on.

Thurgood (252) English: **1.** from the northern Middle English personal name *Thurgod* (Old Norse *þorgautr*), composed of the *þórr*, name of the Norse god of thunder (see THOR) + the ethnic name *Gautr* (see JOSLIN). **2.** nickname from Middle English *thur(og)h* 'completely' + *gode* 'good'.

Thuringer (113) German: regional name for someone from Thuringen.

Thurlow (971) English: habitational name from Thurlow in Suffolk, recorded in Domesday Book as *Tritlawa* and *Tridlauua*, and apparently named with Old English *þrýð* 'troop', 'assembly' + *hlāw* 'burial mound', 'hill'.

Thurm (181) **1.** German: variant of THURN. **2.** Jewish (Ashkenazic): ornamental name from German *Turm* 'tower'.
GIVEN NAMES Jewish 7%; German 4%. *Gershon, Gerson, Meyer, Simcha, Yael; Erwin, Lutz*.

Thurman (7539) **1.** English (East Midlands): from the Middle English personal name *Thurmond*, Old Norse *þormundr*, composed of the elements *þórr*, name of the Norse god of thunder (see THOR) +

mundr 'protection'. Reaney and Wilson suggest that, *Thurmond* having been an uncommon personal name, this surname may also represent the commoner name *Thurmod, Thormod* with the second element derived from Old Norse *móþr* 'mind', 'courage', but assimilated to *-mund* (a common second element in other compound names). **2.** German (**Thurmann**): habitational name for someone from a place called Thur (see THUR). **3.** German (**Thurmann**): occupational name for a watchman, from Middle Low German *torn(e)-man* (*torn(e)* 'tower') or Middle High German *turn, turm* 'tower' + *man* 'man'. **4.** Respelling of Jewish (from Ukraine) **Turman**, a nickname from Yiddish *turman* 'inconstant man'.

Thurmon (323) English: variant spelling of THURMAN.

Thurmond (1910) English: variant of THURMAN.

Thurn (271) German: topographic name for someone who lived near a watchtower or a metonymic occupational name for someone responsible for manning one, from Middle High German *turn, turm* 'tower'. In some cases it may be a habitational name from any of the many places named with this word in the Rhineland, Bavaria, Austria, and Bohemia.
GIVEN NAMES German 6%. *Otto* (3), *Katharina, Milbert*.

Thurnau (143) German: habitational name from Thurnau, a place in Franconia, or from Thürnau in Austria.

Thurner (258) German: variant of THURN, + the suffix *-er* denoting an inhabitant.
GIVEN NAMES German 4%. *Hans* (2), *Otto*.

Thurow (373) Eastern German: habitational name from places so named in Mecklenburg and Pomerania.
GIVEN NAMES German 4%. *Dieter, Guenther, Helmuth*.

Thursby (237) English: habitational name from a place in Cumbria, so named from the Old Norse personal name *þórir*, a derivative of *þórr* (see THOR) + Old Norse *bý* 'farmstead', 'settlement'.

Thurston (5875) English: **1.** from a medieval personal name, Old Norse *þórsteinn*, composed of the elements *þórr*, name of the Scandinavian god of thunder (see THOR) + *steinn* 'stone', 'rock', hence 'altar of Thor' or perhaps 'hammer of Thor'. **2.** habitational name from Thurston in Suffolk, so called from the genitive case of the Old Norse personal name *þóri* (see THOR) + Old English *tún* 'enclosure', 'settlement'.

Thwaites (152) Northern English: topographic name for someone who lived by a clearing or patch of pasture land, Middle English *thwaite* (Old Norse *þveit*), or a habitational name from any of the various places named with this word, in northern England, Norfolk, and Suffolk.

Thwaits (106) English: variant spelling of THWAITES.

Thweatt (679) Variant spelling of English THWAITE.

Thwing (155) Apparently an English habitational name from the place so called in East Yorkshire, named with Old Scandinavian *þvengr* or Old English *þweng* 'narrow strip of land'. The surname, however, does not appear in English sources.
FOREBEARS Martha Thwing (d. 1774) is buried in the King's Chapel Burying Ground in Boston MA.

Thye (100) German: variant of TYE.

Thyen (112) German: patronymic from the personal name THIE.

Thyfault (107) Probably an Americanized form, under the influence of folk etymology, of French THIBAULT.
GIVEN NAMES French 5%. *Alcide, Delphine.*

Thygesen (145) Danish and Norwegian: patronymic from the personal name *Tyge,* Old Danish *Tyki,* a short form of any of various names beginning with *þórr-* (see THOR).
GIVEN NAMES Scandinavian 15%. *Ejnar* (2), *Bent, Birgit, Erik, Helmer, Uffe.*

Thyne (148) English: nickname from Middle English *thin* 'thin', 'slender' (Old English *þynne*).
GIVEN NAME Irish 5%. *Brendan.*

Thyng (103) English (East Anglia): unexplained.

Thyssen (117) German and Danish: variant spelling of THISSEN.
GIVEN NAMES German 10%; Scandinavian 5%; Dutch 4%. *Juergen* (2), *Guenter, Otto; Erik; Cor, Maike.*

Tian (317) **1.** Chinese 田: from a region called Tian, which existed during the Xia dynasty (2205–1766 BC). A ruler of this region changed his surname to the name of the region. **2.** Vietnamese: variant of TIEN.
GIVEN NAMES Chinese 65%; Vietnamese 10%. *Li* (5), *Feng* (4), *Ping* (4), *Bin* (3), *Hui* (3), *Wei* (3), *Xin* (3), *Yi* (3), *Yuan* (3), *Hong* (2), *Jin* (2), *Lei* (2); *Bang, Binh, Dung, Hung, Loi, Loi Van, Long, Ly, Nghiem, Nhuan, Nhung, Than.*

Tiano (356) **1.** Italian: from a reduced form of **Tigano**, which is probably from a dialect term for a frying pan (Old Calabrian *tegánin,* Bovese *tigàni,* Sicilian and southern Italian *tiganu*), presumably applied as an occupational name for a maker of such vessels. **2.** Jewish (Sephardic): habitational name from Tiana in Barcelona province, Spain, or from Teano in Italy, in Campania near Caserta.
GIVEN NAMES Italian 8%. *Biagio, Franca, Giovanni, Pasquale.*

Tibbals (244) English: patronymic from the common medieval personal name *Tebald, Tibalt* (see THEOBALD).

Tibbets (324) English: variant spelling of TIBBETTS.

Tibbett (190) English: from the common medieval personal name *Tibalt, Tebald* (see THEOBALD).

Tibbetts (2703) English: patronymic from the personal name *Tibalt, Tebald* (see TIBBETT).

Tibbits (576) English: variant spelling of TIBBETTS.

Tibbitts (711) English: Variant spelling of TIBBETTS.

Tibbles (156) English: variant spelling of TIBBALS.

Tibbs (2106) English: patronymic from a short form of the medieval personal name *Tibalt, Tebald* (see THEOBALD).

Tiberi (316) Italian: patronymic from the personal name TIBERIO.
GIVEN NAMES Italian 28%. *Lino* (4), *Mario* (4), *Antonio* (3), *Domenic* (3), *Guido* (3), *Angelo* (2), *Dante* (2), *Pasqual* (2), *Pasquale* (2), *Salvatore* (2), *Silvio* (2), *Amedeo, Armando, Attilio, Benito, Carmine, Orlando, Tito.*

Tiberio (295) Italian: from the personal name *Tiberio,* from Latin *Tiberius,* a derivative of the name (of obscure origin) of the Tiber river. This is also found as a Dutch name, as the personal name was also used in the Low Countries during the Renaissance.
GIVEN NAMES Italian 13%. *Carlo* (2), *Angelo, Dante, Gennaro, Marco, Nunzio, Rocco, Sal, Stefano.*

Tibor (138) Hungarian and Jewish (from Hungary): from the common Magyar personal name *Tibor,* from the ecclesiastical name *Tiborc (Tiburc),* derivative of Latin *Tiburtius.*
GIVEN NAMES German 5%; Jewish 4%. *Kurt; Iren.*

Tice (3707) **1.** English: from a female name *Tezia, Teucia, Tietsa,* pet forms of Continental Germanic compound names formed with the unattested element *þeudo* 'people', 'race'. **2.** Americanized spelling of German THEISS or possibly THEUS. **3.** Possibly an altered spelling of Dutch **Tijs**, from a short form of *Matthijs,* Dutch form of MATTHEW.

Ticer (250) Possibly an Americanized spelling of German DEUSER.

Tichacek (101) Czech (**Ticháček**): nickname for a quiet person, from a noun derivative of Czech *tichý* 'quiet', 'calm' (see TICHY).

Tichenor (1067) English: variant of TICKNER.

Ticknell (134) Possibly a variant of English **Ticknell,** a habitational name from Ticknall in Derbyshire, so named from Old English *ticcen* 'young goats' + *halh* 'nook of land'.

Tichy (476) Czech and Slovak (**Tichý**): nickname for a quiet person, from *tichý* 'quiet', 'calm'.

Tick (111) Respelling of Jewish **Tyk**, a metonymic occupational name or ornamental name from Polish *tyk* 'ticking' (textile; of a clock).
GIVEN NAMES Jewish 9%. *Hyman, Miriam, Sol.*

Tickle (668) **1.** English (Lancashire): habitational name from Tickhill in South Yorkshire, so named from the Old English personal name or byname *Tica* (of uncertain origin) or *ticce(n)* 'kid' + *hyll* 'hill'. **2.** Probably an altered spelling of German **Tickel**, from a pet form of *Dick,* from a Germanic personal name formed with Old High German *diot* 'people' (see for example DIETRICH).

Tickner (287) Southern English: perhaps a variant of **Tichner**, a topographic name for someone who lived at a crossroads or a fork in the road, Old English *twicen(e)* (a derivative of *twā* 'two'). This occurs as a place name, particularly in Devon in the form Twitchen, and in one case as Tuchenor.
GIVEN NAMES French 4%. *Amie, Medard.*

Ticknor (406) English: variant spelling of TICKNER.

Tidball (334) English (Devon): variant of THEOBALD.

Tidd (873) English: habitational name from Tydd St. Mary in Lincolnshire or Tydd St. Giles in Cambridgeshire, named probably with an unattested Old English word, *tydd* 'shrubs', 'brush', 'wood'.

Tidmore (694) English: unexplained; possibly a habitational name from a lost or unidentified place.

Tidrick (200) Dutch: from the personal name *Diederik* (see TERRY 1).

Tidwell (7174) English: reduced form of **Tid(e)swell**, a habitational name from Tideswell in Derbyshire, so named from the Old English personal name *Tīdi* + Old English *wella* 'spring'.

Tiede (630) North German: variant spelling of THIEDE.
GIVEN NAMES German 6%. *Otto* (3), *Ernst* (2), *Erwin* (2), *Bernhardt, Gerhard, Kurt.*

Tiedeman (507) Dutch and North German: see TIEDEMANN.

Tiedemann (689) North German: from a Germanic personal name composed of *theod* 'people', 'race' + *man* 'man'.
GIVEN NAMES German 7%. *Hans* (2), *Kurt* (2), *Manfred* (2), *Berthold, Dieter, Gerhardt, Ingeborg, Margarethe, Otto, Waltraud.*

Tiedt (376) North German: variant of THIEDE.
GIVEN NAMES German 5%. *Erwin* (2), *Merwin* (2), *Lorenz, Otto, Theresia.*

Tiefenthaler (192) German and Jewish (western Ashkenazic): habitational name for someone from a place called Tiefental, or from Diefental in Alsace.
GIVEN NAMES German 6%. *Kurt* (2), *Liesl.*

Tiegs (266) North German (including Rhineland): from a reduced form of the personal name *Matthiges,* a form of *Matthias* (see MATTHEW).

GIVEN NAMES German 7%. *Otto* (4), *Florian*, *Kurt*.

Tieken (180) North German: patronymic from a pet form of the personal name *Tiede* (see THIEDE).

Tiell (119) Altered spelling of German and Luxembourgeois **Tiel**, a variant of THIEHL.

Tieman (751) Dutch: variant of TIEDEMAN.

Tiemann (758) North German: variant spelling of THIEMANN.

GIVEN NAMES German 4%. *Otto* (3), *Franz*, *Hans*, *Hermann*.

Tiemeyer (251) North German: distinguishing name for a tenant farmer (see MEYER) whose land was near a meeting place (Middle Low German *tie*).

Tien (446) **1.** Vietnamese: unexplained. **2.** Chinese: variant of TIAN.

GIVEN NAMES Vietnamese 22%; Chinese 18%. *Dao* (2), *Duong* (2), *Hai* (2), *Hoa* (2), *Hung* (2), *Lam Van* (2), *Minh* (2), *Nguyen* (2), *Pham* (2), *Phat* (2), *Quan* (2), *Binh*; *Shu-Hui* (3), *Chi* (2), *Chun* (2), *Fu* (2), *Li* (2), *Liling* (2), *Chan*, *Cheng*, *Chou*, *Jung*, *Lifang*, *Man*.

Tienken (123) North German and Dutch: patronymic from a pet form of the personal names *Augustin* (see AUGUSTINE) or MARTIN.

Tier (137) **1.** Scottish: reduced form of MCINTYRE. **2.** English: variant of TYER. **3.** Dutch: variant of DIER.

Tierce (258) Possibly French: from the feminine form of *Tiers* 'third', probably denoting someone who had a third share in something or who owed a third of their agricultural produce in dues.

Tiernan (1002) Irish (Westmeath and Mayo): reduced Anglicized form of Gaelic **Ó Tíghearnáin** 'descendant of *Tígheárnán*', a diminutive of *Tíghearna*, a byname meaning 'lord', 'master'. Compare TIERNEY, MCKIERNAN. Woulfe believes *Ó Tígheárnáin* to be a variant of **Ó Tíghearnaigh** (see TIERNEY) in both counties.

Tierney (5779) Irish: reduced form of **O'Tierney**, an Anglicized form of Gaelic **Ó Tíghearnaigh** 'descendant of *Tíghearnach*', a byname meaning 'lord', 'master'. The Gaelic name is sometimes 'translated' as English LORD.

GIVEN NAMES Irish 5%. *Brendan* (3), *Eamon* (2), *John Patrick* (2), *Brigid*, *Clodagh*, *Kieran*, *Michael Sean*, *Siobhan*.

Tierno (223) **1.** Italian: habitational name from a place so named. **2.** Sicilian: from Old Sicilian *ternu* 'having three syllables', presumably a nickname bestowed on someone who used long words. **3.** Spanish: nickname from *tierno* 'tender', 'soft' (Latin *tener*).

GIVEN NAMES Italian 19%; Spanish 6%. *Angelo* (2), *Mario* (2), *Domenic*, *Donato*, *Filomena*, *Gennaro*, *Giuseppe*, *Nicola*, *Pasquale*, *Sante*, *Vito*; *Jose* (2), *Carmela*, *Elva*, *Julio*.

Tieszen (204) Probably Dutch or German: variant spelling of **Tiessen**, a variant of THIESSEN.

Tietje (189) North German and Frisian: from a pet form of a compound Germanic personal name from *theod* 'people', 'race' + the diminutive suffix *-ge*.

GIVEN NAMES German 6%. *Erhard*, *Erwin*, *Wilhelm*.

Tietjen (621) North German and Frisian: patronymic from TIETJE.

GIVEN NAMES German 6%. *Kurt* (5), *Dietrich*, *Egon*, *Erwin*, *Johannes*, *Siegfried*.

Tietsort (114) Origin unidentified. Perhaps an altered form of the Belgian name **Tietaert**, **Tistaert**, a nickname for an obstinate man, from Old French *testart* 'stubborn'.

Tietz (1073) North German: from a pet name formed with the stem of the personal name DIETRICH.

GIVEN NAMES German 5%. *Erwin* (2), *Frieda* (2), *Horst* (2), *Kurt* (2), *Otto* (2), *Dieter*, *Egon*, *Fritz*, *Gerhardt*, *Reinhard*, *Wilhelm*.

Tietze (231) North German: variant of TIETZ.

GIVEN NAMES German 12%. *Armin* (2), *Erwin*, *Fritz*, *Georg*, *Hellmut*, *Lothar*, *Wolfgang*.

Tieu (281) Vietnamese (**Tiêu**): unexplained.

GIVEN NAMES Vietnamese 61%; Chinese 11%. *Thanh* (7), *Anh* (4), *Hung* (4), *Nam* (4), *Tuan* (4), *Binh* (3), *Lien* (3), *Minh* (3), *Quang* (3), *Ba Van* (2), *Cang* (2), *Chau* (2), *Duc* (2), *Tuong* (2), *Tam*, *Thai*, *Tuoi*, *Uyen*; *Dong* (2), *Hong* (2), *Chan*, *Chia*, *Cui*, *Fong*, *Ho*, *Meng*, *Song*, *Yan Qing*.

Tiffany (1914) English (Yorkshire): from the medieval female personal name *Tiffania* (Old French *Tiphaine*, from Greek *Theophania*, a compound of *theos* 'God' + *phainein* 'to appear'). This name was often given to girls born around the feast of Epiphany. Compare Italian BIFANO, which is named for the same feast.

Tiffin (354) Northern English (border counties): variant of TIFFANY.

Tifft (305) English: variant of TAFT. Compare TOFT.

Tift (302) English (Midlands): variant of TAFT. Compare TOFT.

Tiger (602) **1.** Irish: variant of TAGGART in County Dublin. **2.** French: from a Germanic personal name composed of the unattested word *þeudo* 'people', 'nation' + *gār*, *gēr* 'spear'. **3.** Jewish (eastern Ashkenazic): ornamental name from German *Tiger*, Yiddish *tiger* 'tiger'.

Tigert (219) Variant of German **Teikert** or **Deikert** (see DYGERT).

Tigges (432) **1.** North German (especially Rhineland): variant of **Thieges** (see TIEGS). **2.** Dutch: patronymic, perhaps from a pet form of a Germanic personal name composed of the unattested word *þeudo* 'people', 'nation' + *gār*, *gēr* 'spear'.

Tiggs (119) English: apparently a variant of **Tigg**, itself a variant of TAGG.

Tighe (2090) Irish: **1.** reduced Anglicized form of Gaelic **Ó Taidhg** 'descendant of *Tadhg*', a byname meaning 'bard', 'poet', 'philosopher'. **2.** In Ulster it is sometimes an Anglicization of *Mac Taidhg*, which is more commonly Anglicized as MCCAIG.

GIVEN NAMES Irish 8%. *Brendan*, *Nuala*.

Tigner (575) Dutch: habitational name for someone from Tignée in the Belgian province of Liège.

Tignor (515) Dutch: variant spelling of TIGNER.

Tigrett (101) Origin unidentified.

Tigue (336) Irish: variant spelling of TIGHE.

Tijerina (1146) Spanish (mainly Mexico): probably a derivative of *tijera* 'scissors' (Latin *tonsoria*), a metonymic occupational name for a maker or seller of scissors or for a user of scissors, i.e. a tailor.

GIVEN NAMES Spanish 44%. *Juan* (20), *Jose* (15), *Manuel* (13), *Raul* (12), *Jesus* (11), *Ramon* (10), *Carlos* (7), *Armando* (6), *Luis* (6), *Mario* (6), *Alfredo* (5), *Fernando* (5).

Tikalsky (103) German: of Czech origin, probably a habitational name.

Tikkanen (149) Finnish: nickname or ornamental name from *tikka* 'woodpecker' + the common surname suffix *-nen*. This name is found mainly in eastern Finland.

GIVEN NAMES Finnish 6%. *Eino*, *Reino*, *Timo*.

Tilbury (280) English: habitational name from Tilbury, a port on the Thames in Essex, which is named from the Old English byname *Tila* (from *til* 'capable') + Old English *burh* 'fortress'.

Tilden (807) English: probably a habitational name from a lost or unidentified place, apparently so named from the Old English byname *Tila* (compare TILBURY) + Old English *denu* 'valley'.

Tiley (199) English: variant spelling of TILLEY.

Tilford (622) Scottish and English: variant of TELFORD.

Tilghman (910) Possibly an altered spelling of German **Tilchmann**, an occupational name for someone who raised or tended trees, from Middle Low German *telge* 'branch', 'young tree', 'seedling'.

Tilkens (103) Dutch: patronymic from a pet form of the personal name *Til*, *Tijl*, of Germanic origin (see THIEL 1).

Till (1654) **1.** English: from the common medieval female personal name *Till*, a pet form of *Matilda* (see MOULD). **2.** North German: variant of THIEL.

Tillema (158) Frisian: patronymic from the personal name *Til*.

Tilleman (103) Dutch and German (**Tillemann**): patronymic from the personal name *Til*.

Tiller (2595) **1.** Southern English: occupational name for a husbandman, from Middle English *til(l)er*, a secondary derivative of Old English *tilian* 'to till or cultivate'. There has been some confusion with **Tiler** (see TYLER). **2.** South German: topographic name of unknown origin. **3.** North German: from a variant of THIEL. **4.** variant of German **Tüller** (see TULLER).

Tillerson (128) English: **1.** Variant of TILLOTSON. **2.** Perhaps also a variant of TILSON.

Tillery (2419) Scottish: habitational name from Tillery in the parish of Orwell, Kinross-shire.

Tilles (193) Jewish (eastern Ashkenazic): metronymic from the Yiddish female personal name *Tile* derived either from Hebrew *tehila* 'splendor' or from *Ottilia*, borrowed from German Christians.
GIVEN NAMES Jewish 8%. *Nurit* (2), *Yaron*, *Zevi*.

Tillett (927) English (Norfolk): from a pet form of the personal name TILL.

Tilley (5588) English: **1.** variant spelling of TILLY. **2.** habitational name from Tilley in Shropshire, named from Old English *telga* 'branch', 'bough' + *lēah* 'wood', 'clearing'. **3.** occupational name for a husbandman, Middle English *tilie* (Old English *tilia*, a primary derivative of *tilian* 'to till or cultivate'). **4.** from the medieval female personal name *Tilly*, a pet form of TILL.

Tillie (128) English: variant spelling of TILLEY.

Tillinghast (508) English: habitational name from Tillinghurst in Sussex, earlier *Tytyngehurst* 'wooded hill of Tytta's family or followers', from the Old English personal name *Tytta* + *-inga-* 'of the family or followers of' + *hyrst* 'wooded hill'.

Tillis (809) **1.** English: metronymic from the medieval personal name TILL. **2.** Jewish (eastern Ashkenazic): variant spelling of TILLES.

Tillison (261) English: variant of TILSON.

Tillman (8360) **1.** English: variant of TILMAN. **2.** Americanized spelling of German TILLMANN.

Tillmann (164) North German and Danish: elaborated form of TILL, with the addition of *-mann* 'man'.
GIVEN NAMES German 13%; Scandinavian 4%. *Fritz* (3), *Ruedi* (2), *Franz*, *Georg*, *Helmut*, *Joerg*; *Holger* (2), *Johan*.

Tillmon (198) Variant spelling of English TILMAN or German TILLMANN.

Tillotson (1758) English (Yorkshire): metronymic from a pet form of TILL.

Tillson (441) English: variant spelling of TILSON.

Tilly (467) **1.** English (of Norman origin) and French: habitational name from any of various places in northern France called Tilly (*Tiliacum* in medieval records). Examples in Eure and Calvados are so called from a Gallo-Roman personal name *Tilius* (perhaps from Latin *tilia* 'lime tree') + the locative suffix *-acum*; one in Seine-et-Oise gets its name from the personal name

Attilius + *-acum*. **2.** Irish: variant of TULLY.

Tilman (275) Jewish (Ashkenazic): possibly a variant of TILLES with the addition of Yiddish *man* 'man', in the sense of 'husband of Tile'.

Tilson (1171) English: metronymic from the medieval female personal name TILL.

Tilton (3230) English: habitational name from Tilton in Leicestershire, named with the Old English personal name *Tila* + Old English *tūn* 'farmstead', 'settlement'.
FOREBEARS William Tilton came to Lynn, MA, in or before 1637. Many of his descendants were master mariners, living on Martha's Vineyard. James Tilton of DE (1745–1822) was a physician who became U.S. surgeon general.

Tim (178) **1.** Cambodian: unexplained. **2.** English: variant of TIMM.
GIVEN NAMES Cambodian 22%. *Yoeum* (2), *Chheang*, *Noeun*, *Phoeun*, *Sambath*, *Soeun*, *Sokhom*, *Sombath*, *Sovann*; *Lach*, *Mau*, *Sophal*, *Thong*, *Thy*; *Leng* (2), *Roeun*.

Timar (114) Hungarian (**Tímár**): occupational name for a cobbler or tanner, Hungarian *tímár*.
GIVEN NAMES Hungarian 7%. *Elek*, *Laszlo*, *Tibor*, *Zsolt*.

Timberlake (1594) English: habitational name from a lost place in the parish of Bayton, Worcestershire, so named from Old English *timber* 'timber', 'wood' + *lacu* 'stream'.

Timberman (227) Dutch: variant of TIMMERMAN.

Timbers (206) English (Norfolk): unexplained.

Timblin (248) English: from a pet form of an Old English personal name (see TIMM).

Timbrook (322) Origin unidentified.

Timbs (245) English: apparently an altered spelling of TIMMS.

Times (112) English: probably a variant of TIMMS.

Timian (121) **1.** Perhaps Irish, an Anglicized form of Gaelic **Ó Tiomáin** (see TIMMONS). **2.** Alternatively perhaps Norwegian, a topographic name for someone who lived where wild thyme grew, from *timian* 'thyme'. **3.** Variant spelling of German **Thimian**, a metonymic occupational name from *thymus* 'thyme' for an herb and spice grocer.

Timken (136) North German: variant of THIEME.

Timko (1004) Hungarian (**Timkó**): from a pet form of the ecclesiastical name *Timót*, from a reduced form of Latin *Tymotheus*.

Timler (103) Altered spelling of German **Timmler**, a variant of **Thümmler**, from either *tumel* 'loud noise' or an agent derivative Middle High German *tumelen* 'to lark about', as a nickname for a restless, lively person; or alternatively from Middle Low

German *tumeler* 'tightrope walker', 'tumbler'.

Timlin (395) Irish: from a pet form of the personal name THOMAS. According to MacLysaght, this was the name of a family of Norman Welsh origin that formed a sept in the Irish fashion in the barony of Tirawley, Co. Mayo. The name is recorded as *Tomilin* in the 17th century and has been Gaelicized as **Mac Toimilin**.

Timm (3900) **1.** English: probably from an otherwise unrecorded Old English personal name, cognate with the attested Continental Germanic form *Timmo*. This is of uncertain origin, perhaps a short form of **Dietmar**. The personal name *Timothy* was not in use in England until Tudor times, and is therefore not a likely source of this surname, which is medieval in origin. **2.** North German and Dutch: from a short form of the medieval personal name **Dietmar**.
GIVEN NAMES German 4%. *Otto* (8), *Erwin* (3), *Ewald* (3), *Helmuth* (3), *Irmgard* (3), *Ernst* (2), *Frieda* (2), *Angelika*, *Arno*, *Bernhard*, *Bernhardt*, *Dieter*.

Timme (263) Variant of TIMM.
GIVEN NAMES German 5%. *Eberhard* (2), *Christoph*.

Timmel (136) German: **1.** variant of THUMMEL. **2.** habitational name from place so named in Lower Saxony.

Timmer (1122) North German: **1.** metonymic occupational name for a carpenter, from Low German *timmer* 'timber'. **2.** from a reduced form of *Thiemer*, a variant of DITTMAR. **3.** habitational name from any of several places called Timmern in Lower Saxony.

Timmerman (2876) **1.** Dutch and English: occupational name for a carpenter or timber merchant, from Middle English *timber*, *tymber*, Middle Dutch *timmer*, Low German *Timmer* 'timber' + Middle English, Middle Dutch *man*, Low German *Mann* 'man'. **2.** Variant spelling of German TIMMERMANN.

Timmermann (308) North German: occupational name for a carpenter, from Low German *Timmer* 'timber' + Low German *Mann* 'man'. Compare German ZIMMERMANN.
GIVEN NAMES German 8%. *Klaus* (3), *Ernst* (2), *Johann*, *Kurt*.

Timmermans (161) Dutch: patronymic from TIMMERMAN.
GIVEN NAMES Dutch 12%; French 5%. *Pieter* (2), *Cornie*, *Frans*, *Jeroen*, *Martinus*; *Adrien*, *Philippe*.

Timmers (252) Dutch: occupational name for a carpenter from Middle Dutch *timmer* 'timber'.

Timmins (944) English (chiefly West Midlands): variant spelling of TIMMONS.

Timmis (112) English: variant of TIMMONS.

Timmons (6532) **1.** Irish: reduced Anglicized form of Gaelic **Mac Toimín** 'son of

Toimín', a pet form of *Tomás*, Gaelic form of THOMAS. **2.** Irish: Anglicized form of Gaelic **Ó Tiomáin** 'descendant of *Tiomán'*, a personal name from a diminutive of *tiom* 'pliant', 'soft'. **3.** Irish: reduced Anglicized form of Gaelic **Ó Tiománaigh** (see TIMONEY). **4.** English: patronymic from a pet form of the personal name TIMM.

Timmreck (101) North German: probably a reduced form of **Timmerhindrich** (equivalent to *Heinrich Timmer(mann)*), a distinguishing occupational name for a carpenter called *Heinrich* (see TIMMER and HEINRICH).

Timms (1355) English (Oxfordshire) and Dutch: patronymic from TIMM.

Timon (131) Irish (Mayo): variant of TIMMONS.

Timoney (173) Irish: reduced Anglicized form of Gaelic **Ó Tiománaigh** 'descendant of *Tiománach'*, a variant of *Tiomán* (see TIMMONS).
GIVEN NAMES Irish 14%. *Conall* (2), *Brendan, Ciaran, Conan, Eamon.*

Timothy (583) **1.** English: from the New Testament Greek personal name *Timotheos*, from Greek *timē* 'honor' + *theos* 'God'. This was the name of a companion of St. Paul who, according to tradition, was stoned to death for denouncing the worship of Diana in Ephesus. This was not in general use in England as a given name until Tudor times, so, insofar as it is an English surname at all, it is a late formation (e.g. in Wales, where surnames came into use only relatively recently). In America it also represents an adoption of the English given name in place of a cognate in Greek (**Timotheou, Timotheopoulos**) or any of various other European languages. **2.** Irish: adoption of the English personal name as an equivalent of TUMULTY.

Timpano (107) Southern Italian: from Italian *timpano*, Sicilian *timpanu* 'drum', 'drummer', Latin *tympanum*.
GIVEN NAMES Italian 27%. *Alfonso, Angelo, Egidio, Gennaro, Ilario, Nazzareno, Orlando Rocco, Salvatore, Sarino.*

Timpe (302) North German: from Middle Low German *timpe* 'tip', 'point', hence a topographic name from a field so called or for someone who lived at the far end of a village.
GIVEN NAMES German 5%. *Gunter, Kurt, Winfried.*

Timperley (133) English: unexplained.

Timpone (175) Italian: **1.** habitational name from any of various places named with this word, probably from Sicilian *timpuni* 'lump of earth', 'clod', as for example Timpone in Sapri, Salerno province, or Timpone Carnalevari in Cutro, Crotone province. **2.** from an augmentative of *Tempo*, a short form of the personal name BONTEMPO.
GIVEN NAMES Italian 11%. *Angelo, Leonardo, Pasquale, Salvatore.*

Timpson (324) English: variant of TIMS.

Tims (998) English: patronymic from the personal name TIMM.

Timson (188) English: variant of TIMS.

Tin (174) **1.** Dutch and French: unexplained. **2.** Chinese: variant of TIAN.
GIVEN NAMES Chinese 27%; Vietnamese 8%. *Maung* (5), *Han* (2), *Wan* (2), *Ying* (2), *Eng, Heang, Heng, Kan, Kwok, Man, Ming, On; Danh, Hung, Lanh, Men, Mui, Nguyen, Quan, Thai, Tun.*

Tinajero (253) Spanish: occupational name from *tinajero* 'landlord', 'innkeeper'.
GIVEN NAMES Spanish 58%. *Jose* (11), *Salvador* (5), *Juan* (4), *Miguel* (4), *Sergio* (4), *Carlos* (3), *Manuel* (3), *Rafael* (3), *Arturo* (2), *Eduardo* (2), *Felipe* (2), *Gustavo* (2).

Tinch (392) English: probably a variant of TENCH.

Tincher (1092) Altered form of German **Tüncher**, a spelling probably influenced by a dialect pronunciation of the surname, which is an occupational name for a whitewasher or painter, Middle High German *tüncher*.

Tindal (508) Variant of TINDALL, Variant of TYNDALL.

Tindall (2321) English: regional name for someone who lived in Tynedale, the valley of the river Tyne, or a habitational name from a place in Cumbria called Tindale, which is situated on a tributary of the South Tyne. The name derives from a British river name *Tina* (apparently from a Celtic root meaning 'to flow') + Old English *dæl* or Old Norse *dalr* 'valley'.

Tindel (211) English: variant spelling of TINDALL.

Tindell (839) English: variant spelling of TINDALL.

Tinder (413) German: of uncertain origin; perhaps from **Tinter, Dinter**, an occupational name for a maker and seller of ink, from an agent derivative of Middle High German *tin(c)te* 'ink' (from Late Latin *aqua tincta* 'colored water').

Tindle (709) English (northeastern): variant spelling of TINDALL.

Tindol (189) Respelling of English TINDALL.

Tine (209) **1.** Italian (Sicily; **Tinè**): most probably an occupational name for a comb maker, from a reduced form of medieval Greek *kteneas*, from *ktenion* 'comb' + the occupational suffix *-eas*. **2.** English (mainly Yorkshire): variant of TYNE. **3.** Perhaps also an Americanized spelling of German THEIN.
GIVEN NAMES Italian 13%. *Pasquale* (3), *Salvatore* (3), *Angelo, Ignazio, Marco, Stefano.*

Tineo (176) Spanish: Castilianized form of Asturian-Leonese **Tíneu**, a habitational name from Tíneu in Asturies.
GIVEN NAMES Spanish 54%. *Jose* (6), *Ramon* (5), *Julio* (4), *Alberto* (2), *Altagracia* (2), *Ana* (2), *Carlos* (2), *Leticia* (2), *Manuel* (2),

Maribel (2), *Mercedes* (2), *Rafael* (2); *Antonio, Carmelo, Rafaelina, Salvatore.*

Tiner (804) Americanized spelling of German **Theiner** or **Theuner**, variants of **Theinert** (see TEINERT).

Tines (168) See TYNES, of which this is probably a variant spelling.

Ting (892) **1.** German, of Lithuanian origin: nickname from Lithuanian *tingus* 'sluggish'. **2.** Chinese 丁: variant of DING.
GIVEN NAMES Chinese 14%. *Li* (5), *Chao* (2), *Chen* (2), *Cheng* (2), *Chien* (2), *Kang* (2), *Keh* (2), *Ming* (2), *Sen* (2), *Yu Chen* (2), *Beng, Chang Sheng.*

Tingen (279) Possibly an Americanized spelling of German **Düngen**, from a short form of the personal name *Anton(ius)* (see ANTHONY).

Tingey (343) Americanized form of French TANGUAY.

Tingle (1683) English: metonymic occupational name for a maker of nails or pins, or nickname for a small, thin man, from Middle English *tingle*, a kind of very small nail (of North German origin).

Tingler (495) **1.** English: occupational name from an agent derivative of Middle English *tingle* (see TINGLE). **2.** German: occupational or status name for a medieval judge or court official, from Old High German *ding* 'legal proceeding'. **3.** German: variant of TENGLER.

Tingley (1254) **1.** Altered spelling of German DINGLE. **2.** Possibly an altered spelling of North German **Tüngler**, a habitational name for someone from Tunglen near Oldenburg (Lower Saxony); or alternatively a topographic name for someone living on a tongue-shaped piece of land, from Middle Low German *tungle* 'tongue'. **3.** English: habitational name, possibly from Tingley in West Yorkshire, named from Old English *þing* 'meeting', 'assembly' + *hlāw* 'mound'. However, this is a predominantly southern name, associated chiefly with Sussex and Kent, which suggests that a different, unidentified source may be involved.

Tingue (106) Of French origin: unexplained.
GIVEN NAMES French 8%. *Delphin, Yvrose.*

Tinker (2185) English (mainly Yorkshire): occupational name for a mender of pots and pans, Middle English *tink(l)er* (of uncertain etymology).

Tinkey (225) Americanized form of French TANGUAY.

Tinkham (727) English (Devon): probably a habitational name from a lost or unidentified place.

Tinkle (442) Probably an altered spelling of German DINKEL, an occupational name for a grain farmer or grain merchant.

Tinklenberg (126) Probably of German origin, a habitational name from Tecklenburg in North Rhine-Westphalia.

Tinklepaugh (129) Americanized spelling of German **Dinkelbach**, a habitational name from a place so named near Neuwied, Rhineland.

Tinkler (372) **1.** Northern English and Scottish: variant of TINKER. **2.** Probably an altered spelling of German **Dinkler**, a metonymic occupational name for a grain farmer or grain merchant, from an agent derivative of Middle High German *dinkel* 'spelt' (a variety of wheat).

Tinley (230) English: apparently a habitational name, probably a variant of TENLEY.

Tinlin (116) Scottish: unexplained; this is a Roxburghshire name, which Black believes to be of local origin.

Tinnel (136) Of French origin: see TINNELL.

Tinnell (329) Probably an altered spelling of French **Tinel**, a metonymic occupational nickname for a porter, from Old French *tinel*, an implement consisting of a pole with two chains on it, carried across the shoulders, with hooks on the ends of the chains, used for moving barrels and the like.

Tinner (123) English: occupational name for a tin worker, Middle English *tinier*, an agent derivative of Middle English, Old English *tin*.

Tinnes (154) German: variant spelling of THINNES.

Tinney (1296) Irish: reduced Anglicized form of Gaelic **Mac an tSionnaigh** 'son of the fox', from *sionnach* 'fox'. Compare SHINNICK.

Tinnin (477) English (Cumbria): unexplained.

Tinnon (130) Origin unidentified; possibly related to TINNIN.

Tino (247) Italian: **1.** from the medieval personal name *Tino*, a reduced form of MARTINO, VALENTINO, or of any of various pet names formed with the suffix *-ino*, as for example *(Al)bertino* from (AL)BERTO, *Clementino* from CLEMENTE, *Fantino* from FANTE, or *Parentino* from PARENTE. **2.** from *tino* 'vat', 'tub' hence probably a metonymic occupational name for someone who made or used such vessels.
GIVEN NAMES Italian 11%. *Salvatore* (3), *Angelo, Antonio, Carmine, Guido, Sal, Silvio.*

Tinoco (541) Spanish and Portuguese (common in Brazil): of uncertain origin; possibly a nickname meaning 'sensible', 'reasonable', from *tino* 'reason', 'sense', 'intellect'.
GIVEN NAMES Spanish 56%; Portuguese 10%. *Jose* (13), *Carlos* (9), *Jesus* (8), *Jorge* (7), *Guillermo* (6), *Juan* (6), *Luis* (6), *Manuel* (6), *Pedro* (5), *Antonio* (4), *Francisco* (4), *Gerardo* (4), *Isidro* (4); *Vasco.*

Tinsley (5171) English: habitational name from a place in South Yorkshire near Rotherham, named in Old English with the genitive case of an unattested personal name *Tynni* + *hlāw* 'hill', 'mound', 'bar-

row'. This name is also established in Ulster.

Tinsman (375) German (**Tinsmann**): **1.** status name for a tax (rent) payer, from Middle Low German *tins* 'tax' + *man* 'man'. **2.** perhaps a habitational name for someone from any of several places in Silesia named Tinz.

Tinson (145) English: unexplained.

Tinti (103) Italian: nickname from Sicilian *tintu* 'evil', 'bad', Calabrian 'unlucky', from Latin *tino* 'stained'.
GIVEN NAMES Italian 4%. *Aldo, Egidio.*

Tintle (145) Probably an altered spelling of German **Tintel** or **Tüntel**, of uncertain origin; possibly a nickname from Low German (Westphalian) *tünte* 'lazy or silly woman' or *tünteln* 'to waste time'. Alternatively, it may be an altered form of German **Tintler**, an occupational name for an ink maker (see TINDER).

Tio (116) **1.** Spanish (**Tío**) and Portuguese: from a byname meaning 'uncle'. **2.** Catalan (**Tió**): nickname from Catalan *tió* 'log', 'stump' (for burning).
GIVEN NAMES Spanish 24%; Italian 6%. *Delfin* (2), *Alberto, Arsenio, Catalina, Jose, Juanita, Julio, Manuel, Mario, Ninfa, Nydia, Pepe*; *Cesario, Emelio, Federico, Romano.*

Tipler (226) English (East Midlands): occupational name from Middle English *tipeler* 'ale-seller'.

Tipp (123) **1.** English: from a short form of the medieval personal name *Tebald, Tibalt* (see THEOBALD). **2.** North German: from Low German *tippe, tibbe* 'wooden pail', 'small tub'.

Tippen (148) **1.** German: from a short form of the Germanic personal name *Theudobrand*, a compound of *theod* 'people' + *brand* 'sword'. **2.** German: reduced form of **Tippenhauer**, an occupational name from Low German *Tippe* 'wooden pail', 'tub' + *houwer* (High German *Hauer*) 'cutter'. **3.** English: variant spelling of TIPPIN.

Tippens (294) **1.** English: variant spelling of TIPPINS. **2.** Probably also a derivative or variant of German TIPPEN.

Tipper (196) **1.** English: probably an occupational name for a maker of arrowheads, from an agent derivative of Middle English *tippe* 'tip', 'head'. On the other hand it may possibly be a bawdy nickname from an agent derivative of Middle English *tÿpe(n)* 'to knock over' (of obscure origin; here with a sexually suggestive sense). The same name has been established in Ireland, in County Kildare, since the beginning of the 14th century. **2.** German: topographic name from a Westphalian field name, *Tippe*, of unexplained etymology.

Tippery (132) English (Durham): unexplained.

Tippet (103) English: variant of TIBBETT.

Tippets (186) Variant of English TIBBETTS.

Tippett (1564) English (Cornwall): variant of TIBBETT.

Tippetts (282) English: variant of TIBBETTS.

Tippie (345) Possibly an altered spelling of German **Tippe**, a metonymic occupational name for a tub maker, from Low German (also Rhineland) *tibbe, tippe* 'wooden tub', 'vat'; or of **Tibbe**, from *Tiebbo*, a short form of a Germanic personal name formed with Old High German *diot* 'people' + *brand* 'sword' or *berht* 'shining'.

Tippin (347) English: from the personal name *Tippin*, a pet form of TIPP.

Tipping (305) English: from a medieval personal name, originally an Old English patronymic from a personal name or byname *Tippa*, for which there is evidence in place names such as Tiptree, but which is of uncertain origin.

Tippins (380) English: patronymic from the personal name TIPPIN, or a variant of TIPPING.

Tippit (436) English: variant of TIBBETT.

Tippitt (188) English: variant of TIBBETT.

Tipple (239) **1.** English (Norfolk): from the medieval personal name *Tebald, Tibalt* (see THEOBALD). **2.** German: from a nickname for a simpleton, from Low German *tippel* 'point', 'corner', 'tag' (possibly a reference to the pointed shape of a fool's cap). **3.** German: from a pet form of a Germanic personal name related to DIETRICH.

Tipps (576) Probably a variant of English TIBBS.

Tippy (184) See TIPPIE.

Tipsword (235) Origin unidentified. It appears to be of English origin, but the name is not found in current English records.

Tipton (8967) English (West Midlands): habitational name from a place in the West Midlands, recorded in Domesday Book as *Tibintone*, probably 'settlement (Old English *tūn*) associated with *Tibba*', an Old English personal name of obscure origin.

Tirabassi (146) Italian: evidently a nickname from a compound of *tirare* 'to move', 'to pull' + *basso* 'low', of uncertain application.
GIVEN NAMES Italian 11%. *Santo* (2), *Amerigo, Gaspare, Guido.*

Tirado (1275) Spanish: probably a nickname for someone with long limbs, from Spanish *tirado* 'stretched' (past participle of *tirar* 'to pull').
GIVEN NAMES Spanish 47%. *Jose* (50), *Carlos* (17), *Juan* (14), *Angel* (11), *Julio* (10), *Luis* (10), *Miguel* (10), *Rafael* (10), *Francisco* (7), *Manuel* (7), *Ruben* (7), *Aida* (6).

Tirey (305) English and Irish: probably a variant of Scottish TYREE.
GIVEN NAME Irish 4%. *Conley* (4).

Tirone (326) Italian: possibly from an augmentative of the personal name *Tiro*, from Calabrian *tiru* denoting a type of snake, but more likely a habitational name for someone from Thiron in France (recorded *c.*1120 as *Tyronium*), or a topographic name from *tirone* 'round hill'.

GIVEN NAMES Italian 19%. *Carmelo* (4), *Carmine* (4), *Salvatore* (4), *Antonio* (2), *Gasper* (2), *Stefano* (2), *Angelo, Carlo, Filiberto, Francesco, Ignazio, Marco*.

Tirpak (314) Hungarian (**Tirpák**): ethnic name for a Slovak.

Tirrell (582) English and Irish: variant spelling of TYRRELL.

Tiscareno (178) Spanish (**Tiscareño**): probably habitational name froma derivative of Tiscar, a village near Seville.

GIVEN NAMES Spanish 55%. *Jesus* (5), *Javier* (4), *Jose* (4), *Juan* (4), *Rafael* (3), *Arturo* (2), *Belen* (2), *Eduardo* (2), *Fernando* (2), *Fidel* (2), *Francisca* (2), *Ruben* (2).

Tisch (339) Jewish (Ashkenazic): metonymic occupational name for a joiner, from German *Tisch*, Yiddish *tish* 'table'.

Tischendorf (105) German: habitational name from Tischendorf in Thuringia or possibly from any of various places named Teschendorf, for example in Lower Saxony.

Tischer (518) German: variant of TISCHLER.

GIVEN NAMES German 6%. *Hans* (3), *Bernd* (2), *Erwin, Fritz, Heinz, Horst, Kurt*.

Tischler (819) German and Jewish (Ashkenazic): occupational name for a joiner, from an agent derivative of Middle High German *tisch*, German *Tisch* 'table'. This became the normal term for the craftsman in northern and eastern Germany and in Austria and Switzerland during the 15th century; before that it had been TISCHER.

GIVEN NAMES German 4%. *Reinhold* (3), *Hans* (2), *Heinz, Ignaz, Rainer, Siegmund*.

Tisdale (3077) English (Shropshire): variant of TEESDALE.

Tisdel (225) English: variant of TEESDALE.

Tisdell (216) English: variant of TEESDALE.

Tise (132) Probably an Americanized spelling of German THEIS or THEISS.

Tish (235) Jewish (Ashkenazic): variant of TISCH.

Tisher (198) Variant of German TISCHER.

Tishler (176) Jewish (Ashkenazic): occupational name for a joiner, from German TISCHLER, or variant of the German name, or Americanized form of Slovenian **Tišler**, with the same meaning.

GIVEN NAMES Russian 5%. *Arkadiy, Raisa, Yuriy*.

Tishman (128) Jewish (Ashkenazic): occupational name for a joiner, from German *Tisch* 'table' + *Mann* 'man'.

Tisinger (124) Probably a variant of German **Teisinger, Deisinger**, a habitational name for someone from Deising in Bavaria or Teising in Upper Austria.

Tisler (131) Slovenian (**Tišler**): occupational name for a joiner, from an agent deriva-

tive of Middle High German *tisch* 'table' (see TISCHLER).

Tiso (138) Italian: of uncertain derivation; possibly from a personal name of Germanic origin, but in some cases at least probably a habitational name from Tiso in Bolzano province.

GIVEN NAMES Italian 30%. *Angelo* (4), *Pasquale* (3), *Marco* (2), *Carlo, Carmine, Cosimo, Enrico, Gaetano, Libero, Luciano, Marcello, Nicoletta*.

Tison (518) **1.** French: nickname from Old French *tison* 'firebrand' (see TYSON 2). **2.** Possibly an altered spelling of German THEISEN.

Tissot (120) French: from a diminutive of **Tissier** (see TESSIER).

GIVEN NAMES French 8%; German 5%. *Emile, Pierre; Otto* (2).

Tissue (155) Altered form of French TISSOT.

GIVEN NAME German 4%. *Otto*.

Titcomb (349) English: habitational name from Titcomb in Berkshire or Titcombe in Gloucestershire.

Tite (108) **1.** English (Northamptonshire): from the Old French form of the Latin personal name *Titus*. Compare TITO. **2.** French: from the Germanic personal name *Tito*, derived from *theudo* 'people', 'race'.

Title (138) Spelling of German and Dutch TITTEL or English TUTTLE.

Titley (105) English (Staffordshire and Shropshire): habitational name from Titley in Hereford, named from an Old English personal name *Titta* + *lēah* 'woodland clearing'.

GIVEN NAMES French 6%. *Jacques, Pascale*.

Titlow (149) English (eastern counties): unexplained.

Titman (144) **1.** English: status name for the head of a tithing, Old English *tēoðingmann* (from *tēoðing* 'tithing', a group of households, originally ten households, + *mann* 'man'). According to the medieval system of frankpledge, every member of a tithing was responsible for every other, so that for example if one of them committed a crime the others had to help pay for it. **2.** English: from the Middle English, Old English personal name *Tideman*, composed of Old English *tīd* 'time', 'season' + *mann* 'man'. **3.** Altered spelling of German **Tittmann**, a variant of DITTMANN.

Titmus (135) English (Hertfordshire): nickname from *titmose* 'tit(mouse)', applied to someone thought to resemble the bird.

Tito (243) Italian: **1.** (also Greek, **Titos**): from the Latin personal name *Titus*, which was borne by a disciple of St. Paul who became bishop of Crete. It is also found as a surname among Spanish speakers. **2.** habitational name from Tito in Potenza province. **3.** in southern Italy, possibly a nickname from Sicilian *titu* 'small'.

GIVEN NAMES Spanish 14%; Italian 5%. *Manuel* (5), *Miguel* (4), *Luis* (2), *Mario* (2),

Carlos, Emilia, Geraldo, Hernan, Imelda, Jose, Juan, Margarita; Antonio (2), *Salvatore* (2), *Dario*.

Titone (263) Italian: from an augmentative of TITO, or possibly from a personal name of Germanic origin.

GIVEN NAMES Italian 21%. *Mario* (2), *Salvatore* (2), *Angelo, Antonio, Carmella, Claudio, Gaspare, Rosario, Sal, Salvatore, Vito*.

Titsworth (446) English: habitational name from Tetsworth in Oxfordshire, from an unattested Old English personal name *Tǣtel* + Old English *worth* 'enclosure'.

Tittel (148) **1.** South German: nickname from Middle High German *tütelen* 'to flatter', or possibly from Middle High German *tütel* 'nipple', 'tit'. **2.** North German and Dutch: from a variant of *Dietel*, a pet form of a personal name formed with *Diet-*, from the unattested Germanic word *þeudo-* 'people'. Compare DIETRICH.

GIVEN NAMES German 9%. *Friedrich, Hans, Helmuth, Jurgen, Klaus, Otto*.

Titterington (188) English (northwestern England and northern Ireland): habitational name from Tytherington in Cheshire, named in Old English as *Tydringtūn*, either 'settlement (*tūn*) associated with *Tȳdre*', an unattested personal name of uncertain meaning, or 'stockbreeding farmstead' (Old English *tȳd(d)ring* + *tūn*).

Tittle (1517) Altered spelling of German TITTEL or TITLE.

Tittsworth (155) See TITSWORTH.

Titus (5701) German: **1.** from the personal name (Latin *Titus*, probably Etruscan in origin). The name was popular in the Middle Ages since it had been borne by a disciple of St. Paul who became bishop of Crete. **2.** from a short form of a Germanic personal name (see TITTEL 2).

Titzer (159) German: variant of TIETZ.

Tiu (151) **1.** Filipino: probably from a personal name. Due to imposition of the Spanish culture in the Philippines, some Filipino names with Tiu were respelt as Tio, by the assimilation to Spanish **Tío** (see TIO). **2.** Chinese: unexplained.

GIVEN NAMES Spanish 35%; Italian 5%. *Wilfredo* (5), *Alfredo* (2), *Domingo* (2), *Ofelio* (2), *Alfonso, Amando, Balbino, Carlos, Elvira, Ernesto, Fortunato, Jaime; Romeo* (2), *Antonio, Enrico, Rossano*.

Tivnan (159) Irish: reduced Anglicized form of Gaelic **Ó Teimhneáin** (see TYNAN).

Tiwari (170) Indian (northern states): altered form of TRIPATHI.

GIVEN NAMES Indian 84%. *Prabhat* (3), *Rajesh* (3), *Ram* (3), *Satish* (3), *Sudha* (3), *Ajit* (2), *Anil* (2), *Indra* (2), *Mamta* (2), *Rakesh* (2), *Ramesh* (2), *Sandeep* (2).

Tix (102) From a short form of any of the many Germanic personal names formed with *theod* 'people'. Compare TIEKEN.

Tjaden (505) North German and Frisian: patronymic from a pet form of the personal name *Tjade* (see TACK).
GIVEN NAMES German 5%. *Kurt* (3), *Claus, Guenter, Jurgen, Otto.*

Tjarks (162) North German and Frisian: patronymic from *Tjark*, a form of the Germanic personal name *Theodoric* (see DIETRICH).
GIVEN NAMES German 4%. *Fritz, Hermann.*

Tkac (107) Sorbian or other Slavic: occupational name for a weaver. Compare TKACH.

Tkach (477) Ukrainian and Jewish (eastern Ashkenazic): occupational name for a weaver, Ukrainian *tkach*, a derivative of *tkaty* 'to weave'.
GIVEN NAMES Russian 10%; Jewish 6%. *Anatoliy* (3), *Boris* (3), *Vladimir* (3), *Arkadiy* (2), *Igor* (2), *Leonid* (2), *Mikhail* (2), *Nadezhda* (2), *Nikolay* (2), *Aleksandr, Galina, Grigory, Aba, Aron, Faina, Irina, Isaak, Jakov, Naum, Reveka.*

Tkachuk (137) Ukrainian and Jewish (eastern Ashkenazic): from a diminutive of TKACH.
GIVEN NAMES Russian 15%; Jewish 5%. *Igor* (2), *Vasily* (2), *Dmytro, Ekaterina, Evgeny, Galina, Grigory, Mikhail, Svetlana; Filipp, Mariya, Semen.*

Tkacz (144) Polish and Jewish (eastern Ashkenazic): occupational name for a weaver, Polish *tkacz*, a noun derivative of *tkać* 'to weave'. Compare TKACH.
GIVEN NAMES Polish 14%. *Bogdan* (2), *Andrzej, Dariusz, Dorota, Jaroslaw, Jerzy, Piotr, Wasyl.*

Tkaczyk (104) Polish: from a diminutive of TKACZ 'weaver'.
GIVEN NAMES Polish 16%. *Krystyna, Maciej, Slawek, Slawomir, Stanislaw, Tadeusz, Wieslaw.*

Tlusty (103) Czech; Slovak (**Tlstý**): descriptive epithet meaning 'plump', 'stout'.

To (1182) **1.** Vietnamese: unexplained. **2.** Chinese 杜: Cantonese variant of DU 1. **3.** Chinese 陶: Cantonese variant of TAO. **4.** Chinese 涂: Cantonese variant of TU 2. **5.** Chinese 屠: Cantonese variant of TU 3. **6.** Chinese 褚: variant of CHU 2. **7.** Korean: there are three Chinese characters for the Korean surname *To*. Of these, two are quite rare, while the third is used by at least fifteen clans. Three clans can be documented, but two of them appear to be practically extinct. Only the Söngju To clan has a significant population in Korea. The origins of the Söngju To clan are unclear. It is certain, however, that the clan was living in the Söngju area by the end of the post-Shilla Three Kingdom period.
GIVEN NAMES Vietnamese 46%; Chinese/Korean 19%. *Minh* (14), *Thanh* (14), *Dung* (10), *Vinh* (10), *Hung* (9), *Son* (9), *Chuong* (6), *Ha* (6), *Hien* (6), *Hoa* (6), *Huong* (6), *Mai* (6); *Wai* (5), *Chi* (3), *Hang* (3), *Hon*

(3), *Lai* (3), *Sang* (3), *Sze* (3), *Chan* (2), *Hing* (2), *Man Ching* (2), *Chen, Cheung.*

Toadvine (123) Origin unidentified.

Toal (542) Irish (County Monaghan): variant of TOOLE.
GIVEN NAME Irish 4%. *Malachy.*

Toalson (162) Origin unidentified.

Toback (221) Possibly a variant of the Ashkenazic Jewish family name **Tobak**, a variant of TABAK.
GIVEN NAMES Jewish 4%; German 4%. *Hyman; Erna* (2).

Tobar (513) Spanish: habitational name from any of the places called Tobar, named with a collective noun derived from *toba* 'tufa' (a kind of light, porous volcanic rock).
GIVEN NAMES Spanish 52%. *Jose* (13), *Carlos* (12), *Juan* (7), *Luis* (6), *Rafael* (6), *Guadalupe* (5), *Jorge* (5), *Julio* (5), *Mario* (5), *Miguel* (5), *Fernando* (4), *Jesus* (4).

Tobe (230) **1.** German: habitational name from a place in Thuringia called Toba. **2.** Frisian and Dutch: from a pet form of a Germanic personal name (see TABBERT 2), or from a derivative of the Biblical name TOBIAS. **3.** Japanese: variously written, usually with characters meaning 'door' or 'earth' for the first character and 'department' or 'side' for the second. None are common in Japan.
GIVEN NAMES Japanese 5%. *Atsushi, Mami, Takao, Tatsuro, Yoshika.*

Tobeck (112) North German: topographic name meaning 'at (the) brook', from Low German *to* 'at' + *beck* 'brook' (see BACH).
GIVEN NAME German 4%. *Jochen.*

Toben (203) **1.** Frisian: patronymic from TOBE. **2.** German and Jewish: patronymic from TOBIAS.

Tober (549) **1.** German: habitational name for someone from Toba in Thuringia or Tober in Styria. **2.** German: from a derivative of *Tobe*, a short form of the personal name TOBIAS. **3.** Jewish (Ashkenazic): variant of TAUBER.
GIVEN NAMES German 7%. *Kurt* (2), *Otto* (2), *Ewald, Heinz, Herta, Horst, Klaus, Merwin, Siegfried.*

Toberman (142) Jewish (Ashkenazic): variant of TAUBER + Yiddish *man* 'man'.

Tobey (1568) English: from the personal name *Toby* (see TOBIAS).

Tobia (376) **1.** Italian: from the personal name *Tobia* (see TOBIAS). **2.** Spanish (**Tobía**): habitational name from Tobía in Logroño province.
GIVEN NAMES Italian 9%. *Giacomo* (2), *Aldo, Angelo, Caesar, Emanuele, Emelio, Enio, Enrico, Gino.*

Tobias (4088) English, French, German, Dutch, Spanish (**Tobías**), Hungarian (**Tóbiás**), and Jewish: from a Greek form of the Hebrew male personal name *Ṭōvyāh* 'Jehovah is good', which, together with

various derivative forms, has been popular among Jews for generations.

Tobiason (202) Respelling of Danish and Norwegian TOBIASSEN or of the Swedish cognate **Tobiasson**.
GIVEN NAMES Scandinavian 9%. *Erik* (4), *Eilif, Thor.*

Tobiassen (115) Danish or Norwegian: patronymic from the personal name *Tobias* (see TOBIAS).
GIVEN NAMES Scandinavian 15%. *Oivind, Thoralf.*

Tobiasz (102) Polish: patronymic from the personal name *Tobiasz* (see TOBIAS).
GIVEN NAMES Polish 13%. *Andrzej, Boleslaw, Tadeusz, Zygmunt.*

Tobie (106) Patronymic from the personal name *Tobias* (see TOBIAS), in an unidentified language.

Tobin (7693) **1.** Irish: reduced Anglicized form of Gaelic **Tóibín**, which is itself a reduced Gaelicized version of a Norman habitational name from Saint-Aubin in Brittany (so called from the dedication of its church to St. ALBIN). **2.** English: from a pet form of the personal name TOBIAS or TOBY. **3.** Dutch: patronymic from TOBIAS.

Tobler (682) South German (especially Swiss): topographic name for someone who lived near a ravine or gorge, from Middle High German southern dialect *tobel* 'gorge' + -*er*, suffix denoting an inhabitant.
GIVEN NAMES German 4%. *Erwin, Hans, Hans-Peter, Johann.*

Tobola (122) Polish (also **Tobola**): **1.** derivative of the personal name *Tobiasz*, Polish form of TOBIAS. **2.** nickname from Polish dialect *tobola* 'bundle'.

Tobolski (179) Jewish (eastern Ashkenazic): habitational name for someone from Toboly in Belarus.

Tobon (161) perhaps Spanish (**Tobón**): possibly a topographic name from a derivative of *toba* 'tufa' (see TOBAR). This is an uncommon name in Spain, but common in Colombia and also Mexico.
GIVEN NAMES Spanish 46%. *Luis* (6), *Carlos* (4), *Francisco* (4), *Jorge* (4), *Juan* (3), *Alvaro* (2), *Guillermo* (2), *Mario* (2), *Alfonso, Amado, Amparo, Asuncion.*

Toburen (137) North German (also **Tobüren**): topographic name from *to buren* 'at the dwelling place(s)', from Middle Low german *bür* 'one who lives in the same community (*bur*)'.

Toby (443) English: from the personal name *Toby* (see TOBIAS).

Toca (115) **1.** Spanish: from *toca* 'cap', 'headgear', a nickname for someone who made or sold headgear or who habitually wore distinctive headgear. **2.** Galician: habitational name from places called Toca, in the Galician provinces of A Coruña and Lugo.
GIVEN NAMES Spanish 23%. *Carlos* (3), *Mario* (3), *Genaro* (2), *Luis* (2), *Orestes*

(2), *Ana, Ana Luisa, Humberto, Jose, Lupe, Marta, Pablo.*

Tocci (578) **1.** Italian: patronymic from the personal name *Toccio*, a short form of a pet name formed with this ending, as for example *(Al)bertoccio* from (AL)BERTO, *Bartoccio* from BARTO(LO), or *Fantoccio* from FANTE. **2.** Greek (**Totsis, Tokis**): from a pet form of the personal name *Theotokēs*, a derivative of *theotokos*, an epithet of the Virgin Mary (from *theos* 'god' + *tokos* 'bearer', 'biological mother', from *tiktein* 'to give birth to').
GIVEN NAMES Italian 17%. *Angelo* (5), *Guido* (4), *Salvatore* (3), *Carlo* (2), *Carmine* (2), *Rocco* (2), *Santino* (2), *Valentino* (2), *Amerigo, Battista, Biagio, Carmelo.*

Tocco (633) Italian: **1.** probably a habitational name from any of various places so named, in particular Tocco Caudio in Benevento province or Tocco da Casauria in Pescara. **2.** alternatively, it could be a nickname from *tocco*, an adjective meaning 'eccentric', or from the noun *tocco* meaning '(judge's) cap', or, in Old Italian, 'piece', 'part'. **3.** from a variant of the personal name *Toccio* (see TOCCI).
GIVEN NAMES Italian 17%; French 4%. *Salvatore* (11), *Sal* (4), *Vito* (4), *Carmela* (2), *Salvator* (2), *Alfonse, Angelo, Carlo, Carmine, Damiano, Dante, Domiano*; *Andre* (2), *Alphonse, Georges, Pierre.*

Toce (152) Italian: unexplained; possibly from a reduced form of a personal name. In Italy the surname is associated chiefly with Corleto Perticara in Potenza province.
GIVEN NAMES Italian 13%; French 8%. *Rocco* (3), *Carmin, Vito*; *Andre* (3).

Tock (169) **1.** English (Lincolnshire) and Scottish: from an Old English personal name *Tocca*. **2.** German: from a short form of the Germanic personal name *Theodicho*, formed with Germanic *theod-* 'people', 'tribe'. Compare DIETRICH. **3.** Jewish (eastern Ashkenazic): metonymic occupational name for a turner, from Yiddish *tok* 'turner's lathe' (see TOKAR).

Toczek (162) Polish: nickname for a person who waddled, from a derivative of *toczyć się* 'to waddle'.
GIVEN NAMES Polish 16%. *Andrzej* (3), *Jacek, Janina, Leszek, Mariusz, Stanislaw, Tadeusz, Wladyslawa.*

Tod (102) Scottish: variant of TODD.

Toda (184) **1.** Japanese: there are three names with this pronunciation. One, written with characters meaning 'door' and 'rice paddy', is found predominantly in eastern Japan; bearers are said to be descended from the northern FUJIWARA clan. Another, meaning 'far rice paddy', can also be pronounced **Enda** and is found in eastern Japan. A third, meaning 'eastern rice paddy', is also pronounced **Higashida** in western Japan. **2.** Catalan: from the female personal name *Tota.*

GIVEN NAMES Japanese 43%. *Shigeru* (3), *Ayako* (2), *Kenji* (2), *Minoru* (2), *Akira, Chisa, Eiko, Hideo, Hirohito, Hiroshi, Hiroyuki, Ikuko.*

Todaro (1014) Italian: from the Greek personal name *Theodōros* (see THEODORE).
GIVEN NAMES Italian 23%. *Salvatore* (10), *Angelo* (7), *Mario* (5), *Sal* (5), *Biagio* (4), *Carlo* (4), *Carmine* (4), *Giuseppe* (3), *Alicia* (2), *Antonio* (2), *Giovanni* (2), *Liborio* (2), *Marcello* (2), *Onofrio* (2), *Rocco* (2).

Todd (26184) English (mainly northern) and Scottish: nickname for someone thought to resemble a fox, for example in cunning or slyness, or perhaps more obviously in having red hair, from northern Middle English *tod(de)* 'fox' (of unknown origin).

Toder (106) Jewish: from the male personal name *Toder*, a pet form of *Todres*, which in turn is related to Greek *Theodoros*.
GIVEN NAMES Jewish 8%; German 5%. *Emanuel* (3), *Iakov, Isadore, Sol*; *Wolf.*

Todhunter (239) English (Cumbria): nickname for a keen hunter of foxes, from Northern Middle English *tod(de)* 'fox' + Middle English *hunter(e)* (see HUNTER).

Todisco (230) Southern Italian: variant of TEDESCO.
GIVEN NAMES Italian 28%. *Mario* (5), *Antonio* (4), *Angelo* (3), *Pasquale* (3), *Lorenzo* (2), *Vito* (2), *Arcangelo, Carlo, Carmine, Franco, Guido, Modesto, Rocco, Salvatore, Sergio, Urbano.*

Todman (106) English: variant of **Tudman**, a habitational name for someone from either of two places in Norfolk and Suffolk called Tuddenham, from the genitive form of the Old English personal name *Tūda* + *hām* 'homestead', 'settlement'.
GIVEN NAMES French 11%. *Lucien, Patrice.*

Todora (132) Italian: feminine form of **Todoro**, a variant of TODARO.
GIVEN NAME Italian 5%. *Santo.*

Todoroff (139) Bulgarian: alternative spelling of **Todorov**, a patronymic from the personal name *Todor*, Bulgarian form of THEODORE.

Todorovich (144) Serbian (**Todorović**): patronymic from the personal name *Todor* (see THEODORE).
GIVEN NAMES South Slavic 21%. *Marko* (2), *Aleksandar, Bosko, Branko, Dragoljub, Mile, Milica, Momir, Slavko.*

Todt (256) German: variant of TOTH 2 and 3.
GIVEN NAMES German 7%. *Christoph, Franz, Hannes, Volker, Wolfgang.*

Toelke (100) German (**Tölke**): variant of **Tolk** or **Tölk**, from a Slavic personal name based on Old Slavic *toliti* 'to soothe' (see TULK).

Toelle (228) **1.** German: from a pet form of the personal name *Bertold* (see BERTHOLD). **2.** German: variant of TOLLE. **3.** Eastern German (**Tölle**): of Slavic origin, from *toliti* 'to soothe or calm'.

GIVEN NAMES German 4%. *Gerda, Reinhold, Willi.*

Toellner (149) North German (**Töllner**): occupational name for a collector of tolls or customs levies, Middle Low German *tol-ner.*

Toenjes (199) North German and Frisian: from a short form of the personal name *Antonius* (see ANTHONY).

Toennies (136) North German, Westphalian (**Tönnies**): from a reduced form of the personal name *Antonius* (see ANTHONY).
GIVEN NAMES German 10%. *Arno, Ewald, Kurt, Otto, Ralf.*

Toensing (122) German (**Tönsing**): probably a variant of **Tonsing**, a patronymic from a short form of the personal name *Antonius* (see ANTHONY).

Toepel (100) German: **1.** (also **Töpel**): habitational name from Töpeln in Saxony. **2.** from Middle High German *top(p)el* 'die', probably applied as a nickname for an inveterate dice player.
GIVEN NAME German 6%. *Arno.*

Toepfer (565) German (**Töpfer**): occupational name for a maker of metal or earthenware pots, from an agent derivative of Middle High German *topf(e)* 'pot', 'vessel' (first attested in the 12th century, and at first found only in the eastern German dialects).
GIVEN NAMES German 4%. *Ernst, Rudi.*

Toepke (115) North German and Frisian: from a pet form of a variant of TEBBE.
GIVEN NAMES German 8%. *Otto.*

Toews (540) North German (**Töws**): variant of TEWS.

Tofani (101) Italian: from *Tofano*, a short form of the personal name *Cristofano*, a variant of *Cristoforo* (see CHRISTOPHER).
GIVEN NAMES Italian 13%. *Angelo* (2), *Dino, Gino.*

Toft (606) **1.** English: habitational name from any of the various places, for example in Cambridgeshire, Lincolnshire, Norfolk, and Warwickshire, named in Old Norse with *topt*, Old Danish *toft* 'curtilage', 'site', 'homestead'. **2.** Scandinavian: habitational name from any of several farmsteads or place names derived from Old Norse *topt* 'curtilage', 'site', 'homestead'.
GIVEN NAMES Scandinavian 4%. *Hjalmer, Nels, Thorval.*

Tofte (318) Scandinavian (mainly Norwegian): variant of TOFT.
GIVEN NAMES Scandinavian 6%. *Erik, Hjalmer, Iver, Steinar, Thora.*

Tognetti (122) Italian: from pet form of *Togni*, a reduced form of the personal name *Antonio* (see ANTHONY).
GIVEN NAMES Italian 8%. *Aldo, Dino, Emo, Gioacchino, Guido, Marino, Omero.*

Toh (112) **1.** Chinese 杜: Cantonese variant of DU 1. **2.** Chinese 陶: Cantonese variant of TAO. **3.** Chinese 涂: Cantonese variant of TU 2. **4.** Chinese 屠: Cantonese variant

of TU 3. **5.** Chinese 褚: variant of CHU 2.
6. Korean: variant of To.
GIVEN NAMES Chinese/Korean 20%. *Hong*
(2), *Seng* (2), *Ailing, Chee, Jung Ja, Kyung
Hwan, Sin, Soon, Wai Ling, Yiu, Yoon.*

Toher (103) Variant of TUCKER.

Tohill (129) Northern Irish (Derry): reduced
variant of O'TOOLE.

Toia (121) Italian: Piedmontese surname associated with the Waldensians, probably an
altered form of French TOYE.
GIVEN NAMES Italian 14%. *Salvatore* (2),
Luciano, Salvator, Vito.

Toigo (120) Origin unidentified.
GIVEN NAMES Italian 13%. *Aldo, Angelo,
Dante, Gino, Leno, Quinto, Stefano.*

Toivonen (140) Finnish: ornamental name
from *toivo* 'hope' + the common surname
suffix *-nen*. It may also be a derivative of
Toivo as a traditional Finnish personal
name. It is found chiefly in western Finland.
GIVEN NAMES Finnish 16%. *Tapio* (2), *Arvi,
Eero, Eino, Pentti, Sulo, Taisto, Toivo,
Urho.*

Tokar (513) Jewish (eastern Ashkenazic)
and Ukrainian: occupational name from
Ukrainian *tokar* 'turner'. Compare Polish
TOKARZ.
GIVEN NAMES Russian 9%; Jewish 5%. *Boris*
(3), *Mikhail* (3), *Michail* (2), *Yefim* (2),
*Andrei, Arkady, Asya, Dmitry, Fedor,
Gennadiy, Iosif, Konstantin; Irina, Naum,
Shika, Sima, Yakov, Zinaida.*

Tokarczyk (197) Polish: occupational name
(pet form) for a turner, from a diminutive of
TOKARZ, or patronymic from TOKARZ.
GIVEN NAMES Polish 6%. *Jerzy, Lucyna,
Tadeusz, Zygmunt.*

Tokarski (319) **1.** Polish, Jewish (eastern
Ashkenazic), and Ukrainian: habitational
name for someone from any of many places
named Tokary. **2.** Jewish (eastern Ashke-
nazic) and Ukrainian: patronymic from
TOKARZ and TOKAR.
GIVEN NAMES Polish 11%. *Zbigniew* (2),
*Andrzej, Czeslaw, Grzegorz, Janina, Jerzy,
Karol, Lucjan, Stanislaw, Tadeusz,
Wojciech, Zygmunt.*

Tokarz (544) Polish and Jewish (from
Poland): occupational name from Polish
tokarz 'turner'.
GIVEN NAMES Polish 6%. *Agnieszka, Casimir,
Czeslaw, Grazyna, Halina, Wladyslaw,
Wojciech.*

Tokash (135) Origin unidentified; possibly
an Americanized form of TOKOS.

Tokos (101) Origin unidentified.

Tokuda (118) Japanese: 'virtuous rice
paddy'. This name is found mostly in west-
ern Japan and in the Ryūkyū Islands.
GIVEN NAMES Japanese 57%. *Junko* (2),
Masatoshi (2), *Shintaro* (2), *Akira, Atsushi,
Emiko, Haruko, Haruo, Hiroaki, Hiromi,
Itsuo, Junichi.*

Tokunaga (270) Japanese: meaning 'virtue
eternal', it is found mostly in the island of
Kyūshū.

GIVEN NAMES Japanese 43%. *Takeshi* (3),
Emiko (2), *Hiroshi* (2), *Keisuke* (2), *Mitsue*
(2), *Yoshiaki* (2), *Chiyoko, Eiji, Fumio,
Hideo, Hiroaki, Hitoshi.*

Tolan (687) Northern Irish: variant of
TOLAND.
GIVEN NAMES Irish 4%. *Brendan, Delma,
Jarlath.*

Toland (1650) Northern Irish: reduced form
of **O'Toland**, an Anglicized form of Gaelic
Ó Tuathaláin 'descendant of *Tuathalán*', a
personal name formed from a pet form of
Tuathal (see O'TOOLE).

Tolar (813) Slovenian (north central
Slovenia): variant of **Dolar**, topographic
name for someone who lived in a valley,
from *dol* 'valley' or variant of the German
form THALER. Compare DOLLAR.

Tolbert (6480) French and English (of
Norman origin): from a Continental Germanic personal name composed of a first
element of uncertain meaning + *berht*
'bright', 'famous'.

Tolchin (111) Jewish (from Ukraine): habitational name from Tulchin in Ukraine.
GIVEN NAMES Jewish 9%. *Hyman, Ilya.*

Tole (213) English: variant spelling of TOLL.

Toledano (180) Spanish and Jewish
(Sephardic): habitational name for some-
one from TOLEDO, from an adjectival form
of the place name.
GIVEN NAMES Jewish 16%; Spanish 14%;
French 4%. *Shlomo* (3), *Igal* (2), *Moshe*
(2), *Shimon* (2), *Ehud, Shmuel, Yehuda;
Alberto* (3), *Gonzalo* (2), *Alina, Carlos,
Conrado, Elena, Enrique, Evelia, Luis,
Manuel, Miguel, Ramona; Gabrielle,
Michel.*

Toledo (1839) Spanish and Jewish
(Sephardic): habitational name from the
city in central Spain, which was the capital
of the Visigothic state between the 6th and
8th centuries. Its role declined for three
centuries after the Muslim invasion of
Spain, until it was taken as the capital of the
kingdom of Castile between the 11th and
16th centuries. It was a major cultural and
political center throughout the Middle
Ages, and was also the home of an important Jewish community. The place name,
first recorded in Latin as *Toletum*, is of obscure etymology, possibly connected with
Toleto in Piedmont; Jewish tradition con-
nects it with Hebrew *toledot* 'generations',
but this is no more than folk etymology.
GIVEN NAMES Spanish 43%. *Jose* (50), *Luis*
(18), *Jorge* (17), *Manuel* (17), *Ramon* (14),
Rafael (13), *Juan* (12), *Antonio* (11), *Jesus*
(11), *Miguel* (11), *Roberto* (10), *Carlos* (9),
Francisco (9).

Tolen (310) Belgian French: metronymic
from a Walloon female personal name.

Tolentino (989) Spanish, Italian, and
Jewish (from Italy): habitational name
from the city of Tolentino in Macerata
province, Italy. It was adopted as a given
name in Spain because of its association

with St. Nicholas of Tolentino (c.1245–
1305).
GIVEN NAMES Spanish 42%; Italian 8%. *Jose*
(13), *Luis* (6), *Manuel* (6), *Pedro* (6),
Lourdes (5), *Rafael* (5), *Ramon* (5), *Ana*
(4), *Arturo* (4), *Carlos* (4), *Dominador* (4),
Ernesto (4); *Antonio* (6), *Donato* (2),
Leonardo (2), *Agnelo, Carmelo, Federico,
Flavio, Heriberto, Lorenzo, Marcellino,
Marcello, Olivero.*

Toler (3110) English: variant of TOLLER.

Tolerico (113) Italian: possibly a variant of
Tallerico, from a Germanic personal name.
GIVEN NAMES Italian 19%. *Angelo* (3),
Carmine (2), *Rocco, Sal.*

Toles (786) **1.** Greek (**Tolis**): from a short
form of the personal name *Apostolis*, variant of APOSTOLOS. **2.** Possibly an altered
form of the English surnames **Tole**, from a
personal name (Old English *Tola*, Old
Norse *Toli*), or **Tolles**, also from a personal
name (Old English *Toll*, an unattested name
found in various place names such as
Tollesbury and Tolleshunt) or Anglo-Scandinavian *Toll*, an unattested short form of
Old Norse *þorleifr*, or perhaps in some
cases a topographic name from a southern
dialect term *toll* 'clump of trees'.

Tolhurst (179) English: habitational name
from Tollhurst in Frittenden, Kent.

Tolin (310) French: from a pet form of a
Nordic personal name, *Tolimer*, composed
of a hypocoristic form of compound names
in *Thor-* (see THOR) + *mar* 'famous'.

Toliver (1737) Variant of TOLLIVER.

Toll (1045) **1.** English: from the Middle
English personal name *Toll*, Old English
Toll, or Old Norse *Tóli*, the latter being derived from a reduced form of a compound
name such as *þorleifr* (composed of the elements *þórr*, name of the Scandinavian god
of thunder (see THOR) + *leifr* 'relic') or
þórleikr (composed of the elements *þórr* +
leikr 'sport', 'play'). **2.** English: topographic name from *toll* 'clump of trees', a
dialect term of Kent, Sussex, and
Hampshire. **3.** German: nickname from
Middle High German *tol, dol* 'foolish', also
'pretty' or 'handsome'. **4.** German: from a
reduced form of the personal name
Bartholomäus (see BARTHOLOMEW).

Tolle (1178) **1.** North German and Dutch:
metonymic occupational name for a collector of tolls or customs, from *toll, tol* 'toll'.
2. German: variant of TOELLE.

Tollefsen (165) Norwegian: from a patronymic from *Tollef*, a variant of *Torleiv*,
from Old Norse *þorleifr*, formed with *þórr*,
name of the Scandinavian god of thunder
(see THOR) + *leifr* 'heir', 'descendant'.
GIVEN NAMES Scandinavian 13%. *Tollef* (2),
Thor.

Tollefson (1792) Americanized spelling of
Norwegian TOLLEFSEN.

Tollefsrud (128) Norwegian: habitational
name from seven farmsteads in southeastern Norway, so named from the personal

name *Tollef* (see TOLLEFSEN) + *rud*, from Old Norse *ruð* 'clearing'.

Toller (294) **1.** English, Scottish, and North German (also **Töller**): occupational name for a toll taker or tax collector, from an agent derivative of Middle English *toll* 'tax', 'payment', Middle Low German *toll* (from Late Latin *toloneum, teloneum*, a derivative of Greek *telos* 'tax'). **2.** English: habitational name from Toller in Dorset, named from a British river name, apparently composed of elements akin to Welsh *toll* 'hollow', 'pierced' + *dw(f)r* 'stream'. **3.** German: from a short form of the personal name *Bartholomäus* (see BARTHOLOMEW). **4.** German: nickname meaning 'foolish one' or 'handsome one'; a noun derivative of TOLL 3.

Tolles (315) English: variant of TOLL.

Tolleson (754) **1.** Swedish: patronymic from a variant of the personal name *Torleiv* (see TOLLEFSEN). **2.** Respelling of Norwegian **Taalesen** or **Tålesen**, cognate with 1.

Tollett (557) English: probably a variant spelling of **Tullet(t)**, apparently a metonymic occupational name for a maker of armor, from Middle English *tuillet* denoting a piece of medieval armor that protects the thigh, from a diminutive of Old French *tieule* 'plaque', 'tile'.

Tolley (2068) **1.** English (chiefly West Midlands): from a pet form of the Middle English personal name *Toll* (see TOWLE). **2.** Probably an altered spelling of German TOLLE.

Tollison (693) Origin unidentified; possibly Scandinavian.

Tolliver (2977) **1.** English: variant of TELFER. **2.** Americanized form of the Italian family name **Taliaferro** (cognate with 1), from *tagliare* 'to cut' + *ferro* 'iron', probably applied as a nickname for a metal worker or a fierce fighter (see genealogical note).

FOREBEARS The Virginia family of **Taliaferro** (pronounced Tolliver) are descended from London-born Robert Taliaferro or Tolliver, who settled in VA by 1647. He was the grandson of a Venetian, Bartholomew Taliaferro, who had settled in London by 1562. Between 1651 and 1673 Robert patented several sizeable holdings in Gloucester Co., England. He married Sarah Grimes, the daughter of an Anglican priest, and had one daughter and four sons, all of whom produced large and prosperous families.

Tolly (189) English: variant spelling of TOLLEY.

Tolman (1406) English (Devon): occupational name for a toll collector, from Middle English *toll* 'tax', 'payment' (see TOLLER) + *man* 'man'.

Tolmie (146) Scottish: habitational name from a lost or unidentified place.

Tolomeo (111) Italian (mainly Calabrian and Sicilian): from a short form of the personal name *Bartolomeo* (see BARTHOLOMEW), or (in the Greek-influenced south of Italy) from the personal name *Tolomeo*, representing Greek *Ptolemaios*.

GIVEN NAMES Italian 8%. *Antonio* (2), *Elisabetta*.

Tolonen (114) Finnish: from *Tolo*, a male forename of uncertain origin (it could be either Germanic or Russian Orthodox) + the common surname suffix *-nen*. This name is found chiefly in north–central regions of Finland.

GIVEN NAMES German 5%; Finnish 5%. *Arno*; *Risto, Vieno*.

Tolsma (197) Frisian: occupational name for a toll collector.

Tolson (1832) English (Yorkshire): patronymic from the personal name TOLL.

Tolton (160) English (Leicestershire): habitational name, possibly from either of two places called Tollerton, in Nottinghamshire and North Yorkshire. The first is named from the Old Norse personal name *Thorleifr* + Old English *tūn* 'settlement', 'enclosure'; the second is from Old English *tolnere* 'tax gatherers' + *tūn*.

GIVEN NAMES French 5%. *Chanel, Damien*.

Tolzman (134) German: possibly an extended form of a habitational name from a place near Stettin (Szczecin in Polish) called Tolz.

GIVEN NAMES German 5%. *Eckhart, Reinhold*.

Tolzmann (106) German: unexplained.

GIVEN NAMES German 4%. *August, Bernhard*.

Tom (2512) **1.** English and Dutch: from a short form of the personal name THOMAS. **2.** Polish: from a short form of the personal name *Tomasz* (see THOMAS). **3.** Chinese: see TAN.

GIVEN NAMES Chinese 6%. *Wing* (7), *Gim* (4), *Ping* (4), *Wah* (4), *Fat* (3), *Fong* (3), *Kwai* (3), *Leung* (3), *Ming* (3), *Wai* (3), *Yee* (3), *Chee* (2).

Toma (751) **1.** Italian, French, Polish, Czech, Hungarian, Romanian, etc.: from a short form of the personal name THOMAS (Italian *Tommaso*, French *Thomas*, Polish *Tomasz*). **2.** Arabic: from *Tūma*, Arabic form of THOMAS. **3.** Japanese (**Tōma**): variously written with characters used phonetically; two such combinations mean 'Tang Chinese space' and 'appropriate truth' and are found mostly in the Ryūkyū Islands.

GIVEN NAMES Arabic 10%; Japanese 9%. *Kamal* (3), *Nabil* (3), *Salem* (3), *Kamil* (2), *Safa* (2), *Samir* (2), *Adil, Adnan, Aziz, Bahjat, Basem, Bashar; Hiroshi* (2), *Hideo, Isako, Izumi, Junichi, Kenji, Kiyoko, Masakazu, Rikuo, Sachi, Shigeo*.

Tomac (128) Croatian and Serbian: from a pet of the personal names *Toma* or *Tomo*, short forms of *Tomislav*, which is a hybrid name composed of the Latin name THOMAS + the Slavic element *-slav* 'glory'.

Tomaino (376) Italian: from a pet form of the personal name *Tomà*, from Greek *Thomas* (see THOMAS).

GIVEN NAMES Italian 14%. *Angelo* (2), *Agostino, Camillo, Concetta, Elio, Franco, Gino, Nicolina, Rocco, Santo*.

Tomala (136) **1.** Polish: from a derivative of the personal name *Tomasz* (see THOMAS). **2.** Puruha-Mochica: in northern Ecuador, unexplained. **3.** probably also from a language from the Philippine Islands, unexplained.

GIVEN NAMES Spanish 11%; Polish 9%. *Carlos* (2), *Alipio, Angel, Augusto, Eduardo, Leokadia, Luis, Marisa, Pilar; Andrzej, Janina, Krystyna, Slawek, Zbigniew, Zofia*.

Toman (1025) **1.** Czech and Slovak: from a pet form of the personal name *Tomáš* (see THOMAS). **2.** Irish: reduced form of **O'-Toman**, an Anglicized form of Gaelic **Ó Tuamáin** 'descendant of *Tuamán*', a personal name based on a diminutive of *tuaim* 'hill'.

Tomanek (162) Czech and Slovak (**Tománek**) and Polish: from a pet form of a derivative of the personal name *Tomáš* (Czech), *Tomasz* (Polish) (see THOMAS).

GIVEN NAMES German 5%. *Otto, Udo*.

Tomaras (101) Greek: occupational name for a tanner, from medieval Greek *tomaras*, agent noun derived from *tomari* 'hide', 'skin' (originally a diminutive of classical Greek *tomos* 'membrane'). The word *tomari* is also found in Greek as a nickname meaning 'rascal' or 'blackguard'.

Tomarchio (100) Italian: status name from medieval Greek *tourmarkhēs* 'commander of a cavalry squadron', from *turma* 'cavalry squadron'.

GIVEN NAMES Italian 14%. *Angelo* (2), *Cirino* (2), *Orazio*.

Tomaro (203) Southern Italian: unexplained.

GIVEN NAMES Italian 21%. *Biagio* (3), *Angelo, Annunziata, Cosmo, Domenic, Gino, Giuseppina, Pasquale, Rocco, Valentino*.

Tomas (807) Spanish and Portuguese (**Tomás**), Catalan (**Tomàs**), Czech and Slovak (**Tomáš**), and Polish: from a personal name equivalent to THOMAS.

GIVEN NAMES Spanish 27%; Portuguese 8%. *Jose* (13), *Manuel* (8), *Francisco* (6), *Luis* (6), *Jorge* (5), *Juan* (5), *Arturo* (4), *Alejandro* (3), *Carlos* (3), *Miguel* (3), *Pedro* (3), *Alberto* (2); *Joao* (2), *Paulo*.

Tomasek (366) Czech and Slovak (**Tomášek**) and German (under Slavic influence): from a pet form of the personal name, Czech *Tomáš* (see THOMAS).

Tomaselli (589) Italian: patronymic or plural form of TOMASELLO.

GIVEN NAMES Italian 16%. *Salvatore* (5), *Angelo* (3), *Deno* (3), *Domenic* (2), *Alfio, Antimo, Attilio, Carmelo, Dante, Giuseppe, Italo, Luigi*.

Tomasello (728) Italian: from pet form of the personal name *Tommaso*, Italian form of THOMAS.

GIVEN NAMES Italian 12%. *Salvatore* (5), *Santo* (4), *Angelo* (3), *Sal* (3), *Antonio* (2), *Giovanna* (2), *Carmine, Giuseppe, Nunzio, Pasquale, Pino, Vito*.

Tomasetti (306) Italian: patronymic or plural form of *Tomasetto*, a pet form of *Tommaso*, Italian form of THOMAS.
GIVEN NAMES Italian 11%. *Angelo* (5), *Caesar* (2), *Amelio, Dino, Gino, Salvatore, Silvio*.

Tomasi (377) Italian: from a plural or patronymic form of the personal name *Tomaso*, Italian equivalent of THOMAS. This is also found as a Greek family name (**Tomasis**).
GIVEN NAMES Italian 9%. *Salvatore* (2), *Biagio, Carlo, Dino, Gino, Luigi, Maurizio, Sal, Sandro, Ugo*.

Tomasic (186) Croatian (**Tomašić**): patronymic from the personal name *Tomaš* (see THOMAS).
GIVEN NAMES South Slavic 4%. *Davor, Drago*.

Tomasik (282) Polish: from a pet form of the personal name *Tomasz* (see THOMAS).
GIVEN NAMES Polish 7%. *Casimir, Halina, Jerzy, Wieslawa, Witold, Zbigniew*.

Tomasini (233) Italian: patronymic or plural form of TOMASINO.
GIVEN NAMES Italian 4%. *Angelo* (2), *Dante, Rinaldo*.

Tomasino (285) Italian: from a pet form of the personal name *Tomaso* (see THOMAS).
GIVEN NAMES Italian 12%; Spanish 10%. *Antonio* (2), *Salvatore* (2), *Attilio, Grazia, Rocco, Sal, Vincenzo, Vito; Angel, Cesar, Jorge, Jose, Juan, Luis, Vidal*.

Tomaski (98) Polish: habitational name for someone from any of several places called Tomaszew, Tomaszewo, or Tomasze; all derived from the personal name *Tomasz* (see THOMAS).

Tomasko (313) Polish (**Tomaszko**) and Slovak: from a pet form of the personal name *Tomas, Tomasz* (see THOMAS).

Tomaso (173) Italian: from the personal name *Tomaso*, (see THOMAS).
GIVEN NAMES Italian 16%. *Carmello* (2), *Benedetto, Biagio, Biago, Carlo, Nicola, Pasquale, Salvatore*.

Tomassetti (209) Italian: from a pet form of the personal name *Tomaso* (see THOMAS).
GIVEN NAMES Italian 12%. *Dino* (2), *Serafino* (2), *Aldo, Dante, Gino, Giovanni, Rocco, Sal, Valentino*.

Tomassi (216) Italian: patronymic or plural form of TOMASO.
GIVEN NAMES Italian 28%. *Angelo* (4), *Ettore* (2), *Giuliano* (2), *Pietro* (2), *Alessio, Antonio, Benedetto, Carlo, Carmel, Domenic, Domenica, Donato*.

Tomassini (112) Italian: from the personal name *Tomassino*, a pet form of TOMASSO.
GIVEN NAMES Spanish 11%; Italian 10%. *Ines, Juan, Juana, Racquel, Ramon, Ramona; Aldo* (2), *Flavio, Geno, Piero, Reno, Santino*.

Tomasso (245) Italian: variant spelling of the personal name *Tommaso*, Italian equivalent of THOMAS.
GIVEN NAMES Italian 6%. *Domenic* (2), *Guido*.

Tomasulo (244) Italian: from a pet form of the personal name *Tommaso*, Italian equivalent of THOMAS.
GIVEN NAMES Italian 12%. *Angelo, Carmine, Filomena, Gennaro, Rocco*.

Tomaszewski (1312) Polish: habitational name for someone from any of the many places in Poland called Tomaszew or Tomaszewo, formed with the personal name *Tomasz* (see THOMAS).
GIVEN NAMES Polish 7%. *Bogdan* (2), *Casimir* (2), *Jozef* (2), *Maciej* (2), *Slawomir* (2), *Zbigniew* (2), *Zigmund* (2), *Andrzej, Dariusz, Grazyna, Irena, Jadwiga*.

Tomb (259) Irish or English: perhaps a variant spelling of TOM.

Tombaugh (111) Altered spelling of North German **Tombach**: **1.** topographic name from *to dem bach* 'at the creek', perhaps a hybrid form as *Bach* is standard German, *bek(e)* being the Low German form. **2.** habitational name from places in Hesse, Baden, and Bavaria called Dombach (earlier *Tunbach*, from *tun, tan* 'mud').

Tomberlin (647) Apparently an altered form of English TOMBLIN.

Tomblin (731) English (East Midlands): variant of TOMLIN, with an intrusive -*b*-.

Tombs (113) English: variant of TOMS, with a late intrusive -*b*-.

Tomczak (967) Polish: patronymic from *Tomek*, a pet form of the personal name *Tomasz* (see THOMAS).
GIVEN NAMES Polish 4%. *Andrzej, Boguslawa, Casimir, Dariusz, Eugeniusz, Ewa, Halina, Jerzy, Jozef, Karol, Krzysztof, Tadeusz*.

Tomczyk (462) Polish: derivative of *Tomek*, a pet form of the personal name *Tomasz* (see THOMAS).
GIVEN NAMES Polish 12%. *Piotr* (2), *Stanislaw* (2), *Andrzej, Bronislaus, Casimir, Jacek, Janina, Jerzy, Kazimierz, Malgorzata, Ryszard, Slawomir*.

Tome (487) **1.** Spanish and Portuguese (**Tomé**): from a personal name equivalent to THOMAS. **2.** Northern Italian (**Tomè**): from a derivative of the personal name *Tommaso*, Italian equivalent of THOMAS. **3.** Slovenian: from a short form of the personal name *Tomaž* (see THOMAS), + the suffix -*e*, usually used of young people.
GIVEN NAMES Spanish 13%. *Luis* (4), *Carlos* (3), *Jose* (3), *Manuel* (3), *Mario* (3), *Miguel* (3), *Adelino* (2), *Lilia* (2), *Vicente* (2), *Wilfredo* (2), *Alberto, Alda*.

Tomei (396) Italian: patronymic or plural form of TOMEO.
GIVEN NAMES Italian 22%. *Mario* (7), *Remo* (3), *Antonio* (2), *Carlo* (2), *Cesare* (2), *Dante* (2), *Dario* (2), *Elena* (2), *Evo* (2),

Mariano (2), *Alberto, Americo, Cataldo, Dino, Ercole, Gildo, Guido, Orlando*.

Tomek (272) Czech and Sorbian: from a pet form of the personal name *Tomáš* (see THOMAS).
GIVEN NAMES German 4%. *Erwin, Guenther, Reinhold*.

Tomeo (263) Italian: from a reduced form of the personal name *Bartolomeo* (see BARTHOLOMEW).
GIVEN NAMES Italian 12%. *Angelo* (3), *Vito* (2), *Carmine, Domenic, Marco, Stefano*.

Tomer (298) Jewish (Ashkenazic): from the Yiddish female personal name *Tomer*, the Biblical name *Tamar* (Genesis 38:6).

Tomerlin (268) Apparently an altered form of English TOMBLIN. Compare TOMBERLIN.

Tomes (776) **1.** English: patronymic from *Tom*, a short form of the personal name THOMAS. **2.** Czech (**Tomeš**): from a variant of the personal name *Tomáš* (see THOMAS). **3.** Spanish (**Tomés**): from a derivative of the personal name *Tomás* (see THOMAS).

Tomey (312) Spanish and Aragonese: probably from a derivative of the personal name *Tomás* (see THOMAS).

Tomhave (104) North German: topographic name for someone who lived 'at the farm', Low German *to dem have* (High German *zu dem Hofe*).

Tomic (138) Croatian (**Tomić**): see TOMICH.
GIVEN NAMES South Slavic 41%. *Ratko* (3), *Mihailo* (2), *Slobodan* (2), *Darko, Dragan, Dusanka, Dusica, Franjo, Goran, Milorad, Slavko, Verica; Josip, Pavlina, Sava, Tatjana; Miroslav* (2), *Milan, Milos, Mirko, Vladislav; Tomo* (2), *Mato*.

Tomich (504) Croatian and Serbian (**Tomić**): patronymic from the personal names *Tomo* or *Toma*, short forms of *Tomislav*, which is a hybrid name composed of the Latin name THOMAS + the Slavic element -*slav* 'glory'.

Tominaga (141) Japanese: 'abundance eternal'; a habitational name taken from villages in Mikawa (now part of Aichi prefecture) and Ōmi (present-day Shiga prefecture), and found mostly in western Japan.
GIVEN NAMES Japanese 55%. *Mitsuru* (2), *Yuji* (2), *Akiko, Akinori, Hayato, Hideo, Hiroshi, Junji, Kanji, Kazunari, Kazuo, Kenichi*.

Tomita (385) Japanese: from a common place name meaning 'abundant rice paddy', found throughout Japan. The surname occurs mostly in eastern Japan.
GIVEN NAMES Japanese 50%. *Yoko* (4), *Koichi* (3), *Masao* (3), *Minoru* (3), *Akira* (2), *Eiji* (2), *Hideo* (2), *Hiroko* (2), *Hiroshi* (2), *Junichi* (2), *Katsuji* (2), *Kenji* (2).

Tomkiewicz (159) **1.** Polish: patronymic from *Tomek*, a pet form of the personal name *Tomasz* (see THOMAS). **2.** Jewish (from Poland): metronymic from the

Yiddish personal name *Tomke*, a pet form of TOMER.

GIVEN NAMES Polish 6%; German 5%. *Katarzyna, Maciej, Zygmunt; Alphons.*

Tomkins (505) English (mainly central England): patronymic from a pet form of the personal name THOMAS.

Tomkinson (272) English: patronymic from a pet form of the personal name THOMAS.

Tomko (987) Slovak and Polish: from a pet form of the personal name *Tomas*, Polish *Tomasz* (see THOMAS).

Tomlin (3825) English: from a pet form of *Tom*, a short form of the personal name THOMAS.

Tomlins (114) Variant of TOMLINSON.

Tomlinson (9256) English: patronymic from the personal name TOMLIN.

Tomme (130) North German: probably from a short form of the personal name THOMAS.

Tompkins (9187) English: patronymic from a pet form of the personal name THOMAS.

Tompson (215) English: patronymic from *Tom*, a short form of the personal name THOMAS.

Toms (1860) English (Devon and Dorset): patronymic from *Tom*, a short form of the personal name THOMAS.

Tomsic (304) Slovenian (**Tomšič, Tomsič**): patronymic from *Tomše*, a derivative of the personal name *Tomaž* (see THOMAS).

Tomson (306) English: patronymic from *Tom*, a short form of the personal name THOMAS.

Ton (574) Vietnamese: unexplained.

GIVEN NAMES Vietnamese 46%; Chinese 16%. *Minh* (7), *Tuan* (6), *Cuong* (5), *Dung* (5), *Thanh* (5), *Son* (4), *Anh* (3), *Doan* (3), *Hieu* (3), *Hoang* (3), *Hung* (3), *Lan* (3); *Ho* (3), *Chi* (2), *Hang* (2), *Chan, Chi Hung, Choi, Dong, Heang, Jin Hong, Ngan Ying, Sang, Song.*

Tondre (113) Possibly an altered form of LETENDRE.

Tondreau (190) French: from a diminutive of Old French *tonder*, an oblique case of *tondeur* 'clipper', hence an occupational name for someone who clipped cloth, or for a sheep-shearer.

FOREBEARS A Tondreau from the Orléans region of France is documented in Beaupré, Quebec, in 1691, with the secondary surname La Souche.

GIVEN NAMES French 15%. *Normand* (3), *Andre, Florien, Laurent, Monique.*

Tone (409) **1.** English: variant of TOWN. **2.** Japanese: variously written, usually with characters meaning either 'sword' or 'benefit' and 'root', the latter version being used for the name of the Tone River, which was formerly the boundary between the provinces of Musashi (now Tōkyō and Saitama prefecture) and Shimōsa (now Chiba prefecture), until it was diverted in

early modern times to become the northern boundary of Chiba. Some families may have taken their name from the name of the river.

GIVEN NAMES Japanese 4%. *Fumihiro, Hideo, Hideshi, Kiyoshi, Masayo, Toshio, Yozo.*

Tonelli (406) Italian: from a reduced pet form of the personal name *Antonio* (see ANTHONY).

GIVEN NAMES Italian 12%. *Dino* (3), *Dante* (2), *Marco* (2), *Antonio, Carlo, Dario, Domenica, Enzo, Giovanna, Luciano, Remo, Stefano.*

Toner (1783) Irish: reduced Anglicized form of Gaelic **Ó Tomhrair** 'descendant of *Tomhrar*', a Norse personal name.

Toney (5067) English: from the medieval personal name *Ton(e)y*, a reduced form of ANTHONY.

Tong (2585) **1.** Chinese 唐: variant of TANG 2. **2.** Chinese 汤: variant of TANG 3. **3.** Chinese 佟: from a modification of the character Zhong (终). In the Xia dynasty (2205–1766 BC), there existed a senior adviser whose name was Zhonggu. Much later, in the Ming dynasty (1368–1644 AD), some descendants settled along a river that became known as the Tong Family river. As the Manchus moved southwards, some took up residence by this river and they too adopted Tong as their surname. **4.** Chinese 童: from *Lao Tong*, the 'style name' given to a son of Zhuan Xu, legendary emperor of the 26th century BC. Two of his sons became important advisers to the next emperor, Ku. Some descendants of Lao Tong adopted a character from his style name as their surname. **5.** Chinese: see also DONG. **6.** English: metonymic occupational name for a maker or user of tongs (Old English *tang(e)*), or a habitational name from one of the places named with this word (there are examples in Lancashire, Shropshire, and West Yorkshire), from their situation by a fork in a road or river, considered as resembling a pair of tongs. **7.** English: topographic name for someone who lived on a *tongue* of land, or a habitational name from a place named with this word (Old English *tunge*, Old Norse *tunga*), for example Tonge in Leicestershire. Alternatively, Reaney suggests that it may have been a nickname from the same word in the sense of a chatterbox or a scold. **8.** Dutch: from a short form of the personal name *Antonius* (see ANTHONY). It could also be from Dutch *tong* 'tongue' and hence a nickname for a chatterbox or scold, or possibly a shortening of **Van Tongeren**, a habitational name for someone from Tongeren in the province of Gelderland.

GIVEN NAMES Chinese 29%. *Wing* (11), *Ming* (8), *Chi* (7), *Lai* (6), *Man* (6), *Hing* (5), *Hung* (5), *Kin* (5), *Kwan* (5), *Wen* (5), *Hong* (4), *Kam* (4), *Ping* (4), *Minh* (5), *Dang* (3), *Doan* (3), *Dung* (3), *Hoang* (3), *Lam* (3),

My (3), *Trung* (3), *Tuan* (3), *Tung* (3), *Be* (2).

Tongate (131) English: variant spelling of TUNGATE.

Tonge (259) **1.** English: variant spelling of TONG, also established in Ireland since the 17th century. **2.** German: from a reduced short form of the personal name *Anton* (see ANTHONY).

Tongue (209) English: variant spelling of TONG.

Toni (103) Italian: from a short form of the personal name *Antonio* (see ANTHONY).

GIVEN NAMES Italian 18%. *Alberto, Aldo, Alessandro, Anselmo, Beto, Eugenio, Italo, Luigi, Sergio, Silva.*

Tonini (169) Italian: from a pet form of *Toni*, a short form of the personal name *Antonio* (see ANTHONY).

GIVEN NAMES Italian 18%. *Melio* (3), *Cesare, Claudio, Dante, Emanuele, Gasper, Julio, Mando, Marcello, Stefano, Tito.*

Tonjes (185) North German (**Tönjes**): patronymic from a reduced pet form of the personal name *Antonius* (see ANTHONY).

Tonkin (781) English (mainly Devon): from a pet form of the personal name THOMAS.

Tonkinson (169) English (West Midlands): patronymic from the personal name TONKIN.

Tonkovich (194) Croatian (**Tonković**): patronymic from *Tonko*, a pet form of *Antun*, Latin *Antonius* (see ANTHONY).

Tonks (213) English (Midlands): patronymic from a pet form of the personal name THOMAS.

Tonn (675) German: metonymic occupational name for a cooper, from Middle Low German, Middle High German *tunne, tonne* 'vat', 'barrel', 'cask'.

GIVEN NAMES German 6%. *Gerhart* (2), *Kurt* (2), *Arno, Erhart, Erwin, Fritz, Kaethe, Lorenz, Reinhard, Reinhardt.*

Tonne (211) German: variant of TONN.

Tonner (189) **1.** Irish and Scottish: variant spelling of TONER. **2.** South German: variant of TANNER.

GIVEN NAMES German 5%. *Heinrich, Kurt, Otto.*

Tonnesen (231) **1.** Norwegian and Danish (**Tønnesen**): variant of TONNESSEN. **2.** Altered spelling of German **Thönnessen**, from a patronymic from the personal name *Ant(h)onius* (see ANTHONY).

GIVEN NAMES Scandinavian 17%. *Erik, Lars, Thor, Thoralf, Torleif.*

Tonnesen (231) **1.** Norwegian and Danish (**Tønnesen**): variant of TONNESSEN. **2.** Altered spelling of German **Thönnessen**, from a patronymic form of the personal name *Ant(h)onius* (see ANTHONY).

GIVEN NAMES Scandinavian 17%. *Erik, Lars, Thor, Thoralf, Torleif.*

Tonnessen (144) Norwegian (**Tønnessen**): patronymic from *Tonne* or *Tønne(s)*, short forms of the personal name *Antonius* (see ANTHONY).

GIVEN NAMES Scandinavian 37%; Dutch 4%. *Arnt* (2), *Nils* (2), *Bjorn, Per, Rigmor, Selmer, Tor*.

Tonti (173) Italian: patronymic from *Tonto*, a nickname meaning 'stupid', 'silly'.

GIVEN NAMES Italian 8%. *Aldo, Angelo, Dino, Domenic, Gino, Guido, Rocco*.

Tony (171) **1.** English and French: from the personal name *Tony*, a short form of ANTHONY. **2.** Americanized form of any of various derivatives of the Latin personal name *Antonius* (see ANTHONY), for example Greek **Antoniou, Antoniadis**.

GIVEN NAMES French 4%. *Andre, Jean Pierre*.

Toogood (194) English: apparently a nickname from Middle English *to* 'exceedingly' + *gode* 'good', perhaps ironic in application.

Toohey (1021) Irish (Cork): reduced Anglicized form of Gaelic **Ó Tuathaigh** 'descendant of *Tuathach*', a byname meaning 'chief', 'lord' (i.e. ruler over a *tuath* 'tribe', 'territory').

GIVEN NAMES Irish 5%. *Brendan* (2), *Siobhan*.

Tooke (449) English (Norfolk): variant spelling of TUCK.

Tooker (705) English: probably a variant spelling of TUCKER.

Tookes (156) **1.** Probably an altered form of English TOOKE. **2.** Perhaps also an altered spelling of Hungarian **Tőkés**, from *tőke* 'trunk'.

Tool (167) Irish: see TOOLE.

Toolan (232) Irish: variant of TOLAND.

Toole (2477) **1.** Irish: reduced form of O'TOOLE, an Americanized form of *Ó Tuathail* 'descendant of *Tuathal*'. **2.** English: variant of TOLL.

Tooley (1571) **1.** Irish: variant of TOOLE. **2.** English (mainly Norfolk): from a pet form of the Middle English personal name TOLL.

Tooman (158) Irish: variant of TOMAN.

Toombs (1600) English: patronymic from a short form of the personal name THOMAS.

Toomer (656) English (Hampshire): unexplained; perhaps related to Old English *tumbere* or Old French *tombeor, tumbeur* 'tumbler', 'dancer'.

Toomey (3023) Irish: reduced form of O'TOOMEY, an Anglicized form of Gaelic **Ó Tuama** 'descendant of *Tuaim*', a personal name apparently derived from *tuaim* 'burial mound'.

GIVEN NAMES Irish 6%. *Aidan, Caitlin, Colm, James Patrick*.

Toon (843) English (Leicestershire): variant of TOWNE.

Toone (548) English (Leicestershire): variant of TOWNE.

Toop (102) English: possibly from the Old Norse personal name *Tópi, Túpi*, a short form of a personal name formed with *þórr*, name of the Norse god of thunder (see THOR) + a second element with initial *b-*, for example *björn* 'bear', 'warrior'. On the other hand, the name is found mainly in Dorset and Devon, which are far from areas of Scandinavian settlement.

Toops (265) English: patronymic form of English TOOP.

Toor (189) Indian (Panjab): Sikh name based on the name of a Jat tribe.

GIVEN NAMES Indian 48%; Muslim 10%. *Pritam* (2), *Amar, Amritpal, Asim, Beant, Bhajan, Chandan, Darshan, Gagan, Karnail, Rakesh, Sabena; Mohammad* (4), *Iqbal* (2), *Aamir, Arifa, Arshad, Hafeez, Irfan, Javed, Qaiser, Saqib, Tahir*.

Toot (165) Possibly an altered spelling of German or Hungarian TOTH.

Toothaker (364) Altered spelling of Swiss German **Totenacher**, a habitational name (recorded in Konstanz in the 14th century) for someone from Todtnacht in Thurgau, Switzerland.

Toothman (748) Probably an altered spelling of German **Todtmann** or **Tödtmann**, from the Germanic personal name *Teutman*, composed of the elements *þeod-* 'people', 'tribe' + *man* 'man'.

Tootle (444) English (Lancashire): variant of TUTHILL.

Top (176) **1.** Dutch and German: from Middle Dutch *top*, Middle Low German *topp* 'crown of the head', 'plait', 'lock of hair', hence a nickname referring to a feature of someone's head, perhaps baldness or a particular hairstyle. **2.** Jewish (eastern Ashkenazic): metonymic occupational name for a potter, from Yiddish *top* 'pot'.

Topa (127) **1.** Polish: nickname from a derivative of Polish *topić się* 'to drown', probably with reference to someone who drowned his sorrows in liquor. **2.** Polish: nickname from Polish dialect *topa* 'slow woman'. **3.** Hungarian: nickname from *topa* 'limp'.

Topalian (142) Armenian: patronymic from Turkish *topal* 'lame', 'crippled'.

GIVEN NAMES Armenian 9%. *Garabed* (2), *Arshag, Mesrop, Shake, Siranoush, Zohrab*.

Tope (526) English (Devon): unexplained.

Topel (488) **1.** German (**Töpel**): habitational name from Töpeln near Leipzig; Bahlow also makes reference to Tepl in Bohemia and Töppeln near Gera, probably all deriving their names from Slavic *topol* 'poplar'. **2.** German: from Slavic *toplu* 'warm', possibly applied as a nickname. **3.** Jewish (from Poland): from Polish *topiel* 'whirlpool'.

GIVEN NAMES German 5%. *Kurt* (3), *Fritz* (2), *Gerd, Heinz*.

Topete (335) Spanish and Portuguese: nickname from Portuguese *topete* 'quiff', 'cockscomb'.

GIVEN NAMES Spanish 58%. *Jose* (9), *Francisco* (7), *Jorge* (7), *Juan* (6), *Pedro* (5), *Guadalupe* (4), *Jesus* (4), *Juan Carlos* (4), *Raul* (4), *Carlos* (3), *Manuel* (3), *Mario* (3).

Topf (152) German: metonymic occupational name for a potter from Middle High German *topf(e)* 'pot'.

Topham (563) English (Yorkshire): habitational name from a place in Yorkshire, near Snaith. The final element is probably Old English *hām* 'homestead', and the first may be an unattested personal name, *Toppa* (see TOPP).

Topinka (117) Czech: occupational name for someone whose job was to stoke a boiler or stove.

Topliff (170) English: habitational name from Topcliff in North Yorkshire or Topcliffe in West Yorkshire. The first was named from *Toppa* (an unattested Old English personal name) + *clif* 'cliff', 'bank', 'slope', and the second from Old Norse *topt* 'enclosure' + Old English *clif*.

Topol (130) Polish and eastern German: topographic name, or perhaps a nickname for a tall person, from *topola* 'poplar'.

GIVEN NAME German 6%. *Franz* (2).

Topolewski (117) Polish: habitational name for someone from any of various places called Topolew, named with *topola* 'poplar'.

Topolski (321) Polish, Ukrainian, Belorussian, and Jewish (from eastern Poland): habitational name for someone from places called Topola or Topole (named with *topola* 'poplar'), in Poland, Belarus, and Ukraine.

Topor (218) Polish (**Topór**) and Jewish (eastern Ashkenazic): from Polish *topór* 'axe', 'battleaxe', presumably a metonymic occupational name for a maker or bearer of such, or in the case of the Jewish name an ornamental adoption. In some instances the Polish name may derive from the same word in the sense 'coat of arms'.

GIVEN NAMES Polish 7%; Jewish 4%. *Bogdan, Genowefa, Janina, Kazimierz, Piotr; Anchel, Erez, Shimon*.

Toporek (154) Polish and Jewish (from Poland): from *toporek* 'hatchet', a diminutive of Polish *topór* 'axe', hence a metonymic occupational name for someone who made hatchets or axes, or used them. The Jewish name may be ornamental.

GIVEN NAMES Jewish 5%; German 4%. *Efrom, Miriam; Detlef*.

Topp (991) **1.** English: from the Old English byname *Topp* meaning 'tuft', 'crest', or the cognate Old Norse *Toppr*. **2.** German: from Low German *topp* 'point', 'tree top', hence a topographic name; or alternatively a metonymic occupational name or nickname from the same word in the sense 'braid'. **3.** German: variant of DOPP. **4.** Jewish (Ashkenazic): variant spelling of TOP.

Toppel (121) German: **1.** from Middle High German *top(p)el* 'game of dice'. **2.** possibly a habitational name from a place so called on the Havel river. **3.** (also **Töppel**) nickname from Slavic *toplu* 'warm'. See TOPEL.

GIVEN NAMES German 8%. *Hans Peter, Kurt, Ulrich.*

Topper (1065) German (**Töpper**): **1.** variant of TOEPFER. **2.** habitational name from Topper, a place near Krossen, Brandenburg. **3.** possibly an occupational name from Sorbian *topár* 'stoker', or from *topor* 'axe handle'.

Toppi (113) Italian: unexplained; possibly a habitational name from Toppo, a common place name.

GIVEN NAMES Italian 18%. *Pasquale* (3), *Dominico, Gino, Marco, Oresto, Rocci, Rocco.*

Toppin (305) English and Irish: variant of TOPPING.

Topping (1341) English (common in Lancashire and northern Ireland): from a patronymic or pet form of TOPP, or possibly from an unattested Old English personal name *Topping*.

Toppins (157) Altered form of TOPPIN; the addition of a final *-s* is a common feature of American surnames.

Topps (164) Altered form of TOPP; the addition of a final *-s* is a common feature of American surnames.

Torain (207) Origin unidentified. Possibly a variant of French TURENNE.

Toral (105) Spanish and Asturian-Leonese: habitational name from places in Asturies named Toral or El Toral.

GIVEN NAMES Spanish 54%. *Juan* (6), *Cesar* (2), *Jose* (2), *Lucila* (2), *Adela, Alfonso, Alfredo, Ana Maria, Armando, Dalila, Elena, Escolastica; Eliseo, Marco.*

Toran (216) **1.** Galician (**Torán**): habitational name from the village of Santa María de Torán in Ourense province. **2.** Irish: reduced form of **O'Toran**, an Anglicized form of Gaelic **Ó Toráin** 'descendant of *Torán*', a personal name formed from a diminutive of *tor* 'lord', 'hero', 'champion'.

Torbeck (190) North German: topographic name from Low German *to der bek(e)* 'at the stream'. Compare TOMBAUGH.

Torbert (633) Probably an altered form of English TORBETT.

Torbet (123) English: variant of TORBETT.

Torbett (450) English and Scottish: apparently from a hybrid Germanic name (introduced from the Continent by the Normans), formed with the name of the Scandinavian god of thunder THOR + Germanic *berht* 'bright', 'famous'.

Torborg (151) **1.** Swedish: from the personal name *Tor* (see THOR) + *borg* 'castle', 'fortress', probably an ornamental name. **2.** North German: topographic name from Low German *to der borg* (*burg*) 'at the fort or castle'.

Torchia (532) Italian: variant of **Torchio**, from *torchio* 'press' (from Latin *torculum*),

hence probably an occupational name for someone who had a wine, oil, or printing press.

GIVEN NAMES Italian 15%. *Salvatore* (4), *Angelo* (3), *Gildo* (2), *Vito* (2), *Alessandro, Amadeo, Dino, Domenic, Franco, Giuseppe, Natale, Pompeo.*

Torcivia (107) Italian: according to Caracausi, a reduced form of *torce la via*, though in what sense this would be applied is unclear.

GIVEN NAMES Italian 15%. *Rocco* (2), *Caesar, Enrico, Santo.*

Tordoff (119) English (Yorkshire): unexplained. This name has had a long association with Wibsey in Bradford, Yorkshire, England, but its etymology is unknown.

Torell (142) **1.** English: topographic name from Old French *torail*, *torel* 'small tower'. **2.** Swedish: ornamental name from the personal name *Tor* (see THOR) + the common adjectival suffix *-ell*, from the Latin adjectival ending *-elius*.

GIVEN NAME German 5%. *Kurt* (2).

Torelli (294) Italian: patronymic or plural form of TORELLO.

GIVEN NAMES Italian 22%; Spanish 5%. *Aldo* (2), *Donato* (2), *Marco* (2), *Antonio, Caesar, Carlo, Cosmo, Dante, Enzo, Ermanno, Laurina, Paola; Diego, Jose, Primitiva, Ramon.*

Torello (221) Italian: **1.** from a pet form of *Tore*, a reduced form of the personal name SALVATORE. **2.** from a pet form of the personal name *Toro* (see TORO 2). **3.** nickname from *torello* 'young bull'.

GIVEN NAMES Italian 7%. *Carmela, Dominico, Marcellina, Martino, Pasquale, Silvio.*

Toren (175) **1.** Dutch (**Van Toren**): habitational or topographic name from Middle Dutch *to(o)rn, tor(r)en* 'tower', which has given rise to many place names (compare TORRE). **2.** Swedish: ornamental name from the personal name *Tor* (see THOR 3) + the common adjectival suffix *-en*, from Latin *-enius* 'descendant of'. **3.** Jewish (Ashkenazic): habitational name from the city of Toruń in Poland, called *Thorn* in German.

GIVEN NAMES Jewish 4%. *Hanoch, Moshe, Shira.*

Torgersen (350) Norwegian: patronymic from *Torger*, a form of Old Norse *þorgeirr*, from *þórr*, name of the Norse god of thunder (see THOR) + *geirr* 'spear'.

GIVEN NAMES Scandinavian 10%. *Thor* (2), *Berger, Erik, Jorgen, Morten, Selmer, Torleif.*

Torgerson (1991) Americanized spelling of Norwegian TORGERSEN.

GIVEN NAMES Scandinavian 4%. *Erik* (6), *Anders* (2), *Arlis, Helmer, Hjalmer, Iver, Ordell, Swen, Toralf.*

Torgeson (324) Swedish form of TORGERSEN.

Torgrimson (114) Scandinavian: patronymic from the Old Norse personal name *Torgrimr*.

Torian (249) Swiss German: most probably an altered form of Italian TORINO.

FOREBEARS Schertorio Torian came from Soglio, Switzerland to Halifax Co., VA in 1740. Peter Torian, presumably a relative, was born in Soglio in 1727, the son of Scher de Toriano.

Toribio (352) Spanish: from a medieval personal name, *Toribio*, Latin *Turibius*, bestowed in honor of two Spanish saints. St. Turibius of Astorga was a 5th-century bishop who championed Catholic doctrine against the Priscillianist heresy. St. Turibius of Palencia was the 6th-century founder of the famous abbey of Liébana in Asturies.

GIVEN NAMES Spanish 51%. *Jose* (8), *Francisco* (6), *Juan* (5), *Julio* (4), *Luis* (4), *Manuel* (4), *Ramon* (4), *Jesus* (3), *Lourdes* (3), *Miguel* (3), *Rafael* (3), *Ramona* (3); *Antonio* (6), *Lorenzo* (2), *Dante, Fausto, Heriberto, Leonardo.*

Toriello (104) **1.** Italian: from a pet form of the personal name SALVATORE. **2.** Asturian-Leonese: habitational name from wither of the places in Asturies named Toriello, in Uviéu and Ribesella districts.

GIVEN NAMES Italian 8%. *Americo, Angelo.*

Torino (147) Italian: **1.** habitational name from the city of Turin (Italian *Torino*) in northern Italy. **2.** from a pet form of the personal name *Tore*, a short form of SALVATORE.

GIVEN NAMES Italian 7%; French 4%. *Carmela, Sal, Salvatore; Alphonse, Dominique.*

Torio (115) Asturain-Leonese: habitational name from Torío, a place in the Asturian district of Cangues.

GIVEN NAMES Spanish 29%; Italian 8%. *Carlito* (2), *Amalia, Angel, Arsenio, Cesar, Eduardo, Fernando, Francisco, Jose, Josefina, Luz, Manuel; Antonio, Carmine, Gino, Romeo.*

Torkelson (980) Swedish and Norwegian (**Torkelsen**): patronymic from a form of the Old Norse personal name *þorketill*, composed of the elements *þórr* (see THOR) + *ketill* 'cauldron', 'helmet'.

GIVEN NAMES Scandinavian 5%. *Erik* (4), *Hjalmer, Selmer.*

Torma (199) Hungarian: metonymic occupational name or nickname from *torma* 'horseradish'.

GIVEN NAMES Hungarian 6%. *Attila* (2), *Laszlo* (2), *Arpad.*

Tormey (549) Irish (Ulster): reduced form of **O'Tormey**, an Anglicized form of Gaelic **Ó Tormaigh** 'descendant of *Tormach*', a Gaelic derivative of the Norse personal name *Thormodr*.

Tornabene (223) Italian (Sicily): from a medieval personal name of good omen meaning 'producing a good result'.

GIVEN NAMES Italian 22%. *Salvatore* (5), *Angelo* (2), *Alfonso, Alonzo, Antonio, Benito, Carmela, Livio, Nunzio, Patria, Rosario, Sal, Salvatrice, Santo.*

Tornatore (280) Italian: occupational name for a turner, from medieval Latin *tornator*.
GIVEN NAMES Italian 12%. *Carmine* (2), *Salvatore* (2), *Carlo, Carmelo, Nino, Pietro, Sal, Santo, Sebastiano.*

Tornberg (105) Swedish: ornamental name from *torn* 'thorn' or *torn* 'tower' + *berg*, 'mountain'.
GIVEN NAMES Scandinavian 12%. *Anders, Nels, Thor.*

Tornes (132) Catalan: respelling of **Torners**, an occupational name from the plural of Catalan *torner*, meaning either 'turner' or 'potter's wheel'.
GIVEN NAMES Spanish 6%. *Luis* (2), *Felisa, Jose, Josefina, Juan, Lilia.*

Tornetta (139) Italian: from a feminized diminutive or pet form of TORNO.
GIVEN NAMES Italian 13%. *Angelo* (2), *Calogero, Giuditta, Matteo.*

Torney (194) **1.** English and northern Irish: habitational name from places called Tournay in Calvados and Orne in northern France. In some cases it could be of English origin, from any of the places called Thorney, in Cambridgeshire, Nottinghamshire, Somerset, and Sussex, mostly named from Old English *þorn* 'thorn tree' + *ēg* 'island', although the Nottinghamshire example is from Old English *þorn* + *haga* 'enclosure'. **2.** Irish: reduced Anglicized form of Gaelic **Ó Torna** 'descendant of *Torna*', a personal name. **3.** German (eastern): topographic name and habitational name derived from a Slavic word, *tarn-*, meaning 'brush made of thorns'.

Torno (151) **1.** Italian: metonymic occupational name for a turner, from *torno*, an old word for a lathe (modern Italian *tornio*), or a habitational name from a place named with this word in the sense 'curved or rounded hill'. **2.** Italian: from a short form of the personal name *Ritorno*. **3.** Spanish (often **Del Torno**): habitational name from El Torno in Cáceres. **4.** Altered spelling of a German or Polish habitational name from Turnów in Poland.

Tornow (296) German (of Slavic origin): habitational name from any of four places so named in eastern Germany, probably of similar origin to TORNEY 3.
GIVEN NAMES German 6%. *Helmuth* (2), *Hans, Lothar, Markus.*

Tornquist (254) Swedish: ornamental name from *torn* 'thorn' or *torn* 'tower' + *quist*, an old or ornamental spelling of *kvist* 'twig'.
GIVEN NAMES Scandinavian 9%; German 6%. *Erik* (4), *Anders, Kerstin, Lennart; Gerd, Heinrich, Helmut, Kurt.*

Toro (1279) **1.** Spanish: habitational name from Toro in Zamora province, called Campos Gotorum in the Middle Ages. **2.** Spanish: nickname from *toro* 'bull'

(usually in the form **Del Toro**). **3.** Italian: nickname for a lusty person or a metonymic occupational name for a tender of bulls, from Italian *toro* 'bull' (Latin *taurus*). **4.** Italian: from a short form of the personal name *Ristoro*. **5.** Estonian or Finnish: unexplained.
GIVEN NAMES Spanish 41%. *Jose* (24), *Carlos* (22), *Luis* (18), *Juan* (12), *Rafael* (10), *Angel* (9), *Raul* (8), *Jaime* (7), *Julio* (7), *Miguel* (7), *Manuel* (6), *Efrain* (5).

Torok (788) Hungarian (**Török**): ethnic name from *török* 'Turkish'. The name was borne by people of ethnic Turkish descent, but also sometimes given to people who were captured by the Turks or someone who had taken part in the wars against the Ottoman Empire. In other cases the surname may be from a habitational name, from the use of a picture of a Turk as a house sign.
GIVEN NAMES Hungarian 6%. *Geza* (3), *Janos* (3), *Tibor* (3), *Elek* (2), *Imre* (2), *Andras, Balint, Bela, Gabor, Sandor.*

Torosian (279) Armenian: patronymic from the personal name *T'oros*, of unknown origin.
GIVEN NAMES Armenian 23%. *Minas* (2), *Sarkis* (2), *Toros* (2), *Vartouhi* (2), *Zaven* (2), *Akop, Aram, Ardemis, Asatour, Azatui, Gevork, Grigor.*

Torossian (101) Armenian: variant of TOROSIAN.
GIVEN NAMES Armenian 50%. *Ara* (2), *Berj* (2), *Hovik* (2), *Artine, Gayane, Gevorg, Hagop, Haik, Hosep, Hovhannes, Karabet, Karnig.*

Torosyan (101) Armenian: variant of TOROSSIAN.
GIVEN NAMES Armenian 73%. *Arutyun* (3), *Avetis* (3), *Sedrak* (3), *Gevork* (2), *Hovsep* (2), *Knarik* (2), *Oganes* (2), *Stepan* (2), *Akop, Anahit, Anait, Araks, Araksi.*

Torp (180) Scandinavian: habitational name from a place named with the word *torp*, from Old Norse *þorp* 'farm'. (In Norway there are 35 places so named.)
GIVEN NAMES Scandinavian 9%; German 4%. *Erik, Fredrik; Erna, Gerd.*

Torpey (548) Irish: reduced Anglicized form of Gaelic **Ó Tarpaigh** (see TARPEY).

Torpy (148) Irish: reduced Anglicized form of Gaelic **Ó Tarpaigh** (see TARPEY).

Torr (172) English: **1.** topographic name for someone who lived by a tor or rocky hilltop (Old English *torr*, of Celtic origin), or a habitational name from any of the places named with this word, for example Torre or Torr in Devon, where the surname is frequent. **2.** nickname for someone thought to resemble a bull, Anglo-Norman French *tor* (Latin *taurus*). **3.** Scottish: perhaps a habitational name from a minor place in Fife.

Torralba (133) Spanish, Catalan, and Aragonese: habitational name from any of several places called Torralba, named with *torre* 'tower' + *alba* 'white'.

GIVEN NAMES Spanish 45%. *Jorge* (3), *Jose* (3), *Manuel* (3), *Juanita* (2), *Ramon* (2), *Agustin, Alfredo, Antolin, Araceli, Arturo, Bernardo, Carlos.*

Torrance (872) Scottish: variant of TORRENCE.

Torre (1195) **1.** Italian: topographic name for someone who lived near a tower, usually a defensive fortification or watchtower (from Latin *turris*), or a habitational name from any of the places named with this word, as for example Torre Annunziata or Torre del Greco in Naples province, Torre de' Passeri (Pescara, Abruzzo), or Torre di Ruggiero (Catanzaro, Calabria). **2.** Galician, Catalan, Aragonese, Spanish, and Portuguese: habitational name from any of the numerous places so named in Galicia (often in the form **De la Torre**), in Catalonia and Aragon (as for example La Torre de Fontalbella, La Torre del Compte, La Torre de Fluvià), or from any of the many places in Spain and Portugal named Torre or La Torre, from *torre* '(watch) tower' (of the same etymology as 1).
GIVEN NAMES Italian 16%; Spanish 12%. *Rocco* (10), *Angelo* (8), *Salvatore* (7), *Carmelo* (5), *Vito* (3), *Antonio* (2), *Carmine* (2), *Pietro* (2), *Sal* (2), *Sebastiano* (2), *Agostino, Bartolo; Jose* (9), *Francisco* (5), *Carlos* (4), *Julio* (3), *Alvaro* (2), *Eduardo* (2), *Elvira* (2), *Ernesto* (2), *Fernando* (2), *Gregorio* (2), *Guillermo* (2), *Jorge* (2).

Torregrossa (214) Italian: topographic name for someone who lived near a distinctively large tower, from *torre* 'tower' + *grossa* 'big'.
GIVEN NAMES Italian 13%; French 5%. *Salvatore* (3), *Lorenzo, Sal, Serafino, Umberto; Alphonse, Emile, Michel.*

Torrence (1849) **1.** Scottish and northern Irish: habitational name from either of two places called Torrance (one near East Kilbride, the other north of Glasgow under the Campsie Fells), named with Gaelic *torran* 'hillock', 'mound', with the later addition of the English plural -*s*. **2.** Irish: reduced Anglicized form of **Ó Toráin** (see TORAN).

Torrens (321) **1.** Catalan: respelling of **Torrents**, a topographic name for someone living by the course of a torrent, from the plural of Catalan *torrent* 'mountain stream', 'torrent' (Latin *torrens*). **2.** Scottish and northern Irish: variant spelling of TORRENCE. **3.** Dutch: patronymic from a reduced pet form of the personal names *Victor* or *Hector* (see HECTOR).
GIVEN NAMES Spanish 16%. *Raul* (4), *Jaime* (3), *Jorge* (2), *Luis* (2), *Manuel* (2), *Aida, Alejandro, Ana, Andres, Anselmo, Benito, Caridad.*

Torrente (119) Spanish: habitational name from any of several places in Spain named Torrente, from *torrente* 'torrent', 'intermittent fast-flowing stream'.

GIVEN NAMES Spanish 24%; Italian 9%. *Ventura* (2), *Adela, Beatriz, Efrain, Emilio, Fernando, Humberto, Irineo, Juan, Juan Antonio, Juana, Manolo; Sal, Saverio.*

Torres (37645) **1.** Galician, Catalan, Spanish, Portuguese, and Jewish (Sephardic): habitational name from any of the numerous places named Torres, all named with the plural of *torre* 'tower' (see TORRE). **2.** Italian: habitational name from Torres in Belluno or Porto Torres in Sassari. In southern Italy the surname is sometimes a borrowing from Spanish (see 1). **3.** Dutch: from a short form of *Victoris*, from the Latin personal name *Victorius*.

GIVEN NAMES Spanish 48%; Portuguese 10%. *Jose* (1063), *Juan* (527), *Luis* (380), *Carlos* (360), *Manuel* (316), *Jesus* (263), *Francisco* (222), *Pedro* (204), *Miguel* (193), *Jorge* (190), *Raul* (189), *Rafael* (176); *Ligia* (5), *Anatolio* (3), *Catarina* (3), *Paulo* (2), *Albeiro, Gonsalo, Joaquim, Lidio, Omero, Wenceslao.*

Torrey (1886) English: probably a variant of TERRY 1.

FOREBEARS A Josiah Torrey was in Boston before 1680. John Torrey (1796–1873) was a botanist and teacher born in NY who catalogued many North American plants.

Torrez (1714) Spanish (**Tórrez**): variant of TORRES.

GIVEN NAMES Spanish 33%. *Manuel* (30), *Jose* (24), *Juan* (9), *Pedro* (9), *Carlos* (8), *Jesus* (8), *Armando* (6), *Raul* (6), *Ruben* (6), *Alfredo* (5), *Alvaro* (5), *Fernando* (5).

Torri (170) Italian: from the plural of *torre* 'tower' (see TORRE).

GIVEN NAMES Italian 8%; French 4%. *Giovanni* (2), *Aldo, Carlo, Fiorella, Geno; Andre, Collette.*

Torrico (140) Spanish: habitational name from Torrico in Toledo province.

GIVEN NAMES Spanish 32%. *Carlos* (3), *Luis* (3), *Mario* (3), *Jorge* (2), *Jose* (2), *Juan* (2), *Pedro* (2), *Rosario* (2), *Sergio* (2), *Blanca, Guadalupe, Gualberto; Antonio, Caterina, Corrado, Romeo, Sandro.*

Torrisi (350) Italian: topographic name for someone living by a tower, from a variant of *torrese*, an adjectival derivative of TORRE. The form is a hybrid of standard Italian *torese* and southern Italian *turrisi*.

GIVEN NAMES Italian 18%. *Salvatore* (7), *Angelo* (3), *Alfio* (2), *Carmelo* (2), *Giuseppe* (2), *Palma* (2), *Sal* (2), *Carmine, Domenic, Mauro, Salvator, Vito.*

Torry (142) **1.** English: variant of TERRY. **2.** Scottish: probably a habitational name from Torry near Aberdeen.

Torsiello (158) Southern Italian (Campania): southern variant of **Torsello**, which is of uncertain derivation; perhaps from the personal name *Torsoas*.

GIVEN NAMES Italian 14%. *Domenic, Emidio, Ezio, Guido, Romeo, Vito.*

Torson (129) Variant spelling of Scandinavian THORSON.

Torstenson (130) **1.** Swedish: variant of T(h)orstensson (see THORSTENSON). **2.** Americanized spelling of Norwegian **Torstensen**, cognate with 1.

GIVEN NAMES Scandinavian 6%. *Lennart, Selmer.*

Torti (177) Italian: nickname from *torto* 'twisted', 'tortured', 'sullen' or Sicilian *tortu* 'bad', 'wicked' (but also in *castru tortu* 'castrated ram'), from Latin *tortus*, past participle of *torquere* 'to turn or twist'.

GIVEN NAMES Italian 7%. *Benedetto, Guido, Luigi.*

Tortora (499) Italian: **1.** from a personal name derived from *tortora* 'turtle dove' (from Latin *turtur*, genitive *turturis*), symbolizing innocence and purity. Compare TURTLE 2. **2.** habitational name from Tortora in Cosenza province.

GIVEN NAMES Italian 14%. *Salvatore* (6), *Aniello* (2), *Sal* (2), *Agostino, Angelo, Antonio, Canio, Carmine, Ciro, Gioia, Luigi, Marco.*

Tortorella (258) Italian: **1.** from a diminutive of TORTORA. **2.** habitational name from Tortorella in Salerno province.

GIVEN NAMES Italian 16%. *Ottavio* (3), *Salvatore* (2), *Angelo, Antonio, Caesar, Domenic, Gino, Giovanna, Nicola, Olympia, Palma, Rocco.*

Tortorelli (214) Italian: patronymic or plural form of TORTORELLO.

GIVEN NAMES Italian 10%. *Aldo, Antonio, Filippo, Francesco.*

Tortorello (182) Italian: from a diminutive of TORTORA.

GIVEN NAMES Italian 13%. *Antonio, Concetta, Onofrio, Rocco, Vito.*

Tortorice (236) Italian (Sicily): variant of TORTORICI.

GIVEN NAMES Italian 6%. *Attillo, Lorenzo, Sal.*

Tortorich (122) Probably an Americanized variant of Italian TORTORICE.

GIVEN NAMES Spanish 7%. *Juanita, Salvador.*

Tortorici (360) Italian (Sicily): habitational name from Tortorici in Messina.

GIVEN NAMES Italian 16%. *Salvatore* (4), *Gasper* (3), *Angelo* (2), *Pasquale* (2), *Antonio, Bartolo, Domenic, Francesco, Pellegrino, Rosaria, Sal, Santo.*

Tortoriello (130) Variant of Italian TORTORELLO.

GIVEN NAMES Italian 8%. *Carmela, Vito.*

Torvik (113) Norwegian: habitational name from any of several farmsteads in western Norway named Torvik, from a first element of varied origin + *vik* 'bay', 'inlet'.

GIVEN NAMES Scandinavian 18%; German 4%. *Hilmar* (2), *Hilma, Lars, Ove, Svein; Gerhard.*

Toscani (100) Italian: patronymic or plural form of TOSCANO.

GIVEN NAMES Italian 24%. *Palma* (2), *Alessandro, Angelo, Antonio, Domenic, Donato, Gennaro, Ivano.*

Toscano (1629) Italian and Spanish: regional name for someone from Tuscany (Italian *Toscana*) in Italy.

GIVEN NAMES Spanish 17%; Italian 13%. *Jose* (12), *Jesus* (9), *Juan* (8), *Mario* (8), *Alfredo* (4), *Guadalupe* (4), *Alfonso* (3), *Carlos* (3), *Cesar* (3), *Jorge* (3), *Miguel* (3), *Salvador* (3); *Antonio* (15), *Salvatore* (8), *Angelo* (6), *Ciro* (3), *Sal* (3), *Santo* (3), *Carlo* (2), *Cosimo* (2), *Domenico* (2), *Filippo* (2), *Gino* (2).

Tosch (154) South German: **1.** probably a habitational name for someone who lived at a house distinguished by the sign of a bouquet of flowers, Middle High German *doste, toste*. **2.** topographic name for someone who lived where wild thyme grew, from the dialect term *dost*.

Tosh (799) **1.** Scottish: reduced form of MCINTOSH, which is also established in northeastern Ulster. **2.** Americanized spelling of German TOSCH. **3.** Americanized spelling of Slovenian **Toš**, a derivative of the personal name *Tomaž* (see THOMAS).

Tosi (393) Italian: patronymic or plural form of TOSO.

GIVEN NAMES Italian 13%. *Angelo* (3), *Primo* (2), *Antonio, Attilio, Dante, Dino, Emanuele, Flavio, Gino, Luigi, Marco, Mauro.*

Toso (308) Italian: nickname for a youth, from *toso* 'clean-shaven', 'close-cropped' (Latin *tonsus*, past participle of *tondere* 'to cut or shear'). In the later Middle Ages it was for some time the fashion for young men to cut their hair close, while their elders preferred a longer style.

Tostado (171) Spanish: nickname for a very dark-skinned person, from the past participle of *tostar* 'to tan', 'to turn brown'.

GIVEN NAMES Spanish 49%. *Jose* (11), *Juan* (3), *Mario* (3), *Carlos* (2), *Edgardo* (2), *Ernesto* (2), *Guillermo* (2), *Javier* (2), *Jorge* (2), *Miguel* (2), *Pedro* (2), *Ricardo* (2); *Antonio, Enedino, Marco Antonio, Silvano.*

Toste (265) Spanish (especially Tenerife) and Portuguese: of uncertain origin; possibly from *tost(e)* 'quick' or alternatively from Portuguese *toste* 'galley bench'.

GIVEN NAMES Spanish 19%; Portuguese 12%. *Manuel* (13), *Jose* (5), *Antonio* (3), *Luis* (3), *Jorge* (2), *Aniceto, Arnaldo, Carlos, Fernanda, Francisco, Lino, Miguel, Osvaldo; Mateus* (2), *Henrique.*

Tostenson (173) Scandinavian: variant of TORSTENSON.

Tosti (273) Italian: patronymic or plural form of TOSTO.

GIVEN NAMES Italian 13%; Spanish 6%. *Angelo, Antonio, Carlo, Chiara, Emidio, Enzo, Gaetano, Giacomo, Giuseppe, Marco, Mario, Nicola, Santina; Manuel* (2), *Angel, Fernando.*

Tosto (234) Sicilian and Southern Italian: nickname from the dialect word *tosto*,

Neapolitan *tuosto*, Sicilian *tostu*, 'obstinate', 'headstrong', or 'impudent'.

GIVEN NAMES Italian 17%. *Salvatore* (3), *Angelo, Antonino, Gino, Giuseppe, Luigi, Martino, Palma, Pasquale, Sal, Vito.*

Tota (146) Italian (Apulia): unexplained.

GIVEN NAMES Italian 9%. *Concetta, Grazia, Leonardo, Vito.*

Totah (124) Arabic: topographic name from *tūta* 'mulberry tree'.

GIVEN NAMES Arabic 26%. *Basem* (2), *Sami* (2), *Abla, Aziz, Faiz, Ibrahim, Kamel, Nabeeh, Nabeel, Nabil, Nadim, Naim.*

Totaro (312) Southern Italian: **1.** variant of TODARO. **2.** nickname from Calabrian dialect *totaru* 'fool', 'idiot'.

GIVEN NAMES Italian 14%. *Angelo* (3), *Gandolfo, Nicola, Olindo, Rosaria, Sal, Salvatore, Vincenzo.*

Toth (7596) **1.** Hungarian (**Tóth**): ethnic name for a Slovak or a Slovenian, Hungarian *tót*. It is also found in Prekmurje, the easternmost part of Slovenia, where it is spelled both **Toth** and **Tot**. **2.** German: nickname from Middle High German *tōt* 'death'. **3.** German: nickname from Middle High German *tote* 'godfather'.

GIVEN NAMES Hungarian 6%. *Zoltan* (18), *Tibor* (16), *Laszlo* (13), *Sandor* (13), *Bela* (10), *Geza* (10), *Attila* (9), *Gabor* (9), *Endre* (8), *Kalman* (8), *Andras* (6), *Jozsef* (6).

Totherow (159) Presumably an altered form of German DOTTERER (see TEDROW). Compare TUTTEROW.

Toti (140) Italian: patronymic or plural form of TOTO.

GIVEN NAMES Italian 11%. *Benedetto, Carlo, Evo, Savino.*

Totin (106) French: from a shortened pet form of a personal name ending in *-tot*, for example *Robertot*, itself a pet form of ROBERT.

Totino (130) Italian: from a pet form of the personal name TOTO.

GIVEN NAMES Italian 29%. *Rocco* (6), *Salvatore* (2), *Vito* (2), *Umberto.*

Totman (366) English: occupational name for a watchman or lookout, Middle English *toteman*.

Toto (453) **1.** Italian: from a personal name of Germanic origin, *Dod(d)o, Totto*. **2.** Italian (Sicily): from the personal name *Toto* (a pet form of SALVATORE or ANTONIO). **3.** Greek (**Totos**): from Albanian *toto* 'priest'. It is sometimes found forming a surname in combination with personal names, as in **Totogiannis** 'John the priest'.

GIVEN NAMES Italian 19%. *Rocco* (4), *Carmine* (3), *Salvatore* (3), *Vito* (3), *Giuseppe* (2), *Luigi* (2), *Nicola* (2), *Angelo, Antonio, Cosmo, Domenic, Donato.*

Totten (2434) English and northern Irish: possibly from a diminutive of the nickname *totte* 'simpleton', 'fool'.

Totton (142) Northern Irish and English: probably a variant spelling of TOTTEN.

Totty (434) English: from a pet form of an Old English personal name, *Tot(t)a*.

Totzke (198) German (under Slavic influence): from a much altered pet form of the personal name DIETRICH.

GIVEN NAMES German 5%. *Eldred, Otto.*

Touch (186) **1.** Scottish: variant of TOUGH. **2.** Cambodian: unexplained.

GIVEN NAMES Cambodian 35%. *Sok* (2), *Bunthoeun, Chhom, Chhum, Choun, Eng, Heng, Hoeun, Koeun, Kosal, Samoeun, Savath, Somaly, Soun, Thoeun; Kao, Kon, Kong, Lim, Lun, Sen; Muon, Nguon, Phal, Phan, Pho, Than, Thy, Ry, Then.*

Touchet (687) French: topographic name from a diminutive of Old French *touche* 'grove', 'thicket' (of unknown origin).

FOREBEARS An immigrant from Normandy, France, is documented as Touchet and Touchette in either Notre-Dame-des-Anges or Charlesbourg, Quebec, in 1666.

GIVEN NAMES French 5%. *Anastasie, Curley, Denys, Evest, Minos, Raywood, Rodolph, Vernice.*

Touchette (510) Altered spelling of TOUCHET, reflecting the Canadian pronunciation, which sounds the final *t*.

GIVEN NAMES French 8%. *Lucien* (2), *Marcel* (2), *Pierre* (2), *Armand, Collette, Euclide, Henri, Hilaire, Huguette.*

Touchstone (752) Possibly Irish: unexplained.

Touchton (480) Origin unidentified. Possibly related to TOUCHSTONE.

Tougas (373) Variant of French **Tougard**, from a personal name composed of the Old Norse personal name *þórr*, the name of the god of thunder in Scandinavian mythology (see THOR), + *gard* 'manor' (cognate with English *yard* and *garden*).

FOREBEARS A Tougas or Tougard from Normandy, France, is documented in Montreal in 1698, with the secondary surname LAVIOLETTE.

GIVEN NAMES French 11%. *Marcel* (2), *Alain, Armand, Cecile, Emile, Gaston, Pierre, Rosaire.*

Tough (126) **1.** Scottish: variant of TULLOCH. In Scotland it is pronounced *tyookh*. **2.** English: nickname for a valiant or stubborn person, from Middle English *togh, tow(e)* 'steadfast'.

Touhey (284) Irish: variant spelling of TOOHEY.

GIVEN NAME Irish 5%. *Brendan.*

Toulouse (214) French and English: habitational name from the city in Haute-Garonne, whose name is of uncertain, apparently Celtic, origin. In Canadian usage, it is a secondary surname for BERTRAND, Crésac, Crisaque, Damours, Fournesse, Galand, LAVIOLETTE, Pitou, RAYMOND, and Rivos.

GIVEN NAMES French 14%. *Andre* (2), *Monique* (2), *Camile, Emile, Gilles, Marcel, Rosaire.*

Toulson (130) English: **1.** variant of TOLSON. **2.** variant of TOMLINSON, from a colloquial pronunciation.

Touma (163) Arabic: variant spelling, under French influence, of **Tūma**, Arabic form of THOMAS.

GIVEN NAMES Arabic 31%; French 9%. *Fadi* (2), *Farid* (2), *Ghada* (2), *Habib* (2), *Sami* (2), *Yousef* (2), *Zaki* (2), *Adnan, Hany, Hayat, Issam, Jamel; Andre* (2), *Antoine* (2), *Alain, Georges, Pierre.*

Toupin (237) French: from *toupin*, which in medieval French meant 'spinning-top', possibly a nickname; in Occitan, however, it denotes a small earthenware pot and was probably a metonymic occupational name for a potter.

FOREBEARS A Toupin of unknown regional origin is documented in Quebec City in 1645. The secondary surnames Du Sault, DUSSAULT, and LAPIERRE are associated.

GIVEN NAMES French 12%. *Andre, Armand, Aurore, Cecile, Emilienne, Julien, Marcel, Maxime, Normand.*

Toups (1155) French: unexplained.

GIVEN NAMES French 8%. *Emile* (8), *Andre* (2), *Irby* (2), *Kearney* (2), *Monique* (2), *Oneil* (2), *Ulysse* (2), *Alphe, Cecile, Clovis, Octave, Prosper.*

Tourangeau (193) French: from a derivative of *Tourange*, an old form of Touraine, hence a regional name denoting someone from the Touraine region, or from its main city, Tours. In Canadian usage, this has principally been a secondary surname, still with its original significance.

GIVEN NAMES French 11%. *Armand* (2), *Cecile* (2), *Marcel, Marjolaine, Normand, Pierre.*

Tourdot (106) French: according to Morlet, from a diminutive of **Tourde**, denoting a species of thrush with black and brown plumage; hence a nickname for someone with graying hair.

GIVEN NAME French 6%. *Marcel* (2).

Toure (180) African (**Touré**) and Muslim: unexplained.

GIVEN NAMES African 38%; Muslim 34%. *Mamadou* (6), *Oumar* (4), *Amadou* (3), *Sekou* (3), *Bakary* (2), *Moctar* (2), *Seydou* (2), *Aboubacar, Aliou, Aminata, Babacar, Boubacar; Abdoulaye* (3), *Ibrahima* (3), *Mohamed* (3), *Askia* (2), *Daouda* (2), *Moussa* (2), *Omar* (2), *Abdullah, Ahmed, Aisha, Cherif, Elhadji.*

Tourigny (213) French: habitational name from Torigni in Manche.

GIVEN NAMES French 13%. *Normand* (2), *Andre, Armand, Gilles, Herve, Laurent, Roch.*

Tourtellotte (124) French: from a diminutive of *tourte*, in Normandy denoting a type of bread, hence a metonymic occupational name for a baker of such bread. It is a Huguenot name, particularly associated with Boston.

GIVEN NAMES French 4%. *France, Georges.*

Tourtillott (125) Variant of French TOUR-TELLOTTE.

Tourville (623) French: perhaps a variant of **Tourneville**, a habitational name from places so named in Eure, Manche, Seine-Inférieure, and Ille-et-Vilaine. In Canada this first appears as a secondary surname for the families Dutaut and Hubout.

Tousey (163) English: unexplained; possibly of French origin.

Tousignant (589) French: unexplained.
FOREBEARS A Tousignant from the Guyenne region of France is documented in Quebec City in 1668 with the variant **Tousillon** and the secondary surname LAPOINTE.
GIVEN NAMES French 12%. *Armand* (3), *Jacques* (3), *Normand* (3), *Andre* (2), *Etienne* (2), *Aime*, *Alphonse*, *Benoit*, *Cecile*, *Celina*, *Gilles*, *Herve*.

Tousley (304) See TOWSLEY, of which this may be a variant.

Toussaint (1348) French: from a nickname or personal name composed of the elements *tous* 'all' (plural) + *saints* 'saints'. The name was given to someone who was born on All Saints' Day (1 November), or chosen as an invocation of the protection of all the saints of the calendar.
FOREBEARS A Toussaint from the Poitou region of France is recorded in Quebec City in 1725.
GIVEN NAMES French 18%. *Jacques* (4), *Armand* (3), *Marcel* (3), *Yves* (3), *Andre* (2), *Gaston* (2), *Jean Claude* (2), *Lucien* (2), *Marcelle* (2), *Pierre* (2), *Raoul* (2), *Serge* (2).

Tout (187) English (Devon): nickname from Middle English *toute* 'buttocks', 'rump', or a topographic name from the same word used in a transferred sense to denote a smooth, rounded hillock.

Toutant (188) French: variant of **Tostain** or **Toutain**, a derivative of the Old Norse personal name *þorsteinn* (see THURSTON).
FOREBEARS A Toutant from the Orléans region of France is documented in Champlain, Quebec, in 1686.
GIVEN NAMES French 13%. *Andre* (4), *Pierre* (2), *Jacques*, *Raynald*.

Tovar (2623) Spanish: variant of TOBAR.
GIVEN NAMES Spanish 51%. *Jose* (89), *Jesus* (41), *Juan* (36), *Francisco* (31), *Manuel* (29), *Carlos* (27), *Jorge* (18), *Luis* (18), *Rafael* (15), *Raul* (15), *Pedro* (14), *Ruben* (14).

Tovey (321) English: from the Old Norse personal name *Tófi*, a reduced form of any of various compound names formed with *þórr*, name of the Norse god of thunder (see THOR), + a second element beginning with *f* or *v*, for example *valdr* 'rule'.

Tow (686) English: perhaps, as Reaney proposes, a variant of TOUGH.

Towe (942) English: variant of TOW.

Towell (543) Irish (County Waterford): variant of TOOLE.

Tower (1966) English: **1.** topographic name for someone who lived near a tower, usually a defensive fortification or watchtower, from Middle English, Old French *tūr* (Latin *turris*). **2.** occupational name for someone who dressed white leather, cured with alum rather than tanned with bark, from an agent derivative of Middle English *taw(en)* (Old English *tawian* 'to prepare, make ready'). **3.** Americanized spelling of German TAUER.

Towers (1534) English: **1.** variant of TOWER, with later *-s*. **2.** habitational name for someone from Tours in Eure-et-Loire, northern France, so called from the Gaulish tribal name *Turones*, of uncertain etymology.

Towery (1199) English (Northumberland and Durham): unexplained.

Towey (377) Irish: **1.** variant of TOOHEY. **2.** (Mayo) reduced form of **O'Towey**, an Anglicized form of Gaelic **Ó Toghdha** 'descendant of *Toghdha*', from *toghdha* 'chosen'.
GIVEN NAMES Irish 8%. *Brendan*, *Malachy*.

Towle (1929) English (Nottinghamshire): variant of TOLL.

Towler (843) English: variant of TOLLER.

Towles (780) English: variant of TOLL.

Town (869) English: variant spelling of TOWNE.

Towne (2581) English: topographic name for someone who lived in a village, as opposed to an outlying farm or hamlet, from Middle English *toun* (Old English *tūn*, which originally meant 'fence' and then 'enclosure', although the sense 'settlement, village' was already firmly established in the Old English period) .

Towner (1327) English (Sussex): **1.** topographic name for one who lived in a township or village, Middle English *toun*, + *-er*, a characteristic topographic ending of Sussex surnames. **2.** occupational name for a toll taker or tax collector, from *tolnere*, an agent derivative of Middle English *toll* 'tax', 'payment'. Compare TOLLER.

Townes (1232) English: variant of TOWNE.

Townley (1531) English (especially northwestern): habitational name from Towneley near Burnley in Lancashire, which is named with Old English *tūn* 'enclosure', 'settlement' + *lēah* 'wood', 'clearing'; or a topographic name for someone who lived at a clearing associated with a farm or village. The surname has also been established in Ireland since the 16th century.

Towns (2124) English (northern) and Scottish: variant of TOWN.

Townsel (272) Variant of TOWNSELL.
GIVEN NAMES French 4%. *Andre*, *Celestine*, *Sylviane*.

Townsell (168) English: unexplained.

Townsend (23214) English: topographic name for someone who lived at the extremity of a village, from Middle English *toun* 'village', 'settlement' + *ende* 'end'.

Townshend (214) English (Norfolk): variant of TOWNSEND.

Townsley (1005) English: variant of TOWNLEY. In Ulster this is sometimes used synonymously with TINSLEY.

Townson (501) English: patronymic from a pet form of the personal name THOMAS.

Townzen (157) English: probably an altered form of TOWNSEND.

Towry (299) Probably a variant spelling of English TOWERY.

Towse (103) English (Yorkshire): possibly a topographic name from Middle English *ate howes* 'at the spur of a hill' (from Old English *hōh* 'heel', 'projecting ridge of land').

Towsley (292) English: unexplained; possibly a habitational name from a lost or unidentified place.

Towson (198) English: probably an old form of TOWNSON, as recorded in the 16th century.
GIVEN NAMES French 4%. *Damien*, *Michel*.

Toy (1818) **1.** English: nickname for a light-hearted or frivolous person, from Middle English *toy* 'play', 'sport' (of uncertain origin), or from an occasional medieval personal name, *Toye*. **2.** French: metonymic occupational name for a sheath maker, from Old French *toie* 'sheath' (Latin *theca*).

Toyama (308) Japanese: 'abundant mountains'; found mostly in eastern Japan. The same characters are pronounced *Tomiyama* in the Ryūkyū Islands. The same name, written with characters meaning 'outer mountain' (and sometimes read *Sotoyama*), is less common. Many bearers of all versions of the name have samurai or noble connections. Yet another name, properly Romanized *Tōyama*, means 'far mountain'. The name is taken from a village in Shinano (now Nagano prefecture) and is found in eastern Japan and the Ryūkyū Islands.
GIVEN NAMES Japanese 48%. *Hiroshi* (2), *Kenji* (2), *Noriko* (2), *Shigemi* (2), *Toki* (2), *Yasuko* (2), *Yoshiko* (2), *Akihiko*, *Akiko*, *Akio*, *Atsuko*, *Emiko*.

Toye (378) **1.** English: variant spelling of TOY 1. **2.** Irish: variant of TOWEY. (The English name is also present in Ireland.) **3.** French: variant spelling of TOY. **4.** French (**Toyé**): habitational name for someone from To(u)ya, a region in southwestern France (Bearn). As a French name, this is associated first with the Waldensians, a group of religious reformers founded by Valdensius of Lyon, France, in the 12th century, and second with the Huguenots.

Toyne (147) English (Lincolnshire): unexplained.

Toyoda (81) Japanese: 'fruitful rice paddy'; a common placename and surname throughout Japan.
GIVEN NAMES Japanese 76%. *Hiroshi* (4), *Futoshi* (2), *Hikaru* (2), *Fumio*, *Hiromi*,

Hiroo, Hitoshi, Junichi, Junji, Kazuo, Keiichiro, Kumiko.

Tozer (451) **1.** English: occupational name for a comber or carder of wool, from an agent derivative of Middle English *tōse(n)* 'to tease'. **2.** Americanized spelling of Hungarian **Tőzsér**, an occupational name for a dealer or tradesman, *tőzsér*, especially one selling cattle.

Tozier (502) Variant of English TOZER.

Tozzi (428) Italian (especially frequent in Tuscany): **1.** from the Germanic personal name *Tozo* (a pet form of a personal name based on the root *dod-*). **2.** from the personal name *Tozzo*, a reduced form of *Albertozzo*, *Robertozzo*, or other pet names with the diminutive suffix *-ozzo*. **3.** nickname from *tozzo* 'squat', 'dumpy'.
GIVEN NAMES Italian 23%. *Gino* (4), *Rocco* (3), *Salvatore* (3), *Amedio* (2), *Carmine* (2), *Enio* (2), *Giorgio* (2), *Luigi* (2), *Raffaele* (2), *Angelo*, *Antonio*, *Carlo*.

Traber (185) Variant of TRABERT.
GIVEN NAMES German 5%. *Armin, Otto.*

Trabert (228) German and Swiss German: nickname from an agent derivative of Middle High German *draben* 'to trot'.
GIVEN NAMES German 4%. *Aloysius, Matthias.*

Trabold (138) German: from a personal name composed of the Germanic elements *trag* (related to Gothic *draban* 'to hit' or *thragjan* 'to run') + *bald* 'bold', 'quick'.
GIVEN NAMES German 5%. *Andreas, Hermann, Karl.*

Trabucco (248) Italian: metonymic occupational name for a trapper, from Old Italian *trabucco* 'trap', 'pitfall', Sicilian *trabbuccu* '(mouse)trap'.
GIVEN NAMES Italian 6%. *Ermanno* (3), *Aldo, Gilda, Lucio, Remo.*

Trabue (208) Possibly of French origin: unexplained.

Trace (368) English: perhaps a variant of TREECE.

Tracey (2883) Irish **1.** (of Norman origin) variant of TRACY. **2.** variant of TREACY.

Trach (135) **1.** Variant of South German DRACH. **2.** Americanized spelling of Jewish and Polish TRACZ. **3.** Vietnamese: unexplained.
GIVEN NAMES Vietnamese 9%; Jewish 4%. *Hoan* (2), *Duc, Hung, Thanh; Reuven.*

Trachsel (268) German (Swiss, Bavarian, and Austrian): variant of DRECHSEL.

Tracht (140) German: **1.** possibly a habitational name from a place so called in Moravia. **2.** possibly from Middle High German *trachte* 'catch (of fish)'. **3.** in northern Germany, a topographic name from *dar achten* 'there, at the back'.

Trachtenberg (491) Jewish (eastern Ashkenazic): ornamental name of uncertain origin; *-berg* 'mountain', 'hill' is a very common ornamental ending of Yiddish surnames; *Trachten-*, however, is unclear. It may derive from Yiddish *trakhtn* 'to think'

or German *Tracht* 'costume', '(national) dress'.
GIVEN NAMES Jewish 7%. *Meyer* (3), *Ari, Avram, Hyman, Mort, Zev.*

Trachtman (160) Jewish (eastern Ashkenazic): nickname from Yiddish *trakhtn* 'to think' + *man* 'man'.
GIVEN NAMES Jewish 8%. *Erez, Hyman, Mendel.*

Tracy (11441) **1.** Irish (of Norman origin): habitational name from Tracy-Bocage or Tracy-sur-Mer in Calvados, both named from the Gallo-Roman personal name *Thracius* (a derivative of Latin *Thrax*, genitive *Thracis*, 'Thracian') + the locative suffix *-eium*. **2.** Irish: variant of TREACY. **3.** Americanized form of some like-sounding Jewish name.

Tracz (181) Polish and Jewish (from Poland): occupational name from Polish *tracz* 'sawyer'.
GIVEN NAMES Polish 13%. *Dariusz* (2), *Zdzislaw* (2), *Bronislaus, Ignatius, Jozef, Zosia.*

Traczyk (152) Polish: occupational name for a sawyer, from a diminutive of TRACZ, or patronymic from TRACZ.
GIVEN NAMES Polish 6%; German 4%. *Czeslaw, Jadwiga, Janusz; Irmgard, Otto.*

Trad (121) Origin unidentified.
GIVEN NAMES Muslim 17%. *Ameen, Assaf, Fouad, Ibrahim, Jamil, Jumana, Karim, Mohamad, Nizar, Sami, Tarek, Walid.*

Trader (1034) **1.** North German (**Träder**): from an agent derivative of North German *trede* 'step', 'stair'; 'path'. **2.** German: habitational name for someone from Trado near Kamenz.

Traeger (566) **1.** German and Jewish (Ashkenazic): variant of TRAGER. **2.** German (**Träger**): variant of DREHER. Compare DRAEGER.

Trafford (287) English: habitational name from any of various places so called. One in Northamptonshire is named with Old English *træppe* '(fish-)trap' + *ford* 'ford'. The places called Trafford in Cheshire have as their first element Old English *trog* 'trough', 'valley'; while Trafford in Lancashire was originally called *Stratford* 'ford on a Roman road' (see STRATFORD). Nevertheless, most cases of the surname probably derive from the last of these places; a landowning family can be traced there to the 13th century.

Traficante (195) Italian: occupational name for a merchant or trader, Sicilian *traficanti*, Italian *trafficante*. This is a common name in Italy, occurring chiefly in the regions of Molise and Apulia.
GIVEN NAMES Italian 18%. *Biagio* (2), *Rocco* (2), *Carmelo, Cosimo, Gerardo, Gustavo, Mario, Philomena, Sal, Vito.*

Trafton (623) English: unexplained; possibly a habitational name from a lost or unidentified place.

Trager (758) German (**Träger**) and Jewish (Ashkenazic): from German *Träger*, Yiddish *treger*, agent derivatives of Middle High German *tragen* 'to carry', hence an occupational name for someone who carried a load, a peddler or porter, or, in the case of the German name, a legal guardian or guarantor.

Trageser (242) German: habitational name for someone from Trages near Leipzig.

Tragesser (175) German: variant of TRAGESER.

Trahan (4693) Altered or variant form of French **Trahand**, a metonymic occupational name for a silkworker who drew out the thread from the cocoons, from a derivative of *traire* 'to draw or stretch'. It has been 'translated' into English as STRONG.
FOREBEARS The LA branches of the Trahan family trace their descent from one Guillaume Trahan, from Bourgueil, France, in the Loire Valley, who arrived in Acadia in the late 17th century. At the time of the expulsion (1755), his numerous descendants were deported and settled principally in the Attakapas country of LA.
GIVEN NAMES French 7%. *Andre* (5), *Marcel* (5), *Monique* (5), *Pierre* (5), *Leonce* (4), *Lucien* (4), *Alcide* (3), *Cecile* (3), *Emile* (3), *Raywood* (3), *Adrien* (2), *Camille* (2).

Trahern (115) Welsh: from the personal name *Trahaearn*, composed of the elements *tra* 'most', 'very' + *haearn* 'iron'. Compare TREHARNE.

Trahey (103) Variant of Irish **Trahy**, itself a variant of **Trohy**, an Anglicized form of Gaelic **Ó Troighthigh** 'descendant of the foot soldier', Gaelic *troightheach*.

Trail (1318) Scottish: probably a habitational or topographic name from northern Scotland; Black mentions a creek named Traill in Gaelic, running into Upper Loch Torridon.

Traill (130) Scottish: variant spelling of TRAIL.

Train (332) English (Devon): **1.** metonymic occupational name for a trapper or hunter, from Middle English *trayne*, Old French *traine* 'guile', 'snare', 'trap'. **2.** topographic name from Middle English *atte trewen* 'at the trees', or a habitational name from any of the places named with this phrase, for example Train, Traine, or Trewyn, all in Devon.

Traina (625) Italian: habitational name from Troina in Sicily, formerly known as Traina.
GIVEN NAMES Italian 14%. *Angelo* (6), *Sal* (4), *Salvatore* (3), *Nunzio* (2), *Bartolo, Carmela, Caterina, Cosimo, Franco, Giovanni, Leonardo, Lia.*

Trainer (1242) **1.** Northern English and Scottish: occupational name for a trapper, from an agent derivative of Middle English *trayne*, Old French *traine* 'guile', 'trickery', 'snare', 'trap'. Compare TRAIN. **2.** Variant spelling of Irish TRAINOR.

3. Altered spelling of German **Trainer**, a habitational name for someone from Train in Bavaria or Trainau in Upper Franconia.

Trainham (126) Probably a respelling of English TRENHOLM.

Traino (125) **1.** Italian (Sicily): variant of TRAINA. **2.** Southern Italian and Greek (**Trainos**): occupational name for a butcher selling goat meat, from Greek *traginos* 'goat meat', from *tragi* 'he-goat', originally a diminutive of classical Greek *tragos*.
GIVEN NAMES Italian 11%. *Vito* (2), *Sal*.

Trainor (2800) **1.** Irish (Ulster): reduced form of **McTraynor**, an Anglicized form of Gaelic **Mac Thréinfhir** 'son of *Tréinfhear*', a byname meaning 'champion', 'strong man' (from *tréan* 'strong' + *fear* 'man'). **2.** English: variant of TRAINER.
GIVEN NAMES Irish 4%. *Aidan* (2), *Brendan* (2), *Ciaran*, *Finbar*.

Trainum (144) Probably a respelling of English TRENHOLM.

Traister (221) Jewish (eastern Ashkenazic): ornamental name from Yiddish *treyster*, central Yiddish *trayster* 'comforter', 'consoler' (see TROST).

Trakas (156) Greek: From the vocabulary word *traka* 'crash, collision', from Italian *attaccare*. The word has come to mean in Greek slang 'sponging', 'living at another's expense', which may be the trait alluded to.
GIVEN NAMES Greek 4%. *Spero*, *Vasilios*.

Tram (189) Vietnamese: unexplained.
GIVEN NAMES Vietnamese 70%. *Minh* (5), *Thanh* (4), *Chau* (3), *Hai* (3), *Hoa* (3), *Binh* (2), *Dung* (2), *Hue* (2), *Hung* (2), *Kiet* (2), *Lan* (2), *Long* (2), *Dong*, *Hong*, *Leong*, *Phoung*.

Trama (101) Italian: unexplained.
GIVEN NAMES Italian 26%. *Francesco* (2), *Gasper* (2), *Antonio*, *Armando*, *Biagio*, *Emanuele*, *Gustavo*, *Marco*, *Nicola*, *Santo*.

Tramble (134) Probably an Americanized form of German **Tremel** (see TRAMMELL).

Trame (130) French: unexplained.

Tramel (594) Variant of TRAMMELL.

Tramell (158) Variant of TRAMMELL.

Trammel (908) Variant of TRAMMELL.

Trammell (3948) Altered spelling of German **Trem(m)el** or **Treml**, a nickname for a rude man, Bavarian dialect *Tremel* 'cudgel', 'club' (from Middle High German *drām*, *trāme* 'beam', 'rafter').

Tramontana (267) Italian: topographic name denoting someone from north of the Alps, Italian *tramontana*, literally '(someone) from over the mountains'.
GIVEN NAMES Italian 23%; Spanish 6%. *Sal* (3), *Americo* (2), *Raul* (2), *Salvatore* (2), *Antonio*, *Camillo*, *Carlo*, *Carmella*, *Gaetano*, *Gianluca*, *Giovanni*, *Luigi*, *Rocco*, *Santo*; *Carmelo*, *Jorge*, *Jose Carlos*, *Rosario*, *Salvador*.

Tramontano (175) Italian: **1.** habitational name for a man from a place named Tramonti or Tramonte (see TRAMONTE). **2.** topographic name for a person who lived at the top of a mountain.
GIVEN NAMES Italian 18%. *Alfonso*, *Alphonso*, *Angelina*, *Camillo*, *Carmelo*, *Natale*, *Raffaela*, *Sal*.

Tramonte (159) Italian: habitational name for someone from a place named Tramonte (in Padova) or Tramonti (in Salerno, Cosenza, and elsewhere). The place name means literally 'over the mountain'.
GIVEN NAMES Italian 11%. *Angelo*, *Antonio*, *Dino*, *Oreste*, *Sal*.

Tramontozzi (111) Italian: probably a suffixed form of TRAMONTE.
GIVEN NAMES Italian 27%; Spanish 5%. *Antonio* (4), *Carlo* (2), *Luciano* (2), *Aldo*, *Amerigo*, *Cesidio*, *Donato*, *Fiore*, *Fiorella*, *Francesco*, *Gino*, *Nunzio*; *Mario* (2), *Gerardo*.

Tramp (171) Variant of TRAMPE.

Trampe (179) German: habitational name from a place so named in Uckermark.
GIVEN NAMES German 5%. *Frieda*, *Otto*, *Wolfgang*.

Tran (19748) **1.** Vietnamese: unexplained. **2.** Scottish: nickname from Old Norse *trani* 'crane'.
GIVEN NAMES Vietnamese 78%. *Hung* (285), *Thanh* (285), *Minh* (219), *Tuan* (191), *Dung* (178), *Hai* (160), *Hoa* (157), *Anh* (134), *Hoang* (123), *Quang* (117), *Cuong* (110), *Son* (108), *Hong* (85), *Chi* (51), *Sang* (51), *Hang* (34), *Dong* (27), *Man* (25), *Chan* (23), *Chien* (22), *Lai* (19), *Ho* (18), *Tong* (16), *Han* (14); *Tam* (129), *Nam* (81), *Phong* (72), *Thai* (52), *Tuong* (37), *Tinh* (36), *Sinh* (20), *Chung* (19), *Vang* (12), *Thach* (11), *Uyen* (11), *Manh* (10).

Trana (109) Swedish: unexplained.

Tranbarger (139) Danish: Americanized form of a habitational name for someone from Tranbjerg in Denmark (see TRANBERG).

Tranberg (164) Danish: habitational name from Tranbjerg in Denmark, named with *tran(e)* 'crane' + *berg* 'mountain', 'hill'.
GIVEN NAMES Scandinavian 13%. *Helmer*, *Jorgen*, *Nels*.

Tranchina (216) Italian: possibly from the personal name *Tranchida*, a metathesized form of *Tancrida*, feminine form of the personal name TANCREDI.
GIVEN NAMES Italian 15%. *Sal* (3), *Salvatore* (3), *Angelo*, *Luigi*, *Sebastiano*.

Tranel (100) German: of uncertain origin.

Trang (340) Vietnamese: unexplained.
GIVEN NAMES Vietnamese 64%; Chinese 7%. *Hung* (9), *Tran* (5), *Dung* (4), *Minh* (4), *Thanh* (4), *Ha* (3), *Hoa* (3), *Loc* (3), *Nguyen* (3), *Phong* (3), *Vinh* (3), *Binh* (2), *Buu* (2), *Nam*, *Tam*, *Tap*, *Thach*, *Thai*, *Tuong*, *Vang*; *Dong* (2), *Chua*, *Ho*,

Hong, *Hua*, *Kong*, *Lian*, *Ming*, *Sang*, *Sen*, *Yung*.

Trani (232) Italian and Jewish (from Italy): habitational name from Trani in Bari province.
GIVEN NAMES Italian 17%; Spanish 5%. *Angelo* (2), *Antonio* (2), *Armando*, *Biagio*, *Carmela*, *Lino*, *Pasquale*, *Salvatore*, *Umberto*; *Ines*, *Jose*, *Mercedes*.

Trank (127) German: nickname for a drinker, from Middle High German *tranc* 'drink'.

Transou (165) Probably an altered form of a Fench Huguenot name (see below).
FOREBEARS Abraham Transou was born about 1700 in Mutterstadt, Rheinland-Palatinate, Germany. He came to America in 1730 aboard *The Thistle of Glasgow*. Abraham, whose parents have not been documented, is believed to be the son of Jacob Trentsols, born about 1657 in Somme, France.

Transue (495) Origin unidentified; compare TRANSOU. Transue occurs predominantly in PA, while Transou is associated chiefly with NC.

Trant (398) **1.** English (Devon): unexplained. **2.** Irish (County Kerry): reduced form of **Tramant**, which MacLysaght describes as 'a family of pre-Norman origin'.

Tranter (348) English (mainly West Midlands): occupational name for a peddler or hawker, especially one equipped with a horse and cart, Middle English *traunter*, *traventer* (Late Latin *travetarius*, of uncertain origin, possibly derived from Latin *transvehere* 'to convey').

Trantham (1141) English: variant of TRENTHAM.

Tranum (160) Scandinavian: habitational name from a place so named; the first element, *Tran-*, may be from *trane* 'crane', or a word meaning 'someone from Trøndelag', while the second element, *-um*, is from Old Norse *heimr* 'home', 'farmstead'.

Traore (140) African: unexplained.
GIVEN NAMES African 45%; Muslim 31%; French 5%. *Mamadou* (8), *Idrissa* (3), *Oumar* (3), *Bakary* (2), *Boubacar* (2), *Moctar* (2), *Aboubacar*, *Aliou*, *Alou*, *Balla*, *Hamidou*, *Lansana*; *Moussa* (5), *Abdoulaye* (4), *Mohamed* (2), *Ahmed*, *Aishah*, *Daouda*, *Ibrahim*, *Ismaila*, *Issa*, *Souleymane*, *Yussuf*, *Zakaria*; *Eloi*, *Jean Francois*.

Trapani (994) Sicilian and southern Italian: habitational name from the city of Trapani in western Sicily.
GIVEN NAMES Italian 28%. *Salvatore* (11), *Mario* (4), *Sal* (4), *Angelo* (3), *Luigi* (3), *Carmelo* (2), *Cosimo* (2), *Cosmo* (2), *Francisco* (2), *Gasper* (2), *Ignazio* (2), *Renato* (2), *Rocco* (2), *Santo* (2), *Vito* (2).

Trapasso (228) Southern Italian: from *trapasso* 'Maundy Thursday', presumably applied as a nickname for someone born on that day or otherwise associated with it.
GIVEN NAMES Italian 22%. *Angelo* (5), *Rocco* (2), *Camillo*, *Nilda*, *Orlando*.

Traphagen (150) Respelling of German **Trapphagen**, apparently from a hypercorrected and enlarged form of *traphan* '(male) bustard'; *hagen*, however, means 'hedge'.

Trapnell (213) English and French: nickname for an impetuous person, from the Old French phrase *trop isnel* 'too swift'.
GIVEN NAMES French 4%. *Cecile*, *Yvon*.

Trapp (3348) **1.** English: metonymic occupational name for a trapper, from a derivative of Middle English *trapp* 'trap'. **2.** German: nickname for a stupid person, from Middle High German *trappe* 'bustard' (of Slavic origin). **3.** German: topographic name for someone living by a step-like feature in the terrain, from Middle Low German *treppe*, *trappe* 'step', or by a flight of steps, standard German *Treppe*.
FOREBEARS Thomas Trapp (b. 1635) was in Edgartown, Martha's Vineyard, MA, by 1659. He or his family probably came originally from Great Baddow, Essex, England.

Trappe (144) Variant of English and German TRAPP.
GIVEN NAME German 5%. *Rainer*.

Trask (2377) English: habitational name for someone from Thirsk in North Yorkshire, named from an unattested Old Scandinavian word, *thresk* 'marsh'.

Traster (142) Perhaps an altered spelling of TRESTER or TRAISTER.

Trathen (103) English (Cornish): unexplained.

Trattner (153) South German: from Middle High German *trat* 'pasture', hence perhaps a topographic name for someone who lived near grazing land.

Traub (1248) German and Jewish (Ashkenazic): metonymic occupational name for a wine-grower, from Middle High German *trübe* 'bunch of grapes', German *Traube*. In some cases the German name may originally have been habitational, for someone who lived at a house marked with the sign of a bunch of grapes, while the Jewish surname was often an ornamental adoption.
GIVEN NAMES German 4%. *Kurt* (3), *Egon* (2), *Ewald* (2), *Frieda*, *Gerda*, *Irmgard*, *Juergen*, *Reinhold*, *Volker*.

Traube (105) German and Jewish (Ashkenazic): variant of TRAUB.
GIVEN NAMES Jewish 12%. *Aron*, *Avraham*, *Chaim*, *Rochel*.

Traudt (215) German: variant of TRAUT.

Trauernicht (121) German: nickname for someone who was never sad or possibly for an insouciant person, from a compound of *Trauer* 'grief', 'sorrow' + *nicht* 'not'.

Trauger (275) Americanized spelling of German TRAGER.

Traugh (152) Possibly an altered spelling of DRACH or alternatively of South German **Trauch**, a metonymic occupational name for a trapper, from Middle High German *drüch* 'trap for game'.

Traughber (435) Probably an altered spelling of German **Tragbar**, which may perhaps be from the personal name *Dragbert*, composed of Germanic *dragan* 'to roam', which could have become confused with *Drake* later on.

Traugott (286) German: from a phrase meaning 'trust (Middle High German *trüwen*) God', presumably a nickname applied to someone who used the expression a great deal.
GIVEN NAMES German 5%. *Fritz* (2), *Kurt*, *Lorenz*, *Ute*.

Traum (217) **1.** German: nickname for a dreamer, from Middle High German *troum* 'dream'. **2.** German: from Bavarian *Traum* (standard German *Tramm*) 'rafter', 'beam', a nickname for a crude man. Compare TRAMMELL. **3.** Jewish (Ashkenazic): ornamental name from German *Traum* 'dream'.

Traurig (108) Jewish (Ashkenazic): ornamental name from German *traurig* 'sad'.

Trausch (240) German: of uncertain origin; possibly Slavic, a variant of *Trauschke*, a nickname from Old Slavic *drugu* 'companion', or alternatively it could be a nickname from Middle Low German *druus* 'sullen', 'dour'.

Traut (456) German: from Middle High German *trūt* 'dear', 'beloved', or from a short form of a personal name formed with the same word. Compare DRAUDT.
FOREBEARS Eight members of a family called Traut arrived in PA in 1719. One branch (known as TROUT) moved to NC at the end of the 18th century.

Trauth (203) German: variant spelling of TRAUT.

Trautman (1437) Altered spelling of TRAUTMANN.

Trautmann (341) German: from a medieval personal name, formed with Middle High German *trūt* 'beloved' + *man* 'man', or from an older stem, Germanic *thrud* 'strength' (Old Norse *thrudr* 'divine being'), from which several personal names were formed.
GIVEN NAMES German 9%. *Horst* (2), *Dieter*, *Elfriede*, *Erwin*, *Frieda*, *Kurt*, *Manfred*, *Markus*, *Otto*, *Reinhold*.

Trautner (186) German: **1.** habitational name for someone from Trautenau in East Prussia or Bohemia. **2.** variant of TRAUTMANN.

Trautwein (429) German: from a medieval personal name composed of Middle High German *trūt* 'beloved' + *win* 'friend'.

Travaglini (186) Italian: **1.** nickname from a diminutive of *travaglio* 'anguish', 'worry', 'distress'. **2.** a derivative of Sicilian *travagghia* 'twitch' (a device for restraining a restive horse while it is being shod).
GIVEN NAMES Italian 18%. *Aldo* (2), *Pasquale* (2), *Dante*, *Domenico*, *Enzo*, *Giuseppe*, *Nicola*, *Stefano*, *Ugo*.

Travelstead (232) Origin unidentified.

Traver (1392) **1.** French: variant of TRAVERS. **2.** Catalan: habitational name from any of the minor places called with Traver, mainly in La Garrotxa and L'Empordà districts but also in other areas.

Travers (2917) **1.** English and French: occupational name for a gatherer of tolls exacted for the right of passage across a bridge, ford, or other thoroughfare, from Middle English, Old French *travers* 'passage', 'crossing', from Old French *traverser* 'to cross'. **2.** Northern Irish: reduced Anglicized form of Gaelic **Ó Treabhair** (see TREVOR).
FOREBEARS A Travers from the Poitou region of France is documented in Quebec City in 1712, with the secondary surname Sansregret.

Traverse (238) French: variant of TRAVERS 1.

Traverso (312) Italian: nickname from *traverso* 'transverse' in any of several transferred senses: 'thick-set', 'broad-shouldered'; less commonly 'cross-eyed', 'squinting', or 'hostile', 'perverse'.
GIVEN NAMES Italian 10%; French 4%. *Giancarlo* (2), *Vito* (2), *Angelo*, *Attilio*, *Carlo*, *Enrico*, *Fulvio*, *Renzo*, *Rinaldo*; *Andre*, *Arianne*, *Normand*.

Travieso (186) Spanish (widespread in Latin America): nickname from *travieso* 'bad', 'mischievous', 'perverse' (from Latin *traversus*, *transversus* 'turned across').
GIVEN NAMES Spanish 54%. *Jose* (8), *Raul* (7), *Manuel* (4), *Alfredo* (3), *Angel* (3), *Jorge* (3), *Margarita* (3), *Carlos* (2), *Eduardo* (2), *Enrique* (2), *Gerardo* (2), *Jesus* (2); *Lorenzo* (2), *Vigilio* (2), *Antonio*, *Elio*, *Luciano*, *Lucio*.

Travis (11565) **1.** English (mainly Lancashire and Yorkshire): occupational name for a gatherer of tolls exacted for the right of passage across a bridge, ford, or other thoroughfare, from Middle English *travis* 'crossing', variant of *travers* (see TRAVERS). **2.** German: Americanized variant of DREWES.

Travisano (148) Italian: variant of **Trevisano**, habitational name for someone from the Venetian city of Treviso.
GIVEN NAMES Italian 12%. *Angelo*, *Gaetano*, *Raniero*, *Vito*.

Traw (155) Possibly an altered spelling of German **Traue**, a variant of TREU.

Traweek (342) See TRAWICK.

Trawick (1140) Probably an altered form, under German influence, of Polish **Trawicki**, a habitational name from a place called Trawice in Gdańsk voivodeship, or some other place named with Polish *trawa* 'grass'.

Trawinski (127) Polish (**Trawiński**): habitational name for someone from a place named for its fine grass (from *trawa* 'grass', 'lawn').

GIVEN NAMES Polish 6%. *Jozef, Mariusz, Zbigniew.*

Traxel (112) South German: variant of **Drechsel** (see DRESSLER).

Traxler (1148) South German (Bavarian and Austrian): occupational name for a wood turner, a variant of **Drechsler** (see DRESSLER).

Tray (109) English: nickname from Middle English *treye* 'grief', 'misfortune', from Old English *trega*.

Trayer (230) Probably an altered spelling of German **Traier**, a variant of DREHER (of which it could also be an altered spelling).

Traylor (4145) English: unexplained.

Traynham (393) See TRAINHAM.

Traynor (1478) Irish: variant spelling of TRAINOR.

Traywick (491) Origin unidentified. Compare TRAWICK.

Trbovich (166) Serbian and Croatian (**Trbović**): derivative of the nickname *trba* 'pot belly' + the patronymic suffix *-ović*.

Trcka (135) Czech, Slovak, and Croatian (**Trčka**): nickname from *trčka* 'partridge' or a derivative of the verb *trčati* (Czech), *trčati* (Croatian) 'to run'.

Treacy (665) Irish: reduced Anglicized form of Gaelic **Ó Treasaigh** 'descendant of *Treasach*', a personal name meaning 'warlike', 'fierce'.

GIVEN NAMES Irish 6%. *Colm, Liam.*

Treadaway (596) English: variant of TREADWAY. In some cases it could perhaps be a variant of the Cornish surname TRETHEWEY, but the complete absence of the surname in the southwest suggests that this is unlikely.

Treadway (2741) English: possibly a phrase name from Middle English *tred(en)* 'to tread' + *weye* 'way', 'path'.

Treadwell (1996) English (chiefly West Midlands): metonymic occupational name for a fuller, from Middle English *tred(en)* 'to tread' + *well* 'well'. Fulling was the process by which newly woven cloth was cleaned and shrunk by the use of heat, water, and pressure (from treading) before finally being stretched and laid out to dry on tenter hooks.

Treanor (655) Irish: variant spelling of TRAINOR.

GIVEN NAMES Irish 9%. *Brendan* (4), *Seamus* (3), *Conley, Declan, James Patrick, Sinead.*

Treas (141) Probably an altered spelling of English TREECE or German DRIES.

Trease (213) 1. English: variant spelling of English TREECE. 2. Possibly an altered spelling of German DRIES.

Treaster (297) Possibly an altered form of Ashkenazic Jewish **Treister**, a variant of TRAISTER.

Treasure (200) English (Bristol, Gwent): from Middle English *tresor* 'treasure', 'wealth', 'riches' (Old French *trésor*, from Latin *thesaurus* 'hoard'), hence a metonymic occupational name for a treasurer or person in charge of financial administration, or an affectionate nickname for a loved or valued person.

Treat (1826) Americanized spelling of German TRITT.

Trebesch (105) German: unexplained.

Trebilcock (204) Cornish: habitational name from a place in the parish of Roche, apparently so named from Cornish *tre* 'homestead', 'settlement' + a lenited form of the Middle English term of endearment *pilicock* 'darling'.

Trebing (100) German: from a Slavic personal name formed with Old Slavic *treb* 'skilled'.

GIVEN NAMES German 11%. *Ralf* (2), *Gerd, Otto.*

Trede (104) North German: from Low German *trede* 'tread', 'step', 'path', hence probably a topographic name for someone who lived by a thoroughfare, by some steps, or on terraced ground.

GIVEN NAMES German 11%. *Egon, Hans, Kurt, Nikolaus, Otto.*

Treder (199) German: 1. from an agent derivative of Low German *treden* 'to tread or stomp', probably a (derogatory) nickname for a peasant, a dancer, or someone who worked the bellows of an organ. 2. topographic name from a noun derivative of Low German TREDE. Compare TRETTER.

Tredinnick (138) Cornish: habitational name from any of various places so called, for example near Bodmin, Liskeard, and St. Issey. Some of these get their name from Cornish *tre* 'homestead', 'settlement' + *dynek* 'fortified' (an unattested derivative of *dyn* 'fort'); in other cases the second element is *eythynek* 'overgrown with gorse' or *redenek* 'overgrown with bracken' (both unattested).

Tredway (543) English: variant spelling of TREADWAY.

Tree (208) English (mainly southeastern): topographic name for someone who lived near a conspicuous tree, Middle English *tre(w)*.

Treece (1521) English: topographic name from the plural of Middle English *tre(w)* 'tree'.

Treen (209) 1. Cornish: habitational name from places so named in the parishes of Zennor and St. Levan, both of which appear earlier in the form *Trethyn*, from Cornish *tre* 'homestead', 'settlement' + *dyn* 'fort'. 2. English: variant of TREECE, from a form with the weak plural ending.

Trees (430) English: variant of TREECE.

Treese (402) English: variant of TREECE.

Treesh (143) Probably a respelling of North German **Driesch**, a topographic name for someone living at an uncultivated field used for grazing.

Trefethen (238) Altered spelling of Cornish TREVETHAN.

Treffinger (117) Probably a variant of **Treffig(er)**, from Middle Low German, Middle High German *treff-* 'fitting', 'excellent', 'hitting the nail on the head', a nickname for a successful person.

GIVEN NAME German 5%. *Fritz.*

Trefry (234) English (Cornish): unexplained.

Trefz (255) South German: nickname for a good-for-nothing, from Middle High German *trefze* 'weed'.

Treger (127) Variant of TRAGER.

GIVEN NAMES Jewish 10%. *Benzion, Faina, Hyman, Tali, Zelman.*

Treglia (211) Southern Italian: from the dialect word *treglia* 'mullet' (standard Italian *triglia*), presumably a nickname for someone thought to resemble the fish or possibly a metonymic occupational name for a fisherman or seller of these fish.

GIVEN NAMES Italian 21%. *Angelo* (4), *Dante* (3), *Antonio* (2), *Enrico* (2), *Salvatore* (2), *Aldo, Carlo, Concetta, Pasquale, Raffaela, Tullio.*

Trego (620) English (Devon): probably an altered form of an unidentified Cornish name.

Tregoning (198) Cornish: habitational name from any of various places so named, from Cornish *tre* 'homestead', 'settlement' + a lenited form of the personal name *Conan*.

Tregre (200) Frenchified form of the German surname TRAEGER, found in LA.

GIVEN NAMES French 8%. *Alcide* (2), *Antoine, Armand, Benoit, Fernand.*

Treharne (115) Welsh: from the personal name *Trahaearn*, composed of the elements *tra* 'most', 'very' + *haearn* 'iron'. This personal name has also given rise to a place name (spelled *Trehaearn* as if containing the element *tre(f)* 'homestead', 'settlement'), and so in some cases the surname may be a habitational name with this origin.

Treiber (622) German and Jewish (Ashkenazic): occupational name from an agent derivative of Middle High German *trīben*, German *treiben*, Yiddish *traybn* 'to drive'. In some cases this name may have denoted someone who floated logs down a river.

GIVEN NAMES German 6%. *Heinz* (2), *Kurt* (2), *Armin, Berthold, Erhard, Fritz, Joerg, Otto, Udo.*

Treible (119) Altered spelling of German **Treibel**: 1. from a diminutive of TRAUB. 2. from Middle High German *tribel* 'mallet', a metonymic occupational name for a cooper, goldsmith, or silversmith.

Treichel (393) Swiss German: from a word meaning 'cow bell', presumably a nickname for a cowherd or farmer, or a metonymic occupational name for someone who made cow bells.

GIVEN NAMES German 5%. *Horst* (2), *Hans*, *Klaus*.

Treichler (217) Swiss German: occupational name from a derivative of TREICHEL.

Treinen (273) German: metronymic from a short form of the personal name *Katrein*, a reduced form of *Katharina*, German form of CATHERINE.

Trejo (2602) **1.** Spanish: habitational name from a place Cádiz named Trejo. **2.** Asturian-Leonese: Castilianized form of Asturian-Leonese **Trexo**, a habitational name from a place in Asturies.

GIVEN NAMES Spanish 51%; Portuguese 10%. *Jose* (61), *Juan* (32), *Francisco* (28), *Manuel* (20), *Mario* (20), *Roberto* (19), *Luis* (18), *Antonio* (17), *Miguel* (16), *Jesus* (15), *Jorge* (14), *Pedro* (14), *Carlos* (13); *Catarina*, *Paulo*.

Trela (219) Polish: **1.** topographic name from *trel* 'place in the forest where felled timber lies'; perhaps also a metonymic occupational name for a lumberjack. **2.** nickname from *trel* 'trill'.

GIVEN NAMES Polish 19%. *Casimir* (2), *Stanislaw* (2), *Tadeusz* (2), *Andrzej*, *Dorota*, *Elzbieta*, *Jacek*, *Jerzy*, *Kazimierz*, *Mariusz*, *Wladyslaw*, *Wojciech*.

Trelease (117) Cornish: habitational name from a place in Cornwall.

Treleven (104) Cornish: habitational name from a place in Cornwall.

Trella (237) Polish: variant of TRELA.

GIVEN NAMES Polish 4%. *Kazimierz*, *Maciej*.

Treloar (384) Cornish: habitational name from Treloar in Cornwall.

Trelstad (123) Norwegian: habitational name from a farmstead in Trødelag named Trelstad, from Old Norse *præll* 'thrall', 'slave' + *staðir*, plural of *staðr* 'farmstead', 'dwelling'.

GIVEN NAMES Scandinavian 6%. *Per*, *Thora*.

Tremain (378) Variant of TREMAINE.

Tremaine (492) Cornish: habitational name from any of various places so named, from Cornish *tre* 'homestead', 'settlement' + *men* 'stone'.

Tremayne (151) Cornish: variant spelling of TREMAINE.

Trembath (209) Cornish: habitational name from a place in the parish of Madron, named in Cornish as *tre an bagh* 'homestead of the corner'.

Tremblay (3386) French: from a collective form of TREMBLE, hence a topographic name for someone who lived near a group of aspen trees. This is a very common name in French-speaking Canada.

FOREBEARS A Tremblay or Tremblé from the Perche region of France was documented in Quebec City in 1657.

GIVEN NAMES French 18%. *Armand* (23), *Marcel* (12), *Normand* (11), *Fernand* (9), *Jacques* (9), *Pierre* (9), *Gilles* (7), *Andre*

(5), *Herve* (5), *Lucien* (5), *Michel* (5), *Cecile* (4).

Tremble (336) **1.** French: topographic name for someone who lived near an aspen, Old French *tremble* (from *trembler* 'to quiver'). **2.** Northern English: variant of TRUMBLE.

Trembley (489) Altered spelling of French TREMBLAY or **Tremblet**, a diminutive of TREMBLE.

GIVEN NAMES French 6%. *Camil*, *Jacques*, *Jean Marie*, *Jean-Francois*, *Jean-Paul*, *Rodrigue*.

Trembly (303) French: see TREMBLAY.

GIVEN NAMES French 4%. *Andre*, *Berard*, *Pierre*.

Tremel (157) German (frequent in Bavaria): variant spelling of TREMMEL.

Tremelling (114) English (Cornish): habitational name for someone from Tremellen in Cornwall.

Treml (283) German: variant of TREMMEL.

Tremmel (366) German (frequent in Bavaria): nickname from *tremel* 'boor', 'ruffian', from Middle High German *Tram*, *Dram* 'beam', 'block', 'cudgel'.

GIVEN NAMES German 4%. *Alois*, *Elke*, *Horst*, *Lothar*.

Tremont (181) French (**Trémont**): habitational name from places in Maine-et-Loire, Meuse, Orne, and Aisne, meaning 'over the hill'.

FOREBEARS In Canada the name is documented in Sorel in 1675, and was borne by an Italian from Piedmont. The name is variously given as **De Trémon** and **Trémont**; it is a secondary surname to a family otherwise known as Salvaye, Salvail, Salvaille, Salvay, and Serail.

Trempe (100) French: unexplained.

GIVEN NAMES French 14%. *Andre*, *Germaine*, *Jean Pierre*, *Lucien*, *Pierre*.

Tremper (418) Altered form of German **Trömper**, an occupational name for a trumpet player or drummer, from Middle High German *trumbe* 'trumpet', sometimes 'drum'.

Trenary (489) Cornish: variant spelling of **Trener(r)y**, a habitational name from a place in the parish of St. Allen, named in Cornish with *tre* 'homestead', 'settlement' + an unexplained second element.

Trench (226) English and Scottish (of French origin): habitational name from La Tranche in Poitou, so named from the Old French topographical term *trenche*, a derivative of the verb *trenchier* 'to cut', which denoted both a ditch and a track cut through a forest. The term is also found in Middle English, and in some cases the surname could be of topographic origin or from minor place, such as The Trench in Kent, named with this word.

FOREBEARS The Trench family that hold the earldom of Clancarty trace their descent from Frederic de la Tranche, who settled in Northumbria from France *c.*1575. They

became established in Ireland in the 17th century, when Frederick Trench went there and purchased an estate in Galway in 1631.

Trenchard (179) French: from Old French *trenche*, a derivative of *trenchier* 'to cut, hack, or slice' (compare TRENCH) + the pejorative suffix *-ard*, hence a metonymic occupational name for a butcher or a nickname for a violent person.

Trenda (111) Czech: unexplained.

Trenholm (343) English: habitational name from Trenholme in North Yorkshire, named from Old Norse *trani* 'crane' + *holmr* 'island'.

Trenkamp (172) **1.** Altered spelling of German **Threnkamp**, a topographic name for someone living by a hummocky field, from Middle Low German *trint* 'round', 'hump' + *kamp* 'enclosed field', 'domain'. The element *trint* occurs frequently in field and place names, such as Drentwede (Hannover), Trendelenburg (Westphalia). **2.** German: perhaps also a topographic name from Middle High German *tren* 'drone', 'bumblebee' + *kamp* 'field', 'domain'.

Trenkle (184) Variant of South German **Tränkle**, **Trenkel**, a nickname denoting a heavy drinker. See also TRINKLE.

GIVEN NAMES German 6%. *Kurt* (2), *Benno*, *Frederich*.

Trenner (100) German: possibly a nickname for a quarrelsome person, from an agent derivative of Middle High German *trennen* 'to separate', 'to divide', or alternatively a nickname for a bowls player, from Middle Low German *trenden* 'to play with balls', 'to bowl'.

GIVEN NAMES German 5%. *Dietrich*, *Otto*.

Trent (6235) **1.** English: topographic name for someone living on the banks of any of the several rivers so called. The river name is of British origin; it may be composed of the unattested elements *tri* 'through', 'across' + *sant-* 'travel', 'journey'; alternatively it may mean 'traveler' or 'trespasser', a reference to frequent flooding. There is a village in Dorset of this name, on the river Trent or Piddle, and the surname may therefore also be a habitational name derived from this. **2.** Scottish: probably of the same origin as 1, though in some cases it may be from a reduced form of Tranent, a place in East Lothian.

Trentham (490) English (Midlands): habitational name from Trentham in Staffordshire, named from the Celtic river name TRENT + *hām* 'enclosure', 'settlement' or *hamm* 'river meadow'.

Trentman (174) Origin unidentified: **1.** possibly a variant of English TRENTHAM. **2.** alternatively a habitational name for someone from the region in Holland called Drenthe.

Trento (111) Italian: habitational name from the city or province of Trento, or a masculinized form of **Trenta**, a habitational name from Trenta in Cosenza province. GIVEN NAMES Italian 23%. *Angelo* (3), *Sal* (3), *Salvatore* (2), *Agostino*, *Marco*, *Rosario*.

Trenton (108) English: unexplained; possibly a habitational name from a lost or unidentified place.

Treon (245) Origin unidentified: perhaps a variant of English TREEN, or an altered spelling of French **Tréand**, a habitational name from any of various minor places so named.

Trepagnier (130) French: variant of TRE-PANIER. GIVEN NAMES French 8%. *Amelie*, *Julien*, *Pierre*.

Trepanier (712) French: from an agent derivative of *trépan* 'auger' (Latin *trepanum*), hence an occupational name for someone who drilled holes in bone or stone, perhaps even someone who practised medical trepanning (of the cranium).
FOREBEARS Documented as Trépanier and Trépagny, a bearer of the name from Normandy, France, is recorded in Quebec city in 1656. GIVEN NAMES French 12%. *Marcel* (9), *Gilles* (2), *Pierre* (2), *Raynald* (2), *Alain*, *Andre*, *Armand*, *Cecile*, *Gaston*, *Gisele*, *Henri*, *Jacques*.

Trepp (112) English: perhaps a variant of TRIPP.

Treptow (328) East German (of Slavic origin): habitational name from places so named in Pomerania and Brandenburg. GIVEN NAMES German 5%. *Eberhard* (2), *Merwin* (2), *Kurt*.

Tresch (159) Swiss German: variant of DRESCH.

Trescott (204) English: variant spelling of TRUSCOTT.

Tresner (106) Origin unidentified.

Tress (264) **1.** English: unexplained. **2.** German: from a short form of the personal name *Andreas* (see ANDREW). **3.** German: from a short form of the female personal name *Theres(e)*. **4.** German: variant of DRESS. **5.** Jewish: unexplained. GIVEN NAMES Jewish 5%. *Mendel* (2), *Avrohom*, *Emanuel*, *Hyman*, *Shmuel*.

Tressel (157) German: occupational name for a wood turner (see DRESSLER).

Tressler (1155) German: **1.** variant of DRESSLER. **2.** Possibly also a variant of **Trissler** (see TRISLER).

Trest (151) Swedish: unexplained.

Trester (260) German: from Middle High German *trester* 'sediment from beer brewing or the pressing or fermentation of grapes' (from *trestern* 'to press grapes'), presumably a nickname for a worthless person.

Tretheway (106) Cornish: variant of TRE-THEWEY.

Trethewey (198) Cornish: habitational name from any of various places so named, from Cornish *tre* 'homestead', 'settlement' + *Thewi*, a lenited form of the personal name *Dewi* (see DAVID).

Trettel (189) Probably a variant of German **Trittel**, a derivative of TRETTER.

Tretter (453) **1.** German: perhaps an occupational name from Middle High German *treter* 'dancer', 'clown', an agent derivative of *treten* 'to step or dance'. **2.** Jewish (Ashkenazic): occupational name from Yiddish *treter*, German *Treter* 'grape presser'.

Trettin (183) German: habitational name from a place so named in Brandenburg. GIVEN NAMES German 8%. *Ernst*, *Hermann*, *Kurt*, *Otto*.

Treu (285) German and Jewish (Ashkenazic): nickname for a trustworthy person, from late Middle High German *triuwe* 'loyal', German *treu*. The Jewish surname is mainly ornamental. GIVEN NAMES German 10%. *Kurt* (3), *Benno*, *Fritz*, *Hans*, *Heinz*, *Manfred*, *Siegfried*, *Willi*.

Trevarthen (113) Cornish: habitational name from places in the parishes of St. Hilary and Newlyn East named Trevarthen, from Cornish *tre(v)* 'homestead', 'settlement' + a personal name equivalent to Welsh *Arthen*.

Trevathan (370) Variant spelling of Cornish TREVETHAN.

Trevena (127) Cornish: habitational name from any of various places so named, from Cornish *tre* 'homestead', 'settlement' + a lenited form of *meneth* 'mountain', 'hill'.

Trevethan (122) Cornish: habitational name from places in the parishes of Budock, St. Eval, and Gwennap, all so named from Cornish *tre* 'homestead', 'settlement' + a second element of uncertain form and meaning (possibly a lenited form of *budin*, *buthyn* 'meadow').

Trevett (167) English: apparently a variant of TRIVETT.

Trevillian (164) English: habitational name from Trevelyan in St. Veep, Cornwall, which probably means 'house at the mill', from Cornish *tre* 'house' + a mutated form of *melin* 'mill'.

Trevino (7629) Spanish (**Treviño**): habitational name from either of the places so named in the provinces of Burgos and Santander. GIVEN NAMES Spanish 45%. *Jose* (168), *Juan* (113), *Manuel* (82), *Jesus* (59), *Carlos* (56), *Ruben* (54), *Raul* (50), *Roberto* (46), *Luis* (45), *Pedro* (42), *Mario* (41), *Guadalupe* (37).

Trevisan (130) Italian: habitational name for someone from the Venetian city of Treviso, from an adjectival form of the place name (compare TRAVISANO). GIVEN NAMES Italian 18%. *Paolo* (2), *Aldo*, *Domenic*, *Francesco*, *Gino*, *Maurizio*, *Rachele*, *Santina*.

Trevithick (149) Cornish: habitational name from any of various places, in the parishes of St. Columb Major, St. Columb Minor, Perranzabuloe, and St Ewe, so named from Cornish *tre* 'homestead', 'settlement' + various personal names; in the case of the last-mentioned place, the second element may be a lenited form of *methek* 'doctor'.

Trevizo (296) Altered spelling (under American Spanish influence) of Italian **Treviso**, a habitational name from Treviso in Veneto. GIVEN NAMES Spanish 55%. *Jesus* (9), *Jose* (9), *Juan* (6), *Manuel* (5), *Raul* (5), *Emilio* (4), *Guadalupe* (4), *Mario* (4), *Ramon* (4), *Alberto* (3), *Adolfo* (2), *Andres* (2).

Trevor (278) **1.** Welsh: habitational name from any of the numerous places in Wales, in particular the one near Denbigh, so named from Welsh *tre(f)* 'homestead', 'settlement' + a mutated form of *mawr* 'large'. **2.** Irish: reduced Anglicized form of Gaelic **Ó Treabhair** 'descendant of *Treabhar*', a byname meaning 'industrious', 'prudent'.

Trevorrow (148) Cornish: habitational name from a place in the parish of Ludgvan, so named from Cornish *tre* 'homestead', 'settlement' + a second element of uncertain form and meaning.

Trew (402) **1.** English: variant of TROW, mainly of 1. **2.** altered spelling of German TREU.

Trewin (126) English (Cornish): habitational name from Trewin in Cornwall.

Trexler (1377) German: variant of **Drechsler** (see DRESSLER).

Treybig (121) East German: variant of **Treubig**, probably of Slavic origin.

Trezise (177) Cornish: habitational name from Trezise in the parish of St. Martin in Meneage or Tresayes in the parish of Roche, both so named from Cornish *tre* 'homestead', 'settlement' + *Seys* 'Englishman'.

Trezza (338) Italian: from medieval Latin *treza* 'braid', 'plait', probably applied as a nickname for someone who wore their hair plaited. GIVEN NAMES Italian 16%. *Carmine* (4), *Cono* (2), *Agostino*, *Angelo*, *Carmela*, *Gennaro*, *Gianfranco*, *Marco*, *Rocco*, *Salvatore*.

Tri (174) Vietnamese: unexplained. GIVEN NAMES Vietnamese 15%. *Binh* (2), *Cao*, *Chau*, *Huan*, *Hung*, *Minh*, *Nguyen*, *Phi*, *Thiem*, *Tran*, *Truong*, *Vinh*.

Trial (125) French: according to Morlet, from a word denoting a stack of sheaves; its application as a surname is unclear. GIVEN NAMES French 7%. *Alain*, *Thierry*.

Triana (505) Spanish and Galician: habitational name from any of the places so called in Galicia, Málaga, and Tenerife, in particular a suburb of Seville. GIVEN NAMES Spanish 40%. *Jose* (13), *Armando* (6), *Jorge* (6), *Rafael* (6), *Juan* (5), *Pedro* (5), *Francisco* (4), *Alberto* (3),

Ana (3), *Carlos* (3), *Humberto* (3), *Miguel* (3); *Antonio* (5), *Lorenzo* (4), *Marco* (2), *Cosimo, Cosmo, Filiberto, Giovanni, Sal.*

Triano (328) **1.** Spanish and Portuguese (a Gypsy name): unexplained. **2.** Spanish: possibly a habitational name from Triano, the Castilianized name of the Basque towns called Abanto and Urtuella, in Biscay province, Basque Country. **3.** Possibly Italian: this is a rare name in Italy, found in Basilicata, and may be a habitational name from a lost or unidentified minor place.
GIVEN NAMES Italian 10%. *Salvatore* (5), *Angelo, Domenica, Gaetano, Pasquale, Rocco.*

Trias (114) Catalan: variant spelling of **Tries**, a topographic name from the plural of Old Catalan *trilla* 'wine arbour' (from Latin *trichila*), or (less likely) a habitational name from a farmstead so named in Catalonia. This name is well established in Uruguay.
GIVEN NAMES Spanish 37%. *Ramon* (5), *Ana* (3), *Fernando* (2), *Jose* (2), *Orlando* (2), *Tomas* (2), *Alejandro, Augusto, Estrellita, Francisco, Jaime, Jesus.*

Tribbett (256) English: variant of TRIPPETT.

Tribbey (195) Perhaps an altered spelling of North German **Tribbe**, of uncertain, probably Slavic, origin (see TRIEBEL).

Tribble (2024) English (Devon): of uncertain origin; perhaps a variant of **Dribbel**, from a nickname from Middle English *drevel, dribil* 'saliva'.

Tribby (252) Origin unidentified. Compare TRIBBEY.

Tribe (233) **1.** Southern English: unexplained. **2.** German: from a Germanic personal name formed with *thrud-* 'strength', 'energy' + *bald* 'bold' or *berht* 'bright', 'shining'.

Tribett (105) English: possibly a variant of TRIPPETT.

Trible (181) English: variant of TRIBBLE.

Tribolet (114) French and Swiss French: nickname from a diminutive of *triboul*, a noun derivative of Old French *tribouler* 'to disturb'; 'to torment'.

Tribou (113) Possibly a variant of French **Tribau**, from the Germanic personal name *Tritbald*, a compound of Old High German *trit* 'step' + *bald* 'bold', 'brave'.

Tricarico (384) Southern Italian: habitational name from Tricarico in Matera, named with the Latin personal name *Tricarius*.
GIVEN NAMES Italian 17%. *Rocco* (5), *Vito* (4), *Donato* (2), *Angelo, Carlo, Gilda, Mauro, Pasquale, Sal, Santo, Serafino.*

Trice (2374) **1.** English (Kent): perhaps a variant of TREECE. **2.** Altered spelling of German **Treis**, a topographic name for someone who lived by or owned an uncultivated piece of land used as pasture, from Middle Low German *drīsch* 'fallow land', or a habitational name from a place named with this word (in Hessian dialect *treis*), in Hesse or on the Mosel river. Alternatively,

in some instances it may be from a short form of the personal name *Andreas* (see ANDREW).

Triche (364) **1.** French: from Old French *triche* 'trickery', 'deception', or, written **Triché**, from the past participle of *tricher* 'to trick or deceive'. Both names may have denoted a cheat or a cunning, deceitful person. **2.** Altered spelling of German **Trisch**, a variant of **Driesch**, a topographic name from Middle High German *driesch* 'uncultivated land used as pasture'. See also TRICE 2.
GIVEN NAMES French 5%. *Clovis, Roch.*

Trichel (140) Respelling of German **Trischl**, a variant of **Drischel**, itself probably a variant of **Dri(e)sch** (see TRICHE). This name is found mainly in LA.

Trick (401) English (southwest and South Wales): metonymic nickname for a cunning or crafty person, from Middle English *trick* 'strategem', 'device' (from a Norman form of Old French *triche*).

Trickel (182) Respelling of German TRICHEL.

Trickett (443) English: from a diminutive of TRICK.

Trickey (498) English (Devon): habitational name from Trickey in Devon, recorded in 1238 as *Trikehle* apparently 'enclosure (Middle English *hey*) of a man nicknamed TRICK'.

Tricomi (113) Southern Italian: possibly of Greek origin but unexplained.
GIVEN NAMES Italian 14%. *Antonio* (2), *Mario* (2), *Alphonso, Carlo, Francesco, Santo.*

Triebel (143) East German (of Slavic origin): **1.** from a personal name from Old Slavic *treb-* 'skillful', 'dexterous'. **2.** habitational name from places near Sorau and Ölsnitz, so named from *trebiti* 'to clear land'.

Triebold (100) Probably an altered spelling of German TRIEBEL.

Triebwasser (100) Jewish (Ashkenazic): from German *Trübwasser* 'cloudy water', one of unflattering names assigned to Jews by government officials when surnames were made compulsory.
GIVEN NAMES Jewish 4%. *Emanuel* (2), *Sol.*

Trier (344) **1.** German, Dutch, and Jewish (Ashkenazic): habitational name from the city of Trier on the Mosel, named in Latin as *Augusta Treverorum* 'city of Augustus among the *Treveri*', a Celtic tribal name of uncertain etymology. Compare DREYFUS. **2.** Dutch: habitational name from a place so called in Poppel in Antwerp province.

Trierweiler (268) German: habitational name from a place so named near Trier.

Triest (103) Dutch and North German: topographic name for someone who lived by uncultivated land or a habitational name from a place named Triest, for example in East Flanders.

Trieu (416) Vietnamese: unexplained.

GIVEN NAMES Vietnamese 77%. *Hung* (12), *Thanh* (10), *Chau* (7), *Minh* (6), *Quang* (6), *Vinh* (5), *Cuong* (4), *Dat* (4), *Long* (4), *Dieu* (3), *Duc* (3), *Dung* (3), *Phong* (3); *Hang* (2), *Chi, Han, Ho, Hon, So, Tong, Young; Chang, Hoa Kim, Sinh, Sun Cha, Thai.*

Trifiletti (138) Italian: topographic name from a diminitive of Greek *triphyllon* 'trefoil', 'clover'.
GIVEN NAMES Italian 23%. *Angelo, Geno, Nunzio, Rosario, Salvatore, Vito.*

Trigg (1338) English: from the Old Norse byname *Triggr* meaning 'trustworthy', 'faithful', a cognate of TROW 1.

Trigger (141) Possibly an altered spelling of German **Dregger**, a variant of DREHER.

Triggs (806) English: patronymic from the personal name TRIGG.

Triglia (110) Italian: from *triglia* 'red mullet', probably applied as a metonymic occupational name for a fisherman or as a nickname for someone thought to resemble the fish.
GIVEN NAMES Italian 11%. *Aldo, Angelo, Rocco, Santina.*

Trigo (184) Spanish and Portuguese: occupational name for a grower or seller of wheat, from Spanish and Portuguese *trigo* 'wheat'.
GIVEN NAMES Spanish 41%; Italian 7%. *Alicia* (3), *Jorge* (3), *Manuel* (3), *Osvaldo* (3), *Alejandro* (2), *Benigno* (2), *Delfino* (2), *Jose* (2), *Julio* (2), *Luis* (2), *Roberto* (2), *Alberto; Antonio* (7), *Flavio, Marcello, Romeo.*

Trigueros (106) Spanish and Portuguese: **1.** habitational name from places in Huelva and Valladolid named Trigueros, from a derivative of *trigo* 'wheat', or possibly *triguero* 'corn merchant'. **2.** nickname from *triguero* 'dark blond', 'corn colored'.
GIVEN NAMES Spanish 50%. *Jose* (6), *Mario* (4), *Carlos* (3), *Manuel* (3), *Eduardo* (2), *Joaquin* (2), *Alcira, Alvaro, Amada, Armando, Braulio, Carlos Ernesto.*

Trilling (176) German: nickname from Middle High German *drīlinc* 'one of three', 'one third', which was also the name of a medieval coin.

Trillo (218) **1.** Spanish: possibly a habitational name from Trillo in Guadalajara province; otherwise, a metonymic occupational name from *trillo* 'threshing sledge' (Latin *tribulum*). **2.** Italian: perhaps from French *trille*, a southern variant of *treille* 'vine arbor'. **3.** English: Reaney believes this to be an altered form of THURLOW, citing as evidence Philip de Trillowe 1279.
GIVEN NAMES Spanish 41%; Italian 8%. *Carlos* (6), *Juan* (6), *Jose* (5), *Manuel* (5), *Cruz* (2), *Francisco* (2), *Rodolfo* (2), *Aida, Alberto, Alfonso, Alfredo, Ana Luz; Antonio* (3), *Angelo* (2), *Carmin, Cecilio, Nazareno, Rocci.*

Trim (579) **1.** English: apparently a nickname for a well-turned-out person, from the adjective *trim* 'well-equipped', 'neatly made'. The word is first attested in the early 16th century, but may well have been in colloquial use much earlier. **2.** English: from an Old English personal name, *Trymma*. **3.** Irish: habitational name, originally **de Truim**, from a place in County Meath named Trim.

Trimarchi (193) Sicilian and southern Italian: occupational name from medieval Greek *tourmarchēs* 'leader of a squadron' or 'governor of a *tourma*' (an administrative region of the Byzantine empire, of which Sicily and southern Italy at one time formed a part) from Latin *turma* 'squadron' + Greek *arkhē* 'lead', 'rule'. The term is attested in 1091 in Greek sources in the form *tromarkhis*.
GIVEN NAMES Italian 24%. *Rocco* (3), *Antonio* (2), *Salvatore* (2), *Amedeo*, *Domenic*, *Gino*, *Nino*, *Piero*, *Sal*, *Santo*.

Trimarco (149) Sicilian and southern Italian: variant of TRIMARCHI.
GIVEN NAMES Italian 6%. *Antonio*, *Giuseppe*.

Trimbach (117) **1.** German: habitational name from Trimbach in Solothurn canton, Switzerland. **2.** French: habitational name from Trimbach in Bas-Rhin, Alsace.

Trimberger (121) German: habitational name for someone from Trimberg in Baden.

Trimble (5888) Scottish and northern Irish: variant of TRUMBLE, recorded in northern Ireland since the 17th century.

Trimboli (333) Italian: variant of TRIPOLI, possibly also of **Triboli**, a nickname from the plural of *tribolo* 'tribulation', 'affliction'.
GIVEN NAMES Italian 24%. *Santo* (3), *Angelo*, *Armando*, *Bartolo*, *Carmela*, *Carmelo*, *Carmine*, *Giovanni*, *Mario*, *Pasquale*, *Pietro*, *Rocco*, *Salvatore*, *Vito*.

Trimbur (143) French (Alsace): unexplained.

Trimm (617) English: variant spelling of TRIM.

Trimmer (1227) English: occupational name, probably for a trimmer of cloth. The verb *trim* is not attested in its modern sense before the early 16th century, but the surname form William le Trymmere is found in the 14th century, and this seems to be continuous with Old English *trymian*, *trymman* 'to strengthen or confirm' (from *trum* 'strong', 'firm').

Trimpe (208) Dutch: possibly a metonymic occupational name, from Middle Dutch *trippe* 'patten', 'wooden over-shoe', with epenthetic *-m-*.

Trimper (121) Origin unidentified.

Trimpey (103) Altered spelling of North German *Trimpe*, of uncertain origin (see TRIMPE).

Trinca (101) Italian: **1.** probably from *Trinca*, an old Tuscan short form of compound names formed with the verb *trincare* 'to drink greedily'. **2.** otherwise from a southern dialect word *trinca* 'piece of a

boulder or rock', a derivative of *trincare* 'to cut stone'.
GIVEN NAMES Italian 24%. *Saverio* (2), *Alfonso*, *Bartolo*, *Gino*, *Mario*, *Remo*.

Trindade (148) Portuguese: from *Trindade*, a religious personal name meaning 'Trinity', often bestowed on someone born or baptized on the feast of the Holy Trinity.
GIVEN NAMES Spanish 26%; Portuguese 13%. *Carlos* (3), *Jose* (3), *Abilio* (2), *Fabio* (2), *Francisco* (2), *Manuel* (2), *Sergio* (2), *Adolfo*, *Alfredo*, *Armindo*, *Ferando*, *Germano*; *Joao*, *Manoel*; *Antonio* (2), *Fausto*, *Ricci*, *Silvio*.

Trindle (128) **1.** English: possibly a variant of TRUMBLE. **2.** Possibly a variant spelling of German **Trindl**, from a Bavarian and Swabian nickname for a slow person, or alternatively an altered spelling of **Drindle**, from a South German short form of the personal name *Katharina* (see CATHERINE).

Trine (181) Dutch: from a short form of the personal name CATHERINE.

Tringale (126) Italian: variant of TRINGALI.
GIVEN NAMES Italian 23%. *Domenic* (7), *Domenico*, *Gasper*, *Santo*.

Tringali (373) Italian: status name from medieval Greek *droungarios* 'commander of a squad of soldiers' (Greek *droungos*, from Latin *drungus*).
GIVEN NAMES Italian 25%. *Salvatore* (6), *Angelo* (5), *Sal* (4), *Vincenzo* (3), *Carmelo* (2), *Gaetano* (2), *Alfio*, *Domenic*, *Domenica*, *Domenico*, *Ezio*, *Filippo*.

Trinh (1879) Vietnamese: unexplained.
GIVEN NAMES Vietnamese 66%; Chinese 10%. *Thanh* (36), *Minh* (34), *Hung* (21), *Long* (20), *Binh* (19), *Hoa* (18), *Dung* (17), *Khanh* (15), *Vinh* (14), *Duc* (12), *Hoang* (12), *Huy* (12), *Phong* (12), *Tam* (11), *Thai* (10), *Nam* (8), *Tinh* (3); *Chan* (5), *Chi* (5), *Sang* (5), *Han* (4), *Hong* (4), *Sen* (4), *Hang* (3), *Man* (3), *Tong* (3), *Dong* (2), *Hon* (2), *Hui* (2).

Trinidad (1052) Spanish: **1.** from the religious personal name *Trinidad* 'Trinity', often bestowed on someone born on the feast of the Holy Trinity. **2.** habitational name for someone from any of the many places named La Trinidad.
GIVEN NAMES Spanish 49%. *Jose* (23), *Juan* (17), *Manuel* (11), *Jesus* (10), *Rafael* (8), *Alejandro* (7), *Roberto* (7), *Miguel* (6), *Ricardo* (6), *Tomas* (6), *Alfredo* (5), *Angel* (5).

Trinka (166) Czech and Slovak (**Trnka**): nickname from a derivative of *trn* 'thorn'.

Trinkle (669) South German: nickname for a drinker, from a diminutive noun derivative of Middle High German *trinken* 'to drink'.

Trinklein (122) German: nickname for an imbiber, from Middle High German *trincklin* 'little drinker'.
GIVEN NAMES German 6%. *Fritz* (2), *Hans*.

Trinko (101) Slovenian: unexplained. Perhaps a metronymic from a short form of the personal name *Katra*, pet form of *Katarina* (see CATHERINE).

Trinque (102) French: unexplained; possibly from Middle French *trinc* denoting a type of game, hence a nickname for an habitual or skilled player of the game.
GIVEN NAMES French 14%. *Armand*, *Fernand*, *Michel*, *Pierre*.

Triola (225) Italian: variant of TRIOLO.
GIVEN NAMES Italian 9%. *Angelo*, *Carmelo*, *Carmine*, *Domenic*.

Triolo (560) Italian: **1.** from a reduced form of **Tiriolo**, a habitational name from a place so named in Catanzaro province. **2.** from a diminutive of **Trio** 'trio', 'triad', 'triplet', presumably a nickname.
GIVEN NAMES Italian 15%. *Carlo* (5), *Salvatore* (5), *Antonino* (3), *Carmelo* (3), *Antonio* (2), *Angelo*, *Carmela*, *Cira*, *Franco*, *Gaspare*, *Gasper*, *Guiseppe*.

Tripathi (137) Indian (northern states): Hindu (Brahman) name, from Sanskrit *tripāṭhī* 'one that has studied the three Vedas' (see TRIVEDI), from *tri-* 'three' + *pāṭha* 'reading', 'studying'.
GIVEN NAMES Indian 93%. *Ram* (3), *Satish* (3), *Ajai* (2), *Chandravadan* (2), *Mahesh* (2), *Manoj* (2), *Raj* (2), *Rakesh* (2), *Ramesh* (2), *Uma* (2), *Ajay*, *Alok*.

Tripi (330) **1.** Italian (Sicily): habitational name from Tripi in Messina region. **2.** Greek (**Tripis**): topographic name for someone who lived in a shack or very poor accommodation, from Greek *trypa* 'hole', 'burrow', 'shack'. This is also a common element in Greek place names.
GIVEN NAMES Italian 17%. *Salvatore* (5), *Sal* (2), *Vito* (2), *Angelo*, *Carlo*, *Carmine*, *Cosimo*, *Gianfranco*, *Giuseppe*.

Triplet (146) Variant spelling of English TRIPLETT.

Triplett (5609) English: unexplained. In part it may be an Anglicized spelling of French **Triplet**, a reduced form of **Tripelet**, from a derivative of the Old French verb *tripier* 'to hop', 'to skip', hence a nickname for a dancer or acrobat.

Tripodi (529) Italian (Calabrian and Sicilian): from Calabrian *tripodi*, *tripodu*, Sicilian *tripoddu*, from medieval Greek *tripodion* 'tripod', 'trivet', possibly a metonymic occupational name for a cook or a metonymic occupational name for a maker of trivets.
GIVEN NAMES Italian 23%. *Rocco* (8), *Antonio* (5), *Carmelo* (5), *Salvatore* (3), *Carlo* (2), *Carmela* (2), *Giuseppe* (2), *Luigi* (2), *Marcello* (2), *Sal* (2), *Angelo*, *Orlando*, *Rosario*.

Tripoli (391) Italian and Greek (**Tripolis**, **Tripolitakis**): habitational name from any of various cities called Tripoli, a place name of Greek origin meaning 'triple city'. In particular, there is a place so named in North Africa (Libya), another in Lebanon, and another in the Peloponnese (capital of Arcadia).

GIVEN NAMES Italian 15%. *Salvatore* (4), *Sal* (2), *Carlo*, *Cosimo*, *Domenic*, *Filippo*, *Francesco*, *Gaspare*, *Giorgio*, *Marino*, *Santo*, *Vincenzo*.

Tripp (7373) **1.** English (mainly southern): metonymic occupational name for a dancer, or a nickname for someone with an odd gait, from Middle English *trip(p)(en)* 'to step lightly, skip, or hop' (Old French *triper*). **2.** English: metonymic occupational name for a butcher or tripe dresser, from Middle English, Old French *trip(p)e* 'tripe' (of unknown origin). **3.** German: metonymic occupational name for a maker of wooden pattens (*trippe*), a type of raised sole that could be strapped to normal footwear for walking in unpaved muddy streets.

Trippe (368) English: variant of TRIPP.

Trippel (153) German: from a pet form of a Germanic personal name formed with *thrud* 'strength' (Old Norse *þrudr* 'divine being', 'valkyrie').

Trippett (213) English: nickname for a schemer or trickster, from Middle English *tripet(t)*, Old French *tripot* 'malicious plot', 'trick'.

Triscari (100) Southern Italian: unexplained.
GIVEN NAMES Italian 21%. *Carmelo* (2), *Luigi* (2), *Carmella*, *Carmello*, *Cirino*.

Triska (151) Czech (**Tříska**, **Tříška**): from *tříska* 'splinter', a nickname for a very thin man. The Czech idiom *hubený jako tříska* means 'as thin as a rake'.

Trisko (101) German (of Slavic origin): probably an altered form of Czech **Tříska** (see TRISKA). This name is found in Austria, and in Bohemia in the early 18th century, but the form is not Czech.

Trisler (354) German (**Trissler**): occupational name from Middle High German *triseler*, *treseler* 'treasurer'.

Trissel (123) German: probably from a nickname for someone with an abnormality of the throat or neck, from Middle High German *drüzzel* 'throat', 'gorge'.

Tristan (403) Spanish (**Tristán**): from the popular medieval personal name *Tristán*, derived from a British Celtic legend which became incorporated into the Arthurian cycle as the story of Tristan and Iseult. The name is of unknown derivation. It was transmitted through Old French and became associated by folk etymology with Latin *tristis* 'sad'.
GIVEN NAMES Spanish 46%. *Jose* (15), *Juan* (12), *Guadalupe* (5), *Carlos* (4), *Pablo* (4), *Andres* (3), *Jesus* (3), *Sergio* (3), *Angel* (2), *Diego* (2), *Domingo* (2), *Felipe* (2).

Tritch (158) Altered spelling of German TRITSCH.

Trites (164) Americanized spelling of German **Treitz**, of Slavic origin.

Tritle (162) Possibly an Americanized form of German **Trittel**, from a Germanic personal name formed with *thrud* 'strength'

(compare TRAUTWEIN), which in medieval times became confused with Middle High German *trût* 'dear', 'beloved'.

Tritsch (196) German: nickname meaning 'flirt' or 'lover', derived from Middle High German *trutschel* 'flirtatious look'.

Tritschler (184) German: **1.** variant of TRITSCH. **2.** possibly a nickname for a skilled board game player, from Middle High German *trütscheln* 'to play a board game'. **3.** nickname for a chatterer, Middle High German *tritscheler*.
GIVEN NAMES German 4%. *Eberhard*, *Klaus*.

Tritt (657) German: apparently from Old High German *tretan* 'to step'. However, a South German family of that name are the descendants of late 16th-century immigrants from Como, Italy who bore the name *de Triddi*.

Tritten (133) Swiss German: topographic name for someone who lived by a step or flight of steps, from Middle High German *trit* 'step'.
GIVEN NAMES German 5%. *Kurt*.

Tritz (206) German: **1.** topographic name for someone who lived by a step or flight of steps, from Middle High German *trit* 'step'. **2.** altered spelling of TRITES.

Trivedi (536) Indian (northern states): Hindu (Brahman) name from Sanskrit *trivedī* 'one that knows the three Vedas', from *tri-* 'three' + *veda* '(sacred) knowledge'. The Vedas are the oldest sacred texts of the Hindu religion. Three of them are regarded as primary but a fourth one was added later. See also TRIPATHI.
GIVEN NAMES Indian 93%. *Bharat* (10), *Mahesh* (8), *Yogesh* (6), *Dilip* (5), *Divyang* (5), *Hitesh* (5), *Kamlesh* (5), *Sanjay* (5), *Amit* (4), *Ashish* (4), *Himanshu* (4), *Ketan* (4).

Trivett (559) English and French: from Middle English, Old French *trivet*, *trevet* 'trivet', 'tripod', presumably a nickname for someone who walked with a stick, or perhaps a metonymic occupational name for someone who made or used such articles.

Trivette (700) French: variant of TRIVETT.

Trivisonno (117) Italian: probably an altered form of **Trivisano**, itself a variant of **Trevisano** (see TREVISAN). In Italy it occurs almost exclusively in Campobasso, Molise.
GIVEN NAMES Italian 12%. *Angelo* (2), *Rocco*.

Trivitt (102) English: variant of TRIVETT.

Trnka (219) Czech and Slovak: **1.** topographic name for someone living by a blackthorn (sloe) bush, Czech *trnka*. **2.** nickname for someone with eyes as dark as sloes, from the same word in a transferred sense.

Troast (139) Probably an Americanized spelling of German TROST.

Trobaugh (456) Americanized form of a German habitational name, probably Trabach (now called Traben-Trabach) on the Mosel River.

Troccoli (129) Italian: possibly a habitational name from a lost place called *Triocala*, medieval Greek *Triokala*, from *tria* 'three' and *kala* 'good things'.
GIVEN NAMES Italian 16%; Spanish 12%. *Angelo* (3), *Domenic* (2), *Antonio*, *Carmelo*, *Carmine*; *Jesus* (2), *Silverio* (2), *Luis*, *Pascual*, *Rosalinda*, *Silvia*.

Troche (286) Galician: of uncertain origin; probably related to the idiomatic expression *a troche y moche* 'all over (the place)', 'left and right'; 'on the off-chance', and may be derived from *trozar* 'to cut up'.
GIVEN NAMES Spanish 37%. *Jose* (9), *Angel* (3), *Manuel* (3), *Ana* (2), *Bernardo* (2), *Domingo* (2), *Fernando* (2), *Juanita* (2), *Luis* (2), *Rafael* (2), *Rogelio* (2), *Roxana* (2).

Trocki (125) Polish and Jewish (eastern Ashkenazic): habitational name for someone from a place in Lithuania (Lithuanian *Trakai*, Polish *Troki*, Russian *Troki*), which had a large Jewish population.
GIVEN NAME Polish 6%; German 4%. *Mikolaj*.

Troeger (203) **1.** German (Saxony, Vogtland): habitational name for someone from Trogen. **2.** Dutch: possibly from a derivative of Middle Dutch *troc* 'trough', 'tub', hence an occupational name for a maker of such items.
GIVEN NAMES German 9%. *Kurt* (2), *Klaus*, *Uwe*.

Troendle (166) German (Württemberg, Baden): apparently from *trenlin* 'tear', hence a nickname for someone who was easily moved to tears.

Troester (350) German: from a variant of TROST.

Trogdon (604) Origin unidentified.

Troglin (121) South German: variant of **Trog**, a topographic name for someone living by a village watering trough, from Middle High German *troc* + diminutive *-l(e)in*.

Troha (221) Slovenian: nickname for a small person, from *troha* 'a scrap', 'a tiny bit of something'.

Troia (412) **1.** Italian: of uncertain origin; most likely a habitational name from Troia in Foggia province, or alternatively nickname from *troia* 'sow'. **2.** Portuguese (**Tróia**): habitational name from any of various places so named.
GIVEN NAMES Italian 25%. *Salvatore* (6), *Antonio* (5), *Santo* (3), *Gaspar* (2), *Luigi* (2), *Mario* (2), *Rosario* (2), *Pasquale* (2), *Vito* (2), *Ambrogio*, *Angelo*, *Carmela*, *Carmelina*, *Carmine*, *Eduardo*, *Elia*, *Erasmo*, *Franco*.

Troiani (252) Italian: patronymic or plural form of TROIANO.
GIVEN NAMES Italian 27%. *Mario* (3), *Angelo* (2), *Marco* (2), *Osvaldo* (2), *Aldo*, *Antonio*, *Armando*, *Carlo*, *Dino*, *Domenic*, *Emedio*, *Emilio*, *Enrico*, *Italo*, *Luca*, *Nazzareno*, *Orlando*.

Troiano (926) Italian: **1.** ethnic name for someone from Troia in Apulia, from an adjectival form of the place name. **2.** outside Apulia, from the personal name *Troiano* 'Trojan', which was borne by a minor saint, a bishop of Saintes in France.
GIVEN NAMES Italian 17%. *Salvatore* (6), *Gino* (4), *Rocco* (4), *Vito* (4), *Gabriele* (3), *Marco* (3), *Antonio* (2), *Domenic* (2), *Guido* (2), *Pasquale* (2), *Aldo, Angelo.*

Troilo (161) **1.** Italian: nickname from *troglio* 'stuttering'. **2.** Perhaps also a metathesized spelling of Italian TRIOLO.
GIVEN NAMES Italian 12%. *Domenic* (2), *Agostino, Rocco.*

Troise (155) Italian: probably a regional name from *Turgisius*, Latin name of a Norman province of Sicily.
GIVEN NAMES Italian 16%; French 5%. *Carlo* (2), *Francesco, Gaetano, Rocco, Salvatore; Armand, Marie Claire.*

Troisi (378) Italian: patronymic or plural form of TROISE.
GIVEN NAMES Italian 16%. *Angelo* (6), *Fiore* (2), *Salvatore* (2), *Cosmo, Dino, Domenic, Guido, Pasquale, Sal, Silvio, Tullio.*

Trojan (491) **1.** Polish: from an Old Slavic personal name, *Trojan*, a derivative of Latin *Traianus*. This was the name of a Roman emperor (53–117), who extended the Roman Empire east into Dacia (modern Romania). In early Slavic records the name is also borne by a mythical creature. **2.** Czech and Slovak: from the Old Czech vocabulary word *trojan* 'triplet', from the numeral *tři* 'three'. This was used as a personal name, bestowed on children born on the Feast of the Holy Trinity, and as a surname for people living at a house distinguished by the sign of a Golden Three. **3.** The surname is also well established in Germany, of Slavic origin. **4.** French: from the Latin personal name *Troianus* (see Italian TROIANO). This gained currency in France as having been the name of a 6th-century bishop of Saintes.

Trojanowski (334) Polish: habitational name for someone from any of various places called Trojanów, Trojanowa, or Trojanowice, all of which are named with the personal name *Trojan*.
GIVEN NAMES Polish 11%. *Casimir* (2), *Zbigniew* (2), *Dymitr, Ewa, Grzegorz, Jerzy, Kazimierz, Stanislaw, Szymon, Tadeusz, Wincenty.*

Trokey (114) Possibly an altered spelling of **Trokey**, **Troquay**, a habitational name from Le Trokay in Chokier, Liège province, Belgium or of French (Picard) **Troquet**, a habitational name from a house so named, from a diminutive of *troque* 'stag's horn'. Origin unidentified.

Trolinger (168) Variant of TROLLINGER.

Troll (262) German: nickname from Middle High German *trolle* 'demon', 'goblin'; 'blockhead'.

Trollinger (391) Swiss and German: of uncertain origin; in some cases probably a variant of DROLLINGER.

Trom (134) North German (**Tromm**), Danish, and Dutch: metonymic occupational name for a drummer, from Middle Low German *tromme* 'drum'.

Trombetta (552) Italian (especially eastern Sicily): metonymic occupational name for a trumpeter or bugler, from *trombetta* 'bugle', a diminutive of *tromba* 'trumpet'.
GIVEN NAMES Italian 19%. *Lorenzo* (3), *Nicola* (3), *Enrico* (2), *Giovanni* (2), *Guido* (2), *Luigi* (2), *Orfeo* (2), *Pietro* (2), *Umberto* (2), *Vito* (2), *Alessandro, Angelo.*

Trombino (224) Italian: metonymic occupational name for a trumpeter or bugler, from a diminutive of *tromba* 'trumpet'.
GIVEN NAMES Italian 15%. *Aldo* (2), *Antonio, Armando, Dino, Gaetano, Italo, Salvatore, Sebastiano.*

Tromblee (110) Americanized spelling of French TREMBLAY.

Trombley (2399) Americanized spelling of French TREMBLAY.

Trombly (615) Americanized spelling of French TREMBLAY.

Trommer (124) German: variant of TRUMMER.
GIVEN NAMES German 5%; Scandinavian 4%. *Gerd, Rudi.*

Tromp (196) **1.** Dutch: metonymic occupational name for a trumpeter or a drummer. **2.** German: habitational name from a place so named near Braunsberg in Brandenburg.
GIVEN NAMES Dutch 10%; German 4%. *Lidwina* (2), *Cornie, Gerrit, Jeroen, Laurens, Marten, Martinus, Maryke; Erwin, Hans, Johannes, Kurt.*

Trompeter (221) **1.** German: occupational name for a trumpeter, messenger, or herald, Middle High German *trum(m)eter*, *trumpter*. **2.** German: habitational name from any of four estates so named in the Rhineland. **3.** Dutch: occupational name for a trumpeter from an agent derivative of *trompet* 'trumpet'.

Tron (107) **1.** Vietnamese: unexplained. **2.** French: possibly a variant of **Trond**, from the personal name *Trond*, of Germanic origin, which was borne by a 7th century saint, the founder of a religious chapter which in the 8th century was to become a celebrated Benedictine abbey.
GIVEN NAMES Vietnamese 8%; French 6%. *Hien Van, Lam, Luong Van, Nguyen, Nhon; Alexandre, Etienne, Henri.*

Troncone (108) Italian: augmentative form of **Tronco**, apparently from *tronco* 'trunk'.
GIVEN NAMES Italian 20%. *Alphonso, Araceli, Ciriaco, Dominico, Iolanda, Marcello, Mario, Sabino.*

Troncoso (300) Galician: habitational name from Troncoso in Ourense province, from a derivative of *tronco* 'tree trunk', 'stump'.
GIVEN NAMES Spanish 50%. *Juan* (8), *Manuel* (5), *Fernando* (4), *Luis* (4), *Ricardo* (4),

Eduardo (3), *Jose* (3), *Mario* (3), *Pedro* (3), *Rafael* (3), *Alberto* (2), *Ana* (2).

Trone (412) English and French: metonymic occupational name, from Middle English, Old French *trone* 'weighing machine'.

Tronnes (104) Norwegian: habitational name from any of about ten farmsteads called Tronnes, from Old Norse *þródr* 'swine', 'boar' + *nes* 'headland', 'promontory'.

Tronolone (130) Italian: unexplained. In Italy this name is found mainly in Potenza.
GIVEN NAME Italian 9%. *Carmine* (2).

Tronson (150) **1.** English: nickname for a short, fat man, from Middle English, Old French *tronchon* 'piece broken off' (Late Latin *truncio*, genitive *truncionis*, from *truncus* 'lopped', 'cut short'). It is just possible that the nickname also denoted someone who carried a staff or cudgel as a symbol of office, but this sense of the word is not attested in English before the 16th century. **2.** French: from Old French *tronson* 'block of wood', perhaps a metonymic occupational name for a woodcutter.

Troop (380) **1.** Scottish: variant of TROUP. **2.** English: variant of THROOP.

Troost (210) Dutch and German: from Middle Dutch *tro(o)st*, Middle High German *trōst*, 'confidence', 'trust', 'solace', 'consolation', a nickname for a comforter or possibly a personal name given to a child born after the death of a sibling.

Tropea (214) Italian (Calabrian and Sicilian): habitational name from Tropea, a place in Vibo Valentia province.
GIVEN NAMES Italian 26%. *Angelo* (2), *Caterina* (2), *Dante* (2), *Gaeton* (2), *Salvatore* (2), *Alfio, Armando, Enza, Marcello, Nicola, Oreste, Rocco, Sal.*

Tropeano (176) Italian (Calabria and Sicily): habitational name for someone from TROPEA.
GIVEN NAMES Italian 30%. *Carmine* (4), *Angelo* (2), *Antonio* (2), *Sarino* (2), *Agostino, Augostino, Elio, Elvio, Francesco, Piero, Rocco.*

Tropf (102) German: nickname for a naïve person, from Middle High German *tropf* (see TROPP).

Tropiano (122) Italian: variant of TROPEANO.
GIVEN NAMES Italian 26%. *Salvatore* (3), *Antonio* (2), *Vito* (2), *Concetta, Cono, Mario, Vincenzo.*

Tropp (311) **1.** North German: nickname for a simpleton, Middle Low German *trop*. **2.** Jewish (eastern Ashkenazic): habitational name from a place in Silesia called Troppau in German (formerly part of Austria-Hungary).
GIVEN NAMES Russian 5%; Jewish 5%. *Vitaly* (2), *Aleksandr, Emiliya, Galina, Vladimir; Miriam* (2), *Emanuel, Ilya, Yetta.*

Trosclair (731) Altered form of German TROXLER, under the influence of the French of LA.

GIVEN NAMES French 5%. *Anatole, Andre, Angelle, Antoine, Camille, Emile, Ketty, Lucien, Sylvain.*

Trosky (112) **1.** Origin unidentified. Possibly an Americanized spelling of German **Troschke**: **2.** from a Low German pet form of a compound personal name formed with *trūt* 'dear'. **3.** habitational name from Troschkau, Droschka(u).

Trosper (601) Origin unidentified; possibly French, or perhaps an Americanized spelling of German TRESPE, a derogatory nickname for a rustic or peasant, from Middle High German *trefze* 'weed'.

Tross (127) German: metonymic occupational name for a carter or carter's man, from Middle High German *trosse* 'baggage'.

GIVEN NAMES German 8%. *Frieda, Horst, Jurgen.*

Trost (1508) **1.** German: from a medieval personal name or byname often bestowed on a child born after the death of a sibling, from German *Trost* 'comfort', 'consolation' (Middle High German *trōst*, 'confidence', 'trust'). This surname is also found in Slovenia, where it is commonly spelled **Trošt**. **2.** Dutch: variant of TROOST. **3.** Jewish (Ashkenazic): ornamental name from modern German *Trost* 'comfort', 'consolation'.

Trostel (163) South German: probably a nickname for someone who enjoyed singing, from Middle High German *trostel* 'thrush'.

Trostle (432) Variant spelling of German TROSTEL.

Troth (315) English (West Midlands): nickname from Middle English *trowthe, trouthe* 'good faith', 'loyalty'. *By my troth* was a common phrase emphasizing the veracity of an assertion, and the nickname may have been bestowed on someone who used it habitually or to excess.

Trotman (769) **1.** English and Scottish: variant of TROTTER 1. **2.** Altered spelling of German **Trotmann**, a variant of TROTTER 2.

Trott (1625) **1.** English and Scottish: variant of TROTTER 1. **2.** South German: metonymic variant of TROTTER 2.

Trotta (1050) Italian: from the feminine form of the personal name TROTTO.

GIVEN NAMES Italian 13%. *Angelo* (5), *Vito* (4), *Aniello* (3), *Attilio* (2), *Carlo* (2), *Marzio* (2), *Nicolina* (2), *Pasquale* (2), *Rocco* (2), *Salvatore* (2), *Amedeo, Carmela.*

Trotter (6360) **1.** Northern English and Scottish: occupational name for a messenger, from an agent derivative of Middle English *trot(en)* 'to walk fast' (Old French *troter*, of Germanic origin, akin to 2 below). **2.** German: occupational name for a grape-treader, from a derivative of Middle High German *trot(t)e* 'winepress'. The word and the surname are confined largely

to Alsace, Lorraine, Switzerland, and Swabia.

Trotti (161) Italian: patronymic or plural form of TROTTO.

GIVEN NAMES Italian 4%. *Luciano, Rocco.*

Trottier (878) French: occupational name from the agent derivative of Old French *troter* 'to walk fast' (see TROTTER 1).

FOREBEARS A Trottier from the Perche region of France is documented in Quebec City in 1646, as lord of Desruisseaux and Desaulniers. The family also bear the secondary surnames Bellecourt and BELCOURT.

GIVEN NAMES French 12%. *Andre* (2), *Armand* (2), *Benoit* (2), *Gilles* (2), *Adrien, Alderic, Edouard, Emile, Emilien, Girard, Jean-Guy, Laurent.*

Trotto (195) Italian: probably from a medieval personal name *Trotto*, of Germanic origin.

GIVEN NAMES Italian 20%. *Angelo* (2), *Carmine* (2), *Cosmo* (2), *Rocco* (2), *Salvatore* (2), *Concetta, Giuseppe, Marco, Tommaso.*

Troublefield (151) Apparently an altered form of TURBERVILLE.

Troudt (167) German: variant of DRAUDT.

Troughton (139) English (Cumbria): habitational name from Troughton Hall in the parish of Kirkby Ireleth, Lancashire, so named from Old English *trog* 'trough', 'hollow' + *tūn* 'enclosure', 'settlement'.

Troung (260) Vietnamese: unexplained.

GIVEN NAMES Vietnamese 62%; Chinese 13%. *Minh* (6), *Hung* (5), *Hoa* (4), *Muoi* (4), *Tam* (4), *Tan* (4), *Hai* (3), *Thanh* (3), *Tuan* (3), *Diep* (2), *Ha* (2), *Hien* (2), *Hoang* (2), *Phong* (2), *Thach, Tuong*; *Chi* (3), *Dong* (2), *Sang* (2), *Chan, Chen, Soung, Tong.*

Troup (1308) **1.** Scottish: habitational name from a place in the parish of Gamrie, near Banff. The place is situated on a headland affording some sheltered anchorage, and is said to get its name from Middle English *true hope*; however, when first recorded in 1296 it already appears as *Trup*, so it is more likely to be of the same origin as THORPE. **2.** English: variant of THROOP.

Troupe (793) Scottish and English: variant of TROUP.

Trousdale (436) English: see TRUESDALE.

Trout (4849) **1.** English: from Middle English *trowte* 'trout', hence a metonymic occupational name for a fisherman, or a nickname for someone supposedly resembling the fish. **2.** Altered spelling of German TRAUT.

Trouten (132) Probably an Americanized spelling of German **Trauten**, a metonymic from a short form of the female personal name *Gertrud* (see TRUDE).

Troutman (4075) Americanized spelling of German TRAUTMANN.

Troutner (266) Americanized spelling of TRAUTNER.

Troutt (687) English: variant spelling of TROUT.

Troutwine (158) Americanized spelling of TRAUTWEIN.

Trovato (625) Italian: nickname for a foundling, literally 'found', from the past participle of *trovare* 'to find'.

GIVEN NAMES Italian 27%. *Salvatore* (9), *Angelo* (5), *Carmelo* (4), *Aldo* (2), *Carmine* (2), *Giuseppe* (2), *Guerino* (2), *Pasquale* (2), *Antonio, Assunta, Dante, Guillermo, Liborio, Rosalia, Zoraida.*

Trover (127) Possibly Irish: from **Trower**, a reduced Anglicized form of Gaelic **Ó Treabhair** (see TREVOR).

Trovillion (122) Variant spelling of Cornish TREVILLIAN.

Trovinger (101) Origin unidentified. Possibly an altered spelling of German TREFFINGER.

Trow (327) **1.** English (chiefly West Midlands): nickname for a trustworthy person, from Middle English *trow(e)*, *trew(e)* 'faithful', 'steadfast'. **2.** English: variant of TREE, from Middle English *trow, trew*. **3.** English: topographic name for someone who lived near a depression in the ground, from Middle English *trow* 'trough', 'hollow'. **4.** Translated form of French **Jetté** (see JETTE). *Trow* represents the French Canadian pronunciation of English 'throw'.

Trowbridge (2734) English: habitational name from Trowbridge in Wiltshire, named from Old English *trēow* 'tree' + *brycg* 'bridge'; the name probably referred to a felled trunk serving as a rough-and-ready bridge.

Trowell (323) English: habitational name from Trowell in Nottinghamshire, named in Old English with *trēow* 'tree' + *wella* 'stream'. Ekwall suggests that this may have referred to a tree bridge. Compare TROWBRIDGE.

Trower (597) **1.** English: variant of THROWER. **2.** Irish: reduced Anglicized form of Gaelic **Ó Treabhair** (see TREVOR). **3.** Americanized spelling of German **Trauer**, a habitational name for someone from Trauen in Lower Saxony.

Troxclair (134) See TROSCLAIR.

GIVEN NAMES French 8%. *Emile* (2), *Prudent.*

Troxel (1217) German: variant of TRAXEL.

Troxell (1724) Altered spelling of TROXEL.

Troxler (576) Swiss German: variant of TRAXLER.

Troy (2935) **1.** Irish (Munster): reduced Anglicized form of Gaelic **Ó Troighthigh** 'descendant of *Troightheach*', a byname meaning 'foot soldier'. **2.** English (of Norman origin): habitational name from Troyes in Aude, France. There was also an Anglo-Norman family of this name in Ireland. **3.** Americanized form of some like-sounding Jewish surname or an Americanized spelling of TREU. **4.** French: habitational name from a place in the Haute-Garonne. **5.** Dutch: from a short form of the female personal name *Geertrui(de)*, Dutch form of *Gertrude* (see TRUDE). **6.** Dutch: from Middle Dutch *troye* 'doublet', 'jerkin', possibly a metonymic occupational name for a tailor, or a nickname for someone who wore a striking garment of this kind.

Troyan (292) **1.** Jewish (from Belarus): habitational name from Troya in Belarus, or from a place called Trojany, of which there are several examples in Poland. **2.** Americanized spelling of TROJAN.

Troyer (3006) **1.** Altered spelling of German **Troier**, **Treuer**, in the south, a topographic name for someone who lived by a cattle track *Treyen* (from Latin *trivium* 'trail'); in the north, from an occupational name from Middle Low German *troye* 'jerkin'. **2.** Dutch (**De Troyer**): occupational name for a maker of jerkins (see TROY 6).

Trozzo (110) Italian: possibly from a reduced form of *Mastrozzo* or a derivative of the Germanic personal name *Truto* (see TROTTO).

GIVEN NAMES Italian 9%. *Romano, Salvatore.*

Truan (105) **1.** Spanish (**Truán**): nickname from *truhán* 'knave', 'joker'. **2.** English (Cornwall): unexplained; possibly a variant spelling of TREWIN.

GIVEN NAMES Spanish 9%. *Carlos* (4), *Jose, Raul.*

Truax (2187) Americanized spelling of French **du Trieux**, a habitational name from Trieux in Meurthe-et-Moselle, in northeastern France.

FOREBEARS This is a Huguenot name, which is frequent in NJ and in the Albany-Schenectady area of NY. It was already well established in North America by the mid 17th century. Philip Truax was born in Monmouth Co., NJ, in 1675 or 1676 (possibly two different people); the father is documented as Jacob DuTrieux.

Trubey (150) **1.** English: variant spelling of Truby; unexplained. **2.** Probably also an Americanized spelling of Swiss German **Trübi** or **Trüby** (see TRUBY).

Trubiano (113) Italian (Pescara): unexplained.

GIVEN NAMES Italian 18%; French 6%. *Reno* (2), *Cono, Dino, Enzio, Fausto, Giacomo, Luciano, Lucio, Paolo, Romeo; Antoine, Pierre.*

Truby (291) **1.** English (Oxfordshire and West Midlands): unexplained. **2.** Swiss German (**Trüby**): of uncertain origin; it may have originated as a nickname, from Middle High German *trüebe* 'dark', 'sad', 'troubled'.

Truchan (145) Ukrainian and Polish: nickname from Ukrainian *truchan* 'turkey', or possibly a metonymic occupational name for a turkey farmer.

GIVEN NAMES Polish 6%. *Casimir, Stanislaw, Wasil.*

Truchon (103) French: unexplained.

GIVEN NAMES French 8%. *Armand, Armande, Emile.*

Truckey (129) Origin uncertain. Possibly an Americanized spelling of **Trokay** or **Troquet** (see TROKEY).

Trucks (167) German: reduced form of **Truchsess**, a status name for a lord high steward, Middle High German *truh(t)sæze*, one of the three most important posts at a medieval court.

GIVEN NAMES German 4%. *Ewald, Helmut.*

Trude (159) Dutch and German: from a short form of the female personal name *Gertrude*, composed of the Germanic elements *gēr* 'spear' + *trud* 'strength', the latter being subsequently reinterpreted as *traut* 'dear', yielding the form *Gertraut* (see DRAUDT).

Trudeau (2177) French: from a pet form of the personal name *Thouroude* or perhaps *Gertrude*.

FOREBEARS A Trudeau from the Aunis region of France is documented in Montreal in 1666 with the variant **Truteau**.

GIVEN NAMES French 8%. *Marcel* (9), *Jacques* (4), *Andre* (3), *Lucien* (3), *Antoine* (2), *Pierre* (2), *Adelard, Adrien, Anatole, Aurore, Benoit, Elphege.*

Trudel (530) French: metronymic derived from *Gertrude*, or perhaps from a pet form of the personal name *Thouroude*. Compare TRUDEAU.

FOREBEARS A Trudel from the Perche region of France is recorded in Quebec City in 1655.

GIVEN NAMES French 19%. *Jacques* (3), *Jean Claude* (3), *Lucien* (3), *Yvon* (3), *Andre* (2), *Gilles* (2), *Philippe* (2), *Adelard, Alban, Colette, Fabien, Jeannot.*

Trudell (1067) Variant of French TRUDEL.

Trudelle (118) Variant of French TRUDEL.

Trudgeon (143) English (Cornwall): habitational name from Tregian in the parish of St. Ewe, earlier *Trudgeon*. The place name is recorded in 1331 in the form *Trehydian*, from Cornish *tre* 'homestead', 'settlement' + a personal name similar in form to the attested *Hedyn*.

Trudo (248) Americanized spelling of French TRUDEAU.

True (3286) English: variant of TROW, mainly of 1.

Trueba (117) Spanish (of Basque origin): probably a habitational or topographic name from the Trueba river in the Cantabria area.

GIVEN NAMES Spanish 35%. *Manuel* (4), *Jose* (3), *Luis* (3), *Carlos* (2), *Francisco* (2), *Mario* (2), *Osvaldo* (2), *Roberto* (2), *Andres, Armando, Elvira, Emiliano.*

Trueblood (1227) English: probably from a nickname for a loyal person, from Middle English *trow(e), trew(e)* 'faithful' + *blode* 'blood'.

Truehart (100) See TRUEHEART.

Trueheart (135) Probably a translated form of Ashkenazic Jewish **Treuherz**, an orna-

mental name composed of German *treu* 'true', 'faithful' + *Herz* 'heart'.

Truell (118) Irish (County Wicklow): probably derived from French **Truelle** (according to Morlet a Norman metonymic occupational name for a mason or builder, from *truelle* 'spatula used for mixing and applying mortar', 'trowel'), or alternatively of the same origin as TROWELL; it was taken from England to Ireland in the 17th century.

Truelock (120) English: nickname from Middle English *treulac* 'fidelity'.

Truelove (965) English: nickname for a lover, from Middle English *trewe* 'faithful' + *loue, love* 'love'.

Truelsen (105) Danish and Norwegian: variant of TRULSON.

GIVEN NAMES Scandinavian 6%. *Asger, Nels.*

Truelson (106) Scandinavian: variant of TRULSON.

GIVEN NAMES Scandinavian 12%. *Nels* (2), *Erik, Tryg.*

Trueman (379) **1.** English (common especially in the Midlands): nickname for a trustworthy man, from Middle English *trewe, trow* 'faithful' + *man* 'man'. This was apparently also used as a personal name during the Middle Ages, and some instances of the surname may derive from this use. **2.** Americanized form of any of the various Jewish surnames derived from German *treu* 'true', 'faithful', for example **Treu(mann)**, **Treiman**; **Getreuer**; **Getroir**, **Getrouer** (from Yiddish *getray*, influenced by German *treu*); **Treuherz** ('true heart').

Truesdale (1335) English: apparently a habitational name from an unidentified place.

Truesdell (1143) English: see TRUESDALE.

Truett (928) English: habitational name from Trewhitt in Northumbria, named from Old Norse *tyri* 'dry resinous wood' + possibly an Old English *wiht* 'river bend'.

Truex (689) Of French Huguenot origin (see TRUAX).

Trufant (122) Origin unidentified. Possibly of French origin, from **Truffand**, a nickname for someone given to mockery or ridicule.

Truglio (153) Italian: possibly a nickname from southern Italian *trugliu*, Sicilian *trugghiu* 'stocky', 'chubby'.

GIVEN NAMES Italian 28%. *Angelo* (3), *Vito* (3), *Stefano* (2), *Aida, Francesco, Mario, Paolo.*

Truhan (118) Czech: unexplained.

Truhlar (101) Czech and Slovak (**Truhlář**): occupational name for a cabinetmaker.

Truitt (3348) English: variant spelling of TRUETT.

Trujillo (9471) Spanish: habitational name from the city so named in Cáceres province, called in Latin *Turgalium*, which is probably of Arabic origin. This place was the home of various conquistadors, hence its great frequency in the Americas.

GIVEN NAMES Spanish 30%. *Jose* (135), *Juan* (80), *Manuel* (64), *Carlos* (59), *Ruben* (33), *Pedro* (31), *Jesus* (28), *Miguel* (28), *Raul* (26), *Jorge* (25), *Alfonso* (23), *Francisco* (22).

Trull (1233) **1.** English: nickname from Middle English *trull* 'slattern', 'prostitute'. **2.** German: nickname for a street entertainer or a cheat, from a noun derivative of Middle High German *trüllen* 'to juggle', also 'to cheat'. **3.** German (also **Trüll**): from a short form of the female personal name *Gertrud* (see TRUDE).

Trullinger (188) Respelling of German TROLLINGER.

Trulock (229) English: variant spelling of TRUELOCK.

Trulove (149) English: variant spelling of TRUELOVE.

Trulson (242) Scandinavian: patronymic from a derivative of Old Norse *þorgils*, from *þórr*, name of the Scandinavian god of thunder (see THOR), + *gils*, a word probably denoting a weapon of some kind.

GIVEN NAMES Scandinavian 11%. *Lars* (2), *Alf*, *Obert*.

Truluck (256) Variant of English TRULOCK.

Truly (150) Probably of English origin but unexplained. This is a predominantly Texan name.

Truman (1895) **1.** English (mainly East Midlands): variant spelling of TRUEMAN. **2.** Jewish (from Latvia): habitational name for someone from a Latvian village, the Russian name of which is Trumany. **3.** Possibly an Americanized spelling of German **Trumann**, a variant of TRAUT-MANN.

Trumbauer (141) **1.** Variant spelling of German **Trambauer**, a distinguishing name for a farmer (see BAUER) living by the Traun river in Upper Bavaria. **2.** German: unflattering nickname from Middle High German *trâme* 'beam', 'rafter' + *bûr* 'farmer', denoting a crude peasant.

Trumble (1073) English and Scottish: from an unrecorded Old English personal name, *Trumbeald*, composed of the elements *trum* 'strong', 'firm' + *beald* 'bold', 'brave'.

Trumbly (105) Americanized spelling of French TREMBLAY.

Trumbo (609) French (Alsatian) form of German TRUMBAUER.

Trumbore (102) Americanized spelling of German **Trambauer** (see TRUMBAUER).

Trumbower (114) Americanized spelling of German **Trambauer** (see TRUMBAUER).

Trumbull (931) English and Scottish: variant of TRUMBLE.

Trumm (152) German: metonymic occupational name for a drummer, from Middle High German *trom(m)e*, *trumpe* 'drum'.

Trummer (108) German: occupational name for a drummer or trumpeter, from the agent derivative of Middle High German *trumme*, *trumbe* 'drum', 'trumpet'.

GIVEN NAMES German 11%. *Wolfram* (2), *Gunther*, *Hans*, *Wolf*.

Trump (1354) **1.** English (Devon): metonymic occupational name for a trumpeter, from Middle English *trumpe* 'trumpet'. **2.** German (Bavaria): metonymic occupational name for a drummer, from Middle High German *trumpe* 'drum'.

Trumper (101) English: occupational name for a trumpeter, from Old French *trumpeur*.

GIVEN NAMES French 8%. *Antoine*, *Vernice*.

Trumpower (142) Americanized form of German **Trambauer** (see TRUMBAUER).

Trumpy (103) Swiss German (**Trümpy**, also **Trümpi**): nickname for a slow, relaxed person.

GIVEN NAMES French 4%. *Colette*, *Monique*.

Trundle (141) **1.** English (Essex, Cambridgeshire): possibly a variant of **Trendall**, a topographic name for someone who lived by a well, earthwork, stone circle, or other circular feature, from Middle English *trendel*, *trandle* 'circle' (Old English *trendel*). **2.** Possibly an altered spelling of South German **Tröndle**, a variant of **Trendle**, a nickname for a tearful person, from *Träne* 'tear' + the diminutive suffix *-l*.

Trundy (120) Possibly of English origin but unexplained.

Trunk (342) **1.** German: nickname for a heavy drinker, from Middle High German *trinken* 'to drink'. **2.** Jewish (Ashkenazic): metonymic occupational name or nickname from German *Trunk* 'drink' (see 1 above).

GIVEN NAME German 4%. *Erhard*.

Trunnell (254) English: unexplained; possibly a variant of TRUNDLE.

Trunzo (315) Italian: possibly a nickname for a worthless person, from Calabrian *trunzu* 'cabbage stalk', 'apple core'.

GIVEN NAMES Italian 11%. *Caesar* (3), *Angelo* (2), *Natale* (2), *Carmine*, *Ceasar*, *Ettore*, *Serafino*, *Vittorio*.

Truong (4064) Vietnamese (**Trương**): unexplained.

GIVEN NAMES Vietnamese 67%; Chinese 11%. *Thanh* (67), *Hung* (59), *Hoa* (47), *Minh* (46), *Tuan* (35), *Dung* (34), *Anh* (31), *Duc* (31), *Hai* (29), *Long* (29), *Quang* (27), *Trung* (27), *Tam* (22), *Phong* (17), *Nam* (16), *Thai* (11), *Tinh* (9), *Sinh* (8), *Tuong* (8), *Manh* (5), *Sieu* (4), *Cho* (3), *Thach* (3); *Hong* (29), *Chi* (10), *Sang* (10), *Man* (6), *Dong* (5), *Ho* (4), *Hon* (4), *Chan* (3), *Chu* (3), *Hang* (3), *Hua* (3), *Tong* (3).

Trupiano (257) Italian (Calabrian and Sicilian): variant of TROPEANO.

GIVEN NAMES Italian 27%. *Vito* (6), *Sal* (4), *Salvatore* (3), *Agostino* (2), *Antonino* (2), *Damiano* (2), *Grazia* (2), *Mario* (2), *Antonio*, *Ciro*, *Cristoforo*, *Gaetano*, *Gaspare*, *Rosario*.

Trupp (260) English: variant of THORPE.

GIVEN NAMES German 4%. *Hans*, *Hermann*, *Reinhold*.

Truran (123) English (Cornish): unexplained.

Truscott (449) Cornish: habitational name from Truscott in the parish of St. Stephens by Launceston, named from Cornish *dres* 'beyond' + *cuit* 'wood'.

Trush (120) Ukrainian: nickname for a coward, from *trush* 'rabbit'.

GIVEN NAMES Russian 4%. *Sergey*, *Vladimir*, *Yevgeniy*.

Truskowski (157) Variant of Polish TRUSZ-KOWSKI.

GIVEN NAME Polish 4%. *Casimir*.

Trusler (239) English: according to Reaney, this is a variant of TRUSLOW.

Truslow (320) English: variant of **Truslove**, a metonymic occupational name for a wolf-hunter, from Old French *tr(o)usser* 'to truss or bind', 'to carry off' + Anglo-Norman French *love* 'wolf'.

Truss (498) **1.** English: occupational nickname for a peddler, from Old French *trousse* 'bundle', 'pack'. **2.** Ukrainian: nickname from *trus* 'rabbit', typically applied to someone thought to be a coward.

Trussell (1472) English (East Midlands): of uncertain origin; perhaps from Old French *troussel*, Middle English *trussel* in the sense 'packet', and hence an occupational nickname for a peddler, or from the same word in the sense 'stamp', 'mould (for stamping coins)', and hence an occupational name for a minter. Alternatively, it may be from a nickname representing a variant of **Thrussell**, from Middle English *throstle* 'thrush', given probably to a cheerful person, the bird being noted for its cheerful song.

Trust (206) **1.** English (Devon): unexplained; perhaps a variant of **Trist**, from Middle English *triste* 'hunting station' (Old French *triste*), hence probably a metonymic occupational name for someone whose job was to look after the hounds or organize the hunt. **2.** Altered form of TROST.

Trusty (1212) English: unexplained.

Truszkowski (194) Polish: habitational name for someone from Truszków in Lublin voivodeship.

GIVEN NAMES Polish 15%. *Jerzy* (2), *Boguslaw*, *Dariusz*, *Eugeniusz*, *Jacek*, *Jadwiga*, *Jozef*, *Ryszard*, *Tadeusz*, *Wieslaw*, *Wladyslaw*.

Truxal (126) Probably an altered spelling of TROXEL.

Truxillo (159) Spanish: variant spelling of TRUJILLO.

GIVEN NAMES French 4%. *Cecile*, *Ulysse*.

Tryba (168) Polish: topographic name, a derivative of *tryb* 'balk', 'strip of raised land between neighboring fields'.

GIVEN NAMES Polish 5%. *Bogdan*, *Halina*, *Jozef*, *Pawel*.

Trybus (163) Polish (also **Trybuś**): nickname from Polish dialect *trybus* 'corpulent man', or from Old Polish *trybus* 'tripod'.
GIVEN NAMES Polish 4%. *Krzysztof, Mariola.*

Trygg (107) **1.** Scandinavian: from the Old Norse byname *Tryggr* 'trustworthy', 'faithful'. **2.** English: variant of TRIGG.
GIVEN NAMES Scandinavian 6%. *Helmer, Hjordis.*

Trygstad (173) Norwegian: habitational name from any of several farmsteads in Trøndelag, so named from the Old Norse personal name *Tryggvi* meaning 'reliable', 'fearless', or an unidentified first element + Old Norse *staðr* 'farmstead', 'dwelling'.
GIVEN NAMES Scandinavian 5%. *Arndt* (2), *Tor.*

Tryon (1549) English: of Dutch origin and uncertain derivation.
FOREBEARS A Northamptonshire, England, family of this name trace their descent from Peter Trieon (d. 1611), who went to England from the Netherlands *c.*1562. His son, Moses Tryon, was high sheriff of Northamptonshire in 1624.
William Tryon (b.1729 in Surrey, England) was the last provincial governor of NY; he gave his name to Tryon Co., the district which took in the Mohawk Valley; after the American Revolution this huge area was split into Montgomery, Fulton, and other counties.

Trzaska (146) Polish: nickname for a thin person, from Polish *trzaska* 'lath', 'chip (or splinter) of wood'; compare the idiom *chudy jak trzaska* 'as thin as a lath'.
GIVEN NAMES Polish 17%. *Witold* (3), *Irena, Krzysztof, Wieslaw, Zdzislaw.*

Trzcinski (341) Polish (**Trzciński**): habitational name from any of various places called Trzcin (in Toruń voivodeship), Trzciniec, Trzcińsko, and other similar names, all derived from *trzcina* 'reed'.
GIVEN NAMES Polish 7%. *Zygmunt* (2), *Agnieszka, Halina, Zigmunt.*

Trzebiatowski (156) Polish: habitational name from a place called Trzebiatów in Szczecin voivodeship, or another near Opoczno.

Trzeciak (235) Polish: from *Trzeciak*, presumably originally a byname for a third child or third son, from Polish *trzeci* 'third'.
GIVEN NAMES Polish 7%; German 5%. *Franciszek, Jerzy, Marcin, Wladyslaw, Zbigniew; Gerda, Gunter, Hannelore, Kurt, Ralf.*

Tsai (2439) **1.** Chinese 蔡: variant of CAI 1. **2.** Chinese 柴: Cantonese variant of CHAI.
GIVEN NAMES Chinese 24%. *Ming* (20), *Ching* (6), *Wei* (5), *Chen* (4), *Chin* (4), *Tsung* (4), *Wen* (4), *Yong* (4), *Cheng* (3), *Chi* (3), *Chih* (3), *Hong* (3).

Tsang (1416) **1.** Chinese 曾: variant of ZENG. **2.** Chinese 臧: variant of CHONG.

GIVEN NAMES Chinese 33%; Vietnamese 5%. *Hing* (9), *Chi* (7), *Wai* (7), *Kwan* (5), *Kwok* (5), *Kwong* (5), *Man* (5), *Sing* (5), *Wing* (5), *Yee* (5), *Cheong* (4), *Ping* (4); *Chung* (9), *Kwok Fai* (2), *Kwok Wai, Moon, Shiu, Tam, Tuk, Tuong, Yiu, Yuet; Hung* (4), *Lap* (3), *Sau* (3), *Hoi* (2), *Lam* (2), *Tung* (2), *Chau, Khanh, Kiet, Lien, Linh, Mau.*

Tsao (619) Chinese 曹: variant of CAO.
GIVEN NAMES Chinese 14%. *Chee* (2), *Cheng* (2), *Chin* (2), *Ching-Chi* (2), *Ding* (2), *Hsi* (2), *Jian Lin* (2), *Chen, Cheng-Chung, Chi Ching, Chin Yu, Ching.*

Tsay (139) Chinese 蔡: variant of CAI 1.
GIVEN NAMES Chinese 30%. *Wenyu* (2), *Chia-Yuan, Ching, Jiunn, Kuen, Lian, Liang, Ming, Sheng, Shin, Ting, Tsong.*

Tschannen (117) South German and Swiss German: from a dialect variant of the French personal name *Jean* (see JOHN).
GIVEN NAMES German 6%. *Erwin, Heinz.*

Tschantz (187) South German and Swiss German: from a dialect variant of the French personal name *Jean* (see JOHN).

Tschanz (140) South German and Swiss German: variant spelling of TSCHANTZ.
GIVEN NAMES French 7%; German 6%. *Etienne* (2), *Alain; Erwin, Otto, Ulrich.*

Tschappat (115) Swiss German (Bern) (**Tschäppät**): unexplained.

Tschetter (487) German (Liechtenstein): unexplained. This name was once also common in Russia.

Tschida (673) German (Austrian) form of an unidentified Slavic name.

Tschirhart (324) German: from a hybrid form of the personal name GERARD, consisting of a representation of the pronunciation of *Gér-*, from the French form of the name (*Gérard*) + the Germanic component *hart* 'hardy', 'brave', 'strong', from the German cognate (*Gerhard*).

Tschoepe (121) Swiss German: variant of TSCHOPP.
GIVEN NAMES Scandinavian 5%; German 5%. *Hilmar* (2); *Erwin* (2).

Tschopp (194) Swiss German: probably from a metonymic occupational name for a jacket maker, from Middle High German *jop(p)e, juppe* 'jacket' (*schōpe, schoppe*), a loanword from Italian *g(i)ubba*; in some instances the surname may have arisen from a nickname for someone who wore jackets that were remarkable.
GIVEN NAMES German 6%. *Erwin, Fritz, Juerg, Manfred.*

Tschudy (183) German: probably a nickname from southern German *Tschaude* 'messy', denoting someone with tousled, untidy hair, or a silly person.

Tse (1323) Chinese 谢: variant of XIE 1.
GIVEN NAMES Chinese 36%. *Wai* (11), *Wing* (11), *Kwok* (8), *Siu* (7), *Kam* (6), *Chung* (5), *Lai* (5), *Man* (5), *Chiu* (4), *Choi* (4), *Chun* (4), *Kin* (4), *Ping* (4), *Yiu* (4), *Pak* (2), *Woon* (2), *Cho, Chong, Moon, Shiu, Sik, Toy, Waiyee.*

Tseng (1143) Chinese 曾: variant of ZENG.
GIVEN NAMES Chinese 21%. *Ching* (3), *Chien* (2), *Hui-Mei* (2), *Kuo* (2), *Kuo-Hua* (2), *Li* (2), *Lung* (2), *Ming* (2), *Yin* (2), *Chen, Cheng, Cheng-Chih.*

Tshudy (103) Americanized spelling of German TSCHUDY.

Tso (394) **1.** Chinese 曹: Cantonese variant of CAO. **2.** Navajo: unexplained.
GIVEN NAMES Chinese 21%. *Chun* (2), *Fong* (2), *Jin* (2), *Li* (2), *Li-Ming* (2), *Man* (2), *Wai* (2), *Wing* (2), *Chao, Cheong, Chuen, Chung Ching.*

Tsoi (203) Chinese 蔡: a Cantonese spelling of CAI.
GIVEN NAMES Chinese 34%. *Wing* (3), *Hing* (2), *Chan, Cheung, Chi, Chi Man, Chuen, Chung Man, Hon, Kam Cheung, Kwan, Lai Ying, Tung.*

Tsosie (176) Navajo: unexplained.

Tsou (212) Chinese 邹: variant of ZOU.
GIVEN NAMES Chinese 16%. *Chi, Chi-Jen, Chia-Lin, Chien-Hung, Ching, Hsuan, Jau, Ji, Kang, Mei Hua, Ming, Ping.*

Tsu (101) Chinese (pinyin **Zu**) 祖: from the character for 'ancestor', *zu*. In ancient China a 'style name' was given when a person reached majority: the twentieth birthday for a boy, and the fifteenth birthday for a girl. During the Shang dynasty (1766–1122 BC), the style name of several kings contained the character *zu*, and the surname was derived from this usage.
GIVEN NAMES Chinese 12%; Vietnamese 9%. *Chen, Chi, Ching, Kin, Kung, Kuo, Yuk; Mui* (2), *Loc.*

Tsuchida (81) Japanese: 'rice paddy of earth'; a habitational name taken from several locations so named in Ōmi (now Shiga Prefecture).

Tsuchiya (187) Japanese: 'earthen house'; taken from a village in Sagami (now Kanagawa prefecture). Bearers are descendants of the TAIRA clan. The name is found mainly in the Tōkyō area and west-central Japan.
GIVEN NAMES Japanese 67%. *Atsushi* (2), *Hiroko* (2), *Kazuo* (2), *Mitsuko* (2), *Shinsuke* (2), *Takashi* (2), *Yoshiaki* (2), *Akihiro, Akio, Akira, Ayako, Daisuke.*

Tsuda (173) Japanese: from a common place name meaning 'harbor rice paddy'. Some bearers are descended from the SASAKI, ODA, and other families. The surname is found mainly in northern Japan.
GIVEN NAMES Japanese 55%. *Takeshi* (3), *Akira* (2), *Kazuo* (2), *Satoru* (2), *Tomio* (2), *Chiyoko, Daisuke, Eishi, Hiroyuki, Hitoshi, Isami, Iwao.*

Tsui (681) **1.** Chinese 徐: variant of XU 1. **2.** Chinese 崔: variant of Cui.
GIVEN NAMES Chinese 34%. *Wai* (4), *Chin* (3), *Ching* (3), *Chun* (3), *Chung* (3), *Kin* (3), *Kwai* (3), *Kwok* (3), *Lam* (3), *Mei* (3), *Chi* (2), *Chun Wah* (2), *Fook* (2), *Hsiang* (2), *Pang* (2); *Chau, Nam, To, Woon, Yuet.*

Tsuji (267) Japanese: 'crossroad'; variously written. The surname is found mostly in western Japan. Some bearers are of samurai origin, particularly descendants of a daimyō family of Hiroshima prefecture.
GIVEN NAMES Japanese 63%. *Yukiyo* (4), *Junko* (3), *Naoki* (3), *Haruo* (2), *Hisako* (2), *Jiro* (2), *Junichi* (2), *Kiyoshi* (2), *Masayuki* (2), *Ryuhei* (2), *Takashi* (2), *Takeo* (2).

Tsukamoto (197) Japanese: 'by the mound'; the name originated in two places: in Kawachi, descending from the Tachibana family, and in Chikugo, with members of the TAIRA clan.
GIVEN NAMES Japanese 63%. *Yuji* (5), *Shigeo* (3), *Takashi* (3), *Yuko* (3), *Akio* (2), *Atsushi* (2), *Jiro* (2), *Keiko* (2), *Minoru* (2), *Shiro* (2), *Yoshio* (2), *Yugi* (2).

Tsutsui (121) Japanese: habitational name meaning 'round well', taken from a village in Yamato, where the name is still found.
GIVEN NAMES Japanese 55%. *Kazuo* (2), *Masaaki* (2), *Nobuyoshi* (2), *Osamu* (2), *Seiichi* (2), *Shinjiro* (2), *Shunichi* (2), *Akinori, Etsuko, Hideo, Izumi, Kinu*.

Tsutsumi (115) Japanese: 'dike'; variously written and common as a place name throughout Japan. The surname is found mostly in the island of Kyūshū. Some bearers have very ancient connections. The name *Shiratsutsumi* is recorded in the Shinsen shōjiroku.
GIVEN NAMES Japanese 62%. *Hideki* (2), *Hiroyuki* (2), *Seiji* (2), *Fumiko, Hideo, Hiro, Hiroki, Hitomi, Kazuhiro, Kazuyoshi, Keiji, Kentaro*.

Tu (1388) **1.** Chinese 涂: from the name of the Tu river, a tributary of the Yangtze. **2.** Chinese 屠: from one of the characters in the name of the ancient city of Zoutu. The legendary emperor Huang Di (2697–2595 BC) used this city as a military base. Both characters of the city name, Zou (see ZOU) and Tu, were adopted as surnames. **3.** Chinese: variant of DU. **4.** Vietnamese: unexplained.
GIVEN NAMES Vietnamese 34%; Chinese 28%. *Muoi* (14), *Anh* (10), *Dung* (8), *Hung* (8), *Minh* (8), *Thanh* (8), *Hue* (7), *Tuan* (6), *Ha* (5), *Hoa* (5), *Lien* (5), *Linh* (5); *Chan* (5), *Chi* (4), *Hong* (4), *Qiang* (3), *Weiming* (3), *Cheng* (2), *Chu* (2), *Chuan* (2), *Hon* (2), *Jin* (2), *Liwei* (2), *Ping* (2); *Chung* (5), *Thai* (4), *Tuong* (4), *Nam* (3), *Phong* (2), *Sinh* (2), *Chang Yol, Min, Shen, Tian, Uyen*.

Tuan (131) **1.** Chinese: see DUAN. **2.** Vietnamese: unexplained.
GIVEN NAMES Chinese 20%; Vietnamese 14%. *Cheng, Chia, Ching, Kao, Kwang, Lian, Mei, Ming, Tsai, Yung*; *Bui* (2), *Nguyen* (2), *Phan* (2), *Bang, Hoang, Huynh, Yen*.

Tuazon (182) Filipino (**Tuazón**): Castilianized variant of Filipino **Tuason** 'eldest grandson'.
GIVEN NAMES Spanish 49%. *Jaime* (3), *Jose* (3), *Angelita* (2), *Angelito* (2), *Prudencio* (2), *Raul* (2), *Regino* (2), *Romeo* (2), *Salvador* (2), *Ador, Almario, Amado, Arturo*.

Tubb (604) English: from the Middle English personal name *Tubbe*, apparently derived from either Old Norse *Tubbi* or Old English *Tubba* (an unattested form, evidence for which is found in the place name Tubney, Berkshire). There is no evidence to support the suggestion that it might be a metonymic occupational name or nickname from Middle English *tub* 'barrel'.

Tubbesing (105) German: Westphalian habitational name from Tubsiek, a local place name composed of *tub* 'bog' + *siek* 'swamp'.
GIVEN NAME Scandinavian 6%; German 4%. *Otto*.

Tubbs (4075) English: patronymic from the personal name *Tubbe* (see TUBB).

Tubergen (113) Dutch (**Van Tubergen**): habitational name from Tubbergen in Overijssel.

Tuberville (155) English: variant of TURBERVILLE.

Tubman (278) English: occupational name for a cooper, from Middle English *tubbe* 'tub' + *man* 'man'.

Tubridy (122) Irish (County Clare): reduced form of **O'Tubridy**, an Anglicized form of Gaelic **Ó Tiobraide** 'descendant of *Tiobraid*', a personal name apparently from *tiobraid* 'well', 'fount'.
GIVEN NAME Irish 8%. *Eamon*.

Tucci (1498) Italian: patronymic or plural form of TUCCIO.
GIVEN NAMES Italian 11%. *Angelo* (6), *Rocco* (4), *Antonio* (3), *Luigi* (3), *Umberto* (3), *Sal* (2), *Aldo, Amedeo, Aniello, Caesar, Carlo, Carmine*.

Tucciarone (249) Italian: from an augmentative form of TUCCIO.
GIVEN NAMES Italian 17%. *Angelo* (4), *Biagio* (3), *Silvio* (2), *Dino, Giuseppe, Pasquale, Salvatore, Vito*.

Tuccillo (249) Italian (Tuscany and Campania): from a pet form of the personal name TUCCIO.
GIVEN NAMES Italian 12%. *Aldo, Angelo, Gabriella, Gilda, Raffaele, Sal*.

Tuccio (146) Italian: from a short form of any of various personal names ending with the hypocoristic suffix *-(t)uccio*, for example *Albertuccio, Robertuccio*.
GIVEN NAMES Italian 10%. *Gilda, Rocco, Salvatore, Vincenza*.

Tucek (169) Czech (**Tuček**): nickname for a plump person, from a diminutive of *tučný* 'fat'.

Tuch (191) **1.** North German (also **Tüch**): metonymic occupational name from Middle Low German *tuch* 'stuff', 'tack', 'clothes'. **2.** German and Jewish (Ashkenazic): metonymic occupational name for a cloth merchant, from Middle High German *tuoch*, German *Tuch*, Yiddish *tukh* 'cloth', 'linen'.

Tuchman (299) German (**Tuchmann**) and Jewish (Ashkenazic): occupational name for a cloth merchant (see TUCH).
GIVEN NAMES Jewish 11%. *Sol* (2), *Hyman, Mayer, Mendel, Miriam, Tzvi, Zvi*.

Tucholski (192) Polish and Jewish (Ashkenazic): habitational name for someone from Tuchola in Bydgoszcz voivodeship.
GIVEN NAMES German 4%. *Florian, Helmut*.

Tuchscherer (153) German: occupational name for a cloth cutter or merchant, from Middle High German *tuoch* 'cloth' + an agent derivative of *schern* 'to cut'.
GIVEN NAMES German 6%. *Ewald, Gerd, Konrad*.

Tuck (3563) **1.** English: from the Old Norse personal name *Tóki*, of uncertain origin, perhaps a short form of *þorkell* (see TURKEL). **2.** Altered spelling of German and Jewish TUCH.

Tucker (56636) **1.** English (chiefly southwestern England and South Wales): occupational name for a fuller, from an agent derivative of Middle English *tuck(en)* 'to full cloth' (Old English *tūcian* 'to torment'). This was the term used for the process in the Middle Ages in southwestern England, and the surname is more common there than elsewhere. Compare FULLER and WALKER. **2.** Americanized form of Jewish To(c)ker (see TOKARZ). **3.** Irish: Anglicized form of Gaelic **Ó Tuachair** 'descendant of *Tuachar*', a personal name composed of the elements *tuath* 'people' + *car* 'dear', 'beloved'. **4.** Possibly also an Americanized form of German **Tucher**, from an occupational name for a cloth maker or merchant, from an agent derivative of Middle High German *tuoch* 'cloth'.

Tuckerman (224) English: variant of TUCKER 1.

Tuckett (223) English (Devon): unexplained. Reaney and Wilson suggest that this may be from an Anglo-Scandinavian personal name *Tukka*, but the distribution in England makes a Scandinavian connection unlikely.

Tuckey (286) English: from the Old Norse personal name *Tóki* (see TUCK).

Tuckman (127) Americanized spelling of German and Ashkenazic Jewish **Tuchmann** (see TUCHMAN).
GIVEN NAMES Jewish 6%; German 4%. *Ari; Frieda*.

Tuckness (108) English: unexplained.

Tudisco (163) Southern Italian: variant of TEDESCO.
GIVEN NAMES Italian 21%. *Alberto, Antonio* (2), *Ciro* (2), *Santina* (2), *Biagio, Carmine, Elio, Gaetano, Nicoletta, Rocco, Sal, Tino, Vito*.

Tudor (2153) Welsh: from the personal name *Tudur*, which is of ancient Celtic origin and unexplained etymology. It has sometimes been erroneously taken as a Welsh equivalent of Latin *Theodorus*,

Greek *Theodōros* (see THEODORE), for which the usual Welsh form is *Tewdwr*.

FOREBEARS The Tudor royal family, English sovereigns from the accession of Henry VII in 1485 to the death of Elizabeth I in 1603, were of Welsh origin, being descended from Owain ap Maredudd ap Tudur, who held lands at Penmynydd in Anglesey.

Tuel (347) **1.** Breton: from a personal name composed of the elements *tut* 'people' + *wal* 'valor'. The name was borne by a Saint Tudal, who came from Britain and became one of the early saints of Brittany. **2.** French: southwestern variant of **Tual**, from an occupational name for a seller of pipes, Old French *tuel*.

Tuell (456) **1.** German (**Tüll**): nickname from Slavic (Old Slavic *toliti* 'to soothe or calm'). **2.** See TULL 3.

Tueller (145) German (**Tüller**): see TULLER.

Tuerk (118) German (**Türk**): see TURK.

GIVEN NAMES German 9%. *Helmut, Markus.*

Tufano (401) Italian: from a variant of the personal name *Teofano*, from Greek *Theophanēs*. Compare TIFFANY.

GIVEN NAMES Italian 19%. *Carmine* (4), *Angelo* (2), *Salvatore* (2), *Vincenzo* (2), *Vito* (2), *Aniello, Biagio, Carlo, Caterina, Crescenzo, Cristoforo, Gaetano.*

Tufaro (121) Italian: occupational name for someone who quarried or sold tufa (a kind of volcanic rock used as a building material), from a derivative of Italian *tufo*.

GIVEN NAMES Italian 15%. *Angelo* (2), *Carmine.*

Tuff (198) English: probably a variant of TUFT.

Tufford (105) English: unexplained; possibly a habitational name from a lost or unidentified place.

Tufo (159) Italian: from *tufo* 'tufa' (a kind of volcanic rock used as a building material), either a topographic name for someone who lived in an area of tufa, or a metonymic occupational name for someone who quarried tufa.

GIVEN NAMES Italian 12%. *Rocco* (2), *Sal* (2), *Angelo, Carlo, Francesca, Vincenzo.*

Tuft (290) **1.** English (Midlands): possibly a topographical name from Middle English *tufte, tuffe* 'clump of trees or bushes'. This is an element of minor place names and field names in various counties. **2.** Norwegian: habitational name from any of several farmsteads so named, from Old Norse *tupt* 'site', 'lot'. **3.** Possibly an altered spelling of South German **Duft**, from a topographic name meaning 'swamp', 'moor'.

Tufte (238) Norwegian: habitational name from any of fifteen or more farmsteads so named, a variant of TUFT.

GIVEN NAME Scandinavian 4%. *Obert* (2).

Tufts (1169) English (Norfolk): variant of TUFT.

Tuggle (2303) Possibly an altered spelling of German **Tügel**, a metonymic occupational name for a saddler or harness maker, from Low German *Tügel* 'rein', 'bridle'; or from *Tögl*, of uncertain origin.

Tugman (144) Northern English: unexplained.

Tugwell (271) English: apparently an occupational nickname for a TUCKER.

Tuhy (121) Irish: variant spelling of TOOHEY.

Tuinstra (228) Frisian: topographic name for someone who lived by a garden or enclosure, Frisian *tuin*, or a habitational name for someone from a place called Tuin.

Tuite (416) Irish (of Norman origin): unexplained; probably a habitational name from an unidentified place in England or northern France.

GIVEN NAMES Irish 5%. *Brendan, Conan.*

Tukes (93) **1.** Probably an altered form of English **Tuke**, from the Old Norse personal name *Tóki*. **2.** Perhaps also an altered spelling of the German personal name **Dux**, or **Düx**, from a short form of *Benedictus* (see BENEDICT).

Tuley (542) English (Yorkshire): unexplained.

Tulin (135) Swedish: unexplained.

GIVEN NAMES Jewish 4%. *Barak, Miriam.*

Tulip (122) English (Northumberland and Durham): unexplained; just possibly a late formation from the plant name, although tulips were not introduced into western Europe until the 16th century.

Tulk (136) **1.** German: variant of **Tolk**, **Tölke**, from the Slavic verb *toliti* 'to soothe'. Compare TOELKE. **2.** Perhaps an altered spelling of German **Tolk**, an occupational name for an interpreter, Middle Low German *tolk, tollik*. **3.** Altered spelling of German **Tölk** or **Tolk**, a habitational name from places so called in former East Prussia.

Tull (2003) **1.** English: of uncertain origin, possibly from an unrecorded late survival of the Old English personal name *Tula*. **2.** South German (**Tüll**): from a nickname for someone who was patient, from Middle High German *dult* 'patience'; or from a personal name formed with the same word; or from Middle High German *tult, dult* 'fair', 'festival' (Bavarian *Dult*). **3.** South German: nickname for a stubborn man, *Tull*. **4.** Altered spelling of German TOLL.

Tullar (219) Variant spelling, under Slavic influence, of German **Tüller** (see TULLER).

Tuller (555) **1.** German (**Tüller**): topographic name from Middle High German *tülle* 'fence'. **2.** Altered spelling of German **Duller**, a nickname for someone who was patient, from an agent derivative of Middle High German *dult* 'patience'; or a habitational name for someone from Dullen in Württemberg; or from an agent derivative of Middle High German *tult* 'fair', 'festival' (Bavarian *Dult*), probably denoting someone who performed or peddled his wares at such events; or (in southern Germany) from a topographic name from *Tull* 'elevation', 'knoll'.

Tulley (353) English: variant spelling of TULLY.

Tulli (100) Italian: patronymic or plural form of TULLIO.

GIVEN NAMES Italian 10%. *Antonietta, Giuseppe, Palma.*

Tullier (283) French: from an occupational name for a maker or layer of tiles, from an agent derivative of Old French *tieule* 'tile', 'plaque'.

GIVEN NAMES French 6%. *Damien, Ignace, Pierre.*

Tullio (156) Italian: from the personal name *Tullio*, Latin *Tullius*, a derivative of the Latin name *Tullus*, which was probably of Etruscan origin.

GIVEN NAMES Italian 10%. *Cesare* (2), *Antonella, Antonio, Domenic, Gilda, Vito.*

Tullis (1506) Scottish: unexplained.

Tullius (193) German or Dutch: humanistic name from the Latin personal name *Tullius* (see TULLIO).

Tullo (252) Italian: variant of TULLIO, or perhaps from a personal name such as *Antullo*, a pet form of *Antonio* (see ANTHONY), or *Robertullo*, a pet form of *Roberto* (see ROBERTO).

GIVEN NAMES Italian 19%. *Vito* (6), *Angelo* (3), *Carmine, Pasquale, Sal.*

Tulloch (513) Scottish: habitational name from a place near Dingwall on the Firth of Cromarty, named with Gaelic *tulach* 'hillock', 'mound', or from any of various other minor places named with this element.

Tullock (314) Variant of Scottish TULLOCH.

Tullos (1115) Probably an altered form, under French influence, of Scottish TULLOCH.

Tulloss (118) See TULLOS.

Tully (3573) **1.** Irish (Ulster): reduced Anglicized form of Gaelic **Ó Taithligh** 'descendant of *Taithleach*', a byname meaning 'quiet', 'peaceable'. **2.** Irish: reduced Anglicized form of Gaelic **Ó Maol Tuile** 'descendant of the devotee of the will of God' (from *toil* 'will of God'). **3.** Scottish: habitational name from any of various places called Tullo in eastern Scotland.

Tulp (116) Dutch: metonymic occupational name for a grower or seller of tulips, Low German *tulp*.

Tuma (939) **1.** Czech (**Tůma**) and Polish: from a variant of the personal name *Tomáš*, Polish *Tomasz* (see THOMAS). This surname is also found in Slovenia. **2.** Arabic: from *Tūma*, Arabic form of THOMAS.

Tuman (237) Polish: probably a derivative of the personal name *Tomasz* (see THOMAS), but perhaps also a nickname meaning 'duffer', 'nitwit', from Polish *tuman* 'cloud of dust'.

Tumbarello (101) Italian: nickname from *tombarello* 'dolphin', perhaps applied to an exuberant person.

GIVEN NAMES Italian 22%. *Angelo* (2), *Vito* (2), *Ignazio, Rocco, Salvatore.*

Tumbleson (348) English: variant spelling of **Tombleson**, a variant of TOMLINSON.

Tumblin (353) Altered spelling of English TOMBLIN.

Tumey (293) Possibly an altered spelling of German **Tümme**, a variant of THIEME, or from a nickname from Middle High German *tumbe* 'dumb', 'inexperienced', 'naive'; 'mute'.

Tuminello (241) Italian: from a pet form of the personal name *Tumino*, itself a pet form of TOMEO.

GIVEN NAMES Italian 6%. *Angelo, Camillo.*

Tumlin (446) English: variant spelling of TOMLIN.

Tumlinson (369) Variant spelling of English TOMLINSON.

Tumminello (311) Italian: variant spelling of TUMINELLO.

GIVEN NAMES Italian 18%. *Santo* (3), *Salvatore* (2), *Carlo, Domenic, Enrico, Gaspare, Giulio, Giuseppe, Matteo, Pietro, Vincenzo.*

Tumminia (138) Italian (Sicily): from Sicilian *tumminia, tumunia*, denoting a type of wheat which ripens in three months, from medieval Greek *trimēnia* 'three months', hence a topographic name or a metonymic occupational name for a grower of or dealer in such wheat.

GIVEN NAMES Italian 13%. *Salvatore* (2), *Angelo, Nicolina, Nicolo, Sal.*

Tummons (106) English: patronymic from a status name meaning either 'man of the village or settlement', Middle English *tuneman* (Old English *tūnmann*), or a status name meaning 'servant (Middle English *man*) of Tom'.

Tumolo (183) Italian: topographic name from *tumolo* 'mound', 'tumulus', a variant of *tomolo*, which is derived from medieval Latin *tomulus, tumulus*.

GIVEN NAMES Italian 9%. *Salvatore* (2), *Giovina, Saverio.*

Tumulty (145) Irish: reduced Anglicized form of Gaelic **Mac Tomaltaigh** or **Ó Tomaltaigh** 'son' or 'descendant of *Tomaltach*', a byname meaning 'glutton', from *tomaltach* 'bulky'.

Tun (123) **1.** Mexican: unexplained; probably from a native American language. **2.** Cambodian or other southeastern Asian: unexplained.

GIVEN NAMES Southeast Asian 15%; Spanish 12%. *Carlos* (2), *Fernando, Fidencio, Julio, Manuel, Orlando, Pablo; Khin* (3), *Sein* (2), *Han, Kyaw, Maung, Hoeun, Sokheng, Ying Kit.*

Tune (717) **1.** English: variant of TOWNE. **2.** French (Champagne): possibly from a shortened form of the personal name *Opportune*, which was borne by an 8th-century abbess of Montreuil.

Tunell (100) English: variant spelling of TUNNELL.

Tung (1004) **1.** Chinese 董: variant of DONG 1. **2.** Chinese: variant of TONG 3. 童 **3.** Chinese: variant of TONG 4. 佟

GIVEN NAMES Chinese 25%. *Wen* (6), *Ling* (4), *Wing* (4), *Chin* (3), *Ching* (3), *Wei* (3), *Chen* (2), *Cheng* (2), *Cheng-Yu* (2), *Chi* (2), *Hang* (2), *Hou* (2).

Tungate (279) English (Norfolk): habitational name from Tungate, a minor place near North Walsham, named from Middle English *toun* 'village', 'settlement' + *gate* 'gate'.

Tunick (222) Belorussian and Jewish (from Belarus): variant of **Tunik**, which is said to be a habitational name from the name of a town near Minsk. The surname is strongly associated with the town of Stolbtsy in Belarus.

GIVEN NAMES Jewish 4%. *Iren, Sol.*

Tuning (143) Possibly a respelling or a variant of German *Thunig*, a pet form of the personal name *Anton* (see ANTHONY).

Tunis (358) Dutch: from a variant of the personal name *Teunis* (see TEUNISSEN).

Tunison (373) Possibly an altered form of Dutch **Tunnesen**, a variant of TEUNISSEN, or of English TENNYSON.

Tunks (216) **1.** English: unexplained; perhaps a variant of **Tongs**, itself a variant of TONG 6. **2.** Possibly an altered spelling of German **Dungs**, a variant of DUNG.

Tunnell (1193) English: from an unrecorded Old English female personal name composed of the elements *tūn* 'settlement', 'village' + *hild* 'strife', 'battle'.

Tunney (496) Irish (Sligo, now rare): reduced form of **O'Tunney**, an Anglicized form of Gaelic **Ó Tonnaigh** 'descendant of *Tonnach*', a personal name meaning either 'billowy' (from *tonn* 'wave') or 'shining'.

Tunnicliff (124) English: habitational name from Tonacliffe in Lancashire, recorded in 1246 as *Tunwal(e)clif*, from Old English *tūn* 'enclosure', 'settlement' + *wæll(a)* 'spring', 'stream' + *clif* 'bank', 'slope'.

Tunstall (1110) English (chiefly in Lancashire and Yorkshire): habitational name from any of the numerous places, for example in Lancashire, North and East Yorkshire, County Durham, Humberside, Kent, Norfolk, Shropshire, Staffordshire, and Suffolk, so named from an Old English *tūn-st(e)all* 'site of a farm'.

Tunstill (115) English: variant spelling of TUNSTALL.

Tuohey (215) Irish: variant spelling of TOOHEY.

Tuohy (691) Irish: variant spelling of TOOHEY.

GIVEN NAMES Irish 8%. *Brendan* (2), *Liam* (2), *Dermot, Niamh, Seamus.*

Tuomala (101) Finnish: habitational name from a farm named with the male personal name *Tuomas* (see THOMAS) + the local suffix *-la*, i.e. 'Tuomas's place'. Found chiefly in southern Finland.

GIVEN NAMES Finnish 8%; Scandinavian 5%. *Taisto, Taito, Tauno, Vilho.*

Tuomi (183) Finnish: **1.** ornamental name from *tuomi* 'choke cherry' (*Prunus padus*). **2.** from the personal name *Tuomi*, a pet form of the male personal name *Tuomas* (see THOMAS). This name is found chiefly in southwestern Finland. Mostly, it is an ornamental name adopted during the name conversion movement in the late 19th and early 20th centuries.

GIVEN NAMES Finnish 10%. *Eino* (2), *Aimo, Alpo, Kalervo, Pirjo, Toivo, Wiljo.*

Tuominen (132) Finnish: **1.** ornamental name from *tuomi* 'choke cherry' + the common surname suffix *-nen*. This name is found chiefly in the southern and western parts of Finland. Mostly, it is an ornamental name adopted in the late 19th and early 20th centuries. **2.** from a derivative of the male personal name *Tuomas* (see THOMAS).

GIVEN NAMES Finnish 27%. *Reino* (3), *Paavo* (2), *Wilho* (2), *Erkki, Jaakko, Olli, Seppo, Tauno, Toivo, Urho, Waino.*

Tupa (252) German: from a short form of the Germanic personal name *Theudobert*, composed of the elements *þeudo* 'people' + *berht* 'bright'.

Tupper (1539) **1.** English: occupational name for a herdsman who had charge of rams, from an agent derivative of Middle English *to(u)pe* 'ram' (of uncertain origin). **2.** German (**Tüpper**): occupational name for a potter, from Middle Low German *duppe*, Rhenish *düppen* 'pot'. This is predominantly a Rhineland surname.

FOREBEARS This is the name of a family descended from two brothers, originally from Kassel, Germany. They fled religious persecution in the 16th century, settling in the Netherlands, where a descendant became burgomaster of Rotterdam in 1813. A branch of the family settled in England at Sandwich, Kent, whence another descendant, Thomas Tupper, went to America in 1635, and helped to found Sandwich, MA, in 1637. Benjamin Tupper, born in Stoughton, MA, in 1738 was a colonial legislator and explorer of OH.

Tupy (208) Czech and Slovak (**Tupý**): unflattering nickname for a dull, insensitive, or apathetic person, from Czech *tupý* 'thick', 'blunt', 'dull'.

Tur (115) **1.** Catalan: probably a topographic name from *tur* 'tufa', 'porous limestone'. This name is very common in the Pitiusses (Eivissa and Formentera) and Balearic Islands (Majorca and Minorca). **2.** Polish, Belorussian and Jewish (eastern Ashkenazic): from the nickname *Tur* meaning 'aurochs', ultimately cognate with Latin *taurus* 'bull' (see TORO). The Jewish surname is generally ornamental in origin. **3.** Jewish (eastern Ashkenazic): habitational name from Tury in Belarus.

GIVEN NAMES Spanish 34%; Polish 5%. *Juan* (4), *Jose* (3), *Angel* (2), *Enrique* (2), *Josefina* (2), *Consuelo, Cristina, Eladio, Eliazar, Gustavo, Jorge, Juana; Andrej, Krzysztof.*

Turan (185) Iranian, Turkish, etc.: ethnic name for someone from *Turan*, a region of central Asia, said to have been named for Tūr, son of Faridun, a legendary king of Persia who ruled around 750 BC.

GIVEN NAMES Muslim 26%. *Kazim* (2), *Abdullah, Ahmet, Emin, Hamza, Hatice, Hayati, Huseyin, Levent, Mete, Metin, Mohammed.*

Turano (545) Italian: habitational name, most probably from Torano Castello in Cosenza, named with the Latin personal name *Thurius*. There are also numerous places named Turano in Lombardy and Tuscany, but these are unlikely to have contributed greatly to the American surname, since most of the migration to the U.S. was from southern Italy.

GIVEN NAMES Italian 17%. *Salvatore* (7), *Angelo* (3), *Costantino* (2), *Giorgio* (2), *Pasquale* (2), *Sal* (2), *Antonino, Antonio, Carmine, Dante, Dino, Giuseppina.*

Turay (158) **1.** Muslim: unexplained. Possibly an adjectival derivative of TURAN. **2.** African: unexplained. **3.** Hungarian: habitational name for someone from a place called Tura.

GIVEN NAMES Muslim 19%; African 12%. *Mohamed* (3), *Zainab* (3), *Ismail* (2), *Ahmed, Hamid, Ibrahim, Isata, Khadijah, Mohammed, Ramatu; Alieu* (2), *Alimamy, Fatmata, Foday, Idrissa, Isatu, Kadiatu, Mamadou.*

Turberville (272) English (of Norman origin): habitational name from Thouberville in Eure, France.

Turbes (112) Origin unidentified. Perhaps a French or Belgian name (originally **Turbe**) that was brought as *Turbes* from Manderfeld, Germany, to North America.

GIVEN NAMES German 4%. *Florian, Mathias.*

Turbett (142) English: variant of TORBETT.

Turbeville (826) English: variant spelling of TURBERVILLE.

Turbin (164) **1.** English: variant of THORBURN. **2.** French: nickname for a disruptive person, from a diminutive derivative of Middle French *turber* 'to disturb' (Latin *torbare*).

Turbyfill (450) Altered spelling of English TURBERVILLE.

Turchi (221) Italian: patronymic or plural form of TURCO.

GIVEN NAMES Italian 15%; French 4%. *Domenic* (2), *Dino, Donato, Francesca, Gino, Giuseppe, Nicola, Pasquale, Premo, Remo, Rinaldo; Camille, Patrice.*

Turchin (200) **1.** Jewish (eastern Ashkenazic), Russian, and Ukrainian: nickname or ethnic name from Russian *turchin*, Ukrainian *turchyn* 'Turk' (see TURK). **2.** Jewish (eastern Ashkenazic): habita-

tional name for someone from Turchiny or Turchino in Belarus.

GIVEN NAMES Russian 7%. *Aleksandr, Arkadiy, Arkady, Leonid, Lev, Pyotr.*

Turcios (385) Hispanic: unexplained. This is predominantly a Latin American surname, occurring in Guatemala, Honduras, and Mexico.

GIVEN NAMES Spanish 62%. *Jose* (22), *Carlos* (10), *Manuel* (6), *Luis* (4), *Roberto* (4), *Francisco* (3), *Juan* (3), *Mario* (3), *Miguel* (3), *Reyes* (3), *Salvador* (3), *Santos* (3).

Turck (292) **1.** Dutch and German (also **T(h)ürck**): from a vocabulary word meaning 'Turk', a nickname for someone who had either fought against the Turks or one who was thought to resemble a Turk in some way, or a habitational name for someone who lived at a house distinguished by the sign of a Turk. **2.** German (Alsace): habitational name from shortened forms of place names such as Türkheim.

FOREBEARS This name is recorded in Beverwijck in New Netherland (Albany, NY) in the mid 17th century. See WESSELS.

Turco (871) Italian: ethnic name for a Turk, Italian *Turco*, or a nickname from the same word in the sense of a non-Christian or, following the medieval ethnic stereotype, a cruel, ferocious, or short-tempered person. See also TURK. This name may also be of Greek origin, from *Tourko-, Tourkos* 'Turk'. It is often found combined with a personal name to form a Greek surname, for example **Tourkantonis** 'Turkish Anthony' (i.e. 'Anthony the Muslim', 'Anthony originally from Ottoman Turkey rather than the Greek state', or 'Anthony the irascible'), **Tourkogeorgis** 'Turkish George', **Tourkomanolis** 'Turkish Emmanuel', etc.

GIVEN NAMES Italian 8%. *Salvatore* (5), *Angelo* (4), *Antonio* (2), *Gaetano* (2), *Patrizio* (2), *Carmin, Concetta, Domenic, Gennaro, Natale, Sal, Santo.*

Turcott (223) **1.** Respelling of French TURCOTTE. **2.** Jewish (from Ukraine): nickname from Ukrainian *turkot* 'grumbler'.

Turcotte (2124) French: from a diminutive of *turc* 'Turk', which may be an ethnic name, but is also found as a nickname for someone who had traveled to the eastern Mediterranean on a crusade. Compare English, Dutch, and German TURK.

FOREBEARS A Turcotte from the Poitou region of France is documented in Trois Rivières, Quebec, in 1651.

GIVEN NAMES French 13%. *Normand* (7), *Marcel* (6), *Armand* (5), *Andre* (4), *Gilles* (4), *Laurent* (3), *Serge* (3), *Alain* (2), *Alphonse* (2), *Cecile* (2), *Donat* (2), *Emile* (2).

Turczyn (114) Polish: ethnic name or nickname from Old Polish *Turczyn* 'Turk', a derivative of *Turek*.

GIVEN NAMES Polish 4%. *Mykola, Zygmund.*

Turek (1562) **1.** Czech, Slovak, Polish, and Jewish (eastern Ashkenazic): from the vocabulary word *Turek* 'Turk', either an ethnic name for a Turk or a nickname for someone who was thought to resemble a Turk in some way. **2.** Croatian (northern Croatia) and Slovenian: nickname for a refugee from the Turks in the 15th and 16th century, from the ethnic term *Turek* 'Turk'. Slovenian territory and the northern parts of present-day Croatia were a refuge for Christians from Bosnia when it was conquered by the Ottoman Empire, and from those parts of Croatia that were a war zone. Refugees were thus not ethnic Turks, but Serbs and Croats from 'Turkey', i.e. the Ottoman Empire. **3.** Slovenian: perhaps also a nickname or occupational name from any of various plants named *turek*, e.g. a kind of flax or a mushroom of the genus Leccinium. **4.** Polish and Jewish (from Poland): habitational name from any of several places named Turek, in particular one in Konin voivodeship.

Turenne (230) French: regional name for someone from the Touraine region.

FOREBEARS In Canada, Turenne is recorded as a secondary surname for a BLANCHARD from Poitiers; it is documented in Trois Rivières, Quebec, in 1727, in the form **Turaine**.

GIVEN NAMES French 19%. *Andre* (3), *Normand* (3), *Donat, Emile, Francois, Oneil, Philomene, Serge, Yves.*

Turetsky (167) Jewish (from Belarus and Lithuania): habitational name for someone from Turets in Belarus.

GIVEN NAMES Jewish 14%; Russian 9%. *Hyman, Isadore, Kolman, Ruvim, Tikva, Yakov; Boris* (4), *Igor, Mikhail, Nikolai, Sergey, Sofya, Yelizaveta, Yury.*

Turgeon (1495) Breton: nickname meaning 'sturgeon', borrowed from French *esturgeon*.

FOREBEARS A bearer of the surname from the Perche region of France was documented in Quebec City in 1661.

GIVEN NAMES French 15%. *Armand* (5), *Normand* (5), *Andre* (4), *Fernand* (4), *Lucien* (4), *Jacques* (3), *Yvon* (3), *Aime* (2), *Emile* (2), *Emilien* (2), *Ghislain* (2), *Herve* (2).

Turi (305) **1.** Hungarian: habitational name for someone from any of several places called Túr in Hungary. **2.** Italian: habitational name from Turi, a place in Bari province. **3.** Central Italian: reduced form of **Venturi**, a patronymic from the personal name *Ventura*, itself short form of *Bonaventura*.

GIVEN NAMES Hungarian 5%; Italian 5%. *Janos, Laszlo, Leszlo, Nandor, Zoltan, Zsuzsanna; Angelo* (2), *Antonio, Fiore, Gabriella, Rocco.*

Turiano (118) Italian: habitational name for someone from Turi (see TURI).

GIVEN NAMES Italian 26%. *Angelo* (2), *Alfredo, Dante, Eriberto, Rosario, Santo.*

Turin (156) **1.** French and northern Italian: habitational name from the city of Turin in Italy (Italian name *Torino*). **2.** French: from a reduced form of the personal name *Art(h)urin*, a pet form of the personal name ARTHUR. **3.** Jewish (eastern Ashkenazic): habitational name from a village called Tury or Turin, now in Belarus.

GIVEN NAMES Jewish 7%. *Avrohom, Bentzion, Isaak, Miriam.*

Turk (4053) **1.** English (mainly Gloucestershire), Dutch, and German (also **Türk**): from Middle English, Old French *turc*, Middle High and Low German *Turc* 'Turk', from Turkish *türk*. In theory this could be an ethnic name but, both in England and northwest Europe, it is generally a nickname for a person with black hair and a swarthy complexion or a cruel, rowdy, or unruly person. The Dutch and German surname also represents a house name, derived from the use of a picture of a Turk as a house sign. It is also found as a nickname for someone who had taken part in the wars against the Turks. **2.** English: from a medieval personal name, a back-formation from TURKEL, misanalyzed as containing the Old French diminutive suffix *-el*. **3.** Scottish: reduced Anglicized form of Gaelic **Mac Tuirc**, a patronymic from the byname *Torc* 'boar'. **4.** Jewish (Ashkenazic): ethnic name denoting someone from Turkey or anywhere in the Ottoman Empire, or a nickname for someone thought to resemble a Turk. **5.** Americanized form of the Greek ethnic name **Tourkos** 'Turk'. See also TURCO.

Turke (110) German: variant of TURK.

Turkel (255) **1.** English: from the Middle English personal name *þorkell*, a reduced form of Old Norse *þórketill*, composed of the elements *þórr* (name of the Scandinavian god of thunder; see THOR) + *ketill* 'cauldron'. The personal name *Thurkill* or *Thirkill* was in widespread use in England in the Middle Ages; in northern England it was introduced directly by settlers from Scandinavia, whereas in the South it was the result of Norman influence. **2.** Jewish (Ashkenazic): unexplained; possibly an ornamental name from Yiddish *turkltoyb* 'turtle dove'.

GIVEN NAMES Jewish 5%. *Chavie, Cohen, Mayer.*

Turkett (109) English: from a pet form of the personal name TURKEL.

Turkington (253) English and northern Irish: variant of **Torkington** (see TALKINGTON), now more common in northern Ireland than anywhere else. It has sometimes been used as an Americanized form of Scottish *McTurk* (see TURK).

Turko (163) **1.** Polish: variant of TUREK. **2.** Also from the Turkish family name *Turko* 'Turk'. The term denotes not merely someone from Turkey, but also a speaker of any of the Turkic languages that stretch right across central Asia, from the Caucasus to China.

GIVEN NAMES Polish 8%. *Slawomir* (3), *Aleksander, Andrzej.*

Turkovich (171) Jewish (from Ukraine): habitational name from a place called Turkovichi in Ukraine.

Turkowski (90) Polish: habitational name for someone from Turków in Opole voivodeship, Turkowo in Poznań voivodeship, or Turkowy in Kalisz voivodeship.

GIVEN NAME Polish 4%. *Bogdan.*

Turley (3823) **1.** Irish: reduced Anglicized form of Gaelic **Mac Toirdealbhaigh**, a patronymic from the personal name *Toirdhealbhach*, a personal name meaning 'like Thor' or 'like thunder', composed of the Old Norse name *þórr* (see THOR) + Gaelic *dealbhach* 'like', 'in the shape of'. Compare MCCURLEY, from the lenited form. **2.** Altered spelling of German **Thurley**, from a personal name formed with Old High German *tiuri* 'dear', 'valuable' + *līh* (?), related to Gothic *leiks* 'body', 'shape'.

Turlington (519) English (Leicestershire): apparently a habitational name. Compare TURKINGTON.

Turman (1606) **1.** Dutch: topographic name from Middle Dutch *turre, torre* 'tower' + *man* 'man', or possibly a habitational name for someone who lived at a house distinguished by the sign of a tower. **2.** Variant of German **Thurmann** (see THURMAN).

Turmel (146) French: from a derivative of Old French *turme*, Old Occitan *turma* 'troop', 'band', also 'flock of animals', so probably an occupational name for a shepherd.

FOREBEARS The name is frequent in New England, but very rare in Canada: the marriage of a Breton so named is recorded in 1762 in Sainte-Foy, Quebec.

GIVEN NAMES French 17%. *Adrien, Antoine, Betrand, Fernand, Francois, Gilberte, Lucien, Normand.*

Turnage (1875) **1.** English: unexplained; in England it is associated chiefly with Essex. **2.** Probably an Americanized spelling of German **Türnich**, of unexplained origin.

Turnbaugh (449) Americanized spelling of German **Dürnbach** (see DURNBAUGH and TURNBOW).

Turnbo (210) Americanized spelling of German **Dürnbach** (see TURNBOW).

Turnbough (408) Americanized spelling of German **Dürnbach** (see TURNBOW).

Turnbow (980) Americanized spelling of German **Dürnbach**, from a habitational name from any of several places so named or from places in Austria and Bavaria named Dürrenbach (meaning 'dry stream').

Turnbull (3357) Northern English (chiefly Northumbrian) and Scottish: variant, altered by folk etymology, of TRUMBLE, on theory that it denoted a nickname for a man thought to be strong and brave enough to turn back a charging bull, from Middle English *turn(en)* 'to turn' + *bul(l)e* 'bull'.

Turner (112377) **1.** English and Scottish: occupational name for a maker of objects of wood, metal, or bone by turning on a lathe, from Anglo-Norman French *torner* (Old French *tornier*, Latin *tornarius*, a derivative of *tornus* 'lathe'). The surname may also derive from any of various other senses of Middle English *turn*, for example a turnspit, a translator or interpreter, or a tumbler. **2.** English: nickname for a fast runner, from Middle English *turnen* 'to turn' + 'hare'. **3.** English: occupational name for an official in charge of a tournament, Old French *tornei* (in origin akin to 1). **4.** Jewish (eastern Ashkenazic): habitational name from a place called Turno or Turna, in Poland and Belarus, or from the city of *Tarnów* (Yiddish *Turne*) in Poland. **5.** Translated or Americanized form of any of various other like-meaning or like-sounding Jewish surnames. **6.** South German (**T(h)ürner**): occupational name for a guard in a tower or a topographic name from Middle High German *turn* 'tower', or a habitational name for someone from any of various places named Thurn, for example in Austria.

Turney (2388) English (of Norman origin): habitational name from places in northern France called Tournai (Orne), Tournay (Calvados), or Tourny (Eure), all named with the pre-Roman personal name *Turnus* (probably meaning 'height', 'eminence') + the locative suffix *-acum*.

Turnham (162) English: habitational name from Turnham in East Yorkshire or Turnham Green in West London, both of which are so named from an Old English *trun* 'circular', probably denoting a U-shaped bend in a river, + *hamm* 'water meadow' or *hām* 'homestead'.

Turnier (103) Probably an Americanized spelling of French **Tournier**.

GIVEN NAMES French 15%; German 4%. *Auguste, Francoise, Kettly, Octavie, Raoul; Ernst.*

Turnipseed (905) translated form of German **Rübsam(en)** 'turnip seed', a nickname for a turnip grower. Turnips were important as staple diet in winter during the Middle Ages.

Turnley (207) English or Scottish: unexplained; possibly a habitational name from a lost or unidentified place.

Turnmire (228) Americanized spelling of German **Dürmeyer** or **Dürrenmayer**, a distinguishing name either for a tenant farmer (see MEYER) who sold his produce at a high price (Middle Low German *düre* 'dear', 'expensive'), or, in the south, a tenant farmer whose farm was by water (Middle High German *dur* 'water' appears in field names).

Turnock (109) English (Midlands): unexplained. There is a Turnock Farm in

Cheshire, but it is not clear whether the surname arose from the place name or vice versa.

Turnquist (778) Swedish: variant of TORN-QUIST.
GIVEN NAMES Scandinavian 5%. *Nels* (2), *Erik, Lennart.*

Turns (144) English: unexplained.

Turo (140) **1.** Italian: of uncertain derivation. The surname is most frequent in Campania and Apulia, where **Ammaturo** is also a frequent family name, suggesting that *Turo* may perhaps be a short form of this name. Alternatively, it may be from a reduced form of the personal name *Arturo* (see ARTHUR). **2.** Hungarian (**Túró**): metonymic occupational name from *túró* 'curd'.
GIVEN NAMES Italian 5%. *Angelo, Romeo.*

Turoff (149) Jewish (eastern Ashkenazic): alternative spelling of **Turov**, a habitational name for someone from a place called Turov in Belarus. The place is named with *tur* 'aurochs' (ultimately cognate with Latin *taurus* 'bull').

Turowski (232) **1.** Polish and Jewish (eastern Ashkenazic): habitational name from any of various places called Turowo or Turów, named with Polish *tur* 'aurochs'. **2.** Jewish (eastern Ashkenazic): habitational name for someone from Turov in Belarus (see TUROFF).
GIVEN NAMES Polish 9%. *Grzegorz* (2), *Krystyna* (2), *Casimir, Mieczyslaw, Tadeusz.*

Turpen (655) English: variant spelling of TURPIN.

Turpin (3971) English and French: from an Anglo-Norman French form of the Old Norse personal name *Þórfinnr*, composed of the elements *Þórr*, the name of the god of thunder in Scandinavian mythology (see THOR) + the ethnic name *Finnr* 'Finn'. This may have absorbed another name, *Turpius, Turpinus* (from Latin *turpis* 'ugly', 'base'), one of the self-abasing names adopted as a mark of humility by the early Christians. It was borne by the archbishop of Rheims in the Charlemagne legend.
FOREBEARS A Turpin of unknown geographic origin is documented in Montreal in 1681.

Turrell (320) English and Irish: variant of TYRRELL.

Turrentine (532) Origin unidentified.

Turri (188) Italian (Sicily): variant of TORRE, from Sicilian *turri* 'tower'.
GIVEN NAMES Italian 7%; Jewish 4%. *Dino, Fabrizio, Giorgio, Pierina, Valentino; Ido, Miriam.*

Turrill (111) English: probably a variant of TYRRELL.

Turrisi (118) Italian (Sicily): variant of TOR-RISI.
GIVEN NAMES Italian 9%. *Francesca, Gaetano, Mauro, Sal.*

Turro (115) **1.** Italian: perhaps a southern dialect variant of TORRE 'tower'.

2. Catalan (**Turró**): variant of **Torró**, probably a nickname or a metonymic occupational name from Catalan *torró*, denoting a hard nougat-like candy made of almond, honey, etc.
GIVEN NAMES Spanish 7%, Italian 6%. *Angel* (4), *Ana, Juan; Fausto* (2), *Berta.*

Tursi (308) Italian: habitational name from Tursi in Matera.
GIVEN NAMES Italian 17%. *Pasquale* (2), *Vito* (2), *Armando, Carlo, Domenic, Gennaro, Lorenzo, Sal, Salvatore.*

Turski (147) Polish: habitational name for someone from any of various places in Poland called Tur, Tursko, or Turza, all named with *tur* 'aurochs'.
GIVEN NAMES Polish 11%. *Jacek* (2), *Andrzej, Tadeusz, Zygmond.*

Turtle (153) English: **1.** variant of TURKEL. **2.** nickname for a mild and gentle or affectionate person, from Middle English *turtel* 'turtle dove'. **3.** nickname for a crippled or deformed person, from Old French *tourtel*, a diminutive of *tourt* 'crooked'.

Turton (366) English: habitational name from Turnton, a place in Lancashire named from the Old Norse personal name *Þórr* (see THOR) + Old English *tūn* 'enclosure', 'settlement'. The surname is now as common in the Midlands as it is in Lancashire and Yorkshire.

Turturro (139) Italian (Sicily): metonymic occupational name for a groom, from *turturo*, a southern form of *tortoro* 'straw or hay plait used for strapping horses'.
GIVEN NAMES Italian 24%. *Angelo* (4), *Nicola* (3), *Antonio, Domenic, Giulio, Vincenzo.*

Turvey (307) English: habitational name from Turvey, a place in Bedfordshire named from Old English *turf* 'turf', 'grass' + *ēg* 'island', 'low-lying land'.

Turville (100) English (of Norman origin): habitational name from Turville-la-Campagne in Eure, France.

Tusa (324) **1.** Italian (Sicily): habitational name from a place so called in Messina province. **2.** Hungarian: from the old secular personal name *Tusa*. **3.** Hungarian: habitational name from a place so called in Zemplén county.
GIVEN NAMES Italian 9%. *Salvatore* (3), *Carmela, Luciano, Pietro, Sal, Vita.*

Tuscano (142) Italian: variant of TOSCANO.
GIVEN NAMES Italian 6%; Spanish 4%. *Nuncio, Pasquale; Juan* (2), *Juanito.*

Tush (114) **1.** Americanized spelling of Slovenian **Tuš**, probably a derivative from the personal name *Tomaž* (see THOMAS). It is found in eastern Slovenia. Compare TOSH. **2.** English: unexplained; possibly a variant of Scottish TOSH.

Tusing (309) Variant of German **Düsing** or **Dusing** (see DUSING).

Tuss (137) German: variant of DUSS, THUS, from short forms of the old personal name *Duso, Tuzzo.*

Tussey (555) Possibly an altered spelling of German **Tusche**, which may be from a nickname for a cheat, from Middle Low German *tüsche* 'deception', or a nickname, perhaps for a ruffian, from Bavarian *tusch* 'blow', 'stroke'; alternatively, it could be of Slavic origin.

Tussing (318) German adaptation of the French surname TOUSSAINT.

Tustin (401) **1.** English: variant of THURSTON. **2.** French: variant of TOUTANT.

Tuszynski (118) Polish (**Tuszyński**): habitational name for someone from places called Tuszyn in Piotrków and Częstochowa voivodeships.

Tuten (905) Scottish: variant of THURSTON.

Tuter (140) Jewish (eastern Ashkenazic): nickname from Yiddish *tuter* 'Tartar'.

Tuthill (1139) English: topographic name for someone who lived by a hill used as a lookout station, from an unattested Old English *tōt hyll* 'lookout hill', or a habitational name from some place named with this word, for example Tootle Heights in Lancashire, Tothill in Lincolnshire, or Tuttle Hill in Warwickshire. This surname became established in Ireland in the 17th century, and is now more common in Ireland than England.

Tutino (195) Italian: from a pet form of Old Italian (Tuscan dialect) *Tuti*, a short form of the personal name *Dietaiuti*, an omen name meaning 'may God assist you'.
GIVEN NAMES Italian 22%. *Rocco* (5), *Vito* (2), *Dino, Gerlando, Nicola, Sal, Santo.*

Tutko (179) Ukrainian: unexplained.

Tuton (119) English: variant of THURSTON.

Tutor (756) Probably a variant spelling of Welsh TUDOR.

Tutt (1147) **1.** English: from an Old English personal name or byname *Tutta*, preserved in place names such as Tutnall (Worcestershire) and Tuttington (Norfolk), and apparently persisting into the Middle Ages. Its origin and meaning are unclear. **2.** German (also **Tütt**): from a short form of a Germanic personal name formed with *Diet-* (see DIETRICH), or from a short form of *Dudo*, originally a name from nursery talk.

Tutterow (201) Probably an Americanized form of German **Teterow**, a habitational name from a place so named in Mecklenburg–West Pomerania.

Tuttle (10803) English and Irish: from the Old Norse personal name *Þorkell*, a contracted form of a name composed of the elements *Þórr*, name of the Scandinavian god of thunder (see THOR) + *ketill* 'cauldron'. The personal name *Thurkill* or *Thirkill* was in use throughout England in the Middle Ages; in northern England it had been introduced directly by Scandinavian settlers, whereas in the South it was the result of Norman influence. This surname and its variants are especially common in East Anglia. In Ireland the Old Norse name was adopted as a Gaelic personal name (*Thorcall*), which generated the surnames MCCORKLE and CORKILL.

Tutton (229) English: variant of THURSTON.

Tutwiler (278) Altered spelling of Swiss German **Duttweiler**, **Duttwiler**, a habitational name from a place so named in the Palatinate, near Neustadt.

Tuxhorn (173) German: unexplained.

Tuzzolino (180) Italian: from a pet form of *Tuzzo*, itself a short form of a personal name formed with the suffix *-uzzo* from a personal name ending in *-te* or *-to*. for example *Robertuzzo*.
GIVEN NAMES Italian 17%. *Salvatore* (3), *Luigi* (2), *Carlo, Santo, Vita.*

Tvedt (238) Norwegian: variant of TVEIT.
GIVEN NAME Scandinavian 8%. *Per* (2).

Tveit (197) Norwegian: habitational name from any of about 60 farmsteads, mainly in western Norway and Agder, so named from Old Norse *þveit* 'small field on a hillside'.
GIVEN NAMES Scandinavian 8%. *Oddmund* (2), *Jorgen, Thor.*

Tvrdik (162) Czech (**Tvrdík**): nickname for an obstinate or severe person, from a derivative of Czech *tvrdý* 'hard'.

Twaddell (182) Scottish and northern English: variant of TWEEDLE.

Twaddle (272) Scottish and northern English: variant of TWEEDLE.

Twait (154) **1.** Americanized form of Norwegian TVEIT. **2.** Possibly an altered spelling of English **Twaite**, a variant of THWAITES.

Twardowski (349) Polish: habitational name for someone from Twardowo in Poznań voivodeship or Twardów in Kalisz voivodeship, named with Polish *twardy* 'hard'.
GIVEN NAMES Polish 8%. *Andrzej, Czeslaw, Eugeniusz, Henryk, Jacek, Janusz, Krzysztof, Mieczyslaw, Waclaw.*

Twardy (151) Polish: nickname for an obstinate or severe person, from *twardy* 'hard'. The name also occurs in Germany.
GIVEN NAMES Polish 5%. *Bronislaw, Mariusz.*

Twardzik (132) Polish: derivative of TWARDY.

Twarog (138) Polish (**Twaróg**): from *twaróg* 'curds', 'cottage cheese', an occupational name or a nickname.
GIVEN NAMES Polish 5%; German 4%. *Halina, Zbigniew.*

Tway (112) Origin unidentified; possibly English or Irish, unexplained.

Twedt (504) Variant of Norwegian TVEIT.
GIVEN NAMES Scandinavian 5%. *Egil, Thor.*

Tweed (1129) Northern English and Scottish: topographic name for someone living on the banks of the river Tweed, which flows between northeastern England and southeastern Scotland, and bears a British name of uncertain meaning.

Tweedie (552) Scottish: habitational name from Tweedie, a place in the parish of Stonehouse, south of Glasgow, the name of which is of uncertain origin.

Tweedle (156) Scottish and northern English: topographic name for someone who lived in the valley (see DALE) of the river TWEED.

Tweedy (1219) **1.** Scottish: variant spelling of TWEEDIE. **2.** English: habitational name from Tweedyhill in Kingwater in Cumbria.

Tweet (265) Americanized spelling of Norwegian TVEIT, or possibly of North German **Twiete**, from a topographical name for someone who lived by a passage or alley.
GIVEN NAMES Scandinavian 7%. *Thor* (2), *Obert, Thorvald.*

Tweeten (160) Respelling of Norwegian **Tveten**, a variant of TVEIT.

Twenter (134) Dutch: unexplained.

Twersky (189) Jewish (eastern Ashkenazic): habitational name from a place in Lithuania called Tvery in Russian, or from Tiberias in Israel, the Yiddish name of which is *Tverye*.
GIVEN NAMES Jewish 40%. *Baruch* (3), *Sholom* (3), *Avraham* (2), *Boruch* (2), *Aharon, Avram, Chaim, Chana, Isadore, Leibel, Mayer, Mordechai.*

Tweten (240) Respelling of Norwegian **Tveten**, a variant of TVEIT.
GIVEN NAMES Scandinavian 6%. *Selmer* (2), *Hjalmer, Obert.*

Twichell (230) English: variant spelling of TWITCHELL.

Twiddy (189) English: unexplained. In part, it may be a variant of TWEEDY, but the concentration of the modern surname in Norfolk suggests another source is also involved.

Twidwell (148) Origin unidentified. This has the form of an English habitational name, possibly from Twydall in Kent, named from Old English *twī* 'two' + *dāl* 'portion of land', but the surname is not found in current English sources.

Twiford (317) English: variant spelling of TWYFORD.

Twigg (1186) English (Midlands): nickname for a thin person, from Middle English *twigge* 'twig', 'shoot'. Since the word occurs only late in the Old English period and was initially confined to northern dialects, it may be a borrowing from Old Norse.

Twiggs (438) English: patronymic from TWIGG.

Twilley (554) English: unexplained.

Twine (367) English: metonymic occupational name for someone who made string or thread, from Old English *twīn* 'thread', 'string'.

Twiner (126) English: occupational name for a maker of thread or twine, an agent derivative of Old English *twīnen* 'to twine'.

Twing (126) Origin unidentified; possibly English, unexplained.
GIVEN NAME German 5%. *Kurt.*

Twining (558) English: habitational name from Twyning in Gloucestershire, which was originally named with Old English *betwēonan* 'between' + *ēam*, dative of *ēa* 'river', with the ending later being assimilated to *-ingas* 'inhabitants', 'people'.

Twisdale (156) Probably a variant of northern English TEESDALE.

Twiss (589) English (mainly Lancashire): **1.** habitational name from Twiss in Lancashire, named from Old English *(ge)twis* 'forking', used as a noun to mean 'fork in a river'. **2.** variant of TWIST.

Twist (468) English (mainly Lancashire): **1.** probably a variant of TWISS, or possibly in a few cases from Twist, a minor place in Devon, or Twist Wood in Brede, Sussex, both named from Old English *twist*, Middle English *twist* 'something twisted or forked'. **2.** possibly a metonymic occupational name for someone in the cotton-spinning industry, whose responsibility was to combine threads into a strong cord, a sense of *twist* recorded from the 16th century.

Twitchell (1152) English: unexplained.

Twite (207) English: **1.** (northern): variant of THWAITES, for example from Twit in Lincolnshire. **2.** nickname from the twite, a moorland finch, or perhaps a metonymic occupational name for someone who sold or kept them as songbirds.

Twitty (805) English: unexplained.

Twohey (112) Irish: variant spelling of TOOHEY.

Twohig (359) Irish (County Cork): reduced form of **O'Twohig**, an Anglicized form of Gaelic **Ó Tuathaigh** (see TOOHEY).
GIVEN NAME Irish 7%. *Declan* (2).

Twohy (103) Irish: variant spelling of TOOHEY.

Twombley (108) Irish: variant of TWOMBLY.
GIVEN NAMES Irish 4%. *Aidan, Donovan.*

Twombly (774) Probably an Americanized form of French TREMBLAY.

Twomey (1402) Irish: variant of TOOMEY.
GIVEN NAMES Irish 6%. *Liam* (5), *Aileen, Brendan, Conor, Cormac, Fintan, Kieran, Niall.*

Tworek (218) Polish: from a pet form of the personal name *Tworzyjan*, a Polish variant of FLORIAN.
GIVEN NAMES Polish 4%. *Boguslaw, Urszula.*

Twyford (235) English: habitational name from any of the numerous places named Twyford, for example in Berkshire, Buckinghamshire, Derbyshire, Hampshire, Leicestershire, Lincolnshire, Middlesex, and Norfolk, from Old English *twī-* 'double' + *ford* 'ford'.

Twyman (850) English (Kent): unexplained; perhaps a metathesized form of **Twynam**, a habitational name from Twinehame in

Sussex or Twinham (now Christchurch) in Hampshire.

Ty (103) **1.** Vietnamese: unexplained. **2.** Filipino: unexplained.
GIVEN NAMES Vietnamese 13%; Other Southeast Asian 10%; Spanish 4%. *Nguyen* (2), *Dang, Du, Mai, Phung, Tan, Thy; Ouk, Seng, Sheng, Tong, Yang, Yao*; *Eleuterio, Marcelo, Mario.*

Tyburski (329) Polish (also **Tyborski**): habitational name for someone from places called Tybory in Łomża voivodeship or Tyborów in Radom or Siedlce voivodeship.

Tydings (171) Irish: adopted as an English equivalent of Gaelic **Ó Tuaruis(c)**, an altered form of **Ó hUarghuis** 'descendant of *Uarghus*' meaning 'cold choice'. The English form is a translation of *tuairisc* 'tidings', a word which is in fact unrelated to the Gaelic name. **Ó hUarghuis** has also been mistranslated as WATERS or CALDWELL, being taken as *Ó Fuaruisce* 'son of cold water'.

Tye (1239) **1.** English (mainly East Anglia): topographic name for someone who lived by a common pasture, Middle English *tye* (Old English *tēag*). **2.** North German: from a short form, *Tide*, of the personal name DIETRICH.

Tyer (503) English: **1.** from the Continental Germanic personal name *Theudhard*, Old French *Thiart*, composed of *theod* 'people', 'race' + *hard* 'hardy', 'brave', 'strong'. **2.** perhaps a topographic name from a derivative of Middle English *tye* 'common pasture'.

Tygart (174) Variant of German **Teikert** or **Deikert** (see DYGERT).

Tyger (146) **1.** Perhaps a variant of German **Teikert** or **Deikert** (see DYGERT). **2.** perhaps a variant of Irish TIGER.

Tyler (20078) English: occupational name for a maker or layer of tiles, from an agent derivative of Middle English *tile* 'tile'. In the Middle Ages tiles were widely used in floors and pavements, and to a lesser extent in roofing, where they did not really come into their own until the 16th century.

Tylicki (109) Polish: habitational name for someone from Tylice in Toruń voivoideship or Tylisz in Nowy Sącz voivodeship, named with *tył* 'back'.
GIVEN NAMES Polish 7%. *Juliusz* (2), *Janusz.*

Tylka (207) Polish: nickname from Old Polish (or Polish dialect) *tylki* 'that size' (i.e. 'that big' or 'that small').
GIVEN NAMES Polish 8%. *Bronislaw* (2), *Zdzislaw* (2), *Kazimierz, Krzysztof, Zofia.*

Tylutki (112) Polish: diminutive of TYLKA.
GIVEN NAMES Polish 6%; French 5%. *Halina, Ludwika; Gabrielle* (2).

Tyma (88) Polish: from the personal name *Tyma*, a derivative of *Tymoteusz*, Polish form of Greek *Timotheos* (see TIMOTHY).

Tyminski (215) Polish (**Tymiński, Tymieński**): habitational name for someone from Tymin in Zamość voivodeship.
GIVEN NAMES Polish 16%. *Jacek* (2), *Zigmond* (2), *Casimir, Czeslaw, Dorota, Jozef, Lech, Mariusz, Stanislaw, Tadeusz, Teofil.*

Tynan (789) Irish: reduced Anglicized form of Gaelic **Ó Teimhneáin** 'descendant of *Teimhneán*', possibly from a diminutive of Old Irish *teimhean* 'dark'.
GIVEN NAMES Irish 6%. *Aileen, Brendan, Patrick Michael.*

Tyndall (1811) English: variant spelling of TINDALL.

Tyne (121) **1.** Irish: reduced Anglicized form of Gaelic **Ó Teimhin** 'descendant of *Teimhean*', from *teimhean* 'dark', an adjective from *teimhe* 'dusk', 'darkness'. **2.** English: probably a habitational name for someone from Tyneside in northeast England.

Tyner (2459) English: unexplained.

Tynes (918) Possibly of English origin but unexplained.

Tyo (394) Origin unidentified.

Tyra (548) Polish: unexplained.

Tyre (860) **1.** Scottish: reduced form of McINTYRE. **2.** English: variant spelling of TYER.

Tyree (3157) Scottish: Anglicized derivative of McINTYRE.

Tyrell (430) English and Irish: variant spelling of TYRRELL.

Tyrer (157) English (Lancashire): of unknown origin. It is possible that it arose as an occupational name for an official in charge of the wardrobe of a great personage, from an agent derivative of Middle English *tire(n)* 'to equip, dress' (a reduced form of Old French *atir(i)er*). However, there is no early evidence for this.

Tyrie (122) Scottish: variant of TYREE.

Tyrone (231) Irish American: probably a habitational name from the county of Tyrone (Gaelic *Tir Eoghain* 'land of Owen') in Ulster. The name was used as a forename among an Irish-American family of actors, of whom the first on record was Tyrone Power (1795–1841) and the most famous was his great-grandson, also called Tyrone Power (1914–58). It is not found as a surname in Ireland.

Tyrrell (2267) English and Irish: of uncertain origin: **1.** perhaps from a Norman nickname for a stubborn person, from Old French *tirel*, used of an animal which pulls on the reins, a derivative of *tirer* 'to pull'. **2.** Woulfe suggests that it may be from the personal name *Thurold*, Old Norse *Thorvaldr*, composed of the elements *þórr*, name of the Norse god of thunder (see THOR) + *valdr* 'rule'.

Tysdal (131) Variant of English and Scottish TEASDALE.

Tysinger (464) Altered spelling of German **Theisinger, Theusinger**, from a habitational name for someone from Theissing in Upper Bavaria, recorded as *Teusing* in the Middles Ages.

Tyska (149) Altered spelling of Polish TYSZKA.
GIVEN NAME Polish 5%. *Zygmunt.*

Tyson (8633) **1.** English: variant of **Dyson** (see DYE). **2.** English: nickname for someone with a fiery temperament, from Old French *tison* 'firebrand'. **3.** Americanized spelling of German THEISSEN or THEISEN.

Tysor (138) Americanized spelling of German **Theuser**, a variant of DEUSER.

Tysver (103) Origin unidentified.

Tyszka (130) Polish: from the personal name *Tyszka*, a pet form of *Tymoteusz*, Polish form of Greek *Timotheos* (see TIMOTHY).
GIVEN NAMES Polish 13%. *Janina* (2), *Casimir, Dariusz, Ryszard, Stas, Zygmunt.*

Tyus (693) Probably an altered spelling of English **Tyas**, from an ethnic name from Old French *tieis* 'German'; or alternatively of German **Thias**, from a short form of the personal name *Matthias* (see MATTHEW).

Tzeng (136) Chinese 曾: variant of ZENG.
GIVEN NAMES Chinese 26%. *Kuo* (2), *Chen, Chien, Chih-Hung, Ching-Hwa, Chu, Chun Yan, Jing, Li-Mei, Liang, Shu Min, Shuen.*

U

U (149) Chinese and Korean: variant spelling of Yu.

Ubben (243) North German (Frisian): patronymic from Frisian *Ubbe*, a reduced form of a Germanic personal name beginning with *od-* 'property', 'possessions'.

Ubel (102) German (**Übell**): variant spelling of Uebel.

Ubelhor (119) Southern German (**Übelhör**): altered form of **Übelherr**, literally 'evil lord'.
GIVEN NAMES French 6%. *Chantelle, Roch.*

Uber (557) German: **1.** from Middle High German *uober* 'active', 'busy', 'enterprising' (from Middle High German *uoben* 'to be busy'), hence a nickname for an active or adventurous person. **2.** from the Germanic personal name *Audoberht*, composed of the elements *od* 'property', 'possession' + *berht* 'bright', 'famous'.

Uberti (117) Italian: from the personal name *Uberto*, of Germanic origin, probably via French Hubert.
GIVEN NAMES Italian 8%. *Angelo* (2), *Amelio, Nino.*

Ubl (131) **1.** German: probably from the Germanic personal name *Ubaldin*, or *Ubbo* (*Oppo*), a short form of various compound personal names beginning with *od* 'property', 'possession'. **2.** German: nickname from Middle High German *ubel* 'bad', 'evil'.

Uccello (118) Italian: nickname from *uccello* 'bird', 'fowl', 'cock'. Compare Auci-ello.
GIVEN NAMES Italian 29%. *Salvatore* (8), *Antonio* (2), *Corrado* (2), *Carmine, Nunzio, Sal, Santo.*

Ucci (168) Italian: from the personal name *Uccio*, a short form of a pet name formed with the suffix *-uccio*.
GIVEN NAMES Italian 13%. *Angelo* (2), *Amedeo, Antonio, Gino, Guilio, Silvio, Vincenzo.*

Uchida (433) Japanese: variously written, mostly with characters meaning 'inner rice paddy', denoting a field within an enclosure. It is a common name throughout Japan and the Ryūkyū Islands, and was adopted by some samurai families. It is listed in the Shinsen shōjiroku.
GIVEN NAMES Japanese 61%. *Hiroshi* (6), *Atsushi* (3), *Kazuko* (3), *Kazuo* (3), *Takao* (3), *Toshi* (3), *Hideo* (2), *Hiroki* (2), *Hiroyuki* (2), *Hisashi* (2), *Hitoshi* (2), *Masaru* (2).

Uchiyama (166) Japanese: 'inner mountain', found mostly in eastern Japan and in the Ryūkyū Islands.
GIVEN NAMES Japanese 64%. *Akiko* (2), *Hiro* (2), *Mikio* (2), *Shigeru* (2), *Susumu* (2), *Takuya* (2), *Daisuke, Goro, Hiroshi, Isao, Katsuhiko, Kazu.*

Uchytil (111) Czech: nickname for a tenacious man, from the past participle of the verb *uchytit* 'to take hold', 'to fasten'.
GIVEN NAMES Czech and Slovak 4%. *Bohumil, Miroslav.*

Udall (229) English: habitational name from Yewdale in Lancashire, so named from Old English *īw* 'yew tree' + Old Norse *dalr* 'valley'.

Uddin (509) Muslim: from Arabic *ud-dīn* (*al-dīn*), meaning '(of) the religion', usually a suffix attached to another word forming a compound Arabic personal name such as *Ṭallāh ud-Dīn* (see Saladin).
GIVEN NAMES Muslim 87%. *Mohammed* (48), *Mohammad* (20), *Kamal* (13), *Nasir* (8), *Shahab* (7), *Zia* (6), *Jalal* (5), *Muhammed* (5), *Syed* (5), *Muhammad* (4), *Qazi* (4), *Salah* (4).

Ude (148) German: from *Udo*, in the Middle Ages a popular short form of various personal names composed with *od* 'property', 'possession'.

Udelhofen (132) German: see Udelhoven.

Udelhoven (116) German: habitational name from Üdelhoven in North Rhine-Westphalia.

Udell (788) English: variant spelling of Udall.

Uden (202) German: patronymic from the personal name *Udo* (see Ude).

Udovich (208) Slovenian (**Udovič**): nickname for the son of a widow, from an old spelling of *vdova* 'widow' + the patronymic suffix *-ič*.

Udy (239) English (Cornwall): unexplained.

Uebel (206) German (also **Übel**): **1.** from a pet form of the personal name *Oppo*, a short form of a Germanic compound name beginning with *od* 'property', 'possession'. **2.** possibly also a nickname for an evildoer, from Middle High German *übele* 'evil', though this may be no more than folk etymology.
GIVEN NAMES German 7%. *Gerhard, Kurt, Ralf, Wilhelmina.*

Uebelacker (102) German (also **Übelacker**): from Middle High German *übel(e)* 'angry', 'bad', 'evil', 'little' + *acker* 'field',

hence a nickname for a farmer with poor or little land to farm.
GIVEN NAMES German 10%. *Klaus, Reinhold, Rudi.*

Uebele (126) German (also **Übele**): variant spelling of Uebel.
GIVEN NAMES German 5%. *Herman, Kurt, Reinhold.*

Uecker (657) North German: **1.** from the Germanic personal name *Audagar*, a compound of *od* 'property', 'possession' + *gar* 'ready' or *gēr* 'javelin', 'spear'. **2.** topographic name from the river Ücker (Uckermark district), or a habitational name from a place called Ückern in Westphalia.
GIVEN NAMES German 4%. *Otto* (3), *Detlef, Erwin, Kurt, Ottmar.*

Ueckert (143) North German: variant of Uecker.

Ueda (306) Japanese: from a common place name meaning 'upper rice paddy'; variously written, and also read **Kamida**. The surname, like the place name, is found throughout Japan and the Ryūkyū Islands.
GIVEN NAMES Japanese 79%. *Keiko* (5), *Toru* (4), *Etsuko* (3), *Shinji* (3), *Akio* (2), *Akira* (2), *Atsushi* (2), *Fumiko* (2), *Hajime* (2), *Haruhiko* (2), *Hiroko* (2), *Hiroshi* (2).

Uehara (318) Japanese: from a common placename meaning 'upper plain'; it is also read **Kamihara** (which can be written to mean 'divine plain'). The surname, like the placename, is found throughout Japan and the Ryūkyū Islands.
GIVEN NAMES Japanese 52%. *Hiroshi* (4), *Hiroki* (2), *Kame* (2), *Masako* (2), *Masaru* (2), *Sadao* (2), *Satoru* (2), *Shinsuke* (2), *Aki, Atsushi, Chiho, Chiyoko.*

Uehlein (100) German (also **Ühlein**): from a pet form of the personal name Uhl.

Uehling (191) German: from a short form of the various Germanic personal names formed with *od* 'property', 'possession'.

Ueland (198) Norwegian: habitational name from any of several farmsteads so named in Rogaland. The first element is of uncertain origin, perhaps from Old Norse *úfr* 'horned owl'; the second element is *land* 'land', 'farmstead'.
GIVEN NAME Scandinavian 7%; German 4%. *Arnulf* (3).

Uemura (155) Japanese: from a common placename meaning 'upper village' or (less commonly) 'planting village'; it is also read **Kamimura** (which can be written to mean 'divine village'). The surname is

515

found in western Japan and the Ryūkyūan island of Amami.

GIVEN NAMES Japanese 60%. *Hiroshi* (3), *Akira* (2), *Kazuyuki* (2), *Akio, Chiyono, Etsuro, Goro, Hideko, Hirotaka, Hiroyuki, Isamu, Jiro.*

Ueno (194) Japanese: from a common place name meaning 'upper field'; it is variously written, and also read *Kamino, Agano* and *Kōzuke.* Several families, some descended from various great clans, have adopted the name.

GIVEN NAMES Japanese 76%. *Hiroshi* (8), *Takashi* (4), *Akira* (2), *Atsushi* (2), *Kazuo* (2), *Masaaki* (2), *Shinji* (2), *Teruo* (2), *Aki, Akiko, Akio, Ayako.*

Ufer (105) German: topographic name for someone who lived on the bank or shore of a river, lake, or sea, late Middle High German *uover,* Middle Low German *over,* or a habitational name from a place named with this word, two examples of which are found in Austria and one in Germany, near Cologne.

GIVEN NAMES German 7%. *Fritz* (2), *Hans.*

Uffelman (203) German (**Uffelmann**): habitational name for someone from any of the six places called Uffeln in Westphalia.

Ufford (130) English: habitational name from places in Northamptonshire and Suffolk, so named from the Old English personal name *Uffa* (of uncertain origin) + Old English *worð* 'enclosure'.

Ugalde (331) Basque: habitational name from Ugalde in Araba province. The first element of place name is *ug-* meaning 'river', 'water'.

GIVEN NAMES Spanish 45%. *Jose* (8), *Juan* (8), *Pedro* (6), *Carlos* (4), *Alfredo* (3), *Guillermo* (3), *Manuel* (3), *Ruben* (3), *Agustin* (2), *Alicia* (2), *Bernardo* (2), *Enrique* (2).

Ugarte (378) Basque: habitational name from any of several places in the Basque provinces named Ugarte. The first element of place name, *ug-,* means 'river', 'water'.

GIVEN NAMES Spanish 50%. *Carlos* (13), *Jose* (9), *Luis* (9), *Jorge* (7), *Manuel* (7), *Juan* (6), *Miguel* (5), *Ricardo* (4), *Salvador* (4), *Angel* (3), *Armando* (3), *Carolina* (3).

Uglow (103) English (Devon and Cornwall): unexplained.

Ugolini (135) Italian (Tuscany): patronymic from the personal name *Ugolino,* a name of Germanic origin, which was particularly popular in the medieval period. It is generally considered to be a pet form of *Ugo* (Italian equivalent of HUGO).

GIVEN NAMES Italian 27%. *Alberto, Aldo, Amerigo, Angelo, Arrigo, Constantino, Corrado, Enrico, Gino, Grazia, Marco, Marino, Olinto, Piero, Valeriano.*

Uhde (200) German: from a short form of various Germanic personal names composed with *od* 'property', 'possession'.

GIVEN NAMES German 8%. *Otto* (3), *Frieda, Wilhelm.*

Uher (326) Czech and German: ethnic name for a Hungarian (see UNGER).

Uhing (121) Origin unidentified.

Uhl (2164) **1.** German and Czech: from a short form of the personal name ULRICH. **2.** North German: nickname from Middle Low German *ule* 'owl'. **3.** Czech: perhaps also a nickname or metonymic occupational name from Czech *uh(e)l* 'coal'.

Uhland (173) South German: from a Germanic personal name composed of the elements *odal* 'inherited property' + *nand* 'daring', 'bold'.

Uhle (176) German: variant of UHL.

GIVEN NAMES German 8%. *Otto* (4), *Alfons, Kurt.*

Uhlenhake (143) North German (Westphalia): topographic name for someone who lived on an estate (Middle Low German *hake;* see HUBER) named for its owls (Middle Low German *ule* 'owl', plural *ulen*).

GIVEN NAME German 4%. *Kurt.*

Uhlenhopp (127) North German: misinterpreted form of **Uhlenhof**, from Middle Low German *ūle* 'owl' + **hof(f)** 'farm', hence a habitational name.

Uhler (742) German: patronymic from a Germanic compound personal name beginning with *odal* 'inherited property'.

Uhles (139) German (Rhineland): topographic name from Middle Low German *ulla* (from Latin *olla* 'earthen pot') + *hūs* 'house'.

Uhlhorn (101) German: habitational name from Uhlhorn on the Hunte river. According to Bahlow, the first element of the place name is *ul,* an old term for 'rot', 'decay', later reinterpreted as Low German *ūle* 'owl' + *horn* 'spit of land'.

GIVEN NAMES German 12%. *Arno* (2), *Gunther.*

Uhlich (139) German: variant of ULRICH.

GIVEN NAMES German 8%. *Kurt* (2), *Gottfried.*

Uhlig (553) German: variant of ULRICH.

GIVEN NAMES German 11%. *Kurt* (4), *Gerhard* (2), *Hans* (2), *Wolfgang* (2), *Arno, Gerhart, Grete, Guenther, Gunther, Helmut, Rainer, Reiner.*

Uhlik (117) Czech (**Uhlík**): diminutive of **Uhlíř** (see UHLIR).

Uhlir (257) Czech (**Uhlíř**) and Slovak (**Uhliar**): occupational name for a coal merchant or, at an earlier date, a charcoal burner, from an agent derivative of Czech *uhlí* 'coal', 'charcoal'.

GIVEN NAMES German 4%; French 4%. *Otto* (3); *Camille* (2).

Uhlman (412) Altered spelling of UHLMANN.

Uhlmann (203) German: from a pet form of a Germanic compound personal name beginning with *odal* 'inherited property'.

GIVEN NAMES German 7%. *Gunther* (2), *Erwin, Kurt.*

Uhls (164) Altered form of German UHL. Addition of *-s* is a common feature of German names in the U.S.

Uhr (154) **1.** German: from a short form of the personal name *Uhrich,* a variant of ULRICH. **2.** German: from Middle High German *ūr* 'aurochs', hence a nickname for someone thought to resemble a bison. **3.** Jewish (Ashkenazic): metonymic occupational name for a watch or clockmaker, from German *Uhr* 'watch', 'clock'.

GIVEN NAMES Jewish 5%; German 4%. *Shimon, Yakov; Horst.*

Uhrich (603) German: variant of ULRICH.

Uhrig (539) German: variant of ULRICH.

GIVEN NAMES German 5%. *Juergen, Jurgen, Kurt, Mathias, Ulrike, Willi, Wolfgang.*

Uhrin (184) Slovak (**Uhrín**): ethnic name for a Hungarian.

Uihlein (116) Variant spelling of German **Ühlein** (see UEHLEIN).

Ulan (102) Polish: **1.** from a vernacular form of the Latin personal name *Julianus* (see JULIAN). **2.** possibly also a nickname from a derivative of Old Polish *ulać* 'to mold or cast'.

Ulanowski (65) Polish: habitational name for someone from any of various places in Poland called Ulany, Ulanów, or Ulanowice. The places are named with the Polish personal name ULAN.

GIVEN NAMES Polish 10%. *Bronislaw, Eugeniusz.*

Ulanski (48) Polish (also **Ułański**): habitational name for someone from Ulany (formerly *Ułany*) in Sieradz voivodeship. The place is named either with the Old Polish personal name ULAN or with the Latinate name JULIAN.

Ulatowski (168) Polish: habitational name for someone from Ulatowo in Ostrołęka voivodeship, a place named with Old Polish *ulot, ulatać* 'to fly away'.

GIVEN NAMES Polish 8%. *Bogdan, Grzegorz, Kazimierz, Piotr, Tomek, Zygmunt.*

Ulberg (170) **1.** German: variant of ULBRICH. **2.** Norwegian: habitational name from any of three farmsteads so named in southeastern Norway. The second element in each case is from Old Norse *berg* 'mountain', 'hill'; while the first element is derived respectively from *ulfr* 'wolf', *urð* 'scree', 'rock-strewn slope', and from an unknown source.

GIVEN NAMES Scandinavian 6%. *Selmer, Thor.*

Ulbrich (455) German: from a Saxon and Silesian dialect form of a Germanic personal name composed of the elements *odal* 'inherited property' + *berht* 'bright', 'famous'.

GIVEN NAMES German 13%. *Konrad* (3), *Klaus* (2), *Kurt* (2), *Lothar* (2), *Wolfgang* (2), *Erhard, Erwin, Georg, Gerhard, Hans Peter, Heinz, Horst.*

Ulbricht (214) German: variant of ULBRICH.

GIVEN NAMES German 10%. *Kurt* (2), *Ernst, Helmut, Helmuth, Otto, Wolfgang*.

Ulch (162) Americanized spelling of German **Ulsch** (see ULSH).

Ulery (578) Probably an Americanized spelling of German ULRICH or its variant **Ullerich** (see ULLERY).

Ulferts (122) Dutch and North German: patronymic from a derivative of the Germanic personal name *Ulfrid*, from *odal* 'inherited property' + *frid-* 'peace'.

Uliano (161) Italian: from a reduced form of the personal name *Iuliano*, southern dialect form of GIULIANO, or possibly from some other name with this ending.

GIVEN NAMES Italian 20%. *Angelo* (4), *Carmine, Francesco, Salvatore*.

Ulibarri (706) Basque: habitational name from a place in Navarre named Ulibarri, from Basque *uri-*, *iri-* 'hamlet', 'village' + *barri* 'new', or in some cases from Ullibarri or Ullivarri, Castilianized variants of several places in Araba province named Uribarri in Basque.

GIVEN NAMES Spanish 16%. *Manuel* (8), *Alfonso* (3), *Orlando* (3), *Armando* (2), *Carlos* (2), *Estela* (2), *Jorge* (2), *Jose* (2), *Juanita* (2), *Ruben* (2), *Adelina, Alejandra*.

Ulicny (135) Czech (**Uličný**): topographic name from *ulice* 'street'.

Ulin (223) Dutch: variant of *Huelin*, a patronymic from *Hue*, a pet form of the French personal name *Hugues* (see HUGO).

Ulinski (114) Polish (**Uliński**): habitational name from Ulina in Kraków vovivodeship, named either with *ul* 'bee hive' or with the personal name *Ul(i)an* (see ULAN).

Ullah (267) Muslim: literally 'of Allah', usually a suffix attached to another word forming a compound Arabic personal name such as *'Abd-Ullah* 'servant of Allah' (see ABDULLAH).

GIVEN NAMES Muslim 87%. *Mohammed* (13), *Mohammad* (9), *Sana* (7), *Habib* (6), *Aman* (4), *Ahsan* (3), *Asif* (3), *Inayat* (3), *Safi* (3), *Saif* (3), *Sami* (3), *Sayed* (3).

Ulland (182) **1.** Norwegian: habitational name from any of several farmsteads probably named in Old Norse as *Ullarland*, denoting land dedicated to *Ullr*, a pagan god who originally occupied a place of great power in the Nordic pantheon, but was overtaken in importance by Odin at an early stage in history. **2.** German: variant of UHLAND.

GIVEN NAMES Scandinavian 17%. *Anders* (2), *Borge, Britt, Oivind*.

Ullery (494) Of German origin: see ULERY.

Ullman (1410) **1.** Respelling of German ULLMANN. **2.** Jewish (Ashkenazic): variant spelling of ULMAN.

Ullmann (448) German: from a pet form of ULRICH.

GIVEN NAMES German 7%. *Klaus* (2), *Kurt* (2), *Fritz, Gunther, Hans, Heinz, Herta, Horst*.

Ullmer (178) **1.** English: variant of **Woolmer** (see WOOMER). **2.** German: variant spelling of ULMER.

Ulloa (1105) Galician: habitational name from either of two places in Galicia named Ulloa (in A Coruña and Lugo provinces).

GIVEN NAMES Spanish 53%. *Jose* (32), *Carlos* (14), *Juan* (12), *Miguel* (12), *Jorge* (10), *Luis* (10), *Francisco* (9), *Julio* (9), *Ramon* (9), *Fernando* (8), *Jesus* (8), *Raul* (8).

Ullom (693) Probably an Americanized form of ULM.

Ullrich (1566) German: variant spelling of ULRICH.

GIVEN NAMES German 6%. *Otto* (4), *Erwin* (2), *Franz* (2), *Hanns* (2), *Bernhard, Dieter, Dietmar, Frieda, Gottfried, Hans, Hartmut, Heino*.

Ulm (617) German: habitational name from the city of this name (see ULMER 1).

Ulman (585) **1.** German: from a pet form of the personal name ULRICH. **2.** Jewish (Ashkenazic): habitational name from the city of Ulm in Baden-Württemberg, with the suffix *-man* 'man', which is occasionally found as a surname-forming element with placenames, denoting a native or inhabitant of a place.

Ulmen (149) German: **1.** perhaps in some cases a respelling of **Ulmann** (see ULMAN). **2.** alternatively, perhaps a habitational name for someone from any of several places named Ulm.

Ulmer (3223) German: **1.** habitational name for someone from the city of Ulm. The placename is from the root *uel*, an unattested word meaning 'turn', 'wind', 'roll' or from *el-* or *ol-* 'flow', a reference in either case to the influx of the Blan river into the Danube. **2.** from the Germanic personal name *Odolmar*, composed of the elements *odal* 'inherited property' + *mār* 'famous'.

Ulrey (471) Variant of ULLERY.

Ulrich (6869) German: from the personal name *Ulrich*, Old High German *Odalrīc*, composed of the elements *odal* 'inherited property', 'fortune' + *rīc* 'power'. The name was borne by a 10th-century saint, bishop of Augsburg, whose fame contributed greatly to the popularity of the personal name in German- and Slavic-speaking areas in the Middle Ages.

GIVEN NAMES German 4%. *Kurt* (11), *Otto* (10), *Erwin* (4), *Hans* (4), *Gerhard* (3), *Klaus* (3), *Frieda* (2), *Fritz* (2), *Reinhard* (2), *Alfons, Alois, Bernd*.

Ulrick (152) Altered spelling of German ULRICH.

Ulsh (309) Americanized spelling of German **Ulsch** a Germanized form of Czech VLK 'wolf' (inflected stem *vlč-*; see VLCEK).

Ulshafer (169) Altered form of South German **Ulshöfer**, habitational name for someone from a place called Ilshofen (old form *Ulleshoven*), near Schwäbisch Hall.

Ulven (128) Norwegian: habitational name from any of about fifteen farmsteads, mainly in Hedmark and Oppland, so named from Old Norse as *Ulfvin*, a compound of either *ulfr* 'wolf' or *alfr* 'gravel' + *vin* 'meadow'.

Ulvestad (105) Norwegian: habitational name from any of five farmsteads, most in western Norway, named from Old Norse *ulfr* 'wolf' + *staðir*, plural of *staðr* 'farmstead', 'dwelling'.

GIVEN NAME Scandinavian 14%; German 5%. *Thor*.

Um (269) **1.** Korean (**Ŭm**): unexplained. **2.** Cambodian: unexplained.

GIVEN NAMES Korean 53%. *Kee* (4), *Jung* (3), *Chung* (2), *In* (2), *Jae* (2), *Jin* (2), *Joon* (2), *Ki Hoon* (2), *Yong* (2), *Young* (2), *Bin, Byung, Chan, Dae Yong, Daeho, Eng, Eunjin, Hak, Jaeyong, Jang, Jin-Young, Joo, Jungwon, Ki Hong*.

Umali (114) from a Filipino language, most probably Ilocano: unexplained.

GIVEN NAMES Spanish 49%. *Amado* (2), *Lucila* (2), *Ramon* (2), *Aida, Angel, Armida, Arturo, Carlito, Ebaristo, Edgardo, Eladio, Enrique*.

Umana (461) **1.** probably Basque (**Umaña**): variant of **Omaña**, topographic name from Basque *oma* 'scallions seed'. **2.** Southern Italian: habitational name from any of various places named with this word, feminine form of *umano* 'human', Latin *humanus*.

GIVEN NAMES Spanish 54%; Italian 14%. *Jose* (22), *Miguel* (7), *Francisco* (6), *Juan* (6), *Pedro* (6), *Ana* (4), *Jesus* (4), *Luis* (4), *Ricardo* (4), *Carlos* (3); *Mario* (8), *Alvaro* (3), *Enrico, Massimiliano*

Umansky (177) Jewish (from Ukraine) and Ukrainian: habitational name for someone from a place called Uman, in Ukraine.

GIVEN NAMES Russian 15%; Jewish 13%. *Anatoly* (2), *Leonid* (2), *Arkady, Boris, Igor, Kirill, Konstantin, Mikhail, Semyon, Vladimir, Yefin, Yelena; Ilya* (2), *Hyman, Irina, Meyer*.

Umanzor (171) Spanish: probably variant of **Almanzor**, a habitational name for somebody who lived by the area of Almanzor, a remarkable mountain in Sierra de Gredos, in Ávila province. The name Almanzor possibly originates from the personal name of Almanzor (arabic al-Mansur), the fearsome vizier and actual ruler of Muslim Spain from 978 to 1002. The variant Umanzor is mainly found in Chile, El Salvador, and Honduras.

GIVEN NAMES Spanish 58%. *Jose* (26), *Consuelo* (3), *Guadalupe* (3), *Julio* (3), *Luis* (3), *Pedro* (3), *Carlos* (2), *Efrain* (2), *Jose Angel* (2), *Oscar Rene* (2), *Telma* (2), *Wilfredo* (2).

Umbach (233) South German, Austrian, and Jewish (Ashkenazic): habitational name from various places called Umbach or Ambach, in Bavaria and Austria.

GIVEN NAMES German 11%. *Eldred* (3), *Erwin, Friedrich, Fritz, Karl Heinz, Uwe*.

Umbarger (497) Altered spelling of German UMBERGER.

Umbaugh (255) Altered spelling of German UMBACH.

Umbel (149) Perhaps an altered spelling of Swiss German **Humbel** (see BUHL) or of German **Hummel, Hümpel**, or some other derivative of the personal name *Hunibald*. See also UMBLE.

Umberger (836) German: topographic or habitational name of unexplained origin.

Umble (175) English: variant of HUMBLE.

Umbreit (115) German: nickname for an unready or uncooperative person, from Middle High German *unbereit* 'unprepared', 'unwilling'.

Umeda (130) Japanese: 'plum rice paddy'; taken as a surname by the Shida branch of the MINAMOTO family from a village in Musashi (now Tōkyō and Saitama prefectures). Other bearers descend from FUJIWARA no Hidesato (10th century).
GIVEN NAMES Japanese 54%. *Kenji* (3), *Yuko* (2), *Akiko, Atsuko, Ayako, Giichi, Hideyuki, Junko, Katsushi, Kazuo, Mamoru, Masaharu*.

Umemoto (111) Japanese: '(one who lives) near the plum tree'. This name is found mostly in western Japan.
GIVEN NAMES Japanese 45%. *Koji* (2), *Kuniaki* (2), *Akira, Haruo, Hisato, Itsuo, Kenji, Masakazu, Masao, Masaru, Mayuko, Michiye*.

Umfleet (206) Altered spelling of English (Worcestershire) **Anfleet** or **Amphlett**, a topographic name from Middle English *an flete* 'by the stream', in this case most probably the River Severn. Old English *flēot* 'stream', 'estuary', 'creek' is a common place-name element in English (see FLEET). *Holt Fleet* 'the wood by the river' is the name of a place on the River Severn near where this surname was established in the 14th century.

Umfress (107) Variant of English and Welsh HUMPHRIES.

Umhoefer (126) German (**Umhöfer**): probably a habitational name for someone from a place called Ummenhofen on the Jagst river.
GIVEN NAMES French 5%. *Firmin, Germaine*.

Umholtz (220) German: **1**. topographic name for someone who lived by a forest. **2**. from *unholz* 'waste, or refuse wood', hence probably a metonymic occupational name for a carpenter.
GIVEN NAME German 4%. *Kurt* (2).

Umland (340) North German: occupational name for a shipowner or mariner who traveled between the Dutch and the Baltic ports, skirting round Skagen in order to do so, Middle Low German *umlandes(varer)*.
GIVEN NAMES German 4%. *Kurt, Otto*.

Umlauf (264) German: occupational name for a policeman in a town or city, from

Middle High German *umbe laufen* 'to make the rounds'.
GIVEN NAMES German 6%. *Erwin* (2), *Gerhardt, Kurt, Otto*.

Ummel (199) Swiss German: unexplained.

Umphenour (134) Origin unidentified.

Umphlett (200) English: see UMFLEET.

Umphress (217) Variant of English and Welsh HUMPHRIES.

Umphrey (403) Variant of English and Welsh HUMPHREY.

Umpleby (97) English (Yorkshire): habitational name from Anlaby in Humberside, recorded 1234 as *Anlaweby* but in Domesday Book as *Umloueby*. The place is named with the Old Norse personal name *Anláfr, Óláfr* (see OLIFF) + Old Norse *býr* 'farm', 'settlement'.

Umscheid (208) German: nickname from Middle High German *unbescheiden* 'improper', 'inconsiderate'.

Umstead (689) Origin uncertain: perhaps an altered form of an unidentified Scandinavian habitational name ending in *-stedt* 'homestead', or of the English surname **Hamstead**, a habitational name from any of several places in England named with Old English *hāmstede* 'homestead', for example Hamstead in the West Midlands and Isle of Wight, Hampstead in London, or Hamstead Marshall and Hampstead Norris in Berkshire.

Umsted (125) See UMSTEAD.

Un (123) **1**. Chinese 阮: variant of RUAN. **2**. Cambodian: unexplained. **3**. probably from a native American language in Mexico, unexplained.
GIVEN NAMES Chinese 37%; Cambodian 10%; Spanish 7%. *Chong* (2), *Young* (2), *Chun, Hang, Ho, In, Jung, Maeng, Mijin, Rong; Hyong, Pong, Then, Yom; Lanh, Nu; Chea, Chhay, Chheng, Chhom, Voeun, Yoeun; Alejandro, Angel, Miguel, Ricardo, Secundino, Tomas*.

Unangst (348) South German: nickname for a fearless person, from Middle High German *angest* 'fear', 'fright', prefixed by *un*, denoting the absence of this quality.

Uncapher (246) Of German origin: see UNKEFER.

Underberg (227) **1**. Dutch, North German, Norwegian, and Danish (**Underbjerg**): topographic name for someone who lived at the foot of a hill. **2**. Swedish and Norwegian: habitational name from a place named with Old Norse *undir* 'under' + *berg* 'mountain', 'hill'.

Underdahl (279) Norwegian: habitational name from any of several farmsteads with similar names (for example *Undredal* in Sogn), which are probably derived from Old Norse *undir* 'under' + *dalr* 'valley', denoting a farm situated in a valley bottom.
GIVEN NAMES Scandinavian 4%; German 4%. *Hans* (2), *Orlo* (2).

Underdown (287) English: topographic name for someone who lived at the foot of

a hill (Old English *dūn*), or a habitational name for someone from a place so named, for example in Kent.

Underhill (2665) English: topographic name for someone who lived at the foot of a hill, or a habitational name from Underhill in Devon, named from Old English *under* 'under' + *hyll*, or from Underhill in Kent, named from Old English *under* + *helde* 'slope'.
FOREBEARS John Underhill (*c*.1597–1672) was born in Kenilworth, Warwickshire, England. His father was a mercenary in the Netherlands, and he himself became a cadet in the Prince of Orange's guards. In 1630 he emigrated to Boston, MA, where he was appointed captain of militia. In 1664–65 he played a significant role in helping to bring the Dutch colony of New Netherland under English control.

Underkoffler (177) Partly Americanized form of German **Unterköfler**, an occupational name for an agent or middleman, Middle High German *underköufel(er)*, a surname found chiefly in the Rhineland and Frankfurt areas.

Underkofler (101) German: variant of UNDERKOFFLER.

Underwood (19831) English and Scottish: topographic name for someone who lived near or in a wood, from Middle English *under* + *wude, wode* 'wood', or a habitational name from any of various places so named, for example in Derbyshire, Nottinghamshire, and the former county of Ayrshire (from Old English *under* + *wudu*).
FOREBEARS Joseph Underwood emigrated from England to Watertown, MA, in 1637. William Underwood came from England to Concord, MA, before 1640, later settling in Chelmsford, MA.
In VA, the name was established by Thomas William Underwood, who came from Norfolk, England, in 1675.

Unfried (117) German: nickname for a quarrelsome or troublesome person, from Middle High German *unvride* 'quarrel', 'restlessness'.
GIVEN NAMES German 8%. *Ignaz* (2), *Manfred*.

Ung (636) **1**. Chinese 王: possibly a variant of WANG 1. **2**. Other Southeast Asian: unexplained.
GIVEN NAMES Chinese 39%; Vietnamese 15%; Other Southeast Asian 5%. *Seng* (5), *Hong* (4), *Kiu* (4), *Leng* (4), *Cheng* (3), *Chou* (3), *Heng* (3), *Khun* (3), *Meng* (3), *Sang* (3), *Chin* (2), *Dong* (2); *Ly* (5), *Mui* (5), *Thong* (4), *Huy* (3), *Long* (3), *Hai* (2), *Ky* (2), *Lenh* (2), *Luong* (2), *Nhi* (2), *Thang* (2), *Anh, Nam* (2), *Jang, Neng, Phong, Ry, Tam, Then*.

Ungar (698) German, Hungarian (**Ungár**), and Jewish (Ashkenazic): ethnic name for a Hungarian or a nickname for someone who had trade relations with Hungary. Paradoxically, as a Hungarian name it is of foreign (probably German) origin. Despite the Finno-Ugric origin of the Magyars in most European languages they were mistakenly named after the Turkic Hun people (English *Hungarian*, German *Ungarisch*, Italian *Ungerese*, Russian *Vengerskij* etc.). The Hungarian ethnic name for a Hungarian is MAGYAR.

GIVEN NAMES Jewish 8%; German 4%. *Aharon* (2), *Akiva* (2), *Emanuel* (2), *Menachem* (2), *Mendel* (2), *Mordchai* (2), *Aron, Miriam, Mort, Motti, Nuchem, Shmuel*; *Egon* (2), *Ernst* (2), *Erwin* (2), *Georg, Otto*.

Ungaro (244) Italian: ethnic name for a Hungarian or a nickname for someone who had some trading or other connections with Hungary, from *ungaro* 'Hungarian' (from Latin *Hungarus*).

GIVEN NAMES Italian 11%; Spanish 7%. *Rocco* (3), *Antonio, Cosmo, Fabio, Nicoletta, Quirino, Vito*; *Carlos, Luis, Manuel, Rocio, Rosario*.

Unger (6231) German, Jewish (Ashkenazic), and Slovenian: ethnic name for a Hungarian or a nickname for someone who had trade relations with Hungary, from the ethnic term *Unger* 'Hungarian' (see UNGAR).

Ungerer (240) German: variant of UNGER 'Hungarian'.

GIVEN NAMES German 5%. *Erwin* (2), *Horst* (2), *Kurt*.

Ungerleider (123) German: unexplained.

Ungerman (140) German (**Ungermann**) and Jewish (Ashkenazic): variant of UNGER.

Unick (115) Probably an Americanized spelling of **Unich**, a rare German family name, or of **Unik**, a Dutch name.

Union (159) English: probably a variant spelling of ONION.

Unis (119) Origin unidentified.

Unkefer (146) Altered spelling of German **Ungefehr**, a nickname for an honorable man, from Middle High German *ān gevœre* 'without deceit', 'without guile'. This name is found chiefly in OH.

Unkel (124) German: habitational name from any of various places so named in the Rhineland and Hessen.

Unland (167) North German (Westphalia): topographic name for someone living in or farming an area of infertile land, from Middle Low German *unland* 'wasteland'.

Unnerstall (118) North German: Low German equivalent of High German **Unterstall(er)**, a habitational name for a farmer whose barn was situated below another farmer's, from *unter* 'below' + Middle Low German *stal* 'barn', 'cattle stand'.

GIVEN NAME German 5%. *Kurt*.

Uno (166) Japanese: written with characters meaning 'roof' (implying the heavenly roof) and 'field'; it is found in western Japan and descended through several branches of the MINAMOTO clan.

GIVEN NAMES Japanese 49%. *Hideo* (3), *Shigeko* (2), *Takao* (2), *Takeshi* (2), *Hidehiko, Hiroshi, Junichi, Kaoru, Katsutoshi, Kazuhiko, Keiko, Kiku*.

Unrath (140) German: nickname for an unfortunate person, from Middle High German *unrat* 'need', 'disaster'.

Unrau (100) German: Low German variant of UNRUH. This is one of the German family names that were established in Russia and Ukraine in the 19th century.

Unrein (358) German: nickname from Middle High German *unreine* 'unclean', 'evil', 'unchaste'.

Unroe (133) Americanized spelling of German UNRUH.

Unrue (169) Americanized spelling of German UNRUH.

Unruh (3094) German: **1.** nickname for a restless or quarrelsome person, from Middle High German, Middle Low German *unrouwe, unrāwa* 'unrest', 'disturbance'. **2.** habitational name from places called Unruh, in East Prussia, or Unrow. **3.** nickname for a careless or casual person, from Middle High German *unruoch* 'careless', 'negligent'.

Unsell (115) Altered spelling of German **Unseld**, from Middle High German *unsaelde* 'misfortune', a nickname for a sad, unlucky person.

Unser (301) **1.** South German (Baden): unexplained. **2.** North German: habitational name for someone from a place called Unsen, near Hameln.

Unsworth (384) English (Lancashire): habitational name from Unsworth, a place in Greater Manchester, named from the genitive case of the Old English byname *Hund* meaning 'dog' + Old English *worð* 'enclosure'.

Unterberger (119) German: habitational name for someone from Unterberg in Styria, Austria.

GIVEN NAMES German 11%; Scandinavian 4%. *Friedrich* (2), *Erwin, Franz, Kurt*; *Hilma* (2).

Unterbrink (111) Dutch and North German: topographic name for someone who lived by a pasture, from Middle Low German *unter* 'under' + *brinc* 'edge', 'slope', 'grazing land', in particular a raised meadow in low-lying land.

GIVEN NAME German 4%. *Armin*.

Unterreiner (191) South German: topographic name for someone who lived below a mountain ridge, from Middle High German *under* 'under' + *rein* 'ridge'.

Unterseher (147) South German: topographic name for someone who lived downhill from a mountain lake, from Middle High German *under* 'under' + *sē* 'lake'.

GIVEN NAME Scandinavian 6%. *Iver* (2).

Unthank (134) English: habitational name for someone from places called Unthank in Cumbria and Northumberland, so named from Old English *unthanc* 'without consent', i.e. a squatter's holding.

Untiedt (178) North German: from Middle Low German *untīt* 'inappropriate time', 'bad time', hence a nickname for someone in the habit of making an untimely appearance.

GIVEN NAME French 7%. *Andre* (2).

Unverferth (130) Respelling of German **Unverfehrt** or **Unverfährt**, a nickname from Middle High German *unverværet* 'intrepid'.

Unverzagt (225) German: nickname from Middle High German *unverzaget* 'undaunted', 'unabashed'.

Unwin (264) English: from the Old English personal name *Hūnwine*, composed of the elements *hūn* 'bear cub' + *wine* 'friend'. Later in the Old English or early Middle English period, this name came to be confused with the word *unwine* 'enemy' (from the negative prefix *un-* + *wine* 'friend'), and this is no doubt the source of the surname in some cases.

Unzicker (211) German (Hessen): perhaps an altered form of **Hunsrücker**, a regional name for someone from the Hunsrück area, situated between the Rhine, Mosel, and Nahe. However, since the surname is now found chiefly in the Bad Wildungen–Edertal area, a different source may be involved.

Upadhyay (119) Indian (northern states and Karnataka): Hindu (Brahman) name from Sanskrit *upādhyāya* 'teacher' (from *upa* 'with', 'under' + *adhyāya* 'studying').

GIVEN NAMES Indian 95%. *Ajay* (3), *Ram* (3), *Satish* (3), *Vijay* (3), *Dipak* (2), *Haren* (2), *Jagadish* (2), *Jayprakash* (2), *Kirit* (2), *Nandini* (2), *Nirmala* (2), *Pankaj* (2).

Upah (117) Origin unidentified.

Upchurch (3455) English: habitational name from Upchurch, a place in Kent, named from Old English *upp* 'up' + *cirice* 'church', i.e. 'church standing high up'.

Updegraff (600) Altered form of a Dutch topographic name for someone who lived near a tomb.

FOREBEARS Two brothers Updegraff were among the thirteen German families who in 1683 founded the first German settlement on American soil, Germantown, PA, near Philadelphia. Their forebears had emigrated to Germany from the Netherlands two generations before.

Updegrove (262) Altered form of Dutch UPDEGRAFF.

Updike (1246) Altered spelling of Dutch **Opdijk**, a topographic name for someone who lived on a dike.

FOREBEARS The American writer John Updike traces his ancestry to Gijsbert Opdijck, commander of the Fort Goede Hoop (now Hartford, CT) in the 1640s.

Updyke (355) See UPDIKE.

Upham (831) English: habitational name for someone from Upham in Hampshire or from minor places so named in Devon and Wiltshire. The first is named with Old English *upp* 'upper' + *hām* 'homestead' or *hamm* 'river meadow', 'enclosure hemmed in by water'.

Uphaus (125) Possibly an altered form of German **Uphu(e)s**, a habitational name from any of various places named Uphusen, for example in Saxony and Lower Saxony.

Uphoff (464) Dutch and North German: topographic name for someone who lived on a farm or manor, from Middle Low German *up* 'on' + *hof* 'farmstead', 'manor farm'.

Uphold (212) English: perhaps a shortened form of **Upholder**, an occupational name for someone who dealt in secondhand clothes and other articles, Middle English *upoldere*.

Uplinger (196) German: habitational name for someone from Üplingen in Saxony-Anhalt.

Upp (297) **1.** English: unexplained. **2.** Probably a variant or variant spelling of **Opp**, from a short form of a Germanic personal name formed with *ōd* 'inherited wealth', or of OPPERMAN.

Uppal (145) Indian (Panjab): Hindu (Jat, Khatri) and Sikh name. The Jats have a tribe and the Khatris have a clan called Uppal.

GIVEN NAMES Indian 84%; Muslim 4%. *Sanjay* (3), *Bal* (2), *Krishan* (2), *Radhika* (2), *Sunil* (2), *Alok, Anuj, Aparna, Archana, Ashwani, Avtar, Balraj*; *Iqbal* (2), *Arifa, Kamal, Mohammed.*

Upperman (217) Americanized form of German OBERMANN.

Upright (308) English: nickname for an honorable man, from Middle English *upri(g)ht* 'erect'.

Upshaw (1804) English (East Anglia): probably a habitational name from a lost or unidentified place named with Old English *upp* 'up(per)' + *sc(e)aga* 'copse', or a topographic name with the same meaning.

Upshur (241) Most probably an altered spelling of English **Upshire**, a habitational name from Upshire in Essex, named with Old English *upp* 'up' + *scīr* 'district'. Alternatively, it may be a variant of UPSHAW.

Upson (688) English (East Anglia): probably a variant of **Upston**, a habitational name for someone from Ubbeston Green in Suffolk, so named from the Old Scandinavian personal name *Ubbi* + Old English *tūn* 'settlement'.

Uptain (301) Perhaps a variant of English UPTON.

Uptegrove (146) Americanized form of Dutch UPDEGRAFF.

Upthegrove (127) Americanized form of Dutch UPDEGRAFF.

Uptmor (103) Origin unidentified.

Upton (5153) English: habitational name from any of the numerous places called Upton. The majority of them are named from Old English *up-* 'upper' + *tūn* 'enclosure', 'settlement'. One in Essex, however, was originally named with the phrase *upp in tūne* 'up in the settlement', i.e. the higher part of the settlement; and one in Worcestershire is probably so called from the Old English personal name *Ubba* + *tūn*.

Uram (297) Hungarian: nickname for someone who habitually used the expression *Uram* 'My Lord!'.

Uran (154) **1.** Slovenian: nickname from an old spelling of *vran* 'raven', 'crow', or 'black horse'. **2.** English: variant spelling of UREN. **3.** probably from a native American language in northern Mexico: unexplaiend.

GIVEN NAMES Spanish 4%. *Carlos* (2), *Alberto, Eduardo, Juan, Leticia, Luz.*

Uranga (227) Basque: topographic name from Basque *ur* 'water', hence a topographic name for someone who lived near a river or lake.

GIVEN NAMES Spanish 40%. *Jose* (4), *Armando* (3), *Luis* (3), *Felipe* (2), *Jaime* (2), *Jesus* (2), *Juan* (2), *Lazaro* (2), *Marisa* (2), *Roberto* (2), *Rodolfo* (2), *Sergio* (2); *Erminio.*

Urbach (473) **1.** German: habitational name from any of numerous places named Urbach. **2.** German: from the personal name URBAN with the Slavic suffix *-ak* (Germanized form *-ach*). **3.** Czech: from a pet form of derivative of the personal name URBAN. **4.** Jewish (Ashkenazic): see AUERBACH.

GIVEN NAMES German 5%. *Gunther, Kurt, Ralf.*

Urbain (180) French: variant of the personal name URBAN.

GIVEN NAMES French 8%. *Henri, Jean-Luc, Monique, Sebastien, Thierry.*

Urban (7911) English, French, German, Czech, Slovak, Polish, Ukrainian, Belorussian, Hungarian (**Urbán**), and Jewish (eastern Ashkenazic): from a medieval personal name (Latin *Urbanus* meaning 'city dweller', a derivative of *urbs* 'town', 'city'). The name was borne by a 4th-century saint, the patron saint of vines, and by seven early popes. The Jewish surname represents an adoption of the Polish personal name.

Urbanczyk (256) Polish (**Urbańczyk**): from a pet form of the personal name URBAN.

GIVEN NAMES Polish 5%. *Czeslaw, Janusz, Kasmier, Krystyna, Zygmunt.*

Urbanek (654) Polish, Czech (**Urbánek**), and Sorbian: from a pet form of the personal name URBAN. The surname is also established in Germany.

Urbani (180) Italian: patronymic or plural form of URBANO.

GIVEN NAMES Italian 19%. *Angelo* (4), *Aldo* (2), *Antonio, Carmela, Dante, Domenic, Luca, Natale, Niccolo, Nicolo, Rinaldo.*

Urbaniak (507) Polish and Ukrainian: patronymic from URBAN.

GIVEN NAMES Polish 6%. *Andrzej* (2), *Dariusz, Feliks, Irena, Jacek, Slawomir, Waclaw.*

Urbanik (226) Polish and Czech (**Urbaník**): from a pet form of the personal name URBAN.

GIVEN NAMES Polish 8%. *Andrzej* (2), *Jaroslaw, Mieczyslaw, Wieslawa.*

Urbano (591) Spanish and Italian: from the personal name *Urbano* (see URBAN), or a nickname from *urbano* 'urbane', 'elegant'.

GIVEN NAMES Spanish 27%; Italian 8%. *Jose* (6), *Juan* (4), *Mario* (4), *Jorge* (3), *Manuel* (3), *Raul* (3), *Adriana* (2), *Alfonso* (2), *Armando* (2), *Arturo* (2), *Eusebio* (2), *Leopoldo* (2); *Antonio* (4), *Leonardo* (3), *Rocco* (2), *Amadeo, Angelo, Federico, Fortunata, Gaetano, Genoveffa, Gino, Guido, Heriberto.*

Urbanovsky (120) Czech (**Urbanovský**): habitational name from a place called Urbanovice, named for the URBAN family.

GIVEN NAMES German 5%. *Alphons.*

Urbanowicz (274) Polish: patronymic from the personal name URBAN.

GIVEN NAMES Polish 14%. *Jerzy* (2), *Andrzej, Bronislaw, Dariusz, Henryk, Krzysztof, Tadeusz, Teofil, Witold, Zygmunt.*

Urbanowski (132) Polish: habitational name for someone from places called Urbanów in Radom voivodeship or Urbanowo in Poznań voivodeship, both named with the personal name URBAN.

Urbanski (1166) **1.** Polish (**Urbański**): habitational name for someone from a place named with the personal name URBAN. Compare URBANOWSKI. **2.** Perhaps an altered spelling of Czech *Urbanský*, habitational name for someone from a place called Urbanice.

GIVEN NAMES Polish 6%. *Casimir* (4), *Jerzy* (4), *Janusz* (2), *Slawomir* (2), *Zygmunt* (2), *Boleslaw, Jozef, Leszek, Lucjan, Stanislaw, Zbigniew, Zigmund.*

Urbas (178) Polish (**Urbaś**), Slovenian, and Jewish (Ashkenazic): from a derivative of the personal name URBAN. The reason for its adoption as a surname by Jews (who never used it as a personal name) is unknown.

GIVEN NAMES Jewish 4%. *Elisheva, Eytan, Yaron.*

Urben (152) French: variant of URBAN.

Urbin (116) French: variant of URBAN.

Urbina (1085) Basque: habitational name from Urbina in Araba province, Basque Country, or a topographic name probably for someone who lived near a confluence, from Basque *ur-* 'water' + *bi* 'two'.

GIVEN NAMES Spanish 52%. *Jose* (24), *Carlos* (16), *Francisco* (16), *Luis* (16), *Manuel*

(15), *Juan* (14), *Jorge* (10), *Jesus* (8), *Raul* (8), *Guadalupe* (7), *Javier* (7), *Julio* (7).

Urbon (108) German: variant of URBAN.

Urch (115) **1.** English (Somerset): unexplained; possibly a shortened form of *Urchfont*, name of a place in Wiltshire, which is named with the Old English personal name *Eohrīc* + *funta* 'spring', 'well'. **2.** Germanized spelling of Slovenian **Urh**, from the personal name *Urh*, Slovenian vernacular form of *Ulrik*, German *Udalrich*.

GIVEN NAME German 4%. *Gunter*.

Urciuoli (164) Italian: probably from *orciuolo* (from Latin *urceolus* 'small pitcher', 'water pot', a diminutive of *urceus*), presumably applied as a metonymic occupational name or perhaps as a nickname.

GIVEN NAMES Italian 14%. *Carlo* (2), *Carmine*, *Domenic*, *Nicoletta*, *Rocco*, *Salvator*.

Urda (203) Spanish: habitational name from Urda in Toledo province.

Urdahl (142) Norwegian: habitational name from any of seven farmsteads, most of them originally named in Old Norse as *Urðadalr*, from *urð* 'scree', 'rock-strewn slope' + *dalr* 'valley'.

GIVEN NAMES Scandinavian 9%; German 5%. *Nordeen*, *Steinar*; *Kurt* (2).

Urdiales (138) Spanish: habitational name from any of the places named Urdiales, in particular León-Urdiales and Castro-Urdiales in Santander province, named with a derivative of Basque *urda* 'field'.

GIVEN NAMES Spanish 36%. *Carlos* (3), *Ricardo* (3), *Celestino* (2), *Jose* (2), *Raul* (2), *Abelardo*, *Alexandro*, *Alicia*, *Benito*, *Francisco*, *Hernan*, *Juanita*; *Dario*, *Dino*, *Lorenzo*.

Ure (352) **1.** Scottish: from the Older Scots personal name *Ure*, a variant of *Ivor*. **2.** Norwegian: habitational name from a place in Hordaland, probably named in Old Norse *Urðvin*, a compound of *urð* 'scree', 'rock-strewn slope' + *vin* 'meadow'.

Uren (433) **1.** Welsh and Cornish: from a Brythonic personal name *Orbogenos* (probably 'of privileged birth'), recorded as *Urbgen* and *Urgen* in Old Welsh and later as *Urien*, and as *Urbien* and *Urien* in Old Breton. The first element is unexplained; the second represents the root *gen* 'birth', 'born'. In Cornwall the name may be a survival from the Celtic period or, more probably, a reimportation from Brittany. **2.** Norwegian: habitational name from any of numerous farmsteads, so named from the definite singular form of *ur*, from Old Norse *urð* 'scree', 'rock-strewn slope'.

Urena (786) Spanish (**Ureña**): habitational name, probably from Urueña in Valladolid province.

GIVEN NAMES Spanish 56%. *Jose* (35), *Ramon* (14), *Rafael* (13), *Jesus* (11), *Juan* (10), *Luis* (9), *Francisco* (8), *Miguel* (8), *Pedro* (7), *Luz* (6), *Ana* (5), *Julio* (5); *Antonio* (2), *Lorenzo* (2), *Adalgisa*, *Clementina*, *Dario*, *Fausto*, *Federico*, *Filiberto*, *Giovanni*, *Guido*, *Marco*, *Santo*.

Urenda (104) Spanish or Basque: most probably a topographic name formed with Basque *ur-* 'water'.

GIVEN NAMES Spanish 45%. *Jesus* (3), *Juan* (3), *Alfonso* (2), *Cesar* (2), *Jose* (2), *Luis* (2), *Ricardo* (2), *Ruben* (2), *Angelina*, *Beltran*, *Dionisia*, *Felipe*.

Ureno (106) Spanish (Mexico; **Ureño**): unexplained; probably a derivative of Spanish **Ureña** (see URENA).

GIVEN NAMES Spanish 59%. *Angel* (4), *Manuel* (4), *Jesus* (3), *Jose* (3), *Juan* (3), *Francisco* (2), *Pedro* (2), *Sotero* (2), *Alberto*, *Apolonio*, *Carlos*, *Enrique*; *Eliseo* (2), *Antonio*, *Lorenzo*.

Uresti (201) Basque: most probably a topographic name formed with Basque *ur-* 'water' + *-ezti* 'sweet, honey'.

GIVEN NAMES Spanish 47%. *Juan* (4), *Enrique* (3), *Gilberto* (3), *Jose* (3), *Alfonso* (2), *Apolonio* (2), *Carlos* (2), *Ezequiel* (2), *Jesus* (2), *Raul* (2), *Adan*, *Amada*.

Urey (220) English and Scottish: from an Anglo-Norman French pronunciation of the Old and Middle English personal name *Wolrich* (see WOOLDRIDGE).

Urfer (167) German: habitational name for someone from Urff near Kassel.

Urgo (171) Italian: according to Caracausi, a reduced variant of **Gurgo**, a topographic name with a variety of meanings, including 'vortex', 'whirlpool', 'mill race', 'ditch where flax was put to soak', 'depression in which water collects'.

GIVEN NAMES Italian 11%. *Saverio* (2), *Donato*, *Rocco*, *Sal*.

Urian (110) Welsh and Cornish: variant of UREN, occurring mainly in Lancashire.

Uriarte (365) Spanish: topographic name formed with Basque *uri-*, *iri-* 'hamlet', 'village', 'settlement'.

GIVEN NAMES Spanish 45%. *Jesus* (7), *Jose* (7), *Luis* (5), *Manuel* (5), *Pedro* (5), *Carlos* (4), *Marcos* (4), *Pablo* (4), *Alejandro* (3), *Jorge* (3), *Juan* (3), *Raul* (3); *Angelo* (2), *Romeo* (2), *Antonio*, *Eliseo*, *Heriberto*, *Lia*, *Luciano*, *Marco Antonio*, *Oreste*.

Urias (713) Spanish (**Urías**): from the Biblical name meaning 'God is light' (English *Uriah*).

GIVEN NAMES Spanish 44%. *Jose* (17), *Juan* (10), *Armando* (8), *Jesus* (6), *Manuel* (6), *Carlos* (5), *Francisco* (5), *Ana* (4), *Ramon* (4), *Alejandro* (3), *Fernando* (3), *Jorge* (3).

Uribe (2165) Basque: **1.** topographic name for someone who lived in the lower part of a village, from Basque *uri* 'settlement' + *be(h)e* 'lower part'. **2.** habitational name from Uribe, a town in Biscay province, Basque Country.

GIVEN NAMES Spanish 52%. *Jose* (57), *Juan* (41), *Luis* (31), *Carlos* (29), *Manuel* (25), *Miguel* (24), *Francisco* (20), *Jorge* (18), *Jesus* (17), *Roberto* (15), *Fernando* (12), *Jaime* (12).

Urich (599) **1.** German: variant of ULRICH. **2.** English: probably from the Old English personal name *Wulfrīc* (see WOOLDRIDGE). **3.** Scottish: reduced form of **McUrich**, itself a reduced form of **McCurrach**.

Urick (456) Variant spelling of URICH; this is found as a Scottish name, but it may also be a respelling of the German surname.

Urie (474) **1.** Scottish and English: variant spelling of UREY. **2.** Scottish: habitational name from Urie in Fetteresso parish, Kincardineshire.

Uriegas (99) Hispanic: unexplained.

Urioste (188) Basque: topographic name for someone who lived outside or on the perimeter of a village, from Basque *uri* 'settlement' + *oste* 'behind'.

GIVEN NAMES Spanish 25%. *Jose* (3), *Fernando* (2), *Juan* (2), *Manuel* (2), *Carlos*, *Carolina*, *Cristina*, *Domingo*, *Eduardo*, *Emilio*, *Fidel*, *Humberto*.

Uriostegui (102) Basque (alongside the Castilianized variant **Urióstegui**): from URIOSTE + the locative suffix *-egi*.

GIVEN NAMES Spanish 68%. *Juan* (5), *Francisco* (3), *Jose* (3), *Aurelio* (2), *Guillermo* (2), *Jesus* (2), *Jorge* (2), *Pablo* (2), *Reyna* (2), *Reynaldo* (2), *Tomas* (2), *Albino*; *Bartolo*, *Filiberto*, *Silvano*.

Urish (104) Origin unidentified.

Urlacher (149) German: habitational name for someone from Urlach.

Urlaub (111) German: from Middle High German *urloup* 'vacation', possibly applied as a nickname for an indolent person.

Urman (240) **1.** Respelling of German **Urmann** or **Uhrmann**, from a pet form of UHR. **2.** Jewish (Ashkenazic): variant of UHR. **3.** Jewish (from Ukraine): nickname from southeastern Yiddish *ureman* 'poor man'.

GIVEN NAMES Jewish 14%; Russian 12%. *Reuven* (2), *Eitan*, *Etya*, *Filipp*, *Haim*, *Haya*, *Isaak*, *Mayer*, *Meyer*, *Naum*, *Semen*; *Yefim* (2), *Aleksandr*, *Boris*, *Dmitriy*, *Galina*, *Gennady*, *Igor*, *Konstantin*, *Leonid*, *Lyuba*, *Lyudmila*, *Michail*.

Urness (317) Norwegian: habitational name from any of several farmsteads, most of them named with Old Norse *urð* 'scree', 'rock-strewn slope' + *nes* 'promontory', 'headland'. In Sogne, the original name is *Ornes*, denoting a farmstead on or near a jutting headland.

GIVEN NAMES Scandinavian 4%. *Bernt*, *Erik*, *Nels*, *Thor*.

Urquhart (1721) Scottish: habitational name from any of four places so called. One in Fife is found in old records (1128) as *Pettnaurcha*, a Pictish-Gaelic name meaning 'the portion of the shot'. Others, including one on Loch Ness, are named with Welsh *ar* 'on', 'by' + *cardden* 'thicket'.

Urquidez (154) Spanish (**Urquídez**): variant of Spanish URQUIDI. This form occurs chiefly in NM and CA, and is not found in present-day Spain.

GIVEN NAMES Spanish 28%. *Armando* (3), *Ofelia* (2), *Ruben* (2), *Alberto*, *Alfonso*, *Alvaro*, *Andres*, *Bernadino*, *Carlos*, *Cesar*, *Cristobal*, *Jose*.

Urquidi (153) Basque: topographic name from Basque *urki* 'birch tree' + the collective suffix *-di*.

GIVEN NAMES Spanish 39%. *Jesus* (4), *Javier* (3), *Donaciano* (2), *Jose* (2), *Juan* (2), *Raul* (2), *Alfonso*, *Amparo*, *Beatriz*, *Chico*, *Eduardo*, *Elodia*.

Urquiza (200) Basque: Castilianized variant of habitational name from a place in Biscay province named Urkiza, from Basque *urki* 'birch tree' + the collective suffix *-tza*.

GIVEN NAMES Spanish 58%. *Manuel* (7), *Rafael* (4), *Sergio* (4), *Carlos* (3), *Eulalio* (3), *Jose* (3), *Juan* (3), *Aida* (2), *Alfredo* (2), *Arturo* (2), *Domingo* (2), *Felipe* (2); *Antonio*, *Federico*, *Lorenzo*.

Urrea (251) Aragonese and Spanish (of Basque origin): habitational name from Urrea de Gaén in Teruel province, or Urrea de Jalón in Zaragoza, of certain Basque influence.

GIVEN NAMES Spanish 44%. *Carlos* (7), *Juan* (6), *Francisco* (4), *Jorge* (4), *Luis* (4), *Miguel* (4), *Gustavo* (3), *Jose* (3), *Alejandro* (2), *Eduardo* (2), *Jaime* (2), *Mario* (2).

Urrutia (862) Basque: habitational name from either of two places in Biscay province called Urrutia, named with Basque *urruti* 'distant' + the definite article *-a*.

GIVEN NAMES Spanish 42%. *Jose* (28), *Carlos* (14), *Juan* (12), *Luis* (10), *Guillermo* (6), *Jorge* (6), *Miguel* (6), *Ruben* (6), *Ana* (5), *Eduardo* (4), *Faustino* (4), *Manuel* (4).

Urry (149) English: variant of UREY.

Urschel (182) German: metronymic from the female personal name *Ursula*, literally 'little bear' (female), a derivative of Latin *ursus* 'bear'.

Ursery (132) English: variant of ESSARY. Compare USSERY.

Ursillo (107) Italian: from a diminutive (southern suffix *-illo* for *-ello*) of **Urso**, from Latin *ursus* 'bear' (see ORSO).

GIVEN NAMES Italian 11%. *Antonio*, *Domenic*, *Guido*, *Luigi*, *Pasco*.

Ursin (191) Danish and Swedish: vernacular form of the humanist name **Ursinius**, a nickname from Latin *ursus* 'bear'. It has been suggested that in some cases this was adopted as an equivalent of Italian ORSINI.

GIVEN NAME Scandinavian 6%; German 5%. *Otto* (3).

Ursini (154) Italian (mainly Sicily): patronymic or plural form of URSINO.

GIVEN NAMES Italian 14%. *Dante* (2), *Domenic*, *Marco*, *Philomena*, *Rocco*, *Salvatore*, *Santina*, *Vito*.

Ursino (137) Italian (mainly Sicily): from a diminutive of URSO.

GIVEN NAMES Italian 31%. *Salvatore* (3), *Angelo* (2), *Antonio* (2), *Benito*, *Carmelo*, *Cosimo*, *Domenico*, *Francesca*, *Liborio*, *Luigi*, *Marco*, *Mario*, *Nicasio*, *Nicola*, *Rocco*.

Urso (953) Italian (mainly Sicily): from the Latin personal name *Ursus* meaning 'bear'. Compare ORSO.

GIVEN NAMES Italian 16%. *Angelo* (10), *Salvatore* (10), *Antonio* (4), *Enrico* (3), *Cataldo* (2), *Giuseppe* (2), *Pio* (2), *Vito* (2), *Carmelo*, *Concetto*, *Domenic*, *Domenico*.

Urton (260) English (Derbyshire): variant of ORTON.

Urtz (107) German: unexplained.

Urwin (166) 1. English, Scottish, and Irish: variant spelling of IRWIN. 2. Variant of Welsh **Urien** (see UREN).

Ury (182) 1. French (Alsace): regional variant of *Oury*, a pet form of the German personal name *Ulrich*. 2. English: variant spelling of UREY. 3. German: variant of ORY. 4. Perhaps an Americanized spelling of Ukrainian **Jury**, from the personal name, Ukrainian form of GEORGE. 5. Jewish: from the Biblical personal name *Uri*.

Urzua (134) Basque: probably nickname from Basque *urzo* 'dove' + the definite article *-a*.

GIVEN NAMES Spanish 56%. *Jose* (7), *Jorge* (3), *Fernando* (2), *Juan* (2), *Manuel* (2), *Adriana*, *Alejandro*, *Alfredo*, *Alicia*, *Amado*, *Ana Lilia*, *Anastacio*.

Uselman (181) Probably an Americanized spelling of German **Uselmann**, **Usselmann**, from topographic names from the Ussel river in Swabia.

Uselton (463) English: perhaps a variant of **Osselton**, a habitational name from a lost or unidentified place, probably in northeastern England, where this name is most common.

Usery (303) English: variant of ESSARY. Compare USSERY.

Usher (2443) 1. English, Scottish, and Irish: occupational name for a janitor or gatekeeper, Middle English *usher* (Anglo-Norman French *usser*, Old French *ussier*, *huissier*, from Late Latin *ustiarius*, a derivative of classical Latin *ostium* 'door', 'gate'). The term was also used in the Middle Ages of a court official charged with accompanying a person of rank on ceremonial occasions, and this may be a partial souce of the surname. This surname has been recorded in Ireland since the 14th century, and has sometimes been used as an equivalent of HESSION. 2. Jewish (from Poland and Ukraine): from a southern Yiddish pronunciation of the Yiddish male personal name OSHER (Hebrew ASHER).

FOREBEARS Hezekiah Usher (d. 1676) is buried in King's Chapel Burying Ground, Boston, MA.

Usilton (137) English: see USELTON.

Usman (119) Muslim (Iranian and Indian subcontinent): from the Persian form of Arabic '*Uthmān*. Compare OSMAN.

GIVEN NAMES Muslim 69%; Indian 8%. *Muhammad* (5), *Khalid* (4), *Mohammad* (3), *Mohammed* (3), *Asif* (2), *Iqbal* (2), *Saleem* (2), *Yousuf* (2), *Agha*, *Ahmed*, *Akhter*, *Aly*; *Anand*, *Asim*, *Ramesh*, *Sahib*, *Seema*, *Sushil*.

Usner (125) German: variant spelling of **Usener**, a habitational name for someone from Usingen on the Use, a tributary of the Wetter river in Hesse.

Usrey (406) English: variant of USSERY.

Usry (664) English: variant of USSERY.

Usselman (148) German (**Usselmann**): variant of **Uselmann** (see USELMAN).

Ussery (1697) English: variant of ESSARY. Many forms of this name are found in North America, ranging from ESAREY to USREY, and probably NECESSARY as well. In the U.S. it is predominantly a southern name.

FOREBEARS John Ussery is recorded in New Kent Co., VA in 1684; he died in 1687. Many bearers are recorded in VA in the early 18th century. In NC several Usserys obtained land grants between 1760 and 1770. William Ussery obtained a land grant in SC in 1772.

Usui (109) Japanese: 'mortar well', referring to a mortar in which things are ground up with a pestle; the name is found mostly in eastern Japan.

GIVEN NAMES Japanese 79%. *Shigeru* (2), *Shoichi* (2), *Takashi* (2), *Tomoko* (2), *Akira*, *Atsushi*, *Chikako*, *Goro*, *Hideo*, *Hirohito*, *Hiroji*, *Ippei*.

Utech (280) German: 1. from a short form of a Slavic personal name composed with *tech* 'consolation'. 2. from Middle Low German *ūt-echtisch* 'outsider', a term denoting someone who was not a member of a particular guild.

GIVEN NAMES German 5%. *Erwin* (2), *Friedrich*, *Klaus*.

Utecht (465) German: 1. variant of UTECH. 2. habitational name from a place so named near Lübeck.

Utesch (137) German: variant of UTECH.

GIVEN NAMES German 4%. *Inge*, *Kurt*.

Uthe (328) German: from a short form of a Germanic personal name formed with *odal* 'inherited property' as the first element.

Uthoff (126) German (Westphalia): topographic name for someone who lived on an outlying farm, from Middle Low German *ūt* 'out' + *hof* 'farmstead', 'court'.

Utke (194) German: from a pet form of UDE.

Utley (2564) English (South Yorkshire): habitational name from Utley, a place in West Yorkshire, near Keighley, named from the Old English personal name *Utta* + Old English *lēah* 'wood', 'clearing'.

Utsey (289) Probably an Americanized spelling of German **Jutze**, **Jütze** (see YOUTSEY).

Utsler (151) German (also **Utzler**): variant of UTZ, or possibly from **Jutzler** (see YOUTSEY).

Utt (845) German: variant of UTHE.

Uttech (178) German: variant spelling of UTECH.
GIVEN NAMES Scandinavian 7%; German 4%. *Hilmer* (2); *Horst, Otto.*

Uttecht (115) Variant of German UTECH.

Utter (1735) Swedish: soldier's name from Swedish *utter* 'otter'.

Utterback (1247) Americanized form of Dutch **Van Utterbeeck**, habitational name for someone from a place called Itterbeek.

Uttley (128) English (Lancashire and Yorkshire): variant spelling of UTLEY.

Utz (1256) South German (**Ütz**): from a pet form of the personal name ULRICH.

Utzig (105) German: variant of **Utzing**, a patronymic from UTZ.

Utzinger (160) South German and Swiss German: habitational name for someone from any of various places in Germany and Switzerland called Utzing or Utzingen.
GIVEN NAMES German 6%. *Kurt, Urs.*

Uva (203) Italian: most likely from *uva* 'grapes'. Compare D'UVA.

GIVEN NAMES Italian 15%; French 4%. *Vito* (2), *Carmino, Gennaro, Marcello, Nichola, Nicolo, Salvatore*; *Alphonse, Armand.*

Uveges (123) Hungarian (**Üveges**): metonymic occupational name for a glassmaker, from *üveg* 'glass'.

Uy (509) Filipino: unexplained.
GIVEN NAMES Spanish 29%. *Manuel* (6), *Mario* (4), *Domingo* (3), *Isidro* (3), *Rolando* (3), *Augusto* (2), *Ernesto* (2), *Gregorio* (2), *Jaime* (2), *Joaquin* (2), *Pancho* (2), *Rodolfo* (2).

Uyeda (453) Japanese: see UEDA. The *-ye* in this spelling represents a sound no longer used in modern Japanese, which is now pronounced and spelled *-e*.
GIVEN NAMES Japanese 30%. *Masao* (5), *Hiroshi* (3), *Susumu* (3), *Toshio* (3), *Aki* (2), *Fumiko* (2), *Hiromi* (2), *Minoru* (2), *Satoru* (2), *Teruko* (2), *Tsutomu* (2), *Atsumi.*

Uyehara (321) Japanese: see UEHARA. The *-ye* in this spelling represents a sound no longer in modern Japanese, which is now pronounced and spelled *-e*.
GIVEN NAMES Japanese 23%. *Masao* (3), *Hiroshi* (2), *Takeo* (2), *Taro* (2), *Emiko, Fumiko, Hidehiko, Hiroko, Isamu, Kazuyo, Kenichi, Kimie.*

Uyemura (117) Japanese: see UEMURA. The *-ye* in this spelling represents a sound no longer in modern Japanese, which is now pronounced and spelled *-e*.

GIVEN NAMES Japanese 34%. *Shizuko* (2), *Chikashi, Hisako, Ichiro, Katsumi, Kazuo, Kikuyo, Manabu, Masayuki, Minoru, Shig, Susumu.*

Uyeno (162) Japanese: see UENO. The *-ye* in this spelling represents a sound no longer in modern Japanese, which is now pronounced and spelled *-e*.
GIVEN NAMES Japanese 38%. *Kiyoshi* (2), *Masato* (2), *Takashi* (2), *Takeo* (2), *Goro, Hiroshi, Junzo, Kayoko, Kinue, Koichi, Masakazu, Masako.*

Uzelac (183) Serbian and Croatian: unexplained.
GIVEN NAMES South Slavic 10%. *Milan* (4), *Branko, Desanka, Dusan, Mirko.*

Uzzell (410) English (Wiltshire and Gloucestershire): nickname for someone thought to resemble a bird, from Old French *oisel* 'bird'.

Uzzle (256) English (Gloucestershire): variant spelling of UZZELL.

Uzzo (102) Italian: unexplained; possibly either from a pet form of a personal name formed with *-uzzo*; or a variant of **Guzzo**, a nickname from Sicilian and Calabrian *guzzo* 'angry little dog'.
GIVEN NAMES Italian 17%. *Ignazio* (2), *Gasper, Nunzio, Salvatore, Santo, Vito.*

V

Vaca (604) **1.** Spanish and Portuguese: from *vaca* 'cow' (Latin *vacca*), probably applied as a metonymic occupational name for a cowherd or as a nickname. **2.** Czech: pet form of the personal name *Václav* (see VACEK).

GIVEN NAMES Spanish 47%. *Jose* (13), *Carlos* (10), *Juan* (10), *Francisco* (7), *Javier* (7), *Miguel* (6), *Salvador* (6), *Jesus* (5), *Luis* (5), *Manuel* (5), *Ramiro* (5), *Alberto* (4).

Vacanti (248) Italian (Sicily): nickname for a simpleton, from Sicilian *vacanti* (Italian *vacante*) 'empty', 'vacant'.

GIVEN NAMES Italian 13%. *Vito* (4), *Salvatore* (3), *Alfio, Arcangelo, Domenic, Francesca.*

Vacca (929) Italian: from Italian *vacca* 'cow' (Latin *vacca*); a metonymic occupational name for a cowherd or in some instances a nickname for a gentle person.

GIVEN NAMES Italian 13%. *Pasquale* (5), *Angelo* (4), *Salvatore* (4), *Sal* (3), *Carlo* (2), *Domenic* (2), *Gennaro* (2), *Rocco* (2), *Aldo, Antonio, Carmelo, Carmine.*

Vaccarella (189) Italian: from a diminutive of **Vaccara**, a feminine form of VACCARO 'cowherd'.

GIVEN NAMES Italian 12%. *Angelo, Carlo, Luigi, Romilda, Sal.*

Vaccarelli (108) Italian: patronymic or plural form of VACCARELLO.

GIVEN NAMES Italian 12%. *Angelo, Antonio, Rocco.*

Vaccarello (125) Italian: from a pet form of the occupational name VACCARO 'cowherd'.

GIVEN NAMES Italian 16%. *Angelo* (2), *Fulvio, Pietrina.*

Vaccari (158) Italian (Sicily): patronymic or plural form of VACCARO.

GIVEN NAMES Italian 24%. *Mario* (3), *Angelo, Armando, Bernardo, Claudio, Dario, Gioia, Marco, Oreste, Raffaele, Renzo, Riccardo, Roberto, Salvo.*

Vaccariello (107) Italian (Campana): from a diminutive of VACCARO.

GIVEN NAMES Italian 20%. *Angelo* (2), *Antonella, Bartolo, Carmine, Pasquale.*

Vaccarino (122) Italian: from a diminutive of the occupational name VACCARO 'cowherd'.

GIVEN NAMES Italian 17%. *Salvatore* (2), *Angelo, Carmelo, Carmine, Sal, Serafino.*

Vaccaro (2437) Italian: occupational name for a cowherd, Italian *vaccaro* (Late Latin *vaccarius*, a derivative of *vacca* 'cow').

GIVEN NAMES Italian 16%. *Angelo* (13), *Sal* (12), *Salvatore* (10), *Vito* (10), *Antonio* (8), *Pasquale* (5), *Gaetano* (4), *Calogero* (3), *Donato* (3), *Enrico* (3), *Guido* (3), *Santo* (3).

Vacchiano (137) Southern Italian (mainly Sicily): unexplained; perhaps a habitational name from an unidentified place named Vacchiano or Bacchiano.

GIVEN NAMES Italian 11%. *Antonio, Luigi, Pasquale, Sabato.*

Vacco (105) Italian: patronymic or plural form of BACCO.

GIVEN NAMES Italian 10%. *Aldo, Angelo, Rocco, Vito.*

Vacek (567) Czech: from a pet form of the personal name *Václav*, Old Czech *Vęceslav* (cognate with Polish *Więcesław*, Latinized as *Wenceslas*). It is composed of the Old Slavic elements *viece* 'greater' + *slav* 'glory'. It was borne by a 10th-century duke of Bohemia who fought against a revival of paganism in his territory, and after his death became patron saint of Bohemia.

Vacha (230) Czech (**Vácha**): from a pet form of the personal name *Václav* (see VACEK).

GIVEN NAMES Czech and Slovak 4%. *Lubos* (2), *Bohumil.*

Vachon (1172) French: from a diminutive of *vache* (from Latin *vacca* 'cow'), an occupational name for a cowherd. In New England, this name is sometimes Americanized as COWAN.

FOREBEARS A Vachon from the Poitou region of France is documented in Quebec City in 1653. Secondary surnames include Desfourchettes, Laminée, and Pamerlaux.

GIVEN NAMES French 16%. *Armand* (6), *Fernand* (5), *Jacques* (3), *Normand* (3), *Pierre* (3), *Adelard* (2), *Edmour* (2), *Emile* (2), *Francoise* (2), *Lucien* (2), *Michel* (2), *Adrien.*

Vaclavik (145) Czech (**Václavík**): from a pet form of the personal name *Václav* (see VACEK).

GIVEN NAMES Czech and Slovak 4%. *Milan* (2), *Zdenek.*

Vacura (125) Czech: from a derivative of the personal name *Václav* (see VACEK).

Vadala (269) Italian (Sicily; **Vadalà**): variant of *Badalà*, a much altered form of Arabic *'Abd Allāh* 'servant of God'. See also BADALAMENTI.

GIVEN NAMES Italian 15%. *Angelo* (2), *Dante, Domenic, Domenico, Gaetano, Nunzia, Nunzio, Pietro, Rocco, Salvatore.*

Vadas (169) **1.** Hungarian and Jewish (from Hungary): from *vad* 'wild', hence a nickname for an unsophisticated person, or someone with crazy ideas, alternatively an occupational name for a hunter. **2.** Americanized spelling of Hungarian and Hungarian Jewish **Vadász**, from the vocabulary word *vadász* 'hunter', from *vad* 'game' + *ász* (*ész*) occupational suffix of Hungarian family names, hence an occupational name for a hunter. **3.** Czech: from a pet form of the personal name *Vadislav*, variant of *Vladislav*. In some cases the Czech family name is a derivative of the Hungarian word *vadász* 'hunter', hence an occupational name for a hunter.

Vadeboncoeur (166) French: secondary surname, common among soldiers, which has been adopted as a principal surname; it means 'Go with a merry heart'.

GIVEN NAMES French 18%. *Emile* (2), *Normand* (2), *Armand, Eudore, Jinette, Lucien, Pierre, Roch, Valmore.*

Vaden (1051) **1.** Apparently of English origin, but of unexplained etymology. **2.** Swedish (**Vadén**): probably an ornamental name from the place-name element *vad* 'ford' + the adjectival suffix *-én*, from Latin *-enius*.

FOREBEARS The earliest recorded bearer of this name in North America is Henry Vaden (1663–1729), of Chesterfield Co., VA.

Vader (284) North German: from Middle Low German *vader* 'father', 'senior'; in the Middle Ages this was used a term of address for someone who was senior in rank or age.

Vadnais (602) French: probably a northern or eastern variant of **Gadonnet**.

FOREBEARS A Vadnais from Paris is documented in 1737, in Saint Sulpice, Quebec.

GIVEN NAMES French 5%. *Rosaire* (2), *Andre, Fernand, Pierre.*

Vadney (166) Americanized form of French VADNAIS.

Vaeth (277) South German (**Väth**): variant of VOGT.

Vagle (133) Scandinavian: variant spelling of WAGLE.

GIVEN NAMES Scandinavian 5%; German 4%. *Arnt; Kurt.*

Vagnoni (128) Italian: from an augmentative of **Bagno**. Compare Spanish BANOS.

GIVEN NAMES Italian 8%; French 4%. *Emidio, Luigi*; *Armand* (2).

Vago (124) Hungarian (**Vágó**): occupational name for a wood- or stonecutter, or butcher, from *vágni* 'to cut'.

GIVEN NAMES Hungarian 6%. *Attila, Bela, Laslo*.

Vagts (138) German: variant of VOGTS.

GIVEN NAMES German 6%. *Kurt, Manfred*.

Vahey (252) Irish (Mayo): reduced Anglicized form of Gaelic **Mac M(h)ic an Bheathadh**, a patronymic from *Mac an Bheathadh*, from a personal name meaning 'son of life'.

Vahl (127) North German: **1.** nickname from Middle Low German *vāl* 'pallid', 'fair'. **2.** from the Germanic personal name *Falho*, a short form of a compound name formed with *fal*, an ethnic name (the etymon of East- and Westphalia).

Vahle (326) North German: variant of VAHL.

Vaidya (250) Indian (northern states): Hindu name from Sanskrit *vaidya* 'scholar', 'physician' (from Sanskrit *vid-* 'to know'). The surname is found among several communities. It is the name of a clan of the Konkanasth Brahmans.

GIVEN NAMES Indian 89%. *Mahesh* (3), *Manish* (3), *Subhash* (3), *Anil* (2), *Ashwini* (2), *Avinash* (2), *Bhasker* (2), *Hemant* (2), *Jitendra* (2), *Kiran* (2), *Kishor* (2), *Krishna* (2).

Vail (4055) **1.** English: variant spelling of VALE. **2.** Scottish: shortened form of **Macvail**, a variant of **Macphail**, an Anglicized form of Gaelic **Mac Phàil** 'son of Paul'. **3.** Irish: variant of VEALE.

Vaile (169) English: variant spelling of VALE.

Vaill (106) Scottish: variant of VAIL.

Vaillancourt (1487) French: variant of **Valencourt**, a topographic name meaning 'low-lying farm'.

FOREBEARS A Vaillancourt, also called Villencourt, from Normandy, France, was documented in Beaupré, Quebec, in 1666.

GIVEN NAMES French 16%. *Emile* (5), *Andre* (4), *Marcel* (4), *Armand* (3), *Gaston* (3), *Lucien* (3), *Normand* (3), *Adrien* (2), *Arsene* (2), *Fernand* (2), *Gilles* (2), *Girard* (2).

Vaillant (140) French, English, and Dutch: nickname for a courageous or robust person, from Old French *vaillant* 'sturdy', 'brave', Middle English *vailaunt*, *valiaunt*, Middle Dutch *valiant* (the latter two being from Old French).

GIVEN NAMES French 14%. *Pierre* (2), *Alphonse, Ambroise, Andre, Normand, Philias, Philippe*.

Vails (123) Scottish and English: variant of VAIL, with English patronymic *-s*.

Vairo (130) Italian: from the personal name *Vairo*, from Latin *varius* 'variegated', or possibly a nickname with the same meaning.

GIVEN NAMES Italian 14%. *Angelo, Guiseppe, Pasquale*.

Vajda (262) Hungarian and Jewish (from Hungary): status name from *vajda* 'leader', 'governor', a word of Slavic origin. The Hungarian name is especially common in Transylvania, where, before the creation of the independent Hungarian principality, the term had denoted the highest ranking administrative and military leader. In medieval times various Romanian village leaders, as well as the leaders of gypsy caravans, were also called *vajda*. As a Jewish name it was ornamental or a name taken by a rabbi.

GIVEN NAMES Hungarian 7%. *Janos* (2), *Arpad, Eszter, Ferenc, Gabor, Sandor, Tibor*.

Vala (115) **1.** Portuguese: habitational name from any of the towns in Portugal named Vala or with Vala. **2.** Indian (Gujarat): Hindu name of unknown meaning. **3.** Italian: unexplained.

GIVEN NAMES Spanish 7%; Indian 5%. *Jose* (2), *Ana, Luis, Manuel, Rosario, Silvino, Valerio*; *Bhupendra, Janardhan, Jyoti*.

Valachovic (123) Americanized spelling of Serbian and Croatian **Vlahović**, a patronymic from the ethnic name *Vlah* 'Wallachian', 'Romanian', also used as a general term for a person of foreign origin, in particular one speaking a Romance language. In Croatia the term *Vlah* is also used to denote a Serb or a member of the Orthodox Church.

Valade (317) French: Occitan variant of **Vallée**, a topographic name for someone living in a valley.

FOREBEARS A Valade from La Rochelle, France, is documented in Quebec City in 1666. The secondary surname LAJEUNESSE was associated with Valade in the 18th century.

GIVEN NAMES French 7%. *Euclide, Laurier, Lucien, Ovila, Yvon*.

Valadez (1822) probably variant of Asturian-Leonese **Valdés** (see VALDES).

GIVEN NAMES Spanish 51%. *Jose* (55), *Juan* (28), *Jesus* (26), *Manuel* (18), *Luis* (14), *Raul* (14), *Miguel* (13), *Rafael* (12), *Ruben* (11), *Francisco* (10), *Salvador* (10), *Carlos* (9).

Valasek (262) Czech (**Valášek**): **1.** from Moravian *Valach*, an ethnic name for a Wallachian (a member of a Carpathian shepherd people), from a Slavic word meaning originally 'foreigner', 'speaker of a Romance language', hence 'Romanian'. **2.** nickname for an idle person, from *valet se* 'to wallow'. **3.** nickname from *valach* 'gelding'.

Valbuena (106) Spanish: habitational name from any of the places named Valbuena, for example in Valladolid, Cáceres, and Salamanca.

GIVEN NAMES Spanish 43%. *Arturo* (2), *Fernando* (2), *Juan* (2), *Julio* (2), *Ricardo*

(2), *Alejandro, Amparo, Ana, Beatriz, Eduardo, Fidel, Isidro*.

Valcarcel (139) Spanish, Galician and Asturian-Leonese (**Valcárcel**): habitational name from any of the places in Logroño province, Galicia and Asturies, named Valcárcel, named in Galician or Old Spanish with *val* 'valley' + *cárcel* 'prison' (Latin *carcer*), the second element being used in the transferred sense of a confined space, i.e. a narrow gorge.

GIVEN NAMES Spanish 44%. *Jorge* (7), *Jose* (5), *Luis* (5), *Manuel* (5), *Aurelio* (2), *Carlos* (2), *Mario* (2), *Pedro* (2), *Aida, Alfonso, Consuelo, Emilio*; *Dario* (2), *Ciro, Eliseo*.

Valcourt (298) French: habitational name from a place so named in Haute-Marne or from Vaucourt in Meurthe-et-Moselle.

GIVEN NAMES French 21%. *Pierre* (3), *Alcide, Alphonse, Andre, Antoine, Armand, Aurelien, Cecile, Dominique, Donat, Francois, Frenel*.

Valder (104) Dutch and North German: topographic name for someone who lived in a forest or wood, Middle Dutch *vald*, or habitational name from a place named with this word.

FOREBEARS The surname Valder has been established in England (Kent and Sussex) since the late 17th century.

GIVEN NAME German 4%. *Otto*.

Valderrama (372) Spanish: habitational name from any of the places named Valderrama, as for example in Burgos province.

GIVEN NAMES Spanish 46%. *Jose* (10), *Carlos* (7), *Alvaro* (4), *Jorge* (4), *Manuel* (4), *Jaime* (3), *Mario* (3), *Octavio* (3), *Alberto* (2), *Alonso* (2), *Anselmo* (2), *Arturo* (2).

Valdes (3037) **1.** Asturian-Leonese and Spanish (**Valdés**): habitational name from either of the two places called Valdés in Málaga and Asturies. **2.** Catalan (**Valdès**): nickname from Catalan *valdès* 'Waldensian', i.e. a member of a Puritan religious sect which was founded in the 12th century by Peter Valdes (died 1205) in southern France. The widespread distribution of the surname in present-day Spain, however, suggests that other sources may also have been involved.

GIVEN NAMES Spanish 51%. *Jose* (61), *Carlos* (50), *Luis* (42), *Juan* (40), *Jorge* (39), *Pedro* (37), *Armando* (31), *Jesus* (26), *Ricardo* (23), *Roberto* (23), *Eduardo* (22), *Julio* (21); *Antonio* (14), *Heriberto* (5), *Leonardo* (4), *Delio* (3), *Guido* (3), *Lorenzo* (3), *Luciano* (3), *Aldo* (2), *Clemente* (2), *Dario* (2), *Fausto* (2), *Rossano* (2).

Valdespino (154) Spanish: habitational name for someone from any of various places named Valdespino.

GIVEN NAMES Spanish 41%. *Juan* (3), *Andres* (2), *Armando* (2), *Emilio* (2), *Jorge* (2), *Marina* (2), *Miguel* (2), *Adelaida, Alfredo, Alicia, Amador, Ana Maria*; *Antonio* (2), *Heriberto*.

Valdez (13211) Spanish: variant spelling of **Valdés** (see VALDES).
GIVEN NAMES Spanish 41%. *Jose* (284), *Juan* (141), *Manuel* (116), *Carlos* (95), *Jesus* (89), *Luis* (67), *Francisco* (58), *Miguel* (55), *Ricardo* (54), *Ruben* (54), *Ramon* (51), *Raul* (49).

Valdivia (1318) Spanish: **1.** in Spain, a widespread family name of uncertain derivation. **2.** in Chile, a habitational name from Valdivia in Chile. **3.** in Ecuador, a nickname from *valdivia* 'bird of prey'.
GIVEN NAMES Spanish 49%. *Jose* (28), *Juan* (26), *Manuel* (18), *Jesus* (13), *Luis* (13), *Carlos* (11), *Miguel* (11), *Pedro* (11), *Francisco* (9), *Javier* (8), *Enrique* (7), *Jaime* (7).

Valdivieso (172) Spanish: probably variant of **Valdivielso**, habitational name from Valdivielso, a region in Burgos province.
GIVEN NAMES Spanish 43%. *Jorge* (6), *Carlos* (5), *Jose* (5), *Luis* (4), *Manuel* (4), *Alfonso* (2), *Ana* (2), *Elba* (2), *Juan* (2), *Julio* (2), *Ramiro* (2), *Alberto*.

Valdovinos (440) **1.** Spanish: from a literary personal name of Germanic origin, composed of *bald* 'bold', 'brave' + *wine* 'friend'. Compare BALDWIN. **2.** Galician (**Valdoviños**): probably a topographic name from Galician *val* 'valley' + *do* 'of' + *viños* 'wines', or a derivateive from the habitational name Valdoviño, in A Coruña, Galicia.
GIVEN NAMES Spanish 64%. *Jose* (20), *Juan* (10), *Jesus* (7), *Manuel* (6), *Miguel* (6), *Angel* (5), *Carlos* (5), *Francisco* (5), *Gonzalo* (5), *Jorge* (4), *Leticia* (4), *Luis* (4).

Vale (998) **1.** English: topographic name for someone who lived in a valley, Middle English *vale* (Old French *val*, from Latin *vallis*). The surname is now also common in Ireland, where it has been Gaelicized as **de Bhál**. **2.** Galician and Aragonese: topographic name from *val* 'valley', or habitational name from any of the places named with this word.
GIVEN NAMES Spanish 7%. *Jose* (5), *Manuel* (4), *Abilio* (2), *Angel* (2), *Fernando* (2), *Jose Joel* (2), *Miguel* (2), *Pedro* (2), *Roberto* (2), *Adriana, Alberto, Alfredo*.

Valek (347) Czech and Slovak (**Válek**): from a pet form of the personal name *Valentin*, from Latin *Valentinus* (see VALENTINE).

Valen (167) Norwegian: habitational name from any of several farmsteads, notably along the coast from Hordaland and northward, so named from Old Norse *vaðill* 'ford', denoting shallow water, for example in a bay or strait.

Valencia (5474) Catalan (**València**) and Spanish: habitational name from any of various places called València or Valencia, principally the major city in eastern Spain, which was formerly the capital of an independent Moorish kingdom of the same name, until it was reconquered in 1239 by

James I, king of the Catalan dynasty, and became part of the Crown of Aragon together with the Principality of Catalonia and the Kingdom of Aragon. The city was apparently named from an honorary title derived from Latin *valens* 'brave'.
GIVEN NAMES Spanish 48%. *Jose* (135), *Juan* (60), *Luis* (50), *Carlos* (49), *Jesus* (45), *Manuel* (36), *Miguel* (36), *Armando* (28), *Francisco* (28), *Rafael* (28), *Jorge* (25), *Jaime* (23).

Valenciano (147) Spanish: habitational name meaning '(inhabitant) of VALENCIA'.
GIVEN NAMES Spanish 52%. *Juan* (7), *Jose* (6), *Enrique* (2), *Fernando* (2), *Ofelia* (2), *Placido* (2), *Alejandro, Alfonso, Arturo, Avelardo, Blanca, Carlos; Antonio* (2), *Annamaria, Lorenzo, Romeo*.

Valencic (106) Slovenian (**Valenčič**) and Croatian (northern Croatia; **Valenčić**): patronymic from the personal name *Valent*, an old short form of *Valentin*, Latin *Valentinus* (see VALENTINE).

Valent (293) **1.** Italian (Friuli): variant of VALENTE. **2.** Slovenian: from an old short form of the personal name *Valentin*, Latin *Valentinus* (see VALENTINE).
GIVEN NAMES Italian 4%. *Antonio* (3), *Angelo, Enzo*.

Valenta (687) Czech: from a pet form of the personal name *Valentin*, Czech form of VALENTINE.

Valente (2178) **1.** Italian, Galician, and Portuguese: nickname from *valente* 'brave', 'valiant'. **2.** Italian: from the personal name *Valente*, of the same origin and meaning as 1, which was borne by a 6th-century bishop of Verona.
GIVEN NAMES Italian 16%; Spanish 8%; Portuguese 4%. *Mario* (19), *Angelo* (11), *Salvatore* (9), *Antonio* (8), *Sal* (7), *Rocco* (5), *Carmine* (4), *Gino* (4), *Carlo* (3), *Enrico* (3), *Gabriele* (3), *Nicola* (3), *Pasquale* (3); *Manuel* (12), *Jose* (11), *Carlos* (9), *Fernando* (4), *Luis* (3), *Renato* (3), *Rigoberto* (3), *Armando* (2), *Claudio* (2), *Francisco* (2), *Jaime* (2); *Joaquim* (5), *Ilidio, Joao*.

Valenti (2915) **1.** Italian (**Valènti**): patronymic from the personal name VALENTE. **2.** Catalan (**Valentí**): from the Catalan personal name *Valentí* (see VALENTINO and VALENTINE).
GIVEN NAMES Italian 15%. *Angelo* (13), *Salvatore* (10), *Vito* (10), *Sal* (6), *Antonio* (5), *Rocco* (4), *Attilio* (3), *Carlo* (3), *Carmelo* (3), *Carmine* (3), *Gino* (3), *Biaggio* (2).

Valentin (1754) French, northeastern Italian, Spanish (**Valentín**), German, Swedish, Danish, and Jewish (western Ashkenazic): from the Latin personal name *Valentinus* (see VALENTINE). The Jewish surname is an adoption of the Christian personal name.
GIVEN NAMES Spanish 43%. *Jose* (38), *Juan* (22), *Luis* (20), *Angel* (19), *Carlos* (18), *Pedro* (16), *Ramon* (13), *Miguel* (11), *Andres* (7), *Rafael* (7), *Javier* (6), *Jesus* (6).

Valentine (12444) English and Scottish: from a medieval personal name, Latin *Valentinus*, a derivative of *Valens* (see VALENTE), which was never common in England, but is occasionally found from the end of the 12th century, probably as the result of French influence. The name was borne by a 3rd-century saint and martyr, whose chief claim to fame is that his feast falls on 14 February, the date of a traditional celebration of spring going back to the Roman fertility festival of Juno Februata. A 5th-century missionary bishop of Rhaetia of this name was venerated especially in southern Germany, being invoked as a patron against gout and epilepsy. It is probably also an Americanization of VALENTIN, VALENTINO, and possibly other European cognates.

Valentini (390) Italian: patronymic or plural form of VALENTINO.
GIVEN NAMES Italian 27%. *Orlando* (3), *Vito* (3), *Giuseppe* (2), *Julio* (2), *Mario* (2), *Remo* (2), *Valerio* (2), *Aldo, Americo, Angelo, Carlo, Cesare, Claudio, Dante, Deno, Dino, Domenico, Florindo, Mondo*.

Valentino (2044) Italian and Spanish: from the personal name *Valentino*, a pet form of VALENTE.
GIVEN NAMES Italian 13%. *Angelo* (9), *Salvatore* (8), *Carmine* (3), *Pasquale* (3), *Romeo* (3), *Antonio* (2), *Dino* (2), *Emedio* (2), *Leno* (2), *Matteo* (2), *Nicola* (2), *Vito* (2).

Valenza (351) Italian: habitational name for someone from the Spanish city of València (see VALENCIA) or from the Italian town of Valenza in Alessandria province.
GIVEN NAMES Italian 24%. *Salvatore* (5), *Angelo* (4), *Mario* (3), *Sal* (2), *Alessandra, Antonio, Carmel, Cesare, Gasper, Gennaro, Gianfranco, Lorenzo, Onofrio, Celestino, Rosario*.

Valenzano (169) Southern Italian: habitational name from a place so called in Bari province, which takes its name from the Latin personal name *Valentius*.
GIVEN NAMES Italian 33%. *Vito* (8), *Angelo* (4), *Guiseppe* (2), *Antonio, Marcello, Nicola, Pasquale, Renzo, Saverio*.

Valenzuela (4933) Spanish: habitational name from places named Valenzuela in Córdoba and Ciudad Real. The place name is a diminutive of Valencia, literally 'Little Valencia'.
GIVEN NAMES Spanish 45%. *Jose* (106), *Jesus* (58), *Juan* (58), *Manuel* (56), *Carlos* (40), *Francisco* (37), *Luis* (36), *Ruben* (29), *Javier* (23), *Jorge* (23), *Fernando* (22), *Mario* (21).

Valera (440) Spanish: habitational name from Valera in Cuenca province and possibly also from a place with the same name in Badajoz.
GIVEN NAMES Spanish 42%; Italian 8%. *Jose* (16), *Juan* (6), *Julio* (5), *Luis* (5), *Ramon* (5), *Carlos* (4), *Manuel* (4), *Marina* (4), *Pablo* (4), *Alberto* (3), *Alejandro* (2), *Alonso* (2); *Lorenzo* (4), *Antonio* (3), *Elio*

(3), *Giraldo* (2), *Angelo, Ceasar, Ciro, Clemente, Heriberto, Ireneo, Silvano, Tarcisio.*

Valeri (385) **1.** Italian: patronymic from the personal name VALERIO. **2.** Catalan: from the personal name VALERI, Catalan form of VALERIO.

GIVEN NAMES Italian 16%. *Angelo* (3), *Luciano* (2), *Luigi* (2), *Aldo, Amerigo, Antonio, Camillo, Dino, Emidio, Enrico, Fiorino.*

Valeriano (228) Spanish and Italian: from the personal name *Valeriano*, Latin *Valerianus*, a derivative of *Valerius* (see VALERIO). The name was borne by various minor Christian saints, most notably 4th-century bishops of Aquileia and Auxerre.

GIVEN NAMES Spanish 35%; Italian 7%. *Jose* (7), *Juan* (3), *Alfredo* (2), *Francisco* (2), *Jesus* (2), *Lauro* (2), *Manuel* (2), *Adalberto, Alicia, Alvaro, Ana, Armando; Amedeo, Armonda, Ciro, Domenic, Donato, Pasquale, Rocco, Romeo.*

Valerio (1818) Spanish and Italian: from the personal name *Valerio* (Latin *Valerius*, a Roman family name ultimately derived from Latin *valere* 'to flourish', 'to be strong and healthy'). The name was borne by several minor Christian saints, among them 4th-century bishops of Trier and Zaragoza and 5th-century bishops of Sorrento and of Antibes.

GIVEN NAMES Spanish 27%; Italian 7%. *Jose* (25), *Juan* (14), *Ana* (10), *Manuel* (9), *Pedro* (9), *Mario* (8), *Luis* (7), *Francisco* (6), *Ramon* (6), *Ruben* (6), *Carlos* (5), *Jesus* (5); *Antonio* (7), *Angelo* (6), *Lucio* (3), *Francesco* (2), *Maurizio* (2), *Niccolo* (2), *Romeo* (2), *Vito* (2), *Amadeo, Anastasio, Aureliano, Carmela.*

Valerius (249) German: from the Latin personal name *Valerius* (see VALERIO).

Valero (475) Spanish and Jewish (Sephardic): habitational name from a place called Valero in Salamanca province.

GIVEN NAMES Spanish 41%. *Jose* (8), *Miguel* (6), *Jesus* (5), *Jorge* (5), *Carlos* (4), *Francisco* (4), *Juan* (4), *Luis* (4), *Ignacio* (3), *Manuel* (3), *Mario* (3), *Rolando* (3); *Antonio* (5), *Dominico, Elio, Francesca, Gabino, Heriberto, Julieta.*

Valery (123) French: from the personal name *Valery*, Latin *Valerius* (see VALERIO). This name was borne by several minor Christian saints, among them a 4th-century bishop of Trier and a 5th-century bishop of Antibes.

GIVEN NAMES French 13%. *Armand, Colette, Pierre, Raoul, Yva.*

Vales (379) **1.** Catalan (**Valès**): respelling of Catalan **Vallès** (see VALLES). **2.** Galician: habitational name from any of the places called Vales in Galicia, or topographic name from the plural of Galician *val* 'valley'. **3.** Czech (**Valeš**): from a pet form of the personal name *Valentin* (see VALENTINE).

GIVEN NAMES Spanish 10%. *Jose* (5), *Carlos* (2), *Ricardo* (2), *Abilio, Agustin, Aldina, Arturo, Diego, Gonzalez, Jorge, Josefina, Juan Francisco.*

Valiante (109) Italian: from a nickname meaning 'brave'.

GIVEN NAMES Italian 10%. *Angelo, Carmine.*

Valiente (228) Spanish: from a nickname based on *valiente* 'brave'.

GIVEN NAMES Spanish 50%. *Jose* (9), *Carlos* (5), *Francisco* (5), *Rafael* (5), *Miguel* (4), *Alfredo* (3), *Roberto* (3), *Alfonso* (2), *Ana* (2), *Arnaldo* (2), *Jesus* (2), *Juan* (2); *Flavio* (2), *Annamaria, Antonio, Lorenzo, Marco.*

Valin (179) French: from a pet form of the personal name *Valier*, a popular French form of the Latin personal name *Valerius* (see VALERIO).

FOREBEARS A Valin from Picardy, France, is documented in Sillery, Quebec, in 1679.

GIVEN NAMES French 10%. *Adrien, Aime, Andree, Gaston, Michel, Serge.*

Valine (181) Perhaps an Americanized form of Czech **Valina**, a pet form of the personal name *Valentin* (see VALENTINE).

Valiquette (232) French: from a pet form of *Valhico*, a personal name of Germanic origin meaning 'foreigner'.

FOREBEARS A person called Valiquette, with the secondary surname LAVERDURE, is documented in Montreal in 1653.

GIVEN NAMES French 10%. *Valmore* (3), *Andre, Jean-Luc, Normand.*

Valis (144) **1.** Czech (**Vališ**): from a pet form of the personal name *Valentin*, from Latin *Valentinus* (see VALENTINE). **2.** Jewish (from Ukrainian): variant of **Volis**, a patronymic from the personal name *Vole*, a pet form of *Volf*, from Yiddish *volf* 'wolf'. **3.** Greek: variant of VALLIS.

Valk (348) Belgian and Dutch (**Van der Valk**): habitational name for someone from any of the places called Valk, in the provinces of Brabant, Antwerp, and East Flanders.

Valko (277) **1.** Czech and Slovak: pet form of the personal name *Valentin* (see VALENTINE). **2.** Hungarian (**Valkó**): from a pet form of the personal name *Valér*, from Latin *Valerius* (see VALERIO). **3.** Hungarian: probably also a habitational name from any of various places called Valkó or a regional name from a former county so named, although in this case the correct form of the surname would be with the suffix *-i* (i.e. **Valkói** or **Valkai**).

Valla (232) **1.** Italian: variant of VALLE. **2.** Norwegian and Swedish: habitational name from any of several places named from the plural of Old Norse *vǫllr* 'field', 'meadow' (Swedish *valla*). In Norway there are several farmsteads so named in Nordland. **3.** Albanian: see VALLAS.

GIVEN NAMES Italian 4%. *Antonio, Attilio, Marco.*

Valladares (811) Galician: Castilianized spelling of **Valadares**, a habitational name

from various places in Galicia, so named from a derivative of *valado* 'boundary wall', 'ditch' (from Latin *vallus, vallum* 'fence', 'barrier', 'bastion').

GIVEN NAMES Spanish 52%. *Jose* (29), *Juan* (14), *Jorge* (13), *Luis* (12), *Carlos* (9), *Manuel* (9), *Mario* (8), *Miguel* (8), *Raul* (8), *Roberto* (8), *Julio* (7), *Rafael* (7); *Antonio* (4), *Marco* (3), *Fausto* (2), *Romeo* (2), *Bartolo, Caesar, Caio, Eliseo, Enedino, Enio, Franco, Gino.*

Valladolid (109) Spanish: habitational name from the city of this name.

GIVEN NAMES Spanish 54%. *Manuel* (5), *Jose* (4), *Raul* (3), *Eduardo* (2), *Gustavo* (2), *Javier* (2), *Mario* (2), *Ramon* (2), *Ana, Aristeo, Armando, Audelia; Antonio* (2), *Paolo, Severino.*

Vallance (402) English and Scottish (of Norman origin): habitational name from Valence in Drôme, France, which probably has the same origin as VALENCIA.

Vallandingham (236) Americanized spelling of German **Willmandingen**, a habitational name from a place so named.

FOREBEARS Bearers of this name are descended from Michael van Landeghem, a Flemish Huguenot, who was in Stafford Co., VA, by 1690.

Vallario (174) Italian: variant of **Ballario**, from a derivative of *ballo* 'dance'.

GIVEN NAMES Italian 17%. *Pasquale* (3), *Salvatore* (3), *Lorenzo* (2), *Franco, Silvestro.*

Vallas (167) Greek and Albanian (**Valla**): from Albanian *valle* 'dance'.

GIVEN NAMES Greek 5%. *Spiro, Theophilos.*

Valle (3220) **1.** Spanish and Italian: habitational name from any of the many places named with *valle* 'valley', or topographic name for someone who lived in a valley (Latin *vallis*). **2.** Norwegian: habitational name from any of several farmsteads so named, from Old Norse *vǫllr* 'field', 'meadow'.

GIVEN NAMES Spanish 42%; Italian 8%. *Jose* (86), *Juan* (37), *Manuel* (32), *Luis* (31), *Ramon* (25), *Carlos* (23), *Jesus* (21), *Jorge* (17), *Roberto* (16), *Mario* (15), *Rafael* (15), *Francisco* (14); *Antonio* (19), *Angelo* (6), *Heriberto* (3), *Pio* (3), *Romeo* (3), *Aldo* (2), *Clemente* (2), *Leonardo* (2), *Marcello* (2), *Marco* (2), *Marco Antonio* (2), *Camillo.*

Valleau (146) French: of uncertain origin; perhaps from **Vallard**, a derivative of **Val**, a topographic name for someone who lived in a valley, from Old French *val*.

FOREBEARS A Valleau from Normandy, France, is documented in Quebec City in 1665.

Vallecillo (129) Spanish: topographic name from Spanish *Vallecillo*, a diminutive of *valle* 'valley'.

GIVEN NAMES Spanish 53%. *Jose* (9), *Carlos* (7), *Luis* (4), *Ricardo* (3), *Alejandro* (2), *Fernando* (2), *Guillermo* (2), *Jorge* (2), *Juan* (2), *Luz* (2), *Angel, Arturo.*

Vallee (928) French (**Vallée**): topographic name for someone who lived in a valley, from Old French *vallée*.
GIVEN NAMES French 15%. *Armand* (8), *Andre* (5), *Normand* (4), *Benoit* (2), *Lucien* (2), *Michel* (2), *Pierre* (2), *Raoul* (2), *Agathe, Alain, Aldee, Camille.*

Vallejo (1812) Spanish: habitational name from any of various places in Burgos, Lleón, and Santander named Vallejo, from a diminutive of *valle* 'valley'.
GIVEN NAMES Spanish 45%. *Jose* (48), *Juan* (25), *Manuel* (20), *Francisco* (14), *Jesus* (14), *Carlos* (12), *Guadalupe* (12), *Luis* (12), *Alfredo* (11), *Arturo* (11), *Fernando* (10), *Jorge* (10).

Vallejos (552) Spanish: plural variant of VALLEJO.

Vallely (308) Irish (Armagh): probably a much altered Anglicized form of Gaelic **Mac Giolla Mhuire** or **Mac Giolla Mhura** (see Gilmore).

Valleroy (109) French: habitational name from any of several place called Valleroy, for example in Franche-Comté, Haute Marne, and Meurthe-et-Moselle.

Vallery (424) French: habitational name from Vallery in Yonne, once a Romano-Gallic estate, recorded in 1218 as Valerianus. The surname is also found in the British Isles and may be of Norman origin, from the same place.
GIVEN NAMES French 4%. *Leonce* (2), *Monique, Yolette.*

Valles (1371) **1.** Catalan (**Vallès**): regional name for someone from a region of Catalonia named with *vallès* 'of or relating to the valley' (from Latin *vallensis*, an adjective derivative of *vallis* 'valley'). This name is very common in Catalonia. **2.** Spanish: habitational name from any of the places named Valles or Los Valles, from *valles*, plural of *valle* 'valley'.
GIVEN NAMES Spanish 41%. *Jose* (26), *Carlos* (13), *Jesus* (13), *Manuel* (13), *Luis* (12), *Juan* (11), *Raul* (11), *Francisco* (9), *Julio* (8), *Alfonso* (7), *Javier* (7), *Roberto* (7).

Vallese (104) Italian: topographic name from an adjectival form of *valle* 'valley', or a habitational name for someone from any of the numerous places named with this word.
GIVEN NAMES Italian 17%. *Carmine, Ezio, Guido, Pasco, Primo, Saverio.*

Vallet (130) **1.** French and English: occupational name for a manservant, Middle English, Old French *vaslet, val(l)et* (a diminutive of *vassal* 'serf'). **2.** French: topographic name from a diminutive of *val* 'valley'.
GIVEN NAMES French 9%. *Dominique, Marcel, Pierre, Prosper.*

Valletta (228) Southern Italian: from a diminutive of VALLE.
GIVEN NAMES Italian 16%. *Angelo, Antimo, Antonio, Caesar, Carmine, Giovanni, Nicola, Rocco, Salvatore, Umberto, Vincenzo.*

Vallette (149) French: from a diminutive of **Val**, a topographic name for someone who lived in a valley, Old French *val*.

Valley (1621) English: topographic name for someone who lived in a valley, Middle English *valeye*.

Vallez (110) Spanish (**Vállez**): variant of VALLES, especially 2.
GIVEN NAMES Spanish 23%. *Emilio* (2), *Adelaida, Francisco, Gregorio, Gustavo, Jaime, Juan, Luis, Manuel, Mario, Pablo, Raul.*

Valli (277) **1.** Italian: variant (plural) of VALLE or a habitational name from a place named with this word, as for example Valli del Pasubio or Valli dei Signori. **2.** Greek: see VALLIS. **3.** Hungarian (**Válli**): habitational name for someone from Vál in Fehér county or Vály in Gömör county, now in Slovakia. **4.** Finnish: see WALLI.
GIVEN NAMES Italian 7%. *Antonio, Caesar, Carmela, Dario, Gildo, Guido, Luigi.*

Valliant (168) Altered spelling of English **Valiant**, a variant of VAILLANT.

Vallie (148) **1.** English: unexplained. **2.** Probably an altered spelling of German **Vallee**, a fairly common surname of French origin denoting someone who lived in a valley. The name in Germany is also spelled **Wallee**.

Vallier (452) **1.** French: from the personal name *Valére*, from Latin *Valerius* (see VALERIO). **2.** English: topographic name for a dweller in a valley, from a noun derivative of Old French *val* 'valley' or possibly Middle English *valeye*.
FOREBEARS A Vallier, also recorded as Valliere and Vallieres, from the Saintonge region of France, is documented in Quebec City in 1667.

Valliere (747) French (**Vallière**): topographic name for someone who lived in a valley, or a habitational name from any of various places named Vallières or La Vallière.
GIVEN NAMES French 8%. *Armand* (4), *Fernand* (2), *Lucien* (2), *Mathieu* (2), *Alcide, Cyrille, Donat, Laurent, Marcel, Normand, Reynald.*

Vallieres (137) French: variant of VALLIERE.
GIVEN NAMES French 33%. *Andre* (3), *Armand* (3), *Lucien* (3), *Gilles* (2), *Alain, Fernand, Jacques, Marcel, Michel, Regean, Simonne, Yvan.*

Vallin (173) **1.** Galician: Castilianized form of Galician **Valín**, a habitational name from any of the places so named in Galicia, from a derivative of *val* 'valley'. **2.** French: topographic name for someone who lived in a small valley, from a diminutive of Old French *val* 'valley', or a habitational name from a minor place so named in Isère. **3.** Swedish: habitational name for someone from a place name formed with *val* (from Latin *vallis* 'valley', representing Swedish *dal*) or *vall* 'grassy bank', 'pasture', + the surname suffix *-in*, from Latin *-inius*.
GIVEN NAMES Spanish 32%. *Jose* (4), *Manuel*

(4), *Jesus* (2), *Juan* (2), *Rafael* (2), *Angel, Cirilo, Delfina, Enrique, Esperansa, Esteban, Francisco.*

Vallis (137) Greek: status name from Greek *valis* 'prefect', Turkish *vali* 'governor'.
GIVEN NAMES Greek 13%. *Dimitrios* (6), *Savvas, Spiro.*

Vallo (212) Hungarian: from Hungarian *valló*, either in the sense 'person who confesses or gives evidence' (from *vallani* 'to confess'), or in the older sense 'shepherd'.

Vallone (721) Italian: **1.** from an augmentative form of VALLE. **2.** habitational name from any of various places named Vallone.
GIVEN NAMES Italian 16%. *Pasquale* (5), *Salvatore* (5), *Vito* (4), *Gaetano* (2), *Lia* (2), *Sal* (2), *Angelo, Annamarie, Benedetta, Carmela, Carmelo, Carmin.*

Vallot (163) French: variant of VALLET.
GIVEN NAMES French 13%. *Curley* (3), *Monique* (2), *Alphe, Eraste, Etienne, Minus.*

Valls (208) Catalan: habitational name from Valls in Tarragona province, so named from *valls*, plural of *vall* 'valley'.
GIVEN NAMES Spanish 32%. *Jose* (6), *Felipe* (4), *Jorge* (4), *Juan* (4), *Enrique* (3), *Luis* (3), *Roberto* (3), *Alfonzo* (2), *Ana* (2), *Eugenio* (2), *Ramon* (2), *Sergio* (2); *Amadeo, Marino.*

Valois (361) French: topographic name for someone who lived in a valley, or a habitational name from any of the various places called Val(l)ois, or regional name from the district in northern France so called, which was once an independent duchy. In all cases the source is an adjective derivative of Old French *val* 'valley' (see VALE).
FOREBEARS A bearer of the name Valois from the Saintonge region of France was documented in Champlain, Quebec, in 1694.
GIVEN NAMES French 18%. *Marcel* (4), *Andre* (3), *Henri* (2), *Normand* (2), *Alcide, Armand, Emilien, Gilberte, Gilles, Herve, Jacques, Lucien.*

Valone (217) Variant of Italian VALLONE.

Valore (126) Italian: from the medieval personal name *Valóre*, an omen name from *valore* 'valor'.
GIVEN NAMES Italian 15%. *Angelo, Benedetto, Dante, Nunzio, Rocco.*

Valtierra (213) Basque: habitational name from Valtierra, a village in Navarre province.
GIVEN NAMES Spanish 51%. *Jose* (7), *Juan* (5), *Guadalupe* (3), *Jesus* (3), *Adolfo* (2), *Alejandro* (2), *Alfonso* (2), *Ana* (2), *Armondo* (2), *Arturo* (2), *Dionisio* (2), *Francisco* (2); *Antonio* (2), *Umberto* (2), *Lorenzo, Valentino.*

Valvano (244) Italian: variant of **Balvano**, a habitational name from Balvano in Potenza province.
GIVEN NAMES Italian 25%. *Rocco* (8), *Angelo* (2), *Carmine* (2), *Vito* (2), *Antonio, Costantino, Gaetano, Giuseppe, Nicola, Sal, Vincenzo.*

Valverde (992) Spanish: habitational name from any of the numerous places named Valverde 'green valley'.
GIVEN NAMES Spanish 35%. *Jose* (16), *Luis* (11), *Manuel* (10), *Carlos* (9), *Roberto* (7), *Juan* (6), *Ana* (5), *Francisco* (5), *Jorge* (5), *Mario* (5), *Pedro* (5), *Angel* (4).

Valvo (301) Italian: variant of BALBO.
GIVEN NAMES Italian 13%. *Salvatore* (3), *Angelo, Giacomo, Giuseppe, Sal, Santo.*

Vamos (138) Hungarian (**Vámos**): occupational name for a collector of tolls, taxes, or levies, from *vám* 'toll', 'tax'.
GIVEN NAMES Hungarian 8%. *Bela, Endre, Geza, Istvan, Zoltan.*

Van (1476) **1.** Vietnamese: unexplained. **2.** Dutch (**De Van**): metonymic occupational name for a winnower or a maker of winnowing fans, from Middle Dutch *van(ne)* 'fan'. **3.** English: Western English variant of FANN. **4.** Czech (**Vaň**): from a pet form of the personal name *Václav*, Old Czech *Vęceslav* (see VACEK). **5.** Ukrainian: from a short form of the personal name *Ivan*, Slavic form of JOHN.
GIVEN NAMES Vietnamese 31%. *Anh* (14), *Thanh* (14), *Hung* (12), *Minh* (7), *Vinh* (5), *Dung* (4), *Hue* (4), *Huong* (4), *Lan* (4), *Quang* (4), *Tan* (4), *Thuy* (4); *Hong* (7), *Chi* (3), *Hang* (3), *Ho* (2), *Pok* (2), *Sang* (2), *Bai, Chin, Ching, Chu, Chuan, Dong.*

Vana (339) Czech (**Váňa**): from the personal name *Váňa*, a derivative of the Old Czech name *Vęceslav* (see VACEK).

Van Acker (296) Dutch: **1.** topographic name for someone who lived next to a field, Middle Dutch *ack(e)re*, or a habitational name for someone from a place named with this word. **2.** Alternatively, it may be a habitational name for someone from Aachen, a variant of VAN AKEN.
GIVEN NAMES French 6%. *Michel* (2), *Alphonse, Andre, Armand, Gaston.*

Vanacore (250) **1.** Italian (Naples): unexplained. **2.** Dutch (**van Acore**): habitational name for someone from a place called Core (from Old French *Caure*, Latin *colrylus, colurus* 'walnut tree').
GIVEN NAMES Italian 15%. *Antonio* (5), *Salvatore* (2), *Alessandro, Enrico, Pasquale, Sal.*

Van Aken (387) Dutch: habitational name for someone from the city of Aachen (Dutch name *Aken*) in Germany, close to the border with the Netherlands and Belgium.

Van Allen (923) Dutch and Belgian: habitational name for someone from Alen or Aalden, in the province of Drenthe, or from a place in northern France called Allan.
FOREBEARS Pieter van Allen came to New Netherland in 1658.

Van Alstine (652) Dutch: origin uncertain; probably an Americanized form of **van Alstein** (see ALSTEEN).

Van Alstyne (505) Variant of Dutch VAN ALSTINE.

Van Aman (339) Dutch: habitational name from Amen in Drenthe.

Van Amburg (217) Dutch: habitational name for someone from HAMBURG or possibly HOMBURG.

Van Amburgh (149) Dutch: variant of VAN AMBURG.

Van Andel (117) Dutch: unexplained.
GIVEN NAMES Dutch 6%. *Cornelis, Gerrit, Renn.*

Van Antwerp (509) Variant of Dutch **Van Antwerpen**, habitational name for someone from the Belgian city of Antwerp.

Van Ark (102) Dutch: habitational name from a place called Ark in Gelderland.

Van Arkel (101) Dutch: habitational name from a place called Arkel in South Holland.
GIVEN NAMES Dutch 12%; German 4%. *Henk* (2), *Antoon, Hendrikus; Hans* (2), *Gerhard.*

Van Arnam (124) Dutch: habitational name for someone from the city of Arnhem.

Van Arsdale (875) Americanized form of an unidentified Dutch habitational name, possibly from a place called Aertsen or Aerssen, + *dal* 'valley'.

Van Arsdall (258) Variant of Dutch VAN ARSDALE.

Van Artsdalen (100) Variant of Dutch VAN ARSDALE.

Van Assche (113) Dutch and Belgian: habitational name from a place called Assche, in Brabant, just north of Brussels.
GIVEN NAMES French 8%. *Monique, Pierre.*

Van Asse (474) Dutch and Belgian: most probably a variant of VAN ASSCHE.
FOREBEARS A Vanasse, coming from Normandy, France, is recorded in Trois-Rivières, Quebec, in 1666.
GIVEN NAMES French 11%. *Lucien* (2), *Ovila* (2), *Pierre* (2), *Anatole, Armand, Emile, Gaetan, Gaston, Gilles, Oliva, Rejean, Serge.*

Van Asten (209) Belgian: habitational name from a place called Asten in Brabant.

Vanatta (954) Dutch: altered form of an unidentified habitational name. **1.** This may be the village of Etten near Zutphen in Overijssel. **2.** Alternatively, it may be a variant of VAN NATTER.

Van Auken (696) Variant of Dutch VAN AKEN.

Van Ausdal (145) Dutch: origin uncertain. Possibly a variant of VAN ARSDALE.

Van Ausdall (154) Dutch: origin uncertain. Possibly a variant of VAN ARSDALE.

Van Bebber (212) Dutch: most probably from a place called Bebbrig in Gelderland.

Van Beek (884) Dutch and Belgian: habitational name for someone from any of various places called Beek, for example in the provinces of Limburg, North Brabant, and Gelderland.
GIVEN NAMES Dutch 5%. *Gerrit* (7), *Dirk* (2), *Willem* (2), *Aart, Albertus, Cor, Cornie, Egbert, Gerritt, Klaas, Marinus, Pieter.*

Van Belle (106) Dutch or Belgian: habitational name from an unidentified place, possibly Bellen in province of Limburg.
GIVEN NAMES French 10%. *Germain, Jacques, Pierre.*

Van Benschoten (222) Dutch: probably a habitational name from a lost or unidentified place called Benschote, or a topographic name for someone who lived by an enclosure for cattle, Middle Dutch *scho(o)t(t)e*, or by a corner of woodland or heathland in a marshy area, Middle Dutch *scoet*. The element *Ben-* is unexplained.
FOREBEARS Theunis Eliasen Van Benschoten's name is found regularly, as both a witness and a principal, on documents from in and around Kingston, NY, from April 1671 until his death in 1725.

Van Benthuysen (110) Dutch: habitational name from Benthuizen in South Holland near Alphen.
FOREBEARS This name is recorded in Beverwijck in New Netherland (Albany, NY) in the mid 17th century.

Van Bergen (232) Dutch and Belgian: habitational name for someone from any of numerous places named with *bergen* 'hills' or 'coal mines'.
GIVEN NAMES German 4%. *Hubertus, Johannes.*

Van Berkum (100) Dutch: variant of **Van Bergum**, a habitational name from Bergum in Freisland.

Van Beveren (115) Dutch: unexplained. It may be a variant of *Bever*, said to be an old name for Beverwijk in the province of Holland.
GIVEN NAMES Dutch 8%. *Marinus, Marten, Meindert.*

Van Bibber (397) Dutch: variant of VAN BEBBER.

Van Blarcom (239) Dutch: variant of VAN BLARICOM.

Van Blaricom (219) Dutch: habitational name for someone from Blaricum, a place northeast of Hilversum in the Netherlands.

Van Boven (119) Dutch: habitational name for someone from Boven, a place in the province of North Brabant.
GIVEN NAME Dutch 4%. *Elfriede.*

Van Boxtel (125) Dutch: habitational name for someone from Boxtel, a place in the province of North Brabant.

Van Bramer (110) Dutch: most probably a habitational name for someone from Breemeer, a place in the province of Drenthe.

Van Brocklin (410) Americanized spelling of Dutch **Van Breukelen**, a habitational name for someone from either of two places so named, in North Brabant and Utrecht.

Van Bruggen (134) Dutch: habitational name for someone from the city of Brugge (Bruges) in northeast Belgium, or from any of several places similarly named, from Dutch *bruggen* 'bridges'.

GIVEN NAMES Dutch 6%; German 4%. *Gerrit* (2), *Adrianus, Hendrick; Johannes.*

Van Brunt (654) Dutch: habitational name from an unidentified place, perhaps Brundt in Jutland, Denmark.

FOREBEARS Rutger Joesten van Brunt emigrated from the Netherlands in 1653 and in 1657 settled in New Utrecht, Long Island, NY.

Van Buren (2084) Dutch and Jewish (from the Netherlands): habitational name for someone from any of the many places in the Netherlands named with Middle Dutch *buur, buer* 'house', 'shed', in particular Buren in Gelderland.

FOREBEARS Cornelis van Buren came to New Netherland in 1631. His descendant Martin van Buren (1782–1862) was 8th president of the U.S. (1836–40).

Johannes van Bueren (*c.*1680–1755), who came to NY from Amsterdam in 1702, was the founder of a famous family of physicians. They are not related to the presidential family.

Van Buskirk (1918) Dutch: habitational name for someone from any of various minor places called *Boskerck* 'church in the woods'.

Van Camp (1313) Dutch and Belgian: topographic name for someone who lived by an open field, from Latin *campus* 'plain', 'uncultivated land', or a habitational name for someone from a place named with this word, in particular the village of Camp in Flanders near Lille.

Van Campen (230) Dutch: variant spelling of VAN KAMPEN.

Vance (16130) English and Irish: topographic name for someone who lived by a fen or marsh, Old English *fenn*. Compare FANN.

Vancil (699) Variant of the Czech personal name *Vancl* or some other derivative of the Old Czech name *Vęceslav* (see VACEK).

Van Cise (133) Dutch: habitational name for someone from a place called Zeist, east of Utrecht.

Van Cleave (1490) Americanized spelling of Dutch VAN CLEVE.

Van Cleef (221) Dutch: variant of VAN CLEVE.

Van Cleve (711) Dutch: habitational name for someone from the city of Cleves (German *Kleve*), in North Rhine-Westphalia, Germany.

Van Cott (286) Probably a variant of Dutch **Van Gat**, a habitational name for someone from either of two places called Gat, in North Brabant and North Holland.

Van Court (152) Dutch: probably a habitational name from a place called *Court*, a French word equivalent in meaning to Dutch *hof* 'farm', 'main farm on an estate'. Compare VANDERHOFF.

Vancura (353) **1.** Czech (**Vančura**): from the personal name *Vančura*, a derivative of the Old Czech name *Vęceslav* (see

VACEK). **2.** Hungarian (**Vancsura**): from a derivative of the Slavic personal name VANA.

Van Curen (280) Dutch: variant of VAN KEUREN.

Van Daele (164) Dutch: variant of VAN DALE.

GIVEN NAMES French 10%. *Marcel* (2), *Chantal, Eugenie, Francoise, Remi.*

Vandagriff (275) Probably an altered spelling of Dutch VANDEGRIFT.

Vandal (257) Dutch and Belgian: variant of VAN DALE.

GIVEN NAMES French 11%. *Andre* (2), *Normand* (2), *Aime, Amedee, Gaston, Germaine, Herve, Lucien.*

Van Dale (129) Dutch: topographic name for someone who lived in a valley, from *van* 'from' + *daal* 'valley', or habitational name from any of various places named with this word, in particular Daal in Utrecht and Limburg.

GIVEN NAMES French 8%; German 4%. *Armand, Camille, Normand; Armin, Hans.*

Van Dalen (171) Dutch: variant of VAN DALE.

GIVEN NAME German, Dutch 6%. *Alfons* (3).

Vandall (256) Dutch: variant spelling of VANDAL.

GIVEN NAMES French 4%. *Armand, Camille.*

Van Dam (859) Dutch and Belgian: habitational name for someone from any of the numerous places called Dam (for example in Utrecht province and in Gennep, Limberg) or Ten Damme (for example in Overijssel), or from other places named for a dam, dike, or pond (for example Stadje Damme in West Flanders).

FOREBEARS Claes Ripse van Dam came to Fort Orange, New Netherland (now part of Albany, NY), before 1658. His son, Rip Van Dam, was a prominent merchant and politician during the colonial era.

GIVEN NAMES Dutch 5%; French 4%. *Andries* (4), *Adrianus* (2), *Gerrit* (2), *Dirk, Harmen, Hendrick, Hendrik, Machiel, Marinus, Neeltje; Jacques* (3), *Henri* (2), *Luc, Marcel.*

Vandamme (292) Belgian: variant, under French influence, of VAN DAM.

GIVEN NAMES French 8%. *Henri* (2), *Alphonse, Andre, Florent, Marcel, Remi.*

Vandaveer (113) Altered spelling of Dutch **Van der Veer**, a habitational name for someone from a place named with Middle Dutch *veer(e)* 'jetty', for example Veere in Zeeland.

Vandeberg (345) Dutch (**Van de Berg**): variant of VANDENBERG.

Van De Bogart (143) Dutch: variant of **van den Bogaard**, a topographic name for someone living by an orchard, Dutch *boomgaard.*

Vandecar (171) Americanized spelling of Dutch **Van de Kar**, a name of uncertain origin.

Van Dee (106) Dutch: habitational name from a place of uncertain identification, perhaps *Die*, name of a stream just south of Alkmaar.

Vandegriff (134) Dutch (**Van de Griff**): variant of VANDERGRIFT.

Vandegrift (864) Dutch (**Van de Grift**): variant of VANDERGRIFT.

Vandehei (218) Dutch (**Van de Hei**): probably a variant of VANDERHEYDEN.

Vandehey (625) Dutch (**Van de Hey**): probably a variant of VANDERHEYDEN.

Vandekamp (159) Dutch (**Van de Kamp**): variant of VANDERKAMP.

Vandelinder (115) Dutch (**Van de Linder**): variant of VANDERLINDEN.

Van Dell (155) Dutch: topographic name for someone who lived in an area of lowland among sand dunes, Dutch *del*, or habitational name from a place named with this word.

Van Dellen (118) Dutch: topographic name for someone who lived in an area of lowland among sand dunes, from the plural of Dutch *del* (see VAN DELL).

Vandeloo (162) Dutch (**Van de Loo**): topographic name for someone who lived in a woodland clearing, from Dutch *loo* 'woodland clearing'.

Vandeman (144) Dutch (**Van Deman**): probably a habitational name from Demen or Deemen, a place in North Brabant.

Vandemark (715) Dutch (**Van de Mark**): topographic name for someone who lived by a border or boundary, from Middle Dutch *marke, merke* 'boundary', 'borderland'.

Vandenakker (129) Dutch (**Van den Akker**): topographic name for someone living by a cultivated field, Dutch *akker*.

Vandenberg (2603) Dutch (**Van den Berg**): topographic name for someone who lived on or by a hill or mountain, Middle Dutch *berghe*.

GIVEN NAMES Dutch 4%. *Dirk* (6), *Marinus* (4), *Gerrit* (3), *Gerritt* (2), *Hendrik* (2), *Jacobus* (2), *Maarten* (2), *Pieter* (2), *Wim* (2), *Albertus, Durk, Hendrick.*

Vandenberge (145) Dutch: variant of VANDENBERG.

Vandenbergh (213) Dutch: variant of VANDENBERG.

FOREBEARS This name is recorded in Beverwijck in New Netherland (Albany, NY) in the mid 17th century.

GIVEN NAMES Dutch 4%; French 4%. *Frans, Henk, Pieter; Constant, Mathieu.*

Vandenberghe (185) Variant, perhaps under French influence, of Dutch VANDENBERG.

GIVEN NAMES French 8%. *Hilaire, Pierre, Yves.*

Vandenboom (187) Dutch (**Van den Boom**): topographic name for someone who lived by a large or conspicuous tree, from Middle Dutch *boom* 'tree', or a habitational name from any of various places named with this word.

Vandenbos (286) Dutch: variant of VAN-DENBOSCH.

Vandenbosch (559) Dutch and Belgian: topographic name for someone who lived by an area of woodland, Dutch *bos(ch)*, or habitational name from a village in Brabant called den Bosch, near Malines.
GIVEN NAMES German 4%. *Kurt* (2), *Hans*, *Otto*.

Vandenbossche (109) Variant, under French influence, of Dutch VANDENBOSCH.

Vandenbrink (249) Dutch (**Van den Brink**): topographic name for someone who lived by a raised pasture in low-lying marshland, from Middle Dutch *brinc* 'edge', 'slope', 'raised grazing land' (see BRINK), or habitational name from a place called den Brink, named with this word, in particular Brink in the Veluwe region of Gelderland.
GIVEN NAMES Dutch 5%; German 4%. *Gerrit* (3), *Coba, Dirk, Gysbert*; *Johannes* (2), *Kurt* (2).

Vandenbroek (157) Dutch (**Van den Broek**): topographic name for someone who lived by a flood plain or a stream that frequently flooded, from *broek*, 'water meadow', 'flood plain', or habitational name from any of several places named with this word, for example den Broek in North Holland, Groningen, North Brabant, and elsewhere.
GIVEN NAMES Dutch 7%; German 4%. *Cornie, Kees, Willem*; *Hans, Johannes, Monika*.

Vandenburg (423) Dutch and Belgian (**Van den Burg**): topographic name for someone who lived by a citadel or stonghold, from Middle Dutch *burch*, or a habitational name from a place named with this word, for example Burch in South Holland or Burcht in Antwerp province, Belgium.

Vandenburgh (311) Variant spelling of Dutch VANDENBURG.

Vandenbusch (102) Dutch: variant of VANDENBOSCH.

Vandenbush (105) Americanized form of Dutch VANDENBOSCH.

Vandenelzen (113) Dutch (**Van den Elzen**): topographic name for someone living among elder trees, from the plural of Dutch *els* 'elder tree', or habitational name from Elsen in Brabant, named with this word.

Vandenheuvel (918) Dutch (**Van den Heuvel**): habitational name from any of several places in Belgium and the Netherlands named De(n) Heuvel or Heuvel, from *heuvel* 'mound', 'small hill', or a topographic name from the same word.

Vandenhoek (135) Dutch (**Van den Hoek**): topographic name for someone living at a corner or in a secluded nook, from *hoek* 'corner', 'nook', or habitational name from

any of the many places named with this word (see VAN HOOK).

Vandenhouten (121) Dutch (**Van den Houten**): topographic name for someone living in a forest, from *houten* 'forest', 'woods', or a habitational name from any of the many places called Ten Houte.
GIVEN NAMES German 4%. *Erna, Hans*.

Vandenlangenberg (151) Dutch (**Van den Langen Berg**): topographic name for someone living by a long hill, from Dutch *lang* 'long' + *berg* 'hill', or habitational name from a place called Langenberg, for example in the Veluwe region of Gelderland.

Vandenplas (111) Dutch (**Van den Plas**): habitational name from de Plas, name of a polder (reclaimed land) in South Holland near Leiden, named with Middle Dutch *plas* 'puddle', 'pool', 'plash'.

Vandepol (134) Dutch (**Van de Pol**): variant of VANDERPOL.
GIVEN NAMES Dutch 8%; German 8%. *Hendrik* (2), *Klaas*; *Johannes* (2), *Kurt* (2), *Gerda*.

Vandeputte (135) Dutch (**Van de Putte**): habitational name for someone from any of various places called (Ten) Putte, in Belgium and the Netherlands, from Middle Dutch *putte* 'well', 'pit', or a topographic name for someone living beside a pit or a well.
GIVEN NAMES French 8%. *Amedee* (2), *Marcel*.

Vander (140) North German and Dutch: unexplained.

Vanderaa (137) Dutch (**Van der Aa**): topographic name for someone living by a waterway, Dutch *aa*, or habitational name from any of the many places named with this word.

Vanderark (110) Dutch (**Van der Ark**): habitational name from a place called Ark in Gelderland near Nijkerk.

Vanderbeck (256) Dutch (**Van der Beck**): variant of VANDERBEEK.

Vanderbeek (383) Dutch and Belgian (**Van der Beek**): habitational name for someone from any of various places in Belgium and the Netherlands named Terbeek, Beek, or (Ter) Beke, from *beke* 'stream', 'creek', or a topographic name from this word.
GIVEN NAMES German 4%. *Fritz, Gerhard, Gerhardt*.

Vanderberg (340) Dutch (**Van der Berg**): topographic name for someone who lived by a hill or mountain, from Middle Dutch *berghe* 'mountain', 'hill'.

Vanderbilt (582) Dutch (**Van der Bilt**) and North German: topographic name for someone living by a low hill, from Middle Low German *bulte* 'mound', 'low hill'. De Bilt is the name of an area just northeast of Utrecht.
FOREBEARS Cornelius van der Bilt came from the Netherlands to Long Island, NY, in the second half of the 17th century. His

descendant Cornelius Vanderbilt (1794–1877), financier and railroad and shipping magnate, was born on Staten Island, NY. He was the founder of a family of powerful financiers.

Vanderbosch (140) Dutch: variant of VANDENBOSCH.

Vanderbrook (106) Americanized form of Dutch VANDENBROEK.

Vanderburg (634) Dutch: variant of VANDENBURG.

Vanderburgh (143) Variant spelling of Dutch VANDENBURG.

Vanderbush (130) Americanized spelling of Dutch **Van der Bussche**, a habitational name from any of various places in the Netherlands and Belgium named with Middle Dutch *bos(ch)*, *bussche* 'wood', 'copse', as for example Den Bosch in the Netherlands.
GIVEN NAME German 4%. *Erwin*.

Vandercook (169) Dutch: unexplained.

Van Deren (112) Dutch (**Van de Ren**): habitational name from a place called de Ren in North Brabant.
GIVEN NAME German 6%. *Kurt* (2).

Vanderford (697) Dutch: **1.** habitational name from a place called De Voerde in Freisland. **2.** Americanized form of VANDERVOORT.

Vandergriff (974) Dutch: variant of VANDERGRIFT.

Vandergrift (514) Dutch (**Van der Grift**): topographic name from Middle Dutch *grifte* 'man-made channel'.

Vanderhart (116) Dutch and Belgian (**Van der Hart**): topographic name from De Hart, name of a hill in Luxemburg.

Vanderheide (159) Dutch (**Van der Heide**): variant of VANDERHEYDEN.
GIVEN NAMES Dutch 5%. *Gerrit, Pieter, Wiebe*.

Vanderheiden (364) Dutch (**Van der Heiden**): variant of VANDERHEYDEN.

Vanderheyden (482) Dutch and Belgian: topographic name from Middle Dutch *heede, heide* 'heath', 'moor', or a habitational name for someone from any of numerous places in Belgium and the Netherlands named with this word, as for example Ter Heide in Belgium or Ter Heijde in the Netherlands.
FOREBEARS This name is recorded in Beverwijck in New Netherland (Albany, NY) in the mid 17th century.
GIVEN NAMES French 4%. *Andre* (3), *Pierre, Thierry*.

Vanderhoef (208) Dutch (**Van der Hoef**): **1.** variant of VANDERHOFF. **2.** habitational name from either of two places, in Gelderland and Utrecht, called De Hoef.

Vanderhoek (117) Dutch (**Van der Hoek**): variant of VANDENHOEK.
GIVEN NAMES Dutch 9%. *Cornelis, Henk, Rutger*.

Vanderhoff (517) Dutch (**Van der Hoff**): topographic name for someone who lived and worked on the main farm or estate in a community, Middle Dutch *hove*.

Vanderhoof (847) Dutch (**Van der Hoof**): variant of VANDERHOFF or VANDERHOEF.

Vanderhorst (442) Dutch (**Van der Horst**): topographic name from Middle Dutch *horst* 'brushwood', 'shrubs', indicating a place that was overgrown, or possibly even a house bearing a stork's nest (storks' nests are large and untidy). Horst occurs as a placename in just about every province of the Netherlands.
GIVEN NAMES German 4%. *Kurt* (2), *Willi*.

Vanderhyde (126) Americanized spelling of Dutch VANDERHEIDE.

Vanderiet (123) Dutch (**Van de Riet**): habitational name from places called De Riet, in North Brabant and Overijssel.

Vanderjagt (148) Dutch (**Van der Jagt**): occupational name for a huntsman, literally 'of the hunt'.
GIVEN NAMES Dutch 5%. *Lourens, Marinus, Pim.*

Vanderkamp (130) Dutch (**Van der Kamp**): topographic name for someone who lived by a field or a particular domain, from Middle Dutch *kamp* 'field', 'domain', or habitational name from der Kamp, a place in North Holland.

Vanderkolk (241) Dutch (**van der Kolk**): topographic name from *kolk*, which has various meanings: 'well', 'pool', 'deep trough', or 'passage'.

Vanderkooi (205) Dutch **Van der Kooi**: habitational name for someone from either of two places, De Kooi in South Holland or De Kooy in North Holland.

Vanderlaan (691) Dutch (**Van der Laan**): topographic name from the same word from *laan* 'lane', 'path', or a habitational name for someone from any of various minor places named with this word: De Laan (in the provinces of North and South Holland, and North Brabant) or Ter Laan (in Groningen).
GIVEN NAMES Dutch 4%. *Dirk* (3), *Gerrit* (2), *Pieter* (2), *Cornelis, Derk, Hilko, Laurens.*

Vanderleest (192) Dutch and Belgian (**Van der Leest**): habitational name for someone from a place called Leest in Antwerp province, or De Leest in North Brabant.

Vanderlinde (282) Dutch (**Van der Linde**): topographic name for someone who lived by a lime tree, Middle Dutch *linde*, or a habitational name for someone from a place named with this word.
GIVEN NAMES Dutch 4%. *Dirk, Henk, Leendert, Marinus.*

Vanderlinden (837) Dutch (**Van der Linden**): topopgraphic name for someone who lived among lime trees or habitational name for someone from places in Belgium and the Netherlands named Terlinden, from Middle Dutch *linden* 'lime trees'.

Vanderlip (251) Reduced form of Dutch **Van de Lippe**, probably a topographic name for someone who lived by the Lippe river.
GIVEN NAMES Dutch 4%. *Henrik, Klaas, Renn.*

Vanderloop (191) Dutch (**Van der Loop**): topographic name for someone who lived by a waterway, Middle Dutch *lo(e)pe*, in particular a waterway called De Loop in North Brabant.

Vanderlugt (127) Dutch: topographic name from Dutch *Lucht* 'cleared area', or habitational name from a place called De Lucht in South Holland.
GIVEN NAMES Dutch 8%. *Gerrit* (3), *Marinus.*

Vandermark (568) Dutch (**Van der Mark**): variant of VANDEMARK.

Vandermay (101) Dutch (**Van der May**): variant of VANDERMEY.

Vandermeer (671) Dutch (**Van der Meer**): topographic name for someone who lived by a lake, Middle Dutch *mere*, or habitational name from any of the numerous places named with this word.
GIVEN NAMES Dutch 7%. *Gerrit* (3), *Diemer* (2), *Albertus, Berend, Dirk, Egbert, Hendrick, Hendrik, Henk, Kees, Maarten, Marinus.*

Vandermeulen (465) Dutch (**Van der Meulen**): topographic name for someone who lived at a mill or, by extension, an occupational name for a miller, a variant of VANDERMOLEN.
GIVEN NAMES Dutch 7%. *Roelof* (4), *Dirk* (3), *Derk, Hendrik, Ineke, Klaas, Pieter.*

Vandermey (141) Dutch (**Van der Mey**): habitational name from a place called De Meije, near Woerden in South Holland.

Vandermolen (613) Dutch (**Van der Molen**) and Jewish (from the Netherlands): topographic name for someone who lived by a mill.

Vanderplaats (128) Dutch (**Van der Plaats**): habitational name from a place called De Plaats in North Brabant.

Vanderploeg (620) Dutch and Belgian (**Van der Ploeg**): habitational name for someone from any of various minor places named (de) Ploeg, in the Belgian provinces of Antwerp, East Flanders, and West Flanders.

Vanderpoel (253) Dutch (**Van der Poel**): topographic name for someone who lived near a pond, Middle Dutch *poele*, or habitational name from any of the many places in the Netherlands named with this word.
FOREBEARS This name is recorded in Beverwijck in New Netherland (Albany, NY) in the mid 17th century.

Vanderpol (376) Dutch (**van der Pol**): topographic name from Middle Dutch *pol* 'area of higher ground in fenland', or a habitational name from a place named with this word, for example De Pol (Overijssel, Drente).

GIVEN NAMES Dutch 4%. *Nelis* (2), *Sybren* (2), *Gerrit, Marinus, Willem.*

Vanderpool (1892) Variant of Dutch VANDERPOEL.

Vanderschaaf (210) Dutch: probably a habitational name from Schaft, a place in North Brabant.

Vanderslice (625) Americanized spelling of Dutch VANDERSLUIS.

Vandersloot (163) Dutch and Belgian (**Van der Sloot**): topographic name from *sloot* 'drainage ditch', 'channel', or a habitational name from a minor place named with this word, for example Slote or Sloten in East Flanders.
GIVEN NAMES Dutch 4%. *Adriaan, Gerritt.*

Vandersluis (184) Dutch (**Van der Sluis**): topographic name for someone who lived by a sluice gate, Middle Dutch *sluis* (Old French *escluse*), or a habitational name from a place named with this word, notably Sluis in Zeeland, which was founded in the 13th century.
GIVEN NAME German 4%. *Kurt* (2).

Vandersteen (144) Dutch and Belgian (**Van der Steen**): habitational name for someone from any of various minor places called Steen or Ten Stene (from *steen* 'stone'), for example in the Belgian provinces of East Flanders and Brabant.
GIVEN NAMES Dutch 11%; German 4%. *Henk* (2), *Joost* (2), *Cornie, Dirk; Kurt* (2).

Vanderstelt (161) Dutch (**Van der Stelt**): topographic name for someone who lived by a *stelt*, an artificial bank constructed on the outside of a dike to give temporary protection to a shepherd and his flock against high tides or inclement weather.
GIVEN NAMES Dutch 6%. *Cornie, Derk, Gerrit, Gerritt.*

Vanderveen (854) Dutch (**Van der Veen**): topographic name from Dutch *veen* 'peat bog', 'fen', or a habitational name from any of various places named (het) Veen.
GIVEN NAMES Dutch 4%. *Kort* (2), *Albertus, Cornelis, Geert, Gerrit, Harm, Klaas, Pieter, Teunis.*

Vanderveer (648) Dutch (**Van der Veer**): topographic name for someone who lived near a ferry crossing, Middle Dutch *vēre*, or a habitational name from a place named with this word.
FOREBEARS Cornelius Janse van der Veer came from the Netherlands to Long Island, NY, in 1659.

Vandervelde (357) Dutch (**Van der Velde**): topographic name for someone who lived on land which had not been brought into cultivation, from *veld* 'pasture', 'open country', or a habitational name from a place named with this word.
GIVEN NAMES Dutch 4%. *Cor, Thys, Wiebe.*

Vandervelden (219) Dutch (**Van der Velden**): variant of VANDERVELDE.

Vanderven (109) Dutch (**Van der Ven**): variant of VANDERVEEN.

Vandervest (112) Dutch: unexplained; possibly an altered form of **Van der Vecht**, a topographic name for someone living by the river Vecht.

Vandervliet (210) Dutch (**Van der Vliet**): topographic name for someone who lived by a stream, Middle Dutch *vliet*.

Vandervoort (482) Dutch (**Van der Voort**): topographic name for someone who lived by a ford or crossing point, Middle Dutch *voorde*, or a habitational name from a place named with this word, for example Tervoort in North Brabant.
GIVEN NAMES Dutch 4%. *Dirk* (2), *Pieter* (2), *Hendrik*.

Vandervort (684) Dutch: variant of VANDERVOORT.

Vanderwaal (121) Dutch (**Van der Waal**): 1. habitational name from any of various places called Waal, or topographic name from Middle Dutch *wal* 'pool, eddy, or mudflat behind a dike (resulting from a breach in the dike)'. 2. topographic name for someone living by a city wall, a variant of VANDERWAL 2. 3. topographic name for someone who lived by the river Waal, a distributary of the Rhine.

Vanderwal (416) Dutch (**Van der Wal**): 1. variant of VANDERWAAL 1 and 2. 2. topographic name from Dutch *wal* 'wall', denoting either a city wall or a wall forming the bank of a river or waterway.
GIVEN NAMES Dutch 6%; German 4%. *Gerrit* (2), *Bartel, Cor, Cornelis, Cornie, Henk, Willem, Wouter; Johannes* (3), *Hilde, Johann*.

Vanderwalker (104) American altered form of Dutch **Van der Werken**, a habitational name from Werken, name of places in Gelderland and Brabant.

Vanderwall (501) Dutch: variant spelling of Dutch VANDERWAAL, in any of its senses.

Vanderweele (172) Dutch (**Van der Weele**): habitational name from Weele in Zeeland, or a similarly named place elsewhere, named with Middle Dutch *wiele*, variant of *wal* 'pool, eddy, or mudflat resulting from a breach in a dike'. See also VANDERWAAL, VANDERWIELEN.

Vanderweide (232) Dutch (**Van der Weide**): topographic name from *weide* 'pasture', 'meadow'.

Vanderwende (113) Dutch: unexplained; possibly from a place called Wendel in Overijssel, near Zwolle.

Vanderwerf (364) Dutch (**Van der Werf**): 1. topographic name from Middle Dutch *werve, wereft*, denoting an uncultivated area of land surrounding a house, farm, dike, or the like, or a place where willows grew, or a habitational name for someone from a place named with this word. 2. topographic name for someone who lived by a wharf, Middle Dutch *werf*.

Vanderwerff (319) Dutch (**Van der Werff**): variant of VANDERWERF.

GIVEN NAMES Dutch 4%. *Gerrit* (2), *Henk* (2), *Cornie*.

Vanderwielen (103) Dutch (**Van der Wielen**): probably a topographic name from the plural of Middle Dutch *wiele*, variant of *wal* 'pool, eddy, or mudflat resulting from a breach in a dike'. See also VANDERWAAL, VANDERWEELE, VANDEWIELE.

Vanderwilt (170) Dutch (**Van der Wilt**): reduced form of **van der Wildert**, a topographic name from Middle Dutch *wildert* 'wilderness', 'uncultivated land', or a habitational name from a place named with this word.

Vanderwoude (432) Dutch (**Van der Woude**): 1. most probably a variant of **Vanderwoud**, topographic name for someone who lived in a wood or forest, Dutch *woud*, equivalent of German WALD. 2. according to Debrabandere, it may be a topographic name for someone living by a patch of weld (a plant yielding a yellow dye), from Middle Dutch *woude, wou(we)* 'weld'.

Vanderzanden (329) Dutch (**Van der Zanden**): topographic name from *zand* 'sand', or a habitational name from any of numerous places in Belgium and the Netherlands (Het Zand), named with this word.

Vanderzee (319) Dutch: literally 'from the sea', a topographic name for someone who lived by the sea, Middle Dutch *zee*, or a name for a child born at sea.
FOREBEARS Storm van der Zee (1636–c.1679), son of Albert Andriessen BRADT, was born aboard the ship *Rensselaerwyck* during a violent storm off the coast of England, en route to New Netherland. He adopted the surname **Van der Zee** in adult life, and had numerous prominent descendants.
GIVEN NAMES Dutch 4%. *Dirk* (2), *Michiel, Pieter*.

Vanderzwaag (133) Dutch (**Van der Zwaag**): habitational name for someone from a place called Zwaag in the province of North Holland or Swaag in Groningen.

Van Deursen (100) Dutch: habitational name for someone from a place called Deursen in North Brabant.

Van Deusen (879) Dutch: habitational name for someone from the German town of Deusen, north of Dortmund, in North Rhine-Westphalia near the Dutch border.
FOREBEARS This name is recorded in Beverwijck in New Netherland (Albany, NY) in the mid 17th century.

Vandevander (202) Dutch: variant of VAN DEVENTER.

Van Devanter (101) Dutch: variant of VAN DEVENTER.

Vandeveer (273) Dutch and Belgian (**van de Veer(e)**): from Middle Dutch *vēre* 'ferry', topographic name for someone who lived by a ferry, occupational name for a ferryman, or habitational name from any

of numerous places in the Netherlands and Flanders named with this word.

Vandevelde (432) Dutch (**van de Velde**): variant of VANDERVELDE.
GIVEN NAMES French 6%. *Julien* (2), *Alberic, Andre, Dominique, Gabrielle, Pierre, Valere*.

Vandeven (279) Dutch (**Van de Ven**): variant of VANDERVEEN.

Van Devender (446) Dutch: variant of Dutch VAN DEVENTER.

Van Deventer (990) Dutch: habitational name for someone from Deventer in Overijssel.

Vandever (495) Dutch (**Van de Ver**): variant of VANDEVEER.

Vandevoorde (190) Dutch (**Van de Voorde**): variant of VANDERVOORT.

Vandevoort (193) Dutch (**Van de Voort**): variant of VANDERVOORT.

Vandewalker (203) Dutch: see VANDERWALKER.

Vandewalle (363) Dutch (**Van de Walle**): 1. topographic name for someone who lived near a rampart or embankment, Middle Dutch *walle* (Germanic *walla*), or a habitational name from a place named with this word. 2. variant of VANDERWAL.
GIVEN NAMES French 4%. *Etienne, Marcel*.

Vandewater (478) Dutch (**Van de Water**): topographic name for someone who lived by the Water river, a branch of the Amstel inside the city of Amsterdam.

Vandeweghe (108) Dutch and Belgian (**Van de Weghe**): habitational name from any of numerous places in the Netherlands and Belgium called Weg or Ten Wege, named with Middle Low German *weg* 'road', 'way'.

Vandewiele (113) Dutch and Belgian (**Van de Wiele**): topographic name from Middle Dutch *wiele*, variant of *wal* 'pool, eddy, or mudflat resulting from a breach in a dike', or habitational name from a place named with this word, for example Te Wiele, in Pittem, Belgium. See also VANDERWAAL, VANDERWEELE.

Vandezande (202) Dutch (**Van de Zande**): variant of VANDERZANDEN.

Van Diest (162) Dutch and Belgian: habitational name for someone from either of two places called Diest, in Brabant and in Gelderland between the Waal and the Maas rivers.

Van Dijk (101) The usual modern Dutch spelling of VAN DYKE.
GIVEN NAMES Dutch 28%; German 9%. *Cornelis* (2), *Gerrit* (2), *Hendrik* (2), *Jacobus* (2), *Derk, Dirk, Frans, Michiel, Pieter, Willem; Hans* (3), *Johannes, Jurgen*.

Vandine (401) Americanized spelling of Dutch **Van Duyn(en)** (see VAN DUYNE).

Vandiver (2148) Americanized form of Dutch **Van Duiver**, a habitational name for someone from Duiven in Gelderland, near Arnhem.

Vandivier (184) Of Dutch origin: see VANDIVER.

Vandivort (114) Variant of Dutch VANDERVOORT.

Van Dolah (119) Dutch: unexplained; possibly a variant of **van Dollard**, topographic name from Dollard, name of a bay in Groningen on the border with Germany.

Van Domelen (178) Dutch: variant spelling of **Van Dommelen**, a habitational name for someone from Dommelen in North Brabant, named for the Dommel river, on which it stands.

Van Dongen (118) Dutch: habitational name from Dongen, near Tilburg.
GIVEN NAMES Dutch 14%. *Dirk* (2), *Cornelis, Hendrika, Henk, Marinus, Pieter.*

Van Doorn (144) Dutch: habitational name for someone from the city of Doorn, near Utrecht, or Apeldoorn, north of Arnhem.

Van Doren (798) Dutch and Belgian: **1.** most probably a variant of VAN DOORN. **2.** according to Debrabandere, it may be a habitational name for someone from places in Belgium and the Netherlands called Deurne, or from Durne in North Brabant.

Van Dorn (520) Dutch and Belgian: topographic name from Middle Dutch *do(o)rne* 'thorn bush', 'gorse', or a habitational name for someone from any of several places in Belgium and the Netherlands called Doorn, from the same word (see VAN DOORN).
FOREBEARS Pieter van Dorn emigrated from the Netherlands to New Amsterdam in the mid 17th century.

Van Dover (126) Dutch: habitational name for someone from Doveren in North Brabant.

Vandre (110) Dutch: habitational name for someone from Dray in Friesland.
GIVEN NAME German 4%. *Erhard.*

Van Driel (131) Dutch: habitational name from a place called Driel near Arnhem.
GIVEN NAMES Dutch 6%; German 5%. *Hendrik, Marinus; Hans* (2), *Erwin, Kurt.*

Van Druff (161) Americanized spelling of Dutch **Vandrouf**, a reduced form of VANDERHOFF.

Van Drunen (140) Dutch: habitational name from a place called Drunen near 's Hertogenbosch.

Van Dunk (125) Dutch: variant of **Van Donk**, a habitational name for someone from Donk in North Brabant.

Van Duren (123) Dutch: variant of VAN DOREN.

Van Dusen (1432) Dutch and Belgian: **1.** most probably a habitational name for someone from Dussen in North Brabant. **2.** possibly a habitational name for someone from Deinze in East Flanders. Debrabandere cites a reference to Jan van Doyse in 1373, probably from this place.

Van Duser (137) Dutch: probably a habitational name for someone from Dussen in North Brabant.
GIVEN NAMES German 4%. *Erhardt, Kurt.*

Van Dusseldorp (104) Dutch: habitational name for someone from the city of Düsseldorf in Germany.

Van Duyn (288) Dutch and Belgian: variant of VAN DUYNE.

Van Duyne (328) Dutch and Belgian: habitational name for someone from any of several places in Belgium and the Netherlands called Duin or Duinen.

Van Duzer (283) Dutch: variant of VAN DUSER.

Van Dyck (320) Dutch: variant of VAN DYKE.
GIVEN NAMES German 4%. *Florian* (2), *Claus, Egmont, Kurt.*

Vandygriff (132) Americanized form of Dutch VANDERGRIFT.

Van Dyk (595) Dutch: variant of VAN DYKE.
GIVEN NAMES Dutch 8%. *Gerrit* (5), *Cornelis* (2), *Gerben* (2), *Albertus, Andries, Dirk, Geert, Harm, Hendrik, Henk, Hilko, Kees.*

Van Dyke (6323) Dutch: topographic name for someone who lived by any of the many thousands of dikes in the Netherlands (Middle Dutch *dike* 'dike'), or a habitational name for someone from any of the many places in Belgium and the Netherlands called Dijk, Dijke, or Dyck, named with this word.
FOREBEARS Jan Thomassen van Dijk, the first mayor of New Utrecht, Long Island (now part of Brooklyn, NY), came from Amsterdam in the Netherlands to North America in 1652. The name was brought to North America independently by many other bearers.

Van Dyken (313) Dutch: variant (plural) of VAN DYKE.

Van Dyne (518) Dutch (**Van Duinen**): habitational name for someone from Duinen in Gelderland.

Vane (257) English: variant of FAYNE.

Van Eaton (243) Dutch: probably a habitational name for someone from Eten in North Brabant.

Vanecek (163) Czech (**Vaněček**): from a pet form of *Váňa*, a derivative of the Old Czech name *Věceslav* (see VACEK).

Van Eck (299) Dutch and Belgian: **1.** habitational name for someone from any of various minor places called ten Hekke, for example in East and West Flanders. **2.** possibly also a habitational name for someone from Eecke (near Ghent) or Eecken (Limburg) in Belgium.

Vanegas (490) Variant spelling of Spanish VENEGAS.
GIVEN NAMES Spanish 52%. *Jose* (19), *Miguel* (8), *Jorge* (7), *Luis* (7), *Carlos* (6), *Manuel* (5), *Amparo* (4), *Juan* (4), *Rodrigo* (4), *Angel* (3), *Guillermo* (3), *Jaime* (3).

Van Egmond (105) Dutch: habitational name for someone from Egmond in the province of North Holland.
GIVEN NAMES Dutch 6%. *Cor* (2), *Dirk.*

Vanek (200) Czech (**Vaněk**): from a pet form of the Old Czech name *Věceslav* (see VACEK).

Van Ek (882) Dutch (also **Vanek**): variant spelling of VAN ECK.

Vanella (130) **1.** Dutch: habitational name for someone from a place or house called Hel or Ter Helle, from Middle Dutch *helle* 'depression', 'low-lying place'. **2.** Italian: of uncertain derivation. It could be a topographic name from Old Italian *venella* 'alley'. Alternatively, it could be from a short form of the personal name *Giovanello* (or the feminine form *Giovanella*) or from a derivative of VANO.
GIVEN NAMES Italian 18%. *Salvatore* (2), *Angelo, Concetta, Eduardo, Gasper, Giuseppe, Lorenzo.*

Van Eman (131) Dutch: habitational name for someone from Emmen, in Overijssel near Zwolle.

Van Engen (168) Dutch: habitational name for someone from Engh near Utrecht.

Van Epps (501) Dutch: probably a habitational name for someone from Epse, a village near Deventer in Overijssel. **Van Epps** was a familiar name in the Schenectady–Albany area; Fultonville, NY, was formerly called Van Epps Swamp.

Van Eps (135) Dutch: variant of VAN EPPS.

Van Ert (162) Dutch: of uncertain origin; possibly a habitational name from *Aard*, name of several places in Gelderland, Drenthe, and North Brabant.

Vanes (87) English: variant of FAYNE.

Van Es (77) Dutch: variant spelling of VAN ESS.
GIVEN NAMES Dutch 8%. *Pieter* (2), *Cornelis, Frans, Piet, Willem.*

Van Ess (436) Dutch: topographic name for someone who lived by a prominent ash tree, Middle Dutch *ess(che)*, or a habitational name for someone from any of various places named Es or Ten Es(sche), from this word.

Van Essen (214) Dutch: **1.** habitational name for someone from places in Belgium and the Netherlands called Essen or Essene, or from the German city of Essen; possibly also a regional name for someone from the German state of Hesse (German *Hessen*). **2.** variant of VAN ESS.
GIVEN NAMES German 5%; Scandinavian 4%. *Hans* (2), *Ingeborg* (2), *Erwin, Otto; Lasse.*

Van Etten (952) Dutch: habitational name for someone from places called Etten in North Brabant and Gelderland.

Van Every (320) Americanized form of Dutch **Van Yvery** or **Van Jeveren**: habitational name for someone from either of two places in Luxembourg called Yvery (Yvery-le-Secq and Yvery-la-Pree), or from Jeveren in Westphalia, Germany.

Van Fleet (974) Americanized spelling of Dutch VAN VLIET.

Van Fossan (145) American variant spelling of Dutch **Van Vossen** (see VAN FOSSEN).

Van Fossen (810) Variant spelling of Dutch **Van Vossen**, a habitational name for someone from Vossem in Brabant, Belgium.

Vang (2845) **1.** Scandinavian (Swedish also **Vång**): habitational or ornamental name from any of numerous farmsteads and other places so named, from Old Norse *vangr* 'field', 'meadow', Swedish *vång*. See also WANG. **2.** Jewish (Ashkenazic): variant of *Wang*. **3.** Laotian: unexplained. **4.** Vietnamese: unexplained.

GIVEN NAMES Southeast Asian 59%; Vietnamese 11%. *Neng* (47), *Pao* (41), *Yer* (37), *Chue* (35), *Chao* (34), *Doua* (29), *Mee* (27), *Kou* (26), *Chou* (23), *Yia* (23), *Chia* (22), *Ying* (22), *Kao* (21), *Seng* (21), *Tong* (21), *Yee* (20); *Chong* (25), *Youa* (23), *Houa* (20), *Thai* (18), *Soua* (16), *Blia* (15), *Toua* (15), *Koua* (14); *Mai* (46), *Bao* (11), *Thao* (11), *Dang* (10), *Long* (10), *Khue* (7), *Mang* (6), *Thong* (6), *Da* (5), *Hue* (5), *Kha* (5), *Khai* (4).

Vangel (144) Shortened form of Greek **Vangelis**, itself from a shortened form of the personal name *Evangelos*, based on New Testament Greek *euangelistēs* 'evangelist' (see EVANGELISTA). It may also be a reduced form of a patronymic derivative of this name, e.g. **Vangelidis**, **Vangelopoulos**, etc.

Van Gelder (547) Dutch and Jewish (from the Netherlands): **1.** habitational name for someone from Gelderland in the east-central Netherlands. **2.** habitational name for someone from Geldern in the Rhineland, Germany.

GIVEN NAMES Dutch 5%. *Annika*, *Dirk*, *Frans*, *Gerben*, *Gerritt*, *Joost*, *Maarten*, *Willem*.

Van Gemert (118) Dutch: habitational name for someone from Gemert in North Brabant.

Vangen (116) **1.** Dutch and Belgian: unexplained; most probably a variant of **Van Geen**, a habitational name fron an unidentified place, possibly Gein in Jutphaas (south of Utrecht), Gene in Vreren (Belgium), or Geem in East Flanders. **2.** Norwegian: habitational name from any of several farmsteads named with the definite singular of *vang*, from Old Norse *vangr* 'field', 'meadow'.

GIVEN NAMES Dutch 4%. *Johan*, *Miek*.

Van Genderen (124) Dutch: habitational name for someone from Genderen in North Brabant.

Van Gerpen (106) Dutch: probably a habitational name for someone from Gorp (Gorep) in North Brabant, near Eindhoven. Compare VAN GORP.

Van Gieson (181) Americanized spelling of Dutch **Van Giesen**, a habitational name for someone from either of two places called Giessen, in North Brabant and South Holland.

Van Gilder (732) Dutch: variant of VAN GELDER.

Van Ginkel (109) Dutch: habitational name for someone from Ginkel in Gelderland.

Van Goethem (109) Dutch and Belgian: habitational name for someone from Gottem in East Flanders, Gotem in Limburg, or Goetem in Sint-Gillis (now a suburb of Brussels).

GIVEN NAMES French 9%; German 4%. *Henri* (2), *Pierre* (2); *Darrold*.

Van Gorden (295) Dutch: habitational name for someone from Garderen in Gelderland, a village near Arnhem.

Van Gorder (594) Dutch: variant of VAN GORDEN.

Van Gordon (132) Dutch: variant of VAN GORDEN.

Van Gorp (304) Dutch and Belgian: habitational name for someone from places called Gorp or Gorep in North Brabant near Eindhoven, and in the Belgian province of Antwerp.

Van Grinsven (136) Dutch (**Van Griensven**): habitational name for someone from Griendtsveen, near Maastricht.

Vangsness (119) Norwegian: variant spelling of WANGSNESS.

GIVEN NAMES Scandinavian 6%. *Ole*, *Uwe*.

Van Guilder (357) Altered form of Dutch VAN GELDER.

Van Gundy (563) Dutch: of uncertain origin; possibly a variant of VAN GENDEREN.

Van Haitsma (118) Dutch: habitational name for someone from Haitsma, a place in Friesland.

Van Hall (124) Dutch: habitational name from any of several places in the Netherlands and Belgium called Hall, Halle, or Ter Halle.

Van Handel (322) Dutch: habitational name for someone from Handel in North Brabant.

GIVEN NAMES Dutch 4%. *Alois*, *Florian*; *Fritz*, *Kurt*.

Van Haren (118) Dutch: habitational name for someone from any of various places called Haren, in Groningen, Friesland, Gelderland, Limburgh, and North Brabant.

Van Hecke (192) Dutch and Belgian: **1.** variant of VAN ECK. **2.** possibly also a habitational name from Hekkum in Groningen or Hekkendorp in South Holland.

GIVEN NAMES French 7%. *Henri*, *Napoleon*, *Raoul*, *Rolande*.

Van Hee (109) Dutch and Belgian: **1.** habitational name for someone from Hee on the island of Terschelling. **2.** from a Flemish dialect pronunciation of Eede in Zeeland. **3.** topographic name for someone living on a heath, from a reduced form of VANDERHEYDEN.

GIVEN NAMES German 4%. *Herta*, *Wolf*.

Van Heel (171) Dutch habitational name for someone from Heel in Limburg (Netherlands) or Hedel in Gelderland.

Van Heest (100) Dutch: habitational name for someone from a place called Heest in Gelderland, near Zutphen.

Van Hemert (144) Dutch: habitational name from any of several places in the Netherlands called Hemert.

GIVEN NAMES Dutch 5%. *Maarten*, *Willem*, *Wim*.

Van Heusen (108) Dutch: variant of VAN HOESEN.

FOREBEARS This name is recorded in Beverwijck in New Netherland (Albany, NY) in the mid 17th century.

Van Hise (178) Americanized spelling of Dutch **Van Huise** (see VAN HOOSE).

Van Hoesen (261) Dutch: habitational name for someone from any of various places named with *hoesen*, variant of Dutch *huisen* 'houses'.

Van Hoff (123) Dutch: habitational name for someone from a place called Hof or Hoff (see HOFF).

Van Hoof (172) Dutch: variant of VAN HOFF.

GIVEN NAME German 5%. *Kurt* (3).

Van Hook (1223) Americanized spelling of Dutch **Van Hoek**, a habitational name for someone from any of various places in the Netherlands and Belgium called Hoek, for example in East and West Flanders, Zeeland, North Brabant, Gelderland, and elsewhere, or from the Hook of Holland (*Hoek van Holland*). Compare VANDENHOEK.

Van Hoose (1122) Americanized spelling of Dutch **Van Huise**, a habitational name for someone from any of the many places in the Netherlands and Belgium named with *huis* 'house'.

Van Hooser (570) Americanized spelling of Dutch **Van Huiser**, variant of **Van Huise** (see VAN HOOSE).

Van Hoosier (105) Americanized spelling of Dutch **Van Huiser**, variant of **Van Huise** (see VAN HOOSE).

Van Hoozer (203) Americanized spelling of Dutch **Van Huiser**, variant of **Van Huise** (see VAN HOOSE).

Van Horn (5339) Dutch: habitational name for someone from any of numerous places in the Netherlands named Hoorn, named with Dutch *hoorn* 'point' or 'nook'.

FOREBEARS Christian Barentsen van Horn emigrated from the Netherlands to New Netherland before 1653.

Van Horne (516) Dutch: variant of VAN HORN.

Van Housen (139) Dutch: variant of VAN HOESEN.

Van Hout (148) Dutch: topographic name for someone living in a forest, Dutch *hout*, or habitational name from a place named with this word.

GIVEN NAMES Dutch 6%. *Thys* (2), *Marinus*, *Maryke*.

Van Houten (1732) Dutch: habitational name for someone from Houten in Utrecht province, named with *hout* 'forest'. Compare VANDENHOUTEN.

Van Hove (237) Dutch: habitational name for someone from any of various places called Hove, named with Middle Dutch *hof* 'farmstead', 'manor farm', 'court'.
GIVEN NAMES French 7%. *Amie, Andre, Desire, Luc, Marcel, Simonne.*

Van Hoven (167) Dutch: variant of VAN HOVE.

Van Hoy (647) Dutch and Belgian: **1.** habitational name for someone from a place called Hoei in the province of Liège, Belgium. **2.** topographic name from Middle Dutch *ooye, oye* 'water meadow', 'pasture'.

Van Huis (102) Dutch and Belgian: habitational name for someone from Huise in East Flanders, Belgium, or from any of numerous other places named with *huis* 'house'. Compare VAN HOOSE.

Van Hulle (126) Dutch: habitational name from any of various places, in particular in Gelderland and Utrecht, called Hulle or Ten Hulle, named with Dutch *hulle* 'hill'.
GIVEN NAMES French 7%. *Henri, Jean-Paul.*

Van Huss (286) Dutch: variant of **Van Huis**.

Van Hyfte (107) Belgian: habitational name from a place called Hijfte in East Flanders.

Van Hyning (138) Dutch: habitational name for someone from either of two places called Heining, in North Holland and North Brabant.

Vanicek (111) Czech (**Vaníček**): from a pet form of the personal name *Vána*, itself a pet form of *Václav* (see VACEK).
GIVEN NAMES Czech and Slovak 5%; German 4%. *Miroslav* (2), *Lubomir*; *Otto.*

Vanier (227) French: variant spelling of VANNIER.
FOREBEARS A Vanier from Picardy, France, is recorded in Quebec City in 1669. Another, from Normandy, France, is documented in Quebec City in 1672 with the secondary surname LAFONTAINE.
GIVEN NAMES French 13%. *Fernand* (2), *Marcel* (2), *Adrien, Andre, Armand, Aurel, Gilles, Jacques, Pierrette, Serge.*

Van Kampen (337) Dutch: habitational name for someone from the port of Kampen in Overijssel, or from any of various other places named with *kamp* 'field', for example in Zeeland, North Brabant, and North Holland.
GIVEN NAMES Dutch 5%. *Gerrit* (3), *Adrianus* (2), *Aad, Gerritt, Pieter.*

Van Kempen (115) Dutch: habitational name from any of several places in the Netherlands and Belgium called Kempen.
GIVEN NAMES German 10%; Dutch 5%. *Ewald* (2), *Karl Heinz, Kurt*; *Cornelis, Gert.*

Van Keulen (102) Dutch: habitational name from *Keulen*, Dutch name of Cologne (*Köln*), Germany.

Van Keuren (448) Dutch: variant of VAN KEULEN.

Van Kirk (1128) Altered form of Dutch **Van (den) Kerck**, a topographic name for someone who lived by a church, Middle Dutch *kerke*, or a habitational name for someone from a place named with this word.

Van Kleeck (243) Dutch: of uncertain origin; possibly a topographic name from a term meaning 'cleft' or 'crevice' (compare Middle High German *klac* 'crevice').

Van Kley (124) Dutch: habitational name for someone from Klei, a place in South Holland.
GIVEN NAMES Dutch 4%. *Gerrit* (2), *Cornie.*

Van Koevering (111) Dutch: habitational name for someone from Koevering(e), a place in North Brabant near Breda.

Van Kooten (136) Dutch: habitational name from any of several places called Koten or Kooten, in particular east of Doordrecht and south of Gorinchem.

Van Kuiken (115) Dutch: **1.** perhaps a habitational name for someone from Cuijk on the Maas, south of Nijmegen. **2.** according to Debrabandere, it may be an occupational name for a cook, literally 'from the kitchen', from Dutch *keuken* 'kitchen'.

Van Kuren (170) Dutch: variant of VAN KEUREN.

Van Laanen (130) Dutch and Belgian: variant of VAN LANEN.

Van Landingham (1234) Belgian: Americanized spelling of **Van Landeg(h)em**, a habitational name for someone from Landegem, near Ghent, in Flanders.

Van Lanen (236) Dutch and Belgian: habitational name for someone from a place called Lanen, in particular a village southeast of Brussels.

Van Langen (103) Dutch: habitational name for someone from Lange, near Zutphen in Gelderland.

Van Laningham (241) Belgian: see VAN LANDINGHAM.

Van Lare (114) Dutch and Belgian: variant of VAN LEER.

Van Lear (138) Dutch and Belgian: variant of VAN LEER.

Van Leer (311) Dutch and Belgian: variant of **Van Laar**, a habitational name for someone from any of numerous places in Belgium and the Netherlands named Laar, from Middle Dutch *lare* 'woodland clearing'.

Van Leeuwen (571) Dutch and Belgian: habitational name for someone from Leeuwen in Limburg, Netherlands, or from any of various places in Belgium and the Netherlands named with Leeuw, denoting a (burial) mound.
GIVEN NAMES Dutch 8%; German 4%. *Gerrit* (6), *Pieter* (3), *Dirk* (2), *Cor, Egbert,*

Frans, Gerritt, Kees, Siebe, Wim; *Harro, Johannes, Rudi.*

Van Lenten (136) Dutch: probably a habitational name from Lent, name of places in Groningen, Gelderland, and North Brabant. The placename is probably a derivative of *linde* 'lime tree'.

Van Lerberghe (104) Belgian: habitational name from Laarberg, near Kortrijk in West Flanders.

Van Leuven (410) Belgian: habitational name for someone from the city of Leuven in Brabant, Belgium.

Van Liere (176) Belgian: habitational name for someone from a place called Lier, in Antwerp province.
GIVEN NAMES Dutch 7%. *Jaap* (3), *Frans, Marinus.*

Van Lieshout (109) Dutch: habitational name from a place called Lieshout in North Brabant.

Van Lieu (119) Belgian: variant of VAN LIEW.

Van Liew (300) Belgian: habitational name for someone from either of two places in Belgium called Lieu, in Nord and Lamain (Hainault), or similarly named places elsewhere.

Van Lith (158) Dutch: habitational name for someone from a place called Lith in North Brabant.

Van Loan (233) Variant of Dutch VAN LOON.

Van Loo (319) Belgian (**Van Loo**): habitational name for someone from Lo in West Flanders, or any of several places named with *lo(o)* 'woodland clearing', such as Korbeek-Lo and Kessel-Lo in Brabant. See also VANDELOO.

Van Loon (451) Dutch (**Van Loon**): habitational name for someone from any of various places called Loon, for example in North Brabant and Drenthe.
GIVEN NAMES Dutch 4%. *Cornelis* (2), *Dirk, Gerritt, Hendrik, Kryn.*

Van Lue (183) Dutch and Belgian: variant spelling of VAN LIEW, VAN LEEUWEN, or VAN LOO.

Van Luven (150) Belgian: variant of VAN LEUVEN.

Van Maanen (212) Dutch: habitational name from a place called Manen in Gelderland, near Arnhem.
GIVEN NAMES Dutch 5%. *Gerrit* (4), *Adriaan.*

Van Marter (147) Dutch: origin uncertain; possibly a habitational name from Martena in Friesland.

Van Matre (528) Dutch and Belgian: variant of VAN METER.

Van Meeteren (122) Dutch: habitational name for someone from Meteren in Gelderland.

Van Meter (3064) Dutch and Belgian: habitational name for someone from Meteren in Gelderland, Netherlands, or from Méteren in Nord, France.

Van Metre (259) Dutch: variant of Van Meter.

Van Middlesworth (115) Probably an Americanized form of Dutch **Van Middelburg**, a habitational name for someone from any of various places called Middelburg in the Netherlands.

Vann (4679) English: topographic name for someone who lived by a fen or marsh (see Fenn).

Van Name (153) Dutch and Belgian: habitational name from Namen in Zeeland or Namen (French name: *Namur*) in southern Belgium.

Vannatta (869) Variant of Dutch Van Natter.

Van Natter (367) Dutch: of uncertain origin; probably a variant of **Van Etter**, a habitational name for someone from Etten in North Brabant (see Van Etten).

Vannelli (137) Italian: patronymic from a pet form of the personal name Vanni.
Given names Italian 5%. *Matteo, Stefano.*

Vanneman (104) Dutch: of uncertain origin; possibly a variant of **Van Emeren**, habitational name from Emeren in Gelderland near Zutphen.

Van Ness (1641) Altered spelling of Dutch **Van Nes** or **Van Nesse**, a habitational name from any of various places in Friesland called Nes, or other places named with this word, denoting a spit of land.
FOREBEARS This name is recorded in Beverwijck in New Netherland (Albany, NY) in the mid 17th century.

Van Nest (467) Dutch: habitational name from a place called Nest in North Brabant.

Van Neste (112) Dutch: variant of Van Nest.
Given names French 7%. *Alphonse, Remi.*

Vannett (106) Scottish: unexplained.

Vanni (275) Italian: from a short form of the personal name *Giovanni*, Italian equivalent of John.
Given names Italian 13%. *Angelo* (3), *Edo* (2), *Renzo* (2), *Bartolomeo, Egidio, Giulio, Luciano, Pasquale, Romolo, Vincenzo.*

Van Nice (254) Americanized form of Dutch Van Ness.

Vannier (130) French: occupational name for a winnower, or more often, since this was a highly seasonal activity, for a maker and seller of winnowing fans, from an agent derivative of Old French *vanne* 'winnowing fan'. Compare English Fonner.
Given name French 6%. *Raoul* (2).

Van Noord (129) Dutch: topographic name for someone 'from the north' (Dutch *noord*) or habitational name from any of the places named with this word, in North Holland, Zeeland, and North Brabant.
Given names Dutch 5%; German 4%. *Hessel; Hans, Kurt.*

Van Norden (121) Dutch: habitational name from Noorden in South Holland, near Leiden.

Van Norman (636) Dutch: of uncertain origin; **1.** possibly an altered form of **de Norman**, an ethnic name for a Norseman. **2.** alternatively, perhaps a habitational name from Normanskerk in Zeeland.

Van Nort (110) Dutch: variant of Van Noord.

Van Nortwick (221) Americanized spelling of Dutch **Van Noortwijk**, a habitational name for someone from any of various places in the Netherlands called Noordwijk, or from Noorderwijk in Antwerp, Belgium.

Van Nostrand (610) Dutch: reduced form of **Van Noordstrand**, a topographic name denoting someone from the 'north shore'.
FOREBEARS Jacob Jansen van Nostrand (alias van Noorstrand) came from the Netherlands to Long Island in 1638.

Van Note (393) Americanized spelling of Dutch **Van (der) Not**, a habitational name for someone from a place called Ter Noot, for example one in French Flanders.

Vannoy (1543) Americanized spelling of Dutch **Van Noye**, a habitational name for someone from a place named with Middle Dutch *ooye, oye* '(water) meadow', as for example Hoye, near Ghent, Belgium. It may also be a Dutch form of French **De la Noye** (see Delano).

Vannucci (228) Italian: patronymic from a pet form of Vanni.
Given names Italian 10%. *Giorgio* (2), *Pasquale* (2), *Amelio, Attilio, Giovanni, Leno, Marco.*

Vano (152) Southern Italian: **1.** habitational name from Vano, a district of Arpino in Frosinone province. **2.** from a short form of a personal name with this ending, for example *Silvano*.
Given names Italian 26%. *Carmine* (2), *Mario* (2), *Silvestro* (2), *Amato, Emilio, Francesco, Gerardo, Santo, Wilfredo.*

Van Oort (129) Dutch: **1.** habitational name from any of various minor places named with Middle Dutch *ort* 'outermost point'. **2.** Alternatively, it may be from a misdivision of **Van Noort**, variant of Van Noord.

Van Orden (766) Dutch: **1.** variant of **Van Oorden**, a variant of Van Oort. **2.** variant of Dutch Van Noorden.

Van Order (289) Variant of Dutch **Van Orderen**, a habitational name for someone from a place named Orderen, near Antwerp, Belgium.

Vanore (117) Italian: unexplained.
Given names Italian 15%. *Amerigo, Lorenzo, Pasquale, Salvatore.*

Van Orman (365) Dutch: variant of Van Norman.

Van Ormer (108) Dutch: of uncertain origin; possibly a habitational name from Orm in Limburg.

Van Ornum (154) Dutch: probably a variant of Van Arna.

Van Os (133) Dutch: variant of Van Oss.

Van Osdol (270) Altered form of Dutch **Van Oostdal**, a topographic name for someone from somewhere known as the 'east valley'.

Van Oss (212) Dutch: habitational name for someone from a place called Oss, in North Brabant.

Van Osten (103) Dutch: topographic name for someone 'from the east'.

Van Ostrand (176) Dutch: reduced form of **Van Oststrand**, a topographic name denoting someone 'from the eastern shore'.

Van Otterloo (119) Dutch: habitational name for someone from a place called Otterloo, in Gelderland near Arnhem.

Van Over (1926) Americanized spelling of Dutch **Van Oever**, a topographic name from Middle Dutch *oever* 'shore', 'river bank', or a habitational name from a place named with this word.

Van Overbeke (175) Belgian: habitational name for someone from any of various minor places in Belgium called Overbeke(n), Overbeek, or Over de Beek, all meaning 'over (the) creek'.
Given names French 5%. *Marcel, Philippe.*

Vanoy (110) Dutch: variant of Vannoy.
Given names French 4%. *Ancil, Cecile.*

Van Parys (124) Dutch and Belgian: habitational name for someone from the city of Paris, France (Dutch name *Parijs*).
Given names French 9%. *Henri, Thierry.*

Van Patten (773) Dutch: variant of Van Putten.

Van Pelt (2563) Belgian and Dutch: habitational name from either of two places in Brabant called Pedele (later Peelt, Pelt), or from Overpelt or Neerpelt in Limburg, Belgium, or possibly from places in the Netherlands called De Bilt, east of Utrecht and in Overijssel.

Van Petten (105) Dutch: variant of Van Putten.

Van Peursem (105) Dutch: habitational name for someone from Peurssum in South Holland.

Van Putten (235) Dutch: habitational name for someone from either of two places called Putten, in Gelderland and North Brabant. The former was the home of Kiliaen van Rensselaer, founder and patron of Rensselaerswijck on the upper Hudson.
Given names Dutch 8%. *Marinus* (3), *Cornelis, Dirk, Gerben.*

Van Riper (774) Dutch: altered form of **Van Rijper**, a habitational name for someone from any of the places in North Holland called Rijp or De Rijp.

Van Roekel (403) Dutch: habitational name for someone from La Rochelle, the Huguenot stronghold in France in the 17th century, which was vigorously supported by the Dutch and had numerous Dutch connections.

Van Rooy (151) Dutch: habitational name from any of several places named with

Middle Dutch *rooi*, *rode* 'clearing in a wood'.

Van Rossum (219) Belgian and Dutch: habitational name for someone from any of the places called Rossem (Brabant, Antwerp) or Rossum (Gelderland, Overijssel).

Van Roy (133) Dutch: variant of VAN ROOY.

Van Ry (116) Dutch: probably a variant of VAN ROOY.

Van Ryn (189) **1.** Dutch: topographic name for someone who lived on the banks of the Rhine, Dutch *Rijn*. **2.** Belgian: habitational name for someone from a minor place in West Flanders called Ten Ryne.
GIVEN NAMES French 8%. *Jacques* (4), *Henri* (2).

Van Ryzin (119) Dutch: topographic name for someone from any of various places named with *rijsen* 'osiers', or habitational name from Rijssen in Overijssel near Deventer, named with this word.

Van Sandt (182) Dutch: variant of VAN ZANDT.

Van Sant (1027) Dutch: variant of VAN ZANDT.

Van Santen (105) Dutch: variant of VAN ZANDT.
GIVEN NAMES Dutch 7%. *Adrianus*, *Gert*, *Willem*.

Van Schaick (208) Dutch: habitational name for someone from Schaijk in North Brabant, the name of which is a reduction of Schadewijck, an area south of Utrecht named after Willem Schade, an official of the Bishop of Utrecht in the Middle Ages.
FOREBEARS Goosen Gerritsen van Schaick was a brewer in Fort Orange (Albany, NY) in the mid 17th century.

Van Schaik (129) Dutch: variant of VAN SCHAICK.
GIVEN NAMES Dutch 7%. *Dirk*, *Gerrit*, *Pieter*.

Van Schoick (129) Dutch: variant of VAN SCHAICK.

Van Schoyck (118) Dutch: variant of VAN SCHAICK.

Van Sciver (221) Dutch: variant of **Van Schieven**, habitational name for someone from Schieven in Gelderland.

Van Scoy (574) American variant of Dutch VAN SCHAICK.

Van Scoyk (117) Dutch: variant of VAN SCHAICK.

Van Scoyoc (158) American variant of Dutch VAN SCHAICK.

Van Scyoc (310) American variant of Dutch VAN SCHAICK.

Van Selow (170) Dutch: habitational name for someone from Selow in Mecklenburg-Schwerin, Germany.

Van Sickel (168) Dutch and Belgian: **1.** habitational name for someone from a place named Sikkel, for example in Asse, Brabant, Belgium, or from a similarly named place in Germany. **2.** Reduced form of **van der Sickel**, a habitational name for

someone who lived at a house distinguished by the sign of a sickle.

Van Sickle (2270) Americanized spelling of Dutch VAN SICKEL.

Van Skike (154) Americanized spelling of Dutch VAN SCHAICK.

Van Skiver (190) Dutch: variant of VAN SCIVER.

Van Slooten (151) Dutch and Belgian: habitational name from a place named with *sloot* 'ditch', 'channel', for example in Friesland near Sneek, Sloten in North Holland, Slote or Sloten in East Flanders.

Van Slyke (996) Dutch: **1.** topographic name from Middle Dutch *slijcke* 'mire', 'marshy place', or a habitational name for someone from a place named with this word, for example Slijkenburg near Berg op Zoom in Brabant or Slijkewijck in Gelderland. **2.** It could also be a diphthongized variant of Slik in North Holland.

Van Soest (135) Dutch: habitational name for someone from either of two places called Soest, in North-Rhine Westphalia and in Utrecht.

Van Someren (102) Dutch: habitational name for someone from Someren in North Brabant.

Vanstone (252) English: habitational name, which Reaney says in from Faunstone in Shaugh, Devon, named as 'farm (Middle English *toun*) of a family called **Faunt**' (from French **le Enfaunt** 'the child').

Van Story (144) Probably of Dutch origin: unexplained.

Van Straten (205) Dutch and Jewish (from the Netherlands): habitational name for someone from any of various minor places called Straten, from *straat* 'road', in particular a place in Limburg.
GIVEN NAMES Dutch 5%. *Dirk*, *Gerrit*, *Joop*, *Willem*.

Van Syckle (165) Americanized spelling of Dutch VAN SICKEL.

Vant (207) English: variant of FANT.

Van Tassel (954) Dutch: habitational name for someone from Texel, the largest of the islands that form a line stretching from North Holland to East Friesland. This was the assembly area for ships of the Dutch West India Company leaving for the New World.

Van Tassell (392) Dutch: variant of VAN TASSEL.

Vanterpool (112) Dutch: variant of VANDERPOL.

Van't Hof (147) Dutch: occupational name for someone who worked 'at the manor farm' (see HOFF).

Van Tiem (104) Dutch: probably a habitational name from either of two places called Diem, in North Holland and Gelderland.

Van Til (183) Dutch: **1.** habitational name for someone from Thys (earlier *Til*) in Liège province, Belgium. **2.** variant of **van**

Tiel, a habitational name for someone from any of several places in Gelderland called Tiel.

Van Tilburg (187) Dutch: habitational name for someone from Tilburg in North Brabant.

Van Tine (437) Probably an altered form of Dutch **Van Tuyn**, a topographic name for someone who lived by an enclosed or fenced-off property, Middle Dutch *tuna*, or a habitational name from a place named with this word. The change in form reflects the characteristic shift of the diphthong from high front to low front (as in the pronunciation of Stuyvesant).

Van Tol (226) Dutch and Belgian: habitational name for someone from a place called Thull in Dutch Limburg or possibly from a place called Thol in French Flanders.
GIVEN NAMES Dutch 7%. *Willem* (2), *Antoon*, *Dirk*, *Gerrit*, *Pieter*.

Van Trease (333) Dutch: probably an altered form of a habitational name for someone from Driesum in Friesland.

Van Treese (148) Dutch: variant of VAN TREASE.

Van Tuyl (322) Dutch: habitational name for someone from either of two places called Tuil, in the provinces of Gelderland and Utrecht.

Van Vactor (156) Dutch: of uncertain origin; possibly a variant of **Van Vechten**, which is probably a topographic name from the Vecht River, which flows through Amsterdam.

Van Valkenburg (874) Dutch: habitational name for someone from either of two places in the Netherlands called Valkenburg, in Limburg and South Holland.

Van Valkenburgh (398) Dutch: variant spelling of VAN VALKENBURG.

Van Veen (233) Dutch: habitational name for someone from any of various place called (het) Veen, for example in North Brabant, or a topographic name for someone who lived by a moor or fen, Middle Dutch *veen*.
GIVEN NAMES Dutch 5%; French 4%. *Dirk*, *Huibert*, *Nicolaas*; *Andre*, *Henri*, *Jacques*.

Van Veldhuizen (138) Dutch: habitational name for someone from any of various places called Veldhuizen, in Drente, Gelderland, and Utrecht.

Van Vickle (127) Dutch: habitational name from Wijckel in Friesland.

Van Vlack (169) Dutch: variant of VAN VLECK.

Van Vleck (351) Dutch: habitational name for someone from Vleek or Vlieck in Limburg.

Van Vleet (697) Variant of Dutch VAN VLIET.

Van Vliet (681) Dutch: habitational name for someone from any of the many places named with *vliet* 'brook', 'stream'.

GIVEN NAMES Dutch 7%. *Frans* (2), *Gerrit* (2), *Klaas* (2), *Leendert* (2), *Pieter* (2), *Willem* (2), *Henk*, *Marinus*, *Mieke*, *Nicolaas*, *Piet*.

Van Volkenburg (122) Dutch: variant of VAN VALKENBURG.

Van Vooren (201) Dutch and Belgian: habitational name for someone from a place called Voorne in South Holland or from any of various places in Belgium called (Ter) Voorde.

GIVEN NAMES French 4%. *Andre*, *Marcelle*.

Van Voorhees (128) Dutch: habitational name for someone from Voorhees in Drenthe (see VOORHEES).

Van Voorhis (641) Dutch: variant of VAN VOORHEES.

Van Voorst (220) Dutch and Belgian: **1.** habitational name for someone from either of two places in Gelderland called Voorst. **2.** habitational name from any of several places named Vorst or Vurste, or a topographic name for someone who lived in a forest, from Middle Dutch *vorst* (from Latin *forestum*).

Van Vorst (197) Dutch and Belgian: variant of VAN VOORST.

Van Vranken (229) Belgian and Dutch: habitational name for someone from a place called Franck in Liège province, Belgium, or from the region of Germany called Franken (Franconia).

FOREBEARS This name is recorded in Beverwijck in New Netherland (Albany, NY) in the mid 17th century.

Van Vuren (119) Dutch: variant of VAN VOOREN.

GIVEN NAME Dutch 8%. *Dirk* (4).

Van Wagenen (311) Altered spelling of Dutch **Van Wageningen**, a habitational name from a place in Gelderland called Wageningen.

Van Wagner (713) Most probably a variant of Dutch **Van Wageningen** (see VAN WAGENEN).

Van Wagoner (394) Most probably a variant of Dutch **Van Wageningen** (see VAN WAGENEN).

Van Wart (221) Dutch: variant of VAN WERT.

Van Weelden (145) Belgian: habitational name for someone from Weelde near Antwerp, Belgium.

Van Wert (314) Dutch and Belgian: habitational name for someone from any of various places in Belgium and the Netherlands called Weert, (De) Weerd, Weerde, or Waarde.

Van Wey (320) Dutch: habitational name for someone from Wijhe in Overijssel, between Zwolle and Deventer.

Van Why (178) Variant of Dutch VAN WEY.

Van Wie (433) Dutch: variant of VAN WEY.

Van Wieren (166) Dutch: habitational name from places called Wieren in Friesland and Groningen.

Van Wingerden (134) Dutch: topographic name for someone living by a vineyard, Dutch *wijngaard*, or habitational name from places called Wijngaard(en), for example in Friesland and South Holland.

GIVEN NAMES Dutch 14%. *Pieter* (3), *Aart* (2), *Gerrit*.

Van Winkle (2781) Dutch (also **Van Winckle**, **Van Winkel**): topographic name for someone who lived on a corner (either a street corner or a corner of land), from Dutch *winkel* 'corner', 'nook', or a habitational name from a place named with this word, for example in North Holland.

FOREBEARS Jacob van Winkle settled in New Netherland in 1634.

Van Woert (115) Dutch: habitational name for someone from Woert in South Holland.

FOREBEARS This name is recorded in Beverwijck in New Netherland (Albany, NY) in the mid 17th century.

Van Wormer (733) Dutch: habitational name for someone from Wormer in North Holland.

Van Wyck (230) Dutch: variant of VAN WYK.

Van Wye (124) Variant of Dutch VAN WEY.

Van Wyhe (190) Dutch: variant of VAN WEY.

Van Wyk (718) Dutch (also **Van Wyck**) and Jewish (from the Netherlands): habitational name for someone from any of the many places in the Netherlands named Wijk, from the Dutch word *wijk* 'district', 'settlement'.

FOREBEARS Cornelius Barendtsen van Wyck came from the Netherlands to Long Island in 1660. His descendant Charles Henry van Wyck (1824–95) was a prominent New York politician.

Vanyo (209) Hungarian (**Vanyó**): from a pet form of the personal name *Iván*, a Slavic form of JOHN.

Van Zandt (1345) Dutch and Belgian: habitational name for someone from any of the places called Zandt, in Gelderland, Friesland, South Holland, and Zeeland; or Zande in Belgium. See also VANDERZANDEN.

Van Zant (1048) Dutch: variant of VAN ZANDT.

Van Zante (146) Dutch: variant of VAN ZANTEN.

GIVEN NAMES Dutch 7%. *Dirk* (3), *Hessel*.

Van Zanten (235) Dutch and Belgian: habitational name for someone from the German city of Xanten in North Rhine-Westphalia, or from Zanten (French *Saintes*), in Belgium.

GIVEN NAMES Dutch 8%; German 4%. *Dirk* (2), *Klaas* (2), *Cornie*, *Gerrit*, *Rutger*; *Erwin*.

Van Zee (561) Dutch: topographic name for someone who lived by the sea, Middle Dutch *zee*.

Van Zeeland (116) Dutch: habitational name for someone from the province of Zeeland in the southwest Netherlands.

GIVEN NAMES French 4%; German 4%. *Alain*, *Michel*; *Alois*, *Kurt*.

Van Zile (361) Dutch: variant of VAN ZYL.

Van Zyl (108) Dutch: topographic name for someone who lived by a sluice or water management system in low-lying land, from *zijl* 'sluice', 'pump', or a habitational name from places in the provinces of South Holland and Utrecht named with this word.

GIVEN NAMES Dutch 8%; French 6%; German 6%. *Johan* (2), *Dirk*, *Frans*, *Roelof*; *Andre*, *Francois*; *Kurt*.

Vap (100) Origin unidentified.

Vaquera (169) Spanish: habitational name from a place called Vaquera, in Andalucia, southern Spain, from a feminine form of the adjective *vaquero* 'of or relating to a cowherd'.

GIVEN NAMES Spanish 54%. *Jose* (8), *Manuel* (5), *Juan* (4), *Jesus* (3), *Efrain* (2), *Gilberto* (2), *Isidoro* (2), *Mario* (2), *Roberto* (2), *Adriana*, *Alberto*, *Alfonso*.

Vara (502) **1.** Galician, Asturian-Leonese and Spanish: habitational name from Vara (Galicia), Vara del Rey (Cuenca), or La Vara (Asturies). **2.** Portuguese and Spanish: from *vara* 'rod', 'stick', 'yard-stick' (Late Latin *vara* 'forked stick'), applied as a nickname or metonymic occupational name in any of various possible senses; it may have been given to a keeper of animals, who used a stick to urge his charges on, or to an official who was responsible for checking weights and measures or who carried a rod as a symbol of his office.

GIVEN NAMES Spanish 28%. *Jose* (7), *Manuel* (7), *Miguel* (5), *Mario* (4), *Alfonso* (3), *Carlos* (3), *Ramiro* (3), *Raul* (3), *Adalberto* (2), *Fernando* (2), *Gerardo* (2), *Jesus* (2); *Carmine* (5), *Fulvio* (2), *Antonio*, *Carmela*, *Cecilio*, *Federico*.

Varady (300) Hungarian (**Várady**): habitational name for someone from one of the various places called Várad (from *vár* 'castle') in Arad, Bars, Bihar, Marosszék, Nyitra, and Somogy counties.

GIVEN NAMES Hungarian 4%. *Attila* (2), *Denes*, *Janos*, *Laszlo*.

Varallo (137) Italian: probably a habitational name from a place in Piedmont named with Varallo, as for example Varallo in Vercelli province and Varallo Pombia in Novara.

GIVEN NAMES Italian 17%. *Carmine*, *Liberato*, *Pasquale*, *Rocco*, *Salvatore*.

Varano (355) Italian: habitational name from any of various places throughout Italy called Varano; the district so named in Castellammare di Stabia (Naples province) and the one in Teramo have probably contributed the most to the American surname.

GIVEN NAMES Italian 19%. *Carmine* (2), *Sal* (2), *Angelo*, *Antonio*, *Concetta*, *Dante*,

Graziella, Nicola, Oreste, Pasquale, Raffaele, Rocco.

Varas (128) Spanish: from the plural of *vara* 'rod', 'stick' (see VARAS), of uncertain application, possibly topographic.
GIVEN NAMES Spanish 37%. *Alberto* (4), *Ernesto* (3), *Raul* (3), *Enrique* (2), *Manuel* (2), *Silvia* (2), *Augusto, Carlos, Cristobal, Fernando, Hernan, Jaime*; *Paolo*.

Varble (281) Origin unidentified. Perhaps an Americanized spelling of Hungarian *Várbeli*, an occupational or status name for a soldier or a servant who lived in a castle (see VARI).

Varco (104) **1.** English (Cornwall): variant spelling of VARCOE. **2.** Possibly an altered form of Portuguese **Vargo**, a habitational name probably related to VARGAS.

Varcoe (127) English (Cornwall): unexplained. Compare VERCOE.

Varda (131) **1.** Italian (Turin): unexplained. **2.** Probably an altered spelling of Hungarian **Várdai**, habitational name for someone from any of several places called Várda in Hungary.
GIVEN NAMES Italian 4%. *Domenic, Gildo.*

Vardaman (249) Origin unidentified.

Vardaro (100) Southern Italian: metonymic occupational name for someone who made or repaired saddles, from a variant of *bardaro*, from Sicilian *bardaru* 'pack saddle'.
GIVEN NAMES Italian 13%; Spanish 10%. *Antonio* (2), *Gaetano, Nunzie, Pellegrino*; *Armando* (2), *Carmella* (2), *Mario* (2), *Adolpho, Alfonso, Angelina.*

Vardell (113) English: unexplained.

Vardeman (222) Swedish: ornamental name, probably from *vard-* 'beacon' (a common place-name element) + *man* 'man'.

Varden (172) English: variant of VERDUN.

Vardy (112) **1.** English: unexplained. Possibly a variant of VERITY. Compare VARTY. **2.** Jewish (Israeli): from Hebrew *vardi* 'of rose', translating any of the many Ashkenazic surnames starting with *Rosen-*.
GIVEN NAMES Jewish 13%. *Nir* (2), *Hagit, Itzik, Moshe, Yehoshua.*

Varela (2544) **1.** Galician: habitational name from any of the places in Galicia named Varela, from a diminutive of *vara* 'rod', 'stick'. **2.** Greek (**Varelas**): from Greek *varela* 'barrel', from Italian *barella* 'barrel'. Accented on the final syllable, *varelás* is a metonymic occupational name for a cooper; with the accent on the middle syllable, *varélas* is a nickname for a large fat man.
GIVEN NAMES Spanish 45%. *Jose* (61), *Manuel* (42), *Juan* (33), *Jesus* (26), *Luis* (25), *Carlos* (18), *Jorge* (17), *Antonio* (16), *Julio* (14), *Mario* (14), *Roberto* (14), *Fernando* (12), *Raul* (11).

Varga (2123) **1.** Hungarian: occupational name from Hungarian *varga* 'cobbler', 'shoemaker'. It is also found as a Slovenian surname in easternmost Slovenia. **2.** Czech and Slovak: nickname for a miserable or

complaining person, from *vargat* 'lament', 'moan', 'complain'. **3.** Slovak and Ukrainian: descriptive nickname from *varga* 'lip'. Compare Polish WARGA.
GIVEN NAMES Hungarian 11%. *Zoltan* (13), *Gyula* (10), *Laszlo* (10), *Tibor* (7), *Imre* (5), *Jozsef* (5), *Endre* (4), *Istvan* (4), *Karoly* (4), *Sandor* (4), *Csaba* (3), *Janos* (3).

Vargas (13723) Spanish and Portuguese: habitational name from Vargas in Santander province, or a topographic name from *vargas*, plural of *varga*, a dialect term used in various senses: '(thatched) hut', 'steep slope', or 'fenced pastureland which becomes waterlogged in winter'.
GIVEN NAMES Spanish 50%; Portuguese 10%. *Jose* (384), *Juan* (191), *Luis* (176), *Carlos* (149), *Manuel* (117), *Pedro* (94), *Francisco* (89), *Jorge* (86), *Jesus* (83), *Rafael* (82), *Miguel* (78), *Roberto* (77); *Paulo* (3), *Ligia* (2), *Vasco* (2), *Catarina, Conceicao, Joao, Omero, Serafim, Wenceslao.*

Vargason (206) Origin unidentified.

Varghese (858) Indian (Kerala): derivative of the Greek personal name *Geōrgios* (see GEORGE), found as a personal name among Christians in Kerala (southern India) and in the U.S. used as a last name among families from Kerala.
GIVEN NAMES Indian 36%. *Babu* (7), *Mathai* (6), *Oommen* (5), *Raju* (4), *Cheriyan* (3), *Eapen* (3), *Shaji* (3), *Annu* (2), *Jayan* (2), *Manoj* (2), *Marykutty* (2), *Reji* (2).

Vargo (2931) Hungarian: variant of VARGA.

Vargus (107) Origin unidentified. **1.** Apparently a respelling of Spanish VARGAS. **2.** Irish: variant of FERGUS.
GIVEN NAMES Spanish 9%. *Angel, Arturo, Carlos, Rafael, Rodolfo, Ruben.*

Vari (158) Hungarian (**Vári**): **1.** habitational name for someone from a place called Vári in Békés or Bereg county. **2.** from *vár* 'castle', hence a topographic name for someone who lived by or within a castle or an occupational name for someone who worked in one.
GIVEN NAMES Italian 9%; Hungarian 4%; Spanish 4%. *Aldo* (2); *Andras, Sandor, Tibor*; *Mario, Pasquale.*

Varian (286) Irish: of uncertain origin. This is a surname associated with county Cork since the mid 17th century; a poet of this name used the Gaelic form **Ó Bhiorráin**.

Varin (227) French: regional variant of GARIN.
GIVEN NAMES French 10%. *Andre, Jacques, Normand, Onezime, Ovide, Pierre.*

Vario (105) Italian: nickname from *vario* 'flecked', 'speckled' (Latin *varius*), perhaps with reference to the eyes, hair, or clothing.
GIVEN NAMES Italian 13%. *Antonino* (2), *Antonio, Sabato, Silvio.*

Varisco (194) Italian: variant of GUARISCO.
GIVEN NAMES Italian 13%; Spanish 6%. *Sal* (2), *Alessandra, Angelo, Biagio, Enrico,*

Salvatore, Vito; *Jaime, Javier, Luis, Rodolfo.*

Varkey (118) Indian (Kerala): pet form of VARGHESE.
GIVEN NAMES Indian 31%. *Mathai* (4), *Babu, Shaila.*

Varland (141) Norwegian: habitational name from either of two farmsteads in Rogaland, named in Old Norse as *Vǫrðuland*, a compound of *varða* 'beacon', 'cairn' + *land* 'land', 'farmstead'.

Varley (934) English: **1.** habitational name from Varley or Varleys in Devon, or any of the other places in southwestern England named in Old English as 'fern clearing' (see FARLEY), the change from *f* to *v* arising from voicing of *f* which is characteristic of that area. **2.** (of Norman origin) habitational name from Verly in Aisne, Picardy, France, so named from the Gallo-Roman personal name *Virilius* + the locative suffix *-acum*, or from Vesly (La Manche); surnames of this origin are recorded in Suffolk from the 13th century. However, the overwhelming preponderance of the modern surname is in West Yorkshire.

Varma (352) Indian (north-central India): Hindu name, from Sanskrit *varman* 'armor', 'protection'. Although it was once associated exclusively with the Kshatriya class, it has now been adopted by many non-Kshatriya communities.
GIVEN NAMES Indian 87%. *Anil* (8), *Ashok* (8), *Sanjay* (8), *Ajay* (5), *Rajiv* (5), *Ravi* (5), *Usha* (5), *Vijay* (5), *Arvind* (3), *Munish* (3), *Prem* (3), *Rajesh* (3).

Varn (352) Swedish: unexplained.

Varnado (966) Americanized form of French **Vernadeau**, a habitational name from a place named with Old French *vern* 'alder grove' (see VERNE).
GIVEN NAMES French 5%. *Alban, Alphonse, Andre, Celestine, Monique, Patrice.*

Varnadoe (315) Of French origin: variant spelling of VARNADO.

Varnadore (505) Of French origin: variant of VARNADO.

Varnedoe (113) Of French origin: variant spelling of VARNADO.

Varnell (981) English: variant of FARNELL belonging to southwestern England, where the change from *f* to *v* arose from the voicing of *f* that was characteristic of this area in Middle English.

Varner (6201) South German: habitational name for someone from Farn near Oberkirch, or Fahrnau near Schopfheim.

Varnes (416) English: variant of FERN.

Varney (3147) English (of Norman origin): habitational name from Saint-Paul-du-Vernay in Calvados or any of various other places in northern France named with Vernay, from the Gaulish element *vern* 'alder' + the locative suffix *-acum*.

Varni (168) Italian: **1.** possibly a habitational name from places named Varni (in Gorreto, Genoa province) or Varna (in

Bolzano province or Florence). **2.** possibly a variant of **Barni**, derived in part from the personal name (a short form of *Barnabei*; see BARNABY); otherwise a habitational name from Barni in Como province.

Varno (107) Origin unidentified. Possibly a respelling of a French surname such as **Varnoux**, a habitational name from any of the places so named in Ain, Ardèche, and Deux-Sèvres.

Varnon (152) English: variant of VERNON.

Varnum (725) Southwestern English: variant of the habitational name FARNHAM, reflecting the voicing of *f* that was characteristic of southwestern dialects of Middle English.

FOREBEARS George Varnum emigrated in about 1635 from Lilbourne, Northamptonshire, England, to Ipswich, MA. The brothers James Mitchell Varnum (1748–89) and Joseph Bradley Varnum (1750/1–1821), both born in Dracut, MA, were revolutionary war soldiers and congressmen.

Varon (388) **1.** Spanish (**Varón**) and Jewish (Sephardic): nickname from *varón* 'man' (from Latin *varo, varonis*). This is often a Castilianized form of the Catalan equivalent, BARÓ. **2.** Galician (**Varón**) and Jewish (Sephardic): in some cases, possibly a habitational name from any of several places in Ourense province (Galicia) named Varón. **3.** French: from the old German personal name *Waro* (from *wara* 'protection'). **4.** Jewish (eastern Ashkenazic): from the personal name ARON.

GIVEN NAMES Jewish 8%; Spanish 8%. *Arye, Bension, Doron, Eti, Etty, Haya, Hyman, Mier, Miriam, Shabtay, Sol*; *Jose* (3), *Alfonso* (2), *Adolfo, Alberto, Alvaro, Eloy, Emilio, Jacobo, Jaime, Jairo, Javier, Juan*.

Varona (246) Spanish: apparently a nickname from *varona* '(courageous) woman'. Compare VARON.

GIVEN NAMES Spanish 45%; Italian 7%. *Jose* (7), *Carlos* (4), *Pedro* (4), *Enrique* (3), *Eugenio* (3), *Alberto* (2), *Amado* (2), *Ana* (2), *Armando* (2), *Domingo* (2), *Eduardo* (2), *Francisco* (2); *Federico* (2), *Alberico, Antonio, Clemente, Elio*.

Varone (280) Italian: variant of BARONE.

GIVEN NAMES Italian 16%. *Carmine* (2), *Rocco* (2), *Angelo, Carlo, Domenic, Domenico, Ennio, Flavio, Franco, Gennaro, Neri, Romeo*.

Varriale (115) Italian: from Spanish **Barrial**, from *barrial* 'clayey, muddy terrain'.

GIVEN NAMES Italian 20%. *Carlo* (2), *Carmine, Domenico, Giulio, Giuseppe, Rosaria, Tullio, Vincenzo, Vito*.

Varricchio (148) Italian (Campania): unexplained.

GIVEN NAMES Italian 22%. *Angelo* (4), *Enrico* (3), *Carmine, Domenic, Mafalda, Pellegrino*.

Varrone (213) Italian: **1.** variant of BARONE. **2.** possibly from an augmentative of the personal name *Varro*.

GIVEN NAMES Italian 24%. *Mario* (3), *Angelo* (2), *Domenic* (2), *Aurelio, Carmine, Emilio, Fausto, Giuseppe, Nichola, Pasquale, Rocco*.

Vars (138) Italian (Turin): unexplained.

Vartanian (625) Armenian: patronymic from *Vartan*, a personal name from Persian *vardan* 'shield'.

GIVEN NAMES Armenian 34%. *Vartan* (19), *Sarkis* (6), *Armen* (4), *Aram* (3), *Haig* (3), *Haik* (3), *Andranik* (2), *Dickran* (2), *Garabet* (2), *Hagop* (2), *Hampar* (2), *Herand* (2).

Varty (133) **1.** English: variant of VERITY. **2.** Indian (Karnataka): Hindu (Brahman) name of unknown meaning, found among Saraswat Brahmans of Goan origin who have migrated to Karnataka.

GIVEN NAMES Indian 7%. *Nikhil* (2), *Kunal, Sangeeta*.

Varughese (341) Indian: variant of VARGHESE.

GIVEN NAMES Indian 33%. *Varughese* (5), *Babu* (3), *Saji* (3), *Mathai* (2), *Raju* (2), *Shaji* (2), *Sheela* (2), *Biju, Binoy, Binu, Mohan*.

Varvaro (145) Italian (Sicily): variant of BARBARO.

GIVEN NAMES Italian 18%. *Angelo* (2), *Natale* (2), *Antonino, Antonio, Caterina, Damiano, Gasper*.

Varvel (284) English (Norfolk): unexplained. In the U.S. this name is found mainly in the southern States.

Vary (173) **1.** English: from a late form of FARROW; it was first recorded in the 17th century. **2.** Hungarian (**Váry**): variant of **Vári** (see VARI).

Vas (117) **1.** Portuguese: patronymic from VASCO, from the genitive form. This name is also common on the west coast of India, where it was taken by Portuguese colonists. **2.** Hungarian: variant of VASS 5. **3.** Slovenian (eastern Slovenia; **Vaš**): from a reduced and altered form of the personal name *Sebastjan* (see SEBASTIAN). Compare BAS. **4.** Dutch: from a short form of the personal name *Servaas*, from Latin *Servatus*. St. Servaas was a bishop of Maastricht and its patron saint.

GIVEN NAMES Spanish 6%; Italian 4%; Hungarian 4%. *Guillermo, Jose, Mario*; *Tibor* (2), *Arpad*.

Vasa (113) Indian (Gujarat): Hindu (Vania) and Jain name of unknown meaning.

GIVEN NAMES Indian 27%. *Dhirendra, Jiten, Kamlesh, Kiran, Kusum, Mukund, Nimish, Nirmala, Paresh, Purnima, Raj, Shaila*.

Vasallo (112) **1.** Spanish: status name or nickname from *vasallo* 'vassal'. **2.** Old or altered spelling of Italian VASSALLO.

GIVEN NAMES Spanish 53%; Italian 8%. *Diego* (4), *Jose* (4), *Angel* (3), *Francisco* (3), *Miguel* (3), *Ana* (2), *Homero* (2), *Jesus* (2), *Pedro* (2), *Raul* (2), *Rolando* (2), *Alberto*; *Antonio* (2), *Ceasar, Clemente, Leonardo, Salvatore*.

Vasbinder (261) Variant of the German occupational name FASSBENDER 'cooper'.

Vasco (182) **1.** Spanish, Galician, and Italian: ethnic name from *vasco* 'Basque', denoting someone from the Basque region, or from a Spanish byname or Italian personal name of the same derivation. The inhabitants of this region, which extends between southern France and northern Spain, are first recorded in Latin sources as the *Vascones*, a word of unknown origin. See also GASCOIGNE. The Basques' own name for themselves is *Euskaldun*. **2.** Greek: see VASKO.

GIVEN NAMES Spanish 15%; Italian 14%. *Jose* (3), *Fernando* (2), *Angel, Arnando, Arturo, Carlos, Dominga, Enrique, Jairo, Luis, Luz, Sergio*; *Carmine* (2), *Dante, Giro, Giuseppe, Michelangelo, Nunzi*.

Vasconcellos (362) **1.** Spanish: probably a variant of **Basconcillos**, a habitational name from Basconcillos in Burgos province. **2.** Variant of Portuguese VASCONCELOS.

Vasconcelos (166) **1.** Portuguese: habitational name from Vasconcelos, a town in Portugal. **2.** Spanish: variant of VASCONCELLOS.

GIVEN NAMES Spanish 36%; Portuguese 20%. *Jose* (13), *Anastacio* (2), *Faustino* (2), *Francisco* (2), *Jorge* (2), *Jose Manuel* (2), *Luis* (2), *Mario* (2), *Nuno* (2), *Adalberto, Alfredo, Carlos*; *Marcio* (2), *Joao, Joaquim, Manoel, Paulo*; *Antonio* (2), *Silvio* (2), *Angelo, Elio, Enio*.

Vasek (269) Czech (**Vašek**): from a pet form of the personal name *Václav* (see VACEK).

Vasel (120) German: variant of FASEL 1.

Vasey (457) English: variant of VEAZEY.

Vasicek (175) Czech (**Vašíček**): from a pet form of *Váša*, a derivative of the personal name *Václav* (see VACEK).

GIVEN NAME Czech and Slovak 5%. *Rostislav*.

Vasil (357) **1.** Greek: reduced form of VASILAKIS or any of various other patronymic or other derivatives of the personal name *Vasilis* (see BASIL), including **Vasilidis, Vasiloglou, Vasilopoulos**, etc. **2.** American reduced form of Serbian **Vasiljević**, from Greek *Vasilis* (see BASIL).

Vasilakis (111) Greek: patronymic from the personal name *Vasilis* (see BASIL). The *-akis* patronymic is particularly common in Crete, where it was adopted massively in the 19th century.

GIVEN NAMES Greek 16%. *Costas, Demetrios, Konstantinos, Spero, Spyros, Xenophon*.

Vasile (421) **1.** Italian (Sicily): from a Sicilian variant, under Greek influence, of the personal name *Basile* (see BASIL). **2.** Romanian: from the personal name *Vasile*, Romanian form of BASIL.

GIVEN NAMES Italian 17%. *Salvatore* (4), *Carmelo* (2), *Carmine* (2), *Vito* (2), *Angelo*,

Benedetto, Francesca, Francesco, Gennaro, Giuseppe, Graziella, Leonardo.

Vasiliou (114) Greek (Cyprus): patronymic from the personal name *Vasilios*, from classical Greek *basileios* 'royal'. This was borne by several saints and martyrs venerated in the Greek Orthodox Church. Compare BASIL.
GIVEN NAMES Greek 25%. *Andreas* (2), *Anastasios, Costas, Demetrios, Eleftherios, Evangelos, Kimon, Konstantions, Kostas, Panagiota, Vasilios, Vasilis.*

Vaske (277) Czech (**Vaške**): from a pet form of *Váša*, a derivative of the personal name *Václav* (see VACEK).

Vasko (542) **1.** Czech and Slovak (**Vaško**): from a pet form of the personal name *Václav* (see VACEK). **2.** South Slavic: from a pet form of *Váso*, a pet form of the personal name *Vasil*, Slavic form of BASIL. **3.** Ukrainian: from a pet form of *Vasyl*, Ukrainian form of BASIL.

Vasques (258) Spanish and Portuguese: variant of **Vásquez** (see VASQUEZ).

Vasquez (20016) Galician and possibly also Spanish: patronymic from the personal name VASCO, reduced form of Spanish **Velásquez** (see VELASQUEZ).
GIVEN NAMES Spanish 47%. *Jose* (561), *Juan* (294), *Carlos* (172), *Manuel* (170), *Jesus* (146), *Luis* (132), *Francisco* (131), *Miguel* (116), *Mario* (106), *Jorge* (102), *Pedro* (93), *Guadalupe* (92).

Vass (962) **1.** English: status name denoting a serf, Middle English, Old French *vass(e)*, from Late Latin *vassus*, of Celtic origin. Compare Welsh *gwas* 'boy', Gaelic *foss* 'servant'. **2.** English: variant of VAUSE. **3.** Swedish: variant of WASS. **4.** South German: variant of FASS. **5.** Hungarian: from *vas* 'iron', hence a metonymic occupational name for a blacksmith, or a nickname for a resilient, tough man.
GIVEN NAMES Hungarian 6%. *Geza* (3), *Laszlo* (3), *Akos* (2), *Arpad* (2), *Elek* (2), *Aranka, Bela, Emese, Ildiko, Janos, Jeno, Jozsef.*

Vassallo (1102) Italian and Greek (**Vassalos**): from the medieval term *vassallo* 'vassal', hence a status name for a nobleman who was in the service of a king or powerful lord.
GIVEN NAMES Italian 15%. *Angelo* (12), *Salvatore* (9), *Domenic* (3), *Giuseppe* (3), *Sal* (3), *Antonio* (2), *Enrico* (2), *Gandolfo* (2), *Orazio* (2), *Agostino, Arcangelo, Baldassare.*

Vassar (994) Altered form of French **Vasseur**, a status name for a vassal in feudal society, from Old French *vasseor, vasseur* 'vassal'. Compare French LEVASSEUR.
FOREBEARS Matthew Vassar (1792–1868), brewer and founder of Vassar College, was born at East Tuddingham, Norfolk, England, and came to Dutchess Co., NY, as a child in 1796. The family were originally French Huguenots called Vasseur, who fled

to England in the late 17th century, to escape the persecution of Protestants in France following the revocation of the Edict of Nantes in 1685.

Vassel (127) English: variant of VASSELL.

Vassell (159) English: status name for a servant or nobleman who was under the protection of a king or powerful lord, Middle English, Old French *vassal* (Late Latin *vazallus*). In the U.S. this is a mainly southern name.

Vasser (411) Variant of English VASSAR or French **Vasseur** (see LEVASSEUR).

Vasseur (324) French: see LEVASSEUR.
GIVEN NAMES French 5%. *Emile, Francois, Laurent.*

Vassey (179) English (of Norman origin): habitational name from Vassy in Calvados, France.

Vassos (100) Greek: from *Vasos*, a pet form of the personal name *Vasilis* (see BASIL).
GIVEN NAMES Greek 9%. *Dimitrios, Konstantinos, Vasiliki.*

Vasta (290) Italian and Albanian: variant of BASTA.
GIVEN NAMES Italian 26%. *Salvatore* (5), *Alfio* (2), *Carmelo* (2), *Mariano* (2), *Pasquale* (2), *Angelina, Carmine, Gaetano, Gerardo, Guillermo, Leonardo, Lucio, Rocco, Rosario, Sal, Sebastiano.*

Vastano (110) Italian: probably a habitational name for someone from Vasto in Chieti province.
GIVEN NAMES Italian 14%. *Angelo, Antonio, Pasquale.*

Vastine (200) French: said to be a French form of German WETZSTEIN.

Vastola (150) Italian (Campania): unexplained.
GIVEN NAMES Italian 15%. *Alfonso, Amedeo, Carmine, Dino, Emileo, Salvator.*

Vaswani (107) Hindu name meaning '(descendant) of Vasu', found among people from Sind, Pakistan. *Vasu* is presumably from a shortened form of an ancestral name beginning with this element, probably *Vasudev* (Sanskrit *vāsudeva* 'son of *vasudeva*'), which is an epithet of the god Krishna and a popular personal name. Krishna's father's name was *vasudeva*.
GIVEN NAMES Indian 85%. *Haresh* (5), *Raj* (4), *Vijay* (4), *Amar* (2), *Kiran* (2), *Lachman* (2), *Prakash* (2), *Ramesh* (2), *Ranesh* (2), *Reshma* (2), *Shyam* (2), *Anil.*

Vatalaro (123) Southern Italian: perhaps from an agent derivative of *badile* 'shovel' (Sicilian *vadili*), hence an occupational name for someone who made or used shovels.
GIVEN NAMES Italian 11%. *Veto, Vito.*

Vatcher (100) English (Hampshire, Dorset): occupational name for a cowherd, from Old French *vachier*.

Vater (283) North German: nickname or status name from Middle Low German *vater* 'father', 'person of seniority or higher rank'.

GIVEN NAMES German 6%. *Gerhard* (2), *Bernhard, Hans, Kurt, Lutz, Reinhard.*

Vath (297) **1.** German: nickname from *fad*, an old stem meaning 'man'. **2.** North German: from Middle Low German *vat* 'barrel', 'keg', hence a metonymic occupational name for a cooper, or a nickname for a fat person.

Vatter (248) German: variant of VATER.
GIVEN NAMES German 5%. *Claus, Dietrich, Hans, Kurt.*

Vaugh (122) Irish: reduced and altered form of MCVEIGH.

Vaughan (15090) Welsh: from *fychan*, a lenited form of *bychan*, a diminutive of *bach* 'little'. This was often used to distinguish the younger of two bearers of the same personal name, typically the son of a father with the same name.

Vaughn (28692) Welsh: variant spelling of VAUGHAN.

Vaughns (174) Variant of Welsh VAUGHAN, with English patronymic *-s*.

Vaught (3475) Americanized spelling of German VOGT.

Vaughter (101) Americanized form of German or Dutch WACHTER.

Vaughters (136) Probably an Americanized form of German or Dutch WACHTER.

Vaupel (288) German: from a dialect pet form of the personal name *Volbrecht* (see VOLLBRECHT).

Vause (406) English and Scottish (of Norman origin): **1.** habitational name, a variant of VAUX. **2.** There are a number of early English examples of the name with articles rather than prepositions, which Reaney explains as being from a southern form of Middle English *faus* 'false', 'untrustworthy' (late Old English *fals*, from Latin *falsus*, reinforced by Old French *fals*, *faus* from the same source).

Vautour (149) French: from Old French *voltor*, Occitan *vautor* 'vulture', hence a nickname for a rapacious man.
GIVEN NAMES French 15%. *Aldea, Alphonse, Francois, Germaine, Lorette, Ovila, Yvon.*

Vautrin (103) French: from a pet form of the personal name *Vautier*, a regional variant of GAUTHIER.
GIVEN NAMES French 9%. *Franck, Lydie, Normand.*

Vaux (213) French, English, and Scottish: habitational name from any of various places in northern France called Vaux, from the Old French plural of *val* 'valley'.
FOREBEARS A Vaux from the Berry region of France is documented in Beaupré, Quebec, in 1666.
    Richard Vaux (1749–90) emigrated from Sussex, England, to Philadelphia, PA, in early youth. He was the descendant of Huguenot refugees who came to England from France in the late 17th century.
    Calvert Vaux, landscape architect, came to America in 1850 and designed several

major U.S. parks, including Central Park in New York City (with Frederick Olmstead).

Vavala (112) Southern Italian: possibly, as de Felice suggests, from the Muslim name ABDULLAH 'servant of Allah'.
GIVEN NAMES Italian 17%. *Antonio, Arturo, Biagio, Dino, Domenic, Isidro, Reno.*

Vavra (821) Czech and Slovak (**Vávra**): from a derivative of the personal name *Vavřinec*, Czech form of Latin *Laurentius* (see LAWRENCE). The surname is also well established in German-speaking lands.

Vavrek (201) Czech (**Vavřek**): from a pet form of *Vávra*, derivative of the personal name *Vavřinec*, Czech form of Latin *Laurentius* (see LAWRENCE).

Vawter (771) Americanized spelling of German VATER.

Vayda (218) Americanized spelling of Hungarian or Slavic VAJDA.

Vayner (113) Jewish (eastern Ashkenazic): respelling of WEINER.
GIVEN NAMES Russian 33%; Jewish 30%. *Boris* (6), *Mikhail* (4), *Arkadiy* (2), *Leonid* (2), *Semyon* (2), *Aleksandr, Efim, Grigori, Grigory, Iosif, Kseniya, Lev; Ilya* (3), *Lyova* (2), *Aron, Gitlya, Inna, Isak, Khaim, Mariya, Naum, Polina, Samoil, Sima.*

Vaynshteyn (132) Jewish (eastern Ashkenazic): respelling of WEINSTEIN.
GIVEN NAMES Russian 40%; Jewish 35%. *Boris* (6), *Mikhail* (5), *Iosif* (4), *Leonid* (3), *Lev* (3), *Vladimir* (3), *Anatoliy* (2), *Fanya* (2), *Igor* (2), *Yefim* (2), *Ayzik, Dmitriy; Ilya* (3), *Moysey* (2), *Semen* (2), *Yakov* (2), *Aron, Genya, Golda, Isak, Josif, Khana, Moisey, Molka.*

Vayo (104) **1.** Catalan (**Vayó**): probably variant of Catalan **Batlló** (alongside the variants **Bayó** and **Balló**), an occupational name from a derivative of Catalan *batlle* 'bailiff' or 'mayor'. This variant is nowadays not found in Catalonia. **2.** Spanish: perhaps variant of **Bayo**, of uncertain origin.

Vaysman (155) Jewish (eastern Ashkenazic): respelling of WEISMANN.
GIVEN NAMES Russian 37%; Jewish 33%. *Mikhail* (6), *Boris* (5), *Vladimir* (4), *Dmitriy* (3), *Grigory* (2), *Yelena* (2), *Aleksandr, Anatoliy, Anatoly, Fanya, Fenya, Gennadiy; Yakov* (4), *Semen* (3), *Moisey* (2), *Naum* (2), *Bronya, Chaim, Faina, Feyga, Izrail, Josif, Khanan, Khanna.*

Vaz (468) Portuguese: variant of VAS. This name is also common on the west coast of India, where it was taken by Portuguese colonists.
GIVEN NAMES Spanish 21%; Portuguese 16%. *Jose* (10), *Antonio* (9), *Manuel* (7), *Luis* (4), *Alfredo* (2), *Alvaro* (2), *Joaquin* (2), *Jorge* (2), *Mario* (2), *Victorio* (2), *Adriano, Aires, Amandio; Joao* (4), *Damiao* (2), *Afonso, Henrique, Joaquim, Ligia, Nelio, Paulo.*

Vaziri (117) Muslim (mainly Iranian): name indicating descent from or association with a vizier, from the Persian form of Arabic

wazīrī, adjectival form of *wazīr* 'vizier', 'minister'.
GIVEN NAMES Muslim 72%. *Ali* (5), *Bahram* (2), *Bijan* (2), *Jaleh* (2), *Ladan* (2), *Mansour* (2), *Masoud* (2), *Nahid* (2), *Ahmad, Alireza, Behzad, Fariba.*

Vazquez (7568) Galician and Spanish (**Vázquez**): variant of **Vásquez** (see VASQUEZ).
GIVEN NAMES Spanish 52%. *Jose* (299), *Juan* (132), *Luis* (105), *Carlos* (84), *Manuel* (75), *Jorge* (63), *Miguel* (62), *Francisco* (58), *Jesus* (56), *Pedro* (52), *Rafael* (52), *Raul* (49).

Vazzana (122) Southern Italian: occupational name, either from Arabic *wazzān* 'someone responsible for weighing things', or Old Sicilian *vazzanu* 'artisan', 'craftsman'.
GIVEN NAMES Italian 18%. *Antonino* (2), *Agostino, Mario, Mario Alberto, Milagro, Natale.*

Vea (173) **1.** Spanish and Galician: habitational name, principally from Vea in Soria province, but in some cases from any of four places with the same name in Pontevedra province, Galicia. **2.** Catalan: habitational name from any of the places named Bea or Vea in the Catalan-speaking areas. **3.** Norwegian: habitational name from any of four farmsteads so named, from the plural of Old Norse *viðr* 'wood', 'tree'.
GIVEN NAMES Spanish 17%; Scandinavian 4%. *Domingo* (2), *Pedro* (2), *Agripina, Alejandro, Angel, Carlos, Constante, Demetrio, Elpidio, Florentino, Hilario, Javier.*

Veach (1745) Scottish: variant of VEITCH.

Veal (2163) English (of Norman origin): **1.** nickname for an old man, or for the elder of two bearers of the same personal name, from Anglo-Norman French *viel* 'old' (Old French *vieil*). **2.** metonymic occupational name for a calf-herd or nickname for a docile, calf-like person, from Anglo-Norman French *ve(e)l* 'calf' (Old French *veel*).

Veale (635) **1.** English: variant spelling of VEAL. **2.** Irish (Waterford): from an unexplained Anglo-Norman name that is common in medieval records, *le Veel*, Gaelicized as **de Bhial** (see VEAL 2).

Vealey (140) English: variant of VELEY.

Veals (160) English: apparently a variant of VEAL.

Veasey (581) English: variant spelling of VEAZEY.

Veasley (245) Probably an altered form of English BEASLEY.

Veatch (940) Scottish: variant of VEITCH.

Veazey (886) English: nickname for a cheerful person, from a reduced form of Anglo-Norman French *enveisié* 'playful', 'merry' (Old French *envoisié*, past participle of *envoisier* 'to sport, enjoy oneself').
FOREBEARS John Veazey came from England to MD in the late 17th century.

Thomas Ward Veazey (b. 1774) was a MD legislator and planter.

Veazie (155) English: variant of VEAZEY.

Vecchi (135) Italian: patronymic or plural form of VECCHIO.
GIVEN NAMES Italian 11%. *Sesto* (2), *Mario* (2), *Antonio, Arrigo, Carlo, Dario, Natale, Quinto.*

Vecchiarelli (198) Italian: from a diminutive of the nickname *vecchio* 'old', 'aged'.
GIVEN NAMES Italian 21%. *Umberto* (2), *Angelo, Cesare, Domenic, Elio, Filomena, Gaetano, Guido, Paolo, Rocco.*

Vecchio (1042) Italian (mainly Sicily): from *vecchio* 'old', 'aged', applied as a status name for the older or oldest son, or as a nickname, possibly for someone who was prematurely gray, bent, or wrinkled.
GIVEN NAMES Italian 24%; Spanish 6%. *Angelo* (9), *Salvatore* (8), *Carmelo* (3), *Carmine* (2), *Dino* (2), *Francesco* (2), *Pasquale* (2), *Sal* (2), *Aldo, Alfio, Antonio, Carmel, Mario, Rafael, Rogelio; Raul* (3), *Eliezar* (2), *Enrique, Ercilia, Francisco, Germano, Jose, Nydia.*

Vecchione (578) Italian: from an augmentative of VECCHIO.
GIVEN NAMES Italian 11%. *Angelo* (2), *Domenic* (2), *Salvatore* (2), *Aldo, Attilio, Carmela, Dante, Donato, Ettore, Gennaro, Guerino, Maurizio.*

Vece (125) Southern Italian: possibly from *vece* 'change', 'mutation', 'alternation' (from Latin *vix, vicis*, plural *vices*), or from a pet form of a personal name formed with this element.
GIVEN NAMES Italian 8%. *Dante, Nicola, Sal.*

Vecellio (175) Italian (Venice): unexplained.
GIVEN NAMES Italian 11%. *Dino* (3), *Aldo, Angelo, Deno, Elio, Leno, Pio, Valentino.*

Vecera (114) **1.** Czech (**Večeřa**), Slovak (**Večera**), and Hungarian (**Vecsera**): from Slavic (Czech and Slovak) *večeře, večera* 'dinner'. **2.** Italian: unexplained.
GIVEN NAME Italian 6%. *Rocco* (2).

Vedder (786) North German: from Middle Low German *vedder* 'cousin', also used to denote any male relative. Compare VETTER.
GIVEN NAMES German 5%. *Wolf* (3), *Hellmuth* (2), *Kurt* (2), *Orlo* (2), *Dietrich, Eckhard, Helmut.*

Vedros (158) Origin unidentified.

Vee (104) Norwegian: habitational name from farmsteads named Ve, for example in Hordaland and Sogn, from Old Norse *vé* 'sacred place'.
GIVEN NAME Scandinavian 8%. *Ordell* (2).

Veech (126) Variant of Scottish VEITCH.

Veeder (362) Frisian: topographic name for someone who lived in a low-lying boggy area, a variant of **Feeder**.

Veen (221) **1.** North German: topographic name for a moorland dweller, from Middle Low German *vēn* 'moor'. **2.** Norwegian: habitational name from any of ten farmsteads named Ven, from Old Norse *vin* 'meadow'.

Veeneman (116) Dutch: variant of **Van Veen** or **Van den Vene**, habitational names from places named Veen or het Veen, from *veen* 'peat', 'peat bog', for example Veen in North Brabant.

Veenendaal (100) Dutch: habitational name for someone from a place so called.
GIVEN NAMES Dutch 4%. *Dirk* (3), *Gerrit* (3), *Klaas* (3), *Gerben, Maryke, Minert*.

Veenstra (450) Frisian: habitational name for someone from a place called Veen, or topographic name from *veen* 'pit', 'moor'. Compare FEENSTRA.

Veerkamp (142) Dutch: probably a variant of VERKAMP.

Vega (10429) Spanish: habitational name from any of the numerous places named Vega or La Vega, from *vega* 'meadow' (of pre-Roman origin, probably originally denoting irrigated land).
GIVEN NAMES Spanish 48%. *Jose* (293), *Juan* (133), *Luis* (131), *Carlos* (109), *Manuel* (106), *Jesus* (84), *Miguel* (61), *Rafael* (60), *Francisco* (59), *Angel* (54), *Ramon* (51), *Jorge* (48).

Vegas (305) Spanish: habitational name from any of the places named Vegas or Las Vegas, from the plural of *vega* 'meadow' (see VEGA).
GIVEN NAMES Spanish 18%. *Manuel* (3), *Raul* (3), *Angel* (2), *Pedro* (2), *Alfredo, Alicia, Angel Luis, Carmelita, Dalia, Eduardo, Genaro, Gustavo*.

Vegh (178) Hungarian (**Végh**): topographic name for someone who lived at the end of a village, from *vég* 'end'.
GIVEN NAMES Hungarian 11%; Jewish 5%. *Attila* (2), *Ferenc* (2), *Laszlo* (2), *Antal, Zsolt; Aron* (3).

Vegter (118) Dutch: occupational name meaning 'fighter', denoting a professional champion or duelist, someone who fought duels for legal purposes, or one who fought for entertainment at fairs.
GIVEN NAMES Dutch 8%. *Marten* (3), *Cornelus*.

Vehrs (141) North German: from the Germanic personal name *Fara*, which is based on the stem *far* 'to go'.
GIVEN NAME German 5%. *Otto*.

Veiga (336) Portuguese and Galician: habitational name from any of the towns called Veiga in Galicia and Portugal, from *veiga* 'meadow', Portuguese and Galician equivalent of Spanish VEGA.
GIVEN NAMES Spanish 25%; Portuguese 17%. *Manuel* (14), *Jose* (8), *Luis* (3), *Armando* (2), *Candido* (2), *Carlos* (2), *Enrique* (2), *Juan* (2), *Marta* (2), *Pedro* (2), *Aida, Ana; Joao* (6), *Duarte, Henrique, Margarida; Antonio* (4), *Giovanni* (3), *Caesar* (2), *Cesario, Iolanda, Leonardo*.

Veigel (141) German: variant spelling of FEIGEL.

GIVEN NAMES German 6%. *Erwin, Gerd, Gerhard, Heinz*.

Veil (144) **1.** German: variant of FEIGEL. **2.** English: occupational name for a watchman, from Anglo-Norman French *veil(le)* 'watch', 'guard' (Latin *vigilia* 'watch', 'wakefulness'). **3.** Jewish (western Ashkenazic): variant of WEIL.
GIVEN NAMES German 6%. *Erna, Hartmut*.

Veillette (215) Altered spelling of French **Veillet**, a diminutive of VEILLEUX.
GIVEN NAMES French 15%. *Lucien* (2), *Alain, Armand, Francois, Germaine, Jacques, Jean-Marie, Marcel, Yves*.

Veilleux (1018) French: occupational name for a watchman, from Old French *veille* 'watch', 'guard' (Latin *vigilia* 'watch', 'wakefulness').
GIVEN NAMES French 20%. *Armand* (6), *Marcel* (6), *Andre* (3), *Gilles* (3), *Jacques* (3), *Laurent* (3), *Lucien* (3), *Normand* (3), *Pierre* (3), *Rosaire* (3), *Cecile* (2), *Donat* (2).

Veillon (311) French: variant of **Vellon**, a nickname meaning 'calf'. This surname is found predominantly in LA.
GIVEN NAMES French 6%. *Emile* (2), *Damien, Jacques, Monique*.

Veirs (146) Variant of VIRES.

Veit (1036) German: from the name of Saint Veit (Latin *Vitus*), patron saint against fire. In many cases this is an altered spelling of the variant **Veith**, written thus to preserve the German pronunciation of *th* as *t*.
GIVEN NAMES German 5%. *Hans* (2), *Helmut* (2), *Kurt* (2), *Otto* (2), *Siegbert* (2), *Alois, Dieter, Eberhardt, Fritz, Manferd, Theodor*.

Veitch (647) Scottish (Norman): from a derivative of Latin *vacca* 'cow', hence a metonymic occupational name for a cowherd or a nickname for a gentle person. FOREBEARS Samuel Veitch (1668–1732), born in Edinburgh, Scotland, the son of William and Mary Veitch, went to central America as a soldier and adventurer, moving to New York in 1699 after the expedition failed.

Veitenheimer (129) German: habitational name for someone from a lost or unidentified place name, perhaps Wittenheim in Alsace.

Veith (873) German: variant of VEIT.
GIVEN NAMES German 4%. *Ernst* (2), *Gerhard* (2), *Hedwig* (2), *Franz, Hans, Helmut, Inge, Kurt, Rainer, Ulrich, Wolfgang*.

Vejar (148) Spanish: either a variant of **Béjar** (see BEJAR) or perhaps a variant of **Véjer**, a habitational name from a place called Véjer, in Cádiz province.
GIVEN NAMES Spanish 33%. *Manuel* (3), *Mario* (3), *Carlos* (2), *Jesus* (2), *Jose* (2), *Alfredo, Apolonio, Armando, Bernardo, Cristina, Edelmira, Eduardo; Antonio, Leonardo, Lorenzo, Marco*.

Veksler (140) Jewish (eastern Ashkenazic): variant of WECHSLER.

GIVEN NAMES Jewish 35%; Russian 33%. *Ilya* (5), *Mendel* (3), *Yakov* (3), *Moisey* (2), *Aron, Benyamin, Etya, Gitlya, Irina, Izya, Khaim, Marat; Anatoly* (6), *Mikhail* (5), *Boris* (4), *Igor* (2), *Aleksandr, Aleksey, Anatoliy, Arkady, Galina, Gennadiy, Iosif, Leonid*.

Vela (2904) **1.** Spanish, Catalan and Galician: of uncertain derivation; it could be from the pre-Roman personal name *Vela* (compare Basque *bela, vela* 'raven'). More likely perhaps, it may be a byname from *vela* meaning either 'sail' or 'watchman'. **2.** Spanish: habitational name from a place name Vela, in Córdoba province. **3.** Portuguese: habitational name from a place named Vela in Portugal. **4.** Czech: from a pet form of either of two personal names, *Velislav* or *Velimir*.
GIVEN NAMES Spanish 49%. *Jose* (49), *Juan* (37), *Carlos* (36), *Raul* (30), *Manuel* (27), *Ricardo* (25), *Roberto* (25), *Ruben* (21), *Jesus* (20), *Luis* (20), *Guadalupe* (18), *Ramon* (13).

Velarde (910) Spanish or Basque: possibly a topographic name from Basque *belar* 'vegetation', 'grass' + the suffix *-de, -di* denoting abundance.
GIVEN NAMES Spanish 36%. *Jose* (16), *Carlos* (8), *Luis* (8), *Jorge* (7), *Cesar* (6), *Guadalupe* (6), *Juan* (6), *Manuel* (5), *Ramon* (5), *Ricardo* (5), *Alberto* (4), *Francisco* (4).

Velardi (321) Southern Italian (mainly Sicily): patronymic or plural form of VELARDO.
GIVEN NAMES Italian 12%. *Sal* (2), *Salvatore* (2), *Antonio, Carlo, Carmelo, Cosimo, Crispino, Domenico, Ottavio, Rocco*.

Velardo (177) Southern Italian (mainly Sicily): variant of **Belardo**, a dissimilated form of BERARDO.
GIVEN NAMES Italian 26%. *Mario* (4), *Antonio* (2), *Claudio, Francisco, Livio* (2), *Rocco* (2), *Antonino, Carmelo, Enrico, Luciano, Luigi, Nicola, Oresto*.

Velasco (2917) Spanish: **1.** from the personal name *Velasco, Belasco*, formed with Basque *bel-* 'raven' + the diminutive suffix *-sco*. **2.** in some cases possibly a habitational name from any of various places in Logroño, Soria, and Seville provinces named Velasco.
GIVEN NAMES Spanish 49%. *Jose* (77), *Juan* (37), *Manuel* (31), *Jesus* (27), *Carlos* (26), *Francisco* (25), *Luis* (25), *Jorge* (17), *Pedro* (16), *Ruben* (15), *Raul* (14), *Enrique* (13).

Velasquez (7072) Spanish (**Velásquez**): patronymic from the personal name VELASCO.
GIVEN NAMES Spanish 46%. *Jose* (197), *Juan* (103), *Carlos* (63), *Francisco* (59), *Jesus* (56), *Manuel* (56), *Luis* (55), *Pedro* (40), *Miguel* (39), *Jorge* (35), *Mario* (35), *Raul* (33).

Velazco (195) Spanish: variant of VELASCO.
GIVEN NAMES Spanish 51%. *Carlos* (7), *Jose* (7), *Jorge* (4), *Juan* (4), *Rafael* (4), *Francisco* (3), *Ana* (2), *Feliciano* (2), *Guadalupe* (2), *Jesus* (2), *Luis* (2), *Manuel* (2).

Velazquez (3463) Spanish (**Velázquez**): variant of VELASQUEZ.

Velde (143) **1.** Norwegian: habitational name from any of several farmsteads named Velle, from *velli*, the dative singular of Old Norse *vǫllr* 'field', 'meadow'. **2.** Dutch: variant of VANDERVELDE.
GIVEN NAMES Scandinavian 11%; German 4%. *Anders, Tryg.*

Veldhuis (103) Dutch: habitational name from Veldhuis in North Holland, or alternatively, perhaps from Feldhaus in Lower Saxony, Germany.
GIVEN NAMES Dutch 6%; German 4%. *Henk*; *Johannes* (2).

Veldhuizen (220) Dutch: habitational name from places so named in Drenthe, Gelderland, and Utrecht.

Veldkamp (121) Dutch: habitational name for someone from Veldkamp in Enschede, Overijssel.

Veldman (289) Dutch: variant of VANDERVELDE.

Veley (203) English: habitational name for someone from Velly in Devon.

Velez (5511) **1.** Spanish (**Vélez**): patronymic from the personal name VELA. **2.** Spanish (**Vélez**): habitational name from any of various places in Andalusia called Vélez. **3.** Portuguese (**Velez, Velêz**): unexplained. It may be a habitational name from Vellés in Salamanca.
GIVEN NAMES Spanish 45%. *Jose* (160), *Carlos* (81), *Luis* (78), *Juan* (63), *Pedro* (39), *Manuel* (38), *Angel* (36), *Jorge* (34), *Rafael* (32), *Francisco* (31), *Miguel* (30), *Ramon* (30).

Velie (271) Origin unidentified.

Velis (110) **1.** Variant of Spanish **Véliz** (see VELIZ). **2.** Greek: from Turkish *veli* 'guardian', a term used to denote various administrative officials in the Ottoman Empire.
GIVEN NAMES Spanish 26%; Greek 6%; Italian 5%. *Juan* (3), *Pedro* (2), *Roberto* (2), *Alejandro, Ana, Caridad, Carlos, Eduardo, Elia, Gerardo, Gregorio, Jorge*; *Despina, Kosta, Speros*; *Deno, Giovanni, Marco, Mauro.*

Veliz (503) Spanish (**Véliz**): variant of **Vélez** (see VELEZ).
GIVEN NAMES Spanish 51%. *Jose* (11), *Juan* (8), *Luis* (8), *Carlos* (6), *Angel* (4), *Arturo* (4), *Jesus* (4), *Julio* (4), *Manuel* (4), *Pedro* (4), *Alejandro* (3), *Marcos* (3).

Velky (114) Slavic: nickname meaning 'big'.

Vella (1262) Southern Italian, Maltese: variant of BELLA.
GIVEN NAMES Italian 12%. *Salvatore* (10), *Angelo* (9), *Reno* (4), *Calogero* (2), *Carmel*

(2), *Nino* (2), *Pietro* (2), *Sal* (2), *Alfonse, Carmine, Gino, Giovanni.*

Vellucci (202) Italian: variant of BELLUCCI.
GIVEN NAMES Italian 20% *Cosmo* (2), *Enrico* (2), *Achille, Angelo, Domenico, Franco, Luigi, Massimo, Rocco, Romeo.*

Velo (132) **1.** Portuguese, Galician and Spanish: possibly from a byname formed with *velo* 'veil' or in some cases perhaps from Galician *belo* 'beautiful'. **2.** Hungarian (**Vélő**): nickname for a thoughtful or intelligent person, from a derivative of *vélni* 'to think'.
GIVEN NAMES Spanish 33%. *Jose* (4), *Enrique* (2), *Jesus* (2), *Lino* (2), *Mario* (2), *Alvaro, Andres, Armando, Catalina, Consuelo, Fruto, Guadalupe*; *Antonio, Heriberto, Primo.*

Veloso (170) Portuguese and Galician: **1.** nickname for a hirsute individual, from Portuguese *veloso* 'hairy' (Latin *villosus*). **2.** habitational name from any of the places in Portugal named Veloso.
GIVEN NAMES Spanish 48%; Portuguese 14%. *Jose* (5), *Manuel* (4), *Roberto* (4), *Juan* (3), *Alfredo* (2), *Carlos* (2), *Fernando* (2), *Luis* (2), *Nicanor* (2), *Abilio, Agustina, Aida*; *Joaquim.*

Velotta (127) Italian: possibly a variant of **Belotta**, which would be from a feminine form of *Belotto*, a reduced pet form of the Biblical name *Abele*.
GIVEN NAMES Italian 8%. *Antonio, Lucio, Nunzio, Pasquale.*

Veloz (426) Spanish (mainly Latin America): from a nickname or byname formed with *veloz* 'fast'.
GIVEN NAMES Spanish 50%. *Jose* (12), *Juan* (8), *Francisco* (6), *Ramon* (6), *Jesus* (5), *Manuel* (4), *Ruben* (4), *Armando* (3), *Arturo* (3), *Carlos* (3), *Javier* (3), *Roberto* (3); *Antonio* (5), *Carmela, Federico, Geno, Geronimo, Heriberto, Lorenzo, Lucio.*

Velte (163) German: variant of VELTEN.

Velten (217) **1.** Dutch and German: from a vernacular form of the personal name *Valentin* (see VALENTINE). **2.** Norwegian: habitational name from any of several farmsteads, mainly in Hedmark, named with *velte* 'log pile'.

Veltkamp (162) Dutch: variant of VELDKAMP.

Veltman (351) Dutch: variant of VANDERVELDE.

Veltre (163) Italian: variant of VELTRI.

Veltri (690) Southern Italian: patronymic from *veltro* 'greyhound' (from Late Latin *vertragus, veltrus*), presumably a nickname for a fast runner or a lean rangy person.
GIVEN NAMES Italian 16%. *Angelo* (3), *Antonio* (3), *Carlo* (3), *Carmine* (3), *Nunzio* (3), *Attilio* (2), *Domenic* (2), *Francesco* (2), *Salvatore* (2), *Albo, Concetta, Enrico.*

Vena (334) Italian: habitational name, most likely from Vena di Maida in Catanzaro province or Vena di Ionadi in Vibo Valentia,

so named from Latin *vena* 'vein', 'vein of water'.
GIVEN NAMES Italian 6%. *Cosmo* (2), *Carmine, Cesare, Concetta, Dante, Luciano.*

Venable (3570) English (of Norman origin): habitational name from a place called Venables in Eure, France, probably named with Late Latin *venabulum* 'hunting ground' (a derivative of *venari* 'to hunt').
FOREBEARS American bearers of this name are descended from Abraham Venables, who came to VA from England in or before 1687.

Venables (246) English: variant of VENABLE.

Venanzi (107) Italian: from the personal name *Venanzio*, from Latin *Venantius* 'hunter'.
GIVEN NAMES Italian 8%. *Angelo, Attilio, Galileo.*

Venard (214) English (Cornwall): unexplained.

Vences (142) Spanish and Portuguese: reduced form of the Slavic personal name *Venceslaus* (see VACEK).
GIVEN NAMES Spanish 63%. *Jose* (6), *Juan* (5), *Roberto* (3), *Jesus* (2), *Marcelo* (2), *Miguel* (2), *Adolfo, Agustin, Alberto, Alejandro, Alfredo, Alicia.*

Vencill (300) Variant spelling of **Vencl**, Czech form of the German personal name WENZEL, which is itself of Slavic origin, from Old Czech *Vęceslav* (see VACEK).

Vender (105) Origin unidentified.
GIVEN NAMES Spanish 5%. *Fernando, Raul, Reyes, Ruben.*

Vendetti (411) Italian: patronymic or plural form from a variant of the personal name BENEDETTO.
GIVEN NAMES Italian 12%. *Angelo* (3), *Rocco* (3), *Carlo* (2), *Aldo, Domenic, Enrico, Filippo, Lucio, Pasquale.*

Venditti (576) Italian: patronymic or plural form of VENDITTO.

Venditto (208) Italian: from a variant of the personal name BENEDETTO.
GIVEN NAMES Italian 14%. *Carlo* (2), *Angelo, Beniamino, Giuseppe, Rocco, Stefano.*

Venegas (1586) Spanish: patronymic from Arabic or Jewish *ben* 'son' + the medieval personal name *Ega(s)*, probably of Visigothic origin. Compare Portuguese VIEGAS.
GIVEN NAMES Spanish 53%. *Jose* (55), *Manuel* (30), *Juan* (20), *Jesus* (18), *Raul* (17), *Francisco* (16), *Luis* (16), *Carlos* (12), *Jaime* (10), *Jorge* (10), *Salvador* (10), *Arturo* (9).

Venegoni (102) Northern Italian: Lombard habitational name from either of two places named Venegono (Superiore and Inferiore).
GIVEN NAMES Italian 20%. *Paolo* (2), *Alfio, Angelo, Caesar, Cesare, Domenic.*

Venema (342) Frisian: topographic name denoting someone who lived by a peat bog, Frisian *ven.*

GIVEN NAMES Dutch 7%. *Cornelis* (2), *Gerrit* (2), *Auke*, *Dirk*, *Harm*, *Hessel*, *Roelf*, *Sjoerd*.

Veneman (118) Dutch: variant of VEENEMAN.

GIVEN NAMES French 8%; Dutch 4%. *Amie*, *Cecile*, *Hancy*; *Dirk*, *Mieke*.

Vener (144) Czech form of German WERNER.

Veness (108) English: variant of VENUS.

Veney (326) English: unexplained.

Venezia (1076) Italian and Jewish (from Italy): habitational name from the city of Venice or a regional name from the region of Venetia, both called *Venezia* in Italian, from Latin *Venetia*. The name derives from the tribal name of the *Veneti*, a probably Celtic tribe which inhabited this area before the Roman expansion.

GIVEN NAMES Italian 12%. *Angelo* (6), *Salvatore* (4), *Antonio* (3), *Rocco* (3), *Domenic* (2), *Pietro* (2), *Vito* (2), *Alessandra*, *Carmine*, *Ferdinando*, *Francesca*, *Francesco*.

Veneziale (111) Italian (Molise): unexplained; perhaps related to the place name *Venezia* (Venice).

GIVEN NAMES Italian 36%. *Antimo* (2), *Antonio* (2), *Dante* (2), *Enrico* (2), *Angelo*, *Carmela*, *Carmine*, *Domenic*, *Elio*, *Ferdinando*, *Guido*, *Libero*.

Veneziano (394) Italian: habitational or regional name from *veneziano* 'Venetian' (see VENEZIA). In the form **Venetsianos**, this is also found as a Greek family name. The Venetians had many possessions in the Ionian islands and the Aegean, including Crete and Naxos, from the 13th to the 17th centuries, and there was a thriving Greek community in Venice itself.

GIVEN NAMES Italian 26%. *Angelo* (4), *Carmine* (3), *Domenic* (3), *Salvatore* (3), *Antonio* (2), *Franco* (2), *Pasquale* (2), *Rocco* (2), *Santo* (2), *Alfio*, *Carmela*, *Domenico*.

Venezio (101) Italian: variant of VENEZIA.

Venhaus (112) German: habitational name from Venhaus in Lower Saxony.

Venhuizen (187) Altered form of Dutch **van Huizen**, a habitational name for someone from Huizen in North Holland.

Venier (173) **1.** French: Norman variant of **Guenier**, from a Germanic personal name, *Wanhari*. **2.** Italian: from the personal name *Venerio* (from Latin *Venerius*), which became popular, especially in Venice, as a result of the cult of San Venerio. The surname is also found in Greece, mainly in the form **Venieris** and the patronymic derivatives **Venierakis** and **Venieratos**.

GIVEN NAMES Italian 5%. *Carlo*, *Dino*, *Matteo*, *Orfeo*, *Vittorio*.

Venis (126) English: variant of VENUS.

Venkataraman (140) Indian (southern states): Hindu name, from Sanskrit *venkaṭeśa* 'lord of Venkata hill', an epithet of the god Vishnu (from *venkaṭa* 'name of

the hill' + *īśa* 'lord'). There is a celebrated temple dedicated to Vishnu on this hill in Andhra Pradesh. This name is found only as a male personal name in India, but has come to be used as a family name in the U.S. among south Indians.

GIVEN NAMES Indian 99%. *Shankar* (6), *Ravi* (4), *Sundar* (4), *Ramesh* (3), *Chandran* (2), *Ganesh* (2), *Jayashree* (2), *Nagarajan* (2), *Natarajan* (2), *Raghu* (2), *Raj* (2), *Srikanth* (2).

Venkatesh (104) Indian (southern states): Hindu name, from Sanskrit *venkatesha* 'lord of Venkata hill', an epithet of the god Vishnu. There is a celebrated temple dedicated to Vishnu on this hill in Andhra Pradesh. This name is found only as a male personal name in India, but has come to be used as a family name in the U.S. among south Indians.

GIVEN NAMES Indian 88%. *Harsha* (2), *Prasanna* (2), *Sudhir* (2), *Viswanath* (2), *Babu*, *Dinesh*, *Gopi*, *Kasturi*, *Kiran*, *Lakshmanan*, *Lalitha*, *Leela*.

Venn (364) **1.** English (southwest): topographic name for someone who lived in a low-lying marshy area, a variant of FENN. **2.** German: topographic name from Middle High German, Middle Low German *venne* 'pit', 'moor', or 'water meadow'.

Vennard (165) French: variant of **Venart**, itself a variant of **Guénard**, from the Germanic personal name *Wanhard*.

Venne (379) **1.** German: variant of VENN. **2.** Reduced form of Dutch **van der** (or **den**) **Venne**, a variant of VAN VEEN.

FOREBEARS A Venne or Voyne is documented in Montreal in 1666.

GIVEN NAMES French 6%. *Andre*, *Celina*, *Luc*, *Philippe*, *Sylvie*.

Venneman (153) **1.** Dutch: topographic name for a fen dweller (see VAN VEEN). **2.** Altered spelling of German **Vennemann**, a topographic name for someone who lived by a pit or bog (see VENN), or a habitational name for someone from a place called Venne, near Osnabrück.

Venner (291) **1.** English (west country): topographic name for someone who lived by a fen or marsh, a variant of FENNER, reflecting the voicing of *f* that was characteristic of southwestern dialects of Middle English. **2.** English: occupational name for a huntsman, from Old French *veneo(u)r* (Latin *venator*, a derivative of *venari* 'to hunt'). **3.** Dutch and North German: topographic name for someone living by a pit, moor, or fen, from VENN + the suffix *-er* denoting an inhabitant, or a habitational name for someone from places called Venn or Venne.

Venneri (149) Italian: patronymic from *Venero*, masculine form of *Venera*, one of the most popular female personal names in Sicily.

GIVEN NAMES Italian 13%. *Cosmo* (2), *Antonio*, *Cosimo*, *Francesco*, *Rocco*, *Valdo*.

Venning (145) English (West Country): topographic name for someone who lived in a low-lying marshy area, from Old English *fenn* 'marsh', 'bog', reflecting the voicing of *f* that was characteristic of southwestern dialects of Middle English.

Veno (276) Italian (mainly Naples): unexplained.

Vensel (240) Americanized spelling of Czech *Vencl*, Hungarian *Vencel*, German WENZEL, or some other name derived from the Slavic personal name *Venceslav* (see VACEK).

Venske (100) Respelling of German WENSKE, a pet form of Slavic *Vęceslav* (see VACEK).

Venson (218) Most probably a variant of English or French VINCENT.

Vent (203) **1.** Dutch (**de Vent**): nickname from Middle Dutch *vennoot*, or *veynoot* 'colleague', 'apprentice', 'mate', 'guy'. **2.** Czech: from a reduced form of the Italian personal name *Bonaventura*.

Venteicher (115) German (Westphalia): unexplained. This surname is found mainly in IA.

GIVEN NAMES German 4%. *Anton*, *Kurt*.

Venter (190) **1.** German: reduced vernacular form of the Italian personal name *Bonaventura*. **2.** Reduced form of Dutch VANDEVENTER.

Venters (534) English and Scottish: probably a nickname for a daring person, from Middle English *aventurous* 'bold', 'venturesome'.

Venti (201) Italian: patronymic from VENTO.

GIVEN NAMES Italian 12%. *Dino* (2), *Antonio*, *Carmela*, *Francesco*, *Rocco*, *Settimio*.

Ventimiglia (526) Italian: habitational name for someone from Ventimiglia in northeastern Italy (Imperia province). The name is most frequent in Sicily through an extensive feudal family associated with Ventimiglia di Sicilia.

GIVEN NAMES Italian 18%. *Salvatore* (5), *Vito* (4), *Carlo* (3), *Gino* (3), *Sal* (3), *Antonio* (2), *Antonino*, *Carmela*, *Carmelo*, *Gaetano*, *Lorenzo*, *Pasquale*.

Vento (753) **1.** Italian: from a short form of the personal name BENEVENTO, or the variant *Bon(i)vento*. **2.** Portuguese and Galician: possibly from Galician and Portuguese *vento* 'wind' or in some cases a habitational name from any of various places in Galicia and Portugal called or called with Vento.

GIVEN NAMES Spanish 15%; Italian 13%. *Jorge* (3), *Jose* (3), *Rosario* (3), *Jaime* (2), *Juan* (2), *Orlando* (2), *Pedro* (2), *Rodolfo* (2), *Rolando* (2), *Adela*, *Amada*, *Anacleto*; *Salvatore* (5), *Constantino* (4), *Elio* (3), *Angelo* (2), *Sal* (2), *Attilio*, *Carmine*, *Ciro*, *Delio*, *Domenica*, *Domenico*.

Ventola (221) Italian (Apulia, Campania): apparently from *ventola* 'fire fan'; however, the term is not attested before the 18th century, which would be very late for surname formation.

GIVEN NAMES Italian 14%. *Giorgio* (2), *Pasquale* (2), *Agostino, Angelo, Carmine, Dante, Enrico*.

Ventre (322) **1.** Italian and French: nickname for a man with a large paunch, from Italian, Old French *ventre* 'belly' (Latin *venter*). **2.** Italian: probably from a short form of the personal names *Bonventre* or *Brazzaventre*. **3.** English: nickname for a bold or daring person, from Middle English *aventure* 'chance', 'hazard'. Compare VENTERS.

GIVEN NAMES Italian 8%; French 6%. *Antonio, Carmelo, Carmine, Francesco, Reno, Rocco, Vito; Emile* (2), *Armand*.

Ventrella (167) Italian: **1.** from a diminutive of **Ventra**, which may be a nickname from *ventra* 'belly', Calabrian dialect form of VENTRE, or from a short form of the personal name *Bonventra*. **2.** reduced form of VENTURELLA.

GIVEN NAMES Italian 17%. *Antonio* (2), *Vito* (2), *Angelo, Egidio, Peppino, Salvatore, Saverio, Vincenzo*.

Ventresca (427) Italian: of uncertain derivation, but probably related to *ventre* 'belly' (see VENTRE).

GIVEN NAMES Italian 32%. *Mario* (6), *Antonio* (5), *Angelo* (4), *Dante* (3), *Gino* (3), *Pietro* (3), *Attilio* (2), *Benito* (2), *Domenic* (2), *Domenico* (2), *Donato* (2), *Giovanni* (2), *Guido* (2), *Panfilo* (2), *Pasquale* (2).

Ventress (203) English: variant of VENTERS.

Ventrone (117) Italian: augmentative form of **Ventro**, which is probably a variant of VELTRI.

GIVEN NAMES Italian 10%. *Angelo* (2), *Pasquale*.

Ventry (104) **1.** English: unexplained. **2.** possibly an Americanized spelling of Italian **Ventre**, a short form of a compound name formed with *ventre* 'belly', 'stomach', such as BONVENTRE.

GIVEN NAMES Italian 4%. *Dino, Santina*.

Ventura (4129) Italian, Spanish, Catalan, Portuguese, and Jewish (Sephardic): from a medieval personal name, a short form of *Bonaventura* or *Buenaventura*, meaning 'good fortune', or, in the case of the Italian name, a nickname from *ventura* 'fortune', 'luck'. The name *Bonaventura* was borne in honor of a saint (1221–74) who was given this nickname by St. Francis of Assisi when he cured him miraculously as a child.

GIVEN NAMES Spanish 31%; Portuguese 8%; Italian 7%. *Jose* (103), *Manuel* (37), *Juan* (31), *Carlos* (25), *Rafael* (20), *Mario* (19), *Luis* (18), *Miguel* (15), *Ana* (13), *Francisco* (13), *Ramon* (11), *Pedro* (9); *Joao* (5), *Joaquim* (2), *Paulo; Antonio* (23), *Salvatore* (13), *Sal* (5), *Angelo* (4), *Carmine* (4), *Vito* (4), *Dante* (3), *Lorenzo* (3), *Luigi* (3), *Marco* (3), *Carmela* (2), *Dario* (2).

Venturella (212) Italian: from a diminutive or pet form of VENTURA.

GIVEN NAMES Italian 11%. *Angelo, Domenic, Gasper*.

Venturelli (111) Italian: from a pet form of VENTURA.

GIVEN NAMES Italian 9%. *Angelo, Riccardo*.

Venturi (249) Italian: patronymic from the personal name VENTURA.

GIVEN NAMES Italian 15%. *Deno* (3), *Gino* (3), *Giuseppe* (2), *Aldo, Dante, Gianni, Guido, Lazzaro, Marino, Primo, Silvio*.

Venturini (393) Italian: patronymic from the personal name VENTURINO.

GIVEN NAMES Italian 21%; Spanish 5%. *Aldo* (3), *Marino* (3), *Americo* (2), *Angelo* (2), *Antonio* (2), *Aurelio* (2), *Claudio* (2), *Dante* (2), *Albino, Amelio, Arduino, Ciro, Emidio, Evo, Francesco, Guerino, Mario, Renato, Sergio; Hermano, Jose, Julio, Miguel, Nestor*.

Venturino (187) Italian: from a pet form of VENTURA.

GIVEN NAMES Italian 14%. *Salvatore* (3), *Angelo, Concetta, Dante, Egidio, Fausto, Gino, Marco*.

Venturo (122) Italian: masculinized form of VENTURA.

GIVEN NAMES Italian 23%; Spanish 10%. *Gennaro* (2), *Antonio, Carmela, Galileo, Renzo, Santo, Vito; Luis, Mariela, Mario, Orlando*.

Venus (240) English (of Norman origin): habitational name from Venoix in Calvados, France. Spelled thus, the surname is now found principally in northeastern England.

GIVEN NAMES French 6%. *Andree, Camille*.

Venuti (382) Italian: patronymic from the personal name VENUTO.

GIVEN NAMES Italian 11%. *Vito* (4), *Angelo, Domenic, Enzo, Giuseppe, Sal*.

Venuto (299) Italian: from the personal name *Venuto*, a short form of BENVENUTO.

GIVEN NAMES Italian 21%. *Dino* (3), *Domenic* (2), *Americo, Antonio, Carmelo, Erminio, Lorenzo, Nino, Rocco, Rosario, Salvatore*.

Venzke (208) German: from a pet form of the personal name WENZEL.

GIVEN NAMES German 4%. *Benno, Otto*.

Venzon (100) Italian: Italianzed form of Friul **Vençon**, a habitational name from a Friul town named Vençon, in northern Italy.

GIVEN NAMES Spanish 15%; Italian 5%. *Raul* (2), *Ricardo* (2), *Alfredo, Crisanto, Ernesto, Juanita, Luz, Perlita, Ponciano, Tino; Angelo, Giacomo*.

Venzor (151) perhaps from a native American language: commonly found in northern Mexico, alongside the variants **Vensor**, **Benzor** and **Bensor**, unexplained.

GIVEN NAMES Spanish 45%. *Jose* (3), *Armando* (2), *Javier* (2), *Manuel* (2), *Norberto* (2), *Oralia* (2), *Socorro* (2), *Ventura* (2), *Alfonso, Alfredo, Alicia, Ana Maria*.

Veon (162) Probably an altered form of Welsh VAUGHAN. It is also found in the spelling **Veyon**.

Vera (3010) Spanish (especially southern Spain): habitational name from any of various places called Vera or La Vera, named with *vera* 'river bank'.

GIVEN NAMES Spanish 50%. *Jose* (84), *Luis* (38), *Juan* (36), *Carlos* (35), *Manuel* (29), *Jesus* (24), *Francisco* (19), *Pedro* (19), *Jorge* (17), *Miguel* (17), *Javier* (16), *Rafael* (15).

Verano (116) Spanish: Castilianized variant of Basque **Berano**, a habitational name from a town in Biscay province, Basque Country.

GIVEN NAMES Spanish 37%. *Ana* (3), *Luis* (3), *Jorge* (2), *Sigifredo* (2), *Alberto, Alirio, Alvaro, Aurelio, Aureo, Eduardo, Faustino, Jaime*.

Veras (259) Spanish: apparently from *veras*, plural of *vera* 'river bank', presumably applied as a topographic name for a river bank dweller.

GIVEN NAMES Spanish 55%. *Jose* (12), *Carlos* (8), *Luis* (6), *Rafael* (6), *Pedro* (4), *Juan* (3), *Altagracia* (2), *Ana* (2), *Juana* (2), *Manuel* (2), *Marina* (2), *Mercedes* (2).

Verastegui (106) Basque (also **Verástegui**): Castilianized variant of Basque **Berastegi**, a habitational name from a place called Berastegi in Gipuzkoa province, Basque Country.

GIVEN NAMES Spanish 49%. *Alfredo* (3), *Juan* (3), *Emilio* (2), *Jesus* (2), *Ricardo* (2), *Adalid, Adela, Alfonso, Ana, Araceli, Armando, Avelina; Antonio* (3), *Dario*.

Verba (264) Jewish (from Ukraine): **1.** ornamental name from Ukrainian *verba* 'willow'. **2.** habitational name from Verba, now in Ukraine.

GIVEN NAMES Russian 5%. *Anatoliy, Anatoly, Arkadiy, Gennadiy, Grigoriy, Mikhail*.

Verbeck (374) Dutch: variant of VANDERBEEK.

Verbeek (179) Dutch: variant of VERBECK.

FOREBEARS This name is recorded in Beverwijck in New Netherland (Albany, NY) in the mid 17th century.

GIVEN NAMES German 5%. *Johannes, Kurt, Otto*.

Verbeke (222) Dutch: variant of VERBECK.

GIVEN NAMES French 5%. *Fernand, Octave, Virginie*.

Verbeten (104) Dutch: habitational name for someone from Betuwe in Tongeren in Limburg province, Belgium.

Verble (237) Probably German or Dutch: unexplained. Compare VARBLE.

Verbrugge (188) Dutch: topographic name for someone who lived near a bridge, *brugge* 'bridge', or a habitational name for someone from a place named with this word, notably Bruges in Belgium (Dutch *Brugge*).

Verburg (376) Dutch: topographic name for someone who lived by a fortification, Middle Dutch *burch(t)*.

GIVEN NAMES Dutch 4%. *Adriaan* (2), *Gerrit*, *Leendert*, *Marinus*, *Rens*.

Vercauteren (110) Dutch: habitational name for someone from any of various places named Kouter (meaning 'cultivated land'), for example in East Flanders, Belgium.

Verch (140) Probably a respelling of German **Werch**, from a Slavic personal name, or in some cases a habitational name from Werchau, Werchow in Brandenburg.

GIVEN NAMES German 7%. *Otto* (2), *Orlo*.

Vercher (375) French: topographic name for someone who lived by farmland (medieval Latin *vercaria*), or a habitational name from Verchère in Haute Savoie, Verchères in Rhône, Les Verchers in Maine-et-Loire, or Les Verchères in Rhône. This is a common surname in LA.

Vercoe (105) English (Cornwall): unexplained. Compare VARCOE.

Vercruysse (140) Dutch and Belgian: topographic name for someone who lived by a cross.

Verde (408) **1.** Spanish, Italian, and Portuguese: from Spanish *verde* 'green' (Latin *viridis*), presumably a nickname for someone who habitually dressed in this color or had green eyes, etc. This is also a common element of place names. **2.** Italian: from the medieval personal name *Verde* (see 1 above).

GIVEN NAMES Spanish 21%; Italian 16%. *Francisco* (5), *Fernando* (4), *Gerardo* (2), *Jose* (2), *Juan* (2), *Manuel* (2), *Mario* (2), *Rafael* (2), *Agustin*, *Alberto*, *Alina*, *Amalia*; *Antonio* (5), *Salvatore* (4), *Angelo* (2), *Antimo* (2), *Heriberto* (2), *Aniello*, *Carlo*, *Carmine*, *Ceasar*, *Ciro*, *Dino*, *Eliseo*.

Verdejo (102) Spanish: habitational name from any of the places so called.

GIVEN NAMES Spanish 52%. *Rafael* (3), *Jose* (2), *Natividad* (2), *Adela*, *Alberto*, *Alicia*, *Ana*, *Angel*, *Candido*, *Carlos*, *Catalino*, *Cruz*; *Antonio*, *Luciano*.

Verderame (169) Italian: from the personal name *Verderame*, a variant of *Beltrame* (see BELTRAMI).

GIVEN NAMES Italian 17%. *Salvatore* (3), *Biagio*, *Carmela*, *Carmine*, *Cataldo*, *Franco*, *Marino*, *Valentino*.

Verderber (210) German: nickname from Middle High German *verderber* 'destroyer', an agent derivative of *verderben* 'to destroy or kill'.

GIVEN NAMES German 8%. *Aloysius*, *Franz*, *Irmgard*, *Kurt*, *Manfred*.

Verderosa (152) Italian: apparently from a medieval female personal name, *Verdirosa*.

GIVEN NAMES Italian 19%. *Rocco* (3), *Carmine* (2), *Angelo*, *Antonio*, *Domenica*, *Salvatore*.

Verdi (663) Italian: patronymic from VERDE.

GIVEN NAMES Italian 14%. *Angelo* (5), *Ciro* (4), *Salvatore* (3), *Carmine* (2), *Pasquale* (2), *Antonio*, *Cesare*, *Gaetano*, *Geno*, *Giuseppe*, *Philomena*, *Rocco*.

Verdier (218) **1.** English (of Norman origin) and French: occupational name for a forester, Old French *verdier* (Late Latin *viridarius*, a derivative of *viridis* 'green'). The medieval officials in charge of a forest were known as *verdiers* on account of their green costumes, which may be regarded as an early example of camouflage. **2.** Southern French: topographic name for someone who lived near an orchard or garden, or an occupational name for someone who was employed in one, from Occitan *verdier* 'orchard' (Late Latin *virid(i)arium*).

GIVEN NAMES French 9%. *Celine*, *Henri*, *Jacques*, *Monique*, *Philippe*.

Verdin (695) **1.** English: variant of VERDUN. **2.** French: habitational name from any of the places so named, for example in Cher, Isère, and Haute-Loire. **3.** Spanish (**Verdín**): nickname from *verdín* 'light green', a diminutive of *verde* (see VERDE).

GIVEN NAMES Spanish 24%. *Jose* (9), *Juan* (6), *Ramon* (4), *Angel* (3), *Luis* (3), *Ruben* (3), *Azael* (2), *Fernando* (2), *Fidel* (2), *Francisco* (2), *Guillermo* (2), *Javier* (2).

Verdon (355) **1.** French: habitational name from a place so named, for example in Dordogne, Gironde, and Marne. **2.** French and English: variant of VERDUN.

FOREBEARS A Verdon, also written Verdun, from the Aunis region of France was documented in Quebec City in 1663.

GIVEN NAMES French 6%. *Lucien*, *Marcel*, *Pierre*, *Renaud*, *Sylvie*.

Verdone (198) Italian: from an augmentative of VERDE.

GIVEN NAMES Italian 20%. *Angelo* (5), *Marco* (2), *Salvatore* (2), *Agostino*, *Carlo*, *Carmine*, *Francesco*, *Gaetano*, *Giuseppe*.

Verdoorn (151) Dutch: variant of **Verdoren**, a habitational name for someone from any of various places in Belgium and the Netherlands named (ten) Doorn, or a topographic name for someone who lived by a thorn hedge or thorn bush, Middle Dutch *do(o)rne*.

GIVEN NAMES Dutch 5%. *Cornie*, *Dirk*.

Verducci (105) Italian: from a diminutive of VERDI (see VERDE).

GIVEN NAMES Italian 22%. *Angelo*, *Nicola*, *Pasco*, *Rocco*, *Vittorio*.

Verdugo (642) **1.** Spanish and Portuguese: from *verdugo*, which has a variety of meanings, ranging from 'switch', 'whip' to 'tyrant', 'hangman', some or all of which may have contributed to the surname. **2.** Galician: habitational name from O Verdugo, a town in Pontevedra province, Galicia.

GIVEN NAMES Spanish 38%. *Jose* (12), *Manuel* (6), *Miguel* (6), *Ruben* (6), *Alberto* (4), *Ernesto* (4), *Francisco* (4), *Gonzalo* (4), *Guadalupe* (4), *Juan* (4), *Raul* (4), *Alfonso* (3).

Verduin (162) French: variant of VERDUN.

Verdun (244) French and English (of Norman origin): habitational name from any of various places in France called Verdun. The place name is probably of Gaulish origin, deriving from *ver(n)* 'alder' + *dūn* 'hill', 'fortress'. Some early bearers of the name certainly came from a place of this name in La Manche, others possibly from one in Eure.

Verduzco (484) Spanish: possibly from *verdusco* 'dark green', hence a nickname for someone who habitually wore dark green clothing.

GIVEN NAMES Spanish 53%. *Jose* (17), *Carlos* (10), *Juan* (8), *Jesus* (6), *Luis* (5), *Miguel* (5), *Pedro* (5), *Guadalupe* (4), *Manuel* (4), *Rafael* (4), *Ramon* (4), *Raul* (4).

Vereb (209) Hungarian (**Veréb**): from *veréb* 'sparrow', hence a nickname for someone thought to resemble the bird.

Vereen (808) Dutch: unexplained.

Veres (497) Hungarian: nickname for someone with red hair or a ruddy complexion, from *veres*, an old form of *vörös* 'red'.

GIVEN NAMES Hungarian 7%. *Imre* (3), *Arpad* (2), *Geza* (2), *Jozsef* (2), *Aranka*, *Csaba*, *Gabor*, *Karoly*, *Sandor*.

Verga (272) Italian and Greek (**Vergas**): metonymic occupational name for a shepherd, from *verga* 'stick', 'cane', 'shepherd's crook'.

GIVEN NAMES Italian 17%. *Vito* (4), *Gaetano* (2), *Sal* (2), *Albertina*, *Aldo*, *Antonino*, *Carlo*, *Enrico*, *Ignazio*, *Nino*, *Salvatore*.

Vergara (1418) Basque: Castilianized variant of Basque **Bergara**, a habitational name from places so called (earlier *Virgara*) in the provinces of Gipuzkoa and Navarre. The place name is of uncertain derivation; the second element is *gara* 'hill', 'height', 'eminence', but the first has not been satisfactorily identified.

GIVEN NAMES Spanish 50%. *Jose* (34), *Luis* (17), *Juan* (16), *Carlos* (14), *Jorge* (14), *Mario* (12), *Francisco* (11), *Fernando* (10), *Manuel* (10), *Miguel* (9), *Eduardo* (7), *Ernesto* (7); *Antonio* (11), *Marco* (4), *Heriberto* (3), *Filomena* (2), *Romeo* (2), *Angelo*, *Carmela*, *Cesario*, *Dario*, *Delio*, *Fausto*, *Federico*.

Verge (269) **1.** English (Kent and London): from Old French *verge* 'half-acre', hence a status name for the owner of that amount of land. **2.** Catalan (**Vergé**): variant of **Verger**, topographic name from Catalan *verger* 'orchard' (Latin *viridiarium*) **3.** Catalan: possibly also a nickname from *verge* 'maiden' (Latin *virgo* 'maiden').

Verges (187) Occitan (**Vergès**) and Catalan (**Vergés**): from the plural of Catalan *verger* and Occitan *vergèr* (or also *vergièr*) 'orchard', topographic name for someone who lived near an orchard or garden, or occupational name for someone who was employed in one (see VERGE 2 and VERDIER 2).

GIVEN NAMES Spanish 8%; French 4%. *Raul* (2), *Carmelita, Gilberto, Jorge, Jose, Juanita, Lourdes, Nieves, Rafael, Ricardo, Vidal*; *Emile*.

Vergin (147) English: variant spelling of VIRGIN.

GIVEN NAMES German 8%. *Hans, Kurt, Otto, Reinhold, Ute*.

Verhaeghe (138) Dutch: variant of VERHAGEN.

GIVEN NAMES French 7%. *Marcel* (2), *Franck*.

Verhage (254) Dutch: variant of VERHAGEN.

Verhagen (408) Dutch: reduced form of **van der Hagen**, a habitational name for someone from places named Haag, Hage, or Ter Hagen in Belgium and the Netherlands.

Verhalen (136) Dutch: unexplained; probably a respelling of **Verhallen**, a reduced form of **Van der Hallen**, a habitational name for someone from any of numerous places named ter Halle ('at the hall').

Verhelst (152) Dutch: reduced form of **van der Elst**, a topographic name for someone who lived by an alder, Middle Dutch *(h)e(e)lst*, or a habitational name for someone from any of various places called Elst.

GIVEN NAMES German 6%. *Kurt* (2), *Wolfgang*.

Verhey (289) Dutch: variant of VANDERHEYDEN.

GIVEN NAMES Dutch 5%. *Cornelis, Cornie, Dirk, Gerrit, Herm, Marinus*.

Verheyen (177) Dutch: variant of VANDERHEYDEN.

Verhoef (151) Dutch: variant of VERHOFF.

GIVEN NAMES Dutch 7%; German 4%. *Gerrit, Hendrik, Pieter, Willem*; *Kurt*.

Ver Hoeven (286) Dutch: reduced form of **van der Hoven**, a variant of **Van der Hoef** (see VANDERHOOF).

GIVEN NAMES German 6%; Dutch 5%. *Rudi* (2), *Erwin, Hans, Johannes, Kurt*; *Marten* (2), *Dirk, Gert, Michiel, Wim*.

Verhoff (260) Dutch and North German (Rhineland): reduced form of **Van der Hoef** (see VANDERHOOF).

Verhulst (290) Dutch: reduced form of **van der Hulst**, a topographic name for someone who lived by a holly bush or grove, Middle Dutch *hulst* 'holly', or a habitational name from any of various places in Belgium and the Netherlands named with this word.

Verissimo (107) Portuguese: literally 'most true', but the reasons for its adoption as a surname are unexplained.

GIVEN NAMES Spanish 20%; Portuguese 16%. *Jose* (5), *Manuel* (5), *Aguinaldo, Armando, Carlos, Fernando, Jorge, Luis, Silvino*; *Joao, Margarida*.

Verity (424) English (Yorkshire): nickname for a truthful person, or perhaps rather for someone who was in the habit of insisting repeatedly on the truth of the stories he told, from Middle English *verite* 'truth(ful-

ness)' (Old French *verité*). The surname may sometimes have been acquired by someone who had acted the part of the personified quality of Truth in a mystery play or pageant.

Verkamp (144) Dutch: reduced form of VANDERKAMP.

Verkler (130) French (Lorraine, Switzerland): probably of German origin but unexplained.

Verkuilen (201) Dutch and Belgian: reduced form of **van der Kuylen**, a topographic name for someone who lived by a pit or hole, or a habitational name for someone from Kuil in East Flanders or Kuilen in Limburg.

Verlander (158) Probably an altered spelling of Dutch **Verlende**, itself a reduced form of **van der Lende**, a variant of VANDERLINDE.

GIVEN NAMES French 4%. *Andre, Leonie*.

Verley (219) 1. English: variant of VARLEY. 2. Dutch: reduced form of **van der Leye**, a topographic name for someone living near the river Leie. 3. French: habitational name from a place called Verlée in Liège province, Belgium.

Verma (607) Indian: variant of VARMA.

GIVEN NAMES Indian 91%. *Anil* (13), *Vijay* (11), *Arun* (8), *Ajay* (7), *Krishna* (7), *Raj* (7), *Rajesh* (7), *Rakesh* (7), *Ravi* (7), *Sanjay* (7), *Ashok* (6), *Peppi* (6).

Vermeer (436) Dutch: reduced form of VANDERMEER.

Vermeersch (129) Dutch: from an adjectival variant of VERMEER.

GIVEN NAME French 8%. *Andre*.

Vermeire (117) Altered spelling of Dutch VERMEER.

Vermette (415) German: variant of METTE.

GIVEN NAMES French 16%. *Armand* (3), *Emile* (3), *Andre* (2), *Lucien* (2), *Marcel* (2), *Michel* (2), *Normand* (2), *Alphonse, Benoit, Chantel, Donat, Jean Pierre*.

Vermeulen (706) Dutch and Belgian: reduced form of VANDERMEULEN, a topographic name for someone who lived at a mill.

GIVEN NAMES Dutch 4%. *Dirk* (2), *Frans* (2), *Gerrit, Hendrik, Leendert, Michiel, Mieke, Pieter*.

Vermillion (1986) Americanized form of Dutch or Belgian VERMEULEN.

FOREBEARS This name was already well established in NC and WV in the 18th century, but its history is unclear.

Vermilya (179) Variant of VERMILLION.

Vermilyea (329) Variant of VERMILLION.

Verna (481) Italian: probably a habitational name from any of various places called Verna; otherwise, a shortened form of **Averna** (unexplained) or a variant of BERNA.

GIVEN NAMES Italian 22%; French 6%. *Mario* (8), *Carmine* (2), *Gennaro* (2), *Antonio, Camillo, Carlo, Carmela, Domenic, Duilio, Emilio, Enrico, Giovanni, Luigi*;

Tito, Tulio; *Armand, Dominique, Gilberte, Lucien, Marie Claire, Monique, Pierre, Yves*.

Verne (176) 1. English: see FERN. 2. French: topographic name for someone who lived near a grove of alders, French *verne*, a word of Gaulish origin.

GIVEN NAMES French 6%. *Henri* (2), *Mimose*.

Verner (1018) 1. Czech or other Slavic respelling of German WERNER. 2. Scottish: of uncertain origin, probably a variant of WARNER.

Vernet (110) 1. Catalan and Occitan: topographic name from *vernet* 'plantation or forest of alders'. 2. Catalan: habitational name from any of the places named Vernet, especially a town in El Conflent district, in northern Catalonia.

GIVEN NAMES French 20%; Spanish 6%. *Yves* (2), *Andre, Herard, Julien, Lucien, Marcel, Raymonde, Wilner*; *Guillermo* (2), *Andres, Lourde, Mario, Nestor, Roberto*.

Vernetti (111) Italian: habitational name from any of various places in Piedmont called Vernetti or Vernetto.

Verney (122) English: variant of VARNEY.

Verni (115) Italian: unexplained; possibly a habitational name from a place named Verni or Vernio, in Tuscany and elsewhere.

GIVEN NAMES Italian 33%. *Gaetano* (3), *Saverio* (3), *Vito* (2), *Francesco, Leonardo, Luca, Luigi, Marco*.

Vernick (202) American spelling of Slovenian **Vernik** (eastern Slovenia), of unexplained origin.

Vernier (465) French: 1. topographic name for someone who lived near an alder tree. 2. hypercorrected form of *Varnier*, the form of WARNER found in eastern France.

FOREBEARS A Vernier, also called Gourville, from the Angoumois region of France is documented in Quebec City in 1721.

GIVEN NAMES French 4%. *Armand, Emile, Jean Michel, Lucien*.

Verno (168) Italian: unexplained; possibly related to VERNA or **Malinverno** meaning 'bad winter'.

GIVEN NAMES Italian 8%. *Angelo, Carmine, Domenic, Donato*.

Vernon (6172) 1. English (of Norman origin): habitational name from Vernon in Eure, France, named from the Gaulish element *ver(n)* 'alder' + the Gallo-Roman locative suffix *-o* (genitive *-ōnis*). 2. French: habitational name from the same place as in 1 or from any of numerous other places in France with the same name and etymology.

Vernor (159) Scottish: of uncertain origin; possibly a habitational name from Vernours in Midlothian, although it seems more likely that this place name is derived from the family name. A branch of this family was established in Ireland in the 17th century.

Vero (120) 1. Italian: nickname from *vero* 'real', 'true' (from Latin *verus*). 2. Italian: possibly from a variant of the Germanic

personal name *Bero*, related to *bera* 'bear'. **3.** Romanian: unexplained. **4.** Hungarian (**Verő**): from *ver* 'hit', 'strike', hence an occupational name probably for a smith or someone who worked with hammer.
GIVEN NAMES Italian 17%; Romanian 4%. *Cosmo* (2), *Fedele, Francesco, Giuseppina, Rinaldo, Salvatore*; *Radu* (2).

Veron (164) **1.** French (**Véron**): nickname for someone with bi-colored eyes, from Latin *varius* 'diverse', 'varying'. **2.** Spanish (**Verón**): unexplained.
GIVEN NAMES French 8%; Spanish 4%. *Oneil* (2), *Desire, Gaston, Michel*; *Ana Maria, Diego, Jorge, Juan, Juan Manuel, Manuel, Raul.*

Verona (185) Italian: habitational name from the city or regional name from the province of Verona in northeastern Italy, Latin *Verona*. The place was an important settlement long before its capture by the Romans in 89 BC; its name is of uncertain origin.

Veronesi (129) Italian: habitational name for someone from VERONA, from an adjectival form of the place name.
GIVEN NAMES Italian 20%. *Aldo* (3), *Angelo* (2), *Agostino, Dante, Geno, Guido, Pietro, Rocco.*

Verplank (121) **1.** Dutch: reduced form of **van der Planken**, a topographic name for someone who lived near a foot bridge, from Middle Dutch *plan(c)ke* 'plank', 'board', or a habitational name for someone from a place named with this word, as for example Ter Planken in Lampernisse, West Flanders. **2.** Altered form, under Dutch influence of the French Huguenot name BLANCK or **Blanque** ('the white one').
FOREBEARS Abraham Verplanck came to New Amsterdam from the Netherlands in about 1635. Gulian Crommein Verplank (1786–1870), a NY legislator was the grandson of the CT statesmen and jurist William Samuel Johnston (1727–1819).

Verran (129) Cornish: reduced form of **Treverran**, a habitational name from Treverran in the parish of Tywardreath, so called from Cornish *tre* 'homestead', 'settlement' + a second element of unknown original form and meaning. Alternatively it may derive from Veryan near Tregony. This latter place name is a shortened version of *Saint Veryan*, itself the result of a misinterpretation of the form *Symphorianus* recorded from 1278 onwards. The church there was dedicated to a certain St. Symphorianus, probably the 2nd-century martyr of Autun revered in France.

Verrastro (167) Italian: of uncertain derivation; possibly from a derivative of *verro* 'boar'.
GIVEN NAMES Italian 26%. *Salvatore* (4), *Canio* (2), *Rocco* (2), *Sal* (2), *Angelo, Donato, Pasquale, Vita, Vito.*

Verret (685) French: from a diminutive of *verre* (see VERRIER).
FOREBEARS A Verret or Verrette, also called

LAVERDURE, from the Saintonge region of France is documented in Charlesbourg, Quebec in 1667. The Verret families of LA trace their foundation to one Michel Joseph Verret, who was born in Canada and was in LA by 1724.
GIVEN NAMES French 7%. *Emile* (2), *Yves* (2), *Antoine, Camille, Collette, Eusebe, Laurent, Maryse, Monique, Raoul, Solange.*

Verrett (434) Variant of French VERRET.

Verrette (198) French: variant of VERRET.
GIVEN NAMES French 10%. *Adrien, Alcee, Anite, Emile, Emilien, Jean-Louis, Rosaire.*

Verrico (130) Italian: unexplained.
GIVEN NAMES Italian 14%. *Aldo, Angelo, Canio, Cosmo, Salvatore.*

Verrier (295) English (of Norman origin) and French: occupational name for a maker of glass objects, Old French *verrie(o)r* (from *verre, voir(r)e* 'glass', Latin *vitrum*).
GIVEN NAMES French 12%. *Monique* (3), *Briand, Fernand, Georges, Jean-Paul, Lucien, Napoleon, Origene, Philippe, Priscille, Viateur.*

Verrill (508) Northeastern English: unexplained.

Verrilli (177) Italian: from a diminutive of **Verri**, a nickname from Calabrian *verre, verru* 'boar'.
GIVEN NAMES Italian 14%. *Rocco* (2), *Salvatore* (2), *Raffaela, Rocchina.*

Verrone (118) Italian: probably a nickname from an augmentative form of *verro* 'boar'.
GIVEN NAMES Italian 13%; French 7%; Jewish 5%. *Angelo* (2), *Enrico.*

Verry (173) English: nickname from Old French *verai* 'true'.
FOREBEARS The widow Bridget Very settled with her children in Salem, MA, in about 1634. She had many prominent descendants, including the poet Jones Very (1813–1880).

Versace (149) Southern Italian (Sicily): from the Greek personal name *Barsakios*, Latin *Bersacius*, probably of Arabic origin.
GIVEN NAMES Italian 28%. *Rocco* (3), *Salvatore* (3), *Antonio* (2), *Gaetano* (2), *Carmela, Carmelo, Viviana.*

Versaw (111) Altered form of Dutch **Versauw**, a habitational name from any of various places named Zuew, Zauw, or Sauw, from Middle Dutch *souw* 'ditch', 'channel', 'canal'.

Verschoor (104) Dutch: reduced form of **Van der Schoor**, a topographic name for someone who lived by a *schoor*, a piece of silted up land suitable for reclamation.
GIVEN NAMES Dutch 4%. *Adriaan, Frans.*

Verser (190) German: perhaps a habitational name for someone from Versen near Meppen on the Ems river.

Versluis (176) Dutch: reduced form of VANDERSLUIS.
GIVEN NAMES Dutch 4%. *Adriaan, Frans, Marinus.*

Versteeg (435) Dutch: topographic name for someone who lived by a gangway, foot-

way, or narrow bridge, Middle Dutch *steg(h)e*.
GIVEN NAMES Dutch 5%. *Dirk* (3), *Henk* (2), *Adriaan, Hendrik, Kees.*

Versteegh (110) Dutch: variant of VERSTEEG.

Verstegen (145) Dutch: variant of VERSTEEG.

Verstraete (219) Dutch and German: reduced form of **van der Straete**, a topographic name for someone who lived by a roadway, or a habitational name for someone from any of various places named with this word.
GIVEN NAMES French 7%. *Andre, Florent, Marcel.*

Vert (177) English and Scottish (of Norman origin): habitational name from any of numerous places named in France named Vert or Le Vert.

Vertefeuille (101) French: unexplained. Ostensibly meaning 'green leaf', this is probably an altered form of some other, unidentified name.
GIVEN NAMES French 10%. *Emilien, Laurent.*

Vertin (154) Origin unidentified: probably a spelling variant of **Vertein**, from the Low German number 'fourteen', a nickname for a tax or service obligation.

Vertrees (290) Altered spelling of Dutch **Vertryce**, a metronymic from a short form of the French female personal name *Béatrice*.

Vertucci (169) Italian: possibly a variant of BERTUCCI.
GIVEN NAMES Italian 9%. *Cono, Domenic, Gennaro, Umberto.*

Vertz (202) Partly Americanized spelling of German **Würtz** (see WURTZ).

Verucchi (45) Italian (Emilia-Romagna and Tuscany): habitational name for someone from Verucchio in Emilia-Romagna or Verrucchio in Forlì.
GIVEN NAMES Italian 13%. *Angelo, Dario, Salvo.*

Verville (451) French: variant of **Vervelle**, which Morlet derives from a word denoting the metal keeper or ring through which a bolt is secured.
GIVEN NAMES French 9%. *Alain* (2), *Andre* (2), *Herve* (2), *Armand, Emile, Gabrielle, Jean-Noel, Normand, Rolande, Yvon.*

Vervoort (124) Dutch: reduced form of VANDERVOORT.

Verwey (150) Dutch: variant of VANDERWEIDE.
GIVEN NAMES Dutch 6%. *Bastian, Marinus, Pieter.*

Vescio (230) Italian: unexplained. In Italy the surname is most frequent in Calabria, specifically in Lamezia Verme in Catanzaro province.
GIVEN NAMES Italian 12%. *Angelo* (2), *Antonio* (2), *Carmela, Ettore, Pasquale, Serafino, Vito.*

Vesco (157) Italian: from *vesco* 'bishop', a north-central variant of *vescovo* (see

VESCOVI), denoting someone in the service of a bishop or alternatively a nickname for a pompous or pious person. In the form **Veskos** this is also found as a Greek family name.

Vescovi (142) Italian: patronymic from *vescovo* 'bishop', a derivative of Greek *episkopos* 'bishop', literally 'overseer'.
GIVEN NAMES Italian 8%. *Dante* (2), *Geno*, *Leno*, *Paolo*.

Vesel (161) **1.** Slovenian: nickname for a cheerful person, from the adjective *vesel* 'merry', 'cheerful'. **2.** Czech: variant of VESELY.

Veselka (205) Czech: **1.** nickname for a cheerful person, from a noun derivative of *veselý* 'cheerful' (see VESELÝ). **2.** from *veselka* 'marriage', an ironic nickname for someone who wanted to marry but could not find a bride.
GIVEN NAME German 4%. *Otto* (2).

Vesely (878) Czech and Slovak (**Veselý**) and Jewish (from central and eastern Europe): nickname for a cheerful person, from Czech and eastern Slavic *veselý* 'merry', 'cheerful'.

Vesey (478) English: variant of VEAZEY.

Vespa (304) Italian: nickname from *vespa* 'wasp'. In parts of Italy and France this was also a nickname for a gravedigger.
GIVEN NAMES Italian 12%. *Nicola* (2), *Carmine*, *Donato*, *Ennio*, *Gennaro*, *Marcello*, *Remo*, *Sal*, *Silvio*.

Vesper (452) German: **1.** nickname from Latin *vesper* '6 o'clock in the evening', 'evening time', originally the second to last canonical hour. **2.** habitational name from a place so called on the Ruhr river.

Vesperman (104) German (**Vespermann**): from Middle High German, Middle Low German *vesper*, originally denoting the penultimate canonical hour; later 'between meals' + *man* 'man'; the reason for its adoption as a surname is unclear.

Vess (755) Probably a respelling of German WESS.

Vessel (185) **1.** Variant of Slovenian VESEL or Czech VESELY. **2.** Variant of English VESSELL.
GIVEN NAMES French 4%. *Jeanpaul*, *Monique*.

Vessell (221) English: metonymic occupational name for a maker or seller of household vessels, from Middle English *vessele*, from Old French *vessel(e)* 'vessell'.
GIVEN NAMES French 5%. *Andre*, *Monique*, *Valdor*.

Vessels (550) Probably an altered form of VESSELL.

Vessey (263) English (of Norman origin): habitational name from a place in Manche, France, so named from the Gallo-Roman personal name *Vessius* or *Vettius* (of uncertain origin) + the local suffix *-acum*.

Vest (4005) **1.** German: variant of FEST. **2.** Probably an altered spelling of WEST.

Vestal (2180) English, of French (Huguenot) origin: altered form of French **Vassal**,

status name for a medieval retainer (see VASSELL).

Vester (488) **1.** German: variant of FEST. **2.** Danish: topographic name for someone who lived to the west of a settlement or who had arrived from the west, from *vest* 'west' (see WESTER). **3.** Slovenian (north central Slovenia): either from a reduced form of the personal name SILVESTER, or from the German surname WESTER.

Vetere (264) Italian: nickname from Latin *vetus*, *veteris* 'old', 'aged'.
GIVEN NAMES Italian 12%. *Alfonse* (3), *Carmine*, *Luigi*, *Nino*, *Salvator*, *Salvatore*.

Veteto (230) Origin unidentified. This is a predominantly southern name, found chiefly in TX, AR, and TN.

Vetrano (494) Southern Italian (mainly Sicily): nickname from Latin *veteranus* 'old man', 'veteran'.
GIVEN NAMES Italian 18%. *Antonino* (3), *Angelo* (2), *Carlo* (2), *Carmine* (2), *Pasquale* (2), *Salvatore* (2), *Aniello*, *Antonio*, *Calogero*, *Francesco*, *Gennaro*, *Gino*.

Vetro (123) Southern Italian (mainly Sicily): probably from a derivative of Latin *vetus*, *veteris* 'old'. Compare VETERE.
GIVEN NAMES Italian 20%. *Salvatore* (3), *Rocco* (2), *Angelo*, *Antonio*, *Armonda*, *Vincenzo*.

Vetrone (123) Italian: unexplained.
GIVEN NAMES Spanish 4%. *Fernando* (2), *Rito* (2).

Vetsch (378) Swiss German: probably an altered spelling of WETSCH.
GIVEN NAMES German 5%. *Kurt* (3), *Niklaus* (2).

Vette (149) German: nickname from an old word *fad* 'man'. Compare VATH.
GIVEN NAMES German 5%. *Heinz*, *Kurt*.

Vettel (162) German (Rhineland): variant of VETTE.

Vetter (3479) German: nickname from Middle High German *veter(e)* 'uncle', 'nephew'. The word is from Old High German *fetiro* (a derivative of *fater* 'father'), which was used more generally to denote various male relatives; the meaning of modern German *Vetter* is 'cousin'.
GIVEN NAMES German 4%. *Kurt* (4), *Hans* (3), *Mathias* (3), *Otto* (3), *Erwin* (2), *Gerhard* (2), *Wendelin* (2), *Balzer*, *Dieter*, *Ernst*, *Ewald*, *Hannelore*.

Vetters (112) German: from the possessive form of VETTER.

Vettraino (124) Italian: unexplained; possibly related to VETRANO.
GIVEN NAMES Italian 25%; Spanish 4%. *Antonio* (7), *Benedetto* (2), *Domenico* (2), *Angelo*, *Carlo*, *Domenic*, *Luigi*, *Marino*, *Riccardo*; *Pepe*, *Ricardo*.

Veum (103) Norwegian: habitational name from farmsteads in Sogn and Telemark named from Old Norse *viðr* 'wood', 'tree', or elsewhere from *viðr* 'wide' + *heimr* 'homestead', 'farmstead'.
GIVEN NAME Scandinavian 8%. *Erik*.

Veurink (110) Dutch: unexplained.

GIVEN NAMES Dutch 8%. *Gerrit* (2), *Gradus* (2), *Marinus*.

Veverka (358) Czech: nickname meaning 'squirrel', applied either to someone thought to resemble a squirrel, in particular someone with red hair. European squirrels were red, until displaced by their imported gray American cousins.

Vey (243) **1.** Irish (eastern Ulster): reduced form of **McVey**, an Anglicized form of Gaelic **Mac an Bheathadh**, a patronymic from the personal name *Mac an Bheathadh* meaning 'son of life'. Compare VAHEY. **2.** Dutch (**de Vey**): from *Vei* 'playful' 'luxuriant', 'sensual'. **3.** German: metronymic from a short form of the personal name *Sophie*.
GIVEN NAMES German 5%. *Kurt*, *Lieselotte*, *Otto*.

Vezina (579) Southern French: topographic name from an Occitan equivalent of *voisinage* 'communal holdings', perhaps, or a literal 'neighbor'.
FOREBEARS A Vezina, also documented as *Voisinat*, from the Aunis region of France is recorded in L'Ange Gardien, Quebec, in 1667.
GIVEN NAMES French 17%. *Andre* (5), *Armand* (3), *Gaston* (3), *Marcel* (3), *Normand* (3), *Herve* (2), *Luc* (2), *Pierre* (2), *Alban*, *Clovis*, *Emile*, *Germain*.

Via (1701) **1.** French (Huguenot): variant of **Viau** (see VIAL). **2.** Southern Italian: from a short form of a personal name or surname ending with *-via*, for example BELLAVIA. **3.** Southern Italian: from a variant of *Bia*, a personal name of Greek origin, a calque of Latin *Vita* 'life'.

Vial (362) English, French, and Italian (Venetia): from a personal name derived from the Latin personal name *Vitalis* (see VITALE). The name became common in England after the Norman Conquest both in its learned form *Vitalis* and in the northern French form *Viel*.
GIVEN NAMES French 5%. *Armand* (2), *Emile*, *Jacques*, *Veronique*.

Viale (124) Italian: from a personal name derived from the Latin personal name *Vitalis* (see VITALE).
GIVEN NAMES French 7%; Spanish 7%; Italian 5%. *Aime*, *Lucien*, *Philippe*; *Enrique* (2), *Emilio*, *Jorge*, *Marina*, *Tiberio*; *Alessandro*, *Angelo*, *Antonio*.

Viall (323) Variant of VIAL.

Vialpando (335) Hispanic (NM): apparently a habitational name, possibly from Villapando in Zamora province, Spain.
GIVEN NAMES Spanish 12%. *Eloy* (2), *Jose* (2), *Manuel* (2), *Marcelo* (2), *Ruben* (2), *Adelmo*, *Andres*, *Benito*, *Elva*, *Felipe*, *Lazaro*, *Mario*.

Vian (220) Italian (Venetia): variant of VIANO.

Viana (255) Portuguese, Galician, and Spanish: habitational name from any of the places in Spain and Portugal called Viana.

GIVEN NAMES Spanish 36%; Portuguese 18%. *Jose* (17), *Fernando* (5), *Manuel* (5), *Carlos* (4), *Luis* (4), *Jorge* (3), *Francisco* (2), *Roberto* (2), *Ana*, *Angelina*, *Armindo*, *Arnaldo*; *Joaquim*, *Manoel*, *Marcio*; *Antonio* (4), *Elvio*, *Ercole*, *Leonardo*, *Marco*, *Quintino*, *Silvio*.

Viands (130) Origin unidentified.

Viani (152) Italian: patronymic or plural form of VIANO.
GIVEN NAMES Italian 10%. *Angelo* (2), *Dante*, *Dino*, *Enrico*.

Viano (175) Italian: **1.** from the personal name, a short form of *Viviano* (Latin *Vivianus*, a derivative of *vivus* 'living', 'alive'). **2.** occasionally a habitational name from any of the places so named, for example in Como and Reggio nell'Emilia.
GIVEN NAMES Italian 5%. *Angelo*, *Dante*, *Giancarlo*.

Viar (446) Variant of VIER.

Viars (352) Variant of VIRES.

Viator (784) Variant of VIETOR.
GIVEN NAMES French 6%. *Etienne* (2), *Aldes*, *Fernand*, *Leonce*, *Monique*, *Octave*, *Pierre*, *Raywood*, *Ulysse*.

Viau (494) **1.** French: variant of VIAL. **2.** German (Silesia): habitational name from a place named Viau near Liegnitz.
FOREBEARS A Viau from Brittany is documented in Montreal in 1665, with the secondary surname LESPERANCE.
GIVEN NAMES French 13%. *Marcel* (2), *Pierre* (2), *Albertine*, *Andre*, *Armand*, *Edouard*, *Francois*, *Gaston*, *Gilles*, *Gisele*, *Jean Marie*, *Jean-Paul*.

Vibbert (304) Respelling of VIBERT.

Vibert (128) French and English: from a variant of the personal name *Guibert*.

Vicari (557) Italian: patronymic or plural form of VICARIO.
GIVEN NAMES Italian 22%. *Salvatore* (9), *Sal* (6), *Angelo* (5), *Vito* (3), *Carlo* (2), *Luciano* (2), *Pietro* (2), *Rocco* (2), *Agostino*, *Antonio*, *Crispino*, *Domenico*.

Vicario (264) Italian and Spanish: status name for an official who carried out duties on behalf of an absentee office-holder or who deputized for a magistrate. In ecclesiastical usage, the word became specialized to denote a priest who carried out duties in a parish on behalf of a bishop. See VICKER.
GIVEN NAMES Spanish 11%; Italian 8%. *Juan* (3), *Manuel* (3), *Abelardo*, *Adali*, *Armida*, *Belen*, *Camila*, *Lourdes*, *Marcelo*, *Mario*, *Mercedes*, *Renato*; *Dante* (2), *Domenic* (2), *Leonardo*.

Vicars (485) English: variant spelling of VICKERS.

Vicary (135) English: variant spelling of VICKERY.

Vice (1851) English (Midlands): probably a variant spelling of VISE.

Vicencio (178) Spanish: from the personal name *Vincencio*, Latin *Vincentius* (see VINCENT).

GIVEN NAMES Spanish 41%. *Jose* (3), *Anamaria* (2), *Javier* (2), *Jesus* (2), *Jorge* (2), *Juan* (2), *Manuel* (2), *Mario* (2), *Adriana*, *Alfonso*, *Amado*, *Baudelio*.

Vicente (731) Spanish and Portuguese: from the personal name *Vicente*, Spanish and Portuguese equivalent of VINCENT.
GIVEN NAMES Spanish 46%; Portuguese 11%. *Jose* (27), *Manuel* (10), *Armando* (8), *Carlos* (8), *Juan* (6), *Antonio* (5), *Sergio* (5), *Enrique* (4), *Jorge* (4), *Luis* (4), *Mario* (4), *Adriano* (3), *Esteban* (3); *Joaquim* (3), *Paulo* (3), *Aderito*, *Anabela*, *Joao*, *Martinho*, *Vasco*.

Vicini (133) Italian: from a patronymic or plural form of VICINO.
GIVEN NAMES Italian 16%; French 4%. *Antonio* (3), *Reno* (2), *Antonietta*, *Baldo*, *Gino*, *Mario*, *Rocco*, *Stefano*, *Tulio*; *Alphonse*, *Armand*.

Vicino (144) Italian: from a short form of the personal name *B(u)onvicino*, literally 'good neighbor', an omen name.
GIVEN NAMES Italian 12%. *Rocco* (2), *Giuseppe*, *Lorenzo*, *Salvatore*.

Vick (5417) **1.** English: nickname or metonymic occupational name, from Anglo-Norman French *l'eveske* 'the bishop', which was wrongly taken for *le vesk*. This in turn became *Vesk*, and later *Veck* or *Vick*. **2.** North German: variant of FICK.

Vicker (164) **1.** English: occupational name for a parish priest, Middle English *vica(i)re*, *vikere* (Old French *vicaire*, from Latin *vicarius* 'substitute', 'deputy'). The word was originally used to denote someone who carried out pastoral duties on behalf of the absentee holder of a benefice. It became a regular word for a parish priest because in practice most benefice holders were absentees. **2.** Irish and Scottish: reduced form of McVICKER, an Anglicized form of Gaelic **Mac áBhiocair** (Scottish) or **Mac an Bhiocaire** (Irish) 'son of the vicar'.
GIVEN NAMES German 4%. *Erna*, *Kurt*.

Vickerman (373) English: occupational name for the servant of a vicar (see VICKER).

Vickers (7740) English: patronymic for the son of a vicar or, perhaps in most cases, an occupational name for the servant of a vicar (see VICKER). In many cases it may represent an elliptical form of a topographic name. Compare PARSONS.

Vickery (3496) English: variant of VICKER, from the Middle English variant *vicarie*, derived directly from Latin *vicarius*. The English surname is also established in Cork, Ireland.

Vicknair (751) Of French origin: unexplained; perhaps an altered form of **Vicaire**, a nickname from Old French *vicaire* denoting a member of the clergy deputizing for or assisting a bishop (from Latin *vicarius* 'substitute').

GIVEN NAMES French 7%. *Antoine*, *Celestin*, *Clovis*, *Etienne*, *Marcel*, *Mederic*, *Michel*, *Monique*, *Nemour*, *Normand*, *Odette*, *Patrice*.

Vickrey (574) English: variant spelling of VICKERY.

Vickroy (285) English: variant spelling of VICKERY.

Vicks (198) Probably an altered form of VICK; the addition of a final *-s* is characteristic of many North American names.

Victor (2994) French: from a medieval personal name (Latin *Victor* meaning 'conqueror', an agent derivative of *vincere* 'to win'). Early Christians often bore this name in reference to Christ's victory over sin and death, and there are a large number of saints so called. Some of the principal ones, who contributed to the popularity of the personal name in the Middle Ages, are a 2nd-century pope, a 3rd-century Mauritanian martyr, and a 5th-century bishop of Cologne.
GIVEN NAMES French 6%. *Jacques* (5), *Remi* (3), *Dominique* (2), *Lucien* (2), *Marcel* (2), *Michel* (2), *Pierre* (2), *Renel* (2), *Yves* (2), *Andre*, *Antoine*, *Armand*.

Victoria (662) **1.** Spanish: from a medieval personal name, Spanish form of VICTOR. **2.** French: from the personal name *Victoria* (female form of VICTOR), which was popularized by a 3rd-century martyr so named.
GIVEN NAMES Spanish 34%. *Jose* (11), *Carlos* (8), *Luis* (6), *Manuel* (6), *Francisco* (4), *Jorge* (4), *Rafael* (4), *Aurelio* (3), *Guillermo* (3), *Juan* (3), *Ricardo* (3), *Roberto* (3).

Victorian (228) French (New Orleans): Americanized form of French **Victorien**, from a personal name that is a derivative of Latin *Victorinus*, a pet form of VICTOR.
GIVEN NAMES French 4%. *Andre*, *Pierre*.

Victorine (120) French: variant of **Victorien** (see VICTORIAN).

Victorino (277) Spanish: from the personal name *Victorino* (from Latin *Victorinus*).
GIVEN NAMES Spanish 27%. *Manuel* (5), *Jose* (4), *Armando* (2), *Enrique* (2), *Miguel* (2), *Agustin*, *Alejo*, *Arcelia*, *Benancio*, *Blanca*, *Carlos*, *Constancio*.

Victory (731) **1.** Irish: adopted, by mistranslation, as an English equivalent of Gaelic **Mac an Anabadha** 'son of the unripe one', translated as if from *Mac na Buadha* 'son of victory'. This name is also found Anglicized as **McNaboe**. **2.** Americanized form of French **Victoire**, a derivative of VICTOR.

Vida (467) **1.** Spanish and Portuguese: either a nickname from *vida* 'life' or possibly from the male personal name *Vida(s)*. **2.** Northern Italian: variant of VITA 1. **3.** Italian: from the female personal name *Vida*. **4.** Hungarian: patronymic form of the ecclesiastical name *Vid*, a derivative of Latin *Vitus* (from *vita* 'life').

GIVEN NAMES Spanish 4%. *Otilio* (2), *Adolfo, Alfonso, Brigido, Carlos, Celedonio, Erlinda, Imelda, Jose, Manuel, Roberto.*

Vidal (2267) Spanish, Catalan, Portuguese, northern Italian, French, and English: from the personal name, a derivative of the Latin personal name *Vitalis* (see VITALE).

GIVEN NAMES Spanish 39%; Portuguese 9%. *Jose* (47), *Juan* (29), *Luis* (21), *Manuel* (20), *Carlos* (18), *Francisco* (15), *Jorge* (15), *Rafael* (14), *Raul* (13), *Pedro* (12), *Ramon* (12), *Mario* (11); *Joaquim* (2), *Duarte.*

Vidales (260) **1.** Spanish: from a vernacular form of the Latin personal name *Vitalis* (see VITALE) or alternatively a habitational name from Los Vidales in Murcia province, meaning 'the Vidals', i.e. 'home of the Vidal family'. **2.** Greek (**Vidalis**): from the Greek form of the Latin personal name *Vitalis* (see VITALE, VITALIS).

GIVEN NAMES Spanish 50%. *Jose* (6), *Manuel* (5), *Fernando* (4), *Pedro* (4), *Carlos* (3), *Felipe* (3), *Francisco* (3), *Jorge* (3), *Rosalinda* (3), *Ruben* (3), *Domingo* (2), *Guillermo* (2).

Vidas (151) Lithuanian: from a short form of the personal name *Vidmantas.*

GIVEN NAMES Latvian 5%. *Arturs, Ilmars, Ojars.*

Vidaurri (270) Basque: Castilianized variant of Basque **Bidaurre**, a habitational name from Bidaurre in Navarre, or a topographic name from Basque *bide* 'road', 'way' + *aurre* 'opposite'.

GIVEN NAMES Spanish 37%. *Jose* (5), *Ruben* (5), *Roberto* (4), *Manuel* (3), *Mario* (3), *Efrain* (2), *Francisco* (2), *Gerardo* (2), *Jesus* (2), *Juan* (2), *Ramiro* (2), *Raul* (2); *Antonio* (2), *Lucio* (2), *Carlo, Donato, Fausto, Leonardo, Sisto.*

Vides (169) Spanish: from the plural of Spanish *vid* 'grapevine', topographic name for somebody who lived by a vineyard, or occupational name for somebody who worked on it.

GIVEN NAMES Spanish 55%. *Carlos* (6), *Jose* (4), *Ana* (2), *Felipe* (2), *Francisco* (2), *Manuel* (2), *Rafael* (2), *Salvador* (2), *Alberto, Alejandro, Alfredo, Amalia*; *Marco* (2).

Vidler (104) English: variant spelling of FIDDLER.

Vidmar (405) Slovenian, Croatian (northern Croatia), Czech, and Slovak: topographic name for someone who lived on land or property belonging to the church, from a Slavic form of German WIDMER 1.

Vidovich (148) Croatian and Serbian (**Vidović**): patronymic from the personal name *Vid*, a derivative of Latin *Vitus* (see VITO).

GIVEN NAMES Italian 4%. *Marco, Romano.*

Vidrine (1124) LA form of French **Vedrine**, a habitational name a place so named in Creuse or La Védrinne in Lozère.

FOREBEARS The LA families Vidrine are said to trace their origins from one Jean Baptiste Lapaise de Vedrine, who had moved from IL to LA sometime between 1763 and 1765.

GIVEN NAMES French 5%. *Alcee, Dominique, Eloi, Elrick, Emile, Jacques, Leandre, Numa, Philippe, Pierre, Raywood, Sylvie.*

Vidrio (111) Spanish: from Spanish *vidrio* 'glass', probably metonymycal occupational name for a glassmaker.

GIVEN NAMES Spanish 62%. *Carlos* (3), *Beatriz* (2), *Francisco* (2), *Jesus* (2), *Jose* (2), *Ramon* (2), *Roberto* (2), *Alfredo, Ancelmo, Conception, Enrique, Ernesto.*

Vieau (236) Altered spelling of French **Viaux** or **Viaud**, from the personal name *Vial*, a vernacular form of Latin *Vitalis* (see VITALE).

Viebrock (185) North German (Bremen area): topographic name from the name of a swampy region on the Weser near Bremen, from *vi* 'swamp'.

GIVEN NAMES German 5%. *Joerg, Lorenz, Mathias.*

Viegas (153) Portuguese: patronymic composed of Semitic *ben* 'son' + the medieval personal name *Ega(s)*, probably of Visigothic origin. Compare Spanish VENEGAS. This name is also found in western India, where it was taken by Portuguese colonists.

GIVEN NAMES Spanish 22%; Portuguese 12%; Italian 7%. *Antonio* (6), *Jose* (6), *Carlos* (2), *Alfredo, Ana, Arlindo, Aurelio, Fernanda, Fernando, Francisco, Haroldo, Joaquin, Julio; Joao, Martinho.*

Viehman (126) Respelling of German VIEHMANN.

Viehmann (119) German: occupational name for a cattle dealer, from Middle High German *vihe* 'cattle' + *man* 'man'.

Viehweg (100) German: variant of FIEBIG.

GIVEN NAMES German 6%. *Erwin, Kurt.*

Vieira (2515) Galician and Portuguese: **1.** religious byname from Portuguese *vieria* 'scallop' (Late Latin *veneria*, a derivative of the name of *Venus*; the goddess was often depicted riding on a scallop). The scallop was a symbol of the pilgrim who had been to the shrine of Santiago de Compostela. **2.** habitational name from any of numerous minor places called Vieiria.

GIVEN NAMES Spanish 20%; Portuguese 13%. *Manuel* (76), *Jose* (54), *Carlos* (23), *Fernando* (11), *Mario* (9), *Francisco* (8), *Americo* (6), *Armando* (6), *Luis* (5), *Jaime* (4), *Jorge* (4), *Alvaro* (3); *Joao* (13), *Joaquim* (6), *Paulo* (4), *Conceicao* (2), *Henrique* (2), *Manoel* (2), *Albano, Aloisio, Batista, Catarina, Duarte, Ilidio.*

Viel (317) **1.** English and French: variant spelling of VIAL. **2.** German: topographic name from *vil*, an old word for a swamp or bog. **3.** Italian (Venetia): from a pet form of VITO.

GIVEN NAMES French 9%. *Gilles* (2), *Jean-Pierre* (2), *Pascal* (2), *Dominique, Jacques, Raoul, Rejean.*

Viele (362) **1.** Dutch: nickname from Old French *vieil, viel* 'old'. **2.** variant of German VIEL. **3.** Southern Italian (Apulia): unexplained.

FOREBEARS Cornelis Volkertszen Viele was an innkeeper in New Amsterdam as early as 1639. Aerout Cornelissen Viele (b. 1640 in New Amsterdam) was a skilled Indian interpreter and negotiator.

Vielma (135) Spanish and Galician: variant of **Viedma**, a habitational name from any of the places called with Viedma.

GIVEN NAMES Spanish 51%. *Jose* (8), *Jesus* (3), *Alfonso* (2), *Felipe* (2), *Francisco* (2), *Guadalupe* (2), *Juan* (2), *Manuel* (2), *Marcos* (2), *Mario* (2), *Raul* (2), *Alberto.*

Vien (234) **1.** Vietnamese: unexplained. **2.** French and Dutch: from a reduced form of the personal name *Vivien*, a vernacular form of the Latin name *Vivianus*.

GIVEN NAMES Vietnamese 27%; French 9%. *Anh* (2), *Kieu* (2), *Long* (2), *Minh* (2), *Mylinh* (2), *Phat* (2), *Phung* (2), *Thi* (2), *Bach, Bien Van, Dao, Dien; Cecile, Celine, Christophe, Fernand, Jacques, Laurent, Marcel, Philippe; Hua.*

Vienneau (194) Variant of French **Viennot**, a habitational name for someone from the city of Vienne; or perhaps a pet name derived from the personal name *Vivien*.

GIVEN NAMES French 4%. *Armand, Phillippe.*

Viens (636) Canadian variant of French VIEN.

GIVEN NAMES French 13%. *Andre* (4), *Lucien* (3), *Armand* (2), *Gilles* (2), *Normand* (2), *Antoine, Camille, Fernand, Fernande, Ferrier, Gabrielle, Ghislain.*

Vier (127) English: of uncertain origin. It has been suggested that this may be an Anglicized form of French (Huguenot) VIA. Another possibility is that it is a reduced form of DEVERE.

FOREBEARS William Vier was transported to VA in 1675.

Viera (1471) Galician and Spanish: possibly a variant spelling of VIEIRA. In Spain the surname is found mainly in the island of Tenerife.

GIVEN NAMES Spanish 36%. *Jose* (25), *Manuel* (16), *Juan* (11), *Luis* (11), *Mario* (11), *Carlos* (10), *Jesus* (10), *Jorge* (9), *Francisco* (8), *Miguel* (8), *Raul* (7), *Ricardo* (7).

Viereck (174) German: **1.** nickname from Middle High German *vierecke* 'burly', 'coarse'. **2.** habitational name for someone from a place called Viereck near Pasewalk.

GIVEN NAMES German 4%. *Fritz, Kurt.*

Viergutz (119) North German: of uncertain origin; possibly a habitational name from a Slavic place name; possibly a variant spelling of **Vielguth**, a habitational name from a place so named near Frankfurt an der Oder.

GIVEN NAMES German 7%. *Klaus, Udo, Uwe.*

Viering (100) **1.** German: topographic name from *vir*, an obsolete word meaning 'swamp'. **2.** In some cases, probably a respelling of North German **Wiering**, from the personal name *Wigrich* (see WIERENGA).

Vierling (455) German: from Middle High German *vierlinc* 'one-fourth of a measure', hence a status name or nickname for someone who had an annual tax liability of this amount.

Viernes (154) **1.** Spanish: possibly from Spanish *viernes* 'Friday'. **2.** Occitan (**Viernés**) and Catalan (**Viernès**): variants of Occitan **Biarnés** and Catalan **Biarnès** or **Bearnès** (alongside the variants **Biernés**, **Biernès**), a regional name for somebody from the region of Biarn (Catalan Bearn), in southern France.
GIVEN NAMES Spanish 42%. *Ricardo* (3), *Ernesto* (2), *Jesus* (2), *Virgilio* (2), *Amante*, *Anacleto*, *Andres*, *Artemio*, *Avelino*, *Bartolome*, *Carlos*, *Carmelito*; *Antonio* (3), *Lorenzo*, *Quirino*, *Romeo*.

Vierra (1127) Origin unidentified; possibly a respelling of Spanish VIERA.
GIVEN NAMES Spanish 4%. *Manuel* (21), *Jose* (2), *Alda*, *Carolina*, *Elena*, *Joaquin*, *Juanita*, *Leopoldo*, *Luis*, *Maria Luisa*, *Osvaldo*, *Pedro*.

Viers (817) Variant of VIRES.

Viertel (174) German: from Middle High German *viertel*, a land measure, hence a status name or nickname for a farmer who owned that much land.
GIVEN NAMES German 10%. *Ernst*, *Hans*, *Kurt*, *Otto*.

Vieth (595) German: variant of **Veith** (see VEIT).

Vietmeier (121) German: distinguishing name for a tenant farmer (MEYER), who was a tenant of or owed some obligation to an estate or monastery named for St. *Veith* (see VEIT).
GIVEN NAME German 5%. *Kurt*.

Vietor (228) German or Dutch: Humanistic name, a Latinized form of any of the various German and Dutch names for a cooper, Latin *vietor*.
GIVEN NAMES German 6%. *Ernst*, *Klaus*, *Wilhelm*.

Vietri (103) Southern Italian: habitational name from Vietri sul Mare in Salerno or Vietri di Potenza in Potenza.
GIVEN NAMES Italian 21%. *Carmine*, *Enrico*, *Gesualdo*, *Pasquale*.

Viets (382) North German: patronymic from **Viet**, North German form of VEIT.

Vietti (151) Italian: from a plural pet form of the personal name *Vio*, a northern variant of VITO.

Vieux (124) French: from *vieux* 'old', probably applied as a nickname but also as a distinguishing epithet for the older of two bearers of the same personal name.
GIVEN NAMES French 24%. *Edouard* (2), *Jacques* (2), *Pierre* (2), *Colette*, *Fernande*, *Georges*, *Germaine*, *Manon*.

Vieweg (114) German: respelling of German **Viehweg**, a topographic name for someone who lived by a drover's path, from Middle High German *vihe*, *vehe* 'cattle' + *weg* 'way', 'path'.
GIVEN NAME German 6%. *Otto*.

Vieyra (275) Portuguese and Galician: variant spelling of VIEIRA.
GIVEN NAMES Spanish 41%. *Roberto* (5), *Jose* (4), *Juan* (4), *Carlos* (3), *Alberto* (2), *Alejandro* (2), *Fernando* (2), *Francisco* (2), *Gustavo* (2), *Miguel* (2), *Pablo* (2), *Adriana*; *Antonio*, *Clementina*, *Primo*.

Vig (384) **1.** Indian (Panjab): Hindu (Khatri) and Sikh name of unknown meaning. **2.** Hungarian: from Hungarian *víg* 'happy', 'cheerful', hence a nickname for a funny or happy-go-lucky person. **3.** Norwegian and Danish: variant spelling of VIK.
GIVEN NAMES Indian 13%. *Ramesh* (2), *Sushil* (2), *Anjana*, *Ashok*, *Deepak*, *Madan*, *Naresh*, *Pradeep*, *Praveen*, *Rajneesh*, *Rakesh*, *Renuka*.

Vigeant (301) French: habitational name from Vigéant in Vienne, so named from Latin *vicanus*, a derivative of *vicus* 'village'.
GIVEN NAMES French 12%. *Armand* (3), *Alphonse*, *Camille*, *Fernand*, *Gilles*, *Jacques*, *Marcel*, *Mederic*, *Normand*.

Vigen (199) Norwegian and Danish: variant spelling of VIKEN.
GIVEN NAMES Scandinavian 5%. *Erik*, *Hartvig*, *Nils*.

Viger (265) French: occupational name for a legal official, Old French *voyer* (Latin *vicarius*).
FOREBEARS A Viger from Normandy, France, is documented in Montreal in 1666. The form **Vigor** is also found, with a secondary surname **Galop**.
GIVEN NAMES French 11%. *Marcel* (2), *Andre*, *Laurent*, *Laurette*, *Lucienne*, *Marcell*, *Normand*, *Pierre*, *Simonne*.

Viggiani (100) Southern Italian: habitational name from Viggiano in Potenza.
GIVEN NAMES Italian 11%; Spanish 5%. *Armando*, *Eduardo*, *Nino*; *Luis*, *Mercedes*.

Viggiano (518) Southern Italian: habitational name for someone from Viggiano in Potenza province, so named from the Latin personal name *Vibius* or *Vivius*.
GIVEN NAMES Italian 15%. *Angelo* (4), *Rocco* (3), *Sal* (3), *Salvatore* (3), *Carmine* (2), *Carlo*, *Carmela*, *Cosimo*, *Dante*, *Donato*, *Nunzio*, *Stefano*.

Vigh (116) Hungarian (**Vígh**): variant of VIG.
GIVEN NAMES Hungarian 15%. *Sandor* (3), *Istvan* (2), *Ildiko*, *Laszlo*, *Tibor*.

Vigil (5468) Castilianized form of Asturian-Leonese **Vixil**, a habitational name from a place named Vixil in the district of Consejo de Siero, Asturies.
GIVEN NAMES Spanish 20%. *Jose* (64), *Manuel* (38), *Juan* (34), *Carlos* (27), *Orlando* (17), *Alfonso* (14), *Luis* (13), *Ramon* (13), *Arturo* (11), *Francisco* (11), *Eloy* (10), *Ricardo* (9).

Vigilante (221) Southern Italian: occupational name from *vigilante* 'guard', 'watchman'.
GIVEN NAMES Italian 21%. *Angelo*, *Antonio*, *Carmella*, *Domenico*, *Elvira*, *Guerrino*, *Lazaro*, *Vivianna*.

Viglione (315) Italian: possibly from **Viglio**, a reduced form of a Germanic personal name such as GUGLIELMO, with the addition of the Germanic suffix *-one*.
GIVEN NAMES Italian 17%. *Carlo* (2), *Gaetano* (2), *Guido* (2), *Salvatore* (2), *Antonietta*, *Antonio*, *Cosimo*, *Domenic*, *Francesca*, *Italo*, *Luca*, *Rocco*.

Vigliotti (384) Italian: from a pet form of the personal name *Viglio* (see VIGLIONE).
GIVEN NAMES Italian 20%; French 5%. *Antonio* (4), *Angelo* (3), *Antimo* (2), *Luigi* (2), *Biagio*, *Clemente*, *Francesco*, *Gennaro*, *Pasquale*, *Rocco*, *Sabato*, *Sal*; *Alphonse* (4), *Camille*.

Vigna (323) Italian: topographic name from *vigna* 'vine', or a habitational name from any of various places named with this word.
GIVEN NAMES Italian 21%. *Franco* (2), *Vito* (2), *Alfonso*, *Angelo*, *Antonio*, *Carmine*, *Elvira*, *Emilia*, *Fedele*, *Gerardo*, *Giovanni*, *Guillermo*, *Luciano*, *Mario*, *Modesto*, *Pietro*, *Rocco*, *Salvatore*.

Vignali (123) Italian (Sicily): variant of **Vignale**, a topographic name from *vignale* 'vineyard' (Latin *vinealis*, genitive of *vinea* 'vine'), or a habitational name from any of various places named with this word, in particular Vignale Monferrato in Alessandria province.
GIVEN NAMES Italian 16%. *Aldo*, *Alessio*, *Dante*, *Dario*, *Geno*, *Salvatore*, *Valdo*.

Vigneau (205) French: **1.** habitational name for someone from a place so named in Vienne, or from places in Aube and Indre called Les Vigneaux. **2.** status name for the owner of a vineyard, from a derivative of Occitan *vinhier* 'vineyard'. This is found as a Huguenot name.
GIVEN NAMES French 7%. *Andre* (2), *Adrien*.

Vigneault (293) French: **1.** habitational name for someone from Vignaud in Creuse, Les Vignauds, in Haute-Vienne or Vignaux in Hautes Alpes. **2.** variant of VIGNEAU.
GIVEN NAMES French 15%. *Alain*, *Andre*, *Armand*, *Benoit*, *Jeremie*, *Laurent*, *Luc*, *Lucien*, *Marcel*, *Michel*, *Normand*, *Yvan*.

Vignes (102) **1.** French: from Old French *vignes* 'vines', a metonymic occupational name for the owner of a vineyard or a vine dresser, or a habitational name from any of several places named with this word. **2.** Norwegian (also **Vigness**): habitational name from a farm name in Ryfylke; the first element is of uncertain origin, the second element is *nes* 'headland', 'promontory'.
GIVEN NAME French 5%. *Jacques*.

Vignola (326) Italian: habitational name from a place named Vignola. There is a sizeable place of this name in Modena province, but the surname is more likely to have arisen from a minor place elsewhere, since in Emilia-Romangna, as in Lombardy, Tuscany, and various other regions, surnames from place names ending in a vowel are invariably regularized to *-i*.
GIVEN NAMES Italian 15%. *Rocco* (6), *Carmine* (2), *Angelo, Annunziato, Gaeton, Nicola, Stefano.*

Vignone (129) Italian: from an augmentative of VIGNA.
GIVEN NAMES Italian 13%; French 7%. *Giustina* (2), *Angelo, Carmela, Dino*; *Prosper* (2), *Achille.*

Vigo (195) Galician: habitational name from any of the numerous places named Vigo, notably the one in Pontevedra province, Galicia, named from *vigo* 'village' (from Latin *vicus*).
GIVEN NAMES Spanish 32%. *Luis* (4), *Andres* (2), *Angel* (2), *Carlos* (2), *Catalina* (2), *Ladislao* (2), *Lazaro* (2), *Miguel* (2), *Rafael* (2), *Ramon* (2), *Alberto, Angeles*; *Silvio* (2), *Francesco, Lorenzo, Umberto.*

Vigorito (171) **1.** Southern Italian: from the personal name *Vigorito*, an omen name from *vigore* 'vigor' or Old Italian *vigorire* 'to draw strength' (physical, moral, or intellectual), which was particularly popular in the medieval period. **2.** Spanish: of uncertain derivation; possibly related to *vigor* 'vigor', 'strength'.
GIVEN NAMES Italian 19%. *Mario* (3), *Aida* (2), *Angelo* (2), *Antonio* (2), *Benito* (2), *Vito* (2), *Aniello, Carmine, Ettore, Guido, Renato.*

Vigue (528) Probably a respelling of French **Viguié**, an occupational name for a court official, from Latin *vicarius* 'substitute'.
GIVEN NAME French 5%. *Damien.*

Vigus (145) Cornish: unexplained.

Vik (401) **1.** Norwegian and Swedish: habitational name from any of numerous farmsteads all over Norway and Sweden, so named with Old Norse *vík* 'small bay', 'inlet'. In Swedish it may also be a topographic or ornamental name. **2.** Czech: from a short form of the personal name *Viktor* (see VICTOR).
GIVEN NAMES Scandinavian 14%. *Alf, Erik, Lars, Lennart, Nels, Nils.*

Viken (158) Norwegian: variant of VIK 1, from the definite singular form.

Vila (509) **1.** Catalan: topographic name for somebody who lived in a *vila*, which in Catalonia denoted a small town or village with certain privileges not common for villages, or habitational name from any of the places called La Vila or Vila. This name is one of the most common names in Catalonia. **2.** Catalan: habitational name from (**Vilá**): variant of VILAR. **3.** in some cases possibly also Galician and Portuguese: habitational name from any of the

numerous places in Galicia named Vila, from *vila* '(outlying) farmstead', '(dependent) settlement'.
GIVEN NAMES Spanish 45%. *Jose* (22), *Carlos* (9), *Luis* (9), *Juan* (8), *Manuel* (8), *Jorge* (6), *Francisco* (5), *Pedro* (4), *Ramon* (4), *Eduardo* (3), *Efrain* (3), *Enrique* (3).

Vilar (144) **1.** Catalan, Galician and Portuguese: habitational name from any of the numerous places called Vilar, which are named from *vilar* 'village' or '(outlying) farmstead', a derivative of *vila* '(outlying) farmstead', '(dependent) settlement'; or topographic name for someone who lived in a *vilar*. **2.** Slovenian (central Slovenia): from an agent noun derived from *vile* 'hayfork', 'dungfork', either a nickname or perhaps an occupational name for a fork maker. It may also be a variant spelling of the surname **Vilhar**, a medieval derivative of the German personal name WILHELM.
GIVEN NAMES Spanish 36%; Portuguese 17%. *Jose* (6), *Manuel* (6), *Miguel* (3), *Alfonso* (2), *Jorge* (2), *Juan* (2), *Alberto, Alfredo, Angel, Bienvenido, Carlos, Concepcion*; *Aderito, Joaquim.*

Vilardi (222) Southern Italian: patronymic or plural form of VILARDO.
GIVEN NAMES Italian 17%. *Carmine* (2), *Salvatore* (2), *Amedeo, Angelo, Antonio, Cira, Dante, Santo, Vito.*

Vilardo (208) Italian: variant of BELARDO.
GIVEN NAMES Italian 9%. *Angelo, Antonio, Carmine, Dante, Domenica, Gilda, Sal.*

Vilas (150) **1.** Catalan (**Vilàs**): variant of **Vilars**, from the plural of *vilar*, a derivative of *vila* 'farmstead', 'village'. **2.** Catalan: in some cases also variant of **Viles**, from the plural form of *vila* '(outlying) farmstead', '(dependent) settlement' (see VILA 1). **3.** in some cases also Galician: habitational name from any of the various places in Galicia named Vilas, from the plural of *vila* '(outlying) farmstead', '(dependent) settlement'. **4.** Czech: from a pet form of the personal name *Vilém*, Czech form of WILHELM (see WILLIAM).
GIVEN NAMES Spanish 11%. *Santiago* (3), *Manuel* (2), *Alfredo, Bernardino, Elena, Gerardo, Jacinta, Jose.*

Vilches (145) Spanish: habitational name from Vilches, a place in Jaén province.
GIVEN NAMES Spanish 43%. *Armando* (3), *Carlos* (3), *Francisco* (3), *Jorge* (3), *Juan* (3), *Luis* (3), *Consuelo* (2), *Jose* (2), *Miguel* (2), *Ricardo* (2), *Roberto* (2), *Adolfo.*

Vilchez (124) Spanish (**Vílchez**): variant of VILCHES.
GIVEN NAMES Spanish 52%. *Jose* (5), *Manuel* (3), *Blanca* (2), *Carlos* (2), *Cesar* (2), *Francisco* (2), *Juan* (2), *Luis* (2), *Mario* (2), *Miguel* (2), *Pablo* (2), *Raul* (2).

Vilchis (100) Spanish: probably variant of VILCHES.
GIVEN NAMES Spanish 57%. *Fernando* (5), *Jose* (3), *Rogelio* (3), *Carlos* (2), *Ernesto*

(2), *Jorge* (2), *Juan* (2), *Manuel* (2), *Mauricio* (2), *Salvador* (2), *Alvino, Angel.*

Vile (161) English: unexplained; possibly a variant spelling of VIAL. Compare VILES.

Viles (617) **1.** English: unexplained; possibly a variant spelling of **Vials**, a variant of VIAL. **2.** Hispanic: unexplained.

Vilhauer (221) German: variant of **Feilhauer**, an occupational name for a file maker, from Middle High German *vîle* 'file' (tool) + agent derivative of *houwen* 'to cut'.

Villa (5124) **1.** Asturian-Leonese and Spanish: habitational name from any of the places (mainly in Asturies) called Villa, from *villa* '(outlying) farmstead', '(dependent) settlement', or from any of the numerous places named with this word as the first element. **2.** Italian: topographic name for someone who lived in a village as opposed to an isolated farmhouse, or in a town as opposed to the countryside, from Latin *villa* 'country house', 'estate', later used to denote of a group of houses forming a settlement, and in some dialects to denote the most important area or center of a settlement or a habitational name from any of various places named with this word.
GIVEN NAMES Spanish 43%. *Jose* (119), *Juan* (66), *Manuel* (48), *Francisco* (39), *Jesus* (39), *Carlos* (37), *Luis* (28), *Mario* (27), *Miguel* (22), *Raul* (22), *Pedro* (20), *Ramon* (18); *Antonio* (36), *Lorenzo* (7), *Angelo* (5), *Dario* (4), *Federico* (4), *Luciano* (4), *Dante* (3), *Leonardo* (3), *Marco* (3), *Mauro* (3), *Salvatore* (3), *Vito* (3).

Villacis (136) Hispanic: unexplained.
GIVEN NAMES Spanish 45%. *Luis* (5), *Angel* (4), *Carlos* (3), *Jose* (3), *Efrain* (2), *Hermes* (2), *Mercedes* (2), *Alejandro, Alfredo, Bernardo, Blanca, Cesar*; *Angelo, Antonio, Giovanni.*

Villacorta (161) Asturian-Leonese and Spanish: habitational name from a place in Lléon province named Villacorta, from *villa* '(outlying) farmstead', '(dependent) settlement' + *corta* 'short'.
GIVEN NAMES Spanish 45%. *Miguel* (3), *Rodolfo* (3), *Cesar* (2), *Jose* (2), *Luis* (2), *Adelfo, Adriano, Alcira, Alfonso, Alicia, Amado, Amador.*

Villafana (255) Spanish (**Villafaña**): unexplained, but undoubtedly from a place name formed with *villa* '(outlying) farmstead', '(dependent) settlement'. This name could be related to **Villafañé** (see VILLAFANE).
GIVEN NAMES Spanish 55%. *Juan* (11), *Jose* (8), *Jesus* (5), *Alfredo* (3), *Fernando* (3), *Javier* (3), *Raul* (3), *Ana* (2), *Andres* (2), *Carlos* (2), *Cesar* (2), *Ernesto* (2).

Villafane (275) Spanish (**Villafañé**): habitational name from Villafañé, a place in Lléon province, named from *villa* 'farmstead', 'settlement' + an old personal name.
GIVEN NAMES Spanish 48%. *Jose* (12), *Carlos* (8), *Juan* (8), *Miguel* (3), *Angel* (2),

Eduardo (2), *Guillermo* (2), *Milagros* (2), *Sergio* (2), *Wilfredo* (2), *Adelina*, *Adiela*.

Villaflor (110) Spanish: habitational name from either of two places, in Ávila and Zamora provinces, named Villaflor, from *villa* 'farmstead', 'settlement' + *flor* 'flower'.

GIVEN NAMES Spanish 28%. *Jose* (4), *Amador*, *Apolonio*, *Ernesto*, *Joaquin*, *Luis*, *Marcelino*, *Patricio*, *Perlita*, *Petronilo*, *Purita*, *Tomas*.

Villafranca (151) Spanish: habitational name from one of various places called Villafranca, from Late Latin *villa* '(outlying) farmstead', '(dependent) settlement' + *franca* 'free' (see FRANK 2). The settlements were so named because they were exempt from certain feudal taxes or obligations, normally as a reward for some special service.

GIVEN NAMES Spanish 43%. *Jose* (5), *Fernando* (3), *Armando* (2), *Carlos* (2), *Evelia* (2), *Joaquin* (2), *Ninfa* (2), *Rafael* (2), *Timoteo* (2), *Adelina*, *Arnaldo*, *Baltasar*; *Mauro* (3), *Antonio*, *Dario*, *Luciano*, *Romeo*.

Villafuerte (256) Spanish: habitational name from Villafuerte, a place in Valladolid province, most probably named from *villa* '(outlying) farmstead', '(dependent) settlement' + the personal name *Fuertes* (rather than the adjective *fuerte* 'strong').

GIVEN NAMES Spanish 47%. *Jose* (5), *Manuel* (5), *Francisco* (4), *Alfonso* (3), *Carlos* (3), *Juan* (3), *Luis* (3), *Alberto* (2), *Consuelo* (2), *Ernesto* (2), *Guadalupe* (2), *Jaime* (2).

Villagomez (714) Spanish (**Villagómez**): habitational name from Villagómez la Nueva in Valladolid province, which is named from *villa* '(outlying) farmstead', '(dependent) settlement' + the personal name GOMEZ.

GIVEN NAMES Spanish 58%. *Jose* (25), *Jesus* (21), *Manuel* (14), *Carlos* (11), *Guadalupe* (10), *Juan* (8), *Raul* (8), *Armando* (6), *Francisco* (6), *Jaime* (6), *Salvador* (6), *Rafael* (5).

Villagran (299) Spanish (mainly southern; **Villagrán**): habitational name, apparently from a lost place called Villa Grande, meaning 'large farmstead or settlement'.

GIVEN NAMES Spanish 55%. *Juan* (9), *Jose* (6), *Carlos* (5), *Raul* (5), *Ruben* (5), *Armando* (4), *Fernando* (4), *Luis* (4), *Manuel* (4), *Mario* (3), *Blanca* (2), *Francisco* (2).

Villagrana (197) Spanish (mainly Latin America): apparently a habitational name from a place named with *villa* '(outlying) farmstead', '(dependent) settlement' + an unexplained second element.

GIVEN NAMES Spanish 58%. *Jesus* (5), *Juan* (4), *Jaime* (3), *Jose* (3), *Manuel* (3), *Refugio* (3), *Ruben* (3), *Santos* (3), *Agustin* (2), *Alfonso* (2), *Francisco* (2), *Ignacio* (2); *Antonio* (3), *Lorenzo* (3), *Fausto* (2), *Mauro*.

Villalba (441) Spanish: habitational name from any of the various places named Villalba, from *villa* '(outlying) farmstead', '(dependent) settlement' + *albo*, feminine *alba* 'white' (Latin *alba*).

GIVEN NAMES Spanish 50%. *Jose* (14), *Juan* (11), *Carlos* (6), *Enrique* (5), *Jorge* (5), *Julio* (5), *Manuel* (4), *Mario* (4), *Alicia* (3), *Angel* (3), *Arturo* (3), *Fernando* (3).

Villalobos (2762) Spanish: habitational name from Villalobos in Zamora province, named from *villa* '(outlying) farmstead', '(dependent) settlement' + *lobos*, plural of *lobo* 'wolf'.

GIVEN NAMES Spanish 54%. *Jose* (96), *Juan* (50), *Jesus* (44), *Luis* (32), *Carlos* (28), *Francisco* (25), *Manuel* (25), *Ruben* (24), *Javier* (19), *Rafael* (19), *Mario* (17), *Ramon* (17).

Villalon (267) Spanish (**Villalón**): habitational name from a place in Valladolid province called Villalón de Campos.

GIVEN NAMES Spanish 51%. *Carlos* (8), *Jose* (7), *Pedro* (6), *Alejandro* (3), *Juan* (3), *Marcos* (3), *Porfirio* (3), *Rolando* (3), *Andres* (2), *Augusto* (2), *Librado* (2), *Luis* (2).

Villalovos (106) Spanish: variant of VILLALOBOS.

GIVEN NAMES Spanish 39%; Italian 7%. *Jesus* (2), *Maurillo* (2), *Adolfo*, *Alfonso*, *Apolonia*, *Arcadio*, *Armando*, *Bernardo*, *Celso*, *Dionicio*, *Domingo*, *Ezequiel*; *Carmelo*, *Tarcisio*.

Villalpando (561) Spanish: habitational name from a place in Zamora province called Villalpando.

GIVEN NAMES Spanish 52%. *Jose* (16), *Juan* (8), *Manuel* (7), *Salvador* (7), *Jesus* (6), *Raul* (6), *Francisco* (5), *Guadalupe* (5), *Jose Luis* (5), *Luis* (5), *Mario* (5), *Miguel* (4).

Villalta (305) Spanish: habitational name from a place in Burgos province named Villalta, from *villa* '(outlying) farmstead', '(dependent) settlement' + *alto* 'high-(lying)'.

GIVEN NAMES Spanish 50%. *Jose* (13), *Manuel* (7), *Jorge* (6), *Mauricio* (5), *Francisco* (4), *Luis* (4), *Carlos* (3), *Fernando* (3), *Gregorio* (3), *Mario* (3), *Rafael* (3), *Ana* (2).

Villalva (201) Spanish: variant of VILLALBA.

GIVEN NAMES Spanish 45%. *Jose* (5), *Juan* (4), *Luis* (4), *Carlos* (2), *Mario* (2), *Ruben* (2), *Socorro* (2), *Alejandro*, *Alina*, *Anastacio*, *Andres*, *Aurelio*.

Villamar (132) Asturian-Leonese and Spanish: habitational name from any of the places called Villamar, from *villa* '(outlying) farmstead', '(dependent) settlement' + *mar* 'sea'.

GIVEN NAMES Spanish 45%. *Jose* (4), *Carlos* (3), *Fernando* (2), *Nilo* (2), *Adelina*, *Alberto*, *Alfredo*, *Ana*, *Arturo*, *Concepcion*, *Eduardo*, *Enrique*.

Villamil (205) Asturian-Leonese: habitational name from Villamil, a place in Asturies.

GIVEN NAMES Spanish 51%. *Jose* (6), *Carlos* (5), *Jorge* (4), *Angel* (3), *Fernando* (3), *Luis* (3), *Rodolfo* (3), *Enrique* (2), *Ernesto* (2), *Rafael* (2), *Adan*, *Adriana*.

Villamor (129) **1.** Spanish: habitational name from any of several places called Villamor (Burgos), from *villa* '(outlying) farmstead', '(dependent) settlement' + an unexplained second element. **2.** in some cases also, Castilianized form of Galician **Vilamor**, a habitational name from any of the towns so named in Lugo and A Coruña provinces, Galicia.

GIVEN NAMES Spanish 39%. *Anacleta* (2), *Ramon* (2), *Alfredo*, *Angel*, *Arnaldo*, *Bernardino*, *Blanca*, *Camilo*, *Chico*, *Eladia*, *Enrique*, *Eusebio*; *Antonio*, *Franco*, *Gilda*, *Romeo*, *Sal*, *Tolentino*.

Villani (924) Italian: patronymic from VILLANO.

GIVEN NAMES Italian 19%. *Angelo* (7), *Carmine* (5), *Luigi* (5), *Vito* (5), *Rocco* (4), *Salvatore* (4), *Gino* (3), *Aldo* (2), *Alessandro* (2), *Antonio* (2), *Dante* (2), *Domenic* (2).

Villano (726) Italian and occasionally Spanish: nickname for someone who lived in the country as opposed to a town, *villano* (Latin *villanus*).

GIVEN NAMES Italian 9%. *Pasquale* (3), *Rocco* (2), *Antonio*, *Caesar*, *Gennaro*, *Giovanna*, *Nunzi*, *Sal*, *Salvatore*, *Vito*.

Villanova (253) **1.** Italian: habitational name from any of the numerous places so called, from Latin *villa nova* 'new settlement', as for example Villanova del Battista (Avellino), Villanova Del Ghebbo and Villanova Marchesanda (Rovigo), Villanova di Camposampiero (Padua), Villanova d'Albenga (Savona). **2.** Spanish: Castilianized spelling of Catalan and Galician **Vilanova** (see VILLANEUVA). However, the lack of associated Spanish forenames indicates that this source has not contributed greatly to the American surname.

GIVEN NAMES Italian 5%. *Remo*, *Vito*.

Villanueva (5179) Spanish: **1.** habitational name from any of the numerous places named Villanueva, from Spanish *villa* '(outlying) farmstead', '(dependent) settlement' + *nueva* (feminine) 'new' (Latin *nova*). **2.** Castilianized spelling of Catalan and Galician **Vilanova**, a habitational name from a frequent place name, of the same derivation as 1 above.

GIVEN NAMES Spanish 48%. *Jose* (134), *Juan* (67), *Luis* (49), *Manuel* (46), *Carlos* (42), *Francisco* (38), *Jesus* (37), *Miguel* (31), *Raul* (28), *Pedro* (26), *Roberto* (23), *Ruben* (23).

Villar (727) **1.** Spanish: habitational name from any of numerous places named Villar, or in some cases a Castilianized spelling of the Catalan and Galician cognates VILAR.

2. English: variant of VILLERS, cognate with **3.** **3.** Southern French: topographic name from Late Latin *villare* 'outlying farm', 'dependent settlement', or a habitational name from any of various places named with this word.

GIVEN NAMES Spanish 45%. *Jose* (18), *Juan* (11), *Luis* (11), *Manuel* (10), *Carlos* (6), *Jorge* (6), *Angel* (5), *Arturo* (5), *Fernando* (5), *Eduardo* (4), *Enrique* (4), *Humberto* (4).

Villard (205) Altered form of German **Hilgard**, from the female personal name *Hildegard*, composed of the Germanic elements *hild* 'strife', 'battle' + *gard* 'fortress', 'stronghold'.

FOREBEARS Henry Villard (1835–1900), journalist and financier, came from Bavaria to North America in 1853, changing his name from Ferdinand Heinrich Hilgard and settling in IL.

GIVEN NAMES French 13%. *Philippe* (2), *Ambroise, Dumas, Marie Therese, Odette, Pierre, Raoul.*

Villareal (1203) Spanish: simplified spelling of VILLARREAL.

GIVEN NAMES Spanish 45%. *Jose* (23), *Manuel* (19), *Jesus* (12), *Juan* (12), *Luis* (7), *Ramiro* (7), *Ramon* (7), *Ruben* (7), *Guadalupe* (6), *Raul* (6), *Roberto* (6), *Armando* (5).

Villari (230) Southern Italian: topographic name from Latin *villarius* 'dweller in the settlement'.

GIVEN NAMES Italian 16%; French 5%. *Salvatore* (3), *Antonio* (2), *Rocco* (2), *Filippo, Guglielmo, Italia, Sal, Umberto; Aurel, Camille.*

Villarreal (7311) **1.** Spanish: habitational name from any of several places named Villar(r)eal, from Spanish *villa* '(outlying) farmstead', '(dependent) settlement' + *real* 'royal' (Latin *regalis*), as for example Villarreal de San Carlos in Cáceres. The places were so named from having some particular connection with the Crown. **2.** in some cases, variant of Catalan **Vila-real**, from the town named Vila-real in Castelló de la Plana province.

GIVEN NAMES Spanish 48%. *Jose* (170), *Juan* (101), *Jesus* (77), *Manuel* (74), *Carlos* (55), *Raul* (53), *Luis* (47), *Ruben* (47), *Guadalupe* (43), *Ricardo* (41), *Roberto* (40), *Armando* (36).

Villarroel (118) Spanish or Portuguese: unexplained. Compare VILLARRUEL.

GIVEN NAMES Spanish 54%. *Juan* (7), *Carlos* (6), *Miguel* (4), *Jaime* (3), *Jose* (3), *Julio* (3), *Armando* (2), *Fernando* (2), *Luis* (2), *Mario* (2), *Adela, Eduardo.*

Villarrubia (114) Spanish: habitational name from Villarrubia (Córdoba), Villarrubia de los Ojos (Ciudad Real), or Villarrubia de Santiago (Toledo), so named from *villar*, a derivative of *villa* '(outlying) farmstead', '(dependent) settlement' + *rubia* 'light red'.

GIVEN NAMES Spanish 9%. *Andres, Aurea, Jose, Luis, Manuel, Mario, Teresita, Wilfredo.*

Villarruel (114) Spanish or Portuguese: unexplained. Compare VILLARROEL.

GIVEN NAMES Spanish 49%; Italian 7%. *Luis* (5), *Francisco* (4), *Roberto* (3), *Alberto* (2), *Amalia* (2), *Jose* (2), *Ramon* (2), *Abelino, Alfredo, Angel, Armando, Efren; Dario, Filiberto, Lucio, Quirino.*

Villars (183) Southern French: habitational name from any of various places called Villars, from Late Latin *villare* 'outlying farm', 'dependent settlement'. Compare VILLERS.

GIVEN NAMES French 4%. *Andre, Henri.*

Villas (105) Spanish: from the plural of Latin *villa* '(outlying) farm', '(dependent) settlement' (see VILLA).

GIVEN NAMES Spanish 15%. *Nestor* (2), *Alejandro, Carmelita, Jorge, Julio, Luz, Manuel, Orlando, Rafaela, Roque.*

Villasana (235) Spanish: habitational name from Villasana de Mena, a place in Burgos province, named from *villa* '(outlying) farm', '(dependent) settlement' + possibly *sano* 'healthy'.

GIVEN NAMES Spanish 51%. *Jose* (8), *Jesus* (5), *Juan* (5), *Arturo* (3), *Francisco* (3), *Luis* (3), *Andres* (2), *Enrique* (2), *Guadalupe* (2), *Jorge* (2), *Manuel* (2), *Manuela* (2).

Villasenor (1111) Spanish (**Villaseñor**): habitational name, apparently a Castilianized spelling of Galician **Vilseñor**, from any of three places in Lugo province named Vilaseñor.

GIVEN NAMES Spanish 51%. *Jose* (30), *Jesus* (15), *Luis* (15), *Manuel* (13), *Francisco* (10), *Roberto* (9), *Alfonso* (8), *Guadalupe* (8), *Ramon* (8), *Salvador* (8), *Arturo* (7), *Jorge* (7).

Villatoro (519) Spanish: habitational name from either of two places, in Ávila and Burgos provinces, named Villatoro, from *villa* '(outlying) farm', '(dependent) settlement' + *toro* 'bull'.

GIVEN NAMES Spanish 55%. *Jose* (42), *Carlos* (8), *Juan* (8), *Mario* (6), *Pedro* (6), *Santos* (6), *Jorge* (5), *Julio* (5), *Angel* (4), *Manuel* (4), *Roberto* (4), *Blanca* (3).

Villaverde (167) Spanish: habitational name from any of the numerous places named Villaverde, from *villa* '(outlying) farm', '(dependent) settlement' + *verde* 'green', or a Castilianized spelling of the Galician cognate **Vilaverde**.

GIVEN NAMES Spanish 41%. *Carlos* (3), *Luis* (3), *Roberto* (3), *Albino* (2), *Ana* (2), *Felipe* (2), *Jose* (2), *Manuel* (2), *Miguel* (2), *Agustin, Angeles, Armando.*

Villavicencio (374) Spanish: habitational name from Villavicencio de los Caballeros, a place in Valladolid province, named from *villa* '(outlying) farm', '(dependent) settlement' + the personal name VICENCIO.

GIVEN NAMES Spanish 50%. *Jose* (7), *Luis* (7), *Miguel* (6), *Cesar* (5), *Jorge* (5), *Juan* (5), *Carlos* (4), *Armando* (3), *Fernando* (3), *Luisa* (3), *Ramon* (3), *Raul* (3).

Villeda (230) Spanish: unexplained. This name is commonly found in Mexico.

GIVEN NAMES Spanish 57%. *Jose* (8), *Roberto* (5), *Jose Luis* (3), *Carlos* (2), *Efrain* (2), *Francisco* (2), *Gilberto* (2), *Guillermo* (2), *Macario* (2), *Manuel* (2), *Marina* (2), *Mario* (2).

Villegas (3710) Spanish: habitational name from Villegas, a place in Burgos province.

GIVEN NAMES Spanish 51%. *Jose* (88), *Manuel* (47), *Jesus* (42), *Juan* (41), *Luis* (39), *Francisco* (32), *Carlos* (27), *Roberto* (26), *Jorge* (25), *Rafael* (25), *Pedro* (24), *Miguel* (20).

Villela (257) Portuguese and Spanish: habitational name, an old spelling of **Vilela**, from any of several places in Portugal and Spain so named, from a diminutive of *vila* '(outlying) farm', '(dependent) settlement'.

GIVEN NAMES Spanish 56%. *Jesus* (8), *Jose* (6), *Pedro* (5), *Francisco* (4), *Felipe* (3), *Javier* (3), *Juan* (3), *Raymundo* (3), *Alfonso* (2), *Eduardo* (2), *Geraldo* (2), *Jose Cruz* (2).

Villella (450) **1.** Italian: possibly from a diminutive of VILLA. **2.** Portuguese and Spanish: variant spelling of VILLELA.

GIVEN NAMES Italian 10%. *Gino* (2), *Caio, Domenico, Gennaro, Giuseppe, Giuseppina, Guido, Natale.*

Villemaire (118) Possibly a variant of French **Villemeyre**, a habitational name from a place so named in Puy-de-Dôme.

GIVEN NAMES French 14%. *Andre, Cecile, Jacques, Lucien, Pierre.*

Villemarette (105) French: unexplained; probably a habitational name from a lost or unidentified place.

GIVEN NAMES French 6%. *Andre, Pierre.*

Villena (110) Spanish: habitational name from Villena, a town in southeastern Spain.

GIVEN NAMES Spanish 47%. *Jose* (5), *Andres* (3), *Fernando* (3), *Luis* (2), *Nestor* (2), *Alfonso, Armando, Carlos, Carolina, Cesar, Dulce, Felipe.*

Villeneuve (627) French: habitational name from any of the numerous places called Villeneuve or Vilneuve, from *ville* 'settlement' + *neuve* 'new'. Most of the places so called were named when they were bestowed upon a new owner.

GIVEN NAMES French 15%. *Marcel* (3), *Andre* (2), *Fernand* (2), *Germain* (2), *Gilles* (2), *Michel* (2), *Pierre* (2), *Alain, Denys, Georges, Jean Pierre, Pascal.*

Villere (101) French: unexplained; perhaps a respelling of **Viller**, a habitational name from any of various places in northern France so named from Latin *villare* 'farmstead'.

GIVEN NAMES French 20%. *Andre* (2), *Henri, Jean-Paul, Monique, Pierre.*

Villers (370) English (of Norman origin) and northern French: habitational name from any of the numerous places in France named Viller(s) or Villier(s), from Late Latin *villare* 'outlying farm', 'dependent settlement'.
GIVEN NAMES French 4%. *Andre, Arsene, Philippe.*

Villescas (135) Spanish: probably a habitational name from a lost or unidentified place. The surname is rare in Spain, occurring mainly in Murcia, but frequent in Mexico.
GIVEN NAMES Spanish 41%. *Jose* (6), *Amado* (2), *Baudelio* (2), *Blanca* (2), *Felipe* (2), *Juan* (2), *Pedro* (2), *Ruben* (2), *Alberto, Albino, Alfonso, Alfredo.*

Villicana (145) probably Spanish (**Villicaña**): unexplained. This name is mainly found in Mexico, and less in present-day Spain.
GIVEN NAMES Spanish 57%. *Jesus* (4), *Salvador* (3), *Francisco* (2), *Javier* (2), *Jose* (2), *Rafael* (2), *Sergio* (2), *Adolfo, Aleyda, Angel, Armando, Arturo; Antonio* (2), *Eliseo, Heriberto.*

Villines (629) French: unexplained. This name is found mainly in AR.

Villone (133) Italian: possibly from an augmentative form of VILLA or alternatively a variant of BELLONE.
GIVEN NAMES Italian 15%. *Rocco* (4), *Carmela, Gasper.*

Villwock (248) North German: of unknown origin.
GIVEN NAMES German 4%. *Guenter, Kurt.*

Viloria (255) 1. Spanish: habitational name from any of the places called Viloria, for example in Valladolid and Burgos provinces. 2. Basque: Castilianized variant of Basque **Biloria**, a habitational name from either of the two towns in Araba and Navarre provinces named Biloria.
GIVEN NAMES Spanish 38%; Italian 9%. *Alberto* (3), *Amable* (3), *Jose* (3), *Alfredo* (2), *Angel* (2), *Artemio* (2), *Jaime* (2), *Juana* (2), *Manuel* (2), *Mariano* (2), *Adelfo, Bonifacio; Romeo* (2), *Antonio, Constantino, Dante, Duilio, Eligio, Enrico, Filomena, Jovencio.*

Vina (116) 1. Galician and Spanish (**Viña**): habitational name from any of numerous places (especially in Galicia and Asturies) named Viña, from *viña* 'vineyard'. 2. in some cases also Castilianized spelling of Catalan **Vinya**, of the same derivation.
GIVEN NAMES Spanish 43%. *Jose* (4), *Amado* (2), *Benito* (2), *Medardo* (2), *Pedro* (2), *Alberto, Alfredo, Ana, Candido, Carlos, Catalino, Cruz.*

Vinal (172) 1. English (Sussex, Essex, and Kent): unexplained. Reaney derives it from Vynall's Farm in Pebmarsh in Essex, but it seems more likely that the surname gave rise to the farm name. 2. Galician and Spanish (**Viñal**): habitational name from

any of six places in Galicia named Viñal, from a derivative of *viña* 'vineyard'. 3. in some cases also a Castilianized spelling of Catalan **Vinyal**, of the same derivation as Spanish **Viñal**.

Vinas (195) Galician and Spanish (**Viñas**): habitational name from any of numerous places named Vinñas (especially in Galicia) or Las Vinñas, from the plural of *viña* 'vineyard'.
GIVEN NAMES Spanish 46%. *Jose* (5), *Jaime* (4), *Carlos* (3), *Francisco* (3), *Luis* (3), *Ricardo* (3), *Enrique* (2), *Juan* (2), *Marcos* (2), *Mario* (2), *Abelardo, Aladino.*

Vince (612) 1. English (East Anglia): from a short form of the personal name VINCENT. 2. Hungarian: variant of VINCZE.

Vincelette (192) French: from a derivative of the personal name VINCENT.
GIVEN NAMES French 8%. *Aime, Alphonse, Fernand, Normand.*

Vincelli (111) Italian: from derivative of the personal name *Vince*, a short form of *Vincenzo, Vinciguerra*, etc.
GIVEN NAMES Italian 10%. *Angelo, Enrico, Vito.*

Vincent (18403) 1. English and French: from a medieval personal name (Latin *Vincentius*, a derivative of *vincens*, genitive *vincentis*, present participle of *vincere* 'to conquer'). The name was borne by a 3rd-century Spanish martyr widely venerated in the Middle Ages and by a 5th-century monk and writer of Lérins, as well as various other early saints. In eastern Europe the name became popular in honor of Wincenty Kadłubek (died 1223), a bishop of Kraków and an early chronicler. 2. Irish: the English surname has been established in the south of Ireland since the 17th century, and has also been adopted as an English equivalent of Gaelic **Mac Dhuibhinse** 'son of the dark man of the island'.

Vincenti (224) Italian: patronymic from the personal name *Vincente* (see VINCENT).
GIVEN NAMES Italian 14%. *Aldo* (2), *Angelo* (2), *Attilio* (2), *Carlo, Dante, Gino, Marco, Querino, Vito.*

Vincenzo (106) Italian: from the personal name *Vincenzo*, a cognate of *Vincente* (see VINCENT).
GIVEN NAMES Italian 17%. *Silvio* (2), *Angelo, Emilio, Fortunato, Mario.*

Vinci (879) Italian: 1. from a short form of a compound personal name formed with *vinci* (from Latin *vincere* 'to conquer') as the first element, as for example *Vinciguerra* or *Vinciprova*. 2. habitational name from a place so named in Firenze (Florence) province.
GIVEN NAMES Italian 15%. *Angelo* (8), *Salvatore* (4), *Sal* (3), *Carlo* (2), *Carmelo* (2), *Cosimo* (2), *Santo* (2), *Saverio* (2), *Antonino, Bartolomeo, Cristoforo, Dante.*

Vinciguerra (433) Southern Italian and French (Corsican): from the popular

medieval personal name *Vinciguerra*, an omen name composed of Latin *vincere* 'to conquer' + *guerra* 'war'.
GIVEN NAMES Italian 11%. *Salvatore* (3), *Carmela* (2), *Angelo, Clementina, Cosmo, Dino, Domenic, Donato, Marco, Nicola, Vito.*

Vincze (115) Hungarian and Jewish (from Hungary): from the personal name *Vince*, Hungarian form of VINCENT.
GIVEN NAMES Hungarian 26%; Jewish 6%. *Arpad* (3), *Laszlo* (3), *Aranka, Attila, Bela, Ildiko, Kalman, Lajos, Mihaly, Miklos, Sandor, Zsolt; Aron* (2), *Irina.*

Vine (880) 1. English: topographic name for someone who lived near a vineyard, or a metonymic occupational name for a vine dresser, from Middle English *vine* 'vine(yard)' (Old French *vi(g)ne*). Vine growing was formerly more common in England than it is now, and there are several minor places in southern England named from their vineyard, any of which may be partial sources of the surname. See also VINEYARD, WINGARD. 2. Spanish (**Viñe**): variant of **Viña** (see VINA).

Viner (492) 1. English: occupational name from Old French *vignour, vigneur, vigneaur*, Anglo-French *viner* 'wine-grower' (see also VINE). 2. Jewish (eastern Ashkenazic): variant of WIENER.
GIVEN NAMES Jewish 8%; Russian 4%. *Aron* (2), *Eran, Irina, Khaim, Molka, Mort, Shimon, Sima, Volf, Yakov, Zinaida; Leonid* (2), *Aleksandr, Boris, Dmitry, Lev, Lyubov, Vlad, Yefim, Yelena, Yevgenia.*

Vines (3184) English: variant of VINE.

Vinet (144) French: occupational name for a wine grower, from a diminutive of *vin*, a noun derivative of Old French *viner* 'to make wine'.
FOREBEARS A Vinet from the Saintonge region of France is documented in Montreal in 1666, with the secondary surname Larente. Other known secondary surnames include LALIBERTE, Préville, and Souligny.
GIVEN NAMES French 18%. *Numa* (2), *Pierre* (2), *Angelle, Antoine, Emile, Lucien, Marcel, Michel.*

Viney (383) English (of Norman origin): probably a habitational name from an unidentified place in northern France named with Late Latin *vinetum* 'vineyard', a derivative of Latin *vinea* 'vine'.

Vineyard (1488) 1. English: topographic name for someone who lived by a vineyard. Compare WINGARD. 2. Perhaps also a translation of a cognate in some other language, for example German WEINGARTEN.

Vinh (150) Vietnamese: unexplained.
GIVEN NAMES Vietnamese 78%. *Nguyen* (4), *Binh* (3), *Hoang* (3), *Hung* (3), *Tan* (3), *Tran* (3), *Tuan* (3), *Cong* (2), *Duong* (2), *Hai* (2), *Hau* (2), *Hong* (2), *Huy* (2), *Sen, Tang, Nam, Vong.*

Vining (1993) English: habitational name for someone from a place called Fyning in Rogate in Sussex.

Vinje (229) Norwegian: habitational name from any of fifteen farmsteads so named, from a form of Old Norse *vin* 'meadow'.
GIVEN NAMES Scandinavian 15%; German 5%. *Alf, Karsten, Svein; Kurt* (2), *Erna*.

Vink (316) **1.** English: variant of FINCH. **2.** German (Rhineland): variant of FINK.
GIVEN NAMES Dutch 7%; French 4%. *Pieter* (3), *Dirk, Gerrit, Hendrik, Henk, Machiel, Marinus; Eugenie* (2), *Dominique, Leonie*.

Vinnedge (101) Origin unidentified.

Vinokur (139) Jewish (eastern Ashkenazic): occupational name for a distiller, Russian *vinokur*, from *vino* 'wine', earlier used also to denote liquor of all kinds, including spirits, + *kurit* 'to distil'.
GIVEN NAMES Jewish 31%; Russian 30%; German 4%. *Yakov* (4), *Amiram* (2), *Aron* (2), *Benyamin* (2), *Esfir, Fayvel, Irina, Pinhas, Sol; Leonid* (7), *Boris* (6), *Mikhail* (4), *Aleksandr* (2), *Igor* (2), *Oleg* (2), *Svetlana* (2), *Yevgeniy* (2), *Arkady, Asya, Grigory, Lyudmila; Berthold*.

Vinsant (152) Variant spelling of VINCENT.

Vinson (8130) English: variant of VINCENT.

Vinsonhaler (103) Origin unidentified.

Vint (285) **1.** English: habitational name for someone from a place called Vint, probably one in Oath, Somerset. **2.** Scottish: variant of WINT, which is of unexplained origin.

Vinton (673) English: unexplained; possibly a variant of FENTON.
FOREBEARS John Vinton was a resident of Lynn, MA, as early as 1648. He had numerous prominent descendants, including Samuel Finley Vinton, who was born in South Hadley, MA, in 1792, and became on OH congressman.

Vinyard (937) English: see VINEYARD.

Vinzant (378) Variant of VINCENT.

Viola (2143) **1.** Italian: from the female personal name *Viola*, from *viola* 'violet' (Latin *viola*). **2.** Catalan: probably from *viola* 'fiddle', 'viol', hence an occupational nickname for a viol player; otherwise a byname from *viola* 'violet'.
GIVEN NAMES Italian 13%. *Salvatore* (10), *Angelo* (5), *Carlo* (4), *Rocco* (4), *Santo* (4), *Antonio* (3), *Saverio* (3), *Aldo* (2), *Baldassare* (2), *Eligio* (2), *Enrico* (2), *Franco* (2).

Violante (284) Southern Italian, Spanish, and Portuguese: from the female personal name *Violante*, probably a derivative of *viola* 'violet'.
GIVEN NAMES Italian 25%; Spanish 8%. *Mario* (3), *Salvatore* (3), *Angelo, Arturo, Carmino, Donato, Elio, Gabriele, Luciano, Nicola, Nino, Onofrio, Vito, Vittoria; Francisco, Guillermo, Isauro, Jose, Juan Manuel, Juana, Lucilia, Manuel*.

Violet (283) French: see VIOLETTE.
GIVEN NAMES French 4%. *Christophe, Pierre*.

Violett (211) French: see VIOLETTE.

Violette (1365) French: perhaps a topographic name from a diminutive of *viol* 'path', itself a derivative of *vie* 'way'. It is more likely, however, that this name is from the secondary surname LAVIOLETTE 'the violet (flower)', which was common among soldiers in French Canada.
GIVEN NAMES French 8%. *Adrien* (2), *Fernand* (2), *Marcel* (2), *Normand* (2), *Aime, Albertine, Alderic, Andre, Armand, Armande, Aurel, Aurele*.

Vipond (255) English (of Norman origin): habitational name from a place called Vieuxpont in Calvados, France.

Vipperman (242) Probably an Americanized spelling of North German **Wippermann**, a topographic name for someone who lived by any of several rivers or streams named Wipper.

Virag (186) Hungarian (**Virág**): from the personal name *Virág* (from Hungarian *virág* 'flower', one of several female names which derived from an affectionate nickname).
GIVEN NAMES Hungarian 5%. *Laszlo* (2), *Katalin, Lazlo*.

Viramontes (448) Hispanic (Mexico): probably a habitational name from an unidentified place.
GIVEN NAMES Spanish 52%. *Jose* (17), *Manuel* (8), *Carlos* (6), *Jesus* (6), *Ruben* (5), *Francisco* (4), *Enrique* (3), *Jaime* (3), *Jorge* (3), *Pedro* (3), *Raul* (3), *Serafin* (3).

Virani (153) Hindu, Muslim, and Jain name found in Gujarat, India, and among people from Sind, Pakistan, meaning '(descendant) of Vir'. Vir (from Sanskrit *vīra* 'hero') must be an ancestral personal name or the initial element of an ancestral personal name such as Virender.
GIVEN NAMES Muslim 82%; Indian 9%. *Amin* (4), *Saleem* (4), *Salim* (4), *Amirali* (3), *Iqbal* (3), *Mansoor* (3), *Zulfiqar* (3), *Ahmed* (2), *Amir* (2), *Asif* (2), *Azim* (2), *Karim* (2); *Ajit, Anisha, Bharti, Dilawar, Gopal, Kanu, Popat, Pravin, Rajeev, Vinesh*.

Virant (113) Slovenian: probably a nickname from the dialect plant name *virant* 'wall rue' (Latin *Asplenium ruta-muraria*).

Viray (199) Southern French (Occitan) and Catalan: variant of Occitan **Verai** and **Veray**, nickname from Occitan *verai* 'honest'. From southern France this name spread to northern Catalonia.
GIVEN NAMES Spanish 41%; Italian 7%. *Fernando* (4), *Jose* (3), *Manuel* (3), *Renato* (3), *Cesar* (2), *Mario* (2), *Alberto, Alfredo, Andres, Arturo, Avelino, Bonifacio; Clemente, Donato, Fausto, Liberato, Primo, Romeo*.

Virden (693) English: probably a variant spelling of VERDUN.

Virella (115) Catalan: variant of **Vilella**, a habitational name from any of the places called Vilella in Catalonia.
GIVEN NAMES Spanish 31%. *Jose* (2), *Luis* (2), *Mariano* (2), *Miguel* (2), *Ana, Angeles,*

Cesar, Edgardo, Elva, Frederico, Idalia, Juan Ramon.

Vires (286) French (Huguenot): of uncertain origin; perhaps a habitational name from Vire in Calvados. Compare VIER.

Virga (320) Italian (Sicily) variant of VERGA.
GIVEN NAMES Italian 11%. *Salvatore* (3), *Ignazio* (2), *Sal* (2), *Angelo, Filippo, Pietro, Santo*.

Virgen (224) Spanish (Mexico): from *virgen* 'virgin' (Latin *virgo*), probably a nickname for someone who had played the part of the Virgin Mary in a pageant.
GIVEN NAMES Spanish 56%. *Jose* (7), *Luis* (5), *Sergio* (4), *Armando* (3), *Juan* (3), *Alberto* (2), *Alejandro* (2), *Alfonso* (2), *Angel* (2), *Cesar* (2), *Francisco* (2), *Guadalupe* (2); *Cecilio*.

Virgil (602) From the personal name *Virgil*, a vernacular form of the Latin personal name *Vergilius, Virgilius*, which was probably of Etruscan origin. The name is famous in particular as that of the Latin poet Publius Vergilius Maro (70–19 BC), author of the *Aeneid*. Virgil was much admired in medieval Europe; there were attempts to make him into an honorary Christian (even though he actually lived before the time of Christ), and Dante made him his guide through the Inferno and Purgatorio, a model of classical moderation and reason. This was also the name of an early saint, a 6th-century bishop of Arles. The forename is popular mainly in the U.S., and it is possible that the surname was coined here in at least some cases.

Virgili (102) **1.** Italian: patronymic or plural form of VIRGILIO. **2.** Catalan: from the personal name *Virgili*, Catalan equivalent to VIRGILIO.
GIVEN NAMES Italian 15%; Spanish 11%. *Vito* (3), *Gino, Luciano, Marino, Romano, Vittorio; Marcelo* (3), *Amadio, Eduardo, Elvira, Esteban, Jaime, Orlando*.

Virgilio (422) Italian: from the personal name *Virgilio* (see VIRGIL).
GIVEN NAMES Italian 14%. *Vito* (7), *Angelo* (2), *Antonio* (2), *Aldino, Carmine, Francesca, Gaetano, Nicola, Nunzio, Pasquale*.

Virgin (667) English: from a medieval vernacular form of VIRGO.

Virginia (112) Italian: from the personal name *Virginia*, a vernacular form of Latin *Verginius*.

Virgo (202) English: of uncertain origin. The surname coincides in form with Latin *virgo*, genitive *virginis* 'maiden', from which is derived (via Old French) modern English *virgin*. It is possible that the surname was originally a nickname for someone who had played the part of the Blessed Virgin Mary in a mystery play. Alternatively, it may have been a nickname for a shy or girlish young man, or possibly ironically for a lecher.

Virk (133) Indian (Panjab): Sikh name based on the name of a Jat clan. The founder of the clan is believed to have been a Rajput called Virak.

GIVEN NAMES Indian 81%. *Jarnail* (2), *Karnail* (2), *Som* (2), *Ajit, Anoop, Darshan, Daya, Gurdarshan, Gurdial, Karm, Malkit, Meena.*

Virkler (180) French (Alsace): probably of German origin but unexplained.

Virnig (294) Variant of German **Virnich**, from a place called Virnich near Cologne. This name occurs chiefly in MN and WI.

Virostek (140) Americanized spelling of Czech and Slovak **Výrostek**, from *výrostek* 'teenager', 'youth', hence a nickname for a youngster.

Virts (199) Dutch: patronymic from a Germanic personal name formed with *virt* 'worth' as the first element. Compare German WIRTZ.

Virtue (454) English and Scottish: nickname from Middle English, Old French *vertu* 'moral worth'; 'goodness' (Latin *virtus* 'manliness', 'valor', 'worth'). This may have been bestowed on a good or pious person, it may alternatively have been a sarcastic nickname for a prig, or it may have been borne by someone who had played the part of Virtue in a medieval mystery play.

Virzi (155) Italian (Sicily and Calabria): occupational name for a tanner, from medieval Greek *virseas*, classical Greek *byrseus*.

GIVEN NAMES Italian 15%. *Salvatore* (3), *Vito* (2), *Angelo, Nicoletta, Vincenzo.*

Vis (288) Dutch (**de Vis**): from *vis* 'fish', a metonymic occupational name for a fisherman or fishmonger, or a nickname for someone thought to resemble a fish.

GIVEN NAMES Dutch 5%. *Gerrit* (3), *Maarten, Teunis, Willem.*

Visage (115) French: from *visage* 'face', presumably a nickname for someone with a beautiful or otherwise remarkable face. The surname was brought to North America via England, no doubt by French Huguenots.

Visalli (138) Italian: possibly an altered form of VASSALLO.

GIVEN NAMES Italian 16%. *Natale, Rocco, Santi, Umberto.*

Viscardi (197) Italian: patronymic from a variant of the personal name *Guiscardo*, from a Germanic name composed of the elements *wisa* 'wise' + *hard* 'hard', 'strong'.

GIVEN NAMES Italian 10%. *Antonio, Salvatore.*

Viscarra (120) Basque: variant of **Bizcarra** (see VIZCARRA).

GIVEN NAMES Spanish 48%. *Jose* (5), *Jesus* (3), *Ricardo* (3), *Arturo* (2), *Ernesto* (2), *Manuel* (2), *Rosario* (2), *Agustin, Alberto, Alfonso, Alfredo, Amalia; Donato, Federico, Philomena.*

Visco (517) Italian: **1.** from southern dialect *visco* 'bishop' (standard Italian *vescovo*), probably a nickname for a pious person or for someone in the service of a bishop. **2.** habitational name from Visco in Udine province.

GIVEN NAMES Italian 14%; French 6%. *Guido* (4), *Donato* (3), *Cesidio* (2), *Alfonse, Angelo, Antonio, Domenic, Enrico, Gaspare, Lucio, Nicola; Alphonse* (2), *Armand, Girard, Patrice, Philomene.*

Viscomi (159) Italian: Sicilian and Calabrian form of VISCONTI, from Greek *biskōmēs*, derived in turn from medieval Latin *vicecomes* 'deputy'.

GIVEN NAMES Italian 25%. *Emilio* (2), *Salvatore* (2), *Antonio, Beniamino, Filomena, Mario, Rodolfo, Santo.*

Visconti (802) Italian: from *visconte*, a title of rank (medieval Latin *vicecomes* 'deputy of a count'). Unusually (since most noble families took their surnames from their estates), the surname was sometimes of literal application, but it is also no doubt in part a nickname for someone who gave himself airs and graces, and in part an occupational name for someone employed by a viscount.

GIVEN NAMES Italian 11%; French 4%. *Salvatore* (3), *Pasquale* (2), *Rocco* (2), *Umberto* (2), *Amerigo, Angelo, Carlo, Domenic, Ennio, Gaetano, Gerlando, Gino; Laurent* (3), *Camille, Girard.*

Viscusi (227) Southern Italian: **1.** patronymic or plural form of VISCUSO. **2.** habitational name from a place so called, named with medieval Latin *biscus* 'butcher's broom' (*Ruscus aculeatus*).

GIVEN NAMES Italian 18%. *Carlo* (2), *Enzo* (2), *Antonio, Arcangelo, Domenico, Giacomo, Guido, Philomena, Pietro, Ricci, Salvatore.*

Viscuso (177) Italian (Sicily): nickname from Sicilian *viscusu* 'tough', 'tenacious'.

GIVEN NAMES Italian 31%. *Sal* (5), *Salvatore* (3), *Pasquale* (2), *Angelo, Antonietta, Antonio, Bartolo, Carmello, Carmelo, Cosimo, Gennaro, Luigi, Mario.*

Vise (458) English: topographic name for someone who lived by a boundary, Old French *devise*.

Visel (103) German: variant of **Viesel**, itself a variant of **Fiesel** (see FEASEL).

Viselli (105) Italian: unexplained.

GIVEN NAMES Italian 19%. *Angelo* (3), *Guido* (2), *Cesidio, Rinaldo, Rocco, Sandro.*

Visger (115) Americanized spelling of Dutch VISSCHER.

Visintainer (118) Probably a respelling of German **Wiesentanner**: unexplained; it could perhaps be a habitational name for someone from Wessentin in Mecklenburg-West Pomerania.

Visscher (252) Dutch: occupational name for a fisherman. Compare German FISCHER. FOREBEARS Harmen Visscher came from Hoorn in the Netherlands to Beverwyck (Albany, NY) in or before 1643.

GIVEN NAMES Dutch 8%. *Pieter* (3), *Gerrit* (2), *Jantje* (2), *Klaas.*

Visser (1835) Dutch and North German: variant of FISCHER.

GIVEN NAMES Dutch 7%. *Dirk* (10), *Pieter* (6), *Gerrit* (5), *Marinus* (3), *Piet* (3),

Willem (3), *Derk* (2), *Durk* (2), *Jacobus* (2), *Klaas* (2), *Nicolaas* (2), *Adrianus.*

Vissers (165) Dutch and North German: patronymic form of **Visser** (see FISCHER).

Viste (103) Norwegian: unexplained.

Viswanathan (223) Indian (Kerala, Tamil Nadu): Hindu name from Sanskrit *viśvanātha* 'lord of the universe' (from *viśva* 'universe' + *nātha* 'lord', an epithet of the god Shiva), + the Tamil-Malayalam third-person masculine singular suffix *-n*. This is only a given name in India, but has come to be used as a family name in the U.S.

GIVEN NAMES Indian 95%. *Ramesh* (5), *Ravi* (5), *Bala* (4), *Kesava* (3), *Meera* (3), *Narayanan* (3), *Aparna* (2), *Ganesh* (2), *Kumar* (2), *Mahesh* (2), *Manoj* (2), *Mohan* (2).

Vita (551) **1.** Italian and Spanish: from a medieval female personal name, originally an affectionate nickname, from Italian *vita* 'life' (Latin *vita*). **2.** Italian: from a short form of the medieval personal name BONAVITA.

GIVEN NAMES Italian 21%; Spanish 5%. *Rocco* (4), *Alfredo* (3), *Angelo* (3), *Domenic* (3), *Mario* (2), *Orlando* (2), *Salvatore* (2), *Angelina, Carmelo, Carmine, Clementina, Francesco, Giovanni, Leonardo, Ottavio, Santo; Edgardo, Eleazar, Ines, Juan, Manuel.*

Vitacco (117) Italian: possibly from a derivative of the personal name VITO.

GIVEN NAMES Italian 14%. *Rocco* (2), *Gennaro, Salvatore.*

Vitagliano (303) Southern Italian (Campania and Calabria): from the personal name *Vitagliano*, a dialect variant of *Vitaliano*, from the Latin personal and family name *Vitalianus*, a derivative of *Vitalis* (see VITALE).

GIVEN NAMES Italian 19%. *Carmine* (4), *Luigi* (3), *Salvatore* (3), *Aldo* (2), *Alessio, Biagio, Bruna, Domenico, Gaetano, Gennaro, Giuseppe, Rocco.*

Vital (581) French, Spanish, Italian, and English: from a vernacular form of the Latin personal name *Vitalis* (see VITALE). The English surname may derive, at least in part, as a nickname from the Middle English word *vital* in the sense 'full of vitality'.

GIVEN NAMES Spanish 26%; French 8%; Italian 7%. *Jose* (6), *Manuel* (6), *Juan* (4), *Rafael* (4), *Fernando* (3), *Jorge* (3), *Luis* (3), *Ruben* (3), *Ana* (2), *Armando* (2), *Francisco* (2), *Guadalupe* (2); *Alphonse* (2), *Patrice* (2), *Pierre* (2), *Alain, Altagrace, Anastasie, Andre, Jean Louis, Magalie, Monique, Octave, Rodrigue.*

Vitale (4226) Italian and Jewish (from Italy): from the medieval personal name *Vitale* (Latin *Vitalis*, a derivative of *vita* 'life'). The name was popular with Christians as a symbol of their belief in eternal life, and was borne by a dozen early saints; it became especially popular in Emilia-Romagna because of two saints,

San Vitale of Bologna and Ravenna. As a Jewish personal name it represents a calque of the Hebrew personal name *Chayim* 'life'. Compare HYAMS.

GIVEN NAMES Italian 19%. *Salvatore* (54), *Angelo* (21), *Rocco* (18), *Sal* (17), *Vito* (14), *Carmine* (9), *Antonio* (7), *Pietro* (6), *Domenic* (5), *Carlo* (4), *Ciro* (4), *Dante* (4).

Vitali (422) Italian: patronymic from VITALE.

GIVEN NAMES Italian 15%. *Angelo* (5), *Achille* (2), *Gino* (2), *Vito* (2), *Albo*, *Aldo*, *Dante*, *Dario*, *Enio*, *Enrico*, *Evo*, *Federico*, *Franco*.

Vitalis (117) Greek: Hellenized form of Italian VITALE. It is also found as a pet form of the personal name *Vitalios* (Latin *Vitalius*), name of a bishop of Ravenna who was martyred under Nero.

Vitanza (184) Italian: from a derivative of VITA.

GIVEN NAMES Italian 26%. *Salvatore* (4), *Angelo* (3), *Amedeo* (2), *Domenic*, *Florinda*, *Gaetano*, *Mario*, *Rosario*, *Sergio*.

Vitatoe (142) Origin unidentified. Many origins have been proposed, none of them convincing.

Vitek (612) Czech (**Vítek**): from the personal name *Vít*, from Latin *Vitus*, a derivative of *vita* 'life'. Compare Italian VITO.

Vitela (152) Italian (Sicily): from a pet form of the Latin name *Vitus* (see VITO).

GIVEN NAMES Spanish 47%; Italian 6%. *Juan* (5), *Carlos* (3), *Jaime* (3), *Jose* (3), *Luis* (3), *Francisco* (2), *Guadalupe* (2), *Salvador* (2), *Adela*, *Alberto*, *Alfredo*, *Angelina*; *Antonio* (2), *Amadeo*, *Ceasar*, *Dario*, *Eligio*, *Leonardo*.

Vitelli (396) Italian: patronymic or plural form of VITELLO.

GIVEN NAMES Italian 11%. *Aldo* (2), *Rocco* (2), *Angelo*, *Carmine*, *Dario*, *Enrico*, *Francesco*, *Gennaro*, *Luigi*, *Sal*, *Salvatore*, *Serafino*.

Vitello (495) Italian: from a pet form of the personal name VITO.

GIVEN NAMES Italian 8%. *Angelo* (3), *Carmine* (2), *Baldassare*, *Carmelo*, *Ciro*, *Salvatore*, *Vincenzo*.

Viteri (160) Basque: variant of **Biteri**, a habitational name from a place so named in the Basque Country.

GIVEN NAMES Spanish 53%. *Blanca* (3), *Carlos* (3), *Diego* (3), *Jaime* (3), *Pablo* (3), *Cesar* (2), *Consuelo* (2), *Galo* (2), *Gonzalo* (2), *Jose* (2), *Juan* (2), *Julio* (2).

Vitez (108) Hungarian (**Vitéz**): nickname from the vocabulary word *vitéz* 'brave soldier'.

GIVEN NAMES Hungarian 10%. *Bela*, *Illes*, *Imre*, *Lajos*, *Laszlo*.

Viti (215) Italian: patronymic from the personal name VITO.

GIVEN NAMES Italian 19%. *Antonio* (5), *Guido* (2), *Rocco* (2), *Stefano* (2), *Attilio*,

Benedetto, *Enzo*, *Federico*, *Giulio*, *Michelangelo*, *Pio*, *Sal*.

Vitiello (486) Italian (Campania): variant of VITELLO.

GIVEN NAMES Italian 29%. *Salvatore* (8), *Gaetano* (4), *Antonio* (3), *Filippo* (3), *Guido* (3), *Luigi* (3), *Mario* (3), *Sal* (3), *Augusto* (2), *Franco* (2), *Giovanni* (2), *Adelmo*, *Alfonse*, *Amadeo*, *Americo*, *Marisa*, *Salvadore*, *Silverio*.

Vititoe (128) Origin unidentified. See VITATOE.

Vitko (139) Ukrainian: from a pet form of the personal name *Vit* (see VITEK).

Vitkus (102) Lithuanian: **1.** from a pet form of the personal name *Výtautas* (a compound of *vyti* 'to guide' + *tauta* 'the people'). **2.** from a pet form of Slavic VITEK or VOYTEK.

GIVEN NAMES Lithuanian 5%. *Gintautas*, *Vytautas*.

Vito (570) Italian: from the personal name *Vito*, Latin *Vitus*, from *vita* 'life'. Compare VITA. The name was popular in the Middle Ages as the result of the cult of an early Christian martyr in southern Italy, about whom very little is known. He was regarded as a patron against epilepsy and the nervous tremor named after him, 'St. Vitus's dance'. His cult spread into Germany and thence through Eastern Europe, where the name was reinforced by native Slavic names such as *Vitoslav* and *Vitomír*, with a first element derived from Old Slavic *vitati* 'inhabit' or 'welcome'. It may also derive in part from the Lombardic name *Wido* or Frankish *Wit(t)o* (see GUIDO).

GIVEN NAMES Italian 9%. *Antonio* (2), *Pasquale* (2), *Angelo*, *Carmine*, *Constantino*, *Gennaro*, *Giuseppe*, *Leonardo*, *Lia*, *Nunzio*, *Remo*, *Salvatore*.

Vitolo (277) Italian: from a pet form of VITO.

GIVEN NAMES Italian 17%. *Carmine* (2), *Dante* (2), *Gennaro* (2), *Salvatore* (2), *Antonio*, *Caterina*, *Franco*, *Marco*, *Nunzio*, *Rino*, *Stefano*.

Vitrano (263) Italian: variant of VETRANO.

GIVEN NAMES Italian 16%. *Santo* (3), *Vito* (3), *Gabriella*, *Giusto*, *Nicolo*.

Vitt (378) German: **1.** variant of VEIT. **2.** habitational name from places called Vitt or Vitte, in Pomerania and on Rügen.

Vittetoe (168) Origin unidentified. See VITATOE.

Vitti (286) Italian: patronymic from the personal name *Vitto*, which is probably a variant of BITTO.

GIVEN NAMES Italian 18%. *Dino* (5), *Vito* (3), *Angelo*, *Antonio*, *Carmel*, *Donato*, *Giovanni*, *Levio*, *Luciano*, *Luigi*, *Oreste*, *Ornella*.

Vittitoe (126) Origin unidentified. See VITATOE.

Vittitow (270) Origin unidentified. See VITATOE.

Vittone (103) Italian: probably from an augmentative form of the personal name *Vitto* (see VITTI).

GIVEN NAMES Italian 14%. *Domenic* (3), *Carmine*, *Dante*, *Ettore*.

Vittori (103) Italian: patronymic or plural form of VITTORIO.

GIVEN NAMES Italian 12%. *Guido* (2), *Amedio*, *Angelo*, *Enrico*, *Quinto*.

Vittoria (130) Italian: **1.** from the personal name *Vittoria*, feminine form of VITTORIO. **2.** habitational name from the Sicilian town of Vittoria.

GIVEN NAMES Italian 34%. *Biagio* (2), *Giuseppe* (2), *Mario* (2), *Vito* (2), *Antonino*, *Antonio*, *Caterina*, *Dino*, *Ettore*, *Falco*, *Gino*, *Nino*, *Rosario*, *Sal*.

Vittorio (171) Italian (Sicily): from the personal name *Vittorio* (see VICTOR).

GIVEN NAMES Italian 15%. *Angelo*, *Benedetto*, *Cosmo*, *Domenico*, *Nino*, *Ricci*, *Salvatore*, *Sante*.

Vittum (141) Origin unidentified.

Vitucci (216) Italian: patronymic from a pet form of the personal name VITO.

GIVEN NAMES Italian 24%. *Rocco* (4), *Vito* (3), *Angelo* (2), *Antonio* (2), *Aldo*, *Carmine*, *Giuseppe*, *Pasquale*.

Vitulli (171) Italian: patronymic or plural form of VITULLO.

GIVEN NAMES Italian 21%. *Domenico* (2), *Marco* (2), *Vito* (2), *Carmela*, *Mario*, *Marisa*.

Vitullo (294) Italian: from the personal name *Vitullo*, a pet form of VITO.

GIVEN NAMES Italian 12%. *Angelo* (4), *Florio* (2), *Antonio*, *Carmel*, *Mauro*, *Onofrio*.

Vitzthum (101) Origin unidentified.

Vivanco (166) Spanish: habitational name from any of the towns called Vivanco, as for example in Burgos province.

GIVEN NAMES Spanish 55%. *Jose* (8), *Carlos* (3), *Lourdes* (3), *Alberto* (2), *Cesar* (2), *Edgardo* (2), *Eduardo* (2), *Mario* (2), *Miguel* (2), *Rafael* (2), *Roberto* (2), *Rogelio* (2); *Marco*.

Vivar (171) Spanish: habitational name from any of the places called with Vivar, specially from Vivar del Cid, in Burgos province, the place where the medieval warrior Rodrigo Díaz de Vivar, also known as El Cid, was born.

GIVEN NAMES Spanish 61%. *Juan* (8), *Jorge* (3), *Jose* (3), *Manuel* (3), *Miguel* (3), *Pedro* (3), *Alejandro* (2), *Arturo* (2), *Felipe* (2), *Francisco* (2), *Jose Antonio* (2), *Julio* (2).

Vivas (284) Catalan: Castilianized form of VIVES.

GIVEN NAMES Spanish 48%. *Carlos* (9), *Jose* (7), *Francisco* (4), *Javier* (3), *Miguel* (3), *Pablo* (3), *Ricardo* (3), *Ruben* (3), *Sigifredo* (3), *Alberto* (2), *Cesar* (2), *Eduardo* (2).

Viveiros (541) Galician and Portuguese: topographic name from the plural of *viveiro* 'tree nursery', '(fish) hatchery', 'breeding ground' (Latin *vivarium*, a derivative of *vivus* 'alive') or a habitational name from a place named with this word.

GIVEN NAMES Spanish 19%; Portuguese 12%. *Manuel* (20), *Jose* (13), *Carlos* (5), *Alvaro* (3), *Luis* (3), *Horacio* (2), *Mario* (2), *Ricardo* (2), *Americo, Angelina, Camilo, Dimas; Albano* (2), *Duarte* (2), *Henrique, Joao.*

Vivenzio (122) Italian: from the personal name *Vivenzio,* Latin *Viventius,* an omen name from the verb *vivere* 'to live'.

GIVEN NAMES Italian 11%. *Gaetano, Silvio, Vincenzo.*

Viverette (205) French: of unknown origin; possibly a derivative of VIVIER.

Viverito (127) Probably a respelling of Italian VIVIRITO.

GIVEN NAMES Italian 14%. *Angelo, Sal, Salvatore, Vita.*

Viveros (286) Spanish: habitational name from Viveros, a place in Albacete province, or a Castilianized spelling of Galician VIVEIROS.

GIVEN NAMES Spanish 49%. *Carlos* (4), *Octavio* (4), *Ruben* (4), *Cruz* (3), *Francisco* (3), *Jaime* (3), *Jorge* (3), *Jose* (3), *Manuel* (3), *Ramon* (3), *Roberto* (3), *Armando* (2).

Vives (181) Catalan: from *Vives* (Latin *Vivas*), a medieval personal name meaning 'may you live', bestowed on children for the sake of good omen.

GIVEN NAMES Spanish 40%. *Angel* (5), *Jose* (5), *Carlos* (3), *Juan* (3), *Pedro* (3), *Alicia* (2), *Ana* (2), *Eduardo* (2), *Ramon* (2), *Wilfredo* (2), *Agustin, Aleida.*

Vivian (920) English and French: from the personal name (Latin *Vivianus,* a derivative of *vivus* 'living', 'alive'). The name was borne by a 5th-century bishop of Saintes, France, and was popular among the Normans, by whom it was introduced to England.

Viviani (197) Italian: patronymic from the personal name VIVIANO.

GIVEN NAMES Italian 21%. *Antonio* (2), *Alessandro, Carmela, Emilio, Geno, Mario, Massimo, Michael Angelo, Ovidio, Ricardo, Vito.*

Viviano (571) Italian: from the personal name *Viviano,* Latin *Vivianus,* a derivative of *vivus* 'living', 'alive'. Compare VITO and VITALE.

GIVEN NAMES Italian 12%. *Antonio* (5), *Vito* (5), *Salvatore* (4), *Sal* (2), *Angelo, Carlo, Cesare, Gaetano, Gaspare, Geno, Lorenzo.*

Vivier (135) French: topographic name for someone who lived by a fish pond, from Latin *vivarium,* a derivative of *vivus* 'alive'.

FOREBEARS A Vivier from the Poitou region of France is documented in Quebec City in 1665.

GIVEN NAMES French 13%. *Marcel* (2), *Pierre* (2), *Jean-Luc.*

Vivirito (103) Italian (Sicily): habitational name for someone from any of various minor places in Sicily named Biviere, from Sicilian *bbiveri, viveri* 'small natural lake'

(from French *vivier* 'fish pond', from Latin *vivarium*).

GIVEN NAMES Italian 19%. *Antonio, Battista, Ignazio, Sal, Salvatore, Santo.*

Vivolo (101) Italian: from the Latin personal name *Bibulus* or Old Tuscan *Vivolus,* from Latin *vivus* 'live', 'alive'.

GIVEN NAMES Italian 23%. *Armando* (2), *Rocco* (2), *Angelo, Aurelio, Domenico, Donato, Lorenzo, Placido, Stefano, Vincenzo.*

Vivona (212) Italian: variant of BIVONA.

GIVEN NAMES Italian 15%. *Antonio* (2), *Aldo, Salvatore, Santo, Vincenzo, Vita, Vito.*

Vix (114) German: variant spelling of FIX.

GIVEN NAMES French 6%. *Christophe, Elrick.*

Vizard (76) Scottish (of Norman origin): variant of WISHART.

Vizcaino (272) Spanish: habitational name or regional name for someone from the town or province of Biscay (Spanish *Vizcaya*) in the Basque Country. The place name derives from Basque *bizkai* 'ridge' + the definite article *-a*. Historically, the term was also used to denote a seafarer and in some cases this may be the meaning behind the surname.

GIVEN NAMES Spanish 57%. *Jose* (10), *Carlos* (8), *Juan* (6), *Ramon* (4), *Jaime* (3), *Luis* (3), *Raul* (3), *Armando* (2), *Edmundo* (2), *Efrain* (2), *Jesus* (2), *Jorge* (2).

Vizcarra (367) Basque: variant of **Bizcarra** (alongside **Viscarra** and **Biscarra**), a topographic name from Basque *bizcar* 'shoulder (of a mountain)' + the definite article *-a*.

GIVEN NAMES Spanish 52%. *Jose* (9), *Manuel* (7), *Salvador* (6), *Carlos* (4), *Jorge* (4), *Ricardo* (4), *Alberto* (3), *Javier* (3), *Juan* (3), *Julio* (3), *Rafael* (3), *Alejandro* (2); *Antonio* (2), *Leonzo* (2), *Sal* (2), *Ceasar, Eliseo, Lorenzo, Marco, Mauro.*

Vizcarrondo (103) Basque: variant of **Bizcarrondo,** from Basque *bizcar* 'shoulder (of a mountain)' + *ondo* 'near to', a topographic name for someone who lived by the shoulder of a mountain.

GIVEN NAMES Spanish 44%. *Jose* (9), *Julio* (3), *Rafael* (3), *Angel* (2), *Carlos* (2), *Felipe* (2), *Manuel* (2), *Alejandro, Aura, Aurelio, Blanca, Jaime.*

Vize (101) English: variant spelling of VISE.

Vizza (104) Italian (Cosenza): unexplained.

GIVEN NAMES Italian 13%. *Carmine, Lorenzo, Orlando, Rosario.*

Vizzini (189) Italian (Sicily): habitational name from a place so named in Catania, Sicily.

GIVEN NAMES Italian 12%. *Salvatore* (5), *Carmelo, Sal.*

Vlach (397) Czech and Slovak: **1.** from *Vlach* 'Italian', 'Romanian', or 'Wallachian'. This vocabulary word originally meant 'foreigner'; it is cognate with German *welsch* meaning 'Latin' or 'Romance-speaking', and ultimately with Old English *wælisc* 'foreign' and modern

English *Welsh.* At the time when surnames were formed, the Czech word was applied chiefly to Italians, but also to Romanians. **2.** from a pet form of any of various personal names beginning with *Vla-,* for example *Vlastislav* or *Vladislav.*

Vlachos (221) Greek: ethnic name for an Aromanian. The Aromanians are traditionally nomadic pastoralists throughout the southern Balkans, speaking a language closely related to Romanian. The Greek name **Vlakhos** is derived from an Indo-European stem meaning 'foreigner'; it is cognate with *Welsh* and *Walloon.* See also VLACH. Through ethnic stereotyping, the Greek term came to denote a highlander, and thence acquired the meaning 'uncouth'. Any of these senses could be involved in the development of the surname. It can also be a reduced form of compound surnames beginning with *Vlacho-,* for example **Vlachogiannis** meaning 'John the Aromanian', 'John the hillbilly', or 'John the uncouth'.

GIVEN NAMES Greek 17%. *Christos* (3), *Constantine* (2), *Dimitrios, Haralambos, Konstantinos, Koula, Labros, Pantelis, Stamatios, Vaios, Vasilios.*

Vlad (98) Czech, Slovak, and Romanian: from a short form of the personal name *Vladislav,* an old Slavic name composed of the elements *volod* 'rule' + *slav* 'glory', Latinized as *Ladislaus* and found in Hungarian as *László* (see LASZLO).

Vlahakis (197) Greek: patronymic from VLACHOS 'Aromanian', also a nickname meaning 'hillbilly'. The *-akis* ending is particularly associated with Crete, where there is no indigenous Aromanian population; so the secondary, pejorative sense is probably more frequent in this instance.

GIVEN NAMES Greek 11%. *Angelos* (2), *Stylianos* (2), *Anastasios, Constantine, Costas, Stavros.*

Vlahos (510) Greek: see VLACHOS.

GIVEN NAMES Greek 16%. *Dimitrios* (4), *Christos* (3), *Anastasios* (2), *Constantine* (2), *Spyros* (2), *Angelos, Athanasios, Demetrios, Eleni, Fotios, Kosmas, Kosta.*

Vlasak (377) Czech (**Vlasák**): nickname for a man with thick or long hair, from Czech *vlas* 'hair' + *-ák* suffix denoting human agents, or an occupational name for a buyer of hair.

Vlasic (123) Serbian and Croatian (**Vlasić**); Slovenian (**Vlašič**): patronymic from the ethnic name *Vlah* 'Wallachian', 'Romanian', also used more widely to denote a person of foreign origin, especially one speaking a Romance language. In Croatia *Vlah* denoted a shepherd of Romanian origin; subsequently it was used as a name for a Serb or a member of Orthodox Church.

Vlcek (316) Czech (**Vlček**): **1.** nickname from a diminutive of VLK, i.e. 'little wolf'. **2.** nickname for a brisk, quick person, from the same word, *vlček*, denoting a simple toy on the flywheel principle. The idiom *točit se jako vlček* 'to turn like a flywheel', is applied to people.

GIVEN NAMES Czech and Slovak 4%. *Bohumil, Milan, Stanislav.*

Vliet (215) Dutch: topographic name for someone who lived by a brook, from *vliet* 'brook', 'stream', or habitational name from a place named with this word. Compare VAN VLIET.

Vlietstra (120) Frisian: topographic name for someone who lived by a brook, from a agent noun based on Dutch *vliet* 'brook', 'stream'.

Vlk (125) Czech and Slovak: from the vocabulary word *vlk* 'wolf', probably from an Old Slavic personal name containing this element, but perhaps also applied as a nickname for someone thought to resemble a wolf or connected with wolves in some other way.

Vo (3486) Vietnamese: unexplained.

GIVEN NAMES Vietnamese 80%. *Hung* (57), *Thanh* (48), *Minh* (39), *Dung* (32), *Hoa* (29), *Hoang* (28), *Hai* (27), *Long* (27), *Anh* (25), *Son* (25), *Duc* (24), *Chau* (23), *Tam* (23), *Hong* (18), *Sang* (18), *Nam* (15), *Chi* (9), *Phong* (9), *Lai* (8), *Chung* (6), *Dong* (6), *Han* (6), *Chin* (5), *Man* (5), *On* (4), *Tao* (4), *Thai* (4), *Tham* (4), *Tong* (4), *Tuong* (4), *Chan* (3), *Tinh* (3), *Tuoi* (3), *Manh* (2), *Sinh* (2), *Thach* (2).

Voce (145) Italian: unexplained; possibly related to Italian *voce*.

GIVEN NAMES Italian 4%. *Marco, Ugo.*

Voci (138) Italian: possibly of Albanian origin, a nickname from *voc, voci* 'boy'.

GIVEN NAMES Italian 28%. *Rocco* (2), *Saverio* (2), *Armando, Domenic, Emilio, Gerardo, Luigi, Paola, Teresina.*

Vock (107) North German and Frisian: from a short form of any of the various male personal names beginning with *volk* 'people'.

GIVEN NAME German 5%. *Manfred.*

Vocke (173) Variant of VOCK.

Voda (164) Czech, Slovak, and Slovenian: topographic name or nickname from *voda* 'water'. Compare Czech VODICKA.

Vodicka (223) Czech and Slovak (**Vodička**): from a diminutive of Czech *voda* 'water', hence a topographic name for someone who lived by water, a nickname for a teetaler or an ironical nickname for an innkeeper.

Voecks (105) German (also **Völcks**): probably a variant of VOCK.

GIVEN NAME German 4%. *Fritz.*

Voegele (512) German (also **Vögele**): see VOGELE.

GIVEN NAMES German 7%. *Dieter* (2), *Otto* (2), *Annice, Erwin, Frieda, Gerhard, Helmuth, Klaus, Kurt, Milbert, Otmar.*

Voegeli (314) South German and Swiss German (also **Vögeli**): from a diminutive of VOGEL.

GIVEN NAMES German 4%. *Kurt, Mathias, Otto.*

Voehl (105) German: variant of **Föhl**, Alemannic dialect variant of FEIL 2.

Voeks (112) German: variant of VOECKS.

GIVEN NAME German 5%. *Frieda* (2).

Voelkel (456) German (also **Völkel**): from a pet form of VOLKMAR.

GIVEN NAMES German 6%. *Angelika, Eldor, Franz, Kurt, Lutz.*

Voelker (2025) German (also **Völker**): variant of VOLKER.

Voeller (408) German (**Völler**): from a variant of VOLLER.

GIVEN NAMES French 4%. *Romain, Vernice.*

Voellinger (124) German (**Völlinger**): habitational name for someone from Völling near Regensburg.

Voeltz (220) German: variant of VOLZ.

Voelz (285) German: variant of VOLZ.

GIVEN NAMES German 4%. *Hans, Klaus.*

Voet (125) Dutch: nickname for someone with a deformity of the foot or with big feet, Middle Dutch *voet* 'foot'.

Vogan (377) Irish: variant of WOGAN.

Voge (282) **1.** North German: from Middle Low German *voge* 'skillful' or 'small', a nickname from either sense. **2.** Americanized form of Norwegian **Våge**, a habitational name from any of thirty or more farmsteads so named, from Old Norse *vágr* 'bay', 'fjord', 'inlet'.

GIVEN NAMES German 5%. *Erwin, Gerhardt, Hans, Kurt, Wilfried.*

Vogel (13278) **1.** German, Dutch, and Jewish (Ashkenazic): nickname for a happy person or someone who liked to sing, or a metonymic occupational name for a bird catcher, from Middle High German, Middle Low German *vogel* 'bird'. This name is found throughout central Europe, not only in German-speaking lands. **2.** Jewish (Ashkenazic): from the Yiddish female personal name *Foygl*, cognate with 1 above.

GIVEN NAMES German 4%. *Kurt* (27), *Hans* (10), *Gerhard* (6), *Manfred* (6), *Wolfgang* (6), *Erwin* (5), *Otto* (5), *Bernhard* (3), *Dieter* (3), *Franz* (3), *Fritz* (3), *Heinz* (3).

Vogele (151) German (**Vögele**): from a diminutive of VOGEL.

GIVEN NAME German 4%. *Gerhard.*

Vogeler (223) German: variant of VOGLER.

GIVEN NAMES German 8%. *Erna, Gerhard, Hellmuth, Kurt, Otto.*

Vogelgesang (250) German: variant of VOGELSANG 2.

Vogelman (132) **1.** German (**Vogelmann**): occupational name for a birdcatcher, from Middle High German, Middle Low German *vogel* 'bird' + *man* 'man'. **2.** Jewish (Ashkenazic): variant of VOGEL 2, in the sense 'husband of Foygl'.

GIVEN NAME German 9%. *Kurt* (3).

Vogelpohl (213) North German: topographic name from Middle Low German *vogel* 'bird' + *pohl* 'pool', 'pond'.

Vogelsang (693) **1.** German: habitational name from any of several places called

Vogelsang. **2.** Jewish (Ashkenazic): ornamental name meaning 'bird song'.

GIVEN NAMES German 6%. *Ingo* (2), *Kurt* (2), *Bernd, Dieter, Erwin, Fritz, Gerhard, Gunther, Joerg, Otto, Willi.*

Vogelsberg (115) German: habitational name from any of various places named Vogelsberg, for example in Thuringia, or Vögelsberg in Tyrol, Austria.

GIVEN NAME German 6%. *Kurt.*

Vogelsong (202) Part translation of German VOGELSANG.

Vogen (121) Americanized spelling of Norwegian **Vågen**, a habitational name from any of numerous farmsteads so named, from the definite singular of *våg* 'bay', 'fjord', 'inlet' (see VOGE).

GIVEN NAME Scandinavian 9%. *Bjorn* (2).

Voges (478) North German: of uncertain origin; possibly a patronymic from VOGT, or alternatively from a short form of Middle High German *vogesser*, a variant of *voche(n)zer*, an occupational name for a pastrycook or confectioner.

GIVEN NAMES German 5%. *Gerd* (2), *Otto* (2), *Hans, Johann.*

Voght (183) Variant of German VOGT.

GIVEN NAME German 5%. *Gunter.*

Vogl (600) German: variant of VOGEL.

GIVEN NAMES German 6%. *Otto* (2), *Beate, Guenther, Herwig, Johann, Kurt, Siegfried, Sigi, Volker.*

Vogle (134) German (**Vögle**): variant of VOGEL.

Vogler (1581) German: occupational name for a fowler or birdcatcher, from an agent derivative of VOGEL.

GIVEN NAMES German 4%. *Kurt* (4), *Otto* (4), *Gunther* (2), *Alfons, Erwin, Frieda, Gerhard, Volker, Wilfried, Wolf.*

Vogt (7568) German: occupational name for a bailiff, farm manager, or other person with supervisory authority, Middle High German *voget*, Late Latin *vocatus*, from Latin *advocatus*, past participle of *advocare* 'to call upon (to help)'. The term originally denoted someone who appeared before a court on behalf of some party not permitted to make direct representations, often an ecclesiastical body which was not supposed to have any dealings with temporal authorities.

GIVEN NAMES German 4%. *Otto* (11), *Kurt* (7), *Hans* (6), *Armin* (5), *Erna* (3), *Fritz* (3), *Gerhard* (3), *Gunter* (3), *Helmut* (3), *Alois* (2), *Erwin* (2), *Guenther* (2).

Vogts (159) German: variant (from the genitive form) of VOGT.

Vogus (116) German: perhaps a respelling of North German **Voges**, a variant of **Fochezer**, an occupational name for a baker (of cakes), from Late Latin *focatia* (Italian *focaccia*) '(kind of) cake', '(kind of) white bread'.

Vohra (185) **1.** Indian (Panjab): Hindu (Khatri) and Sikh name based on the name of a clan in the Khatri community. It is of

uncertain origin, but is popularly thought to derive from Sanskrit *vyūha* 'battle array'. **2.** Muslim (Pakistan): perhaps an occupational name from Urdu *bohora* 'merchant'.
GIVEN NAMES Indian 70%; Muslim 17%. *Ajay* (3), *Meena* (3), *Archana* (2), *Ashok* (2), *Bharat* (2), *Deepak* (2), *Pankaj* (2), *Pran* (2), *Rakesh* (2), *Saroj* (2), *Subhash* (2), *Sunil* (2); *Iqbal* (2), *Ismail* (2), *Sham* (2), *Yusuf* (2), *Abdul*, *Ahmed*, *Aref*, *Arif*, *Asif*, *Beshir*, *Kausar*, *Mohammad*.

Vohs (439) German: variant spelling of German FOSSE.
GIVEN NAMES German 4%. *Gerhard*, *Hans*, *Heinrich*, *Johann*.

Voice (120) English: variant spelling of VOYCE.

Voight (1319) Variant of German VOGT.

Voigt (3046) German and Danish: variant of VOGT.
GIVEN NAMES German 6%. *Kurt* (7), *Arno* (4), *Ernst* (2), *Fritz* (2), *Gerhard* (2), *Hans* (2), *Klaus* (2), *Otto* (2), *Reiner* (2), *Volkmar* (2), *Bernhard*, *Deiter*.

Voigts (178) North German: variant of VOGTS.
GIVEN NAMES German 6%. *Fritz*, *Hellmut*, *Kurt*.

Voiles (363) English, of Welsh origin: variant spelling of VOYLES.

Voils (100) English, of Welsh origin: variant spelling of VOYLES.

Voirol (112) Eastern French and Swiss French: from a personal name of Germanic origin composed of *war(in)* 'guard' + *wulf* 'wolf'.

Voisard (127) French: regional variant of *Vézant*, a nickname from a pejorative of *vézant* 'joyful', 'happy'.

Voisin (374) English (of Norman origin) and French: from Old French *voisin* 'neighbor' (Anglo-Norman French *veisin*). The application is uncertain; it may be a nickname for a 'good neighbor', or for someone who used this word as a frequent term of address, or it may be a topographic name for someone who lived on a neighboring property.
GIVEN NAMES French 6%. *Collette*, *Evest*, *Francois*, *Lucien*, *Pascal*, *Remy*.

Voisine (384) French: **1.** variant of VOISIN. **2.** habitational name from places so named in Haute-Marne and Yonne.
GIVEN NAMES French 15%. *Normand* (3), *Marcel* (2), *Adrien*, *Alcide*, *Alphonse*, *Alyre*, *Aurore*, *Cecile*, *Emile*, *Germain*, *Josephe*, *Lucien*.

Voit (512) German: eastern German dialect variant of VOGT.
GIVEN NAMES German 4%. *Eberhard*, *Erwin*, *Fritz*, *Kurt*, *Otto*, *Reinhard*.

Vojta (120) Czech and Slovak: from a pet form of the personal name *Vojtěch* (see VOYTEK).

Vojtech (100) Czech (**Vojtěch**) and Slovak: see VOYTEK.

Vokes (219) English: variant of FOLK.

Vokoun (125) Czech: **1.** nickname from *(v)okoun* 'perch' (the fish), denoting either a perch fisherman or someone thought to resemble a perch. **2.** from *(v)oko* 'eye', a nickname for someone with expressive eyes.

Voland (202) **1.** French: nickname from the present participle of Old French *voler* 'to fly', in the sense of 'nimble', 'agile'. **2.** Americanized spelling of Norwegian **Våland**, a habitational name from any of four farmsteads so named in Agder and Rogaland, probably from Old Norse *vá* 'bend', 'corner' + *land* 'land', 'farm'.
GIVEN NAMES German 4%. *Florian*, *Guenther*, *Kurt*.

Volante (218) **1.** Italian: nickname from *volante* '(he) who flies' (compare 3, below). **2.** Spanish: unexplained. **3.** English: nickname from the present participle of Old French *voler* 'to fly', in the sense of 'nimble', 'agile'.
GIVEN NAMES Italian 16%; Spanish 5%. *Guido* (3), *Antonio* (2), *Alberico*, *Alfredo*, *Bonifacio*, *Carmine*, *Elio*, *Fortunato*, *Marco*; *Carlos* (2), *Julio* (2), *Josefina*, *Wilfredo*.

Volbrecht (115) German: variant of VOLLBRECHT.

Volcy (123) Of French origin: unexplained.
GIVEN NAMES French 46%. *Gaspard* (2), *Leonce* (2), *Lucien* (2), *Andre*, *Eunide*, *Evens*, *Francois*, *Jean Robert*, *Jean-Claude*, *Landry*, *Mireille*, *Mirlande*.

Vold (443) Norwegian: variant of VOLL.
GIVEN NAMES Scandinavian 5%. *Erik*, *Helmer*, *Oivind*.

Volden (271) Norwegian: habitational name from any of numerous farmsteads so named, from the definite singular form of *voll* 'meadow' (see VOLL).

Volek (153) Czech: **1.** from a pet form of the personal name *Voldřich*, a derivative of *Oldřich*. **2.** from a diminutive of *vůl* 'ox', a nickname for a big clumsy man or an occupational name for an oxherd.

Volentine (140) Variant of VALENTINE.

Volesky (146) Probably Belorussian, a habitational name for someone from a place named with *vol* 'ox'.

Volin (207) Czech: habitational name from a place called Volyně (German *Volin*).

Volino (130) Italian: from a diminutive of *Volo* (see VUOLO).
GIVEN NAMES Italian 20%. *Rocco* (2), *Aniello*, *Antonio*, *Carmela*, *Carmine*, *Giovanni*, *Sabato*, *Santina*.

Voliva (142) Hispanic: perhaps variant of OLIVA.

Volk (3692) **1.** German: from a medieval personal name, a short form of various Germanic personal names with the first element *folk* 'people'. Compare FOULKES. **2.** Czech: variant of the personal name VOLEK. **3.** Slovenian: nickname from *volk* 'wolf'. **4.** Ukrainian: Russianized form of

Ukrainian **Vovk**, a nickname meaning 'wolf'. **5.** Jewish (western Ashkenazic): ornamental name from German *Volk* 'people'. **6.** English: variant of FOULKS.

Volker (784) German: from a Germanic personal name composed of the elements *folk* 'people' + *her* 'army'.
GIVEN NAMES German 4%. *Kurt* (4), *Otto* (2), *Erwin*, *Heinz*, *Monika*.

Volkers (199) German: patronymic derivative of VOLKER.
GIVEN NAMES German 5%. *Hans*, *Kurt*.

Volkert (512) German: from a Germanic personal name composed of the elements *folk* 'people' + *hard* 'hardy', 'strong'.
GIVEN NAMES German 4%. *Fritz* (2), *Otto* (2), *Frieda*.

Volkman (918) Altered spelling of German VOLKMANN.

Volkmann (514) German: from the personal name *Volkmann*, an elaborated form of VOLK, with the addition of *Mann* 'man'.
GIVEN NAMES German 9%. *Kurt* (3), *Bernhard*, *Eldred*, *Erwin*, *Fritz*, *Gerhard*, *Guenter*, *Hermann*, *Hubertus*, *Inge*, *Otto*, *Ralf*.

Volkmar (141) German: variant of VOLLMER.

Volkmer (244) German: variant of VOLLMER.
GIVEN NAMES German 7%. *Kurt* (2), *Erik*, *Hans*, *Reiner*.

Volkov (108) Russian and Jewish (eastern Ashkenazic): patronymic form from Russian *volk* 'wolf'. The Russian name is derived from a nickname or older male personal name. The Yiddish name is in some cases an ornamental name, while in other cases it is a habitational name from places called Volkovo or Volki, now in Belarus, which in turn are derived from the name of the animal.
GIVEN NAMES Russian 39%; Jewish 17%; French 4%. *Igor* (5), *Sergey* (4), *Oleg* (3), *Vladimir* (3), *Boris* (2), *Grigoriy* (2), *Sergei* (2), *Aleksandr*, *Anatoliy*, *Arkadiy*, *Emiliya*, *Evgeni*, *Vladislav*; *Baruch*, *Irina*, *Josif*, *Naum*, *Ruvim*; *Alexandre*, *Anatole*, *Serge*.

Voll (593) Norwegian: habitational name from any of fifty or more farmsteads all over Norway, so named from Old Norse *vǫllr* 'grassy field', 'meadow'.

Volland (217) German: from a Germanic personal name composed of the elements *folk* 'people' + *nand* 'dare'.

Vollaro (113) Italian: unexplained.
GIVEN NAMES Italian 18%. *Angelo*, *Carlo*, *Gaetano*, *Gennaro*, *Guido*, *Philomena*, *Valentino*.

Vollbrecht (253) German: from a Germanic personal name composed of the elements *folk* 'people' + *berht* 'bright', 'famous'. In the U.S. this name is Americanized as FULBRIGHT and FULLBRIGHT.
GIVEN NAMES German 8%. *Kurt* (3), *Eldor*, *Ernst*, *Manfred*.

Volle (195) **1.** German: variant of VOLL. **2.** Norwegian: habitational name from any of several farmsteads so named, from Old Norse vǫllr 'grassy field', 'meadow'.
GIVEN NAME German 4%. *Kurt* (2).

Vollenweider (174) German: topographic name for someone who lived by a field named as being a pasture reserved for foals, from Middle High German *vole* 'foal' (plural *volen*) + *weide* 'meadow', 'pasture'.
GIVEN NAMES German 5%. *Heinz, Kurt, Otto*.

Voller (238) Dutch and German: occupational name for a dresser of cloth, cognate of English FULLER.

Vollman (243) German (**Vollmann**): variant of VOLKMANN.
GIVEN NAMES German 4%. *Kurt* (2), *Inge*.

Vollmar (514) German: variant of VOLLMER.

Vollmer (2723) German: from a Germanic personal name composed of the elements *folk* 'people' + *meri, mari* 'famous'.

Vollrath (513) German: from a Germanic personal name composed of the elements *folk* 'people' + *rāt* 'council'.

Vollstedt (113) German: habitational name from Vollstedt in Schleswig-Holstein.
GIVEN NAMES German 9%. *Kurt* (2), *Otto*.

Volmer (251) German: variant spelling of VOLLMER.

Volner (255) Czech: occupational name for a wool worker, from German WOLLNER.

Voloshin (128) Ukrainian and Jewish (from Ukraine): ethnic or regional name from Ukrainian *voloshin* 'person from Wallachia'.
GIVEN NAMES Russian 25%; Jewish 14%; Czech and Slovak 4%. *Arkady* (2), *Igor* (2), *Leonid* (2), *Vladimir* (2), *Aleksandr, Anatoly, Boris, Dmitry, Galena, Genady, Gennady, Mikhail; Gelina, Moshe, Moysey, Yakov; Alexandr, Pavel*.

Volosin (104) Ukrainian and Jewish (from Ukraine and Russia): variant of VOLOSHIN.

Volpe (3111) **1.** Italian: nickname for a crafty person, from *volpe* 'fox' (Latin *vulpes*). **2.** Jewish (eastern Ashkenazic): habitational name from a place in Belarus, southeast of Grodno, the Yiddish name of which is *Volp(e)* (Belorussian, Russian *Volpa*, Polish *Wołpa*).
GIVEN NAMES Italian 15%. *Angelo* (19), *Rocco* (15), *Salvatore* (15), *Antonio* (10), *Dante* (6), *Vito* (6), *Pasquale* (5), *Sal* (5), *Carmine* (4), *Santo* (4), *Caesar* (3), *Carlo* (3).

Volpert (115) Jewish (from Lithuania): variant of WOLPERT.
GIVEN NAMES Jewish 9%; Russian 7%; French 6%. *Yehuda* (2), *Mendy; Vladimir* (2), *Aleksandr, Grigoriy, Leonid; Auguste, Pierre*.

Volpi (283) Italian: patronymic from VOLPE.
GIVEN NAMES Italian 10%. *Carlo* (2), *Guido* (2), *Silvio* (2), *Ugo* (2), *Angelo, Gino, Luigi, Marco, Nicola, Rocci, Rocco*.

Volpicelli (108) Italian: from a diminutive of VOLPE.
GIVEN NAMES Italian 16%. *Angelo* (2), *Antonio, Gaetano, Vito*.

Voltmer (100) German: variant of VOLLMER.
GIVEN NAME German 4%. *Egon*.

Voltz (622) German (also **Völtz**): variant spelling of VOLZ.

Volz (2124) German (**Völz**): from the personal names *Vol(k)mar* or *Volkmer* (see VOLLMER).

Vona (298) Italian: variant of BONA.
GIVEN NAMES Italian 24%. *Sebastiano* (3), *Armando* (2), *Carlo* (2), *Dino* (2), *Eduardo* (2), *Antonio, Benito, Carmine, Ernesto, Fiore, Gino, Nicola, Ottavio, Sal, Salvatore*.

Vonada (195) German: see NIDA.

Von Allmen (183) Swiss German: topographic name from Middle High German *alm* 'mountain pasture' + the preposition *von* 'from'.
GIVEN NAMES German 8%. *Hans* (2), *Erwin, Fritz, Kurt*.

Von Arx (187) Swiss German: habitational name for someone from Arx, a place near Basel in Switzerland.
GIVEN NAMES German 4%. *Otto, Urs*.

Vonasek (146) Czech (**Vonásek**): from a variant of the personal name *Ondřej*, Czech form of ANDREAS.

Von Bank (107) German: habitational name for someone from a place named Bank, or a reduced form of *von der Bank* 'from the bench', referring to a merchant stall in a market.
GIVEN NAMES German 6%. *Franz, Gerhard*.

Von Bargen (257) German (**von Bargen**): variant of VON BERGEN.
GIVEN NAMES German 6%. *Fritz, Karlheinz, Otto, Siegfried*.

Von Behren (288) German (**von Behren**): habitational name for someone from a place called Behren or Beeren.
GIVEN NAMES German 7%. *Erwin* (2), *Kurt* (2), *Dietrich*.

Von Berg (117) German: habitational name for someone from Berg in North Rhine-Westphalia.

Von Bergen (172) German (**von Bergen**): topographic name for someone who lived in a mountainous area, from Middle High German *berc* 'mountain', 'hill' (dative plural *bergen*).
GIVEN NAMES German 6%. *Fritz, Gerhard, Otto*.

Voncannon (228) Probably an American altered form of Irish CONCANNON. This name occurs predominantly in NC. Compare VUNCANNON, FINCANNON.

Von Der Ahe (133) German: topographic name for someone who lived by a creek, from the old terms *aa* or *ahe* 'running water', 'stream'.
GIVEN NAME German 6%. *Kurt* (2).

Von Der Au (139) German: topographic name from *von der Au* 'from the water meadow or river island'.

Von Der Haar (457) North German: topographic name for a marsh or moorland dweller, from Middle Low German *von der haar* 'from the marsh or moor'.

Von Der Heide (323) German: topogaphic name for a heathland dweller, from Middle High German *von der heide* 'from the heath'.
GIVEN NAMES German 5%. *Kurt* (3), *Hans, Otto*.

Vondra (252) Eastern German and Czech: from the personal name *Vondra(s)*, a Slavic vernacular form of ANDREAS. Compare VONDRACEK.

Vondracek (169) Czech (**Vondráček**): from a pet form of *Vondřej*, a variant of the personal name *Ondřej*, Czech form of ANDREAS.
GIVEN NAME German 4%. *Viktor* (2).

Vondrak (223) Eastern German and Czech (**Vondrák**): from a derivative of the personal name *Ondřej*, Czech form of ANDREAS, or a Sorbian or other Slavic cognate.

Vondran (174) German (of Slavic origin): Germanized form of a Slavic, possibly Sorbian, form of Latin ANDREAS.
GIVEN NAME German 4%. *Ulrich* (2).

Vondrasek (179) Czech (**Vondrásek**): from a pet form of the personal name *Vondrej, Ondřej*, a Czech vernacular form of the New Testament name ANDREAS.

Von Eschen (108) German: habitational name for someone from Eschen in Bavaria.

Von Essen (108) German: habitational name for someone from the city of Essen in North Rhine-Westphalia, or possibly from a similarly named place in Lower Saxony.
GIVEN NAMES German 8%. *Ingrid, Klaus, Nikolaus*.

Von Feldt (283) German (**von Feldt**): topographic name for someone who lived by an area of open country, Middle High German *vëlt*.

Vong (482) **1.** Danish and Swedish (**Vång**): variant of **Vång** (see VANG). **2.** Vietnamese: unexplained.
GIVEN NAMES Vietnamese 58%. *Sang* (16), *Mui* (13), *Chan* (5), *Minh* (5), *On* (5), *Sinh* (4), *Cau* (3), *Cong* (3), *Ly* (3), *Nam* (3), *Yen* (3), *Bao* (2), *Bau* (2), *Cai* (2), *Hin* (2), *Kiu* (2), *Song* (2), *Ha* (2), *Hung* (2), *Khung* (2), *Long* (2), *Phong* (2).

Von Glahn (141) German: habitational name for someone from a place called Glahn near Hannover.
GIVEN NAMES German 11%. *Claus, Fritz, Gerhard, Klaus, Uwe*.

Von Gunten (147) Swiss German: habitational name for someone from Gunten in Bern canton, Switzerland.

Von Haden (115) Apparently a German habitational name from a lost or unidentified place; it could perhaps be a shortened form of Hadenfeld, a place in Schleswig-Holstein.

Von Holten (108) German: habitational name for someone from Holten in North Rhine-Westphalia.
GIVEN NAMES German 11%. *Claus, Gunter, Heinz, Johann.*

Vonk (246) Dutch: from Middle Dutch *vonc, vonke* 'spark', hence probably a metonymic occupational name for a smith.
GIVEN NAMES Dutch 7%. *Dirk* (2), *Henk, Joost, Marten.*

Von Kaenel (120) German (**Von Känel**): probably a habitational name from a lost or unidentified place named Känel, from Middle High German *kenel* 'water channel' (from Latin *canalis*).
GIVEN NAMES German 7%. *Gottlieb, Heinz, Juerg.*

Vonnahme (99) German: topographic or habitational name of unknown origin.
GIVEN NAMES German 4%. *Erwin, Hans.*

Von Ruden (242) German: habitational name for someone from a place called Ruden.

Von Seggern (237) North German: topographic name for someone who lived where sedges grew, from the dative plural of Middle Low German *segge* 'sedge'.
GIVEN NAMES German 4%. *Erna, Hans, Kurt.*

Von Stein (190) German: topographic name for someone from a place distinguished by a rock, Middle High German *stein* or from any of several places named with this word.
GIVEN NAMES German 6%. *Alfons, Armin, Lorenz.*

Von Wald (172) German: topographic name for someone who lived in a forest, Middle High German *walt* or from any of several places named with this word.

Voogd (113) Dutch: occupational name for a bailiff, farm manager, or other personal with supervisory authority, Middle High German *voget*, Late Latin *vocatus*, from Latin *advocatus*, past participle of *advocare* 'to call up (to help)'. Compare German VOGT.
GIVEN NAMES Dutch 8%; Scandinavian 4%; German 4%. *Maarten* (2), *Gerrit*; *Erik*; *Hertha.*

Voong (155) Vietnamese: unexplained.
GIVEN NAMES Vietnamese 55%; Chinese 16%. *Mui* (6), *Bau* (3), *Cong* (3), *Minh* (3), *Phi* (3), *Lan* (2), *That* (2), *Binh, Cuong, Denh, Duong, Henh*; *Sang* (3), *Man* (2), *Tong* (2), *Chan, Hang, In, Kiu, Lai, Leng, Sin, Siu, Song.*

Voorhees (2387) Dutch: habitational name from a place in Drenthe called Voorhees.
FOREBEARS Steven Coertse van Voorhees emigrated from the Netherlands and settled on Long Island, NY, in 1660.

Voorheis (290) Dutch: variant of VOORHEES.

Voorhies (656) Dutch: variant of VOORHEES.

Voorhis (355) Dutch: variant of VOORHEES.

Voos (111) German: from a short form of *Servatius*, a saint's name.
GIVEN NAMES German 6%. *Hans, Klaus, Kurt.*

Vopat (114) Czech: variant of **Opat**, metonymic occupational name for someone in the service of an abbot, from *opat* 'abbot'.
GIVEN NAMES German 5%. *Gottlieb, Otto.*

Vora (315) Indian (Gujarat): Hindu and Muslim name of unknown meaning.
GIVEN NAMES Indian 85%. *Ashok* (4), *Rajesh* (4), *Sanjay* (4), *Varsha* (4), *Ajay* (3), *Amit* (3), *Bharat* (3), *Jayesh* (3), *Mahendra* (3), *Manish* (3), *Navin* (3), *Ramesh* (3).

Voran (101) German: variant of VORNDRAN.

Vorbeck (99) German: habitational name from a place near Altenau in the Harz Mountains.

Vorce (281) **1.** English: variant of FORCE. **2.** Perhaps an altered form of Dutch VOORHEES.

Vorderbruggen (104) German: topographic name for someone who lived 'in front of the bridge'.

Vore (508) English: unexplained.

Vorel (120) Czech: from a variant of *orel* 'eagle', probably a habitational name for someone who lived at a house distinguished by the sign of an eagle (see OREL).

Vorhees (251) Variant of Dutch VOORHEES.

Vorhies (254) Variant of Dutch VOORHEES.

Vorhis (104) Variant of Dutch VOORHEES.

Voris (590) Variant of Dutch VOORHEES.

Vork (101) Danish: variant of WORK 3.

Vorndran (259) German: nickname meaning 'ahead of all'.
GIVEN NAMES German 5%. *Otto* (3), *Kurt.*

Voros (168) Hungarian (**Vörös**): nickname for someone with red hair or skin complexion, from Hungarian *vörös* 'red'.
GIVEN NAMES Hungarian 19%. *Janos* (3), *Attila* (2), *Istvan* (2), *Bela, Endre, Ferenc, Katalin, Lorant, Zsolt.*

Vorpagel (113) German: probably a variant of VORPAHL.
GIVEN NAMES German 5%. *Erwin, Kurt.*

Vorpahl (262) German: topographic name for someone who lived at a boundary marker, from Middle Low German *vorpāl* 'boundary pole'.
GIVEN NAMES German 5%. *Konrad* (2), *Gerhardt, Hans, Otto, Ulrich.*

Vorse (116) English: variant of FORCE.

Vorst (101) Dutch and North German: topographic name for someone who lived in a forest or occupational name for someone who worked in one, from Middle Low German *vorst* 'forest'.

Vorwald (200) German: topographic name for someone who lived 'in front of (Middle High German *vor*) a forest (Middle High German *walt*)'.

Vorwerk (231) German: topographic name from Middle Low German *vōrwerk*,

Middle High German *vorwerc* 'outlying farm (belonging to a manor)', later 'large rural property'.
GIVEN NAME German 4%. *Arno* (2).

Vos (1309) **1.** English: see FOSSE. **2.** Dutch (**de Vos**): nickname for someone with red hair, from *vos* 'fox'. **3.** North German: variant of VOSS.

Vosberg (287) North German and Dutch: topographic name for someone who lived by a hill frequented by foxes, from Middle Low German *vos* 'fox' + *berg* 'hill', 'mountain'.

Vosburg (545) Variant of North German and Dutch VOSBERG, by confusion with the equally common place-name element *burg* 'fortress', 'citadel'.

Vosburgh (704) Americanized spelling of Dutch and German VOSBERG. See also VOSBURG.

Vose (718) **1.** English: variant of FOSSE. **2.** Dutch: patronymic from a reduced form of the Latin personal name *Servatius*.
FOREBEARS Robert Vose emigrated from Lancashire, England, to Dorchester, MA, before 1654.

Voshall (106) English: variant of **Vauxhall**, habitational name from a place in Surrey so called, on the south bank of the River Thames, now part of Greater London. This was named in the 13th century as *Faukeshalle* 'the Hall of Fauke', a reference to Baron Falke de Breaulté, who was granted the manor by King John in 1233. This was the site of a famous pleasure garden frequented by 18th-century Londoners.

Voshell (333) Variant of English **Vauxhall** (see VOSHALL).

Vosika (149) Origin unidentified.

Voskuil (156) Dutch: topographic name from *voskuyl* 'fox-hole'.

Vosler (191) Altered spelling of German VOSSLER.

Vosper (135) English (Cornwall and Devon): unexplained.

Voss (8541) German: variant of FOSSE.
GIVEN NAMES German 4%. *Kurt* (16), *Hans* (11), *Otto* (7), *Erwin* (5), *Heinz* (4), *Dieter* (3), *Ernst* (3), *Fritz* (3), *Gunther* (3), *Helmut* (3), *Ulrich* (3), *Erna* (2).

Vossen (288) North German: from a diminutive of FOSSE.

Vossler (471) South German: variant of FOSSLER.

Vosters (139) Dutch: occupational name for a forester or woodsman, Middle Dutch *voestere*.

Vota (132) Italian: of uncertain derivation. Caracausi proposes a derivation from Sicilian *vota* 'turning', 'bend' or from medieval Latin *vota* 'vault', 'vaulted room'. The surname, however, belongs to the northwest (Liguria and Piedmont), which throws doubt on the first suggestion at least.

GIVEN NAMES Italian 6%; French 6%. *Alfonse, Carmine*; *Emile* (2), *Alphonse*.

Votava (294) Czech: from *(v)otava*, literally 'aftermath', i.e. a second crop of grass from the same field, after a first crop has been mown in early summer. As a surname, this may be a topographic name for someone who lived by a field that yielded two crops a year, or an anecdotal nickname.

Votaw (659) Origin uncertain. Possibly an Americanized form of Czech VOTAVA.

Vote (160) Hispanic (Mexico): unexplained.

Voth (998) North German: from Middle Low German *vōt* 'foot', hence most probably a nickname for someone with some peculiarity or deformity of the foot, but perhaps also a topographic name for someone who lived at the foot of a hill.

Votruba (153) Czech: unflattering nickname from Czech *(v)otruby* 'bran', 'husks', which has the figurative sense 'blockhead'.

Votta (244) Italian: variant of BOTTA.

GIVEN NAMES Italian 6%; French 4%. *Antonio* (3), *Reno* (2), *Rocco* (2), *Domenic*; *Lucien, Monique*.

Vought (600) Americanized spelling of German VOGT.

Vowell (943) English variant of FOWLE.

Vowels (398) English: variant of FOWLE.

Vowles (165) English: variant of FOWLE.

Voyce (111) English (of Norman origin): habitational name from Voise, in Eure-et-Loire, France.

Voyer (175) French: occupational name for a legal official, Old French *voyer*, from Latin *vicarius*.

FOREBEARS A bearer of the name Voyer from the Maine region of France is documented in Château Richer, Quebec, in 1662. **Le Jardinier** is an associated secondary surname.

GIVEN NAMES French 15%. *Emile* (2), *Gaetan, Gilles, Jacques, Jean-Paul, Julien, Marcel, Rosaire, Viateur*.

Voyles (1985) English, of Welsh origin: variant of **Voyle**, a nickname for a bald man or a topographic name for someone living by a treeless hill, from a lenited form of Welsh *moel* 'bald' or 'treeless hill'.

Voytek (219) Americanized spelling of Czech **Vojtek** or **Vojtěch**, Slovak and Bulgarian **Vojtek**, Polish **Wojtek**, or a cognate in any other Slavic language. This is a surname taken from the personal name *Vojtek*, a pet form of Slavic *Vojtěch* (Polish *Wojciech*), meaning 'consoling the host' (from *voj* 'host', 'army', 'force' + *těch* 'comfort', 'consolation'). This, together with the Germanized form *Wozzek*, was a popular personal name among Christians in Eastern Europe, mainly because of the cult of St. Vojtěch (*c*.956–997), bishop of Prague from 982 onwards. In 995 he was expelled from Bohemia and in 996 he went to Poland on a mission to the Prussians (members of a heathen Baltic-speaking people, not the German speakers who later

took their name). He was killed by the Prussians in 997, and was canonized in 999. He is regarded as the first Polish saint; in Polish he is known as St. Wojciech. In German he is known by his second name as St. Adalbert (or Albert) of Prague.

Voytko (180) Ukrainian: from a pet form of the personal name *Vojcech* (see VOYTEK).

Vozar (124) Slovenian; also Croatian (northern Croatia; **Vožar**): occupational name for a driver of a horse-drawn vehicle, from an agent derivative of *voz* 'cart'.

Vozza (129) Southern Italian and Sicilian: variant of BOZZA.

GIVEN NAMES Italian 28%. *Angelo* (4), *Alfredo* (2), *Almerinda* (2), *Carmine* (2), *Antonio, Giovanni, Guilio, Mario, Pasquale*.

Vozzella (157) Italian: from a derivative of **Vozzo**, a variant of BOZZO.

GIVEN NAMES Italian 14%. *Angelo* (3), *Carmela* (2), *Prisco* (2), *Gennaro, Marino, Salvatore*.

Vrabel (563) Czech and Slovak (**Vrábel**): nickname from dialect *vrabec* 'sparrow'.

Vradenburg (127) Altered spelling of VREDENBURG.

Vrana (509) Czech (**Vrána**) and Slovenian: nickname from Czech *vrána*, Slovenian *vrana* 'crow'.

Vranich (107) **1.** Croatian and Serbian (**Vranić**), Slovenian (**Vranič**): patronymic from the surname **Vran**, a nickname from *vran* 'raven', 'male crow', or 'black horse'. **2.** Croatian: also a dialect form of **Franić**, patronymic from the personal name *Franjo*, Latin *Franciscus* (see FRANCIS).

GIVEN NAMES South Slavic 7%. *Branko, Marko, Stanko*.

Vrba (274) Czech and Slovak (**Vŕba**): habitational name for someone from a place named with *vrba* 'willow tree', or a topographic name for someone who lived near willow trees.

Vrchota (106) Czech: topographic name from a derivative of *vrch* 'hill'.

Vredenburg (230) Dutch, German, and Jewish (western Ashkenazic): **1.** habitational name from a place called Vredenburg in Gelderland, Netherlands. **2.** from a Germanic personal name, composed of the elements *frithu* 'peace' + *burg* 'stronghold'.

Vredenburgh (119) Dutch: variant spelling of VREDENBURG.

Vredeveld (133) Dutch: habitational name from a place so named in Drenthe province.

GIVEN NAMES Dutch 6%. *Gerrit, Henk, Hessel*.

Vreeland (1221) Dutch: habitational name from a place so named in Utrecht province.

Vrieze (152) Dutch: ethnic name for a Frisian.

Vroman (817) Dutch: patronymic from a personal name derived from a Germanic personal name composed of the elements

frōda 'clever', 'intelligent' + *mundō* 'protection'.

Vroom (280) Dutch: from a short form of a German personal name.

Vrooman (668) Dutch (**Vrooman**): variant of VROMAN.

Vu (3847) Vietnamese: unexplained.

GIVEN NAMES Vietnamese 68%; Chinese 15%. *Hung* (65), *Tuan* (62), *Thanh* (41), *Dung* (36), *Minh* (32), *Hoa* (30), *Hai* (29), *Cuong* (28), *Long* (28), *Tien* (27), *Binh* (26), *Hoang* (25), *Tam* (20), *Thai* (18), *Phong* (17), *Nam* (10), *Manh* (8), *Sinh* (6), *Tinh* (6), *Chung* (5), *Tuong* (3), *Neng* (2), *Tham* (2), *Thein* (2); *Hong* (15), *Chi* (13), *Hang* (10), *Chien* (8), *Han* (6), *Ho* (6), *Chan* (5), *Dong* (5), *Lai* (3), *Tao* (3), *Choung* (2), *Man* (2).

Vuckovich (117) **1.** Serbian and Croatian (**Vučković**), patronymic from *Vučko*, a pet form of the personal name *Vuk* (see VUKOVICH). **2.** Americanized spelling of Serbian and Croatian **Vuković**, patronymic from the personal name *Vuk*, from *vuk* 'wolf' (see VUKOVICH).

GIVEN NAMES South Slavic 14%. *Milenko* (2), *Dejan, Dragan, Drago, Lazar, Ljubisa, Marko, Vojo*.

Vue (741) Laotian: unexplained.

GIVEN NAMES Southeast Asian 70%; Vietnamese 7%. *Tou* (13), *Chao* (11), *Chue* (11), *Kao* (10), *Nhia* (9), *Tong* (9), *Yia* (9), *Chai* (8), *Mee* (8), *Yee* (8), *Chou* (7), *Xiong* (7); *Neng* (15), *Pao* (12), *Chong* (11), *Vang* (9), *Koua* (8), *Shoua* (8), *Soua* (8), *Yer* (8), *Thai* (6), *Yeng* (6), *Doua* (5), *Toua* (5); *Mai* (14), *Long* (6), *Kha* (3), *Thong* (3), *Dang* (2), *Khue* (2), *Bao, Dao, Ly, Nang, Nu, Pha*.

Vukelich (216) Serbian and Croatian (**Vukelić**): patronymic from a derivative of the personal name *Vuk*, from *vuk* 'wolf'.

Vukich (106) Serbian and Croatian (**Vukić**): patronymic from the personal name *Vuk*, from *vuk* 'wolf'.

Vukovich (352) Serbian and Croatian (**Vuković**): patronymic from the personal name *Vuk*, from *vuk* 'wolf'.

GIVEN NAMES South Slavic 5%. *Dragan, Marko, Miodrag, Rad, Vuk, Zvonko*.

Vulgamore (175) Origin unidentified.

Vullo (197) Italian (Sicily): variant of GULLO.

GIVEN NAMES Italian 19%. *Salvatore* (4), *Enzo* (2), *Adamo, Angelo, Cosmo, Giacomo, Luca, Saverio*.

Vultaggio (160) Italian (western Sicily): habitational name, probably from a lost place named Vultaggio.

GIVEN NAMES Italian 33%. *Giuseppe* (3), *Salvatore* (2), *Agostino, Antonio, Baldassare, Baldo, Bartolo, Biagio, Carlo, Filippo, Gaetano, Nino, Onofrio, Renato*.

Vuncannon (196) Probably an American altered form of Irish CONCANNON. This name occurs predominantly in NC. Compare VONCANNON, FINCANNON.

Vuolo (204) Southern Italian: southern variant of **Volo**, a variant of **Bolo**, which is probably a nickname derived from Greek *bōlos* 'clod', 'sod', 'lump'.
GIVEN NAMES Italian 19%. *Angelo* (2), *Pasquale* (2), *Aniello, Antonio, Ciro, Domenic, Gaetano, Gennaro, Gino, Luigi.*

Vuong (1207) Vietnamese: unexplained.
GIVEN NAMES Vietnamese 64%; Chinese 14%. *Thanh* (23), *Minh* (14), *Chau* (13), *Hung* (13), *Quang* (13), *Anh* (12), *Cuong* (12), *Binh* (10), *Hoa* (10), *Long* (10), *Duc* (9), *Lan* (8), *Phong* (6), *Tam* (6), *Chung* (4), *Nam* (4), *Tinh* (2); *Hong* (9), *Chan* (3), *Sang* (3), *Tong* (3), *Dong* (2), *Fat* (2), *Hon* (2), *Sai* (2), *Cai, Chi Hung, Chou, Han.*

Vuono (138) Italian: variant of BUONO.
GIVEN NAMES Italian 15%. *Angelo* (4), *Gennaro* (2), *Eligio, Natale.*

Vyas (447) Indian (northern states): Hindu (Brahman) name, from Sanskrit *vyāsa* 'compiler'. This was the name of the Sanskrit sage said to have compiled the *Mahabharata*.
GIVEN NAMES Indian 93%. *Dilip* (7), *Ashok* (5), *Hemant* (5), *Rohit* (5), *Girish* (4), *Ramesh* (4), *Vijay* (4), *Anil* (3), *Arvind* (3), *Ashutosh* (3), *Bharat* (3), *Chetan* (3).

Vyskocil (128) Czech (**Vyskočil**): anecdotal nickname from the past participle of *vyskočit* 'to jump or leap'.
GIVEN NAME Czech and Slovak 4%. *Antonin.*

W

Waack (189) **1.** North German: from the medieval personal name *Woke*. **2.** German: variant of WAAG.
GIVEN NAMES German 6%. *Dietrich, Erwin, Ewald, Friederike, Gerhardt.*

Waag (163) **1.** German: topographic name for someone who lived near a lake or marsh, from Middle High German *wāc* 'standing water', 'pool'. **2.** Norwegian: habitational name from any of ten or so farmsteads named Våg, mainly in Nordland, from Old Norse *vágr* 'bay', 'creek'.
GIVEN NAME German 4%. *Kurt.*

Waage (329) **1.** German and Dutch: from Middle High German *wāge*, Middle Dutch *waghe* 'scales', hence a metonymic occupational name for an official responsible for weighing produce, especially produce offered as rent in kind, or else for checking weights and measures used by merchants. **2.** Norwegian: variant of VOGE.
GIVEN NAMES Scandinavian 10%; German 7%. *Enok, Erik, Lars, Ludvig, Selmer, Thor; Otto* (3), *Hans* (2), *Konrad, Kurt.*

Waak (139) German: variant spelling of WAACK.

Waalkes (108) North German: variant of WALKES.

Waara (153) Finnish (**Vaara**): topographic or ornamental name from *vaara* 'hill', 'range of hills'. Found chiefly in northern Finland; occurs in southern Finland as an adopted name.
GIVEN NAMES Finnish 5%. *Oiva, Reino, Vieno.*

Waas (210) **1.** German: from a vernacular short form of the Latin personal name *Gervasius*, which was borne by a martyr and patron saint of Breisach on the Rhine. **2.** Dutch: habitational name from a place named with Middle Dutch *wase, waes* 'marsh', 'wetland'.

Waber (116) German and Jewish: Americanized variant of WEBER.
GIVEN NAMES Jewish 8%; German 4%. *Isadore; Hans, Kurt.*

Wable (104) **1.** Americanized form of German WEIBEL. **2.** Indian (Maharashtra); pronounced as *wah-blay*: Hindu (Maratha) name of unknown meaning.
GIVEN NAMES Indian 7%. *Suresh* (2), *Milind.*

Wacaster (135) Variant of WAYCASTER.

Wacek (120) Polish: from a pet form of the personal name *Wacław* (see VACEK).

Wach (328) **1.** Polish: from a short form of any of various Polish personal names

beginning with *Wa-*, e.g. *Wacław* (see VACEK) and *Wawrziniec*, Polish form of Latin *Laurentius* (see LAWRENCE). **2.** German (of Slavic origin): from a pet form of WENZEL.
GIVEN NAMES Polish 5%; German 4%. *Jadwiga, Marzena, Piotr, Stanisław, Wieslawa; Aloys, Manfred, Orlo.*

Wacha (204) **1.** Polish: derivative of WACH. **2.** Czech: from a Germanized spelling of Czech *Vácha*, a pet form of the personal name *Václav* (see VACEK).

Wachal (156) Polish: derivative of WACH.

Wachholz (246) **1.** German: habitational name for someone from a place called Wachholz ('boggy woods') near Stade. **2.** German: from the Germanic personal name *Wacald*.
GIVEN NAMES German 5%. *Kurt* (2), *Gerhard.*

Wachob (214) Origin unidentified.

Wachowiak (291) Polish: patronymic from the personal name WACH.

Wachowicz (91) Polish: patronymic from the personal name WACH.

Wachowski (243) Polish: habitational name for someone from a place called Wachów in Częstochowa voivodeship.
GIVEN NAMES Polish 5%. *Casimir, Jaroslaw, Kasmier, Piotr, Zygmunt.*

Wachs (663) German and Jewish (Ashkenazic): metonymic occupational name for a gatherer or seller of beeswax, from Middle High German *wahs*, German *Wachs* 'wax'. Wax was important in former times, being used for example to make candles and for sealing letters.
GIVEN NAMES Jewish 4%. *Abbe* (2), *Moshe* (2), *Aviva, Chaim, Eliezer, Hirsh, Hyman.*

Wachsman (223) German (**Wachsmann**) and Jewish (Ashkenazic): occupational name for a gatherer or seller of beeswax, a variant of WACHS, with the addition of the Middle High German and Yiddish suffix *man* 'man'.
GIVEN NAMES Jewish 14%; German 5%. *Chaim* (5), *Benzion* (4), *Ephrain, Mendel, Mendy, Sol; Brendt, Frieda, Rudi.*

Wachsmuth (214) German: from the personal name *Hwasmot* or *Wahsmut*, meaning 'sharp mind'.
GIVEN NAMES German 8%. *Hannelore* (2), *Ernst, Gerhard, Hans.*

Wachtel (983) **1.** German: from Middle High German *wahtel* 'quail', a metonymic occupational name for a bird catcher, or a nickname for a person thought to resemble

the bird. **2.** Jewish (Ashkenazic): ornamental name taken from German *Wachtel* or Yiddish *vakhtl* 'quail'.
GIVEN NAMES German 4%; Jewish 4%. *Hans* (4), *Helmut* (2), *Kurt* (2), *Bernd, Dieter, Gerda, Klaus, Rosl, Siegmund; Emanuel* (2), *Miriam* (2), *Shaul* (2), *Zev* (2), *Hyman, Isadore.*

Wachter (1886) **1.** German (also **Wächter**), and Dutch: occupational name for a watchman, from Middle High German *wachtære, wehtære*, Middle Dutch *wacht(e)re*, German *Wachter* 'watchman', 'guard'. **2.** Jewish (Ashkenazic): from German *Wachter* 'watchman', perhaps an occupational name by a synagogue beadle (Yiddish *shames*).

Wachtler (173) German (also **Wächtler**): occupational name for a bird catcher or dealer, from an agent derivative of WACHTEL.
GIVEN NAMES German 7%. *Siegmund* (2), *Kurt.*

Wachtman (113) German (**Wachtmann**): occupational name for a watchman (see WACHTER).

Wack (325) **1.** German: habitational name from a place called Wacken near Itzehoe. **2.** German: variant of WAACK 1. **3.** French: perhaps derived from an old Flemish word *wacque*, a measure of weight (Middle Dutch *wage* 'weight'), hence an occupational name for an official responsible for weighing produce (in particular produce paid as rent in kind), or else for one who was in charge of checking weights and measures used by merchants in a market.

Wacker (1625) German: nickname for a bold or energetic person, from Middle High German *wacker* 'fresh', 'lively', 'brave', 'valiant'.
GIVEN NAMES German 4%. *Kurt* (4), *Alois, Erwin, Frankl, Frieda, Hans, Heinz, Hermann, Reinhold, Rudi, Wolfgang.*

Wackerle (97) German: from a diminutive of WACKER.

Wackerly (123) Americanized spelling of German WACKERLE.

Wackerman (143) Americanized spelling of German **Wackermann**, a variant of WACKER, with the addition of Middle High German *man* 'man'.
GIVEN NAMES German 7%. *Otto* (2), *Kurt.*

Waclawski (113) Polish (**Wacławski**): habitational name for someone from a place called Wacławice in Przemyśl

voivodeship or from any of the many places in Poland called Wacławów, all named with the personal name *Wacław* (see VACEK).
GIVEN NAME Polish 4%. *Krzysztof.*

Wactor (129) Origin unidentified.

Wada (550) Japanese: 'harmonious rice paddy' (an older, formerly more common reading was *Nigita*, with a meaning similar to that of YOSHIDA). One powerful daimyō family, descended from the TAIRA through the MIURA family, supported the Minamoto against the Taira in the 12th century. They took their name from the village of Wada in the Miura Peninsula.
GIVEN NAMES Japanese 62%. *Yutaka* (6), *Akira* (4), *Hiroyuki* (4), *Koichi* (4), *Yoko* (4), *Hiroko* (3), *Junichi* (3), *Kazuo* (3), *Mamoru* (3), *Masaki* (3), *Osamu* (3), *Akiko* (2).

Wadas (211) Polish: perhaps an unflattering nickname from *wada* 'fault', 'defect'.

Waddel (109) Scottish and English: variant of WADDELL or WEDDLE.

Waddell (7874) **1.** Scottish: variant of WEDDLE. **2.** English: topographic name for someone who lived at the hill where woad grew, from Old English *wād* 'woad' + *hyll* 'hill', or a habitational name from a place so named, as for example Woodhill, Wiltshire.

Waddey (98) Scottish: variant of WALDIE.

Waddill (315) Variant of Scottish WADDLE.

Wadding (158) Southern English: unexplained; perhaps a reduced form of WADDINGHAM or WADDINGTON.

Waddingham (107) English: habitational name from Waddingham in Lincolnshire.

Waddington (785) Northern English: habitational name from any of various places called Waddington. One near Clitheroe in Lancashire and another in Lincolnshire (*Wadintune* in Domesday Book) were originally named in Old English as the 'settlement (Old English *tūn*) associated with *Wada*'.

Waddle (1506) Scottish and northern English: variant of WEDDLE or WADDELL.

Waddoups (155) English (Midlands): unexplained.

Waddy (469) Scottish: variant of WALDIE.

Wade (31204) **1.** English: from the Middle English personal name *Wade*, Old English *Wada*, from *wadan* 'to go'. (*Wada* was the name of a legendary sea-giant.) **2.** English: topographic name for someone who lived near a ford, Old English *(ge)wæd* (of cognate origin to 1), or a habitational name from a place named with this word, as for example Wade in Suffolk. **3.** Dutch and North German: occupational name or nickname from Middle Dutch, Middle Low German *wade* 'garment', 'large net'.
FOREBEARS Jonathan Wade emigrated from Norfolk, England, to Medford, MA, in 1632. Benjamin Franklin Wade (1800–1878), born near Springfield, MA, was a

prominent U.S. senator from OH during the Civil War.

Wadel (190) German: nickname from Middle High German *wadel, wedel* 'tail'.

Wadell (127) **1.** Variant spelling of English WADDELL. **2.** Variant spelling of German WADEL. **3.** Swedish: ornamental or topographic name from *vad* 'ford' + the common surname suffix *-ell*.
GIVEN NAMES French 8%; Scandinavian 4%. *Andre, Gabrielle; Helmer, Lennart.*

Wadford (217) English: habitational name, perhaps a variant of WATFORD.

Wadhams (178) English (Kent): habitational name from a place identified by Reaney as Wadham in Knowstone, Devon.

Wadhwa (120) Indian (Panjab): Hindu (Arora) and Sikh name based on the name of an Arora clan.
GIVEN NAMES Indian 89%. *Ashok* (5), *Vivek* (3), *Anil* (2), *Atul* (2), *Om* (2), *Raj* (2), *Ranjan* (2), *Satish* (2), *Subodh* (2), *Suresh* (2), *Abhay, Ajay.*

Wadhwani (103) Hindu and Muslim name found among people from Sind, Pakistan, meaning '(descendant) of Wadhwa'.
GIVEN NAMES Indian 87%. *Anil* (4), *Ashok* (4), *Deepak* (4), *Sunil* (3), *Prakash* (2), *Ramesh* (2), *Ajay, Amit, Ashish, Ashit, Dilip, Gautam.*

Wadkins (580) English: variant of WATKINS.

Wadle (270) **1.** Variant spelling of German WADEL. **2.** Scottish: variant spelling of WADDLE.
GIVEN NAMES German 4%. *Otto* (2), *Heinz, Rudi.*

Wadleigh (465) English: variant spelling of WADLEY.

Wadler (162) **1.** South German: nickname from an agent derivative of Middle High German *wadelen* 'to wander, roam'. **2.** Jewish (Ashkenazic): unexplained.
GIVEN NAME Jewish 8%. *Dovid* (2).

Wadley (1138) English: habitational name from a place in Berkshire named Wadley, from Old English *wād* 'woad' or the personal name *Wada* + *lēah* 'woodland clearing'. Wadley in Northumberland, which has the same derivation, appears not to have contributed significantly to the modern surname.

Wadlington (471) Perhaps a variant of the English habitational name WATLINGTON.

Wadlow (260) English: habitational name from a lost place, Wadlow in Toddington, Bedfordshire, named with the Old English personal name *Wada* + Old English *hlāw* 'hill', 'barrow'.

Wadman (360) English: occupational name for a gatherer or seller of woad, from an agent derivative of Middle English *wade* 'woad' (Old English *wād*). This plant produces a blue dye, which was widely used in the Middle Ages.

Wadsworth (3913) English: habitational name from Wadsworth near Halifax, West

Yorkshire, named with the Old English personal name *Wæddi* + *worð* 'enclosure'.
FOREBEARS William Wadsworth came from England to Cambridge, MA, in 1632, and in 1636 accompanied Thomas Hooker as one of the founders of Hartford, CT.
John Wadsworth (d. 1787) was a fellow of Harvard College and is buried in the old burial ground in Cambridge, MA.
Peleg Wadsworth, born in Duxbury, MA, 1748, was a revolutionary war general and grandfather of the poet Henry Wadsworth Longfellow.

Wadzinski (170) Polish: probably an altered spelling of **Wądzyński**, a habitational name for someone from a place called Wądzyn in Toruń voivodeship.

Waechter (541) German (**Wächter**): see WACHTER.
GIVEN NAMES German 5%. *Gerhard* (2), *Alfons, Ernst, Fritz, Manfred, Otto.*

Wafer (395) English: **1.** from Anglo-Norman French *wafre* 'wafer', alternating with *wafrer, wafrour* 'waferer', an occupational name for a maker or seller of eucharistic wafers or thin cakes. **2.** from an Old German personal name *Waifar, Waifer*, Old French *Gaifier*.
GIVEN NAMES French 4%. *Camille, Collette, Gregoire.*

Waffle (161) Americanized spelling of Dutch **Waffel**, a metonymic occupational name for a pastrycook.

Wafford (279) English: probably a variant of WATFORD.

Wagaman (624) Americanized spelling of German **Wagemann** (see WAGEMAN).

Wagar (619) English and German: variant spelling of WAGER.

Wage (151) **1.** North German: nickname for an indecisive person, from Middle Low German *wage* 'undecided', 'vaccilating'. **2.** German: (**Wäge**): variant of WAH. **3.** Jewish (Ashkenazic): metonymic occupational name from German *Waage* 'scales'.

Wageman (284) German (**Wagemann**) and Jewish (Ashkenazic): occupational name for an inspector of weights and measures (see WAGER).

Wagemann (136) German: see WAGEMAN.
GIVEN NAMES German 6%. *Erwin, Heinrich, Kurt.*

Wagenaar (178) Dutch: occupational name for a carter or cartwright, from Middle Dutch *waghenare*.
GIVEN NAMES Dutch 4%. *Andries, Dirk.*

Wagenbach (127) German: habitational name from a place so named: there is one in Styria (Austria) and another in Alsace.
GIVEN NAMES German 7%. *Franz, Klaus, Otto.*

Wagenblast (132) German: nickname for a hothead, meaning 'risk a fight'.

Wagener (786) German: variant of WAGNER.

GIVEN NAMES German 5%. *Hans* (3), *Fritz* (2), *Arno, Bernhard, Dieter, Horst, Johann, Klaus, Kurt, Matthias, Willi.*

Wagenknecht (247) German: occupational name from Middle High German *wagenknēht* 'hauler's assistant'.
GIVEN NAMES German 9%. *Erwin* (2), *Gerhard, Guenter, Hans, Kurt, Otto, Uwe.*

Wagenman (106) German (**Wagenmann**): occupational name from Middle High German *wagenman* 'hauler', 'wagoner'.
GIVEN NAMES German 6%. *Gottlieb, Kurt.*

Wager (1294) **1.** English: unexplained. **2.** German (also **Wäger**), Swiss German, and Jewish (Ashkenazic): from Middle High German *wæger* 'weigher', German *Waager*, an occupational name for an official responsible for weighing produce, especially produce offered as rent in kind, or for an official in charge of checking weights and measures used by merchants.

Wagers (943) English and German: variant of WAGER.

Wages (1441) German: unexplained.

Wagg (200) English: **1.** nickname from Old English *wagian* 'to shake or waddle'. **2.** topographic name from Middle English *wagge* 'marsh', 'bog'.

Waggener (533) Americanized form of WAGNER. Compare WAGONER.

Waggett (114) English: from a pet form of WAGG.

Waggle (147) Probably an Americanized spelling of Norwegian WAGLE.

Waggoner (6089) **1.** English: variant of WAGONER. **2.** Americanized form of German WAGNER.

Waggy (171) Americanized form of German WEGE.

Wagle (273) **1.** Norwegian: habitational name from any of several farmsteads in Rogaland named *Vagle*, from the dative singular of Old Norse *vagl* 'perch', 'roost', with reference to a high ridge between two lakes. **2.** Indian (Maharashtra, Goa); pronounced as *wah-glay*: Hindu (Brahman) name found among Saraswat Brahmans. It appears to be derived from Marathi and Konkani *waguļ* 'bat' (Sanskrit *valgula*).
GIVEN NAMES Indian 28%. *Girish* (2), *Maruti* (2), *Prasad* (2), *Raj* (2), *Vasant* (2), *Vijay* (2), *Anagha, Anil, Aparna, Arvind, Chandrakant, Dileep.*

Wagler (527) German: variant of WAGNER.

Wagley (377) Probably an Americanized form of German WAGLER, although the surname is found in England in the 1881 British census.

Wagman (622) **1.** Dutch: occupational name for a carter or cartwright. Compare WAGENAAR. **2.** German (**Wagmann**) and Jewish (Ashkenazic): variant of WAGEMANN.
GIVEN NAMES Jewish 4%. *Izy* (2), *Fira, Hyman, Meyer, Sura.*

Wagner (62299) German (also **Wägner**) and Jewish (Ashkenazic): occupational name for a carter or cartwright, from an agent derivative of Middle High German *wagen* 'cart', 'wagon', German *Wagen*. The German surname is also well established in Scandinavia, the Netherlands, eastern Europe, and elsewhere as well as in German-speaking countries.

Wagnon (806) **1.** French: habitational name from a place in Novion-Porcien (Ardennes), so named from the Germanic personal name *Wanio*. **2.** Northern French: from a diminutive of **Wagneur**, an occupational name for a farmer, from French *gagneur*, Walloon and Picard *wagneu(r)* 'farmer'. Compare GAGNON.

Wagoner (5660) **1.** English: occupational name for a carter, from an agent derivative of Old English *wagen* 'cart', 'wagon'. **2.** Americanized form of German WAGNER.

Wagstaff (1153) English (chiefly Midlands and Yorkshire): **1.** occupational nickname for an official who carried a staff of office, from Middle English *wag(gen)* 'to brandish or shake' + *staff* 'staff', 'rod'. **2.** obscene nickname for a medieval 'flasher', one who brandished his 'staff' publicly.

Wagster (213) English (Lancashire): unexplained. Possibly a variant of WAGSTAFF.

Waguespack (698) Respelling under French influence of German **Wagensbach**. The name occurs predominantly in LA.
GIVEN NAMES French 7%. *Andre* (3), *Leonce* (3), *Pierre* (2), *Aime, Chantal, Colette, Emile, Fernand, Gaston, Michel, Patrice.*

Wagy (194) Americanized form of German WEGE.

Wah (137) **1.** German (**Wäh**): nickname for a smart, good looking person, from Middle High German *wæhe* 'pretty', 'neat'. **2.** Chinese 华: variant of HUA 2. **3.** Other Southeast Asian: unexplained.
GIVEN NAMES Chinese 20%; Other Southeast Asian 5%. *Yung* (2), *Ching, Chiu, Eng, Kwan, Leong, Lok, Mei, Mok, Tsui, Wah; Yick* (2), *Thein, Yook.*

Wahab (179) Muslim: from a personal name based on Arabic *wahhāb* 'giver'. *Al-Wahhāb* 'the All-Giver' is one of the names of Allah (Qur'an 38:35). As a personal name, this is usually found in compounds such as 'Abd al-Wahhāb 'servant of the All-Giver'. Muḥammad ibn 'Abd al-Wahhāb (1703–87) was the founder of the Wahhabi movement for the purification of Islam.
GIVEN NAMES Muslim 65%. *Abdul* (18), *Amin* (3), *Mohammed* (3), *Abdool* (2), *Abdullah* (2), *Hussein* (2), *Khalid* (2), *Nasrin* (2), *Salim* (2), *Abdul Hamid, Ahmad, Bassem.*

Wahba (131) Muslim: from a personal name based on Arabic *wahba* 'gift', 'present'.
GIVEN NAMES Muslim 47%. *Safwat* (3), *Amgad* (2), *Ashraf* (2), *Rafik* (2), *Sameh* (2), *Samia* (2), *Afaf, Ahmed, Atef, Effat, Emad, Ezzat; Matthias* (2); *Emile, Michel.*

Waheed (140) Muslim: from a personal name based on Arabic *waḥīd* 'unique', 'matchless'.
GIVEN NAMES Muslim 80%. *Abdul* (24), *Mohammed* (4), *Amjad* (2), *Hassan* (2), *Khalid* (2), *Mohammad* (2), *Aamir, Adib, Adil, Ahmad, Ahmed, Aisha.*

Wahl (5562) **1.** German and Jewish (Ashkenazic): from Middle High German *Walhe, Walch* 'foreigner from a Romance country', hence a nickname for someone from Italy or France, etc. This surname is also established in Sweden. **2.** North German: from the personal name *Wole*, a short form of *Wol(d)er* (see WAHLER). **3.** Norwegian: habitational name from any of several farmsteads named Val, from Old Norse *vaðill* 'ford', 'shallows'.

Wahlberg (491) **1.** German: topographic name from Middle High German *wal* 'field', 'meadow' + *berg* 'mountain', 'hill'. This surname is also established in Denmark. **2.** Norwegian and Swedish: variant of WALBERG.
GIVEN NAMES Scandinavian 8%. *Erik* (3), *Alf, Anders, Johan, Sven.*

Wahle (212) German: **1.** variant of WAHL. **2.** habitational name from Wahle near Braunschweig. This surname is also established in Sweden.
GIVEN NAMES German 6%. *Frieda, Klaus, Kurt, Otto.*

Wahlen (293) German: **1.** variant of WAHL 2. **2.** variant of WAHLE 2. This surname is also established in Sweden.

Wahler (385) German: **1.** from the personal name *Wol(d)er*, a variant of WALTER. **2.** habitational name for someone from any of various places called Wahl, Wahle, or Wahlen.

Wahlers (275) German: patronymic from WAHLER 1.
GIVEN NAMES German 5%. *Lorenz* (2), *Heinz.*

Wahlert (209) German: from a derivative of WAHLER.

Wahlgren (313) Swedish: variant spelling of WALLGREN.

Wahlig (129) German: unexplained.

Wahlin (150) Swedish: ornamental name composed of the elements *vall* 'grassy bank' + the common suffix *-in*.
GIVEN NAMES Scandinavian 6%. *Lars, Per, Sigvard.*

Wahlman (102) Swedish: ornamental name, a variant of WALLMAN.
GIVEN NAMES Scandinavian 11%. *Erik* (2), *Nels.*

Wahlquist (255) Swedish: ornamental name composed of the elements *wall*, an old spelling of *vall* 'grassy bank', 'pasture', + *quist*, an old or ornamental spelling of *kvist* 'twig'.
GIVEN NAMES Scandinavian 7%. *Erik, Holger, Lennart.*

Wahls (119) German: patronymic from WAHL 2.

Wahlstrom (620) Swedish (**Wahlström**): ornamental name composed of the elements *vall* 'grassy bank', 'pasture' + *ström* 'stream'.

GIVEN NAMES Scandinavian 9%. *Erik* (3), *Nils* (2), *Mats*, *Sig*, *Sven*.

Wai (241) **1.** Chinese 韦: variant of WEI 2. **2.** Chinese 卫: variant of WEI 3.

GIVEN NAMES Chinese 34%. *Chi* (3), *Chan* (2), *Ming* (2), *Chi Kwong*, *Chien*, *Chow*, *Fong*, *Fung Ying*, *Hoi*, *Kam*, *Khin*, *Kin*, *Tha*, *Tin*.

Waibel (581) German: variant of WEIBEL.

GIVEN NAMES German 4%. *Helmut* (2), *Kurt* (2), *Erwin*, *Klaus*, *Otto*.

Waid (1073) German: **1.** variant of WEIDE. **2.** from Middle High German *weit* 'woad', a plant which yields a blue dye.

Waide (294) **1.** English: variant of WADE. **2.** German: variant of WEIDE.

Waidelich (203) German: variant of **Weidelich** (see WEIDLICH).

Waight (142) English: variant spelling of WAITE.

Wailes (196) English: patronymic from WALE 1.

Wain (343) English: variant spelling of WAYNE.

Wainer (263) **1.** English: occupational name for a wagoner or carter, Middle English *wayner*, an agent derivative of Old English *wæg(e)n*, *wæn* 'cart'. **2.** Variant of German WAGNER in Slavic-speaking regions. **3.** German and Jewish (Ashkenazic): variant of WEINER.

GIVEN NAMES Jewish 4%. *Arye*, *Isak*, *Uri*.

Wainio (153) Finnish (**Vainio**): ornamental name from *vainio* 'field'; one of the most common names adopted during the early 20th century. Found chiefly in southern and southwestern Finland.

GIVEN NAMES Finnish 10%. *Sulo* (3), *Reino* (2), *Irja*, *Tauno*, *Toivo*.

Wainman (171) English: occupational name for a carter or cartwright, from Middle English *wain* 'cart' + *man* 'man'.

Wainright (328) English: variant spelling of WAINWRIGHT.

Wainscott (998) English: from Middle English *waynscot* (a word of uncertain etymology), which originally denoted superior quality oak boarding imported from the Continent. The surname presumably arose from a nickname for someone who imported or used such timber.

Wainwright (2540) English (chiefly Lancashire and Yorkshire): occupational name for a maker of carts or wagons, Middle English *waynwright* (see WAYNE + WRIGHT).

Wais (178) Slavic spelling of German WEISS.

GIVEN NAMES German 8%. *Florian*, *Lorenz*, *Uwe*.

Waisanen (233) Finnish (**Väisänen**): topographic name from *väisä* meaning either 'road' or 'sign placed on the ice' + the common surname suffix -*nen*. Alternatively, it may be derived from *Väisä* as a personal name. This name is found chiefly in eastern and north-central Finland.

GIVEN NAMES Finnish 12%; Scandinavian 4%. *Toivo* (2), *Vaino* (2), *Waino* (2), *Aaro*, *Armas*, *Aune*, *Eino*, *Olavi*, *Reino*.

Waisner (167) German: variant (chiefly in Slavic regions) of WEISNER.

Wait (1275) English: variant spelling of WAITE.

FOREBEARS Thomas Wait came to MA from England in 1634. Samuel Wait (1789–1867), a Baptist clergyman, was born in White Creek, NY, organized Baptists in NC and helped found what became Wake Forest College (1838).

Waite (6435) English: occupational name for a watchman, Anglo-Norman French *waite* (of Germanic origin; compare WACHTER), or from the same word in its original abstract/collective sense, 'the watch'. There may also have been some late confusion with WHITE.

Waiters (326) English: unexplained.

Waites (1137) English: patronymic from WAITE.

Waithe (122) English: habitational name from a place named with Old Norse *vað* 'ford', such as Waithe in Lincolnshire, or Wath in North and West Yorkshire. Compare WADE.

Waitkus (217) Lithuanian (**Vaitkus**): from the personal name *Vaitkus*, from Polish *Wojtek* (see WOJTKIEWICZ, VOYTEK).

Waitman (203) English: perhaps a variant of **Waithman**, an occupational name for a hunter, from Old Norse *veiðimaðr*, *veiðimann*.

Waits (2066) English: patronymic from WAITE.

Waitt (253) English: variant spelling of WAITE.

Waitz (124) German. variant of WEITZ.

GIVEN NAME German 4%. *Grete*.

Wajda (354) Polish: status name from Polish *wajda* 'leader of Gypsies'.

GIVEN NAMES Polish 7%. *Andrzej*, *Bogumil*, *Boleslaw*, *Czeslaw*, *Darek*, *Mikolaj*, *Tadeusz*, *Wieslawa*.

Wakabayashi (135) Japanese: 'young forest', found mostly in eastern Japan.

GIVEN NAMES Japanese 60%. *Shigeru* (4), *Isao* (3), *Noriko* (2), *Yoshitaka* (2), *Akira*, *Daisuke*, *Hidehito*, *Hideki*, *Hiro*, *Hiroaki*, *Hiroshi*, *Hisao*.

Wake (849) Northern English and Scottish: from the Old Norse byname *Vakr* meaning 'wakeful', 'vigilant' (from *vaka* 'to remain awake'), or perhaps from a cognate Old English *Waca* (attested in place names such as **Wakeford**, WAKEHAM, and WAKELEY).

Wakefield (5326) English: habitational name from the city of Wakefield in West Yorkshire, and probably also from a place of the same name in Northamptonshire. Both are named from an Old English *wacu*

'vigil', 'festival' (a derivative of *wac(i)an* 'to watch or wake') + *feld* 'pasture', 'open country', i.e. a patch of open land where a fair was held.

Wakeford (120) English: habitational name, possibly a variant of WAKEFIELD; otherwise from a lost or unidentified place.

Wakeham (169) English (Devon): habitational name, primarily from Wakeham in Devon, named from the Old English byname *Waca* (meaning 'watchful') + Old English *hām* 'homestead', and to a lesser extent from either of two other places called Wakeham: one in Sussex, which has the same etymology, and the other on the Isle of Portland in Dorset, which is probably named from an Old English *wacu* 'watch', 'wake' + *cumb* 'valley'.

GIVEN NAME German 4%. *Helmut* (2).

Wakeland (389) English: habitational name, perhaps from Wackland on the Isle of Wight (recorded in 1249 as *Wakelande*), which is named from an Old English *wacu* 'watch', 'wake' + *land* 'cultivated land', 'estate'. The modern English surname, however, is found mainly in the north Midlands, which may point to another source, now lost.

Wakeley (325) English: habitational name from Wakeley in Hertfordshire, named from the Old English byname *Waca*, meaning 'watchful' (see WAKE) + Old English *lēah* 'woodland clearing'.

Wakelin (112) English: variant of WAKELING.

Wakeling (124) English: from the personal name *Walchelin*, an Anglo-Norman French double diminutive of a Germanic personal name *Walho* or *Walico*.

Wakely (208) English: variant spelling of WAKELEY.

Wakeman (1091) English: occupational name for a watchman, from Middle English *wake* 'watch', 'vigil' + *man* 'man'. This was the title of the mayor of Ripon in West Yorkshire until the 16th century.

Waker (133) English: nickname for a watchful person, from Middle English *waker* 'watchful', 'vigilant'.

Wakim (145) Muslim: probably a variant of HAKIM.

GIVEN NAMES Muslim 31%; French 12%. *Salim* (2), *Samir* (2), *Adnan*, *Bassam*, *Fahd*, *Ghassan*, *Hala*, *Hiba*, *Huda*, *Ibrahim*, *Jawad*, *Kalil*; *Pierre* (3), *Antoine* (2), *Jean-Claude*, *Laure*, *Michel*.

Wakley (181) English: variant of WAKELEY.

Waks (106) Jewish (Ashkenazic): variant spelling of WACHS.

GIVEN NAMES Jewish 16%. *Uzi* (2), *Zvi* (2), *Meir*, *Meyer*, *Zahava*.

Walas (128) **1.** Polish: from a derivative of the personal name *Walenty*, Polish form of Latin *Valentinus* (see VALENTINE). **2.** Possibly a reduced and altered form of the Lithuanian family name **Valavičius** or **Valasevičius**.

GIVEN NAMES Polish 14%. *Zbigniew* (2), *Halina, Henryka, Tomasz, Zofia.*

Walbeck (130) German: habitational name from any of various places so named, for example in Saxony-Anhalt and North Rhine-Westphalia.
GIVEN NAME German 8%. *Kurt* (4).

Walberg (511) **1.** Norwegian: habitational name from any of the six or so farmsteads so named, from Old Norse *valr* 'falcon', *varða* 'beacon', 'cairn' or *hváll* 'dome-shaped hill', 'rise' + *berg* 'mountain'. **2.** Swedish: ornamental name composed of the elements *vall* 'grassy bank' + *berg* 'mountain', 'hill'. **3.** German: habitational name for someone from any of several places named Wallberg. **4.** German: variant of WAHLBERG.
GIVEN NAMES Scandinavian 4%. *Erik* (3), *Lars, Nels.*

Walbert (365) German: from the medieval personal name *Waldobert.*

Walborn (372) English: variant of WALBURN.

Walbridge (514) English (Dorset): habitational name, probably from Wool Bridge in East Stoke, Dorset.

Walburg (155) German: from a Germanic female personal name composed of the elements *wald* 'rule' + *burg* 'fortress'. St. Walburga (died 779) was an English missionary who accompanied St. Boniface on his mission to Germany, and became abbess of Heidenheim. Her cult became very popular in northern Germany in the early Middle Ages, with consequent effects on the frequency of the personal name. Her bodily remains were later transferred to Eichstätt, according to legend on 1 May, which thus came to be known as *Walpurgisnacht.* This is also the date of an extremely ancient pagan fertility festival, welcoming the return of summer, and associated with witchcraft and revelry.

Walburn (545) English: from Old French *Walebron* (Langlois).

Walby (189) English: habitational name for someone from a place in East Yorkshire called Wauldby (recorded in Domesday Book as *Walbi* '(village) on the wold') or from Walby in Cumbria ('(village) by the (Roman) wall').
GIVEN NAMES Scandinavian 4%. *Alf, Nels, Sven.*

Walch (811) **1.** Irish: variant spelling of WALSH. **2.** German: from the personal name *Walcho.* **3.** German: ethnic name, a variant of WAHL 1.

Walcher (233) German: variant of WALKER or WALCH.
GIVEN NAMES German 6%. *Gunther, Hans, Horst, Klaus.*

Walck (485) German: variant of WALKER or WALCH.

Walcott (1143) English: habitational name from any of several places called Walcott, Walcot, or Walcote, for example in Lincolnshire, Leicestershire, Norfolk, Oxfordshire, and Wiltshire, all named in Old English with *w(e)alh* 'foreigner', 'Briton', 'Welsh', genitive plural *wala* (see WALLACE) + *cot* 'cottage', 'shelter', i.e. 'the cottage where the (Welsh-speaking) Britons lived'.
FOREBEARS This surname was in MA from an early date. William Walcott emigrated from England to Salem, MA, in 1637; John Wolcott (1632–1690) is recorded in Springfield, MA.

Walcutt (135) English: variant of WALCOTT.

Walczak (1369) Polish: patronymic from the personal name WALEK, *Walerian,* or some other personal name beginning with *Wal-*.
GIVEN NAMES Polish 6%. *Jozef* (3), *Casimir* (2), *Wojciech* (2), *Aleksander, Andrzej, Boguslaw, Darek, Dariusz, Ewa, Henryk, Janina, Janusz.*

Walczyk (246) Polish: derivative of WALEK.
GIVEN NAMES Polish 8%; German 4%. *Grazyna, Henryk, Irena, Ireneusz, Jerzy, Michalina; Meggan.*

Wald (1936) **1.** German and English: topographic name for someone who lived in or near a forest (Old High German *wald,* northern Middle English *wald*). **2.** Jewish (Ashkenazic): ornamental name from German *Wald* 'forest'. Very few Jews would have been living anywhere near a forest at the time when they acquired surnames, so as a Jewish name its origins are unlikely to be topographic.
GIVEN NAMES German 4%. *Fritz* (2), *Arno, Gerhard, Guenther, Gunther, Hans, Inge, Ingeborg, Liesl, Markus, Mathias, Udo.*

Waldbaum (131) Jewish (Ashkenazic): ornamental name from German *Waldbaum* 'forest tree'.
GIVEN NAMES German 6%; Jewish 5%. *Gitta, Otto; Hyman.*

Waldbillig (132) Luxembourgeois: habitational name from a place so named in the Grand Duchy of Luxembourg.

Walde (166) German: variant of WALD.
GIVEN NAMES German 6%. *Dieter, Fritz, Kurt.*

Waldeck (541) German and Jewish (western Ashkenazic): habitational name from a place in Hesse, on the Eder river, probably named from Old High German *wald* 'wood', 'forest' + *ecka, egga* 'corner', 'nook'.

Waldecker (150) German: habitational name for someone from any of various places called WALDECK.

Waldemar (128) German: from the Germanic personal name *Waldemar,* composed of the elements *walt* 'power', 'rule' + *mar* 'fame'.

Walden (8682) English: habitational name from any of the places, in Essex, Hertfordshire, and North Yorkshire, named Walden, from Old English *w(e)alh* 'foreigner', 'Briton', 'serf' (see WALLACE) + *denu* 'valley'.

Walder (638) **1.** English: variant of WALD, with the addition of the habitational suffix -*er.* **2.** German: habitational name from any of several places called Wald, or a topographic name for someone who lived in a forest or wood, Middle High German *walt.*

Waldera (147) Possibly of Polish origin: unexplained.
GIVEN NAMES French 10%. *Aurel, Clemence, Marcel, Marcell.*

Waldie (345) Scottish and northern English: from the Anglo-Scandinavian personal name *Wælþēof* (Old Norse *Valþiófr*), composed of the elements *val* 'battle' + *þiofr* 'thief', i.e. one who snatched victory out of battle. This spelling is found mainly in Scotland.

Walding (312) English: **1.** from an unattested Old English personal name *Wealding.* **2.** topographic name from an unattested Old English word, *wealding* 'forest dweller', from *weald* 'forest'.

Waldinger (159) **1.** German: habitational name for someone from a place called Walding in Upper Austria. **2.** Jewish (Ashkenazic): ornamental name from German *Wald* 'forest' + the suffix -*inger.*
GIVEN NAMES German 5%. *Hermann* (2), *Hans.*

Waldman (2715) **1.** Jewish (Ashkenazic): from Yiddish *wald* 'forest' + *man* 'man'. Very few Jews would have been living anywhere near a forest at the time when they acquired surnames, so in most cases this is probably an ornamental name. In other cases it many be a metonymic occupational name for someone whose job was connected with forestry, such as a woodcutter or lumber merchant. **2.** Americanized spelling of German WALDMANN. **3.** English: topographic name for a forest dweller, from Old English *w(e)ald* 'forest' + *mann* 'man'.
GIVEN NAMES Jewish 7%. *Isadore* (3), *Shmuel* (3), *Chaim* (2), *Emanuel* (2), *Herschel* (2), *Hyman* (2), *Itzchak* (2), *Menachem* (2), *Meyer* (2), *Shimon* (2), *Sol* (2), *Zalman* (2).

Waldmann (313) **1.** German: topographic name for someone who lived in a forest, or alternatively an occupational name for a forest warden, Middle High German *waltman* (literally 'forest man'). **2.** Jewish (Ashkenazic): see WALDMAN.
GIVEN NAMES German 9%; Scandinavian 4%. *Kurt* (3), *Elfriede, Gerhard, Gunter, Hans, Horst, Otto, Winfried; Helgard* (2), *Gunner.*

Waldner (594) **1.** South German: habitational name for someone from Wald, Walda, Walden, or any other place named from Old High German *wald* 'forest'. **2.** German and Jewish (Ashkenazic): topographic name from German *Waldner* 'forest dweller', 'forester', Middle High German *waldenære.* Compare WALDMAN.

Waldo (1781) **1.** English: variant of WALDIE. **2.** German: habitational name for someone from any of several places in Pomerania and Brandenburg called Waldow.

FOREBEARS Cornelius Waldo was living in Ipswich, MA, in 1647. Samuel Waldo (1695–1759) was born in Boston and became a land speculator in ME.

Waldoch (185) German: of uncertain origin.

Waldock (132) Dutch: habitational name for someone from a place named Waldeck in South Holland or one in Germany, near Koblenz.

Waldon (1155) English: variant spelling of WALDEN.

Waldorf (759) German: habitational name from any of at least three places so called, named with Old High German *wald* 'forest' + *dorf* 'village', 'settlement'.

Waldow (168) German: variant of WALDO.

GIVEN NAMES German 7%. *Guenther* (2), *Gerhard*, *Otto*.

Waldren (263) English: variant spelling of WALDRON.

Waldrep (847) Variant of English and Scottish WARDROP.

Waldridge (189) English: habitational name, probably from Waldridge in County Durham (probably named with Old English *wall* 'wall' + *hrycg* 'ridge'). However, in the British Isles, the surname is most common in Suffolk; it may be that another place similarly named, but lost, is the origin.

Waldrip (675) Variant of English and Scottish WARDROP.

Waldron (6780) English: 1. from a Germanic personal name composed of the elements *walh* 'foreigner' + *hrafn* 'raven'. 2. habitational name from a place in Sussex named Waldron, from Old English *w(e)ald* 'forest' + *ærn* 'house', 'dwelling'. The surname is now also common in Ireland, especially in Connacht.

FOREBEARS This is the name of a prominent NH family, established there since the 17th century. Richard Walderne (b. *c.* 1615) came to New England from Alchester, Warwickshire, England, about 1640 and settled at Dover, NH.

Waldroop (176) Variant of English and Scottish WARDROP.

Waldrop (4136) Variant of English and Scottish WARDROP.

Waldroup (411) Variant of English and Scottish WARDROP.

Waldrum (148) English: variant of WALDRON.

Waldrup (475) Variant of English and Scottish WARDROP.

Waldschmidt (482) German: from Middle High German *waltsmit* denoting a blacksmith who smelted iron ore gathered in the forest.

Waldstein (138) 1. German: habitational name from a place in Bohemia called Waldstein, named with Middle High German *walt* 'forest' + *stein* 'stone'. 2. Jewish (Ashkenazic): ornamental name composed of German *Wald* 'forest' + *Stein* 'stone'.

GIVEN NAMES Jewish 6%; Scandinavian 5%; German 5%. *Aviv, Aviva; Dietmar, Erwin.*

Waldvogel (401) 1. German: probably a nickname for a carefree, easy-going person, from Middle High German *waldvogel* 'bird of the forest'. 2. Jewish (Ashkenazic): ornamental name composed of German *Wald* 'forest' + *Vogel* 'bird'.

Wale (117) English: 1. from a Germanic personal name *Walo*, either a byname meaning 'foreigner' (see WALLACE), or else a short form of the various compound names with this first element. 2. nickname for a well-liked person, from Middle English *wale* 'good', 'excellent' (originally meaning 'choice'). 3. topographic name for someone who lived near an embankment, Middle English *wale* (Old English *walu*).

Walega (100) Polish: possibly from a derivative of the Polish personal name *Walenty* (see WALENTA, VALENTINE).

GIVEN NAMES Polish 16%. *Zbigniew* (2), *Aniela, Grzegorz, Wieslaw, Zygmunt.*

Walek (138) Polish, Ukrainian, and German (of Slavic origin): from the personal name *Walek*, a pet form of a vernacular derivative of Latin *Valentinus*, e.g. Polish *Walenty*, Ukrainian *Valenty* (see VALENTINE).

GIVEN NAMES Polish 6%. *Jolanta, Wojciech.*

Walen (276) 1. Dutch: from a short form of a Germanic personal name containing the element *walha-*. 2. Variant of Norwegian VALEN or Swedish WALLEN.

Walenta (163) Polish: from a derivative of the personal name *Walenty*, Polish form of Latin *Valentinus* (see VALENTINE).

Wales (2048) English and Scottish: patronymic from WALE 1.

FOREBEARS Nathaniel Wales came from Yorkshire, England, to Boston, MA, in 1635.

Waleski (87) Polish (also **Walewski**): habitational name from places called Walewice in Piotrków and Skierniewice voivodeships or Walew in Płock voivodeship.

FOREBEARS The surname Walewski is borne by several Polish noble families and can be traced back to the 14th century. Countess Maria Walewska (1789–1817) was Napoleon's mistress and the mother of the emperor's son, A. Colonna Walewski.

Waletzko (108) Of Slavic origin: unexplained.

Walford (332) English: habitational name from any of various places called Walford. Examples in Herefordshire and Shropshire are named with Old English (West Midlands) *wæll(a)* 'spring', 'stream' + *ford* 'ford'. A second place of the same name in Herefordshire was named with Old English *w(e)alh* 'foreigner', 'Briton', 'serf' (see WALLACE) as the first element, and one in

Dorset with Old English *wealt* 'unsteady', 'difficult'.

Walgren (247) Variant spelling of Swedish WALLGREN.

Wali (102) 1. Muslim: from a personal name based on Arabic *walī* 'lord', 'guardian', 'protector', 'saint', or 'friend', often interpreted as a short form of *Walī Allāh* 'friend of God', an epithet of the Prophet Muhammad. 2. Indian (Kashmir): Hindu (Brahman) name, probably ulitmately derived from Arabic *walī* 'lord' (see 1). 3. Indian (Karnataka): Hindu (Lingayat) name of unknown meaning.

GIVEN NAMES Muslim 71%; Indian 10%. *Abdul* (7), *Afzal* (2), *Ahmad* (2), *Ghulam* (2), *Mohammad* (2), *Omar* (2), *Sayed* (2), *Ali, Amin, Bakir, Basem, Bashar; Alaka, Anupam, Ashutosh, Autar, Mohan, Promod, Ramesh, Seema.*

Walia (196) Indian (Panjab): Hindu and Sikh name of unknown origin.

GIVEN NAMES Indian 86%. *Ajit* (6), *Amit* (2), *Anil* (2), *Daman* (2), *Harjeet* (2), *Satish* (2), *Adarsh, Ajay, Amar, Anoop, Ashu, Brij.*

Walicki (153) Polish: habitational name, probably for someone from places called Waliska in Radom and Siedlce voivodeships.

GIVEN NAMES Polish 7%; German 5%. *Andrzej, Wlodzimierz, Zbigniew; Florian* (2), *Hedwig* (2).

Waligora (156) Polish (**Waligóra**): nickname for a big man. Waligóra is the name of a giant in Polish fairy tales.

GIVEN NAMES Polish 10%. *Andrzej, Boguslaw, Wieslaw, Zygmunt.*

Walin (102) Swedish and Danish: variant of WALLEN.

GIVEN NAMES Scandinavian 5%. *Claus, Lennart.*

Walinski (123) Polish: habitational name for someone from a place called Waliny in Radom voivodeship.

GIVEN NAME Polish 5%. *Ludwik* (2).

Walizer (163) Americanized spelling of Swiss German WALLISER.

Walk (1429) 1. German: from the personal name *Walko*. 2. German: occupational name, a variant of WALKE.

Walke (391) German: metonymic occupational name for a fuller, from Middle High German *walke* 'fulling mill'. Compare WALKER.

Walkenhorst (198) German: habitational name from an unidentified place. The second element in the place name is clearly *horst* 'wooded hill'.

Walker (163390) English (especially Yorkshire) and Scottish: occupational name for a fuller, Middle English *walkere*, Old English *wealcere*, an agent derivative of *wealcan* 'to walk, tread'. This was the regular term for the occupation during the Middle Ages in western and northern England. Compare FULLER and TUCKER. As a Scottish surname it has also been used as a translation of Gaelic **Mac an Fhuca-dair** 'son of the fuller'.

FOREBEARS The name was brought to North America from northern England and Scotland independently by many different bearers in the 17th and 18th centuries. Samuel Walker came to Lynn, MA, in about 1630; Philip Walker was in Rehoboth, MA, in or before 1643. The surname was also established in VA before 1650; a Thomas Walker, born in 1715 in King and Queen Co., VA, was a physician, soldier, and explorer.

Walkes (104) German: variant of WALKE.

Walkington (174) English: habitational name from a place in East Yorkshire named Walkington, from an unattested Old English personal name *Walca* + *-ing-* denoting association with + *tūn*.

Walkinshaw (159) Scottish: habitational name from Walkinshaw in Renfrewshire, which was probably named from Old English *wealcere* 'fuller' + *sceaga* 'copse'.

Walkley (244) English: habitational name from Walkley in Sheffield, South Yorkshire, named with an unattested Old English personal name *Walca* + Old English *lēah* 'woodland clearing'.

Walko (459) Ukrainian: from a pet form of the personal names *Walentyn*, Ukrainian form of the Latin personal name *Valentinus* (see VALENTINE) or *Valerian* (see VALERY).

Walkowiak (408) Polish (also found in German-speaking countries): **1.** patronymic from the personal name WALEK. **2.** habitational name from a place called Walków in Sieradz voivodeship.

Walkowicz (111) Polish: patronymic from WALEK.

GIVEN NAMES Polish 7%; German 5%. *Henryka, Mariusz; Erwin.*

Walkowski (255) Polish: habitational name for someone from a place called Walków, in Sieradz voivodeship. This surname is also established in Germany.

GIVEN NAMES Polish 7%; German 5%. *Andrzej, Wlodzimierz, Zbigniew; Florian* (2), *Hedwig* (2).

Walkup (1160) English (Derbyshire): unexplained.

Wall (21352) **1.** English: topographic name for someone who lived by a stone-built wall, e.g. one used to fortify a town or to keep back the encroachment of the sea (Old English *w(e)all*, from Latin *vallum* 'rampart', 'palisade'). **2.** Northern English: topographic name for someone who lived by a spring or stream, northern Middle English *wall(e)* (Old English (Mercian) *wæll(a)*; compare WELL). **3.** Irish: re-Anglicized form of **de Bhál**, a Gaelicized form of *de Valle*, the name of a Norman family established in Munster and Connacht. **4.** German: topographic name for someone who lived by a defensive wall, Middle High German *wal*. **5.** German: variant of WAHL 2. **6.** German: from a

short form of the personal name WALTHER. **7.** Swedish: ornamental name from Swedish *vall* 'grassy bank', 'pasture', 'grazing ground', or in some cases a habitational name from a place named with this element.

Walla (413) **1.** Variant spelling of the Polish personal name *Wala*, a pet form of *Walenty*, Polish form of Latin *Valentinus* (see VALENTINE). **2.** German: from a Slavic form of the personal name *Valentin* (see VALENTINE). **3.** Variant spelling of Swedish and Norwegian VALLA. **4.** Indian (Panjab): Sikh (Jat) name of unknown origin.

Wallace (66195) **1.** Scottish and northern Irish: from Anglo-Norman French *waleis* 'Welsh' (from a Germanic cognate of Old English *wealh* 'foreign'), hence an ethnic name for a Welsh speaker. In some cases this clearly denoted an incomer to Scotland from Wales or the Welsh Marches, but it may also have denoted a Welsh-speaking Scot: in western Scotland around Glasgow, the Welsh-speaking Strathclyde Britons survived well into the Middle Ages. **2.** Jewish: this surname has been adopted in the 19th and 20th centuries as an Americanized form of various Ashkenazic Jewish surnames, e.g. WALLACH.

Wallach (1365) **1.** Jewish (Ashkenazic): from Middle High German *walhe, walch* 'foreigner from a Romance country', most probably a nickname for someone from Italy. **2.** German: habitational name from Wallach, a place near Wesel. **3.** Scottish: variant of WALLACE.

Wallack (364) Variant of German or Jewish WALLACH.

GIVEN NAMES Jewish 4%. *Zalmon* (2), *Ari, Sol.*

Wallander (260) Swedish: variant of WALL, with the addition of the suffix *-ander*, from Greek *anēr, andros* 'man'.

Wallar (124) Swedish: unexplained.

Wallbaum (106) Jewish (Ashkenazic): ornamental name from German *Wall(nuss)-baum* 'walnut tree'.

Wallberg (105) German and Swedish: variant spelling of WALBERG.

Walle (221) English and German: variant spelling of WALL. This name is also established in Mexico.

GIVEN NAMES Spanish 10%. *Alberto, Arnulfo, Efrain, Emilia, Evodio, Frederico, Jaime, Javier, Jesus, Jose, Juan, Justo.*

Wallen (2462) Swedish (**Wallén**): from *vall* 'grassy bank', 'pasture' (see WALL) + the common surname suffix *-én*, from Latin *-enius*.

Wallenberg (137) Swedish: ornamental name composed of the elements WALL + the suffix *- en* (originally German) + *berg* 'mountain', 'hill'.

FOREBEARS While working as a businessman in Budapest in 1944, Raoul Wallenberg (1912–?) was entrusted by the Swedish

government with the protection of Hungarian Jews from the Nazis. Wallenberg helped about 95,000 Jews to escape death by issuing them Swedish passports. When Soviet forces took control of Budapest in 1945, he was arrested, taken to Moscow, and imprisoned. The Soviet authorities stated that he died in prison in 1947.

GIVEN NAME German 5%. *Fritz.*

Wallenhorst (123) German: habitational name from Wallenhorst in Lower Saxony.

Wallenstein (189) German: habitational name from Wallenstein (originally Waldenstein 'forest rock') in Bohemia. This is the name of a famous dynasty of Czech counts. See also WALDSTEIN. It was also adopted as a Jewish name.

GIVEN NAME Jewish 4%. *Benzion.*

Wallentine (148) Variant of VALENTINE in a spelling under German or Polish influence.

Waller (12519) **1.** English: topographic name for someone living near a wall (in particular, the wall of a city), or an occupational name for a mason who built walls (see WALL). **2.** English: topographic name for someone who lived by a prominent wall, for example a Roman wall or the wall of a walled city (see WALL 2). **3.** English: occupational name for someone who boiled sea water to extract the salt, from an agent derivative of Middle English *well(en)* 'to boil'. **4.** English: nickname for a good-humored person, Anglo-Norman French *wall(i)er* (an agent derivative of Old French *galer* 'to make merry', of Germanic origin). **5.** South German: nickname from Middle High German *wallære* 'pilgrim'.

FOREBEARS Col. John Waller came from England to VA in about 1635. The name was brought to North America by several other bearers independently.

Wallerich (124) German: from a Germanic personal name composed of *walt* 'rule' + *rīh* 'powerful'.

Wallerstedt (108) Swedish: ornamental name formed from a place-name element *vall* 'grazing ground', 'pasture' + *stedt* 'place' (of German origin). The infix *er-* is originally German, but not uncommon in newly formed Swedish surnames.

GIVEN NAMES German 6%; Scandinavian 4%. *Fritz* (2); *Nils.*

Wallerstein (215) German and Jewish (Ashkenazic): habitational name from Wallerstein, a place near Nördlingen.

GIVEN NAMES Jewish 8%. *Chanie* (2), *Shmuel* (2), *Eliezer, Pinchus, Yacov.*

Walles (151) English: variant spelling of WALLACE.

Wallett (145) English: perhaps from a pet form of the Anglo-Scandinavian personal name *Wælþēof* (see WALDIE).

Walley (1640) English: variant of WHALEY.

Wallgren (229) Swedish: ornamental name composed of the elements *vall* 'grassy bank', 'pasture' + *gren* 'branch'.

GIVEN NAMES Scandinavian 6%. *Anders, Elof, Erik, Hilmer.*

Walli (119) **1.** Finnish (**Valli**): ornamental name of uncertain origin. **2.** It may be derived from a Germanic personal name, *Walha* or *Wallo*. **3.** Alternatively, it could be from the word *valli*, from Swedish *vall* 'defensive wall'. This name is found chiefly in southwestern Finland.

GIVEN NAMES Finnish 5%. *Helvi, Sulo, Wiljo.*

Wallick (739) Perhaps an altered form of German **Wallich**, a variant of WALCH, or a habitational name from Wallichen in Thuringia.

Wallin (2796) Swedish: variant of VALLIN.

GIVEN NAMES Scandinavian 6%. *Lars* (6), *Erik* (4), *Berger* (2), *Alrik, Alvar, Anders, Astrid, Halvar, Hilmer, Ingegerd, Iver, Johan.*

Walline (110) English: unexplained.

Walling (2739) German (**Wälling**): from the short form of a Germanic personal name formed with *walt* 'rule'.

Wallinger (103) German (**Wällinger**): habitational name for someone from a place called Wällingen.

Wallingford (762) English and Scottish: habitational name from a place in Oxfordshire (formerly in Berkshire), named in Old English as *Welingaford* 'ford of the people of a man called *Wealh*'.

Wallington (219) English: habitational name from any of various places called Wallington. Those in Berkshire, Hampshire, and Greater London are probably all named from the genitive plural of Old English *walh* 'foreigner', 'Briton' (see WALLACE) + *tūn* 'enclosure', 'settlement'. One in Northumberland was originally Old English *Wealingtūn* 'settlement associated with *Wealh*', a personal name or byname. One in Hertfordshire was named as the 'settlement of the people of *Wændel*', an unattested Old English personal name, while one in Norfolk was probably the 'settlement of the dwellers by the wall (Old English *wall*)'.

Wallis (4832) English: from Anglo-Norman French *waleis* 'Welsh' (from a Germanic cognate of Old English *wealh* 'foreign'), hence an ethnic name for a Welsh speaker. Compare Scottish WALLACE.

Wallisch (110) German: from a short form of the medieval personal name *Valentine* (see VALENTIN).

GIVEN NAMES German 7%. *Guenter, Kurt.*

Walliser (102) Swiss German: habitational name for someone from the Wallis (Valais) region of Switzerland, so named from Latin *vallis* 'valley'.

GIVEN NAME German 5%. *Markus.*

Wallman (500) **1.** English: variant of WALL. **2.** Swedish: ornamental name composed of the elements *wall*, an old spelling of *vall* 'grassy bank' + *man* 'man'. **3.** German (**Wallmann**): variant of WALL 4 and 5.

GIVEN NAMES German 4%. *Ernst, Frieda, Fritz, Kurt.*

Wallner (826) German: variant of WALDNER. This name is also established in Sweden.

GIVEN NAMES German 5%. *Alois* (2), *Armin, Erwin, Horst, Ingeborg, Lothar, Markus, Mathias, Othmar, Otto.*

Wallo (167) Finnish: see WALLI.

Walloch (200) German: variant of WALLACH.

Wallock (119) Probably a variant of German WALLACH.

Walls (12335) **1.** English: variant of WALL. **2.** Scottish: most probably a derivative of WALLACE.

Wallschlaeger (114) German: variant spelling of WOLLSCHLAGER.

Wallwork (190) English (Lancashire): habitational name of uncertain origin. Thomas de Wallerwork was living in Lancashire *c.*1324. Throughout the Middle Ages English forms in *-work* alternate with ones in *-worth*, and the surname may derive from places in County Durham or Greater London called WALWORTH.

Wally (188) **1.** English: unexplained. **2.** South German: variant of **Walli**, from a short form of any Germanic personal name formed with Old High German *waltan* 'to rule' as a first part, as in WALTER.

Walmer (343) English: habitational name from Walmer in Kent, so named from Old English *wala* (plural of *walh* 'Briton') + *mere* 'pool', or from Walmore Common in Gloucestershire.

Walmsley (818) English: habitational name from Walmersley in Greater Manchester, which according to Ekwall is named from Old English *wald* 'forest' + *mere* 'lake' or *(ge)mære* 'boundary' + *lēah* 'woodland clearing'. However, it is perhaps more plausibly from the genitive case of an Old English personal name *Walhmær*, meaning 'foreign-famous', or *Waldmær* 'rule-famous' + Old English *lēah*.

Waln (214) English (Lancashire): unexplained.

FOREBEARS Nicholas Waln came from the West Riding of Yorkshire, England, to New Castle, DE, in 1682. A Philadelphia, PA, Waln family flourished in the second half of the 18th century.

Walp (329) Perhaps a respelling of Swiss German **Wulp**: unexplained.

Walper (106) German: from the Germanic personal name *Waldobert*, composed of the elements *walt* 'ruler' + *berht* 'bright', 'famous'.

Walpole (664) English: habitational name from either of two places in Norfolk and Suffolk. The first element of the former is Old English *w(e)all* 'wall', while the first element of the latter is *wealh* 'foreigner', 'Briton' (see WALLACE); they share the second element Old English *pōl* 'pool'.

Walquist (143) Variant spelling of Swedish WAHLQUIST.

Walrath (844) Variant spelling of German **Wallrath**, a habitational name from Wallrath in the Rhineland.

Walraven (708) German and Dutch: from *Walravan*, a personal name composed of the elements *wal* 'battlefield' + *hraban* 'raven'. The personal name was popular among knights and patricians of the Lower Rhine and Upper Swabian region, where the family name is still common. This name is also found in England.

Walrod (260) Variant of German WALRATH, probably altered from **Walrodt**, a habitational name for someone from any of several places named Wallrode, -roth, -roda, all from Waldenrode, a clearing in a forest.

Walrond (148) Origin uncertain: perhaps a variant of German WALRATH or English WALDRON.

Walsdorf (118) German: habitational name from a place so called.

GIVEN NAME German 5%. *Kurt* (2).

Walser (1142) **1.** South German: habitational name for someone from Wals near Salzburg. **2.** German: variant of WALLISER.

GIVEN NAMES German 4%. *Kurt* (4), *Siegbert* (4), *Wilhelm* (2), *Egon, Erwin.*

Walsh (43045) Irish: Anglicized form (translation) of **Breathnach** 'Briton'. It was used in particular to denote the Welshmen who arrived in Ireland in the wake of Strongbow's Anglo-Norman invasion of 1170.

GIVEN NAMES Irish 5%. *Brendan* (30), *Aileen* (6), *Dermot* (6), *John Patrick* (6), *Kieran* (6), *Declan* (4), *Eamonn* (4), *Colm* (3), *Donal* (3), *Seamus* (3), *Siobhan* (3), *Brennan* (2).

Walshe (178) Irish: variant spelling of WALSH.

GIVEN NAMES Irish 9%. *Brendan, Eoin, Murph.*

Walsingham (104) English: habitational name from Great or Little Walsingham in Norfolk, named in Old English as 'homestead (Old English *tūn*) of the family or followers of a man called Waels'.

GIVEN NAME Irish 5%. *Donal.*

Walski (229) Polish: habitational name for someone from any of the many places in Poland named with Polish *waly* 'ramparts', 'dikes'.

Walstad (239) Norwegian: habitational name from any of seven farmsteads named Valstad, probably from Old Norse *vǫllr* 'meadow' + *staðir* 'farmstead', 'dwelling'.

Walstead (103) Americanized spelling of Norwegian WALSTAD.

Walston (1905) English: habitational name from Walsden, a place in West Yorkshire, which is probably named with an unattested Old English personal name, *Walsa*, + *denu* 'valley'.

Walstrom (372) Americanized form of Swedish **Walström** or **Wahlström** (see WAHLSTROM).

Walsworth (271) English (West Yorkshire): variant of WALWORTH.

Walt (529) **1.** Variant of German **Waldt**, a topographic name from Middle High German *walt* 'forest'. **2.** German: short form of WALTHER. **3.** Jewish (Ashkenazic): variant of WALD.

Waltemath (116) German: nickname meaning 'moderate', 'measured', from Low German *wol te mate* 'well to measure' ('well measured').

Waltenbaugh (116) Americanized spelling of German **Waltenbach**, a habitational name from an unidentified place, named with an unexplained first element + Middle High German *bach* 'stream', 'creek'.
GIVEN NAMES German 6%. *Dieter, Kurt.*

Walter (19072) German, Swedish, and English: from a Germanic personal name composed of the elements *wald* 'rule' + *heri*, *hari* 'army'. The personal name was introduced into England from France by the Normans in the form *Walt(i)er, Waut(i)er.*

Walterman (157) German (**Waltermann**): from a pet form of the personal name WALTHER + Middle High German *man* 'man'.

Waltermire (218) Americanized form of German **Walthermeyer**, a distinguishing name for a tenant farmer (see MEYER) whose name was WALTHER.

Walters (38412) English and German: patronymic from WALTER.

Walterscheid (176) German: habitational name from a place so called in the Rhineland.

Walth (210) German: variant of WALT.
GIVEN NAMES German 4%. *Otto* (2), *Erwin, Reinhart.*

Walthall (901) English: unexplained; perhaps a habitational name from a lost or unidentified place.

Walther (2694) German and Dutch (also found in Sweden and Denmark): variant of WALTER.
GIVEN NAMES German 6%. *Kurt* (13), *Hans* (7), *Erwin* (4), *Wolfgang* (4), *Otto* (3), *Gerhard* (2), *Gunter* (2), *Heinz* (2), *Klaus* (2), *Konrad* (2), *Bernd, Bernhard.*

Walthers (241) German: patronymic from the personal name *Walther* (see WALTER).

Walthour (266) Americanized spelling of German **Waldhauer**, an occupational name for a woodsman, from Middle High German *walt* 'woods', 'forest' + agent derivative of *houwen* 'to hew', 'cut', 'chop'.

Waltke (102) German: from a pet form of any of the Germanic personal names formed with Old High German *waltan* 'to rule' as a first element, as in WALTER.
GIVEN NAMES German 6%. *Eldred, Jurgen, Wilhelmina.*

Waltman (1560) German (**Waltmann**) and Jewish (Ashkenazic): variant of WALDMANN.

Waltner (256) South German: variant spelling of WALDNER.

Walton (23734) English: habitational name from any of the numerous places called Walton. The first element in these names was variously Old English *walh* 'foreigner', 'Briton', genitive plural *wala* (see WALLACE), *w(e)ald* 'forest', *w(e)all* 'wall', or *wæll(a)* 'spring', 'stream'.
FOREBEARS George Walton (1741–1804) signed the Declaration of Independence. He was born in Prince Edward Co., VA, whither his grandfather had emigrated from England in 1682. He moved to Savannah, GA, and became governor of GA and a prominent jurist.

Waltrip (600) Variant of English and Scottish WARDROP.

Walts (389) Americanized or Dutch spelling of WALZ.

Waltz (2718) German: variant spelling of WALZ.

Waltzer (203) Variant spelling of German and Jewish WALZER.
GIVEN NAMES German 5%. *Frieda, Kurt.*

Walvatne (108) Origin unidentified.

Walvoord (142) Dutch: perhaps an altered form of **Welvaart**, **Welvaert**, from a Germanic personal name composed of the elements *wolf* 'wolf' + *hart* 'hardy', 'brave', 'strong', or *willo* 'will', 'wish' + *fridu* 'peace'. If this is correct, the second element has been assimilated by folk etymology to the Dutch word *voord* 'ford'.

Walworth (482) English: habitational name from either of two places called Walworth, in Greater London and County Durham, both named with Old English *w(e)alh* 'Briton', genitive plural *wala* (see WALLACE) + *worð* 'enclosure'. The present-day concentration of the name in Yorkshire suggests the latter is the more likely source. Compare WALLWORK.
FOREBEARS A William Walworth of London came to New London, CT, in 1689.

Walz (2913) German: from a pet form of the personal name WALTER.

Walzer (407) South German and Jewish (Ashkenazic): occupational name, a reduced form of **Walzenmüller**, denoting a miller (see MUELLER) who milled by means of rollers, Middle High German *walze*, German *Walze* 'roller'.
GIVEN NAMES German 4%. *Bernhard, Frieda, Kurt, Manfred.*

Wambach (322) German: habitational name from any of various places so called in Hesse, Bavaria, and Baden.
GIVEN NAMES German 4%. *Kurt* (2), *Aloys, Frieda, Jochen.*

Wambaugh (126) Americanized spelling of German WAMBACH.

Wamble (232) English: variant of WOMBLE.

Wambold (395) German: from a Germanic personal name composed *wān* 'hope' + *bald* 'bold'.

Wamboldt (172) German: variant of WAMBOLD.

Wambolt (178) German: variant of WAMBOLD.

Wamhoff (118) German: probably a variant of WEMHOFF.

Wammack (160) Probably a variant of English WOMACK (unexplained).

Wampler (2554) German and French (Alsace): probably a habitational name for someone from Wambel in North Rhine-Westphalia.

Wampole (227) Origin uncertain; probably a variant of English **Wimpole**, a habitational name from Wimpole in Cambridgeshire, named with the Old English personal name *Wina* + *pōl* 'pool'.

Wamser (202) German: from an agent derivative of Middle High German *wambes*, *wambeis* 'jerkin', 'waistcoat' (originally for wearing under armor), hence an occupational name for a maker of such clothing.

Wamsley (1183) English: variant of WALMSLEY.

Wan (1081) **1.** Chinese 万: from a place name, Wan City, that existed during the Zhou dynasty (1122–221 BC) in Shaanxi province. Descendants of a marquise who was granted the territory adopted the city name as their surname. **2.** Chinese 温: variant of WEN 1. **3.** Chinese 尹: variant of YIN 1. **4.** Dutch: occupational name for a maker or seller of winnowing fans, from Latin *vannus*. **5.** Scottish: variant of WANN.
GIVEN NAMES Chinese 30%; Vietnamese 4%. *Hong* (5), *Yi* (4), *Qi* (3), *Qiang* (3), *Wai* (3), *Yiu* (3), *Yuk* (3), *Chien-Min* (2), *Fang* (2), *Hin* (2), *Jichun* (2), *Li* (2), *Man* (2); *Chung* (2), *Min* (2), *Yiping* (2), *Pak, Sik, Sung Man*; *Tin* (2), *Bang, Da, Hien, Hoi, Lan, Minh Quang, Sau, Tich, Tung, Yaping, Yuet.*

Wanamaker (986) Altered spelling of Dutch **Wannemaeker** 'maker of winnowing baskets'. A winnowing basket is a type of object that is now quite unknown, except perhaps in a few museums, but was familiar on every farm in Europe in bygone centuries. Compare the German cognate WANNEMACHER.

Wanat (295) Polish and Ukrainian: of uncertain origin; perhaps from Polish dialect *wanata*, denoting a variety of apple, or from a derivative of a Germanic personal name, *Wānrat*, composed of an unidentified first element + *rat* 'counsel'.
GIVEN NAMES Polish 6%. *Kazimierz* (2), *Mieczyslaw, Waclaw, Witold.*

Wand (381) **1.** English: perhaps a nickname for a shy or short-sighted person, from Old English *wand* 'mole'. Compare

WANT. **2.** German: occupational name for a weaver or cloth cutter, from a reduced form of Middle High German *gewant* 'cloth', 'garment'. Compare WANDER 2. **3.** German: topographic name from Middle High German *want* 'wall', 'steep rock', 'precipice'. **4.** Dutch: metonymic occupational name for a glove maker, from Middle Dutch *wante* 'glove'.

Wandel (265) Dutch and German: variant of WENDEL.
GIVEN NAMES German 6%. *Hans* (2), *Gerhard, Horst, Klaus.*

Wandell (299) Dutch and German: variant of WENDEL.

Wander (459) **1.** German: occupational name for a builder, one who built walls, from an agent derivative of Middle High German *want* 'wall' (from Old High German *wenten* 'to wind or weave'; the earliest domestic walls were of wattle and daub construction, made from woven hurdles packed with clay). **2.** German: occupational name for a maker or seller of cloth, from an agent derivative of a reduced form of Middle High German *gewant* 'cloth', 'garment' (from Old High German *giwant*, likewise a derivative of *wenten* 'to weave'). **3.** Jewish (Ashkenazic): variant of WANDERER, a nickname from Yiddish *vandern* 'to wander or hike'.

Wanderer (120) German and Jewish (Ashkenazic): nickname for someone who moved around a lot.

Wandersee (221) Probably a Germanized alteration of Dutch VANDERZEE.

Wandler (168) Variant of German WENDLER or its Dutch cognate **Wandelaer.**
FOREBEARS The name **De Wandelaer** is recorded in Beverwijck in New Netherland (Albany, NY) in the mid 17th century.
GIVEN NAMES French 6%. *Alphonse, Monique.*

Wandling (209) Perhaps an altered spelling of German WENDLING.

Wandrey (213) Partly Americanized spelling of a German personal name, based on a Slavic form of ANDREAS. Compare Czech VONDRA.

Wands (248) Scottish: unexplained.

Wanek (410) Eastern German: from a borrowing of the Slavic personal name *Vaněk* (see VANEK).

Waner (169) German (**Wäner**): Swabian habitational name for someone from a place called Wain, or from Wahn near Cologne.

Wang (14919) **1.** Chinese 王: from a character meaning 'prince'. There are numerous unrelated Wang clans, descendants of various princes of the Shang (1766–1122 BC) and Zhou (1122–221 BC) dynasties, including in particular descendants of the Shang dynasty prince Bi Gan and descendants of Bi Gonggao, 15th son of the virtuous duke Wen Wang, who was granted the state of

Wei (a different state of Wei than that granted to the eighth son; compare SUN). **2.** Chinese 汪: from the name of a state or area called Wang. From ancient times through the Xia (2205–1766 BC) and Shang (1766–1122 BC) dynasties there existed a state of Wang. Later, during the Spring and Autumn period (722–481 BC), there also existed an area named Wang in the state of Lu. Some descendants of the ruling class of both areas took the place name Wang as their surname. **3.** Korean: there is one Chinese character for the surname Wang. Some sources indicate that there are fifteen Wang clans, but only two can be identified: the Kaesŏng Wang clan and the Chenam Wang clan. The Kaesŏng Wang clan, which originated in China, ruled the Korean peninsula for almost five hundred years as the ruling dynasty of the Koryŏ period (918–1392). There are some indications that the Kaesŏng Wang clan was present in the ancient Chosŏn Kingdom (?194 BC). When the Chŏnju Yi clan seized power in 1392 and established the Chosŏn kingdom, many of the members of the Kaesŏng Wang clan changed their names and went into hiding to avoid being persecuted by the new ruling dynasty. The Chenam Wang clan is also of Chinese origin. The Chenam Wang clan is much smaller than the Kaesŏng Wang clan. **4.** German and Dutch: from Middle German *wang*, Middle Dutch *waenge*, literally 'cheek', but also in southern German having the transferred sense 'grassy slope' or 'field of grass'. It was thus either a topographic name for someone who lived by a meadow or a descriptive nickname for someone with noticeable cheeks (for example, round or rosy). **5.** Jewish (Ashkenazic): either a borrowing of the German name (see 4), or else a regional name for a Jew from Hungary (compare Russian *Vengria* 'Hungary'). **6.** Scandinavian: variant spelling of VANG 1.
GIVEN NAMES Chinese/Korean 44%. *Wei* (89), *Hong* (69), *Jian* (57), *Li* (42), *Yi* (39), *Jing* (38), *Ping* (36), *Ming* (35), *Yang* (35), *Ying* (33), *Jin* (32), *Yan* (31); *Chung* (33), *Min* (15), *Chang* (14), *Chong* (11), *Shen* (7), *Yiping* (6), *Hu* (5), *Tian* (4), *Yiming* (4), *Jang* (2), *Myong* (2), *Neng* (2).

Wangberg (105) **1.** Norwegian: habitational name from a farmstead in Trøndelag, probably named from *Vang*, a river name of unknown origin, + *berg* 'mountain'. **2.** Swedish: ornamental name from a place-name element *vång* 'field', 'meadow' + *berg* 'mountain'.
GIVEN NAMES Scandinavian 8%; German 7%. *Ludvig, Maren*; *Erna* (2).

Wangelin (133) German: habitational name from a place called Wangelin in Mecklenburg.

Wangen (355) **1.** German and Dutch: variant of WANG. **2.** Norwegian: variant spelling of **Vangen**, from the definite singular form of VANG ('meadow').

GIVEN NAMES Scandinavian 6%. *Arlis, Erik, Nels, Obert.*

Wanger (292) **1.** German: habitational name for someone from any of various places called Wang or Wangen (meaning 'grass slope'). **2.** South German: metathesized variant of WAGNER.
GIVEN NAMES German 7%. *Franz* (2), *Aloysius, Frieda, Heinz, Kurt, Manfred.*

Wangerin (281) North German: habitational name from a place called Wangerin near Stettin.

Wangler (516) German (**Wängler**): variant of WANGER.

Wangsgard (106) Danish: habitational name from any of several farmsteads named, Vangsgård or Vangsgaard.

Wangsness (163) Norwegian: habitational name from a farmstead in Sogn named Vangsnes, probably from Old Norse *vangsni* 'plowshare', (indicating a reef of that shape) + *nes* 'headland', 'promontory'.
GIVEN NAMES German 4%; Scandinavian 4%. *Erwin, Otto*; *Erik.*

Waninger (100) Variant spelling of German WANNINGER.

Wank (227) **1.** German pet form of a personal name derived from Slavic *Vęceslav* (see VANEK, WENZEL). **2.** German: from a field named with Middle High German *wanc* 'bend or turn (in the course of a path or river)'. **3.** Jewish (Ashkenazic): variant of WANG.

Wanke (331) German: pet form of a personal name derived from Slavic *Vęceslav* (see VANEK, WENZEL).
GIVEN NAMES German 5%. *Helmut, Jurgen, Kurt, Rainer.*

Wankel (132) German: pet form of WANKE, itself a pet form of a Slavic name represented in German by WENZEL.

Wanko (153) German pet form of a personal name derived from Slavic *Vęceslav* (see VANEK, WENZEL).

Wanlass (134) English: variant of WANLESS.

Wanless (393) English: nickname from Middle English *wanles* 'hopeless', 'luckless'. In the British Isles the surname is found chiefly in Northumberland and Durham.

Wann (722) **1.** English and Scottish: nickname from Middle English *wann* 'wan', 'pale' (the meaning of the word in Old English was, conversely, 'dark'). **2.** German: from the personal name *Wano*, a short form of *Wambald* (see WAMBOLD). **3.** German: topographic name denoting a basket-shaped valley or on a basket-shaped knoll, Middle High German *wann(e)* 'basket' (see WANNER and WANNEMACHER).

Wannamaker (364) Altered spelling of Dutch **Wannemaeker** 'maker of winnowing baskets', or of the German cognate WANNEMACHER.

Wannemacher (257) German: occupational name for a maker of winnowing baskets, from Middle High German *wanne* 'winnowing basket' + *macher* 'maker'. The *wanne* was a kind of tub-shaped basket or trough (alternatively a fan), used to separate grain from chaff.

Wanner (1557) **1.** German: occupational name for a winnower, someone who used a winnowing basket or fan to separate grain from chaff (see WANNEMACHER). **2.** German: topographic name for someone who lived in a basket-shaped valley or on a basket-shaped knoll (see WANN), the suffix *-er* denoting an inhabitant.
GIVEN NAMES German 4%. *Kurt* (6), *Fritz* (5), *Armin*, *Dieter*, *Franz*, *Johann*, *Theresia*.

Wanninger (189) German: habitational name for someone from a place called Wanning near Altötting.
GIVEN NAMES German 9%. *Kurt* (2), *Alois*, *Aloysius*, *Gerhardt*, *Helmut*, *Helmuth*.

Wanous (187) German spelling of Czech *Vanous*, a derivative of the personal name *Václav*, Old Czech *Vęceslav* (see VACEK).

Wanser (170) Dutch: variant of WANZER.

Wansley (314) English: habitational name from Wansley in Devon, named with the Old English personal name *Want* + *lēah* 'woodland clearing', or from Hutton Wandesley in North Yorkshire, named with an unattested Old English personal name (*Wand* or *Wandel*) + *lēah*. The latter seems the more likely source, the surname having been concentrated in Lancashire in the late 19th century. Today there are few if any bearers of the surname in the U.K.

Want (137) **1.** English: from Middle English *want* 'mole', hence a nickname, perhaps for a short-sighted person. **2.** English: topographic name for someone who lived at a crossroad, a dialect form of WENT. **3.** Dutch: variant of WAND.

Wanta (343) Polish: of uncertain origin; perhaps a nickname from Polish dialect *wanta* 'stone', 'rock'.

Wantland (282) Variant respelling of German **Wendlan(t)** (see WENDLAND).

Wantuch (134) German and Polish: occupational name for a maker or seller of heavy linen cloth, German and Old Polish *wantuch*.
GIVEN NAMES German 10%; Polish 7%. *Otto* (3), *Erwin*, *Florian*; *Halina* (2).

Wantuck (102) Americanized spelling of WANTUCH.

Wanty (106) Perhaps an Americanized form of Polish WANTA.

Wantz (359) German and Dutch: from the Germanic personal name *Wanzo*, a short form of a compound name formed with *wan* 'hope', 'expectation' as the first element.

Wanzer (292) Dutch: derivative of the medieval personal name *Wanshart*, formed with the elements *wan* 'hope', 'expectation' + *hart* 'hardy', 'brave'.

Waple (107) Variant of English WALPOLE.

Waples (328) English: derivative of **Waple** (a variant of WALPOLE).

Wapner (141) **1.** German: occupational name from Middle High German *wapener* 'man bearing arms'. **2.** Jewish (eastern Ashkenazic): occupational name for a limestone quarry worker, a Yiddishized form of Polish *wapniarz*.

Wappler (100) South German: occupational name, from Middle High German *waepener* 'man bearing arms' (in the service of a town), 'shield bearer', 'young knight' (in the service of a knight).
GIVEN NAME German 5%. *Reinhold*.

Warbington (212) English (Lancashire): perhaps a variant of WARBURTON; otherwise a habitational name from a lost or unidentified place.

Warble (132) Variant of English WALPOLE.

Warbritton (106) Probably an altered form of English WARBURTON. This spelling is not found in English sources.

Warburton (1148) English: habitational name from a place in Greater Manchester (formerly in Cheshire) called Warburton, from the Old English female personal name *Wǣrburh* (composed of the elements *wǣr* 'pledge' + *burh* 'fortress') + Old English *tūn* 'enclosure', 'settlement'.

Warchol (381) Polish (**Warchoł**): nickname for an quarrelsome person, from *warchoł* 'squabbler'.
GIVEN NAMES Polish 10%. *Dorota* (2), *Andrzej*, *Danuta*, *Jadwiga*, *Jerzy*, *Jozef*, *Karol*, *Krystyna*, *Krzysztof*, *Mieczyslaw*, *Piotr*.

Ward (92242) **1.** English: occupational name for a watchman or guard, from Old English *weard* 'guard' (used as both an agent noun and an abstract noun). **2.** Irish: reduced form of **McWard**, an Anglicized form of Gaelic **Mac an Bhaird** 'son of the poet'. The surname occurs throughout Ireland, where three different branches of the family are known as professional poets. **3.** Surname adopted by bearers of the Jewish surname **Warshawski**, WARSHAWSKY or some other Jewish name bearing some similarity to the English name. **4.** Americanized form of French GUERIN.
FOREBEARS The surname Ward was brought to North America from England independently by several different bearers in the 17th and 18th centuries. Nathaniel Ward (1578–1652), author of the MA legal code, was born in Haverhill, Suffolk, England, and emigrated to Agawam (Ipswich, MA) in 1633. William Ward was one of the original settlers of Sudbury, MA, in about 1638. Miles Ward came from England to Salem, MA, in about 1639. Thomas Ward (d. 1689) settled in Newport, RI, in 1671; among his descendants were two governors of colonial RI.

Warda (225) Polish: descriptive nickname from Polish dialect *warda* 'left-handed person'. This surname is also established in Germany.

GIVEN NAMES Polish 11%. *Slawomir* (2), *Boguslaw*, *Dariusz*, *Lech*, *Maciej*, *Marzena*, *Tadeusz*, *Tomasz*, *Zbigniew*.

Warde (193) Mainly Irish variant spelling of English WARD.
GIVEN NAMES Irish 4%. *Cormac*, *Donal*.

Wardell (1447) English: variant spelling of WARDLE.

Warden (4030) **1.** English, Scottish, and northern Irish: occupational name for a watchman or guard, from Norman French *wardein* (a derivative of *warder* 'to guard'). **2.** English: habitational name from any of various places, for example in Bedfordshire, County Durham, Kent, Northumbria, and Northamptonshire, called Warden, from Old English *weard* 'watch' + *dūn* 'hill'. Compare WARDLAW and WARDLE 1.

Wardenburg (112) German: habitational name from Wardenburg in Lower Saxony.
GIVEN NAME German 4%. *Erwin*.

Warder (321) English: habitational name for someone from a place called Wardour in Wiltshire, named with Old english *weard* 'watch' + *ōra* 'hill slope'.

Wardlaw (1147) Scottish: habitational name from any of several minor places called Wardlaw, from Old English *weard* 'watch' + *hlāw* 'hill'. Compare WARDLOW.

Wardle (897) English: **1.** habitational name from places in Cheshire and Greater Manchester (formerly in Lancashire) called Wardle, from Old English *weard* 'watch' + *hyll* 'hill'. Compare WARDEN 2 and WARDLAW. **2.** regional name from Weardale in County Durham, which takes its name from the Wear river (named with a Celtic word probably meaning 'water') + Old Norse *dalr* 'valley'.

Wardlow (966) English: habitational name from Wardlow in Derbyshire, from Old English *weard* 'watch' + *hlāw* 'hill'. Compare WARDLAW.

Wardman (105) English: occupational name for guard, a variant of WARD.

Wardrip (229) Variant of Scottish and English WARDROP.

Wardrop (310) Scottish: metonymic occupational name for someone who was in charge of the garments worn by a feudal lord and his household, from Norman French *warde(r)* 'to keep or guard' + *robe* 'garment'.

Wardwell (731) English: perhaps a variant of WARDLE or a habitational name from a place called Wordwell in Suffolk, probably named with an Old English *wride* 'bend' + *well* 'stream'.

Ware (14632) English: **1.** topographic name for someone who lived by a dam or weir on a river (Old English *wær*, *wer*), or a habitational name from a place named with this word, such as Ware in Hertfordshire. **2.** nickname for a cautious person, from Middle English *war(e)* 'wary', 'prudent' (Old English *(ge)wær*).
FOREBEARS Robert Ware came to Dedham,

MA, from England in or before 1642. Henry Ware (1764–1845), born in Sherborn, MA, was a Unitarian clergyman and theologian and father of the physician John Ware (b. 1795) and two clergymen, Henry (b. 1794) and William (b. 1797).

Wareham (707) English: habitational name for someone from either of the places called Warham, in Herefordshire and Norfolk, or from Wareham in Dorset. All are named with Old English *wær* 'weir' + either *hām* 'homestead' or *hamm* 'enclosure hemmed in by water'.

Warehime (321) Americanized spelling of German WEHRHEIM.

Wareing (170) English: variant spelling WARING.

Waren (171) Dutch and Belgian (**van der Varen**): habitational name for someone from any of various places in Zeeland, French Flanders, or East and West Flanders, called Waard, Waarde, or Weerd, denoting an area of land surrounded by water, an island.

Wares (255) English: variant of WARE 1.

Warf (531) English: variant spelling of WHARFF.

Warfel (737) German: variant of WERFEL.

Warfield (2573) English: habitational name from a place in Berkshire called Warfield, from Old English *wær* 'weir' + *feld* 'pasture', 'open country'.

FOREBEARS Richard Warfield came from Berkshire, England, to MD in 1662.

Warford (771) English: habitational name, probably from Warford in Cheshire, which is named with Old English *wær*, *wer* 'weir' + *ford* 'ford'. The surname is now more common in Suffolk than in Cheshire.

Warga (243) **1.** Polish and Ukrainian: descriptive nickname from *warga* 'lip', presumably for someone with prominent lips or with a growth on the lips. **2.** Polish or German spelling of Hungarian *varga* 'cobbler' (see VARGA).

Wargel (139) German: pet form of uncertain origin, perhaps from Polish WARGA 'lip' or Hungarian VARGA 'cobbler'.

Wargin (139) Polish: from a derivative of WARGA. This surname is also established in Germany.

Wargo (1744) Polish and Ukrainian: dialect variant of WARGA.

Warhol (182) Variant spelling of Polish **Warchoł** (see WARCHOL).

Warholic (100) Americanized form of Polish **Warcholik**, a diminutive of **Warchoł** (see WARCHOL).

Warhurst (270) English: habitational name, possibly from Warhurst Fold Farm in Derbyshire.

Waring (1717) English: from the Norman personal name *Warin*, derived from Germanic *war(in)* 'guard', and used as a short form of various compound names with this first element. Compare, for example,

WARNER 2. The name was popular in France and among the Normans, partly as a result of the popularity of the Carolingian lay *Guérin de Montglave*.

Wark (706) Scottish and English (Northumberland): habitational name from Wark on the Tweed river, which is named from Old English *(ge)weorc* '(earth)-works', 'fortification'.

Warkentin (436) North German: from a place name of Slavic origin.

GIVEN NAMES German 5%. *Hans* (2), *Otto* (2), *Benno, Dietrich, Helmut, Ute*.

Warlick (946) English: perhaps an altered form of **Warlock**, an English surname of uncertain origin; it is more likely to be from Old Norse *varðlokkur* 'incantations' than from Old English *wǣrloga* 'traitor', 'devil'.

Warling (114) Variant of Swiss German WERLING.

Warm (175) German, Jewish (Ashkenazic), and English: probably a nickname for a warm-hearted or a zealous person, from Middle High German and German *warm* 'warm', Middle English *warme*.

GIVEN NAMES German 10%; Jewish 5%. *Kurt* (3), *Gunter* (2); *Bluma, Sol*.

Warmack (414) Origin unidentified. Possibilities include: **1.** altered form of English WOMACK (itself unexplained). **2.** Americanized form of Polish **Warmiak**, a habitational name or regional name from any of various places in Poland, in particular Warmia, a region of northeastern Poland.

Warman (1086) **1.** English: from the Old English personal name *Wǣrmund*, composed of the elements *wǣr* 'pledge' + *mund* 'protection'. **2.** English: alternatively, perhaps an occupational name for a merchant or trader, from Middle English *ware* 'wares', 'articles of trade' + *man* 'man'. **3.** Jewish (Ashkenazic): probably an ornamental name from German *wahr* 'true' or *warm* 'warm' + *Mann* 'man'. **4.** This name is also found in Swedish, as is **Varman**, both probably of German origin.

Warmath (138) Variant of German WARMUTH.

Warmbier (118) North German: metonymic occupational name for a brewer, from Middle Low German *warm* 'warm' + *bēr* 'beer'.

Warmington (167) English: habitational name from either of two places called Warmington. The one in Warwickshire was named in Old English as *Wǣrmundingtūn* 'settlement (Old English *tūn*) associated with *Wǣrmund*'. That in Northamptonshire was *Wyrmingtūn* 'settlement associated with *Wyrm*', an unattested byname meaning 'serpent', 'dragon'.

Warmke (102) German: short form of any Germanic personal name formed with *wer*, *war* + *berht*, *bald*, as in **Warmbold**.

GIVEN NAME German 4%; Scandinavian 4%. *Alfons*.

Warmkessel (117) German: from Middle High German *warm* 'warm' + *kessel* 'kettle', probably a nickname for a tavern keeper.

Warmoth (195) Dutch: from a Germanic personal name composed of the elements *war* 'guard' + *mut* 'spirit'.

Warmouth (111) Americanized form of Dutch WARMOTH or German WARMUTH.

Warmuth (251) German: from a Germanic personal name composed of the elements *ward* 'guardian' + *mut* 'desire', 'spirit'.

GIVEN NAME German 4%. *Manfred*.

Warn (422) **1.** English: variant spelling of WARNE. **2.** German: from a short form of any of various Germanic personal names formed with *war(in)* 'guard' as the first element.

Warncke (200) German: variant of WARNECKE.

GIVEN NAMES German 6%. *Claus, Eldor, Erwin, Hilde*.

Warne (1009) English: habitational name from a place in Devon, first recorded in 1194 as *Wagefen*, apparently from an Old English derivative of *wagian* 'to shake or quiver' + *fen* 'bog', 'marsh'.

Warnecke (560) North German: from a pet form of the personal name *Warner*, Low German form of WERNER.

GIVEN NAMES German 4%. *Hans* (2), *Kurt* (2), *Dieter, Fritz*.

Warneke (414) German: variant spelling of WARNECKE.

Warnell (164) English: unexplained.

Warner (31357) **1.** English (of Norman origin) and North German: from a Germanic personal name composed of the elements *war(in)* 'guard' + *heri, hari* 'army'. The name was introduced into England by the Normans in the form *Warnier*. **2.** English (of Norman origin): reduced form of *Warrener* (see WARREN 2). **3.** Irish (Cork): Anglicization of Gaelic **Ó Murnáin** (see MURNANE), found in medieval records as *Iwarrynane*, from a genitive or plural form of the name, in which *m* is lenited.

FOREBEARS The name Warner was brought from England to MA independently by several different bearers in the first half of the 17th century and subsequently. Andrew Warner came from England to Cambridge, MA, in or before 1632; William Warner was in Ipswich, MA, by 1637; and John Warner was one of the settlers in Hartford, CT, in 1635.

Warnes (269) English (East Anglia): of uncertain origin. There is a family tradition that the name is of Low German origin; probably a variant of WARNS. There was fairly extensive migration from the Low Counties to East Anglia during the Middle Ages in connection with the wool trade.

Warnick (1388) Variant spelling of German WARNECKE.

Warning (382) German: patronymic from WARNER.

Warnke (1105) German: variant of WARNECKE.

GIVEN NAMES German 4%. *Erwin* (3), *Ernst* (2), *Horst* (2), *Arno*, *Egon*, *Fritz*, *Gunter*, *Hans*, *Reinhold*, *Uwe*.

Warnken (351) German: patronymic from WARNECKE.

Warnock (2063) Scottish (Lanarkshire) and northern Irish: reduced form of **Mac Warnock**, an Anglicized form of Gaelic **Mac Giolla Mhearnóg** 'son of the devotee of St. *Mearnóg*'. St Mearnóg is the patron saint of Kilmarnock.

Warns (163) **1.** Dutch: habitational name from places so named in Friesland and Overijssel. The one in Friesland was the site of a famous victory of Frisians over the Hollanders in the 14th century. **2.** German: patronymic from WARN.

Warr (1002) English (of Norman origin): nickname for a soldier or for a belligerent person, from Old French *(de la) werre*, *(de la) guerre* '(of the) war'. Compare DELAWARE.

Warrell (175) English: variant spelling of WORRELL.

Warren (52256) **1.** English and Irish (of Norman origin): habitational name from La Varrenne in Seine-Maritime, France, named with a Gaulish element probably descriptive of alluvial land or sandy soil. **2.** English: topographic name for someone who lived by a game park, or an occupational name for someone employed in one, from Anglo-Norman French *warrene* or Middle English *wareine* 'warren', 'piece of land for breeding game'. **3.** Irish: adopted as an Englsih form of Gaelic **Ó Murnáin** (see MURNANE, WARNER).

FOREBEARS The surname Warren was brought to North America from England independently by many different bearers in the 17th and 18th centuries. Richard Warren, a London merchant, was one of the Pilgrims on the *Mayflower*. John Warren came to Salem, MA, in 1630 on the *Arbella*, and was the founder of an influential 18th-century Boston family. Arthur Warren emigrated to Weymouth, MA, before 1638.

Warrender (132) Scottish and English: variant of WARRINER.

Warrenfeltz (121) German or Jewish (western Ashkenazic): origin uncertain; perhaps a habitational name from Wallenfels in Bavaria or Wachenfels.

Warrens (117) English: variant of WARREN.

Warrick (2147) English: **1.** variant of WARWICK. **2.** metonymic occupational name for a maker of warrocks, wedges of timber that were used to tighten the joints in a scaffold.

Warriner (882) English and Scottish: occupational name for a gamekeeper, someone whose job was to watch over game in a park, from Old French *warrennier* (central Old French *garennier*) 'warrener'. See also WARREN 2.

Warring (271) English: variant of WARING.

Warrington (1635) English: habitational name from a place of this name in Cheshire (formerly in Lancashire), probably named in Old English as *Wæringtun* 'settlement by the weir', from Old English *wæring* (not independently recorded), a derivative of *wær* 'weir'. Another Warrington, in Buckinghamshire, which may also have given rise to the surname, is recorded in the 12th century as *Wardintone*, probably from an unattested personal name *Wearda* or *Wærheard* + *-ing-*, denoting association, + *tūn* 'settlement', 'estate'.

Warrior (194) **1.** English: occupational name or nickname from Old French *werreieor*, *werrieur* 'warrior'. Compare WARR. **2.** Indian (Kerala): Hindu name based on the name of the *Variar* community. The traditional occupation of this community is performance of temple services.

GIVEN NAMES Indian 5%. *Jogesh*, *Krishna*, *Rahul*.

Warsaw (221) Jewish: Americanized form of Jewish WARSHAW.

Warshauer (197) Jewish (Ashkenazic) and German (**Warschauer**): habitational name for someone from Warsaw, capital of Poland, from the German name of the city *Warschau*.

Warshaw (682) Jewish (Ashkenazic): habitational name for someone from the city of Warsaw, capital of Poland (see WARSHAWSKY).

GIVEN NAMES Jewish 6%. *Isadore* (2), *Yehudit* (2), *Hyman*, *Meyer*, *Miriam*.

Warshawsky (222) **1.** Jewish (eastern Ashkenazic): habitational name for someone from the city of Warsaw (Polish *Warszawa*), which became the capital of Poland at the end of the 16th century, after the destruction of Kraków by fire. **2.** Americanized spelling of the Polish form of this name, **Warszawski**.

GIVEN NAMES Jewish 6%. *Meyer* (2), *Ari*, *Hyman*.

Warstler (262) German: variant of WERSTLER.

Warta (155) Polish: **1.** occupational name for a watchman, from *warta* 'guard'. **2.** habitational name from a place called Warta in Sieradz voivodeship.

Wartell (112) English: perhaps a respelling of the French family name **Wartel**, which is from a pet form of any of various Germanic personal names beginning with the element *war(in)* 'guard', 'preserve'. The surname *Wartell* is recorded in England in the 1881 British census.

Wartenberg (113) German: habitational name from any of numerous places called Wartenberg.

Warters (111) English: variant of WATER 2.

Warth (386) **1.** English: habitational name from for example Warth in Glouceshire or Ward in Devon, which are named with Old English *waroð* 'marshy ground by a shore or stream' or from any of various minor places named with Old Norse *varða* 'beacon' (a derivative of *varða* 'to guard'). **2.** German: habitational name from any of various places named with an Old High German cognate of this element.

Warthan (143) Origin unidentified.

Warthen (469) German: from a short form of the personal name *Wartold*, from Old High German *wart* 'guardian'.

Wartman (313) South German (**Wartmann**): occupational name, from Middle High German *wartman* 'sentinel', 'watchman', 'scout'.

Warton (109) English: variant spelling of WHARTON.

Warwick (2233) English: **1.** habitational name from the county seat of Warwickshire, or a regional name from the county itself. The city was originally named as the 'outlying settlement (Old English *wīc*) by the weir (a hypothetical Old English *wæring*)'. Compare WARRINGTON. **2.** habitational name from a much smaller place of the same name in Cumbria, named with Old English *waroð* 'bank' + *wīc*.

Warzecha (320) Polish: nickname from *warzecha* 'ladle'.

GIVEN NAMES Polish 4%. *Agnieszka*, *Alicja*, *Jerzy*, *Teofil*.

Was (135) **1.** Polish (**Wąs**): descriptive nickname for a man with a particularly fine or noticeable moustache, from *wąs* 'moustache'. **2.** altered spelling of WASS.

GIVEN NAMES Polish 6%; German 4%. *Bogdan*, *Eugeniusz*; *Hedwig*.

Wascher (255) German (usually **Wäscher**): occupational name for a washer, from an agent derivative of Middle High German *waschen*, *weschen* 'to wash'. Numerous trades involved washing processes (see WASHER) and the name may relate to any of these.

GIVEN NAMES German 4%. *Erwin*, *Konrad*, *Uwe*.

Wasco (185) Polish (**Waśko**) and Ukrainian: see VASKO.

Wascom (208) Origin unidentified.

GIVEN NAMES French 4%. *Chantale*, *Idee*.

Wasden (294) English (Sheffield): of uncertain origin; perhaps a habitational name from a lost place name.

Wasdin (160) Variant of English WASDEN.

Wasem (171) **1.** German: variant of WASMER. **2.** Arabic: from a personal name based on *wasīm* 'graceful'.

Waser (139) **1.** German: topographic name for someone who lived by a water meadow, from Middle High German *wase* 'water meadow', 'pasture' + *-er*, suffix denoting an inhabitant. Compare WASMER. **2.** Jewish (Ashkenazic): variant of WASSER.

GIVEN NAMES Jewish 4%. *Shlomo* (2), *Naum*.

Wash (925) Perhaps a variant of English WASS.

Washa (114) Variant of German WESCHE.

Washabaugh (196) Americanized form of German **Weschebach**, a habitational name from a place so named in eastern Germany, or from **Waschenbach** in the Odenwald Mountains.

Washam (774) Origin unidentified; perhaps an Americanized spelling of German WASEM.

Washburn (7941) Northern English: topographic name for someone living on the banks of the Washburn river in West Yorkshire, so named from the Old English personal name *Walc* + Old English *burna* 'stream'. The river name is first recorded as *Walke(s)burna* in the early 12th century. FOREBEARS John Washburn came to MA in 1626 and settled in Duxbury, MA, in 1632.

Washburne (171) English: variant spelling of WASHBURN.
GIVEN NAME Jewish 5%. *Elihu* (3).

Washer (534) **1.** English: from an agent derivative of Middle English *wasch(en)* 'to wash' (Old English *wæscan*), hence an occupational name for a laundryman, or for someone who washed raw wool before spinning. Various other occupations, too, involved washing processes and the name may relate to any of these. For example, it may have denoted a man who washed sheep; some tenants on the manor of Burpham, near Worthing, in Sussex (where the surname is found from an early date), had as part of their feudal service to wash the flocks of their master. **2.** Americanized spelling of the German cognate WASCHER.

Washington (32636) English: habitational name from either of the places called Washington, in Tyne and Wear and West Sussex. The latter is from Old English *Wassingatūn* 'settlement (Old English *tūn*) of the people of *Wassa*', a personal name that is probably a short form of some compound name such as *Wāðsige*, composed of the elements *wāð* 'hunt' + *sige* 'victory'. Washington in Tyne and Wear is from Old English *Wassingtūn* 'settlement associated with *Wassa*'. FOREBEARS George Washington (1732–99), 1st president of the U.S. (1789–97), was born at Bridges Creek, VA. His great-grandfather had settled in the colony after emigrating from England in 1658. With the passage of time, the surname has come to be borne by more African Americans than English Americans. A prominent example was the educator Booker T. Washington (1856–1915), born a slave in VA, who adopted his surname from his stepfather, Washington Ferguson.

Washko (259) Variant of Ukrainian WASKO.

Wasielewski (606) Polish: variant of WASILEWSKI.

Wasik (533) **1.** Polish (**Wąsik**): descriptive nickname from a diminutive of *wąs* 'moustache' (see WAS). **2.** Polish and Ukrainian:

from a pet form of the personal name *Wasyl*, Polish form of Greek *Basileios* (see BASIL). **3.** Eastern German: nickname from Sorbian *wasik* 'crawler'.
GIVEN NAMES Polish 8%. *Zbigniew* (2), *Agnieszka, Casimir, Darek, Ewa, Ignatius, Krzysztof, Mariusz, Tomasz, Witold, Zbig.*

Wasil (166) Polish (**Wasyl**) and Ukrainian: from a vernacular form of Greek *Basileios* (see BASIL).

Wasilewski (789) Polish: habitational name for someone from Wasilew in Siedlce voivodeship, named with the personal name WASIL.
GIVEN NAMES Polish 10%. *Krzysztof* (5), *Piotr* (2), *Andrzej, Bogdan, Bronislaw, Dorota, Eugeniusz, Jacek, Jadwiga, Janina, Jozef, Kazimierz.*

Wasinger (351) German: probably a habitational name for someone from a place called Wasungen in Thuringia.

Waskey (148) Americanized form of Polish WASKO or a similar name.

Waskiewicz (413) Polish (**Waśkiewicz** or **Waszkiewicz**): patronymic from *Wasek*, a pet form of the personal name *Wasyl*, Polish form of Greek *Basileios* (see BASIL).

Wasko (738) **1.** Polish (**Waśko**): from a pet form of the personal name *Wasyl* (see WASIL) or of *Iwan*, a vernacular form of Latin *Johannes* (see JOHN). **2.** Ukrainian: see VASKO.

Waskom (155) Origin unidentified.

Waskow (189) Jewish (Ashkenazic): of uncertain origin; probably a patronymic from a Slavic personal name.
GIVEN NAMES German 5%; Jewish 4%. *Erwin* (2), *Kurt* (2); *Ilan, Shoshana.*

Wasley (292) English: habitational name from an unidentified place.

Wasmer (251) German: topographic name for someone who lived by a water meadow, from Middle High German *wase, wasem* 'water meadow', the suffix *-er* denoting an inhabitant.

Wasmund (298) North German: variant of WACHSMUTH.

Wasmuth (153) North German: variant of WACHSMUTH.

Wason (286) **1.** Scottish: variant of WATSON. **2.** Indian (Tamil Nadu): Anglicized form of a Hindu name that is regularly spelt as **Vasan**, which is an abbreviation of SRINIVASAN and sometimes of **Vasudevan** (see *vāsudeva* under VASWANI).
GIVEN NAMES Indian 4%. *Amit, Ashwani, Sarwan, Satish.*

Wass (692) **1.** Scottish and English: from the Norman personal name *Wazo*, which is probably derived from a compound Germanic name with a first element *wad* 'to go'. Compare WADE 1. **2.** German and Swedish: nickname from Middle High German *was(se)*, Swedish *vass* 'sharp', 'cutting'. The Swedish name is a soldier's name, one of the identifying names adopted by soldiers in the 17th and 18th centuries,

before the use of surnames became general in Scandinavia. **3.** Swedish: ornamental name from *vass* 'reed', 'marsh'. **4.** German: metonymic occupational name for a seller of wax, from Middle Low German *was* 'wax' (see WAX).

Wassel (340) English: variant spelling of WASSELL.

Wassell (347) English: habitational name for someone from a place in Worcestershire named Wasthills, from Old English *weardsetl* 'guardhouse'.

Wassenaar (215) Dutch: habitational name from a place so called in South Holland.

Wassenberg (155) German and Dutch: habitational name from Wassenberg in North Rhine-Westphalia, Germany or from Wassenberg in Temse, East Flanders.

Wasser (878) **1.** German: topographic name from Middle High German *wazzer* 'water'. **2.** Jewish (Ashkenazic): ornamental name or a metonymic occupational name for a water-carrier, from German *Wasser*, Yiddish *vaser* 'water'.

Wasserburger (118) South German: habitational name for someone from any of various places in Austria and Germany named Wasserburg.

Wasserman (3455) German (**Wassermann**) and Jewish (Ashkenazic): German topographic name or Jewish ornamental or occupational name from Middle High German *wazzer*, German *Wasser*, Yiddish *vaser* 'water' + Middle High German *-man* 'man', Yiddish *-man* (see WASSER). This surname is also established in Sweden.
GIVEN NAMES Jewish 4%. *Isadore* (4), *Miriam* (4), *Hillel* (3), *Sol* (3), *Hyman* (2), *Shmuel* (2), *Aron, Chaim, Chana, Dror, Dvorah, Hava.*

Wassermann (138) German: see WASSERMAN.
GIVEN NAMES German 15%. *Kurt* (2), *Franz, Horst, Klaus, Wolfgang.*

Wasserstrom (151) Jewish (Ashkenazic): ornamental name composed of German *Wasser* 'water' + *Strom* 'river', 'current'.
GIVEN NAME German 5%. *Frieda.*

Wassil (102) Altered spelling of English WASSELL.

Wassink (186) German: patronymic from *Waso*, a short form of the Germanic personal name *Wasmod* (see WACHSMUTH).
GIVEN NAMES German 6%; Dutch 4%. *Kurt* (2), *Bernhard; Cornie, Dirk.*

Wassman (134) Americanized spelling of German WASSMANN.

Wassmann (119) German: variant of WACHSMUTH.
GIVEN NAME German 6%. *Ernst.*

Wassmer (227) German: variant spelling of WASMER.

Wassmuth (111) German: variant of WACHSMUTH.

Wassom (194) Origin uncertain; perhaps an altered form of Scottish WASSON or Norwegian WASSUM.

Wasson (3505) Scottish and northern Irish: **1.** from the Norman personal name *Wasso* or *Wazo* (see WASS). **2.** perhaps a variant of WATSON.

Wassum (142) **1.** Norwegian: habitational name from a farmstead in Akershus named Wassum, from Old Norse *vatn* 'lake' + *endi* 'end'. **2.** Probably an altered form of WASSON.

Waszak (252) Polish: from a pet form of the personal names *Wasyl* (see BASIL) or *Iwan*, a vernacular derivative of Latin *Johannes* (see JOHN).

Waszkiewicz (155) Polish: patronymic from the personal names *Waszko*, a pet form of *Wasyl* (see BASIL) or *Iwan*, a vernacular derivative of Latin *Johannes* (see JOHN).
GIVEN NAMES Polish 9%. *Henryk, Janina, Kazimierz, Krzysztof.*

Watanabe (2113) Japanese: one of the ten most common surnames, especially in eastern Japan. The original meaning was occupational: *Wataribe* 'ferrymen's guild'. Some bearers descend from Minamoto no Toru (822–895), a son of Emperor Saga. A common alternate reading is **Watabe**.
GIVEN NAMES Japanese 60%. *Akira* (12), *Hiroshi* (10), *Takashi* (10), *Kazuo* (9), *Kiyoshi* (9), *Takeshi* (9), *Toshio* (9), *Kenji* (8), *Shinichi* (7), *Tadashi* (7), *Atsushi* (6), *Hideo* (6).

Watchorn (145) English (Midlands): unexplained.

Water (131) **1.** English: variant of WALTER, representing the normal medieval pronunciation of the name. **2.** English and German (Rhineland): topographic name for someone who lived by a stretch of water, Middle English, Low German *water*. **3.** Irish: adopted as an English translation of Gaelic **Ó Fuartháin** (see FORAN), being wrongly taken as *Ó Fuaruisce* 'son of cold water'.
GIVEN NAMES German 6%. *Siegfried, Wolf.*

Waterbury (878) English: habitational name of uncertain origin; perhaps from Waterperry in Oxfordshire, which is named with Old English *pyrige* 'pear tree', to which was later added Middle English *water* to distinguish it from nearby Woodperry.

Waterfall (106) English: habitational name from Waterfall, a place in Staffordshire, named from Old English *wætergefall* 'place where a water course disappears below ground'. There is another place so called in Guisborough in North Yorkshire and a lost Waterfall in Pontefract, West Yorkshire, both of which may also have contributed to the surname.

Waterfield (460) English (of Norman origin): habitational name from Vatierville in Seine-Maritime, France, so named from the personal name WALTER + Old French *ville* 'settlement'.

Waterhouse (1477) English (chiefly Yorkshire, Lancashire, and Midlands): topographic name for someone who lived in a house by a stretch of water or perhaps a moated house, from Middle English *water* 'water' + *hous* 'house'.
FOREBEARS Richard Waterhouse, a tanner from Yorkshire, England, emigrated to Portsmouth, NH, in 1669.

Waterman (4844) **1.** English: occupational name for the servant of a man called *Wa(l)ter* (see WATER 1). **2.** English and Dutch: occupational name for a boatman or a water carrier, or a topographic name for someone who lived by a stretch of water (see WATER 2). **3.** Americanized form of German and Jewish (Ashkenazic) **Wasserman(n)**, an occupational name for a water-carrier. Compare 2 above.
FOREBEARS Robert Waterman emigrated from England to Marshfield, MA, in 1636.

Waters (23602) **1.** English: patronymic from an altered form of the personal name WALTER. **2.** English: variant of WATER 2. **3.** Irish: when not the English surname, an Anglicized form of various Gaelic names taken to be derived from *uisce* 'water' (see for example HASKIN, HISKEY, TYDINGS).
FOREBEARS James Waters came from London, England, to Salem, MA, in 1630. Lawrence Waters came to Charlestown, MA, from Lancaster, England, in 1675.

Waterson (387) Scottish and northern English: patronymic from WALTER.

Waterston (111) Scottish: probably a variant of WATERSON, altered by folk etymology to the form of a place name.

Waterstradt (107) Dutch or North German: topographic name (also **Watterstradt** 'water street') for someone who lived by the water or along a canal; or a habitational name from Waterstraat in East Flanders, Belgium, which was carried over to Pennsylvania as the place name Waterstreet.
GIVEN NAME German 4%. *Kurt.*

Waterworth (234) English (chiefly Lancashire): occupational name for a water bailiff, earlier *Waterward*, from Middle English *water* + *ward* 'guard'. All the early examples occur on the banks of Martin Mere, a large freshwater lake (now drained) in western Lancashire.

Wates (103) English: variant spelling of WAITES.

Watford (1286) English: habitational name from Watford in Hertfordshire or from the much smaller place in Northamptonshire, both named with Old English *wāð* 'hunt' + *ford* 'ford'.

Wathen (1266) Welsh: from the personal name *Gwaiddon*, which is found as part of place names in Robeston Wathen, near Narberth, Pembrokeshire, and the nearby Llanwathen (from Welsh *llan* 'church' + *Gwaiddon*).

Watkin (251) English: from a pet form of *Wat(t)*, a short form of WALTER.

Watkins (40138) English (also frequent in Wales): patronymic from the personal name WATKIN.

Watkinson (344) northern English: patronymic from the medieval personal name WATKIN.

Watland (190) Norwegian: habitational name from any of eleven or so farmsteads in Agder and Vestlandet named Vatland, from Old Norse *Vazland*, a compound of *vatn* 'water', 'lake' + *land* '(piece of) land'.

Watler (139) English: occupational name for a wattler, Middle English *watelere*, i.e. someone who made the panels of interwoven twigs that were used to fill the spaces between the structural timbers of a timber frame building. See also DAUBER.
GIVEN NAMES Spanish 4%. *Andres, Carlos, Jose, Melida, Silvia.*

Watley (485) English: variant of WHATLEY.

Watling (191) **1.** English (East Anglia): from a pet form of WATT. **2.** German: from *Wado*, a short form of a Germanic personal name formed with *wadi* 'pledge' as the first element.

Watlington (507) English: habitational name from Watlington in Norfolk or Oxfordshire, or Whatlington in Sussex. All are from an unattested Old (variously *Hwætel, Wacol, Wæcel*) + *-inga* suffix indicating association + *tūn* 'settlement'.

Watne (190) Norwegian: habitational name from any of some twenty or so farmsteads in Agder and Vestlandet, so named from Old Norse *vatn* 'water', 'lake'.
GIVEN NAME Scandinavian 4%. *Knute.*

Watring (124) Origin unidentified.

Watroba (109) Polish (**Wątroba**): from Polish *wątroba* 'liver', used as a nickname in Polish idiom for someone who bore a grudge.
GIVEN NAMES Polish 6%. *Eugeniusz, Jacek, Kazimierz.*

Watrous (867) Altered form of English WATERHOUSE.

Watry (214) Dutch: from the personal name *Waldrich*, composed of the Germanic elements *wald* 'rule' + *rīc* 'powerful', 'rich'.

Watson (82750) Scottish and northern English: patronymic from the personal name *Wat* (see WATT)

Watt (5733) Scottish and English: from an extremely common Middle English personal name, *Wat(t)*, a short form of WALTER.

Wattenbarger (368) Variant of German **Wattenberger**, a habitational name for someone from any of various places called Wattenberg.

Wattenberg (160) **1.** German and Jewish (Ashkenazic): habitational name for someone from any of the various places so named. **2.** Jewish (Ashkenazic): ornamental name from German *Watte* 'wadding', 'cotton' + *Berg* 'montain', 'hill'.
GIVEN NAMES Jewish 4%; German 4%. *Emanuel, Hyman; Benno, Hans.*

Watters (4092) Scottish and northern Irish: patronymic from an altered form of the personal name WALTER. Compare WATERS.

Watterson (1317) Scottish and northern Irish: patronymic from an altered form of the personal name WALTER. Compare WATERSON.

Wattier (133) Northern French and Belgian: variant of **Wautier**, itself a variant of GAUTHIER.
GIVEN NAMES French 4%. *Alexandre* (2), *Henri*.

Wattles (275) English or Scottish: unexplained.

Wattley (112) English: variant spelling of WHATLEY.

Watton (245) English: habitational name from a place called Watton, as for example one in Norfolk, named from the Old English personal name *Wada* + *tūn* 'settlement', or another, in East Yorkshire, which takes its name from Old English *wēt* 'wet' + *dūn* 'hill'.

Watts (28775) English: patronymic from WATT. This surname is also well established in South Wales.

Watwood (206) English (Staffordshire): habitational name from a place in Staffordshire called Wetwood, from Old English *wēt*, *wǣt* 'wet', 'damp' + *wudu* 'wood'.

Watz (185) German: from a short form of a Germanic personal name formed with *war* 'to protect or warn'; 'man'; 'true' as the first element.
GIVEN NAME Scandinavian 4%. *Nels* (2).

Waud (100) English: variant of English or German WALD.

Waugaman (354) Americanized spelling of German WAGEMANN.

Waugh (4272) Scottish and northern English: of disputed origin. It is most likely from Old English (Anglian) *walh* 'foreign' (see WALLACE), perhaps applied originally to the Welsh-speaking Strathclyde Britons, who survived as a separate group in Scotland well into the Middle Ages.

Wauters (189) Dutch (**de Wauters**): variant of WOUTERS.
GIVEN NAMES French 8%. *Henri*, *Jacques*, *Luc*.

Wavra (203) Polish (**Wawra**): from a pet form of the personal name *Wawrzyniec*, Polish form of Latin *Laurentius* (see LAWRENCE).

Wawro (126) Polish: from a pet form of the personal name *Wawrzyniec*, Polish form of Latin *Laurentius* (see LAWRENCE).
GIVEN NAMES Polish 6%. *Krzysztof*, *Ryszard*.

Wawrzyniak (447) Polish: patronymic from the personal name *Wawrzyniec*, from Latin *Laurentius* (see LAWRENCE).
GIVEN NAMES Polish 9%. *Grazyna* (2), *Casimir*, *Ignacy*, *Ignatius*, *Janina*, *Jerzy*, *Krzysztof*, *Piotr*, *Radoslaw*, *Stanislaw*, *Wojciech*.

Wawrzynski (70) Polish (**Wawrzyński**): habitational name for someone from Wawrzynki in Bydgoszcz voivodeship, a place named with a pet form of the personal name *Wawrzyniec*, from Latin *Laurentius* (see LAWRENCE).

Wax (860) **1.** Variant spelling of German and Jewish WACHS. **2.** English: metonymic occupational name for a seller or gatherer of beeswax, Middle English *wax* (from Old English *weax*). In the Middle Ages wax was an important commodity, used among other things for making candles.
GIVEN NAMES Jewish 4%. *Chani*, *Mendel*, *Miriam*, *Nechama*, *Yetta*, *Yigal*.

Waxler (344) Variant of WEXLER.

Waxman (1176) **1.** English: occupational name for a seller or gatherer of beeswax, from WAX with the addition of Middle English *man* 'man'. **2.** Americanized spelling of the German and Jewish (Ashkenazic) cognate **Wachsmann** (see WACHS).
GIVEN NAMES Jewish 6%. *Sol* (6), *Herschel* (3), *Mordecai* (3), *Miriam* (2), *Avi*, *Avrohom*, *Avrom*, *Chaim*, *Chana*, *Hyman*, *Moishe*, *Reuven*.

Way (5366) English (chiefly southern): topographic name for someone who lived near a road or path, Old English *weg* (cognate with Old Norse *vegr*, Old High German *weg*), or a habitational name from some minor place named with this word, as for example any of the places called Way or Waye, in Devon.

Waybright (552) Americanized form of German **Weibrecht** or **Weybrecht**, from a Germanic personal name composed of the elements *wīg* 'battle', 'war' + *berht* 'bright' (see WEYBRIGHT).

Waycaster (296) Probably an Americanized form of German WECKESSER. This name has the form of an English habitational name formed with Old English *cæster* 'Roman walled city', but neither the place name nor the surname are found in English records.

Waychoff (118) Perhaps a variant of Dutch WYCKOFF.

Wayda (119) Polish and Ukrainian: variant of WAJDA.
GIVEN NAME Scandinavian 5%. *Erik* (2).

Waye (246) English: variant spelling of WAY.

Wayland (966) **1.** English: from a Germanic personal name, *Welond*. **2.** English: habitational name for someone from a place called Wayland Hundred in Norfolk. **3.** Perhaps an Americanized spelling of German WEILAND.

Waymack (114) Of uncertain origin. Possibly a variant of English **Waymark**, which probably a derivative of the Old Breton personal name *Wiumarch*, composed of the elements *uuiu* 'worthy' + *march* 'horse'. See also WYMER.

Wayman (1724) English: variant of WYMAN.

Wayment (166) English: variant spelling of **Waymont**, a variant of WYMAN.

Waymire (788) Americanized form of German **Wehmeyer** or **Wehmeier** (see WEDEMEYER).

Wayne (3950) English: metonymic occupational name for a carter or cartwright, from Middle English *wain* 'cart', 'wagon' (Old English *wægen*). Occasionally it may have been a habitational name for someone who lived at a house distinguished with this sign, probably from the constellation of the Plow, known in the Middle Ages as *Charles's Wain*, the reference being to Charlemagne.
FOREBEARS Anthony Wayne and his son Isaac, of English ancestry, came from Ireland to Chester Co., PA, in about 1724. Gen. Anthony Wayne (1745–96), born in Waynesboro, PA, was a prominent military officer in the American Revolution and the Indian war of 1794–95.

Wayner (144) Americanized spelling of German and Jewish WEINER or WEGNER.

Waynick (352) Variant of English WINNICK.

Ways (105) Scottish and English: possibly a variant of **Wace**.

Wayson (201) Scottish and English: patronymic from the Norman personal name *Wazo* (see WASS).

Wayt (314) English: variant spelling of WAITE.

Wazny (124) Polish (**Ważny**): nickname for a self-important man, from *ważny* 'important'.
GIVEN NAME Polish 4%. *Zbignew*.

Weaber (156) Variant of German WEBER.

Wead (138) Irish: probably an Irish spelling of English **Weed**, a nickname for an irascible man, from Middle English *wede* 'rage', 'fury'.

Weadock (119) Origin unidentified.

Weadon (102) English: variant spelling of WEEDON.

Weagle (117) Americanized spelling of German WIEGEL.

Weakland (496) Probably an Americanized spelling of German WICKLAND.

Weakley (1260) English: variant spelling of WEEKLEY.

Weakly (170) English: variant spelling of WEEKLEY.

Weaks (379) English: variant of WEEK.

Wean (161) Scottish: reduced and altered form of McQUEEN.

Weant (199) Variant of Scottish WEAN.

Wear (1316) English (Northumbria): **1.** topographic name for someone who lived by the Wear river in northern England. The river name is ancient, occuring in the form *Vedra* in Ptolemy's *Geographia*; it is probably a Celtic word meaning 'water'. **2.** topographic name for someone who lived near a dam or weir, a variant spelling of WARE 1, or a habitational name from a place called Weare, in Devon and Somerset, from Old English *wær*, *wer* 'weir'.

Weare (206) English: variant spelling of WEAR.

Wearing (146) English: variant spelling of WARING.

Wears (183) English: variant of WEAR.

Weary (416) **1.** Americanized form of Geman WEHRY. **2.** English: nickname from Middle English *wery* 'wicked', 'acursed' (from Old English *wearg*).

Wease (296) Perhaps an Americanized spelling of German WIESE.

Weast (317) English: unexplained.

Weatherall (304) English: variant spelling of WETHERALL.

Weatherbee (517) Variant spelling of English WEATHERBY.

Weatherby (951) English: habitational name for someone from a place in West Yorkshire named Wetherby, from Old Norse *veðr* 'wether (sheep)' + *býr* 'farmstead'.

Weatherford (3199) English: probably a topographic name or a habitational name from a lost or unidentified place.

Weatherhead (291) English and Scottish: of uncertain origin. According to Reaney this is an occupational name for a shepherd, from Middle English *wether* 'wether', 'ram' + *herd* 'herdsman'. His evidence for this interpretation of the final syllable is alternation in the late 15th century between *Weydurherd* and *Wedirhed*. Black speculates that the name may be a topographic name from a hill in Berwickshire.

Weatherholt (327) Americanized form of German WIEDERHOLD.

Weatherholtz (226) Part Americanized form of German WIEDERHOLD.

Weatherill (131) English: variant spelling of WETHERELL.

Weatherington (200) English (Nottinghamshire): variant spelling of WETHERINGTON.

Weatherley (103) English and Scottish: variant spelling of WEATHERLY.

Weatherly (2629) English and Scottish: habitational name from Wetherley in Cambridgeshire, named with Old English *weðer* 'wether', 'ram' + *lēah* 'woodland clearing', or possibly from Wedderlie in Berwickshire, Scotland, which has the same origin.

Weatherman (657) **1.** English: unexplained; perhaps an occupational name for a shepherd, in particular one who castrated rams, from Middle English *weder* 'wether', 'castrated ram' + *man* 'man'. **2.** Americanized form of German **Wettermann**, a variant of WETTER 2, with the addition of the Middle High German suffix *-man* 'man'.

Weathers (4270) English: patronymic from **Weather**, from Middle English *wether* 'wether', '(castrated) ram' (Old English *weðer*), hence a nickname for a man supposedly resembling a wether, or a metonymic occupational name for a shepherd.

Weathersbee (274) English: variant of WEATHERBY.

Weathersby (981) English: variant of WEATHERBY.

Weatherspoon (985) Scottish: variant of WITHERSPOON.

Weatherton (105) Scottish: apparently a habitational name, but no place of this name has been identified. It may be from a lost or unidentified place, or possibly a much-altered variant of WATERSON.

Weatherwax (565) Anglicized spelling of an unidentified North German or Dutch family name.

Weathington (222) Origin unidentified. This has the form of an English habitational name, but no suitable source has been identified and the surname is not found in current English records.

Weaver (50628) **1.** English: occupational name, from an agent derivative of Middle English *weven* 'to weave' (Old English *wefan*). **2.** English: habitational name from a place on the Weaver river in Cheshire, now called Weaver Hall but recorded simply as *Weuere* in the 13th and 14th centuries. The river name is from Old English *wēfer(e)* 'winding stream'. **3.** Translated form of German WEBER.
FOREBEARS Clement Weaver was in Weymouth, MA, by 1643.

Weaverling (142) Americanized form of German **Weberling**, a habitational name from a place named Weferlingen near Helmstedt.

Weavil (168) English (of Norman origin): habitational name for someone from a place called Vauville in Manche, France.

Webb (57791) **1.** English and Scottish: occupational name for a weaver, early Middle English *webbe*, from Old English *webba* (a primary derivative of *wefan* 'to weave'; compare WEAVER 1). This word survived into Middle English long enough to give rise to the surname, but was already obsolescent as an agent noun; hence the secondary forms with the agent suffixes *-er* and *-ster*. **2.** Americanized form of various Ashkenazic Jewish cognates, including **Weber** and **Weberman**.
FOREBEARS Richard Webb, a Lowland Scot, was an admitted freeman of Boston in 1632, and in 1635 was one of the first settlers of Hartford, CT.

Webber (10064) **1.** English (chiefly West Country): occupational name for a weaver, early Middle English *webber*, agent derivative of WEBB. **2.** Jewish (Ashkenazic): variant of WEBER.

Webel (146) German: variant of WEIBEL.
GIVEN NAME German 4%. *Reinhardt*.

Weber (45096) German and Jewish (Ashkenazic): occupational name for a weaver, Middle High German *wēber*, German *Weber*, an agent derivative of *weben* 'to weave'. This name is widespread throughout central and eastern Europe, being found for example as a Czech, Polish, Slovenian, and Hungarian name.

Weberg (259) **1.** German: variant of WEBER. **2.** Norwegian (**Veberg**): habita-

tional name from a farm named with *berg* 'mountain'; the first element is either *vegr* 'road' or *veðr* 'weather'. **3.** Swedish: ornamental name from the same elements as in 1.
GIVEN NAMES Scandinavian 8%. *Nels* (2), *Alf*, *Erik*.

Webert (100) **1.** Probably an altered spelling of German **Wibert**, from the personal name *Wi(g)bert*. **2.** Frenchified form (**Wébert**) of German WEBER, found in the French-speaking area of Belgium.
GIVEN NAME German 5%. *Otto*.

Webley (183) English: habitational name for someone from a place in Herefordshire named Weobley, from an unattested Old English personal name, *Wiobba* + *lēah* 'woodland clearing'.

Webre (346) Frenchified spelling of German WEBER.
GIVEN NAMES French 6%. *Emile* (2), *Cecile*, *Marcel*.

Webster (25639) English (chiefly Yorkshire, Lancashire, and the Midlands) and Scottish: occupational name for a weaver, early Middle English *webber*, agent derivative of WEBB.
FOREBEARS The name Webster was brought to North America from England independently by several different bearers in the 17th and 18th centuries. One John Webster settled in Ipswich, MA, in 1635; another John Webster (d. 1661), ancestor of the lexicographer Noah Webster, emigrated to Cambridge, MA, in about 1631 and later became one of the founders of the colony of CT, of which he was appointed governor in 1656.
Daniel Webster (1782–1852), politician and orator, was born in Salisbury, NH, a descendant of Thomas Webster, a prominent 17th-century citizen of Ipswich, MA, whose family had settled there around 1635, while he was still a child.

Wechsler (1046) German and Jewish (Ashkenazic): occupational name for a money changer, Middle High German *wëhselære*, German *Wechsler*, Yiddish *veksler*.
GIVEN NAMES Jewish 5%. *Sol* (2), *Chaim*, *Hyman*, *Meyer*, *Miriam*, *Yehuda*.

Wechter (291) Variant spelling of German **Wächter** (see WACHTER).

Weck (289) German: **1.** from Middle High German *wecke*, '(wedge-shaped) pastry', 'hard roll', hence a metonymic occupational name for a pastry cook. **2.** from *Waccho*, a short form of a Germanic personal name formed with an initial element related to Old High German *wachēn* 'to wake'.
GIVEN NAMES German 6%. *Heinz* (2), *Dieter*, *Egon*, *Margrethe*.

Wecker (392) German: **1.** occupational name for a pastry cook, from an agent derivative of Middle High German *wecke* '(wedge-shaped) pastry', 'hard roll'. **2.** variant of WECK 2.
GIVEN NAMES German 4%. *Kurt* (2), *Ewald*.

Weckerly (211) Americanized spelling of German **Weckerle**, from a pet form of WACKER.

Weckesser (197) German: occupational nickname for a baker or a nickname for a man with a large appetite, from Middle High German *wecke* '(wedge-shaped) pastry' + *ezzer* 'eater'.

Weckman (135) German (**Weckmann**): variant of WECKER.

Weckwerth (223) German: variant of **Wegwerth** (from German **Wegwarte**), probably a topographic name or a metonymic occupational name for an herbalist, from Middle High German *wegewarte* 'succory', 'wild chicory', a medicinal plant.

Wedde (108) German: topographic name from Low German *wede* 'woods' or from a similar word meaning 'ford in swampy terrain'.
GIVEN NAMES German 4%. *Hans, Ingo.*

Weddel (136) Scottish: variant of WEDDLE.

Weddell (358) Scottish: variant spelling of WEDDLE.

Wedderburn (162) Scottish: habitational name from the lands of Wedderburn in Berwickshire.

Wedding (642) German: **1.** habitational name from any of various places named Wedding or Weddingen. **2.** variant of **Weddig**, a short form of WEDEKIND.

Weddington (731) English: habitational name from Weddington in Warwickshire, recorded in Domesday Book as *Watintune*, from an unattested Old English personal name *Hwæt* + *-ing-* denoting association with + *tūn* 'estate'. However, the surname does not appear in English sources and it may simply be an altered form of WADDINGTON.

Weddle (2375) Scottish: habitational name from a place called Wedale (now Stow) near Edinburgh. The origins of this place name are uncertain. The second element is evidently Old English *dæl* or Old Norse *dalr* 'valley'. The first element might be Old English *wedd* 'pledge', 'security' or its Old Norse cognate *veð* (although this is not found elsewhere as a place name element).

Wedekind (371) North German: from a Germanic personal name composed of the elements *widu* 'wood' + *kind* 'child'. The name became famous as that of a Duke of Lower Saxony who was an opponent of Charlemagne, and was consequently popular in northern Germany as a personal name in the Middle Ages.

Wedeking (278) German (Westphalia): patronymic from WEDEKIND.
GIVEN NAMES German 5%. *Kurt* (2), *Erwin, Horst.*

Wedel (1092) German: **1.** habitational name from any of various places called Wedel or Wedell, all in northern Germany. **2.** (in northwestern Germany) topographic name for someone who lived in a forest, from Middle Low German *wede* 'wood', 'forest' + *lo* 'brush', 'wood'.

Wedell (293) Variant of WEDEL.
GIVEN NAMES French 4%. *Henri* (2), *Andre.*

Wedemeyer (493) **1.** North German: from Middle Low German *wede* 'wood', 'forest' + *meier* 'steward', 'tenant farmer' (see MEYER), hence either an occupational name for a woodland bailiff or a distinguishing name for a tenant farmer living by a wood or forest. **2.** South German: variant of WIEDMEYER.
GIVEN NAMES German 5%. *Kurt* (2), *Hannes, Horst, Juergen.*

Weder (120) German and Swiss German: from a Germanic personal name *Withar,* formed with *witu* 'wood' or *wīt* 'far' as a first element.
GIVEN NAMES German 4%. *Christoph, Erwin, Hans.*

Wedge (959) English: from the Old English personal name *Wegga.*

Wedgewood (126) English: habitational name from Wedgwood in Staffordshire.

Wedgeworth (500) English: probably a perhaps variant of WEDGEWOOD; otherwise a habitational name from a lost or unidentified place.

Wedig (223) German: from a reduced form of WEDEKIND.

Wedin (275) Swedish: ornamental name composed of an uncertain first element (possibly representing a place name formed with *Ved-* 'wood', 'forest') + the common adjectival suffix *-in* (from Latin *-inius*).

Wedlake (119) Variant of Irish and English WOODLOCK.

Wedlock (127) Variant of Irish and English WOODLOCK.

Wedman (121) **1.** Dutch: unexplained; perhaps an altered form of **Weidmann**, a habitational name from a place named Weide, from *weide* 'meadow', 'pasture' or a topographic name from the same word. **2.** Swedish: unexplained.

Wedmore (119) English: habitational name from Wedmore in Somerset, recorded in the 9th century as *Wethmor*, possibly meaning 'marsh (Old English *mōr*) used for hunting (*wæthe*)'.

Wee (353) **1.** Norwegian: variant of VEE. **2.** Dutch: variant of WEI. **3.** Chinese 魏: see WEI.
GIVEN NAMES Chinese/Korean 7%. *Jung* (2), *Sung* (2), *Cheng, Choong, Eun, Hye, Hyunsoo, Jae, Jin Woo, Kee, Kwi, Leong.*

Weeber (187) German: variant of WEBER.
GIVEN NAMES German 4%. *Armin, Dieter.*

Weech (151) **1.** English: variant of WYCHE. **2.** German: nickname for a beautiful person, from Middle High German *wæhe* 'beautiful', 'precious'.

Weed (3231) **1.** English: nickname for an irascible person, from Old English *wēd* 'fury', 'rage'. **2.** Americanized form of Dutch WEEDA.

Weeda (153) Perhaps a shortened form of Dutch **Weedaeg(h)e** or **Wiedaghe**, a habitational name from a place named Ter Wedage ('at the osier hedge').
GIVEN NAMES Dutch 4%; German 4%. *Gerrit* (2), *Dirk; Kurt* (2).

Weede (108) Variant of English WEED or Dutch WEEDA.

Weeden (1133) English: variant spelling of WEEDON.
FOREBEARS James Weeden emigrated from England to Newport, RI, in 1638.

Weeder (129) English: unexplained.

Weedman (480) English: unexplained.

Weedon (470) English: habitational name from places in Buckinghamshire and Northamptonshire called Weedon, named in Old English with *wēoh* '(pre-Christian) temple' + *dūn* 'hill'.

Week (140) **1.** English: variant of WICK, specifically a habitational name from any of various places called Week or Weeke, notably in Cornwall, Hampshire, and Somerset. **2.** Americanized spelling of Norwegian or Swedish VIK.
GIVEN NAMES Scandinavian 8%. *Nils* (2), *Erik, Iver, Knute.*

Weekes (788) English: variant spelling of WEEKS or WICKS.

Weekley (1570) English: habitational name from a place in Northamptonshire called Weekley, from Old English *wīc* 'settlement', perhaps in this case a Roman settlement, Latin *vicus* + *lēah* 'wood', 'clearing'.

Weekly (446) English: variant of WEEKLEY.

Weeks (15885) **1.** English: patronymic from the Middle English personal name *Wikke* (see WICK 2). **2.** English: variant of WICK 1. **3.** It may also be an Americanization of Scandinavian VIK.
FOREBEARS This surname was brought to North America independently by several different bearers in the 17th and 18th centuries. One of the earliest on record is Leonard Weeks, who emigrated from Somerset, England, to Portsmouth, NH, some time before 1656.
William Weeks, recorded in Edgartown, Martha's Vineyard, MA, from 1653 onward, was probably a cousin or other relative of the John Wickes mentioned at WICKES.

Weeldreyer (109) Origin unidentified.

Weeman (148) Perhaps an altered spelling of German WIEMANN.

Weems (3175) Scottish: variant of WEMYSS, reflecting the usual pronunciation of that name.
FOREBEARS David Weems (Wemyss) emigrated from Scotland to Herring Bay, Anne Arundel Co., MD, some time before 1722. Mason Locke Weems, born near Herring Bay in 1759, was a clergyman who wrote a biography of George Washington, in which the first account of the cherry-tree story appeared.

Weers (234) Dutch and German: nickname for someone thought to resemble a ram or wether, from Middle Dutch, Middle Low German *weder*, *weer* 'ram', 'wether'.

Weerts (171) Dutch and German: occupational name for a landlord or innkeeper, Middle Dutch *we(e)rt*, Middle Low German *wert*.

Wees (128) German and Dutch: variant of WEESE.

Weese (1684) **1.** German and Dutch (**de Weese**): descriptive epithet for an orphan, Middle Low German *we(e)se*. **2.** North German: topographic name from Middle Low German *wese* (modern German *Wiese*) 'meadow', 'pasture'.

Weesner (344) Perhaps an altered spelling of German WIESNER.

Weeter (132) Origin unidentified.

Wefel (102) Shortened form of German **Wefels**, a nickname from Middle Low German *wevel* 'weevil'.

GIVEN NAMES German 6%. *Lorenz, Walther.*

Weg (117) Jewish (Ashkenazic): ornamental name from German *Weg* 'path'.

GIVEN NAMES Jewish 16%. *Rivkah* (2), *Sol* (2), *Chaim, Naftali, Shloma, Yehuda.*

Wege (234) German: **1.** topographic name from Middle High German *wēc* 'path', 'street', or habitational name from any of various places named with this word. **2.** short form of WEDEKIND.

FOREBEARS Philip Wege (d. 1812) came to PA in the 1760s from Germany. Descendants of his who moved to VA changed the name to WAGGY, while the brothers John, Jacob, and Philip moved to OH in 1805 and changed their name to WAGY.

GIVEN NAMES German 6%. *Ernst, Hans, Juergen, Jutta, Volker.*

Wegener (1339) German: northern and central German variant of WAGNER.

GIVEN NAMES German 6%. *Gerhard* (3), *Heinz* (3), *Friedrich* (2), *Johannes* (2), *Lorenz* (2), *Armin, Eldor, Erna, Guenther, Hans, Kurt, Manfred.*

Weger (654) German: variant spelling of **Wäger** (see WAGER).

Weghorst (121) German: habitational name from a place so named near Hannover.

GIVEN NAME Scandinavian 4%. *Alf.*

Weglarz (283) Polish (**Węglarz**): occupational name from Polish *węglarz* 'coal merchant'.

GIVEN NAMES Polish 10%. *Casimir* (2), *Krystyna* (2), *Feliks, Halina, Janusz, Kazimierz, Piotr, Wojciech, Zygmunt.*

Wegleitner (132) South German: topographic name for someone who lived beside a path on a mountain slope (see WEG + LEITNER).

GIVEN NAME German 6%. *Kurt* (2).

Wegley (137) South German: variant of WEGE, an Americanized form of the diminutive **Wegle** or **Wegl**.

Wegman (829) Variant spelling of German WEGMANN.

Wegmann (373) German: topographic name for someone living by a main highway, from Middle High German *wēc*, *weg* 'way', 'street' + *man* 'man'.

GIVEN NAMES German 6%. *Urs* (2), *Franz, Gerd, Hans, Ingeburg, Klaus.*

Wegner (3763) German: northern and central variant of WAGNER.

GIVEN NAMES German 5%. *Otto* (9), *Kurt* (5), *Dieter* (3), *Erwin* (3), *Gerhard* (3), *Heinz* (3), *Helmuth* (3), *Bernhard* (2), *Ernst* (2), *Hans* (2), *Alfons, Eldor.*

Wegrzyn (388) Polish (**Węgrzyn**): ethnic name for a Hungarian, derivative of Polish *Węgier* 'Hungarian', *Węgry* 'Hungary'.

GIVEN NAMES Polish 10%. *Witold* (2), *Andrzej, Boguslaw, Jaroslaw, Kazimierz, Lucjan, Piotr, Stanislaw, Tadeusz, Wieslaw, Zygmunt.*

Wehby (124) Origin unidentified.

Wehde (183) North German: from Middle Low German *wede* 'wood', 'forest', hence a topographic name for someone who lived in or by a wood or a metonymic occupational name for a woodcutter or forester.

Wehe (147) German: variant of WEHDE.

Wehinger (100) German (Austria): habitational name for someone from a place named Wehingen, examples of which are found in Baden-Württemberg and Saarland.

Wehking (155) Variant of German WEDEKING.

GIVEN NAME German 5%. *Kurt* (2).

Wehle (138) **1.** German: habitational name from any of various places called Wehlen, for example near Hamburg or near Pirna. **2.** South German: from a pet form of the personal name *Wahho*.

GIVEN NAMES German 9%. *Arno* (2), *Kurt* (2).

Wehler (174) German: habitational name for someone from any of the places mentioned at WEHLE 1, or from any of several places named Wehl, for example near Neuss and near Hannover.

Wehling (396) North German: **1.** topographic name from Middle Low German *wēlinge* 'vortex', 'rapids'. **2.** nickname for someone who was worn out, from Middle Low German *welinge* 'withering', 'decline'.

Wehman (174) North German (**Wehmann**): topographic name from Middle Low German *wede* 'wood', 'forest' + *man* 'man'.

Wehmeier (214) German: variant of WEHMEYER.

GIVEN NAMES German 6%. *Fritz, Kurt, Lothar, Udo.*

Wehmeyer (819) German: variant of WEDEMEYER.

GIVEN NAMES German 5%. *Otto* (3), *Bernhard, Dieter, Erna, Horst, Orlo, Reinhard.*

Wehner (1358) German: central German dialect variant of WAGNER.

GIVEN NAMES German 4%. *Kurt* (4), *Ernst* (2), *Gerd* (2), *Heinz* (2), *Elfriede, Heinrich, Hermann, Horst, Wolf.*

Wehr (1134) **1.** German: topographic name for someone who lived by the defenses of a town or village, for example a wall, ditch, or fence, Middle High German *wer*. **2.** North German: from a reduced form of the personal name *Weder*, composed of the Germanic elements *widu* 'wood', 'forest' + *hari* 'army'.

Wehrenberg (254) German: habitational name from any of several places so named in Lower Saxony.

Wehrer (108) German: **1.** habitational name for someone from any of several places named Wehr, in Baden-Württemberg, North Rhine-Westphalia, and the Rhineland Palatinate. **2.** occupational name for a militia member, from Middle High German *wer(e)n* 'to defend'.

Wehrheim (144) German: habitational name from a place so named near Frankfurt.

Wehring (113) North German: patronymic from any of the Low German personal names beginning with the element *wer* 'to protect or warn'; 'man'; 'true'.

GIVEN NAMES German 11%. *Otto* (3), *Volker.*

Wehrkamp (112) German: topographic name for someone who lived by a military training ground, from Middle High German *wer* 'defense work' + *kamp* 'enclosed field', or a habitational name from a place named with this word.

Wehrle (847) German: from a pet form of the personal name WERNER.

Wehrley (122) Americanized form of South German WEHRLE or Swiss German WEHRLI.

Wehrli (221) Swiss German: variant of WEHRLE.

GIVEN NAMES German 5%. *Hans* (2), *Ernst, Mathias.*

Wehrly (182) Swiss German: variant of WEHRLE.

GIVEN NAME German 4%. *Manfred* (2).

Wehrman (506) Altered spelling of WEHRMANN.

Wehrmann (174) German: **1.** habitational name for someone from any of various place called Wehr, Wehre, or Wehren. **2.** variant spelling of **Wermann** (see WERMAN 1).

GIVEN NAMES German 10%. *Kurt* (3), *Erwin, Helmut.*

Wehrmeister (107) South German: occupational name for an official responsible for overseeing dams or fences, Middle Low German, Middle High German *we(h)r* 'dam', 'barrage', 'barrier' + Middle High German *meister* 'master'; in Bavaria it denoted a forester who oversaw a wild game park or enclosure.

GIVEN NAMES German 4%. *Johannes, Markus.*

Wehrs (123) German: patronymic from WEHR 2.

Wehrung (100) German: patronymic form from WEHR 2.

Wehry (125) German: pet form of WEHR 2.

Wehunt (405) Americanized form of German WEIGAND.

Wei (1382) **1.** Chinese 魏: from the name of the area of Wei in present-day Shanxi province. During the Warring States period (403–221 BC), Hua Wan of the state of Jin repeatedly distinguished himself in battle, and as a reward was granted this area. His descendants subsequently adopted the place name *Wei* as their surname. **2.** Chinese 韦: from the name of an area called Shiwei. A grandson of Peng Zu, who according to tradition lived for over 800 years and came to be a symbol of long life, was granted an area named Shiwei. His descendants adopted the second character of this name, *Wei*, as their surname. **3.** Chinese 卫: from the name of the state of Wei. When the Zhou dynasty was established in 1122 BC, the new ruler Wu Wang left the conquered Shang people their capital, to rule themselves under the supervision of various Zhou appointees. The Shang convinced their overseers to revolt with them, but were soon put down by the Zhou. This time, Wu Wang put his younger brother Kang Shu, the eighth son of Wen Wang, in control of the area, naming it the state of Wei. Many descendants of Kang Shu later adopted Wei as their surname, although others adopted the name Kang (see KANG 1).

GIVEN NAMES Chinese 41%. *Ming* (13), *Wei* (13), *Li* (7), *Chao* (6), *Hong* (6), *Cheng* (5), *Jin* (5), *Ling* (5), *Ping* (5), *Yuan* (5), *Bin* (4), *Dong* (4), *Lan* (3), *Min* (3), *Chang, Chong, Chung, Houa, Pai, Sha, Yiming.*

Weiand (249) Variant of German WIEGAND.

Weibel (771) German: occupational name, from Middle High German *weibel* 'bailiff', 'court usher'.

GIVEN NAMES German 4%. *Brendt* (2), *Katharina* (2), *Hans, Kurt, Markus, Otto.*

Weible (536) German: **1.** from the personal name *Wiibo*, a short form of a compound name formed with *wīg* 'battle', 'fight' as the first element + a second element beginning with *b*, such as *berht* 'bright' or *bald* 'bold'. **2.** variant of WEIBEL.

Weibley (129) Americanized spelling of German WEIBLE.

Weich (179) German: from a short form of any of the various Germanic personal names beginning with the element *wīg* 'battle', 'fight'.

Weichel (287) German: from a pet form of WEICH.

Weichert (256) German: from a Germanic personal name composed of the elements *wīg* 'battle', 'fight' + *hard* 'hardy', 'strong'.

Weichman (184) German (**Weichmann**): from the medieval personal name *Wigman*, from Germanic *wīg* 'battle', 'fight' + *man* 'man'.

Weicht (187) German: from a reduced form of WEIGAND.

Weick (401) German: from a short form of any of the Germanic personal names beginning with the element *wīg* 'battle', 'fight'.

Weickert (110) German: variant of WEICHERT.

GIVEN NAMES German 6%. *Bernhard, Guenther, Manfred.*

Weida (228) German: habitational name from any of the places so named, for example in Saxony or Thuringia (see WEIDE).

Weide (360) **1.** German: topographic name for someone who lived by a conspicuous willow or by a group of willow trees, from Middle High German *wīde* 'willow'. **2.** German: topographic name for someone who lived by a pasture or a hunting ground, Middle High German *weide*. **3.** Jewish (Ashkenazic): ornamental name from German *Weide* 'willow tree'.

Weidel (153) German: topographic name from Middle High German *wīdelin* 'willow twig or shoot', 'willow sapling'.

GIVEN NAMES German 6%. *Fritz, Oskar.*

Weideman (490) Variant of German WEIDMANN 'huntsman'.

Weidemann (431) German: variant of WEIDMANN 'huntsman'.

GIVEN NAMES German 5%. *Achim, Erwin, Hermann, Klaus, Lothar.*

Weiden (122) German: topographic name for someone who lived by a group of willow trees, from the plural of Middle High German *wīde* 'willow', or a habitational name from any of 24 places named Weiden.

GIVEN NAMES German 5%. *Gerda, Mathias.*

Weidenbach (253) German: habitational name from any of numerous places so named, from Middle High German *wīde* 'willow' + *bach* 'stream'.

Weidenfeller (134) German (Rhineland): variant of German **Weidenfelder**, a topographic name based on Middle High German *weide* 'pasture', 'hunting ground' + *feld* 'open country'.

GIVEN NAMES German 7%. *Wolfgang* (2), *Fritz.*

Weidenhamer (110) German: variant of WEIDENHAMMER.

Weidenhammer (130) German: habitational name from a place called Weidenhain near Torgau.

GIVEN NAME German 6%. *Kurt* (2).

Weider (304) **1.** German: variant of WEIDE, meaning either 'willow' or 'open country', + *-er* denoting a person. **2.** Dutch: occupational name for a shepherd or herdsman, Middle Dutch *weider*. **3.** Jewish (Ashkenazic): ornamental name from German *Weide* 'willow tree' (see WEIDE 3).

GIVEN NAMES Jewish 4%. *Moshe* (2), *Mayer.*

Weidert (141) Variant of WEIDER.

Weidig (142) German: habitational name from a place called Weidich in Silesia.

GIVEN NAMES German 6%. *Hans* (3), *Fritz, Kurt.*

Weidinger (259) German: habitational name for someone from any of various places named Weiding or Weidingen, for example in the Rhineland and Bavaria.

GIVEN NAMES German 5%. *Claus, Franz, Johann, Kurt.*

Weidle (115) Variant of South German **Weidl**, from a diminutive of WEIDE.

GIVEN NAMES German 5%. *Gunther, Kurt.*

Weidler (433) German: variant of WEIDNER.

Weidlich (173) German: nickname from Middle High German *weidelīh* 'fresh', 'bold', 'frisky'.

Weidman (1810) Americanized spelling of German WEIDMANN.

Weidmann (216) German: occupational name for a hunter, Middle High German *weidman*, from Middle High German *weide* 'hunting ground' + *man* 'man'.

GIVEN NAMES German 12%. *Armin* (3), *Erhardt, Hans, Heinz, Inge, Jurgen, Monika.*

Weidner (3326) German: occupational name for a hunter, Middle High German *wiedener* (see WEIDMANN).

GIVEN NAMES German 4%. *Kurt* (9), *Fritz* (4), *Arno* (2), *Eldor* (2), *Erna, Gerda, Gotthard, Gunther, Hannelore, Otto, Theodor.*

Weier (515) **1.** North German: variant of WEIHER. **2.** Variant of WEIGER.

Weiers (123) North German: variant of WEIER 2.

Weig (128) German: variant of WEICK.

Weigand (1608) German: variant of WIEGAND.

Weigandt (163) Variant of German WIEGAND.

Weigel (2813) German: from a widespread medieval pet form of the personal name *Wigand* (see WIEGAND).

Weigelt (208) German: variant of WEIGEL.

GIVEN NAMES German 9%. *Alfons, Angelika, Gerhard, Helmut, Johannes, Kurt.*

Weiger (112) German: variant of WEICHERT.

GIVEN NAMES German 8%. *Egon, Erwin, Frieda, Kurt.*

Weigert (183) German: variant of WEICHERT.

GIVEN NAMES German 7%. *Hans, Heinz, Heribert, Otto.*

Weight (511) English: variant of WIGHT.

Weightman (358) English: variant of WIGHTMAN.

Weigl (180) German: variant spelling of WEIGEL.

GIVEN NAMES German 15%. *Otto* (3), *Alfons* (2), *Franz, Georg, Henrich, Horst, Viktor.*

Weigle (826) German: variant of WEIGEL.

Weigman (165) German (**Weigmann**): variant of WEICHMAN.

Weigold (236) German: from a personal name composed of the elements *wīg* 'battle', 'fight' + *walt* 'ruler'.

Weigt (116) German: reduced form of WEIGAND (see WIEGAND).

GIVEN NAMES German 7%. *Hans, Kurt.*

Weigum (117) German (in Russia): probably an altered form of WEIGAND.

Weihe (294) German: **1.** variant of WEICK. **2.** habitational name from places called Weihe (near Hannover and Oldenburg) or Wey (Rhineland).
GIVEN NAMES German 7%. *Erwin, Gunter, Kurt, Otto.*

Weiher (240) **1.** German: habitational name for someone from any of the places called Weier, Weiher, or Weyer. **2.** South German: topographic name for someone who lived by a fish pond, Middle High German *wīher, wī(w)er.*

Weihl (110) German: unexplained; perhaps an altered spelling of WEIL.
GIVEN NAME German 4%. *Gerhard.*

Weihrauch (123) Variant of WEYRAUCH.

Weihs (165) German: variant spelling of WEISS.
GIVEN NAMES German 10%. *Kurt* (2), *Bernhard, Eckhard, Ernst.*

Weik (392) German: variant spelling of WEICK.

Weikart (113) German: variant spelling of **Weickart**, which is a variant of WEICHERT (see also WEIKERT).

Weikel (945) German: variant spelling of WEIGEL.

Weiker (155) German: from the Germanic personal name *Wigheri,* composed of the elements *wīg* 'battle', 'fight' + *heri* 'army'.

Weikert (438) German: variant spelling of WEICHERT.

Weikle (308) Probably an altered spelling of German WEIKEL.

Weikum (112) German (in Ukraine): see WEIGUM.

Weil (3384) South German and Jewish (Ashkenazic): habitational name from any of various places so named in Baden, Bavaria, and Württemberg, from Latin *villa* 'country house', 'estate' (later used of a group of houses forming a settlement).
GIVEN NAMES German 4%. *Kurt* (7), *Otto* (3), *Erwin* (2), *Gunther* (2), *Hans* (2), *Herta* (2), *Lothar* (2), *Manfred* (2), *Arno, Dieter, Elfriede, Fritz.*

Weiland (2607) **1.** German: variant of WIELAND. **2.** Jewish (western Ashkenazic): unexplained.

Weilbacher (161) German: habitational name for someone from any of several places called Weilbach, for example near Frankfurt, Miltenberg, and Schärding, Austria.

Weiler (3079) **1.** German and Jewish (western Ashkenazic): habitational name from any of several places so named in southern Germany. **2.** Jewish (Ashkenazic): variant of WEIL.

Weilert (137) German: variant of WEILER.

Weill (375) German and Jewish (Ashkenazic): variant spelling of WEIL.

GIVEN NAMES French 6%; German 4%. *Pierre* (3), *Aliette* (2), *Marcel* (2); *Hans* (3), *Otto* (2), *Kurt.*

Weiman (397) Variant of German WEIMANN.

Weimann (229) German: **1.** variant of WEINMANN. **2.** variant of **Weigmann** (see WEIGMAN).
GIVEN NAMES German 17%. *Wilhelm* (3), *Kurt* (2), *Fritz, Hans, Helmuth, Juergen, Reinhold.*

Weimar (316) German: **1.** habitational name from any of several places called Weimar in Hesse and Thuringia. **2.** variant of WEIMER 1.
GIVEN NAMES German 5%. *Bernd, Hans, Kurt, Reinhard.*

Weimer (3247) German: **1.** from a Germanic personal name composed of the elements *wini* 'friend' + *mār* 'famous' or from another, composed of the elements *wīg* 'battle', 'fight' + *mār* 'famous'. **2.** variant of WEIMAR 1.

Weimerskirch (116) German: habitational name from an unidentified place named with the personal name WEIMER + *Kirche* 'church'.

Weimert (107) German: variant of WEIMER 1.

Wein (949) **1.** German and Jewish (Ashkenazic): from Middle High German *wīn,* German *Wein* 'wine', hence a metonymic occupational name for a wine merchant or producer, or perhaps for a tavern keeper. As a Jewish name it may also be of ornamental origin. **2.** German: from a short form of any of the various Germanic compound personal names beginning with the element *wini* 'friend', such as *Winifrid* or *Winimar.* **3.** German: altered spelling of WIEN.
GIVEN NAMES Jewish 5%. *Sol* (3), *Tova* (2), *Ahron, Chaim, Hershel, Isadore, Miriam, Mort, Rivka, Zahava, Zev.*

Weinand (263) German: from the medieval personal name *Weinand,* composed of the Germanic elements *wīg* 'battle', 'fight' + *nand* 'courage', 'bravery'.

Weinbaum (238) Jewish (Ashkenazic): ornamental name composed of German *Wein* 'wine' + *Baum* 'tree'.
GIVEN NAMES Jewish 7%. *Batya, Hillel, Rina, Shmuel, Yehuda.*

Weinberg (5492) **1.** German and Jewish (Ashkenazic): habitational name from a place called Weinberg or Weinberge, of which there are numerous examples, especially in Austria and Bavaria. **2.** Jewish (Ashkenazic): ornamental name from German *Wein* 'wine' + *Berg* 'mountain', 'hill'.
GIVEN NAMES Jewish 6%. *Sol* (13), *Hyman* (7), *Chaim* (4), *Yehuda* (3), *Yetta* (3), *Avi* (2), *Ben-Zion* (2), *Meyer* (2), *Miriam* (2), *Moshe* (2), *Rivka* (2), *Shaya* (2).

Weinberger (2038) German and Jewish (Ashkenazic): habitational name for someone from a place called Weinberg or Weinberge (see WEINBERG).

GIVEN NAMES Jewish 8%. *Moshe* (6), *Aron* (5), *Hillel* (5), *Chaim* (4), *Mayer* (4), *Berish* (3), *Chana* (2), *Mendy* (2), *Miriam* (2), *Shlomo* (2), *Ahuva, Bernat.*

Weinblatt (143) Jewish (Ashkenazic): ornamental name from German *Wein* 'wine' + *Blatt* 'leaf'.
GIVEN NAMES Jewish 12%. *Hyman* (2), *Symcha* (2), *Mayer.*

Weinbrecht (108) German: from a Germanic personal name composed of *wini* 'friend' + *berht* 'famous', 'bright'.
GIVEN NAMES German 7%. *Heinz, Karlheinz.*

Weinbrenner (101) German: occupational name for a distiller of brandy, literally 'wine burner'. See WINEBRENNER.

Weindel (148) German: Bavarian and Austrian variant of WEINEL.
GIVEN NAME German 6%. *Otto.*

Weinel (164) German: from a pet form of the Old High German personal name *Wino,* a short form of any of the various Germanic compound names beginning with the element *wini* 'friend' or *wīg* 'battle', 'fight'.

Weiner (8097) **1.** German: occupational name for a cartwright; central German form of WAGNER. **2.** Altered spelling of WIENER. **3.** Jewish (Ashkenazic): occupational name from Yiddish *vayner* 'wine merchant', 'keeper of a wine shop'.
GIVEN NAMES Jewish 5%. *Hyman* (12), *Sol* (10), *Meyer* (9), *Miriam* (7), *Emanuel* (5), *Isadore* (4), *Aron* (2), *Hymen* (2), *Mordechai* (2), *Moshe* (2), *Shoshana* (2), *Aba.*

Weinerman (124) Jewish (Ashkenazic): variant of WEINER.
GIVEN NAME Jewish 8%. *Miriam.*

Weinert (751) German and Jewish (Ashkenazic): variant of WEINER.
GIVEN NAMES German 5%. *Hans* (2), *Otto* (2), *Alfons, Erna, Fritz, Hermann, Lorenz, Monika.*

Weinfeld (254) **1.** Jewish (Ashkenazic): ornamental compound from German *Wein* 'wine' + *Feld* 'field'. **2.** German: habitational name from any of several places in Austria and Switzerland named Weinfelden.
GIVEN NAMES Jewish 17%. *Chaim* (4), *Avrum, Chana, Meier, Mendel, Miriam, Moshe, Rivky, Sholom, Yechiel, Yocheved, Yosef.*

Weinfurter (152) German: habitational name from a place called Weinfurt, or an extended form of the Germanic personal name *Weinforth,* from *wini* 'friend' + *frid* 'peace'.

Weingard (110) German: topographic name for someone who lived by a vineyard, Middle High German *wīngart* or a habitational name from any of numerous places named Weingart or Weingarten, from this word.

Weingarden (125) Partly Americanized form of German and Jewish WEINGARTEN.
GIVEN NAME Jewish 6%. *Lieba.*

Weingardt (116) German: variant of WEIN-GART.

GIVEN NAME Scandinavian 4%; German 4%. *Erik*.

Weingart (689) Variant of German and Jewish WEINGARTEN.

Weingarten (953) **1.** South German: topographic name for someone living near a vineyard, from Middle High German *wīngart*, or a habitational name from any of numerous places named Weingarten. **2.** Jewish (Ashkenazic): ornamental name from German *Weingarten* 'vineyard' (see 1 above).

GIVEN NAMES Jewish 10%. *Aron* (3), *Herschel* (2), *Mendel* (2), *Meyer* (2), *Moshe* (2), *Sol* (2), *Akiva, Bernath, Chaim, Chana, Chayim, Eliezer*.

Weingartner (564) South German: **1.** variant of WEINGARTEN 1. **2.** occupational name for a vintner, from Middle High German *wīngartener*.

GIVEN NAMES German 5%. *Kurt* (2), *Dieter, Friedrich, Otto, Ulrich*.

Weingartz (102) South German: variant of WEINGARTEN 1.

Weinger (124) Jewish (Ashkenazic): of uncertain origin, perhaps an altered form of **Weingart** (see WEINGARTEN).

GIVEN NAME Jewish 6%. *Meyer*.

Weinhardt (148) German: from the medieval personal name *Winhart*, from a Germanic name composed of the elements *wini* 'friend' + *hart* 'hardy', 'strong'.

Weinheimer (539) German: habitational name for someone from any of the places named Weinheim, for example in Baden and Hessen.

GIVEN NAMES German 5%. *Kurt* (3), *Alphons* (2), *Ewald, Franz, Horst*.

Weinhold (580) German: from a Germanic personal name composed of the elements *wini* 'friend' + *walt* 'power'.

GIVEN NAMES German 5%. *Horst* (2), *Kurt* (2), *Wolf* (2), *Gerhard, Guenther, Otto*.

Weininger (164) **1.** South German: habitational name for someone from Weiningen in the Swiss canton of Zurich. **2.** Jewish (Ashkenazic): ornamental name from German *Wein* 'wine' + the suffix -*inger*.

GIVEN NAMES Jewish 4%. *Mandel, Miriam*.

Weinkauf (338) German: occupational name for a wine merchant, Middle High German *wīnkouf(er)*.

GIVEN NAMES German 4%. *Dieter, Ewald, Orlo*.

Weinke (138) German: from a pet form of the personal name WEIN 2.

Weinland (105) German: topographic name for someone who lived in a wine-producing area, from Middle High German *wīn* 'wine' + *land* 'land', or habitational name from a place so named.

Weinman (990) Altered spelling of German and Jewish WEINMANN.

GIVEN NAMES Jewish 4%. *Meyer* (2), *Zvi* (2), *Hyman, Mendel, Tovia, Yael*.

Weinmann (593) German and Jewish (Ashkenazic): occupational name for a viticulturalist or wine merchant, Middle High German *wīnman*, German *Weinmann*.

GIVEN NAMES German 7%. *Ingeborg* (2), *Kurt* (2), *Armin, Bernd, Florian, Gunther, Hans, Heinz, Juergen, Klaus, Lorenz, Otto*.

Weinmeister (111) German: occupational name for a master vintner, literally 'wine master'.

GIVEN NAMES German 7%. *Erik* (2); *Kurt* (2).

Weinraub (132) Jewish (Ashkenazic): variant of WEINTRAUB.

GIVEN NAME German 5%; Jewish 5%. *Meir*.

Weinreb (271) **1.** German: from Middle High German *wīnrëb* 'grapevine', hence a habitational name for someone living at a house distinguished by a sign depicting a grapevine, or a metonymic occupational name for a vintner. **2.** Jewish (Ashkenazic): ornamental name from German *Weinrebe* 'grapevine' (see 1 above).

GIVEN NAMES Jewish 20%. *Zvi* (4), *Avraham* (2), *Ahuva, Aryeh, Chaim, Chana, Eliezer, Moshe, Shlomie, Shmuel, Yaakov, Yaffa*.

Weinreich (369) Variant of WEINRICH.

GIVEN NAMES German 6%; Jewish 4%. *Otto* (2), *Egon, Erwin, Hans, Kurt; Gadi* (2), *Avron, Eitan, Schlomo, Sol*.

Weinrib (110) Variant of Jewish WEINREB.

GIVEN NAME Jewish 7%. *Yonah*.

Weinrich (571) **1.** German: from a Germanic personal name composed of the elements *wini* 'friend' + *rīc* 'rich', 'powerful'. **2.** Jewish (Ashkenazic): ornamental named composed of German *Wein* 'wine' + *reich* 'rich'.

GIVEN NAMES German 5%. *Dieter, Kurt, Otto, Reinold, Ulli*.

Weins (222) Dutch and German: patronymic from a short form of a personal name such as *Walewein* or *Iwein*.

Weinschenk (144) German and Jewish (Ashkenazic): occupational name for an innkeeper, Middle High German *wīnschenke*, German *Weinschenk*, literally 'wine giver'.

GIVEN NAMES German 8%. *Franz, Fritz, Kurt, Otto*.

Weinstein (7916) **1.** Jewish (Ashkenazic): ornamental name composed of German *Wein* 'wine' + *Stein* 'stone'. **2.** Perhaps also German: topographic name for someone who lived by a field named with Middle High German *wīn* 'wine' + *stein* 'stone'.

GIVEN NAMES Jewish 6%. *Hyman* (12), *Emanuel* (8), *Isadore* (7), *Miriam* (7), *Sol* (7), *Mayer* (6), *Meyer* (6), *Zev* (5), *Mandel* (3), *Naftoli* (3), *Ari* (2), *Aron* (2).

Weinstock (1383) **1.** Jewish (Ashkenazic): ornamental name from German *Weinstock* 'grapevine'. **2.** German: from Middle High German *wīnstoc* 'grapevine', hence a habitational name for someone living at a house distinguished by a sign depicting a grape-

vine, or a metonymic occupational name for a vintner. Compare WEINREB.

GIVEN NAMES Jewish 11%. *Chaim* (4), *Miriam* (4), *Amram* (3), *Moshe* (3), *Aron* (2), *Avrohom* (2), *Dov* (2), *Emanuel* (2), *Isadore* (2), *Mendel* (2), *Cheskel, Eliyahu*.

Weintraub (2283) **1.** Jewish (Ashkenazic): ornamental name from German *Weintraube* 'grape'. **2.** German: from Middle High German *wīntrūb* 'grape', hence a metonymic occupational name for a vintner, or a habitational name for someone living at a house distinguished by a sign depicting a bunch of grapes.

GIVEN NAMES Jewish 7%. *Sol* (8), *Emanuel* (6), *Hyman* (3), *Mort* (3), *Zev* (3), *Aron* (2), *Gershon* (2), *Isador* (2), *Ari, Avi, Avram, Chaim*.

Weinzapfel (133) German: from a diminutive form of **Weinzapf**, an occupational name for a tavern keeper, reinterpreted as if the second element were *Apfel* 'apple'.

Weinzetl (114) German (Austria): occupational name for a city scribe who kept the books and records on the importation and distribution of wine, from *Wein* 'vine' + *zettel* 'chit', 'note', Late Latin *cedula* (originally *schedula*) 'slip of paper'.

Weinzierl (242) South German: **1.** occupational name for a vintner, Middle High German *wīnzürl* (from Latin *vinitor*). **2.** habitational name from places in Bavaria and Austria called Weinzierl or Weinzierlein.

GIVEN NAMES German 7%. *Alfons, Franz, Gunter, Helmut, Heribert, Ulrich*.

Weipert (147) German: from the popular medieval personal name *Wīgbert*, composed of the Germanic elements *wīg* 'battle', 'fight' + *berht* 'bright'.

Weippert (129) German: variant of WEIPERT.

GIVEN NAMES German 12%. *Kurt* (2), *Christoph, Reinhold*.

Weir (7622) **1.** Scottish and English: topographic name for someone who lived by a dam or weir on a river. Compare WARE. **2.** Irish: reduced Anglicized form of Gaelic **Mac an Mhaoir** 'son of the steward' (see McNAIR). **3.** Irish: Anglicized form, based on an erroneous translation (as if from Gaelic *cora* 'weir', 'stepping stones'), of various Gaelic names such as **Ó Corra** and **Ó Comhraidhe** (see CORR and CURRY).

Weirauch (162) German and Jewish (Ashkenazic): variant spelling of WEYRAUCH.

Weirich (754) German: from a personal name composed of the Germanic elements *wīg* 'battle', 'fight' + *rīc* 'power'.

Weirick (279) Americanized spelling of German WEIRICH.

Weis (3979) **1.** German: nickname from Middle High German *wīs(e)* 'wise', 'clever', 'experienced', Middle Low German *wīs*. **2.** Respelling of German and Jewish WEISS.

Weisbach (131) **1.** German and Jewish (Ashkenazic): habitational name from any of numerous places named Weisbach or

Weissbach. **2.** Jewish (Ashkenazic): ornamental name from German *weiss* 'white' + *Bach* 'brook'.

GIVEN NAMES Jewish 7%; German 5%. *Avi, Isador, Shira; Heinz, Helmut.*

Weisbeck (177) German: variant of WEISBECKER.

Weisbecker (210) German: occupational name for a baker of white bread, from a reduced form of Middle High German *wizbrōt* 'white bread' + an agent derivative of *backen* 'to bake'.

Weisberg (1679) **1.** German: habitational name from any of various places named with Middle High German *wīz* 'white' + *berc* 'mountain'. **2.** Variant spelling of Jewish WEISSBERG.

GIVEN NAMES Jewish 7%. *Chaim (3), Hyman (3), Meyer (2), Rina (2), Shlomo (2), Ahron, Ari, Avi, Avram, Chana, Devorah, Dov.*

Weisberger (291) **1.** German and Jewish (Ashkenazic): habitational name for someone from any of various places called WEISBERG. **2.** Jewish (Ashkenazic): ornamental name from German *weiss* 'white' + *Berg* 'mountain' + *-er*, suffix denoting an inhabitant.

GIVEN NAMES Jewish 7%. *Avram, Channa, Gittel, Sol, Yisroel, Zev.*

Weisbrod (576) Jewish (Ashkenazic) and German: metonymic occupational name for a baker, from Middle High German *wizbrōt*, German *Weissbrot* 'white bread'; compare WEISBECKER. White bread would have been something of a delicacy in the Middle Ages, when coarse brown bread was the norm. In some instances the Jewish surname is of ornamental origin.

Weisbrodt (116) Jewish (Ashkenazic) and German: variant of WEISBROD.

Weisbrot (158) Jewish (Ashkenazic): variant of WEISBROD.

GIVEN NAMES Jewish 8%; German 4%. *Baruch (2), Sol (2), Ari, Shalom; Erna.*

Weise (1540) **1.** German: variant of WEIS 1. **2.** Altered spelling of German WIESE.

GIVEN NAMES German 6%. *Kurt (5), Wolfgang (3), Gerhard (2), Heinz (2), Manfred (2), Wolf (2), Aloysius, Arno, Dieter, Ewald, Frieda, Fritz.*

Weisel (562) German: **1.** status name, from Middle High German *wīsel* 'leader', 'chief'. **2.** habitational name from any of several places so named in Hessen, the Rhineland, and Württemberg.

Weisenbach (169) German: habitational name from any of numerous places named Weissenbach.

Weisenberg (197) **1.** German: habitational name from any of numerous places named Weissenberg. **2.** Jewish (Ashkenazic): variant of WEISSBERG.

GIVEN NAME Jewish 4%. *Shira.*

Weisenberger (659) German: habitational name for someone from any of numerous places named Weissenberg (see WEISENBERG).

Weisenborn (201) German: habitational name from any of numerous places named Weissenborn.

Weisenburger (304) German and Jewish (Ashkenazic): habitational name for someone from any of numerous places named Weissenburg 'white fortress'.

Weisenfeld (158) German: habitational name from a place in Bavaria called Weissenfeld.

Weisensel (223) German: probably a habitational name from a place called Weissensee, with the addition of the diminutive suffix *-el*.

Weiser (2289) German: **1.** nickname for a wise man, from an agent derivative of Middle High German *wīsen* 'to teach'. **2.** variant of WEISSER.

FOREBEARS Johann Conrad Weiser (1696–1760), the son of a magistrate, came from Gross Anspach, Württemberg, Germany, to Schoharie, NY, in 1710, and became an influential Indian agent among the Iroquois. He left 15 children.

Weisert (110) German: variant of WEISER.

GIVEN NAMES German 7%. *Hilde (2), Franz.*

Weisfeld (164) **1.** German: habitational name from a field name composed of Middle High German *wīz* 'white' + *feld* 'open country'. **2.** Jewish (Ashkenazic): ornamental compound of German *weiss* 'white' + *Feld* 'field'.

GIVEN NAMES Jewish 6%. *Herschel, Shimon.*

Weisgerber (474) German: occupational name for a tanner, Middle High German *wīzgerwer*.

Weishaar (722) German: nickname for someone with white hair, from Middle High German *wīz* 'white' + *hār* 'hair'.

Weishaupt (218) German: nickname for someone with white hair, from Middle High German *wīz* 'white' + *houbet* 'head'.

GIVEN NAME German 4%. *Kurt.*

Weisheit (253) German: nickname for a sagacious man, from Middle High German *wīsheit* 'wisdom', 'understanding'.

GIVEN NAME German 4%. *Kurt.*

Weishuhn (130) German: from Middle High German *wīz* 'white' + *huon* 'hen', 'fowl', hence a metonymic occupational name for a poultry farmer or dealer, or perhaps in some instances a nickname.

Weisiger (109) German: probably a habitational name for someone from any of various places called Weissig, in Saxony, Brandenburg, Thuringia, and Silesia. Although the surname **Weissig** occurs in Germany, there is no record of the form Weis(s)iger.

Weisinger (407) German: variant of WEISSINGER or WEISIGER 2.

Weiske (106) German: diminutive of WEIS.

GIVEN NAMES German 4%. *Hans, Kurt.*

Weiskopf (359) German: nickname for someone with white or very fair hair, from Middle High German *wīz* 'white' + *kopf* 'head'.

Weisler (163) German: occupational name for a painter or plasterer, from an agent derivative of Middle High German *wīze(l)n* 'to whitewash', 'to make white'. Compare WEISSER.

Weisman (2212) Respelling of German and Jewish WEISMANN.

GIVEN NAMES Jewish 4%. *Mayer (2), Meyer (2), Myer (2), Chaia, Dalit, Eliezer, Hyman, Ido, Isidor, Kopel, Nili, Tova.*

Weismann (202) **1.** German: nickname from Middle High German *wīs(e)* 'wise', 'clever', 'experienced' + *man* 'man'. **2.** Jewish (Ashkenazic): variant spelling of WEISSMANN.

GIVEN NAMES German 4%. *Dietrich (2), Anton, Gertrud.*

Weismantel (111) German: from Middle High German *wīz* 'white', 'shining' + *mantel* 'cloak', 'mantle', applied as a nickname for someone who habitually wore a white cloak.

GIVEN NAME German 4%. *Kurt.*

Weismiller (130) Part Americanized form of German **Weissmüller**, from Middle High German *wīz* 'white' + *müller* 'miller', an occupational name for a miller who produced white flour, which was produced as early as the 14th century.

Weisner (667) German: occupational name for a painter or plasterer, from an agent derivative of Middle High German *wīzen* 'to whitewash', 'to make white'.

Weiss (26852) **1.** German and Jewish (Ashkenazic): nickname for someone with white hair or a remarkably pale complexion, from Middle High German *wīz* 'white', German *weiss*. **2.** German: variant of WEIS. **3.** German: habitational name from any of various places named Weis(s) or Weissen. **4.** German: from a short form of a Germanic personal name formed with *wīg* 'battle' or *widu* 'wood' as the first element.

GIVEN NAMES German 4%; Jewish 4%. *Kurt (37), Otto (21), Erwin (19), Hans (17), Gerhard (8), Fritz (6), Manfred (6), Egon (5), Armin (4), Arno (4), Gunther (4), Heinz (4); Sol (18), Chaim (17), Moshe (17), Emanuel (15), Miriam (15), Aron (14), Meyer (13), Mendel (12), Hyman (11), Isadore (9), Zvi (7), Shlomo (6).*

Weissberg (316) **1.** German: variant of WEISBERG. **2.** Jewish (Ashkenazic): ornamental name composed of German *weiss* 'white' + *Berg* 'mountain', 'hill'.

GIVEN NAME German 4%. *Konrad.*

Weisse (257) German: variant of WEISS.

GIVEN NAMES German 12%. *Guenter (2), Bernhard, Erhard, Hilde, Ingeborg, Jochen, Lothar, Otto, Wolfgang.*

Weissenberger (109) German: habitational name for someone from any of various places called Weissenberg.

GIVEN NAMES German 8%; Scandinavian 4%. *Hans, Klaus, Ralf.*

Weissenborn (150) German: habitational name from any of numerous places so named, mainly in central and eastern Germany.

GIVEN NAMES German 8%. *Florian, Juergen, Kurt.*

Weisser (763) **1.** German: occupational name for a painter or plasterer, from an agent derivative of Middle High German *wīzen* 'to make white', 'to whitewash'. **2.** German: variant of WEISER. **3.** German and Jewish (Ashkenazic): nickname for someone with white hair or an exceptionally pale complexion, from an inflected form of Middle High German *wīz* 'white', German *weiss*.

GIVEN NAMES German 4%. *Otto* (2), *Alois, Erwin, Helmut, Helmuth, Manfred.*

Weissert (233) German: variant of WEISSER.

GIVEN NAME German 4%. *Otto.*

Weissinger (322) German: **1.** habitational name from either of two places in Bavaria named Weissingen and Weisingen. **2.** variant of WEISIGER 2.

GIVEN NAMES German 6%. *Dietrich, Gerhard, Kurt, Otto.*

Weissler (121) Jewish (Ashkenazic): probably a topographic name for someone who lived near the Vistula river, from Yiddish *vaysl* 'Vistula' + the Yiddish suffix *-er* denoting an inhabitant.

GIVEN NAMES Jewish 6%. *Aron, Emanuel, Yitzchok.*

Weissman (2426) **1.** Altered spelling of German WEISSMANN. **2.** Jewish (Ashkenazic): variant spelling of WEISSMANN.

GIVEN NAMES Jewish 7%. *Hyman* (3), *Arie* (2), *Meyer* (2), *Miriam* (2), *Moshe* (2), *Syma* (2), *Arnon, Asher, Avi, Avrom, Batya, Hersch.*

Weissmann (249) **1.** German: from WEISS, with the addition of Middle High German *man* 'man'. **2.** Jewish (Ashkenazic): nickname for someone with white hair or a pale complexion, from German *weiss* 'white' + *Mann.*

GIVEN NAMES German 11%. *Erwin* (3), *Gunter* (2), *Florian, Fritz, Juergen, Klaus, Nikolaus.*

Weist (626) German (Silesia): of uncertain, probably Slavic, origin.

Weister (126) German: unexplained.

Weisz (990) **1.** Jewish (from Hungary) and Hungarian (of German origin): Hungarian spelling of WEISS, transcribed according to the Hungarian pronunciation. **2.** German: variant spelling of WEISS.

GIVEN NAMES Jewish 8%; German 4%. *Naftali* (4), *Meir* (3), *Tova* (3), *Eliezer* (2), *Izidor* (2), *Alter, Ari, Chaim, Gitel, Gitty, Hershy, Isador; Erwin* (4), *Kurt* (2), *Otto* (2), *Armin, Egon, Eldor, Frieda, Maximilian, Siegfried.*

Weit (101) Dutch and North German: from the personal name *Weit*, a reduced and altered form of *Wouter*, Dutch form of WALTER.

GIVEN NAME German 5%. *Claus.*

Weitekamp (111) North German: variant of WEITKAMP.

Weith (158) **1.** North German: metonymic occupational name for a grower of wheat, Middle Low German *weite*. **2.** German: metonymic occupational name for a fisherman who used a particular kind of net, Middle High German *weit*. **3.** German: topographic name or a metonymic occupational name for a dyer, from Middle High German *weit* 'woad', a plant which yields a blue dye. **4.** Dutch: from *Weith*, a variant of the personal name WEIT.

Weitkamp (152) North German: topographic name from Middle Low German *weite* 'wheat' + *kamp* 'enclosed field', 'domain'.

Weitman (241) **1.** Dutch and North German: elaborated form of WEIT. **2.** Jewish (Ashkenazic): nickname from German *weit* 'wide' + *Mann* 'man'.

GIVEN NAMES Jewish 5%. *Eliezer, Meyer, Yitzhak, Yossef.*

Weitz (1431) German and Jewish (Ashkenazic): metonymic occupational name for a wheat grower or dealer, from Middle High German *weiz(e)*, Yiddish *veyts* 'wheat'. In some instances the Jewish name is ornamental.

GIVEN NAMES German 4%; Jewish 4%. *Kurt* (2), *Erwin, Hans, Markus, Mathias, Otto, Rainer; Emanuel* (3), *Isadore* (3), *Meyer* (3), *Isidor* (2), *Doron, Eliezer, Hershel, Moshe, Nurith, Pesach, Zeev.*

Weitzel (1888) German: from the personal name *Weitzel*, a pet form of *Wizo*, a short form of any of various Germanic compound personal names beginning with *wīg* 'battle' or *wid* 'wood'.

Weitzman (832) German (**Weitzmann**) and Jewish (Ashkenazic): occupational name for a wheat grower or dealer, from Middle High German *weiz(e)*, Yiddish *veyts* 'wheat' + Middle High German, Yiddish *man* 'man'.

GIVEN NAMES Jewish 7%. *Sol* (5), *Meyer* (2), *Shimon* (2), *Sima* (2), *Ari, Avi, Elihu, Hyman, Moshe, Pincus, Yaffa, Zvi.*

Weitzner (207) German and Jewish (Ashkenazic): occupational name for a wheat grower or dealer, from an agent derivative of Middle High German *weiz(e)* 'wheat'.

GIVEN NAMES Jewish 9%. *Ari, Avrohom, Emanuel, Shalom, Shmuel, Yisroel.*

Weix (101) German: probably a variant spelling of **Weichs**, a patronymic from WEICH or its variant WEICK.

Weixel (136) German: variant spelling of **Weichsel**, a topographic name for someone who lived near a sour cherry tree (St. Luce cherry), from Middle High German *wīhsel* (modern German *Weichsel(n)*, pronounced 'Weiksel'.

Welander (140) Swedish: ornamental name composed of an unexplained first element (possibly from a place name) + the common suffix *-ander*, from Greek *anēr* 'man', genitive *andros.*

GIVEN NAMES Scandinavian 9%. *Bjorn, Hjalmer, Sven, Thor.*

Welbaum (113) Altered spelling of German WELLBAUM.

Welborn (2797) English: habitational name from Welborne in Norfolk, Welbourn in Lincolnshire, or Welburn in North Yorkshire, all named with Old English *wella* 'spring' + *burna* 'stream'.

Welborne (100) English: variant spelling of WELBORN.

Welbourn (115) English: variant spelling of WELBORN.

Welburn (145) English: variant spelling of WELBORN.

Welby (212) English: habitational name from either of two places called Welby, one in Leicestershire and one in Lincolnshire. The last is named from Old English *wella* 'spring' + Old Norse *býr* 'farmstead', 'settlement'.

GIVEN NAME Irish 8%. *Caitlin.*

Welch (39573) **1.** English: ethnic name for someone of Welsh origin. This is the usual form of the surname in England; the usual form in Ireland is WALSH and in Scotland WELSH. **2.** German: variant of WELK. **3.** Perhaps an Americanized spelling of German WELSCH.

Welchel (202) German or Dutch: unexplained.

Welcher (582) German: **1.** variant of WELKER. **2.** habitational name from Welchau near Karlsbad in Bohemia (Czech Karlovy Vary).

Welcome (535) **1.** English: habitational name from places in Devon and Warwickshire called Welcombe, from Old English *well(a)* 'spring', 'stream' + *cumb* 'broad, straight valley'. **2.** English: nickname for a well-liked person or one noted for his hospitality, from Middle English *welcume*, a calque of Old French *bienvenu* or Old Norse *velkominn*. **3.** Translated form of Canadian French BIENVENUE, found in New England.

Weld (629) English: topographic name from Middle English *wold* 'forest' or 'cleared upland' (see WALD, WOLD).

FOREBEARS Thomas Weld (1596–1661), born in Sudbury, Suffolk, England, was an influential Puritan divine who emigrated from Terling, Essex, to Roxbury, MA, in 1632.

Welde (124) **1.** German: habitational name from a place called Welda near Minden. **2.** Norwegian: variant spelling of VELDE.

Welden (521) German: habitational name from any of several places so named, for example near Augsberg and near Kaufbeuren.

Welder (261) German: variant of WALDER.

Weldin (193) **1.** English: perhaps a variant spelling of WELDON. **2.** German: perhaps a respelling of **Welden**, a habitational name from a place so named in Bavaria. **3.** Possibly an altered spelling of Dutch

Welden, a habitational name from a place so named in East Flanders, Belgium.

Welding (149) English: of uncertain origin; perhaps a variant of WELDON.

Weldon (5242) English: habitational name from a place in Northamptonshire called Weldon, from Old English *well(a)* 'spring', 'stream' + *dūn* 'hill'.

Weldy (606) Variant spelling of German **Weldi,** a name of unexplained origin.

Welford (219) English: habitational name from any of the places named Welford, of which there are instances in Berkshire, Gloucestershire, Northamptonshire, and elsewhere. The first is named from Old English *welig* 'willow' + *ford* 'ford'; the latter two seem to have the first element *well(a)* 'spring', 'stream'.

Welge (219) **1.** North German: nickname from Middle Low German *welich* (inflected form *welige*) 'lively', 'upright'. **2.** German: from a short form of a Germanic personal name formed with *Walch* (see WELSCH) as the first element.
GIVEN NAMES German 4%. *Jurgen, Klaus.*

Welhouse (104) Origin unidentified.

Welk (745) German: **1.** variant of WELGE **2.** nickname from Middle High German *welc* 'soft', 'mild'.

Welke (517) German: **1.** variant of WELK. **2.** nickname of Slavic origin, from Slavic *velij* 'big', denoting either a big man or a father with a son of the same name.
GIVEN NAMES German 5%. *Otto* (2), *Erwin, Gerd, Kurt.*

Welker (3201) Variant (probably under French influence, at least in some cases) of English WALKER.

Well (300) **1.** English: topographic name for someone who lived near a spring or stream, Middle English *well(e)* (Old English *well(a)*). **2.** German: from a short form of the personal names *Wallo, Walilo.* **3.** German: nickname from Middle High German *wël* 'round'.

Wellbaum (136) German (Cologne, Ruhr): nickname or occupational name from Middle High German *wëlboum* 'roller (in a mill)', 'axle'.

Wellborn (782) **1.** English: variant spelling of WELBORNE. **2.** German: habitational name from any of several places so named in Saxony-Anhalt and Schleswig-Holstein.

Wellbrock (213) North German: topographic name from Middle Low German *welle* 'spring' + *brōk* 'brush-covered swamp'.

Welle (546) **1.** North German: topographic name for someone who lived by a spring or stream, Middle Low German *welle.* **2.** German: variant of WELL 3. **3.** Dutch: from a short form of the personal names *Willem* (see WILHELM) or *Wouter* (see WALTER).
GIVEN NAMES German 4%. *Bernhard* (3), *Math* (2), *Klaus, Otto.*

Wellen (322) Dutch and Belgian (**van Wellen**): habitational name for someone from a place called Welle, for example in East Flanders and Zeeland, or from Wellen in Limburg.

Wellendorf (179) North German: habitational name from any of several places so named, for example near Osnabrück.

Wellens (204) Dutch and German: variant of WILLENS.

Weller (6926) **1.** Southern English: topographic name for someone who lived by a stream, an agent derivative of WELL. **2.** North German: variant of WELLE, cognate with 1. **3.** German: from an agent derivative of Middle High German *wëllen* 'to roll, revolve, or smear', hence an occupational name for someone who made wattle and daub walls. **4.** German: from Middle High German *wëllen* 'to cause to boil or simmer', hence a metonymic occupational name for a smelter, cook, or the like. **5.** German: from Middle High German *wëlle* 'roll', 'bale', hence a metonymic occupational name for someone who sold cloth or wool, for example.

Welles (726) English: variant of WELLS.

Wellford (106) English: variant of WELFORD.

Wellhausen (102) German: habitational name from Wellhausen in Thurgau canton, Switzerland.
GIVEN NAME German 4%. *Claus.*

Welling (1466) **1.** English: patronymic from the Old English personal name *Wella.* **2.** topographic name for someone who lived near a spring or stream, from a derivative of Old English *well(a)* 'spring', 'stream'. **3.** German: habitational name from any of various places in the Rhineland called Welling or Wellingen.

Wellings (110) English: variant of WELL.

Wellington (1994) English: habitational name from any of the three places named Wellington, in Herefordshire, Shropshire, and Somerset. All are most probably named with an unattested Old English personal name *Wēola* + *-ing-* (implying association with) + *tūn* 'settlement'.
FOREBEARS Roger Wellington came to Massachusetts Bay Colony from England in 1636.

Welliver (564) Of English origin: probably a variant of either GULLIVER or OLIVER.

Wellman (4243) **1.** English: variant of WELL, with the addition of *man* 'man', i.e. 'man who lived by a stream'. **2.** Variant spelling of German WELLMANN. **3.** Swedish: ornamental name composed of an unexplained first element (found as a place-name element, of various possible origins) + *man* 'man'.
FOREBEARS Thomas Welman came to Lynn, MA, from England before 1640.

Wellmann (136) German: variant of WELLE 1, with the addition of Middle High German *man* 'man', i.e. 'man who lived by a stream'.
GIVEN NAMES German 8%; Scandinavian 5%. *Hans* (2), *Helmut, Klaus, Volker.*

Wellmon (121) English: variant of WELLMAN.

Wellner (472) South German: occupational name for someone who prepared wool for spinning, from Middle High German *wollener, woller.* Compare WOLLSCHLAGER.

Wellnitz (380) German: habitational name from any of the various places so named in Brandenburg.

Wellons (497) Altered form of an unidentified English name.

Wells (60845) **1.** English: habitational name from any of several places named with the plural of Old English *well(a)* 'spring', 'stream', or a topoppgraphical name from this word (in its plural form), for example Wells in Somerset or Wells-next-the-Sea in Norfolk. **2.** Translation of French DUPUIS or any of its variants.
FOREBEARS One of numerous early immigrants from England bearing this name was Thomas Welles, governor of colonial CT, who was in Hartford, CT, by 1636.

Welp (339) North German: affectionate nickname from Middle Low German *welp* 'young animal'.

Wels (104) German: habitational name from Wels in Upper Austria.
GIVEN NAMES German 7%. *Horst, Lorenz.*

Welsch (1244) German: from Middle High German *welsch, walsch* 'person from a Romance country (especially Italy)', 'foreigner', hence an ethnic name or in some cases perhaps a nickname for someone who had trading or other connections with the Romance countries.
GIVEN NAMES German 4%. *Gerhard* (3), *Bernd* (2), *Mathias* (2), *Matthias* (2), *Alois, Bernhard, Ernst, Erwin, Florian, Hans, Jochen, Kurt.*

Welser (150) German: habitational name for someone from Wels in Upper Austria.

Welsh (11788) **1.** Scottish and English: ethnic name for someone from Wales or a speaker of the Welsh language. Compare WALSH and WALLACE. **2.** Irish: variant of WALSH. **3.** Americanized spelling of German WELSCH. **4.** Americanized form of Ukrainian *Volosin* (see WOLOSZYN).

Welshans (268) Irish: derivative of WELSH, with Irish diminutive *-an* and English patronymic *-s.*

Welt (258) **1.** German: habitational name from a place so named in Schleswig-Holstein. **2.** Jewish: ornamental name from German *Welt* 'world'.
GIVEN NAME Jewish 4%. *Mendy.*

Welte (474) German: from a pet form of the personal name *Walther* (see WALTER).

Welter (1972) German: from a pet form of the personal name *Walther* (see WALTER).

Weltman (308) German: nickname from Middle High German *wërltman* 'man of the world'.

Weltmer (109) German: reduced form of **Weltmeyer,** a distinguishing name for a tenant farmer, called *Welt* or *Walter* (see WELTE) + MEYER.

Weltner (142) Swiss German: unexplained.

Welton (1753) English: habitational name from any of various places named Welton, for example in Cumbria, Lincolnshire, Northamptonshire, and East Yorkshire, from Old English *well(a)* 'spring', 'stream' + *tūn* 'enclosure', 'settlement'.

Welty (2092) Swiss German: from a pet form of the personal name *Walther* (see WALTER).

Weltz (276) German: variant spelling of WELZ.

Weltzin (166) North German: habitational name from any of several places so named, for example on the island of Usedom.

Welz (321) German: **1.** variant of WALZ. **2.** habitational name for someone from Oberwölz (formerly Welz) on the border between Styria and Carinthia, in Austria; or from the German towns of Welz (near Aachen), Welze (near Hannover), or Wölls (near Landsberg; formerly recorded as *Weltz* and *Welss*). **3.** from Middle High German, Middle Low German *wels* 'catfish', hence probably a nickname for someone thought to resemble the fish.
GIVEN NAMES German 8%. *Angelika* (3), *Gerhardt, Hans, Kurt, Leonhard*.

Wemhoff (200) North German: from a reduced form of Middle High German *widemhof*, Middle Low German *wedemhof* 'farm belonging to a parsonage', hence a topographic name or a nickname for someone who worked on or rented such a place.

Wemmer (150) German: variant of WIMMER.

Wempe (187) German: from the short form of a Germanic personal name composed of Old High German *wān* 'hope' + *bald* 'bold' or *berht* 'shining'.

Wemple (386) Dutch: unexplained. Perhaps a variant of **Wemel**, a nickname for a restless individual, from *wemelen* 'to be teeming with (something)'.
FOREBEARS This was the name of a prominent Dutch family name in the Albany–Schenectady area. Jan Barentsen Wemple arrived in Rensselaerswyck in 1645.

Wemyss (109) Scottish: habitational name from Wemyss in Fife, named from Old Gaelic *uaim* 'cave', with the addition of the Middle English plural suffix *-s*. The name is traditionally pronounced 'weems'.

Wen (781) **1.** Chinese 温: there are two sources for this character for Wen, which also means 'warm'. One is a territory named Wen, and the other an area named Wenyi. Descendants of rulers of these areas adopted Wen as their surname. **2.** Chinese 文: from a character that also means 'literature'. Its origin, however, is from the given name of an ancient personage called Wen. **3.** Chinese 闻: from a character that also means 'hear'. During the Spring and Autumn period (722–481 BC), in the state

of Lu there existed a man who has a supplementary name, Wenren. His descendants adopted the first character of his name, Wen, as their surname. **4.** English: unexplained.
GIVEN NAMES Chinese 48%. *Chi* (4), *Han* (4), *Cheng* (3), *Jin* (3), *Li* (3), *Yen* (3), *Yong* (3), *Chen* (2), *Chih-Hung* (2), *Chin* (2), *Hong* (2), *Jian* (2), *Jung* (2), *Long* (2), *Huan, Hung, Hung Chi, Ly, Quan*.

Wenberg (201) Swedish: ornamental name composed of an unexplained first element (possibly from a place name element) + *berg* 'mountain', 'hill'.

Wencel (129) Partly Slavic spelling of German WENZEL, a personal name of Slavic origin.

Wenck (265) German and Dutch: from a short form of the North German and Frisian personal name *Weneke*, from a pet form of a Germanic compound name beginning with *wini* 'friend'.
GIVEN NAMES German 5%. *Fritz, Otmar*.

Wencl (133) Variant of German or Slavic WENCEL.

Wend (119) German: variant of WENDT.
GIVEN NAME German 4%. *Hans*.

Wende (138) German: variant of WENDT.
GIVEN NAMES German 6%. *Ernst, Hans, Juergen*.

Wendel (2120) **1.** Dutch and German: from a pet form of a short form, *Wando*, of a compound Germanic personal name beginning with *wand* 'to go', 'to migrate'. **2.** German: metonymic occupational name for a turner, from Middle High German *wendel* 'to turn' or Middle Low German *wendelen* 'to turn, twist'. **3.** South German: from a short form of WENDELIN.
GIVEN NAMES German 4%. *Hans* (3), *Helmut* (2), *Otto* (2), *Aloys, Bodo, Egon, Elke, Erwin, Frieda, Gerhard, Jurgen, Katharina*.

Wendelin (117) South German: from the personal name *Wendelin*, the name of a saint venerated in southern Germany.

Wendelken (165) North German: metronymic from the female personal name *Wendelke*, a pet form of *Wendelburg*.

Wendell (1647) Variant spelling of WENDEL.
FOREBEARS A prominent New Netherland merchant family of this name descended from a colonist from Emden, Germany, which was part of the Netherlands in the 17th century.

Wender (243) German: topographic name from the common field name *Wand*, meaning 'wall', or a habitational name from any of several places named *Wenden*.

Wenderoth (123) German: habitational name from any of several places so named, the first part referring to the Wends (Middle High German *Wint, Wende* 'Slav'), the original Slavic population; the element *-roth* (from Middle High German *roden* 'to clear') denotes a settlement on cleared land.

Wendl (104) German: variant of WENDEL.
GIVEN NAME German 5%. *Hans* (3).

Wendland (1136) German: regional name for someone from the area of northeastern Germany inhabited by the Wends (see WENDT).
GIVEN NAMES German 5%. *Otto* (4), *Volker* (3), *Armin, Ernst, Erwin, Gunter, Gunther, Heinz, Juergen, Manfred, Reinhard, Wolfgang*.

Wendlandt (441) German: variant of WENDLAND.
GIVEN NAMES German 5%. *Hans* (4), *Gunter* (2), *Horst* (2), *Wolf*.

Wendle (140) German: variant of WENDEL, or in some cases probably an Americanized spelling of the same name.

Wendler (694) German: **1.** from Middle High German *wandeler* 'traveler on foot' (Middle Low German *wendeler*), hence a nickname for a pilgrim or an occupational name for a peddler. **2.** patronymic from the personal name *Wendel* (see WENDEL 1).
GIVEN NAMES German 8%. *Arno* (3), *Kurt* (2), *Siegbert* (2), *Claus, Erwin, Ewald, Gerd, Hans, Helmut, Helmuth, Otto*.

Wendling (1438) German: **1.** habitational name from any of numerous places called Wendling, notably in Bavaria, or a place called Wendlingen, for example near Stuttgart. **2.** (Westphalia): patronymic from the personal name *Wendel* (see WENDEL 1).

Wendorf (667) North German: habitational name from any of various places named Wendorf.
GIVEN NAMES German 4%. *Kurt* (2), *Ewald, Gerhard, Helmuth, Otto, Wilhelm*.

Wendorff (256) German: variant spelling of WENDORF.
GIVEN NAMES German 5%. *Erna, Erwin, Gunter, Helmuth, Hermann*.

Wendt (5499) German and Danish: ethnic name for a Wend, Middle High German *wind(e)*. The Wends (also known as Sorbians) once occupied a large area of northeastern Germany (extending as far west as Lüneburg, with an area called Wendland), and many German place names and surnames are of Wendish origin. Their Slavic language is still spoken in the eastern part of Germany, around Bautzen and Cottbus.
GIVEN NAMES German 4%. *Otto* (11), *Kurt* (10), *Erwin* (7), *Hans* (3), *Dieter* (2), *Heinz* (2), *Reinhold* (2), *Wolfgang* (2), *Armin, Eldred, Erhard, Ernst*.

Wendtland (100) German: variant of WENDLAND.
GIVEN NAMES German 7%. *Erwin, Kurt*.

Wener (123) German and Danish: variant of WEHNER.
GIVEN NAMES Scandinavian 5%. *Alvar, Erik*.

Weng (587) **1.** Chinese 翁: from the name of a district called Weng that existed during the Zhou dynasty. A son of Zhao Wang, fourth king (1052–1002 BC) of the Zhou dynasty, was granted this district and his descendants adopted the place name as their surname. **2.** German: habitational name from any of several places so named in southern Germany and Austria. **3.** Danish: unexplained.

GIVEN NAMES Chinese 27%. *Wei* (5), *Jian* (3), *Ching Ming* (2), *Guoqing* (2), *Li* (2), *Mei* (2), *Yan* (2), *Yan Qing* (2), *Yang* (2), *Yi* (2), *Ying* (2), *Bin*.

Wengel (102) German: **1.** from a short form of a Germanic personal name based on Old High German *wān* 'hope'. Compare WEMPE. **2.** nickname for someone with a facial peculiarity, from Middle High German *wengel*, diminutive of *wange* 'cheek', 'face'.

GIVEN NAMES German 7%. *Florian*, *Hertha*, *Manfred*.

Wenger (3956) German: habitational name for someone from any of various places in Bavaria named Weng or Wengen.

Wengerd (241) Variant spelling of German WENGERT.

Wengert (435) German: **1.** Swabian variant of the topographic name WEINGARTEN. **2.** variant of WENGER.

Wengler (202) German: **1.** variant of **Wängler** (see WANGLER). **2.** nickname for someone with a facial peculiarity, from Middle High German *wengel(īn)*, diminutive of *wange* 'cheek', 'face'.

GIVEN NAMES German 7%. *Arno* (2), *Heinz*, *Kurt*.

Wenham (111) English: habitational name from a place in Suffolk so called.

Wenhold (140) German: from a Germanic personal name (see WEINHOLD).

Wenig (313) German and Jewish (Ashkenazic): nickname for a small or insignificant man, from, Middle High German *wēnic* 'puny', German *wenig* 'little'.

Weniger (208) German: variant of WENIG.

GIVEN NAMES German 5%. *Arno*, *Erwin*, *Gotthilf*, *Konrad*.

Weninger (349) German: **1.** variant of WENIGER. **2.** variant of WENNINGER.

GIVEN NAMES German 6%. *Christl*, *Ernst*, *Ewald*, *Guenter*, *Kurt*, *Milbert*.

Wenk (507) German: **1.** from the Low German and Frisian personal name *Weneke*, a short form of any of the compound names beginning with the Old High German element *wini* 'friend'. **2.** topographic name for someone who lived by a turning or bend, Middle High German *wenke*. **3.** from Middle Low German *wenke*, *wenneke* 'wide woolen dress', hence a metonymic occupational name for a maker or seller of such garments. **4.** nickname from Middle High German *wenken* 'to stagger or waver', probably applied to someone with a peculiar gait, or to a drinker or someone who was indecisive.

GIVEN NAMES German 5%. *Otto* (2), *Ernst*, *Erwin*, *Maximilian*, *Theodor*.

Wenke (274) German: variant of WENK.

GIVEN NAMES German 5%. *Gerhard* (2), *Fritz*.

Wenker (244) German: **1.** from a Germanic personal name formed with Old High German *wān* 'hope' as a first element. **2.** perhaps a variant of WENGER.

GIVEN NAMES German 4%. *Gunter* (2), *Hans*.

Wenman (109) **1.** English: variant of WAINMAN. **2.** Swedish: ornamental name composed of an unexplained first element, *Venn* or *Vänn* (found as a place-name element, of many possible origins) + *man* 'man'.

GIVEN NAMES Scandinavian 4%. *Johan*, *Nels*.

Wennberg (165) Swedish: variant spelling of WENBERG.

GIVEN NAME Scandinavian 12%. *Erik* (3).

Wenner (1280) **1.** Swedish: ornamental name, probably from the name of lake Vänern. Like *Wenn-*, *Wenner-* was commonly used to form ornamental compounds in Swedish. **2.** German: variant of WANNER.

Wennerberg (108) Swedish: ornamental name composed of the elements WENNER + *berg* 'mountain'.

GIVEN NAMES Scandinavian 14%; German 7%. *Nils*; *Kurt*.

Wennerstrom (183) Swedish (**Wennerström**): ornamental name composed of WENNER + *ström* 'current', 'stream'.

GIVEN NAMES Scandinavian 13%. *Erik*, *Nord*.

Wenning (505) German: patronymic from a short form of the personal name *Wano*.

Wenninger (289) German: habitational name for someone from various places in the Swiss canton of Zürich: Oberweningen, Niederweningen, or Weiningen (formerly Weningen); or from various places in Germany including Wehningen in Hannover and Venningen (formerly Wenningen) in Bavaria.

GIVEN NAMES German 6%. *Alois*, *Dieter*, *Erwin*, *Fritz*, *Herta*, *Otto*.

Wenrich (638) German (of Slavic origin): from the personal name *Wenrich*, a Sorbian form of *Heinrich* (see HENRY).

Wenrick (215) Americanized spelling of German WENRICH.

Wensel (495) German: variant of WENZEL.

Wenske (128) Eastern Germany: from a pet form of the Slavic personal name *Vęceslav* (see VACEK).

GIVEN NAMES German 8%. *Irmgard*, *Kurt*, *Otto*.

Wensley (108) English: habitational name from Wensleydale in North Yorkshire.

Wenstrom (181) Swedish (**Wennström**): ornamental name composed of an unexplained first element (see WENBERG) + *ström* 'current', 'stream'.

GIVEN NAMES Scandinavian 8%; German 4%. *Helmer* (2); *Otto*, *Viktor*.

Wenstrup (108) Danish: unexplained.

Went (108) **1.** Danish and German: variant of WENTE. **2.** English: topographic name from Middle English *went(e)* 'crossroad'.

GIVEN NAME Scandinavian 4%. *Johan*.

Wente (435) German: ethnic name for a Wend, a member of the Slavic-speaking people inhabiting parts of eastern Germany.

Wenthe (135) German: variant of WENTE.

GIVEN NAMES German 6%. *Erwin*, *Fritz*, *Hans*, *Markus*.

Wentland (492) Variant spelling of German WENDLAND.

GIVEN NAMES German 5%. *Reinhold* (2), *Alois*, *Ewald*, *Kurt*, *Otto*.

Wentling (335) Altered spelling of German WENDLING.

Wentworth (3487) English: habitational name from places in Cambridgeshire and South Yorkshire called Wentworth, probably from the Old English byname *Wintra* meaning 'winter' + Old English *worð* 'enclosure'. It is, however, also possible that the name referred to a settlement inhabited only in winter. Compare WINTERBOTTOM.

FOREBEARS William Wentworth came from Rigsby, England, to Exeter, NH, in 1639. Benning Wentworth (1696–1770) and his nephew John Wentworth (1737–1820) were both colonial governors of NH.

Wentz (3271) German: from a pet form of the personal name *Werner*, or, especially in eastern regions, from a short form of the Slavic personal name *Wenceslaw*.

Wentzel (1485) German: variant spelling of WENZEL, or in some cases probably an altered spelling of the same name.

Wentzell (418) German: variant spelling of WENTZEL, or in some cases probably an altered spelling of the same name.

Wenz (768) German: from a short form of the personal name WENZEL.

GIVEN NAMES German 7%. *Otto* (4), *Ernst* (2), *Friedrich* (2), *Kurt* (2), *Bodo*, *Erwin*, *Helmut*, *Herta*, *Horst*, *Inge*, *Ingeborg*, *Manfred*.

Wenzel (4797) German: from the personal name *Wenzel*, a pet form (with the German diminutive suffix *-el*) of the Middle High German personal name *Wenze*, a borrowing from Slavic representing a short form of the Old Czech personal name *Vęceslav* (see VACEK; the borrowing took place before Czech lost its nasal vowels).

GIVEN NAMES German 5%. *Kurt* (12), *Otto* (4), *Fritz* (3), *Hans* (3), *Erna* (2), *Franz* (2), *Friedrich* (2), *Harro* (2), *Helmut* (2), *Benno*, *Bernhard*, *Dieter*.

Wenzell (112) Danish and German: variant of WENZEL.

GIVEN NAMES Scandinavian 7%. *Holger* (2), *Hilmar*.

Wenzinger (112) German and Swiss German: unexplained; possibly a habitational name for someone from Winzingen in Baden-Württemberg.

GIVEN NAME German 4%. *Kurt*.

Wenzl (253) German: variant of WENZEL.

GIVEN NAMES German 5%. *Gerhard*, *Hans*, *Heinz*, *Wilhelm*.

Wenzlaff (125) Eastern German: from the Slavic personal name *Vaclav* (see WENZEL).

GIVEN NAMES German 6%. *Erwin* (2), *Manfred*.

Wenzler (262) German: patronymic from WENZEL.

GIVEN NAMES German 10%. *Otto* (4), *Franz, Fritz, Theresia*.

Wenzlick (166) German: from a pet form of WENZEL.

GIVEN NAME German 5%. *Otto*.

Weppler (184) German: occupational name or nickname for a man who bore arms, from an agent derivative of Middle High German *wāpen* 'weapon', 'shield' (a borrowing from Low German, used alongside the original High German byform *wāfen*).

GIVEN NAMES German 7%. *Kurt, Manfred, Rainer, Udo*.

Werber (202) German and Jewish (Ashkenazic): occupational name for a merchant or entrepreneur, German *Werber*, Middle High German *wërbære*.

GIVEN NAMES Jewish 9%; German 8%. *Yehuda* (2), *Gitla, Meyer, Sol, Yaron; Kurt* (3), *Hermann* (2), *Ilse*.

Werden (256) German: habitational name from a place so named on the Ruhr river.

Werder (223) North German: topographic name from Middle Low German *werder* 'piece of land surrounded by water', '(river) island', or a habitational name from a place named with this word. Compare WERT.

GIVEN NAMES German 7%; Scandinavian 4%. *Fritz, Hasso, Horst, Kurt; Alvar*.

Werfel (109) German: dialect form of **Würfel**, a metonymic occupational name for a dice maker or nickname for a dice player, from Middle High German *würfel* 'die'.

Wergin (170) North German and Swedish: from the Latin personal name *Virginius*.

GIVEN NAMES German 12%. *Klaus* (4), *Juergen* (2), *Erwin, Wolf*.

Werk (161) German: nickname for an artisan or craftsman, from Middle High German *werc(h)* 'work', 'craft'.

GIVEN NAMES German 12%. *Ingo* (2), *Egon, Ernst, Frieda, Gerda, Horst, Kurt, Wolfgang*.

Werkheiser (520) German (**Werkhäuser**): habitational name for someone from Werkhausen in Rhineland.

Werking (174) German: unexplained. The name occurs chiefly in Polch, in the Eifel Moutains.

Werkman (118) German (**Werkmann**): occupational name for a craftsman, artisan, or builder, from Middle High German *wërcman*.

GIVEN NAMES Dutch 9%; German 7%. *Dirk, Harm, Hendrik, Onno; Franz, Fritz*.

Werkmeister (307) German: occupational name for a master craftsman, especially a master builder, from Middle High German *wërcmeister*.

Werle (434) German: from a pet form of the personal name WERNER.

GIVEN NAMES German 4%. *Erwin* (2), *Dieter, Heiner, Heinz*.

Werlein (121) German: variant of WERLE.

Werley (465) Americanized spelling of German WERLE.

Werling (656) German: patronymic from WERLE, from a short form of a Germanic personal name formed with any of several verbs, for instance Middle High German *weren* 'to defend', *warnen* 'to warn', or *wären* 'to protect'.

Werlinger (108) German: habitational name for someone from a place called Werling.

Wermager (111) Norwegian: unexplained.

Werman (149) **1.** German (**Wermann**): status name for a guarantor, Middle High German *werman*. **2.** German: variant spelling of WEHRMANN. **3.** Jewish (Ashkenazic): unexplained.

GIVEN NAME Jewish 5%. *Hyman*.

Wermers (156) German: patronymic from **Wermer**, a compound of a Germanic personal name formed with *war(in)* 'guard' + *māri* 'famous'.

Wermuth (257) German: **1.** metonymic occupational name for someone who gathered or dealt in herbs, from Middle High German *wërmuot* 'wormwood'. **2.** perhaps also from the Germanic personal name *Warmut*.

Wern (103) North German and Danish: from a short form of WERNER.

GIVEN NAME Scandinavian 5%. *Erik*.

Werne (121) North German: variant of WERN.

Wernecke (271) North German: from a pet form of WERNER. See also WARNCKE.

GIVEN NAMES German 9%. *Kurt* (2), *Dietrich, Eldor, Gunther, Heinz, Reinhard*.

Werneke (109) North German: variant of WERNECKE.

Werner (14683) German: from a personal name composed of the Germanic elements *war(in)* 'guard' + *heri, hari* 'army'. Compare WARNER.

GIVEN NAMES German 4%. *Kurt* (30), *Otto* (14), *Hans* (10), *Erwin* (8), *Heinz* (8), *Gerhard* (7), *Ernst* (5), *Helmut* (5), *Horst* (5), *Klaus* (5), *Arno* (3), *Dieter* (3).

Wernert (176) German: variant of WERNER.

Wernet (169) German: unexplained.

Wernette (206) Origin unidentified.

Wernick (405) **1.** Jewish (eastern Ashkenazic): status name for someone who was the secretary of a Jewish administration or a Jewish official responsible for the ratification of community impost treaties, from the Polish term *wiernik*. **2.** German: variant of WERNICKE.

GIVEN NAMES Jewish 5%. *Ahuva, Iddo, Isadore, Morty, Sol, Yetta*.

Wernicke (145) German: variant of WERNER.

GIVEN NAME German 4%. *Dieter*.

Wernig (108) German: variant of WERNICKE.

GIVEN NAMES German 6%. *Kurt, Wilhelm*.

Wernimont (183) Belgian French: habitational name from a place called Warrimont in Liège province.

Werning (175) German: variant of WARNING.

Wernke (140) German: reduced form of WERNECKE.

Wernli (195) South German: from a pet form of WERNER.

GIVEN NAMES German 8%. *Fritz* (3), *Markus, Otto*.

Wernsing (127) German (Westphalia): patronymic from the personal name WERNER.

Wernsman (129) German (**Wernsmann**) or Dutch: perhaps an occupational name for the servant (*man*) of a man named *Wern*, a short form of WERNER.

Werntz (210) German: from a short form of the personal name WERNER.

Werra (100) German: variant spelling of WERRE.

Werre (271) German: topographic name for someone who lived by a turnpike or fence, Middle High German *wërre*.

Werry (190) English: from an unattested Old German personal name *Werric* (Old French *Guerri*).

Wersal (125) German: variant of **Wirsal**, a nickname from Middle High German *wirs* 'bad', 'evil' denoting either an evil or a destitute person.

Werst (231) German: **1.** variant of WERSAL. **2.** perhaps an Americanized form of WURST 'sausage'.

Werstler (147) German: probably a nickname for a pugnacious or athletic person, from Middle Low German *worstelen* 'to wrestle'.

Wert (1636) German: topographic name for someone who lived on an island in a river, or on a riverbank, or on a patch of dry land in a fen, all of which were senses of the Middle High German term *wert, werder*.

Wertenberger (210) Probably of German origin, an altered spelling of **Würtemberger** (or the earlier form **Wirtemberger**, **Würtenberger**), a regional name for someone from Württemberg (earlier *Wirtemberg*) in southwestern Germany.

Werth (1600) **1.** German: variant spelling of WERT. **2.** English: variant spelling of WORTH.

Wertheim (402) German and Jewish (Ashkenazic): habitational name from Wertheim, a place on the Main river, named from Old High German *werid* 'island' (see WERT) + *heim* 'homestead'. The German surname may have arisen from various other places so named.

GIVEN NAMES German 9%. *Kurt* (5), *Manfred* (2), *Erna, Ilse, Otto*.

Wertheimer (593) German and Jewish (western Ashkenazic): habitational name for someone from WERTHEIM.

GIVEN NAMES German 6%; Jewish 4%. *Gunther* (2), *Hans* (2), *Kurt* (2), *Otto* (2), *Ernst, Ilse, Lothar, Zvi* (2), *Aviva, Chana, Emanuel, Mendel, Meyer, Shira, Yosef.*

Werther (140) German: **1.** variant of **Werth** (see WERT), the suffix *-er* denoting an inhabitant. **2.** occupational name from Middle High German *warte* 'lookout', 'observation point'. Compare WARTMAN.

GIVEN NAMES German 10%. *Egon, Herwig, Markus, Rainer, Willi.*

Werthman (134) Altered spelling of German WERTHMANN.

GIVEN NAME German 4%. *Otto.*

Werthmann (145) German: variant of **Werth** (see WERT), with the addition of Middle High German *man* 'man'.

GIVEN NAME German 7%. *Eberhard* (2).

Wertman (636) German (**Wertmann**): variant of WERTHMANN, or in some instances an Americanized spelling of the same name.

Werts (694) Americanized spelling of WERTZ.

Wertz (3255) German: from a short form of the personal name WERNER.

Wertzberger (136) Jewish (Ashkenazic): habitational name for someone from the city of Würzburg in Bavaria.

GIVEN NAMES Jewish 18%. *Benzion, Chaim, Eliezer, Ezriel, Hertz, Mayer, Mazal, Pincus, Yitzchok, Zev.*

Wery (248) Belgian (Walloon): from a Germanic personal name composed of the elements *widu* 'wood' + *rīc* 'power'.

GIVEN NAMES French 7%. *Camille* (2), *Alexandre, Desire.*

Wesby (115) English: variant of WESTBY.

GIVEN NAMES French 6%. *Monique, Vernice.*

Wesch (206) German: variant of WESCHE.

GIVEN NAMES German 6%. *Hans, Heinz, Siegfried.*

Wesche (276) North German: from a much altered short form of the personal name *Wasmod* (see WACHSMUTH).

GIVEN NAMES German 5%. *Ulrich* (2), *Eldor, Erwin.*

Weschler (147) German: variant of **Wäscher** (see WASCHER).

Wescoat (221) Variant of English WEST-COTT.

Wescott (1865) English: variant of WEST-COTT.

Weseloh (148) German: habitational name from a place so named near Hannover.

GIVEN NAMES German 5%. *Heinz, Helmut.*

Wesely (204) Germanized or Americanized form of Polish **Weseli**, nickname from *wesoły* 'cheerful'.

Weseman (253) Variant of German WESEMANN.

GIVEN NAMES German 5%. *Kurt* (2), *Claus, Lorenz.*

Wesemann (153) North German: topographic name for someone who lived by a

meadow, from Middle Low German *wese* 'meadow', 'pasture' + *man* 'man'.

GIVEN NAMES German 12%. *Heinz, Kurt, Manfred, Wolfgang.*

Wesenberg (277) North German: habitational name from any of several places so named, all in northern Germany, for example near Hamburg and Neustrelitz.

Wesler (134) North German: variant of WESSLER.

Wesley (6104) English: habitational name from any of various places named with the Old English elements *west* 'west' + *lēah* 'wood', 'clearing', as for example Westley in Cambridgeshire and Suffolk, and Westleigh in Devon and Greater Manchester.

Wesling (158) North German: variant of WESSLING.

Weslowski (95) Americanized form of Polish **Wesołowski** (see WESOLOWSKI).

Wesner (933) German: variant of WESS-NER.

Wesolek (169) Polish (**Wesołek**): nickname from *wesołek* 'jester', 'prankster', 'merry Andrew'.

Wesoloski (143) Polish: variant of **Wesołowski** (see WESOLOWSKI).

Wesolowski (1221) Polish (**Wesołowski**): habitational name for someone from any of the many places in Poland called Wesoła, Wesołowo, or Wesołów, all named with Polish *wesoły* 'pleasant', 'cheerful'.

GIVEN NAMES Polish 7%. *Casimir* (4), *Andrzej* (3), *Ewa, Ignatius, Jacek, Jadwiga, Janina, Janusz, Jerzy, Jozef, Karol, Krystyna.*

Wesp (139) Dutch: habitational name from a place so named.

Wess (343) German: from a short form of the personal name *Wasmuot.*

Wessel (2574) **1.** Dutch and German: from a pet form of the personal name WERNER. **2.** German: habitational name from Wessel in Saxony.

Wesseler (106) **1.** North German: variant of WECHSLER. **2.** Perhaps a habitational name for someone from Wessel in Saxony.

Wessell (341) Americanized spelling of German WESSEL.

Wessells (194) Variant spelling of Dutch or German WESSELS.

Wesselman (205) Dutch and German (**Wesselmann**): **1.** elaborated form of WESSEL. **2.** habitational name for someone from Wessel in Westphalia or Wesseln near Hildesheim. **3.** occupational name for a money changer, from Middle Low German *wessele* 'trade', 'exchange' + *man* 'man'.

Wesselmann (115) German: **1.** habitational name for someone from Wessel in Saxony or from a place named with Middle Low German *wessele* 'exchange', 'trade'. **2.** from a pet form of the personal name WERNER, which in the forms *Wessela* and *Wessle* is also recorded as a female and a Jewish personal name in th Middle Ages.

Wessels (1494) Dutch and North German: patronymic from the personal name WESSEL 1.

FOREBEARS One of the most prominent fur traders in New Netherland in the 1660s was Dirck Wessels(e) (1637–1717), who probably came to New Netherland before 1650 with his father, Wessel Wesselse, a West India Company employee. He also bore a secondary surname, TEN BROECK.

Wessinger (435) German: habitational name for someone from Wessingen near Tübingen.

GIVEN NAME German 4%. *Gerhardt.*

Wessler (244) North German: occupational name for a money changer, Middle Low German *westere*. Compare WECHSLER.

Wessling (521) German (Westphalia): **1.** patronymic from the personal name WESSEL. **2.** habitational name from Wessling near Munich or Wesseling near Cologne, or Wesselink in Lower Saxony.

Wessman (332) German (**Wessmann**): patronymic from a short form of the personal name *Wasmuot* (see WESS). This surname is also established in Scandinavia.

Wessner (335) German: habitational name for someone from any of several places named Wessen.

Wesson (1916) English (Midlands): variant of WESTON.

FOREBEARS John Wesson came from England to Salem, MA, in 1644.

West (67177) English and German: from Middle English, Middle High German *west* 'west', hence a topographic name for someone who lived to the west of a settlement, or a regional name for someone who had migrated from further west.

FOREBEARS This name was brought to North America independently by many bearers in the 17th and 18th centuries. Thomas West, 12th Baron De La Warre, was captain general of Virginia in 1610–11. The state of DE is named for him. One of the earliest permanent settlers was Francis West (1606–92), who came to Duxbury, MA, from Salisbury, Wiltshire, England, in or before 1638.

Westall (391) English: Black identifies this as a habitational name from the lands of Westhall in the parish of Oyne, Aberdeenshire. However, the surname now occurs predominantly in England, particularly Berkshire, which suggests that an additional or a different source may be involved.

Westbay (147) Origin uncertain. Perhaps an Americanized form of Norwegian and Swedish WESTBY.

Westberg (1003) **1.** Scandinavian: ornamental or topographic name from *väst* 'west' + *berg* 'mountain', 'hill'. In some cases the name could be habitational, from a place so named. **2.** North German: topographic name from Middle Low German *west* 'west' + *berg* 'mountain', 'hill'.

GIVEN NAMES Scandinavian 5%. *Nils* (3), *Anders, Erland, Johan.*

Westberry (698) Americanized spelling of Swedish WESTBERG 1.

Westbrook (6872) **1.** English: habitational name from any of various places named Westbrook, for example in Berkshire, Kent, and the Isle of Wight, from Old English *west* 'west' + *brōc* 'brook'. **2.** Altered spelling of Dutch **Westbroek**, a habitational name from a place so named near Utrecht.

Westbrooks (616) Altered form of WEST-BROOK; the addition of a final *-s* is a characteristic of North American surnames.

Westbury (329) English: habitational name from any of various places named Westbury, for example in Buckinghamshire, Gloucestershire, Hampshire, Shropshire, Somerset, and Wiltshire, from Old English *west* 'west' + *byrig*, dative case of *burh* 'fortress', 'fortified town'.

Westby (855) **1.** English: habitational name from any of various places named Westby, for example in Lancashire, Lincolnshire, and West Yorkshire, from Old Norse *vestr* 'west' + *býr* 'settlement'. **2.** Norwegian: habitational name from any of twenty or more farmsteads, mainly in southeastern Norway, named in Old Norse as *Vestbýr*, a compound Old Norse *vestr* 'west' + *býr* 'settlement'. Compare 1. **3.** Swedish: habitational or ornamental name of the same etymology as 2 above.
GIVEN NAMES Scandinavian 5%. *Selmer* (2), *Alf, Erik, Eyvind, Knut, Mauritz, Orvald, Thor.*

Westcott (2280) English (Devon): habitational name from any of various minor places named with Old English *west* 'west' + *cot* 'cottage', 'shelter', for example Westcott in Surrey, Westcot in Berkshire, or Westcote in Gloucestershire, Hampshire, and Warwickshire.

Westen (158) German, Dutch, and Jewish (Ashkenazic): from Middle High German, Middle Low German, Middle Dutch *westen*, German *Westen* 'west', hence a topographic name for someone who lived to the west of a settlement, or regional name for one who had migrated from further west. The Jewish name may also be of ornamental origin.
GIVEN NAMES Jewish 5%; German 4%. *Shosh, Shoshana; Ulrich.*

Westenberg (132) North German and Dutch: habitational name from any of several places so named, for example in Lower Saxony and Meckenburg.

Westenberger (207) German: habitational name for someone from any of the various places called WESTENBERG.
GIVEN NAMES German 9%. *Kurt* (4), *Fritz, Gerda.*

Westendorf (663) German: habitational name from any of several places so named.

Westenhaver (113) Dutch or North German: habitational name from a place called Westerhaven or Westerhever west of Husum.

Westenskow (101) Dutch: unexplained.

Wester (2108) German: from Middle High German *wëster* 'westerly', hence a topographic name for someone who lived to the west of a settlement, or a regional name for one who had migrated from further west.

Westerbeck (172) **1.** North German: habitational name from any of several places so named, for example near Braunschweig and Osnabrück. **2.** Americanized spelling of Dutch **Westerbeek**, a habitational name from Westerbeek in North Brabant or Westerbeke in Zeeland.

Westerberg (596) **1.** German: habitational name from any of numerous places so named. **2.** Swedish: ornamental or habitational name from *väster* 'western' + *berg* 'mountain', 'hill'.
GIVEN NAMES Scandinavian 5%. *Lars* (2), *Anders, Berndt, Erik, Lennart, Nils, Sten.*

Westerdahl (146) Swedish: ornamental or topographic name composed of the elements *väster* 'western' + *dahl*, an ornamental spelling of *dal* 'valley'.
GIVEN NAMES Scandinavian 5%. *Bertel, Nels.*

Westerfeld (196) German: topographic name from Middle High German, Middle Low German *wester* 'westerly', 'west' + *velt* 'open country'.
GIVEN NAMES German 7%. *Kurt* (2), *Otto* (2), *Egon.*

Westerfield (1311) Probably an Americanized form of WESTERFELD or WESTERVELT.

Westergaard (293) Scandinavian: variant of WESTERGARD.

Westergard (300) Scandinavian (**Westergård**): habitational name from a place so named, from *wester-* 'western' + *gard* 'farm'.
GIVEN NAMES German 4%. *Ewald, Inge, Manfred.*

Westergren (205) Swedish: ornamental name composed of the elements *väster* 'western' + *gren* 'branch'.
GIVEN NAME Scandinavian 5%. *Per.*

Westerhaus (111) German: habitational name from any of various places named Westerhausen or Westerhusen, for example in Lower Saxony, Saxony-Anhalt, and North Rhine-Westphalia.
GIVEN NAME German 4%. *Otto.*

Westerhoff (208) North German (Westphalia): topographic name for someone who lived on a farm situated to the west of a settlement, from Middle Low German *wester* 'westerly' + *hof* 'farmstead', 'manor farm'.
GIVEN NAME German 4%. *Kurt* (2).

Westerhold (184) North German: habitational name from any of the places named Westerholt, for example in Oldenburg, Hannover, and Westphalia, or a topographic name for someone who lived in woods to

the west of a settlement, from Middle Low German *wester* 'westerly' + *holt* 'wood', 'forest'.

Westerholm (115) Swedish: ornamental name composed of the elements *väster* 'western' + *holm* 'islet', 'small island'.
GIVEN NAMES Scandinavian 7%; German 5%. *Erik; Kurt.*

Westerkamp (125) North German and Dutch: topographic name for someone who lived by or owned a piece of land to the west of a settlement, from Middle Low German *wester* 'westerly' + *kamp* 'enclosed field', 'domain'.
GIVEN NAME German 4%. *Gerhard.*

Westerlund (613) Swedish and Danish: ornamental name composed of the elements *väster* 'western' + *lund* 'grove', or a habitational name from a place so named.
GIVEN NAMES Scandinavian 7%. *Erik* (4), *Dagny, Iver, Knute, Nils.*

Westerman (2024) **1.** English: from Old English *wester* or *westerne* 'western' + *mann* 'man', hence a topographic name for someone who lived to the west of a settlement, or a regional name for one who had migrated from further west. **2.** Americanized spelling of WESTERMANN.

Westermann (342) North German: from Middle Low German *wester* 'westerly' + *man* 'man', hence a topographic name for someone who lived to the west of a settlement, or regional name for one who had migrated from further west.
GIVEN NAMES German 5%. *Bernhard, Hermann, Kurt, Otto.*

Westermeyer (190) German: topographic name for a tenant farmer who lived on a farm or estate situated to the west of a settlement, from Middle High German *wester* 'westerly' + *meier* 'tenant farmer'.

Western (943) English: variant of WEST.

Westervelt (921) Dutch and Belgian (**Westerveld**): habitational name for someone from Westvelde in Drente, Westerveld in West Flanders, or Westervelt in Ebblinghem.
FOREBEARS Lubbert van Westervelt came from Meppel on the Zuider Zee, Netherlands, to Bergen Co., NJ, in 1662.

Westfahl (166) German and Dutch: see WESTFALL.

Westfall (4883) German and Dutch: regional name for someone from Westphalia, Middle High German, Middle Low German *Westvāl*.

Westfield (373) English: topographic name for someone who lived by a field (Middle English *feld*) to the west (Middle English *west*) of a settlement, or a habitational name from either of two places named Westfield, in Norfolk and Sussex, from Old English *west* 'west' + *feld* 'open country'.

Westgard (146) **1.** Norwegian: habitational name from any of over fifteen farmsteads, mainly in southeastern Norway, so named from *vest* 'west' + *gard* 'farm'.

2. Swedish (**Westgaard**, **Westgård**): ornamental or habitational name of the same etymology as 1.
GIVEN NAME Scandinavian 6%. *Sten*.

Westgate (679) English: topographic name for someone who lived by the west gate of a city, from Middle English *west* 'west' + *gate* 'gate', or, in northern and eastern areas, 'street' (from Old Norse *gata*), or a habitational name from any of numerous places named Westgate, for example in County Durham, Kent, and Northumberland.

Westhafer (131) Origin unidentified.

Westheimer (123) German: habitational name for someone from any of the numerous places named Westheim, for example in Baden-Württemberg, the Rhineland Palatinate, and Bavaria.
GIVEN NAME German 9%. *Manfred* (3).

Westhoff (752) North German (Westphalia): **1.** topographic name for someone who lived on a farm situated to the west of a settlement, from Middle High German *west* 'west(en)' + *hof* 'farmstead', 'manor farm'. **2.** Dutch: variant of WESTHOVEN.

Westhoven (116) Dutch and Belgian (**van Westhove(n)**): habitational name for someone from Westhof or Westhove in West Flanders, or any of various other places similarly named.

Westin (419) Swedish: ornamental name composed of the elements *väst* 'west' + the common suffix *-in*.
GIVEN NAMES Scandinavian 7%. *Erik, Johan, Tor*.

Westlake (1172) English: topographic name for someone who lived to the west of a stream, from Middle English *by weste lake* (see LAKE). Westlake in Devon derives its name from the surname, rather than the other way around.

Westland (256) Scottish: habitational name from a place so called. 'Westlandis, called the Leyes of Tullochaddie' were granted to the Marquis of Huntly in 1638.

Westley (634) English: variant of WESLEY.

Westling (502) Swedish: ornamental name composed of the elements *väst* 'west' + the common suffix *-ling*.

Westlund (1025) Swedish: ornamental name composed of the elements *west* 'väst' + *lund* 'grove'. In some cases, the name may be habitational, from a farm or settlement so named.
GIVEN NAMES Scandinavian 5%. *Erik, Gunner, Hjalmer, Juel, Nels, Per*.

Westman (1097) **1.** Americanized spelling of German **Westmann**, a variant of WEST, with the addition of Middle High German *man* 'man'. **2.** Swedish: ornamental or topographic name of German origin.
GIVEN NAMES Scandinavian 4%. *Birgit, Erik, Hilmer, Nels*.

Westmark (123) German and Swedish: topographic name for someone who lived in the western part of a municipality, from

Middle High German *west(en)* 'west' + *marc* 'boundary', 'boundary mark'.

Westmeyer (120) German: variant of WESTERMEYER.

Westmoreland (3608) Northern English: regional name for someone from the former country of this name, originally named in Old English as *Westmōringaland* 'territory of the people living west of the moors (i.e. the Pennines)'.

Weston (8899) **1.** English and Scottish: habitational name from any of numerous places named Weston, from Old English *west* 'west' + *tūn* 'enclosure', 'settlement'. **2.** English: variant of WHETSTONE.

Westover (1817) English: habitational name from either of two places called Westover, in Somerset and the Isle of Wight, both named with Old English *west* + *ofer* 'ridge' or *ōfer* 'bank'.

Westpfahl (110) German: variant spelling of WESTFAHL.
GIVEN NAMES German 6%. *Kurt, Otto*.

Westphal (3066) German: variant spelling of WESTFAHL.
GIVEN NAMES German 5%. *Kurt* (6), *Otto* (4), *Klaus* (3), *Reinhard* (3), *Ernst* (2), *Hans* (2), *Heinz* (2), *Uwe* (2), *Bernd, Christoph, Dietrich, Erhardt*.

Westphalen (159) German: variant (dative form) of WESTPHAL.

Westphall (129) German: variant spelling of WESTFAHL.

Westra (689) Frisian: variant of **Westraete** (see WESTRATE).

Westrate (145) Dutch (**Westraete**): from a Germanic personal name composed of the elements *fasta* 'fast', 'fixed' + *rēda* 'counsel', 'advice'.

Westray (141) English: unexplained.

Westrich (478) German: habitational name for someone from a place so named in North Rhine-Westphalia.
GIVEN NAMES German 4%. *Jutta* (2), *Kurt* (2), *Erna*.

Westrick (656) German: habitational name for someone from a place named Westerwick or a variant spelling of WESTRICH.

Westrom (187) Swedish: ornamental name composed of the elements *väst* 'west' + *ström* 'current', 'stream'.

Westrope (134) English: habitational name a place in Wiltshire named Westrop, from Old English *west* 'west' + *þrop* 'village', or perhaps from Westrip in Gloucestershire or Westhorpe in Buckinghamshire, both having the same origin as the place in Wiltshire.

Westrum (269) **1.** Norwegian: habitational name from any of four farmsteads in eastern Norway named *Vestrum* or *Vestrom*, from Old Norse *vestr* 'west' + *heimr* 'homestead'. **2.** German: habitational name from a place so named near Lingen.
GIVEN NAME Scandinavian 4%. *Erik*.

Westrup (176) **1.** German: habitational name from a place so named near Osnabrück. **2.** English: variant of Westrope. **3.** Danish: habitational name from any of several places so named.

Westry (109) English: unexplained. Compare WESTRAY.

Westveer (102) Dutch: unexplained.
GIVEN NAME Dutch 4%. *Dirk*.

Westwater (137) Scottish: habitational name from a minor place so named, now lost, in west Fife.

Westwood (725) English and Scottish: habitational name from any of numerous places named Westwood, from Old English *west* 'west' + *wudu* 'wood'.
FOREBEARS William Westwood was one of the founders of Hartford, CT, (coming from Cambridge, MA, with Thomas Hooker) in 1635.

Wetenkamp (109) German or Dutch: topographic name, a variant of **Wetekamp**, from Middle Low German *wede* 'wood' + *kamp* 'enclosed field', 'domain'.
GIVEN NAME German 4%. *Erwin* (3).

Wetherald (130) English: variant of WETHERELL.

Wetherall (108) English: variant spelling of English WETHERELL.

Wetherbee (785) English: variant spelling of WEATHERBY.

Wetherby (266) English: variant spelling of WEATHERBY.

Wetherell (744) English: habitational name from a place in Cumbria named Wetheral, from Old English *weðer* 'wether', 'ram' + *halh* 'nook', 'recess'.

Wetherhold (102) Americanized spelling of German WIEDERHOLD.
GIVEN NAME German 4%. *Kurt*.

Wetherholt (109) Americanized spelling of German WIEDERHOLD.

Wetherill (319) English: variant of WETHERELL.
FOREBEARS Christopher Wetherill emigrated from England to Burlington, NJ, in 1683.

Wetherington (802) English: habitational name from a place in Wiltshire called Witherington, from Old English *wīðign* 'willow copse' (which is not recorded independently) + *tūn* 'settlement', although the spellings with *-r-* only appear in the 17th century.

Wethington (961) English: habitational name, a reduced form of WETHERINGTON.

Wetmore (1418) English: habitational name from any of various minor places called Wetmore, for example in Staffordshire, Shropshire, and Hereford and Worcester, Wet Moor in Somerset, or Wetmoor Hall Farm in Staffordshire, mostly named with Old English *wēt* 'wet', 'damp' + *mōr* 'moor', 'mashland', although the first element of Wetmore in Staffordshire is Old English *wiht* 'river bend'.

Wetsch (144) German: metonymic occupational name for a manufacturer of travel bags or duffel bags, of uncertain origin, perhaps from Middle High German *wātsac*.
GIVEN NAMES German 4%. *Arno, Bernhard.*

Wetsel (180) Altered spelling of German **Wetzel** (see WETZELL).

Wettengel (162) German: occupational name for a road maker or mender, from Middle High German *wec* 'way', 'street' + *tengelen* 'to break (stones), beat, or knock'.

Wetter (589) **1.** German: from Middle High German *wetter* 'weather', specifically 'stormy weather', perhaps a nickname for someone who made weather predictions. **2.** German: habitational name from any of numerous places so named. **3.** Dutch: from Middle Dutch *wetter* 'grindstone', hence a metonymic occupational name for a knife grinder.

Wetterau (142) German: topographic name for someone from the Wetterau, an area in Hessen.

Wetterer (102) German: unexplained; perhaps a habitational name for someone from a place named Wetter, examples of which are found in Hesse, Lower Saxony, and North Rhine-Westphalia; or from the Wetterau, *q.v.*; or otherwise a respelling of **Witterer**, a nickname from Middle High German *witeren* 'to attack with short words'.

Wettig (124) German: habitational name from either of the places named Weddingen, near Hildesheim or Magdeburg.

Wettlaufer (223) German (**Wettläufer**): from Middle High German *wetteloufer* 'runner', probably a nickname for a fast runner or someone who rushed around.
GIVEN NAME German 4%. *Kurt* (2).

Wettstein (514) North German: variant of WETZSTEIN, from Middle Low German *wetstēn* 'whetstone'.
GIVEN NAMES German 5%. *Otto* (4), *Fritz, Markus, Ulrich.*

Wetz (208) German: from a Slavic personal name.

Wetzel (6225) German: from a pet form of WENZEL.

Wetzell (148) German: variant spelling of WETZEL, or an Americanized spelling of the same name.

Wetzler (514) German: habitational name from Wetzlar on the Lahn.

Wetzstein (170) German: **1.** occupational name for a knife grinder, from Middle High German *wetzstein* 'whetstone'. **2.** habitational name from a lost Wetzstein near Emmendingen. **3.** from a field name, for example Wezstein near Esslingen.
GIVEN NAMES German 12%. *Kurt* (2), *Benno, Hanns, Helmut, Jurgen, Math.*

Wever (389) North German and Dutch: occupational name for a weaver, Middle Low German *wever*, Middle Dutch *wever(e)*. Compare WEBER.

Wexler (2161) German and Jewish (Ashkenazic): variant spelling of WECHSLER.
GIVEN NAMES Jewish 5%. *Sol* (8), *Emanuel* (5), *Hyman* (4), *Morry* (4), *Chaim* (2), *Ari, Arnon, Elisheva, Ilan, Isadore, Miriam, Nurit.*

Wey (359) **1.** English: variant spelling of WAY. **2.** Dutch: variant of WEI.

Weyand (564) Americanized form of German WIEGAND.

Weyandt (420) Americanized form of German WIEGAND.

Weyant (769) Americanized form of German WIEGAND.

Weybright (120) Perhaps an Americanized form of German **Weibrecht** (see WAYBRIGHT).

Weydert (128) Dutch: occupational name from Middle Dutch *weider* 'herdsman'.

Weyenberg (350) German (Lower Rhine): probably a habitational name from an unidentified place.

Weyer (1148) **1.** German: variant of WEIHER. **2.** Dutch: from Middle Dutch *weyen* 'to graze', hence a metonymic occupational name for a herdsman.

Weyers (372) North German: patronymic from a variant of the Germanic personal name *Wigheri*, composed of *wīg* 'battle' + *heri* 'army'.

Weygand (116) German: variant of WEIGAND.

Weygandt (293) German: variant of WEIGAND.

Weyhrich (103) German: variant of WEIRICH.
GIVEN NAME German 5%. *Kurt.*

Weyker (129) Swiss German: variant of WEIKER.

Weyl (180) German: variant of WEIL.
GIVEN NAMES German 4%. *Otto, Woldemar.*

Weyland (222) German: variant of WIELAND.
GIVEN NAMES German 4%. *Hans, Kurt.*

Weyman (240) **1.** English: variant of WYMAN. **2.** Americanized spelling of German **Weymann**, a variant spelling of WEIMANN.

Weymouth (781) English: habitational name from Weymouth in Dorset, named with an ancient pre-English river name + Old English *mūða* 'mouth'.

Weyrauch (332) **1.** German and Jewish (Ashkenazic): from Middle High German *wī(h)rouch*, German *Weihrauch* 'incense', hence an occupational nickname for a priest, or a metonymic occupational name for a seller of incense and spices, or, among Jews, mainly an ornamental name. Incense was not used exclusively for religious ceremonies, but was also burnt in the home, as well as being used for medicinal puposes. **2.** German: variant of WEIRICH.

Weyrich (115) German: variant of WEIRICH.

Weyrick (171) Americanized spelling of German WEIRICH.

Whale (113) English: nickname for a large, ungainly person, from Middle English *hwal* 'whale' (Old English *hwæl*).

Whalen (9553) Irish: variant of WHELAN.

Whaley (7846) English: habitational name from Whaley in Derbyshire, Whalley in Lancashire, or Whaley Bridge in Derbyshire (formerly in Cheshire). The first is probably named with Old English *wælla* 'spring', 'stream' + *lēah* '(woodland) clearing'. The second has as the first element Old English *hwæl* 'round hill', and the last has Old English *weg* 'path', 'road' as the first element, the second element in both cases also being *lēah*.

Whalin (275) **1.** Irish: variant of WHELAN. **2.** Americanized spelling of the Swedish ornamental name **Walin, Valin** (see VALLIN).

Whaling (199) Irish: variant of WHELAN.

Whall (107) English: variant of WHALE.

Whalley (410) English: variant of WHALEY.

Whallon (107) Origin uncertain; perhaps a variant spelling of French **Wallon**, an ethnic name for a Walloon, a member of a French-speaking people living in southern Belgium. Alternatively, it may be an altered form of Irish WHELAN.

Whalon (114) See WHALLON.
GIVEN NAMES French 7%; German 5%. *Jean-Paul, Pierre; Erwin* (3).

Wham (173) **1.** Scottish: variant of WHAN. **2.** English: topographic name for someone who lived in a corner or angle or land, from Old English *hwamm* 'corner', or a habitational name from Wham in County Durham, named with this word.

Whan (200) Scottish: reduced form of **McWhan**, a variant of MCQUEEN, an Americanized form of *Mac Shuibhne* 'son of *Suibhne*' (see SWEENEY).

Whang (400) Korean: variant of WANG.
GIVEN NAMES Korean 49%. *Young* (7), *Byung* (5), *Kyung* (5), *Sun* (3), *Sung* (3), *Won* (3), *Chull* (2), *Hyun Sook* (2), *In* (2), *Jung Soon* (2), *Keum* (2), *Kwan* (2), *Pyung* (2), *Sung Chul* (2), *Tong* (2), *Yong* (2), *Bok Sun, Bok Nam, Chae, Cheol, Chong, Chung, Dong Soo, Eun Joo.*

Wharff (145) English: topographic name for someone who lived by a wharf or an occupational name for someone who worked at one, from Old English *hwearf* 'wharf'.

Wharry (128) Scottish and northern Irish: reduced Anglicized form of Gaelic **Mac Guaire** (see MCQUARRIE, QUARRY).

Wharton (4325) English: habitational name from any of various places called Wharton. Examples in Cheshire and Herefordshire are from an Old English river name *Wæfer* (derived from *wæfre* 'wandering', 'winding') + Old English *tūn* 'settlement'; another in Lincolnshire has as its first element Old English *wearde* 'beacon' or *waroð* 'shore', 'bank'; one in the former county of Westmorland (now part of Cumbria) is from Old English *hwearf* 'wharf', 'embankment' + *tūn*.

FOREBEARS Richard Wharton (d. 1689) emigrated from England to MA in about 1667, in search of fortune (which he did not achieve) rather than religious freedom.

A very different character was the Quaker Thomas Wharton, who came from Westmoreland, England, to Philadelphia, PA, some time before 1689.

Whary (102) Scottish and northern Irish: variant of WHARRY.

Whatley (4018) English: habitational name from any of various places named with Old English *hwǣte* 'wheat' + *lēah* '(woodland) clearing', as for example Whatley in Somerset, Whately in Warwickshire, or any of the places mentioned at WHEATLEY.

Wheadon (137) English: origin uncertain. Perhaps a variant spelling of WEEDON.

Whealton (137) Variant spelling of **Wheelton**, an English habitational name from Wheelton in Lancashire or possibly Whilton in Northamptonshire, both named with Old English *hwēol* 'wheel' (perhaps indicating a waterwheel or similar feature) + *tūn* 'enclosure', 'settlement'. The spelling Whealton does not appear in current English records.

Wheat (3841) English (chiefly Nottinghamshire): metonymic occupational name for a grower or seller of wheat, from Old English *hwǣte* 'wheat' (a derivative of *hwīt* 'white', because of its use in making white flour).

Wheatcraft (141) English: variant of WHEATCROFT.

Wheatcroft (113) English: habitational name from a place so named from Old English *hwǣte* 'wheat' + *croft* 'smallholding'. There is one such place in Derbyshire; it is also a common field name.

Wheatley (4552) English: habitational name from any of various places named Wheatley, for example in Essex, Lancashire, Nottinghamshire, Oxfordshire, and West Yorkshire, from Old English *hwǣte* 'wheat' + *lēah* '(woodland) clearing'.

Wheaton (3113) English: habitational name of uncertain origin, possibly from places in Lancashire and East and West Yorkshire named Weeton, from Old English *wīðig* 'willow' + *tūn* 'settlement'.

FOREBEARS Robert Wheaton came from England to Rehoboth, MA, in about 1636.

Whedbee (175) Origin uncertain. Perhaps a variant of English WHITBY.

Whedon (152) English: variant of WHEATON.

FOREBEARS Thomas Whedon came from Yorkshire, England, to New Haven, CT, in 1657, and later moved to Branford, CT.

Wheelan (129) Irish: variant spelling of WHELAN.

Wheeland (269) Variant of Irish WHEELAN.

Wheeldon (277) English: habitational name from a place in Derbyshire named Wheeldon, from Old English *hwēol* 'wheel' (referring perhaps to a rounded shape) + *dūn* 'hill', or from Whielden in Buckinghamshire, which is named with *hwēol* + *denu* 'valley'.

Wheeler (44923) English: occupational name for a maker of wheels (for vehicles or for use in spinning or various other manufacturing processes), from an agent derivative of Middle English *whele* 'wheel'. The name is particularly common on the Isle of Wight; on the mainland it is concentrated in the neighboring region of central southern England.

FOREBEARS A founder of Salisbury, NH, in 1634 was John Wheeler.

Wheeles (125) English: origin uncertain. Perhaps a variant of WHEELESS, or of **Wheels**, from Old English *hwēol* 'wheel', and so a topographic name for someone who lived near a waterwheel, or a metonymic occupational name for someone in charge of one.

Wheeless (338) English: origin uncertain; possibly an altered spelling of WHEELHOUSE, reflecting a local pronunciation.

Wheeley (130) English: habitational name for someone from Weoley Castle in West Midlands (formerly in Worcestershire), named with Old English *wēoh* '(pre-Christian) temple' + *lēah* '(woodland) clearing', or from Weeley in Essex, which is named with Old English *wilig* 'willow' + *lēah*.

GIVEN NAME German 5%. *Otto* (2).

Wheelhouse (128) English (Yorkshire and East Midlands): topographic name composed of Middle English *whele* 'wheel' + *hous* 'house'. According to Reaney, the reference is often to a house near a dammed-up stream where a cutler ground his knives on a small water-wheel. The compound is not attested as a vocabulary word in this or any other sense before the 19th century, although the surname William de Whelehous is found in 1379.

Wheeling (354) Scottish: unexplained.

Wheelis (280) Reduced form of English WHEELHOUSE.

Wheelock (1649) English: habitational name from a place in Cheshire named Wheelock, from the Wheelock river, which is named with a Celtic word meaning 'winding'.

Wheelus (128) Reduced form of English WHEELHOUSE.

Wheelwright (274) English: occupational name for a maker of wheels, from Middle English *whele* 'wheel' (Old English *hwēol*) + *wyrhta* 'wright'. See also WHEELER.

FOREBEARS John Wheelwright (c. 1592–1679), clergyman, came to Boston, MA, from Lincolnshire, England in 1636. He was banished from Massachusettes for his support of his sister-in-law, Anne Hutchinson, in the antinomian controversy; he set up a community at Exeter, NH.

Wheet (102) Variant spelling of English WHEAT.

Wheetley (120) English: variant of WHEATLEY.

Whelan (4832) Irish (southern provinces): reduced and altered Anglicized form of Gaelic **Ó Faoláin** 'descendant of *Faolán*', a personal name representing a diminutive of *faol* 'wolf'.

GIVEN NAMES Irish 6%. *Brendan* (4), *Dermot* (3), *Declan* (2), *James Patrick* (2), *Niall* (2), *Cahal*, *Ronan*, *Sean Patrick*.

Welchel (839) Dutch or North German: unexplained.

Wheless (380) Reduced form of English WHEELHOUSE. Compare WHEELESS.

Whelihan (120) Irish: Anglicized form of Gaelic **Ó Faoileacháin** 'descendant of *Faoileachán*', a byname from *faoileach* 'joyful'.

Wheller (115) English: variant spelling of WELLER.

Whelpley (277) English: habitational name from Whelpley Hill in Ashley Green, Buckinghamshire or from places called Whelpley in Hailsham, Sussex, and Whiteparish, Wiltshire, all named with Old English *hwelp* 'whelp', 'cub', 'young animal' + *lēah* '(woodland) clearing'.

Whelton (193) **1.** Irish (west Cork): because of the earlier Anglicized form **Houlton**, MacLysaght suggests this may be a variant form of HOULIHAN. **2.** English: possibly a variant spelling of WELTON.

GIVEN NAMES Irish 7%. *Brendan*, *Paddy*.

Wherley (284) English: variant of WHORLEY.

Wherry (790) English (Cornwall): perhaps a variant spelling of WERRY.

Whetham (132) English: probably a variant of WITHAM. Compare WHITHAM.

Whetsel (420) Americanized spelling of German WETZEL.

Whetsell (388) Americanized spelling of German WETZEL.

Whetstine (303) Americanized spelling of German WETTSTEIN.

Whetstone (1801) **1.** English: habitational name from either of two places called Whetstone, in Leicestershire and Greater London (formerly in Middlesex), or from Wheston in Derbyshire. All are named with Old English *hwetstān* 'whetstone' and are sited in areas that provided stone suitable for whetstones, stones used to sharpen knives and blades. **2.** Americanized form of German WETTSTEIN.

Whetten (123) English, Scottish, or northern Irish: variant of WHITTON.

Whetzel (891) Altered spelling of German WETZEL.

Whichard (299) Origin unidentified; perhaps an Americanized spelling of German **Wichardt**, from the personal name *Wīkhart* 'warrior'.

Whicker (581) English: topographic or habitational name, from a derivative of WICK.

Whidbee (142) Variant of English WHITBY.

Whidby (217) English: variant of English WHITBY.

Whidden (774) Variant of WHIDDON.

Whiddon (1109) English: habitational name from any of the numerous minor places in Devon named Whiddon. Some are named with Old English *hwīt* 'white' + *dūn* 'hill' or *tūn* 'settlement'; others with Old English *hwǣte* 'wheat' + *dūn* 'hill' or *denu* 'valley'.

Whiffen (134) English: of uncertain origin. Possibly a habitational name from an unidentified place named with Old English *hwīt* 'white' (i.e. 'phosphorescent') + *fen* 'marsh'.

Whigham (759) Scottish: probably a reduced and altered form of MCGUIGAN.

Whilden (167) Origin uncertain; perhaps a variant spelling of WILDEN.

Whiles (161) English: origin unidentified; perhaps a variant spelling of WILES or of WHEELESS.

Whillock (131) English: variant of WHEELOCK.

Whinery (307) English: probably either a topographic name from Middle English *whin* 'whin', 'gorse' (Old Norse *hvin*) + *wra(y)* 'nook or corner of land' (Old Norse *vrá*), or a habitational name from Whinneray in Gosforth, Cumbria, which may have the same origin.

Whinnery (169) English: variant of WHINERY.

Whipkey (705) Origin unidentified. Perhaps an Americanized spelling of North German **Wiepke**, a short form of *Wiebert* (see WIEBER), or a metronymic from the Frisian personal name *Wiebke* (from *Wigburg*).

Whipp (392) English: perhaps a metonymic occupational name for someone who carried out judicial floggings, from Middle English *whip*, or perhaps, as Reaney suggests, from the Old English personal name *Wippa*.

Whipple (5144) English: of uncertain origin, perhaps, as Reaney suggests, from a pet form of the Old English personal name *Wippa*, or perhaps a topographic name for someone who lived by a whipple tree, whatever that may have been. Chaucer lists *whippletree* (probably a kind of dogwood) along with maple, thorn, beech, hazel, and yew.

FOREBEARS Matthew Whipple came from England to Ipswich, MA, in about 1638. His descendant William Whipple (1730–85) born in Kittery, ME, was a signer of the Declaration of Independence.

A John Whipple was one of the first settlers in Providence, RI.

Whippo (122) Variant of English WHIPPLE.

Whipps (203) English: variant of or patronymic from WHIPP.

Whirley (217) English: variant of WHORLEY.

GIVEN NAMES German 4%. *Kurt* (2), *Otto*.

Whisenand (168) Variant of WHISENANT. GIVEN NAME German 4%. *Fritz*.

Whisenant (1244) Probably a variant of an unidentified Dutch name.

Whisenhunt (1122) Variant of WHISENANT.

Whisler (1178) English: variant spelling of WHISTLER.

Whisman (925) Origin unidentified.

Whisnant (1063) Variant of WHISENANT.

Whisner (233) Perhaps an altered spelling of German WISNER.

Whisonant (158) Variant of WHISENANT.

Whistler (447) English: from an agent derivative of Middle English *whistle* (Old English *hwistle*, of imitative origin), hence an occupational name for a player on a pipe or flute, or possibly a nickname for an habitual whistler.

Whiston (244) English: habitational name from any of various places called Whiston. Examples in Merseyside (formerly in Lancashire) and South Yorkshire are named from Old English *hwīt* 'white' + *stān* 'stone', while one in Staffordshire is from the genitive case of an unattested Old English personal name *Witi* meaning 'white' + Old English *tūn* 'enclosure', 'settlement'. Another place of the same name, in Northamptonshire, was probably named as the settlement associated with the *Hwicce*, the name of an Old English tribe.

Whitacre (1724) English: variant spelling of WHITAKER.

Whitaker (18889) English: habitational name from any of various places named with Old English *hwīt* 'white' or *hwǣte* 'wheat' + *æcer* 'cultivated land', as for example Whitaker in Lancashire and Whitacre in Warwickshire (both 'white field') or Whiteacre in Kent and Wheatacre in Norfolk (both 'wheat field').

Whitbeck (698) English: habitational name from any of several minor places in northern England called Whitbeck. One in Cumbria is named with Old Norse *hvítr* 'white' + *bekkr* 'stream'.

Whitby (828) English: habitational name from the port in North Yorkshire named Whitby, from Old Norse *hvítr* 'white' or the personal name *Hvíti* + *býr* 'farmstead', 'settlement', or from a place of the same name in Cheshire, originally named with Old English *hwīt* 'white' (i.e. stone-built) + *burh* 'manor house', 'fortified place'.

Whitcher (537) English: variant spelling of WITCHER.

Whitchurch (236) English: habitational name from any of several places named Whitchurch from having a 'white' (Old English *hwīt*) church, i.e. probably one built of stone, as for example in Dorset, Hampshire, Shropshire, and Somerset.

Whitcomb (3457) English: habitational name from any of various places called Whitcombe or Witcombe. Whitcombe in Dorset and Witcombe in Gloucestershire

are named with Old English *wīd* 'wide' + *cumb* 'valley'; Whitcombe, Isle of Wight, may have the same etymology or alternatively the first element may be Old English *hwīt* 'white'. Witcombe in Somerset is named with Old English *wīðig* 'willow' + *cumb*.

Whitcombe (108) English: variant spelling of WHITCOMB.

Whitcraft (287) English: variant of WHEATCROFT.

White (217049) **1.** English, Scottish, and Irish: from Middle English *whit* 'white', hence a nickname for someone with white hair or an unnaturally pale complexion. In some cases it represents a Middle English personal name, from an Old English byname, *Hwīt(a)*, of this origin. As a Scottish and Irish surname it has been widely used as a translation of the many Gaelic names based on *bán* 'white' (see BAIN 1) or *fionn* 'fair' (see FINN 1). There has also been some confusion with WIGHT. **2.** Translated form of cognate and equivalent names in other languages, such as German WEISS, French BLANC, Polish **Białas** (see BIALAS), etc.

FOREBEARS Peregrine White (1620–1704), brother of Resolved, was born in Cape Cod harbor on board the *Mayflower*, thus becoming the first child of English descent to be born in New England. His father, William White, was the son of the rector of Barham, near Ipswich, Suffolk, England; he died in 1621 during the first winter at Plymouth Colony.

John White, who came to Cambridge, MA, in 1632 and who was later one of the founders of Hartford, CT, is the ancestor of a noted American family, which included the architect Stanford White (1853–1906). The name was brought to North America from the British Isles independently by many other bearers from the 17th century onward.

Whiteaker (735) English: variant of WHITAKER.

Whitebread (175) **1.** English: metonymic occupational name for a baker or seller of white bread, from Old English *hwīt* 'white' or *hwǣte* 'wheat' + *brēad* 'bread'. White bread, considered the best bread, was made from wheat flour. **2.** In some cases, perhaps a translation of the German cognate WEISBROT.

Whitecotton (499) Origin unidentified; apparently a compound of WHITE + COTTON, but the history is obscure.

Whited (2597) reduced form of English WHITEHEAD.

Whitefield (523) **1.** English: habitational name from places in Greater Manchester and the Isle of Wight, named with Old English *hwīt* 'white' + *feld* 'pasture', 'open country' (see WHITFIELD). **2.** Americanized form of German **Weissfeld** (see WEISFELD).

Whitefoot (106) Altered form of Scottish WHITEFORD.

Whiteford (627) Scottish: habitational name from Whiteford near Paisley, outside Glasgow, named with *hwīt* 'white' + *ford* 'ford', or from some other place similarly named.

Whitehair (424) **1.** English: variant, altered by folk etymology, of WHITTIER. **2.** Americanized form of German WEISHAAR.

Whitehall (247) English: topographic name from Middle English *whit* 'white' + *halgh* 'nook' or *hall* 'hall'.

Whitehead (14303) **1.** English and Scottish: nickname for someone with fair or prematurely white hair, from Middle English *whit* 'white' + *heved* 'head'. **2.** Irish (Connacht): erroneous translation of **Ó Ceanndubháin** 'descendant of the little black-headed one' (see CANAVAN), as if from Gaelic *ceann* 'head' + *bán* 'white'. **3.** Translated form of German *Weisshaupt* (see WEISHAUPT) or *Weisskopf* (see WEISKOPF).

Whitehill (779) Scottish: habitational name from any of various minor places called Whitehill, in Midlothian, Lanarkshire, Kincardineshire, and elsewhere.

Whitehorn (402) Scottish: habitational name from Whithorn near Wigtown, named with Old English *hwīt* 'white' + *ærn* 'house'. The settlement is said to have been established in the 5th century by St. Ninian, and named from the white stone church built by him.

Whitehouse (2426) English (widespread, but especially common in the West Midlands): topographic name for someone who lived in a white house, from Middle English *whit* 'white' + *hous* 'house', or a habitational name from a place named with these elements, as for example Whittas in Cumbria.

Whitehurst (2710) English (mainly Cheshire): habitational name from a place in West Staffordshire named Whitehurst, probably from Old English *hwīt* 'white' + *hyrst* 'wooded hill'.

Whiteis (114) Origin unidentified.

Whitelaw (513) Scottish and northern English: habitational name from any of various places in the Scottish Borders called Whitelaw, from Old English *hwīt* 'white' + *hlāw* 'hill'.

Whiteley (1961) English (chiefly Yorkshire): variant of WHITLEY.

Whitelock (311) English: variant of WHITLOCK.

Whitelow (131) English: habitational name from Whitelow in South Yorkshire, named with Old English *hwīt* 'white' + *hlāw* 'hill'. Compare WHITELAW.

Whitely (477) English: variant of WHITLEY.

Whiteman (2803) **1.** English: variant of WHITMAN. **2.** Translated form of German WEISSMANN.

Whiten (337) English: perhaps a variant of WHITTON.

Whitenack (311) Origin uncertain; perhaps an Americanized form of German Weidknecht (see WHITENIGHT).

Whitener (1747) Americanized form of German WEIDNER or WEISNER.

Whitenight (205) Americanized form of Weidknecht, occupational name for a young hunter, from Middle High German *weide* 'hunting ground' + *knecht* 'youth'. Compare WEIDMANN.

Whitenton (106) English: variant of WHITTENTON.

Whites (159) English: patronymic from WHITE.

Whitescarver (180) Americanized form of German Weissgerber (see WEISGERBER).

Whitesel (440) Americanized form of German WEITZEL.

Whitesell (1497) Americanized form of German WEITZEL.

Whiteside (3831) English (Lancashire) and Scottish (also northern Ireland): probably a habitational name from any of various minor places named Whiteside, from Old English *hwīt* 'white' + *sīde* 'slope (of a hill)'. Reaney, however, quotes early forms without prepositions and derives the surname from a nickname.

Whitesides (669) English: variant of WHITESIDE.

Whitestone (117) English and Scottish: habitational name from any of various places called Whitestone, Whitestone Farm, or Whitstone, in Sussex, county Durham, Perth, and elsewhere.

Whitfield (8369) English: habitational name from any of various places named Whitfield, for example in Derbyshire, Kent, Northamptonshire, and Northumberland, named with Old English *hwīt* 'white' + *feld* 'open country', because of their chalky or soil.

FOREBEARS Henry Whitfield (1597–*c*.1657), preacher and scholar, came from Mortlake, Surrey, England (now part of Greater London) to New Haven, CT, in 1639 and was one of the first settlers in Guilford, CT. He had ten children, some of whom he left in CT when he returned to England in 1650, where he died.

Whitfill (200) English: probably a variant of WHITFIELD.

Whitford (1847) English: habitational name from a place named with Old English *hwīt* 'white' + *ford* 'ford', probably the one in Devon, although there are other places similarly named.

Whitham (536) English (mainly Yorkshire): variant of WITHAM.

Whiting (5905) English: patronymic from WHITE.

FOREBEARS Rev. Samuel Whiting arrived in Boston, MA, in May 1636, and made his home in Lynn, MA.

Whitinger (124) Origin unidentified.

Whitington (103) English: variant spelling of WHITTINGTON.

Whitis (461) Probably a reduced form of English WHITEHOUSE. Compare WHITUS.

Whitlatch (569) Variant of English WHITLEDGE.

Whitledge (231) English: of uncertain origin; perhaps from an unidentified or lost place name, or an arbitrarily altered form of WHITLEY.

Whitler (149) English: perhaps a variant spelling of **Whit(t)la**, itself a variant of WHITLEY.

Whitley (9262) English: habitational name from any of various places named with Old English *hwīt* 'white' + *lēah* 'wood', 'clearing'.

Whitling (187) English: **1.** possibly from an unattested Old English personal name, e.g. *Wihtling* or *Hwītling*. **2.** alternatively, a habitational name from Whitlinge, in Worcestershire, named from Old English *hwīt* 'white' + *hlinc* 'ridge'.

Whitlock (6031) English: **1.** nickname for someone with white or fair hair, from Middle English *whit* 'white' + *lock* 'tress', 'curl'. Compare SHERLOCK. **2.** from an Old English personal name composed of the elements *wiht* 'creature', 'demon' + *lāc* 'play', 'sport'.

Whitlow (2819) English: variant of WHITELAW.

Whitman (7522) English: from Middle English *whit* 'white' + *man* 'man', either a nickname with the same sense as WHITE, or else an occupational name for a servant of a bearer of the nickname WHITE.

FOREBEARS John Whitman settled in Weymouth, MA, in about 1638.

The poet Walt Whitman (1819–92) was descended from Joseph Whitman, who had settled in Stratford, CT, from England around 1660.

Whitmarsh (514) English: habitational name from Whitemarsh, a place in the parish of Sedgehill, Wiltshire, named from Old English *hwīt* 'white' (i.e. 'phosphorescent') + *mersc* 'marsh'. Compare WHITMORE.

Whitmer (2008) **1.** English: variant of WHITMORE 2. **2.** Americanized form of German WITTMEYER.

Whitmeyer (115) Americanized form of German WITTMEYER.

GIVEN NAMES French 5%. *Elmire, Pierre*.

Whitmill (141) English: topographic name for someone who lived at a mill where wheat was milled, from Middle English *whit* 'white' (a reference to the color of wheatflour) + *mille* 'mill'.

Whitmire (2562) Americanized form of German WITTMEYER.

Whitmore (5398) English: **1.** habitational name from any of various places named Whitmore, for example in Staffordshire,

from Old English *hwīt* 'white' + *mōr* 'moor'. **2.** Some bearers of the name are descended from John of Whytenmere, Shropshire, who lived in the 13th century. This form is probably a variant of Whittimere, a place on the Staffordshire–Shropshire border, named in Old English most probably as 'pool associated with someone called Hwīta'.
FOREBEARS Francis Whitmore settled in Cambridge, MA, before 1648.

Whitmoyer (193) Americanized form of German WITTMEYER.

Whitmyer (168) Americanized form of German WITTMEYER.

Whitner (318) **1.** Possibly an Americanized form of German **Wittner**, a habitational name from any of several places named Witten (for example, on the Ruhr) or Wittenau (for example, near Berlin and in Silesia). **2.** Perhaps also an Americanized spelling of German **Weissener** (see WISENER).

Whitney (13831) English: habitational name from a place in Herefordshire, the etymology of which is uncertain. The second element is Old English *ēg* 'island', 'piece of higher ground in a low-lying area'; the first appears to be *hwītan*, which is either the genitive singular of an Old English byname *Hwīta* (meaning 'white'), or the weak dative case (originally used after a preposition and article) of the adjective *hwīt* 'white'.
FOREBEARS John Whitney came from London, England, to Watertown, MA, in 1635, and had numerous prominent descendents.

Whiton (189) English: variant of WHITTON.
FOREBEARS James Whiton of Hingham, Norfolk, England, came to Plymouth, MA, in 1635.

Whitsel (305) Americanized form of German WEITZEL or WITZEL.

Whitsell (380) Americanized form of German WEITZEL or WITZEL.

Whitsett (633) English: of uncertain origin; possibly a habitational name from Witsett Farm near Leominster, Herefordshire.

Whitsitt (434) English: variant of WHITSETT.

Whitson (3473) Scottish: patronymic from WHITE as a personal name, or translation of any of the many Gaelic names based on *fionn* 'fair' (see FINN 1) or *bán* 'white' (see BAIN 1), as for example MCLENNAN and MCBAIN.

Whitt (5391) **1.** English (Nottingham): variant of WHITE. **2.** Possibly also an Americanized spelling of German WITT.

Whittaker (5952) English: variant spelling of WHITAKER.

Whittall (117) English: variant spelling of WHITTLE, found mainly in the Welsh Marches and West Midlands.

Whitted (1238) Scottish: probably a reduced form of WHITEHEAD.

Whittemore (2175) English: variant of Whitemore.
FOREBEARS Thomas Whittemore came from England to Charlestown, MA, in or about 1639. Amos Whittemore, born in Cambridge, MA, in 1759 was an inventor and gunsmith, and another Thomas Whittemore was born in Boston in 1800; he was a Universalist clergyman and MA legislator.

Whitten (5344) Scottish, English, and northern Irish: variant of WHITTON.

Whittenberg (308) Americanized spelling of German WITTENBERG or WITTENBURG.

Whittenburg (635) Americanized spelling of German WITTENBERG or WITTENBURG.

Whittenton (107) English: probably a variant of WHITTINGTON.

Whitter (134) English (chiefly Lancashire): occupational name for a whitewasher, from an agent derivative of Old English *hwītian* 'to whiten'.

Whittet (151) Scottish: probably a reduced form of WHITEHEAD. Compare WHITTED.

Whittier (1066) English: occupational name for a white-leather dresser, from Middle English *whit* 'white' + *taw(i)er* 'tawer' (from an agent derivative of Middle English *taw(en)* 'to prepare').
FOREBEARS John Greenleaf Whittier (1807–92), poet and active opponent of slavery, was descended from Thomas Whittier, who came to MA from England in 1638.

Whitting (92) English: variant of WHITING.

Whittingham (317) English and Scottish: habitational name from places in Lancashire, Northumberland, and East Lothian, originally named in Old English as *Hwītingahām* 'homestead (Old English *hām*) of the people of *Hwīta*', a byname meaning 'white'.
FOREBEARS Richand Whittingham and his son, also called Richard, brass founders from Birmingham, Warwickshire, England, came to New York City in 1791, where they established a successful business.

Whittinghill (185) **1.** Origin unidentified; perhaps an English habitational name from a lost or unidentified place. However, the surname is not found in the British Isles. **2.** Possibly a translation of German **Wittenberg**.

Whittington (6156) English: habitational name from any of a large number of places called Whittington, for example in Gloucestershire, Worcestershire, Warwickshire, Shropshire, Staffordshire, Derbyshire, Lancashire, and Northumberland. The place name could mean 'Hwīta's settlement' (Old English *Hwītantūn*), 'settlement associated with Hwīta' (Old English *Hwītingtūn*), or '(at the) white settlement' (Old English *(æt ðǣm) hwītan tūne*).

Whittle (2709) English (chiefly Lancashire): **1.** habitational name from any of various places named Whittle, especially one in Lancashire, named from Old English

hwīt 'white' + *hyll* 'hill'. **2.** variant of WHITWELL.

Whittlesey (472) English: habitational name from Whittlesey, a place in Cambridgeshire, named from an unattested Old English personal name (*Wittel*) + Old English *ēg* 'island'.

Whittley (104) English: variant spelling of WHITLEY.

Whitton (1239) Scottish and English: habitational name from any of various minor places so called, for example in Morebattle in the Scottish Borders, in county Durham, Greater London, Suffolk, and elsewhere, all named with Old English *hwīt* 'white' (or the Old English personal name *Hwīta*) + *tūn* 'enclosure', 'settlement'.

Whittum (143) English or Scottish: probably a variant of WITHAM or WHITTON.

Whitty (513) English: of uncertain origin; possibly: **1.** habitational name from an unidentified place named with Old English *hwīt* 'white' + *ēg* 'island' or *(ge)hæg* 'enclosure'. **2.** nickname for someone with unusually pale eyes, from Middle English *whit* 'white' + *eye* 'eye'.

Whitus (117) English: probably a reduced form of WHITEHOUSE.

Whitwell (300) English: habitational name from any of various places called Whitwell, for example in Dorset, Hertfordshire, Norfolk, and North Yorkshire, named from Old English *hwīt* 'white' + *well(a)* 'spring', 'stream'.

Whitworth (3629) English: habitational name from any of several places named Whitworth, from the Old English byname *Hwīta* meaning 'white' (or the adjective *hwīt* 'white') + Old English *worð* 'enclosure'. The chief places of this name are in County Durham and Lancashire, but the surname is fairly evenly distributed throughout northern England and the Midlands.

Whobrey (224) Of uncertain origin. There is an English place name, Whoberley, in the West Midlands, which may perhaps have given rise to the surname, although it is not found in current English records.

Wholey (235) Irish: Anglicized form of Gaelic **Ó hUallaigh**, from a nickname, *uallach* 'boastful', 'proud'.

Wholley (111) Irish: variant of WHOLEY.

Whoolery (105) English: unexplained. Compare WOOLERY.

Whooley (105) Irish (County Cork): variant of WHOLEY. According to MacLysaght, this is borne by some O'Driscoll families of Clonakilty, County Cork.
GIVEN NAMES Irish 15%. *Brendan, Finbarr, Seamus.*

Whorley (363) English: variant of WORLEY.

Whorton (1101) English (West Midlands): perhaps a variant spelling of WORTON.

Whritenour (125) Origin unidentified.
GIVEN NAME French 4%. *Mireille.*

Whybrew (119) English: from the Old English female personal name *Wīgburgh*, a compound of *wīg* 'war' + *burgh* 'fortress'.

Whyde (117) English: unexplained; perhaps an altered form of WHYTE or HYDE.

Whyman (109) English: variant spelling of WYMAN.

Whynot (138) Origin unidentified.

Whyte (2215) Scottish, Irish, and English: variant spelling of WHITE.

Wiacek (173) Polish: from a variant of the personal name **Więcek** (see WIENCEK).
GIVEN NAMES Polish 15%. *Kazimierz* (2), *Andrzej, Bronislawa, Casimir, Grazyna, Jadwiga, Janusz, Wladyslawa, Wojciech.*

Wiand (152) German: variant spelling of **Wiandt** (see WIEGAND).

Wiant (344) German: variant spelling of **Wiandt** (see WIEGAND).

Wiard (211) North German and Frisian: from a Germanic personal name composed of the elements *wīg* 'war', 'battle' + *hard* 'hardy', 'brave', 'strong'.

Wiater (239) Polish: nickname for a speedy person, from *wiater*, dialect variant of Polish *wiatr* 'wind'.
GIVEN NAMES Polish 4%. *Jacek, Jerzy.*

Wiatrek (152) Polish: nickname from a diminutive of *wiatr* 'wind' (see WIATER).

Wiatrowski (148) Polish: habitational name from Wiatrowo in Piła voivodeship or Wiatrowiec in Piła and Radom voivodeships, all named with a derivative of *wiatr* 'wind' (see WIATER).
GIVEN NAMES Polish 7%. *Ludwik, Wojciech.*

Wiatt (122) Variant spelling of English WYATT.

Wibbels (104) North German: patronymic form of a short form of a Germanic personal name formed with *wīg* 'battle' + *bald* 'bold' or *berht* 'shining' or *brand* 'fire', 'sword'.

Wibben (111) North German and Dutch: variant spelling of **Wibem**, a patronymic from a derivative of the Germanic personal names *Wibert* (a compound of *wīg* 'battle' + *berht* 'bright', 'shining') or *Wiboud* (a compound of *wīg* 'battle' + *bald* 'bold', 'brave'.
GIVEN NAMES German 5%; Dutch 4%. *Hans* (2), *Claus; Harm.*

Wibbenmeyer (154) German: distinguishing name for a tenant farmer (see MEYER), with an unexplained first element.
GIVEN NAMES German 6%. *Kurt, Othmar.*

Wiberg (470) Swedish: ornamental name from Old Norse *viðr* 'forest' + *berg* 'mountain', 'hill'.
GIVEN NAMES Scandinavian 10%; German 4%. *Nels* (3), *Erik* (2), *Lars* (2), *Sven* (2), *Bjorn, Helmer, Nils; Ewald, Ralf.*

Wible (831) **1.** Americanized spelling of German **Wibel**, from a Germanic compound personal name beginning with *wīg* 'war', 'battle'. **2.** Americanized spelling of WEIBEL.

Wiborg (103) Swedish: ornamental or habitational name from Old Norse *viðr* 'forest' or *vé* '(pagan) sacred place', + *borg* 'castle'.
GIVEN NAME Scandinavian 4%; German 4%. *Liesl.*

Wical (143) Polish: from the personal name *Wical*, a pet form of *Wincenty* (see VINCENT).

Wice (139) English: of uncertain origin. Possibly a variant of WYCHE.

Wich (212) **1.** North German: variant of WEICH or WIECH. **2.** Polish: from the personal name *Wich*, a short form of *Wincenty* (see VINCENT). **3.** English: variant of WYCHE.
GIVEN NAMES German 6%. *Kurt* (2), *Claus.*

Wichern (182) North German (Hamburg): possibly a topographic name from Middle Low German *wīk* 'muddy place', 'bay' + *horn* 'corner'.

Wichers (152) North German: patronymic from the personal name WICHERT.
GIVEN NAMES German 5%. *Arno, Hans, Heinz.*

Wichert (337) German: from a personal name composed of the elements *wīg* 'battle', 'war' + *hard* 'brave', 'hardy', 'strong'.
GIVEN NAMES German 5%. *Otto* (2), *Erhard, Ernst, Lothar.*

Wichman (1059) Americanized spelling of German WICHMANN.

Wichmann (634) North German: from a Germanic personal name composed of the elements *wīg* 'battle', 'war' + *man* 'man'.
GIVEN NAMES German 7%. *Hans* (3), *Ernst* (2), *Heinz* (2), *Horst* (2), *Kurt* (2), *Bernd, Erna, Ingeborg.*

Wicht (141) German: **1.** nickname from Middle High German *wiht* 'dwarf', 'goblin'. **2.** habitational name from any of various places called Wichte, for example near Kassel and Aurich.
GIVEN NAMES German 8%. *Juergen, Klaus, Oskar.*

Wichterman (144) South German: unexplained.

Wicinski (109) Polish (**Wiciński**): habitational name for someone from places called Wicie in Siedlce or Skierniewice voivodeships (named with *wić* 'osier', 'twig') or Wity in Siedlce voivodeship (named with the personal name *Wit*; see WITEK).
GIVEN NAMES Polish 5%. *Edyta, Irena.*

Wick (3603) **1.** English: topographic name for someone who lived in an outlying settlement dependent on a larger village, Old English *wīc* (Latin *vicus*), or a habitational name from a place named with this word, of which there are examples in Berkshire, Gloucestershire, Somerset, and Worcestershire. The term seems to have been used in particular to denote an outlying dairy farm or a salt works. **2.** English and German: from a medieval personal name, Middle English *Wikke*, German *Wicko*, a short form of any of various Germanic personal names

formed with the element *wīg* 'battle', 'war'.

Wicka (100) German: variant of WICK 2.
GIVEN NAMES French 5%. *Cecile, Marcel.*

Wickard (233) Altered spelling of German **Wickardt**, a variant of WICHERT.

Wicke (382) English and German: variant of WICK.

Wickel (114) German: from a short form of a Germanic personal name, for instance WICK.
GIVEN NAMES German 9%. *Gunter, Juergen, Rainer.*

Wicken (103) English: variant of WICK 1, from the Old English dative plural *wīcum* 'at the outlying farm'.

Wickenhauser (139) Variant of German WICKENHEISER.

Wickenheiser (138) German: habitational name for someone from Wickenhaus in Württemberg.
GIVEN NAME German 5%. *Kurt.*

Wickens (362) English: variant of WICKEN, with the addition of the Middle English plural or genitive suffix -*s*.

Wicker (3468) **1.** German: occupational name from Middle High German, Middle Low German *wicker* 'soothsayer', 'magician'. **2.** German: from an Old High German personal name composed of the elements *wīg* 'battle', 'war' + *heri* 'army'. **3.** English: topographic name for someone who lived or worked in an outlying settlement, from a derivative of Old English *wīc* (see WICK).

Wickerham (163) English: probably a variant of WICKERSHAM.

Wickers (107) **1.** German: patronymic from WICKER 2. **2.** English: variant of WICKER.

Wickersham (1000) English: habitational name from a lost or unidentified place.

Wickersheim (107) German: habitational name from a place in the Saar, near the French border.

Wickert (490) German: variant of WICHERT.
GIVEN NAMES German 4%. *Fritz* (4), *Frieda, Hans.*

Wickes (375) English: patronymic from WICK 2, or variant of the habitational name WICK, with genitive or plural -*s*. There has been much confusion between this name and WEEKS.
FOREBEARS In 1638 Richard Wickes (also known as Richard **Atwick**), of Staines, Middlesex, England, died, leaving a bequest to "my son John Wickes now living in New England." This John Wickes came from London, England, to Plymouth, MA, in 1635, and subsequently settled at Portsmouth, RI.
Some American bearers of this name are descended from Thomas Weekes, who came to Long Island, NY, in 1635.

Wickett (387) English: from a pet form of a medieval personal name, *Wikke* (see WICK 2).

Wickey (207) Americanized spelling of German WICKE.

Wickham (2750) English: habitational name from any of various places so called, for example in Cambridgeshire, Suffolk, Essex, Hertfordshire, Kent, Hampshire, Berkshire, and Oxfordshire. It has been established that *wīchām* was an Old English term for a settlement (Old English *hām*) associated with a Romano-British town, *wīc* in this case being an adaptation of Latin *vicus*. Childswickham in Gloucestershire bears a British name with a different etymology. The surname is now also common in Ireland, where it was taken in the 17th century.
FOREBEARS Thomas Wickham is recorded as a freeman of Weathersfield, CT, in 1658.

Wickizer (257) Americanized form of German WICKENHEISER.
GIVEN NAME German 4%. *Kurt.*

Wickland (244) **1.** German: from the personal name *Wigland*, composed of the elements *wīg* 'battle', 'war' + *land* 'land'. See also WIELAND. **2.** Swedish: ornamental name composed of an uncertain first element, probably *vik* 'bay' + *land* 'land'.
GIVEN NAMES French 4%. *Gabrielle, Mathieu.*

Wicklander (165) Swedish: variant of WICKLAND, with the addition of the habitational suffix -*er*.

Wicklein (103) German: from a pet form of the personal name *Wick* (see WICK 2).

Wickliff (153) Variant spelling of English **Wicliffe**.

Wickliffe (394) English: habitational name from Wycliffe, a place in Durham, situated on a bend in the Tees, and probably named from Old English *hwīt* 'white' or *wiht* 'bend' + *clif* 'slope', 'bank'.

Wickline (952) Americanized spelling of German WICKLEIN.

Wicklund (1109) Variant spelling of Swedish WIKLUND.
GIVEN NAMES Scandinavian 4%. *Britt, Erik, Lars, Nels, Sig, Swen, Thora.*

Wickman (1191) **1.** Americanized spelling of Swedish **Vikman**, an ornamental name composed of the elements *vik* 'bay' + *man* 'man'. **2.** German (**Wickmann**): variant of WICHMANN or WEICHMANN.

Wicks (3457) English: patronymic from the Middle English personal name *Wikke* (see WICK 2).

Wickson (112) English: patronymic from the Middle English personal name *Wikke* (see WICK 2).

Wickstrom (992) Swedish: variant spelling of WIKSTROM.
GIVEN NAMES Scandinavian 6%. *Per* (3), *Nels* (2), *Anders, Erik, Lars, Mauritz, Nils, Thor.*

Wickum (102) Probably a variant of English WICKEN.

Wickware (199) English: habitational name from Wickwar in Gloucestershire (Avon), originally called simply *Wick*, from Old English *wīc* 'outlying settlement'. The *war* element is from the name of the de la Warr family (see WARR), who held the manor in the 13th century.
FOREBEARS John Wickware moved from England to New London, CT, in 1675.

Wickwire (413) English: variant of WICKWARE.

Widder (288) German: habitational name for someone who lived at a house distinguished by the sign of a ram, Middle High German *wider* 'ram'.
GIVEN NAMES German 4%. *Erwin, Heinz, Kurt.*

Widdicombe (111) English: habitational name from places in Devon called Widecombe in the Moor, Widdicombe, or Widdacombe, or from Withycombe in Somerset or Withycombe Raleigh in Devon. Both examples of Withycombe are named from Old English *withig* 'willow' + *cumb* 'valley', and Widecombe probably has the same derivation.

Widdifield (137) English: habitational name from an unidentified place, perhaps Widefield in Devon or Buckinghamshire, named in Old English with *wīd* 'wide' + *feld* 'open country'.

Widdison (146) English: variant of WIDDOWSON.

Widdows (169) English: metronymic denoting the son of a widow (see WIDDOWSON).

Widdowson (225) English: patronymic or metronymic denoting the son of a widow, Middle English *widow(e)* (Old English *widewe* feminine, *widewa* masculine).

Widell (232) Swedish: ornamental name composed of the elements *Wid-*, an element of uncertain meaning (see WIDMAN) + the adjectival suffix -*ell*, a derivative of Latin -*elius*.
GIVEN NAME Scandinavian 7%. *Hilmer.*

Wideman (1206) **1.** German (**Widemann**): from the Germanic personal name *Widiman*, composed of *witu* 'wood' or *wīt* 'wide', 'broad' + *man* 'man'. **2.** Americanized form of German WEIDMANN 'huntsman'. **3.** Americanized form of Swedish WIDMAN.

Widen (265) Swedish (**Widén**): ornamental name composed of the elements *Wid-*, an element of uncertain meaning (see WIDMAN) + the common surname suffix -*én*, from Latin -*enius*.
GIVEN NAMES Scandinavian 6%. *Gunnel, Iver, Lennart, Sven.*

Widener (1819) Americanized spelling of German WEIDNER 'hunter'.

Wider (159) Swedish: ornamental name composed of the elements *Wid-*, an element of uncertain meaning (see WIDMAN) + the suffix -*er*.

Widerman (102) Jewish (Ashkenazic): from German *Widder* 'ram' + *Mann* 'man', probably one of the names selected at random from vocabulary words by government officials when surnames were made compulsory.
GIVEN NAME Jewish 4%. *Rivka.*

Widger (366) English (chiefly Devon): from the Old English personal name *Wihtgār*, composed of the elements *wiht* 'elf' + *gār* 'spear'.

Widhalm (233) South German (Austrian): variant of the Germanic personal name *Withelm*, from *witu* 'wood' or *wīg* 'battle' + *helm* 'helmet'.

Widick (270) English: variant spelling of **Widdick**, which is most probably a habitational name from White Dyke in Hailsham, Sussex.

Widing (150) **1.** Swedish: ornamental name composed of the elements *Wid-*, an element of uncertain meaning (see WIDMAN), + the common suffix -*ing*. **2.** North German: unexplained.

Widjaja (149) Origin unidentified.
GIVEN NAMES French 5%; German 5%. . *Andre, Marcel; Bernhard, Johannes.*

Widmaier (150) German: variant spelling of WIEDMEYER.
GIVEN NAMES German 7%. *Eugen, Hans, Kurt.*

Widman (974) **1.** Swedish: ornamental name composed of the elements *Wid-*, an uncertain element, possibly Old Swedish *viþr* 'wood', 'forest' or from a place name formed with Old Swedish *vīd* 'wide' + *man* 'man'. **2.** Altered spelling of German WIDMANN.

Widmann (475) German: **1.** variant of **Wiedmann** 'huntsman'. **2.** variant of WIDMAN 1.
GIVEN NAMES German 8%. *Kurt* (5), *Reinhard* (2), *Armin, Christoph, Gerhard, Klaus.*

Widmar (160) **1.** German: variant of WITTMER 1. **2.** Germanized spelling of Slovenian VIDMAR.

Widmark (126) Swedish: ornamental name composed of the elements *Wid-*, an element of uncertain meaning (see WIDMAN) + *mark* 'land'.
GIVEN NAME Scandinavian 5%. *Erik.*

Widmayer (245) Variant of German and French (Alsatian) WIEDMEYER.

Widmer (1430) **1.** German: from Middle High German *widemer* 'tenant of land or property belonging to a church', an agent derivative of *widem* 'prebend'. **2.** German: variant of WITTMER 1. **3.** English: habitational name from Widmere in Ibstone, Buckinghamshire, named from Old English *wīdig* 'willow' + *mere* 'pool'.
GIVEN NAMES German 5%. *Kurt* (4), *Christoph* (2), *Hans* (2), *Helmut* (2), *Sieg* (2), *Armin, Ernst, Hans Peter, Konrad, Othmar, Siegfried, Ute.*

Widmeyer (125) German and French (Alsatian): variant of WIEDMEYER.
GIVEN NAMES French 5%. *Alphonse, Fanchon.*

Widmyer (118) Americanized form of German and French (Alsatian) WIEDMEYER.

Widner (1346) German: **1.** topographic name for someone who lived by pastureland, from Middle High German *weid(e)* 'grassland', 'pasture' + *-er*, suffix denoting an inhabitant. **2.** variant of WIDMER.

Widney (120) Variant of English WHITNEY.

Widrick (231) Americanized form of German WIDRIG.

Widrig (176) German: from a Germanic personal name composed of the elements *widu* 'wood', 'forest' + *rīc* 'power'.

Wieand (182) German: variant of WIEGAND.
GIVEN NAME German 6%. *Otto* (3).

Wiebe (1266) German: from a short form of any of various Germanic personal names beginning with *wīg* 'battle', 'war'.
GIVEN NAMES German 4%. *Kurt* (3), *Arno, Claus, Franz, Heinrich, Hermann, Horst, Joerg, Klaus, Lothar.*

Wiebelhaus (151) German: habitational name from a lost or unidentified place.

Wieber (475) German: **1.** from a Germanic personal name composed of the elements *wīg* 'battle', 'war' + *berht* 'bright', 'famous'. **2.** southwestern form of WEBER.

Wieberg (225) Swedish: variant of WIBERG.

Wiebers (143) North German: patronymic from the Germanic personal name *Wigberht*, composed of the elements *wīg* 'battle', 'war' + *berht* 'bright', 'famous'.

Wiebke (182) German: from a pet form of *Wibo*, a short form of the Germanic personal name *Wigberht* (see WIEBERS).
GIVEN NAMES German 4%. *Erwin, Kurt.*

Wiebold (177) German: from a Germanic personal name composed of the elements *wīg* 'battle', 'war' + *bald* 'bold'.

Wieboldt (101) German: variant spelling of WIEBOLD.

Wiebusch (202) North German: topographic name for someone who lived by a willow or willows, from a reduced form of Middle High German *wīde* 'willow' + *busch* 'bush'.
GIVEN NAMES German 5%. *Fritz, Klaus, Kurt.*

Wiech (167) **1.** German: from a short form of a Germanic personal name beginning with *wīg* 'battle', 'war'. **2.** Polish: from the personal name *Wiech*, a pet form of any of several Old Polish names beginning with *Wie-*, e.g. *Wielisław*, from *wieli-* 'great' + *sław* 'glory'.

Wiechec (110) Polish: **1.** derivative of the personal name WIECH. **2.** nickname from *wiecheć* 'whisk' or 'wet rag'.

Wiechert (215) German: variant of WICHERT.
GIVEN NAMES German 9%. *Kurt* (2), *Alois, Gerd, Horst, Siegfried, Wolfgang.*

Wiechman (320) Variant of North German WIECHMANN.

Wiechmann (309) North German: from a Germanic personal name composed of the elements *wīg* 'battle', 'war' + *man* 'man' (see WICHMANN).
GIVEN NAMES German 8%. *Dietrich, Eldred, Heinz, Inge, Ingo, Irmgard, Meinrad, Ralf.*

Wieck (427) German: **1.** habitational name from Middle Low German *wīk* 'fortified settlement' (Latin *vicus*). **2.** variant spelling of WICK.

Wieckowski (128) Polish (**Więckowski**): habitational name for someone from any of various places in Poland called Więckowo, Więckowy, Więców, or Więckowice.
GIVEN NAMES Polish 23%. *Andrzej* (2), *Ryszard* (2), *Ewa, Jacek, Miroslaw, Wojciech, Zdislaw, Zdzislaw, Zygmunt.*

Wieczorek (1198) Polish: nickname for someone thought to resemble a bat, from Polish dialect *wieczorek* 'bat', a diminutive of *wieczór* 'evening'.
GIVEN NAMES Polish 8%. *Czeslaw* (2), *Danuta* (2), *Jerzy* (2), *Miroslaw* (2), *Andrzej, Boleslaw, Darek, Eugeniusz, Henryk, Ignacy, Irena.*

Wieczorkowski (74) Polish: habitational name for someone from Wieczorki in Łomża voivodeship, named with *wieczorek* 'bat'.
GIVEN NAMES Polish 17%. *Czeslawa, Janusz, Zbigniew, Zigmunt, Zygmunt.*

Wied (267) German: **1.** topographic name from Middle High German *wīde* 'willow' + *man*. **2.** topographic name from Middle High German *widem* 'prebend', 'land endowed to a church'.
GIVEN NAMES German 5%. *Kurt* (2), *Otto* (2).

Wiedel (193) German: from a diminutive of WIED.

Wiedeman (609) German: see WIDEMAN 1.

Wiedemann (640) German: see WIDEMAN 1.
GIVEN NAMES German 11%. *Hans* (3), *Helmut* (2), *Otto* (2), *Claus, Elke, Ernst, Franz, Friederike, Fritz, Gerd, Guenter, Gunter.*

Wiedemeier (114) German: variant of WIDMEYER.
GIVEN NAMES German 5%. *Ernst, Heribert.*

Wiedemer (119) Variant of German WIDMER.

Wiedenfeld (143) Variant of German **Weidenfelder** (see WEIDENFELLER).
GIVEN NAMES German 8%. *Kurt* (2), *Bodo, Egon.*

Wiedenhoeft (154) North German: from Middle Low German *wide* 'willow' + a variant of *hof* 'farm'. Compare German **Gehöft**.
GIVEN NAMES German 5%. *Kurt* (2), *Erwin.*

Wiedenmann (103) German: variant of **Widemann** (see WIDEMAN).
GIVEN NAMES German 7%. *Hans* (2), *Kurt.*

Wieder (815) **1.** German: habitational name for someone from a place named Wied, Wieden, or Wieda. **2.** variant of German WEDER. **3.** Jewish (Ashkenazic): from German *Widder* 'ram'. Compare WIDERMAN.

GIVEN NAMES Jewish 8%; German 4%. *Baruch* (3), *Mayer* (3), *Aron* (2), *Pincus* (2), *Sol* (2), *Avraham, Ben-Zion, Boruch, Chana, Cheskel, Isador, Mendel; Armin* (2), *Frieda, Horst, Klaus, Willi.*

Wiederhold (416) German: from the medieval personal name *Widerolt*, from a Germanic compound name formed with *witu* 'wood' + *walt(an)* 'to rule'.
GIVEN NAMES German 5%. *Kurt* (3), *Aloysius, Bernhard, Ewald, Konrad, Otto.*

Wiederholt (314) German: variant of WIEDERHOLD.

Wiederkehr (171) German: nickname for someone who had returned to a place on one occasion or more, from Middle High German *widerkēr* 'return'.
GIVEN NAMES German 5%. *Hans, Otto, Urs.*

Wiedmaier (110) German and French (Alsatian): variant of German WIEDMEYER.
GIVEN NAME French 7%. *Marcel* (2).

Wiedman (395) Variant of German WIEDMANN.

Wiedmann (264) North German: variant of **Widemann** (see WIDEMAN 1).
GIVEN NAMES German 7%. *Klaus, Otto, Siegfried.*

Wiedmer (126) French (Alsatian) form of German WIEDMEYER or a variant of WITTMER 1.
GIVEN NAMES German 6%; French 5%. *Ernst, Fritz; Alphonse, Camille.*

Wiedmeyer (185) German: distinguishing name for a tenant farmer (see MEYER) who worked on land that had been endowed to a prebendary (Middle High German *widem*).

Wiedner (172) German: **1.** topographic name for someone who lived in a place distinguished by a willow or willows, from Middle High German, Middle Low German *wīde* 'willow'. **2.** topographic name for a woodland dweller, from Middle Low German *wede* 'wood'.
GIVEN NAMES German 6%. *Benno* (2), *Mathias.*

Wiedrich (155) German: variant of **Widrich** (see WIDRICK).
GIVEN NAMES German 7%. *Gottlieb* (2), *Erna, Frieda, Milbert.*

Wiegand (2467) German: from the Germanic personal name *Wīgant*, originally a byname meaning 'warrior', from the present participle of *wīgan* 'to fight'.
FOREBEARS Michael Wiegand, aged 52, came to North America from the Palatinate in western Germany as part of a group led by the Rev. Joshua Kocherthal. They sailed up the Hudson River and settled on lands at Quassick Creek, then Dutchess Co., NY, 1709. His descendants later left the Hudson River settlement and migrated to Tulpehocken, PA.
GIVEN NAMES German 4%. *Otto* (4), *Kurt* (3), *Hans* (2), *Heinz* (2), *Wilfried* (2), *Arno, Bernhard, Dieter, Frieda, Hedwig, Siegfried.*

Wiegel (519) German: from a pet form of any of the various Germanic personal names beginning with the element *wīg* 'battle', 'war'.
GIVEN NAMES German 4%. *Kurt* (2), *Gottfried, Gottlieb, Juergen.*

Wiegele (102) South German: variant of WIEGEL.

Wieger (101) German: from a reduced form of the personal names *Wighard* or *Wigher* (compounds of the Germanic elements *wīg* 'battle' + *hard* 'hardy', 'strong' or *hari, heri* 'army', respectively).
GIVEN NAME German 4%. *Heino.*

Wiegers (266) North German: patronymic from WIEGERT.

Wiegert (520) North German: variant of WEICHERT.
GIVEN NAMES German 4%. *Kurt* (3), *Hans* (2), *Christoph, Erwin.*

Wiegman (366) Variant spelling of German WIEGMANN.

Wiegmann (276) German: from a Germanic personal name composed of the elements *wīg* 'battle', 'war' + *man* 'man' (see WICHMANN).
GIVEN NAMES German 6%. *Erwin, Hartmut, Heinz, Helmut, Otto, Rainer.*

Wiegner (114) German: probably an occupational name for a scale maker, Middle High German *wiger*, or for a cradle maker, from an agent derivative of Middle High German *wige, wiege* 'cradle', 'crib'.
GIVEN NAME German 4%. *Eberhard.*

Wiehe (243) North German: **1.** topographic name for someone who lived where willows grew, a Low German variant of WEIDE 1. **2.** habitational name from a place so named on the Unstrut river.
GIVEN NAME German 5%. *Kurt* (2).

Wiehl (134) **1.** Southwestern German: topographic name from Middle High German *wuol(lache)* 'drain hole'. **2.** habitational name from a place near Cologne named Wiehl.

Wieland (2300) **1.** German: from a Germanic personal name composed of the elements *wīg* 'war' + *land* 'land', 'territory'. This name was borne by the supernaturally skilled smith of Germanic folk legend, and for this reason it may in part have been given as a nickname to blacksmiths. **2.** Jewish (Ashkenazic): presumably an adoption of the German surname.
GIVEN NAMES German 5%. *Kurt* (5), *Erwin* (4), *Otto* (4), *Heinz* (2), *Dieter, Dietrich, Eldred, Erdmann, Florian, Franz, Fritz, Gerhard.*

Wiele (103) German: probably a habitational name from a place named with an old water word, *wil*, as for example Wiehl in North Rhine-Westphalia or Wielen in Lower Saxony and Schleswig Holstein.

Wielenga (117) Polish (also **Wielęga**): derivative of any of several Slavic and Old Polish compound personal names beginning with *Wiel-*, for example *Wielimir, Wielisław.*

Wieler (139) **1.** German: perhaps a topographic name from Middle High German *wuol, wüele* 'waterhole' + -er suffix denoting an inhabitant. **2.** habitational name for someone from a place named Wiehl or Wielen (see WIELE).
GIVEN NAMES German 5%. *Merwin, Trud.*

Wielgus (218) Polish: nickname from the Old Polish and dialect term *wielgus*, denoting a big, tall, thickset man.
GIVEN NAMES Polish 12%. *Jozef* (2), *Casimir, Ignacy, Jadwiga, Janina, Jarek, Kazimierz, Ludwik, Mieczyslaw, Pawel, Wladyslaw.*

Wieman (299) Altered spelling of German WIEMANN.

Wiemann (349) North German: **1.** variant of WEINMANN, from Middle Low German, Middle High German *wīnman* 'viticulturalist', 'wine merchant'. **2.** variant of WIEDEMANN.
GIVEN NAMES German 5%. *Hans* (2), *Hilde* (2).

Wiemer (431) German: from a Germanic personal name composed of the elements *wīg* 'battle', 'war' + *mar* 'famous'.
GIVEN NAMES German 6%. *Klaus* (3), *Frieda, Hans, Otto, Wolfgang.*

Wiemers (290) North German: patronymic from WIEMER.

Wiemken (102) North German: patronymic from a pet form of the personal name WIEMER.

Wien (265) **1.** German and Jewish (Ashkenazic): habitational name from the city of Vienna (German *Wien*, Yiddish *Vin*). The place name is first recorded in the Latin form *Vindobona*, and is of Celtic origin. Before the Holocaust there was a large Jewish population in Vienna. From the 17th century onwards the Leopoldstadt district was officially designated as a Jewish quarter, and many families bearing this surname no doubt originated there. **2.** Norwegian: habitational name from any of seven farmsteads in eastern Norway named Vien, earlier *Vivin*, from Old Norse *viðr* 'wood', *víðr* 'wide', or *vé* '(pagan) sacred place' + *vin* 'meadow'.
GIVEN NAMES German 5%. *Kurt* (3), *Alois, Fritz.*

Wiencek (302) Polish (also **Więcek**): from the personal name *Więcek*, a pet form of *Więcesław* (Latin form *Venceslaus*; compare Czech VACEK). This name is also well established in German-speaking countries.
GIVEN NAME German 4%. *Florian.*

Wienecke (160) North German: variant of WIENEKE.
GIVEN NAMES German 6%. *Milbert, Otto, Rainer.*

Wieneke (424) North German: from a pet form of the personal name *Wīgnand* (see WEINAND).
GIVEN NAMES German 4%. *Kurt* (2), *Otto.*

Wiener (2696) German and Jewish (Ashkenazic): habitational name for someone from Vienna, Austria (see WIEN).
GIVEN NAMES Jewish 4%. *Sol* (5), *Miriam* (4), *Hyman* (3), *Alter* (2), *Hillel* (2), *Isadore* (2), *Arnon, Ayelet, Leibel, Meyer, Moshe, Yaron.*

Wieners (101) Variant of German WIENER.
GIVEN NAME German 4%. *Bernd.*

Wienke (421) German: reduced form of WIENEKE.

Wiens (1022) German: patronymic from a short form of a Germanic compound personal name beginning with *wini* 'friend'.

Wier (1081) German: from the Germanic personal name *Wigheri*, composed of the elements *wīg* 'battle' + *heri* 'army'.

Wiercinski (132) Polish (**Wierciński**): habitational name for someone from Wiercień in Białystok voivodeship, named with *wiercić* 'to pester somebody', or 'fidget'.
GIVEN NAMES Polish 13%; German 4%. *Bogdan, Irek, Jerzy, Kazimierz, Lucjan, Miroslaw, Pawel; Alfons, Florian.*

Wierda (124) Frisian: variant of WIARD.

Wierenga (423) Frisian: patronymic from a Germanic personal name composed of the elements *wīg* 'battle', 'war' + *rīk* 'powerful'.

Wieringa (149) Variant of WIERENGA.
GIVEN NAMES Dutch 12%. *Onno* (3), *Aaltje, Berend, Dirk, Gerrit, Hendrik.*

Wierman (328) **1.** Dutch: patronymic from a Germanic personal name composed of the elements *warō* 'guard', 'protection' + *man* 'man'. **2.** German (**Wiermann**): variant of WIER, with the addition of Middle High German *man* 'man'.

Wiers (223) North German: patronymic from WIER.
GIVEN NAMES Dutch 6%. *Gerrit* (2), *Dirk, Gerritt, Marinus.*

Wiersema (273) Frisian: variant of WIERSMA.

Wiersma (774) Frisian: patronymic from WIER.

Wierzba (277) Polish: topographic name or nickname from Polish *wierzba* 'willow'.
GIVEN NAMES Polish 8%; German 4%. *Dariusz* (2), *Andrzej, Kazimierz, Marcin, Zbigniew, Zdzislaw; Helmut* (3), *Konrad.*

Wierzbicki (623) Polish: habitational name for someone from any of the many places in Poland called Wierzbica or Wierzbice, named with *wierzba* 'willow'.
GIVEN NAMES Polish 13%. *Andrzej* (4), *Miroslaw* (3), *Boleslaw* (2), *Jacek* (2), *Aleksander, Bronislaw, Czeslaw, Feliks, Grazyna, Grzegorz.*

Wierzbowski (126) Polish: habitational name for someone from any of the many places in Poland called Wierzbowo, named with *wierzba* 'willow'.
GIVEN NAMES Polish 14%; German 4%. *Wieslaw* (2), *Bogdan, Boleslaw, Halina, Stanislaw, Zygmunt; Erwin.*

Wies (219) German: variant of WIESE.

Wiese (3861) German: **1.** topographic name from Middle High German *wise* 'meadow'. **2.** habitational name for someone from any of various places called Wies, Wiese, Wiesa, or possibly also Wiesau.
GIVEN NAMES German 4%. *Kurt* (10), *Hans* (5), *Otto* (5), *Erwin* (4), *Arno* (2), *Fritz* (2), *Gerhard* (2), *Manfred* (2), *Uwe* (2), *Bernhard, Friedrich, Gerhart*.

Wiesehan (137) Origin unidentified.

Wiesel (152) **1.** German and Jewish (Ashkenazic): from German *Wiesel* 'weasel', Middle High German *wisele*. As a German name this is a nickname; as a Jewish name it is generally an ornamental name. **2.** German: from Middle High German *wīsel* 'leader'.
GIVEN NAMES German 7%; Jewish 6%. *Manfred* (3); *Arie, Eliezer, Ephraim, Moshe, Nachum*.

Wieseler (190) German and Jewish (Ashkenazic): variant of WIESEL, with the addition of the agent suffix *-er*.

Wieseman (105) Variant of German WIESEMANN.

Wiesemann (149) German: topographic name for someone who lived by a meadow, from WIESE + Middle High German *man* 'man'.
GIVEN NAMES German 13%. *Dieter* (2), *Claus, Ingeborg, Kurt, Reinhard, Wolfgang*.

Wiesen (434) **1.** German: habitational name from any of various places so named, for example near Aschaffenburg. **2.** German: topographic name from Middle High German *wise* 'meadow'. **3.** Jewish (Ashkenazic): probably an ornamental adoption of German *Wiesen* 'meadows'.

Wiesenfeld (157) **1.** German: topographic name from Middle High German *wise* 'meadow' + *vëlt* 'open country', or a habitational name from any of various places named Wiesenfeld. **2.** Jewish (Ashkenazic): ornamental name composed of German *Wiesen* 'meadow' + *Feld* 'field'.
GIVEN NAMES Jewish 13%. *Aron, Aryeh, Batia, Hadassa, Haim, Shaindy, Yitzchok*.

Wiesenthal (118) **1.** German: habitational name from any of various places called Wiesent(h)al. **2.** Jewish (Ashkenazic): ornamental name from German *Wiese* 'meadow' + *Tal* 'valley'.

Wieser (750) German: topographic or habitational name (see WIESE).
GIVEN NAMES German 5%. *Aloys* (2), *Erwin* (2), *Franz* (2), *Otto* (2), *Alois, Ernst, Heinz, Jochen, Kurt*.

Wiesinger (139) German: habitational name for someone from any of various places in Bavaria and Austria called Wiesing.
GIVEN NAMES German 6%. *Gerhard, Ilse, Wilhelm*.

Wiesler (106) German and Jewish (Ashkenazic): variant of WIESEL, with the addition of the agent suffix *-er*.
GIVEN NAME Jewish 5%. *Mordechai* (2).

Wiesman (299) German (**Wiesmann**): variant of WIESEMANN.

Wiesmann (127) German: **1.** topographic name for someone who lived by a meadow, from Middle High German *wise* 'pasture', 'meadow' + *man*. **2.** Alternatively, it could be an altered form of WEISSMANN.
GIVEN NAMES German 16%. *Traugott* (2), *Fritz, Hans, Heinz, Jurgen, Klaus*.

Wiesner (1259) German: habitational name for someone from a place called WIESEN, or topographic name for someone who lived by a meadow, a derivative of Middle High German *wise* 'meadow'.
GIVEN NAMES German 5%. *Dieter* (2), *Kurt* (2), *Wenzel* (2), *Wilhelm* (2), *Achim, Alois, Bodo, Erhard, Erna, Gerhart, Hans, Jurgen*.

Wiess (142) Variant spelling of German WIES.

Wiessner (169) Variant spelling of German WIESNER.
GIVEN NAMES German 10%. *Frieda, Lutz, Otto, Siegfried, Traude*.

Wiest (1422) German: **1.** variant of **Wüst** (see WUEST). **2.** habitational name from a place named Wiest or Wieste, for example near Meppen.

Wietecha (120) Polish: nickname from a derivative of Polish dialect *wietki* 'flimsy' (standard Polish *wiotki*).

Wieters (124) German: patronymic from a variant of WIEDER 2.
GIVEN NAMES German 4%. *Fritz, Johann*.

Wieting (257) North German: variant of WITTING.

Wiewel (119) German: unexplained.
GIVEN NAMES German 6%. *Kurt, Rainer*.

Wigal (243) Americanized spelling of German WEIGEL or WIEGEL.

Wigand (247) **1.** English: variant of WIGGIN. **2.** German: variant of **Weigand** (see WIEGAND).

Wigdahl (104) Norwegian: habitational name from a farmstead named Vigdal or Vikdal, from *Vig*, probably a river name, or *vik* 'bay', 'inlet' + *dal* 'valley'.

Wigen (238) Norwegian and Danish: variant spelling of VIGEN.

Wigent (135) Origin unidentified; perhaps an altered spelling of WIGAND.

Wiget (109) Swiss German: reduced form of WIEGAND.

Wigfall (392) English (South Yorkshire): habitational name from Wigfield (earlier Wigfall) Farm, Worsbrough, named with the Old English personal name *Wicga* or Old English *wicga* 'beetle' + *(ge)fall* 'forest clearing'.

Wigfield (243) English (South Yorkshire): variant of WIGFALL.

Wigg (145) English (East Anglia): **1.** nickname from Middle English *wigge* 'beetle', 'bug'. **2.** metonymic occupational name for a maker of fancy breads baked in rounds and then divided up into wedge-shaped slices, Middle English *wigge*, from Middle Dutch *wigge* 'wedge(-shaped cake)'.

Wiggans (158) English: variant spelling of WIGGINS.

Wigger (350) German: variant of WICKER.

Wiggers (339) German: patronymic from WIGGER.

Wiggin (782) English: **1.** from the Breton personal name *Wiucon*, composed of elements meaning 'worthy' + 'high', 'noble', which was introduced into England by followers of William the Conqueror. **2.** from the Germanic personal name *Wīgant*, originally a byname meaning 'warrior', from the present participle of *wīgan* 'to fight', likewise introduced to England in the wake of the Conquest.
FOREBEARS Many American bearers of this name are descended from Thomas Wiggin who came to Boston, MA, in 1631.

Wiggington (145) English: variant of WIGGINTON.

Wiggins (15043) English: patronymic from the personal name WIGGIN.

Wigginton (876) English: habitational name from any of the places in Hertfordshire, Oxfordshire, Staffordshire, and North Yorkshire named Wigginton, from the Old English personal name *Wicga* + genitive *-n* or *-ing-* + *tūn* 'enclosure', 'settlement'.

Wigglesworth (373) English (West Yorkshire): habitational name from a place in Ribblesdale, North Yorkshire, recorded in Domesday Book as *Winchelesuuorde*, from the genitive case of the Old English byname *Wincel* meaning 'child' + Old English *worð* 'enclosure'.
FOREBEARS Michael Wigglesworth (1631–1705), Puritan poet and preacher, was brought from Yorkshire to New England as a child in 1638. His first home was in Charlestown, MA; subsequently, he settled in New Haven, CT. From 1651 onward he was a fellow of Harvard College; in 1654 he was appointed minister at Malden, MA. His son and grandson, both named Edward were professors of divinity at Harvard.

Wiggs (1337) English: patronymic from WIGG.

Wight (2027) Scottish and English: nickname from Middle English *wiht*, *wight* 'nimble', 'strong'.

Wightman (1399) Scottish and English: **1.** from an unattested Old English personal name *Wihtmann* meaning 'elf man'. **2.** variant of WIGHT, with the addition of Middle English *man* 'man'.

Wigington (553) English: variant of English WIGGINTON.

Wiginton (421) English: variant of English WIGGINTON.

Wigle (227) Probably an Americanized spelling of German WEIGEL.

Wiglesworth (122) English: variant spelling of WIGGLESWORTH.

Wigley (1103) English: habitational name from places in Derbyshire and Hampshire, named from the Old English byname *Wicga* (meaning 'beetle', 'insect') or Old English *wicga* 'beetle', 'insect' + *lēah* 'wood', 'woodland clearing'.

Wigmore (183) English: habitational name for someone from Wigmore in Herefordshire, so named from Old English *wicga* in the sense 'something moving', 'quaking' + *mōr* 'marsh'.

Wignall (291) English (Lancashire): habitational name from Wignal, a minor place near Holmes in the parish of Croston, so named from the genitive case of the Old English byname *Wicga* (see WIGLEY) + Old English *h(e)alh* 'nook', 'corner', 'recess'.

Wigner (107) German: occupational name from an agent derivative of Middle High German *wigen* 'to weigh'.

Wigren (139) Swedish: ornamental name composed of the place-name element *vi-* (representing either Old Norse *viðr* 'forest' or *vé* '(pagan) sacred place')+ *gren* 'branch'.
GIVEN NAME Scandinavian 8%; German 4%. *Nils.*

Wigton (366) Scottish (Borders) and northern English: habitational name from Wigton in Cumbria, near Carlisle.

Wiig (118) Norwegian and Danish: variant spelling of VIG.
GIVEN NAMES Scandinavian 11%. *Erik, Hilmer.*

Wiita (156) Finnish (**Viita**): ornamental name from *viita* 'forest'; common as an adopted name from the early 20th century. Occurs chiefly in Ostrobothnia.
GIVEN NAMES Finnish 4%. *Ahti* (2), *Eino.*

Wiitala (188) Finnish (**Viitala**): topographic name from *viita* 'forest' + the local suffix *-la*. Found chiefly in Ostrobothnia.
GIVEN NAMES Finnish 8%; Scandinavian 5%. *Eino* (3), *Eero, Sulo, Toivo, Wilho; Erik.*

Wik (286) Norwegian and Swedish: variant spelling of VIK.
GIVEN NAMES Scandinavian 6%. *Nils, Thorvald.*

Wike (884) **1.** Norwegian and Swedish: variant of VIK. **2.** English: variant of WICK.

Wikel (164) **1.** Americanized spelling of German **Weikel**, a variant of WEIGEL. **2.** ornamental name from *vik* 'bay' + the common surname suffix *-el(l).*

Wiker (249) **1.** Norwegian: habitational name from any of ten or more farmsteads so named in eastern Norway, from the plural of *vik* 'bay', 'inlet' (see VIK). **2.** Swedish: ornamental name from *vik* 'bay' + the suffix *-er.*

Wikert (100) German: variant of WEICHERT.

Wikle (274) Possibly an Americanized spelling of German **Weikel**, a variant of WEIGEL.

Wiklund (173) Swedish: ornamental name composed of the elements *vik* 'bay' + *lund* 'grove'.
GIVEN NAMES Scandinavian 10%. *Erik, Fredrik, Nils.*

Wikman (108) Swedish: ornamental name composed of the elements *vik* 'bay', 'inlet' + *man* 'man'.
GIVEN NAMES Scandinavian 10%; German 4%. *Lars* (2), *Johan.*

Wikoff (417) Variant of Dutch WYCKOFF.

Wikstrom (338) Swedish (**Wikström**): ornamental name composed of the elements *vik* 'bay' + *ström* 'river'.
GIVEN NAMES Scandinavian 13%. *Tor* (2), *Alf, Bernt, Erik, Fredrik, Holger, Lennart, Sven.*

Wiland (209) Norwegian: habitational name from any of three farmsteads named in Old Norse as *Viðiland*, a compound of *víðir* 'willow' + *land* '(piece of) land'.

Wilbanks (2975) English: unexplained.

Wilber (2348) English: nickname from Middle English *wild* 'wild' + *bor* 'boar'.

Wilberding (158) German (Westphalia): patronymic from WILBERT.
GIVEN NAMES French 4%. *Luc, Monique.*

Wilberg (177) **1.** Norwegian: habitational name from any of six farmsteads near Oslo named Vilberg, from an unexplained first element + *berg* 'mountain'. **2.** German: habitational name from place so named near Paderborn.

Wilberger (101) German: variant of WILBERG 2.

Wilbers (146) German: patronymic from WILBERT.
GIVEN NAME German 4%. *Aloys.*

Wilbert (840) English and German: from a Germanic personal name composed of the elements *wil* 'will', 'desire' + *berht* 'bright', 'famous'. The native English form, *Wilbeorht*, is attested before the Conquest, but was greatly reinforced in the early Middle Ages by the introduction of the Continental cognate by the Normans.

Wilbon (204) English: see WILBURN.

Wilborn (1324) English: see WILBURN.

Wilbourn (732) English: see WILBURN.

Wilbourne (218) English: see WILBURN.

Wilbur (3880) English: variant spelling of WILBER.
FOREBEARS Samuel Wilbur (also known as **Wilbore** and **Wildbore**) (*c.*1585–1656) is recorded in Boston, MA, before 1633 and purchased Boston Common in 1634. He and other religious exiles from MA purchased and settled Aquidneck Island (now RI) in 1637.

Wilburn (4596) English: unexplained; this surname occurs predominantly in the northeast Midlands of England. It is most

probably a habitational name from a lost or unidentified place.

Wilby (134) English: habitational name from any of the places called Wilby, in Suffolk, Norfolk, and Northamptonshire. The first is probably named from an Old English *wilig* 'willow' + Old English *bēag* 'circle'; the second has the same first element + Old Norse *býr* 'farmstead' or Old English *bēag*, and the last is named with the Old English or Old Scandinavian personal name *Villi* + *býr*.

Wilch (155) German: unexplained.

Wilcher (1090) English: variant of WILTSHIRE.

Wilcock (275) English (chiefly Lancashire and Yorkshire): from a medieval personal name, composed of the elements WILL 1 + the hypocoristic suffix *-cok* (see COCKE).

Wilcott (130) English: habitational name from Wilcott in Shropshire, which is probably from an unattested Old English personal name *Wifela* + Old English *cot* 'cottage', or Wilcot in Wiltshire, which is named in Old English as *Wilcotum* 'cottages by the spring'.

Wilcox (21118) English: patronymic from WILCOCK.

Wilcoxen (476) Variant spelling of English WILCOXSON.

Wilcoxon (417) English: variant spelling of WILCOXSON.

Wilcoxson (826) English: patronymic from WILCOCK.

Wilcutt (92) English: variant of WILCOTT.

Wilczak (153) Polish: patronymic from the personal name WILK.
GIVEN NAMES Polish 9%. *Andrzej, Danuta, Stanislawa, Witold, Wojciech.*

Wilczek (275) Polish: from a diminutive form of the personal name WILK.
GIVEN NAMES Polish 9%; German 4%. *Stanislaw* (2), *Casimir, Ewa, Krzystof, Miroslaw, Zosia; Gunther, Natascha.*

Wilczewski (224) Polish: habitational name for someone from Wilczewo in Łomża voivodeship, named with Polish *wilk* 'wolf'.
GIVEN NAMES Polish 9%. *Czeslaw, Ireneusz, Kazimierz, Krystyna, Wlodzimierz, Zbigniew.*

Wilczynski (505) Polish (**Wilczyński**): habitational name for someone from any of several places called Wilczyn, Wilczyna, or Wilczyno, named with Polish *wilk* 'wolf'.
GIVEN NAMES Polish 6%. *Bogdan, Dariusz, Eugeniusz, Ireneusz, Jerzy, Kazimier, Lucyna, Piotr, Ryszard, Tomasz, Wincenty.*

Wild (3437) **1.** English: from Middle English *wild* 'wild', 'uncontrolled' (Old English *wilde*), hence a nickname for a man of violent and undisciplined character, or a topographic name for someone who lived on a patch of overgrown uncultivated land. **2.** English: habitational name from a place named Wyld, as for example in Berkshire and Dorset, both named from Old English *wil* 'trap', 'snare'. **3.** German and Jewish (Ashkenazic): cognate of 1, from Middle High German *wilde*, *wilt*, German *wild* 'wild', also used in the sense 'strange', 'foreign', and therefore in some cases a nickname for an incomer.

Wilda (161) German: habitational name from any of several places named Wildau.

Wildasin (244) Origin unidentified.

Wilday (102) English: variant of Waldie.

Wildberger (132) German: habitational name for someone from any of the numerous places called Wildberg.

Wilde (4148) **1.** Irish, English, and German: variant of Wild. **2.** Dutch (**de Wilde**) and Jewish (Ashkenazic): nickname for a violent, unruly, and irascible man, from Middle Dutch *wilde* 'wild', German *Wilde* 'wild man', 'savage'.

FOREBEARS The writer Oscar Wilde (1854–1900) was born in Dublin, Ireland, descended from Ralph Wilde, a builder from Walsingham near Durham, England, who had moved to Ireland in the 17th century. Richard Henry Wilde (1789–1847), born in Dublin, emigrated to Baltimore, MD, in 1797 and was raised in GA, where he became a congressman (1815–17, 1827–35). He moved to New Orleans, LA, in 1843 and was a professor at the University of LA (now Tulane).

Wildeboer (110) Dutch: .

GIVEN NAMES Dutch 4%. *Harm, Tonnis.*

Wildeman (230) **1.** Dutch: variant of Wilde. **2.** Altered spelling of German **Wildemann**, a variant of Wild.

Wilden (189) **1.** English: variant of Wilding. **2.** German and Dutch: variant of (De) Wilde. **3.** German: habitational name from a place so named near Siegen. **4.** Swedish (**Wildén**): ornamental name, probably formed with *wild*, old spelling of *vild* 'wild' + the common surname suffix *-én*, from Latin *-enius*.

Wildenberg (174) German: habitational name from any of various places so named in Germany and Switzerland.

Wilder (10601) English, German, Danish, and Jewish (Ashkenazic): variant of Wild.

FOREBEARS Thomas Wilder is recorded as a freeman of Charlestown, MA, in 1640. He had numerous prominent descendents.

Wilderman (330) **1.** Jewish (Ashkenazic): variant of Wild. **2.** Respelling of German **Wildermann**, an elaborated form of Wild, with the addition of Middle High German *man* 'man'.

Wildermuth (677) German: variant of Wild, literally 'wild spirit', from Middle High German *wilder*, inflected form of *wild* + *muot*.

GIVEN NAMES German 4%. *Kurt* (3), *Heinz.*

Wildes (780) English: variant of or patronymic from Wild.

Wildey (389) English: variant of Waldie.

Wildfong (115) Variant of German **Wildfang** (see Wilfong).

GIVEN NAME German 4%. *Orlo* (2).

Wildhaber (136) German: occupational nickname for a farmer, from Middle High German *wilt* 'wild' + *haber* 'oats'.

Wilding (626) **1.** English (now chiefly Lancashire): from an unattested Old English personal name, *Wilding*, a derivative of Old English *wilde* 'wild', 'savage'. It is also possible that it may be from a topographical term derived from the same vocabulary word. Compare Wild, but early forms with prepositions are not found. **2.** German: patronymic from *Wilto*, a short form of a Germanic personal name beginning with *wild* 'wild'.

Wildman (2010) **1.** English: variant of Wild, with the addition of Middle English *man* 'man'. **2.** German (**Wildmann**): from a short form of the Germanic personal name *Wilto* + Middle High German *man* 'man'.

Wildner (118) Variant of Willner.

GIVEN NAMES German 15%. *Gunter, Heinz, Kurt, Ralf, Wolfgang.*

Wildrick (297) Americanized spelling of German **Wildreich**, a medieval personal name, from Old High German *wildi* 'wild'.

Wilds (1013) English: variant of or patronymic from Wild.

Wildstein (109) German: habitational name from Wildstein in Bavaria.

Wildt (353) German: variant of Wild.

Wile (669) **1.** English: metonymic occupational name for a trapper or nickname for a devious man (see Wiles, of which this is the singular form). **2.** Perhaps an Americanized spelling of Weil.

Wileman (325) English: occupational name for a trapper (see Wiles), with the addition of Middle English *man* 'man'.

Wilemon (351) English: variant of Wileman.

Wilen (275) Dutch: variant of Willen.

GIVEN NAME Scandinavian 4%. *Sven.*

Wilensky (443) Polish (**Wileński**) and Jewish (eastern Ashkenazic): habitational name for someone from the Lithuanian city of Vilnius (called *Wilno* in Polish).

GIVEN NAMES Jewish 4%. *Heshy, Isadore, Moshe, Uri.*

Wiler (211) **1.** English: variant of Wheeler. **2.** Perhaps an Americanized spelling of Weiler.

Wiles (4929) English: metonymic occupational name for a trapper or hunter, in particular someone who caught fish, especially eels, by setting up wicker traps in rivers and estuaries, from Middle English *wile* 'trap', 'snare' (late Old English *wīl* 'contrivance', 'trick' possibly of Scandinavian origin), or in some cases probably a nickname for a devious person.

Wiley (16263) **1.** Northern Irish and Scottish: variant of Wylie. **2.** Possibly also English, a habitational name from Wylye in Wiltshire, named for the Wylye river (see Wilton). **3.** English: possibly a variant of Willey.

Wilf (112) Jewish (Ashkenazic): unexplained.

GIVEN NAMES Jewish 6%. *Emanuel, Gittel, Ilan.*

Wilfert (180) German and Dutch: **1.** from a Germanic personal name composed of the elements *wolf* 'wolf' + *hart* 'hardy', 'brave', 'strong'. **2.** from a Germanic personal name composed of the elements *wille* 'will', 'wish' + *fridu* 'peace'. **3.** nickname for a wild or wily man, from Middle High German *wülven* 'to behave like a wolf'.

Wilfong (1466) Americanized spelling of German **Wildfang**, a nickname from Middle High German *wiltvanc* 'stranger'.

Wilford (797) **1.** English: habitational name from either of two places called Wilford, in Nottinghamshire and Suffolk, both probably named with an Old English *wilig* 'willow tree' + Old English *ford* 'ford'. **2.** Dutch: see Williford.

Wilger (133) German: from the Germanic personal name *Williger*, composed of *wil* 'will' + *gār, gēr* 'lance', 'spear'.

Wilgus (523) **1.** Polish: variant of Wielgus. **2.** English: nickname for a wild or unpredictable person, from a variant of **Wildgoose**.

Wilham (137) German: probably a variant of Wilhelm.

Wilharm (119) German: probably a variant of Wilhelm.

GIVEN NAMES German 4%. *Heinz, Udo.*

Wilhelm (8118) German: from the Germanic personal name *Willahalm*, composed of the elements *wil* 'will', 'desire' + *helm* 'helmet', 'protection'.

GIVEN NAMES German 4%. *Kurt* (16), *Otto* (10), *Fritz* (4), *Hans* (4), *Heinz* (4), *Ewald* (2), *Gerhard* (2), *Helmut* (2), *Markus* (2), *Ralf* (2), *Rudie* (2), *Balzer.*

Wilhelmi (552) German: Latinized patronymic from Wilhelm.

Wilhelms (232) German: patronymic from Wilhelm.

GIVEN NAME German 4%. *Otto* (2).

Wilhelmsen (236) Danish, Norwegian, and North German: patronymic from the personal name Wilhelm.

GIVEN NAMES Scandinavian 18%; German 7%. *Alf, Erik; Hans* (4), *Kurt* (2), *Bredt.*

Wilhelmson (101) Partly Americanized spelling of North German, Danish, and Norwegian Wilhelmsen.

Wilhelmy (175) German: variant spelling of Wilhelmi.

GIVEN NAMES German 6%. *Jochen, Viktor, Xaver.*

Wilhide (208) Of German origin: variant of Wilhite.

Wilhite (2827) German: Americanized spelling of **Willeit**, a variant of **Willeitner**, a habitational name from a more recent form of the place name Weillitnen in northern Bavaria. **Willeit** is probably also a topographic name from Middle High German *wīl* 'small settlement' + *leite* 'slope'.

FOREBEARS Johann Michael Wilhoit or Wilheit emigrated in about 1717 from Germany to the Germanna Colony on the Rapidan River, VA (a settlement of Protestant refugees from the Rhineland). Little is known about him and his family, but they had many descendants, and the surname has many variant spellings.

Wilhoit (903) Of German origin: variant of WILHITE.

Wilhoite (486) Of German origin: see WILHITE.

Wiliams (124) Welsh: variant spelling of WILLIAMS.

Wilinski (172) Polish (**Wiliński**) and Jewish (eastern Ashkenazic): variant of **Wileński** (see WILENSKY).

Wilk (2112) **1.** Polish: from Polish *wilk* 'wolf', probably from an Old Slavic personal name containing this element, but perhaps also applied as a nickname for someone thought to resemble a wolf or connected with wolves. **2.** Scottish and English: from a medieval personal name, a back-formation from WILKIN, as if that contained the Anglo-Norman French diminutive suffix -*in*. **3.** North German: variant of WILKE.
GIVEN NAMES Polish 7%. *Mariusz* (4), *Stanislaw* (3), *Tadeusz* (3), *Zygmunt* (3), *Andrzej* (2), *Bogdan* (2), *Boguslaw* (2), *Casimir* (2), *Krzysztof* (2), *Stanislawa* (2), *Boleslaw*, *Darek*.

Wilke (3275) **1.** North German: from a Low German pet form of WILHELM. **2.** English: variant spelling of WILK.
GIVEN NAMES German 5%. *Fritz* (5), *Kurt* (5), *Otto* (4), *Erwin* (3), *Arno* (2), *Bernd* (2), *Gerhard* (2), *Siegfried* (2), *Wilfried* (2), *Wilhelm* (2), *Wolfgang* (2), *Angelika*.

Wilken (1308) **1.** North German: patronymic from a Low German pet form of WILHELM. **2.** English: variant spelling of WILKIN.

Wilkening (608) North German: patronymic from WILKE.

Wilkens (1433) **1.** German: variant of WILKEN. **2.** English: patronymic from WILKIN.
GIVEN NAMES German 4%. *Hans* (2), *Klaus* (2), *Kurt* (2), *Christoph*, *Dietrich*, *Eldor*, *Ernst*, *Ewald*, *Heiner*, *Helmut*, *Ilse*, *Jurgen*.

Wilkenson (132) English: variant spelling of WILKINSON.

Wilker (514) German: variant of WILGER.

Wilkerson (14718) English: patronymic from WILKIN.

Wilkes (6225) **1.** English: patronymic from WILK. **2.** Frisian: from a pet form of the personal name *Will*.

Wilkey (1253) **1.** English (Bristol): from a pet form of the personal name WILK. **2.** Variant of German WILKE.

Wilkie (2778) **1.** Scottish: from a medieval pet form of the personal name WILLIAM. **2.** Altered spelling of German WILKE, written thus to preserve the final syllable.

Wilkin (1168) **1.** English: from the medieval personal name *Wilkin*, a pet form WILLIAM. **2.** Dutch: from a pet form of *Willem* (see WILHELM).

Wilking (230) Dutch and German: patronymic from WILKIN and WILKE.
GIVEN NAMES German 7%. *Erna*, *Kurt*, *Lorenz*, *Otto*.

Wilkins (18701) English and Dutch: patronymic from WILKIN.

Wilkinson (20988) English: patronymic from WILKIN.

Wilkison (426) Probably an altered form of English WILKINSON.

Wilkosz (126) Polish: derivative of WILK.
GIVEN NAMES Polish 8%; German 4%. *Zbigniew* (2), *Henryk*; *Otto*.

Wilkowski (221) Polish: habitational name for someone from any of the many places in Poland called Wilkowo or Wilków, named with Polish *wilk* 'wolf'. This name is also well established in German-speaking countries.

Wilks (2763) English: patronymic from the personal name WILK.

Will (4866) **1.** Scottish and northern English: from the medieval personal name *Will*, a short form of WILLIAM, or from some other medieval personal names with this first element, for example WILBERT or WILLARD. **2.** English: topographic name for someone who lived by a spring or stream, Middle English *wille* (from *wiell(a)*, West Saxon form of Old English *well(a)* 'spring'). The surname is found predominantly in the south and southwestern parts of the country. **3.** German: from a short form of any of the various Germanic personal names beginning with *wil* 'will', 'desire'.

Willadsen (209) Danish: patronymic from the personal name *Villadz*, from English *Willehad*, composed of elements meaning 'will', 'determination' + *hadu* 'fight', 'battle'.

Willaert (100) Dutch: from a personal name composed of the Germanic elements *wil* 'will' + *hard* 'hardy', 'strong'.

Willaman (107) English: unexplained; possibly a variant of WILLIAM.

Willams (223) Variant of English WILLIAMS.

Willan (103) **1.** Swiss German: variant of **Wielan** (see WIELAND). **2.** English: unexplained.

Willard (8314) **1.** English: from a Germanic personal name composed of the elements *wil* 'will', 'desire' + *hard* 'hardy', 'brave', 'strong'. **2.** Probably an Americanized form of the German cognate **Willhardt** (see WILLERT).
FOREBEARS Simon Willard (1605–76) came from Horsmonden, Kent, England, to Boston, MA, in 1634. In that year he became one of the founders of Cambridge, MA, and the following year (1635) was a founder of Concord, MA. Twenty years later, in 1659, he was a founder of Lancaster, MA. Simon Willard was involved in numerous confrontations with the native American Indians, in particular in King Philip's War of 1675–76. He had seventeen children and was the ancestor of many prominent Americans.

Willardson (127) Patronymic from English WILLARD.

Willauer (157) German: habitational name for someone from Willau in the Rhineland.

Willbanks (462) Variant of English WILBANKS.

Willborn (130) English: variant spelling of WILBURN.

Willburn (106) English: variant spelling of WILBURN.

Willcox (962) English: patronymic from WILCOCK, widespread in southwestern England.

Willcoxon (128) English: patronymic from WILCOCK.

Willcut (130) Altered spelling of English WILCOTT.

Willcutt (299) Altered spelling of English WILCOTT.

Willden (215) English: variant spelling of WILDEN.

Wille (1464) German: from a short form of any of the Germanic personal names beginning *Willi-*, as for example, *Willibrant*, *Willihart*.
GIVEN NAMES German 4%. *Kurt* (3), *Armin*, *Detlef*, *Ernst*, *Gerhard*, *Gerhardt*, *Gerhart*, *Otto*, *Reinhard*, *Ulrich*, *Wilhelm*.

Willeford (574) Dutch: variant spelling of WILLIFORD.

Willeke (109) North German and Dutch: from a pet form of the personal name WILHELM.
GIVEN NAME German 4%. *Klaus*.

Willem (104) Dutch form of WILLIAM.
GIVEN NAMES German 8%. *Juergen*, *Kurt*.

Willems (1046) Dutch and North German: patronymic from WILHELM.

Willemsen (261) North German, Dutch, and Danish: patronymic from WILHELM.

Willemssen (109) North German, Dutch, and Danish: patronymic from WILHELM.

Willen (345) German: **1.** variant of WILLE. **2.** habitational name from a place so named near Wittmund. **3.** Dutch: from the personal name *Willin* (see WILHELM).
GIVEN NAME German 4%. *Frieda*.

Willenberg (126) German: habitational name from Willenberg in Silesia.

Willenborg (387) German (from the Cloppenburg area): habitational name from an unidentified place.

Willenbring (214) German: variant of WILLENBRINK.

Willenbrink (128) German (Oldenburg): habitational name for someone from a minor place named with Middle Low German *brinc* 'edge', 'slope', 'grazing land', 'raised meadow in low-lying marshland'. The first element is unexplained.

Willens (202) Dutch: patronymic from the personal name *Willin* or *Willem* (see WILHELM).

Willer (822) **1.** German: from a short form of a Germanic personal name beginning with *wil* 'will'. **2.** Dutch: from a personal name composed of the Germanic elements *wil* 'will', 'desire' + *heri* 'army'.

Willers (261) North German and Dutch: patronymic from WILLER.
GIVEN NAMES German 5%. *Helmuth, Ingeborg, Johann.*

Willert (397) German: from a Germanic personal name composed of the elements *wil* 'will', 'desire' + *hard* 'hardy', 'brave', 'strong'.
GIVEN NAMES German 5%. *Hedwig, Heinz, Kurt, Wendelin, Winfried.*

Willes (184) English: variant spelling of WILLS.

Willet (439) **1.** English: variant spelling of WILLETT. **2.** French: cognate of 1, from a pet form of *Willaume*.

Willets (225) English: variant spelling of WILLETTS.

Willett (5078) **1.** English: from a pet form of WILL 1. **2.** Americanized form of French OUELLETTE.

Willette (1439) **1.** English: from a pet form of WILL 1. **2.** Americanized form of French OUELLETTE.

Willetts (428) English: patronymic from WILLETT.

Willever (119) Of English origin: probably a variant of either GULLIVER or OLIVER.

Willey (5312) English: **1.** habitational name from any of various places so named. Those in Cheshire, Herefordshire, Shropshire, and Warwickshire are named from an Old English *wilig* 'willow' + Old English *lēah* 'wood', 'clearing'; one in Devon probably has Old English *wīðig* 'willow' as the first element, while one in Surrey has Old English *wēoh* '(pre-Christian) temple'. **2.** variant spelling of WILLY 2.
FOREBEARS Isaac Willey is recorded in Boston, MA, in 1640, and went on to be one of the founders of New London, CT. His descendent Samuel Hopkins Willey (1821–1914) was one of the founders of the College of California at Berkeley in 1860.

Willford (262) English: variant spelling of WILFORD.

Wilhelm (184) German: variant spelling of WILHELM.

Willhite (1330) Of German origin: see WIL-HITE.

Willhoit (178) Of German origin: see WIL-HITE.

Willhoite (349) Of German origin: see WIL-HITE.

Willi (215) German: variant of WILLE.

GIVEN NAMES German 7%. *Erwin, Hermann, Markus, Mathias.*

William (2123) English: from the Norman form of an Old French personal name composed of the Germanic elements *wil* 'will', 'desire' + *helm* 'helmet', 'protection'. This was introduced into England at the time of the Conquest, and within a very short period it became the most popular personal name in England, mainly no doubt in honor of the Conqueror himself.

Williams (452360) English (also very common in Wales): patronymic from WILLIAM.
FOREBEARS This very common surname was brought to North America from southern England and Wales independently by many different bearers from the 17th century onward. It has also absorbed some continental European cognates such as Dutch WILLEMS. Roger Williams, born in London in 1603, came to MA in 1630, but the clergyman was banished from the colony for his criticism of the Puritan government; he fled to RI and founded Providence.

Williamsen (264) **1.** Danish and Norwegian: patronymic from the personal name WILLIAM. **2.** Partly Americanized form of North German, Danish, and Norwegian WILHELMSEN.

Williamson (40959) Northern English, Scottish, and northern Irish: patronymic from WILLIAM.
FOREBEARS This surname was brought to North America from northern England and northern Ireland independently by numerous different bearers from the 17th century onward. Timothy Williamson is recorded in Plymouth Colony in 1643. It has also absorbed some continental European cognates such as Dutch WILLEMSEN.

Williard (521) **1.** English: variant of WIL-LARD. **2.** German: variant of **Willhardt** (see WILLERT).

Willick (102) Jewish (Ashkenazic): ornamental name from German *willig* 'willing'.
GIVEN NAMES Jewish 4%. *Rivka, Simcha.*

Willie (1000) **1.** English and Scottish: variant spelling of WILLEY or WYLIE. **2.** Probably also a variant spelling of German WILLI.

Willier (126) Dutch: variant of WILLER.

Williford (2989) Americanized form of Dutch and North German WILFERT.

Willig (483) **1.** German and Dutch: from a pet form of WILHELM. **2.** German: habitational name from Willich near Düsseldorf.

Willing (634) **1.** German: patronymic from WILLE. **2.** German: habitational name from any of several places in Bavaria named Willing or places in Hessen and near Soltau named Willingen. **3.** English: patronymic from the Old English personal name *Willa*.

Willinger (302) German: habitational name for someone from any of the various places called Willing or Willingen (see WILLING 2).

GIVEN NAMES German 4%. *Hans, Helmuth, Kurt.*

Willingham (4355) English: habitational name from a place named Willingham, notably one in Cambridgeshire and one in Suffolk. The first is recorded in Domesday Book as *Wivelingham* 'homestead (Old English *hām*) of the people of a man called *Wifel*'.

Williquette (156) French: from a pet form of the personal name *Williaume*, Norman and Picard form of *Guillaume* (see WILLIAM).

Willis (40768) English: patronymic from the personal name WILL.
FOREBEARS George Willis is recorded in Boston, MA, in the 1630s. Nathianel Willis, born in Boston in 1780, and his son Nathaniel Parker Willis, born in Portland, ME, in 1806, were both prominent journalists.

Willison (1058) English: patronymic from the personal name WILL.

Williston (292) English or Scottish: unexplained. This has the form of a habitational name, but no such place has been identified. It may be an altered form of WILLISON, or possibly a habitational name from *Willesden*, now part of North London.

Willits (870) English: patronymic from *Willet*, a pet form of the personal name WILL.

Willitts (113) English: variant spelling of WILLITS.

Willkomm (149) German: **1.** probably from a nickname for a hospitable man, someone who habitually used the greeting *willkomm* 'welcome', although the epithet may have belonged to a house rather than to a person. **2.** from the personal name *Willcomo*, testified from the 8th century.
GIVEN NAMES German 4%. *Bernhard, Dieter.*

Willman (1596) **1.** English: occupational name for someone who was the servant of a man called Will. **2.** Altered spelling of German WILLMANN.

Willmann (372) German: from a short form of WILHELM or any of the various other personal names beginning with the element *Wil(l)-* (see WILLE) + Middle High German *man* 'man'.

Willmarth (129) Variant of English WILMARTH, itself a variant of WILMOT.

Willmer (125) German: variant of WILMER.
GIVEN NAME German 5%. *Manfred.*

Willmes (113) North German and Dutch: patronymic from a reduced form of the personal name WILHELM.

Willmon (331) English: variant of WILL-MAN.

Willmore (378) English: variant spelling of WILMORE.

Willmott (250) English: from a pet form of the personal name WILLIAM.

Willms (601) North German and Dutch: patronymic from a reduced form of the personal name WILHELM.
GIVEN NAMES German 5%. *Willi* (2), *Elfriede, Fritz, Kurt.*

Willner (699) **1.** German: habitational name for someone from any of various places, for example in Saxony, Upper Franconia, the Upper Palatinate, and Upper Austria, called Wildenau, from Old High German *wildi* 'wild', 'uncultivated' (with the adjective retaining the weak dative ending originally used after a preposition and article) + *ouwa* 'wet land', 'marsh'. **2.** Jewish (eastern Ashkenazic): habitational name from Yiddish *vilner* 'native or inhabitant of the Lithuanian city of Vilnius' (Yiddish *Vilne*).
GIVEN NAMES Jewish 6%; German 5%. *Isadore* (2), *Abbe, Aron, Avrom, Channan, Gershon, Hyman, Miriam, Moshe, Naftali, Shimon, Yaakov; Kurt* (3), *Bernhard, Dieter, Erwin, Ewald, Gerda, Hans, Heinz, Otto.*

Willock (212) English: from the Middle English and Old English personal name *Willoc*, a pet form from a short form of the various compound names with the first element *willa* 'will', 'desire'. In the Middle Ages this came to be used as a pet form of the personal name WILLIAM.

Willocks (129) English: patronymic from WILLOCK.

Willoughby (5809) English: habitational name from any of the various places called Willoughby, for example in Leicestershire, Lincolnshire, Nottinghamshire, and Warwickshire. They are named from an Old English *wilig* 'willow' + Old Norse *býr* 'farm', 'settlement', or perhaps in some cases from *wilig* + Old English *bēag* 'ring'.

Willow (281) English: topographic name for someone who lived in an area where willows grew or by a conspicuous willow tree, from an unattested Old English word, *wilig*.

Willows (125) English: variant of WILLOW.

Willrich (123) German: from a Germanic personal name composed of the elements *wil* 'will', 'desire' + *rīk* 'powerful'.

Wills (10014) **1.** English: patronymic from WILL. **2.** German: patronymic from any of the Germanic personal names beginning with *wil* 'will', 'desire'.

Willsey (501) Variant spelling of WILSEY.

Willsie (112) Variant spelling of WILSEY.

Willson (3424) English: variant spelling of WILSON.

Willwerth (183) German and Dutch: from a Germanic personal name composed of the elements *wil* 'will', 'desire' + *wart* 'guardian'.

Willy (317) **1.** English: variant spelling of WILLEY. **2.** English: from a pet form of the personal name WILL. **3.** Americanized spelling of German WILLI.

Willyard (294) Americanized spelling of German WILLIARD.

Wilm (127) German: from a reduced form of the personal name WILHELM.
GIVEN NAMES German 5%. *Hans, Heinz.*

Wilmarth (385) Variant of English WILMOT.
FOREBEARS Thomas Wilmarth (1620–90) came to America in 1639. He was one of the proprietors of Rehoboth, MA, in 1643.

Wilmer (666) German and English: from the Germanic personal name *Wilmar* (Old English *Wilmǣr*), composed of the elements *wil(l)* 'will' + *mar* 'famous'.
FOREBEARS Simon Wilmer settled in Kent Co., MD, before 1680. William Holland Wilmer, born in Kent Co. in 1782, and his son Richard Hooker Wilmer (b. 1816) were both Episcopal clergymen.

Wilmes (720) North German and Dutch: patronymic from a reduced form of the personal name WILHELM.

Wilmeth (296) Variant of English WILMOT.

Wilmore (576) English: habitational name for someone from Wildmore in Lincolnshire or the Weald Moors in Shropshire, both named with Old English *wilde* 'wild', 'uncultivated' + *mōr* 'moor', 'marsh'.

Wilmot (1784) English: from a pet form of the personal name WILLIAM.
FOREBEARS Benjamin Wilmot and his wife, with their 6-year-old son William, emigrated from England to New Haven, CT, in or before 1640.

Wilmoth (1898) Variant of English WILMOT.

Wilmott (192) English: variant spelling of WILMOT.

Wilmouth (180) Altered form of English WILMOTH.

Wilms (367) North German and Dutch: patronymic from a reduced form of the personal name WILHELM.
GIVEN NAMES German 19%. *Uli* (7), *Hermann* (5), *Heinz* (2), *Ernst, Friedrich, Manfred, Ralf, Udo, Willi.*

Wilner (662) German and Jewish (eastern Ashkenazic): variant of WILLNER.
GIVEN NAMES Jewish 5%. *Chaim, Meier, Meyer, Shlomo, Shmuel, Sol.*

Wilsey (862) **1.** English (Norfolk): unexplained; perhaps a variant of WOOLSEY. **2.** Americanized spelling of Dutch WILTSE.
FOREBEARS Hendrick Wiltsee's son Hendrick, born in 1746, spelled his surname Willse in adult life.

Wilshire (322) English: variant of WILTSHIRE.

Wilshusen (160) North German: probably a habitational name from a place so named, now lost. It was most probably in the Bremervörde area, where the name is now predominantly found.

Wilson (269682) English, Scottish, and northern Irish: patronymic from the personal name WILL, a very common medieval short form of WILLIAM.

Wilt (3027) **1.** German: variant of WILD. **2.** Dutch: variant of **de Wilde** (see WILDE).

Wiltbank (117) Probably of Dutch origin: unexplained.

Wiltfong (178) Altered spelling of German **Wildfang** (see WILDFONG).

Wiltgen (236) Dutch: from a pet form of the personal name *Wouter*, Dutch form of WALTER.

Wilton (1139) English: habitational name from any of various places so called. Most, including those in Cumbria, Herefordshire, Norfolk, and East and North Yorkshire, are named from an Old English *wilig* 'willow' + *tūn* 'enclosure', 'settlement'. One in Somerset and another in Wiltshire have as their first element Old English *wiell(a)* 'spring', 'stream'. The one that has given its name to the county of WILTSHIRE is named for the Wylye river, on which it stands (an ancient British river name, perhaps meaning 'capricious').

Wiltrout (332) Americanized form of German **Wiltraud**, from the female personal name, a compound of *wil* 'will', 'desire' + *drud* 'strength'.

Wilts (112) Of Dutch origin: variant of WILTZ or WILTSE.

Wiltse (906) Dutch: unexplained. This name is recorded in New Netherland before 1675; it is most probably of Danish origin.
FOREBEARS Hendrick Martenzen Wiltsee (c.1623–1712) is believed to have been born in Copenhagen, Denmark. He came to Wiltwyck, New Amsterdam, in or before 1660, after first spending time in the Dutch settlement in Brazil.

Wiltsey (157) Americanized form of Dutch WILTSE.

Wiltshire (1048) English: regional name from the county of Wiltshire in southwest central England, which gets its name from WILTON (once the county's principal town) + Old English *scīr* 'district', 'administrative division'.

Wiltsie (251) Of Dutch origin: see WILTSE.

Wiltz (743) **1.** Luxembourgeois: habitational name from Wiltz in Luxembourg. **2.** German: from a short form of WILHELM or any other of the Germanic personal names formed with *wil* 'will', 'desire' as its first element.
GIVEN NAMES French 5%. *Alcide, Alphonse, Antoine, Curley, Emile, Honore, Maudry, Michel, Monique.*

Wiltzius (100) German: Latinized form of WILTZ.

Wilusz (158) Polish: from a derivative of the German personal name WILHELM.

Wilwerding (113) Luxembourgeois: habitational name from Wilwerdange in Luxembourg.

Wilz (192) German: variant spelling of WILTZ.
GIVEN NAMES German 4%. *Alois* (2), *Hans* (2), *Erwin.*

Wiman (169) **1.** English: variant spelling of WYMAN. **2.** North German: perhaps an altered spelling of WEIMANN. **3.** Swedish: ornamental name from Old Norse *viðr* 'forest' + *man* 'man'.
GIVEN NAMES Scandinavian 4%. *Holger, Sten.*

Wimberley (792) English: see WIMBERLY.

Wimberly (2473) English: origin uncertain. The form is that of a habitational name; it may be a variant of WIMBLEY.

Wimbish (520) English: habitational name from Wimbish, a place in Essex, most probably named from the Old English personal name *Wine* + an Old English *(ge)bysce* 'bushy copse'.

Wimble (111) English (Kent): origin uncertain; perhaps a variant of the habitational name WIMBLEY, or a variant of **Wimple**, a metonymic occupational name for a maker of wimples, from Middle English *wimple* (Old English *wimpel* 'veil').

Wimbley (247) English: apparently a habitational name, perhaps from Wembley in Greater London (formerly Middlesex), which is named with an unattested Old English personal name *Wemba* + *lēah* 'woodland clearing'.

Wimbrow (103) Probably English: unexplained.

Wimbush (422) English: variant of WIMBISH.

Wimer (1399) Altered spelling of English WYMER or German WEIMER.

Wimmer (2594) **1.** German: reduced form of WIDMER. **2.** German: occupational name from Middle High German *wimmer* 'wine maker'. **3.** German: nickname from Middle High German *wim(m)er* 'knotty growth on a tree trunk'. **4.** German: variant of WEIMER 2. **5.** English: from the Old English personal name *Winemǣr*, a compound of *wine* 'friend' + *mǣr* 'famous'.

Wimmers (106) German: variant of WIMMER.
GIVEN NAMES German 12%. *Horst* (2), *Joerg, Otto, Willi.*

Wimp (122) English: unexplained. The derogatory English word *wimp*, denoting a feeble person, is far too recent to be the source of a surname.

Wimpee (191) Variant spelling of English WIMPEY.

Wimpey (132) English: of uncertain origin. Sir Elijah **Impey**, an 18th-century English judge, had an illegitimate son who bore this name.

Wimpy (167) English: variant spelling of WIMPEY.

Wims (236) Variant of Scottish WEMYSS.

Wimsatt (432) English: variant of WIMSETT.

Wimsett (109) English (Kent): unexplained.

Win (175) **1.** Southeast Asian: unexplained. **2.** Dutch: variant of WINNE. **3.** English: variant spelling of WYNN.

GIVEN NAMES Southeast Asian 43%. *Kyaw* (6), *Maung* (5), *Thein* (5), *Tun* (5), *Zaw* (4), *Than* (4), *Khin* (3), *Tin* (3), *Sein* (2), *Soe* (2), *Chan, Cong, Min, Phat, Shwe, Toan.*

Winand (130) Dutch (**Wijnand**): variant of WINANT.

Winans (1568) Dutch: patronymic from the medieval personal name WINANT.
FOREBEARS American bearers of this surname are mostly if not all descended from Jan Wynants, who came to North America from the Netherlands in about 1662.

Winant (172) Dutch: from the medieval personal name *Wynant*, composed of the Germanic elements *wīg* 'battle', 'fight' + *nand* 'courage', 'bravery'.
GIVEN NAMES French 5%. *Anais* (2), *Luc.*

Winarski (113) **1.** Polish: variant of WINIARSKI. **2.** Jewish (from Ukraine): patronymic from Ukrainian *vynar* 'wine merchant' + the possessive suffix *-ski*.
GIVEN NAMES Polish 6%. *Lucjan, Zygmund.*

Winberg (370) **1.** Danish and German: habitational name from a place so named, most probably the one in Mecklenburg, Germany. **2.** Swedish: ornamental name from *vin(d)* 'wind' + *berg* 'mountain', or habitational name from a place named with these elements.
GIVEN NAMES Scandinavian 6%. *Erik* (3), *Lars.*

Winberry (243) Americanized spelling of Danish or Swedish WINBERG.

Winborn (291) English: variant of WINBURN.

Winborne (356) English: variant of WINBURN.

Winburn (644) English: habitational name from any of the various places in Dorset named after the Wimborne river (for example Wimborne Minster, Wimborne St. Giles, Up Wimborne). The river, now called the Allen, was earlier named from Old English *winn* 'meadow' + *burna* 'stream'.

Winbush (369) English: variant of WIMBISH.

Wince (305) Probably an Americanized or Slavicized variant of German **Winz**, a short form of a Germanic personal name beginning with *wini* 'friend' or of *Winzenz*, German form of VINCENT.

Wincek (149) Polish: from the personal name *Wincek*, a pet form of *Wincenty* (see VINCENT).

Winch (705) English: **1.** in examples such as William de la Winche (Worcestershire 1275) evidently a topographic name, perhaps for someone who lived at a spot where boats were hauled up onto the land by means of pulleys, from Middle English *winche* 'reel', 'roller'. However, Old English *wince* as an element of place names may also have meant 'corner' or 'nook', and in some cases the surname may be derived from this sense. **2.** in examples such as William le Wynch (Sussex 1327) it

appears to be a nickname, perhaps from the lapwing, Old English *(hlēap)wince.*

Winchel (181) English: variant of WINCHELL.

Winchell (1822) **1.** English: from Old English *wencel* 'child', perhaps used to distinguish a son from his father with the same forename or perhaps a nickname for a person with a baby face or childlike manner. **2.** Scottish: habitational name for someone from the lands of Windshiel (formerly Winscheill) in Berwickshire.
FOREBEARS Robert Winchell came from England to Windsor, CT, in 1635.
In the case of the broadcaster Walter Winchell (1897–1972) the surname is an Anglicized form of Jewish WINSCHEL.

Winchenbach (138) German: probably an Americanized form of **Wenzenbach**, a habitational name from a place of this name in Bavaria or from Wünschenbach in eastern Germany.

Winchester (3667) English: habitational name from the city in Hampshire, so named from the addition of Old English *ceaster* 'Roman fort or walled city' (Latin *castra* 'legionary camp') to the Romano-British name *Venta*, of disputed origin.
FOREBEARS John Winchester was admitted a freeman in Brookline, MA, in 1637. Oliver Winchester (1810–80), owner of the arms company that produced the Winchester rifle, was his fifth-generation descendant, born in Boston.

Winckler (367) **1.** German: variant spelling of WINKLER. **2.** Dutch: occupational name for a storekeeper, Middle Dutch *windelare*.

Wind (1000) **1.** English: topographic name for someone who lived near a pathway, alleyway, or road, Old English *(ge)wind* (from *windan* 'to go'). **2.** English, German, and Danish: nickname for a swift runner, from Middle English *wind* 'wind', Middle High German *wint* 'wind', also 'greyhound'. **3.** German: variant of WENDT. **4.** Swedish: ornamental name from *vind* 'wind', or a habitational name from a place named with this element.
GIVEN NAMES German 4%. *Erwin* (3), *Gerhard* (2), *Elfriede, Florian, Kajetan, Klaus, Kurt, Reinhold, Wilhelm.*

Windecker (136) South German: habitational name for someone from any of the numerous places named Windeck.

Windell (253) **1.** English: variant spelling of WINDLE. **2.** Swedish: ornamental name composed of the elements *vind* 'wind' + the common suffix *-ell*, from Latin *-elius*.

Windels (121) German: perhaps a patronymic or metronymic from *Wendel*, which in southern Germany and Austria is a short form of the male personal name *Wendelin* and in north Germany of the female personal name *Wendelke*.
GIVEN NAMES German 9%. *Gerhard* (2), *Lothar.*

Winden (105) German: habitational name from any of numerous places so named in Germany and Switzerland.

Winder (1715) English: **1.** occupational name for a winder of wool, from an agent derivative of Middle English *winde(n)* 'to wind' (Old English *windan* 'to go', 'to proceed'). The verb was also used in the Middle Ages of various weaving and plaiting processes, so that in some cases the name may have referred to a basket or hurdle maker. **2.** habitational name from any of the various minor places in northern England so called, from Old English *vindr* 'wind' + *erg* 'hut', 'shelter', i.e. a shelter against the wind.
FOREBEARS John Winder is recorded in Somerset Co., MD, in 1665. William Henry Winder, born in the county in 1775, was blamed for the military defeat that led to the British burning of Washington, DC, in 1814; his son John Henry Winder (b. 1800) was a confederate general who was commander of southern military prisons.

Winders (752) English: metonymic occupational name for a weaver or textile worker, from Middle English *wyndhows* 'winding house'. Compare WINDER 1.

Windes (165) English: variant of WINDERS.

Windham (3678) **1.** English: habitational name from Wyndham in West Sussex, near West Grinstead, probably named from an unattested Old English personal name *Winda* + Old English *hamm* 'water meadow'; or from Wymondham in Leicestershire and Norfolk, named from the Old English personal name *Wīgmund* (see WYMAN) + Old English *hām* 'homestead'. The name de Wyndem is found in Westmorland as early as 1284, and the surname may additionally derive from some unidentified place in northern England. **2.** Irish (Connacht): Anglicized ('translated') form of Gaelic **Ó Gaoithín** 'descendant of *Gaoithín*' (see GAHAN).

Windholz (195) German: topographic name from a field name composed of Middle High German *wint* 'wind' + *holz* 'wood'.
GIVEN NAMES German 4%. *Alois, Otto*.

Windhorst (341) North German: topographic name from Middle Low German *wint* 'wind' + *horst* 'brush', 'wild place', or a habitational name from places so named in Lower Saxony.
GIVEN NAME German 4%. *Fritz* (2).

Winding (116) Danish and Norwegian: unexplained.

Windisch (386) German: ethnic name from *windisch* 'Slovenian'. This surname is found mainly in Austria and in Slovenia itself, where it is commonly spelled **Vindiš**.
GIVEN NAMES German 7%. *Kurt* (2), *Lutz* (2), *Florian, Horst, Manfred, Otto*.

Windish (240) Americanized spelling of WINDISCH.

Windland (113) Variant of German **Wendland**, denoting an inhabitant of the Wendland district near Lüneburg, where Wendish continued to be spoken as late as the 18th century.

Windle (1133) English (Lancashire and Yorkshire): habitational name from Windhill in West Yorkshire or Windle in Lancashire, both named from Old English *wind* 'wind' + *hyll* 'hill', i.e. a mound exposed to fierce gusts. There is a Windhill in Kent (with the same etymology), but this does not appear to have contributed significantly to the modern surname.

Windler (216) German: variant of WENDLER.

Windley (409) English: habitational name from Windley, a place in Derbyshire named from an unattested Old English *winn* 'meadow' + Old English *lēah* 'clearing'.

Windmiller (170) Americanized form of German **Windmüller**, an occupational name for a miller (see MULLER).

Windom (620) Probably an altered spelling of WINDHAM.

Windon (197) English: unexplained.

Windschitl (138) German: probably an altered form of Austrian German **Windschigl**, an occupational nickname for a shoemaker, from Middle High German *winden* 'to turn', 'wind' + *schigl* (equivalent to *schüg(e)l*), a diminutive of *schuoh*, probably a journeyman's name, 'turn the (little) shoe'.

Windsor (2873) English: habitational name from Windsor in Berkshire, Broadwindsor in Dorset, or Winsor in Devon and Hampshire, all named from an unattested Old English *windels* 'windlass' + Old English *ōra* 'bank'.
FOREBEARS Windsor is the surname of the present British royal family, adopted in place of Wettin in 1917 as a response to anti-German feeling during the World War I. The original surname of Edward VII (and hence of George V up to 1917) was Wettin, his father, Prince Albert, being Prince Wettin of Saxe-Coburg-Gotha. The family took the name Windsor from the place in Berkshire, England, where Windsor Castle is a royal residence. There is unlikely to be any royal connection for American bearers, however: the name was an ordinary English habitational surname for centuries before this event.

Windt (184) German: variant of WENDT.

Windus (157) English: variant of WINDERS.

Wine (1628) **1.** English: variant of WYNN. **2.** Americanized spelling of German WEIN.

Winebarger (543) Americanized spelling of German WEINBERGER.

Wineberg (203) Americanized spelling of German and Jewish WEINBERG.
GIVEN NAME Jewish 4%. *Sholom* (2).

Winebrenner (675) Partly Americanized spelling of the German occupational name WEINBRENNER 'distiller' (literally, 'wine

burner'). The original function of the distiller, attested from the 8th century, seems to have been to extract alcohol for medicinal purposes from wine; the modern sense of someone who prepared spirituous liquor for drinking is first recorded in the 14th century.
FOREBEARS American bearers of this surname are descended from Johann Christian Weinbrenner, who came from the Rhineland Palatinate to Hagerstown, MD, in 1753–54.

Winecoff (213) Americanized form of German WEINKAUF.

Winegar (928) Americanized form of Dutch **Wijngaerd**, a topographic name meaning 'vineyard'. This is also a common place name in the Netherlands, and the surname may be a habitational name from one of these places. Also, it could be a metonymic occupational name for a wine producer.

Winegard (131) **1.** Americanized form of Swedish WINGARD. **2.** Americanized form of Dutch **Wijngaerd** (see WINEGAR) or German WEINGART.

Winegarden (229) Americanized form of Dutch **Wijngaarden** 'vineyard' (see WYNGARDEN) or German or Jewish WEINGARTEN.

Winegardner (447) Americanized form of German WEINGARTNER.

Winegarner (123) Americanized form of German WEINGARTNER.

Winegeart (127) Americanized form of Dutch **Wijngaerd** or German WEINGART.

Wineinger (429) Americanized spelling of German WEININGER.

Wineland (510) Americanized form of German WEINLAND.

Wineman (322) Americanized form of Dutch **Wijnman** 'wine merchant' or German WEINMANN.

Winemiller (419) Literal translation of German **Weinmüller**, an occupational name for someone who operated a grape press.

Winer (1080) **1.** Jewish (Ashkenazic): variant of WIENER. **2.** Jewish and German: Americanized spelling of WEINER.
GIVEN NAMES Jewish 6%. *Sol* (4), *Hyman* (2), *Miriam* (2), *Aron, Elihu, Meyer, Myer*.

Wines (1183) English: variant of WINE.
FOREBEARS Barnabas Wines came from Wales to Watertown, MA, in or before 1635.

Winesett (106) Probably a variant of English WINSETT.

Winey (147) English: unexplained; perhaps a variant of WINNEY.

Winfield (2305) English: habitational name from any of various places now called Wingfield. North and South Wingfield in Derbyshire are evidently named with Old English *wynn* 'meadow', 'pasture' + *feld* 'pasture', 'open country'. A place of this name in Bedfordshire may have as it first element a topographical term or bird name *wince* (see WINCH). One in Suffolk was probably either the 'field of the people of *Wīga*' (a short form of any of various compound names formed with *wīg* 'war'), or else derives its first element from Old English *wēoh* '(pre-Christian) temple'.

Winford (350) English: habitational name from either of two places named Winford, in Somerset or in Newchurch on the Isle of Wight, or from Wynford Eagle in Dorset. The first and last are named from a Celtic river name meaning 'white or bright stream', the last having acquired a manorial prefix from the *del Egle* family, who were there in the 13th century. Winford, Isle of Wight, is named from an unattested Old English *winn* 'meadow' + Old English *ford* 'ford'.

Winfree (846) English: variant spelling of WINFREY.

Winfrey (2082) English: from the Old English person name *Winfrið*.

Wing (4905) **1.** English: habitational name from places named Wing in Buckinghamshire and Rutland. The former was probably named in Old English as the settlement of the *Wiwingas* 'the family or followers of a man named *Wiwa*', or alternatively perhaps 'the people of the temple' (from a derivative of Old English *wīg*, *wēoh* '(pre-Christian) temple'). The latter is from Old Norse *vengi*, a derivative of *vangr* 'field'. Compare WANG. **2.** Dutch (**van Wing**): variant of WINGE. **3.** Chinese 荣: variant of RONG 2.

Wingard (1772) **1.** English: from Middle English *winyard* 'vineyard', hence a topographic name for someone who lived by a vineyard, or a metonymic occupational name for someone who worked in one. **2.** Swedish: ornamental name formed with *vin(d)-* 'wind' + *gard* 'farmhouse', or a habitational name from a place so named.

Wingate (2884) Scottish and northern English: habitational name from any of various place so called, for example Wingate in County Durham or Wingates in Northumberland, named in Old English as *windgeat* 'wind gate', i.e. a place where the wind howls through a narrow pass or gap.

FOREBEARS The earliest recorded Wingate in America is Charles Wyngate (born 1613) who came to VA in 1635. John Wingate (b. 1636) came to Dover, NH, about 1658. Family historians also report two brothers (Robert and Andrew) and a third brother whose name is unknown, coming from Scotland to Schenectady, NY, at about the time of the American Revolution. The British general Orde Wingate (1903–44) was from a well-known Stirlingshire family in Scotland.

Winge (312) **1.** German: from a short form of any of the Germanic personal names beginning with *wini* 'friend'. **2.** Belgian (**van Wing**): habitational name from Sint-Joris-Winge in the Belgian province of Brabant. **3.** Belgian: according to Debrabandere, it may also be variant of **van (der) Winden**, a habitational name from Overwinden or Neerwinden, also in Brabant. **4.** Swedish and Danish: ornamental name from *vinge* 'wing'.

Winger (1680) **1.** English: from the Old English personal name *Winegār*, composed of the elements *wine* 'friend' + *gār* 'spear'. **2.** German: habitational name from any of several places in Alsace (now part of France) named Wingen. **3.** Swedish: ornamental name from *ving(e)* 'wing' + the agentive suffix *-er*.

Wingerd (170) Altered spelling of German WINGERT.

Wingert (1189) German: dialect variant of WEINGARTEN.

Wingerter (489) German: variant of WEINGARTNER.

Winget (641) English (Devon): variant of WINGATE.

Wingett (215) English (Devon): variant of WINGATE.

Wingfield (2166) English: variant of WINFIELD.

Wingler (453) German: variant of WINKLER.

Wingo (2055) Probably an Anglicized form of the French Huguenot name VIGNEAU.

Wingrove (433) English: habitational name from Wingrave in Buckinghamshire, probably named in Old English as 'grove (Old English *grāf*) of the family or followers of (-*inga*-) of a man named *Wīga*'.

Winham (131) English: perhaps a variant of **Wingham**, a habitational name from Wingham, a place in Kent named from an unattested Old English personal name *Wiga* or Old English *wīg* 'heathen temple' + -*inga*- 'of the family or followers of' + *hām* 'homestead', i.e. 'homestead of Wiga's people'.

Winiarski (363) Polish: habitational name for someone from Winiary, a place named from Polish *winiarz* 'producer or seller of wine'.

GIVEN NAMES Polish 9%. *Wieslaw* (2), *Andrzej, Ignatius, Janusz, Jerzy, Mieczyslaw, Ryszard, Stanislaw, Wladyslaw, Zdzislaw*.

Winick (346) Variant spelling of WINNICK.

Winiecki (200) Polish: habitational name for someone from Winiec (now Wieniec) in Włocławek voivodeship, named with *wieniec* 'wreath', 'garland'. This name is also established in German-speaking lands.

GIVEN NAMES German 4%. *Bernhard, Kurt*.

Winiger (123) German and Jewish (Ashkenazic): **1.** variant of WEININGER. **2.** variant of WENIGER.

Wininger (865) German: variant of WEININGER.

Winings (212) German: unexplained.

Winjum (106) Norwegian: unexplained.

Wink (923) English: variant of WINCH.

Winke (112) Variant of English WINK or German WINKEL.

Winkel (1058) **1.** German and Jewish (Ashkenazic): topographic name for someone who lived on a corner of land in the country or a street corner in a town or city, from Middle High German *winkel*, German *Winkel* 'corner'. In time this word also came to denote a corner shop (see WINKELMANN). This surname is also established in Denmark, Sweden, and elsewhere in central Europe. **2.** German: habitational name from any of various places named Winkel. **3.** Dutch and Belgian (**van (der) Winkel, van den Winkel**): habitational name from any of numerous minor places named with *winkel* 'corner', for example Ten Winkel in many provinces of Belgium and the Netherlands, or either of two places called Oostwinkel, in East and West Flanders.

GIVEN NAMES German 4%. *Arno* (2), *Gerhardt* (2), *Aloysius, Bernd, Erwin, Gerd, Horst, Kurt, Math, Philo, Theodor*.

Winkelbauer (132) German: topographic name for a peasant (see BAUER) who farmed a corner of land (see WINKEL).

Winkeler (140) German, Alsatian, and Jewish (Ashkenazic): variant of WINKLER.

GIVEN NAMES French 4%. *Alphonse, Marcel*.

Winkelman (1504) German and Jewish (Ashkenazic): variant of WINKELMANN.

Winkelmann (568) German and Jewish (Ashkenazic): topographic name for someone who lived on a corner or kept a corner shop (see WINKEL), with the addition of Middle High German *man*, German *Mann* 'man'.

GIVEN NAMES German 6%. *Erwin* (4), *Klaus* (3), *Otto* (3), *Hans*.

Winkels (282) German and Dutch: variant of WINKEL.

Winker (311) German: nickname for an agitated or nervous person, or one with a nervous tic, from an agent derivative of Middle High German *winken* originally meaning 'to wave or shake' and later 'to wink or blink'.

GIVEN NAMES German 5%. *Ewald* (2), *Kurt* (2), *Lorenz*.

Winkfield (208) English: habitational name from Winkfield, a place in Berkshire named from an unattested Old English personal name *Wineca* + Old English *feld* 'open country'.

Winkle (1441) **1.** Respelling of German and Jewish WINKEL. **2.** English: probably a nickname for a small man, from *winkle*, a kind of small shellfish.

Winkleblack (104) German or Dutch: variant of WINKLEPLECK.

Winkleman (398) Variant of German and Jewish WINKELMANN.

Winklepleck (136) Americanized form of German or Dutch **Winkelbleck**, a topographic name meaning 'corner dwelling' or 'dwelling by the corner field' (see BLECK).

Winkler (9031) German and Jewish (Ashkenazic): topographic name for someone who lived on a corner or occupational name for someone who kept a corner shop or farmed a corner of land, from an agent derivative of WINKEL 1. This name is widespread throughout central and eastern Europe, being found for example as a Czech, Polish, Slovenian, and Hungarian name.
GIVEN NAMES German 4%. *Kurt* (15), *Klaus* (7), *Otto* (7), *Erwin* (6), *Hans* (6), *Gerhard* (4), *Heinz* (4), *Hermann* (4), *Fritz* (3), *Gernot* (3), *Helmut* (3), *Horst* (3).

Winkles (452) **1.** English: variant of WINKLE. **2.** Americanized spelling of German WINKELS.

Winkley (256) **1.** English: habitational name, perhaps from Winkleigh in Devon, named with an unattested Old English personal name *Wineca* + *lēah* 'woodland clearing'. However, the modern surname occurs chiefly in South Yorkshire and Lancashire, which suggests that another, unidentified source may be involved. **2.** Americanized form of German **Winkele**.

Winkowski (192) **1.** Polish: habitational name for someone from Winek in Piotrków voivodeship. **2.** Jewish (eastern Ashkenazic): habitational name from Vinkovtsy (Polish *Winkowce*), in western Belarus.

Winks (219) English (mainly Yorkshire): probably a variant of WINK.

Winland (414) English: unexplained.

Winn (8224) **1.** English: variant spelling of WYNN. **2.** Variant of Welsh GWYNN.

Winne (429) **1.** Dutch: occupational name for an agricultural worker, Middle Low German *winne* 'peasant'. **2.** English: variant spelling of WYNN.
FOREBEARS Pieter Winne (1609–c.1690) was born in Ghent, Flanders, and brought his family to New Netherland in about 1653, where he became a prominent fur trader. He and his wife Tannetje had at least twelve children.

Winner (1503) **1.** English (Norfolk): unexplained. **2.** Jewish (Ashkenazic): variant of WIENER.

Winnett (513) English: from a pet form of WYNN.

Winney (200) **1.** Variant of Dutch WINNE. **2.** English: from an unattested Old English personal name, *Wyngeofu*, composed of the elements *wyn* 'joy' + *geofu* 'battle'.

Winnick (332) **1.** English: habitational name for someone from a place called Winwick, for example in Northamptonshire or Cambridgeshire, both of which are named from the Old English personal name *Wina* + *wīc* 'outlying dairy farm or settlement'. **2.** Jewish (eastern Ashkenazic; **Winnik**): occupational name for a wine seller, from Polish *wino* 'wine' + the agent suffix *-nik*.
GIVEN NAMES Jewish 4%. *Meyer, Sol*.

Winnicki (142) Polish and Jewish (eastern Ashkenazic): habitational name for someone from any of various places called Winnica or Winniki in Poland, or Vinnitsa in Ukraine.
GIVEN NAMES Polish 8%. *Andrzej, Dariusz, Lucyna, Piotr, Tadeusz*.

Winnie (482) **1.** Variant of Dutch WINNE. **2.** Scottish: perhaps a variant of WINNING.

Winning (286) Scottish: Anglicized and altered form of Irish FINAN.

Winningham (1058) English (East Yorkshire): habitational name from a lost or unidentified place.

Winograd (328) Jewish (eastern Ashkenazic): from Polish *winograd*, Russian *vinograd* 'gape(s)', 'raisin(s)'. The name may occasionally have been taken as an occupational name, but for the most part it is ornamental.
GIVEN NAMES Jewish 8%. *Mayer* (2), *Arie, Orah, Pinchas, Shmuel, Yehudah*.

Winokur (387) Jewish (eastern Ashkenazic): occupational name for a distiller, Russian *vinokur* (from *vino* 'wine', earlier used also of spirits, + *kurit* 'to distil').
GIVEN NAMES Jewish 5%. *Emanuel* (2), *Avi, Chana, Gitla, Mandel, Meyer*.

Winquist (281) Swedish: ornamental name composed of the elements *vind* 'wind' or *ving* 'wing' + *quist*, an old or ornamental spelling of *kvist* 'twig'.
GIVEN NAMES Scandinavian 6%. *Tryg* (2), *Erik, Lars, Lennart*.

Winrow (158) English (Lancashire): variant of WHINERY.

Winschel (135) Jewish: unexplained.

Winsett (412) English: unexplained.

Winship (744) English: of uncertain origin. Reaney suggests that it may be habitational name from Wincheap Street in Canterbury, but this origin is not supported by the present-day distribution of the surname, which is heavily concentrated in northeastern England.

Winski (230) Polish (**Wiński**): possibly a habitational name for someone from Wino (now Winna) in Poznań voivodeship.
GIVEN NAMES Polish 5%. *Casimir* (2), *Bronislaw, Ireneusz*.

Winslett (359) English: unexplained.

Winslow (5716) English: habitational name from Winslow, a place in Buckinghamshire named from the genitive case of the Old English personal name or byname *Wine* (meaning 'friend') + Old English *hlāw* 'hill', 'mound', 'barrow'.
FOREBEARS Edward Winslow (1595–1655), one of the founders of the Plymouth Colony who sailed on the *Mayflower* in 1620, was born in Droitwich, Worcestershire, England. He was a governor of the colony and also served as agent of the Massachusetts Bay Company in France. In 1621 he married Susanna, the widow of William White, the first marriage in New England. Their son Josiah (*c*.1629–80) was

governor of Plymouth Colony from 1673 to 1680, the first native-born governor in North America. He had numerous prominent descendents.

Winson (193) English: patronymic from WYNN.

Winsor (1129) **1.** English: variant of WINDSOR. This is the spelling used for places so named in Devon and Hampshire. **2.** Perhaps also an Americanized spelling of German WINZER.

Winstanley (213) English (Lancashire): habitational name from Winstanley, a place near Manchester, named from the Old English personal name *Wynnstān* (see WINSTON 1) + Old English *lēah* 'wood', 'clearing'.

Winstead (3262) English: habitational name, perhaps from Wanstead in Greater London (formerly Esses), recorded in Domesday Book as *Wenesteda* 'site (Old English *stede*) by a mound (Old English *wænn*) or where wagons (Old English *wæn*) are kept', but more likely from Winestead in East Yorkshire, named from Old English *wīf* 'wife' or a female personal name *Wīfa* + *stede* 'homestead'.

Winsted (109) Respelling of English WINSTEAD.

Winstel (117) German: unexplained.

Winston (6055) **1.** English: from an Old English personal name composed of the elements *wynn* 'joy' + *stān* 'stone'. **2.** English: habitational name from any of various places called Winston or Winstone, from various Old English personal names + Old English *tūn* 'enclosure', 'settlement', or, in the case of Winstone in Gloucestershire, Old English *stān* 'stone'. **3.** Americanized form of Jewish WEINSTEIN.

Wint (401) Dutch (**de Wind**): **1.** ethnic name for a Wend, from Middle Dutch *Wi(e)nt* (see WENDT). **2.** possibly also a nickname for someone who rushed around a lot, from Middle Dutch *wint* 'wind'. **3.** English: unexplained.

Winter (13478) **1.** English, German, Danish, and Swedish: nickname or byname for someone of a frosty or gloomy temperament, from Middle English, Middle High German, Danish, Swedish *winter* (Old English *winter*, Old High German *wintar*, Old Norse *vetr*). The Swedish name can be ornamental. **2.** Jewish (Ashkenazic): from German *Winter* 'winter', either an ornamental name or one of the group of names denoting the seasons, which were distributed at random by government officials. Compare SUMMER, FRUHLING, and HERBST. **3.** Irish: Anglicized form (part translation) of Gaelic **Mac Giolla-Gheimhridh** 'son of the lad of winter', from *geimhreadh* 'winter'. This name is also Anglicized **McAlivery**. **4.** Mistranslation of French LIVERNOIS, which is in fact a habitational name, but mistakenly construed as *l'hiver* 'winter'.

Winterberg (156) **1.** German: habitational name from any of several places named with Middle High German *winter* 'winter' + *berg* 'mountain'. **2.** Jewish (Ashkenazic): ornamental name composed of German WINTER + *Berg* 'mountain', 'hill'.

Winterbottom (340) English: from Middle English *winter* 'winter' + *bottom* 'valley', hence a topographic name, especially in the hilly regions of Lancashire and Yorkshire, for someone whose principal dwelling was in a valley inhabited only in winter (the summer being spent in temporary shelters on the upland pasture).

Winterburn (102) English: habitational name from Winterburn in North Yorkshire or any of several places, notably in Dorset and Wiltshire, originally a river name from Old English *winter* 'winter' + *burna* 'stream', i.e. a stream or river that flowed strongly in winter but more or less dried up in summer.

Winterfeld (125) German: topographic name from Middle High German *winter-velt* denoting a winter pasture or a field with an autumn sowing or a winter crop, or a habitational name from any of various places so named, for example near Salzwedel.

GIVEN NAMES German 8%. *Heinrich*, *Heinz*, *Willi*.

Winterfeldt (106) German: variant of WINTERFELD.

GIVEN NAMES Scandinavian 4%; German 4%. *Erik*; *Erwin*, *Hans*.

Winterhalter (333) German: topographic name for someone who dwelt on a north-facing slope, from Middle High German *winterhalde* 'winter slope'.

GIVEN NAMES German 5%. *Kurt* (2), *Erwin*, *Fritz*, *Inge*, *Reinold*.

Wintermute (308) Americanized spelling of German **Wintermut(h)**, a variant of **Wendemuth**, a nickname for an inconstant or fickle person, from Middle High German *wenden* 'to turn' + *muot* 'mind', 'sense', later 'courage'.

Winterroth (106) German: topographic name for someone who lived on the north side of a clearing (see RODE).

Winterrowd (222) Americanized form of German WINTERROTH.

Winters (15346) English and German: patronymic from WINTER.

Wintersteen (308) Variant of German and Jewish WINTERSTEIN.

Winterstein (220) **1.** German: habitational name from a place so named near Eisenach, or perhaps a topographic name from Middle High German *winter* 'winter' + *stan* 'stone'. **2.** Jewish (Ashkenazic): ornamental name composed of German *Winter* 'winter' + *Stein* 'stone'.

GIVEN NAMES German 4%. *Arno*, *Bernd*.

Winterton (275) English: habitational name from either of two places, in Lincolnshire

and Norfolk, named Winterton. The first is named in Old English as 'farmstead (Old English *tūn*) of the family or followers (-*inga*-) of a man called *Winter*', while Winterton-on-Sea in Norfolk is from Old English *winter* 'winter' + *tūn* 'enclosure', 'settlement', referring perhaps to a place inhabited only in winter.

Winther (468) German, Danish, and Swedish: variant spelling of WINTER.

GIVEN NAMES Scandinavian 9%; German 4%. *Niels* (2), *Aksel*, *Anders*, *Bent*, *Jorgen*, *Lars*, *Nels*, *Sven*; *Gerhardt*, *Kurt*, *Otto*.

Winthrop (407) English: habitational name from places in Lincolnshire and Nottinghamshire called Winthorpe. The former is named with the Old English personal name or byname *Wine*, meaning 'friend', + Old Norse *þorp* 'settlement'. In the latter the first element is a contracted form of the Old English personal name *Wigmund*, composed of the elements *wīg* 'war' + *mund* 'protection', or the Old Norse equivalent, *Vígmundr*.

FOREBEARS John Winthrop (1588–1649) was the first governor of the Massachusetts Bay Colony. He kept a detailed journal, an invaluable source for historians. He was born into a family of Suffolk, England, gentry whose fortunes were founded by his grandfather Adam Winthrop (d. 1562) of Lavenham. In 1544 the latter acquired a 500-acre estate that had been part of the monastery of Bury St. Edmunds. John Winthrop emigrated from Groton, Suffolk, England, to Salem, MA, in 1630 because of Charles I's anti-Puritan policies. By the time of his death he had had four wives and 16 children, the most notable of whom was his son John (1606–76), a scientist and governor of CT. His descendants were prominent in politics and science, including John Winthrop (1714–79), an astronomer, and Robert Winthrop (1809–94), a senator and speaker of the House of Representatives.

Wintjen (109) Dutch: from a pet form of a personal name beginning with the element *Wint-*, as for example *Wintbert*.

Wintle (194) English (Gloucestershire): habitational name primarily from Wintle in Worcestershire, named from Old English *wind* 'wind' + *hyll* 'hill', but in some cases perhaps from one of the places mentioned at WINDLE.

Winton (1483) Scottish and English: habitational name from any of various places called Winton. Those near Edinburgh and in North Yorkshire are named from the Old English byname or personal name *Wine* (meaning 'friend') + Old English *tūn* 'enclosure', 'settlement'; one in former Westmorland (now Cumbria) probably has as its first element an Old English *winn* 'pasture'; and one in Lancashire has Old English *wiðigen* 'growing with willows'.

Wintrode (123) Americanized form of German **Winterroth** (see WINTERROWD).

Wintz (318) German: from a short form of any of the Germanic compound names beginning with *wini-* 'friend'.

Winward (294) English (Lancashire): unexplained.

Winwood (107) English (Worcestershire): unexplained.

Winzeler (155) German: habitational name for someone from any of several places named Winzeln, for example near Pirmasens and Rottweil.

Winzenried (105) Swiss German: unexplained; probably a habitational name from a lost or unidentified place.

Winzer (227) **1.** German: occupational name vine-grower or vintner, Middle High German *winzer*. **2.** German: habitational name from any of various places so named in Bavaria. **3.** English: variant spelling of WINDSOR.

GIVEN NAMES German 6%. *Gerhard*, *Ilse*, *Ingo*, *Wilhelm*.

Wion (201) **1.** French and English (of Norman origin): from a Norman French form of the Germanic personal name *Wido* (see GUY). **2.** German: variant spelling of **Vian**, a short form of the medieval personal name *Vivianus* (from Latin, meaning 'lively').

Wipf (499) German: nickname for a lively energetic person, from Middle High German *wipfen* 'to spring, vault, or bound'.

Wipper (106) English: according to Reaney, an occupational name, the meaning of which has not been established.

Wipperfurth (199) German (**Wipperfürth**): habitational name from a place so named in the Rhineland.

GIVEN NAMES German 9%. *Kurt* (6), *Helmut*.

Wipperman (127) German (**Wippermann**): **1.** variant of WEIPERT, with the addition of Middle High German *man* 'man'. **2.** topographic name for someone who lived by a river named Wipper, of which there are several examples.

Wire (408) English: **1.** metonymic occupational name for a wire drawer, from Middle English *wīr* 'wire'. **2.** topographic name for someone who lived where bog myrtle grew, Old English *wīr*. **3.** habitational name from Wyre Forest in Hereford, Worcestershire, and Shropshire, probably named from a Celtic river name meaning 'winding river'.

Wireman (663) Perhaps an Americanized spelling of German **Wiermann**, a variant of WIER, with the addition of Middle High German *man* 'man'.

Wires (183) English: variant of WIRE.

Wirgau (109) German: probably a habitational name from an unidentified place.

GIVEN NAMES German 5%. *Erhardt*, *Reinhardt*.

Wirick (516) North German: probably a respelling of German **Wirich** (see WEIRICH).

Wirkkala (153) Finnish (**Virkkala**): habitational name from a farm named with the personal name *Virkki*, Finnish form of Latin *Virgilius* (see VIRGIL) + the local suffix *-la*. This name is found chiefly in Ostrobothnia.
GIVEN NAMES Finnish 9%; German 4%. *Reino* (2), *Lempi, Urho, Vieno; Hannes*.

Wirkus (263) **1.** Lithuanian (**Virkus**): from derivative of a shortened form of the personal name *Virkavas* or *Virkovas*, or possibly from a derivative of Lithuanian *virkauti* 'to cry'. **2.** Polish: possibly a derivative of Polish dialect *wirk*, a derivative of *wierzch* 'top'.

Wirsing (227) German: nickname from Middle High German *wirsic* 'bad', 'evil', 'worse'.
GIVEN NAMES German 4%. *Klaus* (2), *Bernhard*.

Wirt (973) German: variant spelling of WIRTH.

Wirta (141) Finnish (**Virta**): from *virta* 'stream', used as a topographic name, also as a soldier's name in the 17th century. Also adopted as an ornamental name, especially in western and southern Finland.
GIVEN NAMES Finnish 6%. *Eino* (2), *Wilho*.

Wirtanen (255) Finnish (**Virtanen**): topographic or ornamental name from *virta* 'stream' + the common surname suffix *-nen*. This is the most common of all Finnish surnames.
GIVEN NAMES Finnish 4%. *Arvo, Irja, Onni, Toivo*.

Wirth (4378) **1.** German and Jewish (Ashkenazic): occupational name for an innkeeper, Middle High German *wirt*, German *Wirt*. **2.** German: status name for a man who was head of a family and master of his own household, from the same word in the sense 'provider'. **3.** German: from a short form of *Werdo*, from a Germanic personal name formed with *werd* 'worth' as the first element.
GIVEN NAMES German 5%. *Otto* (8), *Kurt* (7), *Hans* (5), *Erwin* (4), *Gunter* (3), *Dieter* (2), *Ernst* (2), *Gerhard* (2), *Manfred* (2), *Reinhold* (2), *Armin, Erna*.

Wirthlin (155) Swiss German: diminutive of WIRTH.

Wirtjes (114) Dutch: unexplained; perhaps an altered form of **Witjes**, a diminutive of WITTE 2.

Wirts (106) Respelling of German WIRTZ.

Wirtz (1608) German: **1.** from a pet form of the personal name *Wertwein*. **2.** patronymic from WIRTH 3.

Wirz (203) German: variant spelling of WIRTZ.
GIVEN NAMES German 5%. *Hans* (2), *Edeltraut, Ute, Willi*.

Wisbey (103) English: variant spelling of WISBY.

Wisby (162) English: habitational name from Whisby in Lincolnshire, named from the Old Norse personal name *Hvítr* + Old Norse *býr* 'farmstead', 'settlement'.

Wisch (208) North German: topographic name for someone who lived by a meadow, Middle Low German *wisch*, or a habitational name from any of several places so named, all in northern Germany.
GIVEN NAMES German 5%. *Lothar* (2), *Eldor*.

Wischer (110) **1.** German: nickname from an agent derivative of Middle High German *wischen* 'to rush'. **2.** North German: variant of WISCH.

Wischmeier (146) North German: variant of WISCHMEYER.

Wischmeyer (199) North German: distinguishing name for a tenant farmer (MEYER) whose farm was by a meadow (see WISCH).

Wiscombe (111) English (Devon): habitational name from a former place whose name survives in the name of Wiscombe Park, Southleigh, Devon.

Wisdom (2227) English: nickname for a wise or learned person, from Middle English *wisdom* 'wisdom'.

Wise (24145) **1.** English: nickname for a wise or learned person, or in some cases a nickname for someone suspected of being acquainted with the occult arts, from Middle English *wise* 'wise' (Old English *wīs*). This name has also absorbed Dutch **Wijs**, a nickname meaning 'wise', and possibly cognates in other languages. **2.** Americanized form of German and Jewish WEISS 'white'.

Wisecarver (382) Possibly an Americanized spelling of German WEISGERBER.

Wisecup (355) Possibly an Americanized spelling of German WEISKOPF.

Wisehart (317) **1.** Probably an Americanized spelling of German **Weisshardt**, from a Germanic personal name composed of the elements *wīs* 'wise' + *hart* 'strong', 'hard'. **2.** Perhaps an altered spelling of Scottish WISHART.

Wiseley (285) Variant spelling, found mostly in Ireland, of Scottish WISELY.

Wisell (121) Swedish: ornamental name from an unexplained first element (possibly from a place name) + the common surname suffix *-ell*.

Wisely (364) Scottish (Aberdeen): unexplained; most probably a habitational name from a lost or unidentified place.

Wiseman (7226) **1.** English and Scottish: nickname for a wise man, from WISE + *man* 'man'. **2.** Americanized spelling of German WEISMANN.

Wisenbaker (236) Americanized spelling of German **Weis(s)enbacher**, a variant of WEISENBACH or of WEISBECKER.

Wisener (461) Americanized spelling of German **Weis(s)ner**, **Wiesener**, **1.** habitational name from any of several places named Weissen, Weisenau, or Weissenau.

2. or of **Weissener**, an occupational name for an executioner or beadle, from Middle High German *wīzenaere*.

Wiser (1377) **1.** Spelling variant of WIESER. **2.** Probably an Americanized spelling of German WEISER.

Wish (225) **1.** English: topographic name for someone who lived by a water meadow or marsh, Middle English *wyshe* (Old English *wisc*). **2.** Americanized spelling of WISCH.

Wisham (197) Variant of English WORSHAM.

Wishard (358) **1.** variant of Scottish WISHART. **2.** Americanized spelling of German **Weisshardt** (see WISEHART).

Wishart (668) Scottish (of Norman origin): from the Anglo-Norman French form, *Wischard*, of the Old French personal name *Guiscard*. This was formed in Normandy from the Old Norse elements *viskr* 'wise' + *hard* 'hardy', 'brave', 'bold' (or possibly the Old French suffix *-ard*). Compare the French cognate **Guiscard**.

Wisher (228) Americanized spelling of WISCHER.

Wishner (148) Americanized spelling of German **Wischner**, a variant of WISCHER 2.

Wishon (452) Most probably a variant of English WORSHAM.

Wisinski (193) Polish (**Wisiński**): habitational name, possibly from Wisy in Kielce voivodeship.
GIVEN NAME Polish 4%. *Krzysztof*.

Wiskow (164) German: unexplained; probably a habitational name from Weskow in Brandenburg.
GIVEN NAMES German 4%. *Gerhart, Kurt*.

Wisler (508) Variant spelling of German **Wissler** (see WECHSLER).

Wisley (159) Variant of Scottish WISELY.

Wisman (258) Probably an Americanized spelling of North German **Wis(s)mann**, a variant of **Wischmann**, itself a variant of FISCHER.

Wismer (554) German: habitational name from any of various places named Wismer or Wismar, for example in Mecklenburg and Hesse.

Wisner (1632) **1.** German: habitational name for someone from any of various places named Wissen, mostly in the Rhineland, for example near Siegen. **2.** North German: variant of **Wischner**.

Wisneski (621) Variant of Polish WISNIEWSKI.

Wisnewski (328) Variant of Polish WISNIEWSKI.

Wisnieski (286) Polish (**Wiśnieski**): variant of WISNIEWSKI.

Wisniewski (4697) Polish (**Wiśniewski**): habitational name for someone from any of the many places in Poland called Wiśniewo, Wiśniew, or Wiśniewa, named with *wiśnia* 'cherry'.

GIVEN NAMES Polish 6%. *Tadeusz* (6), *Casimir* (3), *Dariusz* (3), *Janina* (3), *Janusz* (3), *Jerzy* (3), *Pawel* (3), *Wieslaw* (3), *Zbigniew* (3), *Zigmund* (3), *Andrzej* (2), *Boleslaw* (2).

Wisniowski (85) Polish (**Wiśniowski**): habitational name for someone from any of the many places in Poland called Wiśniowa or Wiśniowo, named with *wiśnia* 'cherry'.
GIVEN NAMES Polish 26%; German 4%. *Tadeusz* (2), *Bronislaw*, *Casimir*, *Jerzy*, *Jozef*, *Ludwik*, *Lukasz*, *Tomasz*, *Zygmunt*; *Kurt*.

Wisnoski (139) Variant of Polish WISNIOWSKI.

Wisor (308) Polish: from Polish dialect *wisor*, variant of *wisior* 'pendant', or from *wiszor* 'stamp'.

Wisowaty (102) Polish (also **Wiszowaty**): nickname or topographic name from Old Polish *wiszowaty* 'slender', 'stalk-like'.

Wiss (289) **1.** German: variant of WEISS. **2.** North German: nickname for a sure, reliable person, from Middle Low German *wisse* 'sure', 'reliable'.
GIVEN NAMES French 4%. *Amie*, *Lucien*.

Wisse (140) German: **1.** variant of WIESE. **2.** variant of WISS.
GIVEN NAMES German 4%. *Horst*, *Kurt*.

Wissel (354) German: habitational name from a place so named.

Wisser (300) German: **1.** variant of WISCHER 2. **2.** variant of WISNER.

Wissing (268) German: habitational name from Wissingen near Osnabrück or Wissing in Bavaria.

Wissinger (450) German: habitational name for someone from Wissingen or Wissing (see WISSING).

Wissink (218) North German: variant of WISSING.

Wissler (421) **1.** German: variant of WECHSLER. **2.** German: habitational name for someone from Weisel near Friedberg, formerly called *Wissele*. **3.** English: variant spelling of WHISTLER.

Wissman (417) Americanized spelling of German WISSMANN.
GIVEN NAMES German 4%. *Kurt* (3), *Guenter*, *Otto*.

Wissmann (196) German: **1.** nickname from Middle High German, Middle Low German *wis* 'sure', 'safe', 'reliable'. **2.** variant of WISSE, with the addition of Middle Low German *man* 'man'. **3.** variant of WEISEMANN.
GIVEN NAMES German 9%. *Hans*, *Kurt*, *Rudi*, *Siegfried*, *Ulrich*.

Wissner (204) Variant of German WISNER.
GIVEN NAMES German 6%. *Kurt* (2), *Horst*.

Wist (169) **1.** North German: habitational name from any of several places named Wiste in Lower Saxony. **2.** Swedish: probably from a place named Vist or a place name formed with this as the first element.
GIVEN NAME German 6%. *Uwe* (3).

Wistrom (125) Swedish (**Wiström**, **Viström**): ornamental name from Old Norse *viðr* 'forest' + *ström* 'river'.
GIVEN NAME Scandinavian 13%. *Oyvind* (2).

Wiswall (140) English: variant spelling of WISWELL.

Wiswell (384) English: habitational name from Wiswell in Lancashire, named from Old English *wisc* 'marshy meadow' + *wella* 'spring', 'stream'.

Wisz (154) **1.** Polish: from a pet form of *Wisław*, *Wiktor*, or another personal name beginning with *Wi-*. **2.** Polish: topographic name from *wisz* 'thicket'. **3.** Variant of German WISS.

Witbeck (227) Dutch and North German: habitational name from a place named Wittbek in Schleswig-Holstein, formed with *wit* 'white' + *beck* 'stream'.
FOREBEARS This name is recorded in Beverwijck in New Netherland (Albany, NY) in the mid 17th century.
GIVEN NAMES German 6%. *Kurt* (2), *Otto*.

Witcher (1545) English: **1.** occupational name for a chest maker, from an agent derivative of Old English *hwicce* 'chest'. **2.** from an agent derivative of Middle English *wiche* 'settlement', 'farmstead' (Old English *wīc*), hence an occupational name for a dairy farmer or a habitational name for someone who lived at a place called Wich or Wick. **3.** topographic name Middle English *wyche* 'wych-elm' + *hey* 'enclosure'.

Witchey (143) Americanized spelling of Swiss German **Witschy**, **Witschi**, a variant of **Witzsche**, itself a variant of WITZ.
GIVEN NAME German 4%. *Kurt* (2).

Witcraft (107) English: unexplained.

Witczak (239) Polish: patronymic from WITEK.
GIVEN NAMES Polish 10%. *Boleslaw*, *Leszek*, *Ryszard*, *Tadeusz*, *Wieslaw*, *Wlodzimierz*, *Zbigniew*.

Witek (508) Polish: **1.** from the personal name *Wit*, a short form of *Witold*, a derivative of Lithuanian *Vytautas*, a compound of *vyti* 'to guide' + *tauta* 'the people'. **2.** from a pet form of another personal name *Wit* with a different etymology, namely a derivative of Latin *Vitus*, from *vita* 'life'. Compare Italian VITO.
GIVEN NAMES Polish 10%. *Casimir* (2), *Mariusz* (2), *Andrzej*, *Boguslaw*, *Bronislaw*, *Danuta*, *Ireneusz*, *Janina*, *Jerzy*, *Kazimierz*, *Ludwik*, *Malgorzata*.

With (122) **1.** English: variant of WYTHE. **2.** German spelling of the Slavic personal name *Wit* (see WITEK). **3.** Danish and Norwegian: nickname for a broad man, from *wiidh* 'broad', or for a pale or fair-haired person, from German *weiss* 'white'.
GIVEN NAME Scandinavian 10%. *Erik* (3).

Witham (1671) English: habitational name from any of various places so called. North and South Witham in Lincolnshire derive the name from the river on which they stand, which is of ancient British origin and uncertain meaning. Witham on the Hill in Lincolnshire, along with other examples in Essex and Somerset, was probably originally named with an Old English byname *Wit(t)a* (presumably from *wit(t)* 'wits', 'mind') + Old English *hām* 'homestead'. However, the first element may instead have been Old English *wiht* 'bend'.

Withee (351) Altered spelling of English WITHEY.

Withem (232) English: variant spelling of WITHAM.

Witherbee (108) Variant spelling of English WEATHERBY.

Witherell (550) English: variant spelling of WETHERELL.

Witherington (360) English: habitational name from Witherington Down or Witherington Farm in Wiltshire, or Witherenden in Ticehurst, Sussex. The Wiltshire places are named from an Old English *wīðign* 'willow copse' + Old English *tūn* 'settlement'. Witherenden is from the Old English personal name *Wither* + *-ing-* denoting association with + *denn* 'woodland pasture'.

Witherite (133) Origin unidentified.

Witherow (564) English (Cambridgeshire) and Scottish: unexplained. Possibly a variant of WETHERELL.

Withers (3957) English: patronymic from the Old Norse personal name *Viðarr*, composed of the elements *víðr* 'wide' + *ar* 'warrior'.

Witherspoon (3411) Scottish: of uncertain origin, perhaps a habitational name from an unidentified place named with Middle English *wether* 'sheep', 'ram' + *spong*, *spang*, a dialect term for a narrow strip of land.
FOREBEARS John Witherspoon (1723–94), Presbyterian minister and teacher, was a signer of the Declaration of Independence. He was born at Gifford, near Edinburgh, Scotland, and came to North America in 1768 after being recruited as president of the College of New Jersey (now Princeton University).

Withey (484) English: topographic name for someone who lived by a willow tree, Middle English *withy* (Old English *wīðig*).

Withington (410) English: habitational name from any of several places called Withington. The majority, including those in Cheshire, Herefordshire, Lancashire, and Shropshire, are named from an unattested Old English *wīðign* 'willow copse' + *tūn* 'enclosure', 'settlement'; Withington in Gloucestershire appears in Domesday Book as *Widindune*, from the genitive case of an Old English personal name *Widia* + Old English *dūn* 'hill'.

Withrow (2920) English: probably a reduced form of WITHEROW.

Witkin (293) Jewish (eastern Ashkenazic): metronymic from the Yiddish female personal name *Vitke*, a pet form of *Vite* (of

Slavic origin) + the eastern Slavic possessive suffix *-in*.

GIVEN NAMES Jewish 7%. *Miriam* (2), *Mordecai, Yehoshua, Zelig*.

Witko (135) **1.** Polish and Ukrainian: from a pet form of the personal names *Witold* or *Wit* (see WITEK). **2.** Ukrainian: from the personal name *Vytko*, a pet form of *Vyktir*, Ukrainian form of VICTOR.

GIVEN NAMES Polish 5%. *Stanislaw, Zbigniew*.

Witkop (179) North German: variant spelling of WITTKOPP.

Witkowski (2173) Polish: habitational name for someone from any of the places in Poland called Witkowo, Witków, or Witkowice, named with the personal name WITEK.

GIVEN NAMES Polish 5%. *Ignatius* (4), *Tadeusz* (4), *Casimir* (3), *Krzysztof* (3), *Andrzej* (2), *Jerzy* (2), *Stanislaw* (2), *Aleksander, Dorota, Eugeniusz, Halina, Jacek*.

Witman (586) Variant spelling of English WHITMAN or an Americanized spelling of German WITTMANN.

Witmer (2321) Variant spelling of German WITTMER.

Witowski (129) Polish: habitational name for someone from any of the places in Poland called Witowice, Witowo, or Witów, named with the personal name *Witold* or *Wit* (see WITEK).

GIVEN NAMES Polish 7%; German 5%. *Pawel, Ryszard*; *Kurt*.

Witt (12552) **1.** North German: nickname for someone with white hair or a remarkably pale complexion, from a Middle Low German *witte* 'white'. **2.** South German: from a short form of the old German personal name *Wittigo*. **3.** English: variant of WHITE.

Wittbrodt (110) North German form of WEISBROT.

GIVEN NAMES Polish 5%. *Jadwiga, Mariusz*.

Witte (4057) **1.** North German: variant of WITT 1. **2.** Dutch: nickname for someone with white or blonde hair or an unusually pale complexion, from Middle Dutch *witte* 'white'. **3.** English: variant of WHITE.

GIVEN NAMES German 4%. *Otto* (6), *Franz* (5), *Kurt* (5), *Erwin* (4), *Gerhard* (3), *Dieter* (2), *Egon* (2), *Fritz* (2), *Gerhart* (2), *Lorenz* (2), *Eldor, Erhart*.

Wittek (111) Germanized form of a Slavic personal name (see WITEK).

GIVEN NAMES German 11%. *Egon, Hans George, Hilde, Volker, Willi*.

Wittekind (164) North German: variant of WEDEKIND.

Witteman (151) North German and Dutch: variant of WITTE.

Witten (1093) North German: patronymic from WITTE.

Wittenauer (161) German: habitational name from any of several places so named.

Wittenberg (1224) North German: habitational name for someone from a place called Wittenberg, Wittenberge, or Wittenbergen.

GIVEN NAMES German 4%. *Erwin* (4), *Kurt* (3), *Armin, Deiter, Joerg, Lauritz, Ralf, Wolf*.

Wittenborn (149) North German: habitational name from any of several places so named, for example near Bad Segeberg and near Neubrandenburg.

GIVEN NAME German 4%. *Otto*.

Wittenburg (263) North German: habitational name from any of various places called Wittenburg.

Wittenmyer (170) Variant of German WITT-MEYER.

Witter (1522) **1.** German: from a Germanic personal name, composed of the elements *widu* 'wood' + *hari* 'army'. **2.** North German: occupational name for a painter or plasterer, from Middle Low German *witten* 'to make white'.

Witters (337) German: patronymic from WITTER 1.

Witthoft (113) North German (**Witthöft**): nickname for someone with white hair, from Middle Low German *wit(t)* 'white' + *höft* 'head'.

Witthuhn (200) North German: metonymic occupational name for a poultry farmer or dealer, or a nickname for someone thought to resemble a chicken in some way, from Middle Low German *witte* 'white' + *hōn* 'chicken'.

GIVEN NAMES German 8%. *Wilfried* (4), *Gerhard, Heinz*.

Wittich (252) German: variant of WITTIG.

GIVEN NAMES German 9%. *Bernd* (2), *Gunther* (2), *Arno, Gerhard, Guenter*.

Wittie (104) English: variant of WITTY.

Wittig (973) German: **1.** from the personal name *Wittich*, from a short form of a Germanic name beginning with *widu* 'wood'. **2.** nickname from Middle Low German *wittich* 'clever', 'wise'.

GIVEN NAMES German 5%. *Arno* (2), *Gunter* (2), *Hans* (2), *Kurt* (2), *Erwin, Frieda, Lutz*.

Witting (231) **1.** English: patronymic from WHITE. **2.** North German: habitational name from a place named Wittingen, near Braunschweig. **3.** North German: patronymic from WITT 1.

Wittkamp (105) German: habitational name from a place so named near Münster, Westphalia.

GIVEN NAMES German 7%. *Gerhard, Uwe*.

Wittke (212) German: **1.** from a pet form of WITTIG or WITTE. **2.** from a pet form of a Slavic personal name such as *Vitoslav*.

GIVEN NAMES German 12%. *Ernst* (2), *Rudi* (2), *Erna, Erwin, Heinz, Joerg, Kurt, Reinhard, Waltraut*.

Wittkop (144) Dutch and North German: variant of WITTKOPP.

Wittkopf (106) North German: partly standardized form of Low German WITTKOPP.

GIVEN NAME German 4%. *Dieter*.

Wittkopp (144) North German: Low German form of WEISKOPF, from Middle Low German *wit(t)* 'white' + *kop* 'head', a nickname for a white-haired man.

GIVEN NAMES German 4%. *Otto*.

Wittler (229) German: variant of WITTWER.

GIVEN NAMES German 5%. *Kurt* (3), *Erwin*.

Wittlin (113) Jewish (eastern Ashkenazic): name from the Yiddish female personal name *Vitle*, a pet form of *Vite* (compare WITKIN) + the eastern Slavic possessive suffix *-in*.

GIVEN NAME Jewish 7%. *Meyer*.

Wittlinger (120) German: habitational name for someone from either of two places in Baden-Württemberg named Wittlingen.

GIVEN NAMES German 4%. *Fritz, Gerda*.

Wittman (1891) **1.** English: variant of WHITMAN. **2.** Altered spelling of German WITTMANN.

Wittmann (651) German: **1.** occupational name from Middle Low German *witman* 'council member'. **2.** from a short form of the personal name WITTICH + Middle Higher German *man* 'man'.

GIVEN NAMES German 9%. *Erwin* (2), *Heinz* (2), *Wolfgang* (2), *Aloysius, Dieter, Dietmar, Edeltraud, Franz, Guenter, Horst, Juergen, Markus*.

Wittmayer (143) Variant spelling of German and French (Alsatian) WITTMEYER.

Wittmer (665) German: **1.** from the Germanic personal name *Wittimar*, composed of the elements *widu* 'wood', 'forest' + *marī* 'famous'. **2.** habitational name from a place so named near Wolfenbüttel.

Wittmeyer (231) German and French (Alsace): **1.** distinguishing name for a tenant farmer (see MEYER) who lived by a wood or copse (Middle High German *wite*).

2. possibly also a variant of WIDMEYER.

Wittner (277) German: habitational name for someone from any of several places named Witten, for example in the Ruhr.

GIVEN NAME German 4%. *Helmuth*.

Wittrock (637) North German and Dutch: from Middle Low German *witte* 'white', Middle Dutch *wit(te)* + Middle Low German *rok* 'jacket', Middle Dutch *roc(k)*, presumably applied as a nickname for someone who habitually wore a white jacket.

Wittry (140) **1.** Belgian French: habitational name from Witry in Luxembourg province, Belgium. **2.** Perhaps a variant of French **Guitry** (see **Guidry**).

Witts (187) **1.** Dutch: patronymic from the Germanic personal name *Wido*. **2.** English: patronymic from WITT. **3.** Probably an Americanized spelling of German WITZ, cognate with 1.

Wittstock (115) North German: habitational name from any of several places so named, for instance north of Berlin.
GIVEN NAME Scandinavian 5%. *Ove* (2).

Wittstruck (114) Dutch and North German: topographic name for someone who lived near a willow underbrush, from Low German *wīde* + *struck* (High German *Strauch*) 'bush'.

Wittwer (575) German: nickname from Middle High German *witewer* 'widower'.
GIVEN NAMES German 4%. *Erwin* (2), *Bodo*, *Fritz*, *Matthias*, *Otto*.

Witty (781) English: nickname for a bright or inventive person, from Middle English *witty* 'clever', 'ingenious'. It is possible that some early examples may represent a survival into Middle English of Old English *wītega* 'soothsayer', and there may also have been some confusion with WHITTY.

Witucki (276) Polish: variant of WITULSKI.

Witulski (111) Polish: habitational name for someone from either of two places called Witulin, in Bielsko-Biała or Kielce provinces.

Witwer (322) German: variant spelling of WITTWER.

Witz (346) German: **1.** from the medieval personal name *Witzo*, a short form of any of several Germanic compound names beginning with *wīg* 'battle'. **2.** variant of WITZIG.

Witzel (701) German: variant of WETZEL.
GIVEN NAMES German 5%. *Hans* (2), *Fritz*, *Heinz*, *Kurt*, *Otto*, *Rudi*.

Witzig (180) German: nickname from Middle High German *witzic* 'clever', 'prudent', 'knowing'.
GIVEN NAMES German 6%. *Kurt*, *Otto*.

Witzke (435) Eastern German (under Slavic influence): from a pet form of a Slavic personal name.
GIVEN NAMES German 5%. *Horst* (2), *Bernhardt*, *Klaus*, *Reinhold*.

Witzman (115) German (**Witzmann**): from the medieval personal name *Witzeman*, a pet form of *Witzo* (see WITZ 1).

Wivell (161) **1.** English (Devon and Cornwall): according to Reaney a habitational name of Norman origin, from Gouville in Eure, France, recorded earlier as *Wivilla*, but possibly from the Old English personal name *Wifel* or the vocabulary word *wifel* 'weevil', 'beetle'. **2.** Danish: habitational name from the place name Vivild.

Wix (650) English: variant spelling of WICKS.

Wixom (395) English: unexplained. Probably an altered form of WIXON (see WICKSON).

Wixon (291) English: variant spelling of WICKSON.

Wixson (425) English: variant spelling of WICKSON.

Wixted (167) English: habitational name from Wickstead, a place in Cheshire, or Wicksted Farm in Highworth, Wiltshire, both named from Old English *wīc-stede* 'dwelling place', 'habitation'.

Wiygul (116) Probably a variant, under Slavic influence, of German WEIGEL or WIEGEL.

Wiza (157) Americanized form of German WEISER.

Wizner (120) Americanized form of German WEISNER.

Wlodarczyk (272) Polish (**Włodarczyk**): occupational name or status name from a diminutive of *włodarz* 'steward', a derivative of *włodać* 'to govern or rule'.
GIVEN NAMES Polish 24%. *Ryszard* (3), *Janina* (2), *Malgorzata* (2), *Piotr* (2), *Urszula* (2), *Waclaw* (2), *Beata*, *Bogdan*, *Boguslaw*, *Halina*, *Jerzy*, *Jozef*.

Wlodarski (131) Polish (**Włodarski**): **1.** habitational name for someone from Włodary in Opole voivodeship, named with Polish *włodarz* 'steward'. **2.** occupational name for a steward, from Polish *włodarz* (see WLODARCZYK), with the addition of the (originally local) suffix of surnames *-ski*.
GIVEN NAMES Polish 17%. *Andrzej*, *Beata*, *Halina*, *Jerzy*, *Krzysztof*, *Maciej*, *Wojciech*, *Wojtek*, *Zbigniew*.

Wnek (325) Polish (**Wnęk**): from Old Polish *wnęk* 'grandson' (see WNUK).
GIVEN NAMES Polish 7%. *Andrzej* (2), *Agnieszka*, *Janusz*, *Leszek*, *Malgorzata*, *Thadeus*.

Wnorowski (115) Polish: habitational name for someone from places called Wnorów in Tarnobrzeg voivodeship or Wnory in Łomża voivodeship, named with the Old Polish personal name *Wnor*.
GIVEN NAMES Polish 20%. *Tadeusz* (2), *Mieczyslaw*, *Ryszard*, *Stanislaw*, *Wieslaw*, *Zbigniew*.

Wnuk (380) Polish: from *wnuk* 'grandson', possibly a name for someone who was brought up by his grandparents after losing his parents.
GIVEN NAMES Polish 15%. *Stanislaw* (4), *Dorota* (2), *Elzbieta* (2), *Janusz* (2), *Bernadeta*, *Bogdan*, *Boguslaw*, *Casimir*, *Faustyn*, *Halina*, *Ignacy*, *Janina*.

Wobbe (151) North German: from a short form of various Germanic compound names.

Wobig (168) North German: habitational name from a place so named near Stettin (Polish Szczecin).
GIVEN NAMES German 6%. *Fritz*, *Kurt*.

Wobschall (122) German: unexplained.

Wodarski (130) Polish: **1.** possibly a dialect variant of **Włodarski** (see WLODARSKI). **2.** nickname from Polish *wodarz* 'waterman', with the addition of the common surname suffix *-ski*.

GIVEN NAMES Polish 9%. *Casimir*, *Czeslaw*, *Ignatius*, *Zigmond*.

Wodrich (136) North German: unflattering nickname from Middle Low German *woderik* 'madman', 'tyrant'.
GIVEN NAMES German 4%. *Helmut*, *Kurt*.

Wodzinski (93) Polish (**Wodziński**): habitational name for someone from Wodzin in Piotrków voivodeship, named with Polish *woda* 'water.'
GIVEN NAMES Polish 10%. *Jaroslaw*, *Zbigniew*, *Zigmund*.

Woehl (217) South German (also **Wöhl**): variant of **Wölke** (see WOLKE 1).
GIVEN NAMES German 5%. *Reinhold* (2), *Otto*.

Woehler (258) German: variant spelling of **Wöhler** (see WOHLER).

Woehr (177) German: variant spelling of **Wöhr**, from a short form of a Germanic personal name beginning with *war* or *wer*, of various origins.
GIVEN NAME German 6%. *Ekkehard*.

Woehrle (241) South German: Alemannic variant of WEHRLE.

Woelfel (799) German (also **Wölfel**): from a pet form of the personal name WOLF or any of the compound names beginning with this element.
GIVEN NAMES German 4%. *Ernst* (3), *Erwin* (2), *Erna*, *Florian*, *Kurt*, *Othmar*, *Ulrike*.

Woelfle (187) German (also **Wölfle**): variant of WOELFEL.
GIVEN NAMES German 4%. *Hans*, *Kurt*, *Wilhelm*.

Woelk (170) German: variant spelling of **Wölk** (see WOLK).
GIVEN NAMES German 6%. *Erwin*, *Helmut*, *Klaus*, *Reinhold*.

Woelke (114) German: variant spelling of **Wölke**, itself a variant of WOLK.
GIVEN NAMES German 18%. *Gerhard* (2), *Friedhelm*, *Heinz*, *Jurgen*, *Kurt*, *Reinhard*, *Rudi*.

Woerner (1139) German (also **Wörner**): variant of WERNER.
GIVEN NAMES German 6%. *Kurt* (3), *Otto* (3), *Hans* (2), *Erwin*, *Guenther*, *Helmut*, *Wilhelm*, *Wilhelmine*, *Wolfgang*.

Woertz (105) German: variant of **Würtz** (see WURTZ).

Woessner (551) German (also **Wössner**): see WESSNER.
GIVEN NAMES German 4%. *Erwin*, *Gerhard*, *Heinz*, *Otto*, *Ruediger*.

Woeste (228) German: from Middle Low German *wōste* 'void', 'bare', probably a topographic name for someone who lived on barren unfertile ground.

Wofford (2953) English: variant of WOLFORD.

Wogan (272) Irish (of Welsh (Pembrokeshire) origin): from the Old Welsh personal name *Gwgan*, *Gwgon*, originally a byname, probably a diminutive of *gwg* 'scowl', i.e. 'Little Scowler'. Compare CADOGAN. A family of this name settled in County

Kildare following the Anglo-Norman invasion of the 12th century.
GIVEN NAME French 4%. *Andre* (2).

Wogoman (139) Americanized spelling of German **Wagemann** (see WAGEMAN).

Wohl (922) **1.** German: nickname from Middle High German, Middle Low German *wol* 'pleasant'. **2.** North German: topographic name from Middle Low German *wolt* 'wood'. **3.** Jewish (Ashkenazic): ornamental name adopted in a spirit of optimism, from modern German *Wohl* 'well-being'.
GIVEN NAMES German 4%. *Hellmut* (2), *Georg, Helmuth, Kurt, Theodor*.

Wohlberg (130) Jewish (Ashkenazic): ornamental name composed of German *Wohl* 'well-being' + *Berg* 'mountain', 'hill'.
GIVEN NAMES Jewish 5%. *Miriam* (2), *Myers*.

Wohler (345) North German (**Wöhler**): from the personal name *Wolder*, Low German form of WALTER.
GIVEN NAMES German 6%. *Kurt* (3), *Ernst, Ewald, Gerhard, Hans*.

Wohlers (541) North German: patronymic from WOHLER.

Wohlert (131) North German: from the Germanic personal name form *Wolhart*, composed of the elements *wol* 'well' + *hard* 'hardy', 'strong'.
GIVEN NAMES German 9%. *Kurt* (2), *Deiter*.

Wohlfarth (197) **1.** German: nickname from Middle High German, Middle Low German *wolvert* 'well-being', 'health'. **2.** German: variant of WOLFERT.
GIVEN NAMES German 11%; Scandinavian 5%. *Kurt* (3), *Armin, Guenter, Hans, Maximilian; Erik* (2).

Wohlfeil (164) German: occupational nickname for a merchant or trader, from Middle High German, Middle Low German *wol veil* 'worth the price', 'good value'.
GIVEN NAMES German 5%. *Erwin, Gerhard, Margarethe*.

Wohlford (480) Americanized form of German WOHLFARTH.

Wohlgemuth (541) German and Jewish (Ashkenazic): nickname or Jewish ornamental name, from (respectively) Middle High German *wolgemuot* and German *Wohlgemut* 'cheerful'.
GIVEN NAMES German 6%. *Kurt* (3), *Otto* (2), *Dietmar, Ernst, Franz, Klaus, Willi*.

Wohlman (122) German (**Wohlmann**) and Jewish (Ashkenazic): nickname from Middle High German, Middle Low German *wol* 'pleasant', or from modern German *Wohl* 'well-being' (see WOHL), with the addition of Middle High German, Yiddish *mann* 'man'.
GIVEN NAMES German 5%. *Kurt, Otto*.

Wohlrab (104) North German: **1.** habitational name from any of various places named Wallrath or Wallroth (for example in Hesse) **2.** alternatively, from a personal name formed with Middle Low German

wal-rav(e) 'raven of the battle field' (see WALRAVEN).
GIVEN NAMES German 4%. *Gertrud, Hartmut*.

Wohlwend (227) South German: possibly a nickname for a lucky person, from Middle High German *wol* 'well' + *wende* 'turn', 'return'.

Woida (144) Polish (also **Wojda**): from a derivative of any of various Slavic compound personal names beginning with *Woj-*, for example *Wojciech* and *Wojsław*.

Woitas (115) Altered spelling of Polish WOJTAS. This form is established in German-speaking lands.
GIVEN NAMES German 6%. *Gerhard, Gunther*.

Wojack (111) Altered form of Polish **Wojak**, a derivative of the personal name *Wojciech* (see VOYTEK).

Wojahn (227) German: from a Slavic personal name *Woj-ahn*, from *voj* 'man'.
GIVEN NAMES German 6%. *Otto* (2), *Armin*.

Wojciak (213) Polish: **1.** patronymic from the personal name *Wojciech* (see VOYTEK). **2.** patronymic from the status name *wójt* 'village headman' (see WOJCIK).
GIVEN NAMES Polish 10%. *Ewa* (2), *Andrzej, Grazyna, Jacek, Jadwiga, Jozef, Krystyna, Wincenty*.

Wojcicki (271) Polish (**Wójcicki**): habitational name for someone from a place called Wójcice in Sieradz voivodeship.
GIVEN NAMES Polish 12%. *Zbigniew* (2), *Casimir, Czeslawa, Henryka, Janusz, Jerzy, Jozef, Ryszard, Wieslawa, Zigmunt*.

Wojciechowski (1781) Polish: habitational name for someone from any of several places called Wojciechowo or Wojciechów, named with the personal name *Wojciech* (see VOYTEK).
GIVEN NAMES Polish 8%. *Andrzej* (5), *Jerzy* (3), *Beata* (2), *Casimir* (2), *Krzysztof* (2), *Tomasz* (2), *Zbigniew* (2), *Darek, Genowesa, Grzegorz, Janina, Janusz*.

Wojciehowski (111) Polish: variant of WOJCIECHOWSKI.
GIVEN NAMES Polish 5%. *Danuta, Leszek*.

Wojcik (2874) Polish **1.** (**Wójcik**) from a diminutive of **Wójt**, a status name from Polish *wójt* 'village headman', a borrowing of German VOGT. **2.** from a pet form of the personal name *Wojciech* (see VOYTEK).
GIVEN NAMES Polish 10%. *Casimir* (7), *Jerzy* (4), *Kazimierz* (4), *Krzysztof* (4), *Tadeusz* (4), *Andrzej* (3), *Irena* (3), *Krystyna* (3), *Waclaw* (3), *Wojciech* (3), *Zofia* (3), *Zygmunt* (3).

Wojcinski (94) Polish (**Wójciński**): habitational name for someone from any of the many places called Wójcin, or from Wójcina in Tarnów voivodeship, named with *wójt* 'village headman'.

Wojdyla (212) Polish (**Wojdyła**): variant of the personal name *Wojtyła*, a derivative of *Wojciech*, a personal name composed with the element *woj* 'warrior' (see VOYTEK).

GIVEN NAMES Polish 13%. *Waclaw* (2), *Casimir, Czeslawa, Krzysztof, Malgorzata, Pawel, Sylwester, Tadeusz, Zbigniew*.

Wojewoda (69) Polish: nickname or status name from Polish *wojewoda* 'voivode', title of a provincial administrator or governor.
GIVEN NAMES Polish 18%. *Zygmunt* (2), *Andrzej, Ireneusz, Jarek, Zdzislaw*.

Wojick (141) Polish: from a pet form of the personal name *Wojciech* (see VOYTEK).

Wojnar (331) Polish: **1.** occupational name for a warrior or nickname for an aggressive man, from Polish *wojna* 'fight'. **2.** Polonicized form of German WAGNER.
GIVEN NAMES Polish 8%. *Casimir, Czeslaw, Danuta, Ewa, Karol, Tadeusz, Zbigniew*.

Wojnarowski (165) Polish: habitational name for someone from a place called Wojnarowa in Nowy Sącz voivodeship.
GIVEN NAMES Polish 4%. *Agnieszka, Ludwika*.

Wojno (110) Polish: derivative of *wojna* 'fight'.
GIVEN NAMES Polish 15%. *Casimir, Elzbieta, Krzysztof, Maciej, Ryszard, Wieslaw*.

Wojnowski (164) Polish: habitational name for someone from any of various places called Wojnowice, Wojnowo, or Wojnów.
GIVEN NAMES Polish 6%. *Leszek, Mikolaj, Rajmund*.

Wojtalewicz (104) Polish: patronymic from the personal name *Wojtala* (see WOJDYLA).
GIVEN NAMES Polish 6%. *Jacek, Zbigniew*.

Wojtas (248) Polish (also **Wojtaś**): from a pet form of the personal name *Wojciech* (see VOYTEK).
GIVEN NAMES Polish 12%. *Andrzej* (2), *Danuta, Henryka, Iwona, Jozef, Karol, Lucyna, Ludwik, Piotr, Tadeusz, Wieslaw, Zbigniew*.

Wojtaszek (211) Polish: from a pet form of the personal name *Wojciech* (see VOYTEK).
GIVEN NAMES Polish 10%. *Jozef* (2), *Andrzej, Casimir, Henryk, Ignatius, Piotr, Tadeusz*.

Wojtczak (122) Polish: patronymic from *Wojtek*, a pet form of the personal name *Wojciech* (see VOYTEK).
GIVEN NAMES Polish 15%. *Janusz* (2), *Bogdan, Jacek, Jadwiga, Krystyna, Krzysztof*.

Wojtkiewicz (145) Polish: patronymic from *Wojtek*, a pet form of the personal name *Wojciech* (see VOYTEK).
GIVEN NAMES Polish 5%. *Casimir, Wladyslaw*.

Wojtkowiak (105) Polish: patronymic from *Wojtek*, a pet form of the personal name *Wojciech* (see VOYTEK).

Wojtkowski (173) Polish: habitational name for someone from a place called Wojtkowa in Krosno voivodeship, Wojtkowice in Łomża voivodeship, or Wojtków in Częstochowa voivodeship.
GIVEN NAMES Polish 16%. *Tadeusz* (2), *Andrzej, Boguslaw, Gerzy, Jacek, Lucyna, Maciej, Tomasz, Zigmund*.

Wojton (139) Polish (also **Wojtoń**): **1.** derivative of the personal name *Wojciech* (see VOYTEK). **2.** derivative of *wójt* 'village headman' (see WOJCIK).
GIVEN NAMES Polish 7%. *Tadeusz, Zigmund.*

Wojtowicz (849) Polish: **1.** patronymic from the personal name name *Wojciech* (see VOYTEK). **2.** patronymic from *wójt* 'village headman' (see WOJCIK).
GIVEN NAMES Polish 11%. *Andrzej* (2), *Jacek* (2), *Janina* (2), *Ryszard* (2), *Stanislaw* (2), *Beata, Boguslaw, Czeslaw, Dorota, Ewa, Grzegorz, Halina.*

Wojtysiak (101) Polish: **1.** patronymic from *Wojtys*, a pet form of the personal name *Wojciech* (see VOYTEK). **2.** patronymic from *wójt* 'village headman' (see WOJCIK).
GIVEN NAMES Polish 9%. *Jerzy, Krystyna.*

Wolak (534) Polish: patronymic from a short form of *Wolimir* or some other personal name formed with *woli-*, a derivative of *woleć* 'to want' or of *wola* 'will'.
GIVEN NAMES Polish 7%. *Ludwik* (2), *Andrzej, Casimir, Genowefa, Janusz, Jaroslaw, Kazimierz, Krzysztof, Piotr, Teofil.*

Wolan (134) Polish: derivative of *Wolimir* or some other personal name formed with the elements *woli* 'to want', or from *wola* 'will' (from *woleć* 'to prefer').

Wolanin (178) Polish: habitational name for someone from any of various places called Wola, named with the personal name WOLAN.
GIVEN NAMES Polish 10%. *Grzegorz* (2), *Feliks, Halina, Janina, Zdzislaw.*

Wolanski (199) Polish: habitational name for someone from any of various places called Wola or Wolany, named with the personal name WOLAN.
GIVEN NAMES Polish 7%. *Zygmunt* (2), *Ignacy, Zbigniew.*

Wolaver (188) Of English origin: probably a variant of either GULLIVER or OLIVER.

Wolbach (120) German: habitational name from a place named with *bach* 'stream' as the last element.

Wolber (245) German (also **Wölber**): from a Germanic personal name composed of the elements *wolf* 'wolf' or *walt* 'power', 'might' + *bero* 'bear'.
GIVEN NAME German 4%. *Erwin* (3).

Wolberg (117) Jewish (Ashkenazic): **1.** variant of WOHLBERG. **2.** ornamental name from German *Wolle* 'wool' + *Berg* 'hill'.
GIVEN NAMES Jewish 8%. *Hyman, Moshe.*

Wolbers (112) German: patronymic from WOLBER.

Wolbert (493) German: from a Germanic personal name composed of the elements *wolf* 'wolf' or *walt* 'power', 'might' + *berht* 'bright'.

Wolcott (2373) English: habitational name for someone from Woolcot in Somerset, possibly so named from Middle English *wolle* 'spring', 'stream' + *cot* 'cottage', 'shelter'.
FOREBEARS Henry Wolcott (1578–1655), clothier, came from Tolland, Somerset, England, and settled in Windsor, CT, in 1636. His grandson Roger (1679–1767) was colonial governor of CT; his great-grandson Oliver (1726–1797) was a signer of the Declaration of Independence.

Wold (2491) **1.** Norwegian: variant spelling of **Vold** (see VOLL). **2.** English: topographic name for someone who lived on any of the areas of open upland known from Middle English times onwards as *wolds* (e.g. the Yorkshire Wolds or the Cotswolds). This term derives from Old English *wald* 'forest' (see WALD). After the extensive clearance of forests in England, from before the Norman Conquest onward, the Old English term *wald* came to denote open uplands (*wolds*) in Middle English in certain areas of England.
GIVEN NAMES Scandinavian 4%. *Lars* (2), *Alf, Dagny, Erik, Johan, Juel, Thor.*

Wolden (217) **1.** Norwegian: spelling variant of VOLDEN. **2.** English: variant of WALDEN.

Woldt (311) German: from a short form of WALTER.
GIVEN NAMES German 4%. *Alfons, Erwin, Otto.*

Wolek (107) Polish (also **Wołek**): **1.** from a pet form of a personal name such as *Wolimir* (see WOLAK). **2.** nickname from *wołek* 'little bullock', or possibly an occupational name for someone who looked after bullocks.
GIVEN NAMES Polish 21%. *Jozef* (2), *Boleslaw, Halina, Janusz, Krzysztof, Lech, Stanislaw.*

Woleslagle (105) Americanized form of South German **Wollschlegel** (see WOLLSCHLAGER).

Wolever (134) Of English origin: probably a variant of either GULLIVER or OLIVER.

Wolf (29596) **1.** English, Danish, and German: from a short form of the various Germanic compound names with a first element *wolf* 'wolf', or a byname or nickname with this meaning. The wolf was native throughout the forests of Europe, including Britain, until comparatively recently. In ancient and medieval times it played an important role in Germanic mythology, being regarded as one of the sacred beasts of Woden. This name is widespread throughout northern, central, and eastern Europe, as well as in Britain and German-speaking countries. **2.** German: habitational name for someone living at a house distinguished by the sign of a wolf, Middle High German *wolf*. **3.** Jewish (Ashkenazic): from the Yiddish male personal name *Volf* meaning 'wolf', which is associated with the Hebrew personal name *Binyamin* (see BENJAMIN). This association stems from Jacob's dying words 'Benjamin shall ravin as a wolf: in the morning he shall devour the prey, and at night he shall divide the spoil' (Genesis 49:27). **4.** Irish: variant spelling of WOULFE.

Wolfanger (119) German: variant of **Wolffanger** 'wolf catcher', an occupational name for a trapper who caught wolves (see WOLF, FANGER).

Wolfarth (131) Variant spelling of German WOHLFARTH.

Wolfe (32761) Irish, English, and German: variant spelling of WOLF.

Wolfel (103) German (**Wölfel**): from a pet form of WOLF.

Wolfenbarger (548) Altered form of Swiss German **Wolfensberger**, a habitational name for someone from an unidentified place called Wolfensberg.

Wolfenden (236) English: habitational name from Wolfenden, a place in the parish of Newchurch-in-Rossendale, Lancashire, apparently named from the Old English personal name *Wulfhelm* (composed of the elements *wulf* 'wolf' + *helm* 'helmet', 'protection') + Old English *denu* 'valley'.

Wolfer (613) German: **1.** from a reduced form of the Germanic personal names *Wolfher* or *Wolfhart*, composed of the elements *wolf* 'wolf' + *hari* 'army' or *hard* 'hardy', 'brave'. **2.** topographic name for someone who lived in a place frequented by wolves, Middle High German *wolf*, or a habitational name from a place named with this word.

Wolfert (330) German: from the Germanic personal name *Wolfhart*, composed of *wolf* 'wolf' + *hard* 'brave', 'hardy', 'strong'.
GIVEN NAMES German 5%. *Guenter, Kurt, Otto, Wilhelmina.*

Wolff (9988) German, Danish, and Jewish (Ashkenazic): variant spelling of WOLF.
GIVEN NAMES German 5%. *Hans* (17), *Kurt* (16), *Otto* (13), *Erwin* (10), *Fritz* (8), *Helmut* (6), *Franz* (5), *Gerhard* (5), *Guenter* (4), *Gunter* (3), *Heinz* (3), *Klaus* (3).

Wolffe (140) English: variant spelling of WOLF.

Wolfgang (1082) German: from the Germanic personal name *Wolfgang*, composed of *wolf* 'wolf' + *ganc* 'going'. From the late 10th century it became popular in Bavaria and the south as the name of a saint, Bishop Wolfgang of Regensburg.

Wolfgram (703) German: variant of WOLFRAM.

Wolfinbarger (144) See WOLFENBARGER.

Wolfinger (507) German: habitational name for someone from Wolfing in Bavaria.

Wolfington (164) Possibly English: of uncertain origin. Although it has the appearance of a habitational name, no such place is known, and it may simply be a variant of WOLFENDEN.

Wolfley (250) Americanized spelling of German WOELFLE.

Wolfman (269) Jewish (Ashkenazic): variant of WOLF.

GIVEN NAMES Jewish 7%. *Devorah* (2), *Hyman* (2), *Mort*.

Wolfmeyer (100) German: a distinguishing name, from German *wolf* 'wolf' (here probably as a personal name) + MEYER 'tenant farmer'.

GIVEN NAME German 4%. *Kurt*.

Wolford (3764) English: **1.** habitational name from Great or Little Wolford in Warwickshire, named with Old English *wulf* 'wolf' + *weard* 'protector', 'guard'. **2.** from the Old English personal name *Wulfweard*, composed of the same elements as 1.

Wolfram (683) English and German: from the Germanic personal name *Wolfram*, composed of the elements *wolf* 'wolf' + *hrafn* 'raven'. Both these creatures played an important role in Germanic mythology. They are usually represented in battle poetry as scavengers of the slain, while Woden (Odin) is generally accompanied by the wolves Geri and Freki and the ravens Hugin and Munin.

GIVEN NAMES German 8%. *Kurt* (3), *Klaus* (2), *Manfred* (2), *Berthold, Dietmar, Erhard, Ernst, Erwin, Gerhard, Guenter, Helmut, Horst*.

Wolfrey (154) English: from the Old English personal name *Wulffrið*, composed of the elements *wulf* 'wolf' + *frið* 'peace'.

Wolfrom (196) German: variant of WOLFRAM.

Wolfrum (240) German: variant of WOLFRAM.

GIVEN NAMES German 8%. *Franz* (2), *Egmont, Erwin, Fritz*.

Wolfson (2135) **1.** English and Jewish (Ashkenazic): patronymic from WOLF. **2.** Americanized spelling of the Low German cognate **Wolfsen**.

GIVEN NAMES Jewish 6%. *Sol* (5), *Meyer* (4), *Moshe* (3), *Zev* (3), *Bluma* (2), *Hyman* (2), *Isadore* (2), *Miriam* (2), *Abbe, Chaya, Emanuel, Hershel*.

Wolgamott (197) Americanized spelling of German WOHLGEMUTH.

Wolgast (198) German: habitational name from places so named in Brandenburg and Pomerania.

Wolgemuth (195) German: variant spelling of WOHLGEMUTH.

Wolin (403) **1.** Swedish: ornamental name composed of an unexplained first element (probably abstracted from a place-name in *Voll-*, formed with *vall* 'grassy bank', 'pasture') + the adjectival suffix *-in*. **2.** Jewish (American): shortened form of WOLINSKI.

GIVEN NAMES Jewish 4%. *Hyman, Meyer*.

Wolinski (295) Polish, Jewish (eastern Ashkenazic), and Ukrainian: habitational name for someone from Wolin in Szczecin voivodeship or from Wolina in Słupsk and Tarnobrzeg voivodeships, or from the region of Volynia in Ukraine (Ukrainian *Volyn*, Polish *Wołyń*).

GIVEN NAMES Polish 10%. *Slawomir* (2), *Arkadiusz, Jerzy, Krzysztof, Lucjan, Ryszard, Tadeusz*.

Wolinsky (273) Jewish (eastern Ashkenazic) and Ukrainian: variant of WOLINSKI.

GIVEN NAMES Jewish 6%. *Asher, Isadore, Mayer, Yael*.

Woliver (118) Of English origin: probably a variant of either GULLIVER or OLIVER.

Wolk (1207) **1.** German (also **Wölk**): from a Low German short form of WALTER. **2.** Germanized spelling of Slovenian or Czec VOLK.

Wolke (320) German (also **Wölke**): variant of WOLK.

Wolken (475) German: patronymic from WOLK.

Wolking (105) North German: patronymic form of WOLK.

Wolkoff (204) German spelling of Russian VOLKOV.

Wolkow (106) Polish (**Wołków**): from a possessive derivative of *wołek* 'little bullock' (see Wolek 2).

GIVEN NAMES Polish 5%; Scandinavian 4%. *Bronislawa, Wasyl; Helmer*.

Woll (667) **1.** English: variant of WOOL. **2.** German: variant of WOLLE. **3.** Norwegian: spelling variant of VOLL.

Wollam (357) English: possibly a variant of WOOLEN.

Wollan (174) **1.** English: variant of WOOLEN. **2.** Norwegian: habitational name from any of several farmsteads, mainly in Trøndelag, named *Vollan*, from the definite plural form of VOLL ('meadow'). Compare WOLLEN.

GIVEN NAME Scandinavian 6%; German 4%. *Gerhard*.

Wollard (316) English: variant of WOLFORD.

Wollaston (148) English: habitational name from any of various places called Wollaston. Those in Northamptonshire (Domesday Book *Wilavestone*) and Worcestershire (first recorded in 1275 as *Wollaueston*) are named from the genitive case of the Old English personal name *Wulflāf* (composed of the elements *wulf* 'wolf' + *lāf* 'relic') + Old English *tūn* 'enclosure', 'settlement'. The first element of the one in Shropshire (Domesday Book *Willavestune*) is the genitive case of the Old English personal name *Wīglāf* (composed of the elements *wīg* 'war' + *lāf* 'relic').

Wolle (174) **1.** German: metonymic occupational name for worker or dealer in wool, from Middle High German *wolle* 'wool'. **2.** Norwegian: spelling variant of VOLLE.

GIVEN NAMES Scandinavian 4%; German 4%. *Erik, Kerstin; Armin, Ernst*.

Wollen (174) **1.** English: variant of WOOLEN. **2.** Norwegian: habitational name from any of numerous farmsteads named *Vollen*, from the definite singular form of *voll* 'meadow' (see VOLL).

Wollenberg (416) German: habitational name from either of two places so named, in Brandenburg and Rhineland.

Wollenburg (118) German: habitational name, possibly an altered spelling of WOLLENBERG or from a lost or unidentified place.

GIVEN NAMES German 6%. *Gerhard, Lorenz, Otto*.

Wollenhaupt (125) German: nickname for someone with a bushy head of hair, from Middle High German *wolle* 'wool' + *houbet* 'head'.

GIVEN NAME German 5%. *Kurt*.

Wollenweber (146) German: occupational name for a weaver (of wool), Middle High German *wollenweber*.

GIVEN NAMES German 8%. *Guenter, Kurt, Otto*.

Woller (457) **1.** English: occupational name for a worker in wool, from an agent derivative of Middle English *woll* 'wool'. **2.** English: variant of WOOL 2, with the suffix *-er* denoting an inhabitant. **3.** German: occupational name for a wool worker whose job was to prepare wool for spinning, Middle High German *woller*. **4.** German: variant of WALTHER.

GIVEN NAMES German 4%. *Alfons, Erwin, Kurt, Manfred*.

Wollerman (107) German: patronymic or pet form of WOLLER 4.

Wollert (137) North German (also **Wöllert**): variant of WOHLERT.

GIVEN NAMES German 7%. *Dieter* (2), *Otto*.

Wollet (102) English: variant spelling of WOLLETT.

Wollett (117) **1.** English: from the Old English personal name *Wulfgēat* 'wolf Geat'. **2.** German: variant of WOLLERT.

GIVEN NAME German 4%. *Fritz*.

Wollin (365) German: habitational name from any of various places so named, for example in Brandenburg and Pomerania.

Wollitz (103) German: from a Slavic personal name formed with *vol* 'will', 'desire'.

Wollman (580) **1.** English: occupational name for a wool worker (see WOOL). **2.** Respelling of the German cognate WOLLMANN. **3.** Jewish (Ashkenazic): occupational name for a wool worker, from Yiddish *vol*, German *Wolle* 'wool' + Yiddish *man*, German *Mann* 'man'.

Wollmann (116) German: occupational name for a wool worker, Middle Low German *wollmann*.

GIVEN NAMES German 11%. *Gerhardt, Horst, Kurt, Rainer*.

Wollner (234) German: occupational name for a wool worker whose job was to prepare wool for spinning, Middle High German *wollener*. See also WOLLSCHLAGER.

GIVEN NAMES German 8%. *Egon, Horst, Klaus, Kurt, Otmar, Wolf*.

Wollschlager (221) German (**Wollschläger**): occupational name for someone who prepared wool for spinning by washing and combing or carding it, from Middle High German *wolle(n)slaher*, *-sleger*, Middle Low German *wullensleger* (literally 'wool beater').

Wollum (101) Norwegian: unexplained.

Wolman (310) **1.** English: variant of WOOL. **2.** Respelling of Jewish WOLLMAN, or of the German cognate, *Wollmann*.
GIVEN NAMES Jewish 11%; German 4%. *Yosef* (2), *Amnon*, *Aron*, *Hyman*, *Izak*, *Meyer*, *Moshe*, *Shlomo*, *Shmuel*, *Yehuda*; *Otto* (2), *Gerd*.

Wolner (136) Possibly an altered spelling of German WOLLNER.

Wolny (126) Polish: status name for a freedman, one who had been released from the feudal obligations of serfdom, from Polish *wolny* 'free'. It may also have been a nickname meaning 'free'.
GIVEN NAMES Polish 18%. *Ryszard* (2), *Alojzy*, *Grazyna*, *Jerzy*, *Marcin*, *Merek*, *Michalina*, *Zdzislaw*.

Woloshin (104) Jewish (Ashkenazic): variant of VOLOSHIN.
GIVEN NAMES Jewish 6%. *Aaron*, *Meyer*, *Sol*.

Woloszyk (112) Polish: from a diminutive of WOLOSZYN.

Woloszyn (266) Polish spelling of a Ukrainian and Jewish ethnic or regional name for someone from Wallachia. Compare VOLOSHIN.
GIVEN NAMES Polish 8%. *Alicja*, *Bronislaw*, *Grazyna*, *Tadeusz*, *Zbigniew*, *Zigmunt*.

Wolper (164) **1.** German: variant of WOLPERT. **2.** Jewish (eastern Ashkenazic): habitational name from Volpa in Belarus.
GIVEN NAMES Jewish 4%; German 4%. *Abbe*; *Eberhard*.

Wolpert (612) **1.** German: from the personal name *Waldobert*, composed of the elements *waltan* 'rule' + *bërht* 'bright', 'shining'. **2.** Jewish (from Lithuania): assimilation to the German male personal name *Wolpert*, perceived as a variant of the Jewish male name WOLF.

Wolsey (182) English: variant spelling of WOOLSEY.

Wolske (230) Eastern German (of Slavic origin): see WOLSKI.
GIVEN NAMES German 5%. *Erhard*, *Hans*, *Kurt*, *Otto*.

Wolski (717) Polish and Eastern German (of Slavic origin): habitational name for someone from one of many places called Wola, named in Latin as *libera villa* 'free village', i.e. a settlement which was awarded liberty or relieved from certain duties. Compare ZWOLINSKI, also VILLAFRANCA.
GIVEN NAMES Polish 6%. *Irena* (2), *Kazimierz* (2), *Dariusz*, *Jacek*, *Janusz*, *Jerzy*, *Krystyna*, *Miroslaw*, *Piotr*, *Wladyslaw*, *Wojciech*, *Zygmund*.

Wolsky (184) Ukrainian, Belorussian, and Jewish (eastern Ashkenazic): habitational name for someone from places in Ukraine and Belarus called Volya (Polish *Wola*) or Vol'ka (Polish *Wólka*).

Wolstenholme (173) English: habitational name from Wolstenholme, a place in Lancashire named from the Old English personal name *Wulfstān* (see WOOLSTON 1) + Old Norse *holmr* 'island', 'dry land in a fen'.

Wolter (1971) North German form of WALTER.
GIVEN NAMES German 7%. *Kurt* (10), *Otto* (5), *Fritz* (3), *Dieter* (2), *Gerhard* (2), *Hans* (2), *Klaus* (2), *Lothar* (2), *Reinhard* (2), *Reinhold* (2), *Alfons*, *Alois*.

Woltering (128) North German: patronymic from WOLTER.

Wolterman (149) North German (**Woltermann**): patronymic from WOLTER.

Wolters (1362) North German: patronymic from WOLTER.

Wolthuis (145) Dutch: habitational name from a lost or unidentified place.
GIVEN NAMES Dutch 10%. *Marinus* (3), *Gerrit* (2), *Harm*, *Henk*.

Woltjer (143) Dutch: from the Germanic personal name *Waldhar* (see WOUTERS).

Woltman (377) Altered spelling of WOLTMANN.
GIVEN NAME German 4%. *Kurt* (3).

Woltmann (117) German: occupational name for a forester, Middle Low German *woltman*.

Woltz (439) German: from a pet form of any of the various Germanic personal names beginning with the element *wald* 'rule' (see for example WALTER).

Wolven (213) English: from the Old English personal name *Wulfwine* 'wolf friend'.

Wolverton (1494) English: habitational name from any of various places named Wolverton, as for example the one in Buckinghamshire, or from Woolverton in Somerset or Wolferton in Norfolk, all of which are named from the Old English personal name *Wulfhere* + *-ing-* denoting association + *tūn* 'farmstead', 'settlement'.

Wolz (346) German: variant spelling of WOLTZ.
GIVEN NAMES German 5%. *Alois*, *Fritz*, *Kurt*, *Otto*.

Womac (273) Variant of English WOMACK.

Womack (8985) English: unexplained. The surname is well established in England (Yorkshire and Norfolk) as well as North America, and there is a Womack Water in Norfolk, but the name remains unexplained. It may possibly be connected with Dutch **Walmack**, from Middle Dutch *walmac(k)e* 'twig', 'faggot', applied as a nickname for a thin person.

Wombacher (169) German: habitational name possibly for someone from Wambach near Landshut.

Womble (2021) English: habitational name from Wombwell in South Yorkshire, named with the Old English byname *Wamba* meaning 'belly' (or this word used in a transferred topographical sense) + Old English *well(a)* 'spring', 'stream'.

Wombles (158) English: variant of WOMBLE.

Womeldorf (149) German: variant spelling of WOMELSDORF.
GIVEN NAMES Scandinavian 4%. *Erik*, *Selmer*.

Womelsdorf (111) German: habitational name from a place so named near Erndtebrück.

Womer (448) English: probably a variant of **Woolmer** (see WOOMER).

Wommack (476) English: variant of WOMACK (unexplained).

Won (838) Korean (**Wŏn**): there are two Chinese characters for this surname. Although there is some dispute, the founder of the Wŏn clan is believed by many to be Wŏn Kyŏng, a Tang China scholar sent to Shilla in the mid 7th century. The other Wŏn character has only one clan, the Wŏnju Wŏn.
GIVEN NAMES Korean 49%. *Chong* (11), *Jong* (8), *Young* (8), *Yong* (6), *Kwang* (4), *Chun* (3), *Jung* (3), *Sung* (3), *Wai* (3), *Chang Ho* (2), *Dong* (2), *Duk* (2), *Jin* (2); *Chang* (4), *Dae* (3), *Jong Ho* (3), *Jae Hee* (2), *Young Jun* (2), *Chang Jin*, *Chong Ho*, *Chong Sik*, *Chul*, *Chun Soo*, *Chung*.

Wonder (300) Probably a variant of German WUNDER.

Wondergem (112) Dutch: habitational name from Wondelgem or Wontergem, both in East Flanders.

Wonderling (124) Americanized spelling of German **Wunderling**, a derivative from WUNDER.

Wonderly (368) Americanized spelling of German WUNDERLE.

Wonders (375) English (Northumberland and Durham): unexplained; perhaps a variant of Scottish **Wanders**, which Black tentatively derives from a Scottish local pronunciation of *Guinevere*, name of King Arthur's queen, who according to local Angus legend was buried in the parish of Alyth.

Wondra (322) Germanized spelling of Czech and Slovak VONDRA.

Wong (24519) **1.** Chinese: variant of WANG. **2.** Chinese: variant of HUANG.
GIVEN NAMES Chinese 15%. *Wing* (70), *Wai* (66), *Kam* (59), *Kin* (47), *Kwok* (45), *Ming* (41), *Chun* (33), *Chi* (24), *Hong* (24), *Yuk* (23), *Hing* (22), *Mei* (22).

Wonnacott (153) English: habitational name from Wonnacott, a place in Devon, named with an unattested Old English personal name *Wunna* + Old English *cot* 'cottage'.

Wonser (126) Dutch: variant of WANZER.

Wonson (110) English: habitational name from Wonson, Devon.

Woo (2867) **1.** Chinese 吴: variant of Wu 1. **2.** Chinese 胡: Cantonese variant of Hu. **3.** Chinese 武: variant of Wu 3. **4.** Chinese 伍: variant of Wu 4. **5.** Chinese 巫: variant of Wu 5. **6.** Korean: unexplained.
GIVEN NAMES Chinese/Korean 26%. *Young* (15), *Jung* (8), *Sang* (8), *Jin* (7), *Sung* (7), *Wing* (6), *Yong* (6), *Jae* (5), *Chen* (4), *Dong* (4), *Jong* (4), *Kwan* (4); *Chong* (12), *Byung* (7), *Chung* (5), *Young Hoon* (3), *Chang* (2), *Jung Sook* (2), *Kyu Sung* (2), *Moon* (2), *Nam* (2), *Sook* (2), *Young Sik* (2), *Cheol*.

Wood (98424) English and Scottish: **1.** mainly a topographic name for someone who lived in or by a wood or a metonymic occupational name for a woodcutter or forester, from Middle English *wode* 'wood' (Old English *wudu*). **2.** nickname for a mad, eccentric, or violent person, from Middle English *wōd* 'mad', 'frenzied' (Old English *wād*), as in Adam le Wode, Worcestershire 1221.

Woodall (5712) English (chiefly West Midlands): habitational name from any of various places called Woodhall, for example in Hertfordshire, Lincolnshire, North Yorkshire, and Lothian, so named from Old English *wudu* 'wood' + *heall* 'hall'.

Woodard (14473) English: variant of WOODWARD.

Woodbeck (191) Possibly an English habitational name, from Woodbeck, a place in Nottinghamshire, named in Middle English with *wode* 'wood' + *beck* 'stream'. This surname is not found in current English sources.

Woodberry (478) English (Devon and Somerset): variant spelling of WOODBURY.
FOREBEARS William Woodberry, from Somerset, England, was one of the founders of the settlement at Beverley, MA, in 1628.

Woodbridge (433) English: habitational name from Woodbridge in Suffolk or Dorset, both named from Old English *wudu* 'wood' + *brycg* 'bridge', i.e. a bridge made of timber or one near a wood.
FOREBEARS John Woodbridge (1613–95), emigrated in 1634 from Stanton in Wiltshire, England, to Newbury, MA, where he was pastor and magistrate.

Woodburn (1073) Scottish: habitational name from places named Woodburn in Ayrshire, Kincardineshire, and Midlothian, and in Northumberland, all named from Old English *wudu* 'wood' + *burna* 'stream', i.e. a stream flowing through a wood.

Woodbury (2736) English: habitational name from any of various places, notably in Devon, called Woodbury, from Old English *wudu* 'wood' + *byrig*, dative of *burh* 'fortified place', or from either of two places called Woodborough, in Nottinghamshire

and Wiltshire. The Nottinghamshire place name is from Old English *wudu* + *burh*, while Woodborough in Wiltshire is named with the same first element + Old English *beorg* 'hill'.
FOREBEARS John Woodbury emigrated from Somerset, England, to Gloucester, MA, in 1623.

Woodby (374) English: perhaps a reduced form of WOODBURY.

Woodcock (2689) English: **1.** from Middle English *woodcock* (a compound of Old English *wudu* 'wood' + *cocc* 'cock', 'bird'), a bird that is notoriously easy to catch, hence a nickname for a stupid or gullible person. **2.** variant of **Woodcott**, a habitational name from any of various places named with Old English *wudu* 'wood' + *cot* 'cottage', 'shelter', as for example Woodcott in Cheshire and Hampshire or Woodcote in Hampshire, Surrey, Oxfordshire, Warwickshire, and Shropshire.

Woodcox (240) English: variant of WOODCOCK.

Wooddell (394) English: topographic name for someone living in a wooded valley, from Middle English *wode* 'wood' (Old English *wudu*) + *dell* 'dell', 'valley', or a habitational name from some minor place named with these elements.

Woodell (513) English: **1.** variant of WOODDELL. **2.** topographic name for someone living on a wooded hill, from Middle English *wudu* 'wood' + *hyll* 'hill', or a habitational name from any of various minor places named Woodhill.

Wooden (2008) English (mainly Norfolk): variant of WOODING.

Wooderson (120) English (southern counties): from Middle English *woderson* 'son of the woodman'.

Woodfield (315) **1.** English: topographic name for someone who lived in a stretch of open country by a wood, or (as a later formation) someone who lived near a field by a wood, from Middle English *wode* 'wood' (Old English *wudu*) + *feld* 'open country', later with the modern meaning 'field'. **2.** Scottish: habitational name from Woodfield, a place near Annan in Dumfriesshire. A certain Roger Wodyfelde is recorded as holding land in Dumfries in 1365.

Woodfill (178) English: probably a variant of either WOODFIELD or **Woodfull**, which is from an Old English personal name or nickname composed of the elements *wudu* 'wood' + *fugol* 'bird'.

Woodfin (820) English: topographic name for someone who lived at a place where wood was stacked, from Old English *wudu* 'wood' + *fīn* 'pile'.

Woodford (1811) English and Scottish: habitational name from any of various places, as far apart as Essex, Wiltshire, Cornwall, Northamptonshire, Cheshire,

and Roxburghshire, named with Old English *wudu* 'wood' + *ford* 'ford'.
FOREBEARS Thomas Woodford emigrated from Lincolnshire, England, to NY in 1690.

Woodfork (300) English (Derbyshire): topographic name for someone who lived by a fork in the road in woodland.

Woodhall (177) English (mainly West Midlands): variant of WOODALL.

Woodham (1136) English: habitational name from any of various places named Woodham. Most, as for example those in Essex and Surrey, are named from Old English *wudu* 'wood' + *hām* 'homestead'; one in Buckinghamshire, however, probably has as its second element Old English *hamm* 'water meadow', and one in County Durham is from *wudum*, the dative plural of *wudu*, originally used after a preposition.

Woodhams (262) English: variant of WOODHAM.

Woodhead (482) English and Scottish: habitational name from any of various minor places named Woodhead, for example in West Yorkshire and Strathmore, from Old English *wudu* 'wood' + *hēafod* 'head(land)', 'top', 'extremity'.

Woodhouse (1461) English and Scottish: habitational name from any of numerous places named Woodhouse; there are examples in Leicestershire, South and West Yorkshire, and Peebleshire, all named from Old English *wudu* 'wood' + *hūs* 'house'.
FOREBEARS William Woodhouse, a Jacobite, emigrated from Alnwick in Northumberland, England, to Philadelphia in 1766.

Woodhull (357) English: topographic name for someone living on a wooded hill, from Middle English *wode* 'wood' + *hyll* 'hill', or a habitational name from any of various minor places named with these elements.
FOREBEARS Richard Woodhull emigrated to America from Northampton, England, in about 1648, and settled in Mastic, Long Island, NY.

Woodie (539) English: variant spelling of WOODY.

Woodin (642) English: variant of WOODING.

Wooding (462) English: topographic name for someone who lived at a place where wood was cut, Middle English *wo(o)ding*.

Woodington (144) English (Gloucestershire): habitational name from a place named Woodington, of which there are examples in Devon and Hampshire. The Devon place is probably named from the Old English personal name *Odda* (with genitive *-n*) + Old English *tūn* 'farmstead', 'settlement'.

Woodis (156) English: **1.** perhaps a nickname from Old English *wuduwāsa* 'faun', 'satyr'. **2.** alternatively, a reduced form of WOODHOUSE.

Woodke (176) Americanized spelling of German WUTTKE.

Woodland (1340) English: topographic name for someone living in an area of woodland, from Old English *wudu* 'wood' + *land* 'land', or a habitational name from any of the numerous places, for example in Devon, Dorset, Kent, and Somerset, named with these elements.

Woodle (331) Variant of English WOODALL or Scottish WEDDELL.

Woodlee (269) Variant of English WOODLEY.

Woodley (1988) English: habitational name from Woodleigh in Devon, Woodley in Berkshire, or some other place named with Old English *wudu* 'wood' + *lēah* 'clearing', 'pasture'.

Woodlief (412) Probably a variant spelling of English WOODLIFF.

Woodliff (164) English (Lincolnshire): from the Old English personal name *Wuduleof*.

Woodling (292) English (Hampshire): probably an affectionate nickname for someone who lived in the woods.

Woodlock (148) Irish and French: originally English, from an Old English personal name, *Wudlāc*, composed of the elements *wudu* 'wood' + *lāc* 'play', 'sport'.
FOREBEARS The name Woodlock or Wodelock was taken to Ireland as early as 1172 by the brothers Torsten and Reginaldus Utlag, the sons of a Wiltshire, England, landowner named Wudulach. Their descendants held large estates in Tipperary and Co. Dublin until, in the 18th century, they suffered greatly from the restrictions placed on Catholics, and several members of the family emigrated to France and Spain, and in the 19th century to Canada, the U.S., Australia, and New Zealand.
GIVEN NAMES French 5%. *Andre, Michel*.

Woodman (2186) English and Scottish: **1.** occupational name for a woodcutter or a forester (compare WOODWARD), or topographic name for someone who lived in the woods. **2.** possibly from the Old English personal name *Wudumann*.

Woodmancy (111) English (Yorkshire): variant spelling of WOODMANSEE.

Woodmansee (584) English: habitational name from Woodmansey in East Yorkshire, named from Old English *wudumann* 'woodman', 'forester' + *sǣ* 'pool'.

Woodrich (169) Altered form of North German WODRICH.

Woodrick (179) Americanized form of North German WODRICH.

Woodring (1710) English: topographic name for someone who lived in a wood, from an unattested Old English word *wuduring*, a derivative of *wudu* 'wood' (see WOOD).

Woodrome (175) Variant of English WOODRUM.

Woodroof (204) English: variant spelling of WOODRUFF.

Woodrow (1075) English: habitational name from a place named Woodrow, from Old English *wudu* 'wood' + *rāw* 'row', 'line', i.e. a row of cottages near a wood. There are places bearing this name in Buckinghamshire, Dorset, Wiltshire, and Worcestershire, but the surname is found mainly in Norfolk.

Woodruff (9734) English: topographic name for someone who lived on a patch of land where woodruff grew, Old English *wudurofe* (a compound of *wudu* 'wood' with a second element of unknown origin). The leaves of the plant have a sweet smell and the surname may also have been a nickname for one who used it as a perfume, or perhaps an ironical nickname for a malodorous person.
FOREBEARS Two English families brought the name Woodruff to the American colonies: those of Matthew Woodruff and of John and Ann Woodruffe. The latter migrated to Lynn, MA, from Kent, and moved to Southampton, Long Island, NY, before 1640. John and Ann's many descendants were established in NJ, NC, and SC by 1790. The city of Woodruff, SC, is named for this family. The name is variously spelled Woodrove, Woodroffe, Woodruffe, Woodrough, and Woodruff in colonial records.

Woodrum (1141) Variant of English **Wooderham**, a place named in Old English as 'the dwelling of the woodman'.

Woods (52881) **1.** English and Scottish: topographic name for someone who lived in the woods (see WOOD). **2.** Irish: English name adopted as a translation of **Ó Cuill** 'descendant of *Coll*' (see QUILL), or in Ulster of **Mac Con Coille** 'son of *Cú Choille*', a personal name meaning 'hound of the wood', which has also been mistranslated COX, as if formed with *coileach* 'cock', 'rooster'.

Woodside (1393) Scottish and northern Irish: habitational name from any of various minor places named Woodside, for example in Ayrshire, from Old English *wudu* 'wood' + *sīde* 'hillside'.

Woodsmall (153) Apparently English, but unexplained.

Woodson (4860) English (Yorkshire): habitational name for someone from Woodsome in West Yorkshire, named in Old English as *æt wudu-hūsum* '(place at) the houses in the wood'.

Woodstock (166) English: habitational name from Woodstock in Oxfordshire, named from Old English *wudu* 'wood' + *stoc* 'settlement'.

Woodsum (112) Variant of English **Woodsome** (see WOODSON).

Woodward (14889) English: **1.** occupational name for a forester employed to look after the trees and game in a forest, Middle English *woodward* (from the Old English elements mentioned at 2). **2.** perhaps also

from an Old English personal name *Wuduweard*, composed of the elements *wudu* 'wood' + *weard* 'guardian', 'protector'.
FOREBEARS Henry Woodward emigrated from England in 1635 and settled first in Dorchester, MA, and subsequently in Northampton, MA. He had many prominent descendants. Another Henry Woodward, born about 1646 in the British West Indies, was the first English settler in SC (1664).

Woodworth (3684) English (Cheshire, Lancashire, Merseyside): possibly a habitational name from Wadworth in South Yorkshire, named with the Old English personal name *Wada* + *worth* 'enclosure'.

Woody (6032) English: from a derivative of WOOD with an unexplained second element; this may be a diminutive suffix, or the Old English topographic term *ēg* 'island', 'piece of high ground in a fen'.

Woodyard (1080) Scottish: perhaps an occupational name for a woodcutter or wood carrier, from Old English *wudigere*.

Woofter (278) Apparently an altered form of an unidentified English name.

Wool (385) **1.** English: metonymic occupational name for a worker in wool, Middle English *woll* (Old English *wull*). **2.** English: in southwestern England, a topographic name for someone who lived by a spring or stream, from Middle English *wolle*, *wulle* 'spring', 'stream', a western dialect development of Old English (West Saxon) *wiell(a)*. **3.** Americanized form of French HOULE.

Woolard (1922) English: variant of WOLFORD.

Woolbert (114) Americanized form of German WOLBERT.

Woolbright (419) Probably an Americanized form of German **Wollbrecht**, a variant of WOLBERT or of VOLLBRECHT.

Woolcock (141) English: variant of WOLCOTT.

Woolcott (172) English: variant of WOLCOTT.

Wooldridge (3036) English: from the Middle English personal name *Wol(f)rich*, Old English *Wulfrīc*, composed of the elements *wulf* 'wolf' + *rīc* 'power'.

Woolen (211) English: topographic name for someone who lived on a curved or irregularly shaped piece of land, from Old English *wōh* 'curved', 'crooked' + *land* 'land', 'estate', or a habitational name from Woolland in Dorset, named from an Old English *winn*, *wynn* 'meadow', 'pasture' + *land* 'land', 'estate'.

Woolery (980) English (West Midlands): unexplained.

Woolever (484) Of English origin: probably a variant of either GULLIVER or OLIVER.

Wooley (2273) English: variant spelling of WOOLLEY.

Woolf (1890) English: variant spelling of WOLF.

Woolfolk (890) English: unexplained.

Woolford (571) English: variant of WOLFORD.

Woolfork (108) See WOOLFOLK.

Woollard (204) English: variant of WOLFORD.

Woollen (176) English: variant spelling of WOOLEN.

Woolley (2730) English: habitational name from any of various places so called. Most, including those in Berkshire, Cambridgeshire, and West Yorkshire, are named from Old English *wulf* 'wolf' or perhaps the personal name or byname *Wulf* (see WOLF) + *lēah* 'wood', 'clearing'. One example in Somerset, however, has as its first element Middle English *wolle*, *wulle* 'spring', 'stream' (see WOOL 2).

Woolman (422) **1.** English: variant of WOOL. **2.** Americanized form of Jewish WOLLMAN or German **Wollmann** (see WOLLMAN).

Woolridge (834) English: variant of WOOLDRIDGE.

Wools (118) English: variant of WOOL.

Woolsey (2554) English: from the Middle English personal name *Wulsi*, Old English *Wulfsige*, composed of the elements *wulf* 'wolf' + *sige* 'victory'.

FOREBEARS George Woolsey came to New Amsterdam from England via the Netherlands in 1623.

Woolson (246) English: unexplained.

FOREBEARS Thomas Woolson, from England, settled in Cambridge, MA, before 1660.

Woolstenhulme (158) English: variant spelling of WOLSTENHOLME.

Woolston (410) English (chiefly East Anglia): **1.** from the Middle English personal name *Wol(f)stan*, Old English *Wulfstān*, composed of the elements *wulf* 'wolf' + *stān* stone. **2.** habitational name from any of a large number of places called Woolston(e) or Wollston, all of which are named with Old English personal names containing the first element *Wulf* (*Wulfhēah*, *Wulfhelm*, *Wulfrīc*, *Wulfsige*, and *Wulfweard*) + Old English *tūn* 'enclosure', 'settlement'.

Woolum (320) Origin unidentified.

Woolums (273) Origin unidentified.

Woolverton (468) English: variant spelling of WOLVERTON.

Woolwine (530) **1.** Probably an Americanized form of **Volkwein**, from a Germanic personal name composed of *folc* 'people', 'army' + *wini* 'friend'. It is recorded in Lancaster co., PA, in the mid 18th century. **2.** Possibly an altered spelling of English **Walwyn**, from the Old English personal name *Wealdwine* 'power-friend'.

Woolworth (282) English: perhaps a variant of WALWORTH.

Woomer (437) English: variant of **Woolmer**: **1.** from the Old English personal name *Wulfmǣr*, a compound of *wulf* 'wool' + *māri*, *mēri* 'famous'. **2.** habitational name from a lost place named Wolmoor ('wolves' moor'), in Ormskirk, Lancashire; possibly also from Woolmer Forest in Hampshire, Wolmer Farm in Ogbourne St George, Wiltshire, or Woomore Farm in Melksham Wiltshire, all meaning 'wolves' pool'.

Woon (130) **1.** Cornish: habitational name from a place in Cornwall called Woon. **2.** Chinese 温: Hakka and Taishan form of WEN 1.

GIVEN NAMES Chinese 13%. *Chu, Han, Heng, Jung, Kam, Kwan, Seung, Sze, Tong, Wing.*

Woosley (1429) English: habitational name from Wolseley in Staffordshire, named with the Old English personal name *Wulfsige* + *lēah* 'woodland clearing'.

Wooster (1009) English: variant of WORCESTER.

Wootan (228) Variant altered spelling of English WOOTEN.

Wooten (9618) English: habitational name from any of the extremely numerous places named with Old English *wudu* 'wood' + *tūn* 'enclosure', 'settlement', such as Wootton in Northamptonshire or Oxfordshire, Wootton Bassett in Wiltshire, Wotton in Surrey, and Wotton under Edge in Gloucestershire.

Wooters (388) Altered spelling of Dutch WOUTERS.

Wooton (588) English: variant spelling of WOOTEN.

Wootten (587) English: variant spelling of WOOTEN.

Wootton (842) English: variant spelling of WOOTEN.

Worby (104) English: **1.** occupational nickname for a forester, literally 'guard wood', from Old French *garder*, *warder* 'to guard' + *bois* 'wood'. **2.** habitational name from Warboys in Cambridgeshire, possibly from an unattested Old English *Wearda* or alternatively Old English *weard* 'watch', 'protection' + *busc* 'bush'.

Worcester (1021) English: habitational name from the city of Worcester, named from Old English *ceaster* 'Roman fort or walled city' (Latin *castra* 'legionary camp') + a British tribal name of uncertain origin.

FOREBEARS Rev. William Worcester emigrated from England and settled in Salisbury, MA, before 1638. He had many prominent descendants, including Noah Worcester (b. 1758) and Samuel Worcester (b. 1770), both NH Congregational clergymen, and Joseph Emerson Worcester (1784–1865), a noted lexicographer, geographer, and historian.

Word (1999) Perhaps an Americanized spelling of Dutch **van der Woord**, a habita-

tional name from places named Woord, Woerd, or Word.

Wordell (206) English: variant spelling of WARDLE.

GIVEN NAMES German 5%. *Erhardt, Otto.*

Worden (3709) English (chiefly Lancashire): habitational name from a place near Chorley. Early forms consistently show the first syllable as *Wer-*, and the name is probably derived from Old English *wer* 'weir' + *denu* 'valley'.

Work (1531) **1.** Scottish: habitational name from the lands of Work in the parish of St. Ola, Orkney. **2.** English: from Old English *(ge)weorc* 'work', 'fortification', hence probably a topographic name or an occupational name for someone who worked on fortifications or at a fort. **3.** Danish: habitational name from a place so called.

Working (206) Probably an Americanized spelling of German WERKING.

Workinger (198) Variant of German WERKING.

Workman (10584) English: ostensibly an occupational name for a laborer, from Middle English *work* + *man*. According to a gloss cited by Reaney the term was used in the Middle Ages to denote an ambidextrous person, and the surname may also be a nickname in this sense.

Works (967) English: variant of WORK.

Worl (165) **1.** German (**Wörl**): variant of WEHRLE. **2.** English: perhaps a habitational name for someone from Worle in Somerset, which is most probably named with Old English *wōr* 'wood grouse' + *lēah* 'wood', '(woodland) clearing'.

Worland (367) English (Cambridge): unexplained; perhaps a habitational name from a lost or unidentified place. There are two places in England called Warland, in Durham and West Yorkshire, but the distribution of the modern surname suggests that a different souce is most probably involved.

World (111) English: unexplained.

Worlds (135) Origin unidentified. Compare WORLD.

Worley (9090) English: most probably a habitational name, either from a variant spelling of WORTLEY, or alternatively from places in Essex and Somerset called Warley, named in Old English with *wer*, *wer* 'weir' + *lēah* 'wood', 'clearing', or from Warley in the West Midlands, which is named with Old English *weorf* 'draft oxen' + *lēah*.

Worlow (112) Probably a variant of English WORLEY.

Worm (434) **1.** German and Danish: variant of WURM. **2.** English: nickname from Middle English *wurm* 'serpent', 'dragon' (Old English *wyrm*).

Wormald (110) English (Yorkshire): habitational name from Wormald in West Yorkshire or Wormhill in Derbyshire, which is named from an Old English personal name *Wyra* + *hyll* 'hill'.

Worman (788) English: possibly a variant of Warman.

Wormington (240) English: habitational name from a place in Gloucestershire, recorded in Domesday Book as *Wermetune* 'estate (Old English *tūn*) associated with a man called *Wyrma*', and unattested Old English personal name.

Wormley (385) Most probably English: habitational name from places in Hertfordshire and Surrey named Wormley, from Old English *wyrm* 'snake' + *lēah* '(woodland) clearing'. There is, however, a suggestion that the family may be of Dutch origin and that this may be an altered form of an unidentified Dutch name.

Worms (135) German and Jewish (Ashkenazic): habitational name from Worms, on the Rhine.
GIVEN NAME German 4%. *Wolf*.

Wormser (169) German: habitational name for someone from Worms.

Wormuth (218) German: from a Germanic personal name composed of the elements *war* (of various origins) + *mut* 'desire', 'spirit'.
GIVEN NAMES German 4%. *Klaus*, *Manfred*.

Wormwood (156) English: of uncertain origin; possibly a topographic name for someone who lived where wormwood (*Artemesia absinthium*) grew, Middle English *wormod*, or a metonymic occupational name for a herbalist. In the Middle Ages wormwood was variously used as a tonic and vermifuge, in brewing ale, and to protect clothes and linen from moths and fleas.

Worner (247) German (**Wörner**): variant of Werner.
GIVEN NAMES German 4%. *Fritz*, *Gerhard*, *Reinhold*.

Worrall (778) English: variant spelling of Worrell.

Worrel (159) English: variant of Worrell.

Worrell (3838) English: habitational name from Worrall in South Yorkshire, named with Old English *wīr* 'bog myrtle' + *halh* 'nook', 'recess'. The Wirral peninsula in Cheshire has the same origin and may well be the source of the surname in some cases.

Worrick (110) English: variant of Warwick.

Worsham (2208) English: habitational name from either of two places named Worsham, in Oxfordshire and Sussex. The first is named from the Old English personal name *Wulfmǣr* + *hām* 'homestead' or *hamm* 'enclosure hemmed in by water'; the second is from an unattested Old English personal name *Wyrtel* + *hā*.

Worsley (765) English: habitational name from either of two places called Worsley, in Lancashire and Worcestershire. The former, which appears to be the main source of the surname, is probably named from the genitive case of an Old English personal name of uncertain form (probably with a first element *weorc* 'work', 'fortification')

+ Old English *lēah* 'wood', 'clearing'. The first element of the latter is probably from the genitive case of Old English *weorf* 'draft cattle' (a collective noun).

Worst (232) German: variant of Wurst.

Worstell (296) English: topographic name from the dialect term *wormstall* 'summer cattle shelter against gadflies' (from an unattested Old English *wyrm-stall*).

Worster (648) **1.** English: variant of Worcester. **2.** German: variant of Wurster.

Worth (3099) English: habitational name from any of various places named Worth, for example in Cheshire, Dorset, Sussex, and Kent, from Old English *worð* 'enclosure', 'settlement'. The vocabulary word probably survived into the Middle English period in the sense of a subsidiary settlement dependent on a main village, and in some cases the surname may be a topographic name derived from this use.

Wortham (1715) English: habitational name from Wortham in Suffolk, named with Old English *worð* 'enclosure' + *hām* 'homestead'.

Worthan (147) English: variant spelling of Worthen.

Worthen (1377) English: habitational name from Worthen in Shropshire or Worthing in Norfolk, both named from Old English *worðign* 'the enclosure'.

Worthey (419) English: variant spelling of Worthy.

Worthing (320) English: habitational name from either of two places called Worthing, in Sussex and Norfolk. The Norfolk place name is probably from Old English *worðign* 'the enclosure', while the Sussex one is derived from an unattested Old English personal name, *Weorð*, (from Old English *weorð* 'worthy') + *-ingas* 'people of'.

Worthington (5564) English: habitational name from places in Lancashire and Leicestershire named Worthington; both may have originally been named in Old English as *Wurðingtūn* 'settlement (Old English *tūn*) associated with *Wurð*', but it is also possible that the first element was Old English *worðign*, a derivative of *worð* 'enclosure'.
FOREBEARS Nicholas Worthington emigrated from England to Old Saybrook, CT, in about 1650.

Worthley (393) English: unexplained; perhaps a variant of Wortley; otherwise a habitational name from a lost or unidentified place.

Worthman (180) English: possibly an altered form of Wortman.

Worthy (2351) English: **1.** habitational name from any of various minor places called Worthy, from Old English *worðig*, a derivative of *worð* 'enclosure'. **2.** nickname for a respected member of the community, from Middle English *worthy* 'valuable' (a derivative of *worth* 'value', 'merit', Old English *weorð*).

Wortley (214) English: habitational name from either of two places in Yorkshire called Wortley. The one near Barnsley is named with Old English *wyrt* 'plant', 'vegetable' + *lēah* 'wood', 'clearing'; the one near Leeds probably has as its first element an unattested Old English personal name, *Wyrca*, perhaps a short form of a compound name with a first element *weorc* 'work', 'fortification'.

Wortman (1827) **1.** English: metonymic occupational name for a grower or seller of vegetables or of medicinal herbs and spices, from Middle English *wurt*, *wort* 'plant'. **2.** Jewish (Ashkenazic): nickname for a reliable person who could be trusted to keep his word, from Yiddish *vort*, German *Wort* 'word' + *man*, *Mann* 'man'. **3.** Americanized spelling of German Wortmann.

Wortmann (263) North German: topographic name for someone who lived on a raised, secure site, Middle Low German *wort* + *man* 'man'.

Worton (184) English: habitational name from any of various places called Worton. Most are named with Old English *wyrt* 'plant', 'vegetable' + *tūn* 'enclosure', i.e. a kitchen garden, but in some cases the first element may be Old English *worð* 'enclosure' (see Worth), and in the case of Nether and Over Worton in Oxfordshire (*Hortone* in Domesday Book, *Orton* in other early sources), it is Old English *ōra* 'bank', 'slope'.

Wortz (126) German (**Wörtz**): from a pet form of the personal name Werner.

Worzalla (126) Of Polish origin: partly Germanized form of Polish **Worcała**, a nickname of German origin, from German dialect *Worzel*, standard German *Wurzel* 'root'. This may be a nickname for someone from a family that had resided in a particular place for many generations.

Wos (198) Polish (**Woś**): from a pet form of the personal name *Wojciech* (see Voytek).
GIVEN NAMES Polish 12%; German 4%. *Andrzej*, *Genowefa*, *Jadwiga*, *Jerzy*, *Jozef*, *Pawel*, *Tadeusz*; *Konrad* (3).

Woten (114) Variant of English Wooten.

Wotherspoon (166) Scottish: variant of Witherspoon.

Wotring (448) Americanized form of German **Wottreng**, of unexplained origin.

Wotton (242) English: variant of Wooten.

Woulfe (203) **1.** English: variant spelling of Wolf 1. **2.** Irish: translation of Gaelic **Ó Faoláin** (see Whelan).

Wouters (186) Dutch and North German (Lower Rhine): patronymic from the Germanic personal name *Waldhar* (or other forms such as *Walthari*, *Waldheri*, *Waltherus*, *Wolterus*, *Walterus*, *Woutra*) meaning 'mighty army' (see Walter).
GIVEN NAMES French 6%. *Alain*, *Andre*, *Laurent*, *Pascal*.

Wowk (126) German spelling of Ukrainian or Slovenian **Vovk**, a nickname from Ukrainian and Slovenian *vovk* 'wolf'. Compare WOLF.

GIVEN NAME German 4%. *Nikolaus* (2).

Woy (144) Origin unidentified.

Woyak (174) Americanized form of Polish **Wojak**, a derivative of the personal name *Wojtek* (see VOYTEK).

Woytek (118) Americanized spelling of Polish WOJCIK or of Czech *Vojtěk* (see VOYTEK).

Wozney (105) Americanized spelling of Polish WOZNY.

Wozniak (3202) **1.** Polish (**Woźniak**): derivative or patronymic from the occupational or status term *woźny* 'beadle', 'city official' (see WOZNY). **2.** Polish, Ukrainian, and Jewish (from Poland and Ukraine): derivative of *woźny* in its original sense, 'carrier', a derivative of *wozić* 'to carry', hence an occupational name for a carter, driver, or coachman.

GIVEN NAMES Polish 6%. *Tadeusz* (6), *Miroslaw* (3), *Wladyslaw* (3), *Zofia* (3), *Zygmunt* (3), *Andrzej* (2), *Casimir* (2), *Dariusz* (2), *Halina* (2), *Janusz* (2), *Kazimierz* (2), *Wasyl* (2).

Woznick (174) Americanized or Germanized spelling of the Polish occupational name **Woźnik** 'carter', or of its Ukrainian cognate **Voznik**. Compare WOZNIAK.

GIVEN NAMES German 4%. *Frieda, Irmgard.*

Woznicki (313) Polish (**Woźnicki**): habitational name for someone from any of several places called Woźniki.

GIVEN NAMES Polish 4%. *Andrzej* (2), *Jadwiga, Wieslaw.*

Wozny (366) **1.** Polish (**Woźny**): status name for a beadle, usher, or town crier, Polish *woźny* (from *wozić* 'to convey'). The word now means 'caretaker' or 'janitor' in modern Polish. **2.** Ukrainian: occupational name from Ukrainian *voznyj* 'coachman'.

GIVEN NAMES Polish 5%. *Karol* (2), *Andrzej, Ludwik, Teofil, Zofia.*

Wrage (213) North German: nickname from Middle Low German *wrak* 'spoiled', 'damaged', 'useless'.

GIVEN NAMES German 5%. *Claus, Kaethe.*

Wragg (220) English: from the Old Danish personal name *Wraghi*.

FOREBEARS One of the leading figures in colonial Charlestown, SC, during the early 18th century was Samuel Wragg (1714–77), who was made a baron for his services to the colony and the crown; as a Loyalist, he was banished from the colony in 1777.

Wragge (128) **1.** English: variant spelling of WRAGG. **2.** German: variant of WRAGE.

Wratchford (131) Altered spelling of Irish and English RATCHFORD (see ROCHFORD).

Wrather (149) English (Yorkshire): unexplained.

Wratten (122) English (Kent): probably a variant spelling of **Ratten**, from Old French *raton* 'rat', an unflattering nickname for someone thought to resemble a rat, or possibly a metonymic occupational name for a rat catcher.

Wray (5700) English: habitational name from any of various minor places in northern England named Wray, Wrea, or Wreay, from Old Norse *vrá* 'nook', 'corner', 'recess'.

Wrede (361) **1.** North German and Dutch: nickname from Middle Low German *wrede*, 'fierce', 'evil', 'angry'. **2.** English: variant of WRIDE.

GIVEN NAMES German 6%; Scandinavian 4%. *Fritz* (2), *Dieter, Frieda, Ilse, Johann, Wilhelmine; Holger* (2).

Wrege (133) North German: variant of **Wrige**, a nickname from Middle Low German *wrige* 'stiff', 'crazy', 'obstinate', 'wilful'.

Wren (3669) **1.** English: nickname from the bird, Middle English *wrenne*, probably in reference to its small size. **2.** Irish: Anglicized form of Gaelic **Ó Rinn** 'descendant of *Rinn*', a personal name possibly derived from *reann* 'spear'. **3.** Welsh: Anglicized form of Welsh UREN.

Wrench (361) English: nickname from Middle English *wrench* 'wile', 'trick', 'artifice'.

Wrenn (2081) English and Irish: variant spelling of WREN.

Wrice (113) Of uncertain origin; possibly a variant spelling of Welsh RICE.

Wride (154) **1.** Americanized spelling of Dutch and North German WRIEDT. **2.** English: from Old English *wride* 'twist', 'turn', hence a topographic name for someone who lived by a winding stream, or perhaps a nickname for a devious man.

Wriedt (106) North German and Dutch: **1.** nickname from Middle Low German *wrēt, wrede* 'fierce', 'evil', 'angry' (cognate with English *wrath*). **2.** topographic name from Low German *write* 'entangled roots' denoting someone who lived in an overgrown area.

GIVEN NAMES Dutch 4%; German 4%. *Dirk; Hans* (2), *Erwin.*

Wright (148099) **1.** English, Scottish, and northern Irish: occupational name for a maker of machinery, mostly in wood, of any of a wide range of kinds, from Old English *wyrhta, wryhta* 'craftsman' (a derivative of *wyrcan* 'to work or make'). The term is found in various combinations (for example, CARTWRIGHT and WAINWRIGHT), but when used in isolation it generally referred to a builder of windmills or watermills. **2.** Common New England Americanized form of French **Le Droit**, a nickname for an upright person, a man of probity, from Old French *droit* 'right', in which there has been confusion between the homophones *right* and *wright*.

Wrights (103) Variant of English WRIGHT.

Wrightsman (227) Probably English (although no longer found in Britain), meaning 'servant of the wright' (see WRIGHT).

Wrightson (309) English: patronymic from WRIGHT.

Wrigley (845) English (Lancashire): habitational name from Wrigley Head near Salford, the second element of which is presumably Old English *lēah* 'wood', 'clearing'; the first may be a personal name or topographical term from Old English *wrigian* 'to strive', 'to bend or turn'.

Wrinkle (481) English: unexplained; perhaps a variant of RINGLE.

Wrinn (111) Irish: reduced Anglicized form of Gaelic **Ó Rinn** (see WREN).

Wrisley (239) Origin uncertain; perhaps a variant spelling of English RISLEY.

Wriston (222) English: habitational name, probably from Long Riston in East Yorkshire, named from Old English *hrīs* 'brushwood' + *tūn* 'farmstead'.

Writer (143) English: occupational name for a copier of manuscripts, Old English *wrītere*.

Wrobel (1528) Polish and Jewish (eastern Ashkenazic): nickname or Jewish ornamental name from Polish *wróbel* 'sparrow'.

GIVEN NAMES Polish 9%. *Janusz* (3), *Jerzy* (3), *Zbigniew* (3), *Andrzej* (2), *Bogdan* (2), *Halina* (2), *Henryk* (2), *Krzysztof* (2), *Pawel* (2), *Stanislaw* (2), *Cecylia, Elizbieta.*

Wroble (136) Americanized spelling of Polish or Jewish WROBEL.

Wrobleski (446) Polish (**Wróblewski**): variant spelling of WROBLEWSKI.

Wroblewski (1731) Polish (**Wróblewski**) and Jewish (from Poland): habitational name for someone from any of several places called Wróblew or Wróblewo, named with Polish *wróbel* 'sparrow'.

GIVEN NAMES Polish 7%. *Zbigniew* (4), *Jaroslaw* (3), *Zygmunt* (3), *Casimir* (2), *Ireneusz* (2), *Jacek* (2), *Janina* (2), *Jozef* (2), *Krzysztof* (2), *Wojtek* (2), *Aleksander, Andrzej.*

Wroe (190) English: variant of WRAY.

Wrona (547) Polish: nickname for someone thought to resemble a crow in some way, from *wrona* 'crow'.

GIVEN NAMES Polish 11%. *Casimir* (3), *Miroslaw* (2), *Tadeusz* (2), *Andrzej, Bronislaw, Edyta, Halina, Jacek, Janina, Krystyna, Mariusz, Ryszard.*

Wronski (299) Polish (**Wroński**): habitational name from a place called Wronie in Toruń voivodeship or Wrońsko in Sieradz voivodeship, named with *wrona* 'crow'.

GIVEN NAMES Polish 7%. *Rafal* (2), *Grzegorz, Leszek, Stanislaw.*

Wroten (673) Variant of English WRATTEN.

Wrubel (360) Variant spelling of WROBEL.

Wruble (132) Americanized spelling of WROBEL.

GIVEN NAME German 5%. *Bernhardt* (2).

Wruck (320) German: nickname from Middle Low German *wruk*, *wrok* 'cantankerous'.
GIVEN NAMES German 5%. *Kurt* (3), *Inge*, *Karl-Heinz*.

Wrye (244) English: nickname from Middle English *wry(e)* 'bent', 'twisted'.

Wrzesinski (227) Polish (**Wrzesiński**): habitational name for someone from a place called Września in Poznań voivodeship, or a place called Wrzesina or Wrzesiny, named with *wrzos* 'heather'.
GIVEN NAMES Polish 6%. *Bogdan* (2), *Eugeniusz, Przemyslaw, Thadeus*.

Wszolek (113) Polish: unflattering nickname from a diminutive of *wszoł* 'louse'.
GIVEN NAMES Polish 17%. *Zbigniew* (2), *Casimir, Henryk, Mieczyslaw, Teofil, Wojciech*.

Wu (10015) **1.** Chinese 吳: from the name of the ancient state of Wu in what is now Jiangsu province. In the 13th century BC, the state of Zhou was ruled by Tai Wang, who had three sons: Tai Bo, Zhong Yong, and Ji Li. The eldest sons, Tai Bo and Zhong Yong, believing that their father wished the youngest son, Ji Li, to inherit the reins of power, left the Zhou homeland with a group of followers and traveled southeastward to east-central China, where they established the state of Wu. Their descendants eventually adopted Wu as their surname. Ji Li stayed on to rule the Zhou and became the father of the famed virtuous duke Wu Wang, to whom those named Zhou (see CHOW) trace their ancestry. Thus, the surnames **Wu** and **Zhou** are traced to the same ancestor, Tai Wang. **2.** Chinese 胡: Cantonese variant of HU. **3.** Chinese 武: from the name of Ji Wu, a son of Ping Wang (770–719 BC), the first king of the Eastern Zhou dynasty. His descendants adopted the given name Wu as their surname. **4.** Chinese 伍: from the name of Wu Can, an official of the state of Chu during the Spring and Autumn period (722–481 BC). At one time, the states of Chu and Jin were at war. The general of Chu viewed the strong position of the Jin and recommended retreat. However, a minor official, Wu Can, performed an analysis of the situation which concluded that an attack would be better. The prince of Chu agreed with Wu Can, which resulted in a victory over the Jin. Wu Can then became a senior official and used part of his given name, Wu, as his new surname. **5.** Chinese 巫: from the name of Wu Peng, doctor of the legendary emperor Huang Di (2697–2595 BC).
GIVEN NAMES Chinese 37%. *Ming* (40), *Wei* (40), *Jian* (30), *Mei* (26), *Jing* (20), *Ying* (19), *Bin* (18), *Hong* (17), *Jin* (17), *Ping* (17), *Ching* (16), *Wen* (15).

Wubben (193) North German (**Wübben**): from a Frisian short form of a Germanic personal name formed with *walt* 'rule', 'power' or *wolf* 'wolf' as the first element.

Wubbena (120) Variant of North German WUBBEN.

Wuchter (105) German: unexplained; perhaps an altered spelling of WACHTER.

Wuebben (132) North German: variant spelling of **Wübben** (see WUBBEN).

Wuebker (157) German: from a pet form of WUBBEN.

Wuellner (178) German (**Wüllner**): occupational name for a wool worker, a Low German variant of WOLLNER.
GIVEN NAMES German 6%. *Franz, Otto, Wilhelm*.

Wuensch (208) German (**Wünsch**): ethnic name for a Wend (see WENDT).
GIVEN NAMES German 6%. *Dieter, Erna, Siegfried*.

Wuensche (105) German (**Wünsche**): **1.** variant of WENDE (see WENDT). **2.** habitational name from a place in Saxony called Wunscha.
GIVEN NAMES German 12%. *Dieter, Gerhard, Helmut, Reinhard*.

Wuerth (150) German (**Würth**): variant of WIRTH.
GIVEN NAMES German 9%. *Dieter, Erwin, Hans, Irmgard, Juergen, Markus*.

Wuertz (340) German (**Würtz**): variant of **Würtz** (see WURTZ).

Wuest (736) German (**Wüst**): **1.** from Middle High German *wüeste* 'empty', 'uncultivated', hence a topographic name for someone who lived on a piece of waste or fallow land, or a nickname for a coarse or uncultivated man. **2.** habitational name from any of various places called Wust, for example in Brandenburg and Saxony.
GIVEN NAMES German 5%. *Kurt* (2), *Guenther, Hans, Helmut, Horst, Markus, Otto, Wolfgang*.

Wuesthoff (113) German: habitational name for someone from an estate of uncultivated land or a poorly run farm, from Middle High German *wüste* 'deserted', 'neglected', 'derelict', 'abandoned' + *hof* 'farm'.
GIVEN NAME German 4%. *Hans*.

Wuethrich (156) German (**Wüthrich**): unflattering nickname for a tyrannical person, Middle High German *wüetrich* 'tyrant'.
GIVEN NAME German 6%. *Otto* (3).

Wujcik (193) Polish: **1.** from the Polish spelling of Ukrainian *vujchyk*, a diminutive of *vuj* 'uncle', specifically 'mother's brother'. **2.** variant spelling of the diminutive form (here patronymic) of Polish *wójt*, the chief officer of a district or group of villages.

Wujek (142) Polish and Ukrainian: from a diminutive of Polish *wuj*, Ukrainian *vuj* 'uncle', specifically 'mother's brother'.

Wulf (1644) North German and Danish: variant of WOLF.
GIVEN NAMES German 4%. *Hans* (4), *Rainer* (2), *Dieter, Eldor, Ernst, Erwin, Ewald, Franz, Gunter, Harro, Jochen, Kurt*.

Wulfekuhle (105) German: probably a variant spelling of **Wulfekühler**, a habitational name from Wulfskuhl in Mecklenburg-West Pomerania.

Wulff (1136) North German, Danish, and Jewish (Ashkenazic): variant of WOLF.
GIVEN NAMES German 5%. *Kurt* (5), *Hans* (3), *Erwin, Fritz, Helmuth, Johann, Johannes, Klaus, Math, Otto, Siegfried, Ulrich*.

Wullschleger (115) German: variant of WOLLSCHLAGER.
GIVEN NAMES German 5%. *Erwin, Kurt, Manfred*.

Wunder (952) German and Jewish (Ashkenazic): nickname for someone who performed wonders, from German *Wunder* 'miracle', Middle High German *wunderære*. The Jewish name is mainly of ornamental origin. The German name can also be from a nickname for a curious or inquisitive person, from Middle High German *wunder* 'curiosity', 'astonishment'.

Wunderle (141) South German: from a diminutive of WUNDER.

Wunderlich (1545) **1.** German: nickname for an eccentric or moody person, from Middle High German *wunderlīch* 'odd', 'capricious', 'unpredictable' (a derivative of *wunder*, Old High German *wundar* 'puzzle', 'marvel'). **2.** Jewish (Ashkenazic): probably an anecdotal nickname from Yiddish *vunderlekh* 'wonderful', 'marvellous', based on some now irrecoverable event, but possibly also a descriptive nickname from German *wunderlich* 'odd', 'strange'.
GIVEN NAMES German 5%. *Kurt* (4), *Bernhard* (2), *Gebhard* (2), *Benno, Dieter, Eberhard, Erna, Erwin, Gerd, Guenther, Helmut, Klaus*.

Wunderlin (187) German: from a diminutive of WUNDER.

Wunderly (100) Variant spelling of German WUNDERLE.

Wunsch (710) German (of Slavic origin): **1.** habitational name from a place called Wunsch or Wunscha. **2.** (**Wünsch**): see WUENSCH.
GIVEN NAMES German 5%. *Eldor, Ernst, Erwin, Gerhard, Kurt, Manfred, Otto*.

Wunschel (208) South German (also **Wünschel**): nickname for a covetous or greedy person, from Middle High German *wunsch* 'desire', or from a pet form of WUENSCH.
GIVEN NAME German 4%. *Otto*.

Wuollet (112) Finnish (**Vuollet**): ornamental name from *vuolle* 'current'. Found chiefly in Ostrobothnia.
GIVEN NAMES German 6%; Finnish 5%. *Kurt* (2); *Kristiina, Reino, Riitta*.

Wuori (114) Finnish (**Vuori**): ornamental name from *vuori* 'mountain'. It is found throughout Finland. During the name conversion movement in the late 19th and early 20th centuries, this was one of the words denoting natural features taken by Finns as surnames to replace Swedish surnames, in this case particularly Swedish surnames containing the element *berg* 'mountain'. In America, it may also be an abbreviation of

Vourinen, a variant with the surname suffix *-nen*.
GIVEN NAMES Finnish 17%. *Eino* (2), *Armas, Kaarlo, Onni, Sulo, Taisto, Tauno, Urho, Waino.*

Wurdeman (172) **1.** North German (**Wurdemann**, also **Würdemann**): a topographic name from Middle Low German *wurt* 'farm area', 'field', 'woodland'. **2.** German (**Würdemann**): from a Germanic personal name formed with Old High German *wirdi* 'dignity' + *man* 'man'.

Wurgler (119) Swiss German (**Würgel**): occupational name for an executioner or a hangman, from Middle High German *würgel*.
GIVEN NAMES German 4%. *Fritz, Otto.*

Wurl (190) German: variant of **Wörl** (see WORL).
GIVEN NAMES German 7%; Scandinavian 4%. *Gerhard, Hans, Otto, Reinhart; Erik.*

Wurm (683) German: nickname from Middle High German *wurm*, Middle Low German *worm* 'worm', 'snake', 'dragon', 'mythical beast'.
GIVEN NAMES German 5%. *Eldred* (3), *Konrad* (2), *Alois, Florian, Georg, Heinrich, Helmut, Klaus-Dieter, Kurt, Theresia.*

Wurst (843) German: from Middle High German *wurst* 'sausage' (a collective noun), hence either a metonymic occupational name for a butcher who specialized in the production of sausages, or a nickname for a plump person or someone who was particularly fond of sausages.

Wurster (916) German: agent derivative of WURST.
GIVEN NAMES German 5%. *Hans* (2), *Kurt* (2), *Bernd, Dieter, Ernst, Erwin, Fritz, Manfred, Siegfried, Volker.*

Wurtele (118) North German: variant of Wurzel (see WURTZEL), a metonymic occupational name for a greengrocer or vegetable farmer. (*Wurzel* is the North German word for 'carrot').

Wurth (542) German (**Würth**): variant of WIRTH.
GIVEN NAMES German 4%. *Armin, Florian, Gerhard, Jurgen, Kurt, Marliese, Wolfgang.*

Wurts (139) Americanized spelling of WURTZ.

Wurtz (846) German (also **Würtz**): metonymic occupational name for a greengrocer or grower or seller of herbs, from Middle High German *würz* 'herb'.

Wurtzel (221) Variant spelling of German and Jewish WURZEL.
GIVEN NAMES Jewish 8%. *Sol* (3), *Yehuda* (2), *Aviva, Ephraim.*

Wurz (185) German: variant spelling of WURTZ.
GIVEN NAME German 7%. *Kurt* (3).

Wurzbach (110) German: habitational name from Wurzbach in Thuringia or Würzbach in Baden-Württemberg.
GIVEN NAME German 7%. *Otto.*

Wurzel (190) **1.** German: from a diminutive of WURTZ. **2.** Jewish (Ashkenazic): ornamental name from German *Wurzel* 'root'.
GIVEN NAMES German 5%. *Dietmar, Ilse.*

Wurzer (264) German: occupational name for a greengrocer or dealer in herbs, from an agent derivative of Middle High German *würz* 'herb', 'plant' (see WURTZ).
GIVEN NAMES German 6%. *Gerhard* (2), *Ewald.*

Wussow (241) German: habitational name from any of several places so named, notably in Pomerania.
GIVEN NAMES German 5%. *Kurt* (2), *Erna, Ewald.*

Wuthrich (305) German (**Wüthrich**): see WUETHRICH.
GIVEN NAMES German 6%. *Otto* (3), *Friedrich, Gerhardt, Johann.*

Wuttke (154) German: **1.** from a short form of the Slavic personal name *Woitslaw*. **2.** habitational name from Wutike near Neuruppin.
GIVEN NAMES German 19%. *Hans* (2), *Klaus* (2), *Kurt* (2), *Rainer* (2), *Erwin, Fritz, Hedwig, Heinz, Juergen, Manfred.*

Wutzke (145) German: from a short form of the Slavic personal name *Wutschik, Woitzik.*
GIVEN NAMES German 10%. *Gerhard* (2), *Erwin, Frieda, Helmuth, Willi.*

Wyand (222) **1.** English: variant spelling of WYANT. **2.** Americanized spelling of German **Weiand**, itself a variant of WIEGAND.

Wyandt (100) Americanized spelling of German **Weiand**, itself a variant of WIEGAND.

Wyant (2249) **1.** English: from the personal name *Wyun*, a pet form of Old German *Wido*, Old French *Guy*. **2.** Americanized spelling of German **Weiand**, itself a variant of WIEGAND.

Wyatt (17807) English: from the medieval personal name *Wiot, Wyot, Gyot*, which derives from the Old English personal name *Wīgheard*, composed of the elements *wīg* 'war' + *heard* 'hardy', 'brave', 'strong'. Under Norman influence it was also adopted as a diminutive of both GUY 1 and WILLIAM.

Wyble (489) See WIBLE.

Wyche (1151) English: topographic name for someone who lived by a wych elm, Old English *wice*, or habitational name from a minor place named with this word.

Wyckoff (2194) Dutch: topographic name for someone living at the main farm in a district, from Dutch *wijk* 'district' + *hof* 'farmstead', 'manor farm' (see HOF).
FOREBEARS The name is first recorded in North America in 1687, when it was used as a secondary surname for Pieter Claesen (*c.*1619–94), who in 1655 had become superintendent of the Bowery and cattle of Peter Stuyvesant in New Amersfoort, NY, moving into the house in Brooklyn now known as the Pieter Claeson Wyckoff

residence. The surname may have been taken with reference to this house or to some similarly named place in the Netherlands.

Wycoff (808) Dutch: see WYCKOFF.

Wydra (314) Polish: **1.** nickname from Polish *wydra* 'otter'. **2.** possibly from *wydrzeć* 'to pluck', 'to tear away', hence a nickname for someone who seized something from someone else.
GIVEN NAMES Polish 7%. *Stanislaw* (2), *Jurek, Tadeusz, Wladyslaw, Zbigniew, Zdzislaw.*

Wyer (435) **1.** English: variant spelling of WIRE. **2.** Irish: see WEIR.

Wyers (249) English: variant of WIRE.

Wyeth (241) English: unexplained.
FOREBEARS Nicholas Wyeth emigrated from Suffolk, England to Cambridge, MA, before 1645. John Wyeth (1770–1858) was born in Cambridge and became a prominent publisher and editor in Harrisburg, PA.

Wyffels (175) Dutch: patronymic from a Germanic personal name or nickname of uncertain origin. It may be based on the element *wijf* 'woman', 'wife', or possibly *wivel* 'weevil'.

Wygal (221) Variant of German WEIGEL.

Wygant (404) Perhaps an altered spelling of WIGAND.

Wygle (114) Americanized spelling of German WEIGEL.

Wyka (166) Polish: nickname from Polish *wyka* 'vetch', 'tare'.
GIVEN NAMES Polish 12%. *Jozef* (2), *Miroslaw* (2), *Tadeusz* (2), *Casimir, Zosia.*

Wyke (201) English: variant of WICK.

Wykes (202) English: variant of WICK.

Wykle (228) Americanized spelling of German WEIGEL.

Wykoff (422) Dutch: see WYCKOFF.

Wyland (583) German: variant of WIELAND.

Wylde (189) English: variant spelling of WILD.
GIVEN NAMES Irish 5%. *Aidan, Caitlin.*

Wyle (105) English: variant of WILES.

Wyler (344) **1.** English: variant of WHEELER. **2.** Respelling of Jewish WEILER.

Wyles (306) English: variant spelling of WILES.

Wylie (4646) **1.** Scottish and northern Irish: from a pet form of the personal name WILLIAM. **2.** English: variant spelling of WILEY.

Wyllie (630) Scottish: variant spelling of WYLIE.

Wyly (222) English and Scottish: variant of WILEY or WYLIE.

Wyma (110) Frisian: from a personal name of Germanic origin, composed of the elements *wīg* 'battle' + *mār* 'fame'.

Wyman (4661) English: from the Middle English personal name *Wymund*, Old English *Wīgmund* (composed of the elements *wīg* 'war' + *mund* 'protection'), reinforced by the cognate Old Norse form *Vígmundr*, introduced by Scandinavian settlers in northern England.

FOREBEARS John Wyman, from Hertfordshire, England, was one of the founders of Woburn, MA, in 1640.

Wymer (984) English: from the Middle English personal name *Wymer*, Old English *Wīgmǣr* (composed of the elements *wīg* 'war' + *mǣr* 'famous'), reinforced by the cognate Continental Germanic form *Wigmar*, introduced into England from France by the Normans. This also became confused with an Old Breton personal name, *Wiumarch*, composed of the elements *uuiu* 'worthy' + *march* 'horse'.

Wymore (496) English: perhaps a variant of WYMER.

Wynder (174) English: variant spelling of WINDER.

Wyndham (241) English and Irish: variant spelling of WINDHAM.

Wyne (247) **1.** Dutch: variant of WINNE. **2.** English: variant of WYNN.

Wyner (216) Americanized spelling of German and Jewish WEINER.

Wynes (135) English: patronymic from WYNN.

Wyngarden (124) Dutch (**Wijngaerden**): topographic name for someone who owned or lived by a vineyard, or habitational name from any of several places in the Netherlands and Belgium named with this word.

FOREBEARS The name **Wyngaert** is recorded in Beverwijck in New Netherland (Albany, NY) in the mid 17th century.

Wynia (292) Dutch: unexplained.

Wynkoop (765) Dutch: occupational name for a wine merchant.

Wynn (8980) **1.** English: from the Old English personal name and byname *Wine* meaning 'friend', in part a short form of various compound names with this first element. **2.** Welsh: variant of GWYNN.

Wynne (3746) **1.** English: variant spelling of WYNN. **2.** Welsh: variant of GWYNN. **3.** Irish (Connacht): adopted as an English equivalent of Gaelic **Ó Gaoithin** 'descendant of *Gaoithín*' (see GAHAN), because Gaelic *gaoth* also means 'wind', and the English surname *Wynne* was taken as being related to the English vocabulary word *wind*.

Wynns (187) English: patronymic from WYNN.

Wynter (252) English: variant spelling of WINTER.

GIVEN NAMES French 7%. *Camille* (2), *Cecile, Stephane*.

Wyre (140) English: variant spelling of WIRE.

Wyrick (2304) Americanized or Germanized form of Polish **Wyrzyk**, from a personal name of Old Prussian origin.

Wyrzykowski (43) Polish: habitational name for someone from places called Wyrziki in Ciechanów and Łomża voivodeships, named with the personal name *Wyrzyk* (see WYRICK).

GIVEN NAMES Polish 37%; German 5%. *Henryk, Jaroslaw, Radoslaw, Waclaw, Zbigniew, Zygmunt*.

Wyse (948) Irish and English: variant spelling of WISE.

Wysinger (87) Americanized spelling of German WEISSINGER.

Wysocki (1875) Polish and Jewish (from Poland): habitational name for someone from any of various places named with *wysoki* 'high', such as Wysocko, Wysoka, and Wysokie.

GIVEN NAMES Polish 6%. *Andrzej* (4), *Krzysztof* (3), *Boguslaw* (2), *Grzegorz* (2), *Piotr* (2), *Ryszard* (2), *Tadeusz* (2), *Aleksander, Casimir, Ewa, Franciszek, Jacek*.

Wysong (800) Americanized form of German **Weissang**, probably a variant or altered spelling through folk etymology of **Weissaag**, from Middle High German *wīssage* 'prophet', a nickname for a soothsayer.

Wyss (894) Swiss German: Alemannic form of WEISS.

GIVEN NAMES German 5%. *Hans* (2), *Otto* (2), *Willi* (2), *Bernd, Frieda, Fritz, Gerhard, Gottlieb, Kurt, Urs*.

Wyszynski (213) Polish (**Wyszyński**): habitational name for someone from Wyszyny or Wyszyna, both named with the personal name *Wysza*, a derivative of the personal names *Wyszesław* or *Wyszemir*.

FOREBEARS This Polish noble name dates back to the 15th century. Stefan Wyszyński (1901–81) was archbishop of Gniezno and Warsaw and the primate of Poland. Between 1953 and 1956 he was interned in the cloister of Komańcza by the communist regime. In Poland he is known as "The Primate of the Millenium".

GIVEN NAMES Polish 14%. *Andrzej, Bogdan, Casimir, Janina, Jaroslaw, Jerzy, Katarzyna, Mieczyslaw, Tomasz, Zigmund*.

Wythe (135) English: topographic name for someone who lived by a willow tree, Middle English *wythe* (Old English *wiðð e*).

FOREBEARS American bearers of the surname Wythe trace their ancestry to Thomas Wythe, who emigrated from England to VA in 1680. One of his descendants was the statesman and jurist George Wythe (1726–1806), mentor of Thomas Jefferson and one of the signers of the Declaration of Independence.

Wyzykowski (131) Polish: variant of WYRZYKOWSKI.

X–Z

Xander (148) German: from a short form of the personal name ALEXANDER.

Xanders (102) German: variant of XANDER.

Xavier (536) Portuguese and Catalan: from the personal name *Xavier*, Portuguese and Catalan forms of Basque *Xabier* (see JAVIER).

GIVEN NAMES Spanish 14%; Portuguese 10%. *Manuel* (10), *Jose* (7), *Eduardo* (2), *Fernando* (2), *Francisco* (2), *Ramon* (2), *Alberto*, *Alda*, *Alicia*, *Armando*, *Carolina*, *Domingos*; *Joao* (3), *Guilherme*, *Paulo*.

Xenakis (165) Greek: patronymic from XENOS 'stranger', 'newcomer'. The *-akis* patronymic is particularly common in Crete, where it was adopted massively in the 19th century.

GIVEN NAMES Greek 16%. *Nikos* (2), *Antonios*, *Argyro*, *Despina*, *Eleftheria*, *Markos*, *Sotirios*, *Spyros*, *Stamos*, *Stratis*.

Xenos (145) Greek: from Greek *xenos* 'stranger', 'newcomer' (equivalent to English NEWMAN), or short for a composite name such as **Xenocostas** 'Costas the newcomer'. *Xenos* is occasionally found as a personal name.

GIVEN NAMES Greek 9%. *Andreas*, *Antonios*, *Costas*, *Eleftherios*, *Panayiota*, *Savvas*, *Theodoros*.

Xi (90) Chinese 奚: from the name of a man called Xi Zhong, credited with inventing the carriage, who lived during the Xia dynasty (2205–1766 BC).

Xia (345) Chinese 夏: from a name of the model emperor Yu (2205–2198 BC), who was also known as Xia Yu. His descendants adopted the first character of his name as a surname. Xia Yu was a gifted man, chosen by the previous emperor on the basis of merit. His son changed this type of merit-based succession, however, establishing the Xia dynasty (2205–1766 BC), the first dynasty in which the throne was passed on by heredity. The existence of the Xia dynasty has not been confirmed by archaeological evidence, but Chinese historians all accept its existence as fact.

GIVEN NAMES Chinese 71%. *Hong* (6), *Tian* (5), *Wei* (5), *Li* (4), *Ming* (4), *Yang* (3), *Yi* (3), *Bin* (2), *Chu* (2), *Chun* (2), *Fan* (2), *Haiying* (2), *Hui* (2).

Xiang (123) **1.** Chinese 向: there are two accounts of the origin of this surname, which is represented by a character that also means 'to'. The first account derives the name from Xiang Ji, a senior adviser to Wu Wang, the first king (1122–1116 BC) of the Zhou dynasty. The second account traces it to Xiang Fu, a son of a duke of the State of Song during the Spring and Autumn period (722–481 BC). **2.** Chinese 项: from the name of an ancient state of Xiang. Following the defeat of this state, its residents adopted its name as their surname. **3.** Chinese 相: from the name of Xiang, the fifth king of the Xia dynasty (2205–1766 BC).

GIVEN NAMES Chinese 68%. *Hong* (6), *Dong* (3), *Jian* (2), *Kun* (2), *Ning* (2), *Tao* (2), *Cheng*, *Chu*, *Gang*, *Guang*, *Hui*, *Jing*, *Tian*.

Xiao (503) **1.** Chinese 肖: from the name of a territory that existed during the Zhou dynasty (1122–221 BC). **2.** Chinese 萧: from the name of a fiefdom called Xiao (in present-day Anhui province) that existed during the Zhou dynasty (1122–221 BC). A descendant of the ruler of the state of Song was granted this fiefdom and subsequently his descendants adopted the place name as their surname.

GIVEN NAMES Chinese 70%. *Hong* (9), *Dong* (7), *Li* (7), *Yun* (5), *Fei* (4), *Jian* (4), *Yang* (4), *Feng* (3), *Gang* (3), *Jing* (3), *Liang* (3), *Mei* (3), *Min* (3), *Du* (2), *Lan* (2), *Bao*, *Cong*, *Hai*, *Mang*, *Tian*, *Yaping*.

Xie (852) **1.** Chinese 谢: from an area called Xie, in present-day Henan province. Xuan Wang, the penultimate king (827–781 BC) of the Western Zhou dynasty, granted this area to one of his brothers-in-law, and the latter's descendants adopted the place name Xie as their surname. **2.** Chinese 解: from the name of Xie City, which existed in present-day Henan province during the Zhou dynasty (1122–221 BC).

GIVEN NAMES Chinese 75%. *Hong* (6), *Li* (6), *Ming* (6), *Ying* (6), *Min* (5), *Qing* (5), *Yuan* (5), *Bin* (4), *Hui* (4), *Ping* (4), *Wei* (4), *Xiaoli* (4), *Ding* (3), *Chang* (3), *Lan* (2), *Quan* (2), *Cong*, *Dang*, *Hai*, *Tian*, *Yiping*.

Xin (104) Chinese 辛: from the name of a state of Xin that existed during the Xia dynasty. King Qi (2197–2188 BC) granted this state to one of his sons, whose descendants adopted a modified form of the character for Xin as their surname.

GIVEN NAMES Chinese 76%. *Li* (3), *Dapeng* (2), *Fang* (2), *Wei* (2), *Yan* (2), *Chen*, *Chun Lin*, *Feng*, *Fu*, *Guorong*, *Hong*, *Hongbo*.

Xing (108) Chinese 邢: from the name of an area called Xing, which existed during in the Zhou dynasty (1122–221 BC). Descendants of the ruling family of this area adopted Xing as their surname. Another account of the origin of this name derives it from an area named Pingxing.

GIVEN NAMES Chinese 76%. *Gao* (2), *Guoqiang* (2), *Jian* (2), *Jiangang* (2), *Shu* (2), *Yan* (2), *Chao*, *Chu*, *Chun*, *Dongsheng*, *Fan*, *Heming*, *Tian*.

Xiong (2032) **1.** Chinese 熊: this name has at least two origins. The first is from one of the names of the legendary emperor Huang Di (2697–2595 BC), also known as You Xiong; some of his descendants adapted this name as their surname. A second origin traces it to the end of the Shang dynasty in the 12th century BC: at this time there lived in the state of Chu a wise scholar and author, Yu Xiong, who served as teacher to the duke of Zhou, Wen Wang, famous for his virtue. Some of Yu Xiong's descendants adopted their illustrious forebear's given name as their surname. **2.** Laotian and Hmong: unexplained.

GIVEN NAMES Chinese 65%; Other Southeast Asian 11%. *Chue* (31), *Tong* (23), *Ying* (23), *Yia* (21), *Chao* (19), *Mee* (19), *Chou* (18), *Chia* (17), *Kou* (16), *Nhia* (16), *Kao* (14), *Yang* (14); *Neng* (35), *Vang* (29), *Pao* (25), *Yer* (24), *Toua* (18), *Vue* (16), *Blia* (15), *Chong* (15), *Youa* (13), *Blong* (12), *Yeng* (12), *Soua* (11); *Mai* (20), *Hue* (8), *Thao* (8), *Dang* (7), *Long* (7), *Dao* (6), *Bao* (3), *Pha* (3), *Da* (2), *Hai* (2), *Kha* (2), *Khue* (2).

Xu (2328) **1.** Chinese 徐: from the name of the ancient state of Xu. The model emperor Yu (2205–2198 BC) granted this state to one of his retainers. The retainer's family governed the state from this time on until the Western Zhou dynasty (1122–771 BC), when the Xu prince of the time believed it to be God's will that he should oppose the Zhou dynasty, on account of a prophecy associated with a red bow and arrow that he pulled out of a river. The Zhou king, Mu Wang, was far away to the west in the Kunlun mountains, but raced back to confront and defeat the Xu prince (see CHAO 1). Mu Wang then granted the state of Xu to the defeated prince's son, giving him the 'style name' of Xu. Descendants of this new ruler eventually adopted Xu as their surname. **2.** Chinese 许: this name goes back as far as the 23rd century BC. According to tradition, there existed a philosopher named Xu You, who was offered succession to the throne by the model emperor Yao. Having heard this proposal,

Xu You washed his ears in a river to rid them of such defilement. The main stock of this name probably came later, however, when Wu Wang, the first king (1122–1116 BC) of the Zhou dynasty, granted the area of Xu in present-day Henan province to Wen Shu, a descendant of Bo Yi, adviser to the model emperor Shun (who coincidentally accepted the offer of power which Xu You had declined). The descendants of Wen Shu eventually adopted the name of the area of Xu as their surname.

GIVEN NAMES Chinese 78%; Vietnamese 5%. *Wei* (24), *Jing* (19), *Jian* (18), *Ming* (17), *Li* (16), *Yi* (16), *Hui* (15), *Bin* (14), *Gang* (14), *Hong* (14), *Ping* (12), *Jin* (11); *Min* (11), *Chong* (4), *You* (4), *Chang* (2), *Hu* (2), *Neng, Shen, Yiming, Yiping*; *Long* (5), *Hao* (3), *Lan* (3), *Hai* (2), *Bian, Buu, Cong, Dai, Mai, Nu, Quan, Thi.*

Xue (312) Chinese 薛: from the area of Xue, in present-day Shandong province. During the Xia dynasty (2205–1766 BC) an official with the title 'chief of carts' was granted this area. Much later, in the state of Qi during the Warring States period (403–221 BC) the same area was granted to a prince. Descendants of both these men adopted the place name Xue as their surname.

GIVEN NAMES Chinese 72%; Vietnamese 6%. *Hong* (6), *Jian* (5), *Hua* (3), *Liang* (3), *Wei* (3), *Yuan* (3), *Biao* (2), *Chun* (2), *Fei* (2), *Lixin* (2), *Ming* (2), *Qi* (2), *Min, Tian, Yiming*; *Lan* (3), *Hao, Huan.*

Yablon (166) Jewish (Ashkenazic): Americanized spelling of JABLON.

GIVEN NAMES Jewish 8%. *Miriam* (2), *Asher, Hyman.*

Yablonski (243) Americanized spelling of Polish and Jewish JABLONSKI.

Yablonsky (179) Americanized spelling of Polish and Jewish JABLONSKI.

GIVEN NAMES Jewish 6%; Russian 4%. *Alter, Chaim, Irina, Isadore*; *Dmitry, Vasily.*

Yaccarino (108) Americanized spelling of Italian IACCARINO.

Yach (107) Americanized spelling of German or Polish JACH.

Yack (139) Americanized spelling of German JACK 3.

Yackel (247) Probably an Americanized spelling of German **Jackl** or **Jäckel**, from a pet form of the personal name JACH.

Yackley (227) Americanized spelling of German **Jäckle**, from a pet form of the Biblical personal name *Jakob* (see JACOB).

Yacko (146) Americanized short form of any of various surnames beginning with *Jacko-* (see, for example, JACKOWSKI).

Yacono (152) Americanized spelling of Italian IACONO.

GIVEN NAMES Italian 12%. *Salvatore* (2), *Benedetta.*

Yacoub (212) Muslim: from the Arabic personal name *Ya'qūb*, the name of a Prophet

in Islam (the Biblical JACOB). This name is widespread in all Muslim countries.

GIVEN NAMES Muslim 66%. *Fouad* (4), *Hany* (4), *Yacoub* (4), *Adnan* (3), *Khalil* (3), *Baha* (2), *Mahmoud* (2), *Mofid* (2), *Mohsen* (2), *Mourad* (2), *Nabil* (2), *Raad* (2).

Yacovone (119) Americanized spelling of Italian IACOVONE.

GIVEN NAMES Italian 12%. *Dino* (2), *Carmine, Domenico.*

Yadao (123) Filipino: unexplained.

GIVEN NAMES Spanish 44%. *Beatriz* (2), *Jaime* (2), *Manolo* (2), *Ruben* (2), *Alfonso, Amante, Aureo, Bartolome, Benito, Bienvenido, Bonifacio, Carlito.*

Yadav (123) Indian (northern states): Hindu (usually Ahir) name, from Sanskrit *yādava* 'of Yadu', 'descendant of Yadu'. Yadu was a legendary Hindu king, believed to be an ancestor of the god Krishna, who for this reason is sometimes referred to as *Yadava*. Since Krishna is said to have been brought up among Ahirs, who were herdsmen, the surname **Yadav** is popular among them. In Maharashtra, this name is found among the Marathas.

GIVEN NAMES Indian 90%. *Anil* (4), *Rajesh* (4), *Ram* (4), *Sunil* (3), *Ashok* (2), *Dharam* (2), *Mukesh* (2), *Prabhakar* (2), *Sanjay* (2), *Satish* (2), *Satya* (2), *Shiv* (2).

Yaden (170) Probably a variant of English YEADON.

Yadon (391) Probably a variant of English YEADON.

Yaeger (1520) Americanized spelling of German and Jewish surname JAEGER.

Yaffe (481) Jewish (Ashkenazic): variant spelling of JAFFE.

GIVEN NAMES Jewish 8%. *Chaim, Ehud, Eliahu, Ilanit, Meyer, Miriam, Shlomo, Yaacov, Yariv, Yossi.*

Yaffee (101) Jewish (Ashkenazic): variant of JAFFE.

GIVEN NAMES Jewish 9%. *Hyman, Yechezkel.*

Yager (2952) **1.** Jewish (Ashkenazic): Americanized spelling of **Jäger** (see JAEGER). **2.** Americanized spelling of Slovenian **Jager** (see JAGER 3).

Yagi (227) Japanese: 'eight trees'; taken from a valley in Tajima (now part of Hyōgo prefecture) by a branch of the ancient Kusakabe family, which descended from Emperor Nintoku (early 5th century). The name is also found in the Ryūkyūan island of Amami, written with characters used phonetically. The name could also simply mean 'goat'.

GIVEN NAMES Japanese 59%. *Hajime* (3), *Seiichi* (3), *Akira* (2), *Hiroshi* (2), *Kenji* (2), *Kimie* (2), *Koichi* (2), *Masahiro* (2), *Minako* (2), *Morio* (2), *Aki, Asao.*

Yagle (102) Americanized spelling of South German and Swiss **Jaegle** (see JACKLEY).

Yagoda (133) Americanized spelling of Polish and Jewish JAGODA.

GIVEN NAMES Jewish 14%. *Aron* (2), *Meyer* (2), *Hyman, Isidor, Sol.*

Yahn (450) Americanized spelling of German JAHN.

Yahner (151) Americanized spelling of German JAHNER.

Yahnke (283) Americanized spelling of German JAHNKE.

Yahr (215) Americanized spelling of German JAHR, itself a northern variant of GEHR.

Yake (254) Probably an Americanized form of German JACH.

Yakel (255) **1.** Americanized form of German **Jackl** or **Jäckel**, from a pet form of the personal name JACH. **2.** Jewish: from a pet form of JACOB.

Yakes (109) Probably an Americanized form of Czech **Jakeš** (see JAKES).

Yaklin (184) Americanized spelling of South German **Jäcklin**, a pet form of the Biblical personal name *Jakob* (see JACOB).

Yakubov (126) Jewish (from Ukraine, Caucasus, and central Asia): patronymic from the personal name *Yakub*, a variant of JACOB.

GIVEN NAMES Russian 39%; Jewish 21%. *Boris* (8), *Yuriy* (4), *Igor* (3), *Gennadiy* (2), *Grigoriy* (2), *Misha* (2), *Oleg* (2), *Raisa* (2), *Alexey, Evgeniy, Gavril, Grigory*; *Ilya* (3), *Avner* (2), *Ari, Avram, Irina, Isaak, Semen, Yaffa, Yakov.*

Yale (965) Welsh: habitational name for someone who lived in the commote of Iâl (near Wrexham in northeastern Wales), named with Welsh *iâl* 'fertile or arable upland'.

FOREBEARS Yale University in New Haven, CT, takes its name from an early benefactor, Elihu Yale (1649–1721), a merchant of Welsh ancestry. He was born in Boston into a family that originated in Wrexham, Wales; his father, David Yale, had settled in NH in 1637.

Yam (314) **1.** Chinese 任: variant of REN. **2.** Mexican: probably of Mayan origin. **3.** English (Gloucestershire): unexplained.

GIVEN NAMES Chinese 20%. *Chang* (5), *Wai* (2), *Ying* (2), *Boon, Chi, Chi Man, Chong, Chung, Fung, Kan, Kiwon, Ku, Kwun, Lik, Lim.*

Yamada (1524) Japanese: from a place name meaning 'mountain rice paddy'; the surname, like the place name, is very common, so that many of its bearers may be unrelated. The surname is especially common along the eastern seaboard. It is listed in the Shinsen shōjiroku.

GIVEN NAMES Japanese 59%. *Hideo* (8), *Masaru* (8), *Hiroki* (7), *Hiroshi* (7), *Koji* (7), *Takeshi* (7), *Hideki* (6), *Kenji* (6), *Osamu* (6), *Makoto* (5), *Minoru* (5), *Akira* (4).

Yamagata (152) Japanese: variously written, with characters meaning 'mountain shape' or 'mountain district'. Bearers of the first are descendants of the Shiba branch of the MINAMOTO clan, and took the name from a village in Uzen (now Yamagata prefecture). Bearers of the second are of the TADA branch of the same clan, and took their name from a district in Mino (now Gifu prefecture).

GIVEN NAMES Japanese 48%. *Eishi* (2), *Hideo* (2), *Kumiko* (2), *Sayaka* (2), *Tadashi* (2), *Toshiro* (2), *Ako, Ayako, Eiji, Hideki, Hiromi, Hisayo.*

Yamaguchi (938) Japanese: from a very common place name. The meaning as now written is 'mountain entrance', but originally the full meaning was 'entrance to the mountain forest' (*yamabayashi no iriguchi*). The surname occurs most frequently in western Japan. It is listed in the Shinsen shōjiroku.

GIVEN NAMES Japanese 59%. *Kazuo* (6), *Shigeru* (5), *Hiro* (4), *Hiroshi* (4), *Kaoru* (4), *Koji* (4), *Masahiro* (4), *Osamu* (4), *Tadashi* (4), *Takeo* (4), *Takeshi* (4), *Yoshiaki* (4).

Yamakawa (118) Japanese: 'mountain river', listed in the Shinsen shōjiroku and found mostly in western Japan, though the entire country is filled with mountains and rivers. An alternative pronunciation is *Yamagawa.*

GIVEN NAMES Japanese 70%. *Hiroshi* (2), *Takeshi* (2), *Yoshiko* (2), *Akemi, Akio, Akira, Ayumu, Hidehiro, Hisashi, Isao, Jiro, Junya.*

Yamamoto (2457) Japanese: meaning '(one who lives) in the mountains' or 'at the foot of the mountain', this is one of the ten most common surnames; it is found predominantly in central and west-central Japan.

GIVEN NAMES Japanese 53%. *Akira* (11), *Hiroshi* (10), *Hideo* (9), *Takeo* (9), *Satoshi* (8), *Yutaka* (8), *Kazuo* (7), *Susumu* (7), *Tatsuo* (7), *Akiko* (6), *Koji* (6), *Yoko* (6).

Yamamura (136) Japanese: from a place name meaning 'mountain village'; it is an ancient name taken from many villages in the Japanese heartland of Yamato (now Nara prefecture) and surrounding areas. It is found in western Japan and the island of Okinawa, and is listed in the Shinsen shōjiroku.

GIVEN NAMES Japanese 54%. *Hiroshi* (3), *Hiroko* (2), *Kyoko* (2), *Satoshi* (2), *Yuko* (2), *Akemi, Akihiro, Hideshi, Hiroaki, Hirotsugu, Isao, Jitsuo.*

Yamanaka (262) Japanese: topographic name meaning '(one who lives) in the center of the mountains'; it is borne by various descendants of the OGASAWARA, SEKI, SASAKI, and Akamatsu families. It is found chiefly in western Japan and the island of Okinawa.

GIVEN NAMES Japanese 58%. *Hiroyuki* (3), *Koji* (3), *Akira* (2), *Hanayo* (2), *Hideki* (2), *Hiromu* (2), *Kenji* (2), *Masao* (2), *Noboru* (2), *Takeshi* (2), *Akiko, Atsushi.*

Yamane (332) Japanese: meaning 'mountain root'; many bearers are descended from a family which took its name from a location so named in present-day Saitama

prefecture. The name is found mainly in the Tōkyō-Saitama prefectures and west-central Japan, as well as in the island of Okinawa.

GIVEN NAMES Japanese 43%. *Akira* (3), *Noboru* (3), *Eiji* (2), *Kazuo* (2), *Keiji* (2), *Minoru* (2), *Aiko, Akiko, Atsushi, Chisako, Eiko, Emiko.*

Yamaoka (126) Japanese: topographic and habitational name meaning 'mountain hill'; it is found chiefly in western Japan. Bearers from a district in Yamato (now Nara prefecture) are of MINAMOTO origin, while those from Ōmi (now Shiga prefecture) descend from the Ban family.

GIVEN NAMES Japanese 48%. *Hiroshi* (2), *Hisashi* (2), *Kazuya* (2), *Yukio* (2), *Eriko, Fumiko, Haruko, Hideaki, Hiroyuki, Kaoru, Kazuko, Koichi.*

Yamasaki (543) Japanese: alternate pronunciation of YAMAZAKI, found mainly in western Japan and the Ryūkyū Islands. It is the more common form of the name in North America.

GIVEN NAMES Japanese 44%. *Toru* (4), *Tsugio* (3), *Hiroshi* (2), *Kaoru* (2), *Kazuo* (2), *Mamoru* (2), *Midori* (2), *Osamu* (2), *Reiko* (2), *Takeo* (2), *Toshio* (2), *Yoshio* (2).

Yamashiro (317) Japanese: 'mountain castle', taken from the name of the main province of the three which now comprise Kyōto prefecture. The place name originally meant 'behind the mountains' and described the position of the place relative to the more ancient capital city of Nara. When Emperor Kanmu moved the capital there in 794, he changed the second character to its present meaning. Some other families have taken the name from other places with the same name. The surname is mostly found in western Japan and the Ryūkyū Islands, where it is pronounced *Yamagushiku.* It is listed in the Shinsen shōjiroku.

GIVEN NAMES Japanese 30%. *Hisako* (2), *Seiko* (2), *Shigeko* (2), *Shigeru* (2), *Tadao* (2), *Akiyo, Haru, Hide, Hideo, Hiroshi, Isami, Isao.*

Yamashita (826) Japanese: from a common place name meaning '(one who lives) below the mountain'; the surname occurs mostly on the island of Kyūshū. Some bearers are descended from the MINAMOTO or FUJIWARA.

GIVEN NAMES Japanese 58%. *Toshio* (8), *Hiroshi* (6), *Noboru* (5), *Masao* (4), *Takeshi* (4), *Yoshio* (4), *Akira* (3), *Hajime* (3), *Hideo* (3), *Isao* (3), *Kenji* (3), *Koichi* (3).

Yamauchi (371) Japanese: from any of several place names meaning 'within the mountains'. The surname, which is sometimes pronounced **Yamanouchi**, is found mainly in western Japan and the Ryūkyū Islands.

GIVEN NAMES Japanese 49%. *Hiroshi* (4), *Akira* (3), *Kazuya* (3), *Yuki* (3), *Yutaka* (3), *Hiroko* (2), *Kenji* (2), *Koji* (2), *Masaharu* (2), *Takeshi* (2), *Yoichi* (2), *Yoshio* (2).

Yamazaki (248) Japanese: from a common place name meaning 'mountain promontory'. This is a common surname, occurring chiefly in eastern Japan; the alternate pronunciation, **Yamasaki**, is more common in western Japan. Some bearers are of samurai origin.

GIVEN NAMES Japanese 87%. *Hiroshi* (7), *Kenji* (4), *Koichi* (4), *Tomoko* (4), *Akiko* (3), *Akira* (3), *Hiroyuki* (3), *Kazuo* (3), *Kosei* (3), *Masahiro* (3), *Shiro* (3), *Atsushi* (2).

Yambor (122) Americanized spelling of Hungarian JAMBOR.

Yamin (196) **1.** Muslim: from a personal name based on Arabic *yamīn* 'right-hand side' (see the Qur'an 56:38). **2.** Jewish (from Belarus): unexplained.

GIVEN NAMES Muslim 21%; Jewish 6%. *Mohamed* (2), *Mohammad* (2), *Mohammed* (2), *Afshin, Ahmad, Ali, Daud, Hadi, Hasan, Issa, Kamal, Khadijah; Avner, Moshe, Shaul, Sima.*

Yampolsky (149) Jewish (from Ukraine): habitational name from the town of Yampol in Ukraine.

GIVEN NAMES Russian 20%; Jewish 20%. *Igor* (3), *Mikhail* (2), *Semyon* (2), *Vladimir* (2), *Anatoliy, Boris, Grigory, Leonid, Lev, Lubov, Nataly, Sheyva; Ilya* (2), *Chana, Esfir, Mendel, Myer, Volf, Yakov.*

Yan (1395) **1.** Chinese 言: of uncertain origin, originating in Shaanxi province. It may be a variant of another name from the same region and pronounced the same way (see 4 below, 閻). **2.** Chinese 严: the origin of this name is closely tied up with that of ZHUANG. During the Spring and Autumn period (722–481 BC), many members of the ruling class of the state of Chu adopted as their surname *Zhuang*, the posthumously given name of a king of Chu. The name Zhuang was kept until the Eastern Han dynasty (25–220), when, to avoid a taboo on having the same name as the ruler (then Liu Zhuang), many people changed their surname from Zhuang to Yan. **3.** Chinese 颜: from the 'style name' Yan. Yi Fu, a descendant of the grantee of the fief of Zhu (see ZHU 1) during the Zhou dynasty had the 'style name' Yan. Descendants adopted his style name as their surname. **4.** Chinese 閻: there are two accounts of the origin of this name: one a place named Yan Village and the other Yan Town. Both places existed during the Zhou dynasty (1122–221 BC). **5.** Chinese 甄: variant of ZHEN. **6.** Chinese 晏: from the name of a person called Yan An from the state of Qi during the Spring and Autumn period (722–481 BC). **7.** Chinese 殷: variant of YIN 1. **8.** Chinese 鄢: from the name of a state of Yan that existed during the Zhou dynasty (1122–221 BC). **9.** Americanized spelling of JAN.

GIVEN NAMES Chinese 49%; Vietnamese 6%. *Yan* (11), *Hong* (10), *Ming* (8), *Li* (6), *Man* (6), *Chi* (5), *Ying* (5), *Kam* (4), *Siu* (4), *Wai*

(4), *Wei* (4), *Wing* (4); *Chung* (4), *Pak* (4), *Kwok Fai* (2), *Min* (2), *Yuet* (2), *Chong*, *Chun Ho*, *Hu*, *Shen*, *Sook Ja*, *Yeung*; *Lan* (4), *Hai* (3), *Hung* (3), *Sau* (3), *Tin* (3), *Chau* (2), *Chut*, *Dam*, *Dat*, *Hau*, *Huan*, *Lap*.

Yanagi (101) Japanese: 'willows', a surname found mostly in eastern Japan and in the Ryūkyū Islands.
GIVEN NAMES Japanese 65%. *Haruo* (2), *Masa* (2), *Ryohei* (2), *Takeshi* (2), *Eiji*, *Fumi*, *Fumio*, *Hiro*, *Hisao*, *Kazunobu*, *Kimiko*, *Koichi*.

Yanak (106) Americanized spelling of Czech **Janák** (see JANAK).

Yancey (4598) Americanized form of Dutch JANSEN (final -*n* is silent in some dialects of Dutch).

Yancy (1222) Variant of YANCEY.

Yanda (257) Americanized spelling of Czech JANDA.

Yandell (872) English (Somerset): unexplained.

Yandle (407) English: variant of YANDELL.

Yando (140) Americanized form of French GUINDON.
GIVEN NAME French 4%. *Armand* (2).

Yandow (205) Americanized spelling of French GUINDON.
GIVEN NAMES French 8%. *Marcel* (2), *Andre*, *Emile*.

Yanek (111) Americanized spelling of Czech and Polish JANEK.

Yanes (459) Spanish: variant of **Yáñez** (see YANEZ).
GIVEN NAMES Spanish 43%. *Jose* (16), *Juan* (11), *Luis* (7), *Carlos* (5), *Pedro* (4), *Armando* (3), *Felipe* (3), *Francisco* (3), *Manuel* (3), *Margarito* (3), *Mario* (3), *Miguel* (3).

Yaney (174) Americanized spelling of German **Jähne**, from a short form of the personal name *Johannes* (see JOHN).

Yanez (2081) **1.** Spanish (**Yáñez**): patronymic from a variant of the personal name *Juan*, Spanish equivalent of JOHN. Compare IBANEZ. **2.** Americanized spelling of Slovenian **Janež**, a derivative of the personal name *Janez*, Latin *Iohannes* (see JOHN).
GIVEN NAMES Spanish 49%. *Jose* (56), *Juan* (26), *Francisco* (21), *Carlos* (20), *Jesus* (20), *Manuel* (20), *Raul* (20), *Luis* (15), *Miguel* (15), *Rafael* (12), *Roberto* (12), *Mario* (11).

Yang (10178) **1.** Korean: there are four Chinese characters used for the Yang surname, but only two are common enough to consider here; they have between them eight clans. The founding ancestor of the Ch'ŏngju Yang clan was Chinese and stayed in Korea after escorting Koryŏ, King Kongmin's future queen to Korea. The first historical ancestor of the Cheju Yang clan was a Shilla figure named Yang T'ang, but according to legend, his distant ancestor was one of three men who ascended from a cave on the north side of Cheju Island's Halla Mountain. These three men were the founders of the Yang, PU, and KO clans. The legendary founder of the Yang clan was named Yang Ŭl-la. Some days after their emergence, a box washed up on the shore of the island. In the box were three women, horses, cows, and agricultural seed. From these beginnings, the three established Cheju's T'amnaguk kingdom and ruled peacefully for 900 years. Later, descendants of the three men settled throughout Korea, although 40 percent of the Yang clan still live on Cheju island and in Chŏlla province. **2.** Chinese 杨: from the name of the state of Yang during the Zhou Dynasty. The first king of this dynasty, Wu Wang (1122–1116 BC), had a son named Tang Shuyu; a descendant of his was enfeoffed the state of Yang, and later descendants adopted the name of the state as their surname. **3.** Chinese 阳: from a region called Yang that existed in the state of Qi during the Spring and Autumn period (722–481 BC). **4.** Chinese 羊: in the Spring and Autumn period (722–481 BC), there existed in the state of Jin a senior adviser with the surname Yang-she. During the Warring States period (403–221 BC) his descendants fled to escape destruction by the conquering Qin, and simplified their surname to Yang. **5.** Laotian: unexplained.
GIVEN NAMES Chinese 43%; Other Southeast Asian 20%. *Mai* (39), *Chue* (35), *Chia* (34), *Chang* (33), *Chong* (32), *Ming* (32), *Mee* (30), *Wei* (30), *Hong* (29), *Jae* (29), *Kao* (28), *Tong* (28), *Yia* (28), *Chao* (27), *Seung* (26); *Pao* (44), *Neng* (39), *Vang* (32), *Yer* (32), *Pang* (25), *Youa* (22), *Doua* (18), *Shoua* (17), *Koua* (16), *Yeng* (16); *Dang* (10), *Thao* (10), *Bao* (6).

Yanick (144) Americanized spelling of German JANICK or Polish, Czech, and Hungarian JANIK.

Yanik (225) Partly Americanized spelling of Polish, Czech, and Hungarian JANIK and Slovak **Janík**. See also German JANICK.
GIVEN NAME German 4%. *Kurt* (2).

Yanish (144) Americanized spelling of German **Jänisch** (see JANISCH).

Yank (137) Americanized spelling of Dutch or North German **Jank**, itself a variant of JANKE.

Yanke (441) Americanized spelling of Dutch or North German JANKE or JAHNKE.

Yankee (299) Americanized spelling of Dutch or North German JANKE, JAHNKE, or JENKE.

Yankey (240) Americanized spelling of Dutch or North German JANKE, JAHNKE, or JENKE.

Yanko (281) Americanized spelling of Slavic JANKO.

Yankovich (275) Americanized spelling of Serbian and Croatian **Janković** or Slovenian **Jankovič** (see JANKOVIC).

Yankowski (236) Americanized spelling of Polish JANKOWSKI.

Yanni (262) Americanized spelling of Italian IANNI.
GIVEN NAMES Italian 8%. *Palma* (3), *Antonio*, *Valentino*.

Yannone (171) Americanized spelling of Italian IANNONE.
GIVEN NAMES Italian 13%. *Angelo* (5), *Carmin*.

Yannotti (101) Americanized spelling of Italian IANNOTTI.
GIVEN NAMES Italian 16%. *Sal* (2), *Americo*, *Gino*, *Rocco*.

Yannuzzi (178) Americanized spelling of Italian IANNUZZI.
GIVEN NAMES Italian 8%; Spanish 5%. *Alberto* (2), *Angelo*, *Carmin*, *Gilda*; *Carlos*, *Juana*, *Miguel*, *Rosario*.

Yano (342) Japanese: from a common place name, usually written with characters meaning 'arrow field'; the original meaning was 'eighth field', eight being from ancient times the sacred number of completion. The surname is found chiefly in western Japan.
GIVEN NAMES Japanese 45%. *Hiroshi* (5), *Hajime* (3), *Hideki* (3), *Koichi* (3), *Takahiro* (3), *Hiroyuki* (2), *Kazuhiko* (2), *Kazuo* (2), *Keiji* (2), *Masao* (2), *Akiko*, *Akira*.

Yanofsky (137) Americanized spelling of Polish JANOWSKI or Jewish JANOVSKY.
GIVEN NAMES Jewish 8%. *Eliyahu*, *Shimon*.

Yant (452) Variant of YANTZ.

Yanta (140) Origin unidentified.

Yantis (396) Americanized form of Dutch or North German JANZ.

Yantz (206) Americanized spelling of Dutch or North German JANZ.

Yao (1077) Chinese 姚: from the name of an ancient place (Yao Ruins), in present-day Henan province. According to legend, the model emperor Shun (2257–2205 BC) was conceived and born here, after his mother was so greatly moved by the beauty of a rainbow that she became pregnant. Some of Shun's descendants later adopted the place name Yao as their surname.
GIVEN NAMES Chinese 39%. *Jin* (5), *Jing* (5), *Yao* (5), *Yuan* (5), *Cheng* (4), *Hong* (4), *Min* (4), *Gang* (3), *Jia* (3), *Jian* (3), *Li* (3), *Ping* (3), *Ying* (3), *Yiming* (2), *Yiping* (2), *Chung*, *Neng*, *Shen*.

Yap (831) **1.** English: nickname for a clever or cunning person, from Middle English *yap* 'devious', 'deceitful', 'bent'; 'shrewd'. **2.** Americanized spelling of North German JAPP. **3.** Chinese: variant of YE. **4.** Filipino: unexplained.
GIVEN NAMES Spanish 11%. *Enrique* (3), *Jose* (3), *Alberto* (2), *Carlos* (2), *Fernando* (2), *Rodolfo* (2), *Rolando* (2), *Rosalina* (2), *Vincente* (2), *Adela*, *Adoracion*, *Alfredo*.

Yaple (334) **1.** Americanized spelling of Slovenian *Japelj*, derivative of the personal name *Jap*, a dialect short form of *Jakob* (see JACOB). **2.** Americanized form of German **Jäpel**, a pet form of JAPP.

Yapp (200) Variant of YAP.

Yarber (954) English: probably an altered form of English **Yarbord** or **Yerburgh**, both variants of YARBROUGH.

Yarberry (343) English: **1.** variant of YARBROUGH. **2.** possibly a habitational name from any of the places named Arbury (for example in Warwickshire and Cambridgeshire), named from Old English *eorðbyrig*, the dative form of *eorðburg* 'earthworks'.

Yarboro (158) English: variant of YARBROUGH.

Yarborough (2295) English (Lincolnshire): variant of YARBROUGH.

Yarbough (165) English: variant of YARBROUGH.

Yarbro (463) Variant spelling of English YARBROUGH.

Yarbrough (8302) English: habitational name from Yarborough and Yarburgh in Lincolnshire, named with Old English *eorðburg* 'earthworks', 'fortifications', (a compound of *eorðe* 'earth', 'soil' + *burh* 'fortress', 'stronghold').

Yard (507) English: **1.** topographic name for someone who lived by an enclosure of some kind, Middle English *yard(e)* (Old English *geard*; compare GARTH). **2.** nickname from Middle English *yard* 'rod', 'stick' (Old English (Anglian) *gerd*), probably with reference to a rod or staff carried as a symbol of authority. **3.** from the same word as in 2, used to denote a measure of land. The surname probably denoted someone who held this quantity of land, and as it was quite a large amount (varying at different periods and in different places, but generally approximately 30 acres, a quarter of a hide), such a person would have been a reasonably prosperous farmer.

Yarde (167) English: variant spelling of YARD.

Yardley (811) English (West Midlands): habitational name from any of various places, for example Yardley in the West Midlands, Essex, Northamptonshire, etc., or Yarley in Somerset, named with Old English *gerd*, *gyrd* 'pole', 'stick' + *lēah* 'wood', 'clearing'. The compound apparently referred to a forest where timber could be gathered.

Yarger (716) Americanized spelling of German **Järger** or **Jerger**, a patronymic from the personal name *Georg* (see GEORGE).

Yarian (153) Probably of Dutch origin. See YERIAN.

Yarish (118) Americanized form of Czech **Jareš** (see JAROS).

Yarman (121) Americanized spelling of German **Jahrmann**, a variant of GEHRMANN.

Yarnall (541) English: variant of YARNELL.

Yarnell (1278) English: possibly a variant of ARNALL.

Yaroch (160) Americanized spelling of German **Jaroch**, a derivative of Czech and Slovak **Jaroš** (see JAROS).

GIVEN NAMES German 4%. *Gerhard, Oskar.*

Yaros (194) Americanized spelling of Polish JAROSZ or Czech and Slovak **Jaroš** (see JAROS).

Yarosh (164) Americanized spelling of Polish JAROSZ or Czech and Slovak **Jaroš** (see JAROS), or from a Russianized form of these names.

GIVEN NAMES Russian 8%. *Vladimir* (4), *Kseniya, Raisa, Yevgeniy.*

Yarrington (414) English: probably a habitational name from a lost or unidentified place, possibly in the West Midlands, where the surname is now most frequent.

Yarrow (219) Scottish (Borders) and English: **1.** habitational name from a place so called, named for the river on which it stands, one in the Border region of Scotland, the other in Lancashire, both named with Welsh *garw* 'rough'. **2.** topographic name for someone who lived in a place overgrown with yarrow, Old English *gearwe*.

Yarter (110) Origin unidentified.

Yarwood (200) **1.** English: habitational name from Yarwood Heath in Cheshire, earlier Yarwode, from Old English *earn* 'eagle' + *wudu* 'wood'. **2.** Welsh: Anglicized form of the Welsh personal name *Iorwerth*, composed of the elements *iôr* 'lord' + a lenited form of *berth* 'handsome'.

Yasin (199) Muslim: from Arabic *yā sīn*, the first two letters at the beginning of sura 36 of the Qur'an, endowed with mystic significance, being interpreted as a divine address to the Prophet Muhammad. This is a popular personal name throughout the Islamic world.

GIVEN NAMES Muslim 80%. *Ali* (7), *Mohammad* (7), *Mohamed* (6), *Mohammed* (6), *Muhammad* (4), *Naim* (4), *Yousif* (4), *Aishah* (2), *Aleem* (2), *Amin* (2), *Bibi* (2), *Latifah* (2).

Yasko (122) Americanized spelling of JASKO.

Yassin (104) Muslim: variant spelling of YASIN.

GIVEN NAMES Muslim 69%. *Hassan* (4), *Mohamed* (4), *Mohammad* (3), *Mohammed* (3), *Ahmed* (2), *Mahmoud* (2), *Said* (2), *Samir* (2), *Abdel, Abdul, Adem, Akram.*

Yasuda (356) Japanese: from a common place name meaning 'safe (or inexpensive) rice paddy', found throughout Japan and the Ryūkyū Islands. Several families have taken the surname; some are descendants of the MINAMOTO, TAIRA, or other noted families.

GIVEN NAMES Japanese 57%. *Satoshi* (5), *Hiroshi* (3), *Masao* (3), *Takashi* (3), *Akihiro* (2), *Akio* (2), *Hideki* (2), *Hiro* (2), *Hiroyuki* (2), *Katsuya* (2), *Minoru* (2), *Nobuyoshi* (2).

Yasui (142) Japanese: 'safe well'; two families are descended from different branches of the MINAMOTO clan. The name is mostly found in western Japan and the Ryūkyū Islands.

GIVEN NAMES Japanese 49%. *Koichi* (2), *Akihiko, Akira, Eiji, Eizo, Hiroaki, Hiromi, Hisashi, Katsuto, Keisuke, Kenji, Kiyo.*

Yasutake (101) Japanese: 'peaceful warrior', not common in Japan.

GIVEN NAMES Japanese 48%. *Kenji* (3), *Yutaka* (2), *Akinobu, Atsushi, Ayako, Chisako, Hide, Hiroyuki, Hisayo, Kazuyoshi, Masaki, Masao.*

Yater (153) Americanized form of German JETER.

Yates (22026) English: from Middle English *yates* 'gates', plural of *yate*, Old English *geat* 'gate', hence a topographic name for someone who lived near the gates of a walled town, or a metonymic occupational name for a gatekeeper.

Yatsko (294) Origin unidentified.

Yau (630) **1.** Chinese 邱: Cantonese variant of QIU 1. **2.** Chinese: see YOU.

GIVEN NAMES Chinese 28%. *Chi* (3), *Ching* (3), *Chuen* (3), *Chun* (2), *Jee* (2), *Kwok Wing* (2), *Mei* (2), *Sau* (2), *To* (2), *Cheuk, Chi Keung, Chi Kin, Chi Ming, Chi Wei; Chau, Hung, Kwok Kwong, Lam, Mui, Ngan, Tung, Yen.*

Yauch (215) Americanized spelling of the southern German and Swiss surname JAUCH.

GIVEN NAME German 4%. *Kurt.*

Yauger (256) Americanized form of Dutch JAGER.

Yaun (201) Americanized form of Dutch JAHN.

Yavorsky (101) Americanized spelling of Czech and Slovak **Javorský** (see JAVORSKY).

Yaw (506) **1.** Irish: perhaps a reduced and altered Anglicized form of Gaelic **Mac Eochadha** (see McGAFFEY, McGEOUGH). **2.** English: probably a variant of YEO. **3.** Chinese 邱: Cantonese variant of QIU 1. **4.** Chinese: see YOU.

Yawn (848) Americanized spelling of German JAHN.

Yaworski (149) Americanized spelling of Polish JAWORSKI.

Yax (239) Perhaps an Americanized spelling of the German (Frisian) surname **Jaacks**, a patronymic from a reduced form of *Tjadeke*, itself a reduced form of the personal name *Tjadebern* or *Tjadeward*, Frisian forms of *Dietbern* and *Dietward* respectively.

Yazdani (151) Iranian: derivative of *Yazdān*, used in Persian personal names such as *Yazdān Bakhsh* 'gift of God', a name corresponding to Greek *Theodōros* (see THEODORE).

GIVEN NAMES Muslim 80%. *Ali* (2), *Masoud* (2), *Mohammed* (2), *Ramin* (2), *Vafa* (2),

Abbas, Abdi, Afsaneh, Ahmad, Amir, Arezoo, Ata.

Yazdi (114) Iranian: habitational name for someone from the city of Yazd.
GIVEN NAMES Muslim 75%. *Ali* (6), *Farrokh* (4), *Feryal* (2), *Hamid* (2), *Hassan* (2), *Nematollah* (2), *Ramin* (2), *Ahmad, Akram, Alireza, Ebrahim, Erfan.*

Yazel (118) Of Dutch origin: see YAZELL.

Yazell (128) American reduced and altered form of Dutch **van Ysselstein**, a habitational name from the village of IJsselstein, near Utrecht.
FOREBEARS Cornelius Martinse van Ysselstein came to New Netherland in 1658. The name was eventually Americanized as **Yeazel** or **Yazell**.

Yazzie (468) Navajo: unexplained.

Ybanez (240) Spanish (**Ybáñez**): variant spelling of **Ibáñez** (see IBANEZ).
GIVEN NAMES Spanish 37%. *Benito* (3), *Jose* (3), *Luis* (3), *Manuel* (3), *Gustavo* (2), *Jesus* (2), *Mario* (2), *Sergio* (2), *Adolfo, Alfonso, Arturo, Asela.*

Ybarbo (156) perhaps of Basque origin: possibly a derivative of Basque *ibar* 'meadow'. The surname is not found in present-day Spain.
GIVEN NAMES Spanish 10%. *Benito, Domingo, Elvira, Ignacio, Jesus, Lupe, Ramon, Rosendo.*

Ybarra (3203) Basque: variant spelling of IBARRA.
GIVEN NAMES Spanish 37%. *Jose* (50), *Manuel* (45), *Juan* (32), *Jesus* (18), *Lupe* (17), *Raul* (17), *Ruben* (17), *Francisco* (16), *Carlos* (14), *Ramon* (14), *Mario* (13), *Guadalupe* (11).

Ye (858) **1.** Chinese 叶: from the name of the area of Ye, in present-day Henan province. During the Spring and Autumn period (722–481 BC), a senior military adviser of the state of Chu was killed in battle; his son was granted the area of Ye, with the title Duke of Ye. The Duke of Ye was successful in battle, and his descendants adopted the place name Ye as their surname. **2.** Korean: variant of YI.
GIVEN NAMES Chinese/Korean 65%. *Wei* (14), *Hong* (11), *Jian* (9), *Qing* (9), *Feng* (5), *Zhong* (5), *Bin* (4), *Jin* (4), *Li* (4), *Mei* (4), *Min* (4), *Ming* (4), *Wen* (4); *Chol, Dong Sup, Jong Chul, Myong, Neng, Sook Young, Sung Chul.*

Yeadon (242) English (Yorkshire): habitational name from Yeadon, a place in West Yorkshire, named from Old English *gēah* 'steep' + *dūn* 'hill'.

Yeager (9024) Americanized spelling of German **Jäger** (see JAEGER).

Yeagle (268) Americanized spelling of German **Jäggle** or **Jäckle**, from a pet form of the Biblical personal name *Jakob* (see JACOB).

Yeagley (362) Americanized spelling of German **Jäggle** or **Jäckle**, from a pet form

of the Biblical personal name *Jakob* (see JACOB).

Yeakel (355) Americanized spelling of German **Jäckle** or **Jäckel** (see YEAGLEY).

Yeakey (156) Americanized spelling of German **Jäcke**, a pet form of JAKOB.

Yeakle (187) Americanized spelling of German **Jäckle** (see YEAGLEY).

Yeakley (227) Americanized spelling of German **Jäckle** (see YEAGLEY).

Yeaman (335) Scottish and English: variant of YEOMAN.

Yeamans (168) Scottish and English: variant of YEOMANS.
FOREBEARS Sir John Yeamans (1610–74), of Bristol, England, was an early governor of colonial Carolina.

Yearby (186) English: habitational name from Yearby in Cleveland (formerly in North Yorkshire), which Ekwall derives from Old Scandinavian *Efribýr* 'upper village or homestead'.
GIVEN NAMES French 4%. *Celestine, Marcell.*

Yeargain (163) Americanized form of German **Jürgen** (see JURGENS).

Yeargan (264) Americanized form of German **Jürgen** (see JURGENS).

Yeargin (484) Americanized form of German **Jürgen** (see JURGENS).

Yearick (226) Americanized form of Danish **Jorick**, a Danish form of GEORGE, also found in Northern Germany.

Yearous (130) Probably an Americanized form of Dutch **Joris** (see JORISSEN).

Yearout (349) Americanized form of German **Jurreit**, German form of Lithuanian **Jurgaitis**, patronymic from the personal name *Jurĝis*, Lithuanian form of Greek *Geōrgios* (see GEORGE).

Yearsley (245) English: variant of YARDLEY.

Yearwood (874) English: variant of YARWOOD.

Yeary (1003) Origin uncertain. Most probably a variant of Irish GEARY.

Yeast (139) English: unexplained.

Yeater (543) Evidently a variant spelling of the unexplained surname YATER.

Yeates (632) English: variant of YATES.

Yeatman (419) English: extended form of YATES.

Yeaton (487) Probably English: habitational name from Yeaton in Shropshire, named with Old English *ēa* 'river' + *tūn* 'farmstead', or possibly from any of the numerous places called Eaton (see EATON). The surname, however, does not appear in current English records.

Yeats (325) Scottish and northern English: variant spelling of YATES.

Yeatts (707) Scottish and northern English: variant spelling of YATES.

Yeaw (122) English: unexplained; perhaps a variant spelling of YEO.

Yeazel (139) Of Dutch origin: see YAZELL.

Yeboah (108) African: unexplained.
GIVEN NAMES African 21%. *Kwabena* (3), *Kwasi* (3), *Kofi, Kwaku, Kwame.*

Yeck (251) Americanized spelling of German **Jäck** or **Jeck** (see JACK).

Yeckley (172) Americanized form of German **Jäckle** or Swiss German **Jeggli** (see YEAGLEY).

Yedinak (190) Americanized spelling of Polish JEDYNAK or Slovak **Jediník**, a descriptive epithet from Polish *jedynak* or Slovak *jedinácik* 'only child'.

Yee (5194) **1.** Chinese 余: variant of YU 2. **2.** Chinese 俞: variant of YU 4. **3.** Chinese 易: variant of YI 2. **4.** Korean: variant of YI 1. **5.** Filipino: unexplained.
GIVEN NAMES Chinese/Korean 10%. *Wing* (19), *Wah* (8), *Wai* (8), *Gim* (7), *Kam* (7), *Kan* (7), *Ping* (7), *Kwok* (6), *Ming* (6), *Fook* (5), *Lai* (5), *Mei* (5).

Yegge (112) Americanized form of Swiss German **Jäggi**, from a pet form of *Jacob* (see JACOB).

Yeh (1631) Chinese 叶: variant spelling of YE.
GIVEN NAMES Chinese 19%. *Ching* (8), *Ming* (5), *Cheng* (4), *Chin* (3), *Hui* (3), *Hui Chun* (3), *Ping* (3), *Yuan* (3), *Chi* (2), *Chien* (2), *Ching Ling* (2), *Ching Yu* (2).

Yehl (141) Americanized spelling of German **Jehl**, a variant of JEHLE.

Yehle (175) Americanized spelling of German JEHLE.
GIVEN NAMES German 5%. *Otto.*

Yeich (116) Origin unidentified. Possibly an Americanized form of German **Jetsch** or **Jätsch**, variants of JESCH, pet forms of the personal name *Johannes* (see JOHN).
GIVEN NAME German 5%. *Franz* (2).

Yeilding (106) Variant of YIELDING.

Yeiser (166) Probably an Americanized spelling of German **Jeser**, **Jeeser**, or **Jehser**, a topographic name from Sorbian *jezor* 'pond'.

Yeisley (128) Americanized form of German **Jaisle**, a pet form of the medieval personal name *Jodocus* (from Celtic, meaning 'warrior', 'fighter') or from the biblical name *Joash*.

Yeldell (205) Origin unidentified.

Yelder (113) English: probably a variant of ELDER.

Yeley (131) Origin unidentified. It may be a variant of English **Yeoley**, which is most probably from an unidentified place named in Old English with *ēa* 'river' (see YEO) + *lēah* 'woodland clearing'.

Yelich (113) Americanized spelling of Serbian and Croatian **Jelić**, a metronymic from the female personal name *Jela*, short form of *Jelisaveta* (see ELIZABETH) or Croatian *Jelena*. The Croatian female personal name *Jela* could also be of Slavic origin, from *jela* 'fir tree'.
GIVEN NAMES South Slavic 5%. *Branko, Pasko.*

Yelinek (114) Americanized spelling of Czech JELINEK.

Yelk (107) Americanized spelling of Swiss German **Jelk**, a pet form of the personal name JELLE.

Yell (274) **1.** English (Essex): unexplained; perhaps from the personal name *Yuel*, a form of the biblical name *Joel*. **2.** Scottish (Shetland): from the name of the principal island of the Shetlands. According to Black, 'Persons of this name in Shetland have changed to Dalziel, probably from the idea of its being more aristocratic, and spell Deyell or De Yell.'

Yelland (167) English (Devon and Cornwall): habitational name from any of several places named Yelland, as for example near Bideford, Devon, from Old English *ēald* 'old' + *land* 'land'.

Yelle (399) **1.** Americanized spelling of German **Jelle**, from a short form of a personal name beginning with the element *geld* 'to be worth', for example *Gelderich* or *Geldolf*. **2.** Possibly a respelling of Norwegian HJELLE.
GIVEN NAMES French 10%. *Armand* (2), *Sylvain* (2), *Adrien, Andre, Gaston, Gisele, Henri, Normand, Pierre*.

Yellen (314) **1.** English: probably a variant of YELLAND or YELLIN. **2.** Americanized spelling of Norwegian **Hjellen**, from the definite singular form of Old Norse *hjallr* 'terrace', 'ledge' (see HJELLE). **3.** Jewish (Ashkenazic): variant spelling of JELEN.

Yellin (467) **1.** English: perhaps a variant of **Yelling**, a habitational name from Yelling in Cambridgeshire (formerly in Huntingdonshire), probably named with the Old English personal name *Giella* + *-ingas* 'people of'. **2.** Jewish (Ashkenazic): variant of JELEN.
GIVEN NAMES Jewish 5%. *Aviva, Hyman, Reuven, Rina, Sol, Yett*.

Yellott (103) English (Yorkshire): probably a variant of ELLIOTT.

Yelton (1041) Scottish and English: variant spelling of **Yeltoun**, a surname of uncertain origin recorded in Lanarkshire. Black speculates that it may be a habitational name from Youlton in North Yorkshire, which is named from the Old Scandinavian personal name *Jóli* + Old English *tūn* 'farmstead', 'settlement'.

Yelverton (822) English: habitational name from a place in Devon recorded in 1291 as *Elleford* 'elder tree (Old English *ellen*) ford'; *tūn* 'village' is a later addition. Alternatively, the surname may have be from Yelverton in Norfolk, which is probably from the personal name *Geldfriþ* + Old English *tūn* 'village', 'settlement'.

Yelvington (279) English: perhaps an altered spelling of YELVERTON.

Yen (1156) **1.** Chinese: see YAN. **2.** Chinese 甄: see ZHEN.
GIVEN NAMES Chinese 18%; Vietnamese 4%. *Wei* (4), *Chen* (3), *Cheng* (3), *Chi* (3), *Chieh* (3), *Chih* (3), *Ching* (3), *Shing* (3), *Wen* (3), *Chao* (2), *Chimin* (2), *Chung-Cheng* (2); *Anh Thi, Chau, Cuc, Cuong, Giai, Hoanh, Houng, Hue, Hung, Lam, Leang, Ly*.

Yencha (104) Origin unidentified.

Yenney (105) Americanized spelling of Swiss-German JENNY.

Yennie (103) Americanized spelling of Swiss German JENNY.

Yenser (127) Probably an Americanized form of German **Jenzer** or **Jentzer**, probably a variant of **Jantzer**, a pet form of the personal name *Johann(es)* (see JOHN).

Yenter (172) Americanized spelling of German **Jenter**, from a Germanic personal name formed with *gand-* 'magic'.

Yeo (682) **1.** English (chiefly Devon and Somerset): habitational name from any of several minor places in Somerset and Devon named with southwestern Middle English *ya* or *yo* (Old English *ēa* 'stream', 'river', the same word as found in NYE, RYE, and TYE). **2.** Korean: variant of YOH.
GIVEN NAMES Korean 5%. *Yong* (3), *Cheng* (2), *In* (2), *Li* (2), *Youngho* (2), *Bock, Byeong, Chi, Eunsook, Fung, Hoon, In Young*.

Yeoman (806) English and Scottish: **1.** status name, from Middle English *yoman*, *yeman*, used of an attendant of relatively high status in a noble household, ranking between a SERGEANT and a GROOM, or between a SQUIRE and a PAGE. The word appears to derive from a compound of Old English *geong* 'young' + *mann* 'man'. Later in the Middle English period it came to be used of a modest independent freeholder, and this latter sense may well lie behind some examples of the surname. **2.** topographic name, an expanded form of YEO.

Yeomans (1106) English (chiefly Midlands): patronymic from YEOMAN 1.

Yep (158) **1.** English: variant of YAP. **2.** Chinese: see YE.
GIVEN NAMES Chinese 6%. *Jing, Shin, Tong, Wai, Wing Fong*.

Yepes (161) Spanish: habitational name from Yepes in Toledo province (the ancient city of *Hippo* or *Hipona*).
GIVEN NAMES Spanish 57%. *Carlos* (4), *Gustavo* (3), *Hernan* (3), *Julio* (3), *Mario* (3), *Aura* (2), *Cesar* (2), *Efrain* (2), *Francisco* (2), *Guadalupe* (2), *Jaime* (2), *Pedro* (2).

Yepez (401) Spanish (**Yépez**): habitational name for someone from Yepes. See YEPES.
GIVEN NAMES Spanish 56%. *Jose* (9), *Jesus* (6), *Ignacio* (4), *Javier* (4), *Jorge* (4), *Juan* (4), *Rafael* (4), *Raul* (4), *Ruben* (4), *Alberto* (3), *Armando* (3), *Carlos* (3).

Yerby (396) English: variant of YEARBY.

Yerdon (261) Variant of English **Yeardon**, which is of unexplained origin. It may be a variant of YEADON.

Yerger (681) Americanized spelling of German JERGER.

Yerian (257) Origin uncertain. It is probably an Americanized spelling of North German or Dutch **Jurian**, a diminutive of the personal name *Joris*, a Dutch form of GEORGE. The notion that it is Armenian seems to be based on nothing more than the *-ian* ending, which is characteristic of Armenian surnames. It is not known as an Armenian surname.
FOREBEARS Matthias Jerian or Jurian arrived in Philadelphia from the Palatinate, Germany, on the ship *Pleasant*, in October 1732.

Yerk (113) Variant of JERKE.

Yerke (168) Americanized spelling of German JERKE.
GIVEN NAME German 4%. *Theodor*.

Yerkes (731) Americanized spelling of German and Dutch **Jerkes**, a patronymic from the personal name JERKE.

Yerkey (184) Americanized spelling of German and Dutch JERKE.

Yerks (114) Americanized spelling of German and Dutch **Jerkes** (see YERKES).

Yerman (140) Anglicized spelling of: **1.** Slovenian **Jerman**, a variant of the personal name *Herman* (see German HERMANN). **2.** German **Jährmann** or **Jermann**, variants of GEHRMANN.
GIVEN NAME German 4%. *Kurt*.

Yero (101) Spanish: habitational name from Yero in Cuenca province.
GIVEN NAMES Spanish 36%; African 4%. *Luis* (3), *Carlos* (2), *Conrado* (2), *Jorge* (2), *Juan* (2), *Arminda, Arnaldo, Blanca, Candido, Demetrio, Efren, Evelio*; *Mamadou* (2).

Yerton (109) English: unexplained. See YERDON.

Yerxa (134) Americanized spelling of Dutch **Jurckse**, a patronymic meaning 'son of George'. Compare YERKES.

Yeske (252) Americanized spelling of German JESKE.

Yester (135) Origin unidentified.

Yetman (356) English: variant of YEATMAN.

Yett (144) Probably an Americanized spelling of German JETTE.

Yetter (1089) Americanized spelling of German JETTER.

Yetzer (144) Origin unidentified.

Yeung (1476) Chinese: see YANG.
GIVEN NAMES Chinese 35%. *Chun* (7), *Chi* (5), *Ching* (5), *Kwok* (5), *Po* (5), *Wai* (5), *Wing* (5), *Kam* (4), *Ming* (4), *Ping* (4), *Sai* (4), *Chi Hung* (3); *Yiu* (3), *Cho* (2), *Chung* (2), *Kwok Fai* (2), *Moon* (2), *Pak* (2), *Chong, Kok, Kwok Wai, Mi Soon, Nam, Pae*.

Yewell (118) Variant spelling of English YULE.

Yezzi (114) Americanized spelling of Italian IEZZI.

GIVEN NAMES Italian 9%. *Dante* (2), *Mauro* (2), *Luciano*.

Yglesias (191) Altered spelling of Spanish IGLESIAS.

GIVEN NAMES Spanish 35%. *Manuel* (8), *Jose* (5), *Rafael* (3), *Juan* (2), *Orlando* (2), *Angel, Armando, Arturo, Benigno, Eduardo, Elena, Ernesto*.

Yi (3586) **1.** Korean: the second most common surname in Korea, comprising about 16 percent of the total population. It is found in every part of the country. There are three Chinese characters for the surname *Yi*, but two of the three are quite rare, and one of these is not found outside North Korea. Although some sources indicate that there are as many as 546 different clans, only about 100 have been documented. The founder of the oldest clan, the Kyŏngju Yi, was named Yi Al-p'yŏng and lived in AD 32. He was one of the six original governors of pre-Shilla Korea. Aside from a few other Yi families that originated from the Kyŏngju Yi clan, most of the other 100 or so clans were formed at the end of the Koryŏ or beginning of the Chosŏn periods. Some Korean Yi families trace their origins back to China. The founder of the Chosŏn Kingdom, or Yi Dynasty, Yi Sŏng-gye, was a member of the Yi clan from Chŏnju. This clan ruled the Korean peninsula from 1392 to 1910. **2.** Chinese 易: from an area named Yi, probably from Yi county in Hebei province.

GIVEN NAMES Chinese/Korean 71%. *Yong* (49), *Young* (41), *Sung* (31), *Sang* (29), *Kyong* (24), *Song* (23), *Chae* (19), *Jung* (19), *Jong* (17), *Sun* (17), *Kwang* (13), *Chun* (12); *Chong* (76), *Chang* (28), *Pyong* (16), *Myong* (13), *Chung* (11), *Hyong* (8), *Chol* (7), *Kum* (7), *Pong* (7), *Byung* (6), *Min* (6), *Hae* (5).

Yielding (233) English (Sussex): unexplained.

Yilmaz (139) Turkish: from the personal name *Yılmaz* 'unyielding'.

GIVEN NAMES Muslim 70%. *Ali* (4), *Adnan* (2), *Emin* (2), *Ibrahim* (2), *Salih* (2), *Adil, Ahmet, Arzu, Aziz, Bahri, Cafer, Coskun*.

Yim (1263) **1.** Chinese 严: variant of YAN 2. **2.** Chinese 阎: variant of YAN 4.

GIVEN NAMES Chinese 49%. *Yong* (12), *Young* (12), *Sung* (10), *Chong* (9), *Chun* (5), *Dong* (5), *Jung* (5), *Kwang* (5), *Sang* (5), *Chang* (4), *Ho* (4), *Jong* (4), *Kwok* (4), *Song* (4), *Chul* (3), *Myung Ja* (3), *Chong Sun* (2), *Chung* (2), *Min* (2), *Myong* (2), *Pak* (2), *Pong* (2), *Taek* (2), *Ae*.

Yin (858) **1.** Chinese 尹: from the name of Yin City, in present-day Shanxi province, or from a status name of a government official. A grandson of the legendary emperor Huang Di (2697–2595 BC) was granted Yin City and in due course his descendants adopted the name of the city as their surname. Additionally, throughout the Shang (1766–1122 BC) and Zhou (1122–221 BC)

dynasties, there existed a high government position called Yin. Many descendants of Yin officials adopted the status name Yin as their surname. **2.** Chinese 殷: from the name of the Yin dynasty and the city from which it takes its name. Midway through the Shang dynasty (1766–1122 BC), the Shang moved their capital to the city of Yin, in present-day Henan province. Some scholars divide the Shang dynasty into two parts, calling the first half the Shang dynasty, and the second half the Yin dynasty. After the Zhou conquered the Shang, many descendants of the vanquished Yin adopted the city name as their surname. **3.** Cambodian: unexplained.

GIVEN NAMES Chinese 42%; Cambodian 6%. *Feng* (3), *Hong* (3), *Jian* (3), *Kong* (3), *Li* (3), *Man* (3), *Min* (3), *Ning* (3), *Yuan* (3), *Bei* (2), *Chao* (2), *Ching* (2), *Chong* (2), *Chung* (2), *Heng* (2) *Yeng* (2), *Tun, Youn*; *Hai, Phal, Phon, Pu, Samnang, Tho, Thy*.

Ying (442) **1.** Chinese 应: from the name of the state of Ying, which existed during the Zhou dynasty (1122–221 BC). After Wu Wang established the Zhou dynasty in 1122 BC, he granted to his fourth son the state of Ying, along with the title Marquis of Ying. Descendants of the marquis later adopted the state name Ying as their surname. **2.** Chinese 邢: variant of XING. **3.** Chinese 英:there are two accounts of the origin of this surname, the character for which also means 'hero'. One is a territory called Ying that existed during the Zhou dynasty (1122–221 BC) until its defeat by the state of Chu. The other source is a personage named Ying Bu who lived during the Han dynasty (206 BC–220 AD). **4.** Laotian: unexplained. **5.** Americanized form of German JUNG.

GIVEN NAMES Chinese 36%; Other Southeast Asian 5%. *Chen* (4), *Li* (3), *Ho* (2), *Hong* (2), *Jin* (2), *Ming* (2), *Nai* (2), *Wenlong* (2), *Chang-Sheng, Cheng, Chi, Chia*; *Moua* (2), *Siew, Tian, Vang*.

Yinger (438) Americanized form of German **Jünger** (see JUNGER).

Yingling (1668) Americanized form of the German surname **Jüngling**, from a diminutive of JUNG.

Yingst (452) Americanized form of German **Jüngst**, a distinguishing name for the youngest son of a family, from the superlative form of Middle High German *junc* 'young'. Compare JUNG.

Yip (1260) Chinese 叶: Cantonese variant of YE.

GIVEN NAMES Chinese 24%. *Wai* (9), *Wing* (9), *Ching* (4), *Lai* (4), *Chi* (3), *Chi Hung* (3), *Chun* (3), *Kam* (3), *Kan* (3), *Man* (3), *Shu* (3), *Yuk* (3).

Yiu (209) **1.** Chinese 姚: Cantonese variant of YAO. **2.** Chinese 饶: variant of RAO.

GIVEN NAMES Chinese 34%; Other Southeast Asian 4%. *Chun* (3), *Kwok* (2), *Pei* (2), *Wai* (2), *Cheung, Chik, Ching Yi, Chun Man,*

Ho, Hong Yu, Kam, Kin Wing; *Houng, Lap, Ngok, Tin, Tung*.

Ylitalo (134) Finnish: topographic name from *yli* 'upper' + *talo* 'house', 'building'. This name is found chiefly in central and northern Finland.

GIVEN NAMES Scandinavian 5%; Finnish 4%. *Erik* (2); *Aaro, Jaana, Wilho*.

Yniguez (190) Spanish (**Yñíguez**): variant spelling of **Iñíguez** (see INIGUEZ).

GIVEN NAMES Spanish 34%. *Jose* (4), *Juan* (3), *Manuel* (3), *Alfredo* (2), *Amador* (2), *Eduardo* (2), *Silverio* (2), *Alfonso, Andres, Asencion, Aurelio, Carlos*.

Yoak (169) Probably a variant of English OAK.

Yoakam (207) Americanized form of German JOACHIM.

Yoakum (914) Americanized form of German JOACHIM.

Yoast (134) Americanized form of Dutch JOOST or German JOST.

Yob (137) Americanized spelling of German or Hungarian JOB.

Yocham (214) Americanized form of German JOACHIM.

Yochem (125) Americanized form of German JOACHIM.

Yochim (211) Americanized form of German JOACHIM.

Yochum (581) Americanized form of German JOACHIM.

Yock (129) Americanized spelling of southern German **Joch**, a variant of JAUCH.

Yockel (101) Americanized spelling of German **Jockel**, a Bavarian pet form of JAKOB.

Yockey (759) Probably an Americanized form of a German dialect pet form of JAKOB.

Yocom (742) Americanized form of German JOACHIM.

Yocum (2452) Americanized form of German JOACHIM.

Yoder (11269) Americanized spelling of the Swiss surname **Joder**, from a reduced form of the personal name *Theodor(us)* (see THEODORE). This was the name of the patron saint of western Switzerland.

Yodice (153) Americanized spelling of Italian **Jodice**, a variant spelling of IODICE, or of Iodice itself.

GIVEN NAMES Italian 19%. *Angelo* (3), *Carmine* (3), *Carmela, Salvatore*.

Yoe (156) **1.** English: probably a variant of YEO. **2.** Perhaps also an Americanized form of Hungarian **Jó** (see JO).

Yoes (166) Americanized form of Dutch, German, or Hungarian JOOS.

Yoest (109) Americanized form of Dutch JOOST or German JOST.

Yoffe (135) Jewish (eastern Ashkenazic): variant of JAFFE.

GIVEN NAMES Jewish 20%; Russian 12%. *Dov* (2), *Aron, Eliya, Jacov, Shlomo, Yacov, Yonah*; *Boris* (3), *Vladimir* (3), *Dmitry, Fedor, Leonid, Lubov, Yulia*.

Yogi (112) **1.** Japanese: variously written, the name is of Ryūkyūan origin and is usually written with characters meaning 'bestow' and 'ceremony'. **2.** Indian (Gujarat, Maharashtra): Hindu (Brahman) name, from Sanskrit *yogī* 'one who performs yoga', i.e. someone who does exercises designed to promote control of the mind and body.
GIVEN NAMES Japanese 29%; Indian 4%. *Seiko* (2), *Akio*, *Kenji*, *Kishin*, *Masaichi*, *Masayoshi*, *Matsu*, *Satoshi*, *Seichi*, *Setsu*, *Shinji*, *Sumio*; *Anand*, *Hari*.

Yoh (189) Korean (**Yŏ**): there are two Chinese characters for this surname. Only one of them is used by a clan large enough to warrant treatment here. The Ŭryŏng Yŏ clan's founding ancestor is said to have been Yŏ Sŏn-jae, a Song Chinese government officer who migrated from China to Koryŏ. Although members of the Yŏn clan can be found throughout the Korean peninsula, they are concentrated in the Kyŏngsang provinces.

Yohannan (119) Indian (Kerala): from the Hebrew personal name *yōḥānān* (see JOHN), used as a given name among Christians in Kerala (southern India) and in the U.S. found as a last name among families from Kerala.
GIVEN NAMES Indian 25%. *Mathai* (4), *Panna*, *Raju*.

Yohannes (173) **1.** Americanized spelling of German JOHANNES. **2.** Ethiopian: from a personal name based on Latin *Johannes*, Hebrew *Yochanan* (see JOHN).
GIVEN NAMES Ethiopian 54%; Jewish 5%; African 4%. *Lemlem* (3), *Azeb* (2), *Kesete* (2), *Saba* (2), *Tesfay* (2), *Abeba*, *Afework*, *Aklilu*, *Alem*, *Amanuel*, *Araya*, *Bereket*; *Aron*, *Berhe*, *Robel*; *Almaz*.

Yohe (897) Americanized form of North German **Johe**, from a short form of the personal name *Johannes*.

Yohey (121) Americanized form of German **Johe**.

Yohman (103) Variant of German **Johmann**, pet form of JOHE.

Yohn (756) Americanized spelling of North German JOHN.

Yoho (974) Americanized spelling of German and Swiss German **Joho**, unexplained.
FOREBEARS This name was brought to North America by Johannes Joho from Sulzthal in 1738.

Yoke (138) English: status name from Old English *geoc* 'holder of a yoke (a measure of land)'.

Yokel (129) Respelling of German **Jockel** or **Jöckl**, from a pet form of the personal name *Jakob*, German form of JACOB.

Yokley (474) Americanized spelling of German **Jöchle**, from a pet form of the personal name JOACHIM.

Yokom (125) Americanized form of German JOACHIM.

Yokota (209) Japanese: 'rice paddy to the side', also pronounced *Yokoda*; it is found throughout Japan and the Ryūkyū Islands. Several families have samurai or noble connections, and there are two very old families of Suruga (now part of Shizuoka prefecture) and Musashi (present-day Tōkyō–Saitama prefectures).
GIVEN NAMES Japanese 58%. *Hideo* (2), *Hisao* (2), *Koichi* (2), *Masao* (2), *Masaru* (2), *Shiro* (2), *Akiyo*, *Asako*, *Chiyoko*, *Eiko*, *Emiko*, *Fumiko*.

Yokoyama (413) Japanese: 'mountain to the side'; it is found throughout Japan and the Ryūkyū Islands, but mostly in the north.
GIVEN NAMES Japanese 60%. *Kiyoshi* (4), *Shigeru* (4), *Hiroshi* (3), *Yutaka* (3), *Akihiko* (2), *Atsushi* (2), *Katsuhisa* (2), *Kazuhiko* (2), *Kazuo* (2), *Kenji* (2), *Koichi* (2), *Koji* (2).

Yokum (284) Americanized form of German JOACHIM.

Yon (791) **1.** French: from the Latin personal name *Ionis*, which also occurs as an element of place names. The personal name was popularized by a 3rd-century Athenian saint who evangelized Châtres (present-day Arpajon), where he was martyred. As an American family name, it is probably of Huguenot origin. **2.** Korean (**Yŏn**): there are three Chinese characters for the surname *Yŏn*, only one of which occurs frequently enough to be treated here. Some sources indicate that there are thirty Yŏn clans, but they all seem to be descended from the Hapsan Yŏn clan, whose founding ancestor, Yŏn Su–ch'ang, migrated to the Koryŏ kingdom after escorting a princess to the Koryŏ court. The king (probably King Ch'ungyŏl (1274–1308)) gave him some land in the Hapsan area, and so began the Hapsan Yŏn clan. The surname can be found throughout the peninsula, but it is most common in Ch'ungch'ŏng North province.

Yonamine (110) Japanese: possibly meaning 'rice plant peak', the name is found mostly in the Ryūkyū Islands.
GIVEN NAMES Japanese 37%. *Shigeo* (2), *Shigeru* (2), *Chizuko*, *Hideo*, *Kiyomi*, *Kiyoto*, *Koichi*, *Kosei*, *Masa*, *Mika*, *Mutsuko*, *Noboru*.

Yonan (220) Variant spelling of Turkish YOUNAN.

Yonce (405) See YONTZ.

Yoneda (134) Japanese: 'rice paddy', also pronounced *Maita*, *Maida*, or *Kometa*; all forms are found mostly in western Japan and the Ryūkyū Islands.
GIVEN NAMES Japanese 61%. *Kentaro* (3), *Masaru* (2), *Noboru* (2), *Toshio* (2), *Aki*, *Akira*, *Hiromi*, *Izumi*, *Juichi*, *Kayo*, *Kazuo*, *Kenichi*.

Yong (581) **1.** Americanized spelling of Dutch JONG. **2.** Chinese 雍: from the name of the state of Yong, which was granted to the thirteenth son of the virtuous duke Wen Wang (1231–1135 BC). The son also received the title Earl of Yong, and his descendants adopted Yong as their surname. **3.** Korean: there are two characters and two clans associated with the Yong surname; one is too rare to be treated here. The other claims its origins in prehistoric tribal Korea. In this early period, tribes would assume the names of animals. It is said that the Yong surname (which means 'dragon') came into being when the tiger tribe wished to avoid being named after a man-eating beast. The first recorded ancestor was an official in the court of the Koryŏ king Wŏn-jong (1260–73). **4.**
GIVEN NAMES Chinese/Korean 28%; Other Southeast Asian 5%. *Hai Long* (2), *Khee* (2), *Leong* (2), *Seung* (2), *Xinsheng* (2), *Chen*, *Chi Kin*, *Ching*, *Ching-Mei*, *Choi*, *Chang*, *Chong Su*, *Chu*, *Eng*, *Fong*, *Hak Soo*, *Hu*, *Kok*, *Kwang-Soo*, *Min*, *Pak*, *Soon Young*; *Bian*, *Hung*, *Mui*, *Phal*, *Phan*, *Savuth*, *Seong*, *Son*, *Tan*, *Thao*.

Yonge (133) **1.** Americanized spelling of Dutch JONG. **2.** English: variant of YOUNG.

Yongue (148) **1.** English: variant spelling of YOUNG. **2.** Perhaps also an Americanized spelling of Dutch JONG.

Yonke (294) Americanized spelling of German JONKE.

Yonker (693) Americanized spelling of Dutch JONKER.
FOREBEARS This was the title given to Adriaen van der Donck for his service in ending the 1643–45 Indian war in New Netherland; out of gratitude he was given a tract of land north of Manhattan that is now known as Yonkers.

Yonkers (335) Americanized spelling of Dutch **Jonkers**, a variant of JONKER.

Yonts (300) Americanized spelling of Dutch or North German JANZ.

Yontz (318) Americanized spelling of Dutch or North German JANZ.

Yoo (2171) Korean and Chinese: see YU.
GIVEN NAMES Chinese/Korean 68%. *Young* (40), *Jae* (29), *Sung* (19), *Kyung* (16), *Jung* (15), *Kwang* (14), *Seung* (14), *Jin* (12), *Sang* (11), *Won* (8), *Yong* (8), *Ho* (7); *Chung* (17), *Byung* (10), *Chang* (9), *Dae* (4), *Hae* (4), *Jeong* (4), *Kwang Soo* (4), *Sook Ja* (4), *Chong* (3), *Chul* (3), *Do Hyun* (3), *In Suk* (3).

Yoon (2609) **1.** Korean: variant of YUN. **2.** Chinese: see RUAN. **3.** Chinese: see YUN.
GIVEN NAMES Chinese/Korean 65%. *Young* (61), *Jung* (21), *Sung* (21), *Jae* (18), *Won* (15), *Jong* (14), *Sang* (14), *Kyung* (13), *Yong* (13), *Suk* (12), *Dong* (11), *Kwang* (11); *Byung* (16), *Chang* (13), *Chul* (10), *Chong* (9), *Jeong* (7), *Chung* (6), *Dae* (6), *Hae* (6), *Byung Ho* (4), *Nam* (4), *Seok* (4), *Byung Hoon* (3).

Yoos (130) Americanized spelling of Dutch and North German JOOS.
GIVEN NAME German 7%. *Fritz* (2).

Yopp (462) Americanized spelling of German JOPP.

Yordy (324) Americanized form of German **Jorde** or Swiss German **Jordi**, from a pet form of the personal name *Jördan* (see JORDAN).

Yore (205) English and Irish: unexplained.
GIVEN NAME Irish 4%. *Liam.*

Yori (110) **1.** Americanized spelling of Italian **Iori** or **Jori**, patronymics from the personal names IORIO or *Jorio*, a variant. **2.** Yaqui: nickname from Yaqui *yori*, 'white person', 'someone who is not yaqui'.
GIVEN NAMES Spanish 5%. *Fernando, Guerrino, Jaime, Luis, Marina.*

Yorio (188) Americanized spelling of Italian IORIO.
GIVEN NAME Italian 4%. *Beniamino.*

York (18575) English: habitational name from the city of York in northern England, or perhaps in some cases a regional name from the county of Yorkshire. The surname is now widespread throughout England. Originally, the city bore the British name *Eburacum*, which probably meant 'yew-tree place'. This was altered by folk etymology into Old English *Eoforwīc* (from the elements *eofor* 'wild boar' + *wīc* 'outlying settlement'). This name was taken over by Scandinavian settlers in the area, who altered it back to opacity in the form *Iorvík* and eventually *Iork*, in which form it finally settled by the 13th century. The surname has also been adopted by Jews as an Americanized form of various like-sounding Jewish surnames.

Yorke (593) English: variant spelling of YORK.

Yorks (252) English: variant of YORK.

Yorty (119) Probably a variant of YORDY.

Yoshida (1360) Japanese: from a common place name meaning 'lucky (or good) rice paddy'. The surname is variously written; it is very common throughout Japan, especially in the west and the Ryūkyū Islands. It is listed in the Shinsen shōjiroku.
GIVEN NAMES Japanese 62%. *Hiroshi* (14), *Susumu* (8), *Minoru* (7), *Takashi* (7), *Akio* (6), *Akira* (6), *Atsushi* (6), *Kiyoshi* (6), *Tadao* (6), *Hideo* (5), *Hitoshi* (5), *Jiro* (5).

Yoshihara (121) Japanese: from a very old and common place name in Japan and the Ryūkyū Islands meaning 'lucky (or good) plain', which has been taken as a surname by several unrelated families. One family descends from court nobles who took the name in ancient times. It is also pronounced *Yoshiwara*; and in the Ryūkyū Islands as *Yoshibaru*.
GIVEN NAMES Japanese 45%. *Takao* (2), *Taro* (2), *Hideki, Hideo, Hiro, Hiroaki, Hisako, Kensaku, Koichi, Masami, Masanori, Ryo.*

Yoshikawa (276) Japanese: from an ancient and common place name meaning 'lucky (or good) river', which was taken by several families, mostly in western Japan and the Ryūkyū Islands. One family is of

the Kudō branch of the southern FUJIWARA, while others descend from the Ōe family (see OE).
GIVEN NAMES Japanese 64%. *Hiroshi* (4), *Ayako* (3), *Maki* (3), *Takashi* (3), *Atsushi* (2), *Hideo* (2), *Koshiro* (2), *Susumu* (2), *Tetsuo* (2), *Yukio* (2), *Aki, Akio.*

Yoshimoto (286) Japanese: 'lucky (or good) origin'; it is found mostly in west-central Japan and the island of Okinawa.
GIVEN NAMES Japanese 47%. *Kazumi* (2), *Masaya* (2), *Michiko* (2), *Takashi* (2), *Tsugio* (2), *Akihiro, Hanako, Harumi, Haruo, Hideshi, Hiroshi, Hiroyoshi.*

Yoshimura (503) Japanese: 'lucky (or good) village'; it is found mainly in western Japan. Many bearers are unrelated, some having samurai origins.
GIVEN NAMES Japanese 49%. *Haruo* (3), *Hiroshi* (3), *Kazuyuki* (3), *Masao* (3), *Takashi* (3), *Toshiaki* (3), *Akira* (2), *Fumio* (2), *Hitoshi* (2), *Ichiro* (2), *Isao* (2), *Kiyoshi* (2).

Yoshinaga (109) Japanese: 'luck eternal'. The name is not common and is found mostly in western Japan and in the Ryūkyū Islands.
GIVEN NAMES Japanese 45%. *Hiroko* (3), *Koji* (2), *Masayuki* (2), *Atsushi, Fujiko, Fumio, Keiichiro, Makoto, Mitsunori, Miyako, Naoko, Nobuyoshi.*

Yoshino (186) Japanese: ancient name meaning 'lucky (or good) field', taken from the scenic Yoshino region of southern Yamato (now Nara prefecture). It is also written with characters meaning 'fragrant field'. Some bearers are descendants of Emperor Bidatsu (reigned 572–585), while others are of the SATO, MINAMOTO, NITTA, KIKUCHI, and other noted families. It is listed in the Shinsen shōjiroku, and is found in eastern Japan and the island of Okinawa.
GIVEN NAMES Japanese 56%. *Hiroshi* (3), *Tadashi* (3), *Haruo* (2), *Nobuo* (2), *Toshiaki* (2), *Toshihiro* (2), *Yasuo* (2), *Aki, Akihiko, Akio, Eiichi, Genji.*

Yoshioka (412) Japanese: from a number of locations throughout Japan named 'lucky (or good) hill'. Several families have taken the surname, which is found mostly in western Japan and the Ryūkyū Islands.
GIVEN NAMES Japanese 59%. *Takashi* (4), *Masato* (3), *Takae* (3), *Yutaka* (3), *Izumi* (2), *Katsumi* (2), *Kazuo* (2), *Keiko* (2), *Kenji* (2), *Koji* (2), *Kunio* (2), *Makoto* (2).

Yoss (191) Americanized spelling of German JOSS.

Yost (7626) Americanized spelling of German **Jost**, a variant of JOOS, or of Dutch JOOST.

Yosten (103) Americanized spelling of German JOSTEN.

Yother (244) Origin unidentified.

Yothers (149) Origin unidentified.

Yott (170) Probably an Americanized spelling of German **Jott** or **Jotte**, variants of GOTT 2, or short forms of a Germanic per-

sonal name formed with this element, for instance *Gottfried.*

Yotter (133) Americanized espelling of German **Jotter**, variant of **Jott** (see YOTT).

You (589) **1.** Chinese 游: from a byname of a certain Prince Yan, who lived during the Spring and Autumn period (722–481 BC) in the state of Zheng, in modern-day Henan province. He had the byname *Ziyou*, and the second character of this name was adopted as a surname by his descendants. **2.** Chinese 尤: altered form of the surname SHEN. During the Five Dynasties period (907–960) the founder of the state of Min, in present-day Fujian province, was called Wang Shen Zhi. The character in his name for *Shen*, 审, was pronounced in the same way as the character for the surname **Shen**, 沈 (see SHEN 1). This spelled danger for those named Shen, as the culture of the time regarded imitation not as as flattery, but as criminal arrogance. A solution to the problem was developed by dropping from 沈 the portion signifying water, which changed the character into 尤, pronounced *You*. **3.** Korean: variant of YU.
GIVEN NAMES Chinese/Korean 62%. *Young* (7), *Han* (4), *Jin* (4), *Jung* (3), *Kwang* (3), *Li* (3), *Heng* (2), *Hui* (2), *In* (2), *Jae* (2), *Jianyu* (2), *Jong* (2); *Chang Jin, Chul, Chul Ho, Hye Sook, Hyo Sook, Jae Hee, Ji Young, Jung Hyun, Jung Woo, Ki Sook, Min, Moon.*

Youell (182) English: variant spelling of YULE.

Youker (217) Americanized spelling of German JAUKER.

Youman (156) English: variant of YEOMAN.

Youmans (1811) English: variant of YEOMANS.

Youn (284) Korean: variant of YUN.
GIVEN NAMES Korean 59%. *Young* (8), *Chang* (2), *Duk* (2), *Kwang* (2), *Kwang Soo* (2), *Kyong* (2), *Kyung* (2), *Kyung Ho* (2), *Wan* (2), *Byong, Chang Hui, Chang Soo, Dong, Hee, Byung, Chul, Hee Young, Hyun Joo, Jang, Joo Young, Jung Kyu, Kum, Kum Soon, Nam.*

Younan (179) Turkish, Iranian, and Muslim generally: ethnic name for a Greek. It is ultimately derived from Greek *Iōn* 'Ionian', the tribe of Greeks with whom the Persians had first contact. This term was subsequently borrowed into Hebrew and Arabic, and later came to be used in the Muslim world at large to denote a Greek.
GIVEN NAMES Muslim 32%; French 4%. *Younan* (5), *Sami* (2), *Samir* (2), *Amal, Amera, Atour, Bahig, Bushra, Davoud, Emad, Fawzi, Ihab; Andre, Georges, Jean-Claude.*

Younce (721) Americanized form of Dutch or North German **Jauns**, patronymic variant of JAHN.

Younes (253) Muslim: from the Arabic personal name *Yūnus*, name of a prophet, the Biblical *Jonah* (see JONAS). Yūnus is mentioned in the Qur'an (37:139): 'And Yūnus was among those sent'.

GIVEN NAMES Muslim 47%. *Aziz* (3), *Omar* (3), *Walid* (3), *Ahmad* (2), *Ahmed* (2), *Ali* (2), *Anis* (2), *Fouad* (2), *Habib* (2), *Imad* (2), *Khalil* (2), *Mohamad* (2).

Young (160864) **1.** English, Scottish, and northern Irish: distinguishing name (Middle English *yunge*, *yonge* 'young'), for the younger of two bearers of the same personal name, usually distinguishing a younger brother or a son. In Middle English this name is often found with the Anglo-Norman French definite article, for example Robert le Yunge. **2.** Americanization of a cognate, equivalent, or like-sounding surname in some other language, notably German JUNG and JUNK, Dutch (DE) JONG(H) and JONG, and French LEJEUNE and LAJEUNESSE. **3.** assimilated form of French DION or GUYON. **4.** Chinese: see YANG.

Youngbauer (101) Partly Americanized form of German **Jungbauer**, a distinguishing name from Middle High German *junc* 'young' + *būre* 'farmer'. This name has been further Americanized as **Youngbear**.

Youngberg (904) **1.** Americanized spelling of Swedish **Ungberg**, an ornamental name composed of the elements *ung* 'young' + *berg* 'mountain'. **2.** Americanized form of Swedish **Ljungberg**, a compound of *ljung* 'heather' + *berg* 'mountain'. **3.** Americanized form of Ashkenazic Jewish **Jungberg**, an ornamental name composed of German *jung* 'young' + *Berg* 'mountain', 'hill'.

Youngblood (6027) Americanized form of German JUNGBLUTH.

Youngblut (155) Americanized form of German JUNGBLUTH.

Youngdahl (229) Americanized form of Swedish **Ljungdahl**, an ornamental name composed of the elements *ljung* 'heather' + *dahl*, an ornamental (old) spelling of *dal* 'valley'.

GIVEN NAMES Scandinavian 7%. *Erik* (2), *Gunard*, *Hilma*.

Youngdale (112) Americanized form of Swedish **Ljungdahl** (see YOUNGDAHL).

GIVEN NAME Scottish 6%; Scandinavian 5%. *Anders*.

Younge (170) Chiefly Irish variant spelling of English YOUNG.

GIVEN NAMES Irish 4%. *Fitzroy*, *Sinead*.

Younger (3604) **1.** English (mainly Borders): from Middle English *yonger* 'younger', hence a distinguishing name for, for example, the younger of two bearers of the same personal name. In one case, at least, however, the name is known to have been borne by an immigrant Fleming, and was probably an Americanized form of Middle Dutch *jongheer* 'young nobleman' (see JONKER). **2.** Americanized spelling of various cognate or like-sounding names in other languages, notably German JUNGER and JUNKER, or Dutch JONKER.

Youngerman (227) Americanized form of German **Jungermann**, an extended form of JUNGER.

Youngers (177) **1.** Americanized form of German JUNGERS or JONKER or its variant **Jonkers**. **2.** variant of English YOUNGER.

Younggren (116) Swedish: see YOUNGREN.

Younghans (130) Americanized form of German JUNGHANS.

Youngkin (173) Americanized spelling of German **Juncken** or **Jünken**, patronymics from the Low German personal name *Juncke*. Compare YOUNKIN.

Younglove (278) This has the form of an English surname but it is not found in English sources and may rather be an Americanized form of German **Jungleib** (a nickname meaning 'young man'), of which the second element has been mistaken for *Lieb* 'love'.

Youngman (1133) English: from Middle English *yunge man* 'young servant'.

Youngquist (663) **1.** Americanized form of the Swedish ornamental name **Ungquist**, composed of the elements *ung* 'young' + *quist*, an old or ornamental spelling of *kvist* 'twig'. **2.** Possibly an Americanized form of Swedish **Ljungquist**, an ornamental name composed of the elements *ljung* 'heather' + *quist*.

GIVEN NAMES Scandinavian 6%. *Erik* (3), *Lennart*, *Sten*.

Youngren (393) **1.** Americanized form of Swedish **Unggren**, an ornamental name composed of the elements *ung* 'young' + *gren* 'branch'. **2.** Americanized form of Swedish **Ljunggren**, an ornamental name composed of the elements *ljung* 'heather' + *gren* 'branch'.

GIVEN NAME Scandinavian 4%. *Erik*.

Youngs (1873) English: patronymic from YOUNG.

Youngstrom (258) **1.** Americanized form of Swedish **Ungström**, an ornamental name composed of the elements *ung* 'young' + *ström* 'current', 'stream'. **2.** Possibly an Americanized form of Swedish **Ljungström**, an ornamental name composed of the elements *ljung* 'heather' + *ström* 'current', 'stream'.

Youngwirth (104) Americanized form of German JUNGWIRTH.

Younie (100) Scottish (Moray): unexplained.

Younis (174) Muslim: variant spelling of YOUNES.

GIVEN NAMES Muslim 59%. *Mohammad* (11), *Mohamed* (3), *Mohammed* (3), *Abed* (2), *Eyad* (2), *Ghandi* (2), *Muhammad* (2), *Ramzi* (2), *Saeeda* (2), *Sana* (2), *Abdi*, *Abdullah*.

Younk (138) Americanized form of Dutch JONG or JUNG.

Younker (780) Americanized spelling of German JUNKER or Dutch and North German JONKER.

Younkin (681) Americanized spelling of German **Juncken** or **Jünken**, patronymics from the Low German personal name *Juncke*. Compare YOUNGKIN.

Younkins (188) Americanized spelling of German **Juncken** or **Jünken**, patronymics from the Low German personal name *Juncke*. Compare YOUNGKIN.

Yount (3011) French (Alsace): probably a French altered form of Dutch or German JANZ or of German **Jund**, a metronymic from the female personal name *Jutta*.

Younts (551) Americanized spelling of Dutch and North German JANZ.

Youree (160) Americanized spelling of Swiss German **Juri**; unexplained.

Youse (258) Americanized form of German **Jauss** (see JAUS).

Yousef (248) Muslim: see YOUSSEF.

GIVEN NAMES Muslim 77%. *Mohamed* (5), *Hasan* (4), *Mahmoud* (4), *Yousef* (4), *Bassam* (3), *Ibrahim* (3), *Mohammed* (3), *Abdel* (2), *Ahmad* (2), *Anwar* (2), *Ashraf* (2), *Emad* (2).

Yousey (119) Origin uncertain. Most probably an Americanized form of a German or Dutch name, perhaps a variant of YOUSE or YOUTSEY.

Yousif (306) Muslim: see YOUSSEF.

GIVEN NAMES Muslim 63%. *Yousif* (8), *Samir* (5), *Emad* (4), *Saad* (4), *Hashim* (3), *Khalid* (3), *Shamoon* (3), *Thamir* (3), *Abdul* (2), *Akram* (2), *Alaa* (2), *Amer* (2).

Youssef (455) Muslim: from the Arabic personal name *Yūsuf*, name of a prophet (the Biblical JOSEPH). It is the title of the 12th sura of the Qur'an, where it is told that Zulaykha, wife of Aziz, was attracted by the beauty of Yūsuf.

GIVEN NAMES Muslim 70%. *Mohamed* (10), *Ahmed* (9), *Youssef* (9), *Nabil* (6), *Samir* (6), *Fouad* (5), *Ibrahim* (5), *Kamal* (4), *Tarek* (4), *Ashraf* (3), *Ekram* (3), *Emad* (3).

Yousuf (138) Muslim: see YOUSSEF.

GIVEN NAMES Muslim 88%. *Mohammed* (17), *Mohammad* (12), *Syed* (7), *Abdul* (4), *Anwar* (3), *Arshad* (2), *Bashir* (2), *Faisal* (2), *Jawed* (2), *Muhammad* (2), *Murad* (2), *Rauf* (2).

Youtsey (202) Probably an Americanized spelling of German **Jutze**, **Jütze**, a metronymic from the female personal name *Jutta*, a short form of the Biblical name *Judith*.

Youtz (207) Americanized spelling of: **1.** **Jütz**, Swiss and South German form of JUTTE. **2.** German **Jautz**, a variant of JAUS.

Yovino (106) Americanized spelling of Italian IOVINO.

Yow (875) Probably an altered spelling of English YEO.

Yowell (983) Perhaps an altered spelling of English YULE.

Yox (127) Americanized form of German **Jacks**, a variant of JACK.

Yslas (123) Altered spelling of Spanish ISLAS.

GIVEN NAMES Spanish 26%. *Angel* (2), *Jaime* (2), *Juan* (2), *Alfredo*, *Alvaro*, *Armando*, *Fidel*, *Florentino*, *Francisco*, *Gilberto*, *Lino*, *Luis*; *Claudina*.

Yu (7825) **1.** Korean: there are four Chinese characters for the surname *Yu*. Some sources indicate the existence of as many as 230 clans, but only about twenty can be positively documented. Several of the clans are of Chinese origin. The largest Yu clan, the Munhwa Yu, was founded by a man named Ch'a Tal. Ch'a's fifth great-grandfather had been involved in an attempt to overthrow the Shilla king. To avoid prosecution, the ancestor fled to Munhwa and changed his surname, first to that of his maternal grandmother, *Yang*, and then to *Yu*. Many years later, Ch'a Tal assisted Wang Kŏn to establish the Koryŏ Kingdom. Ch'a was recognized for his support and was rewarded accordingly. Ch'a's eldest son began again to use the Ch'a surname, but his younger son continued to use Yu. The Munhwa Yu clan, along with the Andong Kwŏn clan, possesses one of the oldest extant clan genealogies in Korea. **2.** Chinese 余: in the Spring and Autumn period (722–481 BC) there lived in the state of Qin a high counselor called You Yu, whose descendants took part of their forebear's 'style name', *Yu*, as their surname. **3.** Chinese 于: from the name of a territory granted by Wu Wang, the first king (1122–1116 BC) of the Zhou dynasty, to his second son. Some of his descendants adopted a simplified version of the character for Yu as their surname. **4.** Chinese 俞: during the time of the legendary emperor Huang Di (2697–2595 BC), there lived an extraordinary doctor who could cure all manner of diseases. Because of his great abilities, he was called *Yu*, which meant 'to heal'. His descendants adopted a modified form of this character as their surname. 虞: from the name of either of two ancient states called Yu, one located in present-day Henan province and the other in Shanxi province.

GIVEN NAMES Chinese/Korean 49%. *Hong* (29), *Ming* (24), *Yong* (23), *Young* (23), *Ping* (20), *Chi* (19), *Chun* (19), *Jae* (17), *Li* (17), *Sung* (17), *Jin* (15), *Yang* (15); *Chung* (14), *Chang* (11), *Byung* (10), *Chong* (10), *Min* (10), *Pyong* (7), *Myong* (5), *Hyong* (4), *Moon* (4), *Yiu* (4), *Inyoung* (3), *Shiu* (3).

Yuan (1183) **1.** Chinese 袁: from the secondary name, or 'style name', of a certain prince Bo Yuan, who lived during the Warring States period (722–481 BC). A grandson of his adopted the Yuan portion of this as his surname. **2.** Chinese 原: origin unknown. **3.** Chinese 苑: origin unknown. **4.** Chinese 元: the earliest record of this name is of an adviser called Yuan Xi in the 12th century BC, during the later stage of the Shang dynasty. Another source of the name is an adviser who lived in the state of Wei during the Spring and Autumn period (722–

481 BC), who was granted an area named Yuan; his descendants adopted the place name Yuan as their surname.

GIVEN NAMES Chinese 50%. *Wei* (14), *Li* (10), *Jian* (5), *Ying* (5), *Chao* (4), *Chen* (4), *Fang* (4), *Hong* (4), *Ling* (4), *Ting* (4), *Feng* (3), *Gang* (3), *Min* (3), *Chang* (2), *Chong*, *Chung*, *Pao*, *Tian*, *Yeng*.

Yudin (135) Jewish (from Belarus) and Russian: patronymic from the personal name *Yude*, the Yiddish form of *Juda* (see JUDE), or from *Iuda*, the Russian form, + the eastern Slavic possessive suffix *-in*.

GIVEN NAMES Russian 13%; Jewish 7%. *Vladimir* (3), *Igor* (2), *Sergey* (2), *Andrei*, *Boris*, *Dmitriy*, *Veniamin*, *Yevgeny*; *Isaak* (3).

Yue (447) **1.** Chinese 岳: from a title denoting a regional administrator in ancient China. The first of the 'model emperors', Yao, (2357-2257 BC), appointed four princes to administer the North, South, East and West. These were known as the Siyue, or 'four mountains'. The surname Yue is derived from this title. **2.** Chinese 余: variant of YU 2. **3.** Chinese 俞: variant of YU 4.

GIVEN NAMES Chinese 32%. *Chi* (3), *Feng* (3), *Gang* (3), *Wei* (3), *Chun* (2), *Guo* (2), *Jin* (2), *Kin* (2), *Ping* (2), *Yan* (2), *Yun* (2), *Zhang* (2), *Chau*, *Du*, *Hau*, *Hung*, *My*, *Sau*.

Yuen (1794) **1.** Chinese: see YUAN. **2.** Chinese: see RUAN.

GIVEN NAMES Chinese 18%. *Kam* (9), *Wing* (9), *Wai* (6), *Cheuk* (5), *Chi* (5), *Chun* (5), *Kwok* (4), *Kin* (3), *Mei* (3), *Chi Keung* (2), *Choi* (2), *Jin* (2).

Yuhas (927) Americanized spelling of Hungarian JUHASZ.

Yuhasz (351) Partly Americanized spelling of Hungarian JUHASZ.

Yuill (238) Scottish: variant of YULE.

Yuille (165) Scottish: variant of YULE.

Yule (475) Scottish and English: nickname for someone who was born on Christmas Day or had some other connection with this time of year, from Middle English *yule* 'Christmastide' (Old English *gēol*, reinforced by the cognate Old Norse term *jól*). This was originally the name of a pagan midwinter festival, which was later appropriated by the Christian Church for celebration of the birth of Christ.

Yum (188) Korean (**Yŏm**): there is only one Yŏm clan. It was originally known as the Yŏm family from Tanwŏn County (Kyŏnggi Province), but the name of this county was changed to P'aju County. The Yŏm family was very influential throughout the Koryŏ Kingdom until Yŏm Hŭngbang, a powerful court official, was executed for treason by the Koryŏ King U (1374–87). The clan never recovered its former glory.

GIVEN NAMES Korean 54%. *Kyung* (3), *Young* (3), *Dong* (2), *Doo* (2), *Ho* (2), *Jung* (2), *Kyoung* (2), *Byoung*, *Chang*, *Chang Soon*,

Chang Yong, *Chong*, *Choong*, *Chung Nam*, *Heung*, *Hyum*, *Jaehyun*, *Jin Suk*, *Kiho*, *Kum*, *Pyong*, *Sang Chul*, *Sang Soo*, *Seong*.

Yun (1573) **1.** Korean: there is only one Chinese character for the surname Yun. Although some records indicate the existence of 149 clans, only ten can be documented. Each descends from a different ancestor. The largest, that of P'ap'yŏng, descends from a man named Shin Tal. According to legend, an old woman named Yun On, who lived in P'ap'yŏng, saw a rainbow over a lotus pond in the mountains. When she went to investigate, she found a boy in a box. The boy had scales under his arm and seven dark birth marks on his body. She raised him as her own and gave him the surname Yun. The oldest Yun clan, that of Tamwŏn, descends from a man named Shi-yŏng, who lived during the reign of the Shilla King Muyŏl (654–661). **2.** Chinese 云: from the second character of *Jinyun*, a title borne by certain officials under the legendary emperor Huang Di (2697–2595 BC). **3.** Americanized spelling of Czech JUN.

GIVEN NAMES Chinese/Korean 61%. *Yong* (19), *Young* (13), *Jae* (12), *Sang* (11), *Sung* (10), *Song* (8), *Eun* (7), *Jung* (7), *Kyung* (7), *Won* (7), *Hyung* (6), *Kyong* (6); *Chong* (24), *Byung* (8), *Pyong* (5), *Chul* (4), *Seong* (4), *Chang* (3), *Myong* (3), *Song Su* (3), *Wook* (3), *Chong Sok* (2), *Chong Su* (2), *Jeong* (2).

Yund (107) Probably a respelling of German JUNDT.

GIVEN NAME French 7%. *Laurette* (2).

Yundt (158) Respelling of German JUNDT.

Yung (1014) **1.** Americanized form of German JUNG. **2.** Scottish and English: variant spelling of YOUNG. **3.** Chinese 翁: variant of WENG 1. **4.** Chinese 容: variant of RONG 1. **5.** Chinese 雍: variant of YONG 2. **6.** Chinese 戎: variant of RONG 3.

GIVEN NAMES Chinese 12%. *Chun* (5), *Cheuk* (4), *Ming* (4), *Chan* (3), *Ching* (3), *Chiu* (3), *Kin* (3), *Kwok* (3), *Fan* (2), *Foo* (2), *Kwong* (2), *Mei* (2).

Yunger (117) Americanized spelling of German and Jewish JUNGER 'young man'.

GIVEN NAMES Jewish 4%. *Baruch*, *Ilan*, *Semen*.

Yunk (151) Americanized spelling of German *Junk*, variant of JUNG.

Yunker (838) Americanized spelling of German JUNKER.

Yurchak (183) Americanized spelling of Polish JURCZAK.

GIVEN NAMES Russian 4%. *Mikhail*, *Sergei*, *Yuriy*.

Yurek (235) Americanized spelling of Polish JUREK.

Yurick (273) Americanized spelling of Polish JUREK.

Yurk (146) Probably an Americanized form of German JERKE, a derivative of a Slavic form of *Georg* (see GEORGE) or of its German variant *Jörg*.

GIVEN NAMES German 8%. *Arno, Klaus, Otto, Reinhold.*

Yurko (354) Americanized spelling of Slovenian **Jurko**, from the personal name *Jurko*, pet form of *Jurij* (see GEORGE).

Yurkovich (230) **1.** Ukrainian and Belorussian: patronymic from the personal name *Yurko*, a pet form of *Yury* or *Yura*, eastern Slavic equivalents of GEORGE. **2.** Jewish (from Bessarabia): habitational name for someone from Yurkovtsy in Ukraine. **3.** Americanized spelling of Croatian **Jurković** or Slovenian **Jurkovič** 'son of George' (see JURKOVICH).

Yurman (116) Anglicized spelling of Slovenian JURMAN.

GIVEN NAMES Italian 7%; German 6%; Jewish 6%. *Sal* (2), *Gino, Salvatore; Sepp; Moshe, Yetta.*

Yuska (157) Americanized spelling of Lithuanian JUSKA.

Yusko (353) Americanized spelling of Polish JUSKO.

Yust (207) Respelling of JUST, representing the German, Danish, Hungarian, or Czech pronunciation.

Yusuf (242) Muslim: see YOUSSEF.

GIVEN NAMES Muslim 78%. *Mohamed* (7), *Mohammed* (5), *Muhammad* (5), *Abdi* (4), *Ahmed* (3), *Mohamud* (3), *Abdulaziz* (2), *Fatuma* (2), *Jemal* (2), *Lateef* (2), *Mamun* (2), *Mohammad* (2).

Yutzy (359) Probably an Americanized spelling of German **Jutze, Jütze** (see YOUTSEY).

Yzaguirre (270) Respelling of Basque IZAGUIRRE.

GIVEN NAMES Spanish 38%. *Roberto* (6), *Jose* (5), *Ruben* (4), *Carlos* (3), *Guadalupe* (3), *Luis* (3), *Manuel* (3), *Amado* (2), *Margarita* (2), *Mario* (2), *Pedro* (2), *Raul* (2).

Zabala (492) Basque: habitational name from any of various places in Biscay and Araba named Zabala, from Basque *zabal* 'large', 'broad' + the definite article *-a*. In some cases the surname may have arisen as a nickname from the same word.

GIVEN NAMES Spanish 46%. *Luis* (9), *Carlos* (7), *Jaime* (5), *Jose* (5), *Juan* (5), *Manuel* (5), *Angel* (4), *Efrain* (3), *Julio* (3), *Pedro* (3), *Salvador* (3), *Alba* (2).

Zabawa (217) Polish: habitational name from Zabawa in Kraków and Tarnów voivodeships, from *zabawa* 'game', or possibly a nickname from this word.

GIVEN NAMES Polish 5%. *Aleksander, Andrzej, Jerzy, Zbigniew, Zofia.*

Zabel (1552) **1.** German: from a personal name of Slavic origin. **2.** Alternatively, perhaps, from Middle High German *zabel* 'board game' (Latin *tabula*), hence perhaps a nickname for an inveterate game player. **3.** North German: variant of ZOBEL.

Zabielski (169) Polish: habitational name for someone from any of the various places in Poland called Zabiele.

GIVEN NAMES Polish 9%; German 4%. *Wieslaw* (2), *Jacek, Stanislaw; Alfons.*

Zabinski (328) Polish (**Żabiński**): habitational name for someone from Żabin in Ciechanów, Leszno, Ostrołęka, or Suwałki voivodeships, named with Polish *żaba* 'frog'.

GIVEN NAMES Polish 4%. *Witold* (2), *Jacek, Zdzislaw.*

Zabka (109) German (of Slavic origin): nickname from a Slavic word meaning 'frog'. Compare Polish ZABINSKI.

GIVEN NAME German 5%. *Johann.*

Zablocki (351) Polish (**Zabłocki**): habitational name for someone from any of the various places in Poland called Zabłocie, named with Polish *za błotem* 'beyond the mud'.

GIVEN NAMES Polish 7%. *Boguslaw, Halina, Henryk, Jozef, Leszek, Tadeusz, Zygmunt.*

Zaborowski (499) Polish: habitational name from any of several places called Zaborowo or Zaborów, probably named with *za* 'beyond' + *bór* 'forest' + *-owo* or *-ów*, suffix of place names. Alternatively, it could be a topographic name for someone who lived 'on the other side of the forest'.

GIVEN NAMES Polish 5%. *Casimir, Dariusz, Janina, Kazimierz, Leszek, Radoslaw, Teofil, Tomasz, Zbigniew.*

Zaborski (122) Polish: habitational name for someone from any of the various places in Poland called Zaborze, named with *za* 'beyond' + *bór* 'forest'. Alternatively, it may be a topographic name for someone who lived 'on the other side of the forest' (see ZABOROWSKI).

GIVEN NAMES Polish 10%; Hungarian 4%. *Casimir, Kazimierz, Tadeusz, Wladyslaw; Andras, Miklos.*

Zabriskie (458) Altered form of Polish **Zabrzyski** (topographic name for someone who lived 'beyond the birch tree', from Polish *za* 'beyond' + *brzezie* (*brzoza*) 'birch tree') or **Zabrzeski** (habitational name from a place called Zabrzeg, named with *za* 'beyond' + *brzeg* 'bank').

Zabrowski (104) Polish: variant of ZABOROWSKI.

GIVEN NAME Polish 4%. *Stanislaw.*

Zacarias (275) Spanish (**Zacarías**) and Jewish: see ZACHARIAS.

GIVEN NAMES Spanish 54%. *Jose* (14), *Juan* (8), *Carlos* (5), *Juana* (5), *Francisco* (4), *Jesus* (3), *Jorge* (3), *Salvador* (3), *Alejandro* (2), *Alfredo* (2), *Blanca* (2), *Eduardo* (2).

Zaccagnini (148) Italian: patronymic or plural form of ZACCAGNINO.

GIVEN NAMES Italian 12%; Spanish 4%. *Mario* (3), *Silvio* (2), *Antonio, Giulio; Ines, Juanita.*

Zaccagnino (175) Italian: **1.** nickname for a stupid, ignorant servant, Italian *zaccagni-*

no. **2.** from *zaccagnare* meaning in the dialect of Lombardy and Emilia 'to strive', 'to manage', 'to make do'.

GIVEN NAMES Italian 21%. *Angelo* (2), *Rocco* (2), *Sal* (2), *Salvatore* (2), *Canio, Carmela, Emelio, Lia, Pellegrino, Vito.*

Zaccardi (189) Italian (Sicily): probably a variant of **Saccardi.**

GIVEN NAMES Italian 6%. *Antonio, Sal, Silvio.*

Zaccardo (109) Italian: patronymic or plural form of ZACCARDI.

GIVEN NAMES Italian 17%. *Vito* (2), *Antonio, Carmela, Giuseppe.*

Zaccaria (352) Italian: from the Biblical personal name *Zaccariah* (see ZACHARIAS).

GIVEN NAMES Italian 27%. *Angelo* (3), *Attilio* (3), *Gaetano* (2), *Silvio* (2), *Alfonso, Antonino, Carlo, Carmella, Carmelo, Carmine, Concetta, Concetto, Cosmo, Franco, Mario, Paola, Teresina.*

Zaccaro (218) Southern Italian: nickname from the Neapolitan dialect word *zaccaro* 'boy', 'baby' or Sicilian *saccaru* 'dirty'.

GIVEN NAMES Italian 19%. *Giacomo* (2), *Marco* (2), *Cosmo, Francesco, Girolamo, Guiseppe, Lorenzo, Luca, Nunzio, Vito.*

Zaccheo (110) Italian: from the personal name *Zaccheo*, from *Zacchaeus* or *Zakchàios*, respectively Latin and Greek forms of the Biblical name ZACHARIAS.

GIVEN NAMES Italian 27%. *Vito* (3), *Angelo, Attilio, Carmela, Giacomo, Matteo, Nunzio, Pasquale, Vincenzo.*

Zaccone (187) Italian: of uncertain origin. Caracausi proposes that this may be derived from Greek *diakonos* 'deacon', but it is more likely to be from an augmentative of the personal name *Zacco*, pet form of the personal name ZACCARIA.

GIVEN NAMES Italian 19%. *Angelo* (3), *Antonio* (2), *Domenic* (2), *Aldo, Amato, Carmine, Rocco, Romeo, Salvatore.*

Zacek (152) Czech (**Žáček**): from a diminutive of **Žák** (see ZAK).

GIVEN NAMES Czech and Slovak 6%; German 4%. *Milan, Miroslav, Pavel; Florian* (2).

Zach (646) **1.** German and Czech: from the personal name *Zach*, a short form of ZACHARIAS. The Czech form is *Zachariáš*. **2.** German: nickname from Middle High German *zäch* 'tenacious', 'stubborn'.

GIVEN NAMES German 5%. *Alois* (2), *Otto* (2), *Erwin, Franz, Guenther, Ignatz, Rainer, Wilfried.*

Zachar (211) **1.** Czech (also **Zachař**) and Slovak: from the personal name *Zachariáš* (see ZACHARIAS). **2.** Jewish (eastern Ashkenazic): from the personal name *Zakhar*, the eastern Slavic equivalent of ZACHARIAS.

GIVEN NAME German 4%. *Kurt.*

Zacharia (139) Indian (Kerala): variant of ZACHARIAH.

GIVEN NAMES Indian 9%. *Babu, Omana, Oommen, Raju.*

Zachariah (194) Indian (Kerala): from the Hebrew personal name *zakhar'yah* (see Zacharias), found as a personal name among Christians in Kerala (southern India) and in the U.S. used as a last name among families from Kerala.
GIVEN NAMES Indian 24%. *Ajay, Babu, Jaya, Mani, Manorama, Mathai, Raju, Santha, Shaji, Shalini, Sudhir, Sunil.*

Zacharias (1292) German, Greek, English, etc.: from the New Testament Greek Biblical personal name *Zacharias*, Aramaic and Hebrew *Zecharya*, composed of the elements *zechar* 'to remember' + *ya* 'God'. This name was borne by a Biblical prophet and in the New Testament by the father of John the Baptist, for which reason it achieved a modest popularity among Gentiles during the Middle Ages. It is found as a Jewish name, and as a personal name among Christians in India. In the U.S. it is used as a last name among families from southern India.
GIVEN NAMES German 4%. *Erwin* (2), *Gerhard* (2), *Erna, Hannes, Helmut, Irmgard, Kurt, Lothar, Nikolaus, Rudi, Wolfgang.*

Zachary (2060) English and Jewish: from a vernacular form of the Biblical personal name Zacharias.

Zacher (725) German: from a vernacular form of the personal name Zacharias.
GIVEN NAMES German 4%. *Gerhardt* (2), *Aloysius, Erwin, Heinz, Hermann, Ignatz, Maximilian, Rainer.*

Zacherl (136) South German: pet form of Zacher.

Zachery (340) English: variant of Zachary.

Zachman (463) Americanized spelling of German Zachmann.

Zachmann (137) German: extended form of Zach.
GIVEN NAMES German 4%. *Hans, Kurt.*

Zachow (232) Eastern German (of Slavic origin): habitational name from any of various places named Zachow, in Brandenburg and Mecklenburg-West Pomerania.

Zachrich (120) German: irregular variant of German Zacher.

Zachry (424) English: variant of Zachary.

Zack (1592) **1.** Jewish (Ashkenazic): variant spelling of Sack. **2.** Americanized spelling of Zach.

Zacker (136) **1.** Americanized spelling of German Zacher. **2.** German: occupational name for a farmer, from dialect *zackern* 'to plow', from Middle High German *ze acke gän* 'to go to the field'.

Zackery (251) Variant spelling of English Zachary.

Zacks (171) Jewish: altered spelling of Ashkenazic Sachs.
GIVEN NAMES Jewish 7%. *Arieh, Hyman, Meyer.*

Zaczek (111) Polish (Żaczek): nickname meaning 'schoolboy', from Old Polish *żaczek*, a diminutive of *żak* (see Zak).

GIVEN NAMES Polish 10%. *Danuta, Dariusz, Witold.*

Zadeh (139) Muslim (mainly Iranian and Pakistani): from Persian *zāda* 'son'. It is often found added as a suffix to a status name, as in *Shāh-zāda* 'son of the king', or *Nawāb-zāda* 'son of the nawab'. It is also used as a suffix appended to the father's name.
GIVEN NAMES Muslim 63%. *Ali* (5), *Firooz* (3), *Habib* (3), *Hamid* (3), *Abbas* (2), *Hassan* (2), *Mehdi* (2), *Rahim* (2), *Afshin, Ahad, Akbar, Aref.*

Zadra (133) Italian: topographic name from an old Venetian dialect word *zadro* 'theatre'. The term has survived in the names of various Venetian streets and squares which once housed theatres.
GIVEN NAMES Italian 8%. *Leno* (2), *Reno* (2), *Serafino.*

Zadroga (110) Polish: topographic name for someone who lived 'over the road' or 'beyond the end of the road', from Polish *za* 'beyond' + *droga* 'road'.
GIVEN NAMES Polish 8%. *Alicja, Mariusz.*

Zadrozny (168) Polish (Zadrożny): habitational name for someone from Zadroże in Kraków voivodeship, named as *za* 'beyond' + *droga* 'road' (see Zadroga).
GIVEN NAMES Polish 6%; German 4%. *Krzysztof, Wlodzimierz; Fritz.*

Zaeske (103) German (also **Zäske**, **Zaske**): unexplained.
GIVEN NAME German 5%. *Kurt.*

Zafar (178) Muslim: from a personal name based on Arabic *ẓafar* 'victory'. It is sometimes found in compound names such as *Ẓafarullah* 'victory of Allah'.
GIVEN NAMES Muslim 85%. *Syed* (9), *Mohammad* (6), *Mohammed* (4), *Asif* (3), *Iqbal* (3), *Muhammad* (3), *Abdullah* (2), *Karim* (2), *Kashif* (2), *Mahmood* (2), *Muzaffar* (2), *Nadeem* (2).

Zaffino (146) Italian (mainly Sicily): from Old Sicilian *zaffina* 'precious stone' (a variant of *zaffiro*), perhaps applied as a nickname or as a metonymic occupational name for a jeweler or dealer in gem stones.
GIVEN NAMES Italian 19%; French 4%. *Salvatore* (5), *Angelo, Domenico, Gasper, Sal, Saverio; Armand, Camille.*

Zaffuto (126) Italian: most probably of Arabic origin; possibly, as Caracausi suggests, from *saffūd*, 'spit', 'skewer'.
GIVEN NAMES Italian 24%. *Angelo* (5), *Carmelo, Cesare, Gerlando, Ignazio, Maddalena, Nicola, Sal, Salvatore.*

Zagami (139) Southern Italian: probably from a personal name based on Arabic *za'āma* 'leadership'.
GIVEN NAMES Italian 20%. *Salvatore* (3), *Agatino, Dante, Domenic, Gaetano, Marcello, Sal.*

Zagar (377) Slovenian and northern Croatian (**Žagar**): occupational name for a sawyer, from an agent derivative of *žaga* 'saw'.

GIVEN NAMES South Slavic 4%. *Darko* (2), *Marko* (2), *Mladen* (2).

Zagata (122) Polish: metonymic occupational name for someone who plastered external walls to protect them for winter, from *zagata* 'protective coating (somewhat similar to whitewash)'.
GIVEN NAMES Polish 13%. *Danuta, Feliks, Malgorzata, Stanislaw, Stanistaw, Wladyslaw.*

Zager (599) **1.** German: habitational name from Zager, a place near Wollin. **2.** Jewish (eastern Ashkenazic): habitational name for someone from a place called (in Russian) Zhagory, now in Lithuania.
GIVEN NAMES German 4%. *Gerhart, Gunther, Heinz, Kurt.*

Zagorski (467) **1.** Polish (**Zagórski**): topographic name for someone who lived on the other side of a hill from the main settlement, from *za* 'beyond', 'on the other side of' + *góra* 'hill' (see Gorski) + the surname suffix *-ski*. Alternatively, it may be a habitational name from a place named Zagóra or Zagórze, named with this phrase. **2.** Jewish (eastern Ashkenazic): habitational name for someone from Zagorie in Belarus or Zhagory, now in Lithuania.
GIVEN NAMES Polish 8%. *Ludwik* (2), *Mariusz* (2), *Zygmunt* (2), *Andrzej, Casimir, Halina, Henryk, Jacek, Jadwiga, Zbigniew.*

Zaharias (105) Greek form of the New Testament personal name Zacharias.
GIVEN NAMES Greek 6%. *Epaminondas, Kalliopi, Soterios.*

Zaher (117) Muslim: from a personal name based on Arabic *ẓāhir* 'knowing' or 'clear', 'evident'.
GIVEN NAMES Muslim 24%. *Manar* (2), *Maroun* (2), *Mohamad* (2), *Abdul, Ahmed, Atef, Cherif, Mohamed, Samir, Samy, Tarek, Zaher.*

Zahl (125) **1.** German: from a reduced form of Middle High German *zagel* 'tail' or from a reduced form of a compound name formed with this element, as for example **Hasenzahl** ('hare's tail'). **2.** Jewish (Ashkenazic): from the Yiddish personal name *Tsal*, a pet form of the Biblical name *Betzalel*. **3.** Jewish (Ashkenazic): from German *Zahl* 'number'.
GIVEN NAMES German 6%; Scandinavian 4%. *Reiner; Carsten* (2).

Zahler (513) **1.** German (**Zähler**) and Jewish (Ashkenazic): from an agent derivative of German *zahlen* 'to count', Middle High German *zalen*, hence an occupational name for someone who kept count, i.e. a tallyman or clerk; also, for German, a nickname for a debtor. **2.** German: from a reduced form of *zagel* (see Zahl), which also appears as a field name and hence a topographic name.
GIVEN NAMES Jewish 4%. *Avi* (2), *Miriam, Moshe.*

Zahm (367) German: nickname from Middle High German *zam* 'tame'.

Zahn (2678) German and Jewish (Ashkenazic): nickname for someone with a large or peculiar tooth or a re.narkable or defective set of teeth, from Middle High German *zan(t)* 'tooth', German *Zahn*.

GIVEN NAMES German 4%. *Otto* (4), *Heinz* (2), *Helmut* (2), *Markus* (2), *Armin, Dieter, Fritz, Gerhard, Heinrich, Herta, Horst, Joerg*.

Zahnd (114) Variant of German **Zahndt** (see ZAHN).

Zahner (552) German: habitational name for someone from Zahna near Wittenberg.

Zahniser (229) German: **1.** altered spelling of **Zahnhäuser**, a habitational name from a place called Zahnhausen. **2.** from *Zahneiser*, an occupational nickname for a person who provided iron teeth as a replacement, from Middle High German *zan(t)* 'tooth' + *īser* 'iron', 'ironworker'.

Zahnow (163) Eastern German (of Slavic origin): unexplained.

Zahorchak (106) Ukrainian: topographic name for someone who lived 'over the mountain', from *za* 'beyond', 'on the other side of' + *hora* 'hill' + *-chak*, patronymic suffix.

Zahorik (138) Ukrainian: topographic name for someone who lived 'over the mountain', from *za* 'beyond', 'on the other side of' + *hora* 'hill' + the diminutive suffix *-ik*.

Zahorsky (105) Ukrainian: topographic name composed of the elements *za* 'beyond', 'on the other side of' + *hora* 'hill' + the local surname suffix *-ski*.

Zahra (118) Muslim: from the Arabic female personal name *Zahrā'*, feminine of *Azhar* 'bright', 'brilliant', 'radiant'. Zahrā is an epithet of Fatima, daughter of Muhammad.

GIVEN NAMES Muslim 21%. *Mohammed* (2), *Tasneem* (2), *Atef, Basma, Bassem, Majdi, Muhammed, Nazir, Sami, Samir, Shadia, Syeda*.

Zahradka (127) Czech (**Zahrádka**): variant of ZAHRADNIK.

Zahradnik (187) Czech and Slovak (**Zahradník**): status name for a person who farmed on a small scale, from *zahrada* 'smallholding', 'orchard', 'garden'. A *zahradník* held lands larger than those of a cottager (*chalupník*; see CHALUPA) but smaller than those of a farmer (*sedlák*; see SEDLAK).

Zahrt (131) German: unexplained.

Zaidi (306) Muslim: Arabic family name denoting someone descended from an ancestor called Zaid ('increase') or a follower of the Shiite imam Zaid al-Shahid. After the death of the fourth Shiite imam, Zaynul Abidin, a branch of the Shiites chose to follow Zaid as the next imam instead of his brother Muḥammad al–Baqīr. Zaidis are found mainly in Yemen.

GIVEN NAMES Muslim 89%. *Syed* (57), *Ali* (8), *Azhar* (5), *Raza* (5), *Hasan* (3), *Javed*

(3), *Mumtaz* (3), *Qasim* (3), *Sayed* (3), *Abbas* (2), *Akhtar* (2), *Amir* (2).

Zaiger (108) Possibly a respelling of German **Saiger**: **1.** occupational name from Middle High German *sæjære* 'sower'. **2.** habitational name for someone from Saig in Baden-Württemberg. **3.** occupational name for someone who assayed coins, from Middle High German *seigære*.

GIVEN NAME German 6%. *Heinz*.

Zaino (299) Italian: from *zaino* 'knapsack', or alternatively from the dialect word *zaina* 'basket', 'hamper'.

GIVEN NAMES Italian 25%. *Mario* (4), *Aurelio* (3), *Carmine* (3), *Dino* (2), *Rocco* (2), *Angelo, Aniello, Antonio, Odilio*.

Zais (143) Variant of Jewish ZAITZ.

Zaiser (173) South German: from Middle High German *zeiser*, an agent derivative of *zeisen* 'to pick', hence a nickname for a wool plucker, or alternatively a nickname for a quarrelsome person, from the same word in its figurative sense.

GIVEN NAMES German 7%. *Friedrich* (2), *Hartmut, Heinz*.

Zaitz (171) Jewish (eastern Ashkenazic): **1.** ornamental name from eastern Slavic *zayats, zaets* 'hare'. **2.** habitational name for someone from Zajtsy in Belarus, derived from 'hare'.

GIVEN NAMES Jewish 4%. *Hyman, Sol*.

Zajac (1841) Polish (**Zając**) and Czech and Slovak: from Polish *zając* 'hare', Czech dialect *zajac* (see ZAJIC), a nickname for a swift runner or a shy person.

GIVEN NAMES Polish 8%. *Kazimierz* (4), *Andrej* (3), *Andrzej* (3), *Casimir* (2), *Danuta* (2), *Iwona* (2), *Jerzy* (2), *Krzysztof* (2), *Leszek* (2), *Piotr* (2), *Stanislaw* (2), *Wladyslaw* (2).

Zajaczkowski (107) Polish (**Zajączkowski**): habitational name for someone from any of various places called Zajączki, Zajączkowo, or Zajączków, named with *zajączek*, a diminutive of Polish *zając* 'hare'.

GIVEN NAMES Polish 18%; German 4%. *Bogumil, Feliks, Grzegorz, Henryk, Jozef, Kazimierz, Maciej, Waclaw; Dieter*.

Zajdel (215) Polish form of the German personal name SEIDEL.

GIVEN NAMES Polish 9%. *Grazyna* (2), *Casimir, Danuta, Karol, Ludwik, Szymon, Zygmunt*.

Zajic (167) Czech (**Zajíc**) and Slovak (**Zajac**): from *zajíc* 'hare', hence a nickname for a swift runner or a coward, one quick to run away.

GIVEN NAMES German 4%. *Kurt, Willi*.

Zajicek (406) Czech (**Zajíček**) and Slovak (**Zajačik**): from a diminutive of **Zajic** (see ZAJIC).

Zajkowski (177) Polish: habitational name for someone from a place called Zajki in Łomża voivodeship.

GIVEN NAMES Polish 20%; Czech and Slovak 4%. *Andrzej* (2), *Wieslaw* (2), *Bronislaw*,

Casimir, Janusz, Jerzy, Kazimerz, Kazimierz, Krystyna, Miroslaw, Tadeusz, Zygmunt; Bohdan (2).

Zak (1987) Polish (**Żak**), Czech (**Žák**), and Slovak (**Žiak**): nickname for a youthful or studious person, from Polish *żak* 'student', 'schoolboy'. The original meaning of this word was 'novice', 'candidate for the priesthood', and so in some cases it is perhaps a nickname for someone who had been destined for holy orders.

GIVEN NAMES Polish 5%. *Casimir* (2), *Feliks* (2), *Jadwiga* (2), *Janusz* (2), *Stanislaw* (2), *Stanislawa* (2), *Boleslaw, Czeslaw, Darek, Dorota, Genowefa, Jacek*.

Zakaria (138) Muslim: from the Arabic personal name *Zakariā*, name of a Prophet (the Biblical ZACHARIAS), a messenger of Allah, father of the Prophet Yahya (the Biblical John the Baptist).

GIVEN NAMES Muslim 73%. *Mohammed* (4), *Muhammad* (4), *Fadi* (2), *Ramzi* (2), *Aamir, Abdallah, Abdul, Abdul Hamid, Abed, Adil, Ali, Amin*.

Zakarian (225) Armenian: patronymic from the personal name *Zak'ar* (see ZACHARIAS).

GIVEN NAMES Armenian 27%. *Hrair* (3), *Agop* (2), *Arsham* (2), *Harout* (2), *Pogos* (2), *Sarkis* (2), *Zohrab* (2), *Adrine, Anahid, Ararat, Berjouhi, Garo*.

Zaki (217) Muslim: from a personal name based on Arabic *zakī* 'pure', 'chaste', 'sinless'. See the Qur'an 19:19: 'He said: I am only a Messenger of your Lord, to give you (Mariam) a son most pure'.

GIVEN NAMES Muslim 81%. *Ahmed* (8), *Mohamed* (8), *Nagi* (5), *Sherif* (5), *Ashraf* (4), *Nabil* (4), *Tarek* (4), *Ihab* (3), *Mohammed* (3), *Sami* (3), *Samir* (3), *Zaki* (3).

Zakowski (123) Polish (**Żakowski**): habitational name for someone from any of many places in Poland called Żaków, Żakowo, or Żakowice.

GIVEN NAME Polish 6%. *Thadeus* (2).

Zakrajsek (130) Czech: nickname from the expression *zakryj se* 'cover yourself up', from some long-forgotten anecdote.

Zakrzewski (751) Polish: habitational name for someone from any of many places in Poland called Zakrzewo or Zakrzów (named with *za* 'beyond' + *krzew* 'thicket'), or alternatively, a topographic name for someone who lived 'beyond the thicket'.

GIVEN NAMES Polish 8%. *Andrzej, Bronislaus, Cecylia, Dariusz, Halina, Henryk, Jacek, Janusz, Radoslaw, Slawomir, Stanislaw, Stas*.

Zaks (132) Jewish (eastern Ashkenazic): regional name for someone from Saxony (see SACHS).

GIVEN NAMES Jewish 19%; Russian 11%. *Chaim* (2), *Igal* (2), *Shmuel* (2), *Eliyohu, Mayer, Rimma, Yisroel; Yulia* (2), *Boris, Genady, Lev, Misha, Yury*.

Zalar (172) Slovenian: **1.** (mainly eastern Slovenia; **Žalar**) status name from the dialect word *žalar* 'cottager', 'tenant', from the Austrian German word *Söller* (compare SELLNER). This denoted a day laborer who lived in a small house with no agricultural land. **2.** habitational name for a person from the village of Zala.

Zaldivar (329) Basque: Castilianized variant of Basque **Zaldibar**, a habitational name from a place so named in Biscay province. The place name is of uncertain derivation: it may be from *zaldu* 'wood', 'copse' or from *zaldi* 'horse' + *ibar* 'water meadow', 'fertile plain'.
GIVEN NAMES Spanish 50%. *Jose* (10), *Raul* (8), *Francisco* (6), *Miguel* (5), *Ana* (4), *Enrique* (4), *Juan* (4), *Rafael* (4), *Ramon* (4), *Carlos* (3), *Ramiro* (3), *Ricardo* (3).

Zale (341) Polish (**Żale**): of uncertain origin; perhaps a habitational name from Żale in Białystok voivodeship (see ZALESKI).

Zalenski (234) Polish (**Zaleński**): variant of ZALESKI.
GIVEN NAMES Polish 7%. *Casimir, Thadeus, Zygmont.*

Zales (127) Polish: variant of **Zalas**, a topographic name for someone who lived 'on the other side of the wood', from Polish *za* 'beyond' + *las* 'wood'.

Zaleski (1256) **1.** Polish, Ukrainian, and Belorussian: topographic name for someone who lived 'on the other side of the wood', from Polish *za* 'beyond' + *las* 'forest', with the addition of *-ski*, suffix of local surnames, or a habitational name for someone from a place called Zalesie, named with these elements. As a habitational name, it is also found as an Ashkenazic Jewish name. **2.** Polish (**Załęski**): topographic name for someone who lived 'on the other side of the water meadow', from Polish *za* 'beyond' + *łęg* 'water meadow'. **3.** Polish: variant of ZALEWSKI.
GIVEN NAMES Polish 5%. *Tadeusz* (2), *Aleksander, Andrzej, Benedykt, Bronislaw, Czeslaw, Janusz, Jerzy, Karol, Leslaw, Mieczyslaw, Miroslaw.*

Zalesky (187) Ukrainian, Belorussian, and Jewish (eastern Ashkenazic): variant spelling of ZALESKI.

Zalewski (1366) Polish: topographic name for someone who lived by a flood plain or a bay, Polish *zalew*, or a habitational name for someone from a place named with this word, in particular Zalew in Sieradz voivodeship or Zalewo in Olsztyn voivodeship. There has been considerable confusion with ZALESKI.
GIVEN NAMES Polish 14%. *Bogdan* (4), *Krzysztof* (4), *Zbigniew* (4), *Jerzy* (3), *Leszek* (3), *Stanislaw* (3), *Wieslaw* (3), *Witold* (3), *Andrzej* (2), *Boguslaw* (2), *Casimir* (2), *Janina* (2).

Zalkin (110) Jewish (Ashkenazic): from the Yiddish personal name *Zalkind*, a derivative of SALOMON.

Zall (134) Perhaps an altered spelling of ZAHL.

Zalman (110) Jewish (Ashkenazic): variant of SALMON 2.

Zaloudek (158) Czech (**Žaloudek**): nickname meaning 'stomach', probably applied to someone with a sweet tooth or a good appetite.

Zaluski (108) Polish (**Załuski**): habitational name for someone from any of several places in Poland called Załuski, Załuskie, or Załuże, named with Polish *za* 'beyond' + *ług* 'water meadow', a dialect form of standard Polish *łęg*. Alternatively, it may be a topographic name for someone who lived 'on the other side of the water meadow'.
GIVEN NAMES French 4%. *Alphonse, Andre.*

Zaman (399) Muslim: from a personal name based on Arabic *zamān* 'time', 'age', 'era', often used to form names in combination with other words, for example *Nūr uz-Zamān* 'light of the era', *Shams uz-Zamān* 'sun of the time'. *Zaman* is a popular name in the Indian subcontinent.
GIVEN NAMES Muslim 80%. *Mohammed* (17), *Mohammad* (16), *Syed* (8), *Mohamed* (6), *Muhammad* (5), *Ali* (4), *Qamar* (4), *Akhtar* (3), *Anis* (3), *Arif* (3), *Tariq* (3), *Abul* (2).

Zamani (113) Muslim: Arabic family name indicating descent from or association with someone called ZAMAN.
GIVEN NAMES Muslim 84%. *Mohammad* (6), *Ali* (3), *Mahmood* (3), *Abbas* (2), *Fereidoun* (2), *Hossein* (2), *Kaveh* (2), *Marzieh* (2), *Mehran* (2), *Mohammed* (2), *Mostafa* (2), *Payam* (2).

Zamarripa (612) Basque: topographic name from Basque *zama* 'gorge', 'ravine' + *erripa* 'slope', 'incline'.
GIVEN NAMES Spanish 52%. *Jose* (24), *Juan* (15), *Jesus* (7), *Armando* (6), *Raul* (6), *Jaime* (5), *Pablo* (5), *Pedro* (5), *Rafael* (5), *Mario* (4), *Ramon* (4), *Andres* (3).

Zamarron (243) Spanish (**Zamarrón**): **1.** nickname from an augmentative of *zamarra* 'fur or fleece jacket'. **2.** habitational name from Zamarrón in Granada.
GIVEN NAMES Spanish 51%. *Juan* (8), *Jesus* (4), *Jose* (4), *Javier* (3), *Angel* (2), *Carlos* (2), *Fernando* (2), *Josue* (2), *Leticia* (2), *Manuel* (2), *Maria Elena* (2), *Mario* (2).

Zambelli (164) Italian (Venice): from the personal name, a compound of ZANNI + *bello* 'handsome' or the personal name BELLO, from this word.
GIVEN NAMES Italian 11%. *Dino, Fulvio, Gino, Giorgio, Mauro, Romilda.*

Zambito (353) Southern Italian: variant of **Zammito**, a nickname from Arabic *zamīt* 'of serious disposition'.
GIVEN NAMES Italian 22%. *Angelo* (7), *Salvatore* (5), *Ignazio* (4), *Ricardo* (4), *Liborio* (2), *Antonino, Antonio, Galileo, Giovanni, Lorenzo, Paolo, Rocco, Rosario.*

Zambo (155) Hungarian (**Zámbó**): of uncertain origin, perhaps a derivative of the personal name *Zombor*.

Zambon (140) Italian: variant of ZAMBONI.
GIVEN NAMES Italian 11%. *Angelo, Attilio, Francesco, Franco, Giacomo, Tullio.*

Zamboni (151) Italian: from the personal name *Zamboni*, a northeastern variant of *Giambono*, composed of a reduced form of *Gianni* (from GIOVANNI) + BONO or *buono* 'good'.
GIVEN NAMES Italian 9%. *Enzo* (2), *Giovanna* (2), *Albertina, Luciano, Marco, Silvio.*

Zambrana (222) Basque: Castilianized variant of Basque **Zanbrana**, a habitational name from the town called Zanbrana, in Araba province, Basque Country.
GIVEN NAMES Spanish 44%. *Jose* (12), *Fernando* (4), *Jaime* (3), *Juan* (3), *Angel* (2), *Efrain* (2), *Jorge* (2), *Luis* (2), *Luz* (2), *Manuel* (2), *Marina* (2), *Pedro* (2).

Zambrano (1298) **1.** Spanish: habitational name for someone 'from Zamora', from an adjectival form of the place name. **2.** Spanish: possibly also habitational name for someone from Zanbrana, a town in Araba province, Basque Country. **3.** Italian: of uncertain derivation; it is thought by some authorities, on the basis of the form *Zammarano* to be a habitational name for someone from Zammaro, part of San Gregorio d'Ippona in Vibe Valentia province, hypercorrection of *-mm-* to *-mb-* being a characteristic of southern dialect.
GIVEN NAMES Spanish 51%. *Jose* (33), *Luis* (21), *Carlos* (20), *Manuel* (17), *Juan* (16), *Jesus* (13), *Francisco* (11), *Jorge* (11), *Mario* (11), *Sergio* (10), *Ramon* (8), *Angel* (7); *Antonio* (11), *Giacomo* (2), *Marco* (2), *Severino* (2), *Amelio, Carlo, Claudina, Federico, Flavio, Geronimo, Gilda, Guido.*

Zammit (279) Italian (Sicily): variant of **Zammito** (see ZAMBITO), also found in Malta.
GIVEN NAMES Italian 5%. *Carmel, Concetta, Gino, Salvino.*

Zamora (5569) Spanish: habitational name from the city of Zamora in northwestern Spain, capital of the province which bears its name.
GIVEN NAMES Spanish 48%. *Jose* (121), *Juan* (68), *Jesus* (55), *Carlos* (53), *Manuel* (53), *Pedro* (39), *Luis* (37), *Francisco* (36), *Miguel* (32), *Ruben* (32), *Ramon* (31), *Guadalupe* (27).

Zamorano (319) Spanish: habitational name for someone from Zamora, from an adjectival form of the place name. Compare ZAMBRANO.
GIVEN NAMES Spanish 53%. *Manuel* (9), *Jose* (6), *Raul* (5), *Carlos* (4), *Francisco* (4), *Jorge* (4), *Juan* (4), *Esteban* (3), *Luis* (3), *Pedro* (3), *Anabel* (2), *Bonifacio* (2).

Zamorski (127) Polish: habitational name for someone from a place called Zamorze, named with Polish *za* 'beyond' + *morze* 'sea'.

Zampella (112) Italian: possibly a diminutive of a nickname from *zampa* 'foot', 'hoof', 'paw'.

GIVEN NAMES Italian 20%. *Antimo* (2), *Amerigo, Enrico, Gennaro, Salvatore.*

Zampini (163) Italian: patronymic or plural form of ZAMPINO.

GIVEN NAMES Italian 24%. *Dino* (4), *Angelo* (3), *Aldo, Donato, Giuseppe, Guido, Guiseppe, Palma, Pasquale, Pietro.*

Zampino (187) Italian (Sicily): from a diminutive of **Zampa**, from Italian *zampa* 'leg', 'foot', a nickname for someone with a limp or a peculiarity of the foot or leg.

GIVEN NAMES Italian 9%. *Antonio, Domenic, Pasquale, Salvatore.*

Zamudio (710) Basque: habitational name from Zamudio in Biscay province, so named from Basque *zame* 'ravine' + *dio* 'terrain with water'.

GIVEN NAMES Spanish 53%. *Jose* (21), *Francisco* (13), *Juan* (11), *Carlos* (10), *Luis* (8), *Raul* (7), *Jesus* (7), *Jorge* (7), *Ramon* (7), *Manuel* (6), *Alberto* (5), *Ernesto* (5).

Zamzow (334) German: unexplained.

GIVEN NAMES German 5%. *Otto* (3), *Arno.*

Zanardi (124) Italian: probably a pejorative from ZANI or ZANNI.

GIVEN NAMES Italian 6%. *Angelo, Attilio, Silvio.*

Zanca (174) Italian: nickname for a lame or stooped person, from various dialect words, now no longer distinguishable, notably Venetian *zanca* meaning 'turn', 'fold', 'bend', or *zanca*, an old dialect word, associated particularly with Tuscany and Sardinia, meaning 'leg'.

GIVEN NAMES Italian 8%. *Angelo, Gaetano, Sal, Salvatore.*

Zand (134) **1.** Iranian: from a personal name based on Persian *zand* 'interpretation'. In Old Persian the Zand or Zend is the commentary on the *Avesta*, the sacred text of the Zoroastrians. **2.** Jewish (Ashkenazic): variant spelling of SAND. **3.** German: perhaps a nickname for someone with protruding or otherwise remarkable teeth, from Middle High German *zand* 'tooth'.

GIVEN NAMES Muslim 29%; Jewish 9%. *Ali* (3), *Hossein* (2), *Abbas, Behnaz, Gitti, Hamid, Jafar, Mansour, Masoud, Mehdi, Pari, Rana*; *Jechiel* (3), *Bracha, Herschel, Morry.*

Zander (1841) **1.** German: variant spelling of SANDER. **2.** Jewish (Ashkenazic): ornamental name from German *Sander, Zander* 'pike perch'. **3.** South German: occupational name for a barber-surgeon who also pulled teeth, an agent derivative from Middle High German *zan(t)* 'tooth'.

GIVEN NAMES German 5%. *Kurt* (4), *Dieter* (2), *Ernst* (2), *Erwin* (2), *Klaus* (2), *Otto* (2), *Detlef, Eldor, Ewald, Gerhardt, Hans, Helmuth.*

Zanders (425) North German: variant spelling of SANDERS.

Zandi (143) **1.** Iranian: adjectival derivative of ZAND. **2.** Italian (Venetia): of uncertain derivation; perhaps a patronymic from the personal name *Zande*, a short form of

Zadegiacomo, composed of the elements *Gianni* + *de* + *Giacomo*.

GIVEN NAMES Muslim 34%. *Mahmud* (2), *Taher* (2), *Ahmad, Azi, Bahram, Behzad, Farman, Firooz, Hamid, Hossein, Jaleh, Masood.*

Zandstra (212) Frisian: topographic name from a locative agent noun based on Frisian *zand* 'sand'.

GIVEN NAMES Dutch 10%. *Bartel* (6), *Gerrit* (2), *Diederik, Klaas.*

Zane (1025) **1.** English: unexplained. **2.** Italian (Venice and Mantua) and Greek (**Zanes**): from a variant of the Venetian personal name *Z(u)an(n)i* 'John' (see ZANI). **3.** Americanized spelling of German and Jewish ZAHN.

FOREBEARS Robert Zane was a clothmaker of English origin, a founding member of the Quaker colony that was set up at Salem, NJ, in 1676.

Zanella (310) Italian: feminine form of ZANELLI.

GIVEN NAMES Italian 7%. *Aldo* (2), *Amato, Bruna, Fabrizio, Fiorello, Gianluca, Silvano.*

Zanelli (148) Italian: from a pet form of ZANI.

GIVEN NAMES Spanish 12%; Italian 10%. *Mario* (4), *Gabriela* (2), *Luis* (2), *Cesar, Claudio, Enrique, Jose, Roberto*; *Dante* (2), *Aldo, Antonio, Marco, Renzo.*

Zaner (143) Jewish: variant of SANER.

GIVEN NAMES Jewish 4%. *Hyman, Meyer.*

Zanetti (446) Italian: from a pet form of ZANI.

GIVEN NAMES Italian 11%. *Angelo* (3), *Marco* (3), *Gino* (2), *Aldo, Carlo, Domenic, Francesco, Franco, Gilio, Giovanni, Marcello, Maurizio.*

Zang (608) **1.** Chinese 臧: from an area named Zang in the state of Lu, probably during the Zhou dynasty (1122–221 BC). Descendants of the ruling clan of this area eventually adopted the place name Zang as their surname. **2.** South German and Jewish (Ashkenazic): metonymic occupational name for a blacksmith, from Middle High German *zange* 'pliers', German *Zange.*

Zangara (189) Southern Italian: from a feminine form of **Zangaro** (see ZANGARI).

GIVEN NAMES Italian 10%. *Nunzio, Salvatore, Santo.*

Zangari (210) Italian: patronymic from or plural of *zangaro*, an occupational name from medieval Greek *tsangaris* 'bootmaker', from *tsanga* 'boot', a word of Persian origin.

GIVEN NAMES Italian 25%. *Angelo* (2), *Mario* (2), *Carmine, Costantino, Domenico, Francesco, Maurizio, Orlando, Sal, Salvatore.*

Zanger (270) **1.** Dutch: from Dutch *zanger* 'singer', hence an occupational name for a singer or chorister, or nickname for someone who was always singing. Compare German SANGER. **2.** German: variant of

ZENGER. **3.** Jewish (Ashkenazic): metonymic occupational name from German *Zange* 'pincers', 'pliers' + the agent suffix *-er.*

GIVEN NAMES German 5%; Jewish 4%. *Armin, Manfred*; *Meier* (2), *Aron.*

Zanghi (242) Italian: **1.** plural form of **Zanga**, itself a variant of ZANCA. **2.** (**Zanghì**): nickname for a peevish, cantankerous man, from medieval Greek *tsanggos* 'rancid', 'mouldy', 'rank'. **3.** (**Zanghì**): variant of **Zanchi**, a metonymic occupational name for a bootmaker, from medieval Greek *tsanga* 'boot' (see ZANGARI).

GIVEN NAMES Italian 22%. *Angelo* (4), *Sal* (2), *Salvatore* (2), *Carmello, Dario, Domenic, Fortunato, Natale, Rito, Santo.*

Zangrilli (106) Italian (Latium): possibly, as Caracausi proposes, from a diminutive form of an unexplained family name **Zangri** or a reduced diminutive form of ZANGARI.

GIVEN NAMES Italian 26%. *Fabrizio* (2), *Bernardino, Carlo, Francesca, Livia, Piero, Rocco, Sante, Santina, Silvio.*

Zani (193) Italian: from the personal name *Z(u)an(n)i*, a northeastern (Venetian) form of GIANNI (from GIOVANNI, Italian equivalent of JOHN). *Zani* or *Zanni* is a comic figure in the Commedia del'Arte, and the surname may be a nickname derived from this use, which is also the origin of the English word *zany.*

GIVEN NAMES Italian 6%. *Delio* (2), *Agostino, Aldo, Caesar, Francesco, Silvio.*

Zaniewski (164) Polish: habitational name for someone from places called Zanie in Białystok, Suwałki, and Zamość voivodeships.

GIVEN NAMES Polish 12%. *Kazimierz* (2), *Franciszek, Jaroslaw, Jozef, Tadeusz.*

Zanin (153) Italian: from a derivative of ZANI.

GIVEN NAMES Italian 14%; Spanish 4%. *Angelo, Antonietta, Attilio, Flavio, Giacomo, Luca, Lucio, Marco, Renzo*; *Emilio* (2), *Armando, Brunilda, Claudio, Norberto, Zaira.*

Zank (272) South German: nickname for a quarrelsome or cantankerous person, from a noun derivative of Middle High German *zanken, zenken* 'to pick a fight'.

Zanni (197) Italian and Greek (**Zannis**): from the personal name *Zanni*, a northeastern form of GIANNI (from GIOVANNI, Italian equivalent of JOHN). See also ZANI.

GIVEN NAMES Italian 20%; French 4%. *Silvio* (4), *Antonio* (3), *Benedetto* (2), *Carlo* (2), *Aldo, Attilio, Carmine, Egidio, Gino, Guido, Prisco, Vito*; *Francois, Jean-Marc.*

Zannini (105) Italian: diminutive of ZANNI.

GIVEN NAMES Italian 15%. *Gaetano* (2), *Carmine, Domenic, Umberto.*

Zanon (104) Italian (Venezia): variant of ZANONE.

GIVEN NAMES Italian 7%. *Sandro* (2), *Tullio.*

Zanone (152) Italian: from an augmentative of ZANI.

Zanoni (248) Italian: patronymic or plural form of ZANONE.
GIVEN NAMES Italian 11%. *Aldo* (2), *Gino* (2), *Angelo, Attilio, Camillo, Dante, Elio, Geno, Leno, Renzo.*

Zanotti (239) Italian: from a pet form of ZANI.
GIVEN NAMES Italian 22%. *Ferruccio* (2), *Marino* (2), *Mario* (2), *Angelo, Antonio, Eligio, Emilio, Guido, Isidoro, Italo, Libero, Luisa, Nino, Secondo, Sergio.*

Zant (148) **1.** German: variant of ZAND. **2.** Shortened form of Dutch VAN ZANDT.

Zapalac (234) Czech (**Zapalač**): nickname for an arsonist or incendiary, from *zapalovat* 'to set fire to'.

Zapata (2886) **1.** Spanish: metonymic occupational name for a cobbler or shoemaker, from *zapato* 'half boot'. **2.** Spanish and Galician: possibly also a habitational name from the places in Pontevedra and Ávila called Zapata.
GIVEN NAMES Spanish 50%. *Jose* (60), *Juan* (55), *Carlos* (35), *Luis* (27), *Manuel* (23), *Jesus* (18), *Miguel* (16), *Jaime* (15), *Jorge* (15), *Francisco* (14), *Julio* (14), *Mario* (14).

Zapatka (109) Czech: probably from an altered spelling of *západka* 'pawl', 'latch', and so a metonymic name for a locksmith.

Zapf (465) South German: from Middle High German *zapfe* 'bung', 'stopper', hence a metonymic occupational name for a taverner, or perhaps a nickname for an inebriate.
GIVEN NAMES German 7%. *Dieter* (3), *Franz, Fritz, Hans, Irmgard, Jutta, Lothar, Otto.*

Zapien (228) Basque: variant of **Zapiain**, probably habitational name from Zapiain, a neighborhood near Donostia, in Gipuzkoa, Basque Country. This name is nowadays very common in Mexico.
GIVEN NAMES Spanish 50%. *Jose* (7), *Manuel* (5), *Carlos* (4), *Rafael* (4), *Jesus* (3), *Juan* (3), *Ernesto* (2), *Jaime* (2), *Pedro* (2), *Ricardo* (2), *Rodolfo* (2), *Rudolfo* (2).

Zapolski (109) Polish: habitational name for someone from places called Zapole in Rzeszów and Sieradz voivodeships, named with *za* 'beyond' + *pole* 'field', 'open country'. Altenatively, it may be a topographic name for someone living 'beyond the field'.
GIVEN NAMES Polish 5%. *Bronislaw, Slawomir.*

Zapp (392) North German form of ZAPF.

Zappa (419) Italian: metonymic occupational name for an agricultural laborer, from Italian *zappa* 'mattock', 'hoe', or a nickname for a rough, uncultivated person.
GIVEN NAMES Italian 7%. *Aldo* (3), *Onofrio* (2), *Carmine, Domenico, Gasper, Sal, Salvatore.*

Zappala (362) Italian (Sicily; **Zappalà**): occupational name for an agricultural laborer, someone who used a mattock or hoe.
GIVEN NAMES Italian 19%. *Angelo* (3), *Salvatore* (3), *Antonio* (2), *Nunzio* (2), *Orazio* (2), *Alfio, Carmine, Cirino, Dante, Dino, Gaetano, Marco.*

Zappia (398) Southern Italian: metonymic occupational name for a laborer, from *tsapion*, a Greek diminutive of Italian *zappa* 'mattock', 'hoe' (see ZAPPA).
GIVEN NAMES Italian 33%. *Rocco* (9), *Angelo* (3), *Antonio* (2), *Marco* (2), *Natale* (2), *Benito, Carlo, Domenic, Elisabetta, Gino, Guglielmo, Mario, Nunzio, Philomena, Teodoro.*

Zappone (251) Italian: possibly from an augmentative form of ZAPPA.
GIVEN NAMES Italian 15%. *Angelo* (3), *Vito* (2), *Biagio, Domenic, Guiseppe, Rocco.*

Zappulla (191) Italian: metonymic occupational name from southern Italian *zappulla* 'little hoe'.
GIVEN NAMES Italian 22%. *Salvatore* (5), *Angelo* (2), *Antonino, Carmelo, Elio, Gaetano, Giovanni, Giuseppe.*

Zar (155) **1.** Iranian: unexplained. Possibly from a Persian form of Arabic *jār* 'neighbor'. **2.** Jewish: unexplained; presumably a shortened form of some Ashkenazic surname.
GIVEN NAMES Muslim 16%; Jewish 5%. *Abdulrahim* (2), *Amir, Korosh, Mansour, Mohamed, Nasser, Nosratollah, Payam, Saeed; Dror, Mayer, Shlomie, Yael.*

Zara (207) **1.** Italian: habitational name from the Italian name for the city of Zadar on the Dalmatian coast in former Yugoslavia. **2.** Italian: in Sicily, possibly from a variant of *zagara, zagra, zaara* 'orange flower', or, in Venezia, possibly a variant of ZADRA. **3.** Spanish: probably a metronymic from the female personal name *Sara, Zara* (see SARA). **4.** Basque: topographic name from Basque *zara* 'wood', 'thicket'.
GIVEN NAMES Italian 7%; Spanish 6%. *Rocco* (2), *Carlo, Federico, Sabastian; Digna, Erlinda, Graciela, Lucila, Maria Elena, Pedro, Vincente.*

Zaragosa (106) Spanish: variant of ZARAGOZA.
GIVEN NAMES Spanish 53%. *Jose* (3), *Manuel* (3), *Fernando* (2), *Juan Manuel* (2), *Alfredo, Arturo, Carlos, Cristobal, Educardo, Efrain, Enrique, Ernesto.*

Zaragoza (1194) Spanish: habitational name from the city of Zaragoza in northeast Spain, the ancient capital of the kingdom of Aragon. The name derives, via Arabic, from Latin *Caesarea Augusta*, the name bestowed in the 1st century AD by the Emperor Augustus.
GIVEN NAMES Spanish 51%. *Jose* (34), *Juan* (20), *Manuel* (17), *Francisco* (12), *Pedro* (12), *Ignacio* (10), *Jesus* (10), *Fernando* (8), *Javier* (8), *Carlos* (7), *Enrique* (7), *Luis* (7).

Zarate (1426) Basque: habitational name from Zarate, a place in Araba province, named from Basque *zara* 'thicket'.
GIVEN NAMES Spanish 51%. *Jose* (29), *Juan* (24), *Manuel* (19), *Francisco* (16), *Jesus* (12), *Luis* (11), *Miguel* (11), *Carlos* (10), *Alberto* (9), *Salvador* (9), *Sergio* (9), *Arturo* (8).

Zarazua (106) Basque: probably a topographic name from a derivative of Basque *zara* 'thicket'.
GIVEN NAMES Spanish 59%. *Jose* (9), *Juan* (3), *Raul* (3), *Javier* (2), *Jesus* (2), *Alberto, Alvino, Anselmo, Aquilino, Aurelio, Bernabe, Bernardo.*

Zarbock (117) Dialect variant of German *Scharbock* 'scurvy'.
GIVEN NAME German 6%. *Kurt* (3).

Zarco (127) Spanish and Portuguese: nickname from *zarco* 'light blue (eyes)'.
GIVEN NAMES Spanish 57%. *Jose* (4), *Mario* (4), *Jorge* (3), *Alonso* (2), *Carlos* (2), *Esequiel* (2), *Isidoro* (2), *Jesus* (2), *Ricardo* (2), *Alfredo, Amilia, Austreberto; Antonio* (2), *Cecilio, Marco, Marco Antonio, Stefano.*

Zarcone (293) Italian (Sicily): nickname for a peasant, from Arabic *zarqūn* 'ruddy', 'red in the face'.
GIVEN NAMES Italian 9%. *Carmine* (2), *Agostino, Marcello, Pasquale.*

Zarecki (103) Jewish (form Poland): variant of ZARZECKI.
GIVEN NAME Jewish 4%. *Isadore.*

Zarek (158) Polish (**Żarek**): from Polish *żarek*, diminutive of *żar* 'embers', also 'flame of passion'.

Zarella (128) Italian: from a pet form of the personal name ZARA or ZARO.
GIVEN NAMES Italian 8%. *Mario, Salvatore.*

Zaremba (966) Polish (**Zaręba**): **1.** metonymic occupational name for a woodcutter, from a derivative of Polish *zarąbać* 'to hack or chop'. **2.** habitational name from any of various places called Zaręby.
GIVEN NAMES Polish 5%. *Andrzej, Bogdan, Bronislawa, Danuta, Jaroslaw, Slawomir, Wieslawa, Zbigniew, Zigmond, Zigmund, Zygmunt.*

Zaremski (142) Polish: habitational name from any of the many places in Poland called Zaręby.

Zaret (124) Jewish (American): shortened form of ZARETSKY.
GIVEN NAMES Jewish 12%. *Moshe* (3), *Bracha, Sol.*

Zaretsky (275) **1.** Ukrainian and Belorussian: topographic name for someone living 'on the other side of the river'. Compare Polish ZARZECKI. **2.** Jewish (eastern Ashkenazic), Ukrainian, and Belorussian: habitational name for someone from places called Zarechie (meaning 'on the other side of the river'), in Ukraine and Belarus.
GIVEN NAMES Jewish 14%; Russian 11%; German 4%. *Basya, Girsh, Hyman, Ilya, Inna, Meyer, Naum, Sol, Tsilya; Boris* (4),

Iosif (3), *Lev* (2), *Vladimir* (2), *Dmitry, Grigory, Igor, Liliya, Matvey, Mikhail, Natalya, Pinya; Viktor* (2), *Erwin.*

Zarin (100) Jewish (from Belarus): habitational name from the village of Zhary in Belarus + the eastern Slavic possessive suffix *-in*.
GIVEN NAMES Jewish 10%. *Emanuel, Isadore, Reuven, Sol.*

Zaring (239) German (also **Zähring**): habitational name from a place called ZEHRING or nickname for someone who lived at the court of or had connections with the powerful dynasty of the Zähringers in southwestern Germany in the 17th century, whose surname is derived form this place.

Zarins (102) Latvian (**Zariņš**): from Latvian *zars* 'branch', 'twig'.
GIVEN NAMES Latvian 52%. *Zigrida* (3), *Andris* (2), *Daina* (2), *Egils* (2), *Juris* (2), *Arija, Dzintra, Gunars, Gunta, Indulis, Karlis, Laima, Laimonis, Nikolajs, Raimonds.*

Zarlengo (143) Italian: unexplained. This is a rare name in present-day Italy, found in the Naples area.
GIVEN NAMES Italian 7%. *Aldo, Guido, Marco, Serafino.*

Zarling (283) German: unexplained.

Zarn (138) Swiss German: perhaps a habitational name from Sarling in Bavaria.

Zarnowski (119) Polish (**Żarnowski**): habitational name for someone from any of various places called Żarnowo or Żarnów, named with Polish *żarna* 'quern', 'hand mill'.
GIVEN NAMES Polish 6%. *Dariusz, Grzegorz.*

Zaro (195) Italian and Greek (**Zaros**): probably a descriptive nickname from Greek *zaros* 'cross-eyed', 'squinting' or *zaros* 'hawk', both words of unknown etymology.
GIVEN NAMES Italian 12%. *Aldo, Claudio, Elvira, Gaetana, Guido, Guillermo, Margarita, Remo.*

Zarr (272) German and Swiss German: nickname for an autocratic person, from *car* 'tsar'.

Zarra (121) Basque: habitational name from Zarra in Araba province, named from Basque *zarra* 'iron slag'.
GIVEN NAMES Italian 28%. *Angelo* (4), *Carmine* (2), *Vito* (2), *Antonio, Armando, Ernesto, Filomena, Gaetano, Gerardo, Giulio, Mario, Maximo, Rocco.*

Zarrella (215) Italian: from a pet form of the personal name ZARA or ZARO.
GIVEN NAMES Italian 15%. *Angelo, Antonio, Concetta, Dante, Dino, Livio, Pasquale, Salvatore, Sylvio, Vincenza.*

Zarrilli (116) Italian: from a pet form of the personal name ZARA or ZARO.
GIVEN NAMES Italian 11%. *Angelo, Canio, Donato, Giovanni.*

Zarro (182) Italian: probably a variant of SARRO.
GIVEN NAMES Italian 25%. *Amato* (2), *Angelo* (2), *Salvatore* (2), *Amerigo, Antonietta,*

Antonio, Domenico, Gennaro, Giuseppe, Marco, Paolo, Pasquale.

Zarse (100) German: probably a short form of the medieval personal name *Nazarius.*

Zartman (489) German (**Zartmann**): nickname from Middle High German 'lover', 'beloved'.

Zaruba (305) Polish: variant of **Zaręba** (see ZAREMBA).

Zarzecki (134) **1.** Polish: topographic name for someone who lived 'on the other side of the river', from Polish *za* 'beyond' + *rzeka* 'river', with the addition of *-ski*, suffix of local surnames. **2.** Polish and Jewish (from Poland): habitational name from Zarzecze in northeastern Poland.
GIVEN NAMES Polish 17%. *Stanislaw* (2), *Genowesa, Jerzy, Jozef, Kazimierz, Krzysztof, Lucjan, Tadeusz.*

Zarzycki (222) Polish: variant of ZARZECKI.
GIVEN NAMES Polish 15%. *Jurek* (2), *Arkadiusz, Beata, Casimir, Ignatius, Janina, Jozef, Malgorzata, Mieczyslaw, Zofia.*

Zasada (165) Polish: status name for a person who organized a new settlement, Old Polish *zasadźca*. The name has been altered by folk etymology to conform to the modern Polish word *zasada* 'principle', 'basis' (which formerly meant 'trap' or 'ambush').
GIVEN NAMES Polish 4%. *Andrzej, Zigmond.*

Zaske (181) German (of Slavic origin): variant of **Zaschke**, perhaps a habitational name from a place called Zatzschke in Saxony.
GIVEN NAMES German 4%. *Erna, Kurt.*

Zaslavsky (126) Jewish (from Ukraine): habitational name from Zaslav (Izyaslav) in Ukraine.
GIVEN NAMES Russian 27%; Jewish 17%. *Boris* (5), *Leonid* (2), *Vladimir* (2), *Anisim, Dmitry, Igor, Lyudmila, Mikhail, Mily, Pasha, Semyon, Sergey; Ilya* (3), *Hyman, Isaak, Izrail, Khana, Mariya, Moisey, Rakhil.*

Zaslow (218) Jewish: Americanized form of ZASLAVSKY.
GIVEN NAMES Jewish 7%. *Isadore* (2), *Sol* (2), *Gerson.*

Zastoupil (115) Czech: anecdotal nickname from the past participle of *zastoupit* 'to supply or replace'.

Zastrow (1236) German: habitational name from a place so named in western Pomerania, of Slavic origin.
GIVEN NAMES German 4%. *Klaus* (3), *Erwin* (2), *Otto* (2), *Armin, Eldor, Eldred, Franz, Jutta, Kurt.*

Zatarain (126) Basque: unexplained, probably originated in the Donostia area, in Gipuzkoa province, Basque Country.
GIVEN NAMES Spanish 38%. *Jose* (7), *Ernesto* (3), *Cesar* (2), *Emilia* (2), *Juan* (2), *Roberto* (2), *Alicia, Andres, Aurelio, Eduardo, Evelia, Everardo.*

Zatorski (158) Polish: habitational name for someone from Zator near Oświęcim in southern Poland. The word *zator* denotes a

place where a river became blocked by ice in winter.
GIVEN NAMES Polish 10%. *Casimir, Dariusz, Jacek, Jozef, Krystyna, Zdzislaw.*

Zatz (136) Jewish (Ashkenazic): acronym from the Hebrew phrase *Zera TSadikim* 'seed of the righteous', assumed in a spirit of pious respect for one's ancestors.
GIVEN NAMES Jewish 6%. *Meier, Shoshana.*

Zaucha (184) Polish: descriptive nickname from Polish *za uchem* 'behind the ear', denoting someone who had something behind one of his ears.
GIVEN NAMES Polish 12%. *Andrzej, Casimir, Franciszek, Kazimierz, Krzysztof, Mieczyslaw, Rafal, Wojciech.*

Zaugg (301) Swiss German: from an Old High German personal name *Zougo*, perhaps related in meaning to *ziehen* 'to pull'.
GIVEN NAMES German 4%. *Ueli, Ulrich, Urs.*

Zaun (294) German: topographic name from Middle High German *zūn* 'fence', 'hedge'.

Zaunbrecher (177) German: nickname for a violent man, from Middle High German *zūnbrüchel*, literally 'fence breaker', or an altered form of **Zahnbrecher**, from *Zahn* 'tooth' + *Brecher* 'breaker'.

Zauner (266) South German: occupational name for a fence maker, Middle High German *ziūner*. In particular, the term denoted the enclosure surrounding a village as a defense against marauding animals and strangers, and in some cases the name may have been topographic for someone who lived by such a fence.
GIVEN NAMES German 4%. *Alois, Fritz, Otto.*

Zavada (182) Czech (**Závada**): nickname for a troublesome or troubled person, from Czech *závada* 'problem', 'obstacle'. In some cases it may be a topographic name for someone who lived by a physical obstruction.

Zavadil (195) Czech: anecdotal nickname, of uncertain application, from the past participle of Czech *zavadit* 'to touch'.

Zavaglia (104) Italian: possibly related to the common Spanish place name Zaballa.
GIVEN NAMES Italian 33%. *Salvatore* (5), *Angelo* (2), *Attilio, Carmela, Cosmo, Gaetano, Rocco.*

Zavala (3272) Basque: variant of ZABALA 1.
GIVEN NAMES Spanish 53%. *Jose* (125), *Juan* (68), *Jesus* (43), *Manuel* (40), *Miguel* (29), *Luis* (27), *Raul* (21), *Roberto* (21), *Carlos* (20), *Javier* (20), *Francisco* (19), *Guadalupe* (18).

Zavaleta (205) Basque: habitational name from any of places in the Basque provinces named Zabaleta, from Basque *zabal* 'big', 'wide', 'long' + the collective suffix *-eta*.
GIVEN NAMES Spanish 52%. *Luis* (5), *Raul* (5), *Carlos* (4), *Manuel* (4), *Mario* (4), *Francisco* (3), *Jose* (3), *Ricardo* (3), *Alfredo* (2), *Andres* (2), *Asuncion* (2), *Javier* (2).

Zavatsky (117) Czech (**Závatský**): from a derivative of **Závada** (see ZAVADA), denoting a member of the Zavada family.

Zavesky (105) Czech (**Záveský**): topographic name for someone living 'beyond the village', *za vsí*, from *zá* 'beyond' + an inflected form of *ves* 'village'.

Zavitz (119) German: probably an altered form of **Zewitz**, a habitational name from a place so called in eastern Germany.

Zavodny (165) Czech (**Závodný**): topographic name for someone living *za vodou* 'beyond the water'.

Zawacki (794) Polish and Jewish (eastern Ashkenazic): variant of ZAWADZKI.

Zawada (308) Polish and Jewish (from Poland): nickname for a troublesome or troubled person, from Polish *zawada* 'problem', 'obstacle'. In some cases it may be a topographic name for someone who lived by a physical obstruction or a habitational name from a place called Zawada, named with this word (see ZAWADZKI).
GIVEN NAMES Polish 9%. *Wieslaw* (2), *Czeslaw, Danuta, Genowefa, Irena, Jolanta, Tadeusz, Zdzislaw, Zofia.*

Zawadski (127) Polish and Jewish (eastern Ashkenazic): variant spelling of ZAWADZKI.
GIVEN NAMES Polish 5%. *Bogdan, Jurek.*

Zawadzki (427) Polish and Jewish (eastern Ashkenazic): habitational name for someone from any of several places called Zawada or Zawady, in different parts of Poland. The place name is derived from Polish *zawada* 'obstacle'.
GIVEN NAMES Polish 20%; German 4%. *Maciej* (4), *Zbigniew* (3), *Andrzej* (2), *Casimir* (2), *Slawomir* (2), *Zygmunt* (2), *Bogdan, Grazyna, Ireneusz, Jacek, Janusz, Jerzy; Kurt* (2), *Rainer.*

Zawislak (223) Polish (**Zawiślak**): topographic name for someone who lived 'over the Vistula', from *za* 'beyond' + *Wisła* 'Vistula' + *-ak*, suffix of animate nouns.
GIVEN NAMES Polish 8%. *Beata, Boguslaw, Janina, Kazimierz, Piotr, Ryszard.*

Zawistowski (261) Polish: habitational name for someone from places called Zawisty in Łomża and Ostrołęka voivodeships.
GIVEN NAMES Polish 7%. *Bogdan, Dariusz, Jozef, Mikolaj, Miroslaw.*

Zawisza (127) Polish: from the Old Polish personal name *Zawisza*, which is possibly a derivative of *zawist* 'jealousy', 'envy'.
GIVEN NAMES Polish 8%. *Ewa, Mieczyslaw, Piotr.*

Zaworski (114) Polish: habitational name for someone from places called Zawory in Poznań and Gdańsk voivodeships, named with Polish *zawora* 'bolt'.
GIVEN NAMES Polish 5%. *Jacek, Jaroslaw.*

Zay (108) **1.** Hungarian: unexplained. **2.** French (Alsace): Frenchified form of German SEE.

Zayac (166) Partly Americanized spelling of Polish ZAJAC.

Zayas (952) Spanish: habitational name from Zayas de Torre or in some cases from Zayas de Báscones, both in Soria province, which probably derive their names from Basque *zai, zain*, 'guardian', 'vigilante'.
GIVEN NAMES Spanish 44%. *Jose* (24), *Luis* (13), *Carlos* (11), *Juan* (10), *Francisco* (8), *Julio* (8), *Angel* (7), *Enrique* (7), *Jesus* (7), *Roberto* (7), *Fernando* (6), *Mario* (6).

Zazueta (233) Basque: unexplained; apparently topographic.
GIVEN NAMES Spanish 47%. *Jose* (8), *Manuel* (6), *Jesus* (4), *Guadalupe* (3), *Rafael* (3), *Ramon* (3), *Sergio* (3), *Tomas* (3), *Juan* (2), *Pedro* (2), *Susana* (2), *Abelardo.*

Zbikowski (217) Polish (**Żbikowski**): habitational name for someone for any of various places called Żbik, Żbiki, or Żbików, named with *żbik* 'wildcat', which is also found as a personal name.
GIVEN NAMES Polish 6%. *Casimir, Stanislaw, Zygmund.*

Zbinden (180) Swiss German: topographic name in the form of a prepositional phrase, *ze bünden* 'at the enclosure' (i.e., the common property of a village).
GIVEN NAMES German 6%. *Hans* (2), *Otto, Ruedi.*

Zborowski (113) Polish and Jewish (eastern Ashkenazic): habitational name for someone from any of numerous places called Zborów in Poland and Ukraine, named with the personal name *Zbor* (a derivative of *z bor* 'to fight together') or possibly with Polish *zbór* 'herd'.
GIVEN NAMES Polish 11%; Czech and Slovak 4%. *Henryk, Jarek, Maciej, Wladyslaw.*

Zdanowicz (197) Polish: patronymic from the Old Polish personal name *Zdan*, from a word meaning 'bequest' or 'inheritance'.
GIVEN NAMES Polish 8%. *Andrzej, Jaroslaw, Krzysztof, Walenty.*

Zdanowski (113) Polish: habitational name from places called Zdanowice in Kielce voivodeship and Zdanów in Tarnobrzeg voivodeship, named with the vocabulary word *zdan* or the personal name *Zdan* (see ZDANOWICZ).
GIVEN NAMES Polish 6%. *Krzysztof, Wieslaw.*

Zdeb (97) Polish: from Polish *zdeb* 'wildcat', an unflattering nickname for a disagreeable, idle person.
GIVEN NAMES Polish 5%; German 4%. *Ewa; Kurt.*

Zdenek (136) Czech: unexplained.

Zdroik (120) Polish: topographic name for someone who lived by a spring or at a spa, from *zdrój* 'well', 'spring' (later also meaning 'spa'), + the diminutive suffix *-ik*.

Zdrojewski (151) Polish: habitational name for someone from any of several places called Zdroje or Zdrojewo, in particular in Bydgoszcz voivodeship, named with Polish *zdroje* 'springs', 'spa'.
GIVEN NAMES Polish 7%. *Casimir, Zygmund.*

Zea (240) Galician and Spanish: possibly a variant spelling of the habitational name CEA.
GIVEN NAMES Spanish 20%. *Jorge* (3), *Carlos* (2), *Hernando* (2), *Jesus* (2), *Jose* (2), *Juan* (2), *Maria Luisa* (2), *Miguel* (2), *Ramon* (2), *Alba, Alfredo, Alicia.*

Zeagler (148) Americanized spelling of German ZIEGLER.

Zeamer (106) Americanized spelling of German SIEMER.

Zebell (144) Variant of German ZABEL or ZOBEL.

Zebley (228) Americanized form of South German **Zoeble**, variant of ZOBEL.

Zebro (111) Polish (**Żebro**): nickname from *żebro* 'rib'.

Zebroski (123) Variant of Polish ZEBROWSKI.
GIVEN NAME Polish 4%. *Casimir.*

Zebrowski (664) Polish (**Żebrowski**): habitational name from any of various places named with Polish *żebro* 'rib'. The place name Żebry is found mainly in Masovia.
GIVEN NAMES Polish 6%. *Jozef* (2), *Andrzej, Eugeniusz, Maciek, Piotr, Tomasz, Witold, Zigmund.*

Zecca (284) Italian: **1.** nickname from *zecca* 'tick' (the blood-sucking insect). **2.** from *zecca* 'mint', probably a metonymic occupational name for someone who minted coins.
GIVEN NAMES Italian 24%. *Guido* (4), *Alfonso* (3), *Mario* (3), *Aldo, Attilio, Carmine, Domenica, Filomena, Francesca, Italo, Josefina, Livio, Nilda, Oreste, Roberto.*

Zech (580) German: **1.** nickname from Middle High German *zæhe, zæch* 'tenacious'. **2.** from a short form of the personal name ZACHARIAS.
GIVEN NAMES German 5%. *Kurt* (2), *Manfred* (2), *Horst, Klaus, Monika, Wolfgang.*

Zecher (193) German: **1.** occupational name from Middle High German *zëchære* denoting a member of a watch or some other task that was carried out on an organized rota. **2.** variant of ZACHARIAS.

Zechman (327) Jewish (eastern Ashkenazic): occupational name from Yiddish *tsekh* 'guild', 'craft corporation' + *man* 'man'.

Zeck (331) South German: unflattering nickname for an exhausting person, from Middle High German *zëcke* 'wood tick'.
GIVEN NAMES German 4%. *Fritz, Otto, Rainer, Siegfried.*

Zediker (118) Possibly of German origin: unexplained.

Zee (373) Reduced form of Dutch VANDERZEE.

Zeeb (309) South German: dialect variant of ZEE.
GIVEN NAMES German 4%. *Erwin, Otto.*

Zeedyk (111) Dutch: topographic name for someone who lived by a dike built to keep out the sea.

Zeek (309) Perhaps an altered spelling of **Zeeck**, a Frisian short form of a personal name beginning with the element *sigi* 'victory', for example *Sigfrid* or *Sigwart*.

Zeeman (157) Dutch: topographic name for a sailor or for someone who lived by the seashore or beside a lake, Middle Dutch *zee*.

Zeff (207) Jewish (Ashkenazic): from the personal name *Zev*, meaning 'wolf' in Hebrew.

GIVEN NAMES Jewish 5%. *Aron, Isadore, Tova.*

Zegar (103) Possibly of English origin, an altered form of **Segar**, from the Old English personal name *Sǣgār* (meaning 'sea spear').

Zegarelli (140) Italian: **1.** variant of **Zagarella**, from a diminutive of Sicilian *zagara* 'orange flower' (a derivative of Arabic *zahr*). **2.** metonymic occupational name for a maker of ribbons, laces, and the like, from Old Sicilian *zacharella* 'string', 'ribbon', 'lace'.

GIVEN NAMES Italian 25%. *Angelo* (4), *Antonio* (2), *Dino* (2), *Francesco, Guiseppe, Pasquale, Remo.*

Zegarra (112) Spanish: probably a Castilianized form of Catalan SEGARRA.

GIVEN NAMES Spanish 48%. *Jorge* (5), *Carlos* (3), *Hernando* (3), *Miguel* (3), *Ana* (2), *Jose* (2), *Juan* (2), *Julio* (2), *Manuel* (2), *Ricardo* (2), *Albino, Alejandra.*

Zeger (195) Dutch: variant of SEGER.

Zegers (195) Dutch: variant of SEGERS.

Zeglin (103) German: probably an altered spelling of **Sekeli** (see SZEKLER).

Zeh (642) German: **1.** nickname for someone with deformed or otherwise remarkable toes, from Middle High German *zēhe*, *zehe* 'toe', 'claw'. The term also meant 'tough', and in some cases the surname may have arisen from this sense. **2.** variant of ZECH 1.

GIVEN NAMES German 4%. *Ernst, Kurt, Orlo, Otto.*

Zehler (101) German: variant of ZAHLER 1.

Zehm (156) German: **1.** habitational name from the Slavic place names Zehma, near Altenburg, or Zehmen, near Leipzig. **2.** (of Slavic origin) topographic name from Slavic *zemja* 'earth', 'land', probably denoting a new settler.

GIVEN NAMES German 6%. *Otto* (2), *Erwin.*

Zehnder (661) Variant of ZEHNER.

Zehner (880) German (chiefly Bavaria, Austria, Switzerland, and Württemberg): occupational name for an official responsible for collecting, on behalf of the lord of the manor, tithes of agricultural produce owed as rent. The more prosperous tenants had to contribute wine and grain, those with smaller holdings fruit, vegetables, milk, cheese, beer, and poultry. The Middle High German term for this official was *zehendære*, a derivative of *zehende* 'tenth part', 'tithe' (Old High German *zehanto*, from *zehan* 'ten').

Zehr (1033) German: nickname for a big eater or a spendthrift, from Middle High German *zeren* 'to spend a lot of money on food and drink', 'splurge'.

Zehren (204) Swiss German: from a prepositional phrase from Middle High German *ze hĕrren*, an occupational name for someone who was in the service of a lord.

Zehring (181) German: **1.** habitational name from a place so named. **2.** variant of **Zähring** (see ZARING).

Zehrung (128) German: variant of ZEHRING.

Zeichner (131) German: probably a habitational name for someone from Zeichen near Pirna. Bahlow doubts that it is from Middle High German *zeichener* 'one who does signs and wonders'.

Zeiders (281) Altered spelling of German SEIDERS, reflecting the German pronunciation of the initial *s*.

Zeidler (367) South German: occupational name for a beekeeper, Middle High German *zīdeler*.

GIVEN NAMES German 7%. *Kurt* (2), *Reinhold* (2), *Dietmar, Manfred, Udo.*

Zeidman (267) Jewish (Ashkenazic): variant spelling of SEIDMAN.

GIVEN NAMES Jewish 7%. *Bezalel, Hyman.*

Zeien (181) Of German origin: unexplained.

Zeier (165) **1.** German: variant of **Zeiher**, from the medieval personal name *Zyriak* (see ZILCH). **2.** Perhaps an unflattering nickname for a litigious peron or a slanderer, from Middle High German *zīhen* 'to accuse'. **3.** Perhaps an altered spelling of German SEIER, reflecting the German pronunciation of the initial *s*.

Zeiger (651) German: **1.** occupational name for a sign maker, from Middle High German *zeiger* 'sign', 'guide', 'sign at an inn'. **2.** altered spelling of German SEIGER, reflecting the German pronunciation of the initial *s*, or of ZIEGER.

GIVEN NAMES German 4%. *Kurt* (3), *Otto.*

Zeigler (4676) Respelling of German ZIEGLER.

Zeiler (669) South German: topographic name from Middle High German *zīle* 'row of houses', 'alley', or *zīl* 'thorn bush', the suffix -*er* denoting an inhabitant.

Zeilinger (143) German: habitational name for someone from Zeiling in Bavaria.

Zeilman (116) German: habitational name for someone who livd in a row of houses or on a prominent street, from Middle High German *zīl(e)* 'row', 'line', 'street'.

Zeimet (212) Western German and Luxembourgeois: probably a variant spelling of **Zeimert**, a variant of **Zeumer**, an occupational name for a harness maker, from an agent derivative of Middle High German *zoum* 'bridle'.

Zeiner (249) South German: from an agent derivative of Middle High German *zeinen* 'to forge (iron)', also 'to weave basketwork' (from Middle High German *zein* 'cane', 'rod', 'tine'), hence an occupational name for a smith or a basket maker.

Zeinert (128) German: variant of ZEINER.

Zeis (339) Variant spelling of German ZEISS.

Zeise (124) German: **1.** from Middle High German *zīse* 'siskin' (a yellow and black finch), hence a nickname for someone thought to resemble the bird in some way, or an occupational name for a bird dealer or catcher. **2.** variant of ZEISS.

GIVEN NAMES German 8%. *Ingo* (2), *Otto.*

Zeiser (207) German: variant of ZAISER.

GIVEN NAMES German 4%. *Lorenz, Otto.*

Zeiset (108) Of German origin: unexplained.

GIVEN NAME German 7%. *Phares* (2).

Zeisler (287) **1.** South German: occupational name for a bird dealer or catcher, from an agent derivative of Middle High German *zīsel* 'siskin' (see ZEISE). **2.** North German: variant of **Ziesler**, a nickname for a person in a hurry or one who did sloppy work.

GIVEN NAMES German 6%. *Erwin, Kurt, Ulrich, Wolfgang.*

Zeisloft (135) Altered form of German **Zeislof**, a metathesized derivative of the Germanic personal name *Zeissolf*, a compound of *zeiss* 'tender', 'kind', 'graceful' (see ZEISS) + *wolf* 'wolf'.

Zeiss (230) German: nickname for a gentle person, from Middle High German *zeiss* 'tender', 'kind', 'graceful'.

Zeiter (165) Perhaps an altered spelling of German SEITER, reflecting the German pronunciation of the initial *s*.

Zeitler (710) Austrian German: dialect variant of ZEIDLER.

GIVEN NAMES German 5%. *Kurt* (3), *Arno, Hans, Heinz, Inge, Konrad, Markus, Otto.*

Zeitlin (418) Jewish (from Belarus and Lithuania): metronymic from the Yiddish female personal name *Tseytl*, which is of uncertain origin, with the addition of the Slavic metronymic suffix -*in*.

GIVEN NAMES Jewish 6%. *Hillel* (4), *Hyman, Ilya, Josif, Shimon, Shmuel, Yakov.*

Zeitz (498) German: habitational name from either of two place so named, both in Saxony-Anhalt.

GIVEN NAMES German 4%. *Kurt* (2), *Hans, Matthias, Orlo, Reinhold.*

Zelasko (306) Polish (**Żelazko**): from Polish *żelazko* 'flat iron', a metonymic occupational name for someone who ironed or pressed clothes.

GIVEN NAMES Polish 4%. *Kazimierz* (2), *Slawomir.*

Zelaya (826) Basque: variant spelling of **Zelaia**, a habitational name in Biscay province, Basque Country, from Basque *zelai* 'field', 'meadow' + the definite article -*a*.

GIVEN NAMES Spanish 54%. *Jose* (46), *Carlos* (13), *Mario* (10), *Blanca* (9), *Luis* (9), *Juan* (8), *Manuel* (8), *Miguel* (8), *Francisco* (7), *Pablo* (7), *Ana* (6), *Jorge* (6).

Zelazny (239) Polish (**Żelazny**): from Polish *żelazny* 'iron', a nickname for a strong personality or someone who ruled 'with a rod of iron'.
GIVEN NAMES Polish 5%. *Janusz* (2), *Rajmund*.

Zeldin (216) Jewish (eastern Ashkenazic): metronymic from the Yiddish female personal name *Zelde* (from Middle High German *sælde* 'fortunate', 'blessed') + the eastern Slavic possessive suffix *-in*.
GIVEN NAMES Russian 17%; Jewish 13%. *Boris* (3), *Vladimir* (3), *Leonid* (2), *Aleksandr*, *Anatoliy*, *Arkadiy*, *Arkady*, *Asya*, *Dmitry*, *Fedor*, *Lev*, *Luda*; *Ari*, *Hyman*, *Miriam*, *Naum*, *Oded*, *Zinaida*.

Zeledon (180) Variant of Spanish **Celedón**, from a short form of the personal name *Celedonio*.
GIVEN NAMES Spanish 42%. *Carlos* (4), *Luis* (4), *Alvaro* (2), *Francisco* (2), *Jaime* (2), *Juan* (2), *Mario* (2), *Ricardo* (2), *Alejandro*, *Alfredo*, *Alicia*, *Armando*.

Zelek (146) Polish: **1.** (**Żelek**) pet form of the Polish personal names *Żelisław* or *Żelistryj*, derived from Slavic *želěti* 'desire', 'wish'. **2.** occupational name from Polish dialect *zelek* 'rag-and-bone man'.
GIVEN NAME Polish 4%. *Tadeusz*.

Zelenak (319) **1.** Czech and Slovak (**Zelenák**): variant of ZELENKA. **2.** Perhaps an Americanized form of Slovenian **Zelenjak**, a derivative of *zelen* 'green', 'immature' (or perhaps a nickname from Slovenian dialect *zelenjak* 'green woodpecker').

Zelenka (486) Czech and Croatian (eastern and northern Croatia): from a diminutive of *zeleny* 'green'. The application as a surname is uncertain: it may be a nickname for someone who habitually dressed in green or who was 'green' in the sense of being immature or inexperienced, or for someone with a sickly 'greenish' complexion.

Zelenski (108) Polish: variant of **Zieliński** (see ZIELINSKI).
GIVEN NAME Polish 4%. *Aleksander*.

Zeleny (203) Czech and Slovak (**Zelený**): nickname name from *zeleny* 'green'.

Zeleznik (172) **1.** Polish (**Żeleźnik**): occupational name for a metalworker, Polish *żeleźnik*. **2.** Slovenian (**Železnik**): derivative from *železo* 'iron', probably a nickname from the plant name *železnik* (Latin *Lithospermum*), a plant noted for its hard seeds, or an old habitational name for a person from any of places called Železno, named with *železo* 'iron'.

Zeliff (127) Origin unidentified.

Zelinger (102) Jewish: variant of SALINGER.
GIVEN NAMES Jewish 15%. *Yaakov* (3), *Shaul*, *Shira*, *Yehudah*.

Zelinka (138) Czech: **1.** variant of ZELENKA. **2.** nickname from a vocabulary word meaning 'herb'.

Zelinski (544) **1.** Ukrainian and Jewish (from Ukraine): habitational name for someone from Zelenki in Ukraine. The top-

onym is derived from the eastern Slavic root 'green'. **2.** Polish (**Zieliński**): variant of ZIELINSKI.

Zelinsky (379) Americanized spelling of ZELINSKI.

Zelko (169) Altered form of Polish ZYLKA.

Zell (1215) German: habitational name from any of the numerous places named Zell. Compare ZELLE.

Zella (125) Italian: unexplained.

Zellar (147) German or Dutch: variant spelling of ZELLER.

Zellars (190) German or Dutch: variant spelling of ZELLER.
GIVEN NAMES French 5%. *Andre*, *Veronique*.

Zelle (180) German and Dutch: topographic name from Middle High German *zelle* '(hermit's) cell' or habitational name from a place called Zelle or Celle (see ZELLER).

Zeller (4147) **1.** German and Dutch: habitational name from any of the various places called Zelle or Celle, in particular Celle near Hannover, named with German *Zelle* 'cell', Middle High German *zelle* (from Latin *cella* 'small room'), or a topographic name from this word, denoting someone who lived near the site of a hermit's cell. **2.** German and Jewish (Ashkenazic): In other cases it was an occupational name for someone who owned or was employed at a *Zelle* in the sense of a small workshop.

Zellers (1121) Variant of German ZELLER with the addition of *-s*, typical of changes in the U.S.

Zellman (197) **1.** Respelling of German ZELLMANN. **2.** Jewish (Ashkenazic): variant of SELMAN.
GIVEN NAMES German 4%. *Kurt*, *Otto*.

Zellmann (112) **1.** German: occupational name for someone who owned or was employed at a small workshop (see ZELLER). **2.** habitational name for someone from Celle near Hannover. **3.** Jewish (Ashkenazic): variant of SELMAN.

Zellmer (935) German: reduced form of **Zellmeier** (see SELLMEYER).

Zellner (1297) German and Jewish (Ashkenazic): occupational name from German **Zöllner** 'tax collector'.

Zello (114) Italian: **1.** possibly a habitational name from Zello in Bologna or either of two places called Zelo, in Milan and Rovigo. **2.** perhaps from a short form of *donzello* (see DONZE).
GIVEN NAMES Italian 8%. *Angelo* (2), *Rocco*.

Zelman (345) Jewish (Ashkenazic): variant of SELMAN.
GIVEN NAMES Jewish 7%. *Sol* (3), *Gerson* (2), *Noam* (2), *Chaim*, *Yakov*.

Zelmer (158) German: variant of ZELLMER.
GIVEN NAMES German 8%. *Erwin*, *Milbert*, *Otto*.

Zelnick (148) **1.** Jewish (eastern Ashkenazic): occupational name from Yiddish *tselnik* 'haberdashery' or from Polish *celnik* 'tax collector'. **2.** Americanized spelling of

Slovenian Zelnik, a nickname or topographic name from *zelje* 'cabbage'.
GIVEN NAMES French 9%; Jewish 4%. *Henri* (2), *Michel* (2), *Serge*; *Hyman*.

Zelonis (104) Origin unidentified.

Zelt (113) German: perhaps a variant of ZELTNER.
GIVEN NAME German 7%. *Siegfried*.

Zeltner (173) South German: occupational name for a baker, from an agent derivative of Middle High German *zelte* 'flat loaf', 'pastry'.

Zeltser (122) Jewish (eastern Ashkenazic): variant of SELTZER.
GIVEN NAMES Jewish 30%; Russian 30%; Czech and Slovak 5%. *Yakov* (3), *Samoil* (2), *Basya*, *Irina*, *Isaak*, *Izrail*, *Kolman*, *Pinkus*, *Shmuel*, *Sima*, *Sura*, *Zelig*; *Mikhail* (3), *Yefim* (3), *Asya* (2), *Boris* (2), *Leonid* (2), *Lev* (2), *Anatoly*, *Efim*, *Fima*, *Igor*, *Liya*, *Lyudmila*; *Pavel*, *Vladislav*.

Zema (100) Italian: from the dialect word *zema* 'broth'.

Zemaitis (259) Lithuanian (**Žemaitis**): regional name meaning 'lowlander', for someone from the western part of Lithuania.

Zeman (1652) Czech: status name for a yeoman farmer or small landowner, Czech *zeman* (a derivative of *zem* 'land'). This is one of the most common Czech surnames.

Zemanek (237) Czech (**Zemánek**): from a diminutive of ZEMAN.

Zemba (184) Germanized spelling of Polish **Zięba**, from *zięba* 'finch', thus a nickname for someone thought to have some characteristics of a finch.

Zembower (138) Possibly an Americanized spelling of German **Zembacher**, a habitational name or a house name meaning 'at the brook'.
GIVEN NAME German 5%. *Kurt*.

Zemel (239) Jewish (Ashkenazic): variant of SEMMEL.
GIVEN NAMES Jewish 8%; Russian 5%; German 4%. *Irina* (3), *Chain*, *Eitan*, *Fridrikh*, *Sol*, *Tali*, *Yoram*; *Efim*, *Fanya*, *Gennadiy*, *Lev*, *Svetlana*; *Erna*, *Mathias*.

Zemke (549) German: Germanized form of Czech **Zemek**, an old word for a yeoman farmer (see ZEMAN).
GIVEN NAMES German 4%. *Hermann* (2), *Kurt* (2), *Ernst*, *Erwin*, *Otto*.

Zemlicka (136) Czech (**Žemlička**): metonymic occupational name for a baker, from *žemlička*, diminutive of *žemle* 'bread roll'. Compare German SEMLER.

Zemp (111) German: Germanized form of Slavic ZEMBA 'farmer'.
GIVEN NAME German 4%. *Hanspeter*.

Zempel (233) German: diminutive of ZEMP.

Zendejas (330) Spanish: variant spelling of the habitational name CENDEJAS.
GIVEN NAMES Spanish 54%. *Jose* (12), *Luis* (6), *Francisco* (5), *Jesus* (5), *Juan* (5), *Mario* (5), *Javier* (4), *Miguel* (4), *Manuel*

(3), *Margarita* (3), *Raul* (3), *Rigoberto* (3), *Antonio*, *Eliseo*, *Mirella*; *Lorenzo* (2), *Marco* (2), *Silvano*, *Sylvio*.

Zender (344) German: reduced form of ZEHNDER.

Zeng (629) Chinese 曾: from a simplified form of the name of the state of Kuai. During the Xia dynasty (2205–1766 BC) this state was granted to the youngest son of King Shaokang. After being overthrown by another state, the prince fled and adopted a simplified form of the character *Kuai* as his surname.

GIVEN NAMES Chinese 68%. *Ming* (10), *Li* (6), *Rong* (6), *Guang* (5), *Hong* (4), *Lei* (4), *Wen* (4), *Jian Ming* (3), *Jin* (3), *Wei* (3), *Ying* (3), *Zhi* (3).

Zengel (118) South German: from a diminutive of ZANG.

Zenger (265) South German: nickname from Middle High German *zenger, zanger* 'cheeky', 'bold', 'vivacious'.

FOREBEARS John Peter Zenger (1697–1746), printer, came to America from the Palatinate in Germany in 1710.

GIVEN NAMES German 4%. *Helmut*, *Wolfgang*.

Zeni (161) Italian: patronymic or plural form of ZENO.

GIVEN NAMES Italian 13%; Spanish 8%. *Angelo* (3), *Aldo*, *Dario*, *Gino*, *Leno*, *Rino*, *Silvio*; *Albino*, *Jaime*, *Jesus*, *Ramona*.

Zenisek (141) Czech (**Ženíšek**): ironic nickname for an amorous man or a womanizer, from a diminutive of Czech *ženich* 'bridegroom', 'wooer'.

Zenk (423) South German: unflattering nickname for a quarrelsome person, from a derivative of Middle High German *zenken, zanken* 'to provoke'.

GIVEN NAMES German 4%. *Erwin*, *Gunther*, *Lothar*.

Zenker (338) South German: unflattering nickname for a quarrelsome person, from an agent noun derivative of Middle High German *zenken, zanken* 'to provoke'.

GIVEN NAMES German 7%. *Christoph* (2), *Franz*, *Jochen*, *Kurt*, *Otto*, *Wilfried*, *Willi*.

Zenner (618) South German: unflattering nickname for a surly, snarling person, from an agent derivative of Middle High German *zannen* 'to growl or howl' or 'to bare one's teeth'.

Zeno (655) Italian and Greek (**Zenos**): 1. from the personal name *Zeno*, from the Greek personal name *Zēnōn*, an ancient derivative of *Zeus*, name of the king of the gods in Greek mythology. *Zēnōn* is the name of several saints and martyrs venerated in the Greek Orthodox Church, and in the form *Zeno* or *Zenone* it was also the name of a 4th-century saint from Verona. The Greek name may also be a shortened form of a derivative of the above, for example **Zenovi(o)s** or **Zenopoulos**. This is sometimes found as an alternative for LUSIGNAN, a powerful family in the Middle East in medieval times. 2. Also possibly from *tsenos*, Southern Italian Greek form of Greek *xenos* 'newcomer', 'stranger' (see XENOS).

Zenon (177) Greek, Spanish (**Zenón**), and French (**Zénon**): from the Greek personal name *Zēnōn* (see ZENO).

GIVEN NAMES French 10%; Spanish 10%. *Camile*, *Kettly*, *Lydie*, *Ulysse*, *Yves*; *Angel*, *Carmelita*, *Chiquita*, *Efrain*, *Jaime*, *Julio*, *Lorenza*, *Miguel*, *Modesta*, *Ramona*, *Tomas*, *Wilfredo*.

Zenor (276) Americanized spelling of German ZEHNER.

Zens (204) German: variant of ZENTZ.

Zent (380) German (also found in Russia): unexplained.

Zentgraf (124) German: occupational name for the presiding official of a court of justice, Middle High German *zentgrāve*.

GIVEN NAMES German 6%. *Ernst*, *Fritz*.

Zentner (564) German: 1. variant of ZEHNER. 2. occupational name from Middle High German *zentener* 'district judge' (see ZENTGRAF).

GIVEN NAMES German 5%. *Franz*, *Gerhard*, *Kurt*, *Otto*, *Raimund*.

Zentz (469) German: from a short form of the personal name *Vinzentz*, German form of VINCENT.

Zenz (264) German: variant of ZENTZ.

GIVEN NAMES German 4%. *Franz*, *Fritz*, *Manfred*.

Zeoli (272) Italian: probably from a short form of a pet name formed with the suffix *-olo* from a personal name ending with *-zeo*, such as MAZZEO.

GIVEN NAMES Italian 16%. *Angelo* (5), *Geno* (2), *Amedeo*, *Antonio*, *Carmine*, *Donato*, *Guido*, *Leonardo*, *Rocco*.

Zeolla (109) Italian: unexplained. Recorded in Foggia in the 19th century, the name appears to have since died out in Italy.

GIVEN NAMES Italian 42%. *Angelo* (3), *Antonio* (2), *Donato* (2), *Mario* (2), *Salvatore* (2), *Alfredo*, *Carmela*, *Giorgio*, *Giuseppe*, *Nicola*, *Pietro*, *Teo*.

Zepeda (2355) Spanish: variant spelling of CEPEDA.

GIVEN NAMES Spanish 51%. *Jose* (55), *Manuel* (35), *Carlos* (29), *Francisco* (25), *Jorge* (22), *Juan* (22), *Luis* (20), *Jesus* (18), *Enrique* (16), *Pedro* (16), *Rafael* (14), *Roberto* (14).

Zepf (123) German: 1. variant of ZAPF. 2. metonymic occupational name for a grower of or dealer in grapes, corn, or grain, from Middle High German *zepfe* 'grape', 'ear (of a cereal plant)'.

Zepp (674) German: probably a variant of ZAPP.

Zeppieri (104) Italian: unexplained.

GIVEN NAMES Italian 32%. *Duilio* (2), *Massimo* (2), *Angelo*, *Carmine*, *Egidio*, *Elio*, *Giorgio*, *Italo*, *Livio*, *Luigi*, *Santo*, *Silvo*.

Zera (192) 1. Polish (**Żera**): variant of *żyra* 'food', from an old Polish compound name such as *Żyrosław* (from *żyr* 'food' + *sława* 'glory') or *Domażyr* (from *doma* 'home' + *żyr* 'food'). 2. Ethiopian: unexplained.

Zerangue (130) Altered form, under French influence, of German ZEHRING, found predominantly in LA.

Zerba (116) Origin uncertain. Most probably a variant of German ZERBE.

Zerbe (974) German: habitational name from a place near Magdeburg named Zerben.

Zerbel (105) German: pet form of an altered form of ZERVAS.

Zerbo (101) Southern Italian and Sicilian: possibly a nickname from modern Greek *zerbos* 'left-handed', by extension 'treacherous'.

GIVEN NAMES Italian 26%. *Salvatore* (5), *Angelo*, *Carlo*, *Carmelo*.

Zerbst (103) German: habitational namne from Zerbst in Saxony-Anhalt.

Zerby (378) Americanized form of German ZERBE.

Zercher (127) Swiss German: habitational name for someone from the city of Zürich, variant of **Zürcher** (see ZURCHER).

Zerfas (148) German: variant of SERFASS.

Zerfoss (101) German: variant of SERFASS.

Zerger (135) German (also found in Russia): possibly an altered spelling of **Zarger**, a topographic name for someone who lived at the edge of a village or wood, from *zarge* 'edge'.

Zerilli (133) Southern Italian: patronymic or plural form of ZERILLO.

GIVEN NAMES Italian 27%. *Attilio* (2), *Giuseppe* (2), *Salvatore* (2), *Antonino*, *Enrico*, *Francesco*, *Marco*, *Paolo*.

Zerillo (105) Southern Italian: from a pet form of the personal name ZERO.

GIVEN NAMES Italian 16%. *Salvatore* (2), *Vito* (2), *Antonio*, *Leonardo*.

Zeringue (690) Altered form, under French influence, of German ZEHRING, found predominantly in LA.

GIVEN NAMES French 7%. *Alcee* (2), *Andre* (2), *Antoine* (2), *Camille* (2), *Pierre* (2), *Alphonse*, *Angelle*, *Cecile*, *Elmire*, *Etienne*.

Zerkel (141) Variant spelling of German ZIRKEL.

Zerkle (248) Americanized spelling of German ZIRKEL.

Zermeno (299) Spanish (**Zermeño**): variant spelling of **Cermeño**, a nickname from *cermeño* 'fool', 'lout', 'slob'.

GIVEN NAMES Spanish 47%. *Jose* (10), *Roberto* (4), *Carlos* (3), *Francisco* (3), *Juan* (3), *Manuel* (3), *Alberto* (2), *Cirilo* (2), *Consuelo* (2), *Felipe* (2), *Guadalupe* (2), *Ignacio* (2).

Zern (242) German: occupational name for a man who dealt in grain, from Sorbian *zerno, zorno* 'grain'.

Zero (135) **1.** Southern Italian: from the medieval Greek personal name *Xeros*, derived from Greek *xeros* 'dry', 'bare'. **2.** Polish: unflattering nickname for an insignificant or worthless person, from *zero* 'zero', 'nought'.
GIVEN NAMES Polish 7%; Italian 6%. *Dariusz, Leszek, Zdzislaw; Lucio, Sabato.*

Zerr (661) South German: nickname for a rowdy or tough person, from a derivative of Middle High German *zerren* 'to scold or complain'.

Zertuche (239) probably form a native American language in northern Mexico: unexplained.
GIVEN NAMES Spanish 39%. *Jose* (5), *Juan* (4), *Manuel* (4), *Arturo* (3), *Adolfo* (2), *Armando* (2), *Carlos* (2), *Fernando* (2), *Gavino* (2), *Jesus* (2), *Mario* (2), *Ramon* (2).

Zervas (209) **1.** Greek: from a nickname meaning 'left-handed'. **2.** Dutch and North German: from the personal name *Zervas*, a vernacular pet form of Latin *Servatius*. This was the name of the patron saint of Maastricht, a 14th-century bishop of Tongeren.
GIVEN NAMES Greek 16%. *Athanasios, Christos, Demetre, Dionisios, Efstratios, Ioannis, Markos, Photios, Spiro, Tasos, Vasilios.*

Zervos (222) Greek: from the vocabulary word *zervos*, a nickname meaning 'left-handed'.
GIVEN NAMES Greek 10%; Italian 6%. *Thanos* (2), *Christos, Constantine, Constantinos, Diamantis, Spero, Stratis, Theophilos*; *Angelo* (4), *Dino.*

Zesiger (122) Swiss German: unexplained.

Zessin (124) German: habitational name from a place so named on Rügen island.

Zettel (276) **1.** South German: metonymic occupational name for a scribe, from Middle High German *zettel* 'document'. **2.** South German: metonymic occupational name perhaps for a weaver, from Middle High German *zettel(-garn)* 'thread'. **3.** German: reduced form of **Zettelmeier** (see ZETTLEMOYER).

Zetterberg (137) Swedish: ornamental name composed of the elements *Zetter*, an ornamental spelling of the place name element *säter* 'mountain pasture' + *berg* 'mountain'.
GIVEN NAMES Scandinavian 19%. *Erik* (5), *Niklas.*

Zettle (225) Altered spelling of German ZETTEL.

Zettlemoyer (269) Altered spelling of German **Zettelmeier**, a variant of **Sedelmair**, from Middle High German *sedelmeier* 'tenant of a manor (*sededhov*)'.
GIVEN NAMES German 4%. *Erwin* (2), *Kurt.*

Zettler (427) German: occupational name for a scribe or perhaps for a weaver, from an agent derivative of Middle High German *zettel* 'document' or *zettel(garn)* 'thread' (see ZETTEL).

Zetts (104) Origin unidentified.

Zevallos (153) Spanish: variant spelling of CEBALLOS.
GIVEN NAMES Spanish 55%. *Carlos* (7), *Manuel* (5), *Cesar* (4), *Edmundo* (3), *Mario* (3), *Rafael* (3), *Alberto* (2), *Arturo* (2), *Fabricio* (2), *Guillermo* (2), *Jose* (2), *Miguel* (2).

Zevenbergen (118) Dutch and Belgian: habitational name from either of two places named Zevenbergen ('seven hills'): in Antwerp province, Belgium, and North Brabant in the Netherlands.
GIVEN NAMES Dutch 8%. *Cornie* (2), *Janneke, Willem.*

Zewe (106) German: probably from a short form of the personal name *Zevaert*, a Low German variant of *Sievert*, or a variant of **Seebe**, cognate with **Sievert**.
GIVEN NAMES German 7%. *Bernhard, Detlef, Uwe.*

Zezza (102) Italian: variant of ZIZZA.
GIVEN NAMES Italian 15%; French 7%. *Carlo* (3), *Alessandro, Geno*; *Patrice.*

Zgoda (110) Polish: nickname for a peaceful person, from *zgoda* 'concord', 'harmony'.

Zha (32) Chinese 查: from the name of an area called Zha that existed in Shandong province during the Five Dynasties (907–960 AD).

Zhan (131) Chinese 詹: from the name of a territory granted to a son of Xuan Wang (827–781 BC), the twelfth king of the Zhou dynasty.
GIVEN NAMES Chinese 67%. *Yi* (3), *Huimin* (2), *Lei* (2), *Wai Lam* (2), *Bin, Gao, Guo, Guosheng, Haiying, Heping, Hongbin, Huo.*

Zhang (5773) **1.** Chinese 张: the origin of this name goes back 4500 years to a grandson of the legendary emperor Huang Di (2697–2595 BC), surnamed Hui. Hui invented bows and arrows, and was put in charge of their production. In honor of his deeds, he was given as surname the character pronounced Zhang, which is composed of the symbols for 'bow' and 'long', meaning 'to stretch open a bow'. Zhang has now become one of the most common names in China. **2.** Chinese 章: from the name of an area called Zhang in present-day Shandong province. During the Western Zhou dynasty (1122–771 BC) a fief was made of this area. It was later conquered by the state of Qi; at that time the former rulers of conquered states were not allowed to take the name of their state as their surname. The former ruling class of Zhang fortunately were able to drop off a small portion of the character for Zhang and still leave another character also pronounced Zhang. This modified character became their surname.
GIVEN NAMES Chinese 75%. *Wei* (79), *Hong* (52), *Li* (50), *Jian* (41), *Ming* (41), *Yi* (37), *Jing* (34), *Hui* (31), *Yan* (30), *Fan* (26), *Xin* (26), *Ping* (25); *Min* (25), *Hao* (14), *Quan*

(8), *Lan* (6), *Tian* (6), *Chong* (4), *Da* (4), *Huan* (4), *Xuan* (4), *You* (4), *Chang* (3), *Shen* (3), *Yiming* (3).

Zhao (1683) Chinese 赵: from the name of the city of Zhao, in present-day Shanxi province in north-central China. Mu Wang, king of the Zhou dynasty (1001–947 BC), was noted for his campaigns and journeys to distant lands and for his expansion of the Chinese empire. According to legend, he once traveled to the Kunlun mountains, then west of China, to see the Queen Mother of the West. After arriving, he learned of military attacks at home, so his chariot driver, Zao Fu, obtained eight marvelous steeds which took them back at a rate of a thousand li (500 miles) a day, so that they were able to defend the capital. In recognition of his service, Mu Wang granted to the charioteer Zao Fu the city of Zhao, and his descendants subsequently adopted Zhao as their surname.
GIVEN NAMES Chinese 74%. *Ming* (21), *Hong* (16), *Wei* (16), *Hui* (14), *Yi* (12), *Ying* (10), *Gang* (9), *Li* (9), *Yan* (9), *Dong* (8), *Feng* (8), *Jian* (8), *Min* (5).

Zhen (255) Chinese 甄: from a word meaning 'potter'. During the time of the model emperor Shun (2257–2205 BC), the character for Zhen was used as a title for one who made pottery. Descendants of a potter of this period adopted this character as a surname.
GIVEN NAMES Chinese 70%. *Guo* (3), *Chun Lin* (2), *Jian* (2), *Jin* (2), *Li* (2), *Lian* (2), *Lun* (2), *Wan Ping* (2), *Wen* (2), *Yong* (2), *Chao, Chen.*

Zheng (1678) Chinese 郑: from the name of a state of Zheng. Xuan Wang, penultimate king (827–781 BC) of the Western Zhou Dynasty, granted the fief of Zheng to his younger brother, along with the title Duke Xuan of Zheng. In the time of Duke Xuan's son, Duke Gong, the capital of the Zhou dynasty was destroyed and the king was killed, bringing to an end the Western Zhou dynasty. The new Zhou king moved the capital eastward, beginning the Eastern Zhou dynasty. Duke Gong of Zheng moved eastward as well, to an area in present-day Henan province in central China, establishing a new state of Zheng. His descendants later adopted Zheng as their surname.
GIVEN NAMES Chinese 76%. *Jian* (14), *Yi* (10), *Bin* (9), *Hong* (9), *Hua* (9), *Li* (9), *Wei* (9), *Yong* (9), *Ting* (8), *Xin* (8), *Yan* (7), *Hui* (6); *Min* (6), *Hao* (4), *Shen* (4), *Da* (3), *Quan* (3), *Tian* (3), *Chong* (2).

Zhong (447) **1.** Chinese 钟: from the place name Zhongli. During the Spring and Autumn period (722–481 BC), some members of the state of Song adopted Zhongli as their surname, as they considered it to be the place which their ancestors came from. Some descendants later shortened the name to Zhong, while others kept Zhongli. **2.** Chinese 仲: the origin of this name has been attributed to three different people.

One is Zhong Kan, a scholar under the legendary emperor Ku, who lived 4500 years ago. Another is Zhong Sun, who lived in the state of Qi during the Spring and Autumn period (722–481 BC). A third is Zhong Ji, who lived during the Song dynasty (960–1279 AD).
GIVEN NAMES Chinese 66%. *Wei* (8), *Min* (5), *Mei* (4), *Ning* (3), *Sheng* (3), *Zhu* (3), *Jianhua* (2), *Jianping* (2), *Jin Hui* (2), *Lan* (2), *Li* (2), *Ling* (2), *Liping* (2), *Ping* (2), *Xuan*, *Yaping*, *You*.

Zhou (2105) Chinese 周: one of the oldest Chinese surnames, already being the name of the Zhou dynasty (1122–221 BC), when many current Chinese surnames first came into use. According to legend, Jiang Yuan, a concubine of the legendary emperor Ku in the 25th century BC, accidentally stepped in the imprint of a god's big toe, which impregnated her. Not wanting such a child, she abandoned the newborn baby, Hou Ji, in the wilderness. The infant was protected from the elements by the wings of eagles and was suckled on the milk of cows and sheep. He learned how to grow grain, and became the minister of agriculture under the legendary emperor Yao. His clan eventually settled in a city named Zhouyuan, in present-day Shaanxi province in western China. Under the influence of the name of the city, they came to be known as the Zhou, even though their surname was originally Ji. This situation lasted for over a millennium until a descendant, the famed virtuous Duke Wu Wang, changed his surname to Zhou, and his son established the Zhou dynasty. Zhou Enlai, premier of China from 1949 to 1976, belonged to this clan.
GIVEN NAMES Chinese 76%. *Jian* (22), *Yi* (21), *Wei* (20), *Bin* (16), *Hong* (15), *Jing* (13), *Ming* (13), *Zheng* (12), *Jin* (10), *Ping* (10), *Yan* (10), *Feng* (9); *Min* (7), *Lan* (5), *Hao* (4), *Quan* (4), *Long* (3), *Bao* (2), *Huan* (2), *Mai* (2).

Zhu (1857) **1.** Chinese 朱: from the name of the state of Zhu in present-day Shandong province. Wu Wang, the first king (1122–1116 BC) of the Zhou dynasty, granted to Cao Xie, a descendant of the emperor Zhuan Xu of the 26th century BC, lordship of the state of Zhu (see also CAO). Later, this state was conquered by the state of Chu, after which many descendants of the Zhu aristocracy took a modified form of the character Zhu for their surname; the pronunciation is the same. The name has become very common in southern China. **2.** Chinese 祝: following the establishment of the Zhou dynasty in 1122 BC, Wu Wang granted lordship of the area of Zhu to a descendant of the legendary emperor Huang Di. His descendants eventually adopted the place name Zhu as their surname. Additionally, in ancient China the titles of several important governmental positions contained the character for Zhu.

Descendants of some of these officials adopted Zhu as their surname. **3.** Chinese 诸: there are two accounts of the origin of this name, both from the Spring and Autumn period (722–481 BC). One account derives the name from an area named Zhu in the state of Lu. Another account derives it from a senior minister of the state of Yue named Zhu Zhiying. **4.** Chinese 竺: this was part of the ancient word *Tianzhu* 'India'. When Buddhist monks came to China from India, they often used Zhu as part of their name, and it gradually came to be used as a surname.
GIVEN NAMES Chinese 71%. *Li* (14), *Ming* (12), *Wei* (12), *Hong* (10), *Hua* (10), *Jian* (10), *Yan* (10), *Yi* (10), *Ying* (10), *Yong* (10), *Bin* (9), *Ping* (8); *Min* (8), *Chang* (3), *Yiming* (2).

Zhuang (170) Chinese 庄: from the name of a prince of the state of Chu during the Spring and Autumn period (722–481 BC).
GIVEN NAMES Chinese 73%. *Hong* (3), *Lei* (3), *Wei* (3), *Xiaomei* (3), *Jian* (2), *Mei* (2), *Ping* (2), *Yan* (2), *Yong* (2), *Yuan* (2), *Fan*, *Fei*; *Min*.

Zhuo (50) Chinese 卓: from the name of Zhuo Hua, a senior adviser in the state of Chu during the Spring and Autumn period (722–481 BC).

Zia (188) Muslim: from a personal name based on Persian *zia* 'light', from Arabic *ḍīyā* 'light', 'illumination' (Qur'an 10:5). This is used to form names in combinations such as *Zia ul-Haq* 'light of the truth' and *Zia ur-Rahman* 'light of the most gracious'.
GIVEN NAMES Muslim 61%. *Mohammad* (7), *Ahmad* (4), *Tariq* (3), *Amir* (2), *Anjum* (2), *Asif* (2), *Bahram* (2), *Omar* (2), *Rashid* (2), *Sultan* (2), *Syed* (2), *Abdul*.

Zibell (177) German: variant of ZIEBELL or a respelling of SEIBEL.
GIVEN NAMES German 5%. *Hans*, *Reinhold*.

Zicari (109) Southern Italian and Sicilian: from an unattested Arabic personal name *Zik(a)rī*.
GIVEN NAMES Italian 6%. *Alessandro*, *Onofrio*.

Ziccardi (306) Southern Italian: patronymic from *Ziccardo*, a variant of *Siccardo*, a Germanic personal name composed of the elements *sigi-* 'victory' + *hard* 'hardy', 'brave'.
GIVEN NAMES Italian 17%. *Vito* (3), *Pasquale* (2), *Angelo*, *Antonio*, *Dante*, *Dino*, *Enrico*, *Gilda*, *Vincenzo*.

Zich (176) Czech: from a short form of the personal name *Zikmund*, Czech form of SIEGMUND.

Zick (759) Americanized form of ZICH.

Zickafoose (127) Americanized spelling of German ZIEGENFUSS.

Zickefoose (421) Americanized spelling of German ZIEGENFUSS.

Zickert (126) Variant of German SIEGERT.
GIVEN NAMES German 4%. *Juergen*, *Kurt*.

Zickler (108) Variant of German SIGLER.

GIVEN NAMES German 12%. *Kurt* (2), *Christoph*, *Heinz*.

Zidek (214) Czech (**Žídek**): ethnic name for a Jew, from a diminutive of *Žid* 'Jew'.

Zieba (194) Polish (**Zięba**): from *zięba* 'finch', a nickname for someone thought to resemble the bird, or perhaps a metonymic occupational name for a birdcatcher or dealer.
GIVEN NAMES Polish 29%. *Jerzy* (3), *Pawel* (3), *Jozef* (2), *Karol* (2), *Tadeusz* (2), *Andrzej*, *Beata*, *Bogdan*, *Boleslaw*, *Casimir*, *Dariusz*, *Edyta*.

Ziebart (134) North German: variant of SIEBERT.
GIVEN NAMES German 9%. *Arno*, *Kurt*, *Wilhelm*.

Ziebarth (453) North German: variant of SIEBERT.

Ziebell (551) German: metonymic occupational name for an onion grower or seller, from Middle High German *z(w)ibolle*, *zwibel* (from Late Latin *cepula*).

Zieber (129) Altered spelling of German SIEBER.

Zieg (158) Jewish (eastern Ashkenazic): nickname from Yiddish *tsig*, German *Ziege* 'goat'.
GIVEN NAMES Jewish 8%. *Chaim* (3), *Moshe* (2), *Baruch*.

Ziegel (117) German and Jewish (Ashkenazic): metonymic occupational name for a tiler or tile maker, from Middle High German *ziegel*, German *Ziegel* 'roof tile' (see ZIEGLER).

Ziegelbauer (122) German: occupational name for a tiler, from *Ziegel* 'roof tile' (see ZIEGLER) + *Bauer* (see BAUER).

Ziegenbein (171) German: unflattering nickname from Middle High German *zige* 'goat' + *bein* 'leg'.

Ziegenfus (112) Variant spelling of German ZIEGENFUSS.

Ziegenfuss (284) German: unflattering nickname from Middle High German *ziga* 'goat' + *fuoz* 'foot'.

Ziegenhagen (130) German: habitational name from various places so called, for example in Hesse and Saxony-Anhalt, named with Middle High German *ziga* 'goat' + *Hagen* 'hedge'.
GIVEN NAMES German 8%. *Wolfgang* (2), *Wilhelm*.

Ziegenhorn (162) German: topographic or for someone who lived on a hook of land where goats grazed, from Middle High German *ziga* 'goat' + *horn* 'horn'.

Zieger (217) German: metonymic occupational name for a maker or seller of curd cheese, Middle High German *ziger(kæse)*.
GIVEN NAMES German 9%. *Claus*, *Erhard*, *Georg*, *Otto*.

Ziegler (10553) German and Jewish (Ashkenazic): occupational name for a tiler, from an agent derivative of Middle High German *ziegel* 'roof tile' (Old High German *ziagal*, from Latin *tegula*), German *Ziegel*. In the Middle Ages the term came to denote bricks as well as tiles, and so in some cases the term may have denoted a brickmaker or bricklayer rather than a tiler.

Ziehl (164) German: variant of ZIEL.

Ziehm (188) North German: variant of SIEM.
GIVEN NAMES German 9%. *Egon* (2), *Fritz, Heinz, Kurt, Rainer*.

Ziel (220) German: **1.** from a short form of the Slavic personal name *Zilosław*. **2.** topographic name from a field name meaning 'boundary'.
GIVEN NAMES German 6%. *Helmut, Hermann, Kurt, Reinholdt*.

Zielinski (3984) **1.** Polish (**Zieliński**): from *zielony* 'green', in various senses, or from *zioło* 'herb'. As a Polish name it seems primarily to have been a nickname for a person with a sickly 'greenish' complexion. It may also have been a nickname for someone who habitually dressed in green, or who was 'green' in the sense of being immature or inexperienced. Additionally, it may be a habitational name from any of many place named with this word, Zielin, Zielenec, Zielińce, etc. It is also well established as a surname in Germany. **2.** Jewish (from Poland): habitational name for someone from places in Poland called Zielona or Zielonka; the place name derives from a root meaning 'green'.
GIVEN NAMES Polish 6%. *Casimir* (5), *Bogdan* (4), *Janina* (4), *Stanislaw* (4), *Tadeusz* (4), *Andrzej* (3), *Jerzy* (3), *Jozef* (3), *Kazimierz* (3), *Zbigniew* (3), *Zdzislaw* (3), *Beata* (2).

Zielke (768) German: from a pet form of ZIEL 1.
GIVEN NAMES German 7%. *Erwin* (4), *Otto* (4), *Helmut* (2), *Klaus* (2), *Gunter, Heinz, Helmuth, Horst, Reinhold, Siegfried, Volker*.

Zielonka (138) Polish and Jewish (eastern Ashkenazic): habitational name from any of many places in Poland called Zielonka. Compare Polish *zielonka* 'silage', a derivative of *zielony* 'green'.
GIVEN NAMES Polish 16%; German 4%. *Ryszard* (2), *Aleksander, Bogdan, Ewa, Janina, Jerzy, Tomasz, Zdislaw; Fritz*.

Zielsdorf (125) German: habitational name from an unidentified place, perhaps Ziersdorf in Lower Austria.
GIVEN NAMES German 5%. *Kurt, Reinhard*.

Zieman (403) Altered spelling of North German ZIEMANN.
GIVEN NAMES German 4%. *Hertha, Ingeborg, Kurt, Merwin, Otto, Wilhelm*.

Ziemann (432) North German: from a short form of the Germanic personal name *Siegmar* (see SIEMER), with the addition of Middle High German *man* 'man'.
GIVEN NAMES German 11%. *Erwin* (2), *Kurt* (2), *Otto* (2), *Gerhard, Ilse, Jurgen, Manfred, Uwe, Wilhelm*.

Ziemba (1061) Polish: variant of **Zięba** (see ZIEBA).
GIVEN NAMES Polish 4%. *Arkadiusz, Bronislaw, Casimir, Dorota, Urszula, Waclawa, Wladyslawa, Zofia*.

Ziemer (985) North German: variant spelling of SIEMER.
GIVEN NAMES German 4%. *Erwin* (3), *Kurt* (2), *Manfred* (2), *Otto* (2), *Ewald*.

Zieminski (116) Polish (**Zieminski**): habitational name for someone from Ziemin in Poznań voivodeship, named with *ziemin* 'ground'.
GIVEN NAMES Polish 10%. *Andrzej* (2), *Pawel, Stanislaw*.

Ziemke (231) North German: **1.** from a pet form of the personal name SIMON. **2.** from a pet form of the personal name *Siem*, a reduced form of *Siegmar* (see SIEMER).

Ziems (112) German: from a variant pet form of the personal name SIMON.
GIVEN NAMES German 6%. *Kurt, Otto*.

Ziemski (106) Polish: status name for a landowner or someone connected with a landowner, from the adjective *ziemski* 'connected with the land'.
GIVEN NAMES Polish 5%. *Jacek, Pawel*.

Zientara (138) Polish (also **Ziętara**): derivative of Polish *zięć* 'son-in-law'.

Zientek (341) Polish (also **Ziętek**): from a diminutive of Polish *zięć* 'son-in-law'.

Zier (442) German: **1.** nickname from Middle High German *zier* 'beautiful', 'lovely'. **2.** habitational name from a place so named near Düren.

Zierden (162) German: unexplained.
GIVEN NAMES German 4%. *Alfons, Lorenz*.

Zierer (102) German: habitational name for someone from Zier, near Düren (see ZIER).

Zierke (149) German: **1.** from a reduced form of the Germanic personal name *Sīgerik*, composed of the elements *sigi-* 'victory' + *rik* 'ruler'. **2.** habitational name, of Slavic origin, from a place so named near Neustrelitz.

Ziesemer (153) German: **1.** from a Slavic personal name. **2.** possibly a habitational name from Cismar, site of a monastery near Lübeck.

Zieser (130) German: possibly a variant of **Ziese**, an occupational name for a tax collector, from Middle Low German *sise*, Middle High German *zīse* 'consumer tax'.

Zieske (205) Eastern German: from Czech, Sorbian *čižik* 'siskin'; either a nickname for someone thought to resemble the bird in some way, or a metonymic occupational name for a birdcatcher.

Ziesmer (238) Eastern German: variant of ZIESEMER.
GIVEN NAMES German 4%. *Erwin, Kurt*.

Zietlow (335) German: habitational name from a place so named in Mecklenburg-West Pomerania.
GIVEN NAMES German 5%. *Gunter* (2), *Hans, Klaus, Otto*.

Zietz (237) Eastern German: from a Slavic personal name or habitational name.

Ziff (301) Jewish (eastern Ashkenazic): variant of SIFF.
GIVEN NAMES Jewish 6%. *Sol* (2), *Hyman, Isadore*.

Ziglar (339) Variant spelling (in Slavic-speaking regions) of German ZIEGLER.

Zigler (670) Eastern German and Jewish (Ashkenazic): variant of ZIEGLER.

Zigman (170) Jewish (eastern Ashkenazic): variant spelling of SIEGMAN.
GIVEN NAMES Jewish 7%. *Sol* (2), *Hyman, Naum*.

Zigmond (113) Variant of German SIEGMUND.

Zigmont (104) Variant of German SIEGMUND.
GIVEN NAMES French 6%. *Celine, Michel*.

Zika (217) **1.** Czech (also **Zíka**): from a short form of the personal name *Zikmund*, Czech form of SIEGMUND. **2.** Greek (**Zikas**): from a pet form *Zikas*, of the male personal name *Zissis*, an omen name from the phrase *na zissis* 'may he live', given to a male child born after the death of an elder brother.

Zike (216) Germanized form of Czech ZIKA.

Zikmund (104) Czech: from the Czech form of the German personal name SIEGMUND.

Zilberman (188) Jewish (eastern Ashkenazic): eastern variant of SILBERMAN.
GIVEN NAMES Jewish 36%; Russian 29%. *Ilya* (3), *Yakov* (3), *Moysey* (2), *Aron, Elik, Eliyahu, Esfir, Feyga, Fishel, Gersh, Gershon, Isaak; Boris* (5), *Vladimir* (4), *Arkady* (3), *Iosif* (3), *Leonid* (3), *Lev* (3), *Yefim* (3), *Aleksandr* (2), *Mikhail* (2), *Semyon* (2), *Arkadiy, Dmitry*.

Zilch (158) German: from a pet form of the personal name *Zyriak*, vernacular form of Greek *Kyriakos* 'belonging to the Lord'. The name was borne by two saints; Cyriacus the Recluse, born at Corinth in the 5th century, is reputed to have lived to the age of 108. The other saint of this name was a Roman martyr, of whom nothing is known except that he was buried on the road to Ostia.

Zilinski (129) Polish (**Ziliński**): variant of ZIELINSKI. This is also a well-established surname in German-speaking lands.

Zilka (275) Czech and Slovak (**Žilka**): from Czech *žilka*, diminutive of *žíle* 'vein', nickname for someone with noticeable veins, or from the same word in the sense 'sinew', 'tendon', applied as a nickname for a resilient or quick-witted individual.

Zill (205) German: **1.** metonymic occupational name for someone who piloted a river barge, from Middle High German *zülle, zulle, zille* 'river barge'. **2.** from the personal name *Cyliak* (a variant of *Cyriak*; see ZILCH) or of the female personal name *Cäcilie* (German form of *Cecilia*).

Ziller (231) German: **1.** occupational name for a bargeman, from an agent derivative of Middle High German *zülle, zulle, zille* 'river barge'. **2.** variant of ZILL 2.

Zilles (122) German: probably a variant of **Zillies**, a vernacular form of *Cyriakus* (see Zilch).

GIVEN NAME German 4%. *Kurt.*

Zilliox (132) German: from a vernacular form of the personal name *Zyriacus* (see Zilch).

Zillman (109) **1.** Jewish (from Ukraine): variant of Selman. **2.** German (**Zillmann**): variant of Zill 1, with the addition of Middle High German *man* 'man'.

GIVEN NAME Jewish 4%. *Herschel* (2).

Zillmer (354) German: from a Slavic personal name.

Zills (126) German: vernacular form of *Cyriakus* (see Zilch).

Zima (527) **1.** Czech and Slovak: from *zima* 'winter', 'cold', probably a nickname from someone with a gloomy or unapproachable personality, but possibly also a topographic name for someone living in a particularly cold spot. **2.** Czech: from a short form of the personal name *Erazim* (see Rasmus). **3.** German: from a Slavic short form of the personal name Simon.

Ziman (147) Jewish (Ashkenazic): variant spelling of Siman.

Zimbelman (332) Jewish (Ashkenazic): occupational name for a dulcimer player, from Yiddish *tsimbl* 'dulcimer' + *man* 'man'.

Zimdars (238) Variant of German **Zimdarse**, a habitational name from a place so named in Pomerania.

GIVEN NAMES German 6%. *Gerhard* (2), *Kurt* (2), *Florian, Heino.*

Zimet (140) German and Jewish (Ashkenazic): from Middle High German *zinment, zi(ne)mīn* 'cinnamon', German *Zimmet*, hence an occupational name for a spicer. In some instances the Jewish surname is ornamental.

GIVEN NAMES Jewish 5%. *Elihu, Tova.*

Ziminski (122) Polish (**Zimiński**): variant of Zieminski.

GIVEN NAMES Polish 4%. *Jadwiga, Wladyslaw.*

Zimmel (157) **1.** Jewish (eastern Ashkenazic): from the Yiddish personal name *Ziml*, a pet form of Simon. **2.** German (Austria): short form of a Germanic personal name formed with Old High German *sigu* 'victory' (*Sigismund*, for instance), or a pet form of *Simon* (see sense 1).

Zimmer (7270) German: metonymic occupational name for a carpenter, either from Middle High German *zim(b)er, zimmer* 'wood', 'wooden building' or a shortening of Zimmermann.

GIVEN NAMES German 4%. *Hans* (12), *Erwin* (8), *Kurt* (7), *Franz* (4), *Fritz* (3), *Mathias* (3), *Otto* (3), *Bernhard* (2), *Dieter* (2), *Georg* (2), *Horst* (2), *Markus* (2).

Zimmerer (362) German: variant of Zimmermann.

GIVEN NAMES German 4%. *Dieter, Egon, Kurt.*

Zimmerle (249) South German: occupational name for a carpenter, from a diminutive of Zimmer.

Zimmerlee (100) Americanized form of South German Zimmerle.

Zimmerli (133) Swiss German: variant of Zimmerle.

GIVEN NAMES German 7%. *Kurt* (2), *Otto.*

Zimmerly (350) Variant of German Zimmerle.

Zimmerman (32869) Americanized or Jewish spelling of Zimmermann.

Zimmermann (2822) German and Jewish (Ashkenazic): occupational name for a carpenter, Middle High German *zimbermann* (a compound of *zimber, zim(m)er* 'timber', 'wood' + *mann* 'man'), German *Zimmermann*.

GIVEN NAMES German 11%. *Kurt* (12), *Otto* (6), *Erwin* (5), *Hans* (5), *Fritz* (4), *Gerhard* (4), *Hermann* (4), *Klaus* (4), *Gerd* (3), *Manfred* (3), *Wolfgang* (3), *Bernhard* (2).

Zimmers (224) German: derivative of Zimmer.

Zimmerschied (116) altered spelling of German **Zimmerscheid**, a habitational name from a place so named in the Rhineland-Palatinate.

Zimney (119) Americanized spelling of Polish Zimny.

Zimny (264) Polish: from *zimny* 'cold', 'bleak', presumably a nickname for someone with a distant or dour disposition, but perhaps also a topographic name for someone living in a cold or exposed spot.

GIVEN NAMES Polish 10%. *Stanislaw* (2), *Ewa, Jacek, Jaroslaw, Jozef, Miroslaw, Zygmunt.*

Zimpel (121) **1.** North German: habitational name from Zimpel in Saxony. **2.** South German: variant of **Zimpfer**, which Brechenmacher derives from the personal name *Symphorian*, but which Bahlow believes to be an adjective meaning 'finicky', 'squeamish'.

GIVEN NAMES German 5%. *Hans, Kurt.*

Zimpfer (170) South German: **1.** nickname for a finicky, affected, or squeamish person, late Middle High German *zimpfer*. **2.** from the personal name *Symphorian*.

Zinck (325) German: variant of Zink.

GIVEN NAMES German 5%. *Uwe* (2), *Aloys, Beate, Wolfgang.*

Zinda (313) Polish: of uncertain origin; possibly an occupational name for a sawyer, from a derivative of the dialect verb *zyndać* 'to saw'.

Zindel (138) **1.** German: from Middle High German *zindal, zindel* 'silk', hence a metonymic occupational name for a dealer in silk or perhaps a nickname for a flamboyant dresser. **2.** German: habitational name from places so named, for example in Schleswig and Silesia. **3.** Americanized spelling of Hungarian **Zsindely** (see Sindel).

Zindler (120) German: **1.** occupational name for a silk merchant, variant of Zindel with the agent noun suffix *-ler*. **2.** habitational name for someone from any of several places called Zindel.

Zingale (231) Italian: from a variant of *zingaro* 'gypsy' (see Zingaro).

GIVEN NAMES Italian 19%. *Nunzio* (2), *Sal* (2), *Salvatore* (2), *Gaetano, Santo.*

Zingarelli (129) Italian: **1.** patronymic from *Zingarello*, a diminutive of Zingaro. **2.** perhaps a habitational name from Zingarello, a district of Monopoli in Bari province.

GIVEN NAMES Italian 12%. *Carlo, Donato, Gaetano.*

Zingaro (161) Italian: ethnic name or nickname from *zingaro* 'gypsy'.

GIVEN NAMES Italian 13%. *Angelo* (2), *Antonio, Giuseppe, Nunzio, Rocco.*

Zinger (338) **1.** Jewish (Ashkenazic): variant of Singer. **2.** Dutch: variant of Zanger.

GIVEN NAMES Jewish 11%; Russian 6%. *Bentsion, Dorit, Eyal, Hanon, Mayer, Moisey, Moysey, Rakhil, Rozalya, Sarra, Semen, Yakov; Leonid* (2), *Mikhail* (2), *Aleksandr, Anatoliy, Beyla, Grigoriy, Vladimir, Yevgeniya, Yuriy.*

Zingg (205) South German variant of Zink 2.

Zingler (198) German: topographic name for someone who lived close to a city wall, from Middle High German *zingel* 'belt' (Latin *cingula*), the suffix *-er* denoting an inhabitant.

Zingsheim (119) German: habitational name from an unidentified place.

Zini (114) Italian: patronymic or plural form of Zino.

GIVEN NAMES Italian 18%. *Primo* (3), *Aldo* (2), *Anello, Cesare, Gildo, Secondo.*

Zink (3466) German: **1.** from Middle High German *zinke* 'peak', acquired either as a topographic name by someone who lived on or near a crag or on a pointed piece of land or as a nickname for a man with a singularly pointed nose. Compare modern German slang *Zinken* 'hooter'. The same word was used to denote the cornet, although the semantic development is not clear, and the surname may sometimes have been metonymic for a player of this instrument. It was not until the 16th century that the metal *zinc* was discovered and named (apparently from its jagged appearance in the furnace), so this is unlikely to be the origin of the surname. **2.** from *Jacinctus*, which derives from *Hyacinthus*, a saint's name. Compare Spanish Jacinto, Italian Giacinto.

Zinke (426) German: variant of Zink.

GIVEN NAMES German 4%. *Kurt, Otto, Reinold, Siebert.*

Zinman (155) Jewish (Ashkenazic): metonymic occupational name from German

Zinn, Yiddish *tsin* 'pewter' + German *Mann*, Yiddish *man* 'man'. Compare ZINN.

Zinn (2352) German and Jewish (Ashkenazic): metonymic occupational name for a worker in pewter, Middle High German *zin*; German *Zinn*, Yiddish *tsin*.

Zinna (112) Southern Italian: from the feminine form of ZINNO.
GIVEN NAMES Italian 11%. *Cosimo, Gabriella, Salvatore, Silvestro.*

Zinnecker (105) German: of uncertain origin.
GIVEN NAMES German 6%. *Hans* (2), *Hartmut.*

Zinnel (107) German: metonymic occupational name for a worker in pewter, from a diminutive of German ZINN.
GIVEN NAMES French 4%. *Clemence, Germaine.*

Zinner (242) German: occupational name for a worker in pewter, from an agent derivative of Middle High German *zin* 'pewter' (see ZINN).
GIVEN NAMES German 4%. *Ernst, Ingo, Kurt.*

Zinni (186) Italian: patronymic or plural form of ZINNO.
GIVEN NAMES Italian 14%. *Nichola* (2), *Nunzi* (2), *Angelo, Carmine, Rocco.*

Zinno (158) Italian: possibly a nickname from the southern dialect word *zinnu* 'small'.

Zino (116) Italian: from the personal name *Zino*, an independent form but in some cases a reduced form of a pet name ending with *-zino*, for example *Bonifazzino, Lorenzino, Vincenzino.*
GIVEN NAMES Italian 12%; Jewish 4%; Spanish 4%. *Angelo* (3); *Haim* (2); *Mario* (2), *Jaime.*

Zins (399) German: **1.** nickname for a tenant farmer, from Middle High German *zins* 'dues', 'tribute'. **2.** from a short form of the personal name *Vinzenz*, German form of VINCENT.

Zinser (533) German: occupational name for a tenant farmer, or occasionally for a collector of rents or taxes, from an agent derivative of Middle High German *zins* 'dues'.
GIVEN NAMES German 7%. *Kurt* (4), *Volker* (4), *Otto* (3), *Eugen.*

Zinsmeister (220) German: occupational name for a collector of ground rents or taxes, Middle High German *zinsmeister* (a compound of *zins* 'dues', 'rent' + *meister* 'master').
GIVEN NAME German 4%. *Dieter.*

Zinter (188) German: variant of **Zinder**.

Ziobro (261) Polish: nickname from Old Polish and Polish dialect *ziobro* 'rib' (see ZEBRO).
GIVEN NAMES Polish 8%; German 4%. *Casimir* (2), *Danuta, Grazyna, Jozef, Malgorzata; Alfons.*

Ziolkowski (823) Polish (**Ziółkowski**): habitational name for someone from Ziółków in Lublin voivodeship or Ziółkowo

in Leszno and Włocławek voivodeships, named with Polish *ziółko* 'herb' (diminutive form). This surname is also found in Germany.
GIVEN NAMES Polish 6%. *Casimir* (4), *Bogdan, Dorota, Eugeniusz, Ignatius, Jacek, Jadwiga, Jerzy, Karol, Krystyna, Pawel, Wiktor.*

Ziomek (245) Polish: nickname from Polish *ziomek* 'countryman'.
GIVEN NAMES Polish 4%. *Casimir, Stanislaw.*

Zion (544) Jewish: ornamental name from Hebrew *tsion* '(Mount) Zion', the hill in Jerusalem on which the city of David was built, or from the male personal name derived from the name of the mount.
GIVEN NAMES Jewish 4%. *Moshe* (3), *Ari* (2), *Chaim, Ephraim, Hyman, Shabtai.*

Zipay (111) Probably Czech: unexplained.

Zipf (255) **1.** German: from late Middle High German *zipf, zipfel* 'point', 'tip', 'corner', hence a topographic name for someone who occupied a narrow corner of land, as for example between converging channels of a stream. **2.** South German: nickname for a simpleton.
GIVEN NAMES German 6%. *Bernhard, Otto, Raimund.*

Zipfel (243) German: from a diminutive of ZIPF.

Zipkin (158) Jewish (eastern Ashkenazic): metronymic from the Yiddish female name *Tsipke*, a pet form of the Biblical name *Zipporah*, meaning 'bird' (Exodus 2:21).
GIVEN NAMES Jewish 8%. *Ilan, Ronen, Yetta.*

Zipp (402) German: **1.** variant of ZIPF. **2.** from a short form of the personal name *Sippo.*

Zipper (225) **1.** Jewish (Ashkenazic): metronymic from a short form of the female Biblical name *Zipporah*, meaning 'bird' (Exodus 2:21). **2.** German: vernacular form of the personal name *Cyprianus*. **3.** East German (of Slavic origin): occupational name for a thresher, from Sorbian *cepař.*
GIVEN NAME Jewish 4%. *Orah.*

Zipperer (429) German: variant of ZIPPER 3.

Zipprich (107) German: variant of **Sipprich**, from a Germanic personal name composed of the elements *sigi* 'victory' + *rīc* 'power(ful)'.

Zipse (107) German: variant of ZIPSER.

Zipser (119) German: habitational name from any of several places called Zips, in Bavaria and Silesia; also the name of a district in Hungary.
GIVEN NAMES German 8%; Hungarian 5%; Scandinavian 4%. *Otto; Aladar* (3); *Birgit.*

Zirbel (431) German: pet form of an altered form of ZERVAS. Compare ZERBEL.
GIVEN NAMES German 4%. *Kurt* (2), *Fritz.*

Zirbes (176) German: variant of ZERVAS.

Zirk (184) German: variant of ZIERKE.

Zirkel (183) German: occupational name for a watchman in a town or city, from Middle

High German *zirkeler* 'someone who does the rounds'. **Zirkel** also means 'compass' in German, and the name may also be an occupational name for a compass maker.

Zirkelbach (191) German: habitational name from Zirkenbach (Fulda), recorded in the 12th century as *Cirkumbach*, presumably because of the arching course of a nearby stream.
GIVEN NAMES German 4%. *Erwin, Kurt.*

Zirkle (1066) Variant of German ZIRKEL.

Zirpoli (107) Italian: unexplained.

Zisa (165) Italian (Sicily): most probably from a female personal name based on Arabic *zīzah* 'chrysalis'.
GIVEN NAMES Italian 13%. *Filippo, Giuseppe, Rino, Salvatore.*

Zisk (157) Possibly a reduced form of Jewish ZISKIN.

Ziska (245) **1.** Czech (**Žiška**) and Slovak (**Šiška**): variant of **Šiška** (see SISKA). **2.** Slovenian (south central Slovenia; **Žiška**): nickname from *šiška* 'gallnut'. This name is also established in Austria and Germany.

Ziskin (128) Jewish (Ashkenazic): variant of SUSSKIND.
GIVEN NAMES Jewish 15%; Russian 10%. *Yakov* (2), *Yetta* (2), *Hersch, Naum; Yefim* (2), *Aleksandr, Boris, Dmitry, Igor, Leonid, Vladimir.*

Ziskind (135) Jewish (Ashkenazic): variant spelling of SUSSKIND.
GIVEN NAMES Jewish 18%; Russian 6%. *Shalom* (2), *Sholem* (2), *Elihu, Irina, Isadore, Izia, Tzvi, Yechiel; Efim, Mikhail, Semyon, Yefim.*

Zisman (152) Jewish (eastern Ashkenazic): from the Yiddish personal name *Zisman*, a dialect variant of *Zusman* (see SUSSMAN).
GIVEN NAMES Jewish 17%; Russian 9%. *Berka, Dror, Ilya, Isadore, Jefim, Meyer, Naftali, Naftoli, Sima; Leonid* (2), *Aleksandr, Boris, Brukha, Galina, Raisa, Vladimir, Zhanna.*

Zitek (157) Czech: from a diminutive of Old Czech *zít* 'son-in-law'.

Ziter (104) German: variant of ZEITER.

Zitnik (110) Czech (**Žitník**): from a derivative of *žito* 'rye', hence an occupational name for a dealer in rye or a baker who made rye bread.

Zito (1967) Southern Italian: from the medieval personal name *Zito*, originally a nickname from the southern Italian dialect word *zito, zite, zitu* 'boy', 'young bachelor', 'fiancé'.
GIVEN NAMES Italian 12%. *Salvatore* (10), *Rocco* (7), *Angelo* (6), *Vito* (4), *Antonio* (3), *Sal* (3), *Santo* (3), *Carmine* (2), *Pasquale* (2), *Alfonse, Aniello, Calogero.*

Zittel (233) German: nickname for a lazy, unambitious person, a dawdler.
GIVEN NAMES German 6%. *Guenter, Otto, Reinhold.*

Zittle (112) Variant of German ZITTEL.

Zitzer (111) Variant of German SITZER, found especially among the German settlers of the Volga Basin in Russia.

Zitzmann (127) Variant of German SITZMANN, found especially among the German settlers of the Volga Basin in Russia.

GIVEN NAMES German 11%. *Heinrich, Kurt, Wolf.*

Ziv (115) Jewish (mainly Israeli): ornamental name from Hebrew *ziv* 'brilliance', 'charm'.

GIVEN NAMES Jewish 41%. *Moshe* (4), *Meir* (2), *Noam* (2), *Yaron* (2), *Anat, Avi, Doron, Elad, Ilan, Mordechi, Nurit, Ofer.*

Zivkovich (106) Serbian and Croatian (**Živković**): patronymic from the personal name *Živko*, from *živ* 'alive' or 'lively', equivalent of Latin *Vitalis*.

GIVEN NAMES South Slavic 14%. *Milos, Radmila, Vladislav; Milorad, Miodrag, Radomir.*

Zizza (148) Southern Italian: **1.** from the feminine form of ZIZZO. **2.** variant of ZISA.

GIVEN NAMES Italian 26%. *Rocco* (2), *Americo, Angelo, Carmelo, Concetta, Domenico, Donato, Sal, Salavatore, Salvatore.*

Zizzi (112) Italian: patronymic or plural form of ZIZZO.

GIVEN NAMES Italian 14%. *Angelo, Emanuele, Enrico, Vito.*

Zizzo (260) Italian (Sicily): nickname from Sicilian dialect *zizzu* (feminine *zizza*) 'ostentatiously elegant youth'; also 'unmarried', from Arabic *'azīz* 'beloved', 'beautiful', 'mighty' (see AZIZ).

GIVEN NAMES Italian 22%. *Salvatore* (3), *Angelo, Antonio, Francesco, Gino, Giuseppe, Lucrezia, Mario, Salvator, Silvio, Vito.*

Zlotnick (213) Americanized spelling of Jewish and Slavic ZLOTNIK.

GIVEN NAMES Jewish 8%. *Dov, Zalman.*

Zlotnik (113) Jewish (eastern Ashkenazic), Belorussian, Ukrainian, and Polish (**Złotnik**): occupational name for a goldsmith, Polish *złotnik*, Belorussian *zlotnik*, Ukrainian *zlotnyk*, from *zloto* 'gold'.

GIVEN NAMES Jewish 17%; Russian 9%. *Meyer* (2), *Asher, Feyga, Hinda, Khana, Yakov; Grigory, Igor, Leonid, Lev, Vitaly, Yefim.*

Zmijewski (143) Polish (**Żmijewski**): habitational name for someone from a place called Żmijewo in Ciechanów or Ostrołęka voivodeships, named with Polish *żmija* 'viper'.

GIVEN NAMES Polish 12%. *Slawomir* (2), *Boleslaw, Janusz.*

Zmolek (110) Czech: topographic name for someone who lived by a ravine, Czech dialect *zmol* 'ravine'.

Zmuda (400) Polish (**Żmuda**): nickname for an earnest, hard-working person, from Polish *zmudny* 'toilsome'.

GIVEN NAMES Polish 7%. *Tadeusz* (2), *Beata, Dariusz, Fryderyk, Janina, Jaromir, Malgorzata, Wojciech.*

Zobel (729) German: **1.** metonymic occupational name for a furrier or fur trader, from Old High German *zobel* 'sable fur'. **2.** nickname from Middle High German *zoblen* 'to tease', 'to scrap or fight'. **3.** from a personal name, *Zobelo*.

GIVEN NAMES German 5%. *Gerlinde* (2), *Kurt* (2), *Wilhelm* (2), *Ernst, Erwin, Heinz, Wolfgang.*

Zobrist (298) Swiss German: topographic name for someone who lived at the highest or furthest point of a settlement.

GIVEN NAMES German 4%. *Arno, Erwin, Kurt.*

Zocchi (104) Italian: patronymic or plural form of ZOCCO.

GIVEN NAMES Italian 13%. *Aldo, Angelo, Carlo, Carmine, Salvatore.*

Zocco (135) Italian: from *zoco* or *zoch* 'tree stump', perhaps a nickname for a stockily built man or a slow person of limited intellect; alternatively, it may have been a topographic name for someone who lived by a tree stump.

GIVEN NAMES Italian 22%. *Salvatore* (3), *Giuseppe* (2), *Giancarlo, Giorgio, Giovanni, Matteo, Natale, Piero, Sebastiano.*

Zoch (397) **1.** German: nickname from Middle High German *zoche* 'cudgel', 'club'. **2.** Eastern German: habitational name from a place in Saxony named Zochau.

GIVEN NAMES German 7%. *Erwin* (6), *Otto* (3), *Benno, Eldor, Hans.*

Zoda (112) Italian: of uncertain derivation; perhaps related to a Bovese (Reggio Calabria) dialect word *zooda* 'girl'.

GIVEN NAMES Italian 8%. *Salvatore* (2), *Santo.*

Zodrow (124) Eastern German: habitational name from a place named with Slavic *zode* 'marshy district', a cognate of **Söder** (see SODER).

GIVEN NAME German 4%. *Horst.*

Zody (175) Origin unidentified. Possibly German.

Zoeller (792) German (**Zöller**): variant of ZOLLER.

GIVEN NAMES German 6%. *Kurt* (3), *Guenter* (2), *Inge* (2), *Otto* (2), *Wolfgang* (2), *Alois, Arno, Ewald, Franz, Helmut.*

Zoellick (154) German (**Zöllick**): from a pet form of the Slavic personal name *Zulimir*.

Zoellner (603) German (**Zöllner**): occupational name for a customs officer (see ZOLLER).

GIVEN NAMES German 5%. *Franz* (2), *Kurt* (2), *Gunther, Hedwig, Horst, Lorenz, Monika, Wilhelmina.*

Zoerb (142) German (**Zörb**): unexplained.

Zoerner (113) German (**Zörner**): nickname for a man with an irascible temperament, from an agent derivative of *Zorn* 'rage'.

GIVEN NAMES German 5%. *Albrecht, Heinz.*

Zoet (102) Dutch: nickname meaning 'sweet'.

Zogby (112) Arabic: apparently a derivative of Arabic *zaghab* 'fluff', 'fuzz', 'down'.

GIVEN NAME Muslim 9%. *Brahim* (3).

Zogg (177) South German: probably a nickname for a crude or violent man, from Middle High German *zoche* 'cudgel'.

GIVEN NAMES German 5%. *Leonhard, Wilfried, Willi.*

Zografos (100) Greek: occupational name for a portrait painter or miniaturist, Greek *zōgraphos*, from *zōē* 'life' + *graphein* 'to write'.

GIVEN NAMES Greek 16%; Italian 5%. *Andreas, Antonios, Constantine, Dimitrios, Kalliope, Kostas, Pantelis; Dino* (3).

Zohn (148) Jewish (Ashkenazic): **1.** variant of SOHN. **2.** nickname from Yiddish *tson* 'tooth' (German *Zahn*).

GIVEN NAMES Jewish 7%. *Ahron, Boruch, Elchonon, Hershel.*

Zola (406) **1.** Italian: habitational name from any of various minor places named with Zol(l)a, from a dialect term for a mound or bank of earth, as for example Zola Predosa (Bologna) or Zolla in Monrupino (Trieste). **2.** Italian: from a reduced form of the personal name *Anzola*. **3.** Italian: from the old Venetian dialect word *zola* 'female kid'.

Zoladz (108) Polish (**Żołądź**): nickname from Polish *żołądź* 'acorn'.

GIVEN NAMES Polish 5%; German 5%. *Aloysius, Markus; Eugeniusz, Janina.*

Zoldak (117) Polish (**Żołdak**): nickname from Polish *żołdak* 'scornful or arrogant soldier'.

GIVEN NAMES Polish 4%; German 4%. *Casimir, Jozef; Kurt.*

Zolezzi (131) Italian: unexplained. In Italy the name occurs chiefly in Genoa and Liguria.

GIVEN NAMES Spanish 10%; Italian 7%. *Raul* (2), *Rodolfo* (2), *Eduardo, Gustavo, Mario, Renaldo; Angelo* (2), *Dino.*

Zoll (546) German: metonymic occupational name for a customs officer, from Middle High German *zoll* 'toll', 'duty'.

Zolla (123) Italian: **1.** possibly from a reduced form of *Pizzolla*, a feminine diminutive of PIZZO. **2.** variant of ZOLA.

Zollars (285) Dutch and German: variant of ZOLLER.

FOREBEARS Friedrich Zollars came to OH from Germany or the Netherlands in about 1735.

Zoller (1179) German (also **Zöller**) and Jewish (Ashkenazic): occupational name for a customs officer, Middle High German *zoller*, German *Zoller*.

GIVEN NAMES German 4%. *Bernd, Christoph, Fritz, Gerhard, Hannelore, Hans, Heinz, Klaus, Kurt, Manfred, Rudi.*

Zollicoffer (120) Americanized spelling of Swiss German **Zollikofer**, a habitational name for someone from a place called Zollikofen, in Bern canton.

FOREBEARS Jacob Christoph Zollicoffer came to the U.S. from Switzerland in the early 18th century; he was one of the leading figures associated with the settlement of New Bern, NC.

Zollinger (642) German: habitational name for someone from some place called Zollingen, probably named with German *Zoll* 'customs post'. There were customs posts at river ports as well as at national frontiers.

Zollman (306) Variant spelling of German **Zollmann**, an occupational name for a customs officer (see ZOLLER).

Zollner (295) German (also **Zöllner**): occupational name for a customs officer, a variant of ZOLLER.
GIVEN NAMES German 6%. *Kurt* (3), *Hans* (2), *Dieter, Otto*.

Zollo (405) Italian: unexplained; possibly related to dialect *zolle, zulle* 'baby'.
GIVEN NAMES Italian 12%. *Pasquale* (2), *Angelo, Carmine, Corrado, Enrico, Gioacchino, Giuseppe, Luciano, Marino, Maurizio, Pellegrino, Santo*.

Zolman (257) Variant spelling of German **Zollmann** (see ZOLLMAN).

Zoltowski (117) Polish (**Żółtowski**): habitational name for someone from Żółtowo in Płock voivodeship, named with *żółty* 'yellow'.
GIVEN NAME Polish 4%; German 4%. *Aloysius*.

Zombek (103) Polish (**Ząbek**) and Jewish (from Poland): nickname from Polish *ząbek* 'little tooth', 'denticle'.
GIVEN NAME Polish 4%; Jewish 4%. *Moshe*.

Zombro (109) Variant of Swiss German ZUMBRO.

Zomer (100) **1.** Dutch: from *zomer* 'summer', a nickname for someone of a warm disposition, or for someone associated with the season in some other way. **2.** Polish spelling of German SOMMER.
GIVEN NAMES Dutch 9%; Polish 7%; German 4%. *Cornie, Egbert, Hendrik, Henk*; *Halina* (2), *Zygmunt*.

Zona (544) Italian: topographic name from *zona* 'zone', 'area'.
GIVEN NAMES Italian 7%. *Angelo, Antonio, Carmela, Naldo, Pasquale, Rocco, Sabatino, Saverio, Vito*.

Zone (113) **1.** Dutch: from *zoon* 'son', a distinguishing epithet for a son who shared the same personal name as his father. **2.** English (southwestern): variant of SON.

Zong (70) Chinese 宗: from the first part of the name of Zong Bo, a high counselor who lived during the Zhou dynasty (1122–221 BC). His descendants adopted the first part of his name as their surname.

Zook (2151) **1.** Respelling of Swiss German **Zug**, a habitational name from the city and canton so named in Switzerland. This is a frequent surname among Amish and Mennonites in the U.S. **2.** Respelling of Ashkenazic Jewish **Zhuk**, an ornamental from eastern Slavic *zhuk* 'beetle', or a habitational name for someone from a place in Belarus or Lithuania called Zhuki, from the same word.

Zopf (129) German: nickname for someone who wore his hair in a pigtail or plait, Middle High German *zopf, zoph*, or from a field name from same word in the sense 'tail', 'end', 'narrow point'.

Zopfi (129) Swiss German: variant of ZOPF.

Zoppi (101) Italian: nickname from *zoppo* 'lame', 'unsteady'.
GIVEN NAMES Italian 12%. *Carina, Carlo, Ezio*.

Zorger (113) Jewish (Ashkenazic): variant of SORGE.
GIVEN NAMES Jewish 4%. *Chaim, Naftali*.

Zorich (226) Anglicized spelling of Croatian and Serbian **Zorić**, metronymic from the female personal name *Zora*, from *zora* 'aurora', 'dawn'.

Zorn (1869) **1.** German and Jewish (Ashkenazic): nickname for a short-tempered man, from Middle High German *zorn* 'wrath', 'anger'. **2.** from a Slavic word (e.g., Sorbian *corny* 'black'). Compare CZERNY. **3.** Slovenian (western Slovenia): of uncertain origin. It may be connected with the Friulian dialect personal name *Zorz* (see GEORGE).
GIVEN NAMES German 4%. *Kurt* (4), *Manfred* (3), *Alphons, Christoph, Erwin, Ewald, Hans, Irmgard, Klaus, Leonhard, Markus, Otto*.

Zornes (521) German: unexplained.

Zornow (127) German (of Slavic origin): habitational name from Zornow in Mecklenburg-West Pomerania.

Zoromski (127) Polish: probably a variant of **Żeromski**, a habitational name for someone from any of the various places called Żeromin, in Konin, Piotrków, and Ciechanów provinces. The place name is from *żeremię* 'settlement of beavers'.

Zorrilla (171) Spanish: probably a variant of *zorra* 'vixen', *zorro* 'fox', applied as nickname either for a crafty or devious person, or possibly a lazy one, the Spanish term for the fox meaning literally 'the lazy one', from Old Spanish *zorro* 'lazy' (from *zorrar* 'to drag').
GIVEN NAMES Spanish 56%. *Jose* (9), *Andres* (5), *Jorge* (5), *Francisco* (3), *Miguel* (3), *Raul* (3), *Carlos* (2), *Juan* (2), *Lazaro* (2), *Luis* (2), *Luz* (2), *Maximo* (2).

Zortman (210) Variant spelling of German **Zartmann** (see ZARTMAN).

Zorzi (131) Italian: patronymic from the personal name *Zorze*, Venetian form of *Giorgio* (see GEORGE).
GIVEN NAMES Italian 4%. *Gaeton, Reno*.

Zoss (158) Swiss German: unexplained.

Zotter (124) **1.** South German: from an agent derivative of Middle High German *zotte, zote* 'shaggy wool', hence perhaps an occupational name for someone who kept sheep or was employed in the wool trade, or alternatively a nickname for someone who habitually wore a sheepskin or who had unkempt hair. **2.** German: nickname for a clumsy or distracted person, from a derivative of Middle High German *zotten* 'to stroll or amble'.

Zotti (113) **1.** Italian: patronymic from the personal name *Zotto*, which may derive in part from an old Germanic personal name and in part from a variant of *Giotto* or a pet form of *Ambrogiotto, Angelotto*, etc. **2.** Italian: possibly a nickname from an old Venetian word, *zoto* 'lame'. **3.** Albanian: from *zot, zoti* 'lord', 'master'. This was either a status for a landowner or a nickname for someone who frequently used this word as an oath.
GIVEN NAMES Italian 8%. *Angelo, Dino, Guido, Luigi*.

Zottola (140) Italian: from a feminine diminutive of **Zotto**, which is of uncertain derivation. It may be from *zoto* 'lame', a Venetian form of *zoppo* (see ZOPPI), or otherwise from a short form of a personal name ending with the hypocoristic suffix *-otto*, such as *Lorenzotto* (from LORENZO) or *Zorzotto* (from *Zorze*, ZORZI).
GIVEN NAMES Italian 17%; French 7%. *Antonio, Carlo, Luigi, Raffaele, Sal, Salvatore*; *Armand* (6).

Zou (304) Chinese 邹: from the name of the ancient city of Zoutu. The legendary emperor Huang Di (2697–2595 BC) used this city as a military base. Both characters forming its name, *Zou* and *Tu* (see TU), were adopted as surnames.
GIVEN NAMES Chinese 70%. *Hui* (4), *Qin* (4), *Wei* (4), *Chu* (3), *Ming* (3), *Cheng* (2), *Jian* (2), *Jing* (2), *Liqun* (2), *Mei* (2), *Qun* (2), *Wei Xiong* (2); *Chang, Min*.

Zoubek (124) Czech: from a diminutive of **Zub**, a nickname for someone with something odd or noticeable about his teeth, from *zub* 'tooth'.

Zoucha (148) Polish: dialect variant of ZAUCHA.

Zuba (170) Polish: nickname for someone with a prominent or noticeable tooth, from Slavic *zub* 'tooth' (Polish *ząb*), or possibly from the Polish dialect verb *zubać* 'to peck'.
GIVEN NAMES Polish 5%. *Agnieszka, Miroslaw*.

Zubal (117) Polish: derivative of *zub* 'tooth' (see ZUBA).

Zube (144) Germanized form of Polish ZUBA or a cognate (meaning 'tooth') in some other Slavic language.

Zubek (115) Polish: nickname from a diminutive of *zub* 'tooth' (see ZUBA).
GIVEN NAMES Polish 24%. *Andrzej* (2), *Krystyna* (2), *Tadeusz* (2), *Irena, Jadwiga, Jozef, Jozefa, Ludwik, Stanislaw, Wojciech*.

Zuber (1574) **1.** German: metonymic occupational name for a cooper or tubmaker, from Middle High German *zuber* '(two-handled) tub', or a habitational name from a house distinguished by the sign of a tub. **2.** Swiss German: habitational name from a place so named, denoting an alpine stream.

Zubia (208) **1.** Spanish: habitational name from Zubia in Granada province or either of two smaller places in Málaga province, so named from *zubia* 'rich in water' (from Arabic). **2.** Basque: Pyrenean topographic name from Basque *zubi* 'bridge' + the definite article -*a*.

GIVEN NAMES Spanish 53%. *Jesus* (7), *Jose* (7), *Manuel* (4), *Ruben* (4), *Juan* (3), *Raul* (3), *Catalina* (2), *Cruz* (2), *Ernesto* (2), *Esteban* (2), *Miguel* (2), *Ramon* (2).

Zubiate (122) Basque: habitational name from Zubiate in Biscay province, so named from Basque *zubi* 'bridge' + *ate* 'gorge', 'ravine'.

GIVEN NAMES Spanish 44%. *Jose* (5), *Carlos* (4), *Pablo* (3), *Ricardo* (2), *Alvaro*, *Armando*, *Benito*, *Blanca*, *Elvira*, *Enrique*, *Francisca*, *Graciano*.

Zubke (161) German: from the Slavic personal name *Subek*, a pet form of *Subislaw*.

Zubrod (165) Variant spelling of German **Zubrot**, which Brechenmacher explains as a Swabian nickname for someone who was never satisfied with what he had; he wanted something (butter, dripping, cheese) to go 'with (his) bread'.

Zucca (151) Italian (Sicily): **1.** in part a metonymic occupational name for a grower and seller of gourds (squashes or marrows), from Italian *zucca* 'gourd' (Late Latin *cucutia*, for classical Latin *cucurbita*). More often, however, it is a nickname from the same word used in its colloquial transferred sense 'head', in particular 'empty head'. **2.** possibly also a topographic name of Albanian origin, from *zhukë*, *zhuka* 'marsh', 'rush'.

GIVEN NAMES Italian 10%. *Angelo*, *Enrico*, *Marcello*, *Salvatore*, *Silvio*.

Zuccarelli (138) Italian: patronymic or plural form of ZUCCARELLO.

GIVEN NAMES Italian 23%. *Mario* (3), *Aldo*, *Alessandro*, *Biagio*, *Ettore*, *Fiore*, *Rocco*, *Tommaso*, *Umberto*.

Zuccarello (116) Italian: **1.** from a diminutive of ZUCCARO. **2.** habitational name from Zuccarello in Savona province.

GIVEN NAMES Italian 28%. *Mario* (4), *Gregorio* (2), *Corrado*, *Giovanni*, *Guiseppe*, *Sal*, *Salvatore*.

Zuccaro (383) Italian: from *zucchero* 'sugar', a nickname for a sweet natured person or a metonymic occupational name for a dealer in sugar or for a confectioner or seller of sweetmeats.

GIVEN NAMES Italian 22%. *Rocco* (5), *Salvatore* (4), *Amerigo* (3), *Angelo* (3), *Dante* (2), *Reno* (2), *Santo* (2), *Domenic*, *Ezio*, *Geno*, *Gino*, *Giuseppe*.

Zucco (372) Italian (Sicily): from *zuccu* 'base of a tree', 'stump', possibly a topo-

graphic name for someone who lived where a coppice had been cut down for timber.

GIVEN NAMES Italian 22%. *Angelo* (5), *Geno* (2), *Rocco* (2), *Silvio* (2), *Carmelo*, *Demetrio*, *Donato*, *Emilio*, *Gino*, *Sal*.

Zuch (175) Eastern German: topographic name for someone who lived on dry ground, from Slavic *suchy* 'dry', or a habitational name from any of various places named with this word, such as Zuch and Zuchen in Pomerania, or Züchen in Silesia.

Zuchowski (310) Polish (**Żuchowski**): habitational name for someone from Żuchowo in Włocławek voivodeship.

GIVEN NAMES Polish 4%. *Mieczyslaw*, *Wieslaw*.

Zuck (501) **1.** German: from a Slavic personal name, *Zuk* 'beetle'. **2.** South German: from dialect *sucke* 'sow', an occupational name for a hog raiser. **3.** Americanized form of ZUCH or of Swiss German ZUG.

Zucker (2035) **1.** German and Jewish (Ashkenazic): metonymic occupational name for a dealer in sugar or a confectioner, or a nickname for someone with a sweet tooth, from Middle High German *zu(c)ker*, German *Zucker*, Yiddish *tsuker* 'sugar'. In some cases the Jewish surname is ornamental. **2.** German: offensive nickname for someone thought to be a thief, from Middle High German *zücker*, *zucker* 'thief', an agent derivative of *zucken* 'to snatch or grab'.

GIVEN NAMES Jewish 6%. *Miriam* (3), *Sol* (3), *Hyman* (2), *Kieve* (2), *Moshe* (2), *Anchel*, *Avram*, *Chanie*, *Dov*, *Elihu*, *Gerson*, *Liba*.

Zuckerberg (113) Jewish (Ashkenazic): ornamental name composed of German *Zucker* 'sugar' + *Berg* 'mountain', 'hill'.

GIVEN NAMES Jewish 9%. *Hyam*, *Miriam*, *Shaul*.

Zuckerman (2018) German (**Zuckermann**) and Jewish (Ashkenazic): occupational name for a dealer in sugar or a confectioner, or (as a Jewish name) an ornamental name formed with German *Zucker* 'sugar' (see ZUCKER).

GIVEN NAMES Jewish 6%. *Sol* (5), *Mayer* (3), *Arnon* (2), *Emanuel* (2), *Isadore* (2), *Meyer* (2), *Aryeh*, *Boruch*, *Chana*, *Shira*, *Shoshanah*, *Yetta*.

Zuege (145) South German (**Züge**): from a field name with the sense 'branch', 'line', 'path'.

GIVEN NAME German 4%. *Kurt* (2).

Zuehl (121) German (**Zühl**): from a pet form of a Slavic personal name, e.g. *Zulimir* or *Zulislaw*.

Zuehlke (577) German (**Zühlke**): from a pet form of a Slavic personal name, e.g. *Zulimir* or *Zulislaw*.

GIVEN NAMES German 6%. *Erwin* (3), *Kurt* (3), *Adelheid*, *Fritz*, *Heinz*, *Helmuth*, *Horst*.

Zuelke (199) Variant spelling of German ZUEHLKE.

GIVEN NAMES German 4%. *Kurt*, *Otto*.

Zuercher (463) German (**Zürcher**): see ZURCHER.

Zufall (232) **1.** German: from Middle High German *zuoval* 'benefit', 'windfall', hence a nickname for a lucky person or a status name for someone to whom a particular plot of communal land had been allotted. **2.** occupational name for a tax collector, from an administrative term denoting a kind of tax.

Zufelt (265) German: topographic name for someone who lived by a stretch of open country, from German *zu* 'at' + *Fel(d)t* 'open country'.

Zug (153) Swiss German: habitational name from the Swiss city of Zug.

Zuhlke (248) German (**Zülke**): see ZUEHLKE.

GIVEN NAMES German 4%. *Kurt*, *Otto*.

Zuidema (468) Frisian: patronymic from the old Germanic personal name *Sudhari*.

Zuk (486) Polish (**Żuk**): nickname from *żuk* 'beetle', denoting someone thought to resemble a beetle.

GIVEN NAMES Polish 5%. *Piotr* (2), *Andrzej*, *Beata*, *Bogdan*, *Boleslaw*, *Elzbieta*, *Mariusz*.

Zukas (182) Lithuanian: **1.** nickname from *zukas* 'white rabbit'. **2.** reduced form of **Žukauskas** (see ZUKAUSKAS).

Zukauskas (102) Lithuanian (**Žukauskas**): nickname from a Lithuanian derivative of Polish *żuk* 'beetle'.

GIVEN NAMES Lithuanian 9%; German 4%. *Vito* (2), *Vladas* (2), *Liudas*, *Romualdas*; *Viktor*.

Zuker (162) Jewish (Ashkenazic): variant spelling of ZUCKER.

Zukerman (171) Jewish (Ashkenazic): literally 'sugar man', an occupational name for a dealer in sugar or a confectioner, a nickname for someone with a sweet tooth, or an ornamental name (see ZUCKER).

GIVEN NAMES Jewish 11%. *Arie*, *Asher*, *Itai*, *Miriam*, *Yossef*.

Zukoski (121) Polish (**Żukoski**): variant spelling of Polish ZUKOWSKI.

Zukowski (1110) Polish (**Żukowski**): habitational name from any of many places called Żukowo or Żuków, named with *żuk* 'beetle'. This surname is also established in German-speaking countries.

GIVEN NAMES Polish 7%. *Andrzej* (3), *Leszek* (2), *Boleslaw*, *Bronislaw*, *Dariusz*, *Franciszek*, *Jerzy*, *Lech*, *Mariusz*, *Radoslaw*, *Ryszard*, *Stanislaw*.

Zulauf (268) South German: nickname for an inquisitive person, from Middle High German *zuolouf* 'great rush or run'.

Zuleger (230) German: occupational name from Middle High German *zuoleger* 'assistant', 'helper', in some cases perhaps used ironically.

Zulick (149) Perhaps an Americanized spelling of German **Züllich**, **Züllig**, which in the east is from a pet form of the Slavic personal names *Zulimir* or *Zulislaw* (compare ZUEHLKE) and elsewhere from the personal name *Zyriacus* (see ZILCH).

Zulli (138) Italian: patronymic from ZULLO.
GIVEN NAMES Italian 19%. *Rocco* (2), *Carmine, Giovanni, Mauro, Nicola, Pasquale, Philomena, Pompeo.*

Zullo (721) Italian: probably from a short form of a hypocoristic personal name formed with this suffix, as for example *Marzullo* or *Vincenzullo.*
GIVEN NAMES Italian 11%. *Rocco* (3), *Antonio* (2), *Aldo, Angelo, Carmela, Carmine, Cosmo, Dario, Domenic, Donato, Ferdinando, Franca.*

Zuluaga (178) Basque: variant of **Zuloaga**, a habitational name from Zuloaga in Biscay province, which is named from Basque *zulo* 'opening' + *-aga* 'place'.
GIVEN NAMES Spanish 54%. *Carlos* (6), *Jose* (5), *Ana* (3), *Jorge* (3), *Luis* (3), *Luz* (3), *Alvaro* (2), *Fabio* (2), *Gustavo* (2), *Humberto* (2), *Jaime* (2), *Mario* (2).

Zumalt (107) German: unexplained.

Zumbach (108) German: topographic name for someone who lived 'by the stream'.
GIVEN NAMES German 4%. *Hans, Kurt.*

Zumbo (122) Italian: a nickname for a squat, fat, or stubborn person, from Calabrian *zumbu* 'lump', from Calabrian Greek *dzomba, tsoumba,* from Medieval Greek *gombos,* itself in turn from Venetian *gobo* 'hunchbacked'.
GIVEN NAMES Italian 28%. *Domenic, Erminio, Giancarlo, Lorenzo, Orazio, Salvatore, Vincenzo.*

Zumbro (175) Americanized form of Swiss German **Sommerau**, a habitational name from a place so called.

Zumbrun (180) German (**Zumbrunn**): topographic name for someone who lived 'at the spring or well', from Middle High German *brunne* 'fount', 'well'.

Zumbrunnen (142) German: topographic name for someone who lived 'at the springs', from the plural of Middle High German *brunne.*

Zummo (250) Italian: probably an assimilated form of ZUMBO.
GIVEN NAMES Italian 24%. *Salvatore* (3), *Alfonso* (2), *Angelo* (2), *Carmelo* (2), *Natale* (2), *Antonio, Ciro, Cosmo, Enrico, Filippo, Francesca, Giovanni, Nunzio, Rico.*

Zumpano (160) Italian (Sicily): status name for a district administrator in the Byzantine Empire, from Slavic *zupan* 'leader', 'chief', 'headman' (see ZUPAN).
GIVEN NAMES Italian 18%. *Sal* (3), *Caesar, Alberto, Emilio, Enrico.*

Zumstein (189) German: topographic name for someone who lived 'at the rock' or 'at the castle', from Middle High German *stein* 'rock', also used to refer to a stone-built castle.

Zumwalt (1118) German: topographic name for someone who lived 'by the forest', from Middle High German *walt*

'woods', 'forest' + the fused preposition and article *zum* (*zu dem*) 'at the'.

Zundel (380) German (also **Zündel**): from a diminutive of **Zunder**, a metonymic occupational name for a seller of kindling wood, from Middle High German *zunder* 'tinder'.

Zunich (109) Croatian and Bosnian (**Žunić**); Slovenian (eastern and southern Slovenia; **Žunič**): patronymic from a nickname based on Croatian and Slovenian dialect *žuna* 'woodpecker'.

Zuniga (3923) Basque (**Zuñiga**): habitational name from a place in Navarre province named Zuñiga, from Basque *zuin* 'cultivated field' + *iga* 'incline', 'slope'.
GIVEN NAMES Spanish 52%. *Jose* (88), *Juan* (69), *Manuel* (49), *Luis* (47), *Carlos* (43), *Jesus* (34), *Jorge* (29), *Miguel* (26), *Pedro* (25), *Alberto* (22), *Francisco* (22), *Javier* (19).

Zunino (196) Italian: unexplained. In Italy this surname is found chiefly in Liguria and Piedmont.
GIVEN NAMES Italian 7%. *Lorenzo* (2), *Aldo, Angelo, Gianni, Italo, Pompeo.*

Zunk (116) German: variant of ZUNKER.

Zunker (358) German: topographic name for someone living by a crag, from South German dialect *Zunke.*
GIVEN NAMES German 7%. *Berthold, Erwin, Fritz, Heinz, Horst, Klaus, Kurt, Manferd, Otto.*

Zupan (456) Slovenian, Slovak, (also **Župan**), and Croatian (**Župan**): from Slavic *župan,* historic term for a village headman, a derivative of Old Slavic *župa* 'district' or 'community'. The modern Slavic word *župan* means 'mayor', 'burgomaster', or (in Croatia) 'head of an administrative district'.

Zupancic (437) Slovenian (**Zupančič**, **Župančič**) and Croatian (northern Croatia; **Župančić**): patronymic from *župan* (see ZUPAN).

Zupko (166) Slovak: diminutive of ZUPAN.

Zupon (107) Probably an altered spelling of Slovenian and Croatian **Zupan** or **Župan** (see ZUPAN).

Zur (111) Jewish (Israeli): ornamental name from Hebrew *tsur* 'rock'. In some cases it may also be a translation of some Ashkenazic surname with similar meaning (e.g. FELS or STEIN).
GIVEN NAMES Jewish 16%; German 6%. *Ofer* (2), *Yael* (2), *Amikam, Amram, Ari, Uri; Gerhard, Otto.*

Zuraw (131) Polish (**Żuraw**): nickname for a tall, gangling person, from Polish *żuraw* 'crane'. The term was also used as a nickname for a chimneysweep, referring to the crane's habit of nesting on chimneys.
GIVEN NAMES Polish 5%. *Krzysztof, Piotr, Wladyslaw.*

Zurawski (585) Polish (**Żurawski**):
1. habitational name for someone from any of many places called Żuraw, Żurawa, or Żurawia, named with *żuraw* 'crane'.

2. nickname for a tall, gangling person, a variant of ZURAW.
GIVEN NAMES Polish 7%. *Bogdan, Casimir, Darek, Dariusz, Jacek, Janina, Jerzy, Kazimierz, Lech, Tadeusz, Zdzislaw, Zofia.*

Zurbuchen (110) German: topographic name for someone who lived 'at the beech trees'.
GIVEN NAMES German 8%. *Erwin, Kurt, Otto.*

Zurcher (452) German (**Zürcher**): habitational name for someone from the Swiss city of Zurich.

Zurek (550) Polish (**Żurek**): from Polish *żurek* 'sour soup', probably a nickname for someone who had a special liking for sour soup. This name is also established in German-speaking countries.
GIVEN NAMES Polish 9%. *Janusz* (3), *Wojciech* (2), *Andrzej, Janina, Jolanta, Mieczyslaw, Ryszard, Slawomir, Wlodzimierz, Zofia.*

Zurfluh (178) South German: topographic name for someone who lived 'at the cliff', Middle High German *zur* 'at the' + *vluo* 'cliff'.

Zurick (106) Americanized spelling of German **Zürich**, habitational name for someone from the Swiss city of Zurich (see ZURCHER).

Zurita (302) Spanish and Aragonese:
1. nickname from Spanish *zurita* 'dove'.
2. habitational name from either of two places, in Uesca and Santander, named Zurita, possibly from Basque *zuri* 'white'.
GIVEN NAMES Spanish 54%. *Manuel* (10), *Jose* (9), *Fernando* (6), *Pedro* (6), *Juan* (5), *Jorge* (4), *Jesus* (3), *Ricardo* (3), *Alejandro* (2), *Alfonso* (2), *Armando* (2), *Arturo* (2).

Zurlo (157) Italian (both southern and Venetian) and Greek (**Zourlos**): nickname for a mad enthusiast or a wild, unpredictable person, from Italian *zurlo* 'mad enthusiasm', Greek *zourlos* 'crazy', 'enthusiastic', 'unpredictable', from medieval Greek *svourlos* 'spinning top', from *svourizesthai* 'to spin'.
GIVEN NAMES Italian 9%. *Livio, Marino.*

Zurn (367) German (**Zürn**): nickname for an irascible man, from Middle High German *zurn* 'angry'.

Zurowski (154) Polish (**Żurowski**): habitational name for someone from Żur in Bydgoszcz voivodeship or Żurowa in Tarnów voivodeship.
GIVEN NAMES Polish 8%. *Janusz, Jozef, Stanislaw, Tadeusz.*

Zusman (121) Jewish (Eastern Ashkenazic): variant of SUSSMAN.
GIVEN NAMES Jewish 20%; Russian 7%. *Aba* (2), *Isaak* (2), *Berka, Iser, Ronit, Zeev; Anatoliy, Anatoly, Boris, Leonid.*

Zussman (135) Jewish (Ashkenazic): variant of SUSSMAN.
GIVEN NAMES Jewish 13%. *Amiram* (2), *Elimelech* (2), *Mendel* (2), *Eliezer.*

Zutter (100) Swiss German: variant of **Sutter**, an occupational name for a shoemaker.

Zutz (108) German: unexplained; possibly from *Zutz* 'warlike attack' or Slavic *czucz* 'dog'.
GIVEN NAME German 4%. *Frieda.*

Zuver (178) German: variant of ZUBER.
GIVEN NAME German 4%. *Kurt* (2).

Zuvich (122) Croatian (**Žuvić**): patronymic from the personal names *Žuva* or *Žuvo*, old Croatian dialect forms of the Italian personal name *Giovanni* (see JOHN). This surname originates from the Adriatic islands of Krk and Brač.

Zwack (197) German: **1.** from a Bavarian dialect variant of **Zweck** (see ZWICK). **2.** possibly from Middle High German *zwac* 'bite' (from *zwacken* 'to tear off'), presumably as a nickname perhaps for someone with a huge appetite or a ferocious temper.
GIVEN NAME German 4%. *Ernst* (2).

Zwahlen (169) Swiss German: topographic name for someone living 'at the water channels', from a dialect word *wa(h)l* 'channel', in particular one used for irrigation.
GIVEN NAMES German 7%. *Helmut* (2), *Gerda, Hans, Lotti.*

Zwald (130) Reduced form of German ZUMWALT.
GIVEN NAME German 6%. *Gottlieb.*

Zwanziger (113) German: status name for a member of a committee of twenty (from German *zwanzig* 'twenty').
GIVEN NAME German 5%. *Otto.*

Zwart (436) Dutch: from Middle Dutch *zwart* 'black', hence a nickname for someone with black hair or a dark complexion.
GIVEN NAMES Dutch 9%. *Dirk* (3), *Gerrit* (3), *Hendrik* (3), *Derk* (2), *Durk, Laurens, Pieter, Teunis.*

Zweber (197) German: probably from Middle Low German *swebbe* 'blatherer', 'ditherer', 'coward', an unflattering nickname.

Zweifel (577) German: nickname for a fickle or indecisive person, from Middle High German *zwīvel* 'equivocation'.
GIVEN NAMES German 4%. *Erwin* (2), *Kurt* (2), *Hanspeter, Kaspar, Monika.*

Zweig (626) German and Jewish (Ashkenazic): from Middle High German *zwīg* 'branch', 'bough', 'twig', 'graft', German *Zweig*, applied perhaps as a nickname for a thin person or as an occupational name for a horticultural expert. The Jewish surname is ornamental.
GIVEN NAMES Jewish 8%; German 5%. *Avrohom* (3), *Miriam* (3), *Isadore* (2), *Yochanan* (2), *Akiva, Arie, Aron, Elchanan, Hyman, Moishe, Moshe, Shimon*; *Gerd* (2), *Hans* (2), *Manfred* (2), *Reinhold* (2), *Arnulf, Herta, Kurt.*

Zwerling (122) German: nickname for a small person, from an altered form of **Zwergling**, a diminutive of *Zwerg* 'dwarf'.
GIVEN NAME German 5%. *Hermann.*

Zwick (960) South German: metonymic occupational name for a nailsmith or occupational nickname for a shoemaker, from Middle High German *zwic, zwëc* 'tack', 'nail'. In some instances it may have been applied as a nickname for a small person or a topographic name for someone who lived on a wedge-shaped piece of land.

Zwicker (534) German: **1.** occupational name from an agent derivative of Middle High German *zwicken* 'to secure with nails', 'to peg'; this could denote a leather or textile worker, a cooper, or someone performing a similar function in a wide variety of other industries including, or example, salt extraction and mining. **2.** nickname for a small person or a topographic name (see ZWICK). **3.** habitational name for someone from a place called Zwickau.
GIVEN NAMES German 5%. *Kurt* (2), *Otto* (2), *Fritz, Reinhold, Rudi.*

Zwicky (169) Swiss German: variant of ZWICK.

Zwiebel (284) **1.** German: variant of ZIEBELL. **2.** Jewish (Ashkenazic): from German *Zwiebel* 'onion', a metonymic occupational name for a grower or seller of onions, or just one of the large number of Jewish ornamental names referring to plants.
GIVEN NAMES Jewish 6%. *Eliezer* (2), *Chaim, Isidor, Mayer, Naftali, Yitzhak.*

Zwiefelhofer (189) Swiss German: Bavarian variant of **Zwiebelhofer**, a habitational name for someone from a farm named *Zwiebelhof* 'onion farm' (see ZWIEBEL).

Zwieg (191) South German: variant of ZWEIG.

Zwiener (127) South German variant of **Zweiner**, a nickname for a quarrelsome person, from an agent derivative of *zweinen* 'to have a falling out with someone'.

Zwiers (157) Variant of Polish **Zwierz**, an unflattering nickname for an uncouth person, from Polish *zwierz* 'wild beast'.

Zwilling (223) German and Jewish (Ashkenazic): identifying epithet for a twin, from Middle High German *zwillinc*, German *Zwilling*, Yiddish *tsviling*.
GIVEN NAMES German 4%. *Gerhard, Helmut, Math.*

Zwirn (164) German and Jewish (Ashkenazic): metonymic occupational name for a yarn or twine maker, from German *Zwirn* 'twine', 'yarn'.
GIVEN NAMES Jewish 6%; German 6%. *Aaron, Isidor* (3); *Hermann, Otto.*

Zwolinski (299) Polish (**Zwoliński**): habitational name for someone from any of the various places in Poland called Wola (see WOLSKI), with the fused preposition *z*; *z Woli* means 'from Wola'.
GIVEN NAMES Polish 8%. *Aleksander, Casimir, Dionizy, Piotr, Wieslaw, Witold, Zdzislaw.*

Zych (509) Polish: from a short form of the personal name ZYGMUNT.
GIVEN NAMES Polish 9%. *Miroslaw* (2), *Andrze, Andrzej, Dorota, Eugeniusz, Jadwiga, Jolanta, Krzysztof, Lech, Mariusz, Stanislaw, Stanislawa.*

Zychowski (104) Polish: habitational name for someone from Zychy in Kielce voivodeship, named with the personal name *Zych*.

Zygmont (101) Polish: variant of ZYGMUNT.

Zygmunt (273) Polish: from the personal name *Zygmunt*, Polish form of SIEGMUND.
GIVEN NAMES Polish 10%. *Casimir, Elzbieta, Janina, Janusz, Krystyna, Lech, Mieczyslaw, Stanislaus, Zbigniew, Zofia.*

Zyla (206) Polish (**Żyla**): nickname from Polish *żyla* 'vein', in the transferred sense 'bore'.
GIVEN NAMES Polish 7%. *Aleksander, Danuta, Karol, Krzysztof, Piotr, Stanislaw.*

Zylka (181) Polish (**Żylka**): nickname from a diminutive of *żyla* 'vein' (see ZYLA).

Zylstra (664) Frisian: topographic name for someone who lived by a sluice, from an agent noun based on *zijl* 'sluice', 'pump'. Compare VAN ZYL.
GIVEN NAMES Dutch 4%. *Gerrit* (4), *Arjen, Dirk, Egbert, Gerben, Hessel, Mieke, Pieter.*

Zynda (193) Polish (**Zynda**): from a pet form of the Polish personal name *Zyndram*, a Polish form of the rare Germanic name *Sindram*, composed of the elements *sind* 'journey' + *hrabn* 'raven'.

Zysk (210) Polish: nickname for someone who got something out of something, an opportunist or a shrewd dealer, from Polish *zyskać* 'to gain'.
GIVEN NAMES Polish 10%; German 8%. *Andrzej, Krzysztof, Leszek, Mariola, Tadeusz, Wladyslawa, Zofia; Elke* (2), *Eckhard, Helmut, Kurt.*

Zyskowski (176) Polish: this has the form of a habitational name, but is more probably an elaborated form of ZYSK, with the common surname ending *-owski*.
GIVEN NAMES Polish 19%. *Tadeusz* (2), *Casimir, Dariusz, Grzegorz, Ireneusz, Marcin, Ryszard, Zdzislaw, Zygmund, Zygmunt.*

Zywicki (189) Polish (**Żywicki**): habitational name for someone from a place called *Żywy*, or possibly a nickname from Polish *żywy* 'live wire'.